I-Z
VOLUME 2

ENCYCLOPEDIA OF BUSINESS

I-Z
VOLUME 2

Jane A. Malonis,
Editor

Foreword by
Martin S. Fridson, CFA
Managing Director,
Merrill Lynch

ENCYCLOPEDIA OF BUSINESS

SECOND EDITION

Detroit
San Francisco
London
Boston
Woodbridge, CT

Encyclopedia of Business

Jane A. Malonis, *Editor*

Donna Craft, Andrea DeJong, Sheila Dow, Sonya Hill, Terrance Peck, Nader Qaimari, Amanda C. Quick, Brian Rabold, *Contributing Editors*

Erin Braun, *Managing Editor*

Mary Beth Trimper, *Production Director*
Evi Seoud, *Assistant Production Manager*

Cynthia Baldwin, *Product Design Manager*
Michelle DiMercurio, *Senior Art Director*

Library of Congress Cataloging-in-Publication Data

Malonis, Jane A.
Encyclopedia of business / Jane A. Malonis.—2nd ed.
p. cm.
Includes bibliographical references and index.
ISBN 0-7876-2438-1 (set : alk. Paper) — ISBN 0-7876-2439-X (vol.1) — ISBN 0-7876-2440-3 (vol.2)
1. Business—Encyclopedias. 2. Commerce—Encyclopedias. 3. Finance—Encyclopedias. 4. North America—Commerce—Encyclopedias. 5. Finance—North America—Encyclopedias. I. Title.

HF1001 .E466 1999
650′.03—dc21 99-047471

The paper used in this publication meets the minimum requirements of American National Standard for Information Sciences—Permanence Paper for Printed Library Materials, ANSI Z39.478-1984.

Printed in the United States of America

ISBN 0-7876-2438-1, ISBN 0-7876-2440-3, ISBN 0-7876-2439-X

I

ILLITERACY IN THE WORKPLACE

"Workplace illiteracy" is considered a business and social problem when workers are not able to read or write well enough to function optimally on the job. While illiteracy occurs in many fields, it is most prevalent among clerical and traditional blue-collar industrial workers. Contrary to popular perceptions, illiteracy in the workplace is not solely a result of large numbers of immigrants in the work force. Moreover, while the perception of illiteracy in the workplace has increased recently it does not mean that employees of the past were more literate or better educated.

Strictly defined, illiteracy means the inability to read and write. Nuanced definitions take into account the context and purpose of the reading task; simple tasks may only require recognizing individual printed words, whereas complex skills involve comprehending the words and logic of a substantial piece of prose. Some experts would include the inability to perform simple arithmetic, a deficiency also labeled "innumeracy." Together these rudimentary language and math abilities are often described collectively as "basic skills."

LITERACY STATISTICS

Some studies have reported that the basic skills deficit in the workplace is widespread and costly. According to statistics published in 1998 by the National Institute for Literacy, a federal agency established by the National Literacy Act of 1991, businesses lose more than $60 billion annually—an amount comparable to Mobil Corporation's 1997 worldwide revenues—because of skill deficiencies.

According to a **United Nations** survey of worldwide adult literacy, of the 158 participating nations, the United States ranks 49th. In 1992 the U.S. Education Department's National Center for Education Statistics conducted a National Adult Literacy Survey to assess the depth and breadth of literacy problems in the United States. The survey suggested that 20 percent or more of U.S. adults possess no better than a fifth-grade reading capacity.

There is some general agreement on what constitutes functional illiteracy—reading and writing below the sixth grade level. In 1993, the Education Department determined that as many as 30 percent of unskilled and semiskilled industrial workers (approximately 14 million) were below even a fourth grade level of reading and writing. This would make it almost impossible to read required safety manuals, product labels, and even written warning signs. A commonly cited incident involved an apparently illiterate worker taking a cigarette break: unable to read the danger sign on the door of an empty room, the worker set off a lethal explosion after he entered the room and ignited his cigarette.

Since a high school level of literacy is usually necessary in order to read newspapers and magazines fluently, some experts insist that anyone who reads and writes below secondary school level is functionally illiterate. If one accepts this broad definition of functional illiteracy, then as many as 72 million adults are affected, making functional illiteracy a truly gargantuan problem in this country. Perhaps most alarming is the fact that the highest levels of functional illiteracy can be found among the young, specifically, in the 18- to 30-year-old age bracket.

The majority of this age group has already entered the workplace or hopes to become employed. Job applications have exposed the high level of illiteracy in the current adult population. Estimates by the National Institute for Literacy reckon that as much as 75 percent of the unemployed have literacy shortcomings. In the state of Nevada, it was estimated in 1994 that two out of three recently hired employees had at most an eighth-grade reading level. In 1990, Southwestern Bell received 15,000 job applications; of these applicants only 800 could pass the company's basic skills test.

EVOLUTION OF LITERACY IN THE UNITED STATES

Illiteracy—which in this essay will be considered functional illiteracy—has always existed in this country and cannot be blamed on immigrant labor. The industrial manufacturing sector of the economy has been employing immigrants since the early 19th century. While newly arrived immigrants for the most part read and write English poorly or not at all, the majority—over 50 percent—are literate in their own native languages and do not require literacy programs as much as they do ESOL (short for English for Speakers of Other Languages) training.

Hence at the heart of the illiteracy problem in this country is rapidly changing technology, and most importantly, the computerization of business and industry. As recently as the 1960s, what mattered in most industrial jobs was physical endurance. More recently, automation has reduced physical labor and increased the need for semiskilled labor to operate and maintain the equipment that actually completes the manufacturing tasks.

It is not only computerization that has changed the workplace, however. Thirty years ago, business and industry for the most part had to contend only with domestic competitors. With **trade barriers** falling all over the globe, international **competition** has grown intense. Only the most streamlined, cost-efficient, and quality-conscious companies will survive and make a profit. Competition from Japan in particular has compelled American businesses to become more productive and create new products. Moreover, the internal structures of many businesses are changing. For decades, a company would be neatly divided between managers, who did the thinking, and the rank-and file-employees, who carried out management's ideas and plans. Nowadays, input and, especially, creative thinking are sought at all levels. Many believe meeting these challenges necessitates a literate, if not highly literate, work force.

SHORTFALLS IN EDUCATION AND TRAINING

A Senate Labor Committee report in 1990 maintained that while a fourth-grade education had always been sufficient for most skilled and unskilled jobs since World War II, current working conditions demanded that high school or the equivalent be the new minimum required level of education for the marketplace. Unfortunately, nearly 2 million students graduating from high schools annually are functionally illiterate. To American business and industry, which must pay high property taxes to support the public education system, this is a frustrating reality.

How is it that students can graduate from high school while reading and writing far below the 12th grade level? One reason is that students are often automatically promoted to the next grade even if they have not learned to read. Additionally, more inner-city students graduate functionally illiterate than do students at suburban schools. Hence illiteracy is also caused by economic disparity and social breakdown; students who have not learned to read very often come from broken and impoverished homes. Students from minority groups are far more likely to be semiliterate than whites. At least 40 percent of minorities under 18 are believed to be functionally illiterate. Educational studies have failed to prove that merely keeping a student behind a grade or two has helped him or her learn to read.

Despite the problems illiteracy poses, few employees seek out the help offered by literacy programs, even if they are free and easily accessible. This phenomenon has been closely studied by literacy experts, who posit that the social stigma of illiteracy is far greater than it is for drug or alcohol abuse. Moreover, should an older man or woman enroll in a literacy class, more often than not, he or she has to use materials geared for high school or even grade school-aged children, clearly inappropriate for older adults. Lastly, even if he or she is lucky to have adult-level learning materials, an illiterate person is often daunted at the length of time it takes to learn to read fluently—often several years, sometimes even longer. For this reason alone, most adults who are functionally illiterate bluff their way through their job by greatly exaggerating their reading and writing abilities.

Where rank-and-file employees are poorly educated and reluctant to seek out the help of community-based literacy programs, companies are increasingly looking inward for solutions. As of 1995, U.S. businesses spent an estimated $53 billion each year on all forms of training, including basic skills programs. That's on top of approximately $1.3 billion (1997 figure) invested each year in adult literacy programs by federal and state agencies. Not only do these programs attempt to reach functionally illiterate workers, but also those who have been on the job for years and need to upgrade their job knowledge and skills (which often includes literacy).

Currently, at least one in five organizations (businesses as well as nonprofit concerns) sponsor and pay for programs that teach basic literacy skills. This translates into only 20 percent of organizations with a minimum work force of 100 employees. Of the 80 percent without such programs, almost all require testing to ensure job applicants have the appropriate, job-related skills. Most companies want to weed out the semiliterate applicants and hire only those who are fully qualified, although some believe this is increasingly becoming a luxury. According to some labor data, to pass up intelligent, hardworking, and ambitious applicants because of deficient skills hazards the risk of running out of applicants altogether. This was the conclusion in 1987 of the farsighted chairman of Xerox Corp., David Kearns, who acknowledged even then the necessity of hiring unqualified employees if the company was to expand. According to Kearns, businesses throughout the United States could end up hiring upwards of one million entry-level employees annually who were unable to read or write. More recent figures support Kearns' prognosis: between 1995 and 1998 government statistics recorded a surge in the number of companies suffering shortages of skilled labor.

The larger the company, the more apt it is to implement some kind of on-the-job training to combat declining skills, including the fundamentals—basic reading, writing, and math skills. Polaroid led the way in establishing the first on-the-job basic skills program in the early 1970s. Since then, other companies have followed. Nonetheless, 90 percent of American companies still lack such job training programs. An exception is Hershey Foods in Pennsylvania, which automatically sends any employee without a high school diploma to GED classes; it also provides employees desiring extra math and science training with tutors. In 1993, more than half of the 1,340 firms in Illinois responded positively on a questionnaire asking if their employees needed to upgrade their skills—but only 24 percent of these firms offered training courses.

The cost of implementing such programs can be prohibitive. Start-up costs can range anywhere from as low as $2,500 to a high of $100,000. Not all companies can afford to pour into basic literacy programs the $35 million that Motorola, Inc. had expended by 1993. By then, Motorola had decided that the time had come to turn away job applicants whose reading and writing skills fell below the seventh-grade level. While even an eighth-grade literacy level increasingly disqualifies one for the growing demands of the work place, training employees at this level requires much less time, and therefore, saves the company more money.

When Magnavox was faced with an increase in the number of immigrants seeking and obtaining work in the early 1990s, the firm installed a pilot literacy program that also included English as a second language courses. To mitigate the prohibitive cost of this program, Magnavox turned to the Department of Education's National Workplace Literacy Program for matching grant funds (the Education Department allocates the funds to the states, which in turn make them available to qualified applicants). In this way, the pilot program became a permanent success story emulated by other companies. However, the state governments administering the literacy grants are overwhelmed with applications each year, leading to stiff competition. Between fiscal years 1990-94, the budget for literacy programs in the state of Illinois alone increased from $119,000 to nearly half a million dollars, but the number of grant applications still exceeded the budget.

The literacy program at Magnavox initially offered only evening classes, but the company discovered, not surprisingly, that employees were far more encouraged to take the classes if they were conducted during work time. Despite the time lost in productivity, the long-term gain to the company offset the loss. Other innovations have included tapes of adult-level reading material, which students listen to until they can recognize and read the corresponding text, and interactive computer software that simulates the work environment and challenges some adults to overcome their fear of computers. What used to take several years to master in some cases can now take as little as ten months. Workplace literacy programs offered during work hours have provided the most effective incentive to eradicate serious as well as functional illiteracy, when compared to community-based programs.

So many benefits accrue to companies that implement successful on-the-job literacy training programs that they become a form of investment, rather than an extraneous expense. For instance, there are improvements in job morale, in company loyalty (reducing the **employee turnover** rate), and in overall productivity.

FURTHER READING:

Davis, Mack. "Getting Workers Back to the Basics." *Training & Development,* October 1997.

Hull, Glynda A., ed. *Changing Work, Changing Workers: Critical Perspectives on Language, Literacy, and Skills.* New York: State University of New York Press, 1997.

National Institute for Literacy. "Fact Sheet: Workforce Literacy." Washington, 1998. Available from www.nifl.gov.

IMPLICIT PRICE DEFLATOR

The implicit price deflator is an **index** that is used to gauge the extent of price level changes or **inflation** in the economy. This index is essentially one of three different methods by which inflation in the economy is measured. Knowledge of two concepts, the notions of inflation and price index, is crucial to understanding the implicit price deflator.

INFLATION AND DEFLATION

Inflation is understood to be an increase in price level. It is actually defined as the rate of change in the price level. Thus, an inflation rate of five percent per annum means that the price level is increasing at the rate of five percent. However, inflation need not always be positive. It may be a negative number, in which instance the price level would be declining. Negative inflation rates (deflation) are very uncommon. Most economies face positive rates of inflation year after year.

PRICE INDEX AND THE MEASUREMENT OF THE INFLATION RATE

The inflation rate is derived by calculating the rate of change in a **price index**. A price index, in turn, measures the level of prices of goods and services at any point of time. The number of items included in a price index varies depending on the objective of the index. Usually three kinds of price indices are periodically reported by government sources. The first index is called the **consumer price index (CPI)**. This index measures the average retail prices paid by consumers for goods and services. There are approximately 400 items included in this index including several thousand products. These items are selected on the basis of their inclusion in the household budget of a consumer. Each of the 400 prices is assigned a weight based on the importance of the item in the household budget. As a result, the consumer price index reflects the changes in the cost of living of a typical household (consumer). The CPI is considered the most relevant inflation measure from the point of view of the consumers, as it measures the prices of goods and services that are part of their budgets. However, the consumer price index will not measure the changes in the cost of living of every consumer precisely due to the differences in consumption patterns.

A second price index used to measure the inflation rate is called the producer price index (PPI). It is a much broader measure than the consumer price index, in that it measures the wholesale prices of approximately 3,000 items. The items included in this index are those that are typically used by producers (manufacturers and businesses) and thus contain many raw materials and semi-finished goods. A change in the producer price index reflects a change in the cost of production, as encountered by producers. Since producers may pass on part or all of the increase in the cost of production to consumers, movements in producer price index indicate future movements in the consumer price index. The producer price index can thus forewarn consumers of coming increases in the cost of living.

The implicit price deflator is the third measure of inflation. This index measures the prices of all goods and services included in the calculation of the current output of goods and services in the economy, known as **gross domestic product (GDP)**. It is the broadest measure of the price level. This index includes prices of fighter bombers purchased by the U.S. Department of Defense as well as paper clips used in common offices. Thus, the implicit price deflator is a measure of the overall or aggregate price level for the economy. Movement in the implicit GDP price deflator captures the inflationary tendency of the overall economy.

CALCULATIONS OF THE IMPLICIT PRICE DEFLATOR AND THE INFLATION RATE

Calculation of the consumer price index (CPI) and producer price index (PPI) is direct—indexes are calculated from price data on the items included. The implicit price deflator, on the other hand, is inferred indirectly from the estimates of gross domestic product in nominal terms (in current dollars) and in real terms (when the nominal value of gross domestic product is adjusted for inflation by re-evaluating the GDP in prices that prevailed during a chosen base year).

Currently, 1992 is being used as the base year to calculate the real value of gross domestic product in the United States. Thus, the 1998 U.S. output of goods and services is first evaluated at prices prevailing in 1998. Once this is done, 1998 output of goods and services is also evaluated at prices that prevailed in 1992 (thus, the terms gross domestic product in 1992 dollars or constant dollars). One can easily see how the ratio of gross domestic product in 1998 prices and gross domestic product in 1992 prices would yield a measure of the extent of the rise in price level between 1992 and 1998. According to the federal government statistics, this ratio is estimated at 1.1307, or 113.07 when multiplied by 100 (as is customarily done to determine the extent of price increase more conveniently). The value of implicit price deflator of 113.07 implies that the price level increased by 13.07 percent over the 1992-1998 period (note that the base year, currently 1992, value of implicit price deflator is equal to 100).

This method of expressing nominal or current gross domestic product into its value in 1992 prices is routinely done every year (of course, sometimes the base year itself, may be changed to a later year to keep the data series closer to the current period). Thus, we have 1997, 1996, 1995 (and so on) gross domestic products expressed in 1992 prices. This helps to calculate the inflation rate between subsequent years. For example, the implicit price deflator stood at 112.08 at the end of 1997. Given that the deflator was at 113.07 at the end of 1998, we arrive at the annual inflation rate of roughly 0.88 percent during 1998 (1998 inflation rate = [(113.07 - 112.08) / 112.08] * 100).

Since the implicit price deflator is derived from the nominal and real values of the gross domestic product (GDP), it is also called implicit GDP price deflator. One should also notice that the term *deflator* is not used in consumer and producer price indexes. This is because, if one knows the implicit price deflator for 1998, and the 1998 gross domestic product in current prices, one could arrive at the gross domestic product in 1992 prices by deflating the 1998 gross domestic product in current prices by the deflator for 1998 (expressed in plain ratio form, rather than the one multiplied by 100). Despite the use of term deflator, one should not lose sight of the fact the implicit price deflator is essentially a price index.

SEE ALSO: Index/Indexes; Inflation

[Anandi P. Sahu, Ph.D.]

FURTHER READING:

Froyen, Richard T. *Macroeconomics: Theories and Policies.* 6th ed. Upper Saddle River, NJ: Prentice Hall, 1998.

Gordon, Robert J. *Macroeconomics.* 7th ed. Addison-Wesley, 1998.

Sommers, Albert T. *The U.S. Economy Demystified.* Lexington, MA: Lexington Books, 1985.

IMPORTING

Importing is the purchasing side of trade and takes place when one region acquires goods or services from another region. The region that sells the goods or services is the exporter, whereas the region the buys the goods or services is the importer. Importing most often refers to purchases from other countries. Importing is linked with international trade and generally is distinguished from trade within a specific nation because importing involves government regulation, whereas interstate importing does not. While the U.S. government can impose a variety of **trade barriers** and quotas on other countries in accordance with various trade agreements, a state cannot impose such trade barriers on other states, because the Constitution reserves this power for Congress only.

Because certain regions can produce and manufacture goods that other regions cannot (e.g., petroleum, precious metals, minerals, and agricultural products), countries lacking these resources and goods must import them from the regions that have and produce them. In addition, various economic factors may facilitate producing goods or offering services in one region or country, but not in another.

Importing in contemporary society is bound by several multinational trade agreements and their regulations as well as by respective national trade policies. National trade policies generally include tariffs and **duties** on imported goods, expect for countries with ''**most-favored nation**'' status or countries participating in mutual trade agreements. National trade policies tend to restrict importing certain products from certain countries, whereas trade agreements encourage importing certain products from certain countries.

Countries import both raw materials such as aluminum, steel, glass, and wood, as well as finished products such as automobiles, appliances, furniture, and clothing. In addition, countries import partially finished products, which they in turn finish and sell domestically or export to other countries.

Examination of a country's imports in relation to its **gross national product** indicates the approximate significance of imported goods to its economy. The U.S. ratio was about 10 percent in the early 1990s, while Germany's was 23 percent and Japan's 6.5 percent. In addition, imports generally increase in tandem with exports as countries become accustomed to international trade and trading with specific partners.

THE EVOLUTION OF TRADE AND TRADE THEORY

Since ancient times, nations and other organized societies have relied on importing and **exporting** goods to meet their needs. Because certain regions could not produce certain goods or could not produce enough of them, they had to import them from outside regions. In addition, city-states, such as those of ancient Greece, lacked diversified economies and therefore needed to import goods and resources from other areas.

The beginning of European colonialism around 1500 marked the beginning of modern international trade. At this point, trade became part of national policy. European countries attempted to gain as much **wealth**—precious metals in particular—as possible from their colonies and trading partners as inexpensively as possible. This method of international trade, referred to as **mercantilism**, remained in place from the 16th through the 18th centuries. The mercantilist philosophy typically held that one country's gain through international trade was another country's loss. Hence, mercantilists commonly believed that international commerce always had a loser. European empires of this period attempted to increase and maintain their power by amassing gold and silver coins. Simultaneously, these empires imposed numerous trade restrictions and protectionist policies to ensure that they exported more than they imported—i.e., to maintain a positive **balance of trade**.

With the development of nation-states in the 17th and 18th centuries, international trade continued to evolve towards its present state. Leaders of the nation-states realized they could increase not only their wealth but also their power by promoting and facilitating trade, thereby solidifying the power and stability of their respective nations.

During this period, economists began formulating theories of international trade and conceiving of liberalized trade policies. Scottish economist Adam Smith (1723-1790) is usually credited with founding the theoretical study of international trade. Based on some doctrines of the French economist François Quesnay (1694-1774), Smith developed the theory of ''absolute advantage,'' arguing that, given the limited supply of natural resources and materials, countries should produce only those products they can manufacture more cheaply and efficiently than their trading partners. Consequently, Smith postulated that countries should import the products they cannot produce cheaply and efficiently and export the products they can. Smith believed that international trade also brought about greater productivity by introducing a greater division of labor, allowing workers to specialize in the production of particular goods.

English economists Robert Torrens (1780-1864) and David Ricardo (1772-1823) modified this theory in 1815, proposing that countries import and export goods according to the principle of ''comparative advantage.'' This principle stipulates that a country can still produce and export a product even though it cannot produce the product as cheaply as some of its trading partners, if this more expensively produced product can garner stronger revenues in a foreign market than in the domestic market. Conversely, a country may choose to import a product, even if it costs more than its domestic counterpart, if the country can earn greater profits importing the product than selling it in the country's own home market.

In addition, economists of this period reasoned that international trade was inherently beneficial in that it brings about greater and more efficient world production and allows countries with limited natural resources to consume more than they would if they were not importing goods from other countries.

Another key step in the development of contemporary international trade theory was the rise of ''national'' economists who proposed theories primarily aimed at benefiting their respective nations. In the late 18th and early 19th centuries, these theories began to unfold based on the ideas of American politician Alexander Hamilton (1755-1804) and others. Hamilton helped develop the notion of political economy, which refers to active government involvement in economics, including international trade. Hamilton argued that the Congress should enact policies that would make the United States self-sufficient in the area of essential goods and resources, such as military supplies and equipment, in order to avoid reliance on importing these essential goods.

Early in the 20th century, the Heckscher-Ohlin theory of international trade became the most influential version of the comparative advantage theory. Borrowing from their predecessors, Eli Heckscher and Bertil Ohlin predicted that countries would export goods that they could produce efficiently given their land, labor, natural resources, and production technology, and import goods they could not produce efficiently given the same factors. Consequently, Heckscher and Ohlin believed countries achieved comparative advantage through a combination of factors such as financial resources, natural resources, and production technology, in contrast to Ricardo's formulation of comparative advantage, which attributed the advantage to labor productivity.

Some economists, however, have dispensed with the principle of comparative advantage altogether because it has failed to account for a variety of economic and trade phenomena, including several U.S. industries' lack of competitiveness. Despite its skilled **workforce**, leading scientists, and financial resources, the United States has seen its market share decline in industries such as appliances, electronics, machine tools, and semiconductors—industries where the country appears to have a comparative advantage.

Instead, more modern explanations of why countries export and import specific products rely on concepts such as competitive advantage, overlapping demand, **economies of scale**, and **economies of scope**. According to the competitive advantage theory of Michael E. Porter, a country can excel at trading if it has the right demand conditions, competitive environment, production factors, related and supporting industries, structure, and strategy. If a country lacks these conditions for a particular industry or product sector, however, it will most likely rely on importing these goods. Focusing on manufactured goods, Staffan Linder's theory of overlapping demand holds that after a company launches a product in response to domestic market demands, it will seek markets with similar consumer demands and similar per capita income with which to trade. Consequently, countries import goods from other countries with similar consumer tastes and levels of income, according to this theory.

The ''new trade theory'' assumes that the global economy can support only a limited number of companies producing any given good. Hence, the first companies to produce certain goods will capture a significant share of the market, hold **patent** rights, lead in development, and achieve economies of scale and scope. Economies of scale afford countries trade advantages, because companies can charge less for products when they increase the size of their production facilities, since this increase will enable them to produce more goods. Economies of scope refer to the integration of supplier, manufacture, and retail activities into a single company, with such integration allowing the company to produce and sell goods less expensively than independent manufacturers and retailers can. Once companies hold these advantages, other companies face formidable obstacles trying to compete against them.

Finally, the growth of multinational corporations, especially in the 1980s and 1990s, contributed to the importance and necessity of international trade. With production and **marketing** operations in many countries, these corporations account for a significant amount of the world's sales, assets, and human resources in both their home countries and in their host countries and their divisions trade materials and products between home and host countries. Many contemporary economists view multinational corporations as the facilitators of efficient international trade. Multinational corporations also have access to the raw materials and natural resources of a number of countries, which traditional comparative advantage theories do not take into consideration.

THE BENEFITS AND DRAWBACKS OF IMPORTING

Many economists, businesses, and politicians continue to rely on the principle of comparative advantage and it still influences import theories and policies. Consequently, countries continue to import products because they can obtain them less expensively abroad. Moreover, while trade policies, regulations, and theories have undergone numerous changes over the centuries, a basic motivation for countries to import goods from other countries remains the same. When certain countries lack goods and resources, they either must import them or make do without them.

In addition, given the technology, labor costs, government incentives, and **subsidies** of different countries, one country may be able to produce goods more efficiently than other countries. Hence, other countries will seek to import these goods because of price and perhaps quality advantages. For example, other countries import aircraft from the United States, while the United States imports clothing from other countries such as India and the Philippines.

Importing allows countries to achieve higher standards of living by obtaining products and resources that cannot be obtained domestically. For example, in order for the United States to maintain its standard of living, it must import petroleum, since the country cannot produce a sufficient amount to satisfy consumer demand. In addition, the United States also depends on imports for many of its cars, obtaining many of them from Japan. Japan, on the other hand, relies on imports for raw materials to produce and export finished goods such as cars and appliances; such imports help Japanese workers earn higher wages and the Japanese economy prosper.

Events of the 20th century provide evidence that international trade leads to greater productivity, consumption, and living standards. During periods of trade expansion such as the boom after World War II, the global economy has grown dramatically. Conversely, during periods of trade declines such as the Great Depression of the late 1920s and 1930s, the global economy has slowed down. Although trade growth accompanies global economic growth, economists cannot say for certain what the causal relationship is—that is, whether global trade expansion causes global economic growth or vice versa. Nevertheless, most governments and economists believe trade is vital to national and international economic growth.

Despite the advantages of importing, many economists and governments believe that importing goods can lead to the erosion of their national economies—especially when imports exceed exports. In the case of the United States, for example, some contend that importing goods such as cars and appliances leads not only to the loss of jobs for U.S. workers but also to a host of related consequences such as higher welfare reliance, the devaluation of **real estate**, the closure of plants, and the decline of cities and states. Estimates suggest that the United States loses 20,000 jobs for every $1 billion in the **trade deficit**.

Importing goods poses other problems such as the tacit acceptance of social values that conflict with domestic values. Importing goods from countries that pay low wages, for instance, can cripple domestic industries that cannot compete because they have a minimum wage, obligations to **labor unions**, and so forth; such importing also allows the exporting countries to continue to keep their workers impoverished. Furthermore, importing cheap goods, especially textiles, from countries that force employees—even children—to work in sweatshop conditions overlooks the type of treatment of employees that the United States and many other countries condemn.

IMPORT REGULATIONS AND TRADE AGREEMENTS

IMPORT REGULATIONS AND RESTRICTIONS. Because countries consider it in the interest of their national economies to export more than they import, they rely on a number of methods designed to restrict imports and protect their markets from **international competition**. In addition, countries also attempt to increase the amount of money they hold in their reserves and reduce the amount of their respective national currencies held by other countries. These concerns have led countries to impose a variety of trade restrictions such as import quotas, tariffs, and trade barriers, especially in the first half of the century. But countries have also established preferential trade agreements with favored nations that granted such nations reduced tariffs and trade barriers.

In order to limit the flow of goods from elsewhere, countries implement import quotas, which set maximum limits on the number of various goods a country will import. When confronted with a trade deficit, countries impose trade quotas as a quick remedy to prevent the growth of the trade imbalance. Countries also use import quotas to protect their markets from competition. In addition, countries have resorted to prohibiting of certain imports altogether, especially during the mercantile period.

Nations also impose tariffs, or **taxes**, on imported goods to limit the number of imports that are entering the country. The buyer of imported products pays the tariffs, making the price higher for the goods in the country that imported them. The higher price from the tariffs decreases any price advantage these goods might have over similar domestic products. Governments increase their revenues through tariffs and tariffs also subsidize domestic producers, providing them with motivation to produce the goods other countries try to export. Tariffs take the form of duties calculated as a percentage of the value of the goods imported—usually about 4 percent—and as fixed tariffs applied to a specific quantity of an imported product. But tariffs often benefit one sector of a domestic economy while harming another. Tariffs on imported steel, for example, protect the domestic steel industry from international competition, but they force car manufacturers to pay higher steel prices, and the car manufacturers in turn pass the higher prices on to consumers.

Countries also restrict imports by using nontariff barriers, that is, by establishing voluntary restraint agreements. With these agreements, exporters voluntarily limit the quantity of goods they ship to importing countries. Japanese car manufacturers, for example, reached a voluntary restraint agreement with the United States in the early 1980s to restrict the number of automobiles they export, thereby decreasing U.S. imports of Japanese cars.

Besides these direct methods of limiting imports, various domestic policies and programs work indirectly—and sometimes unintentionally—to restrict imports; these policies and programs function therefore as trade barriers. These trade barriers take the form of health and safety regulations, tax policies, and product labeling laws. Government support of certain industries, such as agriculture, also functions as a trade barrier, giving domestic producers an advantage over outside producers.

TRADE AGREEMENTS. By the middle of the 20th century, countries began to reach trade agreements limiting tariffs and trade barriers on specific products for all participating countries. In addition, countries in various regions such as Western Europe, North America, and Central America began to form trading blocs that eliminated tariffs and trade barriers for member nations.

The **General Agreement on Tariffs and Trade** (GATT) stands out as the most expansive trade agreement, involving 123 countries with numerous other countries seeking to participate. Originally, GATT governed trade from 1948 to 1994 and was among the first trade agreements that sought to promote importing by reducing tariffs and other trade barriers. A revised version of GATT took effect in 1994 as a result of the Uruguay Round of negotiations which occurred between 1986 to 1994. The new version of GATT called for continued liberalization of international markets and the reduction and elimination of tariffs and trade barriers. The agreement mandates the reduction and elimination of tariffs designed to impede and to control competition in favor of domestic businesses. GATT also established a formal organization for the implementation of systematic global trade policies, the **World Trade Organization**.

One of the most important trading blocs to the United States is the one that resulted from the **North American Free Trade Agreement** (NAFTA). Implemented in 1994, NAFTA will gradually eliminate trade barriers such as tariffs and trade restrictions among Canada, Mexico, and the United States enabling freer trade among these nations. Its main policies include the reduction and elimination of tariffs on a variety of products and the establishment of initial trade quotas to protect individual countries from overimporting while the agreement is being implemented. Most of the safeguard tariffs and quotas will end in 2004 and the rest will expire in 2005.

The democracies of North, Central, and South America plan to create a trading bloc for the entire Western Hemisphere that will reduce and eliminate tariffs and trade barriers restricting imports. These countries began negotiating the new trade agreement known as the Free Trade Area of the Americas (FTAA) in 1998 with the goal of implementing the agreement by 2005. The 34 participating countries are attempting to develop multilateral trade policies that will provide all countries in the Western Hemisphere with the same kind of trading privileges afforded to NAFTA members.

IMPORTING SERVICES

While the discussion, theory, and practice of trade and importing has focused on products over the centuries, importing services has become a common occurrence, fueled in part by the General Agreement on Trade in Services (GATS). GATS, the **service industries** counterpart of GATT, covers almost all commercial services including financial services, telecommunications services, air transportation services, and maritime transportation services. Financial services in particular have undergone **globalization** enabling various countries to import and export **credit**, **investment banking**, insurance, and related services. For example, international insurers accounted for about 10 percent of total U.S. premiums in the late 1990s.

Ratified in 1994 and implemented in 1995, GATS includes legislation that will reduce barriers to the trade of services in much the same way as GATT will reduce barriers to the trade of goods. Under the agreement, participating countries will gradually reduce trade barriers for specific service sectors according to schedules that are unique to each country. Furthermore, GATS provides the rules that govern the trade of services and prohibits national policies that discriminate in favor of domestic services over imported ones. In addition, the FTAA also will have a component devoted to the trade of services.

THE U.S. IMPORTATION PROCESS

To import products, companies must first establish agreements with international producers in accordance with national and international regulations and trade covenants. Companies considering importing products often begin their research into what products to import by contacting various international consulates, which can offer information on the manufacturers and distributors in their respective countries that are interested in exporting products to the United States. Furthermore, some countries have special agencies to promote international trade and the respective consulates can provide information on these agencies, too.

Importers must obtain the appropriate licenses from the government, which authorizes them to import goods. The importation of certain goods, such as pharmaceuticals and alcoholic beverages, is restricted and controlled by related government agencies such as the Food and Drug Administration and the Bureau of Alcohol, Tobacco, and Firearms. Importers then must follow the procedures of the U.S. Customs Service to bring about the legal "entry" of imported goods. When the shipment of these goods arrives at one of the country's officially designated ports of entry, the importer must file entry documents with the port director. The U.S. Customs Service must authorize the delivery of the goods and then the importer must pay all relevant duties.

Importers must provide evidence of their right to enter imported goods. Under U.S. Custom Service regulation, only the owner, the purchaser, or a licensed customs broker can enter imported goods. Importers can enter goods for consumption, storage at the port of arrival, or transportation to another port of entry following the same procedures as for the port of arrival. The entry of imports for consumption involves two steps. First, importers must file the mandatory documents within five days of the arrival of the goods to have the goods released from customs' custody. Second, importers must file documents for duty assessment. If importers want to store the incoming merchandise at the port of entry, they may have it placed in a customs warehouse as a warehouse entry for up to five years. During this period, importers may enter the stored merchandise for consumption following the appropriate procedures.

Customs officials usually examine portions of all incoming goods in order to assess duties, to ensure compliance with regulations governing the imported goods, to determine if these goods require special labeling or **packaging**, to see if the goods are accurately invoiced, and to prevent drug trafficking by intercepting any smuggled drugs. The U.S. Customs Service considers certain kinds of merchandise such as textiles trade-sensitive and, therefore, tends to examine them more thoroughly and frequently than other goods.

An invoice must accompany all imported goods and the invoice must be prepared following the regulations of the U.S. Customs Service. The invoice must include essential information such as the port of entry, the names of the importer and exporter, a detailed description of the goods, the quantity of the goods, the value of the goods, the currency, and the country of origin. Specific products or kinds of products may require the inclusion of additional information in the invoice.

SEE ALSO: Exporting

[Karl Heil]

FURTHER READING:

Cloney, Gordon J. "It's a Small World After All for Insurers." *National Underwriter Property and Casualty—Risk and Benefits Management,* 6 July 1998, 11.

Ekelund, Robert B., Jr., and Robert D. Tollison. *Mercantilism as a Rent-Seeking Society.* College Station, TX: Texas A&M University Press, 1981.

Hall, Kevin E. "34 Nations Begin to Bargain over Free Trade." *Journal of Commerce,* 1 June 1998, 10A.

Lanze, L. B. *Import/Export Can Make You Rich.* Englewood Cliffs, NJ: Prentice Hall, 1988.

Maneschi, Andrea. *Comparative Advantage in International Trade: A Historical Perspective.* Cheltenham, United Kingdom: Edward Elgar, 1998.

Markusen, James R., and others. *International Trade: Theory and Evidence.* New York: McGraw-Hill, 1995.

Moon, Bruce E. *Dilemmas of International Trade.* Boulder, CO: Westview Press, 1996.

Porter, Michael E. *The Competitive Advantage of Nations.* New York: Free Press, 1990.

U.S. Customs Service. *Importing into the United States.* Washington: GPO, 1994.

Weiss, Kenneth D. *Building an Import/Export Business.* New York: Wiley, 1987.

Yoffie, David B. *Beyond Free Trade: Firms, Governments, and Global Competition.* Boston: Harvard Business School Press, 1993.

INCOME AND REVENUE

Income is an important concept in **economics** as well as in **accounting**. Accountants prepare an **income statement** to measure a company's income for a given accounting period. Economists are concerned with measuring and defining such concepts as national income, personal income, disposable personal income, and money income versus real income. In each field the concept of income is defined in slightly different terms.

For accounting purposes, income is distinguished from revenues. A company's revenue is all of the money it takes in as a result of its operations. Another way of defining a company's revenue is as a monetary measure of outputs, or goods sold and services rendered, with expense being a monetary measure of inputs or resources used in the production of goods or services. On the other hand, a company's net income or profit is determined by subtracting its expenses from its revenues. Thus, revenues are the opposite of expenses, and income equals revenues minus expenses. For example a store may sell $300 worth of merchandise, for which it originally paid $200. In that example the company's revenue is $300, its expense is $200, and its net income or profit is $100. Other expenses that are typically deducted from sales or revenues include salaries, rent, utilities, **depreciation**, and interest expense.

When looking at a company's income statement, it is easy to distinguish between revenues, which appear at the top of the statement, and net income, which appears at the bottom. In other contexts, however, it is easy to confuse the two through improper usage. It is misleading to refer to revenues as income, for a company with revenues of $1 million is much different than a company with net income of $1 million.

Since revenues increase owners' equity in a company, and expenses decrease owners' equity, income can also be defined as the increase in owners' equity due to transactions and other events and circumstances from nonowner sources. If we recognize that income results in an increase in owners' equity, then it becomes clear that income is not the same as a company's cash receipts. For example, a company may increase its cash account by taking a **loan** from a **bank**. Such an increase in cash does not increase owners' equity, though, because there is also an increase in the company's **liability** to the bank.

For personal income tax purposes, gross income is money received by an individual from all sources. Many of the items that the Internal Revenue Code defines as income and that are called income on tax form 1040 are actually revenues, such as dividend income, investment income, and interest income. The Internal Revenue Code also provides for exclusions and exemptions as well as for nontaxable types of income to arrive at the concept of taxable income.

While accountants measure a single company's income for a specific accounting period, economists are concerned with the aggregate income for an entire industry or country. In looking at an entity as a whole, economists define its gross income as the total value of all claims against its output. That is, when goods are produced and services are rendered by the entity, workers, investors, the government, and others have a claim against those goods and services. Workers are paid wages or salaries, investors receive interest payments for their investment, and the government collects **taxes**. The total value of these claims represents the entity's gross income and is equal to the total value added through activities that have contributed to the production of the entity's goods and services.

In looking at the economy as a whole, economists view gross national income as the total of all claims on the **gross national product**. These include employee compensation, rental income, net interest, indirect business taxes, capital consumption allowances, incomes of proprietors and professionals, and corporate profits. National income includes all compensation paid to labor and for productive property that is involved in producing the gross national product. In addition, about 20 percent of national income includes such items as depreciation or capital consumption allowances, indirect business taxes, subsidies less surpluses of government enterprises (such as the U.S. Postal Service), and business transfer payments to employees not on the job.

Personal income includes all payments received by individuals, including wages, transfer payments such as sick pay or vacation pay, and the employer's contribution to Social Security. Personal income differs from national income in two important aspects: (1) some national income is received by entities other than individuals, and (2) some individuals receive personal income from social insurance programs that are not connected with producing the current gross national product.

Disposable personal income is the amount of personal income that remains after an individual's taxes have been paid. It is estimated that approximately 70 percent of the gross national income ends up as disposable personal income. The remaining 30 percent includes such items as depreciation, retained corporate profits, and the government's net tax revenue.

Economists also distinguish between money income and real income. While money income is measured in terms of the number of dollars received, real income is measured by the purchasing power of those dollars. After all, what is important is not how much money you earn, but how much you can buy with that money. Economists use a deflator based on a **price index** for personal goods and services to calculate an individual's real income from his or her money income. Since rising prices reduce the dollar's purchasing power, real income provides a truer measure of buying power than does money income.

SEE ALSO: Accounting; Economics; Income Statement

[David P. Bianco]

FURTHER READING:

Meigs, Robert F., et al. *Accounting: The Basis for Business Decisions.* 11th ed. Boston: Irwin/McGraw-Hill, 1999.

INCOME STATEMENT

An income statement presents a company's revenues and expenses for a given **accounting** period, e.g., a month, quarter, or year. Also called a statement of earnings or a statement of operations, the income statement compares a company's revenues with its expenses during a specific period. The difference between the two is a company's net **income** (or net loss). A company's net **income** for an accounting period is measured as follows:

Net income = Revenues − Expenses + Gains − Losses

The income statement provides information concerning return on investment, **risk**, financial flexibility, and operating capabilities. Return on investment is a measure of a firm's overall performance. Risk is the uncertainty associated with the future of the enterprise. Financial flexibility is the firm's ability to adapt to problems and opportunities. Operating capability relates to the firm's ability to maintain a given level of operations.

The current view of the income statement is that income should reflect all items of profit and loss recognized during the accounting period, except for a few items that would be entered directly under retained earnings on the **balance sheet**, notably prior period adjustments (i.e., correction of errors). The following summary income statement illustrates the generally accepted accounting principles used when preparing these **financial statements**:

Revenues	$1,000,000
Deduct expenses	(400,000)
Gains (losses) that are not extraordinary	(100,000)
Other gains (losses)	20,000
Income from continuing operations	520,000
Gains (losses) from discontinued operations	75,000
Extraordinary gains (losses)	20,000
Cumulative effect of changes in accounting principles	10,000
Net income	$625,000
Pretax earnings per share (2,000 shares)	$3.13

Although income statements measure revenues, expenses, etc. in terms of dollars, these figures do not necessarily correspond to specific amounts of cash a company has. For example, a company most likely does not have the amount of cash corresponding to its net income on an income statement. Instead, this figure represents both the actual cash the company has received as well as promises from customers and clients to pay the company for products and services purchased on **credit**. Nevertheless, companies record revenues when they earn them and expenses when they incur them, not when they actually receive cash. This practice is referred to as the accrual basis of accounting.

ELEMENTS OF INCOME STATEMENTS

The **Financial Accounting Standards Board** (FASB) establishes the definitions of key elements of the income statement, such as revenues, expenses, gains, and losses. Revenues (sales) refer to the total amount of money a business earns by selling its products or by providing its services during a specific period. Revenues also include money earned from **dividends**, interest, and royalties. Expenses refer to the total **costs** a company incurs for doing business in a specific period, such as the cost of materials, supplies, labor, leases, and utilities. In addition, expenses must directly relate to generating revenues for a company. Materials and utilities are obvious expenses, because a company needs both materials and utilities to manufacture and sell products.

Gains are increases in the excess of what a company owns over what it owes (owners' equity) from peripheral or incidental transactions of a business entity and from all other transactions and events affecting the company during the accounting period, except those that result from revenues or investments by owners. Examples are a gain on the sale of a building and a gain on the early retirement of long-term **debt**. Losses are decreases in owners' equity from peripheral or incidental transactions of a business entity and from all other transactions and events affecting the entity during the accounting period, except those that result from expenses or distributions to owners. Examples are losses on the sale of investments and losses from litigation.

Discontinued operations are those operations of an enterprise that have been sold, abandoned, or otherwise disposed. The results of continuing operations must be reported separately in the income statement from discontinued operations. In addition, any gain or loss from the disposal of a segment must be reported along with the operating results of the discontinued separate major line of business or class of customer.

Extraordinary gains or losses are significant events and transactions that are both unusual in nature and infrequent in occurrence. Both of the following criteria must be met for an item to be classified as an extraordinary gain or loss:

- Unusual in Nature: The underlying event or transaction should possess a high degree of abnormality and be clearly unrelated to, or only incidentally related to, the ordinary and typical activities of the business, taking into account the environment in which the business operates.
- Infrequency of Occurrence: The underlying event or transaction should be of a type that would not reasonably be expected to recur in the foreseeable future, taking into account the environment in which the business operates.

Extraordinary items could result if gains or losses were the direct result of any of the following events or circumstances: a major casualty, such as an earthquake; an expropriation of property by a foreign government; and a prohibition under a new act or regulation.

Gains and losses that are not extraordinary refer to significant financial transactions that are unusual or infrequent, but not both. Such items must be disclosed separately above ''income (loss) before extraordinary items.''

An accounting change refers to a change in accounting principle, accounting estimate, or reporting entity. Changes in accounting principles result when an accounting principle is adopted that is different from the one previously used. Changes in estimate involve revisions of estimates, such as the useful lives or residual value of depreciable assets, the loss for bad debts, and **warranty** costs. A change in reporting entity occurs when a company changes its composition from the prior period, as occurs when a new **subsidiary** is acquired.

Net income, or the ''bottom line,'' is the excess of all revenues and gains for a designated period over all expenses and losses of that period. Conversely, net loss is the excess of expenses and losses over revenues and gains for a designated period.

Generally accepted accounting principles—the principles and conventions that govern accounting—require the disclosure of earnings per share amounts on the income statement of all **publicly held companies**. Earnings per share data provides a measure of the enterprise's **management** and past performance and enables users of income statements to evaluate future prospects of the enterprise and assess dividend distributions to shareholders. Disclosure of earnings per share for effects of discontinued operations and extraordinary items is optional, but it is required for income from continuing operations, income before extraordinary items, cumulative effects of a change in accounting principles, and net income.

THE RECOGNITION PRINCIPLE

The revenue recognition principle provides guidelines for reporting revenue in the income statement. The principle generally requires that revenue be recognized in the financial statements when: (1) realized or realizable and (2) earned. Revenues are realized when products or services are exchanged or performed for cash or claims to cash. Revenues also are realizable when a company's things of monetary value (assets), such as products and debts owed to the company, are readily convertible into cash. Revenues are considered earned when a business has substantially accomplished what it must do to be entitled to the benefits represented by the revenues. Recognition through sales or the providing (performance) of services provides a uniform and reasonable test of realization. Limited exceptions to the basic revenue principle include recognizing revenue during production (on long-term construction **contracts**), at the completion of production (for many **commodities**), and subsequent to the sale at the time of cash collection (on installment sales).

In recognizing expenses, accountants rely on the matching principle because it requires that efforts (expenses) be matched with accomplishments (revenues) whenever it is reasonable and practical to do so. For example, matching (associating) the cost of goods sold with revenues from the interrelated sales that resulted directly and jointly from the same transaction as the expense is reasonable and practical. To recognize costs for which it is difficult to adopt some association with revenues, accountants use a rational and systematic allocation policy that assigns expenses to the periods during which the related assets are expected to provide benefits, such as **depreciation**, **amortization**, and insurance. Some costs are charged to the current period as expenses (or losses) merely because no future benefit is anticipated, no connection with revenue is apparent, or no allocation is rational and systematic under the circumstances, i.e., under an immediate recognition principle.

The current operating concept of income includes only those value changes and events that are controllable by management and that are incurred in the current period from ordinary, normal, and recurring operations. Any unusual and nonrecurring items of income or loss would be recognized directly in the statement of retained earnings. Under this concept of income, investors are primarily interested in continuing income from operations.

In the late 1990s, however, the FASB moved closer to adopting all-inclusive or comprehensive income reporting. The all-inclusive concept of income includes the total changes in equity recognized during a specific period, except for dividend distributions and capital transactions. Unlike the previous concept of income, this concept requires companies to include unusual and nonrecurring income or loss items in their income statements for the appropriate accounting period.

CONSOLIDATED INCOME STATEMENTS

Accountants prepare consolidated income statements by combining the revenues, gains, expenses, and losses of a parent company's accounts the accounts of its subsidiary operations. A subsidiary is a company with more than 50 percent of its voting **stock** owned by a parent company. Revenues and expenses that result from transactions between parent and subsidiary companies—intercompany transactions—are not included or are eliminated because they do not affect the assets of the overall company, when viewed as a consolidated operation. Intercompany transactions include sales between parent and subsidiary companies and rent received from or paid by affiliated companies to each other.

FORMATS OF THE INCOME STATEMENT

The income statement can be prepared using either the single-step or the multiple-step format. The single-step format lists and totals all revenue and gain items at the beginning of the statement. All expense and loss items follow the revenue and expense items. Finally, the total expenses and losses are deducted from the total revenues and gains, yielding the net income.

The multiple-step income statement, on the other hand, presents operating revenue at the beginning of the statement and nonoperating gains, expenses, and losses near the end of the statement. Various items of expenses, however, are deducted throughout the statement at intermediate levels, providing useful subtotals along the way. The statement is arranged to show explicitly several important amounts, such as gross margin on sales, operating income, income before **taxes**, and net income. At the first step, the cost of products sold is deducted from the net revenues. At the second step, operating expenses are deducted. At the final step, nonoperating revenues are added and nonoperating expenses are subtracted resulting in the net income. Extraordinary items, gains and losses, accounting changes, and discontinued operations are always shown separately at the bottom of the income statement ahead of net income, regardless of which format is used.

Each format of the income statement has its advantages. The advantage of the multiple-step income statement is that it explicitly displays important financial and managerial information that the user would have to calculate from a single-step income statement. The single-step format has the advantage of being relatively simple to prepare and to understand.

SEE ALSO: Financial Statements

[Charles Woelfel, updated by Karl Heil]

FURTHER READING:

Eisen, Peter J. *Accounting.* 3rd ed. Hauppauge, NY: Barron's Educational Series, 1994.

Financial Accounting Standards Board. *Statements of Financial Accounting Concepts.* Homewood, IL: Irwin, 1986.

Hendriksen, Eldon. S., and M. F. Van Bred. *Accounting Theory.* Homewood, IL: Irwin, 1992.

Label, Wayne A. *10-Minute Guide to Accounting for Non-accountants.* New York: Alpha Books, 1998.

Lueke, Randall W., and David T. Meeting. "How Companies Report Income." *Journal of Accountancy,* May 1998, 45.

Meigs, Robert F., and Walter B. Meigs. *Accounting: The Basis for Business Decisions.* 11th ed. Homewood, IL: Irwin, 1998.

Weiss, Donald. *How to Read Financial Statements.* New York: AMACOM, 1986.

INCUBATORS, BUSINESS

Business incubators are literally what they sound like, a warm nurturing environment for new, small, entrepreneurial businesses to start and grow. Incubators are usually located in older, sometimes abandoned offices or industrial buildings. Incubators give starting businesses inexpensive space to rent, shared office support such as telephone receptionists/secretaries, office services and equipment such as photocopiers, technology support services, financing assistance, and most important, other people who are in the same situation of starting their own businesses. A budding entrepreneur can frequently walk a few steps to someone in the same situation to ask questions and advice. Overall, an incubator program aims to produce businesses that are financially viable and freestanding by the time they leave the incubator, after a typical stay of two to three years.

The stakes are high as studies show that up to 90 percent of new **small businesses** fail within five years of their founding. According to a 1997 study conducted by the Athens, Ohio-based National Business Incubation Association (NBIA), about 87 percent of companies that graduated from an incubator since the 1970s are still in business. Furthermore, during their stay in the incubators, these companies recorded an average sales increase of more than 400 percent.

Incubators are relatively new concepts, born in the late 1950s in Batavia, New York, when the city leaders decided to help businesses without much capital grow into job producers. During the 1980s and 1990s, the concept took off. In 1980 the NBIA reported there were 12 incubators in operation in North America. By 1998 that number had grown to 587.

The concept appears to be most popular in both rural areas, where farmers and other small town residents fill them when not working full time on the farm, and in the inner city. According to the association, 36 percent of North American incubators are in rural areas. Urban-based incubators make up 45 percent of the total while suburbs (to where many of the former urban jobs moved) have just 19 percent.

The ''big'' business community has not yet embraced incubators as a way to build a network of vendors or as a system for developing future new products. Only 8 percent of all incubators have a for-profit company as a sponsor. About 51 percent of all incubators are sponsored by government agencies and nonprofit organizations, sometimes as an effort to boost economic development in an area, or as a means of encouraging those laid off from ''big business'' to go into commerce for themselves. Four-year colleges and universities sponsor 27 percent of the incubators, sometimes aiming to provide faculty with research opportunities or to offer start-up business opportunities to alumni, faculty, and associated groups. Another 16 percent of North American incubators are hybrid facilities, run through joint efforts of government, nonprofit, and/or for-profit organizations. The remaining 5 percent are sponsored by a variety of other entities, such as American Indian tribal governments, church groups, and **chambers of commerce**.

Business incubators shelter as many types of businesses as exist in the cold world outside them. Each incubator, however, is unique in regard to the type of business accepted into its program. A 1998 study conducted by the NBIA found that 43 percent of all incubators accept businesses from a mix of industries; 25 percent specialize in technology companies; 10 percent focus on manufacturing; 9 percent are targeted on helping start-ups from a specific industry, such as biomedicine, the arts, or fashion; 6 percent center on **service industry** firms; and 5 percent are categorized as ''**empowerment**'' incubators, helping to launch women- and/or minority-owned companies.

During 1997, again according to the NBIA, the average incubator served 20 entrepreneurial firms. The association has also estimated that in their relatively short span of existence North American incubators have created nearly 19,000 companies that are still in business and more than 245,000 jobs.

One of the advantages of incubators is that the concept works in all size communities and in urban or rural areas. The incubator takes on the character of the community in which it is located. Rural-based incubators may launch companies based on the agriculture present in the area. For example, an incubator based in the heartland might build its expertise around turning grain and corn into products other than foodstuffs. An urban-based incubator in Miami might draw on the Cuban culture to produce ethnic foods. In both cases, the small business people in the community would know more about how to start and operate such businesses than major corporations that focus on mass production.

SEE ALSO: Entrepreneurship

[Clint Johnson, updated by David E. Salamie]

FURTHER READING:

Buss, Dale. ''Bringing New Firms Out of Their Shell.'' *Nation's Business,* March 1997, 48-50.

Evanson, David R. ''Fertile Ground: Providing Access to Investors Is Just One Way an Incubator Can Help Your Business Take Flight.'' *Entrepreneur,* August 1997, 55-56.

Hayhow, Sally, ed. *A Comprehensive Guide to Business Incubation.* Athens, OH: National Business Incubation Association, 1996.

National Business Incubation Association. ''NBIA: National Business Incubation Association.'' Athens, OH: National Business Incubation Association, 1999. Available from www.nbia.org.

Rice, Mark P., and Jana B. Matthews. *Growing New Ventures, Creating New Jobs: Principles and Practices of Successful Business Incubation.* Westport, CT: Quorum, 1995.

INDEPENDENT CONTRACTORS

Independent contractors, also known as freelance employees, are individuals who work on their own, without a long-term contractual commitment to any one employer. An independent contractor usually performs services or completes work assignments under short-term contracts with several employers, or clients, who have the right to control only the final result of the individual's work, rather than the specific means used to get the work done. Examples of positions held by independent contractors range from doctors and computer programmers to maids and farm workers. Freelance employment can offer a number of advantages to individuals, including flexible work arrangements, independence, variety, and some tax deductions. It can also hold some pitfalls, however, such as assuming risk in business dealings, paying **self-employment** taxes, and taking personal responsibility for **health insurance**, disability, and retirement coverage.

Specifically, individuals who are classified as independent contractors can deduct work-related expenses for tax purposes. In contrast, the first 2 percent of expenses are not deductible for those classified as employees, plus the deduction is phased out above $55,900 in **income**. In addition, independent contractors often qualify for tax deductions for using part of their home as an office and for salaries paid to other people, while employees usually do not. Independent contractors also have the benefit of sheltering 15 percent of their annual income, or up to $30,000, for retirement, while employees are limited to $9,500 annually. Finally, independent contractors must pay the full amount of Social Security and Medicare taxes and make quarterly estimated tax payments to the federal government. Employers must withhold **taxes** for their employees and pay half of their Social Security and Medicare taxes.

Freelance employment boomed in the United States during the 1980s, as many companies sought to reduce their payroll **costs** in order to remain competitive. Instead of hiring new employees and paying an additional 30 percent or more in payroll taxes and benefits, many companies chose to make ''work-for-hire'' arrangements with independent contractors. Businesses, and especially **small businesses**, can gain several advantages from such arrangements. For example, employers are not responsible for paying taxes for independent contractors, and they avoid the high costs of providing health insurance, paid vacation and sick leave, and other benefits often granted to regular, full-time employees. Instead, employers simply file Form 1099 with the government to report the total compensation paid to each independent contractor for the year.

FREELANCE TREND CAUSES CONTROVERSY

The boom in freelance employment led to increased scrutiny by the U.S. **Internal Revenue Service** (IRS) in the early 1990s. Section 1706 of the Internal Revenue Code provides a 20-part test to determine whether workers are employees or independent contractors. The IRS began using this test to reclassify many independent contractors—particularly those engaged in high-paying professions—as employees in order to eliminate tax deductions and increase tax revenues. This practice ''leaves virtually everyone angry, and that includes the IRS,'' according to David Cay Johnston in the *New York Times.* ''The agency is trying to apply tax laws that were largely written for an age of manual work and factories to an era of intellectual labor, often conducted in home offices.'' The IRS would argue that the law also protects individuals from unfair treatment by employers—such as being fired and then rehired as an independent contractor without benefits—but few of the reclassifications have involved exploited low-wage laborers, because they generate minimal tax revenues. Since the issue could potentially affect up to 5 million self-employed Americans, Johnston called it ''the most contentious employment tax issue in the nation today.''

Although the controversy surrounding freelance employment has received increased attention in recent years, it is not new. As early as the 1960s, the IRS started looking more closely at household employees—such as maids, nannies, and gardeners—who often received income ''under the table'' and thus did not pay taxes. The main cause of dissention over current application of the law, according to the *New York Times,* is that it often tends to penalize individuals who wish to be classified as independent contractors and take advantage of tax breaks (as well as the small businesses that depend on them), while it often fails to protect individuals who should be classified as employees and be eligible for benefits. For example, the IRS would be likely to review the case of a highly paid engineer who markets her services to several companies as an independent contractor and deducts various expenses of doing business. But the IRS would be unlikely to review the case of a migrant farm worker who is employed by a large producer but, as an independent contractor, makes less than minimum wage and receives no disability or old-age benefits.

ELEMENTS OF THE IRS TEST

The IRS applies a 20-part test in order to determine whether a certain worker should be classified as an employee or an independent contractor. The main issue underpinning the test is who sets the work rules: employees must follow rules set by their bosses, while independent contractors set their own rules. The hours during which a job is performed is one determination of work rules. For example, if the employer dictates an individual's work hours or pays an individual by the hour rather than by the job, that individual is likely to be considered an employee rather than an independent contractor. Likewise, if the employer requires that an individual work full-time or not be employed by another company simultaneously, that individual would appear to be an employee. On the other hand, an individual who sets his own hours, receives payment by the job, and divides his time between work for several different employers would probably be classified as an independent contractor.

Other criteria involve who provides the tools and materials needed to complete the work. For example, an individual who works at an employer's facility and uses the employer's equipment would be considered an employee, while one who works at a separate location and provides her own equipment would be classified as an independent contractor. Another element of the IRS test involves termination of the work relationship. Employees can usually quit their jobs at will, and can also be fired by their employers. An independent contractor, however, would have a contractual obligation to complete a specific amount of work for an employer, and neither party could break the agreement without cause. Finally, an independent contractor usually pays his own expenses of doing business and takes the risk of not receiving payment when work is not completed in accordance with a contract, while an employee is usually reimbursed for business-related expenses by the employer and receives a paycheck whether his work is completed or not.

Despite such specific guidelines, the IRS test has generated criticism. ''This 20-factor test has frustrated both the IRS and the small-business owner,'' said an accountant quoted in *Crain's Small Business Detroit.* ''Ten different revenue agents could review the same case, and ten different responses could result.'' The IRS recognized that the test was sometimes applied inconsistently, and was evaluating whether to modify or eliminate it. But while a 1998 *U.S. News and World Report* article noted that the agency has ''mellowed in the last couple of years (legislative pressure helped),'' the IRS still tries to reclassify certain independent contractors as employees because of the potential gains in tax revenue. Reclassification can cost businesses that rely on independent contractors huge sums in penalties, back taxes, and interest—and can even force some out of business.

INDEPENDENT CONTRACTORS AND SMALL BUSINESSES

The rules governing independent contractors affect small businesses in two significant ways. First, many entrepreneurs are themselves independent contractors, and they must understand and adhere to the IRS guidelines in offering services to clients. Otherwise, they risk being reclassified by the IRS. An entrepreneur who is reclassified as an employee of a major client loses a variety of tax breaks and other advantages of self-employment.

In order to be considered independent contractors, entrepreneurs must establish that they are in business for themselves for the purpose of making a profit. They might demonstrate that their enterprise is a business—rather than a hobby or the work of an employee—by registering a business name, obtaining an occupational permit or license, establishing an office, soliciting clients, and printing stationery and business cards. Even if the majority of work will be performed for one client, entrepreneurs should make clear their intention of soliciting work from other clients.

Next, the entrepreneur should subject his or her business activities to the IRS 20-step test in order to avoid the appearance of being an employee. For example, the entrepreneur should be certain that the client does not set his or her hours, determine the location where work is performed, pay withholding taxes on his or her income, or provide needed equipment, tools, supplies, or transportation. Instead, the entrepreneur should sign a contract specifying an amount of work that will be completed by a certain deadline. The contract should include a specific disclaimer stating that this work will be performed as an independent contractor. For tax purposes, the entrepreneur should also be certain to obtain from the client a 1099 form (a statement of miscellaneous income), rather than a W-2 form (a statement of income from employment).

The rules governing independent contractors affect small businesses in another significant way. Many small businesses lack the resources to hire permanent employees to provide support for short-term projects or to provide expertise in highly technical fields, so instead they enlist the services of independent contractors. In these cases, it is to the benefit of the small business owner as well as the independent contractor to spell out the details of the work arrangement in a contract. Small business owners should also choose independent contractors carefully to be sure that they present themselves as in business to make a profit.

[Laurie Collier Hillstrom]

FURTHER READING:

Brodsky, Ruthan, and Marsha Stopa. ''Sneak a Tax.'' *Crain's Small Business Detroit,* July 1994, 1.

Hand, Larry E. *Freelancing Made Simple.* New York: Doubleday, 1995.

Internal Revenue Service. ''Employee vs. Independent Contractor'' (IRS publication no. 937). Washington: Internal Revenue Service, 1994. Available from www.irs.ustreas.gov.

Internal Revenue Service. ''Tax Guide for Small Business'' (IRS publication no. 334). Washington: Internal Revenue Service, 1998. Available from www.irs.ustreas.gov.

Johnston, David Cay. "Are You Your Own Boss? Only if the IRS Says So." *New York Times,* 19 March 1995, F13.

King, Julia. "Independent Contractors an Endangered Species." *Computerworld,* 27 January 1997, 63.

Laurance, Robert. *Going Freelance: A Guide for Professionals.* New York: Wiley, 1988.

Saunders, Laura. "Attention, Income Hiders." *Forbes,* 2 March 1992, 64.

Spragins, Ellyn E. "Protecting Independent Contractor Status." *Inc.,* March 1992, 98.

Szabo, Joan C. "Contract Workers: A Risky Business." *Nation's Business,* August 1993, 20.

Wiener, Leonard. "Sure You're Hired—On a Contract Basis." *U.S. News and World Report,* 26 October 1998, 68.

INDEX/INDEXES

Various kinds of indexes or index numbers are used by the scientific and academic communities, and the popular media. In fact, some indexes are so commonly used that one does not even recognize that they are *index* numbers, not absolute values of the variable or the item of interest. Changes in stock prices associated with several **stock markets**, for example, are quoted in terms of index numbers. Thus, when the media reports that the Dow fell by 200 points on a particular day, the reference is to the fall in the value of the index representing 30 industrial stocks included in the Dow Jones Industrial Average index, sometimes called the Dow 30. Suppose that the Dow Jones Industrial Average was at the 8,000 mark before it fell by 200 points. This implies that the average price of the 30 stocks included in the Dow index fell by 2.5 percent in one day ([200/8,000]*100 = 2.5 percent). In order to understand index numbers, it is useful to have some idea of the methods of constructing indexes, and to be able to relate these methods to some common examples of index numbers.

THE WIDESPREAD USE OF INDEXES IN BUSINESS AND ECONOMICS

A wide variety of sources generate the various indexes in the fields of business and economics. Many government agencies in the United States regularly produce information in index number form on a variety of variables. The Bureau of Labor Statistics under the U.S. Department of Labor reports data on various price indexes that are used to measure the inflation rate in the economy. The **U.S. Department of Commerce** also reports economic data on a regular basis. In addition to government sources, economic data are also reported (many of them in index number form) by private sources and by partisan and nonpartisan research organizations. Most business-related indexes can be categorized within two broad categories—those associated with the financial markets and those that describe the state of the economy.

INDEXES ASSOCIATED WITH THE FINANCIAL MARKETS. There are many indexes associated with financial markets. These indexes measure different attributes of the financial markets at various degrees of depth and rigor. The majority of them track two major components of the financial markets: stock markets and bond markets.

Several index numbers measure the changes in stock prices at different levels of aggregation (that is, with respect to the number of stocks included in an index). The Dow Jones Industrial Average (DJIA), an index of 30 industrial stocks, is one of the most commonly followed stock price indexes. The DJIA includes major U.S. industrial stocks (such as Coca-Cola, IBM, General Motors, du Pont, Eastman Kodak, Disney, Sears, Goodyear, Merck, and AT&T) listed on the New York Stock Exchange (NYSE). There are also index numbers that represent stock price changes at a particular stock exchange or a stock-trading network. Thus, pertaining to the three trading mediums NYSE based in New York, the American Stock Exchange also based in New York (AMEX), and the computer-linked stock trading network of the National Securities Dealers Association (NASDAQ)—there are separate indexes called NYSE, AMEX, and NASDAQ, respectively. In addition to these so-called exchange-based indexes, there are several other stock price indexes that include an increasing number of stocks. For example, the S&P100 index, maintained by Standard & Poor's, measures stock price movements of 100 important stocks. Similarly, the S&P500 index measures the change in the aggregate price level of 500 selected stocks. The Wilshire 5000 index measures the change in the aggregate price level of the 5,000 stocks it monitors—a large number of stocks are included in this index to give a better picture of the overall stock market, rather than a narrow group of stocks.

By contrast, the bond market has far fewer indexes. The most widely used bond price index is the Lehman Brothers' bond price index; it measures changes in prices of long-term bonds included in the index. Changes in bond prices convey information regarding changes in interest rates. Thus, the bond price index is also closely watched by financial market participants.

INDEXES ASSOCIATED WITH THE ECONOMY. Information and data on a large number of economic variables are regularly reported. Some of these data are reported in index number form. All price data in the economy are reported in index number form—as will be explained later, this is out of necessity, rather than choice. Three major price indexes are: **Con-**

sumer Price Index, Producer Price Index, and Implicit Gross Domestic Product Price Deflator. Similarly, the Federal Reserve Bank computes the Index of Industrial Production on a monthly basis to gauge the pace of industrial production.

Other regularly reported indexes that describe the state of the economy (current or future) include: Index of Leading Indicators (LEI), which indicates the pace of economic activity in the economy in the near future; Consumer Confidence Index, which captures consumer sentiment and thus suggests consumers' willingness to spend; the Housing Affordability Index, which tracks the cost of being able to afford a home. Some indexes are not reported regularly, but occasionally crop up. For example, George Bush during his reelection campaign kept referring to the Misery Index, which captures the combined effects of inflation and unemployment.

THE NEED FOR AN INDEX. Most economic variables are measured in absolute terms. For example, 12 million cars were produced in 1994 in the United States, or the gross output of goods and services in the United States was estimated at $8.7 trillion during 1998. It is not possible, however, to measure the price associated with a group of commodities in absolute terms; it can only be done so long as we refer to one commodity. We thus can say that the average price of a loaf of bread in the United States was $1.75 in 1998. But when dealing with a number of commodities together (as in the calculation of an individual's cost of living from year-to-year, one cannot simply compute the average price of all the goods and services bought in each year. Since most people buy a different set of commodities each year, the resulting averages would not be comparable. An index helps us out of this quandary. In the most basic terms, an index usually attaches weights to the prices of items in order to track the resulting collective price movement.

TYPES OF INDEX MEASUREMENTS

All indexes in the business and economics fields can be broadly placed in two categories: **price indexes** and quantity indexes. Price indexes measure changes in prices of a set of commodities, while quantity indexes measure changes in quantities of a set of commodities. Most common index numbers are price indexes, such as the Dow Jones Industrial Average and the Consumer Price Index.

CONSTRUCTION OF AGGREGATE PRICE INDEXES

In its simplest form, a price index may be used to monitor changes in the price of one commodity over time—the price index shows how the current price of a given commodity compares with its price in a chosen base year (and in any other year in the past). Consider the example shown below from *Statistics for Business and Economics,* in which the price per gallon of unleaded gasoline is given for a nine-year period from 1982 to 1990:

Year	Price per Gallon of Gasoline ($)
1982	1.30
1983	1.24
1984	1.21
1985	1.20
1986	0.93
1987	0.95
1988	0.95
1989	1.02
1990	1.16

To understand the changes in the gasoline price over the nine-year period, simple index numbers, called price relatives, are calculated. In this example, 1982 is considered the base period from which the price relatives will be calculated. A price relative for any particular year is then the price in that period divided by the base period price times 100. Thus, for 1982, the price relative is 100 ([1.30/1.30] * 100 = 100). For year 1983, the price relative is equal to 95 ([1.24/1.30] * 100 = 95). Thus, using simple price relatives, a series of price indexes for unleaded gasoline can be calculated as shown in the next table.

Year	Price Relative (Base Period = 1982)
1982	100
1983	95
1984	93
1985	92
1986	72
1987	73
1988	73
1989	78
1990	89

From this series of indexes, meaningful information about changes in the price of unleaded gasoline can be obtained. For example, between 1986 and 1990, the price relative for unleaded gasoline increased from 72 to 89. This suggests that gasoline prices increased by roughly 23.6 percent ({[89-72]/72} * 100 = 23.6) during that period. Similarly, one can examine year-to-year changes in the price of gasoline, as well as compute price changes between any two years (or periods), using such a price relative series. Price relatives are very helpful in understanding changing economic and business conditions over time. They also form the basis for understanding the idea of index numbers.

AGGREGATE PRICE INDEXES. Price relatives can only be used for individual items. In the real world, we are often concerned with the price change for a group of items taken together. For example, the DJIA uses a group of stocks to indicate the change in the average price of those stocks. Similarly, if we want an index that measures changes in the overall cost of living over time, we have to use a group of commodities (e.g., goods and services—food, clothing, medical care, etc.) that are bought by the individuals whose cost of living is being measured. In these instances, an aggregate price index is computed for the specific purpose of measuring the combined change in the prices of a group of items.

To illustrate the development of an aggregate **price index** for a group of items, one can consider the example of tracking changes in normal automotive operating expenses. For the sake of simplicity, only four items—gasoline, oil, tire, and insurance expenses—are included in the this example from *Statistics for Business and Economics.* Table 1 shows expense data in these categories for two years (1982 and 1996).

Table 1

Automotive Operating Expenses ($)

Item	1982	1996
Gasoline per gallon	1.30	1.23
Oil per quart	1.50	2.20
Tires	80.00	145.00
Insurance policy	300.00	700.00

Using 1982 as the base, an aggregate price index for automotive operative expenses can be calculated that will measure the change in operating expenses between 1982 and 1996. The simplest way of calculating an aggregate price index is to calculate an unweighted aggregate index. An unweighted aggregate index is found by simply summing the unit prices in the period of interest and then dividing the resulting amount by the sum of the unit prices in the base period. The ratio of the two sums is also multiplied by 100, a tradition followed in index number construction. Since in the present example 1996 expenses are being compared with the 1982 base, the unweighted price index for 1990 is equal to 249 ({[1.23 + 2.20 + 145.00 + 700.00]/[1.30 + 1.50 + 80.00 + 300.00]} * 100 = 222). Based on the calculated unweighted price index number for 1996, the price of normal automotive operating expenses increased by 122 percent between 1982 and 1996.

It can easily be seen that the unweighted aggregate index attaches the same weights to large per-unit price items in the group (such as insurance policy) and small per-unit price items (such as a gallon of gasoline). As a consequence, an unweighted aggregate price index is heavily influenced by items that have high per-unit price. This will be the case even if a large per-unit price item does not play a big role when one looks at the overall picture. In the present example, automotive operative expenses are too heavily influenced by price changes in tires and insurance coverage. It is because of the sensitivity of an unweighted aggregate price index to high-priced items that this measure of index is seldom used. A weighted aggregate price index corrects for the distortions caused by the unweighted aggregate price index.

WEIGHTED AGGREGATE PRICE INDEX. The weighted aggregate price index improves on its unweighted counterpart by assigning a weight to each item in the group, in accordance with its importance in the overall group. In most instances, quantities of items used are employed as weights, as the quantity of usage provides the best indication of its importance in the group. To illustrate the construction of the weighted aggregate price index for the normal automotive operating expenses example, Table 2 provides data on annual usage of the four expense items. The weights provided are based on the assumption that a typical owner of a midsize automobile drives approximately 15,000 miles per year.

Table 2

Annual Usage Information

Item	Quantity Weights
Gasoline per gallon	1000
Oil per quart	15
Tires	2
Insurance policy	1

The weighted aggregate price index is calculated in the same manner as unweighted aggregate price index, except that the unit price of a product is multiplied by its appropriate weight before the unit prices are summed up. The weighted aggregate price index for 1990 for the automotive expenses example is thus equal to 127 ({[(1.23 * 1000) + (2.20 * 15) + (145.00 * 2) + (700.00 * 1)]/[(1.30 * 1000) + (1.50 * 15) + (80.00 * 2) + (300.00 * 1)]} * 100 = 126). Based on this value, the price of automotive operating expenses increased by 26 percent between 1982 and 1996.

One can easily see that a weighted aggregate price index can yield a vastly different result than one that is unweighted. In the example, a 122-percent unweighted increase became a 26-percent weighted increase. The weighted aggregate price index provides a more accurate estimate of the magnitude of the price change for the group as a whole. While gasoline cost only $1.23 per gallon in 1996, a typical automotive operation involved 1,000 gallons of gasoline, resulting in a total expenditure of $1,230 on gasoline—much more than the $700 spent on automotive insurance. While the unweighted aggregate price index does not capture this effect, the weighted one does. As a general rule, quantities of usage are widely used as weights in constructing weighted aggregate price indexes for groups of items.

IMPORTANT ECONOMY-WIDE PRICE INDEXES

Price indexes are used to measure the rate of **inflation** in the economy. There are three key price indexes that are routinely calculated and reported to the public by government sources in the United States. These three measures differ with respect to the number of items they take into account.

The inflation rate is derived by calculating the rate of change in a price index. The number of items included in a price index vary depending on the objective of the index. Usually three kinds of price indexes are periodically reported by government sources. They all have particular advantages and uses. The first index is called the consumer price index (CPI), which measures the average retail prices paid by consumers for goods and services bought by them. Several thousand products, grouped into 207 sets of items, are included in this index. These items are selected on the basis of their inclusion in the budget of a consumer (household). Each of the product prices is assigned a weight based on the importance of the item in the household budget. As a result, the CPI reflects the changes in the cost of living of a typical urban household. The CPI is considered the most relevant inflation measure from the point of view of the consumers, as it measures the prices of goods and services that are part of household budgets. Nevertheless, the CPI does not precisely measure the changes in the cost of living for every consumer because of differences in consumption patterns.

A second price index used to measure the inflation rate is called the producer price index (PPI). It is a much broader measure than the CPI. The PPI measures the wholesale prices of approximately 3,000 items. The items included in this index are those that are typically used by producers (manufacturers and businesses) and thus contain many raw materials and semi-finished goods. A change in the PPI reflects a change in the cost of production, incurred by producers. Since producers may pass a part or all of the increase in the cost of production to consumers, movements in the PPI indicate future movements in the CPI. The PPI can thus forewarn consumers of coming increases in the cost of living.

The **implicit price deflator** is the third measure of inflation. This index measures the prices of all goods and services included in the calculation of the current output of goods and services in the economy, known as **gross domestic product** (GDP). The implicit price deflator is the broadest measure of the price level. This index includes prices of fighter bombers purchased by the U.S. Department of Defense as well as paper clips used in offices. Thus, the implicit price deflator is a measure of the overall or aggregate price level for the economy. Movements in this index reflect the inflationary tendency of the overall economy.

The three measures of the inflation rate are most likely to move in the same direction, though not to the same extent. Differences can arise due to the differing number of goods and services included for the purpose of compiling the three indexes.

CALCULATIONS OF THE CONSUMER PRICE INDEX AND THE INFLATION RATE

The construction of the **consumer price index** employs an index number technique, in which a fixed basket of commodities (a collection of goods and services considered relevant to the index) is valued using prices at different points of time. First, a point of reference or base is selected. Normally, a particular year is selected as the base. Currently, however, the 1982-84 period is used as the base in construction of the CPI in the United States. So, the average price of a commodity over the three-year period is used as the base price for the commodity for comparing to other periods. The price of each item in the basket of commodities selected is attached a weight in accordance with its importance in the budget of a typical urban family. In other words, the government must first identify the goods and services that are used by a typical urban consumer. Then, it must assign a weight to each of the items in the fixed basket—the basket thus contains a collection of goods and services in quantities that, presumably, a representative consumer consumes. Next, the government evaluates the fixed basket of commodities using prices at successive points and compares its costs (or values) with the cost to buy the same basket in the base year or period. This process generates a series of price ratios, which are usually multiplied by 100 for convenience. Thus, the price index is 100 in the base year or period, which the price index for other points of time reflect movements in the price level, which can be used to calculate the inflation rate between any two points.

With 1982-84 as the base, the consumer price index stood at 161.3 at the end of 1997, and at 163.9 at the end of 1998. The latter two values of the CPI imply that the cost of the fixed basket of commodities, compared to the base, had gone up by 61.3 percent by the end of 1997, and by 63.9 percent by the end of 1998. They also imply that the inflation rate during

1998 was roughly 1.6 percent on an annual basis (inflation rate = {(163.9 - 161.3)/161.3} * 100).

ITEMS INCLUDED IN THE CONSUMER PRICE INDEX. The consumer price index is calculated by the U.S. Bureau of Labor Statistics (BLS), and it is published on a monthly basis. The broad categories of items that are included in construction of the CPI are: food and beverages, housing, apparel and upkeep, transportation, medical care, entertainment, and other goods and services. In reality, however, the CPI is based on several thousand products that are grouped into 207 sets of items. BLS employees visit thousands of stores in 85 geographical areas every month and collect more than 100,000 prices. Then, the average prices of related items, say, poultry and honey, are combined to yield group indexes—in this particular case, food and beverages. Next, the group indexes are combined to yield the overall price index called the ''all-items CPI.''

USEFULNESS OF THE CONSUMER PRICE INDEX. The consumer price index is widely used, both in the private and public sectors. The CPI is most commonly used in calculating the inflation rate for general purposes. The movement in the consumer price index reflects the changes in the cost of living for urban consumers. **Labor unions** often use the CPI in bargaining for wage increases. Also, most government **pensions**, including the level of Social Security benefits, are indexed to the CPI.

CALCULATIONS OF THE PRODUCER PRICE INDEX AND THE INFLATION RATE

The producer price index is also published by the U.S. Bureau of Labor Statistics (BLS) on a monthly basis. For the PPI, the BLS collects prices on more than 3,000 commodities that are purchased by businesses, not directly by consumers. In a simplified form, the producer price index can be thought of as having the following broad categories: (1) finished goods; (2) intermediate materials, supplies, and components; and (3) crude materials for further processing. Each of these broad categories is further subdivided in smaller groups. For example, the finished goods category consists of foods, energy, and finished goods excluding food and energy (the last subcategory includes capital equipment).

The producer price index uses an index number construction methodology similar to the consumer price index. While in case of the CPI the price data are directly collected by the BLS workers, the actual prices for the PPI are obtained from questionnaires mailed to thousands of firms that sell the products included in the PPI.

Currently, 1982 is used as the base for the producer price index series. The interpretation of the PPI series is similar to the CPI series—the PPI can also be used to calculate the inflation rate.

USEFULNESS OF THE PRODUCER PRICE INDEX. One should recognize that the producer price index serves as an index relevant to the producers' cost. In other words, the PPI reflects what is happening to the cost of production. If the cost of production is rising, however, producers may also increase the prices at which they sell. This, in turn, is likely to increase the retail prices that consumers pay in stores across the nation. The PPI, thus, has an important information function—it forewarns coming changes in the consumer price index.

CALCULATIONS OF THE IMPLICIT PRICE DEFLATOR AND THE INFLATION RATE

The implicit price deflator is arrived at in an indirect—or implicit—manner. Calculation of the consumer price index and the producer price index are explicit or direct; indexes are calculated from price data on the items included. The implicit price deflator, on the other hand, is inferred indirectly from the estimates of gross domestic product in nominal terms (in current dollars) and in real terms (when the nominal value of the GDP is adjusted for inflation by reevaluating it in prices that prevailed during a chosen base year).

Currently, 1992 is being used as the base year to calculate the real value of gross domestic product in the United States. Thus, the 1998 U.S. output of goods and services is first evaluated at prices prevailing in 1998. Once this is done, 1998 output of goods and services is also evaluated at prices that prevailed in 1992 (thus, the terms gross domestic product in 1992 dollars or constant dollars). One can easily see how the ratio of gross domestic product in 1998 prices and gross domestic product in 1992 prices would yield a measure of the extent of the rise in price level between 1992 and 1998. According to the federal government statistics, this ratio is estimated at 1.1307, or 113.07 when multiplied by 100 (as is customarily done to determine the extent of price increase more conveniently). The value of implicit price deflator of 113.07 implies that the price level increased by 13.07 percent over the 1992-1998 period (note that the base year, currently 1992, value of implicit price deflator is equal to 100).

This method of expressing nominal or current gross domestic product into its value in 1992 prices is routinely done every year (of course, sometimes the base year itself, may be changed to a later year to keep the data series closer to the current period). Thus, we have 1997, 1996, 1995 (and so on) gross domestic products expressed in 1992 prices. This helps to calculate the inflation rate between subsequent years. For example, the implicit price deflator stood at 112.08 at the end of 1997. Given that the deflator was at 113.07 at the end of 1998, we arrive at the annual inflation rate of roughly 0.88 percent during 1998 (1998 inflation rate = [(113.07 - 112.08) / 112.08] * 100).

Since the implicit price deflator is derived from the nominal and real values of the gross domestic product (GDP), it is also called implicit GDP price deflator. One should also notice that the term *deflator* is not used in consumer and producer price indexes. This is because, if one knows the implicit price deflator for 1998, and the 1998 gross domestic product in current prices, one could arrive at the gross domestic product in 1992 prices by deflating the 1998 gross domestic product in current prices by the deflator for 1998 (expressed in plain ratio form, rather than the one multiplied by 100). Despite the use of term deflator, one should not lose sight of the fact the implicit price deflator is essentially a price index.

USEFULNESS OF THE IMPLICIT GDP PRICE DEFLATOR. As noted, the implicit price index is the broadest measure of price level. Although changes in it reflect the inflation pressure underlying the whole economy, since this index is all-inclusive, it may not be directly useful to ordinary households and even businesses. The CPI and PPI are more relevant to these units.

USEFULNESS OF THE THREE PRICE INDEXES

As mentioned earlier, all three price indexes can be used to calculate the inflation rate. There are, however, two important differences among these indexes. First, the consumer and producer price indexes are published every month, whereas the implicit GDP price deflator figures are reported on a quarterly basis. Thus, more frequent users of inflation data would be inclined to use the CPI or the PPI. Second, coverage of the three indexes varies dramatically. Thus, one of these price index series can be more suitable than the other two in particular cases. To measure the cost of living of an urban consumer, for example, the CPI will be overwhelmingly preferred to the PPI and the implicit GDP price deflator. Nevertheless, one must be aware that even the CPI is an average price measure that is based on certain weights. While the CPI may reflect the cost of living changes of consumers on average, it cannot precisely reflect changes in the actual cost of living of a particular consumer; his or her consumption pattern may be quite different from that assumed in assigning weights to the fixed basket of commodities. One thus needs to interpret the price index numbers carefully.

Despite the slight caution one must exercise in interpreting the price indexes, a good understanding of the inflation rate, that all three price indexes are designed to yield, is important for every individual and household. Most economies face positive rates of inflation year after year. If the inflation rate is positive and an individual's income remains constant, his or her real standard of living will fall as the individual's income will be worth less and less in successive periods. Let us assume that a household earns $50,000 per year and the income remains fixed at this level in the future. If the inflation rate persists at 10 percent per year, the purchasing power of the household income will also keep declining at the rate of 10 percent per year. At the end of the five-year period, prices will be one and a half times greater. This will lead to the household being able to buy only two-thirds of the goods and services it was able to buy at the beginning of the period.

An understanding of inflation is also crucial in making plans to save for retirement, children's education, or even a luxury purchase. One must use an appropriate price index in calculating the funds required for a given purpose. The consumer price index is a good guide for retirement purposes. If one is saving to buy a boat, however, even the CPI may not produce a good result—the individual may want to know the way boat prices are increasing. Nevertheless, an understanding of the price indexes prepares an individual to explore such scenarios further.

QUANTITY INDEXES

Another use of index numbers, in addition to measuring changes in prices, is to measure changes in quantity levels over time. This type of index is called a quantity index. In discussing price indexes, emphasis was placed on the weighted aggregate price index as an index number methodology of choice. A set of weights are also used to compute quantity indexes. The weighted aggregate quantity index is computed essentially in a manner similar to that for a weighted aggregate price index. As a weighted aggregate quantity index seeks to measure changes in quantities, it obviously cannot use quantity usage as weights. Analogous to weighted aggregate price indexes, the weighted aggregate quantity index uses fixed price weights—that is, quantities are weighted by associated prices. Except for the weights used, construction of price and quantity indexes employs the same index number methodology.

A well-known example of the quantity indexes is the Index of Industrial Production (IIP), developed by the central bank of the United States (the **Federal Reserve** Bank). This index is designed to measure changes in production levels for a variety of items in the manufacturing, mining, and utilities sectors. In general terms, the IIP Production is used to monitor the pace of economic activity in the industrial sector, considered to be the core sector of the U.S. economy. This index is reported on a monthly basis and it uses

1992 as the base year. Since the GDP, a comprehensive measure of economic activity in the United States, is reported only on a quarterly basis, the IIP provides more frequent measures of changes in production levels in the economy.

SEE ALSO: Consumer Price Index (CPI); Price Indexes

[Anandi P. Sahu, Ph.D.]

FURTHER READING:

Anderson, David R., Dennis J. Sweeney, and Thomas A. Williams. *Statistics for Business and Economics.* 7th ed. St. Paul, MN: West Publishing Company, 1999.

Froyen, Richard T. *Macroeconomics: Theories and Policies.* 6th ed. Upper Saddle River, NJ: Prentice Hall, 1998.

Gordon, Robert J. *Macroeconomics.* 7th ed. Reading, PA: Addison-Wesley, 1998.

Sommers, Albert T. *The U.S. Economy Demystified.* Lexington, MA: Lexington Books, 1985.

INDIA, DOING BUSINESS IN

India is the world's largest democracy and is rapidly becoming one of the most attractive developing nations for doing business. This attractive business environment came about largely because of political and economic reforms that provide foreign investors with incentives for doing business in India. India brought about major economic reforms in the early 1990s, making it possible for business firms located outside India to make **direct investments** in the Indian marketplace. Due to these reforms, U.S. firms and businesses from other countries have taken advantage of the opportunities there; today the United States is currently the largest foreign investor in India. And while opportunities for doing business in India have led to many success stories, particularly from many large U.S. multinational business organizations, there remain numerous challenges in doing business effectively with India. To understand these challenges and to learn how to effectively do business in India, it is important first to learn how Indian firms and their managers conduct business. Business, as practiced in India, provides a useful model for Western business organizations planning to enter the Indian marketplace.

In contrast to many Western transnational corporations with high technology capabilities and proprietary product systems, many Asian Indian managers rely extensively upon long-term relationship building in their international business encounters. Indian business styles are based upon long-term, vis-à-vis short-term, priorities in the context of several cultural and functional dimensions. This knowledge should be useful to Western businesses in the development of strategies for India, or for researchers interested in learning more about the way business is conducted in India. To describe the Indian business approach, several organizational dimensions are included to provide an understanding of these issues.

ORGANIZATIONAL DIMENSIONS

POWER DISTANCE. According to Geert Hofstede, organizations can be defined as "high power distance" instances when less powerful members *accept* a standard of unequally distributed power and believe that their superiors make sound leadership decisions due, in large part, to the superior's position of power. In contrast, subordinates in low power distance organizations attribute high quality decisions to leadership skills, rather than positions of power. India is a high power distance society. Due to the vertical structure in most Indian business organizations, someone from the United States working in an Indian business environment will need to be willing to accept authority in a more complete sense than he or she is perhaps accustomed to.

INDIVIDUALISM-COLLECTIVISM. Collectivist organizations nurture group interdependence; in turn the organization has a greater responsibility for its individual members. Collectivist persons give primary attention to the needs of their group and are willing to sacrifice opportunities for personal gain, since their sense of self is an extension of the group. Conversely, individualistic employees see themselves primarily as engineers, managers, professors, etc., and secondarily as group members of specific organizations or institutions. Persons from individualistic cultures pay more attention to their own needs, taking advantage of opportunities for personal gain or enrichment.

An interesting business phenomenon takes place in India. As one doing business in India quickly learns, independence is welcome in carrying out one's assignments, but at the same time supervisors are looked up to and respected for their managerial wisdom (high power distance). An interesting collectivist value in India, as well as most of Asia, is that of "filial piety." This value relates to the obedience to, respect for, and financial support of parents, and the honoring of ancestors as a collectivist value system. In India, according to Sunil H. Rathi, director for Rathi Dye Chem Ltd., "elderly people are very respected. We look to them for advice because they are people who have experienced life and they have more wisdom. An 80-year-old person will have greater wisdom because he has lived a long, practical life. So for them I touch their feet when I greet them," (from an interview with Rathi).

Filial piety within many of India's industries is shown, in large part, in an entrepreneurial spirit, including a group of companies founded by the former J.R.D. Tata—synonymous with India's very best.

While outside investors are often welcome, Indian families retain financial and administrative control. In India, society revolves around the entire family rather than an individual's personal priorities. This carries over into the business setting. Top management positions are reserved for family members, although this is changing somewhat, particularly within the ranks of middle management. Still, the family remains very strong in the entrepreneurial functions and investment areas.

LANGUAGE AND SOCIOLINGUISTICS. Due to the long-term colonization of India, the British Raj cultural traits remain strong to this day. While many languages and multiple dialects are spoken in India, the language of international business is English. While English is the language of industry and large business, it is mixed with Hindi and state dialects, creating somewhat different connotations from British or American English. Thus, miscommunication can occur even between those sharing the same language. The sharing of the same native language is not necessarily sufficient for effective interpretation of business documents.

Beyond simple language differences, paralinguistic meaning can also vary significantly from culture to culture. Speakers of Indian English, for example, routinely increase their voice volume for recognition purposes in business negotiations and other encounters; this paralinguistic behavior can be misinterpreted by standard British or American English negotiators as an expression of anger. In addition to paralinguistics, other nonverbal behavior can also be understood differently.

Nonverbal management symbols relate, for example, to power relationships such as seating patterns at management meetings, body posture, dress, and personal greetings. In India, *namaste* is a greeting of choice (with hands together as if in prayer and just under the chin). This greeting is appreciated, particularly when a visiting Western businessperson greets a woman in India. Also, respect to elders is shown through the custom of touching of feet and at the same time looking into their eyes. Indian nonverbal responses often vary significantly from other country's norms. For example, moving the head sideways in the United States denotes a negative response; in India, a sideways movement of the head carries a positive connotation of understanding. And while nonverbal cues should be supportive of parallel verbal messages, this is not always the case, as conflicting verbal and nonverbal signals are commonplace.

MARKETING AND POLITICAL CHALLENGES. While worldwide tastes are becoming more standardized, demand is coming from a more diverse marketplace. For example, in India there are approximately 250 million middle-class people with various Western tastes in the selection of products and services. The Indian middle-class culture, however, is still very much Eastern and also differs from other classes within India. This poses complex **marketing** challenges for business organizations planning initiatives within India's expanding marketplace.

Political events in India have an impact on all business. As mentioned earlier, a more relaxed investment climate has developed in India, changing the rules for foreign direct investment in the country. With support from the prime minister and legislative bodies, investment by foreigners in India is now encouraged. There is a sense of excitement in the Indian financial and industrial communities as transnational organizations enter into Indian **joint ventures**. Political challenges, however, remain real and strong. According to Mohan R. Limaye, writing in *Business Horizons,* American companies need to be aware of the complexities of the Indian political environment including India's multiparty democracy, the growing power of India's states vis-à-vis the federal government, and a growing Indian political nationalism.

TIME CONSIDERATIONS. In India, most **management** persons are time-conscious, meaning that they regulate their business life according to the clock. Many Indian managers tend to follow a linear time frame as is the practice in much of Western Europe or the United States. That is, businesspeople are expected to be punctual for appointments and it is mandatory for workers to arrive on time for work. It can also be noted, however, that trains run on a more flexible schedule and are routinely late. This is important to keep in mind when scheduling appointments; extra time needs to be scheduled to reach business destinations on time. Social contacts can differ from business protocol in relation to time; flexible behavior is much more the norm in social settings.

NEGOTIATIONS. Successful negotiations are customer oriented in India and follow a long-term communication strategy. When negotiating in Japan, for instance, Indian executives and managers approach business negotiations according to the Japanese communication style; the Indian negotiator presents the proposal in such a way that the Japanese counterparts will be attracted to doing business. Dr. Ramchandra Rathi, managing director of Sudarshan Chemical Industries, Ltd., stated that to accomplish their business objectives, there must first be an understanding of the Japanese culture and then a plan to adjust the negotiating strategy accordingly (in a conversation with the author). In labor **contracts**, which are generally for three-year periods in India, one rarely refers to the contract prior to the negotiations, as trust between the parties is developed first.

ACADEMIC AND GOVERNMENT COLLABORATIONS. Currently in India there are relatively few developed collaborations between academic institutions and business practitioners. **Consultants** are utilized in professional management areas such as legal matters, technology, and marketing. The Indian government offers grants to do so, thus it is profitable to use consultants under grant arrangements. When grants are not available, few Indian companies take advantage of consultants, since they are not viewed as being cost effective.

India is a very bureaucratic country and everything is monitored by government. **Banking** is nationalized in India as well. Better financing is available through the banking system in India than is normally found in the United States, as Indian banks provide credit of up to 75 percent on inventory **loans** against **export** orders.

QUALITY ASSURANCE. Sudarshan L. Rathi, managing director of Sun Engichem Ltd., believes his charge at all times is to "look after the plant," reflecting a long-term orientation to quality. "The key ingredient for any production success rests with the person in charge—every detail of the plant must be known. This is done by moving around and having dialog with the people. The supervisor must communicate that the people are critical to the organization's success. Teamwork is very important. This must be communicated; then anything is possible" (paraphrase of selected remarks obtained in an interview with Rathi).

LONG-TERM ORIENTATIONS

CONFUCIAN VALUES. In an article in the *Journal of Business Communication,* Moyan R. Limaye and David A. Victor discussed the limitations of Western linear paradigms for international business encounters that ignore the uniqueness of other worldviews. The Eastern worldview is worthwhile to examine due to the remarkable economic growth that many of these economies have experienced over the last couple of decades. And while India does not share a heritage of Chinese Confucian philosophy, many connections can be made between Hinduism, as practiced by the majority in India, and the cultures of East Asia.

Confucianism is a set of rules focusing on a long-term versus a short term lifestyle. Confucian teaching includes obligations of relationships, family collectivities, virtuous behavior toward others, and moderate living, i.e., preserving resources—as individuals and as economies. The shared heritage of East Asia provides strong evidence that culture may indeed be a contributing factor for economic growth. The link between Confucian values and economic growth was intuitively thought to be the case for some time: economic growth of Japan, South Korea, Taiwan, Hong Kong, and Singapore (the "Five Dragons") was due in large part to certain key traits that derive their social ideals from Confucian tradition. Proponents of such an argument attribute the economic success of East Asia to common cultural roots; roots providing conditions that contribute to the region's post-World War II competitive business accomplishments.

LONG-TERM ORIENTATION INDEX. The correlation between long-term Confucian values and economic growth over the past few decades was examined empirically in what Geert Hofstede and Michael Bond call the long-term orientation (LTO) index. The LTO index is a survey designed to quantify certain Confucian values within selected countries. The original survey was titled the "Chinese Value Survey" (CVS). A number of ethnic Chinese social scientists from Hong Kong and Taiwan designed 40 questions listing ten basic Chinese cultural values.

An interesting finding, aside from business practice, is that the LTO index appears to correlate positively with certain economic growth data published by the International Bank for Reconstruction and Development (the **World Bank**) for the period 1965 to 1987. While Hofstede in his 1991 book showed a correlation coefficient between a country's LTO level and percent average **gross domestic product** (GDP) growth, his statistical method was based upon an assumed linear relationship between these two parameters during the period from 1965 to 1987. While a compelling case can be presented in support of LTO cultural values as being an integral component for economic growth, other factors are also determinants to economic growth; market, economic, and political factors clearly come to bear on GDP results.

Among the first nine countries on the LTO index, however, are China (1), Hong Kong (2), Taiwan (3), Japan (4), South Korea (5), and Singapore (9). All these economies are experiencing rapid economic growth. India is very high and is seventh on the LTO index. While India's economic growth was not as great over the last decade in comparison to some of the East Asian countries, this is now changing, as discussed earlier, due to relaxed financial constraints upon foreign direct investments. There is a widespread sense of excitement within Indian industrial circles, as it is anticipated their country will become a member of the community of rapidly growing nations. The cultural environment that fosters a long term outlook, in addition to the necessary factors of a rapidly expanding middle-class market, and a favorable political environment that encourages investment in India, points toward India as a key growth area over the next several years. Major global corporations are expanding rapidly into India, taking advantage of this window of opportunity.

While the LTO attributes are not all directly related to international business issues, of direct significance is the contrast of quick results versus perseverance towards slow results. The Chinese have a term relating to interpersonal perseverance: *guanxi,* defined as the linking of people with highly developed relationships through mutual dependencies. This value system includes the concepts of personal connections and mutual dependencies and is a strong trait in Chinese interrelational systems. In effect, *guanxi* is a value for long-term relationships that combine practical needs with a closeness going much deeper than surface relationships; characteristics necessary to doing business in India. There is no direct translation into English describing the word's meaning, yet the rich semantic intrigue surrounding the concept can be somewhat captured within the creative term ''peopleizing'': A communication process that develops mutual relationships. But the definition of the term involves much more. Peopleizing is a strategy that prioritizes long-term relationship building over that of the completion of short-term functional business tasks and is a useful strategy for doing business in India.

INDIAN LONG-TERM RELATIONSHIPS. The success of leading Indian businesses is attributable, in large part, to this strategy of long-term relationship building: Madhu Rathi, a leading industrialist in India, shared the following high context thoughts in a conversation: ''Our networking is built on trust. There is some initial risk, of course, but trust builds through very close relationships. What is needed is to find out what the needs are in a country and fulfill those needs. This means knowing the culture and studying the market. We look to the long-term not the short-term. If you look to the short term and fail, there is no long-term.''

Providing additional flavor to the long-term cultural values prevalent in Indian business, are remarks by Sunil H. Rathi (a truly international person), director for Rathi Dye Chem Ltd. (from an interview conducted with Rathi):

> We have seven industries [in the Rathi Group]. My uncle [Dr. R. J. Rathi] deals with sales at the international level for Sudarshan Chemical Industries. He travels to America, Russia, Europe, France, and elsewhere to develop these markets. He has many friends in all of these places. When people come to India, we show them all of India. These are our potential agents, and through them we get more and more business. And, if you have open-mindedness, lasting business connections can be formed.

CONCLUDING THOUGHTS

The organizational dimensions described above and supported by remarks from leading Indian executives are pertinent to doing business successfully in India; they illustrate Indian relationships that are significant for international business in India as well as to help foster greater human understanding in the global village. Future Western international business accomplishments in India will go to organizations motivated to developing long-term communication strategies. While there may be disagreement with this conviction, arguing that culture and communication are not determinants to business success, many in top U.S. management ranks are becoming more convinced that this is indeed the case. Western international business practice is undergoing radical change, reflecting the belief that a focus for the future ought to be, in part, on culture and communication. The connections between long-term strategies and business success, afford rich possibilities for discovering and providing knowledge to international business practitioners entering, or planning to enter, the burgeoning Indian marketplace.

[William B. Chapel]

FURTHER READING:

Chapel, William B. ''Developing International Management Communication Competence.'' *Journal of Business and Technical Communication* 11, no. 3 (1997).

Hofstede, Geert. *Cultures and Organizations: Software of the Mind.* London: McGraw-Hill, 1991.

——, and Michael Harris Bond. ''The Confucius Connection: From Cultural Roots to Economic Growth.'' *Organizational Dynamics* 16 (Spring 1988).

Limaye, Mohan R. ''Doing Business in India: Aspects of the Political Dimension.'' *Business Horizons,* November/December 1998.

——, and David A. Victor. ''Cross-Cultural Business Communication Research: State of the Art and Hypotheses for the 1990s.'' *Journal of Business Communication* 28, no. 3 (1991).

Selmer, Jan, ed. *International Management in China: Cross Cultural Issues.* London and New York: Routledge, 1998.

INDIVIDUAL RETIREMENT ACCOUNT (IRA)

Created under federal **tax** law, an individual retirement account (IRA) is a tax-deferred retirement program in which any employed person can participate. The extent of annual contributions and the tax deductibility thereof are, however, dependent on the individual worker's situation.

IRAs were authorized by Congress in 1974 as part of a broader effort to reform laws governing **pensions**. Subsequent legislation, in particular the Tax Reform Act of 1986, has refined the scope, provisions, and requirements of IRAs so that currently not only the basic, individual ''contributory'' IRA but also other forms of the plan are available. As outlined by W. Kent Moore in *The Guide to Tax-Saving Investing,* these include: spousal IRAs, enabling a working spouse to contribute to an IRA opened for a nonworking partner; third-party-sponsored IRAs, used by employee organizations, unions, and others wishing to contribute on workers' behalf; **simplified employee pensions** (SEPs), enabling employers to provide retirement benefits by contributing to workers' IRAs; and so-called rollover contributions, allowing distributions from an IRA or an employer's qualified plan to be reinvested in another IRA.

While the rules and regulations are quite specific, employees using the basic contributory IRA can generally contribute up to $2,000 per year until they reach the age of 70 1/2. Whether or not these contributions are tax deductible depends on the worker's income level and eligibility for an employee pension plan; nevertheless, the **dividends** and interest earned by the investment accumulate in the account on a tax-free basis. Typically, IRA funds are invested in varied ways, including **stocks** and **bonds**, money market accounts, treasury bills, **mutual funds**, and certificates of deposit.

The Small Business Job Protection Act of 1996 (SBJA) and the Taxpayer Relief Act of 1997 (TRA) liberalized many of the rules governing IRAs, and, in general, made IRAs more attractive investments than ever before. Under the SBJA, spouses filing jointly were able to contribute up to $4,000 per year, even if one spouse had no earnings for the year. The TRA removed penalties for premature withdrawal of IRA funds in cases of medical or dental expense or unemployment, and enabled self-employed individuals to deduct their health-insurance costs. It also created two new types of IRA: the Roth IRA, contributions to which are taxable, but can be made after the owner reaches the age of 70 1/2, and is not taxed upon withdrawal; and the Education IRA, into which contributors can place a nondeductible total of $500 per child per year to defray future educational expenses.

Those interested in opening an IRA should familiarize themselves with the regulations governing the amounts that may be contributed, the timing of contributions, the criteria for tax deductibility, and the penalties for making early withdrawals. They should also shop around when investigating financial institutions that offer IRAs, in as much as fees vary from institution to institution, ranging from no charge to a one-time fee for opening the account to an annual fee for maintaining the IRA. Still, as Moore noted, "The advantages of IRAs far outweigh the disadvantages. . . . Earnings for either deductible or nondeductible IRAs grow faster than ordinary savings accounts, because IRA earnings are tax deferred, allowing all earnings to be reinvested. Even when withdrawals are made, the remaining funds continue to grow as tax-deferred assets."

[Roberta H. Winston, updated by Grant Eldridge]

FURTHER READING:

Block, Sandra. "Reap a Richer Retirement with a Roth Account." *USA Today*, 19 September 1997, B4.

Downes, John, and Jordan Elliot Goodman. *Barron's Finance and Investment Handbook.* 5th ed. Hauppage, NY: Barron's, 1998.

Gitman, Lawrence J., and Michael D. Joehnk. *Fundamentals of Investing.* 7th ed. Reading, MA: Addison-Wesley, 1999.

Kistner, William G. "Tax Reforms Benefit Retirement Plans and IRAs." *Healthcare Financial Management* 51, no. 2 (February 1997): 84.

Mazawey, Louis T. "1997 Tax Law Changes Affecting Retirement Plans." *Journal of Pension Planning and Compliance* 23, no. 4 (winter 1998): 72.

Moore, W. Kent. "Deferring Taxes with Retirement Accounts." In *The Guide to Tax-Saving Investing,* by David L. Scott. Old Saybrook, CT: Globe Pequot Press, 1995.

Napach, Bernice. "Tax Relief That Will Bloom in Spring." *Medical Economics* 75, no. 19 (5 October 1998): 38.

Stevenson, Richard W. "Socking It Away for College, with Uncle Sam's Help." *New York Times,* 10 August 1997, F5.

"Tax Bill Expands IRAs, Extends Tax Exclusions." *Employee Benefit Plan Review* 52, no. 3 (September 1997): 18.

INDONESIA, DOING BUSINESS IN

Indonesia is comprised of more than 6,000 inhabited islands. The nation's total land area is just over 700,000 square miles, or just under three times the size of Texas. With a population of more than 185 million (1994), Indonesia is the fourth-most populous nation in the world.

Since its independence in the wake of World War II, Indonesia transformed itself from a primarily subsistence economy, to emerge as a growing industrial and commercial force in the world economy. Indonesia's economic emergence was due in large part to the efforts of Suharto, its dictatorial president since 1966. Suharto upon gaining power introduced a pro-Western policy, called the New Order, that promoted **foreign investment** and development in Indonesia.

In economic terms, the policy worked well throughout the 1970s; Indonesia maintained a real **gross domestic product** (GDP) growth rate averaging approximately 7.5 percent annually. During the collapse of oil prices in the early 1980s, that figure slipped briefly (but remained on average well over 5.5 percent), recovering by the end of the 1980s and into the 1990s to a real GDP annual growth rate of over 8 percent. Indonesia became a major site for operations of Japanese companies in the 1980s and of U.S. and Western European companies in the early 1990s.

Indonesia's strong economic performance, however, masked serious social divisions and governmental corruption. These both came heavily to the forefront in 1997; the country collapsed both economically and socially.

INDONESIA AND THE EAST ASIAN ECONOMIC CRISIS

When Thailand's currency collapsed in July 1997, an economic crisis enveloped the whole region. The economic instability spread almost immediately to Indonesia, whose political corruption and unsustainably high levels of foreign **debt** in private hands made it particularly susceptible to an economic downturn. The Indonesian banks unsuccessfully attempted to stabilize the rupiah, but on August 14, 1997, Indonesia gave up its attempt at a managed exchange rate and let the currency float. Almost immediately, the rupiah slipped from 2,400 to the dollar to 2,640, then continued slipping in the following days to 2,800 rupiahs to the dollar.

In response to this monetary disaster, Indonesia canceled 15 of its largest projects. While the cancellations helped conserve foreign currency, they had a domino effect on the economy as a whole, and Indonesia entered a full-scale **recession**.

In response, Indonesia sought assistance from the **International Monetary Fund** (IMF). On October 31, 1997, Indonesia received a $42 billion IMF assistance package. By that point, the rupiah had fallen to 3,680 to the dollar.

Indonesia, however, refused to adhere to the reforms demanded by the IMF. This both undercut the bailout's effectiveness and further shook outsiders' confidence in Indonesia's ability to recover. Much of the reason for Indonesia's resistance to the IMF measures, however, derived from the corrupt interrelationship between the nation's business interests and the government. Through government interventions, the vast majority of Indonesia's business interest had been channeled into the hands of President Suharto's family and close friends. The IMF measures thus directly affected the private **wealth** of the nation's political leadership, including that of President Suharto himself. Under such conditions, it became nearly impossible for the government to agree to follow IMF reforms that would, if adopted, destroy the personal wealth of the very people who would have had to enforce the IMF measures.

As a result, while the IMF package might have staved off further disaster, little could be done about Indonesia's outstanding foreign debt since the majority of that debt lay not only in private hands but in the hands of President Suharto's family and close friends. The amount of debt itself has been subject to debate, with the Indonesian government officially admitting to just over half of what European analysts calculated. The French firm Indosuez, for example, estimated Indonesia's foreign debt in December 1997 as approximately $200 billion. Additionally, one-third of this was due for repayment in the first quarter of 1998. Consequently, the rupiah continued to plummet, falling to 80 percent of its precrisis value before stabilizing and regaining some of its strength. By 1998 the nation was in shambles, unemployment had topped 15 percent, and President Suharto began to lose control of the government.

THE GREAT FIRE OF 1997-98

As if its economic troubles were not enough, Indonesia was struck by one of the largest uncontrolled forest fires in world history. Beginning in August 1997, the same month that the economic crisis reached Indonesia, the fire burned out of control well into 1998. The fire resulted from unusual weather patterns, uncontrolled rainforest logging, and poor plantation management. The smoke haze it emitted spread over the whole nation as well as the nearby countries of Singapore, Brunei, Malaysia, the Philippines, and Thailand. The smoke was so severe that it resulted in shipping accidents and airplane crashes from reduced visibility.

The fire gutted an already battered economy, with at least $3 billion in damage to timber and agricultural production in Kalimantan and Sumatra. Additionally, the fire conservatively cost Indonesia $90 million in lost or canceled tourism. Finally, the fire was responsible not only for revenues lost, but for expenses undertaken by the government as well. Thus, Indonesia's state-run clinics and hospitals were filled beyond capacity for nearly a year with patients suffering from the effects of smoke-related illnesses. Estimates made by the Indonesian government jointly with the World Wildlife Fund and Canada's Economy and Environment Programme for South East Asia placed the fire's economic impact at a staggering $4.4 billion for 1997 alone. This amounted to 2.5 percent of Indonesia's **gross national product** (GNP) before the economic crisis began; occurring as it did simultaneously with the crisis, the fire was economically devastating.

Yet the economic cost was only a fraction of the overall impact of the fire. Tens of thousands of people were displaced, losing their homes and businesses. Additionally, the loss of rainforest habitat has decimated Indonesia's wildlife (the fire affected the majority of the world's orangutan population, for instance), which in turn has brought worldwide condemnation from wildlife organizations, and the loss from potential tourism and conservation funds.

THE FALL OF SUHARTO

By March 1998, faced with the economic collapse of his nation and the effects of the fire, President Suharto began to lose control of the government. Over 30,000 antigovernment demonstrators took to the streets of Jakarta to protest his rule. By the end of April, the situation had become critical, and Suharto began to fear that a concerted uprising would take place on May 21, Indonesia's National Day commemorating liberation from Dutch rule. In response, Suharto announced on May 1, 1998, that he would restructure the government.

Seeking a scapegoat for their frustrations, the Indonesian populace began to target the Chinese community. Student protests began to spread into looting of Chinese stores. On May 5, 1998, rioters burned a Chinese shopowner to death in his store in Medan. The Medan incident, however, turned out to be a predictor of coming events.

On May 12, rioting broke out in Jakarta against Chinese shopowners. Soon the rioting spread against ethnic Chinese across the nation. The looting, arson, and murder raged uncontrolled through May 15, leaving in its wake an estimated 1,200 dead, most of them ethnic Chinese. The damage to Chinese-owned businesses and homes totaled approximately $1 billion (10 trillion rupiahs).

Government forces not only made little attempt to stop the attacks, but in some cases actively contributed to them. Most notably, Indonesia received worldwide condemnation for the alleged rape of 150 ethnic Chinese women by Indonesian armed forces.

During the rioting, thousands of ethnic-Chinese Indonesian citizens fled the country for their lives. This added to Indonesia's economic woes. Before the crisis, the Chinese community dominated in the food and consumer goods distribution areas of the economy. As a result, the destruction or closing of the ethnic Chinese-owned businesses has severely compromised Indonesia's distribution network, resulting in food shortages in many parts of the nation.

Faced with massive student uprisings, interethnic violence, and a currency that had lost 80 percent of its value in ten months, President Suharto resigned on May 21, 1998. His successor was Dr. Bacharuddin Jusuf Habibie, a German-educated engineer and close political ally of Suharto.

ETHNICITY

To understand the current tensions in post-Suharto Indonesia, it is necessary to address its multiethnic makeup. Ethnicity has always been a central issue of Indonesian business, not just since the interethnic violence that surfaced during the economic crisis. Indeed, since independence, and especially during the Suharto periods, Indonesia made concerted efforts to promote appreciation for ethnic diversity.

Indonesia's national motto espouses "unity in diversity" with good reason. Indonesia has hundreds of ethnic groups. Each group has its own customs, traditional dress, and usually distinctive names. Indonesians hold stereotypes of the behaviors of most groups, and know the business practices of the major ethnic groups. These stereotypes affect business expectations among Indonesians, and merit the attention of foreign business executives as an insight into Indonesian business culture as a whole.

Most ethnic groups are tied to a specific region of a particular island. Thus, the Batak live primarily in central Sumatra and the Acehnese in northwest Sumatra. The Balinese live primarily on Bali. The Ambonese live primarily on Ambon. The Sundanese are found mostly in West Java, and so forth.

By contrast, some important groups are found widely scattered throughout Indonesia. The Bugis inhabit the river port cities throughout Kalimantan and Sulawesi and on the many smaller islands off their coasts.

Similarly widely scattered are the ethnic-Chinese Indonesians. The ethnic-Chinese Indonesians, who have been scapegoated for Indonesia's economic woes, have traditionally played a large role in much of Indonesian business. While ethnic Chinese are present throughout the country, they are most concentrated in the urban areas of Java as well as the port cities of Kalimantan and of eastern Sumatra.

Whether geographically discrete or scattered, though, virtually all of Indonesia's ethnic groups are represented in large numbers in the capital city of Jakarta. The capital's multicultural mix of the various groups helps to sustain the sense of national unity in the country. As a result, foreigners conducting business in Indonesia should at the minimum attempt to familiarize themselves with as many of these groups as possible.

THE ETHNIC CHINESE. None of Indonesia's ethnic groups are as important relative to their size as the ethnic Chinese. The Chinese are not considered an indigenous group to the nation, although they have been present in varying degrees for centuries.

The Chinese are few in number but dominate Indonesia's business sector. They represent only 2.5 percent of Indonesia's total population yet they control 60 percent of all wholesale business and 75 percent of all retail business in the country. Moreover they own or control 68 percent of the largest Indonesian-headquartered businesses.

The position of the ethnic Chinese in Indonesian society has for decades been ambivalent. Resentment against the Chinese for their business success and dominance has led to frequent outbursts of anti-Chinese sentiment and riots both after independence as well as during colonial times. Conversely, the Chinese have also received considerable appreciation for their introduction of business techniques. Moreover, during the Dutch and Japanese occupations of Indonesia, it was the ethnic Chinese who contributed most heavily to the independence movement of the nation.

The situation of the ethnic-Chinese Indonesians seems unlikely to improve soon. While to some degree the violent persecutions have abated since the resignation of President Suharto, his successor, President Habibie, has only added to the troubles of the ethnic Chinese. In one of his first acts as president, Habibie joined in the scapegoating of the Chinese community. Instead of attempting to encourage the ethnic-Chinese Indonesian citizens who fled the country to return, President Habibie instructed the government to give their trading licenses to what he called ''indigenous Indonesians'' (nonethnic Chinese).

EAST TIMOR. East Timor was for centuries a colony of Portugal. When the Portuguese withdrew from East Timor in 1975, it declared independence. Disregarding this, however, Indonesia occupied East Timor in December 1975, over the objections not only of the East Timorese but of Portugal and the **United Nations**. While the number of East Timorese killed in the Indonesian occupation is not fully known, conservative estimates place the death toll at 100,000.

Anti-Indonesian sentiments ran high throughout the 1980s, but it was not until 1991 that violence again erupted. Indonesian troops fired on pro-independence demonstrators. This led to guerilla activities against the Indonesians. East Timor attracted world attention in 1996 when two leading East Timorese dissidents, Bishop Carlos Ximenes Belo and Jose Ramos Horta, won the Nobel Prize.

Following the collapse of the Suharto government, East Timorese resistance intensified. On June 9, 1997, less than a month after coming to office, President Habibie announced that he would grant a special status to East Timor with greater internal autonomy. This proposal, however, was rejected by Portugal. In part inspired by the Portuguese response, thousands of students held pro-independence marches throughout East Timor the next day. In response, Indonesia attempted to work with Portugal to define a workable alternative but before the two nations could agree on an action, the student demonstrations erupted into violence.

In June 1998 government troops shot a student demonstrator in the East Timorese city of Dili. This led to violent outbreaks against the troops by hundreds of students. Two days later in the East Timorese city of Baucau, another student was killed during a visit by a **European Union** envoy. To quiet the international condemnation of its actions, Indonesia announced that it would withdraw its troops. In return, the United Nations sponsored talks between Portugal and Indonesia over East Timorese autonomy. At the end of October, however, the situation erupted again when it became known that Indonesia had withdrawn no troops despite public statements that all troops were withdrawn months earlier.

In November 1998, East Timorese rebels claimed that Indonesian troops had killed 44 civilians. Then on January 4, 1999, more violence erupted in East Timor in which two people were killed in a clash between pro-Indonesian and pro-independence groups. In response, Australia became the first nation to officially announce its support for East Timorese independence (as opposed to autonomy). Violence erupted again on February 25, 1999, during which Indonesian armed forces killed three more pro-independence demonstrators. In March 1999, Indonesia agreed to allow the East Timorese to hold a referendum on independence to be held in July, but before the vote could be held, anti-independence erupted into violence, killing 17 civilians. In response, pro-independence groups announced their intention to escalate their guerilla war against Indonesia.

THE AMBONESE. In November 1997, Moslems burned a Christian church in Jakarta and hacked five ethnic Ambonese Christians to death. This seemed to have sparked Moslem-Christian tensions on the island of Ambon itself.

On January 19, 1998, Moslems and Christians broke into fighting on the island of Ambon. The fighting began on a small scale but had escalated to the point that by the end of February, over 160 people were killed, and several villages had been entirely burned and thousands of Ambonese have fled. Ambon, which is approximately 50 percent Christian and 50 percent Moslem soon found itself in a state of siege. On March 3, President Suharto sent in 3,000 soldiers with orders to shoot rioters on sight. Despite this, by year's end the death toll had passed 300.

OTHER ETHNIC TENSIONS. The scapegoating of the Chinese Indonesians and the revolt among the East Timorese, however, are not the only sources of ethnic tensions. In the 1980s, ethnic groups seeking autonomy began to surface on a small scale in many areas. The Acehnese on Sumatra's northernmost point have maintained an underground liberation front for years. Similarly, in response to Javanese immigration to Irian Jaya (the Indonesia half of New Guinea), Papuans have formed a Free Papua movement.

NAMES AND TITLES

Because of the extreme diversity of ethnic groups in Indonesia, a wide range of naming patterns exists in the country. This mix of naming systems may prove to be confusing for foreigners; nonetheless, it is especially important to use the names of Indonesians properly since, throughout the nation, most ethnic groups hold to the tradition that one's name is sacred.

The most common naming patterns follow the Javanese system. Most common people have a single name. No surname on the Western model is used. For example, President Suharto's full name is Suharto, with no first or last name attached. Indeed, the only major ethnic groups using family surnames similar to the Western pattern are the Minahasa and the Bataks. In recent times, many middle-class Indonesians in the business sphere have adopted second names roughly equivalent to the Western first and last name.

Most Indonesians, particularly in Jakarta, use titles from Bahasa Indonesia. This is common even when speaking in English. The two main courtesy address forms are Bapak for a man and Ibu for a woman. Both titles reflect considerably more respect than their rough English equivalents of Mr. and Ms. Because these honorifics reflect high respect, some English speakers use Bapak and Ibu for business equals or superiors and revert to Mr. and Ms. for subordinates of considerably lower rank.

Most academic honorifics in Indonesia are taken directly from the Dutch. These are usually never dropped in business settings. The most common of the Dutch-derived academic titles are for men Doktorandus (Drs) and for women Doktoranda (Dra) referring to any graduate degree received outside of law or engineering. The title Insingjur (male or female) is used for those with degrees in engineering. The non-Dutch title Sarajana Hukum (male or female) refers to those with law degrees.

BUSINESS PRACTICES

LANGUAGE. Indonesia is home to an unequaled array of linguistic and ethnic groups. In all, more than 990 languages are native to its islands.

Bahasa Indonesia was consciously selected as the national language in an attempt to unify the nation. It is spoken as a first language by only 12.1 percent of the population. Still, an additional 58 percent of the people speak or read Bahasa Indonesia as a second language. Moreover, since Bahasa Indonesia developed as a marketplace version of Malay used throughout the islands during the colonial occupation, it has a strong history as a language of business communication. Today, all **advertising** and official communication must be in Bahasa Indonesia. Moreover, while English—and to a lesser extent Dutch—remain widespread, foreigners usually find learning Bahasa Indonesia useful for the same reason Indonesians learn it: to open opportunities and demonstrate commitment to the nation. Finally, since the majority of the nation speaks Bahasa Indonesia as a second language, foreigners' proficiency level becomes less of a factor than with many other languages.

For business purposes, the use of English is widespread. Still, because English is a third or even fourth language for many Indonesians, proficiency is less common than in many countries of similar importance in global trade. Among older Indonesians, the use of Dutch as the foreign business language of choice is still fairly common.

VIEWS OF TECHNOLOGY AND THE ENVIRONMENT

The traditional Indonesian attitude toward technology differs significantly from that of the United States. The United States is a control culture, while Indonesian is traditionally a subjugation culture. This means that U.S. culture views technology as consistently positive and reinforces a belief that people can control their environment to conform to their needs. By contrast, Indonesian groups traditionally view technology with some skepticism and conform their behavior to existing environmental conditions. The traditional Indonesian view of technology is changing toward the culture stance in the most developed urban and industrial areas around Jakarta. These traditional norms, however, remain firmly in place in most of the rest of the country.

SOCIAL ORGANIZATION

Social organizational factors in Indonesia affecting business include the influence of the government, the importance of religion, the concept of family, and group ties.

THE INFLUENCE OF GOVERNMENT. The Indonesian government plays a considerably more active role in business than does government in the United States or Canada. The importance of government officials, in particular, far exceeds that of their North American counterparts in status and power. Generally, the Indonesian government official has taken over the traditional position of *tua* or village headman. Unlike the North American public servant, the Indonesian government official is unlikely to be seen as "serving" the needs of constituents or businesspeople. Rather Indonesian officials are public leaders served by those they govern or oversee.

The importance of the government official is reinforced, in turn, by the power of Indonesian nationalism as a force in business. Despite their ethnic and linguistic diversity, Indonesians are united by a common conception of themselves as a unified whole who in their unity were able to wrest power from exploitive foreign colonizers. As a result, Indonesians are considerably more concerned with how their business activities (particularly when conducted with foreigners) will likely affect the nation as a whole. This concern with nationalism emerges in several ways in business, including long-term coordination of business activities with government goals and protective **labor laws**.

RELIGION. Religion plays an important role in Indonesian business. While a religion is required by law, which religion is left to the individual. Hinduism, Christianity, and Buddhism all have substantial followings in Indonesia, but for the vast majority of Indonesians, religion is synonymous with Islam. As the nation with the world's largest Moslem population, Indonesian Moslems have been able to forge a national variation of the religion emphasizing the concept of *rukun* or societal and interpersonal harmony at the familial, community, and societal level. While *rukun* is universally recognized as a principle of Islam, Indonesians have blended it with East Asian concepts of harmony, conflict avoidance, and surface tranquillity to give it a greater emphasis than practiced anywhere else in the Moslem world.

Additionally, because of the influence of Hindu and Chinese spiritual beliefs, Indonesian Moslems are more likely than Moslems elsewhere to believe in ghosts and the spirit world. While remaining true to the essential monotheistic beliefs of Islam, Indonesians nonetheless recognize spiritual forces or attributes of the soul in a variety of day-to-day objects, trees, flowers, animals, and rice as well as human blood, nail cuttings, and hair. The presence of ghosts, witches, or other spiritual entities remains a real part of life for the majority of Indonesians, and the need to placate or avoid these spirits affects all aspects of life, including work. A common mistake of foreigners is to view Indonesia as a traditional Islamic society and therefore to play down the importance of these supernatural forces, to criticize such beliefs, or to mistakenly reduce their importance to that of mere superstition. Fear of ghosts or the believed presence of spiritual forces can prevent employees from coming to work or prevent the conclusion of a business deal.

Because Islam is so widespread, its major holidays are state holidays and its calendar is observed nationwide. Moreover, Islamic bans on activities (alcohol consumption, for example) affect some areas of business. Finally, the Friday service at the mosque is one of the main areas for solidifying business relationships—a resource often outside of the reach of the non-Moslem foreigner.

FAMILY AND GROUP TIES. Most Indonesians hold considerably stronger and more extended kinship bonds than those in the United States. Family connections and obligations influence hiring, deal making and other business issues. Moreover, the definitions of immediate relationships reach far beyond the nuclear family to those who would be considered distant relatives in a North American conception.

For several Indonesian ethnic groups, **nepotism** extends beyond direct kin relationships to clan ties. This is particularly the case for the various clans of much of Indonesia's influential ethnic-Chinese communities. Finally, for such groups as the Bataks and Minahasa, preference is extended to include preference for all ethnic group members in a form of nepotism called *suka-ism.*

CONTEXTING. Indonesia is a high-context society and the United States is a low-context culture. This means that Indonesians are more likely to rely on implicit communication rather than on explicit messages. Indonesians as a result read more into what is said than the words themselves may actually mean. For most Indonesians, what is meant matters more than what is actually said.

In Indonesia, meaning is usually communicated indirectly, especially in the delivery of bad news. As a result, Indonesians are likely to agree to things with which they disagree, allowing the context of the discussion or past relationship to convey their disagreement. This is clear to Indonesians but to those from low-context cultures such as the United States, such indirect communication is often misread as dishonesty. Conversely, the direct style of communication practiced by most U.S. businesspeople in Indonesia is perceived as rude and often causes others to lose face.

Indonesians, as a high-context culture, place a strong value on face-saving, while most North Americans place little emphasis on face-saving. The Indonesian conception of face-saving takes the form of the avoidance of *malu,* or shame. Most low-context U.S. business practice is controlled by the following of the law and adherence to written agreements. Indonesians are considerably less bound by the law and the specific terms of **contracts**. Instead, Indonesian business practice is controlled by the desire to avoid *malu.* In other words, one holds to a contract to maintain appearances rather than from fear of a lawsuit. The North American businessperson in Indonesia is thus viewed as lacking honor, having no sense of *malu* (and therefore dangerous to deal with) and being foolishly litigious. The Indonesians in turn are viewed by their North American counterparts as dishonoring their contracts and ignoring their own laws. In reality both perceptions are accurate when viewed through the context of the values of the other's culture.

Still, to succeed in business in Indonesia, the foreigner will need to view contracts and other legally binding arrangements as ongoing rather than definitive. Moreover, the foreigner will have to be willing to allow some inconsistencies to stand at times to maintain appearance and avoid forcing *malu* on the Indonesians who would otherwise terminate the business relationship.

AUTHORITY CONCEPTION

Indonesian business is conducted in a strict hierarchy. The traditional **management** system, known as *bapakism,* consists of heavily paternalistic control in the form of a benevolent authoritarianism that tolerates little direct questioning of authority. The basic tenet of *bapakism* is summarized in the commonly repeated phrase *apal bapak senang* (''keep the boss, father, or headman happy''). Bad news is rarely shared with superiors directly or is toned down to the level that it may be incomprehensible for many non-Indonesian managers. Moreover, no two people are equal—everyone has a relative status of higher or lower to any other person. One's boss (*bapak*), therefore, has a boss as well. Heads of companies have bosses in the form of government leaders, and so on.

Related to this is the responsibility for the *bapaks* to defend and protect their subordinates. The *bapak*'s authority rests in his power to take care of his employees. The price for this protection is their unquestioning respect and the outward honor they show him.

Indonesian custom demands that all managers or *bapaks*—whether foreign or Indonesian—forgive any subordinate who sincerely apologizes, regardless of the offense. Indeed, the national holiday of Lebaran is a formal day for granting apologies, although the practice is far from limited to that day alone. Moreover, a boss must accept an apology without bringing shame (*malu*) on the employee, or the manager (not the employee) will risk losing all authority over others by losing their respect. Since this is diametrically opposed to the custom in many Western countries, foreign managers often find this mandatory forgiveness difficult. It remains nonetheless necessary to succeed in a managerial role in Indonesia. While the strict Indonesian labor laws would in any case prevent firing in such situations, it is customary after an apology is accepted that the manager and subordinate must never again raise the situation directly. The effect of maintaining such appearances is as essential to authority conception as the act of forgiveness itself.

TEMPORAL CONCEPTION

Indonesia is a polychronic culture. Time is more fluid than in monochronic societies such as the United States. The Indonesians value friendship, personal commitments, and the completion of tasks at hand at the expense of preset schedules.

The Indonesian term for this polychronic orientation is *jam karet* or ''rubber time.'' Time is seen as malleable. Appointment times are approximate. Work hours are variable. Consequently, the monochronic foreigner needs to adjust his or her concepts of scheduling, deadlines, and other time-linked activities in Indonesia.

[David A. Victor]

FURTHER READING:

Draine, Cathie, and Barbara Hall. *Culture Shock: Indonesia.* Portland, OR: Graphic Arts Center Publishing, 1990.

Jackson, Karl D., and Lucien W. Pye, eds. *Political Power and Communication in Indonesia.* Berkeley: University of California Press, 1978.

MacIntyre, Andrew. *Business and Politics in Indonesia.* North Sydney, Australia: Allen & Unwyn, 1991.

Palmier, Leslie, ed. *Understanding Indonesia.* Brookfield, VT: Ashgate Publishing, 1985.

INDUSTRIAL RELATIONS

Industrial relations refers to processes and outcomes involving **employment** relationships. Frequently the term is used in a narrower sense, for employment relationships involving collective representation of employees in the form of a **labor union** or employee association, especially in the United States. At the other extreme, industrial relations has been defined by Thomas A. Kochan, in his book *Collective Bargaining and Industrial Relations,* as ''all aspects of people at work,'' but there are clearly some aspects of people at work that entail highly technical subjects (e.g., industrial hygiene, **ergonomics**) which are not normally regarded as falling within the mainstream of industrial relations study.

As an academic subject area, industrial relations is often defined as an interdisciplinary field of applied study. This conception recognizes that employment relationships entail practical problems and other phenomena that transcend any one traditional discipline (e.g., economics). To fully appreciate the multifaceted nature of many industrial relations issues, one must draw from a variety of perspectives, including economics, psychology, sociology, political science, and law, among others. For example, employee compensation issues may be usefully addressed in terms of **economic theory**, but psychological theories offer useful insights on employee attitudes toward and reactions to compensation matters. Whether the nature of industrial relations issues is sufficiently unique to justify considering industrial relations a ''true discipline'' has been controversial, but most scholars appear to favor the interdisciplinary subject view. Nevertheless, John Dunlop, a key figure in industrial relations theory, continues to argue (in a 1998 article in *Advances in Industrial and Labor Relations*) for the advantages of ''industrial relations systems theory'' over other theoretical disciplines (e.g., economics), and contends that industrial relations is a genuine discipline.

BACKGROUND

In *The Origins and Evolution of the Field of Industrial Relations in the United States,* Bruce E. Kaufman attributed the popularization of the term ''industrial relations'' to a Commission on Industrial Relations created by the federal government in 1912. That commission was created to investigate and report on conditions in ''industry'' that gave rise to labor problems, including conflict between employers and employees (and their organizations) that often erupted in violence and strikes. Thus the term ''industrial relations'' referred to ''relations'' between employers and employees in ''industry.'' Better industrial relations were seen as the solution to labor problems.

Although the term ''industry'' or ''industrial'' (as in ''industrial relations'') connotes for many ''heavy'' industry (e.g., steel mills, auto assembly plants), this connotation is much narrower than the field's conception of industrial relations. At least to most industrial relations scholars, the term ''industrial'' is used broadly, as in distinguishing industrialized societies from agrarian societies. As noted by Dunlop (in *Industrial Relations Systems*) and his colleagues, industrialization gives rise to employment relationships as we know them today, in which large numbers of people work for and in large part follow the direction of others in exchange for wages or salaries and other compensation. This is in contrast to agrarian societies where the farmer is typically self-employed, directing his or her own labor and obtaining his or her livelihood as the difference between revenues and expenses. Thus industrial relations refers to relations between employers and employees not only in heavy industry but also in retailing, government, financial services, education, and recreational services, for example. In fact, even agricultural production, when organized in a form where an employer relies extensively on the services of hired workers, as is increasingly the case, can be said to fall within the purview of industrial relations.

Similarly, industrial relations is not limited to formal employment relationships, but rather to what one might call ''functional employment relationships.'' There are many instances where workers are technically classified as self-employed ''**independent contractors**,'' and yet for practical purposes these workers are essentially employees. The construction industry provides many examples of this. Many laws governing employment are limited to formal employment relationships, and independent contractor status is often used by firms as a means of cutting labor costs, possibly by avoiding or evading legal obligations to employees. Related to this, **temporary employment** services whereby firms contract for workers with another firm (which technically employs the workers, paying their wages and possibly benefits such as **health insurance**), have grown dramatically in recent years. Many firms have found this a cost-effective alternative to traditional employment arrangements. These two types of arrangements are part of a larger and growing work phenomenon that many refer to in terms of the ''contingent workforce.'' This phenomenon contrasts with traditional employment relationships in which one is employed by the firm that controls the work site as a matter of law as well as in a practical sense, and in which the work relationship is generally assumed to be relatively permanent. Some would include many part-time workers as well as many independent contractors and temporary employees in a definition of the contingent **workforce**. In any case, conceptions of industrial relations as the study of ''all aspects of people at work'' clearly do not limit the field to formal or legal definitions of employment.

As noted earlier, in the United States especially, the term industrial relations is sometimes viewed more narrowly as referring solely to relations between employers and employee representation organizations, i.e., labor unions, and related phenomena such as union organizing, collective bargaining (negotiations between employers and unions over work matters), and the effects of unions on employment terms and society. In this view, the importance of industrial relations in the United States has fallen apace with the decline of unions over the past four decades. Since the mid-1950s, when unions represented roughly one-third of employees, U.S. union representation has declined so that today unions represent about one-seventh of employees (13.9 percent in 1998). (This overall unionization rate conceals considerable variation across industries. To illustrate, the unionization rate, according to the U.S. Department of Labor's Bureau of Labor Statistics, is about 10 percent in private sector employment, but close to 38 percent in public sector employment.)

The terms ''human resources'' and ''**human resources management**'' have emerged as preferred labels referring to employment issues in the absence of unions, although these terms are not always sharply distinguished from industrial relations. For some, industrial relations is a field within human resources while for others human resources is a field within industrial relations. Clearly, however, the human resources terms have become more popular and the industrial relations term has become less popular as unions have declined. It would be a mistake to regard these changes as merely semantic. Perhaps at the heart of the substantive matter, in simplified form, is the question of whether employment matters will be determined unilaterally by **management** (the human resources view) or jointly by employers and employees through negotiations with employee representation organizations. Unilateral management determinations tend to be viewed as the norm in setting employment terms or at least specifying the conditions and limitations of employee influence under the human resources view, and collective bargaining tends to be seen as exceptional and often stemming from management's failure to manage properly its human resources (i.e., unions are seen as a result of management's mistakes). In contrast, industrial relations specialists tend to view collective bargaining (and other forms of joint determination) as a normal and legitimate process, or even a preferable process, for determining the bulk of employment matters. Legislation, such as minimum wage laws or bans on **child labor**, is also seen as a means to remedy labor problems. (It is noteworthy that federal laws declare collective bargaining to be a favored national labor policy although many question the effectiveness of laws promoting this policy [see *Restoring the Promise of American Labor Law,* edited by Sheldon Friedman and others].) Of course, markets, laws, technology, worker attitudes, and social norms present constraints on determining employment matters in any case.

CURRENT STATUS OF THE FIELD

At this time industrial relations remains the preferred term for describing the field among scholars. One indicator of this is that the major professional association among scholars, which also includes many practitioner members (especially in its local chapters), is the Industrial Relations Research Association. Many industrial relations scholars are also active in the Academy of Management's Human Resources Division, in discipline-based professional associations such as the American Economics Association or the American Psychological Association, or in more specialized professional associations (e.g., for dispute resolution specialists). There has, however, been controversy concerning whether the field has become too closely associated with the narrower conception of industrial relations, i.e., union-management relations, and there have been calls for name changes with the intent of better conveying the broad sense of the field (e.g., "employment relations") or to signal that the field recognizes and wishes to keep in step with trends toward a greater predominance of nonunion employment settings. In the 1980s and 1990s especially, many firms and academic programs tended to play down or even eliminate reference to industrial relations terms, and instead tended to elevate or adopt human resources terms in their job titles, department names, etc. In *The New Look in Wage Policy and Employee Relations,* Audrey Freedman documented many changes in managerial approaches to industrial relations in leading U.S. firms during the late 1970s and early 1980s.

Apart from this trend, the industrial relations field, like many, has associated with it a large number of alternative or closely related terms, including labor relations, collective bargaining, employee relations, and union-management relations. The collective bargaining term may be particularly significant. As noted earlier, collective bargaining, whereby employers negotiate with unions representing employees to establish **contracts** specifying terms and conditions of employment, holds a central and legitimate place in the view of most industrial relations specialists. In broad conceptions of industrial relations, it is merely one of a number of alternative mechanisms for establishing terms and conditions of employment. Yet to many, collective bargaining is or at least has traditionally been the "heart" of industrial relations in the United States. Thus it is not unusual to find introductory courses and texts in industrial relations referencing collective bargaining in their titles. In a sense, the view this terminology suggests is that union formation, **labor law**, and certain other matters are essentially preludes to collective bargaining, whereas contract administration (especially grievance procedures and grievance arbitration whereby employee complaints of contract violations are resolved through union-management negotiations or a neutral party's decision in the event negotiations fail), union effects on employment matters, and so on, are consequences of collective bargaining. Yet in much of the world, and increasingly over recent decades in the United States, collective bargaining per se occupies a less central place in industrial relations.

In addition, the disciplinary areas that contribute to industrial relations often have their own terms that refer to industrial relations but which also may include additional related subjects within the discipline. These include **labor economics**, industrial psychology, industrial sociology, labor law, and labor history. Similarly, management scholars often regard human resources management as a field within management that includes industrial relations or labor relations as one of its more specialized areas.

Whether one defines industrial relations broadly or narrowly of course influences which topics one would consider specializations within industrial relations. Under a narrower definition of industrial relations, specialized subjects could include industrial relations theory; labor organizations (unions and employee associations); management of industrial relations; labor and management history; labor and business law; collective bargaining and negotiations; industrial conflict (especially strikes); grievance procedures, **arbitration and mediation**, and other dispute resolution techniques; worker participation or industrial democracy; the effects of unions on employment terms and on society more broadly; and "comparative" or internationally oriented perspectives on industrial relations. A broader definition of industrial relations would include not only these but also topics that fields such as human resources tend to see as their domain, including **training and development**, workforce diversity, compensation, selection and staffing, and other employment legislation (laws and regulations directly affecting employment terms, such as laws on **pensions**, safety, and minimum wages, as opposed to ''labor law,'' which mainly governs relations between employee organizations and employers).

As an academic subject, industrial relations tends to be taught either as a subject within management (what one might call ''the business school model'') or as a separate subject within an institute or school devoted primarily to industrial relations or industrial relations and human resources. After World War II, when unions were still in ascension and had already established themselves as a major power in the U.S. political economy, many of the more industrialized states established or expanded specialized institutes or schools for industrial relations at their major universities. Typically, a major force for this movement was the state's organized labor movement (unions and employee associations), arguing that just as business schools at public universities served the needs of industry, schools were needed to servé the needs of workers. The political compromises struck in state legislatures generally produced a more neutral institution with an emphasis on studying how to maintain and promote industrial peace as well as training students in industrial relations to be employed by industry, government, and labor organizations. In addition to research and more traditional academic degree programs, these institutions often included a ''labor education'' or ''labor studies'' component aimed clearly at the needs of organized workers and their organizations. Examples of these institutions include the Institute of Labor and Industrial Relations at the University of Illinois, the School of Labor and Industrial Relations at Michigan State University, the Industrial Relations Research Institute at the University of Wisconsin, and the New York State School of Industrial and Labor Relations at Cornell University. Similar programs were established or expanded in many other states in the Great Lakes region, the Northeast, and on the West Coast. These programs tend to stress graduate and professional level education, although some offer undergraduate courses and degrees.

With the decline of unions in recent decades and the tremendous expansion of business schools at many universities and colleges, at least two important changes in the research and teaching of industrial relations have occurred. First, the specialized industrial relations institutions have tended to follow industry's call for more emphasis on human resources management and less on union-management relations. Second, business schools have become major centers of industrial relations research and teaching, but more as a result of their sheer size and number than as a result of its emphasis within the business school curriculum. In fact, due to its distinctive values and assumptions (see below) industrial relations has often been something of an awkward fit within business schools, which have found human resources management a more comfortable fit. In any case, currently both business schools and specialized schools or institutes in industrial relations are major centers for research and teaching of industrial relations. In addition, some traditional discipline programs (e.g., economics, psychology) are major centers for research and teaching on some aspects of industrial relations.

VALUES AND ASSUMPTIONS WITHIN THE FIELD

In *Collective Bargaining and Industrial Relations,* Kochan suggested that an important factor distinguishing industrial relations from its contributing disciplines and related applied areas of study (e.g., human resources) is a distinctive set of values and assumptions. These include the following propositions:

1. Labor is more than a commodity. That is, unlike inanimate factors of production such as machinery and raw materials, the work of human beings raises questions about the impact of work and work relations upon employees, questions that are societal concerns. Some industrial relations scholars (such as Roy J. Adams, in an 1992 article in *Labor Studies Journal*) take this assumption a step further in arguing that a society cannot be truly democratic if it does not provide mechanisms by which employees can influence their working lives, i.e., a means for industrial democracy.

2. There are inherent conflicts of interest between employers and employees not only in terms of economic matters (e.g., wages versus profits), but also in terms of inherent friction in superior-subordinate relations.

3. There are large areas of common interests between employers and employees despite their conflicting interests, and important interdependencies (e.g., firms need workers and workers need jobs). These compel employers and employees to resolve their conflicting interests for the sake of mutual benefits.

4. There is an inherent inequality of bargaining power in most individual employer-employee relationships, and thus collective representation of employees (e.g., unions) is often necessary to establish true freedom of contract. That is, it is not sufficient to argue

that since employer and employee are each legally free to establish or terminate an employment relationship, that they are then on equal footing.

5. Pluralism—the notion that there are multiple competing interest groups in society, each with valid interests. Thus in the workplace and in the larger society the goals of workers, employers, and society should be accommodated in an equitable balance. This contrasts with the often implicit assumption in business areas that the goals of the firm or its shareholders are supreme. Similarly, it contrasts with economists' stress on efficiency as a supreme goal, although some labor economists (such as Richard B. Freeman and James L. Medoff, authors of *What Do Unions Do?*) have updated and expanded upon earlier arguments for the efficiency of collective voice mechanisms (e.g., collective bargaining and other forms of worker representation) relative to individualistic market mechanisms (e.g., the worker's choice to enter or exit an employment relationship).

Some of these assumptions (e.g., inherent conflict of employer-employee economic interests) can be traced at least as far back as the 19th century and the work of German political philosopher Karl Marx (1818-1883); in fact, some regard Marx as the intellectual father of industrial relations. In the United States, however, the "Wisconsin School" of institutional economics, led by John R. Commons (1862-1945) and Selig Perlman (1888-1959) in the early 20th century, rejected Marx's prediction of pathological conflict escalating into inevitable class warfare between workers and capitalists and the ultimate demise of **capitalism**. Instead, Commons and his followers argued that collective bargaining and legislation could temper the excesses of capitalism, allowing workers and management to resolve their conflicts for the sake of greater common interests within the capitalist economic system. Commons is generally regarded as the intellectual father of American industrial relations.

INDUSTRIAL RELATIONS SYSTEMS MODEL

The dominant paradigm or conceptual framework for the study of industrial relations is the "Industrial Relations Systems" model advanced by Dunlop in his book of the same name. The concept of a system is applied in the sense that industrial relations, according to Daniel Quinn Mills, author of *Labor-Management Relations,* consists of the "processes by which human beings and organizations interact at the workplace and, more broadly, in society as a whole to establish the terms and conditions of employment." In other words, certain inputs (e.g., human labor, capital, managerial skill) from the environment are combined via alternative processes (e.g., collective bargaining, unilateral management decisions, legislation) to produce certain outcomes (e.g., production, job satisfaction, wage rates). Consistent with the definitions of industrial relations noted above, the study of industrial relations and the systems model focus on outcomes most closely related to the interaction of employees and employers and the "web of rules" concerning employment that they and their organizations, along with government, establish to govern employer-employee relations. Thus production per se is a system outcome, but not a principal focus of industrial relations. It has been noted that the industrial relations system concept may fall short of the definition of a system in the physical or biological sciences, but nonetheless the concept has proved useful and endured. Dunlop, in *Industrial Relations Systems,* noted that industrial relations systems can be thought of as being embedded in broader social systems. In *Collective Bargaining and Industrial Relations,* Kochan observed that like any complex social system, industrial relations systems are best understood by identifying and analyzing their various components and how they interact with one another to produce certain outcomes.

The major components of the industrial relations system are:

1. The actors (workers and their organizations, management, and government).
2. Contextual or environmental factors (labor and product markets, technology, and community or "the locus and distribution of power in the larger society" [from Dunlop's *Industrial Relations Systems*]).
3. Processes for determining the terms and conditions of employment (collective bargaining, legislation, judicial processes, and unilateral management decisions, among others).
4. Ideology, or a minimal set of shared beliefs, such as the actors' mutual acceptance of the legitimacy of other actors and their roles, which enhance system stability.
5. Outcomes, including wages and benefits, rules about work relations (e.g., standards for disciplinary action against workers), job satisfaction, employment security, productive efficiency, industrial peace and conflict, and industrial democracy.

The basic purposes of the industrial relations systems concept are to provide a conceptual framework for organizing knowledge about industrial relations and for understanding how various components of an industrial relations system combine to produce particular outcomes (and hence why outcomes vary from one setting to another or over time). Thus for example, wage rates for a particular group of workers might be understood as reflecting the interactions of their unions with management via collective bargaining within the constraints of a particular market, technological, and community environment.

The precise specification of system components may vary with the level of analysis and from one system to another. For example, when applied to a particular work site, legislation may be best understood as an environmental constraint upon the immediate parties to the employment relationship (workers, management, and possibly unions). But when speaking of a nation's industrial relations system or systems, legislation can be viewed as a process by which the parties (via government) establish terms and conditions of employment or the rules workers and management must follow in establishing those terms and conditions. As another example, when comparing industrial relations systems at a given level of analysis, the roles of the various actors may differ. Unions may play a critical role in one system, and virtually no role in another. In some national systems (e.g., within certain Latin American countries), other actors such as the military or organized religious institutions may play influential roles. The nature of actor roles may also vary across industries within a nation, perhaps as best illustrated by public sector employment, where government is also the employer.

CRITICISMS OF THE INDUSTRIAL RELATIONS SYSTEMS MODEL

Although it has endured, the industrial relations systems concept has been criticized and challenged. Criticisms have included charges that it is too static, failing to specify how change occurs in industrial relations; that its treatment of ideology is too simplistic; and that it is too deterministic or does not encourage sufficient appreciation for strategic choices made by the actors.

All of these criticisms have been embodied in recent writings arguing that U.S. industrial relations have been undergoing profound transformations in recent years. Kochan, Harry C. Katz, and Robert B. McKersie—the authors of *The Transformation of American Industrial Relations*—although not rejecting the systems concept entirely, argue that as it has been widely understood, the systems concept has not prepared us to appreciate the nature and extent of the transformation taking place. In particular, they stress how the strategic choices of management to avoid and oppose unions (both legally and illegally), often in conjunction with decisions to open or close facilities or locate production abroad or in areas where unions are weak, have fundamentally altered U.S. industrial relations. They note for example, that in the 1950s, when unions represented roughly one-third of U.S. workers, the unionized sector of the economy was often the leader in introducing workplace **innovations**, including innovations in employment terms and work methods. Further, that level of unionization was sufficiently high to provide a compelling model (or perhaps threat) for nonunion firms, such that they tended to follow the lead of the unionized sector. By the 1980s, however, innovation came to be associated more with the nonunion sector, and with unionization falling, the power of the unionized sector as a model to be emulated by nonunion firms was diminished in tandem. For example, although unions themselves represent a form of employee participation, many of the recent innovations in employee participation at the workplace level (e.g., employee involvement programs, **team** concepts, **quality circles**, employee **empowerment**, etc.) are more closely associated with the nonunion sector. In addition, Kochan and his coauthors stress that there are multiple levels of interaction between employers and employees—strategic (e.g., top executives' decisions to open or close facilities), functional (e.g., collective bargaining), and workplace (e.g., day-to-day supervisor-subordinate relations)—arguing that the industrial relations systems conception has tended to encourage excessive preoccupation with the functional level and thereby neglect of the other levels.

During the same time, public policy on employment matters had shifted from a reliance on collective bargaining (and markets) to more of an emphasis on individual worker rights established by statute and judicial decisions. **Equal employment** opportunity laws and judicial decisions narrowing the notion of employment-at-will (the notion that employer and employee are free to enter or terminate an employment relationship at any time for good reason, bad reason, or no reason in the absence of a formal contract) are prominent examples of this trend.

Reflecting its temporal origins, Dunlop's industrial relations systems concept had tended to portray or least be perceived as portraying collective bargaining as the principal mechanism for setting employment terms, although this is not inherent in the industrial relations systems concept. By the 1980s and 1990s, this tendency (or interpretation) was clearly open to question, if not clearly inaccurate.

Although not denying change, several scholars have argued that even though major transformations in industrial relations may be occurring, they are not inconsistent with traditional understandings of industrial relations or the systems concept. For example, in his essay "Industrial Relations as a Strategic Variable," which was published in *Human Resources and the Performance of the Firm,* David Lewin noted that many managerial decisions that have been called strategic choices can easily be viewed as managerial responses to environmental imperatives. Thus to the extent that increased domestic and foreign **competition** put cost-cutting pressures on employers, these can be seen as strongly influencing employer choices to avoid and oppose unions as well as influencing other employer choices about how to organize production to improve quality and minimize costs. In a recent study of possible industrial relations system transformation in several countries, which was published in *Industrial and Labor Relations Review,* Christopher L. Erickson and Sarosh Kuruvilla noted that the "transformation debate" persists partly because there is no clear consensus on what constitutes transformation.

RECENT TRENDS AND FUTURE PROSPECTS

Whether attributable to employer strategic choices or more fundamental environmental changes that govern those choices, U.S. industrial relations have clearly undergone significant change in recent years and are likely to experience further dramatic change in the years ahead. As already noted, unionization has declined dramatically. With that decline, collective bargaining has diminished in importance as a mechanism for setting employment terms of U.S. workers; rates of increases in wages and benefits for unionized workers frequently lag behind those of their nonunion counterparts (although the union-nonunion wage differential is still estimated to be fairly sizable, in the range of 10 to 20 percent with a higher differential for benefits); strike activity has set new record lows; and union political "clout" is seriously questioned. Many U.S. unions have undergone unprecedented soul-searching in their efforts to develop strategies to respond to these changes. Mergers between unions, new forms of membership and new membership benefits, and new organizing, bargaining, and political strategies and tactics have been proposed and implemented as part of union efforts to reverse their decline. In the 1994 report *The New American Workplace: A Labor Perspective*—compiled by the Committee on the Evolution of Work of the American Federation of Labor-Congress of Industrial Organizations (AFL-CIO)—unions expressed a much more positive stance toward union-management cooperation than is usually attributed to them. But in 1995, John Sweeney, then-president of the Service Employees International Union, launched an almost unprecedented and successful challenge to the incumbent leadership of the AFL-CIO, stressing a renewed commitment to organizing as a central theme. Since Sweeney's election as AFL-CIO president, the federation has made substantial changes in staff, strategies, and tactics. The AFL-CIO and some of its affiliates seem to have taken more aggressive approaches to organizing, bargaining, and politics under Sweeney's leadership. As yet there has not been a dramatic turnaround in union organizing success. In fairness to Sweeney, the contemporary decline of unionization has been in the making for roughly 50 years, and expectations for a quick turnaround might be unrealistic. In bargaining, a large-scale strike in 1997 by the Teamsters against the United Parcel Service was hailed by some as indicating that labor still had clout, as the Teamsters were able to achieve some important gains. But attempts to play a larger role in the 1996 national elections achieved only limited success, and appear to have spurred efforts by union opponents to limit union political activity.

Public policy makers have also considered other significant changes. Early in his first term, President Bill Clinton appointed a Commission on the Future of Worker-Management Relations (headed by Dunlop and including many academics as well as union and management representatives) to offer recommendations for public policy changes. Some scholars argue that the present legal framework governing union formation and union-management relations in most of the private sector (e.g., the National Labor Relations Act of 1935 or Wagner Act, as amended by the Labor Management Relations Act or **Taft-Hartley Act** of 1947, and other legislation) may have been reasonably well-suited to the United States of the 1930s and 1940s, but that subsequent economic and social changes necessitate significant amendments or even a major overhaul. Among the issues the commission considered were whether current legal bans on company-dominated unions unduly intrude on legitimate employee participation programs in nonunion firms; whether statutory protections of employee rights to join and form unions are adequate, and how to effectuate those rights in the face of intense employer opposition; and whether public policy can promote a more cooperative and less adversarial relationship between employers and employee organizations.

Some scholars (such as Bruce E. Kaufman and Morris M. Kleiner, editors of *Employee Representation: Alternatives and Future Directions*) assert that employee representation is a more fundamental issue than representation of employees by unions, noting that many nonunion firms willingly establish some form of representation system, and that the public is more supportive of this principle than of union representation. Coupling these observations with the current low level of union representation (and perhaps with the conclusion that the decline of unions is irreversible), some have proposed that the United States should seriously consider establishing **works councils** similar to those in many European nations.

Works councils are legally mandated employee representation mechanisms independent of unions which require that all employees (usually in establishments with a minimum number of employees, perhaps ten) elect representatives to the works council to confer with management and to ensure that workers' statutory rights are observed. Although they generally do not bargain over wages and benefits, works councils address many of the issues that U.S. unions have traditionally addressed, including **layoffs**, discipline systems, and workplace safety.

Even in a Democrat-controlled Congress, any major changes to labor relations law could face stiff opposition. After more business-friendly Republicans gained a slight majority in Congress in the 1994 elections, prospects for any significant changes in legislation appeared to evaporate. Relatively strong performance for the economy during most of the 1990s probably contributed to Congressional inaction as well.

(Acknowledgment: The author thanks Roy J. Adams, William P. Anthony, Daniel G. Gallagher, Paul Jarley, and Bruce E. Kaufman for helpful comments, but retains sole responsibility for any errors.)

SEE ALSO: Labor-Management Relations

[Jack Fiorito, Ph.D.]

FURTHER READING:

Adams, Roy J. ''Efficiency Is Not Enough.'' *Labor Studies Journal* 17, no. 1 (Spring 1992): 18-28.

——, and Noah Meltz, eds. *Industrial Relations Theory.* Metuchen, NJ: Scarecrow Press, 1994.

American Federation of Labor-Congress of Industrial Organizations. Committee on the Evolution of Work. *The New American Workplace: A Labor Perspective.* Washington: American Federation of Labor-Congress of Industrial Organizations, 1994.

Dunlop, John T. *Industrial Relations Systems.* New York: Holt-Dryden, 1958.

——. ''Industrial Relations Theory.'' *Advances in Industrial and Labor Relations* 8 (1998): 15-24.

Erickson, Christopher L., and Sarosh Kuruvilla. ''Industrial Relations System Transformation.'' *Industrial and Labor Relations Review* 52 (1998): 3-21.

Freedman, Audrey. *The New Look in Wage Policy and Employee Relations.* New York: Conference Board, 1985.

Freeman, Richard B., and James L. Medoff. *What Do Unions Do?* New York: Basic Books, 1984.

Friedman, Sheldon, Richard W. Hurd, Rudolph A. Oswald, and Ronald L. Seeber, eds. *Restoring the Promise of American Labor Law.* Ithaca, NY: ILR Press, 1994.

Heckscher, Charles C. *The New Unionism.* New York: Basic Books, 1988.

Katz, Harry C., and Thomas A. Kochan. *An Introduction to Collective Bargaining and Industrial Relations.* New York: McGraw-Hill, 1992.

Kaufman, Bruce E. *The Origins and Evolution of the Field of Industrial Relations in the United States.* Ithaca, NY: ILR Press, 1993.

Kaufman, Bruce E., and Morris M. Kleiner, eds. *Employee Representation: Alternatives and Future Directions.* Madison, WI: Industrial Relations Research Association, 1993.

Kochan, Thomas A. *Collective Bargaining and Industrial Relations: From Theory to Policy to Practice.* Homewood, IL: Irwin, 1980.

Kochan, Thomas A., Harry C. Katz, and Robert B. McKersie. *The Transformation of American Industrial Relations.* New York: Basic Books, 1986.

Lewin, David. ''Industrial Relations as a Strategic Variable.'' In *Human Resources and the Performance of the Firm,* edited by Morris M. Kleiner and others. Madison, WI: Industrial Relations Research Association, 1987.

Mills, Daniel Quinn. *Labor-Management Relations.* 5th ed. New York: McGraw-Hill, 1994.

Strauss, George, Daniel G. Gallagher, and Jack Fiorito, eds. *The State of the Unions.* Madison, WI: Industrial Relations Research Association, 1991.

U.S. Department of Labor. Bureau of Labor Statistics. ''Union Members in 1998'' (press release 99-21). Washington: U.S. Department of Labor, 1999. Available from stats.bls.gov/newsrels.htm.

Walton, Richard E., and Robert B. McKersie. *A Behavioral Theory of Labor Negotiations: An Analysis of a Social Interaction System.* New York: McGraw-Hill, 1965.

INDUSTRIAL SAFETY

Safety problems in work settings range from immediate threats like toxic substances and grievous bodily injuries to subtle, progressive dangers such as repetitive motion injuries, high noise levels, and air quality. In general, workplace hazards can be categorized into three groups:

1. Chemical hazards, in which the body absorbs toxins.
2. Ergonomic hazards, in which the body is strained or injured, often over an extended period, because of the nature (design) of the task, its frequency, or intensity.
3. Physical hazards, in which the worker is exposed to harmful elements or physical dangers, such as heat or moving parts.

In many cases companies are not only ethically bound to ensure the safety of their workers against all such hazards, but also legally and financially liable to do so. In most industrial settings safety precautions are highly regulated by federal and state agencies, a compliance regime that many business leaders resent. The stiff regulatory burden in part reflects the complex and serious nature of safety issues. Some believe that smaller companies, in particular, would have a hard time staying abreast of the myriad safety issues if not for legal requirements, which, according to the theory, educate employers about work hazards. However, the labyrinth of safety laws and regulations has also risen in response to the historical pattern of corporate resistance in adopting comprehensive, proactive safety policies and in providing adequate compensation once an injury has occurred. There is a marked tendency for businesses to do as little as possible in these areas until prodded by laws or organized labor.

Thus, the issue of industrial safety has evolved concurrently with industrial development in the United States. Two events were most important: the passage of workers' compensation laws at the start of the 20th century, and the Occupational Safety and Health Act, enacted in 1970. Over time, the issue of industrial safety has been marked by a shift from compensation to prevention as well as toward an increasing emphasis on addressing the long-term effects of occupational hazards.

In the modern context, corporate management increasingly has viewed industrial safety measures as an investment—one that may save money in the long run by way of reducing disability pay, improving productivity, and avoiding lawsuits. This approach lends itself to greater professionalization of safety management, instead of rote compliance, and to more proactive policies. Rather than viewing an injury as a fluke or a random mistake, management today is more likely to look for systemic problems, such as:

- the way equipment is designed or used;
- the way workflow is configured;
- how workers are trained;
- whether unsafe behaviors are tacitly encouraged by other corporate practices or goals; and
- whether there is a gap between official policies and employee practices.

Table 1

Components of a Safety Program

The following are techniques and policy areas identified by the National Safety Council in its publication *14 Elements of a Successful Safety & Health Program.*

1. Hazard recognition, evaluation, and control
2. Workplace design and engineering
3. Safety performance management
4. Regulatory compliance management
5. Occupational health
6. Information collection
7. Employee involvement
8. Motivation, behavior, and attitudes
9. Training and orientation
10. Organizational communications
11. Management and control of external exposures
12. Environmental management
13. Workplace planning and staffing
14. Assessments, audits, and evaluations

STATISTICAL PROFILE

INJURIES AND ILLNESSES. According to figures compiled by the U.S. Bureau of Labor Statistics, in 1997 there were 7.1 workplace injuries and illnesses for every 100 full-time workers, corresponding to a total of 6.1 million incidents in the private sector. Injuries constitute more than 90 percent of these cases, as workplace-induced illnesses are relatively rare. The overall injury/illness rate was down by about 15 percent from levels in the early 1990s. Indeed, the 1997 level was the lowest ever recorded.

The most common non-lethal occupational hazard is by far repetitive motion. Repetitive motion injuries are caused by tasks such as typing and repetitive use of tools. In 1997, these accounted for nearly two-thirds of all reported workplace injuries in the private sector. Skin disorders were second, representing 13.4 percent of all injuries. They included rashes, boils, inflammations, and hives, among other ailments. Other major injury categories included respiratory conditions and other illnesses brought on by exposure to toxins, such as digestive disorders. Just under half of all such illnesses and injuries result in lost work time.

FATALITIES. In a typical year in the 1990s there were also more than 6,000 fatalities in U.S. workplaces. The rate of work-related deaths has declined significantly over time. The death rate in 1980 was a tenth of that in 1910; from 1974 to 1994 alone the rate fell by 50 percent. In 1997, some 40 percent of the 6,218 deaths were caused by transportation equipment, mostly due to vehicle collisions. Other leading causes of workplace fatalities include worksite violence (most often in the course of a robbery or other crime), being accidentally struck by an object, machine-related accidents, falls, and exposure to deadly substances and environments (e.g., poisons, oxygen shortage, electrical shock, fire). Perhaps contrary to general perceptions, a large percentage of all occupational fatalities occur at small companies.

PUBLIC SECTOR. While workplace injuries are most commonly associated with private industry, even the federal government is not immune workplace hazards. In fiscal 1998, 152,053 workplace injuries and illnesses and 146 deaths were reported. Among the most dangerous federal agencies were defense-related departments, the prison system, the Food Safety Inspection Service, the Immigration and Naturalization Service (INS), the Mine Safety and Health Administration, the Bureau of Engraving and Printing, and the U.S. Postal Service. (OSHA had a somewhat below average rate of workplace injuries.)

HISTORICAL DEVELOPMENT

Many of the important developments in promoting industrial safety were initially implemented at the state level. Massachusetts, then the leading textile production center in the United States, was the first state to introduce industrial safety measures. It introduced factory inspection in 1867, established the Bureau of Labor Statistics in 1869 to study factory accidents, and enacted the first legislation requiring protective guards over dangerous machinery in 1877.

These measures resulted from demands made by the labor movement. Another key demand was for **workers' compensation**. Prior to the late 19th century, the courts consistently favored employers in cases in which workers attempted to gain compensation for injuries occurring in the workplace. The defenses used on behalf of employers were that the employee assumed the risk of employment by accepting the job and that either the injured worker's or a fellow worker's negligence was responsible for an accident. The principles behind these defenses were referred to as assumption of risk, contributory negligence, and the fellow servant rule.

By the late 19th century, a number of states enacted employer's liability acts, for which courts made awards to injured workers or their survivors on the finding of employer **negligence**. Yet these acts still required litigation, a practice that was often costly and time-consuming for both employers and employees, and fewer than 30 percent of industrial accidents in the United States were compensated prior to workers' compensation legislation. Workers' compensation was first developed in the 19th century under the German chancellor Otto von Bismarck. The German system compensated workers on a no-fault basis. The system spread to most other European countries by the turn of the century. The first workmen's compensation legislation in the United States was enacted in 1908, but covered only certain federal employees and provided low benefits. New Jersey passed the first state-level workers' compensation legislation in 1911, and many other states shortly followed suit. The last state to enact workers' compensation legislation was Mississippi in 1948.

Workers' compensation laws vary widely from state to state but have key objectives in common. Employers are required to compensate for work-related injuries or sickness by paying medical expenses, disability benefits, and compensation for lost work time. Workers are barred, on the other hand, from suing their employers in most cases, protecting employers from large liability settlements. In his *Industrial Safety: Management and Technology,* David Colling writes that, "Workmen's compensation laws have done more to promote safety than all other measures collectively, because employers found it more cost-effective to concentrate on safety than to compensate employees for injury or loss of life."

As employers came to rely on insurance companies to protect them from the costs of workers' compensation, insurers came to be increasingly involved in promoting industrial safety programs and researching industrial safety issues. The right of organized labor to negotiate with management was vindicated by the National Labor Relations Act of 1935 (the Wagner Act), and a number of improvements in company safety programs followed in its wake.

THE CREATION OF OSHA

One of the key developments in industrial safety legislation was the Occupational Safety and Health Act of 1970. The Act was the first comprehensive, industrial safety legislation passed at the federal level and passed nearly unanimously through both houses of Congress. One of the factors contributing to strong support for the act was the rise in the number of work-related fatalities in the 1960s and particularly the Farmington, West Virginia mine disaster of 1968, in which 78 miners were killed. The distinguishing characteristic of the act was its emphasis on the prevention of rather than compensation for industrial accidents and illnesses. The act provided for the establishment of the **Occupational Safety and Health Administration (OSHA)** and the National Institute of Occupational Safety and Health (NIOSH). Among the key provisions of the act were the development of mandatory safety and health standards, the enforcement of these standards, and standardized record-keeping and reporting procedures.

OSHA POLICIES AND REGULATIONS

Among the types of OSHA regulations are safety standards, designed to prevent accidents, and health standards, designed to protect against exposure to toxins and to address the more long-term effects of occupational hazards. So-called "horizontal" standards apply to all industries whereas "vertical" standards apply to specific industries or occupations. Some of OSHA's standards were adopted from private national organizations, such as the American National Standards Institute, the National Fire Protection Association, and the American Society of Mechanical Engineers. Other standards are developed by OSHA itself, often based on recommendations from NIOSH.

Prior to their being issued, OSHA must publish the proposed standards, after which the public has 30 days to respond. In the case of objections to proposed standards, OSHA holds public hearings to determine whether the standard should be issued or withdrawn. Court rulings upheld OSHA's enforcement of standards through surprise inspections. Given the high ratio of workplaces to OSHA inspectors, however, the agency often is compelled to inspect worksites after an accident has occurred. A program of voluntary compliance was also developed in which employers invite OSHA inspectors to provide assistance in identifying and correcting violations of standards.

Right-to-know laws were an important development in industrial safety legislation. The first of these laws was OSHA's Hazard Communication Standard, enacted in 1983. The **Environmental Protection Agency (EPA)** is also engaged in the administration of right-to-know laws as a result of the Superfund Amendments and Reauthorization Act of 1986. Right-to-know laws require that dangerous materials in the workplace be identified and that workers be informed of these dangers as well as trained in their safe use.

OSHA INSPECTION TRENDS

In fiscal 1998, OSHA conducted some 34,442 inspections of U.S. companies. In addition, state agencies performed 55,699 workplace inspections. More than three-quarters of federal inspections were done at construction and manufacturing sites. OSHA inspections uncovered 76,980 violations, or an average of 2.2 violations per inspection. Of these, two-thirds were classified as serious. Total penalties levied by OSHA that year surpassed $79 million.

POLITICS AND FUNDING

OSHA's effectiveness in reducing industrial injury and illness has been debated since its earliest years. There was a 27 percent decline in the actual number of workplace fatalities from 1974 to 1986 and a 40 percent decline in the rate of fatalities over these same years. However, in his *Cooperation and Conflict in Occupational Safety and Health,* Richard Wokutch cites several studies that argue that these declines are not readily attributable to OSHA's actions. Consistent with the anti-regulatory agenda of the Reagan administration, OSHA suffered substantial cutbacks in the 1980s. In the budget for fiscal year 1982, OSHA funding fell to $195 million, down from $205 million in fiscal year 1981, and the number of funded positions was reduced by 19 percent. During the 1990s OSHA's budget was restored under the Clinton administration; by 1999 it was at $350 million a year, supporting a staff of 2,200.

BASIC SAFETY POLICIES AND PROCEDURES

One of the important aspects of industrial safety programs is the identification of hazards. Managers typically determine hazards by the examination of accident records, interviews with engineers and equipment operators, and the advice of safety specialists, such as OSHA or insurance companies.

Approximately one-fourth of workers' compensation claims result from the handling of materials, including not only manual handling, but also semi-automated handling and material handling with powered equipment, such as forklifts. Fully 80 percent of injuries resulting from the handling of materials are injuries to the lower back. Most back injuries result not from a single incident, but from prolonged repetition. The development of automatic palletizing machinery has eliminated one of the tasks most responsible for causing lower back injury.

Based on a NIOSH study, the Kaiser Aluminum and Chemical Corporation undertook a safety program for forklift operators. One of Kaiser's and NIOSH's findings was that most forklift accidents occurred when operators were backing up. After identifying this hazard, Kaiser developed an operating procedure that required a redesign of the exhaust systems on their propane-fueled forklifts, such that forklift operators could improve their visibility when backing up without breathing in exhaust.

About one-tenth of industrial accidents result from operating machinery, and these accidents often result in severe injury. Among the most dangerous types of machinery are power presses and woodworking tools, which most commonly cause injury to the hands. A number of mechanisms have been developed to safeguard against such injuries. The simplest of these are barrier guards, in which the moving parts of machinery are enclosed in a protective housing. These safeguards are typically used in conjunction with sensors so that the machine cannot be operated without them. Other types of safeguards include those that prevent a machine from operating unless a worker has both hands properly in place, automated material feeding devices, warning labels, and color coding.

Table 1 lists a more comprehensive set of policy areas and management practices for a safety program, as published by the National Safety Council, a broad-based safety advocacy organization.

SEE ALSO: Comprehensive Environmental Response, Compensation & Liability Act (CERCLA) of 1980 (Superfund)

[David Kucera]

FURTHER READING:

Colling, David A. *Industrial Safety: Management and Technology.* Englewood Cliffs, NJ: Prentice Hall, 1990.

Hantula, Donald A., and Susan M. Hilbert. "Safety Isn't Simple." *Academy of Management Executive* 11, no. 2 (1997).

Kohn, James P., Mark A. Friend, and Celeste A. Winterberger. *Fundamentals of Occupational Safety and Health.* Rockville, MD: Government Institutes, 1996.

Mansdorf, S.Z. *Complete Manual of Industrial Safety.* Englewood Cliffs, NJ: Prentice Hall, 1993.

Marsh, Barbara. "Workers at Risk: Chance of Getting Hurt is Generally Far Higher at Small Companies." *Wall Street Journal,* 3 February 1994.

National Safety Council. *14 Elements of a Successful Safety and Health Program.* Itasca, IL, 1998. Available from www.nsc.org.

Occupational Safety and Health Administration. *OSHA Home Page.* Washington, 1999. Available from www.osha.gov.

Wokutch, Richard E. *Cooperation and Conflict in Occupational Safety and Health: A Multination Study of the Automotive Industry.* New York: Praeger, 1990.

INDUSTRIAL/ORGANIZATIONAL PSYCHOLOGY

Industrial/organizational (I/O) psychology is the application or extension of psychological methods and principles to the solution of organizational and workplace problems. Most commonly, I/O psychology is concerned with those problems caused by human performance and those which affect human performance within organizational contexts. Specifically, this entails, among other things,

- conducting studies on **organizational behavior** and worker-management interactions,
- analyzing **corporate culture** and individual/group interactions
- developing and evaluating employee selection and appraisal techniques
- assessing corporate leadership and **employee motivation** strategies
- identifying causes of—and resolutions to—internal conflicts
- advising management of the potential psychological and social impact of corporate policies

I/O psychologists employ psychological measurement and research findings related to human abilities, motivation, perception, and learning in seeking to improve the fit between the needs of the work organization and those of the people who populate it.

Normally training in I/O psychology requires a master's degree or Ph.D. Practitioners may also be affiliated with one or more professional associations for the field. The Society for Industrial-Organizational Psychology (SIOP), the major professional organization which represents I/O psychologists and a division of the American Psychological Association, had about 2,000 members as of 1999.

HISTORY

ORIGINS. I/O psychology has its roots in the late 19th century movement to study and measure human capabilities and motives. Some early psychologists, noting the practical nature of psychological research, sought to apply the findings to business problems. In response to the urging of some **advertising** executives, one such early psychologist, Walter Dill Scott, *The Theory of Advertising* (1903), generally considered to be the first book linking psychology and the business world. It was followed by *The Psychology of Advertising* (1908). Another founder of the field was Hugo Münsterberg (1863-1916), a German-born psychologist teaching at Harvard University who in 1913 published *The Psychology of Industrial Efficiency.* Münsterberg's book was heavily influenced by the fascination with human efficiency so well represented in the work of Frank and Lillian Gilbreth and Frederick W. Taylor (1856-1915).

When the United States entered World War I in 1917, applied psychology truly came into its own. Committees of psychologists investigated soldier morale, motivation, and the prevalence of psychological impairment. Moreover, psychologists developed a group-administered intelligence test called the Army Alpha. While 1,726,000 enlisted men and officers were tested, little use was made of the results at the time since the war ended a mere three months after the testing program was authorized. However, research studies did show that the test scores were related to soldier performance.

After the war, in 1919, the first university-based center for studying the applications of psychology to business was established at the Carnegie Institute of Technology. Called the U.S. Bureau of Salesmanship Research, it was funded largely by the life insurance industry for the purpose of conducting research for the selection and development of clerical and executive personnel as well as sales people.

NEOCLASSICAL SCHOOL. In 1924, a change in direction was heralded by the **Hawthorne experiments**, named after Western Electric Company's Hawthorne plant in Chicago where the studies were conducted. Originally conceived as a test of some aspects of Taylor's principles, the researchers sought the optimal level of illumination necessary for workers to produce telephone equipment. Instead of finding Taylor's assumed "one-best-way," the researchers found that productivity increased after each change in lighting no matter how bright or dim they made it. Eventually, they concluded that the workers were responding to the attention they were getting as part of the special research study and this phenomenon came to be known as the *Hawthorne effect.* Up to this point, thinking about work organizations had been dominated by classical (i.e., bureaucratic or machine) theory. Workers were viewed as extensions of the job and the aim was to arrange human activity to achieve maximum efficiency. Moreover, these classical views of organization assumed a top-down management point of view, emphasizing the authority structure of the organization. The object was to get top management's wishes translated into practice on the shop floor. So the task was to design the job according to scientific precepts and then provide an incentive (usually piecework) to get workers to comply with the will of management and the industrial engineers.

The Hawthorne researchers came to embrace a very different view of the business enterprise. They concluded that friendship patterns among the workers were the guts of the organization, and also that people would work harder for an organization that they believed was interested in their. The Hawthorne researchers eschewed economic incentives as the driving force behind work and painted a rich picture of the informal relationships (i.e., those not specified in the organizational chart or job specifications) among workers themselves, in addition to those among workers and the managers, which was the focus of the classical view. People, in other words, came to work not for money, but for the social rewards and satisfactions inherent in human organization.

Management was no longer the controlling force for the Hawthorne researchers (also called neoclassical theorists). Rather, they argued that management can govern only with consent of the workers and that workers actually influence management decisions by controlling the impression that management had of a proper day's work. For example, workers might slow up the pace when the time-motion man (the one with the stopwatch) came into view. The Hawthorne researchers became convinced that job performance could be influenced in ways that could not be achieved with either money or job design. They proposed motivating workers with a set of techniques called human relations, which involved providing considerate supervision and management as a means of persuading the workers to conform to management's expectations by convincing them that the company was indeed concerned about them. In other words, the goal was to change employee attitudes rather than job design or pay. In return, productivity and reliable job performance would presumably increase. Thus, motivation was seen as a function of the satisfaction of social needs for acceptance, status within one's group, and humane supervision. They recognized that workers may not be performing effectively, not because they are immoral, but because they perceive that they are being treated indifferently or even shabbily by management. To motivate workers, therefore, one changes those perceptions.

Contemporary I/O psychologists no longer feel they have to choose between classical bureaucratic theory or scientific management on the one hand and neoclassical human relations on the other. The common view today is that taken together, they provide a comprehensive picture of organizational functioning. Environmental forces such as management directives, human capabilities, the state of technology, and economic considerations are potent forces on worker performance and cannot be denied. Likewise, human motivation, perceptions, and job attitudes are influential as well and are ignored at management's peril.

I/O psychologists recognize that there is an inherent conflict between the needs of organizations and the needs of individuals. Organizations seek regularity and so attempt to reduce human behavior to predictable patterns. That's what organizing is. Humans, on the other hand, do not take well to having their behavior reduced to only those acts required by the job, preferring instead to add spontaneity and expression to the equation. This conflict will never be eliminated, only alleviated. It requires constant, ongoing effort and vigilance to contain the unnatural arrangement we call social organization.

GROWTH AND PROFESSIONALIZATION. During World War II, psychologists contributed heavily to the military by developing the Army General Classification Test for the assessment and placement of draftees, as well as specific skills and ability tests, and leadership potential tests. Psychologists also conducted studies of accidents and plane crashes (which led to the field of engineering psychology), morale, and soldier attitudes.

Following World War II, I/O psychology emerged as a specifically recognized specialty area within the broader discipline of psychology. And even within I/O psychology, subspecialties emerged such as personnel psychology, engineering psychology, and organizational psychology. In the late 1950s and into the 1960s, a renewed thrust toward studying organizations with psychological precepts emerged as social psychologists and I/O psychologists gained the conceptual tools needed to model and understand large, task oriented groups including work organizations. From this line of inquiry came the work of I/O psychologists in assessing the effects of organizational structure and functioning on employees. Related applications appeared under the rubric of *organization development* (e.g., participative management, socio-technical systems, self-managing work groups, team building, survey feedback, and related approaches).

MODERN APPROACHES. Contemporary I/O psychologists no longer feel they have to choose between classical bureaucratic theory or scientific management and neoclassical human relations. The common view today is that taken together, they provide a comprehensive picture of organizational functioning. Environmental forces such as management directives, human capabilities, the state of technology, and economic considerations are potent forces on worker performance and cannot be denied. Likewise, human motivation, perceptions, and job attitudes are influential and are ignored at management's peril.

I/O psychologists recognize that there is an inherent conflict between the needs of organizations and the needs of individuals. Organizations seek regularity and so attempt to reduce human behavior to predictable patterns. Humans, on the other hand, do not take well to having their behavior reduced to the acts required by a job, preferring to add spontaneity and expression to the equation. This conflict will never be eliminated, only alleviated. It requires constant, ongoing effort and vigilance to contain the unnatural arrangement we call social organization.

The most recent major thrust in I/O psychology began in the 1970s following court decisions interpreting the 1964 Civil Rights Act. The courts placed a heavy burden on employers to defend the validity (i.e., job relevance) of their recruiting, selection, and promotional procedures. Many employers concluded that complying with this and subsequent antidiscrimination legislation required the skills of I/O psychologists as their best defense against lawsuits brought by employees who claimed they were victims of illegal employment discrimination. Evidence of the validity of selection criteria as provided by I/O psychologists is often essential in defending against charges of civil rights violations brought by government or employees against employers.

WHERE I/O PSYCHOLOGY IS USED

According to a 1997 membership survey of the Society for Industrial-Organizational Psychology, nearly two-thirds of U.S. I/O psychologists are employed by academic institutions and consulting firms. Employment at consulting firms has been the growth category in the profession, while the percentage of I/O psychologists employed by academia and private organizations has declined somewhat. About 15 percent work for private companies, and the rest work at government agencies or other organizations.

Large organizations are the primary users of I/O psychological methods, either directly by employing an I/O psychologist's services or indirectly by using information from the field (e.g., published articles, books, seminars). Numerous large American corporations such as AT&T, IBM, Unisys Corp., General Motors Corp., Ford Motor Co., PepsiCo, Inc., to name just a few, maintain a staff of I/O psychologists. Many other companies regularly use I/O psychologists as consultants on an as-needed basis. I/O psychologists are also employed by government. The federal Office of Personnel Management has an active test development program for civil service test construction, and all branches of the military employ I/O psychologists to conduct research and applications in leadership, personnel placement testing, human factors, and for improving motivation and morale. The U.S. Army Research Institute is an example of one such military agency. State and municipal governments also employ psychologists, especially for personnel selection purposes in the context of local civil service requirements. Abroad, I/O psychology is widely employed in England, Australia, Germany, Japan, and China.

In these various settings, the most common activities of I/O psychologists are in the areas of personnel selection and performance appraisal; management, leadership, and organizational psychology; motivation and employee satisfaction; and **training and development**.

HOW I/O PSYCHOLOGY IS USED

In the process of diagnosing an organization's problems, recommending or implementing changes, and evaluating the consequences of those changes, contemporary I/O psychologists employ one or more of four non-mutually exclusive emphases in addressing:

1. *Personnel psychology.* Personnel psychology is concerned with individual differences and therefore deals with all aspects of recruiting and selecting personnel.
2. *Training.* Training is applying the principles of human learning to teaching employees skills, techniques, strategies, and ideas for improving their performance.
3. *Motivation and leadership.* This deals with incumbent employees and seeks to create an environment that provides employees with a clear view of what they are supposed to accomplish and promotes the creation of conditions conducive to encouraging people to give their best.
4. *Engineering psychology.* The engineering psychologist addresses the human problems of organization through the design of machinery and tools that take human limitations specifically into account.

PERSONNEL PSYCHOLOGY

Personnel psychology is the most distinctive and potent approach available to I/O psychologists in alleviating the person-organization dilemma (i.e., the resistance of humans to have their behavior artificially reduced to recurring predictable patterns). Simply put, personnel psychology attempts to identify the best candidate for an available position using rigorous methods that have been shown to be accurate in the past. The thrust of personnel psychology is to study a job and the traits of individuals who hold the job, and then use this information to predict what kinds of individuals would do well in the future. Personnel psychology is based on the psychology of individual differences (i.e., that people vary in their interests, skills, and abilities). Since various jobs require different combinations of these human qualities, matching the person to the job involves assessing human characteristics and job characteristics alike in an objective manner in order to achieve a satisfactory person-job fit.

JOB ANALYSIS. Job analysis refers to a set of techniques for describing (a) the actual tasks, activities, arrangements, and working conditions a job involves; (b) the employee traits (knowledge, skills, other qualifications) needed to perform the job effectively; and (c) the procedures used to hire the existing employees. Job analysis yields a job description that portrays the actual job as it is done, not as management wants it to be done or as management imagines it is done.

There are a variety of methods and data sources available for uncovering the knowledge, skills, and abilities necessary to perform a job. Chief among these are observation (when the job activities are observable), interviews, and/or questionnaires administered to employees performing the job, their supervisors, as well as subject matter experts (SMEs) who are individuals carefully chosen because of their expertise in the target job. Other methods are activity logs, examination of training manuals, personnel records, and performance reviews. Choosing among these will obviously be influenced by such factors as whether the job is largely observable (i.e., manual) or not readily observable (i.e., primarily knowledge work).

CRITERION DEVELOPMENT. Following the job analysis is the establishment of job performance criteria for the target job. The object is to set measurable standards that include a complete representation of demonstrably relevant job facets (criterion sufficiency) and exclude those not essential to proper performance (criterion contamination). Performance criteria may be objective or subjective. Examples of objective criteria are numbers of units produced, amount of scrap, number of errors made, and similar objectively measurable criteria. Subjective criteria consist of methods such as supervisory ratings, peer ratings, and sometimes subordinate ratings. The challenge in developing useful performance criteria is to resist the temptation to try to force objective performance criteria on jobs that are not amenable to such criteria.

I/O psychologists, moreover, recognize that setting performance standards means making sure that apples are being compared with apples. If the same standards apply to several employees, even if their job titles are the same, it is critical they are doing precisely the same job under the same conditions—another reason why the job analysis is so important. If some workers are using old model machine tools while others are using newer models, it could make a performance difference that has nothing to do with the individual worker.

PERFORMANCE EVALUATION. Once performance criteria are established, the next step is the process of evaluating the performance of existing employees. Performance evaluation may be used for two purposes: personnel decisions and feedback to the employee to help improve performance (i.e., **performance appraisal**). In the former instance, performance evaluations are used in making decisions about promotions, transfers, pay increases, layoffs, granting performance awards, evaluating recruiting procedures, and validating personnel selection devices.

PERSONNEL SELECTION. For selection devices to be useful they have to be related to the job. While the point is obvious, it is often overlooked or distorted in practice. Commonly used selection devices include personal interviews, application blanks, paper and pencil tests, situational tests (such as incorporated in assessment centers and work samples), biographical inventories. For any given job, a selection device can be validated by showing that performance on the device is statistically related to subsequent job performance (empirical validity) or logically related to job performance based on the results of the job analysis itself (job content validity). Generally, validity studies of some of the most popular selection devices reveal the following:

PERSONAL INTERVIEWS. The unstructured personal interview is usually an unreliable selection device because research has shown, with few exceptions, that different interviewers draw different conclusions about the same candidate. Without adequate reliability, a selection device cannot be valid. The commonly used unstructured personal interview is based on the assumption that one person can size up another in a brief and unsystematic chat. For most selection purposes, there is no evidence that humans have that ability. Studies of the unstructured interview reveal that different candidates are often asked different questions, or the order of questioning varies from candidate to candidate. Often questions are asked for which the answers are usually uninterpretable with regard to the job (e.g., "Why do you want to work here?"). It should be no surprise, then, that some studies have actually found the unstructured interview to be a negative selector. That is, it increases the probability of picking the wrong candidate for the job. Most of the information garnered from the personal interview can be obtained by other means.

For employers who want to use interviews, the structured or standardized interview is preferred. In the structured interview all candidates are asked the same questions in the same order. Newer developments in structured interviewing include the situational interview and experience interview where candidate are presented with situations and then are asked how they would (or actually did) respond to them. The situations presented are derived from job analyses and the answers are scored based on validated coding schemes.

PAPER-AND-PENCIL TESTS AND QUESTIONNAIRES. Paper-and-pencil tests are used to measure human skills, interests, abilities, and personality attributes. Such tests are economical to administer and, when judiciously chosen and validated, are an objective and efficient aid in the selection of employees. Evidence collected over many decades indicates that cognitive ability (intelligence) tests generalize across many different jobs and predict performance for a substantial variety of jobs. This is because virtually all human endeavor requires at least some logical reasoning and problem solving ability. The more reasoning ability a job requires, the more valid will be cognitive ability tests. Other tests measure such abilities as perceptual speed and accuracy which is essential to effective clerical work, perception in three dimensions necessary for certain technical jobs, reading and vocabulary skills, numerical ability, interests, specialized aptitudes, and knowledge.

Biographical inventory questionnaires tap applicants' background and experiences and have proven highly valid in many settings. Additionally, if properly designed and validated, the application blank can also serve as a useful selection device. A relative newcomer to personnel selection is the integrity or honesty test, which has come to replace the polygraph. In 1988, polygraph testing became illegal for use in personnel testing by private employers, but not by government agencies. Preliminary validation studies of paper-and-pencil integrity tests that have come to replace the polygraph show they have promise in identifying employees prone to theft, absenteeism, drug abuse, and malingering. Honesty tests are relatively inexpensive to administer and perhaps 15 million employees a year are asked to take such tests.

WORK SAMPLES, SIMULATIONS, AND ASSESSMENT. Another set of methods for assessing job applicants is the use of tests which attempt to sample or simulate situations that the employee might encounter on the job. For some jobs, such as word processing, it is often only necessary for the applicant to demonstrate the ability to create a document meeting certain requirements using a word processing program. On a more elaborate scale one of the most widely used examples of this type of test is the assessment center method, which requires candidates for a job or promotion to perform exercises before observers who rate their performance. Originally, developed by the Office of Strategic Services, forerunner of the Central Intelligence Agency (CIA), assessment centers are used to identify leadership talent. In the private sector their use was pioneered beginning in the 1950s by AT&T. They are currently used by over 2,000 organizations for identifying managerial talent as well as for training and feedback.

LETTERS OF RECOMMENDATION. Letters of recommendation are usually poor indicators of future job performance, and many organizations refuse to write them for departing employees for fear of legal reprisal if the employee discovers the letter contains uncomplimentary statements. Letters of recommendation are somewhat like unstructured personal interviews in that, without a specific guide for the writers, they are non-comparable. Letters also suffer from a leniency bias in that writers are usually too eager to say good things about the candidate whether or not they are accurate.

RECRUITING. Finding satisfactory employees can be simplified by identifying recruiting sources that yield the most successful employees. Research by I/O psychologists has shown that, in general, rehires and recommendations of existing employees are the best sources, while employment agencies, college placement offices, walk-ins, and replies to newspaper ads have the least chance of working out. This varies with the nature of the job, however.

TRAINING

I/O psychologists are keenly interested in employee training for a number of reasons. For one, new employees often need instruction about the job or the organization's particular rules, procedures, or facilities. Another reason is that training involves the application of theories and techniques of human learning developed mainly by experimental and cognitive psychologists over the years and in which all psychologists, including I/O psychologists, are well versed as part of their education. Thus, applying learning principles such as reinforcement, feedback, knowledge of results, and learner motivation in an organizational context are all within the purview of I/O psychology.

One of the major concerns of I/O psychologists has to do with training outcomes. While no one is sure how much American organizations spend on training employees every year, there is wide agreement that the amount is probably in the tens of billions. Very little money or time, however, is spent evaluating the training to see what the organization is getting for its money and effort. This is especially true of management training. It would seem that for most organizations, training is a ritual: it's something they feel they are supposed to do and questions of results are irrelevant

I/O psychologists are rarely trainers, but they can be heavily involved in establishing training needs through the job analysis and performance evaluation processes as well as employee attitude surveys. They are, moreover, well placed to judge if an organizational problem can be alleviated by training. Knowing that training does not reliably overcome differences in ability, I/O psychologists address questions such as "who, if anyone, needs training?" and "are the present employees likely to improve with training or would an improved selection or motivational program be more fruitful?" Once the I/O psychologist determines that training is the appropriate course, he or she then attempts to define the best content and format for the training, where it should be held, and what measures will be used to evaluate its effectiveness.

EMPLOYEE MOTIVATION AND SATISFACTION

Despite the best efforts of I/O psychologists to design recruitment, selection, and training programs to reduce the inherent conflict between the needs of people and those of organizations, problems still arise. Just because people can do the job and know how to do the job does not mean they will do it as required. At this point it becomes necessary to motivate employees not merely to do management's bidding, but, in many cases, to take responsibility themselves for improving the way the work is done and creating satisfying work experiences. I/O psychologists influence this process by identifying to what degree employees are satisfied and motivated, what factors contribute most to this status, and what the company might to do improve the situation.

There are four major approaches I/O psychologists employ to assist organizations in creating conditions conducive to high effort and effective performance:

1. *Motivation.* Creating organizational conditions conducive to bringing out the best in employees requires making assumptions about what motivates employees or why people work. One of the I/O psychologist's tasks, therefore, is to apply theories of work motivation in the development of working conditions and a reward structure that will motivate good performance. A number of such theories have been found useful for these purposes which can be classified as psychodynamic theories (which emphasize common human attributes), job content theories, and job context theories.
2. *Job satisfaction.* Related to motivation is the matter of employee job satisfaction. Since there is no necessary relationship between job satisfaction and productivity, and since job satisfaction is only weakly related to employee turnover and absenteeism, assessing satisfaction reflects a general assumption that since so many people spend a third or more of their waking hours at work, it ought to be satisfying rather than a noxious experience. Studies may consider overall satisfaction or, increasingly, task satisfaction. Satisfaction levels can provide a rich picture of the mood of employees which management can use as a guide to improving reward, benefit, and motivational conditions.
3. *Leadership.* The task of creating working conditions through administration and policy-making rests with management and supervisors. As a consequence, the study of leadership and leader behavior is of keen concern to I/O psychologists. Discovering what leaders do, how people come to be leaders, and how to prepare employees for leadership positions are all topics addressed by I/O psychologists.
4. *Organization development.* Finally, many I/O psychologists work in the area known as organization development, which is defined as the various activities, including job design, to help employees work better together as a group. This includes team building, leadership exercises, socio-technical approaches, quality of work life, self-managing work groups, survey feedback, and related techniques for enhancing group cohesiveness and effectiveness.

ENGINEERING PSYCHOLOGY

The last of the major specializations within I/O psychology is engineering psychology, also known as human engineering, human factors, or ergonomics. In a number of important ways engineering psychology is the opposite of personnel psychology. While personnel psychologists concentrate on the measurement of individual differences to improve the fit between people and jobs, engineering psychologists largely assume that people are the same.

Bearing much in common with industrial engineering, engineering psychology focuses traditionally on person-machine systems but has branched into other aspects of the workplace as well. It has two prominent thrusts. One focuses on the design of machinery and workspaces to be compatible with human limitations and capabilities. It includes the design of controls, displays, furniture, and related aspects of work environments. Applications of human factors principles can be found in the design of aircraft cockpits, automobiles, punch presses, kitchen ranges, computer keyboards and displays, just to name a few examples.

The other thrust is the allocation of decision-making between the machine and the operator. The object is to design machines, tools, and equipment to reduce the number of decisions the operator needs to make; engineering psychologists assume that when people are confronted with choices, they will make the wrong decision. When a human makes an error operating a machine or performing a task, the engineering psychologist is likely to blame the machine or the work layout, not the operator. The goal then is to design foolproof, fail-safe machinery and work spaces that inhibit error commission and transfer as many decisions from the operator to the machine as the current state of technology allows. Anti-lock brakes on automobiles are an example of such a transfer of decision making from the person to the machine. With conventional brakes the operator must decide when to pump the brake pedal when driving on a slippery surface to prevent wheel lockup, skidding, and loss of steering ability. Anti-lock brakes reassign the decision on when the brakes need pumping to the machine itself. It is a ''fly-by-wire'' type of system where the operator's action (applying the brakes) is relayed directly to a computer, which takes over the rest of the decisions necessary to avoid a lockup.

Designing such easy-to-use, safe, and error-proof machinery requires a thorough knowledge of human perceptual and sensory processes, human physical limitations, and human physical proportions and capabilities. Additionally, engineering psychologists concentrate on the causes of machine-related accidents (preventable human error is often the cause) to create working environments that remain within the boundaries of human abilities to see, hear, feel, move, and remain alert. Additional elements of study are noise, light, human attention span, fatigue, the effects of shift work, the placement and height of machinery and furniture, and the efficacy of feedback systems that tell the operator when an error has been made or a problem is occurring or impending.

SEE ALSO: Employee Motivation; Employment Services; Hiring Practices; Industrial Safety; Leadership; Organizational Behavior; Organizational Growth; Training and Development

[Cary M. Lichtman]

FURTHER READING:

Aamodt, Michael G. *Applied Industrial/Organizational Psychology.* 3rd ed. Pacific Grove, CA: Brooks/Cole, 1999.

Lawson, Robert B., and Zheng Shen. *Organizational Psychology: Foundations and Applications.* New York: Oxford University Press, 1998.

Muchinsky, Paul M. *Psychology Applied to Work.* 6th ed. Belmont, CA: Wadsworth, 1999.

Personnel Psychology, quarterly.

Schultz, Duane P., and Sydney Ellen Schultz. *Psychology and Work Today.* 7th ed. Upper Saddle River, NJ: Prentice Hall, 1998.

Society for Industrial and Organizational Psychology. *Welcome to the SIOP Homepage.* Bowling Green, OH, 1999. Available from www.siop.org.

Stone, Philip, and Mark Cannon. *Organizational Psychology.* Brookfield, VT: Ashgate Publishing Co., 1997.

INFLATION

Inflation is commonly understood as an increase in the price level. Formally, it is defined as the rate of change in the price level. Thus, an inflation rate of 5 percent per annum means that the price level is increasing at the rate of 5 percent. Inflation, however, need not always be positive. It could be a negative number, in which case the price level would be declining. Of course, a negative inflation rate, termed deflation, is very uncommon. Most economies face positive rates of inflation year after year.

If the inflation rate is positive and an individual's **income** remains constant, his or her real standard of living will fall as the individual's income will be worth less and less in successive periods. Let us assume that a household earns $50,000 per year and the income remains fixed at this level in the future. If the inflation rate persists at 10 percent per year, the **purchasing power** of the household income will also keep declining at the rate of 10 percent per year. At the end of the five-year period, prices will be one and a half times greater. This will lead to the household being able to buy only two-thirds of the goods and services it was able to buy at the beginning of the period.

MEASUREMENT OF THE INFLATION RATE

The inflation rate is derived by calculating the rate of change in a **price index**. A price index, in turn, measures the level of prices of goods and services at any point of time. The number of items included in a price index vary depending on the objective of the index. Usually three kinds of price indexes are periodically reported by government sources. They all have their particular advantages and uses. The first index is called the **consumer price index** (CPI), which measures the average retail prices paid by consumers for goods and services bought by them. Several thousand items are included in this index. The second price index used to measure the inflation rate is called the producer price index. It is a much broader measure than the CPI because it measures the wholesale prices of approximately 3,000 items. The items included in this index are those that are typically used by producers (manufacturers and businesses) and thus contain many raw materials and semifinished goods. The third measure of inflation is the called the **implicit price**

deflator. This index measures the prices of all goods and services included in the calculation of the current output of goods and services in the economy, known as **gross domestic product**. It is the broadest measure of the price level.

The three measures of the inflation rate are most likely to move in the same direction, even though not to the same extent. Differences can arise due to the differing number of goods and services included for the purpose of compiling the three **indexes**. In general, if one hears about the inflation rate number in the popular media, it is most likely to be the one based on the CPI.

[Anandi P. Sahu, Ph.D.]

FURTHER READING:

Froyen, Richard T. *Macroeconomics: Theories and Policies.* 6th ed. Upper Saddle River, NJ: Prentice Hall, 1998.

Gordon, Robert J. *Macroeconomics.* 7th ed. Reading, MA: Addison-Wesley, 1998.

Sommers, Albert T. *The U.S. Economy Demystified.* Lexington, MA: Lexington Books, 1988.

INFOMERCIALS

An infomercial is a 30- or 60-minute broadcast commercial that delivers extensive sales messages in a natural format. It differs from the typical television commercial in the amount of time, amount of information, and amount of ''reality.'' It is, in short, an elaborately orchestrated sales pitch. The modern-day infomercial originated in 1984 when the U.S. **Federal Communications Commission** (FCC) revoked its ban on ''program-length commercials.'' Deregulation freed television stations and cable networks to sell entire half-hour blocks of air time for **advertising**. What they sold initially were ''remnants,'' the unprofitable, late-night slots that had been the domain of 1950s horror flicks and test patterns. By the late 1990s, according to one estimate, infomercials generated some $1.7 billion in direct sales, and possibly more indirectly because of increased sales through retail channels.

The evolution of infomercials included some dramatic success stories. In 1987, for example, American Telecast Corp. of Pasli, Pennsylvania, produced ''Where There's a Will There's an A,'' hosted by John Ritter. Since then, more than a million audio and videocassette of the study program have been sold for $60 to $90 apiece. Similarly, 70-year-old fruit-juice fanatic Jay Kordich was nothing more than an oddity at local trade shows until Trilium Health Products of Seattle put him in an infomercial as its ''Juiceman'' and launched a nationwide juicing craze. Finally, Mike Levy went from obscurity to self-proclaimed ''most-watched man on television'' with his ''Amazing Discoveries'' infomercials. Among his more amazing feats: selling more than $40 million each year of tooth whitener and car wax.

In the early 1990s, infomercials earned the interest and respect of a more upscale audience. Companies such as Volvo, IBM, AT&T, General Motors, and Time Warner have all made infomercials. Further, traditional ad agencies such as Foote, Foote, Cone and Belding, Ketchum Communications, and Hal Riney have either established their own infomercial departments or have formed partnerships with infomercial production houses.

Three interrelated reasons have been proposed for this growth in infomercials. The first is cost; infomercials became attractive because of the relatively cheap air time, averaging $50,000 to $500,000 per week for a half-hour slot, and the relatively small amount they cost to produce, usually somewhere between $110,000 and $650,000 for 30 minutes. Second, the tremendous need for alternative programming as the nation's cable system expands to a capacity of as many as 150 channels apiece by the mid-1990s has spurred advertisers to capitalize on these openings with infomercials. A third reason is increased strategic credibility. As more prestigious companies have become involved with infomercials, an improvement in product quality and implementation has resulted. Celebrity endorsements also augment credibility. Vanna White has cashed in on her famous smile by endorsing Perfect Smile teeth whitener. She helped generate over $20 million in sales for the product in just a few months. A mid-range celebrity can make $25,000 on an infomercial, plus up to 5 percent of gross sales. The recognized and proven commercial pull of celebrities has transferred well to the infomercial industry. Consequently, infomercials are increasingly viewed as a legitimate part of a company's communication strategy.

By the late 1990s, the infomercial industry had evolved into a $1.7 billion market. The most successful and prevalent products pitched by infomercials were related to diet, fitness, and appearance concerns. Indeed, half of the top ten grossing infomercials in 1998 advertised products in these categories. Television sales generated $80 million in sales for Bioslim, which sat atop the list for its infomercial assembled by Thane Marketing. Salton Maxim's infomercial for George Foreman's Lean Mean Grilling Machine cashed in on the heavyweight's star appeal to rank second place. One company, Quantum, placed three shows in the top ten, while TruVantage maintained two slots. National Media Corporation remained the largest publicly traded infomercial company.

A study by InfoCision Marketing Corp. found that the gender gap among infomercial customers has widened even as the medium has matured. Whereas 69 percent of infomercial buyers in 1995 were women, by 1997 that figure had leaped to 85 percent. Higher-income consumers also increasingly figure into infomercial demographics. NIMA International (formerly National Infomercial Marketing Association) found that 13 million U.S. adults purchased at least one item from infomercial offers in 1997. Moreover, the average U.S. television viewer spent about 14 minutes per week watching infomercials. Thus, a quite viable market exists; the challenge to advertisers is to implement strategies whereby more males are drawn to infomercials as a standard shopping medium, and to tap the vast lower-income brackets.

The dramatic growth of Internet-based shopping poses a further challenge to the infomercial industry. Infomercial producers may need to find ways to transfer a recognizable motif to the World Wide Web or in some other fashion address this booming medium. Analysts also expect that "cause marketing," in which infomercials are produced with the intention of raising funds for specific charities, rather than for profit, will continue its steady growth to become a larger force in the infomercial arena.

SEE ALSO: Advertising; Marketing

FURTHER READING:

Culpepper, Kenneth M. "A Significant Part of the New Marketing Convergence." *Direct Marketing,* September 1998, 56-7.

Hampe, Barry. *Making Videos for Money: Planning and Producing Information Videos, Commercials, and Infomercials.* New York: H. Holt, 1998.

Hawthorne, Timothy R. "Opening Doors to Retail Stores." *Direct Marketing,* January 1998.

——. *The Complete Guide to Infomercial Marketing.* Lincolnwood, IL: NTC Business Books, 1997.

INFORMATION MANAGEMENT AND PROCESSING

Many business scholars consider information processing, in all of its forms, the lifeblood of organizations. Information in this context is defined broadly to encompass ideas, documents, records, personal communications, and most of all, knowledge shared within an organization. According to some experts, in fact, information processing is primarily concerned with knowledge acquisition and dissemination.

The management and processing side is what businesses do with their information. (Although there are subtle differences, management and processing will be considered synonymous in this discussion.) Information may be retrieved and distributed over computers or on paper, or it may simply reside in the consciousness of employees at the company. Much information processing can be aided by computers, but ultimately a great deal of organizational information must be processed by individual decision makers in some fashion. Successful information management is widely seen as a harbinger of a successful business enterprise; if a company is able to sift through the glut of available information, amplifying what is relevant and suppressing what isn't, it may enjoy a competitive advantage over other firms.

As an academic field, information processing first gained prominence in the 1970s through the work of **organization theory** specialists like Jay R. Galbraith, David Nadler, and Michael L. Tushman. It is now related to a wide number of management specializations, including organization theory and design, managerial cognition, **communication in organizations**, and technology management. Recent academic inquiries into information management and processing have focused on how information processing impacts the development of organizational knowledge.

BASIC PRINCIPLES OF INFORMATION PROCESSING

As highlighted by John L. Kmetz in *The Information Processing Theory of Organization,* there are four main stages of processing information: (1) acquisition or retrieval, (2) storage, (3) transformation, and (4) transmission. They generally occur in this order, but not always. First, acquisition and retrieval is the phase in which an individual seeks—or is given—some piece of information or knowledge. It may originate from inside the organization, outside the organization, or even within the mind of the individual who came upon it. Second, storage may occur in the individual's memory, or via computer or media. When information is stored (and/or disseminated) so that a wide number of employees, present and future, can retrieve it over time, it may lead to organizational learning and become part of the organizational memory. Third, transformation happens when individuals modify the information they receive for various purposes. They may analyze it to arrive at a judgment or inference about the information, or they may expand on it or condense it for some specific need, such as reporting a synopsis to colleagues or management. Fourth, transmission is the means by which the information is disseminated to others, beginning the acquisition process for them anew.

Kmetz also identified four components in what he termed the framework of information processing. These components specify the structure of an information processing system, whether human or machine. They are (1) sensors, (2) memory, (3) processing mechanisms, and (4) access mechanisms. Some of these correspond directly to stages of information processing, but there is some crossover. Sensors are input channels for acquiring information. They may include computer devices (e.g., a keyboard for data entry) or simply human senses like eyes and ears. Similarly, memory involves using the human mind or computer storage media for saving information for future use, whether it is needed for a few seconds or a few years. Related to the transformation stage, processing mechanisms are tools to control, organize, and modify information. The human mind and computer processors running application software are the most important kinds of information processing mechanisms. Lastly, access mechanisms allow retrieval and additional processing of information that has already been acquired and processed. Again, the human brain can serve as its own access device, but these mechanisms also include printed publications, computer interfaces, and other information retrieval tools.

SCOPE OF INFORMATION MANAGEMENT

The subject of information processing can be difficult to grasp because it is so general and pervasive. Indeed, according to information processing theory, organizational control is exercised through information management, and all business activities center around one form of information or another. Sometimes information management is presented as providing managers—particularly decision makers—with all the information they need in a timely fashion. This is of course an essential function, but it's only one aspect of how businesses must channel information in order to be effective. Other examples include training and educating employees, handling feedback from customers and vendors, unearthing details about market forces, and communicating innovations and changes.

COMMUNICATION CHANNELS. Communication is at the heart of information management. An otherwise valuable idea is useless if the right individuals don't know about it at the right time. At the same time, irrelevant information clogs communication channels and can cause more important information to be lost or ignored. Importantly, most businesses now recognize that the flow of information isn't simply from the top down. An organization that is effective at processing information will be able to regularly accommodate information flowing from the bottom up and laterally within peer groups, not to mention information entering the organization from the outside and information being sent to the outside by the organization.

INFRASTRUCTURE AND POLICIES. To enable effective information processing, channels of communication must be supported by at least two additional resources: technology infrastructure and management policies. In the modern business climate, it's hard to overstate the value of an efficient **information technology** infrastructure. This includes everything from being able to store and retrieve information on computers to being able to disseminate information to others through the use of e-mail, corporate intranets, extranets, and other means. In their own right, computers have always been used to process raw data and routine information into more meaningful forms, and this ability is growing ever more sophisticated through the use of **expert systems**, neural networks, data mining programs, and other advanced software applications. Ultimately, however, high-level information must be processed by humans, and therefore management policies and practices must be in place to facilitate the flow of appropriate information, and in some cases, to discourage the flow of inappropriate information. Such policy areas might include:

- the frequency and nature of meetings and conferences;
- how management encourages employee collaboration and knowledge sharing;
- specific technology the company uses to manage operations information, such as how customer databases, accounting systems, and quality control systems are used;
- formal mechanisms to promote the acquisition of new knowledge, such as training programs, mentorships, and so forth; and
- the organizational hierarchy of the firm.

Thus, communication channels, facilitated by information infrastructure and management policies, are the basis for nearly all information processing. Even when information is being processed in the mind of a sole actor, say a sales representative dealing with a customer, it's critical that the appropriate infrastructure and policies be in place to allow that individual to perform in a manner most consistent with corporate objectives.

EXAMPLE. For example, if the company wishes to maintain a liberal customer satisfaction policy, customer service representatives must be trained not to refuse customers who want to return merchandise under unusual circumstances not be specifically documented in training manuals. If the corporate objective is to always provide amicable, hassle-free customer service, these employees must be taught the broad customer service philosophy and probably should be empowered to evaluate specific circumstances using that basic knowledge. In other words, assuming that generous customer service is consistent with the business strategy, information processing in this case probably should involve disseminating to employees broad objectives that they then can process themselves and apply to specific instances—a targeted decentralization of information processing.

The primary alternatives would be to try to devise a detailed, comprehensive customer service policy manual covering each return scenario, which could omit some obscure scenarios, or to have employees direct questions about unusual situations to a manager who is empowered to make such a judgment. Depending on the specifics, any combination of these three alternatives—employee empowerment, detailed manuals, and manager intervention—could be the most cost-efficient or deliver the highest quality service, and yet under other circumstances could lead to inefficiencies and poor service. The choice is largely one based on information processing abilities, specifically those of the frontline representatives. The greatest efficiencies are likely to be found in empowering these individuals by providing them with selected information, through training and reinforcement exercises, to make the best decisions using their own judgment, i.e., processing the information themselves. Too much reliance on manuals or managers would slow the customer service process, making it more time-consuming for customers, more costly for the company, and possibly demoralizing for the workers. Hence, this small application of information processing can affect any number of strategic objectives.

INFORMATION PROCESSING AND ORGANIZATIONAL CONTROL

As noted earlier, certain kinds of information processing are considered fundamental to maintaining effective control over business organizations. Control in this sense is ensuring that members of the organization (i.e., employees) behave in ways consistent with management policies and business objectives. Usually the concern here is not to micromanage employees' actions in a disciplinarian manner, but rather to coordinate diverse human activities in order to maximize quality, productivity, efficiency, and other measures of organizational effectiveness.

Research on this aspect of information processing suggests that the kind of control mechanisms an organization should employ depend on the information processing involved in the tasks to be regulated. Specifically, Richard Leifer and Peter K. Mills proposed in a 1996 *Journal of Management* paper that managers should consider to what degree tasks involve a high degree of uncertainty or variability. They argue that formal, explicit rules work best when there is minimal uncertainty or variance in the task (i.e., routine work), and conversely, implicit rules (communicated through organizational norms, for instance) work best when high uncertainty and variance create the need for individual discretion (e.g., research, creative or complex processes). Naturally, in practice business use a combination of formal and informal controls, but the lesson is that information processing plays a fundamental role in corporate management and operations.

SEE ALSO: Communication in Organizations; Organization Theory

FURTHER READING:

Anand, Vikas, Charles C. Manz, and William H. Glick. ''An Organizational Memory Approach to Information Management.'' *Academy of Management Review,* October 1998.

Garud, Raghu, and Joseph F. Porac, eds. *Advances in Managerial Cognition and Organizational Information Processing,* vol. 6. Greenwich, CT: JAI Press, 1999.

Kmetz, John L. *The Information Processing Theory of Organization.* Brookfield, VT: Ashgate Publishing Co., 1998, 18-19.

Leifer, Richard, and Peter K. Mills. ''An Information Processing Approach for Deciding upon Control Strategies and Reducing Control Loss in Emerging Organizations.'' *Journal of Management,* spring 1996, 113.

INFORMATION TECHNOLOGY

Information technology (IT) is the lifeblood of most businesses. It is used to fulfill administrative and production requirements, and it crosses all industries. Generally, the larger the enterprise, the greater the need for a sophisticated and professionally managed information technology infrastructure.

Computers are at the core of IT, but to say information technology is just computers is to ignore the complexity and diversity of the technologies businesses need to stay afloat in the 21st century. A more complete definition of IT is this: all of an organization's hardware and software for storing, retrieving, transmitting, and managing electronic information. Information in this context is in its broadest sense and includes images and digitized sound and video. Among the tools companies use to manage their information are:

- personal computers, terminals, and workstations
- network servers (including Internet) and other networking hardware
- mainframes
- scanners, printers, and other peripherals
- all forms of software, including proprietary systems and site licenses for off-the-shelf packages.

These technologies serve many purposes in a business. Some are purely logistical or convenient and thereby save time and resources. Others are essential to the company's output or its competitive advantage. Examples of IT's benefits to different areas of an enterprise include:

- timely and efficient delivery of products and services
- higher sales through better understanding of customer behaviors
- cost savings from fewer staff hours and reduced human or machine error
- better resource planning through detailed, accurate, and timely financial information.

Medium to large corporations oversee their often substantial investments in these technologies through a specialized department that may be known simply as IT, or as information systems (IS) or **management information systems** (MIS). This area may be under the direction of a **chief information officer** (CIO), but many IT departments report ultimately to the company's chief financial officer (CFO).

ACQUISITIONS AND UPGRADES

Most large organizations must purchase and install new hardware and software on a regular basis. In order to do so effectively, IT managers must be familiar simultaneously with business needs and available technologies. Some purchases may be very routine; the corporation may only need additional units of existing devices it has already implemented, or, as is the case with software upgrades, there may only be one logical course of action. However, many IT-acquisition decisions demand strategic vision for the organization. IT decision-makers must be able to match present and future needs with technological solutions, often in the face of rapidly changing technologies and severe financial repercussions from choosing the wrong technology.

The acquisition process can be especially troublesome when custom software is being implemented. These projects are notorious for exceeding cost estimates and taking longer than planned. Moreover, custom software clients must be wary, after added time and expense, of whether the new system will serve all of the needs it was intended to satisfy—and without loosing the essential strengths and capabilities of the system it is replacing.

SERVICE AND MAINTENANCE

Another requisite to owning information technology is ensuring that it is compatible with other technologies already in place and that it functions properly. Compatibility issues extend from making software applications work together on a single computer to allowing substantially different computer systems to share information. A mix of new and old technology can present special challenges. Over time, most computer equipment requires some form of servicing, usually due to component failures, user mistakes, or obsolescence. This aspect of IT isn't trivial: performing routine service and maintenance in a large IT environment may require a substantial investment in technical staff hours (or outside services) and replacement equipment.

SEE ALSO: Computer Networks; Computers and Computer Systems; Electronic Data Interchange (EDI); Geographic Information Systems (GIS); Graphical User Interface (GUI); Internet and World Wide Web; Management Information Systems; Microcomputers in Business; Office Automation; Optical Character Recognition Devices (OCR); Software

FURTHER READING:

Bologna, Jack, and Anthony M. Walsh. *The Accountant's Handbook of Information Technology.* New York: John Wiley & Sons, 1997.

Computerworld, weekly.

Galliers, Robert D., and Walter R.J. Baets, eds. *Information Technology and Organizational Transformation: Innovation for the 21st Century Organization.* New York: John Wiley & Sons, 1998.

Information Strategy: An Executive's Journal, quarterly.

Klepper, Robert, and Wendell O. Jones. *Outsourcing Information Technology, Systems, and Services.* Upper Saddle River, NJ: Prentice Hall, 1997.

Sauer, Christopher, and Philip W. Yetton. *Steps to the Future: Fresh Thinking on the Management of IT-Based Organizational Transformation.* San Francisco: Jossey-Bass Publishers, 1997.

INFRASTRUCTURE

Infrastructure refers to a wide variety of systems in place to support the prevailing industrial society, in both the public and private sectors. The public infrastructure encompasses a number of basic structures and services, including wastewater systems, power plants, dams, housing, and education. It includes the basic transportation system of mass transit, railroads, aviation (airports and air traffic control systems), highways, roads, and bridges. In addition, communication systems, **computer networks**, and information superhighways are also included in the definition of infrastructure. Similarly, corporations have their own physical infrastructures of basic structures and systems that support the firm's ongoing business activities.

In the United States, about 85 to 90 percent of public infrastructure activity is accounted for by state and local governments. To build, oversee, and maintain the full range of public works, state and local governments provide fiscal, governmental, and technological services. Additionally, these governments sometimes enter into arrangements with private companies to help them perform these tasks. State and local investments in the infrastructure can be divided into three groups: (1) the core infrastructure (water supply facilities, sewers, and utility and transit systems); (2) buildings (schools and hospitals); and (3) water resource projects (especially flood control).

The U.S. infrastructure is arguably the most extensive in the world and, after years of technological development and construction, has become a tangible asset improving the quality of life for the nation's population. Most facilities and structures comprising U.S. infrastructure were built as a series of separate and distinct projects by federal, state, and local agencies, as well as by independent authorities and private corporations. Because many of the investments were made in earlier decades and because there was little coordination between the agencies involved, the U.S. infrastructure is aging, inefficient, and inadequate.

HISTORICAL ASPECTS

From 1929 to 1969 investment in public infrastructure increased consistently. This increase can be attributed to rapid growth in the overall **gross national product** (GNP) as well as an increase in the percentage of GNP spent on infrastructure investments. The reason that a great deal of attention was given to infrastructure needs can be attributed to the demographic demands of the day. For example, during the 1950s and 1960s, U.S. investment in its infrastructure rose sharply, in part to meet the increased educational demands of the baby boom generation. Initiatives such as the interstate highway system and the space program as well as later federal programs that invested in education for the poor also accounted for consistent increases in infrastructure spending.

Since the 1970s there has been a drastic decline in funding that supports the infrastructure of the United States, as well as in funding for other countries' infrastructures. In constant dollars, federal grants that support state and local efforts have remained stable, representing a decline in the real amount of federal funding. Real federal spending peaked in 1980 with increased funding for mass transit, rail, wastewater treatment, and various educational and training programs. The decline in federal infrastructure funding continued during the 1980s as most of the wealth of the United States was devoted to consumption rather than to the enhancement of the nation's infrastructure (or any other form of future investment). Thus, the current infrastructure has not kept pace with the growing population.

Some of this decline in spending was in response to budget pressures felt in all levels of government, but much of it can be attributed to an inattention to the importance of top-quality public amenities and to a shortsighted perspective about the value of investing in the future. This perspective began to change somewhat during the 1990s, a decade marked by the end of the Cold War. During this time, officials in the federal government started to discuss alternative ways to spend the funds formerly spent on the military, although these discussions were waylaid somewhat by the Persian Gulf conflict. There seemed to be a growing realization, however, that additional money should be devoted to repairing the existing infrastructure and adding to it.

ECONOMIC IMPLICATIONS

The state of the nation's economy plays a large role in infrastructure needs. Obviously, a very direct impact on the economy are the federal, state, and local tax bases available to pay for the needed infrastructure investments. Changes in the pace and areas of economic growth, however, are also very important—critical to both the demand for and the ability to support infrastructure investments. Economic growth has numerous effects on the demand for a nation's infrastructure. First, in a fast-growing economy, infrastructures are placed under great use, deteriorate quickly, and require replacement frequently. In slower economies, the opposite is true. Second, as the economy changes, modifications must be made to capital outlays. For example, as the U.S. economy changes from reliance on manufacturing to reliance on high-tech industries, the mix of infrastructure needs changes. Ensuring that an infrastructure is in place to facilitate communications has become as important as planning for highways. Third, changes in the economy cause shifts in the population that, in turn, require modified infrastructure investments. Thus, in some areas of the country, rapidly growing economies and populations strain existing infrastructures; at the same time, areas of the country experiencing minimal growth may have situations of overcapacity.

DECLINING INVESTMENTS: THE REAL IMPACT

In 1960 U.S. federal public spending on infrastructure was 5 percent of **gross domestic product** (GDP); by the mid-1990s, this figure was down to 2.5 percent. But when state and local government funding of infrastructure and educational institutions, plus private funding of **research and development** (R&D), is added to federal spending, the total was fairly stable from 1970 to 1994 as a percentage of the U.S. GDP. During that period total spending on infrastructure and R&D remained around 10 percent of the GDP, according to a 1998 study by the Congressional Budget Office.

Similarly, the capital spending on the building of infrastructures worldwide has declined. The reasons behind this decline in spending can be attributed to numerous factors. First of all, many countries have experienced large budget deficits in recent years and thus do not have the extra capital to spend on their infrastructures. Second, tax revenues in many countries have been stagnant since the oil crisis of the 1970s. Third, many countries have increased their spending on welfare, using money usually spent on the public sector, and have underestimated the increasing burden that population growth and other societal changes place on existing infrastructures. The long delays in the planning and implementation of major projects is a fourth significant problem. Delays are caused by the increasingly complex nature of many of these major projects as well as by the increased scrutiny and opposition by environmental advocacy groups and landowners.

The decline in government spending, however, may not be as significant as it first seems. For instance, the prices associated with some aspects of major infrastructure projects have declined due to better technology. Furthermore, in some areas of the nation's infrastructure, new investments have been made by the private sector, especially in the areas of telecommunications and the generation and distribution of electric power. Indeed, in some places, there is actually overcapacity of substructure services.

As one may expect, however, the spending decline of the last two and one-half decades is not without negative consequences. In the 1990s there was almost a certainty that the increasing population combined with other events, such as **globalization** and regional economic integration, would increase worldwide demand for transportation, telecommunications, waste disposal, energy, and other elements associated with infrastructure over the years to come. For example, in the United States, the increased use of automobiles led to congestion on public highways that was projected to cause traffic delays of four billion vehicle hours by the year 2005. In the **European Union** (EU), similar traffic delays were projected as European borders continued to come down; in fact, travel between the EU countries was projected to grow about 130 percent by 2015. Similarly, studies projected that the use of the railroad system in Europe was likely to triple by 2005.

When finances are short, most infrastructure needs have to be met by the public sector. Governments all over the world are in **debt**, averaging 40 percent of GDP in countries belonging to the **Organisation for Economic Co-operation and Development**. Although budget deficits were projected to decline in the latter part of the 1990s, there are other factors, such as the projected rising health costs associated with aging populations, that will require increased spending. Thus, governments in the United States and abroad are faced with the tasks of repairing existing infrastructures and building new ones to meet future needs, even though, economically, they will have a very difficult time meeting very basic needs.

OUTLOOK: THE STAGGERING BURDEN OF INFRASTRUCTURE INVESTMENT

The infrastructure investment necessary to meet projected demands is staggering. To meet the projected needs of the U.S. infrastructure until the year 2000, the U.S. Congressional Budget Office projected that it would cost taxpayers approximately $800 billion. And the United States was not alone in these cost projections. In Europe and Asia, countries face proportionately large costs.

According to Rebuild America, a coalition of organizations and agencies concerned about the U.S. infrastructure, the United States should increase its annual spending on the transportation system, including highways and mass transit, from $30 billion to $60 billion. Approximately $20 billion was spent on roads and bridges in 1997.

Wastewater infrastructure costs are expected to result in massive funding gaps at the local government level well into the 21st century. The Association of Metropolitan Sewerage Agencies and the Water Environment Federation projected that it would cost $330 billion over 20 years in wastewater treatment plants and collection systems to maintain water quality standards.

In 1998 the Rebuild America Coalition estimated U.S. infrastructure costs to be $850 billion to maintain and improve roads, bridges, transit systems, airports, ports, schools, water works, sewers, dams, solid waste disposal, and more. That included $358 billion to improve roads, highways, and bridges; $72 billion to improve mass transit systems; $33 billion to $60 billion to expand and modernize airports; $112 billion to bring school facilities up to good condition; $138 billion to improve the drinking water infrastructure; and $140 billion to improve wastewater systems.

[Kathryn Snavely, updated by David P. Bianco]

FURTHER READING:

Congressional Budget Office. *The Economic Effects of Federal Spending on Infrastructure and Other Investments.* Washington: Congressional Budget Office, 1998. Available from www.cbo.gov.

Gould, James P., and Andrew C. Lemer. *Toward Infrastructure Improvement.* Washington: National Academy Press, 1994.

Magid, Larry. *The Economic Importance of Transportation Infrastructure Investment.* Washington: National Governors' Association, 1997.

Munnell, Alicia H., ed. *Is There a Shortfall in Public Capital Investment?* Boston: Federal Reserve Bank of Boston, 1991.

Organisation for Economic Co-operation and Development. *Assessing Structural Reform: Lessons for the Future.* Paris: Head of Publications Service, Organisation for Economic Co-operation and Development, 1994.

——. *Infrastructure Policies for the 1990s.* Paris: Head of Publications Service, Organisation for Economic Co-operation and Development, 1993.

——. *Urban Infrastructure: Finance and Management.* Paris: Head of Publications Service, Organisation for Economic Co-operation and Development, 1991.

Perry, David C. *Building the Public City.* Thousand Oaks, CA: Sage Publications, 1995.

Rebuild America Coalition. ''Key Facts about America's Road and Bridge Conditions and Federal Funding.'' Rebuild America Coalition, 1999. Available from www.rebuildamerica.org/reports/conditions.html.

——. ''Nation Needs to Increase Its Federal Transportation Spending, Says Chairman of National Infrastructure Coalition Called Rebuild America.'' Rebuild America Coalition press release, 4 February 1997. Available from www.rebuildamerica.org/reports/feb4-98.html.

——. ''National Public Works Week: Celebration of Nation's Infrastructure Becomes Wake-Up Call for Burgeoning Needs.'' Rebuild America Coalition press release, 19 May 1998. Available from www.rebuildamerica.org/reports/may19-25.html.

——. ''Nationwide Poll Shows Strong Support for Infrastructure Investment.'' Rebuild America Coalition press release, 27 January 1999. Available from www.rebuildamerica.org/reports/jan27-99.htm.

——. ''Unless We Act Now . . . Wastewater Infrastructure Costs Will Swamp America's Communities.'' Rebuild America Coalition press release, 31 March 1999. Available from www.rebuildamerica.org/reports/mar31-99.htm.

Stein, Jay M., ed. *Public Infrastructure Planning and Management.* Thousand Oaks, CA: Sage Publications, 1988.

INJUNCTION

An injunction is a court order, issued by a judge, that prohibits an individual, business firm, labor union, or other type of organization from engaging in a specified action, or that requires them to resume an action. An injunction is intended to protect the property rights of an individual or business from being violated. It is not used to punish violations of the law, although it may be used to enforce a breach of contract.

A preliminary injunction may be issued when a lawsuit is initiated to protect property rights while the litigation is in progress. Such an injunction is often issued on a temporary basis without a hearing. Preliminary injunctions are frequently sought in **patent** infringement cases, where the plaintiff alleging a patent violation obtains a preliminary injunction against the party who is charged with infringing on the plaintiff's patent rights. In such cases a judge may issue a preliminary injunction prohibiting the defendant from manufacturing or distributing the product or products alleged to be in violation of the plaintiff's patent rights. The effect of such an injunction may be to put the competitor out of business, especially if it is a smaller company and the patent suit takes a long time to resolve. Consequently, judges may grant such preliminary injunctions only when there is a reasonable likelihood that the patent infringement claim will be successful.

In trademark infringement cases, courts typically consider four factors before deciding whether or not to grant a preliminary injunction. These include the strength of the plaintiff's case and the overall probability of its success; whether the plaintiff is likely to suffer irreparable harm if the injunction is not granted; whether the plaintiff's injury outweighs the potential harm the injunction would cause the defendant; and the effect of an injunction on the public interest. In addition, courts may consider the likelihood of future infringement—whether the infringement was an isolated case and not likely to occur again in the future. That is, the court may refuse to issue a preliminary injunction on the basis that the defendant is not likely to violate the plaintiff's trademark rights again in the future.

Under the European Treaty Convention, cross-border injunctions may be granted in patent infringement and other **intellectual property** cases. In one case, a Dutch judge granted an injunction that covered Belgium, the Netherlands, and Luxembourg.

LABOR INJUNCTIONS

In the early 20th century injunctions were frequently used by big business to prevent **labor unions** from going on strike. The Norris-LaGuardia Act of 1932 limited the ability of federal courts to issue injunctions in labor disputes. The Labor-Management Relations Act of 1947, also known as the **Taft-Hartley Act**, allowed the president of the United States to seek an injunction to prevent a strike when a labor dispute threatened national health or safety. After issuing an unfair labor-practices complaint, the **National Labor Relations Board** (NLRB) may seek injunctive relief in federal court to compel a party to either desist or resume an action under Section 10(j) of the National Labor Relations Act.

Since it settled the baseball strike of 1994 with an unfair labor practices charge and an injunction against the major-league owners, the NLRB has used its power to seek injunctive relief to a greater extent. In order to obtain a labor injunction, the NLRB must show that irreparable harm would be caused and that injunctive relief would be ''just and proper.'' The most common situations in which the NLRB has sought an injunction include management interference with a union's organizing campaign, owners subcontracting work to avoid bargaining obligations, owners refusing to recognize an incumbent union, unions using coercion to meet an illegal objective, and the occurrence of mass picketing violence.

OTHER COMMON USES OF INJUNCTIONS

In the realm of **contracts**, an injunction may be used to enforce a negative covenant (an agreement not to perform certain acts or services) when there is a breach of contract. For example, a recording company may seek an injunction against a recording artist who is under contract, to prevent the artist from recording for another label or performing in violation of specific articles of the contract.

Preliminary injunctions are also commonly used by the **Securities and Exchange Commission** (SEC), especially in factually or legally difficult cases and in cases where it can demonstrate ''irreparable harm.'' Many franchise terminations result in litigation alleging wrongful termination of franchise rights, and it is not unusual for plaintiff franchisees to seek a preliminary injunction allowing them to continue to operate as a franchisee until the case is decided.

SEE ALSO: Copyright

[David P. Bianco]

FURTHER READING:

Berkowitz, William N. ''Defeating Requests for Preliminary Injunctive Relief in Franchise Termination Cases.'' *Franchise Law Journal,* winter 1995, 57-63.

Koen, Clifford M., Jr., and others. ''10(j) Injunctions: A Shift in NLRB Approach.'' *Labor Law Journal,* November 1995, 699-707.

Koen, Clifford M., Jr., and others. ''The NLRB Wields a Rejuvenated Weapon.'' *Personnel Journal,* December 1996, 85-86.

Lans, Maxine S. ''To Enjoin or Not to Enjoin: A Tough Question.'' *Marketing News,* 13 February 1995, 5.

Miller, Charles E., and Bart J. Van Den Broek. ''European Patent Makes Its Debut.'' *Journal of Commerce and Commercial,* 8 January 1997, 7A.

Northrup, Herbert R., and H. Lane Dennard Jr. ''The Return of 'Government by Injunction?' Public Policy and the Expansive Uses of Section 10(j) of the NLRA.'' *Employee Relations Law Journal,* summer 1996, 101-31.

Pitt, Harvey L., and others. '' 'Court-ing Disaster': The Factors that Prompt the SEC to Seek Injunctive Relief.'' *Annual Institute on Securities Regulation,* summer 1995, 269-74.

Retsky, Maxine Lans. ''Watch Out for This New Legal Hurdle in Trademark Litigation.'' *Marketing News,* 5 January 1998, 28-29.

INNOVATION

Innovation is the act of introducing something new or doing something in a different way. Innovation in business differs from creativity in that the latter is generally associated with the generation of new ideas. In contrast, innovation refers to taking those new ideas and actually implementing them in the marketplace. Thus, creativity is simply one element of the innovation process through which new ideas lead to new products, procedures, or services. Business scholars often attribute company success to innovation. Because of growing **international competition**, innovation became even more vital for companies toward the end of the 20th century.

Innovation usually results from trial-and-error experimentation and sometimes occurs incidentally where researchers produce something other than what they intended. Nevertheless, because of the growth of and accessibility to knowledge and information through the technology and information revolutions, researchers of the late 20th century generally could move from ideas to innovations much more quickly than their predecessors. A confluence of factors contributes to innovation in the business setting, including the research environment, market need, company strategy, and company resources.

HISTORY OF INNOVATION IN BUSINESS

While innovation has existed as long as the species has, early innovations penetrated society and became established more slowly. For example, printing technology, various transportation innovations, and the use of gunpowder took centuries to reach most levels of society and become part of everyday life, according to Basil Blackwell and Samuel Eilon, authors of *The Global Challenge of Innovation.*

The penetration and acceptance of various innovations began to accelerate with the gradual collaboration and cooperation of science and assorted crafts and industries, especially in the 19th century. The partnership between science and industry allowed scientists to produce practical, reproducible technologies, which businesses could reasonably afford. Because of this collaboration, innovation grew quickly.

Despite the partnership, however, science and businesses still remained separate entities. Researchers worked either independently or as members of companies that specialized in developing, producing, and **marketing** innovations during this period. Consequently, many of these innovations failed to make it to the market.

Companies, however—especially power, chemical, and communications companies—began creating in-house **research and development** divisions early in the 20th century. In addition, they enhanced and marketed the innovations of others, breaking down the barrier between innovator and company. As a result, companies, not individuals, began controlling the **patents** to new inventions. Furthermore, teams of company researchers, not lone inventors, became the primary innovators.

THE INNOVATION PROCESS

While necessarily highly simplified, the ''market model'' of innovation highlights some of the significant steps in the development of new products and services. This model assumes that innovation arises from a market need and that the steps are not strictly linear, but recursive. Given this foundation, according to this model, developers create an invention designed to satisfy an existing market need. Next, developers assess the feasibility of the innovation in terms of both sales and production potential. If deemed feasible, they develop a prototype and obtain the technology needed to produce it in large quantities. After this step, developers conduct research in order to manufacture the product successfully and to ensure that the product will satisfy market demand.

At this point, developers hone the product's definition and seek to prove that the product specification fits. In addition, they make sure that the product complies with all relevant regulations. While the product definition process is underway, production begins along with marketing campaigns, which facilitate the movement of the product from the factories to the stores. Here, developers establish sales targets, delivery dates, and sales goals. Finally, the new product is launched and its success is gauged. If needed, the product's marketing plan can be modified or the product itself improved.

FUNCTIONS AND ATTRIBUTES OF INNOVATIVE COMPANIES

Entrepreneurs, scientists, and other innovators in business have always assumed that creativity and innovation are necessary to succeed and advance in a constantly changing world and marketplace. Highly successful industrial pioneers, such as Henry Ford (1863–1947), support this theory. Ford achieved great success by innovating mass production techniques that boosted productivity and output. But the Ford Motor Co. also demonstrated the results of failing to innovate—because Ford's organization failed to retain its creative edge, other manufacturers (e.g., General Motors Corp.) managed to exploit Ford's manufacturing breakthroughs with additional innovations of their own, eventually eclipsing the success of Ford.

The fast-paced technological advancement of the late 20th century and the opening of markets around the world through various trade agreements motivated companies to launch a profusion of new products and services, in many cases exploiting the advancing technology. As a consequence, innovation became a crucial part of corporate **strategy** during this period as companies tried to remain competitive and not lose market shares to more innovative companies. To attain this level of competitiveness, companies require not only the technology, but also the management skills and corporate vision to implement the technology successfully, according to Blackwell and Eilon.

To help identify factors that lead to creativity and inventiveness, U.S. researchers began to study innovation and creativity during the mid-1900s. A plethora of research and observation, particularly during the 1960s, served to highlight the importance of innovation in organizations, identify characteristics of innovative companies and groups of workers, and establish a framework for fostering creativity and inventiveness.

For example, Andrall E. Pearson (1925-), business analyst and former CEO of PepsiCo, argued in the *Harvard Business Review* that consistent innovation and constant changes to meet customers' needs distinguish the most successful companies from the rest. In order for businesses to promote consistent innovation and achieve this level of competitiveness, Pearson contended that they must engage in the following five activities simultaneously:

1. Establishing and maintaining a business environment that values innovation or stronger performance.
2. Creating a corporate structure where innovation is the top priority.
3. Developing a company strategy that encourages realistic innovations that will prove successful in the market.
4. Figuring out where to find innovative ideas and how to implement them once they are found.
5. Pursuing innovative ideas with full company support and resources.

CHARACTERISTICS OF GROUPS THAT PROMOTE INNOVATION

Businesses and groups of workers exhibit certain characteristics that reflect a propensity to innovate. For instance, companies in which employees are given a lot of responsibility for initiating new projects tend to be more innovative, as do companies that offer their workers a high degree of job security (i.e., the freedom to make mistakes without fear of disciplinary action or dismissal). Minimal interference from superiors also enhances creativity. The most innovative companies, however, successfully match the skills and interests of their workers to job tasks.

In general, companies in the United States that are more likely to be considered innovative are those that score highly in comparison to other firms in the following trait categories, in rough order of importance: freedom, risk taking, idea support, time to generate ideas, freedom to debate and challenge, and trust. More specifically, ten stimuli to creativity have been identified in the *Handbook for Creative and Innovative Managers.*

The five most commonly occurring stimuli are: (1) freedom and control to get a job done with minimal supervision; (2) good project management, including the supervisor's ability to match individuals to tasks and protect the group from destructive outside intervention; (3) sufficient resources to realize ideas; (4) encouragement, or the support of upper **management** and peers to take risks; and (5) a corporate climate that is generally amenable to making suggestions and trying new things. Other important organizational attributes include recognition and feedback, sufficient time to execute ideas, and a challenging environment.

In addition to these attributes of innovative company environments, various worker personality types also promote and advance innovation. Three particular personality types—risk takers, caretakers, and undertakers—are found in most groups, all of which can contribute positively to the organizational creative process. Most people lean toward one personality type but occasionally exhibit traits of all three categories.

Risk takers are the innovators in an organization. They possess the creative traits described earlier. Caretakers, in contrast, try to maintain the status quo. They tend to see changes as threats, rather than opportunities, and typically respond to outside influences only when forced to do so. Finally, undertakers are those people who are extremely resistant to change and are even willing to bury projects or sabotage ideas to maintain the status quo. They are often a detriment to the innovation process but may assume certain organizational roles that facilitate the innovation process.

WORKER ROLES IN THE INNOVATION PROCESS

Business innovation benefits from a diversity of personality types that fill different roles. After all, if every person in a company is extremely innovative, free-spirited, and nonconformist, the company might lack balance and grounding. Thus, a multiplicity of personality types and traits can be accommodated by the innovation process, which requires at least five general personality types. The first role of the innovation process is idea generator, someone who seeks to satisfy market needs by thinking of new ideas, developing solutions to problems, and identifying opportunities. Idea generators are often experts in one or two fields and are therefore able to recognize niche opportunities. They often enjoy working alone and are able to think abstractly and conceptually.

Champions, the second role in the innovation process, sell the ideas to others in the organization and secure resources to execute ideas. Individuals who play this role sometimes are referred to as **intrapreneurs**. In contrast to idea generators, champions are more apt to possess a wide range of interests, have general knowledge about several areas of a company or industry, and like to work with and influence other people. They are also more likely to be very energetic and to take risks.

Project leaders perform the third role in the process. They coordinate activities such as leading **teams**, planning and organizing projects, and balancing project goals with available resources and organizational needs. Effective project leaders are good at working with other people and fostering group cooperation. They are also adept at company politics and have a broad knowledge of company functions, such as **finance**, production, and marketing.

Gatekeepers, the fourth role in the innovation process, take charge of tracking influences outside of the organization through conferences, journals, friends at other companies, and similar sources. Gatekeepers pass the information on to others and serve as an information source, and sometimes critic, to idea generators, champions, and leaders. They facilitate group communication and project coordination. Good gatekeepers typically enjoy working with other people, are personable, and have a relatively high degree of technical competence. The gatekeeper role is one in which a non-innovative personality may still function to the benefit of the group.

Finally, the coaching role of the organizational innovation process involves encouraging and assisting team members, protecting the team from destructive outside forces (e.g., undertakers in other departments or groups), and securing the support of top-level management. Employees who fill the coaching role in the innovative process are usually good listeners. In addition, they tend to be less opinionated than their coworkers, a characteristic not ascribed to the stereotypic creative personality. Effective coaches are also proficient at politicking and have proven experience sponsoring new ideas.

SOURCES OF INNOVATION

Innovation is occasionally the result of a stroke of genius. More often, though, it occurs in response to a problem or opportunity that arises either inside or outside of an organization. Management guru Peter Drucker (1909-) has identified four internal and three external impetuses for innovation. Internal prompts include unexpected occurrences, incongruities, process needs, and industry or market changes.

INTERNAL IMPETUSES. Unexpected occurrences include mishaps, such as a failed product introduction. It is often through such unexpected failures (or successes) that new ideas are born from new information brought to light. For instance, Ford's failed Edsel gave the company new information about marketing that allowed it to achieve stellar gains with succeeding products. Unexpected occurrences can also take the form of accidents. For example, the hugely successful NutraSweet artificial sweetener was created by an accident during a project completely unrelated to sweeteners.

Incongruities result from a difference in a company's or industry's perception and reality. For example, although the demand for steel continued to grow between 1950 and 1970, profits in the steel industry fell. This incongruity caused some innovators to develop the steel minimill, a less expensive method of making steel that was also more conducive to changing market demands.

Innovations inspired by process needs are those created to support some other product or process. For example, **advertising** was introduced to make mass-produced newspapers possible. Newspaper publishers devised ads to cover the expense of printing the newspapers on the new equipment that made such printing possible.

Industry and market changes, the fourth internal impetus to innovate, often result in the rise (and decline) of successful innovators. For example, innovation and business savvy allowed International Business Machines Corp. (IBM) to effectively dominate the **computer** industry during the 1970s and early 1980s. It failed, however, to respond to a market switch during the 1980s from mainframes to smaller computer systems, particularly workstations and personal computer networks. As a result, IBM's share of the computer market plummeted and profits plunged as more innovative newcomers emerged.

EXTERNAL IMPETUSES. External impetuses to innovate include demographic changes, shifts in perception, and new knowledge. Demographic changes affect all aspects of business. For instance, an influx of Asian and Mexican immigrants into the United States has created new market niches for companies. Likewise, an increase in the level of education of Americans has resulted in a dearth of qualified workers for some low-paying jobs, causing many companies to develop new automation techniques.

Changes in perception also open the door to innovation. For example, despite the fact that health care in the United States has continually gotten better and more accessible, people have become increasingly concerned about their health and the need for better and more accessible care. This change in perception has generated a huge market for health magazines, vitamin supplements, and exercise equipment.

Finally, one of the strongest external impetuses for innovation is new knowledge, or technology. When a new technology emerges, innovative companies can profit by exploiting it in new applications and markets. For example, the invention of Kevlar, a synthetic material, has spawned thousands of new product innovations, ranging from improved canoes and bulletproof vests to better tires and luggage.

INNOVATION STRATEGIES

Two types of strategies for innovation in business are internal and market-based approaches. Internal strategies include programs and initiatives implemented by companies to foster a creative and innovative environment, whereas market-based strategies—such as the leader, quick follow, and slow follow strategies—refer to different approaches to delivering innovations to the market.

INTERNAL INNOVATION STRATEGIES. Internal strategies usually seek to develop and nurture the attributes of innovative corporations, such as prioritizing and encouraging innovation. Specific approaches to encouraging innovation differ by company and industry. For example, an integral aspect of Dow Corning Inc.'s strategy is to form ''research partnerships'' with its customers that solicit creative input from consumers and help the company benefit from new market opportunities. Other companies that employ customer-partnering programs include Black & Decker Corp. and General Electric.

Rubbermaid, Inc. encourages innovation by requiring that 30 percent of its sales come from products developed during the past five years. An important element of its program is searching for new ideas in other industries, such as the automotive business. Similarly, researchers at Hewlett-Packard Company (HP) are encouraged to spend at least 10 percent of their time toying with pet projects. HP also keeps its labs open 24 hours each day and utilizes small divisions and decentralized decision making to promote innovation. Likewise, pharmaceutical giant Merck & Co., Inc. gives its researchers time and money to pursue high-risk, high reward projects—a strategy that has profited the company handsomely.

One of the most innovative firms in the United States, 3M Company, sustains its creative environment by following a set of simple rules. By keeping its divisions small, division managers know the first names of all their subordinates, and, moreover, the company splits up divisions before their sales surpass $250 million to $300 million. It tolerates failure by promoting risk taking and experimentation. In fact, divisions must derive at least 25 percent of their profits from products developed during the past five years. 3M also ties salaries and bonuses to the success of new ideas and allows people who generate viable ideas to recruit an action team to develop them. In addition, 3M seeks customer input, shares technology throughout its different divisions, and never ''kills'' a project in which an employee has faith.

One of the best illustrations of the benefits of 3M's innovation program is Post-it notepads. 3M researcher Spencer Silver (1941-) developed an adhesive that the company was unable to find an application for, for five years. Company support slipped and Silver's project was eventually abandoned. 3M allowed Silver, however, to continue to spend 15 percent of his time looking for a way to use his creation. Finally, the adhesive was used to create one of 3M's most successful consumer innovations, Post-it pads.

One of the most renowned strategies to generate innovation in organizations is the ''Office of Innovation'' model developed by Eastman Kodak Company in the late 1970s. It has since been implemented by several leading organizations, including Amoco Corp., Union Carbide, the U.S. Air Force, and Bell Canada. The Office of Innovation provides a mechanism for drawing people together to brainstorm on ideas that may not even be related to their departments or expertise. In fact, its chief benefit is that it promotes cross-fertilization and free-flow of ideas within a company.

Although implementation varies, the model prescribes the use of a decentralized network of individual offices located in different functional areas, such as marketing, finance, and production. Staff members are encouraged to seek employees in other sectors who will come to the office and provide feedback on new ideas. The process is founded on the importance of giving credence to workers' ideas. It involves a five-step process that mimics the five-stage innovation process detailed earlier: idea generation, initial screening, group review, seeking sponsorship, and sponsorship. Kodak estimated that in just one year its Office of Innovation program harvested ideas eventually worth more than $300 million.

MARKET-BASED STRATEGIES. Even companies with the most innovative organizational environments will languish if they fail to effectively market their innovations. For example, just because a firm improves its product doesn't mean that it should necessarily take the improvement to the market. From a strategic standpoint, the company could lose money if it has invested a lot of resources in marketing the original product because the improved version might cannibalize sales. On the other hand, if the company waits too long to introduce the improved version, a competitor may produce such an innovation earlier and capture market share. Consider the inventors of items such as the air conditioner or electric lamp. The innovators of those concepts died before their creations were widely accepted by the marketplace.

Although there are a number of product- and industry-specific strategies that companies may employ to promote their innovations, three of the most common market-based innovation strategies include the leader, quick follow, and slow follow (or no follow) strategies, according to William E. Rothschild, author of *Strategic Alternatives.* A company that adopts a **leadership** strategy for its invention becomes the first to introduce the innovation to the market. The obvious risk of such a move is that the product or service will be rejected by the marketplace at a potentially enormous cost to the company.

The leadership strategy, however, also may provide a variety of different benefits. For instance, companies often introduce an innovation to an existing product or service, calling it ''new'' or ''improved,'' to breathe new life into it. Or they may bring out an improved product to discourage the competition from trying to steal market share, or to ''leapfrog'' their competitors. In the case of completely new products or ideas, a company may introduce the innovation in an effort to establish market dominance and attain leadership status.

The quick-follow strategy is often used by established competitors that already lead an industry or market niche. Rather than assume the risk inherent to the leadership strategy, the company will simply wait for one of its competitors to introduce an innovation. Shortly thereafter, the company will follow the leader with a substitute or improvement of the innovation. Quick followers are usually relatively sure of their ability to crush the competition with their established reputation and marketing and distribution channels.

The risk of the quick-follow tactic is that the follower will be unseated by a hugely successful introduction, or that it will lose its reputation as an innovator over time. Quick followers often include smaller competitors that are simply trying to keep up with the competition. They may try to target select market niches. For example, a company may follow with a cheaper version of a new innovation in an effort to lure buyers who can't afford the leader's product or service.

A company that adopts a slow- or no-follow strategy may do so for a number of reasons. It may feel that existing competitive pressures or lackluster market growth make an investment in following an innovation unappealing. Or, the company may realize that it simply lacks the resources or technology necessary to compete with the new innovation. Some companies refuse to introduce or adopt an innovation because they fear that they will lose customers. For instance, a manufacturer of industrial air conditioners may delay introducing a substantially different technology because it knows that its existing customers have made large capital investments in its existing product line and will be hesitant to buy new equipment. Finally, some companies are so strong in marketing or manufacturing that product innovation is simply not a chief concern—they would prefer to wait until the new innovation is accepted by the market before they follow.

[Dave Mote, updated by Karl Heil]

FURTHER READING:

Blackwell, Basil, and Samuel Eilon. *The Global Challenge of Innovation.* Boston: Butterworth-Heinemann, 1991.

Brown, John Seely, ed. *Seeing Differently: Insights on Innovation.* Boston: Harvard Business School Press, 1997.

Diebold, John. *The Innovators: The Discoveries, Inventions, and Breakthroughs of Our Time.* New York: Dutton, 1990.

Henry, Jane. *Managing Innovation.* London: Sage Publications, 1991.

Kanter, Rosabeth Moss, John Kao, and Fred Wiersema, eds. *Innovation: Breakthrough Ideas at 3M, DuPont, GE, Pfizer, and Rubbermaid.* New York: HarperBusiness, 1997.

Katz, Ralph, ed. *Managing Professionals in Innovative Organizations.* Cambridge, MA: Ballinger, 1988.

Kotter, John P. *The Leadership Factor.* New York: Free Press, 1988.

Kuhn, Robert L. *Handbook for Creative and Innovative Managers.* New York: McGraw-Hill, 1988.

Mescon, Michael H., Michael Albert, and Franklin Khedouri. *Management.* 3rd ed. New York: Harper & Row, 1988.

Pearson, Andrall E. "Tough-Minded Ways to Get Innovative." *Harvard Business Review* 66, no. 3 (May/June 1988): 99+.

Rothschild, William E. *Strategic Alternatives.* New York: AMACOM, 1979.

Sayles, Leonard R. *Leadership: Managing in Real Organizations.* 2nd ed. New York: McGraw-Hill, 1989.

Terkel, M. *Integrative Management, Innovation, and New Venturing: A Guide to Sustained Profitability.* New York: Elsevier, 1991.

INPUT-OUTPUT ANALYSIS

Input-output analysis is a basic method of quantitative economics that portrays macroeconomic activity as a system of interrelated goods and services. In particular, the technique observes various economic sectors as a series of inputs of source materials (or services) and outputs of finished or semi-finished goods (or services). The field is most identified with the work of Wassily Leontief (1906-1999), who was awarded the 1973 Nobel Prize in Economics for his pioneering work in the area. Leontief once explained input-output analysis as follows: "When you make bread, you need eggs, flour, and milk. And if you want more bread, you must use more eggs. There are cooking recipes for all the industries in the economy." And hence, one industry's output is another's input, and the chain continues.

INFLUENCE OF CLASSICAL ECONOMICS

Leontief's approach was based in large part on classical theory economics. During the 18th and first half of the 19th centuries the theoretical perspectives of classical school economists held sway in the field. Many of its principal contributors resided or gained notoriety in England. In general, classical theory economists approached the study of economics from the vantage point of its systematic operation, attempting to understand the mutual interaction between parts and whole. This major distinction set them apart from the core theoretical approach taken by present day neoclassical economics which has dominated formal economic analysis since the 1870s. In direct contrast to classical theory, neoclassical theory builds from the level of individual economic agents and conducts its analysis in terms of the operation of individual markets.

The theoretical works of Adam Smith (1723-1790) and David Ricardo (1772-1823) figure most prominently within the school of classical theory. And, while he was critical of and rejected some of their major theoretical propositions, Karl Marx (1818-1883) duly acknowledged the contributions of Smith and Ricardo as instrumental to his own investigation into the systematic operation, as opposed to individual market analysis, of a capitalist economy.

While reviving the methodological approach analogous to classical theorists, Leontief's overriding concern focused on how economic systems were structured, the way an economy's component parts interrelate and mutually influence one another. To a limited extent, because input output analysis deals with aggregate categories, it falls within the purview of **macroeconomics**. Yet because it is applied within the realm of observable and measured phenomena, input-output analysis is considered a branch of **econometrics**. As such, much of the existing literature on the subject is highly technical in nature. Practitioners of input-output analysis converse in a seemingly arcane language that few outside its profession know how to interpret. It draws heavily upon mathematics, especially matrix algebra, and, in the construction of input-output tables (see Table 1), strives to be in strict conformity with a bevy of statistical properties. For these reasons alone many students, academics, professionals, and other interested parties find input-output analysis intimidating. Yet the basic approach to the construction of input-output tables and their analysis is highly accessible.

A salient feature of Leontief's early input-output work resided in its highly disaggregated nature. This allowed for a comprehensively detailed, quantitative grasp of the structured linkages between an economic system's component parts. Parallel to his efforts of compiling a highly disaggregated database, Leontief formulated an equally disaggregated theoretical

Table 1
Sample Input-Output Table from Leontief

	Industry Consuming								
Industry Producing	Agriculture	Food & beverages	Textiles	Apparel	Lumber & wood	Furniture & fixtures	Paper & allied products	. . .	Total output
Agriculture	10.86	15.70	2.16	0.02	0.19		0.01		44.26
Food & beverages	2.38	5.75	0.06	0.01			0.03		40.30
Textiles	0.06		1.30	3.88		0.29	0.04		9.84
Apparel	0.04	0.20		1.96		0.01	0.02		13.32
Lumber & wood	0.15	0.10	0.02		1.09	0.39	0.27		6.00
Furniture & fixtures			0.01			0.01	0.01		2.89
Paper & allied products		0.52	0.08	0.02		0.02	2.60		7.90
. . .									
Total Outlays	44.26	40.30	9.84	13.32	6.00	2.89	7.90		

Figures in billions of U.S. dollars

Source: Based on Wassily Leontief's analysis of Bureau of Labor Statistics data, 1947.
Excerpted from Input-Output Economics, 2nd ed., by Wassily Leontief (Oxford, 1986).

model. For its time, the empirical implementation of his model presented an unsurpassed challenge. Its numerical computations, both in terms of their complexity and scale, were virtually unknown within the field of economics or, for that matter, within any other empirically grounded social science discipline.

Ironically, around the same time Leontief was busy developing input output tables, complete with their aggregative and disaggregative capabilities, the general direction of economic research, under the influence of John Maynard Keynes (1883-1946), became increasingly dominated by a highly aggregative approach. The foremost concern of Keynesian economics was countering the effects of chronic unemployment. This cast a decade's long shadow over Leontief's pathbreaking efforts. Nevertheless, during a time when all the world's advanced capitalist economies were mired in the Great Depression, the emphasis on aggregates, at least from a public policy standpoint, made practical sense.

During the mid-1940s, Leontief acted as a consultant for the U.S. Bureau of Labor Statistics (BLS) when it undertook the first construction of a national input-output table. The effort culminated in the 1947 publication of a 50-sector table of interindustry relations followed shortly thereafter by a 200-sector table with more highly detailed industrial and sectoral classifications. One important practical result of the table was its projections for postwar employment growth until the year 1950 along with policy recommendations should the economy fall short of full employment.

By the early 1950s, though, government appropriations for the BLS's continued development of input-output analysis ceased. A short time later, in 1953, the U.S. Department of Defense abandoned plans to conduct a departmental study using input-output analysis. These decisions were influenced by some businessmen who cast the BLS's program as a step toward socialist ''push-button planning.'' No further work on government sponsored input-output projects transpired until after the Census of Manufactures of 1958. The interindustry results of the input-output study were eventually published in 1964.

Despite its languish in the United States, not long after World War II the use of input-output analysis began to gain an institutional presence throughout the world. Its application soon incorporated major traditional areas of economic analysis such as short-term **forecasting**, dynamic input-output modeling, income and employment multipliers, regional and interregional analysis, environmental impacts, international trade, underdeveloped economics, and social demography. By 1986, about 90 countries had constructed input-output tables.

HISTORICAL FORERUNNERS

The historical precursors to input-output analysis were in evidence as far back as the first half of the

17th-century. Most economic historians cite François Quesnay's (1694-1774) *Tableau Economique* as the earliest recorded examples to depict the importance of mutual interindustry flows or, in more modern parlance, systematic economic interdependence. Quesnay was one of the leading theoreticians whose work inspired the formation of a group of French agrarian social reformers called the Physiocrats. Though its central focus was on agriculture, the *Tableau* represents a basic working model of an economy and its extended reproduction. It highlighted the processes of production, circulation of money and **commodities**, and the distribution of **income**. And, despite having originally appeared in a cumbersome zigzag form, the *Tableau's* easy adaptability to Leontief's input-output or double-entry table format has been demonstrated.

The Physiocrats divided society into three classes or sectors. First, a productive class of cultivators engaged in agricultural production were solely responsible for the generation of society's surplus product, a part of which formed net investment. Second, the sterile class referred to producers of manufactured commodities. The term sterile was applied not because manufacturers did not produce anything of value, but because the value of their output (e.g., clothes, shoes, cooking utensils) was presumed to be equal to the necessary costs of raw materials received from the cultivators plus the subsistence level of the producer wages. According to the Physiocrats no surplus product or profits were thought to originate in manufacturing. Lastly came landlords or the idle class who through the money they received as rent consumed the surplus product created by the productive cultivators.

Of particular relevance to the contemporary method of input-output analysis is the *Tableau's* lengthy depiction of the three classes' transactions. Once the landlord class received their money rents, account was made of the transactions that lead to distribution of products between the agricultural and manufacturing sectors. In short, the *Tableau* illustrated the two sectors' interdependence as the output from each sector served as a necessary input for the other. These are exactly the type of interindustry relationships that form the core theoretical foundation upon which modern day input-output analysis rests. Here, money's role as a medium of circulation was also critical since it functioned to maintain a fluid means of product allocation. Finally, with the passage of one year, the *Tableau*'s entire socioeconomic process came to an end and the transactions were aggregated. Given the *Tableau*'s postulated assumptions, it could then be shown that the economy arrived back at its initial static state.

Some of the outstanding ideas expressed in Quesnay's *Tableau* were to exercise an enduring impact, even up to the present day, on the study of economics. Among these were: (1) the notion of productive and unproductive labor and their relationship to an economic surplus, (2) the mutual interdependence of production processes, and (3) the circular flows of money and commodities and the potential for economic crises that arise from the hoarding of money. Of these, the second point clearly resonates closest to the object of input-output analysis, while the concern raised by the third point has been addressed by the creation of central banking institutions. However, with the notable exception of two economists, Anwar Shaik and Ertugrul Amhet Tonak, little in the way of integrating the first and second point has been attempted. This is somewhat unsettling as once this distinction has been drawn, comparisons in the measurement of commonly used aggregate macroeconomic input and output variables estimated across the postwar period diverge both in terms of the direction and magnitude of their trends.

Though they were active in England instead of France, the economists who figured most prominently in the development of classical theory themselves drew heavily from theoretical insights of the Physiocratic school. Adam Smith's seminal work, *An Inquiry into the Nature and Causes of the Wealth of Nations,* borrows wholesale, and proceeds to extend upon, the Physiocrats' major theoretical propositions. And, as Luigi Pasinetti indicated, the analytical roots of Ricardo's now widely used one sector corn model or two sector gold and corn model, depicting economic growth or capital accumulation, takes its notion of economic surplus from the Physiocrats. Both of Ricardo's models also emphasize the Physiocratic notion of production as a circular process, or, in accord with Leontief's definition, of an economy's "general interdependence."

Most of the economic history literature covering the early forerunners of input-output analysis contain a curious omission—hardly any mention of Marx's work. Indeed, of all the economists typically associated with developing the early groundwork out of which input-output analysis was to emerge, probably none spent more time in exploring the interdependence of economic life, along with a host of other related matters, than Marx.

For instance, all the material covered in Volume II of *Capital* (some 550 pages), analyzes the complete process by which one industry's output serves as another's input. Marx readily acknowledged the debt he owed to Quesnay's *Tableau.* Called the "reproduction schema," Marx divided total social reproduction into two basic departments: production of the means of production and production of the means of consumption. He then proceeded to elaborate a simple mathematical model to explore what happens when the entire surplus product is totally consumed or used for further accumulation, while in either case balance (equilibrium) between each department is maintained. Simple reproduction referred to the above case where the entire surplus product was consumed while extended reproduction designated the instance where a fraction or all of the surplus product was employed for accumulation purposes.

In his *Theories of Surplus-Value,* Parts I and III, Marx also devotes over 100 pages to a critique of Quesnay's *Tableau* and other issues related to Physiocratic theory. Both the *Theories of Surplus-Value,* and the three volumes of *Capital* contain much qualified praise for Quesnay's *Tableau* and other Physiocratic writings which, as Marx pointed out, were to form the theoretical foundation upon which Smith and Ricardo drew.

Leon Walras represents the last link in the chain leading up to Leontief's formulation of input-output analysis. Despite having worked within a neoclassical framework, Walras is credited with introducing the use of production coefficients, a concept that closely resembles one of the core ideas contained in Leontief's work. Yet unlike Leontief's approach, Walras's model of a pure exchange market economy's ability to arrive at an equilibrium state analytically trivialized the production sector. It treated production as nothing more than an intermediate phase sandwiched between simultaneous acts of utility maximization and the optimal allocation of exogenously given stock of scarce resources. Though it makes little sense to the uninitiated, Walras's use of production coefficients grafted onto this theory of a pure exchange equilibrium suffered from a major limitation. He erroneously treated the stock of resources as a flow variable that occurred within a current period and failed to take account of its existence from previous periods. As a result, Walras was never able to develop a coherent theory of capital accumulation.

LEONTIEF'S DEVELOPMENT OF INPUT-OUTPUT ANALYSIS

Born 5 August 1906 in St. Petersburg (known as Leningrad during the Communist era), Russia, Leontief received a degree of "Learned Economist" from the University of Leningrad. He received his Ph.D. in 1928 while attending the University of Berlin. Taking up an offer to join the staff of the prestigious National Bureau of Economic Research, Leontief arrived in the United States in 1931. Within a few months he had accepted an appointment at Harvard University where he was to remain and attain worldwide recognition for his invention and application of input-output analysis.

Growing impatient with the penchant of his economist peers for "implicit theorizing," Leontief set out to pursue a dictum that has served as a guiding thread throughout his career: that economic concepts were of little validity unless they could be observed and measured. He was convinced that not only was a well-formulated theory of utmost importance but so too was its application to real economics. To be of use, an economic theory must yield interesting behavioral predictions whose results were subject to verification. With this in mind, Leontief's early extensions of input-output analysis were intended to demonstrate that: (1) production coefficients, expressing relationships among the industrial sectors of an economy, lent themselves to statistical estimation; (2) that the estimated coefficients were sufficiently stable so as to be used in comparative static analyses, i.e., different equilibrium states; and, given the above two points, (3) that on a quantitative level, the merits of different economic policies could be evaluated by taking into consideration both their direct and indirect feedback effects (or multiplier impact) on interindustry flows.

At the time, Leontief's grandiose input-output efforts encountered two major stumbling blocks. First, only part of the information needed for his production coefficients was available (through the U.S. Census of Manufactures) while the remainder had to be arduously gleaned from trade journals and other dispersed sources. Second, underlying Leontief's input-output method was the assumption that production coefficients remained largely constant for extended periods. This proposition was hard to reconcile with the dominant neoclassical theory of production that held that factors of production, (i.e., different quantities of labor and machines expressed in isoquants), were readily substituted for one another as their relative prices changed (i.e., the changing slopes of isocost curves).

Undaunted, around 1934 Leontief began to surmount these self-admitted difficulties. He compiled a 44-sector industrial table containing about 2,000 coefficients in addition to mapping out a plan for their analysis and tests for their validity. To ascertain the coefficients' stability, tables were constructed for the years of 1919 and 1929. The first test results on the coefficients' stability proved inconclusive. This lack of decisiveness was rectified in 1944, however, when Leontief calculated a table of coefficients for 1939, comparable in scope to his 1919 and 1929 tables. He arrived at a satisfactory degree of stability for most coefficients across the two decades.

In 1948, Leontief founded and became the director of the Harvard Economic Research Project established for the purposes of applying and extending the field of input-output analysis. During his 25-year tenure as its director, Leontief remained a driving force in developing interregional input-output analysis and in introducing capital-coefficient matrices meant to depict the investment response to changes in final demand. Given these developments, input-output analysis proved adept at generating an economic system's forecasted growth path as well as its various static equilibrium positions. Leontief's work at the project led to the publication of two books, *The Structure of American Economy 1919-1939,* in 1951, and *Studies in the Structure of the American Economy,* in 1953.

Other significant extensions of input-output analysis included estimates of the inflationary consequences of wage settlements, the direct and indirect impact of armament expenditures, estimates of capital requirements for economic development, and methods intended to forecast the individual growth-paths of industrial sectors in a developing economy. In more recent years input-output analysis has been applied to the issue of worldwide economic growth, its environmental consequences, its impact on the world's reserve of natural resources, and the political-economic ramifications for relations between the economies of developed and less-developed countries. Under a project funded by the **United Nations**, Leontief managed a study on the growth of the world economy until the year 2000. The multiregional input-output model extended across 15 regions consisting of 45 sectors each with balanced trading accounts.

The results were published in 1977 as *The Future of the World Economy.* Based on a broad set of reasonable assumptions, it provisionally concluded that only small progress would be made in closing the gap between rich and poor regions unless current policies dealing with international trade and finance were abandoned. As policy alternatives the study recommended a marked increase in multinational aid and a significant increase in the flow of imports from the developing economies to industrial economies.

DEVELOPMENTS AND EXTENSIONS

A standard input-output table contains an equal number of rows and columns, as depicted in Table 1, which is based on an early input-output table produced by Leontief in 1951. Tables can measure dollars or physical units of produced goods and services, such as tons of steel, bushels of wheat, or gallons of fuel. Following the construction of an annual input-output table, it is possible to derive a second table of input or technical coefficients. The term ''technical coefficients'' refers to the quantity of inputs required from each industry to produce one dollar's worth of a given industry's output. Because it represents the entire domain of wealth-producing activities, computation of the technical coefficients are restricted to the processing sector industries only. The coefficients can be denominated in either monetary or physical units. The basic formula for determining coefficients is

$$a_{ij} = \frac{x_{ij}}{x_j}$$

where a_{ij} = the input coefficient of industry i into industry j,
x_{ij} = the amount of industry i's output used by industry j, and
x_j = the total output from industry j

Using this formula, the coefficient a_{ij} can be obtained for all the industries in an input-output table. Once a transaction table of direct and indirect coefficients (or a coefficient matrix) has been obtained, several common economic analyses can be performed.

FORECASTS BASED ON COEFFICIENTS. The first concerns the use of static input-output tables to consistently forecast projections of both industry and final sector demands. Typically, for periods of up to two or three years, these are reliable short-term forecasts over which it makes sense to assume that the production coefficients change very little. But the existence of stable technical coefficients within a longer term forecast is tenuous. Integration of disturbances related to relative input price changes, the appearance of new industries during the projection period, and the effects of technological change on technical coefficients, require more complex, dynamic models of input output analysis. Around 1953 Leontief initially formulated a dynamic input-output model. Later, Copper Almon also achieved significant results working with dynamic input-output models.

INCOME MULTIPLIERS. A second area extending the use of input-output analysis concerns the use of income multipliers. Their construction requires appending the households row and column to a coefficient table followed by the calculation of their direct and indirect effects. While Keynes first introduced and applied multipliers as a concept central to the study of macroeconomics, it was R.S. Kahn who originated their theoretical development. Nevertheless, credit goes to input-output analysis for making it possible to disaggregate the highly aggregated multipliers in order to detail how multiplier effects ramify throughout an economic structure. If, for instance, it becomes a question as to whether a given level of public investment should be directed toward the construction or military industries, then, based on their different multiplier impacts, input output analysis provides policy makers with a tool to evaluate the merits of either project. Or, in international trade, should the problem concern easing import restrictions, input-output analysis can indicate how imports might affect industries supplying domestic inputs and outputs.

In short, when based on the assumption that each industry's output expands by the same amount, then input-output augmented multipliers reveal that varying amounts of income are generated by different industries. In general, for the case of international trade, the greater the degree of the domestic economy's interdependence, the greater will be the direct effects of income change. But in terms of both the direct and indirect effects the results could be reversed, neutralized, or strengthened.

EMPLOYMENT MULTIPLIERS. Third, the existence of an input-output table combined with a projected change in aggregate final demand also allows for the calculation of employment multipliers. Computation of employment multipliers differ from the method used for income multipliers. Two methods, the Isard-Kuene and Moore-Peterson approach, were the first to tackle the subject. The Isard-Kuene method sought to measure the total employment impact within a region based on the establishment of a new basic industry within it borders. It drew from national coefficients to estimate the inputs of both the basic industry and the accompanying industries expected to locate around the new industry. The Moore-Peterson method, by contrast, uses regional—instead of national—coefficients to estimate both the direct, indirect, and induced employment effects. Assuming a change in the final demand for the output of one or more industries within the region, calculation of total employment changes was performed across all industries.

REGIONAL INPUT-OUTPUT ANALYSIS. Developments in both regional and interregional models of input-output studies have loomed large in the post-World War II era. During this time the trend in economics has moved to quantitative research, a task for which input-output analysis is well suited. The distinction between the two models is straightforward, a region comprises one geographical area while an interregional model spans several regions. From here two further complementary distinctions apply—that between a balanced regional and pure interregional model. A balanced regional model is constructed through disaggregation of a national input-output model into component regions. Conversely, a pure interregional model is designed by aggregating a number of regional tables, which may or may not include all the regions in a national economy.

Interregional models have been used to analyze regional **balance of trade** payments and interregional trade flows. Interregional models are more complex than either national or regional models. This stems from having to sort out interindustry and interregional economic flows. As a result many have tended to be highly aggregated since reliable data on industry sales and purchases by region are hard to come by.

Regional models cover geographic areas of varying size. Some have encompassed **Federal Reserve** districts, others, metropolitan areas, states, counties, or an area specified across two or more states. For the most part, regional input-output models are considered more ''open'' than a national economy model. The quality of openness derives from the tendency of regions to be more highly specialized in terms of their processing sectors, thus more inclined to transact exchanges from without.

CURRENT STATUS AND TRENDS

Input-output analysis remains an active branch of economics, and one with numerous offshoots. Some of its most popular applications are those that Leontief helped pioneer, including national accounts and trade, environmental studies, and technological change forecasts. In addition to the many input-output studies published from time to time in general economics journals, there are a number of academic journals devoted specifically to input-output analysis. For economists who specialize in input-output work, there are also several professional associations worldwide, the most prominent being the International Input-Output Association (IIOA), based in Vienna, Austria. As of the late 1990s, the IIOA had some 300 individual members and 20 institutional members representing 49 nations.

Input-output analysis has sustained such interest in the professional community because of its versatility and its strong grounding in empirical evidence. While it is most associated with grand macroeconomic studies like those of Leontief, input-output analysis can be equally valuable to research on a single firm. And unlike some areas of economics, input-output analysis does not come with a great deal of theoretical baggage that is hard to prove in real life. Of course, it is susceptible to distortions from measurement error or inaccurate modeling, but its underlying strength lies in being driven by real data.

[Daniel E. King]

FURTHER READING:

Correa, Hector, and James Craft. ''Input-Output Analysis for Organizational Human Resources Management.'' *Omega,* February 1999.

Galbraith, James. ''Wassily Leontief: An Appreciation.'' *Challenge,* May-June 1999.

Kurz, Heinz D., Erik Dietzenbacher, and Christian Lager, eds. *Input-Output Analysis.* Cheltenham, UK: Edward Elgar Publishing, 1998.

Leontief, Wassily. *Input-Output Economics.* 2nd ed. New York: Oxford University Press, 1986.

Shaik, Anwar, and Ertugrul A. Tonak. *Measuring the Wealth of Nations: The Political Economy of National Accounts.* New York: Columbia University Press, 1994.

Sohn, Ira, ed. *Readings in Input-Output Analysis: Theory and Applications.* New York: Oxford University Press, 1986.

INSTITUTIONAL INVESTMENTS

An institutional investor is an organization that trades large volumes of **securities** on behalf of a collection of individual investors. Institutional investors include commercial **banks**, **savings and loan associations**, investment trusts, insurance companies, **pension funds**, and, most notably in recent years, **mutual funds**.

Such an organization offers individual investors two primary benefits. First, by trading in aggregate—or utilizing the collective financial resources of many individual investors—the institutional investor may realize tremendous **economies of scale** in securities trades. For example, such high-volume trades typically qualify the institutional investor for discounts on commissions and "soft dollar" rebates from brokerage firms that find their business very profitable.

Second, the financial largesse of the assets of the investment firm enables the firm to retain highly qualified money managers, or professional investment advisers, who may devote more time and attention to thoroughly investigate investment opportunities than any single investor could afford.

Institutional investment firms have their origin in investment trusts that came into being in European financial centers, principally London, Amsterdam, and Paris, during the 18th and 19th centuries. Such firms later formed in other financial centers, such as New York, Chicago, Hong Kong, and Frankfurt, and today may exist in virtually any city in the world.

The growth of institutional investors was fueled to a great extent during the 1980s by growth strategies of firms that sought new sources of investment capital. By marketing new, more customized investment vehicles and services to smaller investors, institutional investment firms brought the benefits of participation in large financial markets to investors who previously lacked the financial resources necessary for cost-effective participation. As individuals, they lacked sufficient capital to enter certain markets or profit fully from trades in those markets. As members of investment collectives, however, various entry and operating costs could be widely distributed and reduced.

It is estimated that securities trading by institutional investment firms now accounts for about 90 percent of all trades in financial markets. This does not represent the waning of the individual investor, but merely a trend in which individual investors participate in markets through institutional investment intermediaries rather than as direct investors.

According to one study, firms that managed $100 million or more in securities controlled 51 percent of the capitalization of U.S. **stock markets** at the end of 1996, up from just 26.7 percent in 1980. Another 1998 finding by the Conference Board found that the 25 largest institutional investors controlled a growing share of the U.S. equity market, some 19.7 percent of total outstanding equities in 1997, up from 16.7 percent in 1996. Among all institutional investors, the 25 largest institutions accounted for 40.9 percent of all equities managed by institutional investors.

It has been suggested, particularly after the October 1987 market collapse, that the influence of institutional investors over markets is too strong. The collapse in 1987 resulted in a decline in the Dow Jones Industrial Average of more than 500 points, representing devaluation of about 20 percent.

At the time of the collapse, market values for shares were generally agreed to be inflated, and a correction was necessary. Nevertheless, the actions of institutional investors were governed largely by computer programs, set to sell in increasing volumes as market prices declined. Therefore, a small number of highly sensitive programmed trades caused the entire community to bail out of the market all at once. Market prices fell, but far beyond what was necessary for a proper correction. Regulatory safeguards were subsequently enacted to blunt the effect of programmed trading by institutional investors.

[John Simley, updated by David P. Bianco]

FURTHER READING:

Blommestein, Hans J., and Norbert Funke. "The Rise of the Institutional Investor." *OECD Observer,* June/July 1998, 37-42.

"Institutional Investors Continue to Gain Control of U.S. Corporations." *Directorship,* October 1998, 14.

Kover, Amy. "The Perfect Price—Every 15 Minutes." *Fortune,* 15 March 1999, 208.

McNamee, Mike. "A Big Break for Big Caps?" *Business Week,* 11 January 1999, 34.

Palmer, Jay. "Going Soft." *Barron's,* 28 September 1998, 14.

Vickers, Douglas. *Economics and Ethics: An Introduction to Theory, Institutions, and Policy.* Westport, CT: Greenwood, 1997.

Wipperfurth, Heike. "Full Steam Ahead for Institutional Equity Unit at Shaw." *The Investment Dealers' Digest,* 8 February 1999, 11.

INTANGIBLE ASSETS

In **accounting** and law, intangible assets are nonphysical assets or things of value, such as trademarks, **patent** rights, **copyrights** (known collectively as **intellectual property**), **franchise** rights, leasehold interests, and noncompete agreements, as well as unquantifiable assets often referred to as goodwill or deferred **costs**, such as **corporate culture** and **strategy**, customer satisfaction, and employee loyalty. Although they lack physical substance, intangible assets—also called intangible property—may represent a substantial, or even a major, portion of a company's total assets.

Intangible assets are usually shown on a company's **balance sheet** under noncurrent assets, falling after fixed assets and before or among other assets. Generally they are recorded at their historical cost, and amortized—i.e., gradually written off as expenses over their useful lives. The period of **amortization**, however, cannot exceed 40 years under the current rules of the **Financial Accounting Standards Board**. The balance sheet lists such assets only if a company incurs a cost when acquiring them. Hence, nonphysical assets acquired without a cost are not included in a company balance sheet. Moreover, not all assets lacking substance are classified as intangible assets. Money owed a company or an account receivable, for instance, is considered a current account, even though it has no substance.

Furthermore, in order for an expenditure to qualify as an intangible asset, a company must expect benefits in the following years and support that expectation with evidence. Expenditures such as those on **advertising**, for example, may promise future benefits, but the benefits are so uncertain and unpredictable that companies classify them as current expenses.

TYPES OF INTANGIBLE ASSETS

Patent rights entitle their owners to a 17-year monopoly to manufacture or use a certain product or process. The capitalized value of the intangible asset usually includes the legal costs involved with filing the patent application and perfecting and enforcing the patent rights. **Research and development** costs incurred in discovering the patent are typically excluded from the intangible asset, as accounting rules require such expenditures to be charged to expense in the year incurred. If part of the patent utility involves a cross-license arrangement with another company, any money paid to that other company would be included in the capitalized value of the intangible asset. Although patents have a technical length of 17 years, as a practical matter, inventions and innovations are often replaced by new technologies in much shorter periods. The amortization period should be the shorter of 17 years or until the patent no longer offers a competitive or marketable advantage.

Trademarks are the exclusive rights to proprietary symbols, names, and other unique properties of a product, such as packaging, style, and even color in some instances. The trademark is established by active use in the marketplace and registration with the U.S. Patent and Trademark Office. Capitalized costs will include the original design work plus the legal expense and filing fees to record the trademark. Any costs incurred to enforce the exclusive use of the mark are included as well. Trademarks have an indefinite life, provided the owner continues to actively use them, and, therefore, are not necessarily amortized.

As sanctioned by the Copyright Act of 1976, copyrights represent the legal right, for a period of 50 years after the author's death, to sell, copy, or perform a piece of literary, musical, or art work. Copyrights protect both published and unpublished works from reproduction or derivative use without the consent from the copyright owner (usually the author or publisher). This intangible asset will normally be recorded at its acquisition price, if the rights were bought, or simply the cost to file the copyright notice. This asset is amortized over its useful life, but not for more than 40 years.

Sometimes in connection with the purchase and sale of a business, the former proprietor(s) will agree not to engage in a similar business within a defined geographic area and for a defined period of time (generally two to five years). Such agreements are called noncompete agreements. The parties may also agree to allocate a portion of the purchase price to the noncompete provision. In these circumstances, the amount allocated becomes the intangible asset, which is amortized over the prescribed noncompete period.

Licenses are the contractual rights to use another's property, whether it be a patent, trademark copyright, **real estate** (usually called a lease), or exploration for natural resources. Often such licenses provide for ongoing payments assessed as a payment for the benefit gained by the licensee from the use of the property. These payments are known as royalties. In some cases, however, an up-front payment is extracted by the licensor, in which case that amount can be recorded as an intangible asset by the licensee. As with other intangible assets, its value should be amortized over the useful or contractual life, whichever is shorter.

Franchise rights constitute another kind of intangible asset. Franchises provide their holders with the right to practice a certain kind of business in a certain geographical location as sanctioned by the franchiser, usually a company or government agency. Fast-food restaurants, for example, often expand by selling franchise rights, which allow the franchisees to use a restaurant name and format in a specific locale. Since franchise costs vary dramatically, the period of amortization may be very short (one or two years) or very long (up to 40 years).

Goodwill refers to the price or value above the **market value** of the tangible assets of a company. When a company is bought, the price paid will often be above the market value of its facilities, equipment, inventory, etc. A company cultivates this intangible asset by establishing a strong business track record and by establishing many beneficial relationships, including those with customers, distributors, and suppliers. In addition, goodwill covers other valuable albeit intangible aspects of a company, such as its credit rating, location, reputation, and name. Goodwill also may manifest itself in the form of trademarks, manufacturing processes, and license rights.

In any event, goodwill reflects the buyer's perception that the company as a whole is worth more than the sum of the identifiable physical assets. On occasions, companies even sell their goodwill without the sale of other assets. For instance, a company planning to relocate may sell the right to use its name and facilities. Goodwill, as an intangible asset, is amortized for accounting purposes over no more than 40 years. Current **tax** provisions do not allow a deduction for the amortization of goodwill.

Deferred costs generally include any remaining miscellaneous intangible assets acquired for some future benefit. Examples include moving costs, formulas, restructuring costs, **loan** acquisition costs, capitalized interest, name lists, and movie rights. These intangible assets are amortized over the period the assets continue to yield benefits.

SEE ALSO: Inventory Accounting; Licensing Agreements

[Christopher C. Barry, updated by Karl Heil]

FURTHER READING:

Meigs, Robert F., et al. *Accounting: The Basis for Business Decisions.* 11th ed. Boston: Irwin/McGraw-Hill, 1999.

Parrott, Mark D. ''Intangibles and Profits.'' *Do-It Yourself Retailing,* May 1996, 10.

INTELLECTUAL CAPITAL

Intellectual capital provides a conceptual platform from which to view, analyze, and hopefully quantify the nontangible (but nonetheless extremely valuable) assets of a corporation. Defining the function of intellectual capital is often easier than defining intellectual capital itself. Compounding this difficulty are the ever-changing or expanding definitions of intellectual capital that have been developed in the wake of a 1991 *Fortune* article by Thomas Stewart. ''Every company depends increasingly on knowledge—patents, processes, management skills, technologies, information about customers and suppliers, and old-fashioned experience. Added together this knowledge is intellectual capital,'' Stewart wrote in his seminal article. Paraphrased definitions of intellectual capital proffered by other writers include: the sum total of the useful knowledge of an organization's employees and customers (*Human Resources Glossary*); a measurement that equals the product of competence and commitment (Ted Gautschi); sum and synergy of a company's knowledge, experience, relationships, processes, discoveries, innovations, market presence, and community influence (William Miller); gap between the **market value** and book value of a company's equity (*Economist*); sum of **human capital** plus structural capital plus customer capital (Petrochemical Open Software Corporation); and the combined **intangible assets** that enable a company to function (Annie Brooking).

Although the first usage of the term ''intellectual capital'' is generally attributed to Hugh McDonald, who worked for a British computer manufacturer, the concept was introduced to the American business community in Stewart's 1991 *Fortune* article. Between 1991 and 1997 intellectual capital began receiving more and more attention from the business community, the business media, and publishers of business books. In 1997 Stewart's *Intellectual Capital: The New Wealth of Organizations* was published and went a long way in showing how people, technology, and corporations can be viewed through an intellectual capital perspective. In the book's first chapter Stewart clarifies the extraordinary theory of intellectual capital via a rather mundane object—the aluminum beer can.

By the early 1950s virtually all beer cans were made of steel. Aluminum, although lighter than steel, was more expensive and thus less competitive, because its production required costly amounts of electricity. Aluminum was, however, more malleable than steel. If a very thin but strong aluminum can could be produced, the differential between the amount of aluminum going into the thinner can would offset the high energy cost needed to produce aluminum. By the early 1990s, because of technological advances in the aluminum industry, a beer can weighed .48 of an ounce and was 25 percent lighter than Reynold's first .66-ounce aluminum can produced in 1963. The aluminum can was now cheaper than the steel can. By 1997 aluminum's share of the beer can market had also grown to an amazing 99 percent. Stewart calculated that the new can was 75 percent aluminum and 25 percent knowledge or intellectual capital. This turnaround in the fortunes of the aluminum industry was due to intellectual capital—a nontangible asset. It is important to note that while the aluminum in the new can was virtually unchanged from the aluminum introduced to the public at an international exposition in 1855, it was intellectual capital that led aluminum to decisively dominate the beer can market.

Intellectual capital as a concept is clearly a product of the Information Age and the Information Economy. Stewart again provided examples. The quintessential manufactured product of the Information Age is the **computer** and the quintessential component of the computer is the microchip. The component parts of a microchip, mostly silicon made from sand, are relatively inexpensive, if not downright cheap. The inherent value and resultant cost of a microchip is, however, a product of the technology or knowledge that goes into its production—the technology needed to turn beach sand into RAM. Stewart also borrowed from Brian Arthur, a Stanford University economist. Arthur put forth the idea of ''congealed resources'' and "congealed knowledge." Congealed resources are symbolic of the old or pre-information economy. Congealed resources are represented by small amounts of knowledge holding together a lot of material. An ingot of aluminum (a lot of material) is "held together" or produced by a little bit of knowledge—a smelting process that has remained relatively unchanged over the decades. The Information Age introduced the concept of congealed knowledge. Congealed knowledge exemplifies a tremendous amount of knowledge or intellectual capital producing or holding together small amounts of material. A **software** program is a prime example of Information Age congealed knowledge. The value of a software program lies in the intellectual capital that went into its creation, not the component physical parts of the diskette or hard drive on which it is stored.

Intellectual capital is not to be confused with **corporate culture**. Whereas corporate culture attempts to answer the question: "Who are we?," intellectual capital, in regards to nontangible assets, attempts to answer the question: "What is our worth?" Just as it is easier to describe the function of intellectual capital than to define it, so is it easier to describe the function of intellectual capital than to quantify it—although many people are trying. How does one quantify such nontangible items as customer goodwill, technological strategies, workplace creativity, and knowledge management? How does one quantify "brainpower"?

As reported in the *Economist,* Leif Edvinsson of Skandia, one of Sweden's largest financial services firms, measured intellectual capital as the difference between the market value of a corporation and the book value of its equity. Edvinsson stated that the **balance sheet** is an outmoded way of measuring a company's worth. He cited data showing that over the past dozen years or so (and perhaps not coincidentally coinciding with the Information Age) the relationship between share prices and reported equity value has been weakening. To measure worth, Edvinsson said that he starts with a corporation's market value (a good estimate of the corporation's true worth) and then breaks it down into hierarchical categories of assets. Intellectual capital is first categorized as the difference between market value and the "financial capital," or market value, of the corporation's physical assets. Intellectual capital is then further broken down into subcategories such as "human capital" ("the value of its **training**") and "structural capital" ("the ability to make money out of all these trained people"). Structural capital is further subdivided and value is assigned to such things as customer loyalty, product development, and trademarks. Edvinsson does not assign dollar values to the categories—their value is rather measured in terms of their rank in the hierarchal structure. This method thus allows a way to determine the relative worth of each category of a corporation's assets.

Other methods that include intellectual capital in measuring a corporation's worth are the "balanced scorecard" and Skandia Navigator. The **balanced scorecard** method was introduced by Robert S. Kaplan and David P. Norton in 1992 in an article in the *Harvard Business Review.* This method attempts to measure knowledge and worth by scoring four categories:

- Customer: customers needs, expectations, satisfactions, etc.
- Internal processes: those processes that drive the company on a day-by-day basis, those processes that best respond to the customer category, etc.
- **Innovation** and learning: looking to the future to increase value.
- Financial: the result of the first three categories, the extent to which the company is creating value for shareholders, etc.

The Skandia Navigator as described by David J. Skyrme and Debra M. Amidon in *Journal of Business Strategy* views intellectual capital as the "hidden value of a corporation." The Navigator is similar to the balanced scorecard and provides a taxonomy of five categories: financial, customer, human, process, and renewal.

Intellectual capital provides a new way to measure the worth of a corporation. Under intellectual capital, worth and value are not synonymous. The challenge of intellectual capital is not so much in defining it or understanding its function but rather to quantify it and once quantified to use it effectively.

SEE ALSO: Intangible Assets; Intellectual Property

[Michael Knes]

FURTHER READING:

Brooking, Annie. *Intellectual Capital.* London: International Thomson Business Press, 1996.

Edvinsson, Leif, and Michael S. Malone. *Intellectual Capital: Realizing Your Company's True Value by Finding Its Hidden Brainpower.* New York: HarperBusiness, 1997.

Gautschi, Ted. "Develop Your Intellectual Capital." *Design News* 53, no. 14 (20 July 1998): 170.

Kaplan, Robert S., and David P. Norton. "The Balanced Scorecard: Measures that Drive Performance." *Harvard Business Review* 70, no. 1 (January/February 1992): 71-79.

Miller, William. "Building the Ultimate Resource." *Management Review,* January 1999, 42-45.

Petrotechnical Open Software Corporation. "Intellectual Capital." Petrotechnical Open Software Corporation, 1997. Available from www.posc.org/presentations/km_archer/sld041.htm.

Roos, Johan. "Exploring the Concept of Intellectual Capital (IC)." *Long Rang Planning: Journal of Strategic Management* 31, no. 1 (February 1998): 150-53.

——. *Intellectual Capital: Navigating in the New Business Landscape.* New York: New York University Press, 1998.

Skyrme, David J., and Debra M. Amidon. "New Measures of Success." *Journal of Business Strategy* 19, no. 1 (January/February 1998): 20-24.

Stewart, Thomas A. "Brainpower: Intellectual Capital Is Becoming Corporate America's Most Valuable Asset and Can Be Its Sharpest Competitive Weapon." *Fortune,* 3 June 1991, 44+.

——. *Intellectual Capital: The New Wealth of Organizations.* New York: Doubleday, 1997.

Tracey, William R. ed. *The Human Resources Glossary.* Boca Raton, FL: St. Lucie Press, 1998.

"A Viking with a Compass." *Economist,* 6 June 1998, 64.

INTELLECTUAL PROPERTY

A major component of what many posit is the emerging knowledge economy, intellectual property consists of items that represent the expression of ideas or intellectual pursuits and that are assigned certain rights of property. It is an intangible creation of the human mind usually expressed or translated into a tangible form. Examples of intellectual property include an author's **copyright** on a book or article, a distinctive logo design representing a soft drink company and its products, or a patent on the process to manufacture chewing gum. Intellectual property law covers the protection of copyrights, **patents**, trademarks, and trade secrets, as well as other legal areas such as unfair competition. Patents, trademarks, and similar business-oriented creations are sometimes known as industrial property.

The concept of intellectual property developed and evolved through its individual components. There is no history of intellectual property per se, but the history of trademarks, for example, extends back to the medieval period.

The laws protecting intellectual property in the United States exist at both the state and federal level. State laws cover a broad spectrum of intellectual property fields from trade secrets to the right of publicity. Laws differ somewhat from state to state. At the federal level, the Constitution and legislation cover patents, copyrights, and trademarks and related areas of unfair competition.

U.S. intellectual property laws were most recently modified through the Digital Millennium Copyright Act of 1998, which granted broader and more explicit protections to information on digital media, notably movies on digital versatile discs (DVD) and sound recordings. Greater protection of industrial designs was another provision of the legislation. The act also ratified the World Intellectual Property Organization (WIPO) Copyright Treaty and the WIPO Performances and Phonograms Treaty, two major new international treaties.

INTERNATIONAL PROTECTION

Intellectual property is recognized internationally through a system of treaties and international organizations. The most important organization is the World Intellectual Property Organization (WIPO), a special agency of the United Nations. Founded in 1967, the Geneva-based organization administers most of the current international treaties concerning intellectual property issues. The World Trade Organization, a trade dispute resolution and trade negotiation body founded in 1995, is also involved in certain intellectual property matters.

PARIS CONVENTION. In the late 19th century, intellectual property protection at an international level became an important issue in trade and tariff negotiations and has remained so ever since. One of the first international treaties relating to intellectual property in the broadest sense was the International Convention for the Protection of Industrial Property, commonly known as the Paris Convention. First signed in 1883, the Paris Convention provided protection for such properties as patents, industrial models and designs, trademarks, and trade names. As of 1998, 151 countries had signed the Paris Convention, including several nations such as China that are often cited publicly as poor enforcers of intellectual property rights.

Two of the most important provisions of the treaty relate to the right of national treatment and the right of priority. The right of national treatment ensures that those individuals seeking a patent or trademark in another Convention country will not be discriminated against and will receive the same rights as a citizen of that country. The right of priority provides an inventor one year from the date of filing a patent application in his or her home country (six months for a trademark or design application) the right to file an application in a foreign country. The legal, effective date of application in the foreign country is then retroactively the legal, effective filing date in the home country, provided the application is made within the protection period. If the invention is made public prior to filing the home country application, however, the right of priority in a foreign country is no longer applicable.

The Paris Convention is supported by a number of additional treaties that provide for protection and registration of industrial property. Among the most important are the Madrid Agreement Concerning the International Registration of Marks (1891), the Patent Cooperation Treaty (1970), and the Hague Agreement

Concerning the International Deposit of Industrial Designs (1925).

BERNE CONVENTION. The central international agreement on copyright protection is the **Berne Convention** for the Protection of Literary and Artistic Works (1886). As of 1998, 133 nations were party to this agreement. The Berne Convention outlines principles of protection similar to those of the Paris Convention: 1) member states enforce copyrights originating in other member states; 2) copyright protection is automatic and not dependent on formalities of registration; 3) protection of a work in one country is independent of its protection status in its country of origin (until the minimum period of protection expires).

WIPO COPYRIGHT TREATY. Because older copyright conventions were ambiguous concerning how computer software and electronic information would be protected, the World Intellectual Property Organization Copyright Treaty was concluded in 1996 to clarify the protections for ideas expressed via electronic media. This agreement was intended to eliminate potential loopholes and uncertainties regarding the protection of intellectual creations on electronic media and their various modes of dissemination, including the Internet. As of 1999 the treaty was not yet in effect because it hadn't been ratified by a sufficient number of countries.

OPPOSING PERSPECTIVES

Various industry and professional groups disagree about the ideal levels of intellectual property protection. Parties that tend to hold copyrights or patents, such as publishers, recording labels, and innovative manufacturers, usually favor strong property rights and stiff penalties for violators. Meanwhile, some users of copyrighted or patented goods, including consumers, libraries, and educators, favor looser regulations so that one party's commercial interests don't override the fair use and intellectual freedom of others. A number of free-speech advocates go further, suggesting that copyrights shouldn't be viewed as property at all, but as protected free speech that cannot be censored economically or otherwise.

SEE ALSO: Intangible Assets; Intellectual Capital

FURTHER READING:

Elias, Stephen, and Lisa Goldoftas. *Patent, Copyright & Trademark: A Desk Reference to Intellectual Property Law.* 2nd ed. Berkeley: Nolo Press, 1997.

Guthrie, Lawrence S., III. ''Copyright: Free Speech or Property Right?'' *Information Outlook,* August 1997.

Miller, Arthur R., and Michael H. Davis. *Intellectual Property: Patents, Trademarks, and Copyright in a Nutshell.* 2nd ed. St. Paul, MN: West/Wadsworth, 1990.

Reid, Calvin. ''AAP Hails WIPO Bills; Libraries, Consumer Groups Voice Opposition.'' *Publishers Weekly,* 22 September 1997.

Roos, Johan, ed. *Intellectual Capital: Navigating in the New Business Landscape.* New York: New York University Press, 1998.

World Intellectual Property Organization. ''What Is WIPO?'' Geneva, Switzerland, 1998. Available from www.wipo.org.

INTEREST RATES

It is human nature to prefer immediate gratification. We dislike postponing consumption. If we are requested to delay our satisfaction, we demand a reward. This reward often takes the form of increased consumption at the later time. This same idea applies to money. Money, it has been observed, is only as good as what you can use it for. Whether dollars, rubles, or drachmas, money is a measure of the ability to consume. If we lend money we give up the possible immediate consumption it represents, and we expect a reward in the form of a greater return than the amount originally lent. In the case of money, the reward, or difference between what was lent and what is returned, is referred to as interest. Alternately, interest may be considered as rent.

A similar argument for interest is that the money could have been used to purchase assets. Those assets could then be rented to other parties (or used directly to produce a return). Interest, then, is compensation for rent or return foregone. More directly, interest is the cost of ''renting'' the money itself.

MEASUREMENT

For reasons of comparability, interest is normally specified as a percentage rate of increase, rather than as an absolute amount. The ''interest rate'' is the percentage increase:

$$\begin{array}{l}\text{Percent}\\ \text{Interest Rate}\end{array} = \frac{\text{Amount Returned \&minus Amount Lent}}{\text{Amount Lent}} \times 100$$

The interest rate is also sometimes described in terms of ''basis points,'' with one basis point being one hundredth of 1 percent. The difference between the interest rate of 10.25 percent and the interest rate of 10.00 percent is 25 basis points.

The specification of the interest rate is not complete unless the period over which the increase occurs is specified. Although interest rates are stated in terms of an annual rate, interest may be computed and become due more often than annually. The period over which interest is calculated is called the compounding period. The standard period for compounding is one year, but other intervals such as quarterly, daily, or even continuous compounding are not unusual.

Where the compounding period is shorter than one year, the per period rate must be converted to an annual rate. The simplest method of annualizing is called "simple interest" or annual percentage rate (APR), which is computed by simply multiplying the per period rate by the number of periods in a year. The "yield" or interest rate on **bonds**, for instance, is normally computed on a semiannual basis and then converted to an annual rate by multiplying by two. Although this rate is incorrect when the compounding period is less than one year, it has become convention, a holdover from days of hand calculation. The realized or "effective" annual interest rate will be higher than the stated annual rate due to the interest on interest effect. For example, suppose that $100 is borrowed at 10 percent compounded semiannually. At the end of six months, $50 is paid. The reduces the amount in the hands of the borrower over the next six months to $95.00. The borrower thus pays $10.00 annual interest to borrow an average of $97.50—an actual rate of about 10.25 percent. Alternately, if $100.00 is invested for one year at 6 percent compounded annually, the lender will receive $106.00 at the end of the year, a return of 6 percent to the lender. The same $100.00 invested at 6 percent compounded semiannually would lead to interest payments of $3.00 at six months and at one year. The $3.00 payment received at six months would be added to the principal amount and reinvested at 6 percent, however, so that the interest payment over the second six months would be $3.30. Under semiannual compounding, the investor's account at the end of the year would have the original investment of $100.00, the six-month interest payment of $3.00, and the one-year interest payment of $3.30—a total of $106.30. This would be an actual or realized rate of return of 6.3 percent. The extra $0.30 is interest on the interest. The effect of interest on interest and compounding more often than once a period is not large for any one period, but over long periods the realized amount can be significantly different. If the above $100.00 had been invested at 6 percent for 20 years at simple interest—i.e., with no compounding, ignoring reinvestment of interest payments—the final amount would be the original $100.00, plus 20 years' interest payments amounting to $120.00, a total of $220.00. If the interest payments are reinvested at 6 percent compounded annually, the final amount would be $320.71, with interest on interest amounting to $100.71. The same $100 invested for 20 years at 6 percent compounded semiannually would increase to $326.20. The $5.49 increase over the amount earned under annual compounding would arise from interest on interest.

The interest rate computation that includes the compounding effect is called the annual percentage yield (APY), and is considered a superior measure of annualized interest rates. The APY is computed by compounding or multiplying the per period rates over the year to arrive at the effective annual rate:

$$\text{APY} = R_1 \times R_2 \times R_3 \times \ldots \times R_N$$

where R_N is the per period rate and there are N periods per year.

Another misleading form of interest computation is "discounted in advance." In this form, the interest is deducted from the principal, and the borrower receives the net amount. This form can severely understate the interest rate. In our example, a one-year borrower would receive $9.00, or $10.00 principal less $1.00 interest for one year, and would owe $10.00 at the end of the year, effectively paying the interest at the time of borrowing. This is equivalent to paying $1.00 to borrow $9.00, a compound annual rate of 11.11 percent.

DETERMINANTS OF INTEREST RATE LEVELS

The level of interest rates is set by supply and demand—i.e., when the amount of money supplied is equal to the amount that other economic units wish to borrow. The interesting question, however, is what factors influence supply and demand. Since interest is in the nature of a reward for postponing consumption, a higher interest rate can be expected to result in a greater supply of funds. Under different conditions, however, a given interest rate may result in a differing supply. Attitudes toward consumption are important, as shown by the differences between savings rates in different countries. Uncertainty about the economy may prompt more saving, as shown by the different attitudes of the "depression generation" and their children. Demand, on the other hand, depends on the investments available, and will be downward sweeping since more investments are profitable at lower interest rates. In periods of high growth or technological advancement, there will be more acceptable investment and greater demand. Future economic growth is affected by the rate of increase of population, the **workforce**, and the educational and skill level. Economic conditions and production possibilities set the general level of demand for funds.

The economic and other variables set the interest rate as a rate of increase in ability to consume. This rate of increase in ability to consume is called the "real" rate of interest. The "nominal" or dollar rate of interest measures the increase in dollars. Money is a measure of ability to consume, but the yardstick itself changes over time due to **inflation**. Inflation is a decrease in the purchasing power, or amount of consumption that can be acquired per monetary unit. Since it is the real rate of interest that controls the supply and demand of funds, the nominal interest rate must include a premium that compensates for any expected loss of purchasing power. The stated or nominal interest rate is then expressed as the real rate of interest plus an inflation premium:

$$R_N = R_R + I + IR_R$$

where R_N = the nominal rate of interest,
R_R = the real rate of interest,
I = the expected rate of inflation.

For small rates of inflation the inflation rate itself is a good approximation of the premium required, and the last term is often ignored. For higher rates of inflation the last term becomes significant, and should be included. The higher level of interest rates in the early 1980s is partially due to the effects of actual or feared inflation.

Interest rates are also affected by and are an instrument of government policy. The **Federal Reserve** manages the amount of money in circulation, and affects the interest rates. Too rapid growth of the amount of money will have an immediate effect of decreasing interest rates, since supply is increased. Over the longer run, however, too rapid growth in the amount of money may result in inflation. Interest rates, reacting to the expectation of inflation, will increase. Too low a rate of growth in the amount of money, on the other hand, will result in a reduction of supply and higher interest rates. This in turn may hamper economic growth. If the economy stagnates, the eventual result may well be decreased interest rates.

Over time the Federal Reserve has placed varied emphasis on two policy targets. The first is the growth of the amount of money, while the second is interest rates. It would be incorrect to say that the Federal Reserve has ''control'' over either of these variables. This would be impossible in a dynamic economy such as that of the United States. Given the number of money-like arrangements, the definition of ''money,'' much less its measurement, is difficult. The monetary tools of the Federal Reserve work most directly on short-term interest rates. Interest rates for longer maturities are indirectly affected through the market's perception of government policy and its economic effects. More recently, expectations of possible inflation have been a major concern to lenders and policy makers. Economic forces shape the level of interest rates, while governmental policies have some effect on economic forces. Foreign interest rates have become increasingly important. Major firms now routinely borrow in foreign markets, and lenders are increasingly willing to hold foreign **debt**. This forces some alignment of interest rates worldwide, and reduces the amount of control any nation has over its domestic conditions.

There are many forms of borrowing, and thus many interest rates. Borrowing and lending arrangements include personal **loans**, credit cards, **mortgages**, various federal and municipal government obligations, corporate bonds, and multiple other forms. Investors borrow when they trade on margin, firms borrow by using **trade credit**. The interest rate on different borrowing arrangements will be different, which is why the plural is used here. While economic and other variables set the general level of interest rates, specific interest rates are affected by other variables. While there are a multitude of factors affecting interest rates, they are generally grouped under differences in maturity, quality, and tax status.

THE TERM STRUCTURE OF INTEREST RATES

Interest rates are also related to the maturity, or length of commitment, of the arrangement. The relationship is often described by a **yield curve** showing the interest rates for various maturities. There are several theories to explain this ''**term structure of interest rates**.'' The first is called the ''expectations theory.'' This theory holds that interest rates over longer periods are dependent on the series of short-term interest rates expected over that period—i.e., lenders are indifferent to the length of commitment, but require the same expected ending **wealth** regardless of whether they lend money once for ten years or they make a series of ten-year loans, each for one year. The motivation here is that if this relationship did not hold, investors would prefer the alternative with the higher ending wealth, forcing a readjustment of interest rates. Alternately, if the relationship did not hold, investors could **arbitrage**, selling the lower yielding alternative and investing the proceeds in the higher yielding alternative. This arbitrage would allow the arbitrager to make a return from a net zero investment. Under this theory, the yield curve would be upward sweeping if short-term interest rates were expected to increase in the future, and downward sweeping if short-term interest rates were expected to decrease in the future.

A second approach, called the ''liquidity theory,'' suggests that investors are not indifferent as to the length of commitment. This argument suggests that lending for longer periods is more risky than short-term lending. The longer period makes prediction less accurate, and permits more opportunities for negative results. Investors prefer more liquid, shorter-term lending, and will not commit the funds for longer periods unless given a ''liquidity premium'' to compensate for this higher risk. Under only this approach, the yield curve would be upward sweeping at all times. Empirical observation of decreasing yield curves does not refute this theory, however, if it is combined with other theories. If the liquidity premium is superimposed on the expectation that short-term interest rates will decrease in the future, the result can be a yield curve that is still downward sweeping but less steep.

A third approach is called the ''segmented markets'' theory. As we have noted, interest rates depend on supply and demand. Segmented markets builds on this obvious statement, adding the idea that lenders and borrowers will have a ''preferred habitat,'' or length of commitment. This preferred habitat comes about because of the desire of lenders and borrowers to reduce risk by matching the maturity of assets and **liabilities**. A lender with a liability that will come due in ten years, for example, avoids risk by lending with a maturity of ten years; a borrower whose use of the funds will pay off in ten years will borrow with a maturity of ten years. Borrowers and lenders are thus reluctant to leave their preferred maturity, and will not arbitrage. As a result, the interest rate for any given maturity will depend on the supply and demand for that given maturity.

In actuality, all of these theories are to some extent correct. Empirically, since World War II the yield curve has been predominantly upward sweeping, with long-term rates higher than short-term rates. Inverted, or downward sweeping yield curves in which long-term rates are lower than short-term rates, have been observed over shorter intervals. Long-term rates tend to have less volatility, and to move over a smaller range, than short-term rates.

THE QUALITY STRUCTURE OF INTEREST RATES

The ''quality'' structure of interest rates describes the effect of uncertainty about receiving the specified reward. In the face of uncertainty about payments, lenders will demand a higher rate of return or ''risk premium.'' The interest rate to a particular borrower will be the sum of a ''risk-free'' rate plus the risk premium. **Default** risk is not simply the failure to pay principal, but is rather a matter of degree. There are many possibilities short of complete loss, sometimes as small as a ''skipped'' or late payment. Loan arrangements with little probability of a problem are said to be of high quality.

The higher the severity and probability of a problem, or the lower the quality, the higher will be the risk premium. Treasury obligations, which are direct obligations of the U.S. government and assumed to have no default risk, are of the highest quality. Bonds issued by agencies of the government, which are not direct government obligations, are of only slightly lower quality since it is assumed the government would assume the responsibility. State and local bonds, called ''municipals,'' vary widely in quality depending on the characteristics of the security and the issuer. The same variation is true of corporate bonds. These **securities** are sometimes ''rated'' as to quality by independent firms such as Standard & Poor's, Moody's, Duff & Phelps, and Fitch Investors Service. These ratings are widely used to classify bonds and are important factors in the interest rate, or ''yield,'' provided to investors. Bonds below a certain rating are often referred to as **junk bonds**, and carry a higher interest rate.

This quality structure is also apparent in **bank** loan interest rates. The **prime rate** is the rate charged to large customers with established relationships. Borrowers with less admirable **credit** records (or smaller accounts that are comparatively more expensive) will pay a higher rate. Collateral is also important. Unsecured personal loans, such as credit card credit, will ordinarily pay a higher rate than car loans, which will in turn pay more than home mortgages. An important characteristic of loan arrangements is liquidity. An asset that can be converted to cash quickly at a fair price is liquid; if price concessions are required for rapid sale the asset is illiquid. Many loans have been relatively illiquid, so that once the loan is made the creditor was locked in. This lack of freedom of action increased the risk of the lender, resulting in higher interest rates. More recently, a number of classes of loans have been ''securitized'' by being bundled into portfolios against which securities are issued. This added liquidity reduces lender risk and lowers the interest rate on the underlying loan classes.

TAX STATUS

The interest rate on bonds issued by state and local governments, called ''municipal bonds,'' is lower than the interest rate on corporate bonds of the same quality. The reason for this difference is that the interest on these debt obligations is generally exempt from federal taxation. They are also often exempt from **taxes** of the state of issue. The real rate of increase in purchasing power from taxable federal and corporate debt instruments will be reduced by the taxes:

$$\text{After-Tax Rate of Return} = (\text{Pretax Rate of Return}) \times (1 - \text{Tax Rate})$$

Since interest rates reflect the real rate or increase in purchasing power, taxable and nontaxable debt will have the same after-tax rate of return. This equilibrium will not hold for all investors because of differing tax rates. For investors with high tax rates, the after-tax rate of return on municipals may be higher, while for investors with low tax rates the return on corporate debt may be higher.

Another tax effect comes about because of the tax deductibility of some interest payments on personal taxes. The tax deductibility of interest on home mortgages effectively lowers the interest rate. This is reflected in the rapid increase in mortgage-based loans after interest on consumer debts was no longer tax deductible.

[David E. Upton]

FURTHER READING:

Reilly, Frank K., and Keith C. Brown. *Investment Analysis and Portfolio Management.* 5th ed. Fort Worth, TX: Dryden Press, 1997.

Van Horne, James C. *Financial Market Rates and Flows.* 5th ed. Upper Saddle River, NJ: Prentice Hall, 1998.

INTERNAL AUDITING

Most large companies, major institutions, governmental agencies, and federal, state, and local governments have established internal auditing functions. Job titles other than ''internal auditor''—such as internal **consultants**, compliance officers, quality assurance managers, or operations analysts—are sometimes given to those performing internal audit functions. Regardless of the position title, it is the character of service that classifies it as internal auditing. From their organization's point of view, ''internal'' auditors serve in a self-evaluative or self-assessing function. They compare existing conditions (''what is'') to a standard (''what should be'') and suggest how to achieve the ideal.

A governing body, the Institute of Internal Auditors (IIA), operates to bring uniformity and consistency to the practice of internal auditing. The IIA is an international association with chapters operating in approximately 120 countries. By 1999, the IIA had grown to 70,000 individual members. The IIA provides performance standards for internal audit professionals and serves as a source for education, training, research, and reference materials. The Association also administers a Certified Internal Auditor program, which leads to an internationally recognized certification—CIA.

In June 1999, the IIA Board of Directors unanimously approved the following definition of internal auditing produced by their Guidance Task Force:

> Internal auditing is an independent, objective assurance and consulting activity designed to add value and improve an organization's operations. It helps an organization accomplish its objectives by bringing a systematic, disciplined approach to evaluate and improve the effectiveness of risk management, control, and governance processes.

There is theoretically no restriction on what internal auditors can evaluate and report about within an organization. But, internal audit projects tend to vary from one company to another, reflecting particular objectives of owners, directors, and senior management. Internal auditors typically operate under a board-approved charter that defines their role, objectives, and scope. The following five directives from the IIA's *Statement of Responsibilities of Internal Auditing* are included in most charters:

- Review the reliability and integrity of financial and operating information and the means used to identify, measure, classify, and report such information;
- Review the systems established to ensure compliance with those policies, plans, procedures, laws, regulations, and contracts which could have a significant impact on operations and reports, and determine whether the organization is in compliance;
- Review the means of safeguarding assets and, as appropriate, verify the existence of such assets;
- Appraise the economy and efficiency with which resources are employed; and,
- Review operations or programs to ascertain whether results are consistent with established objectives and goals and whether the operations or programs are being carried out as planned.

HISTORY AND BACKGROUND

The double-entry **bookkeeping** system invented in the 13th century provided the means for those engaged in commerce to control transactions with suppliers and customers, and check the work of employees. Historical records suggest that internal auditors were being utilized prior to the 15th century. These auditors, employed by kings or merchants, were charged with detecting or preventing theft, fraud, and other improprieties. Control techniques such as separation of duties, independent verification, and questioning (i.e. ''auditing'') to detect and prevent irregularities are thought to have originated during that time. Thus, control assessment and fraud detection have become known as the ''roots'' of internal auditing.

As industry and commerce evolved, so did control methods and auditing techniques. These methods migrated to the United States from England during the industrial revolution. Managerial control through auditing continued to gain favor up to and through the 20th century. Many events contributed.

The economy of the United States was growing rapidly after World War I and required better techniques for planning, directing, and evaluating business activities. Unfortunately, the growth was accompanied by a rise in price-fixing, interlocking directorates, stock manipulations, and false statements of business performance. Regulatory actions followed and auditing was used as a means to confirm that laws were being followed. The **Federal Trade Commission (FTC)** was created in 1914. The Great Depression and the 1930s brought more regulatory action for publicly traded securities. The **Securities Act of 1933**, the **Securities and Exchange Act of 1934**, the Public Utilities Holding Company Act of 1935, and the Investment Company Act of 1940 were enacted by the United States Congress.

As the need for auditing grew, corporations realized that they could no longer rely solely on external auditors from public **accounting** firms. Corporations began hiring auditors as their own employees to verify financial transactions and test compliance with accounting controls. Many of these internal auditors were hired from external auditing firms. They brought to the companies that hired them auditing methods used by public accountants with a **financial statement** focus. These internal auditors concentrated on financial auditing. Management viewed these internal auditors as a means to reduce external audit fees while maintaining the same level of financial audit coverage. Within some organizations this image of internal auditing still persists.

Internal auditing started to emerge as a function distinctly different from external auditing about the middle of the 20th century. Then, a significant event brought internal auditing to the forefront—the **Foreign Corrupt Practices Act** of 1977. The Act was the government's response to outcries as news of corporate wrong-doings increased. The Act was passed to prevent secret funds and bribery. It specifically prohibited offering of bribes to foreign officials. It required organizations to maintain adequate systems of internal control and maintain complete and accurate financial records. While the Act did not specifically call for an internal auditing function, internal auditors were poised and ready to help **management** fulfill the requirements of this Act. Testing and evaluation of internal controls within companies increased significantly. The role of internal auditors was viewed with new importance.

In the mid-to-late 1980s there were a number of large **business failures** and financial statement frauds. On several occasions external auditing firms failed to detect those frauds. The issues of fraudulent financial reporting were examined by a group of private sector organizations which included the American Institute of Certified Public Accounts (AICPA), the American Accounting Association (AAA), the Financial Executives Institute (FEI), the Institute of Internal Auditors (IIA), and the National Association of Accountants (NAA). This group of organizations, known as the Treadway Commission, issued its final recommendations in 1987. Several recommendations of the Treadway Commission were of great significance to internal auditors. Among other recommendations, the Commission's report directs companies to maintain adequate internal control systems, to establish effective and objective internal audit functions staffed with adequate qualified personnel, and to coordinate internal auditing with the external audit of the financial reports. The Commission's report also directed internal auditors to consider whether their findings of a non-financial nature could impact the financial statements. The Treadway Commission also directed its sponsoring organizations to develop guidance on internal control. That sponsoring group did so, issuing its report *Internal Control—Integrated Framework* in 1992, which again emphasized the importance of internal controls in organizations.

The evolution of internal auditing tracks changing business practices and concepts of internal control. At the most basic level, internal controls are individual preventive, detective, corrective, or directive actions that keep the operations functioning as intended. Basic controls, when aggregated, create whole networks and systems of control procedures, which are known as the organization's overall system of internal control. During the 1990s, business process "reengineering" and downsizing, removed layers of management and flattened organizational hierarchies. Traditional controls were loosened or dismantled to improve efficiency and lower costs. In response, internal auditing's control orientation moved away from evaluating individual process controls toward assessing the overall control environment—integrated control frameworks, **corporate governance**, and the ethical climate—within the organization. Internal auditors increased their use of risk assessments and aligned their activities with broader organizational goals to deploy their own scarce audit resources. Internal auditing's focus shifted to risk prevention and to promoting change. Even so, control assessment and fraud detection, the "roots" of internal auditing, still retained a place in the internal audit function.

THE INSTITUTE OF INTERNAL AUDITORS

In 1941, the Institute of Internal Auditors (IIA) was founded in New York by a small group of practicing internal auditors. The group recognized that they had many commonalities in the way they worked despite the fact that they worked in different businesses and industries. They agreed that merely applying external auditing techniques internally was not sufficient. They felt the need for a formal approach to sharing and organizing their body of knowledge and their mutual concerns. They began the long process of achieving an identity for internal auditing as a distinct profession concerned with providing independent appraisals for all activities within an organization. The first textbook for the practice, *Brinks Internal Auditing* (United States), was published in 1941. A technical journal for the field, *Internal Auditor,* distributed its first issue in 1943. The Institute developed the first version of a *Statement of Responsibilities* in 1947 and has continued to revise it (1957, 1971, 1976, 1981, 1990) as internal auditing practices matured. In 1978 the IIA published the *Standards for Professional Practice* to serve as the primary source of reference for directing an internal audit function. The Institute has modified or amended the Standards by issuing *Statements on Internal Auditing Standards* and Administrative Directives. Also, a Guidance Task Force, chartered by The IIA board of directors in 1997, has been reviewing the *Standards* to ensure that they reflect the current practices.

In 1974 the Institute began a certification program—Certified Internal Auditor (CIA). The credential requires a combination of education and work experience with successful completion of a four-part comprehensive exam which tests: Internal Audit Process; Internal Audit Skills; Management, Control and Information Technology; and, Audit Environment. In 1992 the IIA completed and published an in-depth study—*A Common Body of Knowledge for the Practice of Internal Auditing.* It identified 334 competencies in 20 different disciplines needed by practicing internal auditors. The study lists needed disciplines in the following order of perceived importance: reasoning, communications, auditing, ethics, organizations, sociology, fraud, computers, financial accounting, data gathering, managerial accounting, government, legal, finance, taxes, quantitative methods, marketing, statistics, economics, and international business.

The IIA Research Foundation subsequently planned to update and expand the *Common Body of Knowledge.* But, the project expanded to study, document, and define internal auditing and its competencies on a global level. The research, *Competency Framework for Internal Auditing (CFIA),* led by William P. Birkett, was published in six separate modules: 1) *Internal Auditing: The Global Landscape*; 2) *Competency: Best Practices and Competent Practitioners* ; 3) *Internal Auditing Knowledge: Global Perspectives*; 4) *The Future of Internal Auditing: A Delphi Study*; 5) *Assessing Competency in Internal Auditing: Structures and Methodologies*; and, 6) *Conceptual Foundations of Internal Auditing.*

The CFIA study found a need for a universal definition of internal auditing. The study observed that internal auditing had moved beyond control evaluation and **risk management** toward risk prevention, even though risk issues had become more complex with complicated business relationships, new products and services, rapid advances in information and network technology, and global commerce. ''Organizations are moving toward an ideal where they will review and seek assurance for their risk exposures in totality,'' Birkett said. ''Thus, areas that were previously viewed as separate in terms of risk management—quality assurance, environmental management, occupational health and safety, and internal auditing—are likely to be amalgamated.'' CFIA predicts internal auditors in the future ''will provide advice, promote understanding, facilitate change, and sponsor continuous improvement programs, in addition to the traditional role of providing assurance.''

KEY ASSUMPTIONS ABOUT THE INTERNAL AUDIT FUNCTION

There are three important assumptions implicit in the definition, objectives, and scope for internal auditing. First, is the assumption that internal auditors can evaluate objectively, free from conflicts of interest, political, or monetary pressures that could inhibit their questioning, bias their reporting, or compromise their recommendations. This is called auditor independence. Independence and objectivity should exist in appearance and in fact for a credible work product. Related to independence is the assumption that internal auditors have unrestricted access to whatever they might need to make an objective assessment. That includes unrestricted access to plans, forecasts, people, data, products, facilities, and records necessary to perform their independent evaluations. Second, is the assumption that the internal auditing function is staffed with people possessing the necessary education, experience, and proficiency to perform competently. Third, is the presumption that the evaluations and conclusions contained in internal auditing reports are directed internally to management and the board, not to stockholders, regulators, or the public.

It is presumed that management and the board can resolve issues that have surfaced through internal auditing and implement solutions. After internal auditors present conclusions, management and the board have responsibility for subsequent decisions—to act or not to act. If action is taken, management has responsibility to assure progress is made. Internal auditors later can determine whether the actions had the desired results. If no action is taken, internal auditors have responsibility to determine if management and the board understand and have assumed risks of inaction. Under all circumstances, internal auditors have the direct responsibility to notify management and the board of significant matters that the internal auditors believe need their attention.

INTERNAL AUDITING VS. EXTERNAL AUDITING AND INDUSTRIAL ENGINEERING

The industrial engineer studies methods of performing work, suggests improvements, designs and installs work systems, and evaluates results. Internal auditors do utilize some of the analytical techniques belonging to industrial engineers, but do not focus on them. Further, internal auditors do not design and install systems.

Internal auditors and external auditors both audit, but have different objectives. Internal auditors generally consider operations a whole relative to objectives. External auditors focus primarily on financial systems that have a direct, significant effect on the amounts reported in financial statements. Internal auditors consider even small amounts of fraud, waste, and abuse as symptoms of underlying issues. The external auditor considers just what materially affects the financial statements since that is the nature of their engagement. *Sawyer's Internal Auditing* summarizes the differences in the following way.

> Management controls over financial activities have been greatly strengthened throughout the years. The same cannot always be said of controls elsewhere in the enterprise. Embezzlement can hurt a corporation; the poor management of resources can bankrupt it. Therein lies the basic difference between external auditing and modern internal auditing; the first is narrowly focused and the second is comprehensive in scope. True, the external auditor performs services for management and submits letters to management, which recommend improvement in systems and controls. By and large, however, these are financially oriented. Also, the external auditor's occasional sally into nonfinancial operations may not benefit from the same depth of understanding as does the resident internal auditor, who is intimately familiar with the organization's systems, people, and objectives.

"OUTSOURCING" OR "CO-SOURCING" THE INTERNAL AUDIT FUNCTION

The previous comparison of internal auditing to external auditing considers only the external auditors' traditional role of attesting to financial statements. During the 1990s a number of the large professional service firms (the ''Big 5'' public accounting firms) began establishing divisions offering internal auditing services in additional to tax, financial planning, actuarial, external auditing, and management consulting. New firms also emerged offering internal auditing services but not attestation (external audits) of financial statements. Predictably, the arrival of ''outside'' consultants ready to do ''internal'' audits caused a flurry of debate about independence, objectivity, depth of organizational knowledge, operational effectiveness, and long run costs to the organization. Regardless, the trend continued throughout the rest of the decade. Initial protests gave way to acknowledgment that non-employees can indeed perform internal audits. Orderly analyses of outsourcing's pros and cons followed. ''Co-sourcing'' (using outsiders for selected projects) became a useful compromise. That option provided access to an outside firm's resources while retaining a knowledgeable core of internal auditors to direct and manage co-sourced projects.

However, perceptions of impaired independence continued when public accounting firms providing opinions on financial statements also staffed the internal auditing function. In 1998, the American Institute of Certified Public Accounts (AICPA) decided that professionals from the same CPA firm could serve as external auditors of the financial statements and still perform internal auditing functions (called ''extended services'') without impairing independence if certain conditions were met. The AICPA required that outside professionals not act as employees and not assume ongoing control or other functions. It required management to retain responsibility for internal audit scope, planning, and risk assessments and to designate a competent executive to retain responsibility for the overall internal audit function. In New Zealand and several European countries, external auditors of financial statements in public sector companies may not provide internal audit services to the same company.

TYPES OF AUDITS

Various types of audits are used to achieve particular objectives. The types of audits briefly described below illustrate a few approaches internal auditing may take. The examples are not all inclusive.

OPERATIONAL AUDIT. An operational audit is a systematic review and evaluation of an organizational unit to determine whether it is functioning effectively and efficiently, whether it is accomplishing established objectives and goals, and whether it is utilizing all of its resources appropriately. Resources in this context include funds, personnel, property, equipment, materials, information, intellectual property, or space. Operational audits often include evaluations of the work flow and propriety of performance measurements. These audits are tailored to fit the nature and objectives of the operations being reviewed.

PROGRAM AUDIT. A program audit evaluates whether the stated goals or objectives for a project or initiative have been achieved. It may include an appraisal of whether an alternative approach can achieve the desired results at a lower cost. These types of audits are also called performance audits or management audits.

FRAUD AUDIT. A fraud audit investigates whether the organization has suffered through misappropriation of assets, manipulation of data, omission of information, or illegal acts. It assumes that deceptions were intentional.

ETHICAL BUSINESS PRACTICES AUDIT. An ethical business practices audit determines the extent to which the organization, management, and employees support established codes of conduct, policies, and standards of ethical practices. Topics that may fall within the scope of such audits include procurement policies, conflicts of interest, gifts and gratuities, entertainment, political **lobbying**, **patents**, copyrights, and licenses (including software use), or fair trade practices

COMPLIANCE AUDIT. A compliance audit determines whether a process or transaction is or is not following applicable rules. Such rules can originate internally as corporate bylaws, policies, and procedures or externally as laws and regulations. Characteristic of compliance audits are the yes/no aspects of the evaluation. For each process or transaction examined, the auditor must ultimately decide whether it complies with the rule or not. Reaching that conclusion is not necessarily simple in domains governed by complex regulations (e.g. occupational health and safety, environmental, federal grants and contracts, employee pensions and benefits, or federal tax). Compliance auditors and attorneys specializing in these fields may be engaged to assist with evaluations if such specialists are not part of the internal audit staff.

SYSTEMS DEVELOPMENT AND LIFE CYCLE REVIEW. A systems development and life cycle review is an information systems audit conducted in partnership with operating personnel who are implementing a new information system. The objective is to appraise and independently test the system at various stages throughout the design, development, and installation. The approach intends to identify issues and correct problems early because modifications made during developmental stages are less costly. and some problems can be avoided altogether. The concern about this type of audit is that the internal auditor could lose objectivity through extended participation in the system design and installation.

CONTROL SELF-ASSESSMENT AUDIT. A control self-assessment audit enlists management to share audit responsibility by evaluating and reporting on the state of controls and levels of risks under their **supervision**. Internal auditors provide training and act as facilitators. In effect this become a problem solving partnership and can be a cost-effective. Its inherent risk is that management's self-evaluation may be biased. Although, the internal auditor can retain the right to independently verify any reported conclusions.

FINANCIAL AUDIT. A financial audit is an examination of the financial planning and reporting process, the conduct of financial operations, the reliability and integrity of financial records, and the preparation of financial statements. Such a review includes an appraisal of the system of internal controls related to financial functions.

INTERNAL AUDIT PLANNING

A prerequisite to successful internal audit planning is a keen understanding of the organization, its strategic plan, and how it operates. In that context, the internal auditor can develop audit priorities and strategies that take into account significance of activities, and relative risk. The planning process is dynamic. Departures of key people, shifts in markets, new demographics, or drastic upheavals in the business environment can totally transform a company. Organizational processes can become obsolete with new technology. Laws and regulations may change, as well as attitudes about the degree of compliance necessary. Consequently, organizational objectives and related audit strategies will change. The person directing the internal audit function is usually the one responsible for creating a comprehensive audit plan. It is customary for senior management to review the plan and submit it to the board for approval.

SEE ALSO: Auditing; Compliance Auditing

[Aldona Cytraus]

FURTHER READING:

Association of Certified Fraud Examiners. Available from www.cfenet.com.

Birkett, William P. *Competency Framework for Internal Auditing (CFIA).* Alamonte Springs, FL: The Institute of Internal Auditors Research Foundation, 1999.

Committee of Sponsoring Organizations of the Treadway Commission (COSO). *Internal Control—Integrated Framework: An Executive Summary.* Ernst & Young, 1992.

Fargason, James Scott. *Law and the Internal Auditing Profession.* Alamonte Springs, FL: The Institute of Internal Auditors, 1992.

Frigo, Mark L., Krull, George W., and Stephen V.N. Yates. *The Impact of Business Process Reengineering on Internal Auditing.* The Institute of Internal Auditors Research Foundation, 1995.

The Information Systems Audit and Control Association & Foundation. *COBIT: Control Objectives for Information and Related Technology, 1996-99.* Available from www.isaca.org.

The Institute of Internal Auditors. ''Internal Auditing: All in a Day's Work.'' Available from www.theiia.org/.

Reider, Harry R. *The Complete Guide to Operational Auditing.* New York: John Wiley & Sons, Inc., 1994.

Rittenburg, Larry, Moore, Wayne, and Mark Covaleski. ''The Outsourcing Phenomena.'' *Internal Auditor.* April 1999, 42.

Sawyer, Lawrence B. *Sawyer's Internal Auditing.* Alamonte Springs, FL: Institute of Internal Auditors, Inc., 1988.

Selim, Georges M. and David McNamee. *Risk Management: Changing the Paradigm.* Alamonte Springs, FL: The Institute of Internal Auditors Research Foundation, 1998.

INTERNAL REVENUE SERVICE (IRS)

The Internal Revenue Service (IRS), part of the U.S. Department of the Treasury, is mandated by federal law to enforce the tax laws of the United States. In addition to collecting income tax from individuals and corporations—the largest source (55 percent) of the government's income—the IRS also collects such major revenues as Social Security taxes, excises (taxes on commodities), gift taxes, and estate taxes. Internal revenues derived from the sale of alcohol, tobacco, and firearms are no longer collected by the IRS.

HISTORICAL DEVELOPMENT

For the most part, the revenue history of this country has consisted of tariffs levied on imported goods and, in colonial times, various property taxes. The extreme reaction to ''taxation without representation'' might have been due to the abhorrence of taxation in general. Raising revenue to fund George Washington's army turned out to be a thankless task; when Americans finally installed a government that represented them in 1781, they made sure that the Articles of Confederation deprived the central government all right to levy taxes.

The stinginess of the state treasuries and obvious need for revenue led the founding fathers to insert into the new federal Constitution a clause (Article I, Section 8) granting the federal government the right to raise taxes. As the first Secretary of the Treasury, Alexander Hamilton (1755-1804) exerted every effort to strengthen the taxing power of the government, and thanks to his initiative, Congress passed the first revenue bill in U.S. history, the Revenue Act of 1791. This created the office of the Commissioner of Revenue, predecessor to today's IRS. The commissioner was empowered to collect the excise tax not only on distilled liquor, but also excises on all manner of other goods, as well as a progressive tax on property.

Judging from the fierce opposition to these taxes, especially the one on liquor, taxation with representation proved to be every bit as unpopular as without. Thomas Jefferson, who became president in 1801 and led the opposition, helped to repeal the act and disband the commissioner's office. The federal government subsequently relied on the lucrative revenues derived from tariffs, and the Treasury recorded surpluses annually until the eve of the Civil War.

The War of 1812 necessitated levying a new internal tax that resembled a sales tax on purchased goods. The office of Commissioner of Revenue was restored. When the war ended in late 1814, Treasury Secretary Albert Gallatin hoped the taxes would continue, but Congress abolished them, as well as the commissioner's office, in 1817. There was enough money in the treasury to fund the Mexican War 29 years later without an internal tax.

The real birth of the IRS, or the U.S. Bureau of Internal Revenue as it was originally called, had to wait until the Civil War. With $2 million per day going to fund the public debt, the need for more revenue was desperate. In July 1862, President Lincoln signed the largest revenue bill in U.S. history. Once again, it revived the office of Commissioner of Internal Revenue. The commissioner was empowered to establish a system to collect a progressive income tax based on income withholding (a tax return form was duly created), as well as to collect numerous other internal taxes. For the first time, failure to comply with the tax laws could result in punishment: prosecution and confiscation of assets most extreme cases. Tax returns had to be signed under oath.

Operating in a tiny room in the U.S. Treasury Building in Washington, the new commissioner, George S. Boutwell, read every letter from anxious new taxpayers and kept his office open day and night to accommodate the crush of inquiries. The income tax forms seem simple by today's standards but were complicated to most new taxpayers then: even Abraham Lincoln failed to understand his form and unnecessarily overpaid (a sizable refund arrived posthumously). By the end of fiscal year 1863, the new revenue bureau took in, through its assessors and collectors, nearly $40 million.

By war's end, the Bureau of Internal Revenue had grown from 1 employee to more than 4,000. Despite the revenue garnered, the public deficit stood at an unprecedented $3 billion in 1865. Surprisingly, the income tax was discontinued after the Civil War, including the lucrative inheritance tax. The bureau, however, was not dismantled along with the taxes. Until 1913, most of the nation's revenue derived from taxes on fermented and distilled liquor and tobacco. The bureau was put in charge of collecting the liquor and tobacco taxes, and a rather odd tax on oleomargarine that Congress levied in 1886 to protect the butter interest. In 1890, to control the sale of opium, a tax on it was also collected by the bureau.

How is it that the Bureau of Internal Revenue became identified almost exclusively with the income tax? In 1894, a bill restoring the progressive income tax passed Congress, in response to the agitation and lobbying efforts of Populists, Greenbackers, and other reformers who believed the rich should pay their dues to society. The next year the U.S. Supreme Court, in *Pollack v. Farmers Loan and Trust Co.,* struck down the income tax as unconstitutional, to the dismay of reformers. The newly created Income Tax Division of the Bureau of Internal Revenue was duly disbanded.

Lobbying on behalf of a progressive income tax intensified after 1895. The vast majority of Americans would be exempt from paying income tax, with only the well-to-do expected to pay. President Taft (1909-13) supported the idea of an amendment to the Constitution that would specifically allow the government to implement such a tax. The amendment he supported was quickly adopted by the states, and in February 1913, under President Woodrow Wilson, who had defeated Taft in the interim, the 16th Amendment inaugurated the income tax. In October followed a revenue bill establishing a progressive income tax for those earning over $3,000, only 1 percent of the population. Corporations also were subject to a tax on net income. Almost immediately, the Income Tax Division, heir to the one dismantled in 1895, was revived.

World War I, which cost the nation nearly $35 billion, was financed in part (33 percent) by internal revenues. Even before the United States became involved in the war, the Revenue Act of 1916 enlarged the number of taxpayers and created other internal taxes. The bureau was charged for the first time with publishing income tax statistics.

Following the 1916 tax law, other laws were swiftly passed to raise revenue for the war. The War Revenue Act of 1917 created new excess profits and estate taxes and other revenue measures. The bureau was a beneficiary of some of this windfall, as its budget increased from $8 million in 1917 to nearly $15 million in 1918. In that same period, revenue collectors in the field increased from 4,500 to 7,400.

During World War I, the bureau for the first time made a determined effort to educate the public about the patriotism of paying taxes. Clergyman were encouraged to preach the morality of income tax filing from the pulpit. The bureau also established its first intelligence division, with specially trained officers to detect tax fraud (a system of withholding tax money from paychecks had been repealed by Congress in 1916, undoubtedly making evasion easier).

Postwar agencies maintained the need office for revenue, so that by 1920, the bureau collected a record $5.5 billion in revenue, compared to $350 million in 1913. From a total of 4,000 employees in 1913, its bureaucracy sprawled to 15,000 seven years later.

In 1919 the 19th Amendment, outlawing alcoholic beverages, became part of the Constitution. Prohibition occasioned the establishment of a prohibition unit in the Bureau of Internal Revenue. Oddly, the Prohibition Law of October 1919 gave the Commissioner of Internal Revenue the authority to enforce the criminal aspects of the ban on liquor. Although distilleries were illegal, they were subject, if detected, to prosecution for tax evasion. The Bureau of Internal Revenue in 1925 alone made over 77,000 arrests, besides seizing and impounding property. After 1930, the U.S. Department of Justice took over these duties. When the 19th Amendment was repealed in late 1933, the bureau switched to collecting a liquor revenues again.

In that year the Great Depression reached its height. The trauma of that experience ushered in the New Deal, which was committed to the philosophy that the government should spend money, even at the risk of an unbalanced budget, to get people back on the job. Another concern in those desperate times was the elderly indigent, whose plight resulted in the Social Security Act of 1935. Two years later, the Social Security Tax Division was up and running in the Bureau of Internal Revenue.

By 1941, the number of employees at the bureau, thanks to the New Deal, rose to an all-time high of 27,000. Because of five major tax cuts in the 1920s, revenues stood at only $1.6 billion in 1933. In 1941, because of government spending, tax revenues of necessity increased to a record $7.4 billion. Four years later, the cost of the war had driven revenues up to $45 billion.

Despite $7.4 billion collected by the IRS in 1941, still only a segment of the U.S. population filed income tax returns—at most 8 million, including corporations. The huge demands of wartime spending changed that. More and more individuals earning modest salaries, previously excluded from taxation, were required to pay. While in 1939 those earning less than $5,000 made up only 10 percent of the taxpayers, by 1948 these accounted for at least 50 percent. After 1941, therefore, the number of taxpayers increased greatly—from 8 million in 1941 to 60 million in 1945—and unlike the decade following World War I, there would not be a reduction in taxation after 1945.

The final building block to the creation of a modern revenues state was the reintroduction (after it was repealed in 1916) of tax withholding in July 1943. This money was sent directly from the place of employment to the bureau. A year later, the "standard deduction" came into force for the first time also. Such a massive number of tax returns were coming into the bureau that it was collapsing under the strain, despite the debut of an abbreviated tax form in 1941, and tax refunds were taking over a year to be processed. This gave rise to bitter public criticism.

The result of the 1951 House subcommittee investigation of the bureau was the 1952 Reorganization Plan No. 1, inaugurating the most extensive restructuring of this agency in its history. All politically appointed posts within the bureau, except for the commissioner and deputy commissioner, were replaced by civil service positions. The agency was significantly decentralized, with headquarters in Washington determining policy, while field offices were given wide latitude in decision making. In addition, electronic machines—predecessors of the computer—were introduced to speed up processing of forms, which in turn were further simplified. Lastly, the name of the agency was changed officially to the Internal Revenue Service.

The organization of the IRS remained basically unaltered from 1952 until the late 1990s, when new reforms were enacted. Reporting to the headquarters in Washington were seven regional IRS offices headed by a regional commissioner, and 64 district offices headed by a district director. It was at the district level that the tax laws are interpreted and applied, and often no two districts applied the laws alike. Ever since the U.S. Bureau of Alcohol, Tobacco, and Firearms became a separate division within the Treasury Department in 1972, the IRS has no longer been responsible for collecting revenue on these items.

THE TAX COLLECTION PROCESS

Tax collection can be uncomplicated: most pay their taxes through payroll deductions. Tax returns are sent processing centers, where a computer scans each one for errors. For error-free returns, this is the end of the line, with the exception of processing a refund for those eligible. Unlike in Sweden, where the majority of tax returns are audited, in the United States only a small proportion—around 10 percent—are audited. This is mainly because of the expense involved. If tax fraud is discovered through an audit, any one of a range of 150 penalties can be assessed against the taxpayer. The severest is the seizure of one's property. In 1990, nearly 3 million seizures took place. Taxpayers have the right to appeal such seizures.

Detecting such fraud is an important and expensive pursuit on the part of the IRS, requiring specialized computer equipment and skilled research staff to pour over complex financial transactions. The IRS has the legal authority to request information from any bank and to inquire into any type of vehicle registration or business activity. This uncovers a huge amount of information on businesses or individuals, particularly as financial transactions and records are increasingly automated.

The IRS can also legally transmit taxpayer information to a variety of other government agencies. In this way, a person who has defaulted on a student loan or who has failed to pay child support can be ferreted out and forced to pay.

BUSINESS OBLIGATIONS

Businesses generally have two kinds of tax obligations to the IRS: payroll and income. Federal payroll taxes are mostly withheld from employee wages and submitted to the IRS on a regular schedule that depends on the size of the business. (State and local taxes may also be withheld, but these are not processed by the IRS.) Larger businesses, e.g., with more than $50,000 in payroll tax liabilities per year, are required to deposit withholding taxes more frequently, and in some cases, electronically. In addition to deductions from wages, employers must match employee Social Security contributions.

While almost any company has payroll liabilities, not all companies pay corporate income tax. Net income (profit) at subchapter **S corporations**, or small business corporations, is not taxed separately from the owners' personal income tax. The same is true of sole proprietorships and most partnerships (limited liability partnerships may be taxed as corporations under some circumstances). In addition, if a regular C corporation has no net profit for the year, there generally is no corporate tax at the federal level. When a corporation is liable for federal income tax, the basic tax rate is between 15 and 35 percent, depending on the amount of income. If a C corporation distributes profits in the form of dividends to shareholders, the shareholders are usually also taxed, creating double taxation.

As with individual income tax, business taxes paid to the IRS are "voluntary" in the sense that the company is responsible for determining the correct amount to pay and for meeting the appropriate deadlines. Companies that underpay or fail to file in a timely manner are usually subject to stiff penalties and interest charges.

RECENT TRENDS

As of 1997, the IRS received income tax returns from nearly 1.8 million partnerships, 5.2 million corporations, and approximately 17 million sole proprietorships. Employer wage withholdings and contributions accounted for around two-thirds of the IRS's $1.5 trillion in net collections. Corporate income tax that year made up just 12.3 percent, or $182 billion, of total collections.

In 1997 a labor force of 101,703 carried out the collection and processing of federal taxes at the IRS. Nearly 93 percent of these employees worked in field offices, and the remainder staffed the IRS national headquarters in Washington, D.C. This employment level, which was at its lowest point since 1986, reflected the Clinton administration's efforts to downsize the federal government. IRS staffing reached its apex in 1992, when the bureau employed 116,673 workers, including more than 9,000 at its headquarters.

The IRS cost $7.2 billion to run in 1997. Cost-containment measures during the mid-1990s improved the bureau's overall efficiency, as measured by the ratio of operating costs to dollars collected. The IRS's cost efficiency had waned in the late 1980s and early 1990s as its expenditure growth outpaced revenue growth. By 1997 the cost of collecting each $100 in taxes was back down to $0.44, from a peak of $0.60 in 1993. Over the previous 30 years, the IRS's most cost-efficient year was 1981, when operating costs ran at just $0.41 per $100 of revenue.

Always the object of public scrutiny and mistrust, the IRS during the 1990s underwent a number of reform initiatives—some voluntary and some legislated by Congress—to improve its performance and accountability to taxpayers. Perhaps the most sweeping of these was the bureau's decision in 1999 to abandon its long-standing geographical organization, which granted significant latitude to regional offices. In a move mandated by the Restructuring and Reform Act of 1998, the bureau announced that it would create instead four operating units to specialize in various revenue categories. The four were (1) the Wage and Investment Income Operating Division, based in Atlanta; (2) the Small Business and Self Employed Operating Division, based in Washington, D.C.; (3) the Tax Exempt Operating Division, also based in Washington; and (4) the Large and Mid-Size Business Operating Division, based in New Jersey. These divisions replaced the geographic structure of four regions containing 33 district offices. Other reforms included placing a greater burden of proof on the IRS when it brings cases in U.S. Tax Court and creating an oversight board for the bureau.

FURTHER READING:

Burnham, David. *A Law unto Itself: The IRS and the Abuse of Power.* New York: Vintage Books, 1989.

Fay, Jack R. "What Form of Ownership Is Best?" *CPA Journal,* August 1998.

Internal Revenue Service. *1997 Internal Revenue Service Data Book.* Washington, 1999. Available from www.irs.gov.

Philips, Bernie. "Are the IRS Districts Being Eliminated?" *National Public Accountant,* March-April 1999.

Saunders, Laura. "Congress Giveth—With Strings." *Forbes,* 23 March 1998.

Worsham, James. "IRS Overhaul Is Good News for Small-Business Owners." *Nation's Business,* September 1998.

INTERNATIONAL ACCOUNTING STANDARDS COMMITTEE (IASC)

The International Accounting Standards Committee (IASC) is an independent private-sector organization that in its own words is a "body working to achieve uniformity in the accounting principles that are used by businesses and other organizations for financial reporting around the world." As stated in its constitution the IASC's goals are to "formulate and publish in the public interest accounting standards to be observed in the presentation of financial statements and to promote their worldwide acceptance," and to "work for the improvement and harmonization of regulations, accounting standards and procedures relating to the presentation of financial statements." The IASC was founded in London in 1973 and by 1998 its membership included 143 **accounting** organizations representing 2 million accountants in 103 countries.

The IASC is not the first organization on either a national or international level to attempt the harmonization of accounting standards. The English Institute of Chartered Accountants in 1942 and the Committee on Accounting and Auditing Research of the Canadian Institute of Chartered Accountants in 1946 studied harmonization on the national level; the Accountants International Study Group—which was sponsored by British, American, and Canadian professional accountants—viewed standardization from a global perspective and compared the accounting practices and procedures of the three countries. In 1977 the International Federation of Accountants was established by IASC members, and is closely allied with the IASC.

Standardized accounting procedures are important in order to make financial reports comparable, especially from country to country. It is even possible, however, for accounting procedures to vary within a country. It often falls upon investment services or companies doing business in more than one country to harmonize different accounting procedures. This can prove to be an expensive and time-consuming task. Standardized accounting procedures are especially important for multinational companies which need a consistent accounting procedure for evaluating operations from different countries. External reports coming into a multinational's headquarters must also be harmonious with internal assessments of performance. International accounting standards can also be important to developing countries, since establishing national accounting standards can be an expensive and arduous process.

International accounting standards are becoming increasingly important in a financial world dominated by global traders. Between 1991 and 1997, for instance, non-U.S. equity holdings of American investors surged from $200 billion to more than $1 trillion. Of the approximately 13,000 companies registered with the U.S. **Securities and Exchange Commission** (SEC), nearly 1,000 are foreign companies.

Adoption of a harmonized accounting procedure has also been an objective of the **European Union**, which has closely associated itself with the IASC. Other groups and nations supporting the IASC include the Arab Society for Certified Accountants, which represents 22 Arab nations; Australia, which was working to harmonize its accounting standards with the IASC in the late 1990s; as well as Canada, the South African Accounting Practices Board, and the Malaysian Accounting Standards Board, all of which are pursuing similar policies. Notable holdouts to the adoption of IASC standards are the United Kingdom, which prefers procedures set by the United Kingdom Accounting Standards Board but still makes attempts at IASC harmonization; Japan, whose government sets accounting standards and often politicizes the process; and finally the United States.

In the United States, accounting standards, which are mostly set by the private sector, operate under the authority of the SEC and various state certified public accountant licensing laws. The SEC is considering allowing issuers of foreign securities to use IASC standards. Currently, these issuers must use either U.S. Generally Accepted Accounting Procedures (GAAP) or reconcile their **financial statements** to GAAP. Items that need to be reconciled include such things as pension cost measurement, **employee benefits**, and deferred income **taxes**.

The IASC is also attempting to develop standardized accounting procedures that will be recognized by the International Organization of Securities Commissions (IOSCO), a worldwide association of securities commissions including the SEC. Although the IOSCO and the IASC reached an agreement on core standards in 1993, a full endorsement of IASC standards has yet to be achieved. If the IOSCO were to fully adopt IASC standards, the SEC would probably do an independent evaluation. Both of these processes could last well into the 21st century.

[Michael Knes]

FURTHER READING:

Epstein, Barry Jay. *Interpretation and Application of International Accounting Standards.* New York: Wiley, 1997.

Financial Accounting Standards Board. *IASC-U.S. Comparison Project: A Report on the Similarities and Differences between IASC Standards and U.S. GAAP.* Norwalk, CT: Financial Accounting Standards Board, 1996.

International Accounting Standards Committee. ''International Accounting Standards Committee (IASC).'' London: International Accounting Standards Committee, 1998. Available from www.iasc.org.uk.

Pacter, Paul. ''International Accounting Standards: The World's Standards by 2002.'' *CPA Journal* 68, no. 7 (July 1998): 14 18+.

INTERNATIONAL COMMERCIAL ARBITRATION

Arbitration is the process by which parties to a dispute submit their differences to the binding judgment of an impartial third person (or group of persons) selected by mutual consent. The perceived advantages of arbitration in a domestic context are magnified in an international transaction; savings in time and expense may be considerable, and preventing litigation in the other party's ''home'' judicial system is often far more preferable than exposure to the uncertainties of a different nation's laws and procedures. Accordingly, **arbitration** has become the primary method for resolving international business disputes.

The most important advantage of arbitration over litigation in the international context is the relative ease with which an award can be enforced. An international arbitral award can be enforced without further judicial inquiry into the merits of the dispute in more than 100 countries around the world. These are countries that have signed the 1958 **United Nations** Convention on the Recognition and Enforcement of Arbitral Awards (also known as the New York Convention). Under the New York Convention, the winning party can enforce the arbitration award much more easily than a court judgment in a foreign country.

For example, suppose that Merit Systems, Inc. of New York has a contract dispute with an firm in India, and there is no arbitration agreement, either in their **contract** or subsequent to their dispute. Whose law applies? New York law? U.S. law? Do both India and the United States have jurisdiction over the case and the parties? If a judgment is taken in the United States without the Indian firm's participation, would the courts in India honor the judgment? All such questions are set aside in the event the parties agree to arbitrate in, say, Geneva, Switzerland, under the rules of the International Chamber of Commerce, and applying Indian law (or whatever law the parties choose). An award by the arbitral panel in Geneva would also be enforceable by Indian courts, since India has signed the New York Convention.

THE ARBITRAL PROCESS

How does the international arbitration process work? In the typical case, the parties agree in writing to refer their dispute to arbitration. That agreement may take place either before or after the dispute arises. Second, the arbitral tribunal must make a decision (not just a recommendation) that is final, and within the scope of its authority. Third, with very few exceptions that provide a basis to appeal an arbitration award, the award can generally be enforced through court orders if the losing party does not voluntarily satisfy the terms of the award. Each of these steps is discussed in greater detail below.

THE AGREEMENT TO ARBITRATE. An arbitration agreement establishes by mutual consent the willingness of the parties to be bound by an arbitrator's decision, and also defines the issues on which an arbitrator may render an award. The parties may determine the number of arbitrators (usually one or a panel of three), the place of arbitration, the rules under which the arbitration will take place, and the applicable law.

There are two basic types of arbitration agreements. The most common is an agreement to submit future disputes to arbitration (a predispute arbitration agreement). Generally, this will be a relatively short clause in the more general contract between the parties. For example, the Balfour Corporation, based in Massachusetts, might contract with Mitsubishi Heavy Industries, based in Japan, using the following single paragraph agreeing to submit to arbitration any future disputes relating to the contract:

> The parties to this contract agree that, in the event of any dispute or disagreement of any kind arising out of this contract or matters pertaining to this contract, that such disputes be settled by arbitration before a panel of three arbitrators in Geneva, Switzerland, under the auspices of the International Chamber of Commerce.

If there is no predispute arbitration agreement and a dispute arises, the parties may draw up a set of questions to be decided along with procedural rules specifically suited to the dispute at hand to guide the arbitral tribunal. This is called a "submission." More often, however, the agreement to arbitrate precedes any dispute, and it is customary to incorporate the procedural rules of an institution such as the American Arbitration Association, the Inter-American Commercial Arbitration Association, the International Chamber of Commerce (ICC), the International Center for the Settlement of Investment Disputes, or the London Court of International Arbitration. By incorporating the rules of these institutions, parties adopt an administering agency to assist the arbitral process.

As an example, consider the above predispute arbitration agreement between Balfour and Mitsubishi. Among other contingencies, the ICC Court will: (1) decide if there appears to be a binding arbitration agreement under which the ICC is authorized to act; (2) decide whether there should be one or three arbitrators, if the parties have not specified the number; (3) appoint arbitrators in accordance with its rules; (4) determine the place of arbitration, if not already agreed upon by the parties; (5) set time limits; (6) review the draft of the arbitral tribunal's award; and (7) administer issues of fees and expenses of the arbitrators. The reader is cautioned, however, that arbitrations conducted under institutional auspices may be more expensive than an arbitration where the rules and procedures have been crafted by the disputants to ensure the greatest efficiency.

Where the parties do not incorporate a set of institutional rules, an arbitration clause should—at a minimum—contain the following:

- The place of arbitration (naming a certain city or nation). This will have the effect of establishing which nation's laws will govern the formation and maintenance of the arbitration. The law of the place of arbitration—or *lex arbitrii*—controls a number of key issues, including the validity of the arbitration agreement, appointment or removal of arbitrators, time limits, interim protective measures, and form of the arbitral award.
- The number of arbitrators (whether one or three).
- The choice of substantive law to be applied to any issue between the parties; in contrast to the *lex arbitrii,* the choice of a substantive or proper law for the arbitration is meant to reach the merits of the controversy to invoke some rule of decision.
- The issues to be decided and any time limits for the award to be rendered.

Where parties to a dispute are unlikely to agree on such details after the dispute has arisen, making reference to arbitral institutional rules is nearly essential.

THE ARBITRATOR'S POWERS AND THE ARBITRAL DECISION. The arbitral tribunal—whether it be a single arbitrator or a panel—obtains its power from the agreement to arbitrate and the willingness of a legal system to enforce that agreement or any arbitral award made pursuant to that agreement. Hence, if the arbitrator or arbitral panel decides a matter that is beyond the scope of the arbitration agreement, recognition and enforcement of the award may be refused. Also, certain kinds of agreements to arbitrate may be invalid under national law. For many years, U.S. courts refused to honor agreements to arbitrate certain kinds of disputes, such as claims based on violations of federal **securities** or **antitrust** statutes. Public policy, it was felt, was better served by having such federal law-based claims heard in the judicial system rather than by arbitrators. Gradually, however, the U.S. Supreme Court led the way in allowing arbitration of such claims. At present, arbitration of claims based on federal employment discrimination, antitrust, racketeering, and securities laws are all arbitrable. Few, if any, restrictions remain in U.S. law as to the kinds of controversies that can be arbitrated.

In other countries, however, the kinds of disputes that can lawfully be arbitrated may be limited. In Latin America, for example, commercial arbitration has not been generally accepted. A **government contract** may not be arbitrable in some countries unless a statute expressly allows it, and there are sometimes difficult issues involved in holding a particular government to its agreement to arbitrate disputes arising under a contract; issues of sovereign immunity and its waiver are often involved.

Even when there is little doubt about the arbitrability of a particular kind of claim, there may yet be some doubt as to whether the parties' predispute arbitration agreement was intended to cover certain issues. That is, the ''scope'' of the arbitrator's decisional powers as given by the parties may be contested. But predispute arbitration agreements are generally phrased rather broadly (''all disputes arising under or in relation to this contract'') and are generally interpreted liberally by the courts. In any case, it is the arbitrator who makes the initial determination as to whether a particular issue or set of issues is within the scope of his or her arbitral authority, and not the court.

Much could be said about the arbitral hearing itself, and the kinds of evidence that are allowed and the kinds of procedures that are typical. But the reader is best advised to consult the more extended references at the end of this article, and to bear in mind that, in general, arbitrations are often conducted with fairly strict time limits, that informality is the norm, that not all evidence is heard, and that the well-known judicial rights of cross-examination and discovery are largely absent under most international institutional arbitral rules. Moreover, by custom and law in many countries, the arbitrator is not required to state the judicial equivalent of ''findings of fact'' or ''conclusions of law''—it is sufficient that the arbitrator make a decision in writing, but not that he or she defend it.

This was probably appropriate in simple disputes where, for example, the arbitrator was called upon to render a prompt decision as to whether delivered goods did or did not correspond to a sample or to a known trade description or industry standard. Nevertheless, with the increasing complexity of arbitrations to include claims in securities, antitrust, employment discrimination, and the like, there is a discernible trend that favors giving reasons in awards. And since the arbitrator or panel has a duty to ensure that the award, once made, is valid and enforceable, the particular institutional rules (whether they are the UNCITRAL rules, the ICC rules, or some other set of institutional rules) must be consulted to see that the award is in proper form (and, thus, enforceable).

Under the UNCITRAL arbitration rules (formulated by the United Nations Commission on International Trade Law), for example: (1) the award must be in writing; (2) the reasons for the award must be stated; and (3) the award must be signed by the arbitrators and must bear the date and place of the decision. Under rules of the International Center for the Settlement of Investment Disputes, there are additional requirements for a valid award, such as designating counsel for the parties, a summary of the proceedings, and a statement of facts as found by the tribunal.

The tribunal must issue its award within any time limits set forth in the submission or the institutional rules incorporated by the parties. For example, if parties submit a dispute to arbitration and require that a decision be made within 60 days, then any arbitral award taking place after 60 days would not be valid and enforceable. Under rules of the American Arbitration Association, the award must be made no later than 30 days from the close of the hearings; unless an extension had been obtained, an award dated beyond the 30-day period would not be valid and enforceable.

JUDICIAL REVIEW AND ENFORCEMENT OF ARBITRAL AWARDS. Once the arbitrator or arbitral tribunal has made its award it seldom has any further function with respect to the parties. The award, being final and binding, does have important legal consequences, and may be enforced against a nonpaying party or enforcement of the award may be delayed when the losing party seeks to ''vacate'' the award. But even if the losing party succeeds (which is relatively rare) the arbitrator or arbitral tribunal does not generally rehear the dispute unless the losing party: (1) appeals to the courts in the country where the arbitration was held; and (2) obtains an order requiring resubmission of all or part of the dispute. Almost always, however, the award marks the end of the tribunal's involvement with the parties on that particular dispute.

After the arbitration, the winning party may wish to register or deposit the award with a court in the country where the arbitration took place. In theory, this should not be necessary: the parties have agreed that an arbitrator should render a final and binding award, and implicit in that agreement is that no further action needs to be taken by the winning party. But not all awards are promptly and voluntarily paid; the losing party, after all, is likely to disagree with the tribunal's decision, and may well be looking for grounds on which to resist enforcement of the award. Registration or deposit of the award with a court of competent jurisdiction can in some cases put additional psychological pressure on the losing party to comply sooner rather than later, and in some cases, registration or deposit may be a necessary prerequisite to enforcement.

The winning party can often use the award to put pressure on the losing party, whether through explicit or implicit threats of commercial reprisal or noncooperation, or through the threat of adverse publicity. If such pressure fails, the winning party may have to seek execution by court proceedings on the bank accounts or other assets of the losing party. If the award has been deposited or registered, it may thereafter be enforced as though it were a judgment of the court. In many countries, however, and as envisioned by the New York Convention, a final and binding award may be enforced in a country other than where the arbitration took place, provided that the two countries are both signatories to the New York Convention.

A losing party can comply with the award, use it as a basis for negotiating a settlement, or may challenge the award. The bases for challenge, however, are few indeed. Aside from showing bias or favoritism on the part of arbitrators, the principal means of successfully challenging an arbitration award deal with procedural issues. Challenges on procedural issues may be made, for example, where the arbitrator failed to decide an issue submitted by the parties, failed to allow a continuance of the hearing even though good cause was shown, or considered and decided issues beyond the scope of the agreement or submission by the parties. It is abundantly clear as of 1999 that, internationally, challenges to arbitral awards based on the merits (in contrast to procedural challenges) will seldom succeed. In some countries, a tribunal's decision that is in manifest disregard of the law may be set aside by judicial review. This is not, however, a generally recognized basis for setting aside an arbitral award in the United States.

An award may be challenged in at least two ways. One way is for the losing party to ask a court to modify or set aside the award, while another way is to ask the court to remit the award to the arbitral tribunal for reconsideration and revision. If an award is set aside, the award loses its legal validity in the country where it was made, and also any country adopting the New York Convention.

Under the New York Convention, recognition and enforcement of the award may be refused where the losing party offers proof:

1. That the agreement on which the arbitration is based involves one or more parties with a legal incapacity, or that the agreement is not valid under the proper law of the contract or the *lex arbitrii* (the law of the country where the award was made).
2. The losing party was not given proper notice of the appointment of the arbitrator or of the arbitration proceedings or was otherwise unable to present its case.
3. The award contained decisions on matters beyond the scope of the tribunal.
4. The composition of the arbitral tribunal was not in accordance with the agreement of the parties.
5. The subject matter of the decision is not capable of settlement by arbitration under the law of the country where the arbitration is held.
6. Recognizing and enforcing the award would be contrary to the public policy of the country whose court is asked to enforce the award.

These objections are largely procedural—none of them attacks the correctness of the particular decision (such as "Was delivery of the goods timely? And, if not, what are appropriate damages to the buyer?"). Rather, these objections largely concern whether the tribunal exceeded the scope of its authority or ignored basic rules of procedural fairness or its own set of procedural rules. When they lead to nonenforcement of an arbitral award, these objections serve to remind us that private international arbitration can operate only within the broader context of public laws and institutions.

SEE ALSO: International Law

[Chris A. Carr and Donald O. Mayer]

FURTHER READING:

Born, Gary B. *International Commercial Arbitration in the United States: Commentary and Materials.* Boston: Kluwer Law and Taxation Publishers, 1994.

Carter, James H. "International Commercial Arbitration." Chap. 19 in *The International Lawyer's Deskbook,* edited by Lucinda A. Low, Patrick M. Norton, and Daniel M. Drory. Washington: Section of International Law and Practice, American Bar Association, 1996.

Convention on the Recognition and Enforcement of Foreign Arbitral Awards (New York Convention). U.S. Code. Vol. 9, secs. 201-8 (1958).

Craig, W. Laurence, William W. Park, and Jan Paulsson. *International Chamber of Commerce Arbitration.* 2nd ed. New York: Oceana, 1990.

Redfern, Alan, and Marin Hunter. *Law and Practice of International Commercial Arbitration.* 2nd ed. London: Sweet & Maxwell, 1991.

INTERNATIONAL COMPETITION

International competition is a fact of life for today's companies. Manufacturers in the United States, for example, must compete not only with **exports** from other countries, but also with American **subsidiaries** of foreign corporations. The same is true for manufacturers and other companies in Japan and the **European Union** (EU). Newly industrialized countries such as China, Singapore, South Korea, Taiwan, Brazil, and Mexico are also competing for a share of the international marketplace. In short, international competition is the driving force behind the **globalization** of production and markets.

International trade in the 1990s has been dominated by the United States, Japan, and the European Union (EU). Together they generate 80 percent of all world trade and account for 65 percent of all foreign **direct investment**. One sign of increased international competition has been the growth of **imports** and exports. In the United States, for example, exports increased from less than 10 percent of manufacturing output in the 1960s to more than 20 percent in the 1990s. Similarly, imports of manufactured products increased from 5 percent of domestic output in the 1960s to more than 25 percent in the 1990s.

FOREIGN DIRECT INVESTMENT

The growth of foreign direct investment is another sign of increased international competition. Since the 1980s, foreign direct investment has increased four times faster than world output. Trade between parent companies and their foreign subsidiaries in the early 1990s accounted for approximately 80 percent of all trade between the United States and Japan, 40 percent of all trade between the United States and the EU, and 55 percent of all trade between the EU and Japan.

Foreign direct investment is a strategy used by multinational enterprises to create international production networks. Through an equity investment by a parent company in a branch, subsidiary, or affiliate located in another country, the parent company gains managerial control of an enterprise located in another country.

Foreign direct investment is primarily used by companies to establish foreign subsidiaries that will produce goods and services for sale in local and international markets. In the early 1990s U.S. subsidiaries of foreign companies accounted for approximately 20 percent of all U.S. exports and 33 percent of all U.S. imports. Foreign subsidiaries of U.S. parent companies accounted for approximately 33 percent of U.S. exports and 20 percent of U.S. imports.

There is a tendency toward regional clustering of foreign direct investment. That is, Japanese firms tend to invest in Asian countries, EU firms in other European countries, and U.S. firms in North and South American countries. Among the three dominant international trading groups, the United States is the principal direct investor in the EU and Japan, and the EU is the principal direct investor in the United States.

The elimination of trade and investment barriers can encourage foreign direct investment. The **North American Free Trade Agreement** (NAFTA), for example, involves the United States, Canada, and Mexico. It eliminated many of the trade and investment barriers that existed among the three signatories. With the adoption of NAFTA, foreign direct investment by the United States increased in Mexico, just as foreign direct investment by U.S. companies in Canada increased following the passage of the **U.S.-Canada Free Trade Agreement of 1989**. In other parts of the world, though, foreign direct investment can be discouraged through protectionist policies that regulate the amount of allowable investment. For example, Malaysia requires foreign partners to limit their investments to less than 50 percent, so that control of such ventures remains with a local partner.

HOW BUSINESSES COMPETE IN FOREIGN MARKETS

There are three basic methods by which companies can compete in foreign markets: exporting, licensing and other contractual agreements, and investment. Each method has its own advantages and disadvantages. One method may be more appropriate for a certain line of business than another. For example, exporting works for best for physical goods. Licensing and other contractual arrangements are more appropriate for intangibles, services, and the transfer of technology. Investment involves the transfer of an entire enterprise to another country.

EXPORTING. Exporting is limited to physical goods. When a company exports goods to another country, those goods are manufactured outside of the target market. Companies that export can use intermediaries located in their own country to facilitate exports, or they can use no intermediaries or only those located in the target country. International freight forwarders, **banks**, and other specialists can assist companies wishing to export by handling many of the details regarding documentation and financing.

Exporting is often the way a company initially becomes involved in international trade. Companies can gain valuable experience in international markets through exporting without being exposed to large capital losses. A recent variation on traditional exporting is mail-order exporting. **Mail-order businesses** based in the United States, for example, have found that with the use of fax machines, international **toll free telephone calls**, credit cards, and air courier delivery, consumers in Europe, Japan, and elsewhere are willing to place orders from catalogs and other **direct-mail** promotions.

LICENSING AND OTHER CONTRACTUAL AGREEMENTS. International licensing is another way for domestic companies to compete internationally. Under an international **licensing agreement**, domestic companies provide foreign companies with rights to some of their intangible assets, such as their **patents**, trade secrets, know-how, trademarks, or even their company name and logo. Domestic companies often provide some type of technical assistance to make sure the licensed properties are used properly. Similar contractual agreements may include **franchising**, technical agreements, service or management **contracts**, and other variations.

Licensing and other contractual agreements are typically long-term associations between an international company and an entity in the host country. They typically involve the transfer of technology or human skills. Characteristically there is no equity investment by the international company in such agreements.

Licensing and other contractual arrangements can offer several advantages over or alternatives to exporting. Exports are often subject to another country's import barriers, such as tariffs and quotas. Licensing agreements can circumvent such barriers, since only intangible assets and services are being exchanged. When exports are no longer profitable, companies can enjoy incremental income from licensing agreements. In some cases a country's currency may experience a prolonged **devaluation**, making exports no longer profitable. Licensing agreements can overcome some of the risks associated with such currency fluctuations. There is also less of a political risk with licensing, which avoids the risks associated with expropriation of the international company's investment by the host country's government. Licensing can also provide the host country with much-desired **technology transfer**, so that its government is likely to view such agreements as beneficial.

INVESTMENT. Investment is the third way in which companies can compete in other countries. Typically, foreign direct investment involves ownership by an international company of a manufacturing plant or other production facility in a target country. Investments may be sole ventures, with full ownership and control by the parent company; or they may be **joint ventures**, with ownership and control shared with one or more local partners. Investment may be in a new establishment, or it may involve the acquisition of an existing enterprise.

International companies generally make direct investments in foreign countries for one of three reasons. One reason is to obtain raw materials from the host country. Such investors are known as extractive investors. Very little of the extracted resource is sold in the host country. Most of it is either exported back to the international company's home country for use in manufacturing there, or sold on the world market. The steel, aluminum, and petroleum industries are examples of this type of investment.

A second reason for foreign direct investment is to source products at a lower cost. Sourcing investors establish manufacturing or assembly operations in a foreign country for the purpose of obtaining components or finished goods more cheaply than they could in their home country. These components or finished goods are then exported back to the investor's home country or shipped to other countries. In the U.S. consumer electronics industry, for example, assembled products are obtained by U.S. companies from Mexico, Taiwan, or elsewhere for sale in the United States.

The third and most prevalent reason for foreign direct investment is to penetrate local markets and compete internationally. As noted above, international companies use direct investment to establish a production base in another country for the purpose of competing in that country's marketplace.

FINANCING INTERNATIONAL TRADE THROUGH COUNTERTRADING

Countertrading is a type of contractual agreement in international trade that provides special arrangements for financing an exchange of goods and services. There are many forms of countertrading, ranging from simple **barter** agreements to complex offset deals that involve the exporter agreeing to compensatory practices with respect to the buyer. Countertrading commonly takes place between private companies in developed nations and the governments of developing countries, although countertrading also occurs between developed nations. It has become popular as a means of financing international trade to reduce risks or overcome problems associated with various national currencies.

Buybacks are a common form of countertrading that typically take place between a private corporation from a developed country and the government (or government agency) of a developing nation. Under the first contract of a buyback arrangement, the exporting private corporation agrees to provide a production facility or other type of capital goods to the developing nation. Then, under the second contract, the developing nation repays the exporting private corporation with output produced at the facility or derived from the originally exported capital goods. The exporter, in effect, buys back the output of the facility it has constructed.

Buybacks are used to finance direct investment in developing countries. They are popular because they meet the needs and objectives of both parties. From the developing country's viewpoint, buybacks expand the country's export base, provide **employment**, and help it meet its goals for industrialization and development. From the point of view of a private corporation, the buyback may help it gain a market presence in the country and provide it with a source of products it can use or sell. If the particular output of the facility is not needed by the corporation, it can involve a third party to help it meet its countertrade obligations.

Another type of countertrade is the compensation trade. An exporter and importer agree to make reciprocal purchases of specific goods. The exchange is covered under a single contract. It may or may not take place simultaneously. Each delivery is invoiced in an agreed currency, with payments going either to the supplier or to a clearing account. A third party may be involved to fulfill the purchase commitment of one of the parties. There are many other types of countertrading; it has become firmly established as a method of financing international trade. For developing countries that have hard currency shortages, or whose national currencies are not readily convertible to other types of foreign exchange, countertrading offers them a means of financing imports.

International companies from developed countries who are willing to countertrade have found that it provides them with a competitive edge. By being flexible in the type of payment they are willing to receive, companies that are willing and able to countertrade have a stronger position in competitive bidding for projects involving emerging markets in developing countries. Many such companies are eager to find outlets for their products in emerging markets such as China and Mexico, for example.

POLITICAL FACTORS IN INTERNATIONAL COMPETITION

International competition can be affected by political policies beyond the control of international companies. While various international trade agreements have served to reduce or eliminate **trade barriers**, such barriers continue to exist. The most common form of trade barrier in international trade is a tariff or **duty** that is usually imposed on imports. There is also a category of nontariff barriers that also serve to restrict global trade and affect international competition.

Governments can give international companies based in their own countries significant advantages by establishing trade barriers. Protecting domestic producers against foreign competitors—especially in infant industries—improving a nation's terms of trade, reducing domestic unemployment, and improving a nation's balance-of-payments position are some of the reasons given for imposing import tariffs on foreign-made goods.

In addition to duties and tariffs, there are also nontariff barriers (NTBs) to international trade. These include quantitative restrictions, or quotas, that may be imposed by one country or as the result of agreements between two or more countries. Examples of quantitative restrictions include international **commodity** agreements, voluntary export restraints, and orderly **marketing** arrangements.

Administrative regulations constitute a second category of NTBs. These include a variety of requirements that must be met in order for trade to occur, including fees, licenses, permits, domestic content requirements, financial **bonds** and deposits, and government procurement practices. The third type of NTB covers technical regulations that apply to such areas as packaging, labeling, safety standards, and multilingual requirements.

In 1980 the Agreement on Technical Barriers to Trade, also known as the Standards Code, came into effect for the purpose of ensuring that administrative and technical practices do not act as trade barriers. Additional work on promoting unified standards to eliminate NTBs was conducted by the **General Agreement on Tariffs and Trade** (GATT) Standards Committee.

Government **subsidies** are another way in which government policies can provide assistance to domestic companies involved in international trade. Export subsidies are given to domestic producers of goods that will be exported. Export subsidies may take the form of a variety of government benefits, including direct payments, support prices, tax incentives, and funds for **training**. Export subsidies are given on the condition that the goods being produced will be exported. In the European Union (EU), export subsidies are called variable subsidies. Rules affecting variable subsidies of EU countries are found in the Common Agricultural Policy of the EU.

GATT contains restrictions on the use of export subsidies. Developed countries are forbidden to use subsidies to support the export of most manufactured goods, for example. Under GATT, less-developed nations are permitted to subsidize manufactured goods that will be exported, provided the subsidies do not significantly damage the economies of developed countries. GATT also provides for remedies, such as countervailing duties, when it has been determined that one trading partner is unfairly using export subsidies.

INTERNATIONAL COMPETITION AND THE WORLD TRADE ORGANIZATION

The **World Trade Organization** (WTO) was established in January 1995 as a successor to GATT, which officially ended in April 1994. The WTO's main function has been to resolve trade disputes, and it developed procedures for handling trade disputes that were much improved over the GATT procedures.

In its first 18 months the WTO settled more than 50 trade disputes.

The WTO has encouraged international competition in several ways. It adopted a competition policy that promotes international competition and seeks to eliminate national policies that hinder international competition. At its December 1996 summit meeting in Singapore, more than 60 member nations agreed to eliminate tariffs on more than 300 high-technology products including telecommunications and **computer** equipment. The WTO also opened the telecommunication sector to international competition when its members agreed to eliminate national telecommunications monopolies.

THE FUTURE OF INTERNATIONAL COMPETITION

It is clear that many factors will contribute to the growth of international competition. These include technological and political factors as well as economic factors. Industries that are experiencing rapid technological advancements are already global in nature. Production facilities can and are being located virtually anywhere in the world. As a result, consumer demand in the different industrial countries is converging, so that consumers in Germany, for example, want the benefits of the same technologies as consumers in Japan.

Politically it seems clear that international and multinational trade agreements are being written for the purpose of facilitating international trade. The formation of the European Union, the North American Free Trade Agreement, the General Agreement on Tariffs and Trade, and the World Trade Organization indicate that political leaders not only have realized the benefits of less restricted international competition, they have also been able to convince their constituents of those benefits.

It is likely that international competition will continue to increase. Companies will continue to enter international markets by exporting and through direct investment and licensing and other contractual agreements. International trade agreements will facilitate their efforts and potentially make them more profitable. Consumers throughout the world will benefit with a higher standard of living from access to a wider range of goods and services.

[David P. Bianco]

FURTHER READING:

"Co-operate on Competition: Competition Policy Increasingly Overlaps with Trade Policy." *Economist,* 4 July 1998, 16.

Feinerman, James V. "A New World Order." *China Business Review.* March/April 1995, 16-18.

Fliess, Barbara, and Anthony Kleitz. "Trade Policy in 2000." *OECD Observer,* April/May 1998, 7-11.

"Landmark Deal." *Business Korea,* March 1997, 26-27.

Lindsey, Brink. "Freedom to Trade: WTO's Promising Anniversary." *Regulation,* winter 1997, 19.

McCulloch, Wendell. *International Business: The Challenge of Global Competition.* 7th ed. New York: McGraw-Hill, 1998.

Nelson, Carl A. *Managing Globally: A Complete Guide to Competing Worldwide.* Burr Ridge, IL: Irwin Professional Publishing, 1993.

Porter, Michael E. *On Competition.* Boston: Harvard Business School Press, 1998.

Root, Franklin R. *International Strategic Management: Challenges and Opportunities.* Bristol, PA: Taylor & Francis, 1992.

"The Way It Was." *Economist,* 20 June 1998, S5 S6.

Williams, Frances. "Antagonists Queue for WTO Judgment." *Financial Times,* 8 August 1996, 6.

Zarocostas, John. "A Summit Triumph." *Journal of Commerce and Commercial,* 6 January 1997, C28-C29.

INTERNATIONAL EXCHANGE RATE

A **foreign exchange** (FX) rate or international exchange rate is the price of one country's money (currency) in terms of another's. Technically, this is known as the nominal exchange rate, as contrasted with the real exchange rate, which is the relative price of comparable goods between two countries. In general usage, however, when someone refers to the exchange rate, he or she is referring to the nominal rate. Due to government interventions, some currencies also have multiple exchange rates for different purposes.

Exchange rates are determined by the supply of and the demand for currencies, many of which are traded on foreign exchange markets. Such trading is fundamental to the modern market-based global economy, as it enables a rapid and relatively fair exchange of goods or services across national borders.

As nations and their economies have become increasingly interdependent, the FX market has emerged as a global focal point. With an estimated daily FX turnover exceeding $1 trillion, equal to around one-eighth of U.S. annual gross domestic product, this is by far the world's largest market. In order to remain competitive in the world economy, it is vital for businesses dealing in international markets to manage the risk of adverse currency fluctuations.

EXCHANGE RATE MECHANISMS

Nations have used three main mechanisms to establish exchange rates for their currencies: 1) the gold standard, in which a currency is denominated in a unit of gold; 2) pegged rates, under which governments denominate their currencies in units of a strong global currency—often the U.S. dollar; and 3) free-floating rates, which are set by free (or relatively free) market forces.

Most countries abandoned the gold standard in the 1970s; however, pegged and free-floating methods are used widely. Pegged rates are usually sought by countries with emerging economies that want the stability of a major currency but may not have the economic presence to ensure that stability on their own. This method is by no means flawless, though, and countries with pegged currencies still face currency crises even when the currency to which they are pegged remains stable. Floating rates are employed by most of the world's largest economies, including that of the United States, most of the industrial economies, and some of the emerging economies. Some governments participate in the market system, but also attempt to insulate their currencies by placing certain arbitrary restrictions on trading, such as specifying a ''band'' or range of acceptable trading values.

MARKET INFLUENCES

Several factors influence exchange rates, including:

- relative rates of **inflation**
- comparative **interest rates**
- growth of domestic money supply
- size and trend of balance of payments
- economic growth, as measured by **gross domestic product** and other indicators
- dependence on outside energy sources
- central bank intervention
- government policy and political stability

All of these, and possibly other, factors can affect the market's perception of the strength of the foreign currency. Analogous to the buying and selling of corporate stocks, if signs loom that a national economy could be weakening or troubled, traders may quickly reduce their holdings of its currency. This typically causes the currency to loose value relative to other currencies the market favors.

Because exchange rates express one currency in terms of another, a change in the rate may be triggered by positive or negative influences from either side. For instance, if the U.S. dollar weakens versus the yen, it's not necessarily because there is bad news about the U.S. economy. Rather, it could simply mean there is good news about the Japanese economy and no change in the perception of U.S. economic health.

Currency trading is not always grounded in cautious, rational analysis, however. Since currency investors make many short-term decisions about how best to position their assets, a small item in the daily news may trigger an onslaught of buying or selling of a particular currency, which on a macro scale could result in a an exchange rate fluctuation of several U.S. cents or more per unit.

EXCHANGE RATES AND FOREIGN TRADE

Exchange rates can significantly alter a particular country's trade position by changing the relative value of its exports and imports. In general, when the currency in Country A is strong relative to Country B, Country A's exports are more expensive and less attractive to buyers in Country B, but imports from Country B may be at a favorable price in Country A. Conversely, if Country A's currency is weak, its exports would likely be more robust and imports from Country B would be less attractive.

As these converse relationships illustrate, there are advantages and disadvantages to a nation having a currency that is considerably stronger or weaker than those of major trading partners. Certainly, a rapid weakening of a currency can produce an economic crisis, as noted below in the discussion on Asia, but a stable yet weak currency can be a boon to an export-based economy because exporters from a weak-currency country tend to have a price advantage over competitors based in a stronger-currency economy. Still, the market nature of exchange rates usually ensures there is no great imbalance between a country's broader economic health and the strength of its currency; when a currency remains weak compared to others, it often reflects a lack of investor confidence in that country's economy.

THE LATE 1990S ASIAN CRISIS

While any nation can suffer from a volatile or weak exchange market for its currency, smaller, emerging economies tend to be most susceptible to wide, and potentially catastrophic, fluctuations. Some of the most dramatic recent examples of this phenomenon ravaged east Asian economies in the late 1990s Asian financial crisis. While the roots of the region's economic malaise were diverse and complex, much of the tangible damage occurred when currency traders—mostly from outside the region—balked at perceived weaknesses and sold off Asian currencies at a frenetic pace. The resulting drop in value of currencies such as South Korea's won and Indonesia's rupiah had devastating consequences for individuals, businesses, and even governments.

One of the most immediate effects of these currency devaluations was the appreciation of foreign-denominated debt relative to the local currencies. For example, consider an Indonesian company with a \$1 million loan, denominated in dollars, from a U.S. bank. If the monthly payment on the loan were

$10,000, at pre-crisis exchange rates (approximately 2,500 rupiahs to the dollar) the company would have paid 2.5 million rupiahs per month. However, once the Indonesian currency plummeted in 1997 to 10,000 rupiah to the dollar, the amount needed to service this debt would instantly skyrocket to 10 million rupiahs per month. Assuming the company had no substantial assets or revenue streams denominated in dollars to help insulate it, its revenues in rupiahs would at best remain flat, thus creating a shortfall of 7.5 million rupiah per month. In effect, the company's debt would have quadrupled without any corresponding change in its local business conditions. If anything, its revenues would likely drop as its customers faced similar hardships and cut back on spending, leading to a cycle of mounting debts and falling revenues.

SEE ALSO: Foreign Exchange

FURTHER READING:

Chong-Tae, Kim. "Critical Condition?" *Business Korea,* September 1997, 20.

Isard, Peter. *Exchange Rate Economics.* New York: Cambridge University Press, 1995.

Rosenberg, Michael R. *Currency Forecasting: A Guide to Fundamental and Technical Models of Exchange Rate Determination.* New York: Irwin/McGraw-Hill, 1995.

INTERNATIONAL FINANCE

International finance is the examination of institutions, practices, and analysis of cash flows that move from one country to another. There are several prominent distinctions between international finance and its purely domestic counterpart, but the most important one is exchange rate **risk**. Exchange rate risk refers to the uncertainty injected into any international financial decision that results from changes in the price of one country's currency per unit of another country's currency. Examples of other distinctions include the environment for direct **foreign investment**, new risks resulting from changes in the political environment, and differential taxation of assets and **income**.

The level of international trade is a relevant indicator of economic growth worldwide. **Foreign exchange** markets facilitate this trade by providing a resource where currencies from all nations can be bought and sold. While there is a heavy volume of foreign exchange between some countries, such as the United States and Canada, other countries with little international trade may have only intermittent need for such transactions. Current exchange rates of one country's currency versus another are determined by supply and demand for these currencies. As an example of an exchange rate, consider a recent rate at which U.S. dollars (US$) could be exchanged for Canadian dollars (C$): US$0.65 per C$1. This implies that a Canadian dollar can be purchased for US$0.65 and conversely, a U.S. dollar can be purchased for C$1.54 (or 1/0.65). These current rates are also called spot rates.

In addition to international trade, there is a second motivation for international financial activity. Many firms make long-term investments in productive assets in foreign countries. When a firm decides to build a factory in a foreign country, it has likely considered a variety of issues. For example: Where should the funds needed to build the factory be raised? What kinds of **tax** agreements exist between the home and foreign countries that may influence the after-tax profitability of the new venture? Are there any government-imposed restrictions on moving profits back to the home country? Do the forecasted cash flows of the new venture enhance the parent firm's exposure to exchange rate fluctuations or does it lessen this exposure? Are the economic and political systems in the foreign country stable?

The short-term motive for foreign exchange (trade) and the long-term motive (capital formation) are related. For example, for most of the 1980s Japan maintained a sizable **balance of trade** surplus with the United States. This is because Japan exports more to the United States than they import from the United States, resulting in a **flow of funds** from the United States to Japan. This was also a period, however, when Japan provided considerable capital investments in automobile plants and other U.S. **securities**. These investment funds from Japan far outweighed the flow of investment funds moving from the United States to Japan. While some motivation for Japan's large investment in U.S. assets is strategic, the overall result is an inflow of investment funds from Japan that offsets the outflow created by the trade imbalance.

By the late 1990s the Japanese economy was in a deep recession. This made the trade imbalance even more extreme as demand for U.S. exports declined precipitously. The lack of appealing domestic investment alternatives in Japan, however, encouraged Japanese investors to pursue international options. Again, the flow of investment funds tends to offset the trade imbalance. While the two motives for foreign exchange do not always offset, they typically do for major trading partners over longer periods.

THE NATURE OF EXCHANGE RATES AND EXCHANGE RATE RISK

Consider two developed countries, A and B. If A and B are trading partners and make investments in each other's country, then there must also be a well-developed market for exchange of the two currencies. From A's perspective, demand for B's currency will depend on the cost of B's products when compared with domestic substitutes. It will also depend on investment opportunities in B compared with those available domestically in A. Likewise, the supply of B's currency depends on the same issues when examined from B's perspective.

Ignoring everything else, A will demand more of B's currency if it can buy it more cheaply. For example, if the exchange rate moves from 2 B per 1 A to 3 B per 1 A, imports from B become cheaper since it costs A's residents fewer units of their own currency to buy them. Conversely, if the exchange rate moves to 1.5 B per 1 A, the cost of imports has risen and demand for B's currency will fall. The supply of B's currency will change for the same reasons, but the change will be in the opposite direction. If B's citizens can trade the same number of their own currency units for fewer units of A's currency, they will offer less currency for exchange. At some exchange rate, the supply of B's currency will exactly satisfy the demand and an equilibrium, or market-clearing rate, will be established.

This market-clearing exchange rate does not stay in one place. This is because of a variety of events including: (1) changes in the relative **inflation** rates of the two countries, (2) changes in the relative rates of return on investments in the two countries, and (3) government intervention. Examples of government intervention include quotas on imports or restrictions on foreign exchange. As a brief example of how the market-clearing exchange rate can move, suppose that the current equilibrium exchange rate is 2 B per 1 A. Next, consider new information that indicates investors can achieve a higher rate of return on investments in B while returns on investments available domestically in A remain the same. As investors in A realize this, they have greater interest in making investments in B. This increases the demand for B's currency and means that investors in A are now willing to pay more for a unit of B's currency. B's investors, however, now see that investment prospects in A have deteriorated in relative terms. They are less interested in making these investments and will supply fewer units of B's currency in exchange for A's currency. The dual influences of A's investors becoming more eager to buy B's currency and the increased reluctance of B's investors to offer their currency indicates that the market clearing exchange rate must be different than the prior rate of 2 B per 1 A. In this example, to reach equilibrium, the rate should move to a point where 1 unit of A's currency can be exchanged for less than 2 units of B's currency. This movement can be interpreted as a weakening of A's currency and a strengthening of B's currency.

Specific movements in the market-clearing exchange rate can be modeled by a several economic equalities called parity conditions. Three specific parity conditions are commonly used to model exchange rate equilibrium. Purchasing power parity indicates that currencies experiencing high inflation are likely to weaken while those experiencing low inflation are likely to strengthen. The international Fisher effect indicates that currencies with high **interest rates** will tend to strengthen while currencies with low levels of interest will weaken. A third parity condition, interest rate parity, indicates that exchange rates must move to a level where investors in either country cannot make a riskless profit by borrowing or lending a foreign currency.

EXAMPLES OF EXCHANGE RATE RISK

Since forecasts of future inflation rates, interest rates, and government actions are uncertain, exchange rates are also uncertain. This means that an investment that will pay its return in units of a foreign currency has an uncertain return in the home currency. For example, suppose an investor in A bought a security B for 100 B. This one-year investment has a guaranteed return of 10 B, or 10 percent. If the exchange rate remains at a constant 2 B per 1 A over the life of the investment, the investor must initially commit 50 A to exchange for 100 B to make the investment. After one year, the 110 B returned (including the 10 B in interest) is exchanged for 55 A. The profit of 5 A on an investment of 50 A represents a 10 percent return to the investor from A. If, however, the exchange rate moved to 1.8 B per 1 A during the year, the investor would now receive the same 110 B from the investment, but when converted to the home currency, 61.1 A is received. This represents a profit of 11.1 A on an investment of 50 A, or 22.2 percent. Note that the return is amplified because B's currency strengthened during the holding period. Likewise, if the exchange rate moved to 2.2 B per 1 A, the return of 110 B translates to 50 A and a rate of return of 0 percent.

As another example, suppose an importer in country A purchases a quantity of goods from an exporter in country B and agrees to pay 1,000 B in 90 days. The importer is now obligated to make a foreign exchange transaction and must purchase the units of B's currency at the exchange rate that prevails in 90 days. Since that rate is likely to be different from the current rate, the importer is exposed to exchange rate risk. One common method for reducing this exposure is to enter into a forward **contract** to buy B's currency. A forward contract is an agreement to trade currencies at a specified date in the future at an exchange rate determined today. By purchasing the needed currency through a forward contract, the importer can eliminate concern with exchange-rate volatility by locking in a specific rate today.

TYPES OF EXPOSURE TO EXCHANGE RATE RISK

Exposure to exchange rate fluctuations can be placed into three categories: translation, transaction, and economic. Translation exposure refers to the changes in **accounting** profits that result from reporting requirements. Transaction exposure is created when the firm enters into agreements that will require specific foreign exchange transactions during the current period. The example of the importer in the previous paragraph would be classified as transaction exposure. Economic exposure is the need for foreign exchange transactions and exposure to exchange rate fluctuations that results from future business activities.

If a firm can measure its transaction exposure, it has the option to reduce or eliminate this risk by netting payments and receivables among foreign **subsidiaries** and other trading partners. Any exposures that cannot be eliminated by netting can be hedged by taking various positions in foreign currency forward or **futures contracts**. Suppose the importer used in a previous example had agreed to make payments in several different foreign currencies during the upcoming 90-day period. An initial measure of transaction exposure could be obtained by computing the value of each of the obligations using the spot exchange rate for each currency. The sum of these values, measured in the home currency, would provide a gross measure of transaction exposure. This measure, however, may overstate the true level of exposure if the importer also has receivables in these same currencies. Since foreign currency receivables offset payment obligations in the same currency, the more relevant measure of exposure is the net of payables less receivables.

Once a firm has properly measured its transaction exposure to exchange rate fluctuations, it can opt to reduce the risk by engaging in a practice called **hedging**. Hedging is a technique of eliminating or limiting losses due to unfavorable movements in exchange rates. For example, a U.S. importer with a large payment denominated in Canadian dollars due in 90 days may enter into a forward contract to purchase that currency when needed. A forward contract is an agreement to exchange currencies at a specific date in the future for a specific exchange rate determined at the time the agreement is made. Although the spot rate 90 days later may be materially different from the forward rate specified in the contract, both parties now know exactly what the other currency units will cost. In this way exchange rate risk can be effectively neutralized. Other financial instruments such as futures contracts and **options** can also be used to reduce transaction exposure. Foreign currency futures contracts are similar to forward contracts but are more standardized and, as a result, can be purchased or sold very quickly. This means that futures contracts can be used when transaction exposure is likely to change. For example, if a firm agrees to purchase two million Canadian dollars using a futures contract and subsequently finds out that they will only need one million, they can quickly sell some of the contracts and reduce their protective hedge to the proper level. Forward contracts do not offer that flexibility. Foreign currency options can also be used to build a cap on the potential cost of an upcoming foreign currency purchase or a floor under the value of revenue from an upcoming foreign payment.

Economic exposure to exchange rate fluctuations is often more difficult to manage. The Japanese automobile manufacturer Toyota provides a prominent example of this exposure and its management. This company developed a very sizable market in the United States by initially producing an inexpensive, fuel-efficient vehicle. As time passed, Toyota developed a broader line of products to expand its share of the U.S. automobile market. Beginning in the early 1980s, however, the yen began to appreciate relative to the dollar. Even with constant dollar sales in the U.S. market, Toyota's revenues began to drop significantly when converted back to yen. Since the majority of their production costs were already yen denominated, this hurt their profitability. Toyota was reluctant to raise the dollar price of their products because they feared that they would lose market share. The firm had significant economic exposure because a large proportion of its revenues were denominated in dollars while most of its costs were denominated in yen. Toyota responded to this problem by building manufacturing facilities in the United States. This generated dollar-denominated production costs that could be used to offset dollar revenues. The result was a reduced need for foreign exchange and more stable corporate earnings in Toyota's home country of Japan.

Note that economic exposure results from having revenue and cost streams that have different sensitivities to exchange rate changes. This is very different from measuring the need for foreign exchange transactions during an upcoming period and hedging the cost. Economic exposure to exchange rate fluctuations cannot be hedged with simple financial instruments. It must be managed more dynamically and requires actions such as relocating production facilities, borrowing in foreign countries, and developing product markets in a more diverse set of countries.

COUNTRY RISK

Layered on top of the other sources of risk that make international business decisions unique from a financial perspective are the concerns with country risk. Country risk can be divided into two parts, economic risk and political risk. Economic risk refers to the stability of a country's economy. It embodies concerns such as dependence on individual industries or markets, the ability to sustain a vibrant level of activity and to grow, and the supply of natural resources and other important inputs. Political risk is more concerned with the stability of the government that manages the economy. It encompasses concerns such as the ability to move capital in and out of the country, the likelihood of a smooth transfer of power after elections, and the government's overall attitude toward foreign firms. Obviously, these two branches of country risk overlap significantly. There are a variety of services that provide in-depth assessments of country risk for virtually every country; multinational firms make considerable use of these services to form their own decisions regarding international projects.

In summary, the basic objective of international finance is no different than that of its purely domestic counterpart. The firm should attempt to identify profitable business opportunities that will provide benefit to the owners of the corporation. When these opportunities traverse an international border, a variety of new complexities arise in the financial analysis. Many of the new concerns with this analysis stem from the risk that is introduced by the need for foreign exchange transactions in an environment of fluctuating exchange rates. Once these risks are identified, steps can be taken to address them. Short-term, specific sources of exchange rate risk can often be hedged using standard financial contracts. Longer term exposure to exchange rate risk requires more strategic management. Additional risks arise due to the potential for major shifts in foreign economic or political climates. It is the recognition, assessment, and management of risks such as these that provides the unique character of financial **decision making** in an international context.

SEE ALSO: International Exchange Rate

[Paul Bolster]

FURTHER READING:

Madura, Jeff. *International Financial Management.* 5th ed. Cincinnati: SouthWestern, 1998.

Shapiro, Alan C. *Foundations of Multinational Financial Management.* 3rd ed. Upper Saddle River, NJ: Prentice-Hall, 1998.

Solnik, Bruno H. *International Investing.* 3rd ed. Reading, MA: Addison-Wesley, 1995.

INTERNATIONAL LABOR ORGANIZATION (ILO)

Since its founding in 1919 the International Labor Organization (ILO) has worked to improve the working and living conditions of people worldwide by promoting standards that reduce social injustice in the areas of employment, pay, health, and working conditions. The ILO also believes that workers have the right to freedom of association. Central to the ILO's philosophy is the belief that the promotion and implementation of these standards on a global scale will greatly reduce if not eliminate the injustice and unrest that leads to conflict, social upheaval, and war. Since 1946 the ILO has been a specialized agency of the **United Nations**. In keeping with its global operations the ILO is headquartered in Geneva, Switzerland, and has regional offices in Africa, the Arab states, Asia, the Caribbean, Europe, North America, and Latin America that are responsible for reporting, regional analysis, and policy implementation.

During the 1800s there were numerous but largely unsuccessful efforts to establish an international labor movement in Europe. The short-lived and unaligned endeavors began as early as the 1814-15 Congress of Vienna and continued through the end of the century with international labor conferences in Berlin in 1890, London in 1896, and Zurich and Brussels in 1897. In 1900 the establishment of the International Association for Labor Legislation brought together a loose coalition of government representatives, labor organizations, and private citizens interested in labor affairs. Although it lacked the wherewithal to institute sweeping labor reforms, it had limited success in promoting better working conditions for women in select industries. Headquartered at the University of Basel in Switzerland, the International Association for Labor Legislation served largely as a center for labor research and a clearinghouse for labor information before growing in influence and prestige. By 1912 its conference in Zurich attracted 22 government delegations and private delegates from 24 countries. The outbreak of war in Europe in 1914, however, brought a sudden end to its activities.

After World War I delegates to the Paris Peace Conference were mindful of agitation throughout Europe for an international labor organization. The Paris conference organized a commission headed by Samuel Gompers (1850-1924), then president of the American Federation of Labor, to study the issue. Rather than favoring an organization with legislative authority, the commission proposed an organization administered by representatives of government, labor, and industry that would make recommendations to national governments on issues of labor reform. The ILO was thus created pursuant to the Treaty of Versailles. In many respects the ILO was modeled after the now-defunct International Association for Labor Legislation and was designated soon thereafter as an affiliated agency of the now defunct League of Nations.

From its inception to the end of World War II, the ILO was involved in numerous legislative and research projects related to labor reform. During the 1930s it dealt with problems arising from the worldwide economic depression and subsequent unemployment. With the end of World War II the ILO became the first specialized agency of the United Nations after overcoming initial objections from the United States and the Soviet Union. Under an agreement with the United Nations, the ILO—although affiliated with that body—retained policy-making and budgetary autonomy. In 1997 174 member countries were represented in the ILO by their respective workers, employers, and governments.

The ILO sets forth its labor standards in its ''conventions.'' There are seven core conventions that go to the heart of the ILO's philosophy of an economically and socially stabilized world through the promotion of human rights in the workplace, employment and job creation, and fair trade among nations. These seven core conventions are: the Forced Labor Convention, which, excepting for compulsory military service and humane convict labor, denies forced compulsory labor in all of its forms; the Freedom of Association and the Right to Organize Convention, which protects the rights of workers to organize and form beneficial labor associations without prior authorization; the Right to Organize and Collective Bargaining Convention, which recognizes the right of labor to engage in the collective bargaining process; the Equal Remuneration Convention, which calls for equal pay for men and women for equal work; the Abolition of Forced Labor Convention, which prohibits forced or compulsory labor for political or educational purposes or for punishment for political reasons or for participation in a strike; the Discrimination Convention, which seeks national policies to prevent discrimination in the workplace; and the Minimum Age Convention, which seeks to abolish **child labor**, defined as an age not less than the final age of compulsory schooling.

ILO policy is set by its executive council which meets three times a year at the Geneva headquarters. The council is composed of 28 government members, 14 employers' members, and 14 workers' members. Ten of these seats go to Brazil, the People's Republic of China, France, Germany, India, Italy, Japan, Russia, the United Kingdom, and the United States, all members regarded as ''states of chief industrial importance.'' The remaining 18 seats are elected from other member countries every three years. The International Labour Office in Geneva is regarded as the ILO's secretariat, headquarters, and publishing house. The ILO is staffed by about 1,700 employees with regional, area, and branch offices in 40 countries. ILO's budget for the two years 1998 and 1999 is a projected $481 million.

The ILO maintains relations with such international economic institutions as the **International Monetary Fund**, the **World Bank**, and the **World Trade Organization** in an effort to keep current with labor-related issues and world trade. In a 1997 interview published in *HR Magazine,* Anthony Freeman, director of the Washington office of the ILO, said that world trade has greatly increased with the fall of international communism and the move of many Eastern European countries toward a free market economy. As a result the ILO has found itself preoccupied with establishing international labor standards for this new and emerging world economy based on global trade. To meet these new needs and demands the ILO has restructured many of its operations in order to offer better service to clients, members, and developing economies. Part of this restructuring is strategically located multidisciplinary teams consisting of a standards person and an education or labor market specialist. In cooperation with members representing the private sector, the ILO has launched debates, examinations, and annual studies dealing with issues related to employment creation on a global scale. Concurrent is an effort to move worker members away from a protectionist philosophy and toward a way of thinking that parallels the trade liberalization. Freeman also urges employers to offer up-to-date technical training to their employees in an effort to make them more employable and more productive.

[Michael Knes]

FURTHER READING:

Ekstrom Library. ''International Labor Organization (ILO).'' Louisville, KY: University of Louisville, 1997. Available from www.louisville.edu/library/ekstrom/govpubs/subjects/labor/.

International Labor Organization. ''International Labor Organization.'' Geneva: International Labor Organization, 1998. Available from www.ilo.org.

——. ''International Labor Organization.'' Washington: International Labor Organization, 1998. Available from us.ilo.org/aboutilo/index.html.

Leonard, Bill. ''An Interview with Anthony Freeman of the ILO.'' *HR Magazine,* August 1997, 104-9.

Morse, David A. *The Origin and Evolution of the ILO and Its Role in the World Community.* Ithaca, NY: New York State School of Industrial and Labor Relations, Cornell University, 1969.

INTERNATIONAL LAW

International law is often defined as the body of rules and norms that regulate activities carried on outside the legal boundaries of states. More particularly, it is the law that applies to three international relationships: (1) relations among nation-states; (2) relations among individuals (including corporations) and foreign nations; and (3) relations among individuals from different nations.

LEGAL RELATIONS AMONG NATION-STATES

Much of the law governing relations among nation-states developed from history, customs, and traditions that found their way into legal precedents. In cases where nations disagreed over their rights and duties toward one another, consensus slowly developed. For example, when a citizen attempted to bring a lawsuit in his home country against a foreign sovereign, the court would typically deny relief on the ground that the foreign sovereign had immunity as a generally recognized custom of international law.

Customary international law, however, could not answer all of the questions and needs of nation-states and their citizens. Agreements between nations were needed to improve alliances in times of war, or to promote international trade and commerce in times of peace. Thus, countries often entered into treaties of ''friendship, commerce, and navigation'' (FCN) with other countries. Such treaties define the reciprocal rights and duties of each nation in furtherance of each nation's self-interest. Most FCN treaties cover issues such as the entry of individuals, goods, ships, and capital into the other nation's territory, acquisition of property, repatriation of funds, and protection of each nation's persons and their property in the treaty-partner's nation.

To further improve alliances, trade, and commerce, countries also enter into conventions—a legally binding agreement between states sponsored by an international organization. Examples of international law conventions include the **United Nations**-sponsored Convention on Contracts for the International Sale of Goods and the Treaty of Rome (which eventually led to the creation of the European Community). Of course, not all conventions are under the auspices of the United Nations (UN), but the UN has sponsored various multilateral agreements among nation-states.

One organization within the United Nations that has fostered the growth of international law is the International Court of Justice (ICJ). The ICJ hears and rules on disputes between nation-states but usually does so only where the respective nations agree that the ICJ has jurisdiction. The ICJ relies on customary international law, treaties, and conventions in making its decisions.

After World War II, when the United Nations was organized, it was envisioned that a **World Bank** and International Trade Organization (ITO) would also be established. The World Bank came into being as an international lending and development agency to which industrialized nations make contributions for the ostensible purpose of promoting development globally. But in 1948 the U.S. Congress had serious reservations about the wisdom of surrendering any of its sovereignty or discretion over trade matters to an international organization. Under powers delegated to the president in the Reciprocal Trade Agreements Act of 1934, the United States joined in the **General Agreement on Tariffs and Trade** (GATT), which had been drafted in 1947 in Geneva. The basic purpose of GATT was to move the nations of the world toward lower trade barriers (**free trade**).

Under GATT, member nations were obligated to give ''**most-favored nation**'' treatment to all goods originating in member countries. That is, trade concessions to one member nation would automatically be extended to all others. A series of ''negotiating rounds'' since 1947 progressively lowered tariff barriers among GATT signatory nations. In the most recently concluded Uruguay Round of GATT, both tariff and nontariff barriers were further reduced. Moreover, the original vision of a global trade organization such as the ITO has been at least partially realized in the agreement to replace GATT with a **World Trade Organization** (WTO). The WTO incorporates GATT rules, but has considerably more power to set and enforce standards than the previous GATT secretariat in Geneva.

The institutionalization of free trade principles has also been furthered by regional free trade arrangements, such as the **European Union** and the **North American Free Trade Agreement** (NAFTA). Nations who belong to either group are also members of the WTO, whose provisions allow that concessions given to other members of a regional trading block do not have to be given to other WTO-member nations. The People's Republic of China, which had not participated in the trade liberalization process of GATT, seems eager to join the WTO, to which 134 nation-states were members as of 1999.

As of 1999, a strong sentiment existed in the U.S. business community to support the admission of China to the WTO in order to open up the Chinese market by lowering or removing tariff and nontariff barriers. China's membership in the WTO would bind it to the dispute resolution process seen in cases such as the U.S.-European Union ''banana dispute'' or the U.S.-European ''beef hormone'' dispute.

Under the WTO's dispute resolution procedures, a member-state believing that free trade has been undermined or blocked by another state or group of states can seek to have such barriers (be they tariff or nontariff barriers) declared a violation of WTO principles. If the WTO's Dispute Settlement Body (DSB) agrees with the complaining state, it can authorize retaliatory measures (tariffs, typically) to equal the cost of the trade barriers wrongly imposed.

To illustrate, the United States complained that the European Union (EU) was giving preferential treatment to the importation of bananas from its member-states former colonies in the Caribbean. U.S.-based banana merchants, such as Chiquita and Dole, grew bananas primarily in Central America rather than the Caribbean, and persuaded the executive branch of the U.S. government to ask that the EU abandon its preferential treatment. The DSB ruled that the EU's policies were a violation of its obligations under the treaty, and allowed the United States to impose retaliatory tariffs of up to $191 million. Subsequent to the DSB ruling, Brussels indicated that it would revise its policies, in consultation with Washington and growers in the Caribbean and Latin America, rather than appeal the ruling within the WTO.

The new dispute resolution mechanisms of the WTO have thus met an early test. Nonetheless, in the aftermath of the U.S.-EU trading tensions such as the ''banana dispute,'' there was some concern that the free trade regime is somewhat fragile and cannot withstand frequent and abrasive disputes between major trading partners. Time will tell how well the WTO dispute resolution procedures will settle such turbulent tensions.

LEGAL RELATIONS AMONG INDIVIDUALS AND NATION-STATES

One of the traditional principles of international law is that rights granted under international law are given to nations, not individuals. Violations of international law by nations that affect individuals (or corporations) must be raised, if at all, by a nation on behalf of its citizen.

A ''citizen'' of a country normally includes individuals and corporations. While many corporations doing business globally tend to think of themselves as multinational (having no particular allegiance or duties toward any particular country), the reality is that corporations must often depend on national governments to protect their rights. For example, where patented or trademarked products are counterfeited, the company whose **patent** or trademark has been misused will have to seek the protection of a certain country's laws. If that protection is not forthcoming, the company will often request that its home government (with whom it has the closest or most powerful connections) advocate its interests in treaty or convention negotiations. Protection of **intellectual property**, for example, was one of the principal areas of concern for industrialized nations in the Uruguay Round of GATT.

Similarly, where a corporation chooses to engage in foreign **direct investment** in a foreign country, political uncertainties and legal risk have frequently resulted in a loss of assets through expropriation or nationalization. In such cases, diplomatic efforts of the home country have been enlisted to recover adequate compensation. Or, if a corporation with a large number of employees in the United States experiences a serious competitive threat from products originating in another country, one time-honored strategy has been to seek protective legislation from the home country government.

The free trade movement has at least partially limited the success (or validity) of such efforts, but even GATT allowed exceptions for member nations to impose antidumping duties or countervailing duties where the country of origin has provided unfair **subsidies** for the product, or the product is being sold at below home country cost to establish a foothold in a new foreign market. The WTO rules preserve these exceptions.

Companies seeking to do business outside their home country have encountered many legal difficulties other than tariffs, antidumping duties, or countervailing duties. Technical and nontariff barriers to trade often exist in the export market, barriers such as government procurement rules (requirements that a certain percentage of business must be given to home countries), byzantine licensing and procedural requirements, and restrictions on the mobility of key personnel. Exports may also be limited by political and strategic considerations: since the 1950s, for example, the United States has had various statutes and executive orders establishing export controls for political reasons.

Some of the export control laws include the Export Administration Act of 1969, the International Emergency Economic Powers Act, the Trading with the Enemy Act, and various executive orders under each. When U.S. Embassy personnel were held hostage in Iran, President Jimmy Carter ordered a cessation of all trade with Iran. A number of U.S. companies with **contracts** pending in Iran were adversely affected. When the Soviets invaded Afghanistan in 1980, U.S. companies with subsidiaries abroad were ordered by President Carter to cease doing business on the Soviet oil pipeline that was to serve Europe and bring much-needed hard currency to the Soviets. A French **subsidiary** of the U.S. company, Dresser Industries, had a pending contract with the U.S.S.R. Dresser U.S. was informed by the U.S. government that it must act to prevent its subsidiary from dealing with the Soviets. Dresser, its French subsidiary, and the government of France all resisted the application of U.S. law to a French company, and ultimately their resistance succeeded after the subsidiary was restructured to reduce formal control by Dresser U.S. When President George Bush ordered cessation of all business with Iraq after its invasion of Kuwait, a number of U.S. companies were affected.

These incidents illustrate a principal difficulty of international law: much of it is made by national legislatures and courts, and one nation's laws may reach beyond its own boundaries, or attempt to. When, for example, the U.S. public learned that many U.S. corporations were obtaining and retaining business in foreign countries by means of bribes or kickbacks, the U.S. Congress enacted the **Foreign Corrupt Practices Act** (FCPA). The FCPA criminalized the act of making payments to foreign government officials for the purpose of obtaining or retaining business. A U.S. company found to have made such payments could be prosecuted in the United States for actions taken outside U.S. territory. Thus, the FCPA is an example of "extraterritorial" application of U.S. law.

Under customary international law, the basic principle of sovereign jurisdiction to prescribe and enforce law is territorial. International law also recognizes the nationality principle—the right of a sovereign to make and enforce law with respect to its own citizens (nationals). Not only the FCPA, but also U.S. **antitrust law**, securities law, and employment discrimination law may apply to actions of U.S. companies outside U.S. territory. In the case of U.S. antitrust law, the action alleged to be a violation of the Sherman Act or the Clayton Antitrust Act must have a "direct effect" on the United States for extraterritorial application to be upheld. For employment discrimination cases, a U.S. company must adhere to the provisions of Title VII of the Civil Rights Act of 1964 (as amended) with respect to a U.S. citizen employed by that company overseas.

Conflicts between U.S. law and the law of foreign states has led to certain nations blocking the application of U.S. law by statute. Blocking statutes typically limit the extent to which U.S. plaintiffs can obtain evidence through discovery and make it difficult to enforce a U.S. judgment outside of the United States. For example, French blocking statutes make it extremely difficult for the plaintiff in a U.S. court proceeding to obtain the requisite documents to prove his or her case. Even where Congress clearly intends U.S. law to have extraterritorial application, U.S. courts are reluctant to apply it where doing so would raise a clear conflict or implicate foreign policy concerns in any way.

Where U.S. companies and individuals actually have an adversarial relationship with a foreign nation, either sovereign immunity or the Act of State Doctrine may apply. In the case of a claim in U.S. courts against a foreign sovereign, plaintiffs must show that the case falls within one of the exceptions to sovereign immunity listed in the Foreign Sovereign Immunities Act of 1976 (FSIA). Under the FSIA, which adopts the restrictive theory of sovereign immunity (rather than the absolute theory), governmental activities are generally immune, whereas private or commercial kinds of activities are not. Under the FSIA, a foreign sovereign that engages in a commercial activity that has a direct effect on the United States cannot avail itself of the sovereign immunity defense in U.S. courts. The majority of industrialized nations follow the restrictive theory of sovereign immunity, either by statute or judicial precedent.

In certain cases, deciding a lawsuit in U.S. courts may require that the public act of a foreign sovereign (on its own territory) be declared invalid by the court. In such cases, the Act of State Doctrine may be invoked by the court to avoid coming to a decision on the merits in a way that would discredit the public act of the foreign sovereign. The Supreme Court has declared in numerous cases that it is not constitutionally proper for a U.S. court to decide a case in a way that would invalidate the public act of a foreign sovereign; this, it believes, would infringe upon the proper prerogatives of the executive and legislative branches of U.S. government. For the Act of State Doctrine to apply, it is not necessary that the foreign sovereign be a named defendant; it is only necessary that the court be unable to find for a certain party without questioning the lawfulness of a public act of a foreign sovereign on its own territory.

LEGAL RELATIONS BETWEEN INDIVIDUALS FROM DIFFERENT NATIONS

Quite apart from governing relations among nation-states, or between individuals and nation-states, international law began centuries ago to develop rules for dispute resolution between citizens of different states. When Europe entered the Renaissance period, Roman and Germanic legal systems were not adequate to handle the needs of a growing transnational commercial community. As a result, the guilds and merchant associations began forming their own customs and rules for fair dealing, and soon had their own courts. These rules, sometimes known as *lex mercatoria* (or Merchant Law), became influential and were eventually applied in both church and governmental courts. Many of the *lex mercatoria* concepts can be found today in the United Nations Convention on Contracts for the International Sale of Goods.

One of the common problems that arise in international commercial transactions is determining where the dispute between citizens of different states should be heard. Without a contractual choice of forum, issues of personal jurisdiction often arise. For example, a Japanese company may find itself sued in a U.S. court for a small valve that was incorporated in a wheel by a Taiwanese manufacturer, then incorporated in a motorcycle by a different Japanese company. If the motorcycle is sold in the United States, and the wheel malfunctions, the tire valve manufacturer may find itself in a U.S. court. The U.S. Supreme Court has declared that, in fairness, a company must deliberately target the U.S. market to be held legally accountable in the United States. Mere predictability that its product may wind up in a certain market is insufficient to give the court valid personal jurisdiction over the nonresident company. Of course, if a company goes to another country to do business (either directly or through agents) and is sued there, courts generally will assume personal jurisdiction over the nonresident company.

For disputes between parties to a contract, the parties may have chosen to avoid any questions of personal jurisdiction by specifying the judicial forum where any disputes arising between them will be settled. Courts have typically upheld these "choice of forum" clauses in commercial contracts, as well as clauses that specify which law (e.g., German law, U.S. law, or **Mexican law**) will be applied in resolving the dispute.

International companies may entirely avoid judicial settlement of their dispute by choosing **arbitration**. This can be done prior to any disagreement by including a pre-dispute arbitration clause in the contract, or may be done after a dispute arises. In this way, a more neutral forum is often selected, so that the "home court" advantage does not favor either disputant. Often, the parties will have preselected a set of procedural rules to follow, such as those of the International Chamber of Commerce, or those of United Nations Commission on International Trade Law. The arbitration process is aided by the UN-sponsored United Nations Convention on Recognition and Enforcement of Arbitral Awards (sometimes known as the New York Convention), which has been ratified by most major trading nations. If a Japanese and German firm agree to arbitrate their dispute in Los Angeles, California, for example, either party may proceed under the agreed-upon rules (even without the cooperation of the other party), obtain an arbitral award, and have it enforced in any signatory nation without the need to rehear the facts and issues of the dispute.

SEE ALSO: International Commercial Arbitration

[Chris A. Carr and Donald O. Mayer]

FURTHER READING:

August, Ray. *International Business Law: Text, Cases, and Readings.* Upper Saddle River, NJ: Prentice Hall, 1997.

"The International Practice of Law." In *The International Lawyer's Deskbook,* edited by Lucinda A. Low, Patrick M. Norton, and Daniel M. Drory. Washington: Section of International Law and Practice, American Bar Association, 1996.

Richards, Eric L. *Law for Global Business.* Burr Ridge, IL: Irwin, 1994.

Schaffer, Richard, Beverley Earle, and Filiberto Agusti. *International Business Law and Its Environment.* Cincinnati: West Publishing, 1999.

INTERNATIONAL MANAGEMENT

As trade barriers recede and businesses in developed economies increasingly pursue market opportunities abroad, competency and effectiveness in international management are paramount skills at many companies. The issues involved in international management span the whole gamut of those concerning management in general, but there are several areas of special interest, including:

- international finance and currency matters
- cross-cultural communication and understanding (including **international marketing** implications)
- foreign legal requirements and accounting practices
- **global strategy**
- **international competition**

To ignore such issues in an international business is to open the door to risks like inappropriate (and hence ineffective) marketing approaches, poor **labor-management relations**, adverse currency fluctuations, and other problems. Conversely, companies that are able to successfully manage these issues have greater potential to extend their marketing reach, increase market share, improve efficiency and profitability, decrease costs, and enjoy other competitive advantages.

THE EMERGENCE OF THE GLOBAL ECONOMY

In the 1980s, the world's leading industrialized nations began an era of cooperation in which they capitalized on the benefits of working together to improve their individual economies. They continued to seek individual comparative advantages, i.e., a nation's ability to produce some products more cheaply or better than it can others, but within the confines of international cooperation. In the 1990s these trends continued, and in many cases accelerated. Countries negotiated trade pacts such as the **North American Free Trade Agreement (NAFTA)**, and the **General Agreement on Tariffs and Trade (GATT)**, or formed economic communities such as the **European Union**. These pacts and communities created new marketing opportunities in the respective markets by decreasing trade duties and other barriers to cross-border commerce. They opened the door through which companies of all sizes and in various aspects of business entered the international market. The United States benefited extensively from the expanded global economic activity.

U.S. trade figures from the 1990s illustrate the rapid expansion of cross-border business. In 1992, the United States exported $448 billion worth of goods and services, while importing more than $532 billion worth from other countries. By 1998, exports had more than doubled (in current dollars) to approximately $930 billion, and imports approached $1.1 trillion. Adjusting for inflation, the value of exports grew over the seven-year period by 78 percent, and the value of imports rose by 77 percent.

INTERNATIONAL BUSINESS MODELS

Prospective international managers must first realize there is no single way to enter a foreign market. Businesses must choose the model appropriate to their level of resources, market potential, and experience operating in the international sphere. The various categories of international business models include export/import businesses, independent agents, licensing and franchising agreements, direct investment in established foreign companies, joint ventures, and multinational corporations (MNC). The differences among these options are sometimes subtle in nature.

IMPORT/EXPORT BUSINESSES. For instance, an export firm is one that sells its domestically made products to a very small number of countries. In contrast, import firms import foreign-made goods into the country for domestic use. Often, export and import firms are operated by a small group of people who have close ties with the countries in which they do business. Some such firms may begin as export or import specialists, but eventually expand their operations to production of goods overseas. IBM and Coca-Cola Co. exemplify companies that have used that approach.

INDEPENDENT AGENTS, LICENSES, AND FRANCHISES. Independent agents are businesspeople who contract with foreign residents or businesses to represent the exporting firm's product in another country. Closely related are firms with **licensing agreements**, in which domestic firms grant foreign individuals or companies the right to manufacture and/or market the exporter's product in that country in return for royalties on sales. Another variation is a franchising arrangement, in which the parent company grants a franchise upon payment of a franchise fee by a local business operator, who then agrees to follow a prescribed methodology and marketing plan using the company's name. The local franchisee may have to pay royalties or annual franchise fees, but otherwise remains independent of the franchisor. In each of these models, assuming the partner in the target market is competent, the risks to the originating company are usually low, as it is not setting up operations of its own in the foreign country, but rather relying on independent businesses or individuals that are already there.

JOINT VENTURES. Joint ventures help distribute the risk of entering foreign markets and can provide hands-on experience for a company just initiating its presence in a particular country. Joint ventures can be formed with another domestic company to do business in another country, e.g., two Japanese companies collaborate in a Chinese business venture, or between one company from outside the target market and one from within, e.g., a Mexican firm and a Vietnamese firm create a new venture to do business in Vietnam. Having a local partner, as in the latter example, can be especially beneficial to a company that is relatively unfamiliar with the market it is trying to enter. This sort of arrangement can serve as a validation mechanism to reduce the chance of making foolish mistakes by not knowing local customs, preferences, laws, and so on.

BUYING A STAKE IN A FOREIGN AFFILIATE. Buying part or all of a foreign company is a common form of foreign direct investment and carries with it the advantages of having an experienced partner to help do business in the foreign market. The foreign affiliate may be left to operate as a relatively independent entity, functioning more like a partner, or it may be more tightly integrated into the parent organization as a division or subsidiary.

MULTINATIONAL CORPORATIONS. Multinational firms are relatively new in the business world, yet they are becoming increasingly important. There is no specific definition of a MNC. Nor is it easy to differentiate an MNC from a company that simply has offices or factories in multiple countries. Some experts define an MNC as a company that derives at least 25 percent of its sales from foreign sources. However, that is an arbitrary figure. Others define an MNC by its size. There is general agreement that large, multibillion-dollar enterprises, such as General Electric Company, Mitsubishi Corporation, DaimlerChrysler AG, and so forth, constitute MNCs.

Experts predict that the numbers of MNCs, joint ventures, and other international operations will rise as businesses seek to take advantage of **economies of scale** and the growth of new markets as a way of reducing costs and increasing profits. As the geographic boundaries over which individual companies operate become less defined, the need for people who are able to manage international activities becomes more acute. Thus, international managers are becoming more important in the business world, and their success can directly affect a company seeking to compete in the global market. As a result, business leaders are placing increased emphasis on the development of managers with expertise in international management.

INTERNATIONAL MANAGERS NEED SPECIAL SKILLS

Contemporary international managers will need to demonstrate a higher level of skill than those exhibited by the traditional manager in the past. They must be multilingual, sensitive to cultural differences, and knowledgeable about current global management theory, philosophy, psychology, and their practical applications. Acquiring the skills needed to become a successful international manager is a demanding, albeit necessary, process—especially since the global market will continue to expand for the foreseeable future.

APPROACHES TO INTERNATIONAL MANAGEMENT

There are three approaches to international management: ethnocentric, polycentric, and geocentric. Each has its advantages and disadvantages. None of these theories can be successful, however, unless managers understand completely the nuances involved in their applications.

The ethnocentric approach is one in which management uses the same style and practices that work in their own headquarters or home country. Such an approach may leave managers open to devastating mistakes, because what works in the United States, for example, may not necessarily work in Japan. There are many cases in which companies made grievous errors when they attempted to transfer their management styles to foreign countries. For example, Procter & Gamble Co. lost $25 million in Japan between 1973 and 1986 because its managers would not listen to Japanese advisors. The company ran ads for its Camay soap in which a Japanese man meeting a Japanese woman for the first time compared her skin to that of a porcelain doll. That would never happen in Japan, which is exactly what an **advertising** adviser told Procter & Gamble's managers. Procter & Gamble, however, ignored the advice. They assumed that if a similar ad worked well in the United States and other countries (which it did), it would also be successful in Japan, but it was not. In fact, the ad infuriated the Japanese people, who refused to buy Camay. The Procter & Gamble executives learned a lesson, but at a high cost.

In contrast to ethnocentric management is the polycentric management theory. In this approach, management staffs its **workforce** in foreign countries with as many local people as possible. The theory is simple: local people know best the host country's culture, language, and work ethic. Thus, they are the ideal candidates for management. This approach works well in some countries. However, in countries without well-developed economies, it may not be the best approach because the workers may not always have the necessary business acumen or management skills.

The third style of international management is the geocentric approach. This theory holds that the best individuals, regardless country origin, should be placed in management positions. This philosophy maintains that business problems are the same regardless of where in the world they occur. Therefore, competent managers who are able to apply logic and common sense to resolve them will be successful; specific cultural knowledge is not necessary. This is the most difficult of the three approaches to apply, since managers must be able to understand the local and global ramifications of the business.

The Boeing Corporation provides evidence that the geocentric approach can be successful. When sales of its 737 plane dropped precipitously in the early 1970s, Boeing's senior management asked a group of engineers to bolster sales of the plane. Management indicated that if they were unable to increase sales, production would be discontinued. The engineers seized the opportunity.

Their first step was to examine foreign markets for the aircraft. They recognized that what attracted buyers in the United States may not necessarily lure foreign buyers. So, they visited different countries to determine which characteristics might be useful to incorporate into the redesign of the 737. They found many differences in flight operations. For example, many foreign airports, especially those in developing countries, had shorter runways than those in the United States. Moreover, many were constructed of softer materials than concrete, the standard material used in the United States. As a result of their study, the engineers redesigned the plane's wings to allow for shorter landings on asphalt runways and altered the engines so takeoffs would be quicker. Finally, they designed new landing gears and switched to low-pressure tires. Shortly after they made the changes, 737 sales rose dramatically, and so did sales of Boeing's other models. In fact, the 737 eventually became the largest selling commercial jet in aviation history. The key to the engineers' success lay in their ability to think globally and assess the business environment in different parts of the world.

ASSESSING THE GLOBAL ENVIRONMENT

It is extremely important that managers involved in international business recognize the opportunities available in different countries. They must be prescient enough to recognize potential, as well as immediate opportunities. For example, there are three types of countries with which there are potential business opportunities: developed, less developed, and newly industrialized. Once managers have assessed which group a certain country belongs in, they must then analyze the country's **infrastructure**, too.

Developed countries, such as Canada, Italy, Japan, Germany, the United States, and United Kingdom, are those that have a high level of economic or industrial development. Less developed countries, frequently called third world countries, are relatively poor nations with low per capita income and little industry. Many of these countries, however, have the potential to become lucrative trade partners, so international managers cannot afford to overlook them when analyzing business opportunities. Finally, there are countries labeled as newly industrialized, such as Taiwan, South Korea, and Vietnam. These countries are quickly becoming major exporters of manufactured goods. For example, the Hyundai Corporation has made great inroads into the United States through the sales of its cars. Hyundai's success provides ample evidence that more and more countries are taking their places in the industrialized world—and increasing the need for qualified managers who can oversee the business relations involved. There are also transition economies, primarily in eastern Europe, which have some industrial infrastructure, albeit often outdated, and little experience with market-based economics. The transition economies include those of the former Soviet Union and other ex-communist states in eastern Europe.

WHAT INTERNATIONAL MANAGERS NEED TO KNOW

Managers must be trained in facets of international business that are not normally the concern of domestic managers. On a broad scale, these issues include a knowledge of other countries' infrastructures, business practices, and foreign trade dynamics. In addition, international managers must be knowledgeable about **international exchange rates** and the legal-political and sociocultural traits of other countries.

BRIBERY AND RELATED PRACTICES. For example, there is the issue of ethics in international operations. Managers must know when they are confronted with the subtleties of legal and illegal payments, for instance. In some countries, bribes in the form of money or valuables given to influential people are common. So is extortion, or payments made to protect a business against some threatened action, such as the cancellation of a franchise. In such cases, international managers may be torn between U.S. law and foreign culture. However, there is an American law that provides guidance in such cases.

The U.S. Foreign Corrupt Practices Act prohibits most types of questionable payments involving American companies operating in other countries. The law in itself, however, does not make the international manager's job any easier when U.S. legislation and foreign cultures clash. Therefore, international managers are often faced with ethical dilemmas not common to their domestic counterparts. The solutions to these dilemmas can have a major impact on companies' operations and individual managers' careers—which is just one of the disadvantages of an international manager's job.

POLITICAL CLIMATE. Politics are also an important aspect of the international manager's job. International managers must be able to assess political risks inherent in particular countries. Developed countries tend to be relatively stable from a political and an economic standpoint, while less developed countries may be more susceptible to political strife. Governments may come and go or may decide to nationalize companies. Such was the case in the 1960s when Chile's President Eduardo Frei "Chileanized" the country's copper mines. Many American companies lost their holdings, although they were compensated for their losses. International managers must also be prepared for similar events, such as expropriation.

Expropriation is not unheard of for American industries. For example, Iran seized an estimated $5 billion worth of American companies' holdings in 1979. The companies involved included Xerox Corp., R.J. Reynolds, and United Technologies. Events such as this mandate that international managers learn about the legal-political element of foreign business affairs. Their knowledge in this area must also include such things as tariffs, import quotas, and administrative protections (a type of **trade barriers** in the form of various rules and regulations that make it more difficult for foreign firms to conduct business in a particular country).

CULTURAL SENSITIVITY. Equally important to the international manager are sociocultural elements. These include the attitudes, values, norms, beliefs, behaviors, and demographic trends of the host country. Learning these things frequently requires a good deal of self-awareness in order to recognize and control culturally specific behaviors in one's self and in others. International managers must know how to relate to and motivate foreign workers, since motivational techniques differ among countries. They must also understand how work roles and attitudes differ. For instance, the boundaries and responsibilities of occupations sometimes have subtle differences across cultures, even if they have equivalent names and educational requirements. Managers must be attuned to such cultural nuances in order to function effectively. Moreover, managers must keep perspective on cultural differences once they are identified and not subscribe to the fallacy that all people in a foreign culture think and act alike.

The Dutch social scientist Geert Hofstede divided sociocultural elements into four categories: (1) power distance, (2) uncertainty avoidance, (3) individualism-collectivism, and (4) masculinity-femininity. International managers must understand all four elements in order to succeed.

Power distance is a cultural dimension that involves the degree to which individuals in a society accept differences in the distribution of power as reasonable and normal. Uncertainty avoidance involves the extent to which members of a society feel uncomfortable with and try to avoid situations that they see as unstructured, unclear, or unpredictable. Individualism-collectivism involves the degree to which individuals concern themselves with their own interests and those of their immediate families as opposed to the interests of a larger group. Finally, masculinity-femininity is the extent to which a society emphasizes traditional male values, e.g., assertiveness, competitiveness, and material success, rather than traditional female values, such as passivity, cooperation, and feelings. All of these dimensions can have a significant impact on a manager's success in an international business environment.

The inability to understand the concepts Hofstede outlined can hinder managers' capacity to manage—and their companies' chances of surviving in the international arena.

INTERNATIONAL MANAGEMENT STRATEGY

Equally important is the manager's ability to choose the right strategy and organization applicable to individual companies operating in the international business arena. There are four strategies involved in international management. They include globalization, rationalization, national responsiveness, and the multifocal approach. Whether or not these strategies are implemented depends on a company's size and the number of countries in which it operates. For example, a small export company is not likely to employ a rationalization program. On the other hand, an MNC might utilize all four strategies.

Globalization involves the development of relatively standardized products with worldwide appeal. Rationalization is the process of assigning activities to those parts of the organization best suited to produce specific goods or desired results, regardless of where they are located. National responsiveness allows subsidiaries latitude in adapting products and services to conform to the special needs and political realities of the countries in which they operate. Finally, the multifocal approach tries to achieve the advantages of globalization while attempting to be responsive to important national needs. Competent international managers must be able to analyze the business and political environments endemic to the countries in which they are operating and adapt the strategies, either individually or in combination, that best suit their needs.

INTERNATIONAL ORGANIZATION

Companies operating internationally tend to use the same types of organization they do domestically. They may operate functionally (by task), geographically (by country or region), or by product. Or, they may combine organizational strategies. Again, international managers will make those determinations based on their companies' products or services. Regardless of organizational strategy, international managers must pay particular attention to human resources issues, since there are vast cultural differences among citizens of different countries.

THE INTERNATIONAL MANAGER AND HUMAN RESOURCES

One of the most critical factors in the success of a company's international success is its hiring program. Generally, hiring production workers is not a major problem, companies recruit locals to perform the daily work. In all likelihood, first-level supervisors and possibly some of the middle managers will also be members of the local community. Hiring upper-level management, however, is another matter—one that must be handled with care and sensitivity.

International companies have several primary approaches to recruiting and assigning upper-level managers. For example, they can rely strictly on local residents or use expatriates (individuals who are not citizens of the countries in which they are assigned to work). If they assign expatriates to foreign operations, they must make sure those individuals relate well to the local population. Relying strictly on employees' technical skills, to the detriment of interpersonal skills and sensitivity, can harm a company's reputation and destroy its operation in the process.

Another hiring tactic is to assign people to key managerial positions without regard to their native countries. For instance, they might place a foreign resident who was educated in the United States in a management position simply because that individual is best qualified for the job. Whichever options they choose, companies must be sensitive to local customs and cultures, lest they risk alienating the local community and inhibiting cooperation and productivity.

The bottom line is that international managers must be more cognizant of the differences in local social customs and work ethics than are their domestic counterparts. This is simply one more indication that companies involved in international operations must pay strict attention to the quality of the managers they assign to their overseas facilities. As the global economy expands, it is going to become even more critical that international managers be trained specifically for the special nuances involved in worldwide business activities.

HOW AMERICAN COMPANIES TRAIN INTERNATIONAL MANAGERS

Many U.S. companies sponsor special preparation programs for international managers. For example, IBM conducts internal executive development programs at its management development centers in

Australia, Singapore, Japan, and Belgium. The company operates a six-week training program that includes a wide variety of international topics. Some companies use cultural assimilators, programmed learning approaches that expose members of one culture to some of the basic concepts, attitudes, customs, and values of another. There are also many resources within the United States, including business schools offering graduate degrees in international management. In addition to conventional university business school programs, a well-known specialty school in this area is the American Graduate School of International Management, also known as Thunderbird, in Glendale, Arizona. Whatever approach individual companies use to prepare managers for overseas assignments, one thing is essential: the amount and intensity of training is proportionately related to the manager's success—and the company's.

THE FUTURE OF INTERNATIONAL MANAGEMENT

Individuals searching for careers in the field of international management will find numerous opportunities available to them. The field is becoming a specialty of its own. Virtually every management textbook being used in business curricula today has at least one chapter devoted entirely to international management. Colleges and universities are offering degrees ranging from associates to Ph.D.s in the field. As more and more companies enter the international business arena, the number of management opportunities will grow.

SEE ALSO: International Marketing; Global Strategy

[Arthur G. Sharp]

FURTHER READING:

Deresky, Helen. *International Management: Managing Across Cultures.* 2nd ed. Reading, MA: Addison-Wesley, 1997.

Earley, P. Christopher, and Miriam Erez. *The Transplanted Executive.* New York: Oxford University Press, 1997.

Griffen, Ricky W., and Michael W. Pustay. *International Business: A Managerial Perspective.* Reading, MA: Addison-Wesley, 1996.

Hodgetts, Richard M., and Fred Luthans. *International Management.* 2nd ed. New York: McGraw-Hill, 1994.

Rhinesmith, Stephen H. *A Manager's Guide to Globalization.* Chicago: Irwin Professional Publishing, 1996.

Schneider, Susan, and Jean-Louis Barsoux. *Managing Across Cultures.* New York: Prentice Hall, 1997.

INTERNATIONAL MARKETING

International **marketing** occurs when a business directs its products and services toward consumers in more than one country. While the overall concept of marketing is the same worldwide, the environment within which the marketing plan is implemented can be drastically different. Common marketing concerns—such as input costs, price, advertising, and distribution—are likely to differ dramatically in the countries in which a firm elects to market. Furthermore, many elements outside the control of managers, both at home and abroad, are likely to have a large impact on business decisions. The key to successful international marketing is the ability to adapt, manage, and coordinate a marketing plan in an unfamiliar and often unstable foreign environment.

Businesses choose to explore foreign markets for a host of sound reasons. Commonly, firms initially explore foreign markets in response to unsolicited orders from consumers in those markets. In the absence of these orders, companies often begin to export to: establish a business that will absorb overhead costs at home; seek new markets when the domestic market is saturated; and to make quick profits. Marketing abroad can also spread corporate risk and minimize the impact of undesirable domestic situations, such as **recessions**.

While companies choosing to market internationally do not share an overall profile, they seem to have two specific characteristics in common. First, the products that they market abroad, usually patented, have high earnings potential in foreign markets; in other words, the international sale of these products should eventually generate a substantial percentage of the products' total revenue. Also, these products usually have a price or cost advantage over similar products or have some other attribute making them novel and more desirable to end users abroad. Second, the management of companies marketing internationally must be ready to make a commitment to these markets. They must be willing to educate themselves thoroughly on the particular countries they choose to enter and must understand the potential benefits and risks of a decision to market abroad.

MODERN U.S. HISTORY OF INTERNATIONAL MARKETING

Marketing abroad is not a recent phenomenon. In fact, well-established trade routes existed three or four thousand years before the birth of Christ. Modern international marketing, however, can arguably be traced to the 1920s, when liberal international trading was halted by worldwide isolationism and increased barriers to trade. The United States furthered this trend by passing the Smoot-Hawley Tariff Act of 1930, raising the average U.S. tariff on imported goods from 33 to 53 cents. Other countries throughout the world imposed similar tariffs in response to the United States' actions, and by 1932 the volume of world trade fell by more than 40 percent. These protectionist activities continued throughout the 1930s, and the Great Depression, to which many say protectionism substantially contributed, was deeper and more widespread than any other depression in modern history. Furthermore, according to the **United Nations**, this protectionism undermined the standard of living of people all over the world and set the stage for the extreme military buildup that led to World War II.

One result of the Great Depression and World War II was strengthened political will to end protectionist policies and to limit government interference in international trade. Thus, by 1944 representative countries attending the Bretton Woods Conference established the basic organizational setting for the post-war economy, designed to further **macroeconomic** stability. Specifically, the framework that arose created three organizations: the International Trade Organization (ITO), the **World Bank**, and the **International Monetary Fund (IMF)**.

Although negotiations undertaken for the ITO proved unsuccessful, the United States proposed that the commercial policy provisions that were originally be included in the ITO agreements should be temporarily incorporated into the **General Agreement on Tariffs and Trade (GATT)**. In 1947, 23 countries agreed to a set of tariff reductions codified in GATT. Although GATT was at first intended as a temporary measure, because ITO was never ratified, it became the main instrument for international trade regulation. GATT was succeeded by the **World Trade Organization (WTO)**, which was established in January 1995 after GATT officially ended in April 1994. The WTO's main function has been to resolve trade disputes, and it developed procedures for handling trade disputes that were much improved over the GATT procedures. In its first 18 months the WTO settled more than 50 trade disputes.

In the 1960s and 1970s, world trading patterns began to change. While the United States remained a dominant player in international trade, other less developed countries began to manufacture their own products. Furthermore, the United States became more reliant than ever on imported goods. For example, by 1982 one in four cars sold in the United States was foreign-made and more than 40 percent of electronic products were produced or assembled abroad. To make matters worse, the United States consistently imported a sizable portion of its fuel needs from other countries. All of these elements created a U.S. dependency on world trade.

As free market policies continued to be the dominant political force concerning trade around the world, a host of new markets opened. Specifically, in the late 1980s, Central and Eastern European markets opened with the dissolution of the Soviet Union. By the 1990s, world trade began with China, as well as with countries in South America and the Middle East—new markets that looked quite promising. In spite of the changes in the world trade arena, the United States, Japan, and Europe continued to play a dominant role, accounting for 85 percent of the world's trade.

Interestingly, while the trend of opening new world markets continued, there was another trend toward regional trade agreements. These agreements typically gave preferential trade status to nations that assented to the terms of a pact over those nations that did not participate. Two examples are the creation of a unified European Market and the ratification of the **North American Free Trade Agreement (NAFTA)**. Created in 1958, and renamed most recently in 1993, the **European Union (EU)** is a regional organization designed to gradually eliminate customs duties and other types of trade barriers between members. Imposing a common external tariff against nonmember countries, EU countries slowly adopted measures that would unify and, theoretically, strengthen member economies. Member nations include Belgium, France, Germany, Great Britain, Italy, Luxembourg, the Netherlands, Denmark, Ireland, Greece, Spain, and Portugal.

Comprised of Canada, the United States, and Mexico, NAFTA was passed by the U.S. House and Senate in November 1994. In total, 360 million consumers are subject to the agreement, with spending power of about $6 trillion. Therefore, NAFTA is 20 percent larger than the EU.

With non-European multinational corporations facing tariff barriers put up by the EU, the most attractive international markets were those emerging in the developing countries of Asia, Russia, and Latin America. According to Christopher Miller, professor of international marketing at the Thunderbird Graduate School of International Management, "There's nowhere else to go. With the advent of the EU, it's harder and harder for non-European companies to get into Europe. Anyone within the boundaries has no tariffs, and those outside it have more barriers." In emerging markets, companies could expect to achieve 30 to 40 percent growth rates, according to Miller.

DEVELOPING FOREIGN MARKETS

There are four general ways to develop markets on foreign soil. They are: exporting products and services from the country of origin; entering into joint venture arrangements with one or more foreign companies; licensing patent rights, trademark rights, etc. to companies abroad; and establishing manufacturing plants in foreign countries. A company can commit itself to one or more of the above arrangements at any time during its efforts to develop foreign markets. Each method has distinct advantages and disadvantages and, thus, no single method is best in all instances.

Companies taking their first steps internationally often begin by exporting products manufactured domestically. Since the risks of financial losses can be minimized, exporting is the easiest and most frequently used method of entering international markets. Achieving export sales can be accomplished in numerous ways. Sales can be made directly, via mail order, or through offices established abroad. Companies can also undertake indirect exporting, which involves selling to domestic intermediaries who locate specific markets for the firm's products or services. While having numerous benefits, exporting can place constraints on marketing strategies. The exporter often knows little about typical consumer-use patterns or, if using an intermediary, may have little influence over product pricing.

International licensing occurs when a country grants the right to manufacture and distribute a product or service under the licenser's trade name in a specified country or market. Common examples are granting foreign firms rights to technology, trademarks, and patents. Although large companies often grant licenses, this practice is most frequently used by small and medium-sized companies. Often seen as a supplement to manufacturing and exporting activities, licensing may be the least profitable way of entering a market. It can be advantageous, however, because it allows domestic firms to avoid certain obstacles. To illustrate, companies can use licenses when their own money is scarce, when foreign import restrictions forbid other ways of entering a market, or when a host country is apprehensive about foreign ownership.

Two particular types of licensing are franchising and management contracts. Similar to franchising domestically, world franchising occurs most often in fast foods, soft drinks, hotels, and car rentals. The major benefit of this type of license is the ability to standardize foreign operations with minimal investment. A second type of licensing arrangement is referred to as a management contract, often resulting from external pressures from a host government. This contract can occur when the host government nationalizes strategic industries for political or economic purposes. Rather than banish the company completely, the country hires the foreign owner to manage the firm and to give technical and managerial knowledge to the local population.

A third way to enter a foreign market is through a joint venture arrangement, whereby a company trying to enter a foreign market forms a partnership with one or more companies already established in the host country. Often, the local firm provides expertise on the intended market, while the multinational firm is better able to accomplish general management and marketing tasks. Use of this method of international investing has accelerated dramatically in the past 20 years. The biggest incentive to entering this type of arrangement is that it reduces the company's risk by the amount of investment made by the host-country partner. Other potential advantages to a joint venture arrangement are that: (1) it may allow firms with insufficient capital to expand internationally; (2) it may allow the marketer to use the partner's preexisting distribution channels; and (3) it may let the marketer take advantage of special skills possessed by the host country partner. While this method of market entry often results in the loss of total control over business operations, it is the only method of foreign investment that some host governments (especially less developed countries) will allow.

A company can also expand abroad by setting up manufacturing operations in a foreign country. This method is optimal when the foreign demand for a product justifies the costly investment required. Other benefits to manufacturing abroad can be the avoidance of high import taxes, the reduction of transportation costs, the use of cheap labor, and better access to raw materials. When a company chooses to manufacture abroad, the markets of the host country are serviced by that particular manufacturing facility. Moreover, often products from the same facility are sent to other countries—even back to the original home country—for distribution.

INCREASED UNCERTAINTIES ASSOCIATED WITH MARKETING ABROAD

Although firms marketing abroad face many of the same challenges as firms marketing domestically, international environments present added uncertainties which must be accurately interpreted. Like domestic marketing, international marketing requires managers to make decisions that are within the firm's control, such as which product to market, what price it should command, the optimal promotion strategy, and the best distribution channels. Furthermore, like firms marketing domestically, firms marketing internationally must be prepared to react to factors in the home country which might affect their ability to do business. Examples include domestic politics, competition, and economic conditions.

International marketers face a host of issues that are out of their direct control, both at home and abroad. For instance, although domestic policies on foreign trade cannot be controlled by individual businesses, firms marketing abroad must be aware of how domestic policies help or hinder foreign trade activities. Firms marketing abroad must also be prepared for uncertainties presented solely by the business environment in the host country as well. Four very important issues to note in a host country are its laws, politics, economy, and competition. Other issues are the host country's geography, infrastructure, currency, distribution channels, state of technological development, and cultural differences.

The legal and political environments of the host countries are two of the most important variables faced by international marketers. First, companies operating abroad are bound by both the laws of host and home countries; moreover, legal systems around the world vary in content and interpretation. These laws can affect many elements of marketing strategies, particularly when they are in the form of product restrictions or specifications. Also, politics can be a huge concern for companies operating abroad and is, perhaps, the most volatile aspect of international marketing. Unstable political situations can expose businesses to numerous risks that they would rarely face at home. When governments change regulations, there are usually new opportunities for both profits and losses, and firms must usually make modifications to existing marketing strategies in response. For instance, the opening of Central and Eastern Europe presented both high political risks and huge potential market opportunities for companies willing to take the risks.

Economic conditions, per capita **gross national product (GNP)**, and levels of **economic development** vary widely around the world. Before entering a market, firms marketing abroad must be aware of the economic situation there; the economy—not to mention individual standards of living—has a huge impact on the size and affluence of a particular target market. Furthermore, marketers must educate themselves on any trade agreements existing between countries as well as on local and regional economic conditions. Being aware of economic conditions and the likely direction that those conditions will take can help marketers better understand the profitability of potential markets. For example, many companies had to reevaluate international marketing strategies as international financial crises affected the economies of Southeast Asia, Russia, and Latin America in 1997-98.

Competition overseas can come from a variety of sources as well. Further, it has the potential to be much fiercer than competition at home. Often, if a market is ready to accept foreign goods, numerous manufacturers—both indigenous and foreign-based—will be willing to risk entry into that market. Making the situation more intense, the governments of many other countries may subsidize manufacturers to help them enter a particular market.

Obviously, the more foreign markets in which a firm enters, the more of these uncontrollable events the firm must consider. To make the situation more interesting, the solutions to problems occurring in one country are often inapplicable to problems occurring in a second country because of differences in the political climates, economies, and cultures. The uncertainty of different foreign business environments creates the need to closely study the environment within each new market entered.

Companies that are truly global competitors employ a long-term international marketing strategy to overcome the uncertainties associated with conducting business abroad. Their long-term strategies enable them to weather short-term economic or political crises, such as the peso devaluation in Mexico. Such companies are prepared to make increased investments during downturns, and as a result they are better prepared when economic conditions improve.

SEPARATING CULTURAL VALUES

Culture is a very important aspect of international marketing because the elements that compose it affect the way consumers think. The language a population speaks, the average level of education, the prevailing religion, and other social conditions affect the priorities the inhabitants have and the way they react to different events.

With this in mind, it is easy to see that managers of firms operating only in the domestic market are often able to react to many market uncertainties correctly and automatically because they intuitively understand the culture and the impact of changing conditions. In foreign markets, however, this is not the case. Because they were not raised in the country in which they are trying establish a market, managers abroad often do not fully understand the culture and lack the proper frame of reference. Thus, decisions that they would make automatically at home could be dramatically incorrect when operating abroad. Unless special efforts are made to understand the cultural meanings for activities in each foreign market, managers will likely misinterpret the events taking place and risk making the wrong decisions.

This problem is so real that some authorities in international marketing believe that unconscious references to a firm's domestic cultural values contribute to most international business problems. To overcome these potential disastrous decisions, firms must understand the cultural factors existing in both their domestic country and the host country. Business problems and goals must be defined in terms of the host country's culture. Being able to separate home-country norms from those in the host country can be a very challenging task. Often, the influence of one's own culture is underrated.

American multinational corporations have been in the forefront of developing international brands that cut across local cultural differences. Companies such as Coca-Cola, IBM, and McDonald's have created international brands to sell their products to large market segments worldwide. Other American examples of global icons include Intel, MTV, CNN, and Disney. The advertising and marketing campaigns that built these international brands took a universalist approach, building on the American tradition of assimilation. However, as culturally diverse emerging markets become more important to international marketing, campaigns targeted to specific cultures will appear more frequently.

SEE ALSO: Cross-Cultural/International Communication; Exporting; Globalization

[Kathryn Snavely, updated by David P. Bianco]

FURTHER READING:

Bradley, Frank. *International Marketing Strategy.* Paramus, NJ: Prentice Hall, 1998.

Cateora, Philip R. *International Marketing.* 9th ed. New York: McGraw-Hill Professional Book Group, 1995.

Fellman, Michelle Wirth. "Globalization: Worldwide Economic Woes Force Global Marketers to Seek New Opportunities or Ways to Ride out the Storm." *Marketing News,* 7 December 1998.

Gibb, Richard, and Wieslaw Michalak, eds. *Continental Trading Blocs: The Growth of Regionalism in the World Economy.* New York: John Wiley & Sons, 1994.

Gowa, Joanne. *Allies, Adversaries, and International Trade.* Princeton, NJ: Princeton University Press, 1995.

Herbig, Paul A. *Handbook of Cross Cultural Marketing.* Haworth Press, 1997.

Jain, Subhash C. *International Marketing Management.* 6th ed. Storrs, CT: Digital Publishing Co., 1998.

Mitchell, Alan. "Wake up, Uncle Sam." *Management Today,* June 1996.

Paliwoda, Stanley J. "International Marketing: An Assessment." *International Marketing Review,* January-February 1999.

Sletten, Eric. *How to Succeed in Exporting and Doing Business Internationally.* New York: John Wiley & Sons, 1994.

Terpstra, Vern. *International Dimensions of Marketing.* 4th ed. Cincinnati, OH: South-Western College Publishing, 1999.

——. *International Marketing.* 8th ed. Forth Worth, TX: Harcourt Brace College Publishers, 1999.

INTERNATIONAL MONETARY FUND (IMF)

The International Monetary Fund (IMF) is perhaps one of the most misunderstood economic institutions operating on a worldwide scale. The IMF, as is often thought, is not a global **central bank**, it is not a development bank for Third World nations, nor does it dictate monetary policy to its members. Likewise, it is not to be confused with the **World Bank**. The IMF was founded as a result of the **United Nations** Monetary and Financial Conference held at Bretton Woods, New Hampshire, in July 1944. The conference was attended by 45 countries including the United States. The IMF was established to promote worldwide monetary cooperation, international trade, and most importantly, stability in **foreign exchange**. By December 1945 enough countries had ratified the charter to make it a viable institution. The IMF, which in 1998 had 182 member countries, is headquartered in Washington, D.C.

One of the first and most important acts of the newly formed IMF was to establish a method for standardizing the par value of each member nation's currency. It was felt by many economists, most notably John Maynard Keynes (1883-1946) of Great Britain and Harry Dexter White of the U.S. Department of the Treasury, that the Great Depression was exacerbated by currency inconvertibility. During the depression there was a tremendous demand for gold because of a lack of trust in paper currency. Those national treasuries that exchanged their currency for gold could not meet this demand and many countries, most notably the United Kingdom, were forced to abandon the gold standard against which they pegged the value of their currency. This made foreign exchange unstable because the value of these various currencies was no longer pegged to a fixed standard—the price of gold. Especially problematic was establishing a currency exchange rate between those countries still on the **gold standard** and those who had abandoned it. This situation led to nations hoarding gold or currency that could be converted to gold on demand, thus shrinking monetary exchange, foreign trade, and jobs dependent on foreign trade. As a result the world economy faltered with the worldwide prices of goods falling by 48 percent between 1929 and 1932 and the value of international trade falling 63 percent.

The ability to exchange currency is a central feature of world trade. The currency of each country has a value in terms of the currency of every other country. This exchange value is in a constant state of flux but in late 1946 the IMF standardized the par value of its members' currencies and developed various strategies for easing currency convertibility. Par values were standardized using gold. Since the United States also pegged the value of the dollar to gold at $35 per ounce, the value of other currencies for practical purposes became pegged to the dollar. Members of the IMF were required to value their currency within 1 percent of this par value and any deviation required IMF consent. This policy continued for nearly 25 years until the early 1970s when the Nixon administration ceased converting dollars for gold.

With the discontinuance of a par value system based on gold IMF members now use a variety of ways of valuing their currency. One way is to allow the currency to float freely with its value being determined on currency markets, a method favored by many industrial nations. In another method, a country may choose to manipulate currency markets in its favor by buying and selling its own currency. In a third alternative, a country may choose to peg the value of its currency to that of another currency. Regardless of the method used, IMF members may not peg the value of their currency to gold and the criteria used to establish the par value of their currencies must be divulged. In spite of national currencies going off the gold standard, the IMF is generally regarded as still being an important international regulatory agency that promotes an environment for orderly and stable currency exchange arrangements.

In addition to overseeing the international monetary system, the IMF also makes loans to its members during financial crises. In 1983 and 1984 the IMF lent $28 billion to member countries that were in arrears to other IMF members. In 1995 it lent Mexico $17 billion and Russia $6.2 billion. The money for these loans comes from quota subscriptions or membership fees that are based on the wealth of each nation. The wealthier the country, the higher the quota subscription. Quotas are reviewed every five years and can be raised or lowered depending on the economic health of the country. The United States, which is the IMF's wealthiest member, contributes about $38 billion while the Marshall Islands, the least wealthy, contributes about $3.6 million. There is also a specific correlation between the amount of money a member country can borrow and the amount of that country's quota subscription. In the event that the quota subscriptions cannot meet demand, the IMF has an established line of **credit** with governments and **banks** throughout the world. This line of credit is known as the General Arrangements to Borrow. The IMF can also borrow money from member governments for specific programs and uses. Oftentimes the IMF will borrow money for a member country at a more favorable rate than the country could do on its own. The IMF lends money only to member countries with foreign currency payment problems. A member country can withdraw 25 percent of its quota that was paid in gold or a readily converted currency. If this is not sufficient it is possible for the country under certain prescribed conditions to borrow three times its quota subscription over a period of time. In these cases, however, the IMF will insist on concurrent economic reforms to alleviate the underlying problems.

By 1998 the IMF held quotas worth $210 billion. This figure, however, is not a real figure in that 75 percent of each member's quota is paid in its own national currency. Since most of these currencies are not in demand outside of the issuing country, the real value of the IMF quota fund is somewhere around $105 billion. Those member countries that borrow from the IMF invariably ask for currency that can be readily converted, such as the dollar, yen, deutsche mark, pound sterling, or the French franc.

The IMF, despite the goodwill it has accumulated since its establishment, is not without its critics. Many such critics feel that the Asian crisis of the late 1990s was caused in part by IMF policies. The IMF (along with Western governments and banks) stood accused of encouraging Asian governments to loosen controls on foreign borrowing by their private domestic companies. This led to an escalation of foreign debt and when things got shaky a subsequent outflow of this Western money. The result was a devaluation of currencies and economies. Critics feel that IMF policies should promote domestic rather than foreign borrowing (even if it's more expensive) and hold foreign banks more responsible for "reckless lending." The IMF has also been criticized for "intruding" into the political process of Asian debtor nations and ignoring the "moral hazards" that accompany quick bailouts.

The governing authority of the IMF is the board of governors of which each member country contributes a governor and an alternate governor. The board of governors is responsible for the admission of new members, adjustment of quotas, and the election of executive directors. The board of executive directors oversees the managing director and the administrative staff. The interim committee of the board of governors was established in 1974 to analyze the international monetary system and make recommendations to the board of governors.

[Michael Knes]

FURTHER READING:

Culpepper, Roy, ed. *Global Development Fifty Years after Bretton Woods: Essays in Honour of Gerald K. Helleiner.* New York: St. Martin's Press, 1996.

Driscoll, David D. "What Is the International Monetary Fund?" Washington: International Monetary Fund, 1998. Available from www.imf.org.

Fischer, Stanley. "In Defense of the IMF: Specialized Tools for a Specialized Task." *Foreign Affairs* 77 (1998).

Levinson, Mark. "The IMF in Asia: Its Solution Is the Cause of the Crisis." *Dissent* 45 (1998).

INTERNATIONAL MONETARY MARKET (IMM)

The International Monetary Market (IMM) was opened in May 1972 by the Chicago Mercantile Exchange and provides a forum for trading in foreign currency **futures**. The Chicago Mercantile Exchange began in 1919 as a nonprofit organization providing a marketplace for trading in agricultural commodity spot and forward contracts. Other **commodity exchanges**, however, had been operating since the mid-1800s in various large American cities. Trading in these early commodity exchanges was based largely on spot and forward contracts. Spot contracts call for immediate delivery of a commodity at an agreed-upon price. A forward contract calls for the delivery of a commodity at a future date but at a price and quantity determined when the contract is agreed upon. As commodity trading increased over the decades, forward contracts became more and more standardized and incorporated commonly used dates and quantities for delivery. These standardized contracts soon became known as futures contracts. Present-day futures contracts are also characterized by financial obligations, margin requirements, federal and state regulations, and commodity exchange rules that structure and guarantee the contract. The Chicago Mercantile Exchange, like other commodity exchanges, is regulated in part by the **Commodity Futures Trading Commission**, a federal agency. The purpose of a futures contract is to provide, at a predetermined future date, a set amount of a commodity at a guaranteed price. Such guarantees provide a hedge against an uncertain and potentially catastrophic future which may be caused by drought, floods, political uncertainty, fluctuations in **foreign exchange** rates, or a host of other reasons.

There are three basic reasons for dealing in futures contracts: price discovery, which helps predict future spot prices; **hedging**, which protects against future price declines and anticipates future rising prices; and **speculation**. The Chicago Mercantile Exchange and other commodity exchanges, such as the Chicago Board of Trade and the New York Mercantile Exchange, bring together speculators, hedgers, and ''scalpers.'' A speculator does not own or take possession of the commodity, he or she only hopes to profit from the rise or fall of the price of the contract. Hedgers are traders that actually own the underlying commodity. Hedgers use future contracts to protect themselves against price changes that could represent a loss. A farmer guaranteeing to deliver a predetermined number of bushels of wheat on a particular date at a particular price can be considered a hedger. A flour manufacturer who agrees to buy a predetermined number of bushels of wheat on a particular date at a particular price is also a hedger. ''Scalpers'' are those floor traders who buy and sell contracts and thus hope to profit from their trades. Commodity exchanges bring these people together—but not necessarily face-to-face.

Impetus for the creation of the IMM was fueled by world events and many of the Nixon administration's monetary and fiscal policies, including the **devaluation** of the dollar, price and wage controls, the discontinuation of converting dollars to gold on demand, and the withdrawal of the United States from the Bretton Woods agreement which sought to stabilize and maintain foreign exchange rates. Another factor was the general turmoil of monetary systems worldwide. This disarray created a need for hedge services among financial institutions, other borrowers and lenders, and businesspeople dependent on a guaranteed future exchange rate. In essence, foreign currency was assuming the characteristics of more familiar **commodities** such as grain, lumber, and precious metals. The 1970s and 1980s also ushered in futures contracts for stock **indexes** and **bonds**. Collectively these three ''commodities'' are known as financial futures.

Currency futures markets, such as the IMM, quote the number of U.S. currency units (dollars and/or cents) that must be paid to purchase a unit of a foreign currency. This is more a reflection of the value of one currency in relation to another, not necessarily the absolute value of either currency. There are a number of determinants that affect the relationship between two currencies including balance of payments, **interest rates**, economic strength, **inflation**, and political stability.

When the IMM opened for trading it allowed 500 charter members; this number was increased in 1976 to a maximum of 750. The membership fee at that time was $10,000. Currencies traded on the IMM and contract sizes are: British pound sterling (62,500), Canadian dollar (100,000), German deutsche mark (125,000), Japanese yen (12,500,000), Swiss franc (125,000), and the euro (1,000,000). Delivery or trading months are March, June, September, and December and delivery is on the third Wednesday of the contract month. If for whatever reason the third Wednesday is not a business day, then delivery is made on the next business day. All price quotes are in U.S. dollars except the yen and the euro. The yen is quoted in U.S. cents while the euro price quote is based on an IMM index.

[Michael Knes]

FURTHER READING:

Chicago Mercantile Exchange. ''Chicago Mercantile Exchange.'' Chicago: Chicago Mercantile Exchange, 1998. Available from www.cme.com.

Heady, Christy. *The Complete Idiot's Guide to Making Money on Wall Street.* New York: Alpha Books, 1998.

Melamed, Leo. *Leo Melamed on the Markets: Twenty Years of Financial History as Seen by the Man Who Revolutionized the Markets.* New York: Wiley, 1993.

Powers, Mark. ''The Day the IMM Launched Financial Futures Trading.'' *Futures* 21, no. 6 (May 1992): 52-58.

Teweles, Richard J., and Frank J. Jones. *The Futures Game: Who Wins? Who Loses? Why?* New York: McGraw-Hill, 1987.

INTERNATIONAL ORGANIZATION FOR STANDARDIZATION (ISO)

The International Organization for Standardization (ISO) is a private (nongovernmental) worldwide federation, which was founded to promote the creation and implementation of uniform standards facilitating international exchange of goods and services. The ISO's members are elected representatives from national standards organizations in more than 120 countries. The U.S. representative is the American National Standards Institute (ANSI), a private standards organization. U.S. trade associations, professional societies, and government agencies are also involved in the work of the ISO through their membership and participation in technical advisory groups (TAGs), which work with the ISO's technical committees to draft international standards.

Since the ISO was created in 1947, its Central Secretariat has been located in Geneva, Switzerland. Between 1951 (when it published its first standard) and 1998, the ISO issued over 10,060 standards. Standards are documents containing technical specifications, rules, guidelines, and definitions to ensure that equipment, products, and services conform to their specifications. The ISO covers all fields involving goods, services, or products with the exception of electrical and electronic engineering. The ISO is one of three major international standards bodies. The other two are the International Electrotechnical Commission (IEC) and the International Telecommunication Union (ITU).

The IEC was created in 1906 and it also has its central offices in Geneva. The IEC's members include technical committees from 42 participating countries and represent the interests of their respective countries with regard to electrotechnical matters. The IEC and the ISO coordinate their work through a Joint Technical Programming Committee. The IEC handles all matters regarding worldwide electronic engineering and electrical standards.

The third major international standardization body, the ITU, is also headquartered in Geneva and it frequently works with the ISO. The ITU's work covers communications including the **Internet**, radio, cable television, and related industries.

MEMBERSHIP

Only one standards organization per country may be an ISO member, and more than 70 percent of ISO members are representatives of government institutions. But the U.S. representative, ANSI, is a private standards organization. ANSI is actively involved in the ISO, holding participant or observer status on 95 percent of ISO's technical committees (TCs) and subcommittees.

There are three types of membership in the ISO: full members, correspondent members, and subscriber members. There are currently over 85 full members. They have full rights of voting and participation. There are currently at least 24 correspondent members. Correspondent members are usually developing countries that do not have a national standards body. They are entitled to attend General Assembly meetings but do not have voting rights. Subscriber membership is for very small countries that want to be kept informed of ISO activities. There are currently at least nine subscriber members.

ORGANIZATIONAL STRUCTURE

The ISO operates through various governing bodies and policy-making committees. A small Central Secretariat coordinates and oversees the work of the various ISO bodies, and it publishes ISO standards.

The General Assembly (GA) is the highest authority within the ISO. Each ISO member nominates a delegate to the GA. The GA acts on policy, budget, the business agenda, and other important matters. It also oversees all ISO policy committees. There are four major policy committees, each of which is open to all ISO members as participants or observers. They include the following: the Committee on Conformity Assessment, the Committee on Consumer Policy, the Committee on Developing Country Matters, and the Committee on Information Systems and Services.

The ISO Council is made up of 13 elected and 5 appointed members. The council sets the Central Secretariat's annual budget. It also appoints 12 members and a treasurer to the Technical Management Board. The board, in turn, oversees operations of the ISO technical committees.

The ISO operates two information networks. The first is the ISO Information Network (ISONET). ISONET has 72 members, and those members are responsible for disseminating information about ISO standards, technical regulations, and matters related to the standards and regulations. The second is ISO Online. ISO Online is an **Internet** service available to the general public on the World Wide Web in English and French. It provides information about various activities of the ISO including, but not limited to, facts about the ISO, a catalog of all ISO standards and drafts, a list of all ISO members and committees, and copies of all press releases.

DEVELOPMENT OF INTERNATIONAL STANDARDS

COMMITTEES AND GROUPS. The Technical Management Board oversees all technical management committees (TCs). There are 185 TCs, 636 subcommittees (SCs), 1,975 working groups (WGs), and 36 ad hoc committees that develop the international standards that are, in turn, distributed by ISO members throughout the world.

The ISO's standards are drafted by the TCs, each of which is charged with the development of standards in a specified area. As it drafts standards, each TC solicits the input of producers, customers, governmental bodies, and scientists. TCs establish SCs and WGs to assist with the development of standards.

The Technical Management Board coordinates work among various TCs. It also establishes technical advisory groups (TAGs). The TAGs advise the board and committees in planning, coordination, and the development of new standards.

PROCESS: FROM COMMITTEE DRAFT TO STANDARD. Development of a new standard can be viewed as a five-step process. First, there is a proposal, called a new work item proposal, before a TC or SC. If the proposal is accepted by the TC or SC, the second step is the preparation stage during which groups of experts prepare a working draft (WD). When the WD is forwarded to the TC or SC, the third step, the committee draft (CD) stage, begins. At this stage, various additional drafts are prepared until a consensus is reached among the participating members within the TC or SC. The fourth step is the draft international standard (DIS) stage. At this point, the CD becomes a DIS, which is circulated to all ISO members for voting and comment within six months. It is adopted as a standard if two-thirds of participating members approve and no more than 25 percent of those voting oppose it. The fifth and final step is publication by the ISO Central Secretariat.

EXAMPLES OF MAJOR SETS OF STANDARDS

Until about 1979, the ISO had focused on product technical standards. The ISO standards cover a wide variety of subjects. For example, standards cover road vehicles, petroleum products and lubricants, agricultural food products, codes for film used in cameras, measurements, pumps, acoustics, and many other areas.

In 1979 the ISO developed the first of two major sets of standards that cover far more than product technical standards. First was, and is, the 9000 series, which was developed by the Technical Committee on Quality Assurance and Quality Management (TC 176). The **ISO 9000** series was developed between 1979 and 1986 and was published in 1987. Its purpose is to describe the basic requirements of a quality management system and to provide guidance in implementing such a system. The series has been adopted widely by U.S. companies as well as companies around the world. The second is the **ISO 14000** International Environmental Management Series. It covers nearly every aspect of a company's environmental management activities. Its goal is to help any company deal with environmental issues in a systematic way and, through that systematic approach, to help the company improve its environmental performance.

CONCLUSION

The ISO is an international organization that has had and will continue to have significant effects on business in many areas including, but not limited to, quality management and environmental performance. Although it is a private organization, it has had significant effects on the behavior of businesses around the world and it has received significant input and attention from governments around the world. In the process of **globalization** of business, the ISO is playing a significant role in working to harmonize business practices.

[Paulette L. Stenzel]

FURTHER READING:

International Organization for Standardization. ''ISO Online.'' Geneva: International Organization for Standardization. Available from www.iso.ch.

Tibor, Tom, and Ira Feldman. *ISO 14000: A Guide to the New Environmental Management Standards.* Irwin Professional Pub., 1996.

Von Zharen, W. M. *ISO 14000: Understanding the Environmental Standards.* 1996.

Voorhees, John, and Robert E. Woellner. *International Environmental Risk Management.* CRC Press, 1998.

Zuckerman, Amy. *International Standards Desk Reference.* New York: Amacom, 1997.

INTERNATIONAL PRIVATIZATION

Privatization is the transfer of government-owned assets to the private sector. As a result of changing economic policies, **privatization** took place at a significant pace around the world during the last decade of the 20th century. Ranging from the desire to downsize government in developed countries, to the demise of communism in Eastern and Central Europe, and to the opening of the economies of various Latin American countries, privatization has significant direct and indirect effects on international business and **international law**.

Privatization opens unprecedented opportunities for investment throughout the world. Thus, it is a major force in the **globalization** of business, and it is of great interest to investors and businesses around the world.

Privatization is taking place in various kinds of economies. Prior to revolutions during the late 1980s and early 1990s, private ownership of property was not allowed in the communist countries of Eastern and Central Europe. In accordance with Marxist theory, communist governments owned virtually everything. Privatization is, therefore, a necessary tool for those countries converting to market-based economies. As a result, in the 1990s, the formerly communist countries of Central and Eastern Europe have been engaged in an unprecedented number of transfers of assets to private persons and entities.

In Latin America, a parallel movement has taken place. As early as the 1930s and again during the 1960s and 1970s, huge segments of the economies of various Latin American countries were nationalized. Segments of the economy that were reserved to government included electric power, telecommunications, and development of natural resources. One result was that international investors were kept out of major segments of the economies of Latin American countries. Yet, from the perspective of the Latin American countries, nationalization was not a success. A majority of the nationalized industries were inefficient and caused a severe drain on the countries' finances. Latin American governments were compelled to subsidize the industries, which, in turn, caused the governments to fall more deeply in **debt** internationally. For example, the **World Bank** calculates that in the early 1990s, state-owned businesses were responsible for about 60 percent of the external debt of Latin American countries. As a result of heavy debt loads, various Latin American countries defaulted on their **loans** to international **banks**. Huge restructuring programs and bailout programs were negotiated. In turn, international lenders were hesitant to extend additional credit to Latin American countries. As a result, Latin American economies became stagnant; they could not attract significant amounts of long-term capital investment. In response, in the 1990s, Latin American governments turned to privatization and actively sought investment by foreign businesspeople and organizations.

WHICH COUNTRIES PRIVATIZE AND WHY?

Reasons for privatization vary and depend on the history, politics, and needs of each country involved. It is helpful, however, to look at whether a country is developed or undeveloped. In addition, its history as a capitalistic, communist, or **closed economy** affects the decision to privatize.

Although privatization is most frequently discussed with respect to developing countries, it is also taking place in developed, democratic, market-oriented countries. Privatization was conceived by Great Britain's Thatcher government, and it has many advocates in other developed countries such as the United States. In the United States, privatization is seen as a mechanism to be used to "downsize" government, cut costs for government, cut **taxes** for citizens, and promote balanced government budgets. Thus, in the United States, on a federal level, there is pressure on government from some parties (not including environmentalists) to sell oil drilling rights to federal lands and on offshore fields. In addition, there are proposals that the federally run air traffic control system be privatized. On the state and local levels, in some states and municipalities there has been privatization of garbage collection, health care, and ambulance services, usually under **contracts** between the government and a privately owned business. In some states, the government contracts to place prisoners in privately owned and operated detention facilities. Schools have been another target for privatization in the 1990s. Demand for spaces in public schools decreases when government-subsidized vouchers are given to students who, in turn, use them at private schools. Or, for example, privately run charter schools in Michigan receive government funding under the theory that they can provide more choice and better education to students than that which is offered through the public schools.

In developing countries, privatization is creating unprecedented opportunities for investment by businesses and businesspeople from around the world including, but not limited to, those based in the United States. In formerly communist countries of Eastern and Central Europe, conversion to a market-based economy, with privately owned and operated businesses, has resulted in massive privatization programs. There are multiple benefits of such privatization, including the following eight. First, sale of government-owned businesses can generate cash for the government. Second, following sale of an unprofitable business, the government can discontinue **subsidies** to it. A third, related benefit is that the government gets rid of inefficient labor and "hidden" unemployment. Communist governments were obliged to retain nonproductive workers and operate inefficient facilities in order to provide **employment**, but privately owned businesses have incentives and opportunities to release nonproductive workers. Fourth, privatized businesses can provide employment for workers released from inefficient state-owned businesses. Fifth, privatized businesses can become tax-paying entities, which, in turn, generate sorely needed funds for local and national governments. Sixth, privatized businesses promote **competition**. Seventh, as government-owned monopolies are privatized and competition increases, the public gains access to higher quality goods and services at lower prices. Eighth, privatization can facilitate **foreign investment** and trade. (Or, in the alternative, through laws allowing the sale of formerly government owned businesses, privatization can be used to promote domestic investment and restrict the inflow of foreign business.)

Various Latin American countries chose to privatize state-owned businesses during the last two decades of the 20th century as a way to revitalize debt-ridden and stagnant economies. Countries in which substantial numbers of businesses have been privatized include **Argentina**, Chile, and **Mexico**. For example, throughout most of the 20th century, Mexico operated a state-dominated economy using an "import substitution" model. Mexico closed its doors to foreign investment in many sectors of its economy, such as energy, natural resources, and telecommunications. In other areas, foreign investment was severely restricted. In addition, heavy tariffs were used to discourage imports. For example, tariffs on automobiles, auto parts, and light trucks were as high as 100 percent in the early 1980s. The Mexican government expected Mexican businesses to produce the goods needed by Mexicans. The result was, however, that Mexican-made goods were often of a poor quality, and many products were unavailable. Only the wealthiest citizens could afford imported goods with high tariffs. High quality clothing, electronics, and other goods were hard to obtain and extremely expensive. In addition, certain services such as telephone services were costly and hard to obtain. For example, it often took years to get a telephone installed in a home. As a result, in the mid- to late 1980s, Mexico's leaders decided to shift away from the import-substitution model of production and away from government ownership of major businesses.

Simultaneously, Mexican leaders were aware of the growing movement toward the globalization of business as they watched the expansion of international trade alliances such as the **European Union** (EU, then called the European Community) and the **U.S.-Canadian Free Trade Agreement**. Mexico's leaders decided to open Mexico's economy in an effort to stabilize it. One major step was Mexico's decision to join the **General Agreement on Tariffs and Trade** (GATT) in 1996. Another was negotiation of the **North American Free Trade Agreement** (NAFTA) with the United States and Canada, which took effect on January 1, 1994. Pursuant to NAFTA the three countries are phasing out nearly all tariffs among themselves over a 15-year period ending in 2009. Another major tool for opening Mexico's economy is the privatization of government-owned businesses.

The benefits of privatization for Latin American countries parallel the reasons of formerly communist countries. Mexico provides a good example. From 1989 to 1994, President Carlos Salinas privatized 252 state companies including major banks and TELMEX, the government-owned company that monopolized telephone services. Sales of Mexican businesses have generated sorely needed funds for the Mexican government, which faced a major debt crisis in 1995-96. Mexico has been able to discontinue subsidies to unprofitable state-owned businesses. Companies have been restructured, getting rid of unneeded employees. Privatized businesses are becoming tax-paying entities. And privatized businesses, such as in telecommunications, have encouraged competition. In turn, at least in some areas, prices are down and quality is improving. For example, the quality of telephone services in Mexico has improved dramatically since 1994, while prices have been cut significantly. In conjunction with the provisions of NAFTA, privatization has led to foreign investment by U.S. and Canadian firms in areas including, but not limited to, telecommunications, certain types of energy production such as cogeneration power plants, pharmaceuticals, agriculture, automobile manufacturing, and automobile parts. Foreign investments in various areas have allowed Mexico to convert from a country that relied on oil exports (from Pemex, the state-owned oil monopoly) for 78 percent of its foreign income in the early 1980s, to a country that, in the early 1990s, was receiving at least 80 percent of its foreign income from the export of manufactured goods produced by privately owned businesses.

Pressure from international organizations has been another force leading to privatization. The **International Monetary Fund** (IMF) and the **World Bank** have required privatization of unprofitable government-owned businesses as a prerequisite to obtaining loans sought by debt-ridden governments. In the early 1980s the Mexican government controlled sugarcane production, milling, and selling through a state-owned company called Colima. The company, however, was supported by substantial state subsidies. In 1988 Mexico privatized Colima's sugarcane mills when the World Bank pressured it to do so as a precondition to receiving loans. Similarly, the EU requires that countries applying for membership in the EU divest themselves of unprofitable government-owned businesses as a means of demonstrating the economic reform and stability required. Thus, various Central and Eastern European countries including, but not limited to, Romania and the Czech Republic, are privatizing state-owned businesses as they prepare for membership in the EU.

EXAMPLES OF HOW PRIVATIZATION IS ACCOMPLISHED

Because the focus of this article is on international privatization, this section does not include discussion of mechanisms used for privatization in the United States. Included are examples of privatization in formerly communist countries and in Latin America.

FORMERLY COMMUNIST ECONOMIES: THE CZECH REPUBLIC AND RUSSIA. The Czech Republic was the first of the formerly communist countries to begin to convert to a market-based economy through extensive use of privatization. It deserves study, because it has served as a model for other formerly communist countries.

Privatization in the Czech Republic has had far-reaching effects on that country's economy. In 1989 the private sector accounted for less than 1 percent of the **gross domestic product** in the Czech Republic in 1989. That figure had reached 22 percent by the start of 1993 and 44 percent by the start of 1994.

The Czech Republic instituted a four-part privatization program. First, more than 100,000 properties that had been confiscated by the government since 1948 were returned to their former owners. The properties included houses, retail shops, farmland, and small factories. Second, a "small" privatization plan was instituted. It began with a five-year auction of leases on about 22,000 stores and workshops to private bidders. Foreign buyers were not allowed. In addition, as a second step in this part of the program, health care facilities are being sold to staff members. The staff members are assisted with subsidized loans. Third, the Czech government lifted the prohibition on private enterprise that had been in place under communism. Soon, over 1.1 million people (about 10 percent of the population) registered as self-employed. Most of these people are in retailing and services.

The fourth and most significant part of the privatization program was a plan to sell large state-owned enterprises. Starting in 1992, each of about 3,500 state-owned firms was required to prepare its own privatization plan. One of three avenues could be chosen. First, there could be direct sale to a foreign or domestic buyer. Second, there could be a public auction. Third, sale could be through use of vouchers (explained below). In response to the plan prepared by a firm, others (e.g., groups of managers within a plant) could submit rival plans. A newly established Ministry of Privatization selected the "winning" plan to be implemented for each firm.

The voucher system was innovative and has been used as a model by other formerly communist countries, including Russia and Romania. Under the Czech voucher program, the finance minister issued vouchers for the relatively nominal sum of 1,000 crowns (about US$33). Vouchers could be pooled to bid on blocks of shares. The program has had mixed results. About 72 percent of vouchers issued ended up being invested with about 220 investment funds. (The funds were able to buy significant numbers of vouchers by offering up to 15,000 crowns—the equivalent of about US$500.) Czech banks, which were themselves privatized using the voucher system, ended up owning five of the six largest investment funds. The end result is that many privatized firms are owned by investment funds, which, in turn, are owned by banks. Thus, ownership of these firms is concentrated in the hands of a limited number of banks, and many of the firms remain heavily in debt. On the other hand, the successful side of the story is that the program succeeded in transferring ownership of firms from the state to private entities.

Russia modeled its privatization program after the Czech experience. The program began in 1992, and, like the Czech program, it has four parts. First, Russia privatized about 102,000 small businesses, including shops and restaurants. About 73 percent were purchased by employees at nominal prices. Second, mass privatization was ordered in July 1992. About 25,000 firms were ordered to convert to "joint-stock" companies, and they were ordered to draw up plans to distribute shares. Third, in November 1992, the government ordered that 148 million vouchers be issued, each with a nominal value of 10,000 rubles. The vouchers were issued to Russian citizens and could be sold or used to buy shares in companies. (They sold for about US$10.) There were problems with the program. By May 1994 it appeared that not enough shares were being issued to meet the supply of outstanding vouchers. Therefore, the government pressured various companies, including oil, gas, and electricity companies, to make some of their shares available in exchange for vouchers. The voucher program for privatization ended on June 30, 1994. The fourth part of the Russian plan involved sales to workers. Firms were given the option to sell 51 percent of their shares to workers, and about 75 percent of firms opted to do so. In firms in which 51 percent of shares went to workers, another 20 percent went to the Russian Property Fund (a state-owned fund), and 29 percent remained to be auctioned to those holding vouchers.

Comparing the Russian program to the Czech program, each had strengths and weaknesses. The Czech government installed a sophisticated computerized program for distribution of vouchers. Thus, vouchers were distributed more evenly in the Czech Republic than in Russia, where, regionally, elite parties were able to control distribution. The Russian program for worker ownership made it easier for managers to gain sufficient equity in their firms to control them, while the Czech program lacked provisions that provided specifically for worker ownership. On the other hand, public interest in the Czech program was greater because the cash value of the vouchers reached US$300 to US$500, while the cash value reached only US$10 to US$20 per voucher under the Russian program.

FREEING A MARKET IN LATIN AMERICA: MEXICO. In Latin American countries, privatization plans are, generally, more simple in their design and implementation than in formerly communist countries. Firms are sold by the government to private investors and the funds are returned to the government. For example, the 252 companies privatized by Mexico between 1989 and 1994 were sold to private individuals and firms; some of them were Mexican-owned and others were foreign-owned. The sales produced more than US$23 billion that went into government reserves. In addition, the government was able to reduce or eliminate its massive subsidies to those firms.

Not all privatization in Mexico has been of privately owned businesses. Under Mexico's 1917 constitution, peasants, their children, and their grandchildren, have lived on cooperative farms called *ejidos*. Under the constitution, the farmers had lifelong rights to use of the *ejido* property; those rights could not be sold, leased, or rented. Under reforms designed to facilitate domestic and foreign investment, the Mexican government amended the constitution in 1992 to allow for sale, rental, or lease of the *ejido* properties. This privatization is good for investors who need land for industrial projects or large-scale farming. It is also viewed as a positive step by those economists who believe that *ejidos* have resulted in inefficient use of land. Families that have lived on *ejido* lands, however, are being compelled to move elsewhere, and the compensation they receive is usually insufficient to buy land or homes elsewhere. Thus, privatization of *ejidos* is highly controversial.

CHALLENGES AND PROBLEMS

Privatization has led to challenges and problems. One set of challenges involves the need for bodies of contract law, real property law, and personal property law. Problems stem from corruption and abuse that have arisen in some countries engaged in privatization.

A CHALLENGE: THE NEED FOR NEW BODIES OF LAW. First, rules of law must be changed to accommodate new ways. Foreign investors buying assets from a foreign government want a solid legal structure on which to rely. Many assets being sold by governments in Latin America and in formerly communist countries were expropriated from private parties earlier in the 20th century. Therefore, a legal mechanism to ensure that clear title is conveyed to the new investor is crucial. Under communism, the concept of ownership of private party contradicted the foundations of the economic system. Therefore, privatization in a formerly communist state requires an entirely new body of law as well as legal mechanisms for enforcement of that body of law. New laws must cover acquisition and transfer of title to real and personal property; filing systems to register **mortgages** and other interests in real property; finance regulations; and numerous other areas. In addition to property laws, contract laws are needed.

Further, lawyers and judges who are trained in administering the new laws are needed. This has been a particular problem in Russia, where businesspeople complain that the courts have been unprepared to enforce the new laws passed in connection with Russia's efforts to convert to a market-based economy.

THE POTENTIAL FOR ABUSE AND CORRUPTION. Unfortunately, privatization has resulted in abuse and scandal in various developing countries. Self-dealing and corruption in Russia, India, Pakistan, and Mexico have caused the governments (and people) of those countries to lose billions of dollars and to halt some projects. For example, in 1993 in Russia, there was a major scandal in connection with plans to transfer a 51 percent voting share in Norilsk Nickel to Uneximbank, the fourth largest financial institution in Russia. In India, a planned privatization of telecommunications was halted in the early 1990s as a result of allegations of attempted **bribery** and other corruption.

It is recognized that the conversion of state-controlled monopolies to private enterprise has created the potential for abuse. Free markets need restraint. Therefore, as we enter the 21st century institutional changes and careful surveillance are needed to curtail abuse as communist and other closed economies are converted to market-based economies.

CONCLUSION

This essay has provided examples of privatization in various areas of the world including North America, formerly communist countries (using the Czech Republic and Russia as examples), and Latin America (using Mexico as an example). Yet, privatization is taking place throughout the world. Studies have been published discussing privatization in various regions of the world, including Eastern Europe (e.g., Poland and Hungary), Asia (e.g., India and Pakistan), Latin America (including Chile and Argentina), and Africa. And much remains to be observed and studied. Therefore, this essay serves only as an introduction to the privatization movement. Privatization will continue to have significant effects on the global economy as we enter the 21st century.

[Paulette L. Stenzel]

FURTHER READING:

Celarier, Michelle. "Privatization: A Case Study in Corruption." *Journal of International Affairs* 50 (1997): 531-43.

Fainaru, Steve. "NAFTA Cited as Mexicans Get to Pick a Phone Firm." *Boston Globe,* 27 August 1996, A1.

Oppenheimer, Andres. *Bordering on Chaos: Mexico's Guerrillas, Stockbrokers, Politicians, and Road to Prosperity.* Boston: Little, Brown, 1996.

Rutland, Peter. "Privatization in East Europe: Another Case of Words that Succeed and Policies that Fail?" *Transnational Law and Contemporary Problems* 2 (1995): 1-20.

Schaffer, Richard, Beverly Earle, and Filiberto Agusti. *International Business Law and Its Environment.* 4th ed. West/Wadsworth, 1999.

Stanford, Lois. "The Privatization of Mexico's Ejidal Sector: Examining Local Impacts, Strategies, and Ideologies." *Urban Anthropology* 23 (1994): 97-119.

INTERNET AND WORLD WIDE WEB

By now it's almost cliché to take note of the Internet's vast potential as a business resource, but triteness doesn't diminish the fact that this once-obscure **computer network** has changed—and will continue to change—business and society profoundly. A number of estimates pegged the value of Internet commerce in 1998 around $100 billion for the United States, and more than one projection for the early 2000s foresaw worldwide **e-commerce** surpassing a trillion dollars within the first five years of the 21st century. Although much attention has been devoted to the vast consumer market accessible via the Internet (which is a multibillion-dollar franchise in its own right), business-to-business transactions make up the large majority of e-commerce sales in terms of value. Total U.S. 1998 economic activity surrounding the Internet, including computer hardware purchases, Web authoring services, commerce, and so forth, was estimated at more than $300 billion in sales and 1.2 million jobs. And these statistics don't even address the non commerce efficiencies and savings that Internet-based technologies bestow on businesses in areas such as **supply-chain management**.

Whereas during the Internet's early commercialization companies were consumed with simply getting online, perhaps without much forethought about what to do once they got there, increasingly corporations are formulating exacting Internet strategies to capitalize on the network's strengths as well as to cope with its shortfalls. Despite the popular metaphor of a virtual store serving all the same functions as a physical store, conventional transaction-based commerce is not the appropriate Internet business model for all companies. Rather, businesses must evaluate the financial and competitive advantages of using the Internet as a primary vehicle for communication and exchange versus traditional and hybrid options. Some firms may find, for example, that it's more profitable to provide users with Internet tools to help make a purchasing decision than to try to facilitate the entire transaction electronically. Meanwhile, other types of companies will find that doing business exclusively over the Internet is the best approach. No blanket policy is likely to work across dissimilar business lines; the key to determining which model is best is intricately tied to the specific market being served, the logistics of delivering the product or service being offered, and what other non-Internet alternatives exist.

A SHORT HISTORY OF THE INTERNET

ARPANET. The Internet originated as an experimental communication system funded by the U.S. Department of Defense and hosted by several universities. Its impetus was a defense experiment to create a cost-efficient, decentralized, widely distributed electronic communications network for linking research centers. This network was named Arpanet, after its sponsoring agency, the Defense Advanced Research Projects Agency (DARPA). Arpanet began operating in 1969, but it took several years before it became reliable, thanks to packet switching (breaking information into small manageable pieces that could each be routed separately and reassembled at the receiving computer), and acquired familiar functions like **electronic mail**. Arpanet's first international links were established in 1973, when hosts in Great Britain and Norway signed on.

EARLY COMMERCIAL NETWORKS. The Internet's first commercial forebear was called Telenet and was run by Bolt, Beranek & Newman (BBN), a defense contractor with close ties to the Arpanet project. Intro-

Figure 1
Growth of Internet Host Computers in the 1990s

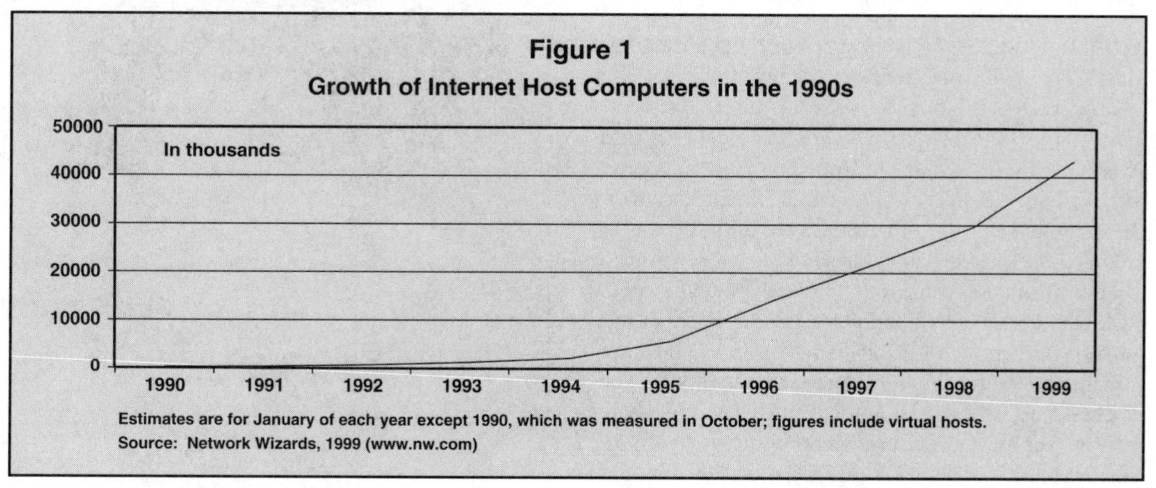

Estimates are for January of each year except 1990, which was measured in October; figures include virtual hosts.
Source: Network Wizards, 1999 (www.nw.com)

duced in 1974, Telenet enjoyed only a lukewarm reception and its founders couldn't keep up with the steep level of investment needed to make it truly commercially viable. Five years later BBN sold Telenet Communications Corp., by then a publicly traded company, to General Telephone & Electronics, better known as the telecommunications company GTE Corp. GTE would eventually spin Telenet off in a joint venture that formed US Sprint, the long-distance and networking giant, but Telenet never became a dominant player. More important were the originally closed (proprietary, non-Internet) networks of CompuServe, Prodigy, and America Online, which would provide the commercial model for consumer Internet service providers (ISPs) and Web content centers, and large commercial network backbone operators, which would give businesses fast access to the Internet and eventually take over the Internet's operation.

EMERGENCE OF THE MODERN INTERNET. Despite its relative obscurity at the time, the 1980s were the Internet's most defining years. By the early 1980s Arpanet had adopted the TCP/IP communications standards that would become commonplace on the Internet, and more importantly, other interconnected research networks began to spring up, both within the United States and abroad. One of the most important was the National Science Foundation's NSFNET, which came online in the mid-1980s to link several supercomputing laboratories with U.S. universities. In this period the collective network was increasingly known as the Internet, although the generic term of internetworking, or connecting networks to other networks, had existed since at least the mid-1970s. Enjoying rapid growth and technical upgrading, the NSF's network became the official backbone of the Internet by the late 1980s, eclipsing Arpanet, which by that time was comparatively small, slow, and outmoded. From just 213 host computers on Arpanet in 1981, the Internet had burgeoned to include some 10,000 hosts by 1987, and topped 300,000 by 1990, the year Arpanet was officially decommissioned.

WORLD WIDE WEB. The final major breakthrough of the 1980s—and one that would decidedly set the course for the 1990s and beyond—was a 1989 proposal at the Swiss physics lab CERN to create a World Wide Web. The idea came from Tim Berners-Lee, a British-born physicist working at CERN at the time. His plan, which was not well received initially, was to allow colleagues at laboratories around the world to share information through a simple hypertext system of linked documents. Eventually gaining CERN's approval, Berners-Lee and others at the research center began developing the now familiar standards for the Web: hypertext transfer protocol (HTTP) to delineate how servers and browsers would communicate; hypertext mark up language (HTML) to encode documents with addressed links to other documents; and a uniform resource locator (URL) format for addressing Internet resources (e.g., http://www.cern.ch or mailto:webmaster@domain.com). By 1990, Berners-Lee had likewise created the first Web browser and server software to feed information to the browser.

Although Berners-Lee's vision was for a collaborative, informal medium of information exchange, perhaps that typified in chat rooms and newsgroups and whiteboard applications, more commercially motivated Web innovations soon followed. Most important was Marc Andreessen's Mosaic browser, which he developed as an undergraduate employee at the National Center for Supercomputing Applications (NCSA) of the University of Illinois at Urbana Champaign. Mosaic, which debuted in early 1993, was more graphical and user friendly than other Web applications up to that point. It was an instant success, albeit not a money maker because it was mostly distributed for free. Andreessen finished his degree in computer science later that year, and in early 1994 established Netscape Communications Corp. with Silicon Valley titan Jim Barksdale, founder of the high-end computer hardware maker Silicon Graphics. Netscape's Navigator quickly became the dominant browser on the Internet, at one point claiming 75 percent of all users. Curiously, the NCSA claimed rights to Mosaic and wrangled with Andreessen over the commercial use of the browser application code and its name; the NCSA would later license Mosaic to Microsoft Corp. to use in a competing browser, en-

Figure 2

Leading Internet Domain Types Worldwide

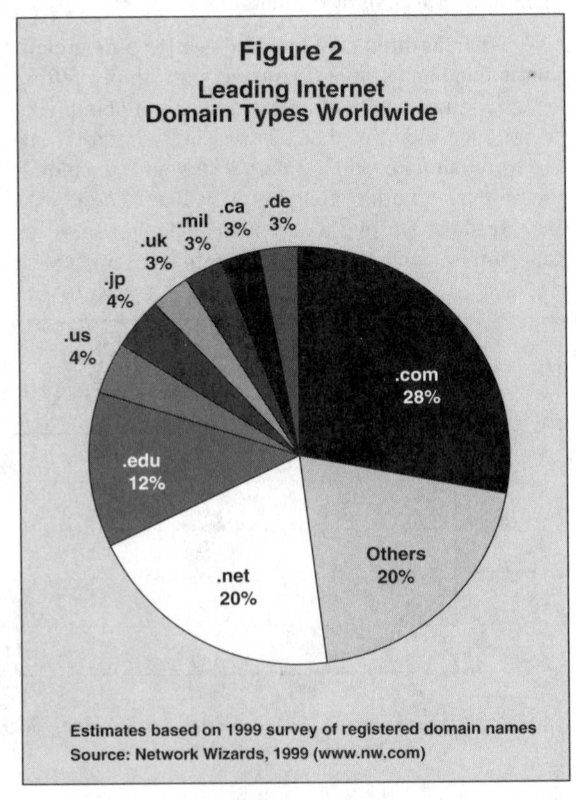

Estimates based on 1999 survey of registered domain names
Source: Network Wizards, 1999 (www.nw.com)

abling the software giant to outmaneuver Netscape within a couple years with its Internet Explorer product. By this time the Web was nearly synonymous with the Internet.

As the browser wars fed on the phenomenal public interest in the Internet in the mid-1990s, the network became a predominantly commercial entity, as businesses set up Internet sites in droves and millions of new users—both private individuals and corporate users—began logging on. The NSF officially bowed out of running the Internet backbone in 1995, when commercial operators took over; however, the NSF continued its policies of funding research into advanced networking applications that could improve the Internet and newer high-speed research networks.

BUSINESS USES OF THE INTERNET

Although there are scores of specific Internet applications that benefit businesses, they can all be grouped under two broad categories: (1) information exchange and dissemination, and (2) facilitating e-commerce.

INFORMATION EXCHANGE. The information exchange function is the broader of the two and includes such diverse applications as:

- e-mail and other person-to-person communications, e.g., **computer conferencing**
- online marketing and brand building
- employee recruitment
- investor and public relations information distribution
- intranets for employee knowledge sharing and collaboration
- extranets to enable outsourcing and supply-chain integration

The economic value of these applications is difficult to measure, but for large organizations they have the potential to save millions of dollars in **costs**, and depending on the application, to stimulate sales as well. Only a couple of the possibilities will be discussed here.

The internal information management and knowledge-sharing abilities of corporate intranets can be substantial. Intranets, which are corporate information networks based on Internet technology but are usually restricted access sites available only to select users, allow central storage and versatile dissemination of diverse information, including corporate **handbooks and manuals**, customer or marketing databases, employee databases, project discussion boards, and other internal documentation. Intranets are substantially more efficient than circulating paper copies of documents, both in terms of immediacy of information and, in most cases, maintenance costs. Because they rely on simple, Web-based client/server technology, they're also typically easier to implement and use than proprietary databases.

The extranet, which enables supply-chain integration and automation, is an especially powerful use of the Internet, and one that is increasingly being adopted by large corporations. Although there are many variations, supply-chain management is generally a hybrid of data exchange and electronic commerce that allows companies to better coordinate their procurement and distribution practices with those of their suppliers and clients. Based on the efficiency principles of **electronic data interchange** (EDI) and just-in-time inventory, this coordination can afford several benefits. The streamlining effects can include eliminating paperwork, reducing staff hours, and improving data accuracy. Web-based ordering systems likewise tend to be easier to use than their old-line counterparts, which also contribute faster and more accurate results. Such automated systems can also provide management with more timely and detailed information about corporate purchasing habits and needs, allowing better resource planning and even providing a blueprint for **cost control**. Extranets can also be established to provide customer service and other external communications functions.

As an information source, the Web is also a particularly efficient means of comparison shopping for business procurement. With relative ease, a procurement officer can find price quotes from several vendors, some of which may not even be aware the other exists. The buyer can then use this information to either choose the low-cost vendor or to gain concessions from established vendors. The downside to this, of course, is when companies are on the receiving end of this informed negotiation, which usually leads to tighter profit margins.

E-COMMERCE. There are also multiple facets to e-commerce, although they are much more closely integrated than information-exchange functions. Specifically, businesses may focus on one or more of these aspects of commerce:

- preparing customers for the sale
- facilitating the actual transaction
- managing any follow-up to the sale

It may not be feasible or profitable to do all three in equal proportion, or even at all. For example, the most logical commerce-related application for Federal Express and similar companies is delivery tracking, which is done after the transaction is completed. It also makes sense to provide pre-transaction services, such as account set-up and drop-off center locators, on the site. However, in this example the transaction itself is more difficult to accomplish. It consists of two main parts, dropping off a package and arranging for payment. The latter could easily be done over the Internet, but it's less clear how the company would profitably obtain the packages for delivery. Federal Express offers pick-up services, but it's uncertain whether it would be profitable for the company to pick up the majority of the parcels it carries, which are traditionally dropped off at local retail centers.

In other trades, of course, the Internet may well be the ideal locus of transaction. The case is particularly compelling for products or services that can be delivered online, such as software applications via high speed connection, musical recordings, or databases. But strong—if not initially profitable—business models have also been adopted in many other fields, notably by booksellers such as Amazon.com and auction houses like eBay, not to mention vendors that electronically service the mundane but lucrative business-to-business supply chain.

Thus, while e-commerce is commonly the more celebrated business application, as noted above it isn't the appropriate model for all types of trade. Companies contemplating a new e-commerce initiative would do well to consider this maxim: all e-commerce is not the same. Internet-era mythology holds that (1) competitors big and small are all on equal footing on the Internet, and (2) anything and everything can be sold online.

Equal footing is only possible in the limited sense that minor players in some line of business can, assuming they have the funding (in 1998 the median development price for a mid-sized Web site was estimated at $100,000 and rising briskly) and technical resources, build Internet sites that are as good as—or better than—those of their major competitors, as measured by site convenience, functionality, marketing tactics, and so forth. However, this doesn't mean that the smaller company will be any more effective in the larger sense. The smaller company must also have a cost-efficient system for order fulfillment, a powerful marketing operation that ensures potential customers are reached, and many other supporting capabilities in order to succeed. For instance, say a small Internet-only start-up wants to sell high-end home appliances online. They may create the best site in the business, but will they be equipped to serve a national market? Probably not. For such large and expensive products, traditional retailers like Sears, Roebuck and Co. and the so called appliance superstores have tremendous competitive advantages in the online arena as well, not the least of which is an established and already profitable physical distribution system. That's not to mention that the marketing model may be off target; Internet transactions may not appeal to potential buyers of expensive appliances, as these people might value the ability to see the product in the showroom and talk with sales staff. While that conclusion in this example is arguable, there are clearly some product and service transactions in which customers place a high value on in-person contact and immediate fulfillment (real life examples being health care, video rental, and grocery shopping), and these so far haven't been good candidates for an Internet-only approach.

The point here is not to deny the Internet's revolutionary implications for the business world, or to suggest that its entry barriers can't be significantly lower than in traditional industries. Instead, the lesson is that many traditional business principles and practices still apply to successful e-commerce. **Market research**, customer service before and after the sale, **cost-benefit analysis**, and return on investment all have essential roles in fashioning an Internet commerce strategy.

THE INTERNET MARKETING ENVIRONMENT

As a point of commerce, the Internet has a number of unique features that must be reckoned with in order to successfully compete in its terrain. Most importantly, customers, whether individuals or businesses, tend to associate different values and expectations with online commerce versus traditional means. Many of these can be summarized under the heading of value. Put simply, many customers expect to come away with something of greater value from an Internet transaction than they do from a conventional physical purchase. Value may present itself in many forms. Examples include greater convenience, better information about the purchase, reliability of service, personalization/customization, security of the transaction, and lower costs. If an online vendor fails to offer better value—perhaps it is only as good as the real-life alternative—it is likely to have trouble making the grade in Internet markets.

Value creation is but one of several aspects of Internet marketing that many ill-conceived Internet ventures fail to address. A technically competent Web site is only a starting point, a baseline. Effective Internet **business plans** must also identify a clear market need, be highly sensitive to competition from all sources, articulate a strong value proposition for customers, and be flexible to respond to market changes.

THE FUTURE

MARKET GROWTH. Divining exactly what the future holds for the Internet is no easy task—and all such projections must be taken with a grain or two of salt—but it is possible to observe a number of trends that are likely to influence that future. Perhaps the broadest and most obvious is the continued growth of the Internet by all measures. As mentioned at the outset, the value of commerce conducted over the Internet will probably be measured in the trillions of dollars within the first few years of the 2000s. Compared to late 1990s levels, this will represent a geometric annual growth rate in the multi-thousand percent range. By some estimates Internet commerce may constitute nearly 10 percent of U.S. gross domestic product by 2005. While it often has a higher profile, some observers expect retail commerce to account for only a small fraction, perhaps only 3-5 percent, of that total. Meanwhile, the number of Web users worldwide is expected to reach a half a billion or more people by then, up from 170 million as of 1999.

TECHNICAL ADVANCEMENTS. Not surprisingly, another noteworthy area of development will be technological. Since the mid-1990s there have been several government and commercial ventures to develop a new, faster breed of technology for the Internet, which has been straining under the aggressive demands of modern networking. More precisely, the research efforts are looking to build new internets, which will ultimately transfer technology to the public Internet, either in the direct sense, as was the case historically, or in a knowledge transfer scenario in which the government provides a roadmap for commercial developers to follow.

The main thrust of U.S. government efforts is behind a program called the Next Generation Internet (NGI) initiative, a high-speed government research network being created under the direction of an interagency committee. The NSF, the National Institutes of Health, the Department of Defense (through DARPA), the Department of Energy, NASA, and the National Institute for Technology and Standards are the primary agencies contributing to NGI. The NGI was scheduled to reach the advanced development and testing stages by 2002, at which time it was intended to demonstrate transfer speeds up to a trillion bits (terabits) per second. Some $300 million in federal grants has been earmarked for NGI and related initiatives.

The NGI project is also feeding funds to a separate Internet research project known as Internet2 (I2), a collaboration between some 154 U.S. colleges and universities. I2 is intended to return institutions of higher learning to the days when they had a relatively private, high-speed network to themselves, i.e., before the commercialization of the Internet. There are also about a dozen and a half commercial firms participating in the I2 effort, mostly from the telecommunications services and network hardware sectors. A related effort being undertaken by many of the same organizations was called Abilene.

While these new networks were being conceived, the NSF, and its contractor MCI WorldCom, deployed a limited-use system known as the Very High Speed Backbone Network Service (vBNS). The vBNS project was the immediate successor to NSFNET when it was transferred to the commercial domain in 1995. Since then, the NSF has financed ongoing upgrades to keep it current with the highest performance standards of current commercial networking technology, including fiber optics. Access to vBNS is restricted to NSF computing centers and merit-based research centers. As a result, only a handful of mostly academic institutions use vBNS. In 1999, an upgrading project brought its bandwidth up to 2.2 gigabits per second (Gbps), but overall it is a much less ambitious endeavor than that of the new Internet projects.

SEE ALSO: Computer Conferencing; Computer Fraud; Computer Networks; Computer Security; Electronic Commerce; Electronic Mail; Local Area Networks (LANs); Wide Area Networks (WANs)

[Scott Heil]

FURTHER READING:

Anders, George. ''Click and Buy: Why and Where Internet Commerce Is Succeeding.'' *Wall Street Journal,* 7 December 1998.

''Creating a Business Model for E-Commerce.'' *CIO,* 1 May 1999.

Friel, Daniel. ''Electronic Commerce on the Web: Digital Drivers for 1999.'' *Business Economics,* January 1999.

Gascoyne, Robert J. *Corporate Internet Planning Guide.* New York: Van Nostrand Reinhold, 1997.

Hanrahan, Timothy. ''Lessons Learned: A Guide to What Does and Doesn't Sell on the Internet.'' *Wall Street Journal,* 7 December 1998.

''How to Survive the Cyber-Revolution.'' *Business Week,* 5 April 1999.

Hunt, Laura. ''Past.com: An Internet Timeline.'' *Computerworld,* 10 May 1999.

''Internet Insights, 1999.'' *Computer Industry Report,* 23 March 1999.

Internet Society. *All About the Internet.* Reston, VA, 1999. Available from www.isoc.org.

MCI WorldCom, Inc. *MCI and NSF's Very High Speed Backbone Network Service.* Jackson, MS, 1999. Available from www.vbns.net.

Mougayar, Walid. *Opening Digital Markets: Battle Plans and Business Strategies for Internet Commerce.* New York: McGraw-Hill, 1998.

National Coordination Office for Computing, Information, and Communications. *Next Generation Internet (NGI) Initiative.* Washington, 1999. Available from www.ngi.gov.

Overly, Michael R. *E-Policy: How to Develop Computer, E-mail and Internet Guidelines to Protect Your Company and Its Assets.* New York: AMACOM, 1999.

''Report Quantifies Economic Impact of U.S. Internet-Related Companies.'' *Wall Street Journal,* 10 June 1999.

University Corporation for Advanced Internet Development. *The Internet2 Project.* Washington, 1999. Available from www.internet2.edu.

INTERNSHIPS

Internships, the temporary and often unpaid entry-level positions companies offer college students and recent graduates, are an increasingly important tool for young workers to gain job experience and make professional contacts. By definition internships are intended to be learning opportunities in some career path, rather than menial or dead-end jobs, even if the tasks assigned to interns aren't always the most challenging. Some internships actually lead to college credit.

Although there are no definitive statistics collected on internships, there is some evidence that the use of internships grew during the 1990s. This trend likely stemmed in part from the tight labor market in the latter half of the 1990s. Traditionally popular in certain professional career tracks, such as MBA and law programs, internships are now common in a diverse range of fields.

A widely cited annual survey published by the Internet career guidance site VaultReports.com reported in 1999 that over 80 percent of all college seniors completed at least one internship. According to Samer Hamadeh, one of the authors of the Vault Reports, as recently as the mid-1980s only 3 percent of college students took part in an internship. With approximately 2.5 million U.S. college seniors each year as of the mid-1990s, the 80 percent estimate translates into some 2 million internships. Moreover, the survey found, many undergraduates don't stop at just one internship. Indeed, a full two-thirds of the same college seniors had undertaken two or more internships—and this doesn't even begin to account for the internships done by graduate students. Princeton Review's *The Internship Bible* boasts 100,000 internship directory listings; *Peterson's Internships* lists some 50,000 positions nationally.

WORKER BENEFITS

Internships can confer three main benefits to workers. First, they provide relatively low-risk opportunities to sample different occupations and work environments. Second, they help build up workers' skills and can thereby make them more attractive candidates for future employment. In a general sense, an internship can help the worker learn effective work habits and practices, such as how to manage time, get along with other people, and use standard business tools like fax machines, **electronic mail** for business correspondence, and so forth. In a more focused sense, internships can also teach workers occupation-specific skills. The third primary benefit of internships is for developing professional contacts. The simple fact that a person has worked for a company in the past is, assuming there were no major problems, often a compelling reason for that person to be rehired into a permanent position. More importantly, beyond the relationship the worker establishes with a particular company during an internship, he or she may also form beneficial relationships with managers or co-workers who may one day be in a position to recommend, refer, or even hire the former intern at another company.

COMPANY BENEFITS. Internships can also serve corporate interests. An obvious, albeit somewhat misleading, example would be the unpaid internship, which allows a company to obtain full-time labor, at least temporarily, at little or no cost. While this perhaps fuels some internship programs, some companies actively eschew unpaid internships, believing that they fail to motivate young workers and send the wrong messages about the company's values. Probably the most important benefit of internship programs to companies comes in providing them with a regular supply of potential new workers. Arguably, many college interns may be more aggressive and motivated employees by virtue of their choosing an internship while in school rather than taking low-skill jobs or not working at all. But more than anything, an internship program provides a means for companies to try out entry- or mid-level employees before establishing a more permanent relationship with them.

If the management is pleased with the intern's performance, rehiring him or her as a regular employee can also be considerably cheaper and easier than bringing in someone new. Some research further suggests that companies with various kinds of youth-worker programs, including internships and local school initiatives, tend to have significantly lower **employee turnover**.

SEE ALSO: Apprenticeship Programs; Training and Development

FURTHER READING:

De Lisser, Eleena. "School-Business Partnerships Help Retain Workers." *Wall Street Journal,* 24 November 1998.

Filipczak, Bob. "The New Interns." *Training,* April 1998.

"Internships." New York: Vault Reports, Inc., 1999. Available from www.vaultreports.com.

Messmer, Max. "Establishing a Successful Internship Program." *Business Credit,* April 1999.

Oldman, Mark, and Samer Hamadeh. *The Internship Bible.* New York: Princeton Review, 1999.

Peterson's Internships. 19th ed. Princeton, NJ: Peterson's Guides, 1999.

Wong, Alex. "Climbing the Ladder of Success Often Begins with Internships." *Record* (Hackensack, NJ), 17 July 1998.

INTERSTATE COMMERCE COMMISSION (ICC)

The Interstate Commerce Commission (ICC)—which was abolished in 1995 and replaced by the Surface Transportation Board—was established as an independent regulatory agency by the Interstate Commerce Act of 1887. The ICC was originally limited to regulating interstate commerce by railroad or by a combination of water and rail. Subsequent pieces of legislation serving to amend the original act broadened the regulatory powers of the ICC to include all surface transportation involved in interstate commerce and foreign commerce to the extent that it took place in the United States.

Surface transportation regulated by the ICC eventually included railroads, trucking, buses, freight forwarders, water carriers, transportation brokers, and those pipelines that were not regulated by the Federal Energy Regulatory Commission. Since there were various exemptions from ICC regulations, in practice the ICC regulated approximately one-third of all interstate trucking operations and only about one-tenth of interstate water carrier operations. Exemptions applied to such areas as water transportation of products in bulk, school buses, hotel buses, national park buses, taxicabs, newspaper distribution vehicles, and vehicles incidental to air transportation.

CHANGES TO JURISDICTION

While most legislation passed from 1903 to the early 1970s served to strengthen the ICC's authority and broaden its areas of jurisdiction, the Railroad Revitalization and Regulatory Reform Act of 1976 and subsequent legislation served to provide for less regulation over carrier rates and practices. Responding to concerns of the railroad industry over the effect of ICC regulations on competitiveness, the Staggers Rail Act of 1980 eliminated many of the regulatory requirements of the ICC for railroads.

That same year the Motor Carrier Act reduced the ICC's regulatory authority over the trucking industry, which the ICC had regulated since long-distance trucking began to compete with railroads in the 1930s. As a result the ICC no longer had as much control over such areas as entry into the trucking business, routes served, and commodities carried. Since part of the trucking industry was concerned about the negative impact of such deregulation, the law provided for phasing in regulatory changes gradually and formally reviewing the impacts of those changes. Other legislation in the 1980s provided for similar regulatory reforms affecting bus lines and surface freight forwarders.

ICC regulations encompassed transportation economics, transportation service, and consumer protection. In the area of transportation economics the ICC had regulatory power over rates and charges among regulated carriers, shippers, receivers of freight, and passengers, among others. It set standards for reasonable rates and in its final years was concerned with the practice of undercharging. It also had approval power over proposed **mergers and acquisitions** and sales of regulated carriers. It administered laws, prescribed **accounting** rules, and awarded reparations relating to railroad bankruptcy. In addition it had jurisdiction over a range of matters concerning railroad equipment.

During the Carter administration the ICC's power to set rates was taken away, a power that dated back to the administration of Theodore Roosevelt. During the 1980s the Reagan administration attempted to abolish the ICC, without success. Subsequently, President Bill Clinton, in his 1995 State of the Union speech, mentioned the ICC as an agency that should be eliminated. This time the goal was accomplished, by means of the Interstate Commerce Commission Termination Act of 1995 (ICCTA), which abolished the ICC effective December 31, 1995.

NEW BOARD CREATED

The passing of the ICC into history, however, did not mean that railroads and motor carriers were completely deregulated. The ICCTA created the Surface Transportation Board (STB) as part of the U.S. Department of Transportation to replace the ICC and take care of the loose ends of rail and motor-carrier regulation.

The STB is a three-member panel whose first appointees were the last ICC commissioners. Its principal responsibilities are concerned with mergers, consolidations, and trackage rights in the railroad industry. It also has regulatory power over a company's ability to enter or leave the railroad business. New railroads require an STB certificate, with approval based on the public interest. Line sales also fall within the STB's jurisdiction, with approvals based on public convenience and necessity.

The STB also inherited the ICC's power to approve or reject abandonment of a rail line. Using the "public convenience and necessity" standard, the STB may require the abandoning carrier to sell the line for other public purposes if continued rail use is not required. The STB may also reject the request to abandon a line and require the carrier to accept financial assistance for its continued operation, again based on public convenience and necessity. Thus, railroad companies do not have the freedom to enter and leave markets at will.

In the area of mergers and consolidations, the ICCTA granted the STB authority to approve or reject proposed mergers in the railroad industry. If the railroad industry were completely deregulated, then such power would vest in the U.S. Department of Justice under provisions of **antitrust** legislation. The ICCTA, however, gave that power to the STB, which in its first years of existence approved the Union Pacific takeover of Southern Pacific as well as the plan by CSX and Norfolk Southern to acquire and divide up Conrail.

By the time the ICC was abolished, federal regulation of motor carrier rates was practically nonexistent. Following the ICCTA, motor carriers were subject to common law rather than federal regulation. Motor carriers, however, still had to register and obtain operating authority from the new Section of Licensing in the Federal Highway Administration of the Department of Transportation. The ICCTA also reclassified surface freight forwarders as motor carriers, placing them under the jurisdiction of the Department of Transportation.

[David P. Bianco]

FURTHER READING:

Best, Samuel, and others. ''Terminating the Oldest Living Regulator: The Death of the Interstate Commerce Commission.'' *International Journal of Public Administration,* December 1997, 2067-96.

Giermanski, James R. ''Changes Loom on the Horizon.'' *Logistics Management,* May 1997, 79-80A.

Gordon, John Steele. ''R.I.P., ICC.'' *American Heritage,* May-June 1996, 22-23.

Marien, Edward J. ''Contract Carriage with Less Regulation.'' *Transportation and Distribution,* July 1996, 76-77.

Thoms, William E. ''Son of the ICC.'' *Trains Magazine,* December 1997, 36-37.

INTRAPRENEURSHIP

Coined by Gifford Pinchott in 1986, ''intrapreneur'' refers to someone who possesses entrepreneurial skills and uses them within a company, instead of using them to launch a new business. Intrapreneurs—also called corporate entrepreneurs—can help established companies implement innovative policies and procedures or introduce innovative products or services. Intrapreneurs, however, must have a fair amount of latitude within a company in order to effect any significant changes. Workers who earn the title ''intrapreneur'' usually go well beyond their narrow job descriptions, providing invaluable help in innovating some aspect of their companies.

Intrapreneurship differs from **entrepreneurship** in that intrapreneurs constantly must overcome barriers and negotiate obstacles and have opportunities to work with greater financial, technological, and human resources offered by an established company. In contrast, entrepreneurs largely work independently and often lack the resources of large companies. People with entrepreneurial skills also may choose to work within a company because they value job security, would like to practice launching a new business inside a company before launching one outside, and wish to take advantage of a company's established marketing channels.

Companies benefit from intrapreneurship because it can function as a means of overcoming aspects of corporate bureaucracy that impede **innovation**, allowing companies to remain creative and hence competitive. Moreover, intrapreneurship can remedy the loss of challenging and rewarding jobs, which can lead to greater job satisfaction and productivity.

Workers who are given freedom to experiment are often associated with the innovation process and the development of new products, services, or businesses within corporations. Intrapreneurship researchers refer to this freedom to experiment as innovative culture. According to Howard Oden in *Managing Corporate Culture, Innovation, and Intrapreneurship,* research indicates that intrapreneurship succeeds when companies provide their innovators with support, encouragement, and an atmosphere that promotes innovation. Specifically, Oden enumerated a host of attributes often found in innovative cultures, including:

1. Long-term strategic and cultural leadership: upper-level **management** provides long-term strategies and challenging goals for the company's innovation.
2. Promotion of innovation and intrapreneurship: the company encourages new ideas and new ways of doing things at all levels and promotes risk taking.
3. Flexibility and adaptability: the company does not have a hierarchical structure, rather a flat structure, and the innovation process involves different **teams** of workers, not different levels of management.
4. Collaboration and teamwork: the company encourages teamwork and collaborative innovation.
5. Ongoing learning: workers are expected to improve their skills and learn new ones continuously.
6. Toleration of failure: since some innovations fail to bear fruit, companies must ac-

cept failure as part of the innovation process in order to keep intrapreneurs free from the fear of failure.

Companies that foster innovation usually possess these and other related characteristics that allow intrapreneurs to seek solutions and generate new ideas, processes, products, or services, while not disrupting the regular flow of business. Although innovation can and does occur in any environment, too rigid and authoritarian **corporate cultures** definitely can stifle the initiative and creativity of intrapreneurs.

Intrapreneurs must possess a variety of skills themselves in order to be innovative—no matter what the corporate culture is like. In general, intrapreneurs have many of the skills that entrepreneurs have—such as market savvy, intuitiveness, creativity, **leadership** skills, and the ability to work independently and collaboratively. They notice opportunities—for new products, services, businesses, and so forth—and they pursue them. In addition, they also must have a certain amount of political savvy and be able to negotiate agreements with resistant or skeptical coworkers and managers, according to Lakshmanan Prasad in *SAM Advanced Management Journal.* Intrapreneurs must play organizational politics and reconcile the interests of different company teams or departments in order to bring about their innovations.

While many workers can develop technical plans for innovations, far fewer can have them implemented. Hence, intrapreneurs must possess strong social skills and knowledge of company politics and power, which entails identifying influential coworkers, managers, and groups within a company, evaluating their likely responses, and developing strategies to influence them.

The intrapreneurial process begins with a new idea or an innovation, and follows the steps of development, implementation, and modification. Intrapreneurs may conceive of an innovation serendipitously or deliberately. Either way, after intrapreneurs have an idea for an innovation they must begin to develop it—whether a product, service, procedure, or company—by determining its feasibility. They assess the market and need for the innovation to determine if implementing it will pay off. Once intrapreneurs are certain they can feasibly introduce the innovation, they make general plans to execute the innovation, develop the innovation, and test it.

If the innovation withstands development and testing, then intrapreneurs implement the innovation. To ensure that the innovation will be successful, however, intrapreneurs gather feedback and make any necessary modifications to the innovation in order to improve it.

INTRAPRENEURIAL TECHNIQUES

Oden identified a number of strategies or techniques for intrapreneurs, which allow them to be innovative and creative while functioning inside a corporation. *Wall Street Journal* columnist Timothy D. Schellhardt included some of these techniques in his article ''Small Business: David in Goliath,'' where he referred to them as part of his ''Intrapreneur's Ten Commandments'':

1. Seek approvals creatively: ask managers for small decisions, to keep the importance of the decisions minimal and to help ensure approval. In addition, use customers and suppliers interested in the potential innovation for leverage in obtaining approval.
2. Find and use allies: recruit the support of employees within the company, especially ones with knowledge and skills relevant to the innovation as well as ones with considerable influence in the company.
3. Establish coalitions: intrapreneurs can realize their goals by forming coalitions to support their innovations. Coalitions involve both supportive coworkers and managers or executives.
4. Persuade management to be flexible: with the help of customers, allies, and coalitions, intrapreneurs should strive to change rigid company policies in order to facilitate innovation and they should point out to senior-level managers that the policies and procedures that work for a mature company, product, or service are not necessarily suitable for a budding company, product, or service.
5. Share credit: intrapreneurs should recognize all those who participate in an innovative project to promote further collaboration in the innovation process.
6. Control time expectations: keep projects low profile until **research and development** is completed and the innovation is nearly ready for the market.

[Karl Heil]

FURTHER READING:

Bygrave, William D. *The Portable MBA in Entrepreneurship.* New York: Wiley, 1994.

Kuratko, Donald F., and Ray V. Montagno. ''The Intrapreneurial Spirit.'' *Training and Development,* October 1989, 83.

Oden, Howard W. *Managing Corporate Culture, Innovation, and Intrapreneurship.* Westport, CT: Quorum Books, 1997.

Prasad, Lakshmanan. ''The Etiology of Organizational Politics: Implications for the Intrapreneur.'' *SAM Advanced Management Journal,* summer 1993, 35.

Schellhardt, Timothy D. ''Small Business: David in Goliath.'' *Wall Street Journal,* 23 May 1996.

INVENTORY ACCOUNTING

A company's inventory is all of its merchandise intended for sale to its customers in the normal course of business. Inventories are considered current assets in that they usually are sold within a year or within a company's operating cycle. Furthermore, inventories make up the most valuable current asset for most retailers. Inventory accounting is the process of determining and keeping track of the inventory costs. Inventory costs refer to all the **costs** a company incurs to obtain merchandise, including the actual merchandise costs as well as transportation costs. Proper inventory accounting enables companies to represent their net **income** accurately. To do so, accountants must use the appropriate methods for measuring inventory, because inaccurate inventory amounts or values can make a company seem more profitable than it really is and can misrepresent a company in its **financial statements**.

A starting point for inventory accounting is determining the cost of merchandise that has been sold within a given **accounting** period, which is referred to as the ''cost of goods sold.'' The cost of goods sold is the net acquisition cost of merchandise obtained and sold to customers during an operating period and is calculated by adding the value of the beginning inventory, the cost of new inventory items, and transportation costs, and then by subtracting the ending inventory amount (see Table 1).

Table 1

Beginning Inventory		$20,000
Add: Net Cost of Purchases	$62,000	
Add: Transportation	1,000	
		63,000
		$83,000
Less: Ending Inventory		18,000
Cost of Goods Sold		$65,000

When measuring inventories, accountants consider two variables—quantity and price—and refer to inventories by their dollar value (quantity multiplied by price). While the principle of taking inventory is simple—counting all items available for sale, pricing them, and calculating their value—the practice of it can be complicated and time consuming. The complications arise because even medium-sized companies often have numerous items in a host of sizes, types, and qualities, which they purchased at different unit prices and which they store at different sites. In addition, measuring inventory may involve including items that have not been delivered yet, which companies nonetheless technically own. Such items are called ''goods in transit.''

INVENTORY ACCOUNTING METHODS

SPECIFIC IDENTIFICATION METHOD. Inventory pricing also becomes complicated when unit prices for inventory items fluctuate during an accounting period. Nevertheless the basic idea of inventory pricing is uncomplicated: a retailer should determine the value of its inventory by figuring out what it cost to acquire that inventory. When an inventory item is sold, the inventory account should be reduced (credited) and cost of goods sold should be increased (debited) for the amount paid for each inventory item. This method works if a company is operating under the Specific Identification Method. That is, a company knows the cost of every individual item that is sold. This method works well when the amount of inventory a company has is limited, the value of its inventory items is high, and each inventory item is relatively unique. Companies that use this method include car dealerships, jewelers, and art galleries.

Problems arise when a company has a large inventory and each specific inventory item is relatively indistinguishable from other items. Some retailers, for example, sell only one line of products, such as blue jeans. Such a retailer may have an inventory that includes various styles and sizes, but the inventory on the whole is similar. Suppose this retailer buys the inventory from a wholesaler or manufacturer and pays $3,000 for 300 pairs of jeans. Hence, the cost per pair is $10. If the cost never changes, then inventory costing is simple. Every pair of jeans costs the exact same amount. Because of **inflation** as well as discounts and sales, however, prices tend to fluctuate. For instance, this retailer might buy 100 pairs of jeans on Monday for $1,000 ($10 per pair), and 200 pairs of jeans on Friday for $2,150 ($10.75 per pair). Under the Specific Identification Method, the retailer would have to mark or code every pair of jeans, to determine which purchase a particular pair of jeans came from. This method is far too cumbersome for companies with large and even medium-sized inventories, although it is the most precise way of determining inventory prices. As a result, other inventory **valuation** methods have been developed.

WEIGHTED AVERAGE METHOD. Under the Weighted Average Method, a company would determine the weighted average cost of the inventory. In the example above, the weighted average cost would be $3,150 / 300 pairs which equals $10.50 per pair of jeans. Therefore, every pair of jeans would have the inventory price of $10.50, regardless of whether they were actually bought in the $10 purchase or the $10.75 purchase. This weighted average would remain unchanged until the next purchase occurs, which would result in a new weighted average cost to be calculated. This inventory accounting method is used primarily by companies that maintain a large supply of undifferentiated inventory items such as fuels and grains.

FIFO METHOD. Another method used by companies is called the FIFO Method (first-in, first-out). Under FIFO, it is assumed that the oldest inventory—i.e., the inventory first purchased—is always sold first. Therefore, the inventory that remains is from the most recent purchases. So for the given example, the first 100 jeans that are sold will reduce inventory and increase cost of goods sold at a rate of $10 per pair. The next 200 sold will have an inventory price of $10.75 per pair. It is irrelevant whether customers actually buy the older pairs of jean first. Under FIFO, a company always assumes that it sells its oldest inventory first and that ending inventories include more recently purchased merchandise. Companies selling perishable goods such as food and drugs tend to use this method, because cash flow closely resembles goods flow with this method.

LIFO METHOD. The final method that a company can use is the LIFO Method (last-in, first-out). Under LIFO, it is assumed that the most recent purchase is always sold first. Therefore, the inventory that remains is always the oldest inventory. So for the given example, the first 200 jeans that are sold will reduce inventory and increase cost of goods sold at a rate of $10.75 per pair. Again, It does not matter if customers actually buy the newer pair of jeans first. Under LIFO, a company always assumes that it sells its newest inventory first. Nevertheless, this method represents the true flow of goods for very few companies.

COMPARISON OF THE METHODS

These different methods will affect cash flow, the actual or assumed association of inventory unit costs with goods sold or in stock—not goods flow, the actual movement of goods. Therefore, gross profits will vary among the different methods. The example of 250 pairs of jeans sold at $15 each in Table 2 demonstrates this phenomenon. Suppose that 80 pairs of jeans remain unsold during this period, making up the ending inventory, and apply the inventory prices supplied above for each method: the first 100 pairs of jeans were bought for $10 and the next 200 for $10.75—or $3,150.

Table 2

Differences in Gross Profit on Sales for Each Pricing Method

	Specific Identification	Avg.	FIFO	LIFO
Sales 250/$15	$3,750	$3,750	$3,750	$3,750
Beginning Inventory	500	500	500	500
Purchases	3,150	3,150	3,150	3,150
Goods for Sale*	3,650	3,650	3,650	3,650
Ending Inv.	837.50	840	860	820
Cost of Goods	2,812.50	2,810	2,790	2,830
Gross Profit	$ 937.50	$ 940	$ 960	$ 920

*Goods available for sale include the beginning inventory as well as additional purchases within the accounting period.

The differences in value of the ending inventory stem from the different ways each method calculates the ending inventory—by determining whether newer or older jeans were left, determining the weighted average for the two purchases, assuming the remaining 80 pairs are newer pairs, or assuming the remaining pairs are older pairs, respectively. Consequently, the differences in gross profit shown in Table 2 reflect the assumptions made about cash flow using the various inventory pricing methods, not the actual goods flow.

Of these four inventory methods, the most popular methods used are FIFO and LIFO. Even though LIFO does not reflect the actual flow of goods in most cases, approximately 50 percent of major companies use this method. The FIFO Method may come the closest to matching the actual physical flow of inventory. Since FIFO assumes that the oldest inventory is always sold first, the valuation of inventory still on hand is at the most recent price. Assuming inflation, this will mean that cost of goods sold will be at its lowest possible amount. Therefore, a major advantage of FIFO is that it has the effect of maximizing net income within an inflationary environment. The downside of that effect is that income **taxes** will be the greatest.

The LIFO Method is preferred by many companies because it has the effect of reducing a company's taxes, thus increasing cash flow. Nevertheless, these attributes of LIFO are present only in an inflationary environment. Under LIFO, a company always sells its newest inventory items first. Given inflation, these items will also be its most expensive items. So cost of goods sold will always be at its greatest amount; therefore, net income before taxes will be at its lowest amount, and taxes will be minimized, which is the major benefit of LIFO.

Another advantage of LIFO is that it can have an income smoothing effect. Again, assuming inflation and a company that is doing well, one would expect inventory levels to expand. Therefore, a company is purchasing inventory, but under LIFO, the majority of the cost of these purchases will be on the **income statement** as part of cost of goods sold. Thus, the most recent and most expensive purchases will increase cost of goods sold, thus lowering net income before taxes as well as lowering taxes and net income. Net income may still be high, but not as high as it would if FIFO had been used.

On the other hand, if a company is doing poorly, it will have a tendency to reduce inventories. To do so, the company will have to effectively sell more inventory than it acquires. Since a company using LIFO assumes it sells its most recent purchases first, the inventory that remains is older and less expensive (given inflation). So when a company shrinks its inventory, it sells older, less expensive inventory. Therefore, the cost of goods sold is lower, net income before taxes is higher, and net income is higher than it otherwise would have been.

A disadvantage of LIFO is the effect it has on the **balance sheet**. If a company always sells its most recent inventory first, then the balance sheet will contain inventory valued at the oldest inventory prices. For instance, if a company were to switch from FIFO to LIFO in 1955, then unless the inventory was zeroed out at some point in time, there may be units of inventory valued at 1955 prices, even though the physical inventory is comprised of the most recent units. As a result, the inventory account can be dramatically undervalued if a company has adopted LIFO, and if during that time, the cost of inventory has increased.

The LIFO Method is justified based upon the matching principle, as the most recent cost of inventory is matched against the current revenue generated from the sale of that inventory. FIFO does not, however, distort the valuation of inventory on the balance sheet like LIFO can potentially do.

Companies generally disclose their inventory accounting methods in their financial statements, usually as a footnote or a parenthetical note in the relevant sections. Therefore, when examining financial statements, it is imperative that the inventory notes be read carefully, to determine the method of inventory valuation chosen by a company. It is most likely that either FIFO or LIFO would have been chosen. Assuming inflation, FIFO will result in higher net income during growth periods and a higher and more realistic inventory balance. In periods of growth, LIFO will result in lower net income and lower income tax payments, thus enhancing a company's cash flow. During periods of contraction, LIFO will result in higher income levels. LIFO also has the potential to greatly undervalue inventory over time.

PERPETUAL INVENTORY PRICING

The previous discussion and examples applied to periodic inventory accounting where a company records the purchases it makes, makes no record of the cost of goods sold at the time of sale, and periodically updates its inventory account. Companies that make numerous sales of products with relatively small unit costs usually employ the periodic accounting method. Such companies include grocery stores, department stores, and drug stores. Companies that make fewer sales of products with higher unit costs, however, use a perpetual inventory system. The perpetual inventory system is updated continuously, not periodically. This systems requires that companies keep track of merchandise purchases at the time of acquisition and the cost of goods sold at the time of sale. Hence, companies using this system have an account for merchandise acquisitions and for the cost of goods sold.

The same four pricing methods apply to this system. With specific identification, the actual cost of the goods sold makes up the cost of goods sold and the value of the remaining inventory equals the specific cost of each unsold item. The average method is called the moving average in the perpetual system. The average is determined each time a new inventory item is purchased. The cost of goods sold for each sale is calculated by multiplying the moving average at the time by the number of items sold.

When using the FIFO method with this system, a company determines the cost of goods sold each time a sale is made by multiplying the cost of the oldest goods on hand by the number of items sold. Finally, when using the LIFO method, a company computes the cost of goods sold each time a sale is made by multiplying the cost of the most recent purchases by the number of goods sold.

The use of the perpetual inventory accounting system requires a company to maintain a detailed perpetual record of inventory transactions, either manually or by **computer**. This record must include information on the inflow and outflow of inventory items as well as the quantities and prices of items at any given time. While these records are updated continuously, companies generally check their accuracy at least once a year by physically counting available merchandise.

[William H. Coyle, updated by Karl Heil]

FURTHER READING:

Harper, Robert M., and Denise M. Patterson. ''An Alternative Approach for Computing Dollar-Value LIFO.'' *National Public Accountant,* December 1998, 20.

Hoffman, Raymond A., and Henry Gunders. *Inventories: Control, Costing, and Effect upon Income and Taxes.* New York: Ronald Press, 1970.

Meigs, Robert F., et al, eds. *Accounting: The Basis for Business Decisions.* 11th ed. Homewood, IL: Richard Irwin, 1998.

Walgenbach, Paul H., et al. *Principles of Accounting.* 5th ed. San Diego: Harcourt Brace Jovanovich, 1990.

INVENTORY CONTROL SYSTEMS

Inventory control (also known as inventory management) refers to the systems and strategies businesses use to ensure that they have adequate supplies of raw materials for production and finished goods for shipment to customers, while also minimizing their inventory carrying costs. Storing excess inventory is costly, because the space and financial resources invested in the goods can often be put to better use elsewhere. At the same time, however, inadequate inventory stores can result in costly production shutdowns or delays in filling customer orders. Inventory control systems help companies to find the delicate balance between too little and too much inventory.

''It is nearly impossible to overemphasize the importance of keeping inventory levels under control,'' Ronald Pachura wrote in an article for *IIE Solutions.* ''Whether the problems incurred are caused by carrying too little or too much inventory, manufacturers need to become aware that inventory control is not just a materials management or warehouse department issue. The purchasing, receiving, engineering, manufacturing, and accounting departments all contribute to the accuracy of the inventory methods and records.''

Pachura created a checklist to aid companies in assessing their inventory controls. He recommended that business managers examine the accuracy and effectiveness of their: bills of materials (BOM); receiving policies; engineering changes; scrap reporting; vendor lead times; reorder triggers; and warehouse locator systems. The inventory turnover ratio is a tool that can help companies to determine whether they are producing and carrying too much inventory. The basic measure of inventory turnover is defined as cost of goods sold divided by average inventory on hand. But Pachura noted that managers may gain more information by segmenting average inventory into raw materials, work in process inventory, and finished goods, and then computing a separate turnover figure for each. Comparing these figures often reveals opportunities for improving inventory controls.

COMPUTERS AND INVENTORY

In today's business environment, even many smaller businesses have come to rely on computerized inventory management systems. Certainly, there are plenty of small retail outlets, manufacturers, and other businesses that still rely on manual means of inventory tracking. Indeed, for some businesses—such as convenience stores, shoe stores, or nurseries—the purchase of an electronic inventory tracking system might constitute a wasteful use of financial resources. But for firms operating in industries that feature high volume turnover of raw materials and/or finished products, computerized tracking systems have emerged as a key component of business strategies aimed at increasing productivity and maintaining competitiveness. Moreover, the recent development of powerful **computer** programs capable of addressing a wide variety of record-keeping needs—including inventory management—in one integrated system have also contributed to the growing popularity of electronic inventory control options.

Given such developments, it is little wonder that business experts commonly cite inventory management as a vital element that can spell the difference between success and failure in today's keenly competitive business world. Writing in *Production and Inventory Management Journal,* Godwin Udo described telecommunications technology as a critical organizational asset that can help a company realize important competitive gains in the area of inventory management. According to Udo, companies that make good use of this technology are far better equipped to succeed than those who rely on outdated or unwieldy methods of inventory control.

Automation can dramatically affect all phases of inventory management, including counting and monitoring of inventory items; recording and retrieval of item storage locations; recording changes to inventory; and anticipating inventory needs, including inventory handling requirements. This is true even of stand-alone systems that are not integrated with other areas of the business. But many analysts indicate that productivity—and hence profitability—gains that are garnered through use of automated systems can be increased when a business integrates its inventory control systems with other systems, such as **accounting** and sales, to better manage inventory levels.

According to Dennis Eskow in *PC Week,* business executives are ''increasingly integrating financial data, such as accounts receivable, with sales information that includes customer histories. The goal: to control inventory quarter to quarter, so it doesn't come back to bite the bottom line. Key components of an integrated system . . . are general ledger, **electronic data interchange**, database connectivity, and connections to a range of vertical business applications.'' David Cahn, a director of product strategy for business applications at a firm in New York, confirmed this view in an interview with Eskow: ''What drives business is optimization of working capital. The amount of control you have on inventory equals the optimization of the capital. That's why it's so important to integrate the inventory data with everything else.''

THE FUTURE OF INVENTORY CONTROL SYSTEMS

In the late 1990s many businesses were investing heavily in integrated order and inventory systems designed to keep inventories at a minimum and replenish stock quickly. But as Eskow noted, business owners have a variety of system integration options from which to choose, based on their needs and financial liquidity. ''Integrated inventory systems may range in platform and complexity,'' he noted.

At the same time that these integrated systems have increased in popularity, business observers have suggested that ''stand-alone'' systems are falling into disfavor. Tom Andel and Daniel A. Kind, for instance, cited a study by the International Mass Retail Association in *Transportation and Distribution:* ''The study concludes that stand alone Warehouse Management System (WMS) packages acquired today to perform individual functions will probably be abandoned in just a few years because they do not integrate well with other systems. Systems investments must be considered in context of future systems objectives.''

Another development of which business vendors should be aware is a recent trend wherein powerful retailers ask their suppliers to implement vendor-managed inventory systems. These arrangements place the responsibility for inventory management squarely on the shoulders of the vendors. Under such an agreement, the vendors obtain warehouse or point-of-sale information from the retailer and use that information to make inventory restocking decisions.

WAREHOUSE LAYOUT AND OPERATION

The move toward automation in inventory management naturally has moved into the warehouse as well. Citing various warehousing experts, Sarah Bergin contended in *Transportation and Distribution* magazine that ''the key to getting productivity gains from inventory management . . . is placing real-time intelligent information processing in the warehouse. This empowers employees to take actions that achieve immediate results. Real-time processing in the warehouse uses combinations of hardware, including material handling and data collection technologies. But according to these executives, the intelligent part of the system is sophisticated software which automates and controls all aspects of warehouse operations.''

Another important component of good inventory management is creation and maintenance of a sensible, effective warehousing design. A well-organized, user-friendly warehouse layout can be of enormous benefit to business owners, especially if they are involved in processing large volumes of goods and materials. Conversely, an inefficient warehouse system can cost businesses dearly in terms of efficiency, customer service, and, ultimately, profitability.

Transportation and Distribution magazine cited several steps that businesses using warehouse storage systems can take to help ensure that they get the most out of their facilities. It recommended that companies utilize the following tools:

- Stock locator database: ''The stock locator database required for proactive decision making will be an adjunct of the inventory file in a state-of-the-art space management system. A running record will be maintained of the stock number, lot number, and number of pallet loads in each storage location. Grid coordinates of the reserve area, including individual rack tier positions, must therefore be established, and the pallet load capacity of all storage locations must be incorporated into the database.''
- Grid coordinate numbering system: The warehouse numbering system should be developed in conjunction with the storage layout, and should be user-friendly so that workers can quickly locate currently stocked items and open storage spaces alike.
- Communication systems: Again, this can be a valuable investment if the business's warehouse requirements are significant. Such facilities often utilize forklift machinery that can be used more effectively if their operators are not required to periodically return to a central assignment area. Current technology, however, makes it possible for the warehouse computer system to interact with terminal displays on the forklifts themselves. ''Task assignment can then be made by visual display or printout, and task completion can be confirmed by scanning, keyboard entry, or voice recognition,'' observed *Transportation and Distribution.*
- Maximization of storage capacity: Warehouses that adhere to rigid ''storage by incoming lot size'' storage arrangements do not always make the best use of their space. Instead, businesses should settle on a strategy that eases traffic congestion and reduces

problems associated with ongoing turnover in inventory.

OUTSOURCING WAREHOUSE RESPONSIBILITIES

Some companies choose to outsource their warehouse functions. ''This allows a company that isn't as confident in running their own warehousing operations to concentrate on their core business and let the experts worry about keeping track of their inventory,'' wrote Bergin. ''There are third party services available for managing warehouse operations. SonicAir, for one, provides companies with an analysis of products and spare parts, evaluations of their time sensitivity, and current installations and locations of vendor's distribution centers.'' Inventory control systems such as the one utilized by SonicAir, said Bergin, provide businesses with the ability to do real-time updating of inventory, cross-docking and dispatch, verification, and up-to-the-minute tracking of inventory item location. Such systems are also capable of providing ''a strategic stocking analysis which looks at the customer's equipment locations to determine which strategic stocking locations should be used, the expected transit time, and projected fill rate,'' added Bergin. Of course, businesses weighing whether to outsource such a key component of their operation need to consider the expense of such a course of action, as well as their feelings about relinquishing that level of control.

SEE ALSO: Inventory Accounting

[Kevin Hillstrom, updated by Laurie Collier Hillstrom]

FURTHER READING:

Andel, Tom, and Daniel A. Kind. ''Flow It, Don't Stow It.'' *Transportation and Distribution,* May 1996.

Bergin, Sarah. ''Make Your Warehouse Deliver: New Developments in Warehouse Management Systems Inspire New Productivity in Needy Operations.'' *Transportation and Distribution,* February 1997.

Betts, Mitch. ''Manage My Inventory or Else!'' *Computerworld,* 31 January 1994.

Eskow, Dennis. ''Rising Stock: Integrated Inventory Systems Help Companies Shoot Economic Rapids.'' *PC Week,* 5 June 1995.

Pachura, Ronald. ''When Is Enough, Enough? Inventory Control Contributes Directly to a Company's Profitability.'' *IIE Solutions,* October 1998.

Udo, Godwin J. ''The Impact of Telecommunications on Inventory Management.'' *Production and Inventory Management Journal,* spring 1993.

Weisfeld, Barry. ''Automated Ordering Puts Profits in Sight.'' *Transportation and Distribution,* February 1997.

INVESTMENT ADVISERS ACT OF 1940

The Investment Advisers Act (IAA) was passed in 1940 in order to monitor those who, for a fee, advise people, **pension funds**, and institutions on investment matters. Impetus for passage of the act began with the Public Utility Holding Company Act of 1935 which authorized the **Securities and Exchange Commission** (SEC) to study investment trusts. The thrust of this study, which led to the passage of the Investment Company Act of 1940 and the Investment Advisers Act, was to provide a closer look at investment trusts and investment companies. The study, however, found many instances of investment adviser abuse such as unfounded ''hot tips'' and questionable performance fees. The IAA sought not to regulate investment advisers so much as to keep track of who was in the industry and what their methods of operation were. The IAA does not mandate qualifications for becoming an investment adviser but it does require registration for those using the mails to conduct investment counseling business.

The IAA mandated that all persons and firms receiving compensation for serving as investment advisers must register with the SEC (this requirement was altered somewhat with the passage of the Investment Advisers Supervision Coordination Act of 1996). There are, however, three general exceptions to the registration requirement: investment advisers whose clients all reside in the same state as the adviser's business office and who do not provide advice on securities listed on national exchanges; investment advisers whose clients are solely insurance companies; and investment advisers who had fewer than 15 clients in any previous 12-month period. The IAA was amended, however, in 1996 with the presidential signing of the Securities Reform Bill. Title III of this bill, known as the Investment Advisers Supervision Coordination Act (IASCA) changed the registration criteria of the IAA. The IASCA, which went into effect on July 8, 1997, basically requires the SEC to supervise and register those investment advisers managing $25 million or more in client assets. Those managing less than this amount are to be registered with and supervised by their proper state regulatory agency. If an investment adviser managing client assets of $25 million or less resides in a state that does not require registration, he or she must then register with the SEC.

A hallmark of the IAA is the required registration of virtually all investment advisers. Much verbiage, however, has gone into exactly what constitutes an investment adviser and his or her corollary—investment advice. The act defines an investment adviser as ''any person who, for compensation, engages in the business of advising others, either directly or through publications or writings, as to the value of securities or as to the advisability of investing in, purchasing, or selling securities, or who for compensation and as part of a regular business, issues or promulgates analyses or reports concerning securities.'' The SEC further refined its definition of an adviser in its Release 1092, which stated that the ''giving of advice need not constitute the principal business activity or any particular portion of the business activities in order for a person to be an investment adviser.'' Release 1092 went on to state that the ''giving of advice need only be done on such a basis that it constitutes a business activity occurring with some regularity. The frequency of the activity is a factor, but is not determinative.''

Whether or not a person is considered to be an investment adviser under the IAA generally depends on three criteria: the type of advice offered, the method of compensation, and whether or not a significant portion of the ''adviser's'' income comes from proffering investment advice. Related to the last criterion is the consideration of whether or not a person leads others to believe that he or she is an investment adviser, as for example through advertising.

Under the act a person is generally considered to be an investment adviser through the offering of advice or the making of recommendations on **securities** as opposed to other types of investments. Securities may be defined under the act as including but not necessarily limited to notes, **bonds**, **stocks** (both common and preferred), **mutual funds**, money market funds, and certificates of deposit. The term ''securities'' does not generally include commodity contracts, **real estate**, insurance contracts, or collectibles such as works of art or rare stamps and coins. Even those who receive finder's fees for referring potential clients to investment advisers are considered to be investment advisers themselves.

Generally excluded from coverage under the act are those professionals whose investment advice to clients is incidental to the professional relationship. The IAA excepts ''any lawyer, accountant, engineer, or teacher whose performance of such services is solely incidental to the practice of his profession.'' ''Solely incidental'' is the key phrase. An accountant, for instance, who acts as an investment adviser is in fact considered to be an investment adviser under the act. If professionals are not to be considered investment advisers under the IAA: they must not present themselves to the public as investment advisers; any investment advice given must be reasonably related to their primary professional function; and fees for the ''investment advice'' must be based on the same criteria as fees for the primary professional function. The IAA, however, excludes from its definition of an investment adviser ''any broker or dealer whose performance of such [advisory] services is solely incidental to the conduct of his business as a broker or dealer and who receives no special compensation thereof.'' **Banks**, publishers, and government security advisers are also excepted from the act. People who call themselves ''financial planners'' may under certain circumstances be considered financial advisers under the act. The difference between a financial planner and an investment adviser as it relates to the IAA is also addressed in the aforementioned Release 1092.

Under the act, investment advisers must register using Form ADV accompanied by a $150 filing fee (as of 1996). The form asks for such information as educational background, experience, exact type of business engaged in, assets, information on clients, past history of a legal and/or criminal nature, and type of investment advice to be offered. Registration under the act does not constitute an endorsement of the investment adviser nor can the person or firm advertise as such.

Registered investment advisers are required to update their ADV form annually and file operating reports with the SEC or state regulatory agency. The investment adviser must also provide to clients and prospective clients a written disclosure statement and allow inspection by the SEC or state regulatory agency of any books and records relating to investment advisory activities. Advisers generally cannot receive compensation based on the performance of their advisement, nor can they engage in excessive trading or profit from market activity resulting from their advice to clients. Investment advisers must also act in the best interest of their clients at all times and take into consideration their clients' financial positions and financial sophistication. There are also many provisions in the act dealing with fraud in terms of **advertising**, control of client assets, soliciting clients, and information disclosure.

[Michael Knes]

FURTHER READING:

Bernzweig, Eli P. *The Financial Planner's Legal Guide.* New York: Prentice Hall, 1986.

Institute of Certified Financial Planners. ''To Be or Not to Be: Are You an Investment Adviser Rep?'' Denver: Institute of Certified Financial Planners, 1997. Available from www.icfp.org.

Kirsch, Clifford E. *Investment Adviser Regulation: A Step by-Step Guide to Compliance and Law.* New York: Practising Law Institute, 1996.

U.S. Securities and Exchange Commission. ''Frequently Asked Questions about Changes in the Regulation of Investment Advisers.'' Washington: U.S. Securities and Exchange Commission, 1997. Available from www.sec.gov/rules/othern/advfaq.htm.

——. ''The Great Divide: Amendments to the Investment Advisers Act and Related Commission Rulemaking.'' Washington: U.S. Securities and Exchange Commission, 1998. Available from www.sec.gov/rules/extra/gdiv398.htm.

Vazzana, John. "New Legislation Means Some Relief for Investment Advisers." *CPA Journal* 67 (June 1997): 65-66.

INVESTMENT ANALYSIS

Investment analysis is an ongoing process of evaluating current and potential allocations of financial assets and choosing those allocations that best fit the investor's needs and goals. The two opposing considerations in investment analysis are growth rate and risk, which are usually directly proportionate in any given investment vehicle. This means that investments with a high degree of certainty, such as U.S. Treasury securities, offer a very modest rate of return (e.g., 5 percent annually), whereas high-risk stock investments could double or quadruple in value over a few months. Through investment analysis, investors must consider the level of risk they're able to tolerate and choose investments accordingly.

Beyond weighing the return of an individual investment, investors must also consider **taxes**, transaction costs, and opportunity costs that erode their net return. Taxes, for instance, may be reduced or deferred depending on the type of investment and the investor's tax status. Transaction costs may be incurred each time an individual purchases or sells shares of stock or mutual funds. These fees are usually a percentage of the dollar amount being transferred. Such fees may sift 3-6 percent or more off the initial investment and final return. If they don't seem warranted, such expenses may be avoided by choosing no load mutual funds and dealing with discount brokers, for instance. Much more nebulous is **opportunity cost**, which is what the investment could have earned had it been deployed elsewhere. Opportunity cost is largely the downside of investing too conservatively given one's means and circumstances. Again, both risk and growth factor into opportunity costs. For example, low risk comes at a price of low returns, but it may be worth the lost opportunity if the investor is retired and will be depending on the invested funds for living expenses in the near future.

INTEREST-BEARING INVESTMENTS AND TREASURIES

Among the lowest risk—and lowest return—investments are interest-bearing notes such as money market funds, certificates of deposit from banks and **U.S. Treasury bills**, notes, and bonds. These pay the investor a guaranteed periodic interest payment, or, in the case of T-bills, a lump sum based on a guaranteed discount rate. To choose between the various options the investor need only consider the comparative interest rate (some pay more than others) and the term (many of these investments are based on fixed periods such as three months or a year). These sorts of investments are popular because they are fairly liquid—they can be bought and sold at any point in a financial cycle without adverse timing effects—and they offer a nearly risk-free option for investors who need certainty of return.

MUTUAL FUNDS

Mutual funds lure investors with the promise of stock market-like returns in a lower risk and more novice-friendly environment. These funds pool their members' investments in professionally managed portfolios of stocks, bonds, and other investments. As a result, they can provide individual investors with the kind of investment diversification that would otherwise require a much greater amount of money to be invested and much more effort in reviewing the many choices. In the 1980s and 1990s mutual funds were increasingly used for employee-managed retirement savings programs such as **401(k) plans**.

Most funds have an investment objective and, as with stocks, the choices range from conservative, low risk funds that mirror a market index like the Standard & Poor's 500 to high-stakes aggressive growth funds that focus on small and unproven companies. Also like stocks, many funds perform poorly in a given year or even over a period of years, a fact that fund marketers sometimes gloss over. Thus choosing mutual funds involves many of the same considerations as choosing stocks.

FUTURES AND OTHER DERIVATIVES

While investments like oil **futures** and **options** are often seen as some of the riskiest forms of investment, ironically a key use for these market-traded contracts is for **hedging** against adverse movements in cash markets. In other words, investors buy futures or options contracts in part to reduce their risk of facing a devastating price fall (or increase, as the case may be) in another market. Collectively, futures, options, and similar instruments are known as derivatives because they derive from price movements in other markets, including commodities, currencies, and stocks. Of course, many investors also use derivatives for speculation. By nature the individual contracts are short-term investments, although some investors, mainly corporations and other institutions, maintain a regular portfolio of derivatives on underlying commodities or assets that affect their business.

Analyzing futures and options involves analyzing the expected direction of price movements for the underlying goods. However, in contrast to stock or mutual fund analysis, which is usually best done with an eye to the long term, derivative analysis requires making a short-term (less than a year) forecast of what might happen to prices in the cash markets. If the forecast proves accurate the investor can make money, but if it's wrong the losses could be substantial. With the practice of buying on margin, which involves taking out a loan to increase the amount of the investment, the profits or losses can be multiplied.

SECURITIES

A security is a financial asset representing a claim on the assets of the issuing firm and on the profits produced by the assets. The term security analysis pertains to the process of identifying desirable investment opportunities in such financial assets. In the case of corporate **stocks** and **bonds**, the analysis flows from the interpretation of **accounting** and financial data regarding operations, profitability, net worth, and the like. Investment alternatives are identified based on (1) the investor's risk/reward ratio, (2) a specified time horizon, and (3) current market prices.

Security analysts, in essence, are the catalysts which drive the efficient market hypothesis. That is, ''smart'' money will logically and efficiently distribute itself in such a way that security prices reflect all available information. As new information becomes available, analysts assess it and recommend market price adjustments according to changes they anticipate for price levels. The cumulative impact of price adjustments moves the market to equilibrium so that the price of any security approximates true investment value.

Security analysts operate in three arenas, each reflecting a different set of goals and objectives. Investment banking and brokerage firms represent the ''sell'' side of security analysis. Their clients are fee and commission paying institutional and individual investors.

Investment management organizations conduct security analysis for the portfolios they manage. Since portfolio managers purchase securities, they represent the ''buy'' side of the street.

Finally, a number of investment publishing services provide security analysis for all investors subscribing to their reports. The most popular investment services are available through Value Line Inc., Standard & Poor's, Moody's Investors Service, and Dun & Bradstreet.

METHODOLOGY

There are two basic methodologies: fundamental analysis and technical analysis. In their own way, each approaches investment decisions from the top-down and from the bottom-up.

THE TOP-DOWN APPROACH. The top-down approach, the traditional methodology, begins with a broad perspective and ends with a specific analysis of a stock or a bond. The top-down approach initially analyzes macroeconomic data, filters it into more specific sectors, and finally distills the results with respect to a specific security.

Analysts determine the important economic conditions and forces at work and their potential impact on the markets. Analysts examine corporate profitability, the direction and magnitude of **interest rates**, money supply, fiscal policy, **employment**, migration, export/import trends, etc., to evaluate the future performance of individual economic sectors and industries.

Security analysts also utilize the top-down approach to allocate available funds within portfolios between short-term and long-term investments, between risky and risk-free securities, and between stocks and bonds. Sector-to-sector and market-to-market comparisons purport to identify where investors should look for superior returns. Analysts recommend investing in favorable industries or sectors, and suggest specific stocks within each sector.

THE BOTTOM-UP APPROACH. A major drawback to the top-down approach is the likelihood of overlooking certain stocks that offer significant investment opportunities but which are outside the favorable sectors. To remedy this, analysts also utilize the bottom-up approach which identifies superior performers without regard to industry.

This approach identifies advantageous investments according to performance and financial criteria. The criteria are applicable across industry and sectors, establishing performance and financial benchmarks which companies must meet or exceed in order to be considered. Analysts also develop criteria to separate the top performers by various degrees of risk, e.g., conservative versus aggressive.

Once the screens have filtered out the appropriate securities, the analyst conducts a fundamental analysis of the company.

FUNDAMENTAL ANALYSIS

Fundamental analysts look for superior returns from securities that are mispriced by the market. To identify them the analyst engages in various calculations using data from **financial statements** and **balance sheets** to determine the future earnings and **dividends** of a company, the degree to which these exceed the expected average for the industry, and the potential for the stock to move closer to a correct or fair value. Fundamental analysts would recommend buying undervalued, or underpriced, stocks. When a stock is believed to be overvalued, the analyst would advise selling or taking a short position because the market would be expected to correct the price downward in the future.

THE OPERATING ENVIRONMENT. Some of the external conditions affecting a company's performance are:

1. Demographic changes: sex, age, absolute numbers, location, population movements, educational preparation.
2. **Economic conditions**: employment level, regional performance, wage levels, spending patterns, consumer debt, capital investment.
3. Government fiscal policy and regulation: spending levels, the magnitude of entitlements, debt, war and peace, tax policies, environmental regulations.
4. **Competition**: market penetration and position, market share, commodity, commodities **marketing strategies**, and niche products.
5. Vendors: financial soundness, quality and quantity of product, R&D capabilities, alternative suppliers, just-in-time capabilities.

Industry- and firm-specific characteristics important to the fundamental analyst are: profitability; market presence; productivity; product type, sales, and services; financial resources; physical facilities; **research and development**; quality of **management**.

The analyst approaches these indicators in two ways: first, as trends within an industry, and secondly as features of a particular firm. To do this, analysts use a series of ratios constructed from the financial statements. Ratios represent the percentage or decimal relationship of one number to another. Ratios facilitate the use of comparative financial statements, which provide significant information about trends and relationships over two or more years. Analysts compare a company's ratios to industry ratios, as well as cross-sectionally to other companies.

Structural analysis compares two financial statements in terms of the various items or groups of items within the same period. **Time series analysis** correlates ratios over time, measured in years or by quarters.

Since ratios are relative measures, they furnish a common scale of measurement from which analysts construct historical averages. Thus, analysts are able to compare companies of different sizes and from different industries based on performance and financial condition by (a) establishing absolute standards, (b) examining averages, and (c) using trends to forecast future results. To increase predictability, the analyst considers the impact of external factors on internal trends.

PIONEERS. In 1934 Benjamin Graham and David Dodd published *Security Analysis.* This book is considered the bible of fundamental practitioners. In the 1920s, Graham became a successful portfolio manager by stressing capital preservation by investing proportionately in high quality stocks and in low risk credit instruments. With Dodd, his student from UCLA, Graham laid out vigorous investment procedures in the book.

Graham and Dodd primarily appraised stocks according to their earning power. They recommended an extensive list of **financial ratios** to measure a company's performance according to:

1. Projected future earnings
2. Projected future dividends
3. A method for valuing expected earnings
4. The value of the asset

In the belief that investors tended to overreact to near-term prospects, Graham and Dodd designed formulas to keep the disparity between P/E's for different companies within sharp focus. Analysts continue to apply these principles today.

FINANCIAL ANALYSIS. Financial analysis is necessary in determining the future value of a company. Financial analysis concentrates on the condition of the financial statements: the income statement, the balance sheet, the statement of changes in shareholders' equity, and the funds flow statements. From these the analyst determines the values of the outstanding claims on the company's **income**.

Financial analysts measure past performance, evaluate present conditions, and make predictions as to future performance. This information is important to investors looking for superior returns. Creditors use this information to determine the risk associated with the extension of credit.

RATIO ANALYSIS. The most common method used by analysts is financial ratios. Composition ratios compare the size of the components of any accounting category with the total of that category, for example, the percentage of net income to net sales. Composition ratios:

- Indicate the size of each of the components relative to their total and to each other.
- Make historic comparisons and trending possible.
- Point to cause-and-effect relationships between the individual components and their total.

FUNDAMENTAL WEAKNESSES. Although widely used, financial analysis does have some fundamental weaknesses. Since it is based on data from financial reports, its findings are subject to distortions resulting from **inflation**, wild business swings, changes in accounting practices, and undisclosed inner-workings of the firm. Management can manipulate important key ratios by changing inventory valuations, **depreciation** schedules, and expense recognition practices. Furthermore, since the financial statements are static, the analyst cannot account for the impact of seasonal variations. Finally, the ratios are meaningless unless compared to performance benchmarks.

TECHNICAL ANALYSIS

Technical analysis examines stock price trends in an attempt to predict future prices. Technical analysts believe that all the relevant information about economic fundamentals of an industry and of a stock are reflected in the direction and volume of prices. Therefore, technical analysts look to the past, for they believe that markets are cyclical, forming specific patterns, and these patterns repeat themselves over time. They further believe that it is only necessary to compare short-term and intermediate price movements to long-term trends in order to predict market direction.

Two major techniques form the basis of technical analysis: the study of key indicators, and the charting of market activity.

KEY INDICATORS. Common key indicators utilized by technical analysts include the following:

1. Trading volume is based on supply-demand relationships and indicates market strength or weakness. Rising prices with increased buying generally signals uptrends. Decreasing prices with increasing demand, and increasing prices with decreasing volume, signal downtrends. Trading volume applies best to the short-term (three to nine months).
2. Market breadth examines the activity of a broader range of securities than do highly publicized indices such as the Dow Jones Industrial Average. The breadth index is the net daily advances or declines divided by the amount of securities traded. The breadth index is calculated by either the number of securities, the dollar volume, or nominal volume. Breadth analysis concentrates on change rather than on level in order to evaluate the dispersion of a general movement in prices. The slope of the advance/decline line indicates the trend of the breadth index. Breadth analysis points to the prime turning points in bull and bear markets.
3. Confidence indices evaluate the trading patterns of bond investors who are regarded as more sophisticated and more well-informed that stock traders and, therefore, spot trends more quickly. Other confidence theories measure the sentiment among analysts themselves, the breadth trends in options and futures trading, and consumer confidence. Analysts consider these to have predictive value in the near and intermediate term.
4. The put-call ratio divides the volume of puts outstanding by the volume of calls outstanding. Investors generally purchase the greatest number of puts around market bottoms when their pessimism peaks, thus indicating a turnaround. Call volume is greatest around market peaks, at the heights of investor enthusiasm—also indicating a market turn.
5. The cash position of funds gives an indication of potential demand. Analysts examine the volume and composition of cash held by institutional investors, pension funds, **mutual funds**, and the like. Because fund managers are performance driven, analysts expect them to search out higher returns on large cash balances and, therefore, will invest more heavily in securities, driving prices higher.
6. Short selling represents a bearish sentiment. Analysts in agreement with short sellers expect a downturn in the market. Analysts particularly watch the action of specialists who make a market in a specific stock. In addition, analysts look at odd-lot short sellers who indicate pessimism with increased activity. However, many technical analysts express a ''contrarian'' view regarding short sales. These analysts believe short sellers overreact and speculate because of the potential profits involved. In addition, to close their positions, short sellers will purchase the securities in the future, thus putting upward pressure on prices. Short selling analysis is based on month-to-month trends.
7. Odd-lot theory follows the trends of transactions involving less than round lots (less than 100 shares). This theory rests on a contrarian opinion about small investors. The theory believes the small trader is right most of the time, and begins to sell into an upward trend. However, as the market continues to rise, the small investor re-enters the market as the sophisticated traders are bailing out in anticipation of a top and a pull back. Therefore, an increase in odd-lot trading signals a downturn in the market.

Odd-lot indices divide (1) odd-lot purchases by odd-lot sales, (2) odd-lot short sales by total odd-lot sales, and (3) total odd-lot volume (buys + sales) by round-lot volume.

CHARTING. Charting is useful in analyzing market conditions and price behavior of individual securities. Standard & Poor's *Trendline* is a well known charting service which provides data on companies. This data shows the trend of prices, insider sales, short sales, and trading volume over the intermediate and long-term. Analysts have plotted this data on graphs to form line, bar, and point-and-figure charts.

Chart interpretation requires the ability to evaluate the meaning of the resulting formations in order to identify ranges in which to buy or sell. Charting assists in ascertaining major market down- turns, upturns, and trend reversals.

Analysts use moving averages to analyze intermediate and long-term stock movements. They predict the direction of prices by examining the trend in current prices relative to the long-term moving average. A moving-average depicts the underlying direction and degree of change.

The relative strength of an individual stock price is a ratio of the average monthly stock price compared to the monthly average index of the total market or the stock's industry group. It informs the analysts of the relationship of specific price movements to an industry or the market in general. When investors favor specific stocks or industries, these will be relatively strong. Stocks that outperform the market trend on the upside may suddenly retreat when investors bail out for hotter prospects. Stocks that outperform in a declining market usually attract other investors and remain strong.

As analysts construct charts, certain trends appear. These trends are characterized by a range of prices in which the stock trades.

The lower end of the range forms a support base for the price. At that end a stock is a ''good'' buy and attracts additional investors, and thus forms a support level. As the price increases, a stock may become ''unattractive'' when compared to other stocks. Investors sell causing that upper limit to form a resistance level. Movements beyond the support and resistance levels require a fundamental change in the market and/or the stock.

RANDOM WALK THEORIES

Random-walk theorists do not believe in the cyclical nature of markets although they analyze the same data as do chartists. **Random walk theory** maintains that technical analysis is useless because past price and volume statistics do not contain any information by themselves that bode well for success. Random walkers believe choosing securities randomly will result in returns comparable to technical and fundamental analysis.

Through a series of illustrations, academicians in the 1960s and 1970s demonstrated that there is no basis in fact for technical analysis. They found that price movements were random and displayed no predictable pattern of movement, as did the Frenchman Louis Bachelier at the turn of the century. Therefore, prices have no predictive value. Since all the studies indicated randomness in price, the proponents of this hypothesis called it the ''random walk theory.''

Random walkers use time-series models to relate efficient markets to the behavior of stock prices and investment returns. They believe that changes in prices are independent of new information entering the market, and that these prices changes are evenly distributed throughout the market. Since this means that the distribution of price changes is constant from one period to the next, investors are not able to identify ''mispriced'' securities in any consistent fashion. Experience and empirical evidence contradict this assumption, suggesting that the random walk properties of returns (or price changes) are too restrictive.

Technicians maintain the validity of their practices especially with regards to the timing of investments. Since computer-based trading programs incorporate some timing technique into their matrix, intra-day trading has increasingly become characterized by dramatic movements in the indices. These movements represent a consensus among traders of the applicability of technical theories despite of the evidence of random walkers. A market driven by similarly configured indices, no matter what the basis, becomes more predictable over time.

In practice, computer programs execute trades not only in anticipation of a market move, but to provide fund managers the opportunity to change positions ahead of the others.

DOW THEORY

Although Charles Dow—publisher of the *Wall Street Journal*—was a fundamentalist, he published a series of articles which laid the foundation for William P. Hamilton's 1908 work that formalized the Dow Theory. Hamilton theorized that the stock market is the best gauge of financial and business activity because all relevant information is immediately discounted in the prices of stocks, as indexed by the Dow Jones Industrial Average and the Dow Jones Transportation Average. Accordingly, both averages must confirm market direction because price trends in the overall market points to the termination of both bull and bear markets.

Three movements are assumed to occur simultaneously:

1. A primary bull or bearish trend, typically lasting 28 to 33 months.
2. A secondary trend goes counter to the primary trend, typically lasts three weeks to three months, and reflects a long-term primary movement.

3. Day-to-day activity makes up the first two movements of the market, confirming the direction of the long-term primary trend.

The primary trend must be supported by strong day-to-day activity to erase the effects of the secondary trend, otherwise, the market will begin to move in the opposite direction. If day-to-day activity supports the secondary trend, the market will soon reverse directions and develop a new primary trend.

If the cyclical movements of the market averages increase over time, and the successive lows become higher, the market will trend upward. If the successive highs trend lower, and the successive low trend lower, then the market is in a downtrend. Computer programs have fully integrated Dow theory into their decision-making matrix.

SEE ALSO: Portfolio Management Theory; Valuation

FURTHER READING:

Bauer, Richard J., and Julie R. Dahlquist. *Technical Market Indicators: Analysis & Performance.* New York: John Wiley & Sons, 1998.

Journal of Portfolio Management, quarterly.

Konoshi, Atsuo, and Ravi E. Dattatreya, eds. *The Handbook of Derivative Instruments.* Chicago: Irwin Professional Publishing, 1996.

Radcliffe, Robert C. *Investment: Concepts, Analysis, Strategy.* Reading, MA: Addison-Wesley Publishing Co., 1996.

Woolley, Suzanne. ''Technicians Take Center Stage.'' *Business Week,* 19 October 1998.

INVESTMENT BANKING

Investment banking involves raising money (capital) for companies and governments, usually by issuing **securities**. Securities or financial instruments include equity or ownership instruments such as **stocks** where investors own a share of the issuing concern and therefore are entitled to profits. They also include **debt** instruments such as **bonds**, where the issuing concern borrows money from investors and promises to repay it at a certain date with interest. Companies typically issue stock when they first go public through initial **public offerings** (IPOs), and they may issue stock and bonds periodically to fund such enterprises as research, new product development, and expansion. Companies seeking to go public must register with the **Securities and Exchange Commission** and pay registration fees, which cover accountant and lawyer expenses for the preparation of registration statements. A registration statement describes a company's business and its plans for using the money raised, and it includes a company's **financial statements**.

Before stocks and bonds are issued, investment bankers perform **due diligence** examinations, which entail carefully evaluating a company's worth in terms of money and equipment (assets) and debt (**liabilities**). This examination requires the full disclosure of a company's strengths and weaknesses. The company pays the investment banker after the securities deal is completed and these fees often range from 3 to 7 percent of what a company raises, depending on the type of transaction.

Investment banks aid companies and governments in selling securities as well as investors in purchasing securities, managing investments, and trading securities. Investment banks take the form of brokers or agents who purchase and sell securities for their clients; dealers or principals who buy and sell securities for their personal interest in turning a profit; and broker-dealers who do both.

The primary service provided by investment banks is **underwriting**, which refers to guaranteeing a company a set price for the securities it plans to issue. If the securities fail to sell for the set price, the investment bank pays the company the difference. Therefore, investment banks must carefully determine the set price by considering the expectations of the company and the state of the market for the securities. In addition, investment banks provide a plethora of other services including financial advising, acquisition advising, divestiture advising, buying and selling securities, interest-rate swapping, and debt-for-stock swapping. Nevertheless, most of the revenues of investment banks come from underwriting, selling securities, and setting up **mergers and acquisitions**.

When companies need to raise large amounts of capital, a group of investment banks often participate, which are referred to as syndicates. Syndicates are hierarchically structured and the members of syndicates are grouped according to three functions: managing, underwriting, and selling. Managing banks sit at the top of the hierarchy, conduct due diligence examinations, and receive management fees from the companies. Underwriting banks receive fees for sharing the **risk** of securities offerings. Finally, selling banks function as brokers within the syndicate and sell the securities, receiving a fee for each share they sell. Nevertheless, managing and underwriting banks usually also sell securities. All major investment banks have a syndicate department, which concentrates on recruiting members for syndicates managed by their firms and responding to recruitments from other firms.

A variety of legislation, mostly from the 1930s, governs investment banking. These laws require public companies to fully disclose information on their operations and financial position, and they mandate the separation of commercial and investment banking. The latter mandate, however, has been relaxed over the intervening years as commercial **banks** have entered the investment banking market.

HISTORY AND DEVELOPMENT OF INVESTMENT BANKING

Investment banking began in the United States around the middle of the 19th century. Prior to this period, auctioneers and merchants—particularly those of Europe—provided the majority of the financial services. The mid-1800s were marked by the country's greatest economic growth. To fund this growth, U.S. companies looked to Europe and U.S. banks became the intermediaries that secured capital from European investors for U.S. companies. Up until World War I, the United States was a debtor nation and U.S. investment bankers had to rely on European investment bankers and investors to share risk and underwrite U.S. securities. For example, investment bankers such as John Pierpont (J. P.) Morgan (1837-1913) of the United States would buy U.S. securities and resell them in London for a higher price.

During this period, U.S. investment banks were linked to European banks. These connections included J.P. Morgan & Co. and George Peabody & Co. (based in London); Kidder, Peabody & Co. and Barling Brothers (based in London); and Kuhn, Loeb, & Co. and the Warburgs (based in Germany).

Since European banks and investors could not assess businesses in the United States easily, they worked with their U.S. counterparts to monitor the success of their investments. U.S. investment bankers often would hold seats on the boards of the companies issuing the securities to supervise operations and make sure **dividends** were paid. Companies established long-term relationships with particular investment banks as a consequence.

In addition, this period saw the development of two basic components of investment banking: underwriting and syndication. Because some of the companies seeking to sell securities during this period, such as railroad and utility companies, required substantial amounts of capital, investment bankers began underwriting the securities, thereby guaranteeing a specific price for them. If the shares failed to fetch the set price, the investments banks covered the difference. Underwriting allowed companies to raise the funds they needed by issuing a sufficient amount of shares without inundating the market so that the value of the shares dropped.

Because the value of the securities they underwrote frequently surpassed their financial limits, investment banks introduced syndication, which involved sharing risk with other investment banks. Further, syndication enabled investment banks to establish larger networks to distribute their shares and hence investment banks began to develop relationships with each other in the form of syndicates.

The syndicate structure typically included three to five tiers, which handled varying degrees of shares and responsibilities. The structure is often thought of as a pyramid with a few large, influential investment banks at the apex and smaller banks below. In the first tier, the ''originating broker'' or ''house of issue'' (now referred to as the manager) investigated companies, determined how much capital would be raised, set the price and number of shares to be issued, and decided when the shares would be issued. The originating broker often handled the largest volume of shares and eventually began charging fees for its services.

In the second tier, the purchase syndicate took a smaller number of shares, often at a slightly higher price such as 1 percent or 0.5 percent higher. In the third tier, the banking syndicate took an even smaller amount of shares at a price higher than that paid by the purchase syndicate. Depending on the size of the issue, other tiers could be added such as the ''selling syndicate'' and ''selling group.'' Investment banks in these tiers of the syndicate would just sell shares, but would not agree to sell a specific amount. Hence, they functioned as brokers who bought and sold shares on commission from their customers.

From the mid-1800s to the early 1900s, J. P. Morgan was the most influential investment banker. Morgan could sell U.S. bonds overseas that the U.S. Department of the Treasury failed to sell and he led the financing of the railroad. He also raised funds for General Electric and United States Steel. Nevertheless, Morgan's control and influence helped cause a number of stock panics, including the panic of 1901.

Morgan and other powerful investment bankers became the target of the muckrakers as well as of inquiries into stock speculations. These investigations included the Armstrong insurance investigation of 1905, the Hughes investigation of 1909, and the Money Trust investigation of 1912. The Money Trust investigation led to most states adopting the so-called blue-sky laws, which were designed to deter investment scams by start-up companies. The banks responded to these investigations and laws by establishing the Investment Bankers Association to ensure the prudent practices among investment banks. These investigations also led to the creation of the **Federal Reserve System** in 1913.

Beginning about the time World War I broke out, the United States became a creditor nation and the roles of Europe and the United States switched to some extent. Companies in other countries now turned to the United States for investment banking. During the 1920s, the number and value of securities offerings increased when investment banks began raising money for a variety of emerging industries: automotive, aviation, and radio. Prior to World War I, securities issues peaked at about $1 million, but afterwards issues of more than $20 million were frequent.

The banks, however, became mired in **speculation** during this period as over 1 million investors bought stocks on margin, that is, with money borrowed from the banks. In addition, the large banks began speculating with the money of their depositors and commercial banks made forays into underwriting.

The **stock market** crashed on October 29, 1929, and commercial and investment banks lost $30 billion by mid-November. While the crash only affected bankers, brokers, and some investors and while most people still had their jobs, the crash brought about a **credit** crunch. Credit became so scarce that by 1931 more than 500 U.S. banks folded, as the Great Depression continued.

As a result, investment banking all but frittered away. Securities issues no longer took place for the most part and few people could afford to invest or would be willing to invest in the stock market, which kept sinking. Because of crash, the government launched an investigation led by Ferdinand Pecora, which became known as the Pecora Investigation. After exposing the corrupt practices of commercial and investment banks, the investigation led to the establishment of the Securities and Exchange Commission (SEC) as well as to the signing of the **Banking Act of 1933**, also known as the Glass-Steagall Act. The SEC became responsible for regulating and overseeing investing in public companies. The Glass-Steagall Act mandated the separation of commercial and investment banking and from then—until the late 1980—banks had to choose between the two enterprises.

Further legislation grew out of this period, too. The Revenue Act of 1932 raised the tax on stocks and required **taxes** on bonds, which made the practice of raising prices in the different tiers of the syndicate system no longer feasible. The **Securities Act of 1933** and the **Securities Exchange Act of 1934** required investment banks to make full disclosures of securities offerings in investment prospectuses and charged the SEC with reviewing them. This legislation also required companies to regularly file financial statements in order to make known changes in their financial position. As a result of these acts, bidding for investment banking projects became competitive as companies began to select the lowest bidders and not rely on major traditional companies such as Morgan Stanley and Kuhn, Loeb.

The last major effort to clean up the investment banking industry came with the *U.S. v. Morgan* case in 1953. This case was a government **antitrust** investigation into the practices of 17 of the top investment banks. The court, however, sided with the defendant investment banks, concluding that they had not conspired to monopolize the U.S. securities industry and to prevent new entrants beginning around 1915, as the government prosecutors argued.

By the 1950s, investment banking began to pick up as the economy continued to prosper. This growth surpassed that of the 1920s. Consequently, major corporations sought new financing during this period. General Motors, for example, made a stock offering of $325 million in 1955, which was the largest stock offering to that time. In addition, airlines, shopping malls, and governments began raising money by selling securities around this time.

During the 1960s, high-tech electronics companies spurred on investment banking. Companies such as Texas Instruments and Electronic Data Systems led the way in securities offerings. Established investment houses such as Morgan Stanley did not handle these issues; rather, Wall Street newcomers such as Charles Plohn & Co. did. The established houses, however, participated in the conglomeration trend of the 1950s and 1960s by helping consolidating companies negotiate deals.

The stock market collapse of 1969 ushered in a new era of economic problems which continued through the 1970s, stifling banks and investment houses. The **recession** of the 1970s brought about a wave of mergers among investment brokers. Investment banks began to expand their services during this period, by setting up retail operations, expanding into international markets, investing in **venture capital**, and working with insurance companies.

While investment bankers once worked for fixed commissions, they have been negotiating fees with investors since 1975, when the SEC opted to deregulate investment banker fees. This deregulation also gave rise to discount brokers, who undercut the prices of established firms. In addition, investment banks started to implement computer technology in the 1970s and 1980s in order to automate and expedite operations. Furthermore, investment banking became much more competitive as investment bankers could no longer wait for clients to come to them, but had to endeavor to win new clients and retain old ones.

RECENT TRENDS IN INVESTMENT BANKING

In the early 1980s, the SEC introduced and made law a rule that permits well-known companies to register securities without a set sale date and delay the sale of the securities until the issuers expect their securities will have strong prices in the market. These registrations are known as ''shelf'' registrations and have become an important part of investment banking.

Shelf financing also contributed to the decline of the historic connections between specific corporations and investment banks. Nevertheless, it did not change the basic structure of the industry, which has retained the pyramid shape. The apex investment houses before the introduction of shelf financing by and large remained the apex houses afterwards.

Contemporary investment banking is also influenced by the growth of institutional investors as key players in the securities market. Whereas institutional investors accounted for 25 percent of securities trade in the 1960s, they accounted for over 75 percent in the 1990s. In addition, the securities market has become more global. For example, U.S. companies raised more money in London in the early 1980s than in New York. Moreover, U.S. investors are buying more European and Asian securities than in previous decades.

New technology—including telecommunications technology, computers, and computer networks—has enabled investment bankers to receive, process, organize, and circulate large amounts of diverse information. This technology has helped investment banks become more efficient and complete transactions more quickly.

The increased **competition** within the investment banking arena has further quelled the establishment of long-term relationships between corporations and investment houses. Company executives receive offers from a variety of investment banks and they compare the offers, choosing the ones they believe will benefit their company the most. Large corporations generally have transactions with four or more investment banks. Nevertheless, corporations still favor their traditional investment banks and about 70 percent of the executives surveyed in a study said they do most of their business with their traditional investment banks, according to *The Investment Banking Handbook.*

In the 1980s and 1990s, the investment banking industry continued to consolidate. As a result, a few investment banks with large amounts of capital dominated the industry and offered a wide array of services, earning the name ''financial supermarkets.'' This trend also altered the structure of the industry, affecting the size and roles of syndicates. Syndicates became dependent on the type and volume of the securities being offered as a result. For small offerings, syndicates are usually small and the managing banks sell the majority of the securities. In contrast, for large offerings, the managing banks may create a syndicate including more than 100 investment banks.

Investment houses continued to be innovative and introduce new financial instruments for both issuers and investors. Some of the most significant innovations include fixed-income and tax-exempt securities, which have grown in popularity since their inception in the 1980s. Some key fixed-income securities have been debt **warrants**, which are bonds sold with warrants to buy more bonds at a specific time; and debt-equity swaps, where companies offer stock to existing bondholders.

With a growing number of mergers and acquisitions as well as **corporate restructurings**, investment banks have become increasingly involved in the process of arranging these transactions as part of their primary services. Because of changing economic, competitive, and market conditions, several thousand small and mid-sized companies as well as a handful of large corporations agree to merger and acquisition deals each year. Investment banks facilitate this process by providing advice on such transactions, negotiating on behalf of their clients, and guaranteeing the purchase of bonds for acquisitions that rely on debt, known as **leveraged buyouts**.

The rapid expansion of the **Internet** in the mid-to-late 1990s provided an impetus for stockbrokers to begin offering trading services through the Internet. Because of the popularity of online trading, brokers began offering investment banking services. Early in 1999, E-Trade established the online investment bank ''E-Offering,'' which provides online initial public offering services.

Since the passage in 1933 of the Glass-Steagall Act, the U.S. banking industry has been closely regulated. This act requires the separation of commercial banking, investment banking, and insurance. In contrast to investment banks, commercial banks focus on taking deposits and lending. Nevertheless, there have been recent endeavors to repeal the act and to relax its measures. While the act has not been overturned even with efforts continuing in 1999, the Federal Reserve, which oversees commercial banking, has allowed commercial banks to sell insurance and issue securities. Consequently, investment banks and insurers support the latest round of activity to overturn the act. Japan and the United States are the only major industrial countries that require the separation of commercial and investment banking.

SEE ALSO: Banks and Banking

[Karl Heil]

FURTHER READING:

''American Financial Regulation: Twelfth Time Lucky.'' *Economist,* 13 February 1999, 71.

Benston, George J. *The Separation of Commercial and Investment Banking.* New York: Oxford University Press, 1990.

Berss, Marcia. ''Tough New Kid on the Block.'' *Forbes,* 2 October 1989, 42.

Hoffman, Paul. *The Deal Makers.* Garden City, NY: Doubleday, 1984.

''The Road to Investment Banking Is Long and Stony.'' *Economist,* 17 April 1999, 8.

Taylor, Dennis. ''E-Trade Move May Lead to Discount Investment Banking.'' *Business Journal,* 15 January 1999, 1.

Williamson, J. Peter, ed. *The Investment Banking Handbook.* New York: Wiley, 1988.

INVESTMENT MANAGEMENT

Investment management comprises a broad spectrum of topics ranging from the workings of **capital markets**, to **valuation** of financial **securities**, to the construction of portfolios of assets to meet the objectives of investors. Investment itself can be considered any activity that requires the commitment of current **wealth** to some set of specified assets for the purpose of enhancing future wealth. These assets can be either real (e.g., gold, art, **real estate**) or financial (e.g., **stocks**, **bonds**). The enhancement of future wealth can be derived from appreciation in the value of the asset itself, referred to as **capital gains**, or as **income** provided to the owner of the asset.

There are well-developed financial markets around the world that have evolved to assist in the transfer of funds from investors to individuals and organizations who have a need for capital. These markets can be divided into primary and secondary categories. Primary markets capture the initial transfer of funds from investors to those with viable projects requiring additional cash. For example, a corporation may sell stock to the public in order to raise needed funds for an expansion of productive capacity, or to undertake new initiatives in new markets. This type of transaction is typically mediated by an investment banker who will assist the corporation in the sale of its securities. Other than the fee charged by the investment banker, the corporation actually receives the cash generated from the stock sale. The investor receives shares of stock representing partial ownership of the firm.

Secondary markets are resale markets where financial securities are traded among investors. Although corporations receive no additional cash flow from the purchase or sale of their securities in secondary markets, these markets provide the important ingredient of liquidity to investors. Liquidity refers to the ability to quickly exchange assets and cash at reasonable prices. The New York Stock Exchange (NYSE) is the largest example of a secondary market in the world. On the floor of the NYSE, traders exchange shares of corporations after agreeing on the proper price. Other major stock exchanges in the world are located in Tokyo, London, Frankfurt, Toronto, Paris, and in most other developed economies. In addition, there are significant markets that have no physical location. The **over-the-counter** (OTC) market in the United States, is one such example. This market is really a **computer** network of dealers who maintain inventories of various securities and serve as market makers. Dealers post prices at which they would be willing to purchase additional securities (the bid price) and prices at which they would be willing to sell securities that they hold (the ask price).

Investors who want to buy or sell financial assets typically engage the services of a broker. The broker transmits orders to buy or sell to the trading floor of the appropriate exchange or views price quotes provided by dealers and executes the order at the best available price. Investors can submit either market orders or limit orders. A market order is an instruction to buy or sell at the current market price. A limit order carries conditions that must be met before the transaction can be carried out. These conditions relate to the price level of the security and the time period during which the order remains valid.

Additionally, investors can hold a long position in a security, by purchasing a quantity and holding it, or a short position, by borrowing securities and selling them. While the motivation behind the long position is clear—the investor expects the value of the security to increase or expects it to provide income in the future—the motivation for short selling requires further explanation. By borrowing securities now, selling them at the current price, and agreeing to replace them at a later date, the investor is clearly **forecasting** a decrease in price. If the price does decline, then the investor can purchase securities at this lower price, repay the loan that is denominated in securities, not money, and profit from the decline. If the price rises after the initial sale, however, the investor will sustain a loss when the shares are eventually purchased and replaced. Brokers will assist in this transaction by locating shares that can be borrowed and sold.

Brokers will also lend funds to investors for the purchase of shares. This is called margin trading. Current regulations in the United States allow an investor to borrow up to 50 percent of the value of securities purchased. Note that the investor's profits are amplified since only a fraction of the purchase was financed with personal funds. Likewise, losses will accumulate at a more rapid rate if the value of the securities purchased declines. If the drop in value is considerable, the investor will be contacted by the broker and instructed to provide additional cash in order to secure the position. This is referred to as a margin call.

There are a variety of financial assets for the investor to consider. Shares of **common stock**, often referred to as equity, represent a claim of ownership of the firm's future earnings. Common stockholders are the legal owners of a corporation and typically carry voting rights regarding matters of **corporate governance**. The shares have value if the firm is expected to generate significant future cash flows that will be sufficient to cover expenses and allow for a profit that can be distributed to shareholders. These future cash flows to shareholders can take the form of **dividends**, direct cash payments, or capital gains. Capital gains represent the change in the value of the shares themselves. This value will change as investors reassess the ability of the firm to generate future cash flows for shareholders. Closely related to common stock is a second category, **preferred stock**. This stock pays a dividend that is either fixed or varies with some indicator of **interest rates**. The term ''preferred'' refers to the fact that dividends must be paid to this class of shareholders before any dividend payments are made to common shareholders. While it is also considered equity, and its holders are also considered owners of the firm, preferred shareholders can vote on matters of corporate governance in only very limited circumstances.

A second category of financial assets is represented by **debt**. Debtholders are creditors of the firm, not owners. Therefore, an investment in a firm's debt is inherently less risky than an investment in its equity. All obligations to debtholders must be met before any payments can be made to preferred or common shareholders. Debt is often classified by the life of the liability it entails. At the shortest end of the maturity spectrum are highly liquid corporate and government obligations that must be paid within one year. Highly creditworthy corporations may issue commercial paper. Commercial paper carries a stated par, or face value, which represents the amount that the corporation agrees to repay when the obligation matures. This asset is sold at a discount, or for less than its face value. The return to the investor is the difference between this initial discount price and the face value. Similar instruments, called **U.S. Treasury bills**, are issued by the U.S. Department of the Treasury and by governmental units of other foreign nations. Notes are medium-term obligations that typically have a life of more than one year and less than five years. Notes also have a face value and usually provide periodic payments of interest at a rate expressed as a percentage of the face value.

Bonds are the most prominent securities in the debt category. They include any obligation with a life of more than five years. Bonds are commonly issued for 20-year periods. There are, however, many examples of 30-year bonds and a U.S. corporation, Disney, has issued bonds with a 100-year life. Regardless of longevity, bonds are similar to notes in that they make periodic payments of interest to holders. These payments are referred to as coupon payments and are typically expressed as a percentage of the bond's face value. For example, a 20-year bond with an 8 percent coupon rate and a $1,000 face value would make payments of $80 per year. Most coupon bonds commonly divide this interest payment into semiannual installments. There are many types of bonds that differ from the fixed rate coupon bond just described. Floating-rate bonds have no fixed coupon rate. Instead, interest payments are adjusted to move with some broader indicator of interest rates. Zero coupon bonds pay no interest whatsoever. They are sold at some fraction of their face value and, unless resold, will generate no cash inflow until they mature. Convertible bonds are typically coupon paying bonds that also provide the holder with the option of exchanging the bond for a specified number of shares of common stock. This option can be very valuable if the firm's stock price rises significantly.

Another class of financial assets is represented by **derivative securities**. These are securities whose value is directly tied to the value of another asset. One prominent example is the stock option. **Options** are traded securities that allow the holder to purchase or sell a specified quantity of shares of an individual stock for a predetermined price, called the strike or exercise price, during a specified period. The holder of a **call option** may purchase stock at the exercise price. Therefore, the call option becomes more valuable as the value of the stock itself increases. Conversely, the holder of a put option has the right to sell stock at the exercise price and will profit if the stock's value falls. A second prominent category of derivative securities is the **futures contract**. In a futures contract, the buyer agrees to take delivery of a specified commodity or financial instrument at a specified time and price. Therefore, the buyer profits if the value of the commodity rises above this price. The seller has incurred a loss since there is an obligation to deliver the commodity for a price that is lower than the current market price. The situation is reversed, however, if the value of the commodity falls below the price specified in the futures contract. In this case, the seller profits and the buyer loses. Futures contracts are used to hedge, or transfer, risk associated with the underlying commodity of the contract; they are used by speculators to take risky positions regarding the future price movements of the **commodities** themselves. Futures contracts are available on many agricultural commodities (e.g., corn, wheat, soybeans, cattle), industrial commodities (e.g., crude oil, copper), precious metals (e.g., gold, silver, platinum), interest rate sensitive securities (e.g., **U.S. Treasury notes**, bonds, and bills), foreign currencies, and a variety of market **indexes**.

Regardless of the assets chosen as investments, the investor must always consider the duality of **risk and return** associated with each. Rate of return refers to the percentage of wealth appreciation or **depreciation** associated with a particular investment. Rate of return can be considered in a historical or an expectational sense. That is, it can be measured for some prior period or it can be forecast for some upcoming period. Risk refers to the cloud of uncertainty surrounding the expected future return. It is common in **investment analysis** to use measures of historical return, such as an arithmetic average over multiple periods, and historical risk, such as statistical variance or standard deviation, to serve as a proxy for expected future returns and risk. But this is just a convenient starting point and investment analysis commonly modifies the forecast drawn from historical data to reflect more relevant information derived from a broader array of sources. So, it is the future risk and return that truly matters and it is reasonable to assume that as investors compare various alternatives, they will prefer higher expected returns and lower expected risk.

Analysis of individual investment alternatives is carried out in a variety of ways. One interesting dichotomy is the distinction between fundamental and **technical analysis**. Fundamental analysis is an attempt to build a model of security value by careful scrutiny of the characteristics of the firm (or government) that has issued the security. Such an assessment will draw upon **financial statements** of a corporation and other pertinent sources of information regarding the firm's activities. The assessment will also rely upon judgments made regarding the prospects of the industry in which the firm resides and on the outlook for the economy in general. The objective is to forecast the future cash flows that will be available to the various security holders in the firm and to subsequently assess whether these expected cash flows will be sufficient to compensate the investor for the associated risk. Clearly, there is no one methodology for fundamental analysis even though there is a common objective.

Technical analysis attempts to forecast future security values by exploiting patterns in past security prices, and in the relationship between prices and other relevant variables. This technique requires careful identification and exploitation of trends that provide an unambiguous clue regarding future price movements. Technical analysts do not rely on information regarding financial characteristics of the firm itself, but instead examine both psychological and institutional determinants of supply and demand of the firm's stock. As with fundamental analysis, there is no one mode of technical analysis.

Acting as an umbrella over these two modes of investment analysis is the idea of market efficiency. A market is considered efficient if security prices fully reflect all available information. Furthermore, new and relevant information will be rapidly incorporated into the price. If there are many fundamental analysts searching for relevant information that can be used to value a security, then financial markets should be informationally efficient. On the other hand, if markets are imperfect and investors exhibit irrational behavior (e.g., systematically overreacting to bad news or exhibiting "herd" behavior), then markets will not be efficient. The question is really one concerning the level of efficiency. There are many studies that have scrutinized the predictive ability of past stock prices and other historical relationships. By and large, these studies have found no significant "memory," or forecasting ability using such data. Other studies have indicated that an unanticipated disclosure of information relevant to the future cash flow stream of the firm evokes a rapid and complete adjustment to a new price level for the firm's securities. There are small, yet undeniable, examples that suggest financial markets are not perfectly efficient and that investors sometimes act on information that should have no economic consequence. It is reasonable, however, to say that financial markets in most developed economies exhibit a high degree of informational efficiency.

The large body of research on market efficiency has generated a relatively new specialty called quantitative investment management. This style of management generates models using both fundamental and technical data. The objective is to rank securities based on expected future performance and to assess the risk of any portfolio resulting from such a ranking.

Given well-functioning global security markets, a broad array of securities, and many sources of information for assessing alternatives, investors are presented with the difficult choice of what combination of securities to hold. The first step in addressing this fundamental problem requires an examination of investment objectives. A clarification of investment objectives and other relevant information regarding the investor's specific situation will lead to effective screening of investment alternatives, proper portfolio construction, and ultimately, a suitable set of investments for the investor. Investment objectives can be described in a number of ways. One useful scale is based upon risk and return.

Consider the following broad categories of investment objectives ranging from low to high risk: (1) preservation of capital, (2) growth and income, (3) capital appreciation, and (4) aggressive growth. The first category, preservation of capital, would consider only the highest-quality, lowest risk, investment alternatives. Primary consideration is given to avoidance of loss, not to an increase in wealth. This objective could be met by holding Treasury bills, commercial paper, and other short-term, low-risk instruments. The second category, growth and income, would screen to find a set of securities that also have low risk, but which are expected to provide a reasonable level of current income. This would suggest a significant component of stocks paying a high dividend and coupon-paying bonds. In addition, the growth component of this objective may be met by holding a proportion of securities in industries that are expected to exhibit moderate growth over some upcoming period. Capital appreciation refers to an objective where current income is a minor consideration at best. Common stock (and possibly convertible bonds) in companies expected to exhibit average and above-average growth would be appropriate to include. On the high-risk, high-expected-return end of the spectrum is the aggressive growth objective. Here, an investor would screen out all but those firms expected to generate above-average growth. This portfolio may include stocks of relatively small companies in new industries, bonds from firms that are considered moderate to high credit risks, and derivative securities such as options.

In addition to these simple objectives, the investor's portfolio may be influenced by other characteristics. For example, an institutional investor managing a **pension fund** will have different concerns than an individual investor designing his or her own personal retirement plan. Other investors will want the portfolio to address their other sources of income, or lack thereof, tax status, age, need to provide for dependents, level of sophistication regarding investment alternatives, and many other attributes. These attributes and attitudes regarding risk will immediately exclude some investment alternatives and implicitly suggest others.

At this point, many investors—individual and institutional—will look toward **mutual funds** to provide them with a proper package of appropriate investments. Mutual funds are companies that hold portfolios of securities and sell shares in the portfolios that they hold. There are nearly as many mutual funds in the United States as there are publicly listed stocks. Mutual funds can be categorized by risk-return objective or by the subset of securities they hold. For example, there are many funds in each of the four categories previously described. In addition, there are sector funds (specializing in individual industries), country funds (specializing in the securities of an individual country), global funds, bond funds, real estate development funds, funds holding tax-exempt securities, and many others. Such categorization is often referred to as a fund's ''style.'' Managers of these funds charge a fee, but relieve investors of the need to scrutinize individual investments.

After settling on an investment objective and screening the vast number of investment alternatives to a manageable number, there is still a major consideration that remains. **Portfolio management theory** indicates that an investor can reduce overall exposure to risk by holding a group of securities selected from a diverse set of industries or countries. This **diversification** of risk occurs because any individual security is subject to unique sources of risk. The unique sources of risk in one security, however, are distinct from the unique sources of risk in another security. This means that when the securities are held together, they tend to stabilize one another since unique surprises from one source are not compounded by similar surprises from another source. This lack of correlation among sources of risk for individual securities means that the investor can minimize, even eliminate, the risk unique to individual securities, by holding a large number of diverse securities. This set could span a number of different industries or regions of the world. This does not eliminate all risk for the investor, however. There is still risk that results from factors common to all securities in the sample. For example, all securities are subject to the risk of changes in overall economic conditions. An investor who wished to reduce risk further could choose securities that have lower sensitivity to such changes.

SEE ALSO: Investment Analysis

[Paul Bolster]

FURTHER READING:

Bodie, Zvi, Alex Kane, and Alan J. Marcus. *Investments.* 4th ed. Boston: Irwin/McGraw-Hill, 1999.

Fabozzi, Frank J., and Franco Modigliani. *Capital Markets: Institutions and Instruments.* 2nd ed. Upper Saddle River, NJ: Prentice Hall, 1996.

Sharpe, William F. ''Asset Allocation: Management Style and Performance Measurement.'' *Journal of Portfolio Management* 18, no. 2 (winter 1992): 7+.

IRA

SEE: Individual Retirement Account

ISO

SEE: International Organization for Standardization; ISO 14000; ISO 9000

ISO 14000

The ISO 14000 Series International Environmental Management Standards are receiving significant attention from business managers and their legal and economic advisers, and it is said that the standards may be a ''watershed in the annals of environmental regulation.'' Business managers view ISO 14000 as a market-driven approach to environmental protection that provides an alternative to ''command and control'' regulation by government. Therefore, the standards are of significant interest to business organizations and their legal representatives; environmental groups and their members; and governments, their agencies, and their officials.

The ISO 14000 standards were issued in September 1996 by the **International Organization for**

Standardization (ISO), a major, private organization involved in standardization of industrial management practices. Although the ISO 14000 standards are the product of a nongovernmental organization and compliance with the standards is voluntary, one of the primary purposes of the standards is to ensure that businesses comply with applicable **environmental law**. Businesses view implementation of ISO 14000 as a means to self-regulate, thereby minimizing their exposure to surveillance and sanctions by the U.S. **Environmental Protection Agency** (EPA) and its state-level counterparts. Part II of this article explores reasons for the development of ISO 14000. Part III describes the provisions of ISO 14000, and Part IV describes the perspectives of various parties on the utility of ISO 14000. Finally, Part V surveys the overall strengths and limitations of ISO 14000.

REASONS FOR DEVELOPMENT OF ISO 14000

Several converging factors relating to the developing global marketplace led to the development of the ISO 14000 Series International Environmental Management Standards. As industrialization has spread to countries throughout the world, citizens and their governments have voiced their concerns about the effects of that industrialization on the environment. As a result of such concerns, the concept of **sustainable development** was developed. Its pursuit has been adopted as a goal by governments and business groups around the world.

Sustainable development was articulated as a goal and defined in 1987 by the World Commission on the Environment and Development (World Commission), a body established by the **United Nations**. In *Our Common Future,* the World Commission defined sustainable development as development which ''meets the needs of the present without compromising the ability of future generations to meet their own needs.''

For more than a decade, sustainable development has been at the center of discussion of environmental issues, especially with respect to the effects of increased trade on the environment. Sustainable development was the focus of discussion at the United Nations Conference on the Environment and Development held in Rio de Janeiro in 1992, and it was listed as one of ten goals in the Environmental Side Agreement to the **North American Free Trade Agreement** (NAFTA), which took effect on January 1, 1994. And in 1996, the ISO incorporated the attainment of sustainable development as a major goal in its new ISO 14000 Series International Environmental Management Standards.

Another impetus for ISO 14000 was the desire of businesses to self-regulate and minimize their exposure to government regulation. Such regulations can be burdensome. For example, in the United States, environmental regulations fill more than 20,000 pages of the *Federal Register,* and there are thousands of additional environmental regulations at the state and local levels.

A third impetus for the ISO 14000 Series Standards came from the United Nations Conference on the Environment and Development (UNCED), which was held in Rio de Janeiro in 1992 and attended by representatives of more than 100 nations. In response to documents issued by UNCED, the international business community adopted a ''Business Charter for Sustainable Development.'' The document includes 16 proposals that set out basic elements for any environmental management system (EMS).

A fourth source of inspiration for development of the standards comes from environmental management programs proposed by groups of concerned citizens around the world. For example, in response to a major oil spill off the coast of Alaska by a ship called the *Exxon Valdez,* a group of environmentalists, investors, government agencies, and economists formed the Coalition for Environmentally Responsible Economies (CERES). The CERES group issued a set of principles that was first known as the Valdez Principles and was later renamed the CERES Principles. The CERES Principles give guidelines designed to lead to an international standard for EMS. CERES has been recognized as a direct impetus for the ISO 14000 series and similar programs.

A fifth impetus for the ISO 14000 series is the need for harmonization among various environmental management and auditing programs. Such harmonization is needed within the United States. For example, the EPA has designed several different environmental management programs, including the XL Program, the Star Track Programs, and the Environmental Leadership Program (ELP). ELP is a voluntary program in which a participating business creates its own EMS according to EPA guidelines. The incentive for participation is that the EPA may treat the company leniently in instances of noncompliance, and, upon certain conditions, the EPA refrains from conducting routine enforcement inspections at the company's facilities. Various state-level counterparts to the EPA have developed similar programs.

In addition, there are industry-specific environmental review programs such as the Chemical Manufacturers Association's (CMA's) Responsible Care program (also known as CARE). All members of the CMA are required to participate in the program, which sets out conformance standards in the areas of pollution prevention, emergency response, and employee health and safety protection and awareness.

Harmonization is also needed internationally. Companies must deal with EMSs originating in the various countries in which they operate. For example, in 1995 the British Standards Institute (BSI) became the national standards setting organization for the United Kingdom. In that same year it became the first national organization to implement a program recognizing independently verified EMSs. In 1995 the **European Union** (EU) implemented an Eco-Management and Audit Regulation (EMAR) program. EMAR includes the Eco-Management and Audit Scheme (EMAS), which took effect in 1995. It is a voluntary program through which a company may register a site as being in compliance with the system. The objectives of the program are to promote adherence to standards for environmental management and to inform the public about the environmental performance of companies.

Businesses are searching for a way to harmonize EPA standards, state standards, private industry standards (such as the CARE program), and requirements of other countries and trade organizations. They want to avoid the record keeping involved in compliance with multiple environmental systems and other management systems, such as **quality control** systems. In addition, they want to avoid dealing with conflicts between and among substantive provisions of such systems. Elimination of multiple sets of standards or, at least, harmonization of such standards became particularly important in the late 20th century in connection with the **globalization** of business. Today, large and small companies deal with the laws and regulations of multiple countries and must comply with the requirements of various trade organizations. It is an essential part of doing business as we move into the 21st century.

WHAT DOES ISO 14000 REQUIRE?

ISO 14000 PROVISIONS. The initial standards in the 14000 series include numbers 14000, 14001, 14004, 14010, 14011, and 14012. They were developed by ISO Technical Committee (TC) 207 Environmental Management and were adopted by the ISO in 1996.

A company must fulfill the following three requirements to comply with ISO 14000:

1. It must create an environmental management system (EMS).
2. It must demonstrate its compliance with the environmental statutes and regulations of countries in which it does business.
3. It must demonstrate its commitment to continuous improvement in environmental protection and pollution prevention.

ISO 14000 sets up criteria pursuant to which a company's EMS may be certified. The EMS is a set of procedures for assessing compliance with applicable environmental laws. It must also include procedures for assessing the company's own procedures for identifying and resolving environmental problems, and for engaging the company's **workforce** in a commitment to improved environmental performance.

ISO 14001 describes two types of documents (guidance documents and specification documents), and it sets out standards used to evaluate a company's EMS. For example, the EMS must include an accurate summary of the laws and legal standards with which the company must comply. Applicable laws include federal, state, and local laws. Applicable legal standards include permit stipulations and provisions of administrative or court-certified consent judgments.

To be certified to ISO 14001, the EMS must include five elements. First, it must establish an environmental policy. Second, it must set environmental goals and establish plans to comply with legal requirements. Third, it must provide for implementation and operation of the policy including training of personnel, communication, and document control. Fourth, it must set up monitoring and measurement devices and an audit procedure to ensure continuing improvement. Finally, it must provide for **management** review to take place on a regular, planned basis.

The EMS must be certified by a registrar who has been qualified under ISO 13012, which is a standard that predates the ISO 14000 series. If a company chooses not to undergo third-party EMS certification, it may decide to use ISO 14001 as a basis for self-declaration. It is important to note that ISO 14001 is the only standard in the ISO 14000 series that leads to certification. The others support 14001 or provide guidance only.

The ISO 14004 standard gives advice only; compliance with its provisions is not required. It includes five principles, each of which corresponds to one of the five areas of ISO 14001 listed above. First, the company should define its environmental policy and take steps to ensure its commitment to the EMS. Second, the company should develop a written plan to implement its environmental policies. Third, it should provide support mechanisms to implement its environmental policies. Fourth, the company should monitor and evaluate its environmental performance. Fifth, the company should review and revise its EMS periodically with the objective of improving its overall environmental performance.

ISO 14010, 14011, and 14012 are **auditing** standards. ISO 14010 gives general principles of environmental auditing, and ISO 14011 provides guidelines for auditing of an EMS. ISO 14012 gives guidelines for establishing qualifications for environmental auditors called ''registrars.''

PLANS FOR ADDITIONAL ISO 14000 STANDARDS. The ISO is considering various proposals for additions to the ISO 14000 series standards. (Documents providing proposals are designated by the prefix "CD.") CD 14021 gives terms and definitions for use in self-declaration through environmental labeling. The proposed standard has two goals. First, it establishes guidelines for environmental claims made in connection with the supply of services and goods. Second, it defines specific terms used in environmental claims and provides rules for their use.

Several draft documents address other concerns. CD 14024 provides guidelines, practices, and certification procedures related to environmental labeling. CD 14040 deals with life-cycle assessment of a product. CD 14050 provides a comprehensive set of definitions of terms used in environmental management.

In addition, an ISO working group is reviewing the needs and concerns of small and medium sized enterprises (SMEs). The group is preparing CD 14002 Environmental Management Systems—Guidelines on Special Considerations Affecting Small and Medium Size Enterprises.

DISTINGUISHING ISO 14000 FROM ISO 9000

It is important to note that the ISO issued a separate set of management standards in 1987 called the **ISO 9000** series. It is a series of standards designed to lead to quality in design, development, production, inspection, testing, installation, and servicing of products. In short, the standards are designed to promote quality management practices.

The ISO 9000 series and the ISO 14000 standards are process standards, not performance standards. Both series promote management systems that focus on prevention rather than corrective action. But the ISO 14000 series can be distinguished from the 9000 series in at least four major aspects. First, the 9000 series is designed to help an organization maintain quality as it designs, produces, and delivers a product or service to a customer. Thus, it focuses on the customer-supplier relationship. The ISO 14000 series is of concern to various groups of interested parties or "stakeholders." It concerns businesses and their customers as well as government, environmental organizations, consumer groups, and others. Second, the ISO 14000 series involves more strategic planning; it prompts businesses to pursue continuous improvement in their environmental performance. Third, the subject of the 14000 series (environmental protection) is heavily regulated by government through thousands of statutes and regulations. Noncompliance with environmental law can result in substantial fines or even imprisonment of business managers. Thus, a major goal of the ISO 14000 series is to ensure that businesses are in compliance with their own national and local applicable environmental laws and regulations. Quality of management is less directly tied to law. Fourth, the ISO 14000 series covers a broad area (the environment) and takes a holistic approach to that area, focusing on the business organization's activities and how they affect the land, water, and air. The quality of management area covered by ISO 9000 is more limited.

Certification to ISO 9000 is not a precondition to ISO 14000 certification, but coordination of the two sets of standards has been addressed by the U.S. Technical Advisory Group, which provides advice to the ISO's Technical Committee charged with formulation of the ISO 14000 standards.

Many organizations that are already registered to ISO 9000, however, have decided to seek ISO 14000 registration, also. As they do so, they are seeking ways to integrate ISO 14000 systems into their existing ISO 9000 systems.

PERSPECTIVES OF BUSINESS ON THE ISO 14000 STANDARDS

The benefits and detriments of the ISO 14000 standards depend on the perspectives of the speaker. Therefore, this section looks at the ISO 14000 standards from the perspectives of business organizations, governments, and environmentalists.

BENEFITS TO THE INDIVIDUAL BUSINESS. ISO 14001 certification may bring various rewards to a company, most of which can ultimately provide a financial advantage to the company. Seven potential rewards are explored below, but this list could be expanded.

First, many firms are hoping that, in return for obtaining ISO 14001 certification (and the actions required to do so), regulatory agencies such as the EPA will give them more favorable treatment. For example, businesses are hoping for less stringent filing, or less monitoring, or even less severe sanctions for violations of environmental laws.

Many state regulatory agencies have suggested that the ISO 14001 certificate may be classified as a voluntary audit program that will, in turn, qualify a business for leniency in filing or monitoring requirements or even, less severe sanctions for violations of environmental regulations. In fact, some states have already acted to provide such leniency. For example, the Pennsylvania Department of Environmental Protection (PA DEP) grants regulatory relief to companies that conduct voluntary environmental compliance audits. If a company, local government body, or an individual completes an environmental compliance audit and discovers a problem, discloses the problem to the PA DEP, and takes action to correct the problem, the DEP will not take civil or criminal action. James M. Seif, secretary of the PA DEP stated, ''Our policy is centered on one simple premise: You find it, you fix it, you tell us—no penalty.'' At least 14 other states have adopted legislation or policies to encourage voluntary environmental audit programs and to limit penalties associated with violations discovered in the process of those audits. Those states include Arkansas, Colorado, Idaho, Illinois, Indiana, Kansas, Kentucky, Minnesota, Mississippi, Oregon, Texas, Utah, Virginia, and Wyoming.

In a state that has not adopted legislation or policies to provide regulatory relief to businesses that implement an EMS, a business can at least benefit from an enhanced relationship with environmental regulatory agencies and regulated businesses. A cordial and cooperative relationship between the business and regulators can be valuable in many instances.

A second benefit to businesses that choose to become certified to ISO 14001 is that substantial numbers of citizens can be influenced in their buying decisions. Obtaining ISO 14000 certification is a way for companies to demonstrate their environmental stewardship and accountability to the public.

Third, ISO 14000 certification can attract investors to the business organization. A growing number of individual investors as well as investment managers and managers of **mutual funds** search for environmentally responsible businesses.

Fourth, the company may save money on insurance premiums. For example, some insurance companies give reduced rates on insurance to cover accidental pollution releases if the insured company has successfully implemented an EMS.

Fifth, actions taken in the process of implementing the EMS are likely to reduce the likelihood of toxic spills endangering employees and members of the community.

Sixth, financial institutions are sensitive to environmental risks and their impact on collateral. ISO 14001 may help a corporation obtain **loans** and protect it from allegations of investor fraud.

Seventh, by implementing an EMS, a company may realize internal cost savings as a result of waste reduction, use of fewer toxic chemicals, reduced energy use, and recycling.

COSTS AND DETRIMENTS TO THE INDIVIDUAL BUSINESS. A company's costs in becoming ISO 14001 certified depend on the scope of the EMS. For example, the EMS might be international, national, or limited to individual plants operated by the company. National and international systems can be very costly. With respect to a company operating in more than one legal jurisdiction (whether that means two states of the United States or two countries, such as the United States and Mexico), it will be necessary to assess the company's compliance with the laws of all national, state, and local jurisdictions involved.

Lawyers studying the ISO 14000 standards are discussing a number of legal issues related to use of environmental audit documents prepared as a part of the ISO 14001 certification process. There are serious questions as to whether a governmental regulatory agency can require disclosure of information discovered during a self-audit by a company. The use of a third-party auditor may weaken a company's argument that information is privileged. In view of the fact that some companies conducted environmental audits for various reasons prior to the creation of ISO 14001, this is not a new area of the law. It is still developing, however, and questions specific to ISO 14001 must be resolved. Taking one step to deal with such problems, the EPA has implemented an Interim Environmental Audit Policy that encourages business organizations to conduct environmental audits. It provides the potential for eliminating or reducing civil penalties and avoiding criminal prosecution when specified conditions are met. Similarly, various states have adopted some form of environmental audit privilege.

The ISO 14000 series has potential consequences with respect to international trade, also. ISO 14000 is designed to provide a series of universally accepted EMS practices and lead to consistency in environmental standards between and among trading partners. It has the potential to lead to two kinds of cultural changes: one of them would be within individual companies and the other would be a global change. First, within the corporation, the ISO 14000 Series can promote consideration of environmental issues throughout the company's operations. Managers of companies that have implemented ISO 9000 have learned to view their companies' operations through a ''quality of management'' lens. Similarly, it is hoped that implementation of ISO 14000 will lead to use of an ''environmental quality'' lens by businesses. Second, the ISO 14000 series has the potential to become part of a global culture as the public comes to view ISO 14001 certification as a **benchmark** connoting good environmental stewardship.

PERSPECTIVES OF GOVERNMENT ON THE ISO 14000 STANDARDS

PERSPECTIVES OF DEVELOPING COUNTRIES. The perspectives of developing countries differ substantially from those of industrialized countries such as the United States and Britain for a variety of reasons. The ISO 14000 Series standards were developed by business representatives from industrialized countries. Developing countries from Latin America, Africa, and elsewhere had little input. As compared to developed countries, developing countries and their businesses suffer from limited financial resources, and they have less experience in environmental law enforcement. In many cases, control of industrial sources of pollution is seen as a ''luxury'' as compared to other more pressing needs of citizens. Their citizens' needs include food, basic housing, clothing, electricity, and clean drinking water.

Because their attentions have been on even more pressing matters, the governments of many developing countries have not developed and consistently enforced environmental legislation. Thus, there has been much discussion about whether the ISO 14000 series standards can be used as an alternative to environmental law in those countries. Some commentators even argue that it could be adopted as law. Some developing countries such as Mexico are reviewing the ISO 14000 series standards and considering incorporating their provisions within their own environmental laws and regulations. Zimbabwe has incorporated ISO 14001 into its national regulatory system. It is important to note, however, that Zimbabwe's plan is to use ISO 14001 in conjunction with its additional legislation and a ''tuned up'' monitoring system.

On the other hand, various commentators as well as the governments of some developing countries argue that the ISO 14000 environmental standards are functioning as nontariff barriers to trade. This assertion is based on the fact that costs of ISO 14000 registration are prohibitively high for poorly funded companies. Thus companies in developing countries, especially small to medium size companies, will suffer disproportionately if ISO 14000 standards become a ''de facto'' requirement of doing business with other nations.

VARYING APPROACHES BY VARIOUS COUNTRIES. Governments' approach to the standards varies widely from one industrialized country to another. Within the EU, efforts are under way to minimize such variance. The European Commission (EC) is the primary legislative body for the EU, and harmonization of standards is a primary missions of the EC. Various European governments provide backing to privately run standards organizations; some grant government charters to their standards organizations. Portugal's primary standards organization is part of its Ministry of Industry, and in Germany and Britain the government makes **contracts** to obtain standards services as a part of its efforts to serve the public.

Because the countries of the EU are, collectively, the United States's largest trading partner, its standards activities are important to U.S. businesses that trade with its members. U.S. companies doing business with Europe must design their products and ensure that their management practices conform to the requirements of the EU.

PERSPECTIVES OF THE U.S. GOVERNMENT. The perspectives of the U.S. government merit separate examination because of the dominant place the United States occupies in world commerce. But it is important to remember that U.S. perspectives are those of a wealthy, highly industrialized society with a highly developed regulatory law system.

Agencies of the U.S. government have been actively following the development of the ISO 14000 series standards and have provided input in various contexts. For example, the EPA, the Department of Defense, and the Department of Energy provide representatives to the U.S. Technical Advisory Group (U.S. TAG). The U.S. TAG, in turn, provides input to TC 207, the ISO technical committee responsible for the ISO 14000 series.

The United States has a highly developed regulatory system designed to protect the environment. The EPA, in conjunction with state-level counterparts, enforces a myriad of environmental protection statutes including, but not limited to, the **Clean Air Act**; the **Clean Water Act**; **Comprehensive Environmental Response, Compensation, and Liability Act** (Superfund); and the Toxic Substance Control Act. Thus, unlike a developing country, which may lack a comprehensive regulatory scheme in the area of environmental protection, the United States does not view the ISO 14000 series as a potential substitute for statutes and regulations. Nevertheless, implementation of an EMS by a company certified to ISO 14001 does have the potential to improve that company's rate of compliance with state and federal environmental law.

PERSPECTIVES OF ENVIRONMENTALISTS ON THE ISO 14000 STANDARDS

Environmentalists and their organizations were active in debate and discussion before the United States joined the NAFTA. As a consequence of their concerns the Environmental Side Agreement was added to NAFTA before the United States joined the agreement.

In contrast, environmentalists have not been outspoken with respect to the benefits and limitations of ISO 14000. Their quiet approach to ISO 14000 can be explained, however, by the differing nature of the two sets of documents. The ISO 14000 series standards are not laws. The standards were prepared by business representatives for use by businesses, and environmentalists were not parties in the drafting of the standards.

Yet, as consumers and investors, environmentalists can play an important part in the success (or lack of success) of ISO 14000. At a minimum, the ISO 14000 series will provide environmentalists with further information to enable them to choose to "do business" with environmentally responsible companies. They can choose to purchase the products and services of companies certified to ISO 14001, and they can invest in those companies by purchasing their **stock** offerings.

Certification to ISO 14001 standards by a business serves one of the purposes of community right-to-know (RTK) and worker right-to-know (RTK) laws. Community RTK and worker RTK laws provide citizens with some of the information they need in order to make decisions about their exposure to toxic chemicals. Similarly, knowledge of the fact that a company's facility is certified to ISO 14000 can provide citizens with useful information as they choose products and services and invest their savings.

THE STRENGTHS AND LIMITATIONS OF ISO 14000

WHAT CAN THE ISO 14000 SERIES PROMOTE OR ACCOMPLISH? On a limited basis, certification to ISO 14001 can help reduce the workload of environmental inspectors. To the extent that businesses regulate themselves, government will not have to do as much work to identify violations of environmental law. In days of reduced budgets, the EPA may be able to allocate enforcement personnel and funds to investigation of companies that do not implement self-imposed EMSs.

ISO 14000 series standards require a participating company to review environmental statutes and regulations as it prepares its EMS and as it undergoes periodic review of its environmental practices under the EMS. Self-assessment is likely to increase compliance rates.

Further, the ISO 14000 series can provide a company with a systematic approach for implementing an EMS that will qualify it for participation in the EPA's Excellence in Leadership (ELF) program. Participation in the ELF program can result in leniency by the EPA toward a company that self-discovers violations of environmental law and makes timely efforts to comply with the law. In addition, participation in ELF will exempt the company from certain routine enforcement inspections.

LIMITATIONS OF ISO 14000. A limitation of the ISO 14000 series is that participants are self-selecting. Because participation is voluntary, it covers only a limited segment of the business community.

A second major limitation of the ISO 14000 series is that it depends on self-enforcement. Thomas Ott, corporate manager for environment, safety, and industrial hygiene with Motorola Corporation, is the U.S. chairperson of the ISO's working group on environmental auditing. He observed, "Having a certificate doesn't mean you have a clean company. . . . The bad guys who pollute today will still do it, and they'll have a certificate." The successful implementation of an EMS within an individual company will depend substantially on the **leadership** of the managers of the company. The organization must show its commitment through its statement of policy in the EMS, articulation of goals, and communication of the policy and goals to its personnel. Further, the company must allocate adequate funds for implementation of its goals and for training of personnel.

A related limitation is that the quality of the environmental audit depends on the qualifications and integrity of the registrar who performs the audit. As increased numbers of companies seek certification to ISO 14001, increased numbers of auditors will be needed for initial audits and continuing, periodic audits. Certification of registrars depends on the accrediting body or bodies of individual countries. For example, in the United States, the American National Standards Institute operates as a partner with the U.S. Registrar Accreditation Board (RAB). RAB is a nonprofit organization that accredits ISO 9000 registrars, and many of those same registrars are beginning to provide ISO 14000 audit services. Even with the services of an accreditation board, a company must choose its auditors and other consultants carefully.

A fourth limitation is that certification to ISO 14000 series standards does not serve as a substitute for conformance to environmental management standards that have been adopted by other organizations. For example, the CMA's Responsible Care (RC) program is not as broad as ISO 14001; an organization meeting RC requirements must do more before it can also be certified to ISO 14001. Because membership in the CMA requires conformance with RC, a chemical company may not wish to undergo the number of audits (and costs) involved in conformance with RC and certification to ISO 14001.

CONCLUSION

The effects of ISO 14000 around the world will vary depending on the needs and perspectives of participating companies, their governments, and individual citizens. In developing countries, adoption of ISO 14000 is likely to lag because of limited resources of developing businesses and their governments. ISO 14000 may even act as a nontariff barrier to trade for those companies.

The perspectives of companies from developed, industrialized countries such as the United States and the members of the EU are different. Overall, the ISO 14000 series can provide a useful supplement to governmental environmental regulation in such countries. It will cause companies to engage in self-examination and self-correction of many environmental problems.

That, in turn, may free government environmental enforcement personnel to concentrate on companies that are not in compliance with environmental law.

Even in industrialized countries with highly developed regulatory systems, however, ISO 14000's reach is limited. It is a voluntary program and, as such, can provide only a supplement to governmental environmental regulation. The effectiveness of ISO in promoting environmental stewardship within individual companies depends on the leadership of the company's managers and the creation of a **corporate culture** in which environmental management permeates the daily operations of the business in all areas. Further, a company must hire well-qualified **consultants** and registrars (auditors) as it formulates and implements its EMS. In the end, the success of the ISO 14000 series program depends on qualified, committed people and the allocation of sufficient resources to accomplish the goals identified in the company's EMS.

SEE ALSO: International Organization for Standardization; ISO 9000

[Paulette L. Stenzel]

FURTHER READING:

''ISO 14000 Standards Make Official Debut: May Be a Watershed in Environmental Regulation.'' *New York Law Journal 53,* (1996).

Tibor, Tom, and Ira Feldman. *ISO 14000: A Guide to the New Environmental Management Standards.* Homewood, IL: Irwin Professional Pub., 1996.

Voorhees, John, and Robert E. Woellner. *International Environmental Risk Management.* CRC Press, 1998.

World Commission on Environment and Development. *Our Common Future.* Cambridge: Oxford University Press, 1987.

Zuckerman, Amy. *International Standards Desk Reference.* New York: AMACOM, 1997.

ISO 9000

INTRODUCTION

The ISO 9000 Series Standards for Quality Management and Assurance were issued by the **International Organization for Standardization (ISO)** in 1987. They reflect an important trend in business practice. Early in the 20th century, quality was viewed by businesses as an additional cost of production. However, as businesses realized that high quality leads to more efficient and less expensive production processes, the pursuit of quality became a desirable goal. Businesses began to implement quality control programs, and they began to require such programs of their suppliers. Quality control programs proliferated at the same time that businesses were being globalized. This led to the realization that international quality assurance standards were needed to avoid the need to comply with multiple, conflicting systems. The ISO responded to the need for harmonization by publishing the ISO 9000 series standards.

The ISO 9000 series is a set of standards for quality management and quality assurance. The standards apply to processes and systems used to produce products; they do not apply to the products themselves. Further, the standards provide a general framework for any industry; they are not industry-specific. A company that has a quality management system (QMS) that is ''certified to'' ISO 9000 has demonstrated that it has a documented QMS in place and that it is applied consistently. The ISO 9000 series emphasizes prevention of problems and meeting customers' needs. ISO 9000 standards apply to all companies large or small, whether in services or manufacturing.

Before discussing quality standards, it is important to discuss the meaning of quality. Quality refers to the combined features of a product that contribute to its ability to meet identified needs. Quality assurance processes must balance the needs of the consumer with the needs of the producer, however, the consumer is the ultimate judge of quality. The process by which quality is achieved is called *quality assurance.* Quality assurance includes quality control procedures, quality plans, and other mechanisms. The process of implementing quality assurance standards is called *quality management.* Quality assurance and quality management are the areas covered by the ISO 9000 series.

More than 200,000 companies around the world have been certified to ISO 9000, and nearly 1,000 additional businesses per month seek registration. Competitive pressure is considered the primary reason for adopting ISO 9000, and in some markets adoption is obligatory. For example, in the European Union, ISO 9000 certification is a legal requirement in the medical devices, high-pressure valves, and public transportation markets.

This essay provides an introduction to the ISO 9000 series standards. Background is provided including the history of the standards. The contents of the standards are summarized, and the certification process is then described. Reasons to adopt the standards and benefits of adoption are later discussed, followed by weaknesses of the standards. This essay concludes by stating that ISO 9000 series standards meet important needs and have changed the daily operations of many businesses. But, if the standards are to continue to meet the needs of industry and society they must be continually reviewed and revised.

BACKGROUND

International standardization began early in the 20th century with the creation of the International

Electrotechnical Commission (IEC) in 1906 and the establishment of the International Federation of National Standardizing Associations (ISA) in 1926. The ISA focused primarily on mechanical engineering.

The idea of quality assurance dates back to World War II. To deal with quality problems related to manufacturing of defense equipment, the U.S. Department of Defense instituted one of the first formal **quality control** programs in the world. The United Kingdom, influenced by the United States, developed its own quality standards for its defense industry. U.S. and U.K. standards later spread to other countries and formed the basis for a set of quality assurance standards adopted by other members of the **North Atlantic Treaty Organization (NATO)**. Those standards were called the Allied Quality Assurance Publication (AQAP). After World War II, the U.S. government continued to develop quality standards. These standards were conveyed to defense contractors who were expected to implement them to ensure quality defense equipment.

The idea of industry standards continued to spread and develop throughout the world. At the close of World War II, in 1947, the **International Organization for Standardization (ISO)** was created with headquarters in Geneva, Switzerland. The ISO published its first standards in 1951, and by 1998 it had published over 10,060 standards. ISO Standards cover a multitude of topics including, but not limited to, paper sizes, a uniform system of measurement, symbols for automobile controls, film speed codes, and an internationally standardized freight container.

In 1979, the British Standards Institute (BSI) submitted a proposal to the ISO calling for the development of international quality assurance and quality management standards. Twenty member nations of the ISO participated on the ISO/TC 176, the technical committee that drafted the standards, with another 14 nations serving as observers. In 1987, eight years after the BSI proposal, the ISO published its first quality assurance standards, called the ISO 9000 Series. Since then more standards have been added to the series.

WHO HAS ADOPTED THE STANDARDS? Over 200,000 companies have been certified to ISO 9000, and those numbers are increasing rapidly. Companies in the United Kingdom and the rest of the European Union were the first to seek certification in large numbers, while progress in the United States was initially slower. For example, as of January 1993, 893 companies in the U.S. had been certified, and by December of 1997, over 18,500 U.S. companies had been certified. In contrast, over 20,000 companies in the United Kingdom were registered by 1993. The United States was catching up quickly, however. For example, the ''Big Three'' auto makers in the United States created an industry-specific system, called QS 9000, that incorporates the ISO 9000 series standards. Since 1997, Chrysler (now Daimler-Chrysler) and General Motors (GM) have required that Tier I suppliers (numbering over 13,000) be certified to QS 9000. QS9000 requires compliance but not necessarily registration to do so. In some cases, those automakers are pressuring Tier I suppliers to require *their* suppliers (the Tier II and Tier III suppliers) to adhere to QS 9000. In addition, the automakers have been working on a version of the ISO 9000 series standards (the TE supplement) for tooling companies and equipment suppliers.

ISO 9000 series standards have been adopted by at least 90 countries around the world. In 1992, the European Union established the European Council for Standardization (CEN). The Council's mission is to set a single set of standards for manufacturers to simplify trade among its 15 member states. The CEN, in turn, adopted the ISO 9000 series provisions verbatim as EN 29000. Within the EU, products such as medical devices, industrial safety equipment, telecommunications equipment, and construction-related products require ISO 9000 series certification. As a result, study of the ISO 9000 series standards is a standard part of the curriculum in European trade schools.

The American National Standards Institute (ANSI), working with the American Society for Quality Control (ASQC), has adopted the ISO 9000 series for use by businesses in the United States as ANSI/ASQU Q-90. The Q-90 series includes five books, each of which corresponds to one of five parts of the ISO 9000 Series. (The five parts are ISO 9000 through ISO 9004). The standards are available for purchase through ANSI or the ASQC. It should be noted, however, that the ANSI/ASQU harmonized variant of ISO 9000 is not sponsored by the U.S. government.

MAJOR PROVISIONS OF THE STANDARDS

The ISO 9000 Series standards are created as generic standards in order to allow them to be applied to every industry. They help businesses plan, control, and document issues related to quality. They are based on the assumption that if a quality management system is properly designed, then quality assurance programs will also be properly designed. However, it is important to note that the ISO 9000 standards relate to the quality of production processes only. They do not include provisions for evaluating the quality of the product. This means that three companies following ISO 9000 standards, each producing the same product, could produce three products of varying qualities. This fact has been the basis for criticism of the ISO 9000 series standards.

There are more than five standards in the ISO 9000 series, but five contain most of the crucial provisions. They include ISO 9000, ISO 9001, ISO 9002,

ISO 9003, and ISO 9004. In addition, ISO 8402 is often grouped with the ISO 9000 series. ISO 8402, which covers vocabulary, was passed in 1986 in anticipation of the ISO 9000 series. ISO 9000 and ISO 9004 provide guidelines. To develop a quality system, a company must choose to become certified to one of three standards: ISO 9001, ISO 9002, or ISO 9003. Below is a summary of each of the six standards.

1. ISO 8402 "Quality Vocabulary." This standard provides definitions of quality assurance terms. It is useful in choosing terminology when drafting quality control manuals.
2. ISO 9000 "Quality Management and Quality Assurance Standards—Guidelines for Selection and Use." This standard provides an overview of the other ISO 9000 series standards. It includes guidelines for choosing the applicable ISO 9000 standards, and describes the purpose and application of quality assurance programs. ISO 9000 provides quality management guidelines for all industries.
3. ISO 90001 "Quality Systems—Model for Quality Assurance in Design/Development, Production, Installation, and Servicing." This standard sets out 20 element requirements and is the most comprehensive of the five ISO 9000 series standards. Although it is designed to apply to all industries, it is particularly useful in manufacturing and related industries in which a company designs, produces, installs, and services its own products.
4. ISO 9002 "Quality Systems—Model for Quality Assurance in Production and Installation." This standard includes 18 element requirements. It is used primarily by companies responsible for production and installation of their own products, but not the design. These standards apply to suppliers and subcontractors for ISO 9001-certified companies.
5. ISO 9003 "Quality Systems—Model for Quality Assurance in Final Inspection and Test." This standard includes 12 element requirements. It is the least complex of the five ISO 9000 series standards. Its primary users are companies that perform tests on and do final production inspections such as calibration. In general, a company that does not add any value to the manufacturing process should use ISO 9003.
6. ISO 90004 "Quality Management and Quality System Elements—Guidelines." This standard is similar to the ISO 9000 standard in that it provides guidelines for implementation of other standards within the ISO 9000 series. It is used for auditing purposes, and it contains guidelines that assist a company as it develops its own quality systems.

REVISIONS. To better serve certain industries, the original 1987 standards have been modified; a major set of revisions was published in 1994. In fact, ISO 9000 includes a provision allowing the quality provisions found in ISO 9001, 9002, and 9003 to be customized to make the system applicable to certain products or services. Areas in which customized standards have been developed include, for example, ISO 9004-2, which applies to service industries; and ISO 9000-3, which covers the development and supply of computer software.

DEVELOPING A QUALITY ASSURANCE SYSTEM

Implementation of ISO 9000 series standards and certification to them is a lengthy and detailed procedure, but this section will provide a brief overview of the process. A series of six steps lead to the development of an internal quality assurance system. That system must include but is not limited to, a quality systems manual.

It is a misperception that preparation of the manual creates mountains of paperwork; the ISO quality manual is typically about 20-35 pages long. It is a major tool in developing and implementing an internal quality assurance system. The manual is to be used for training new personnel as well as in the day-to-day operations of the company.

The process of developing a system can be described in six steps.

1. Management must decide which ISO standards apply to their company and which element requirements must be implemented.
2. All personnel directly involved in the ISO 9000 implementation process must be trained. In turn, staff must develop policies and objectives necessary to meet the element requirements of the applicable ISO series 9000 standards.
3. Procedures and documentation must be developed to carry out the policies and objectives that have been laid out. Examples of documentation include organization charts, quality plans, log books, inspection and test reports, purchase orders, and corrective action reports.
4. Each employee is interviewed on how he she does his or her job, and a description of procedures is created for each job. The description must include safety procedures.

5. Industry-wide standards and specifications must be documented.
6. The company must establish an internal audit system. The system must be used to continually check whether the quality system is functioning properly.

The quality system process is an organization-wide process. There is no such thing as a partial quality assurance system; it is either for all of a company or none of it. The documentation gathered through these steps is used as a basis to develop the company's quality management system; and the system is described in the quality management manual.

After the quality assurance system has been developed, the next step is for the company to perform a preliminary internal assessment to measure how closely it conforms to the relevant standard (ISO 9001, ISO 9002, or ISO 9003).

CERTIFICATION

There are three types of certification for ISO 9000 series standards. The ISO intended the 9000 series standards to be voluntary, and so no certification process was included in the standards issued in 1987. As a result, individual countries have developed certification procedures.

There are three ways to become certified: via first, second, or third party certification. First party certification is when a company certifies itself. Thus, it is sometimes called "self-declaration." This is accomplished using a formal internal quality assessment audit. The audit is performed by an internal quality manager or representative who examines whether the company is in conformance with the applicable ISO 9000 series standards.

Second party certification is performed by a customer of the company seeking certification. (In some cases, it is by large-scale buyers of the company's goods or services.) It is the customer's job to perform an internal audit and decide whether the company is complying with the ISO 9000 series standards. Often, when a company becomes certified through this second party process, an agreement is drawn up documenting the certification process. This agreement is used as part of the basis for future transactions.

Third party certification is done by a disinterested third party, usually a firm that specializes in ISO 9000 certification. The third party provides a registrar (also called an auditor) who performs an intensive internal audit of the company to verify its compliance with ISO 9000 standards. The process, which is described below, is similar to the review process under first or second party certification.

In practice, most companies choose third party certification. With respect to first party certification, there are credibility problems. A company that certifies itself has many opportunities to cheat in the certification; there is no enforcement or verification mechanism in the certification process. Second party certification is sometimes undesirable because of inefficiency and high costs. Every time a company wants to do business with a supplier, it must spend time and money to do an audit of the potential supplier. Yet, it can be less costly than third party certification for small and mid-size companies. Third party certification, in spite of its own inherent limitations (discussed below), is used most often, at least at present.

CERTIFICATION WITH A THIRD PARTY REGISTRAR. The company desiring certification should hire a registrar who has been certified by a national accreditation body. The registrar will then conduct the assessment in several stages. First, there is a pre-assessment. The registrar will review the quality system manual and other documents. The auditor will focus on the management system's ability to document the quality of the process of producing goods and services; he or she will not focus on the quality of the actual product. Based on this review the company may choose to proceed, or it may delay further assessment until deficiencies are corrected.

Second, there is a formal assessment. The registrar reviews documents and interviews company personnel. The objective is to determine whether written procedures are being implemented. Third, the audit report is issued. The registrar summarizes results of the audit and lists areas in which corrective action, if any, is needed. If deficiencies must be corrected, the company can do so and submit a report to the registrar. Corrections must be documented in that report.

The registrar can award certification based on an initial, favorable audit report or upon the initial report accompanied by the report verifying corrective action. After certification, the company can use the ISO 9000 seal on its letterhead and in advertising.

SURVEILLANCE AFTER CERTIFICATION

Following certification, twice annually the registrar will return to the company to verify that the company continues to be in compliance. Such visits will be with little or no notice. During such "spot checks," the registrar will focus on areas that were noted as weaknesses in the original report. The registrar will perform a complete audit and issue a new report every three years.

In addition, the company is expected to implement an internal auditing program to ensure the company continues to conform to ISO 9000 series requirements. A strong internal auditing program ensures that all goes well when the third party registrar visits periodically.

REASONS TO ADOPT ISO 9000 STANDARDS

Compliance with ISO 9000 series standards is voluntary in most, but not all cases. When compliance is voluntary, incentives come from a variety of internal and external benefits. An internal benefit comes from within the company and relates to the day-to-day operations of the organization. An external benefit, on the other hand, comes from outside the company and relates to other entities and factors such as customers and markets. Internal benefits can be realized by any company that uses the ISO 9000 series standards. However, external benefits are limited to those companies that are certified by a second or third party entity. This occurs because customers may not be willing to accept a company's word that it complies with ISO 9000 series and may require second or third party certification.

REQUIRED COMPLIANCE. In some instances, ISO 9000 certification is a requirement for doing business. This may be due to the requirements of a customer, as is the case with respect to Tier I suppliers dealing with U.S. auto makers. Or, it may be due to requirements of laws of a country or trading bloc.

For example, the North American Treaty Organization (NATO) requires that its contractors be ISO 9000 certified. The U.S. Department of Defense does the same.

Some countries have passed laws requiring compliance with ISO 9000. As was discussed above, the **European Union** has passed directives that require ISO 9000 compliance for safety products, medical devices, and other specified products.

INTERNAL BENEFITS. Whether certification is required or not, ISO 9000 series certification provides a variety of internal benefits. First, ISO 9000 certification leads to better documentation of company processes. This, in turn, leads to more efficient production processes and less waste. Both save money for a company.

Second, managers and other employees become more aware of quality. They begin to view operations through a ''quality of management'' lens. This leads to a more efficient company that can be more competitive in the marketplace.

Third, employee morale improves. When employees feel that they are part of the process, they accept responsibility for quality. This creates an incentive for workers to do a better job and makes the company more efficient.

Fourth, cooperation and communication are improved. Documenting procedures facilitates communication and promotes cooperation.

Fifth, production processes can be made more efficient. When there is better coordination of processes, there is less ''down time,'' and resources are shared among departments more efficiently.

Sixth, fewer defective products are produced. Better quality results in fewer defects, less scrap, and, therefore, lower production costs. Finally, documentation of safety standards results in fewer accidents. In turn, there is less downtime for employees. The ultimate results are more efficient workers and lower costs of production.

EXTERNAL BENEFITS. Similarly, there are many potential external benefits. The first is that company prestige increases. Companies following ISO 9000 series standards are perceived as ''good corporate citizens'' that produce higher quality products. Thus, they gain prestige that can help retain old customers and attract new ones.

Second, it improves customer satisfaction. Higher quality means higher customer satisfaction. Further, the manufacturer of a product is certified, a customer may feel better about the product even if it is, in fact, of no higher quality than that of a non-certified manufacturer.

Third, it creates a higher level of trust. Customers perceive a certified company as being more trust worthy than a non-certified company.

Fourth, it reduces the need for customer audits. With certification, a company has already been audited. Therefore, customers will not feel a need to audit every time they want to do business with a company. This can result in major savings. For example, it is reported that in some industry segments in the United States, a facility may be subject to dozens of audits per year; in some cases it may be as many as 30 per month.

Fifth, it can help a company increase its market share. Certified companies gain access to markets that require ISO certification, and they can deepen penetration of existing markets. Finally, the company can respond more quickly to market needs. With better quality procedures, it is easier to develop and market new product lines. Being the first to reach a market results in higher profits for the company.

COSTS AND PROBLEMS RELATED TO ISO 9000

There are costs in time and money for companies becoming certified to an ISO 9000 series standard. For example, an ISO program may take three months to over one year to implement, and it requires continual efforts to review progress and pursue improvement. Further, it costs money to develop a certification program and attain certification. There may be benefits in terms of increased sales resulting from public perception that the firm produces quality goods, but sometimes non-ISO certified companies may be able to produce a similar product more cheaply.

ISO certification does not mean that a firm's product is better than that of a non-ISO certified firm. For example, ISO 9000 series certification does not prevent design defects. To reiterate, the ISO series 9000 standards are process standards; they are not product standards.

The quality of an audit performed for ISO certification purposes depends on the qualifications and honesty of the auditor, and whether the auditor is acting in a first, second, or third party capacity. In addition, there are numerous problems inherent in the third party certification process.

First, the ISO does not have standard procedures for certification. As a result, various countries have developed different certification procedures. For example, in the United States, the national body of accreditation is the Registrar Accreditation Board (RAB). At present, the European Union (EU) does not regulate registrars. Instead, they are accredited through national certification boards. This divergence contributes to a lack of understanding of the certification process. Without an international certification procedure, companies and members of the public are uninformed about what is involved in certification. And, of course, standards for certification are not uniform.

Second, certification is not always recognized across borders of countries. Therefore, a registrar should be chosen in view of the company's customer base. One practice that facilitates operations of companies in various countries is that some U.S. registrars have signed memoranda with registrars in Europe. As a result of such agreements, a company can become ISO-certified in several countries through the completion of a single certification process.

Third, there is no centralized record of registrations. This makes proof of certification difficult, and potential customers must rely on documents in the possession of the certified firm or the auditing firm hired by the firm.

Fourth, certification is costly. It costs from $10,000 to $20,000 or more, and may take six to 18 months to perform, depending on the size of the company. This can be prohibitive for small companies and for companies with severely limited resources. Such companies tend to come, in disproportionate percentages, from developing countries as compared to companies from industrialized countries.

Another set of objections to the ISO 9000 series standards is based on the assertion that the standards function as a non-tariff barrier to trade. The adoption of ISO 9000 series by the EU is viewed by some commentators as a trade barrier to companies from outside the EU. In other cases, it has been asserted that, as ISO 9000 certification becomes a *de facto* requirement for doing business, it operates as a non-tariff barrier to trade with respect to struggling companies from developing countries. This argument is based on the premise that ISO certification is an expense that is beyond the means of firms with extremely limited funds.

TRANSITIONAL ISSUES

As implementation of the ISO 9000 series standards proceeds, additional issues arise. One important set of issues relates to how ISO 9000 will be coordinated with parallel, yet slightly divergent, sets of standards that are being developed. One of these sets of standards is the QS-9000 standard developed by Ford, General Motors, and Chrysler (now DaimlerChrysler). QS-9000 incorporated the ISO 9000 series, but it added customer-specific and sector-specific guidelines. The members of TC 176 (the ISO technical committee that developed the ISO 9000 series) emphasize that the ISO 9000 series must maintain its generic character if it is to continue to be useful over a long term.

In the summer of 1995, proposed standards developed by the Japanese caused a clash between the United States and Japan. The Japanese Accreditation Board (JAB) had announced the JIS Z9901, a variant on ISO 9000, that would be applied to software manufacturers. It included a provision that required certification through registrars who would be trained and accredited under the JAB's system. U.S. software manufacturers and electronics companies were outraged at the special registration requirements. They viewed JIS Z9901 as a potential non-tariff barrier to trade, as a mechanism through which trade secrets might be stolen, and as a mechanism that would cut their market share. After ANSI, the American Electronics Association (AEA), the Informational Technology Industry Council (ITIC), and major multinational corporations such as Apple Computer, IBM, Motorola, and others became involved. Through negotiations with ANSI, JAB agreed with ANSI to conform to ISO norms for ISO 9000 rather than create special registration requirements for software manufacturers. The JAB withdrew JIS Z9901 and averted an international trade crisis.

The ISO 9000 series standards involve potentially high economic stakes. Therefore, there must be continuing, careful surveillance by various industries throughout the world, as standards are developed and refined, and, especially, as variants on the ISO 9000 system are developed.

CONCLUSION

Certification of businesses to the ISO 9000 series standards is increasing rapidly around the world. Many companies see implementation of the standards as an investment in the future. They are convinced that the program will pay for itself as it results in lower production costs and greater efficiency in operation as well as access to new markets and new customers. In many industries, certification has almost become a necessity for doing business. And in some countries, such as in the EU, certification is mandatory in certain industries.

Yet, the ISO 9000 series standards are process standards, not product standards. Their widespread use throughout the world is creating desirable harmonization in terms of providing goods to the public. But the ISO 9000 series standards do not guarantee quality products from the companies that participate in the program.

SEE ALSO: International Organization for Standardization (ISO); ISO 14000

[Paulette L. Stenzel]

FURTHER READING:

Badiru, Adedeji Docunde. *Industry's Guide to ISO 9000.* New York: John Wiley & Sons, Inc., 1995.

Johnson, Perry L. *ISO 9000: Meeting The International Standards.* 2nd ed. New York: McGraw-Hill, 1997.

Label, Wayne A., and Wilbur Priester. ''Expanding Your Role in ISO.'' *The CPA Journal,* June 1996.

Mirams, Mike, and Paul McElheron. *Gaining and Maintaining the New Quality Standards: The BS EN 9000 Tool Kit.* Pitman Publishing, 1995.

''Using International Standards To Build A Better Business.'' *Business Standards.* British Standards Institute (BSI). Available at www.businessstandards.com.

Vloeberghs, Daniel, and Jan Bellens. ''Implementing The ISO 9000 Standards in Belgium.'' *Quality Standards,* June 1996.

Zuckerman, Amy. *International Standards: Desk Reference.* New York: Amacom, 1997.

ITC

SEE: U.S. International Trade Commission

JAPAN, DOING BUSINESS IN

INTRODUCTION

Japan is one of the economic superpowers of global trade. Japan's **gross national product (GNP)** is second only to the United States'. Indeed, at the time that Japan's economy began to stumble during the mid-1990s, its GNP per capita was at $28,470, well exceeding other G7 nations such as the United States at ($24,901), Germany ($24,762), France ($22,871), or Britain ($17,545).

Geographically, Japan is an isolated island nation, trailing along the northeast Asian coast. Japan has four major islands: Hokkaido (in the north), Honshu (the central and most populous island), Shikoku, and Kyushu (both in the south). Additionally, the nation controls Okinawa at its southernmost end and 6,847 minor islands in the overall archipelago.

POPULATION DENSITY. Japan is among the world's most densely populated nations. It's population size and density is so extreme that it significantly affects business in a host of areas, from the comparatively large domestic market size in so geographically small a country to the high cost of real estate and limited agricultural capability.

Japan's population of over 125 million people is squeezed into an area smaller than Montana. Additionally, dozens of Japanese islands are sparsely inhabited, and several regions even on Honshu and Hokkaido are largely uninhabitable due to mountains or other treacherous terrain. Consequently, Japan's cities are home to some of the most crowded conditions in the world. Japan has 11 cities with populations of more than 1 million. By comparison, the United States has only 8 cities of that size and Germany only 1.

Moreover, these numbers correspond only to the populations within the official city limits. Several additional cities have greater metropolitan areas exceeding 1 million, while the greater metropolitan areas of the largest 11 cities are among the most populous anywhere. In fact, Tokyo's greater metropolitan population (including Japan's second largest city, Yokohama) ties with Mexico City as the largest in the world with a population of roughly 29 million people, or nearly the population of Canada.

The Japanese home has an average of under 30 square meters per person (compared to 64 square meters per person in the United States), making Japan the most crowded among the G7 nations.

ETHNIC HOMOGENEITY. Japan is one of world's most homogeneous nations. Limited immigration and centuries of nearly total isolation have resulted in a population that is over 97 percent Japanese in ethnicity. From this extreme homogeneity, Japan has evolved into a society with an unusual degree of cultural and behavioral uniformity.

HISTORICAL OVERVIEW

Japan is an ancient civilization, dating back at least to 660 BC when the first Japanese emperor was enthroned. By the 11th century, Japan had perfected its famous samurai tradition based on powerful military classes. In 1192, Japan's first military government or shogunate came to power. Under the shogunate, shoguns were stronger than the emperor. The rule of the shogunates went on for hundreds of years, reaching its most powerful manifestation under the Tokugawa shogunate, which dominated Japan from 1603 to 1867. It was the Tokugawa shogunate that intentionally sent Japan off into isolation, severing Japan from foreign trade. Not until the latter half of the 19th century, with the accession of Emperor Meiji, did the shogunate system finally end. The replacement of the shogunate system with direct Imperial rule is called the Meiji Restoration, named so since Emperor Meiji restored Imperial power. During the Meiji Restoration, Japan broke from its isolation and plunged itself into world affairs. The result was an era at the close of the 19th century in which Japan introduced new ideas and practices in all walks of life. In economic terms, the Meiji Restoration brought Japan into a period of swift industrialization, the introduction of previously unknown technology, and governmental encouragement of global trade.

Following the Meiji Restoration, Japan began to expand in other areas besides economics. Japan adopted European imperialism with the same vigor it had adopted European business and manufacturing practices. Following the European model of militarily conquering other cultures and converting them into colonies, Japan rapidly extended its empire at the close of the 19th century. The Japanese invaded China in 1894 and established territories there. Next, in the first major defeat of a European nation by an Asian power in modern times, Japan decisively defeated Russia in the Russo-Japanese War of 1905. In a peace brokered by U.S. President Theodore Roosevelt, Japan was forced to return to Russia the territory the Russians had lost. While the reasons why Japan had to give back the Russian territory are debatable (and subject to accusations of European and American racism), the Russo-Japanese War clearly placed Japan on par with its European and North American counterparts in virtually all regards from military power to manufacturing ability. By 1909, Japan occupied Korea. In 1931, Japan overran much of northern China. Finally, in the final stage of its expansionism, Japan conquered most of Southeast Asia and the Pacific islands. These conquests included most of the British, French, and Dutch colonies in Asia, as well as the Japanese attack on Pearl Harbor in 1941 (which brought the United States into World War II).

World War II devastated Japan. Virtually every major city was attacked and several (including Tokyo) were almost entirely destroyed. Most significantly, Japan remains today the only nation to have ever suffered the effects of nuclear weapons. In 1945, the United States dropped atomic bombs on Hiroshima and Nagasaki.

THE KEIRETSU. U.S. occupation of Japan had profound consequences on Japan's current business system. This is because the U.S. occupation led directly to the dominant business structure, the *keiretsu.*

Following World War II, the United States formally occupied Japan, ruling the nation under a military government from 1945 until 1952. Before the United States left, it made Japan adopt a new constitution based on the U.S. Constitution. The United States also made Japan dismember all remaining offensive military forces and had Japan place in its new constitution a prohibition to remilitarizing. The United States also outlawed Japan's great business concerns, the *zaibatsu.*

This last measure was meant to harm Japan economically and punish its major business enterprises. Ironically, the scheme backfired, as it freed up Japanese businesses from many long-standing but unprofitable alliances. The now illegal *zaibatsu* simply reformed as Japan's *keiretsu,* and having shed their ties to these unproductive firms began one of the most dramatic economic recoveries in history. Japan transformed itself in less than 30 years from almost complete economic ruin into the world's second largest economy (after the United States) by the 1970s. While other factors contributed to Japan's success, much of it rise to economic prominence, as well as some of Japan's struggles with corporate-government corruption in the late 1990s can be attributed to the *keiretsu* and their domination of postwar Japanese business.

The *keiretsu* are not single entities. All *keiretsu* are made up of an interdependent group of nominally independent member firms composing a sort of mosaic from which emerges a joint enterprise.

The *keiretsu* can be viewed as a family of member firms, each tied to one another through cross-shareholdership. Thus, every member firm within a *keiretsu* possesses a sizable amount of stock shares within many (and in some cases every) of the other *keiretsu* members. Individual member firms, in turn, are at least nominally independent even if joined together by cross-shareholdership. *Keiretsu*members are not subsidiaries of holding companies, as the United States forced Japan to outlaw holding companies during its postwar occupation. Consequently, while cross-corporate shareholder control is coordinated, technically, the stock of every member company belonging to an individual *keiretsu* is traded independently.

The outlawing of the prewar holding company structure, or *zaibatsu,* freed Japanese prewar corporate families from propping up the less profitable member companies. This did not, however, limit the size of the interwoven collection of companies that were resurrected after the war as the new *keiretsu.* At the close of the 20th century, most *keiretsu* averaged well over 100 member firms, and many of the most significant *keiretsu* are composed of many more than that. For example, by the mid-1990s the giant *keiretsu* Hitachi was comprised of more than 680 member companies and their subsidiaries.

LANGUAGE

The official language of Japan is Japanese. Despite the importance of Japan within the global economy, comparatively few non-Japanese speak the language. Arguably three reasons have led to this linguistic isolation. First, unlike such multinational languages as English, Spanish, French, or Arabic, Japanese as a language is limited to only one country. Additionally, Japanese is one of only three orphan languages (the others being Korean and Basque). In other words, Japanese has no true ties to any other linguistic family. As a result, Japanese is equally difficult to learn regardless of one's native language, since no language shares cognates with Japanese that the Japanese have not themselves borrowed first.

Finally, Japanese writing is significantly more complex than most other languages. Traditional Japanese is written in vertical columns that read from right to left. Today, however, many books and especially signs are written horizontally from left to right.

Another point that complicates Japanese writing for many non-Japanese is the fact that the language employs three independent systems of writing. The first system, known as *kanji,* uses thousands of characters adapted from Chinese. The Japanese did not have a common writing system of their own at the time that large scale missionary Buddhist missionary efforts came to Japan, bringing with them Chinese writing, which was then applied to Japanese.

Normally, this would have posed a problem for translating the books and sacred texts in cases using an alphabetic system. Chinese, however, is not an alphabetic system, and the Chinese monks introduced the Japanese to Chinese characters. Since Chinese characters are non-phonetic (that is, they represent pictures or ideograms rather than an alphabet), the fact that Chinese and Japanese have nothing in common linguistically did not impose a barrier. It is much the same way that a picture of boiled fish on a restaurant menu conveys the concept of boiled fish to an English speaker or a Japanese speaker. Pointing to the picture, the English-speaking customer perfectly communicates what is wanted. The difference comes when the customer says ''boiled fish'' and the server responds ''nizakana.''

At first, the Japanese limited *kanji* to Chinese classical works and religious writings. Soon, however, the Japanese started adapting *kanji* to Japanese words as well. Because Chinese grammar has nothing in common with Japanese, however, the Japanese had to add things—such as word suffixes and so forth—to the characters. To do this, the Japanese invented a series of symbols that they appended to the *kanji* that added syllables. This syllabary (not an alphabet, but a system of common syllables) grew into the remaining two systems (together known as *kana*).

Japanese has two sets of *kana: hiragana* (a stylized form roughly equivalent to cursive) and *katakana* (a block form roughly equivalent to printing). Yet the comparison to block printing and cursive in Latin-based letters is misleading, since the two systems serve differing functions. This is complicated even further by the fact that some words are a combination of both kanji and phonetic symbols.

Finally, the Japanese have adopted a fourth system of writing, using an alphabet. This is *Romaji* (that is, Roman lettering). This is a phonetic transcription of Japanese into English letters. *Romaji* is particularly easy for Americans to pronounce, as it was developed by an American, the missionary James Curtis Hepburn. While Japanese runs *kanji* and *kana* together, *Romaji* is careful to separate words, as well as the divisions between parts of words that are *kanji* and *kana. Romaji,* however, serves an additional function in Japan beyond making Japanese pronounceable to foreigners. Because most computer programs require an alphabetic keyboard, *Romaji* provides a means for using computers employing Japanese with relatively little modification.

THE WORK ENVIRONMENT

The most significant factor affecting the business environment in Japan is the immense population occupying a very limited space, as discussed above. One result of this crowding has been the rise of the so-called open-system office. In most Japanese offices, space is not subdivided into cubicles or individual rooms as is commonly practiced in Europe and the Americas. While generally each person sits at an assigned spot, space is shared, often at long joint tables, with shared telephones and computers and with no individual walls.

Crowding has also influenced Japanese commuting time, which is among the longest in time worldwide. This has also contributed to Japan's highly efficient mass transportation system, including the famous bullet trains.

Other factors are also at play in the business environment besides crowding. To a large extent, Japan is devoid of most natural resources. It must import virtually all of its oil, gas, and other energy resources, driving the cost of energy to a level much higher than in most other industrialized nations. It is possible to argue that to some extent Japan's emphasis on quality control and human resource management directly result from the need to compensate in other areas for this lack of natural resources.

RELIGION

Japanese religion is not directly involved in business aside from annual holidays and corporate gift-giving. Yet indirectly, religion plays a major role in business in a number of aspects.

Japanese religion is unique in that many Japanese hold to more than one religion simultaneously. This differs from the approach most others take toward religions as being absolute. Thus in the United States, for example, it is not customary that a person could at the same time be a Jew, a Roman Catholic and a Moslem; in Japan, such a combination would be more conceivable. At the very least, Japanese religion is mixture of multiple theological influences. To some extent, one can argue that this has helped create the Japanese business tendency to be at least temporarily comfortable with multiple interpretations of a situation (as opposed to the European and American tendencies to demand resolution of conflicting views as they occur).

Japan's indigenous religion, Shintoism, is limited to Japan and focuses on the spiritual forces of nature and of specific mountains, trees, bodies of water, streams, and other geographic spots imbued with religious significance. This has led to, among other practices, *sangaku shinko* (worship of mountains), and *chinju no kami* (local tutelary deities). Perhaps more significantly for business, Shintoism leads most Japanese to respect for nature in its own right, where both humans and *kami* (spirits) coexist and must find their proper place. This contrasts with the North American and north European view that people control nature to their own profit. Finally, the Shinto belief that stating negative outcomes may encourage their realization has limited the ''what if'' problem-solving technique so widespread in American and European brainstorming strategies.

Missionaries from the Asian mainland brought Mahayana Buddhism to Japan in the Middle Ages. The religion evolved during the centuries of Japanese isolation into peculiarly Japanese formulations, such as Zen, with its belief in sudden enlightenment and Shingon Buddhism, with its belief in *sokushin jobutsu* (literally ''Buddhahood in this very body''), a sort of organic pantheism stressing enlightenment as both a bodily and spiritual process. This philosophy may influence the way business is conducted in Japan, as expressed through a greater acceptance of intuitive decision-making as one legitimate criterion for action.

Other major influences on Japanese society from the Asian mainland were Confucianism and Taoism, which like Buddhism, took on uniquely Japanese characteristics. Thus, Confucianism was transformed during the late Middle Ages into the Japanese warrior code (and in modern times arguably transferred to the code of the Japanese business executive) with its emphasis on self-control and *akirame* (or resignation to one's place in a strictly hierarchical society). Taoism, in turn, took root in Japan as *ommyoryo* (the balance of the yin and yang blended with the five Chinese elements), which by the 7th century was even regulated by an official government bureau. Its influence is still evident in Japanese beliefs in lucky and unlucky days, numerology, and the auspiciousness of particular directions in combination with certain physical elements or shapes.

GENDER DIFFERENCES

The differentiation between the sexes in the Japanese work place has remained among the most sharply contrasted in the industrialized world. While significant numbers of women have entered the work force since the late 1980s, this has not traditionally been an option for them.

Japan passed its first law dealing with equal opportunity for women only in 1986. That law, however, held virtually no actual protection for women who felt that employers had discriminated against them, but rather allowed only for the opportunity to engage in arbitration provided that both sides agreed that the situation merited attention.

The first substantial change in Japanese law to protect women in employment situations was put into effect only in April 1999 when Japan revised the law to allow mediation at either party's request. The new law also institutes revisions that require employers to prevent overt sexual harassment and eliminates formal bans on women working in formally prohibited professions. Special restrictions on the amount of holiday and overtime allowances made for women were also eliminated.

While these changes in the employment status of women are likely to change substantially the legal recourse women can pursue in the face of overt discrimination, women and men remain far from equal in the work place.

CONTEXTING AND FACE-SAVING

Japan is considered a ''high context'' culture. Edward Hall has observed that the Japanese are the most highly contexted of all industrialized cultures. In practical terms, this means that the Japanese are as likely to read the context surrounding what is said as they are to rely on the words spoken. As a result, for many Japanese, what is actually spoken is not necessarily the entire message.

This indirect communication style contrasts sharply with business communication in the United States and other lower contexted nations, where what is said represents on the whole what is meant. To some extent, low context cultures also have occasions where so-called ''white lies'' are used to protect someone's feelings. The difference comes in the degree to which people use such ''white lies;'' in Japan, such white lies are much more common than in most other cultures. Business people from more literal low context cultures such as the United States, however, may misunderstand such rhetorical flourishes as dishonesty. Yet even though the Japanese may appear to be saying one thing when meaning another, they are not necessarily dishonest, since the context of the situation clearly indicates (at least to other Japanese and those accustomed to high context communication) the actual meaning. Thus, where an individual from a lower contexted culture might flatly decline to do something by clearly saying ''no,'' many Japanese might be likely to say that the request posed some difficulty or even seemingly agree to do something with a ''yes'' when his or her behavior conveyed the actual message of ''no.''

The process of determining what message is actually being conveyed becomes clear only when simultaneously analyzing both the words spoken and the stored information that one has collected regarding an individual's behavior and goals. This process, in turn, is further complicated by face-saving concerns.

Face or *kao* is a central component in the Japanese work place, and indeed in virtually all Japanese interpersonal relationships. The very word *kao* is used in many expressions that give an idea of its importance. Thus, one says that a person's face is ''broad'' (*kao ga hiroi*) if he or she has a far-reaching web of acquaintances. Most Japanese try very hard to avoid ''smearing dirt'' on one another's face (*kao o yogosu*) or even strong having one's face ''crushed'' (*kao o tubusareru*), as it is very difficult to recover from such a humiliation. On the other hand, much of Japanese interaction centers on face-saving (*kao o tateru* or having one's face ''made to stand''). While people from many other cultures place importance on maintaining their good name or on doing the honorable thing, in Japan the maintenance of face and protection from public shaming or humiliation have arguably reached a level more central to their culture than evident elsewhere.

For reasons of saving face, many Japanese may find that a conflict exists between their real intentions (or *honne*) and the official position (or *tatemae*) that they feel obligated to hold publicly. While often a person's *honne* and *tatemae* are identical, the situation becomes complicated when the two conflict. In such cases, the negotiator must be sensitive to the actual needs of the individual (his or her *honne*) without sacrificing (at least overtly) the *tatemae* he or she feels obligated to uphold (such as an official company policy or a previous commitment).

As in other high context cultures, most Japanese rely on the full context of the communicators' relationship with one another to ascertain fully the meaning of their business communication. This particularly affects the importance for social etiquette, ranging from the simple exchange of business cards to the complex inter-relationship of duty and obligations. The importance of reading the context also affects Japanese formality in official situations (including business meetings) with a particular emphasis on face-saving.

ATTITUDES TOWARD THE WORK PLACE AND INDIVIDUALISM

The general perception of the work place differs fundamentally between Japan and the West. In the Americas and Europe, considerably more emphasis is placed on one's occupation and individual role in an organization than in Japan. Thus, most Americans and Europeans view themselves as individuals with a particular set of job skills, who secondarily happens to work for a particular company. This is diametrically opposed to the view held by most Japanese. As Katsuyuki Hasegawa (1995) has observed, ''Ask most Japanese about what they do and they will answer, 'I am a company employee' and add, 'I work for Toshiba.' They give their company's name. Few people answer with a job title such as accountant or salesman.''

Hasegawa goes on to explain that, ''For Japanese, the company name is more important than the job title . . . For Japanese people, the community they belong to is much more important than what they do.''

AUTHORITY CONCEPTION

The traditional Japanese work place is highly structured and hierarchical. While Japan itself is a remarkably uniform nation economically and with regard to social classes and offers considerable latitude for social advancement based on merit, the nation is not egalitarian in the same way that, for example, one finds in Canada or the United States. By contrast, most Japanese are highly conscious of relative rank and status within their organizations. This rank-consciousness has deep roots in Japan; as Boye DeMente (1997) has noted, ''Japanese concern with rank evolved from their vertically structured feudal society.'' Because seniority is closely tied to rank in Japan, age and rank are also positively correlated. Rank is reflected in the formalized etiquette used by most Japanese in the work place. Rank is especially apparent in the nature of the type of language used since Japanese changes form to differentiate between superiors and subordinates. In a related manner, people of higher rank are customarily addressed using their rank and name, or even at times by rank alone, not only when discussing them in the third person, but even when addressing them personally.

NONVERBAL BEHAVIOR

Japanese nonverbal behavior is generally fairly reserved. Rapid or frequent hand movements common among business people in the Americas, the Middle East, and southern Europe may appear to be extreme by Japanese standards, and thus may prove distracting.

The Japanese greet each other by bowing rather than the handshake. The depth of bow reflects rank, with the lower ranking individual bowing lower than the higher ranking person.

Because the handshake is a foreign custom used only with foreigners, many Japanese shake hands with little firmness. This has led to some misunderstanding among some non-Japanese who have misinterpreted this inadvertently weak handshake as communicating a lack of sincerity.

Eye contact in Japan also differs from that practiced widely elsewhere. Traditionally, Japanese lower their eyes to show respect. Younger people lower their eyes to people older than themselves, women lower their eyes to men, and subordinates lower their eyes to superiors. The lowering of eyes as a sign of respect, however, is often misunderstood in countries such as the United States, where lowering the eyes is a sign of dishonesty or insincerity and direct eye contact is a means for showing respect, regardless of rank.

[David A. Victor]

FURTHER READING:

Beasley, W.G. *The Rise of Modern Japan : Political, Economic and Social Change Since 1850.* 2nd ed. New York: St. Martin's Press, 1995.

De Mente, Boye Lafayette. *The Japanese Have a Word for It: The Complete Guide to Japanese Thought and Culture.* Lincolnwood, IL: Passport Books/NTC, 1997.

Gerlach, Michael L. *Alliance Capitalism : The Social Organization of Japanese Business.* Berkeley: University of California Press, 1997.

Hasegawa, Katsuyuki. *Secrets of the Japanese.* Tokyo: Hira-Tai Books, 1995.

''Japan in Figures 1999.'' Management and Coordination Agency of Japan, 1999. Available at: www.stat.go.jp/16.htm.

Keys to the Japanese Heart and Soul. Tokyo: Kodansha Bilingual Books, 1996.

McAlinn, Gerald Paul. *The Business Guide to Japan.* Butterworth-Heinemann, 1997.

Michihiro, Matsumoto. *Discover Japan: Words, Customs and Concepts.* Tokyo: Kodansha International, 1997.

Nakamura, Akemi. ''New Equal Opportunity Law Called A Start.'' *Japan Times,* 16-30 April 1999.

Victor, David A. *International Business Communication.* New York: Harper Collins, 1992.

JAPANESE MANAGEMENT TECHNIQUES

In the post-World War II era a set of Japanese cultural patterns and managerial practices came to be known collectively as the Japanese management style or Japanese management techniques. Many of these techniques were credited with helping vault the Japanese economy to its status as the world's second largest, behind only the United States, and with making Japanese businesses, particularly in the manufacturing sector, more competitive than their international counterparts. In the wake of Japan's prolonged and arduous struggle with recession throughout much of the 1990s, however, many observers—both inside and outside Japan—have called into question the effectiveness of some traditional Japanese management practices. As a result, at the dawn of the 21st century Japanese management techniques are more than ever in a state of flux, as scholars and business leaders alike reconsider which practices work and which don't.

HISTORICAL CONTEXT

Although Japanese management techniques and economic strategies came to be recognized in Western countries only during the postwar period, their origins are considerably older. Most directly, their origins can be traced to at least the latter part of the 19th century, when a Western influenced modernization program began under the new monarchy created in the 1868 Meiji restoration. In part as a response to the bitter European colonization experiences of its Asian neighbors, the new Japanese government began to open the Japanese economy and society to controlled outside influences in order to stave off any Western conquerors.

Some recognizably modern practices arose during the Meiji period. Even then, when the Japanese economy was still shedding the trappings of feudalism after centuries of closure to foreigners and slow technological development, heavy emphasis was placed on developing domestic imitations of—and innovations on—Western goods, rather than relying on imports. The practice was summarized well under a slogan of the era, ''Japanese spirit, Western technology.''

This ambition to preserve the character of the Japanese culture and the autonomy of the economy can be seen in 20th-century practices at both the macro- and microeconomic levels. In the national economy it is evidenced by long-standing restrictions (direct and indirect) on imports into Japan and the concomitant trade surplus Japan has maintained for years. At the company level, the same motive helps explain the prevalence of the Japanese *keiretsu,* the large and complex families of interdependent companies centered around their own banks (e.g., Sumitomo, Hitachi, Mitsubishi). In theory, at least, these firms can avoid ''importing'' their raw materials, components, or even capital from ''foreign'' (i.e., unaffiliated) companies by sourcing these goods from within their extensive organizations.

PROFILE OF TRADITIONAL JAPANESE MANAGEMENT PRACTICES

Rooted in these and other historical traditions, some of the other key practices commonly associated with Japanese management techniques include:

- in-house training of managers
- consensual and decentralized decision-making
- extensive use of quality control methods
- carefully codified work standards
- emphasis on creating harmonious relations among workers
- lifetime employment and seniority-based compensation

It is important to note that these are generalizations according to a conventional formula. There have always been variations, and, as noted above, some aspects of these practices have been increasingly reconsidered in recent years.

MANAGEMENT EDUCATION. The education of managers in Japan traditionally takes place on a relatively informal basis within firms. The percentage of Japanese chief executives who have attended university is high, similar to that in the United States and Western Europe. However, very few Japanese executives have attended graduate schools compared to their U.S. and European counterparts. In fact, only one Japanese university offers a degree analogous to an MBA, a key credential for managers in the United States.

Formal education for managers is also not well developed at the undergraduate level. Undergraduate education is not viewed by firms as a means of attaining business skills, and firms base their hiring decisions less on a recruit's knowledge than on general attributes such as character and ambition. Firms do not hire recruits to fill specific occupations. Rather, recruits are expected to be malleable, identifying with the general interests of the firm rather than with their specific role within it. The mentor system is widely used in the early training of management recruits and involves middle-level and senior managers serving as teachers and role models.

The emphasis on in-house education is related to the traditional lifetime employment system, in which management recruits are hired each April following university graduation; they typically would stay with the firm until retirement. The lifetime-employment system makes it probable that a firm will benefit from its investment in training, and also enables the firm to develop long-range plans for training recruits.

Management training is based on regular rotation through a broad range of a firm's operations. Management recruits also frequently begin their careers as ordinary workers on a production line. The pattern of regular rotation enables managers to develop a detailed understanding of a number of varied operations, and thus over time to attain a rich general knowledge of the firm.

Linked with the lifetime-employment system is the emphasis on seniority in compensation and promotion—often over what Americans would take to be ''qualifications'' for the job. This results in a higher average age and less variation in age among top executives in Japan. Compared to the United States and Europe, for instance, relatively few company presidents are under age 50. This practice is believed to equip Japanese executives with an intricate knowledge about their particular business.

Japanese managers typically take a more long-term interest in their firms than do their American counterparts, partly a result of the lifetime employment and seniority systems. In the United States, managers are typically compensated on the basis of their divisions' performance. This bonus system is not used for Japanese managers, as it is considered detrimental to a long-term perspective and an interest in the firm as a whole.

CAPITAL AND PRIORITIES. The long-term view of Japanese managers is also based on sources of finance. While American firms rely heavily on capital from the stock markets, Japanese firms tend to rely more heavily on borrowing from banks and generally have much higher debt-to-equity ratios. Consequently, Japanese managers are under less pressure to maximize short-term earnings to please shareholders. By contrast, in the United States there is intense market pressure for companies to meet quarterly earnings expectations—even exceed them—or else face a sell-off of their shares. In general, Japanese firms are more likely to focus on productivity, growth, and market share, whereas U.S. firms are more inclined to concentrate first on profitability.

CORPORATE GOVERNANCE. While directors from outside the company are common in the United States, they are rare in Japan. The decision-making process in Japanese firms is highly decentralized. In publicly held U.S. corporations, power is concentrated in a board of directors, with each director having one vote. In Japan, both middle and senior management serve as directors. Japanese directors typically retain production-line responsibilities. For example, in the early 1970s, 14 of Hitachi's 20 directors were engineers. This represents another facet of the strong production orientation of Japanese management.

THE RINGI SYSTEM

The traditional decision-making process in Japanese firms is referred to as the *ringi* system. The system involves circulating proposals to all managers in the firm who are affected by an impending decision. Proposals are generally initiated by middle managers, though they may also come from top executives. In the latter case, an executive will generally give his idea to his subordinates and let them introduce it. Managers from different departments hold meetings and try to reach an informal consensus on the matter. Only after this consensus is reached will the formal document, or *ringi-sho,* be circulated for approval by the responsible managers.

The ringi system requires long lead times, and thus is problematic in a crisis. In recent years the focus on speeding up decision making has made this approach unpopular at many firms. Nonetheless, one of its underlying principles remains prevalent. That is, when a decision proves beneficial, the middle-level managers who initially advocated it receive credit; when a decision proves unsuccessful, responsibility is taken by top-level executives. This practice is intended to promote aggressiveness in younger managers.

ENTERPRISE UNIONS

One distinctive characteristic of **labor-management relations** in Japan is the enterprise union, which is organized around a single plant. Consequently, any given company may have several enterprise unions representing various portions of its workforce. Enterprise unions generally belong to a larger federation, but the balance of power is at the local level. Japanese unions are distinct not only because of their highly decentralized nature, but also because they represent both white-collar and blue-collar workers, with union membership open to managers up to the section chief level. The fact that many upper-level managers have moved up through union ranks and may have even served as union officials highlights the generally less antagonistic relationship between labor and management in Japan. Combined with a relatively narrow income gap between managers and workers and the willingness of manager recruits to work on production lines as part of their training, the open membership policies of Japanese unions contributes to the fairly harmonious interaction between unions and management.

Union membership is generally associated with lifetime employment guarantees. Membership varies widely by firm size, and relatively few workers in firms with fewer than 100 employees receive lifetime employment guarantees. Nonetheless, in large firms the lifetime employment guarantee creates an environment in which workers are less likely to feel threatened by technological change. As a consequence, changes in the production process are likely to be undertaken by management and workers on a cooperative basis. More generally, since semiannual bonuses and annual wage negotiations are based on a firm's competitive strength, workers have a large stake in their firm's long-term success.

QUALITY CIRCLES

The extensive use of **quality circles** is another distinguishing characteristic of Japanese management. The development of quality circles in Japan in the early 1960s was inspired by the lectures of American statisticians W. Edwards Deming and J.M. Juran, in which they discussed the development of wartime industrial standards in the United States. Noting that American management had typically given line managers and engineers about 85 percent of responsibility for quality control and only 15 percent to workers, Deming and Juran argued that these proportions should be reversed. Production processes should be designed with quality control in mind, they contended, and everyone in the firm, from entry level workers to top management, should be familiar with statistical control techniques and undergo continuing education on quality control. In general, Deming and Juran argued that quality control should focus on prevention, with the ultimate goal being to improve the production process until no defective parts or products are produced. Quality circles were one method of reaching these goals.

In Japan, quality circles consist of groups of about 10 workers who meet weekly, often on their own time. The groups typically include foremen, who usually serve as circle leaders. Quality circles focus on concrete aspects of the operations in which they are directly involved, using tables and graphs to communicate the statistical details of their quality issues. In one common format, problems are categorized by materials, manpower, and machines.

Quality circles provide a means for workers to participate in company affairs and for management to benefit from worker suggestions. Indeed, employee suggestions play an important role in Japanese companies. Two associations, the Japanese Association of Suggestion Systems and the Japan Human Relations Association, were developed to encourage this process. Japanese employee suggestions reportedly create billions of dollars' worth of benefits for companies.

SCIENTIFIC MANAGEMENT

Japanese management techniques have been strongly influenced by the tenets of scientific management. Like quality circles, scientific management originated in the United States, only to be more systematically adopted in Japan. The pioneering figure of scientific management is Frederick Jackson Taylor (1856-1915). Taylor is best known for his time and motion studies of workers as part of an effort to optimize and standardize work efforts, but he also argued for a system of bonuses to reward workers based on productivity. These ideas were implemented by Japanese firms as early as 1908, and a translation of his *Principles of Scientific Management* sold 2 million copies in Japan.

In the post-World War II years, carefully codified work standards and the use of semiannual bonuses for workers became common practices in Japan. Consistent with the Japanese emphasis on teamwork, bonuses are generally allotted to a work group rather than an individual worker. Scientific management emphasizes the role of management in the production process. This is reflected in the more hands-on approach in Japanese management training, as well as the relatively high share of managers directly involved in the production process.

PERVASIVENESS OF ENGINEERS

As with managers, Japanese industrial engineers are more directly involved with production processes than their counterparts in the United States. In his book *The Japanese Industrial System,* Charles J. McMillan explained that most Japanese companies make few distinctions between engineers and blue-collar workers, although engineers do tend to earn more. They work closely alongside production workers. In addition, Japan produces up to three times as many engineers a year as the United States. Japan's emphasis on production oriented engineering is consistent with its dominant competitive strategy in the postwar years—indeed, since the Meiji era—of focusing on improving existing products or processes rather than developing completely new ones.

NEW DIRECTIONS

While many of the patterns just described continue unabated at some Japanese companies, a variety of forces have caused them to change, often toward Western practices. Since the 1980s, for example, the predominance of seniority-based raises has been gradually giving way to a Western style regime of merit-based pay. Indeed, as of 1995, three-quarters of Japanese companies surveyed allocated at least some of their reward pay based on skills or achievements as opposed to tenure. And more than a few Japanese companies have attacked seniority more directly, explicitly revising policies to diminish or even eliminate it as a criterion in the compensation structure. This trend may be evidence of a cultural shift from valuing length of service to valuing quality of service.

Also mirroring Western trends, labor union membership in Japan has dropped considerably since the 1970s, falling from 35.4 percent of the workforce in 1970 to just 22.4 percent by 1998, according to figures compiled by the Japanese Ministry of Labor. Union participation remains the highest in large companies (those with 1,000 or more workers), where in 1998 membership was still nearly 57 percent. This share was down from 68 percent in 1987, the first year statistics by company size were kept.

Other traditional Japanese practices appear more enduring, notably lifetime employment. Although Japan's economic troubles have meant that some employees have lost their jobs, a continuing commitment to the principle of lifetime employment seems to remain at many companies and in the society as a whole. Still, younger workers (e.g., those under age 30) are decidedly less loyal to companies than in decades past, and there is growing evidence of a rise in professional identification over corporate identification among workers (i.e., ''I'm a tax accountant'' instead of ''I'm a Toyota worker'').

Nonetheless, even at the depths of the Japanese recession during the late 1990s Asian financial crisis, companies went to great lengths to avoid outright **layoffs**. One of the most common practices instead was to reassign workers, either within the corporate family or to other companies, such as vendors the company does business with. These transfers (known as *shukko*) could be temporary, in which case the worker is still officially employed by the company that has loaned him or her out, or permanent, where the company essentially finds a new job for the employee at another company. Employees who were never considered part of the lifetime staff, such as part-time help, usually didn't enjoy such privileges.

Although most agree that Japanese management has been moving in new directions, academics who study Japanese management practices are divided on how profound the shifts in the Japanese business paradigm really are. Indeed, the gamut of opinions has ranged from declaring the death of the Japanese management system to asserting its overarching continuity and strength. A number of observers see a continued convergence with Western practices, but many believe that, as in the past, the adoption of Western principles and practices will never be wholesale, but will blend with prevailing norms and beliefs in Japanese business and the broader culture.

SEE ALSO: Japanese Manufacturing Techniques

FURTHER READING:

Dirks, Daniel, Jean-François Huchet, and Thierry Ribault, eds. *Japanese Management in the Low Growth Era.* Berlin: Springer Verlag, 1999.

Harukiyo, Hasegawa, and Glenn D. Hook. *Japanese Business Management.* London: Routledge, 1998.

Herbig, Paul, and Laurence Jacobs. ''A Historical Perspective of Japanese Innovation.'' *Management Decision,* September-October 1997.

McMillan, Charles J. *The Japanese Industrial System.* 3rd rev. ed. Berlin: De Gruyter, 1996.

Mroczkowski, Tomasz, and Masao Hanaoka. ''The End of Japanese Management: How Soon?'' *Human Resource Planning,* September 1998.

JAPANESE MANUFACTURING TECHNIQUES

Japanese manufacturing techniques, as an area of influential practices and philosophies, emerged in the post-World War II era and reached the height of their prominence in the 1980s. Many adaptations of Japanese methods, and indeed, Japanese manufacturing vocabulary, have made their way into U.S. and worldwide manufacturing operations. Distinguishing characteristics associated with Japanese manufacturing include an emphasis on designing processes to optimize efficiency and a strong commitment to quality.

Perhaps the most widely recognized collection of Japanese manufacturing techniques is what is known as the Toyota Production System (TPS), the core of which is just-in-time (JIT) production or so-called lean manufacturing. The pioneers of these methods were Taiichi Ohno, a former Toyota executive, and Shigeo Shingo, an eminent engineer and consultant. In his 1989 book *The Study of the Toyota Production System from an Industrial Engineering Perspective,* Shingo identified these basic features of TPS:

1. It achieves cost reductions by eliminating waste, be it staff time, materials, or other resources.
2. It reduces the likelihood of overproduction by maintaining low inventories (''nonstock'') and keeps labor costs low by using minimal manpower.
3. It reduces production **cycle time** drastically with innovations like the Single-Minute Exchange of Die (SMED) system, which cuts downtime and enables small-lot production.
4. It emphasizes that product orders should guide production decisions and processes, a practice known as order-based production.

These and other practices form a contrast to traditional (e.g., pre-1980s) Western manufacturing, which tended to emphasize mass production, full capacity utilization, and the economies of scale that were presumed to follow.

ELIMINATING WASTE

The driving force behind the Japanese system of production is eliminating waste, thereby maximizing process efficiency and the returns on resources. A wide number of principles and practices can be employed to achieve this goal. As Shingo once noted, people instinctively know to eliminate waste once it is identified as such, so the task of reducing waste often centers first around identifying unnecessary uses of human, capital, or physical resources. After waste is targeted, new processes or practices can be devised to deal with it.

PROCESS IMPROVEMENT. An important aspect of eliminating waste is designing efficiency into production processes and methods. For example, in the Toyota system heavy emphasis was placed on lowering the time and complexity required to change a die in a manufacturing process. A time-consuming die-changing process is wasteful in two ways. First, while it is happening production is often at a standstill, increasing cycle times and all the costs associated with longer cycle times. (However, it is important to note that idle time for individual machines in a system is not always viewed as wasteful under the TPS philosophy.) Second, workers' time and effort are spent on activities that aren't directly related to production (i.e., no value is being added by changing a die). As a result of such concerns, the push at Toyota was to reduce significantly the time it took to change dies.

Major process improvements often occur through a series of smaller initiatives, summarized in the Japanese word *kaizen,* or continuous improvement. In the classic example, Toyota dramatically reduced its die-changing time over a two-year period. In 1970 it took the company four hours to change a die for a 1,000-ton stamping press. Six months later, the changing time had been cut to one and a half hours. The management then, under the leadership of Taiichi Ohno, set the formidable goal of reducing the time further to just three minutes.

Shigeo Shingo, already a highly regarded manufacturing consultant, was employed to design a process that would meet this objective. He approached the problem with two guiding principles: lowering the complexity of the changeover process and standardizing the tools used in it. Shingo looked at such factors as what kinds of fasteners were used to hold dies in place and how much time and variability was involved in performing various tasks during changeover. The result of his work was that by 1971 Toyota had indeed achieved its goal of a three-minute die change.

Other kinds of process improvements resulted from such philosophies as well. Whereas process improvement in many Western firms focused on training workers to master increasingly complicated tasks, the drive in Japanese manufacturing was to selectively redesign the tasks so they could be more easily and reliably mastered. One example is the concept of *poka-yoke,* also pioneered by Shingo in the 1960s, which involves designing a foolproof process to eliminate the chance of errors. Such a process usually consists of a simple yet definitive physical test of whether something is being done correctly. One type of poka-yoke, for instance, is when a part is designed to only be inserted into an assembly right-side up (i.e., it won't fit otherwise), removing the possibility that it can be inserted the wrong way. Three-and-a-half-inch computer diskettes contain this kind of poka-yoke. Other kinds of poka-yokes test the shape of manufactured products for defects or monitor steps in a production process to ensure all are completed and in the correct sequence. Poka-yokes have been widely developed to minimize worker error and improve quality control.

VALUE ADDED. TPS and similar Japanese manufacturing techniques distinguish between activities that add value to a product and those that are logistical but add no value. The primary—even the sole—value-added activity in manufacturing is the production process itself, where materials are being transformed into progressively functional workpieces. Most other activities, such as transporting materials, inspecting finished work, and most of all, idle time and delays, add no value and must be minimized. When processes are examined for potential improvements and cost cutting, reducing non-value-added activities is often the highest priority. Conversely, processes that add the most value, even if they are expensive, will usually not be compromised to achieve lower costs at the expense of quality.

OVERPRODUCTION AND EXCESS INVENTORY. Another area of waste that is a special concern in the Toyota system is excess inventory. The ideal is to produce without accumulating inventory, a condition known as non-stock or just-in-time production. In such a process the company produces goods at the exact quantity and schedule that they are required by its customers. To produce more than customers actually need—or sooner than they need it—is considered overproduction, leading to a build-up of stock or inventory. Overproduction can also occur internally when different steps of a manufacturing process aren't synchronized and excess materials or semi-finished products accumulate. Systems like the Japanese *kanban* established a set of often simple visual cues in the factory (e.g., when no work-in-progress is waiting in a painted square on the floor, it is a signal to advance the next item into the process) to help coordinate and synchronize the flow of materials and work.

Carrying inventory is wasteful because the company must store it or perform other additional handling that increases the total cost of its operations. By minimizing the need for such storage and handling, the company can reduce both the direct costs of holding/handling inventory as well as the indirect costs of tying up capital in the form of excess inventory.

ORDER-BASED PRODUCTION. A natural and necessary extension of the non-stock goal is that manufacturers need specific customer information to drive their production decisions. Obtaining this information necessitates effective market research/forecasting and communication with customers. As much as possible, production under the Japanese system is guided by actual orders, rather than anticipated demand based on less reliable information such as past sales. The order-based system is said to provide production "pull" from the actual market, as opposed to "push" that stems only from the manufacturer's conjecture.

TRANSPORTATION. The Toyota Production System also recognizes waste in the excess movement of items or materials. In general, the more transportation required, the less efficient the process, since moving goods back and forth is normally not a value-adding procedure. Transport waste is usually addressed by changing the layout of a factory, its geographic location relative to its customers, and so forth. While sometimes transportation problems can be mitigated through automation, the ideal under the Japanese system is to minimize it altogether. Cell and **flexible manufacturing** layouts are one approach to controlling transport waste.

It is important to note that reducing transportation costs may be at odds with other goals of the Japanese system, particularly small-lot, order-based production, which leads to smaller, more frequent batches of work and thus more deliveries of materials or finished goods. This can potentially increase the amount of resources devoted to the transportation function, aggravating the need for transportation efficiency. Ideally, the overall process chosen will minimize total costs by striking a balance between the wish to eliminate inventory and the wish to reduce transportation costs.

QUALITY BY DESIGN

Another feature thought to be defining in Japanese manufacturing is a marked attention to quality throughout the production process. Specifically, under the influence of such luminaries as W. Edwards Deming and Joseph M. Juran, Japanese manufacturers have sought to achieve quality by designing it into the production process rather than simply trying to catch all the errors at the end. As noted, poka-yokes can serve this function either by halting/correcting a faulty process or by alerting a worker to a problem as it occurs. While plenty of traditional, defect-monitoring sorts of quality controls are still used, philosophies such as TPS hold that the results of quality inspections should be used to inform—and improve—the manufacturing process, not just to describe it. This means the feedback from a quality inspection is expected to be immediate and, often, to result in some change in the process so that the likelihood of similar problems in the future is reduced.

MARKET-DRIVEN PRICING

In contrast to the traditional practice of setting prices by marking up some percentage over the cost of manufacturing, the Japanese system attempts to identify the market-determined price for a good and then engineer the manufacturing process to produce at this price profitably. Under this principle, increases in costs are not passed on to the consumer in the form of higher prices. As a corollary, the only way for a firm to increase profitability is by lowering costs; lower costs may also allow the company to be profitable yet deliver products at the low end of the pricing spectrum, a practice central to the rise of the Japanese auto manufacturers in the U.S. market.

WORKER FLEXIBILITY

Maximizing returns on human capital is another goal of Japanese manufacturing practices. Driven by the theory that human time is more valuable than machine time, the Japanese system attempts to optimize labor efficiency by deploying workers in different ways as order-based production requirements fluctuate. The main two dimensions of this flexibility are skills and scheduling. More so than in the United States, for example, Japanese manufacturers have emphasized cross-training workers to perform various functions as needed, rather than tying them to a particular machine or process. This is believed not only to improve the subjective work experience, but also to create well-rounded employees who can be assigned exactly where needed in the process without creating delays or diminishing the quality of work (this also feeds into the wish to keep worker tasks simple and foolproof).

In practice, this often translates into individual workers running several machines simultaneously, a practice called *jidoka,* with the machines designed to eliminate both error and the need for constant supervision. Having multiple responsibilities also gives rise to the need for special safety accommodations to reduce the chance of injury in an integrated work environment. In the legendary Toyota production reforms, converting to a multi-machine worker system reportedly achieved 20 to 30 percent gains in worker productivity.

In scheduling under the Japanese system, as long as a process is functioning on a just-in-time basis, the manufacturer will tend to structure the process to optimize the use of human labor, even if it means leaving machines idle. Overtime and temporary labor are used to accommodate short-term spikes in production requirements.

IMPACT OF JAPANESE MANUFACTURING TECHNIQUES

Many of these practices and principles began to attract a serious following outside Japan in the late 1970s, although their implementation continues to the present. During the 1980s many large U.S. manufacturers began to adopt just-in-time practices to improve efficiency. By the late 1980s and early 1990s this and related practices were commonly termed "lean manufacturing," highlighting the role of reducing waste in the production process. In many cases hybrid approaches were developed that embodied some of the principles of the Japanese techniques but also maintained some of the historical differences. More recently, methods like JIT have been increasingly influential in non-manufacturing industries such as retailing and services.

Although critics have rued the wholesale adoption of Japanese manufacturing techniques in the United States on grounds that some aspects are particular to the Japanese culture and economy, the Japanese system is widely recognized as delivering many of the efficiencies and cost reductions it sets out to. Indeed, evaluating the success of attempts to transplant Japanese methods can be difficult for U.S. firms at first, as some companies have found that their traditional accounting concepts obscure some of the economic benefits these methods confer.

SEE ALSO: Japanese Management Techniques

FURTHER READING:

Abo, Tetsuo. *Hybrid Factory: The Japanese Production System in the United States.* New York: Oxford University Press, 1994.

Kenney, Martin, and Richard Florida. *Beyond Mass Production: The Japanese System and Its Transfer to the U.S.* New York: Oxford University Press, 1993.

Liker, Jeffrey K., ed. *Becoming Lean: Inside Stories of U.S. Manufacturers.* Portland, OR: Productivity Press, 1998.

Schonberger, Richard J. *Japanese Manufacturing Techniques: Nine Hidden Lessons in Simplicity.* New York: Free Press, 1983.

Shingo, Shigeo. *The Study of the Toyota Production System from an Industrial Engineering Perspective.* Rev. ed. Cambridge, MA: Productivity Press, 1989.

Wheatley, Malcolm. "Asian Lessons in the Art of Manufacturing." *Management Today,* April 1998.

JOA

SEE: Joint Operating Agreement

JOINT OPERATING AGREEMENT (JOA)

When two or more companies agree to combine some of their operations as a means of sharing costs and reducing operating expenses, they enter into a joint operating agreement (JOA). Benefits involve cost savings and **economies of scale**. Joint operating agreements enable the participating companies to operate with fewer employees; eliminate duplicate facilities, equipment, and functions; and save through bulk purchases of supplies and materials.

Joint operating agreements typically take one of two forms. In some cases a **joint venture** is formed. The companies involved in the JOA form a third company that is jointly owned. The joint venture is capitalized by the participating companies and managed by a **board of directors** consisting of executives from, or individuals selected by, each of the participating companies. If all of the companies contribute equal amounts of capital, they generally share equally in ownership and profits of the joint venture.

This type of integrated JOA was being used by health-care systems that wanted to integrate operations but that also wanted to maintain their separate corporate existences. Two or more health-care systems would form a jointly managed organization, with governance shared among the new entity and the existing entities. Under a contractual agreement, revenues were shared and capital expenditures were made according to a predetermined formula. Such a JOA did not violate **antitrust laws**, because it was viewed as an integrated joint venture, with each partner sharing the risk. As a result, the affiliated entities could engage in joint negotiations and strategic planning through the jointly managed organization. The **Internal Revenue Service** (IRS) ruled in 1996 that such integrated joint ventures among nonprofit health-care providers could retain their nonprofit status. That is, the IRS considered the joint venture an extension of the tax-exempt affiliated entities, rather than as a new entity subject to taxation.

The second form of a joint operating agreement involves an operating **partnership**. One of the companies acts as the operating partner for the other firms, providing shared services on a contract basis. Secondary partners may contribute facilities, equipments, cash, and other items to the operating partner. Under this type of joint operating agreement, no third-party joint venture is created.

JOAs should be distinguished from mergers. In the case of **mergers and acquisitions**, ownership is combined in the new corporate entity. When one company merges with another, the result is single ownership. In the case of joint operating agreements, the two or more companies involved remain separately owned.

Joint operating agreements do not necessarily involve antitrust violations. It is only when joint operating agreements involve price fixing, market allocation, and **profit sharing** that they violate the antitrust laws of the United States. JOAs that are limited to combined operations for the purpose of cost savings and economies of scale are permitted.

In some cases special legislation has been passed by Congress to provide antitrust exemptions for joint operating agreements in specific industries. In 1970 Congress passed the Newspaper Preservation Act, which granted antitrust exemption to joint operating agreements established by two daily newspapers that competed in the same geographic markets.

JOAS IN THE NEWSPAPER INDUSTRY

Perhaps the most widely known, discussed, and analyzed JOAs are those involving newspapers. The first-known JOA between two competing newspaper was formed in 1933 in Albuquerque, New Mexico. Three other newspaper JOAs were established in the 1930s, four in the 1940s, 16 in the 1950s, and four in the 1960s. In 1965 the U.S. Department of Justice challenged the JOA between the *Star* and *Citizen* in Tucson, Arizona, on the grounds that it violated federal antitrust laws. In 1969 the U.S. Supreme Court upheld that challenge.

The Newspaper Preservation Act (NPA) was passed by Congress as a result of extensive lobbying on the part of the newspaper industry. Under the NPA, antitrust exemption was granted to JOAs established by competing newspapers. That meant that under an approved JOA, which included all JOAs currently in existence, newspapers could engage in antitrust practices such as price fixing, profit pooling, and market allocation.

Under the NPA, newspapers that desired to establish new JOAs needed to obtain approval from the attorney general of the United States and the U.S. Department of Justice. In order for a newspaper JOA to be approved, one of the newspapers must be failing. Among the criteria that are considered when determining whether or not a newspaper is failing, are degree of market share disparity between the two newspapers, a downward circulation spiral, and the extent of the failing newspaper's financial losses.

Some newspaper JOAs were not affected by the NPA. These included newspapers in different geographic markets that established centralized facilities to handle operations. Joint newspaper monopolies, where a single company owns two newspapers in a single geographic market, were also not affected by the NPA. In addition there were joint operations that did not violate antitrust laws. For example, newspapers are allowed to combine advertising and circulation operations. They may share printing and production facilities. They may also merge administrative functions, such as accounting and human resources. These types of joint operations do not require an antitrust exemption.

Essentially two factors make it difficult for more than one daily newspaper to publish successfully in a single market. One is that economies of scale heavily favor the larger of the two newspapers. Secondly, many advertisers place ads only in the largest circulating newspapers in any one market, making it difficult for smaller newspapers to compete with larger ones for advertising dollars. Newspaper JOAs offer a way to reduce the high costs associated with newspaper production and distribution as well as the marketing and promotion costs associated with commercial competition.

Following passage of the NPA, two newspaper JOAs were created in the 1970s, three in the 1980s, and several have been established in the 1990s. While newspaper JOAs are designed to preserve editorial competition between two daily newspapers in a single market, whether or not they have been successful has remained a matter of controversy. The number of newspaper JOAs in effect declined from 34 in 1997 to 15 in 1998. As has been noted, several types of joint operations do not require antitrust exemptions, and the benefit of granting specific antitrust exemptions has been questioned by some experts. In addition other market forces appear to be at work against struggling newspapers. These include the growth of television viewing and overall declining readerships for many newspapers. Many newspaper JOAs have been dissolved, resulting in only one daily newspaper serving a particular geographic market.

[David P. Bianco]

FURTHER READING:

Burda, David. "Joint Operating Agreement Gets IRS Nod." *Modern Healthcare,* 17 June 1996, 6.

Busterna, John C., and Robert G. Picard. *Joint Operating Agreements: The Newspaper Preservation Act and Its Application.* Stamford, CT: Ablex, 1993.

Hilts, Elizabeth. "Death by JOA? Sad End for Struggling Web Site: A Web Editor Laments the Demise of Nashvillebanner.com." *Editor and Publisher,* 28 February 1998, 20-21.

O'Hare, Patrick. "Joint Operating Agreements: A New Integration Model." *Healthcare Financial Management,* September 1996, 35.

Stein, M. I. "State Law Does Not Affect JOA." *Editor and Publisher,* 18 January 1997, 17.

——. "Unusual JOA Heats Up." *Editor and Publisher,* 8 March 1997, 9-12.

Wieffering, Eric. "Northwest, KLM Seek Joint Cargo Operating Agreement." *Knight-Ridder/Tribune Business News,* 19 August 1997.

JOINT VENTURES

Joint ventures are domestic or international enterprises involving two or more companies joining temporarily to undertake a particular project. They have grown in popularity in recent years—joint ventures between U.S. and foreign firms, for example, have increased at an average of 27 percent since 1985. Certainly, not all of them will be successful; estimates of the failure rate of joint ventures reaches as high as 70 percent. Nonetheless, companies persist in initiating them for a variety of reasons.

REASONS FOR JOINT VENTURES

Joint ventures may involve companies in one or more countries. International joint ventures in particular are becoming more popular, especially in capital-intensive industries such as oil and gas exploration, mineral extraction, and metals processing. The basic reason is simple: to save money. For example, just to start a mining operation in the United States in 1984, a company would have had to spend one to two billion dollars. Few companies then (or now) could finance such an expenditure on their own, so joint ventures became more attractive as a way to share risks and costs and create scale economies.

Another factor that contributed to the expansion in joint ventures in the past few decades was the cost involved for capital-intensive industries to continue their operations. Companies in these industries depend heavily on advances in technology to reduce costs. By pooling their money and personnel, companies enhanced their chances of developing advanced technological methods that would reduce exploration and production costs and increase profit margins. Joint ventures became a favored method of doing business for such industries.

Joint ventures between American and international companies are increasingly common. Estimates suggest that approximately one-quarter of American companies' direct investments, i.e., the establishment of operating facilities in a foreign country, were in joint ventures. Ideally, the partners contribute approximately equal amounts of resources and capital into each business. The word "approximately" is important in foreign joint ventures, since some countries, such as **China**, will not allow outside companies to own the majority of a domestic business (although they do encourage joint ventures). In some countries, joint ventures are the only way companies can engage in foreign business. For instance, **Mexico** requires that all foreign firms investing there have Mexican joint venture partners. In addition to government regulations, other reasons for multinational joint ventures include cutting the costs of doing business, sharing risks, and acquiring technological information and management expertise from other companies.

International joint ventures have also been fostered by international financial institutions such as the **International Monetary Fund**, the **World Bank**, and the **World Trade Organization**, who have instituted policies to eliminate trade barriers and deregulate foreign ownership restrictions and the international flow of capital. These policies have helped create a business climate in which international investment and partnerships are an increasingly attractive, and often necessary, means by which companies seek to expand profit margins and market share. In addition, regional trade areas such as the **North American Free Trade Agreement** (NAFTA), the **European Union** (EU), and the **Association of South and East Asian Nations** (ASEAN) have created particularly favorable conditions for joint ventures within specific, relatively localized regions.

Joint ventures are extraordinarily helpful to some companies in gaining access to foreign markets. Neither party may really be interested in the primary project, but they participate simply to gain access to the new market. Such projects generally represent a direct investment, which is sometimes limited by laws in the country in which the operation takes place. One of the aims of a partner in a joint venture is to have a majority interest in it; that way, it maintains control over a project. This explains why some countries do not permit foreign companies to hold majority interests in their domestic business ventures.

Companies seeking to cut the costs of doing business see joint ventures as a way to save money. In effect, they are sharing the risks should a particular project fail. For example, if two oil companies wish to produce a new drilling platform to search for oil in swamps or ocean areas, and neither one can finance the project on its own, they might join forces. That way, they are sharing the costs of the projects and reducing their individual risk should they find no oil. That is a decided advantage to many business people.

TYPES OF JOINT VENTURES

Joint ventures fall into several categories. Among them are equity based operations that benefit foreign and/or local private interests, groups of interests, or members of the general public. There are also non-equity joint ventures, also known as cooperative agreements, in which the parties seek technical service arrangements, franchise and brand use agreements, management contracts or rental agreements, or one-time contracts, e.g., for construction projects. Quite often, non-equity joint ventures are used simply to provide access for the participants into foreign markets.

Equity type arrangements involve two sides: one that provides the capital, and one that receives it. Since there is money involved, there are also inherent risks, particularly with equity ventures launched in less developed countries. The biggest risk is that the business will fail and the money invested will be lost. There is also the risk that some foreign governments will nationalize certain industries in order to protect their own domestic interests. For example, the Chilean government nationalized its copper industry in the 1960s to prevent foreign companies from gaining control over the ore. In 1988, Peru took over Perulac, a local milk producer owned by Nestle, because of a national milk shortage. However, such risks are (or should be) included in both the cost of doing business and in joint venture participants' contingency planning.

Participants do not always furnish capital as part of their joint venture commitments. There are, for example, non-equity arrangements in which some companies are more in need of technical services or technological expertise than they are of capital. They may want to modernize operations or start new production operations. Thus, they limit partners' participation to technical assistance. Such arrangements often include some funding as well, albeit limited.

There is also a growing prevalence of franchising joint ventures. American companies such as McDonald's, Coca-Cola Co., and Stained Glass Overlay have opened foreign franchise operations at an increasing rate. The emergence of new markets such as China and Vietnam have made such operations lucrative and have attracted more and more businesses to joint venture participation. A logical extension of franchising and brand-use agreements is the need for managerial expertise. Consequently, companies in developed countries form joint ventures with businesses in emerging countries in which they provide management expertise through contractual agreements. Such arrangements benefit both parties immeasurably, which is one of the goals of joint ventures.

Not all joint ventures involve private companies—some include government agencies. This is most common in less developed countries, but there are notable exceptions. For example, the British and French governments combined their resources in conjunction with privately owned firms to develop a supersonic transport (SST) intended to revolutionize transatlantic flying between the two countries and the United States. The project did not realize its financial goals. The flights were too expensive for average flyers, costing as much as $3,368 one way between London and Washington D.C. As a result, most flights were discontinued, although some between European and New York City still exist. Such are the risks of joint ventures, whether they involve private business or government agencies.

Generally, joint venture participants in the private sector furnish the capital, resources, and management and technological expertise involved in the operation. In less developed countries, however, government agencies are often active in business enterprises. They may provide or arrange for funding; own or manage certain industries, such as utility companies and airlines; or act as agents in attracting foreign investment or participation in businesses. They are no less active than privately held businesses in joint ventures, however. The rules for all participants remain the same, and strategies do not change.

JOINT VENTURE STRATEGIES

Businesses should not engage in joint ventures without adequate planning and strategy. They cannot afford to, since the ultimate goal of joint ventures is the same as it is for any type of business operation: to make a profit for the owners and shareholders. A successful company in any type of business is often recruited heavily for participation in joint ventures. Thus, they can pick and choose in which partnerships they would like to engage, if any. They follow certain ground rules, which have been developed over they years as joint ventures have grown in popularity.

For example, experience dictates that both parties in a joint venture should know exactly what they wish to derive from their partnership. There must be an agreement before the partnership becomes a reality. There must also be a firm commitment on the part of each member. One of the leading causes for the failure of joint ventures is that some participants do not reveal their true intentions in the partnerships. For example, some private companies in advanced countries have formed partnerships with militant governments to supply technological expertise and develop products such as chemicals or nuclear reactors to be used for allegedly peaceful purposes. They learned later that the products were used for military purposes. Such results can be detrimental to the companies involved and adversely affect their bottom lines and reputations, to speak nothing of the direct victims of the military development.

Businesses should form joint ventures with experienced partners. If the partners do not have approximately equal experience, one can take advantage of the other, which can lead to failure. Joint ventures generally do not survive under this imbalanced dynamic. Nor do they survive if companies jump into them without testing the partnership first.

Partners in joint ventures would often be better off participating in small projects as a way to test one another instead of launching into one large enterprise without an adequate feeling-out process. This is especially true when companies with different structures, corporate cultures, and strategic plans work together. Such differences are difficult to overcome and frequently lead to failure. That is why a ''courtship'' is beneficial to joint venture participants.

WHY JOINT VENTURES FAIL

Joint ventures fail for many reasons. In addition to those mentioned above, other factors include: disappearing markets, lagging technology, partners' inability to honor the contract, cultural differences interfering with progress, or governmental and macroeconomic de-stabilizing factors. However, many of these reasons can be eliminated with careful planning.

Inconsistent government interference is a difficult problem to overcome. For example, the United States government has long maintained restrictions against exporting certain technologies to selected foreign countries, such as those utilized to produce jet engines and computers. These restrictions place American companies at a competitive disadvantage, since other countries do not place similar constraints on their businesses. Thus, American companies are unable to engage in certain joint ventures.

Companies that engage in military-oriented joint ventures are often subject to unanticipated risks. The federal government may allocate funds for the production of certain weapons, sign contracts with manufacturers, and then discontinue the project due to changing needs, budget restrictions, or election results. Such government actions are a common risk to these joint ventures. They introduce an element of insecurity into the projects, which is something that partners try to avoid as much as possible.

Another problem with joint ventures concerns the issue of management. The managers of one company may be more adept at decision making than their counterparts at the other company. This can lead to friction and a lack of cooperation. Projects are doomed to failure if there is not a well-defined decision-making process in place that is predicated on mutual goals and strategies.

For example, if two auto manufacturing companies engage in a joint venture, it is imperative that they be similar in their structures and approach to business. If one company relies heavily on nonunionized workers who operate in an autonomous team-building environment, and the other comprises a unionized workforce oriented toward assembly line production in which workers specialize in narrow tasks, the chances of success are poor. The workers at the first plant would be prone to making decisions and solving problems on their own, which would reduce the levels of bureaucracy needed to manage production. Conversely, the workers at the second plant would likely defer to higher-level managers to make decisions. The differences would be difficult to overcome and would lead to higher costs and slower production. While the differences could be alleviated through planning before the actual manufacturing process began, the time expended might lead to technology gaps and other impediments to earning a profit. Most companies engaging in joint ventures would prefer not to deal with such problems after a project was implemented. Rather, they aim to eliminate them through careful planning. Doing so increases profits in the long run, which is one of the many benefits of successful joint ventures.

BENEFITS OF JOINT VENTURES

Among the most significant benefits derived from joint ventures is that partners save money and reduce their risks through capital and resource sharing. Joint ventures give smaller companies the chance to work with larger ones to develop, manufacture, and market new products. They also give companies of all sizes the opportunity to increase sales, gain access to wider markets, and enhance technological capabilities through **research and development** (R&D) underwritten by more than one party. In fact, funding for R&D today is often provided by government agencies in a myriad of countries operating under all types of economies, ranging from capitalist to socialist and hybrid. This is particularly true in the United States.

Until recently, U.S. companies were reluctant to engage in research and development partnerships, and government agencies tried not to become involved in business development. However, with the emergence of countries that feature technologically advanced industries (such as electronics or computer microchips) supported extensively by government funding, American companies have become more willing to participate in joint ventures. Likewise, the U.S. government, along with state governments, has become more generous with its financial support.

Government's increased involvement in the private business environment has created more opportunities for companies to engage in domestic and international joint ventures, although they are still legally limited in what they can do and where they can operate. Nonetheless, more and more companies are involving themselves in joint ventures, and the trend is to increase their participation, since the advantages outweigh the disadvantages.

DISADVANTAGES OF JOINT VENTURES

The disadvantages of joint ventures include: potential financial losses if a project fails, expropriation or nationalization, disagreements among partners, and less-than-anticipated results. For instance, in the 1980s, American Motors Corp., which has since been acquired by Chrysler Corp., entered a joint venture with the Chinese government to produce Jeeps in Beijing. The Chinese government, which did not allow joint ventures before 1980, created many complications that prevented American Motors from operating efficiently. The result was greatly reduced profits for American Motors.

THE FUTURE OF JOINT VENTURES

It is almost certain that the number of joint ventures will continue to increase in the near future. More and more companies are adopting the joint venture approach as a part of their growth strategies, particularly in the international arena. Foreign companies can benefit mutually by combining their technological and monetary resources and taking advantage of respective market conditions. Thus, international joint ventures are becoming the norm rather than the exception—and in more industries than ever before.

Joint ventures may grow in importance so much in the next few years that many companies could lose their national identities. There could be a growth in the activities of multinational corporations to the point where joint ventures will be virtually unrecognizable. In fact, some companies, especially those in capital-intensive industries, have already lost sight of the fact that they engage constantly in joint ventures because they have become so commonplace.

Finally, the wave of privatization, on a global scale, of state-owned industries and enterprises promised an added catapult for joint venture formations. The estimated worth of world-wide state-owned industry sales in 1995 reached $65 billion. This trend will make investment and inroads by companies into previously closed, and still relatively unfamiliar and structurally adverse, countries such as China and the former eastern bloc nations increasingly attractive.

[Arthur G. Sharp]

FURTHER READING:

Beamish, Paul, and J. Peter Killing. *Cooperative Strategies,* vol. 1-3. San Francisco: New Lexington Press, 1997.

Bendaniel, David J. *International M&A, Joint Ventures, and Beyond: Doing the Deal.* Englewood Cliffs, NJ: Prentice Hall, 1998.

Child, John, and David Faulkner. *Strategies of Cooperation: Managing Alliances, Networks, and Joint Ventures.* Oxford, U.K.: Oxford University Press, 1998.

Tesler, Lester G. *Joint Ventures of Labor and Capital.* Ann Arbor, MI: University of Michigan Press, 1998.

JUNK BONDS

Junk bonds are **corporate debt** securities of comparatively high credit risk, as indicated by ratings lower than Baa3 by Moody's Investors Service or lower than BBB- by Standard & Poor's. This usually excludes obligations that are convertible to equity **securities**, although the bonds may have other equity-related **options** (such as **warrants**) attached to them. Junk bonds are also known as high-yield, noninvestment-grade, below-investment-grade, less than-investment-grade, or speculative-grade **bonds**.

HISTORY

The term ''junk bonds'' dates to the 1920s, apparently originating as traders' jargon. Financial publisher John Moody applied the less pejorative label, ''high-yield bonds,'' as early as 1919, but noninvestment-grade **debt** received little attention outside a small circle of professional specialists prior to the mid-1980s. For a few years during that period, high-yield bonds were employed extensively in financing of **mergers and acquisitions**, including two controversial variants—**leveraged buyouts** (LBOs) and hostile **takeovers**. Junk bonds, by virtue of their name alone, became convenient targets for critics of the merger and acquisition boom and its perceived excesses. Public awareness continued to grow as a number of excessively debt-laden LBOs collapsed, causing **default** rates to surge and high-yield bond prices to plummet in 1989-90. See Exhibit 1.

Notwithstanding the sudden notoriety they achieved in the 1980s, high yield bonds by then had been a fixture of the **capital markets** for several decades. During the 1920s, noninvestment-grade paper accounted for 15 to 20 percent of total corporate bond issuance. Additionally, ''fallen angels,'' i.e., bonds originally issued with investment grade ratings but subsequently downgraded, offered an attractive niche for a few investors and market makers.

Demand for higher-risk, higher-return debt remained limited, however, until the establishment of several new **mutual funds** specializing in the high-risk sector, beginning in 1969-70. The assets of these funds grew dramatically during the bond bull market of 1975-76. At the same time, the supply of lower-rated issues shrank through upgradings and **refinancings**. **Investment banks** responded by stepping up new issues from the modest level observed in the early 1970s. By the late 1980s, annual primary volume exceeded $30 billion.

Although Drexel Burnham Lambert was not the first underwriter to capitalize on this market opportunity, it did become the dominant player in junk markets. Under the leadership of Michael Milken, Drexel's high-yield operation accounted for nearly half of all **underwriting** volume during the 1980s. As the decade ended, Milken was first dislodged from the firm and then convicted of several securities law violations. Drexel went bankrupt during the high-yield market's severe slump in 1990, apparently a victim of excessive concentration in a single line of business and a precarious **capital structure**. Supporters contended, however, that Milken and Drexel had been undone by a vendetta of entrenched corporate managers and government regulators, who supposedly felt threatened by the freer access to capital that ''junk bonds'' provided.

By 1991, the high-yield market was healthy once again. Total returns remained strong for the next few years (see Figure 2), aided by declining **interest rates** and the rehabilitation of many distressed issuers. The use of proceeds in new offerings shifted from mergers and acquisitions to more conventional corporate purposes. Replacement of shorter-term bank borrowings and older, higher-cost public high-yield debt were frequently observed applications of funds. Another notable change was the increased prominence of issu-

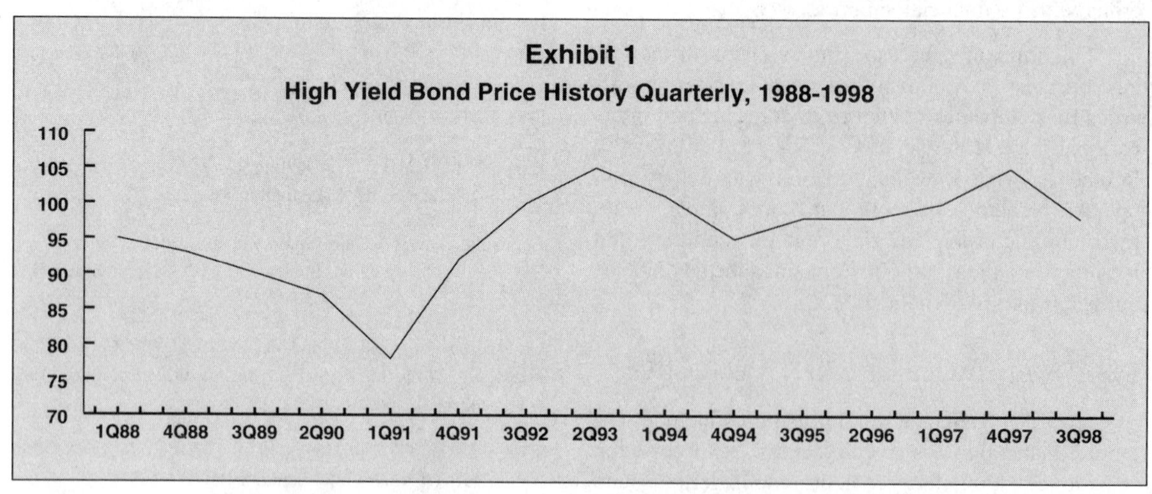

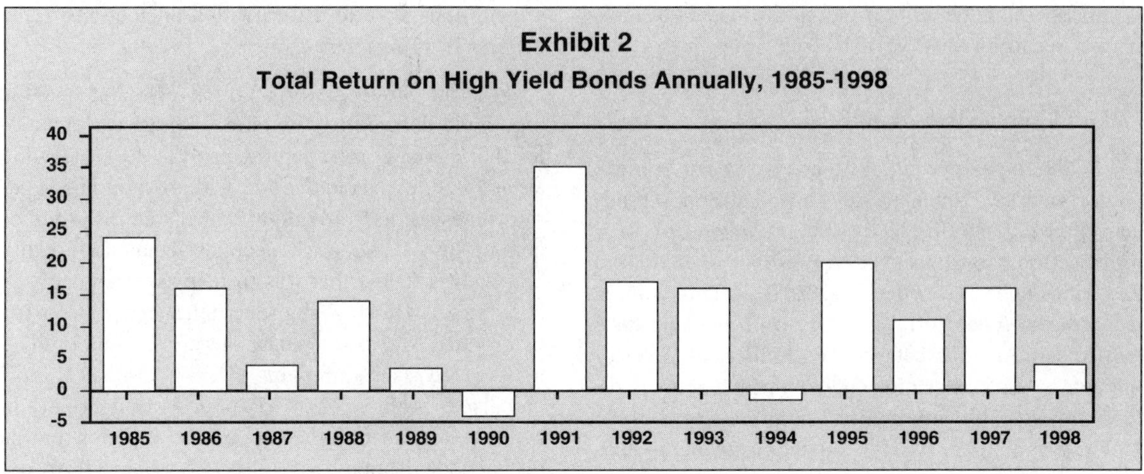

ance in the United States from noninvestment-grade companies based in Europe, as well as developing countries in Asia and Latin America. By the late 1990s, home-grown investor and issuer markets in high-yield bonds had appeared in Canada and Europe.

ADVANTAGES AND DISADVANTAGES

Junk bonds offer corporations several distinct advantages over other types of financing. They avoid the equity dilution that can result from the issuance of new common shares. In addition, high-yield bonds can be a less costly source of funds on an aftertax basis than equity. Compared to private debt (whether in the form of commercial bank **loans** or private placements with insurance companies or other **financial institutions**), high-yield bonds generally impose less stringent **restrictive covenants** on the issuer. Furthermore, longer maturities are available in the high-yield market than the commercial **banks** offer.

An offsetting disadvantage, vis-a-vis equity financing, is the higher level of fixed charges that results from issuing high-yield debt. For privately owned companies that would not otherwise have to comply with **Securities and Exchange Commission** registration and financial reporting requirements, floating public noninvestment-grade bonds in lieu of private debt entails incremental expenses. Also, such companies may not wish, for competitive reasons, to disclose as much information about their operations as high-yield bond issuance necessitates.

The substantial fixed charge requirement created by issuing noninvestment grade bonds makes them best suited to well-established companies with fairly predictable levels of **cash flow**. Accordingly, high technology industries, which are characterized by potentially wide swings in earnings and which generate only modest amounts of cash from **depreciation**, have historically accounted for a minor portion of high-yield issuance. Equity and convertible bonds have represented the more appropriate vehicle for such classes of issuers.

In other respects, however, noninvestment-grade debt has proved adaptable to the borrower's needs, as well as to market conditions. For example, zero-coupon (or deferred-interest) bonds meet the requirements of companies that expect to be large net users of cash in the near term, but substantial cash generators in the future. During the late 1990s, many early-stage telecommunications companies fit this description and turned to zero-coupon high-yield bonds as an alternative to **venture capital**. Zero-coupon instruments pay no cash coupons, but instead are offered at a discount, with the appreciation to par at maturity providing the investor's return. Uneven or unpredictable cash generation patterns can also be accommodated by allowing the coupon rate to vary with the general level of interest rates or with the price of a specified **commodity**.

From the investor's viewpoint, high-yield bonds provide both **income** and potential for **capital gains**. The latter tends to be limited by early redemption provisions, which allow issuers to retire the obligations prior to maturity, at modest premiums to par. Significant appreciation may occur, however, in bonds trading at steep discounts to par, reflecting either past credit deterioration or a rise in the general level of interest rates since issuance. Additional returns to high-yield bondholders arise from **tender offers** and payments offered for consent to modification of financial covenants.

Noninvestment-grade bond funds generally emphasize the income feature. They ordinarily offer small investors higher yields than they can earn on alternatives such as savings accounts, certificates of deposit, money market funds, or investment-grade bonds. In addition, high-yield funds provide a diversification benefit, otherwise impractical for an investor of modest means to achieve. By holding portfolios of many different issues, a fund cushions the investor against possible default or underperformance of individual securities.

WHO USES JUNK BONDS?

Other types of mutual funds also invest in high-yield bonds. Medium quality corporate bonds funds are typically permitted, by the provisions of their prospectuses, to allocate a portion of their assets to securities rated lower than Baa3/BBB-. This latitude enables the funds to raise the overall yield on their portfolios. Another category of high-yield investor includes ''asset allocation funds,'' which achieve diversification by combining noninvestment-grade holdings with other fixed-income investments such as foreign bonds or **mortgage-backed securities**. Some equity mutual fund managers participate in the high-yield market as well. Their objectives include speculating in specific issues and increasing the income in their funds during periods in which the **stock market** offers little potential for capital gains.

Life insurance companies represent a major market for high-yield bonds, which they hold in conjunction with a variety of other fixed-income investments. Some states limit the percentage of assets that insurers can allocate to bonds rated less than investment grade. In all states, reserving requirements of the National Association of Insurance Commissioners effectively establish ceilings on the ownership of high-yield debt, while also generally skewing such ownership toward the better-quality portion of the market.

Pension funds face few specific restrictions on their high-yield investments. On the other hand, the diversification benefits are substantial. High-yield bonds are comparatively insensitive to general movements in interest rates, so they tend to stabilize the performance of portfolios composed of other fixed-income instruments.

The upheavals of the late 1980s left many plan sponsors wary of the sector, but by 1995, an extended period of strong performance had erased many of the old concerns. A growing number of pension plans began to allocate a portion of their assets to specialized high-yield managers. Many other sponsors authorized their generalist fixed-income managers to invest 10 or 15 percent of their fixed-income assets in high-yield bonds.

ARE THEY WORTH IT?

For all classes of investors who bear the risk of owning high-yield bonds, the central question is whether the rewards represent sufficient compensation. Properly speaking, the analysis should consider not only potential losses through default, but also the risks related to illiquidity in the secondary market, redemptions prior to maturity, and fluctuations in the general level of interest rates.

Arthur Stone Dewing effectively launched the high-yield debate in 1926, citing slightly earlier studies that covered bond returns back to 1900. Dewing argued that lower-rated issues had proved to be superior investments, providing higher returns—net of default losses and price declines—than top-quality bonds. In a theme that was to reappear frequently in later years, Dewing suggested that most investors irrationally despised and therefore undervalued lower-rated issues, allowing more level-headed individuals to profit at their expense. Harold Fraine, in contrast, argued that the supposedly superior returns on high-yield bonds were illusions arising from period-specific changes in interest rates and risk premiums. Later, Milken took Dewing's side in the debate. He frequently cited the work of W. Braddock Hickman, who was actually more reserved in his conclusions than many subsequent high-yield enthusiasts believed.

None of these observers addressed risk in the sense in which contemporary financial theory defines it. Marshall E. Blume and Donald B. Keim made an important advance by considering the variance of returns. They found high-yield bonds to have higher returns and less variance than long-term U.S. Treasury securities. Blume and Keim hypothesized, however, that the anomaly would disappear if the results were controlled for differences in maturity. Kevin Maloney, Richard Rogalski, and Lakshmi Shyam-Sunder further challenged the alleged undervaluation of high-yield bonds. They noted that the upside (limited by earlier redemption provisions) was less than the downside (a 100 percent loss), a disparity for which rational investors would require additional compensation. On balance, the evidence points to a generally correct valuation of high-yield bonds relative to their fully elaborated risk. The securities represent neither a bargain, as alleged by their advocates, nor an inferior investment, as the critics maintain.

[Martin S. Fridson, CFA]

FURTHER READING:

Alcaly, Roger. ''The Golden Age of Junk.'' *New York Review of Books,* 26 May 1994, 28-34.

Altman, Edward I., ed. *The High-Yield Debt Market: Investment Performance and Economic Impact.* Homewood, IL: Dow Jones-Irwin, 1990.

Asquith, Paul A., David W. Mullins Jr., and Eric D. Wolff. ''Original Issue High Yield Bonds: Aging Analysis of Defaults, Exchanges, and Calls.'' *Journal of Finance,* September 1989, 923-52.

Becketti, Sean. ''The Truth about Junk Bonds.'' *Economic Review.* Federal Reserve Bank of Kansas City, July/August 1990, 45 54.

Blume, Marshall E., and Donald B. Keim. "The Risk and Return of Low-Grade Bonds: An Update." *Financial Analysts Journal,* September/October 1991, 85-89.

Cornell, Bradford, and Kevin Green. "The Investment Performance of Low-Grade Bond Funds." *Journal of Finance,* March 1991, 29-48.

Dewing, Arthur Stone. *The Financial Policy of Corporations.* Rev. ed. New York: Ronald Press, 1926.

Fabozzi, Frank J., ed. *The New High-Yield Debt Market: A Handbook for Portfolio Managers and Analysts.* New York: HarperCollins, 1990.

Fons, Jerome S. "The Default Premium and Corporate Bond Experience." *Journal of Finance,* March 1987, 81-97.

Fraine, Harold G. "Superiority of High-Yield Bonds Not Substantiated by 1927-1936 Performance." *Annalist,* October 1937, 533, 547.

Fraine, Harold G., and Robert H. Mills. "Effects of Defaults and Credit Deterioration on Yields of Corporate Bonds." *Journal of Finance,* September 1961, 423-34.

Fridson, Martin S. *High Yield Bonds: Identifying Value and Assessing Risk of Speculative Grade Securities.* Chicago: Probus Publishing, 1989.

——. "What Went Wrong with the Highly Leveraged Deals? (Or, All Variety of Agency Costs)." *Journal of Applied Corporate Finance,* fall 1991, 57-67.

Hickman, W. Braddock. *Corporate Bond Quality and Investor Experience.* Princeton, NJ: Princeton University Press, 1958.

Jefferis, Richard H., Jr. "The High-Yield Debt Market: 1980 1990." *Economic Commentary.* Federal Reserve Bank of Cleveland, 1 April 1990, 1-6.

Lederman, Jess, and Michael P. Sullivan, eds. *The New High Yield Bond Market: Investment Opportunities, Strategies, and Analysis.* Chicago: Probus Publishing, 1993.

Maloney, Kevin J., Richard J. Rogalski, and Lakshmi Shyam-Sunder. "An Explanation for the Junk Bond Risk/Return Puzzle." *Working Paper.* Amos Tuck School of Business Administration, December 1992.

Odean, Kathleen. *High Steppers, Fallen Angels, and Lollipops.* New York: Dodd Mead, 1988.

Shulman, Joel, Mark Bayless, and Kelly Price. "The Influence of Marketability on the Yield Premium of Speculative Grade Debt." *Financial Management,* autumn 1993, 132-41.

Yago, Glenn. *Junk Bonds: How High Yield Securities Restructured Corporate America.* New York: Oxford University Press, 1991.

K

KOREA, DOING BUSINESS IN THE REPUBLIC OF

The Republic of Korea (South Korea) from the early 1960s through the mid-1990s was among the fastest-developing economies in the industrialized world. By the 1990s South Korea's **gross national product** was well over $290 billion annually, with an annual growth rate consistently maintained for three decades at over 8 percent. In 1962 South Korea's total export of goods was a mere $60 million; by 1993 its exports had reached $82 billion. The South Korean general business climate thus was arguably among the most favorable in the world.

South Korea began its economic climb by concentrating on straightforward industries with little value added, such as textile and plastics. As the economy grew in the 1970s, South Korean companies began to shift to heavy industries such as shipbuilding and steel. By the 1980s the economy was fully industrialized, and South Korean firms became world leaders in a range of products from microwaves and televisions to automobiles and major home appliances. By the early 1990s South Korean firms expanded vigorously into high technology products, for example, taking the world leadership in DRAM (dynamic random access memory) chips.

As Korea's economy grew, however, so did the demands of its labor market. As Korea's authoritarian government began to loosen its grip in the late 1980s, Korea's **labor unions** became more active, gaining benefits for their members through highly effective strikes. In 1989, for example, manufacturing labor costs rose 25 percent. This in turn raised overall manufacturing costs, and manufacturers began to leave Korea in order to seek lower manufacturing costs. They took advantage of the comparatively inexpensive labor pool elsewhere in Asia, notably the People's Republic of China and Indonesia.

To counter its loss of labor-intensive manufacturing jobs, South Korean firms invested heavily to provide cutting-edge technology. As a result, in 1996, South Korea officially became the 29th member of the **Organisation for Economic Co-operation and Development**. This brought South Korea out of the category of developing nation and fully into **competition** with the major industrial nations of Western Europe, North America, and Japan. This heavy investment in state-of-the-art capital goods and equipment, however, came with a heavy price attached. By 1995 Korea's current account deficit had reached just under $9 billion, and its terms of trade took a sharp downward turn in 1996, adding to a current account deficit of $23.7 billion. This, in turn, made South Korea particularly vulnerable to any economic downturn.

SOUTH KOREA AND THE EAST ASIAN ECONOMIC CRISIS

When Thailand's currency collapsed in July 1997, South Korea was largely unprepared for the economic maelstrom into which it was pulled along with the rest of East Asia's major economies. South Korea's companies had remained competitive not only by maintaining state-of-the-art technology funded by high levels of foreign debt, but by keeping **profit margins** to a minimum. This policy was sustainable only for a rapidly growing economy, which Korea had, in all fairness, come to expect after 35 years of consistently high annual growth.

Nevertheless, under these conditions, even a minor economic downturn would have created great instability in Korea, and the Asian economic crisis of 1997 was anything but minor. In the last two quarters of the year, the won (Korea's currency) sank to half its precrisis value against the U.S. dollar. Even more staggering, in the last six months of 1997, total stocks listed on the Korean stock exchange lost a full 40 percent of their value, for a loss of $60 billion.

The result was a torrent of corporate bankruptcies and the weakening of even Korea's strongest *chaebol* (giant trading company). These, in turn, caused a near collapse of South Korea's banking industry. To counter this, the South Korean government orchestrated a $53 billion restructuring of the nation's financial institutions. One year following the beginning of the crisis, South Korea saw the closure of 5 commercial **banks**, 16 merchant banks, 10 leasing firms, 6 security companies, 4 life insurance companies, and 2 trust-investment firms. Additionally, Korea's unemployment rate nearly quadrupled from roughly 2 percent at the time the crisis began in July 1997 to 7.6 percent a year later in July 1998.

Faced with the threat of near total economic collapse, South Korea turned to the **International Monetary Fund** (IMF). In late 1997 the IMF put together a $60 billion package for South Korea. The initial results of the bailout seemed favorable. In 1998 Korea's trade surplus reached a record high point of $40 billion, a dramatic contrast to 1997's $8 billion **trade deficit**. Still, as the decade closed, South Korea's economy faced a difficult road to full recovery.

OVERVIEW OF THE KOREAN ENVIRONMENT FOR BUSINESS

The success of South Korea's economy during its 35-year climb to success, from the 1960s until the economic crisis of 1997, is all the more noteworthy since the Korean peninsula has very few natural resources and the Republic of Korea is among the most densely populated of nations. South Korea is an extremely crowded country. The entire nation—including Cheju Island in the East China Sea—is only 38,316 square miles, an area that would fit easily into the state of Kentucky. Crowded into this area are more than 42 million people, well over ten times Kentucky's population.

The extreme population density is made even more a factor by the fact that 80 percent of the country is heavily mountainous, providing difficulties for farming and transportation. These rugged regions remain relatively sparsely populated. By contrast (and in part as a result), roughly three-fourths of the country's people live in urban areas. Indeed, nearly one in every four South Koreans lives in the capital city of Seoul—which has a population of just less than 11 million people. Chief among the other major cities are Pusan (4 million people), Taegu (2.2 million), and Inchon, Kwangju, and Taejon, each with well over 1 million people.

The Republic of Korea consists of roughly the lower 45 percent of the Korean Peninsula in northeastern Asia. At its furthest point, South Korea comes within less than 50 miles from Japan's Tsushima Islands in the Strait of Korea, and within approximately 120 miles of the main Japanese island of Honshu. Dividing the peninsula about 600 miles from the tip to the north is the approximately 150-mile long demilitarized zone that has separated the Republic of Korea from the hostile Democratic People's Republic of Korea (communist North Korea).

HISTORY OF SOUTH KOREA

Korea has a long and ancient history. The region was inhabited as early as 3000 B.C. The state of Chosen, occupying a major portion of the peninsula, was well established by the fourth century B.C. During the first century B.C., the numerous tribes of Korea centralized into three kingdoms. By the late seventh century A.D. the three kingdoms had united through a series of wars under the kingdom of Silla, which lasted roughly until the late eighth century A.D. During this period, both Buddhism and Confucianism took firm root in Korea and the foundation of much of modern Korean culture was laid. By the early ninth century A.D., Silla weakened by provincial rebellions, again divided into three—a period known as the Later Three Kingdoms. These three kingdoms were again reunited under the Koryo dynasty in A.D. 935. It was this dynasty that gave the country its English name. Four centuries later, following internal reforms, the Koryo dynasty was supplanted by the Yi dynasty, which ruled Korea through 26 monarchs from its founding in 1392 until the Japanese conquest of Korea in 1910. Korea was liberated from Japan by Allied forces following World War II.

In 1948 Korea was divided into a communist North and a noncommunist South. The Korean War broke out in 1950 after North Korea invaded South Korea in an attempt to reunify the country. The war—never officially ended—established a cease-fire and a demilitarized zone that has divided the two Koreas since 1953. In 1991 North and South Korea set up their first commercial relations, but continuing tensions in the 1990s regarding the development of nuclear weapons in North Korea and the death in July 1994 of Kim Il Sung (the first and until his death only chairman of the North Korean Communist Party) have lent a degree of political instability to the peninsula as a whole.

POLITICAL AND ECONOMIC STRUCTURES

South Korea is a republic. The Constitutional Referendum of 1980 established what is generally called the Fifth Republic. The basic model for the republic is the U.S. tripartite system of government with a separate executive branch led by a president, a legislative branch in the form of the National Assembly, and a judiciary branch with a supreme court. While the Republic of Korea is a democracy, the Democratic Justice Party (formerly the Democratic Republican Party) has held power since it was established in 1963. Trends toward a greater freedom in election results were seen in the December 1992 election. In that election—following a series of scandals connecting government, military, and major business leaders—South Korea elected to the presidency Kim Young Sam, an outspoken dissident with no previous ties to the military.

In February 1998, amidst the worst of the Asian Economic Crisis, South Korea maintained its commitment to increased liberalization, electing to the presidency Kim Dae-Jung. It is significant that Kim Dae-Jung did not use the crisis as an excuse to reimpose more authoritarian rule on Korea. As a result, despite the economic disaster the country faced in the first years of his presidency, Kim Dae-Jung maintained approval ratings as high as 80 percent.

Still, the government of South Korea has had and continues to have a strong influence on business development in the nation. Beginning in the 1960s the government of South Korea began to formulate an industrial policy by which it established target industries and even target companies. These target industries and companies received special aid from the government to help nurture their growth. Under both Presidents Park Chung Hee and Chun Doo-Hwan, five-year plans were established to ensure the economic well-being of these companies through **subsidies**, tax relief, and protective tariffs. These policies contributed in part to the subsequent success of the Korean giant trading companies or *chaebols.* Following the economic crisis, the South Korean government forced the restructuring of the financial industry of the nation. More importantly, the government has forced the great *chaebols* to concentrate more on core businesses, pressured them to trade less profitable divisions among themselves to consolidate, and banned their practice of maintaining mutual **debt** payment guarantees among *chaebol* member firms.

THE CHAEBOL

South Korean business is dominated by a collection of industrial groups whose corporate organization is unique to Korea. These industrial groups are known as *chaebols.* Richard M. Steers, Yoo Keun Shin, and Gerardo R. Ungson defined the Korean *chaebol* as ''a financial clique consisting of varied corporate enterprises engaged in diverse businesses and typically owned and controlled by one or two interrelated family groups.'' Steers, Shin, and Ungson indicated that there are six main characteristics of the *chaebol:* (1) family control and **management**, (2) paternalistic leadership, (3) centralized planning and coordination, (4) an entrepreneurial orientation, (5) close business-government relations, and (6) strong school ties in hiring policies.

Currently there are roughly 50 *chaebols* in Korea of varying strength and size. Over 60 percent of South Korea's gross national product (GNP) comes from the largest five of these: Samsung, Hyundai, the LG Group (formally the Lucky-Goldstar Group), Daewoo, and Sunkyong.

Chaebols consist of numerous companies tied together by internal affiliations, shared boards, and family connections. This federation of interrelated companies is often difficult to understand in the Americas and Europe since no counterparts exist in those regions.

For example, Samsung, the largest *chaebol,* consists of over 30 individual enterprises, each of which would be considered an independent company in the United States. Some of these Samsung ''firms'' are publicly held and others are privately held. The enterprises themselves cover an enormous array of industrial areas ranging from Samsung Electronics (the second-largest semiconductor manufacturer worldwide) to insurance companies (Samsung Life Insurance, Ankuk Fire & Marine Insurance); from shipbuilding to petrochemicals, and so on.

The other *chaebols* are similar in organization both in the number of affiliated companies and in the diverse sectors in which their affiliated firms are involved. Thus the LG Group consists of nearly 40 firms ranging from consumer electronics to financial services to oil refineries. The Hyundai group consists of over 25 member companies ranging from automobile to elevator manufacturing. Daewoo has more than 20 firms in its family of companies—ranging from overseas construction projects to heavy equipment manufacturing and personal **computer** production.

CONDUCTING BUSINESS IN KOREA

LANGUAGE. Korean, the language of Korea, is limited to Korea and has few cognates with Western languages. As a result, many Korean businesspeople are accustomed to Westerners being unable to speak Korean. English is spoken by many educated Koreans, and due to favorable ties to the United States both in trade and militarily, the use of English is often well-received. Nonetheless, the businessperson unable to understand Korean is at a severe disadvantage in Korea. As Boye DeMente observed, the businessperson "who does not learn Korean is greatly limited in both his professional and social contacts in Korea. Those who cannot communicate at all in Korean are severely handicapped in their ability to relate to and participate in life outside the confines of the foreign community and world of international business."

Korean itself as a language has several factors affecting translation into Western languages. For example, the language reinforces hierarchical differences that are untranslatable. The businessperson unable to understand Korean therefore misses both subtle clues to levels of respect directed toward him or her, and the hierarchy established among the Koreans with whom the business is conducted.

Koreans also share the same family names in numbers virtually inconceivable in Western languages. Fifty percent of all Koreans share the same family names: Pak or Park, Lee, Choi, and Kim. The need to memorize a business partner's full name, therefore, becomes a necessity. This situation takes on even more importance when one considers the importance of family ties in hiring in many Korean companies.

GENDER ROLES. Gender roles remain traditionally differentiated along Confucian lines in Korea. Korean women, consequently, are rarely in positions of importance in government or business. Increasingly, Korean women are receiving employment in Western companies, although their role in interacting with Korean men in Korea remains subject to socially learned value systems. Western women are also subject to these traditional attitudes as well, although significantly less so than are Korean women. To some extent, as more and more Western businesswomen play an active role in Korean business with foreigners, they are afforded what amounts to a third gender status outside of the traditional male-female dichotomy.

CONTEXTING. Korea is what is called a high-context culture. As a result, Koreans place a strong emphasis on how a message is said rather than on just the words used. Messages are understood in terms of the full context of the communicators' relationship with one another. This particularly affects the importance for social etiquette and formality in official situations (including business meetings) and creates an emphasis on face-saving.

As a direct consequence of the high-context nature of Korean communication, it is necessary to build a personal relationship in conducting business with Koreans. Without the context of that personal relationship, little if any substantive communication can take place, and necessary levels of trust are inadequate to undertake most business arrangements.

As in most high-context cultures, Korean behavior is more likely to be governed by individual interpretation and the need to save face rather than on external rules and regulations. As a result, in Korea, personal understandings are more binding than **contracts**. Indeed, contracts in Korea are often seen as the beginning of a relationship that can be modified as the business progresses. This contrasts with the view of low-context cultures (such as the United States) in which the contract is viewed as not subject to change.

Finally, in high-context societies, understood or unofficial rules are often as (or even more) important as written rules. This holds true even in relations with government officials. These unwritten rules, called *naekyu* in Korean, are subject to the context of the situation to which they are applied. As a result, *naekyu* may be employed in some instances and overlooked in others, depending on the context of the individuals involved and of the situation particular to the incident at hand.

STATUS AND AUTHORITY CONCEPTION. Status differences are strongly recognized in Korea. These differences are reinforced through language and traditional Confucianist views of authority as well as such factors as place of education, rank in the organization, and family **wealth**. Acknowledging differences in rank, showing respect for titles and other symbols of authority, and acting appropriately to one's own social class are important in conducting business in Korea. Foreigners, including those from ostensibly egalitarian societies, are not exempt from these standards, although most foreign business executives are perceived as belonging to the upper-middle or higher class.

NONVERBAL COMMUNICATION. Because face-saving is so important and because contexting is so high, considerable emphasis is placed on nonverbal cues in Korean business communication. *Nunch'i* or the reading of facial expression is particularly important to determine negative reactions or reservations regarding a proposal. This is because the fear of making another person lose face in Korea makes most Korean businesspeople very hesitant about openly saying something disagreeable or unpleasant.

LEGAL CONSIDERATIONS. The framework of Korea's modern legal system was laid out under the Japanese occupation of the first part of the 20th century. Like Japan, South Korea follows the civil and commercial codes of Continental Europe. As with other civil codes in Japan and Europe, Korea's civil code is comprised of general legal principles and is subject to considerably more interpretation by courts than the case law system of common law practice in the United States. Unlike older civil code countries, however, South Korea's post-occupation Civil Code was officially only put into place in 1960. This poses additional difficulties. As Kyu Wha Lee noted, "Korean courts and lawyers must interpret the laws based on only some 30 years of modern Korean legal history and a sparse body of either case decisions or commentaries by legal scholars.'' As a result, as Lee concluded, ''from an American viewpoint, it may create an impression of too little predictability in the interpretation of laws.''

Additionally, as with many high-context cultures, Korean laws are not as strictly consistent or enforceable as in low-context cultures. This is reinforced by the Confucian tradition in which lawsuits are generally brought as a last resort; most conflicts are expected to be resolved outside of the courts. As DeMente pointed out, ''Lawyers in Korea do not look upon themselves as owing their primary allegiance to a client . . . they put the welfare of Korean society in general (and by extension, the country itself) above the interests of their clients.'' Lawyers in Korea are peacemakers and maintainers of harmony rather than client advocates.

CONCLUSION

The Republic of Korea maintains consulates and trade advisories in most Western nations. Many Western nations additionally maintain **chambers of commerce** and trade consulates in South Korea. The Republic of Korea's Ministry of Trade and Industry maintains a Korean Trade Promotion arm and the Korean Chamber of Commerce and Industry, both useful to foreign business involved in South Korea. Finally, many other organizations exist that can help the new business in Korea, such as the nonprofit Korean-American Business Institute. These organizations may be contacted for a more thorough follow-up to this brief introduction.

SEE ALSO: Cross-Cultural/International Communication

[David A. Victor]

FURTHER READING:

Biggart, Nicole Woolsey. ''Deep Finance: The Organizational Bases of South Korea's Financial Collapse.'' *Journal of Management Inquiry* 7, no. 4 (December 1998): 311-20.

DeMente, Boye. *Korean Etiquette and Ethics in Business.* 2nd ed. Lincolnwood, IL: NTC Business Books, 1994.

Ehrlich, Craig P., and Jay K. Lee. ''Governance of Korea's Chaebols: Role in Crisis, Coming Changes.'' *East Asian Executive Reports* 20, no. 3 (15 March 1998): 9, 23.

Lee, Kyu Wha. ''International Business Negotiations in Korea.'' In *The ABA Guide to International Business Negotiations,* edited by J. R. Silkenat and J. M. Aresty. Chicago: American Bar Association, 1994, 157-63.

Steers, Richard M., Yoo Keun Shin, and Gerardo R. Ungson. *The Chaebol: Korea's New Industrial Might.* New York: Harper & Row/Ballinger, 1989.

Victor, David A. *International Business Communication.* New York: HarperCollins, 1992.

L

LABELING

SEE: Packaging

LABOR ECONOMICS

Labor economics is the branch of economics that studies the nature and determinants of employment and compensation. Particular emphasis is placed on the role played by social institutions and different types of market structures that jointly determine the pattern and mobility or speed of adjustment in the labor market where human labor inputs are bought and sold.

Labor markets are relatively slow to adjust in comparison to those markets for nonlabor inputs and **commodities**. For reasons best attributed to human behavior, worker movement from relatively low wage areas to high-wage locations is sluggish. Worker retraining aimed at eliminating wage differentials also requires a substantial amount of time, which is generally not the case for nonlabor inputs and commodities. As a result, the duration of wage differentials has tended to outlast those of other price differentials.

Another prominent distinction exists between internal and external labor markets. Internal labor markets refer to the determinants of pay and employment within a firm, while external labor markets refer to the determinants of pay and employment between firms or within and across industries. Many labor economists place substantial theoretical weight on these distinctions when trying to explain how labor markets work. As to the question of which type is more efficient or inefficient in the allocation of labor however, unanimity has been absent.

GENERAL OVERVIEW

Almost from its inception (and especially during the post-World War II period), the analytical scope of labor economics mushroomed far outside the domain of traditional economics, making it a difficult field to define in a strict economic sense. Many labor economists caution that the word ''labor'' should not be understood as exclusively linked to the discipline of ''economics.'' Instead, they advocate a more interdisciplinary approach that draws critically from insights provided by the disciplines of sociology, political science, psychology, and organizational theory and behavior. As a result, labor economics has concerned itself with a large range of topics, including race and gender discrimination; labor-management relations; demographic economics; personal or social expenditures on education, medical care, and training (referred to as human capital investments); and a multitude of issues surrounding behavior in the workplace, a subject area germane to industrial and human relations schools.

During the last two decades of the 20th century labor economics has been preoccupied with the problem of understanding and reversing a general economic productivity slowdown in the United States. As a proposed solution, a majority of labor economists and concerned others have recommended the widespread implementation of a ''new'' set of nonadversarial, democratic workplace industrial relations called labor-management cooperation schemes. Largely influenced by ideas gleaned from producer cooperative theory, future workplace relations under these schemes will be designed to "empower" workers in all facets of a firm's activities.

To solicit their participation in these new schemes, workers have been offered more than a token voice in shaping company policy, along with the right to exercise higher-level decision-making responsibilities formerly reserved for upper management. Labor-management schemes are also supposed to substantially reduce overall unit labor costs by eliminating management surveillance designed to detect on-the-job shirking. On the other hand, workers are expected to forego a rigid job classification system, and corresponding wage structure, and agree in turn to a more flexible job-assignment environment. The compelling argument is that worker satisfaction and motivation will increase with the challenge of learning and mastering new jobs, as opposed to the older environment of routine jobs that tended to lower morale over time. For unionized workplaces, this also means eliminating the traditional grievance procedures handled by elected union representatives in favor of nonelected joint labor-management committees that no longer have the option of turning to outside arbitrators to settle disputes.

Labor-management cooperation schemes are theoretically designed to flatten decision making so as to improve communication and spread technical knowledge without supervisory surveillance. Workers, imbued with a greater sense of self-determined voice and responsibility, should come to associate their own work efforts with their firm's success, from which individual or team rates of pay will be calculated. The influence of a more flexible job structure conducted according to democratic principles was expected to impart a long-term positive influence on productivity, but there have been problems after cooperation schemes were implemented. Because this new set of workplace relations often blurs the established, legally recognized separation between worker and management functions, a legal question has developed concerning whether these new types of relations are tantamount to "company unions," which are illegal under the National Labor Relations Act. Unions and management continue to struggle with this new environment.

TWO PREVAILING THEORIES

Up until the period of the Great Depression and World War II, the study of labor economics was confined to the dominant orthodox framework of pure neoclassical economic theory. Analytical concepts familiar to micro and macroeconomists were the guiding precepts. A fundamental theoretical conclusion emerged which held that in a labor market where the competitive forces of supply and demand operated, a uniform industry-wide wage would prevail for laborers with similar skill or occupational characteristics. Any aberrations were thought to be short-lived and generally dismissed. This established theory remained unquestioned until a comprehensive empirical research project conducted by the War Labor Board yielded opposite conclusions. It found that wage rates for similar occupations varied greatly within and across many of the same labor markets. The most ironic finding of the report involved unions. According to established theory, the forces of free competition were thought to be least active in unionized labor markets, which represented the antithesis of neoclassical free competition. The study showed that, in reality, it was only in these unionized markets that anything approaching a uniform industry wage prevailed. Faced with this split between reality and theory, postwar labor economics developed into two schools of thought. The orthodox neoclassical school continued to push ahead with the development of theoretical models, while the institutionalist school conducted empirical research whose results typically clashed with the prevailing conclusions reached by theorists. The following sections will explore the history of the theoretical movement and then detail the key institutionalist beliefs.

HISTORY OF THE THEORETICAL SCHOOL

Labor economics as a separate branch of economics emerged out of the political turmoil swirling around two major theoretical traditions and their competing theories of wage determination. On one side stood classical political economy, on the other neoclassical or marginalist political economy. In general, answers to two key questions divide the two traditions. First, do capitalist market forces function to guarantee that workers will receive their "fair share" of the output they generate? Second, if not, is it possible through collective/union efforts to gain a larger share, given the constraints imposed by capitalist market forces?

Classical political economy, which flourished and dominated the field of economic theory and analysis from the 18th century until the middle of the 19th, would have answered no to the first question and, under certain conditions, yes to the second. The field found its most cogent expression in Adam Smith's (1723-1790) *Wealth of Nations* in 1776, which is popularly demarcated as the founding work of modern political economy. The tradition extended through other major figures such as David Ricardo (1772-1823) and Karl Marx (1818-83); these three brought the field to its highest development. Marx developed his labor theory of value and exploitation to demonstrate how workers received only a portion of their product, with the remainder forming an economic surplus appropriated by capitalists for the maintenance of their consumption and investment activities.

For reasons more political than economic, neoclassical theory displaced classical political economy in the 1870s, and has remained the dominant framework for conducting formal economic analysis ever since. The works of utilitarian social philosopher Jeremy Bentham (1748-1832), were highly influential in the formation of early neoclassical economics. Bentham maintained that all human motivation could be reduced to a single principal: the individual's desire to maximize utility or satisfaction. Contrary to the class-conflict conclusions reached by classical political economy, **utilitarianism** espoused an economic doctrine of class harmony where the satisfaction of individual preferences informed all economic decisions. The appeal to class harmony resided in the ''rational'' notion that if capitalists and workers were brought to understand that they each received only a portion of what they had jointly created, then social justice would prevail. Several early attempts at constructing an economic theory of value and exchange on the basis of a utilitarian approach failed. Only with the separate publication of economic texts by William Stanley Jevons (1835-82) and Carl Menger in 1871, and by Leon Walras three year later, did neoclassical theory emerge as an internally coherent theoretical tradition. A short time later, the work of Alfred Marshall (1842-1924) provided additional support of neoclassical theory.

Neoclassical wage theory developed in response to Marx's critique and in reaction to a burgeoning, often hostile, trade union movement. Its overriding concern was to try to affirm that capitalist market forces were capable of paying workers their ''rightful share'' of the net product. With that in mind, John Bates Clark's influential book, *The Distribution of Wealth,* did just that. In his book, Clark argued that workers received wages that were equivalent to the value of their marginal labor product. From there, it followed that wage differentials simply reflected individual differences in skill and ability and the nonmonetary advantages and disadvantages between numerous jobs. Any of the factors that caused the productivity of labor to increase, thus shifting the demand curve for labor upwards, would be met with appropriate wage increases. Clark and other neoclassical labor economists concluded that Marx was wrong and that unions were unnecessary. In fact, they argued that successful union strategies that raised wages above the value of their marginal product would have a negative effect by lowering employment within unionized sectors while increasing the labor supply and lowering wages in nonunion sectors.

By the mid-1940s, neoclassical economists felt secure within their long-run equilibrium interpretation of wage determinants. At that time, however, empirical economists attempting to reconcile real-life labor market phenomena with neoclassical theory encountered unsettling data. When confronted by a growing number of studies suggesting flaws in their theories, neoclassical economists reacted by simply developing several ad hoc explanations to account for these exceptions. Empirical economists, on the other hand, found themselves shunning theoretical models constructed to guide them in their research. Without any theoretical structure to inform their work, they also resorted to ad hoc explanations. As a result a growing schism emerged within labor economics between theory and practice.

INSTITUTIONALIST LABOR ECONOMISTS

In order to address the widening gulf between theory and reality, a new breed of ''Institutionalist'' labor economists arose at the end of World War II. Recognition of four major economic developments largely explained why this happened. First, the disturbing impact of the Great Depression rattled every branch of economics related to the theories of pure competition and general equilibrium. Second, the publication of John Maynard Keynes's (1883-1946) *General Theory* and its insightful analysis of effective demand posed intriguing questions that were difficult to reconcile with standard neoclassical theory. Third, industrial unions were being formed at an unprecedented pace. Fourth, the development of the theory of imperfect competition in the 1930s seemed better suited to account for the fact that labor and capital markets reflected very large powerful bargaining units that were fewer in number, as opposed to the very large number of small powerless markets assumed by the neoclassical theory of perfect competition.

One of the earliest postwar institutionalists to attempt to explain inter-industry wage differentials based on real economic conditions was John Dunlop. In 1948, he proposed four reasons for their existence: unequal productivity levels; the proportion of labor to total costs; the relative degree or absence of competitive product market pressures; and an industry's changing skill and occupational composition of the workforce. Similar institutionalist studies soon followed. Though their points of emphasis varied, all those studies significantly departed from the prevailing neoclassical theory of perfect competition tied to marginal productivity.

Not content to sit on the sidelines, upholders of neoclassical orthodoxy criticized institutionalist theory on methodological grounds. Institutionalist theory, they claimed, was overly dependent on short- as opposed to long-run determinations. Institutionalists replied that orthodox neoclassical theory had yet to explain the widespread and persistent pattern of interindustry wage differentials between workers with nearly identical productivity characteristics, an undeniable fact uncovered repeatedly by institutionalist research.

Neoclassical theory appeared to be vindicated with the publication in 1964 of Gary Becker's book on human capital theory. Becker's human capital approach, for which he was awarded a Nobel Prize in economics in 1993, argued that workers could upgrade their economic status if they made the rational individual choice to invest in more education and skill training. Once completed, their marginal productivity would increase and competitive pressures within the labor market would operate to raise their income. If they chose to do otherwise, it signaled that they somehow preferred the existing distribution of wages and were willing to live with its consequences, no matter how inequitable. Armed with human capital theory, confident neoclassical labor economists entered the realm of empirical research intent on explaining the persistence of inter- and intra-industry differentials among workers with identical productive characteristics. They anticipated the restoration of marginal productivity theory to its former prominence, arguing that wage differentials simply reflected individual differences in skill and effort, hence productivity. Liberal economists also jumped on the bandwagon, viewing human capital theory as a means for justifying larger government expenditures on training programs for the poor and disadvantaged.

Not long after the rise of human capital theory, real problems revealed its promises to be empty. Despite human-capital-inspired government programs, the continued fragmentation of the economy into low- and high-wage sectors proved intractable, as did wage differentials between black and white, and male and female workers. According to the logic of human capital theory, the economy's competitive pressures should have operated to eliminate those discriminatory forces, yet with the passage of time they had grown more pronounced. Closer empirical scrutiny of human capital theory raised serious questions concerning the use of average years of schooling as the critical variable used to explain wage differentials. Other factors such as large-scale manufacturing, on-the-job training, and reliance upon studies that separated production from skilled workers offered more credible explanations.

The early 1970s saw another institutionalist theoretical upsurge intended to explain the persistence of race and gender wage discrimination and the growth of a newly emergent "working poor" category. Reviving and building upon a previous institutionalist concept of internal labor markets (ILMS), two "new institutionalist" labor economists, Peter Doeringer and Michael Piore (1942-), led the effort to tackle those issues. They emphasized two major theoretical issues pertinent to ILMS theory: the growth of job-specific skill training and the notion of a modern "dual economy." In support of their job-specific skill approach, they argued that the development of large manufacturing firms provided the impetus for stable internal labor markets. So structured, firms could minimize the rising costs associated with skill training and worker turnover. Being somewhat sheltered from competitive external labor market pressures, firms could develop mutually beneficial internal job ladders. These would allow experienced workers to reap seniority benefits, be more inclined to stay within the firm, and train new workers.

Advancing a more detailed version of the dual economy approach first put forward by Robert Averits in 1968, Piore and Doeringer also argued that the labor market was divided into a primary and secondary market. Jobs in primary markets were distinguished by sophisticated technologies, skilled and semi-skilled labor, high wages, good working conditions, chances for advancement, employment stability, fairness, and due process in the administration of work rules. On the other hand, jobs in the secondary markets were subject to external competitive pressures; lacked technological sophistication; were performed by unskilled labor; and featured low wages, little or no fringe benefits, high labor turnover, absenteeism and tardiness, higher levels of petty theft, little chance of advancement, and typically autocratic and capricious supervisors.

Proponents of ILMS argued that the existence of dual labor markets, especially its primary component, did not fit well within the orthodox model of pure competition determining wages. The idea that labor mobility would lead to a reduction in wage differentials was flawed, if not altogether wrong, because of the discriminatory barriers that faced blacks, other ethnic minorities, and women. When it came to the subject of unions however, Piore and Doeringer's ILMS model encountered difficulty in explaining how supposedly secondary labor markets were able to transform themselves into primary markets through unionizing efforts. Nor were they ever able, like older institutionalist labor economists, to ultimately reject the overriding authority of marginal productivity theory.

In the more liberal academic environment of the 1970s, radical and Marxian ideas began to spread in labor economics. Drawing upon a rich historical legacy of industrial organization under capitalism, Harry Braverman's groundbreaking 1974 publication, *Labor and Monopoly Capital,* painstakingly detailed the de-skilling effects of modern capitalism. Consistent with Karl Marx, Braverman argued that this course was undertaken so that capitalist-inspired management could take control of the labor process away from skilled workers in order to raise the level of exploitation. Influenced by Braverman, many radicals took issue with the assumed connection between highly capital-intensive modern technology and the high skill levels said to be found in the high-wage primary labor markets, which was a primary part of the dual labor market theory. Others rejected the harmonious view of the labor process held by the new institutionalist school, especially when frequent strikes and productivity slowdowns seemed to indicate a lack of harmony. Most radical labor market theorists did not entirely reject new institutionalist reasoning, however. Instead, they insisted that dual market structures arose from class struggle over the internal organization of the labor processes. They called this labor segmentation theory.

Though essentially restatements of imperfect competition theories from the 1930s, the new Marxist and radical versions of monopoly capital were advanced to explain how market power served to prop up long-standing, above-average rates of profit. These rates were considered to be the sustaining lifeblood separating high-wage, primary markets from low-wage secondary markets. Interestingly, while reviving the importance of class struggle (once the centerpiece of classical political economy), many radicals were either ignorant of, or rejected outright, Marx's theory of the law of value. Marx considered this law as absolutely critical—it held the key to understanding the objective limits of a theory of inter and intra-industry profit and wage differentials tied to his dynamic theory of capitalist accumulation. With the lone exception of Howard Botwinick's contribution, *Persistent Inequalities,* no radical or Marxian work in labor economics has systematically broken away from the underpinnings of neoclassical theory, in either its perfect or imperfect versions, to formulate a theory of wage differentials consistent with Marx's law of value.

Leftist criticisms of radical segmentation theory were several. On theoretical grounds, it was argued that segmentation theory was overly dependent upon ad hoc explanations and lacked theoretical clarity. Even results from empirical studies were contradictory, indicating that overall patterns of working class division and segmentation were broadly diffused, tending to transcend neatly compartmentalized boundaries. This was true not only for the United States, but especially in Europe where significant numbers of immigrants gained entrance into primary labor markets in Germany, France, and Italy instead of entering the secondary markets as segmentation theory would have expected. Moreover, when it came to the historical development of dual economic structures, more attention was paid to capitalist' s motivations than to those of workers, especially unionized ones.

Beginning in the late 1970s, primary sector industries such as the automobile and steel industries suffered huge losses and went through periods of labor upheaval. In response to falling profit rates, which were once virtually guaranteed by near monopoly power, former primary market high-wage firms were behaving much like secondary ones. Tactics included forcing concessions in wage and working conditions, threatening to or actually relocating firms to low-wage areas, defeating strikes through the use of ''scab'' labor as permanent striker replacements, actively lobbying for passage of trade pacts that threatened high wages, and instituting two-tier wage packages for the same job.

Faced with these difficulties and criticisms, many radical labor economists unceremoniously abandoned ship. Indeed, by the 1990s, many leading radical proponents were no longer touting class struggle as a determinant factor. They had instead joined forces with the orthodox consensus on the need for joint labor-management schemes designed to counter the slowdown in productivity.

A NEW THEORY DEVELOPS

As the 20th century came to a close, a development called ''efficiency wage theory'' was gaining popularity. Efficiency wage theory was initiated by neoclassically oriented labor economists who acknowledge the failure of their traditional competitive framework to explain persistent real-world inter- and intra-industry wage differentials for workers with identical productive characteristics, as well as its inability to account for the growth of chronic unemployment. Efficiency wage theory has elicited considerable unanimity among the previously feuding groups of radical, institutional, and orthodox neoclassical labor economists.

Though many different versions abound, the central premise of efficiency wage theory is that the payment of wage rates above the assumed market equilibrium wage will result in a profit-maximizing outcome and permit capitalist firms to minimize total unit labor costs. Accordingly, above-equilibrium wage rates are thought to induce increased effort and productivity and a reduction in worker shirking; reduced turnover costs; perceived greater costs of termination; improved worker morale; and the attraction and retention of better quality personnel.

In the long run, if all firms pursue a similar higher-than-equilibrium wage strategy, unemployment will result. And neither is there reason for firms to lower wages, since this will slacken worker effort and increase unit labor costs. The prospect of an extended period of unemployment is posited as the safeguard against employee shirking. This approach to employee motivation, however, depends on the fostering of a long-time employer-employee relationship, which in turn creates a new set of factors for labor economists to consider.

Depending, then, on the conditions unique to each industry or firm, different levels of efficiency wages will be necessary so that workers with identical productive characteristics will not receive the same wage. With this logic in mind, orthodox labor economists apparently have a plausible answer to the puzzling question of how above-equilibrium wage firms manage to survive in a competitive economy.

SEE ALSO: Economic Theories

[Daniel E. King]

FURTHER READING:

Botwinick, Howard. *Persistent Inequalities: Wage Disparity Under Capitalist Competition.* Princeton, NJ: Princeton University Press, 1994.

Ehrenberg, Ronald G. *Modern Labor Economics: Theory and Public Policy.* 6th ed. Reading, MA: Addison-Wesley, 1997.

Lippit, Walter, ed. *Radical Political Economy.* Armonk, NY: M.E. Sharpe, 1996.

Reynolds, Lloyd George. *Labor Economics and Labor Relations.* 11th ed. Upper Saddle River, NJ: Prentice Hall, 1998.

Tilly, Chris. *Work Under Capitalism.* Boulder, CO: Westview Press, 1998.

LABOR FORCE

SEE: Human Capital; Intellectual Capital; Multicultural Workforce; Workforce

LABOR LAW AND LEGISLATION

Attempting to strike a balance between assuring fair and humane treatment of workers and micromanaging business affairs, labor legislation is one of the often contentious battlegrounds over which the interests of employees and employers are negotiated. For more than a century a virtual state of war existed between labor and employers. Not until 1935, when meaningful labor law was passed acknowledging the legal rights of independent union organizations, did a climate of relative industrial calm prevail.

Today, labor law and legislation remains a highly contentious and divisive issue, with neither side finding the status quo to their liking. Such partisanship has traditionally not confined itself only to the workplace but also permeates numerous areas of civil society such as academia, the legal profession, the courts, management associations, major media, editorial boards, and religious groups.

When discussing labor law, a critical distinction can be made regarding laws that are binding only on organized labor and those that apply to labor as whole, whether organized or not. For instance certain sections in the **Taft-Hartley Act** apply specifically to organized labor while sections of the Social Security Act of 1935 are enforced for all employees. In most (but not all) instances, organized labor in the 20th century has endorsed legislation aimed at covering all employees regardless of their organizational status. For example, organized labor has played an instrumental role in proposing, endorsing, and defending legislation meant to improve the general public welfare. These include: social security, Medicare and Medicaid, unemployment compensation, education funding, mine safety and health laws, black lung disability funds, parental leave, universal single-payer health insurance, occupational safety and health laws, minimum wage laws, civil rights legislation, and progressive tax law.

LABOR LAW REVIEW

Prior to the passage of comprehensive federal labor legislation in the 20th century, U.S. labor relations were regulated by state law. Laws governing labor relations were largely handled by state courts on a case-by-case basis. In legal terminology such a process of judicial decision making is referred to as "common law." On the other hand, laws made by state legislative bodies or administrative agencies are referred to as "statutory laws." Throughout most of the 19th century, common law rulings were upheld whenever they came into conflict with statutory decisions. Frequently any action taken on the part of workers to form a union was met with judicial hostility. Acting on an employer's request, judges were quick to issue labor injunctions. At the time, the prevailing judicial doctrine held that workers who formed organizations to better their working conditions were guilty of unlawful conspiracy charges.

Even as some state courts began to recognize the rights of workers to form organizations in the mid-19th century, the legal environment in which workers were allowed to operate was highly circumscribed. While some courts recognized the right of workers to strike, they also recognized the employer's right to continue operations using striker replacements (referred to by striking or unionized workers as "scabs"), along with the right of an employee to remain at work if he or she chose not to honor the strike. At the same time courts frequently issued labor injunctions prohibiting unions from peaceful picketing on the grounds that such actions interfered with the rights of the employer to continue operations. Under these terms the "right to strike" was seriously undermined if not rendered ineffective altogether.

The centerpiece of U.S. federal labor law is the National Labor Relations Act of 1935. The act was declared constitutional by the Supreme Court in 1937 and established employee rights and employer unfair labor practices. The **National Labor Relations Board (NLRB)** was established to administrate the NLRA. Its limited jurisdiction extends only to unfair labor practices and union elections covered in Sections 7-9 of the NLRA. In these matters it adheres to set procedures established by the statute and by regulations established by the board. Besides the NLRB, other government agencies play an important role in the administration of labor law. For instance, the U.S. Department of Labor administers portions of the Labor Management Reporting and Disclosure Act of 1959, the **Fair Labor Standards Act of 1938**, the Occupational Safety and Health Act of 1970, and the Employee Retirement Income Security Act of 1974 (ERISA). The **Equal Employment Opportunity Commission (EEOC)** administers Title VII (the statute regulating equal employment opportunity) of the Civil Rights Act, as well as the Equal Pay and Age Discrimination in Employment Acts.

The NLRB's Board has five members appointed by the president and confirmed by Senate vote. The president selects one of the five members to serve as chairperson subject to Senate confirmation. Each member serves five years; member appointments are staggered, and do not expire simultaneously. Along with the board, the statute set up a separate, independent general counsel, also appointed by the president subject to Senate approval for a four-year term. The relationship between the five member board and general counsel imitates that of prosecutor and judge in cases of unfair labor practice only (Section 8), where the board acts as judge and the general counsel as prosecutor. Matters related to election procedures (Section 9) are handled solely by the board and have nothing to do with the general counsel.

In 1947, under conservative political pressure, Congress passed the Taft-Hartley Act. In an attempt to redress the significant labor victories of Wagner, the Taft-Hartley Act, officially known as the Labor-Management Relations Act of 1947, dramatically altered the pro-labor provisions of the NLRA. Controversial aspects of this act are the statutory restrictions contained in Sections 8(b)(4) and 8(b)(7), which comprehensively regulate the right to engage in picketing. The U.S. Constitution permits a limited right to picket as a matter of free speech. But union challenges to overturn the LMRA's picketing statues have been unsuccessful. The courts have maintained that picketing is a form of action, not just speech, thus subject to regulation. The Supreme Court has upheld this argument and ruled that a union's right to picket is determined by the LMRA and not based on constitutional grounds.

Since the 1970s, U.S. union leaders and organizers have routinely voiced concerns about legal obstacles set up to discourage unionization. They are quick to mention that many companies that domestically oppose union organizing drives here have no trouble recognizing unions abroad at their foreign operations. Unfavorable comparisons between U.S. labor laws and those of other industrial democracies do not escape U.S. union advocates.

In mid- to late 1980s, during the Reagan and Bush administrations, pro-labor forces charged that the NLRB had become stacked with administration appointees intent on obstructing union certification campaigns. At first the Reagan administration practiced a policy of benign neglect. Over an extended period of time, cases piled up as vacant NLRB seats went unfilled. This added prolonged delays to a certification process that already worked to an employer's advantage. Moving from benign neglect to calculated activism, Reagan appointed four corporation lawyers and a chair to the board. Sounding very much like a throwback to the days when public officials were virtually indistinguishable from employers, they openly declared that "collective bargaining frequently means the destruction of individual freedom," that "unionized labor relations" figured as one of "the major contributors to the decline and failure of our healthy industries," and characterized strikes as "a concerted effort employing violence, intimidation and political intervention to prevent people who want to work from working." During the board's tenure, complaints against employers that were dismissed increased 300 percent while dismissed complaints filed against unions decreased 40 percent.

Indeed, by 1995, findings released by The Dunlop Commission, convened during the Clinton administration, confirmed this apparent anti-union bias. In the area of labor law, the commission reported the following: illegal firings occurred in one out of four union election campaigns compared to one in every twenty elections in the 1950s; only two-thirds of union-certified elections were recognized by employers agreeing to negotiate contracts, while employers incur no monetary penalty for refusing to engage in good faith bargaining; and, in general, recourse to legal relief through the courts was not an option for a majority of employees, whose low income levels precluded them from paying the high costs and contingency fees required by private lawyers.

PRE-NLRA HISTORY AND DEVELOPMENT

The history and development of U.S. labor law legislation based on independent and legally recognized union organizations divides into two periods—before and after the NLRA. In the pre-NLRA period, roughly 1800-1935, the dominant employer methods used to combat and deny the legal formation of independent unions took two forms: the threat or actual use of private and public armed force and espionage;

and employer recourse to a punitive legal system that served as little more than an appendage to employer property interests.

As early as 1806, Pennsylvania courts found cordwainers (shoemakers) guilty of a criminal conspiracy when they combined for the purpose of raising their wages. In 1842, the Massachusetts Supreme Court in *Commonwealth vs. Hunt* repealed criminal conspiracy laws imposed on unions, but left them with little room to function legally. Following the Civil War, especially during the period of a resurgent labor movement in the 1870s and 1880s, labor conspiracy prosecutions soared. These, along with the upsurge in labor injunctions, proved effective weapons by which employers thwarted the formation of a legally constituted labor movement. By the early 20th century, many state courts were in agreement over the individual laborer's uncontested ''right to strike.'' But then, echoing the 1906 opinion of the Massachusetts Supreme Court, state courts continued to declare many strikes illegal because of the ''increase in power which a combination of citizens has over the individual citizen.'' In short, in most instances a combination of workers was outlawed from doing what one individual worker could do alone.

The use of labor injunctions (a court order prohibiting numerous union actions) rose to prominence during the upsurge in labor activities during the late 1870s and the unrest that was to follow. Just before the Haymarket Square confrontation in 1886, the focal rallying point of one of the first genuine national strikes in U.S. labor history, union strength had reached an all-time high. Leading the way were the Knights of Labor, with more than 700,000 members.

The use of labor injunctions continued well past the 1880s. During the period of 1880-1930, 1,845 labor injunctions were handed down by federal and state courts. And, for approximately the last 10 years of this period, a total of 921 were issued. Among the more notable were the injunctions issued in 1919 during the miners' strike, in 1922 against the national railway shopmen's strike, and in 1922 during the United Mine Workers' campaign to organize West Virginia and Kentucky miners. During the entire period of strife, the U.S. Supreme Court steadfastly upheld injunctions served up by the lower courts.

The Sherman Antitrust Act of 1890 outlawed combinations in restraint of interstate trade and commerce including labor. The Sherman Act was invoked 12 times in the first seven years of its passage. It was first used on a national level in breaking the American Railway Strike of 1894. The courts ruled that the union's national strike in solidarity with the Pullman workers violated the Sherman Act. Injunctions were issued, the U.S. Army intervened, and eventually Eugene Debs and other strike leaders were imprisoned.

Between 1908 and 1914, the Sherman Act was used some 20 times. But on the eve of World War I, a respite arrived in the form of the Clayton Antitrust Act. It declared that ''the labor of a human being is not a commodity or article of commerce.'' Not long after the war's end, however, the courts ruled that the Clayton act did not prevent ''private parties'' from obtaining antitrust injunctions, only the federal government. As a result, antitrust actions against unions reached a new high in the 1920s. Unions and unionists were charged with some 72 violations. Nearly all the injunctions requested under law were obtained, and more than half of the cases resulted in convictions and lengthy prison terms.

Criminal prosecutions were meted out liberally during the 1920s and early 1930s. Felony charges typically included murder, riot, assault, criminal libel, unlawful assembly, malicious mischief, and sedition. Misdemeanor charges included trespassing, loitering, disorderly conduct, assembling without permit, and disturbing the peace. In many instances, hobos riding trains in search of work were charged with any one of these misdemeanors and then required to work for little or no pay as a punishment. In mining states like Idaho, Colorado, Montana, and West Virginia that were policed by national guard units, a person could be arrested without any charge save for ''military necessity'' and frequently held in prison for long periods of time.

From the 1900s to early 1930s, a common, legally sanctioned tactic was the discharge of an employee for union activities. It was used repeatedly by employers as a means of discouraging unionization. Some states eventually did make the tactic illegal, but courts routinely invalidated these laws. Early in the 1900s, federal legislation was passed that prohibited interstate carriers from discharging employees for union activities, but it was declared unconstitutional by the U.S. Supreme Court in 1908. Existing laws gave an employer the right to coerce or threaten employees who wanted a union. They also empowered an employer with the right to fire an employee that joined a union, to refuse to bargain with a union if it did exist, and the right to form a company union and force employees to join it. During this period arose the term ''yellow dog contract,'' which was a written, legally enforceable contract that forbade workers from joining unions. Most courts faithfully enforced these contracts. The penalty for violation was automatic dismissal, and, since the contract was legally binding, unions were outlawed from organizing yellow dog contract workers. With some success, unions agitated for legislation against yellow dog contracts. But, the U.S. Supreme Court struck down these laws with passage of the Norris-LaGuardia Act of 1932.

Prior to labor's formation of the Congress of Industrial Organizations (CIO) in 1932, it was not unusual for employers to finance their own private "armies" or else contract out services intent on crushing new labor organizations. Through mercenaries and spies, employer agencies engaged in subversion, violence, and deliberate lawbreaking. Upon infiltrating a union organization, employer agents identified union activists, gathered information on union organizing drives, fomented factional and ethnic strife among employees, and gained leadership positions with the intent of undermining other elected leaders. By assuming militant postures, these agents incited others to sabotage the union process or provoke violence in order to publicly discredit unions and invite employer retaliatory violence. Employers had no difficulty legally deputizing agents and mercenaries for strikebreaking and union-busting purposes.

Despite the scale and length of this war-like climate, no official casualty figures of those involved in labor disputes were ever kept, despite the fact that this was a time when the recording of statistics for all types of social and scientific phenomena was commonplace. However, one report, limited to reviewing newspaper coverage of strikes from 1877 to 1968, tallied 700 dead and thousands of others suffering serious injuries; the overwhelming majority the dead and injured were workers.

In 1912, the Congressional Commission on Industrial Relations investigated the activities of labor espionage agencies. A second investigation was conducted in the mid-1930s by the LaFollette Civil Liberties Committee of the U.S. Senate. Despite being conducted in two different time periods, both investigations uncovered similar patterns of corporate spying practices and private police activities. Their findings proved influential in framing the legal substance of what was soon to emerge as federal labor law.

In the pre-NLRA period employers also turned to public armed force as a means of intervening against labor unions. At times, because of a sanctioning legal system, the difference between private and public armed forces was indistinguishable. Intervention occurred from local and state police, sheriffs, deputies, state militia (later to be national guard units), and all branches of the U.S. armed forces, including air corps mobilization. The advantages gained by employer use of public force were several: in the eyes of the populace, public force struck a chord of legitimacy; they were empowered to arrest, jail, and punish strikers; and usually, but not always, being publicly financed and equipped for violence, such units were less costly to employers. At other times, employers used state militia that proved less than reliable due to lengthy call-up time and lack of loyalty. Most books dealing with labor history amply document the use of public armed forces to intervene in labor disputes. Even after the passage of NLRA, public armed forces were used in labor disputes although for different reasons. For example, President Richard Nixon used 30,000 federal and national guardsmen to replace postal workers during a 1970 strike and, 11 years later, President Reagan used military personnel to break the air controllers' strike.

Unlike past strikes, when public armed forces were used to break strikes by using their authority and violence, public forces were used in these two cases to maintain services that were deemed essential to the U.S. economy.

American labor began with the legal system clearly stacked against it. One historical study (as noted by Klaus van Beyme, 1980) analyzing comparative labor law legislation throughout Europe and the United States covering the same time period, concluded that, most often, U.S. employers "have made and enforced their own laws, acquired the services of public officials and law enforcement agents, resisted labor's claim to legal legitimacy, and assumed an imperial 'We are the law' posture."

THE NLRA AND ITS LEGISLATIVE AFTERMATH

Enacted during the later years of the Great Depression, the NLRA was prompted by a rising wave of labor union militancy and a sympathetic Roosevelt Administration. It is often referred to as the Wagner Act after the New York Senator who sponsored the legislation. The NLRA established employee rights to organize, join unions, and participate in collective bargaining or mutual aid activities. It also established unfair labor practices, making employer interference with an employee's right to join a union and participate in concerted union activities unlawful. By law, employers were obliged to bargain in good faith with the union and refrain from discharging or otherwise discriminating against workers due to their involvement in union activities. Prior to the NLRA's passage, workers secured bargaining rights in two ways: through a forced strike or recognition based on the voluntary approval of their employer. In matters related to the enforcement of labor law, Congress created the administrative agency of the NLRB in full recognition of the dismal historical performance of the common law courts. At the time this was unheard of, since enforcement of all earlier law had been solely the domain of the courts.

The Taft-Hartley Act, passed in 1947 over President Truman's veto, cited the restoration of "balance" and "individual rights over collective rights" to rationalize its revision of the NLRA's "unfair labor practices." As a result, the NLRA was officially renamed the Labor Management Relations Act. At the time of Taft-Hartley's passage, the United States was caught up in the hysteria of what came to be known as McCarthyism. The House's Dies Committee, later known as the House Un-American Activities Committee (HUAC), took seriously charges that the pro-labor LaFollette Civil Liberties Committee, communists, the CIO, the NLRB, and the Democratic National Committee had all conspired to engage (in the words of steel tycoon Tom Girdler) in a ''cold-blooded plot'' against business. Among one of its provisions was the requirement that union officers sign noncommunist loyalty oaths as a precondition for using the NLRB. Within the ranks of organized labor, a divisive factionalism resulted over how to best respond to the implementation of Taft-Hartley.

Out of such a political atmosphere did Taft-Hartley emerge. Its provisions prohibited unions from interfering with **employee rights**, from coercing or discriminating against employees through the unions' activities, and required union bargain in good faith. With respect to the employee rights provision, an employee could not be forced to engage in collective bargaining or any such union activities against their will. Subsequent restrictions on secondary boycotts and free speech and picketing were also an outgrowth of Taft-Hartley.

In 1959, Congress passed the next substantial piece of labor law legislation, the Landrum-Griffin Act. Named after its two Congressional co-sponsors, the legislation is formally called the Labor Management Reporting and Disclosure Act of 1959 and primarily governs internal union affairs. It established a ''Labor Bill of Rights'' for union members, such as internal union election procedures and reporting and disclosure stipulations for unions, union officers, and employers. It also added Section 8(e) to the LMRA, prohibiting ''hot cargo'' clauses whereby one employer was forbidden from dealing with other employers who were nonunion or on strike.

Soon to follow was passage of the Civil Rights Act of 1964. Under Title VII of the act, discriminatory wage differentials based on race, color, religion, sex, and national origin were prohibited. The Occupational Health and Safety Act (OSHA) was passed in 1970 to the applause of organized labor. Yet disillusionment with OHSA soon set in; both labor and management were critical of it, but for different reasons. For management, it was costly and overly regulatory. Labor complained that with fewer than 3000 inspectors available to visit five million places of work, each establishment would be inspected once every 75 years. At the same time, the average penalty per violation amounted to $25. In 1981, the Reagan administration cut the number of inspectors to 1,100. Exacerbating this trend in the 1980s, OSHA employed inspection procedures that provided incentives for employers to underreport injuries, and was known more generally as a ''hands-off'' agency. As a result, on-the-job injuries and lost work days rose substantially. Debate over the effectiveness and necessity of the OSHA, either as it exists now or altogether, is nowhere near settlement.

In 1974 Congress enacted the Employee Retirement Income Security Act (ERISA). With respect to private pension plans, ERISA was passed to curb administrative misuse and the discharge or permanent layoff of employees just prior to being vested. To further ensure that employees would receive retirement pension benefits, ERISA set up the employer-funded Public Benefit Guaranty Corporation government agency. In 1986 it guaranteed pensions up to $1,858 per month should the employer go out of business and/or terminate the plan.

In 1993, the Family and Medical Leave Act of 1993, endorsed by organized labor, finally became law. It permitted workers at firms of 50 or more employees to take up to 12 weeks of unpaid, but job-protected, leave for the birth or adoption of a child; the critical illness of a child, spouse, parent; or worker illness. In addition, health benefits would continue for the duration of the leave (if the worker had been receiving health benefits prior to the leave). By contrast, most workers in other advanced economies of the world have had this benefit (with pay and for longer periods) since at least World War II.

The Occupational Safety and Health Administration Compliance Assistance Authorization Act of 1998 amended the Occupational Safety and Health Act of 1970 (OSHA), calling on the Secretary of Labor to develop programs in cooperation with the states and allowing employers to consult with state officials about compliance with occupational safety and health requirements. The act requires states to provide on-site consultation, which must be independent of enforcement activities, upon employer request; such consultation, moreover, can exempt employers from certain types of inspection

Legislators sympathetic to labor causes have countered with measures seeking to provide workers with a greater deal of freedom and autonomy. The Right to Organize Act of 1999, introduced in the Senate in 1999, would amend the National Labor Relations Act (NLRA) to provide unions significant access to employers' facilities for purposes of the dissemination of information and other activities related to labor organizing. Furthermore, the act takes specific measures to prohibit employers from discharging employees for exercising rights protected under the NLRA. Whether or not this action results in a public law, it does demonstrate that the push and pull that has characterized labor legislation since the 1930s is hardly at an end.

[Daniel E. King]

FURTHER READING:

Feldacker, Bruce. *Labor Guide to Labor Law.* 3rd ed. Englewood Cliffs, NJ: Prentice-Hall, 1990.

Kaufman, Bruce, ed. *Government Regulation of the Employment Relationship.* Madison, WI: Relations Research Association, 1997.

Nelson, Daniel. *Shifting Fortunes: The Rise and Decline of American Labor, from the 1820s to the Present.* Chicago: Ivan R. Dee, 1997.

Van Beyme, Klaus. *Challenge to Power.* Beverly Hills, CA: Sage, 1980.

LABOR UNIONS

A labor union is an organization of wage earners or salary workers established for the purpose of protecting their collective interests when dealing with employers. Though unions are prevalent in most industrialized countries, and in many less developed countries, union representation of workers has generally declined in most countries over the past 30 to 40 years. For example, in the United States, unions represented about one-third of all workers in the 1950s. Today, unions represent only about 16 percent of the total labor force. There have also been significant declines in many of the Western European countries and in Japan. Countries where unions have maintained or increased strength include Canada, Germany, and some of the emerging economies of East and Southeast Asia. Although weakened in many areas, labor unions continue to be an important force in many aspects of the economy.

TYPES OF UNIONS

Unions can be categorized according to ideology and organizational forms. Ideology refers to the union's **goals** and objectives: what its members see as its mission. A distinction is often made between political unionism and ''bread and butter unionism'' (also termed business unionism). Although the goals and objectives of politically oriented unions may overlap those of business unions, political unions are primarily related to some larger working-class movement. Most political unions have some formal association with a working-class political party, usually socialist or Marxist.

Political unions range from those dedicated to revolutionary activity (rarely found today) to those seeking change through the electoral process (as in the case of labor unions associated with labor and social democratic parties in Western Europe). In most instances, politically oriented unions see fundamental conflicts between the interests of workers and the capitalist system. The more radical political unions may advocate nationalization of key industries and substantial limitations on free enterprise. In contrast, the mainstream political unions common in Western Europe advocate greater worker voice in business **decision making**. One example is the German codetermination system. This system requires, by law, the appointment of worker representatives to a company's **board of directors**. Companies in Germany must also establish **works councils**, which are shop-floor-level worker committees that provide input into organizational **problem solving** and decision making.

In contrast to Western Europe and a number of developing countries, contemporary American labor unions are best viewed as reflecting a business unionism ideology. Business unions generally support free market systems and focus their attention on protecting and enhancing the economic welfare of the workers they represent, usually through some form of collective bargaining. By law in the United States, unionized employers need only bargain with unions over wages, hours, and working conditions.

This does not mean that business unions are not involved in the political process. Most large national unions, as well as the American Federation of Labor and Congress of Industrial Organizations (AFL-CIO)—which is an association of national unions—are involved in lobbying and electoral activities at all levels of government. Such political efforts, however, serve to supplement their principal economic goals. Political objectives are usually reformist in nature. For example, many unions campaigned against passage of the **North American Free Trade Agreement** (NAFTA). The labor movement feared that NAFTA would undercut jobs of union workers and weaken the ability of unions to negotiate favorable **contracts** with employers. Although many American unions are active in the Democratic party, they are not formally affiliated with that party. In fact, some unions regularly support Republican candidates, including presidential candidates. Consequently, the political complexion of American labor unions is varied and driven primarily by economic concerns.

There are several different organizational forms characteristic of labor unions. The earliest unions in the United States were craft unions. Craft unions represent employees in a single occupation or group of closely related occupations. The members of craft unions are generally highly skilled workers. Examples of craft unions include the various skilled trades in the construction industry. Separate unions exist for each major skill (e.g., carpenters, electricians, plumbers). Craft unions are most common in occupations in which employees frequently switch employers. A construction worker is usually hired to complete work at a specific job site and then moves on to work elsewhere (often for another employer). In addition to collective bargaining, craft unions often serve as a placement service for members. Employers contact the union's hiring hall and union members currently out of work are referred to the job.

Closely related to craft unions, though distinct in many respects, are professional unions. A professional is generally understood to be an employee with advanced and highly specialized skills, often requiring some credential, such as a college degree and/or a license. Professional unions are much more recent than craft unions and are most common in the public sector. The American Federation of Teachers is one of the oldest professional unions. Many professional unions began as professional associations, then became more union-like in character (e.g., the National Education Association).

Most unionized workers in the United States belong to industrial unions. An industrial union represents workers across a wide range of occupations within one or more industries. A good example of a typical industrial union is the United Auto Workers (UAW). It represents skilled craft workers, assembly-line workers, and unskilled workers in all of the major American automobile companies. The UAW negotiates separate contracts for workers in each of these companies. Although most industrial unions began by organizing workers in a single industry or group of related industries, most have diversified over the past 30 to 40 years. For example, the UAW represents workers in the tractor and earth-moving equipment industry (e.g., Caterpillar and John Deere) and in the aerospace industry (e.g., Boeing Corporation).

Another organizational form is the general union. General unions organize workers across all occupations and industries. Although some highly diversified unions, such as the Teamsters, appear to be general unions, this form of organization does not really exist in the United States. Because they are typically politically oriented, general unions are more common in Europe and developing countries. There were some general unions in the United States in earlier times (such as the Knights of Labor in the late 1800s), but none of these continue to exist.

UNION GROWTH AND DECLINE

Union membership in the United States has varied considerably throughout the country's history. Although American unions have, at times, exerted considerable economic and political power, the level of unionization has generally been considerably lower than in many other advanced industrialized countries (e.g., Britain, Germany, Japan, and Scandinavia). Although there have been unions in the United States for nearly 200 years, prior to the 1930s unions represented, at most, 10 to 12 percent of the labor force. Union membership prior to the Great Depression era rose and fell often, generally corresponding to fluctuations in the **business cycle**.

The period from about 1935 to the mid-1950s was one of sustained economic growth. The unionization rate went from about 12 percent of the labor force in 1935 to between 32 percent and 35 percent in the mid-1950s. A number of factors were responsible for this unprecedented growth. By the 1930s the American economy had shifted from an agricultural to an industrial base. Industrial workers were concentrated in urban areas and most were native born and English-speaking. Consequently, there was a common culture among workers absent in earlier generations. The depression created a backlash against big business, which was largely viewed as the cause of the country's economic difficulties. Another very important factor was the election of Franklin D. Roosevelt in 1932. Active support for organized labor was an integral part of Roosevelt's New Deal. The most important change was the passage of the National Labor Relations Act (NLRA) of 1935 (see below). The NLRA provided a means for official recognition of labor unions. Once recognized, an employer was legally bound to bargain with the union, enforceable by government action. Economic growth during World War II and in the postwar era also facilitated union growth.

By the mid-1950s, the most union-prone sectors of the American economy had largely been organized. Unions maintained their strength at around one-third of the labor force until about 1960. Union membership declined gradually, decreasing to about 25 percent of the labor force in the mid-1970s. In the period 1970 to 1996 there was clearly a very strong downward trend in unionization in the private sector. Interestingly, there has been a corresponding increase in the unionization rate in the public sector, though this has not compensated for the substantial private sector decline. The overall unionization rate for the economy as a whole was about 14 percent in 1998.

Why has union membership and its corresponding economic and political power declined so much in recent years? There have undoubtedly been many factors. The changing nature of the global economy has been a leading cause. Over the past 20 to 30 years, American companies were increasingly exposed to foreign **competition**. This especially affected many sectors of the economy that were heavily unionized (e.g., automobiles, steel, and textiles). As these industries became more competitive globally, employer resistance to unions often increased. In addition, it became feasible for employers to relocate production facilities to areas of the country that have traditionally been less supportive of unionism (such as the southern and mountain states) or overseas to less developed countries that have low wages and few unions.

Another important factor has been the shifting nature of the labor force. In the 1930s, blue-collar workers represented a large proportion of the labor force. Now white-collar workers (i.e., managers, professionals, and clericals) are a very large component of the labor force. In general, white-collar workers have been difficult to organize (except in the public sector). There are also more service employees working in industries that are highly competitive (e.g., fast food) and thus less easily organized (since employers that recognize unions and make concessions to them are apt to be driven out of business because of higher costs).

The role of the government in relation to unions has changed considerably since the New Deal era. As early as 1947, amendments were added to the NLRA that significantly expanded employer rights and limited the rights of unions. This law, called the **Taft-Hartley Act**, is considered by many scholars to weaken the position of organized labor. Individuals appointed to the **National Labor Relations Board** (NLRB; the agency that enforces the NLRA) by the Nixon, Reagan, and Bush administrations often took positions unfavorable to labor unions in board rulings. This, coupled with a substantial increase in **management** opposition to unions in the 1980s, made it increasingly difficult for unions to organize new members. In addition, many unionized employers, confronting increasing competitive pressures, began to take especially hard bargaining positions in dealing with unions. Such an approach was not seen as a violation of NLRA standards by the new generation of NLRB appointees. Consequently, unions often lost ground in established areas. A number of consulting firms specializing in union avoidance activities became highly visible in the late 1970s and throughout the 1980s. Termed "union busters" by a scornful labor movement, there is considerable evidence that these **consultants** have played a substantial role in the decline of the contemporary labor movement.

Unions have traditionally been strong in four sectors of the American economy: manufacturing, mining, construction, and transportation. They have lost substantial ground in all four of these sectors in the last 20 years. In the transportation sector, an important factor has been deregulation, particularly in the trucking and airline industries. Substantial increases in competition in those industries have made it difficult for unions to negotiate favorable contracts or organize new units. In construction, the growth of nonunion contractors, able to hire qualified workers outside of the union hiring hall system, undercut union contractors. At one time, more than 80 percent of all commercial construction in the United States had been unionized; today, that figure is no more than 25 percent of commercial construction. Foreign competition and technological change have weakened mining unions. In manufacturing, the whole range of factors previously discussed has been responsible for union decline.

The only sector of the economy where unions have gained strength in recent years has been public **employment**. Financial stringency in the public sector has severely impacted public employees. Although public sector unions engage in collective bargaining with employers, they play an even more important role in lobbying legislative bodies regarding the financing of government agencies. Consequently, the relative success of public sector unions is most likely attributable to their role as a lobbying force rather than because of success at the bargaining table. Currently, more than one-third of public employees at all levels of government—local, state, and federal—are unionized.

INTERNAL STRUCTURE AND ADMINISTRATION

Labor unions are complex and vary considerably with respect to internal structure and administrative processes. It is easiest to differentiate among three distinct levels within the labor movement: local unions, national and international unions, and federations.

LOCAL UNIONS. Local unions are the building blocks of the labor movement and represent the interface between the union and its rank-and-file members. Although there are some free-standing local unions, the vast majority of locals are in some way affiliated with a national or international union. Most craft unions began as local unions, which then joined together to form national (or international) organizations. Some major industrial unions also began as amalgamations of local unions, though it was generally more common for national organizations to be formed first, with locals to be established later. At present, there are around 71,000 local unions in the United States.

The duties of a local union almost always include the administration of a union contract, which means assuring that the employer is honoring all of the provisions of the contract at the local level. In some instances, local unions might also negotiate contracts, although unions vary considerably in terms of the degree to which the parent national or international union is involved in the negotiation process.

Another important function of the local union is servicing the needs of those represented by the union. If a worker represented by the union believes his or her rights under the union contract have been violated, then the union may intervene on that person's behalf. Examples of such situations include the discharge of an employee, failure to promote an employee according to a contract seniority clause, or failure to pay an employee for overtime. Virtually any provision of a contract can become a source of contention. The local union may try to settle the issue informally. If that effort is not successful, the union may file what is known as a grievance. This is a formal statement of the dispute with the employer and most contracts set forth a grievance procedure. In general, grievance procedures involve several different steps, with higher levels of management entering at each step. If the grievance cannot be settled through this mechanism, then the union may, if the contract allows, request a hearing before a neutral arbitrator, whose decision is final and binding.

Most craft unions have **apprenticeship programs** to train new workers in the craft. The local union, usually in cooperation with an employers' association, will be responsible for managing the apprenticeship program. In addition, local unions with hiring halls are responsible for making job referrals.

The jurisdiction of a local union depends to a large extent on the organizational form of the parent organization. Locals of industrial unions most often represent workers within a single plant or facility of a company (and thus are termed plant locals). For example, in the case of the UAW, each factory or production facility of each automobile manufacturer has a separate local union. In some instances, a factory may be so big that it requires more than a single local, but this is not usually the case.

In contrast to plant locals, local craft unions (as well as some industrial unions) are best described as area locals. An area local represents all of a union's members in a particular geographical region and may deal with many different employers. Area locals are typically formed for one of two reasons. First, members may in the course of a year work for a number of different employers, as in the case of craft unions. Consequently, it would be difficult, if not impossible, to establish and maintain a separate local in each work location. Second, members may work continuously for a single employer, but each employer or location may be too small to justify a separate local union. The latter case is more typical of some industrial unions. An example is the United Food and Commercial Workers (UFCW), which represents, among others, clerks in retail outlets. Although an industrial union, the UFCW may have only a few members in each store, so a single local is established to serve an entire region. The size of the region served by a local union depends on the number of members available. In large metropolitan areas, an area local might serve only members in a particular city. In less densely populated regions, an area local may have a jurisdiction that covers an entire state (in a few cases, more than one state).

Internal structures and administrative procedures differ between plant and area locals. In almost all local unions, the membership meeting represents the apex of power, as the officers of the union are accountable to the members much as the officers of a corporation are accountable to stockholders. In practice, however, membership participation in union affairs is usually quite limited, so local union officers often enjoy considerable power.

Plant locals have a number of elected officials, usually a president, vice president, secretary, and **treasurer**. In almost all cases, the officers are full-time employees of the company the union represents, and the contract generally allows some release time for union affairs. In addition to the principal officers of the local, there are also a number of stewards. Stewards may be elected or appointed, depending upon the union. The steward serves as the everyday contact between the union and its rank-and-file members. If members have concerns about the affairs of the union, these may be voiced to the steward. The steward's most important responsibility is handling grievances. Should a worker represented by the union have a dispute with the employer over his or her rights under the contract, the steward has the initial responsibility of representing the worker. Usually the steward will discuss the matter with the employee's supervisor to see if the dispute can be resolved. If not, then a formal grievance may be filed and it then proceeds through the grievance system. At higher levels in the grievance system the employee may be represented by a chief steward or union officers.

Area locals typically have more complex internal structures than plant locals. This is usually because of the large geographical region under the local's jurisdiction, along with the greater dispersion of members within the region. As in the case of plant locals, area locals hold periodic meetings in which the officials of the union are accountable to members. There are also elected officers in area locals, as well as stewards for the various work sites in the local's jurisdiction. The principal difference between a plant local and an area local is that the latter typically employs one or more full-time staff members to handle the affairs of the union on a daily basis. These staff members are usually called business agents. Given the dispersion of members over a large geographical area and the possibility that the local may be responsible for administering many different contracts, it is the business agent's responsibility to visit work sites regularly and deal with problems that may arise. The business agent may also be responsible for managing any apprenticeship programs and the union's hiring hall. Contracts are often negotiated directly by local unions and the business agents are usually responsible for these negotiations. In some unions, elected officers may serve as business agents, but normally business agents are separate staff members. Depending on the size of the local union, there may be a number of assistant business agents.

NATIONAL AND INTERNATIONAL UNIONS. There are approximately 150 national unions in the United States, along with about 30 professional associations that carry on union activities. National unions are composed of the various local unions that they have chartered. Some unions have locals in Canada and therefore call themselves international unions. The terms ''international union'' and ''national union,'' however, are generally used interchangeably.

As with local unions, the administrative structures of national unions vary considerably in complexity. One important factor is the size of the union: larger unions are structurally more complex. Structural complexity also differs between craft and industrial unions. Not only do craft unions tend to be smaller, but decision making tends to be decentralized. Contracts usually have a limited geographical scope and are negotiated by local unions. The national union pools the resources of local unions, thus helping out with things such as strike funds. The national union may also provide research services and be involved politically at the national and state levels. In general, there are few intermediate units between the national office and the local craft unions. National officers, elected periodically, generally work on a full-time basis for the union. Such unions also hold national conventions, most often every couple of years. The officers of the national union are accountable to the convention, much as the officers of a local are accountable to membership meetings.

National industrial unions are typically more complex. They tend to be larger and have a more heterogeneous membership than craft unions (both in terms of skills and demographic traits). Although there are exceptions, contracts in industrial unions tend to be negotiated primarily by staff members from the national office. In many cases, the bargaining unit will include all locals from a particular company (across the entire country). Even if contracts are negotiated by locals, representatives from the national union will often participate in talks to assure that the contract conforms to patterns established by the national organization.

As with craft unions, national unions have periodic conventions and national officers. Depending upon the union, the national officers may be elected directly by rank-and-file members or by some other body (such as convention delegates). National unions generally have a substantial paid staff who provide a variety of different services (e.g., research, legal representation, organizing new members, negotiating contracts, and servicing locals). National unions may also have one or more layers of hierarchy between the local unions and the national offices. For example, in the case of the UAW, there are different divisions responsible for the major industries in which that union represents workers (see above). Within the automobile industry, there are divisions that correspond to each of the major producers. There are other divisions that deal with the needs of special groups within the union (such as minority workers and skilled craft workers). Consequently, the structures of large industrial unions are often as complex as the companies with which they deal.

With the decline in union activity in the United States, the number of national and international unions has also decreased. Some unions have simply ceased to exist, while others have merged with different labor organizations. More than 50 such mergers occurred between 1985 and 1997.With the decline in union activity in the US, the number of national and an international unions has also decreased. Some unions have simply ceased to exist, while others have merged with different labor organizations. More than fifty such mergers occurred between 1985 and 1997 (Gifford 1998, 6-7).

FEDERATIONS. A federation is an association of unions. It is not a union in the usual sense of the term. Rather, it provides a range of services to affiliated unions, much as an organization such as the National Association of Manufacturers provides services to its member firms. The AFL-CIO is currently the only national federation in the United States. The AFL-CIO formed in the mid-1950s as the result of the merger of what were then two competing federations: the American Federation of Labor (AFL) and the Congress of Industrial Organizations (CIO). The AFL was established in the 1880s and consisted almost exclusively of craft unions. Craft unionists feared that industrial unions might undercut their position, thus they generally opposed formation of industrial unions. The most famous of the AFL's early leaders was Samuel Gompers (1850-1924), who is generally viewed as the ''father'' of the American labor movement.

Pressures during the Great Depression seemed to favor industrial unionism, so several unions within the AFL broke away to form the rival CIO. Most influential in formation of this federation was John L. Lewis (1880-1969), long-time president of the United Mine Workers (UMW). Initially, the competition between the two federations, which chartered competing unions, probably helped the labor movement to grow in the United States. As it became apparent, however, that further competition was only self-defeating, the merger was ultimately negotiated.

There are about 70 national unions affiliated with the AFL-CIO; these unions represent about 13 million workers, or about 81 percent of the 16 million American union members. In addition, there are about 60 independent local unions that are also directly affiliated with the federation. A guiding principle of the AFL-CIO is ''national union autonomy.'' That is, the federation does not control the affiliates nor dictate their internal policies (though it often tries to influence affiliates).

The federation serves a range of functions. It acts as a lobbying body in the political arena and uses its financial resources in election campaigns. It works to resolve conflicts between affiliated unions, such as disputes between construction craft unions over jurisdiction of different areas of work and disputes between affiliated unions that may be competing in efforts to organize new members. It provides research services to affiliated unions and also helps unions organize new members. The diversity of AFL-CIO standing committees reflects the range of federation functions. These include the Legislative Committee, the Organization and Field Services Committee, the Civil Rights Committee, and the Community Services Committee.

The structure of the AFL-CIO is quite complex and also reflects the federation's multiple functions. The federation holds a convention every two years. Each affiliated union sends delegates to the convention. The day-to-day business of the federation is handled by its principal officers (president and secretary-treasurer), who confer regularly with an executive council consisting of more than 30 vice presidents, virtually all of whom are drawn from the ranks of the affiliated unions. In addition to the standing committees, the federation has several staff units. There are also several different departments within the federation that serve the specialized needs of different affiliates. An affiliate can choose to associate with those departments relevant to its particular needs, such as the Building Trades Department, the Industrial Union Department, the Metal Trades Department, and the Public Employees Department.

The national AFL-CIO offices are in Washington, D.C. There are state-level bodies of the AFL-CIO, however, in all 50 states. These bodies duplicate the federation's national activities at the state level (e.g., lobbying state legislatures and supporting pro-labor candidates in state elections). There are also AFL-CIO central bodies in more than 700 communities. Local unions are affiliated with the city centrals and these organizations provide services at the community level.

The influence of the AFL-CIO has varied over time. George Meany (1894-1980), the first president of the federation, exerted considerable power and influence within the labor movement. Many feel, however, that Meany worked to maintain an old guard within the labor movement that prevented organized labor from fully appreciating the implications of the many political, economic, and social changes that have taken place over the past 30 years. Lane Kirkland (1922-), the president of the federation from 1979 until 1995, had worked hard, along with many staff members, to introduce innovative policies and programs. The leadership of Kirkland's group, however, was challenged by an insurgent slate of younger and more militant leaders in the AFL-CIO's 1995 election. John Sweeney, president of the Service Employee's International Union (SEIU), became the federation's president. The SEIU has been one of the few U.S. unions to be quite successful in expanding its membership in recent years and Sweeney's platform promised new efforts to facilitate organizing by affiliates. Linda Chavez-Thompson (1944-), elected AFL-CIO executive vice president, is the first woman to hold one the federation's top leadership posts. Yet despite change and a recommitment to the organizing process, union membership in general, and membership in AFL-CIO unions in particular, continues to decline. Policy initiatives undertaken by the Sweeney administration would appear to have had little impact in reversing years of union decline.

[John J. Lawler]

FURTHER READING:

Elkouri, F., and E. Elkouri. *How Arbitration Works.* Washington: Bureau of National Affairs, 1997.

Freeman, R., and J. Medoff. *What Do Unions Do?* New York: Basic Books, 1984.

Gifford, C. D. *Directory of U.S. Labor Organizations.* 1998 ed. Washington: Bureau of National Affairs, 1998.

Hirsch, Barry T., and David Macpherson. *Union Membership and Earnings Data Book: Compilations from the Current Populations Survey.* 1998 ed. Washington: Bureau of National Affairs, 1998.

Kochan, T. A., H. C. Katz, and R. B. McKersie. *The Transformation of American Industrial Relations.* New York: Basic Books, 1994.

Lawler, John. J. *Unionization and Deunionization: Strategy, Tactics, and Outcomes.* Columbia, SC: University of South Carolina Press, 1990.

Lipsky, D. B., and C. B. Donn. *Collective Bargaining in American Industry.* Lexington, MA: Lexington Books, 1987.

Mills, Daniel Quinn. *Labor-Management Relations.* 5th ed. New York: McGraw-Hill, 1994.

Sayles, Leonard, and George Strauss. *The Local Union.* New York: Harcourt, Brace, and World, 1967.

Taylor, B. J., and F. Witney. *Labor Relations Law.* Englewood Cliffs, NJ: Prentice-Hall, 1987.

Wallihan, J. *Union Government and Organization.* Washington: Bureau of National Affairs, 1985.

LABOR-MANAGEMENT RELATIONS

The majority of key turning points in labor-management relations in the United States have been associated with periods of economic hardship. The Great Depression saw the establishment of comprehensive federal legislation designed to protect workers' right to organize. With the slowdown in economic growth and the intensification of global competition after the early 1970s, a number of labor-management cooperation programs were advocated to improve the efficiency of U.S. firms. In 1993, the Clinton administration established the Commission on the Future of Worker-Management Relations to address a broad range of issues, among them labor-management cooperation programs and the reform of U.S. labor law.

The federal government first guaranteed the right to organize and bargain collectively for railroad workers with the passage of the Railway Labor Act of 1926. The National Industrial Recovery Act of 1933 (NIRA) was part of the New Deal policies of the Great Depression era. The NIRA was intended to protect workers' right to unionize. It stated "That employees shall have the right to organize and bargain collectively through representatives of their own choosing . . . ." The NIRA had several shortcomings, among them a lack of enforcement provisions, and the act did little to promote workers' rights.

The basic law regulating labor-management relations and collective bargaining in the United States is The National Labor Relations Act of 1935, commonly referred to as the Wagner Act. A key provision of the act guarantees the right of nonmanagerial employees who work for firms engaged in interstate commerce to join unions and bargain on a collective basis. The legally protected right of workers to unionize was first established at the state level. In Massachusetts, for example, the state Supreme Court recognized this right in an 1842 decision.

The Wagner Act was primarily the work of Robert Wagner, a Democratic Senator from New York who wished to address the shortcomings of the NIRA. In 1933, Wagner began meeting with representatives from the American Federation of Labor and the National Labor Board, which was set up to administer the NIRA. These meetings culminated in the writing of the Wagner Act in February of 1934. The act failed to receive congressional support when initially introduced, but passed after the Democrats made substantial gains in the congressional elections of 1934; it was signed into law by President Roosevelt in July of 1935.

The most controversial part of the Wagner Act was Section 8, which prohibited what it called "unfair labor practices" on the part of employers. Under Section 8, employers could not legally fire workers for joining unions, could not refuse to bargain with a union that represented a majority of workers, and could not establish company unions. In large part due to the Wagner Act, union membership increased from 4 million in 1935 to 12 million in 1947. The National Labor Relations Board (NLRB) was established to administer the Wagner Act and is still the key agency regulating labor-management relations at the national level.

The constitutionality of the Wagner Act was affirmed in 1937 by the Supreme Court in *National Labor Relations Board vs. Jones and Laughlin Steel Corporation.* Shortly thereafter, pro-business organizations such as the National Association of Manufacturers sought to amend the Wagner Act. The Wagner Act was not amended, however, until the record wave of strike activity that followed World War II, in which President Truman personally intervened to settle disputes in the coal mining, railroad, and steel industries.

The National Labor Relations Act of 1947, also called the **Taft Hartley Act**, became law over the objections of the **National Labor Relations Board (NLRB)** and Truman's veto. Important amendments were made to Section 8, clarifying what were considered unfair labor practices by unions and employees; the Wagner Act had covered only unfair practices by employers.

Another key amendment was the addition of Section 14(b), which legalized what came to be called right-to-work laws. These laws, enacted at the state level, prohibited what is known as a union shop, in which *all* workers in a unionized factory are forced to join the union and pay dues. Right-to-work laws make union organizing much more difficult and continue to be opposed by organized labor into the late 1990s. Labor interests reject the term "right-to-work" as pertains to these laws as a cynical misnomer. They contend that since a union acting as a bargaining agent is compelled to represent all the workers in question (and not just those belonging to the union), it is only fair that all those employees should pay their share for the benefits of union representation by being dues-paying union members.

Attempts to overturn Taft-Hartley began just after its passage and intensified with the merger of the American Federation of Labor and the Congress of Industrial Organizations in 1955, forming the AFL-CIO. These efforts were greatly weakened by investigations into union corruption by the McClellan Committee of the Senate from 1957 to 1959 that culminated in the Labor Management Reporting and Disclosure Act of 1959, also known as the Landrum-Griffin Act. Landrum-Griffin outlined a Bill of Rights for union members. It did not, however, greatly weaken those elements of Taft-Hartley that opposed unions, and was devoted in large part to regulating the internal affairs of unions in response to the McClellan Committee's findings of widespread union corruption.

Union membership expanded steadily in the post-World War II years until the recession of the late 1950s, when it declined from just over 17.5 million to 16.5 million members by the early 1960s. The period from the mid 1960s to the late 1970s saw a steady and substantial growth in the number of union members, peaking at about 24 million workers in 1977. From 1978 through the 1990s, however, union membership plummeted, reaching lower levels than in the worst years of the early 1960s. Looking at union membership as a percentage of the private sector labor force yields a somewhat less dramatic picture, since this ratio declined in almost all years after 1955, though at an accelerated rate after the mid-1970s. In 1997, only 14.1 percent of full-time wage and salaried employees were unionized.

Moreover, strike activity has paralleled the downward membership trends. In 1997, there were 29 strikes involving 1,000 or more workers; these strikes were able to draw a total of 339,000 workers. By way of comparison, 255 strikes of similar scale took place in 1979, involving a total of 1,021,000 workers.

The decline in union membership was associated with a number of other factors that led to a substantial transformation of labor-management relations in the United States. Among these factors were intensified global competition, substantially slower average growth rates for the economy as a whole, declining real wages, the deregulation of key industries, the shift in employment from the industrial to the service sector and from the union strongholds of the Midwest and Northeast to the Sunbelt states, greatly increased anti-union efforts on the part of employers, and reduced resources devoted to organizing on the part of unions.

In the face of their reduced power, unions were compelled to make substantial bargaining concessions beginning in the early 1980s. These included wage and benefit givebacks, the acceptance of two- and three tiered wage systems, and greater demands by employers for flexibility and cooperation.

Numerous ideas regarding labor-management cooperation came into vogue among managers during the 1980s and continued into the 1990s. Modeled on Japanese labor-management relations and systems of production, these practices were referred to variously as joint programs, team concept, lean production, employee involvement, and labor-management participation, among others. These programs typically advocated non adversarial relations between management and labor, the establishment of work groups or quality control circles, and soliciting workers' input regarding the efficiency of the production process. Many advocated greater flexibility in the production process and workers' schedules.

The rise of employee stock ownership plans (ESOPs) marked another change in labor-management relations in recent years. One of the largest ESOPs went into effect at United Airlines in 1994. The plan gave United employees ownership of 55 percent of outstanding shares in exchange for wage cuts averaging 14 percent. In addition, the two unions involved were each to get a representative on the 12-member board of directors.

Robert Reich, the first Clinton administration's Secretary of Labor, created a Commission on the Future of Worker-Management Relations in mid-1993. This was commonly referred to as the Dunlop Commission after its chairman, John Dunlop, Secretary of Labor under President Ford. The Dunlop Commission studied a broad range of labor-management issues for the purpose of making policy recommendations, in particular with amending federal labor legislation.

The commission's fact-finding report from mid-1994 stated that "stagnation of real earnings and increased inequality of earnings is bifurcating the U.S. labor market, with an upper tier of high-wage skilled workers and an increasing 'underclass' of low-paid labor." The report noted the shift from high-paying production work to low-paying service work, the large number of full-time workers whose income did not provide an adequate standard of living, and the fact that workers in the United States put in longer work weeks than workers in any other advanced industrialized country except Japan. The report also noted that an increasing number of workers were illegally fired for union organizing activities.

The Dunlop Commission was generally supportive of labor-management cooperation programs but noted that many firms were reluctant to implement them because of Wagner Act restrictions on company unions. In 1993, the AFL-CIO expressed to the Dunlop Commission its willingness to accept weakening of restrictions on company unions in exchange for reforms that would make union organizing easier. In hearings held in August of 1994, the AFL-CIO backed off on this offer.

In the mid-1990s, amidst continued deflation of union membership and a general sense of decline in the significance of unions in general, situations emerged signaling that rumors of organized labor's demise had been premature. From 1995 to 1996, Bridgestone/Firestone Company squared off with the United Rubber Workers union in a case that achieved symbolic dimensions for the state of labor-management relations in the United States. The URW struck to maintain "pattern bargaining," whereby Bridgestone workers were to receive compensation and conditions on a par with workers at Goodyear, Bridgestone's more profitable competitor. Bridgestone rejected any such agreement, and the dispute evolved into a 27-month quagmire that saw the URW, by turns, nearly epitomize the death of organized labor and then symbolize its resurgence.

In 1995, when Bridgestone mobilized several thousand strike breakers, some union locals voted to return to work without any concessions, though few workers were actually rehired initially. When Bridgestone registered a significant recovery through 1995 and more strikers were called back to work, the URW regrouped and allied with the sympathetic United Steel Workers, who had decided to take up the cause. Subsequent pressure on the company threatened contagion, and proved embarrassing to the thriving

Bridgestone. Soon all workers were re-hired by the company with massive concessions.

Following this display of union vitality, major strikes were undertaken by workers for United Parcel Service in 1997 and General Motors in 1998. While the results of these strikes were varied, they did manage to demonstrate that management-labor relations were hardly a dying issue.

[David Kucera]

FURTHER READING:

Ballot, Michael. *Labor-Management Relations in a Changing Environment.* 2nd ed. New York: John Wiley & Sons, 1996.

Handbook of U.S. Labor Statistics. 2nd ed. Lanham, MD: Bernan Press, 1998.

Journal of Labor Research, quarterly.

Kovach, Kenneth A. *Strategic Labor Relations.* Lanham, MD: University Press of America, 1997.

Labor Notes, monthly.

LAIA

SEE: Latin American Integration Association

LAISSEZ FAIRE

The centuries-old doctrine known as laissez-faire is a government policy of economic (and social) nonintervention and is a cornerstone of capitalist economic philosophy. Phrases like "rugged individualism," "**free trade**," "market economics," "free enterprise," and "free competition" reflect a posture of laissez-faire, as does Thomas Jefferson's observation that "the least governed are the best governed."

While sources translate the term *laissez-faire* variously—as "allow to do," "leave it alone," "let things alone," and "let go and let pass," among other things—most agree that the expression originated with a 17th century French merchant, François Legendre, who was protesting his government's overregulation of commerce and industry. Subsequently, a group of late 18th century French economists known as the Physiocrats developed and popularized laissez-faire as a principle.

In essence, the Physiocrats believed that the laws of nature, and not of governments, would foster economic and social prosperity. Their efforts and formulations represented a reaction against the widespread practice of mercantilism, a system in which the state exerts significant controls over industry and commerce, particularly foreign trade. Pervading much of Western Europe from the 17th to the 19th centuries, mercantilism manifested itself in the form of a host of navigation laws, tariffs, and other measures constraining merchants' activities.

The concept of laissez-faire was further boosted in the 18th century when the Scottish economist Adam Smith (1723-1790), often called the "father of modern economics," published *The Wealth of Nations* in 1776. In this pathbreaking volume Smith advocated a free enterprise system that was grounded in private ownership, driven by individual initiative, and unencumbered by governmental bureaucracy. In the same work, Smith argued that the "invisible hand" of naturally arising competition would monitor and regulate individual enterprise far more effectively than governmental restrictions would; he, like the Physiocrats, believed in a natural harmony that, if allowed to operate free of institutional restraints, would lead to a beneficent economy and promote the welfare of individuals and communities alike.

As a formal and widely accepted economic and political doctrine, laissez-faire came into full flower during the 19th century, especially in the United Kingdom, where it served to embody the ideas propounded by the English classical school of economists. In his 1828 work *Principles of Political Economy,* the British economist and political philosopher John Stuart Mill (1806-1873) argued vigorously for a society ruled by natural law. Espousing the individual's right to be free of governmental interference in economic pursuits, Mill asserted that "laissez faire . . . should be the general practice: every departure from it, unless required by some great good, is a certain evil."

During the 20th century, especially in the wake of the Industrial Revolution, laissez-faire lost much of its force, giving way to policies and philosophies favoring collective action, as evidenced by the growth of trade associations and trade unions. With the rise of big business, state controls were increasingly seen as a way of breaking up monopolies, advancing international trade, and promoting "the good of all." Resulting from these developments was a multitude of antitrust and other legislation, as well as numerous government policies and regulations addressing such issues as worker safety, the environment, and employment discrimination. While President Ronald Reagan and others initiated a variety of deregulatory actions in the latter part of the 20th century, laissez-faire became just one of several doctrines influencing western economic thought.

In practical terms, it should be noted that although laissez-faire endorses a "hands-off" economic and political posture on the part of government, few economists past or present have embraced the doctrine in a literal sense. Rather, most have supported some form of governmental involvement to promote and safeguard the nation's welfare. Adam Smith, for example, conceded the importance of government's role in protecting certain home industries against encroachment by foreign competitors and in maintaining a system of national defense. Similarly, many of the British classical economists favored government's involvement in such areas as child labor legislation. Other economists have endorsed a primary role for government in spheres ranging from sanitation to education, and from public utilities to national transportation networks.

Laissez-faire remains a part of the modern economic lexicon, but to some it has a negative connotation, conjuring images of industrial barons exploiting ordinary people. Even when it's not used by name, the general theory behind laissez-faire is still widely accepted by many economists, policy analysts, and politicians. Evidence of laissez-faire principles may be observed in such international trade pacts as the **North American Free Trade Agreement** and the **General Agreement on Tariffs and Trade**, as well as in national governments' recent deregulation programs in sectors like telecommunications and utilities.

SEE ALSO: Antitrust Acts and Laws

[Roberta H. Winston]

FURTHER READING:

Fried, Barbara H. *The Progressive Assault on Laissez Faire.* New York: Harvard University Press, 1998.

Mill, John Stuart. *Principles of Political Economy and Chapters on Socialism.* New York: Oxford University Press, 1994.

Smith, Adam. *An Inquiry into the Nature and Causes of the Wealth of Nations.* New York: Oxford University Press, 1998.

LAN

SEE: Local Area Networks

LATIN AMERICAN INTEGRATION ASSOCIATION (LAIA)

The Latin American Integration Association (LAIA) was established as a result of the Montevideo Treaty of 1980. While succeeding the Latin American Free Trade Association (LAFTA) of 1960, LAIA nonetheless strived to keep intact the economic integration process begun by LAFTA. The signatories to the 1980 treaty were Argentina, Bolivia, Brazil, Chile, Colombia, Ecuador, Mexico, Paraguay, Peru, Uruguay, and Venezuela. The goal of LAIA is to reduce restrictions on trade between its members. It is hoped that this will be accomplished through the implementation of economic complementarity agreements that are "specific tariff reduction programs for lists covering just about all products." It is believed that LAIA programs will lead to balanced and complementary social and economic development for the region.

LAFTA was formed following negotiations that took place throughout 1958 under the direction of the **United Nations** Economic Commission for Latin America. These negotiations culminated in the signing of the Montevideo Treaty of 1960 by Argentina, Brazil, Chile, Mexico, Paraguay, Peru, and Uruguay. LAFTA membership increased throughout the 1960s with Colombia and Ecuador joining in 1961, Venezuela in 1966, and Bolivia in 1967. LAFTA did not originally call for a common external tariff nor did it immediately seek to form an economic union. A Latin American common market was discussed but only as a long-term goal. The newly formed association did call for the dismantling of tariffs and other **trade barriers** between member states. In 1969, however, in a meeting in Caracas, rancor developed over proposals to begin working toward a common market. Although consideration of the proposal was postponed until 1980, Colombia and Uruguay continued to disagree with the thrust of the 1969 meeting. Because of continuing internal dissension LAFTA became little more than a trade and marketing association. By 1980 only 14 percent of trade between LAFTA members could be related to the Montevideo agreement. One of the accomplishments of LAFTA, however, was the creation of the Multilateral Compensation and Reciprocal Credit Mechanism. The agreement was signed by the **central banks** of member countries in 1965 and began operating in June 1966.

In June 1980 representatives met in Acapulco and later in Montevideo, and voted to dissolve LAFTA and replace it with the Latin American Integration Association. It was decided that the new association would have less closely defined goals, no specific timetable for goal implementation, and fewer strictures overall. The aim of LAIA is to reduce or remove trade barriers while leaving members free to enter into separate trade and tariff agreements. While LAIA does not call for all-inclusive tariff reductions, there are preferential tariffs for regional products and regional agreements on matters related to agricultural products, technology exchange, and environmental and tourism affairs. LAIA also recognizes an economic hierarchy and its trade and tariff agreements take into account the level of economic development of each country. Member nations are divided into three categories: Argentina, Brazil, and Mexico are considered to be most developed; Chile, Colombia, Peru, Uruguay, and Venezuela are considered to be in a stage of intermediate development; and Bolivia, Ecuador, and Paraguay are the least-developed members. An "eventual objective" of LAIA is, however, is the establishment of a regional common market.

In 1982 LAIA members signed a Reciprocal Payments and Credit Agreement that set in place bilateral lines of **credit** between each pair of central banks. The lines of credit are pegged to the U.S. dollar. In 1984 LAIA ratified the Regional Tariff Preference program which was subsequently expanded by protocols in 1987 and 1990. This program is a series of tariff cuts based on the level of development of participating countries. During this period LAIA also approved various financial and monetary cooperative programs for less-developed member countries, and ended various nontariff barriers to trade. Also in 1984 an important LAIA proposal was the Regional Trade System. This program was aimed at enhancing intraregional trade and controlling bilateral trade agreements. In 1986 LAIA issued the "Buenos Aires Letter" and in 1987 the association expanded the Regional Tariff Preference program. Both of these plans were aimed at furthering trade between members and lessening sanctions and trade barriers. In 1988 LAIA expanded its areas of activity to include construction, transportation, information services, tourism, and insurance. By the 1990s LAIA members had signed 104 bilateral commercial agreements and 20 agreements with non-LAIA countries, and substantially increased trade between member states.

The principal governing organ of LAIA is the Council of Ministers of Foreign Affairs. This body is composed of the ministers of foreign affairs of the 11 member countries unless an official other than the Foreign Minister is responsible for LAIA matters. The council meets annually to review activities and set policy. LAIA's Evaluation and Convergence Conference reviews activities, promotes new programs, makes recommendations to the secretariat, and reviews preferential arrangements. The political body of the LAIA is the Committee of Representatives that is made up of a permanent representative of each member country and the representative's deputy. The committee is responsible for concluding agreements, implementation of treaty provisions, and convenes the council and conference. The aforementioned secretariat is headed by a secretary-general who is elected by the council for a renewable three-year term and is responsible for most LAIA technical and administrative tasks.

[Michael Knes]

FURTHER READING:

Inter-American Development Bank. "Latin American Integration Association." Washington: Inter-American Development Bank, 1997. Available from www.iadb.org/int/spa/index.htm.

International Monetary Fund. "Latin American Integration Association." Washington: International Monetary Fund, 1998. Available from www.imf.org/external/np/sec/decdo/laia.htm.

LAYOFFS

Layoffs refer to either temporary or permanent **employment** reductions. Prior to the 1980s, layoffs generally resulted from **business cycle** downswings, which primarily affected industries such as manufacturing and mining. When the economy improved during this period, employers often recalled laid-off workers. Beginning in the 1980s and extending through the late 1990s, however, a greater proportion of layoffs resulted from plant and office closures, **workforce** reductions, or job eliminations. Consequently, these layoffs were permanent and workers who are laid off permanently are sometimes referred to as "dislocated workers."

Many of the layoffs in the 1980s and 1990s stemmed from reengineering, restructuring, and downsizing efforts to make U.S. firms more efficient and profitable in the face of intensified **international competition**. Layoffs resulting from reengineering and restructuring were unique in that restructuring affected a large proportion of white-collar, managerial, executive positions. For example, the American Management Association found that two-thirds of employees laid off in 1994 were salaried, college-educated workers.

Growth of foreign and domestic **competition**, stagnant earnings, and a slow economy motivated the first round downsizing and layoffs in the early 1980s. As the U.S. economy improved in the mid-1990s and remained strong in the late 1990s, large-scale layoffs continued at about the same rate—even at highly profitable firms—marking a break with historical layoff patterns. During the late 1990s, many of the largest companies in the country underwent reengineering or downsizing, despite greater profits. General Motors, for example, continued to reduce its workforce, announcing in 1998 that it would cut 50,000 jobs to remain competitive, even though the company's profits rose 35 percent in 1997.

AT&T led U.S. companies in 1998 layoffs with 18,000, followed by Compaq with 15,000, Motorola with 15,000, Raytheon with 14,000, and Xerox with 9,000. Furthermore, McDonald's Corp. laid off workers for the first time ever during this period as the company began to reduce its overhead and management personnel in an effort to increase productivity.

A flurry of bank **mergers**—more than 370 of them—in the late 1990s also led to additional layoffs. The top five mergers of 1998 alone resulted in 20,000 job cuts. According to *Fortune,* **banking** along with media/entertainment and utilities jobs were the most prone to layoffs in the mid-to-late 1990s because of mergers, accelerated competition, and government deregulation.

Layoffs resulting from downsizing continued throughout 1990s, despite low unemployment, a strong economy, and the lack of proven economic benefits from downsizing. According to a Wharton School report, downsizing typically failed to boost earnings or **stock market** performance consistently. Moreover, other studies indicate that downsizing tends to cause low employee morale and tarnish a company's image. In addition, some reports found that a number of companies eventually are forced to fill positions left open by layoffs by paying premium wages.

Skilled workers such as computer programmers, **software** engineers, and tool-and-die manufacturers, however, remained insulated from the effects of downsizing during the late 1990s because of a nationwide shortage, according to *Industry Week.*

Unlike other advanced capitalist countries, firms in the United States faced with demand variations generally relied on changes in employment rather than changes in working hours. From 1970 to 1983, for example, variations in employment due to fluctuations in production were substantially greater in the United States than in Japan or West Germany. Changes in employment in the United States resulted mostly from temporary layoffs during downswings and recalls of laid-off workers during upswings. The greater reliance on overtime work in Japan and West Germany, rather than layoffs and recalls, may have been due to the fact that overtime is paid only a 25 percent premium in these two countries, compared with 50 percent in the United States. Furthermore, U.S. companies tend to layoff workers to avoid shareholder losses, whereas companies in other countries tend to pass both earnings and losses on to shareholders in order to bypass frequent layoffs.

SENIORITY AND LAYOFFS

According to a U.S. Bureau of National Affairs survey on layoff provisions in labor agreements, most labor agreements have some type of layoff provision, which specifies the terms and conditions of layoffs. Furthermore, when companies have labor agreements, seniority usually plays a role in determining who will be laid off—and seniority plays the only role in many cases. In addition, some labor agreements with layoff provisions allow a senior employee to ''bump'' or displace a junior employee in a different department or job classification should the senior employee's job be subject to layoff.

Senior employees are favored not only in layoffs but also in recalls, as the laid-off employees with the greatest seniority generally get called back to work first. In many labor agreements, all laid-off workers had to be recalled before any new employees were hired. Violations of such layoff provisions often resulted in union grievance procedures. Seniority also played an important role in the layoff criteria of nonunion firms. A 1982 survey revealed that 42 percent of nonunionized firms followed strict seniority rules in determining layoffs.

Most **labor unions** favored the use of seniority as the only criteria in determining who would be laid off. In addition, many unions favored ''superseniority'' in which union officers and stewards were granted highest seniority. Superseniority was favored on the grounds that union officers and stewards must be working in order to protect the rights of fellow workers. In contrast, firms generally preferred to first lay off workers they regarded as least productive. Firms were also generally opposed to bumping, as this often resulted in less-experienced workers taking over an operation.

UNIONS AND LAYOFFS

In their volume *What Do Unions Do?,* Richard B. Freeman and James L. Medoff addressed the question of why unionized workers were more affected by temporary layoffs than were nonunionized workers and responded as follows:

> Why do unionized workers and firms [in the United States] choose temporary layoffs rather than reductions in wages or hours? Perhaps the most important reason is that temporary layoffs mean laying off junior workers, not the senior employees who have a greater influence on union policies than they would on the policies of a non-union firm. . . . Except in the cases where mass layoffs are threatened, this will lead him or her to prefer layoffs to other forms of adjustment.

Freeman and Medoff argue that union members' preference for temporary layoffs, rather than work-sharing, increased in the post World War II years, noting the decreasing number of union **contracts** with work-sharing provisions. In the face of plant shutdowns, however, unions have accepted not only work-sharing measures but also substantial give backs in terms of wages and benefits.

LEGISLATION

The National Employment Priorities Act, which proposed that firms be required to give advance notice to workers of impending layoffs or plant closures, was first introduced in Congress in 1974. This legislation, introduced by Congressmen Walter Mondale from Minnesota and William Ford from Michigan, failed to gain sufficient congressional support. Similar laws were passed at the state level, however, with Maine and Wisconsin among the first states requiring firms to give advance notice. Congressman Ford reintroduced layoff notification legislation at the national level with the proposed Labor-Management Notification and Consultation Act of 1985. Advance notification legislation eventually passed in the form of the Worker Adjustment and Retraining Notification Act (WARN) of 1988. In general, WARN requires companies with more than 100 permanent, full time employees to give their workers from 60 days to six months of prior notice for plant closures and large-scale layoffs. If employers fail to comply with WARN, then laid-off employees or their unions can sue employers, following the 1996 Supreme Court ruling in *United Food and Commercial Workers Union Local 751 v. Brown Shoe Co.*

SEE ALSO: Corporate Restructuring

[David Kucera, updated by Karl Heil]

FURTHER READING:

Addison, John T., ed. *Job Displacement: Consequences and Implications for Policy.* Detroit: Wayne State University Press, 1991.

Blumenstein, Rebecca. ''GM May Need to Cut Over 50,000 Jobs to Become as Competitive as Its Rivals.'' *Wall Street Journal,* 7 July 1998, A4.

Cross, Michael. *U.S. Corporate Personnel Reduction Policies: An Edited Collection of Manpower Layoff, Reduction, and Termination Policies.* Aldershot, England: Gower, 1981.

Downs, Alan. *Corporate Executions: The Ugly Truth about Layoffs.* New York: AMACOM, 1995.

Freeman, Richard B., and James L. Medoff. *What Do Unions Do?* New York: Basic Books, 1984.

Gold, Jacqueline S. ''Layoffs Mount in Wake of Big Bank, Thrift Deals.'' *American Banker,* 6 October 1998, 1.

Koretz, Gene. ''The Downside of Downsizing: New Evidence of Layoffs' Damage.'' *Business Week,* 28 April 1997, 26.

Sandver, Marcus H. *Labor Relations: Process and Outcomes.* Boston: Little, Brown, 1987.

Smith, Lee, and Erin M. Davies. ''Riskiest Industries.'' *Fortune,* 1 April 1996, 76.

Staudohar, Paul D., and Holly E. Brown. *Deindustrialization and Plant Closure.* Lexington, MA: Lexington Books, 1987.

''Study: Layoffs Haven't Boosted Profits, Productivity.'' *Washington Post,* 26 September 1993.

Tachibanaki, Toshiaki. ''Labour Market Flexibility in Japan in Comparison with Europe and the U.S.'' *European Economic Review,* April 1987.

LBO

SEE: Leveraged Buyout

LEADERSHIP

A plethora of information on leaders and leadership can be found in libraries, bookstores, journals, and business magazines and periodicals. The body of this material is often intensely scholarly, such as the article ''A Meta-analysis of the Relation between Personality Traits and Leadership Perceptions: An Application of Validity Generalization Procedures,'' written by R. G. Lord and others, which appeared in the *Journal of Applied Psychology.* Other material is often intensely popular, such as *Leadership Secrets of the Rogue Warrior: A Commando's Guide to Success* by the consummate ''Rogue Warrior'' and ex-navy seal Richard Marcinko; or *Semper Fi: Business Leadership the Marine Corps Way* by Dan Carrison and Rod Walsh. In between these two extremes are books such as *Leadership: Theory and Practice* by Peter Northouse, a professor of communication at Western Michigan University. Books such as the latter are strongly based in leadership theory but nonetheless take a practical approach to the presentation of this data and information. In essence, books like these bridge scholarship and a more popular approach to leadership. They are well suited for those seeking a serious but not necessarily a strict scholarly approach to the subject.

TRAIT AND PROCESS APPROACHES

Leadership can be defined in numerous ways depending on the theoretical telescope one uses to view the subject. From the 19th century to the present day there have been two general approaches to leadership—trait and process. The trait approach preceded the process approach and is best described by the popular phrase—''He's a born leader.'' The trait perspective put forth the concept that some people are born with certain qualities necessary to leadership roles. These innate personality characteristics or traits are thus an integral part of leadership. Based on this conception of leadership, numerous investigators began compiling lists of personality traits and ancillary ''ability characteristics'' associated with leadership. Two summations were done of the approximately 190 trait-related leadership studies done between 1904 and 1970. The first summation done in 1948 found that leaders differed from other group members in terms of intelligence, alertness, insight, responsibility, initiative, persistence, self-confidence, and sociability. The second summation, done in 1970, found leaders having the following ten characteristics: drive for responsibility and task completion; vigor and persistence in pursuit of goals; ''venturesomeness'' and originality in problem solving; drive to exercise initiative in social situations; self-confidence and sense of personal identity; willingness to accept consequences of decision and action; readiness to absorb interpersonal stress; willingness to tolerate frustration and delay; ability to influence other people's behavior; and the capacity to structure social interaction systems to the purpose at hand. Intelligence, self-confidence, determination, integrity, and sociability are the five leadership traits that consistently reappear in many of these studies. Lists of ability and physical characteristics included such things as speech fluency and height or body type.

In the post-World War II period, criticism of the trait approach to leadership began mounting. While not denying that leaders often displayed certain predictable traits, critics claimed that this approach failed to take into account environmental or situational factors affecting leadership. Why, critics asked, do people with leadership traits become leaders in some situations but not others? Why is it that some people embodying leadership qualities never become leaders? One approach to leadership theory that attempts to answer these questions is the style approach.

''Whereas the trait approach emphasizes the *personality characteristics* of the leader, the style approach emphasizes the *behavior* of the leader,'' Northouse wrote. The style approach attempts to analyze how leaders act in certain situations and what they do to attain and maintain their leadership positions in certain situations. In this context, leadership began being studied not only in terms of the leader but also in terms of those being led and the environment in which leadership activities take place. The style approach views leadership as a process and thus ushers in a ''modern'' definition of leadership: ''Leadership is a *process* whereby an individual influences a group of individuals to achieve a common goal.'' Leadership is thus a process that occurs within the context of a group and is marked by influence and goal attainment. Leadership is a transactional event. Leadership is interactive, occurring between a leader and his or her followers—it is not just the result of innate characteristics or traits.

It is important to note that leadership, while sharing some of the characteristics of **management**, is nonetheless a much different activity. Management seeks to avoid chaos by pursuing order and stability; leadership, however, seeks ''adaptive and constructive change.''

LEADERSHIP STYLES

As they relate to leadership, two types of behavior, task and relationship, are apparent from studies investigating the style approach. Task behavior is associated with goal attainment while relationship behavior is synonymous with interpersonal relations. Interpersonal behavior of this sort is generally associated with creating a comfortable psychological environment for subordinates, especially as it relates to how subordinates feel about themselves, other group members, and the general circumstances they find themselves in. Closely related to relationship behavior are two issues—a leader's concern for production and a leader's concern for people. In attempting to map these issues, researchers construct a leadership or management grid that correlates five major leadership styles: authority compliance; country club management; impoverished management; middle of-the-road management; and **team** management.

The first style, authority-compliance, emphasizes task completion over people and is result driven. A leader choosing this style, according to Northouse, is controlling, demanding, hard-driving, and often overpowering. The antithesis of authority-compliance is country club management, which is marked by concern for interpersonal relationships and an agreeable and uncontroversial work climate. An impoverished manager is distant, oftentimes indifferent, and equally unconcerned with task fulfillment and interpersonal relationships. Middle-of-the-road managers, as the term implies, seek expediency and a balance between task achievement and interpersonal relationships. The team management style is equally concerned with interpersonal relations and task fulfillment. Team management encourages full participation, which encourages subsequent commitment and involvement. Two offshoots are the paternal/maternal style of leadership, which employs both authority compliance and country club styles but manages to keep them separate. ''This is the 'benevolent dictator' who acts in a gracious manner but does so for the purpose of goal accomplishment,'' Northouse wrote in his book. An opportunistic leader or manager uses all five styles, either alone or in various combinations, as the situation demands.

SITUATIONAL APPROACH

Another approach to leadership studies is the situational approach, the basic premise of which is that different situations demand different types of leadership. A situation, within this context, is a ''set of values and attitudes with which the individual or group has to deal in a process of activity and with regard to which this activity is planned and its results appreciated. Every concrete activity is the solution of a situation.'' Situations can be complicated affairs and generally have five elements: the structure of interpersonal relationships within the group; the characteristics of the group as a whole; the characteristics of the group's environment from which members come; physical constraints on the group; and the perceptual representation, within the group and among its members, of these elements and the ''attitudes and values engendered by them'' (from the *International Ency-*

clopedia of the Social Sciences, edited by David L. Sills). Situational influences thus constrain the leader who must adapt his or her style of leadership to the situation at hand. Situational leadership, according to Northouse, has both a directive and a supportive dynamic. A situationally motivated leader realizes that the skills and motivation of any group member are not static and the mix of the leader's supportive and directive activities must likewise change with the situation.

CONTINGENCY THEORY

Closely related to the situational approach is what has become known as contingency theory. The contingency theory of leadership was formulated by University of Illinois research psychologist F.E. Fiedler in his landmark 1964 article, ''A Contingency Model of Leadership Effectiveness.'' Contingency theory posits that effective leadership is contingent on the proper meld of leadership style and situation. Fiedler and his associates studied leaders in a variety of contexts but mostly military. ''After analyzing the styles of hundreds of leaders who were both good and bad,'' according to Northouse, ''Fiedler and his colleagues were able to make empirically grounded generalizations about which styles of leadership were best and which styles were worst for a given organizational context.''

Within the outline of contingency theory there are two styles of leadership: task-motivated and relationship-motivated. Task, of course, refers to task accomplishment, and relationship-motivation refers to interpersonal relationships. Fiedler measured leadership style with his ''Least Preferred Co-Worker Scale'' (LPC scale.) Those leaders scoring high on this scale are relationship motivated while those scoring low are task oriented. According to Fiedler those leaders scoring low on this scale are most effective in very favorable and very unfavorable situations—when things, according to Northouse, are either going well or are out of control. Leaders who score high on this scale are most effective in moderately favorable situations. An important point of contingency theory is that any one leader will not necessarily be effective in all situations.

Central to contingency theory is concept of the situation, which is characterized by three factors. The first, leader-member relations, deals with the general environment of the group and the positive feelings (or lack thereof) such as loyalty and confidence that the group has for its leader. The second, task structure, is related to task clarity, the means to task accomplishment, and task finalization. The third, position power, relates to the amount of reward-punishment authority the leader has over members of the group.

Contingency theory has survived over the decades as a viable measurement of leadership effectiveness because it is grounded in empirical research; researchers who have followed Fiedler have likewise validated contingency theory with their own research. Contingency theory has also been proved to have ''predictive powers'' in determining the probability of success of specific individuals acting as leaders in specific situations. Contingency theory is also popular among leaders or potential leaders as it does not expect leaders to be equally effective in all situations. ''Contingency theory matches the leader and the situation,'' wrote Northouse, ''but does not demand that the leader fit every situation.''

Contingency theory, although providing some answers, generally falls short in trying to explain why individuals with certain leadership traits are effective in some situations but not others. For instance: Why are task motivated leaders most effective in extreme situations but not as effective in moderately favorable situations? Fiedler's contingency theory has also come under criticism (some self-imposed) because of the awkwardness and input shortfalls of the LPC scale.

EVOLUTION OF LEADERSHIP THEORY

It is important to keep in mind how leadership theory has evolved over the decades. The trait approach focused entirely on innate characteristics of leaders—personality characteristics that the individual had little direct control over. The trait approach was modified somewhat by the style approach that looked at the behavior of people in leadership roles rather than their personality characteristics. The situational approach and the subsequent contingency theory represented a major shift in the approach to leadership theory by looking at the context or situation in which leadership activities took place and environmental influences on leadership effectiveness. Since Fiedler's contingency theory there have been numerous other approaches to leadership studies, such as the path-goal theory, the leader-member exchange theory, transformational leadership, the team leadership theory, and the psychodynamic approach. These, like the contingency theory, have moved away from emphasizing the individual leader and instead look at various environmental and interpersonal influences on leadership.

These various theories of leadership have spilled over into related fields such as social and political biography and especially leadership analyses of women and minorities. ''Leaders are essentially individuals who have the ability to understand their own times, who express or articulate programs or policies that reflect the perceived interests and desires of particular groups, and who devise instruments or political vehicles that enhance the capacity to achieve effective change,'' wrote Manning Marable in the introduction to his book, a study of leadership in the black community. This definition closely parallels the definition given earlier by Northouse, who described leadership as a process during which the leader influences change in pursuit of common group goals.

WOMEN AND LEADERSHIP

Following World War II women began entering and staying in the job market in greater and greater numbers for a wide variety of social and economic reasons. As women stayed in the job market they likewise began working in positions of leadership, which prompted gender-based studies of leadership styles and effectiveness. Generally speaking it was found that women in leadership positions tend to adopt an interpersonal style of leadership. Based on numerous studies, a list of leadership characteristics generally shared by women includes: the use of consensus in **decision making**; viewing power in relationship terms as something to be shared; encouraging productive approaches to conflict; the building of supportive work environments; and the promotion of diversity in the workplace. This contrasts with the general leadership styles of men, which tend to be more hierarchical and authority oriented. One researcher believes that these gender-based differences in leadership styles are due to women traditionally working in ''service'' roles, such as mothers, teachers, nurses and volunteers. These are roles in which women are generally cooperative, gentle, understanding, and supportive, whereas men have traditionally occupied roles that have been more competitive and authoritative.

In many ways women are also redefining leadership. Mary S. Hartman, director of the Institute for Women's Leadership at Rutgers University, has edited *Talking Leadership: Conversations with Powerful Women.* In this book 13 well-known women, often regarded as leaders, are interviewed on a variety of topics—including leadership. The women interviewed are socially and politically active and range from New Jersey Governor Christine Todd Whitman to Susan Berresford, the first woman president of the Ford Foundation. Surprisingly, Hartman found that while some of the women interviewed relished their role as leaders, others were troubled with the label. The latter were either uncomfortable with the traditional and oftentimes negative associations with the term or were wary of the media habit of building up leaders only then to turn and demolish them. Others regarded leaders as non-egalitarian. All of the women interviewed, however, saw themselves as agents of change fulfilling at least in part the definition of a leader. Carrison and Walsh, in a chapter entitled ''A Few Good Women,'' however, maintain that ''gender has absolutely nothing to do with leadership.''

As stated earlier, the popular press is replete with books and articles on leadership. Generally speaking these sources can be informative and often entertaining to read. They often inform through the use of analogy (i.e., building your leadership tripod) and anecdotes while seldom backing up their contentions, regardless of validity, with hard facts or data. The major shortcoming of these books and articles, which are largely based on narrow and oftentimes specific personal experiences, is their lack of an encompassing theoretical framework to which a reader can plug in a variety of situations or scenarios. The award, however, for succinct advice to potential leaders goes to Richard Marcinko, who maintains that the most meaningful statement an effective leader can utter is ''follow me!''

[Michael Knes]

FURTHER READING:

Carrison, Dan, and Rod Walsh. *Semper Fi: Business Leadership the Marine Corps Way.* New York: AMACOM, 1999.

Dotlich, David L., and James L. Noel. *Action Learning: How the World's Top Companies Are Re-Creating Their Leaders and Themselves.* San Francisco: Jossey-Bass, 1998.

Fulmer, Robert M., and Stacey Wagner. ''Leadership: Lessons from the Best.'' *Training Development* 53, no. 3 (March 1999): 28-33.

Hartman, Mary S., ed. *Talking Leadership: Conversations with Powerful Women.* New Brunswick, NJ: Rutgers University Press, 1999.

Lippitt, Mary. ''How to Influence Leaders.'' *Training Development* 53, no. 3 (March 1999): 18-22.

Lord, R. G., DeVader, C. L. and G. M. Alliger. ''A Meta-analysis of the Relation between Personality Traits and Leadership Perceptions: An Application of Validity Generalization Procedures.'' *Journal of Applied Psychology* 71 (1986): 402-10.

Marable, Manning. *Black Leadership.* New York: Columbia University Press, 1998.

Marcinko, Richard. *Leadership Secrets of the Rogue Warrior: A Commando's Guide to Success.* New York: Pocket Books, 1996.

Miller, Clifford. ''The Renaissance Manager: Embracing the Three Dimensions of Dynamic Leadership.'' *Supervision* 60, no. 2 (February 1999): 6-8.

Northouse, Peter G. *Leadership: Theory and Practice.* Thousand Oaks, CA: Sage Publications, 1997.

Parachin, Victor M. ''Ten Essential Leadership Skills.'' *Supervision* 60, no. 2 (February 1999): 13-15.

Sills, David L., ed. *International Encyclopedia of the Social Sciences.* New York: Macmillan, 1968.

LEADING ECONOMIC INDICATORS

A leading economic indicator is a statistic, such as housing starts, that is considered to signal the future direction of economic activity. Leading indicators tend to reach cyclical high and low points earlier than corresponding peaks and troughs in the overall economy, which makes them useful for predicting economic downturns or recoveries. In contrast, lagging indicators, such as the average prime interest rate charged by **banks**, generally trail behind changes in the business cycle. Coincident indicators, such as manufacturing and trade sales, tend to rise and fall along with overall economic activity.

The most popular forecasting tool of this type is the Composite Index of Leading Economic Indicators (CLI), which is published monthly by the **U.S. Department of Commerce**. The CLI was created in the late 1950s by a group of economists led by Geoffrey Moore. It appears in numerous magazines and newspapers across the country and is monitored closely by government policymakers, financial analysts, and business leaders who seek to predict and prepare for the future direction of the economy. The CLI is composed of a series of 11 indicators from different segments of the economy selected specifically for their tendency to predict **business cycles** in the near future. The Commerce Department periodically revises the data, definitions, and procedures used to construct the CLI to ensure its accuracy. For example, the percent change in sensitive materials prices was eliminated from the **index** in 1996.

The specific components of the CLI are: the average length of a work week for manufacturing employees; the average number of initial claims for unemployment insurance in state programs; the dollar value of new orders placed with manufacturers in the consumer goods and materials industries; the percentage of vendor deliveries that are slower, or require a longer lead time; the dollar value of **contracts** and orders for industrial plants and equipment; the number of new private housing units authorized by local building permits; the dollar change in manufacturers' unfilled orders in the **durable goods** industries; the average prices of 500 common **stocks**; the dollar change in the M2 **money supply** measure; and the change in consumer expectations.

In order to successfully predict cyclical changes in economic activity, leading indicators must be interpreted using a filtering rule. One popular rule of thumb for interpreting the movement of leading indicators is that three successive periods of decline signal an imminent **recession**, while three successive periods of increase signal the beginning of a recovery. Economists apply much more sophisticated statistical models to interpret the performance of individual leading indicators or the CLI.

In an analysis for the *Journal of Forecasting,* K. Lahiri and J. G. Wang found that the CLI predicted turning points in the economy successfully, with a lead time of about three months using real-time data, but also sent some false signals of impending downturns. Evan F. Koenig and Kenneth M. Emery, in an article for *Contemporary Economic Policy,* found that the CLI predicted peaks in the business cycle an average of 8.2 months in advance and troughs an average of 4.2 months in advance. They still claimed, however, that the CLI ''failed to provide reliable advance warning of both recessions and recoveries'' for several reasons: there is usually a one-month delay in publication of the CLI; the peaks and troughs are gradual and difficult to recognize in real time; and the index is subject to frequent revisions.

Still, the researchers emphasized that their results do not necessarily mean that the CLI is useless. Instead, the index may be relied upon to a great extent by government policymakers. These officials may respond to changes in the CLI by enacting policies to counteract the cyclical trends in the economy. For example, the **Federal Reserve** might raise **interest rates** in order to slow an economic expansion that is accompanied by **inflation**. Any successful countercyclical actions would make the CLI appear less reliable as a predictor.

[Laurie Collier Hillstrom]

FURTHER READING:

''Composite Indexes: Leading Index Components.'' *Survey of Current Business,* March 1995.

Koenig, Evan F., and Kenneth M. Emery. ''Why the Composite Index of Leading Indicators Does Not Lead.'' *Contemporary Economic Policy,* January 1994.

Koretz, Gene. ''Commodities Fall from Grace: They're Out as a Leading Indicator.'' *Business Week,* 2 December 1996, 34.

Lahiri, K., and J. G. Wang. ''Predicting Cyclical Turning Points with Leading Index in a Markov Switching Model.'' *Journal of Forecasting* 13, no. 3 (May 1994): 245.

Linden, Dana Wechsler. ''Sentinel on the Inflation Watch.'' *Forbes,* 12 September 1994, 126.

LEARNING CURVES

SEE: Experience and Learning Curves

LEASING

A lease is a form of financing under which the owner of an asset (the lessor) temporarily transfers the right to use, and sometimes other ownership rights and obligations, of an asset to another party (the lessee). The lessor typically makes the lease for a specified time in return for a lump sum or periodic rental payments from the lessee.

The basic concept of leasing dates back to at least 1800 B.C., when the Babylonian king Hammurabi described the transaction in his Code of laws, stating that use—rather than ownership—of equipment is what produces wealth. Leasing has been employed for centuries in different forms and for different applications, but by the early 1990s it was confined primarily to **real estate** rentals, although leasing was also used to finance other expensive assets such as cars and farm equipment.

As a result of several factors, including tax code changes and improved efficiency in the financial markets, leasing became a common financing tool after 1950. By the mid-1990s people and companies were leasing everything from airplanes and oil rigs to televisions and office furniture. In fact, in the United States leasing was the most common way to finance plant and equipment for manufacturing companies, and it was being used in a growing number of consumer purchases.

ADVANTAGES TO LESSEES

The chief advantage to leasing is that it provides an alternative to ownership. The party that leases also benefits from not having its resources invested in equipment. Indeed, many companies that lease equipment do so because they believe higher productivity and profits are derived from productive use of equipment, rather than its ownership. A trucking company, for example, might benefit from investing its limited resources in **marketing** or inventory tracking operations instead of in trucks. Similarly, an individual who leases a car may believe that her money would provide a better return invested in stocks. In turn, companies that lease equipment to others believe that they can do a better job of buying, financing, servicing, and selling equipment than their customers.

But there are also numerous logistical motivations behind leasing. A company that leases an office machine, for example, avoids the risk of investing its resources in an asset that may soon become technologically obsolete. The company may also benefit from having access to the machine for only a short time, to complete a big project for example, without having to invest larger sums in the equipment and soon after dispose of it. In addition, companies can reduce their apparent debt burden by leasing. Finally, for individuals who cannot afford to buy or who are unable to obtain **loans** for consumer goods such as furniture, leasing provides an important financing alternative.

Importantly, lessees also benefit from a number of tax advantages. A firm that leases equipment or real estate, for example, will be able to deduct its lease payments from its taxable income immediately rather than deducting the cost of purchasing equipment as depreciation over time.

ADVANTAGES TO LESSORS

Lessors also benefit in several ways. Compared to lessees, they are often able to acquire equipment at a low cost, liquidate it efficiently, and obtain acceptable financing terms. These advantages result from various **economies of scale**, such as increased buying power with sellers of equipment. Lessors are also better positioned to take advantage of certain tax laws, such as depreciation allowances and investment tax credits.

TYPES OF LEASES

The two primary types of leases are financial leases (also known as capital leases) and operating leases. Financial leasing companies essentially sell equipment to their customers. The lessee typically rents the item for its entire useful life, or agrees to eventually pay for and own the item through a lease-to-own arrangement. The agreement effectively involves transfer of ownership to the lessee, who cannot cancel the lease without penalty. The payments typically amortize most of the economic value of the asset. Most financial leases are net leases, meaning that the lessee is responsible for maintaining and insuring the asset and paying all property taxes. Financial leases are often used for heavy capital equipment such as airplanes and earth-moving machines, as well as for consumer items such as furniture and electronics.

In contrast, operating leases, or service leases, mimic short-term loans. Lessors typically rent an item more than once during its useful life, and lessees do not commit to purchase the equipment in the lease. Unlike a financial leasing arrangement, a lessee usually can cancel an operating lease, given some minimum notification, without a major penalty. Furthermore, the lessor is usually responsible for maintenance, insurance, and taxes related to the asset. Motor vehicles are often leased under operating leases, as are computers, copiers, and other office machines.

Several types of leases, each of which combine different financial and tax advantages, are actually hybrids of financial and operating leases. The dollar-out lease and the bargain lease, for example, both give the user the option of acquiring the equipment for a negligible or undetermined amount at the end of the lease. Among the most popular hybrid leases is the sale-and-leaseback, whereby a company sells its own assets and then leases them back from the buyer. Sale-and-leasebacks are most commonly used to finance the use of real estate. The seller/lessor benefits from an infusion of cash, and may also enjoy certain tax advantages.

TYPES OF LESSORS

Lessors generally come in one of four varieties:

1. *Captive leasing companies.* These are usually subsidiaries of a parent company that manufactures the product being leased, e.g., IBM Credit Corp. leases IBM computers.
2. *Commercial banks.* Companies enter into leasing agreements with banks they already do business with or by other means. Sometimes banks buy and sell their lease portfolios, or serve as the front end for an outside leasing service.
3. *Independent leasing companies.* These firms typically are unaffiliated with the manufacturer or the lessee and derive most of their business from leasing to businesses, e.g., GE Capital provides general leasing and financing services for a diverse range of commercial and industrial equipment.
4. *Brokers.* Leasing brokerages act as intermediaries to link lessees and lessors.

Within these categories, many lessors target particular markets, such as the small business market, the medical equipment market, and so forth. Leasing veterans recommend that businesses obtain quotes from at least five different providers. Since there are a host of terms and financing options available—as well as competitors in the leasing business—many companies are able to bargain with lessors rather than accepting the first offer.

LEASING INDUSTRY TRENDS

As of the late 1990s, industry estimates placed the annual value of equipment leasing in the United States at some $180 billion. As much as 80 percent of all businesses lease some kind of equipment, and overall a little less than a third of all business equipment (in value) is reportedly leased. Some of the most popular leased items for businesses are transportation equipment, office machines (especially computers), and general manufacturing/industrial equipment.

Based on 1997 figures compiled by the Equipment Leasing Association, transportation equipment and office machines constituted more than half of all leased equipment by dollar value. Within transportation equipment, railroad equipment was the largest category, representing 16.3 percent of all leasing dollars. Computers were second, at 10.6 percent, followed by aircraft (9.7 percent), trucks and trailers (6.6 percent), electrical power equipment (6.4 percent), agricultural equipment (5.8 percent), general office machines (5.4 percent), general industrial/manufacturing equipment (5.3 percent), and construction equipment (4.9 percent). The foregoing categories together made up over 70 percent of all business leasing by dollar volume.

[Dave Mote]

FURTHER READING:

Contino, Richard M. *Handbook of Equipment Leasing.* 2nd ed. New York: AMACOM, 1996.

——. *Negotiating Business Equipment Leases.* 2nd ed. New York: AMACOM, 1998.

Equipment Leasing Association. *Equipment Leasing Association Online Home Page.* Arlington, VA, 1999. Available from www.elaonline.com.

Parra, Elizabeth V. ''How to Avoid Some of the Biggest Traps in Leasing.'' *Business Credit,* September 1998.

Powell, Edwin. ''Equipment Leasing.'' *OfficeSystems,* November 1998.

LEAST SQUARES

The least squares criterion is a statistical approach used to provide the most accurate estimate of relationships between sets of variables in sample data. It is used to define regression lines and planes that yield estimates of a dependent variable, given values for an independent variable.

Least squares analysis is the most popular approach to the computation of regression lines because it is relatively simple and highly accurate. Particularly in linear relationships, it provides the best linear unbiased estimator (BLUE), of sample data. It also gives the maximum likelihood estimator (MLE), in regressions where errors from the regression line form a normal bell-shaped distribution.

In order to understand how a least squares analysis is performed, it is important to first understand the properties of a **regression analysis**. Simply described, regression analysis uses algebraic formulas to estimate the value of a continuous random dependent variable, using other independent variables as indicators. These formulas produce an estimate of the dependent variable that is most correct (or least incorrect), given any value of an independent variable.

The least squares approach is nearly 100 years older than regression analysis. It was independently developed between 1805 and 1809 by French mathematician Adrien-Marie Legendre (1752-1833) and German mathematician and astronomer Carl Friedrich Gauss (1777-1855). These mathematicians were working on ways to estimate the paths of comets.

Astronomical observations had suggested that these comets maintained highly erratic orbits. In fact, the deviations were due to observational errors. This led the discoverers to develop a method, the least

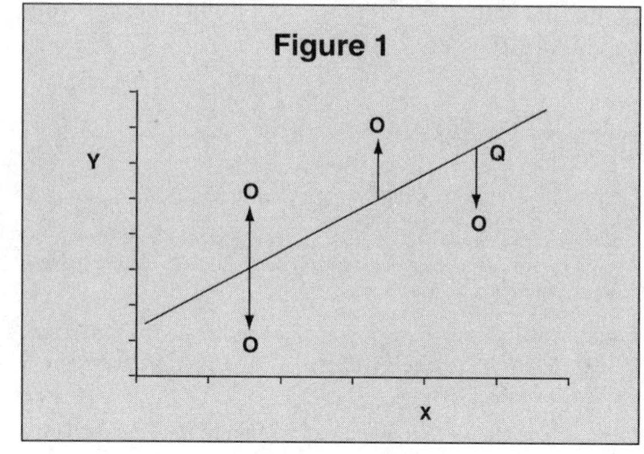

squares criterion, that would factor out these errors and produce a correct prediction of a comet's path.

The mathematicians work yielded important insights into estimating relationships between other types of graphical coordinates—specifically, how to rationalize deviations from a theoretical line of best fit. By the definition of such an estimated line, there are as many negative deviations as positive ones. As a result, all deviations must be expressed as absolute values, a condition met through squaring (the square of any number, whether positive or negative, is positive).

The least squares criterion produces a line in which the sum of the squared deviations of every value Y from the line are lowest. The line represents a continuous *estimate* of Y values for every value of X, based on the sample data (see Figure 1).

This simple example demonstrates that it is impossible to draw a straight line, or linear regression, that touches all four points on the graph. Instead, we use the least squares criterion to determine the location of a straight line (Q) that comes closest to the points.

Squaring also places the regression line precisely where deviations from the line are lowest. If the sums of deviations were not squared, the line may drift upward or downward until it meets a coordinate. Increased deviation on one side of the line would be made up exactly by decreases on the other side of the line (see Figure 2).

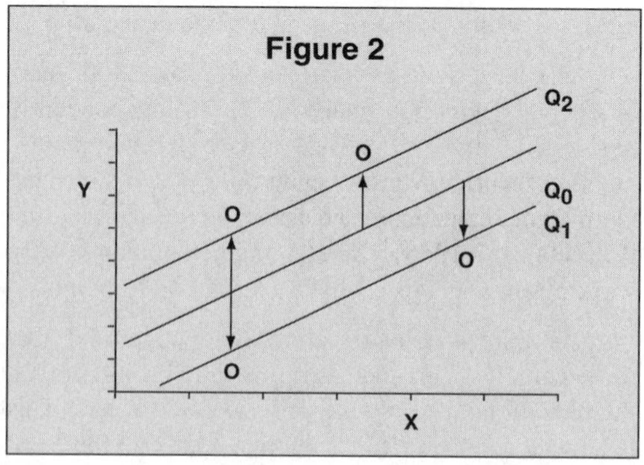

When the deviations are squared, the degree of their deviation is amplified. The difference between 2.5, 3.5, 4.5, and 5.5 is 1, but the difference between their squares—6.25, 12.25, 20.25, 30.25—increases incrementally, 6, 8, and 10.

As a result, the least squares formula indicates a specific slope β, and places that slope at a specific reference point α, the Y intercept.

[John Simley, updated by Kevin J. Murphy]

FURTHER READING:

Foster, D. P., R. A. Stine, and R. P. Waterman. *Business Analysis Using Regression.* New York: Springer-Verlag, 1998.

Lawson, Charles L., and Richard J. Hanson. *Solving Least Squares Problems.* Society for Industrial and Applied Mathematics, 1995.

Lind, Douglas A., and Robert D. Mason. *Basic Statistics for Business and Economics.* New York: McGraw-Hill Higher Education, 1996.

LETTERS OF CREDIT

A letter of credit is a bank's written commitment ensuring that payment will be made to a seller of goods according to conditions specified by the buyer. A letter of credit allows the seller to draw on the issuing bank for payment. The term ''letter of credit'' was legally defined in the case of *American Steel Company v. Irving National Bank* as: ''A letter requesting one person to make advances to a third person on the credit of the writer.'' The decision went on to state that letters of credit may be general or specific. ''They are general if directed to the writer's correspondents generally. They are special if addressed to some particular person.'' Letters of credit involve four parties: the buyer, and the buyer's bank that issues the letter of credit, the seller, and the seller's bank.

Letters of credit work through the following steps:

1. A buyer and seller reach a commercial agreement.
2. The buyer applies to a bank for a letter of credit.
3. The buyer's bank approves the line of credit and forwards this information to the seller's bank.
4. The seller's bank confirms the letter of credit and so notifies the seller.
5. The seller transfers the goods to the buyer.

6. The seller notifies the buyer's bank that the goods have been transferred to the buyer.
7. The seller is paid by his or her bank.
8. The seller's bank apprises the buyer's bank of the transaction.
9. The seller's bank is reimbursed by the buyer's bank.
10. The buyer's bank notifies the buyer of the transaction.
11. The buyer reimburses his or her bank.

In order to comply with these aforementioned steps, letters of credit are generally consistent with proscribed attributes and responsibilities. A letter of credit must clearly state that it is in fact a letter of credit. A letter of credit must have an expiration date and a set credit line. The buyer's bank is not required to reimburse the seller's bank without proper documentation of the transaction, and the buyer's bank is not obligated to referee any legal disputes that may arise between the parties. Finally, the buyer has a total obligation to reimburse his or her bank.

In letters of credit the buyer's bank is often referred to as the ''issuing bank'' and the seller's bank is often referred to as the ''corresponding bank'' or ''confirming bank.'' The ''applicant'' is the buyer or party applying for the letter of credit and the ''beneficiary'' is the seller or the party ''in whose favor the letter of credit is issued.'' The ''amount'' is the maximum sum of money for which the letter of credit is issued and is stated in terms of a specific currency. The ''terms'' are the requirements that must be met by both parties and the ''expiry'' is the final date by which the beneficiary must present a demand against the credit.

All of these components must be present for a letter of credit to be valid. The term ''letter of credit'' is often abbreviated as ''LC'' or ''L/C.'' A revocable letter of credit allows the buyer or applicant to amend or cancel the letter without prior approval of the seller or beneficiary. This type of letter of credit can be hazardous for the seller. An irrevocable letter of credit cannot be amended without the consent of the buyer, seller, and issuing bank. There is also a ''confirmed irrevocable letter of credit'' by which a bank other than the issuing bank agrees to irrevocably honor the letter of credit providing the seller satisfies the terms of the agreement.

Letters of credit are most often involved in commercial transactions in which the buyer and seller reside in different countries and thus are involved in international trade. According to Ideacom International, potential hazards in international trade that letters of credit help to alleviate include: geographical distance, cultural differences, a host of intermediaries such as customs officials and freight forwarders, a myriad of regulations and procedures, and political instability. Other hazards that are also lessened by letters of credit are: economic risks such as changes in currency exchange rates or **interest rates**; political risks such as labor strikes, insurrections, and **boycotts**; natural disasters such as earthquakes and floods; transport risks such as shipwrecks, fire, and theft; and commercial risks such as default of payment and insolvency or bankruptcy.

Letters of credit are thus advantageous to both the buyer and the seller. Payment to the seller is guaranteed by either the issuing bank or the confirming bank, or sometimes by both. The buyer's funds are not immediately tied up by the transaction and, because payment is guaranteed, a discount price can often be negotiated. Since letters of credit have expiration dates, the delivery of goods is usually guaranteed before that date occurs. The respective **banks** profit from the fees they collect for their services. Bank charges are usually based on risk factors rather than a predetermined list of fees.

An international code of rules pertaining to letters of credit is known as the Uniform Customs and Practices for Documentary Credits (UCP). This code is issued by the International Chamber of Commerce headquartered in Paris. Although there is no formal legislative or judicial enforcement of the code, it is adhered to worldwide by most banks and commercial enterprises. A similar code in the United States that governs letters of credit is the **Uniform Commercial Code** (UCC). Like the UCP, there is no formal judicial or legislative enforcement of the UCC. Most deliberative bodies in the United States, however, write applicable legislation based on the UCC.

Generally the above information applies to commercial letters of credit. There are also traveler's letters of credit. These are letters of credit issued by a bank to a traveler and are meant to serve as an introduction of the holding party to banks in foreign countries. There are actually two variations of traveler's letters of credit, circular and specially advised. Specially advised letters of credit are addressed to a particular foreign bank, while a circular letter of credit is issued to foreign banks in general. The holder of a traveler's letter of credit generally makes payment to an issuing bank in advance and in an amount equal to the line of credit. The holder, however, may make arrangements to have withdrawals made from a deposit account as drafts are received by the issuing bank.

[Michael Knes]

FURTHER READING:

Aster, Charles E., and Katheryn C. Patterson. *A Practical Guide to Letters of Credit.* New York: Executive Enterprises Publications, 1990.

Cotton Council International. "Letter of Credit." Washington: Cotton Council International, 1998. Available from www.cottonusa.org.

Dolan, John F. *The Law of Letters of Credit.* Boston: Warren, Borham & Lamont, 1996.

Ideacom International Inc. "The Letter of Credit—Introduction." London: Ideacom International, 1998. Available from www.tradewinds-tv.com/program6/en0610.html.

LEVERAGE

In physics, leverage denotes the use of a lever and a small amount of force to lift a heavy object. Likewise in business, leverage refers to the use of a relatively small investment or a small amount of **debt** to achieve greater profits. That is, leverage is the use of assets and **liabilities** to boost profits while balancing the risks involved. There are two types of leverage, operating and financial. Operating leverage refers to the use of fixed **costs** in a company's earnings stream to magnify operating profits. Financial leverage, on the other hand, results from the use of debt and **preferred stock** to increase stockholder earnings. Although both types of leverage involve a certain amount of **risk**, they can bring about significant benefits with little investment when successfully implemented.

OPERATING LEVERAGE

Operating leverage is the extent to which a firm uses fixed costs in producing its goods or offering its services. Fixed costs include **advertising** expenses, administrative costs, equipment and technology, **depreciation**, and **taxes**, but not interest on debt, which is part of financial leverage. By using fixed production costs, a company can increase its profits. If a company has a large percentage of fixed costs, it has a high degree of operating leverage. Automated and high-tech companies, utility companies, and airlines generally have high degrees of operating leverage.

As an illustration of operating leverage, assume two firms, A and B, produce and sell widgets. Firm A uses a highly automated production process with robotic machines, whereas firm B assembles the widgets using primarily semiskilled labor. Table 1 shows both firm's operating cost structures.

Highly automated firm A has fixed costs of $35,000 per year and variable costs of only $1.00 per unit, whereas labor-intensive firm B has fixed costs of only $15,000 per year, but its variable cost per unit is much higher at $3.00 per unit. Both firms produce and sell 10,000 widgets per year at a price of $5.00 per widget.

Firm A has a higher amount of operating leverage because of its higher fixed costs, but firm A also has a higher breakeven point—the point at which total costs equal total sales. Nevertheless, a change of 1 percent in sales causes more than a 1 percent change in operating profits for firm A, but not for firm B. The "degree of operating leverage" measures this effect. The following simplified equation demonstrates the type of equation used to compute the degree of operating leverage, although to calculate this figure the equation would require several additional factors such as the quantity produced, variable cost per unit, and the price per unit, which are used to determine changes in profits and sales:

$$\text{Degree of Operating Leverage} = \frac{\text{Percentage Change in Profits}}{\text{Percentage Change in Sales}}$$

Operating leverage is a double-edged sword, however. If firm A's sales decrease by 1 percent, its profits will decrease by more than 1 percent, too. Hence, the degree of operating leverage shows the responsiveness of profits to a given change in sales.

FINANCIAL LEVERAGE

Financial leverage involves changes in shareholders' income in response to changes in operating profits, resulting from financing a company's assets with debt or preferred stock. Similar to operating leverage, financial leverage also can boost a company's returns, but it increases risk as well. Financial leverage is concerned with the relationship between operating profits and earnings per share. If a company is financed exclusively with **common stock**, a specific percentage change in operating profit will cause the

Table 1
Illustration of Operating Leverage

	Firm A (High Automation)	Firm B (Low Automation)
Units Produced	10,000	10,000
Sales price per unit (P)	$5.00	$5.00
Variable cost per unit (V)	$1.00	$3.00
Fixed costs (F)	$35,000	$15,000

Table 2
Asset Financing

	Firm A	Firm B
Long-term debt (8%)	$10,000	$ 0
Stockholders equity	30,000	40,000
Total liabilities & equity	40,000	40,000

same percentage change in shareholder earnings. For example, a 5 percent increase in operating profit will result in a 5 percent increase in shareholder earnings.

If a company is financed with debt or is ''leveraged,'' however, its shareholder earnings will become more sensitive to changes in operating profit. Hence, a 5 percent increase in operating profits will result in a much higher increase in stockholder earnings. Nevertheless, financial leveraging makes companies equally susceptible to greater decreases in stockholder earnings if operating profits drop.

For example, recall the two firms, A and B. At production levels of 10,000 widgets, they both had operating earnings (profits) of $5,000. In addition, assume that both firms have total assets of $40,000. Table 2 shows how the $40,000 of assets are financed for both firms. Firm A is financed with $10,000 of debt which carries an annual interest cost of 8 percent, and $30,000 of stockholders' equity (3,000 shares), firm B is financed entirely with $40,000 of stockholders' equity (4,000 shares).

Firm A is leveraged and uses some debt to finance its assets, which can increase earnings per share but also risk. Table 3 shows the results of financial leverage on the firm's earnings.

Panel A shows that as a result of the $800 interest expense from the debt ($10,000 × .08 = $800), firm A's earnings per share are lower than firm B's. Because firm A is financially leveraged, however, an increase in profits will result in a greater increase in stock earnings. Panel B shows the results of a 10 percent increase in profits for both firms. Firm A's stockholder earnings increased from $0.84 to $0.94, an 11.9 percent increase, while firm B's stockholder earnings increased from $0.75 to $0.825, or 10 percent, the same as the increase in profits.

Table 3
Illustration of Financial Leverage

Panel A Operating Income = $5,000

	Firm A	Firm B
Operating income (EBIT)	$5,000	$5,000
Less: interest expense	(800)	(0)
Earnings before taxes (EBT)	4,200	5,000
Less: taxes (40%)	(1,680)	(2,000)
Net profits after taxes (NPAT)	2,520	3,000
Divided by number of shares	3000	4000
Earnings per share (EPS)	$0.84	$0.75

Panel B Operating Income = $5,500

	Firm A	Firm B
Operating income (EBIT)	$5,500	$5,500
Less: interest expense	(800)	(0)
Earnings before taxes (EBT)	4,700	5,500
Less: taxes (40%)	(1,880)	(2,200)
Net profits after taxes (NPAT)	2,820	3,300
Divided by number of shares	3000	4000
Earnings per share (EPS)	$0.94	$0.825
Increase in EPS	$0.10	$0.94
Percentage increase in EPS	11.90%	10.0%

Companies with significant amounts of debt in contrast with their assets are referred to as being highly leveraged and their shareholder earnings are more unpredictable than those for companies with less debt. Lenders and financial analysts often measure a company's degree of financial leverage using the ratio of interest payments to operating profit.

From the perspective of shareholders, financing using debt is the riskiest, because companies must make interest and principal payments on debt as part of their contract with their lenders, but they need not pay preferred stock **dividends** if their earnings are low. Nevertheless, financing with preferred stock will have the same kind of leveraging effect as debt financing as illustrated above.

Firms that use financial leverage run the risk that their operating income will be insufficient to cover the fixed charges on debt and/or preferred stock financing. Financial leverage can become especially burdensome during an economic downturn. Even if a company has sufficient earnings to cover its fixed financial costs, its returns could be decreased during economically difficult times due to shareholders' residual claims to dividends.

Generally, if a company's return on assets (profits ÷ total assets) is greater than the pretax cost of debt (interest percentage), the financial leverage effect will be favorable. The opposite, of course, is also true: if a company's return on assets is less than its interest cost of debt, the financial leverage effect will decrease the returns to the common shareholders.

TOTAL LEVERAGE

The two types of leverage explored so far can be combined into an overall measure of leverage called total leverage. Recall that operating leverage is concerned with the relationship between sales and operating profits, and financial leverage is concerned with the relationship between profits and earnings per share. Total leverage is therefore concerned with the relationship between sales and earnings per share. Specifically, it is concerned with the sensitivity of earnings to a given change in sales.

The degree of total leverage is defined as the percentage change in stockholder earnings for a given change in sales, and it can be calculated by multiplying a company's degree of operating leverage by its degree of financial leverage. Consequently, a company with little operating leverage can attain a high degree of total leverage by using a relatively high amount of debt.

IMPLICATIONS

Total risk can be divided into two parts: business risk and financial risk. Business risk refers to the stability of a company's assets if it uses no debt or preferred stock financing. Business risk stems from the unpredictable nature of doing business, i.e., the unpredictability of consumer demand for products and services. As a result, it also involves the uncertainty of long-term profitability. When a company uses debt or preferred stock financing, additional risk—financial risk—is placed on the company's common shareholders. They demand a higher expected return for assuming this additional risk, which in turn, raises a company's costs. Consequently, companies with high degrees of business risk tend to be financed with relatively low amounts of debt. The opposite also holds: companies with low amounts of business risk can afford to use more debt financing while keeping total risk at tolerable levels. Moreover, using debt as leverage is a successful tool during periods of **inflation**. Debt fails, however, to provide leverage during periods of deflation, such as the period during the late 1990s brought on by the Asian financial crisis.

[James A. Gerhardinger, updated by Karl Heil]

FURTHER READING:

Brigham, Eugene F. *Fundamentals of Financial Management.* Fort Worth, TX: Dryden Press, 1995.

"Choosing the Right Mixture." *Economist,* 27 February 1999, 71.

Dugan, Michael T., and Keith A. Shriver. "An Empirical Comparison of Alternative Methods for Estimating the Degree of Operating Leverage." *Financial Review,* May 1992, 309-21.

Jaedicke, Robert K., and Alexander A. Robichek. "Cost-Volume-Profit Analysis under Conditions of Uncertainty." *Accounting Review,* October 1964, 917-26.

Krefetz, Gerald. *Leverage: The Key to Multiplying Money.* New York: Wiley, 1988.

Shalit, Sol S. "On the Mathematics of Financial Leverage." *Financial Management,* spring 1975, 57-66.

LEVERAGED BUYOUT (LBO)

During the 1980s, leveraged buyouts (LBOs) became increasingly common and increased substantially in size. In a leveraged buyout, a company or division is purchased by a group of private investors, which frequently includes the **management** of the economic unit. To demonstrate their commitment, the managers will normally be expected to purchase a significant equity stake in the transaction. This will usually be a proportion of the equity since the transaction is financed with large amounts of **debt** and little equity. After an LBO, the firm ceases to be publicly traded. The interest and borrowings are expected to be repaid from the target's cash flow, particularly with tax benefits obtainable for the interest payments. Subsequently, once the debt is paid down, the organizers of the buyout attempt to take the firm public again.

The nature of the debt used in LBOs is typically subordinated debentures. In fact, most LBOs are financed with a high proportion of so-called ''**junk**'' (i.e., high-yield) **bonds**. The remainder of the financing usually comes from a mix of private sources and **banks**.

A successful buyout candidate has certain characteristics that can increase its chances of surviving and providing returns to lenders, investors, and managers. Factors that can be found in a successful LBO include: proven earnings growth; a strong market position; an asset base indicating unused debt capacity; an established, unconcentrated customer base; proven management; and a significant opportunity for cost reductions.

The occurrence of LBOs is positively related to the existence of target firms that have large and stable cash flows and the possibility of future tax savings. Finally, LBO incidence increases when there is potential for employment reductions and redeployment, particularly among corporate staff. Therefore, after the LBO, there should be significant improvements in profitability and operating efficiency.

Empirical studies indicate that the acquired firms' shareholders earn large positive abnormal returns from leveraged buyouts. Similarly, the postbuyout investors in these transactions often earn large excess returns over the period from the buyout completion date to the date of an initial **public offering** or resale.

An outstanding introduction to LBOs is the film *Barbarians at the Gate.* This movie, which loosely chronicles the LBO of RJR Nabisco, has found its way into many **finance** classrooms.

SOURCES OF VALUE IN LBOS

Studies have identified several potential sources of value in leveraged buyout transactions. These include: **wealth** transfers from old public shareholders to the buyout group; wealth transfers from public bondholders to the investor group; wealth creation from improved incentives for managerial **decision making**; and wealth transfers from the government via tax advantages. These potential motivations for leveraged buyout transactions are not mutually exclusive; it is possible that a combination of these may occur in a given LBO.

Much controversy regarding LBOs has resulted from the concern that senior executives negotiating the sale of the company to themselves are engaged in self-dealing. On one hand, the managers have a **fiduciary duty** to their shareholders to sell the company at the highest possible price. On the other hand, they have an incentive to minimize what they pay for the shares. Accordingly, it has been suggested that management takes advantage of superior information about a firm's intrinsic value. The evidence, however, indicates that the premiums paid in leveraged buyouts compare favorably with those in interfirm **mergers** that are characterized by arm's-length negotiations between the buyer and seller.

Since leveraged buyout transactions are financed largely with debt, the existing debt of the buyout company, if not covenant protected, becomes more risky and less valuable. Accordingly, it has been argued that there is a transfer of wealth from bondholders to pre- and postbuyout equity investors. The empirical evidence, however, indicates that the transfers from bondholders do not appear to be a major source of value. These studies find that many leveraged buyout companies do not have any publicly traded debt in their capital structures. Moreover, the losses experienced by those firms with non-covenant-protected, publicly traded debt are much smaller than the positive abnormal returns earned by equity investors.

Another potential source of value in LBOs is derived from the reduction in agency costs that accompanies management's increased ownership stake in the company. In a publicly traded company, managers typically own only a small percentage of the common shares, and therefore can share only a small fraction of the gains resulting from improved managerial performance. After an LBO, however, executives can realize substantial financial gains from enhanced performance. This improvement in financial incentives for the firm's managers should result in greater effort on the part of management. The empirical evidence is consistent with efficiency gains in leveraged buyout transactions.

Because of the greater interest expense related to the increased levels of debt that the new company supports after the LBO, taxable income, everything else remaining equal, will decline, leading to lower tax payments. Therefore, the interest tax shield resulting from the higher levels of debt should enhance the value of firm. Studies indicate that these tax advantages are a significant source of value in LBO transactions.

CRITICISM OF LBOS

Critics of leveraged buyouts argue that these transactions harm the long-term competitiveness of the firms involved. First, these firms are unlikely to replace operating assets since the firms' cash flow must be devoted to servicing the LBO-related debt. Thus, the property, plant, and equipment of the LBO firms are likely to have aged considerably during the time when the firm is privately held. In addition, expenditures for repair and maintenance may have been curtailed as well. Finally, it is possible that

research and development expenditures have also been controlled. As a result, the future growth prospects of these firms may be significantly reduced.

Others argue that these transactions have a negative impact on the stakeholders of the firm. In many cases, LBOs lead to downsizing of operations, and many employees lose their jobs. In addition, some of the transactions have negative effects on the communities in which the firms are located.

Towards the end of the 1980s, the prices paid in leveraged buyouts increased, and buyout organizers invested less equity. As a result, a number of high-profile buyouts, such as Revco Drug Stores, filed for bankruptcy protection. Lenders reacted by tightening the supply of LBO credit and demanded changes in deal structures to lower risk.

SEE ALSO: Junk Bonds; Management Buyouts; Restrictive Covenants

[Robert T. Kleiman, updated by Ronald M. Horwitz]

FURTHER READING:

Baker, George P., and George D. Smith. *The New Financial Capitalists.* Cambridge University Press, 1998.

Blair, Margaret M. *The Deal Decade.* Brookings Institute, 1993.

Schwarf, Charles A. *Acquisitions, Mergers, Sales, Buyouts, and Takeovers: A Handbook with Forms.* 4th ed. Upper Saddle River: Prentice Hall Trade, 1991.

Sirower, Mark L. *The Synergy Trap: How Companies Lose the Acquisition Game.* Free Press, 1997.

LEVERAGED RECAPITALIZATIONS

During the latter half of the 1980s, leveraged recapitalizations (recaps) emerged as a popular response of U.S. companies to the increasingly competitive operating environment. In a leveraged recapitalization, a firm replaces the majority of its equity with a package of debt **securities** consisting of both senior bank **debt** and subordinated debentures. Although these transactions could be either defensive or preemptive maneuvers, the vast majority of leveraged recapitalizations were employed as defensive tactics to ward off hostile **takeovers**. The financial leveraging of the firm discouraged corporate raiders who could no longer borrow against the assets of the target firm to finance the acquisition.

Candidates for a leveraged recapitalization should have a relatively debt-free **capital structure**, steady and predictable cash flows, and an experienced and capable **management** team. The majority of firms undertaking these transactions are in mature, slow growth, non-technology-based industries that do not require substantial ongoing capital expenditures to remain competitive.

TYPES OF LEVERAGED RECAPITALIZATIONS

There are two generic categories of leveraged recapitalizations: leveraged cashouts and leveraged share repurchases. A leveraged cashout (LCO) involves a debt-financed special **dividend** paid by a firm to its shareholders. In addition, existing shareholders also receive a ''stub,'' a stock certificate that represents ownership in the restructured company. Since the stubs are publicly traded, shareholders continue to have the opportunity to share in the future gains (or losses) of the firm. LCOs also allow management to increase their proportional shareholdings instead of receiving the cash payout.

In a leveraged share repurchase (LSR), the company repurchases a significant percentage of its **common stock** through a **tender offer** in a transaction financed with **bank** and/or high-yield debt. Like the LCO, an LSR replaces outside equity with debt that has the impact of significantly increasing the financial **leverage** of the firm. Assuming that the firm is able to earn a return on its operating assets greater than the after-tax cost of debt, LSRs should result in higher earnings per share due to the reduction in the number of shares outstanding after the transaction. Whether this, in turn, increases the **market value** of the company's common stock depends upon how the market assesses the new level of **risk** in the company's capital structure.

The structure of leveraged recapitalization transactions is similar to that employed in **leveraged buyouts** (LBOs). In both cases, the firm significantly increases its financial leverage, and senior managers/employees generally receive additional equity ownership in the corporation. The tax shields associated with the interest expense of the additional debt used to finance the transactions are one source of additional value. Moreover, the additional equity interests of managers and employees should improve incentives to enhance productivity since the new organizational structure more closely links managerial rewards to employee performance. Both LBOs and recaps are accompanied by a restructuring in which the company sells off assets that are redundant or no longer a strategic fit in order to reduce debt. Studies of leveraged recapitalization announcements indicate that these transactions, like leveraged buyouts, are associated with increases in firms' **stock** prices. Furthermore, the **wealth** of bondholders declines because of the additional debt in the capital structure, but not by a significant amount.

Leveraged recapitalizations, however, differ from LBOs in a number of fundamental ways. First, following a leveraged recapitalization, the firm remains publicly traded. This differs from an LBO in which the firm is taken private. With a recap, the company continues to incur the costs of providing information to shareholders as well as the expenses associated with satisfying reporting requirements of the **Securities and Exchange Commission** for publicly held firms. Second, companies that undertake leveraged recapitalizations still maintain access to the public **capital markets** that may permit these firms to raise capital on more attractive terms than private firms. Third, in comparison to leveraged recapitalizations, leveraged buyouts may impose costs on managers by forcing managers to hold portfolios that are poorly diversified and/or illiquid due to reduced share marketability of the nonpublic shares. Thus, there is less potential for costly disagreements among stockholders in a recap since shareholders can readily sell their holdings if they disagree with corporate policies.

LEVERAGED RECAPITALIZATIONS AND OPERATING PERFORMANCE

Financial theory suggests that leveraged recapitalizations should result in greater operating efficiency. First, corporate managers' percentage of ownership normally increases in LCOs because executives receive new shares of equivalent value in lieu of cash. Consequently, managers have a reduced incentive to take advantage of corporate perquisites (such as large expense accounts or support staffs) in a manner that reduces corporate profitability. The additional equity ownership also provides performance incentives to managers and employees since their economic well-being is now more closely linked to the firm's performance. Second, the debt taken on in leveraged recapitalizations effectively compels management to pay out future free cash flows. Accordingly, these transactions reduce the cash flow available for discretionary spending making it less likely that management will spend money on subpar investment projects. Third, high levels of financial leverage have a powerful disciplining effect since **default** on the debt could cost managers their managerial independence and even their jobs. Risk-averse managers, fearing the high debt level of the newly recapitalized company, should have a strong motivation to generate additional cash flows.

The principal disadvantage associated with these transactions is the risk incurred from the large amount of debt. In considering a recap, the company must ensure that its cash flows are sufficient to service the additional debt. In order to meet its debt obligations, a highly leveraged company needs steady and predictable cash flows. A firm that encounters cash flow problems jeopardizes its future operating flexibility, and may be forced to sell assets or declare bankruptcy. Therefore, following a recapitalization, management needs to focus on the fundamentals of the business, selling underperforming or underutilized assets and paying down debt quickly.

Empirical studies indicate that managers significantly improve their management of the firm's **working capital** after undertaking a leveraged recapitalization. Managers substantially decrease days of sales outstanding and improve inventory turnover. In addition, firms are able to generate more sales per dollar of assets. The results for profitability measures that are calculated before interest expense indicate that both the operating return on assets and operating **profit margin** increase. This suggests that firms increase their gross profit margins and reduce their selling, general, and administrative expense following recapitalizations.

Improvement in postrecapitalization cash flows, however, appears to be achieved at the expense of long-term viability. Following recaps, firms experience significant decreases in sales and capital expenditures reflecting lower levels of discretionary investment spending and asset sales. This reduction in capital expenditures could have negative implications for the long-term value of these firms.

[Robert T. Kleiman, updated by Ronald M. Horwitz]

FURTHER READING:

Baker, George P., and George D. Smith. *The New Financial Capitalists.* Cambridge University Press, 1998.

Gupta, Atul, and Leonard Rosenthal. ''Ownership Structure, Leverage, and Firm Value: The Case of Leveraged Recapitalizations.'' *Financial Management,* autumn 1991, 69-83.

Handa, Puneet, and A. R. Radhakrishnan. ''An Empirical Investigation of Leveraged Recapitalizations with Cash Payout as Takeover Defense.'' *Financial Management,* autumn 1991, 58-68.

Wasserstein, Bruce. *Big Deal: The Battle for Control of America's Leading Corporations.* New York: Warner Books, 1998.

LIABILITIES

A liability is a **debt** assumed by a business entity as a result of its borrowing activities or other fiscal obligations (such as funding **pension plans** for its employees). Liabilities are paid off under either short-term or long-term arrangements. The amount of time allotted to pay off the liability is typically determined by the size of the debt; large amounts of money usually are borrowed under long-term plans.

Payment of a liability generally involves payment of the total sum of the amount borrowed. In addition, the business entity that provides the money to the borrowing institution typically charges interest, figured as a percentage of the amount that has been lent.

A company's liabilities are critical factors in understanding its status in any industry in which it is involved. As John Brozovsky noted in *Journal of Commercial Lending,* ''a basic understanding of accounting for liabilities is necessary to assess the viability of any company. Companies are required to follow certain accounting rules; however, the rules allow considerable flexibility in how a company accounts for liabilities.''

By the late 1990s, it was even possible within the rules for companies to hide liabilities from investors and analysts. For example, according to Gretchen Morgenson in *Forbes,* some **banks** and investment firms routinely transfer some of their positions to another entity—such as a hedge fund—for a week or so at the end of their quarterly **accounting** periods through a combination **derivative** and **repurchase agreement**. In exchange for holding the liabilities, the second firm receives an amount 25 to 30 basis points over the **interest rate** on the transferred **securities**. Although such transactions are legal, Morgenson asks whether financial firms ''should be spending shareholders' money to hide things from shareholders.''

CURRENT LIABILITIES

Current liabilities are short-term financial obligations that are paid off within one year or one current operating cycle, whichever is longer. (A normal operating cycle, while it varies from industry to industry, is the time from a company's initial investment in inventory to the time of collection of cash from sales of that inventory or of products created from that inventory.) Typical current liabilities include such accrued expenses as wages, **taxes**, and interest payments not yet paid; accounts payable; short-term notes; cash **dividends**; and revenues collected in advance of actual delivery of goods or services.

Economists, creditors, investors, and other members of the financial community all regard a business entity's current liabilities as an important indicator of its overall fiscal health. One financial indicator associated with liabilities that is often studied is known as **working capital**. Working capital refers to the dollar difference between a business's total current liabilities and its total current assets. Another financial barometer that examines a business's current liabilities is known as the current ratio. Creditors and others compute the current ratio by dividing total current assets by total current liabilities, which provides the company's ratio of assets to liabilities. For example, a company with $1.5 million in current assets and $500,000 in current liabilities would have a three to-one ratio of assets to liabilities.

LONG-TERM LIABILITIES

Liabilities that are not paid off within a year, or within a business's operating cycle, are known as long-term or noncurrent liabilities. Such liabilities often involve large sums of money necessary to undertake opening of a business, conduct a major expansion of a business, replace assets, or make a purchase of significant assets. Such debt typically requires a longer period of time to pay off. Examples of long-term liabilities include notes, **mortgages**, lease obligations, deferred income taxes payable, and pensions and other postretirement benefits.

When debt that has been classified as long-term is paid off within the next year, the amount of that paid-off liability should be reported by the company as a current liability in order to reflect the expected drain on current assets. An exception to this rule, however, comes into effect if a company decides to pay off the liability through the transfer of noncurrent assets that have been previously accumulated for that very purpose.

CONTINGENT LIABILITIES

A third kind of liability accrued by companies is known as a contingent liability. The term refers to instances in which a company reports that there is a possible liability for an event, transaction, or incident that has already taken place; the company, however, does not yet know whether a financial drain on its resources will result. It also is often uncertain of the size of the financial obligation or the exact time that the obligation might have to be paid.

Contingent liabilities often come into play when a lawsuit or other legal measure has been taken against a company. An as yet unresolved lawsuit concerning a business's products or services, for example, would qualify as a contingent liability. Environmental cleanup and/or protection responsibility sometimes falls under this classification as well, if the monetary impact of new regulations or penalties on a company is uncertain.

Companies are legally bound to report contingent liabilities. They are typically recorded in notes that are attached to a company's **financial statement** rather than as an actual part of the financial statement. If a loss due to a contingent liability is seen as probable, however, it should be included as part of the company's financial statement.

[Laurie Collier Hillstrom]

FURTHER READING:

Brozovsky, John. ''A Review of Changes Affecting Accounting for Liabilities.'' *Journal of Commercial Lending* 76, no. 7 (March 1994): 48.

Morgenson, Gretchen. ''Now You See It, Now You Don't.'' *Forbes,* 9 February 1998, 44.

Williams, Georgina, and Thomas J. Phillips Jr. ''Cleaning Up Our Act: Accounting for Environmental Liabilities.'' *Management Accounting* 75, no. 8 (February 1994): 30.

Winicur, Barbara. ''Long Term Liabilities.'' *National Public Accountant* 38, no. 1 (January 1993): 6.

LICENSING AGREEMENTS

Businesses use licensing agreements to simultaneously protect and exploit **intellectual property**. Many well-known companies grant or receive licenses. For the business granting use of its intellectual property, be it a brand name, a patent, or a copyright, a license to another company is a mechanism for investing **intellectual capital** while preserving the ultimate control over it. To the licensee, the agreement is a way to obtain something of value that the licensee may not be able to produce on its own, but the licensee may have expertise or market position to generate revenue that the licensor isn't well equipped to do on its own. Licensees are distinguished, however, from vendors or outside contractors that simply perform a service for the originating company; licensing agreements involve the assignment of certain rights to the intellectual property.

As this simplification suggests, licensing is a symbiotic relationship between companies that are in a sense mismatched with intellectual property. Firms with intellectual assets that are more valuable than their current marketing structure can support look to outside partners to maximize the returns on their assets. An owner of a well-known trademark, for instance, may not possess the manufacturing capacity to produce and distribute all of the merchandise that could be marketed under the trademark. Moreover, it may not be in the company's strategic interest to get involved in various types of manufacturing if those activities are outside its sphere of competency. Meanwhile, other companies may be technically skilled at manufacturing such products, but might lack the name recognition and access to distribution channels that a major brand name enjoys. Through a licensing agreement, each may capitalize on its strengths.

Licensing agreements generally are legal contracts that stipulate the rights and responsibilities of each party. Thus, if a copyright is being licensed, it is usually for a limited purpose and the licensee can't simply use the material as it pleases. The agreement also specifies the financial terms under which the grantor will be compensated for the use of its assets. The finances usually take into account the value of the market for the licensed product, the costs of producing the licensed product, and what the licensor might be losing by not pursuing a different use of its assets. Any number of financial arrangements may be worked out, but requiring a percentage royalty on sales is a common practice. The contract may also require a minimum payment to the licensor. In other words, the licensee typically assumes a greater out-of-pocket expense risk in a licensing agreement, whereas the licensor often risks a greater opportunity cost if the anticipated returns don't pan out.

According to Robert C. Megantz in *How to License Technology,* alternative strategies to licensing include forming a joint venture, acquiring a company with the needed expertise, developing internal capacity to perform whatever functions would be licensed, and allowing another company to buy and administer the intellectual property rights altogether. Each of these methods carries different risks and potential returns for the business.

Licensing agreements can be divided into three basic categories:

- copyright licensing
- patent licensing
- trademark licensing

They may be further distinguished as licenses between business partners (loosely defined) versus licenses between property owners and end users. End-user agreements are common in certain types of copyright licensing, notably for software and music. In this scenario, the end user simply pays for the limited right to use the property and usually does not transform or resell the property in any way. Most other types of licenses are part of a business strategy between separate companies, neither of which may be an end user of the licensed property, that will generate new sales from third-party end users. In partner licenses the licensee is expected to resell the property in some form.

COPYRIGHT LICENSING

Copyrights apply primarily to original works of artistic merit such as books, plays, magazine and newspaper articles, musical recordings, photography, paintings, and sculpture. The U.S. Copyright Act of 1976 clearly defined the following exclusive rights of a copyright owner:

1. The right to make copies of the work.
2. The right to prepare derivatives (arrangements) of the work.
3. The right to distribute copies of the work to the public.
4. The right to perform the work publicly.
5. The right to display the work publicly.

These rights also suggest some of the ways in which copyrighted material may be licensed. If a publisher owns the copyright to a book, for example, it may assign limited rights to another company to adapt and market the book for another audience. This may be advantageous for producing international editions of books or releasing copyrighted materials in a format other than the copyright holder's specialty, e.g., marketing an electronic version of a print product.

MUSIC. Musical recordings and scores are fully protected by copyright law, but face unique challenges regarding infringement and licensing. Put simply, there is a wide and varied market for playing and distributing music in many settings, many of which are informal and don't require direct contact with licensors. Most music licensing is a very simple transaction of paying predetermined royalties, and no special negotiations may be necessary. The American Society of Composers, Authors, and Publishers (ASCAP) and Broadcast Music, Inc. are the United States' largest music licensing organizations, together collecting well over $500 million in royalties each year. These organizations distribute licensing royalties to the copyright holders after deducting a handling fee.

Companies that license music include almost any that uses music to enhance its products (such as using music in movies) or business atmosphere (such as playing music in restaurants). Some examples of licensees are television networks, cable channels, movie studios, radio stations, airlines, concert halls, and shopping centers. The royalties for playing copyrighted music—which includes most recorded music currently on the market—vary with the size and type of establishment. Generally, the larger the business and the larger the audience, the higher the rate. Very small businesses, including restaurants under 3,750 square feet, are legally exempt from paying royalties. The controversial Fairness in Music Licensing Act of 1998 came down on the side of small businesses in this respect, reducing the number of firms subject to music licensing requirements.

Enforcing music licenses is particularly problematic because retail musical recordings are readily available and copyright holders often literally must police unauthorized infringements in public places. The sliding royalty scale can also lead to disputes when licensees believe they qualify for a lower rate than the licensing agency requests. Historically, this has sometimes provoked antagonism between music licensors like ASCAP and licensees like restaurants. Recently, however, ASCAP has tried to promote cooperation over confrontation with licensees.

SOFTWARE. As with music, software presents special problems for copyright holders. By nature it is easily duplicated, but unlike music, software is typically not used in places open to the general public. This poses enormous challenges for enforcing software copyrights, as so-called pirated copies of software applications are believed to account for anywhere from 10 to 40 percent of the software installed on a typical business computer. The problem is possibly more widespread in the consumer market.

As with most copyright holders, software publishers have tried to closely restrict duplication and distribution of their products. As end user agreements, software licenses come in two forms: single user and multi-user site licenses. With a few exceptions, single user licenses allow only one installation of the program for use by one person. Multi-user licenses usually specify a numeric range of permissible installations, such as up to 1,000 simultaneous users, and may restrict the physical space over which the software may be deployed, e.g. within one building. Some software installation programs include anti-piracy protections, but the same features that allow legal reuse of a program, for example, reinstalling the program after a system crash, tend to also permit illegal uses.

License infringements may occur at any of several stages in the software distribution process, and thus end users may not even know when they're using pirated copies. Some retailers and computer services install illegal copies of software on computer systems for sale as a means of attracting customers or boosting their profits by not paying licensing fees. There is also a thriving global **black market** for software in which illegal copies are transmitted for free or at minimal cost, with none of the proceeds returning to the publisher.

Businesses are generally liable for any illegal software on their computers, however, regardless of its origin. Watch-dog organizations like the Software & Information Industry Association (formerly the Software Publishers Association) conduct surprise audits at businesses to ensure their compliance. Individual software publishers also have methods of identifying piracy, such as through registration verification. When violations are found, large companies may be subject to fines in the hundreds of thousands of dollars.

Part of the solution to software licensing problems, some believe, is for businesses to implement sophisticated resource-tracking systems that monitor the installed base of programs—perhaps in real time—and identify when an unauthorized application has been installed. As of yet, there are few, if any, widely accepted tools for this, but it is an area of development likely to attract support from both software users and publishers.

Aside from the contentious issues surrounding end-user software licenses, partner licensing is also a common practice within the software industry. This occurs when one software developer licenses an application or, more often, an application component for use in conjunction with another developer's software. Most major off-the-shelf software titles include some licensed components. For example, a graphics conversion filter in a word processing application may have been developed by an outside firm and purchased for either exclusive or nonexclusive use in the word processor.

PATENT LICENSING

Patents, legally protected unique product concepts or processes, may be licensed under a variety of circumstances as well. One of the more common reasons is when two businesses claim rights to an invention. When one of them is ultimately determined to have the legitimate claim, the other must either license the patent from the its owner or give up the infringing portion of the work it has done on the competing version. The parties may choose to litigate it in court, or they may evaluate on their own the evidence and costs involved and settle with a licensing agreement. A similar negotiation must occur when a company creates a patentable innovation that is based on someone else's patented product. In order for either company to use the innovation, the innovator must license its idea to the original patent holder, or the original holder must license its patent to the innovator.

As with other kinds of licensing agreements, patent licenses may be used for all sorts of business purposes. Sometimes the patent owner is a start-up inventor who needs an experienced partner to produce and market the invention. For example, in the pharmaceutical and biotechnology industries, it is not uncommon for leading manufacturers to license some of their best-selling drugs from smaller firms, which in turn may derive a great deal of their revenue from licensing out their ideas rather than marketing them on their own. At the same time, larger firms may wish to leverage their valuable patents in markets or applications that are outside their focus or expertise; for this they may choose smaller companies with unique credentials or other large firms with complementary market placement.

The semiconductor industry uses a special kind of engineering drawing known as a mask work to produce integrated circuits on semiconductor chips. Covered in the United States by the Semiconductor Chip Protection Act of 1984, mask works enjoy somewhat of a cross between copyright and patent protection. When they are registered they enjoy extended protection from duplication and competition.

TRADEMARK LICENSING

Trademark and service mark licensing involves selling the rights to use a distinctive, and usually well-known, name and logo in conjunction with a product or service. Real-world cases include:

1. Walt Disney Company licenses a variety of its cartoon characters to Timex Corporation for use in character-themed watches bearing Timex's name.
2. The food manufacturer ConAgra, Inc. licenses its popular Healthy Choice brand name to Kellogg Co. for use in a line of breakfast cereals, a product line that is outside ConAgra's own marketing strongholds in refrigerated foods, canned foods, and food ingredients.
3. Major universities license their athletic team logos to apparel producers in order to satisfy the strong public demand for college sports clothing and accessories and stimulate further interest in—and royalty revenue for—their athletic programs.

As any observer of American culture can attest to, entertainment companies like Disney maintain some of the most exhaustive trademark/copyright licensing programs. Each new character Disney creates in its animated movies is potentially licensed for dozens of merchandising applications such as toy figures, clothing, lunch boxes, and so forth. (Depending on the circumstances, however, with licensed characters it may technically be a copyright that is licensed rather than a trademark.) The process is similar, if less visible, with most kinds of trademark licensing, whether for the consumer market or the industrial market.

Still, trademark licensors must also defend against unauthorized uses of their names and icons. Particularly with apparel, they must contend with an extensive cottage industry of unlicensed apparel producers that use famous names and images to sell caps, T-shirts, and the like, often at a discount to ''official'' merchandise. Indeed, in some cases, as was true of Anheuser-Busch, it was out of defense against such abuses that companies first hit upon the idea of licensing their names and logos for profit.

Because trademark licensing builds on an already strong brand identity, once obvious precautions are taken against abuses it can represent one of the lowest-risk forms of licensing for both licensor and licensee alike. Care must be taken, of course, to ensure that the licensed uses of the trademark don't tarnish the image they are based on. In many cases, though, the primary and the licensed uses of the trademark can benefit each other, as an advertisement for one is an indirect promotion of the other.

SEE ALSO: Brands and Brand Names; Copyright; Patent Law/Patents; Service Marks

FURTHER READING:

Megantz, Robert C. *How to License Technology.* New York: John Wiley & Sons, 1996.

Revoyr, Jack. *A Primer on Licensing.* 2nd ed. Stamford, CT: Kent Press, 1995.

LICENSING AND CERTIFICATION, OCCUPATIONAL

In the United States, occupational licensing and certification is largely a function of state government. There are literally hundreds of occupations and professions that are regulated in one form or another, but not every state regulates every occupation. Licensing requirements for the same occupation or profession often vary from state to state. Individuals licensed for an occupation in one state may not qualify for licensure in another.

In some cases the federal government has passed legislation that requires states to set up licensure or certification programs for specified occupations. In these instances there is a greater degree of uniformity among the different states regarding licensing or certification requirements. **Real estate** appraisers, asbestos contractors and workers, wastewater and water treatment plant operators, and pesticide operators are some of the occupations that are currently licensed or certified at the state level as a result of federal legislation.

Some occupations are licensed at the federal level. These are typically occupations that take individuals into more than one state, such as airline pilots, who are licensed by the Federal Aviation Administration (FAA), or that are subject to federal laws, such as air traffic controllers. Many water transportation occupations are licensed by the U.S. Coast Guard. Coastal states and those adjacent to large bodies of water may also regulate water transportation occupations. Generally, state regulations must be at least as restrictive as the applicable federal regulations.

THREE LEVELS OF STATE OCCUPATIONAL REGULATION

There are essentially three levels of state regulation of occupations and professions: licensing, certification, and registration. While these terms are used interchangeably on occasion and definitions are not strictly adhered to, it is useful at least to recognize the three levels of occupational regulation.

Licensing is the most restrictive form of occupational regulation. When states issue licenses under licensure laws, it is illegal for individuals to engage in the licensed profession or occupation without a license. Physicians, nurses, and attorneys are examples of professions that are licensed and heavily regulated by state governments. States usually administer occupational licensing through independent boards, with a separate board set up for each licensed profession.

Certification is a somewhat less restrictive form of state regulation. Like licensing, certification requires individuals to meet certain standards that have been established by the state. Uncertified individuals, however, are often allowed to engage in the same profession as long as they do not present themselves to the public as certified practitioners. This type of state regulation affords "title protection" to certified individuals. For example, if psychologists were certified but not licensed as defined above in a certain state, then uncertified individuals could not advertise themselves as psychologists or use psychologist as a title. Uncertified individuals, however, could practice under a different title and provide clients with services similar to those of a certified psychologist.

The least restrictive form of state regulation is registration. Registration usually involves providing a state agency with one's name and address and paying a registration fee. Minimal standards—or no standards at all—might have to be met, such as age, citizenship, and moral character. For public protection the state agency would maintain a registry of all practitioners who have registered with it. In some cases the agency may handle complaints and be able to take disciplinary action.

MANDATORY REGULATION AND VOLUNTARY CERTIFICATION

Whatever level of state regulation is in place for a particular occupation, those regulations have the force of law. They are mandatory. Individuals engaging in occupations that are regulated must comply with the state's laws, rules, and regulations governing those occupations. Such regulations not only set standards for individuals entering an occupation, they also usually spell out acts and conduct that are illegal and subject to disciplinary action.

Individuals in many occupations may have the opportunity to become certified on a voluntary basis. Voluntary certification is typically administered by a trade or professional association. In the absence of state regulation, voluntary certification enables a profession to set its own standards. While certification standards vary from profession to profession, they usually involve having some experience in the field and demonstrating competency or proficiency by passing a written and/or practical certification examination. Certified individuals are then allowed to use a certain title, designation, or other indication that they are in fact certified by a nationally recognized professional association. Acupuncturists, social workers, automotive mechanics, and athletic trainers are a few of the occupations that have voluntary certification.

REASONS FOR OCCUPATIONAL LICENSING AND CERTIFICATION

If there is one principle behind the maze of state occupational regulations, it is that certain occupations and professions must be regulated in order to protect public health, safety, and welfare. Licensing and certification protect the public from being victimized by individuals who are either incompetent or unethical. As noted above, licensing agencies have disciplinary authority. Their rules and regulations have the force of law. Complaints from the public can be directed to the appropriate licensing agencies. Practitioners who have violated the standards of conduct as set forth in the rules and regulations of the licensing agency may be subject to fines and other penalties including loss of license.

Occupational licensing and certification is not without its costs, however. While the public may be protected from incompetent and unethical practitioners, strict licensing and certification standards may have the unfortunate effect of causing shortages of qualified professionals in certain geographic areas or in certain professions. Often the costs associated with obtaining the necessary education and meeting other licensing and certification requirements are passed along to consumers in the form of higher fees.

IMPLICATIONS FOR BUSINESS

Occupational licensing and certification is in a constant state of flux. It is also a highly decentralized activity that is typically spread out among many different state departments, divisions, agencies, and boards. Determining what regulations apply to a specific business, profession, or occupation can often mean contacting several different state agencies to determine who has jurisdiction. Fortunately, professional and trade associations are often good sources of information about state licensing requirements for specific occupations.

Businesses need to know what occupational licensing and certification regulations apply to them. These licenses are usually separate from those business licenses and permits required to operate in a particular state. Building contractors, funeral home directors, private investigators, barbers, cosmetologists, engineers, architects, investment advisers, plumbers, and electricians are just some of the many occupations and businesses that are subject to separate occupational licensing and certification requirements in many states.

[David P. Bianco]

FURTHER READING:

Bianco, David P. *Professional and Occupational Licensing Directory.* 2nd ed. Detroit: Gale Research, 1996.

Burch, Audra D.S. "Florida May Remove Licensing Requirements for Seven Professions," *Knight-Ridder/Tribune Business News,* 30 January 1996.

Guglielmo, Wayne J. "Medical Boards: Facing a Disciplinary Dilemma." *Medical Economics,* 10 May 1999.

Mills, Patti A., and Joni J. Young. "From Contract to Speech: The Courts and CPA Licensing Laws, 1921-1996." *Accounting, Organizations and Society,* April 1999.

Pare, Michael. *Certification and Accreditation Programs Directory.* Detroit: Gale Research, 1998.

LOANS

A loan is the purchase of the present use of money with the promise to repay the amount in the future according to a pre-arranged schedule and at a specified rate of interest. In banking and finance, loan contracts formally spell out the terms and obligations between the lender and borrower.

In 1999, commercial banks in the United States carried more than $3.3 trillion in loans and leases outstanding. More than 40 percent of these loans were for commercial and industrial purposes, including lending for construction and land development. General commercial and industrial loans on the books averaged approximately $950 billion during the first half of 1999, representing a 10 percent nominal increase from the year earlier period, as the relatively strong U.S. economy spurred banks to ease credit. This was in stark contrast to the early 1990s, particularly in the commercial real estate segment, when bank lending was extremely tight. The ten largest commercial lenders represent only between 10 and 15 percent of all business lending by value.

Based on selected short-term averages published quarterly by the Federal Reserve, the average business loan between mid-1998 and mid-1999 was approximately $750,000. The average duration of all business loans during that period was about one year.

LOAN CHARACTERISTICS

TIME TO MATURITY. The length of the loan contract is the time to maturity; therefore, loans vary according to maturity. Short-term debt is from one day to one year. Intermediate debt ranges from one to seven years. Long-term debt is more than seven years.

Revolving credit and perpetual debt have no fixed date for retirement. **Banks** provide revolving credit through extensions of a line of credit. Brokerage firms supply margin credit for qualified customers on certain securities. While the borrower may always be in debt, the borrower constantly turns over the line of credit by paying it down and reborrowing the funds when needed. A perpetual loan, on the other hand, requires only regular interest payments. The borrower, who usually issued such debt through a registered offering, determines the timing of the debt retirement.

REPAYMENT SCHEDULE. Payments may be required at the end of the contract or at set intervals, usually on a monthly or semiannual basis. The payment generally consists of two parts: a portion of the outstanding principal and the interest costs. With the passage of time, the principal amount of the loan is amortized, repaid little by little until completely retired. As the principal balance diminishes, the interest on the remaining balance also declines.

Interest-only-loans do not pay down the principal. The borrower pays interest on the principal loan amount and is expected to retire the principal at the end of the contract through a balloon payment or through refinancing.

INTEREST. Interest is the cost of borrowing money. The interest rate charged by lending institutions must be sufficient to cover operating costs, administrative costs, and an acceptable rate of return. Interest rates may be fixed for the term of the loan, or adjusted to reflect changing market conditions. A credit contract may adjust rates daily, annually, or at intervals of 3, 5 and 10 years. Floating rates are tied to some market index and are adjusted regularly.

SECURITY. Assets pledged as security against loan loss are collateral. The asset purchased by the loan often serves as the only collateral. For example, **real estate** or land collateralizes mortgages. In other cases the borrower puts other assets, including cash, aside as collateral. Credit backed by collateral is thus known as secured debt, while unsecured debt relies on the earning power of the borrower. Government survey figures suggest that around 40 percent of all commercial and industrial loans are collateralized.

SHORT-TERM LOANS

A special commitment loan is a single purpose loan with a maturity of less than one year. Its purpose is to cover cash shortages resulting from a one-time increase in current assets, such as a special inventory purchase, an unexpected increase in accounts receivable, or a need for interim financing.

Trade credit is extended by a vendor who allows the purchaser up to three months to settle a bill. In the past it was common practice for vendors to discount trade bills by one or two percentage points as an incentive for quick payment.

A seasonal line of credit of less than one year is used to finance inventory purchases or production. The successful sale of inventory repays the line of credit.

A permanent **working capital** loan provides a business with financing from one to five years during times when cash flow from earnings does not coincide with the timing or volume of expenditures. Creditors expect future earnings to be sufficient to retire the loan.

INTERMEDIATE-TERM LOANS

Term loans finance the purchase of furniture, fixtures, vehicles, and plant and office equipment. Maturity generally runs more than one year and less than five. Consumer loans for autos, boats and home repairs and remodeling are typically intermediate term.

LONG-TERM LOANS

Mortgage loans are used to purchase real estate and are secured by the asset itself. Mortgages generally run 10 to 30 years.

A bond is a contract held in trust with the obligation of repayment. An indenture is a legal document specifying the terms of a bond issue including the principal, maturity, date, **interest rates**, any qualifications and duties of the trustees, and the rights and obligations of the issuers and holders. Corporations and government entities issue **bonds** in a form attractive to both public and private investors.

A debenture bond is unsecured. Mortgage bonds hold specific property in lien. A bond may contain safety measures to provide for repayment, such as a **sinking fund**.

LOAN AVAILABILITY

As with all credit markets, loan accessibility varies greatly depending on the amount, the borrower's characteristics and purposes, and the general economic and competitive climate in the lending industry.

SMALL BUSINESS LOANS. Traditionally, small businesses—especially those owned by women and minorities—have had a difficult time obtaining loans, even for fairly small amounts, such as under $100,000. For very small businesses, banks are usually more interested in the owner's personal credit history than in the company's, which can be an obstacle for some business owners. Smaller, community-based banks tend to be more willing to make loans to small start-up companies that aren't particularly capital intensive.

The U.S. Small Business Administration (SBA) runs several programs to make loans more available to small businesses, including special programs for firms owned by women and minorities. The typical SBA program loan is administered by a commercial lending institution, but the SBA guarantees at least a percentage of the loan (often 50-90 percent) against default.

In the mid-1990s there were hopes that a secondary market for business loans, including small business loans, would develop in the same way that the secondary market for residential mortgages has flourished. This would add stability to the primary market by distributing risk and ultimately increase the availability of funds to small business borrowers. The commercial mortgage segment has benefited greatly from this trend (see **Mortgage Backed Securities**). However, as of the late 1990s, for small business loans this effort had made only modest headway, as would-be investors found it harder to evaluate the riskiness of business loans than of traditional residential mortgages.

GENERAL BUSINESS LOANS. For larger and more established companies, banks are mostly concerned with the firm's finances, quality of management, and market prospects. Specific considerations may include credit history, assets and liabilities, cash flows, orders, inventories, accounting practices, management experience, marketing strategy, and the general market outlook for the company's products or services.

LOAN ALTERNATIVES

Medium-size and larger businesses often have a variety of alternative methods for raising capital instead of taking out loans. Normally businesses will seek to minimize their cost of capital by choosing the method that most reduces costs or risks based on the length of time and purposes they need the money for. The options include both debt and equity financing. The primary debt alternatives are issuing **bonds** and commercial paper, while equity financing entails selling shares of stock to investors, such as private investors, **venture capital** firms, or the general public through a **public offering**. As another alternative to loans, companies may wish to pursue **joint ventures** with other firms to reduce their level of investment in a project.

SEE ALSO: Banks and Banking; Credit; Leasing

FURTHER READING:

Federal Reserve. ''Report to the Congress on Markets for Small Business and Commercial Mortgage-Related Securities.'' Washington, September 1998. Available from www.federalreserve.gov.

——. ''Survey of Terms of Business Lending.'' Washington, 21 June 1999. Available from www.federalreserve.gov.

Fraser, Jill Andresky. ''How to Finance Anything.'' *Inc.*, March 1999.

''Top 10 Bank Holding Companies in Commercial and Industrial Loans.'' *American Banker,* 25 June 1998.

LOBBYING

Lobbying refers to the activities of individuals, acting either for themselves or on behalf of others, that attempt to influence political decision makers. Lobbying as an activity is usually informal, that is, communication between lobbyists and political decision makers is seldom public. Lobbying has come to be synonymous with so-called special interests, the implication being that lobbying and lobbyists somehow work against ''the will of the people.'' The term has also gained pejorative connotations, because of lobbying's close association in the past with such high-pressure and corrupting tactics as **bribery**. Generally, lobbyists now employ lower-pressure tactics—such as presenting information, research, and expert opinion—that reenforces their view on a particular subject or piece of pending legislation. Somewhere in between are lobbying tactics such as campaign contributions and other persuasive but nonthreatening techniques.

Seeking to persuade political decision makers to act in particular ways has always been part of the human condition. Unique to the United States, however, is the height to which this persuasive process has been institutionalized. Two factors influencing this institutionalization of lobbying practices are the guarantee of freedom of expression found in the Constitution and the belief that elected politicians—be they presidents, senators, representatives, or county drain commissioners—are elected to represent the views of the electorate. Thus they are open to influence by the electorate. In fact the term ''lobbying'' originated from the practice of people attempting to persuade or influence legislators in the lobbies of voting and deliberative chambers.

In the United States early lobbying efforts were aimed almost exclusively at state and federal legislative bodies. Bribery was not unheard of. The first congressional investigation of lobbies was in 1913 against the National Association of Manufacturers. In 1935 as the result of a scandal over a public utilities bill, all utility lobbyists were required to be register. By the end of World War II, however, there were two major shifts in lobbying activities. Because of various lobbying scandals, tactics such as bribery became much less common and lobbyists began resorting to more low-pressure strategies. The post-World War II era saw a tremendous growth in the power and activities of federal administrative agencies; following the lead of President Franklin Roosevelt, it became commonplace for the executive branch to propose federal legislation. As a result of these shifts lobbyists began to form closer relationships with the executive branch of government and the federal administrative bureaucracy.

The need for regulatory mechanisms to control lobbyist activities paralleled the growing pervasiveness of lobbying throughout the federal government structure. As a result, the Federal Regulation of Lobbying Act became a component of the Legislative Reorganization Act (LRA) of 1946. This was the first comprehensive piece of federal legislation aimed at the regulation of lobbying. This act prescribed rules governing who must register as lobbyists and the reporting of their receipts and expenditures. The act was soon challenged in the federal court system and by 1953 had been declared unconstitutional. The government, however, carried the case to the Supreme Court. Defendants' lawyers claimed the act violated First Amendment guarantees of free speech and the right to petition while being too vague to satisfy due process. In a 5-3 ruling, however, the high court upheld the LRA.

The LRA nevertheless came under almost immediate criticism for being vague, largely unenforceable, and without compliance. Despite mounting criticism from many circles it was not until the early 1990s that major new regulatory legislation became viable. In 1993 the independently wealthy political gadfly H. Ross Perot vociferously attacked the lack of effective regulatory mechanisms on lobbyists. In response to criticism by Perot and others, the Senate in 1993 passed a bill that would have required thousands of lobbyists to register while concurrently disclosing who they worked for, how much they were being paid, and to what ends they were lobbying. Gifts to senators and their staff worth $20 or more would also require disclosure. In 1994 the House passed similar legislation but included a ban on gifts and meals. Republicans, however, soon killed a House-Senate compromise bill, claiming it would inhibit lobbying at the grassroots level. In 1995, after much political maneuvering, Congress passed a subsequent compromise bill. Known as the Lobbying Disclosure Act (LDA) of 1995 it was signed into law by President Bill Clinton.

The 1995 act defines a lobbyist as any person (or entity) who for financial (or other) compensation has been retained by a client to make more than one lobbying contact on the client's behalf. A lobbying contact is an oral, written, or electronic communication with a "covered individual" regarding legislative or administrative policy-making or regulatory matters. Individual lobbyists who expect to receive more than $5,000 in compensation in a six-month period, or organizations that expect to spend more than $20,000 on lobbying in a six-month period, must disclose their activities. Organizations that use their own employees as lobbyists and spend more than $20,000 in a six-month period are also required to report their activities. The definition of a covered individual is quite broad and includes political appointees, senators, representatives, the president, and executive branch officials, as well as their respective staffs and employees. The act requires lobbyists to disclose twice a year the issues they lobbied on, the amount of money they spent, and the specific federal agencies and chambers of Congress they had contact with. Under the act, registrants are generally the lobbyist's employer rather than the individual lobbyist. Self-employed individuals, however, are also required to register if they qualify as lobbyists under the act. There are 19 exceptions to what constitutes a lobbying contact, including such things as subpoenas and contacts requiring compliance as specified by statutes, regulations, etc.

The LDA does not specifically define grassroots lobbying nor does it explicitly dismiss its authority over grassroots lobbying. Legislative history, however, seems to imply that grassroots lobbying does not constitute lobbying contact or lobbying activity as defined in the act. What is evidently important under the act is not the activity per se, but rather the driving force behind the activity. For example, whether or not an organized letter-writing campaign is considered to be grassroots lobbying is largely dependent on how the campaign was orchestrated or inspired. For instance, a speech made to the general public during which the speaker implores members of the audience to write letters to government officials advocating a particular position would probably be regarded as grassroots lobbying and thus not subject to LDA compliance. A letter-writing campaign by employees of a corporation that was instigated by the employer, however, would probably not be considered grassroots lobbying and thus would be subject to LDA compliance.

Despite these regulatory measures, lobbyists are still quite active in Washington—especially when they have deep pockets. According to the Center for Responsive Politics, the oil industry, which is affected by most government policies and decisions, spent $62 million in lobbying efforts in 1997. As large as this sum was, big oil nevertheless came in fourth behind the telephone lobby, which spent $62.1 million; insurance concerns, which spent $65.9 million; and the pharmaceutical and health products industry, which disbursed $74.4 million in its lobbying efforts.

[Michael Knes]

FURTHER READING:

Brown, William P. *Groups, Interests, and Public Policy.* Washington: Georgetown University Press, 1998.

Clymer, Adam. "Congress and Reform: Over the Years, Hits and Misses." *New York Times,* 30 June 1996, 23.

de Kieffer, Donald E. *The Citizen's Guide to Lobbying Congress.* Chicago: Chicago Review Press, 1997.

Luneburg, William V., ed. *The Lobbying Manual: A Compliance Guide for Lawyers and Lobbyists.* Chicago: American Bar Association, Section of Administrative Law and Regulatory Practice, 1998.

Wayne, Leslie. "Companies Used to Getting Their Way: Greasing the Wheels." *New York Times,* 4 December 1998, C1+.

Webster, George D. "Understanding the Lobbying Disclosure Act." *Association Management* 48, no. 8 (August 1996): 222+.

LOCAL AREA NETWORKS (LANS)

The Institute of Electrical and Electronics Engineers, which establishes network standards, defines a local area network (LAN) as a data communications system that enables a number of independent devices to communicate with each other in a limited geographic area. In other words, a LAN is a network of **computers** linked together via cable within a limited area. LANs are proprietary systems limited to a finite number of users. Consequently, LANs are not connected with public telephone and cable systems. They also generally serve an area of less than one mile, and are usually confined to a single building. Nevertheless, a **computer network** spanning a university campus or a large industrial site with multiple buildings also can be classified as a LAN. LANs also permit workers—isolated in separate offices—to operate off the same system, as if they were all sitting around a single computer. In addition, they allow audio, video, and data communication and have higher bandwidth connections than traditional **wide area networks**. Besides linking computers, a LAN also may include one or more servers as well as several printers and other computer equipment, depending on the number of network users.

One of the great attributes of a LAN is that it may be installed simply, upgraded or expanded with little difficulty, and moved or rearranged without disruption. Perhaps most importantly, anyone initiated in the use of a personal computer can be trained to communicate or perform work over a LAN. Moreover, LANs can improve productivity by enabling workers to share information and databases and can save companies money by allowing them to purchase fewer computer peripherals such as printers and plotters, which can be shared via a LAN.

HISTORICAL DEVELOPMENT

Local area networks have their genesis in distributed computing systems that were introduced during the 1960s. Initially, they consisted of ''dumb'' terminals connected to a single mainframe processor via a wiring system. Instructions entered on the terminal keyboard were registered at the mainframe, where they were processed, and a visual representation of these instructions was sent back to the terminal for display on a screen.

The first protocols for these distributed computer workstations were proprietary, meaning that they were designed specifically for equipment designed by a certain company. As a result, IBM equipment could not be mixed with Digital Equipment Corp. (DEC), Xerox Corp., Wang, or any other manufacturer's machinery.

By the late 1970s, however, several companies proposed ''open'' standards under which equipment from one manufacturer could be made to emulate the operating system of another. This allowed manufacturers to compete for business in systems that had previously been closed to all but the system designer.

The first of these standards was Ethernet, a ''listen-and-transmit'' protocol developed by DEC, Intel Corp., and Xerox. Ethernet identified the type of instructions being generated and, if necessary, conditioned them so they could be read by the mainframe on a common terminal, or bus.

In 1980 the Institute of Electrical and Electronics Engineers determined that continued reluctance to open protocols would seriously retard the growth of distributed computer systems. It established a group called the 802 committee to establish networking standards for the entire industry. This would ensure that customers could migrate from one vendor to another without sacrificing their considerable investments in existing systems. The standards also compelled manufacturers to follow the standards, or risk being dealt out of the market.

Ethernet was offered to the 802 committee as a standard. Several manufacturers balked because Ethernet did not work well under heavy traffic. Instead, the Ethernet standard was adapted into three versions, corresponding to network designs. Still, these standards could support 1,024 workstations over an end-to-end distance of two kilometers.

Processor manufacturing technology, however, had progressed so far that entire computers could be condensed into a single desktop unit. The first of these ''personal computers'' (PCs) was introduced by IBM in 1981.

IBM's PC featured an open bus architecture, meaning that IBM provided design specifications to other manufacturers in the hope that they would design compatible equipment and **software** for the system. IBM could impose this architecture on the market because it had very high market penetration and was the leading manufacturer in the industry.

The PC changed the type of information sent over office computer networks. Terminals were no longer ''dumb,'' but contained the power to perform their own instructions and maintain their own memories. This took considerable pressure off the mainframe device, whose energies could now be devoted to more complex tasks.

An analysis of common office tasks revealed that as much as 80 percent of the work performed by the average employee never left the room in which it was produced. This factor established demand characteristics for individual, worker-specific PCs.

The remaining 20 percent of office tasks required transmission of data for access by other workers. LANs enabled this data to be directed to a common printer, serving a dozen or more workers. This eliminated the need for each worker to have a printer and ensured that the one printer provided was not underutilized.

In addition, LANs allowed data to be called up directly on other workers' computers, providing immediate communication and eliminating the need for paper. The most common application was in interoffice communications, or **electronic mail** (e-mail). Messages could be directed to one or several people and copied to several more over the LAN.

As a result, an e-mail system became something of an official record of communications between workers. Addressees became obligated to respond to e-mail messages in a timely manner because their failure to answer could be documented for supervisors.

PCs transformed LANs from mere shared processors to fully integrated communication devices. In fact, developments in processing technology endowed some PCs with even greater capacity than the mainframe computers to which they were attached. For some applications, the need for a mainframe was completely eliminated. With processing power distributed among PCs, the mainframe's main role was eclipsed. While still useful for complex processing, administrative functions and data file storage became the job of a new device, the file server.

PHYSICAL COMPONENTS

A local area network generally requires three principal components besides the computers being connected: network cards, cable or wire, and software. While software-driven, the physical properties of a LAN include interfaces, called network access units, which connect computers to networks. These units are actually network cards installed on computer motherboards. Their job is to provide a connection, monitor availability of access, set or buffer the data transmission speed, ensure against transmission errors and collisions, and assemble data from the LAN into usable form for the PC. A LAN consisting of two to four computers, however, can be created without a network card and this kind of network is called a slotless system. In a slotless system, the computers' serial and parallel ports are connected to each other. Such LANs are very inexpensive and businesses use them largely for sharing hard-drive space and printers, but they cannot support high-speed data transmission.

The next part of a LAN is the wiring, which provides the physical connection from one PC to another, and to servers and printers and other peripherals. The properties of the wiring determine transmission speeds.

The first LANs were connected with coaxial cable, a variety of the type used to deliver cable television. Certain kinds of coaxial cable are relatively inexpensive and coaxial cable is simple to attach. More importantly, these cables provide great bandwidth (the system's rate of data transfer), enabling transmission speeds up to 20 megabits per second.

During the 1980s, however, AT&T introduced a LAN wiring system using ordinary twisted wire pair of the type used for telephones. The primary advantages of twisted wire pair are that it is very cheap, simpler to splice than coaxial, and is already installed in many buildings as obsolete or redundant wiring. In fact, many buildings were left with stranded 25-pair wiring once used for key telephone systems.

But the downside of this simplicity is that its bandwidth is more limited, meaning that twisted pair, designed for voice communication, transmits data at a slow rate. For example, AT&T's first LAN product, StarLAN, had a capacity of only one megabit per second. Subsequent improvements expanded this capacity tenfold and eliminated the need for shielded, or conditioned, wiring.

A more recent development in LAN wiring is fiber distributed data interface (FDDI) or fiber-optic cable. This type of wiring uses thin strands of glass to transmit pulses of light between terminals. Its advantages are that it provides tremendous bandwidth and thus allows very high transmission speeds: data transmission at a rate of up to 100 megabits per second. And, because it is optical rather than electronic, it is impervious to electromagnetic interference. Fiber optics also supports a network of up to 1,000 computers and can transmit signals up to 50 miles. Its main drawbacks, however, are that splicing is difficult and requires a high degree of skill and that it costs far more than its counterparts.

The primary application of fiber is not between terminals, but between LAN buses (terminals) located on different floors. As a result, FDDI is used mainly in building risers. Within individual floors, LAN facilities remain coaxial or twisted wire pair.

Where a physical connection cannot be made, such as across a street or between buildings where easements for wiring cannot be secured, microwave radio may be used. It is often difficult, however, to secure frequencies for this medium.

Another alternative in this application is light transceivers, which project a beam of light similar to fiber-optic cable, but through the air, rather than over cable. These systems do not have the frequency allocation or radiation problems associated with microwave, but they are susceptible to interference from fog and other obstructions.

The software needed for a LAN depends on the kind of network being created: whether slotless, peer-to-peer, or server-based. Slotless system software usually enables users to perform the rudimentary tasks associated with slotless systems: sharing hard-drive space and printers. In addition, this software may provide e-mail and security features. Basic slotless system utilities are included in standard operating systems such as Windows 95 and Windows 98.

Peer-to-peer software facilitates peer-to-peer networks, which allow all users to access and use the resources of all computers attached to the network, including hard drives and printers. Peer-to-peer LANs, however, generally lack security and administration capabilities of server-based LANs, as well as the capacity for large data transmissions. Nevertheless, they are less expensive than their server-based counterparts.

Client/server software is designed for networks that designate a computer as the hub or server of the LAN. The server computer is linked to all the other computers of the network—the client computers—and it carries out the majority of the server duties, such as user access control and coordinating user tasks. The server cannot be used as a workstation, however, without special software allowing it to function as one. The client computers use the programs and data stored on the server. Server-based networks are best for companies with heavy network traffic.

TOPOLOGIES

LANs are designed in several different topologies or physical patterns of connecting terminals. The most common topology is the bus, where several terminals are connected directly to each other over a single transmission path. Its layout is linear and it resembles a street with several driveways. The bus network requires cables that allow signals to flow in either direction, called a full duplex medium. Each terminal on the bus LAN contends with other terminals for access to the system. When it has secured access to the system, it broadcasts its message to all the terminals at once. The message is picked up by the one terminal or group of terminal stations for which it is intended. The bus network's lack of routing and central control make it very reliable, because failure of one of the network's computers generally will not impede the flow of other network traffic.

A second topology, the star network, also works like a bus in terms of contention and broadcast. But in the star, stations are connected to a single, central node that administers access. The central node knows the path to all the other nodes, which makes routing easy. The central node also enables access control and establishing a priority status for users. Several of these nodes may be connected to one another. For example, a bus serving 6 stations may be connected to another bus serving 10 stations and a third bus connecting 12 stations. The star topology is most often used where the connecting facilities are coaxial or twisted wire pair.

The ring topology connects each station to its own node, and these nodes are connected in a circular fashion. Node 1 is connected to node 2, which is connected to node 3, and so on, and the final node is connected back to node 1. Messages sent over the LAN are regenerated by each node, but retained only by the addressees. Eventually, the message circulates back to the sending node, which removes it from the stream. Consequently, this configuration does not require routing.

TRANSMISSION METHODS USED BY LANS

LANs are effective because their transmission capacity is greater than any single terminal on the system. As a result, each station terminal can be offered a certain amount of time on the LAN, like a time-sharing arrangement. To take advantage of this window of opportunity, stations organize their messages into compact packets that can be quickly disseminated.

In contending for access, a station with something to send stores its data packet in a buffer until the LAN is clear. At that point the message is sent out. Sometimes, two stations may detect the opening at the same time and send their messages simultaneously. Unaware that another message has been sent out, the two signals will collide on the LAN. When this happens it is up to the software to determine who should go first and ask both machines to try again.

In busy LANs, collisions would occur all the time, slowing the system down considerably. To solve the problem, the LAN software circulates a token. This works like a ticket that is distributed only to one station at a time. Instead of waiting for the LAN to clear, the station waits to receive the token.

When it has the token, the station sends its packet out over the LAN. When it is done, it returns the token to the stream for the next user. Tokens, used in ring and bus topologies, virtually eliminate the problem of collisions by providing orderly, noncontention access.

The transmission methods used on LANs are either baseband or broadband. The baseband medium uses a high-speed digital signal consisting of square wave DC voltage. While it is fast, it can accommodate only one message at a time. As a result it is suitable for smaller networks where contention is low. It also is very simple, requiring no tuning or frequency discretion circuits. As a result, the transmission medium may be connected directly to the network access unit and is suitable for use over twisted wire pair facilities.

In contrast, the broadband medium tunes signals to special frequencies, much like cable television. Stations are instructed by signaling information to tune to a specific channel to receive information. The information within each channel on a broadband medium may also be digital, but they are separated from other messages by frequency. As a result, the medium generally requires higher capacity cables, such as coaxial cable. Suited for busier LANs, broadband systems require the use of tuning devices in the network access unit that can filter out all but the single channel it needs.

SERVERS

File and printer servers provided the initial impetus for companies to develop LANs so that they could share databases and expensive peripherals such as printers. Furthermore, the heart of the LAN, the administrative software, generally resides either in a dedicated file server (which functions as a server only) or, in a smaller, less busy LAN, in a computer acting as a file server (which also can function as a workstation). In addition to acting as a kind of traffic cop by controlling and regulating user access, this server holds files for shared use in its hard drives, administers applications such as operating systems, and coordinates tasks such as printing.

Where a single computer is used both as a workstation and a file server, response times may lag because its processors are forced to perform several instructions at once. In addition, the system will store certain files on different computers connected with the LAN. Consequently, if one machine is down, the entire system may be crippled. Moreover, if the system were to crash due to undercapacity, some data may be lost or corrupted.

The addition of a dedicated file server may be costly, but it provides several advantages over a distributed system. In addition to ensuring access even when some machines are down, it is unencumbered by multiple duties. Its only jobs are to hold files and provide access.

Since 1990 one of the most notable developments in LANs has been the growth of communication servers that allow LANs to communicate with networks outside of the LANs themselves. Communication servers enable remote LAN access, e-mail, fax, and other communication services. Like other servers, this one controls access and facilitates use of communications software and hardware. As with file and printer servers, a separate computer may be designated as a dedicated server to enhance reliability.

Furthermore, the LANs of the late 1990s began to include servers devoted other applications such as those for decision support, transaction processing, and data warehousing. The number of application servers is forecast to increase significantly as more companies add dedicated application servers to their LANs.

SPEED MEASUREMENTS

The speed of the LAN is measured in terms of throughput, a figure different from transmission speed because it takes into account the capacity of the wiring and the distance between stations. The data rate, which most directly represents response time, is determined by throughput and other factors such as overhead bits and other signals, error and collision recovery, software and hardware efficiency, and the memory capacity of disk drives.

OTHER EQUIPMENT

As mentioned earlier, LANs are generally limited in size because of the physical properties of the network: distance, impedance (a kind of electrical resistance), and load. Some equipment, such as repeaters, can extend the range of a LAN. Repeaters have no processing ability, but simply regenerate signals that are weakened by impedance.

Other types of LAN equipment with processing ability include gateways, which refer to the hardware and software necessary to enable technologically different networks to communicate with each other. A gateway, for example, can compensate for dissimilar protocols to pass information by translating them into a simpler code, such as ASCII. A bridge works like a gateway, but instead of connecting technologically different networks, it connects networks employing the same kind of technology. Similar to a bridge, a router is the hardware and software connection between two (or more) networks or subnetworks that routes traffic from one network or subnetwork to another. But routers primarily control the transmission of packets to their destinations.

Gateways, bridges, and routers can act as repeaters, boosting signals over greater distances. They also enable separate LANs located in different buildings to communicate with each other.

In some cases, separate LANs located in different cities—and even separate countries—may be linked over a public network. Whether these are ''nailed up'' dedicated links or switched services, the connection of two or more such LANs in separate geographic locations is referred to as a wide area network (WAN).

WANs require the use of special software programs in the operating system to enable dial-up connections that may be performed by a router. Unless limited to modem speeds, these connections may require special services, such as integrated services digital network (ISDN), to ensure efficient transmission, particularly of large data files. Increasingly, companies employing LANs in separate locations also operate WANs.

Another device, which can be used to create LANs, is the private branch exchange. Private branch exchanges (PBXs) are telephone switching systems that generally serve one company or network and route data and information to specific servers, rather than broadcasting to all stations. PBXs are oblivious to operating systems and use only twisted pair. As a result, PBX networks are somewhat slower and their applications are more limited than other kinds of LANs.

DIFFICULTIES

LANs are susceptible to many kinds of transmission errors. Electromagnetic interference from motors, power lines, and sources of static, as well as shorts from corrosion, can corrupt data. In addition, different kinds of cables are more susceptible to these problems than others. Software bugs and hardware failures can also introduce errors, as can irregularities in wiring and connections.

LANs generally compensate for these errors by working off an uninterruptible power source, such as batteries, and using backup software to recall most recent activity and hold unsaved material. Some systems may be designed for redundancy, such as keeping two file servers and alternate wiring to route around failures.

In addition, as computer software evolves requiring faster processors and faster rates of transmission, LAN technology also must evolve. Multimedia and video applications in particular force companies to upgrade their LANs in order to use such applications in a network environment. Consequently, LANs increasingly need to transmit data at gigabit, not megabit, speeds and hence older technology must be upgraded or replaced.

PURCHASING A LAN

When purchasing a LAN, or even investigating the possibility of installing one, several considerations must be kept in mind. The **costs** involved and the administrative support needed often far exceed reasonable predictions.

Three general concerns when considering a LAN include administration, security, and productivity. Administration utilities regulate and coordinate file, application, peripheral, and resource use, while security utilities control access to the network. Productivity refers to the tasks a company wants to perform via a LAN, which may include file, database, and printer sharing. Moreover, thorough consideration of potential costs should include such factors as purchase price of equipment, spare parts and **taxes**, installation costs, labor and building modifications, and permits. Operating costs include forecasted public network traffic, diagnostics, and routine maintenance. In addition, the buyer should seek a schedule of potential costs associated with upgrades and expansion of the network, since company LANs tend to require new technology and to expand periodically.

The vendor should agree to a **contract** expressly detailing the degree of support that will be provided in installing and turning on the system. In addition, the vendor should provide a maintenance contract that binds the company to make immediate, free repairs when performance of the system exceeds prescribed standards. All of these factors should be addressed in the buyer's **request for proposal**, which is distributed to potential vendors.

[John Simley, updated by Karl Heil]

FURTHER READING:

Daines, Bernard. "The Future of Gigabit LANs." *Telecommunications,* January 1997, 15.

Derrick, Dan. *Network Know-How: Concepts, Cards, and Cables.* Berkeley, CA: Osborne/McGraw-Hill, 1992.

Green, Harry James. *The Business One Irwin Handbook of Telecommunications.* 2nd ed. Homewood, IL: Business One Irwin, 1991.

Madron, Thomas W. *Local Area Networks.* New York: John Wiley & Sons, Inc., 1994.

Rhodes, Peter D. *Building a Network.* New York: McGraw-Hill, 1996.

LOGISTICS MANAGEMENT

SEE: Business Logistics; Channels of Distribution; Physical Distribution Management (Transportation)

M

MAASTRICHT TREATY

The Maastricht Treaty, which is formally known as the Treaty on European Union, was signed in Maastricht, the Netherlands, on February 7, 1992. It represented a major step by its signatories towards European economic, political, and social—but especially monetary—integration. The treaty was signed by Belgium, Denmark, France, Germany, Greece, Ireland, Italy, Luxembourg, the Netherlands, Portugal, Spain, and the United Kingdom—the 12 member countries of the European Community. The main proviso of the treaty was the immediate creation of the **European Union** and by the late 1990s the establishment of the Economic and Monetary Union.

The Maastricht Treaty is part of an evolutionary economic process that began in Europe following the devastation of World War II. Under the prodding of Jean Monnet (1888-1979) and Robert Schuman (1886-1963) of France, and Paul-Henri Spaak (1899-1972) of Belgium, many European leaders came to the conclusion that if economic growth and social and political stability were to be realized then there must be a formal plan for political and economic cooperation between the various nations of western Europe. This plan would also serve as a nonmilitary bulwark against the expansionist threats of the Soviet Union and its Eastern European communist allies.

The first step towards inter-nation cooperation was the formation of the European Coal and Steel Community (ECSC). Established by the Treaty of Paris in 1951, the ECSC united Belgium, France, Italy, Luxembourg, the Netherlands, and West Germany into a single common market that did away with trade barriers relating to coal, steel, scrap metal, and iron ore. The ECSC also allowed the free movement of labor between its signers respective to these industries. The success of the ECSC led to the 1957 signing of the Treaty of Rome and the subsequent establishment of the European Atomic Energy Community and the European Economic Community. In 1967 the executive agencies of these three institutions were combined to form the European Community (EC), which was also known as the European Common Market. Shortly thereafter tariffs relating to trade between member nations were eliminated and a common tariff on goods from nonmember nations was instituted. In 1973 Denmark, Ireland, and the United Kingdom became full members of the EC, as did Portugal and Spain in 1986 and a united Germany in 1990.

The European Economic Community began as a common market whose purpose was to eliminate **trade barriers** between member countries. As the institution matured over the decades, however, it began moving towards not just economic but also social, political, and monetary integration. This evolution is reflected in the name changes from European Economic Community, to European Community, and finally to European Union. In negotiating the Maastricht Treaty, EC members agreed to a number of key provisions. A common currency was to be established by the end of the 1990s, to be overseen by an Economic and Monetary Union (EMU). The EMU would be responsible for instituting the common currency and establishing a central bank which would supervise the EU's monetary policy. An important part of this plan is the exchange rate mechanism (ERM) which supervises and seeks to stabilize currency exchange rates between member countries.

Other provisions of the Maastricht Treaty called for moving towards a common defense and foreign policy as well as a shared social policy. The treaty gives the EU the right to ''support and complement'' the activities of member countries in areas of worker health, safety, and sexual equality. There was, however, much dissension and subsequent compromise over parts of the treaty. The United Kingdom, for instance, felt these provisions would compromise existing British law. As with the common currency provision, Great Britain retained the option of unilateral decision making in these regards. The Maastricht accord also authorized EU activities to include: environmental and consumer protection; energy conservation; and education, health, and cultural issues.

Under the treaty, greater aid and assistance was granted to Greece, Ireland, Portugal, and Spain, the so-called poorest nations of the EU. The powers of the European Parliament, an advisory agency of the EC, were expanded in the EU to include the establishment of various ''watchdog'' committees, input in the appointments of European commissioners, and greater control over legislation passed by the Council of Ministers. The treaty also created an advisory Community of the Regions that represents local and regional governing units.

Ratification of the Maastricht Treaty took two years and numerous compromises and national legislative debates before the 12 EC members voted approval amidst an economic downturn in Europe and growing public disenchantment. The United Kingdom was concerned over loss of sovereignty—especially over the issues of common social policies and a single unit of currency. The French National Assembly had to amend the country's constitution because of treaty provisions dealing with transnational voting rights, visa policies, and the common currency. The German parliament also had concerns over the currency issue as well as discomfort with the ambiguous powers of the European Union and the relative powers of the European Parliament. Ireland's referendum became tied to a controversy over abortion strictures and travel rights. In spite of these roadblocks, Germany in October 1993 became the 12th and final EC member to ratify the Maastricht Treaty, which became effective on November 1 of that year. The Economic and Monetary Union, the most far-reaching provision of the Maastricht accord, will begin formal operations in January 1999.

SEE ALSO: Euro; European Union

[Michael Knes]

FURTHER READING:

''EMU: An Awfully Big Adventure'' (special section). *Economist,* 11 April 1998.

Facts on File News Service. ''Key Event: Maastricht Treaty Sets Closer Union for Europe.'' New York: Facts on File, 1997.

Panarella, Alfredo. *The Maastricht Treaty and the Economic and Monetary Union.* Leuven, Belgium: Leuven University Press, 1995.

Peet, John. ''Maastricht Follies.'' *Economist,* 11 April 1998, 8-10.

Princeton Economic Institute. ''Maastricht Treaty.'' Princeton, NJ: Princeton Economic Institute, 1998.

MACROECONOMICS

Macroeconomics is a social science that studies an economy at the aggregate (or economy-wide) level. For the sake of simplicity, one can consider the discipline of macroeconomics as being composed of three interrelated components: the key attributes that characterize a macroeconomy; the key macroeconomic theories that explain how these attributes behave over time; and the key macroeconomic policy recommendations that emerge from the macroeconomic theories.

THE KEY CHARACTERISTICS OF AN ECONOMY

The characteristics that describe a macroeconomy are usually referred to as the key macroeconomic variables. The following four variables are considered to be the most important in gauging the state or health of an economy: aggregate output or income, the unemployment rate, the **inflation rate**, and the **interest rate**. These will be briefly discussed shortly. It is, however, prudent to point out that numerous additional measures or variables are collected and used to understand the behavior of an economy. In the United States, for example, these additional measures include: the index of leading economic indicators (provides an idea where the economy is headed in the near future); retail sales (indicates the strength of consumer demand in the economy); factory orders, especially for big-ticket items (indicates the future growth in output, as orders are filled); housing starts (usually a robust increase in housing starts is taken as a sign of good growth in the future); the consumer confidence index (indicates how likely consumers are to make favorable decisions to buy durable and nondurable goods, services, and homes). Sometimes, the variables tracked are more innocuous than those included in the preceding list, such as: aluminum production, steel production, paper and paperboard production, industrial production, hourly earnings, weekly earnings, factory shipments, orders for durable goods, new factory orders, new-home sales, existing-home sales, inventories, initial jobless claims, married and jobless, help-wanted advertising, purchasing manager's survey, and the U.S. **trade deficit**.

As is apparent from the preceding list, economists and financial observers use observations on numerous variables to understand the behavior of an economy. Nevertheless, the four key macroeconomic variables summarize the most important characteristics of a macroeconomy.

OUTPUT/INCOME. An economy's overall economic activity is summarized by a measure of aggregate output. As the production or output of goods and services generates income, any aggregate output measure is closely associated with an aggregate income measure. The United States now uses an aggregate output concept known as the **gross domestic product** or GDP. The GDP is a measure of all currently produced goods and services valued at market prices. One should notice several features of the GDP measure. First, only currently produced goods (produced during the relevant year) are included. This implies that if you buy a 150-year old classic Tudor house, it does not count towards the GDP; but the service rendered by your real estate agent in the process of buying the house does. Secondly, only final goods and services are counted. In order to avoid double counting, intermediate goods—goods used in the production of other goods and services—do not enter the GDP. For example, steel used in the production of automobiles is not valued separately. Finally, all goods and services included in the GDP are evaluated at market prices. Thus, these prices reflect the prices consumers pay at the retail level, including indirect taxes such as local sales taxes.

A measure similar to GDP is the **gross national product** (GNP). Until recently, the government used the GNP as the main measure of the nation's economic activity. The difference between GNP and GDP is rather small. The GDP excludes income earned abroad by U.S. firms and residents and includes the earnings of foreign firms and residents in the United States. Several other measures of output and income are derived from the GNP. These include the net national product (NNP), which subtracts from the GNP an allowance for wear and tear on plants and equipment, known as **depreciation**; the national income, which mainly subtracts indirect taxes from the NNP; the personal income, which measures income received by persons from all sources and is arrived at by subtracting from the national income items such as corporate profit tax payments and social security contributions that individuals do not receive, and adding items such as transfer payments that they do receive but are not part of the national income; and the personal disposable income, which subtracts personal tax payments such as income taxes from the personal income measure. While all these measures move up and down in a generally similar fashion, it is the personal disposable income that is intimately tied to consumer demand for goods and services—the most dominant component of the aggregate demand—and the total demand for goods and services in the economy from all sources.

It should be noted that the aggregate income/output measures discussed above are usually quoted both in current prices (in ''nominal'' terms) and in constant dollars (in ''real'' terms). The latter quotes are adjusted for inflation and are thus most widely used since they are not subject to distortions introduced by changes in prices.

UNEMPLOYMENT. The level of employment is the next crucial macroeconomic variable. The employment level is often quoted in terms of the unemployment rate. The unemployment rate itself is defined as the fraction of labor force not working (but actively seeking employment). Contrary to what one may expect, the labor force does not consist of all able-bodied persons of working age. Instead, it is defined as consisting of those working and those not working but seeking work. Thus, it leaves out people who are not working but also not seeking work—termed by economists as being ''voluntarily'' unemployed. For purposes of government macroeconomic policies, only people who are ''involuntarily'' unemployed are of primary concern.

For different reasons, it is not possible to bring down the unemployment rate to zero in the best of circumstances. Realistically, economists normally expect a fraction of labor force to remain unemployed—this fraction for the U.S. labor market has been estimated to be 6 percent. The 6 percent unemployment rate is often referred to as the benchmark unemployment rate. In effect, if the unemployment level is at 6 percent, the economy is considered to be at full employment.

INFLATION RATE. The inflation rate is defined as the rate of change in the price level. Most economies face positive rates of inflation year after year. The price level, in turn, is measured by a price index, which measures the level of prices of goods and services at given time. The number of items included in a **price index** vary depending on the objective of the index. Usually three kinds of price indexes, having particular advantages and uses are periodically reported by government sources. The first index is called the consumer price index (CPI), which measures the average retail prices paid by consumers for goods and services bought by them. A couple of thousand items, typically bought by an average household, are included in this index.

A second price index used to measure the inflation rate is called the producer price index (PPI). It is a much broader measure than the consumer price index. The producer price index measures the wholesale prices of approximately 3,000 items. The items included in this index are those that are typically used by producers (manufacturers and businesses) and thus it contains many raw materials and semi-finished goods. The third and broadest measure of inflation is the called the implicit GDP price deflator. This index measures the prices of all goods and services included in the calculation of the current output of goods and services in the economy, the GDP.

The three measures of the inflation rate are most likely to move in the same direction, even though not to the same extent. Differences can arise due to the differing number of goods and services included for the purpose of compiling the three indexes. In general, if one hears about the inflation rate number in the popular media, it is most likely to be the number based on the CPI.

THE INTEREST RATE. The concept of **interest rates** used by economists is the same as the one widely used by ordinary people. The interest rate is invariably quoted in nominal terms—that is, it is not adjusted for inflation. Thus, the commonly followed interest rate is actually the nominal interest rate. Nevertheless, there are literally hundreds of nominal interest rates. Examples include: savings account rate, six-month certificate of deposit rate, 15-year mortgage rate, variable mortgage rate, 30-year Treasury bond rate, 10-year General Motors bond rate, and commercial bank prime lending rate. One can see from these examples that the nominal interest rate has two key attributes—the duration of lending/borrowing involved and the identity of the borrower.

Fortunately, while the hundreds of interest rates that one encounters may appear baffling, they are closely linked to each other. Two characteristics that account for this linkage are the risk worthiness of the borrower and the maturity of the loan involved. So, for example, the interest rate on a 6-month Treasury bill is related to that on a 30-year Treasury bond, as **bonds/loans** of different maturity levels command different rates. Also, a 30-year General Motors bond will carry a higher interest rate than a 30-year Treasury bond, since a General Motors (GM) bond is riskier than a Treasury bond.

Finally, one should note that the nominal interest rate does not represent the real cost of borrowing or the real return on lending. To understand the real cost or return, one must consider the inflation-adjusted nominal rate, called the real interest rate. Tax and other considerations also influence the real cost or return. Nevertheless, the real interest rate is a very important concept in understanding the main incentives behind borrowing or lending.

MACROECONOMIC THEORIES AND ASSOCIATED POLICY RECOMMENDATIONS

Macroeconomics essentially examines the factors that lead to changes in the main characteristics of the economy—output, employment, inflation, and the interest rate. A set of principles that describes how the key macroeconomic variables are determined is called a macroeconomic theory. Typically, every macroeconomic theory comes up with a set of policy recommendations that the proponents of the theory hope the government will follow. Currently, there are four competing macroeconomic theories: Keynesian economics, **monetarism**, the new classical economics, and supply-side economics. All four theories are based, in varying degrees, on classical economics, which preceded the advent of Keynesian economics in the 1930s. Classical economics, as well as the other four theories are briefly described below.

THE CLASSICAL ECONOMICS

The macroeconomic theory that dominated capitalist economies prior to the advent of Keynesian economics in 1936 has been widely known as ''classical macroeconomics.'' The classical economists believed in free markets—for example, they held that the economy would always achieve full employment through forces of supply and demand. Classical economists did not see any role for government in economic policy. For example, since market forces led to full employment, there was no need for a government intervention to bring it about. Classical economists recommended the use of neither monetary policy nor fiscal policy by the government. This hands-off policy recommendation is known as the laissez faire policy.

KEYNESIAN ECONOMICS. Keynesian economics was born during the Great Depression of the 1930s and has been, for the most part, followed in most capitalist countries ever since. English economist John Maynard Keynes (1883-1946) argued that self-adjusting market forces would take a long time to restore full employment. He held that the government should intervene to increase aggregate demand through the use of fiscal policy, which involves government spending and taxation. By increasing government spending, for instance, jobs will be created which will increase income levels, which will increase the aggregate demand for goods and services and thus create new jobs.

Modern Keynesians (also, known as neo-Keynesians) recommend monetary policy, in addition to fiscal policy, to manage the level of aggregate demand. An increase in the **money supply**, for example, leads to a decrease in the interest rate which increases private investment and consumption, boosting the aggregate demand in the economy.

An increase in aggregate demand under the Keynesian system, however, not only generates higher employment but also leads to higher inflation. This causes a policy dilemma—how to strike a balance between employment and inflation. According to laws that were enacted following the Great Depression, policy makers are expected to use monetary and fiscal policies to achieve high employment consistent with price stability.

MONETARISM. Monetarism was an attempt by conservative economists to reestablish the classical laissez faire recommendation. Proposed by Milton Friedman (1912—) in the 1960s, **monetarism** holds that while it is not possible to have full employment of the labor force all the time, it is better to leave the macroeconomy to market forces. Friedman contended that the government's use of monetary and fiscal policies to stabilize the economy around full employment leads to greater instability in the economy. He argued that while the economy would not achieve a state of bliss in the absence of the government intervention, it will be far more tranquil. Under monetarism, the only policy recommendation is that the money supply should be allowed to grow at a constant rate.

THE NEW CLASSICAL ECONOMICS. The 1970s saw a further push to revive classical orthodoxy. The new classical economists (also known as proponents of rational expectations) provided a theoretical framework and empirical evidence to support the view that neither fiscal nor monetary policy can be effective in altering the output and employment levels in a systematic manner. The concept of rational expectations can simply be considered the use of all available information by economic agents (consumers, businesses, and others). Proponents of the new classical economics argue that if economic agents used rational expectations regarding government policies, they would frustrate any anticipated policy action by the government by altering their own behavior. Thus, there was no point in conducting monetary and fiscal policies—market forces are not amenable to such manipulation.

SUPPLY-SIDE ECONOMICS. While supply-side economics became popular during the Reagan era, it had been a part of U.S. macroeconomic policies for some time. This theory is also rooted in classical economics, even though it accepts some Keynesian demand management policy. Basically, supply siders emphasize enhancing economic growth by augmenting the supply of factors of production (such as labor and capital). This, in turn, is done through increased incentives which mainly takes the form of reducing taxes and regulatory burdens. Reagan used a major tax cut as part of his fiscal policy. The supply siders, in general, want a greater role for market forces and a reduced role for government.

RECENT DEVELOPMENTS IN MACROECONOMICS

Followers of New Classical Economics have further built on the rational expectations concept and have developed "real business cycle models." Assuming that output is always at its natural level, they attempt to explain movements of the natural level of output. New Keynesian Economics, on the other hand, is the result of the effort by the followers of neo-Keynesian economics, who further refined Keynesian Economics by explaining imperfections in different markets. New Growth Theory is the third component of recent developments in macroeconomics. It further refines growth theory, the intellectual basis of supply-side economics.

SEE ALSO: Economic Theories; Microeconomics

[Anandi P. Sahu, Ph.D.]

FURTHER READING:

Blanchard, Oliver. *Macroeconomics.* Upper Saddle River, NJ: Prentice Hall, 1997.

Froyen, Richard T. *Macroeconomics: Theories and Policies.* 6th ed. Upper Saddle River, NJ: Prentice Hall, 1998.

Gordon, Robert J. *Macroeconomics.* 7th ed. Reading, PA: Addison-Wesley, 1998.

Mayer, Thomas. *The Structure of Monetarism.* New York: W.W. Norton & Company, 1978.

Sommers, Albert T. *The U.S. Economy Demystified.* Lexington, MA: Lexington Books, 1985.

MAIL-ORDER BUSINESS

A mail-order business is one that receives and fulfills orders for merchandise through the mail. One often hears the terms "mail order," "**direct mail**," and "**direct marketing**" used as if they were synonymous, when in fact they have different meanings. While a mail-order business may solicit orders using a variety of direct mail packages and catalogs, there are also many businesses, organizations, and agencies that use direct mail that are not mail-order businesses. Direct mail is simply an **advertising** medium that delivers its message through the mail, in much the same way that television, radio, newspapers, and magazines are advertising media.

Direct marketing is a broader term than direct mail and encompasses other media. Mail-order businesses usually use direct-marketing techniques to reach potential customers and make sales. Direct marketing may be distinguished from other types of **marketing** by the fact that it always makes an offer and solicits a direct response. While direct marketing makes heavy use of direct mail, it also employs a range of other advertising media to get its message across to target audiences.

Mail order is simply a way of doing business. While mail-order businesses originally took orders primarily through the mail, the advent of lower long-distance rates and **toll-free telephone numbers** has made it more convenient for customers to place orders over the telephone. In the early 1990s there were an estimated 200,000 toll-free WATS (wide area telecommunications service) lines, and the number continues to grow. Mail-order businesses also use the telephone to solicit orders from potential customers.

Mail-order businesses represent a growing segment of the U.S. economy. Estimates of the amount of consumer and business products purchased from mail-order firms vary. The government does not publish statistics on the volume of business done by mail or telephone. Arnold Fishman, as cited in *How to Start and Operate a Mail-Order Business,* estimated that consumers purchased nearly $100 billion of products by mail in 1990, and more than $50 billion of business products were sold through the mail. According to a study of the catalog industry conducted by the WEFA Group for the Direct Marketing Association, catalog sales were expected to total more than $87 billion in 1998, a 7.7 percent increase over 1997 sales.

THE DEVELOPMENT OF MAIL-ORDER BUSINESSES

How old is mail order? Garden and seed catalogs were known to be distributed in the American colonies before the Revolutionary War. Benjamin Franklin is said to have offered a catalog of books in 1744. The Orvis fishing catalog began in 1856 and is America's oldest mail-order catalog still in circulation. Mail-order shopping in the area of consumer goods entered a period of growth in the 1880s, when mail-order houses began to fiercely compete with local stores. Their marketing contest centered on three major issues—price, inventory, and assurances—the very factors that made mail-order houses successful.

Aaron Montgomery Ward (1843-1913), regarded as the first of the consumer goods catalogers, started his catalog business in 1872, while Richard Warren Sears (1863-1914) mailed his first flyers in the 1880s. These catalogs had a liberating effect on 19th-century consumers. They were no longer captive to their local stores, which had limited inventories and charged higher prices because they were not big enough to receive large volume discounts from their suppliers. With the advent of mail order, consumers could get attractive goods and prices whether they lived in the middle of Manhattan or a remote rural setting.

The postal system allowed direct-mail companies to operate on a national basis. With **economies of scale** working in their favor, mail order houses could undercut the pricing of local stores. In 1897 bicycles were selling for $75 to $100 and more, until Sears started offering them for $5 to $20 in its catalog. Sears could offer those low prices because it sold thousands of bicycles every week.

The large volume of business also allowed catalogers to offer a wider variety of goods. Consumers not only wanted low prices, they also wanted variety—20 kinds of dresses rather than 2. Here again, the enormous volume generated by leading mail-order houses made huge inventories not only possible but also practical. But price and variety, while important, have only limited value if the goods themselves are shoddy or poorly made. So the mail-order firms protected consumers with powerful guarantees. Montgomery Ward was one of the first companies to offer a money-back guarantee, and the Sears, Roebuck and Co. pledge of ''satisfaction guaranteed or your money back'' is one of the best-known commitments in American business.

Another successful cataloger, L. L. Bean of Freeport, Maine, began in 1913 when Leon Leonwood Bean mailed his first single-sheet flyer advertising his Maine hunting boots. Perhaps he got the idea of using direct mail from his brother, Guy Bean, who was the Freeport postmaster. L. L. Bean targeted his mailing to individuals who had hunting licenses.

MAIL-ORDER BUSINESSES TODAY

Mail-order businesses today offer consumers a wide array of products and services. Magazine subscription sales represent the largest segment of mail-order sales. Nearly 10 percent of all direct-mail advertising is done on behalf of magazine subscriptions. Books and newspapers also account for a significant portion of mail-order business.

The fastest-growing segment of the mail-order business is that of specialty catalogs. They are fast replacing the large general merchandise catalogs with which consumers are familiar. In fact, several of the major merchandise catalogs have been discontinued and replaced with a series of specialty catalogs. The list of specialty goods sold through the mail is endless and encompasses virtually hundreds of categories. Kitchenware, fancy foods, outdoor clothing, health products, gardening products, sporting goods, records, collectibles, and computer software and equipment are but a few of the more popular categories.

THE GROWTH AND ATTRACTION OF MAIL-ORDER

People order through the mail for a variety of reasons. Historically, mail-order businesses became successful because they offered a wider variety of goods than could be found in local retail outlets. Goods purchased through the mail were often cheaper than those available locally. Mail order shopping offered consumers more convenience than shopping at retail stores. Individuals pursuing a hobby or special interest were more likely to locate those hard-to-find items in a specialty catalog than in a store.

In addition, several recent socioeconomic factors have contributed to the growth of "at-home shopping." These include changing lifestyles, most notably an increase in the number of women working outside the home. Increased consumer acceptance of the telephone as a way to place orders has also helped mail-order businesses. Coupled with telephone-based ordering are faster order fulfillment and the elimination of delays previously associated with the mail. Today, placing an order by phone offers almost the same "instant gratification" as picking up a piece of merchandise at the store. This has been made possible largely through the widespread use of credit cards and toll-free telephone numbers.

MARKETING AND ADVERTISING A MAIL-ORDER BUSINESS

Mail-order businesses have a wide range of media to choose from when marketing and advertising their products. Mail-order advertisements are commonly found in direct mail (including catalogs), classified ads, and display ads. Other media that can be used to advertise a mail-order business include television, radio, matchbooks, package stuffers, bill stuffers, transit advertising, comic books, daily newspapers, and free-standing inserts in Sunday newspapers.

Mail-order advertising is usually direct-response advertising. Direct response advertising is a type of direct marketing. Like all direct marketing, direct-response advertising makes an offer and asks the reader for a response, such as placing an order or requesting more information. The response to any mail-order advertisement can be precisely measured. It is this measurability that allows direct marketers to test a variety of lists, offers, and media before committing valuable resources to a specific campaign.

Mail-order businesses are also using the **Internet** to display their merchandise without incurring postage and paper costs associated with catalog mailings. While estimates vary widely, one source reported that online retailers generated about $518 million in sales in 1996, up from only $200 million in 1994. That's certainly a small percentage of the overall $75 billion in mail-order sales generated in 1996, but the potential for growth is there.

Certain types of merchandise seem to sell better on the Internet than others. For example, items such as books, software, and music tend to sell well, because they can be described with words rather than pictures. Less successful are items such as apparel and gifts, which require an element of "romance" as part of their sell. Food and flowers, however, have reportedly done well over the Internet.

REGULATIONS THAT AFFECT MAIL-ORDER BUSINESS

Mail-order businesses must comply with the regulations of the **Federal Trade Commission** (FTC) and the U.S. Postal Service. In addition mail-order businesses may be subject to applicable state laws. While recent court decisions have questioned the applicability of state-use tax laws to mail-order businesses, it is still necessary to be aware of state regulations concerning the collection of **sales tax**.

The FTC has issued several directives, guidelines, and advisory opinions concerning mail-order businesses. These and other relevant regulations are published in the Code of Federal Regulations (CFR), Title 16, Chapters 1 and 2, which is available in most large libraries or directly from the FTC. It is worth summarizing a few of the rules that mail-order firms must observe in the conduct of their business.

The Mail-Order Merchandise Rule, also known as the 30-Day Rule, is designed to protect consumers from unexpected delays in receiving merchandise ordered through the mail. When there is a shipping delay, mail-order businesses are required to notify customers before the promised shipping date or within 30 days after the order was received. The notice of delay must provide the customer with the option of canceling the order for a full refund or consenting to the delay. Among other things, the rule also requires that the option notice be sent by first-class mail.

Another FTC rule requires all mail-order advertising to indicate the country of origin of the product being advertised, but only if the product has fabric as part of its content. This rule was designed to protect domestic textile and wool producers. Product **warranties and guarantees** are the subject of additional FTC guidelines that apply to all businesses, not just mail-order businesses.

Mail-order advertising frequently contains endorsements or testimonials. Under FTC guidelines, any endorsement must reflect the views of the endorser, must not be reworded or taken out of context, and the endorser must be a bona fide user of the product. If the endorser has been paid, the ad must disclose that fact, unless they are celebrities or experts. Additional FTC rules apply specifically to endorsements by average consumers and expert endorsements.

The FTC has issued guidelines to help mail-order businesses avoid deceptive pricing. These rules affect two-for-one offers, price comparisons, and other issues. Use of the words "free" and "new" are subject to FTC review. Advertising products that have yet to be manufactured, while legal, is subject to FTC requirements. Also called dry testing, such advertising must clearly state that sale of the product is only planned and that it is possible that consumers who order the product may not receive it. In addition, if the product is not manufactured, consumers who ordered it must be notified within four months of the original ad or mailing, and they must be given the opportunity to cancel their order without obligation.

In addition to FTC regulations, mail-order businesses must also be aware of USPS regulations concerning materials that should not be mailed. Lotteries, for example, are illegal under USPS regulations. A lottery includes the element of chance, consideration, and a prize. Consideration means that consumers must pay something to enter the lottery. Consequently, mail-order businesses often offer consumers the opportunity to enter a sweepstakes that does not require any consideration, payment, or purchase on the part of the consumer. While sweepstakes have proved to be an effective method of advertising mail order merchandise, many states have laws affecting their use. Particularly deceptive practices in the area of sweepstakes have also drawn the attention of postal officials as a possible violation of laws concerning frauds and swindles.

THE FUTURE OF MAIL-ORDER BUSINESS

The mail-order industry has grown during the 1990s, and there is every indication it will continue to do so into the 21st century. Catalog revenues, which account for a significant portion of all mail-order sales, grew at an annual rate of approximately 7 percent from 1987 to 1993, according to a 1994 survey conducted by the WEFA Group for the Direct Marketing Association. The same survey forecast that catalog revenues would grow nearly 6.8 percent annually through 1997, reaching a total of $69.5 billion. In actuality, catalog sales reached $75 billion in 1996, and an update to the WEFA study predicted catalog sales of $87 billion in 1998, on catalog advertising expenditures of nearly $11 billion.

As consumers become more accustomed to at-home shopping, though, they are also showing increasing concern over such issues as privacy and deceptive mail practices. These concerns may lead to increased regulation of mail order businesses. A variety of federal and state regulations have been proposed to protect consumer privacy. Thus far the mail-order industry has been successful at efforts to regulate itself. Mail-order businesses, however, must remain aware of the constantly changing regulatory environment in which they operate.

SEE ALSO: Catalog Marketing

[David P. Bianco]

FURTHER READING:

Bruce, Ian. *Successful Mail Order Marketing: How to Build a Really Cost Effective Operation from Scratch.* Philadelphia: Trans Atlantic Publications, 1997.

Keup, Erwin J. *Mail-Order Legal Guide.* 2nd ed. Grants Pass, OR: PSI Research, 1993.

Muldoon, Katie. *How to Profit through Catalog Marketing.* Lincolnwood, IL: NTC/Contemporary Publishing, 1995.

Simon, Julian L. *How to Start and Operate a Mail-Order Business.* 5th ed. New York: McGraw-Hill, 1993.

Sroge, Maxwell. *Inside the Leading Mail Order Houses.* 4th ed. Lincolnwood, IL: NTC/Contemporary Publishing, 1996.

MALAYSIA, DOING BUSINESS IN

Malaysia is a major developing nation in Southeast Asia. It is comprised of two distinct regions: Peninsular Malaysia and East Malaysia. The South China Sea separates the two regions by over 540 miles. The nation's total land area is 127,317 square miles, or just over the size of New Mexico. Of the two regions, East Malaysia—consisting of the two states of Sabah and Sarawak on the northern half of the island of Borneo—is disproportionately the larger, covering well over 76,400 square miles. East Malaysia is sparsely populated and relatively undeveloped. By contrast, more than 80 percent of Malaysia's 19 million (1994) people live in the rapidly developing Peninsular region. Peninsular Malaysia comprises the southern portion of the Malay Peninsula, bordered on the north by Thailand. Directly off the peninsula's tip is the island nation of Singapore. Just to the west, the Straits of Malacca separates the peninsula from Sumatra in Indonesia.

Since its independence in the wake of World War II, Malaysia had transformed itself from a British colony with an economy almost completely dependent on rubber plantations, tin mining, and agriculture, to emerge as a growing industrial and commercial force in the world economy. The nation remained one of the world's most rapidly expanding economies throughout the 1980s and well into the 1990s, before succumbing to the East Asian economic crisis.

MALAYSIA AND THE EAST ASIAN ECONOMIC CRISIS

When Thailand's currency collapsed in July 1997, the economic crisis it spawned spread rapidly to its neighbors, including Malaysia. To some extent, Malaysia was better prepared to face the crisis. At $29 billion, Malaysia's foreign **debt** was significant but considerably less than such other affected nations as Indonesia ($59 billion) or Thailand ($69 billion). Also, while Malaysia had, like Thailand, fallen victim to a **real estate** and building frenzy, much of the development (such as the port facilities at Klang) created much needed **infrastructure** beyond the confines of the capital. While the real estate speculation had caused unsustainable projects in the capital Kuala Lumpur, in short, the development was not limited to one city. This differentiated Malaysia from the development fever in Thailand that had centered primarily on the Thai capital, Bangkok.

As a consequence, the Malaysian prime minister, Mahathir bin Mohamad, was able to avoid calling on the **International Monetary Fund** (IMF) for help, while Indonesia and Thailand did. Yet Prime Minister Mahathir's general economic policies seemed mostly centered on scapegoating external sources and denial of the actual issues of outstanding debt and unrestrained development. Mahathir asserted that simply by refusing to accept IMF assistance, Malaysia could avoid the economic collapse that Thailand and Indonesia had experienced, indicating that it was the IMF austerity measures that caused (rather than solved) the problem.

By August 1997 Malaysia's worsening economic situation could no longer be ignored. In response, Mahathir focused his attentions on foreign currency speculators, announcing Malaysia's intention to institute currency controls to limit speculators. In response, Deputy Prime Minister and Finance Minister Anwar Ibrahim openly spoke out against Mahathir, and several key **banking** ministers, including the **central bank** governor, resigned in protest. Regardless, on September 1, 1997, Malaysia instituted controls. Immediately after this, Mahathir insisted that Anwar resign. When Anwar refused, the government fired Anwar on grounds of sexual misconduct. Since the charges were widely believed to be false and since when Anwar appeared for trial later in the month, he was bruised from obvious beatings, the incident provoked widespread political unrest with police having to battle thousands of demonstrators in Kuala Lumpur.

By October, Mahathir was in an increasingly weak position politically from pro-Anwar groups, the Malaysian **stock market** was in crisis and its currency, the ringgit, had fallen by 35 percent. Seeking another scapegoat, Mahathir claimed that ''We may suspect that they, the Jews, have an agenda, but we do not want to accuse.'' Blaming the economic problems of Malaysia on a Jewish conspiracy was difficult since Malaysia has no Jewish community. Mahathir, however, indicated that U.S. currency speculator George Soros was Jewish, and gave the rationale that Jews would not want to see a predominantly Moslem nation prosper (this despite the fact that most other nations affected by the crisis were not Moslem). Mahathir's anti-Semitic comments received worldwide condemnation and shook foreign confidence in his leadership.

Ironically, as Malaysia grew economically more stable in early 1999, it became politically more unstable. On April 4, 1999, Anwar's wife, Wan Azizah Wan Ismail, formed an opposition multiethnic party, opposed to Mahathir's New Economic Order, which among other policies has required preferential treatment for Bumiputeras (ethnic Malays). On April 14, 1999, Anwar was sentenced to prison. Awaiting the verdict for the trial, followers erupted in widespread rioting which continued after his sentencing; the trial was widely condemned as highly questionable.

BUSINESS PRACTICES

MALAYSIA AND ITS ETHNICITY. Malaysia is a multicultural nation with three dominant ethnic groups: ethnic Chinese, ethnic Indian (primarily Tamil), and Bumiputera (comprised of ethnic Malays as well as Dayaks and other indigenous people of northern Borneo). Under British rule, the ethnic Chinese grew economically dominant in Malaysia's business sector. This led to tensions between ethnic Chinese and Bumiputera Malaysians following independence. Interethnic tensions grew so marked that predominately Chinese Singapore broke with the Malaysian Federation soon after independence.

In an attempt to equalize business power more equitably between the dominant Chinese minority and Bumiputeras, the country adopted the New Economic Policy. The New Economic Policy was instituted by Mahathir bin Mohamed soon after he first gained office in 1981. The policy gave preferences to Bumiputeras over ethnic Chinese; for example, companies over a certain size were required to have a Bumiputera partner. While the policy was, expectedly, not welcomed by the ethnic Chinese minority, and was liberalized in the early 1990s, the system of preferences may have contributed to the absence of anti-Chinese sentiment after the 1997 economic crisis. Indeed, Malaysia was an exemplary model of interethnic harmony during the economic crisis, especially when compared to Indonesia where thousands of Chinese Indonesians were massacred in anti-Chinese rioting in May 1997.

LANGUAGE. The official language of Malaysia is Bahasa Melayu (literally, ''the language of Malaysia''). This is a standardized form of the many Malay dialects and is—with mild differences—nearly identical to Bahasa Indonesia spoken in neighboring Indonesia.

While Bahasa Melayu is the language required in all governmental communication, and most **advertising**, it is not the only language of the country. Approximately 29.7 percent of Malaysia's population are Chinese, speaking various dialects of Chinese. Additionally, just over 8 percent of Malaysians are ethnic Indians, primarily Tamil-speaking but encompassing a wide range of other Indian languages as well.

Additionally, because of long association with Great Britain, most Malaysians of all ethnic groups speak English as their second language. Indeed, government documents generally have an English translation following the Bahasa Melayu version, both for foreigners and for Chinese and Indian Malaysians.

VIEWS OF TECHNOLOGY AND THE ENVIRONMENT. The attitudes of the three main Malaysian ethnic groups—the Bumiputeras, the Chinese, and the Indians—regarding technology significantly differ from that of the United States. The United States is a control culture, while both Bumiputera and Indian Malaysians traditionally are a subjugation culture. This means that U.S. culture views technology as consistently positive and reinforces a belief that people can control their environment to conform to their needs. By contrast, Malaysian groups traditionally view technology with some skepticism and conform their behavior to existing environmental conditions. This traditional view of technology, though still present, is changing toward the control stance in the most-developed urban and industrial areas around the capital city of Kuala Lumpur. These traditional norms, however, remain firmly in place in most of the rest of the country.

Chinese Malaysian culture is more accurately described as a harmonization culture. Here the emphasis is on one's integration into a natural order rather than one's control of that order. This is most evident in the ethnic Chinese following of *feng shui* (an ancient geomancy dealing with the balance of spiritual forces). The importance of location, lucky or unlucky dates, and numerous other factors determined by *feng shui* experts guide many of Malaysia's Chinese community. For example, many Chinese would confer with a *feng shui* expert before deciding on an office location or signing an important agreement. Such practices are important to those who adhere to them, and should be accorded the same respect one would give to a religion, rather than be misinterpreted as the equivalent of minor superstition.

The location of the nation tends to affect certain aspects of Malaysian behavior as well. Work—particularly that conducted outdoors or in areas without air conditioning—is affected by the climate. Malaysia is tropical with high temperatures year-round and unrelentingly high humidity. Additionally, the wet season consists of daily and often torrential rains from roughly September to December.

SOCIAL ORGANIZATION

Social organizational factors in Malaysia affecting business include the importance of religion, the concept of family, and group ties.

RELIGION. Religion plays an important role in Indonesian business. Virtually all Bumiputeras and many of the ethnic Indians are Moslem. Most Malaysian Moslems take Islam very seriously, and follow its precepts as a lifestyle as much as a religion. Because the mosque is regularly visited, it may serve as a place to socialize and nurture business contacts within the Moslem community. Additionally, Moslem sensibilities affect attitudes toward business attire, with most Malaysian women dressing more modestly than their U.S. counterparts.

Five of Malaysia's states (Perlis, Kedah, Kelantan, Terengganu, and Johore) follow the Islamic workweek. In these five states, business offices are open six days a week, Saturday through Thursday, with business closing after a half day on Thursday and the Islamic Sabbath (Friday) off. In the remaining states, the workweek follows non-Islamic norms of Monday through Friday, and half days on Saturdays. Still, employers give Moslems time to go to the mosque on Thursday afternoons and part of the day on Friday. As in all Moslem nations, the Islamic holy days are followed. For example, the fasting month of Ramadan is followed, with a resulting effect on work performance.

The ethnic Chinese generally follow a wide range of Buddhist and Taoist practices blended with the precepts of Confucianism. Their observances range from strict adherents to loose practitioners. The Chinese New Year and the importance of *feng shui,* however, are nearly universally observed.

Most of the non-Moslem Indians are Hindu. The Thomian Indians, however, are among the world's oldest practitioners of Christianity. Additionally, the Sikhs follow their own religion, and some followers of nearly all of India's religions are evident among some Indian Malaysians.

Additionally, because of the influence of Hindu and Chinese spiritual beliefs, Malaysian Moslems (like their Indonesian coreligionists to the south) are more likely than Moslems elsewhere to believe in ghosts and the spirit world. While remaining true to the essential monotheistic beliefs of Islam, Malaysians nonetheless recognize spiritual forces or attributes of the soul in a variety objects. The presence of ghosts, witches, and other spiritual entities remain a real part of life for many Malaysians, and the need to placate these spirits affects all aspects of life, including work. A common mistake of foreigners is to view Malaysia as a traditional Islamic society and therefore to play down the importance of these supernatural forces, to criticize such beliefs, or to mistakenly reduce their importance to that of mere superstition. Fear of ghosts or the believed presence of spiritual forces can prevent employees from coming to work or prevent the conclusion of a business deal.

FAMILY AND GROUP TIES. Most Malaysians hold considerably stronger and more extended kinship bonds than those in the United States. Family connections and obligations influence hiring, deal making and other business issues. Moreover, the definition of immediate relationships reaches far beyond the nuclear family to those who would be considered distant relatives in a North American conception.

For all Malaysian ethnic groups, **nepotism** extends beyond direct kin relationships to clan ties. This is particularly the case for the various clans of the ethnic Chinese communities.

CONTEXTING

Malaysia is a high context society and the United States is a low context culture. This means that Malaysians are more likely to rely on implicit communication rather than on explicit messages. Malaysians as a result read more into what is said than the words themselves may actually mean. For most Malaysians, what is meant matters more than what is actually said.

In Malaysia, meaning is usually communicated indirectly, especially in the delivery of bad news. As a result, Malaysians are likely to agree to things with which they disagree, allowing the context of the discussion or past relationship to convey their disagreement. This is clear to Malaysians but to those from low context cultures such as the United States, such indirect communication is often misread as dishonesty. Conversely, the direct style of communication practiced by most U.S. businesspeople in Malaysia is perceived as rude and often causes others to lose face.

Malaysians, as a high context culture, place a strong value on face saving, while most North Americans place little emphasis on face-saving. The Malaysian conception of face-saving takes the form of the avoidance of shame. Most low context U.S. business practice is controlled by the following of the law and adherence to written agreements. In Malaysia, one commonly holds to a **contract** to maintain appearances rather than from fear of a lawsuit.

The North American businessperson in Malaysia is thus viewed as lacking honor, having no sense of face (and therefore dangerous to deal with) and being foolishly litigious. The Malaysians in turn are viewed by their North American counterparts as dishonoring their contracts and ignoring their own laws. In reality both perceptions are accurate when viewed through the context of the values of the other's culture.

Still, to succeed in business in Malaysia, the foreigner will need to view contracts and other legally binding arrangements as ongoing rather than definitive. Moreover, the foreigner will have to be willing to allow some inconsistencies to stand at times to maintain appearance and avoid shaming the Malaysians who would otherwise terminate the business relationship.

TEMPORAL CONCEPTION

Malaysia is a polychronic culture. Time is more fluid than in monochronic societies such as the United States. The Malaysians value friendship, personal commitments and the completion of tasks at hand at the expense of preset schedules.

Time is seen as malleable. Appointment times are approximate. Work hours are variable. Consequently, the monochronic foreigner needs to adjust his or her concepts of scheduling, deadlines, and other time-linked activities in Malaysia.

SEE ALSO: Cross-Cultural/International Communication

[David A. Victor]

FURTHER READING:

Andaya, Barbara Watson, and Leonard Y. Andaya. *A History of Malaysia.* London: Macmillan, 1982.

Brooks, Guy, and Victoria Brooks. *Malaysia: A Kick Start for Business Travelers.* North Vancouver, BC: Self-Counsel Press, 1995.

Crouch, Harold. *Government and Society in Malaysia.* Ithaca, NY: Cornell University Press, 1996.

Gomez, Edmund Terence, and K. S. Jomo. *Malaysia's Political Economy: Politics, Patronage, and Profits.* Cambridge: Cambridge University Press, 1997.

Leete, Richard. *Malaysia's Demographic Transition: Rapid Development, Culture, and Politics.* London: Oxford University Press, 1996.

Munan, Heidi. *Culture Shock: Malaysia.* Portland, OR: Graphic Arts Center Publishing, 1991.

Munro-Kua, Anne. *Authoritarian Populism in Malaysia.* New York: St. Martin's Press, 1997.

Schlossstein, Steve. *Asia's New Little Dragons: The Dynamic Emergence of Indonesia, Thailand, and Malaysia.* Chicago: Contemporary Books, 1991.

Victor, David A. *International Business Communication.* New York: HarperCollins, 1992.

MANAGEMENT

Business management can be defined as the acquisition, allocation, and utilization of resources through planning, organizing, staffing, leading, and controlling. Management involves the coordination of human, financial, material, and information resources in order to realize company goals and operate a business efficiently. Managers are the employees charged with these responsibilities. Managers play a variety of roles in a company, summarized as interpersonal roles, information roles, and decision-making roles. Managing entails five functions: planning, organizing, staffing, leading, and controlling. The day-to-day tasks of management include: considering problems and making decisions in how to deal with them, implementing courses of action, and reviewing decisions and actions and making any necessary changes.

BACKGROUND

The basic elements of modern management practices can be traced to ancient times. The Egyptians, for example, developed advanced management techniques related to labor division, hierarchy of authority, and **teams**. They developed complex bureaucracies to measure and forecast river levels and crop yields, distribute revenues within the government, manage trade, and complete massive construction projects such as the pyramids. The Babylonians, Greeks, Romans, Chinese, and other cultures made similar contributions to **management science**.

Although management systems existed long before the modern era, it was not until the late 18th and 19th centuries that advanced business management techniques emerged in response to the Industrial Revolution. The Industrial Revolution resulted in the formation of extremely large organizations characterized by job specialization and the administration of large amounts of human resources. A new breed of middle-level managers were needed to plan and direct human efforts and to administer large pools of capital.

Among the most influential American contributors to management practice during the Industrial Revolution was Daniel C. McCallum (1815-1878), the superintendent of the Erie Railroad during the mid-1800s. To more efficiently manage the vast human and capital resources involved with construction of the railroad, he established a set of guiding management principles that emphasized: a specific division of labor and responsibilities, the **empowerment** of managers to make decisions in the field, compensation based on merit, a clearly delineated managerial hierarchy, and a detailed system of data gathering, analysis, and reporting that would foster individual accountability and improve **decision making**.

SCHOOL APPROACHES TO MANAGEMENT

The efforts of McCallum and other managers of his era were reflected in the first of five schools of management that emerged during the early and middle 1900s. The first of these schools was scientific management, which dominated management philosophy between the 1890s and the early 1920s. Scientific management concepts were heavily influenced by the ideas of American efficiency engineer Frederick W. Taylor (1856-1915). Taylor believed that organizational efficiency could be achieved by using statistics, logic, and detailed analysis to break jobs and responsibilities down into specific tasks. The chief contribution of scientific management was that it successfully applied modern techniques of science and engineering to the management of resources and organizational systems.

Scientific management principles were displaced during the 1920s by the classical management school of thought. Classical management theory is largely attributable to Henri Fayol, who is also known as the father of management. Classical management emphasized the identification of universal principles of management which, if adhered to, would lead to organizational success. Universal principles encompassed two broad areas. The first was identifying business functions and the second was structuring organizations and managing workers.

In essence, classical theory holds that management is a process consisting of several related functions, such as planning and organizing. Thus, by identifying specific business functions—including **marketing**, **finance**, production, and subfunctions within those and other major categories—companies can efficiently divide an organization into departments that work as a process. Furthermore, by carefully structuring chains of authority and responsibility, an entity can successfully facilitate the performance of individuals within departments to achieve company goals.

Importantly, Fayol is credited with identifying five basic management functions: planning, organizing, commanding, coordinating, and controlling. In addition, his 14 principles of management established a framework for management that continues to influence modern management theory. Those principles included: unity of command, meaning a worker should be responsible to only one superior; unity of direction, which implies that each group of activities having a single goal should be unified in a department or work group, or at least under one manager; centralization, or centralized control and decision making; and stability of tenure of personnel, which suggests that, for efficiency reasons, **employee turnover** should be kept to a minimum even if that means sacrificing quality for long-term loyalty.

The classical school of management remained dominant from the 1920s until the 1940s. It was gradually supplanted, however, by theories that focused on the importance of individual needs and group interaction in organizations. Human relations management arose in the 1930s, largely as a result of studies and experiments (including the classic **Hawthorne experiments**) conducted by Harvard University psychologist and researcher Elton Mayo (1880-1949) and his contemporaries. To the surprise of classical theorists, Mayo's research demonstrated that mechanistic, efficiently designed processes did not necessarily create more efficient organizations. Instead, the research demonstrated that success could be attained by showing more concern for workers' psychological needs. The human relations school advocated such techniques as employee counseling, feedback, and communication with coworkers, superiors, and subordinates.

Both the classical and human relations management ideologies were eclipsed during the 1950s by the behavioral management school of thought. It also emphasized the importance of the human psyche in management. It differed, however, from the human relations approach in that it stressed behavior over interaction. It sought to rationalize and predict behavior in the workplace through scientific analysis of social interaction, motivation, the use of power and influence, **leadership** qualities, and other factors. Behaviorists believed that a chief goal of managers should be to increase the effectiveness of workers through motivational techniques, such as empowerment and participation in decisions, and to redesign jobs to take advantage of individuals' strengths and weaknesses.

Demonstrating the gradual transition from mechanistic management theory to a more humanistic approach was the renowned Theory X and Theory Y, which American management theorist Douglas McGregor (1906-1964) posited in the 1950s. Theory X depicts the old, repressive, pessimistic view of workers. It assumes that people are lazy and have to be coerced to produce through tangible rewards. It also presumes that workers prefer to be directed, want to avoid responsibility, and treasure financial security above all else. In contrast, Theory Y postulates that: humans can learn to accept and seek responsibility; most people possess a high degree of imagination and problem-solving ability; employees will self-govern, or direct themselves toward goals to which they are committed; and, notably, satisfaction of ego and self-actualization are among the most important needs that organizations should address.

Coinciding with the behavioral management ideology, which gained acceptance throughout the 1950s (and remained relevant into the 1990s), was the fifth school of thought, quantitative management. Quantitative management theorists believe that, while the behavioral dimension of organizations merits attention, scientific and analytical techniques related to process and structure can help organizations be much more efficient. Quantitative management entails the application of statistical analyses, linear programming, and information systems to assist in making decisions, allocating resources, scheduling processes, and tracking money. Specifically, it advocates the substitution of verbal and descriptive analysis with models and symbols, particularly those that are computer-generated. In fact, it is because of advanced electronic information systems that quantitative management techniques were broadly applied in the 1980s and 1990s.

COMPLEMENTARY MANAGEMENT APPROACHES

In addition to the school approaches that dominated much of the 20th century are three other approaches to management theory and application: systems, contingency, and process. They emerged during the mid-1900s, gained widespread appeal during the latter part of the century, and continued to influence management thought and practice through the 1990s. These approaches differ from most of the schools of management thought in that they are not posited as a wrong or right ideology, but rather are complementary—they can exist and be applied simultaneously depending on the particular internal and external environment of individual organizations.

THE SYSTEMS APPROACH

The systems management approach emphasizes the importance of educating managers to understand the overall system so that they will realize how actions in their department affect other units. An organization can be likened to a mobile: if you touch one part, the entire apparatus swings into motion. For example, the hiring of a single individual into a marketing department is bound to have some degree of impact on other divisions of the organization over time. Similarly, incorporating behaviorist theory, if managers are given more autonomy and responsibility they are likely to perform at a higher level. As a result, subordinates in their departments are likely to perform better, which may cause other departments to be more effective, and so on.

The systems approach to management recognizes both open and closed systems. A closed system, such as a clock, is self-contained and operates relatively free from outside influences. In contrast, most organizations are open systems and are thus highly dependent on outside resources, such as suppliers and buyers. Specifically, systems are impacted by four spheres of outside influence: education and skills (of workers), legal and political, economic, and cultural. Management processes must be designed to adapt to these influences. This acknowledgment of outside factors represents a meaningful departure from the earliest school approaches that viewed management within the context of closed systems.

Importantly, the systems approach also recognizes that all large organizations are comprised of multiple subsystems, each of which receives inputs from other subsystems and turns them into outputs for use by other subsystems. At least five types of subsystems, according to systems theory, should be incorporated into management processes in larger organizations. Production subsystems are the components that transform inputs into outputs. In a manufacturing company this subsystem would be represented by activities related to production. In most business organizations all other subsystems are built around the production subsystem.

Supportive subsystems perform acquisition and distribution functions within an organization. Acquisition activities include securing resources, such as employees and raw materials, from the external environment. Human resources and purchasing divisions would typically be included in this group. Distribution (or disposal) activities encompass efforts to transfer the product or service outside of the organization. Supportive subsystems of this type include sales and marketing divisions, **public relations** departments, and **lobbying** efforts.

Maintenance subsystems maintain the social involvement of employees in an organization. Activities in this group include providing **employee benefits** and compensation that motivate workers, creating favorable work conditions, empowering employees, and other forms of satisfying human needs. Similarly, adaptive subsystems serve to gather information about problems and opportunities in the environment and then respond with **innovations** that allow the organization to adapt. A firm's research lab or a product development department would both be part of an adaptive subsystem. Finally, managerial subsystems direct the activities of other subsystems in the organization. These managerial functions set goals and policies, allocate resources, settle disputes, and generally work to facilitate the efficiency of the organization.

THE CONTINGENCY APPROACH

Like the systems approach, the contingency approach to management views the organization as a set of interdependent units operating in an open system. It differs from all other management approaches, though, in that it is based on the idea that every organization and situation is unique. Its situational perspective implies that there is no single best way to manage. Therefore, specific techniques and managerial concepts must be applied in different ways and in different combinations to achieve organizational or departmental effectiveness. In fact, the contingency theory has been described as a sort of amalgam of all other ideologies. Its chief contribution to modern management theory is its identification of critical internal and external variables that affect management processes.

THE PROCESS APPROACH AND THE BASIC FUNCTIONS OF MANAGEMENT

Perhaps the most widely accepted organizational management theory is the process approach. It also serves as a descriptive overview of the various tasks and responsibilities management faces, and it draws on many of the theories contained in the five schools of management as well as the systems approach and contingency approach described above. For example, the process approach derives from Fayol's ideas, particularly his five management functions. And, like the systems approach and the later schools of management thought, the process approach emphasizes the point that management is an ongoing series of interrelated activities rather than a one-time act.

The process approach also recognizes other management theories that have gained acceptance in the late 1900s. Of import is the generally accepted management pyramid model, which is comprised of three hierarchies based on experience and education. At the top of the pyramid is top management, or the executive level that handles long-term **strategy**. At the center is middle management, which translates top management objectives into more specific goals for individual work units. Finally, line managers and supervisors fill the bottom of the pyramid. They handle the day-to-day management of employees and operations.

Adherents to the process approach have altered and elaborated on Fayol's original functions, usually in an attempt to incorporate behaviorist philosophies. Management theorists commonly recognize five management functions: planning, organizing, staffing, leading, and controlling. The five process management functions are linked together by communication and decision-making activities common to all of them.

PLANNING. Planning is the development of specific strategies designed to achieve organizational goals. Forward-looking managers use planning to develop strategies, policies, and methods for achieving company objectives. Moreover, managers who rely on planning can anticipate problems before they even arise and therefore can implement solutions quickly. In addition, planning serves as the foundation for the other management functions—organizing, staffing, leading, and controlling—by providing direction for a company; and increases a company's potential for success in accomplishing its goals.

Planning occurs at all three management levels: top, middle, and line. As indicated earlier, top managers are charged with making long-term plans that define the mission and policies of the organization while lower level managers implement them. In the planning process, top-level managers concentrate on the questions of what and how much. Middle managers implement mission and policy objectives, usually by focusing on the where and when. Finally, line managers effect the specific plans of the middle managers by addressing the pressing questions of who and how.

For example, top executives at a nail factory may decide that the company should become the most productive, highest-quality, largest-volume producer in the world. Middle managers in the production division may decide that accomplishment of this goal requires that over the next 12 months they cut **costs** by 20 percent, decrease flaws to .01 percent, and increase capacity 40 percent. Likewise, managers in the marketing department may decide that they need to increase sales by 80 percent during the next year. Finally, line managers would have to figure out how to achieve those goals and who would do the actual work. They might increase bonuses for salespeople who boosted volume, for instance, or lower **profit margins** (and prices) to increase sales. Or, production line managers might implement a new quality management program and increase investments in cost-saving **automation**.

Another way of viewing the planning process in an organization is by categorizing planning activities as strategic (top management), tactical (middle), or operational (bottom). The overall process usually entails at least six steps: setting goals, analyzing the external and internal environment to identify problems and opportunities, identifying and evaluating alternatives, choosing a plan, implementing the program, and controlling and judging the results of the implementation. Different stages of the process should ideally overlap management hierarchies, thus fostering organizational unity and informed planning.

In addition to the stages of the planning process and hierarchical responsibilities, most planning activities and responsibilities can be categorized, according to *Corporate Planning: An Executive Viewpoint,* into one of four planning roles: (1) resource allocation, (2) environmental adaptation, (3) internal coordination, (4) and organizational strategic awareness. Resource allocation entails decisions related to the distribution of funds, expertise, labor, and equipment. For instance, a **chief executive officer** (CEO) might decide to not pay shareholder **dividends** as a way to increase funds for new product development. Or, a production line manager may elect to shift laborers from one product line to another to better match fluctuating output requirements.

Environmental adaptation planning activities are those that serve to improve the company's relationship to its external environment, including such influences as governments, suppliers, customers, and public opinion. These activities address problems and opportunities that arise from such external factors. For example, gas station company managers that choose to attach point-of-sale (credit card) machines to their pumps are reacting to a public demand for convenience. Similarly, a CEO of a coal mining company might have to plan to reduce toxic emissions in an effort to satisfy government regulators or to appease public sentiment.

Internal coordination planning activities are those that respond to internal influences. They coordinate internal strengths and weaknesses in an effort to maximize profitability (in the case of for-profit companies). Finally, planning activities categorized as organizational strategic awareness strategies create systematic management development systems that allow an organization to evaluate the effects of past plans.

In order to be effective, plans and goals developed and executed at any level will generally exhibit basic characteristics. The plans should be specific and measurable, for example, meaning that they will have definite goals that can be measured against definite results. Plans should also be time-oriented, or should be devised with deadlines for accomplishing parts of the entire goal and a final deadline for completion. Plans should also be attainable. Insufficient resources or impossible goals can thwart motivation and result in underperformance. Finally, plans should be mutually supportive, meaning that plans made in or for one part of an organization should complement other plans and objectives.

ORGANIZING. Organizing is the second major managerial function. It is the process of structuring a company's resources—its personnel and materials—in a way that will allow it to achieve its objectives. Specifically, organizing entails a fundamental three-step process: developing tasks, labor units, and positions. First of all, managers must determine the exact actions that have to be taken to implement plans and achieve objectives. Second, they must divide personnel into teams with areas of responsibility. Third, managers must delegate authority and responsibility to individuals and establish decision-making relationships. Once management accomplishes the first step, it can take a number of different routes to organize teams and delegate authority. Most organizations are arranged by either function or division.

The most common approach to organizing teams and delegating authority in organizations is by function. Under the functional approach, activities are broken down into primary business functions, such as finance, operations, and marketing. Within each major functional group are numerous subfunctions. In the marketing division, for example, might be the sales and promotions departments. The functional approach results in a comparatively efficient division of labor and an authority hierarchy that is easy for workers to understand. It may lead, however, to internal rivalries between departments or myopia because different divisions are not aware of the goals and actions of other parts of the company.

In addition to functions, many companies are organized by division. There are several different divisional approaches to structuring teams and delegating power to managers. For example, some companies take a product line approach, whereby the company is broken down into different product or service groups. For instance, an appliance producer may break its organization down into dishwashers, clothes washers and dryers, and vacuum cleaners. Other companies might use a customer approach—industrial products, consumer products, government products, etc. The advantage of both approaches is that they allow managers and the entire company to be focused on the product or customer rather than on support functions, such as marketing. This organizational approach may result, however, in an inefficient division of labor (i.e., overlap) because each group is forced to supply their own support functions.

Another common means of organizing a company by divisions is the geographic approach, whereby activities or groups are divided by region. For instance, a multinational **bank** may have three major divisions: North America, Asia, and Europe. Those divisions, then, might be divided into subregions, such as northeast, south, and west. The geographic approach is often used by companies that specialize in marketing, finance, or some other major business function and operate in a number of different geographic areas. It allows flexibility in relation to different laws, exchange rates, and cultures, and fosters a responsiveness to local markets not attainable under other divisional approaches. The chief drawback of geographic organizations is that they can be relatively expensive to maintain.

A less conventional and increasingly popular approach to structuring organizations is known as the matrix system. In essence, a matrix system creates both functional and divisional groups to form multidisciplinary, integrated teams that combine staff and line authority. The main advantage of the matrix is that it reduces myopia in an organization, fosters cooperation, and promotes a free flow of information. But the matrix approach may also create an ambiguous power structure and may have limitations for many types of companies.

In addition to the basic structure, management authority and responsibility will also be dictated by the level of centralization in a company. In general, companies with more centralized management will be figuratively tall, meaning that power flows down through a chain of command. Decisions are made by a few people and handed down to the masses. In contrast, decentralized, or flat, organizations push management authority down. In flat organizations, many managers (and subordinates) are empowered to independently make decisions within their area of expertise in the company. Because of the trend toward flatter organizations during the 1980s and 1990s, traditional middle levels of management have become obsolete in many companies. Effectively, all workers become managers to some degree in the flattest organizations.

STAFFING. Staffing, the third major organizational function, encompasses activities related to finding and sustaining a labor force that is adequate to meet the organization's objectives. First, managers have to determine exactly what their labor needs are and then go into the labor force to try and recruit those skills and characteristics. Second, managers must train workers. Third, they have to devise a method of compensating and evaluating performance that complements objectives. This includes designing pay and benefits packages, conducting **performance appraisals**, and promoting employees. Finally, managers usually must devise a system of firing ineffective employees or reducing the **workforce**. In addition, management duties related to staffing often entail working with organized **labor unions** and meeting federal and state regulations.

LEADING. Leading, or motivating, is the fourth basic managerial function identified by the process approach to management. It is defined as the act of guiding and influencing other people to achieve goals. Leading involves leadership, communication, and motivation skills. In addition, the leadership role for most managers entails four primary duties: educating, evaluating, counseling, and representing. Educating includes teaching skills and showing workers how to function within the company and how to perform their assigned tasks. They do so through both formal and informal means. Examples of informal education are attitudes, work habits, and other behavior that sets an example for subordinates to follow.

Evaluating activities that are part of a manager's leadership responsibilities include settling disputes, creating and enforcing standards and policies, evaluating output, and dispensing rewards. In fact, much of the respect and esteem that a manager gets from subordinates is contingent upon the ability to evaluate effectively.

A manager's ability to counsel will also impact his or her effectiveness. Counseling involves giving advice, helping workers solve problems, soliciting feedback from subordinates, and listening to voluntary input or employee problems. Finally, managers lead through representation by voicing the concerns and suggestions of their subordinates to higher authorities. In other words, managers must show a willingness to back their workers and represent their needs and goals.

Numerous theories have been posited to explain the leadership function and to describe the traits of successful leaders. For example, John P. Kotter, author of *The Leadership Factor,* identified six traits considered necessary for managers in large organizations to be effective leaders: (1) motivation, (2) personal values, (3) ability, (4) reputation and track record, (5) relationships in the firm and industry, and (6) industry and organizational knowledge. Contrary to traditional beliefs about leadership, which hold that leadership ability is innate, these trait groups are acquired through combinations of early childhood experiences, education, and career experiences.

In addition to developing leadership traits, effective managers must adopt a style of leadership that complements their position, personality, and environment. In general, managers practice some combination of four recognized leadership styles: directive, political, participative, and charismatic. The directive leadership style emphasizes the use of facts, sound strategy, and assertiveness. This type of manager focuses on gathering information, establishing objectives through a careful assessment of data, devising strategies to accomplish goals, and then directing subordinates and coworkers to achieve those ends. Managers who subscribe to a directive leadership style are less concerned about building a consensus for their vision than they are about motivating others to achieve it. They are more likely to confront resistance to their goals and to have less patience in pursuing objectives than other types of leaders.

In contrast, managers who embrace a political leadership style believe that their ability to lead requires the power to manipulate forces within the entity toward common objectives. Importantly, they assume that the company is a political arena fraught with deception, in-fighting, and selfish goals. Therefore, they often must push, bargain, and manipulate to advance the interests of their departments and themselves. Although such leaders may be well-intentioned, honest, and acting in the best interests of the company, they may be willing to deceive others and act selfishly in order to achieve a desired result. Common tactics include keeping goals flexible or vague, advancing their agendas patiently, and manipulating channels of influence and authority.

The participative, or values-driven, style of leadership emphasizes joint decision making, decentralization, the sharing of power, and democratic management. Managers who are participative leaders assume that their subordinates are highly motivated by work that challenges them, builds skills, and is accomplished with teams of people that they respect. Thus, unlike directive leadership, the participative style focuses on building a consensus during the decision-making process. It also stresses bottom-up management—information and expertise is gleaned from workers in lower levels of the organization and used to direct decisions and goals—and the empowerment of subordinates to make decisions.

The fourth basic managerial style of leadership, charismatic leadership, differs from the other three styles in that it is more suited to realizing radical visions or handling crises. It is less concerned with influencing behavior toward the attainment of long-term goals or day-to-day management activities. Charismatic leadership in business organizations is a style often used by entrepreneurs who are starting new companies, or by transformational managers seeking to revitalize established organizations.

CONTROLLING. The fifth major managerial function, controlling, is comprised of activities that measure and evaluate the outcome of planning, organizing, staffing, and leading efforts. Controlling is an essential part of management because it helps managers determine the fruitfulness of the other functions (planning, organizing, etc.); helps guides employee efforts towards company goals; and helps a company distribute its resources efficiently and effectively. Controlling is typically viewed as an ongoing management process that ensures that the organization is moving toward its goals. The process includes establishing performance standards, evaluating ongoing activities, and correcting performance that deviates from the standards.

Managers begin by establishing specific criteria outlining how they want a company's tasks performed. Based on company objectives, managers determine the performance standards in order for the company to attain its goals. Performance standards may take the form of qualitative and quantitative criteria. Examples of performance standards are **budgets**, projections, **pro forma statements**, and production, sales, or quality initiatives. Successful managers usually rely on a feedback system to see how employees are responding to performance standards; this allows managers to identify problems before they develop into crises.

During the second stage of the control process, evaluation, managers determine how closely their subordinates' or department's performance matched up with preset standards. Of import is the manager's acceptable range of deviation, or the degree to which actual performance can vary from the standard before corrective action is necessary. In addition, managers must factor into the performance comparison influences outside of the control of their unit. They must also devise a means of communicating results to subordinates in a constructive manner.

If measured results deviate outside of an acceptable range, the manager must take corrective action. Corrective action may mean simply readjusting the preset standards to reflect more realistic goals. Or, the manager may have to analyze the process that lead to the deviation and then act to make changes. For instance, if a production line fails to meet quality goals the manager may choose to rearrange work teams or change the financial incentive system to emphasize quality. The manager may also determine that the departmental budget needs to be revised to increase spending on **quality control**.

To be effective, managers must design control systems that are based on meaningful and accepted standards. If standards are too high, subordinates are likely to lose motivation or become frustrated. Standards should also be based on the overall goals of the organization rather than on the narrow objectives of one department or division. The control process should emphasize two-way communication so that controls are understood by subordinates and managers are able to effectively set standards and evaluate performance, taking into account the workers' perspective. In addition, standards and controls should be flexible enough to accommodate emerging problems and opportunities. Most importantly, controls should be used only when necessary so that they don't unnecessarily obstruct creativity and drive.

MANAGERIAL ROLES AND SKILLS

In addition to the five basic managerial functions defined by the process approach, a number of ancillary roles can be identified (depending on the position and responsibilities of individual managers) that are necessary to perform the functions. These roles take the form of interpersonal roles, information roles, and decision maker roles. As part of their interpersonal roles, managers are generally expected to act as figureheads and leaders for their units or organizations, which entails performing ceremonial duties or entertaining associates. Managers also act as liaisons, working with peers in other departments or contacts outside of the organization. The liaison role requires managers to have contact with peers, customers, executives, and others.

As part of their information role, managers monitor the business environment and gather information that affects their departments. In addition to gathering information, managers also distribute it among their employees. Managers play the information role by acting as spokespersons by providing information about the company to the public. Furthermore, top-level managers often must interact with the government, consumer groups, industry associations, and other organizations.

As part of the decision maker role, managers constantly oversee and observe their units, resolving problems and disturbances, and developing a big picture of the department and its place in the organization. Likewise, managers must be negotiators to help secure resources for their team or group and to elicit cooperation from other groups or individuals inside and outside the company. As decision makers, managers also allocate resources, determining how to distribute limited resources within specific units to achieve maximum effectiveness. This role also involves entrepreneurial skills, because managers must generate ideas about improving their units' performance.

To succeed in their various roles, managers must possess a combination of skills from three broad groups: technical, conceptual, and relationship. Technical skills refer to knowledge of processes, tools, and techniques particular to a company or industry. For instance, sales managers who have never worked as field representatives might lack knowledge that would be important in setting sales goals and compensations systems. Conceptual skills allow managers to view each unit as part of the entire organization, and the company as part of a larger industry. Conceptual skills are particularly important for developing long-range goals and solving problems. Finally, relationship skills are those that the manager uses to communicate effectively and work with others.

Effective managers at all levels typically possess an advanced set of relationship skills, particularly in management structures that stress communication and cooperation (e.g., matrix). In general, managers at the top of the management pyramid require a higher degree of conceptual skills. In fact, as managers assume more responsibility and become less involved with day-to-day activities, technical knowledge becomes secondary. Middle managers, on the other hand, usually must possess a roughly equal amount of conceptual and technical knowledge. Finally, line managers near the bottom of the pyramid depend primarily on technical, rather than conceptual, skills.

CONTEMPORARY ISSUES IN MANAGEMENT

In the 1990s, two different types of senior manager began to emerge in response to the general trend toward specialization and downsizing: the specializing generalist and the generalizing specialist. Because of the **stock market** crash in 1987, companies in the 1990s sought upper-level specializing generalist managers, that is, general managers who specialized in one area, **corporate restructuring** and cost cutting, in particular. These managers focused largely on implementing policies that led to reducing costs, such as closing plants and laying off workers. Entrepreneurs who launch multiple businesses sometimes are referred to specializing generalists. Entrepreneurs often learn an array of general business skills because they perform a variety of tasks during the company start-up phase.

Alternatively, generalizing specialist managers generalize an area of expertise across the various management functions. For example, a senior manager with a marketing background might generalize the marketing management approach across an entire company. As a consequence, for example, such a manager might allocate funds only for research projects that have a proven potential market.

Moreover, with the **globalization** of many industries in the 1980s and 1990s, managers increasingly must possess a global perspective as well as the skills to work with managers and employees from other countries. More and more managers must be able to collaborate with companies from other countries when U.S. companies form multinational alliances with other companies. Consequently, managers must be able to perform their five basic functions—planning, organizing, staffing, leading, and controlling—in multinational settings. Economic globalization makes skills such as influence, negotiation, and conflict resolution indispensable.

Other contemporary issues in management include productivity, quality, innovation, and ethics, some of which also stem from globalization. Since other countries such as Japan have surpassed the United States in productivity, managers of companies of all sizes must address the problem of productivity in order to remain competitive. **International competition** also has caused renewed concern for quality, forcing managers of a variety of companies, such as automobile, computer, and electronics manufactures, to strive for greater quality. In addition, innovation became a key issue in management in the 1990s in response to a host of factors, including changes in the economy, various industries, consumer preferences, and international relations. Finally, because of the growing demand from customers and workers that companies act in a socially responsible manner, managers must make sure that a company's actions and policies are ethical, particularly in the areas of the environment and human rights.

SEE ALSO: Human Resource Management; Management Science; Managerial Economics; Matrix Management and Structure; Operations Management; Organization Theory; Organizational Development; Problem-Solving Styles; Supervision

[Dave Mote, updated by Karl Heil]

FURTHER READING:

Bolman, Lee G., and Terrence E. Deal. *Modern Approaches to Understanding and Managing Organizations.* San Francisco: Jossey Bass, 1984.

Cherrington, David J. *Organizational Behavior: The Management of Individual and Organizational Performance.* 2nd ed. Boston: Allyn and Bacon, 1994.

Kotter, John P. *John P. Kotter on what Leaders Really Do.* Cambridge, MA: Harvard Business School Press, 1999.

Plunkett, Warren R., and Charles R. Greer. *Supervision: Diversity and Teams in the Workplace.* 9th ed. Upper Saddle River, NJ: Prentice Hall, 1999.

MANAGEMENT AUDIT

Simply defined, the management audit is a comprehensive and thorough examination of an organization or one of its components. The audit is implemented to identify problems or significant weaknesses in the organization or corporation, thus providing **management** with a tool to address and repair the problem area.

The audit is not a new or recent idea. History tells us of the presence of auditors in Pharaoh's Egypt and the classical periods of Greek and Roman history. As businesses developed and grew over the centuries of recorded history, the need for controls became increasingly important. Financial **auditing** became a standard in American businesses and, following the lead of New York State, certification for accountants was enacted as legislation in many states. The financial audit is now fully integrated into business practices. The internal audit follows the spirit of financial auditing and surpasses it to examine operational matters as well. Another natural extension is operational auditing. While **internal auditing** is conducted by employees within the organization, an operational audit is generally completed by an internal task force or external analysts.

The management audit is now widely accepted in the business field. For more than 40 years, corporations and nonprofit organizations have utilized the management audit as a comprehensive tool. In 1932 T. G. Rose, a lecturer in management at Cambridge University and former manager for Leyland Motors, embraced the concept of an annual organizational and management audit; Queens University School of Business professor William P. Leonard followed suit, urging a comprehensive examination of the business entity. Additional credibility stemmed from the **General Accounting Office** of the federal government, an office charged with independent audits of government agencies.

The management audit is defined by its scope and objectives. The scope is broad and generally includes all functions of the organization, including objectives and **strategy**, corporate structure, organizational planning, the **budgeting** process, human and financial resources management, **decision making**, **research and development**, **marketing**, equipment and operations, and **management information systems**. This breadth extends to recent, present, and future operations and covers external issues as well as internal concerns. Objectives of the management audit include the development of recommendations and improvements, as well as increased awareness of the credibility and acceptance of the audit's results. The process is more an audit of management, in order to enhance **corporate profits** and financial stability.

The audit follows a logical, step-by-step format, including initial interviews with key managers. A study team uses the interview process to define the scope of the audit, including the areas or functions to be studied. Next, the team requests various forms of documentation, including budgets, planning documents, corporate reports, **financial statements**, policy and procedure manuals, biographical material, and various other documents. Following this stage, the study team then prepares a schedule and detailed plan of study, all aimed at proceeding to the internal fact finding step. Fact-finding relies once again on interviews, documentation, and personal observation of facilities and organizational work patterns. By the time these steps are completed, the study team develops a thorough understanding of organizational structure and operations.

The team generally turns next to an external review, using interviews to determine the opinions and attitudes key people outside the organization have about its operations. Examples of those interviewed are customers, representatives of **financial institutions**, and employees of federal agencies having contact with the audited organization. These interviews provide the team with more objective evaluations, and lead to an analysis of all the information and data now gathered. Organizational performance is profiled, then efficiency and effectiveness are evaluated and compared against industry norms. While many criteria can be measured quantitatively, team members have to use sound judgment and objectivity when evaluating issues that cannot be measured. In turn, the organization's management has to be receptive to the audit process and demonstrate clear acceptance of audit findings.

The study team then develops conclusions and recommendations which are communicated to the organization's management. These final two stages—conclusions/recommendations and communication—are essential to the management audit process. The audit is expected to identify corporate strengths and weaknesses, sources of problems, and potential problem areas. Recommendations for correction are presented to top management. The final report comes in the form of an overall plan of action, which includes prioritized recommendations, the specific units and individuals expected to carry out the recommendations, a schedule for action, and expected results. When conducted with thoroughness, objectivity, and timeliness, the management audit becomes a powerful tool for corporate and organizational executives who seek to improve effectiveness and efficiency.

An important aspect of the management audit is the composition of the study team. Both internal and external analysts are frequently used on audit teams; the composition depends on several factors, including the need for independent appraisal, the lack of human or financial resources to conduct the audit, and the need to provide an external audit to contrast against internal findings. In some instances, associations such as the American Institute of Management (AIM) provide audit teams. The AIM has developed ten categories of the management audit, and many audits apply these same categories. They include:

1. economic function
2. corporate structure
3. health of earnings
4. service to stockholders
5. research and development
6. directorate analysis
7. fiscal policies
8. production efficiency
9. sales vigor
10. executive evaluation

Management audits are not limited to business corporations. Nonprofit organizations—including educational institutions, hospitals, and churches—often use the management audit to attempt to improve operations. When conducted effectively, and when recommendations are applied properly, the management audit has proved its usefulness as a management technique.

[Boyd Childress]

FURTHER READING:

Craig-Cooper, Michael. *The Management Audit: How to Create an Effective Management Team.* Financial Times Pitman Publishing, 1993.

Leonard, William P. *The Management Audit: An Appraisal of Management Methods and Performance.* Englewood Cliffs, NJ: Prentice Hall, 1962.

McNair, Carol Jean. *Benchmarking: A Tool for Continuous Improvement.* New York: HarperBusiness, 1992.

Rose, Thomas G. *The Management Audit.* Gee and Co., 1944.

Sheldon, Debra R. *Achieving Accountability in Business and Government: Managing for Efficiency, Effectiveness, and Economy.* Westport, CT: Quorum Books, 1996.

Talley, Dorsey J. *Management Audits for Excellence: The Manager's Guide to Improving the Quality and Productivity of an Organization.* Milwaukee, WI: ASQC Quality Press, 1988.

Torok, Robert M. *Operational Profitability: Conducting Management Audits.* New York: Wiley, 1997.

MANAGEMENT BUYOUTS

A management buyout occurs when incumbent **management** takes ownership of a firm by purchasing a sufficient amount of the firm's **common stock**. These transactions vary due to the conditions under which the firm is offered for sale and the method of financing employed by the managers.

Consider the conditions that may encourage managers to purchase a controlling interest in the firm's stock. The owners of a corporation are its stockholders. These stockholders are concerned with increasing the value of their investment, not only in one specific firm, but for all investments. Therefore, if a majority of the firm's stockholders perceive that the value of their investment will be enhanced by agreeing to be acquired by another firm, they will elect to sell their stock to the acquiring firm at a price they consider fair. Managers of a firm may consider this transfer of ownership a benign event. They may also, however, be concerned that the new owners will not manage the firm most efficiently, that they will have less control over the management of the firm, or that their jobs will be less secure. In this situation, the current managers of the firm may consider purchasing the firm themselves.

Another situation that frequently leads to management buyouts is the case of financial distress. If the firm is having serious difficulties meeting its financial obligations, it may choose to reorganize itself. This can be done by closing failing operations to slow the drain on financial resources and by selling profitable operations to an outside party for the cash needed to restore financial viability to remaining operations. It is not uncommon for firms in this situation to give managers of the divisions being divested the opportunity to buy the assets. This makes sense for two reasons. First, management probably has the greatest expertise in managing the subset of assets offered for sale. Second, it saves the cost of searching for an external party with an interest in the division for sale.

Once incumbent management has decided it is interested in purchasing the firm or a particular portion of the firm, they must raise the capital needed to buy it. Managers in many corporations are encouraged to become stockholders in the firm by including stock and the option to buy more stock as part of their compensation package. The nonmanagement stockholders, however, will expect some compensation from this sale and the value of manager-owned stock is not likely to be sufficient to finance the purchase of the firm or one of its divisions. This means that managers must raise cash from other sources such as personal **wealth**. If managers have sufficient capital in other investments, these can be sold and used to finance the remainder of the purchase price.

While a management buyout is relatively straightforward when managers have sufficient personal capital to meet the purchase price, the more common scenario requires managers to borrow significant amounts. It is not uncommon for managers to **mortgage** homes and other personal assets to raise needed funds, but in many transactions these amounts are still not sufficient. In these cases, managers will borrow larger amounts using the assets of the firm they are acquiring as collateral. This type of transaction is called a **leveraged buyout**, or LBO. The LBO is a common form of financing for large transactions. It provides the management team with the financing needed to control the assets of the firm with only a small amount of equity. Nevertheless, the new firm that emerges from this transaction has very high financial risk. The large amounts of **debt** will require large periodic payments of interest. If the firm can't meet this obligation during any period, it can be forced into bankruptcy by the debtholders.

This description of a management buyout can be generalized to define an employee buyout. In some situations, it is feasible that all employees, not just a small group of managers, can collectively purchase a controlling interest in a firm's stock. This may be the long-term result of a carefully designed employee stock ownership plan (ESOP), that management has instituted. It may also result from the pressures of financial distress. In 1994 United Airlines was faced with declining profits and strained relations with labor. Management and labor eventually agreed on a swap of wage concessions for a 55 percent equity stake in the firm. In the five following years, the firm became more profitable, the stock price rose significantly, and employees retained a controlling interest in United's common stock.

It is important to note that managers (or employee owners) are no different than other investors. They will assess the **risk** and rewards associated with a buyout, leveraged or otherwise, and will act in their own best interests. As managers, they have specialized knowledge of the firm that may prove advantageous in charting a future course of action for the acquired firm. By assuming ownership of the acquired firm, they will also assume a riskier position personally. If the potential rewards associated with control are perceived as adequate compensation for this risk, then the management buyout will be consummated.

[Paul Bolster]

FURTHER READING:

Baker, George P., and George D. Smith. *The New Financial Capitalists.* Cambridge University Press, 1998.

Blair, Margaret M. *The Deal Decade.* Brookings Institute, 1993.

Schwarf, Charles A. *Acquisitions, Mergers, Sales, Buyouts, and Takeovers: A Handbook with Forms.* 4th ed. Upper Saddle River: Prentice Hall Trade, 1991.

Sirower, Mark L. *The Synergy Trap: How Companies Lose the Acquisition Game.* Free Press, 1997.

MANAGEMENT EDUCATION

SEE: Business Education; Continuing Education; Executive Development; Leadership

MANAGEMENT INFORMATION SYSTEMS

Although management information systems (MISs) vary considerably in scope and function, they are all **software** applications used to support basic business management activities, such as reporting, planning, and controlling. More broadly, the MIS label is also applied to the computer systems that run this software, but strictly speaking an MIS is considered software rather than hardware. In addition, some corporate **information technology** (IT) departments are named MIS, and the term may also be used to describe the overall management of IT resources. For purposes of this discussion, though, MIS will refer only to software systems.

HISTORICAL DEVELOPMENT

MISs have existed since the 1960s, when mainframe computers began making significant inroads in automating information-based activities at large corporations. Historically, they represent roughly the second generation of business software applications, an intermediate step between the very basic, large transaction-centered systems of the 1950s and early 1960s and the more specialized software tools that started taking root in the 1970s, such as **word processing** and **decision support systems**. The first MISs, however, often weren't particularly useful because of equipment shortcomings, a lack of computer literacy among the intended users, and poor planning for which functions the MIS would best serve. As computers continued to grow cheaper and the software more user friendly, MISs gained wider acceptance in the 1970s.

The diversity of software suites and applications that followed, particularly in the 1980s and 1990s, substantially blurred many of the distinctions between MISs and other types of management support applications, particularly as MISs began delivering data nearly in real time. Today, systems that serve in traditional MIS-like roles may or may not be known as MISs; indeed, very few new software packages are called MISs.

DEFINING FEATURES AND COMPONENTS

Nonetheless, MISs are still widely used and have a few distinguishing characteristics. First, they are generally used to generate routine reports for functional areas of a business, e.g., payroll statistics, financial reports, or sales reports. As such, they are mostly intended to be used by middle managers rather than entry-level staff or senior management. Finally, most MISs are linked with one or more additional business systems, such as transaction processing systems (TPSs) or executive information systems (EISs). Often this integration is achieved through networking, enabling the MIS to pull data from diverse systems such as the corporate accounting system, the human resources system, and so on.

MISs are no longer the exclusive domain of mainframes, although these powerful computers are still used effectively to house many corporate MISs. Often minicomputers, also known as midrange systems, run MISs instead, and even workstations and desktop PCs are capable of running small MISs.

The core of any MIS is a **database management system** (DBMS) and a series of data reporting, retrieval, and manipulation tools. Some of these tools are standardized for common or routine actions, such as generating monthly sales reports. Often these tools also allow output to be customized for special analyses. Examples of standard MIS output might include historical reports, short-term forecasts, and exception reports. Exception reports, related to the managerial philosophy of "management by exception," are triggered when some predefined unusual or problematic event occurs, such as an uncommonly large transaction, extremely high or low sales volume, or a statistical discrepancy that suggests a data error or an unexplained use of resources. Exception reports are intended to alert managers to circumstances that are either much better or much worse than normal. Custom reports may be completely user-defined, in which the user chooses which information to see and how it should be displayed, or they may be fairly standard reports executed in special ways, such as tallying weekly or daily sales rather than an end-of-the month summary.

RECENT TRENDS OVERSHADOW MIS

As information technology has grown more powerful and ubiquitous in business settings, the role of the traditional MIS has been obscured by newer software applications. For example, since the mid-1990s a suite of various applications known collectively as enterprise resource planning (ERP) software has taken a dominant position among large corporations' critical business applications. These packages, which typically come in functional modules such as an accounting module, a human resources module, and a manufacturing supply chain module, serve many of the functions that a traditional MIS would, and they tend to be more flexible, integrated, and user-friendly than legacy MISs. While early implementations of ERP suites were largely cross-functional databases with minimal high-level management tools, later upgrades have added decision support and data manipulation tools to facilitate a wide range of management-level—and even executive-level—analyses.

Another trend supplanting conventional MISs since the 1980s has been the adoption of executive information systems (EISs) and other high-level decision support systems. EISs are designed for top executives to glean important information from all major business systems (finance, inventory, payroll, and so on), process it in very sophisticated ways, and possibly even integrate it with outside data such as competitive intelligence or industry statistical norms. By providing such highly refined control over strategic information, EISs have diminished the importance of the more routine kinds of analyses available from an MIS.

FURTHER READING:

Laudon, Kenneth C., and Jane Price Laudon. *Management Information Systems: New Approaches to Organization and Technology.* 5th ed. Upper Saddle River, NJ: Prentice Hall, 1998.

Turban, Efraim, Ephraim McLean, and James Wetherbe. *Information Technology for Management: Making Connections for Strategic Advantage.* 2nd ed. New York: John Wiley & Sons, 1999.

MANAGEMENT SCIENCE

Management science is the application of the scientific method to address problems and decisions that arise in the business community and other organizations, such as government and military institutions. This field of study, which is also commonly known as operations research (OR), operates on the understanding that business managers can make informed decisions only when they have access to scientifically acquired knowledge. To gain such knowledge, practitioners of management science undertake the major steps of scientific inquiry: (1) identify the issue or problem, (2) formulate a hypothesis (theory) about possible solutions to the problem, (3) construct appropriate models to test the hypothesis, (4) collect and analyze the results of the tests, and (5) determine the best way to resolve the issue or address the problem based on the final results.

J. C. Hsiao and David S. Cleaver commented in *Management Science* that "mathematical models that show interrelationships among decision variables are indispensable to management science. In particular, mathematical models facilitate analysis of the overall structure of the problem and help the decision maker predict the relative effects of alternative courses of action." As **computers** have grown more sophisticated and powerful, they have been used with increasing frequency by those undertaking such complex analysis. By the 1990s, computers were well established as integral tools in the execution of management science methods.

Proponents of management science note that the practice and implementation of its information-gathering methods are not intended to replace the valuable insights that people can bring to business decisions based on their own personal experiences. As Shiv K. Gupta and John M. Cozzolino wrote in *Fundamentals of Operations Research for Management,* "the need for insight and intuition will always be present." They point out, however, that a full understanding of all aspects of a business is increasingly difficult to accomplish in a technologically advanced world of diverse industrial enterprises.

Some scholars admit that management science/operations research is often misunderstood. As R. Nichols Hazelwood observed in *International Science and Technology:* "OR defies easy definition because it is a way of using some of the tools of scientific research to study things that often are not conventionally the province of scientists. As its techniques become accepted they become part of everyone's way of research. Then there is a tendency to dismiss OR as simply plain 'horse sense.' True. But such fancy horses!" Indeed, efforts to use management science to find a quantitative basis for making optimal business decisions has become a fundamental cornerstone of corporate and industrial strategy over the past 50 years.

THE EMERGENCE OF MANAGEMENT SCIENCE

Modern management science, declared Hsiao and Cleaver, "was born during World War II when the British military management called a group of scientists together to study the strategies and tactics of various military operations. The goal was efficient allocation of scarce resources for the war effort. The name operations research came directly from the context in which it was used and developed: research on (military) operations."

Hsiao and Cleaver noted that the efforts of the British scientific community prompted the United States to initiate similar research activities. Use of the military technology required the knowledge of American scientists. "After many successes during that war," wrote Gupta and Cozzolino, "operations research began to be transplanted to the industrial environment." The post-World War II period was one wherein the private sector of the United States and other nations experienced explosive growth in technology and economic **wealth**. Armed with capital and scientific advances, corporations expanded the size of their operations. ''The new business opportunities set the stage for scientific methods to augment the personal experiences of the business managers,'' according to Gupta and Cozzolino.

Management science continued to grow during the 1950s and 1960s as business managers discovered that its use could help reduce problems of huge scale to manageable dimensions. Robert Hayes contended in 1969 in the *Harvard Business Review* that ''quantitative analysis is facilitating communication where it never existed before. When a problem has been stated quantitatively, one can often see that it is structurally similar to other problems . . . And once a common structure has been identified, insights and predictions can be transferred from one situation to another, and the quantitative approach can actually increase communication.''

By the 1990s, management science/operations research was well established as a useful tool in all areas of the business community. It was entrenched in government institutions as well, and continues to be used in attacking problems associated with municipal and regional planning, mass transit routes such as highways and airports, and crime prevention and investigation.

SEE ALSO: Decision Making; Operations Management

[Laurie Collier Hillstrom]

FURTHER READING:

Ahire, Sanjay L. ''Management Science-Total Quality Management Interfaces: An Integrative Framework.'' *Interfaces,* November/December 1997, 91.

Bell, P. C. ''Strategic Operational Research.'' *Journal of the Operational Research Society,* April 1998, 381.

Carney, D. Philip, and Russell Williams. ''No Such Thing as . . . Scientific Management.'' *Management Decision,* September/October 1997, 779.

Filippini, Roberto. ''Operations Management Research: Some Reflections on Evolution, Models, and Empirical Studies in OM.'' *International Journal of Operations and Production Management,* July/August 1997, 655.

Gupta, Shiv K., and John M. Cozzolino. *Fundamentals of Operations Research for Management.* San Francisco: Holden-Day, 1975.

Hayes, Robert H. ''Qualitative Insights from Quantitative Methods.'' *Harvard Business Review,* August 1969, 108.

Hazelwood, R. Nichols. ''Operations Research.'' *International Science and Technology,* January 1966, 36.

Hsiao, J. C., and David S. Cleaver. *Management Science.* Boston: Houghton Mifflin, 1982.

MANAGEMENT SUCCESSION PLANNING

Management succession planning is the process of preparing an organization for a transition in **leadership**. Succession planning is helpful when a **management** change occurs due to unforeseen circumstances, such as the sudden death of a corporation's **chief executive officer** (CEO). But it is also important in ensuring a smooth transfer of power under normal circumstances. ''Management succession planning will allow an institution to keep moving forward when the inevitable occurs,'' consultant Rhonda Cooke told *America's Community Banker.* ''Retirement, career mobility, ill health, termination, or death will require the appointment of a new chief executive officer at some point.''

One important aspect of management succession planning involves evaluating the skills of people in the organization and identifying those employees who have the potential to ascend to top management roles. In this way, succession planning encourages staff development and sends a message to employees that the organization is serious about developing people. It may also persuade talented employees to remain with the company rather than looking elsewhere for growth opportunities. Grooming a successor from within the company can save the time and expense of hiring a new leader from outside. It also aids in continuity, as an insider might be more likely to follow through with current plans and strategies.

The key to management succession planning is preparing a written succession plan. This document provides for the continued operation of a business in the event that the owner—or a key member of the management team—leaves the company, is terminated, retires, or dies. It details the changes that will take place as leadership is transferred from one generation to the next. In the case of **small businesses**, succession plans are often known as continuity plans, since without them the businesses may cease to exist. Succession plans can provide a number of important benefits for companies that develop them. For example, a succession plan may help a business retain key employees, reduce its tax burden, and maintain the value of its **stock** and assets during a management or ownership transition. Succession plans may also prove valuable in allowing a business owner to retire in comfort and continue to provide for family members who may be involved with the company.

Despite the many benefits of having a succession plan in place, many companies neglect to develop one. This oversight may occur because the CEO or business owner does not want to confront his or her own mortality, is reluctant to choose a successor, or does not have many interests beyond the business. Although fewer than one-third of family businesses survive the transition from the first generation to the second—and only 13 percent remain in the family for more than 60 years—just 45 to 50 percent of business owners establish a formal succession plan. ''Succession and the planning it entails is equivalent to planning one's own wake and funeral,'' as Ernesto J. Poza, president of an Ohio-based family business consulting firm, remarked in *Industrial Distribution.* ''But the fact is that the transfer of power from the first to the second generation seldom happens while the founder is alive and on the scene. The succession transition is the most agonizing change I have ever seen CEOs and top management teams confront.'' Up to 40 percent of American businesses may be facing the management succession issue at any given time.

PREPARING FOR SUCCESSION

Experts claim that management succession planning should ideally begin when the CEO or business owner is between the ages of 45 and 50 if he or she plans to retire at 65. Since succession can be an emotionally charged issue, sometimes the assistance of outsider advisers and mediators is required. Developing a succession plan can take more than two years, and implementing it can take up to ten years. The plan must be carefully structured to fit the company's specific situation and goals. When completed, the plan should be reviewed by the company's lawyer, accountant, and **bank**.

''One of the main reasons business owners should take the time to create a successful continuity plan is that they should want to get out of the business alive, with as much money as possible,'' Joanna R. Turpin noted in *Air Conditioning, Heating, and Refrigeration News.* To do this, the business owner has three basic options: sell the company to employees, family members, or an outsider; retain ownership of the company but hire new management; or liquidate the business. An employee stock ownership plan (ESOP) can be a useful tool for the owner of a corporation who is nearing retirement age. The owner can sell his or her stake in the company to the ESOP in order to gain tax advantages and provide for the continuation of the business. If, after the stock purchase, the ESOP holds over 30 percent of the company's shares, then the owner can defer capital-gains taxes by investing the proceeds in a qualified replacement property (QRP). QRPs can include stocks, **bonds**, and certain retirement accounts. The income stream generated by the QRP can help provide the business owner with **income** during retirement.

FOUR STAGES OF SUCCESSION

In the **Small Business Administration** publication *Transferring Management in the Family-Owned Business,* Nancy Bowman-Upton emphasizes that succession should be viewed as a process rather than as an event. She describes four main stages in the management succession planning process: initiation, selection, education, and transition. In the initiation phase, possible successors learn about the business. It is important for the CEO or business owner to speak openly about the business, in a positive but realistic manner, in order to transmit information about the company's values, culture, and future direction to the next generation.

The selection phase involves actually designating a successor among the candidates for the job. Because rivalry often develops between possible successors—who, in the case of a family business, are likely to be siblings—this can be the most difficult stage of the process. For this reason, many business owners either avoid the issue or make the selection on the basis of age, gender, or other factors besides merit. Instead, Bowman-Upton recommends that the business owners develop specific objectives and goals for the next generation of management, including a detailed job description for the successor. Then a candidate can be chosen who best meets the qualifications. This strategy helps remove the emotional aspect from the selection process and also may help the business owners feel more comfortable with their selection. The decision about when to announce the successor and the schedule for succession depends upon the business, but an early announcement can help reassure employees and customers and enable other key employees to make alternative career plans as needed.

Once a potential successor has been selected, the company then enters the **training** phase. Ideally, a program is developed through which the successor can meet goals and gradually increase his or her level of responsibility. The owner or CEO may want to take a number of planned absences so that the successor has a chance to actually run the business for limited periods. The training phase also provides the business owner or **board of directors** with an opportunity to evaluate the successor's **decision-making** processes, leadership abilities, interpersonal skills, and performance under pressure. It is also important for the successor to be introduced to the business owner or CEO's outside network during this time, including customers, bankers, and business associates.

The final stage in the process occurs when the business owner or CEO retires and the successor formally makes the transition to his or her new leadership role. Bowman-Upton stresses that the business owner can make the transition smoother for the company by publicly committing to the succession plan, leaving in a timely manner, and eliminating his or her involvement in the company's daily activities completely. In order to make the transition as painless as possible for himself or herself, the business owner should also be sure to have a sound financial plan for retirement and to engage in relationships and activities outside of the business.

ALTERNATIVE SUCCESSION MODELS

In their book *Family Business Succession: The Final Test of Greatness,* Craig E. Aronoff and John L. Ward outline a number of steps companies should follow in preparing for succession. These steps include:

- Establishing a formal policy regarding family participation in the business.
- Providing solid work experience for all employees, to ensure that succession is based on performance rather than heredity.
- Creating a family mission statement based on the members' beliefs and goals for the business.
- Designing a leadership development plan with specific job requirements for the successor.
- Developing a strategic plan for the business.
- Making plans for the preceding generation's financial security.
- Identifying a successor or determining the selection process.
- Setting up a succession transition team to keep decision makers informed about their role in the changes.
- Completing the transfer of ownership and control.

Throughout all these stages of preparation, Aronoff and Ward note, communication is key.

Turpin described several steps involved in developing a written succession document. These steps include:

- Gathering information, on both the personnel involved and the company itself.
- Choosing advisers, including continuity specialists and people who will be involved internally.
- Deciding upon the company's objectives, including financial and personal goals, as well as those related to ownership and control.
- Laying out the components of the plan.
- Preparing the formal documents and obtaining funding as needed.
- Reviewing the plan every one to three years or whenever the company's personnel or structure changes.

A final consideration in succession planning is for the owner or CEO to decide what he or she will do after concluding involvement in the business. This step, which is something like a personal succession plan, is important in helping the business leader make a successful transition. ''It's so much easier to let go of something when you have a new direction in which to move,'' psychiatrist Barrie Greiff explained in *Industrial Distribution.*

SUMMARY

Although management succession planning can be problematic and even painful, it is vital to ensuring the continuity—and perhaps even the continued existence—of businesses following the departure of the owner or CEO. Many business leaders are reluctant to plan for what will happen when they are no longer with the company, usually because they find it unpleasant to confront their retirement or mortality. It may be helpful to consider succession planning as an extension of employee development programs. ''Succession planning,'' William T. Marshall wrote in *America's Community Banker,* ''should reach deeply into an institution's management ranks to prepare managers at all levels for career advancement, perhaps to the very top.''

SEE ALSO: Employee Stock Options and Ownership; Family-Owned Businesses

[Laurie Collier Hillstrom]

FURTHER READING:

Aronoff, Craig E., and John L. Ward. *Family Business Succession: The Final Test of Greatness.* Business Owner Resources, 1992.

Bowman-Upton, Nancy. *Transferring Management in the Family Owned Business.* Washington: U.S. Small Business Administration, 1991.

Drury, James J. ''Looking beyond the CEO for Management Succession.'' *Corporate Board* 17, no. 101 (November/December 1996): 6+.

Dutton, Gail. ''Future Shock: Who Will Run the Company?'' *Management Review* 85, no. 8 (August 1996): 19+.

Frieswick, Kris. ''Successful Succession.'' *Industrial Distribution* 85, no. 4 (April 1996): 61+.

Lea, James W. ''Dad May Not Know Best When Planning Succession.'' *Washington Business Journal,* 27 March 1998, 53.

Leibman, Michael. ''Succession Management: The Next Generation of Succession Planning.'' *HR Planning* 19, no. 3 (September 1996): 16+.

Marshall, William T. ''How to Succeed with Management Succession Planning.'' *America's Community Banker* 6, no. 6 (June 1997): 20+.

Rothwell, William J. *Effective Succession Planning.* New York: AMACOM, 1995.

Shanney-Saborsky, Regina. ''Why It Pays to Use an ESOP in a Business Succession Plan.'' *Practical Accountant* 29, no. 9 (September 1996): 73+.

Turpin, Joanna R. "Succession Planning Requires Long-Term Strategy, Implementation." *Air Conditioning, Heating, and Refrigeration News,* 28 April 1997, 8+.

MANAGERIAL ACCOUNTING

Managerial accounting, or management accounting, is a set of practices and techniques aimed at providing managers with financial information to help them make decisions and maintain effective control over corporate resources. For example, managerial accounting answers such questions as:

- What is the company's average cost per unit of labor (enterprise wide or within specific departments)?
- How many dollars in sales does each marketing dollar bring in?
- What is the required rate of return to make a new investment worthwhile?
- Which activities require the greatest expenditures and which earn the greatest profits (and how can the organization maximize the former and minimize the latter)?

Managerial accounting procedures are intended primarily to supply knowledge to decision makers within an organization. Financial accounting, in contrast, is concerned with providing information to stockholders, government agencies, creditors, and others who are outside the organization. A corollary of that difference is that financial accounting procedures generally must conform to external standards, such as those developed by the **Financial Accounting Standards Board (FASB)**, while management accounting methods are left almost completely to the discretion of individual organizations.

Cost accounting, the third major sphere of accounting, is the process of determining the cost of a specific output or activity. Although it is sometimes confused with the managerial accounting function, cost accounting information is used by decision makers both inside and outside an organization. Cost and managerial accounting differ in that the latter goes beyond the role of cost accounting by combining multiple **management** disciplines with financial information to facilitate internal decision making. Thus, cost accounting may be seen as a necessary component of managerial accounting, but its focus is much narrower.

BACKGROUND

The earliest recorded accounting records date back to about 3500 B.C., when ancient Egyptian and Sumerian businessmen recorded agricultural production, tax collection, and storehouse inventories. The first evidence of more advanced accounting practices, such as property **depreciation**, has been traced to ancient Greek and Roman record keepers. The earliest accounting records that expressed accounts in terms of common monetary units (currency) date back to 1340 and come from Genoa. In fact, it was during the Middle Ages that an emphasis on arithmetic and writing in commercial trade allowed accounting practices to advance significantly.

The popularization of property ownership and money lending during the Renaissance in Europe necessitated the creation of performance measurement methods to help bankers and investors rate the success or failure of business ventures. Thus, the first advanced accounting procedures evolved that accounted for interest, depreciation, fixed assets, inventory turnover, and other factors that still represent the core of managerial accounting practices. Luca Pacioli, a Venetian, was the first to document accounting practices in his 1494 book, *Summa de Arithmetica, Geometria, Proportioni et Proportionalita.*

Modern accounting practices emerged during the Industrial Revolution, when the very nature of business activity began to change. Complicated financing techniques and huge capital investment expenditures resulted in the formalized distinction between such factors as income and capital, and fixed assets and inventory. It also prompted the creation of advanced means of allocating **overhead** and accurately determining **liabilities** and net worth within companies.

After the Great Depression, and particularly following World War II, the delineation between financial and managerial accounting became more defined, as government regulations and professional groups began to mandate accuracy and standardization in financial reporting and accounting. The dominant trend in managerial accounting during the latter half of the 20th century has been the use of increasingly detailed, internally generated accounting data to help steer management decisions and improve profitability. An important reason for the rapid growth in the use of detailed internal accounting information since the 1970s has been the proliferation of computerized information systems that have allowed managers to quickly access and process vast amounts of data.

MANAGERIAL ACCOUNTING THEORY

Professionals within an organization who perform the managerial accounting function generally support two primary purposes. First of all, they generate routine reports containing information regarding **cost control** and the planning and controlling of operations. Second, managerial accountants produce special reports for managers that are used for strategic and tactical decisions on matters such as pricing products or services, choosing which products to emphasize or de-emphasize, investing in equipment, and formulating overall policies and long-range planning.

Managerial accounting activities include some or all of the following: recognizing and evaluating transactions and economic events; quantifying and estimating the value of those events; recording and classifying appropriate transactions and events; and analyzing the reasons for, and relationships between, the transactions and events. Managerial accountants also assist decision makers who use the information they generate, and evaluate the implications of past and future events on proposed plans or decisions. They also work to ensure the integrity of the information that they produce and strive to implement a system of reporting that contributes to the effective measurement of management's performance.

MANAGERIAL ACCOUNTING APPLICATION

The practical role of managerial accounting is to increase knowledge within an organization and therefore reduce the risk associated with making decisions. Accountants prepare reports on the cost of producing goods, expenditures related to employee training programs, and the cost of marketing programs, among other activities. These reports are used by managers to measure the difference, or ''variance,'' between what they planned and what they actually accomplished, or to compare performance to other benchmarks.

For example, an assembly line supervisor might be interested in finding out how efficient his/her line is in comparison to those of fellow supervisors, or compared to productivity in a previous time period. An accounting report showing inventory waste, average hourly labor costs, and overall per-unit costs, among other statistics, might help the supervisor and superiors to identify and correct inefficiencies. A detailed report might evaluate the assembly line data and estimate trends and the long-term effects of those trends on the overall profitability of the organization.

As another example, a product manager for a line of hair care products at a corporation that manufactured beauty aids would probably want to know how much overhead each of the products is consuming. A report that breaks down the amount of overhead attributable to each product might help the manager better determine the profitability of each item in the line of goods and to find out if the sales and profit goals for each item are being met. For instance, a certain type of shampoo may be selling very well and generating large amounts of cash flow. However, a close accounting of that product's actual costs within the organization may reveal that its contribution to overall profits significantly lags that of other offerings in the hair care line. Armed with that information, the product manager might elect to adjust marketing expenditures to emphasize more profitable items, or to concentrate on reducing expenses related to the shampoo.

Because of the need for detailed information about specific operations within a company, management accounting reports are typically much more in-depth than traditional financial accounting reports, such as balance sheet ratios and net income calculations. Most managerial reports also differ from financial reports in their frequency. Many internal reports, in fact, are generated monthly, weekly, or even daily in the case of information such as cash receipts and disbursements. Despite their emphasis on detail, a critical characteristic of most managerial accounting reports is that they are presented in summary format. Managers can read the summaries, efficiently identify possible problem areas, and then examine the details within those areas to determine a course of action.

PLANNING AND CONTROLLING

In the examples described previously, just as in most managerial accounting applications, information produced for managers is used to make decisions about the future and to judge the effectiveness of past decisions and actions. In managerial accounting, the process of setting goals, determining resource requirements, and devising a means of achieving goals is referred to as ''planning.'' Monitoring financial results and measuring the outcome of planning processes within the enterprise is called ''controlling.'' The person in charge of an entity's accounting department is usually called the ''controller.'' The controller generally plays a key role in both planning and controlling endeavors throughout the organization.

The plans of management are formally communicated as budgets, and the term ''**budgeting**'' typically refers to management planning. The controller oversees the development of budgets by the accounting department, usually on annual basis. Budgets are commonly prepared not only for the overall organization, but also for divisions and departments within a company or institution. Budgets are important to the goal-setting function of an organization because they express the wishes and objectives of management in specific, tangible, quantitative terms.

Once a company's plans, or budgets, have been established, managerial accountants begin gathering information generated by the organization that indicates whether or not the company is achieving its goals. The accounting department presents its findings in the form of performance reports tailored for individual executives or departments. The detailed performance reports essentially compare budgets with actual results for a given time period, allowing managers to identify problem areas. For instance, a company's store managers may utilize data such as inventory levels and sales volumes to direct advertising and promotional programs.

Besides producing routine reports, management accountants also create special reports for other managers that help them to make decisions about proposed projects or problems that arise. Special reports are often created to analyze the relationship between costs and benefits related to different alternatives in the decision-making process. For instance, if a company's competitor drops its prices, management may ask the accounting department to produce a report comparing possible competitive responses, such as lowering prices, increasing advertising, or even changing its product or service. Such reports often involve forecasting as well as the collection of outside information.

COST INFORMATION

Information gathered by cost accounting methods within an organization make up most of the detailed data used to create managerial accounting reports (and financial accounting reports). Understanding the costs associated with producing goods and services is vital to the decision-making process because that comprehension can help place a measurable value on the results of a company's individual decisions.

Four basic cost accounting activities that support the managerial accounting function are

1. cost determination, which involves determining the actual cost of a product or an activity, such as marketing;
2. cost recording, whereby costs are recorded in journals and ledgers;
3. cost analyzing, which refers to accountants and managers analyzing the data to help solve problems and make plans; and
4. cost reporting, which entails showing the costs in detail, including showing how the costs were measured, what characteristics the costs have, and what the costs actually mean and how they should be interpreted.

NEW ROLES

Significant advances in automating routine transaction-related accounting tasks, combined with a strong corporate emphasis on value creation, have signaled new directions for managerial accounting. This trend had been building since the 1980s and accelerated in the mid-1990s. The thrust of the changes have been to make management accountants strategic partners and analysts in management decision making, rather than simply suppliers of data. Many companies now expect their managerial accounting staff to assist in developing strategies to enhance shareholder wealth and to participate on cross-functional teams with managers from operating departments throughout the organization, among other things. If the old analogy was supplying endless data for management to sift through, the new analogy has been providing value-added information that is directly to the point and suggests options that management might not otherwise have considered. Indeed, at some companies the work of management accountants has increasingly been labeled ''finance'' rather than ''accounting'' to suggest a broader set of skills and expectations.

To facilitate this increasingly interactive role, some observers of the profession believe that management accountants will need broader business underpinnings in their academic and professional background. This means studying a wider array of management topics in school, but also gaining hands-on knowledge of their companies' operating units and competitive climate in order to tailor accounting information to narrowly defined needs.

A related trend has been redesigning finance and accounting departments themselves to reduce costs and make all of their operations more efficient and timely. Accountants are expected to take the lead in demonstrating the practices of lean management and continuous improvement.

PROFESSIONAL GROUPS AND DESIGNATIONS

Numerous professional groups and designations exist for accountants. Chief among the professional designations for management accounts is the Certified Management Accountant designation, offered by the Institute of Management Accountants (formerly the National Association of Accountants). The CMA is the management accounting equivalent of the **Certified Public Accountant** (CPA) designation. Accountants earn the certificate after passing a two-and-one-half-day, five-part examination, and by meeting certain accounting experience requirements. CMAs early in their careers often hold staff and supervisory positions, while more experienced CMAs serve as **controllers**, **chief financial officers**, or in other executive financial positions.

One of former NAA's objectives in establishing the CMA designation was to increase the recognition of management accounting as a professional discipline with an identifiable, underlying body of knowledge, and to outline a course of study by which that knowledge could be attained. Among other goals, the designation helps employers, educators, and students by establishing objective measurements of an individual's knowledge and competence in the management accounting field. The NAA has also promulgated complementary ethical standards related to competence, confidentiality, integrity, and objectivity in the management accounting process.

COMPENSATION

Pay in management accounting and related fields varies considerably with education, experience, and even sex. For entry-level management candidates with a bachelor's degree and no professional certification, the average salary as of 1998 was around $39,850 for women and $45,550 for men, according to an annual survey by the Institute of Management Accountants. For middle managers holding the CMA credential and a master's degree, pay was significantly higher, averaging $72,640 for women and $78,140 for men. Top earners in senior/executive management, mostly men, took in $100,000 or more on average when they held a master's degree.

SEE ALSO: Accounting; Cost Accounting

[Dave Mote]

FURTHER READING:

Bisgay, Louis. ''Trends in Financial Management.'' *Management Accounting,* May 1997.

Bruns, William J. *Accounting for Managers: Text and Cases.* 2nd ed. Cincinnati: South-Western, 1999.

Garrison, Ray H. *Managerial Accounting.* 8th ed. Boston: Richard D. Irwin, Inc., 1996.

''IMA '98 Salary Guide.'' *Strategic Finance,* June 1999.

Raiborn, Cecily, Jesse T. Barfield, and Michael R. Kinney. *Managerial Accounting.* 3rd ed. Cincinnati: South-Western, 1998.

Randall, Robert F. ''New Challenges in Finance.'' *Strategic Finance,* March 1999.

MANAGERIAL ECONOMICS

Decisions made by managers are crucial to the success or failure of a business. Roles played by business managers are becoming increasingly more challenging as complexity in the business world grows. Business decisions are increasingly dependent on constraints imposed from outside the economy in which a particular business is based—both in terms of production of goods as well as the markets for the goods produced. The impact of rapid technological change on **innovation** in products and processes, as well as in **marketing** and sales techniques, figures prominently among the factors contributing to the increasing complexity of the business environment. Moreover, because of increased **globalization** of the marketplace, there is more volatility in both input and product prices. The continuous changes in the economic and business environment make it ever more difficult to accurately evaluate the outcome of a business decision. In such a changing environment, sound economic analysis becomes all the more important as a basis of decision making. Managerial economics is a discipline that is designed to provide a solid foundation of economic understanding in order for business managers to make well-informed and well-analyzed managerial decisions.

THE NATURE OF MANAGERIAL ECONOMICS

There are a number of issues relevant to businesses that are based on economic thinking or analysis. Examples of questions that managerial economics attempts to answer are: What determines whether an aspiring business firm should enter a particular industry or simply start producing a new product or service? Should a firm continue to be in business in an industry in which it is currently engaged or cut its losses and exit the industry? Why do some professions pay handsome salaries, whereas some others pay barely enough to survive? How can the business best motivate the employees of a firm? The issues relevant to managerial economics can be further focused by expanding on the first two of the preceding questions. Let us consider the first question in which a firm (or a would-be firm) is considering entering an industry. For example, what led Frederick W. Smith the founder of Federal Express, to start his overnight mail service? A service of this nature did not exist in any significant form in the United States, and people seemed to be doing just fine without overnight mail service provided by a private corporation. One can also consider why there are now so many overnight mail carriers such as United Parcel Service and Airborne Express. The second example pertains to the exit from an industry, specifically, the airline industry in the United States. Pan Am, a pioneer in public air transportation, is no longer in operation, while some airlines such as TWA (Trans World Airlines) are on the verge of exiting the airlines industry. Why, then, have many airlines that operate on international routes fallen on hard times, while small regional airlines seem to be doing just fine? Managerial economics provides answers to these questions.

In order to answer pertinent questions, managerial economics applies economic theories, tools, and techniques to administrative and business **decision-making**. The first step in the decision-making process is to collect relevant economic data carefully and to organize the economic information contained in data collected in such a way as to establish a clear basis for managerial decisions. The goals of the particular business organization must then be clearly spelled out. Based on these stated goals, suitable managerial objectives are formulated. The issue of central concern in the decision-making process is that the desired objectives be reached in the best possible manner. The term "best" in the decision-making context primarily refers to achieving the goals in the most efficient manner, with the minimum use of available resources—implying there be no waste of resources. Managerial economics helps the manager to make good decisions by providing information on waste associated with a proposed decision.

APPLICATIONS OF MANAGERIAL ECONOMICS

Some examples of managerial decisions have been provided above. The application of managerial economics is, by no means, limited to these examples. Tools of managerial economics can be used to achieve virtually all the goals of a business organization in an efficient manner. Typical managerial decision making may involve one of the following issues:

- Deciding the price of a product and the quantity of the commodity to be produced
- Deciding whether to manufacture a product or to buy from another manufacturer
- Choosing the production technique to be employed in the production of a given product
- Deciding on the level of inventory a firm will maintain of a product or raw material
- Deciding on the advertising media and the intensity of the advertising campaign
- Making employment and training decisions
- Making decisions regarding further business investment and the mode of financing the investment

It should be noted that the application of managerial economics is not limited to profit-seeking business organizations. Tools of managerial economics can be applied equally well to decision problems of nonprofit organizations. Mark Hirschey and James L. Pappas cite the example of a nonprofit hospital. While a nonprofit hospital is not like a typical firm seeking to maximize its profits, a hospital does strive to provide its patients the best medical care possible given its limited staff (doctors, nurses, and support staff), equipment, space, and other resources. The hospital administrator can use the concepts and tools of managerial economics to determine the optimal allocation of the limited resources available to the hospital. In addition to nonprofit business organizations, government agencies and other nonprofit organizations (such as cooperatives, schools, and museums) can use the techniques of managerial decision making to achieve goals in the most efficient manner.

While managerial economics is helpful in making optimal decisions, one should be aware that it only describes the predictable economic consequences of a managerial decision. For example, tools of managerial economics can explain the effects of imposing automobile import quotas on the availability of domestic cars, prices charged for automobiles, and the extent of competition in the auto industry. Analysis of managerial economics will reveal that fewer cars will be available, prices of automobiles will increase, and the extent of competition will be reduced. Managerial economics does not address, however, whether imposing automobile import quotas is good government policy. This latter question encompasses broader political considerations involving what economists call value judgments.

ECONOMIC CONCEPTS USED IN MANAGERIAL ECONOMICS

Managerial economics uses a wide variety of economic concepts, tools, and techniques in the decision-making process. These concepts can be placed in three broad categories: (1) the theory of the firm, which describes how businesses make a variety of decisions; (2) the theory of consumer behavior, which describes decision making by consumers; and (3) the theory of market structure and pricing, which describes the structure and characteristics of different market forms under which business firms operate.

THE THEORY OF THE FIRM

Discussing the theory of the firm is an useful way to begin the study of managerial economics, since the theory provides a broad framework within which issues relevant to managerial decisions are analyzed. A firm can be considered a combination of people, physical and financial resources, and a variety of information. Firms exist because they perform useful functions in society by producing and distributing goods and services. In the process of accomplishing this, they use society's scarce resources, provide employment, and pay taxes. If economic activities of society can be simply put into two categories—production and consumption—firms are considered the most basic economic entities on the production side, while consumers form the basic economic entities on the consumption side.

The behavior of firms is usually analyzed in the context of an economic model, an idealized version of a real-world firm. The basic economic model of a business enterprise is called the theory of the firm.

PROFIT MAXIMIZATION AND THE FIRM. Under the simplest version of the theory of the firm it is assumed that profit maximization is its primary goal. In this version of the theory, the firm's owner is the manager of the firm, and thus, the firm's owner-manager is assumed to maximize the firm's short-term profits (current profits and profits in the near future). Today, even when the profit maximizing assumption is maintained, the notion of profits has been broadened to take into account uncertainty faced by the firm (in realizing profits) and the time value of money (where the value of a dollar further and further in the future is increasingly smaller than a dollar today). In this more complete model, the goal of maximizing short-term profits is replaced by goal of maximizing long-term profits, the present value of expected profits, of the business firm.

Defining present value of expected profits is based on first defining "value" and then defining "present value." Many concepts of value, such as book value, **market value**, **going-concern** value, break-up value, and liquidating value, are encountered in business and economics. The value of the firm is defined as the **present value** of expected future profits (net cash flows) of the firm. Thus, to obtain an estimate of the present value of expected profits, one must identify the stream of net cash flow in future years. Once this is accomplished, these expected future profit values are converted into present value by discounting these values by an appropriate interest rate. For illustration, assume that a firm expects a profit of $10,000 in one year and $20,000 in the second year—it is assumed that the firm earns no profits after two years. Let us assume that the prevailing interest rate is 10 percent per annum. Thus, $10,000 in a year from now is only equal to about $9,091 at the present ([$10,000/(1 +0.1)] = $9,091)—that is, the present value of a $10,000 profit expected in a year from now is about $9,091. Similarly, the present value of an expected profit of $20,000 in two years from now is equal to about $16,529 (since [$20,000/(1 + 0.1)^2] = $16,529). Therefore, the present value of future expected profits is $25,620 (equal to the sum of $9,091 and $16,529). The present value of expected profits is a key concept in understanding the theory of the firm, and maximizing this profit is considered the primary goal of a firm in most models.

It should be noted that expected profit in any one period can itself be considered as the difference between the total revenue and the total cost in that period. Thus, one can, alternatively, find the present value of expected future profits by subtracting the present value of expected future costs from the present value of expected future revenues.

THE CONSTRAINED PROFIT MAXIMIZATION. Profit maximization is subject to various constraints faced by the firm. These constraints relate to resource scarcity, technology, contractual obligations, and laws and government regulations. In their attempt to maximize the present value of profits, business managers must consider not only the short-term and long-term implications of decisions made within the firm, but also various external constraints that may limit the firm's ability to achieve its organizational goals.

The first external constraint of resource scarcity refers to the limited availability of essential inputs (including skilled labor), key raw materials, energy, specialized machinery and equipment, warehouse space, and other resources. Moreover, managers often face constraints on plant capacity that are exacerbated by limited investment funds available for expansion or modernization. Contractual obligations also constrain managerial decisions. Labor contracts, for example, may constrain managers' flexibility in worker scheduling and work assignment. Labor contracts may also determine the number of workers employed at any time, thereby establishing a floor for minimum labor costs. Finally, laws and regulations have to be observed. The legal restrictions can constrain decisions regarding both production and marketing activities. Examples of laws and regulations that limit managerial flexibility are: the minimum wage, health and safety standards, fuel efficiency requirements, antipollution regulations, and fair pricing and marketing practices.

PROFIT MAXIMIZATION VERSUS OTHER MOTIVATIONS BEHIND MANAGERIAL DECISIONS. The present value maximization criterion as a basis for the study of the firm's behavior has come under severe criticism from some economists. The critics argue that business managers are interested, at least partly, in factors other than the firm's profits. In particular, they may be interested in power, prestige, leisure, employee welfare, community well-being, and the welfare of the larger society. The act of maximization itself has been criticized; there is a feeling that managers often aim merely to "satisfice" (seek solutions that are considered satisfactory), rather than really try to optimize or maximize (seek to find the best possible solution, given the constraints). This question is often rhetorically posed as: does a manager really try to find the sharpest needle in a haystack or does he or she merely stop upon finding a needle sharp enough for sewing needs?

Under the structure of a modern firm, it is hard to determine the true motives of managers. A modern firm is frequently organized as a corporation in which shareholders are the legal owners of the firm, and the manager acts on their behalf. Under such a structure, it is difficult to determine whether a manager merely tries to satisfy the stockholders of the firm while pursuing other goals, rather than truly attempting to maximize the value (the discounted present value) of the firm. It is, for example, difficult to interpret company support for a charitable organization as an integral part of the firm's long-term value maximization. Similarly, if the firm's size is increasing, but profits are not, can one attribute the manager's decision to expand as being motivated by the increased prestige associated with larger firms, or as an attempt to make the firm more noticeable in the marketplace? As it is virtually impossible to provide definitive answers to these and similar questions, the attempt to analyze these issues has led to the development of alternative theories of firm behavior. Some of the preeminent alternate models assume one of the following: (1) a firm attempts primarily to maximize its size or growth, rather than its present value; (2) the managers of firms aim at maximizing their own personal utility or welfare; and (3) the firm is a collection of individuals with widely divergent goals, rather than a single common, identifiable goal.

While each of the alternative theories of the firm has increased our understanding of how a modern firm behaves, none has been able to completely take the place of the basic profit maximization assumption for several reasons. Numerous academic studies have shown that intense competition in the markets for goods and services of the firm usually forces the manager to make value maximization decisions; if a firm does not decide on the most efficient alternative (implying the need to seek the minimum costs for each output level, given the market price of the commodity the firm is producing), others can outcompete the firm and drive it out of existence. Competition also has its effects through the **capital markets**. As one would expect, stockholders are primarily interested in their returns on **stocks** and stock prices, which in turn, are determined by the firm's value (the discounted present value of expected profits). Thus, managers are forced to maximize profits in order to maximize firm value, an important basis for returns on **common stocks** in the long run. Managers who insist on goals other than maximizing shareholder wealth risk being replaced. An inefficiently managed firm may also be bought out; in almost all such hostile **takeovers**, managers pursuing their own interests will most likely be replaced. Moreover, a number of academic studies indicate that managerial compensation is closely correlated to the profits generated for the firm. Thus, managers themselves have strong financial incentives to seek profit maximization for their firms.

Before arriving at the decision whether to maximize profits or to *satisfice,* managers (like other economic entities) have to analyze the costs and benefits of their decisions. Sometimes, when all costs are taken into account, decisions that appear merely aimed at a satisfactory level of performance turn out to be consistent with value-maximizing behavior. Similarly, short-term firm-growth maximization strategies have often been found to be consistent with long-term value maximization behavior, since large firms have advantages in production, distribution, and sales promotion. Thus, many other goals that do not seem to be oriented to maximizing profits may be intimately linked to value or profit maximization—so much so that the value maximization model even provides an insight into a firm's voluntary participation in charity or other socially responsible behavior.

BUSINESS VERSUS ECONOMIC PROFITS. As discussed above, profits are central to the goals of a firm and managerial decision making. Thus, to understand the theory of firm behavior properly, one must have a clear understanding of profits. While the term profit is very widely used, an economist's definition of profit differs from the one used by accountants (which is also usually used by the general public and the business community). Profit in accounting is defined as the excess of sales revenue over the explicit **accounting** costs of doing business. This surplus is available to the firm for various purposes.

An economist also defines profit as the difference between sales revenue and costs of doing business, but includes more items in figuring costs, rather than considering only explicit accounting costs. For example, inputs supplied by owners (including labor, **capital**, and space) are accounted for in determining costs in the definition used by an economist. These costs are sometimes referred to as implicit costs—their value is imputed based on a notion of **opportunity costs** widely used by economists. In other words, costs of inputs supplied by an owner are based on the values these inputs would have received in the next best alternative activity. For illustration, assume that the owner of the firm works for ten hours a day at his business. If the owner does not receive any salary, an accountant would not consider the owner's effort as a cost item. An economist would, however, value the owner's service to his firm at what his labor would have earned had he worked elsewhere. Thus, to compute the true profit, an economist will subtract the implicit costs from business profit; the resulting profit is often referred to as economic profit. It is this concept of profit that is used by economists to explain the behavior of a firm. The concept of economic profit essentially recognizes that owner-supplied inputs must also be paid for. Thus, the owner of a firm will not be in business in the long run until he recovers the implicit costs (also known as normal profit), in addition to recovering the explicit costs, of doing business.

As pointed out earlier, a given firm attempts to maximize profits. Other firms do the same. Ultimately, profits decline for all firms. If all firms are operating under a competitive market structure, in equilibrium, economic profits (the excess of accounting profits over implicit costs) would be equal to zero; accounting profits (equal to explicit costs), however would be positive. When a firm makes profits above the normal profits level, it is said to be reaping above-normal profits.

HOW A FIRM ARRIVES AT A PROFIT-MAXIMIZING POINT. Let us assume throughout the discussion that a firm uses an economist's definition of profits. Assume that profit is the excess of sales revenue over cost (now assumed to be composed of both explicit and implicit costs). It can also be assumed, as discussed above, that the profit maximization is the firm's primary goal. Given this objective, important questions remain: How does the firm decide on the output level that maximizes its profits? Should the firm continue to produce at all if it is not profitable?

A manufacturing firm, motivated by profit maximization, calculates the total cost of producing any given output level. The total cost is made up of total fixed cost (due to the expenditure on fixed inputs) and total variable cost (due to the expenditure on variable inputs). Of course, the total fixed cost does not vary over the short run—only the total variable cost does. It is important for the firm to also calculate the cost per unit of output, called the average cost. In addition to the average cost, the firm calculates the marginal cost. The marginal cost at any level of output is the increase in the total cost due to an increase in production by one unit—essentially, the marginal cost is the additional cost of producing the last unit of output.

The average cost is made up of two components: the average fixed cost (the total fixed cost divided by the number of units of the output produced) and the average variable cost (the total variable cost divided by the number of units of the output produced). As the fixed costs remain fixed over the short run, the average fixed cost declines as the level of production increases. The average variable cost, on the other hand, first decreases and then increases; economists refer to this as the U-shaped nature of the average variable cost. The U-shape of the average variable cost curve is explained as follows. Given the fixed inputs, output of the relevant product increases more than proportionately as the levels of variable inputs used increase. This is caused by increased efficiency due to specialization and other reasons. As more and more variable inputs are used in conjunction with the given fixed inputs, however, efficiency gains reach a maximum—the decline in the average variable cost eventually comes to a halt. After this point, the average variable cost starts increasing as the level of production continues to increase, given the fixed inputs. First decreasing and then increasing average variable cost lead to the U-shape for the average variable cost. The combination of the declining average fixed cost (true for the entire range of production) and the U-shaped average variable cost results into an U-shaped behavior of the average total cost, often simply called the average cost.

The marginal cost also displays a U-shaped pattern—it first decreases and then increases. The logic for the shape of the marginal cost curve is similar to that for the average variable cost—both relate to variable costs. But while the marginal cost refers to the increase in total variable cost due to an increase in the production by one unit, the average variable cost refers to the average variable cost per unit of output produced. It is important to notice, without going into finer details, that the marginal cost curve intersects the average and the average variable cost curves at their minimum cost points.

In a graphic rendering of this concept there would be a horizontal line, in addition to the three cost curves. It is assumed that the firm can sell as many units as it wants at the given market price indicated by this horizontal line. Essentially, the horizontal line is the demand curve a perfectly competitive firm faces in the market—it can sell as many units of output as it deems profitable at price ''p'' per unit (p, for example, can be $10 per unit of the product under consideration). In other words, p is the firm's average revenue per unit of output. Since the firm receives p dollars for every successive unit it sells, p is also the marginal revenue for the firm.

A firm maximizes profits, in general, when its marginal revenue equals marginal cost. If the firm produces beyond this point of equality between the marginal revenue and marginal cost, the marginal cost will be higher than the marginal revenue. In other words, the addition to total production beyond the point where marginal revenue equals marginal cost, leads to lower, not higher, profits. While every firm's primary motive is to maximize profits, its output decision (consistent with the profit maximizing objective), depends on the structure of the market it is operating under. Before we discuss important market structures, we briefly examine another key economic concept, the theory of consumer behavior.

THE THEORY OF CONSUMER BEHAVIOR

Consumers play an important role in the economy since they spend most of their incomes on goods and services produced by firms. In other words, they consume what firms produce. Thus, studying the theory of consumer behavior is quite important. What is the ultimate objective of a consumer? Economists have an optimization model for consumers, similar to that applied to firms or producers. While firms are assumed to be maximizing profits, consumers are assumed to be maximizing their utility or satisfaction. Of course, more goods and services will, in general, provide greater utility to a consumer. Nevertheless, consumers, like firms, are subject to constraints—their consumption and choices are limited by a number of factors, including the amount of disposable income (the residual income after income taxes are paid for). The decision to consume by consumers is described by economists within a theoretical framework usually termed the theory of demand.

The demand for a particular product by an individual consumer is based on four important factors. First, the price of the product determines how much of the product the consumer buys, given that all other factors remain unchanged. In general, the lower the product's price the more a consumer buys. Second, the consumer's income also determines how much of the product the consumer is able to buy, given that all other factors remain constant. In general, a consumer buys more of a commodity the greater is his or her income. Third, prices of related products are also important in determining the consumer's demand for the product. Finally, consumer tastes and preferences also affect consumer demand. The total of all consumer demands yields the market demand for a particular commodity; the market demand curve shows quantities of the commodity demanded at different prices, given all other factors. As price increases, quantity demanded falls.

Individual consumer demands thus provide the basis for the market demand for a product. The market demand plays a crucial role in shaping decisions made by firms. Most important of all, it helps in determining the market price of the product under consideration which, in turn, forms the basis for profits for the firm producing that product.

The amount supplied by an individual firm depends on profit and cost considerations. As mentioned earlier, in general, a producer produces the profit maximizing output. Again, the total of individual supplies yields the market supply for a particular commodity; the market supply curve shows quantities of the commodity supplied at different prices, given all other factors. As price increases, the quantity supplied increases.

The interaction between market demand and supply determines the equilibrium or market price (where demand equals supply). Shifts in demand curve and/or supply curve lead to changes in the equilibrium price. The market price and the price mechanism play a crucial role in the capitalist system—they send signals both to producers and consumers.

THEORIES ASSOCIATED WITH DIFFERENT MARKET STRUCTURES

As mentioned earlier, firms' profit maximizing output decisions take into account the market structure under which they are operating. There are four kinds of market organizations: perfect competition, monopolistic competition, **oligopoly**, and **monopoly**.

PERFECT COMPETITION. Perfect **competition** is the idealized version of the market structure that provides a foundation for understanding how markets work in a capitalist economy. Three conditions need to be satisfied before a market structure is considered perfectly competitive: homogeneity of the product sold in the industry, existence of many buyers and sellers, and perfect mobility of resources or factors of production. The first condition, the homogeneity of product, requires that the product sold by any one seller is identical with the product sold by any other supplier—if products of different sellers are identical, buyers do not care from whom they buy so long as the price charged is also the same. The second condition, existence of many buyers and sellers, also leads to an important outcome: each individual buyer or seller is so small relative to the entire market that he or she does not have any power to influence the price of the product under consideration. Each individual simply decides how much to buy or sell at the given market price. The implication of the third condition is that resources move to the most profitable industry.

There is no industry in the world that can be considered perfectly competitive in the strictest sense of the term. However, there are token examples of industries that come quite close to having perfectly competitive markets. Some markets for agricultural **commodities**, while not meeting all three conditions, come reasonably close to being characterized as perfectly competitive markets. The market for wheat, for example, can be considered a reasonable approximation.

As pointed out earlier, in order to maximize profits, a supplier has to look at the cost and revenue sides; a perfectly competitive firm will stop production where marginal revenue equals marginal cost. In the case of a perfectly competitive firm, the market price for the product is also the marginal revenue, as the firm can sell additional units at the going market price. This is not so for a monopolist. A monopolist must reduce price to increase sales. As a result, a monopolist's price is always above the marginal revenue. Thus, even though a monopolist firm also produces the profit maximizing output, where marginal revenue equals marginal cost, it does not produce to the point where price equals marginal cost (as does a perfectly competitive firm).

Regarding entry and exit decisions; one can now state that additional firms would enter an industry—whenever existing firms are making above normal profits (that is, when the horizontal line is above the average cost at the profit maximizing output). A firm would exit the market if at the profit maximizing point the horizontal line is below the average cost curve; it will actually shut down the production right away if the price is less than the average variable cost.

MONOPOLISTIC COMPETITION. Many industries that we often deal with have market structures that are characterized by monopolistic competition or oligopoly. Apparel retail stores (with many stores and differentiated products) provide an example of monopolistic competition. As in the case of perfect competition, monopolistic competition is characterized by the existence of many sellers. Usually if an industry has 50 or more firms (producing products that are close substitutes of each other), it is said to have a large number of firms. The sellers under monopolistic competition differentiate their product; unlike under perfect competition, the products are not considered identical. This characteristic is often called product differentiation. In addition, relative ease of entry into the industry is considered another important requirement of a monopolistically competitive market organization.

As in the case of perfect competition, a firm under monopolistic competition determines the quantity of the product to produce based on the profit maximization principle—it stops production where marginal revenue equals marginal cost of production. There is, however, one very important difference between perfect competition and monopolistic competition. A firm under monopolistic competition has a bit of control over the price it charges, since the firm differentiates its products from those of others. The price associated with the product (at the equilibrium or profit maximizing output) is higher than marginal cost (which equals marginal revenue). Thus, production under monopolistic competition does not take place to the point where price equals marginal cost of production. The net result of the profit maximizing decisions of monopolistically competitive firms is that price charged under monopolistic competition is higher than under perfect competition, and the quantity produced is simultaneously lower.

OLIGOPOLY. Oligopoly is a fairly common market organization. In the United States, both the steel and automobile industries (with three or so large firms) provide good examples of oligopolistic market structures. Probably the most important characteristic of an oligopolistic market structure is the interdependence of firms in the industry. The interdependence, actual or perceived, arises from the small number of firms in the industry. Unlike under monopolistic competition, however, if an oligopolistic firm changes its price or output, it has perceptible effects on the sales and profits of its competitors in the industry. Thus, an oligopolist always considers the reactions of its rivals in formulating its pricing or output decisions.

There are huge, though not insurmountable, barriers to entry to an oligopolistic market. These barriers can exist because of large financial requirements, availability of raw materials, access to the relevant technology, or simply existence of patent rights with the firms currently in the industry. Several industries in the United States provide good examples of oligopolistic market structures with obvious barriers to entry, such as the automobile industry, where significant financial barriers to entry exist.

An oligopolistic industry is also typically characterized by **economies of scale**. Economies of scale in production implies that as the level of production rises, the cost per unit of product falls from the use of any plant (generally, up to a point). Thus, economies of scale lead to an obvious advantage for a large producer.

There is no single theoretical framework that provides answers to output and pricing decisions under an oligopolistic market structure. Analyses exist only for special sets of circumstances. One of these circumstances refers to an oligopoly in which there are asymmetric reactions of its rivals when a particular oligopolist formulates policies. If an oligopolistic firm cuts its price, it is met with price reductions by competing firms; if it raises the price of its product, however, rivals do not match the price increase. For this reason, prices may remain stable in an oligopolistic industry for a prolonged period.

MONOPOLY. Monopoly can be considered as the polar opposite of perfect competition. It is a market form in which there is only one seller. While, at first glance, a monopolistic form may appear to be rarely found market structure, several industries in the United States have monopolies. Local electricity companies provide an example of a monopolist.

There are many factors that give rise to a monopoly. Patents can give rise to a monopoly situation, as can ownership of critical raw materials (to produce a good) by a single firm. A monopoly, however, can also be legally created by a government agency when it sells a market franchise to sell a particular product or to provide a particular service. Often a monopoly so established is also regulated by the appropriate government agency. Provision of local telephone services in the United States provides an example of such a monopoly. Finally, a monopoly may arise due to declining cost of production for a particular product. In such a case the average cost of production keeps falling and reaches a minimum at an output level that is sufficient to satisfy the entire market. In such an industry, rival firms will be eliminated until only the strongest firm (now the monopolist) is left in the market. Such an industry is popularly dubbed as the case of a natural monopoly. A good example of a natural monopoly is the electricity industry, which reaps the benefits of economies of scale and yields decreasing average cost. Natural monopolies are usually regulated by the government.

Generally speaking, price and output decisions of a monopolist are similar to a monopolistically competitive firm, with the major distinction that there are a large number of firms under monopolistic competition and only one firm under monopoly. Nevertheless, at any output level, the price charged by a monopolist is higher than the marginal revenue. As a result, a monopolist also does not produce to the point where price equals marginal cost (a condition met under a perfectly competitive market structure).

MARKET STRUCTURES AND MANAGERIAL DECISIONS. Managerial decisions both in the short run and in the long run are partly shaped by the market structure relevant to the firm. While the preceding discussion of market structures does not cover the full range of managerial decisions, it nevertheless suggests that managerial decisions are necessarily constrained by the market structure under which a firm operates.

TOOLS OF DECISION SCIENCES AND MANAGERIAL ECONOMICS

Managerial decision making uses both economic concepts and tools, and techniques of analysis provided by decision sciences. The major categories of these tools and techniques are: optimization, statistical estimation, **forecasting**, numerical analysis, and **game theory**. While most of these methodologies are fairly technical, the first three are briefly explained below to illustrate how tools of decision sciences are used in managerial decision making.

OPTIMIZATION. Optimization techniques are probably the most crucial to managerial decision making. Given that alternative courses of action are available, the manager attempts to produce the most optimal decision, consistent with stated managerial objectives. Thus, an optimization problem can be stated as maximizing an objective (called the objective function by mathematicians) subject to specified constraints. In determining the output level consistent with the maximum profit, the firm maximizes profits, constrained by cost and capacity considerations. While a manager does not solve the optimization problem, he or she may use the results of mathematical analysis. In the profit maximization example, the profit maximizing condition requires that the firm choose the production level at which marginal revenue equals marginal cost. This condition is obtained from an optimization exercise. Depending on the problem a manager is trying to solve, the conditions for the optimal decision may be different.

STATISTICAL ESTIMATION. A number of statistical techniques are used to estimate economic variables of interest to a manager. In some cases, statistical estimation techniques employed are simple. In other cases, they are much more advanced. Thus, a manager may want to know the average price received by his competitors in the industry, as well as the standard deviation (a measure of variation across units) of the product price under consideration. In this case, the simple statistical concepts of mean (average) and standard deviation are used.

Estimating a relationship among variables requires a more advanced statistical technique. For example, a firm may want to estimate its cost function, the relationship between a cost concept and the level of output. A firm may also want to know the demand function of its product, that is, the relationship between the demand for its product and different factors that influence it. The estimates of costs and demand are usually based on data supplied by the firm. The statistical estimation technique employed is called **regression analysis**, and is used to develop a mathematical model showing how a set of variables are related. This mathematical relationship can also be used to generate forecasts.

An automobile industry example can be used for the purpose of illustrating the forecasting method that employs simple regression analysis. Suppose a statistician has data on sales of American-made automobiles in the United States for the last 25 years. He or she has also determined that the sale of automobiles is related to the real disposable income of individuals. The statistician also has available the time series (for the last 25 years) on real disposable income. Assume that the relationship between the time series on sales of American-made automobiles and the real disposable income of consumers is actually linear and it can thus be represented by a straight line. A fairly rigorous mathematical technique is used to find the straight line that most accurately represents the relationship between the time series on auto sales and disposable income.

FORECASTING. Forecasting is a method or a technique used to predict many future aspects of a business or any other operation. For example, a retailing firm that has been in business for the last 25 years may be interested in forecasting the likely sales volume for the coming year. There are numerous forecasting techniques that can be used to accomplish this goal. A forecasting technique, for example, can provide such a projection based on the experience of the firm during the last 25 years; that is, this forecasting technique bases the future forecast on the past data.

While the term ''forecasting'' may appear to be rather technical, planning for the future is a critical aspect of managing any organization—business, nonprofit, or otherwise. In fact, the long-term success of any organization is closely tied to how well the **management** of the organization is able to foresee its future and develop appropriate strategies to deal with the likely future scenarios. Intuition, good judgment, and an awareness of how well the economy is doing may give the manager of a business firm a rough idea (or ''feeling'') of what is likely to happen in the future. It is not easy, however, to convert a feeling about the future outcome into a precise number that can be used, for instance, as a projection for next year's sales volume. Forecasting methods can help predict many future aspects of a business operation, such as forthcoming years' sales volume projections.

Suppose that a forecast expert has been asked to provide quarterly estimates of the sales volume for a particular product for the next four quarters. How should one go about preparing the quarterly sales volume forecasts? One will certainly want to review the actual sales data for the product in question for past periods. Suppose that the forecaster has access to actual sales data for each quarter during the 25-year period the firm has been in business. Using these historical data, the forecaster can identify the general level of sales. He or she can also determine whether there is a pattern or trend, such as an increase or decrease in sales volume over time. A further review of the data may reveal some type of seasonal pattern, such as, peak sales occurring around the holiday season. Thus by reviewing historical data, the forecaster can often develop a good understanding of the pattern of sales in the past periods. Understanding such a pattern can often lead to better forecasts of future sales of the product. In addition, if the forecaster is able to identify the factors that influence sales, historical data on these factors (variables) can also be used to generate forecasts of future sales.

There are many forecasting techniques available to the person assisting the business in planning its sales. For illustration, consider a forecasting method in which a statistician forecasting future values of a variable of business interest—sales, for example—examines the cause-and-effect relationships of this variable with other relevant variables, such as the level of consumer confidence, changes in consumers' disposable incomes, the interest rate at which consumers can finance their excess spending through borrowing, and the state of the economy represented by the percentage of the labor force unemployed. Thus, this category of forecasting techniques uses past time series on many relevant variables to forecast the volume of sales in the future. Under this forecasting technique, a regression equation is estimated to generate future forecasts (based on the past relationship among variables).

SEE ALSO: Economic Theories

[Anandi P. Sahu, Ph.D.]

FURTHER READING:

Anderson, David P., Sweeney, Dennis J., and Thomas A. Williams, *An Introduction to Management Science: Quantitative Approaches to Decision Making.* 8th ed. West Publishing Co., 1997.

Hirschey, Mark, and James L. Pappas, *Managerial Economics.* 8th ed. Harcourt Brace Jovanovich College Publishers, 1996.

Mansfield, Edwin, ed. *Managerial Economics and Operations Research: Techniques, Applications, Cases.* 5th ed. New York: W. W. Norton & Co., 1987.

Mansfield, Edwin. *Principles of Microeconomics.* 9th ed. New York: W. W. Norton & Co., 1997.

MANAGING MACHISMO: U.S. WOMEN VS. FOREIGN MEN ABROAD

Most Americans perceive macho behavior as a problem, but only as a "woman's problem." It occurs when men act in such fashion as to magnify their roles so as to diminish the roles of women. When U.S. managers go abroad, however, machismo may become a business problem for both sexes. What foreigners perceive as local custom can inhibit our commercial impact.

Most Americans feel that both sexes should get equal treatment. That, however, is a minority view. Most people in many other global regions see machismo as a good idea. Islamic nations come initially to mind, but Latinos, Africans, many Asians, and even Southern Europeans also segregate, control, and limit female behavior, particularly in commerce. In rural Bangladesh, for instance, no woman may even enter local markets, let alone sell goods or services. Many may never even leave their husband's compounds. Saudi women are forbidden to drive, even though many learn how to do so while in England. Indonesian women may not rent a car and Swahili women may not even ride bicycles.

Foreign forms of machismo become a problem when U.S. businesswomen seek assignments overseas. They then begin to wonder if these limits will apply to them. Their supervisors, often male, begin to wonder too—then hesitate to send these women lest they prove ineffective in the male dominated cultures. How many women are barred from decision-making posts abroad by a male boss concerned about machismo? Worse, how many women eventually decide not to go abroad, due to their own fears of gender discrimination? In every instance, both sexes suffer from overseas machismo, as do their firms.

HOW MACHO ARE U.S. EXECUTIVES?

Current research suggests that most male American senior executives *privately* believe in gender equality, both here and abroad. In one study, 60 percent of those polled felt a woman could successfully lead their operation overseas. Few U.S. executives, for instance, would approve a decision by Japan's Security Dealers that bars high-risk investment opportunities to female clients, or the refusal of most Bangladeshi **banks** to make any **loans** at all to women.

Nonetheless, that *private* disapproval becomes *public* tolerance, when faced with the realities of machismo abroad. As U.S. firms move overseas, those that seek acceptance into foreign business circles face the need to outwardly respect each local culture as host nationals define it. This applies even when foreign women are relegated to subordinate positions that American women who work in that culture cannot easily evade.

As a result, male **chief executive officers** (CEOs) may oppose sending female staff to such regions, out of concern for the reactions of foreign male clientele. Some fear foreign nationals would assign too little status to a U.S. woman manager, thereby demeaning both her and their firm. Others believe male clients might feel their own commercial status downgraded, merely by having to deal with our female decision makers. One American female manager once received a fax explaining that the male managers of a Middle Eastern firm would be willing to negotiate with her (''even if she was a woman''), if she in turn would forgo either shaking hands or looking directly into their faces.

In consequence, many male bosses just say ''no,'' despite their private feelings, to women seeking posts of consequence abroad. In one study, 72.7 percent of the male managers surveyed felt that foreign versions of machismo posed barriers to the assignment of women overseas. One 1975 survey of 171 American firms reported that all but one of the women sent abroad stayed less that 30 days. In 1985, 3 percent of those American managers on long-term foreign assignment were female. In theory, that represents ''improvement.'' In practice, the overseas potential of most female decision makers remains virtually untapped.

MACHISMO ABROAD: "RESPECT" OR RESEARCH IT

U.S. women who seek foreign posts in ''macho regions'' have two options. One is to accept the judgment of those executives who feel that gender bias in a potential market is too great. Here, the woman concerned may simply decide to ''respect'' the existing situation, either by staying home, accepting short-term (often 30-day) assignments, or restricting her overseas work to an in-house ''safety zone,'' with routine tasks that limit contact with host nationals.

The bolder option, of course, is to challenge that same situation by researching machismo itself, analyzing a foreign variant in the same way as any other business problem. U.S. women seeking posts in any foreign region should certainly examine every aspect of host culture that may affect their work. In nations known for machismo, this should include male-female relationships. Such research should have three goals:

1. Research local practice. By interviewing foreign nationals of both sexes, you should gradually find yourself able to learn:
    - What they do—how men and women are expected to behave.
    - Why they do this—historical origins of this behavior.
    - What they expect of you, an American female decision maker, within their business setting.
2. Thereafter, predict potential conflicts—social and commercial situations in which their expectations will predictably clash with yours, simply because you are American.
3. Finally, design specific ways for you to either neutralize or actively ''manage'' the macho elements of each potential conflict, by adjusting to foreign expectations in ways compatible with American self-respect.

RESEARCH LOCAL PRACTICE

Consider, as an illustration, the Islamic variations of male/female interaction that most Americans would describe as macho. Many Americans equate Islamic practice with the Arabian peninsula, forgetting that significant Moslem populations are found not only in the Middle East, but North, West, and Eastern Africa; East, South, Southeast, and Central Asia; on Europe's Mediterranean fringe, and even in U.S. cities such as Detroit.

Assume an American female manager is assigned to launch a first-time venture in a Moslem region. Obviously, so many diverse peoples practice their religion in varied ways. Many Moslem businessmen have had sufficient contact with Western cultures to adjust to Western concepts, including those pertaining to relationships between the sexes.

Nonetheless, many modern Moslems still embrace traditional ideals. Five of these remain so much a part of current Islamic culture that they impinge repeatedly upon contemporary commerce. It thus seems imprudent for U.S. businesswomen to ignore them. Rather, the American female manager who hopes to create relationships with male Moslem counterparts will find it useful to investigate the beliefs that follow.

FEMALE VIRTUE (IRD). Female virtue implies both spiritual and sexual purity. A woman is born with it. It is the spiritual counterpart to physical virginity, and thus subject to similar behavioral restrictions. Both *Ird* and virginity are intrinsic to being female. A woman *must* preserve both. That is a sacred duty, for once lost, neither can be regained. Thus every woman has two lifelong tasks. The first is to guard her own *Ird.* The second is to actively place herself under the additional protection of socially appropriate men (i.e., members of her family).

MALE HONOR (SHARAF). *Sharaf* is an outward reflection of male behavior. Unlike *Ird,* however, it can be lost and then regained. A man can gain or lose *sharaf* through acts of bravery, cowardice, generosity, inhospitality, etc. A proverb declares that each man wears *sharaf* upon his shoulders, like a brightly colored, tightly woven, constantly glittering cloak, for all of his (male) peers to admire. Without his cloak, he becomes an object of their scorn. He *must,* therefore, behave in such fashion as to retain both his own honor and that of his extended family.

A man's *sharaf,* however, depends not only on his own behavior but that of every woman in his extended family—mother, sisters, daughters, nieces, cousins, etc. Should any of these commit an act that calls their virtue into question, the *sharaf* of every male in that family would be lost. Male honor, therefore, carries with it the obligation of lifetime protection of female kin, thereby preserving the collective *sharaf* of the extended family to which they all belong.

SEXUAL ATTRACTION. The need to constantly protect women is based on belief in the virtually unlimited power of sexual attraction. In contrast with contemporary America, this power is perceived as being far greater than any man or woman can resist, despite fear of punishment. Thus, traditionalists believe that whenever a man and woman find themselves alone, regardless of circumstance, they will be irresistibly drawn to one another. The man will be unable to restrain himself; the woman, unable to resist. Many Moslem cultures reflect this belief with a proverb: ''When man and woman are alone, Shetan (Satan: the Devil) is also there.'' As a result (if the transgression becomes known), the *sharaf* of the woman's extended family is obliterated.

CLAN REVENGE. Traditional Moslems believe the consequences of such sexual attraction *must* be severe if *sharaf* is to be restored. To restore it, men must respond as tradition demands. This concept was expressed most clearly by an elderly Egyptian, as we debated Islam and Christianity while trapped in a Cairo traffic jam: ''The curse of your Christianity is that it gives you (nothing but) choice. The beauty of our Islam is that is does not allow (us to have) choice. It guides us in *all* things. Thus, if adultery occurs we *know* what do. Our religion guides us into righteous acts.''

Thus, in earlier times, since sexual transgression meant loss of family honor, men of that family were obligated to restore the loss by killing the woman (their own kin) who had caused it. Meanwhile, the woman's husband was obligated to kill his wife's seducer. This murder, in turn, would anger male kinsmen of the slain man, thereby triggering what might become an endless blood feud. Over time, as the inevitability and power of sexual attraction caused these incidents to multiply, more and more extended families might be drawn into such feuds. As a result, the consequences of sexual transgression could become so great as to damage the fabric of society. Wise men therefore, looked for an alternative.

PROTECTIVE SEGREGATION. It is to avoid triggering this unending cycle of violence that Moslem males protect women. It is to shield women from power stronger than themselves that they are physically segregated, socially secluded, geographically limited, economically controlled—and thereby removed from sexual temptation. Every woman has the right (and duty) to spend her life in safety and security, under the protection (and thus, jurisdiction) of a man. A virtuous woman, therefore, is one who dwells contentedly under the protection of her father, her husband (and his family), her sons and finally grandsons.

Conversely, a nonvirtuous woman is one who moves outside those overlapping jurisdictions, thereby inviting sexual desire, sexual contact, clan revenge, unending retaliation, and the disruption of society. Men can only provide this level of permanent protection by restricting female mobility, earning power, and independent action—thereby also reducing them to the level of perpetual children by ensuring their perpetual dependence. Viewed from this perspective, the decisions of Afghanistan's Taliban, in barring women from work, education, medical care from males, and even from going outdoors without a male relative is simply the expression of this traditional Islamic ideal, carried to its logical extreme.

Islamic tradition provides two tools to achieve this protective cocoon—physical segregation and visual segregation. Historically, the need for physical segregation has meant creating a dual society of protectors and protected, in which both sexes live essentially separate lives, both before and after marriage. Moslem peoples often strive for this ideal, sometimes with considerable innovation.

In Oman, for instance, the National University combines Western theories of coeducation with Islamic theories of gender segregation. Classes have separate doors for men and women, as well as segregated seating within. Buildings connect by slender skyways, built to let women pass between them unseen by male students, who walk between classes on the ground. Libraries not only post separate reading hours for each sex, but segregate the bookshelves—lest students pass notes to one another by hiding them in texts. The purpose of all this, as the Omani see it, is not feminine repression but mutual protection, both of the students and society.

Visual segregation, the second tool required to protect the sexes, forbids public display of the human form. Even the eyes must be restricted. Consider how traditional Moslems cope with public space within the twisting, narrow streets that form the core of many cities. In Zanzibar, for instance, men walk leisurely down the middle of each path. Women cling to the sides, eyes averted and down as men pass. Both sexes wear cultural blinders. Neither side can officially ''see'' the other. Loudly chatting groups of women invariably fall silent as men draw near. By virtue of their veiling, the women are publicly invisible.

Nevertheless, Americans who walk these streets may also wear cultural blinders. We see the system's outward vestiges: segregation, seclusion, restrictions. We see that Saudi women must walk behind men, may not drive, shop only in groups, and enter hotels only with letters of permission from male kin. We see the morals police accost anyone who seems to violate these restrictions. We do not see the system's purpose, however, and thus do not understand that men and women alike may support it—not to suppress femininity, but protect it. These feelings extend through much of the Moslem world, including regions Westerners consider ''liberal.'' Consider the single Turkish female legislator who dared, in 1999, to wear her veil into the Turkish parliament, in effect demonstrating her support for traditional ways in a modern secular Turkish society. (Turkey banned the veil in 1922.) She was publicly reviled by nearly every male parliamentarian.

Consider the thoughts of a wealthy, educated, and quite Westernized Turkish woman, who declared, in a national magazine: ''Modern Turks no longer believe we are a man's property, but we feel safer when we obey the laws of Islam and allow ourselves to be protected by men.''

Most American businesswomen disagree, particularly when these allegedly protective restrictions are applied to them, while doing business abroad. The sheer number of foreign markets influenced by Islamic ideals, however, make this variant of machismo impossible to avoid. Moreover, too many similar systems operate in non-Islamic regions. Consider Japan, South Korea, Greece, Italy, Kenya, and the Ukraine. In different ways, each nation limits women within business. Our response should be to research male-female relationships anywhere we are assigned, to the point where we can understand the expectations of practitioners. Only after we see their side, can we adjust to it.

PREDICT POTENTIAL CONFLICTS

One reason to research machismo's foreign variants is to identify potential conflicts that may occur. Through research, you may foresee specific problems our female decision makers pose to foreign colleagues by adhering to American customs. You may then predict specific actions those same colleagues may take that we would label ''macho.'' In such cases, advance knowledge of both behaviors may minimize or even neutralize each misunderstanding.

To illustrate, consider three possible conflicts between American businesswomen and Saudi businessmen. Each is predictable, in that our women can expect to trigger what they will consider macho responses, just by adhering to normal U.S. business practices.

DOING BUSINESS ALONE. Consider the problem posed for traditional Saudis by a woman who conducts business alone. All American women do this; indeed, they pride themselves on this independence, believing it reflects their competence in business settings. Nonetheless, women with feminist mind-sets may lose sight of the problems they cause in foreign settings, by refusing to adapt. Consider the female executive, sent to Saudi Arabia at a time when no unaccompanied women were allowed into the country. At the airport, she displayed a transit visa, walked unseen out an airport door, then made her way to her foreign contact's firm.

The decision seemed right, from an American perspective, in that it facilitated business for both sides. From a Saudi perspective, it was wrong in that it violated both legal and social norms. Legally, the woman was forbidden to be there, a situation that placed her Saudi contacts in legal jeopardy. Socially, a woman alone is perceived as either immoral or endangered. Away from appropriate male protection, she can be courted, harassed, or even abused. Once, in Libya, an American woman who left her hotel to go shopping alone was stoned by street boys until she fled back into her hotel. Were they trying to hurt her or (speaking no English) simply driving her back into a place of safety? American women see both erotic and hostile responses as proof of machismo. Islamic men may regard them as a protective alternative to social violence.

OVERSEAS IMAGE/PHYSICAL ATTRACTION. American women who enter foreign business settings can create images that will predictably enhance their physical attractiveness, by disregarding nuances in local dress. Consider the impact on host nationals that could be created by a U.S. female executive assigned to today's rural Iran. If generally aware of Islamic sensibilities, she might ''cover up'' by wearing a tailored business suit that covers arms and legs to wrists and ankles. To complete her intended image of efficiency, however, she might carefully style her hair, if only to avoid loose ends.

In so doing, she creates quite predictable problems. Key foreign colleagues might prejudge this woman as immodest and perhaps immoral. Traditional Moslems believe that clothing should not merely cover the female body but conceal its outlines. A tailored business suit, however, is meant to enhance the female figure. Similarly, female hair should be covered. In more conservative regions even hairlines are concealed. One Persian mullah has declared that women's hair gives off a unique gleam that entrances and thus seduces men. Western hairstyles, however, are created to emphasize the wearer's femininity. In consequence, both clothes and hair will predictably detract from the commercial image she means to present. Notwithstanding, to ask her colleagues to set aside these beliefs due to her nationality and corporate status would be as awkward as them asking her to set aside her own beliefs and don a veil.

CREATING COMMERCIAL CREDIBILITY. The need to create credibility is prerequisite to every foreign venture. Americans and many Moslems resolve this in different ways. We start by sending relevant professional data to future foreign contacts in advance, including what we feel they need to know about ourselves. We then reinforce this first professional impression at an initial meeting, by turning instantly to business, using the discussion to establish our commercial expertise.

American women who follow this pattern, however, can pose problems for their Islamic hosts. Moslem businessmen establish credibility by taking private time to forge personal bonds. This can mean long hours spent in ''personal'' conversation—something American women bent on doing business might find disconcerting. It can also entail long hours of entertainment at restaurants, clubs, or private homes. But what if male-female behavioral codes prohibit all aspects of this process? How and where do these Moslems form social relationships, when barred by custom to socialize with those representatives we send them?

Faced with this conflict, some clients prefer not to deal with U.S. women at all. When forced to do so, they retreat into formality, providing empty courtesies to female representatives, and substantive conversations for male colleagues. We condemn this as macho. They regard this as a display of respect for their tradition. Since habits rarely change when crossing foreign borders, our businesswomen may create this type of conflict just by behaving like Americans.

DEVELOP COUNTERSTRATEGIES

Once potential conflicts are identified, outbreaks of machismo can be managed, both before and as they occur. To do this, both the overseas appointee and her corporate superiors should work in tandem to promote her commercial image in the foreign setting. In Islamic areas, for instance, the four strategies outlined below may prove useful.

DEVELOP AREA EXPERTISE BEFORE DEPARTURE. Research the most probable cultural pitfalls. Before departure, become your company's in-house expert on the assigned region. In Moslem areas, that means beginning to explore not only history, geography, culture, and language, but religion—including the Koran. Few Moslem males believe our businesswomen even think about these things. Yet, displaying even the most basic interest in them can undermine a sexist stereotype by creating the first feelings of mutual respect and personal empathy that Moslems everywhere consider the prerequisites for doing business.

An American female colleague, for instance, found herself unable to speak Arabic grammatically during her stay in the United Arab Emirates, despite persistent study. Nonetheless, impressed by her efforts, local women taught her the formal ''courtesy phrases'' used traditionally by ''proper'' women in conversation with men, to convey female respect. Male business contacts proved delighted when she used them appropriately, thereby contradicting their earlier stereotype of American women as inherently disrespectful to males. They subsequently held her in far higher personal (and thus commercial) esteem.

I found that same degree of empathy could be created by inquiring into either local or theological aspects of Islamic history. Knowing too little to converse with authority, I turned what I had learned into questions. As a result, my very lack of knowledge pleased every Moslem contact, permitting them to assume the dual roles of tour guide and teacher. Here too, an earlier stereotype of U.S. ignorance and arrogance was replaced by common interest in a mutually cherished culture—once again an Islamic prerequisite for conducting business.

Commercial empathy intensifies when we show interest in the Koran. To Moslems, it is more than a ''holy book.'' It is the direct communication of a higher intelligence (Allah), providing mankind with a practical guide to every facet of human behavior. In fact, it is not a ''book'' at all; it is a ''reading,'' to be read aloud in classical Arabic, where the resonance and eloquence of the chanted words are said to attain the level of exquisite poetry. Consider that description. It is astounding to Moslems everywhere that we Americans can never find the time to pick up, open, and read something of such extraordinary beauty, let alone of such extraordinary significance to one-fifth of the world's population. To learn (even a little) Koran, therefore, allows you to ask the type of perceptive questions that allow you to learn more. To apply Koran to modern business situations, under the guidance and leadership of male hosts, may significantly shift their initial gender stereotyping to opinions more appropriate to your professional expertise.

DEVELOP ON-SITE STATUS. Once foreign expertise has been acquired, it should be used to create sufficient on-site status to allow the new appointee to do her job. This means the appointee and her corporate supervisors must become a **team**. On making an overseas appointment, the CEO can first assist the appointee to create a high on-site status by providing her a higher hob-title, to match whatever level of **decision making** will be required.

The CEO's next step is to assure that prior knowledge of both her title and professional expertise arrives on-site before the appointee herself. Initially, this means he or she must:

- Locate foreign (host-nation) colleagues, now working in the United States, who may be useful to the appointee before departure. The goal, at this stage, is to help the appointee create a web of contacts at a higher economic and social level then she might achieve alone.
- Ask each of these higher level colleagues to guide the new appointee, not only by providing data, but by contacting other colleagues within the host-nation itself, asking if they might be helpful once the new appointee arrives. Here, the goal is to create a second web of higher level overseas connections.
- Contact the most useful of these higher level foreign colleagues, asking if each might be willing to advise his appointee on arrival. If they agree, he should e-mail sufficient advance data to enhance the status of the firm, its project, and the appointee herself.

DEVELOP ON-SITE CONTACTS. Thereafter, you (the appointee) take over. Begin by interviewing each U.S. contact supervisors provide, as well as those you develop on your own. Ask each what you should know, why, and who you should meet on arrival—including those high-level colleagues with whom introductions have been arranged. Next, contact these individuals by e-mail. Introduce yourself, the firm, your mission abroad, and the time you'll arrive. Then, request professional advice and personal guidance upon arrival. Finally, ask if you can be of service to them before leaving the United States. Your goal, simply, is to place each one under obligation to you.

Plan to spend the first few weeks upon arrival interviewing and visiting (to the degree each culture allows) each contact you have made. Use your on-site inexperience as a business tool to learn the local rules for doing business. Use the social interaction as a means to meet key players in your field. Forget your product for this period. Put it aside, along with your time schedule and marketing plan. Only by investing the time to acquire expertise on-site can you reinforce the initial status provided by your firm, to the point where you are ready to do business.

LOCALIZE YOUR BUSINESS IMAGE. You can further enhance on-site status by "localizing" two aspects of your business image to conform with foreign feelings: feminine appearance and behavior. This does not mean adopting local dress. To do that undermines the professional image you mean to present. Nonetheless, perceptive inquiry into local expectations may lead to both physical and behavioral changes that can visibly enhance your potential for commercial progress.

The tailored business suit, mentioned earlier, should be replaced by a long, loose-fitting dress. High heels should be lowered. Makeup should be minimized. The hair, hairline, forehead and even the throat should be covered by a scarf. These changes may seem obvious, but only if prior research sensitizes you, both to local expectations and the reasons they exist.

The American female vocal pattern may also create conflict. Behaviors that we consider feminine may be perceived as masculine abroad. Consider how our women have been trained to use their voice in business situations: to compel attention (and thus, respect) it should grow deeper, louder, and more decisive—the better to be both listened to and reckoned with. In contrast, many cultures restrict female voices to higher pitch, lower volume, and softer tones. Japanese women, for instance, use a special "woman's language," with different grammar, higher pitch, and lower volume. Similarly, Moslem women lower their voices and soften their tones, to reflect their femininity.

In these settings, therefore, American women face a two-edged sword. The quasi-masculine vocal traits they need at home constrain them when abroad. Nor are they culturally able to adapt: Which American woman would "raise her vocal pitch and drop the volume" on masculine request? In consequence, Moslem men may react negatively to what they perceive as masculinity, while U.S. women label those reactions as machismo. Once more, only prior research can suggest more subtle changes that can modify one's vocal image while retaining inner dignity.

USE SYMBOLIC MALES. In areas where men hesitate to work alone with women, it may prove useful to work with male partners, both real and symbolic. One option is to send male-female project teams abroad, in which the man both implements his part of the venture and facilitates hers. Here, the man might assist his partner in a symbolic capacity, accompany her both when her expertise is in demand (in offices, during working hours) and when cultural norms (such as evening gatherings) prohibit her to appear alone.

In Oman, for instance, day-long business sessions may end with invitations from the host for the U.S. representatives to visit private homes. Though politeness requires such invitations to include everyone, it is in fact a gathering of males, all related to the host and therefore interested in making contact with his (male) foreign guest. To ask a single woman becomes awkward. A foreign pair, however, may find a local welcome. The symbolic presence of the man makes the woman "unavailable" for courtship, thus allowing her to develop business ties in ways no different than her partner.

U.S. men may also have symbolic value as fictitious husbands. Moslem women gain status through marriage and the birth of sons. Thus American assigned to these regions who are single or divorced may find it useful to imply married status, complete with ring and pictures of an alleged spouse and children. A female colleague did this in the United Arab Republic without telling lies. The ring spoke for itself, while she displayed the pictures (her brother and his sons) with the phrase ''my family.'' The deception illustrates a larger point: in cultures where unattached women cause male anxiety, even a symbolic male presence (in a picture) can transform the status of an American female manager so as to move more closely towards conformity to local custom.

CAN MACHISMO BE MANAGED?

The American tradition of tolerance does not extend to machismo. We intensely disapprove of customs that limit women, even if motivated by desire to protect them. Nor do we leave our own biases behind once sent abroad. Nonetheless, when dealing commercially with such behavior, it seems commercially prudent to move beyond passive disapproval and toward active management. The tool that makes such management effective is prior research—examining specific variants of this behavior as we examine any foreign business problem—then adjusting our behavior in ways that still sustain our dignity. Thus, when working with Islamic businessmen, American businesswomen should consider four guidelines:

- Accept that fact that belief systems restricting local women may restrict you. If so, neither private resentment nor public tolerance will be as effective as active management of those aspects of that system that impede the flow of business.
- Each local variant must thus be analyzed before arrival. Research machismo's inner logic. Examine local practice from the perspective of practitioners, learning both how it works and why they feel it should.
- Do not assume that either your nationality or their Western education provides exemption from centuries of tradition. Rather, identify specific expectations that potential colleagues may hold for U.S. women who work within the local business setting. Next, identify specific points of conflict, situations where these expectations will—predictably—clash with yours.
- Finally, develop strategies to manage each potential conflict so that, ideally, none occur. Dress appropriately; act accordingly; react temperately. Only when forewarned can we arrive forearmed.

Above all, do not be held back by your biases. Many of us privately condemn machismo. Some fear it, when assigned abroad. These beliefs are our prerogative. Beyond these fears and disapproval, however, whole worlds of foreign thought and feeling cry out for further exploration, including those of which we disapprove. To do business in their world, we must explore them, transforming both our private disapproval and passive tolerance into active inquiry and professional concern. Only then will we be able to ''manage'' machismo so artfully as to prove acceptable to both our colleagues and ourselves.

SEE ALSO: Gender Discrimination; Women in Business

[Jeffrey Fadiman, with Evylyne Meier]

FURTHER READING:

Adler, Nancy. ''Expecting International Success: Female Managers Overseas.'' *Columbia Journal of World Business,* fall 1984.

——. ''Five Pacific Basin Managers: A Gaijin, Not a Woman.'' *Human Resources Management* 26, no. 2 (summer 1987).

——. ''Women as Androgynous Managers: A Conception of the Potential for American Women in International Management.'' *International Journal of Intercultural Relations* 3, no. 4 (1979).

——, and Dafna Izraeli. ''Where in the World Are the Women Executives?'' *Business Quarterly* 59 (autumn 1994).

Alizira, Marianne. ''Women of Saudi Arabia.'' *National Geographic,* October 1987.

Breen, Katie. ''Arabia behind the Veil.'' *Marie Claire* (U.K.), September 1989.

Edelman, Karen. ''X—Not Y—Marks the Spot.'' *Across the Board* 35, no. 5 (May 1998).

Feltes, Patricia, Ross Fink, and Patricia Robinson. ''American Female Expatriates and the Civil Rights Act of 1991: Balancing Legal and Business Interest.'' *Business Horizons* 36 (March/April 1993).

Fisher, Anne. ''Overseas, U.S. Businesswomen May Have the Edge.'' *Fortune,* 28 September 1998.

Gilsenan, Michael. *Recognizing Islam: Religion and Society in the Modern Arab World.* Random House, 1982.

Hashmi, M. S., and K. L. Foutz. ''Marketing in the Islamic Context.'' Academic conference paper, Eastern Michigan University, Ypsilanti, MI, spring 1987.

Kupfer, Andrew. ''How to Be a Global Manager.'' *Fortune,* 14 March 1988.

Morgenthaler, Eric. ''Women of the World: More U.S. Firms Put Females in Key Posts in Foreign Countries.'' *Wall Street Journal,* 16 March 1978.

Stasio, Marilyn. ''Beyond the Veil.'' *New Woman,* November 1987.

Sullivan, Constance. ''Machismo and Its Cultural Dimension.'' In *Towards Internationalism,* edited by L. Luce and E. Smith. Harper and Row, 1986.

Taylor, M., M. Odjogov, and E. Morely. ''Experienced Women in Overseas Business Assignments.'' *Academy of Management Proceedings,* 1975.

Thal, Nancy, and Philip Caetora. ''Opportunities for Women in International Business.'' *Business Horizons,* 24 (December 1979).

Wah, Louisa. ''Surfing the Rough Sea.'' *Management Review,* 87, no. 8 (September 1998): 25-29.

MANUALS

SEE: Handbooks and Manuals

MANUFACTURERS' REPRESENTATIVES

Manufacturers' representatives are independent contractors who develop long-term relationships with their client companies (or ''principals'') to sell the latter's products. They do not function under the immediate supervision of the manufacturers they sell for; therefore the relationship is not like that between a boss and employee, but is a business-to-business relationship.

A manufacturers' rep firm, sometimes called a multi-line field sales company, can be run by one person or it can be a much more extensive organization with numerous sales persons covering specific territories. The typical agency is a corporation employing about six people, including those to handle office duties, that sell for an average of 10 different principals, according to the Manufacturers' Agents National Association (MANA). The average rep agency handles annual sales volume of about $8.9 million.

The MANA directory lists approximately 7,000 manufacturers' rep firms and 30,000 agents in the United States, located in all 50 states. The firms represent every conceivable product line, from automotive to rubber products, from arts and crafts to jewelry, from electronics to energy, from food and beverage processing equipment to furniture. Virtually any product that is made and sold can be handled by rep firms.

Beyond sales duties, however, manufacturers' representatives provide an array of services to for their clients in an effort to strengthen the relationship between rep and manufacturer and to increase the mutual benefits of the relationship. These services include (depending on the size, scope, and specialization of the particular sales agency) warehousing, installation and maintenance activities, and, increasingly in the 1990s, consulting on such matters as the identification and definition of clients' needs and problems, efficiency solutions, and a host of other issues. Most rep firms provide one or more of these services in addition to their specialization in field sales.

Smaller companies that can't afford to have their own sales staff use agencies, as do billion-dollar firms that want to ensure maximum coverage for their products. Some large companies even sell exclusively through manufacturers' representatives.

Representatives generally handle sales for several different companies that offer compatible, but not competing, products to the same industry. This method reduces the cost of sales by spreading the rep's cost over the different products touted to each customer. As a result, manufacturers' agents view themselves not as middlemen, but as a cost-effective alternative to a company's hiring of a full-time salaried sales force. Tens of thousands of small- and medium-size manufacturers in the United States use agents to sell their products. This is particularly true of new products where a direct salaried force is cost prohibitive. Because reps are paid by commission, the manufacturer incurs no cost until a sale is made.

At different times, however, some large customers—such as Wal-Mart, Rite Aid, and General Electric—have tried to bypass representatives and buy only directly from manufacturers in an effort to cut costs. This practice, opposed by MANA, was the subject of a hearing in 1994 before a U.S. House committee.

HISTORY

Some sales agencies have been around since the turn of the century, but the manufacturers' representative business really began to grow and develop just after World War II. Industry was taking off at that time, and many new companies were just getting started and needed ways to get their products to market. These new companies especially liked the economics of the rep business: no cost until a sale was made.

The rep business has grown steadily over the years. While the economics have had a lot to do with the growth, agencies often offer much more than just a salaried sales force. They can bring continuity; manufacturers and representatives can build relationships that last years and years. While a salaried sales person may move from company to company, many reps and their principals maintain business relationships that go back decades.

ADVANTAGES AND DISADVANTAGES

One of the obvious advantages of utilizing a manufacturers' representative is the economic benefits it offers. A manufacturer has no fixed overhead. Rep firms are paid commissions when they sell products. When they don't sell anything, they aren't paid. When a manufacturer hires salaried sales people, it has to pay salaries, Social Security taxes, and fringe benefits, regardless of sales performance. Hiring a rep firm entails no such up-front costs.

While field sales calls cost an average of $250, a rep trying to sell several products to an individual customer proves an efficient and reasonable alternative. Agents who have created a complete line of products often get more time (and money) from a buyer who is interested in several of the products. The system of agency selling is geared to be highly efficient, since the agency will only receive payment if it sells products.

Another significant advantage is especially relevant to start-up firms, firms trying to launch a new product, or firms trying to penetrate a new geographic area. By contracting with a manufacturers' rep, a company gains instant access to either industry expertise or knowledge of a particular country or region. This type of knowledge could take a company years to develop on its own, and it could be very expensive. Contracting with a rep bypasses those negatives.

There are other distinct advantages as well. For manufacturers with narrow product lines, agencies offer one of the best ways to access the market. Because they normally sell compatible products to a single market, the rep firms usually are well-connected with the manufacturers' prospects and customers. This offers manufacturers immediate entry to markets that may be hard to reach with a direct sales force.

Many of the owners of start-up companies have backgrounds in production, engineering, and finance, and have little idea of what goes into sales and marketing; they still see making a superior product as the only thing that matters. Most start-up firms face stiff competition and have to work harder to get noticed. By using manufacturers' reps that handle complementary lines, these firms usually can establish valuable contacts with the people they need to influence more easily than by employing their own sales agents who don't have customers in place in the territory.

Rep firms also can give new firms ideas of where to advertise, comment on what the competition is doing, and provide estimates of a given territory's potential. Many reps also do service calls for less cost than if it had to be handled from the factory.

There are certain disadvantages to using rep firms, however. Probably the most important drawback is the lack of control. Reps are independent contractors doing business for more than one manufacturer. Because of this, no one manufacturer gets full-time attention from the agent, as he or she must split time among various principals. Manufacturers seeking to take advantage of a rep firm's services only for the perceived cost-savings generally would do well to weigh the importance of direct control over salespeople for their particular operations

There are also times when it is preferable to have a direct sales person instead of a manufacturers' representative, especially when a product needs highly technical service. When highly skilled technical people are needed for a sale, a direct sales person may have an edge, although some reps have fairly sophisticated backgrounds in the areas in which they specialize.

Some agents also may be reluctant to provide service beyond selling. Such things as start-up assistance and service often are needed and must be supplied by the factory.

AVERAGE AGENCY PROFILE

According to MANA's 1998 survey of manufacturers' agencies, the association's composite profile of the average agency shows the typical agency handled gross sales of about $8.89 million a year. The average agency had been in operation for more than roughly 20.5 years, represented 10 manufacturers, and covered nearly six states in their territories.

Additionally, a typical agency has either one or two offices, employs 3.7 sales people, a little more than two office staff employees, and almost two warehouse workers. Nearly half the firms surveyed announced that they planned to add to their sales staff within a year. More than 76 percent of the agencies were owned by the original founder of the firm, while 24 percent had been acquired, 5 percent as the result of a merger.

About 45 percent of the agencies represent foreign manufacturers in the United States, but only 19 percent actually sell product in foreign countries. Among the markets sold to by manufacturers' representatives, by far the top one was original equipment manufacturers, with 61 percent of reps aiming products there. The second most popular area was the wholesaler/distributor market at 44 percent, followed by capital equipment manufacturing at 27 percent. Other main markets included capital goods in primary industry (19 percent), contractors/architects (19 percent), government/municipalities (15 percent), and retail/mass merchandisers (9 percent).

The MANA survey showed a strong correlation between the number of years a rep firm had been in business and the financial results of the company, save for those firms who had been in business the longest. Fledgling agencies, those in business just 1 to 3 years, handled on average just $1.763 million in total sales and collected gross commissions before costs of about $132,300. For those in business 4 to 10 years, the gross sales rose to $4.8 million, with commissions of nearly $306,650. Agencies in existence 11 to 25 years handled on average $12.72 million in sales, with gross commissions topping $798,900, and rep firms in business more than 25 years had sales of more than $9.1

million and commissions of about $616,100. The slight drop in sales of the oldest firms is quite likely due to the large variation in business structures among these firms; while many have branched out continuously over the years into new markets, others have opted to remain focused on their small, long-term client lists, without an eye toward expansion.

There also was distinct differences discerned in the survey between agencies established as corporations versus those established as sole proprietorships. The corporate rep firms—the more common of the two—averaged $10.34 million in sales and collected $714,300 in commissions, compared with just $4.635 million in sales and less than $211,400 in commissions for the sole proprietors. Corporations typically maintained a greater number of offices, covered more states, had double the number of sales personnel, and had been in business an average of 24.7 years, compared with about 14 for sole proprietors. A greater percentage of corporate-run businesses also represent foreign manufacturers or sell overseas. Moreover, corporations, though not registering a dramatic widening of the scope of their operations, outpaced proprietorships in revenue growth since the 1994 survey, a feature MANA attributes to a greater efficiency model among corporations.

Proprietorships, however, showed a far greater consistency of ownership; 88 percent of sole proprietors established their rep firms, with only 12 percent acquiring the agency, whereas just 66 percent of corporate owners established the firm, with 34 percent acquiring them. It also should be noted that principal owners and partners involved in a sole proprietorship take home net income that is a greater percentage of gross sales than their counterparts at corporate rep firms. This likely is because they have less overhead with fewer employees and less office space and warehousing capability.

SELECTING AN AGENCY

Manufacturers have many factors to consider when selecting a manufacturers' representative. They typically will want someone who is knowledgeable about their products and applications. They'll want reps who respond quickly to calls, present the product in terms of how it will meet customer needs, and represent lines fairly, giving enough time to each regardless of how much income each line accounts for.

Manufacturers also need to decide whether to go with a new agency or an established rep firm. Some want agents who are younger while others want the complete coverage they think comes with an established agency that has a large staff. The best rule of thumb for manufacturers is to be patient and do plenty of preliminary research; they should treat the selection process with as much importance as the hiring of a new vice-president. MANA suggest the following guidelines:

1. The manufacturer should define its own needs. If replacing an agency that did well and had a reputation for good service, the replacement better do an equally good job. If appointing a rep for the first time, it's a good idea to make a profile of the customers, their needs, and the way they do business. The manufacturer should ask prospective reps about such things as likely call cycle, problems in the territory, prospective buyers in the area, and how aggressive are the people who sell for competitors.
2. The company should create a profile of the ideal agency. This profile should be clear, but also flexible enough that it never reaches the point that no one ever gets hired because it's impossible to meet all of the criteria set down on paper.
3. The manufacturing firm should create a comprehensive profile of itself. Many rep firms can be selective and won't take on product lines without knowing quite a bit about their principals. The profile should be honest and touch on growth plans, real advantages of the product, why the territory is open, and what a realistic goal of the territory's potential is.
4. Referrals from other agencies can give the firm a feel for their available options. Manufacturers' representatives are a close-knit fraternity in the United States, and many can provide the names of several agencies that would be a good fit for the line.
5. For the same ends, a manufacturer should obtain referrals from other manufacturers. Companies in the same area that sell similar but noncompetitive products can be a good source in finding potential reps. Some may even recommend their own agencies, while others may be reluctant to have their reps take on additional lines.
6. Manufacturers can create their own agency. Some companies know they have people who won't stay once they've hit the top of the sales department. One way to keep them is by helping them set up their own sales agencies. One maker of roofing supplies had seven regional managers who called on distributors and lumber yards. A marketing executive of the roofing firm knew that once they realized the full potential of the territories, they likely would leave. He offered to help them set up as a rep firm by locating other lines to round out their packages. Within five years, all

seven were in business for themselves but still selling the roofing lines.

7. Patience is a virtue. While manufacturers often don't have the luxury of waiting forever when filling rep openings, doing preliminary research usually is a good idea. Many manufacturers who've admitted making mistakes in hiring agents say it was because they didn't take the time to get to know the prospective rep. In general, it's better to take the needed time to select the right prospect than to rush into a bad situation and have to rectify it later.
8. Manufacturers should be flexible in setting up territories. Reps must have exclusive rights within a territory, but rather than assign arbitrary territories based on geography, it's often preferable to select the agents that best fit the firm's line and let their coverage determine the territories.

DEALING WITH REPS

Manufacturers must remember that their rep firms are independent sales agencies that are not employees of any of its principals, but business partners with each of them. As such, the manufacturers can't have the same type of direct control as they do over their own personnel. For this as well as for other practical reasons, it is crucial for manufacturers to fully support their relationships with their representatives if the endeavor is to prove worth the effort of contracting with an agency in the first place.

From a legal standpoint, it is important to remember that the manufacturers pay nothing to a rep until a sale is made. They also pay no withholding taxes or Social Security. It also means there is none of the bookkeeping or record keeping done by a direct sales staff. This is an important distinction for the Internal Revenue Service. The IRS typically uses as one of its tests the amount of direct control exercised over sales reps. If regular reports are demanded of independent agents, the IRS can declare the rep an employee and require the accordant withholding taxes.

Communication remains an integral part of the relationship between reps and their principals. The process of communicating, though, is different than when a salaried sales person is involved. Manufacturers still need field information, but because of the legal ramifications, the question centers on how it will be supplied. Some agents make regular calls to each of their principals once a month, which is allowable as long as it's not a requirement to keep the line. For the representative, it is often a matter of continually ''selling'' the relationship as much as the products that ensures a successful venture for both parties.

The key is that both parties need to know enough about what the other is doing with respect to the program. Reps should let their principals know what they are doing for them in the field, regardless of the level of sales at that particular moment, while agents need updated information on matters such as product specifications and pricing. Manufacturers should expect loyalty, with no conflict in product lines; knowledge of the territory and/or industry; knowledge of product lines after a reasonable amount of exposure; quick response to suggestions; regular follow-up; and a fair share of the agent's time. Reps, on the other hand, should expect a fair contract that recognizes performance and rewards success and longevity; access to customer service, training, and technical backup; a quality product; timely delivery; and a true commitment to build business in their territory.

DISPUTES AND TENSION

One legal issue involving the use of manufacturers' representatives has evolved over a number of years. It concerns the growth of superstores—such as Wal-Mart—that represent tremendous buying power. Many of these discount stores have tried to circumvent the normal chain by telling their suppliers they won't deal with independent reps, but only directly with the manufacturer.

The superstores argue that their economies of scale allow them to undersell small local competitors. They say that ''going direct'' will help them sell at a lower price by eliminating the commission paid to the rep.

MANA said that large retailers have tried this tactic numerous times since 1980. The association filed a complaint against Wal-Mart in 1992 and testified in late 1994 before a U.S. House committee studying the impact of superstores on sales agents.

More recently, the major retailing firm Rite Aid, Inc. announced in October 1998 that it would cease to conduct business with suppliers who employ manufacturers' representatives. Rite Aid's decision was based on much the same reasoning as Wal-Mart's, adding that Rite Aid intended to utilize emerging technology, particularly the Internet, to cut out the sales rep's role in dealing with smaller suppliers, and instead reaching out to customers directly via online stores and the like. Rite Aid's decision sparked an outcry by manufacturers' reps; some went so far as to call for a veritable boycott by rep firms and affiliated businesses against Rite Aid.

MANA argues that the practice is ''unethical and illegal,'' causing a domino effect that inhibits the ability of smaller companies that depend on manufacturing reps. The group said that in the American system of marketing, someone makes the sale—be it a direct salaried person or a rep firm—and that this selling function is part of the cost of the product.

Internet technology also took center stage in the industry in 1999 when a handful of manufacturers' reps were discovered selling their clients' products directly to customers over the Internet. This violation of the rep-principal relationship had yet to ignite a clear-cut policy for firms' retail accounts as they pertain to Internet selling, but as Web commerce assumes its inevitably increasing role in the economy, such guidelines are likely to be drawn.

Another emerging point of contention stems from the internal dynamics of the manufacturers' representatives industry itself. As more and more rep agencies acquire the product lines of other agencies, a growing concern has centered around the distinction between certain products. Since a rep firm's strength relies on its ability to sell related, but not competitive, products, this consolidation trend has caused many industry insiders to call for a more clearly articulated definition of ''non-competitive'' in order to avoid feeding a potentially self-defeating impulse.

EMPLOYEE COMPOSITE

At multiperson sales agencies, 56 percent of firms consider all sales personnel to be employees, according to another MANA survey. About 16 percent of firms use only independent contractors, while 26 percent use a combination of employees and contractors.

A little more than half of the firms, 57 percent, compensate sales people by a combination of salary and commission. A total of 19 percent utilize salary only, while 24 percent pay commission only. The remainder employ any combination of a variety of compensation methods, including car allowances, expense accounts, bonuses, and profit sharing. Comparing compensation between those paid only by salary and those making a salary plus commission, the study indicates that sales people paid with a combination of both generally make more money.

Average compensation for those making just a salary were: sales trainee, $25,286; 1 to 3 years' experience, $32,460; 4 to 6, $42,575; 7 to 10 years, $47,694; and over 10 years, $68,071. For those making a base salary and commission, compensation averaged: sales trainee, $25,905; 1 to 3 years, $36,088; 4 to 6, $55,192; 7 to 10, $63,568; and over 10 years, $89,500.

[Bruce Meyer]

FURTHER READING:

''Do It Right the First Time.'' Part of Special Report in *Directory of Manufacturers' Sales Agencies,* Manufacturers' Agents National Association, 1999.

Johnson, John R. ''A New Breed of Reps.'' *Industrial Distribution,* May 1999, 86-89.

Keenan, Bill. ''Selling's New Breed.'' *Industry Week,* 21 September 1998, 40-42.

Marshall, George. ''An Idea Whose Time Has Come.'' *Supply House Times,* October 1998, 127-130.

''Selling Your Company to Your Agents.'' *Agency Sales Magazine,* June 1999, 47-48.

Silliphant, Leigh. *Making $70,000+ a Year as a Self-Employed Manufacturers' Representative.* Berkeley, CA: Ten Speed Press, 1988.

''Your Selling Force: Profile of a Manufacturers' Sales Agency.'' *Agency Sales Magazine,* January 1999, 8-17.

MARKET RESEARCH

Market research is the process of gathering and interpreting information about customers and potential customers. Research is needed because buying behaviors are sometimes difficult to predict or explain. If a marketer fails to take into account the customers' interests and motivations, which are learned through market research, the marketer may be trying to sell a product or service that is ill-suited for its target users. People may buy only after carefully studying a product's features and benefits. They may buy after seeing a well-executed advertisement over and over again. Or, they may buy after hearing about a good product from their friends and colleagues. They may even purchase on a whim without knowing anything at all about the product because the packaging caught their eye while walking down the supermarket aisle.

Research attempts to understand and explain buying patterns so that a company's **marketing strategy** can attract the most customers (or more accurately, the highest profits) per dollar spent on marketing. As John Wanamaker, the famed New York department store owner who hired the first **advertising** copywriter, said in the 1880s, ''I know half the money I spend on advertising is wasted, but I can never find out which half.'' Market research tries to solve that dilemma.

Corporations come to understand their markets in many different ways. A few common methods include:

- using company intelligence to learn competitors' strategies
- analyzing past sales data to glean purchasing trends
- surveying present customers or a target audience
- evaluating demographic data, such as from the U.S. census, to infer market shifts

Market research is critically important but remains imperfect. Although new products are usually researched before introduction, more than 80 percent fail. Campbell Soup Co. once conducted an exhaustive market research study on sales of their products and on their customers. They discovered that the company wasted more than 60 percent of its marketing dollars targeting people who never buy from a particular product category or those were loyal to other brands. They also found that the small segment that were loyal Campbell's customers delivered three times the profits that occasional Campbell's buyers did. This meant that the coupons delivered to regular Campbell's customers took money away from the bottom line since those people would have bought the product anyway.

HISTORY OF MARKET RESEARCH

Advertising was not tested in the United States until the 1920s. Until that time copywriters would write what they thought an ad should be, publish it, and hope that readers acted upon the information. During the 1920s, Daniel Starch began expanding his educational surveys into advertising. From those surveys he developed a theory that effective advertising must be seen, read, believed, remembered, and acted upon. By the 1930s he had launched a company that interviewed people in the streets, asking them if they read certain magazines. If they did, his researchers would show them the magazines and ask if they recognized and remembered ads in them. He then compared the number of people he interviewed with the circulation of the magazine to extrapolate how effective those magazine ads were in reaching readers.

Various market research companies started following Starch's example and improved on his techniques. George Gallup (1901-84) developed a rival system of ''aided recall'' that prompted people to recall the ads they had seen without actually showing the ads. Gallup was able to adapt this system to measure radio and television advertising.

Throughout the last 70 years, market research has grown much more sophisticated as well as pervasive. One survey of surveying activity found that 73 percent of Americans said they had participated in a survey with 42 percent having been also surveyed in the previous year.

TYPES OF MARKET RESEARCH

AUDIENCE RESEARCH. Research on who is listening, watching, and reading are all important to marketers in order to determine which media are best suited for reaching a target audience. Television and radio ratings determine popularity of shows and how large of an audience can be reached during show broadcasts. Publication subscription lists are audited by tabulating companies that cross-check magazine subscription records to make sure the people receiving the publications have either subscribed or requested the publication.

In the early days of television, selected viewer families kept diaries or logs of their viewing habits. Completed logs were mailed to the A.C. Nielsen Company, which then compiled the results. In 1986 the log gave way to a people meter that allows viewers to punch buttons on a remote control-like device that records viewers' choices automatically.

While not yet in place, inventors are experimenting with devices that will no longer depend on viewers, listeners, or readers to actively tell researchers about their habits. The researchers may soon be able to get all the information they need from devices placed in the home. One device under study would be a television capable of looking back at viewers. It would store digitized images of its ''television family'' in its memory banks then regularly record if they are in the room. The device would even record whether their faces are turned toward the TV to prove they are looking at the show and its accompanying commercials.

Another device under development would not only monitor when people are watching television, but would know when they are reading advertising-filled magazines. The device would record pulses coming from a television or radio and from a transmitter cleverly hidden in the publication's bindings.

The devices sound Orwellian, which is what is slowing their development and implementation. Broadcasters are not sure they want to cooperate with the transmission of the imperceptible pulses, while advertisers are leery about appearing too eager to know everything their customers do in the privacy of their own homes.

PRODUCT RESEARCH. Simple in-person research such as taste tests conducted in malls and in the aisles of grocery stores is market research. So is elaborate, long-term ''beta testing'' of high-tech products, particularly software, by experienced users. While advertising agencies formerly conducted much of the product research, that function has also moved into the marketing department of advertisers.

Product research can be simple: tweaking the taste of an existing product, then measuring consumers' reactions to see if there is room in the market for a variation. Or, it could be more extensive: developing prototypes of proposed new products that may be intended for market introduction months down the road. Other kinds of product research include:

- researching the appeal of a new product's proposed name
- testing new packaging

- identifying new markets or selling points for an existing product
- testing new pricing
- testing an advertising campaign

As in all research, there is a danger to paying too much attention to the wrong things. The introduction of New Coke in the 1980s was based on the outcome of taste tests that showed the public wanted a sweeter product. Once introduced, an angry public, outraged that Coca-Cola changed the familiar formula, forced the company to ignore its misdirected market research and leave the original Coke on the market. The company had looked closely at taste test studies, but failed to factor in research that showed consumers were happy with the product as is.

BRAND RESEARCH. Brands, the named products that advertising pushes and for which manufacturers can charge consumers the most money, are always being studied. Advertisers want to know if consumers have strong brand loyalty (''I'd never buy another brand, even if they gave me a coupon''); if the brand has any emotional appeal (''My dear mother used only that brand''); and what the consumer thinks could be improved about the brand (''If only it came in a refillable container'').

Brand research has its perils. Campbell's Soup once convened a focus group comprised of its best soup customers. One of the findings was that those customers saw no need for a low-salt alternative soup Campbell's wanted to market. Concerned that the general public seemed to want low-sodium products, Campbell's retested groups other than their best customers. This research found a market interested in a low-sodium soup. The loyal Campbell's customers loved the saltier product as is, while a larger group of potential customers preferred the low-salt alternative.

PSYCHOLOGICAL RESEARCH. Perhaps the most controversial type of market research is psychological research. This research tries to determine why people buy certain products based on experimentally derived profiles of the way consumers live their lives. One company has divided all Americans into more than 60 psychological profiles. This company contends that the lifestyles these people have established by past buying habits and their cultural upbringing influence their buying decisions. The researchers assert that individual differences can sometimes be negated.

This research continues to be controversial since it measures attitudes about buying and not the buying itself. Critics point to conflicting information uncovered through other market research studies. In one series of research projects researchers asked people what they were planning to buy before entering a store. After the people surveyed left the store, the same researcher examined what was actually in the shopping cart. In one such study only 30 percent of the people bought what they said they were going to buy just a half hour earlier.

SCANNER RESEARCH. There is no fooling the checkout scanner at the supermarket or the department store. It records what was actually purchased. This is valuable information advertisers use to help plan ongoing marketing strategies.

Scanners have changed the way advertisers have typically thought about the sale of consumer products. Before scanners, advertisers received sales information when retailers reordered stock, generally every two weeks. Advertisers had no way to quickly measure the effect of national advertising-supported sales promotions, store sales promotions, or the couponing of similar products by their competitors.

Now, computer technology can send scanner information to advertisers within days or even hours. What scanners have so far confirmed is that consumers are fickle. They may try a product heavily promoted through national television one week. Then the next week they may switch brands based on local promotions from the competition.

DATABASE RESEARCH. Virtually every type of consumer shows up on thousands of lists and databases that are regularly cross-referenced to mine nuggets of marketing research. Such database research, associated with **database marketing**, is growing in popularity among marketers because the raw data has already been contributed by the purchaser. All the marketer has to do is develop a computer program to look for common buying patterns.

Database research can be thought of as the ultimate in market segmentation research. For example, from zip codes lists, marketers may determine where the wealthy people live in a city. That list can be merged with a list of licensed drivers. The resulting list can be merged with another list of owners of cars of a certain make older than a certain year. The resulting list can be merged with another list of car enthusiast magazine subscribers. The final compiled and cross-checked list will deliver a potential market for a new luxury car soon to be introduced and profiled in the car magazines. The people on the potential buyers' list would then be mailed an invitation to come see the new car.

Database research and marketing allow companies to build personal relationships with people who have proven from past purchases that they are potential customers. For example, a motorcycle manufacturer such as Harley-Davidson may discover from database research that a family with a motorcycle has a teenage son. That son is a potential new customer for everything from clothes to a new motorcycle of his own. In another example, movie rental giant Blockbuster Entertainment can suggest titles its customers might want to rent based on a check of its database for the types of movies people have rented in the past.

This personal relationship also provides a basis for more detailed and economical market research than might be possible from conducting random calling. From that research, marketing sometimes follows. For example, General Motors Corp., which has collected a database of 12 million GM MasterCard cardholders in just two years, surveys them to determine what they are driving now and when they might buy a new car. GM's logic: why spend millions of dollars trying to sell to total strangers when you have a list of millions of people you already know?

POST-SALES OR CUSTOMER SATISFACTION RESEARCH. Companies no longer believe that the sale ends their relationship with a customer. Nearly one-third of the research revenues generated by the leading U.S. research companies concern customer satisfaction. Many companies are now waiting a few days or weeks, then surveying customers by telephone. Companies want reassurance that the customer enjoyed the buying experience and that the product or service lived up to the buyer's expectations.

One research company uses a one dollar check to encourage customer satisfaction responses. It prints a customer survey on the back of the check that is returned when the customer cashes the check. The survey company thus secures a short, but complete, survey of customer satisfaction. Such research can be even more personal. Honda once developed a program in which assembly line workers called new Accord owners to ask them what improvements could be made in the car.

The reason for this sort of research is to ensure current customers are happy and will consider themselves future customers. One study found that 70 percent of customers believe it is important that companies stay in contact with them, but that less than a third of those same customers reported that they had heard from companies whose products they purchased. Nearly 90 percent of those surveyed said they would choose a company's products if it stayed in touch with them and sought their satisfaction.

METHODS OF PERSONAL RESEARCH

CLOSED-ENDED QUESTIONS. The type of research most people experience is filling out a comment card or questionnaire at a restaurant or hotel asking about the service they received. Another common research method is a telephone survey in which interviewers read from a carefully prepared list of questions designed so answers can be categorized and tabulated by computer.

Both of these are considered closed-ended, meaning that the person being surveyed cannot expound on their answer. Such surveys usually ask for ''yes'' or ''no'' answers or several measures of multiple choice opinion (e.g., ''extremely interested,'' ''somewhat interested,'' or ''not interested at all''). This type of market research is generally conducted to elicit opinions and beliefs of the public. It is commonly used for political polling and to determine the awareness or popularity of a product or service.

The inherent problem with multiple-choice questionnaires that ask for clear-cut answers is that many people do not think in a clear-cut fashion. If not carefully prepared, closed-ended questions may elicit answers that do not provide a clear view of the person being surveyed. Sometimes, the company conducting the survey may intentionally or inadvertently write questions that elicit the answers it wants to get rather than a true picture of what is happening in the marketplace.

OPEN-ENDED QUESTIONS. Although they are useful for soliciting insights or concerns that the marketer hasn't anticipated, open-ended questions tend to be frowned upon in market research. They present two challenges: (1) they can produce answers that are ambiguous and hard to compare because the respondents aren't relying on a fixed vocabulary to describe their thoughts and behaviors, and (2) they require more time and effort to analyze. Some marketers may favor open-ended questions in hopes of uncovering significant new feedback from their current or potential customer base, but experienced market researchers have found that this rarely occurs. Particularly if the research involves an established product or service, researchers find there is usually a predictable spectrum of opinions or responses to a given question; few respondents volunteer profound new ideas. As a result, in most kinds of research experts prefer to keep open-ended questions to a minimum and use them only when they serve a specific purpose.

DRAWBACKS. There is a problem in both closed- and open-ended questionnaire research, particularly that conducted over the telephone. The person answering the questions could grow increasingly bored or, worse, annoyed at the time it takes to answer the questions. Once they become bored or annoyed, people stop giving true opinions.

One company that has researched the problem of bored interviewees found that falloff in attention can begin as soon as one minute after the person starts answering questions. This also held even when people filled out questionnaires on their own time. The company believes that the longer the person is annoyed, the higher the likelihood that the value of the questionnaire is reduced.

Another study showed that 31 percent of Americans say they refuse to answer marketing research surveys. The survey conductors speculate that the high resistance is a result of consumers lumping telemarketing and survey calls together. Both frequently come at the dinner hour, when many people do not want to participate.

FOCUS GROUPS. In-person, sit-down sessions around a table with groups of consumers, would-be consumers, never-buyers, or any other demographic group a company wishes to bring together are called **focus groups**. This can be the most inexpensive type of research when handled on a local basis by a small business wanting to get a handle on its customers. Or, it can be one of the most expensive if a major corporation wants to test its plans in all sections of the country.

Small businesses may invite a focus group to a neighborhood home to sit around the dinner table to discuss how the company can develop new markets. Major corporations conduct their focus groups in a controlled environment, sometimes with a one-way mirror at one end. This allows executives to unobtrusively watch the proceedings and/or to videotape the session for further study.

The key to gathering good information from a focus group is for the moderator to keep the conversation flowing freely without taking a side. If a company is interested in launching a new product, the moderator usually does not even mention the company that is hosting the focus group, not wanting opinions already formed about the company's other products to influence the discussion. The moderator's job is to involve everyone in the session and prevent any individuals from dominating the conversation. The latter danger is called ''The Twelve Angry Men,'' named after a Henry Fonda movie in which a talkative, persuasive Fonda slowly influences 11 other jury members to acquit a man being tried for murder.

Researchers agree that focus group research should be accompanied by other types of research and not be the sole basis for launching new products. The reason is that opinions expressed among strangers may not always reflect the way people would react when alone. For example, a focus group discussing low-fat foods may garner an enthusiastic response from people who want to be publicly perceived as being concerned about their health. The same people, however, might say they never buy low-fat products if questioned during an anonymous phone interview.

RESEARCH AGENCIES

Marketers often outsource their research to outside agencies when they lack the staffing or the expertise to conduct extensive research on their own. Numerous market research firms exist, many of which are quite specialized to a particular trade. These outside suppliers of research range from small one-person consultancies to large multibillion-dollar corporations. Working with a research supplier is often a highly interactive process. The marketer needs to determine if the research agency has sufficient knowledge and skills to produce reliable results; the supplier needs a great deal of information about the product being marketed, its strengths and weaknesses, the marketer's goals, and so forth in order to construct an effective research project.

RESEARCH STANDARDS AND ETHICS

Most professional market research organizations abide by some formal or informal code of ethics. Many of the marketing trade groups like the American Marketing Association and the Marketing Research Association have published standards of ethical practices and require their members to adhere to them. Managers should be aware of ethical standards as they supervise in-house research and contract out to other firms. Some examples of unethical research methods:

- leading a respondent toward a specific answer in a survey, either directly or indirectly
- disclosing a respondent's name or other personal information if they have been told it was an anonymous survey
- interviewing young children without parental consent
- disguising a sales or fundraising pitch as market research, or using research participants subsequently as sales leads based on information obtained from the research

ANALYZING MARKET RESEARCH

Once market data have been collected by reliable means, the goal of market research is to extract as much meaning from the information as possible. Usually this starts by tabulating results, e.g., 34 percent of respondents have heard of the brand and 60 percent represent middle-income households, but only 13 percent buy it regularly. Depending on the type of questions asked and the marketer's objectives for the research, the analysis may involve a host of more sophisticated statistical analyses. Statistical methods may be used to answer the following questions, among many others:

- are the apparent relationships between variables in the study statistically significant or could they easily occur at random?
- what is the margin of error for the findings?
- what kind of patterns could be projected into the future based on past indications?

- what demographic factors best predict a loyal customer and which ones appear irrelevant?
- what are the meaningful segments in the market?
- which aspects of the product or service are most valued by consumers?

Knowledgeable answers to such questions require an understanding of both the data and appropriate statistical methods. Consequently, introductory textbooks on market research often include a heavy dose of statistical theory.

REPORTING MARKET RESEARCH

The final step in most formal research projects is to present the findings to the decision makers. Though it may include many pages of supplementary tables and charts, the essential research report for management is usually one or two pages. The report explains the nature of the research—what it was trying to learn and by what methods—and conclusions from it—what was learned and how it affects the company. A good report not only summarizes the statistics compiled from the research, but goes further to cautiously interpret their significance for the business and what they suggest for the future.

SEE ALSO: Market Segmentation; Marketing; Regression Analysis; Statistical Analysis for Management

FURTHER READING:

Blankenship, A.B., George Edward Breen, and Alan Dutka. *State of the Art Marketing Research.* 2nd ed. Lincolnwood, IL: NTC Business Books, 1998.

Lehmann, Donald R., Sunil Gupta, and Joel H. Steckel. *Marketing Research.* Reading, MA: Addison-Wesley, 1998.

McQuarrie, Edward F. *The Market Research Toolbox: A Concise Guide for Beginners.* Thousand Oaks, CA: Sage Publications, 1996.

Percy, Larry, ed. *Marketing Research That Pays Off: Case Histories of Marketing Research Leading to Success in the Marketplace.* New York: Haworth Press, 1997.

MARKET SEGMENTATION

Market segmentation is the process of identifying key groups or segments within the general market that share specific characteristics and consumer habits. Once the market is broken into segments, companies can develop **advertising** programs for each segment, focus advertising on one or two segments or niches, or develop new products to appeal to one or more of the segments. Companies often favor this method of **marketing** to the one-size-fits-all mass marketing approach, because it allows them to target specific groups that might not be reached by mass marketing programs.

To identify segments, marketers examine consumers' interests, tastes, preferences, and socioeconomic characteristics in order to determine their patterns of consumption and how they will respond to various **marketing strategies**. The primary information marketers seek is why consumers purchase specific products or services but not others. Catalog retailers and **direct-marketing** firms make up some of the key users of market segmentation, although many other kinds of companies and organizations use this technique.

Market segmentation—also called micromarketing—simplifies the marketing process, because it allows marketers to concentrate their advertising on groups of consumers who share significant characteristics. Marketers, therefore, can produce specific advertising geared towards specific segments; otherwise marketers have to create very general advertising and hope that it will appeal to a diverse audience. Market segmentation also can be more efficient than traditional marketing techniques such as product differentiation. Because marketers focus their advertising on specific segments, they can expect better results from each segment than they could expect from these consumer groups if treated as a whole.

Catalog clothing stores, for example, convincingly illustrate these advantages of market segmentation. If a catalog marketer provides both men's and women's clothes, it would have to produce a very large catalog to include all of its merchandise, which would cost a lot to produce and mail. By sending such a catalog to all potential customers, the company could fail to capture the attention of many potential customers simply by having a man on the cover and sending it to women or a woman on the cover and sending it to men. At one point catalog marketers relied on this approach. But contemporary catalog retailers produce numerous versions of their catalogs designed for specific market segments, such as men between 20 and 35, women between 20 and 35, men between 35 and 50, and women between 35 and 50.

Market segmentation, however, works effectively only for certain kinds of products and services. First, to determine whether to segment a market, marketers must find out if the market can be identified and measured, which entails determining which consumers belong to specific market segments. Second, marketers must determine if the segments are large enough to be profitable. While marketers can easily divide the total market into smaller groups, these groups might be so small that they do not justify the expenses associated with market segmentation. Third, marketers must be able to reach the segments through their advertising. If the members of a particular segment do not share interest in a common magazine or television show, for example, then marketers have no way of reaching the segment and so the segment is superfluous.

Fourth, marketers must gauge the responsiveness of the segments and find out if a proposed segment would likely respond to a marketing campaign. If it is not probable that a segment will react to a promotion, then the segment is not useful. Fifth, marketers must determine if the segments will change in the near future. Since it takes time to prepare a marketing strategy for specific segment and since it takes time for market segmentation to be profitable, creating segments where consumer needs and wants are likely to change would not be productive.

SEGMENTATION BASES

The market can be divided into segments by using four ''segmentation bases'': psychographic, behavioristic, geographic, and demographic bases. Psychographic and behavioristic bases are used to determine preferences and demand for a product and advertising content, while geographic and demographic criteria are used to determine product design and regional focus.

Psychographic bases include personality traits such as consumer attitudes, lifestyles, and interests, while behavioristic bases include attitudes towards products such as the frequency of use, brand loyalty, benefits sought in a product, and readiness to purchase the product.

Geographic bases focus on preferences contingent on regional factors, such as region (e.g., North or South), county, population density, urban or rural location, and climate. Demographics include personal characteristics such as gender, age, marital status, social attributes (such as ethnicity and religion), and income level.

Other bases for segmentation include occasions and consumer knowledge of and interest in particular brands. Marketers can use various occasions such as marriage, graduation, anniversaries, birthdays, and holidays to promote products. Marketers can advertise an assortment of products including candy, cards, and flowers to various segments based on occasions. In addition, marketers can create segments based on consumer knowledge and interest, targeting novices and veterans with different promotions for their products or brands. But whatever segmentation bases marketers use, they analyze their data and group consumers in order to determine consumer behavior.

THE SEGMENTATION PROCESS

Once a company has gathered information from these segmentation bases, it must decide how to divide the market, bearing in mind that market segmentation seeks to minimize the differences within a segment and maximize the differences among segments. Consequently, depending on the product or service to be marketed, simple divisions along age, gender, or geographic lines alone may yield segments that are too vague to be of use. Instead, marketers may have to consider several characteristics or clusters of characteristics in order to divide the market into useful segments. When considering beer consumption, for example, marketers must look at both age and gender: the majority of beer drinkers are both young and male.

Hence, to begin segmenting the market, marketing managers must select the segmentation bases they will use to develop the segments, depending on the products or services to be marketed. Marketers may select a few segmentation bases they believe are the most relevant at the outset and develop market segments using them. On the other hand, they may compile a large array of information using all the segmentation bases and use this information to group consumers in various segments.

Next, marketers conduct any primary market analysis they may need, by preparing questionnaires and samples and by assessing the response to them. Using this information, marketers try to determine the most fruitful segments—the ones with greatest similarities within them. Because this process can be labor-intensive and require advanced knowledge of statistics, companies often rely on outside firms or **artificial intelligence** technology to produce meaningful market segments.

Once relevant, stable, reachable, profitable market segments are established, marketers can target the segments they believe will offer the best opportunities for growth given their products and resources and the ones they believe that correspond to the products being marketed the best. Finally, marketers can develop and launch advertising campaigns that appeal to the various segments.

Companies tend to choose the largest segments, although the segments with the most consumers are not always the most profitable and usually have the most **competition**. Consequently, marketers might benefit from considering targeting smaller segments or segments ignored by competitors, such as low-income consumers, which is frequently referred to as ''niche marketing.''

METHODS OF SEGMENTATION

Companies can implement market segmentation in three general ways: through differentiation, concentration, and atomization. Differentiation refers to marketing products or services to different market segments based on each segment's individual needs as well as to developing new products for different segments. For example, a **computer** maker could market its products to home users, corporations, **small businesses**, and government agencies, thereby differentiating the needs of each of these four segments and appropriately targeting them.

A company also may opt to target just one segment of the market, employing the market segmentation method of concentration. After considering various segmentation bases and conducting research, a company might find that its competitors are not reaching specific segments and decide to target this segment or niche exclusively. A computer maker, for instance, could concentrate solely on the home-user segment of the market and ignore the needs of the other segments. To do so, the computer maker would have to offer products that meet home-user needs at prices these consumers could afford. Since concentrated marketing costs less than differentiated marketing, it may appeal to small businesses in particular.

Atomization involves dividing the market into very small segments, which may include a single customer in some cases. Although rare, some companies offering expensive and highly customized products or services rely on this method. If a computer maker focused on government clients, it might have to build special computers for various government branches based on their individual needs. Some marketing analysts predict that atomization will grow in the coming millennium as companies strive to offer more individualized service.

When choosing a method of market segmentation, marketers must take several factors into consideration. First, they must select a method consistent with company resources, because differentiated marketing, for example, has a significant **cost** and some companies may not be able to afford it. Second, marketers must consider the product line they are trying to sell. If the product line is limited, marketers usually choose the concentrated marketing method. If the product line is expansive, however, then marketers usually opt for the differentiated marketing method.

After choosing a method of market segmentation, marketers must integrate the method into an overall marketing strategy. The marketing strategy will try to make the target product or service appeal to the target segment through an advertising campaign developed based on segmentation information such as age, gender, or location. Marketers also consider what a company's strategic position in a market is—e.g., if it is a computer supplier to home users or businesses—and create a marketing program that will help a company achieve or maintain this position. If the segment is properly defined for a specific product or service, then developing promotional strategies and reaching the target segment should be relatively easy. The information used to help create the market segments should help marketers choose among promotional techniques (e.g., direct marketing, advertising, publicity, and **sales promotion**), pricing strategies, and distribution strategies. This information also should help marketers choose among various advertising media.

Companies using market segmentation techniques typically strive to maintain a relationship with their customers, instead just making an isolated sale. After collecting a large amount of information about their customers, marketers can plan promotions and products that will appeal to various segments over a long time by determining what products a segment wants in the future and offering them at the appropriate time.

SEE ALSO: Catalog Marketing

[Karl Heil]

FURTHER READING:

Cohen, Eric. "How to Target Smarter." *Target Marketing,* May 1998, 58.

Haim, Alexander, and Charles D. Schewe. *The Portable MBA in Marketing.* New York: John Wiley & Sons, 1992.

Moschis, George P., Lee Euehun, and Anil Mathur. "Targeting the Mature Market: Opportunities and Challenges." *Journal of Consumer Marketing,* fall/winter 1997, 282.

Sandhusen, Richard L. *Barron's Business Review Series: Marketing.* 2nd ed. Barron's Educational Series, 1993.

Weinstein, Art. *Market Segmentation.* Chicago: Probus Publishing, 1987.

MARKET VALUE

Market value is the concept of how much something—a business, a piece of property, or anything of value—is presently worth under relatively free conditions of exchange. For tax and legal purposes, the standard definition of market value, or so-called fair market value (FMV), was articulated in the IRS Revenue Ruling 59-60, where it is equated with the price paid for a given property under the construct of a willing buyer and willing seller, both with full knowledge of pertinent facts, and neither being under a compulsion to act. Put simply, market value is the price at which goods trade in an open and competitive market.

For many types of property, the market value is an easily observed quantum. It can be examined by reference to comparable assets that have sold under similar circumstances, such as time, location, condition, terms, and the nature of buyer and seller. In the case of **commodities**, one need only look at the Chicago Board of Trade figures to determine at what price crude oil, cotton, pork bellies, etc. are trading on a given day. Similarly, for financial assets, such as shares in publicly traded companies, the New York Stock Exchange, **Nasdaq Stock Market**, or American Stock Exchange stock quote listings can be consulted. The same is true for many debt securities, including corporate, municipal, state, and government **bonds**.

A loaf of bread, a pair of socks, and various consumer products have observable market prices which can be easily determined by sampling prices charged at various retail stores. The same is true, to a lesser extent, about goods sold in other venues. Because the information about competitive products and competitive dealers is often less than perfect, different buyers may pay different amounts for the same or similar things. The precision with which market value is defined diminishes as the property becomes more unique and when the relevant information is limited.

Real estate is an example of how apparently similar properties can fetch dramatically different prices. Each parcel of real estate is in some way unique from all others, and the circumstances under which a given buyer approaches the negotiation may be quite varied. Some potential buyers may have a desperate need to buy soon or an emotional attachment to the neighborhood that may encourage them to pay more than could be obtained from another buyer. Thus, a seller may list the property at an unrealistically high price and get ''lucky'' with a particular buyer at the right time and place. Technically, the high trading price establishes a ''market value.'' If the buyer needed to sell shortly thereafter, however, he might find that the property can only be sold for somewhat lower than he recently paid. This price disparity has sparked a philosophical argument over which is the true market value.

The above discussion highlights this fact about determining market value: it is easier to quantify and support a market valuation for generic, non-unique property than for unique property. An easily understood example is the case of a new car versus the same model several years later. At the time of a new car sale, identical cars can be found (or ordered) and picked up by buyers with zero miles, no dents or dings and a full manufacturer's warranty. Here the variance of actual transactions should be low; that is, the market values should be within a tight tolerance of some mean price. Four years later, a subset of the same group of cars may be for sale in the used car market. With used cars, many variables can affect value. The cars' condition and mileage can vary. Availability is more spotty. Therefore, uniqueness is higher, knowledge is less perfect, and comparing competitive options is not as readily done. As a result, the variance of prices paid for the same model used car, at the same point in time, will be much wider about the mean.

For publicly traded companies, one form of market value (more accurately termed market capitalization) is the total value of all outstanding shares of **common stock** at the current share price. This is often different from how the same business would be valued if it were actually being acquired by another company, when frequently shareholders of the acquired company are given by the acquirer some form of premium over the current trading price of their shares. Alternatively, if the shares being valued are in a privately held company, the stock market price (of a comparable company) may need to be discounted to reflect the lack of marketability, sometimes known as illiquidity.

SEE ALSO: Valuation

[Christopher C. Barry]

FURTHER READING:

Jones, Gary E., and Dirk Van Dyke. *The Business of Business Valuation.* New York: McGraw-Hill, 1998.

Yegge, Wilbur M. *A Basic Guide for Valuing a Company.* New York: John Wiley & Sons, 1996.

MARKETING

Marketing is a very general term that refers to the commercial functions involved in transferring goods and services from a producer to a consumer. It is commonly associated with endeavors such as branding, selling, and **advertising**, but it also encompasses activities and processes related to production, product development, distribution, and many other functions. Furthermore, on a less tangible level, marketing facilitates the distribution of goods and services within a society, particularly in free markets. Evidence of the pivotal role that marketing plays in free markets is the vast amount of resources it consumes: about 50 percent of all consumer dollars, in fact, pay for marketing-related activities.

This text recognizes a chief delineation of the subject of marketing, micro- and macro-marketing. The latter pertains to the flow of goods and services within and between societies. Micro-marketing, in contrast, encompasses specific activities performed by an organization as it attempts to transfer its particular offerings to consumers, primarily through targeted marketing techniques. Case studies and a discussion of multinational marketing nuances complement the very basic review of micro and macro principles.

BACKGROUND

Marketing, as a means of transferring goods and services from suppliers to consumers, predates recorded history. It was born by the transition from a purely subsistence-based society, in which families and tribes produced their own consumables, to more specialized and cooperative societal forms. The simple act of trading a piece of meat for a tool, for example, entails some degree of marketing. The term ''marketing,'' of course, derives from the word ''market,'' a group of sellers and buyers that cooperate to exchange goods and services. The term ''marketing'' in the modern business sense is believed to have come into use during the first decade of the 20th century.

ERAS OF MARKETING. Some scholars and marketing texts have divided the history of marketing into three and sometimes four distinct eras corresponding to the main emphases and practices of those times. Periods commonly cited include, in chronological order, the production era, the sales era, the marketing era, and in some cases, the relationship era.

The production era refers to the period leading up to the 1930s or, more broadly, the pre-World War II period, when emphasis was placed on simply producing a satisfactory product and informing potential customers about it through catalogs, brochures, and advertising. In the sales era, corresponding roughly to the decade or so after the war, companies reportedly recruited customers more actively by trying to develop persuasive arguments or pitches to encourage customers to choose their products. By the late 1950s and early 1960s this evolved further, the theory goes, into the marketing era, when companies grew increasingly sensitive and responsive to consumer preferences and to exactly what motivated purchasing decisions. Finally, in the 1980s, some argue that the notion of relationship marketing began to take hold as a guiding tenet, where companies moved away from courting simple transactions and toward facilitating more complex long term relationships with customers. The concept of relationship marketing is still quite popular today.

Although such era distinctions derive from classic marketing texts from as early as the 1960s, some observers believe the differences are overstated because of the particular marketing fads and vocabulary of more recent times, when there has been a wish by some corporate marketers to ''reinvent'' how they approach their craft and demonstrate that their newer practices are a departure from the past. These scholars argue that while the specific tools and vehicles of marketing have evolved over time, there has in fact been greater continuity in the historical approaches to marketing (at least within the 20th century) than these era designations suggest. In particular, several scholars have concluded that cultivating enduring relationships, purportedly the newest phase in marketing, has existed as a priority at large companies since at least the 1920s.

MACRO-MARKETING

Macro-marketing refers to the social process that directs the flow of goods and services from producer to consumer—an economic system that determines what and how much is to be produced and distributed by whom, when, and to whom. Economists and marketing scholars often identify three broad macro-marketing spheres and eight functions within them that make up the economic process:

A. *Exchange*
   1. *Buying* refers to consumers seeking and evaluating goods and services.
   2. *Selling* involves promoting the offering.

B. *Distribution and Logistics*
   3. *Transporting* refers to the movement of goods from one place to another.
   4. *Storing* involves holding goods until customers need them.

C. *Support and Facilitation*
   5. *Standardization and grading* entails sorting products according to uses, markets, and other shared attributes.
   6. *Financing* delivers the cash and credit needed to perform the first five functions.
   7. *Risk-taking* involves bearing the uncertainties that are part of the marketing process.
   8. *Market information* refers to the gathering, analyzing, and distributing of the data necessary to execute the other marketing functions.

All of the eight basic macro-marketing functions exist in some form in both command economies and in free markets. In both systems, in fact, consumers have different needs, preferences, and patterns of resource allocation. Similarly, producers have different resources, goals, and capabilities. Although virtually every society has some sort of marketing system that serves to match this heterogeneous supply and demand, the success of any macro-marketing system is judged by its ability to accomplish the society's objectives, whether the chief goal is equality of wealth, as in a command economy, or the greatest good for the greatest number regardless of equal distribution, as is the case in a free market system.

In a command economy, government planners perform most of the marketing function for society. The planners tell producers what and how much to provide and at what price. The goal of the producers is primarily to meet government quotas. Such a system may work well in a small and simple economic system or during a crisis like a war. In a larger economy, however, the process of matching supply and demand tends to become so extraordinarily complex that planners are simply overwhelmed. The complicated dynamics of consumer demands and the capabilities of suppliers elude planners, the result being that many consumer needs are left unfulfilled. Nevertheless, the marketing function may still achieve a primary goal, such as equal distribution of wealth.

In a free-market economy the marketing function is carried out by individual consumers and producers who essentially act as economic planners by means of numerous day-to-day decisions. In most modern economies, consumers register their purchasing decisions with dollars. Providers of goods and services respond primarily to consumer input in determining what and how much to provide, and at what price. They are motivated by competition rather than incentives to meet government quotas.

The marketing function of free market economies also tends to be characterized by a greater emphasis on middlemen, or parties that specialize in trade rather than production. They bring buyers and sellers together and charge a fee or commission for their services. Likewise, facilitators serve free market economies by providing producers with adjunct services. Examples of facilitators include advertising agencies, transportation firms, banks and other financial institutions, and market research companies.

Although the marketing function in a free economy is generally effective when judged by its ability to provide the greatest good for the greatest number, it may fail to achieve other goals. For example, some members of society may fail to compete effectively, thus reducing their dollar ''vote'' in the economy and diminishing their ability to acquire basic necessities. As another example, some producers may profit by providing goods and services, such as addictive drugs, that are detrimental to society as a whole.

Critics of free market systems cite several other flaws. Advertising, for instance, can be used to promote products that are unhealthy, bad for the environment, or cause consumers to make unwise decisions by clouding the facts. Also, the extreme emphasis on promotion consumes vast amounts of resources that are not put to any tangible consumer use. Furthermore, some people believe that the marketing function in a free economy leads to materialism, or an emphasis on things rather than social values.

To overcome some of the negative effects that may result from purely free market economies, most societies without a command economy adopt a market-directed economy that reflects a compromise between the two systems. Market-directed economies use government constraints to temper free markets. In the United States, for example, the federal government sets interest rates, creates import and export rules, regulates advertising medium, mandates safety and quality controls, and even limits wages and prices in some instances.

MICRO-MARKETING

Micro-marketing is the formal term for marketing activities in specific businesses; it is what most people mean when they use the word ''marketing.'' Micro-marketing refers to the activities performed by the providers of goods and services within a macro-marketing system. Those organizations use various marketing techniques to accomplish objectives related to profits, market share, cash flow, and other economic factors that can enhance the organization's well being and position in the marketplace. The micro-marketing function within an entity is commonly referred to as marketing management. Marketing managers strive to get their organizations to anticipate and accurately determine the needs and wants of customer groups. Afterward they seek to effectively respond with a flow of need satisfying goods and services. They are typically charged with planning, implementing, and then measuring the effectiveness of all marketing activities.

Academic discussions of the marketing management function are often presented within the context of behaviorist Abraham Maslow's famous hierarchy of needs. Maslow (1908-1970) posited that all peopled respond first to vital physical needs, such as food and shelter. Only after those needs have been met, he argued, do people strive to meet social and emotional needs that are important to their psychological well-being. Examples of those needs are security, belonging, and self-esteem. It is these basic biological needs that shape the buying behavior of all consumers.

Because the way that people choose to satisfy their needs can be shaped by past experiences, different groups and individuals may have different ''wants'' to satisfy the same need. Comprehension of this basic tenet of human behavior reveals an important aspect of the micro-marketing function—that producers are not capable of creating or shaping basic needs, but rather achieve marketing success by influencing wants. In other words, a chief goal of a marketing manager's job is to stimulate customers' ''wants'' for a product or service by persuading the consumer that the offering can help them better satisfy one or more of their needs.

An implication of Maslow's theory for marketing managers is that customers view products and benefits differently; customers don't buy products (services), they buy the benefits that they believe they will get from them. For instance, when trying to get a consumer to purchase an automobile, marketers must remember that they are selling an image. Car buyers with strong needs for social acceptance might seek a prestigious looking automobile, for example, or be willing to pay more for a particular name brand. This product-versus-benefit element is best evidenced by the strategic marketing of relatively homogenous goods, such as fruit juices, which are differentiated from competing products in the marketplace almost solely on the basis of perceived benefits attached to the product through advertising and promotion.

THE TARGET MARKETING CONCEPT

Micro-marketing encompasses a profusion of related activities and responsibilities. Marketing managers must carefully design their marketing plans to ensure that they complement related production, distribution, and financial constraints. They must also allow for constant adaptation to changing markets and economic conditions. Perhaps the core function of a marketing manager, however, is to identify a specific market, or group of consumers, and then deliver products and promotions that ultimately maximize the profit potential of that targeted market. Often, it is only by carefully selecting and wooing a specific group that an organization can attain profit margins sufficient to allow it to continue to compete in the marketplace.

For instance, a manufacturer of fishing equipment would not randomly market its product to the entire U.S. population. Instead, it would likely conduct research to determine which customers would be most likely to purchase its offerings. It could then more efficiently spend its limited resources in an effort to persuade members of its target group(s). Perhaps it would target males in the Midwest between the ages of 18 and 35. The company may even strive to further maximize the profitability of its target market through **market segmentation**, whereby the group is further broken down by age, income, zip code, or other factors indicative of buying patterns. Advertisements and promotions could then be tailored for each segment of the target market.

There are infinite ways to satisfy the wants, and subsequently the needs, of a target market. For example, in the case of a product the packaging can be designed in different sizes and colors, or the product itself can be altered to appeal to different personality types or age groups. Producers can also alter the warranty or durability of the good or provide different levels of follow-up service. Other influences, such as distribution and sales methods, licensing strategies, and advertising media may also play an important role. It is the responsibility of the marketing manager to take all of these factors into account and to devise a cohesive marketing program that will appeal to the customer.

THE FOUR Ps

The different elements of micro-marketing strategy can be divided into four basic decision areas that marketing managers may use to devise an overall marketing strategy for a single product or a line of products, often dubbed the ''four Ps'':

- product (concept and attributes)
- place (distribution)
- promotion
- price

These four decision groups represent all of the variables that a company can control. But those decisions must be made within the context of outside variables that are not entirely under the control of the company, such as competition, economic and technological changes, the political and legal environment, and cultural and social factors.

PRODUCT. Marketing decisions related to the product (or service) involve conceiving of and realizing the right product for the selected target group. This typically encompasses **market research** and data analysis to determine how well the product meets the wants and needs of the target group. Numerous determinants factor into the final choice of a product and its presentation. A completely new product, for example, will entail much higher promotional costs, whereas a product that is simply an improved version of an existing item likely will make use of its predecessor's image. A pivotal consideration in product planning and development is branding, whereby the good or service is positioned in the market according to its brand name. Other important elements of the complex product planning and management process may include selection of features, warranty, related product lines, and post-sale service levels.

PLACE. Considerations about place, the second major functional group, relate to actually getting the good or service to the target market through the right channels, at the right time, and in the proper quantity. Strategies related to place may utilize middlemen and facilitators with expertise in joining buyers and sellers, and they may also encompass various distribution channels, including retail, wholesale, catalog, and others. Marketing managers must also devise a means of transporting the goods to the selected sales channels. Decisions related to place typically play an important role in determining the degree of vertical integration in a company or how many activities in the distribution chain are owned and operated by the manufacturer. For example, some companies elect to own their trucks, the stores in which their goods are sold, and perhaps even the raw resources used to manufacture their goods. On the other hand, the company may determine that its strengths are not in physical distribution, and it may contract other firms to perform all distribution-related activities.

PROMOTION. Decisions about promotion, the third target market functional area, relate to sales, advertising, **public relations** and other activities that communicate information intended to influence consumer behavior. Often promotions are also necessary to influence the behavior of retailers and others who resell or distribute the product. Three major types of promotion typically integrated into a target market strategy are personal selling, mass selling, and sales promotions. Personal selling, which refers to face-to-face or telephone sales, usually provides immediate feedback for the company about the product and instills greater confidence in customers. Mass selling encompasses advertising on traditional mass media, such as television, radio, direct mail, and newspapers, and is beneficial because of its broad scope. It also entails the use of unpaid media exposure, known as publicity, such as feature articles about a company or product in a magazine or related interviews on television talk shows. Finally, **sales promotion** efforts include free samples, coupons, contests, and other miscellaneous marketing tactics. These approaches are used to stimulate interest in products, encourage first-time trials, or help build brand loyalty, among other objectives. While such tactics have generally been shown effective at increasing unit sales, their overall impact is debatable because they can be seen as needlessly subsidizing or rewarding customers who would have bought the product anyway.

PRICE. Determining price, the fourth major marketing activity, entails using discounts and long-term pricing goals, as well as considering competitive, demographic, and geographic influences. From the buyer's perspective, the price must be within certain boundaries (especially the upper limit) and must be commensurate with the perceived value of the item. For the producer, the price of a product or service generally must at least meet some minimum level that will cover a company's cost of producing and delivering its offering; however, even if a company were to price its items exactly at the break-even point on a unit basis, there is no guarantee there will be sufficient demand at that price. The break-even price at the aggregate level will, of course, vary with how many units are sold when the sum of fixed and variable costs for production and overhead are considered. Thus, pricing is an implicit (and sometimes explicit) negotiation between supplier and customer, with competition as an intervening factor that colors the nature of this negotiation.

A firm would logically price a product at the level that maximizes profits. While this seems obvious, it is often difficult for companies to determine the profit-maximizing price because they can't be certain how strong the demand is for their products at a given price level or how a competitor will respond to a price change. Cutting prices to stimulate sales volume, for example, can simply be a ''race to the bottom'' if competitors respond in kind, diminishing profits for both without improving either's competitive position. In general, depending on the exact nature of demand, such as whether it is relatively elastic (fickle) or inelastic (constant), and the availability of substitute products (competition), profits can be maximized either by (1) pricing the product high and moving fewer units, or (2) pricing the product lower and selling more units. In rare cases, such as for certain perceived luxury goods, increased prices can actually lead to higher unit volume, but this is usually regarded as an exception to the norm.

Still, there are a number of other factors that influence pricing, both financial and nonfinancial. In a few cases pricing decisions may be largely out of a firm's control, such as when government controls are in effect or when items (usually raw materials and agricultural commodities) are sold through a competitive bidding system. In most cases, though, a company has a high degree of control over its pricing, at least in a formal sense; in practice it will still be confined by market forces, as it can't set a price that no one will pay.

The price that a company selects for its products will generally vary according to its long-term marketing strategy. For example, a company may underprice its product in the hopes of building market share and ensuring its competitive presence, or simply to generate a desired level of cash flow (however, in some cases extreme underpricing can be illegal, especially in international trading settings). Another producer may price its goods extremely high in the hopes of conveying to the consumer that it is offering a premium product. Another reason a firm might offer a product at a very high price is to discount the good slowly in an effort to maximize the dollars available from consumers willing to pay different prices for the good, a practice known as market skimming. In any case, price is used as a tool to achieve comprehensive marketing goals.

COMPETITIVE STRATEGIES

Often times, decisions about product, place, promotion, and price will be dictated by the competitive stance that a firm assumes in its target market. According to Michael Porter's well-received book *Competitive Strategy* (1980), the three most common competitive strategies are

- low-cost supplier
- differentiation/uniqueness
- niche development

Porter believed that the strategy a company chooses is shaped in large part by its current position within its industry and by the industry's current stage of development. Competitors in mature industries, for example, are more likely to find market advantages through niche strategies because the broad markets are already tapped out.

LOWEST COST. Companies that adopt a low-cost supplier strategy are usually characterized by a vigorous pursuit of efficiency and cost controls. A company that manufactures a low-tech or commodity product, such as wood paneling, would likely adopt this approach. Such firms compete by offering a better value than their competitors, accumulating market share, and focusing on high-volume and fast inventory turnover.

DIFFERENTIATION/UNIQUENESS. Companies that adhere to a differentiation strategy achieve market success by offering a unique product or service. They often rely on brand loyalty, specialized distribution channels or service offerings, or patent protection to insulate them from competitors. Because of their uniqueness, they are able to achieve higher-than-average profit margins, making them less reliant on high sales volume and extreme efficiency. A company that markets proprietary medical devices would likely assume a differentiation strategy.

NICHE DEVELOPMENT. Firms that pursue a niche market strategy succeed by focusing all of their efforts on a very narrow segment of an overall target market. They strive to prosper by dominating their selected niche. Such companies are able to overcome competition by aggressively protecting market share and by orienting every action and decision toward the service of its select group. An example of a company that might employ a niche strategy would be a firm that produced floor coverings only for extremely upscale commercial applications.

BUSINESS VERSUS CONSUMER MARKETS

An important micro-marketing delineation is that between industrial and consumer markets. Marketing strategies and activities related to transferring goods and services to industrial and business customers are generally very different from those used to lure other consumers. The industrial, or intermediate, market is made up of buyers who purchase for the purpose of creating other goods and services. Thus, their needs are different from those of general consumers. Buyers in this group include manufacturers and service firms, wholesalers and retailers, governments, and nonprofit organizations.

In many ways, it is often easier to market to a target group of intermediate or industrial customers. They typically have clearly defined needs and are buying the product for a very specific purpose. They are also usually less sensitive to price and are more willing to take the time to absorb information about goods that may help them do their job better. Nonetheless, marketing to industrial customers can be complicated. For instance, members of an organization usually must purchase goods through a multi-step process involving several decision makers. Importantly, business buyers will often be extremely cautious about trying a new product or a new company because they don't want to be responsible for supporting what could be construed as a poor decision if the good or service does not live up to the organization's expectations.

A chief difference between marketing to intermediate and consumer markets is that consumers are typically considering purchasing goods and services that they might enjoy but don't really need. As a result, they are more difficult to sell to than are business buyers. Consumers are generally

- less sophisticated than intermediate buyers
- less willing to spend time absorbing individual marketing messages of interest to them
- more sensitive to the price of a good or service

However, consumers typically make a buying decision on their own, or at least through an informal decision-making process involving family members or friends, and are much more likely to buy on impulse than are industrial customers.

Despite the differences, a dominant similarity between marketing to both intermediate buyers and consumers is that both groups ultimately make purchases based on personal needs, as described earlier. Consumers tend to react strongly to a desire to belong, have security, feel high self-esteem, and enjoy freedom and status. Similarly, business and industrial consumers react more strongly to motivators such as fear of loss, fear of the unknown, the desire to avoid stress or hardship, and security in their organizational role.

MICRO-MARKETING CASE STUDIES

An example of micro-marketing that demonstrates the importance of the marketing function in relation to other business functions, such as production and distribution, is Rubbermaid, Inc.'s strategy. Rubbermaid continued to produce and sell a line of plastic home products for several decades in an industry characterized as undynamic and even stagnant. Nevertheless, Rubbermaid's savvy marketing strategy allowed it to post continuous gains in sales and market share during the 1980s when the company's sales rocketed more than sixfold. The company achieved its stellar gains by focusing on new product introductions and by tailoring its existing products to meet new consumer wants and needs. While it amassed market share, Rubbermaid managed to post strong profit margins by charging high prices. It commanded premium prices because it had positioned its products as unique and high in quality in comparison to competing products. An emphasis on a field sales force and a high level of service to its retailers augmented Rubbermaid's overall stratagem.

The success of Domino's Pizza, Inc. during the 1980s shows how a company that targets a particular market and is sensitive to its customer's needs can achieve success in the marketplace. Tom S. Monaghan opened his first store in 1960 with $500 and grew his tiny enterprise to a chain of four stores by 1965. Strong competition and the lack of a cohesive marketing strategy, however, forced him into bankruptcy. Monaghan researched pizza consumers and entered the pizza business again in 1971. He decided to target residential customers between the ages of 18 and 34 who preferred to have pizzas delivered to their door. He found that consumers were generally dissatisfied with the taste and reliability of delivery available from other pizza shops. As a result, Monaghan developed a pizza that his customers liked and then promised delivery within 30 minutes from the time the order was placed. His restaurants were strictly delivery and carry-out. By the 1990s, the chain had expanded internationally with thousands of outlets worldwide and sales in the billions of dollars.

One of the most dynamic and telling of all marketing case studies is the U.S. ''cola wars.'' Those battles, which have been waged by major soft-drink manufacturers since World War II, demonstrate the effects of competition on marketing strategies in a free market. Although numerous soft-drink makers competed during the 1950s and 1960s, by the late 1980s the industry had consolidated to just six companies that controlled more than 80 percent of the entire market. The two fiercest competitors, Coca Cola Co. and PepsiCo, Inc. each spend hundreds of millions of dollars each year to promote their products and to avoid loss of market share. Pepsi bludgeoned Coke during the early 1980s with a taste-test promotion. It challenged consumers to taste both colas, which were not labeled, and select the one they believed tasted better. Despite the taste test, both companies have emphasized an emotional appeal to consumers, touting their drinks as fun, youth-oriented, or ''American,'' for example.

Marketing efforts at General Electric (GE) exhibit some of the differences between marketing to industrial and consumer markets. Although GE is generally associated with its production of consumer goods, particularly appliances, only about 25 percent of GE's sales are garnered from consumer markets. Most of its profits come from sales of power generation, heavy industrial, and aerospace equipment. The general public still views GE as a provider of appliances, however, because the company's marketing strategy entails promoting that image in the mass media and through various consumer promotions. In contrast, GE markets its core industrial and technical products primarily through a direct sales force, which consists mostly of highly trained technical sales engineers. GE's marketing program also stresses an extensive lobbying effort at the federal level to secure government contracts and influence policies related to defense spending.

MARKETING FAILURES

Despite a company's best attempts to research and devise effective marketing plans, even the largest and most astute marketing divisions sometimes commit serious marketing mistakes that fail to lure customers and ultimately cost their companies millions of dollars. Such flops illustrate the subjective and complex nature of the micro-marketing process and often show how influences outside of the company's control can play an integral role in the success of any marketing endeavor.

One well-known marketing failure occurred at the Korvette chain of discount department stores. Started in 1948 by Eugene Ferkauf, Korvette grew during the mid-20th century by undercutting department store prices by 10 to 40 percent on appliances and other heavy goods. Ferkauf, who grew Korvette to more than $700 million in revenues by 1965, is credited with revolutionizing merchandising and retail marketing techniques and paving the way for mass discount merchandisers like Kmart and Wal-Mart. But Ferkauf began to change the market position of his stores in the mid-1960s. He tried to upgrade the image of the chain by bringing in higher-priced merchandise, food, and clothing. The new products did not complement Korvette's existing distribution and management infrastructure, however, causing the profitability of the stores to lag. At the same time, moreover, Korvette failed to respond to increased competition in the discount industry. By the late 1960s, Korvette's market presence was quickly fading and Ferkauf was forced out of his management position.

The failure of the Burger Chef hamburger chain to mimic the success achieved by McDonald's exemplifies the importance of a comprehensive and well-executed marketing plan. General Foods purchased the 700-store Burger Chef chain in 1967 with the intent of growing it into a national fast-food powerhouse. By 1969 General Foods had added nearly 600 stores to the chain, primarily through franchising. Unfortunately, the rapid expansion only exacerbated underlying problems that plagued the chain.

Burger Chef developed a red and yellow sign and a menu that was a near clone of its leading competitor. Despite Burger Chef's attempt to copy the vastly successful McDonald's, it lacked key marketing elements that had made McDonald's so successful. Its sign, for example, lacked the distinction of McDonald's golden arches, and its chain of restaurants lacked uniformity, thus reflecting an image of inconsistency to consumers.

Furthermore, Burger Chef had failed to concentrate enough restaurants in a single area, which would have allowed them to increase the efficiency of local promotions. Most importantly, McDonald's had centered its marketing efforts on a creed of quality, service, and cleanliness, three virtues that Burger Chef failed to adequately imitate. In fewer than four years, General Foods amassed a loss of $83 million from its Burger Chef operations. Many of its stores soon closed.

Perhaps the most widely identified marketing flop was Coca-Cola Co.'s introduction of New Coke in the mid-1980s, an effort to diminish gains made by its arch rival, Pepsi, in the youth market. Coke changed its long-revered cola recipe in an attempt to boost interest in its product and to appeal to younger soft-drink consumers who were seeking a sweeter drink. Coca-Cola, long known for its canny marketing prowess, seemingly misread public reaction to the modification. Outraged at the company's tinkering with what they viewed as an American icon, many consumers rejected the change. Fewer than three months after embarking on its new version, Coca-Cola decided to bring back its old ''Classic'' Coke, which was soon outselling New Coke by a margin of 10 to 1. Coca-Cola apparently failed to comprehend both the historical value of, and consumer loyalty to, Coke, both of which it had spent millions of dollars trying to cultivate during much of the 20th century. Still, some marketing specialists have advanced the alternative view that the New Coke episode did in fact help significantly revitalize the brand because it drew intense scrutiny to the product and made consumers more conscious of its uniqueness and their loyalty to it.

MULTINATIONAL MARKETING

As the rapid growth experienced by the U.S. economy during the post World War II boom years faded during and after the 1970s, many companies began to focus on overseas markets for continued growth. While the basic goals of global marketing are the same as marketing a product or service domestically, important differences exist. For example, a product that sells well in the United States may require an entirely different marketing plan to achieve success in another country. General Motors Corp. discovered this when it tried to sell its Nova model in Mexico, where the company learned that the word ''Nova'' in Spanish is similar to ''no go.''

Besides obvious language barriers, cultural subtleties in a country or region can easily thwart a marketing program that has achieved success elsewhere. Other risks associated with global marketing include currency fluctuations, political instability, and unforeseen legal ramifications. Furthermore, the lack of existing market research in many countries and the lack of means to gather information poses a serious roadblock for many would-be competitors. Nevertheless, rampant market growth in emerging countries, as well as relatively untapped markets in established economies, often provide great incentives for U.S. marketers to risk overseas ventures.

Marketers may utilize several different approaches to market their goods to foreign target groups. A common, relatively low-risk strategy is exporting goods through distributors and importers. This technique reduces the company's participation in a foreign country and essentially limits marketing initiatives to various middlemen and their buyers. Retailers and wholesalers in the host country can then select appropriate marketing media, utilize established distribution channels, set prices, and handle other localized marketing endeavors. A second marketing strategy is licensing and franchising, whereby a company sells the right to manufacture or sell its products to a foreign producer. Although this involves a minimal commitment, the company often maintains limited control over the company that purchases the license.

Joint ventures with enterprises in the host country, a third method of overseas marketing, entail a greater commitment on the part of the company trying to sells its goods. Joint ventures reduce political and cultural risks, however, and may help the company compete against local producers. Finally, some manufacturers choose to produce and market their products independently through a wholly owned subsidiary in another country. Although this last method exposes the organization to greater risk and represents a significant commitment to business in the country or region, it allows more control over operations and provides greater profit opportunities should the venture succeed.

Regardless of the ways a company selects to market its products or services abroad, once it makes the decision to go global it typically must establish two separate marketing strategies. First of all, it needs a global strategy that will direct the organization's overall goals abroad—to establish a market presence in Scandinavia, for example, or to control X percent of the East Asian market within five years. Secondly, the company usually devises a separate marketing program tailored to each country or region in which it becomes active—a strategy that is sensitive to the marketing nuances of that particular locale.

Aside from market research, pricing, distribution, advertising, and other marketing activities, the three primary product options available to a company active in overseas markets are: (1) marketing a single ''global'' product to all countries in which it is active; (2) adapting its product to reflect local markets within a region, such as Asia or Europe; or, (3) changing the product to suit individual countries and locales within each country.

SEE ALSO: Database Marketing; International Marketing; Market Research; MaxiMarketing; Multilevel Marketing; Telemarketing

[Dave Mote and Scott Heil]

FURTHER READING:

Kotler, Philip. *Marketing Management: Analysis, Planning, Implementation, and Control.* 9th ed. Englewood Cliffs, NJ: Prentice Hall, 1996.

Levitt, Theodore. *The Marketing Imagination.* New York: Simon & Schuster, 1986.

Petrof, John V. "Relationship Marketing: The Wheel Reinvented." *Business Horizons,* November-December 1997.

Porter, Michael E. *Competitive Strategy.* New York: Free Press, 1980.

Taylor, James W. *Marketing Planning: A Step-by-Step Guide.* New York: Simon & Schuster, 1996.

MARKETING STRATEGY

While all marketers do not agree on a common definition of marketing strategy, the term generally refers to a company plan that allocates resources in ways to generate profits by positioning products or services and targeting specific consumer groups. Marketing strategy focuses on long-term company objectives and involves planning **marketing** programs so that they help a company realize its goals. Companies rely on marketing strategies for established product lines or services as well as for new products and services.

While marketing practices no doubt have existed as long as commerce has, marketing did not become a formal discipline until the 1950s. At this point, businesses began to investigate how to better serve and satisfy their customers and deal with **competition**. Consequently, marketing became the process of focusing business on the customer in order to continue providing goods or services valued by consumers. Marketing includes a plethora of decisions that affect consumer interest in a company: **advertising**, pricing, location, product line, promotions, and so forth. The majors concerns of marketing are usually referred to as the "four Ps" or the "marketing mix": product, price, place, and promotion.

Hence, marketing involves establishing a company vision and definition and implementing policies that will enable a company to live up to its vision or maintain its vision. Marketing strategy is the process of planning and implementing company policies towards realizing company goals in accordance with the company vision. Marketing strategies include general ones such as price reduction for market share growth, product differentiation, and **market segmentation**, as well as numerous specific strategies for specific areas of marketing.

Competition is the primary motivation for adopting a marketing strategy. In industries monopolized by one company, marketing need only be minimal to spur on increased consumption. Utilities long enjoyed monopolized markets, allowing them to rely on general mass marketing programs to maintain and increase their sales levels. Utility companies had rather fixed market positions and steady demand, which rendered advanced concern for marketing unnecessary. Now, however, most companies face some form of competition, no matter what the industry, because of deregulation and because of the **globalization** of many industries. Consequently, marketing strategy has become all the more important for companies to continue being profitable.

ORIGIN OF THE MARKETING STRATEGY CONCEPT

MARKETING AND STRATEGY. Marketing strategy has its roots in the basic concepts of marketing and **strategy**. Marketing strategy was probably used the first time that two humans engaged in trade, i.e., an "arm's-length" transaction. Certainly, early civilizations, such as the Babylonians, the Chinese, the Egyptians, the Greeks, the Romans, and the Venetians, had developed marketing strategies for their trading activities. They probably discussed appropriate strategies for given situations, and even taught these strategies to friends, family members, and subordinates. The actual function of marketing, i.e., the distribution function, was performed whenever exchange occurred.

STRATEGY IS A MEANS TO AN END. Marketing strategy is a conscious approach to accomplishing something. Strategy precedes marketing and marketing strategy. The first time a human planned an approach for achieving a desired end—a goal or objective—he or she was developing strategy. Strategy can be formulated by individuals, groups, and organizations. The organizations can be families, corporations, nations, or groups of nations. In modern times, strategy can be formulated by complicated and sophisticated programmed **software** operating on computerized systems, personal **computers**, or computer networks.

Original, formalized discussions of strategy or strategy theory are associated with politics, war, and the military. The term "strategy" comes from the Greek word *stratigiki,* meaning generalship. It also can mean approach, scheme, design, and system, and is associated with terms such as intrigue, cunning, craft, and artifice.

BUSINESS STRATEGY. Business strategy is usually discussed and developed in the context of competition. It is associated with a struggle for scarce resources. The aim of the ''aggressor'' organization is to improve its position vis-à-vis ''competitors.'' The competitors, i.e., ''defenders,'' can be other organizations, suppliers, distributors, or customers. The competition is the enemy. Words such as ''campaign,'' ''attack,'' ''battle,'' and ''defeat'' are frequently used. There is an ''I win, you lose''—sometimes called a ''zero-sum game''—mentality. This, of course, is also the operating framework for individuals, families, groups, countries, and alliances when formulating political or military strategy. Hence, business and marketing strategy is frequently associated with political and military strategy.

THE DEVELOPMENT OF MARKETING STRATEGY. Modern discussion of marketing strategy can be traced back to a discussion of marketing management by Leverett S. Lyon (1885-1959) in 1926. Marketing management was perceived as the business function that developed marketing strategy. Lyon argued that marketing management involves ongoing planning of a company's marketing activities in response to the constantly changing internal and external conditions. In the 1950s Peter Drucker (1909-) and others advanced theories of **management** that emphasized a customer-centered business strategy. They held that this orientation should be long term, not temporary.

Since World War II, marketing strategy has developed from four approaches to strategic thinking in business: **budgeting**, long-term planning, formula planning, and strategic thinking. During the 1950s, budgeting—the **accounting** task of distributing funds within a company—began to take on a strategic component. Budgets strategically assigned company projects specific amounts of funds in order to control spending on an annual basis. In the 1960s, however, budgeting began to focus on long-term planning: allocating funds to achieve financial goals according to a specific schedule, e.g. to achieve results from a project within five to ten years.

By the middle part of the 1970s, long-range planning had lost its prominence because of problems with long-range **forecasting** and resource allocation. Companies found it difficult to predict how much money to assign various units and when to expect results from research projects. Instead, businesses in the 1970s relied on formulas for planning as part of their company strategies. Because of the conglomeration wave of the 1960s, many managers found themselves with diverse companies and they did not know how to allocate resources prudently to the multifarious units. Instead, they turned to **consultants** to provide advice based on various formulas for planning. The formulas, however, tended to stem from business theory and not from practice. Hence, they largely proved to be ineffectual.

Consequently, strategic thinking grew in the 1980s and 1990s in response to the formulaic, theoretical approach to marketing theory in the 1970s. Strategic thinking focuses on competitive advantage, consumer needs and wants, creativity, and flexibility. Competitive advantage refers to gaining a superior market position and therefore higher profits by offering better products, prices, promotions, convenience, or service than competing companies. In a sense, competitive advantage includes all the other elements of strategic thinking—customer satisfaction, creativity, and flexibility—in that each of them can provide a company with a competitive advantage.

THE NATURE OF MARKETING STRATEGY

DECISION MAKING. Marketing strategy is the result of **decision making** by corporate executives, marketing managers, and other decision makers. In general, the formal organizational titles or jobs of decision makers, or the nature or purpose of the organization, are irrelevant to the formulation of marketing strategy. When the decisions concern products or markets, the results—i.e., the decisions—are all considered marketing strategy.

NARROW PERSPECTIVE. In a narrow sense, marketing strategy is a specified set of ways developed by marketers to achieve desired market ends. E. Jerome McCarthy and William D. Perreault Jr., authors of *Basic Marketing,* stated that a marketing strategy defines a target market as well as an appropriate marketing mix and an overview of what a company will exploit a given market. In a marketing planning context, where marketing strategy tends to be developed, McCarthy and Perreault indicated that marketing strategy planning means finding attractive opportunities and planning ways to capitalize on such opportunities.

BROAD PERSPECTIVE. In a broad sense, marketing strategy is composed of objectives, strategies, and tactics. Objectives are ends sought. Strategies are means to attain ends, and tactics are specific actions—i.e., implementation acts. A marketing objective of increasing market share is linked to the marketing strategy of altering the product line in order to reach new market segments and to the marketing tactic of introducing a new brand name and various promotions for a targeted portion of the market.

STRATEGY LEVELS. Marketing strategy is developed at different levels of an organization (the hierarchical dimension), across core marketing functions (the horizontal dimension), and for marketing execution and control functions (the implementation dimension). Strategy is usually developed in a hierarchical fashion from top to bottom; for example, there could be several layers of objectives where each objective is a function of a superstructure of superior objectives, and a determinant of subordinate objectives (except for the highest and lowest levels of objectives).

Higher-level decisions—the superstructure—act as constraints on the one hand, and guides or aids for decision making on the other. The organization levels could include the overall corporate level, strategic business units, product markets, target markets, and marketing units, depending on the complexity of the organization.

MARKETING MIX STRATEGY. Strategy is also developed across the core functional areas of marketing: product, price, place/distribution, and promotion strategies. Any functional level of marketing, in turn, can have additional levels of marketing strategy decisions where refinement of the strategy might take place. For example, in the advertising component of the promotion function, the organization might develop marketing strategy consisting of advertising objectives, advertising strategies, advertising themes, advertising copy, and media schedules. In addition, because of the growing customer emphasis of marketing, marketers have added new customer-oriented components to the marketing mix: customer sensitivity, customer convenience, and service.

MARKETING STRATEGY TYPES

ORIENTATIONS. Contemporary approaches to marketing often fall into two general but not mutually exclusive categories: customer-oriented marketing strategies and competitor-oriented marketing strategies. Since many marketers believe that striving to satisfy customers can benefit both consumers and businesses, they contend that marketing strategy should focus on customers. This strategy assumes that customers tend to make more purchases and remain loyal to specific brands when they are satisfied, rather than dissatisfied, with a company. Hence, customer-oriented marketing strategies try to help establish long-term relationships between customers and businesses.

Competitor-oriented marketing strategy, on the other hand, focuses on outdoing competitors by strategically manipulating the marketing mix: product, price, place, and promotion. Competitor-oriented strategies will lead companies to imitate competitor products, match prices, and offer similar promotions. This kind of marketing strategy parallels military strategy. For example, this approach to marketing strategy leads to price wars among competitors. Successful marketing strategies, however, usually incorporate elements from both of these orientations, because focusing on customer satisfaction alone will not help a company if its competitors already have high levels of customer satisfaction and because trying to outdo a competitor will not help a company if it provides inferior products and customer service.

GENERAL STRATEGIES. Marketing strategies can be identified by the goals they attempt to accomplish in order to boost company profits. The three basic marketing strategies include price reduction (for market share growth), product differentiation, and market segmentation. The market share strategy calls for reducing production **costs** in order to reduce consumer prices. Via this strategy, companies strive to manufacture products inexpensively and efficiently and thereby capture a greater share of the market. According to this strategy, companies avoid diverse products lines and marginally successful products and allocate minimal funds to product development and advertising. The competitive advantage this strategy offers is the ability to provide products at a lower price than competing companies. Companies implementing this strategy cut their **profit margins** and rely on sales volume to generate profits. The price reduction strategy, however, has three drawbacks: finding markets without or with few low-cost retailers, losing flexibility because of limited product line and limited market, competing with other companies using the same strategy.

The product differentiation strategy involves distinguishing a company's products from its competitors' by modifying the image or the physical characteristics of the products. Unlike the market share strategy, product differentiation requires raising product prices to increase profit margins. Companies adopting this strategy hope that consumers will pay higher prices for superior products (or products perceived as superior). As a result of this strategy, companies usually either achieve high profit margins and a low market share (such as luxury car manufacturers) or they achieve slightly higher profit margins and a moderate to large market share (such as popular food brands such as Kraft and Heinz). This strategy depends on the production of quality goods, brand loyalty, consumer preference for quality over cost, and ongoing product **innovation**. Nevertheless, product differentiation has a couple of disadvantages. First, competing companies often can easily imitate products thereby undercutting product differentiation efforts. Second, companies cannot raise their prices too high without losing customers, even if they provide better products.

Market segmentation refers to the process of breaking the entire market into a series of smaller markets based on common characteristics related to consumer behavior. Once the market is divided into smaller segments, companies can launch marketing programs to cater to the needs and preferences of the individual segments. Moreover, companies can choose to court all the segments of the market through ''differentiated marketing,'' to concentrate on one or two of the smaller segments overlooked by other companies through concentrated marketing (niche marketing), or to focus on very small markets or even individual customers through atomized marketing. Market segmentation also can involve the other two strategies, because marketers can target various segments using a price reduction strategy or a product differentiation strategy. If a segment grows, however, large competitors can begin targeting it as well. Companies that focus on one or two segments also are vulnerable to changes in the segment's size and preferences. Hence, if the segment dwindles or its tastes no longer correspond to a company's offerings, a company's revenues can fall precipitously.

SPECIFIC STRATEGIES. Furthermore, marketers also have developed specific strategies for specific kinds of marketing obstacles, which may serve as part of a general marketing strategy. Moreover, parts of general marketing strategies can be implemented for narrower ends. For example, in *Marketing Strategy,* Orville C. Walker, Harper W. Boyd Jr., and Jean-Claude Larreche identified marketing strategies for various marketing problems and activities such as new markets, growth markets, mature and declining markets, and international markets. Their marketing strategies included a plethora of specific marketing strategies for a host of situations: pioneer strategy, follower strategy, fortress strategy, flanker strategy, confrontation strategy, market expansion strategy, withdrawal strategy, frontal attack strategy, leapfrog attack strategy, encirclement strategy, guerrilla attack strategy, **divestment** strategy, global strategy, national strategy, **exporting** strategy, pricing strategy, channels strategy, and promotion strategy.

In addition, Joseph P. Guiltinan and Gordon W. Paul, authors of *Marketing Management,* outlined primary demand strategies and selective demand strategies. They also developed product-line marketing strategies, including strategies for substitutes (line extension strategies and flanker strategies) and strategies for complements (leader strategies, bundling strategies, and systems strategies). The primary demand strategies included user strategies (increasing the number of users) and rate of use strategies (increasing the purchase quantities). User strategies were, in turn, divided into willingness strategies (emphasis on willingness to buy) and ability strategies (emphasis on ability to buy). The rate of use strategies were divided into usage strategies (increasing the rate of usage—such as brushing your teeth after each meal) and replacement strategies (increasing the rate of use by replacement—such as replacing your toothbrush every month).

The selective demand strategies included retention strategies (retaining the organization's existing customers) and acquisition strategies (acquiring customers from the competition). Retention strategies were divided into:

1. Satisfaction strategies, which include ways to maintain or improve customer satisfaction levels, such as reducing delivery time from three days to 24 hours.
2. Meeting competition strategies, which include matching or ''bettering'' competitive approaches, such as charging the same price or a price stipulated at a percentage lower than the competition.
3. Relationship marketing strategies, which include establishing enduring relationships with customers, such as developing a computer-based automatic inventory replenishment system.

On the other hand, acquisition strategies were divided into:

1. Head-to-head strategies, which include direct, aggressive competitive tactics, such as using comparative advertising copy.
2. Differentiated strategies, which include making an organization's offering different from the competition, such as being the only firm to have a wireless feature on a notebook computer.
3. Niche marketing strategies, which include concentrating on narrow markets—such as a **direct-marketing** mail catalog of premium priced female clothing targeted at large females in the upper-middle and upper classes.

These marketing strategies are not mutually exclusive. They can be used in combination. They also are not exhaustive. In general, additional dimensions and levels can be generated. In other words, other levels and types of strategies at any level can be developed. The actual wording of the final and most refined level of strategy will probably be unique in each situation for each organization for each decision maker. Marketing strategy development is a creative act, requiring an application of science and art.

The decision maker should eventually arrive at a specific stratagem or set of strategies designed to achieve the stated objective. The entire articulated set of decisions (selected strategies) is called the marketing strategy. If the marketing strategy is part of a marketing plan, some or all of the strategy decisions could be formally stated. In some cases, only the lowest level of strategy is indicated. The formal articulation of marketing strategy is a function of the decision maker's preferences, the organization's policy, user needs, and resources available.

PRINCIPLES. The basic principles or theories of marketing appropriate to the successful development of marketing strategy are universal. They can be applied by anyone at any time in any kind of organization to any type of marketing problem in any part of the world. They are relevant to international marketing strategy as well as domestic marketing policy. They are useful in both profit-oriented organizations and nonprofit institutions, and are appropriate for both services and products.

MARKETING STRATEGY PROCESS

Marketing strategy is produced by the following basic decision process: (1) defining the marketing problem (or opportunity); (2) gathering the facts relevant to the problem (this includes defining the appropriate sources of useful facts or information); (3) analyzing the facts (perhaps with the aid of decision models and computer software); (4) determining the alternatives or choices to solve the problem; and (5) selecting an alternative—i.e., making the decision.

DETERMINANTS. Marketing strategy is determined by internal and external uncontrollable environmental forces. The internal environment (the environment within the organization) includes previous and higher-level strategies as well as resources (such as products, processes, **patents**, trademarks, trademark personnel, and capital). An example of an internal environmental influence on marketing strategy is when a previous strategic decision (such as the choice of a product market for a strategic business unit of an organization) affects current marketing decisions (such as market segmentation and target market selection). Likewise, an organization's financial strength (such as current cash flow) influences its formulation of marketing strategies (such as target market selection, positioning choices, and marketing mix decisions).

The external environment has domestic and global dimensions. The domestic dimension contains home country environments (such as a country's cultural environment). The global dimension consists of international forces (such as global demand and competition) affecting home country environments. The external environment includes the immediate task environment as well as legal and political environments, economic environments, **infrastructures**, cultural and social environments, and technological environments. An example of an external environmental influence on marketing strategy is when advertising strategy development is affected by such variables as customer media habits and governmental regulations.

TOOLS AND TECHNOLOGY. Marketing strategy can be developed with the aid of such tools as marketing concepts, marketing models, and computers. A marketer uses these tools to facilitate decision making. The computer-based method of marketing strategy generation, for example, is usually a quantitative approach starting with marketing theory and ending with the processing of data through a specialized computer program that analyzes variables and relationships.

The computer-based method begins with a segment of marketing theory. Marketing theory can be broken down into concepts and subconcepts. A concept is a set of related ideas or variables. For example, the product life cycle is a major concept in marketing. It describes market response (in terms of sales or revenues) to a product over the product's commercial life. It depicts four life stages of the product, namely: introduction (or commercialization), growth, maturity, and decline. Each stage of the product life cycle corresponds to the degree of competition it faces and the maturation of the market. Marketing strategy changes over the life of the product. In general, there is an appropriate set of marketing strategies or alternatives for each phase of the product life cycle. Market response, stages of the product life cycle, and other ideas constituting the concept are all variables that can assume different values and represent different relationships across the variable set. A marketing model articulates and quantifies the variables and variable relationships of a marketing concept. The marketing model also has inputs, processes, and outputs, which allow marketers to determine the effects of their strategies and decisions on both consumers and competitors.

Prepackaged marketing and **spreadsheet** software can facilitate the production of marketing models. A marketer needs only to change the values of the variables based on the facts that have been gathered in the situation analysis in order to use the output to arrive at a decision. When necessary, the decision maker can add or delete variables and change the functional relationships of the marketing model. Of course, it is also quite easy to assume different situational facts and consider the net impacts on the marketing strategy, or the results of implementing the marketing strategy. Thus, it is relatively easy, using computer software, to develop a marketing strategy and to perform sensitivity (degree of impact of changes) and contingency analyses (alternative scenarios).

SEE ALSO: Strategy Formulation

[Lawrence Dandurand, updated by Karl Heil]

FURTHER READING:

Bartels, Robert. "Development of Marketing Thought: A Brief History." In *Science in Marketing,* edited by George Schwartz. New York: John Wiley & Sons, Inc., 1965.

Cohen, William A. *The Practice of Marketing Management.* New York: Macmillan, 1991.

Cravens, David W., and Charles W. Lamb Jr. *Strategic Marketing Management Cases.* Boston: Irwin, 1993.

Gardner, David, and Howard Thomas. "Strategic Marketing: History, Issues, and Emergent Themes." In *Strategic Marketing and Management,* edited by Howard Thomas and David Gardner. New York: John Wiley & Sons, Inc., 1985.

Gladish, Alan W. "Plan to Market for Long-Term Prosperity." *Marketing News,* 7 December 1998, 14.

Graham, John R. "Making Marketing Work." *Direct Marketing,* September 1998, 40.

Guiltinan, Joseph P., and Gordon W. Paul, et al. *Marketing Management.* 6th ed. New York: McGraw-Hill College Div., 1996.

Hiam, Alexander, and Charles D. Schewe. *The Portable MBA in Marketing.* 2nd ed. New York: John Wiley & Sons, Inc., 1998.

Lynn, Robert A., and John M. Thies. "Marketing Strategy and Execution." In *Dartnell Marketing Manager's Handbook,* edited by Stewart Henderson Britt and Norman F. Guess. Dartnell Corp., 1984.

McCarthy, E. Jerome, and William D. Perreault Jr. *Basic Marketing.* 13th ed. New York: McGraw-Hill College Div., 1998.

Schnaars, Steven P. *Marketing Strategy: A Customer-Driven Approach.* Reference ed. New York: Free Press, 1995.

Walker, Orville C., Boyd, Jr., Harper W., and Jean-Claude Larreche. *Marketing Strategy: Planning and Implementation.* 3rd ed. New York: McGraw-Hill College Div., 1998.

MASS PRODUCTION

SEE: Assembly Line Methods

MATCHING CONCEPT

The matching concept is an **accounting** principle that requires the identification and recording of expenses associated with revenue earned and recognized during the same accounting period. Accordingly, under the matching concept the expenses of a particular accounting period are the costs of the assets used to earn the revenue that is recognized in that period. It follows, therefore, that when expenses in a period are matched with the revenues generated for the same period, the result is the net income or loss for that period.

ACCOUNTING TERMS

While in everyday vernacular, the terms "cost," "expenditure," and "expense" are used almost interchangeably; in discussing accounting principles, these terms have distinctly different meanings. A **cost** is the amount of money, or other resources, used for a specific purpose. When a cost is incurred, it is associated with an expenditure; expenditures can either result in the decrease of an asset, such as cash, or the increase of a liability, such as accounts payable. Thus, expenditures result in either assets or expenses. If the expenditure will benefit future periods, such as the purchase of office equipment, it is an asset. If it will benefit the current period, such as the purchase of supplies needed to fill immediate manufacturing needs, it is an expense of that period. Logically, then, it follows that an expense is a cost item that is specifically applicable to the current accounting period used during that period to earn revenue.

THE CONSERVATISM CONCEPT

Oftentimes, when deciding which revenues and expenses to match in a given accounting period, accountants have a difficult time recognizing which revenues and expenses are certain for that period. Like many people, accountants and other business professionals tend to be overly optimistic concerning the revenues that their companies generate but tend to be more realistic concerning the associated expenses. Thus, certain accounting principles have been developed to offset the tendency toward optimism. These principles recognize that increases in reported net **income** require stronger proof than do increases in expenses. Therefore, when deciding which expenses and revenues to acknowledge during a given accounting period, accountants are supposed to apply the conservatism concept. This concept has two conditions associated with it—firms can recognize *expenses* as soon as they are reasonably *possible,* and firms can recognize *revenues* as soon as they are reasonably *certain.*

Usually, a company applies the matching concept by being reasonably certain which items will generate revenue and matching them with any possible expenses for those items. To illustrate, if a company produces an item costing $100 that it later sells for $150, the company must decide the accounting period in which it is reasonably certain to receive the $150. When this is decided, the company must match the $100 cost with the $150 revenue as an expense, resulting in $50 income from sales. Interestingly, not all companies take these steps in the same order; sometimes expenses are first identified and later revenues are matched to them.

REVENUE AND EXPENSE RECOGNITION

The best matching of revenues and expenses occurs under the accrual basis of accounting. Under the accrual basis, revenue (as well as expenses, and other changes in assets, **liabilities**, and equity) is generally recognized in the period in which the economic event takes place, usually at the point of sale—not when the cash actually changes hands. Revenue recognition occurs at this time because the earnings process is complete and there is evidence supporting the sale price. Earnings, however, can be identified at other times, such as during an item's production, at the end of an item's production but prior to its sale, or when the money is collected, as with payments made on installments. Costs are recognized as expenses in a particular period if (1) there is a direct association between costs and revenues for the period or (2) the costs cannot be assigned to the generation of revenues of any period in the future.

The recognition of revenues and expenses can become more complicated, however, because companies often spend money or assume liabilities for nonmonetary assets affecting more than one accounting period. Examples of transactions affecting more than one period are: (1) supplies purchased in a prior accounting period but used for several later periods; (2) insurance premiums paid that cover more than one period; (3) buildings and equipment; and (4) expenses—such as salaries—paid after a service has been rendered. Initially, these expenses are recorded at their original amounts, which represents the future benefit that the company anticipates receiving from these items. As they are used, the related costs must be matched against the revenues earned for the particular period. For example, for equipment and buildings, accountants gradually expense the costs of these assets over their estimated service life, a concept known as **depreciation**.

In accounting, adjusting entries are completed at the end of the accounting period to update the accounts for internal business transactions. Adjusting entries are commonly used to effect the matching of revenues and expenses. For example, the amount of materials used during a particular accounting period would be recorded by an adjusting entry at the end of each period. Expenditures made in the current period for assets not yet used would be recorded as assets and included in the current period's **balance sheet**, not recorded as expenses in the current period. As the assets are used, the related costs would be matched against revenues for that period by making an adjusting entry at the end of that period. If a company fails to make these adjustments at the proper time, the net income and assets of the company could be dramatically overstated.

As businesses have gotten more complex because of **globalization**, creative sales, and customer financing techniques, the proper period in which to recognize revenue has become less clear. Because, under the matching concept, the recognition of revenue triggers the recognition of the related expenses, this can have serious effects on a company's **financial statements**.

As a result, in recent years, there has been a dramatic increase in the number of companies restating prior years' earnings. In most instances, this has been prompted by the discovery that the original timing of the recognition of revenues and, therefore, the related expenses (the matching concept!) had been in error.

[Kathryn Snavely, updated by Ronald M. Horwitz]

FURTHER READING:

Anthony, Robert N., and James S. Reece. *Accounting: Text and Cases.* 8th ed. Homewood, IL: Irwin, 1989.

Diamond, Michael A., Eric G. Flamholtz, and Diana Troik Flamholtz. *Financial Accounting* 2nd ed. Boston: PWS-Kent, 1990.

Eskew, Robert K., and Daniel L. Jensen. *Financial Accounting.* 4th ed. New York: McGraw-Hill, 1992.

Meigs, Robert F., et al. *Accounting: The Basis for Business Decisions.* 11th ed. Boston: Irwin/McGraw-Hill, 1999.

Solomon, Lanny M., Larry M. Walther, and Richard J. Vargo. *Financial Accounting.* 3rd ed. New York: West Publishing, 1992.

MATRIX MANAGEMENT AND STRUCTURE

Matrix management is a technique of managing an organization (or, more commonly, part of an organization) through a series of dual-reporting relationships instead of a more traditional linear management structure. In contrast to most other organizational structures, which arrange managers and employees by function or product, matrix management combines functional and product departments in a dual authority system. In its simplest form, a matrix configuration may be known as a cross-functional work team, which brings together individuals who report to different parts of the company in order to complete a particular project or task. The term ''matrix'' is derived from the representative diagram of a matrix management system, which resembles a rectangular array or grid of functions and product/project groups.

The practice is most associated with highly collaborative and complex projects, such as building aircraft, but is also widely used in many product/project management situations. Even when a company does not label its structure a matrix system or represent it as such on an organization chart, there may be an implicit matrix structure any time employees are grouped into work teams (this does not normally include committees, task forces, and the like) that are headed by someone other than their primary supervisor.

NEW ORGANIZATIONAL MODELS

In the late 1800s and early 1900s, during the U.S. industrial revolution, a need emerged for more formalized structures in large business organizations. The earliest models emphasized efficiency of process through managerial control. Described as ''mechanistic,'' those systems were characterized by extensive rules and procedures, centralized authority, and an acute division of labor. They sought to create organizations that mimicked machines, and usually departmentalized workers by function, such as finance and production. Important theories during that era included German sociologist Max Weber's (1881-1961) ideal bureaucracy, which was based on absolute authority, logic, and order.

During the 1920s and 1930s, new ideas about the structure and nature of organizations began to surface. Inspired by the work of thinkers and behaviorists such as Harvard researcher Elton Mayo, who conducted the famed **Hawthorne Experiments**, theories about management structure began to incorporate a more humanistic view. Those theoretical organizational structures were classified as ''organic,'' and recognized the importance of human behavior and cultural influences in organizations. While the mechanistic school of thought stressed efficiency and production through control, organic models emphasized flexibility and adaptability through employee empowerment. From a structural standpoint, mechanistic organizations tended to be vertical or hierarchical with decisions flowing down through several channels. Organic models, on the other hand, were comparatively flat, or horizontal, and had few managerial levels or centralized controls.

Many proponents of organic organizational theory believed it was the solution to the drawbacks of mechanistic organizations. Indeed, mechanistic organizations often stifled human creativity and motivation and were generally insensitive to external influences, such as shifting markets or consumer needs. In contrast, companies that used organic management structures tended to be more responsive and creative. However, many organizations that adopted the organic approach also discovered that, among other drawbacks, it sometimes lacked efficiency and personal accountability and failed to make the most productive use of some workers' expertise.

As an alternative to basic organic structures, many companies during the mid-1900s embraced a model that minimized the faults and maximized the benefits of different organic management structures, as discussed below. Possibly the first application of what would later be referred to as the ''matrix'' structure was employed in 1947 by General Chemicals in its engineering department. In the early 1960s a more formalized matrix method called ''unit management'' was implemented by a large number of U.S. hospitals. Not until 1965, however, was matrix management formally recognized.

The first organization to design and implement a formal matrix structure was the National Aeronautics and Space Administration (NASA). NASA developed a matrix management system for its space program because it needed to simultaneously emphasize several different functions and projects, none of which could be stressed at the expense of another. It found that traditional management structures were too bureaucratic, hierarchical, slow-moving, and inflexible. Likewise, basic organic structures were too departmentalized (i.e. myopic), thus failing to productively use the far-reaching expertise NASA had at its disposal. NASA's matrix solution overcame those problems by synthesizing projects, such as designing a rocket booster, with organizational functions, such as staffing and finance.

Despite doubts about its effectiveness in many applications, matrix management gained broad acceptance in the corporate world during the 1970s, eventually achieving fad status. Its popularity continued during the 1980s as a result of economic changes in the United States, which included slowing domestic market growth and increasing foreign competition. Those changes forced many companies to seek the benefits offered by the matrix model.

MATRIX BASICS

FUNCTIONAL ORGANIZATION. Most organizational structures departmentalize the work force and other resources by one of two methods: by products or by functions. Functional organizations are segmented by key functions. For example, activities related to production, marketing, and finance might be grouped into three respective divisions. Within each division, moreover, activities would be departmentalized into subdepartments. The marketing division, for example, might encompass sales, advertising, and promotion departments.

The chief advantage of functionally structured organizations is that they usually achieve a fairly efficient specialization of labor and are relatively easy for employees to comprehend. In addition, functional structures reduce duplication of work because responsibilities are clearly defined on a company-wide basis. However, functional division often causes departments to become short-sighted and provincial, leading to incompatible work styles and poor communication.

DIVISIONAL ORGANIZATION. Companies that employ a product or divisional structure, by contrast, break the organization down into semiautonomous units and profit centers based on activities, or ''projects,'' such as products, customers, or geography. Regardless of the project used to segment the company, each unit operates as a separate business. For example, a company might be broken down into southern, western, and eastern divisions. Or, it might create separate divisions for consumer, industrial, and institutional products. Again, within each product unit are subdivisions.

One benefit of product or project departmentalization is that it facilitates expansion (because the company can easily add a new division to focus on a new profit opportunity without having to significantly alter existing systems). In addition, accountability is increased because divisional performance can be measured more easily. Furthermore, divisional structures permit decentralized decision making, which allows managers with specific expertise to make key decisions in their area. The potential drawbacks to divisional structures include duplication of efforts in different departments and a lack of horizontal communication. In addition, divisional organizations, like functionally structured companies, may have trouble keeping all departments focused on an overall company goal.

MATRIX ORGANIZATION. Matrix management structures combine functional and product departmentalization. They simultaneously organize part of a company along product or project lines and part of it around functional lines to get the advantages of both. For example, a diagram of a matrix model might show divisions, such as different product groups, along the top of a table (See Figure 1). Along the left side of the same table would be different functional departments, such as finance, marketing, and production. Within the matrix, each of the product groups would intersect with each of the functional groups, signifying a direct relationship between product teams and administrative divisions. In other words, each team of people assigned to manage a product group might have an individual(s) who also belonged to each of the functional departments, and vice-versa.

Theoretically, managers of project groups and managers of functional groups have roughly equal authority within the company. As indicated by the matrix, many employees report to at least two managers. For instance, a member of the accounting department might be assigned to work with the consumer products division, and would report to managers of both departments. Generally, however, managers of functional areas and divisions report to a single authority, such as a president or vice president.

Although all matrix structures entail some form of dual authority and multidisciplinary grouping, there are several variations. For example, Kenneth Knight identified three basic matrix management models: coordination, overlay, and secondment. Each of the models can be implemented in various forms that differ in attributes related to decision-making roles, relationships with outside suppliers and buyers, and other factors. Organizations choose different models based on such factors as competitive environments, industries, education and maturity level of the workforce, and existing corporate culture.

In the coordination model, staff members remains part of their original departments (or the departments they would most likely belong to under a functional or product structure). Procedures are instituted to ensure cross-departmental cooperation and interaction towards the achievement of extra-departmental goals. In the overlay model, staff members officially become members of two groups, each of which has a separate manager. This model represents the undiluted matrix form described above. In the third version, the secondment model, individuals move from functional departments into project groups and back again, but may effectively belong to one or the other at different times.

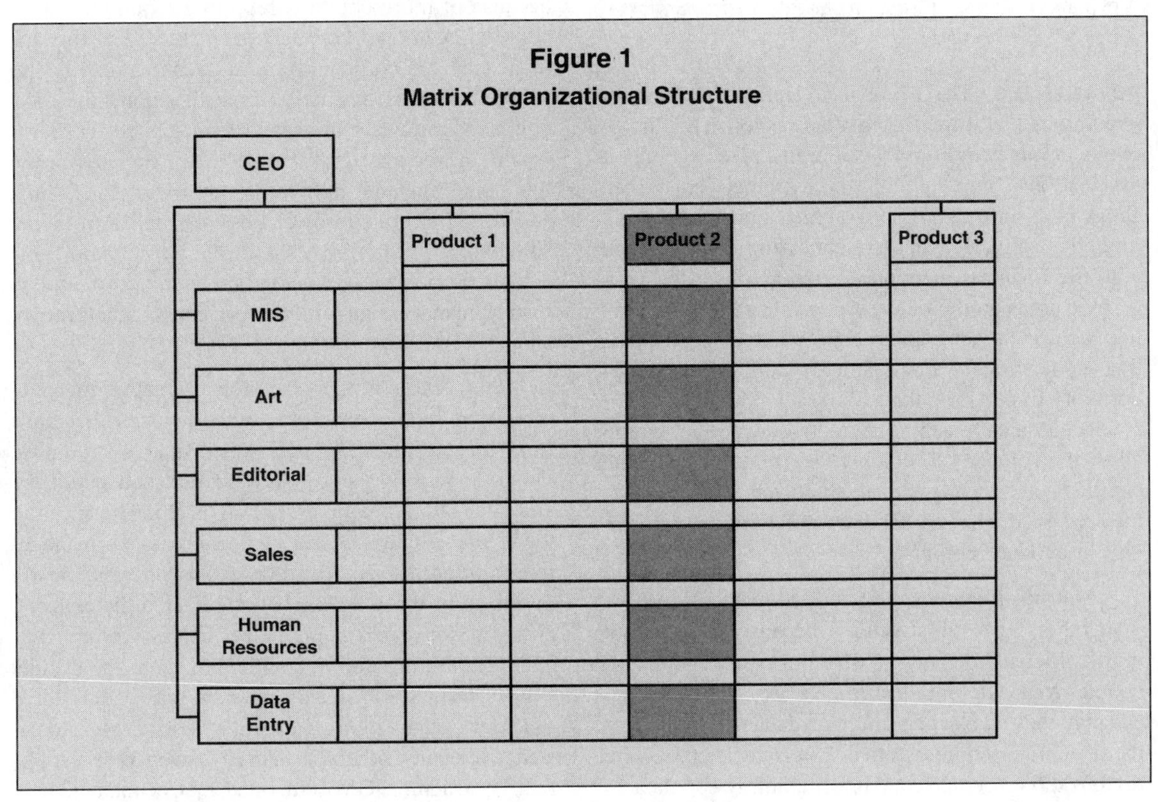

TEMPORARY VERSUS PERMANENT. As these examples and models suggest, matrix structures are more likely than other structures to exist on a temporary or ad hoc basis. Indeed, some scholars group matrix structures under a broader category of organizational forms called ''adhocracies,'' or temporary work configurations, created to deal with a particular problem or project. Large-scale use of adhocracies dates to U.S. military practices during World War II, when the war effort required flexible teams of experts to be convened on short notice and delegated certain tasks, often without a great deal of micromanagement by military brass. Once the objectives were reached, the team would be disbanded and the members reassigned to other duties. A similar rationale and process exist in the business world, and thus many formal matrix structures fall into the ad hoc category.

Permanent matrix structures are centered on more enduring aspects of business operations, such as product lines or processes. A common practice is to have a product or brand manager who is responsible for overseeing the development and production of an ongoing product, but staff who work on the product may also contribute to other products from time to time. This permanent set-up creates accountability, coordination, and perhaps most of all, continuity for the product as a whole, while enabling staff, who generally have a direct supervisor who is not a product manager, to be flexibly assigned where they are needed most.

ADVANTAGES, DISADVANTAGES, AND APPLICATIONS

ADVANTAGES. The cardinal advantage of a matrix structure is that it facilitates rapid response to change in two or more environments. For instance, a telecommunications company might be extremely concerned about both unforeseen geographic opportunities and limited capital. By departmentalizing its company with the financial function on one axis and the geographic areas on the other, it might benefit from having each of its geographic units intertwined with its finance department. For example, suppose that an opportunity to purchase the cellular telephone rights for a specific area arose. The matrix structure would allow the company to quickly determine if it had the capital necessary to purchase the license and develop the area, or if it should take advantage of an opportunity in another region.

Matrix structures are flatter and more responsive than other types of structures because they permit more efficient exchanges of information. Because people from different departments are cooperating so closely, they are eager to share data that will help them achieve common goals. In effect, the entire organization becomes an information web; data is channeled both vertically and horizontally as people exchange technical knowledge, marketing data, product ideas, financial information to make decisions.

In addition to speed and flexibility, matrix organization may result in a more efficient use of resources than other organic structures. This occurs because highly specialized employees and equipment are shared by departments. For example, if the expertise of a computer programmer is needed in another department, he or she can move to that department to solve its problems, rather than languishing on tasks of low priority as might happen in a nonmatrix setting.

Other benefits of matrix management include improved motivation and more adept managers. Improved motivation results from decision-making within groups becoming more democratic and participatory because each member brings specialized knowledge to the table—and since employees have a direct impact on day-to-day decisions, they are more likely to experience higher levels of motivation and commitment to the goals of the departments to which they belong. More adept management is the result of top decision makers becoming more involved in, and thus better informed about, the day-to-day operations of the company. This involvement can also lead to improved long-term planning.

DISADVANTAGES. Despite their many theoretical advantages, matrix management structures have been criticized as having a number of weaknesses. For instance, they are typically expensive to maintain, partly because of more complex reporting requirements. In addition, many workers become disturbed by the lack of a chain of command and a seeming inability to perceive who is in charge. Indeed, among the most common criticisms of matrix management is that it results in role ambiguity and conflict. For instance, a functional manager may tell a subordinate one thing, and then a product/project boss will tell him or her something different. As a result, companies that change from a comparatively bureaucratic structure to matrix management often experience high turnover and worker dissatisfaction.

Supporting critics' derision of matrix management are several examples of companies that have implemented and later abandoned matrix structures. For example, one study showed that between 1961 and 1978 about one-quarter of all teaching hospitals in the United States moved to unit or matrix management structures. By the late 1970s, though, nearly one-third of those hospitals had rejected the concept, citing reasons such as high costs, excessive turnover, and interpersonal conflict. Although the hospital study suggested that matrix management was better suited to larger organizations, General Motors Corp.'s experience indicated otherwise. After a seven-year test of a matrix structure, GM jettisoned matrix management in the 1980s in favor of a more traditional, product oriented organizational structure. It cited managers' lack of control over incentives as a primary shortcoming of the matrix system.

Although matrix management was often viewed during the 1970s as a cure-all for organizational design, the perceived breadth of its potential for application has gradually diminished. In general, matrix structures are assumed to be most appropriate for larger corporations that operate in unique or fast-paced environments; a coal-mining company, for example, might be less likely to benefit from a matrix structure than would a pharmaceutical company. Matrix management also works best for organizations that are managed and staffed mostly by professionals or semi-professionals, e.g., engineers and scientists. Matrix management further requires a workforce that has a diverse set of skills and employees that have strong interpersonal abilities. Finally, matrix management is usually more effective when a project manager, who is technically working under the authority of a product and a functional boss, is given the authority to make critical decisions.

Because of their limitations, matrix management structures frequently are integrated into an organization as one facet of a larger plan. For example, a research team organized to develop a new product might be placed in a division of the company that is set up as a matrix. After the initial stages of the project are completed, the ongoing management of the product might be moved to a division of the company that reflects a more conventional functional or product/project structure. Indeed, as evidenced by NASA's successes in the 1960s, matrix management is particularly effective in accomplishing ''crash'' and high-tech projects, such as those related to medical, energy research, aerospace, defense, and competitive threats.

MATRIX STRUCTURE IN INTERNATIONAL SETTINGS

A special and popular application of matrix management is in the overseas operations of an international firm. This is sometimes known as a three dimensional matrix when management intersects along product/market, function, and country lines. Under such an arrangement there is typically a worldwide product manager, a local or worldwide functional manager, and a country specific manager; however, many variations of the international matrix exist. The product manager is generally concerned with product-specific issues that cut across regional or national boundaries. Depending on the type of task and the company's preference, the functional manager may focus on international issues (e.g., worldwide finance) or local concerns (e.g., domestic finance). Finally, the country manager is concerned with all the implications—both product and function—of producing and/or marketing the goods or services in a particular locale.

As with other uses of the matrix structure, the international format is not without its weaknesses. A particular concern is the role of ambiguity across international lines, and especially when it pits managers of different nationalities against one another. If the system is not handled carefully and the potential for cultural bias recognized by top management, it could lead to favoritism of some international managers while disenfranchising others, thereby defeating the purpose of a matrix structure. In addition, international matrix structures may be unacceptably inefficient and costly to maintain.

CASE STUDY

Bayer AG of Germany—the company best known in the United States for its Bayer aspirin products—is one of the largest and oldest chemical and health-care products companies in the world. Because of massive sales gains and increased activity overseas in the early 1980s, Bayer announced a reorganization in 1984. Bayer had been successful with a conventional organizational structure that was departmentalized by function. However, in response to new conditions the company wanted to create a structure that would allow it to achieve three primary goals: (1) shift management control from the then-West German parent company to its foreign divisions and subsidiaries; (2) restructure its business divisions to more clearly define their duties; and (3) flatten the organization, or empower lower level managers to assume more responsibility, so that top executives would have more time to plan strategy.

Bayer selected a relatively diverse matrix management format to pursue its goals. It delineated all of its business activities into six groups under an umbrella company called Bayer World. Within each of the six groups were several subgroups made up of product categories such as dyestuffs, fibers, or chemicals. Likewise, each of its administrative and service functions were regrouped under Bayer World into one of several functions, such as human resources, marketing, plant administration, or finance. Furthermore, top managers who had formally headed functional groups were given authority over separate geographic regions, which, like the product groups, were supported by and entwined with the functional groups. The net effect of the reorganization was that the original nine functional departments were broken down into 19 multidisciplinary, interconnected business groups.

After only one year of operation, Bayer management lauded the new matrix structure as a resounding success. Not only did matrix management allow the company to move toward its primary goals, but it had the added benefits of increasing its responsiveness to change and emerging opportunities, and of helping Bayer to streamline plant administration and service division activities.

SEE ALSO: Organization Theory

[Dave Mote]

FURTHER READING:

Burton, Richard M., and Børge Obel. *Strategic Organizational Diagnosis and Design.* 2nd ed. Boston: Kluwer Academic Publishers, 1998.

Knight, Kenneth, ed. *Matrix Management: A Cross-Functional Approach to Organization.* New York: PBI-Petrocelli Books, 1977.

Kramer, Robert J. *Organizing for Global Competitiveness: The Matrix Design.* New York: Conference Board, 1994.

Nissan, David. "A Regional Slice of the Global Pie." *Financial Times,* 14 August 1995.

Robbins, Stephen P. *Organization Theory: The Structure and Design of Organizations.* Englewood Cliffs, NJ: Prentice Hall, 1983.

Tailan Chi, and Paul Nystrom. "An Economic Analysis of Matrix Structure, Using Multinational Corporations as an Illustration." *Managerial & Decision Economics,* May 1998.

MAXIMARKETING

MaxiMarketing is set of marketing strategies developed by Stan Rapp and Thomas L. Collins in their 1987 book *MaxiMarketing: The New Direction in Advertising, Promotion, and Marketing Strategy.* The authors, who had extensive background in direct marketing, later expanded on the subject in three follow-up books.

Responding to a mass advertising culture within the business community that dated back to the 1950s, Rapp and Collins presented a series of consumer marketing strategies and philosophies—directed at CEOs as much as marketing personnel—that they believed characterized an effective, modern, and holistic approach to marketing. Many of their ideas focused on the efficiency and differentiation of advertising. They contrasted their philosophy with more monolithic marketing strategies that employed conventional media, such as television, and targeted consumers generally rather than in defined segments.

THE STRATEGY

The MaxiMarketing model was built upon nine points:

1. *Maximized targeting.* This was essentially segmenting the market narrowly by demographics and geography in order to understand and reach the best sales prospects.
2. *Maximized media.* In order to reach the more narrow consumer groups, Rapp and Collins argued, marketers needed to send their message through many different media channels, not just mainstream television and radio.
3. *Maximized accountability.* Accountability referred to ensuring, through formal tracking, that specific marketing efforts were actually delivering results.
4. *Maximized awareness.* This meant developing creative ways to reach consumers with the marketing message, such as sponsoring sporting events.
5. *Maximized activation.* Activation was a code word for promotional strategies that involved consumer participation, such as contests.
6. *Maximized synergy.* The authors suggested that businesses could accomplish multiple objectives through a single advertising vehicle. Examples included cross-promoting two different products, building a sales database from a direct-response campaign, and promoting two distribution channels through one ad.
7. *Maximized linkage.* Linkage was a means of developing and maintaining personal contact with customers, such as through consumer help lines and correspondence.
8. *Maximized sales.* MaxiMarketing emphasized increasing sales through long-term customer relations rather than solely through short-term promotions.
9. *Maximized distribution.* Rapp and Collins also advocated pursuing multiple channels of product distribution, such as combinations of retail and direct selling.

ANALYSIS

While the MaxiMarketing books (and newsletters) have sold hundreds of thousands of copies, and no doubt influenced many readers, it is not clear whether Rapp and Collins have made an enduring contribution to marketing theory or practice. The term MaxiMarketing has not been widely adopted or even cited in the professional literature. And while most of their recommended approaches to marketing are widely accepted, Rapp and Collins certainly were not the first to advocate most of these notions—despite the authors' claims, book reviews at MaxiMarketing's debut admitted as much—and were arguably not always the most persuasive.

It seemed, rather, that they were arguing in 1987 against the state of marketing theory circa the 1950s, ignoring the intervening developments. For example, detailed and well-known studies of market segmentation and niche marketing, the essence of "maximized targeting," existed well before MaxiMarketing was articulated. Likewise, the principles of **database marketing**, which underlie a portion of the writers' theories, were widely being explored by authors during the mid-1980s, when MaxiMarketing first appeared, as personal computers to support database marketing efforts came of age. To their credit, of course, all of the best marketing theories were not in wide practice when they wrote the original book.

The legacy of MaxiMarketing, which as of the late 1990s was still actively being pitched by its entrepreneurial founders, is perhaps as a tool for getting managers to adopt a set of effective marketing techniques that were already in practice.

SEE ALSO: Market Segmentation

FURTHER READING:

Hatch, Denny. "How the MaxiMarketing Gurus Go to Market." *Target Marketing,* January 1996.

Pearlstein, Steven. Review of *MaxiMarketing: The New Direction in Advertising, Promotion, and Marketing Strategy,* by Stan Rapp and Thomas L. Collins. *Inc.,* February 1988.

Rapp, Stan, and Thomas L. Collins. *MaxiMarketing: The New Direction in Advertising, Promotion, and Marketing Strategy.* New York: McGraw-Hill, 1987.

Review of *MaxiMarketing: The New Direction in Advertising, Promotion, and Marketing Strategy,* by Stan Rapp and Thomas L. Collins. *Sales & Marketing Management,* July 1987.

MEASUREMENT

SEE: Metrics and Measurement

MERCANTILISM

Mercantilism is a political and economic system that arose in the 17th and 18th centuries. It purports that a country's economic strength is directly related to the maintenance of a positive **balance of trade**. That is, in order to remain economically and politically viable a country must **export** more than it **imports**. Such a positive balance of trade, according to mercantilist thought, results in a surplus of gold in the practicing country's treasury.

Although not a proponent of mercantilism, noted 18th century Scottish economist Adam Smith (1723-1790) was responsible for coining the term "mercantile system." Mercantilism was in opposition to Smith's concepts of **free trade**, free enterprise, and the free movement of people and goods. In other words, it went against the precepts of a **laissez-faire** economy. One of the key assertions of mercantilism is that national **wealth** will come through the import and accumulation of gold or other precious metals such as silver. Smith was highly critical of this theory of wealth and he clearly understood the class bias in the merchant system that supported it. In fact, Smith expressed great concern about colonialism and the monopoly trade routes instituted by the merchant class, which often worked against the economic interests of the citizenry.

Mercantilism as an economic system is generally held in low regard today. Japan, however, with its structural barriers to foreign **competition** and its discouragement of foreign **direct investment** has been accused of practicing a late 20th century form of mercantilism.

Mercantilism as a historical period has been associated with the rise of a particular form of European **capitalism** often referred to as merchant capitalism. Mercantilism was also a doctrine advanced by various economic writers of the period, who tended to call for a powerful alliance between merchants and the monarchial system, which was then in decline. The term *mercantilism* is often used today to describe protectionist trade policies which, when coupled with other government policies, directly or indirectly subsidize particular industries in order to gain national or regional trade advantage. Japan, as stated above, is a late 20th century example of such policies. Mercantilism has thus come to be associated with nationalistic economic policies and is shunned by free trade advocates who argue for minimal state interference in the domestic and international marketplace.

The mercantile system advocated various nationalistic trade policies thought to enhance the wealth of the respective nation. This wealth was to be achieved via mercantilism's five essential elements, as noted in the work of writer David L. Sills:

- Nationalism and policy go hand in hand, with all policy being directed towards nationalism.
- Foreign trade should always be thought of in terms of its effect on the country's stock of precious metals.
- Lacking domestic gold or silver mines, these precious metals must be accumulated by an excess of exports over imports.
- Government trade authorities, through policy, should strive to restrict imports and encourage exports.
- Economic foreign policy and political foreign policy should be coordinated toward the achievement of these ends.

While most closely associated with 18th century Europe, the term mercantilism has also been used to refer to the general principle of the aggrandizement of state power for the economic gain of its capitalist class by manipulating and controlling trade. During colonial times, for example, this took the form of military control over trade routes, large tariffs on imported goods (especially manufactured products), and outright plundering of colonies in pursuit of gold and raw materials.

The rationale for mercantilist practices, aside from the imperatives of empire and colonial conquest, was reflected in 18th century notions of the origin of profit and the nature of exchange. From a merchant's perspective, profit originated from "buying cheap and selling dear." While this is the goal of any for-profit entity, mercantilists applied this view to the nation as a whole. This is in contrast to the sacred belief of marketplace ideology held by classical economists—that exchange should be made on the basis of equivalents. Mercantilists believed, moreover, that the seller gains via the buyer's loss. Therefore, a nation will only become richer if it exports or sells more than it imports or buys. Gold or other "money commodities" will thus be amassed to the benefit of the state. The view that profit or surplus originates in the unequal exchange of **commodities** was therefore perfectly consistent with the mercantilist policy of controlling the terms of trade.

Mercantilism played an important but not necessarily dominant role in the transition from feudalism to industrial capitalism. Mercantilism, however, did greatly benefit large merchant enterprises such as the British East India Company, which shipped home goods over trade routes protected and maintained by the state. Foreign trade was thought to be necessary for the accumulation of gold because domestic trade could not generate a net surplus or profit. Armed with this view of the origin of profits, merchants promoted exports as a necessary means of gaining surplus profits. Like all good policy makers, the merchants argued that this policy would in turn benefit the state as a whole.

Policies to these ends involved state **subsidies** of export industries; high tariff walls to encourage home production; a prohibition on the sale of gold to foreigners; subsidization of key industries when necessary; control over certain types of capital; and the relentless import of gold and raw materials from colonies. Most of these policies involved strict control over trade routes and the stabilization of prices by state fiat.

During the mercantilist period, merchants controlled the trading system but not the production of goods and services. Before the advent of industrial capitalism, production was along the line of a crafts system, which embodied remnants of the old feudal order. As industrial capitalism emerged the power of the merchant class declined. Merchants would eventually come to see that taking over or being more involved in the means of production would enhance their profits by giving them control over the productivity of labor. For the most part, however, merchants did not control the means of production, as their primary concern was buying and selling. Mercantilist policies encouraged the importation of raw materials, which in turn could be manufactured into various products. Now carrying an added value, these finished goods could subsequently be exported and sold for a high price relative to their original cost. Thus would gold ultimately find its way to the nation's treasury.

The rise of the mercantile system coincided with the beginnings of capitalism in 16th and 17th century Europe. By this time Spain, France, and the low countries of Belgium and Holland had been transformed into merchant-dominated economies. Concurrently, modern nation-states were emerging as a political complement of the merchant economy. It was this coalition of merchants and monarchs that eventually led to the dissolution of the old feudal order. A system evolved that was instead regulated by a competitive labor market. This led to the eventual formation of a class of people who found themselves free from feudal ties to the land only to be forced to sell their labor in order to ensure subsistence. Also emerging was a class of industrial and manufacturing entrepreneurs who were "recruited" from the now declining merchant class.

The merchant class eventually gave way and lost control of the new economic order to the emerging forces of capitalist competition where price and profits were regulated by the production and accumulation of capital. While trading was essential to the emerging industrial capitalist system, transactions were seen as merely a sharing out of the total selling price among the buyers and purchasers, including the merchant. The mercantile idea that trade led to profits for the system as a whole gave way to the classical economist's view that production and the reinvestment of profit was the true source of a nation's wealth.

In addition to the shift in focus from trading to production, the new social and economic dynamic of capital accumulation, in turn, led to devastating critiques of the mercantilist doctrine by English classical economists, such as Adam Smith, and the French Physiocrats. Mercantilist doctrine was pushed aside by the doctrine of comparative advantage which enshrined the idea that free and open trade would be the most beneficial system for all who participate.

While the general perception of mercantilism is one of a long cohesive chapter in the history of economic thought, mercantilist authors were typically business and professional people who haphazardly wrote and made known their thoughts—long before economics came to be an academic discipline. To paraphrase one writer of the time, merchants were proselytizing and pamphleteering men of affairs, rather than philosophers, and had no pretensions to science. This is in contrast to their antecedents, such as Italian religious and philosopher Thomas Aquinas (1225-1274), who sought to understand a just or fair price.

Most representative of mercantilist writings were the French and English writers of the 17th century. These eminently practical thinkers sought the order, protection, and stability that was essential for the expansion of their activities, which in turn would benefit the state. In exchange for military protection of their trading routes, they often succeeded in gaining monopolistic subsidization from the crown while the state expanded its material means for colonization. Wealth accrued to both the state and the merchant elite in the form of gold and various raw materials to which value could be added and then exported in the form of finished goods. Mercantilists viewed production as being important only in so far as it led to an export surplus.

While the merchant class was far from cohesive, disagreements about policy within the merchant class were subservient to the aims of the common goal of expanding the trade surplus. Mercantilists vigorously encouraged exports, except machinery and plant and equipment that might aid foreign competitors. They also discouraged imports, except raw materials and of course precious metals. The colonies, including the Americas, served as a prime export market and a source of **tax** revenue, military bases, and of course a source of gold, silver, and raw materials. A strong navy and a military war machine was vital to the implementation and maintenance of these policies.

As production became relatively more important, capitalists realized that by controlling production, it would be possible to cut **costs**, raise productivity, and undercut competitors by lowering prices. This line of reasoning led economists such as Adam Smith to reject the idea that gold (i.e., money) constituted wealth. In a powerful critique of mercantilists, Smith pointed out that money merely reflected the wealth produced by production while expressing the value of commodities and services offered in the marketplace. Furthermore, struggles between merchants over trade monopolies and prices fostered conflict to the detriment of all concerned. Merchants as a class were thus compelled to become full-fledged capitalists or fade into the newly emerging working class. The many criticisms of mercantilism culminated in a devastating critique known as the specie-flow mechanism. Scottish philosopher and political economist David Hume (1711-1776) pointed out that the very success of a nation's mercantilist policies—a trade surplus—would set in motion forces that would tend to reverse the trade surplus, all through the normal operation of markets. Allowing for the free flow of money, at this time mostly gold, it was argued, would tend to result in a balance of trade equilibrium.

While Hume's specie-flow mechanism is the most well known critique of mercantilist thought, opposition to mercantilist thinking began as early as the late 17th century. The main idea here was that the very success of mercantilist policies would trigger unintended consequences. As argued by Hume and others, a positive trade balance implies a positive net flow of money, because more money is coming in than going out. A situation would soon evolve where too much money is chasing too few goods, as the system is operating at full capacity and money is not generally hoarded but kept in circulation. The only logical effect of this is a rise in prices. In deficit countries, as opposed to the mercantilist surplus countries, money is flowing out, which results in falling prices. The deficit countries will thus become more competitive over time and trade will shift their way resulting in a trade equilibrium. This doctrine later became known as the quantity theory of money.

In terms of its historical influence, mercantilist policy accelerated the breakup of the feudal economy and the guild crafts system of production. State policy and the merchant system complemented one another. The main objective was to foster growth of foreign trade (along with shipping and export industries such as textiles) while encouraging the inflow of precious metals and raw materials to which value could be added for export. Mercantilism thus served to accelerate the transition of Europe from a land-based economy to a monetary economy. Although pure mercantilism is a dead economic issue today, vestiges of it remain. As author and historian Paul Johnson wrote in *Commentary,* "To trade freely is not a human natural propensity."

[John A. Sarich, updated by Michael Knes]

FURTHER READING:

Blaug, Mark. *Great Economists before Keynes.* Atlantic Highlands, NJ: Humanities Press International, 1997.

Johnson, Paul. "Arguing for Free Trade." *Commentary* 100, no. 2 (August 1995): 50-51.

Magnusson, Lars. *Mercantilism: The Shaping of Economic Language.* London: Routledge, 1994.

Sills, David L. ed. *International Encyclopedia of the Social Sciences.* New York: Macmillan Company, 1968.

Spiegel, Henry William. *The Growth of Economic Thought.* Durham, NC: Duke University Press, 1983.

Steele, G. R. "The Money Economy: Mercantilism, Classical Economics, and Keynes' 'General Theory.'" *American Journal of Economics and Sociology* 57, no. 4 (October 1998): 485-98.

Tyson, Laura D'Andrea. "Don't Worry: China Isn't Following in Japan's Footsteps." *Business Week,* 20 April 1998, 26.

Viner, Jacob. *Essays on the Intellectual History of Economics.* Princeton, NJ: Princeton University Press, 1991.

MERCHANDISING

Merchandising is a branch of marketing theory and practice concerned with maximizing product sales by designing, packaging, pricing, and displaying goods in a way that stimulates higher sales volume. The underlying assumption in merchandising is that consumers may have a general need for (or interest in) a certain class of product, and it is the merchandiser's task to present the product in a way that best captures consumers' attention and persuades them that the product will fulfill their needs and wants. Merchandising employs a wealth of theories about consumer behavior to accomplish this.

A particular merchandising campaign can involve myriad considerations, such as

- product packaging
- signage
- location in the store
- shape, size, color, and other physical characteristics of the display
- advertising (in-store and other means)
- discounts, prizes, or other promotional offers

DIFFERENT VIEWS OF MERCHANDISING

Although they all revolve around these basic principles, several different definitions and uses of the term ''merchandising'' exist.

MERCHANDISING AS A PROCESS. First, and most broadly, some view merchandising as an entire set of economic activities, conducted by firms that may be labeled merchandisers, extending from an initial product idea to a finished product on display in a store. In this sense, merchandising is the process of bringing products successfully to market, especially in retail settings. In order to complete this process, the merchandising function requires coordination of many areas of a business, including marketing, procurement, accounting, production, and warehousing/distribution. The entire process is guided by what the company perceives as a market need, and this need will dictate whether there is will be one uniform product or many variations, how it will look, whether it will be produced seasonally or year round, and so on.

MERCHANDISING AS RETAILING. Second, merchandising is sometimes seen as equivalent to **retail trade**, particularly for stores that sell a large volume of popular items (i.e., ''mass merchandisers'' such as Wal-Mart Stores, Inc.). This view emphasizes merchandising as a function of choosing product lines to carry that are likely to move quickly, organizing the store to maximize traffic past profitable lines, and maintaining visual displays and advertisements that turn traffic into sales.

MERCHANDISING AS MASS MARKETING OF INTELLECTUAL PROPERTY. A third and rather narrow notion of merchandising is the familiar practice of creating and marketing a product line centered around a popular theme (usually associated with a piece of **intellectual property**), such as a movie, a television show, a brand name, a corporate identity, a celebrity, or a fictitious character. This is often described as the merchandising side of the entertainment business, although non-entertainment companies also market these kinds of products.

BRIEF SURVEY OF THEORIES

A large body of theory and empirical evidence informs many merchandising decisions. The factors that must be considered when developing a merchandising plan span from **market research** to consumer behavior to competitive intelligence.

Product pricing is a good example of how many considerations can go into merchandising. Prices can be set in various ways to serve different objectives, with the ultimate goal usually being to maximize profitability. In a retail setting, this often means taking a slim profit on certain items while taking a generous profit on others. For instance, in a practice known as price signaling, many grocery stores consciously price certain common staple items, such as milk, at a very competitive low price. The reasoning, supported by empirical research, is that consumers see these staples as a bellwether for the overall value paradigm of that store. In other words, if the consumer sees that the price of milk is low, he or she tends to draw the conclusion that most things at the store are fairly priced. The retailer's hope, however, is that while the customer is there to get milk, he or she will also purchase any number of other items—which tend to be more prominently displayed—that carry a higher price margin. In contrast, even if a convenience store buys its milk at the same wholesale price as the grocery store, it generally doesn't need to practice the same type of price signaling. This is because its customers implicitly derive their value from convenience and are willing to pay more at the register for this convenience.

Another common application of merchandising theory is the practice known as cross-merchandising. This occurs when a manufacturer or retailer links the marketing of one product to the marketing of another. A simple yet powerful example is the use of food displays at grocery stores. Say a store wishes to promote the sales of deli cheeses, which carry an attractive profit margin. To improve the likelihood of selling cheese, the store may locate items consumed with cheese nearby, e.g., crackers and breads, and may even display them directly together or offer samples. All of these things tend to shore up sales. Another alternative frequently used in higher-end grocery stores is to display interesting facts or information pertaining to the product alongside it. The information may answer common questions about the product (e.g., to reduce uncertainty about buying or using it) or it might be something catchy to stimulate the shopper's interest. For example, the cheese stand might include creatively worded reviews and wine suggestions for each type of cheese (provided that the store stocks wines). If the cross-merchandising works, the customer will not only buy the cheese but also the crackers or wine.

Although these examples focus mostly on one factor at a time, usually merchandisers must plan the full array of options in a merchandising program. For instance, in addition to merely determining which products have cross-merchandising potential, the company may also decide whether the appropriate emphasis in the display is (1) price, e.g., using a large sign advertising the low price and a utilitarian display; (2) convenience, e.g., locating the items on the main aisle; or (3) luxury, e.g., emphasizing quality, status, mood, or enjoyable experience with a creative or elaborate display.

SEE ALSO: Marketing

FURTHER READING:

Kunz, Grace I. *Merchandising: Theory, Principles, and Practice.* New York: Fairchild Books, 1998.

MERCOSUR

Mercosur is a customs union coordinating the economies of Argentina, Brazil, Paraguay, and Uruguay. Mercosur (in Portuguese, Mercosul) resulted from the 1991 Treaty of Asunción, and began taking effect on January 1, 1995. Since then, two additional nations have joined as associate members: Chile (in 1996) and Bolivia (in 1997).

Mercosur eliminates the majority of tariffs among the four member states as well as the two associate member nations. Additionally, the original four nations share a single external tariff throughout the region. The tariff is intended to spur interregional growth and interregional investment.

Following political upheavals in Paraguay in the mid-1990s, the four Mercosur presidents met in San Luis, Argentina, in June 1996. At the San Luis meeting, Mercosur added the so-called democratic clause, in which they indicated that respect for democratic institutions is a prerequisite to Mercosur membership.

COMPARISON TO OTHER INTERNATIONAL TRADE BLOCS

Mercosur differs substantially from both the **North American Free Trade Agreement** (NAFTA) and the **European Union**. To some extent, in terms of member integration, Mercosur can be seen as being somewhere between NAFTA and the European Union.

The Mercosur members have as their goal greater economic integration than their NAFTA counterparts. The two blocs are similar in creating a **free trade** zone among their members. Thus, both Mercosur and NAFTA share a common goal in eliminating all barriers to trade among their members. Mercosur, however, extends this cooperation by creating shared external tariffs to third-party members; NAFTA members do not.

The European Union, in turn, goes beyond the integration of member states' economies that characterizes Mercosur. Thus, European Union members share a common trade policy and the free movement of labor and capital among member states; Mercosur does not. Additionally, the European Union leaves open the possibility of coordinating independent national legislative activity; Mercosur does not.

SIZE AND GROWTH OF MERCOSUR

Together, the four member nations represent 59 percent of the land mass of Latin America. Additionally, Mercosur joined together a population of approximately 190 million, or 44 percent of the Latin American total. By 1997, following the associate memberships of Bolivia and Chile, that figure had grown to a population of 220 million people. At the time of the Treaty of Asunción, the combined **gross national product** (GNP) of the four nations was approximately $437 billion. By 1997, the combined GNP of the six Mercosur states (including the two associate members) had reached $1.3 trillion.

Though the customs union formally took effect on January 1, 1995, trade in the entire region had already exploded in anticipation. Trade among the four Mercosur nations grew from $4.7 billion in 1991 to over $10 billion by the end of 1994. Despite world economic crises, growth within Mercosur has continued to grow. Consequently, Mercosur experienced more rapid growth than any other trade bloc, with a 400 percent increase in trade growth between 1990 and 1997.

While some of this growth reflects **foreign investment** in Mercosur member nations, much of this growth can be attributed to the elimination of tariffs and other **trade barriers** among the members. For example, Paraguay, a leading producer of cotton, traditionally shipped 90 percent of its product to Brazil, but in the form of raw cotton. In the wake of Mercosur, Paraguay's textile industry expanded dramatically as—for the first time—it could ship manufactured cotton products (such as thread, cloth, and clothing) to Brazil duty-free. The resultant demand for cotton goods in the form of value-added garment production, in turn, boosted the Paraguayan economy and created a supporting manufacturing **infrastructure**.

While foreign investment has remained substantial among the Mercosur members, the common external tariff for the region has also successfully encouraged interregional investment. In the four-year period from Mercosur's signing in 1991 to its enactment at the close of 1994, for example, investment from Brazil into Argentina reached $1 billion. Additionally, the member states have undertaken a proposal to build the world's longest bridge of its kind, at the Uruguayan city of Colonia, crossing the Río de la Plata. The proposed bridge will join Uruguay with the Argentine capital of Buenos Aires on the opposite river bank. In addition to allowing for construction costs previously far in excess of Uruguay's pre-Mercosur ability, the bridge will radically slash the overland trucking time between Argentina's most important economic center and Brazil's major industrial center of São Paulo. Additionally, Uruguay will reinforce its position as a trade crossroads, increasing **employment** at the least and opening its own opportunities to build on the trade traffic between Argentina and Brazil.

Investment from foreign multinational corporations—including the United States—in the Mercosur has resulted in an estimated $3.5 billion, ranging from investment in factories to franchise operations. While some officials in Mexico, Canada, and the United States see opportunities for expanding NAFTA to the Mercosur nations, the direction of the Mercosur members at present is leaning away from ties to North America. The Mercosur nations have set the goal of first strengthening their own regional economy and then expanding, if at all, to other South American nations in order to form a South America-wide customs union as a counterbalance to, not in cooperation with, the North American free trade partners.

SEE ALSO: Andean Pact Nations, Doing Business in the; Argentina, Doing Business in; Brazil, Doing Business in

[David A. Victor]

FURTHER READING:

Coffey, Peter, ed. *Latin America-Mercosur.* Dordrecht, Netherlands: Kluwer Academic, 1998.

Roett, Riordan, ed. *Mercosur: Regional Integration, World Markets.* Boulder, Co: Lynne Rienner, 1999.

MERGERS AND ACQUISITIONS

A merger occurs when one firm assumes all the assets and all the **liabilities** of another. The acquiring firm retains its identity, while the acquired firm ceases to exist. A majority vote of shareholders is generally required to approve a merger. A merger is just one type of acquisition. One company can acquire another in several other ways, including purchasing some or all of the company's assets or buying up its outstanding shares of **stock**.

In general, mergers and other types of acquisitions are performed in the hopes of realizing an economic gain. For such a transaction to be justified, the two firms involved must be worth more together than they were apart. Some of the potential advantages of mergers and acquisitions include achieving **economies of scale**, combining complementary resources, garnering **tax** advantages, and eliminating inefficiencies. Other reasons for considering growth through acquisitions include obtaining proprietary rights to products or services, increasing market power by purchasing competitors, shoring up weaknesses in key business areas, penetrating new geographic regions, or providing managers with new opportunities for career growth and advancement. Since mergers and acquisitions are so complex, however, it can be very difficult to evaluate the transaction, define the associated costs and benefits, and handle the resulting tax and legal issues.

''In today's global business environment, companies may have to grow to survive, and one of the best ways to grow is by merging with another company or acquiring other companies,'' consultant Jacalyn Sherriton told Robert McGarvey in an interview for *Entrepreneur.* ''Massive, multibillion-dollar corporations are becoming the norm, leaving an entrepreneur to wonder whether a merger ought to be in his or her plans, too,'' McGarvey continued.

When a business owner chooses to merge with or sell out to another company, it is sometimes called ''harvesting'' the business. In this situation, the transaction is intended to release the value locked up in the business for the benefit of its owners and investors. The impetus for a business owner to pursue a sale or merger may involve estate planning, a need to diversify his or her investments, an inability to finance growth independently, or a simple need for change. In addition, some businesses find that the best way to grow and compete against larger firms is to merge with or acquire other businesses.

In principle, the decision to merge with or acquire another firm is a **capital budgeting** decision. But mergers differ from ordinary investment decisions in at least five ways. First, the value of a merger may depend on such things as strategic fits that are difficult to measure. Second, the **accounting**, tax, and legal aspects of a merger can be complex. Third, mergers often involve issues of **corporate control** and are a means of replacing existing **management**. Fourth, mergers obviously affect the value of the firm, but they also affect the relative value of the **stocks** and **bonds**. Finally, mergers are often ''unfriendly'' or ''hostile.''

TYPES OF ACQUISITIONS

In general, acquisitions can be horizontal, vertical, or conglomerate. A horizontal acquisition takes place between two firms in the same line of business. For example, one tool and die company might purchase another. In contrast, a vertical merger entails expanding forward or backward in the chain of distribution, toward the source of raw materials or toward the ultimate consumer. For example, an auto parts manufacturer might purchase a retail auto parts chain. A conglomerate is formed through the combination of unrelated businesses.

Another type of combination of two companies is a consolidation. In a consolidation, an entirely new firm is created, and the two previous entities cease to exist. Consolidated **financial statements** are prepared under the assumption that two or more corporate entities are in actuality only one. The consolidated statements are prepared by combining the account balances of the individual firms after certain adjusting and eliminating entries are made.

Another way to acquire a firm is to buy the voting stock. This can be done by agreement of management or by **tender offer**. In a tender offer, the acquiring firm makes the offer to buy stock directly to the shareholders, thereby bypassing management. In contrast to a merger, a stock acquisition requires no stockholder voting. Shareholders wishing to keep their stock can simply do so. Also, a minority of shareholders may hold out in a tender offer.

A bidding firm can also buy another simply by purchasing all its assets. This involves a costly legal transfer of title and must be approved by the shareholders of the selling firm. A takeover is the transfer of control from one group to another. Normally, the acquiring firm (the bidder) makes an offer for the target firm. In a proxy contest, a group of dissident shareholders will seek to obtain enough votes to gain control of the **board of directors**.

TAXABLE VERSUS TAX-FREE TRANSACTIONS

Mergers and acquisitions can be either tax-free or taxable events. The tax status of a transaction may affect its value from both the buyer's and the seller's viewpoints. In a taxable acquisition, the assets of the selling firm are revalued or ''written up.'' Therefore, the **depreciation** deduction will rise (assets are not revalued in a tax-free acquisition). But the selling shareholders will have to pay **capital gains** taxes and thus will want more for their shares to compensate. This is known as the capital gains effect. The capital gains and write-up effects tend to cancel each other out.

Certain exchanges of stock are considered tax-free reorganizations, which permit the owners of one company to exchange their shares for the stock of the acquirer without paying taxes. There are three basic types of tax-free reorganizations. In order for a transaction to qualify as a type A tax-free reorganization, it must be structured in certain ways. In contrast to a type B reorganization, the type A transaction allows the buyer to use either voting or nonvoting stock. It also permits the buyer to use more cash in the total consideration since the law does not stipulate a maximum amount of cash that can be used. At least 50 percent of the consideration, however, must be stock in the acquiring corporation. In addition, in a type A reorganization, the acquiring corporation may choose not to purchase all the target's assets.

In instances where at least 50 percent of the bidder's stock is used as the consideration—but other considerations such as cash, **debt**, or nonequity **securities** are also used—the transaction may be partially taxable. Capital gains taxes must be paid on those shares that were exchanged for nonequity consideration.

A type B reorganization requires that the acquiring corporation use mainly its own voting **common stock** as the consideration for purchase of the target corporation's common stock. Cash must comprise no more than 20 percent of the total consideration, and at least 80 percent of the target's stock must be paid for by voting stock by the bidder.

Target stockholders who receive the stock of the acquiring corporation in exchange for their common stock are not immediately taxed on the consideration they receive. Taxes will have to be paid only if the stock is eventually sold. If cash is included in the transaction, this cash may be taxed to the extent that it represents a gain on the sale of stock.

In a type C reorganization, the acquiring corporation must purchase 80 percent of the fair **market value** of the target's assets. In this type of reorganization, a tax liability results when the acquiring corporation purchases the assets of the target using consideration other than stock in the acquiring corporation. The tax liability is measured by comparing the purchase price of the assets with the adjusted basis of these assets.

FINANCIAL ACCOUNTING FOR MERGERS AND ACQUISITIONS

The two principal accounting methods used in mergers and acquisitions are the pooling of interests method and the purchase method. The main difference between them is the value that the combined firm's **balance sheet** places on the assets of the acquired firm, as well as the depreciation allowances and charges against **income** following the merger.

The pooling of interests method assumes that the transaction is simply an exchange of equity securities. Therefore, the capital stock account of the target firm is eliminated, and the acquirer issues new stock to replace it. The two firms' assets and liabilities are combined at their historical book values as of the acquisition date. The end result of a pooling of interests transaction is that the total assets of the combined firm are equal to the sum of the assets of the individual firms. No goodwill is generated, and there are no charges against earnings. A tax-free acquisition would normally be reported as a pooling of interests.

Under the purchase method, assets and liabilities are shown on the merged firm's books at their market (not book) values as of the acquisition date. This method is based on the idea that the resulting values should reflect the market values established during the bargaining process. The total liabilities of the combined firm equal the sum of the two firms' individual liabilities. The equity of the acquiring firm is increased by the amount of the purchase price.

Accounting for the excess of cost over the aggregate of the fair market values of the identifiable net assets acquired applies only in purchase accounting. The excess is called goodwill, an asset that is charged against income and amortized over a period that cannot exceed 40 years. Although the **amortization** ''expense'' is deducted from reported income, it cannot be deducted for tax purposes.

Purchase accounting usually results in increased depreciation charges because the book value of most assets is usually less than fair value because of **inflation**. For tax purposes, however, depreciation does not increase because the tax basis of the assets remains the same. Since depreciation under pooling accounting is based on the old book values of the assets, accounting income is usually higher under the pooling method. The accounting treatment has no cash flow consequences. Thus, value should be unaffected by accounting procedure. Some firms, however, may dislike the purchase method because of the goodwill created. The reason for this is that goodwill is amortized over a period of years.

HOW TO VALUE AN ACQUISITION CANDIDATE

Valuing an acquisition candidate is similar to valuing any investment. The analyst estimates the incremental cash flows, determines an appropriate risk-adjusted **discount rate**, and then computes the net present value. If firm A is acquiring firm B, for example, then the acquisition makes economic sense if the value of the combined firm is greater than the value of firm A plus the value of firm B. Synergy is said to exist when the cash flow of the combined firm is greater than the sum of the cash flows for the two firms as separate companies. The gain from the merger is the **present value** of this difference in cash flows.

SOURCES OF GAINS FROM ACQUISITIONS

The gains from an acquisition may result from one or more of the following five categories: revenue enhancement; cost reductions; lower taxes; changing capital requirements; and a lower cost of capital. Increased revenues may come from **marketing** gains, strategic benefits, and increased market power. Marketing gains arise from more effective **advertising**, economies of distribution, and a better mix of products. Strategic benefits represent opportunities to enter new lines of business. Finally, a merger may reduce **competition**, thereby increasing market power. Such mergers, of course, may run afoul of **antitrust** legislation.

A larger firm may be able to operate more efficiently than two smaller firms, thereby reducing **costs**. Horizontal mergers may generate economies of scale. This means that the average production cost will fall as production volume increases. A vertical merger may allow a firm to decrease costs by more closely coordinating production and distribution. Finally, economies may be achieved when firms have complementary resources—for example, when one firm has excess production capacity and another has insufficient capacity.

Tax gains in mergers may arise because of unused tax losses, unused debt capacity, surplus funds, and the write-up of depreciable assets. The tax losses of target corporations can be used to offset the acquiring corporation's future income. These tax losses can be used to offset income for a maximum of 15 years or until the tax loss is exhausted. Only tax losses for the previous three years can be used to offset future income.

Tax loss carry-forwards can motivate mergers and acquisitions. A company that has earned profits may find value in the tax losses of a target corporation that can be used to offset the income it plans to earn. A merger may not, however, be structured solely for tax purposes. In addition, the acquirer must continue to operate the preacquisition business of the company in a net loss position. The tax benefits may be less than their ''face value,'' not only because of the time value of money, but also because the tax loss carry-forwards might expire without being fully utilized.

Tax advantages can also arise in an acquisition when a target firm carries assets on its books with basis, for tax purposes, below their market value. These assets could be more valuable, for tax purposes, if they were owned by another corporation that could increase their tax basis following the acquisition. The acquirer would then depreciate the assets based on the higher market values, in turn, gaining additional depreciation benefits.

Interest payments on debt are a tax-deductible expense, whereas **dividend** payments from equity ownership are not. The existence of a tax advantage for debt is an incentive to have greater use of debt, as opposed to equity, as the means of financing merger and acquisition transactions. Also, a firm that borrows much less than it could borrow may be an acquisition target because of its unused debt capacity. While the use of financial **leverage** produces tax benefits, debt also increases the likelihood of financial distress in the event that the acquiring firm cannot meet its interest payments on the acquisition debt.

Finally, a firm with surplus funds may wish to acquire another firm. The reason is that distributing the money as a dividend or using it to repurchase shares will increase income taxes for shareholders. With an acquisition, no income taxes are paid by shareholders.

Acquiring firms may be able to more efficiently utilize **working capital** and fixed assets in the target firm, thereby reducing capital requirements and enhancing profitability. This is particularly true if the target firm has redundant assets that may be divested.

The cost of debt can often be reduced when two firms merge. The combined firm will generally have reduced variability in its cash flows. Therefore, there may be circumstances under which one or the other of the firms would have defaulted on its debt, but the combined firm will not. This makes the debt safer, and the cost of borrowing may decline as a result. This is termed the coinsurance effect.

Diversification is often cited as a benefit in mergers. Diversification by itself, however, does not create any value because stockholders can accomplish the same thing as the merger by buying stock in both firms.

VALUATION PROCEDURES

The procedure for valuing an acquisition candidate depends on the source of the estimated gains. Different sources of synergy have different risks. Tax gains can be estimated fairly accurately and should be discounted at the cost of debt. Cost reductions through operating efficiencies can also be determined with some confidence. Such savings should be discounted at a normal weighted average cost of capital. Gains from strategic benefits are difficult to estimate and are often highly uncertain. A discount rate greater than the overall cost of capital would thus be appropriate.

The net present value (NPV) of the acquisition is equal to the gains less the cost of the acquisition. The cost depends on whether cash or stock is used as payment. The cost of an acquisition when cash is used is just the amount paid. The cost of the merger when common stock is used as the consideration (the payment) is equal to the percentage of the new firm that is owned by the previous shareholders in the acquired firm multiplied by the value of the new firm. In a cash merger the benefits go entirely to the acquiring firm, whereas in a stock-for-stock exchange the benefits are shared by the acquiring and acquired firms.

Whether to use cash or stock depends on three considerations. First, if the acquiring firm's management believes that its stock is overvalued, then a stock acquisition may be cheaper. Second, a cash acquisition is usually taxable, which may result in a higher price. Third, the use of stock means that the acquired firm will share in any gains from merger; if the merger has a negative NPV, however, then the acquired firm will share in the loss.

In valuing acquisitions, the following factors should be kept in mind. First, market values must not be ignored. Thus, there is no need to estimate the value of a publicly traded firm as a separate entity. Second, only those cash flows that are incremental are relevant to the analysis. Third, the discount rate used should reflect the risk associated with the incremental cash flows. Therefore, the acquiring firm should not use its own cost of capital to value the cash flows of another firm. Finally, acquisition may involve significant **investment banking** fees and costs.

HOSTILE ACQUISITIONS

The replacement of poor management is a potential source of gain from acquisition. Changing technological and competitive factors may lead to a need for **corporate restructuring**. If incumbent management is unable to adapt, then a hostile acquisition is one method for accomplishing change.

Hostile acquisitions generally involve poorly performing firms in mature industries, and occur when the board of directors of the target is opposed to the sale of the company. In this case, the acquiring firm has two options to proceed with the acquisition—a tender offer or a proxy fight. A tender offer represents an offer to buy the stock of the target firm either directly from the firm's shareholders or through the secondary market. In a proxy fight, the acquirer solicits the shareholders of the target firm in an attempt to obtain the right to vote their shares. The acquiring firm hopes to secure enough proxies to gain control of the board of directors and, in turn, replace the incumbent management.

Management in target firms will typically resist **takeover** attempts, either to get a higher price for the firm or to protect their own self-interests. This can be done a number of ways. Target companies can decrease the likelihood of a takeover though charter amendments. With the staggered board technique, the board of directors is classified into three groups, with only one group elected each year. Thus, the suitor cannot obtain control of the board immediately even though it may have acquired a majority ownership of the target via a tender offer. Under a supermajority amendment, a higher percentage than 50 percent—generally two-thirds or 80 percent—is required to approve a merger.

Other defensive tactics include **poison pills** and dual class recapitalizations. With poison pills, existing shareholders are issued rights that, if a bidder acquires a certain percentage of the outstanding shares, can be used to purchase additional shares at a bargain price, usually half the market price. Dual class recapitalizations distribute a new class of equity with superior voting rights. This enables the target firm's managers to obtain majority control even though they do not own a majority of the shares.

Other preventive measures occur after an unsolicited offer is made to the target firm. The target may file suit against the bidder alleging violations of antitrust or securities laws. Alternatively, the target may engage in asset and liability restructuring to make it an unattractive target. With asset restructuring, the target purchases assets that the bidder does not want or that will create antitrust problems, or sells off the assets that the suitor desires to obtain. Liability restructuring maneuvers include issuing shares to a friendly third party to dilute the bidder's ownership position or leveraging up the firm through a **leveraged recapitalization** making it difficult for the suitor to finance the transaction.

Other postoffer tactics involve targeted share repurchases (often termed ''**greenmail**'')—in which the target repurchases the shares of an unfriendly suitor at a premium over the current market price—and **golden parachutes**, which are lucrative supplemental compensation packages for the target firm's management. These packages are activated in the case of a takeover and the subsequent resignations of the senior executives. Finally, the target may employ an exclusionary self-tender. With this tactic, the target firm offers to buy back its own stock at a premium from everyone except the bidder.

A **privately held company** is not subject to unfriendly takeovers. A publicly traded firm ''goes private'' when a group, usually involving existing management, buys up all the publicly held stock. Such transactions are typically structured as **leveraged buyouts** (LBOs). LBOs are financed primarily with debt secured by the assets of the target firm.

WHO BENEFITS FROM MERGERS AND ACQUISITIONS?

Mergers and acquisitions proceeded at a record pace during the late 1990s. Up until 1996, the most expensive corporate merger ever was the $25 billion deal between RJR Nabisco and Kohlberg Kravis Roberts that was completed in 1989. But this record has been surpassed numerous times since then. By the middle of 1998, the most expensive merger was the $78.2 billion deal between the Travelers Group and Citicorp. In fact, according to Jeff Rundles in *Colorado Business,* 8 of the 10 largest corporate mergers in history were announced during the first half of 1998. Some experts claimed that these enormous deals would reduce competition by creating highly consolidated industries controlled by a few major players. They argued that the huge corporations created by such mergers would focus on large accounts to the detriment of smaller customers. Individuals and **small businesses** would likely face higher prices and reduced services.

There is also a question about whether stockholders gain from mergers and acquisitions. Empirical evidence suggests that the shareholders in acquired firms benefit substantially. Gains for this group typically amount to 20 percent in mergers and 30 percent in tender offers above the market prices prevailing a month prior to the merger announcement. The target company's stock price tends to rise following a merger announcement, while the acquiring company's stock price tends to remain flat. Therefore, the gains that accrue to acquiring firms are difficult to measure. The best evidence suggests that shareholders in bidding firms gain little. Losses in value subsequent to merger announcements are not unusual. This seems to suggest that overvaluation by bidding firms is common. Managers may also have incentives to increase firm size at the potential expense of shareholder wealth. If so, merger activity may happen for noneconomic reasons, to the detriment of shareholders.

SEE ALSO: Management Buyouts

[Robert T. Kleiman,
updated by Laurie Collier Hillstrom]

FURTHER READING:

Auerbach, Alan J. *Corporate Takeovers: Causes and Consequences.* Chicago: University of Chicago Press, 1988.

Coffee, John C., Jr., Louis Lowenstein, and Susan Rose-Ackerman. *Knights, Raiders, and Targets: The Impact of the Hostile Takeover.* New York: Oxford University Press, 1988.

Gaughan, Patrick A. *Mergers and Acquisitions.* New York: HarperCollins, 1991.

Lajoux, Alexandra Reed, and J. Fred Weston. "Do Deals Deliver on Postmerger Performance?" *Mergers and Acquisitions,* September/October 1998.

McGarvey, Robert. "Merge Ahead: Before You Go Full-Speed into a Merger, Read This." *Entrepreneur,* October 1997.

Morgenson, Gretchen. "When Big Fish Eat Little Fish." *New York Times,* 29 November 1998.

Rundles, Jeff. "When Mergers Collide: The Ultimate Impact of Corporate Mixes May Not Bode Well for the Little People—or Companies." *Colorado Business Magazine,* October 1998.

METRICS AND MEASUREMENT

Metrics and measurement is comprised of two major bodies of knowledge, both studying the quantitative assessment of performance using test statistics. The first area includes the test measurement (primarily education-oriented), opinion survey, and **market research** survey industries. The second area is **software** engineering whereby the technical specifications of **computer** programs are appraised for execution.

EDUCATION TESTS, OPINION SURVEYS, AND MARKET RESEARCH

In the education industry, student intelligence measurement is a key concern for several reasons, including resource scarcity and pressure to keep up with a world that's becoming increasingly technological. The market research industry finds corporations striving to reach their customers through **advertising** and direct contact as well through niche **marketing**, whereby firms are able to reach consumers by way of preferred select offerings. This increased focus has driven firms to increase their knowledge of their customers and produce or provide services to meet specific consumer demands. Research methodologies used for measuring student learning and consumer preferences and profiles are similar.

The reporting and interpretation of tests and surveys is becoming more of a matter of presentation than content. For example, if a simple spelling test was administered and the number of words correctly spelled was 67, what would this raw score mean? By itself, not much. Questions that would arise include: How many words were asked to be spelled on the test? How many difficult and easy words were there? What is the age and education of the person being tested? Raw scores (absolute standards) typically need to be transformed into a test statistic for the purposes of measurement. Likewise, a survey designed to poll people on their preference for capital punishment will generate varying results depending on who is asked, the circumstances of when the question is asked, and so on. For example, the time period surrounding an emotionally charged event, such as the murder of a child, may cause sentiment in favor of capital punishment to rise. The way capital punishment is carried out (hanging, electric chair, lethal injection, firing squad) can affect public opinion as well. Researching consumer tastes will produce different results depending on the consumer group, season of the year, state of the economy, and so on.

The units of measurement are the test (or survey) scores. There are two major types of scores: norm-referenced scores and content-referenced scores. Norm-referenced scores—which include same group (inter-individual) and growth (intra-individual) norms—measure the raw scores relative to a statistical norm. Same-group norms measure the performance compared to a reference group—the benchmark. Growth norms are used to interpret scores over time, and are relevant when observing an individual or group that is changing because of **training**, aging, disease progression, etc.

Content-referenced scores provide insight into how specific test questions were answered. Examples of metrics that provide this information are raw, percent correct, and criterion (e.g., pass/fail, healthy/sick, satisfied/unsatisfied) scores.

Of these two types of scores, norm-referenced scores, in general, have become much more popular as opposed to content-referenced scores. Of course, which is the most appropriate depends on the situation.

Another rationale for scales and norms to interpret tests (and surveys) is that the number of questions answered correctly is not necessarily a meaningful measure. First, it assumes each unit (question) is of equal value. Second, it may depend on the purpose (e.g., minimal knowledge or ability). One assumes the test (or survey) results are transferable to other situations (or places) and are therefore generalizable. For example, passing a competency test, such as a driver's license test, denotes competence; that is, you can perform a specific task, such as driving, adequately. Similarly, a marketing survey conducted in San Diego, California, that finds a preference for red-painted cars is more useful if it holds true for people living in Chicago, Atlanta, and elsewhere.

Metrics that may be used to report and interpret test scores include:

- Percent score (or percentage): This is calculated by dividing the number correct by the total number of questions.

- Letter Grade: In education, a letter is often used to denote performance. A, B, C, D, and E represent excellent, good, satisfactory, marginal, and failing performance, respectively. Sometimes letter grades have a plus or minus to create a more precise measure. Letter grades may be used to categorize a percent score, such as 90 percent and above being an A.
- Rank: The relative performance of an individual within a group is placed in descending order from the best (one), to the next best (two), and so on to the worst performance.
- Percentile Rank: This statistic combines the concept of percent and rank whereby the best performance by an individual in a group is 100 percentile and the worst is 0 percentile. For those in between the percentile rank is the percentage of people in the group you outperformed. One hundred less the percentile rank is the percentage of people who did better than that individual.
- Decile Rank: This is similar to percentile score except the precision is in 10 percentile increments.
- **Z-Score**: As most sample or population distributions fit a bell-shaped normal curve, the raw score is converted into a Z-statistic. This transformation is done by taking the raw score and subtracting the mean and then dividing this difference by the standard deviation.
- T-Score: This is not to be confused with the T-scaled score. The T-score is a variant of the **Z-Score**, where $T = 10z + 50$.
- Stanines: Fast becoming a popular metric, as it classifies individuals in a group into categories one through nine. If the group adheres to a normal distribution the stanines match up to the percentile ranks shown in Table 1.

SOFTWARE ENGINEERING METRICS

The impact of computers on business and society increased exponentially in the latter part of the 20th century. Methods of measuring the quality of software programs are continually being developed. Much of the metrics to measure and distinguish software quality focus on conformance to explicit development standards, functional and performance requirements, and features expected of all software. The measurement of software quality can be classified into those variables that can be directly measured (e.g., errors per billion calculations) and indirectly measured (e.g., maintainability).

Important quality factors include the following measures:

- Correctness: The degree to which a program meets its specification and satisfies the client's goals.
- Efficiency: The amount of computing resources and code needed by the program to perform its tasks.
- Flexibility: The effort needed to change a program.
- Integrity: The ability to prevent unauthorized access to the program.
- Maintainability: The effort needed to find and fix program errors.
- Interoperability: The effort needed to attach one system to another system.
- Portability: The effort needed to transfer the program from hardware to hardware and/or to another software system.
- Reliability: The degree to which a program performs its function to expectations.

Table 1

Stanine	1	2	3	4	5	6	7	8	9
Percentile Rank	0-4	4-11	11-23	23-40	40-60	60-77	77-89	89-96	96-100

- Reusability: The extent to which the program, partially or wholly, can be used in other applications.
- Testability: The extent of testing needed to verify that the program performs satisfactorily.
- Usability: The amount of training required to learn how to use the software.

The metrics to grade (on a scale of 0 [low] to 10 [high]) the previous measures are as follows:

- Auditability: The ease of compliance to standards can be audited.
- Accuracy: The precision of calculations.
- Communication Commonality: The extent to which standard protocols, interfaces, and bandwidth are employed.
- Completeness: The extent to which the function is achieved.
- Conciseness: The brevity of the program measured by lines of code.
- Consistency: The use of uniform documentation and design methods.
- Data Commonality: The use of standard data types.
- Error Tolerance: The harm that occurs when errors are encountered.
- Execution Efficiency: The run-time program performance.
- Expandability: The extent to which procedural design and data can be extended.
- Generality: The breadth of program applications.
- Hardware Independence: The degree to which the hardware and software are operationally separated.
- Instrumentation: The extent to which the program evaluates its own functioning and identifies errors.
- Modularity: The functional independence of program components.
- Operability: The degree of complexity in operating the software.
- Security: The ability to protect data and programs.
- Self-Documentation: The extent to which relevant documentation is provided.
- Simplicity: The ease with which the program can be understood.
- Software System Independence: The extent to which the software is independent of nonstandard features such as program language and operating system.
- Traceability: The capacity to trace a program design component to its requirements.
- Training: The amount of assistance provided by the software to new users.

As both software and hardware engineering evolve, new metrics and measurements will be created to evaluate the performance quality.

The purposes of the measurement of the metrics are to help evaluate the software models, indicate the complexity of the procedural designs and source code, and aid in the construction of more testing. This measurement process follows five steps:

1. Formulation of metrics appropriate to evaluate the software.
2. Collection of data needed to compute the chosen metrics.
3. Analysis and calculation of metrics.
4. Interpretation of the metrics to provide understanding.
5. Feedback given to the system designers of the software.

In these ways, metrics and measurement can provide a quantifiable gauge of quality for software, facilitating the improvement of the product by the software engineer.

[Raymond A. K. Cox]

FURTHER READING:

Ebel, R. L. *Essentials of Educational Measurement.* Englewood Cliffs, NJ: Prentice-Hall, 1979.

Grady, R. B. *Practical Software Metrics for Project Management and Process Improvement.* Englewood Cliffs, NJ: Prentice-Hall, 1992.

Lorenz, M., and J. Kidd. *Object-Oriented Software Metrics.* Englewood Cliffs, NJ: Prentice Hall, 1994.

Sheppard, M. *Software Engineering Metrics.* New York: McGraw-Hill, 1992.

METROPOLITAN STATISTICAL AREA (MSA)

Metropolitan Statistical Area (MSA) is a designation the U.S. government uses to refer to a region that, broadly speaking, consists of a city and its suburbs, plus any surrounding communities that are closely linked to the city economically and socially. MSAs were known as Standard Metropolitan Statistical Areas (SMSAs) from 1959 to 1983 and, before that, as Standard Metropolitan Areas (SMAs). Having some familiarity with MSAs is useful to businesspeople, since data about these regions can be helpful in devising marketing strategies, delineating sales territories, and determining the locations of plant and operating facilities.

DEFINITIONS

The government uses the designation "MSA" for the purpose of applying uniform and consistent standards to the wealth of data collected, analyzed, and published by its myriad departments and agencies. Official definitions for what constitutes an MSA are developed, issued, and periodically revised by the federal Office of Management and Budget (OMB), following public commentary and hearings and in conjunction with the Federal Executive Committee on Metropolitan Areas. And because MSA and similar designations figure prominently in the compilation of statistics for the national census, the U.S. Department of Commerce's Bureau of the Census also plays a part in refining the definitions. Census data, both from the major decennial censuses and smaller interim ones, are used to revise MSA definitions.

Although the OMB's official standards for defining these regions are highly complex, detailed, and marked by qualifications, in general MSAs can be viewed as part of larger entities known as Metropolitan Areas (MAs). MAs are regions composed of one or more counties and containing either (a) a city whose population is at least 50,000 or (b) a Census Bureau-defined "urbanized area" whose population, together with that of its component county or counties, totals at least 100,000. An important exception to how MAs are defined concerns the New England states, where towns and cities rather than counties are used to designate regions as MAs.

Within the broad category of MAs are three elements, or subcategories: (a) MSAs, generally constituting free-standing MAs whose surrounding counties are nonmetropolitan; (b) Consolidated Metropolitan Statistical Areas (CMSAs), representing the largest metropolitan regions, those with populations of more than one million; and (c) Primary Metropolitan Statistical Areas (PMSAs), consisting of the individual urbanized counties or county clusters within CMSAs. It is, however, possible for an MSA to be larger than a CMSA, depending on the geographic dispersion of the population in a particular metropolitan area.

SELECTED FIGURES

Population figures reflect the importance of these categories for statistical and demographic purposes. Based on 1996 Census Bureau estimates, 212 million of the United States' 265 million residents—just under 80 percent—lived in 273 metropolitan areas, as defined by MSAs and CMSAs. The top 20 areas alone reported 112 million people, or 42 percent of the U.S. population. The New York City CMSA, which includes portions of northern New Jersey and Connecticut, is the largest, with approximately 20 million inhabitants. The other top five consolidated areas include Los Angeles-Long Beach, with 15.5 million; Chicago-Gary-Kenosha, with 8.6 million; Washington, D.C.-Baltimore, with 7.2 million; and San Francisco-Oakland-San Jose, with 6.6 million.

There are 18 such CMSAs in total, and they support some 103 million residents. Between 1990 and 1996, these areas combined added more than 5.4 million residents to their populations. According to tabulations published in 1998 by the magazine *Industry Week,* the CMSAs accounted for around 43 percent of all U.S. manufacturing activity in value.

FOR MORE INFORMATION

Information on the OMB's standards for defining MSAs and other such designations can be obtained from the Statistical Policy Office of the Office of Information and Regulatory Affairs, Office of Management and Budget in Washington, D.C. Information on the Census Bureau's application of these standards is available from the Secretary of the Federal Executive Committee on Metropolitan Areas, Population Division, U.S. Bureau of the Census, also in Washington, D.C.

[Roberta H. Winston]

FURTHER READING:

Office of Management and Budget. "Revised Standards for Defining Metropolitan Areas in the 1990s; Notice." *Federal Register.* April 10, April 30, and 10 May 1990.

Purdi, Traci, and Edward W. Hill. "Generating Wealth: Eighteen CMSAs Contribute a Huge Chunk of Manufacturing Value in the U.S." *Industry Week,* 6 April 1998. Available from www.industryweek.com.

U.S. Bureau of the Census. *Estimates of the Population of Metropolitan Areas.* Washington, annual. Available from www.census .gov/population/www/estimates/metroarea.html.

MEXICAN LAW

As a result of the **North American Free Trade Agreement** (NAFTA) that took effect on January 1, 1994, U.S. businesspeople began trading with Mexico's businesspeople, investing in business opportunities in Mexico, and establishing business facilities in Mexico in unprecedented numbers and ways. As a result, as of 1998, Mexico and the United States achieved a level of trade that makes Mexico the United States's second-largest trade partner, second only to Canada. On a daily basis U.S. businesses are involved with Mexico's legal system, which, like most legal systems, is inextricably linked with its economic system and its history. Failure to understand at least the basic elements of Mexico's legal system can pose a significant barrier to U.S. businesspeople trading with or investing in Mexico, because Mexico's legal system is significantly different from that of the United States. Mexico's legal system is a civil law system, which can be traced to 16th century law brought by the Spaniards to the land that later was named Mexico. But, it is not the same civil law as exists in other civil law countries, because various aspects of Mexico's legal system can be traced to pre-Colombian indigenous law as well as to its unique history, social institutions, and economy.

In fact, use of the term ''civil law'' represents a generalization, because the legal system of each civil law system in the world varies according to the unique social, economic, political, and historical background of the individual country. A civil law system is a system in which, in general, laws are ''codified,'' i.e., society relies on a legislative body (or bodies) to pass statutes spelling out their law. Those statutes are then organized, topic by topic, into codes. The codes become the primary resource (research tool) for lawyers and their clients in such a system. In Mexico, the hierarchy of laws is as follows: (1) the federal constitution, (2) legislation (found in the ''Codes'' or ''*Códigos,*'' in Spanish), and (3) regulations interpreting the statutes. Provisions of the constitution supersede any legislation or regulations, and legislation supersedes any regulations. A final source of law in Mexico, which is least compelling in terms of hierarchy of laws, is ''custom.''

An important consideration for businesses dealing with Mexico is that, unlike Mexico's civil law system, the U.S. legal system is a ''common law'' system. In this system, the roots of which can be traced to England, the federal constitution as well as legislation and regulations are recognized as being law just as such documents set down law in a civil law system. A crucial difference between the two systems, however, is that a common law system recognizes the decisions of courts as creating ''law.'' Thus, in the United States, our courts create rules of law to fill in the gray areas not clearly covered by legislation or regulations, and they create law where no statutes or regulations exist. For example, entire bodies of law such as tort law (which includes the law of **negligence** and strict liability for defective products) and contract law (other than **contracts** for the sale of goods) have been covered in the United States as rules of law established through courts' decisions. Thus, U.S. businesspeople are dealing with a very different way of doing things when dealing with the Mexican legal system.

ATTORNEYS

To do business in Mexico, U.S. businesspeople nearly always need to hire a Mexican attorney. Reciprocity that would allow U.S. licensed attorneys to practice law in Mexico and vice versa is not a part of NAFTA. This is not surprising in view of the significant differences between the two legal systems and their laws. Further, it is helpful to remember that even in the United States, licensing of attorneys is done by the individual states. Thus, most attorneys in the United States take a bar exam and seek admission to practice law in only one state; only a small percentage of U.S. attorneys go through the extensive efforts necessary to become licensed to practice law in two or more states.

U.S. businesses usually use their own U.S. attorneys for matters related to U.S. law and hire Mexican attorneys to work with their U.S. attorneys and to handle legal practice in Mexico. While U.S. attorneys are not allowed to practice law before Mexican courts, they are permitted to register as legal **consultants** and establish offices in Mexico from which they can advise their clients. Beyond the need for a licensed attorney who is knowledgeable about Mexican law and legal practice, working with Mexican attorneys makes good practical sense. Mexicans place great value on contacts and relationships with people they know and trust as they do business. Thus, working with a Mexican attorney can facilitate business transactions in informal, yet important, ways going beyond legal requirements.

Mexican legal education and licensing are different from those processes in the United States. In Mexico, there are two levels of attorneys. At the first level, a student of law obtains a five-year degree in law. (This is roughly equivalent to the four-year undergraduate programs in the United States.) After passing courses and oral exams at his or her university, the prospective attorney becomes a *licenciado* and *abogado* (attorney). (The term *licenciado* is applied to graduates of various programs of study at that level in Mexico, not just law. Mexican *abogados* do not take a bar exam such as the exam required of U.S. attorneys in most states.) The *abogado* can practice law in any part of Mexico. The *abogado*'s powers are limited, however, and many kinds of significant legal transactions, such as transfers of real property, can be handled only by a *notario público.* Although the words *notario público* translate literally to ''notary public'' in English, the *notario público* is not at all the equivalent of the notary public in the United States. The *notario público* has received advanced education and training beyond that of an *abogado* and has been appointed to serve in a specific geographical area within one of Mexico's states. He or she can move to another part of that state or to another state in Mexico only by applying and competing for another opening in that new location.

THE MEXICAN POLITICAL AND LEGAL SYSTEMS

Mexico has a federal system of government with a national government and 31 states. Mexico's national government, however, is far more powerful than those of the United States and Canada.

Mexico's president plays an extremely important role in its legal system. Nearly all federal laws in Mexico are initiated by the president, and his powers (there has been no woman president in Mexico) are such that most laws he proposes are passed with little or no alteration. Further, the president, as the leader of the powerful PRI (the political party of every Mexican president elected since 1928), plays a strong role with respect to policy and enactment of law in the various Mexican states. (PRI stands for the *Partido Revolucionario Institucional,* or Revolutionary, Institutional Party.)

The structure of Mexico's court system is similar to that in the United States. In each state there are trial and appellate courts. The federal level includes trial courts, circuit courts of appeal, and a Supreme Court. The Supreme Court is divided into four ''chambers'' with five justices each. Each chamber handles one of four areas of law: criminal, administrative, civil, or labor. It is important to note, however, that the role of the courts in a civil law system such as Mexico's differs from the role of courts in a common law system. In a civil law system, attorneys and judges look to sets of codes in which statutes are set down as their primary source of law. In contrast, in a common law system, attorneys and judge rely on statutes and rules of law and their interpretation as they are set down in prior-written court opinions.

OVERVIEW OF MEXICAN LAW

The most important legal document in Mexico is its federal constitution, which is the basis for all of Mexican law. The current constitution is the 1917 Political Constitution of the United Mexican States (*Constitución Política de los Estados Unidos Mexicanos*). Although the constitution contains many provisions that parallel guarantees found in the U.S. Constitution, such as the right to due process, there are important philosophical differences underlying the two documents. The Mexican Constitution is far longer than that of the United States. It includes economic, social, and cultural rights of the Mexican people and calls for a federal government that takes an active role in promoting those rights. Many of the specific provisions of Mexico's constitution are so detailed that in the United States they would be covered through legislation rather than in the constitution itself.

Mexico's current constitution, which was adopted in 1917, was a product of the Mexican Revolution of 1910-17. The Mexican Revolution followed a period of history from 1877 to 1911 known as the *Porfiriato* for the ruler of Mexico at that time, Porfirio Díaz. During the *Porfiriato,* Díaz and very few other Mexican people lived in **wealth** at the expense of the poor, attempting to emulate the lifestyles of the rich in France and the United States. Díaz encouraged and facilitated extensive foreign investment and involvement in Mexico's economy, and he governed the country with an iron hand. There was little or no social or political mobility. Mexican citizens resented foreign ownership of Mexico's railroads and extensive foreign control over Mexico's mining and oil industries.

The revolution ended these social inequities, and led to sweeping changes. Various crucial sections of the constitution of 1917 were written in reaction to the Díaz era. Among such provisions were Article 27, dealing with agrarian reform and the use and ownership of land, and Article 123, dealing with labor and social reform. Both articles have maintained their importance as Mexico moves into a new era and new economy pursuant to NAFTA.

Article 27 gives the Mexican government the power to expropriate private property for public use, and gives all subterranean land—including all minerals, gases, and hydrocarbons—to the Mexican government. It also prohibits foreign ownership of any land within 100 kilometers of Mexico's border and within 50 kilometers of Mexico's shoreline. Further, the Mexican nation itself has control over the transfer of land to private persons. The objective of Article 27 was to break up the monopolies on land, water, and natural resources held by a privileged few.

As a result of Article 27, large parcels of land formerly owned by rich individuals, companies, and religious organizations were taken over by the Mexican government. Many of the lands were converted to use as *ejidos. Ejidos* are blocks of land that are operated and farmed by Mexican families who have resided on those lands since the implementation of the 1917 constitution.

Prior to the early 1990s, *ejidos* were viewed as a major block to investment in Mexico because, pursuant to Mexican law, such land could not be sold or leased to others. In addition, economists argued that small parcels of land farmed by people on *ejidos* contributed to low productivity. Therefore, in 1992, the Mexican government amended the 1917 constitution to permit the sale or lease of *ejido* lands. Use of this new legal option, however, has not been a simple process. In general, titles to the land do not exist; the land has simply been used by peasant families since the 1920s. This has resulted in several kinds of problems. It is difficult to transfer land because officials are unable to establish ownership. In other cases, land parcels have been transferred and payments made to those who must leave as a result of the transfer. Unfortunately, payments are minimal and are usually insufficient for peasant farmers and their families to establish themselves elsewhere. Further, it is reported that many peasant farmers are simply being pushed from the land, unable to establish sufficient claim to share in payments being made. Thus, acquisition of land by investors can be a difficult, politically controversial project.

Article 123 of the 1917 constitution places nearly all labor matters under federal jurisdiction. Article 123 will be discussed below in conjunction with discussion of Mexico's **labor laws**.

The remainder of this essay will review three areas of Mexican law that are of particular importance to businesses: (1) investment law, (2) labor law, (3) and **environmental law**.

MEXICO'S INVESTMENT LAWS

HISTORICAL DEVELOPMENT. In reaction to the regime of Porfirio Díaz, the Mexican Constitution of 1917 reserved control of land ownership and the exclusive rights to petroleum and other minerals to the Mexican federal government. Thus, throughout most of the 20th century, Mexico has been functioning under a constitution that severely restricts foreign investment. Restrictions have been loosened in the 1990s, however, in preparation for and as a part of NAFTA.

In 1973 the Law to Promote Mexican Investment and Regulate Foreign Investment (also known as the Foreign Investment Law) was passed. It mandated that Mexican enterprises could have a maximum of 49 percent foreign ownership. Thus, the rule became known as the "51-49 percent rule." In 1984 the law was changed to allow majority foreign ownership of Mexican corporations in certain industrial and tourism-related industries. Such investment, however, was slow and cumbersome and was permitted only with the approval, on a case-by-case basis, of the Mexican Foreign Investment Commission (FIC).

Moving into the 21st century, the FIC continues to oversee and regulate **foreign investment** in Mexico, but restrictions on investment have been eased considerably. Under new regulations established in 1989, with the exception of specified industries, foreign investment in Mexico in amounts less than US$100 million could proceed without prior approval from the FIC, and those limits are being raised gradually.

THE MAQUILADORA PROGRAM. The *maquiladora* program represented a major step by Mexico toward opening its borders to foreign investment. The program was started in 1966, but was not officially authorized by Mexican law until 1983. Under the program, a foreign company may establish a manufacturing facility in northern Mexico and can import equipment, components, and materials to Mexico duty-free, provided that a substantial percentage of the goods produced are exported from Mexico. A plant that operates under the program is called a *maquila,* and the legal structure for the manufacturing program is the *maquiladora.* Most *maquilas* in Mexico are operated in conjunction with a twin plant across the U.S. border. Thus, labor intensive production is done in the Mexican plant, while other aspects of production, **marketing**, and distribution are handled by the plant in the United States. The 1983 Mexican law required that *maquilas* export at least 80 percent of their production, but new regulations in 1989 allowed up to 50 percent to be sold in Mexico under certain conditions. Beginning in 1994, *maquiladoras* are allowed to sell all or part of their production directly into the Mexican market. This is being accomplished with a phase-in period. Starting in 1994, a plant was allowed to sell 55 percent of its previous year's production directly into the Mexican market. The phase-in ends in 2001, when 100 percent of the production of the year 2000 can be sold directly into the Mexican market. (It should also be noted that *maquilas* are also required to export their hazardous wastes generated in the production process to the home country of the investor or business. This requirement is set down in a bilateral agreement between the United States and Mexico.)

For Mexico, the *maquiladora* program has generated much needed employment. As of 1990, there were approximately 1,500 *maquilas* operating in Mexico; as of 1999 there were at least 3,000 *maquiladoras.* U.S. businesses benefit from low labor costs in Mexico and duty-free export of the product from Mexico. Special U.S. tariff schedules place a **duty** only on the value added by Mexican components and labor. This reduction in tariff costs was a major benefit to U.S. companies operating *maquiladoras* prior to 1994. It has decreased in significance, however, as the United States, Mexico, and Canada phase out tariffs among themselves pursuant to NAFTA.

NEW POLICIES, LAWS, AND REGULATIONS

Under the leadership of Carlos Salinas de Gortari, who served as president of Mexico from 1988 to 1994, Mexico negotiated and approved NAFTA with the United States and Canada. During the Salinas administration, several provisions of the Mexican Constitution were amended and new statutes and regulations were passed to facilitate Mexico's move from a protectionist economy to a global one. President Ernesto Zedillo Ponce de León took office in January

1994 and has continued the economic policies instituted under former President Salinas de Gortari.

Under President Salinas, major changes facilitating foreign investment were made in at least four areas. First, Mexico's new agrarian laws included provisions allowing for foreign ownership of land that was formerly communally owned. Second, amendments to Mexico's **copyright** law and a new industrial property law were passed in order to promote investment and prevent unfair **competition**. The changes also permit **joint ventures** between landowners and private investors to develop the land for industry or for farming. Third, hundreds of businesses owned by the Mexican government were ''privatized,'' that is, they were sold to private investors. Privatization of those businesses raised funds that were used to help stabilize Mexico's economy. Fourth, foreign investment regulations issued in 1989 amended the 51-49 percent rule that limited foreign investment in an enterprise to 49 percent, allowing up to 100 percent foreign ownership in specified areas. Restrictions were further loosened in the 1993 Foreign Investment Law and in a decree published in 1996. (A decree in Mexico is similar to a set of regulations promulgated by an administrative agency in the United States. The decree creates law.)

Under the 1993 law and the decree of 1996, foreign investments are classified as: (1) reserved to the State of Mexico; or (2) open to foreign investment in amounts up to 10 percent, 25 percent, 30 percent, 49 percent, or more than 49 percent. More than 49 percent ownership by the foreign company, however, requires prior FIC approval. Areas in which investment is still reserved exclusively for the Mexican government include, but are not limited to, the following: petroleum and other hydrocarbons; generation of nuclear energy; mail service; railways; issuance of banknotes; minting of coins; and control and supervision of ports, airports, and heliports. Up to 10 percent foreign investment is allowed in production cooperatives. Up to 25 percent foreign investment is allowed in firms providing domestic air transportation and air-taxi transportation. Up to 30 percent foreign investment is allowed in areas including, but not limited to: nationwide **banking** institutions; **securities** firms, and **stock** exchange services. Areas open to up to 49 percent foreign investment include, but are not limited to: insurance companies; bonding companies; **factoring** companies; firms that print and publish periodicals for national distribution; and ancillary railway services including operation of terminals, engine and car repairs, and loading and uploading services.

NAFTA'S LIBERALIZING EFFECT. NAFTA eliminates or lessens restrictions on many kinds of investment by U.S. and Canadian citizens and businesses in Mexico. (U.S. or Canadian investors in Mexico are referred to as ''NAFTA investors.'') Areas where increased opportunities for investment have been created include automotive goods, energy-related services and goods, transportation services, and financial institutions.

When NAFTA became effective on January 1, 1994, Mexico immediately removed investment restrictions to allow ''NAFTA investors'' to invest up to 100 percent in Mexican ''national suppliers'' of parts. Up to 100 percent foreign ownership of other auto-parts businesses was allowed as of 1999.

Pursuant to NAFTA, the Mexican state reserves to itself exclusive control of investments in oil, gas, refining, basic petrochemicals, electricity, and nuclear energy. But NAFTA creates opportunities for NAFTA investors in ''nonbasic'' petrochemical goods and in cogeneration and independent power production.

New opportunities for investment in bus and trucking services were created under NAFTA, also. As of 1997, Mexico allowed NAFTA investors to hold up to a 49 percent investment in bus companies and truck companies that provide international cargo services. That percentage is being increased gradually until 2004, when Mexico will permit 100 percent ownership of such companies by NAFTA investors. As of January 1, 1994, Mexico began to allow NAFTA investors to own 100 percent of port facilities such as cranes, piers, and terminals for their own cargo. For businesses handling other companies' cargo, 100 percent ownership by NAFTA investors is allowed contingent upon approval by the FIC.

Under NAFTA, Mexico allows financial institutions organized according to the laws of the United States or Canada to establish such institutions in Mexico. Certain market share limitations were applied initially, but they were phased out by the year 2000. Mexico is increasing its limits on foreign investment in banking (based on an aggregate market share) to 15 percent by 2004. For securities firms, the limit will increase to 20 percent by 2004. NAFTA investors will be permitted to invest in Mexico in two ways. First, they may participate in joint ventures with Mexican insurers, with a phase-in period that reached 100 percent by the year 2000. Second, insurers from the United States or Mexico may establish **subsidiaries**, which will be subject to limits on market share that will be phased out gradually. Those limits were eliminated as of January 1, 2000.

MEXICO'S LABOR LAWS

Mexico's labor laws include extensive rights for workers, and, in theory, are designed to provide a mechanism promoting a ''just'' society. Some of the constitutional provisions do give workers rights and protections that U.S. businesses are not required to provide to their employees in the United States. Actual application and operation of Mexico's guarantees, however, does not always live up to the words of the Mexican Constitution and its statutes. Thus, a description of Mexico's labor laws, such as is given in the paragraphs below, does not provide an accurate picture of actual working conditions for most Mexican workers. Most of Mexico's workers receive insufficient incomes to support their families comfortably, and many work under conditions that threaten their health or safety on a daily or long-term basis. Further, certain guarantees can be circumvented. For example, it is said that Mexican employers avoid hiring women in many cases in order to avoid paying maternity and child-care benefits.

The cornerstone of Mexico's labor laws is Article 123 of the constitution of 1917. Article 123, entitled "Labor and Social Security," was written in response to conditions under the regime of Porfirio Díaz, during which working conditions were abysmal and unions and strikes by workers were suppressed with violence. Article 123 states that every person "is entitled to suitable work that is socially useful. Toward this end, the creation of jobs and social organizations for labor shall be promoted in conformance with the law." Article 123 provides various protections and guarantees to workers, including an eight-hour work day, a maximum workweek of six days, equal pay for equal work, and mandatory childbirth and maternity leave. Mexico's Congress is authorized to enact laws to implement these guarantees and protections and is directed to establish a minimum wage with the authority to consider occupation and geographical areas. According to Article 123, workers are entitled to double pay for overtime work. Also, employers are required to provide employees with a safe workplace and disability pay for work-related injuries. Further, workers are guaranteed the right to form unions and bargain collectively. Workers' rights to organize strikes are recognized, and the rights of employers to impose a lockout, under certain conditions, are recognized. A provision that is unexpected by most U.S. businesspeople is that workers are legally entitled to an 8 percent share of the taxable income of their employers. A second section of Article 123 guarantees the rights of government employees, giving them most of the same rights given to other Mexican workers, although there is no right for them to join unions.

Pursuant to Article 123, all Mexican workers are protected from arbitrary dismissal (unjustifiable discharge). Thus, to some extent, job security is constitutionally guaranteed to the Mexican people. If a business is sold, the new owner must adhere to any existing contract with the workers. These provisions and others in Article 123 illustrate that Mexico's 1917 Constitution is far more detailed than that of the United States, and, for its time, it set forth remarkably progressive social goals and policies.

Various federal labor "decrees" supplement the provisions of Article 123 of Mexico's constitution. The most extensive of these is the Mexican Federal Labor Act of 1970 (FLA), which is a lengthy, detailed statute strengthening the constitutional rights of Mexican workers and placing additional restrictions and duties on employers. Collective bargaining agreements are enforced with the same force as if they were law. A collective bargaining agreement may contain a "closed shop" clause, so long as it is not applied against nonunion workers who were employed prior to the adoption of the agreement.

There are more than 20 million workers in Mexico. Observers say that between 30 and 70 percent of Mexico's workers are unionized. The FLA provides that upon a showing of a minimum of 20 workers, workers can form a union that must be recognized by the employer. Unionization is more prevalent in manufacturing than in service-related work. Most Mexican unions are affiliated with regional or national federations, the largest of which is the Mexican Workers Confederation (*Confederacion de Trabajadores Mexicanos,* or CTM). It is estimated that up to 70 percent of all unionized workers in Mexico are affiliated with the CTM.

Although unions are prohibited by statute from "interfering in political matters," in practice that prohibition is ignored. Most trade unions in Mexico work closely with the dominant PRI political party. The PRI has won all presidential elections since 1928, and it has won most Mexican state elections since then also. The CTM rallies labor support for the PRI and is viewed as a significant factor in the PRI's steady record in maintaining political control in Mexico.

Through legal and political mechanisms, Mexico's government maintains a significant degree of control over union operations and affairs. Mexican law requires that **labor unions** and their leaders be recognized by the government. Thus, independent labor unions can exist, but they are at a disadvantage in dealing with government because often they are not recognized by the Ministry of Labor. On the other hand, a union that is recognized by the PRI and that has leaders who support the PRI has distinct advantages. The CTM was formed in the 1930s by Fidel Vásquez, who led the union until his death in 1997 at the age of 97. Under the leadership of Vásquez, the CTM has worked closely with the PRI political. Various *pactos* (agreements) between the CTM and the Mexican government have, over the years, promoted the stability of Mexico's government and ensured the success of CTM's initiatives, such as NAFTA.

A labor leader can maintain his or her position and power in the union by maintaining close ties with the PRI. Leaders of the CTM who cooperate with the PRI are often offered positions within the federal government as well as in state and local government. Further, there are many reports regarding union leaders who have received substantial bribes from managers, contractors, and others as a result of their public positions.

Collective bargaining agreements generally include provisions on grievance procedures and job security, and they set wages and fringe benefits. Although most agreements set wages that are somewhat higher than the minimums set by Mexican law, even wages agreed upon through collective bargaining are generally only 20 percent (or less) of the amounts typically paid for similar work in the United States. As of 1949 minimum wages set by the Mexican government equaled only about US$2.60 per day, although rates are higher in the U.S.-Mexican border region. During the 1980s and early 1990s, wage agreements were consistently negotiated at levels significantly below the rate of **inflation** in Mexico. (Mexico experienced severe inflation in the late 1980s, which peaked at a rate of about 150 percent around 1986-87.) Those inflation rates have slowed in the late 1990s to rates averaging between 10 and 15 percent annually, but wages remain very low in Mexico as compared to in the United States. Therefore, U.S. businesses are attracted to Mexico to take advantage of low labor costs.

In theory, a U.S. business establishing a manufacturing facility within Mexico can choose its own workers. In practice, however, at least in some cities, political pressures will be such that the U.S. business is compelled to work with the local union and the PRI and to hire workers chosen by the union.

OVERVIEW OF MEXICO'S ENVIRONMENTAL LAW AND ENFORCEMENT

In recent decades, Mexico has been considered a ''pollution haven'' for companies wishing to avoid the more stringent federal and state environmental laws and enforcement in the United States. The worst offenders appear to be the *maquiladora* factories located along the U.S.-Mexican border. Pursuant to the *maquiladora* program, raw materials are brought from the United States and assembled in the Mexican plant, with the final product shipped back to the United States. Cancer and birth defect rates are notoriously high in both northern Mexico and in U.S. cities across the border from the plants as a result of air and water pollution.

U.S. companies contemplating doing business in Mexico should be aware that enforcement of Mexican environmental laws and regulations has become more vigorous since 1988, and that trend is expected to continue. From 1988 to 1993, Mexico's environmental enforcement budget increased from US$6.6 billion to US$77 billion, and the number of Mexican environmental inspectors in the border area was increased from 50 to 200. During the six years preceding 1993, environmental compliance inspections resulted in orders closing about 2,000 facilities temporarily for noncompliance. Between June 1992 and early 1994, Mexican officials conducted more than 16,000 inspections of industrial facilities, 2,400 of them in the area of Mexico's border with the United States. Over 100 facilities have been closed permanently, including a large PEMEX plant near Mexico City. (PEMEX is the Mexican government-owned business that controls the production and sale of petroleum products throughout Mexico.)

In 1992 the United States and Mexico agreed to a comprehensive plan to clean up environmental contamination along the 2,000 mile U.S.-Mexican border. They committed a total of about $700 billion to programs to improve pollution control, strengthen environmental enforcement, and increase planning and education. In 1993 Mexico obtained a $1.8 billion **loan** from the **World Bank** to strengthen its enforcement of environmental laws in the border area.

In response to concerns about the massive environmental problems in the U.S.-Mexican border area, the United States and Mexico entered into two additional agreements that were approved in conjunction with NAFTA. The agreements establish a North American Development Bank (NAD Bank) and a Border Environmental Cooperation Commission (BECC). The NAD Bank provides financing for environmental **infrastructure** in the border area. The United States and Mexico are each contributed US$56 million in paid in capital for each of the first four years of operations. The BECC works with states, local governments, and nongovernmental organizations to provide technical and **financial planning**.

PROVISIONS OF MEXICO'S ENVIRONMENTAL LAWS

Mexico's *Código Ecológico,* known in English as the ''General Ecology Law,'' was adopted in 1988. It is a comprehensive environmental statute addressing water, air, and ground pollution; resource conservation; and environmental enforcement. The General Ecology Law was modeled on U.S. environmental laws, and its provisions closely parallel those of the **Clean Air Act**, **Clean Water Act**, and **Resource Conservation and Recovery Act** (which regulates handling and storage of wastes). For example, in the area of waste disposal, Mexico's regulations require that generators of waste register with the Registry of Hazardous Waste Generators. They must also store, handle, and label hazardous waste in accordance with government standards. Mexican law requires that polluters pay for cleanup of industrial waste sites, although that requirement, to date, is not actively enforced. Mexico, however, does not have community right to know and emergency planning and response provisions such as those included in the 1986 amendments to the U.S. **Comprehensive Environmental Response, Compensation, and Liability Act** (CERCLA, also known as Superfund).

It must be noted, however, that Mexico is in its infancy in terms of environmental enforcement as compared to the United States. As of 2000, the General Ecology Law is only 12 years old, and there has been a lot of restructuring over those years. On the positive side, the General Ecology Law was amended in 1992 and its accompanying 83 sets of environmental standards (that function like regulations promulgated by the U.S. **Environmental Protection Agency** [EPA]) were reevaluated and reissued. One hundred or more additional standards are being issued. In addition, the 31 Mexican states have been directed to establish ''delegations'' to establish regional environmental policies. Most of the states had done so as of 1999.

During its short history the General Ecology Law has been administered by various agencies. The law and regulations implementing it were placed under the jurisdiction of the Secretary of Urban Development and Ecology (SEDUE) in 1988. In 1992 SEDUE was abolished and enforcement and administration of the General Ecology Law were also restructured and placed under the Secretariat of Social Development (*Secretar-a de Desarrollo Social*). Also in 1992, the *Procurarduria Federal De Proteccion al Ambiente* (Federal Attorney General for Environmental Protection) was created. Further restructuring followed in 1997 with the creation of the Secretariat of the Environment, Natural Resources and Fisheries (SEMARNAP), a new agency charged with enforcement of the General Ecology Law. At the present, the *Instituto Nacional de Ecología* (INE, known in English as the National Institute for Ecology), an arm of SEMARNAP, is responsible for formulating environmental policy and setting regulations implementing the General Ecology Law. It also issues standards, known in English as ''NOMS,'' which stands for ''*Normas Oficiales Mexicanos.*'' The Federal Attorney General for Environmental Protection is responsible for enforcement of the law and regulations implementing it.

All industrial facilities, including *maquiladoras,* must comply with Mexico's environmental registration, licensing, and reporting requirements. The Mexican attorney general's office carries out inspections and works with the INE to decide how to handle cases in which a company is not in compliance with environmental laws.

It should be noted that Mexico's environmental laws are becoming more accessible to U.S. businesspeople due to the efforts of the Commission for Environmental Cooperation (CEC). That commission, which was established by the United States, Mexico, and Canada pursuant to the Environmental Side Agreement to NAFTA, is in the process of compiling the environmental laws of the three countries. That information is becoming available to businesspeople and their attorneys through the **Internet**, first in English, and later in Spanish and French.

All industrial facilities, including *maquiladoras,* must comply with Mexico's environmental registration, licensing, and reporting requirements. In order to operate legally, each facility must obtain an environmental operating license. The application for such a license must be accompanied by a statement describing the facility's potential impact on the environment. The attorney general has the authority, based on information in that statement, to require that a full environmental impact study be conducted as a precondition to issuing the license.

The General Ecology Law regulates air pollution from both stationary sources (such as industrial facilities) and mobile sources (such as automobiles and buses). For industrial facilities, the General Ecology Law establishes ambient air quality standards called Maximum Permanent Levels that are identical to those in the U.S. EPA's National Ambient Air Quality Standards. Mexico uses a source permitting system that is administered by the federal SEMARNAP. This regulatory structure differs from that used in the United States where, under the Clean Air Act, air quality attainment is administered pursuant to State Implementation Plans. Mexico's standards for many chemical emissions, such as sulphur dioxide, are much lower than those set by the EPA. It is in the process, however, of developing higher standards.

The General Ecology Law regulates water pollution resulting from a wide range of activities including: (1) releases from municipalities and industrial, agricultural, and livestock activities; (2) use of pesticides and fertilizers; (3) use of toxic substances at industrial facilities; (4) solid waste dumping; and (5) discharges seeping into aquifers. It should be noted that unlike U.S. federal environmental law, Mexico's law also applies to discharges into groundwater. SEMARNAP is in the process of developing regulations covering wastewater treatment facilities. (A lack of such facilities is a major problem throughout Mexico at present.)

Mexico's regulation of hazardous wastes is similar to regulation in the United States pursuant to RCRA. Hazardous wastes and even raw materials must be stored according to the INE's regulations. Any plant generating wastes considered to be ''hazardous'' must obtain a generator's license and number from the attorney general. Mexico regulates the handling and transportation of hazardous materials, products, or wastes in a manner that is similar to the "Manifest" system used in the United States pursuant to RCRA. In Mexico, each shipment of hazardous materials must be accompanied by an "Ecological Waybill" that is used to document the shipment's contents, its handling, and its destination. Each industrial facility must keep a permanent record of all hazardous materials on its premises. Companies generating hazardous waste must file a report every two years with Mexican officials. As of 1999, however, Mexico's hazardous waste disposal system is in complete disarray. As of 1999, there was only one licensed hazardous waste disposal facility in all of Mexico. The site, located in Nuevo Len, is located 12 hours (by truck) north of Mexico City. Tens of millions of dollars have been spent by U.S. companies trying to develop and obtain licenses for seven major waste-treatment facilities at various locations in Mexico, all have been canceled or delayed indefinitely.

CONCLUSION

As U.S. businesses increase their trade with Mexico and locate their facilities within Mexico, an understanding of Mexican law and Mexico's legal system is crucial. Further, as the economies of the two countries become increasingly intertwined thanks to NAFTA, changes in Mexico's laws and more stringent enforcement of Mexico's existing laws are becoming the norm.

SEE ALSO: Mexico, Doing Business in

[Paulette L. Stenzel]

FURTHER READING:

Avalos, Francisco A. *The Mexican Legal System.* New York: Greenwood Press, 1992.

Bartow, Ann M. "The Rights of Workers in Mexico." *Comparative Labor Law Journal* 11 (1990): 182-202.

Goldin, Amy H. "Collective Bargaining in Mexico: Stifled by the Lack of Democracy in Trade Unions." *Comparative Labor Law Journal* 11 (1990): 203-25.

Jamar, Christen, and Angelo Young. "NAFTA at Five." *MB,* April 1999, 26-43.

Krumholz, Dennis J. "Under NAFTA, Mexico No Safe Haven for Polluters." *New Jersey Law Journal* 133 (5 April 1993): 4, 18-19.

Levy, Charles S., and John J. Kim. "Outline of NAFTA-Related and International Environmental Issues." Paper distributed at the 23rd Annual Conference on Environmental Law of the American Bar Association Section of Natural Resources, Energy, and Environmental Law, Keystone, CO, March 1994.

Mexico Business: The Portable Encyclopedia for Doing Business in Mexico. 2nd ed. San Rafael, CA: World Trade Press, 1999.

North American Free Trade Agreement (NAFTA). Washington: GPO, 1993.

Quínones, Sam. "Mexico's Wastelands." *MB,* April 1999, 38-46.

Silva, Jesus, and Richard K. Dunn. "A Free Trade Agreement between the United States and Mexico: The Right Choice?" *San Diego Law Review* 27 (1990): 937-92.

Villegas, Daniel Cosio, and others. *A Compact History of Mexico.* 2nd ed. Mexico City: Colegio de Mexico, 1985.

MEXICO, DOING BUSINESS IN

Mexico is, after Brazil, the second-largest economy in Latin America. At its high point, at the time the Canadian prime minister and the U.S. president signed the **North American Free Trade Agreement** (NAFTA) with Mexico in 1992, Mexico had a **gross national product** of well over $250 billion, with pre-NAFTA exports (75 percent of which went to the United States) of just less than $40 billion.

Mexico is also, again after Brazil, the second-biggest country in Latin America both geographically and in terms of population. Mexico covers approximately 760,000 square miles divided into 31 states and the federal district of Mexico City, its capital. Mexico City is the world's largest city, with a population of more than 20 million people and an estimated greater metropolitan area population of 32 million people. Mexico's two other great industrial cities, Guadalajara and Monterrey, both have exploded from being relatively small cities to having populations of approximately 5 million and well over 3 million, respectively. The nation as a whole has a population of approximately 97.5 million, making it the most populous Spanish-speaking nation in the world.

Mexico has been the focus of considerable attention in the business world with the signing of NAFTA in 1992 and its legislative approval in Canada and the United States in 1994. NAFTA represents an arrangement by which the three nations of North America agreed to reduce tariffs and coordinate limited facets of their trade policy.

NAFTA was of particular importance for Mexico as it represented the first instance in which any developing nation entered into an economic arrangement with two major developed nations. In essence, NAFTA thrust Mexico from a developing-nation status to the status of the 67 developed nations. For Mexico too, NAFTA cemented for the long term its economic relationship with the United States and Canada while paving the way for increased trade and investment.

CURRENT ECONOMIC EVENTS IN MEXICO

The last decade and a half of the 20th century saw Mexico enter its most significant period of economic prosperity, then collapse in the worst economic crisis in its history. While Mexico has always experienced a certain degree of economic fluctuation, this particular period was not a typical boom and bust cycle. The degree of fluctuation was unprecedented and arguably set into motion the world economic crisis that followed, first in South America and later in East Asia and Russia.

THE ECONOMIC BOOM. Well before the flurry of attention surrounding NAFTA, Mexico had much to commend itself in the economic sphere. Reaching a postwar low point tied to the collapse of oil prices in the early 1980s, Mexico officially indicated that it had to default on its **debt** payments and **foreign investment** fled Mexico while the Mexican peso was devalued by almost 50 percent. By 1987, Mexico was experiencing an annualized **inflation** rate of over 130 percent.

Following the election of President Carlos Salinas de Gortari in 1988, Mexico transformed itself. President Salinas negotiated debt relief from the United States, including a $3.5 billion ''debt bridge'' loan. Under the Salinas presidency, Mexico privatized more than 100 of its 1,100 state-owned firms in dozens of areas ranging from **telecommunications** to **banking**. Mexico's debt reduction and **privatization** coupled with an anticorruption campaign and tax restructuring transformed Mexico dramatically, cutting its inflation rate, attracting foreign investment from around the globe, spurring a rebirth of private enterprise, and supporting a thriving stock exchange. All of this culminated with the full legislative approval of the three NAFTA nations in 1994.

THE MEXICAN ECONOMIC CRISIS. The roots of the crisis may have begun with two unrelated events in 1994: an uprising in Chiapis and two political assassinations.

In January 1994, an uprising took place in the southernmost Mexican state, Chiapas, under the banner of the Zapatista Army of National Liberation (EZLN). Chiapas, historically once independent from Mexico as part of the United Provinces of Central America, has long been among Mexico's economically poorest states, and the insurgents protested lack of Mexican concern about poverty. The insurgents also raised issues such as the rights of indigenous ethnic groups. The EZLN and the Mexican government clashed militarily, but soon reached a ceasefire. While no further armed insurrections have taken place in Chiapas, the state still remains politically unstable.

The second event that led to political turmoil surrounded the assassinations of presidential candidate Luís Donaldo Colosio and PRI Secretary General José Francisco Ruíz Massieu. Not only did this lead to political instability in itself, but the murder investigations resulted in charges filed against the brother of President Salinas. The most immediate result of the assassinations, however, was the replacement as PRI presidential candidate of the highly charismatic Colosio by the relatively unknown Ernesto Zedillo Ponce de Leon. Zedillo was then duly elected president, but carried little enthusiasm among the electorate or confidence from foreign investors.

The combination of the Chiapas uprising and a newly elected president with little public experience caused experienced investors in Mexico to grow a bit cautious.

Even this, in itself, would not have caused an economic disaster of the magnitude of the crisis that followed. It was the panic of inexperienced investors that caused the crisis. For the first time, small-scale individual investors had begun to play a marked role in the Mexican stock market. For many of these investors, mostly from the United States, their Mexican stocks represented their first time investing not just in Mexico, but in any foreign market. Unaccustomed to the volatility of international investment and buoyed up in their expectations from over six years of unimpeded growth, these investors grew alarmed when the Mexican market initially stumbled.

Confusing the essentially stable Mexican political landscape with more significant historical political uprisings elsewhere in Latin America, many of these novice investors misinterpreted what was an essentially short-lived and localized uprising as a full-scale revolution. Even this panic might have been stemmed had President Salinas not been so immediately involved in the assassination investigations involving his brother, or had a more politically experienced successor been elected the next president. President Zedillo, however, did not have President Salinas's flair for public relations and handling the press. Indeed, Zedillo's initial days in office seemed only to add to the panic when, after first promising not to devalue the peso, he did just that.

The widescale panic that exploded in the Mexican stock market following the peso devaluation was the worst in Mexico's history. Inexperienced investors felt deceived, and fled not only the Mexican market, but many other Latin American markets. This rash flight of investment served to destabilize such essentially stable markets as Argentina and Chile, even though their economies were unrelated in any significant way to the events occurring in Mexico. The panic itself fueled further destabilization and fears of a default. The peso went into a rapid decline. In December 1994 alone, the peso fell from 3.5 to 6.5 to the U.S. dollar. For most of 1995, the peso continued to decline, averaging over 7 pesos to the dollar, sinking to 8 pesos to the dollar by March 1996.

POLITICAL AND ECONOMIC RECOVERY. Mexico faced the crisis in several ways. To battle charges of corruption, President Zedillo entirely replaced the Mexican Supreme Court.

Moreover, Mexico clearly demonstrated that it was politically more open than ever before. Zedillo's own party, the PRI, faced enormous opposition, losing several state governorships and for the first time in history, it lost its majority in Mexico's Chamber of Deputies. Moreover, the first election for mayor of Mexico City since 1928 was held. For the previous 70 years, the Mexican president appointed the mayor to what is arguably the second-most powerful political position in the nation after the presidency itself. Elections were indisputably freely run as the strongest opponent of the PRI won: the leftist PRD party's leader Cuauhtèmoc Cardenas. These victories, though bad for the ruling PRI party, nonetheless gave foreign investors confidence in the free electoral process of Mexico.

An uprising of terrorists, separate from the Chiapas uprising, took place in the summer of 1996 in the states of Guerrero, Puebla, and Oaxaca. The leaders of the Zapatistas, as well as political opposition leaders such as Cardenas, denounced the uprising as the work of terrorists rather than as a political movement. With support across the political spectrum, the Mexican government quickly put down the uprising. Because of the unity of political opinion toward the uprising as terrorist-led, the incidents led to none of the political instability associated with the Chiapas Zapatista movement.

More significantly, from an economic perspective, the United States, finding its economy heavily integrated through NAFTA and other increased trade ties to Mexico, faced a crisis of its own. The Clinton administration, over heavy opposition from NAFTA critics, opened a $20 billion line of credit to Mexico in 1995. The U.S. loan package was coordinated with a $1.5 billion loan from the **International Monetary Fund** (IMF). Using the line of credit to stabilize the economy, Mexico almost immediately began repaying the U.S. loan, paying $700 million back as early as October of the same year. Well ahead of schedule, by January 1997, Mexico had fully paid back both the U.S. and the IMF loans. Not only did the repayment silence critics of the loan (the United States earned $560 million in interest on the loan) but renewed confidence in the stability of Mexico. Since 1997, the peso had begun to gradually strengthen and the Mexican economy showed a growth rate of over 4 percent.

BUSINESS PRACTICES

With the close integration of the U.S. and Canadian economies to Mexico under NAFTA, coupled with the clear need to understand Mexico in more depth in the aftermath of the Mexican peso crisis, considerable interest in Mexican business practices has developed.

Mexican business culture differs from any other in the Americas due to its unique history. Moreover, it is profoundly different from the United States with whom Mexico shares its long northern border.

LANGUAGE. Mexico is the largest Spanish-speaking country in the world. Its form of Spanish is distinctive, drawing heavily on speakers of pre-Columbian native languages, and filled with many idioms unique to Mexican Spanish.

Spanish as a language is a useful tool when doing business in Mexico both because it gives access to the large number of Mexicans who speak only Spanish or who speak other languages poorly.

Nevertheless, English is extremely widespread, especially among the educated and the middle class who constitute the majority of the business class in Mexico. Many government officials and business leaders have earned degrees from U.S. or Canadian universities, increasing the number of people in leading positions who speak English with great fluency. Indeed, many Mexicans may view the ability to conduct business in English as a sign of their education—suggestions that their use of English is less than fluent or even absent may be a source of loss of face.

While speaking the language of the country in which one conducts business is always advisable for gaining market insight and building relationships, the use of Spanish in Mexico by U.S. businesspeople is of particular value since Mexicans have come to expect that the majority of U.S. businesspeople with whom they come in contact will speak little or no Spanish. For this reason alone, it is an advantage for the U.S. businessperson to learn to speak Spanish as it will likely reflect a presumed interest in and commitment to Mexico that the non-Spanish speaker would have to demonstrate in other ways.

ENVIRONMENT AND TECHNOLOGY. Mexico traditionally has been more ambivalent toward the use of technology than the United States and other control cultures. Mexicans, particularly in nonurban areas, are more likely to see themselves as subject to the forces of nature around them than as controllers of that environment.

Current severe difficulties with pollution and other environmental problems have brought the cost of rapid industrialization further into question in urban areas as well, reviving some traditional skepticism toward the use of technology for its own end. Still, Mexico is rapidly increasing its technological standards. Its **infrastructure**—**telecommunications**, transportation, and electronics—have all seen dramatic improvement in the last two decades.

SOCIAL ORGANIZATION

FAMILY TIES. Family ties are considerably stronger in Mexico than they are in the United States. ''Family,'' as Eva S. Kras explained, ''takes precedence over work and all other aspects of life.'' Moreover, family ties are not only stronger but broader in Mexico than in the United States. The family in the United States consists of a spouse and children (and occasionally one's parents). In Mexico, family ties are equally strong for kinship relationships such as cousins, in-laws, uncles and aunts, nephews and nieces, as well as *compadrazco,* or godparent relationships.

This has far-reaching effects on Mexican-U.S. interactions. The majority of Mexicans define themselves as belonging to a particular family; the majority of people in the United States define themselves by what they do for a living. Thus a Mexican manager is likely to respond first to a query for a self-description with the fact that he or she is a member of the families of his or her father, mother, and spouse. By contrast the average U.S. manager would respond to the same query with the fact that he or she is a manager of some area of specialty. This has direct business application in the way these familial connections are used in the workplace. As John C. Condon explained, ''In Mexico credibility is demonstrated more through position and connections than in the U.S., where one's track record of personal achievements tends to command attention.''

The effect of family on business, however, goes much further than self-definition. Family ties provide access to business **joint ventures**, to favorable terms on negotiations, and to reaching people in power in Mexico. Family ties provide little of this in the United States. The result is that many U.S. businesspeople in Mexico may not be able to reach people in power in Mexico because they do not know how to employ such connections, while many Mexicans in the United States may place greater faith on such connections than their situation merits.

Finally, **nepotism**—the hiring of relatives—is considered desirable in Mexico and undesirable in the United States. In Mexico, relatives one employs are likely to work harder and be more dedicated than strangers. In the United States, relatives are likely to work less hard and be less dedicated than strangers. In Mexico, nepotism ensures access and loyalty through family ties while fulfilling familial obligations to other family members related to the individual hired (even further strengthening and extending the reach of connections with relatives who are not employees). Nepotism, by contrast, is disdained in the United States where family ties are assumed to cover up the relative's incompetence; indeed, many organizations in the United States have explicit antinepotism policies.

GENDER ROLES. The genders are more clearly differentiated in Mexico than in the United States. This especially holds true in Mexican social settings where men are more likely than in the United States to rule their households with little open disagreement from wives and where any unchaperoned male female meetings may be called into question in a way that they would not north of the border.

Machismo does exist in Mexico. Nevertheless, the concept of ''machismo'' is largely misunderstood and exaggerated in the United States. Machismo—essentially the state of acting in a manly manner—is usually misinterpreted in the United States as male boasting of a sexual nature (which is extremely uncommon in the Mexican corporate setting) and a more blatant use of sexually charged stares and innuendos (which do occur at an arguably greater rate but no more so than in, for example, French or Italian culture for which the same concerns are not widely held in the United States). Machismo, however, also includes a man's sense of earned respect through education (including knowledge of the liberal arts—a distinctly unmacho assumption in the United States), titles, and other distinctions. Finally, machismo includes a sense that men must be decisive and unwilling to show fear—a gender distinction still widely practiced in the United States.

While gender distinctions are more strongly delineated in Mexico than in the United States, Mexico is undergoing a transition as well. Many Mexican women, particularly in the large urban centers, are increasingly active in professional settings ranging from university professors to government leaders and entrepreneurs. Finally, many Mexicans are growing accustomed to the large number of women in the United States and Canada in leading business positions and have become increasingly familiar with working with these foreign businesswomen in positions of authority.

CLASS STRATIFICATION. In general, most people in the United States are highly uncomfortable with class distinctions. While it is not uncommon in the United States to talk about good and bad parts of town, someone coming from a good family, or someone's position demanding more respect than another (high-level executives, judges, physicians, etc.), the average person in the United States holds an egalitarian ideal and is uncomfortable in the face of social or even workplace distinctions. Mexicans, by contrast, are much more comfortable with these social realities. Most Mexicans view the world as a whole and the workplace in particular as innately unequal. Mexicans, therefore, are more comfortable than their counterparts north of the border with existing class stratification into good families, powerful positions, and other social and workplace distinctions.

EDUCATION. Advanced education is very widespread in the corporate United States. Indeed, graduate and doctoral degrees are very common in the workplace. Higher education in Mexico is common among business leaders but is nowhere as widespread among the general population as it is in the United States. Among the educated elite, however, the quality and breadth of education is likely to be very high, often including study abroad in the United States, Canada, or Europe, as well as domestically in Mexico.

Educational ties may play a greater role in Mexico than in the United States. Alumni ties as common bonds are strong as they represent a shared experience—a factor that is important in the more personalized nature of business in Mexico described below. The nature of the university is important as well. Foreign education is much more common among upper level Mexican executives than among their counterparts in the United States, and those educated abroad, of course, are likely to reflect the emphases of the educational institutions of the countries in which they studied. Domestically in Mexico, private universities differ markedly from public universities in their educational emphasis; a distinction almost wholly absent in U.S. public and private colleges. Such private institutions of higher education as the prestigious Instituto Tecnologico y Estudios Superiores de Monterrey (ITESM) and La Salle University in Mexico City emphasize analytical approaches applied to business, legal, and technical education. Public universities, by contrast, reflect a more European-based generalist education with a highly theoretical emphasis by U.S. business or technological education standards.

REGIONALISM. Mexico is divided into numerous regions, each with distinctive histories, accents, and loyalties. Most Mexicans are very proud of their region, and many Mexicans claim ties to the region of their parents even if they themselves were born in a distant urban center such as Mexico City. Mexicans themselves carry many stereotypes and beliefs regarding characteristics of these regions. For example, people from Nuevo Leon are perceived as being very business-oriented and thrifty; people from Oaxaca may be proud of the influence of native Indian cultures, and so forth. Whether true or not, these generalizations are more strongly held than comparable divisions of northerners and southerners in the United States and represent very real points of connection for the businessperson aware of their significance.

In recent decades, many Mexicans have been attracted to Mexico's urban centers in the search for jobs and opportunities. While all of Mexico's major cities have seen influxes from the countryside, Mexico City—now the world's largest city—has grown at a pace unmatched anywhere in the industrialized world. Less dramatic but still major migrations of people to Monterrey and Guadalajara have also occurred. These magnet cities represent a major demographic shift for Mexico and break with traditional ties to region and family.

THE CHURCH. Mexico is among the most uniformly Roman Catholic nations. While several hundred-thousand Protestants and several thousand Jews represent significant minorities, Mexico has nowhere near the mix of religion as the United States. Also, while technically Mexico has a separation of church and state (including a period of heavy anticlerical activity early in the 20th century), the role of religion may seem pervasive by U.S. standards. Conflict of religion in the workplace is negligible since Catholicism is so widely shared; consequently such practices as having a priest bless a new office building or corporate sponsorship of a religious procession are well accepted. Display of religious imagery in the workplace is likewise common and well accepted; by contrast, religion is usually intensely personal in the United States, a fact that makes many Mexicans view their U.S. counterparts as irreligious or at least highly secularized. Widespread belief in God's influence in the workplace (as in all aspects of life) may also provide some Mexicans with more of a sense of acceptance of events that might be fought against in the United States.

CONTEXTING. Mexico is what is called a high context culture As a result, Mexicans place a strong emphasis on how a message is said rather than on the words used alone. The eloquence of the words used are themselves part of the message. Something may be exaggerated in a way known to be an exaggeration but spoken because it is rhetorically satisfying; this is often understood to be lying in the literal understanding of low context cultures such as the United States.

Messages are also understood in terms of the full context of the communicators' relationship with one another. This particularly affects the importance for social etiquette and formality in official situations (including business meetings) and creates an emphasis on face-saving.

As a direct consequence of the high context nature of Mexican communication, it is necessary to build a personal relationship in conducting business with Mexicans. Without the context of that personal relationship, little if any substantive communication can take place, and necessary levels of trust are inadequate to undertake most business arrangements.

As in most high context cultures, Mexican behavior is more likely to be governed by individual interpretation and the need to save face rather than on external rules and regulations. As a result, in Mexico, personal understandings are more binding than **contracts**. Indeed, contracts in Mexico are often seen as the beginning of a relationship that can be subject to change as the business progresses. This contrasts to the view of low context cultures (such as the United

States) in which the contract is viewed as not subject to change.

Finally, in high context societies, understood or unofficial rules are often as important (or even more important) than written rules. This holds true even in relations with government officials. These unwritten rules deal often with issues of respect and family loyalty in Mexico, and remain subject to the context of the situation to which they are applied. As a result, these unwritten rules may be employed in some instances and overlooked in others, depending on the context of the individuals involved and of the situation particular to the incident at hand.

NONVERBAL COMMUNICATION

As with all nations, Mexico has distinctive nonverbal communication unique to itself. It contrasts markedly with the United States in the four areas described below.

PERSONAL SPACE. Mexican concepts of personal distance are considerably closer than in the United States. The average workplace distance while standing face to-face between two people in the United States is roughly arm's length. While regional differences are notable in Mexico (with interpersonal distance greater as one moves north), the average distance is approximately three to four inches closer than in the United States.

TOUCHING BEHAVIOR. The United States is an ahaptic (or non-touching) culture. Mexico, by contrast, is a much more haptic culture. Most workplace touching in the United States is limited to the handshake. Even the handshake is minimal, limited to one hand and a relatively short duration. Mexican touching behavior is considerably more extensive. Common workplace interactions would likely include back-patting, greeting hugs between men as well as women, and handshakes using both hands often reaching to the upper arm.

MOVEMENT. Movement (kinesics) differs somewhat in Mexico and the United States. Lacking the large waves of immigration that have influenced U.S. body language, Mexicans are more uniform in the sorts of body movement they use when speaking. Generally speaking, Mexicans are more expressive with the hands than many of their U.S. counterparts. Also, most U.S. movement is limited to the arms and head; movement from the torso is not uncommon in Mexican conversation. Finally, most people in the United States, even in formal situations, tend to slouch while sitting; slouching in Mexico is usually a sign of boredom and is thus subject to misinterpretation.

DRESS. Mexicans tend to dress more conservatively in Mexico City than elsewhere in the country. Still, as a whole, business as well as social dress is somewhat more conservative throughout Mexico than it is in the United States. Details—such as shined shoes or well-groomed hair—are often more important in business dress in Mexico than they are in the United States.

TIME CONCEPTION

Mexico and the United States are extremely different in the way each conceives of time. Mexico is what Edward T. Hall termed a polychronic culture; the United States, a monochronic one. Mexico, like all polychronic cultures, ranks personal involvement and completion of existing transactions above the demands of preset schedules. The United States, like other monochronic cultures, adheres to preset schedules that take precedence over personal interaction or the completion of the business at hand.

Because Mexican businesspeople generally complete tasks at the expense of scheduling, people in high authority may become easily overwhelmed with multiple tasks. To prevent overloading, people in positions of high authority rely heavily on subordinates to screen for them. Once a person gets past the screeners, the person in authority will generally see the task to completion regardless of its relative importance. By contrast, in the United States, the scheduling of appointments acts as the screen; not the person's subordinates. If a task is not completed within a scheduled time, a new meeting is scheduled.

Because people rather than appointment books act as the screens in Mexico, personal relationships flourish within close circles. In the United States, personal relationships are discouraged or at least are not allowed to interfere with maintaining the schedule. As a result, in the United States, personal relationships are determined by the terms of the job in a manner that is nearly incomprehensible in Mexico. Conversely, personal relationships are emphasized in the Mexican workplace in a manner that is difficult for most U.S. businesspeople to comprehend. Mexicans make distinctions between insiders and those outside their existing personal relationships. Appointments are secondary. In the United States, one needs only to schedule a meeting with the appropriate people; little or no preference is given to those one knows over complete strangers. In the United States (in direct contrast to Mexico), the outsider is treated in exactly the same fashion as the close associate.

SEE ALSO: Mexican Law

[David A. Victor]

FURTHER READING:

Condon, John C. *Good Neighbors: Communicating with the Mexicans.* Yarmouth, ME: Intercultural Press, 1985.

Hall, Edward T. *The Dance of Life: The Other Dimension of Time.* Garden City, NY: Anchor Press/Doubleday, 1984.

Kras, Eva S. *Management in Two Cultures: Bridging the Gap between U.S. and Mexican Managers.* Yarmouth, ME: Intercultural Press, 1988.

Paz, Octavio. *The Labyrinth of Solitude: Life and Thought in Mexico.* New York: Grove Press, 1961.

Riding, Alan. *Distant Neighbors: A Portrait of the Mexicans.* New York: Vintage Books, 1984.

Victor, David A. *International Business Communication.* New York: HarperCollins, 1992.

MFN

SEE: Most Favored Nation

MICROCOMPUTERS IN BUSINESS

Commonly known as desktop computers or personal computers (PCs), microcomputers provide decentralized computing power for a wide number of business functions, especially those involving individual productivity tasks. The category ''microcomputer,'' though somewhat of an anachronism now, distinguishes these machines from the traditionally larger, more powerful mainframes and minicomputers (also called midrange computers) that dominated business computing before the 1980s. While modern microcomputers are more powerful than the earliest mainframe and midrange systems, the latter two classes of computers—both recent models and legacy models from decades ago—are still widely used for memory-intensive and distributed computing applications such as hosting **management information systems**, corporate Web sites and intranets, **local area network** file servers, and other enterprise-wide and critical data resources.

Popular business applications available for microcomputers include **spreadsheets**, **word processing**, **database management systems**, **decision support systems**, graphics, communications, and networking software. Illustrations of business use include transactional, knowledge-based, office automation, management information, decision support, and executive support systems. Spanning the continuum of financial, marketing, managerial, production, and personnel activities, microcomputers pervade almost every aspect of business operations.

HISTORICAL BACKGROUND

In the 17th century, the French mathematician Blaise Pascal (1623-62) and the German mathematician Gottfried Leibnitz (1646-1716) almost simultaneously developed the adding machine. Because all mathematical operations in a microcomputer are based on addition and subtraction, the microcomputer owes a great debt to the efforts of such early pioneers. In 1833, British mathematician Charles Babbage (1792-1871) introduced an analytical machine capable of automatically executing a series of mechanized instructions.

By the 1940s and 1950s, computer development accelerated to create the first generation of computing: the vacuum tube age. Electric signals transmitted through vacuum tubes created the first mainframe computers, including the ENIAC computer. By virtue of their size, however, vacuum computers remained large and expensive. The vacuum tube soon gave way to smaller and less expensive transistors. A transistor is a small solid state semiconducting device that relays binary code. Smaller and more cheaply produced, transistor technology fueled the downward spiral of computer costs.

By the 1960s, the third generation of computing was well underway with the advent of integrated circuitry. Integrated circuits etch physical pathways onto a semiconducting material, most notably silicon, to relay binary information. This integrated circuitry accommodated greater complexity of transmission patterns and control.

Another milestone came in 1981, when International Business Machines (IBM) introduced its Personal Computer, or PC, in response to a growing undercurrent of increasingly versatile, small desktop computers from other manufacturers. IBM didn't invent the microcomputer, but its adoption of the format opened the floodgates for rapid innovation and adoption of these machines. Combined with increasingly smaller and cheaper components and improved software applications, these personal computers became affordable and easier to use in the 1980s. The trend toward cheaper, more powerful PCs surged throughout the 1990s, so that by the end of the century, individuals or businesses could purchase for less than $1,000 a system more powerful than those costing tens of thousands a few decades earlier.

PCS IN THE CORPORATE IT STRATEGY

When PCs first revolutionized corporate computing in the 1980s, many prophesied that they would soon replace other types of computers, most notably mainframes. The logic was that PCs were so powerful and inexpensive, there would be no need for bulky, expensive, and complex mainframes. Instead, the story went, PCs on high-speed LANs would take mainframes' place. This perspective continued to persist into the early 1990s, when mainframe titan IBM was faltering and even its own executives had lost faith in the mainframe.

Contrary to those gloomy forecasts, however, the rest of the 1990s saw a more healthy equilibrium between the different classes of computers. Despite PC advocates' hubris, few if any PCs (or LANs) rivaled the stability and reliability of high-end systems, and moreover, powerful centralized machines were still needed as repositories and safe havens for major corporate systems. Indeed, mainframe sales began to flourish again, thanks in part to innovations that made them cheaper. More important, PCs and mainframes have been shown to be complementary technologies with different strengths and weaknesses. As impressive as PC advances have been, mainframes still offer many advantages for large, multi-user computing environments. Whereas PCs were originally touted as cost savers over mainframes, in the wake of PCs' heavy maintenance requirements, mainframes are again seen as cost-effective for certain situations. Meanwhile, some corporate technology managers have begun to realize that many corporate users have a limited range of microcomputer applications they use regularly and their PCs' full resources are never utilized.

By the mid-1990s, in fact, there was much talk of whether PCs might be replaced with an Internet-generation hybrid computer known as the network computer (NC). NCs combined elements of the PC world—graphical interfaces, Web browsers, customizable applications, limited local processing—with a few from the mainframe world—powerful centralized computers accessed by weaker, ''dumb'' terminals. NCs run Web browsers and software fed from the network, rather than storing programs and data files on each individual machine. The NC was not a major success in its first few years, but has begun to develop a niche market among some corporations seeking to contain their PC costs. In response to corporate concerns about cost of ownership, some PC vendors have attempted to market full fledged PCs that they claim are optimized for low maintenance.

A separate trend impacting PC use has been the proliferation of smaller, portable devices like personal digital assistants and so-called palm-top computers. These all technically classify as microcomputers, but they represent a fundamental shift from the conventional desktop format. Portable computing devices are normally used to supplement larger computers rather than as a replacement, however.

In short, corporate **information technology** strategies are deploying the various classes of computers with increasing selectivity. For most corporations, microcomputers are still a central component of their strategy, and probably will remain so for a while. However, the trend toward integrating PCs with other kinds of devices over networks, whether larger computers like mainframes or more specialized network appliances, will also continue.

SEE ALSO: Computers and Computer Systems; Computer Networks

FURTHER READING:

Albrecht, Michael C. *Computerizing Your Business.* Upper Saddle River, NJ: Prentice Hall, 1997.

Erickson, Fritz, and John A. Vonk. *Modern Microcomputers.* 2nd ed. New York: WCB/McGraw-Hill, 1996.

Evans, Dave. ''Back to the Future.'' *Computing,* 5 June 1997.

Hibbard, Justin, and April Jacobs. ''PCs Cost Too Much to Maintain.'' *Computerworld,* 25 November 1996.

Jones, Phil. ''Iron Age Monsters Come in from the Cold.'' *Computing,* 28 January 1999.

Kelly, Shan. ''Analysts Disagree over the Future Shape of IT.'' *Computer Weekly,* 5 September 1996.

Kirkpatrick, David. ''Is the PC Dead? Not Even Close.'' *Fortune,* 21 December 1998.

MICROECONOMICS

Microeconomics, or price theory, covers the economic activity of individual consumers or producers or groups of consumers and producers, and the markets in which they interact. Therefore, microeconomics is the study of buyers, sellers, prices, profits, and wages. The field is devoted to the examination of choices and motivations of these individual economic elements. In contrast, **macroeconomics** covers the economic activity of entire populations, or aggregates, of consumers and producers.

Nevertheless, the distinction between microeconomics and macroeconomics is somewhat artificial. While macroeconomics traditionally has addressed economic issues such as **inflation** and unemployment, current economic thought attributes inflation just as much to microeconomic factors as to macroeconomic factors.

Traditionally, the supply and demand model serves as the foundation of microeconomics, along with a basic set of interrelated principles, including markets, **competition**, production, **cost**, and distribution. Together, these principles account for microeconomic phenomena such as price changes, **profit margins**, and wage differences.

HISTORICAL BACKGROUND

The terms microeconomics and macroeconomics have their origin in the early 1930s, when economists strove to gain an understanding of factors that created the Great Depression. Separate mechanisms to describe the actions of individuals and aggregate populations were first described by the Norwegian economist Ragnar Frisch (1895-1973) in 1933.

Frisch called these mechanisms ''micro-dynamic'' and ''macro-dynamic.'' He wrote that micro-dynamic analysis seeks to ''explain in some detail the behavior of a certain section of the huge economic mechanism'' within specific parameters, while macro-dynamics gives ''an account of the whole economic system taken in its entirety.''

John Maynard Keynes (1883-1946), in his seminal 1936 publication *The General Theory of Employment, Interest, and Money,* established a popular scientific basis for the separate analysis of micro- and macro-dynamic activity. Economists adopted many of Keynes's assumptions about equilibrium, assumptions required to make the models simple enough to work, and subsequently developed these separate methodologies into often unresolvably dissimilar sciences.

The Dutch economist Peter de Wolff was the first to publish the term ''micro-economics'' in a 1941 article on the income elasticity of demand. Others began using the term in their own works, and by the late 1950s microeconomics and macroeconomics made their way into textbooks. Thus, the division of analysis along two different lines of assumptions about the market was institutionalized as a central feature of the study of economic systems.

THE MARKET ECONOMY

Market economy refers to the developed, industrialized economies found throughout most of the world, in which people specialize in the production of a limited array of goods or services and meet their food and material needs through exchange. In market economies, because of specialization and agricultural advances, farmers can produce far more agricultural products than they need, which allows them to sell the surplus to others, who consequently do not have to produce food of their own. Instead, the rest of the population can specialize in other goods, or in services. Hence, farmers, for example, can trade agricultural products for furniture and clothing made by people who specialize in these products and vice versa. While early exchanges were done with barter—trading corn for clothes, for instance—contemporary exchanges are done with money, which facilitates trade in that farmers with corn do not have to find clothing makers seeking corn in order to obtain clothing.

SUPPLY AND DEMAND

Some of the central questions of microeconomics are why certain products or services—**commodities**—cost more than others and why prices change. In order to answer these questions, economists developed the model of supply and demand. Commodities, which include cars, clothing, food, and gas, are scarce relative to their uses. Commodities have prices because they are both useful and scarce. For example, although air is useful, it is not scarce and hence is free. In contrast, corn is both scarce and useful. In economics, usefulness and scarcity take the form of demand and supply, respectively, since consumers demand commodities because they are useful and merchants cannot supply infinite quantities of commodities because they are scarce. Therefore, market prices result from the relationship between supply and demand.

As a result, a commodity that is very scarce will cost far more than a commodity that is not as scarce, because consumers will be willing to pay more money given the small supply. In most cases, however, when a commodity's price is high, demand will fall, because consumers will meet their needs with alternative products. For example, if the lettuce crop is small because of frost damage and the price of lettuce is high, consumers will buy less lettuce and more cabbage, assuming it has a lower price. In other words, if supply exceeds demand prices decrease and if demand exceeds supply prices will increase.

EQUILIBRIUM. Equilibrium refers to the effect of the economic forces supply and demand in balancing each other's influence so that there is no tendency for change. The price of a commodity will be in equilibrium if the quantity demanded equals the quantity supplied; that is, if the amount of a commodity consumers are willing to buy equals the amount sellers are willing to supply. Economists call the price in such a scenario the ''equilibrium price'' and the quantity the ''equilibrium quantity.'' At the equilibrium price, buyers and sellers can trade as much of a commodity as they want.

If the price is not in equilibrium, however, quantity demanded will not equal the quantity supplied. If the price rises above the equilibrium price, consumers will buy less of a commodity than they would at the equilibrium price, and so supply would exceed demand. Consequently, there would be a surplus or excess supply. Conversely, if the price falls below the equilibrium price, the consumers will buy more of a commodity than would they would at the equilibrium price, and so demand would exceed supply. Consequently, there would be a shortage or excess demand.

SHORT-RUN AND LONG-RUN SCENARIOS. Supply and demand are not static; they will change over time. For that reason, microeconomists use two time frames for their considerations, the short run and the long run. Short-run scenarios assume no movement in supply or demand because the time frame involved is too brief to allow sellers to alter their supply and for consumers to change their demand.

In the long run, however, sellers and consumers may exercise changes in supply and demand: sellers by offering more or less of a product to maximize profit, and consumers by reacting to these changes in supply.

The common denominator for both sellers and consumers is the price mechanism. Excess demand in the short run yields high profits, inspiring greater supply in the long run. This increases the supply and dries up excess demand, forcing prices down and lowering the margin of profit.

THE PRICE ELASTICITY OF DEMAND. As previously illustrated, the quantity demanded rises with a commodity's price falls and vice versa. Consequently, the quantity demanded is responsive or sensitive to price changes. Nevertheless, some commodities are more responsive to price changes than others, depending on the availability of alternatives, the necessity of the commodity, and the percentage of a consumer's income spent on the commodity. For example, as Miltiades Chacholiades points out in *Microeconomics,* consumption of salt is not very responsive to prices changes, because there is no direct substitute and because consumers spend only small percentage of their incomes on salt.

Consequently, businesses and governments must take into account the responsiveness of demand to price changes in order to plan budgets and strategies prudently. For example, a store cannot raise its prices arbitrarily without considering how many customers it will lose to competitors because of the price increases.

Economists measure the degree of responsiveness in demand for a commodity to price changes by using the concept of the price elasticity of demand, which is also called the elasticity of demand or just demand elasticity. Economists define this concept as:

$$\text{Elasticity} = \frac{\text{Percentage change in quantity demanded}}{\text{Percentage change in price}}$$

PRICE ELASTICITY OF SUPPLY. The quantity supplied—the total quantity of a commodity merchants are willing to sell—stems from a commodity's price. The price elasticity of supply measures the responsiveness of the quantity supplied to prices changes. Economists calculate the degree of responsiveness in a quantity supplied to price changes using the following equation:

$$\text{Elasticity} = \frac{\text{Percentage change in quantity supplied}}{\text{Percentage change in price}}$$

MARKETS AND COMPETITION

Since microeconomics generally involves capitalist economies, economists study the role competition plays in supply and demand. Competition manifests itself in markets differently and therefore has different effects in different markets. One of the most important markets is the perfectly competitive market, which refers to a market where there are many sellers offering the exact same goods, where all buyers know the price of every seller, and where there are no barriers to entry. As a result, all sellers offer their goods at the same price. Since all the buyers know the sellers' prices, they would buy the goods from the cheapest seller if the prices were not the same.

Moreover, the perfectly competitive market prohibits any seller from earning an extraordinarily high profit. If the goods were extremely profitable, then many new sellers would enter the market, since there are no barriers to entry. Presumably, the new sellers would keep prices low to attract customers and these efforts would cause established sellers to lower their prices to compete, driving profits down to a normal level.

On the other hand, a seller that is alone in a market with no competitors is a monopoly. Monopolies exist because they own proprietary rights to their product (for example, a pharmaceutical company with a patented drug formula), because competition would raise average costs in the industry (such as with electrical power distribution), or because there are significant barriers to entry.

A monopoly will determine a price based on demand elasticity. In other words, it would lower its price only if that would increase its total revenues. For example, electricity is very nearly a necessity in daily life. The utilities that provide it operate in a natural monopoly (where competition could only raise costs, rather than lower them). If they were allowed to set a high price for electricity, demand might drop only slightly. For this reason, governments have created regulatory agencies not only to police monopolies' costs but also to set their prices at affordable levels.

Somewhere between competition and monopoly is monopolistic competition, where several firms compete in the same market, but with appreciably unique products. For example in the pharmaceutical industry, a number of companies may produce different drugs that combat the same affliction. But each may work better for certain types of patients, affording its maker a monopoly in limited areas of the wider market.

Another type of market is the **oligopoly**, where a small number of firms dominate the market, operating with quasi-monopolistic power. The automobile, appliance, aircraft, and steel industries, among others, fall into this category. While competition may exist and even be intense in oligopolies, governments have enacted **antitrust acts and laws** to prevent them from price fixing.

CONSUMPTION

The demand side of the supply and demand equation is influenced by consumption and consumers. In economics, consumers can refer to both individuals and households. For example, automobile purchases are usually analyzed on a household basis, whereas restaurant purchases are usually analyzed on an individual basis. Economists study consumer spending habits and patterns, because consumer tastes and preferences help determine the demand for various commodities. Microeconomics relies on three assumptions about consumers:

1. Consumers may prefer commodity A over commodity B, may prefer commodity B over A, or may be indifferent and have no preference.
2. Consumers' preferences are transitive, meaning if consumers prefer commodity A over B and commodity B over C, then they prefer commodity A over C.
3. Consumers prefer more of a commodity than less.

Using these assumptions, economists plot out consumer preferences on graphs or indifference maps to represent how consumers rank various commodities or groups of commodities. In addition, economists attach numbers or utilities to these commodities to reflect their levels of preference by consumers. This approach to analyzing and representing consumer preferences enables economists to determine consumer preferences by glancing at their numbers or utilities. For example, if commodity A has a higher number or utility than commodity B, consumers will prefer commodity A over B.

But consumer preferences are only half the picture. Economists assume that consumers strive to maximize the utility of their purchases. Consequently, commodity prices and consumer income also come into play, since both factors will influence the kinds of commodities a consumer will buy. Economists call the amount of money a consumer has to spend in a specific period of time, such as a month, ''money income.'' Hence, the higher the commodity price, the smaller the quantity a consumer can purchase, regardless of consumer preferences.

PRODUCTION AND COST

Identifying consumer preferences and discussing the effects of consumer income levels provides an overview of the demand-side factors. In contrast, discussing issues related to production and cost provides an overview of the supply-side factors. The commodities desired and supplied result from production of some sort, whether it is manufacturing, recording, printing, farming, teaching, writing, or any number of other forms of production. Firms take inputs of raw materials and convert them into outputs of products and services. The production process includes not only the actual creation of the commodities, but also the storage and transportation of them.

The production process generally involves a variety of inputs or production factors, which economists divide into four categories: labor services, capital goods, land, and managerial skills. Labor services are provided by a plethora of different kinds of workers including construction workers, doctors, farmers, lawyers, plumbers, teachers, and writers. Capital goods refer to the equipment, goods, and other materials companies use to make their end products and include buses, trucks, machinery, tools, wood, fuel, and grain. While all firms need land to some extent, some enterprises such as farming and mining require land with specific characteristics such as fertility and the presence of mineral deposits, respectively. Finally, the production process must have people or groups of people to provide a firm with coordination, leadership, strategy, and supervision.

Economists assume that firms attempt to coordinate the factors of production so that they can generate commodities as efficiently as possible, which will enable them to maximize their profits. In addition, economists use the concept of the ''production function'' to indicate a firm's technical capability. A firm's production function refers to its ability to produce its commodities efficiently and covers the relationship between labor and capital goods for a given unit of time, for example.

The other part of the supply side is cost. Simply put, the amount paid for all the inputs such as labor, land, and materials a firm needs to produce a specific output is the ''total cost.'' Total cost includes total fixed cost and total variable cost. Total fixed cost remains the same no matter if 10 units are produced or 10,000. On the other hand, total variable cost fluctuates with the level of production, increasing with greater production and decreasing with less production. Firms choose methods of production that maximize the cost efficiency of the inputs; that is, they seek the method of production with the lowest total cost to produce a certain output—a specific quantity of a commodity. Firms achieve this efficiency by calculating their revenues at various levels of output at minimal total costs and choosing the level of output at which revenues exceed total cost the most.

DISTRIBUTION

Economists examine distribution in order to explain how the prices for the factors of production are established. Therefore, distribution covers the payment of wages for labor services as well as the rent paid for land and capital goods. Just as supply and demand determine commodity prices, so they also determine prices of the factors of production. For example, the supply of nuclear physicists is scarce relative to the demand, and so nuclear physicists can earn high wages in the labor market. In contrast, unskilled general laborers are not nearly as scarce; hence, they earn far lower wages. A number of factors determine the supply and hence the wage differences for various job including education, training, experience, and market structure (e.g. union versus non-union jobs). In addition, state and federal laws also influence the cost of labor services. For example, the federal minimum wage guarantees that workers receive at least the federally mandated minimum hourly wage. Supply and demand also determine levels of employment: unemployment is high when demand for workers is low.

The cost of capital goods such as raw materials, industrial equipment, tools, and fuel also are set by supply and demand factors, similar to those that determine commodity prices paid by consumers.

Businesses usually use the factors of production indirectly; that is, the demand for the factors of production is derived demand. Businesses generally do not simply hire workers and buy raw materials for their own sake. Instead, they hire workers and buy raw materials to produce goods, which they will sell for profit. For example, the demand of butchers stems from the demand for meat. Hence, payment for the factors of production depends on what is being produced.

[John Simley, updated by Karl Heil]

FURTHER READING:

Baumol, William J. *Economics: Principles and Policy.* 7th ed. New York: Harcourt Brace College Publishers, 1997.

Chacholiades, Miltiades. *Microeconomics.* New York: Macmillan, 1986.

Fielder, Edgar R. ''Does Macroeconomics Matter?'' *Across the Board,* October 1998.

Hornbusch, Rudiger. *Economics.* 4th ed. New York: McGraw-Hill, 1994.

Lipsey, Richard B., et al. *Microeconomics.* New York: Harper-Collins College Publishers, 1993.

Mansfield, Edwin. *Microeconomics: Theory/Applications.* 7th ed. New York: W. W. Norton & Co., 1997.

MINORITY-OWNED BUSINESSES

Businesses owned by women and minorities in the United States represent a significant and rising percentage of all business enterprises. Estimates from the Census Bureau's Economic Census, which is conducted every five years, reckoned women's and minorities' share of U.S. businesses in 1992 at 41 percent of the national total. Nonwhite business ownership, including firms owned by persons of black, Hispanic, Asian, and Native American descent, characterized more than 11 percent of all sole proprietorships, **partnerships**, and subchapter **S corporations**. Standard C corporations, which include publicly traded companies, were not included in these estimates because their ownership tends to be more dispersed. These 2.15 million minority-owned businesses together recorded 1992 sales in excess of $200 billion, or approximately 3 percent of U.S. gross domestic product at that time. The average minority business employed seven people.

Local evidence from areas with large minority populations, such as southern California, where in some counties the count of Hispanic businesses reportedly doubled between 1992 and 1997, suggested that the number and value of minority businesses continues to rise briskly. Early estimates from the 1997 Economic Census suggested that the number of minority businesses was growing at better than twice the rate of white-owned businesses, indicating a 67 percent jump in minority businesses for the five-year period. Based on these estimates, by 1997 there were approximately 3.6 million minority-owned businesses, or close to 15 percent of all businesses, with Asian- and Hispanic-owned enterprises growing the fastest. Revenues at these companies are fast approaching $500 billion and total employment is close to 4 million workers.

A BRIEF HISTORY OF EARLY MINORITY-OWNED BUSINESS

Minorities have owned businesses in the United States since colonial times. In the early 1700s, for example, historical records show that several blacks owned their own businesses. Historian Carl Bridenbaugh, in his book *Cities in the Wilderness,* wrote that in early 18th century Charles Town (now Charleston, South Carolina), ''there were many black artisans, like Jack, the ship carpenter, and Prince, 'well known . . . as a Plaisterer [sic] and Bricklayer by trade.' '' He also cited Philadelphia and New York as cities that had many black business owners.

Of course, they were not appreciated by their white competitors. As Bridenbaugh wrote, ''Philadelphians also objected to blacks who underbid them in servile work. Although harsh legislation in every town restricted his movements, especially at night, the Negro was of too great use and value to be dispensed with as a source of cheap labor.''

Similarly, Lorenzo Greene mentioned several black business owners in his book *The Negro in Colonial New England.* For instance, he cited Jim Riggs, of Framingham, Massachusetts, a jobber and basket maker, who also fought in the U.S. Revolutionary War (1775-1783). Squire Nep, a Connecticut resident, owned his own barbershop. These men were the exceptions to the rule, though. Minority business owners were not numerous, but they did exist.

Cases abound of blacks who ran successful businesses in the South after the Civil War (1861-1865). In virtually every large Southern city, blacks were butchers, barbers, and artisans. They ran successful restaurants and hotels. For example, Jehu Jones ran one of Charleston's most successful hotels. In 1883, Solomon Humphries, a prosperous grocer in Macon, Georgia, was worth about $20,000—and he had more credit than anyone in town. Thomy Lafon, of New Orleans, accumulated real estate estimated to be worth almost half a million dollars.

RECENT TRENDS AND DEMOGRAPHICS

In 1998 nonwhite and Hispanic minorities constituted 28 percent—some 76 million people—of the U.S. population. By a slim margin, blacks are the largest U.S. minority group, accounting for somewhere between 12 and 13 percent of the population. Hispanic people, including some individuals who may also be considered black, Asian, or white, account for 11-11.5 percent; and persons of Asian, Pacific Island, and Native American heritage represent 3.4-3.8 percent.

Geographically, more than half of U.S. minority businesses are concentrated in just four states: California, Florida, New York, and Texas. Other places with strong minority business presence, measured as a percentage of total firms, include Hawaii, the District of Columbia, New Mexico, Maryland, Louisiana, and New Jersey.

HISPANIC-OWNED BUSINESSES. Hispanic entrepreneurs have statistically been the most prodigious minority business owners in the United States, with an estimated 1.6 million businesses as of 1997. Hispanic businesses in 1997 made up 43 percent of all minority enterprises, and this proportion was up by more than 3 percentage points since 1992. The vast majority of Hispanic-owned firms are held by individuals with Mexican, Cuban, or Central American backgrounds. Revenues at U.S. Hispanic businesses reached nearly $77 billion in 1992, almost tripling since 1987, and this amount more than doubled again by 1997, at $187 billion. Some of the largest economic sectors for Hispanic businesses included retailing and wholesaling, construction, health services, and business services.

BLACK-OWNED BUSINESSES. Black-owned firms have been multiplying as well. The number of black owned businesses rose by nearly 50 percent from 1987 to 1992, and by another 50 percent from 1992 to 1997. By 1997 there were approximately 906,500 black-owned businesses in the United States. These firms represented 27.5 percent of all minority businesses, a slight percentage drop from previous years as the number of Hispanic and Asian businesses has expanded even more rapidly. According to government figures, in 1997 African American businesses (excluding C corporations) brought in revenues approaching $60 billion, twice that of just five years earlier. The black business magazine *Black Enterprise,* which tracks a few hundred of the country's largest black-owned or controlled businesses, estimated that the top 25 black-owned businesses (those with 51 percent or more ownership by black persons) had sales of $4.85 billion as of 1997. Many of these medium to large companies, the smallest of which made $80 million a year, are not included in Census Bureau figures for minority businesses because they are C corporations. Sectors with strong black business participation include retailing and wholesaling, health services, construction, business services, personal and professional services, and real estate.

ASIAN- AND NATIVE AMERICAN-OWNED BUSINESSES. As of 1997 some 1.1 million U.S. businesses were owned by people of Asian, Pacific Island, and Native American descent. This represented a 61 percent increase from 1992 levels. Based on 1992 statistics, Chinese Americans owned 22 percent of these businesses; Korean Americans, 15 percent; Native Americans, 13 percent; Indian (Asian) Americans, 13 percent; Japanese Americans, 10 percent; Filipino Americans, 10 percent; and Vietnamese Americans, 8 percent. Business ownership among Asian and Native Americans is extraordinarily high when compared with these groups' population figures. The numbers suggest that 1 out of every 10 Asian and Native American persons in the United States owns a business, a proportion similar to that in the white non-Hispanic population. This compares with approximately 1 in 20 among Hispanics and with 1 in 40 among blacks. In 1997 Asian and Native American businesses reported revenues of more than $275 billion. The largest economic sectors for Asian- and Native American-owned enterprises include retailing and wholesaling, health services, real estate, business services, and lodging facilities.

GROWING OPPORTUNITIES

As the figures show, the number of start-up businesses among minorities increased dramatically in the last part of the 20th century; there is every sign the trend will continue in the 21st century. This phenomenal growth is due in part to the widespread economic changes that began to occur in the United States in the 1980s. Companies began major restructuring projects that displaced large numbers of workers. Since small business growth often occurs in times of economic slowdown, there was a natural tendency among displaced workers to open their own enterprises. Their timing was good, as many government agencies at the local, state, and federal levels expanded their attempts to encourage the establishment of minority-owned businesses.

Many members of minority groups established themselves as business owners in urban areas. That was due largely to historical demographic patterns. For the most part, each succeeding group of immigrants that entered the United States (e.g., Irish, Chinese, Italian, Polish) has settled in large urban areas. Many times they did so simply because that was where job opportunities existed, but cities also have been centers of ethnic enclaves where new immigrants could interact with relatives, friends, and others who hailed from the same place of origin. So, entrepreneurial members of these communities opened service businesses of all types to satisfy the consumer demands of the local ethnic groups. Certain categories of business became attractive for minority entrepreneurs. Among the most common business opportunities available to minorities were bowling alleys, contract construction, dry cleaning, furniture stores, real estate brokerages, savings and loan associations, and supermarkets.

Despite opportunities in these and other fields, limitations existed that affected minorities attempting to start their own businesses. One of the most significant problems concerned financing, particularly prior to the 1960s. Until that time, banks were not anxious to loan minorities money. However, the civil rights movement that began in the 1960s theoretically made it easier for minorities to obtain financing. Unfortunately, there was not always enough money to go around. The federal government intervened to alleviate that problem.

GOVERNMENT INTERVENTION

Government agencies became more helpful to minority business owners after the civil rights movement began. President Nixon established the Office of Minority Business Enterprises (OMBE) in 1969 as part of his initiative to spearhead minority capitalism. The agency's purpose was to provide management and technical assistance, information, and advocacy in the private sector for minority business development. OMBE has since been renamed the Minority Business Development Agency, and has become part of the U.S. Department of Commerce. Its six regional offices disperse technical advice and information to a network of over 100 local business development centers around the country.

The **Small Business Administration (SBA)** also stepped up efforts to help minority business owners obtain needed financing. The agency initiated two types of programs—loan assistance and preferential procurement of federal contracts, called ''set-asides.'' Many state and local governments set up similar preferential procurement contracts to assist minority contractors.

Set-asides were created in 1953, when the U.S. government passed a law that set aside 5 percent of all procurement contracts for small businesses owned by socially and economically disadvantaged people. The SBA has defined and redefined the term ''socially and economically disadvantaged'' many times since then, adding different groups and deleting others. The core group under the original law included African Americans, Hispanics, Native Americans, Asian Pacific Americans, and other minorities. In 1982 the SBA added Asian Indians. Six years later, it added Sri Lankans. By 1989 the SBA included Tongans and Indonesians. The agency deleted Hasidic Jews in 1980 and took Iranians off its list when they could not prove long-term bias against them. Decisions such as these led to arguments against the effectiveness and fairness of ''set-aside'' programs. Exacerbating the arguments, the courts did not always view ''set-asides'' as legal.

ARGUMENTS OVER SET-ASIDES

Large cities like Atlanta, Baltimore, Detroit, and Philadelphia established their own ''set-aside'' programs. Many minority business owners argued that such programs were necessary if they were to survive. Others disagreed.

In the early 1990s, a judge in San Diego, California, ruled that these programs were unconstitutional. San Diego had an equal opportunity contracting program that mandated that 20 percent of city-funded construction projects had to be awarded to companies owned by ethnic minorities. Without such mandates, some people argued, the minority-owned companies could not stay in business. In 1993, a U.S. district judge struck down the ordinance. That upset many minority business owners, but others were relieved. They argued that ''set-asides'' were not helpful to minorities.

John Robinson, who was president and CEO of the New York-based National Minority Business Council, suggested that minority-owned companies that wanted to become successful should ignore ''set-asides.'' They would be better off, he said, entering mainstream business competition. As proof, he cited a black-owned company, TLC Beatrice International, which at the time had annual sales of more than $1.5 billion (the company later downsized substantially with divestitures in the late 1990s). Proponents of ''set-asides'' argued that companies as large as TLC Beatrice did not need such programs. However, they said, smaller businesses such as construction companies and supply distributors did. Forward thinking business experts disagreed.

Opponents of "set-asides" argued that minority-owned business operators in the late 20th century could no longer rely on "mom-and pop" operations to sustain themselves. They argued that minority owned businesses were coming of age and could compete in the mainstream economy. In fact, they said, "set-asides" impede minority-owned businesses' chances of success, because companies came to depend on them to the detriment of seeking contracts through competition. The success of many minority entrepreneurs supported that argument.

LOANS AND OTHER AID

There is no doubt that the federal government's increased involvement in minority business proved valuable. By 1984, the government had provided $9.5 billion in contracts, grants, and loans to minority businesses. That figure may sound impressive, but it does not offer help to as many companies as the government would like. The SBA, in particular, has made several efforts in the 1990s to improve its service to minority-owned businesses. Between 1992 and 1998, the percentage of SBA loans to minority concerns rose from 15 percent to 24 percent. In the late 1990s, the SBA redoubled its efforts to reach out to minority businesses that need funding, particularly those owned by African Americans and Hispanics.

Other organizations upon which minorities can rely for assistance include the NAACP's Community Development Resource Centers, the U.S. Hispanic Chamber of Commerce, the U.S. Pan Asian American Chamber of Commerce, and the National Black Chamber of Commerce (NBCC). The latter organization was influential in getting the Indianapolis Power and Light Company and PSI Energy, Inc., both of Indianapolis, Indiana, to reexamine their policies regarding minority contractors. At the NBCC's urging, PSI stated that it would like to deliver 4 percent of its business, worth $32 million annually, to minority- and women-owned firms. Help like this is invaluable to minority-owned businesses. More importantly, it bodes well for the future, as more and more minorities establish their own businesses.

MINORITY BUSINESS OWNERS SEIZE OTHER OPPORTUNITIES

More and more minorities are starting to take advantage of government programs, private sector assistance, and established business practices such as networking to assist them in opening their own firms. Networking—interactions among business people for the purpose of discussing mutual problems, solutions, and opportunities—is extremely important to minority business owners. It can take place within a company, an industry, or a group with common characteristics, e.g., race, sex, or religion. One example of a thriving network exists in Cleveland, where the growing Council of Smaller Enterprises of Cleveland comprises over 1,800 members. Organizations such as this are invaluable to minority business owners.

Many companies taking advantage of the assistance available to them have grown quietly into large and respectable firms. One prime example is TRESP Associates Incorporated, a management information systems firm located in Alexandria, Virginia. Owner Lillian Handy started the company from her home. Her only financing was a credit card. She relied on SBA loans through the 8a program to underwrite her business in the early years of the company's business. Only nine years after she started the company, it outgrew the 8a program. The company had 260 employees by 1994 with revenues of $15 million. Ms. Handy projected contracts worth $50 million by 1999.

By the late 1990s there was also heightened interest in minority businesses among venture capital firms and investment funds, some of which were targeting minority enterprises exclusively.

NEW GROWTH STRATEGIES

Some minority business advocates are encouraged by new developments such as the Internet. In contrast to traditional businesses, Internet businesses often require less start-up money, reducing entrepreneurs' dependence on potentially biased lenders. Some believe that electronic commerce also renders business transactions more color blind, improving minority-owned businesses' sales prospects—not to mention that there are yet large untapped markets for Internet-based services.

Another key growth area is in exporting, an activity in which minority businesses tend to be underrepresented. The SBA and the International Trade Administration's export assistance services have begun programs to encourage minority business participation in cross-border trade.

SEE ALSO: Women in Business

[Arthur G. Sharp]

FURTHER READING:

Bridenbaugh, Carl. *Cities in the Wilderness: Urban Life in America, 1625-1742.* New York: Capricorn Books, 1964.

"The Color of Money." *Business Week,* 26 April 1999.

Crockett, Roger O. "Invisible—And Loving It." *Business Week,* 5 October 1998.

Gallop, Gerda D. "The State of Small Black Business." *Black Enterprise,* November 1998.

Greene, Lorenzo Johnston. *The Negro in Colonial New England.* New York: Atheneum, 1969.

Minority Business Entrepreneur, bimonthly. Available from www.mbemag.com.

"Minority-Owned Businesses Growing, But Their Global Markets Remain Untapped." *Jet,* 29 March 1999.

National Black Chamber of Commerce. *National Black Chamber of Commerce.* Washington, 1999. Available from www.nationalbcc.org.

U.S. Hispanic Chamber of Commerce. *United States Hispanic Chamber of Commerce.* Washington, 1999. Available from www.ushcc.com.

U.S. Pan Asian American Chamber of Commerce. *Welcome to USPAACC.* Washington, 1999. Available from www.uspaacc.org.

U.S. Small Business Administration. Office of Advocacy. *Minorities in Business.* Washington, 1999. Available from www.sba.gov.

Wadley, Jared O. "Growth in Hispanic-Owned Businesses Is Strong in California." *Press-Enterprise,* 3 November 1998.

MIS

SEE: Management Information Systems

MISSION

SEE: Strategy Formulation

MIXED ECONOMY

The "mixture" in a mixed economy is one of private enterprise and public-sector controls and supports, of capitalism and socialism. That is to say, most economies that we think of as being "capitalist" are in fact mixed economies, including that of the United States. A similar term, often used to describe the transition economies of eastern Europe and elsewhere, is "market socialism."

To purists, government intervention might seem out of place in **capitalism**, which in theory puts great stock in the enterprising individual making personal decisions in the marketplace. But, in practice, members of capitalist societies also value economic security. The result is the mixed economy, offering government a voice in sustaining economic growth, while at the same time protecting people from the worst excesses of unfettered competition in the marketplace.

Some examples of intervention by the government include:

- agricultural **subsidies** or price supports for farmers
- protective tariffs for steelmakers
- deposit insurance for bank depositors
- social security for retirees
- quotas for fishermen

All such measures instituted by government restrain or control competition and the free exchange of goods in an economy—and yet provide security in different ways. Therefore, under a mixed economy, neither unfettered capitalism nor centralized government control is practiced or necessarily desirable. Instead, the public and private sector combine to make economic decisions on what is produced and distributed in an economy, and how. Society as a whole pursues its interests via individual and collective action.

OPPOSING PERSPECTIVES TESTED

Various economic theories prescribe what kind of government intervention is appropriate in the economy and when. In the first half of the 20th century, a popular theory was derived from the work of British economist John Maynard Keynes. Keynesians believed that in a market economy, such as the United States, government should increase spending and/or the money supply during times of economic slowdown to stimulate growth. In times of economic prosperity, by contrast, spending and capital may be tightened by the government, they argue. Such notions were in part a stimulus for Depression-era government works programs under the New Deal.

However, by the early 1970s, government spending in Western economies had grown significantly, producing **inflation**, while economic growth stagnated. Suddenly, "stagflation" became the economic buzzword of the day, especially when the 1973 oil embargo inspired fears of concurrent rising inflation and unemployment.

In contrast to the Keynesian prescription, monetarist economists argued that high taxes, controls, and regulation imposed by government would suffocate growth. Monetarists believe in strict controls over the **money supply** as a means to economic stability. Only when government intervention was minimized, they reasoned, would significant economic growth resume. Now individuals were no longer encouraged to shift their economic risks to the government—relying on crop insurance or remaining on welfare—but rather to take more responsibility for their economic destiny in the marketplace.

Put simply, monetarists believed government was more of a problem than a solution when it came to sustaining economic growth. During the 1980s, governments turned to stimulating or restraining an economy on the supply side by adjusting the available money supply. This they did, once again, through **taxes**. Specifically, Western governments looked to reducing the tax burden as the impetus for releasing private sector energies.

However, bending to political realities, exceptions were made, and government subsidies grew. The mixed economy was alive and well during the 1980s, despite the wishes of supply-side economists. Indeed, their fears were realized when rising public spending led to higher government borrowing and deficits. This, in turn, led to inflation and higher **interest rates** as the public sector competed with the private sector to borrow on international markets.

In response to the recession of the early 1990s, the monetarists went back on the defensive. Control of the money supply, they argued, would reduce the rate of inflation, foster stability, and further economic growth. This time, however, somewhat of a hybrid policy was implemented in the United States. The money supply was loosened via lowered central bank interest rates, following a Keynesian monetary policy, but the government's fiscal policy was skewed heavily toward controlling spending and, in some cases, modest tax relief. The combination proved advantageous, as a period of robust economic growth ensued.

SEE ALSO: Capitalism; Laissez Faire; Socialism and Communism

FURTHER READING:

Arnold, N. Scott, ed. *The Philosophy and Economics of Market Socialism: A Critical Study.* New York: Oxford University Press, 1995.

Freeman, John R. *Democracy and Markets: The Politics of Mixed Economies.* New York: Cornell University Press, 1989.

Ikeda, Sanford. *Dynamics of the Mixed Economy: Toward a Theory of Interventionism.* New York: Routledge, 1997.

MLM

SEE: Multilevel Marketing

MONETARISM

Monetarism asserts that monetary policy is very powerful, but that it should not be used as a macroeconomic policy to manage the economy. There is thus an apparent contradiction—if monetary policy is so powerful, why not use it, for example, to create more employment in the economy?

HISTORY AND BACKGROUND

First of all, it should be noted that monetarism was an attempt by conservative economists to reestablish the wisdom of the classical **laissez faire** recommendation and was an attack on the *activist* macroeconomic policy recommendations of the Keynesian economists. It is thus helpful to briefly examine the historical background against which monetarism developed as a new school of macroeconomic thought.

THE CLASSICAL ECONOMICS. The macroeconomic thought dominating capitalist economies prior to the advent of Keynesian economics in 1936 has been widely known as classical **macroeconomics.** Classical economists believed in free markets. They believed that the economy would always achieve full **employment** through forces of supply and demand. So, if there were more people looking for work than the number of jobs available, the wages would fall until all those seeking work were employed. Thus, market forces guaranteed full employment. The full employment level of employment resulted in a fixed aggregate output/income. The price level (and thus the inflation rate) was determined by the supply of money in the economy. Since, the output level was fixed, a 10 percent increase in money supply would lead to a 10 percent increase in the price level—too many dollars chasing too few goods. The real interest rate was also determined by forces of supply and demand in the market for funds that could be loaned out. The nominal interest rate was then simply the sum of the real interest rate and the prevailing **inflation** rate. Classical economists thus had an unwavering faith in the self-adjusting market mechanism. However, it was crucial for the working of the market mechanism that there was perfect competition in the market, and that wages and prices were fully flexible.

Classical economists did not see any role for the government. As market forces led to full **employment** equilibrium in the economy, there was no need for government intervention. Monetary policy (increasing or decreasing the **money supply** would only affect prices—it would not affect important real factors such as output and employment. Fiscal policy (using government spending or taxes), on the other hand, was perceived as harmful. For example, if the government borrowed to finance its spending, it would simply reduce the funds available for private consumption and investment expenditures—a phenomenon popularly termed as "crowding out." Similarly, if the government raised taxes to pay for government spending, it would reduce private consumption in order to fund public consumption. Instead, if it financed spending by increasing the money supply, it would have the same effects as an expansionary monetary policy. Thus, classical economists recommended use of neither monetary nor fiscal policy by the government. This hands-off policy recommendation is known as *laissez faire.*

KEYNESIAN ECONOMICS. Keynesian economics was born during the Great Depression of the 1930s. The classical economists argued that the self-adjusting market mechanism would restore full employment in the economy, if it deviated from full employment for some reason. However, the experience of the Great Depression showed that market forces would not work as well as the classical economists had believed. The unemployment rate in the United States rose to higher than 25 percent of the labor force. Hard working people were out in the street looking for nonexisting jobs. Wages fell quite substantially. However, the lower wages did not re-establish full employment.

Economist John Maynard Keynes argued that the self-adjusting market forces would take a long time to restore full employment. He predicted that the economy would be stuck at the high level of unemployment for a prolonged period, leading to untold miseries. Keynes explained that classical economics suffered from major flaws. Wages and prices were not as flexible as classical economists assumed—in fact, nominal wages were very sticky in the downward direction. Also, Keynes argued that classical economists had ignored a key aspect that determined the level of output and employment in the economy—the *aggregate demand* for goods and services in the economy from all sources (consumers, businesses, government, and foreign sources). Producers create goods (and provided employment in the process) to meet the demand for their products and services. If the level of aggregate demand was low, the economy would not create enough jobs and unemployment could result. In other words, the free working of the macroeconomy did not guarantee full employment of the labor force—the deficient aggregate demand was the cause of unemployment. Thus, if aggregate private demand (i.e., the aggregate demand excluding government spending) fell short of the demand level needed to generate full employment, the government should step in to make up for the slack.

The central issue underlying Keynesian thought was that those individuals who have incomes demand goods and services and, in turn, help to create jobs. The government should thus find a way to increase aggregate demand. One direct way of doing so was to increase government spending. Increased government spending would generate jobs and incomes for the persons employed on government projects. This, in turn, would create demand for goods and services of private producers and generate additional employment in the private sector. Keynesian economists thus recommended that the government should use fiscal policy (which includes decisions regarding both government spending and taxes) to make up for the shortfall in the private aggregate demand to reignite the job creating private sector. Keynesian economists even went so far as to recommend that it was worthwhile for the government to employ people to in meaningless jobs, as long as they were employed.

The Roosevelt administration did follow Keynesian recommendations, although reluctantly, and embarked on a variety of government programs aimed at boosting incomes and the aggregate demand. As a result, the Depression economy started moving forward. The really powerful push to the depressed U.S economy, however, came when World War II broke out. It generated such an enormous demand for U.S. military and civilian goods that factories in the United States operated multiple shifts. Serious unemployment disappeared for a long period of time.

Modern Keynesians (also, known as neo-Keynesians) recommend utilizing monetary policy, in addition to fiscal policy, to manage the level of aggregate demand. Monetary policy affects aggregate demand in the Keynesian system by affecting private investment and consumption demand. An increase in the money supply, for example, leads to a decrease in the interest rate. This lowers the cost of borrowing and thus increases private investment and consumption, boosting the aggregate demand in the economy.

An increase in aggregate demand under the Keynesian system, however, not only generates higher employment but also leads to higher inflation. This causes a policy dilemma—how to strike a balance between employment and inflation. According to laws that were enacted following the Great Depression, policy makers are expected to use monetary and fiscal policies to achieve high employment consistent with price stability.

THE MONETARIST COUNTERREVOLUTION

By 1950, Keynesian economics was well established. Keynesian macroeconomic thought became the new standard in place of the old classical standard. The birth of monetarism took place in the 1960s. The original proponent of monetarism was Milton Friedman, now a Nobel Laureate. The monetarists argue that while it is not possible to have full employment of the labor force all the time (as classical economists argued), it is better to leave the macroeconomy to market forces. Friedman modified some aspects of the classical theory to provide the rationale for his noninterventionist policy recommendation. In essence, monetarism contends that use of fiscal policy is largely ineffective in altering output and employment levels. Moreover, it only leads to crowding out. Monetary policy, on the other hand, is effective. However, monetary authorities do not have adequate knowledge to conduct a successful monetary policy—manipulating the money supply to stabilize the economy only leads to a greater instability. Hence, monetarism advocates that neither monetary nor fiscal policy should be used in an attempt to stabilize the economy, and the money supply should be allowed to grow at a constant rate. Friedman contends that the government's use of *active* monetary and fiscal policies to stabilize the economy around full employment leads to greater instability in the economy. He argues that while the economy will not achieve a state of bliss in the absence of the government intervention, it will be far more tranquil. The monetarist policy recommendations are similar to those of the classical economists, even though the reasoning is somewhat different.

A detailed discussion of the key elements of monetarism follows. In particular, an effort is made to explain the theoretical framework that monetarists employ and how they arrive at policy recommendations regarding the use of monetary and fiscal policies.

KEY MONETARIST PROPOSITIONS

Based on Richard Froyen in *Macroeconomics: Theories and Policies,* the key propositions advanced by monetarist economists (in particular, Milton Friedman) can be summarized as follows.

1. The supply of money has the dominant influence on nominal income. Two economic concepts enter this proposition—money supply and nominal income. Money supply can be narrowly defined as the sum of all money (currency, checkable deposits, and travelers checks) with the nonbank public in the economy. The **money supply** so defined is technically called M1 by monetary authorities and economists. Nominal income can simply be understood as the **gross domestic product** (GDP) at current prices. GDP is thus made up of a price component and a real output component. The current value of the GDP can go up due to an increase in the prices of goods and services included in the GDP or due to an increase in the actual production of goods and services included in the GDP or both.

The above proposition then states that the stock of money in the economy is the primary determinant of the nominal GDP, or the level of economic activity in current dollars. The proposition is vague regarding the breakdown of an increase in nominal gross domestic product into increases in the price level and real output. However, the proposition does assume that, for most part, a change in the money supply is the *cause* of a change in the GDP at current prices or nominal income. Also, the level and the rate of growth of the money supply are assumed to be primarily determined by the actions of the central monetary authority (the **Federal Reserve** Bank in the United States).

2. In the short run, money supply does have the dominant influence on the *real* variables. Here, the real variables are the real output (the real GDP) and employment. The first proposition only alluded to real output—implied in the break up of the nominal GDP into the real and price components. Where does the employment variable come from? Employment is basically considered a companion of real output. If real output increases, producers must generally employ additional workers to produce the additional output. Of course, sometimes producers may rely on overtime from existing workers. But, generally an increase in employment eventually follows an increase in real output. The second proposition, however, is not confined to real output and employment—prices are influenced as well. Thus, the second proposition effectively states that changes in money supply strongly influence both real output and price level in the short run. Proposition two, therefore, provides a break down of a change in the nominal income, induced by a change in the money supply, into changes in real output and price level components mentioned in the first proposition.

3. In the long run, the influence of a variation in the money supply is primarily on price level and on other *nominal* variables such as nominal wages. Price level is a nominal variable in the sense that a change in price level is in sharp contrast to a change in real output and employment—it does not have the advantages that are associated with the latter two. In the long run, the *real* macroeconomic variables, such as real output and employment, are determined by changes in real factors of production, not simply by altering a nominal variable, such as the money supply. Real output and employment are, in turn, determined by real factors such as labor inputs, capital resources, and the state of technology. As was indicated in the second proposition, in the short run, a change in the stock of money affects both real output and price level. This, in conjunction with proposition three, leads to the implication that the long-run influence of money supply is only on the price level.

4. The private sector of the economy is inherently stable. Further, government policies are primarily responsible for instability in the economy. This proposition summarizes the monetarist economists' belief in the working of the private sector and market forces. The private sector mainly consists of households and businesses that together account for the bulk of private sector demand, consumption, and investment. This monetarist proposition, then, states that these components of the aggregate demand are stable, and are thus not a source of instability in the economy. In fact, monetarists argue that the private sector is a self-adjusting process that tends to stabilize the economy by absorbing shocks. They contend that it is the government sector that is the source of instability. The government causes instability in the economy primarily through an unstable money supply. Since the

money supply has a dominant effect on real output and price level in the short run, and on price level in the long run, fluctuations in the money supply lead to fluctuations in these macroeconomic variables—i.e., instability of the macroeconomy. Moreover, the government, by introducing a powerful destabilizing influence (changes in the money supply), interferes with the normal workings of the self-adjusting mechanism of the private sector. In effect, the absence of money supply fluctuations would make it easier for the private sector mechanism to work properly.

The above four propositions lead to some key policy conclusions. Based on Froyen, the four monetarist propositions provide the bases for the following two policy recommendations:

First, stability in the growth of money supply is absolutely crucial for stability in the economy. Monetarists further suggest that stability in the growth of money supply is best achieved by setting the growth rate at a constant rate—this recommendation has been termed as the constant money supply growth rule. The chief proponent of monetarism, Milton Friedman, has long advocated a strict adherence to a money supply rule. Other monetarists favor following a less inflexible money supply growth rate rule. However, monetarists, in general, are in favor of following a rule regarding the money supply growth rate, rather than tolerating fluctuations in the monetary aggregate (caused by discretionary monetary policy aimed at stabilizing the economy around full employment). This policy difference from the activist economists (primarily, the Keynesians) is at the heart of the monetarist debate. This component of the debate is known among professional economists as ''rule versus discretion'' controversy.

One should note that while monetarists are adamant about following a money supply rule, they are not so rigid regarding the rate at which the money supply growth rate should be fixed. A general rule of thumb suggests that the money supply should grow between 4 and 5 percent. How do economists arrive at these numbers? It is assumed that the long-term economic growth potential of the U.S. economy is about 3 percent per annum, i.e., the real GDP can grow at about 3 percent. So, the money supply has to grow at about 3 percent just to keep the price level from falling—economists do not like falling prices because they cause other problems in the economy. An inflation rate of 1-2 percent per annum is considered acceptable. To generate 1-2 percent inflation, the money supply must grow at 1-2 percent above the growth rate of the real GDP. In effect, then, to have a modest 1-2 percent inflation, the money supply should grow at about 4-5 percent. The issue of the money supply growth rule will be further clarified when theoretical principles underlying monetarism are discussed later.

Second, fiscal policy is ineffective in influencing either real or nominal macroeconomic variables. It has little effect, for example, on either real output/employment or price level. Thus, the government can't use fiscal policy as a stabilization tool. Monetarists contend that while fiscal policy is not an effective stabilization tool, it does lead to some harmful effects on the private sector economy—it crowds out private consumption and investment expenditures.

THEORETICAL UNDERPINNINGS OF MONETARISM

The four monetarist propositions discussed in the preceding section, from which the two policy recommendations follow, are supported by theoretical reasoning and support. In general, the theoretical framework employed by monetarist economists is a modified version of classical macroeconomic theory. The modifications were needed to address the Keynesian criticisms of the classical theory and to establish monetarist policy conclusions. Theoretical support for each of the four propositions will be briefly discussed in this section.

PROPOSITION ONE. This proposition—that money supply has a dominant effect on nominal income—is the most basic part of the theoretical structure of the monetarist counterrevolution. Proposition one is based on a key classical theoretical framework known as the *quantity theory of money.* Classical economists had argued that the quantity (or the supply) of money determines only price level (a *nominal* variable), not *real* variables such as output and employment. The quantity theory of money is used to establish the link between the quantity of money and the price level, and thus its name simply emphasizes the importance of the quantity of money. The quantity theory of money was written in the form of the equation: $MV = Py$, where M is the quantity or stock of money; P is the aggregate price level; y is a measure of the aggregate real output, say, the gross domestic product; and V stands for the income *velocity* of money that is defined as:

$$V = \frac{(Py)}{M}$$

Apart from the notion of the velocity of money, the other variables that enter the quantity theory of money are relatively straightforward. Noting that ''Py'' is nothing but the nominal aggregate output (the value of the gross domestic product at current prices), the income velocity of money can be thought of as the number of times each dollar in the nation's money supply circulates to finance the current nominal income. The velocity, then, is just the turnover rate of money. Necessarily, the income velocity of money is greater than one. The gross domestic product at current prices in 1998 was about $8,200 billion, and a narrowly defined measure of the money supply (called M1) was about $1,100 billion. These numbers suggested the income velocity of money was approximately 7.5 in 1998.

How does the classical quantity theory of money provide the linkage between changes in the money supply and changes in the price level? In order to translate the equation ''MV = Py'' into the quantity theory of money, two main assumptions are made. First, it is argued that velocity is constant. Classical economists, in particular Irving Fisher, argue that the velocity of money is determined largely by payment technology and payment habits of the society. For example, frequent use of charge cards, rather than money (such as cash or checks) increases the velocity of money. Similarly, if workers are paid on a weekly rather than a monthly basis, the velocity will be greater. It is however, argued that the foregoing are examples of institutional characteristics, and institutional factors that determine the equilibrium level of the velocity change very slowly. As a result, the velocity of money can be regarded as fixed or constant in the short run.

The second key classical assumption (in fact, an inference of classical macroeconomic theory) was that real output (measured by real gross domestic product) is constant or fixed. As alluded to in the previous sentence and discussed under a brief overview of classical theory, the constancy of real output is a result of classical macroeconomic reasoning, rather than a simple assumption. The fixed output is a result of the full employment level. The full employment of the labor force, in turn, is assured by a set of assumptions about the labor market. In particular, perfect **competition**, perfect information, and wage/price flexibility always result in the full employment of workers.

Once the above two assumptions are made (i.e., velocity and real output are fixed), the classical quantity theory of money, given by the expression MV = Py, easily connects the changes in money supply to changes in price level. More specifically, a money supply change leads to a proportionate change in price level. For example, if money supply increases by 10 percent, price also increases by 10 percent. The reasoning behind this linkage between the money supply and the price level is as follows: An increase in the money supply would lead to an increase in spending by individuals. However, given that real output is assumed to be constant, the increased spending can only lead to an increase in the price level. This explanation is often summarized as ''too many dollars chasing too few goods.''

While monetarists, led by Nobel Prize winner Milton Friedman, initially wanted to use the classical quantity theory of money to explain the linkage between the money supply and the nominal GDP/income, in light of the Keynesian theory and the experience of the Great Depression, they could no longer assume that real output level was fixed. Thus, Friedman modified the classical quantity of money to allow for variations in real output. However, if velocity is assumed constant, ''MV = Py'' still means that an increase in money supply will lead to a proportionate change in ''Py.'' Friedman even argues that the velocity of money does not have to be assumed constant. Instead, he argues that the velocity can be allowed to change. However, the changes in velocity are predictable. This complicates the explanation of the linkage between money supply and nominal income somewhat. It no longer means that an increase in the money supply will lead to a proportionate increase in the nominal GDP, because now the velocity can also undergo a change. However, the modified quantity theory of money still links money supply and nominal income. It should be noted that this linkage between money supply and the nominal income does not separate the effects of money on nominal income into changes in the price level (P) and changes in the real output (y). This issue is further dealt with in propositions two and three.

PROPOSITION TWO. As illustrated above, proposition one does not breakdown a change in nominal output into price and real output components. Friedman argues that, in the short run, both price level and real output increase when the money supply increases. As real output increases, the employment level will change as well, since the increased output has to be produced by a greater number of workers (the level of technology is assumed to remain unchanged in the short run). Monetarists explain the increase in employment and real output as an increase in money supply leads to an increase in price level. However, workers do not ask for increases in nominal wages to offset the price increase, as they are initially unaware of it. However, producers know the increased prices their goods and services are commanding. Thus, from the producers' (employers') point of view, the real wage paid actually falls (i.e., the dollar wage paid remains the same whereas the price level increases). This effectively lowers the cost of hiring workers and they employ an increased number of workers, leading to higher employment and higher real output.

An important implication of this proposition is that a change in money supply does more than influence nominal variables such as price level—it affects real variables such as the employment of labor and real output of goods and services. Monetarists further argue that money, of all the sources of demand in the economy, has the most dominant influence on real variables.

PROPOSITION THREE. While proposition two deals with the effects of short-term changes in the money supply, proposition three discusses its long-term effects. Crucial to increases in output and employment in proposition two is the decline in real wages paid to workers. However, the decline in real wage was caused due to workers being unaware of the increase in price levels. It is argued that workers cannot remain uninformed about the price level increase, as they pay higher prices for the goods and services they consume. Once workers understand the true extent of the increase in the price level, they will demand an increase in nominal wages (wages in current dollars) to compensate for the increase in the price level. Strictly speaking, they would want nominal wages to increase by the same percentage as the increase in the price level to restore the previous level of their real wage. Once the real wage paid to workers rises to the level it was before the increase in the price level, employers no longer enjoy a cost savings due to lower real wages and, as a result, they cut back labor employment to the level that existed before the price increase. Consequently, the real output level also falls back to the previous level.

The foregoing implies that once enough time passes for workers to adjust their price expectations, the effects of money supply on real variables such as employment and real output evaporate. Does this mean that changes in money supply have no effect on the economy? According to monetarists, this is not the case. The effect is only on the nominal variables—in this case the price level and nominal wage rate, both of which rise proportionate to the initial rise in the money supply. As workers recognize the increase in prices and receive nominal wage adjustments, employment and output levels return to long-term levels, similar to classical fixed output and employment levels. Even as the real variables do not change over the long-term, the increased levels of prices and nominal wages remain.

An important implication of proposition three is that an increase in money supply has no useful effect on the economy, since real variables such as output and employment remain unaffected but prices and wages increase.

PROPOSITION FOUR. The fourth proposition re-emphasizes the monetarists' faith in the private sector and free market. Monetarists rely on a macroeconomic model that illustrates that the private sector of the economy is not prone to massive fluctuations and is inherently stable. On the other hand, the public sector (as reflected by the behavior of the Federal Reserve Bank in manipulating money supply) is unstable. At a more theoretical level, proponents of monetarism argue that investment (a component of private sector demand) is very sensitive to changes in **interest rates**, whereas the demand for money (the amount of money people want to hold in cash and checkable deposits for various purposes) is not very sensitive to changes in interest rates. While the exact theoretical explanation is quite involved, the preceding assumptions regarding the opposite responses of investment and money demand to interest rates lead to a important theoretical outcome—manipulating the money supply leads to instability in the economy in terms of output, employment, and inflation, whereas changes in the levels of consumption and investment lead to minimal fluctuations in the economy.

A corollary of the foregoing argument involves the third component of aggregate demand, government spending. Aggregate demand is considered to mainly comprise consumption, investment, and government spending. Therefore, like consumption and investment, change in government spending does not trigger large fluctuation in the economy. This also means that fiscal policy in the form of government deficit spending is not very effective in influencing employment and real output in the economy. Monetarists, however, do infer that government deficit spending is not harmless. It leads to increases in interest rates, which reduce private sector spending on consumption and investment—a phenomenon popularly called crowding out.

In sum, the fourth proposition implies that the private sector in itself is stable—instability is introduced by fluctuations in money supply (monetary policy), and fiscal policy, while not causing instability, leads to the crowding out phenomenon.

MONETARIST POLICY RECOMMENDATIONS AND THEIR FOUNDATIONS

Monetarist policy recommendations basically assert that the government should not use monetary and fiscal policies to stabilize the economy. This, not surprisingly, sounds like the *laissez faire* recommendation of classical economists. However, the reasoning behind the policy recommendations advanced by the proponents of monetarism are somewhat different from those used by classical counterparts.

The monetarist policy recommendations have two key aspects—one relates to the use of monetary policy and the other relates to the use of fiscal policy. The four propositions discussed above form the major foundations for monetarist policy recommendations with respect to the conduct of monetary and fiscal policies. The monetarist reasoning behind policy recommendations is briefly discussed below.

With respect to monetary policy, monetarists emphatically recommend that monetary authorities (the Federal Reserve System in the United States) should not use discretionary monetary policy. That is, the nations's money supply should not be manipulated to stabilize or fine tune the economy. The notion of stabilization in turn implies an effort to create stable economic growth with low or no inflation. Such a stabilization policy, if successful, would smooth out the bumps in the path of economic growth—both recessions and booms would be moderated and the economy would grow at a rate consistent with its long-term potential. Monetarists do not believe that the Federal Reserve can conduct a successful monetary policy aimed at stabilizing the economy. They admit that monetary policy does have a dominant effect on nominal GDP (see proposition one). However, monetary policy affects real variables such as employment and real output, whose growth is considered desirable, only in the short-term (see proposition two). In the long term, real output and employment are determined at the equilibrium level, and thus a money supply increase ultimately only affects the price level and inflation, which is not a desirable outcome (see proposition three). Monetarists, therefore, argue that beneficial effects of monetary policy are short-lived and harmful effects prevail. This is one of the reasons monetarists do not recommend using discretionary monetary policies.

Monetarism supporters further argue that the use of discretionary policy destabilizes the economy even further, rather than stabilizing the economy around full employment with low inflation. Monetarists use propositions one and two to support this contention. However, they argue that the monetary instrument is too powerful to be used successfully in stabilizing the economy. Monetary authorities do not have enough knowledge of the way the economy and monetary policy work to use the policy successfully. In particular, they contend that monetary policy affects the economy with long and variable lags. This implies that we do not know exactly when the effects of a dose of monetary policy will show up in the economy. As a result, use of monetary policy can exacerbate the economic fluctuations in the economy, and the resulting instability would be far greater than that found if no monetary policy were used at all.

Consider, for example, that the economy is in recession and that it is going to come out of recession on its own in three months. However, the Federal Reserve, not knowing when the recession will end, conducts an expansionary monetary policy by increasing money supply to eliminate the recession. Now, suppose that the effects of this monetary policy show up in the economy in six months when the economy has already rebounded and is growing rapidly on its own. The powerful push from the monetary policy could have a negative effect—the economy could overheat, leading to unwanted inflation. Thus, monetarists argue that the monetary authorities, even with good intentions, do not have the knowledge to successfully conduct stabilization using monetary policy. Of course, monetarists also argue that the Federal Reserve is not to be trusted with the manipulation of money supply. They say that the Federal Reserve has made a number of costly mistakes in the past in the conduct of monetary policy. The most infamous example is the decrease in money supply during the Great Depression when the economy needed an increase in money supply to cope with the economic crisis. The proponents of monetarism, therefore, advocate that the Federal Reserve should be kept from tampering with monetary policy—instead of manipulating money supply to stabilize the economy, the Federal Reserve should allow money supply to grow at a constant rate. In other words, the Federal Reserve should follow a rule rather than exercising its discretion. This will keep the Fed from being a source of instability. While monetarists agree that following a rule does not imply that the economy would attain *nirvana* (a state of bliss in which there are no fluctuations), the economy would experience smaller fluctuations.

Finally, monetarists insist that ultimately, there is no need to stabilize the economy because the private sector is inherently stable (proposition four). It is discretionary monetary policy that introduces instability into the economy. The proponents of monetarism use the inherent stability argument to further strengthen their recommendation of following a constant money supply growth rule.

With respect to fiscal policy, monetarist's policy recommendations are broadly similar to those of the classical economists. The monetarists argue that government fiscal policy (especially deficit spending) is ineffective in affecting employment and real output in any significant manner in either the short or long term (an indirect implication of proposition four). Fiscal policy also does not appreciably influence price level. Thus, on the surface, the conduct of fiscal policy may appear inconsequential. However, monetarists point out that borrowing by the government will lead to an increase in interest rates which, in turn, reduces private expenditures on consumption and investment—government spending crowds out private sector spending. Thus, fiscal policy based on borrowing is not harmless. Increased government spending, financed by printing money, of course, has effects similar to expansionary monetary policy.

Monetarists thus advocate using neither discretionary monetary or discretionary fiscal policy to stabilize the economy—they would like to see money supply grow at a constant rate.

WHO DOES THE GOVERNMENT FOLLOW?

While proponents of monetarism have staged a very vocal and visible attack on the activist policy recommendations of Keynesian economists, they have not been successful in dethroning the Keynesians. One can safely argue that the United States and many other capitalist countries largely follow Keynesian policy recommendations at the current time. In fact, following the Keynesian revolution, the U.S. Congress has enacted laws that commit the U.S. government to promoting high employment consistent with a stable price level. Officially, both fiscal and monetary policies are considered effective instruments of macroeconomic policies aimed at stabilizing the economy through full employment. However, due to the slow speed at which fiscal policy reacts to developments in the U.S. economy, monetary policy has come to shoulder the major burden of stabilizing the economy.

Does this mean that monetarism has completely failed to influence the conduct of macroeconomic policies? Monetarists did fail in having their key recommendation, the constant money supply growth rule, accepted by monetary authorities. However, they have succeeded in driving home the point that manipulating the money supply has powerful consequences and that it can potentially be harmful to the economy. The monetary policy authorities of today realize the limitations of monetary policy. As a result, they do not take rash steps in either direction. The Federal Reserve watches the economy carefully and collects a great deal of information about the state of the economy before taking a major monetary policy action. Thus, monetarists should not be considered as having failed completely—they have succeeded in, at least, adding a note of caution in the conduct of monetary policy.

SEE ALSO: Federal Reserve System; Money Supply

[Anandi P. Sahu, Ph.D.]

FURTHER READING:

Friedman, Milton, and Anna Schwartz. *Monetary Trends in the United States and United Kingdom.* Chicago: University of Chicago Press, 1982.

Froyen, Richard T. *Macroeconomics: Theories and Policies.* 6th ed. New York: Prentice Hall, 1998.

Gordon, Robert J., ed. *Milton Friedman's Monetary Framework.* Chicago: University of Chicago Press, 1974.

——. *Macroeconomics.* 7th ed. Reading, PA: Addison-Wesley, 1998.

Mayer, Thomas. *The Structure of Monetarism.* New York: W.W. Norton & Company, 1978.

Modigliani, Franco. ''The Monetarist Controversy, or Should We Forsake Stabilization Policies?'' *American Economic Review,* March 1977.

MONEY MARKET INSTRUMENTS

The money market is the arena in which financial, nonfinancial, and banking institutions make available to a broad range of creditors, borrowers and investors, the opportunity to buy and sell, on a wholesale basis, large volumes of bills, notes, and other forms of short-term credit. A typical money market instrument is worth $1 million or more. These instruments have maturities ranging from one day to one year (the average is less than three months) and are extremely liquid. Consequently, they are considered to be near-cash equivalents—indeed, even part of the **money supply** by some definitions—hence the name money market instruments.

Money markets exist to facilitate efficient transfer of short-term funds between holders and borrowers of cash assets. For the lender/investor, the market provides a modest rate of return on funds that are not being used presently, but cannot be tied up in less liquid or less certain investments. For the borrower, the money market enables rapid and relatively inexpensive acquisition of cash to cover short-term liabilities.

The suppliers of funds for money market instruments are institutions and individuals with a preference for the highest liquidity and the lowest risk. Often, money market instruments are a parking place for temporary excess cash of investors and corporations. Interest rates on money market instruments are typically quoted on a bank discount basis.

Retail money market dealers work independently or in syndicated groups to efficiently distribute available supplies of money market instruments to securities dealers, **banks**, and other financial intermediaries who broker them to retail clients. In addition to dealers, institutions and funds repackage money market instruments into money market **mutual funds** to allow participation at almost any level.

Major categories of money market instruments include the following:

- federal funds loaned to banks
- certificates of deposit
- repurchase agreements
- U.S. Treasury bills
- municipal securities
- commercial paper
- bankers acceptances
- money market **futures** and **options**

FEDERAL FUNDS

Federal funds are short-term loans, mostly overnight, exchanged between banks that have reserve accounts in the Federal Reserve system. The Federal Reserve is not the source of the funds, but its regional banks provide the infrastructure for this market. A federal funds loan is generally arranged in one of two ways: (1) a wire transfer over the Fedwire system from the lending bank's account to the borrowing bank's account, or (2) when the two banks have a respondent/correspondent relationship, a respondent bank can allow the correspondent bank to temporarily reclassify the former's deposits as a federal funds purchase on the books. A broker may also mediate a federal funds transaction by linking a borrower and a lender for a commission. Federal funds borrowing pays interest at a market-determined federal funds rate, although the rate is closely influenced by Federal Reserve monetary policy.

REPURCHASE AGREEMENTS

Repurchase agreements, also known as repos or RPs, are somewhat more complex transactions that involve selling one or more securities, typically Treasury instruments, to receive short-term cash, but with an agreement to buy them back at a specified time and price. In effect, repos function like special-purpose collateralized **loans** between institutions. Most repos (they may be called reverse repos depending on which party's perspective is considered) last only overnight or for several days, but they may extend for up to six months. Interest paid to the cash lender under a repo is determined by a number of general market conditions, but in general the rate is somewhat lower than the federal funds rate.

CERTIFICATES OF DEPOSIT

Certificates of deposit (CDs) are certificates issued by a federally chartered bank against deposited funds that earn a specified return for a definite period of time. Large denomination (jumbo) CDs of $100,000 or more are generally negotiable and pay higher interest than smaller denominations. However, such certificates are insured by the FDIC only up to $100,000. A Yankee CD is a CD issued by domestic branches of foreign banks. Eurodollar CDs are negotiable certificates issued against U.S. dollar obligations in a foreign branch of a domestic bank.

Brokerage firms have a nationwide pool of bank CDs and receive a fee for selling them. Since brokers deal in large sums, brokered CDs generally pay higher interest rates and offer greater liquidity than CDs purchased directly from a bank, since brokers maintain an active secondary market in CDs.

COMMERCIAL PAPER

Commercial paper (CP) refers to unsecured short-term **promissory notes** issued by financial and nonfinancial corporations. CP has maturities of up to 270 days (the maximum allowed without SEC registration requirement), but more often it expires within 30 days. Dollar volume for CP exceeds the amount of any money market instrument other than **U.S. Treasury bills**.

CP is typically issued by large, credit-worthy corporations with unused lines of bank credit and, therefore, carries low **default** risk. As of year-end 1998, more than 77 percent of commercial paper in the United States was issued by domestic financial institutions, mostly nonbank financial companies (although some banks also participate). Approximately one-sixth was issued by domestic nonfinancial companies, and the remainder came from foreign companies, both financial and nonfinancial.

Standard & Poor's and Moody's provide risk ratings on various issues of commercial paper. The highest ratings are A1 and P(Prime)1, respectively. A2 and P2 paper is considered high quality, but usually indicates that the issuing corporation is smaller or more debt burdened than A1 and P1 companies. Issuers earning the lowest ratings find few willing investors.

Commercial paper can be issued directly by the company to creditors, using internal transactors or a bank as an agent. The bank assumes no principal position and is in no way obligated with respect to repayment of the CP. Companies may also sell CP through dealers who charge a fee and arrange for the transfer of the funds from the lender to the borrower.

BANKERS ACCEPTANCE

Bankers acceptances are generally used to finance foreign trade. A buyer's promise to pay a specific amount of money at a fixed or determinable future time (usually less than 180 days) is issued to a seller. A bank then guarantees or "accepts" this promise in exchange for a claim on the goods as collateral. The seller may obtain immediate cash in lieu of future payment by selling the acceptance at a discount.

MONEY MARKET FUNDS

While money market instruments themselves are usually available only to corporations or other institutions, smaller investors can participate indirectly by buying shares of money market funds. These are mutual funds that pool investors' resources to create a portfolio of money market instruments. Hence, they are highly liquid mutual funds (i.e., investors can get in and out easily without worry of taking a loss) that generally do not appreciate or depreciate very much, but maintain the value of an investor's principal as well as paying a small interest fee. The typical fund holds its share price close to $1 at all times, and some—particularly those geared toward institutions—have minimum investment requirements. Both taxable and tax-exempt money market funds are available, with the latter holding mostly state and municipal securities. Money market funds are often used as temporary holding accounts for funds that are in between investments, such as for uninvested cash on hand in a stock brokerage account, or as interest-bearing checking accounts. In the late 1990s more than $1 trillion was held in U.S. money market funds.

MONEY MARKET FUTURES AND OPTIONS

Active trading in money market futures and options occurs on a number of **commodity exchanges**. These contracts function like any other futures or options contract, only the underlying security is one or more money market instruments. Investors, hedgers, and speculators can either buy or sell options or futures based on the direction they believe the market will take over a specified period. Futures contracts require the initiating party to reconcile or offset the transaction when the contract expires (or typically sooner), whereas options give the party the right, but no obligation, to do so. Some of the most common money market futures contracts are traded on three-month Treasury bills, three-month Eurodollars, and short term interest rates.

[Roger J. AbiNader]

FURTHER READING:

Cook, Timothy Q., and Robert K. Laroche. *Instruments of the Money Market.* Rev. ed. Richmond, VA: Federal Reserve Bank of Richmond, 1993. Available from www.rich.frb.org/instruments/.

Livingston, Miles. *Money and Capital Markets.* 3rd ed. Cambridge, MA: Blackwell, 1996.

Stigum, Marcia. *The Money Market.* 3rd ed. Homewood, IL: Dow Jones-Irwin, 1990.

Stigum, Marcia, and Frank L. Robinson. *Money Market and Bond Calculations.* Chicago: Irwin Professional, 1996.

MONEY SUPPLY

The supply or stock of money consists of all the money held by the nonbank public at any point of time. Money is defined as the generally accepted medium of exchange, i.e., whatever is generally accepted in paying for goods and services and repaying debt. It must, however, be emphasized that an economist's notion of money differs from the conventional usage of the term.

Commonly, people recognize currency (consisting of notes and coins) as money, since currency in one form or another has been used as a medium of exchange since ancient times. In modern advanced societies, cash is still ''king,'' but currency is not the dominant part of what economists consider money. The other key component of money is the amount of checkable deposits in the banking system, as people can write checks on their bank accounts (deposits) to pay for goods and services or to repay debt. The third, and a relatively minor, component of the money supply is the amount of outstanding traveler's checks. The sum of currency held by the nonbank public, checkable deposits, and traveler's checks yield a measure of money supply officially known as the M1 (or money aggregate) measure of money supply in the United States. At the end of 1998, the M1 measure of money supply was estimated at about $1,115 billion, only 42 percent of which was in currency; 47 percent was in checkable deposits and less than 1 percent was in traveler's checks.

It may be somewhat surprising that credit cards are not considered part of the money supply. After all, people use credit cards in numerous ordinary transactions? Some individuals even refer to credit cards as ''plastic money.'' The main reason for excluding credit cards is fairly straight forward—using a credit card is equivalent to buying on **credit**, at least temporarily. In other words, payment by credit card is inherently different from payment by cash or check.

MONEY AND ITS KEY FUNCTIONS

To properly understand how the money supply is measured by the federal monetary authorities, one needs to understand the functions of money. While money is defined as anything accepted in payment for goods and services or repayment of debts, it serves several additional functions, such as unit of account and store of value. All three major functions of money are briefly discussed below.

MEDIUM OF EXCHANGE. The definition of money itself refers primarily to the medium of exchange as its key characteristic. Certainly, money in the form of currency or checks serves this function. One can appreciate the contribution of money in facilitating exchanges if one looks into the consequences of doing without money—that is, depending on a **bartering** system. Imagine a person working at a farm and being paid in corn that he helped to produce. Further, say this worker does not like to eat corn and has to buy food and nonfood items (such as, clothing, shoes, books, etc.) to satisfy his and his family's needs from his earnings at the farm. He will have to find individuals who will provide him with rice, potatoes, shirts, tennis shoes, children's books, etc. in exchange for his corn. There must always be a double coincidence of wants for a transaction to be consummated. One can easily see that, in the absence of money, the farm worker will have to spend quite a bit of time just converting his earnings in corn into the items he actually wants to consume. When money is introduced into the picture, the farm worker gets paid in dollars. He then takes his earnings in dollars and buys different items with his income. People who receive the farm worker's dollars also do the same. Thus, the need to find an individual, for example, who wants to exchange shirts for corn is avoided. Use of money as a medium of exchange reduces waste and inefficiency by eliminating much of the time spent in exchanging goods and services. As a result, money also promotes specialization, with different individuals specializing in different trades or professions without having to worry about how to trade services or output to assemble all the items that their incomes can afford. The need for money is so strong that all societies, except those that are extremely primitive, invent some form of money. Money has taken the form of strings of beads (used by American Indians), cigarettes (used in prisoner-of-war camps), gold coins (used by Romans,) and traveler's checks used by modern tourists.

UNIT OF ACCOUNT. The second important function of money is to serve as a unit of account—just as we measure weight in pounds or height in inches, the values of goods and services are expressed in terms of money. For example, a shirt costs $45 at a department store, and a crystal ashtray costs $90 at the same store. Thus, the ashtray is twice as expensive as the shirt. The convenience of money can again be seen by contrasting it with a barter economy scenario. Assume that there are only 10 **commodities** in the economy. With 10 commodities, one must know 45 prices (economic worth of each commodity expressed in terms of the 9 other commodities). However, if money is used to quote values of the 10 commodities, one needs to know only 10 prices to accomplish the same objective that the barter system will do with 45 prices. As the number of commodities increases, the complexity of the barter system multiplies immensely. For example, with 1,000 items, nearly half a million prices will be needed in the barter system. Most supermarkets have many more than 1000 items—a total nightmare even for a mathematically inclined shopper. Money thus performs an important function as a unit of account by reducing the transactions costs due to a much smaller number of prices that have to be considered.

STORE OF VALUE. Money also functions as a store of value, although not in all circumstances. Serving as a store of value means that wealth can be held in terms of money for future use—to be spent on items or to be passed on to heirs. Money is not the only asset that functions as a store of value. Many assets, such as **stocks**, **bonds**, **real estate**, and gold, can also be used as a store of value. Money has a minor advantage over competing **assets** in one respect—it is already in the form that can be spent, while the others first have to be converted into money before being spent. In this sense, money is the most liquid of all assets that can be used to store wealth—stocks and bonds are less liquid than money, but more liquid than real estate. However, money as a store of value has two major disadvantages. First, other assets may yield returns that are far greater than money—say, one individual earns 20 percent a year on stocks and only 3 percent on his checking account. Thus, wealth will multiply faster when held in assets other than money. Secondly, during periods of rapid **inflation**, money may not serve as a useful store of wealth. The decline in the usefulness of money as a store of wealth depends on the rate of inflation. Inflation erodes the **purchasing power** of money. If price levels double in one year, the stored money will buy only half as much the next year. There are real world examples in history where money became worthless rather quickly. Germany after World War I provides an example of an extreme inflationary environment—the inflation rate sometimes exceeded 1000 percent per month. If a worker did not spend his or her income in the morning, it lost much of its value by the evening.

As the German example illustrates, money is almost useless as a store of value in a highly inflationary environment. Even with a 10-15 percent annual inflation rate, money is not considered a good store of value. Because of these difficulties, money is not widely used as a store of value for a prolonged period of time—other assets, despite their relative lack of liquidity, have an edge over money.

DIFFERENT MEASURES OF MONEY SUPPLY

Money as defined above yields the most narrowly defined measure of money supply known as M1. This M1 measure of money supply most closely corresponds to the ordinary definition of money (i.e., something that is commonly accepted in payment of goods and services).

THE CENTRAL MONETARY AUTHORITY. Every country has a central bank that monitors the money supply and almost always determines the level of money supply in the economy. In the United States, the **Federal Reserve System** serves as the central bank of the country. The Federal Reserve, commonly referred to as the Fed, uses three different measures of money supply—M1, M2, and M3. M2 and M3 measures of money supply build on the narrowly defined M1 measure by successively broadening the money supply measure. Thus, M1 is the narrowest measure of money supply, M2 is broader than M1, and M3 is the broadest measure.

In order to understand why the **Federal Reserve System** uses successively broader measures of money supply, one has to go back to the ordinary definition of money and then consider what else can be converted into ordinary money with minimum difficulty. The example of savings account deposits can be used to demonstrate why the M1 measure of money supply is broadened. Remember, the narrow M1 definition of money supply includes checkable deposits, but not savings account deposits. The reason for excluding savings account deposits is the inability of a savings account to be directly used in making payments, unlike a checking account. However, with just a phone call to one's bank, one can transfer money from savings into checking and then make the payment by writing checks on the checking account. Alternatively, one can drive to bank and withdraw money in cash from his or her savings account, thus converting resources in the savings account into ordinary money. As this illustrates, there is very little difference between the ''moneyness'' of checkable and savings deposits. Savings account deposits are therefore called near-money. Not considering items that are considered near-money, means that M1 does not properly reflect the extent of true money supply in the economy. The Federal Reserve thus coined broader measures of money supply (M2 and M3) to capture the characteristics of money in items other than those included in the M1 measure of money supply.

THE M1 MEASURE OF MONEY SUPPLY. As pointed out earlier, M1 is the narrowest measure of money supply and closely corresponds to the common definition of money. M1 monetary aggregate can be defined as follows:

M1 = Currency
+ Demand deposits
+ Other checkable deposits
+ Traveler's checks

Currency simply consists of notes (bills of different denominations) and coins. Currency currently accounts for less than one-third of the M1 money supply in the United States. Checkable deposits make up nearly two-thirds of the M1 money supply. The checkable deposits category itself is normally split into demand deposits and other checkable deposits. While both these components of checkable deposits can be used to write checks to make payments for goods and services, there is an important distinction between demand and non-demand checkable deposits. Demand deposits are normally maintained by businesses and carry no interest payments. They are termed demand deposits because the entire amount in a demand deposit is payable to the deposit holder or a designated person *on demand.* Moreover, some banks charge a service fee from holders of demand deposits, fees that are often waived if the amount in a demand deposit exceeds a certain level. The category ''other checkable deposits'' includes different kinds of checkable deposits that pay interest to the deposit holders—NOW (negotiated order of withdrawal) accounts, super-NOW accounts and ATS (automatic transfer from savings) accounts. Therefore, if non-demand checkable deposits can be used both to write checks and to earn interest, why maintain checkable deposits in the demand deposit form? The answer lies in a restriction associated with non-demand checkable deposits—while balances in demand deposits are payable on demand, checks written on balances in non-demand checkable deposits are negotiated orders of withdrawal. That is, the payment may be delayed for a while, depending on the amount of withdrawal. Even though most people have never experienced this delay in payments from an interest bearing non-demand checking account, it can happen in extreme circumstances. Because businesses deal in larger amounts of money, they cannot entertain this uncertainty and have to maintain demand deposits.

Traveler's checks constitute a very small fraction of the M1 money supply—less than 1 percent of the total M1. Traveler's checks can be used to make payments even outside one's home country, as the issuer of the traveler's checks guarantees payments to the individual or business that receives them (so long as they are properly signed). One can thus consider traveler's checks as checks with added features designed to increase widespread acceptance.

One can now see how all three components of the M1 measure of money supply—currency, checkable deposits and traveler's checks—are clearly money in the ordinary sense of the term, as they can be directly used in payment of goods and services. One warning about money as it is defined above—it is not universally acceptable (especially beyond a nation's borders). To make the currency universally acceptable within a country, the government of that country usually provides its currency with legal backing. In the United States, for example, every denomination of paper currency carries the following notice: ''THIS NOTE IS LEGAL TENDER FOR ALL DEBTS, PUBLIC AND PRIVATE.'' Thus, declining to accept a genuine Federal Reserve note is literally in violation of the federal law. However, this doesn't mean that U.S. currency would automatically have value in foreign countries, nor does it mean that the currency of other nations is valid in the United States. In fact, stores in U.S. cities bordering Canada often state that Canadian money is not accepted without violating any rules.

THE M2 MEASURE OF MONEY SUPPLY. The M2 measure of money supply is made broader than the M1 monetary aggregate by adding additional items that fall under the near-money category. M2 is formally defined as follows:

M2 = M1
+ Savings deposits
+ Small-denomination time deposits
+ Money market deposit accounts
+ Money market mutual fund shares (noninstitutional)
+ Overnight repurchase agreements
+ Overnight Eurodollars
+ Consolidation adjustment

Basically, four additional assets are added to the narrow measure of money supply known as M1 (the seventh item is merely an adjustment). These items will be briefly discussed below.

SAVINGS DEPOSITS. Savings deposits are maintained by households and individuals. These deposits pay a varying interest based on the balance in an account. Money can be withdrawn from these accounts without penalty. The major inconvenience of savings accounts is that checks can't be written on them. Banks have found a way around this inconvenience by permitting automatic transfer of funds from a savings account to pay for checks written on the checking account maintained by the individual. These are called ATS (automatic transfer from savings) accounts. Because of this, ATS accounts are included as part of the M1 money supply. Only the non-ATS portion of savings account deposits is added to the M1 measure when broadening it into the M2 monetary aggregate.

SMALL-DENOMINATION TIME DEPOSITS. Time deposits are commonly known as certificates of deposit. A certificate is issued for a fixed period of time with a specified maturity date and a specified interest rate. Certificates of deposits that are for less than $100,000 are called *small-denomination* time deposits. Unlike household savings accounts, certificates of deposits (CDs) have a predetermined maturity date and a financial penalty for early withdrawal of funds, making CDs somewhat less liquid. In order to make certificates of deposits more liquid, banks have begun issuing CDs that are negotiable. Instead of suffering a severe financial penalty, a holder of a negotiable CD can sell it on the secondary market without penalty. Before 1961, bank certificates of deposits were non-negotiable—they could not be sold to others and had to be redeemed, if necessary, from the issuing bank at a substantial penalty. In 1961, Citibank introduced the first negotiable CDs in large denominations ($100,000 or above). Negotiable CDs are now issued by almost all major commercial banks.

MONEY MARKET DEPOSIT ACCOUNTS. **Money market** deposit accounts are interest bearing accounts where the interest paid on balances in the accounts depends on the interest rate prevailing in the money market. The money market itself consists of short-term financial instruments (those that have maturity periods of one year or less). The key feature of a money market instrument is that its yield reflects the current interest rate and inflation in the economy. A money market deposit thus allows the holder of the account to participate in the money market. Usually, large sums are needed to participate in the money market directly, which means most individual investors are not able to do so. Banks and other financial institutions, through money market accounts, provide an individual one way to participate in the money market. There is often a minimum investment that an individual must make to use the money market route, although it is less than other investment options.

Most money market deposit accounts also carry limited check-writing privileges and thus resemble interest bearing checking accounts, to a degree. Therefore, many academic scholars in the field believe that money market accounts should be part of the M1 measure of money supply. However, at the current time, listed as a component of M2, not M1.

MONEY MARKET MUTUAL FUND SHARES (NONINSTITUTIONAL). Money market **mutual funds** are mutual funds that invest in money market instruments. For reasons described above, individuals have difficulty in directly participating in the money market. Opening a money market deposit account at a bank is one way to participate in the money market. Buying shares of a money market mutual fund is another. Money market mutual funds basically pool individual investors' resources and invest them in money market instruments. After subtracting costs, they distribute the gains from the investments to those who contributed to the pool of funds through the purchase of shares. Like money market deposit accounts at banks, most money market mutual funds also provide limited check writing privileges. Checks frequently cannot be written for less than a certain minimum, and a substantial amount of money is initially required to open an account with a money market mutual fund. These restrictions are generally quite similar to those that apply to money market deposit accounts at banks.

CONSOLIDATION ADJUSTMENT. The consolidation adjustment is merely a statistical adjustment applied to the M2 measure to avoid double counting. It is not a fundamental component of the M2 monetary aggregate in the same sense that other elements are. The kind of double counting the consolidation adjustment is designed to avoid can be illustrated with the help of an example—the M2 consolidation adjustment subtracts short-term **repurchase agreements** and Eurodollars being held by money market mutual funds, because they are already included in the balances of money market mutual funds.

One can assert that the M2 measure of money supply is a somewhat lower on the liquidity scale, compared to the M1 measure, which is the most liquid. Assets that are added to the M1 aggregate to arrive at the M2 measure are items that are the most easily and most frequently transferred into checking accounts or can otherwise be converted into cash quickly.

THE M3 MEASURE OF MONEY SUPPLY

The M3 measure of money supply further broadens the M2 monetary aggregate by adding additional assets that are less liquid than those included in M1 and M2. Formally, M3 is defined as follows:

M3 = M2
+ Large-denomination time deposits
+ Money market mutual fund shares (institutional)
+ Overnight and *term* repurchase agreements
+ Overnight and term Eurodollars
+ Consolidation adjustment

Many of the items that are added to the M2 measure of money supply to arrive at the M3 monetary aggregate are similar in name to those added to the M1 measure to arrive at the M2 measure, except that the maturity periods associated with the M1 measures are shorter. The four items that are added to the M2 measure to arrive at the M3 measure are briefly discussed below.

LARGE-DENOMINATION TIME DEPOSITS. Certificates of deposits issued in denominations of $100,000 or above are called large-denomination time deposits. These are like small-denomination time deposits (issued in denominations of less than $100,000), with a scheduled maturity date and a specified interest rate. However, large-denomination certificates of deposits are usually negotiable CDs that can be sold in the secondary market before they mature. Thus, large-denomination negotiable CDs serve as an alternative to investing in Treasury bills for corporate treasurers who have idle funds to invest for a short time.

MONEY MARKET MUTUAL FUND SHARES (INSTITUTIONAL). Money market mutual fund shares that are added to M2 to arrive at M3 are the same as those that are added to the M1 measure to arrive at the M2, with a minor difference. Money market mutual fund shares held by institutions also are included when the M3 measure of money supply is calculated, whereas only money market mutual fund shares held by noninstitutional investors were included when the M2 measure of money supply was constructed.

OVERNIGHT AND TERM REPURCHASE AGREEMENTS. Repurchase agreements are essentially short-term loans backed by U.S. **Treasury bills** as collateral. Usually, the maturity period of a **repurchase agreement** is less than two weeks, although it can be as short as overnight. A repurchase agreement transaction can be illustrated as follows: A large corporation has some idle cash and a bank wants to borrow some funds overnight to make up for the shortfall in the amount of required reserves that it must have at the Federal Reserve. Assume that the corporation uses $10 million to buy Treasury bills from the bank, which agrees to repurchase Treasury bills the next morning at a price slightly higher than the corporation's purchase price. The additional price that the bank pays is a way of paying interest on the overnight use of the $10 million. Should the bank not buy back the Treasury bills that the corporation is holding, the latter can sell those bills to recover its loan. Transferred Treasury bills thus serve as collateral, which the lender receives if the borrower does not pay back the loan.

Repurchase agreements are a relatively new financial instrument. They have been in existence only since 1969. However, they constitute an important source of funds for banks, where large corporations are considered the most important lenders.

Because of extremely short time to maturity, overnight repurchase agreements are considered very liquid—the instrument turns back into cash the very next day. However, because it is less liquid than currency or checkable deposits, it is included in the M3 measure.

Repurchase agreements that have maturity periods of more than one night are called *term* repurchase agreements. Thus, term repurchase agreements also facilitate borrowing and lending in which Treasury bills are essentially used as collateral. By nature, term repurchase agreements are less liquid than overnight repurchase agreements. Term repurchase agreements are included in M3 as well.

OVERNIGHT AND TERM EURODOLLARS. The term Eurodollar originates from the fact that U.S. dollars were at one time deposited at banks in Europe by certain individuals and countries. The tradition of Eurodollar deposits was first established when the Soviet Union deposited U.S. dollars in Europe rather than in the United States—it wanted the security that the U.S. dollar provided, along with interest income from its deposits, without exposing the cash to the uncertainty that a deposit in the United States may have entailed. Depositing U.S. dollars outside the United States is no longer confined to Europe—U.S. dollars are now deposited in a variety of locations, including Hong Kong, Singapore, Sydney, and Tokyo. For this reason, Eurodollars are sometimes also referred to as overseas dollars.

Eurodollar deposits are specially attractive to American banks. The advent of Eurodollar deposits was one of the major reasons that so many banks based in the United States opened branches in foreign countries. They can borrow Eurodollar deposits from their own foreign branches or from other banks when they need additional funds. Inclusion of Eurodollar deposits in M3 is recognition on the part of the Federal Reserve System that Eurodollar deposits abroad can be converted into dollar holdings in the United States, thereby affecting the U.S. money supply.

Like term repurchase agreements, term Eurodollars have a maturity period greater than one night. While the maturity period of a term Eurodollar can vary, a majority of them mature in a few weeks. Obviously, term Eurodollars are less liquid than overnight Eurodollars. Term Eurodollars are included in M3 as well.

CONSOLIDATION ADJUSTMENT. An adjustment, similar to that made to the M2 measure of money supply, is made to the M3 monetary aggregate to avoid double counting.

In sum, one can consider the M3 monetary aggregate to be lower on the liquidity scale than the M2 measure, when all components of M3 are considered together.

WHICH MONETARY AGGREGATE DOES THE FED USE?

As was discussed above, the M2 and M3 measures of money supply are successively lower on the liquidity scale than M1. While M1 closely corresponds to the ordinary notion of money, M2 and M3 capture ''moneyness'' not included in M1. To monitor the supply of money in the economy, the Federal Reserve looks at all three measures of the money supply but tends to focus on the M2 measure. There is a considerable debate among economists regarding the value of the Fed's emphasis on the M2 monetary aggregate.

While growth rates of all three measures of money supply do have a tendency to move together, there also exist some glaring discrepancies in the movements of these monetary aggregates. For example, according to the M1 measure, the growth rate of money supply did not accelerate between 1968 and 1971. However, if the M2 and M3 measures are used as the guide, a different story emerges—they show a significant acceleration in the growth rate of the money supply. Because of this kind of divergent behavior, the battle to find the true measure of money supply continues. Often a weighted average of monetary aggregates—one that captures the moneyness in all assets included in M2 and M3 (remember, M1 is already money in the strict sense of the term)—has been suggested to arrive at the true measure of the money supply.

CONTROLLING THE NATION'S MONEY SUPPLY

As was mentioned earlier, in every free market economy the money supply is controlled by the nation's central bank, the chief monetary authority for the country. A central bank is known by different names in different countries—often, even the adjective ''central'' may be missing. For example, in the United States, the central bank is known as the Federal Reserve System; in England, it is known as the Bank of England; and in Germany, it is called the Bundesbank.

The Federal Reserve System in the United States uses three different methods to control and manipulate the nation's money supply. However, before discussing these methods, it will be useful to understand the players that participate in increasing or decreasing the levels of monetary aggregates.

MONEY SUPPLY AND THE BANKING SYSTEM

All definitions of money supply underscore the fact that deposits at commercial banks, **savings and loan associations**, **credit unions**, and mutual savings banks (collectively known as depository institutions) are an integral part of the money supply. Depository institutions are in the money supply business because they profit by taking deposits from individuals and businesses and making loans to a variety of borrowers. The difference between what they earn from the loans made and the amount paid to depositors (in additional to the operating costs) constitutes the basis for profits to the depository institutions. This logic will induce banks and other depository institutions to loan out as much of depositors' funds as possible. However, the Federal Reserve has put a restriction on this behavior—the depository institutions are required to keep a fraction of the deposits in reserves at the Federal Reserve. Thus, depository financial institutions can only lend out the excess reserves—reserves (vault cash and cash deposits at the Federal Reserve) over and above the reserves required, by law, to be kept at the Federal Reserve Bank.

In manipulating the money supply, it is the level of the excess reserves that the Federal Reserve attempts to influence to affect the growth rate of the nation's money supply. To illustrate this, let us assume that through some mechanism the Fed is able to increase the amount of excess reserves in the banking system. Banks, faced with the extra resources, want to lend them prudently to earn interest on loans made. Further, assume that loans are made by simply creating deposits (which are part of the money supply) in borrowers' names. Creating additional deposits results in an increase in the money supply. While the preceding logic may appear like an academic concoction, this is what happens in the real world. The only question that remains to be answered is as to how the Federal Reserve manipulates the level of excess reserves in the banking system.

There are three instruments available to the Federal Reserve Bank that it can use to manipulate the excess reserves in the banking system and thus the level of money supply—the reserve requirement ratio, the discount rate, and open market operations.

THE RESERVE REQUIREMENT RATIO. The reserve requirement ratio is the legal ratio determined by the Federal Reserve (within limits established by the Congress) required of the depository institutions in calculating the minimum reserves they must keep to conform to the federal banking law. Thus, if the Fed increases the reserve requirement ratio, it automatically reduces the amount of excess reserves in the banking system. This can be explained as follows: Suppose, a bank has $100 million deposits and the reserve requirement ratio is 10 percent. Further, assume that it has $18 million in reserves. Since the bank is required to keep a minimum of $10 million in required reserves (the 10 percent reserve requirement ratio applied to $100 million in deposits), it has an excess reserve of $8 million. If the Federal Reserve increases the reserve requirement ratio from 10 percent to 15 percent, would then have to keep $15 million in legal reserves. This leads to a decrease in the level of excess reserves from $8 million to $3 million. A decrease in the amount of excess reserves reduces the ability of the bank to make loans, to create additional deposits and to increase the money supply. In this example, the bank started from positive excess reserves and then increased the reserve requirement ratio. If it had started from zero excess reserves and then increased the reserve requirement ratio, the levels of deposits and money supply would be forced to fall—banks caught with deficient minimum legal reserves would have to reduce the level of deposits, consistent with available reserves.

The Federal Reserve can both lower and raise the reserve requirement ratio to affect money supply. However, raising the legal reserve ratio is especially powerful when the banking system has no excess reserves.

Despite the apparent potency of the reserve requirement ratio as an instrument of money supply manipulations, it is seldom utilized by the Federal Reserve in influencing money supply. A change in the reserve requirement ratio is a legal change and it is not advisable to change the rules of the game frequently. Thus, while the reserve requirement ratio may be utilized in a financial emergency, the Federal Reserve does not use the ratio to manipulate the nation's money supply on a regular basis.

THE DISCOUNT RATE. The **discount rate** is the interest rate the Federal Reserve Bank charges banking institutions for the loans it makes to them. The Federal Reserve was initially created as a lender of last resort—its function was to lend to banks in need of funds through discounting banks' holdings of, say, Treasury bills. Essentially, the Fed made loans to banks with Treasury bills serving as collateral.

Of course, if banks can borrow from the Federal Reserve at a low rate of interest and lend to its borrowers at higher interest rates, it will be clearly profitable for them. By lowering the discount rate, the Federal Reserve lowers the cost of borrowing and increases banks' willingness to borrow. This can potentially increase the level of excess reserves in the banking system and, consequently, the money supply. Raising the discount rate can have the opposite effect on the level of excess reserves and the money supply.

While the discount rate can potentially be used to influence the levels of excess reserves and money supply in the economy, the Federal Reserve does not use this method to induce increased borrowing by banks. The Federal Reserve dislikes profit-based borrowing by the depository institutions, i.e., borrowing at a lower interest rate from the Fed and then lending at higher interest rates to banks' customers. The Federal Reserve Bank does not mind need-based borrowing by banks (when banks, due to some unanticipated factors, fall short of funds). Even then, Federal Reserve closely monitors any bank that borrows from the Fed too frequently.

The preceding discussion suggests that the Federal Reserve does not like to use the discount rate as an instrument to manipulate the level of money supply in the economy on a regular basis (by manipulating the level of excess reserves in the banking system). The Fed, however, does utilize this instrument in an indirect way in manipulating money supply—it uses the discount rate as a signaling device. When the Federal Reserve Bank lowers the discount rate, it signals to the banking system and the financial market that it is in favor of increasing money supply. When the Fed increases the discount rate, it sends out the opposite message. In fact, banks often take the Fed's announcement of the discount rate change quite seriously—if the Federal Reserve raises the discount rate, for example, major banks follow up by raising their prime rates (the rate a bank charges its best customers).

THE OPEN MARKET OPERATIONS. Open market operations are the third and the most frequently used instrument by the Federal Reserve in manipulating the money supply. In open market operations, the Federal Reserve Bank uses market forces to manipulate the level of the excess reserves and thus the money supply in the economy.

In open market operations, the Federal Reserve either buys Treasury securities (bills and bonds) from banks or sells Treasury securities to them. When the Federal Reserve sells **Treasury bonds** to banks, the Fed receives cash in exchange for bonds—the excess reserves in the banking system go down and thus the money supply will, potentially, go down also. The opposite is the case when the Federal Reserve sells Treasury securities to the banking system.

The Federal Reserve uses open market operations to manipulate the nation's money supply on a regular basis—the open market operations are considered the main instrument of monetary policy (increasing or decreasing the money supply with a view to influence the state of the economy).

THE MONEY SUPPLY UNCERTAINTY. While the Federal Reserve is fairly successful in manipulating the money supply, there are some uncertainties regarding the magnitude of a monetary aggregate or the exact time when the increase in the money supply materializes after the Fed initiates the process of expanding the money supply. For example, the Federal Reserve increases the level of excess reserves in the banking system to increase the money supply. However, banks are reluctant to loan (and thus to increase the money supply) because of lack of creditworthy borrowers or their desire to wait for better opportunities. Thus, the Federal Reserve's attempt to increase money supply is frustrated. Despite this uncertainty, the Fed is able to determine changes in the money supply since banks have to report periodically to the Federal Reserve.

SEE ALSO: Federal Reserve System

[Anandi P. Sahu, Ph.D.]

FURTHER READING:

Froyen, Richard T. *Macroeconomics: Theories and Policies.* 6th ed. Upper Saddle River: Prentice Hall, 1998.

Mishkin, Frederic S. *The Economics of Money, Banking and Financial Markets.* 5th ed. Reading, PA: Addison-Wesley, 1998.

Ritter, Lawrence S., William L. Silber, and Gregory F. Udell. *Principles of Money, Banking and Financial Markets.* 9th ed. Reading, PA: Addison-Wesley, 1997.

MONTE CARLO METHOD

Monte Carlo methods—named after the famous European gambling casino—are a means of numerically simulating chance events in order to predict the most likely future outcome. In other words, Monte Carlo simulations are used to predict a range of different outcomes from a given set of decisions. The decisions are held constant, but the outcomes are allowed to vary depending on changes in some key influence, such as sales volume, interest rates, market volatility, and so forth. Monte Carlo simulations are distinguished from other types of simulation techniques by their extensive use of random numbers and repeated trials. The predictive value of Monte Carlo simulations lends itself to a diverse field of business applications, ranging from risk management to financial planning to economic modeling.

Monte Carlo simulations can be used in **decision making** to provide potential solutions to complex problems. As intimated above, the simulations effectively provide an understanding of the possible outcome of a given decision. They are useful when the environment surrounding a problem is too complex for the effects of a decision or set of decisions to be described with a single outcome. Indeed, Monte Carlo simulations can provide a range of potential results based on the same decision(s). As shown in the example below, the simulations typically involve (1) a decision variable that is chosen and changed by the person running the simulation; (2) a randomly changing variable; and (3) a key performance indicator that is influenced by the decision variable and the random variable.

As a simple example, assume that the owner of a rolling hot dog stand earns an average of $75 in profit per day. He sells hot dogs for $3 each, and expects daily sales to vary between 100 and 200 hot dogs. All hot dogs that do not sell spoil and are a total loss, and he puts 200 hot dogs in his stand each morning just in case he has a big day. Using Monte Carlo analysis techniques, the owner could study the effects of various business decisions based on the performance of a key indicator, such as daily profit. For example, he could test the profit impact of the decision to start each day with only 175 hot dogs in his cart. He could then generate a series of random numbers to represent daily hot dog sales over a given period to determine his average daily profits. He may find, for instance, that profits rise when he starts out with only 175 hot dogs, despite the fact that he will run out of hot dogs on some days.

The party running a Monte Carlo simulation must adhere to several parameters for the simulation to be useful. For example, the random variable(s)—the number of hot dogs sold in a day in the above example—must reflect the underlying uncertainty of the problem. For this reason, Monte Carlo simulations can be highly complex and require the application of advanced statistical techniques. Because they allow the modeling of complex environments, they are often used to simulate difficult scientific and financial problems. Advanced Monte Carlo methods involve the use of Markov chains and the Gibbs sampler, statistical tools that consider the probability of moving through a multistage process given multiple variables and uncertainties. Because Monte Carlo simulations are by nature computationally intensive, they are usually done on a computer.

FURTHER READING:

Chorafas, Dimitris N. *Chaos Theory in the Financial Markets: Applying Fractals, Fuzzy Logic, Genetic Algorithms, Swarm Simulation & the Monte Carlo Method to Manage Market Chaos and Volatility.* Chicago: Probus Publishing Co., 1994.

Fishman, George S. *Monte Carlo: Concepts, Algorithms, and Applications.* New York: Springer-Verlag, 1996.

Sobol, Ilya M. *A Primer for the Monte Carlo Method.* Boca Raton: CRC Press, 1994.

MORTGAGES/MORTGAGE-BACKED SECURITIES

A mortgage-backed security (MBS) is a derivative debt issue secured by groups, or pools, of home or commercial mortgages. The mortgages are grouped together by lenders or other institutions and then either sold to investors who purchase ownership shares in the pool or used to back a debt issue. MBSs shift risks related to changes in **interest rates**, prepayment and refinancing of mortgages, and **default** or nonpayment, and thus trends in these same areas affect the market for mortgage securities. The investors receive the interest and principal payments in the form of distributions as the loans are paid off by the mortgage holders (or by the federal government in some cases of default), or simple cash disbursements from the institution that owns the mortgages.

Besides providing an investment alternative, MBSs serve the important function of bringing additional funding into the mortgage industry that can be used to finance residential or commercial real estate. In addition to debt financing obtained by securitizing pools of mortgages, capital flows into the secondary mortgage market via equity shares in mutual funds and mortgage-buying companies such as Freddie Mac and Fannie Mae, which are government-sponsored quasi-private-sector companies. These publicly traded stocks (Freddie Mac and Fannie Mae are both traded on the New York Stock Exchange) aren't MBSs in the formal sense, but are closely related and serve very similar functions.

MBSs are a major component in a broader market known as the asset backed securities market, which also includes securities based on other forms of loans. In the late 1990s the mortgage-backed securities market was worth some $2 trillion, representing a major segment of the U.S. economy and serving as a primary money supply for the home mortgage industry. Freddie Mac, Fannie Mae, and Ginnie Mae, the trio of government-chartered mortgage securitizers, account for roughly two-thirds of that capitalization. At more than $3 trillion, the entire asset-backed securities market rivals the size of the bellwether U.S. Treasury debt market. Internationally, markets for MBSs are also forming rapidly, notably in places like Australia and the United Kingdom, but none are as developed as that in the United States. Common buyers of MBSs include pension funds, **mutual funds**, and individual investors.

DEVELOPMENT AND MECHANICS

FANNIE MAE. The MBS market emerged during the 1970s as the result of U.S. government initiatives related to the secondary mortgage market. The secondary mortgage market was created in 1938, when the federal government created Federal National Mortgage Association (Fannie Mae) to purchase government-backed mortgages, which include Federal Housing Administration (FHA) and Veterans Administration loans. The effort was designed to supply banks and other financial institutions with cash to make new mortgage loans; the banks continued to profit from servicing the mortgages, but Fannie Mae effectively paid the **banks** cash and assumed ownership of the loans. Fannie Mae was privatized in 1968.

GINNIE MAE. In the same year, a similar entity—the Government National Mortgage Association (Ginnie Mae)—was created with the power to purchase and/or provide payment guarantees (timely payment of principal and interest) on securities backed by FHA and VA mortgages. That effectively made it more feasible for loan originators (i.e., banks and other financial institutions) to begin creating securities backed by pools of mortgages. A bank, for example, could package all of its mortgages together into a debt security backed by Ginnie Mae. Unlike Fannie Mae, however, Ginnie Mae is a government agency with a narrow scope of operations.

FREDDIE MAC. In 1970 Congress chartered the Federal Home Loan Mortgage Corporation, or Freddie Mac, to create competition in the MBS industry and better position it for growth. As part of a related reform effort, both Fannie Mae and Freddie Mac were authorized to purchase conventional, non-government mortgages on the secondary market. Freddie Mac continues to be somewhat smaller than Fannie Mae, but it has grown quickly and some observers believe its more aggressive buying strategy will one day allow it to overtake its older sibling.

SECURITIZATION PROCESS AND INSTRUMENTS. Typically, an investment firm underwrites the security for the institution and sells it to investors. The original lender continues to make money servicing the mortgage, and uses the money from the sale of the security to fund new mortgage loans that may also eventually be securitized. Rather than pool the mortgages themselves, lenders can also sell their mortgages to Fannie Mae or Freddie Mac, which use the mortgages to create their own securities. Indeed, Fannie Mae and Freddie Mac typically function as market rivals.

By the 1980s the MBS industry had expanded to include four major investment vehicles: mortgage pass-through securities (MPTs); mortgage-backed bonds (MBBs); mortgage pay-through bonds (MPTBs); and collateralized mortgage obligations (CMOs).

MPTs were initiated by Ginnie Mae in 1968. They most closely represent the MBS structure—the securities are issued by the mortgage originator and backed by the federal government. In MPTs, as in most MBSs, investors receive participation certificates (PCs), which come with different interest and principal payment configurations.

MBBs are used by private mortgage companies such as banks and savings and loans, and may include mortgages not backed by a government entity. They are similar to MPTs, but the cash flows from interest and principal payments do not pass through directly to the security holders. Instead, the entity that creates the security retains ownership of the mortgages in the pool—the mortgages are usually placed in trust with a third party that ensures that the issuer adheres to the bond provisions—and makes predetermined, periodic cash payments to the bondholders. The net effect is that investors are exposed to different kinds of risk; for example, the risk of mortgage prepayment, which reduces income from interest, is borne by the issuer rather than the security holder, as is the case with an MPT. Underwriters are typically used to sell the securities, and the securities are often rated by a bond rating agency. As with other **bonds**, the value of MBBs is influenced by their riskiness and yields in relation to other securities, and by interest rate fluctuations.

MPTBs are a hybrid of MPTs and MBBs. The MPTB is a bond, but the principal and interest payments are passed through to the owners of the securities. Like the MBB, the issuer retains ownership of the mortgages in the pool and the bond is rated by an agency. The MPTB must be overcollateralized to provide protection against default of some of the underlying mortgages. Still, investors are exposed to various risks inherent to both MBBs and MPTs.

CMOs, created in the early 1980s, are complicated versions of MPTBs. The issuer retains ownership of the mortgages, and principal and interest is passed through. The chief difference is that the mortgages in the pool are separated into different groups, or tranches, based on the date the mortgage matures. By separating the mortgages, the issuer can use the pool to create a number of securities with different characteristics. For example, tranches can be designed to simulate low risk, short-term coupon bonds, or higher risk, long-term zero coupon bonds. The different risk classes theoretically maximize the value of the mortgage pool to the overall investment market.

Related to CMOs are real estate mortgage investment conduits (REMICs). A REMIC is essentially a legally recognized entity that creates a CMO. REMICs evolved following Congress' passage of the Tax Reform Act of 1986. The act allowed CMOs, through REMICs, to be issued with a minimum of tax complications. Among other functions, REMICs are used by companies like Freddie Mac to resecuritize a class of MBSs to provide alternative investment vehicles to investors.

COMMERCIAL MBSS

Commercial MBSs (CMBSs) are simply securities based on commercial real estate loans. They are relatively new—and outside the sphere of residential MBS giants like Fannie Mae and Freddie Mac—but have been an area of rapid development since the mid-1980s. Between 1985 and 1994, the value of annual new CMBS issues jumped tenfold, from just over $1 billion to more than $10 billion. By 1997, it had more than quadrupled again, topping $45 billion; however, a volatile 1998—though still record-setting at $79 billion—was expected to hold 1999 issues at around $50 billion. As of 1998, approximately half of all CMBSs took the form of REMICs.

This explosion in CMBS issues was in part set off by deregulatory policies of the federal government. The REMIC tax advantage, for one, has contributed to its popularity as an investment vehicle. Another important factor was the 1998 decision by the Federal Financial Institutions Examination Council (FFIEC) to ease restrictions on higher risk portfolios in CMOs. The regulatory body cited improvements in accounting standards and unintended consequences of its risk test as reasons for abandoning the much maligned test. In addition to the favorable regulatory climate, the parsimonious commercial real estate lending environment of the early 1990s, triggered by the real estate bust of the late 1980s and early 1990s, created a liquidity crunch that CMBSs helped relieve.

Still, particularly in light of deregulation, the CMBS market places a heavy burden on investors to scrutinize the make-up of the securities in order to determine whether the risk level is acceptable.

SEE ALSO: Bonds; Derivative Securities; Real Estate Investment Trusts (REIT)

[Dave Mote]

FURTHER READING:

Byrt, Frank, and Steven Vames. "Bonds Rise as Evidence of Slowing Economy, Mortgage Investor Demand Spur Steady Buying." *Wall Street Journal,* 15 October 1998.

"Competition and Refi Boom Put REMIC Market in Orbit." *American Banker,* 26 May 1998.

Erb, Debra. "A Flowering of Opportunities." *Mortgage Banking,* January 1998.

Gordon, Sally. "A Lesson from the Capital Markets." *Mortgage Banking,* February 1999.

Levy, John B. "For Mortgage-Backeds, It's Almost Like Old Times." *Barron's,* 11 January 1999.

"MBS Goes Global." *Mortgage Banking,* May 1996.

Silverman, Gary, and Debra Sparks. "A $2.5 Trillion Market You Hardly Know." *Business Week,* 26 October 1998.

MOST-FAVORED NATION (MFN)

The term ''most-favored nation'' (MFN) refers to a trade status granted by countries to one another as part of a formalized and reciprocal trade agreement. Under an MFN clause a country that grants trade concessions to one party of the agreement must grant the same concessions to all signatories of the agreement. The impetus for such a trade agreement is the reduction of tariffs and import **taxes**. This reduction of tariffs fosters international trade by opening and expanding markets. Reciprocal trade agreements and their all-important MFN clauses serve as the basis for the foreign trade policies of most nations.

The idea of granting reciprocal concessions to encourage trade probably began with Islamic and Byzantine commerce. In an effort to persuade European merchants (mostly from Spanish, French, and Italian commercial areas and ports) to settle in eastern trading centers, foreign merchants were granted the same rights and guarantees as the citizens of host countries.

At the outset of the American Revolution, John Adams suggested that a commercial treaty—with what today would be called MFN language—between the colonies and France would keep that country on the side of the Americans against the British. Adams felt a commercial treaty would be beneficial to both sides and less entangling than a political treaty. In his ''Farewell Address of 1796,'' George Washington, however, advised his fellow countrymen to trade impassionately and without regard to political discrimination.

Future generations of American policy makers, however, often disregarded Adams's and Washington's advice. In the late 1700s and through much of the 1800s, the United States drew a distinction between unconditional MFN and conditional MFN status. Unconditional MFN charges a country to grant a trading partner all concessions it grants to a third party. With conditional MFN status, however, only the opportunity to be the recipient of trade concessions is guaranteed. Concessions are available only if the potential recipient is willing to replicate reciprocities granted by a third state. If the United States, for instance, grants a trade concession to France in **reciprocity**, under conditional MFN status the United States will grant the same concessions to Great Britain—but only if Great Britain matches French reciprocity. Under unconditional MFN language, Great Britain obtains the concessions granted by the United States to France without having to match French reciprocity (Cline 1982). Although still abiding by treaty arrangements, the United States has routinely and for political reasons revoked its MFN agreements with many socialist countries including at one time or another the former Soviet Union, Poland, Hungary, Romania, and Nicaragua.

The granting of MFN status to a country can also be used to induce or at least attempt to induce a country to a particular course of action. This strategy can turn trade policy into an impassioned political football. In the 1970s the Soviet Union routinely prohibited many of its Jewish citizens from immigrating to Israel. In 1974 Senator Henry ''Scoop'' Jackson linked Soviet-American trade to that country's treatment of Jews. According to the Jackson-Vanik Amendment to the Trade Act of 1974, the status of most-favored nation was to be granted at the discretion of the president. Since 1980 when the People's Republic of China was granted MFN status, American presidents and Congressional policy makers have been at odds over this issue. At stake is tens of billions of dollars in trade. Both Presidents George Bush and Bill Clinton have renewed China's MFN status but not without Congressional battles. China, for its part, has often felt humiliated and compromised by the wrangling. In 1994 Clinton sought to separate MFN status from China's dismal human-rights record, claiming China was too powerful a country and too big of a trading partner to be isolated from the world community. In 1997 Clinton reiterated his stance claiming that renewing MFN status is the ''best way to integrate China further into the family of nations and to secure our interest and ideals.'' Representative Frank Wolf differed, claiming that the People's Republic of China has ''tortured and killed Buddhist monks and nuns,'' and that they have ''more gulags than the Soviet Union.'' Wolf also said that Saddam Hussein used Chinese-manufactured weapons against U.S. forces during the Gulf War. Under Jackson's ''freedom-of-emigration'' legislation, China's MFN status must be renewed annually. If it were not renewed, China would have to pay substantially higher duties on 95 percent of its exports to the United States—which in 1995 totaled $45,555 million.

The most comprehensive reciprocal trade agreement is the **General Agreement on Tariffs and Trade** (GATT). GATT was signed in Geneva in 1947 by 23 countries, including the United States. By the early 1990s there were 90 signatories to the trade accord. An integral part of GATT is the unconditional MFN clause.

[Michael Knes]

FURTHER READING:

Cline, William R. *Reciprocity: A New Approach to World Trade Policy?* Washington: Institute for International Economics, 1982.

Neff, Stephen C. *Friends but No Allies: Economic Liberalism and the Law of Nations.* New York: Columbia University Press, 1990.

Omicinski, John. "'Most-Favored-Nation Trade' Legislation Got Start in the 1970s with Jackson's Help." Seattle: Seattle Times Company, 1997. Available from www.seattletimes.com/extra/browse/html97/althist_052097.html.

Online Newshour. "Favoring China." Alexandria, VA: Public Broadcasting Service, 1997. Available from www.pbs.org.newshour/.

Pregelj, Vladimir N. "Most-Favored-Nation Status of the People's Republic of China." Washington: Congressional Research Service, 1996. Available from www.fas.org/man/CRS/92-094.htm.

MOTIVATION

SEE: Employee Motivation

MSA

SEE: Metropolitan Statistical Area

MULTICULTURAL WORKFORCE

The phrase "multicultural workforce" refers to the changing age, sex, ethnicity, physical ability, race, and sexual orientation of employees across all types and places of work in the United States. Multicultural workforce as a descriptive term or phrase has, however, largely been supplanted by the term "diversity" in describing the increasing heterogeneity of the workplace through the inclusion of different groups of people. While "multicultural workforce" is still sometimes used in reference to employees of varying social, racial, and ability characteristics, the scope of diversity goes further and includes not only the personal characteristics of an organization's employees but also the way an organization responds to a multicultural or diverse **workforce**. Thus Roosevelt Thomas, founding president of the American Institute for Managing Diversity, qualified *diversity* as a "comprehensive managerial process for developing an environment that works for all employees." Likewise the *Portable MBA Desk Reference* ended its definition of "diversity" in a similar manner. "The challenge posed by diversity, then, is to accommodate different groups by addressing their lifestyles, values, work style, and family needs without compromising the goals and operations of the organization." And Joan Crockett, vice president for human resources at Allstate Insurance Co., viewed a diverse workforce as being about "unlocking the potential for excellence among all workers." Allstate's diversity vision statement summed up this belief: "Diversity is Allstate's strategy for leveraging differences in order to create a competitive advantage."

The American workforce has been historically dominated by the white, male majority of the labor pool. For a variety of complex social and economic reasons, white women began entering the workforce more and more in the late 1800s—in many cases against most of the social norms and mores of the last 200 years. Women, as a percentage of the labor force, continued to grow, although sometimes sporadically, during the 20th century. Following World War II, however, the **employment** of women—especially white women—steadily increased. These demographic changes in the labor force have continued to accelerate as minority men and women have followed white women into the workplace. Based on figures published by the U.S. Bureau of Labor Statistics, the *Handbook of U.S. Labor Statistics* estimated that the U.S. labor force will have increased by about 11 percent, or 15 million persons, from 1996 to 2006, bringing the total workforce up to 149 million. In 2006 the median age of the labor force will be close to 41 years. Women will be expected to increase as a percentage of the labor force but at a lower rate of growth than in past decades. There will also be, "Significant compositional shifts . . . along racial/ethnic lines." White non-Hispanics will still constitute the largest share of the labor force in 2006 at 73 percent, although this will be a drop from 75 percent in 1996 and 80 percent in 1986. The rate of growth of white non-Hispanics in the labor force, however, will be considerably below that for African American, Asian, and Hispanic groups. It is also expected that by 2006 Hispanics will represent the second-largest ethnic segment of the labor market, surpassing African Americans. The Asian percentage of the labor market is also expected to grow relatively fast but will still be a small percentage of the total.

Assimilation of minorities into the workplace, or the practice of suppressing cultural differences to conform to the majority culture, meant that previously many of these minority workers had to lose a part of their heritage in order to obtain and hold gainful employment. Stereotypes of African Americans, Hispanic Americans, Asian Americans, and women permeated the corporate and industrial culture until well into the 1960s, when federal laws were established to prevent discrimination. Some of the more important pieces of federal antidiscrimination legislation are: Title VII of the Civil Rights Act of 1964, which prohibits employment discrimination based on race, religion, sex, and national origin; the Equal Pay Act of 1963; the Age Discrimination Act in Employment of 1967; and the **Americans with Disabilities Act** of 1990. While these pieces of legislation are aimed at preventing discrimination rather than promoting diversity per se, they do help in maintaining a diverse workplace.

Diversity and multiculturalism, however, should not be confused with **affirmative action**. The most striking difference between the two social schemes is that affirmative action is initiated by government regulation and legislation, whereas diversity is voluntary although various governmental agencies may pressure companies under certain circumstances to diversify their workforce. Affirmative action is also legally driven, quantitative, problem focused, assimilated, and reactive, whereas diversity is productivity driven, qualitative, opportunity focused, integrated, and proactive. Janice L. Dreachslin, a Pennsylvania State University management professor and author of *Diversity Leadership,* stated that diversity programs should be differentiated from affirmative action programs. ''Affirmative action means using an individual's group identity as a criterion for making selecting decisions.'' She went on to state that if diversity is to be valued, it must be viewed as a strategic advantage.

Likewise, the focus of diversity programs and diversity **training** should not be on the historical workplace inequalities between men and women and majority and minority segments of the labor force. Such a focus often leads to a condescending atmosphere, according to employee-relations consultant Richard Hadden. ''It's a bit patronizing.'' Hadden told *Workforce* magazine's Gillian Flynn. ''It's like, 'Well what can we do to fix these poor black folk and poor women who obviously don't really know very much about what's going on because, poor things, they haven't been given a chance.''' Many diversity trainers and **consultants** thus feel that although diversity may have some antecedents in affirmative action, it's time for diversity and affirmative action to go separate ways.

Multiculturalism was originally associated with initiatives for race and gender equality in the workplace. Primary dimensions of diversity, however, certainly include race and gender, but also age, ethnicity, physical ability, and increasingly, sexual orientation. Additionally, secondary factors such as education, geographic location, income, marital status, military experience, parental status, religious preference, and work experience also reflect the elements of a diverse or multicultural workforce. Both primary and secondary characteristics significantly affect an individual's interaction in the workplace.

DEMOGRAPHIC CHANGES

All of the diverse characteristics of a multicultural workforce can be used to a strategic advantage by those companies with the creativity to make use of them. The changing demographics of the U.S. population and the resulting shifts in corporate markets offer new competitive opportunities for American businesses. To put it simply, a multicultural workforce makes good business sense. Concurrent with changing demographics in the United States are new patterns in spending power. In 1999 African American buying power was expected to reach over $530 billion—an increase of nearly 73 percent since 1990. Hispanic buying power likewise was expected to increase to $383 billion, an 84 percent increase over 1990 and Asian American spending is expected to jump in the same decade from $113 billion to $229 billion, representing a growth rate of 102 percent. ''Those companies that are able to tap into this growth now, with the right products and services as well as the work force expertise to serve these markets, are looking at an unbelievable business opportunity,'' according to Thomas McInerney, president of Aetna Retirement Services and that company's diversity steward, in an interview with DiversityInc.com.

The rise in the spending power of these minority groups has increased employment opportunities for minorities by ironically creating positive stereotyping, or what Frederick R. Lynch, author of *The Diversity Machine,* called ''identity politics.'' According to Lynch, companies spend a great deal of money and marketing energy on the idea that Mexican Americans can best sell products and services to other Mexican Americans and that African Americans can best sell products and services to other African Americans. *Workforce* editor Gillian Flynn concurred, ''These companies have a stake in the belief that people of a certain race or gender think similarly, and they favor diversity programs that support that belief.''

MANAGING DIVERSITY

Programs or corporate environments that value multiculturalism must answer hard questions about managing diversity. For example, can diversity be best promoted by equal treatment or differential treatment? Antidiscrimination laws prohibit employers from treating applicants differently, yet some argue that this premise seems to ignore those fundamental differences between individuals that form the basis of diversity. On the other hand, treating people differently often creates resentment and erodes morale with perceptions of preferential treatment. Other questions to be answered are: Will the company emphasize commonalities or differences in facilitating a multicultural environment? Should the successful diverse workplace recognize differentiated applicants as equals or some as unequals? How does the company achieve candor in breaking down stereotypes and insensitivity towards women and minority groups? These questions pose difficult dilemmas for companies seeking to create an environment conducive to diverse workers and productivity.

GOOD BUSINESS SENSE

But perhaps the biggest question that companies must face is: Will diversity make good business sense for our company? Evidently it does. *Fortune* magazine in 1999 published its ''America's 50 Best Companies for Asians, Blacks, and Hispanics,'' and found that many of the companies on the list were some of Wall Street's top performers. The companies matched the Standard & Poor's 500 index (S&P 500) over the past year and beat it in three of the past five years. The top ten companies on the *Fortune* list were: Union Bank of California, Fannie Mae, Public Service Co. of New Mexico, Sempra Energy, Toyota Motor Sales, Advantica, SBC Communications, Lucent Technologies, Darden Restaurants, and Wal-Mart. Rich McGinn, **chief executive officer** (CEO) of Lucent Technologies, linked success to talent. ''We are in a war for talent,'' he told *Fortune.* ''And the only way you can meet your business imperatives is to have all people as part of your talent pool—here in the United States and around the world.'' The CEO went on to say that diversity gives a company a competitive advantage because different people approach similar problems from different perspectives. Ivan Seidenberg, CEO of Bell Atlantic (which ranked 28th on the *Fortune* list) put it even more simply: ''If everyone in the room is the same, you'll have a lot fewer arguments and a lot worse answers.'' A diverse **management** team means ''more diversity of thinking.''

Another Wall Street plus for diversity and the success of diverse companies is the Domini Social Equity Fund, which is a **mutual fund** investing in companies on the socially screened Domini 400 Social Index. As reported by HemisphereInc., the Social Equity Fund placed in the top 10 percent of the 4,412 domestic equity funds tracked by Morningstar. In 1998 the fund had almost a 33 percent return and beat the S&P 500 index by nearly 3.5 percent. Nationwide, socially responsible investing grew at a rate of 227 percent from 1995 to 1997, and 9 percent or about $1.2 trillion of all total investment assets are invested in portfolios screened for social responsibility.

STARTING A PROGRAM

How does a company initiate a multicultural or diversity program? Many different elements may be necessary to create a climate of inclusion and to incorporate genuine value for diversity in the workforce. Four common elements in diversity initiatives that strengthen diverse programs are training, communication, task forces, and mentoring.

Many major companies conduct diversity training for managers and almost half conduct training for all employees. The key to success lies in viewing training as an ongoing process rather than a single event. Core components of diversity training may include valuing diversity, cultural literacy, corporate inculturation, global perspectives, and individual self-development.

Communications about the value of inclusion and diversity that come from the top of the organization are critical in the success of a diversity initiative. While this communication is frequently written, companies such as Allstate Insurance employ teleconferenceing to communicate multicultural values across the country. Additionally, the creation of special multicultural manager positions communicates with actions the real value of diversity from the top.

Task forces engage management and employees in the process of dealing with multicultural conflicts, needs, and organizational dynamics. Many task forces operate at high levels within organizations. Yet, increasingly many companies involve employees at all levels of the company in formulating policies and guidelines. Mentoring programs directly connect multicultural employees with traditional employees across racial and gender lines. IBM, for instance, uses a formal mentoring program while Corning employs a more informal ''coaching'' program.

Even the most well-intentioned diversity programs can, however, sometimes go awry. Deleyte Frost, senior associate of a Philadelphia **organizational development** firm offered a number of tips for instituting diversity programs. Frost felt that diversity programs should focus on the real issues of group identity, be they race, gender, age, etc., and not be covered up by such phrases as ''all individual differences.'' Frost also did not approve of euphemisms such as ''lifestyle'' when the issue is sexual orientation. Opposition to diversity programs should be met with ''energy, caring, and thoughtfulness and not deflected by intellectual arguments,'' although baseline data is needed to jump-start such programs. True change in **corporate culture** begins at the top and diversity programs cannot succeed without long-term commitment from top officers and a forward-thinking implementation team. Everything the diversity program does must be linked to business success, diversity strategies must be part of ''the business purpose and vision.'' Do not waste time trying to create a plan that will make everyone happy, it just won't happen. Finally, do not assume that training will change behavior, and do not focus diversity efforts only on customers and external **public relations**.

There are a number of organizations and commercial enterprises that are involved with diversity on a national scale. The American Institute for Managing Diversity is located in Atlanta and was founded in 1984 as a nonprofit organization. The institute helps organizations understand the business imperative for managing diversity. It also provides insights into the strategic implementation of diversity and suggests new areas of research critical to the successful application of diversity programs. DiversityInc.com is an online magazine that provides news, resources, and commentary on the role of diversity in strengthening the corporate bottom line.

Laurie Dougherty, one of the editors of *The Changing Nature of Work,* noted that the image of the American workforce is rapidly changing from essentially a white male image, as exemplified by the ''man in the gray flannel suit'' and the hard-hatted construction worker, to one of men and women of all nationalities and races—in essence, a change from a homogenous image to one much more diverse or multicultural. The greatest challenge of this new and diverse image is to ''balance the respect for diversity against the danger of discrimination based on differences.'' Only when this balance is achieved can our human resources be used effectively and productively.

SEE ALSO: Diversity Culture

[Tona Henderson, updated by Michael Knes]

FURTHER READING:

Ackerman, Frank, and others, eds. *The Changing Nature of Work.* Washington: Island Press, 1998.

American Institute for Managing Diversity. ''American Institute for Managing Diversity.'' Atlanta: American Institute for Managing Diversity, 1999. Available from www.aimd.org.

Argenti, Paul A. *The Portable MBA Desk Reference.* New York: John Wiley & Sons, Inc., 1994.

Colvin, Geoffrey. ''The Best Companies for Asians, Blacks, and Hispanics.'' *Fortune,* 19 July 1999, 53-70.

Crockett, Joan. ''Diversity as a Business Strategy.'' *Management Review,* May 1999, 62.

Digh, Patricia. ''Coming to Terms with Diversity.'' *HR Magazine* 43, no. 12 (November 1998): 117-20.

Dreachslin, Janice L. *Diversity Leadership.* Chicago: Health Administration Press, 1996.

Fernandez, John P. *Race, Gender, and Rhetoric: The True State of Race and Gender Relations in Corporate America.* New York: McGraw-Hill, 1998.

Flynn, Gillian. ''Diversity Programs.'' *Workforce* 77, no. 12 (December 1998): 27-35.

Frost, Delyte. ''Review Worst Diversity Practices to Learn from Other's Mistakes.'' *HR Focus,* April 1999, 11-12.

HemisphereInc. ''Diversity: The Bottom Line. Part 1: Building a Competitive Workforce'' (special advertising section). *Forbes,* 3 May 1999.

——. ''DiversityInc.com.'' Somerset, NJ: HemisphereInc., 1999. Available from www.diversityinc.com.

Jacobs, Eva E., ed. *Handbook of U.S. Labor Statistics.* Lanham, MD: Bernan Press, 1999.

Lynch, Frederick R. *The Diversity Machine: The Drive to Change the ''White Male Workplace.''* New York: Free Press, 1997.

MULTILEVEL MARKETING

Multilevel marketing (MLM), or network marketing, is a system of direct selling that relies on networks of independent distributors, usually private individuals, to reach customers by word-of-mouth. Multilevel systems provide an alternative to conventional arrangements that involve wholesalers and retailers. Besides eliminating costs associated with middlemen, network marketing reduces advertising and promotion expenses and, in theory, passes savings to the independent distributors and customers.

However, because MLM frequently involves constant recruiting of new distributors and a pyramid-like financial structure, it has been a controversial practice for most of its history. In scores of mass-market books aimed at would-be **entrepreneurs** it is presented as little more than a get-rich-quick scheme—gushing about achieving ''financial independence'' through MLM—and historically MLM organizations have more than once crossed the line into criminal activity.

According to the Direct Selling Association (DSA), the leading trade group for MLM and other direct-selling organizations, as of 1998 MLM in the United States generated more than $17 billion in annual sales. MLM that year accounted for 73.5 percent of all U.S. direct-selling revenues. Nearly 8 million people were involved in selling via MLM, for a national average of just $2,125 a year in sales per worker, highlighting how little the typical MLM salesperson actually makes—and this is before deducting the cost of the merchandise. By contrast, most other areas of **retail trade**, such as grocery stores, clothing stores, or health and beauty stores, tend to bring in well over $100,000 per worker, although admittedly these businesses have a much higher **overhead**. Based on DSA statistics, approximately 58 percent of the direct-selling workforce (including MLM and other direct selling) was female, and almost 83 percent worked fewer than 30 hours a week at direct selling.

Household products such as cleaning preparations and kitchen utensils are by a slim margin the most popular direct-selling products, according to the DSA. Personal care products like cosmetics and toiletries rank second, followed by wellness products (e.g., vitamins), household leisure and educational products, and a variety of other products and services. The first three categories—household, personal, and wellness items—represent a full 76 percent of all direct sales by value. Nearly 70 percent of all direct sales occur face-to-face in homes, while 10.9 percent are conducted over the phone (usually as a follow-up to a personal demonstration), 10.7 percent at the salespeople's other workplaces, and the remaining 9 percent in various other ways.

Some of the largest MLM-based companies in the United States (and in some cases, the world) are Amway Corp., Excel Communications, Inc., Herbalife International, Inc., Mary Kay Inc., Nu Skin Enterprises, Inc., Pampered Chef, Ltd., Shaklee Corp., and Sunrider International.

ORIGINS AND DEVELOPMENT

MLM was pioneered in the 1940s by Carl F. Rehnborg, an American. Rehnborg learned about the value of nutrition while scavenging for food in a Chinese internment camp in the 1920s. After he was freed, he started Nutrilite Products Inc., a manufacturer of vitamin-enriched food supplements. Rehnborg was extremely successful at marketing his products through an innovative distribution process that would become known as multilevel marketing. Nutrilite flourished throughout the 1940s and 1950s and was eventually purchased in 1959 by Amway Corp., a company founded by former Nutrilite distributors. Using similar MLM tactics, Amway, now a multibillion-dollar enterprise, thrived and spawned a string of imitators during the 1960s and 1970s.

During the 1960s and 1970s, fraudulent pyramid schemes exploited the success of MLM companies. Although they closely resembled MLM organizations, pyramids bilked investors and members out of millions of dollars. A mass of legislation passed during the 1970s almost ended MLM altogether, including organizations like Amway. However, laws were eventually modified to accommodate legitimate multilevel marketers and similar organizations.

Tupperware, for example, achieved stellar sales during the 1960s and 1970s with techniques that mimicked MLM systems. In fact, network marketing has traditionally been associated with cosmetics and household items. Still considered in its infancy, MLM was increasingly used in the 1980s and early 1990s to sell products and services ranging from vacations and books to software and food items. During the 1990s, services were an increasingly important growth category for MLM, which made inroads into such **service industries** as legal services, broadcasting and computer network services, and long-distance telephone services.

MLM BASICS

In essence, MLM uses customers to distribute products (or services). A company begins by selling its product to selected customers in specific geographic areas. Those customers then become salespeople by telling friends, associates, and contacts about the product and trying to get them to buy. The salespeople are usually paid a commission for the products that they sell. More importantly, they also receive commissions for the products that their customers, or recruits, sell. In other words, new customers are added to the sales network, many of whom also become distributors. As the number of levels of customers grows, so does the distribution network. Thus, by trying to sell the products themselves, customers also become recruiters for the company that represents the products.

MLM organizations are based on commissions that accumulate exponentially. For example, assume that Sandy buys some products from a distributor in the MLM company. She then sells the product to five of her friends and receives a commission. Next, three of her friends sell the products to six of their friends. Not only would those three salespeople receive a commission, but Sandy would also receive a (usually smaller) commission for each of the sales. If four of the six new customers each sold to four contacts, the number of people that could potentially be selling products to Sandy's benefit would suddenly lurch past 15. It is easy to see how the sales network originated by Sandy could quickly jump into the hundreds or thousands. In theory, all of the people in the network would benefit from the efforts and purchases of the people below them.

The compensation system is the infrastructure that supports and drives a MLM program. Sellers in the network usually receive relatively large commissions on sales that they make personally. The commission is the difference between what the salesperson sells the products for and what he (she) must pay to buy them from the company. In addition, purchases made by the same customer at a later date will often result in "residual income" to the person that made the first sale to that buyer. As sellers build a network of customers that also become sellers, they also earn group bonuses, or "overrides." An override is the fraction of sales that is paid to the originator of a network. In general, sales made by distributors further down the network, or at lower levels, pay a lower bonus.

Sellers may also get a "leadership bonus," which is effectively a bonus paid to sellers that help distributors in their network to achieve specific levels of sales success. Leadership bonuses provide an incentive for sellers to train and help their customers to become better distributors and recruiters. "Usage" bonuses are provided to sellers based on the total purchases (product usages) by members of their network. Usage bonuses usually take the form of discounts on air travel or long distance telephone service. They provide an impetus for people in the organization to continue purchasing the goods themselves.

ADVANTAGES AND DRAWBACKS

The obvious enticement for members of a MLM network is the seemingly unlimited profit potential. By purchasing as little as, say, $100 worth of a product, they can become distributors in a network that can pay them thousands or, theoretically, millions of dollars. In addition, MLM sellers get to be their own boss, make their own hours, and choose their own course to success or failure. They also get the advantage of buying the product at nearly the wholesale price.

The company that initiates and supports the network and supplies the products or services may also benefit significantly. It will likely incur costs associated with supporting the organization, including those related to making training videos and audio tapes, warehousing, transportation, and printing brochures. However, even after paying commissions, its advertising and promotion costs may be much lower than those of traditional marketing and distribution channels. Start-up capital requirements are usually much lower because the bulk of the marketing costs are not incurred until the products are actually sold. And the company benefits from strong customer loyalty and a solid base of repeat customers. Furthermore, MLM is more effective for some types of products than is traditional mass media because sales are conducted face-to-face.

Despite its many advantages, network marketing possesses several drawbacks that make it undesirable for many companies. For instance, it usually takes a long time to develop a large, profitable customer base compared to selling techniques like advertising through print and broadcast media. Furthermore, administrative duties and paperwork are usually much greater for MLM operations. Perhaps the greatest disadvantage of network marketing, though, is that the company loses control of its distribution process. It may have no idea of the types of people that are representing (or misrepresenting) its products. A corporate or product image can become quickly tarnished by overly enthusiastic or dishonest salespeople hungry for commissions.

MLM also has several disadvantages for sellers. Long hours are typically required to get a sizable network started, particularly if the product or service is perceived to be of average value by potential consumers. Because of poorly contrived or fraudulent MLM schemes, moreover, many people have attached a stigma to network marketing that sellers must overcome. Indeed, a major drawback of MLM to distributors is risk—they may lose their initial investment or be lured into purchasing additional goods or services that they will never use if the company backing the network is ill-willed or poorly operated.

PYRAMID SCHEMES

Numerous laws exist that regulate MLM organizations to protect consumers against fraud. Most of those laws are designed to discourage pyramid schemes, which closely resemble legitimate MLM systems. The difference between pyramids and legal network marketing is that the latter derives income from the sale of products. In contrast, pyramid organizations get most of their income by bringing new members into the network, or pyramid, and charging them fees.

The classic pyramid scheme is the chain letter. For example, a person might send letters to ten individuals asking for a $1. He would give each person ten names to which they should send the same letter. Theoretically, as the chain multiplies into a pyramid massive sums of money will flow from the people at the base of the pyramid to those at the top. As the pyramid continues to expand, people that were at the bottom see levels added, effectively moving them away from the bottom and bringing them cash from newcomers. Unfortunately, pyramids inevitably collapse. People at the top profit from the misfortune of those at the base. The problem is obviously more serious than the chain letter example when larger amounts of money and effort are required of pyramid members and promises of wealth go unfulfilled.

Some pyramid organizations disguise their objective by mimicking MLM companies. They integrate into the scheme a product or service that they "sell" to newcomers—a strategy known as inventory loading—or they simply charge sellers a fee to join the network. Then they encourage members to recruit, rather than sell the product to, other people.

PROTECTIONS FOR SELLERS

Because of potential abuses in MLM, there are a number of protections for sellers, in addition to criminal laws which outlaw true pyramid schemes. The Direct Selling Association maintains a code of ethics that its 140 member companies must abide by. DSA members include many of the largest MLM companies in the United States. The ethics code requires that member companies buy back distributors' excess inventory at least 90 percent of the purchase price, forbids misleading representations to salespeople and consumers, and discourages high entry barriers that can inflate upstream revenues while leaving downstream sales representatives stuck with excess inventory. The DSA also maintains a complaint resolution process for consumers who believe they've been cheated by direct-selling companies.

CASE STUDY

The case of Bios Lite Diet exemplifies a successful, legitimate MLM effort. Bios Lite Diet is a vitamin supplement marketed in the early 1990s by Rexall Showcase International, a division of Rexall created explicitly to sell products through MLM. Rexall Sundown, Inc., a leading vitamin and nutritional supplement marketer in traditional retail settings, is headed by Carl DeSantis, who started the company from his bedroom and financed it with a second mortgage on his house. Although DeSantis achieved success with traditional marketing methods during the 1980s, he determined that those techniques were not suited to marketing his newer and more complex Bios Lite Diet.

DeSantis decided to sell his new vitamin using MLM. Because MLM involves face-to-face selling, he reasoned, he would have a better chance of communicating the complicated biochemical benefits of the vitamin to potential customers. Within three years Rexall Showcase was growing twice as fast as Rexall's mail-order and retail divisions and was generating a surprising $36 million of Rexall's sales. By fiscal 1997, Rexall Showcase sales topped $100 million, representing one-fifth of the entire company's sales. DeSantis attributed the success to the seller motivation inherent in MLM.

[Dave Mote]

FURTHER READING:

Buss, Dale D. "A Direct Route to Customers." *Nation's Business,* September 1997.

Direct Selling Association. "Industry Facts." Washington, 1999. Available from www.dsa.org.

King, Charles W. "Services: The New Front in the MLM Revolution." *Success,* October 1996.

MULTIVARIATE ANALYSIS

Multivariate analysis deals with the mathematical application of statistics to a regression function to determine the effects of changes in a group of variables on other variables in the function. As a result, multivariate analysis can suggest, with a degree of predictive capability, what can be expected to happen when those variables change.

While it involves many kinds of tools, multivariate analysis is primarily a mathematical approach to **decision making**. It has many applications, including problems in engineering, traffic management, biology, economics, **marketing**, and even ethics and behavioral psychology. It can quantify how changes in one or more areas of a complex problem will affect an outcome over time, and indicate whether those changes will alleviate or exacerbate a problem.

For example, an airline company may use multivariate analysis to determine how revenue from a certain route might be affected by different fare prices, load factors, **advertising** budgets, aircraft choices, amenities, scheduling choices, fuel prices, and employee salaries. An agricultural engineer would use multivariate analysis to gauge crop yields based on different soil qualities; choices of seed, fertilizer, insecticides and planting schedules; amounts of sunlight and rain; and changes in temperature.

In these examples, route revenue and crop yields are dependent variables determined by sets of independent variables, such as fare prices and seed choices. A change in any one of the independent variables will produce a change in the dependent variable. But in some cases, independent variables may affect other independent variables.

For example, lowered airplane fares may affect load factors, and these might affect aircraft choices. Similarly, different fertilizers might affect seed choices, and these might affect planting schedules. Attempts at improving the outcome of the independent variable may have a short-term positive impact but may prove deleterious in the long term.

Multivariate analysis is not synonymous with classical simultaneous equations methodology, although this form of modeling is an essential component of the analysis. Multivariate analysis includes prescriptions for simplifying parameters and drawing relationships between data over different time periods.

The application of **computer** processing power greatly advanced the science of multivariate analysis by freeing analysts from the tedious task of computation. As a result, computer programs have become the necessary basic instrument of multivariate analysis.

One of the greatest problems faced by analysts of multivariate data is overparameterization. An overzealous analyst may be inclined to include many types of microphenomena into the analysis that may have little or no bearing on the result.

Part of the art of multivariate analysis is knowing what variables may be excluded. While this simplifies the computations involved, it may also create greater variation in the observed data, making it difficult to identify reliable regression lines. The only way to work past these dilemmas is to repeatedly test the models.

One form of overparameterization has to do specifically with **time series analysis**. This becomes evident in multivariate analysis of biological and sociological phenomena; current conditions may be primarily dependent on the results of previous time series.

For example, the rate of reproduction of trees in a forest depends not only on how many trees there are, but how many there *were,* and how many there were in successive time series before that. Weather conditions 10,000 years ago may be responsible for climatological changes that affect present rates of growth. In some cases, the analyst may be faced with a practically infinite regress. When faced with such chicken-and-egg problems, the analyst must determine where to draw the line, or limit the parameters of the analysis, without corrupting the reliability of the analysis.

[John Simley, updated by Kevin J. Murphy]

FURTHER READING:

Binder, Michael, and M. Hashem Persaran. "Decision Making in the Presence of Heterogeneous Information and Social Interactions." *International Economic Review* 39, no. 4 (November 1998): 1027.

Kurtz, Norman R. *Statistical Analysis for the Social Sciences.* Revised ed. Allyn & Bacon, 1998.

Lind, Douglas A., and Robert D. Mason. *Basic Statistics for Business and Economics.* New York: McGraw-Hill Higher Education, 1996.

MUTUAL FUNDS

A mutual fund is an investment trust in which investors may contribute funds in exchange for a share of that trust. Contributed funds are, in turn, invested in various **securities**, such as **stocks**, **bonds**, **commodities**, **money market instruments**, **guaranteed investment contracts**, Treasury bills, and other vehicles. Ninety percent of the fund's **income** must be derived from **dividends** and interest, and 90 percent of its sales must be distributed to shareholders. Corporate **taxes** are paid on any undistributed income.

Mutual funds are administered by companies, which employ an investment management board, which is in turn regulated by a **board of directors**. These companies collect an investment fee—normally about .5 percent of invested capital—and are provided an administrative expense budget, usually 1 percent of invested capital.

Mutual funds generally feature low minimum investment requirements. Investors may enter a fund with an initial investment of as little as $500 or regular investments of as little as $50 or $100 per month, withdrawn automatically through investor checking or savings accounts.

As a result, mutual funds permit individual investors with smaller amounts of investment capital to build a diversified portfolio of investments. They enable small investors to employ investment managers used by wealthy investors and investment institutions such as **pension funds**. As a result, individual investors may take advantage of the pooling of assets to retain skilled investment managers capable of making shrewd investment decisions.

For example, without a mutual fund an individual wishing to invest in a broad number of stocks and bonds would require substantial capital to take maximum advantage of the **economies of scale** associated with purchasing investments. Because its assets are invested in dozens of companies, a mutual fund enables an investor to contribute a much smaller amount, say $1,000, and gain holdings through the fund in all those companies. Consequently, the $1,000 investment may be comprised of $40 worth of shares in one company, $25 in another, $10 in another, and even 40 cents in yet another. The investor could not otherwise gain such small positions in these companies.

Each month, quarter, or year, the fund declares a dividend to its holders. This dividend reflects dividend distributions from each of the companies in its portfolio. In effect, it is the average dividend of all the shares in the portfolio.

The price of each share of a mutual fund is based on the aggregate value of all the shares in the portfolio. In other words, if the value of the shares owned by the fund rises by 5 percent during a quarter, the mutual fund share price may be expected to rise by 5 percent as well.

Mutual funds came into existence as investment clubs during the 1920s, when public interest in the **stock market** was growing strongly. Due to their popularity, mutual funds came under regulatory authority of the **Securities and Exchange Commission** through the Investment Company Act of 1940. The act established strict fiduciary standards for mutual funds, requiring reporting and disclosure statements similar to those required for **publicly held companies**.

In the late 1990s, there were more than 7,000 mutual funds trading. This demand created opportunities for market segmentation in the investment community. Fund managers have tailored investment portfolios to economic and social screens. For example, investors may participate in funds concentrated on power utilities, telecommunications, or biotechnology; on companies with good environmental records; on companies that are not involved in tobacco, alcohol, or defense; or on companies whose performance mirrors the performance of the broader market. Many funds are geared specifically toward share price appreciation, while others concentrate on dividend income.

The majority of mutual funds are "open-ended," meaning that they may be purchased or sold based on published closing prices. These values are printed in newspaper financial sections, listed first under the management company, and then by fund name. Open-ended funds are sold directly through the fund or its sales reps and can issue as many shares as the market demands. Excess funds can be held as cash or invested in other vehicles such as money market securities or additional stocks. (See Table 1).

Table 1

Mutual Fund Quotations

Name	NAV (Net Asset Value)	Offer Price	NAV Change
AAL: Mutual			
Bond p	10.50	11.02	...
CaGr p	14.03	14.73	+.02
MuBd p	10.61	11.14	-.01
AARP Invst:			
CaGr	29.88	NL	-.01
GiniM	16.08	NL	+.02
Gthinc	28.06	NL	-.03

Each share is listed first by net asset value (NAV)—calculated as the value of assets in the fund, less management charges, divided by the number of shares outstanding—and second by purchase price, which is higher to reflect **marketing** and other management charges.

Dividends may be collected by holders either as payments (dividend checks) or reinvested to purchase additional shares. As a result, the number of shares in open-ended funds may be constantly increased.

Other funds are ''closed-end'' funds. While also listed in newspapers, these funds include a finite number of shares and are publicly traded on a stock exchange. Because no additional shares are issued, dividends are distributed as cash and shares trade based purely on demand. Shares are traded at whatever price sellers and buyers agree upon.

Loads, or management charges, are figured into share prices through the spread between NAV and purchase price. No-load funds do not feature these spreads, but charge management fees directly out of profits from the portfolio.

[John Simley, updated by Wendy H. Mason]

FURTHER READING:

Boroson, Warren. *Keys to Investing in Mutual Funds.* Hauppauge, NY: Barron's Educational Series, 1997.

Griffin, Ricky W., and Ronald J. Ebert. *Business.* 2nd ed. Englewood Cliffs, NJ: Prentice-Hall, 1991.

Laderman, Jeffrey M. *Business Week Guide to Mutual Funds.* New York: McGraw-Hill, 1997.

N

NAFTA

SEE: North American Free Trade Agreement

NAICS

SEE: North American Industry Classification System

NASDAQ STOCK MARKET

The Nasdaq Stock Market is a computerized communication system that provides the bid and asked prices of more than 5,000 over-the-counter (OTC) **stocks** that have met the market's registration requirements. Originally known as the National Association of Securities Dealers Automated Quotations system, the name was changed in 1990 to the Nasdaq Stock Market, commonly referred to simply as Nasdaq. Introduced in 1971 by the National Association of Securities Dealers (NASD), Nasdaq enjoyed explosive growth during the 1980s and 1990s. From 1983 to 1993 Nasdaq grew from $153 billion in annual trading volume and 4,097 listed companies, to $1.3 trillion in annual trading volume and 4,861 listed companies. In mid-1995 the market capitalization of listed firms on Nasdaq surpassed $1 trillion.

By late 1997 Nasdaq had approximately 5,500 listed companies, compared to some 3,000 listed on the New York Stock Exchange (NYSE). Even though Nasdaq had many more listed firms than the NYSE, market capitalization of NYSE-listed firms was around $8.7 trillion in late 1997 compared to $1.95 trillion for Nasdaq-listed firms. Nasdaq has been known as the market for smaller companies and especially for technology firms. Approximately 35 percent of Nasdaq's 1997 market capitalization came from technology companies.

Trading volume on Nasdaq surpassed that of the NYSE sometime in 1994. For the first eight months of 1997, average trading volume on Nasdaq was 696 million shares, compared to 513 million shares on the NYSE. From 1982 to 1992 Nasdaq increased its share of stock trades from 32 percent to 47 percent, while the NYSE's share of trading dropped from 63 percent to 50 percent.

NASDAQ'S MARKET MAKER SYSTEM

OTC stocks are traded differently than stocks that are listed on the NYSE or the American Stock Exchange (AMEX). Stocks listed on the NYSE or AMEX are traded using the auction method. In the auction method, specialists handle all trades in specific stocks and either passively match orders from buyers and sellers or take a position in the stocks themselves. OTC stocks, on the other hand, are traded using a multiple market maker system. There are approximately 500 member firms that make markets in OTC stocks traded on Nasdaq. Some stocks may have 60 market makers, while smaller stocks may have only two. The multiple market maker system, it is argued, provides companies with greater liquidity than the auction system.

Under the multiple market maker system, dealers make markets in OTC stocks by making bids to buy and offers to sell. A dealer's bid price is the highest price at which someone would buy a stock, and the asked price is the lowest price at which someone would sell the stock. The difference between the market's bid and asked prices is known as the bid-asked spread.

The bid-asked spread, which can range from an eighth of a point ($.125) to half a point ($.50) per share, results in an additional trading cost for investors. Since 1996, when the **Securities and Exchange Commission** (SEC) accused Nasdaq's market makers of colluding to set prices, spreads have declined. During 1997 there was a 30 percent decline in spreads due to new SEC rules, which resulted in savings to investors of an estimated $1.3 billion in trading costs.

Prior to the introduction of Nasdaq in 1971, bid-asked prices were circulated using daily "pink sheets" that were issued by the National Quotation Bureau in three regional editions (East, Midwest, West). During the trading day there was no centralized data on bid and asked prices. Trading in the OTC market was slower, and the bid-asked spreads were higher than under Nasdaq. Nasdaq facilitated OTC trading by providing continuous, up-to-the-minute quotations on bid and asked prices through a centralized computer system.

MEMBERS AND SERVICES

The approximately 500 member firms that trade on Nasdaq do so using computers and telephone lines. Unlike the NYSE, there is no trading floor where dealers gather to execute their transactions. Rather, it is all done electronically. In some cases trades can be executed without individual dealers calling each other on the telephone.

Nasdaq offers its dealers three levels of service. Level One service provides bid and asked prices in all **securities** to all salespersons and dealers through approximately 200,000 terminals. It also provides sales price and volume information on the OTC stocks included in Nasdaq's National Market System. The terminals are usually leased by subscribers from vendor firms such as Quotron. Level Two service utilizes Nasdaq-owned terminals to provide subscribers with a variety of information on the OTC market. Level Three service allows registered market makers to report their trades and daily volume as well as to receive Level Two service.

Other dealer services offered by Nasdaq include the Small Order Execution System (SOES). For trades involving 1,000 shares or less of stocks listed on Nasdaq's National Market System, or 500 shares or less for other Nasdaq issues, trades can be executed electronically under SOES without any telephone calls between dealers. Nasdaq also offers Trade Acceptance and Reconciliation Services, which assists member firms in resolving their uncompared and advisory OTC trades.

Not all securities that trade over-the-counter are listed on Nasdaq. In order to be listed on Nasdaq a **common stock** must be registered under section 12(g) of the **Securities Exchange Act of 1934**, or the equivalent, and must also meet minimum levels for total assets, capital and surplus, public float, number of dealers, and number of shareholders. Those OTC securities that are not listed on Nasdaq trade infrequently and continue to rely on "pink sheets" to disseminate information on their bid and asked prices.

NASDAQ-AMEX MERGER

A merger between Nasdaq and AMEX was completed in November 1998 after it was approved by AMEX members. The two exchanges would continue to be run separately by a newly formed unit, the Nasdaq-AMEX Market Group. The new Nasdaq-AMEX planned to build a globally linked marketplace.

SEE ALSO: Over-the-Counter Securities Markets; Stock Market

[David P. Bianco]

FURTHER READING:

Dwyer, Paula. "Tough Love at Nasdaq." *Business Week,* 3 November 1997, 150-51.

Elliott, Heidi. "'Market of Markets' in Offing." *Electronic News,* 9 November 1998, 50.

"Marry in Haste." *Economist,* 21 March 1998, 88 89.

Nasdaq Stock Market. "Nasdaq-AMEX." Washington: Nasdaq Stock Market, 1999. Available from www.nasdaq.com.

"Nasdaq Wins a Hand." *Economist,* 12 August 1995, 59-60.

"NYSE vs. Nasdaq: Investors Will Win." *Business Week,* 4 August 1997, 96.

Schroeder, Michael. "Nasdaq: An Embarrassment of Embarrassments." *Business Week,* 7 November 1994, 122-24.

NATIONAL ASSOCIATION OF SECURITIES DEALERS AUTOMATED QUOTATIONS SYSTEM

SEE: Nasdaq Stock Market

NATIONAL DEBT

When a national government, such as the federal government of the United States, spends more money than it takes in from taxes, tariffs, and other revenue sources it must borrow from the private sector to meet its financial obligations. If this goes on year after year the accumulated debt is referred to as the national debt. The national debt includes not only the money the government has borrowed, but also the interest it must pay on the borrowed money. The U.S. government, for instance, finances its deficit spending through the issuance of IOUs in the form of Treasury bills, notes, and bonds. Deficits not paid by the end of the fiscal year must be carried over to the next year. If this practice continues year after year with the government borrowing money not only to meet expenses but also to repay interest and principal from previous years the national debt soon balloons. The terms "deficit" and "debt" are sometimes used interchangeably, but are not the same thing. Spending more money in one year than revenues for that year results in a deficit or deficit spending. If deficit spending is allowed to go on year after year the result the large accumulated debt becomes known as the national debt.

The idea of a national debt is controversial with some economists and government officials, who argue that there is nothing inherently wrong with federal government expenditures exceeding revenue. Others, however, find the idea abhorrent and the height of fiscal and political irresponsibility. The debate over deficit spending and a resultant national debt is not new to American economic history and goes back to the beginnings of the country. In 1781 Alexander Hamilton wrote a letter to a friend in which he discussed government spending. "A national debt, if it is not excessive, will be to us a national blessing," Hamilton wrote. Thomas Jefferson, however, took quite a different view. Jefferson said that public debt was a danger and to be greatly feared. In 1798 he wrote a letter to his friend John Taylor in which he addressed amendments to the constitution. "I mean an additional article taking from the government the power of borrowing," he wrote.

Many Americans have always lived under federal deficit spending and a national debt, especially those Americans born after the 1930s. But federal deficit spending and the national debt are not unique to the twentieth century. According to economist Alan Murray, in the 150 years prior to 1932 the federal budget was balanced or showed a surplus in two of every three years. Hamilton, as stated before, favored deficit spending and thought that the ability of a country to borrow and invest made economic sense for the country and its citizens. Jefferson, however, took a more moralistic view and believed public borrowing was akin to public corruption. America's wars have always been costly, have always strained the federal budget, and they have always been financed through deficit spending. Andrew Jackson loathed public borrowing and quickly eliminated the debt leftover from the War of 1812. The Republicans likewise quickly rid the United States of its Civil War debt. In fact the fervor with which these Civil War debts were retired prompted a British diplomat to write back to England: "The majority of Americans would appear disposed to endure any amount of sacrifice rather than bequeath a portion of their debt to future generations." Thus Americans in the past were willing, albeit reluctantly, to endure deficit spending for reasons of national sovereignty, but once the crisis had passed every effort was made to retire the debt as quickly as possible.

This view of deficit spending and national indebtedness changed dramatically when the federal government began following fiscal policies set forth by the British economist John Maynard Keynes. In 1936 Keynes published his *General Theory of Employment, Interest, and Money*. In doing so he replaced Adam Smith, the 18th century British economist who wrote *The Wealth of Nations,* as the world's most influential economist. Smith believed in a balanced budget, but when this was unavoidable any resultant public debt should be paid off as quickly as possible. Smith also believed that an "invisible hand" was always at work in capitalist economies and working to correct market place shortcomings sans government interference. Keynes conversely believed that under certain circumstances Smith's "invisible hand" did not work or worked to slowly. During a depression, for instance, people do not spend money to purchase goods and services because there are not enough workers with disposable income. This causes companies to lay off more and more workers who likewise cannot spend money they do not have. Keynes' solution for breaking this cycle calls for the government borrowing and government spending to "kickstart" the economy.

Upon arrival in 1936 Keynes' theories did not, as is commonly believed, have much affect on the fiscal policies of the Roosevelt administration and America during the Great Depression. In fact Roosevelt found Keynes to be "a little wacky." It wasn't until after World War II that Keynesian economics took hold in the United States. Keynes believed that economic cycles—periods of inflation and periods of recession/depression—could be obviated by the government reducing the money supply (cooling inflation) or by the government borrowing and spending money (boosting the economy.) Keynes saw nothing wrong with government borrowing because in essence it borrowed from itself—from the citizens and institutions that make up the nation and the body politic. This is unlike a family or a business that cannot borrow from itself—it must borrow from outside itself. Following World War II federal fiscal policy under the influence of Keynesian economists, became, for the first time in America's history, aimed at something other than eliminating a war induced national debt. Keynes' ideas became ''... commonplace, at least in Democratic administrations,'' according to Murray. ''By the time of the Kennedy and Johnson administrations, Keynesian-trained economists enjoyed considerable influence in the executive branch, offering advice on how to use budget deficits to spur the economy in times of weakness,'' Murray continues. Republicans generally preferred economic policies that came to be known as ''supply-side economics.''

Because of the unpopularity of imposing higher taxes to finance military spending during the Cold War, deficit spending returned by the 1960s. Lyndon Johnson, for instance, was loathe to raise taxes to finance the Vietnam War and his Great Society social programs. Although it must be said that America's last budget surplus was in 1969 during the Johnson administration. During the 1980s the Reagan administration simultaneously cut taxes and further escalated military spending causing the national debt to continue to grow. By the end of 1981 the national debt had risen to an all time high of $1 trillion; five years later it had doubled. The 1985 Gramm-Rudman Balanced Budget and Emergency Deficit Control Act, which set ceilings on the national debt beyond which the government could not borrow, failed to eliminate deficit spending.

By 1995 the national debt had grown to more than $4 trillion. That figure represents the amount of accumulated deficit since 1969, the last year the federal budget operated in the black (a budget surplus was expected in 1999 but as of this writing it was only a projection.) Not only has the national debt gone unpaid from year to year, but each year since then, the federal government has overspent, forcing it to borrow with interest. In fiscal year 1995, for instance, the federal government overspent by more than $192 billion with billions more in interest added to this sum. In 1995 the accumulated national debt was $4,961,529,000,000.

In 1998 the Congressional Budget Office released a study entitled *Long-Term Budgetary Pressures and Policy Options,* which predicts America's economic situation well into the 21st century. The report was analyzed by N. Gregory Mankiw for *Fortune.* According to Mankiw, the report predicts that the next few decades will show approximately balanced budgets if not a few years with small surpluses. Government debt is likely to drop from today's 47 percent of Gross Domestic Product (GDP) to about 17 percent by 2020. After 2020, however, America's baby-boomers will start drawing on entitlement programs, especially Social Security, Medicare, and Medicaid. Currently these programs are 8 percent of GDP, but by 2040 they are expected to be 17 percent of GDP. While federal government receipts will remain constant at 20 percent of GDP by 2050, the government debt is expected to be 206 percent of GDP, higher even then the national debt at the end of World War II. After 2050 the debt is expected to continue to increase. The solution, according to the Congressional Budget Office is an immediate 8 percent cut in spending or an 8 percent increase in taxes. ''Frightening though that solution is, what's even worse is the probability that no one will act on it,'' Mankiw writes.

[Michael Knes]

FURTHER READING:

Cavanaugh, Francis X. *The Truth About the National Debt: Five Myths and One Reality.* Boston, MA: Harvard Business School Press, 1996.

Coy, Peter. ''Debt is Shrinking. Is That Good?'' *Business Week,* 22 February 1999.

Gordon, John Steele. *Hamilton's Blessing: The Extraordinary Life and Times of Our National Debt.* New York: Walker and Co., 1997.

Mankiw, N. Gregory. ''Government Debt: A Horror Story.'' *Fortune,* 3 August 1998.

Sandak, Cass R. *The National Debt.* New York: Twenty-First Century Books, 1996.

Thompson, Kenneth W. ed., *The Budget Deficit and the National Debt.* New York: University Press of America, 1997.

NATIONAL LABOR RELATIONS BOARD (NLRB)

An independent, quasi-judicial federal agency, the National Labor Relations Board (NLRB) regulates union-employer relations in the United States. Its jurisdiction is the private sector, where it has the power to intervene in unfair labor practices (see Table 1 for examples) by employers or unions. Each year the NLRB receives some 35,000 allegations of unfair practices, a third of which it determines to have merit. The NLRB has a remedial, rather than punitive, focus; hence, it places heavy emphasis on settlement and the vast majority of its cases are settled without going to court.

CREATION OF THE NLRB

The National Labor Relations Act (NLRA), also known as the Wagner Act, was passed by Congress in 1935, but was rooted in decades of unrest over labor unions. Before the NLRA, labor unions had an ambiguous legal standing and were subject to many abuses both by their leadership and by the companies they tried to organize. Establishing a series of legal rights for employees wishing to organize for collective bargaining, the NLRA was by far the strongest and most comprehensive piece of federal legislation concerning unions. The statute created the NLRB as the primary mechanism for enforcing its provisions. The NLRA was subsequently amended several times, notably through the **Taft-Hartley Act** of 1947, thus altering the NLRB's jurisdiction and functions over time.

NLRB STRUCTURE

The principal components of the NLRB are the board itself and the general counsel. The agency is also supported by a network of 50 regional and subregional offices and a bench of administrative law judges who make initial rulings when parties refuse to settle on their own.

THE BOARD. The board is made up of five members, one of whom serves as the chair, appointed by the president and confirmed by the Senate. Board members, who tend to mirror the political leanings of the president who nominates them, serve staggered five-year terms. They can also be re-appointed after their term expires. The board's function is to decide cases when an NLRB administrative law judge's decision is appealed. Usually the board only hears cases with significant policy considerations or other far-reaching effects.

THE GENERAL COUNSEL. Largely independent of the board, the general counsel follows the same nomination process but serves a four-year term. The office of the general counsel functions as the prosecutor for cases that the NLRB regional offices deem valid and that can't be settled through mediation or arbitration. Charges that are dismissed as lacking merit at the regional level may be appealed to the general counsel. The general counsel may bring its cases before the NLRB's administrative law court or, with the consent of the board, may pursue a temporary injunction from the U.S. district courts. The latter course of action is reserved for extreme situations when allowing the dispute to run through the normal litigation process would have severe consequences, particularly when those consequences would hurt the alleged victim of the unfair practice. If there are several stages of appeal, the general counsel presents the NLRB's case at each step of the process.

INTERVENTION PROCESS

The NLRB only gets involved in labor activities when a request to do so has formally been filed with one of the NLRB's regional offices. The requests take two forms:

- petitions to conduct a secret-ballot vote on unionizing
- charges that an employer or union is engaging in illegal activities under the NLRA

In its first role, the NLRB serves as an impartial third party to supervise employee votes on whether to unionize. When properly petitioned by interested employees or a union, the NLRB conducts a secret-ballot vote of all employees in the company and announces the results. This process was created to allow workers to vote their consciences without fear of election rigging or reprisal from the union or the company based on how they vote. There are several kinds of petitions that may be used for different purposes, but most require supporting signatures of at least 30 percent of the work force in order to be considered by the NLRB. The petitioning process is also used to decertify a union by majority vote in a particular workplace.

The bulk of the NLRB's work is in its second role, evaluating and pursuing charges of unfair labor practices. Charges are first investigated by the regional NLRB office, and if they are found to have merit, the regional office tries to broker a settlement by encouraging the party accused of unfair practices—either company or union—to revise its stance. If the alleged violator refuses, the NLRB issues a formal complaint and the case is heard before an administrative law judge at the NLRB, with the NLRB's office of general counsel presenting the case against the purported violator. If either party in the case is unsatisfied with the judge's decision they may appeal it to the NLRB's five-member board; board decisions may be taken up with the U.S. appeals courts and, ultimately, the Supreme Court if necessary.

Table 1

Examples of Prohibited Unfair Labor Practices

For companies and unions under the NLRB's jurisdiction, the following practices are considered illegal:

Employer Practices

- **firing workers for unionizing**
- **threatening to cut compensation or benefits if an employee joins a union**
- **singling out employees involved with union activities for unusual penalties or otherwise unenforced rules ostensibly unrelated to unionizing**
- **offering incentives to employees expressly for not joining a union**
- **screening out employees with union sympathies**

Union Practices

- **threatening that employees will lose their jobs if they don't support the union**
- **discriminating against union members because they don't support the union leadership**
- **requiring employees to pay union dues after they have been expelled from the union**

Source: National Labor Relations Board publications and case literature

SEE ALSO: Labor Law and Legislation; Labor Unions

FURTHER READING:

National Labor Relations Board. "Fact Sheet on the National Labor Relations Board." Washington, December 1998. Available from www.nlrb.gov.

——. *The National Labor Relations Board and You.* Washington, n.d. Available from www.nlrb.gov.

NATIONAL TECHNICAL INFORMATION SERVICE (NTIS)

The National Technical Information Service (NTIS), an agency of the U.S. government, serves as a repository and clearinghouse for scientific, technical, engineering, and business-related information. The information that the NTIS collects and disseminates is generated by U.S. government contractors, U.S. and foreign governments, and various other foreign sources. Although the NTIS falls within the Technology Administration of the **U.S. Department of Commerce** it is entirely self-supporting. In that regard the NTIS is a nonappropriated agency and all its costs are paid for through the sale of its products and services.

The NTIS was preceded by the Publication Board which was created by President Harry Truman's Executive Order 9568 in 1945. The Publication Board reviewed technical and scientific reports and literature generated by the federal government and decided which material could be shared with the public without compromising national security. The board also reviewed similar material captured from the Axis powers during World War II. The thinking that led to the creation of the Publication Board centered on the idea that dissemination of noncompromising government technical information to the private sector would stimulate industrial, economic, and technical growth. In 1950, pursuant to Public Law 776, the Department of Commerce became responsible for overseeing Publication Board activities. In 1970 the board was renamed the National Technical Information Service.

Since its inception the scope of subject matter gathered by the NTIS has continually expanded. In the 1950s NTIS began gathering business and statistical information. In 1954 the Comptroller General of the United States issued an opinion that ''technical information'' (the original purview of the NTIS) was any information deemed useful to business and industry. By the 1990s the NTIS was gathering information related to medicine, the natural sciences, computer science, and many of the social sciences. Under the American Technology Preeminence Act of 1991 all federal agencies are required to transfer to the NTIS all unclassified scientific, technical, and engineering information that results from research and other activities funded by the government. This information must be transferred to the NTIS in a timely fashion, within 15 days of it being made public by the originating agency.

Throughout its history there have been attempts to privatize the NTIS—but especially during the Reagan administration. In 1988, however, Congress passed the Omnibus Trade and Competitiveness Act and the National Institute of Standards and Technology Authorization Act. These acts kept the NTIS under federal stewardship (subject to Congressional review) and made the NTIS part of the Technology Administration of the Department of Commerce.

The NTIS has a collection exceeding 2.5 million items covering 375 technical and business-related subject areas. These items are available through the products division of the NTIS as are the approximately 75,000 to 100,000 new titles added annually. The NTIS has a staff of 370 information processing professionals who are responsible for indexing, cataloging, and abstracting this data. The information is then made available in various formats including printed reports, CD-ROMs, computer tapes and diskettes, online services, audiocassettes, videocassettes, and microfiche. Users of NTIS products and services can be broken down as follows: U.S. business (both large and small), 64 percent; foreign organizations, 20 percent; federal and state governments, 6 percent; academic and public libraries, 6 percent; and individuals, 4 percent. By policy, the NTIS charges federal government agencies for its services just as other users are charged.

In addition to domestic sources the NTIS gathers about 30 percent of its information from foreign sources. It has arrangements with 19 cooperating organizations in foreign countries to acquire information for U.S. distribution. These countries include: Austria, Canada, China, Finland, France, Germany, Italy, Japan, the Netherlands, Norway, Sweden, Taiwan, and the United Kingdom. The NTIS also receives data from science counselors at U.S. embassies as well as military personnel and National Science Foundation personnel assigned to foreign countries. As a result of the Japanese Technical Literature Act of 1986 the NTIS acquires technical reports from approximately 80 Japanese corporations and various Japanese government agencies.

Since 1992 the NTIS has operated FedWorld, an electronic information service that operates through the Internet. FedWorld provides access to government documents, Federal online systems and services, and NTIS products. As part of FedWorld, the NTIS Preview Database displays all titles entered into the NTIS collection in the previous 30 days. FedWorld has been criticized for its awkward format but it has received praise for being a gateway to over 100 U.S. government **bulletin board systems**. The NTIS also offers various information services to federal agencies on a fee basis, including imaging and reproduction, fax management, virtual warehousing and inventory control, program management, and microfiche production and distribution.

[Michael Knes]

FURTHER READING:

Antrim, Patricia. ''NTIS (National Technical Information Service).'' Warrensburg, MO: Central Missouri State University, 1997. Available from library.cmsu.edu/paa/ntis2.htm.

Johnson, Donald R. ''National Technical Information Service.'' Washington: U.S. Department of Commerce, 1996. Available from www.ta.doc.gov/itp/usa/ntis.htm.

Maxwell, Bruce. ''The 10 Best Federal Government Internet Sites.'' *Database* 18 (August/September 1995): 42-47.

National Technical Information Service. ''NTIS: National Technical Information Service.'' Springfield, VA: National Technical Information Service, 1998. Available from www.ntis.gov/ntishome.html.

National Technical Information Service. *NTIS, National Technical Information Service: 40 Years, a Brief History.* Washington: U.S. Department of Commerce, 1985.

NATIONAL TRANSPORTATION SAFETY BOARD (NTSB)

The National Transportation Safety Board (NTSB) is an independent agency of the federal government responsible for investigating civil aviation accidents and serious railroad, highway, marine, and pipeline accidents. The NTSB also reviews **licensing and certification** matters related to the U.S. Department of Transportation (DOT) and, in an effort to prevent accidents, issues transportation-related safety recommendations. The NTSB, however, has no regulatory or enforcement powers nor does it make a determination as to the rights and **liabilities** of parties involved in the accidents it investigates.

The NTSB was established in 1967 as an independent agency but initially relied on the DOT for funding and administrative support. The NTSB became truly independent on April 1, 1975, when the Independent Safety Board Act of 1974 went into effect. This act dissolved all ties between the board and the DOT. The NTSB is administered by five board members appointed by the president for five-year terms.

The NTSB is responsible for investigating a wide range of transportation and pipeline accidents. During an investigation, the agency determines the probable cause, reports the facts and circumstances of the accidents, and when necessary issues safety recommendations. The NTSB has the authority to investigate all U.S. civil aviation accidents; all railroad accidents where there is a fatality, substantial property damage, or a passenger train involved; all pipeline accidents where there is a fatality or substantial property damage; and, in cooperation with the U.S. Coast Guard, major marine casualties and marine accidents involving both public and nonpublic vessels. These investigations, reports, and recommendations are made in relation to the NTSB's mission of saving lives through the prevention of transportation-related accidents. Besides the U.S. Coast Guard, the NTSB works closely with many federal agencies including the DOT, the Federal Aviation Administration, and the National Highway Traffic Safety Administration. Rules governing NTSB activities can be found in Chapter VIII, Title 49, of the Code of Federal Regulations.

When accidents occur that appear to fall within the NTSB's authority, the parties involved must notify the agency, as stipulated in the Code of Federal Regulations. These regulations specify when notification is mandated, outline the time parameters on notification, and specifically define such terms such as ''accident.'' These regulations also prescribe information that must be included in the notification. The notification is made to the NTSB's National Response Center which then passes it on to the relevant NTSB office such as the Office of Aviation Safety. A decision is quickly made as to whether or not more information is needed and whether the accident falls under NTSB jurisdiction. If the accident is to be investigated, it may be treated as a major or regional investigation.

In all major investigations a NTSB team of technical experts is sent to the accident site. Major investigations are broad and far-reaching in scope and the team is often accompanied by one of the five board members. A major investigation usually takes nine months to a year to complete. Regional investigations are headed by an investigator from one of three regional NTSB offices and the report takes about six months to complete. All accidents reports, be they regional or major, are made public.

The first step in any investigation is to designate parties to the investigation and their responsibilities as described in the Code of Federal Regulations. Parties to the investigation are defined as ''those persons, government agencies, companies and associations whose employees, functions, activities, or products were involved in the accident and who can provide qualified technical personnel to actively assist in the field investigation.'' Teams investigating accident sites often test equipment and components involved in the accident; review records and interview witnesses and technical experts; and conduct on-scene tests such as simulations and reenactments of the accident.

In pursuit of its mission the NTSB has investigated more than 100,000 aviation accidents and thousands of surface transportation accidents. The board has also issued more than 10,000 transportation-related safety recommendations of which approximately 80 percent have been adopted. NTSB safety recommendations are based on its own studies and investigations and range from special training for flight attendants in emergency situations to the construction of railroad tank cars that carry chemicals.

The NTSB also evaluates the safety policies and procedures of other government agencies with respect to transportation safety and accident prevention. In the area of hazardous materials, for instance, the NTSB reviews and investigates safeguards and procedures concerning their transportation and evaluates the performance of government agencies charged with the safe transportation of these materials.

[Michael Knes]

FURTHER READING:

Goglia, John. "The Investigation Process." *Mass Transit,* March/April 1998, 54.

National Transportation Safety Board. "National Transportation Safety Board." Washington: National Transportation Safety Board, 1998. Available from www.ntsb.gov.

NATO

SEE: North Atlantic Treaty Organization

NEGLIGENCE

Lawsuits based on negligence are the most common kind of civil action in the area of tort law. Negligence is usually defined as the failure to exercise the degree of care that a reasonable, prudent person would have exercised under the circumstances. This is sometimes called a lack of "due care." If such lack of care causes harm (physical, mental, or economic) to the plaintiff, the defendant may be liable to pay damages. If the plaintiff has also been negligent, however, and such negligence contributes to the harm he or she complains of, his or her recovery may be reduced or lost entirely. (See "Contributory and Comparative Negligence" below.) This demonstrates the "fault" basis that characterizes this area of tort law.

In the United States, tort law in generally defined by state rather than federal law. Negligence cases often get to federal court through diversity jurisdiction, but the case will be tried with some state's negligence law as the basis for decision. Moreover, the state law of negligence is usually common law rather than statutory law, with the effect that what is determined to be a lack of due care will differ from state to state. Even within a particular state, certain kinds of acts found negligent by a court in one community may not be found to constitute negligence in another community. Outcomes will often depend on the differing sensibilities of the juries in various communities, the advocacy talents of attorneys for plaintiffs and defendants, the particular judge, the tenor of the times, and the personalities of the jury sitting in judgment on a negligence case.

NEGLIGENCE DISTINGUISHED FROM OTHER TYPES OF TORT

Negligence is unintentional neglect, in contrast to intentional torts or strict liability torts. In most states, strict liability applies to the seller of a product in a defective condition that is unreasonably dangerous because of that condition and causes harm. The seller may not intend harm or even be negligent, yet where the doctrine of strict liability applies, plaintiffs may obtain a damages award without proving the manufacturer was negligent in the design, production, or marketing of the product. Negligence actions also differ from intentional torts (such as assault, malicious prosecution, or defamation) since negligence usually involves offending acts that are careless rather than deliberate or malicious. In most states, courts consider intentional torts to be more blameworthy than negligent torts, and are thus more likely to bring requests for punitive damages (damages that greatly exceed the actual loss to plaintiff).

A BASIC CASE OF NEGLIGENCE

To succeed in any negligence case in the United States, the plaintiff must prove that the defendant had a legal duty, and breached that duty, causing harm and damages to the plaintiff. Proving all four elements of a negligence case requires that the plaintiff introduce some credible evidence for each element. Failing to do so will ordinarily result in the judge granting the defendant's motion to dismiss the plaintiff's case, usually by means of a directed verdict at the close of plaintiff's evidence.

THE ESSENCE OF A NEGLIGENCE CASE—DUTY AND BREACH OF DUTY. The first two elements establish the core of defendant's negligence: the defendant's duty and the breach of that duty. These elements can be established in one of three ways. Usually, a plaintiff will allege that the defendant had a duty to act as a reasonably prudent person would act. (Corporations are also considered "persons" for purposes of civil lawsuits.) The "reasonably prudent" person standard is a phrase common to most judges when they instruct juries to decide whether the defendant's acts were negligent. Thus, if a defendant fails to warn of a known danger that a reasonably prudent person would have known and warned of, the defendant will likely be found to have breached a legal duty to warn.

In some cases, the burden on the plaintiff to establish the breach of a duty of reasonably prudent care is practically impossible. For a few such cases, the doctrine of *res ipsa loquitur* ("the thing speaks for itself") may help a plaintiff establish duty and breach of duty. In a seminal case, *Escola v. Coca-Cola Bottling Co. of Fresno* (1944), a waitress had sustained severe injuries to her wrist while transferring freshly delivered bottles of Coke from their cases to the restaurant's refrigerator. One of the bottles exploded. The cause of this explosion could not be explained by the way that the bottles were handled after their delivery. The court noted that if the product causing the injury had not been mishandled by the plaintiff and was recently under the exclusive care, custody, and control of the defendant, the events described by plaintiff would ordinarily not occur without some lack of due care on the part of the defendant. In this way, plaintiff could establish breach of duty without specifying in what way the defendant's conduct had been negligent. Application of the doctrine requires that (1) only the defendant controls the cause of the harm, (2) the event would not ordinarily have occurred without some negligence as its cause, and (3) the event must not have been due to any actions of the plaintiff.

Duty and breach of duty can also sometimes be proven by means of a doctrine known as *negligence per se.* In many cases the defendant's conduct is a violation of a state or federal law. The law establishes the defendant's duty, and the failure to comply with some specific law is the breach of that duty. Taken together, this amounts to *negligence per se.* In such cases, the judge and/or jury need not consider whether the defendant's conduct has been that of a reasonably prudent person. Rather, the law has set standards of conduct and care (reasonable or not) that people are expected to meet, and failing to do so may not only result in sanctions for noncompliance, but may separately be actionable as a tort by those who are harmed by the noncompliance.

ACTUAL AND PROXIMATE CAUSE. Causing harm is critical to the third and fourth elements of a negligence case, causing harm and damages to the plaintiff. The failure to act as a reasonably prudent person, or to comply with some applicable law, may or may not cause harm. A reasonably prudent company would not carelessly produce a product that would cause harm to the ordinary user. But, having negligently produced such a product, the company will not be liable to any consumers unless the product is sold, is used or consumed in the expected manner, and results in actual harm.

Actual harm may often be absent. When a restaurant cooks up supposedly boneless chicken nuggets and one of them has a small bone inside capable of choking a patron, the negligently produced nugget may be discovered by the patron before trying to swallow it. In most courts, the patron's shock at discovering the potential harm will not amount to the kind of harm ordinarily compensated by damages. But if the bone is discovered after it has lodged in the patron's throat, then some damages are likely to be awarded. The amount of such damages will vary greatly, depending on the location of the court, the amount of sympathy that can be generated for the plaintiff, and (often) the apparent ability of the defendant to pay damages.

Even if there is demonstrable harm, however, causation may still be an issue in negligence cases. The harm to plaintiff must be actually *and* proximately caused by the defendant's actions. Actual cause means that without (or ''but for'') the defendant's negligence, the harm to plaintiff would not have occurred. Thus, where a delivery van exceeds the posted speed limit by ten miles per hour and collides with a car that stops suddenly ahead, the jury may reasonably find that the driver's negligence (in this case, *negligence per se*) has actually caused the injuries to occupants inside the vehicle he struck. But if one of the occupants (a young child, say) is killed or seriously injured, and grandparents far from the scene of the accident become consumed with grief, their pain and suffering will not be compensated, even though they would not be so aggrieved ''but for'' the negligence of the driver. In such a case, actual cause is established, but not proximate cause. Proximate cause (sometimes known as ''legal cause'') sets limits on the legal consequences of negligent acts, and is most often decided by the judge (deciding on legal cause) rather than the jury (which determines more factual matters).

Proximate cause limits the legal liability for negligent acts by allowing plaintiffs to recover only in cases where the harm is a reasonably foreseeable result of the negligence. Assume an architect's design for an elevated walkway in a hotel atrium is defective, and the walkway collapses two years after its construction, injuring hotel patrons both on and under the walkway. Assume also that the design defect is the result of the architect's failure to use that degree of care that is usual and customary among members of his profession and is, therefore, a breach of the generalized duty of due care. Finally, assume that three blocks from the hotel, a pedestrian is startled upon hearing the loud crash of the atrium walkway and involuntarily jumps off the curb where he awaits a crossing signal. Struck by a passing car and injured, he later sues the architect in a negligent tort case, and proves duty, breach of duty, and harm. But the third element, cause, is only partly present: although the harm most likely would not have occurred ''but for'' the negligence of the architect, the doctrine of proximate cause would limit the architect's liability to those consequences that were reasonably foreseeable. The pedestrian's injuries from a passing car are consequences too remote and unforeseeable for the law to pin on the architect's original negligence.

THE VARIETIES OF NEGLIGENCE

Businesses may be held liable in a negligence case for providing goods or services. Slightly different standards apply for each kind of case, and liability for negligent goods will be discussed first.

In practice, negligence by a business entity selling goods can mean the failure to properly (1) design the product, (2) select the materials, (3) produce, assemble, inspect, and/or test the product, and (4) place warnings adequate to the average consumer regarding any hazards of which an ordinary person might not be aware. For product design, the usual and customary design practices of an industry will be relevant evidence in establishing the appropriate degree of care. Where a company's product embodies ''state of the art'' design, a finding of negligent product design would be most unlikely.

Manufacturers, distributors, and retailers all have some duties to carefully assemble or inspect merchandise where doing so would be within the realm of reasonably prudent behavior. For example, a car dealership might be held liable for negligently putting customized wheels on a car by failing to properly tighten the lug nuts, so that within twenty miles of operation the car loses a wheel and the driver is seriously injured. But a grocery store will not be liable for failing to inspect all its canned peas for possible metal objects hidden in the cans. (Liability may attach, however, on the basis of strict liability, or on some contractual bases such as the implied warranty of merchantability.)

For services, exposure to claims of negligence will typically arise where the service provider has failed to exercise that degree of care that is usual and customary (a) for members of that profession (b) in the community where such services are delivered. Malpractice is the usual name given to a professional's failure to provide that degree of care, and an aggrieved patient, client, or customer must allege and establish the appropriate level of care for the particular community and also show that the defendant's conduct fell short. Anyone offering a service to the public may be liable, including doctors, lawyers, bankers, insurance agents, hair stylists, architects, or designers.

DEFENSES TO CLAIMS OF NEGLIGENCE

Even where the defendant has breached a duty of due care, the plaintiff must establish measurable harm *caused* (both actually and proximately) by the defendant's conduct. The plaintiff's failure to do so will typically result in a directed verdict in defendant's favor.

Apart from any defects in plaintiff's part of the case, the defendant can (in appropriate cases) affirmatively plead contributory negligence, comparative negligence, or assumption of risk.

Proving such matters can reduce or avoid legal liability even where the defendant has been negligent.

CONTRIBUTORY AND COMPARATIVE NEGLIGENCE. If a defendant can prove that the plaintiff failed to exercise due care for his or her own protection, and that this failure was a contributing cause to plaintiff's injuries, a few jurisdictions will recognize this contributory negligence as a complete defense. Under this defense the plaintiff's conduct is found to fall below a level reasonable for his or her own protection. For example, suppose that a fast-food restaurant serves its coffee at a dangerously high temperature but does not inform its customers that their coffee is considerably hotter than other restaurants or that customers have often been burned by coffee spills. A drive-through customer who is burned in a careless attempt to open the lid with his teeth while driving in traffic may be found to have demonstrated a lack of due care (i.e., he is negligent, too). Moreover, if that failure is found to contribute to plaintiff's injuries, some states' laws would deny any recovery to plaintiff.

Where one party is clearly much more negligent than another, the doctrine of contributory negligence has sometimes led to unjust results. One attempt by states to meet this problem was the doctrine of comparative negligence, which in most states has replaced contributory negligence. In such states, comparative negligence does not bar recovery, but reduces it. The jury is asked to assign a particular percentage for the negligence of both plaintiff and defendant.

Consider a case in which the driver of a pizza delivery vehicle (A) negligently speeds through an intersection and collides with another vehicle. Suppose the driver of the other vehicle (B) was also negligent, but for a different reason: he failed to heed a stop sign. A and B have breached the duty of due care. In comparative negligence states, if A and B are seriously injured and sue each other for damages under a negligence theory, the jury will determine the proportionate degree of fault and adjust their damages accordingly.

If the jury determines that B was responsible for 60 percent of the negligence that injured A and B, any damages that B can prove in a negligence case against the pizza company or its driver/agent (A) would be reduced by 60 percent. If B sues A (and the pizza company) for $100,000 in provable damages, the court could award B no more than $40,000 in a ''pure comparative negligence'' state. If A sues (or counterclaims against) B and has $100,000 in provable damages, this amount will be reduced by 40 percent, leaving a recovery of $60,000. In a state where contributory negligence (rather than comparative negligence) is the rule, neither A nor B would recover anything.

In a substantial number of states, pure comparative negligence is modified so that a litigant who is 50 percent negligent or more (or, in some states, is more than 50 percent negligent) would recover nothing. A jury that cannot decide comparative percentages to a precise degree will sometimes decide which litigant it favors, and determine that one was 49 percent negligent and the other was 51 percent negligent. Thus, in a mixed comparative negligence state, a finding that the plaintiff was 49 percent negligent would minimize the plaintiff's recovery and foreclose any counterclaim by the defendant. As suggested above, some states would allow a litigant to recover even if the jury assigned a share of negligence as high as 50 percent, but no comparative negligence state would allow a litigant who was found to be 51 percent negligent to recover.

ASSUMPTION OF RISK. While contributory negligence is characterized by the plaintiff's failure to use proper care for his or her own safety, the assumption of risk defense arises from the plaintiff's knowing and willing undertaking of an activity generally known to be dangerous. A patron at a baseball game may be injured by a sizzling line drive, and while a cautious ballpark might provide continuous netting to separate players from fans, none do. Knowing this, a patron may elect to sit behind the partial netting in back of home plate, or take the risks inherent in a less protected part of the field. Assumption of the known risk, where found, will negate liability for any finding that the defendant was less than reasonably prudent in its activities. Similar cases involve the well-known risks of colliding with other skiers on a busy slope, watching a stock-car race from temporary grandstands near the pit-stop area, or attending a hockey game and sitting where pucks are likely to clear the protective glass.

Assumption of risk is different from contributory negligence in that it involves a conscious or presumed decision on the part of the plaintiff to encounter a known risk. As such, where a defendant shows that the plaintiff assumed a known risk, and the defendant's activities were not unusually careless or negligent, plaintiff will not recover. some states with comparative negligence decisions, however, have transformed assumption of risk into a question of comparative fault, and if the plaintiff is able to prove that the defendant was negligent, a process of relative faultfinding may lead to some recovery for plaintiff.

Some businesses attempt to protect themselves against claims of negligence by giving customers a statement to the effect that they enter the premises or engage in certain activities entirely at their own risk. Where the risks are of the kind not generally known to the public, however, or where the statement about the risk is hidden in a mass of fine print, the court's acceptance of assumption of risk as a defense is far from automatic. Maximum protection is gained under this doctrine where the risks are well-known to the public or clearly articulated to the customers, and where the customers acknowledge receiving and understanding the extent of the risk they are about to assume.

LIMITS ON RECOVERIES BASED ON DEFENDANT'S NEGLIGENCE

As mentioned at the outset, tort law has traditionally been the province of state rather than federal law. In negligence cases, state laws have generally allowed recovery of consequential damages and, occasionally, punitive damages. Consequential damages include compensation for personal injuries and property damage, as well as indirect economic losses (lost wages as a result of disabling injuries, for example). Consequential damages also have included noneconomic losses, such as pain and suffering, mental distress, and loss of companionship or consortium. Such noneconomic losses are generally part of a plaintiff's personal injury claim. Recently, several states have limited noneconomic damages by imposing dollar "caps."

More recently, the Supreme Court for the first time placed limits on states' imposition of punitive damage awards. In *BMW of North America, Inc. v. Gore* (1996), an owner of a BMW was apprised nearly a year after his purchase that the car had been repainted before it ever arrived at the showroom. Such a repainting was considered by BMW to be a minor repair, costing less than 3 percent of the car's overall value ($40,000). Nonetheless, had such a repainting been disclosed, the market value of the car would have been 10 percent less. Dr. Gore, the owner, argued (successfully) that he was entitled to $4,000 compensatory damages (the amount he paid in excess of the market value of the car). Dr. Gore's attorney argued that BMW of North America had systematically been defrauding customers in its failure to disclose such repairs. BMW argued that such no state specifically required disclosure unless the repairs exceeded 3 percent of the car's value; the Alabama jury, however, sought to punish BMW for its actions in the U.S. market by imposing a punitive damages award that was 1,000 times the compensatory award of $4,000.

In so doing, the Supreme Court found a Constitutional problem with such an "excessive" award. Due process under the 14th Amendment to the Constitution could not arbitrarily deprive BMW of North America of its property through a punitive damages award that appeared to punish BMW for behavior that was presumably lawful in most other states. More challenges to punitive damage awards will ultimately give more definition to the Court's admonishment, but at present, states may not deprive defendants of due process by imposing "grossly excessive" punitive damage awards.

Even so, punitive damage awards will continue, especially where businesses act for profit in ways that offend the sensitivities and ethics of ordinary lay jurors. This is most likely in cases where the defendant's conduct is perceived as deliberate, willful, reckless, or wanton. Business has lobbied, with some success, to put caps or limits on the multiples by which punitive damages can exceed compensatory damages. Most proposals for tort reform at the federal level have such proposed limitations, but have languished in Congress since 1994.

SEE ALSO: Product Liability

[Donald O. Mayer]

FURTHER READING:

Phillips, Jerry J. *Products Liability: In a Nutshell.* 5th ed. St. Paul, MN: West/Wadsworth, 1998.

NEGOTIABLE INSTRUMENTS

Negotiable instruments are written orders or unconditional promises to pay a fixed sum of money on demand or at a certain time. **Promissory notes**, bills of exchange, checks, drafts, and certificates of deposit are all examples of negotiable instruments. Negotiable instruments may be transferred from one person to another, who is known as a holder in due course. Upon transfer, also called negotiation of the instrument, the holder in due course obtains full legal title to the instrument. Negotiable instruments may be transferred by delivery or by endorsement and delivery.

One type of negotiable instrument, called a promissory note, involves only two parties, the maker of the note and the payee, or the party to whom the note is payable. With a promissory note, the maker promises to pay a certain amount to the payee. Another type of negotiable instrument, called a bill of exchange, involves three parties. The party who drafts the bill of exchange is known as the drawer. The party who is called on to make payment is known as the drawee, and the party to whom payment is to be made is known as the payee. A check is an example of a bill of exchange, where the individual or business writing the check is the drawer, the bank is the drawee, and the person or business to whom the check is made out is the payee.

To be valid a negotiable instrument must meet four requirements. First, it *must be in writing and signed* by the maker or drawee. Second, it must contain an unconditional promise (promissory note) or order (bill of exchange) to pay *a certain sum of money* and no other promise except as authorized by the **Uniform Commercial Code** (UCC). Third, it must be *payable on demand* or at a definite time. Finally, it must be *payable either to order or to bearer.*

The laws governing negotiable instruments are spelled out in Article 3 of the UCC. Modeled after the Negotiable Instruments Law, Article 3 has been adopted as law by all 50 states and the District of Columbia. It spells out the basic requirements for valid negotiable instruments and covers such matters as the rights of the holder, types of endorsement, **warranties** given to subsequent holders, forgeries, dating, and alterations.

A negotiable instrument is said to be dishonored when, upon presentation, payment or acceptance has been refused. To qualify as a holder in due course, an individual or business must have taken the negotiable instrument before it was overdue and without notice that it had been previously dishonored, if such was the case. The negotiable instrument must also be complete and regular upon its face; that is, all of the necessary information must be present. The holder must also take the instrument in good faith and for value. At the time it was negotiated, the holder in due course must have had no notice of an infirmity in the instrument or a defect in the title of the person negotiating it.

If these conditions are met, then the holder in due course generally holds the instrument free from any defect of title of prior parties involved with the instrument. The holder in due course may enforce payment of the instrument for the full amount against all parties liable thereon, free from any defenses available to prior parties among themselves.

Negotiable instruments may be endorsed in various ways, and some negotiable instruments do not require any endorsement. If a negotiable instrument is a bearer instrument, then it may be negotiated by simply delivering it from one person to another with no endorsement required. Such negotiable instruments typically have a blank endorsement consisting of a person's name only. If the negotiable instrument is an order instrument, then the payee must first endorse it and deliver it before negotiation is complete. For example, if the instrument says, ''Pay to the order of Jane Smith,'' then it is an order instrument and Jane Smith must endorse it and then deliver it to the payer or drawee.

Endorsements such as ''Pay to the order of Jane Smith'' are known as special endorsements and have the effect of making the instrument an order instrument rather than a bearer instrument. Restrictive endorsements (''Pay to Jane Smith only'') and qualified endorsements (''Pay without recourse to the order of Jane Smith'') also have the effect of requiring the payee to endorse the negotiable instrument. Qualified endorsements also affect the nature of implied warranties associated with endorsement.

Under the UCC, an unqualified endorser who receives payment or consideration for a negotiable instrument provides a series of implied warranties to the transferee and any subsequent holder in due course. An unqualified endorser warranties that he or she has good title to the instrument or represents a person with title, and that the transfer is otherwise rightful. The endorser also warranties that all signatures are genuine or authorized, that the instrument has not been materially altered, that no defense of any prior party is good against the endorser, and that the endorser has no knowledge of any insolvency proceeding involving the payer.

Other issues concerning negotiable instruments are also covered in Article 3 of the UCC. In the case of a forgery, the negotiable instrument becomes inoperative. Antedated or past-dated instruments are not invalid, provided the dating was not done for fraudulent or illegal purposes. Negotiable instruments that have been materially altered without the permission of all parties involved are void. But a holder in due course who is not party to the material alteration can enforce payment according to the instrument's original terms. Also covered in Article 3 are interpretations of contradictions that may appear from time to time in negotiable instruments.

[David P. Bianco]

FURTHER READING:

Gallinger, George W., and Jerry B. Poe. *Essentials of Finance: An Integrated Approach.* Englewood Cliffs, NJ: Prentice Hall, 1995.

NEPOTISM

Nepotism in the business world is the showing of favoritism toward one's family members or friends, in both economic and employment practices. The term ''nepotism'' is applied to the practice of granting favors or jobs to friends and relatives, without regard to merit. Oppositely, ''antinepotism'' describes the practice of not allowing relatives (by blood or marriage) to work in the same office or firm. On the political scene, ''nepotism'' is being loosely applied to the phenomenon of ''dynasty building''—members of the same political family running for office and trading on their famous name to gain votes.

The word ''nepotism'' is derived most immediately from the French *népotisme* and the Italian *nepotismo.* These in turn have their origin in the Latin word *nepote,* meaning nephew. The use of the word is passed down from fragmentary information that Roman emperors and generals appointed their nephews to high positions in the empire. In the 14th through 17th centuries ''nepotism'' was used to describe the documented practice of French nobility naming their ''nephews'' (many of whom were their own illegitimate offspring) as prelates and to high office, and of many popes doing the same.

The principle of nepotism migrated to the American colonies along with other political and business concepts. The mainly agrarian economy of the United States was dominated by the family farm. For members of a merchant family to follow in the family business was a given as it was in most of Europe in the 18th century. Nepotism on the political scene was not unheard of, but it was not until the election of Andrew Jackson that the practice was seen as rampant on the American political landscape. Jackson extended patronage farther down the scale than just cabinet positions and other high offices. His use of patronage was so widespread that a supporter, Senator William L. Marcy (1786-1857), said in a speech justifying such extensive patronage that there is ''nothing wrong in the rule that to the victor belong the spoils of the enemy,'' thus coining the phrase ''spoils system.''

The excesses of that era and later administrations led to reforms in the civil service area. The Civil Service Act of 1883 created the basis for the merit hiring system used in the federal service today. Many states followed suit. Nepotism is still a factor on the political scene, in both positive and negative aspects.

While in the **family-owned business** ''nepotism'' is seen as ''succession,'' many businesses in the modern world try to avoid even the appearance of nepotism, by forbidding relatives from working together, including husbands and wives as well as blood relatives. As women have entered the **workforce** in greater numbers and have taken on more significant jobs, rules regarding nepotism have begun to change. Both the man and the woman in a marriage often are now too valuable for a company to lose. The current general outlook is that these family members can be accommodated within a merit system, especially if there is not a direct or indirect supervisory link between the positions of related employees.

Family businesses—estimated to represent 95 percent of all businesses in the United States—are the embodiment of nepotism. In the nonfamily business, reasons given for excluding relatives from working together have historically been that the emotional ties of these relationships may negatively affect **decision making** and growth at the office. The family business, however, encourages participation by all members of the family and the use of emotional ties to bond the relationships more tightly. Recent studies have shown that in the successful family business these bonds are healthy emotionally and good for the business as well. In the family business where there are problems, the type of fears that regular business rightly has concerning nepotism have proven to undermine the family firm. Resources have been developed to help families sort these issues out and to promote the positive aspects of this type of nepotism—the ability to move ahead when all are linked emotionally and mentally and are going in the same direction. The January 1993 issue of *Nation's Business* offered a very thorough "how-to" on policies and practices that forestall the negative aspects of family business and emphasize the positive. The article concludes that family businesses need to set rules and standards for training and succession by experience, much like the outside world of merit competition, to guide family participation and avoid problems.

A company often cited as an example of a firm where nepotism "works" is Thomas Publishing Company, a New York-based publisher of industrial buying guides, such as the *Thomas Register of American Manufacturers.* Thomas has been a family-owned and family-run business for more than 100 years; seven third- and fourth-generation family members were working at the 500-employee company in the late 1990s. The company, however, encourages nepotism beyond the founding family. According to *Sales and Marketing Management* magazine, for example, members of the Gural family have been working as independent sales contractors for Thomas for more than 50 years. Thomas keeps hiring fair by making all prospective employees go through the same process, including interviews with the human resources department. New hires—even those who had benefited from the company's nepotism policy in their hiring—are encouraged to leave if they fail to perform up to expectations. As Thomas's president, Tom Knudsen, explained to *Nation's Business,* "Once in the door . . . you're expected to produce the same as anybody else."

SEE ALSO: Career and Family Issues

[Joan Leotta, updated by David E. Salamie]

FURTHER READING:

Aronoff, Craig E., and John L. Ward. "Rules for Nepotism." *Nation's Business,* January 1993, 64-65.

Baldwin, Deborah. "It's a Small Town After All." *Common Cause Magazine,* Fall 1993, 10-13.

Kaydo, Chad. "Does Nepotism Work?" *Sales and Marketing Management,* July 1998, 16.

Mehta, Ved. *A Family Affair: India under Three Prime Ministers.* New York: Oxford University Press, 1992.

Nelton, Sharon. "The Bright Side of Nepotism." *Nation's Business,* May 1998, 72.

Thomas, Paulette. "An Ohio Design Shop Favors Family Ties." *Wall Street Journal,* 8 September 1998, B1, B4.

NEW PAY

SEE: Strategic Pay/New Pay

NLRB

SEE: National Labor Relations Board

NONDURABLE GOODS

Nondurable, or soft, goods are those which are consumed immediately or within a short time. The **U.S. Department of Commerce** uses three years as the consumption period to distinguish nondurable from durable goods. Nondurable goods consist of food, clothing, and other items that are consumed within three years. Some soft goods, though, are expected to last longer than three years when purchased, such as an expensive suit or coat.

The production of nondurable goods is a component of a country's **gross domestic product (GDP)**. As reported in the *Survey of Current Business* by the Bureau of Economic Analysis, nondurable goods that are sold to consumers appear under personal consumption expenditures. The other two categories of personal consumption expenditures are durable goods and services.

Nondurable goods that are produced but not sold are reported as changes in business inventories. Changes in business inventories also include durable goods. If more goods are produced than sold, then business inventories increase. On the other hand, when more goods are sold than are produced during a given period, business inventories decline. The category of changes in business inventories is used as an economic indicator to gauge the direction of a country's economy. Increases in business inventories may signal a weakening of consumer demand or a strengthening of productive activity. Finally, the production of nondurable goods also appears in the GDP as part of a nation's exports and as part of national, state, and local government purchases.

The category of personal consumption expenditures for nondurable goods is not used as an economic indicator. Most nondurable goods are purchased when needed. Changes in the level of consumer expenditures for nondurable goods tend to reflect population growth rather than economic conditions.

The purchase of nondurable goods by consumers represents a significant portion of the United States' GDP, although it is by no means the largest category of expenditures. Personal consumption expenditures in 1997, including durable goods, nondurable goods, and services, amounted to $5.49 trillion in 1997 out of a total GDP of $8.11 trillion, or 68 percent of GDP. Of that total, consumers spent $1.60 trillion on nondurable goods (19.8 percent of GDP), $673.1 billion on durable goods (8.3 percent of GDP), and $3.22 trillion on services (39.7 percent of GDP). In addition, nondurable goods contributed to the GDP in the categories of exports and government purchases.

SEE ALSO: Durable Goods; Gross Domestic Product (GDP)

[David P. Bianco]

FURTHER READING:

U.S. Department of Commerce. *Survey of Current Business.* Washington, DC: Bureau of Economic Analysis, U.S. Department of Commerce, GPO, 1992.

NONPARAMETRIC STATISTICS

Many statistical methods apply solely to populations having a specified distribution of values, such as the normal distribution. Naturally, this assumption is not always reasonable in practical applications. The need for techniques that may be applied over a wide range of distributions of the parent population has led to the development of distribution-free or nonparametric statistical methods. In place of parameters such as means and variances and their estimators, these methods use ranks and other measures of relative magnitude—hence the term ''nonparametric.'' Distribution-free statistical procedures do not require the normality of underlying populations or that such populations have any particular mathematical form. Although they do require certain assumptions, nonparametric tests are generally valid whatever the population distribution.

Nonparametric counterparts to standard statistical testing procedures are typically used either when an assumption violation that invalidates the standard test is suspected, or in situations where the response variable of interest is not susceptible to numerical measurement, but can be ranked. A common example of this second setting is provided by studies of preference in **marketing**. For instance, in a taste test, a consumer may be asked to rank a new product in order of preference among several current brands. While the consumer probably has a preference for each product, the strength of that preference is difficult to measure. The best solution may be to have the consumer rank the various products (1 = best, 2 = second best, and so forth). The resulting set of ranks cannot be appropriately tested using standard procedures. Thus, nonparametric methods are often employed when measurements are available only on a nominal (categorical) or ordinal (rank) scale.

NONPARAMETRIC TESTS AND PROCEDURES

Sums of ranks are the primary tools of nonparametric statistics. When comparing samples, the statistician ranks the observations in order, and then considers statistics based on those ranks, rather than on the raw data. Most statistical computer packages will calculate a wide array of nonparametric statistical procedures. The most common rank-based tests are the Wilcoxon rank sum and Wilcoxon signed-rank statistics, used for comparing two populations in, respectively, independent sampling experiments and paired-difference experiments.

For independent samples, another nonparametric analog to the two-sample t test is the Mann-Whitney test, which may be extended, in the case of more than two samples, to the Kruskal-Wallis test. The Kruskal-Wallis test (which tests location) and Friedman two-way ANOVA (which compares variation) are often used as alternatives to the analysis of variance for comparing several populations in a completely randomized experimental design. The Kolmogorov-Smirnov two-sample test is also used for testing differences between sample cumulative distribution functions.

For one-sample tests, a Kolmogorov-Smirnov procedure has been developed to compare the shape and location of a sample distribution to a reference distribution, such as a normal or uniform. The Lilliefors procedure tests standardized values of the sample data (values that have been centered at zero, by subtracting the mean, and also divided by the standard deviation) to see whether they are normally distributed. Also, the Wald-Wolfowitz runs test detects serial patterns in a run of values. In the study of correlation between two variables, methods such as Spearman's rank correlation coefficient (a nonparametric alternative to Pearson's product-moment correlation coefficient), Kendall's tau, and the Goodman-Kruskal gamma statistic may be used to estimate relationships using noninterval data.

NONPARAMETRIC REGRESSION AND SMOOTHING

A **regression** curve describes a general relationship between one or more predictor variables X and a response variable Y. Parametric regression procedures specify a functional form (such as a straight line with unknown slope and intercept) for the relationship between Y and X. In nonparametric regression, neither the functional form nor the error distribution of the regression curve is prespecified. Instead, a smoothing estimate is developed, often through the use of kernel smoothers, allowing for extremely versatile and flexible methods of presenting and analyzing data. Nonparametric smoothing procedures may be used to model kinks in nonlinear relationships between, for instance, sales projections for heating-oil use and temperature. Additionally, smoothing methods may be used, without reference to a specific parametric model, in the diagnosis of outliers, and in the analysis of missing data.

THE MISUSE OF NONPARAMETRIC STATISTICS

Some researchers fall back on nonparametric procedures as a substitute for collecting good data. There are, however, explicit assumptions involved in nonparametric analyses, as there are for parametric tests. In most cases, these procedures were designed to apply to data that were categorical or ranked in the first place. Rank-based nonparametric methods may lose much of the information contained in the observed data. Data that violate distributional assumptions for standard probability models may be more effectively transformed using logarithms, roots, or powers than by ranking.

[Thomas E. Love, updated by Kevin J. Murphy]

FURTHER READING:

Conover, W. J. *Practical Nonparametric Statistics.* New York: John Wiley & Sons, Inc., 1998.

Hettmansperger, T. P., and J. W. McKean. *Robust Nonparametric Statistical Methods.* Edward Arnold, 1998.

Hollander, M., and D. Wolfe. *Nonparametric Statistical Methods.* New York: John Wiley & Sons, Inc., 1999.

Randles, R. H., and D. Wolfe. *Introduction to the Theory of Nonparametric Statistics.* Krieger Publishing, 1991.

NORTH AMERICAN FREE TRADE AGREEMENT (NAFTA)

The North American Free Trade Agreement (NAFTA) is an international agreement among the United States, Canada, and Mexico. Much has changed in the years since NAFTA took effect on January 1, 1994. The biggest effect of NAFTA has been on trade volumes. From 1993 to 1997, US.-Canadian trade increased more than 80 percent and U.S.-Mexican trade increased more than 90 percent. Mexico is now the second-largest trading partner of the United States, being second only to Canada.

NAFTA phases out tariffs among the three countries over a period ending in 2009, and it liberalizes rules related to investment in Mexico. NAFTA's adoption was supported strongly by most businesses and investors in the United States. Many other citizens, however, opposed its adoption and continue to be wary of its consequences. Debate continues as to whether NAFTA's effects have been negative or positive. Labor representatives say that NAFTA has encouraged more U.S. companies to move their operations to Mexico, where wages are lower than in the United States, workers receive fewer protections in terms of occupational safety and health, and enforcement of **environmental laws** is less stringent in many, but not all, cases.

Many, but not all, environmental groups opposed NAFTA prior to its adoption, and such opposition continues. As a result of opposition prior to Congress's approval of NAFTA, side agreements on labor, the environment, and import surges were negotiated. Following heated debate and serious concern about whether NAFTA would be approved, NAFTA and the side agreements were approved by the U.S. Congress in November 1993. As we enter the 21st century, environmentalists allege that increased trade resulting from NAFTA has led to further degradation of the environment in Mexico and the Southwest United States.

NAFTA'S PROVISIONS

NAFTA liberalizes rules for investment by businesses from one NAFTA country in another NAFTA country. It also eliminates tariffs and other barriers to trade among the United States, Canada, and Mexico over a 15-year period that began January 1, 1994. Thus, it creates what some commentators are calling "the world's largest trading bloc." As of December 31, 1993, there were tariffs on approximately 9,000 products being traded between the United States and Mexico. Approximately 4,500 tariffs were eliminated on January 1, 1994, and by 1999 tariffs remained in effect on only about 3,000. The remaining tariffs will be gradually phased out, with the last of them being terminated by the year 2009. NAFTA is a two-volume document covering more than 1,200 pages with extremely detailed, complex provisions specifying how tariffs and other barriers for a multitude of different industries will be altered. The following description of NAFTA summarizes some of its salient provisions with respect to selected sectors of the economy.

REMOVAL OF BARRIERS TO INVESTMENT. NAFTA removes certain investment barriers, protects NAFTA investors, and provides process for settlement of disputes between investors and a NAFTA country. Coverage includes anticompetitive practices, financial services, **intellectual property**, temporary entry for businesspersons, and dispute settlement procedures. One of the most significant aspects of NAFTA is that it minimizes or eliminates many requirements of foreign government approval, which formerly posed significant barriers to investment.

NAFTA includes provisions on anticompetitive practices by monopolies and state enterprises as well as on such practices by privately owned businesses. It also sets out principles to guide regulation of financial services. Under NAFTA, financial service providers from one NAFTA country may establish banking, insurance, **securities** operations, and other types of financial services in another NAFTA country. The advantage of this for investors is that they are able to use the same financial service providers for both domestic and international transactions.

NAFTA provides U.S. and Canadian firms with greater access to Mexico's energy markets and energy-related services. Pursuant to NAFTA, U.S. and Canadian energy firms are now allowed to sell their products to PEMEX, Mexico's state-owned petroleum company, through open, competitive bidding. Under NAFTA, for the first time Mexico is allowing foreign ownership and operation of self-generation, cogeneration, and independent power plants.

Transportation among the three countries is becoming more efficient and less costly due to changes in investment restrictions. Pursuant to NAFTA, Mexico is removing its restrictions on **foreign investment** for trucking firms. Since 1995, U.S., Mexican, and Canadian trucking companies have been allowed to establish cross-border routes. Bans on such routes prior to NAFTA made shipping across the U.S.-Mexican border costly and inefficient; goods had to be unloaded from one truck and put onto another truck as they were moved from Mexico to the United States, or vice versa. As we enter the 21st century, trade is flowing more freely between the United States and Canada for a variety of reasons. For example, as of January 1999, a driver-record database is available for use by law enforcement officers in each of the three NAFTA countries. But crossing procedures at the U.S.-Mexican border continue to be inefficient. In January 1996, an agreement was to take effect that would allow U.S. and Mexican carriers to pick up and deliver international shipments in states adjacent to the U.S.-Mexican border, but the agreement was blocked by the United States. Commentators believe that the decision was based on organized labor's opposition to NAFTA. In addition, the United States and Mexico are still working to harmonize safety standards for motor carriers.

Under NAFTA, Mexico's pharmaceutical market is being opened to U.S. investors. Mexico has removed its import restrictions on pharmaceutical products, and it will phase out tariffs on such products by 2004. Mexico has opened its government procurement contracts for pharmaceuticals to bids from U.S. and Canadian companies.

NAFTA builds on the work of the **General Agreement on Tariffs and Trade** (GATT), providing substantial protection for intellectual property. Covered are **copyrights**, including sound recordings; **patents** and trademarks; plant breeders' rights; industrial designs and trade secrets; and integrated circuits (semiconductor chips). NAFTA includes details regarding procedures for enforcement of intellectual property rights and for damages in the event of violations of such rights. Mexico divides its intellectual property laws into two areas: intellectual property and industrial property. Mexico adopted its new Industrial Property Law as of 1994 and its new Federal Copyright Law took effect in 1997. Mexico has a history, however, of weak enforcement of intellectual property rights, and this area of law is developing slowly.

NAFTA does not create a common market for movement of labor. Thus, provisions in NAFTA deal with temporary entry of businesspeople from one NAFTA country into another. On a reciprocal basis, each of the three countries admits four categories of businesspersons: (1) business visitors dealing with research and design, growth, **marketing** and sales, and related activities; (2) traders and investors; (3) intracompany transferees—provided that such transferees are employed in a managerial or executive capacity or possess specialized knowledge; and (4) specified categories of professionals who meet minimum educational requirements or possess specialized knowledge.

ELIMINATION OF TARIFFS. NAFTA's provisions on farm products were of great concern to agriculture businesspeople in the United States. Pursuant to NAFTA, tariffs on all farm products will be phased out, but producers of certain "sensitive" products will be allotted extra time to adjust gradually to **competition** from products of other NAFTA countries. Tariffs for those sensitive products will be phased out over a period of 15 years ending in 2009. "Sensitive products" receiving such treatment include corn and dry beans for Mexico, and sugar, melons, asparagus, and orange juice concentrate for the United States.

Provisions related to the automobile industry were also of special concern in the United States. Pursuant to formulas set out in NAFTA, as of 1995, cars must contain 50 percent North American content to qualify for duty-free treatment. By 2002, they will be required to contain 62.5 percent North American content to receive such treatment. Also, U.S. automobile manufacturers have gained greater access to Mexican markets. During a transition period, limits on numbers of vehicles imported to Mexico are being phased out, as are duties on automobiles, light trucks, and automobile parts. As of 1999, according to Brenda M. Case, "The auto industry is already one of the great success stories of the Mexican economy, and most of the world's auto makers have plans to make it bigger and better. Auto plants, suppliers, and dealers make up 20 percent of Mexico's exports and 2.5 percent of its **gross domestic product** (GDP)."

Mexico's telephone system was severely underdeveloped prior to NAFTA. Prices were high, service was irregular, and private customers often waited for years to get telephones installed. As of NAFTA's effective date, Mexico abolished tariffs on all telecommunications equipment except telephone sets and central-switching equipment, and tariffs on even those products were phased out by 1998. Now, U.S. companies compete for certain **contracts** for Mexico's telephone system. In addition, foreign investors are allowed to form **joint ventures** with Mexican companies in the area of telecommunications, although foreign participation in telecommunications is limited to 49 percent in most cases. As a result of the new joint ventures and lowered tariffs, the quality of telephone service in Mexico has improved tremendously.

DISPUTE RESOLUTION. Administration of NAFTA is handled by a commission composed of ministers (cabinet-level officers) designated by each NAFTA country. A secretariat serves the commission and assists with the administration of dispute resolution panels.

Whenever a dispute arises with respect to a NAFTA country's rights under the agreement, a consultation can be requested at which all three NAFTA countries can participate. If consultation does not resolve the dispute, the commission will seek to settle the dispute through mediation or similar means of alternative dispute resolution procedures. If those measures are unsuccessful, a complaining country can request that an **arbitration** panel be established. The panel is composed of five members selected from a trilaterally agreed upon list of trade, legal, and other experts. After study, the panel issues a confidential initial report. After receiving comments from the parties, a final report will be prepared and conveyed to the commission. If the panel finds that a NAFTA country violated its NAFTA obligations, the disputing parties have 30 days to reach an agreement. If none is reached, NAFTA benefits may be suspended against the violating country in an amount equivalent to the panel's recommended penalty until the dispute is resolved.

ENVIRONMENTAL PROVISIONS AND SIDE AGREEMENT

NAFTA has more provisions relating to the environment and, at least on paper, is more protective of the environment than any other international agreement or treaty ever before entered into by the United States. Former U.S. **Environmental Protection Agency** (EPA) Administrator William K. Reilly observed that it is ''the most environmentally sensitive . . . free trade agreement ever negotiated anywhere.'' Yet consideration and adoption of NAFTA led to a painful division within the environmental community. A coalition of eight major environmental organizations supported it, yet other major environmental groups opposed its approval.

NAFTA's environmental provisions are complex, lengthy, and yet-to-be interpreted as they are implemented. Questions arise in two directions. First, does NAFTA do enough to safeguard *existing* environmental laws and standards? Second, does NAFTA require or at least promote upward harmonization of the environmental laws of the three NAFTA countries?

ENVIRONMENTAL PROVISIONS IN THE PREAMBLE. The environment and the pursuit of what is called ''**sustainable development**'' are mentioned three times in NAFTA's preamble. Nevertheless, in NAFTA's Statement of Objectives, which is part of the agreement itself, they are not mentioned at all. Thus, sustainable development is a goal of NAFTA, but there are no substantive provisions in NAFTA to require its pursuit or achievement. ''Sustainable development'' is a term used often in environmental discussions today. It refers to measures designed to ensure that the needs of the present are met without compromising the ability of future generations to meet their own needs.

ENVIRONMENTAL PROVISIONS WITHIN NAFTA. In terms of our ability to safeguard the ''status quo'' in environmental regulation in the United States, there are two key articles in NAFTA: Articles 7 and 9. Article 7 covers sanitary and ''phytosanitary'' measures. (''Phytosanitary'' refers to measures related to plant and food safety.) Article 7 reserves to each party (the United States, Mexico, and Canada) the ''right'' to set its ''appropriate level of protection'' for human, animal, or plant life or health. It confirms that a party may adopt a measure more stringent than an ''international standard, guideline or recommendation.'' Further, adoption of these ''more stringent'' measures may be by federal, state, or local governments.

A major concern of U.S. environmental groups is the ability of the United States to maintain its own health and environmental standards. For example, Article 7 says that any trade measure used to achieve a party's level of protection must be ''necessary'' for the protection of human, animal, or plant life. Some environmentalists are concerned that the term ''necessary'' might be interpreted very narrowly, as has been the case recently under interpretation of GATT.

Article 9 of NAFTA gives each party the right to establish the levels of protection that it considers to be appropriate so long as the choice is made based on a ''legitimate'' objective. Environmental measures cannot be used to promote unfair discrimination or to serve as a disguised barrier to trade. NAFTA allows only those trade regulations involving ''product *characteristics* or their *related* processes and production methods.'' Thus, a process standard must be related to the characteristics of a product, and a party can't prohibit trade in products grown or manufactured using ''unsustainable'' methods. Analyzing such provisions of NAFTA, environmentalists fear that specific, individual U.S. environmental laws or regulations might be challenged under NAFTA as being a nontariff barrier to trade without a legitimate objective.

PROVISIONS OF THE ENVIRONMENTAL SIDE AGREEMENT. The North American Agreement on Environmental Cooperation, also known as the ''Environmental Side Agreement,'' was adopted as a part of NAFTA along with two other side agreements, covering labor and import surges.

Part one of the Environmental Side Agreement lists two objectives: (1) to promote environmental concerns without harming the economy, and (2) to open discussion of environmental issues to the public.

Part two outlines the obligations of the three countries. It confirms that each party has the right to set its own standards and states that the governments of each country are responsible for monitoring and enforcing their environmental laws. It also states that private parties can request government intervention and can seek remedies through the courts of their respective countries.

Part three establishes a Commission for Environmental Cooperation (Environmental Commission) that is based in Montreal, Canada. The Environmental Commission consists of a council, a secretariat, and a Joint Public Advisory Committee. The council consists of cabinet-level representatives who will meet at least once a year. Its function is to implement the environmental side agreement. The secretariat provides a support system for the Council.

Nongovernment organizations or private citizens may assert that a country ''has shown a persistent pattern of failure to effectively enforce its environmental laws'' by filing a complaint with the commission. Thus, private citizens can serve as watchdogs for the commission. This is important to U.S. environmental groups because such groups have played an active role in overseeing enforcement of U.S. environmental laws and regulations.

The Joint Public Advisory Committee may advise the council on any relevant matter and may provide relevant technical information. The committee consists of 15 members, 5 of whom are appointed by each of the NAFTA countries.

Pursuant to part four of the Environmental Side Agreement, each party agrees to cooperate and to provide information to the secretariat upon request.

Part five allows a party to request consultation with a second party concerning the party's failure to enforce its environmental laws if such a failure is shown to be part of a persistent pattern. If a mutually satisfactory resolution is not reached within 60 days, a party can request a special session of the council, which must meet within 20 days. If the council is unable to resolve the dispute, it can convene a panel for arbitration of the dispute. The panel will issue an initial report within 180 days, and the parties are allowed to submit comments within 60 days. Next, the panel will submit a final report, which will be made public within 5 days after it is received by the council. The parties are given an opportunity to reach their own settlement based on the report, and if they cannot reach an ''action plan'' within 60 days, the panel can be reconvened to establish one. If the offending country does not follow the plan, a fine can be imposed. If the fine is not paid, NAFTA benefits can be suspended.

Thus, the Environmental Side Agreement allows citizens and their organizations to serve as ''watchdogs'' by bringing complaints to the attention of the Environmental Commission. Nevertheless, citizens do not have standing to take action on their own. A NAFTA party, however, can file a complaint with the council in cases in which another party has shown a persistent pattern of failure to enforce its environmental laws and regulations. Ultimate sanctions against an offending party may include suspension of trade benefits; such sanctions, however, have not been used during the first six years of NAFTA, and it is unlikely that they will be invoked in the near future.

At the time NAFTA and the Environmental Side Agreement were adopted, commentators predicted that suspension of trade benefits would seldom be invoked as a sanction. That prediction ''come true'' over NAFTA's first six years. As of mid-1995 the Environmental Commission had not issued even a draft of its procedures for handling complaints from citizens. As of 1999 it is clear that the Environmental Commission is poorly funded (with a budget of under $10 million for all three countries), its complaints process makes it difficult for private citizens to file and pursue complaints, and it lacks authority to force member countries to participate in many of its activities. For example, in 1998, the Environmental Commission issued a detailed pollution report detailing types and quantities of hazardous substances emitted into the air in the United States and Canada. Mexico, however, was not included in the report, because data on emissions from that country were not available.

The Environmental Commission's accomplishments have been limited to date. Its greatest accomplishment so far has probably been that it has promoted communication about environmental problems among governments, citizens, and environmental groups from the three NAFTA countries.

SIDE AGREEMENT ON LABOR

The North American Agreement on Labor Cooperation, commonly known as the ''Labor Side Agreement,'' was negotiated in response to concerns that NAFTA itself did little or nothing to protect workers in Mexico, the United States, or Canada. U.S. labor groups have maintained their opposition to NAFTA even with the addition of the Labor Side Agreement. Representatives of labor groups assert that the Labor Side Agreement does little to protect workers in the United States, Canada, or Mexico. The structure and provisions of the Labor Side Agreement parallel those of the Environmental Side Agreement. Included are a preamble, objectives of the agreement, and obligations of the parties. There are also provisions for a Commission for Labor Cooperation, dispute resolution mechanisms, and sanctions against a NAFTA country found to be in violation of the agreement's provisions.

The preamble affirms the three parties' desire to create new employment opportunities and to protect, enhance, and enforce basic workers' rights while, at the same time, affirming their respect for each party's constitution and laws.

Part one lists the objectives of the agreement. Its basic goals include the desire to improve labor conditions and encourage compliance with **labor laws**. Another goal is to encourage open sharing of information (transparency) among the three countries regarding their respective labor laws and their enforcement of those laws.

Part two of the Labor Side Agreement discusses the obligations of the parties. Each party is responsible for enforcement of its own labor laws, but the parties agree that proceedings dealing with enforcement of labor laws will be "fair" and tribunals will be "impartial." Labor laws and information about their enforcement are to be made public, and public education will be promoted.

Part three establishes a Commission for Labor Cooperation. It will consist of a council and a secretariat. The council meets at least once a year or upon the request of one of the parties. Its primary tasks are to oversee implementation of the Labor Side Agreement and to promote cooperation among the parties on various labor issues.

The secretariat is headed by an executive director, and that position is rotated among the three countries. The secretariat's tasks are to assist the council, make public the labor policies of each country, and prepare studies requested by the council.

The United States, Mexico, and Canada have each established a National Administrative Office (NAO) led by a secretary. NAOs are responsible for gathering information within their respective countries and conveying it to the secretariat and the other two NAFTA parties. In addition, the Labor Side Agreement allows the NAOs in each country to review each other's labor laws (and enforcement) in response to complaints from workers.

In the event of a dispute related to the Labor Side Agreement, the leader of one of the NAFTA parties may request a meeting with another leader to attempt to resolve the dispute. The allegation cannot be based on a single failure to enforce its own laws. Instead, any complaint must be based on a "persistent pattern of failure by the Party complained against to effectively enforce its occupational safety and health, child labor, or minimum wage technical labor standards." All three NAFTA parties are allowed to participate in such a meeting. If the matter is not resolved by those leaders, a party-country may request that an Evaluation Committee of Experts (ECE) be established. The ECE will study the matter and submit a report to the council. The purpose of this report is to allow a party to obtain information about the practices and enforcement of labor laws by another NAFTA party.

After the ECE's report is presented, the parties will try to resolve any dispute between themselves. If this fails, the council may attempt to assist the parties in resolving the dispute. Finally, if the matter is not resolved, the council may convene an arbitration panel, chosen from a roster of 45 people chosen pursuant to qualifications outlined in the Labor Side Agreement. The panel convenes, receives input from each of the disputing party-countries, and prepares an initial report. After reviewing comments from each of the parties, a final report is prepared. If it is found that a party "persistently failed" to enforce its laws, the disputing parties will prepare an action plan. If the parties do not agree or if the plan is not fully implemented, the panel can be reconvened. If the panel finds that the plan was not implemented, the offending party can be fined. If the fine is not paid, NAFTA trade benefits can be suspended to pay the fine. As of 1999, however, such a sanction has not been ordered.

Thus, the Labor Side Agreement provides a mechanism for dealing with a party-country that shows a "pattern of practice" of failing to enforce its occupational safety and health, **child labor**, or minimum wage technical labor standards. The Labor Commission is supposed to pressure NAFTA countries into enforcing their own labor laws, but it lacks a meaningful method for punishing them. For example, managers at the ITAPSA brake parts factory in the State of Mexico, Mexico, fired assembly-line workers in retaliation for voting for an independent union. The U.S. and Canadian NAOs issued reports recommending that the former workers be restored to their jobs, but, according to Robert Donnelly, that has not happened.

As we enter the 21st century, organized labor in the United States continues to oppose NAFTA; labor representatives view the Labor Side Agreement as an ineffective mechanism that is unenforceable. The most significant achievement of the Labor Side Agreement to date is similar to that of the Environmental Side Agreement: complaints before the Labor

Commission and the NAOs of the three countries have attracted media attention. And that media attention, in turn, may be compelling countries to enforce their own labor laws to a greater extent than might otherwise occur.

TRADE AND ECONOMIC CONSEQUENCES

NAFTA is facilitating an unprecedented level of economic integration in North America. It is creating opportunities for investment and growth by private business, and it is promoting more stable relations between and among the United States, Mexico, and Canada. Nevertheless, NAFTA is not welcomed by all people in the three countries. Overall, NAFTA is neither a complete success nor a complete failure. Its benefits vary for each of the three countries.

The effects of NAFTA on trade between the United States and Canada have not been as dramatic. The **U.S.-Canada Free Trade Agreement** was enacted in 1989, and tariffs between the United States and Canada were completely eliminated (with a few minor exceptions) as of 1998. Therefore, under NAFTA, trade observers have focused on effects on Mexico.

Mexico has benefited from NAFTA in substantial ways including, but not limited to, the following: First, as of 1998 Mexico passed Japan to become the second-largest trading partner of the United States. Second, exports from *maquiladoras* (in Mexico) to the United States are up about 135 percent comparing 1994 to 1999. (The *maquiladora* program was established pursuant to an agreement between the United States and Mexico. The agreement allows U.S. businesses to operate manufacturing facilities in northern Mexico, with restrictions, including the condition that all products produced be returned to the United States.) Third, direct foreign investment in Mexico has grown tremendously. It was at about $4 billion before NAFTA and reached over $10 billion in 1998. Fourth, Mexico is beginning to enjoy a more diversified economy. Before NAFTA, oil production was its primary source of revenue; now the manufacturing sector is becoming its primary source.

NAFTA's effect on the United States has not been as dramatic. In 1993, in his book *Save Your Job, Save Our Country,* former U.S. presidential candidate and businessperson H. Ross Perot (1930-) warned workers of a ''giant sucking sound'' that would be the flow of American jobs to Mexico. In reality, NAFTA's effect on jobs in the United States has varied. The jobs that have been most vulnerable are those that require unskilled labor and those that were, in the past, protected by high U.S. tariffs. Such industries include the clothing industry, glassware, and manufacture of ceramic tiles. The American Textile Manufacturers Association strongly opposed and continues to oppose NAFTA because lower labor costs in Mexico make it hard for U.S.-manufactured clothing to compete with low-priced garments made in Mexico. On the other hand, it is reported that NAFTA led to the creation of 100,000 jobs in the United States during the first half of 1994, and that as of January 1995 there were at least 700,000 U.S. jobs that depended on exports to Mexico. Trade officials say that 2.6 million U.S. jobs were supported by exports to Mexico and Canada in 1998.

Economic consequences of NAFTA for Mexico are more significant than those for the United States because Mexico has a much smaller economy. As of 1993, the $6 trillion American economy was 20 times the size of Mexico's. As of 1998, U.S.-Mexico trade totaled $173.3 billion in a U.S. economy with a GDP of $8.5 trillion. In contrast, Mexico had a GDP of about $381 billion in 1998.

FACTORS AFFECTING CONTINUING DEVELOPMENT OF TRADE WITH AND WITHIN MEXICO

NAFTA does not represent a blessing for Mexico's unskilled workers and their families. Workers are obtaining employment at low wages in new manufacturing facilities. Their wages, however, are not sufficient to enable them to purchase decent housing, clothing, and good food for their families. Due to a lack of potable water, inadequate sewage facilities, inadequate or unavailable electricity, and other inadequate or unavailable services in the areas around new industrial facilities, life for workers and their families is often a miserable existence. Diseases and illness due to a lack of sanitary facilities and due to industrial pollution are prevalent and are increasing.

There have been scandals within Mexico's government. On March 23, 1994, Luis Donaldo Colosio, the leading candidate for election to Mexico's presidency, was assassinated during a political rally. In August 1994, Ernesto Zedillo was elected to the presidency. His election was reassuring to investors who were awaiting the results of the election, because he advocated economic and political policies similar to those of former President Carlos Salinas, who led Mexico in approving NAFTA. During 1995, however, there were additional scandals within Mexico's government. The brother of former President Salinas was arrested in March 1995 and convicted in 1998 of planning the murder of José Francisco Ruíz, who had been governor of the Mexican state of Guerrero from 1987 to 1993. In the aftermath of his brother's arrest, and accusations Salinas himself embezzled millions of dollars, he left Mexico and went into exile in Europe.

In addition, on January 1, 1994, the effective date of NAFTA, there was an uprising in Chiapas, Mexico, led by Zapatista rebels. (The rebels take their name from the early 20th-century Mexican revolutionary leader Emiliano Zapata [1879-1919].) After the initial fighting, which resulted in at least 145 deaths, the rebellion has continued to simmer, with occasional armed conflicts, for over six years. The Zapatistas are protesting political injustices, extreme poverty, and ethnic oppression of the indigenous people of Chiapas. They are also protesting NAFTA and the environmental degradation resulting from increased industrialization of Mexico.

Foreign investments in Mexico have been stemmed by Mexico's financial crisis of 1995-96 and its continuing financial problems since then. In November 1994, the Mexican peso was trading for slightly over three pesos per U.S. dollar. But the exchange rate had dropped to a low of 7.7 pesos per dollar as of March 9, 1995. Further, **inflation** in Mexico reached an annualized rate of 64 percent as of February 1995. In March 1995, the United States extended $20 million in **loans** and loan guarantees to Mexico. In return, Mexico instituted an economic plan that included sweeping budget cuts, increased taxes, and approved provisions allowing the United States to oversee Mexico's handling of its economy. The loans have been repaid, but the agreement caused Mexican citizens accuse President Zedillo of "trading his nation's sovereignty" for American dollars.

Meanwhile, Mexico's response to the **debt** crisis included creation of an official **bank** bailout program called Bank Fund for Savings Protection (*Fondo Bancario para Proteccin de Ahorro*—also known as *Profoba* or *Fobaproa*). But, according to Angelo Young, the program has been plagued by scandal and allegations of illegal practices. In early 1999, the Mexican Congress passed a set of reforms to replace *Profoba* with a new Bank Savings Protection Institute (IPAB) that is modeled after the **Federal Deposit Insurance Corporation** in the United States. IPAB is charged with administering a debt-relief package that will discount amounts owed on loans from 16 percent to 60 percent, depending on the type of loan. It is expected that business, agricultural, and small domestic debtors will benefit from the plan.

ENVIRONMENTAL CONSEQUENCES

Environmentalists, business representatives, and the governments of the three NAFTA countries agree that environmental contamination has reached serious proportions in northern Mexico, where U.S. businesses have been operating for nearly three decades under the *maquiladora* program and where industrial development has continued to grow under NAFTA.

The hazardous waste treatment industry was expected to be a major area for U.S. investors under NAFTA. The United States could offer experience and expertise that Mexicans lacked. Sadly, however, "five years into NAFTA, Mexico's hazardous waste industry is in total disarray," as reported by Sam Quínones. Of seven major waste-treatment projects in which tens of millions have been invested, all are "stalled." "As it stands, Mexico has less landfill infrastructure than it had before NAFTA," Quínones related.

A few observers are guardedly optimistic that, in the long term, NAFTA may result in better environmental conditions in Mexico and in the U.S.-Mexican border area. Such optimism rests on the belief that the success of NAFTA itself will help the environment. If jobs are created in Mexico, and wages increase, and Mexico's economy improves, there should be more money available for what is needed environmentally. Money is needed for personnel to enforce Mexico's environmental laws; money is needed for **infrastructure**, including waste disposal facilities, water treatment and sewage facilities; and technology and equipment are needed to create safer working conditions inside and outside the walls of industrial facilities.

LOOKING AHEAD

What happened during the first six years of NAFTA? The effects of NAFTA on trade between Canada and the United States were visible but not unexpected, because the United States and Canada already had a **free trade** agreement that eliminated nearly all tariffs as of 1998. Meanwhile, Mexico has seen significant increases in trade with the United States and Canada since 1994.

On the other hand, NAFTA has not been a success for labor interests and the environment. The Labor Commission created under the Labor Side Agreement has had little success in improving the status of workers. And the Environmental Commission has had similar limited results. Further, the environmental contamination in Mexico is escalating.

Meanwhile, NAFTA is being watched closely by observers throughout the world, because it is being used as a model for other agreements. For example, in December 1994, the United States and 33 other Western Hemisphere countries met in Miami, Florida, for a "Summit of the Americas." At the summit, the 34 countries agreed to create a Free Trade Area of the Americas (FTAA) by the year 2005. The FTAA will be modeled after NAFTA. As an immediate step, at the close of the 1994 Summit of the Americas, the United States, Canada, and Mexico announced their plans to admit Chile to NAFTA by 1996, but that did not happen for a variety of political and economic reasons.

Therefore, NAFTA's provisions and its implementation will continue to be watched closely. NAFTA must be monitored to determine whether its provisions need modification and to determine whether its provisions provide a suitable model for additional trade agreements, such as the FTAA.

[Paulette L. Stenzel]

FURTHER READING:

Alexander, Dean C. "The North American Free Trade Agreement: An Overview." *International Tax and Business Lawyer II,* 1993, 48-71.

Case, Brenda M. "Two Speed Industry: The Automobile and Auto Parts Businesses Are Booming, but Only for Some." *US/Mexico Business,* November 1998, 48-49.

Davis, Bob. "Some Questions and Answers Concerning NAFTA." *Wall Street Journal,* 19 November 1993, 14.

Donnelly, Robert. "On the Side: Nafta's Side Accords on Labor and the Environment Struggle to Have an Influence." *MB,* April 1999, 28-34.

Guillermoprieto, Alma. "Zapata's Heirs." *New Yorker,* 16 May 1994, 52-63.

Hofgard, Kurt C. "Is This Land Really Our Land?: Impacts of Free Trade Agreements on U.S. Environmental Protection." *Environmental Law* 23, 634-81.

Jamar, Christen, and Angelo Young. "Nafta at Five." *MB,* April 1999, 26-34.

North American Free Trade Agreement (NAFTA). Washington: GPO, 1993.

Oppenheimer, Andres. *Bordering on Chaos: Mexico's Guerrillas, Stockbrokers, Politicians, and Road to Prosperity.* Boston: Little, Brown, 1996.

Quínones, Sam. "Mexico's Wastelands." *MB,* April 1999, 38-46.

Torres, Craig. "How Mexico's Behind-the-Scenes Tactics and a Secret Pact Averted Market Panic." *Wall Street Journal,* 28 March 1994, A10.

Young, Angelo. "Settling the Bill: The Nightmarish Specter of Debt Left from the Crash is Finally Confronted." *MB,* March 1999, 14-17.

NORTH AMERICAN INDUSTRY CLASSIFICATION SYSTEM (NAICS)

Introduced in 1997, the North American Industry Classification System (NAICS) is a collaboration between the governments of Canada, Mexico, and the United States stemming mostly from the **North American Free Trade Agreement (NAFTA)**. Its purpose is to categorize narrowly defined economic activities, or industries, in a consistent manner among the three trading partners, although the system does leave room for fine level customization within each country. NAICS is a replacement for the United States' 1987 **Standard Industrial Classification (SIC)** system, which is gradually being phased out in most new federal statistical studies and publications. In Canada, it replaces the 1980 SIC, and in Mexico NAICS replaces the 1994 Mexican Classification of Activities and Products. The NAICS is broadly compatible with the United Nations' International Standard Industrial Classification (ISIC) of 1989, although it differs greatly in the specifics.

The underlying philosophy behind NAICS is a production-oriented model of the economy, which groups activities by how similar their goods- or service-producing processes are. This is distinguished from a product orientation, which groups activities by the similarity of the output. The SIC system followed a hybrid approach, with some industries defined more by process and others defined by product. Neither the SIC nor the NAICS are intended to be product classification systems. Other systems like the Standard International Trade Classification and the Harmonized System, both international standards used for trade classification, exist for this purpose. However, a NAICS-related effort known as the North American Product Classification System (NAPCS) was initiated in 1999. Scheduled to be released in 2002, NAPCS would include both products and services, unlike most of the older merchandise-based classification schemes.

MAJOR CHANGES UNDER NAICS

In addition to aligning the three countries' classification schemes, NAICS also portrays the structure and specificity of economic activity differently from its predecessors. In the U.S. version, for instance, NAICS identifies 358 new industries that weren't considered separate industries in the SIC—a few weren't even mentioned. Examples of newly recognized industries include fiber-optic cable manufacturing (NAICS 335921), warehouse clubs and superstores (NAICS 45291), fast-food restaurants (NAICS 722211), credit card issuing (NAICS 52221), and marketing consulting services (NAICS 541613).

There are differences in the broader structure as well. Special emphasis is placed on service industries, which were often neglected under the manufacturing-dominated SIC. Indeed, well over half of the new industries fall under service headings, as do eight of the top-level sectors (or nine including information-related industries). Under the SIC there was only one broad service sector encompassing all service industry groups and industries. NAICS likewise revises how retail and wholesale businesses are distinguished so that any business that advertises to the general public is considered a retailer, regardless of whether its primary customers are businesses or private individuals. Finally, NAICS also recognizes entirely new sectors of the economy, notably information industries, which were formerly divided among the manufacturing, communications, and service sectors.

NAICS STRUCTURE

NAICS is a hierarchical numerical coding system that begins with broad economic sectors at the top and winnows them down to narrow industries at the bottom (see Figure 1 for an example). In between there are either two or three intermediate levels. Each level is associated with a numerical code and a title. Sectors, such as manufacturing, agriculture, and construction, are designated by the first two digits in the code. Table 1 contains a listing of all 20 NAICS sectors and their codes.

Table 1
Economic Sectors under NAICS

Code	Title
11	Agriculture, Forestry, Fishing, and Hunting
21	Mining
22	Utilities
23	Construction
31-33	Manufacturing
41-43	Wholesale Trade
44-46	Retail Trade
48-49	Transportation and Warehousing
51	Information
52	Finance and Insurance
53	Real Estate and Rental and Leasing
54	Professional, Scientific, and Technical Services
55	Management of Companies and Enterprises
56	Administrative and Support and Waste Management and Remediation Services
61	Educational Services
62	Health Care and Social Assistance
71	Arts, Entertainment, and Recreation
72	Accommodation and Food Services
81	Other Services (Except Public Administration)
91-93	Public Administration

The next level down is the subsector, which indicates major groupings within the sector. For example, in the Real Estate and Rental and Leasing sector (53), the NAICS subsectors are Real Estate (531), Rental and Leasing Services (532), and Lessors of Other Nonfinancial Intangible Assets (533). The number of subsectors varies with the diversity of activities categorized under the whole sector. Altogether there are 96 subsectors.

The third level from the top is the industry group level, represented by four digits. In some cases, NAICS industry groups correspond to industry definitions used by trade associations or in common language, e.g., Household Appliance Manufacturing (3352) and Clothing Stores (4481). NAICS recognizes 311 such industry groups.

The five-digit level represents the most narrow definition of an industry that the three North American nations agree on (although there are some exceptions when only subsectors or industry groups are mutually recognized). There are 721 five-digit industries in total. Some of these serve as the final industry definition used by each country, but in other cases a sixth digit is added for country-specific detail. An example is Small Electrical Appliance Manufacturing (33521). This is the definition accepted by all three countries; however, to it the United States adds at the six-digit level Electric Housewares and Fan Manufacturing (335211) and Household Vacuum Cleaner Manufacturing (335212). Hence, once you reach the six-digit level, it's important to know which version of the system you're using, e.g., U.S. version, Mexican version, because they may differ in the sixth digit. In the U.S. version, there are 659 six-digit NAICS industries, for a total of 1170 five- and six-digit industries at their most detailed level.

Figure 1
The NAICS Hierarchy

Sector →	51	Information
Subsector →	514	Information Services and Data Processing Services
Industry Group →	5141	Information Services
North American Industry →	51419	Other Information Services
Country-Specific Industry →	514191	On-line Information Services

For economic activities that are fairly discrete and homogeneous, such as running a gas station, the subsector, industry group, and even industry may be very similar. Gas stations, which fall under the retail sector, are in the Gasoline Stations (447) subsector, the Gasoline Stations (4471) industry group, and are divided at the five-digit level between Gasoline Stations with Convenience Stores (44711) and Other Gasoline Stations (44712). In this case there is no six-digit defined.

DETERMINING A COMPANY'S NAICS CODE

The method for determining an organization's code is essentially the same in NAICS as in any other classification scheme. Officially, the unit of analysis is by the ''establishment,'' a term used to describe the smallest separate permanent unit of a company's activities, usually a single physical location. The alternative would be an enterprise-based classification. The establishment basis means that large corporations typically have several, and potentially dozens, of NAICS codes enterprise wide. When a single location performs activities covered under more than one NAICS category, the primary NAICS is assigned based on which activity consumes the most capital (if it can be determined) or generates the most revenue (more commonly used). In other words, industry assignment is based on the location's most important business activity in terms of value.

Since NAICS codes are assigned by the location, large corporation headquarters represent a special case. Intuitively, a person might identify General Motors Corp.'s primary industry as NAICS 336111, Automobile Manufacturing, but technically the headquarters should be classified under NAICS 551114, Corporate, Subsidiary, and Regional Managing Offices. While such distinctions mainly exist to satisfy the rigors of conducting economic censuses, in common usage, and hence in some non-government publications, the headquarters code is ignored and industry codes are assigned based on the activities that contribute the most revenue enterprise-wide. Thus, while NAICS is intended as an establishment-based system for government purposes, it also serves as an enterprise-based system for general purposes.

THE FIVE/SIX DIGIT DILEMMA

The use of both five and six digits as the most specific level can create problems for understanding and storing data under NAICS. If the industry code is only expressed as five digits in a publication or database, a reader can't be sure at a glance whether it's at the most detailed level or not. Instead, he or she would either need to know the source's policy on industry codes (for example, whether they only use the five digit form when it's the most specific) or would need to refer to a master list of NAICS codes to see whether there's anything more specific.

In some database environments, it may also complicate things to store both five- and six-digit codes. For instance, it may wreak havoc on relational databases in which the code references the full industry title in a master table. Or, if a report from a database is to be sorted by NAICS, all the five-digit codes may sort first rather than where they fall in the hierarchy (this problem could be easily fixed with programming intervention).

One solution to storage and presentation problems is the practice of adding a zero to the end of five-digit codes to signify that the five digit level is the most specific. This was a common practice under the U.S. SIC for showing higher level categories, and it solves the storage/sorting problem. But this can create data interpretation troubles, to wit: in the U.S. version of NAICS, there appear to be at least two instances when zero is used as part of a six-digit code, apparently when the digits 1 through 9 were used up. Either way, the zero still represents the most detailed level, and for many users this discrepancy will not be concern; however, when the sixth digit is a zero there is no immediate way to distinguish categories that are accepted in all three countries from those accepted only in one.

Under the SIC, zeros were used mainly to signify that data had been aggregated to a higher level than the lowest. For example, SIC 2810 designated all inorganic chemical manufacturers, encompassing chlor-alkali producers (2812), industrial gas producers (2813), and so on. However, using NAICS, the zero in the final position is more ambiguous: does it mean that five digits is the lowest level or that the six-digit data have been aggregated to a higher level? It's back to the same interpretation problem as when no zeros are added.

Official U.S. government publications have equivocated on the subject. Some NAICS documentation suggests that a zero in the sixth position ''generally'' means there is no U.S. sixth digit defined, but in various tables the official documentation presents five-digit NAICS both ways—with and without trailing zeros—in different sections.

Despite these concerns, for most general-purpose uses of NAICS it's probably safest and easiest to use the trailing zero on five-digit codes to avoid other potential problems. This will have minimal impact on most kinds of research. Data providers will need to put forth extra effort in their documentation to inform users exactly how NAICS codes are being cited.

CROSS-BORDER COMPARABILITY

Although in general terms NAICS categories are intended to be comparable down to the five-digit level, there is a surprisingly long list of exceptions. These are areas where the three countries could not agree on a descriptive framework for the narrower areas of economic activity. For instance, in construction-related activities, the three national systems agree only at the two-digit sector level, diverging at the three-digit subsector level; the same is true in retailing, wholesaling, and public administration. Meanwhile, in finance activities, the systems diverge at the four-digit industry group level, as is the case with personal services, nonprofit organizations, and waste management services. Finally, in insurance and real estate activities, the systems agree down to the four-digit level and then differ at the five-digit level.

PHASE-IN AND FUTURE REVISIONS

Use of NAICS is already underway in a number of government and nongovernment statistical publications. Most notably, the 1997 Economic Census, which was conducted during 1998 and is gradually being released, used NAICS to classify all businesses. Publications based on the census also provide limited SIC backward-compatibility. Other government reports, such as annual industry surveys and employment data, have also been converted to NAICS, but the overall transition was expected to last until at least 2004.

Similar to the SIC before it, NAICS is scheduled to be revised at five-year intervals, with the first update slated for 2002.

SEE ALSO: Standard Industrial Classification System (SIC)

[Scott Heil]

FURTHER READING:

Ambler, Carole A. ''NAICS: The 'S' Doesn't Stand for Services (But It Could).'' *Business America,* April 1998.

Office of Management and Budget. *North American Industry Classification System (NAICS)—United States, 1997.* Washington: NTIS, 1998.

U.S. Census Bureau. *North American Industry Classification System.* Washington, 1999. Available from www.census.gov/epcd/www/naics.html.

NORTH ATLANTIC TREATY ORGANIZATION (NATO)

The North Atlantic Treaty Organization (NATO) was established April 4, 1949, in Washington, D.C., with the signing of the North Atlantic Treaty by Belgium, Canada, Denmark, France, Iceland, Italy, Luxembourg, the Netherlands, Norway, Portugal, the United Kingdom, and the United States. The original stated purpose of NATO as put forth in the treaty's preamble was to ''safeguard the freedom, common heritage, and civilization of their peoples, founded on the principles of democracy . . . promote stability and well-being in the North Atlantic area,'' and ''unite their efforts for collective defense and for the preservation of peace and security.'' In fact NATO was created as a defensive political and military association. Its purpose was to protect the democracy, peace, and security of its members from the Soviet Union and its allies who were then joined together in the Warsaw Pact, NATO's Eastern nemesis.

The end of World War II found the nations of Western Europe—with the exception of Sweden, Switzerland, Spain, and Portugal—in a state of economic, political, and social turmoil. This turmoil was heightened by internal and external threats of communism. These threats emanated in large part from the expansionist-minded Soviet Union which by virtue of its military forces had annexed the Baltic states of Estonia, Latvia, and Lithuania and incorporated the nations of Eastern and Central Europe into the Soviet bloc. Numerous Cold War incidents and events including the founding of the Communist Information Bureau (Cominform) in 1947, the 1948 communist coup in Czechoslovakia, and the 1948 Berlin crisis and airlift fueled further fear of the Soviet Union. The invasion of South Korea by North Korea and the subsequent intervention by the People's Republic of China in the early 1950s also raised fears in the West of Soviet imperialism. Although taking place outside the European theater, events in Asia led many Western political strategists to believe that the Soviets were directing these and other events so as to test the resolve of the West on a global scale. In 1952 Turkey and Greece joined NATO and in 1955 the Federal Republic of Germany (West Germany) joined after earlier rejections. NATO was thus created for the eventuality of fighting a major war against the Soviet Union and its allies. The war as envisioned would be conventional in the sense that formidable air, land, and naval forces would do battle across the breadth of the European continent and its ocean boundaries. If such a war were to come about it would definitely not be a brushfire, or a hit-and-run guerrilla war.

Throughout its history the forces of nationalism often played havoc with NATO unity. In 1966 and 1967 France under President Charles de Gaulle (1890-1970) distanced itself from its NATO allies by demanding the withdrawal of NATO forces not under direct French command from home soil. In 1996, however, France again became, from a military standpoint, selectively involved in NATO. In 1976 Iceland nearly withdrew its NATO membership in a fishing-rights dispute with Great Britain, and throughout much of the 1970s Greece and Turkey were bitterly divided over ethnic tensions on the island nation of Cyprus. Greece's problems with NATO were exacerbated in 1981 when a socialist government acceded to power in that country. The Soviet threat and the cajoling of the United States, however, overcame the divisive nationalist tendencies of NATO members and the organization remained largely intact.

For an organization founded for such an overt military purpose NATO has a unique dual military and civilian administration. The highest administrative organ of NATO is the North Atlantic Council, which is made up of representatives of member countries and has final decision-making authority. The council is chaired by NATO's secretary-general. The Defense Planning Committee is responsible for providing guidance to NATO's military arm. All members countries except France are represented on the committee. The Military Committee is made up of the chiefs-of-staff, or their representatives, from member countries and is the supreme military authority in NATO answerable only to the council. It directs Allied Command Europe and Allied Command Atlantic.

By the early 1990s NATO had nearly 4.3 million personnel under arms. They were generally considered to be well trained, well equipped, and of high morale. With the implosion of the Soviet Union beginning in 1989 and the disbanding of the Warsaw Pact in 1991, however, many questions arose and still continue to confront NATO: Who is NATO now to defend western Europe against?; What will be the role of NATO in the "new" Europe?; Should NATO extend membership to former communist bloc countries and the constituent republics of the former Soviet Union? Ironically, by 1994 Estonia, Latvia, Lithuania, Poland, Bulgaria, Hungary, and the Czech and Slovak Republics began clamoring for NATO membership.

NATO claims that with the end of the Cold War it has been "restructured to enable it to participate in the development of cooperative security structures for the whole of Europe," and that it has "transformed its political and military structures in order to adapt them to peacekeeping and crisis management tasks in cooperation with countries which are not members of the Alliance and with other international organizations." U.S. Secretary of State Madeleine Albright in 1998 told the North Atlantic Council Ministerial that NATO's "primary mission must remain collective defense against aggression," and that it must continue to adapt to the realities of Europe in the post-Cold War era. She went on to say that NATO must reach out to the emerging democracies and that a new "strategic concept" will include such activities as military intervention in Bosnia in defense of common interests. She supported President Bill Clinton's belief that NATO must guard against the spread of weapons of mass destruction, ethnic violence, and regional conflict. NATO's future role in Europe is thus envisioned as not to fight a major war but rather to serve in various peacekeeping roles and when necessary to militarily intervene in areas torn by ethnic hostilities and fighting—such as Bosnia and possibly Kosovo in Central Europe. It has even been suggested that NATO be responsible for the economic security of Europe. If for instance should future events in the Middle East threaten Europe's oil supply, then NATO might militarily intervene "out of area."

Many Europeans, however, feel that the United States is attempting to turn NATO into a global policeman assigned to patrol and protect American interests. Part of the American strategy in implementing this new role for NATO is seen as trying to scare Europe with the threat of expanded terrorism. A European diplomat voiced this concern to the *New York Times* in anticipation of NATO's April 1999 50th-anniversary summit meeting in Washington, stating: "But we worry that America may be creating a new 'threat perception' that will scare our populations with visions of anthrax and gangrene, while allowing NATO to become a global organization."

Albright, Clinton, and the U.S. Senate all agree that NATO membership should be expanded to include those European countries that can demonstrate the political, economic, and military readiness to contribute to the collective security of Europe. This is made in reference to the former communist but now emerging democracies of Central and Eastern Europe and the constituent republics of the former Soviet Union, such as the Ukraine. There are many critics to this policy who claim that these countries need not be rewarded for becoming democratic as democracy is its own reward; that the needs of these countries are much better served by their joining the **European Union**; that to bring these countries up to NATO's military standards would ultimately cost the United States between $30 and $100 billion; and finally that to completely encircle the western portion of Russia with NATO countries (especially the Baltic States) would create a diplomatic nightmare and further fuel Russian geopolitical paranoia. Poland, Hungary, and the Czech Republic, however, are expected to join NATO in 1999.

[Michael Knes]

FURTHER READING:

Albright, Madeleine. "The NATO Summit: Defining Purpose and Direction for the 21st Century." *Dispatch* (U.S. Department of State), June 1998, 7-10.

Coffey, Joseph I. *The Future Role of NATO*. New York: Foreign Policy Association, 1997.

Cohen, Roger. "Policy Battle within NATO as U.S. Talks of Wider Scope." *New York Times,* 28 November 1998, A4.

Gordon, Philip H., ed. *NATO's Transformation: The Changing Shape of the Atlantic Alliance*. Lanham, MD: Rowman & Littlefield, 1997.

Mandelbaum, Michael. "The Wrong Idea at the Wrong Time? The Case against NATO Expansion." *Current History,* March 1998, 132-36.

North Atlantic Treaty Organization. "NATO: North Atlantic Treaty Organization." Brussels: North Atlantic Treaty Organization, 1998. Available from www.nato.int.

NTIS

SEE: National Technical Information Service

NTSB

SEE: National Transportation Safety Board

O

OAS

SEE: Organization of American States

OAU

SEE: Organization of African Unity

OCC

SEE: Options Clearing Corporation

OCCUPATIONAL LICENSING AND CERTIFICATION

SEE: Licensing and Certification, Occupational

OCCUPATIONAL MOBILITY AND RETRAINING

The extent of occupational mobility is indicated by the number of workers who change occupations over a given period of time. Occupational mobility can be upward or downward, depending on whether a worker moves to a higher paying, higher status occupation, or vice versa. Since the early 1970s, the growth of higher paying, higher status occupations has slowed in the United States. This includes industrial occupations as well as (more recently) professional positions and occupations in military related industries. Combined with a trend towards downsizing and the increased use of temporary workers, these changes greatly magnify the problem of retraining displaced workers. Worker retraining in the United States is in large part administered under federal government legislation, most recently by the Comprehensive Employment and Training Act of 1973 and the Job Training Partnership Act of 1982.

Occupational mobility is one of the means by which American workers have been able to improve their economic and social circumstances in the post-World War II years. Occupational mobility can be broken down into two types: mobility resulting from overall shifts in the occupational structure, such as from a growing proportion of white-collar occupations; and mobility resulting from workers changing occupations independently of shifts in the occupational structure. The former is referred to as *structural mobility* and the latter as *circulation mobility.*

Until the economic slowdown in the U.S. economy after the early 1970s, there was a tendency towards upward occupational mobility for male workers. While a number of social and cultural changes, particularly beginning in the 1960s, contributed to a broadening of mobility opportunities for historically underrepresented segments of the population, such as women and ethnic minorities, it was, according to some historians, primarily a more favorable occupational structure that maintained the positive mobility opportunities for men. With the slowdown in the economy, the rate of structural mobility also slowed, and with it the tendency towards upward mobility.

Through the second half of the 1990s, U.S. unemployment and inflation remained low while the economy expanded, productivity increased, and profits skyrocketed. Wages, however, had barely kept pace with the cost of living—real wages in 1999, in fact, were slightly below their 1979 level. Meanwhile, temporary jobs had come to represent six percent of available occupations, and were increasing. The smashing of labor unions in the 1980s, overtly supported by the Reagan and Bush administrations, as well as increasing globalization and free trade agreements, helped breed what Federal Reserve Chairman Alan Greenspan praised as a central factor in the economic boom of the mid- and late 1990s; namely, the "restraint on compensation increases . . . mainly the consequence of greater worker insecurity."

As a result of this and other factors, job tenure in the United States is the shortest of all industrialized nations. Between 1991 and 1996, the time average male aged 25 to 64 worked at a single occupation decreased 19 percent. Women's job tenures remained fairly stable since the early 1980s, though in large part this was due to the relatively embryonic stage of workplace infiltration by women in the early 1980s compared to the late 1990s. The tendency toward downsizing, outsourcing, and temporary workers, despite the much-heralded economic boom, was a major factor in this trend, which shows no sign of mitigation.

On the other hand, no small amount of this mobility was, in fact, voluntary. Higher-skilled workers found that shopping their skills around tended to offer greater opportunities for financial improvement than did a long-term relationship with a single company. In accordance with downsizing trends, moreover, companies increasingly demanded workers with a variety of skills; thus, a variety of jobs in a relatively short period of time was not necessarily an unfavorable resume characteristic, as it had been in earlier days.

Despite tremendous gains by minorities and women between the 1960s and 1990s, most studies find persistent institutional biases and obstacles to upward mobility for these groups. While women's penetration of the workforce and educational investment have grown tremendously, the gender wage gap remains stubborn, though it has narrowed incrementally. A number of studies on advancement among African American workers, moreover, have detected severe racial disparities in mobility in the upper-tier occupations. White management hierarchies continue to dominate and set the decision making frameworks, in which African American managers are typically placed onto racially delineated and relatively disenfranchised mobility tracks. Such patterns, while allowing for some financial gains for African Americans, nonetheless install a barrier on the degree of job autonomy, creative freedom, and substantive decision-making capacity and authority they may expect to enjoy. In addition, African Americans tend to generate lower returns on their investments of education and work experience compared to their white counterparts.

Analysts attribute these findings to institutional and social factors. For example, corporate executives and managers tend to enact decisions regarding recruitment and promotion that exclude minorities from advancing to prestigious positions. Qualification for such positions is generally based on such ambiguously determined attributes such as character, judgment, leadership potential, and perceived loyalty. The subjectivity with which such characteristics are judged results in the comparative disadvantage for minorities. To a significant extent, this is born of the fact that, due to historical and pervasive necessity, minorities, and African Americans in particular, rely on racially segregated job networks, thereby severely limiting the sort of interaction with whites in which they could demonstrate these vaguely defined attributes.

The U.S. Bureau of Labor Statistics determined that occupational growth rates would increase at only half the annual average rate from 1986 to 2000 as they had from 1972 to 1986. Higher paid and higher status occupations, such as those in the executive, administrative, and managerial category, were found to grow particularly slowly. Occupations in this category grew 74 percent between 1972 and 1986 but were projected to grow by only 29 percent from 1986 to 2000. In contrast, lower paid and lower status service occupations grew 46 percent between 1972 and 1986 and were projected to grow 33 percent from 1986 to 2000.

Whereas one-half of men were upwardly mobile in 1962, only about one third were in 1999. This decline was attributed to the slower rate of growth for higher status occupations. The projected decline in upward mobility was a continuation of existing patterns through the 1980s. That is, between 1962 and 1989, the rate of upward occupational mobility declined by 7 percent for men. Almost all of this decline occurred after the period of slower economic growth beginning in the early 1970s. Structural mobility for men decreased from 35 percent in the early 1970s to 23 percent in the late 1980s, a reflection of the less-rapid change in the overall occupational structure of the U.S. economy. For women, structural mobility decreased from 51 percent to 43 percent from the early 1970s to the late 1980s. That is, women's rate of structural mobility was higher than men's and decreased at less than one-half the rate of men, indicating that women were less affected by the less-rapid changes in the occupational structure than were men. Circulation mobility for men increased from 30 percent to 41 percent over these same years. Circulation mobility for women also increased, although at a more rapid rate, from 21 to 31 percent.

While men's occupational mobility was higher then women's in the mid-1960s, the pattern was reversed by the early 1990s. Furthermore, the occupational mobility rate declined as workers got older, regardless of sex or time period. This was consistent with the view that older workers had more to lose by changing their occupations, especially in seniority, pay, and pensions, among other factors.

RETRAINING

Retraining is generally associated with displaced workers, those who permanently lose their jobs as a result of structural transformations and regional shifts in the economy. The 1,150 community colleges in the United States were the largest providers of workforce retraining in 1998. Many of these received corporate financing for retraining purposes. Community colleges were generally 10 to 20 percent less expensive than firms offering professional training. Community colleges often provide basic retraining of adult workers to accommodate the estimated 40 million American adults who experience some level of illiteracy.

The overwhelming majority of public and private education in the United States is geared toward children and young adults. The private sector spends about $40 billion each year on education and training. The Twentieth Century Fund Task Force, however, speculated that four times that amount would need to be spent in order for U.S. companies to genuinely maintain the level of training consistent with their emphasis on high-skilled competitiveness, resulting in a ''training gap'' of $120 billion. Less than one percent of U.S. firms spend roughly 90 percent of all training dollars, most of which is geared toward sharpening the skills of executives and high-level technicians.

Since 1982, the primary retraining programs in the United States have been administered under the Job Training Partnership Act (JTPA). JTPA programs are part of the overall government system of aiding unemployed workers. Prior to JTPA, retraining programs were largely run by community organizations, but, consistent with the views of the Reagan administration, private industry came to play a greater role under JTPA. JTPA programs are administered by Private Industry Councils; more than one-half of the council representatives are from private industry, while the remainder are divided among state and local government officials, unions, and community groups.

Unlike earlier government-sponsored training programs, such as those administered under the Manpower Development and Training Act of 1962 (MDTA) and the Comprehensive Employment and Training Act of 1973 (CETA), JTPA programs are performance based. That is, job trainers are funded not on the basis of how well they train workers, but on whether those workers receive employment. In spite of these changes, the overall effectiveness of JTPA programs has been similar to CETA programs.

A number of JTPA retraining programs are designed to assist displaced industrial workers, a group that has been particularly hard hit as a result of the declining growth of industrial occupations. One of these programs was developed in 1983 to assist displaced miners in the Minnesota Iron Range. Training was provided by community organizations, local government agencies, regional vocational schools, and community colleges. Regional firms also provided short-term training in data processing, truck driving, and welding. The program also provided job-search help. For those participating in the program between October of 1983 and June of 1984, 62 percent were able to find new jobs, although one-half of these jobs were outside of the seven-county region in which the miners lived. Among the many similar programs administered under JTPA is one developed at the Cummins Engine Company in Columbus, Ohio, and the Metropolitan Pontiac Retraining and Employment Program in Pontiac, Michigan, a project jointly managed by General Motors Corp. and the United Auto Workers.

Facing declining growth after the end of the Cold War, the aerospace industry has posed a significant challenge for worker retraining programs. Starting in 1991, thousands of employees from Martin Marietta's Electronics and Missile Systems and Information Systems divisions in Orlando, Florida lost their jobs as a series of cuts were made in defense spending. With few defense contractors hiring, high regional unemployment, and skepticism towards defense workers on the part of commercial firms, many of these laid-off workers were unable to find new employment. A program was established in 1993 that was administered by the U.S. Department of Labor and partly funded by the U.S. Department of Defense. Additional funds were provided under the Job Training Partnership Act. Managers, engineers, and assembly workers were included in the program, which involved evaluating each worker's skills and trying to match them with available openings in the area, particularly in the high-tech medical and entertainment industries. Retraining took place in local community colleges and included education in computer-aided design and computer-integrated manufacturing.

Other programs in which displaced defense engineers were retrained had little success. Two months after an engineer retraining program in Long Island, only one participant out of a total of 44 had been able to find employment as a result of the program. In Los Angeles, a similar program was established to retrain defense engineers to become environmental engineers. Four months after retraining, only six of the 26 participants had found permanent employment as a result of the program and only two of the six had found employment as environmental engineers.

The approach to worker retraining under the Job Training Partnership Act was called into question during the Clinton administration. Under Secretary of Labor Robert Reich, the Department of Labor issued a draft of a bill in 1994 called the Re-Employment Act. The bill encouraged states to set up one stop worker training centers and would have extended unemployment compensation for displaced workers undergoing retraining. This faced heavy opposition from business groups, who argued that it would increase the federal unemployment tax, and the bill was ultimately defeated.

[David Kucera]

FURTHER READING:

Blumfield, Michael, Jack Gordon, Michael Picard, and David Stamps. ''The New Job Mobility.'' *Training,* May 1997, 12-14.

Davis, Steven J. *Job Creation and Destruction.* Cambridge, MA: MIT Press, 1996.

Knell, Suzanne. *Learn to Earn: Issues Raised by Welfare Reform for Adult Education, Training, and Work.* Washington: National Institute for Literacy, 1998.

No One Left Behind: The Report of the Twentieth Century Fund Task Force on Retraining America's Workforce. New York: Twentieth Century Fund Press, 1996.

Wilson, George, Ian Sakura-Lemessy, and Jonathan P. West. ''Reaching the Top: Racial Differences in Mobility Paths to Upper-Tier Occupations.'' *Work and Occupations,* May 1999, 165-186.

OCCUPATIONAL SAFETY AND HEALTH ADMINISTRATION (OSHA)

The Occupational Safety and Health Administration (OSHA) was established by the Williams-Steiger Occupational Safety and Health Act (OSH Act) of 1970, which took effect in 1971. OSHA's mission is to ''assure, in so far as possible, every working man and woman in the nation safe and healthful working conditions.'' With the exception of operators of mines, the OSH Act covers every nonpublic U.S. employer whose business affects interstate commerce. Thus, nearly every private employer in the United States is covered. Operators of mines are exempt from the OSH Act because they are regulated separately pursuant to the Mine Safety and Health Act of 1977. Because OSHA is an administrative agency within the U.S. Department of Labor, it is administered by an assistant secretary of labor.

OBJECTIVES AND STANDARDS SETTING

OSHA seeks to make workplaces safer and healthier by making and enforcing regulations, which the OSH Act calls ''standards.'' The OSH Act itself establishes only one workplace standard, which is called the ''general duty standard.'' The general duty standard states: ''Each employer shall furnish to each of his employees employment and a place of employment which are free from recognized hazards that are causing or are likely to cause death or serious physical harm to his [or her] employees.'' In the OSH Act, Congress delegated authority to OSHA to make rules further implementing the general duty standard.

Standards made by OSHA are published in the *Code of Federal Regulations* (*CFR*). The three types of regulations are called interim, temporary emergency, and permanent. Interim standards were applicable for two years after the OSH Act was passed. For this purpose, OSHA was authorized to use the standards of any nationally recognized ''standards setting'' organization, such as those of professional engineering groups. Such privately developed standards are called ''national consensus standards.'' Temporary emergency standards last only six months and are designed to protect workers while OSHA goes through the processes required by law to develop a permanent standard. Permanent standards are made through the same processes as the regulations made by other federal administrative agencies. As OSHA drafts a proposal for a permanent standard, it consults with representatives of industry and labor and collects scientific, medical, and engineering data as appropriate. A proposed standard is then published in the *Federal Register.* A comment period is held, during which input is received from interested parties including, but not limited to, representatives of industry and labor. At the close of the comment period, the proposal may be withdrawn and set aside, withdrawn and reproposed with modifications, or promulgated as a final standard. (Promulgated means that it has been made into a permanent standard and has the force and effect of law.) All promulgated standards are first published in the *Federal Register* and are then compiled and published in the *Code of Federal Regulations.* It is important to note that many of OSHA's permanent standards originated as national consensus standards developed by private professional organizations such as the National Fire Protection Association and the American National Standards Institute. Examples of permanent OSHA standards include limits for exposure of employees to hazardous substances such as asbestos, benzene, vinyl chloride, and cotton dust.

In the OSH Act of 1970, in addition to creating OSHA, Congress established a research institute called the National Institute of Occupational Safety and Health (NIOSH). Since 1973 NIOSH has been a division of the Centers for Disease Control and Prevention. The purpose of NIOSH is to gather data documenting incidences of occupational exposure, injury, illness and death in the United States. After gathering and evaluating data, NIOSH develops "criteria documents" for specific standards giving doctors' and scientists' conclusions about specific hazards. For example, they evaluate how much noise is likely to cause deafness or how much exposure to benzene is likely to cause leukemia. Some OSHA standards specifying permissible amounts and levels of exposure to toxic substances are based on criteria documents. The administration, however, also considers data gathered by representatives of industry, labor, and other groups.

RECORD-KEEPING REQUIREMENTS

As a means of identifying workplace hazards and as a means of identifying violations of OSHA's standards, all employers covered by the OSH Act are required to keep four kinds of records. These records include: (1) records regarding enforcement of OSHA standards; (2) research records; (3) job-related injury, illness, and death records; and (4) records regarding job hazards.

ENFORCEMENT OF STANDARDS

OSHA inspectors conduct planned or surprise inspections of work sites covered by the OSH Act to verify compliance with the OSH Act and standards promulgated by OSHA. The OSH Act allows the employer *and* an employee representative to accompany OSHA's representative during the inspection. It should also be noted that in 1978, in *Marshall v. Barlow,* the U.S. Supreme Court declared that in most industries, employers have a right to bar an OSHA inspector from their premises if the inspector has not first obtained a search warrant.

If violations are found during an inspection, an OSHA citation may be issued in which alleged violations are listed, notices of penalties for each violation are given, and an abatement period is established. The abatement period is the amount of time the employer has to correct any violation(s). Penalties for a violation can be civil or criminal and vary depending on whether the violation is nonserious or serious, willful or nonwillful, or repeated. For serious, repeated, willful violations, possible civil penalties range up to $70,000. Ironically, however, monetary criminal penalties range up to only $10,000. A six-month jail sentence can be imposed if an employee death results from a violation. Because OSHA must refer cases to the U.S. Justice Department for criminal enforcement, it has not made extensive use of criminal prosecution as an enforcement mechanism.

An employer has 15 days to contest an OSHA citation, and any challenge is heard by an administrative law judge (ALJ) within OSHA. The ALJ receives oral and written evidence, decides issues of fact and law, and enters an order. If the employer is dissatisfied with that order, it can be appealed to the **Occupational Safety and Health Review Commission**, which will, in turn, enter an order. Finally, within 30 days of the issuance of that order, the employer or the secretary of labor can take the case to the U.S. federal court system by filing an appeal with a U.S. court of appeals.

OSHA AND ITS STATE COUNTERPARTS

Pursuant to the OSH Act, an individual state can pass its own worker health and safety laws and standards. If the state can show that its counterpart to OSHA will regulate as stringently as or more stringently than the federal agency, the state counterpart will be certified to assume OSH Act administration and enforcement in that state. As of 1999, counterparts to OSHA were authorized in at least 25 states. Therefore, businesses in those states deal on a day-to-day basis with the state agency instead of the federal administration.

Businesses should be aware that in recent years state attorneys general and prosecutors have brought increasing numbers of criminal prosecutions against employers for crimes ranging from battery to murder. Thus, although the OSH Act provides for maximum penalties of six months of jail for willful violation of a standard, state prosecutors can and do seek much more serious penalties using state criminal statutes.

HISTORY OF THE RELATIONSHIP BETWEEN OSHA AND BUSINESS

OSHA has traditionally used "command and control" kinds of regulation to protect workers. "Command and control" regulations are those which set requirements for job safety (such as requirements for guardrails on stairs) or limits on exposure to a hazardous substance (such as a given number of fibers of asbestos per cubic milliliter of air breathed per hour). They are enforced through citations issued to violators.

In 1984 OSHA promulgated the Hazard Communication Standard (HCS), which is viewed as a new kind of regulation differing from "command and control." The HCS gives workers access to information about long-term health risks resulting from workplace exposure to toxic or hazardous substances. The HCS requires manufacturers, importers, and distributors to provide employers with evaluations of all toxic or hazardous materials sold or distributed to those employers. For each chemical, this information is compiled in a material safety data sheet (MSDS). The MSDS describes the chemical's physical hazards such as ignitability and reactivity, gives associated health hazards, and states the exposure limits established by OSHA. In turn, the employer must make the MSDSs available to its employees. In addition, the employer must establish a hazard communication program that educates employees about the HCS, explains the potential hazards of materials in their workplace to employees, and trains employees in methods of using those materials safely. The employer must also label all containers with the identities of hazardous substances and appropriate warnings. Worker Right-to-Know, as implemented on the federal level through the HCS, is designed to give workers access to information which, in turn, may enable workers to make choices about their exposure to toxic chemicals.

OSHA has been criticized by businesses throughout its history. In the 1970s it was criticized for making job-safety regulations that businesses considered to be vague or unnecessarily costly in time or money to enforce. For example, a 1977 OSHA regulation contained detailed specifications regarding irregularities in western hemlock trees used to construct ladders. In the Appropriations Act of 1977, Congress directed OSHA to get rid of certain standards that it described as "trivial." As a result, in 1978 OSHA revoked 928 job-safety standards and increased its efforts to deal with health hazards.

On the other hand, OSHA has been criticized throughout its history for doing too little to protect workers. It has been and continues to be criticized for issuing too few new standards, for failing to protect workers who report violations of OSHA standards, for failing to adequately protect workers involved in the clean up of toxic-waste sites, and for failing to enforce existing standards. For example, in September 1993, 25 men and women perished in a fire in a chicken processing plant in North Carolina. The workers died because they were trapped inside the burning building behind emergency exits that had been bolted by managers of the plant in violation of OSHA standards. During 11 years of operation in North Carolina, the plant had never been inspected by OSHA inspectors.

The alleged reasons for such failures to protect workers range from inadequate funding for research and enforcement to lack of will to enforce. During the 1980s Presidents Reagan and Bush publicly supported efforts to keep agencies such as OSHA "off the backs" of business. Therefore, workers' advocates place at least partial blame for lax enforcement on those administrations. During the 1990s the goal of the Clinton administration has been to reduce the adversarial relationship between businesses and OSHA. For example, OSHA has established a Voluntary Protection Program (VPP), in which about 500 businesses participated in 1999. The program gives official recognition to partnerships between regulated businesses and OSHA. The VPPS are designed to lead to effective safety and health programs in more than 180 industries, saving money for the VPP participants as a result of reduced injury rates.

REFORM LEGISLATION

Although OSHA's HCS and similar state Worker Right-to-Know laws give today's workers access to far more information about their exposure to toxic chemicals than they received in the early 1980s, knowledge alone does not prevent illness, injury, or death. As a result of workers' and other citizens' increased awareness of hazards, however, there are calls for OSHA to do more to protect workers, and there are proposals for new mechanisms to allow workers themselves to take action to protect themselves.

Various OSHA reform bills were considered by the 105th Congress before it adjourned in 1998; several were enacted as law. One authorized a program providing incentives for states to offer on-site consultations and **training** and education for businesses. The bill included funding for consultative visits by officials from OSHA and its state counterparts. A second addition to OSHA prohibits the secretary of labor from considering issuance of citations or penalties as a performance measure when evaluating OSHA employees. Third, the Postal Employees Safety Enhancement Act extended OSHA coverage to the U.S. postal service. In addition, OSHA received an additional $16.3 million in funding for 1999, bringing its total funding for fiscal year 1999 to a total of $353 million.

Bills providing for comprehensive reforms of OSHA failed. In addition, legislation to permit electronic access to MSDSs was blocked by opponents.

On the other hand, although some Republicans advocated a measure barring OSHA from moving forward with an **ergonomics** rule, that measure failed. (Ergonomics involves fitting the job to the worker. It is designed to prevent work-related musculoskeletal disorders [WMSDs].) In late 1998 OSHA proposed a new rule that will require employers to establish ergonomics programs to prevent WMSDs. OSHA will take public comments in various cities in late 1999, and it is expected that a final rule will be published in 1999.

The OSH Act is three decades old, and criticisms of the OSH Act and OSHA abound. Further, OSHA faces new challenges related to the **globalization** of business as it enters the 21st century. For example, in October 1998, the United States and the **European Union** (EU) held a joint safety and health conference in Luxembourg as a part of a new transatlantic agenda. The United States and the EU agreed to continuing joint meetings in the future which will include work on asbestos and the need for ergonomics programs to protect workers from WMSDs. As we enter the 21st century, debate regarding the role of OSHA and its activities continues to be vigorous. The outcome of that debate will be significant for our society.

SEE ALSO: Industrial Safety

[Paulette L. Stenzel]

FURTHER READING:

Abrams, Jim. ''House Approves Two Bills to Ease OSHA Regulation of Businesses: Cooperation Is Goal of Clinton-Backed Plans.'' *San Diego Union-Tribune,* 18 March 1998.

Bodwin, Amy. ''Work-Safety System Clogged: State Audit.'' *Crain's Business Detroit,* 12 April 1993, 1.

Boggs, Richard F. ''OSHA Can't Do It All.'' *Safety and Health,* 5 April 1992, 25.

Occupational Safety and Health Act of 1970. U.S. Code. Vol. 29, secs. 651-78. Washington: GPO, 1988.

Stenzel, Paulette L. ''Right to Act: Advancing the Common Interests of Labor and Environmentalists.'' *Albany Law Review* 57, no. 1 (1993).

Tyson, Patrick R. ''OSHA Reform: The Sequel.'' *Safety and Health,* December 1991, 17.

——. ''OSHA Reform Under Way.'' *Safety and Health,* November 1991, 23.

U.S. Department of Labor. Occupational Safety and Health Administration. ''Ergonomics.'' Washington: Occupational Safety and Health Administration, 1999. Available from www.osha-slc.gov/SLTC/ergonomics/index.html.

——. ''Occupational Safety and Health Administration.'' Washington: Occupational Safety and Health Administration, 1999. Available from www.osha.gov.

OCCUPATIONAL SAFETY AND HEALTH REVIEW COMMISSION (OSHRC)

The Occupational Safety and Health Review Commission (OSHRC) rules on cases arising from contested enforcement actions of the **Occupational Safety and Health Administration (OSHA)**. Its purpose is to provide a timely and fair resolution of those cases, which involve the alleged exposure of workers to unsafe or unhealthy working conditions.

The OSHRC was established by the Occupational Safety and Health Act of 1970. It is an independent, quasi-judicial agency headquartered in Washington, DC, with regional offices in Atlanta, Boston, Dallas, and Denver. The agency consists of three commissioners, one of whom is designated as chairperson, a legal staff, national and regional judges, and assorted other staff. In November 1998, Thomasina Rogers became the first African American to serve as one of the OSHRC commissioners.

The Occupational Safety and Health Act affects virtually every employer in the United States. The act is enforced by the Secretary of Labor primarily through OSHA. It requires employers to provide workers with a safe and healthy environment. In recent years specific areas of concern have included, among others, exposure to hazardous materials and process safety management in the oil and gas industries.

OSHA conducts safety and health inspections to insure compliance with the act. Cases are forwarded to the OSHRC by the Department of Labor when OSHA's rulings and enforcement actions are contested either by an employer, an employee, or an employee representative. An employer may contest any alleged job safety or health violation found during an OSHA inspection as well as the penalties assessed and the time allowed for correction of such violations. Employees or their representatives may also challenge the appropriateness of the time allowed to correct a hazardous situation. All such challenges must be made within 15 working days after OSHA has issued a citation against an employer.

Within the OSHRC there are two levels of adjudication. If the case requires a hearing, it is assigned to an administrative law judge, usually in the community where the alleged violation has occurred. In such a hearing the Secretary of Labor usually has the burden of proving a violation has occurred. Upon completion of the hearing the judge issues a decision based on the facts presented.

In many cases the decisions of the administrative law judges are final. However, each decision may be reviewed at the discretion of one of the three OSHRC commissioners within 30 days. In cases where such a review takes place the OSHRC issues its own decision, which supersedes that of the administrative law judge. Once a case has been decided, either by a judge or by the commission, it may be appealed to the United States Courts of Appeals.

As an independent agency, the OSHRC does not always agree with OSHA. A 1998 decision required OSHA to revise its rules regarding personal protective equipment before OSHA could require employers to pay for such equipment. In what one writer called ''the most significant Review Commission decisions of the last 15 years,'' the OSHRC blocked OSHA's attempt to obtain a ''per employee'' penalty for a safety violation. That decision resulted in a modification to OSHA's policy of obtaining penalties based on the number of employees affected by violations so willful that they were considered ''egregious.''

The main office of the Occupational Safety and Health Review Commission is located in Washington, DC and has a site on the World Wide Web. The rules and regulations of the OSHRC are contained in Title 29, Section XX, of the Code of Federal Regulations.

SEE ALSO: Occupational Safety and Health Administration (OSHA)

[David P. Bianco]

FURTHER READING:

''OSHRC Clamps Down on Egregious Policy,'' *Occupational Hazards,* November 1995.

Sapper, Arthur G. ''Will Arcadian and Hartford Roofing End Per-Employee Penalties?'' *Occupational Hazards,* February 1996.

"Thomasina Rogers Named to Federal Job Safety, Health Tribunal," *Jet,* 23 November 1998.

Wheeler, Susan V. "OSHA Will Not Appeal PPR Ruling," *Boating Industry,* February 1998.

Yokay, Stephen C., and Arthur G. Sapper. "Recent Significant Decisions by the Occupational Safety and Health Review Commission," *Employee Relations Law Journal,* Spring 1996.

OCR

SEE: Optical Character Recognition

OECD

SEE: Organisation for Economic Co-operation and Development

OFFICE AUTOMATION

Office automation refers to the varied computer machinery and software used to digitally create, collect, store, manipulate, and relay office information needed for accomplishing basic tasks and goals. Raw data storage, electronic transfer, and the management of electronic business information comprise the basic activities of an office automation system. In its basic form, information exists as letters, memos, graphs, records, messages, and so on. When that information is electronically transferred, raw data is exchanged between two or more office employees, either at the same or different locations.

The history of modern **office automation** began with the typewriter and the copy machine, which mechanized previously manual tasks. However, increasingly office automation refers not just to the mechanization of tasks but to the conversion of information to electronic form as well. The advent of the personal computer in the early 1980s revolutionized office automation. Popular operating systems like DOS (Disk Operating System) and user interfaces like Microsoft Corp.'s Windows dominate office computer systems. Today, most offices use at least one commercial computer business application in the course of daily activity. Some large companies like AT&T maintain extensive and complex office automation systems, while smaller companies may employ only a word processor.

In order to process information, office automation systems must allow input of new information and the retrieval of stored information. Input of new information refers to the physical transfer of text, video, graphics, and sound into a computer. Input can be typed into the computer or scanned (digitally reproduced) from another document or source. New advances in input devices frequently allow direct handwritten input or voice dictation. Input of pre-existing information means retrieving the electronic materials from an existing storage area. These storage areas can be finite and local, such as the hard drive on the office PC, or as seemingly infinite and global as the Internet, the worldwide collection of computer networks that is growing every year.

THE BASICS OF OFFICE AUTOMATION

Generally, there are three basic activities of an office automation system: storage of raw data, data exchange, and data management. Within each broad application area, hardware and software combine to fulfill basic functions.

DATA STORAGE AND MANIPULATION. Data storage usually includes office records and other primary office forms and documents. Data applications involve the capture and editing of a file, image, or spreadsheet. Word processing and desktop presentation packages accommodate raw textual and graphical data, while spreadsheet applications enable the easy manipulation and output of numbers. Image applications allow the capture and editing of visual images.

Text-handling software and systems cover the whole field of word processing and desktop publishing. Word processing is the inputting (usually via keyboard) and manipulation of text on a computer. Word processing is frequently the most basic and common office automation activity. Popular commercial **word processing** applications include WordPerfect (Corel) and Word (Microsoft). Each provides the office user with a sophisticated set of commands to format, edit, and print text documents. One of the most popular features of word processing packages are their preformatted document templates. Templates automatically set up such things as font size, paragraph styles, headers and footers, and page numbers so that the user does not have to reset document characteristics every time they create a new record.

Desktop publishing adds another dimension to text manipulation. By packaging the features of a word processor with advanced page design and layout features, desktop publishing packages easily create documents with text and images, such as newsletters or brochures.

Image-handling software and systems are another facet of office automation. Images, or digital pictures, are representations of visual information. Visual information is an important complement to textual information. Examples of visual information include pictures of documents, photographs, and graphics such as tables and charts. These images are converted into digital files, which cannot be edited the same way that text files can. In a word processor or desktop publishing application, each word or character is treated individually. In an imaging system, the entire picture or document is treated as one whole object. One of the most popular uses of computerized images is in corporate presentations or speeches. Presentation software packages simplify the creation of multimedia presentations that use computer video, images, sound, and text in an integrated information package.

Spreadsheet programs allow the manipulation of numeric data. Early popular spreadsheets like VisiCalc and Lotus 1-2-3 greatly simplified common financial record keeping. Particularly useful among the many spreadsheet options is the ability to use variables in pro forma statements. The pro forma option allows the user to change a variable and have a complex formula automatically recalculated based on the new numbers. Many businesses use spreadsheets for financial management, financial projection, and accounting.

DATA EXCHANGE. The exchange of stored and manipulated information is an equally important component of an office automation system. Electronic transfer is a general application area that highlights the exchange of information between more than one user or participant. Electronic mail, voice mail, and facsimile are examples of electronic transfer applications. Systems that allow instantaneous or ''real time'' transfer of information (i.e. online conversations via computer or audio exchange with video capture) are considered electronic sharing systems. Electronic sharing software illustrates the collaborative nature of many office automation systems. The distinction between electronic transfer and electronic sharing is subtle but recognizable.

Electronic transfer software and systems allow for electronic, voice, and facsimile transmission of office information. Electronic mail uses computer-based storage and a common set of network communication standards to forward electronic messages from one user to another. It is usually possible to relay electronic mail to more than one recipient. Additionally, many electronic mail systems provide security features, automatic messaging, and mail management systems like electronic folders or notebooks. Voice mail offers essentially the same applications, but for telephones rather than computers. Facsimile transmissions are limited to image relay and have suffered in popularity with the increase in the use of the personal computer. One popular alternative, for example, is to send and receive faxes by modem.

Electronic sharing systems offset the limitations of a store-and-forward electronic mail system. Office automation systems that include the ability to electronically share information between more than one user simultaneously are often called groupware. One type of groupware is an electronic meeting system, which allows geographically dispersed participants to exchange information in real time. Participants may be within the same office or building or thousands of miles apart. Long-distance electronic sharing systems usually use a telephone line connection to transfer data, while sharing in a localized area often involves just a local area network of computers (no outside phone line is needed). An interesting byproduct of the electronic sharing functions of an office automation system is telecommuting. A telecommuter works for a business from another location (often home) using a computer and a connection to the office automation system. Telecommuting is an increasingly popular style of work for many office workers and companies.

DATA MANAGEMENT. The last major component of an office automation system offers planning and strategic advantages by simplifying the management of stored information. Task management, tickler systems or reminder systems, and scheduling programs monitor and control various projects and activities within the office. Electronic management systems monitor and control office activities and tasks through timelines, resource equations, and electronic scheduling. As in data exchange, groupware is gaining in popularity for data management. Each member of the work group or larger group may share access to necessary information via the automated office system and groupware.

OFFICE AUTOMATION: PEOPLE, TOOLS, AND THE WORKPLACE

When considering office automation three main areas need further discussion: people, and how automation affects them; the constantly changing tools used in automation; and the ways in which automation has changed the workplace.

People involved with office automation basically include all users of the automation and all providers of the automation systems and tools. A wide range of people—including software and hardware engineers, management information scientists, and secretaries—use office automation. All are also involved with providing information. This dual role of both provider and user gives rise to two critical issues. First, training of personnel to effectively use an office automation system is essential; the office automation system is only as good as the people who make and use it. Second, overcoming workplace resistance is a must if the full benefits of automation are to be realized. Change is difficult for some workers, yet must occur for a business to remain competitive.

Practical tools for office automation include computer hardware and software currently available in a number of models, applications, and configurations. Two basic microcomputer platforms are DOS (Disk Operating System)-compatible computers and Apple Macintosh systems. Applications such as word processing, database management, and spreadsheets are common and constantly changing. Standards are increasing but still not yet completely integrated into all aspects of office automation. Office automation tools may stand alone (without access to information at other computers) or be networked (with such access). Configuring complex office systems to share information is difficult and involves a considerable staff commitment. Popular local area network software includes Novell NetWare and Lantastic.

Practical workplace issues of office automation often involve the budget and physical considerations involved with creating, exchanging, and managing information. Equipment, rewiring, training, security, and data entry all cost money and require space. Newly recognized medical problems such as repetitive motion syndrome are a significant issue for some people using office automation systems. Repetitive motion syndrome is a medical disorder associated with lengthy keyboard inputting and seating arrangements. Likewise, environmental safety concerns might also include vision and overall health considerations related to electromagnetic computer emissions.

Telecommuting advances enable an increasing percentage of the workforce to maintain an office at home and, at the same time, provoke considerable debate on the future of the central office. Businesses must comply with software licenses or face lawsuits. Office automation systems can be complex to acquire and costly to administrate for large organizations. The availability of vital office information in such an easily obtained digital format requires considerable thought and preparation for data security.

By integrating raw information with exchange mechanisms and management structuring and guidance, office automation creates advantages as well as disadvantages. Benefits in using electronic management systems include savings in production and service costs as information is quickly routed for optimal office performance. Office automation can also be cost effective, as powerful microcomputers continue to drop in price. While office automation often mirrors actual paper transaction and activity, an office automation system may also complement the paper system and provide output only available in digital format. Thus, office automation extends the information activities of the office to surpass physical or geographic limitation.

By far the fastest growing segment of the office automation industry is for multifunction peripherals. These machines incorporate a combination of functions into one. The first such machines included a plain paper fax and a color printer in one unit. These products grew quickly to incorporate scanners and related functions. By the late 1990s, these items registered over 100 percent growth rates.

[Tona Henderson]

FURTHER READING:

''Evolution of Multifunction Office Automation Devices.'' *Finance Week,* 29 May-3 June, 1998, 47-8.

Kobielus, James G. *Workflow Strategies.* Foster City, CA: IDG Books Worldwide, 1997.

Lively, Lynn, and Mary Glenn. *Managing Information Overload.* New York: AMACOM, 1996.

Schill, Alexander. *Cooperative Office Systems.* Chichester, U.K.: Ellis Howard, Ltd., 1996.

OFFICE MANAGEMENT

Office **management** is generally described as organizing and administering the auxiliary, day-to-day chores of the front office—chores that are often the responsibility of an office manager. Possible duties of an office manager include ordering and purchase approval of office supplies and services, hiring and supervision of front office workers, handling customer service, managing **accounting** functions, and analyzing sales—but office management can be virtually anything the company owner wants it to be. According to **chief executive officers** responding to a survey from *Inc.* magazine, good office management and office managers are the grease that keep the wheels of business rolling smoothly. In a similar vein, an author in *Medical Economics* magazine wrote that the main function of an office manager of a medical practice is to ''free you [the doctor] from hassles and let you concentrate on medicine.''

There is no traceable history of office management. The job of ''office manager'' is generally found in smaller companies where the owner depends on a single person who performs a variety of tasks to keep the office functioning. As a company grows into a corporation, office managers seem to disappear, while other departments such as purchasing and human resources expand. The office manager is usually not considered to be a member of the management team. She or he probably would not participate in management strategy sessions on how to increase sales, but would participate in sessions on how to cut operating expenses.

In the area of supplies and services, an office manager is usually responsible for buying short-term supplies such as photocopy paper, envelopes, and letterhead, longer-term purchases such as telephone systems, and other ongoing necessities such as making sure the postal meter has enough postage. This person usually handles the company's service purchases, such as long distance telephone service and photocopier service agreements. Ideally, office managers will be given the authority to accept bids and negotiate **contracts** so that they may tell salespeople that they make the decisions. Office managers must also be savvy enough to recognize fraudulent business practices.

Another responsibility of office managers is staffing. They will recruit, interview, and hire employees for the office. Office managers need to know how to select the right people and train them. For example, the telephone receptionist will need to be skilled in telephone etiquette and customer service.

Office managers sometimes take on the role of monitoring customer service. They may listen to calls, or answer the phone themselves. They may also ask the customers directly how the company is doing in this area. They then report their findings to the company owner on a regular basis. They also know enough to turn over particularly thorny problems to the company owner immediately so faithful customers do not become angry if they think the company owner is ignoring them and passing them off to an office manager. The key to being successful as a customer service manager is to convince customers that all collected information—good and bad—will go directly to the president for review.

Accounting functions are often handled by office managers, provided they have some background in handling money, or can be trained to do so. They may keep track of accounts payable and accounts receivable, assign vendor bills to be paid during specific weeks, prepare outgoing bills as customer orders or jobs are finished, and control the company's petty cash. Many office managers are reluctant to actually sign checks, however, as that could make them appear to be a link in the chain of financial liability if the company were to run into financial problems. Conversely, many owners are reluctant to turn over check-writing duties to their office managers, fearing for **embezzlement**. Owners who do charge their office managers with this responsibility typically set a limit on the amount of the checks, based on the company's average daily expenses. Some owners also secure fidelity bond coverage for their office managers; a fidelity bond is purchased from an insurance company and will pay the insured company for money or property lost from the dishonest actions—including embezzlement, forgery, and theft—of its bonded employees.

Office managers also frequently take on the job of time accounting, particularly for small service companies such as **advertising** agencies or law firms that depend on the billing of time as a source of revenue. The officer manager collects the time sheets from billable employees in order to assign the hours to specific jobs. This task is slowly being replaced by **software** that automatically tracks and assigns time.

A final possible area of responsibility for office managers is to compile and analyze sales information. This might involve calculating the profitability of the company and specific projects or tracking various expenditures. This knowledge is critical to the performance of a company, but too detailed for the company owner to know off the top of his or her head. An office manager performing these duties must be able to retrieve all the necessary documents and be able to analyze the information.

An office manager position can sometimes lead a person up the corporate ladder without a formal business degree. The experience gained from organizing and running the front office successfully can provide a person with a variety of transferable skills.

[Clint Johnson, updated by David E. Salamie]

FURTHER READING:

Greco, Susan. "What Office Managers Really Do." *Inc.*, January 1992, 114.

"Hiring an Office Manager." *American Medical News,* 27 January 1992, 9.

Patrick, Alan. "How to Make the Office Work." *Management Today,* January 1993, 54.

Preston, Susan Harrington. "What a Great Office Manager Can Do for a Small Practice." *Medical Economics* 75, no. 11 (15 June 1998): 62+.

OID

SEE: Original Issue Discount

OLIGOPOLY

An oligopoly is a market condition in which the production of identical or similar products is concentrated in a few large firms. Examples of oligopolies in the United States include the steel, aluminum, automobile, gypsum, petroleum, tire, and beer industries. The introduction of new products and processes can create new oligopolies, as in the **computer** or synthetic fiber industries. Oligopolies also exist in **service industries**, such as the airlines industry.

An oligopoly may be categorized as either a homogeneous oligopoly or a differentiated oligopoly.

In a homogeneous oligopoly the major firms produce identical products, such as steel bars or aluminum ingots. Prices tend to be uniform in homogeneous oligopolies. In a differentiated oligopoly, similar but not identical products are produced. Examples include the automobile industry, the cigarette industry, and the soft drink industry. In differentiated oligopolies companies attempt to differentiate their products from those of their competitors. To the extent that they are able to establish differentiated products, companies may be able to maintain price differences.

Being part of an oligopoly affects a company's competitive behavior. In a competitive market situation that is not an oligopoly, firms compete by acting for themselves to maximize profits without regard to the reactions of their competitors. In an oligopoly, a firm must consider the effects of its actions on others in the industry. While smaller firms may operate at the fringes of an oligopoly without affecting the other firms in the industry, the actions of a major firm in the oligopoly typically cause reactions in the other firms in the industry. For example, if one company in the oligopoly attempts to undersell the others, then the other firms will respond by also lowering prices. As a result, price cuts in oligopolies tend to result in lower profits for all of the firms involved.

Prices in oligopolistic industries tend to be unstable to the extent that companies will shade, or lower, their prices slightly to gain a competitive advantage. It must be remembered that collusion between firms to fix prices is illegal under U.S. **antitrust laws**, so oligopolies must reach industry agreements on pricing indirectly. Companies can signal their pricing intentions indirectly in a variety of ways, such as through press releases, speeches by industry leaders, or comments given in interviews. In some cases there is a recognized price leader in the oligopoly, and other firms in the oligopoly set their prices according to that of the industry's price leader.

Industrial concentration is a matter of degree. This means that there is no absolute definition of an oligopoly in terms of the number of firms accounting for a certain percentage of an industry's output. In the United States the *Census of Manufacturers* reports on each industry's four-firm concentration ratio. This figure indicates what percentage of an industry's output is accounted for by its four largest companies. It is not uncommon for the four largest firms to account for 30 percent or more of an industry's output, and in some cases they account for more than 70 percent of production.

In the United Kingdom, for example, the top four food retailers accounted for 45 to 67 percent of the nation's $150 billion grocery market in 1998. In Russia, economic development under Boris Yeltsin has been described as a "new oligarchy," in which government officials and business leaders join together to gain control of industries such as **banking**, television, the business press, and other companies.

Oligopolies tend to develop in industries that require large capital investments. Studies have shown that industries with high four-firm concentration ratios tend to have higher margins than other industries. In order to maintain an oligopoly, potential investors must be discouraged from establishing competing companies. Oligopolies are able to perpetuate themselves and discourage new investments in several ways. In some cases the oligopoly is the result of access to key resources, which may be either natural resources or some patented process or special knowledge. New firms cannot enter the industry without access to those resources.

The established, experienced firms in an oligopoly also enjoy significant cost advantages that make it difficult for new firms to enter the industry. These cost advantages may be the result of the large scale of production required as well as of experience in keeping manufacturing or operating costs down. Another factor that tends to perpetuate oligopolies is the difficulty of introducing new products into an oligopoly characterized by a high degree of product differentiation. Prohibitively large expenditures would be required of a new firm to overcome consumer reluctance to try a new product over an established one. Finally, oligopolies perpetuate themselves through predatory practices such as obtaining lower prices from suppliers, establishing exclusive dealerships, and predatory pricing aimed at driving smaller competitors out of business.

SEE ALSO: Competition

[David P. Bianco]

FURTHER READING:

"Behind the Throne." *Economist,* 12 September 1998, 76.

Lanchner, David. "A Russian 'Too Big to Topple.'" *Global Finance,* January 1997, 20.

Morais, Richard C. "Squeezed Lemons." *Forbes,* 14 December 1998, 150-52.

Zachary, G. Pascal. "Let's Play Oligopoly!: Why Giants Like Having Other Giants Around." *Wall Street Journal,* 8 March 1999, B1.

ON-THE-JOB TRAINING

On-the-job training focuses on the acquisition of skills within the work environment generally under normal working conditions. Through on-the-job training, workers acquire both general skills that they can transfer from one job to another and specific skills that are unique to a particular job. On-the-job training, typically includes verbal and written instruction, demonstration and observation, and hands-on practice and imitation. In addition, the on-the-job training process involves one employee—usually a supervisor or an experienced employee—passing knowledge and skills on to a novice employee.

On-the-job training is the oldest form of training. Prior to the advent of off-site training classrooms, the only practical way of learning a job was working along side an experienced worker in a particular trade or profession—as evinced by the practice of **apprenticeship** during the Middle Ages when master craftsmen passed on skills and knowledge to novices who worked along side them.

On-the-job training is still the predominant form of job training in the United States, particularly for nonmanagerial employees. Numerous studies indicate that it is the most effective form of job training. The largest share of on-the-job training is provided by the private sector, though the most widely studied training programs are those sponsored by federal legislation.

On-the-job training programs range from formal training with company supervisors to learning by watching. In this sense, the most formal types of on-the-job training are distinct from classroom training largely in that they take place within the firm. In the face of increased international competition and the more widespread use of computers in production processes, the implementation of more formal and sophisticated kinds of on-the-job training has become a critical issue for firms in the United States.

TYPES OF ON-THE-JOB TRAINING

Two different types of on-the-job training are frequently distinguished in the professional literature: structured (planned) and unstructured (unplanned). Unstructured is the most common kind and refers to loose on-the-job training programs that largely involve a novice employee working with an experienced employee, who serves as a guide or mentor in an observe-and-imitate training process. The new workers largely learn by trial and error with feedback and suggestions from experienced workers or supervisors. Unstructured training is designed based on work requirements (e.g. manufacturing products), not on imparting job skilled needed by new workers (e.g. the specific skills needed to manufacture products). Consequently, unstructured on-the-job training often fails to impart needed skills fully or consistently, because experienced employees sometimes are unable to articulate clearly the proper methods for performing a job and they sometimes use different training methods each time train new workers.

In contrast, structured on-the-job training involves a program designed to teach new workers what they must know and do in order to complete their tasks successfully. On-the-job training represents a significant investment considering that roughly 30 percent of a new worker's time is spent in on-the-job training during the first 90 days of employment, that productivity of experienced workers assigned to train new workers may decrease during the training period, and that new workers may make expensive mistakes, according to William J. Rothwell and H.C. Kazanas in *Improving On-the-Job Training.* Hence, it behooves companies to design and implement systematic training programs.

One of the first structured on-the-job training programs was launched during World War I in the shipbuilding industry by Charles ''Skipper'' R. Allen, who based the program on the ideas of the psychologist Johann Friedrich Herbart. Allen sought to make training more efficient by having trainees undergo four steps:

1. Preparation: show workers what they are required to do.
2. Presentation: tell workers what they are required to do and why they are required to do it.
3. Application: let workers perform the required tasks.
4. Inspection: provide feedback, informing workers of what they have done right and what they have done wrong.

On-the-job training received renewed interest during World War II when Allen's program was expanded to include seven steps:

1. Demonstrate how to complete a task.
2. Review important points.
3. Demonstrate task again.
4. Let workers perform easier parts of the task.
5. Help workers perform the entire task.
6. Allow workers to perform the entire task, while being monitored.
7. Allow workers to perform the task on their own.

The seven-step approach to on-the-job training became known as ''job instruction training'' and studies indicated that this approach led to increased productivity during World War II.

Contemporary approaches to on-the-job training emphasize the training of novice workers by experienced workers who possess not only the skills necessary for the tasks to be learned but also the skills as a trainer. By selecting such trainers, companies can achieve consistency in training content, methods, and results. In addition, structured on-the-job training is viewed as a process that includes training inputs (novice employees, experienced employees, and tasks to be learned), a training program, and training outputs (job performance and novice employee development).

The process begins with the selection of qualified trainers and trainees: trainers must know the tasks and know how to communicate how to perform them and the trainees must be able to learn the tasks. In addition, the tasks to be learned and the training goals must be identified. Based on this information, companies can establish a training program. Next, the training program is implemented: the experienced worker prepares to train the novice worker and takes steps to ensure that the trainee understands the tasks to be learned and that the trainee actually learns to perform these tasks. The implementation of the training program also should follow a specific timetable and hence it should help new employees learn needed skills more quickly and systematically than unstructured programs. Finally, the training outputs result from the training inputs and the training program. If all goes well the training outputs should include the trainee being able to complete assigned tasks adequately in accordance with the training goals. After a training program is finished and new employees begin to work on their own, the training process—inputs, the training program, and outputs—must be assessed to make sure that it successfully prepared workers for their tasks and any necessary modifications should be made.

LEGISLATION

Federal legislation has played a large role in the provision of on-the-job training. Title I of the Comprehensive Employment and Training Act of 1973 (CETA) provides for on-the-job training and "work experience" for disadvantaged workers. This includes the establishment of subsidized government jobs in an effort to encourage regular work habits and develop job skills for those with little or no previous experience in the labor market.

Several studies of CETA programs have sought to determine the relative effectiveness of classroom versus on-the-job training in improving participants' earnings. These studies have concluded that on-the-job training is generally more effective, especially for minority participants. This results in part from the fact that participants receiving on-the-job training are often able to continue working at the place of training.

CETA expired in 1982, during one of the deepest U.S. recessions since the 1930s. CETA was replaced by the Job Training Partnership Act (JTPA) of 1982. JTPA has three main titles. Title II provides job training for disadvantaged adults and youths as well as summer jobs for these youths. Title III provides job training for displaced workers whose jobs are eliminated by transformations in the economy. Title IV provides training for Native Americans, veterans, and migrant workers.

Unlike CETA, programs under JTPA are intended to train and place workers in the private sector. This is in response to the political unpopularity of subsidized government jobs developed under CETA. JTPA programs also contrast with CETA programs in that they are largely regulated at the state level, give private sector representatives a large administrative role, and focus more on job training than income maintenance.

The **General Accounting Office (GAO)** conducted a nation-wide survey of Title III JTPA programs between 1982 and 1985. The survey indicated that 80 percent of program participants received job search assistance, compared with only 26 percent who received classroom training and 16 percent who received on-the-job training. The low proportion of participants actually receiving training resulted from the fact that trainers were largely funded on the basis of job placement, not long-term labor market preparedness or earnings improvement. Based on the General Accounting Office survey and an additional year of study, the U.S. Department of Labor recommended greater emphasis on job training to meet the needs of specific employers and particularly on on-the-job rather than classroom training.

The Department of Labor's recommendations were realized with the passage of the Economic Dislocation and Worker Adjustment Assistance Act of 1988. The act greatly increased funding for job training programs under JTPA, even though the level of spending was only one-tenth of that under CETA in its peak year. The effectiveness of on-the-job training was examined for four JTPA programs in the late 1980s. Contrary to the emphasis of the new legislation (and in contrast with more comprehensive studies of CETA programs), on-the-job training was not found to significantly improve employment rates or earnings of trainees.

INTERNATIONAL INFLUENCES

Japanese production and management techniques had a large influence in the American workplace in the 1980s and 1990s. One element of this was the increased use of statistical control techniques and **quality circles**, which required more sophisticated on-the-job training for production workers. Firms such as the Victor Products Division of the Dana Corporation, the First Chicago Corporation, Nestle Foods Corp., and Motorola, Inc. provided basic training to low-skilled and unskilled workers in computers and statistical process controls. In addition, these firms provided on-the-job training in basic skills, including reading and math. An increasing number of firms came to provide such training in basic skills in response to dramatic changes in production techniques, for which such skills were essential.

At the same time, management training also shifted directions. U.S. firms placed increased emphasis on interaction with stockholders, customers, and suppliers. This required greater management knowledge of the details of their firm's products and production processes, knowledge gained through intensified on-the-job training.

On-the-job training programs can be distinguished by the level of centralization at which they occur. Most on-the-job training in the United States is decentralized, occurring at or near the job itself. Centralized training departments generally play a more important role in larger firms, but even in these cases it is estimated that more than half of on-the-job training takes place at a decentralized level. The extent of decentralization depends also on the generality of knowledge that the firm desires in an employee, and this depends on whether the employee is among the managerial, technical, marketing, or production occupations. The Japanese-influenced emphasis on quality control after the 1970s brought with it a greater emphasis on decentralized on-the-job training. This resulted from the implementation of quality circles, in which production workers assume a much larger role in quality control. Previously in the United States, quality control had been largely the domain of management.

In spite of the Japanese influence, however, U.S. firms continue to rely less on on-the-job training and more on formal education for management training than do Japanese firms. Masters in Business Administration (MBA) degrees provide an important credential for managers in the U.S., whereas only one Japanese university offers a degree similar to an MBA Japanese managers often begin their careers by doing production work and are trained by being rotated through a broad range of a firm's operations until they become top-level managers.

The German system of job training is also an influential model in job-training policy debates in the United States The German system relies heavily on on-the-job training, but in a more formal manner than in the U.S. or Japan. About 80 percent of Germans have completed vocational education programs, which prepares them for one of 400 occupations. The system supports approximately 1.5 million apprentices at a time, with an estimated $8,400 (U.S. dollars) spent per year for each apprentice. Though vocational education is overseen by a federal government agency, training takes place largely within firms. These firms take responsibility for the daily supervision of trainees and for the administration of certification exams.

Unlike the Japanese system, trainees in Germany generally do not become employees at the firms in which they received their training. That is, trainees are prepared for the job market at large, not the so-called internal labor market within the firm as in the Japanese system. This difference is a reflection of the lifetime employment system in Japan, in which firms benefit directly from investments made in entry-level on-the-job training. Germany and Japan both have lower employee turnover rates than in the United States, however. In this sense, U.S. firms run a higher risk in investing in ongoing on-the-job training for their workers, in that they are less able to secure returns from that training.

JOINT TRAINING PROGRAMS

During the 1980s and 1990s, there was a rapid expansion in the number of joint union-management training programs in the United States These programs were most extensive in the automotive, communications, steel, and construction industries, as well as in the public sector. Joint programs offer general worker education as well as on-the-job training, including apprenticeships, certifications, and licensing. The growth of joint training programs is a reflection of the greater emphasis that firms placed on training after the 1970s. This was based on the rapid pace of technical change that often required new forms of work organization, such as flexible and just-in-time production. In these forms of production, workers generally are required to perform a greater number of tasks than with traditional mass production techniques.

Joint on-the-job training programs have also been established between labor unions and institutions of higher education in the form of joint apprenticeship training. The pioneering programs were established under a grant by the U.S. Department of Labor to the International Union of Operating Engineers in 1972. These programs typically give college credits to apprentices engaged in on-the-job training, and these apprentices enroll in college courses for related education. Courses are taken mainly in two-year colleges but also in university labor education centers. An increasing number of these programs emphasize background education in labor studies in addition to the more technical aspects of the apprenticeship.

[David Kucera]

FURTHER READING:

Chase, Nancy. ''OJT Doesn't Mean ''Sit by Joe.'' *Quality,* November 1997, 84.

Cook, James and Carol Panza. ''ROI, What Should Training Take Credit For?,'' *Training,* January 1987.

Cook, Robert (ed.). *Worker Dislocation: Case Studies of Causes and Cures.* W.E. Upjohn Institute for Employment Research, 1987.

Jacobs, Ronald L. and Michael J. Jones. *Structured On-the-Job Training.* San Francisco: Berrett-Koehler Publishers, 1995.

Leigh, Duane. ''Public Policy to Retrain Workers: What Does the Record Show?,'' in John Addison (ed.), *Job Displacement: Consequences and Implications for Policy.* Wayne State University Press, 1991.

''On Being an Employee-Oriented Company,'' *Industry Week,* 1 November 1993.

Rothwell, William J., and H.C. Kazanas. *Improving On-the-Job Training.* San Francisco: Jossey-Bass Publishers, 1994.

OPEC

SEE: Organization of Petroleum Exporting Countries

OPEN ECONOMY

An open economy is the opposite of a managed economy. It is one that is characteristically market-oriented, with free market policies rather than government-imposed price controls. In an open economy industries tend to be privately owned rather than owned by the government. In the area of international trade an open economy is one whose policies promote **free trade** over protectionism.

On the other hand, a managed or **closed economy** is characterized by protective tariffs, state-run or nationalized industries, extensive government regulations and price controls, and similar policies indicative of a government-controlled economy. In a managed economy the government typically intervenes to influence the production of goods and services. In an open economy, market forces are allowed to determine production levels.

A completely open economy exists only in theory. For example, no country in the world allows unlimited free access to its markets. Most nations have fiscal and monetary policies that attempt to improve their economies. Many economies that are open in some respects may still have government owned, monopolistic industries. A country is considered to have an open economy, however, if its policies allow market forces to determine such matters as production and pricing.

Chile and **Argentina** are examples of two countries that have moved or are moving from a managed economy to an open economy. Chile has led the way for South America and Central American countries in adopting open economy and free market policies that have led to greater prosperity. As a result of its open economy, Chile became the fastest-growing economy in Latin America from 1983 to 1993.

Among the steps Chile took to make its economy more open was a reduction of its protective tariffs to a uniform 11 percent, which was one of the lowest rates in the world. Such a reduction in tariffs forced its domestic producers to become more competitive in the international market. As a result Chile improved its balance of payments to the point of enjoying a surplus of $90 million in 1991, compared to a deficit of $820 million in 1990. The country became less dependent on its copper exports as the economy diversified under new policies. Chile also improved its international trade by negotiating a series of bilateral trade agreements.

In Argentina similar measures were taken to promote an open economy, including more favorable treatment of foreign investors. An open economy provides the same treatment to foreign investors as it gives to its own investors. Price controls were eliminated for most products, and several government-owned industries were privatized. As a result, Argentina's **gross domestic product** increased by 18 percent between 1991 and 1995. By 1997, however, a widening gap between the country's richest and poorest inhabitants caused widespread social unrest.

The transition from a managed economy to an open economy can be a difficult one. Following the collapse of the Soviet Union, efforts to establish free trade and an open economy in Russia resulted in widespread hardship among the nation's middle class and a failed **bank** system. In Southeast Asia a full-scale financial, economic, and social crisis erupted in 1998, revealing how difficult it was to maintain a small open economy in countries such as Thailand, Indonesia, Malaysia, the Philippines, and Singapore. In South Korea, the nation's president asked its citizens to accept widespread unemployment and bankruptcies in order to move the country toward an open economy by selling off government-owned industries. Germany's transition to an open economy resulted in high levels of unemployment throughout the nation.

Social, political, and economic instability can be avoided in countries moving toward open economies, but domestic conditions must be favorable. For example, states with powerful bureaucracies can establish favorable domestic economic conditions if they have the proper ideology, accept diversity, and achieve legitimacy in the eyes of their citizens. For open economies to succeed in small countries that formerly had managed economies, favorable domestic conditions include a working education system, legal system, judicial system, and low inflation. Such conditions provide the stability necessary for an open economy to flourish.

While the United States supports free trade and an open economic policy, it has never been a completely open economy. The imposition of tariffs and

duties has always been a source of revenue for the U.S. government, as it has been for other governments of the world. The conflict between an open economic policy and the need to protect domestic industries from unfair **international competition**, was illustrated during 1998 as low-priced steel imports into the United States from Japan tripled. President Clinton was forced to warn other nations that they must "play by the rules"—rules that covered **dumping** and other trade practices—or the United States would press other nations to restrict their exports to the United States.

Economists recognize an open economy as being more efficient than a managed economy. In the 18th century, economist Adam Smith (1723 1790) wrote *Inquiry into the Nature and Causes of the Wealth of Nations* to explain the benefits of an open economy and free trade. He wrote that interventions in international trade, such as tariffs and duties, serve only to reduce the overall **wealth** of all nations. Similarly, interventions in the domestic economy are also regarded as inefficient. Smith developed the concept of "the invisible hand," which in effect stated that when individual enterprises work to maximize their own profits and well-being, then the economy as a whole also operates more efficiently. He argued that the economy does not require government intervention, because the operations of domestic producers are guided, as if by an invisible hand, to benefit the economy as a whole.

SEE ALSO: Argentina, Doing Business in; Closed Economy

[David P. Bianco]

FURTHER READING:

Koenig, Robert. "German Jobless Struggle On." *Journal of Commerce,* 20 January 1998, 5A.

Landers, Jim. "U.S. Official Urges Japan to Open Economy to Imports." *Knight-Ridder/Tribune News Service,* 3 November 1998.

Orr, Deborah. "Can South Korea Save Itself?" *Institutional Investor,* July 1998, 125.

Parker, Stephen. "Out of the Ashes?" *Brookings Review,* summer 1998, 10-13.

Sanger, David E. "Clinton Warns U.S. Will Fight Cheap Imports." *New York Times,* 11 November 1998, 1.

Yergin, Daniel. "Don't Write Off Russia—Yet." *Fortune,* 28 September 1998, 99-102.

Zonis, Marvin. "What's the World Coming To?" *Chief Executive,* September 1997, 60-61.

OPERATIONS MANAGEMENT

Do you drive a car, write checks, have a savings accounts, or get medical treatment? If so, you are directly affected by operations and operations management. Operations are the processes within organizations that transform inputs (labor, capital, materials, and energy) into outputs (services and goods) consumed by the public. Services are intangible products, and goods are physical products. According to the classification scheme used by the **U.S. Department of Commerce** and the U.S. Department of Labor, services include transportation, utilities, lodging, entertainment, health care, legal services, education, communications, wholesale and **retail trade**, banking and **finance**, public administration, insurance, **real estate**, and other miscellaneous services. Goods are described as articles of trade, merchandise, or wares. Manufacturing is a specific term referring to the production of goods.

Operations employ people, build facilities, and purchase equipment in order to provide services such as automobile insurance or to change materials—such as glass, plastic, and electrical components—into finished goods, such as **computer** hardware. Hospitals, **banks**, and fire departments, as well as steelmakers and oil refiners, have operations that engage in these transformation processes. The operating arms of these organizations produce the billions of banking transactions, thousands of fire runs, and millions of gallons of gasoline consumed each day, and they do so very efficiently.

The people working in operations are capable of much greater output than they would be working alone because organizations have developed sophisticated facilities and equipment that greatly increase worker productivity. Firms also provide education and **training** to their **workforces** to increase their knowledge and improve their capabilities. As a result of these productivity improvements and training enhancements, more outputs are produced and the standard of living increases for everyone.

Operations management (which is also known as production management and as production and operations management) is a multidiscipline field that focuses on managing an organization's operations. The scope of operations management includes decision making about the design, planning, and **management** of the many factors that affect operations. Decisions include: what products to produce, how large a facility to build, where to locate the facility with respect to customers and suppliers, what techniques and equipment to use to make the goods or to provide the services, how many units to produce next month, how employees should be trained, and what methods to use to enhance product quality. Operations managers apply ideas and technologies to increase productivity and reduce **costs**, improve flexibility to meet rapidly changing customer needs, shorten delivery time, enhance product quality, and improve customer service.

KEY ISSUES IN OPERATIONS

As an organization develops plans and strategies to deal with threats and opportunities present in its environment, it should consider issues related to: designing a system that is capable of producing the services and goods in the demanded quantities, planning how to use the system effectively, and managing key elements of the operations. Each of these topics is described briefly in the following sections.

DESIGNING THE SYSTEM. Designing the system begins with product development. Product development involves determining the characteristics and features of a product. For example, should a bank offer fund transfers via a touch-tone phone? Should a car be equipped with side air bags? Product development begins with an assessment of customer needs and includes a detailed product design. The facilities and equipment that will produce the service or good, as well as the information systems needed to monitor and control performance, should be designed. Product development is a cross-functional decision-making process that requires teamwork to design and implement the **marketing**, financial, and operating plans needed to successfully launch a product.

Product design is a critical activity because it determines the characteristics, features, and functionality of the product. Product design determines a product's cost and quality as well as its features and performance, and these are important factors on which customers make purchasing decisions. Techniques such as design for manufacturing and assembly are being implemented to improve product quality and lower costs by focusing on operating issues during product design. This is critical even though design costs are a small part of the total cost of a product because design may determine up to 90 percent of the total production costs. For example, when a police department designs a procedure for booking a suspect, the procedure dictates the amount of time spent by the police officers, clerical staff, and management each time a booking takes place. A procedure that wastes time and duplicates effort will substantially affect the department's costs.

Quality functional deployment (QFD) can be an important method for improving product design because it focuses design efforts on customer needs. QFD is a set of planning and communication routines that focuses attention on customer wants and describes design constraints that affect these wants. QFD procedures provide a framework for product design that enhances learning and coordinates actions.

Process design describes how the product will be made. The process design decision has two major components: a technical or engineering component and a scale economy or business component. The technical component includes selecting equipment and sequences for production. For example, a fast food restaurant should decide whether its hamburgers will be flame-broiled or fried. A decision to flame-broil would affect the equipment design and selection decision. Decisions are made about the sequence of operations. For example, should a car rental agency immediately inspect a car that has been returned by the customer, or first send it to be cleaned and washed by maintenance? Most likely, the car should be inspected first so that damage that might occur in the cleaning process would not be counted against the customer.

The scale economy or business component involves applying the proper amount of mechanization (tools and equipment) to make the organization's workforce more productive. This includes determining: (1) if the demand for a product is large enough to justify mass production, such as a fast food restaurant that purchases specialized equipment to make a large volume quickly; (2) if there is sufficient variety in customer demand so that flexible production systems are required, such as a full-service restaurant that purchases general-purpose equipment to produce its diverse menu; or (3) if demand for a product is so small that it cannot support a dedicated production facility, such as demand for the handmade luges used in the Olympics.

Mass customization is a process alternative to mass producing standardized products. Customers are demanding both greater product variety and lower prices for goods and services. To enhance value to their customers, firms are searching for ways to realize these apparently conflicting objectives. Mass customization enables firms to quickly design, produce, and deliver a high volume of differentiated products that meet specific customer needs at mass production prices. Mass customization provides an impressive return on investments by producing products for many small market segments on the same equipment and facilities.

Facility design involves determining the capacity, location, and layout for the facility. Capacity is a measure of an organization's ability to provide the demanded services or goods in the quantity requested by the customer and in a timely manner. Capacity planning involves estimating demand, determining the capacity of facilities, and deciding how to change the organization's capacity to respond to demand.

Facility location is the placement of a facility with respect to its customers and suppliers. Facility location is a strategic decision because it is a long-term commitment of resources that cannot easily or inexpensively be changed. When evaluating a location, management should consider: customer convenience, initial investment for land and facilities, government incentives, operating costs, and transportation costs. In addition, qualitative factors, such as recreational activities for employees, adequate transportation **infrastructure**, and a favorable labor environment may be important.

Facility layout is the arrangement of the work space within a facility. It considers which departments or work areas should be adjacent to one another so that the flow of product, information, and people can move quickly and efficiently through the production system.

Job design specifies the tasks, responsibilities, and methods used in performing a job. For example, the job design for a **word processing** specialist at a publishing company would describe the equipment needed and would explain the standard operating procedures.

PLANNING THE SYSTEM. Planning the system describes how management expects to use the existing resource base that was created during the original design of the production system. One of the outcomes of this planning process may be to change the system design to cope with changes in the environment. For example, management may decide to increase or decrease capacity to cope with changing demand, or rearrange layout to enhance efficiency.

Decisions made by production planners depend on the time horizon. Long-range decisions could include the number of facilities required to meet customer needs, how facilities could be altered to produce new products, or how technological change might affect the methods used to produce services and goods. The time horizon for long-term planning varies with the industry and depends on how long it would take an organization to build new facilities or make major technological changes. For example, in the aircraft industry it may take five to ten years to design a new aircraft and build a facility to produce it. So management must plan at least that far into the future. A car rental agency, on the other hand, would need a much shorter time horizon for production planning because it can make changes more quickly.

In medium-range production planning, which is normally about one year, organizations find it difficult to make major changes in facilities. At most, modest expansion may be achieved or some new equipment installed. Here, production planning may involve determining workforce size, developing training programs, working with suppliers to improve product quality and improve delivery, and determining how much material to order on an aggregate basis.

Scheduling has the shortest planning horizon. As production planning proceeds from long range to short range, the decisions become more detailed. In scheduling, management decides what products will be made, who will do the work, what equipment will be used, which materials will be consumed, when the work will begin, and what will happen to the product when it is complete. All aspects of production come together to make the product a reality. Think of the many factors that must be coordinated to prepare a schedule of classes at a college or university: faculty availability and knowledge, student demands based on graduation requirements, availability of appropriate classrooms, and other resources such as audiovisual equipment.

MANAGING THE SYSTEM. Managing the system involves working with people to encourage participation and improve organizational performance. Participative management and teamwork are becoming essential parts of successful operations. Motivation, **leadership**, and training are receiving new impetus. In addition, material management and quality are two key areas of concern.

Material management includes decisions regarding the procurement, control, handling, storage, and distribution of materials. Materials management is becoming increasingly important because in many organizations the costs of purchased materials are more than 50 percent of the total product cost. How much material should be ordered, when should it be ordered, and which supplier should it be ordered from are some of the important questions.

Quality management programs and high product quality are essential to compete in today's business environment. Quality has progressed from an era of inspection in the 1960s to one of building quality at the source today. Quality is increasingly becoming customer-driven with emphasis put on obtaining a product design that builds quality into the product. Then, the process is designed to transform the product design into a quality product and the employees are trained to execute it. The role of inspection is not to enhance quality but to determine if the designs are effective.

BUILDING SUCCESS WITH OPERATIONS

To understand operations and how they contribute to the success of an organization, it is important to understand the strategic nature of operations, the emerging **supply chain management** ideas, the value-added nature of operations, the impact technology can have on performance, and the globally competitive marketplace.

Organizations can use operations as an important way to gain an advantage on the **competition**. What factors influence the buying decision? For most services and goods, price, quality, product performance and features, product variety, and availability of the product are critical. All these factors are substantially influenced by actions taken in operations. When productivity increases, product costs decline and product price can be reduced. As better production methods are developed, quality and variety may increase.

By linking operations and operating strategies with the overall strategy of the organization (including engineering, financial, marketing, and information system strategies) synergy can result. Operations become a positive factor when facilities, equipment, and employee training are viewed as a means to achieve organizational objectives, rather than suboptimal departmental objectives. The criteria for judging operations is changing from cost control, which is a narrowly defined operating objective, to more global performance measures such as product performance and variety, product quality, delivery time, and customer service. When flexibility is designed into operations, an organization is able to rapidly and inexpensively respond to changing customer needs.

The application of supply chain management is an essential ingredient for competition in the 21st century. Organizations are focusing on their core competencies and relying more heavily on their suppliers for the design and production of services and goods. As a result, organizations are managing their supply chains as an extension of their production system. Progressive organizations have recognized that competition is not between individual firms such as Ford and Honda, rather, it is between their supply chains. The development, design, production, marketing, and delivery of a new car is a **team** effort that begins with extracting raw materials from the earth; continues through design, fabrication, and assembly; and ends with fit and finish in the dealer's showroom. When a customer buys a car from Ford, the customer chooses the output of the entire supply chain and pays all of the participants, including Ford. Ford's success depends on developing methods to manage the supply chain from its roots in basic material (such as iron ore, sand, and crude oil) to the dealer network. This does not mean ownership or even direct control of the entire supply chain, but it does imply putting mechanisms in place that influence **decision making** and affect performance.

Operations should always be a value-added activity. This means that customers should be willing to pay more for the finished product than the total costs of the inputs. In the private sector, the difference between the price consumers pay and the cost of production is profit; profit can be reinvested to build new and better products, thus creating **wealth** for society. In the public sector, the benefits added by designing and producing a new product should always be greater than the costs. This added value, once again, represents an increase in wealth for society. For example, effective fire protection should reduce fire insurance premiums, decrease the number of fires because of successful fire prevention programs, and cut the losses from fires because of rapid response and better fire-fighting techniques and equipment. Value-added fire protection would have more benefits to society than the sum of the costs of providing it. Training firefighters, purchasing equipment, and selecting a new location for a fire station should all be undertaken with this value-added approach in mind. All operating decisions, indeed all the decisions made by the organization, should consider how customers or potential customers will value the outcome of the decision.

Technology is the application of knowledge—usually in the form of recently developed tools, processes, and procedures—to solve problems. Advances in technology make it possible to build better products using fewer resources. As technology fundamentally changes a product, its performance and quality can increase dramatically. For example, an electronic watch is cheaper, more reliable, and takes less care than a mechanical watch.

It is impossible to ignore the impact that the emerging global marketplace and **free trade** are having on organizations and their operations. The **North American Free Trade Agreement** and the **General Agreement on Tariffs and Trade** are increasing the opportunities for countries to focus on areas of trade and commerce in which they have a relative advantage. It will be increasingly common for finished products to have component parts from many different countries. Global sourcing and production of goods and services will become more common.

Over time, operations management has grown in scope and increased in importance. Today, it has elements that are strategic; it relies on behavioral and engineering concepts; and it utilizes **management science** /operations research tools and techniques for systematic decision making and problem solving. As operations management continues to develop, it will increasingly interact with other functional areas within the organization to develop integrated answers to complex interdisciplinary problems.

SEE ALSO: Costing Methods (Manufacturing); Facility Management; Quality Control

[Mark A. Vonderembse]

FURTHER READING:

Blackburn, Joseph D. *Time-Based Competition.* Homewood, IL: Business One Irwin, 1991.

Blackstone, J. H. *Capacity Management.* Cincinnati: South-Western Publishing, 1989.

Chase, R. B., and D. A. Garvin. "The Service Factory." *Harvard Business Review* 67, no. 4 (1989): 61-69.

Clark, K. B., and T. Fujimoto. *Product Development Performance.* Boston: Harvard Business School Press, 1991.

Doll, W. J., and M. A. Vonderembse. "The Evolution of Manufacturing Systems: Towards the Post-Industrial Enterprise."

OMEGA International Journal of Management Science 19, no. 5 (1991): 401-11.

Garvin, David A. *Managing Quality.* New York: Free Press, 1988.

Hayes, Robert H., Gary P. Pisano, and David M. Upton. *Strategic Operations: Competing through Capabilities.* New York: Free Press, 1996.

Nicholas, John M. *Competitive Manufacturing Management.* Boston: Irwin/McGraw-Hill, 1998.

Skinner, W. "Manufacturing: Missing Link in Corporate Strategy." *Harvard Business Review* 52, no. 3 (1969): 136-45.

Sule, D. R. *Manufacturing Facilities: Location, Planning, and Design.* Boston: PWS-Kent Publishing, 1988.

Tersine, R. J. *Principles of Inventory and Materials Management.* New York: Elsevier Science Publishing, 1982.

Umble, M. M., and M. L. Srikanth. *Synchronous Manufacturing.* Cincinnati: South-Western Publishing, 1990.

Vonderembse M. A., and G. P. White. *Operations Management: Concepts, Methods, Strategies.* St. Paul, MN: West Publishing, 1996.

Wheelwright, Steven C., and Kim B. Clark. *Leading Product Development.* New York: Free Press, 1995.

OPPORTUNITY COST

Simply stated, an opportunity cost is the cost of a missed opportunity. Applied to a business decision, opportunity cost might refer to the profit a company could have earned from its capital, equipment, and **real estate** if these assets had been used in a different way. The concept of opportunity cost may be applied to many different situations. It should be considered whenever circumstances are such that scarcity necessitates the election of one option over another. Opportunity cost is usually defined in terms of money, but it may also be considered in terms of time, person-hours, mechanical output, or any other finite, limited resource.

Although opportunity costs are not generally considered by accountants—financial statements include only explicit **costs**, or actual outlays—they should be considered by managers. Business managers should factor in opportunity costs when computing their operating expenses in order to provide a bid or estimate on the price of a job. Opportunity costs increase the cost of doing business, and thus should be recovered as a portion of the **overhead expense** charged to every job. Ignoring opportunity costs may lead managers to undercharge for their services and overestimate their profits.

EXAMPLES OF OPPORTUNITY COSTS

One way to demonstrate opportunity cost lies in the employment of investment capital. For example, a private investor purchases $10,000 in a certain security, such as shares in a corporation, and after one year the investment has appreciated in value to $10,500. The investor's return is 5 percent. The investor considers other ways the $10,000 could have been invested, and discovers a bank certificate with an annual yield of 6 percent and a government bond that carries an annual yield of 7.5 percent. After a year, the bank certificate would have appreciated in value to $10,600, and the government bond would have appreciated to $10,750. The opportunity cost of purchasing shares is $100 relative to the bank certificate, and $250 relative to the government bond. The investor's decision to purchase shares with a 5 percent return comes at the cost of a lost opportunity to earn 6 or 7.5 percent.

Expressed in terms of time, consider a commuter who chooses to drive to work, rather than using public transportation. Because of heavy traffic and a lack of parking, it takes the commuter 90 minutes to get to work. If the same commute on public transportation would have taken only 40 minutes, the opportunity cost of driving would be 50 minutes. The commuter might naturally have chosen driving over public transportation because he could not have anticipated traffic delays in driving. Once the choice has been made to drive, it is not possible to change one's mind, thus the choice itself becomes irrelevant. Experience can create a basis for future decisions, however: the commuter may be less inclined to drive next time, now knowing the consequences of traffic congestion.

In another example, a business owns the building in which it operates, and thus pays no rent for office space. But this does not mean that the company's cost for office space is zero, even though an accountant might treat it that way. Instead, the business owner must consider the opportunity cost associated with reserving the building for its current use. Perhaps the building could have been rented out to another company, or demolished in order to make room for a strip mall. The foregone money from these alternative uses of the property is an opportunity cost of using the office space, and thus should be considered in calculations of the business's expenses.

[John Simley, updated by Laurie Collier Hillstrom]

FURTHER READING:

Baumol, William J., and Alan S. Blinder. *Economics: Principles and Policy.* 6th ed. Forth Worth, TX: Dryden Press, 1994.

Fischer, Stanley, Rudiger Dornbusch, and Richard Schmalensee. *Economics.* 2nd ed. New York: McGraw-Hill, 1988.

Miller, Bruce L., and A. G. Buckman. "Cost Allocation and Opportunity Costs." *Management Science* 33, no. 5 (May 1987): 626+.

Primeaux, Patrick, and John Stieber. "Managing Business Ethics and Opportunity Costs." *Journal of Business Ethics* 16, no. 8 (June 1997): 835+.

Saint-Paul, Gilles. ''Business Cycles and Long-Run Growth: An Opportunity Cost Approach to Corporate Production Decisions.'' *Oxford Review of Economic Policy* 13, no. 3 (autumn 1997): 145+.

Silver, Gerald A. ''When Opportunity Knocks, It Costs.'' *Graphic Arts Monthly* 62, no. 6 (June 1990): 116+.

OPTICAL CHARACTER RECOGNITION DEVICES (OCR)

Optical character recognition (OCR) refers to a computer's ability to recognize printed letters, numerals, or symbols (optical characters) as discrete entities rather than as simply an image containing lines, curves, and shading. Useful for document management, form processing, and a host of other commercial applications, this powerful tool allows businesses to convert paper documents into electronic files that can then be manipulated and retrieved at will. Although the earliest OCR devices debuted in the late 1950s, it was in the 1980s when OCR technology first reached the mass market, spurred by the increasing power of personal computer systems.

The OCR process is simple in theory. When a printed page of text is scanned, the scanner delivers an image of the text to OCR software stored in the attached computer. The software then attempts to identify each letter of each word in the image in order to covert it to an editable text document or to process the information in whatever format is needed.

Companies often use OCR to reduce human data entry, as in bill processing, and for a wide number of other applications that save time and improve accuracy. Newer uses under development have included non-contact scanning from a distance (for instance, scanning license plate numbers) and recognition of handwriting as opposed to printed text. Likewise, OCR is increasingly used in conjunction with **bar coding** and other forms of **automatic identification systems**.

ORIGINAL PROBLEMS WITH OCR

One of the problems with OCR when it was first developed was that the computer was frequently baffled by what the human eye and mind readily accepts. For example, the letter ''e'' might be interpreted as the letter ''o.'' Early OCR software programs achieved accuracy rates of more than 90 percent. Though a seemingly high percentage, this rate, measured on a character-by-character basis, in practice meant that in approximately every second or third word, that is, in every tenth character, an error would occur. As a result, the document would have to be carefully proofread and corrected by a typist, who would use the original paper document as a guide.

What usually confused the OCR software were imperfections on the printed page like stains, extraneous marks, fading, and blurring. Letters had to be crisply printed. Unusual fonts were impossible for the OCR to understand and duplicate. Strikeovers also confused OCR programs. Even slightly blurry, shiny type from thermal fax paper could throw the software into fits.

RECENT OCR TRENDS

Modern scanners for commercial purposes can achieve under ideal conditions accuracy rates in the range of one error per tens of thousands of characters, or more than 99.99 percent accuracy. Still, when one considers that a single article of several pages may contain over 10,000 characters, for large scanning projects this rate will allow many errors to pass if other quality control methods aren't practiced.

To maximize accuracy, OCR software developers try to find a happy medium between making recognition of characters too strict and too flexible. Too strict an interpretation of OCR means mistakes when a letter collects a little bit of dirt or suffers a slightly broken letter form. Too flexible, and it will make the same mistakes as it tries to interpret anything it sees as a letter. Uncommon or highly stylized typefaces only compound recognition problems. Also, too many variations of typefaces on one page can confuse the software as it looks through its programming for something that it recognizes. When companies have control over the typeface, such as that on their own forms, they can print with consistent fonts or even special OCR fonts that help maximize accuracy. OCR fonts tend to be more angular or square in shape and have slightly wider spacing between letters (kerning) to reduce the likelihood of misreading.

The biggest problem, however, remains with ''degraded'' text, such as a slight bit of dirt on the paper that causes the OCR software to interpret a lower case ''h'' as a ''b.'' Faxes remain a problem because faxed text frequently has poor resolution and thus confuses OCR software. Research and development continues to focus on ways to improve OCR performance under such circumstances.

On the plus side, OCR developers are working to train their software to handle potential problems. This often involves interpreting characters in their broader context, e.g., a word or sentence, rather than solely on an individual basis, to achieve greater accuracy. Faster computers with greater memory capacity have enabled such complex processing. Some OCR programs are designed to recognize correct grammar and common spellings so they automatically highlight words that they have copied, but that they also find questionable. The software, in effect, tells its user that it may have made a mistake, but it does not know what to do about it. In the end the machine may turn control of the scanning back over to the human to make the final decision about how to handle what it considers a problem.

OCR DEVICE CHOICES

An effective OCR system depends heavily on both the physical scanner and the software used to interpret the scanner's input. A good scanner can be undermined by weak software and vice versa. Entry-level and mid level scanners and their software can be obtained readily through retail channels; specialized and high-power systems may require contacting a regional distributor or even custom manufacturing and programming.

The most common type of scanner is flatbed. Flatbed scanners look and act much like photocopy machines, with pages being scanned placed flat on the scanner's glass. They generally copy single pages at a time. Advanced scanners have feeding systems for scanning large batches of documents without requiring a human operator to switch pages. These scanners may digitize dozens of pages per minute. Drum scanners are high end devices for capturing fine details, and therefore are often used more for graphic images than for OCR. Instead of bringing the page to the scanner, a handheld scanner allows the scanner to go to the page. Software allows wide images to be "stitched" together from two passes of a handheld over a large image. Generally, however, handheld devices are not as effective at full-page scanning as flatbeds. Finally, one of the newest types of scanners looks like a pen. It allows the user to select certain lines of type in a book for scanning. This type of scanner connects to a computer printer port without the addition of any other computer boards, which may be necessary with other types of scanners.

[Clint Johnson]

FURTHER READING:

Callan, Tim. "Putting OCR Where It's Not: Opportunities for New Expansion." *Advanced Imaging,* April 1997.

Davis, Andrew. "Industrial OCR: Machine Vision Takes on New Characters." *Advanced Imaging,* April 1997.

Koulopoulos, Thomas M., and Carl Frappaolo. *Electronic Document Management Systems.* New York: McGraw-Hill, 1995.

Ross, Fred F. *OCR with a Smile.* Englewood, CO: House of Scanning, 1998.

OPTIONS CLEARING CORPORATION

Established in 1973, the Options Clearing Corporation (OCC) is an **options** clearinghouse that is owned by the four securities exchanges that make markets in listed **stock** options. These exchanges are the Chicago Board of Options Exchange (CBOE), the American Stock Exchange (AMEX), the Philadelphia Stock Exchange (PHLX), and the Pacific Stock Exchange (PSE). All four exchanges clear all of their option transactions through the OCC. The OCC is regulated by the **Securities and Exchange Commission** (SEC), and is vital to the operations of the exchanges.

The main role of the OCC is to act as a performance guarantor for all stock options. An option buyer and seller who agree on a price for a standardized stock option will negotiate a deal. The OCC then interposes itself between the buyer and seller, becoming the party to whom delivery is made, and from whom delivery is taken. By becoming the opposite party to every **contract**, the OCC is substituting its own ability to deliver on the contract for the option writer's ability to deliver, thus guaranteeing performance and eliminating counterparty risk.

For example, the seller, or writer, of an IBM **call option** with a three-month expiration date is obligated to deliver 100 shares of IBM stock to the buyer at the striking price, if the buyer decides to exercise his or her option. Buyers of call options will exercise their options when it is economically advantageous to do so. Normally, this occurs at the expiration date, if the current stock price exceeds the striking, or exercise, price. Such an option is said to be "in the money," meaning that the buyer will immediately profit from exercising the option. Since an option is an agreement or contract between two parties, the buyer's profit will equal the writer's loss. There is an incentive, however, for the writer of a call that is in the money at the expiration date to simply ignore his or her obligation to deliver the 100 shares of stock. This could occur because of bankruptcy by the writer, or simply his or her unwillingness to incur the financial loss. (Recall that the potential loss from writing call options is virtually unlimited because the stock value has no price ceiling.)

Because the OCC becomes the counterparty to all option trades, the buyer of a call option need not worry about the integrity or financial means of the writer. If the writer of the option defaults on his or her obligation, the buyer is unaffected because the OCC will make the delivery. This, in effect, increases the secondary marketability of stock options. It also reduces transaction costs, since buyers will not need to investigate the writer's credit.

The same is true for buyers and sellers of put options. The writer of a put option agrees to purchase the 100 shares of stock from the put buyer at the exercise price on or before the expiration date, if the buyer so decides to exercise. Put buyers will exercise their options when the current stock price is below the exercise price. Although the put writer's loss is limited, because the stock value can drop only to zero, there is still a financial incentive for the writer to **default**. But since the OCC is, in effect the counterparty to both sides, the buyer need not worry about the writer's integrity. If the writer defaults, the OCC will purchase the shares from the buyer and take legal action against the writer.

In addition to guaranteeing the performance on all option contracts, another way the OCC increases option marketability and liquidity is by enabling option buyers and writers to terminate their positions in the market at any time, by making an offsetting transaction. A buyer of a call option can in effect, close out his or her position by simply writing a call option with the same exercise price and expiration date. The same holds true for puts; buyers and writers of put options can terminate their positions by taking the opposite position with the same exercise price and expiration date. Because of this possibility, more participants are likely to enter the market, thereby improving the marketability and liquidity of options. Another factor that aids marketability and liquidity is the standardized contract.

The OCC also maintains the financial integrity of the option exchanges and markets through margin requirements that are imposed on option writers. The actual margin requirements are established by the SEC and **Federal Reserve** Board, with the OCC acting as the clearinghouse. Put or call buyers pay a premium to the writer at the time the contract is entered into. The buyers do not need to post any margin because they will only exercise the option if it is profitable. In other words, after purchasing the put or call option, no further money is at risk. Put and call writers, however, have a future financial obligation if the option expires in-the-money. Therefore, option writers are required to post margins equal to the market value of their obligation as a performance guarantee.

While other clearinghouses also serve traders on the options exchanges, the OCC is the world's largest clearinghouse for financial derivatives. It has a daily liability of $30 billion. It began converting its computer systems for **year 2000 compliance** in 1985 and has been Y2K compliant since 1996. In June 1998 it became the first clearinghouse to receive a AAA rating from Standard & Poor's, reflecting its leadership in clearance, settlement, and **risk management** systems.

[James A. Gerhardinger, updated by David P. Bianco]

FURTHER READING:

''ABN AMRO Chicago Corporation to Acquire Sage Clearing.'' *Harvard Business Review,* November/December 1997, 157.

Bailey, Fred. *Practical Strategies in Stock Options.* Grove City, PA: Center for Futures Education, 1997.

Bere, Carol. ''The OCC Sets the Pace.'' *Global Finance,* June 1998, 94.

Connors, Laurence A. *Connors on Advanced Trading Strategies.* Malibu, CA: M. Gordon Publishing, 1998.

Gross, LeRoy. *The Conservative Investor's Guide to Trading Options.* New York: Wiley, 1998.

Options Traders. 3rd ed. New York: Simon & Schuster, 1998.

Szala, Ginger. ''Less Is More: OCC Goes to Institutions.'' *Futures,* November 1993, 24-25.

''Y2K Stats: The Options Clearing Corp.'' *PC Week,* 6 July 1998, 88.

OPTIONS/OPTIONS CONTRACTS

An option is the right to choose a particular action among alternatives. A financial option contract is the right, but not the obligation, to buy or sell a specified amount of an asset at a specified price, for a specified time period. The term is most often associated with **stock**, but options are available on other assets. There are also a number of other financial instruments, such as **warrants** and callable or convertible **bonds**, which include option features. Options and instruments with option features are sometimes called **derivatives**, or contingent claims, since the value of the instrument is derived from or contingent upon the value of some underlying asset. Options have become important tools for managing **risk**. More recently, **financial engineering** has produced an array of innovative financial instruments and strategies that employ options or exhibit option characteristics.

An option contract may be a ''put'' or a ''call.'' The buyer, or ''holder'' of a call has the right to buy (call in), the underlying asset. The holder of a put has the right to sell (put onto someone else), the underlying asset. Although the underlying asset, the price of the trade, and the time period are fixed, the holder of the option is not obligated: the alternatives of choice are to ''exercise'' the option or to let the option expire. The seller, or ''writer,'' of a put (call) is, however, obligated to buy (sell) at the strike price if the buyer decides to exercise the option. The fixed price at which the purchase or sale can be executed is called the ''strike price'' or the ''exercise price.'' Since the right to decide is valuable, the buyer of an option purchases the option at a price referred to as the ''premium.'' Options may be ''European'' or ''American,'' but this label does not refer to where the option is traded. Rather, European options may be exercised only at expiration, while the more prevalent American option may be exercised at any time on or before expiration.

Conventional option **contracts** are available over-the-counter from put and call dealers, who provide individualized option contracts. In 1973, however, the Chicago Board Options Exchange began trading standardized options contracts. These exchange-traded or ''listed'' options are less flexible and are available only on certain assets, but are easier and cheaper to trade, provide greater trading depth and have an active secondary market. Standardized options are now traded on several exchanges and account for the bulk of options trading. Listed options are available on many **common stocks**, various foreign currencies, and several stock **indexes**. Listed options are also available on **futures contracts** for agricultural **commodities**, precious metals, foreign currencies, and **interest rates**.

An additional attraction of listed options is that there is no risk of seller default. Performance is guaranteed by the **Options Clearing Corporation** (OCC). The OCC enters each transaction, becoming a buyer to the seller and a seller to the buyer, but maintaining a zero net position. When an option is exercised before expiration, the OCC will deliver on the option. In order to maintain the zero balance, the OCC will at the same time exercise the option contract with a seller. In this case the exercise is randomly assigned to a broker or dealer, who will in turn assign the exercise to a client who has written the contract. The OCC charges a small fee on each transaction for providing this service.

TYPES OF OPTIONS

The exact terms of standardized option contracts vary with the nature of the underlying asset. For options on common stock, the contract size is 100 shares. Not all strike prices are traded. Strike prices are set by the exchange, most often at multiples of $5.00. The exchange will begin trading options of a given expiration at a strike price or prices that are close to the market price. If the price of the stock changes, however, the exchange will initiate trading in contracts at other strike prices. Eventually, there may be many contracts traded with the same expiration but different strike prices. Strike price and contract size are adjusted for stock splits, and for stock **dividends** of more than 10 percent, using the split factor, e.g., a three-for-two stock split would result in an option on 150 shares at two-thirds of the original strike price. Cash dividends have no effect on the option. The maturity of stock options is usually identified by the month of expiration, with all options expiring on the Saturday following the third Friday of the month. Options with maturities up to two years, called ''long-term equity anticipation securities'' (LEAPS) are available on some blue-chip stocks. Most stock options have maturities of eight months or less, however, and fall into one of three expiration cycles: (1) January, April, July, and October; (2) February, May, August, and November; or (3) March, June, September, and December. Generally, options with expiration in the next two calendar months, plus the next two closest months in the expiration cycle, are available.

Option terms on other assets are set similarly—options on wheat, for instance, call for delivery of 5,000 bushels of a stated type and quality at a stated location. Foreign currency options are written on a set amount of the foreign currency, with expiration on the Saturday before the third Wednesday of the month. Maturities available include the next two months, and March, June, September, and December. Interest rate options are written on a specific amount (usually $100,000) of a specific **U.S. Treasury note** or bond. They are available with original maturities of three and six months, but normally options on a given instrument are traded for only one expiration cycle. Rather than introducing new options on the same **securities**, they are replaced with options on recent issues.

Options on indexes include broad stock market indexes and industry-specific indexes. Expiration dates are similar to those of stock options. An importance difference here is the nature of delivery. The contract is written on 100 units of the underlying index. Since it would be impractical or even impossible for writers to deliver the exact assets and proportions specified in the index, cash settlement is used. At exercise, the writer delivers cash equal to 100 times the (positive) difference between the index value and the strike price. Another important difference is that an order to exercise is executed after the close of trading at the ending price, rather than at the time and the price when the order is given. Although the cash settlement is a desirable feature, it may increase the price volatility of the underlying stock. This occurs because institutional investors with large portfolios use index options to hedge against losses, or to take advantage of small price imbalances. As the options approach expiration, attempts to restructure these positions cause large transactions with attendant price swings.

The options discussed so far are based on the spot price, the price for immediate delivery of the asset. A futures contract, however, calls for delivery of the underlying asset at a fixed price at some time in the future. An important difference between an option and a futures contract is that the buyer of a futures contract assumes the obligation to perform. An option on a futures contract, or ''futures option,'' provides the option feature based on the trading price at some time in the future. Futures options are available on agricultural **commodities**, precious metals, fixed-income securities (called ''interest rate options'') and stock indexes. Trading volume in futures options sometime exceeds trading volume in the spot contract. The exact maturities and expiration dates vary among the underlying assets traded.

OPTION PAYOFFS

The key to the analysis of gains and losses on option positions is that the buyer of the option has the right, but not the obligation, to exercise. The buyer would not exercise the option if exercise would result in a loss. For this reason, many options are never exercised and simply expire. This also implies that the maximum possible loss for the buyer, and the maximum gain for the writer, is the premium. Consider a listed call option on XYZ stock with a strike price of $30, purchased for a premium of $200, which is about to expire. The net payoffs at expiration for both the writer and the buyer are given in Table 1 for a range of market values of the underlying stock. At any price below $30, the buyer will not exercise the call option because to do so would be to buy the stock above market—the option is said to be ''out of the money.'' Expiration is preferable to exercise because by not exercising the buyer limits the loss to the premium paid to obtain the option, in this case $200. At $30, the option is ''at the money,'' and the buyer is indifferent about exercise. Above $30, the buyer could exercise the option and buy the stock at a price below market—the option is ''in the money.'' Note that this may still result in a net loss, since the premium must be deducted. The loss would be higher, however, if the option was not exercised. At $32, the buyer breaks even, and any further increases in the value of the stock result in proportional ($100 for each $1 change) net gains limited only by the maximum stock price. The payoffs of the buyer and the writer are always a mirror image, as depicted in Figure 1. The writer thus has a maximum gain of $200, and an indefinite maximum loss.

This same type of analysis can be applied to the payoffs from a put, as shown in Figure 2 for a put with

Table 1

Strike Price = $30.00, Premium = $200.00

CALL OPTION:

Stock Price	WRITER exercise	+	premium	=	net	BUYER exercise	+	premium	=	net
$00.00	NEX*		+$200		+$200	NEX*		-$200		-$200
29.00	NEX*		+$200		+$200	NEX*		-$200		-$200
30.00	-0-		+$200		+$200	-0-		-$200		-$200
31.00	-$1 X 100		+$200		+$100	+$1 X 100		-$200		-$100
32.00	-$2 X 100		+$200		-0-	+$2 X 100		-$200		-0-
33.00	-$3 X 100		+$200		-$100	+$3 X 100		-$200		+$100
34.00	-$4 X 100		+$200		-$200	+$4 X 100		-$200		+$200
35.00	-$5 X 100		+$200		-$300	+$5 X 100		-$200		+$300

*not exercised

PUT OPTION:

Stock Price	WRITER exercise	+	premium	=	net	BUYER exercise	+	premium	=	net
$00.00	-$30 x 100		+$200		-$2800	+$30 x 100		-$200		+$2800
26.00	-$4 X 100		+$200		-$200	+$4 X 100		-$200		+$200
27.00	-$3 X 100		+$200		-$100	+$3 X 100		-$200		+$100
28.00	-$2 X 100		+$200		-0-	+$2 X 100		-$200		-0-
29.00	-$1 X 100		+$200		+$100	+$1 X 100		-$200		-$100
30.00	-0-		+$200		+$200	-0-		-$200		-$200
31.00	NEX*		+$200		+$200	NEX*		-$200		-$200

*not exercised

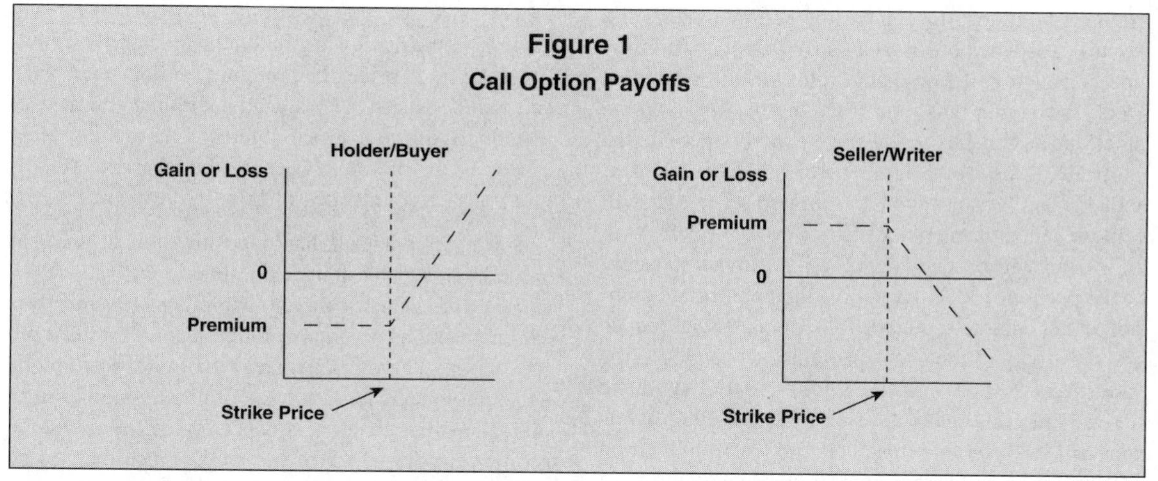

a strike price of $30 and a premium of $200. Again, the payoffs to writer and buyer are mirror images, and again the buyer's maximum loss and the writer's maximum gain are equal to the premium. The buyer's maximum gain and the writer's maximum loss are limited to $2,800 ($30 × 100 less the $200 premium), which will occur if the stock price goes to zero.

OPTION STRATEGIES

The payoffs to various option strategies involving writing or buying combinations of puts, calls, and other assets can also be analyzed by combining the payoffs at various prices. A ''straddle'' is the combination of a put and a call on the same stock with the same strike price and expiration. For a buyer, a straddle will produce a loss of the two premiums if the price of the stock is at the strike price. If the price moves far enough away from the strike price in either direction, one of the options becomes in the money. The buyer will realize a gain if the price of the stock moves far enough away from the strike price, either up or down, so that the gain on exercise of the in-the-money option will more than equal the premiums. The opposite straddle position—sale, or ''shorting'' both a put and a call will result in mirror image payoffs. Variations on a straddle include strips (two puts and one call) and straps (two calls and one put). Spreads involve combination of calls or puts on the same underlying stock, but with differing strike prices or expirations.

A position involving only the option itself is called a naked option, while an option position combined with a long position in the underlying stock is called a covered option. Sales of covered calls, the sale of a call on a stock being held by the investor, has been a popular **strategy**. The seller of the covered call will lose the possibility of **capital gains**, but will receive additional income from the premium. This strategy would be appropriate if the seller does not expect a price increase, or planned to eventually sell the stock at the call price. Purchase of a put on a stock held long is termed a ''protective put.'' The value of the put will increase as the stock price drops, so that the holder has reduced or ''hedged'' the potential loss.

Use of options is not limited to individual investors. Index options are widely used as a **portfolio**

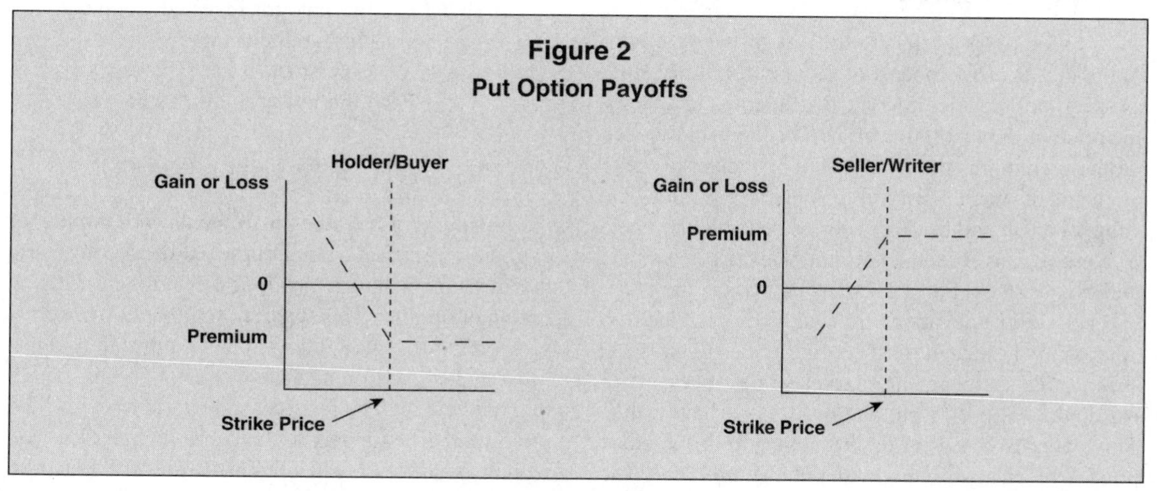

management tool to change the return pattern and control risk. The portfolio can provide portfolio insurance, analogous to protective puts on an individual stock, by buying puts on a stock index. Although the stock index will likely not move exactly opposite the portfolio value, for a large portfolio the movement will be similar and even this imperfect hedge will remove much of the risk of loss. Similarly, sale of an index call will produce payoffs that move oppositely to the portfolio value. By selling the appropriate number of call contracts, the portfolio manager can reduce the sensitivity of the portfolio value to changes in the index. Options may also be used to create ''synthetic assets,'' or combinations of options and other assets that have a different return pattern. The combination of a put and a call at the same strike price would have a payoff pattern at expiration that would be the same as that of the underlying asset, at the cost of the premiums paid.

RISK IN OPTION TRADING

There is no definitive answer to the question of the riskiness of option trading. As shown in Figure 1, the possible outcomes vary widely, and the strategy being followed must also be considered. Sale of a naked put or call exposes the writer to extreme losses, whereas purchase of the call or put has sharply limited loss possibilities. Covered options present limited risk, and protective puts or portfolio **hedging** are meant to reduce risk. There is no doubt, however, that some options trades can present significant risk. One reason for the popularity of options as investment vehicles is that they provide **leverage**. For the amount of the premium, the buyer ''controls'' 100 shares of stock, so that a $1 change in the value of the stock underlying and in-the-money option results in a much larger change in the premium. Because of the inherent risk, the OCC requires to option writer to post and maintain margin.

OPTION PRICING

Option pricing refers to the size of the premium. There are financial models of option premiums, such as the Black-Scholes Model, that attempt to specify the price on a quantitative basis. The largest influence on the premium is the relationship between the strike price and the market price of the underlying asset. The value of a call will be positively related, and the value of a put negatively related, to the market price of the underlying stock. For a given market price, the value of a call will be negatively related, and the value of a put positively related, to the strike price. Even if the strike price is above the market value of a call, or below the value of a put, the option will have value. This value is based on the possibility that the stock price will change enough to put the option in the money. Because the possibility that the option will become in the money is greater, the greater the volatility of the stock price, the premium for both a put and a call will be positively associated with the volatility of the underlying stock price. Interest rates are positively related to the premium because the leverage effect is more attractive in times of high interest rates.

The option itself has a positive value, and this value is greater the longer the time to expiration. Because of the value of time to expiration, few investors exercise options before expiration, but will instead sell the option. Option sellers can exit the position by engaging in an offsetting trade of purchasing the same option, which results in a canceling of the investors' position on the books of the OCC. Since there is no adjustment for dividends, which have a tendency to decrease stock price, the value of a call is negatively related, and the value of a put is positively related, to the dividend yield of the stock. As an exception to the general avoidance of early exercise, if a dividend is to be recorded before expiration, investors may wish to exercise calls to capture the dividend.

The relationship between the price of a put and the price of a call is referred to as the ''**put-call parity**'' relationship. At maturity, a protective put will have a value equal to the greater of the strike price or the stock price. An investor could, however, purchase a call on the same stock at the same strike price and expiration, and invest enough in **U.S. Treasury bills** (T-bills) to equal the strike price at expiration. At expiration, this portfolio also has a value equal to the greater of the strike price or the stock price. Since both of these positions have the same outcome, they should have the same price or **arbitrage** is possible. Therefore,

$$C + \frac{X}{(1 + r_f)^{-T}} = S + P$$

where C = the call premium,
X = the strike price,
$(1 + r_f)^{-T}$ = the **present value** factor for an amount invested at time T in T-bills at rate r_f,
S = the stock price,
P = the put premium.

ASSETS WITH OPTION FEATURES

Analysis of financial instruments with implicit or explicit option features can proceed by decomposing the instrument into a nonoption instrument plus an option or options. This separation provides a different perspective that may allow new insights into value. Most bonds, for instance, are ''callable.'' This means that the bond can be repurchased by the issuer for the price of the bond plus a ''call premium.'' The call feature is simply a call option held by the issuer. A callable bond can be analyzed as a purchase of a noncallable bond, plus the sale of a call on the bond—a covered call position in the bond. The value of a call feature would be affected by the same factors affecting other call options.

Rights arise in stock offerings and are sometimes associated with the preemptive right of common stockholders to maintain their proportional ownership of the firm. The existing shareholders of the firm are given one right for every share that they own. Purchase of one share of the new stock then requires *R* rights plus $\$S_e$. $\$S_e$ is set at a value below the expected post-offering stock price $\$S_p$. The *R* rights required for subscription then have a value $\$S_p - \$S_e$, so that the value of one right will be:

$$\frac{\$S_p - \$S_e}{R}$$

There is a market for rights, and investors who do not wish to subscribe or who have odd numbers of rights may capture their value. The lifetime of rights is typically short, and they may be considered as options on the to-be-issued shares.

Warrants are options to buy a fixed number of newly issued shares at a fixed price, written by the firm. They often are included in bond offerings as "sweeteners" in order to make an issue more attractive, or in executive compensation. They typically have an extended lifetime, some even being perpetual, and originally are "deep" out of the money, carrying an exercise price well above market. The value of a warrant would be affected by the same factors affecting other call options.

Convertible bonds may be converted into common stock at some fixed ratio or face value per share. The conversion feature is in essence a call option on the common stock, and convertible bonds are sometimes analyzed as the combination of a bond and an option. A convertible will be valued at the higher of its value as a straight (i.e., nonconvertible) bond, or its conversion value as the underlying stock, plus an added premium for the value of the call option feature.

Financial engineering is the term applied to the creation of innovative financial instruments, and the options feature has been widely used in this activity. Analysis of the instruments often requires sophisticated mathematical treatment. Some of these instruments are individualized, while others are traded to varying degrees. These traded instruments include putable bonds, certificates of deposit with payoffs based on various indexes, and LYONS (zero coupon, convertible, callable, and putable bonds).

SEE ALSO: Call and Put Options; Options Clearing Corporation

[David E. Upton]

FURTHER READING:

Bodie, Zvi, Alex Kane, and Alan J. Marcus. *Investments.* 4th ed. Boston: Irwin/McGraw-Hill, 1999.

Chance, Don M. *An Introduction to Derivatives.* 4th ed. Fort Worth, TX: Dryden Press, 1998.

Kolb, Robert W. *Futures, Options, and Swaps.* 3rd ed. Malden, MA: Blackwell Publishers, 1999.

Reilly, Frank K., and Keith C. Brown. *Investment Analysis and Portfolio Management.* 5th ed. Fort Worth, TX: Dryden Press, 1997.

ORGANISATION FOR ECONOMIC CO-OPERATION AND DEVELOPMENT

The Organisation for Economic Co-operation and Development (OECD) began in 1948 as the Organisation for European Economic Co-operation (OEEC). The OEEC was established by 16 Western European nations to coordinate policy, make recommendations, and manage aid received through the Marshall Plan. Named after U.S. Secretary of State George C. Marshall, the Marshall Plan began in 1947 when the administration of President Harry Truman came to the realization that the dire situation in Europe following World War II—disease, cold, and hunger—required an immediate and massive U.S. response. On July 12, 1947, representatives of Austria, Belgium, Denmark, France, Greece, Iceland, Ireland, Italy, Luxembourg, the Netherlands, Norway, Portugal, Sweden, Switzerland, Turkey, and the United Kingdom met in Paris to produce a four-year recovery program and to form the Committee of European Economic Co-operation (CEEC). On April 16, 1948, these 16 countries formally established the OEEC and named as its head noted French economist Robert Marjolin.

The founding principles of the OEEC were based on the idea that the economic systems of member countries are interrelated and that the prosperity of each individual country is based on the prosperity of all. The OEEC subsequently flourished as "recovery spurred further recovery" and it soon became a champion of free industrial democracies and free market economies while also serving as a bulwark against communist expansion.

The OEEC continued to operate long after the Marshall Plan had ended and in a way was the victim of its own success. By the end of the 1950s, Western Europe had recovered but other parts of the world were in crisis. This was especially true in many parts of what soon became known as the Third World. Not incidentally many of these emerging countries were former colonies of European nations. In 1959, amidst some opposition, U.S. President Dwight Eisenhower, Chancellor Konrad Adenauer of Germany, and President Charles de Gualle of France sought to have the

OEEC become active on a global rather than a regional scale. The United States and Canada joined the OEEC as full members in 1960 and on September 30, 1961, the OEEC ceased to exist and the OECD was born. Since then nine more countries have joined the OECD: Japan (1964), Finland (1969), Australia (1971), New Zealand (1973), Mexico (1994), the Czech Republic (1995), Hungary (1996), Poland (1996), and Korea (1996). The main goal of the OECD is to "exchange information and harmonize policy with a view to maximizing economic growth with member countries and assisting non-member countries to develop more rapidly."

Originally the OECD was concerned with trade and the economic and financial policies of its members. It has over the decades expanded its sphere of responsibilities to include agriculture, energy, the environment, science and technology, social matters, communications, and even global corruption. To implement policy in these areas the OECD has created advisory committees and agencies such as the International Energy Agency; the Nuclear Energy Agency; the Environmental Policy Committee; the Directorate for Science, Technology, and Industry; the Employment, Labour, and Social Affairs Committee; the Trade Committee; the Committee for Agriculture; the Committee for Fisheries; and the Committee on Capital Movements and Invisible Transactions.

The OECD is also quite concerned with international corruption and financial crimes. In 1989, for instance, the OECD established the Financial Task Force on Money Laundering, which sets forth a comprehensive plan for taking action against money laundering. The task force meets several times every year and brings together legal, financial, and law enforcement policy makers from 26 countries. The task force also monitors the progress of its members to implement anti-money-laundering policies; assesses and reports on trends in money-laundering schemes and activities; and promotes its policies among nonmember countries.

In another attempt to fight international crime the OECD's Convention on Combating Bribery of Foreign Public Officials went into effect in early 1999. The convention and resultant treaty, which has been signed by 29 countries, publicizes and promotes national legislation making the bribing of public officials a crime. The OECD treaty especially promotes the criminalization of the "supply side" of the act, that is legislation aimed at prosecuting those who offer bribes. U.S. companies that bribe foreign public officials can already be prosecuted under provisions of the U.S. Foreign Corrupt Practices Act.

Although the OECD mostly interacts with countries it is also concerned with consumer protection. Its Directorate of Science and Technology has, for instance, a Committee on Consumer Policy which is attempting to establish guidelines for protecting consumers who purchase goods and services online. This committee has developed a declaration on "Consumer Protection in the Context of Electronic Commerce."

The OECD is also recognized worldwide for its extensive publications program highlighted by the biannual *OECD Economic Outlook.* This publication forecasts global economic trends with information on each member country. The OECD also publishes information dealing with specific economic activities. Such publications include *Agricultural Outlook, Indicators of Industrial Activity,* and *Oil and Gas Statistics.* These publications are highly regarded and often quoted and discussed in relevant media outlets.

The council is the governing organ of the OECD. It meets at least once a year and each member country is represented. The council is responsible for OECD policy and for achieving the organization's aims. The chairman of the council is the government minister from the country elected to the chairmanship for that year. The council designates on an annual basis a 14-member executive committee which administers and readies the work of the council. The council and other OECD bodies are assisted in their duties by an independent international secretariat headed by the secretary general. The majority of the funding for the OECD (approximately 60 percent) comes from regular contributions by member states, with the rest generated from special sources and project participants.

[Michael Knes]

FURTHER READING:

Campbell, A. J. "OECD: Providing Consumer Protection in Electronic Commerce." *Business America* 119, no. 9 (September 1998): 28 29.

Kaltenheuser, Skip. "Schmiergeld: "Grease Money" in International Commerce May Soon Be Drying Up." *Across the Board* 35, no. 10 (November/December 1998): 36-42.

Organisation for Economic Co-operation and Development. "Organisation for Economic Co-operation and Development." Paris: Organisation for Economic Co-operation and Development, 1998. Available from www.oecd.org.

Sullivan, Scott. *From War to Wealth: Fifty Years of Innovation.* Paris: OECD Publications, 1997.

Vogel, Frank. "The Supply Side of Global Bribery." *Finance and Development* 35, no. 2 (June 1998): 3.

ORGANIZATION OF AFRICAN UNITY (OAU)

The Organization of African Unity (OAU) was established on May 25, 1963, by representatives of 30 African nations meeting in Addis Ababa, Ethiopia. The conference was held at the invitation of Haile

Selassie I, then emperor of Ethiopia. An earlier meeting the same year, the Conference of Addis Ababa, set the groundwork for the subsequent establishment of the OAU. Foreign ministers of 32 African nations attended this earlier conference and despite regional, political, and linguistic differences they managed to come together on many issues. Most important was the agreement that a pan-African organization was needed. The primary aim of such an organization would be to promote African unification and economic development while fighting colonialism and apartheid. Also discussed were relations between the **United Nations** and various African countries, disarmament, and the creation of a permanent conciliation commission. As a result of this conference, 30 of the original 32 representatives attended a Heads of State Conference and wrote the Charter of the Organization of African Unity.

The OAU was not the first attempt at inter-African unity. A 1958 conference of independent African states was held in Ghana resulting in a charter that would eventually serve as a model for the OAU. A 1961 conference was held in Casablanca that dealt with the possibilities of an African common market and an African military command. Nations attending this conference became known as the ''Casablanca Group.'' In 1960 and 1961, 12 French-speaking African countries not attending the Casablanca conference signed a charter establishing the Union africaine et malgache which later became known as the Organization commune africaine et mauriciene (OCAM). Also in 1961, another conference was held in Monrovia, Liberia, which resulted in the formation of the Organization of Inter-African and Malagasy States. Nations attending this conference became known as the ''Monrovia Group.''

Although these two groups had similar goals—pan-Africanism—they had divergent ways of reaching this goal. The Casablanca Group took a more radical approach to unity. They favored socialistic planned economies for members and viewed strident anticolonialism as a unifying force. The Monrovia Group was more moderate, placing more emphasis on economic cooperation and less on politics and ideology. This group also took a regional approach to problem solving but a hands-off approach to members' internal affairs and problems. Despite these differences, the two groups came together in 1963 and subsequently established the OAU. Although the new inter-African organization resembled the more conservative Monrovian Group, ideological compromises were made. To mollify the Casablanca Group the OAU gave limited support to liberation movements and passed resolutions condemning apartheid and existing remnants of colonialism.

The principles and objectives of the OAU as stated in its charter are: to promote the unity and solidarity of the African states; to coordinate and intensify their various efforts so as to have the peoples of Africa achieve a better life; to defend the sovereignty, territorial integrity and independence of its members; to work to eradicate colonialism from Africa; and finally, to maintain due regard for the Charter of the United Nations and the Universal Declaration of Human Rights. To achieve these goals, OAU members pledged to harmonize their policies in regard to political, economic, diplomatic, educational, cultural, scientific, defense and security, and health, sanitation, and nutritional cooperation. The OAU also recognized the sovereignty and independence of its members; agreed to noninterference in regards to member's internal affairs; forbade political assassination and political subversion; supported the peaceful settlement of disputes through mediation, conciliation, and arbitration; supported the total emancipation of African states that continue to be ''dependent''; and finally, affirmed a policy of nonalignment.

By 1984 all independent African nations except South Africa belonged to the OAU, bringing its membership up to 50. In its battle against apartheid and racial discrimination, the OAU succeeded in excluding South Africa from the Economic Commission for Africa and from UNESCO. The OAU nearly succeeded in having South Africa expelled from the United Nations while showing strong support for Nelson Mandela's African National Congress. (With the fall of apartheid, however, South Africa became the OAU's 53rd member in May 1994.)

The OAU has also promoted economic development and cooperation on numerous fronts. In 1980 it held the African Economic Summit which resulted in the Lagos Plan of Action that called for economic independence of OAU members by the year 2000. The Lagos plan also envisioned a continent wide African Economic Community. In 1989 there was another economic summit, which involved discussion of external debt obligations and economic reforms mandated by the **International Monetary Fund** and the **World Bank**. In 1991 the OAU Assembly met in Abuja, Nigeria, and prepared a draft of the African Economic Community (AEC) treaty. This treaty dealt with the long-term economic deterioration of the continent and called for the implementation of six steps through the year 2025 to deal with these problems. Through these six steps the OAU hopes to gradually remove **trade barriers** while integrating the economies of member countries. The plan also calls for the establishment of an OAU court of justice, an inter-African economic union, a uniform currency, a parliament, and a **central bank**.

As the OAU evolved, one of its major roles on the African continent has been that of a peacekeeper. Over the decades the OAU has mediated conflicts in Somalia, Rwanda, Burundi, Liberia, Angola, Mozambique, and Sudan. Many of these conflicts have been territorial and boundary disputes that reflected artificial borders created by colonial powers.

At a 1993 Cairo Summit the OAU set up its Central Mechanism for the Prevention and Management of Conflict. One purpose of the new mechanism was to make OAU nations less dependent on outside mediators. This peacekeeping role was also a focal point of the 32nd OAU summit held in Yaounde, the capital of Cameroon, in 1996. The resultant Yaounde Declaration, among other things, set up a new and more efficient mechanism for handling conflicts between members and contained a mutual nonaggression treaty signed by 11 Central African nations. Some experts in conflict resolution feel, however, that a continent-wide peacekeeping initiative cannot be strong enough to overcome nationalism, and that various regional approaches are more guaranteed of success. In the late 1990s there were stirrings in some Western countries—namely France, Great Britain, and the United States—to have these countries train an African peacekeeping force. Again because of nationalism, however, it was feared that these peacekeeping forces could quickly revert into private armies of African ruling parties and presidents.

On the agenda for the 1998 54th OAU/African Economic conference were discussions on reparation and debt forgiveness, dual citizenship, a single currency, and the formation of an Africa mineral exporting countries bloc and an African export-import bank. Also scheduled for discussion was the creation of an artificial nation-state that could become the OAU's 54th member. This nation-state would be comprised of an estimated 60 million people of African descent now living in other parts of the world, including African Americans. Such a nation-state would better allow those of the African diaspora, especially those who have been exposed to Western technology, to help "develop a vehicle for transitional change and regional reciprocal trade between Africans globally who seek to have an impact on the economic growth of Africa."

The chief policy-making body of the OAU is the Assembly of Heads of State and Government. The assembly meets annually and each member nation is allotted one vote. The Council of Ministers meets biannually and is made up of the foreign ministers of each member country. The Council of Ministers advises the assembly on budgetary matters, policy implementation, inter-African affairs, and relations with nonmember countries. The General Secretariat carries out those duties assigned to it by the OAU charter and by the agreements and treaties of the OAU. The Secretariat has numerous departments including: Economic Development and Cooperation, Administration and Conference, Political, Finance, and Culture and Social Affairs.

[Michael Knes]

FURTHER READING:

"An African Answer to African Wars." *Economist,* 18 October 1997, 45-46.

Ali, Abdur-Rashid. "A 54th State of Africa?" *African Business,* February 1998, 33-34.

da Costa, Peter. "Keeping the Peace." *Africa Report* 40, no. 3 (May/June 1995): 26-29.

El-Ayouty, Yasin. *The Organization of African Unity after Thirty Years.* Westport, CT: Praeger, 1994.

Gongyuan Chen. "Organization of African Unity: Solidarity that Works." *Beijing Review* 39, no. 21 (20 May 1996): 11.

Harris, Gordon. *Organization of African Unity.* New Brunswick, NJ: Transaction Publishers, 1994.

International Monetary Fund. "Organization of African Unity." Washington: International Monetary Fund, 1998. Available from www.imf.org/external/np/sec/decdo/oau.htm.

Lu Zong. "OAU Summit Calls for Peace, Development." *Beijing Review* 39, no. 31 (29 July 1996): 7-8.

Oloniskan, Funmi. "African 'Homemade' Peace-keeping Initiatives." *Armed Forces and Society* 23 (spring 1997): 349 71.

Organization of African Unity. "Organization of African Unity." Addis Ababa, Ethiopia: Organization of African Unity, 1998. Available from www.oau-oua.org/index.htm.

ORGANIZATION OF AMERICAN STATES (OAS)

The charter of the Organization of American States (OAS) was signed in Bogotá, Colombia, in 1948 and went into force in December 1951. The purpose of the OAS is to strengthen the peace and security of the Western Hemisphere; promote and strengthen democratic governments; prevent and resolve conflict between member states while respecting principles of nonintervention; and prevent aggression against member states. To a lesser extent the OAS is also charged with finding solutions to the economic, political, and social problems of member states; promoting social, economic, political, and cultural development; and limiting the proliferation of arms so as to devote resources to economic and social development. The OAS thus advances peace, security, understanding, and development among it members. In 1998 OAS members were: Antigua and Barbuda, Argentina, Bahamas, Barbados, Belize, Bolivia, Brazil, Canada, Chile, Colombia, Costa Rica, Dominica, Dominican Republic, Ecuador, El Salvador, Grenada, Guatemala, Guyana, Haiti, Honduras, Jamaica, Mexico, Nicaragua, Panama, Paraguay, Peru, St. Kitts-Nevis, St. Lucia, St. Vincent and the Grenadines, Suriname, Trinidad and Tobago, the United States, Uruguay, and Venezuela. Cuba's membership in the OAS was suspended in 1962 following the removal of Soviet missiles from that island country.

Although not established until 1948 the OAS can trace its ideological beginnings to the First Congress of the United States which was convened in Panama City by the Venezuelan revolutionary Simón Bolívar (1783-1830). This meeting resulted in the Treaty of Perpetual Union, League, and Confederation, which was signed by Colombia, the United Provinces of Central America, Peru, and Mexico. The Congress ultimately failed as only one government ratified the agreement.

In 1889, however, representatives of 18 American republics met in Washington, D.C., at the behest of U.S. Secretary of State James G. Blaine. As a result of this conference, the Bureau of American Republics, the purpose of which was to collect and exchange commercial information, was created. The OAS can trace its descent directly from this organization. In 1910 the organization's name was changed to the Union of American Republics with the Pan-American Union being its principal organ. By 1913 the Pan-American Union was maintaining a permanent staff and headquarters in Washington. In 1923 the name was again changed, this time to the Union of Republics of the American Continent; the Pan-American Union became its permanent organ. In 1945 and in 1947 the organization agreed to the Act of Chapultepec and the Inter-American Treaty of Reciprocal Assistance, respectively, which established collective security, defense, and peacekeeping agreements for the Western Hemisphere. In 1948 the OAS charter was agreed upon in Bogotá during the Ninth International Conference of American States; transition from the Pan-American Union to the OAS proceeded smoothly.

A major function of the OAS over the decades has been that of a hemispheric peacekeeper as authorized by the Treaty of Reciprocal Assistance. The OAS played an important role in resolving border conflicts between Costa Rica and Nicaragua in 1948 and 1978; Peru and Ecuador in 1981; and Honduras and El Salvador in 1969, 1970, and 1976. In 1964 the OAS imposed sanctions against Cuba for fomenting revolutionary activity in Venezuela; in 1965 it sent an inter-American peacekeeping force to the Dominican Republic. OAS peacekeeping activities have also been involved in maritime and naval disputes between Colombia and Venezuela in 1988 and Trinidad and Venezuela in 1989. The OAS served as a forum for the denunciation of Manuel Noriega's drug trafficking in Panama in 1989, monitored elections in Nicaragua in 1990, and monitored human-rights violations in Haiti in 1993.

Since its inception the OAS has received strong political and financial support from the United States. American foreign policy, however, has often run afoul of OAS stands on hemispheric issues. This was especially true concerning the Panama Canal prior to the 1977 Panama Canal Treaty, America's support of Great Britain retaking the Falkland Islands from Argentina in 1982, and the American invasion of Grenada in 1983. In 1995 the Inter-American Commission on Human Rights declared the United States to be in violation of OAS principles concerning the **embargo** of food and medicine to Cuba. In 1996 the Inter-American Judicial Committee ruled that the American Helms-Burton legislation—which allows punitive measures against foreign companies trading with Cuba—did not conform to international law. The OAS was also at odds with President Bill Clinton's continuing ''decertification'' of countries deemed unreliable allies in the U.S. war on drugs. Many Latin American countries have been or are threatened with decertification, including Peru and Bolivia, which grow coca; and Colombia and Mexico, which process it and transport the finished product to the United States. Decertification carries with it the threat of visa refusals, loss of financial aid, and blockage of commerce.

The OAS has also been active in promoting inter-American aid and development. In 1958 a massive financial cooperation plan, the Operação Pan Americana, was proposed. The purpose of the plan was to foster, through public investment, economic and social conditions that would then attract private investment. This plan culminated in President John F. Kennedy's 1961 Alliance for Progress. As a result, nearly $16 billion worth of external assistance was generated between 1958 and 1970.

In another effort to aid the various peoples of OAS countries, the Telecommunications Commission (CITEL) was created in 1993. CITEL is the telecommunications agency of the OAS and its purpose is to promote a modern telecommunication **infrastructure** within OAS member countries.

The chief administrative body of the OAS is the General Secretariat. The secretariat is responsible for implementing policy set by the General Assembly and the two councils. The Permanent Council is responsible for relations with other international organizations and promoting harmony amongst OAS members. The Inter-American Council for Integral Development (CIDI) replaced the Inter-American Economic and Social Council and the Inter-American Council for Education, Science, and Culture in 1996. The CIDI is responsible for accelerating regional economic and social development. The General Assembly is the supreme policy-making body of the OAS; it meets annually and when called into special sessions by the Permanent Council.

[Michael Knes]

FURTHER READING:

Albright, Madeleine. ''The OAS and the Road to Santiago: Building a Hemispheric Community in the Americas.'' *U.S. Department of State Dispatch* 9, no. 2 (March 1998): 1-3.

Blois, Roberto. ''The Hemisphere Hooks Up with CITEL.'' *Américas* 49, no. 4 (July/August 1997): 52-53.

Conway, Janelle. ''A Forum for the Future.'' *Américas* 50, no. 3 (May/June 1998): 52-55.

''Foundations for a Golden Anniversary.'' *Américas* 50, no. 2 (March/April 1998): 25-40.

Organization of American States. ''Organization of American States.'' Washington: Organization of American States, 1998. Available from www.oas.org.

Sheinin, David. *The Organization of American States.* New Brunswick, NJ: Transaction Publications, 1996.

''To Decertify, or Not? There Are Better Ways for the United States to Battle against Drugs.'' *Economist,* 21 February 1998, 16.

U.S. Department of State. Bureau of Public Affairs. Office of Public Communication. *Background Notes: Organization of American States.* Washington: GPO, 1994.

ORGANIZATION OF PETROLEUM EXPORTING COUNTRIES (OPEC)

The Organization of Petroleum Exporting Countries (OPEC) was established on September 14, 1960, at a conference in Baghdad, Iraq. The aims of the new organization were to prevent fluctuations in the price of oil, to raise the price of oil to its pre-1960 level, to make the multinational oil companies more accountable when determining the price they pay for oil, to ensure a steady income from oil for OPEC members and a steady supply of oil for their customers, and to remain steadfast and united should oil companies seek to sanction individual OPEC countries for any role they might play in implementing OPEC policies. OPEC thus became a **cartel** that maintained to its members' advantage the production, supply, and price of crude oil. In order to accomplish these objectives, OPEC was responsible for coordinating the petroleum policies of its members. The founding members of OPEC were Iran, Iraq, Kuwait, Saudi Arabia, and Venezuela. Other countries joining OPEC were Algeria (1969), Indonesia (1962), Libya (1962), Nigeria (1971), Qatar (1961), and the United Arab Emirates (1967). Ecuador and Gabon both joined OPEC in 1973, but withdrew in 1992 and 1995, respectively.

After years of agitation by Juan Pablo Pérez Alfonso, Venezuela's minister of mines and hydrocarbons, an Arab Petroleum Congress was organized by the Arab League and held in Cairo in 1959. The congress called for oil companies to adopt the policy of notifying and discussing with the governments of the oil-producing countries changes in their posted bids for oil. This request was largely ignored, further embittering the oil producing countries. Pérez Alfonso argued that prorationing the production of crude oil would allow the oil producers, not the oil companies, to control the price of oil. Prorationing would assign production quotas to the various members of the cartel. Opponents argued that prorationing circumvents market forces of supply and demand (it must be remembered that not all oil-exporting countries joined OPEC) and was ultimately doomed to failure. Pérez Alfonso's arguments, however, found a ready audience in the angry Arab states and OPEC was founded the following year. The immediate impetus for the oil cartel was a soft buyer's market in the early 1960s. The supply of crude oil was greater than the demand, prices were depressed, and prospects of price increases were unrealistic. In spite of OPEC, however, prices remained depressed until the early 1970s when the growing strength and unity of OPEC coupled with the increased demand for oil by the Western industrialized nations brought about a seller's market. This state of economic affairs together with growing Israeli/Arab tensions set the stage for the infamous 1973-74 oil **embargo**.

The embargo was not fashioned by OPEC but rather OAPEC (the Organization of Arab Petroleum Exporting Countries). Membership in the two organizations overlapped somewhat, but in the public's mind long lines at the gas pumps were caused by OPEC and all OPEC members profited from the embargo. Oil embargoes had been attempted by the Arab oil-producing countries in 1956 in reaction to the Suez Canal crisis and again in 1967 following the outbreak of war between Israel and Egypt. Both efforts were futile primarily because of U.S. resolve to break the embargo by making its own oil more available on the world market and the maneuvering of oil supplies by the multinational oil companies. By 1973, however, rapidly changing political and economic trends (the rise of Arab nationalism, growing enmity towards Israel, growing global demand for oil, lessening of the ability to manipulate prices by oil companies) made the embargo much more workable. The 1973 embargo had overtly political goals: the withdrawal of Israel from Arab territory it had occupied since the 1967 war and recognition that a Palestinian homeland needed to be restored. The embargo was applied to oil-importing countries on a sliding scale depending on each country's relationship with Israel. The United States, the Netherlands, and South Africa were Israel's strongest supporters and thus bore the brunt of the embargo—a total ban on the shipment of Arab oil. OPEC acted concurrently with OAPEC by raising the price of oil to \$5.11 a barrel in October 1973, and on January 1, 1974, raising it again to \$11.65 a barrel. Announced oil-production cutbacks were to be at the rate of 5 percent per month but were held in December at 15 percent.

The strategy of OPEC and OAPEC had a depressing but not devastating effect on the economies of the Western industrialized nations and Japan. In the United States, for instance, the **gross national product** fell \$10 billion from the same 1973 quarter and accounted for a .5 percent drop in employment (approximately 500,000 jobs) and a 30 percent rise in the **consumer price index**. This caused the U.S. economy to enter into a period of ''stagflation''—economic stagnation coupled with **inflation**. By March 1974, however, most but not all of OAPEC members felt that the United States and its allies were moving in a positive direction towards easing Arab/Israeli tension and the embargo was lifted. OPEC, however, did not lower prices.

When OPEC was established the price of a barrel of crude oil (42 gallons) was selling for less than $5. By the 1980s, in the aftermath of the embargo, the price of that same barrel of crude had risen to around $40. Much of this increase was due to a rising global demand for oil, as well as OPEC's initial controls over production and price. By the mid-1980s, however, the price of oil began dropping due to overproduction and a worldwide recession. There was also a concerted effort among non-OPEC oil-producing countries and other industrialized nations to increase oil exploration, develop new and more efficient oil-drilling technology, and implement long-term energy-conservation projects. By 1985 the price of a barrel of crude had dropped to $25. Many OPEC members continued to exceed their production quotas because of demands of a growing population in their countries, foreign debt, and **foreign exchange** shortages. In 1987, for instance, the OPEC quota for all members was set at 16.5 million barrels a day, but in fact total OPEC production often exceeded 20 million barrels. Problems with production quotas continued to plague OPEC well into the 1990s.

The price of oil continued to drop throughout the 1990s in spite of area disruptions such as the Persian Gulf War and United Nations's sanctions on Iraq. By 1998 OPEC countries accounted for only 55 percent of crude oil **exports** and 40 percent of world oil production. There are numerous reasons for this downturn in OPEC's fortunes: oil exploration has opened new areas such as the Caspian Sea and offshore West Africa for resource exploitation, new technology has made it feasible to profitably exploit areas that were once considered to be marginally profitable, the use of natural gas in the total energy scheme is on the rise, the Asian monetary crisis has stifled demand, and relatively mild winters have lessened the demand for heating oil. In mid-1998 oil was selling for a little more than $13 a barrel, a 12-year low. OPEC plans for what remains of the 1990s call for production cutbacks to stabilize if not increase the price of oil. Analysts feel, however, that planned production cutbacks will do little more than end the production of oil that was going into storage for lack of buyers. There are many other reasons OPEC will not soon regain the market control it enjoyed during the embargo. Many Arab oil-producing countries have become notorious for surreptitiously increasing oil production beyond their quotas. Norway, a non-OPEC member and the world's second largest oil-exporting country, refuses to go along with cutbacks, while Venezuela, an OPEC member opposed to quotas, has long-term plans to boost production to the level of some Arab states. Perhaps most important cartels such as OPEC dismiss, to their ultimate dismay, the influence that supply and demand has on market prices. According to an oil-industry analyst, quoted in a 1998 issue of *World Press Review,* ''To free-market economists, the fall of OPEC is a textbook case of the futility of price fixing cartels.''

[Michael Knes]

FURTHER READING:

Ahrari, Mohammed. *OPEC: The Failing Giant.* Lexington, KY: University of Kentucky Press, 1986.

Karl, Terry Lynn. *The Paradox of Plenty: Oil-Booms and Petro States.* Berkeley: University of California Press, 1997.

Knott, David. ''OPEC at the Crossroads with Non-OPEC Nations.'' *Oil and Gas Journal,* 15 June 1998, 19-25.

——. ''Venezuela Looks to New OPEC Role.'' *Oil and Gas Journal,* 25 May 1998, 20.

Magnus, Ralph H. ''Middle East Oil.'' *Current History,* February 1975, 49-53, 86-88.

''Once and Future OPEC.'' *World Press Review,* June 1998, 31-32.

Organization of Petroleum Exporting Countries. ''OPEC Online.'' Vienna: Organization of Petroleum Exporting Countries, 1998. Available from www.opec.org/welcome.htm.

Salpukas, Agis. ''Challenges Inside and Out Confront OPEC.'' *New York Times,* 23 June 1998, 50.

U.S. Department of Energy. ''OPEC Fact Sheet.'' Washington: U.S. Department of Energy, 1998. Available from www.eia.doe.gov/.

Yergin, Daniel. ''How OPEC Lost Control of Oil.'' *Time,* 6 April 1998, 58.

ORGANIZATION THEORY

An organization, by its most basic definition, is an assembly of people working together to achieve common objectives through a division of labor. People form organizations because individuals have limited abilities. An organization provides a means of using individual strengths within a group to achieve more than can be accomplished by the aggregate efforts of group members working individually. Business organizations (in market economies) are formed to profit by delivering a good or service to consumers.

Over the years there have been countless theories and models of how business organizations function and what their essential characteristics are. One widely held view, for example, is that at their core organizations are information processing systems, where information includes knowledge about products, markets, production methods, management techniques, finance, laws, and the many other factors involved in running a business. A successful organization, the theory goes, acts on relevant information and ignores the irrelevant. Ultimately, the organization that excels at processing information facilitates learning and the development of new knowledge. Other models of organizations focus on traits such as power and subordination, culture and adaptation, and efficiency.

Organization theory is examined here primarily from a historical perspective that briefly summarizes its evolution. The open-systems theory—the dominant school of thought throughout most of the 20th century—is examined in greatest detail, while organizational characteristics and structures are also reviewed.

BACKGROUND

Modern organization theory is rooted in concepts developed during the Industrial Revolution in the late 19th and early 20th centuries. Of import during that period was the research of Max Weber (1864-1920), a German sociologist. Weber believed that bureaucracies, staffed by bureaucrats, represented the ideal organizational form. Weber based his model bureaucracy on legal and absolute authority, logic, and order. In it, responsibilities for workers are clearly defined and behavior is tightly controlled by rules, policies, and procedures. In effect, Weber's bureaucracy was designed to function like a machine; the organization was arranged into specific functions, or parts, each of which worked in concert with the other parts to form a streamlined process.

Weber's theories of organizations, like others of the period, reflected an indifferent and impersonal attitude toward the people in the organization. Indeed, personal aspects of human behavior were considered unreliable and were viewed as a potential detriment to the efficiency of any system. Humans were likened to a bundle of skills that could be inserted into the system like a cog in a machine. Although his theories are now considered mechanistic and outdated, Weber's views on bureaucracy provided important insight into process efficiency, division of labor, and hierarchy of authority.

Another important contributor to organization theory in the early 1900s was Henri Fayol. He is credited with identifying four basic managerial functions that characterize successful organizations:

1. Planning—thinking before acting
2. Organizing—setting up policies and procedures that regulate employee behavior
3. Staffing—recruiting a suitable work force
4. Controlling—motivating workers to pursue the goals of the organization

Weber's and Fayol's theories found broad application in the early and mid-20th century, largely as a result of the work of Frederick W. Taylor (1856-1915). In a 1911 book entitled *Principles of Scientific Management,* Taylor outlined his theories and eventually implemented them on American factory floors. Taylor's theory of scientific management mimicked the four basic managerial functions identified by Fayol, and adopted the same basic attitudes about process efficiency championed by Weber. Although elements of Taylor's research and findings have been criticized, he is credited with helping to define the role of training, wage incentives, employee selection, and work standards in organizational performance.

HUMAN-CENTERED APPROACHES. Researchers began to adopt a less mechanical view of organizations and to pay more attention to human influences in the 1930s. This development was motivated by several studies, particularly the Hawthorne experiments, that shed light on the function of human fulfillment in organizations. Primarily under the direction of Harvard University researcher Elton Mayo, the **Hawthorne Experiments** were conducted in the mid 1920s and 1930s at a Western Electric Company plant known as the Hawthorne Works. The company wanted to determine the degree to which working conditions affected output.

Surprisingly, the studies failed to show any significant positive correlations between workplace conditions and productivity. In one study, for example, worker productivity escalated when lighting was increased, but it also increased when illumination was decreased. The results of the studies demonstrated that innate forces of human behavior may have a greater influence on organizations than do mechanistic incentive systems. The legacy of the Hawthorne studies and other organizational research efforts of that period was an emphasis on the importance of individual and group interaction, humanistic management skills, and social relationships in the workplace.

The focus on human influences in organizations was reflected most noticeably by the integration of Abraham Maslow's "hierarchy of human needs" into organization theory. Maslow's theories had two important implications for organization theory: (1) people have different needs and are therefore motivated by different incentives to achieve organizational objectives; and (2) people's needs change predictably over time, meaning that as the needs of people lower in the hierarchy are met, new needs arise. These assumptions led to the recognition, for example, that assembly-line workers could be more productive if more of their personal needs were met, whereas past theories suggested that monetary rewards were the sole, or primary, motivators.

THEORY X AND THEORY Y. Douglas McGregor contrasted the organization theory that emerged during the middle of the 20th century with previous views. In the 1950s, McGregor offered his renowned Theory X and Theory Y to explain the differences. In a nutshell, Theory X depicts the old, repressive, pessimistic view of workers. It assumes that people are lazy and have to be coerced to produce with tangible rewards. In fact, McGregor argued that the old view assumed that workers preferred to be directed, wanted to avoid responsibility, and cherished financial security (i.e., jobs) above all else.

McGregor believed that organizations that embraced Theory Y were generally more productive. Theory Y adopted a more optimistic view of human nature. Among other things, it theorized that (1) humans can learn to accept and seek responsibility; (2) most people possess a high degree of imaginative and problem-solving ability; (3) employees will self-govern, or direct themselves toward goals to which they are committed; and, importantly, (4) satisfaction of ego and self-actualization are among the most important needs that have to be met by (profit-maximizing) organizations.

OPEN-SYSTEMS THEORY

Traditional theories regarded organizations as closed systems—autonomous and isolated from the outside world. In the 1960s, these mechanistic organization theories, such as scientific management, were spurned in favor of more holistic and humanistic ideologies. Recognizing that traditional theory had failed to take into account many environmental influences that affected the efficiency of organizations, most theorists and researchers embraced an open-systems view of organizations.

The term ''open systems'' reflected the newfound belief that all organizations are unique and should therefore be structured to accommodate unique problems and opportunities. For example, research during the 1960s showed that traditional bureaucratic organizations generally failed to succeed in environments where technologies or markets were rapidly changing. They also failed to realize the importance of regional cultural influences in motivating workers.

Environmental influences that affect open systems can be described as either specific or general. The specific environment is a network of suppliers, distributors, government agencies, and competitors. An organization is simply one element of that network. To succeed, or profit, the organization must interact with these influences. They use suppliers, for example, when they purchase materials from other producers, hire workers from the labor force, or secure credit from banks or other companies.

CULTURAL INFLUENCES. The general environment encompasses four influences that emanate from the geographic area in which the organization operates. The first is cultural values, which determine views about what is right or wrong, good or bad, and important or trivial. Companies in the United States will likely be influenced by the values of individualism, democracy, individual rights and freedoms, and a puritan work ethic, among many others. In addition, regional and local values will affect organizations. For instance, workers and consumers in southern and northwestern states are more likely to be ideologically conservative.

ECONOMIC CONDITIONS. Economic conditions make up the second cluster of general environmental influences on open systems. These influences include economic upswings, recessions, regional unemployment, and many other factors that affect a company's ability to grow and prosper. Economic influences may also partially dictate an organization's role in the economy. For example, as the economy grows the organization will likely become not only larger but more specialized.

POLITICAL CONDITIONS. A third influence on organizations is the legal/political environment, which effectively helps to allocate power within a society and to enforce laws. The legal and political system in which an open system operates determines, most importantly, the long-term stability and security of the organization's future. For instance, a national government can add stability by maintaining a strong defense force. But legal and political mechanisms can also hamper a company's success by burdening it with regulations, taxes, employee rights laws, and other rules. In general, the larger and more powerful the local, regional, or national government, the less attractive will be the general environment to nongovernment organizations.

EDUCATIONAL CONDITIONS. The fourth general environmental influence on open systems is educational conditions. For example, businesses that operate in countries or regions with a high education level will have a better chance of staffing a complex organization that requires specialized skills and a precise division of labor.

KATZ AND KAHN

Daniel Katz and Robert L. Kahn developed a framework for open-systems theory that encompasses: (1) energic inputs into the organizations; (2) the transformation of those inputs within the system; (3) energic outputs; and (4) recycling. Energic inputs, or external influences, include familiar resources like employees, raw materials, and capital. However, they also include intangible external influences, such as status, recognition, satisfaction, or other personal rewards.

The transformation process involves using energies, or inputs, to (in the business context) create products or services. Energic outputs are simply the products or services that are distributed to consumers. Finally, recycling refers to the fact that outputs are indirectly recycled back into the organization. For instance, when a company sells a toaster the revenue becomes an input into the organization that is used, for example, to pay workers or buy materials.

In addition to identifying the four phases of an open system, Katz and Kahn cataloged several other organizational characteristics that support the open-systems theory and have implications for the design of successful organizations. For example, they recognized the universal law of entropy, which holds that all organizations move toward disorganization or death. However, an open system can continue to thrive by importing more energy from the environment than it expends, thus achieving negative entropy. For example, a failing company might be able to revitalize itself by bringing in a new chief executive who improves the way the company transforms energic inputs.

Another characteristic of organizations is dynamic homeostasis, which infers that all successful organizations must be able to achieve balance between subsystems. For example, a sales department might grow very quickly if it is very successful or demand for its products jumps. But if the manufacturing arm of the company is unable to keep pace with sales activity, the entire organization could break down. Thus, subgroups must maintain a rough state of balance as they adapt to external influences.

Katz and Kahn also characterize open systems by equifiniality. This concept suggests that organizations can reach the same final state by a number of different paths. In fact, the course is not fixed and may develop organically as both internal and external influences intervene.

SUBSYSTEMS

Open-systems theory assumes that all large organizations are comprised of multiple subsystems, each of which receives inputs from other subsystems and turns them into outputs for use by other subsystems. The subsystems are not necessarily represented by departments in an organization, but might instead resemble patterns of activity.

An important distinction between open-systems theory and traditional organization theory is that the former assumes a subsystem hierarchy, meaning that not all of the subsystems are equally essential. Furthermore, a failure in one subsystem will not necessarily thwart the entire system. By contrast, traditional mechanistic theories imply that a malfunction in any part of a system would have an equally quashing effect. This could be likened to pulling one cotter pin from the wheel of a go-cart; doing so would make the entire vehicle inoperable.

At least five subsystems identified by Katz and Kahn are important to the success of any business organization. Each of these subsystems may also be comprised of subsystems. For example, production subsystems are the components that transform inputs into outputs. In a manufacturing company this subsystem would be represented by activities related to production. In most business organizations, all other subsystems are built around the production subsystem.

Maintenance subsystems maintain the social involvement of employees in an organization. Activities in this group include providing benefits and compensations that motivate workers, creating favorable work conditions, empowering employees, and fulfilling other employee needs.

Adaptive subsystems serve to gather information about problems and opportunities in the environment and then respond with innovations that allow the organization to adapt. A firm's research lab or a product development department would both be part of an adaptive subsystem.

Supportive subsystems perform acquisition and distribution functions within an organization. Acquisition activities include securing resources, such as employees and raw materials, from the external environment. Human resources and purchasing divisions are typically included in this group. Distribution, or disposal, activities encompass efforts to transfer the product or service outside of the organization. Supportive subsystems of this type include sales and marketing divisions, public relations departments, and lobbying efforts.

Managerial subsystems direct the activities of other subsystems in the organization. These managerial functions set goals and policies, allocate resources, settle disputes, and generally work to facilitate the efficiency of the organization.

BASIC ORGANIZATIONAL CHARACTERISTICS

Organizations differ greatly in size, function, and makeup. Nevertheless, three characteristics of nearly all organizations with more than a few members are: (1) a division of labor; (2) a decision-making structure; and (3) formal rules and policies.

Organizations practice division of labor both vertically and horizontally. Vertical division includes three basic levels—top, middle, and bottom. The chief function of top managers, or executives, typically is to plan long-term strategy and oversee middle managers. Middle managers generally guide the day-to-day activities of the organization and administer top level strategy. Low-level managers and laborers put strategy into action and perform the specific tasks necessary to keep the organization operating.

Organizations also divide labor horizontally by defining task groups, or departments, and assigning workers with applicable skills to those groups. Line units perform the basic functions of the business, while staff units support line units with expertise and services. For instance, the marketing department (line unit) might be supported by the accounting department (staff unit). In general, line units focus on supply, production, and distribution, while staff units deal mostly with internal operations and controls or public relations efforts.

Decision-making structures, the second basic organizational characteristic, are used to organize authority. They vary in their degree of centralization and decentralization. Centralized decision structures are referred to as "tall" organizations because important decisions usually emanate from a high level and are passed down through several channels until they reach the lower end of the hierarchy. Bosses at all levels have relatively few employees reporting directly to them.

In contrast, flat organizations, which have decentralized decision making structures, employ only a few hierarchical levels. The few bosses or authority figures have many employees reporting directly to them. Such organizations, however, usually practice some form of employee empowerment whereby individuals make decisions autonomously. Decentralized structures are more representative of humanistic organization theories, while traditional tall organizational structures are more mechanistic. Besides meeting human needs, flat structures yield faster response times to internal and external influences.

Formalized rules and policies is the third standard organizational characteristic. Rules, policies, and procedures serve as substitutes for managerial guidance. For example, they may indicate the most efficient means of accomplishing a task or provide standards for rewarding workers. The benefit of formalized rules is that managers have more time to spend on other problems and opportunities. The disadvantage of rules is that they sometimes stifle workers' creativity and autonomy, thereby reducing their satisfaction and effectiveness.

Thus, organizations can be categorized as informal or formal, depending on the degree of formalization of rules. In general, formal organizations are goal-oriented and rational, and the relationship between individuals and the organization is comparatively impersonal. Subordinates have less influence over the process in which they participate, with their duties more clearly defined. The extreme case of a formal organization would resemble Weber's ideal bureaucracy.

Informal organizations are those that have relatively few written rules or policies. Instead, individuals are more likely to adopt patterns of behavior that are influenced by a number of social and personal factors. Changes in the organization are less often the result of authoritative dictates and more often an outcome of collective agreement by members. Informal organizations tend to be more flexible and more reactive to outside influences. But they may also diminish the ability of top managers to effect rapid change.

BASIC ORGANIZATIONAL STRUCTURES

FUNCTIONAL STRUCTURE. In addition to the three root characteristics of business organizations, there are two main types of structures: functional and divisional. Most companies represent an amalgam of both, and many variations exist. Functional organizational structures are more traditional. They departmentalize the company based on key functions. For example, activities related to production, marketing, and finance might be grouped into three respective departments. Within each, moreover, activities would be departmentalized into subdepartments. Within the marketing department, for example, might be the sales, advertising, and promotions departments.

The advantage of functionally structured organizations is that they typically achieve an efficient specialization of labor because people with specific skills can follow a career path within their department. In addition, this type of structure is relatively easy for employees to comprehend. Therefore, they are more likely to identify with their group and enjoy a sense of accomplishment through the gains of the department. Finally, functional structures reduce duplication of work because responsibilities are clearly defined.

On the other hand, functional structures are often divisive, causing departments to become adversarial and employees to engage in behavior that benefits their department at the expense of the overall organization. Furthermore, employees in departments often become myopic, losing sight of the goals of the entire organization. In addition, functional structures typically fail to make full use of the talents of workers and they are often less reactive to environmental influences.

DIVISIONAL STRUCTURE. Companies that employ a more divisional structure break the organization down into semiautonomous units and profit centers based on activities related to products, customers, or geography. Regardless of the activity group used to segment the company, each unit operates as a separate business. For example, a company might be broken down into southern, western, and eastern divisions. Or, it might create separate divisions for consumer, industrial, and institutional products. Again, within each division are subdivisions.

One benefit of a divisional structure is that it facilitates expansion because the company can easily add a new division to focus on a new profit opportunity without having to significantly alter exiting systems. In addition, accountability is increased because divisional performance can be measured more easily. Furthermore, divisional structures permit decentralized decision making, which allows managers with specific expertise to make key decisions in their area.

The potential drawbacks to divisional structures include duplication of efforts and a lack of communication. For example, separate consumer and industrial divisions of the same air-conditioner company may both be trying to develop a better compressor. In addition, divisional organizations, like functionally structured companies, may have trouble keeping all departments focused on an overall company goal. A corollary is that top management sometimes loses touch with the goals and inner-workings of each division.

SECTOR STRUCTURE. A variation on the divisional structure is known as the sector structure. This is employed typically by very large and diversified companies. One of the best known examples is General Electric Co., which pioneered the format in the mid-1970s. Sectors are usually broad market-defined operating areas and they may combine several conventional divisions that produce related goods or services. For instance, some of GE's sectors include aircraft engines, lighting, and capital services. The logic behind the sector structure is to strike a medium between extreme centralization and extreme decentralization. If a company has dozens of divisions it might be impractical to have all the division heads report directly to the CEO. On the other hand, because the company is so large, it may not be possible or desirable to merge divisions and centralize it more. By grouping similar divisions into coherent sectors, the sector approach attempts to make large organizations more focused and manageable.

MATRIX STRUCTURE. A less traditional (and less common) approach is the matrix structure, which emphasizes collaborative relationships between different parts of an organization. Under a matrix structure, individuals or departments have multiple reporting relationships, or at least multiple consulting relationships. This is particularly useful on large projects that require inputs from many different functional areas of the organization. For example, a company may have a product manager for each of its product lines, and these individuals may work both with marketing staff and with production staff in order to fulfill their role. In addition, each may collaborate periodically with other product managers in order to maintain a unified product strategy. If drawn on paper, this structure would appear as a grid with reporting or consulting lines connecting the product managers to the marketing department, the manufacturing or production department, and each other.

INTERNATIONAL STRUCTURES. Since the late 1980s, companies have been paying greater attention to how their activities are organized across national borders. Interest in such **international management** issues has grown as global market strategies increasingly dominate corporate objectives. The primary issues in international structures are local autonomy/uniqueness and how international units relate to each other and to the headquarters.

Christopher Bartlett and Sumantra Ghoshal have done important work in this area, summarizing their findings in the 1989 book *Managing Across Cultures,* which was updated and re-released in 1998. They argue that the oldest—and least effective—form of international structure is the "global" structure, in which international divisions or subsidiaries follow detailed and relatively inflexible supervision from the corporate headquarters. As a result, the company tends to operate in a similar manner in all places following a centrally determined formula. At the other end of the continuum, Bartlett and Ghoshal cited the "transnational" organization, which allows local conditions and strengths to influence both local practices and, if appropriate, worldwide practices. In essence, the transnational enterprise tries to use all of its resources to their fullest potential, regardless of their country of origin.

For example, if a company opens or acquires a new research facility in another country and finds that the labor and legal conditions in that country are ideal for research and development activities (e.g., access to a highly skilled workforce, minimal government intervention), the company may decide to do all of its R&D at that location. At the same time, regional marketing units in a transnational organization have the flexibility to tailor products or marketing to the local audience in order to ensure relevancy. Both of these scenarios would be unlikely under the so-called global structure.

SEE ALSO: Organizational Behavior; Organizational Development; Organizational Growth

[Dave Mote]

FURTHER READING:

Bartlett, Christopher, and Sumantra Ghoshal. *Managing Across Borders.* 2nd ed. Boston: Harvard Business School Press, 1998.

Burton, Richard M., and Børge Obel. *Strategic Organizational Diagnosis and Design.* 2nd ed. Boston: Kluwer Academic Publishers, 1998.

Daft, Richard L. *Organization Theory and Design.* 6th ed. Cincinnati: South-Western, 1997.

Katz, Daniel, and Robert L. Kahn. *The Social Psychology of Organizations.* 2nd ed. New York: Wiley, 1978.

Morgan, Gareth. *Images of Organization.* 2nd ed. Thousand Oaks, CA: Sage Publications, 1996.

Northcraft, Gregory B., and Margaret A. Neale. *Organizational Behavior: A Management Challenge.* Chicago: The Dryden Press, 1990.

Robbins, Stephen P. *Organization Theory: The Structure and Design of Organizations.* Englewood Cliffs, NJ: Prentice Hall, 1983.

ORGANIZATIONAL BEHAVIOR

Organizational behavior is an academic discipline concerned with describing, understanding, predicting, and controlling human behavior in an organizational environment. The field is particularly concerned with group dynamics, how individuals relate to and participate in groups, how leadership is exercised, how organizations function, and how change is effected in organizational settings. When organizational behavior theory is directed specifically at ways in which management can control an organization, it is sometimes known as *organizational behavior management,* or OBM.

Organizational behavior is a fairly new discipline, dating back to the early 20th century, although some experts suggest that it came into existence right after the U.S. Civil War. Organizational behavior has evolved from early classical management theories into a complex school of thought, and it continues to change in response to the dynamic workforce in which today's businesses operate.

THE CLASSICAL MANAGEMENT SCHOOL

In 1911, Frederick W. Taylor's book, *Principles of Scientific Management,* was published. This book marked the first serious attempt to publish the results of scientific management studies aimed at motivating workers to produce more. Taylor was the best known of a group of people, primarily mechanical engineers, who applied time-and-motion study concepts in the workplace. These engineers focused on the task concept to show that workers could be motivated to produce more, especially if they were offered an incentive to do so.

The task concept centered around the idea that if managers planned workers' tasks at least one day in advance, production would increase. Taylor devised a differential piece-rate system based on two different rates of pay. His system was simple: workers who did less than the expected output received a low rate of pay. Those who exceeded the standard earned more money. That was a radical idea for the time. It separated the worker from the machine and indicated that employees could control how much they produced. Taylor also suggested in his approach that money motivated workers. This, too, was a unique idea. This approach became known as Theory X, and it would later be distinguished from other theories that took a different view of worker motivation and human nature. What Taylor did not do, however, was take into account group behavior. He, like most classical managers, had no concept of the importance of workers as members of groups. The next wave of theorists, the human relations experts, addressed the issue of group behavior.

THE HAWTHORNE EXPERIMENTS

Human relationists tried to add a human dimension to classical theory in their studies. They did not try to refute the classical management proponents. Rather, they introduced the idea that workers would be willing to accept as part of their reward humane treatment, personal attention, and a chance to feel wanted. To prove their point, human relationists embarked on a series of experiments.

Perhaps the most significant experiments were the **Hawthorne experiments**. The studies began in 1924 at the Hawthorne Works, part of the Western Electric Company, located in Cicero, Illinois. The researchers' original goal was to measure the effect of illumination on output. In simplified terms, what they actually learned was that an individual's work performance, position, and status in an organization are determined not only by the individual, but by group members, too. They also learned that workers formed cliques that affected their production and that there were certain codes of conduct members of individual cliques were expected to follow. The Hawthorne studies opened the door to more experiments by other human relationists.

HUMAN RESOURCES THEORY

The next group to take center stage in the organizational behavior arena postulated that a manager's role was not to control workers, but to facilitate employee performance. According to human resources experts, people work to make a living, but their efforts go far beyond just laboring. They also work to fulfill certain needs, e.g., contributing to organizational objectives, attaining a feeling of accomplishment, and using their creativity in the work environment. Managers were well advised to keep all these needs in mind when dealing with workers. According to the human resources theorists, managers should apply mutual goal-setting and problem-solving approaches to their workforce members. Their approach has been termed Theory Y.

Managers were encouraged to make use of whatever training was necessary to ensure maximum performance. The training could take a variety of forms, i.e., technical, human, or conceptual. They were also advised to open communication lines in all directions to promote organizational effectiveness. After all, the theorists emphasized, workers welcome self-direction and self-control and will perform well when managers take an interest in their lives. In short, the human resources advocates said, managers should place their primary emphasis on using workers as if they are important human assets.

THE SYSTEM APPROACH TO ORGANIZATIONAL BEHAVIOR

Modern theorists apply a five-part system approach to organizational behavior:

- the individual
- the formal organization
- the informal organization
- the fusion process, in which the first three modify and shape one another
- the physical environment

Each part is essential. None can exist alone in the system. This system approach is the basis for modern organizational theory, which is founded on behavioral science studies.

THE BEHAVIORAL SCIENCES

There are three behavioral sciences: psychology (the study of individual behavior), sociology (the study of social behavior within societies, institutions, and groups), and anthropology (the study of the origin, cultural development, and behavior of humans). Each has made important contributions to the study of organizational behavior.

From an organizational standpoint, psychologists are concerned with the processes of learning, perception, and motivation. Sociologists study the various organizations that compose society, e.g., political, legal, business, governmental, and religious bodies. Finally, anthropologists are interested in the impact of culture on behavior. The three disciplines have had a major impact on the study of organizational behavior.

Organizational behavior scientists study four areas: individual behavior, group behavior, organizational structure, and organizational processes. They investigate facets of these areas like personality and perception, attitudes and job satisfaction, group dynamics, politics and the role of leadership in the organization, job design, the impact of stress on work, decision-making processes, the communications chain, and company cultures and climates. They use a variety of techniques and approaches to evaluate each facet and its impact on individuals, groups, and organizational efficiency and effectiveness.

In regard to individuals and groups, researchers try to ascertain why people behave the way they do. They have developed a variety of models designed to explain individuals' behavior. They investigate the factors that influence personality development, including genetic, situational, environmental, cultural, and social factors. Researchers also look at personality types such as authoritarian (people who adhere closely to conventional values) and dogmatic (people who are extremely rigid in their beliefs). They want to find out what causes a person to form either type of personality and learn whether one or the other—or neither—is a positive trait for people in the business world.

Researchers have also studied a number of concepts, including:

1. Stereotyping—the process of categorizing people based on limited information
2. Halo effect—the use of known personal traits as the basis for an overall evaluation
3. Perceptual defense—the process of screening out or distorting information that is disturbing or that people do not care to acknowledge
4. Projection—people attribute their own undesirable traits or characteristics to others.

They evaluate perception versus reality, individuals' locus of control (whether they believe they or outside forces are in control of their lives), and common problems resulting from these personality traits and characteristics. Finally, they look at an individual's attitudes and correlate them to job satisfaction and job performance.

THE IMPORTANCE OF JOB SATISFACTION STUDIES

The study of job satisfaction is central to organizational behavioral scientists. Companies want to know why their employees are or are not satisfied. If they are not happy, executives look to the behavioral scientists for ways to improve individuals' attitudes and to suggest ways of improving the work environment. This implies that the theorists have to look well beyond the tangible factors influencing job satisfaction, such as pay, benefits, promotional opportunities, and working conditions. They have to study how groups influence the workplace and individuals' expectations.

THE DYNAMICS OF GROUP BEHAVIOR

Perhaps the most basic issue scholars have addressed in the area of group behavior is the definition of ''group.'' They have agreed that there is no one definition. Therefore, they have looked more at why people join groups, types of groups, and group activities and goals. Studies have focused on group norms, individuals' behavior within groups and how it changed, their roles within groups, and what groups could accomplish that individuals could not. Many researchers believe that a group is more than the sum of the individual members, even though its goals, interactions, and performance are determined primarily by the individuals within it.

In an era when teamwork and collaboration figure prominently in many corporations' stated values, organizational behavior theory suggests some models for how people work together well, and conversely, how collaboration breaks down. As in most social science theories, there is no exact formula for how people collaborate in a work environment, but there are some significant social and psychological dimensions that influence these behaviors. Many of them relate to communication styles and methods. While **electronic mail** has been extolled as an important tool for efficient, speedy, and inexpensive communications, some evidence (mostly anecdotal at this stage) suggests that mechanical means of communication like e-mail hinder effective group work by fostering feelings of mistrust, distance, and apathy. By contrast, removing hierarchical and personal barriers and engendering open, face-to-face discussion appear to improve group interactions.

In another important area, organizational behavior scientists draw a distinction between leadership and management. They define management as the process of accomplishing tasks, whereas leadership is the process of getting things done by influencing other people. Another question is whether leaders are "born or made." In order to answer that question, researchers have sought common characteristics shared by leaders. They have found a few—intelligence, dependability, responsibility, social activity, and high originality—but there appear to be too many competing variables to form any universal conclusions of common leadership characteristics.

POWER, POLITICS, AND CONFLICT

Organizational behavior scientists have identified five basic types of power managers and leaders use to influence their subordinates: reward, coercive, legitimate, referent, and expert.

Reward power, which is based on an individual's expectation of receiving desired outcomes, was found to be a positive force. However, if the members of a group do not believe they will be rewarded for their efforts, the person in a position to offer rewards will not be able to influence the individuals. Similarly, managers who rely on coercive power, which is based on fear, will probably be unable to influence workers, especially group members, for a long period of time.

The other three types of power also have advantages and disadvantages. For instance, legitimate power, which exists as part of a manager's position in the hierarchy, is often ignored by workers who do not respect the individual filling the role. Referent power, which is based on the manager's charisma, influences only those individuals or group members who are swayed by the charismatic leader. Finally, expert power, which is power acquired from experience and learning, is a positive force, but only to the degree managers can convince individuals and group members that their leadership skills go beyond expertise alone.

People attempting to exercise power in the organization often resort to political tactics to do so. They blame others for mistakes, form power coalitions, praise co-workers and subordinates when they think it will help them achieve goals and reinforce their images. In short, they use every stratagem possible to win friends and influence people. In the process, however, they often create conflict. This prompted researchers to study conflict and its possible solutions.

Organizational behavior scientists recognize that conflict exists at both the individual and group levels. They have devised a number of ways to deal with it. Among them are mutual problem solving, compromise, and avoidance. Significantly, they discovered that conflict resolutions are most often temporary, and they have looked for ways to make them more permanent. In order to find permanent solutions, they have performed more in-depth studies of organizational structure and processes and how both affect individuals and groups.

ORGANIZATIONAL DESIGN AND PROCESSES

Organizational behavior scientists have conducted extensive studies on job definitions and the tasks a job comprises. They have looked at how each job fit into different groups within the organization, a process called departmentalization. The researchers have studied managerial spans of control, i.e., the number of people an individual manager can manage most effectively. The process required that researchers reduce to its most basic level each task performed and then find ways to perform jobs more efficiently and effectively.

Many researchers have suggested viable ways that organizations could restructure jobs and relationships to stimulate job satisfaction and productivity simultaneously. They have devised better communications programs, identified the elements that create stress, and explained how it could be better managed.

Organizational behavior scientists performed extensive studies on company cultures and climates with an eye to upgrading employees' quality of life in the workplace. They have sought ways to include more people in the managerial and decision-making processes. Their suggestions have included such techniques as **quality circles** and participative management programs.

Quality circles, which are team approaches to identifying and resolving work-related problems, became popular in some businesses. So, too, did participative management efforts, which gave a wider variety of people opportunities to comment on—and implement—new ideas in the workplace. One prominent organizational behavior scientist, William Ouchi, recommended that American companies integrate more Japanese management concepts into their management practices. His approach became known as Theory Z.

The ideas promulgated by organizational behavior scientists have caught on in managerial circles. Not surprisingly, not all of the programs can be used by all companies. If there is one thing that researchers have recognized, it is that no two companies are alike. To compensate for the dissimilarities, behavioral scientists reformed detailed cultural profiles to determine which programs fit individual companies' needs. These profiles have illustrated the importance of culture in the field of organizational behavior. Researchers have examined how company cultures control individual and group behavior, promote innovation, foster personnel commitment, and so on.

ORGANIZATIONAL CHANGE

Another subject of special interest to organizational behavior scholars is how change affects people in an organization and how the process of change can be managed to maximize its success and minimize unintended disruptions. Change is compelled by many sources: social and demographic trends, economic cycles, competition, technology, and politics and regulation, to name a few. Scholars distinguish between change that is incremental and ongoing, sometimes called first-order change, and change that is radical and episodic, termed second-order change. While each form can have both positive and negative consequences, radical changes are commonly seen as requiring the most caution and skill at pulling off.

For example, one of the most visible trends in corporate America since the 1980s has been the rise of sudden mass layoffs at large corporations, or downsizing. This clearly represents one of the largest kinds of changes a company might face, and its scope affects not only the workers who lose their jobs but also those who remain.

Researchers have found that downsizing can have both positive and negative effects on the employees who stay on. In some cases, for example, layoffs can induce employees to work harder and engage in other behaviors that benefit the company. One obvious explanation is that these workers might fear losing their jobs if they don't improve their performance, but there are likely other reasons as well, such as a move to fill a performance vacuum left by the departing workers. Still, other workers may respond by diminishing their performance; they may be demoralized by the corporate policies and may lower their mental and emotional investment in their jobs.

However, studies in organizational behavior suggest that all of these responses aren't inevitable. Scholars have suggested that the way in which the company goes about managing the change, in this case, the events leading up to and following downsizing, can have a significant effect on how employees react. This is not to say all negative reactions can be eliminated, but that there is a good chance they can be reduced. In the downsizing example, taking actions that foster trust in the management (such as open communication or demonstrating objective and consistent criteria for decision making) and that increase employee feelings of empowerment (letting workers have a say in some aspects of change) have been posited as methods of reducing some of the negative shocks of massive organizational change. Similar principles apply to managing other forms of organizational change.

More broadly, scholars like psychologist Kurt Lewin have identified basic models for managing change in organizations. In Lewin's widely cited three-step process, outlined in his 1951 classic *Field Theory in Social Science,* management must first ''unfreeze'' the status quo in the organization, facilitate a move to a new set of practices or environment, and then solidify or ''refreeze'' the new practices or environment into a permanent state. The process of unfreezing the current status involves introducing new policies or initiatives that begin to actively move employees away from the old way of doing things and/or removing policies or practices that tie them to the old. The second step, the shift to the new practices, is the formal implementation of the changes, for example, reorganizing a division or closing a branch office. Third, during refreezing management must solidify the changes by ensuring all the policies and practices are now geared toward maintaining the new equilibrium, and not throwbacks to the supplanted practices or lingering transition measures that create an atmosphere of instability or uncertainty.

THE FUTURE OF ORGANIZATIONAL BEHAVIOR

The international economy has taken on added importance in organizational behavior circles in recent years, as international companies have special requirements and dynamics to contend with. Researchers currently are studying such things as communications between and among foreign business operations, cultural differences and their impact on individuals, language difficulties, motivation techniques in different cultures, as well as the differences in leadership and decision-making practices from country to country.

Today, organizational behavior scientists are dealing with a wide range of problems confronting the business world. For instance, they continue to study downsizing, career development in the global economy, social issues such as substance abuse and changes in family composition, and the global economy. They are trying to determine just what effects such factors are having on the workplace and what can be done to alleviate associated problems.

SEE ALSO: Industrial/Organizational Psychology; Organization Theory; Organizational Development; Organizational Growth

[Arthur G. Sharp]

FURTHER READING:

Mintzberg, Henry, et al. "Some Surprising Things about Collaboration—Knowing How People Connect Makes It Work Better." *Organizational Dynamics,* spring 1996.

Mishra, Aneil K., and Gretchen M. Spreitzer. "Explaining How Survivors Respond to Downsizing: The Roles of Trust, Empowerment, Justice, and Work Redesign." *Academy of Management Review,* July 1998.

Nahavandi, Afsaneh, and Ali R. Malekzadeh. *Organizational Behavior: The Person-Organization Fit.* New York: Simon & Schuster, 1998.

Robbins, Stephen P. *Organizational Behavior: Concepts, Controversies, and Applications.* 8th ed. Upper Saddle River, NJ: Prentice Hall, 1998.

ORGANIZATIONAL DEVELOPMENT

Organizational development (OD) is an application of behavioral science to organizational change. It encompasses a wide array of theories, processes, and activities, all of which are oriented toward the goal of improving individual organizations. OD stresses carefully planned approaches to changing or improving organizational structures and processes, in an attempt to minimize negative side effects and maximize organizational effectiveness.

OD differs from traditional organizational change techniques in that it typically embraces a more holistic approach that is aimed at transforming thought and behavior throughout an entity. Like many other organizational change techniques, the basic OD process consists of gathering data, planning changes, and then implementing and managing the changes. However, OD initiatives are usually distinguished by the use of "action research," change agents, and "interventions."

BACKGROUND

Organization development is rooted in behavioral research that proliferated in the United States after World War II. That research led to the development in the late 1940s and 1950s of behavioral development strategies like sensitivity training, survey feedback, sociotechnical systems, and quality management.

Chief among the early endeavors in the field of behavioral science were Kurt Lewin's contributions to sensitivity training, or T-groups, during the mid-1940s (Lewin was the director of the Research Center for Group Dynamics at the Massachusetts Institute of Technology). Lewin's research showed that informal discussions about individual and group behavior, when combined with feedback, were more educational for group members than were lectures and seminars. T-groups ("T" stands for training) became popular with several major corporations as a means of improving group performance. In fact, during the 1950s and 1960s, organizational change and development was often considered synonymous with sensitivity training.

Also emerging in the mid-1940s were the behavioral techniques of survey research and feedback, many of which were originally developed by Rensis Likert and fellow researchers at the University of Michigan Survey Research Center. Likert and his associates used questionnaires, statistical samples, and feedback to managers to improve organizations. They found that when managers shared the information with subordinates and discussed potential routes to improvement, overall group performance was enhanced.

Also of import to the evolution of OD were sociotechnical system models developed during the 1950s and originating from England's Tavistock Institute. These models were developed to help sustain meaningful social interaction and fulfill workers' social needs in the face of technological change. Such methods of responding to change were later adapted to help manage organizational turbulence caused by other factors, such as restructuring or layoffs, and to create more efficient management structures. In the context of modern OD, a sociotechnical system approach usually involves work teams.

Although they weren't integrated into OD in the United States until the 1980s, quality management philosophies and processes were also formulated during the 1940s and 1950s. W. Edwards Deming and J.M. Juran are generally credited with developing continuous quality improvement techniques that they successfully implemented in many corporations. Both Deming and Juran achieved great success with their programs in Japan following World War II before returning to the United States to help American firms. Their contributions to OD have included statistical analysis techniques and methods for creating conditions of perpetual improvement in organizations.

During the 1950s and 1960s, researchers and managers began to pull together different elements of the behavioral development strategies described above to create more comprehensive processes for planning and executing change in organizations. For example, Lewin (1951) devised a renowned three-step change process that entailed "unfreezing," changing, and then "refreezing" the behavior of individuals and groups within organizations. In fact, it was during the 1960s and 1970s that the term "organizational development" was popularized to describe a multidisciplinary approach to achieving organizational change and improvement. OD evolved during the 1970s and 1980s to encompass a variety of change techniques and processes.

Interest in OD was bolstered in the United States during the 1980s by global and domestic economic influences. As domestic market growth slowed and foreign competition increased, many U.S. companies were forced to implement extensive changes in their organizations. For example, in their pursuit of quality and productivity, many corporations slashed payrolls, introduced new technology, adopted new management structures, and altered worker incentive systems. In an effort to effect change, many companies utilized OD techniques.

ORGANIZATIONAL DEVELOPMENT BASICS

Although the field of OD is broad, it can be differentiated from other systems of organizational change by its emphasis on process rather than problems. Indeed, traditional group change systems have focused on identifying problems in an organization and then trying to alter the behavior that creates the problem. OD initiatives, in contrast, focus on identifying the behavioral interactions and patterns that cause and sustain problems. Then, rather than simply changing isolated behaviors, OD efforts are aimed at creating a behaviorally healthy organization that will naturally anticipate and prevent (or quickly solve) problems.

OD programs usually share several basic characteristics. For instance, they are considered long-term efforts of at least one to three years in most cases. In addition, OD stresses collaborative management, whereby managers and workers at different levels of the hierarchy cooperate to solve problems. OD also recognizes that every organization is unique and that the same solutions can't necessarily be applied at different companies—this assumption is reflected in an OD focus on research and feedback. Another common trait of OD programs is an emphasis on the value of teamwork and small groups. In fact, most OD systems implement broad organizational changes and overcome resistance largely through the efforts of small teams and/or individuals.

An integral feature of most OD programs is the change agent, which is the group or individual that facilitates the OD process. Change agents are usually outside consultants with experience managing OD programs, although companies sometimes utilize inside managers. The advantage of bringing in outside OD consultants is that they often provide a different perspective and have a less biased view of the organization's problems and needs.

The drawback of outside change agents is that they typically lack an in-depth understanding of key issues particular to the company (or institution). In addition, outside consultants may have trouble securing the trust and cooperation of key players in the organization. For these reasons, some companies employ a external-internal team approach, which combines the advantages of internal and external change agents.

IMPLEMENTING OD PROGRAMS

OD efforts basically entail two groups of activities; "action research" and "interventions." Action research was originated in the 1940s by Lewin and another U.S. researcher, John Collier. It is a process of systematically collecting data on a specific organization, feeding it back for action planning, and evaluating results by collecting and reflecting on more data. Data gathering techniques include everything from surveys and questionnaires to interviews, collages, drawings, and tests. The data is often evaluated and interpreted using advanced statistical analysis techniques.

Action research can be thought of as the diagnostic component of the OD process. But it also encompasses the intervention component, whereby the change agent uses actions plans to intervene in the organization and make changes, as discussed below. In a continuous process, the results of actions are measured and evaluated and new action plans are devised to effect new changes. Thus, the intervention process can be considered a facet of action research.

A standard action research model was posited by W.L. French in his essay "Organization Development: Objectives, Assumptions, and Strategies" in *Sloan Management Review,* (1969, Vol. XII, No. 2.). As shown in the chart, the first step in the OD process is recognition of a problem by key executives. Those managers then consult with a change agent (a group or individual), which gathers data, provides feedback to the executives, and then helps them determine change objectives. Next, the agent does new research within the context of the stated OD goals, gives more feedback, devises a plan of action, and then intervenes in the company to effect change. After (or during) the intervention(s), data is gathered, feedback is supplied, actions are planned and implemented, and the process is repeated.

INTERVENTIONS

OD interventions are plans or programs comprised of specific activities designed to effect change in some facet of an organization. Numerous interventions have been developed over the years to address different problems or create various results. However, they all are geared toward the goal of improving the entire organization through change.

In general, organizations that wish to achieve a high degree of organizational change will employ a full range of interventions, including those designed to transform individual and group behavior and attitudes. Entities attempting smaller changes will stop short of those goals, applying interventions targeted primarily toward operating policies, management structures, worker skills, and personnel policies.

OD interventions can be categorized in a number of ways, including function, the type of group for which they are intended, or the industry to which they apply. In fact, W.L. French identified 13 major "families" of interventions based on the type of activities that they included—activity groups included team-building, survey feedback, structural change, and career-planning.

Figure 1

An Action Research Model for Organizational Development

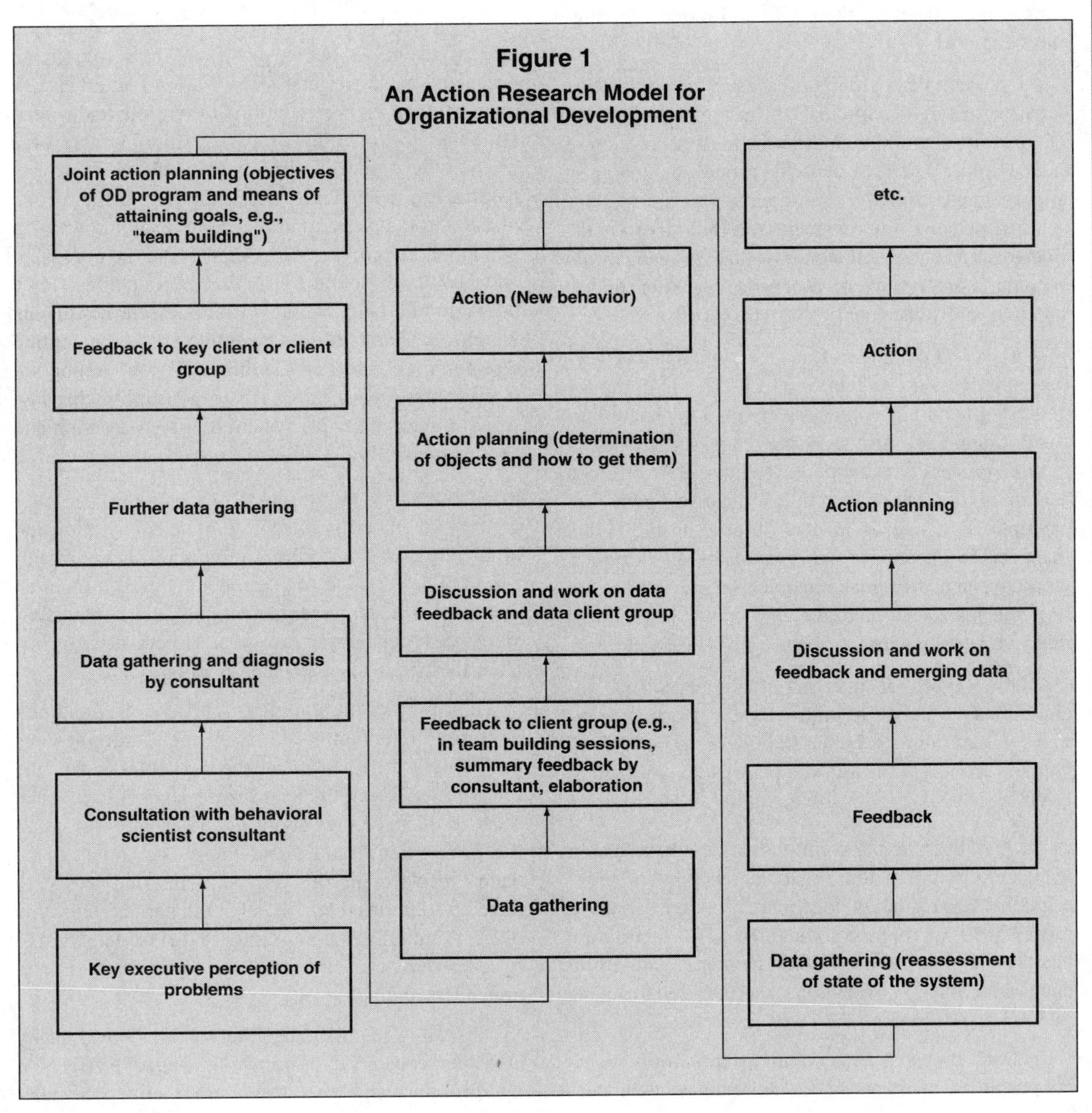

One convenient method of classifying OD interventions is by group size and interrelationship, including: interpersonal relationships, group processes, intergroup systems, and the entire organization. Typically, an OD program will simultaneously integrate more than one of these interventions. A few of the more popular interventions are briefly described below.

INTERPERSONAL. Interpersonal interventions in an OD program are designed to enhance individual skills, knowledge, and effectiveness. One of the most popular interventions in this class are T-groups, which help workers become more aware of their own and their coworker's behavior patterns. A typical T-group consists of 10 to 20 volunteers. They usually meet at a specific time for one or two weeks. The meetings are unstructured, leaving the group to determine subject matter within the context of basic goals stipulated by a facilitator. As group members try to exert structure on fellow members, anxiety ensues and the group becomes more aware of their own and other's feelings and behaviors.

For example, a group of managers in a marketing department might participate in a T-group together. The members would then describe their perception of each member's behavior and the group might suggest improvements. Finally, each member would identify areas of personal improvement and then act to make changes. The end result would be that the team would become more proficient because of greater understanding and subsequent efforts to improve.

A second example of an interpersonal intervention is process consultation, which helps a company understand and alter processes by resolving interpersonal dilemmas. Although they are similar to T-groups, process consultations are more task-oriented and involve greater input by the change agent. For example, a change agent may observe an individual manager in meetings and conversations during a workday, and then make specific suggestions as to how the manager could alter his or her behavior to improve performance.

Other types of interpersonal interventions include those designed to improve the performance review process, create better training programs, help workers identify their true wants and set complementary career goals, and resolve conflict.

GROUP. OD group interventions are designed to help teams and groups within organizations become more effective. Such interventions usually assume that the most effective groups communicate well, facilitate a healthy balance between both personal and group needs, and function by consensus as opposed to autocracy or majority rule.

Group diagnostic interventions are simply meetings wherein members of a team analyze their performance, ask questions about what they need to improve, and discuss potential solutions to problems. The benefit of such interventions is that members often communicate problems that their coworkers didn't know existed (or were perceived to exist). As a result, many problems are resolved and group dynamics are improved simply as a result of the meeting(s).

Team-building meetings are similar to diagnostic interventions, but they usually involve getting the group away from the workplace for a few days. In addition, the group members go a step further than diagnosing problems by proposing, discussing, and evaluating solutions. The purpose of the meetings is to formulate specific procedures for addressing problems. The chief advantage of such interventions is that they help the team reach a consensus on solving problems (away from the pressures of the workplace), thus eliminating incongruent actions and goals that diminish the group's efficiency.

Role analysis technique (RAT) is used to help employees get a better grasp on their role in an organization. In the first step of a RAT intervention, people define their perception of their role and contribution to the overall company effort in front of a group of coworkers. Group members then provide feedback to more clearly define the role. In the second phase, the individual and the group examine ways in which the employee relies on others in the company, and how they define his or her expectations. RAT interventions help people to reduce role confusion, which can result in either conflict or the perception that some people aren't doing their job. A popular intervention similar to RAT is responsibility charting, which utilizes a matrix system to assign decision and task responsibilities.

INTERGROUP. Intergroup interventions are integrated into OD programs to facilitate cooperation and efficiency between different groups within an organization. For instance, departmental interaction often deteriorates in larger organizations as different divisions battle for limited resources or become detached from the needs of other departments.

Conflict resolution meetings are one common intergroup intervention. First, different group leaders are brought together to get their commitment to the intervention. Next, the teams meet separately to make a list of their feelings about the other group(s). Then the groups meet and share their lists. Finally, the teams meet to discuss the problems and to try to develop solutions that will help both parties. This type of intervention helps to gradually diffuse tension between groups caused by lack of communication and misunderstanding.

Rotating membership interventions are used by OD change agents to minimize the negative effects of intergroup rivalry that result from employee allegiances to groups or divisions. The intervention basically entails temporarily putting group members into their rival groups. As more people interact in the different groups, greater understanding results.

OD joint activity interventions serve the same basic function as the rotating membership approach, but it involves getting members of different groups to work together toward a common goal. Similarly, common enemy interventions achieve the same results by finding an adversary common to two or more groups and then getting members of the groups to work together to overcome the threat. Examples of common enemies include competitors, government regulation, and economic conditions.

COMPREHENSIVE. OD comprehensive interventions are used to directly create change throughout an entire organization, rather than focusing on organizational change through subgroup interventions. One of the most popular comprehensive interventions is survey feedback. This technique basically entails surveying employee attitudes at all levels of the hierarchy and then reporting the findings back to them. The employees then use the data in feedback sessions to create solutions to perceived problems. A number of questionnaires developed specifically for such interventions have been developed.

Structural change interventions are used by OD change agents to effect organizational alterations related to departmentalization, management hierarchy, work policies, compensation and benefit incentives programs, and other elements. Often, the implemented changes emanate from feedback from other interventions. One benefit of change interventions is that companies can often realize an immediate and very significant impact as a result of relatively minor modifications.

Sociotechnical system design interventions are similar to structural change techniques, but they typically emphasize the reorganization of work teams. The basic goal is to create independent groups throughout the company that supervise themselves, including administering pay and benefits, disciplining team members, and monitoring quality, among other responsibilities. The theoretic benefit of sociotechnical system design interventions is that worker and group productivity and quality is increased because workers have more control over (and subsequent satisfaction from) the process in which they participate.

A fourth OD intervention that became extremely popular during the 1980s and early 1990s is **total quality management** (TQM), which is largely a corollary of Deming's work. TQM interventions utilize established quality techniques and programs that emphasize quality processes, rather than achieving quality by inspecting products and services after processes have been completed. The important concept of continuous improvement embodied by TQM has carried over into other OD interventions.

RECENT DEVELOPMENTS

ORGANIZATIONAL LEARNING. While TQM has lost some of its popularity since then, other OD trends and theories have come to the forefront since the early 1990s. One of the major new developments has been the notion of the ''learning organization,'' or a continuously adapting and growing organization that actively embraces its own evolution to develop new capabilities or competencies. A key impetus behind this new approach was the critically acclaimed 1990 book *The Fifth Discipline: The Art and Practice of the Learning Organization* by MIT organizational studies lecturer Peter Senge. While the academic study of organizational learning and related phenomena originated a couple decades earlier, this book did much to popularize the idea and stimulate a host of academic studies into organizational learning, as well as corporate initiatives geared toward building learning organizations.

The basic analogy for organizational learning is, of course, human learning. Just as individuals can amass knowledge and skills through both deliberate attempts to acquire knowledge (reading, attending school) and inadvertent discoveries (experimentation, failure, insights from experiences), so too can groups of people, according to the theory. Clearly, the methods by which an organization ''learns'' are different from those of the individual, but the process is seen as similar. Various models of organizational learning posit key stages as knowledge acquisition, knowledge sharing, and knowledge utilization as the core mechanisms of this collective learning process.

The specific kind of learning that this discipline is concerned with is on a fundamental, organization-wide level. OD scholars distinguish between single-loop learning, double-loop learning, and triple-loop learning. Single-loop learning, the most common, is in essence localized learning within departments or subunits of the organization, but has few if any implications for the entire company. Policies and rules remain unchanged. This kind of learning goes on in virtually all organizations and isn't sufficient to create what most OD specialists would term a learning organization. Double-loop learning occurs when a discovery or insight causes not only localized change, but a general revision in corporate policy or strategy that takes into account this new insight. Triple-loop learning goes one step further, causing management to rethink the entire business paradigm and make major organizational changes based on the new insight. Proponents of organizational learning focus on ways to create organizational structures, processes, and policies that encourage second- and third-loop learning.

While in some ways organizational learning has taken on some of the trappings of a management fad, its disciples, including Senge, bristle at this suggestion because they believe it's an enduring and valuable principle for understanding and influencing organizational development.

APPRECIATIVE INQUIRY. A less widely known innovation that also garnered attention in the field during the 1990s was appreciative inquiry, developed by organizational behavior professor David Cooperrider. First conceived during the 1980s, the approach centers around examining organizational practices that have proven successful as a way of addressing broad-based development issues. Cooperrider believed that traditional OD approaches focused too much on hunting down problems and looking for new solutions, whereas many organizations have numerous successes or strengths that might hold a better key to an organization's development.

Appreciative inquiry is still an interventionist approach to OD, but its emphasis is on discovering and identifying current strengths and envisioning a positive future building on those strengths. Appreciative inquiry also places marked emphasis on the human experience in organizational development, asking employees to recount their best experiences in the organization and imagine new possibilities. Usually this approach is reserved for large, company-wide development issues, including redefining the corporate mission and strategy.

Critics of appreciative inquiry charge that it's too simplistic to be used in very many contexts. Many advocates also agree that it is a supplement to, rather than a replacement of, established OD theories and practices.

OD CASE STUDY

A classic example of how OD can change an organization for the better is the initiative undertaken by General Motors Corp. at its Tarrytown, New York, auto assembly plant in the 1970s. By the late 1960s, Tarrytown had earned a reputation as one the least productive plants in the company. Labor relations and quality were at an all-time low, and absenteeism was rampant, when GM finally decided to take action.

Realizing the seriousness of the situation, plant managers tried something new—they sought direct input from laborers about all aspects of the plant operations. Then they began to implement the ideas with success, sparking interest in a more comprehensive OD effort. Thus, in the early 1970s, GM initiated a quality-of-work-life (QWL) program, an OD program that integrates several types of interventions. The goal of QWLs is to improve organizational efficiency through employee well-being and participative decision-making.

In 1973, the union leaders signed a ''letter of agreement'' with management in which both groups agreed to commit themselves to exploring specific OD initiatives that could improve the plant. The plant hired an outside consultant to oversee the change process. The initial research stage included a series of problem-solving training sessions, during which 34 workers from two shifts would meet for eight hours on Saturdays. Those meetings succeeded in helping plant managers to improve productivity. Therefore, in 1977 management increased the scope of the OD program by launching a plantwide effort that included 3,800 managers and laborers.

Although the OD program eventually cost GM more than $1.5 million, it paid off in the long run through greater productivity, higher quality, and improved labor relations. For example, the number of pending grievances plummeted from 2,000 in 1972 to only 32 by 1978. Absenteeism dropped as well, from more than seven percent to less than three percent. In fact, by the late 1970s the Tarrytown plant was recognized as one of the most productive and best run in the entire GM organization.

[Dave Mote]

FURTHER READING:

French, Wendell L., and Cecil H. Bell. *Organizational Development: Behavioral Science Interventions for Organization.* 5th ed. Englewood Cliffs, NJ: Prentice Hall, 1994.

Fulmer, Robert M., and J. Bernard Keys. ''A Conversation with Peter Senge: New Developments in Organizational Learning.'' *Organizational Dynamics,* autumn 1998.

Ivancevich, John M., and Michael T. Matteson. *Organizational Behavior and Management.* 5th ed. New York: McGraw-Hill, 1998.

Robbins, Stephen P. *Organizational Behavior: Concepts, Controversies, and Applications.* 8th ed. Upper Saddle River, NJ: Prentice Hall, 1998.

Zemke, Ron. ''Don't Fix That Company!'' *Training,* June 1999.

ORGANIZATIONAL GROWTH

Growth is something for which most companies, large or small, strive. Small firms want to get big, big firms want to get bigger. Organizational growth, however, means different things to different organizations. How, then, is growth defined? How is it achieved? How does a company survive it?

PHASES OF GROWTH

A number of scholars and management theorists have developed models of how organizations change and grow. One such model is that of Larry E. Greiner, a management and organization professor at the University of Southern California. In his 1998 *Harvard Business Review* article entitled "Evolution and Revolution as Organizations Grow," Greiner outlined five phases of growth punctuated by what he termed "revolutions" that shook up the status quo and ushered in the successive stage. Based on observations of historical company patterns, his phases were as follows:

1. Creative phase—when a company or subunit of a company is first formed, most attention and activity is focused on developing a product and reaching its market.
2. Direction phase—when the company begins to formalize business management methods and "professionalize" its practices, usually including centralizing power in the organization.
3. Delegation phase—when centralization proves too cumbersome for a large organization, it begins to delegate power and decision-making in various ways, such as by creating semi-autonomous business units/divisions and moving the reward/risk paradigm down to lower level managers and employees in general.
4. Coordination phase—when decentralization becomes seen as excessive or inefficient, management attempts to rein in the organization by merging or coordinating the activities of various fragmented parts of the company, demanding more accountability and creating unifying incentives such as profit sharing.
5. Collaboration phase—when central coordination efforts prove bureaucratic and inflexible, management adopts a team-based, cross-functional structure and more fluid policies that empower workers and promote dialog, experimentation, and negotiation.

Greiner believed that many organizations stall at certain stages because management is unable or unwilling to shift its organizational paradigm, or especially, because individuals at the top are reluctant to give up power once it's in their hands.

MEASURING GROWTH

In addition to such qualitative notions of organizational growth, there are many more tangible parameters a company can select to measure its growth. The most meaningful yardstick is one that shows progress with respect to an organization's stated goals as in the following examples.

NUMBER OF EMPLOYEES. Some businesspeople boast of the number of employees in their companies or departments. Employees in and of themselves, however, cost money. A better employee-based measure of growth is change in company or departmental revenue or profit generated per employee. This becomes a valuable measure of increasing (or decreasing) productivity, rather than a measure of labor and salary expense.

REVENUES. Every business magazine or newspaper describes a company by its revenues as an "X million dollar company." Although this is probably the most commonly cited measure of corporate growth, the pitfall of relying on gross revenue or gross margin as a measure of growth for an organization is that it completely ignores the expenses associated with generating those revenues. Greater revenues do not necessarily mean greater profitability. In periods of very quick "growth," expenses can spiral upward and out of control leaving a company strapped for cash and facing an uncertain future, at best.

More useful, revenue-based measures of growth are increases (or decreases) in net profit or net margins. These methods account for the expenses incurred in generating revenues for the firm and identify the portion that is truly added to the bottom line. Special analyses of profit margins include calculating the return on investment (ROI), either for the company as a whole or for individual units or product lines. ROI tells management whether the profits being generated are enough to compensate for the opportunity costs, the risks, and the time value of the money that the company has invested to produce those profits. A related metric is return on assets (ROA), which evaluates profits against the value of all the assets (capital, plant, equipment, etc.) the company has channeled into generating its income.

For many companies, especially publicly held ones, the ultimate measure of growth is the creation of wealth for owners/investors. While net profits are an indication of wealth creation, companies (or their observers) may scrutinize their finances further to determine whether they are actually generating an **economic profit**, or a profit that exceeds the implicit cost of the capital invested in them. It is only after the **cost of capital** is met that the company may be said to create new wealth. This growth may also be expressed in terms of market value added, a more direct measure of shareholder wealth creation.

ACHIEVING GROWTH

While there are many academic models depicting the growth stages of a company, management guru Tom Peters strongly suggests several real-world ways for companies large and small to achieve organizational growth. The business press routinely reports on the activities of companies employing these suggestions.

JOINT VENTURE/ALLIANCE. This strategy is particularly effective for smaller firms with limited resources; however, in a business environment where changing demand, supply, and manufacturing or service conditions are an everyday occurrence, ''partnering'' makes sense for the large organization as well. Forming joint ventures or alliances gives all companies involved the flexibility to move on to different projects upon completion of the first, or restructure agreements to continue working together. Subcontracting, for example, allows firms to concentrate on those portions of their businesses which they do best.

Joint ventures and alliances inject partners with new ideas, access to new technologies, new approaches, and new markets, all of which can have positive implications for the growth of all firms involved. Creating ventures with upstart or overseas firms may present the best opportunities for accomplishing this.

LICENSING. ''License your most advanced technology,'' advised Tom Peters. The idea behind this is that no technologies can be truly proprietary today. A rival or an outsider will soon copy whatever a company has developed. Save competitors the hassle of and profit from copying by selling current technology. This creates cash flow for the company to fund future **research and development** and creates switching costs by making others dependent upon a firm's applications.

SELL OFF OLD WINNERS. Getting rid of the **cash cow** operations to focus on growing newer enterprises can make sense for organizations trying to grow. Even though it sounds contradictory at first, top dollar is commanded in the market for this kind of business and the necessary capital to fuel growth of other operations is generated. The decline of a sold cash cow is left up to the new owner. Meanwhile, ventures that were new at the time of that sale may now be cash cows ripe for picking. An addendum to this line of thinking is the divesting of older technology or products. Emerging markets such as Latin America and Eastern Europe have been favorite places for companies to get rid of outdated products or technology. These markets may not yet be able to afford state-of-the-art goods, but can still benefit from older models.

NEW MARKETS. Entering new markets is an obvious way to expand a company. Creating additional demand for a firm's product or service, especially in a market where competition has yet to fully develop, is a much sought after experience for growing enterprises. As more and more U.S. companies move parts of their operations off-shore, more opportunity and awareness is created for other companies to serve the markets in those foreign locations.

NEW PRODUCT DEVELOPMENT. Some of the strategies suggested here benefit the firm in generating cash. Product or service development is a smart place to use that cash in order to create future growth for the firm. Many companies reinvest part of their profits in developing new products, either completely new products or extensions or adaptations of existing ones. For some companies, such as pharmaceutical manufacturers, maintaining a robust new product pipeline is essential to long-term growth (and even basic stability) because their drug patents will eventually expire and they will face daunting competition from producers of generic and copycat drugs. Other companies such as toy and clothing producers face highly fickle and changing markets that demand a constant flow of new products. While all **research and development** into new products doesn't turn up major new product launches, in the long run new products often prove to be some of a company's most important assets.

VENTURE CAPITAL/IPO. For companies small or large, growth must be funded, but where can one get the money? Where large public firms issue stock or **debt**, smaller private firms search for capital from **banks**, private investors, or **venture capital** firms. A venture capital firm will provide cash to firms it expects will have extremely fast growth. The venture capital firms will expect to be rewarded for its capital infusion with large payoffs at an initial public offering (IPO), the point at which the small private firm issues public stock.

ACQUISITION. Both small and large firms get bigger by buying other companies. Merger-mania cyclically sweeps the business world as a preferred method to increase a company's size, revenues, product or service offering, etc. The takeover frenzy of the 1980s has returned to Western markets. Successful **mergers and acquisitions** will blend resources to create a synergy while improving existing core competencies.

For any company that has achieved growth, the work has just begun. Managing and sustaining that growth is imperative if the initial progress is to have any lasting positive effects for the company.

SEE ALSO: Organizational Development

FURTHER READING:

Churchill, Neil C., and Virginia A. Lewis. ''The Five Stages of Small Business Growth.'' *Harvard Business Review.* May-June, 1983, 30-42.

Greiner, Larry E. ''Evolution and Revolution as Organizations Grow.'' *Harvard Business Review,* May-June 1998.

Peters, Tom. ''Get Innovative or Get Dead, Part I.'' *California Business Review,* fall 1990, 9-26.

Weinzimmer, Laurence G., Paul C. Nystrom, and Sarah J. Freeman. ''Measuring Organizational Growth: Issues, Consequences, and Guidelines.'' *Journal of Management,* March-April 1998.

ORGANIZATIONAL LIFE CYCLE

Organizational life cycle (OLC) is a model that proposes that businesses, over time, progress through a fairly predictable sequence of developmental stages. This model is linked to the study of **organizational growth** and development. It is based on a biological metaphor of living organisms, which have a regular pattern of development: birth, growth, maturity, decline, and death. Likewise, the OLC of businesses has been conceived of as generally having four or five stages of development: start-up, growth, maturity, and decline, with diversification sometimes considered to be an additional stage coming between maturity and decline.

During the start-up stage, companies accumulate capital, hire workers, and start developing their products or services. Toward the end of this stage, companies often experience explosive growth and begin to hire new employees rapidly, because business opportunities exceed **infrastructure** and resources.

This expansion continues into the growth stage where companies increase their resources and **workforces** dramatically. The financial situation of companies usually improves during this stage, as company revenues grow and as companies establish strong customer bases. Despite their expansion, companies may still need additional funds to exploit all the available growth opportunities, so many go public at this point, too.

The maturity stage is marked by security and by a slight slowdown. By this stage, companies have amassed assets and solid profits, by becoming established in the market. The primary area of business has become a **cash cow** because it controls a sizable market share and continues to yield profits, but experiences slow or stagnant growth. In order to avoid the decline stage, mature companies often take a variety of actions to renew their growth, such as acquiring other companies and expanding product lines. Some business theorists consider the foray into new markets a separate stage, namely, the diversification stage.

If companies fail to implement measures to improve growth, they will most likely enter the fourth and final stage of the OLC: decline. In this stage, not only company hiring drops, but also company sales and profits. Furthermore, demand for a company's products or services decreases. To compensate for the decline, companies launch downsizing or reengineering campaigns during this stage. If these efforts do not succeed, however, companies look for a buyer or shut down.

As companies progress through the organizational life cycle the criteria for their effectiveness change. Companies tend to change their **management** styles, reward systems, organization structures, communication and decision-making processes, and corporate strategies. As companies mature, they usually strive to become more innovative or they diversify by making acquisitions.

Despite the usefulness of this model, business scholars point out that companies do not always develop linearly as the OLC model suggests. Instead, companies may experience little growth initially and then experience decreasing sales, before moving into a stage of growth. Or they may undergo spurts of growth and decline, which makes it difficult to place them in any particular stage. Nevertheless, the model represents general patterns companies experience while developing.

THE DEVELOPMENT OF THE OLC MODEL

While a number of business and management theorists alluded to developmental stages in the early to mid-1900s, Mason Haire, editor of the 1959 volume *Modern Organization Theory,* is generally recognized as one of the first theorists to use a biological model for organizational growth and to argue that organizational growth and development follows a regular sequence. A. Chandler, author of the 1962 book *Strategy and Structure,* influenced later OLC research with his argument, based on a study of four large U.S. firms, that as a firm's **strategy** changed over time, there must be associated changes in the firm's structure. Since the early 1970s the number of life cycle stages proposed by business scholars has ranged from three to ten, but most OLC models have four or five stages.

OLC is an important model because of its premise and its prescription. The model's premise is that requirements, opportunities, and threats both inside and outside the business firm will vary depending on the stage of development in which the firm finds itself. For example, threats in the start-up stage differ from those in the maturity stage. As the firm moves through the developmental stages, changes in the nature and number of requirements, opportunities, and threats exert pressure for change on the business firm. L. Baird and I. Meshoulam argued in an article in *Academy of Management Review* that organizations move from one stage to another because the fit between the organization and its environment is so inadequate that either the organization's efficiency and/or effectiveness is seriously impaired or the organization's survival is threatened. The OLC model's prescription is that a company's managers must change its business goals, strategies, and strategy implementation devices to fit the internal and external characteristics of each stage. Thus, different stages of the company's life cycle require alterations in the firm's objectives, strategies, managerial processes (planning, organizing, staffing, directing, controlling), technology, culture, and **decision making**.

REASONS FOR BUSINESS CHANGE

A variety of factors contribute to the passage of companies through the OLC. To begin with, companies usually follow the development stages of the industries in which they operate. Hence, most companies in a mature industry are also mature, and so such companies must launch new products or services or more competitive **marketing** strategies.

Changes in customer preferences may cause both companies and their respective industries to move into another development stage. For example, consumers may choose alternative products that have superior technology, have more features, or are easier to use.

A closely related factor, therefore, is change in products or services. Consumer needs and wants can cause products and services to change and innovative products and services can cause consumer needs and wants to change. Industries that depend on technology, research, and **innovation** are the most susceptible to maturing and declining as a result of product changes. Furthermore, products and services have their own life cycles, which involve the passage through the same stages: start-up, growth, maturity, and decline. In addition, if there are significant barriers to entry in an industry, it will tend to be more stable than industries without such barriers.

PROMOTING NEW GROWTH

To avoid declining, companies can take a variety of corrective actions during the maturity or declining stages in order to start a new development cycle or at least to stave off going out of business. Beginning in the maturity stage companies can bypass decline by focusing on product or service positions and implementing new methods of attracting and retaining customers. To promote new growth, companies also must attempt to introduce innovations and hence company management must emphasize creativity at this point, according to LeRoy Thompson Jr., author of *Mastering the Challenges of Change.*

As a company matures, it must focus more and more on external factors that can lead to decline. If a company fails to take the initiative during the maturity stage, it may face an even more formidable task of trying to reverse its descent later on. Furthermore, if companies anticipate maturation and implement policies that will help them become more innovative during this stage, they can reduce the effects of the maturity stage and more easily spark a new start-up or growth stage (e.g., through **intrapreneurship**).

Maturity and decline tend to result from companies becoming habituated to doing business a certain way during the start-up and growth stages and being unable to break these business habits when they cease to be fruitful. If a business strategy has been successful, companies tend not to make changes until it is too late, until they start to decline. To avoid losing ground, Thompson recommends that companies maintain a marketing attitude, which entails determining customer needs and wants and striving to meet them.

MANAGEMENT STYLES

Thompson, L. Greiner, Lawrence M. Miller, and others correlate the stages of the life cycle with different management styles needed to continue growing. The start-up stage, which involves growth through creativity and vision, eventually leads to **leadership** and organizational problems. More sophisticated and more formalized management practices must be adopted that emphasize action and control. If the founders can't or won't take on this responsibility, they must hire someone who can, and give this person significant authority. The growth stage is successful because of control and direction, but this management style can cause a crisis of autonomy. Lower-level managers must be given more authority if the organization is to continue to grow. The crisis involves top-level managers' reluctance to delegate authority.

During the maturity stage, companies can grow through delegation, yet delegation can lead to control problems within diversified companies. Since lower-level managers prefer to take charge of their own divisions and departments without interference from the rest of the organization, upper-level managers perceive that they are losing control of their diversified company. Companies also implement systems of coordination to enable their various business units and departments to work together. These efforts, however, tend to cause an influx of red tape. Coordination techniques such as product groups, formal planning processes, and corporate staff become, over time, a bureaucratic system that causes delays in decision making and a reduction in innovation. At this stage, companies may become too large and diversified to function effectively with inflexible regulations and dense bureaucracy.

During the final stage, companies must emphasize growth through collaboration, which includes using **teams**, empowering workers, removing red tape, reducing corporate staff, simplifying formal systems, increasing conferences and educational programs, and introducing more sophisticated information systems. Because decline and closure is likely if companies proceed in the same direction as in the maturity stage, they must adopt these kinds of policies and implement these kinds of changes to ward off shrinking sales and employee apathy. Hence, companies must relaunch or recast themselves at this final stage in the organizational life cycle.

SEE ALSO: Corporate Restructuring; Going Public

[John G. Maurer, updated by Karl Heil]

FURTHER READING:

Adler, Karen R., and Paul M. Swiercz. ''Taming the Performance Bell Curve.'' *Training and Development,* October 1997, 33.

Baird, L., and I. Meshoulam. ''Managing Two Fits of Strategic Human Resource Management.'' *Academy of Management Review* 13, no. 1 (January 1988): 116-28.

Chandler, A. *Strategy and Structure: Chapters in the History of the Industrial Enterprise.* Cambridge, MA: MIT Press, 1962.

Churchill, N., and V. Lewis. ''The Five Stages of Small Business Growth.'' *Harvard Business Review* 61, no. 3 (May/June 1983): 30-50.

Greiner, L. ''Evolution and Revolution as Organizations Grow.'' *Harvard Business Review* 50, no. 4 (July/August 1972): 37-46.

Haire, Mason. ''Biological Models and Empirical Histories of the Growth of Organizations.'' In *Modern Organization Theory,* edited by Mason Haire. New York: John Wiley & Sons, Inc., 1959, 272-306.

Hanks, S., et al. ''Tightening the Life-Cycle Construct: A Taxonomic Study of Growth Stage Configurations in High-Technology Organizations.'' *Entrepreneurship Theory and Practice* 18, no. 2 (winter 1993): 5-29.

Miller, Lawrence M. *Barbarians to Bureaucrats: Corporate Life Cycle Strategies.* New York: Clarkson N. Potter, 1989.

Quinn, R., and K. Cameron. ''Organizational Life Cycles and Shifting Criteria of Effectiveness: Some Preliminary Evidence.'' *Management Science* 29, no. 1 (January 1983): 33-51.

Smith, K., T. Mitchell, and C. Summer. ''Top Level Management Priorities in Different Stages of the Organizational Life Cycle.'' *Academy of Management Journal* 28, no. 4 (December 1985): 799-820.

Thompson, LeRoy, Jr. *Mastering the Challenges of Change: Strategies for Each Stage in Your Organization's Life Cycle.* New York: AMACOM, 1994.

Tyebjee, T., A. Bruno, and S. McIntyre. ''Growing Ventures Can Anticipate Marketing Stages.'' *Harvard Business Review* 61, no. 1 (January/February 1983): 62-66.

ORIGINAL ISSUE DISCOUNT (OID)

Original issue discount (OID) refers to a **debt** instrument initially issued at a price substantially below its face amount (i.e., at a deep discount). OIDs can also be **bonds** issued as zero coupon bonds. A zero coupon bond (also referred to simply as a zero) has no stated or coupon interest rate and therefore pays no periodic interest. Non-zero deep discounted bonds are priced well below par at issuance but have regular semiannual or annual interest payments based on their stated interest rate.

BACKGROUND

In the late 1970s and early 1980s, **interest rates** were at historic highs. In an attempt to reduce their periodic cash outflows for interest, borrowers, both corporate and governmental, began issuing bonds carrying very low stated or coupon interest rates relative to those prevailing in the marketplace. During the 1980s many **leveraged buyouts** were financed with deep discount bonds of questionable creditworthiness and earned the name **junk bonds**. These bonds are now called ''high-yield'' bonds.

The U.S. Treasury has been selling zero coupon bonds for many years in the form of Series EE U.S. savings bonds. For example, a $25 investment in a U.S. savings bond can return $50 at its maturity with no periodic interest payments. The interest return to the investor is implied in the difference between the deep discounted price ($25) and the maturity value of the bond ($50). The U.S. Treasury adjusts their yield by changing the time to maturity.

By 1982 the popularity of zeros encouraged the U.S. Treasury to allow U.S. government **securities** dealers to strip the semiannual interest coupons from a group of bonds, and to sell blocks of same-maturity coupons and principal to investors as a zero coupon bond derivative (ZCBD). Broker/dealers developed portfolios of ZCBDs bearing the name of aggressive, coy animals:

- LIONs: Lehman Brothers' Lehman Investment Opportunity Notes
- TIGRs: Merrill Lynch's Treasury Investment Growth Receipts
- CATS: Salomon Brothers' Certificate of Accrual on Treasury Securities

In 1985 the U.S. Treasury began issuing notes and bonds tailored as zeros known as Separate Trading of Registered Interest and Principal Securities (STRIPS).

Municipalities also worked zeros into their debt structures. The high interest rates during the 1980s made it almost impossible to issue municipal bonds. The Tax Reform Act of 1986 lowered the maximum tax bracket to 33 percent, making the tax-free aspects of municipals less attractive. In the face of high debt costs, declining demand, and decreasing bond ratings, municipalities began issuing zeros with U.S. Treasury-backed zeros as collateral.

PROS AND CONS OF OIDS

There are advantages of OIDs and zeros for both issuers and investors and a distinct tax disadvantage for the investors. The tax effects are discussed below.

ISSUERS. The major advantage to an issuer is that because of the lower coupon or stated interest rates, the issuing firm's periodic interest payments are considerably smaller than would otherwise be the case. Another advantage to the issuer is that OIDs tend to carry original yields to maturity that are less than those of similar quality non-OID bonds. One major disadvantage is that OIDs, especially zeros, are rarely callable. This effectively prevents the issuer from taking advantage of lower market interest rates by calling in an outstanding issue. Another disadvantage is the very large cash outflow required at maturity compared to the original proceeds of the issue (but, of course, the firm didn't have to make all of the usual periodic interest payments).

INVESTORS. OIDs, whether purchased at issue or in the secondary market, are convenient and affordable in that they require a low initial investment and provide an implied automatic reinvestment of interest. There are some special tax rules, however. Investors are also attracted to deep discount or zero coupon bonds because they have very little reinvestment rate risk. One of the problems facing an investor in securities that pay periodic returns to their holders (either **dividends** or interest) is how to reinvest those payments in instruments yielding at least as much as the anticipated yield to maturity of the original security. When interest rates are declining, this becomes an increasingly difficult task. By purchasing a zero coupon bond, an investor eliminates this problem because there are no periodic interest payments. Therefore, there is no reinvestment rate risk.

Aside from the adverse tax ramifications discussed below, the major disadvantage of an OID is that because of its very low interest rate relative to the prevailing market rate, the price volatility of these instruments is much greater than traditional debt instruments (see illustration).

PRICING AND YIELDS

The pricing of a zero coupon bond is a straightforward present value computation. It is simply the present value of the face amount of the bond discounted for the time remaining to maturity at the prevailing market rate of interest for bonds of similar risk. For example, assume a 20-year, $10,000 face value zero is issued in a market demanding a 7 percent yield to maturity, compounded semiannually. Its price would be 0.2526 of par, or $2,526, plus commissions. Investors purchasing at that price are able to lock in a compounded rate of interest of 7 percent regardless of what subsequently happens to market rates until the bond matures. This should be recognized as a two-edged sword: an upward change in interest rates, of course, will decrease the market value of zeros and OIDs just as a decrease in interest rates will increase market value. Further, because it has no coupon rate, a zero coupon bond's price volatility, as market rates change, is substantial. And, the longer the maturity of the zero, the greater that volatility will be.

Assuming market interest rates remain at 7 percent, our 7.0 percent, 20-year zero, compounded semiannually, per $10,000 face value, if held by the original purchaser, would have the values shown in Table 1.

Table 1
Value of Zero Coupon Bond

End of Year	Theoretical Value
At Issuance	$2,526
1.	$2,706
2.	$2,898
5.	$3,563
10.	$5,026
20.	$10,000

Recalling the statement made earlier about the price volatility of OIDS, note that if interest rates should rise to 8 percent at the end of the first year, this bond would decline in value to $2,253, or −16.7 percent. Had the bond been originally issued with a 7 percent coupon, its price would fall from $10,000 to only $9,032, or −9.7 percent.

The yield to maturity of an OID is calculated the same as for any other bond. The yield to maturity is that interest rate that equates the present value of the remaining interest payments and the face amount of the bond to the bond's current market price. The yield to maturity can be derived from present value tables, bond yield tables, or by using internal rate of return programs in financial calculators or in computer spreadsheets.

The yield to maturity for a zero is even easier to calculate. It is simply the interest rate that equates the present value of the face of the bond to its current market price, given the time remaining to maturity.

It is usually easy to spot a zero in published bond quotations since the coupon rate of interest will be replaced with "zr."

TAX CONSIDERATIONS

OIDS WITH A COUPON. Investors in OID debt with a coupon or stated interest rate will pay income **taxes** on both the periodic interest payments received and the annual **amortization** of the OID. The amortization is calculated using the compound, or effective, interest rate implied in the bond. Both components are taxed at ordinary (i.e., non-capital gain) income tax rates. Investors purchasing previously issued OID bonds at less than face are also subject to this provision.

Brokers who sell OIDs are responsible for keeping a list of OIDs, their issue dates, and issue price to facilitate taxpayers' filing requirements, and are required to file a form 1099-OID to accounts holding OIDs. This form may be insufficient if OIDs are purchased after the issue date in the secondary market, and also because the reporting requirements have periodically changed, as explained in IRS Publication 1212. Publication 1212 also contains a list of OIDs as does *Moody's Municipal Bond Guide.*

The simplest reporting of OID involves an investor who holds an original issue. The 1099-OID will indicate the taxable portion of the OID for the period. Publication 1212 provides the per-diem rate to use if the bond was sold during the year.

There are special rules for: (1) the reporting of OID for bonds that were originally issued with OID and are then purchased in the secondary market, and (2) the determination of the gain or loss on the sale of a bond with OID. Holders of either taxable or tax-exempt OIDs are referred to **Internal Revenue Service** Publication 550, ''Investment Income and Expense.'' OID rules do not apply to U.S. savings bonds or to OID bonds or obligations with a maturity date of one year or less from the date of issue.

ZEROS. The taxation of both the related implied interest income and interest expense on zeros is covered by special provisions within the Internal Revenue Code.

Since zeros have no stated or coupon interest rate, no interest is either paid or received annually. Nevertheless, the taxpayer must report and pay taxes on the amount accrued each year as though received, and the issuer takes a deduction for the accrued amount as though paid. Using the above example, in the first year of the bond, an investor would report interest income and the issue would report interest expense of $180 ($2,706 - $2,526). Because of the need to pay tax on income never received in cash and the increase in marginal tax rates between 1987 and 1995, the demand for taxable zeros has dried up in recent years. Even taxables, however, may be appropriate investments if they are going to be used to fund **individual retirement accounts** (IRAs) or Keogh plans since no tax is paid on the earnings in these accounts. Recent changes in the Internal Revenue Code that lowered long-term **capital gains** tax rates to (generally) a maximum of 20 percent, are causing many investors to reexamine their investing strategies in tax-deferred accounts.

Some, but very few, of the more generous zeros and OIDs have call provisions that issuers would exercise if the refunding would reduce their overall **liabilities** in the long run. If an OID bond is issued with the intention of calling the debt before maturity, any gain on the retirement or refunding is treated an ordinary income to the investor.

Corporate borrowers find zeros very attractive for the opposite reason: they are able to take annual tax deductions for the implied interest they never pay, even though the cash outflow will not occur until the bond matures. Because they are enjoying the tax deductions for the implied interest before any payments are made, they are effectively lowering their time-value adjusted, after-tax cost of borrowing.

MUNICIPAL ZEROS. The market discount and the OID income of municipal zeros are exempt from federal income tax. As a result, except for their use in tax-exempt retirement plans, investors now find taxable zeros much less attractive than nontaxables. (Note: changes in the Internal Revenue Code have limited the tax-exempt status of many municipal bonds and rules for taxation at state and local levels are different.)

SEE ALSO: Refinancing

[Ronald M. Horwitz]

FURTHER READING:

Bierman, Harold, Jr., and Seymour Smidt. *Financial Management for Decision Making.* New York: Macmillan, 1986.

Moyer, R. Charles, James R. McGuigan, and William J. Kretlow. *Contemporary Financial Management.* 7th ed. Cincinnati: South-Western, 1998.

Sharpe, William F., Gordon J. Alexander, and Jeffery V. Bailey. *Investments.* 6th ed. Upper Saddler River, NJ: Prentice Hall, 1998.

Shillinglaw, Gordon, and Kathleen T. McGahran. *Accounting: A Management Approach.* 9th ed. Homewood, IL: Irwin, 1993.

OSHA

SEE: Occupational Safety and Health Administration

OSHRC

SEE: Occupational Safety and Health Review Commission

OTC

SEE: Over-the-Counter Securities Markets

OUTPLACEMENT

SEE: Employee Outplacement

OUTSOURCING

A company is outsourcing when it purchases products or services from an outside supplier, rather than performing the same work within its own facilities, in order to cut **costs**. The decision to outsource is a major strategic one for most companies, since it involves weighing the potential cost savings against the consequences of a loss in control over the product or service. Some common examples of outsourcing include manufacturing of components, **computer** programming services, **tax** compliance and other **accounting** functions, and payroll and other human resource functions. A relatively new trend in outsourcing is employee leasing, in which specialized vendors recruit, hire, train, and pay their clients' employees, as well as arrange health care coverage and other benefits. A study quoted in *Industrial Management* indicated that the global outsourcing market was growing at a rate of 10 percent per year, and was expected to reach $121 billion by the year 2000.

The growth in outsourcing is partly the result of a general shift in business philosophy. Prior to the mid-1980s, many companies sought to acquire other companies and diversify their business interests in order to reduce risk. As more companies discovered that there were limited advantages to running a large group of unrelated businesses, however, many began to divest **subsidiaries** and refocus their efforts on one or a few closely related areas of business. Companies tried to identify or develop a ''core competence,'' a unique combination of experience and expertise that would provide a source of competitive advantage in a given industry. All aspects of the company's operations were aligned around the core competence, and any activities or functions that were not considered necessary to preserve it were then outsourced.

Successful outsourcing thus requires a strong understanding of the organization's capabilities and future direction. As William R. King explained in *Information Systems Management,* ''Decisions regarding outsourcing significant functions are among the most strategic that can be made by an organization, because they address the basic organizational choice of the functions for which internal expertise is developed and nurtured and those for which such expertise is purchased. These are basic decisions regarding organizational design.'' Outsourcing based only upon a comparison of costs can lead companies to miss opportunities to gain knowledge that might lead to the development of new products or technologies. *Business Week* called companies that had outsourced too many of their core functions ''hollow corporations,'' and claimed that they had relinquished their reason for existence.

Outsourcing can be undertaken to varying degrees, ranging from total outsourcing to selective outsourcing. Total outsourcing may involve dismantling entire departments or divisions and transferring the employees, facilities, equipment, and complete responsibility for a product or function to an outside vendor. In contrast, selective outsourcing may target a single, time-consuming task within a department, such as preparing the payroll or manufacturing a minor component, that can be handled more efficiently by an outside specialist. The opposite of outsourcing is insourcing, when a staff function within a company markets its product or service to external as well as internal customers.

By the late 1990s, 93 percent of executives in North America and Europe reported outsourcing at least one business function. Some business leaders took outsourcing further than ever before, forming intricate partnerships with other companies and outsourcing more than just mundane tasks. ''Today, outsourcing relationships have evolved from one-dimensional contracts based on cost savings to multi-dimensional partnerships that support the core business of client corporations,'' CEO Bill Concannon stated in *Industrial Management.* ''The trend is for outsourcing relationships to function more and more like partnerships. Outsourcing providers are taking increasing responsibility in realms that have traditionally remained in-house, such as corporate strategy, information management, business investment, and internal quality initiatives.''

ADVANTAGES AND DISADVANTAGES OF OUTSOURCING

Companies that decide to outsource do so for a number of reasons. The primary reason is to achieve cost savings or better cost control over the outsourced function. Companies usually outsource to a vendor that specializes in a given function and performs that function more efficiently than the company could. On average, outsourcing companies realize a 9 percent cost savings and a 15 percent increase in capacity and quality, according to the Outsourcing Institute. Anticipated cost savings sometimes fail to materialize, however, because the vendor must make a profit and because the company incurs additional **transaction costs** when interacting with the vendor. Another common reason for outsourcing is to achieve headcount reductions or minimize the fluctuations in staffing that may occur because of to changes in demand for a product or service. Companies also outsource in order to reduce the workload on their employees, or to provide more development opportunities for their employees by freeing them from tedious tasks.

Some companies outsource in order to eliminate distractions and force themselves to concentrate on their core competencies. Still others outsource to achieve greater financial flexibility, since the sale of assets that formerly supported an outsourced function can improve a company's **cash flow**. A possible pitfall in this reasoning is that many vendors demand long-term **contracts**, which may reduce flexibility. A common reason for outsourcing computer programming and other **information technology** functions is to gain access to new technology and outside expertise. Some experts claim, however, that companies are exposed to new technology by vendors anyway, and that they could simply hire people with the expertise they seek. But this is not true for **small businesses**, which often cannot afford to hire computer experts or develop the in-house expertise to maintain high-level technology. When such tasks are outsourced, the small business gains access to new technology that may help it compete with larger companies.

Company politics is another common reason for outsourcing. For example, some companies might begin outsourcing initiatives after observing the successful efforts of a competitor. Others might be pushed toward outsourcing by managers seeking personal gain or by a desire to eliminate troublesome departments. Finally, outsourcing provides an attractive option for start up firms as they grow. In these instances, outsourcing can free the entrepreneur from tedious and time-consuming tasks, such as payroll, so that he or she can concentrate on the **marketing** and sales activities that will enable the firm to make money.

Some of the major potential disadvantages to outsourcing include poor **quality control**, decreased company loyalty, a lengthy bid process, and a loss of strategic alignment. There may also be inherent advantages in maintaining certain functions internally. For example, company employees may have a better understanding of the industry, and their vested interests may mean they are more likely to make decisions in accordance with the company's goals. A general rule of thumb is that companies should never outsource any function that directly affects quality or service.

STEPS IN SUCCESSFUL OUTSOURCING

Once a company has made the decision to outsource, there are still a number of factors it must consider in making a successful transition and in forming a partner relationship with the vendor. In *National Underwriter Life and Health,* Ethel Scully recommended a series of steps for companies to follow. First, the company should determine what sort of outsourcing relationship will best meet its needs. Some businesses share strategic **decision making** with their vendors, while others outsource only on a limited, as-needed basis.

Next, the company needs to obtain the support of key personnel for the decision to outsource. Many companies encounter resistance from employees who feel that their jobs are threatened by outsourcing. This is particularly important in businesses where workers are represented by **labor unions**. In the mid-1990s, the issue of outsourcing was key in several strikes by the United Auto Workers against American automobile manufacturers. Scully suggested forming a **team** consisting of an outsourcing expert, representatives from senior **management** and human resources, and the managers of all affected areas of the company to help address employee concerns about the decision. To maintain the loyalty and productivity of remaining workers, it may also be helpful to design programs to assist any workers that may be displaced due to outsourcing.

After people issues have been addressed, the company can begin contacting potential vendors, either formally or informally, and asking specific questions about the services provided and the terms of the contract. Ideally, the vendor will have experience in handling similar business and will be able to give the client's needs the priority they deserve. "Consider the service company's knowledge of the entirety of your business, its willingness to customize service, and its compatibility with your firm's business culture, as well as the long-run cost of its services and its financial strength," said service provider Carl Schwenker in *Money.*

Finally, the company should select a vendor it trusts in order to develop a mutually beneficial partner relationship. It is important for the company to develop tangible measures of job performance before entering into an agreement, as well as financial incentives to encourage the vendor to meet deadlines and control costs. The contract should clearly define responsibilities and performance criteria, outline confidentiality rules and ownership rights to new ideas or technology, and include a means of severing the relationship if necessary. Since the vendor is likely to have more experience in preparing outsourcing agreements than a small client company, it may also be helpful to consult with an attorney during contract negotiations.

[Laurie Collier Hillstrom]

FURTHER READING:

Buss, Dale D. "Growing More by Doing Less." *Nation's Business,* December 1995, 18.

Byrne, John A. "Has Outsourcing Gone Too Far?" *Business Week,* 1 April 1996, 26.

Elliot, Vince. "Outsourcing without Risk." *Journal of Property Management,* January/February 1995.

Elmuti, Dean, Yunus Kathawala, and Matthew M. Monippallil. "Outsourcing to Gain a Competitive Advantage." *Industrial Management* 40, no. 3 (May/June 1998): 20.

Evans, David, Judy Feldman, and Anne Root. "Smart New Ways to Manage Subcontractors." *Money,* 15 March 1994, 42.

Field, Anne. "Outer Resources." *Inc.,* 15 November 1997, 67.

Foxman, Noah. "Succeeding in Outsourcing." *Information Systems Management* 11, no. 1 (winter 1994): 77.

Greco, JoAnn. "Outsourcing: The New Partnership." *Journal of Business Strategy* 18, no. 4 (July/August 1997): 48.

Guteri, Fred. "How to Manage Your Outsourcer." *Datamation,* March 1996, 79.

Hammonds, Keith H. "The New World of Work." *Business Week,* 17 October 1994, 76.

Heywood, Peter. "Global Outsourcing: What Works, What Doesn't." *Data Communications International,* November 1996.

King, William R. "Strategic Outsourcing Decisions." *Information Systems Management* 11, no. 4 (fall 1994): 58.

Lacity, Mary, Rudy Hirschheim, and Leslie Willcocks. "Realizing Outsourcing Expectations: Incredible Expectations, Credible Outcomes." *Information Systems Management* 11, no. 4 (fall 1994): 7.

Lonsdale, Chris, Andrew Cox. "Falling In with the Out Crowd." *People Management,* 15 October 1998, 52.

Meyer, N. Dean. "A Sensible Approach to Outsourcing: The Economic Fundamentals." *Information Systems Management* 11, no. 4 (fall 1994): 23.

Peterson, Yule S. "Outsourcing: Opportunity or Burden?" *Quality Progress* 31, no. 6 (June 1998): 63.

Scully, Ethel. "Many Factors to Weigh in Decision to Outsource." *National Underwriter Life and Health—Financial Services Edition,* 16 January 1995, 10.

OVER-THE-COUNTER SECURITIES MARKETS

An over-the-counter (OTC) securities market is a secondary market through which buyers and sellers of securities (or their agents or brokers) consummate transactions. Secondary markets (securities markets where previously issued securities are re-traded) are mainly organized in two ways. One is to form an organized exchange, where buyers and sellers of securities (mostly represented by their agents or brokers) meet at a central place to conduct transactions. The New York Stock Exchange (NYSE), the American Stock Exchange (located in New York) and the Chicago Board of Trade for Commodities are examples of major organized exchanges in the United States. An over-the-counter securities market provides an alternative way of organizing a secondary market—in this, dealers with inventories of securities at different geographical locations are in contact with each other through a computer network. In other words, these dealers of securities are ready to buy or sell securities over the counter to anyone who contacts them and accepts their quoted price. One may thus describe an over-the-counter securities market as an electronic market. The **National Association of Securities Dealers Automated Quotations System** (now generally referred to simply as "the Nasdaq") is an example of an over-the-counter securities market in the United States.

THE EVOLUTION OF THE OVER-THE-COUNTER MARKETS

The NASDAQ over-the-counter market was established in 1971. Before the NASDAQ was instituted, trading in OTC securities used to be a rather haphazard operation—individual broker/dealer firms bought and sold securities for their own accounts. In doing so, they acted as dealers, not brokers. For larger OTC **stocks**, a dozen or so firms quoted bid and asked prices for securities—account executives relied on these quoted prices in buying and selling securities for customers. However, for many small over-the-counter securities, only a couple of firms made a market—that is, quoted bid and asked prices. Thus, one could never be sure if one got the best price. Moreover, record keeping was done on "pink sheets" that recorded bids and offers, not actual trades. The computer system replaced the telephone communications mechanism in 1971 and provided a far better method of uncovering the best price.

EFFICIENCY OF THE OTC MARKETS

Since over-the-counter securities dealers are in computer contact with each other, they know the prices set by one another. As a result, an OTC market is very competitive and is not significantly different from a securities market that utilizes an organized exchange. Nevertheless, it is fair to say that the stocks of many large and well known corporations are traded on the NYSE, often called the Big Board. This provides the NYSE with high visibility—it is considered the *real* marketplace. The trading in shares of approximately 2,000 corporations takes place on the floor of the exchange; transactions are recorded on an electronic ticker tape flashed on the floor itself as well as in brokerage offices throughout the country. As a consequence of the emphasis on Big Board stocks, the common stocks listed on over-the-counter markets are often called secondary issues.

OTC MARKETS FOR DIFFERENT SECURITIES

There are over-the-counter securities markets for a variety of financial securities or instruments. The most widely followed is the over-the-counter market in common stocks. While many large corporations have their stock traded at the New York Stock Exchange, not all common stocks traded in the NASDAQ market are small. For example, IBM Corp., AT&T, or General Motors Corp. stocks (that are also part of the 30 common stocks included in the widely followed Dow Jones Industrial Average index) are traded on the Big Board. However, many widely known common stocks, such as Intel Corp. or MCI Communications Corp., are traded in the over-the-counter stock market. Both the NYSE and the NASDAQ market have a large number of small common stocks.

The financial market in U.S. government **bonds** is also set up as an over-the-counter market. It is important to note that the U.S. government bond market has a larger trading volume than the NYSE. The OTC market in government bonds was established by approximately 40 dealers in Treasury bonds who were ready to buy and sell Treasury securities.

Over-the-counter securities markets exist in other financial instruments, in addition to common stocks and government bonds. Markets for several money-market financial instruments are also established as over-the-counter markets. For example, negotiable certificates of deposit, banker's acceptances, and federal funds are all traded in over-the-counter securities markets. There are OTC markets in non-money market instruments as well. These include trading in a **foreign exchange**.

DERIVATIVES AND THE OTC MARKETS. The relatively newly issued financial instrument known as a derivative is also traded in the OTC securities markets. Peter Abken (in *Economic Review*) discusses the implications of **derivative securities** trading in the over-the-counter markets. He points out that, aside from their complexity, the largely unregulated character of the OTC derivatives markets sets them apart from the financial markets for other securities, due to their extremely rapid growth and fast pace of innovation. In recent years, over-the-counter derivatives have become a mainstay of financial risk management and are expected to continue growing in importance, according to Abken. The current structure of the OTC markets is being closely examined, and a set of recommendations has been made. The central policy question in derivatives regulation debated by Abken is whether further federal regulation is appropriate, or whether the existing structure can oversee these markets.

BID-ASK PRICES AND THE DEALER'S SPREAD

The bid price is the amount that a securities dealer must pay to obtain a security, while the ask price is the amount that a securities dealer receives after selling it. Frederic S. Mishkin commented in *The Economics of Money, Banking, and Financial Markets* that "you might want to think of the bid price as the 'wholesale price' and the asked price as the 'retail' price."

The ask price for securities is higher than the bid price. The difference between the two prices provides the dealer with his profit margin, compensating the dealer for his work. This compensation amount is known as the dealer's spread. Since securities can rise or fall in price during the period that the dealer owns them, thus impacting a dealer's ability to secure an acceptable asking price, this business can be a tricky one.

SEE ALSO: Going Public; Nasdaq Stock Market; Stock Market; Stocks

[Anandi P. Sahu, Ph.D.]

FURTHER READING:

Abken, Peter A. "Over-the-Counter Financial Derivatives: Risky business?" *Economic Review* [Federal Reserve Bank of Atlanta], March/April 1994.

Mishkin, Frederic S. *The Economics of Money, Banking, and Financial Markets.* 5th ed. Reading, PA: Addison-Wesley, 1998.

Ritter, Lawrence S., William L. Silber, and Gregory F. Udell. *Principles of Money, Banking, and Financial Markets.* 9th ed. Reading, PA: Addison-Wesley, 1997.

OVERHEAD EXPENSE

Although other types exist as discussed below, overhead expenses can be easily explained in terms of indirect manufacturing costs-that is, costs not associated with direct materials or direct labor. Overhead expenses—also called indirect manufacturing costs and factory overhead—encompass three general kinds of costs: those for indirect materials, indirect labor, and all other miscellaneous production expenses such as **taxes**, insurance, **depreciation**, supplies, utilities, and repairs. Direct material expenses are those for materials that become part of the finished product. For example, the cost of wood used to build furniture is a direct material expense. In contrast, indirect expenses are those that do not become part of the finished product. For example, electricity used to power equipment is an indirect manufacturing cost or overhead expense. Likewise, wage and salaries paid to workers who are directly involved with production are direct costs, whereas those paid to workers who repair and maintain equipment are indirect costs. In addition, overhead costs may include minor direct costs when they are so insignificant that they cannot be practically treated as direct expenses. Therefore, overhead expenses are part of the total costs of maintaining and staffing a business.

TYPES OF OVERHEAD COSTS

Overhead expenses can divided into three general categories: company overhead, selling overhead, and administrative overhead. These expenses cannot be directly linked with manufacturing products or providing services. These expenses constitute some of the most frequently discussed and illustrative kinds of overhead such as equipment maintenance and repair as well as utilities. Selling overhead refers to the costs related to product or service distribution and marketing. Hence, this type of overhead includes packaging and shipping, public relations, and sales staff expenses. Finally, administrative overhead expenses encompass expenses associated with general business operations such as office supply costs, management expenses, and labor costs from administrators and office workers who do not work directly for marketing and production departments. For purposes of explanation, the following discussion and examples will center on company overhead.

In addition, managers distinguish between variable, fixed, and mixed overhead costs in order to obtain information necessary for determining, planning, and controlling product costs. These types are differentiated based on the way changes in the level of production affect them—but these classifications tend to vary from industry to industry. Variable overhead costs are those that change depending on production levels. The cost of production supplies might be variable in that the more a company produces, the more supplies it needs. Fixed overhead costs are those that are constant even when production levels vary. Fixed overhead, for example, might include manager salaries, which remain constant when production levels fluctuate. Finally, mixed (or semivariable) overhead costs are those that are both partially variable and partially fixed. Some utilities, for instance, might be mixed costs if they have a connection fee (fixed cost) as well as a usage fee (variable cost). Consequently, determining the type of overhead cost requires examining whether and to what extent costs are dependent on production levels.

OVERHEAD APPLICATION

Accurate **accounting** and allocation of overhead expenses are very important in calculating the total cost of manufacturing a product and hence in setting a profitable selling price. The accounting of overhead is part of the control established during the budget process.

Because managers may not know total overhead costs until the end of an accounting period and because they generally need detailed information on costs before the end of an accounting period, accountants and managers use a series of steps called the *overhead application* to determine the overhead costs to allocate to production units. This process involves estimating an overhead rate and production volume that will apply to the coming fiscal year:

1. The type of overhead costs must be determined and classified as variable, fixed, or mixed. Then a projection of total overhead expenses must be made.
2. An activity base is chosen as a means for allocating overhead costs to production units. Activity bases are measures of production that can closely account for any differences in the amount of overhead actually incurred. Activity bases include direct labor costs, direct material costs, direct labor hours, machine hours, and units of production.
3. A budget is prepared to show the total projected volume of the activity base for the next period. For example, if direct labor costs are selected as the activity base, then the total amount expected to be spent on direct labor costs for the coming year would be budgeted.
4. Finally, an overhead application rate is determined by dividing the total budgeted overhead into the total budgeted activity level. Based on this rate, overhead costs are assigned to production units. Since this overhead application rate is determined while preparing a budget and not from actual production results, it is called a predetermined overhead rate.

A simple illustration of step four can be constructed by using units of production as the activity base. If the estimated overhead expenses were $400,000 and the projected number of units was 350,000 ($400,000/350,000), then the per unit overhead expense would be $1.14. Hence, if a company had a production goal of 100,000 units, it would assign overhead expenses of $140,000 ($1.14 multiplied by 100,000) to this goal.

However, this process can be far more complicated, especially if a company manufactures more than one product and if a company's different product processes vary considerably. For example, one product may require a labor-intensive finishing process, while another relies more on machinery. The relationships apparent between the finished product and these production processes provide accounting an activity base upon which to calculate the allocation of overhead, which would be divided by the number of direct labor hours and the number of machine hours, respectively. A company provides for overhead absorption by combining a number of these activity-based overhead rate allocation methods.

ABSORPTION AND OVERHEAD VARIANCES

The monthly job cost ledger may indicate that, in applying the predetermined rate, the allocation either exceeded or fell short of actual costs. This variance, termed the "burden variance," means that overhead was either (1) overabsorbed (overapplied): the application of the predetermined rate exceeded the actual overhead used, or (2) underabsorbed (underapplied): the application of the predetermined rate fell short of the actual overhead used.

Burden variance can result from the following spending variations, or budget variance:

1. The total amount actually spent for production overhead varied from the budget.
2. The price paid for units of overhead factors varied from the budgeted prices.
3. The quantity of overhead factors per unit of finished product varied from the quantity per budgeted unit.
4. The mix of overhead factors used changed so that the average cost of overhead per unit of product varied from the amount budgeted.

Burden variance also results from the following volume variances:

1. Actual volume varied from the volume used to set the predetermined overhead rates.
2. Seasonal fluctuations distorted the averages.

Underabsorbed overhead exists as a debit balance in the production overhead clearing account at the end of the year. Overabsorbed overhead is a credit balance. To report these balances in the **financial statements**, the accountant examines the cause of the variance and chooses a method to satisfy the reporting objective. In reporting the variances the accountant considers at least three alternatives:

1. Divide the under- or overabsorption in any period between the **income statement** and the **balance sheet** in direct proportion to the distribution of the overhead absorbed during the period. The objective of this method is to have inventory cost and the cost of goods sold approximate the average costs of production in the period.
2. Report the variance in full as a loss or a gain on the income statement for the period in which it arises. The purpose of this method is to measure the inventory at its normal cost, with the income statement accounting for all variances from the budget. Inefficiencies due to overspending or underproduction are costs of the period rather than costs of the products manufactured during the period. When plant utilization falls short of budget, there is a loss (or an expense for idle capacity) to be reported in the income statement for the period.
3. Carry all burden variances to the balance sheet for the end of the period to be added to or offset against similar amounts arising in preceding or succeeding periods. Management exercises this option when it expects that a portion of the burden variance may be offset. **Management** does not extend this practice to the annual reporting, however, where it splits the burden variance between inventory and the cost of goods sold if the variance is (1) large enough to have a material effect on the financial statement and if it represents overabsorption, or (2) likely to be recoverable from the sale of the inventory in later periods.

COST CLASSIFICATION PROBLEMS

In some instances the cost of classifying production costs to specific units may be prohibitive. Therefore, management recognizes them as part of the production overhead to be absorbed on a per-unit basis and may devise some arbitrary method of allocation. Some examples of these costs are:

- Glue, staples, nuts, bolts, nails, plastic wrap, tape, etc., elements common to a variety of products without specific measurements.
- Shared time and travel expenses resulting from performing services at a number of customer sites.
- Overtime premiums, resulting from over-scheduling, are averaged over the entire production for the period.

SEE ALSO: Budgeting; Cost Control; Costing Methods (Manufacturing)

[Roger J. AbiNader]

FURTHER READING:

Cherrington, J. Owen, et al. *Cost and Managerial Accounting.* Dubuque, IA: Wm. C. Brown Publishers, 1985.

Fultz, Jack. *Overhead: What It Is and How It Works.* Cambridge, MA: Abt Books, 1980.

Meigs, Robert F., and Walter B. Meigs. *Accounting: The Basis for Business Decisions.* 8th ed. New York: McGraw-Hill, 1990.

Rao, Srikumar S. "Overhead Can Kill You." *Forbes,* 10 February 1997, 97.

Shillinglaw, Gordon, and Philip E. Meyer. *Accounting: A Management Approach.* 7th ed. Homewood, IL: Irwin, 1983.

Welsch, Glenn A. *Budgeting: Profit Planning and Control.* Englewood Cliffs, NJ: Prentice Hall, 1976.

P

P/E RATIO

SEE: Price/Earnings Ratio

PACKAGING

Packaging is the container or wrapper that holds a product or group of products. Types of commercial packaging include shipping cartons, containers for industrial goods, and holders for consumer products. Besides protecting the product from damage and protecting consumers from hazardous products, packaging can function as a crucial **marketing** tool, helping companies attract new customers and retain established ones. This second function became even more important for companies in the 1990s as the reach and effectiveness of **advertising** began to shrink. Simultaneously, packaging makers have had to weigh the need for attractive, promotional packaging with consumer demands for environmentally friendly packaging and less packaging altogether.

BACKGROUND

Before World War II, packaging was used primarily to surround and protect products during storage, transportation, and distribution. Some packages were designed with aesthetic appeal and even for ease-of-use by the end consumer, but package design was typically left to technicians. Since the beginning of the Industrial Revolution in the mid-1800s, the "build it and they will come" maxim had prevailed. After World War II companies became more interested in marketing and promotion as a means of enticing customers to purchase their products. As a result, more manufacturers began to view packaging as a way to lure buyers.

During the mid-1900s, several influences contributed to turn packaging into an integral part of most companies' marketing mix. Consumers became better educated, and **wealth** and expectations generally increased. Consequently, consumers began to rely much more heavily on manufactured goods and processed food items. New technologies related to production, distribution, and preservatives led to a massive proliferation in the number and type of products and brands available in industrialized nations. Thus, packaging became a vital means of differentiating items and informing inundated consumers.

The importance of consumer packaging was elevated in the United States during the late 1970s and 1980s. Rapid postwar economic expansion and market growth waned during that period, forcing companies to focus increasingly on luring consumers to their product or brand at the expense of the **competition**. Package design became a marketing science. And, as a new corporate cost-consciousness developed in response to increased competition, companies began to alter packaging techniques as way to cut production, storage, and distribution expenses. Furthermore, marketers began to view packaging as a tool to exploit existing product lines by adding new items and to pump new life into maturing products.

PACKAGE DESIGN

Consumer packaging serves to contain and communicate. A product's "packaging mix" is the result of several requirements that determine how a package accomplishes those two basic functions. Robert D. Hisrich identified eight major package requirements that dictate the mix. A package must: protect the product, be adaptable to production-line speeds, promote or sell the item, increase the product's density, help the consumer use the product, provide reusable value to the user, satisfy legal requirements, and keep packaging-related expenses low. Two classes of package design criteria are: functional requirements and sales requirements.

FUNCTIONAL REQUIREMENTS

Package design must meet five groups of functional criteria: in-home, in-store (or warehouse), production, distribution and safety, and legal. In-home requirements usually dictate that packaging be easy to use and store, remind users when and what to repurchase, reinforce consumers' expectations of the product, and tell them how to safely and effectively use the product. In addition, increasing numbers of consumers expect packaging to be recyclable and environmentally sensitive.

In-store criteria require that packaging attracts attention on the shelf, instill confidence in the buyer, identify the product or brand and differentiate it from the competition, communicate benefits and uses, and entice customers to actually purchase the item. The product must also be easy for retailers to store and stock on the shelves or the floor, and simple to process at a check-out counter or other final point of distribution. For instance, packaging that is oddly shaped and takes up a large amount of space may draw attention, but it may also be shunned by mail-order sellers concerned about shipping costs or space-conscious store retailers.

Production demands, the third group of functional criteria influencing packaging, are primarily based on cost. A designer may create a fantastic package that would perform excellently in the marketplace, but if the company can't find a way to produce the package cost-effectively, the design is useless. Among the most important considerations is production line speed. If a container is too long, wide, or short, it could significantly slow the speed of the production machines. Or, if the top or spout of a container is too small or is oddly shaped, the product may not flow easily into the package.

Packaging considerations related to distribution and safety are important and numerous. If an unacceptable portion of the goods are damaged during storage, transportation, or distribution, the package has failed. Likewise, if the package injures the user, future sales could be lost or the company could be liable for damages. As a result, engineers are faced with numerous technical considerations that have a residual impact on the final look and feel of the package. For instance, packages must be able to withstand the pressure of several other crates stored on top of them. They must also be able to resist moisture, adapt to temperature changes, and withstand rough handling. From a cost standpoint, packages must also be designed to suit standardized transportation requirements related to weight, size, and durability.

In addition, packaging must be tamper-proof, which is to say tamper-evident, since it is extremely difficult to make a package truly tamper-proof. Because of the deaths in 1982 from tampered-with Tylenol containers, providing tamper-evident packaging became another major concern of packagers. As a result of this tragedy, the U.S. Food and Drug Administration requires the use of tamper-evident packages for certain products, and companies adopted tamper-evident packages to avoid being liable for tampering incidents. Tamper-evident packaging comes in a variety of forms including seals, plastic bands, layers of sealed packages, and innerseals. Similarly, harmful substances such as cleaning agents and pharmaceuticals also must be childproof.

Furthermore, packages should ideally be designed to handle normal use by consumers. For example, a vegetable-oil container must be able to fall from a counter without breaking and to have very warm oil poured back into it without melting. Examples of packages that may result in harm to consumers include: those with sharp edges, such as some pull-top canisters; glass containers that hold products made for use in the shower, which could cause serious injury if dropped; and heavy item boxes that might break when the customer is carrying them or cause strain or injury to the consumer when picked up or set down.

The fifth basic group of packaging requirements is laws and legislation. Various federal laws have been passed to protect consumers from misrepresentation and unsafe products. For instance, some laws require that containers for potentially dangerous goods, such as gasoline or drugs, be stored in specially constructed containers. Other laws forbid producers from misrepresenting the product quality or quantity through misleading packaging. Perhaps the most influential class of laws that affect packaging, however, is that related to labeling.

PRODUCT LABELING. The label is the text printed on a product package or, in the case of items such as clothing, attached to the product itself. Legally, labels are all written, printed, or graphic material on the container of products that are involved in interstate commerce or held for sale. The main body of legislation governing packaging and labeling is the Fair Packaging and Labeling Act of 1966. It mandates that every product package or label specify on its ''principal display label'' (the part of the label most likely to be seen by consumers): (1) the product type, (2) the producer or processor's name and location, (3) quantity (if applicable), and (4) number and size of servings (if applicable). Furthermore, several restrictions apply to the way that the label is displayed. For example, information required by the act must be in boldface type. Also, if the company is not listed in the telephone book, the manufacturer's or importer's street address must be displayed.

Other information required by the act relates to specific foods, toys, drugs, cosmetics, furs, and textiles. For instance, under the act, labels for edible products must provide sodium content if other nutritional information is shown. They must also show ingredients, beginning with the one of highest quantity and descending in order. Certain food items, such as beef, may also be required to display qualitative ''grade labels'' or inspection labels. Likewise, ''informative labeling'' may be required for products such as home appliances. Informative label requirements mandate information about use, care, performance capability, life expectancy, safety precautions, gas mileage, or other factors. Certain major home appliances, for example, must provide the estimated cost of running each make and model for one year at average utility rates.

Congress passed significant new labeling legislation in 1990, the Nutrition Labeling and Education Act of 1990, that became effective in the mid-1990s. This act is intended primarily to discourage misleading labeling related to health benefits of food items. Specifically, many package labels subjectively claimed that their contents were ''low-fat,'' ''high-fiber,'' or possessed some other health virtue when the facts indicated otherwise. Basically, the new laws require most food labels to specify values such as calorie and cholesterol content, fat and saturated fat percentages, and sodium levels.

PACKAGING AND THE ENVIRONMENT. According to a 1991 survey by the Roper Organization, consumers are willing to pay 4.6 percent extra for environmentally friendly products. Moreover, estimates indicate that about a third of all U.S. landfills were full by the mid-1990s and that packaging accounts for a third of the country's solid waste. Consequently, packagers have to juggle environmental concerns with functional and marketing concerns. In response to consumer demands, companies adopted the use of recycled materials as part of their packaging and offered products in packages that are recyclable. Furthermore, companies reduced their packaging or implemented more environmentally friendly kinds of packages. For example, McDonald's replaced its polystyrene shells with paper packaging, which, while not recyclable, has a far shorter life cycle than the foam containers or other alternatives.

Besides accommodating consumer concerns, some forms of environmentally sound packaging also benefit companies in other ways. By reducing their packaging in the late 1980s and early 1990s, companies found that they saved significant amounts of money. For example, by removing the cardboard packaging from deodorant containers and by introducing concentrated and refillable laundry detergent containers, companies have substantially reduced the packaging costs of these products, according to *Brandweek.*

SALES REQUIREMENTS

In addition to functional requirements, product packaging must be designed in a way that will appeal to buyers. The four principal merchandising requirement areas are: apparent size, attention drawing power, impression of quality, and brand-name readability.

Apparent size entails designing packaging to look as large as possible without misrepresenting the actual contents. This objective can be achieved by ensuring that the panels or dimensions of the package most likely to be viewed by the consumer are the largest, and that the product or brand name is shown on the most visible areas in large letters. In addition, the package can be made to look larger by using solid colors and simple, bold designs free of borders, superfluous art work, and unnecessary print. The pretense of largeness is particularly important for packages containing commodity items, such as rice, driveway salt, and canned fruit or vegetables.

Attention drawing power refers to the aesthetics and conspicuousness of the package design. Depending on the product and the goals of the marketers, the package may be made to appear attractive, exciting, pure, soft, sexy, scary, intriguing, or to evoke some other emotion. In most cases, though, the product is displayed on the front of the package in the form of a picture, art, or see-through window. In addition, bright colors, glossy stock, obtrusive carton displays, and other elements can garner positive attention if used prudently.

A quality impression is an important sales requirement for packaging because items that are perceived to be of low quality are usually assumed to be a poor value, regardless of price. Examples of packaging mistakes that convey low quality or poor value include: faded lettering or colors, tacky designs or strange typeface, outdated pictures and designs, and cheap construction.

Readability, the fourth basic sales requirement for successful package design, means that the package must be extremely simple and easy to read. This is of paramount importance for products such as breakfast cereal that are shelved next to numerous competing brands and products. If the package attempts to convey too many messages, it will likely fail to connect with the consumer. Because of the mass of buying choices, buyers typically do not take time to absorb messages on packaging, with the possible exception of high-priced specialty items. Among other guidelines, letters or logos should be large and printed in the same type style as that used in complementary print and television advertising. The requirement of readability contributes to the difficulty in packaging completely new products.

PACKAGING STRATEGY

Packagers and researchers of consumer perception, such as Mona Doyle, contend that packaging began to play a greater role in selling products during the 1990s. They argue that companies can no longer rely solely on advertising to communicate information about packaged products to consumers. Instead, packaging has taken on a greater share of this responsibility. With scarce shelf space in stores, packagers must provide packaging that differentiates a company's products from its competitors or packaging that simply catches the eye of the consumer, especially for new products.

Indeed, just as ease-of-use and readability are elements of the strategic packaging mix, packaging has become an even more important part of a company's strategic marketing mix. Most packages for consumer products are designed for one of three purposes: (1) to improve the packaging of an existing product, (2) to add a new product to an existing product line, or (3) to contain an entirely new product.

Redesign of packaging for existing products may be prompted by several factors. Many times, a company may simply want to breathe new life into a maturing product by updating its image or adding a new gimmick to the package, such as an easy-pour spout. Or, a company may redesign the package to respond to a competitive threat, such as a new product that is more visible on the shelf. Other strategic reasons for package redesign include:

- changes in the product
- reduction in packaging costs
- product line restructuring
- alterations in market strategy, such as aiming the product at a different age group
- trying to promote new uses for a product
- theft prevention
- accommodation of consumer needs, wants, or complaints
- legal or environmental requirements
- the advent of new materials or technologies

Even small packaging changes for established brands and products typically require careful consideration, since millions of dollars are often at risk if a company alienates or confuses customers. In 1988, for example, the Adolph Coors Co. changed the words "Banquet Beer" on its beer container labels to "Original Draft." Although the label change was generally successful, sales dropped in southern California and west Texas, the two regions where Coors beer had been sold since the 1940s. Many customers there were confused by the change and assumed that Coors had altered the product. Coors changed the label back to "Banquet Beer" in those two areas and sales recovered.

A second reason for package design is to extend a product or brand line. An example of a product line extension is Anheuser-Busch Companies' Busch Light beer, which is an extension of the Busch beer product line. Another example is the Tide detergent brand line, which was extended to include Tide Free, a detergent without dyes or perfumes. In the case of product extensions, the packaging strategy is usually to closely mimic the established brand or product, but to integrate the benefits of the new feature into the existing package in such a way that customers will be able to easily differentiate it from other products in the line. There are, however, significant risks inherent in packaging for extensions because a new package may confuse customers or frustrate retailers.

The third impetus for package design is the need to generate housing for an entirely new product. This is the most difficult type of packaging to create because it often requires the designer to instill consumer confidence in an unknown product or brand, and to inform the buyer about the product's uses and benefits. Packaging for products and brands that are entirely new to the marketplace require the most education, and are therefore the most challenging to develop. In contrast, packaging for goods that are entering established product categories require less education, they must, however, overcome established competition. In general, packaging strategies for such products entail mimicking the packaging of leading products, which helps to assure the buyer that the product is "normal." For instance, packaging strategies of salad dressing, soda, eggs, toothpaste, and milk are all similar.

An example of a new product launch that demonstrates the importance of packaging in the marketing mix is Ore-Ida Foods, Inc.'s introduction of Deep Fries in the early 1970s. Deep Fries were frozen, oil-coated french fries that were cooked in the oven. Although they were comparatively expensive, Deep Fries were more convenient to prepare and better tasting than other frozen fries. The package was designed to convey to consumers that the product was premium and it offered "Deep Fried flavor and crispness without deep frying."

The initial launch was successful and Deep Fries soon cultivated a small group of loyal customers. Nevertheless, sales growth failed to meet projections. Consumer research showed that the Deep Fries package succeeded in conveying a premium image but had failed to inform customers of the benefits of Deep Fries. In fact, many customers had purchased the product simply because of the quality of the packaging. Other would-be customers never tried the product because they were unable to justify its high price. Those that did buy the product realized its benefits, were satisfied, and continued to buy.

Ore-Ida developed two new packages and eventually selected one that proved, through market tests, to achieve the desired sales growth. Its new package changed the quote ''Deep Fried flavor and crispness without deep frying'' to ''The Self Sizzlers, they make your oven work like a deep fryer.'' In addition, the Ore-Ida name was replaced with Ore-Ida's parent company name, H.J. Heinz Co., which served to soften the expensive, premium image. The phrase ''Heinz, Self Sizzling Deep Fries'' was also added to the package. The product eventually captured a loyal groups of customers characterized as working women who habitually purchased the best, most convenient products.

[Dave Mote, updated by Karl Heil]

FURTHER READING:

Boyd, Harper W., Jr., and Orville C. Walker Jr. *Marketing Management: A Strategic Approach.* Boston: Irwin, 1990.

Doyle, Mona. *Packaging Strategy: Winning the Consumer.* Lancaster, PA: Technomic Publishing, 1996.

Erwin, Lewis, and L. Hall Healy Jr. *Packaging and Solid Waste.* New York: American Management Association, 1990.

Hisrich, Robert D. *Marketing.* New York: Barron's Business Library, 1990.

McCarthy, E. Jerome, and William D. Perreault Jr. *Basic Marketing.* 13th ed. New York: McGraw-Hill College Div., 1998.

Mehegan, Sean. ''Green on Green.'' *Brandweek,* 20 May 1996, 43.

Rosette, Jack L. *Improving Tamper-Evident Packaging.* Lancaster, PA: Technomic Publishing, 1992.

Schoell, William F., and Joseph P. Guiltinan. *Marketing: Contemporary Concepts and Practices.* 5th ed. Boston: Allyn and Bacon, 1992.

Stern, Walter. *Handbook of Package Design Research.* New York: Wiley, 1981.

PARTNERSHIPS

In the United States, the partnership is one of the three most commonly used types of business organizations; the other two are the corporation and the sole proprietorship. The sole proprietorship is the oldest and simplest business organization. It is formed when one person goes into business and has sole control and responsibility for the business; the corporation is the most complex of the three types of business organizations. A partnership is an association of two or more persons who carry on a business, as co-owners, for profit. It is more complex and usually requires more legal formalities than a sole proprietorship, but, in general, it is less complex than a corporation.

There are two main types of partnerships: the general partnership and the limited partnership. This article describes how each type of partnership is created. It also discusses the law governing each, relationships among partners, partners' potential legal liability, duration of the partnership, and termination of the partnership. In addition, there is brief discussion of two special designations that are allowed under the laws of some states for partnerships involving professionals: the limited liability partnership (LLP) and the limited liability limited partnership (LLLP).

GENERAL PARTNERSHIPS

A general partnership can be based on an oral or written agreement among the partners. However, for reasons discussed below, it is always advisable to have a written partnership agreement signed by all partners.

The formation and operation of business organizations are governed primarily by state law. Thus, each of the individual 50 states has unique partnership laws. However, the law of partnerships is relatively uniform throughout the 50 states, because most states have based partnership statutes on the Uniform Partnership Act (UPA), a model act created by the National Conference of Commissioners on Uniform State Laws (Uniform Law Commissioners). The Uniform Law Commissioners have approved various model laws for business organizations including the UPA, the Uniform Limited Partnership Act (ULPA), and others. These model acts are drafted by panels of practitioners, legal scholars, and judges who are respected and experienced in the area of law involved.

The UPA dates from 1914, and the Revised Uniform Partnership Act (RUPA) was adopted by the Uniform Law Commissioners in 1994. The Commissioners approved amendments to the RUPA in 1996 to provide limited liability for partners in a general partnership. Because they became effective in 1997, those amendments are referred to as the ''1997 Amendments.'' As of mid-1999, the RUPA of 1994 had been adopted by at least 25 states; 23 of those states had adopted it with the 1997 amendments. In addition, the RUPA has been introduced as legislation in Hawaii and Indiana.

Under the UPA, a partnership is defined as a voluntary organization formed by two or more persons to carry on a business as co-owners for profit. Most rules set down in the UPA and RUPA apply only if there is no partnership agreement or if an existing partnership agreement is silent with respect to a certain issue or question.

CREATION OF PARTNERSHIP

When lawyers use the term ''partnership,'' they are usually referring to a general partnership, and in this section of this article, I will do the same. The act of doing business together, for profit, creates the partnership. In some states, but not all, a partnership may file a Partnership Agreement or Statement of Authority with the office of a designated state official such as the Secretary of State. However, such filings are not required.

A general partnership is a legal entity for limited purposes only. For example, it can have its own assumed (or fictitious) name, and title to real or personal property can held be in the name of the partnership. However, in a lawsuit, the individual partners will be named as defendants.

Depending on the business or profession of the partners, some filings that are not related to partnership status may be required. For example, if the partnership uses a name other than the names of the partners, it must file for an assumed name. (This requirement also applies to sole proprietorships.) In some states, such as Michigan, the filing is done county by county. In other states, such as Montana, one filing can be made to reserve the name for use throughout the state. In addition, occupational licenses must be obtained, such as in the building industry and cosmetology. Similarly, professionals such as medical doctors, lawyers, and accountants, among others, must meet professional licensing requirements. In states that impose a retail sales tax, the business must obtain a sales tax license, collect sales taxes, and remit them to the state.

ADVANTAGES AND DISADVANTAGES OF THE PARTNERSHIP AS A BUSINESS ORGANIZATION

As compared to the limited partnership or corporation, a major advantage of the general partnership is that it can be organized with minimal paperwork and at a relatively low cost. The partnership, unlike a corporation, can operate in more than one state without having to obtain a license to do business in each state. In general, partnerships are subject to less government supervision and fewer regulations than is true for corporations.

There are some disadvantages to use of a general partnership as a business organization. First, practical considerations limit the number of people who can be involved; a corporation may be needed to accommodate a large number of owners. Second, a partnership can be dissolved at any time. Third, a partner's liability is unlimited. Use of a limited partnership or a corporation may be advisable if some or all of the owners are unwilling to be subject to such liability.

PARTNERS' CONTRIBUTIONS TO AND BENEFITS DERIVED FROM PARTNERSHIP

Under the UPA and RUPA, unless a written partnership agreement stipulates otherwise, certain general rules apply with respect to management, profits, and losses. First, unless otherwise stipulated in writing, each partner has an equal voice in the management of the partnership's business. Second, unless otherwise stipulated in writing, all partners share equally in profits and losses of partnership. If Sam and Mary form a partnership to run a pizza business, each makes contributions, whether in cash, or real or personal property. Each is expected to contribute services (work for the partnership). However, regardless of the contributions (in property or services) of each partner, Sam and Mary share equally in the profits and losses.

These general rules underscore the need for a written partnership agreement (sometimes called ''articles of partnership'') even though it is not legally mandated. With a written agreement, the partners can design management and profit-sharing arrangements that meet specific needs. Almost any terms are permissible so long as they are not illegal or contrary to public policy.

THE PARTNERSHIP AGREEMENT

Certain kinds of provisions should go into any partnership agreement. Here are some categories that should be covered:

1. Names and addresses of the partnership and of individual partners
2. Terms of partnership and events that lead to termination (e.g., death, retirement, insanity, bankruptcy, resignation, or disability)
3. Financial contributions and financial decision-making including:
    - Contributions of each partner (such as cash, real or personal property, or services)
    - Loans from partners to the partnership
    - Borrowing policies
    - Who has authority to borrow money on behalf of the partnership?
    - Banking—Where? Who has authority make withdrawals?

- Sharing of profits and division of losses each year (percentage share of profits)
- Distribution of profits after winding up and liquidation of the partnership

4. Financial record-keeping including:
   - Keeping and maintaining financial records (books)
   - Definition of fiscal year (e.g. January 1 to December 31)
   - Right of access to records
5. Management
   - Voting rights of partners
   - Are all partners equal, or will certain partners be designated as ''controlling'' partners and others as ''minority'' partners?
   - Who has authority to hire and fire employees?
6. Duties of each partner
7. Dispute resolution methods (such as arbitration, mediation, or choice of venue and forum)

TAXATION

Each year, a partnership must file an ''information return'' with the Internal Revenue Service to report the partnership's profits or losses. The information return must also report all dividend income and capital gains or losses. However, the partnership does not pay taxes. If there is a profit, each partner reports his or her share on his or her personal income tax return, and the partner pays taxes on the those amounts as personal income. If there are losses, each deducts those losses from his or her personal income. When there are losses, the partnership form for doing business provides an advantage for partners, because the losses can be used to reduce the total amount of the partner's income. However, the partners' profits are taxed each year whether they are distributed or not. For example, if a partnership with two partners has $50,000 in profits and decides to retain those profits and use them to expand the business, each must report $25,000 as personal income and pay taxes on that amount. In such cases, the partnership creates a disadvantage for the individual partners.

TORT AND CONTRACT LIABILITY OF PARTNERS

The main disadvantage of a partnership is that, if the business fails, each partner can be sued by creditors for contract or tort debts. The law says that the partners are ''jointly and severally'' liable for the debts of the partnership. This means that all partners or even just one partner can be forced to pay all of the partnership's debts out of his or her personal income and resources. For example, if the partnership owes $200,000 to a creditor, the creditor can sue all three creditors jointly for that amount. Or, the creditor can sue one partner or any combination of two partners for the entire $200,000. A partner who pays all of a debt or an unequal share of a debt has a right to seek contribution from the remaining partner or partners who have not paid. However, joint and several liability creates a major risk for a partner who has substantial resources such as real property, income, or other assets. If he or she enters a partnership with a partner who has few or no resources outside of the partnership, the wealthier partner may end up paying all of the partnership's debts if the partnership fails. A right to contribution is of no practical value if the other partners have no assets.

RELATIONSHIPS BETWEEN AND AMONG PARTNERS

The partners in a general partnership are agents and principals of one another. The UPA and RUPA state that each partner has a fiduciary relationship to the partnership and must act in good faith and for the benefit of the partnership. (The RUPA gives more details on this than does the UPA.) In management decisions, each partner has one vote, and most decisions are based on a majority vote. However, certain major decisions, such as a decision to merge with another partnership, require a unanimous vote.

DURATION, DISSOLUTION, AND TERMINATION OF PARTNERSHIP

Unlike a corporation, a general partnership does not have ''perpetual'' existence. Under the UPA, the death, retirement, personal bankruptcy, or insanity of any one partner causes the dissolution of the partnership. This is an area in which the RUPA differs from the UPA. Under the RUPA, dissolution does not occur automatically when a partner leaves. Under the UPA, if a new partner is added, the organization is dissolved and the surviving partnership is considered a new legal entity. Even if a written partnership agreement stipulates that the partnership will continue for a set number of years, the partnership can be dissolved upon petition of one of the partners. The partnership's business, however, is not terminated upon dissolution. Dissolution means the legal organization under which the partnership has been operating ceases to exist.

However, dissolution can lead to termination after winding up unfinished business and liquidating business assets. Contracts are completed or settled, and debts are paid. Finally, any remaining profits and assets are distributed among the partners. During this process, no new business can be transacted.

To prevent problems when a partner dies or leaves the partnership for any reason, a partnership agreement should include a buy-sell agreement provision. By law, this provision must be in place when the partnership is created. It describes the manner of compensation for the survivors of a deceased partner or for the withdrawing partner. A formula is established to determine the amount of payment, and a payment schedule is established. Often, partners provide for the possible death of a partner by taking out a life insurance policy on the life of each partner. The policy is made payable to the partnership or to the surviving partners, enabling the partners to pay the amount required in the buy-sell agreement to the survivors of the deceased partner, and remaining partners are financially able to continue to do business.

The Revised Uniform Partnership Act (RUPA) includes a formula for valuing a partner's interest during a buyout. (This was not included in the UPA.) As with other UPA and RUPA provisions, this formula is applied only if this topic is not covered in a written partnership agreement.

LIMITED PARTNERSHIPS

The limited partnership is an alternative to the general partnership. Use of limited partnerships increased substantially during the 1970s when investors were seeking tax shelters. However, since the 1970s tax reform legislation has reduced the value of the tax shelter afforded to limited partnerships. In 1999, the primary reasons for choosing limited partnership today were based on investment return, cash flow, and the ability to protect some of the investors from unlimited personal liability for the partnership's debts. In many instances, a potential partner for a new partnership wishes to contribute financially to a partnership, but he or she does not want to risk unlimited personal **liability** for its debts. The Revised Uniform Limited Partnership Act (RULPA) has been adopted in 48 states, providing a great deal of uniformity in this area of law throughout the United States.

COMPARING LIMITED PARTNERSHIPS TO CORPORATIONS AND GENERAL PARTNERSHIPS

The limited partnership shares some of the characteristics of a general partnership and some characteristics of a corporation. Like a corporation, the limited partnership must be formed pursuant to state statute. The applicable law is the individual state's version of the RULP as well as the written partnership agreement. Unlike a general partnership, a limited partnership must be based on a written agreement that is signed by all partners (limited and general) and is filed with the designated state office such as the Secretary of State or Corporations and Securities Bureau. Forms must be completed supplying information about the partners, assets and resources of the limited partnership, the purpose of the business, and other relevant information. Statutory requirements must be followed ''to the letter'' before the forms will be accepted and approved by the state office. Upon approval, a certificate of limited partnership is issued and the limited partnership comes into existence. In the event that the forms and agreement are filed but not approved, the business will be treated as a general partnership, and all partners will be treated as limited partners.

One filing for the entire state (through the designated state office) is needed to acquire an assumed name for the limited partnership. Thus, in states such as Michigan, where filing for an assumed name for a general partnership is done county by county, obtaining an assumed name for use throughout the state is easier for the limited partnership than for the general partnership.

However, in many ways, the limited partnership is similar to a general partnership. The managers of the limited partnership are called general partners and their potential liabilities are the same as those of partners in a general partnership. Also, general and limited partners share in the profits of the business in the same way as is done among partners in a general partnership.

THE RIGHTS OF LIMITED AND GENERAL PARTNERS. Under the RULPA, the limited partnership must have at least one general partner who manages the business and is subject to unlimited personal liability for the liabilities of the business. It may also have one or more limited partners who contribute capital only (cash or assets) and do not participate in management. The one or more limited partners are subject to liability only to the extent of their individual investments.

This protection from unlimited liability applies so long as the limited partner does not participate in management in any way. This means that the limited partner, unlike a shareholder in a corporation, cannot vote on business matters and cannot have any say in management decisions. This prohibition on participation in management must be observed carefully and stringently. If a limited partner participates in the partnership's business *or* investment activities, he or she loses his or her status as a limited partner and is treated as a general partner with respect to the partnership's liabilities. For example, at least one state's courts have held that the act of speaking to a potential creditor on behalf of the partnership constitutes participation in management. Further, the partnership name cannot include the surname of a limited partner. The overall objective is to avoid any act or representation that might lead the public to believe that the partner participates in some way in management of the business.

TAXATION. With the exception of specific liabilities attributed to the partnership itself, the tax treatment of limited partnerships and of individual partners is almost identical to the treatment extended to general partnerships and their partners.

MASTER LIMITED PARTNERSHIPS. A recent development in partnership law is the creation of "master limited partnerships." In such arrangements, a promoter gathers interested parties who own a number of smaller limited partnerships and combines them into a new, larger limited partnership. The interests in the master limited partnership are then publicly traded over-the-counter or on a stock exchange. (When limited partnership interests are offered to the public, the offering as well as the limited partnership interests being sold must be registered with the **Securities and Exchange Commission (SEC)**.) Master limited partnerships have been used, for example, for oil drilling ventures. In addition, some corporations have done "spin-offs" of segments of their operations to form master limited partnerships.

SPECIAL DESIGNATIONS: LLP AND LLLP

In 1991, Texas became the first state to offer a new option to professionals in a partnership; it is called the Limited Liability Partnership (LLP). The LLP is treated like a partnership except that partners are protected from personal liability for the torts of partners in the firm. By 1997, a majority of the states had adopted some kind of LLP law, although those laws differ from state to state. By 1999, at least 18 states or jurisdictions had adopted the 1997 amendments to the RUPA that provide for LLPs, thus creating more uniformity. Those states and jurisdictions include: Alabama, Arkansas, Colorado, the District of Columbia, Idaho, Iowa, Kansas, Maryland, Minnesota, Montana, Nebraska, New Mexico, North Dakota, Oklahoma, Oregon, The U.S. Virgin Islands, Vermont, and Washington. Also by 1999, Arizona, California, and Virginia had adopted LLP equivalents.

Going further, a more limited number of states offer another alternative called the Limited Liability Limited Partnership (LLLP). The LLLP designation is similar to the LLP, except that it is available to limited partners in a limited partnership.

THE LLP. If one of the partners in a Limited Liability Partnership (LLP) is sued for a tort (malpractice), his or her partners are not jointly and severally (meaning separately) liable for that partner's debt. This protection applies so long as the partners are not supervising, directing, or otherwise involved in the negligent activity. This is significant when the firm does not have enough insurance coverage to pay all of a large judgment against the offending partner. The partner who engages in malpractice is, however, personally liable for his or her own tort.

For an LLP to exist, the LLP must be registered with the state office designated by statute (usually the Secretary of State or the State Corporations and Securities Bureau). The filing is called a "statement of qualification." In addition, LLP status must be indicated in the partnership's name using the words "Limited Liability Partnership" or the initials "L.L.P." In general, it is relatively easy to convert a general partnership into an LLP.

The LLP is treated like a general partnership for tax purposes. Comparing the LLP to a Professional Corporation (a corporate form that protects professionals from the torts of co-owner professionals), the LLP provides a tax advantage to its owners, because earnings are taxed as personal income, as is the case with other partnerships. In a professional corporation, the corporation pays taxes on earnings before they are distributed to the owners (shareholders). The shareholders, in turn, pay personal taxes on what they receive. Thus, the LLP can provide a tax advantage to partners.

If a partnership is considering seeking LLP status, the provisions of each state's laws must be studied carefully, because the laws vary. In most cases, LLP laws are in the form of amendments to a state's existing partnership laws.

THE LLLP. The Limited Liability Limited Partnership (LLLP) is a type of limited partnership. The difference between the LLLP and a limited partnership is that a general partner in the LLLP enjoys the same protection from liability as a limited partner with respect to the torts of his or her professional partners. The tort liability of each partner, whether he or she is a general or limited partner, is limited to the amount of the partner's investment in the firm. Only a few states have adopted LLLP laws. They include Colorado, Delaware, Florida, Missouri, Texas, and Virginia.

CONCLUSION

Choice of a form for doing business is a decision that must be based on the needs of its owners as well as legal and tax considerations. This article has provided general descriptions of general partnerships and limited partnerships, and it introduces the reader to the Limited Liability Partnership (LLP) and the Limited Liability Limited Partnership (LLL). However, a form for doing business should be chosen only after careful consultation with an attorney who is familiar with the relevant business association laws of the state(s) in which the owners wish to do business and the client's needs. Further, competent legal help will be needed to advise on the filing requirements for limited partnerships as well as on-going, periodic reports to state agencies and the **Internal Revenue Service**. In addition, an accountant can help business owners examine the tax consequences that may result from the choice of a business form.

[Paulette L. Stenzel]

FURTHER READING:

Corley, Robert N., et al. *The Legal and Regulatory Environment of Business.* 11th ed. New York: McGraw-Hill College Division, 1999.

Cross, Frank B., and Roger Leroy Miller. *West's Legal Environment of Business.* 3rd ed. West/Wadsworth, 1998.

Kubasek, Nancy K., et al. *The Legal Environment of Business: A Critical Thinking Approach.* 2nd ed. Upper Saddle River, NJ: Prentice Hall College Division, 1999.

"Revised Uniform Partnership Act (1994) (1997)." National Conference of Commissioners on Uniform State Law.

Windish, David F. *Investor's Guide to Limited Partnerships.* New York: Institute of Finance, 1998.

PASSIVE MANAGEMENT (FIXED INCOME)

Passive bond portfolio management takes advantage of the implications of bond market efficiency. Because bond markets are efficient, investors are not able to use past price and volume data or publicly available information to achieve superior rates of return. The limitations on **portfolio management** imposed by market efficiency preclude achieving superior rates of return by either superior **bond** selection or superior market timing. Investors achieve market rates of return by buying a randomly diversified bond index fund, or investors immunize the bond portfolio by taking advantage of the concept of **duration**.

The simplest approach to creating a bond index fund is to buy a market-weighted random selection of **bonds** in each of the major bond categories in the domestic bond market: Treasury bonds, federal agency bonds, corporate bonds, state and municipal bonds, and mortgage-backed bonds. This portfolio, with proper rebalancing, will provide the investor with the bond market rate of return. If the objective of the investor is narrower, a bond portfolio could be constructed to meet a specific need. For example, a bond portfolio consisting of only corporate bonds could be constructed. The rate of return for this portfolio would mirror the rate of return for corporate bonds in general. A smaller sector of the bond market, such as AAA-rated bonds, could be used to construct an index that would mirror only the highest quality bonds.

Portfolio immunization is more complex than indexation and takes advantage of bond duration to eliminate **interest rate** risk from the bond portfolio. When the interest reinvestment rate rises (falls), the value of the principal repayment falls (rises) and the value of the interest on interest rises (falls). A bond portfolio is immunized when the duration of the bond portfolio is equal to the duration of the **liabilities** hedged by the bond portfolio Thus, total interest rate change effects are offset.

An investor with multi-period obligations can take advantage of duration on a period-by-period basis. This technique is known as dedication.

The duration of the bond portfolio will vary over time. Changes in the bond portfolio duration can be rebalanced by reinvesting coupon payments or replacing longer duration bonds with shorter duration bonds.

[Carl B. McGowan, Jr., updated by David P. Bianco]

FURTHER READING:

Bodie, Zvi, Alex Kane, and Alan J. Marcus. *Investments.* 4th ed. New York: Irwin/McGraw-Hill, 1999.

Hirt, Geoffrey A., and Stanley B. Block. *Fundamentals of Investment Management.* 6th ed. Boston: Irwin/McGraw-Hill, 1999.

Investments and Portfolio Management. Paramus, NJ: Prentice Hall, 1993.

Livingston, Miles. *Bonds and Bond Derivatives.* Malden: Blackwell Publishers, 1999.

PATENT LAW/PATENTS

A patent is a grant of property right issued by the federal government that grants an inventor the exclusive right to manufacture and sell his or her invention for a period of 20 years. Any infringement of this right is punishable by law. Hence a patent is a monopoly that the government protects for the purpose of encouraging inventors and inventorship. Sole rights to an invention allow the inventor (or joint inventors, as the case may be) to profit from it. He or she can then commercialize the invention, often selling the monopoly in the form of a license to other manufacturers, who in turn must abide by the inventor's stipulations. At the conclusion of the 20-year period, other manufacturers have a right to make the product and sell it to their advantage, without permission. Ideally, the inventor by then has enjoyed the commercial benefits of his or her invention, and has a market edge over any new competitor.

Reality, however, often falls short of this ideal. The giant Xerox Corp., for example, fostered the invention of xerography. When the Xerox patent expired in 1979, the Japanese company Canon Inc. quickly seized and overtook Xerox's market share, and nearly destroyed the company in the process. Hence a patent is meant to encourage invention; what the inventor does with the patent depends on his or her business acumen.

The patent document itself is written by the inventor and describes the invention in great detail, underscoring its uniqueness and setting forth its advantages. The Patent and Trademark Office (PTO) then publishes the document. Nowadays all U.S. patents are accessible online as well as in print. Each year the PTO issues over 100,000 patents to U.S. citizens as well as to foreigners seeking American patents.

The overwhelming majority (80,295) of the 90,649 patents granted by the PTO in 1998 fell under the category of utility patents, which embody the traditional, common-sense concept of an invention, including technical objects, instruments, applications, and formulas (as in chemical compounds in medicine) that are of use to the general public. Design patterns, issued for unique and innovative ornamental designs for an item of manufacture, accounted for 9,914 grants in 1998. The design patent does not protect the functional features of the product, only its appearance. Plant patents, of which 245 were granted in 1998, protect unique, usually asexually produced plants and seeds. The final classification is the reissue patent. Reissues are modifications of previously granted patents that more acutely define specifics that were deemed defective in the original. The PTO granted 195 reissue patents in 1998.

Besides patents, the PTO also registers trademarks, which is a quite different matter. For a business that uses trademarks (brand names and corresponding logos) to identify its products or services, trademark registration does not secure monopoly rights. There is also confusion between patents and copyrights. A copyright, issued by the Library of Congress, is similar to a patent in that it grants to the author of a book, the composer of music, or a sculptor, choreographer, sound recorder, or motion picture producer an exclusive right to not have their work copied without their permission. This right lasts for the lifetime of the creator of the work plus 50 years thereafter.

Hence patents do not cover written works, music, or art, but do include computer software products, because of their technical applications. Both patents and copyrights fall under the rubric of **intellectual property**. Almost all countries have patent laws. In the absence of patents, there would be little financial incentive for an individual to create an original product or design or a unique plant. Moreover, there would likely be a paralyzing number of lawsuits in the United States if there were no specific patent laws. In the U.S., patents historically have always been awarded to the original inventor, and not to the "first filer," as in all other countries. Hence if an inventor files for a patent in the United States, he must prove that he or she is the first to invent rather than the first to file the invention.

The U.S. Constitution in 1789 explicitly granted Congress the right to authorize patents to inventors. Patents in those days were quite familiar to the general public, and were characteristic of the most advanced countries. Patents in these formative years of the republic were modeled on those of Great Britain; some colonies, most notably Massachusetts and South Carolina, had granted patents to inventors as early as the 1640s. Britain, however, had not been the originator of patents: the Italian merchant republics, specifically Venice and Florence, awarded the earliest known patents in the mid-fifteenth century. The first patents in the British Isles were awarded a century later, in Elizabethan England.

As a result of Article 1, Section 8 of the Constitution that specified "the Congress shall have power . . . to promote the progress of science and useful arts, by securing for limited times to authors and inventors the exclusive right to their writings and discoveries," the first patent law was passed in 1790. This law spelled out the criteria for granting patents: they were to go to the original inventor; that the invention was not to have been "known before or used"; and that the invention or discovery be useful. The first inventor to be awarded an American patent under the new law was Samuel Hopkins, for his formula for making "Pot and Pearl Ashes."

The patent law of 1790 would be widely imitated. The law, however, did not establish a separate office or administrator to award patents. Instead, examining and awarding patents was considered a part-time job that the secretaries of war and state and the attorney general could perform in their spare time. It was up to them to give patents, deciding either collectively or individually. Secretary of State Thomas Jefferson, himself an inventor, had perhaps the keenest interest in this sideline. However, soon he, too, was inundated, bringing many public complaints about the slowness and cumbersomeness of the patenting process. Nonetheless, in three years, 57 patents were issued for such inventions as type punches, a machine for manufacturing nails, and various steam-power innovations.

To streamline the patenting process and cut down on the time it took to award patents, Congress passed a new law in 1793 that effectively nullified the previous one. This law was decidedly inferior to the one it replaced, since all it did was require a person to register an invention without the stipulation that it be examined and determined to be original or useful. While this certainly simplified the patenting process, it opened the door for all kinds of chicanery, which gave rise to a large number of lawsuits. For the next few decades, however, this law remained in force, until a backlash produced a reformed and stronger patent law in 1836.

The new law reinstated the requirement that an invention's originality had to be proven, which in essence was a restatement of the 1790 patent statute. The 1836 version, however, distinguished itself from its predecessor by its provision for a separate patent bureau with its own staff that worked full-time on patent processing. While Congress in 1802 had created a discrete patent office within the State Department, this one-person office was mandated to do little more than register patents. Hence the 1836 reformed patent statute set up what amounted to a modern patent office, headed by a commissioner of patents; and for the first time, an inventor had the right to appeal if his patent application was rejected.

This new law reinstated the 1790 patent statute's liberal stance toward foreign inventors, who were once again eligible for patents. As in the 1790 and 1793 laws, the inventor, and not the first to file an invention, had the sole right to apply for a patent. That meant that an inventor could freely sound out her ideas or attempt the commercialization of her invention as long as this occurred within 12 months of the first filing date of her patent application.

Even by 20th-century standards, the 1836 patent statute ushered in a modern system of patent processing that was liberal in application, protecting the inventions of foreigners as well as citizens of the United States for a period of 14 years and granting them the right of appeal. While the law would be superseded by another law in 1870 and by the codification of 1952, these later laws would incorporate the features of the 1836 statute. Other changes in patent law occurred in 1842, when design patents were granted for the first time; and 1861, when the 14-year limitation on a patent was extended to the current seventeen years. In 1930, plant patents went into effect, while in 1952, all patent laws were codified.

The United States was so far ahead in its patent application procedure in the 19th century that in 1869 the Patent Office issued seven times as many patents (13,997) than Great Britain, which at that time was considered the world's ''workshop.'' The kinds of inventions no doubt presaged this country's industrial supremacy in the 20th century. Some of the most notable patents were the steam-powered engine (1811), the mechanized reaper (1834), the telegraph (1840), the sewing machine (1846), the typewriter (1868), the telephone (1876), the phonograph (1878), the electric light bulb (1880), and the motion picture projector (1893). Eli Whitney's cotton gin went into use in the first half of the 19th century, but was patented in 1794. In addition, Charles Goodyear's vulcanization of rubber—an example of a process, rather than an instrument or object—received a patent in 1844 and later made the modern bicycle and car tire possible.

Meanwhile, one industrializing country after another was adopting patenting statutes. In 1900 Japan sent an observer to the United States to learn about patenting, and adopted many of the features of the American patent system, including the first-to-invent criterion rather than first to-file. In 1883 those countries which had patent laws in place agreed to the Paris Convention, which meant that an inventor who filed for a patent in one member country could use that same filing date in the other member countries. An American who applied for a patent outside of the United States or its territories, however, would have to file before he or she could disclose the invention publicly. The Paris Convention was followed 87 years later with the Patent Cooperation Treaty of 1970. In this treaty, only a single application had to be filed for a patent, which could be made in English, and was automatically applicable in other member nations.

The U.S. Patent Office, established in its own building as a result of the 1836 patent law, burned to the ground that year, and with it, all of its records, numbering in the thousands. It was quickly rebuilt, becoming part of the Interior Department in 1849. No doubt because of this catastrophe, all patent applications since then, along with their drawings, had to be submitted in duplicate. The Patent Office remained a division of the Interior Department until 1925; since then, it has been a part of the Commerce Department.

Basically, the U.S. patent law and supplements, amalgamated into one single patent law in 1870, remained unchanged until 1952. On 19 July 1952, the new patent statute, which is still in force, became law and went into effect on 1 January 1953. It codified all previous patent laws, modifications and amendments, specified what was patentable, and spelled out the application procedure and the duration of patents. For the first time, it established the principle of ''nonobviousness,'' which meant that an invention not only had to be original, but ingenious, and not obvious to a practitioner or expert on the subject. Excluded from patents was any invention contrary to the public welfare, and any patent that utilized nuclear material for weapons purposes. The Patent Office was renamed the Patent and Trademark Office (PTO), its most important activity being the time consuming, exhaustive study of each patent application.

The Uruguay Round of the General Agreement on Tariffs and Trade (GATT) included provisions for patent legislation that went into effect shortly after the enactment of the World Trade Organization (WTO) Agreement on 1 January 1995. These included measures to guard against discrimination pertaining to the country or territory of inventive activity in issuing patents. In addition, the duration of patent protection was extended from 17 to 20 years, with a possible extension of up to five years in cases involving significant delays stemming from interferences and appeals in the patent process.

Inventions in all categories (utility, design, plant, and reissue) must meet the basic legal criteria for patentability: an invention must be useful, original (beyond what would seem a common-sense or ''obvious'' advancement, even to a practitioner or expert in the field), and cannot have been publicized more than one year prior to filing. The application process for a patent is not difficult. Typically an inventor hires a patent attorney to assist in writing up the application and in researching the possibility that the invention, or some form of it, might have existed prior to the application (known as the ''prior art''), which would disqualify it. An application is not judged ready until there is a workable model, in the form of a drawing or actual model, of the invention. The written application must contain the date of the invention's conception, and must be signed by a witness.

Once the application is submitted to the PTO, the application undergoes detailed examination. To facilitate this, the PTO began an extensive, billion-dollar computerization program in 1984 that will be in place by the turn of the century. It rigorously scrutinizes the prior art of the invention in order to establish its originality, even though the inventor has already done so. This entails researching all previous U.S. patents ever filed, as well as foreign patents, and relevant literature on the topic.

Often an invention is original, but not so ingenious that an expert in the field could not have deduced it. In such cases, it is rejected, and the inventor has the right to appeal the decision. The PTO has its own board of appeals, and from there, an inventor can go even higher, to the Court of Appeals of the Federal Circuit of the District of Columbia (CAFC). Theoretically, it is possible to bring a rejected patent application all the way up to the Supreme Court; surprisingly, this has not yet happened.

A person can apply for more than one patent, and multiple individuals can file a joint patent. In the case of the latter, there is joint ownership of the patent, with neither owner obligated toward the other. This can create problems if one of the owners only contributed marginally to the invention, and sells his or her share, which the joint patentee has the legal right to do. To avoid possible future conflict, joint filers usually have a written agreement between them. Patents are legally considered property, and hence inheritable by law, should the patentee (or one of them) die before the expiration of the patent.

A patented invention is no guarantee of future commercial success. Statistically, the number of successful inventions is minuscule. One avenue of commercialization open to a patentee is licensing his or her patent to a company, or a number of companies, provided a firm is willing to risk investing in a wholly untried product or process. The patent holder, however, cannot demand that royalties from the product continue beyond the stipulated 17-year patent period, nor can the patentee set the product's price or determine its use.

Often an American inventor will seek a foreign patent. The Paris Convention, adhered to by over 90 countries, gives foreign patentees the same rights as their own citizens. Nonetheless, most foreign countries require that a product be manufactured in the country for a stipulated period. Many countries, especially in Asia, Eastern Europe, and Russia, have patent laws that are either not strictly enforced or not as advanced as the heavily industrialized Western nations. This has troubled many manufacturers of commercial software products, who cannot profit from their products in these countries because of lax patent laws or patent laws that do not cover software and computer applications.

The controversy over intellectual property was raging in the late 1990s, particularly as regards more sensational products such as biologically engineered seeds and even life forms. These issues raise serious ethical considerations over, for example, the monopolization of life strains and forms of sustenance. The United States has been a leader in the effort to secure such intellectual property rights, and business leaders have long lobbied for the inclusion of such provisions into international trade agreements.

There is great international pressure on the United States to harmonize its patent criteria with the rest of the world's—i.e., the stipulation that the first to file for a patent is the one who is eligible for a patent, whether or not this person is the original inventor. The PTO also has recommended this change, which would save taxpayer dollars because it would simplify the patent review process. If implemented, the first-to file principle would be a radical change from the tradition of recognizing only the inventor's right to file, first established over 200 years ago in the patent law of 1790. Moreover, it would eliminate the one-year grace period prior to filing, which allows the inventor to publicize or even commercialize his or her invention. Critics of ''harmonization,'' mainly from the academic world, charge that it would benefit only big business, which has ample resources to file first. Filing a patent application costs little—under one hundred dollars. Engaging a patent attorney, however, is expensive. While do-it-yourself patent books abound, few inventors take the risk of filing without assistance. With Congress taking a hard look at patent harmonization and cost cutting, adoption of the first-to-file principle is gaining favor.

Despite the fact that the PTO is considered to be one of the most cost-effective agencies of the government and one of the most efficient, it is subject to criticism on all sides. This has usually preceded major changes in patent law. The criteria for patentability are becoming outmoded, as so much of the world is moving toward technological inventions that defy the traditional concepts of what is useful and tangible, especially in the fast-growing realm of biotechnology and software.

In 1999, for example, the U.S. Supreme Court upheld a lower court's decision in the case of *State Street Bank & Trust Co. v. Signature Financial Group, Inc.* which struck down long-standing methods of denying patents on such innovations as methods for conducting business and mathematical concepts that were merely abstract ideas. While the case dealt specifically with the legality of rejecting patents for certain types of software, the decision carried implications for most U.S. businesses, intellectuals, and researchers. The ruling immediately initiated a rush to the patent office, as companies sought to safeguard the rights to a vast array of products, concepts, and even marketing techniques, many of which could effectively restrict other companies from even entering into certain types of business.

[Sina Dubovoy]

FURTHER READING:

Borge, David A. *Patent and Trademark Tactics and Practice.* New York: John Wiley & Sons, 1999.

Chisum, Donald S. *Principles of Patent Law: Cases and Materials.* Westbury, NY: Foundation Press, 1998.

Fowler, Mavis. *The Law of Patents.* Dobbs Ferry, NY: Oceana Publications, 1996.

Halpern, Sheldon, Craig Allen Nard, and Kenneth L. Port. *Fundamentals of United States Intellectual Property Law: Copyright, Patent, and Trademark.* The Hague: Kluwer Law International, 1999.

PAY-PER-CALL TELEPHONE SERVICE (900 NUMBERS)

Calls to 900 telephone numbers, or pay-per-call services, are paid for by the caller. The charge is greater than, or added to, the carrier's charge for the transmission of the call. Under the 900 Number Rule adopted by the **Federal Trade Commission**, the 900 prefix became the only one through which interstate pay-per-call services could be offered, effective November 1, 1993. Pay-per-call services for local or intrastate calls often use other prefixes, such as 976 or 560. A 1992 survey found that between one-third and one-half of all adult Americans did not realize that they had to pay for calls to 900 telephone numbers.

Pay-per-call services offer a variety of audio information, audio entertainment, simultaneous voice conversations, and other services ranging from product offerings to personal dating services. The operator of a pay-per-call service is known as an information provider (IP). IPs determine the information or service to be provided, the amount of the charge, and whether it will be assessed on a per-call or time-interval basis, and how the service will be advertised. IPs typically use service bureaus to handle incoming calls.

PAY-PER-CALL APPLICATIONS

900 telephone numbers have a variety of applications. Since the caller pays a charge for making a 900 call, many IPs have established 900 services as money-making ventures. In the political arena, one of the first applications of the 900 number was to poll voters. Following the Reagan-Carter debates in 1980, viewers were given the opportunity to call one of two 900 numbers to cast a vote for the presidential candidate of their choice. Similarly, television networks have established 900 numbers to allow viewers to cast votes for programs that were scheduled to be canceled. Television programs airing rock videos have allowed viewers to call 900 numbers to cast their votes for their favorite videos. When an incentive was added to the call, one NBC program received more than 450,000 responses during a 90-minute show.

Since 900 telephone numbers are an effective means of establishing a caller's involvement, they have been used in **marketing** and **sales promotion** campaigns. These applications are not designed to make money from the 900 number. Rather, they are used to create an affinity between the consumer and a particular company or product. In one example, a record company offered a special CD and other merchandise to consumers who called a 900 number. In addition to the 900 charge, callers also paid for the merchandise, some of which could be obtained only by calling the 900 number.

The use of a 900 telephone number in a marketing or sales promotion campaign provides a variety of benefits. In terms of lead generation, 900 numbers provide better qualified leads than do toll-free numbers. If the marketer wants to create a mailing list or database of callers, it is easy to obtain the necessary information using the audiotext, or prerecorded message, feature of the 900 call. When 900 numbers are used in television **advertising**, they usually provide an indication of the response rate within minutes or hours. Finally, the charges associated with a 900 number can help the company recoup its promotional costs.

With the growing use and acceptance of prepaid phone cards, some companies have offered access to helplines and hotlines through both 900 pay-per call lines and prepaid phone cards. In early 1998 IBM established a helpline to answer questions about different types of **software** from a variety of vendors. A five-call plan cost about ten dollars and was offered through computer resellers, with consumers purchasing a prepaid phone card. Digital Equipment Corp. launched a similar service using a pay-by-the-minute format. Pay-per-call helplines providing technical support are common in the **computer** and software industry.

REGULATING PAY-PER-CALL SERVICES

As a result of widespread abuses of 900 telephone numbers by IPs, their use is now subject to regulation by the Federal Trade Commission (FTC) and the **Federal Communications Commission** (FCC). Under the authority of the Telephone Disclosure and Dispute Resolution Act of 1992, the FTC and FCC set up rules governing 900 numbers and pay-per call services effective November 1, 1993. These rules apply to IPs, service bureaus, and carriers. They are limited to interstate services, but individual states may adopt and enforce more stringent regulations.

The FTC regulations cover the preamble, advertising disclosures and prohibitions, and billing rights and responsibilities. The preamble is an introductory message that a caller hears at the beginning of the call. It must include the name of the IP, a description of the service, the cost of the call, and a statement that gives the caller the opportunity to hang up within three seconds to avoid any charge. A preamble is not required when the call costs two dollars or less, or when it is made between data devices and no human is involved.

The FTC requires that all advertisements for pay-per-call services include the cost adjacent to the 900 number. In television advertising, both video and audio disclosures of the cost must be made, unless the ad is 15 seconds or less or contains no audio information about the 900 service. Either the total cost of the call must be given, or the cost per minute and any minimum charges. In the case of **infomercials**, the cost and other disclosures must be made at least three times during the infomercial—at the beginning, middle, and end.

For sweepstakes advertising that employs a 900 number, disclosures that must be made include the odds of winning and alternate methods of entry. Advertising a 900 service to children under 12 years of age is prohibited unless it is a bona fide educational service. Advertising aimed at individuals between 12 and 18 years of age must disclose that parental consent is required.

The FTC also created rules affecting billing rights and responsibilities, including the right of consumers to have 60 days from the date of billing to communicate errors to carriers. Toward the end of 1998 the FTC issued a proposal to add an additional provision aimed at stopping the growing practice of ''cramming,'' or adding unauthorized charges to a phone bill. The new provision would give consumers the same rights in disputing telephone bill charges that they have when dealing with credit card companies. Under the proposed provision, consumers would be able to question any charge appearing on their bill, and the vendor would be required to provide proof of consumer authorization of the charge.

The FCC rules apply mainly to carriers. Consumers must be able to request their carriers block interstate 900 services. Carriers must also provide consumers with local or toll-free numbers from which to obtain information about 900 services. Carriers may not terminate telephone service for failure to pay for 900 calls. Both the FTC and the FCC will enforce a rule prohibiting callers from being charged for calls to an 800 number in any manner without a presubscription agreement.

The rules and regulations covering 900 telephone numbers are designed to protect consumers from fraudulent and deceptive practices. Such practices in the past have tarnished the image of 900 numbers, to some degree slowing their acceptance in the marketplace as legitimate marketing and sales promotion tools. There are many legitimate for-profit IPs providing 900 services. The future of 900 services is dependent on a number of factors that include consumer acceptance, the ability of the industry to police itself, and the effect of federal and state regulations on legitimate providers.

SEE ALSO: Toll-Free Telephone Calls (800 Numbers)

[David P. Bianco]

FURTHER READING:

Lowry, Tom. ''Sweepstakes Firm Pays $3M.'' *USA Today,* 12 January 1999, 6B.

Perine, Keith. ''FTC Offers Plan to Intensify Crackdown on Unauthorized Local-Phone Charges.'' *Wall Street Journal,* 26 October 1998, A24.

Weintraub, Arlene. ''IBM Drives Pay-Per-Call Market.'' *Home Office Computing,* February 1998, 15.

PENSIONS/PENSION FUNDS

A pension plan is an agreement calling for an employer or an employee organization such as a **labor union** to contribute benefits to retired employees or retired members of the organization. These benefits usually come from an annuity, which is an investment program that yields fixed payments. There are both contributory and noncontributory pension plans. In the former, both employee and employer contribute to the plan. In the latter, only the employer contributes. Another distinction is between the defined contribution plan and the defined benefit plan. Defined contribution plans operate by having contributions invested for employees who in turn ''own'' a share of the value of the investments. The retirement benefits thus rise and fall with the value of the fund. Under a defined benefit plan, employee benefits are predetermined and usually based on the earnings and years of service of the employee.

In the United States there are a plethora of pension plans entailing a wide variety of benefit packages. Most pension plans, however, are characterized by two features—vesting and income deferral. Income deferral means that employees cannot begin receiving pension benefits until they retire or if their pension is vested, resign. Vesting refers to the legally binding nonforfeitable right of an employee to receive a pension. Vesting is generally related to length of employment. In order for one's pension to be vested, the participant must be employed by the company or organization for a specified number of years. The percentage of the total benefit package the employee is entitled to is also usually related to length of employment. Generally the longer a participant is employed, the greater the pension benefit up to a predetermined maximum. Once a pension is vested, it is nonforfeitable whether or not the employee continues to work, retires from the **workforce**, or leaves for another job. To be eligible for a pension plan, employees are usually required to work 1,000 hours a year, and their income must be subject to Social Security **taxes**.

The idea of quitting work once one reaches a certain age and still continue to receive benefits is a late 19th-century phenomena. By the latter half of the 19th century most of the American labor force was still agrarian and there was no such thing as retirement or pensions. As farm workers became aged, their workload decreased; it was at first shared and then taken over by younger family members. Aged workers continued to be supported by family members until their deaths. As the U.S. economy became less agrarian and more industrial and service oriented in an urban setting, the demographics of the workforce also changed. According to Dora L. Costa, 78 percent of men were still working past the age of 64 in 1880. By 1900 that figure was 65 percent, in 1930 it was 58 percent, and in 1990 it had fallen to less than 20 percent.

The first pension program for the disabled and those of old age in the United States was the Union army pension plan for Civil War veterans and their widows and dependents. This program was considered to be quite generous in that its benefits approximated 30 percent of the wages of a contemporary unskilled laborer—roughly analogous to present-day Social Security benefits. The first private pension plan in the United States was instituted by American Express in 1875; by 1900, 11 more private pension plans were providing retirement benefits. In 1920 the federal government began its pension program and by 1930 nearly 2.7 million workers, approximately 10 percent of the private wage and salary workforce, were covered under pension plans. Once the idea of a pension had gained a foothold in American society it quickly spread, hastened by the Social Security Act of 1935. By the mid-1980s nearly half of the American workforce was covered by pension plans.

The idea that at 65 one is ''old'' had its beginnings in Germany in 1883 when that age became synonymous with a decline in the ability to labor. In the United States in 1890, Civil War veterans could begin collecting their pensions at age 65 unless they were ''unusually vigorous.'' In 1920 post office letter carriers became eligible for retirement benefits once they reached 65, as did railroad workers in 1933. In 1934 the Commission on Economic Security decided that under Social Security provisions, 65 would be the age to begin receiving Social Security retirement benefits.

By the 1990s the planning and managing of pensions had become a huge industry. In 1993 pension funds could claim $3.4 trillion in assets making private and state and local government pension funds the largest single institutional participants in **capital markets**. Pension funds control approximately 20 percent of U.S. financial assets by holding approximately 30 percent of all U.S. traded equities and about 25 percent of the value of U.S. corporate **bonds**, according to R. Glenn Hubbard. There are three reasons why there has been such a rapid growth of managed pension funds as opposed to individual planning and saving. First, pension funds can generally be managed more efficiently and cheaply than individual accounts. Second, life annuities are costly for an individual to participate in and proportionately less costly for institutional investors. Third, there are **tax** advantages to a managed pension fund. For instance, an employer's matching contribution to a pension plan is generally tax deductible.

As previously mentioned, there are a multitude of pension plans available for U.S. salary and wage earners and a number of options for the self employed. There is not, however, a ''laundry list'' of plans for all potential retirees. Whether or not a particular plan is available for a specific individual depends on the circumstances of the participant and the employer.

A very popular pension plan is the **401(k)**. Under this plan employees may choose to have a portion of their pretax wages or salary contributed by the employer to a qualified plan. In 1998 the maximum contribution was $10,000 per annum although this amount is reviewed in terms of **inflation** every year by the **Internal Revenue Service**. Employers may also choose to match a percentage of the employees' contribution, usually 25 cents to the dollar, although it may be as little as 10 percent or as great as 100 percent. There are several options for investment including bond and stock **mutual funds**, money market funds, or company **stock**. Participant withdrawals from a 401(k) plan prior to age 59 1/2 are subject to a 10 percent penalty except for death, disability, termination of employment, or qualifying hardship. Withdrawals after the participant has reached 59 + are subject to taxes in the year the funds were withdrawn. The 401(k) plan receives its authorization from the Small Business Job Protection Act of 1996.

The **individual retirement account** (IRA) is a personal, tax-deferred retirement account which can be set up by an individual. Contributions to an IRA are tax deductible only if the participant or the participant's spouse is not eligible for an employer maintained retirement plan. Individuals who are participating in an employer maintained retirement plan can also open an IRA on their own, but contributions are not tax deductible, with one qualified exception. If the participants are covered by an employer maintained retirement plan, they may deduct contributions to a personal IRA if their adjusted gross income is less than $30,000 ($50,000 for a joint return). Until the IRA participant reaches the age of 70 1/2, annual contributions up to $2,000 ($4,000 for a married couple filing a joint income tax return) are allowed. IRA withdrawals prior to the age of 59 1/2 are usually subject to a 10 percent penalty tax on the principal. IRA withdrawals must begin no later than age 70 1/2, at which time they are subject to being taxed. Partial withdrawals are allowed, but they are based on an IRS schedule related to life expectancy.

A variation on the IRA is the Roth IRA (named after Senator William Roth of Delaware), which was established in 1997. As with a traditional IRA, individuals can invest $2,000 a year in a Roth. Earnings and principal can be withdrawn tax free after the participant has reached 59 1/2 providing the funds have been in the account for five years. Unlike a regular IRA, participants do not have to begin withdrawing funds by age 70 1/2. In fact, funds do not have to be withdrawn at all and may be passed on to beneficiaries tax free. Participants, however, are not allowed a tax deduction for their contributions. Withdrawals up to $10,000 are allowed without penalty if the money is used for the purchase of a first home, college expenses, or disability expenses. There is also an Education IRA that allows parents to contribute $500 per year per child up to the age of 18. Eligibility and contributions are, however, qualified by income.

Self-employed individuals or employees of unincorporated businesses are eligible to establish a Keogh plan, set up and maintained by the participant. Keogh plans are also available for workers who have full time jobs with a pension plan, but freelance on the side. Those eligible for a Keogh plan may contribute 25 percent of earned income up to a maximum of $30,000. Investment earnings are tax deferred until withdrawal, which can begin as early as age 59 1/2 but must start no later than age 70 1/2. Like the 401(k), most any investment plan is acceptable for a Keogh except for collectibles (art, coins, stamps, antiques, etc.) and precious metals. The plan is named after U.S. Representative Eugene J. Keogh and was established by Congress in 1962.

The Pension Benefit Guaranty Corporation (PBGC) is a self-financing, wholly owned government corporation established by Title IV of the Employee Retirement Income Security Act of 1974. The purpose of the PBGC is to protect the pension funds of American workers who participate in a defined benefit pension plan. In 1998 that included nearly 42 million workers in approximately 45,000 different defined benefit pension plans. The PBGC is financed by premiums collected from companies sponsoring insured pension plans, investment returns on PBGC assets, and recoveries from employers responsible for underfunded terminated plans. In 1998 the PBGC was paying monthly retirement benefits to about 260,000 retirees of 2,150 terminated plans. If an insured pension plan terminates without sufficient assets to continue paying benefits, the PBGC will continue the benefits. For single employer plans terminated in 1999, the PBGC guarantees a monthly maximum of $3,051.14.

[Michael Knes]

FURTHER READING:

Costa, Dora L. *The Evolution of Retirement: An American Economic History, 1880-1990.* Chicago: University of Chicago Press, 1998.

Hardy, C. Colburn, and Howard J. Wiener. *Pension Plan Strategies: A Comprehensive Guide to Retirement Planning for Physicians and Other Professionals.* C. Colburn Hardy and Howard J. Weiner, 1995.

Hubbard, R. Glenn. *Money, the Financial System, and the Economy.* Reading, MA: Addison-Wesley, 1995.

Pension Benefit Guaranty Corporation. ''Pension Benefit Guaranty Corporation.'' Washington: Pension Benefit Guaranty Corporation, 1999. Available from www.pbgc.gov.

Schweitzer, Carole. ''Retirement Plans to Ponder.'' *Association Management* 50, no.12 (November 1998): 70-75.

Sunoo, Brenda. ''Match Pension Plans to Work Goals.'' *Workforce* 77, no. 12 (December 1998): 106-8.

Thompson, Lawrence H. *Older and Wiser: The Economics of Public Pensions.* Washington: Urban Institute Press, 1998.

PER CAPITA INCOME

Per capita income is the average amount of money each person in a nation makes during the course of a year. It is calculated by dividing national income, which is the sum of all the individual and corporate **income** arising from a nation's production of goods and services, by the total population of the nation. Per capita real income is the same figure, but adjusted to eliminate changes in prices or **purchasing power** over time. Many economic terms are commonly divided by population and expressed as per capita, or per person, amounts. Examples include per capita **gross national product** and per capita savings.

It is important to remember that per capita income figures represent a national average; in reality, income is not distributed evenly among all members of the population. Income varies by geographical region, for example, because the primary source of income in one area might be industry while in another it might be agriculture. For example, Connecticut reported the highest per capita income in the United States in 1997 at $36,263, while Kentucky reported the lowest at $20,657. Another geographical difference is based on the fact that wages tend to be higher in large cities than in small towns or rural areas. Income also tends to differ between individuals with different educational backgrounds.

Due to the difficulties of interpreting per capita income figures within a nation, per capita income is most often used to compare the standard of living in different countries. Per capita income varies greatly around the world, and the gap between relatively poor and relatively rich countries is becoming larger all the time. According to Susan Dentzer in *U.S. News and World Report,* in 1988 the top 20 percent of countries worldwide (based on annual national income) reported per capita income figures an average of 65 times greater than the bottom 20 percent of countries. In a 1997 article for *Forbes,* Peter Brimelow found that countries with free-market **economic policies** tended to have higher per capita income figures than other countries.

In the United States, per capita income for 1997 was $25,598, an increase of 5.7 percent from the previous year. Throughout the 1990s, there were many indications that Americans had more money and were living better than before. Three times as many newly constructed homes contained more than two bathrooms in 1992 than in 1970, for example, while the average square footage of new houses increased by one-third over the same period. In an article for *New York,* however, Ben Stein argued that such statistics are misleading. After adjusting for **inflation**, Stein found that per-hour private-sector earnings, excluding agricultural work, rose only .3 percent per year, or 10.6 percent since 1960. In addition, he reported that inflation-adjusted weekly earnings had actually declined by 2 percent since 1959.

Stein attributed the decline in real income in part to the fact that the overall American labor force has increased significantly since the 1950s. An increase in the number of people working means that national and per capita income tends to rise, even though the average income per worker remains the same or declines because it is divided among more people. In addition, Stein noted that the government figures for per capita income growth include nonmonetary benefits received by workers, such as health care and retirement coverage. These payments, which have increased markedly in recent years, tend to inflate per capita income figures and hide underlying trends affecting wages. Other factors Stein found to reduce per capita income growth include fewer people pursuing higher education and companies keeping wages low in order to compete with foreign firms.

[Laurie Collier Hillstrom]

FURTHER READING:

Bailey, Wallace K. ''Local Area Personal Income, 1969-96.'' *Survey of Current Business,* May 1998, 28.

''BEA Current and Historical Data.'' *Survey of Current Business,* March 1998, D1. Available from www.bea.doc.gov.

Brimelow, Peter. ''Freedom Pays.'' *Forbes,* 16 July 1997, 142.

Dentzer, Susan. ''The Wealth of Nations: A Growing Slice of the World Economy is Now in the Hands of the Affluent.'' *U.S. News and World Report,* 4 May 1992, 54.

Stein, Ben. ''Whining and Dining: Why We're Richer and Poorer.'' *New York,* 11 April 1994.

Tran, Duke. ''Personal Income and Per Capita Income by State and Region, 1997.'' *Survey of Current Business,* May 1998, 7.

PERESTROIKA

''Perestroika'' is a Russian word, meaning ''restructuring'' or ''reconstruction.'' It refers to the series of political, economic, and social reforms and foreign policy changes undertaken by the Soviet Communist Party in the years 1985 to 1991. During this period the Soviet Union was transformed from a tightly controlled communist state to a fledgling parliamentary democracy with a developing free-market economy. In the process, the Soviet Union was dissolved and the 15 former communist republics achieved independence. The largest of these is the Russian Federation, which is 8.5 million square miles in size. While this federation includes the vast expanse of Siberia, for the first time in Russian history, it excludes the Ukraine. The architect of perestroika as an official policy was Mikhail Gorbachev, who became party secretary in 1985, and thus head of state. While initially envisioned as a few minor reforms of the machine tool industry and the central planning process, perestroika evolved into a plan to overhaul the Soviet Union when it became clear the earlier reforms could not bring about the necessary economic changes.

Unlike the preceding five communist party heads, all of whom had died of old age or illness, Gorbachev was a relatively young and vigorous man of 53. He had come to the helm of the Soviet Union when, to all the world, the country appeared to be militarily invincible, stable, and changeless. The sizable cracks in the facade of the U.S.S.R. were visible to only a very few outsiders.

Nearly seven decades of control by the communist party of the Soviet Union (CPSU) had isolated the country from the world economy and caused an aggressive Cold War with the United States that was a serious financial drain on the Soviet Union. The state-controlled system of "collective" farming introduced under the Stalin administration had produced a perpetual agrarian crisis, leading to dependency on American and Canadian grain imports to avoid a shortage of bread. In 1979 the U.S.S.R. imported a record 25 million tons of grain from the United States alone, whereas Russia was a leading exporter of grain earlier in the century.

State control of the Soviet Union's industries also led to their stagnancy and decline, after some of them briefly experienced a high growth period in the 1950s. Soviet industries struggled to keep pace with their free-market counterparts, but largely failed to do so. By 1985 free-market countries had long entered the "microchip era," with economies and business life anchored to **computers** and sophisticated **telecommunications** systems. In contrast, in the Soviet Union, state-controlled businesses still widely employed the ancient abacus and the **banking** system was outdated and inefficient. Furthermore, widespread environmental damage caused by antiquated manufacturing industries was carefully hidden from the outside world, until the Chernobyl nuclear plant disaster in 1986.

Real progress in these years occurred in education, with a nearly 100 percent adult literacy rate and 99 percent of high school age children in school. Urbanization also had made rapid strides, with a majority of Soviet citizens living in cities. The restlessness of this educated population, denied the right to travel abroad or the right to freedom of expression, was evident in the growing dissident movement, whose spiritual leader was former communist physicist Andrei Sakharov (1921-1989), who had been sentenced without trial to exile and isolation in the Russian city of Gorky.

Outwardly a loyal communist who had risen through the ranks, Mikhail Gorbachev was determined to reverse the downhill spiral of the Soviet Union when he became secretary general. At the Twenty-Seventh Party Congress in 1986, Gorbachev proposed restructuring and reorganization plans to revitalize the Soviet Union's economy. Gorbachev attempted to undo the nationalization of agriculture, industry, and commerce that ultimately had a stifling effect. Against party opposition he launched the policies that would be known as perestroika and glasnost.

Glasnost (or "openness") took the form of greater freedom of expression (i.e., relaxed censorship), culminating in Gorbachev's personal invitation to dissident Andrei Sakharov to return from his exile in 1989 to help in the reconstruction of his homeland. Perestroika involved a series of political and economic reforms that, modest at the outset, unleashed a torrent of change that led to the collapse of the Soviet Union.

At first, the perestroika program focused on improving the Soviet Union's machine tool industry and ensuring the growth of the industry. In addition, perestroika also brought about a reduction of bureaucracy in the Soviet Union's planning committees. By creating superministries, Soviet planners could bypass intermediate bureaucrats and work solely on strategic planning.

Gorbachev soon realized, however, that these reforms would fail to strengthen the Soviet Union's economy because they remained superficial changes. Consequently, perestroika came to refer to far more substantial reorganizations affecting the economy, government, and society beginning in 1987. This more profound version of perestroika called for reforms that would allow private property and private business, end central planning, and focus on making consumer goods and food more available.

This later form of perestroika ultimately brought about the introduction of a limited free market economy for the first time since 1917. Furthermore, the conversion to a free market economy involved the gradual elimination of communist party control and ownership of the economy. To effect these changes, Gorbachev turned to Western capitalist countries for financial assistance. On the political front, perestroika involved the introduction of multi-candidate elections, eventually ending the monopoly of political control by one party. In foreign policy, the changes brought about by perestroika were very radical, with significant, lasting repercussions. Renouncing the Brezhnev Doctrine that gave the Soviet Union the right to intervene militarily in Warsaw Pact countries, communist governments in Eastern Europe were overthrown; the Berlin Wall collapsed; and the breakup of the Soviet Union itself ensued, with the former Soviet states proclaiming their right to self-determination. The world watched in amazement as the U.S.S.R. and the United States became allies in many areas.

The beginning of liberal reforms in the Soviet Union revealed the weaknesses of the totalitarian system that had been in power for seven decades. Unfortunately, the changes instigated by perestroika took on an uncontrollable momentum, leaving chaos and disruption in their wake and lowering the already low standard of living in the former Soviet Union. A new nostalgia for the stability and even the prosperity of the Soviet Union appeared even among the well educated, leading to political polarization. Diehard communist sympathizers staged a surprise coup in August 1991, while Gorbachev vacationed with his family. This reversion was foiled by the timely support of Boris Yeltsin's (1931-) followers, who called for reforms more radical than perestroika. Gorbachev, who had received the Nobel Peace Prize in 1990, resigned as president of the near-defunct Soviet Union in December 1991, officially bringing perestroika to an end. Under his successor, Yeltsin, the communist party was outlawed, and the loosely organized "Commonwealth of Independent States," whose political capital was not even in Russia, replaced the former monolithic Soviet Union.

[Sina Dubovoy, updated by Karl Heil]

FURTHER READING:

Boznak, Rudolph. "Moscow Diary: Momentum Unleashed by Perestroika Can't Be Reversed." *Industrial Engineering* 22, no. 11 (November 1990): 31+.

Castro, Janice. "Perestroika to Pizza." *Time,* 2 May 1988, 52.

Davidow, Mike. *Perestroika: Its Rise and Fall.* New York: International Publishers, 1993.

Dowlah, A. F. *Perestroika: An Inquiry into Its Historical, Ideological, and Intellectual Roots.* Stockholm: Bethany Books, 1990.

Goldman, Marshall I. *What Went Wrong with Perestroika.* New York: Norton, 1991.

Gorbachev, Mikhail. *Perestroika: New Thinking for Our Country and the World.* New York: Perennial Press, 1988.

Shlapentokh, Vladimir. "Privatization Debates in Russia, 1989-1992." *Comparative Economic Studies* 35, no. 2 (summer 1993): 19+.

"The Sixth Wave." *Economist,* 5 December 1992, S3.

Steele, Jonathan. *Eternal Russia: Yeltsin, Gorbachev, and the Mirage of Democracy.* Cambridge: Harvard University Press, 1994.

Taranovski, Theodore, ed. *Reform in Modern Russian History: Progress or Cycle?* Washington: Woodrow Wilson Center Press, 1995.

PERFORMANCE APPRAISAL AND STANDARDS

Performance appraisal is a process by which organizations evaluate employee performance based on preset standards. The main purpose of appraisals is to help managers effectively staff companies and use human resources, and, ultimately, to improve productivity. When conducted properly, appraisals serve that purpose by: (1) showing employees how to improve their performance, (2) setting goals for employees, and (3) helping managers to assess subordinates' effectiveness and take actions related to hiring, promotions, demotions, **training**, compensation, job design, transfers, and terminations.

In the early part of this century performance appraisals were used in larger organizations mostly for administrative purposes, such as making promotions and determining salaries and bonuses. Since the 1960s, however, companies and researchers have increasingly stressed the use of employee evaluations for motivational and organizational planning purposes. Indeed, for many companies performance appraisal has become an important tool for maximizing the effectiveness of all aspects of the organization, from staffing and development to production and customer service.

That shift of focus was accompanied during the 1970s, 1980s, and 1990s by a number of changes in the design and use of appraisals. Those changes reflected new research and attitudes about **organizational behavior** and theory. In general, employee evaluation systems have recognized the importance of individual needs and cultural influences in achieving organizational objectives. For example, traditional appraisal systems were often closed, meaning that individuals were not allowed to see their own reports. Since the mid-1900s, most companies have rejected closed evaluations in favor of open appraisals that allow workers to benefit from criticism and praise.

Another change in appraisal techniques since the mid-1900s has been a move toward greater employee participation. This includes self-analysis, employee input into evaluations, feedback, and **goal setting** by workers. Appraisal systems have also become more results-oriented, which means that appraisals are more focused on a process of establishing **benchmarks**, setting individual objectives, measuring performance, and then judging success based on the goals, standards, and accomplishments. Likewise, appraisals have become more multifaceted, incorporating a wide range of different criteria and approaches to ensure an effective assessment process and to help determine the reasons behind employees' performance.

Performance appraisals and standards have also reflected a move toward decentralization. In other words, the responsibility for managing the entire appraisal process has moved closer to the employees who are being evaluated; whereas past performance reviews were often developed and administered by centralized human resources departments or upper-level managers, appraisals in the 1990s were much more likely to be conducted by line managers directly above the appraisee. Because of the movement toward more decentralized approaches, performance appraisals also began to involve not only lower-level managers, but also coworkers and even customers. Known as multirater feedback or 360 degree feedback, this form of performance appraisal uses confidential assessments from customers, managers, coworkers, and the individual employees themselves. Furthermore, the appraisal process has become increasingly integrated into complementary organizational initiatives, such as training and mentoring.

In addition to reflecting new ideas about personal needs and cultural influences, performance appraisal systems evolved during the late 1900s to meet strict new federal regulations and to conform to **labor union** demands. A flurry of legislation during the 1970s and 1980s, for example, prohibited the use of performance appraisals to discriminate against members of selected minority groups. Other laws established restrictions related to privacy and freedom of information. The end result of new laws and labor demands was that companies were forced to painstakingly design and document their appraisal programs to avoid costly disputes and litigation.

Finally, with the booming economy in the late 1990s, many managers throughout the country began to move away from performance appraisals, according to Marilyn Moats Kennedy in *Across the Board.* Because of high **employee turnover** during this period, managers felt that conducting performance appraisals was not worth the effort since appraisals have the potential to irritate and drive off badly needed employees and since employees' time at a company might be short-lived. Moats argued, however, that managers should continue to conduct appraisals to assess and retain competent employees, because appraisals inform employees of how they can improve their skills, how they can advance within a company, and how their skills have improved (or failed to improve) over time.

THE ROLE OF PERFORMANCE APPRAISAL

Competent appraisal of individual performance in an organization or company serves to improve the overall effectiveness of the entity. According to D. McGregor, author of *The Human Side of Enterprise,* the three main functional areas of performance appraisal systems are: administrative, informative, and motivational. Appraisals serve an administrative role by facilitating an orderly means of determining salary increases and other rewards, and by delegating authority and responsibility to the most capable individuals. The informative function is fulfilled when the appraisal system supplies data to managers and appraisees about individual strengths and weaknesses. Finally, the motivational role entails creating a learning experience that motivates workers to improve their performance. When effectively used, performance appraisals help employees and managers establish goals for the period before the next appraisal.

Appraisees, appraisers (managers), and companies all reap benefits from effective performance appraisals. Appraisees benefit in a number of ways; for example, they discover what is expected of them and are able to set goals. They also gain a better understanding of their faults and strengths and can adjust behavior accordingly. In addition, appraisals create a constructive forum for providing feedback to workers about individual behavior, and for allowing workers to provide input to their managers. Finally, appraisees are (ideally) given assistance in creating plans to improve behavior, and are able to get a better grasp on the goals and priorities of the company.

Appraisers gain from evaluations as well. They are able to effectively identify and measure trends in the performance of their employees, and to more accurately compare subordinates. They also get a better understanding of their workers' needs and expectations. Managers are able to use the information to assist their subordinates in planning long-term and short-term goals and career objectives, and to tailor their job responsibilities to make fuller use of their skills. Importantly, the appraisal process helps managers to make informed decisions about promotions and assignments based on applicable facts.

Chief benefits that can accrue to the entire organization from the appraisal process include: improved communication, which results in more cooperation and better **decision making**; greater staff motivation; and a more informed and productive **workforce**, which leads to a greater organizational focus on comprehensive goals. Specifically, the performance appraisal process allows the organization to achieve a more productive division of labor, develop training and education programs, eliminate bias and irrelevant data from evaluations and decisions, and design effective compensation and reward systems.

PERFORMANCE APPRAISAL SYSTEMS

Most effective systems of appraising performance are: (1) pragmatic, (2) relevant, and (3) uniform. Pragmatism is important because it helps to ensure that the system will be easily understood by employees and effectively put into action by managers. Appraisal structures that are complex or impractical tend to result in confusion, frustration, and nonuse. Likewise, systems that are not specifically relevant to the job may result in wasted time and resources. Indeed, most successful appraisal programs identify and evaluate only the critical behaviors that contribute to job success. Systems that miss those behaviors are often invalid, inaccurate, and result in discrimination based on nonrelated factors. Finally, uniformity of the appraisal structure is vital because it ensures that all employees will be evaluated on a standardized scale. Appraisals that are not uniform are less effective because the criteria for success or failure becomes arbitrary and meaningless. Furthermore, uniformity allows a company to systematically compare the appraisals of different employees with each other.

Keeping in mind the three key traits of effective performance appraisal programs, companies must address four decisions when structuring their appraisal systems: (1) What should be assessed?; (2) Who should make the appraisal?; (3) Which procedure(s) should be utilized?; and (4) How will the results be communicated? In determining what to evaluate, designers of an appraisal system usually consider not only results, but also the behaviors that lead to the results.

The actions and results that are measured will depend on a variety of factors specific to the company and industry. Most importantly, criteria should be selected that will encourage the achievement of comprehensive corporate objectives. This is accomplished by determining the exact role of each job in accomplishing company goals, and which behaviors and results are critical for success in each position. Furthermore, different criteria for success should be weighted to reflect their importance. Some performance appraisal analysts recommend concentrating assessment on productivity and quality, which can be objectively measured and compared. Focus on these two factors enable companies to determine if workers are performing their tasks at an acceptable pace and if they are performing their tasks at an acceptable level of quality. By assessing these factors, evaluators also can avoid biased appraisals.

In determining who should address performance, managers of the performance appraisal system usually select an employee's immediate supervisor to provide the assessment, which is then reviewed by a higher-level manager or the personnel department. In addition, other appraisers may be selected depending on: their knowledge of, and opportunity to observe, the appraisee's behavior, their ability to translate observations into useful ratings, and their motivation to provide constructive input about the employee's performance. Other evaluators may include coworkers, subordinates, customers, or even the employees themselves.

After selecting performance appraisal criteria and evaluators, the designers of the system must determine which assessment techniques to use. Numerous methods may be applied depending on the nature of the industry, company, or job. As noted earlier, many organizations utilize a combination of several techniques throughout the organization. In general, the most popular rating techniques fall into one of four categories: (1) rating, in which evaluators judge workers based on different characteristics; (2) ranking, whereby supervisors compare employees to one another; (3) critical incidents, in which evaluators create descriptions of good and bad behavior and then assign those descriptions to employees; and (4) techniques that use multiple or miscellaneous criteria, such as employee-directed standards.

In addition to selecting evaluation techniques, managers of appraisal systems must devise a means of effectively communicating the results of assessments to employees. Often, the communication process is built-in to the appraisal technique, but sometimes it isn't. Feedback about performance is important for improving worker behavior. For instance, a worker who receives a very positive appraisal will likely become motivated to perform. On the other hand, a poor appraisal could have the opposite effect. For that reason, assessors have a number of feedback techniques at their disposal to help ensure that the end result of any assessment is constructive. Examples of feedback methods are written follow-ups, goal setting to overcome deficiencies, and allowing workers to have input into their appraisal to explain reasons for success or failure. Importantly, most feedback techniques stress a relationship between employees and their negative behavior (i.e., employee still have value, despite their inadequate behavior).

Furthermore, to be productive, the performance appraisal process must contain general three steps: evaluation and job analysis, appraisal interview, and post-appraisal interview. During the first step, both the appraiser and the appraisee should prepare for the interview by considering job performance, job responsibilities, employee career goals, goals for improving performance, and problems and concerns about the job. Sometimes both the appraiser and the appraisee will fill out forms with questions addressing the previously mentioned topics. Next, managers and employees meet to discuss what they have prepared and to establish goals for the period before the next performance appraisal. It is important that the appraisal interview be an exchange, not a speech. Both parties must be able to share their perceptions of the appraisee's performance. The third step, the post-appraisal interview, gives managers the opportunity to discuss salaries and promotions with employees. By not addressing this issue during the appraisal interview, both managers and employees can focus on performance and goal setting, instead of money. The post-appraisal meeting also can serve as a time for reiterating employee goals.

After appraising the performance of employees, an organization must evaluate the system itself to determine if it is helping to achieve designated organizational objectives (and conforming with legal guidelines, as discussed below). Managers of the appraisal system need to determine whether or not the system is being implemented properly:

- Are managers being rewarded for conducting appraisals?
- Are they being trained to perform the evaluations properly?
- Are evaluations based on specific job-related criteria?

Furthermore, they need to take action to determine whether or not the system is producing measurable results:

- Are the results of individual appraisals valid?
- Is the system producing consistent and reliable information for use in making decisions?
- Are employees developing and achieving goals as a result of appraisal and feedback?

BIAS AND ERRORS

Even when a performance evaluation program is structured appropriately, its effectiveness can be diluted by the improper use of subjective, as opposed to objective, measures. Objective measures are easily incorporated into an appraisal because they are quantifiable and verifiable. For example, fast-food workers may be rated on the number of cars they can serve at a drive-through window during an eight-hour period. Other objective measures commonly include error rates, number of complaints, frequency of failure, or other tangible gauges. In contrast, subjective measures are those that cannot be quantified and are largely dependent on the opinion of an observer. For example, an appraisal of fast-food workers' courteousness and attitude would be subjective.

Subjective measures have the potential to dilute the quality of worker evaluations because they may be influenced by bias, or distortion as a result of emotion. To overcome the effects of prejudice, many organizations train appraisers to avoid six common forms of bias: cross-cultural, error of central tendency, halo effect, leniency and strictness, personal prejudice, and recency effect. The recency effect is a corollary of the natural tendency for raters to judge an employee's performance based largely on his most recent actions rather than taking into account long-term patterns.

Cross-cultural bias is a consequence of an evaluator's expectations about human behavior. Those expectations often clash with the behavior of appraisees who have different beliefs or cultural values. For instance, an evaluator with an Asian heritage may be more likely to rate an older employee higher because he has been taught to revere older people. Likewise, personal prejudice results from a rater's dislike for a group or class of people. When that dislike carries over into the appraisal of an individual, an inaccurate review of performance is the outcome. For example, according to Kurt Kraiger and J. Kevin Ford writing in the *Journal of Applied Psychology,* studies have shown that black raters and white raters are much more likely to give high rankings to members of their own race.

Like cross-cultural and personal prejudice biases, the halo effect is caused by a rater's personal opinions about a specific employee that are not job-related. The term ''halo'' stems from the distortion that the appraisee, like an angel with a halo over its head, can do no wrong. This type of bias, however, also applies to foes of the rater. The effect is particularly pronounced when the appraisee is an enemy or very good friend of the evaluator.

Leniency and strictness bias results when the appraiser tends to view the performance of all of his employees as either good and favorable or bad and unfavorable. Although these distortions are often the result of vague performance standards, they may also be the consequence of the evaluator's attitudes. For example, some evaluators want their subordinates to like them (leniency bias) or want to feel like they are being a ''tough judge'' (strictness). Similarly, the error of central tendency occurs when appraisers are hesitant to grade employees as effective or ineffective. They pacify their indecisiveness by rating all workers near the center of the performance scale, thus avoiding extremes that could cause conflict or require an explanation.

In addition to bias, flaws in the execution of an appraisal program can be destructive. For instance, managers may be downgrading their employees because high performance reviews would outstrip the department's budget for bonuses. Or, some managers may be using performance appraisals to achieve personal or departmental political goals, thus distorting assessments. Problems are usually indicated, for example, by extremely high numbers of poor or positive appraisals, or by a general lack of individual improvement over the long term. In any case, appraisal managers must identify and overcome the causes of these flaws to ensure the usefulness of the system. This is typically accomplished through a formal process of evaluating the effectiveness of the appraisal program itself, as discussed above.

PERFORMANCE APPRAISAL TECHNIQUES

In addition to separating them into the four general categories discussed above, different performance appraisal techniques can be classified as either past-oriented or future-oriented. Past-oriented techniques assess behavior that has already occurred. They focus on providing feedback to employees about their actions, feedback that is used to achieve greater success in the future. In contrast, future-oriented appraisal techniques emphasize future performance by assessing employees' potential for achievement and by setting targets for both short- and long-term performance.

PAST-ORIENTED. Some of the traditional forms of performance appraisals such as rating scales and checklists remain popular despite their inherent flaws. They entail an assessor providing a subjective assessment of an individual's performance based on a scale effectively ranging from good to bad or on a checklist of characteristics. Typically, basic criteria such as dependability, attitude, and attendance are listed. For the rating scale, the evaluator simply checks a box beside each factor to indicate, for example, excellent, good, fair, or poor. A value may be assigned to each level of success—a rating of fair, for instance, might be worth two points—and the appraisee's score totaled to determine his or her ranking. For the checklist, the evaluator simply marks statements such as "works well with others" believed to describe the worker being appraised. The obvious advantage of these techniques is that they are inexpensive and easy to administer. Primary disadvantages include the fact that they are: highly susceptible to all forms of bias; often neglect key job-related information and include unnecessary data; provide limited opportunities for effective feedback; and fail to set standards for future success. Furthermore, subjective techniques such as rating scales are vulnerable to legal attack.

A fairer approach to performance appraisal is behaviorally anchored rating scales (BARSs), which are designed to identify job-related activities and responsibilities and to describe the more effective and less effective behaviors that lead to success in specific jobs. The rater observes a worker and then records his or her behavior on a BARS. The system is similar to checklist methods in that statements are essentially checked off as true or false. BARSs differ, however, in that they use combinations of job-related statements that allow the assessor to differentiate between behavior, performance, and results. Therefore, BARSs can be more effectively utilized in the goal-setting process. The advantage of BARSs is that they are extremely job specific, easy to administer, and eliminate most biases. Nevertheless, they can be difficult and expensive to develop and maintain.

Forced-choice appraisals consist of a list of paired (or larger groups of) statements. The statements in each pair may both be negative or positive, or one could be positive and the other negative. The evaluator is forced to choose one statement from each pair that most closely describes the individual. An example of a pair of statements might be "Always on Time" and "Never on Time." By incorporating several question groups that test different levels or degrees of the same behaviors, evaluators are able to generate an accurate representation of the individual's learning ability, interpersonal competence, drive, and other characteristics. Forced-choice appraisals are typically easy to understand and inexpensive to administer. But they lack job relatedness and provide little opportunity for constructive feedback.

Critical incident evaluation techniques require the assessor to record statements that describe good and bad job-related behavior (critical incidents) exhibited by the employee. The statements are grouped by categories such as cooperation, timeliness, and attitude. An advantage of this system is that it can be used very successfully to give feedback to employees. Furthermore, it is less susceptible to some forms of bias. On the other hand, critical incident assessments are difficult because they require ongoing, close observation and because they do not lend themselves to standardization and are time consuming.

Field review appraisal techniques entail the use of human resource professionals to assist managers in conducting appraisals. The specialist asks the manager and sometime coworkers questions about an employee's performance, records the answers, prepares an evaluation, and sends it to the manager to review and discuss with the employee. This type of system improves reliability and standardization because a personnel professional is doing the assessment. For the same reason, it is less susceptible to bias or to legal problems. But field reviews are generally expensive and impractical for most firms, and are typically utilized only in special instances—to counteract charges of bias, for example.

FUTURE-ORIENTED. One of the most popular future-oriented performance appraisal techniques utilizes the management by objectives (MBO) approach. In MBO, managers and employees work together to set goals. In fact, MBO is usually goal oriented, with the intent of helping employees to achieve continuous improvement through an ongoing process of goal setting, feedback, and correction. As a result of their input, employees are much more likely to be motivated to accomplish the goals and to be responsive to criticism that arises from subsequent objective measurements of performance. To be successful, MBO depends on specific and measurable goals and a definite time frame. Although it achieved fad status in the late 1970s and into the 1980s, critics of MBO cite its propensity to focus on objectively measured behaviors, such as quantity of output, at the expense of subjective criteria, such as quality of output. The result can be employee frustration or lackluster performance.

Assessment center evaluation is a more complex assessment method that is usually applied to managerial or executive prospects. It is a system of determining future potential based on multiple evaluations and raters. Typically, a group meets at a training facility or evaluation site. They are evaluated individually through a battery of interviews, tests, and exercises. In addition, they are evaluated within a group setting during decision-making exercises, **team** projects, and group discussions. Psychologists and managers work together to evaluate the employees' future management potential and to identify strengths and weaknesses. Assessment centers are susceptible to bias, have been criticized as not being specifically job related, and are extremely costly. But they have also proven effective and have achieved broad appeal in the corporate world.

Psychological tests are a much less intricate method of determining future potential. They normally consist of interviews with the employee and his supervisors and coworkers, as well as different types of tests and evaluations of intellectual, emotional, and work-related characteristics. The psychologist puts his or her findings and conclusions in a report that may or may not be shared with the employee. Psychological testing is slow and costly, and must be administered extremely carefully because of the long-term implications of the evaluation on the employee's future. Success is largely dependent on the skill of the psychologist.

Another appraisal technique included in the future-oriented category is self-appraisal, which entails employees making evaluations of their own performance. Although self-assessment techniques may also be coordinated with past-oriented evaluations, they are particularly useful in helping employees to set personal goals and identify areas of behaviors that need improvement. The advantage of such appraisals, which may be relatively informal, is that they provide an excellent forum for input and feedback by superiors. In addition, they allow supervisors to find out what employees expect from themselves and from the organization or department. Furthermore, because the employee is much less defensive about the criticism, self-improvement is much more likely.

In addition, evaluators often combine various future- and past-oriented techniques, forming hybrid approaches to performance appraisal, according to Patricia King in *Performance Planning and Appraisal.* Using several different techniques enables managers to measure both behavior and results and to set goals for employees to improve their performance and to increase their motivation. For example, an evaluator might use both the BARSs and MBO techniques to reap the benefits of both and compensate for the drawbacks of each.

LEGAL INFLUENCES

Federal laws related to performance appraisals, such as the Civil Rights Act of 1964 and the Equal Employment Opportunity Act of 1972, and a plethora of court decisions have turned the evaluation process into a legal mine field for many companies. Most of the federal laws are enforced by the **Equal Employment Opportunity Commission** (EEOC), which was created by the Civil Rights Act. In addition, surveys indicate that employees in the late 1980s had a greater awareness of their legal rights, since employees were three times as likely to sue employers during this period as they were in the early 1980s, according to the Rand Corporation.

Because appraisals are used to make promotions and demotions, give raises, establish salaries, and terminate and transfer workers, they must conform to strict EEOC Uniform Guidelines on Employee Selection Procedures. Specifically, the law requires that performance appraisals: (1) are job related and utilize behavior-oriented, rather than trait-oriented, criteria; (2) use tests, measurements, scales, feedback, and other evaluation tools derived from an analysis of each individual job; (3) not reflect a bias based on race, color, sex, religion, age, or nationality; and (4) be conducted by persons that have distinct knowledge of the position.

In addition to explicit federal guidelines, court cases have also had an impact on appraisal processes. For example, court decisions have demonstrated that, even if it designs its appraisal system according to legal guidelines, a company may be at fault if the numeric results of its appraisal system reflect bias against a protected minority group. Suppose, for example, that statistics showed that a company's appraisal system resulted in a disproportionate number of employees of Mexican descent receiving promotions and raises, while a disproportionate number of African American workers did not receive the same rewards. Unless the organization could prove that its decisions were based only on specific job-related factors, its appraisal system could be judged as biased in the courts. Therefore, managers of appraisal systems must be careful to monitor results as well as structure.

In addition to legal ramifications related to bias, numerous other laws affect appraisal systems. Evaluations must conform to a battery of privacy laws, for example. Companies are not allowed to divulge personal information to outside sources, for instance, and are required to make most information gathered during the evaluation process available to employees at their request. Likewise, evaluators must be careful to steer clear of protected personal information that does not relate specifically to the ability of the worker to perform his or her job. Such questions include inquiries about pregnancy, age, sexual practices, family, and health. For instance, a company would be leaving itself open to legal attack if it asked an employee whether or not she planned to have children in the near future and then made a decision not to promote her based on that answer.

An organization could opt out of conducting any type of appraisal program as a way of avoiding litigation risks. But even that option becomes risky if the company's promotion/salary practices can be shown to be statistically discriminatory (because the company is left with no documentation to prove the legal validity of its decisions). A safer approach is to structure the performance appraisal system in accordance with EEOC guidelines, and to:

- Carefully record all decisions related to staffing, promotions, bonuses, and other actions impacted by appraisals.
- Create specific job requirements and evaluate objective criteria.
- Share appraisals only with staff members and people who have an interest in the assessment that is specifically related to the job.
- Document and follow procedures that eliminate bias and errors from the process.
- Conduct periodic evaluations of the program to ensure that the appraisal process is producing unbiased results.
- Have an attorney review appraisal policies and procedures.

SEE ALSO: Human Resource Management; Supervision

[Dave Mote, updated by Karl Heil]

FURTHER READING:

Jones, Bodil. ''How'm I Doin'?'' *Management Review,* May 1997, 9.

Kennedy, Marilyn Moats. ''The Case for Performance Appraisals.'' *Across the Board,* February 1999, 51.

Kraiger, Kurt, and J. Kevin Ford. ''A Meta-analysis of Ratee Race Effects in Performance Ratings.'' *Journal of Applied Psychology,* 1985.

Latham, Gary P., and Kenneth N. Wesley. *Increasing Productivity through Performance Appraisal.* 2nd ed. Reading, MA: Addison-Wesley, 1994.

McGregor, D. *The Human Side of Enterprise.* New York: McGraw-Hill, 1960.

Werther, William B., Jr., and Keith Davis. *Human Resources and Personnel Management.* 3rd ed. New York: McGraw-Hill, 1989.

PERSONAL INCOME TAX

A tax is a compulsory payment levied by a government for its support and services. There are various kinds of **taxes**, such as taxes on the sale of goods, taxes on imported products (known as tariffs), and income taxes. Incomes taxes are levied against the earnings of estates and **trusts**, but especially against the earnings of corporations and individuals. The latter is known as an individual or personal income tax. Personal income taxes are most often associated with the federal government and the **Internal Revenue Service** (which is part of the U.S. Department of the Treasury), but personal income taxes can also be levied by state and local governments against their citizens or people earning income within their jurisdiction but living elsewhere.

Personal income taxes had a haphazard evolution prior to the passage of the 16th or ''income tax'' Amendment in 1912. A few states had a personal income tax before 1850. To help finance the Civil War, the federal government collected personal income taxes between 1863 and 1872. In 1894 Congress passed another personal income tax bill but this legislation was declared to unconstitutional by the Supreme Court. The high court ruled that in order to be constitutional, personal income taxes had to be levied in proportion to the population of the various states. In 1909 Congress passed a corporate income tax and in 1913 the 16th Amendment eliminated the proportional population requisite that stymied the 1894 legislation.

Present-day personal income tax rates in the United States are progressively based on an individual's personal income. Currently there are five rates based on taxable income: 15 percent, 28 percent, 31 percent, 36 percent, and 39.6 percent. This means that as one's income increases so does the percentage subject to being taxed. There are, however, numerous ways to lower one's taxable income. For instance, income earned as interest from certain types of municipal **bonds** is generally not taxable. Such an income item is called an exclusion. Income less exclusions results in one's gross income. Gross income less certain expenses, such as business or moving expenses, results in one's adjusted gross income. From an adjusted gross income a taxpayer may claim a wide variety of deductions. One of the most popular deductions is the interest paid on home mortgages, but deductions may also be taken for such things as state and local taxes and medical expenses. Another subtraction from adjusted gross income is an exemption. An exemption is a set dollar deduction given in the tax tables. In 1998 the exemption for each individual, spouse, or dependent was $2,700 per person. A husband and wife with one child were thus allowed to subtract $8,100 from their adjusted gross income in 1998. Also affecting income tax rates is the filing status or category. For filing purposes there are four categories: a single person, a married couple filing jointly, a married couple filing separately, and a head of household. The latter is a single person who maintains a household and who, under certain legally defined circumstances, is responsible for supporting others in that household. Each category is taxed at a different rate. Individual income tax returns must be filed by April 15 using Form 1040 as provided by the Internal Revenue Service (IRS).

Individuals, however, are not allowed to wait until the end of the tax year, April 15, to pay their entire tax bill. The IRS requires payments to be made throughout the year. If by April 15 one has paid more than what is owed, then a refund from the government is in order. If by April 15, however, money is still owed, then to avoid interest penalties, the balance must be submitted when the tax form is filed. Personal income taxes are collected by the government in two ways throughout the year. If an individual works for wages or a salary, taxes are deducted from each paycheck by the employer and sent to the government. This is referred to as one's withholding tax or simply withholding. The government does not pay interest on the withholdings it collects and holds throughout the year. People who do not work for wages or for a salary but are paid in other ways must file an estimated tax return by April 15 for each upcoming year. They must then make quarterly tax payments (April 15, July 15, October 15, and January 15) based on their estimated income. Anyone who earns income but does not pay a withholding tax is required to file an estimated return. Income earners who are self-employed, work as **consultants** or on a contractual basis, or who have a substantial income from **dividends**, investments, or **capital gains** often fall into this category. It is also possible to pay the entire estimated tax at the beginning of the tax year. People in this category who severely or purposefully underestimate their income may be subject to a penalty.

Over the decades the personal income tax code has been changed, amended, revised, and reformed countless times, but it has nevertheless always expanded to cover more people and lessen their deductions. When the personal income tax was instituted in 1913, fewer than 1 percent of working people filed returns. By 1940 this figure had risen to 11 percent and by the end of World War II virtually all working people were paying a personal income tax as they do today. The Tax Reform Act of 1986 reduced tax rates and increased the size of personal exemptions but also restricted deductions and exclusions. The next major piece of tax legislation was the Taxpayer Relief Act of 1997, which among other things instituted the Roth IRA, a child tax credit, new regulations on gains from the sale of a personal residence, new capital gains provisions, educational individual retirement accounts, new regulations on home-office deductions, a welfare-to-work credit, and a host of other changes and innovations.

There is growing but not yet overwhelming sentiment that the personal income tax code has become too burdensome, too political, too unfair, too complicated, too abused, too manipulative, too full of loopholes and special provisions, and used for too much ''social engineering.'' Some people feel that instead of continually revising the old system, the only solution is to abandon it in its entirety and replace it with something else. This ''something else'' usually takes two radical but simple forms—a flat tax or a national sales tax. A flat tax, as envisioned by Senator Dick Armey of Texas and businessman Steve Forbes, would eliminate all deductions and everyone would be taxed at a flat rate of 20 percent above a personal exemption of $11,000 per individual and another $5,000 exemption per child. After two years the rate would fall to 17 percent. There would be no additional taxes or higher rates on dividends, interest, or capital gains. Thus an individual earning $50,000 annually would pay a personal income tax of $7,800 ($50,000 $11,000 = $39,000 × .20 = $7,800). Simplicity is the keyword Armey's plan and he boasts that everyone's return could be filed on a postcard.

A national sales tax as proposed by Representative Bill Tauzin of Louisiana would scrap all individual and corporate income taxes. In their stead would be a 15 percent tax on the sale of all goods and services including government purchases, homes, and retail level financial transactions. A 15 percent tax credit would be provided for poor working families. A family of four whose income is below the poverty level would thus receive a tax credit of nearly $2,500. Tauzin's plan is even simpler than Armey's—there would be no tax forms, no tax filing deadlines, and no IRS. Many analysts feel, however, that a flat tax would favor those earning over $300,000 and adversely affect poor working families, while a national sales tax would favor the rich and the poor at the expense of middle-income families.

[Michael Knes]

FURTHER READING:

Adams, Charles. *Those Dirty Rotten Taxes: The Tax Revolts that Built America.* New York: Free Press, 1998.

Carson, Gerald. *The Golden Egg: The Personal Income Tax—Where It Came From, How It Grew.* Boston: Houghton Mifflin, 1977.

Dowd, Ann Reilly. ''Get the Facts on Tax Reform.'' *Money,* January 1998, 86-87.

Sease, Douglas R., and Tom Herman. *The Flat-Tax Primer.* New York: Viking, 1996.

Turville, Mary A. ''Making Sense of the Taxpayer Relief Act of 1997.'' *National Public Accountant* 42, no. 10 (December 1997): 18-24.

PERSONAL SELLING

Personal entails the face-to-face pitching of a product or service to a prospective buyer. The main thing that sets personal selling apart from other methods of commerce is the intensive inter-personal skills required, given that that the salesperson conducts his or her business with the customer in person.

Personal selling dates back to the Bronze Age. Traveling sales kits made up of bones and stones have actually been found from this era. In the United States, the first salesmen were Yankee peddlers who carried their goods from the east on their backs. They traded clothing, spices, pots and pans, and other household goods to settlers on the western frontier. The father of modern selling techniques is considered to be John Henry Patterson, the head of National Cash Register company. As far back as the late 1800s he was implementing sales training programs, quotas, and sales territories for his sales staff. He also introduced the notion of canned sales talks.

Personal selling is one part of the promotion mix, the various ways businesses choose to reach or communicate with their customers. The main elements in a promotion mix are advertising, sales promotion, public relations, and personal selling. **Advertising** is any form of paid presentation or promotion that is not done face-to-face, such as television commercials. Sales promotion is the use of incentives, such as **coupons**, to entice a customer to buy a product or service. Public relations is the act of building up the image of a company in the eyes of the community in the hopes of translating the feelings of goodwill into sales. An example of public relations is a company sponsoring a charity event. The final component of the promotion mix is personal selling, in which a demonstration or presentation to a potential customer is performed in person.

Settling on a promotion mix involves many factors. Businesses may choose to use any or all of the promotion mix tools and must decide how to allocate resources for each component. Some of the things organizations should consider when deciding on a promotion mix are the type of product or service sold, the unit value of the product or service, and the budget allotted for the promotion mix. Of all the industries involved in the promotion mix, the personal selling industry involves the most people. As a comparison, there are about 500,000 people involved in the advertising industry but more than 13 million people in personal selling.

In general, if a product has a high unit value and requires a demonstration, it is well suited for personal sales. For example, an encyclopedia is a high-priced item and most people do not feel they need one. After a demonstration, however, most people agree it would be a useful item to have. Therefore, encyclopedias are well suited to a promotion mix that emphasizes personal selling. Highly technical products are also primarily sold through personal sales methods. Computers and copiers are good examples of technical products that are best sold through personal sales. Products that involve a trade-in are also best sold through personal selling to help facilitate the trade-in process. Automobile sales often involve a trade-in and almost always involve a personal sales transaction. Finally, an organization that cannot afford an advertising campaign (which is a very expensive endeavor) might consider personal selling as an alternative to advertising. A personal **sales force** is a relatively inexpensive alternative to advertising, as the primary cost is the sales-force compensation. Since sales-force compensation is largely based on actual sales, a sales force is an investment that requires much less money up front than do other forms of the promotion mix that need time to pay off.

Personal selling as a career is unique and offers many benefits. It is, however, not for everyone. In general it involves long, irregular work hours and extensive travel. A personal salesperson should also be able to handle rejection face to face, which is a large component of the job. On the other hand, personal sales offers great rewards for those who are successful. Because most compensation involves commissions based on completed sales, the potential for income is great. With personal sales, there is no ceiling on what a person can earn, as there is with other salaried jobs. Also, many people enjoy the freedom of flexible hours and the fact that a personal salesperson has little contact with a supervisor. A career in personal sales offers a person the chance to develop interpersonal, communication, organizational, and time-management skills.

COMPENSATION

Sales-force compensation varies from one organization and industry to another. All compensation plans, however, contain one or more of the following components: commission, bonuses, **expense accounts**, incentives, benefits, and a salary or draw. Commissions, by which a salesperson is paid a percentage of the sale he or she makes, is the most common type of sales force compensation because it directly ties compensation to performance. Bonuses based on performance are often employed as well. With expense accounts or allowances, some companies will reimburse salespeople for business expenses incurred. Another form of compensation, and one that can be extremely motivating for some people, is incentive prizes earned through sales contests. Cars, trips, cash, and a number of other prizes are offered in exchange for meeting certain sales goals. Many companies offer benefits such as life and health insurance, although these benefits too can be tied to sales performance. Finally, some companies pay a base salary or draw, usually in conjunction with one or some of the other compensation elements. A draw is a fixed amount that is held against a salesperson's future sales earnings. This is usually offered to a new salesperson in order to foster earnings stability while he or she is learning the business. Usually if the salesperson does not make future sales, he or she is not held responsible for the amount.

In general, the tighter the control a company has over a salesperson, the larger the role salary plays in compensation. For example, an IBM salesperson, based in a branch office and receiving extensive training and supervision, may have a large part of his beginning compensation plan made up of a base salary or draw. At the other end of the spectrum you may find a *World Book* salesperson, based in her home, with little training and supervision. She may never even see a branch office and will be compensated entirely in commissions and bonuses.

TYPES OF PERSONAL SALES JOBS

Noted industrial psychologist Robert McMurry identified the main types of personal sales jobs:

- Driver-sales person: this person merely delivers the product and has few selling responsibilities.
- Inside order taker: In this position a person takes orders from within a selling environment. Examples include a sales clerk in a retail store, or a phone representative working for a catalog sales company. Some selling skills are required.
- Outside order taker: These salespeople go to the customer's place of business and take orders. Most of these sales are repeat business. Some selling is required, especially to establish new accounts.
- Missionary sales person: This type of sales involves selling goodwill but not any actual product or service. This salesperson's goal is to make a customer feel good about the company, products, or services the salesperson represents. Companies in the pharmaceutical and liquor industries, for example, typically employ missionary salespeople.
- Sales engineer: These positions are found in technical industries such as computers and copiers. Sales engineers provide technical support, explain the products, and adapt the product to the customer's needs.
- Creative sales person: These salespeople attempt to sell goods (vacuum cleaners or encyclopedias), services (insurance), or causes (charities). These salespeople are usually dealing with customers who are unaware of their need for the service or product, and so, the salespeople must possess the most refined selling skills.

Although there are many different types of salespeople, they all go through the same basic steps when making a sale: prospecting and qualifying, preapproach, approach, presentation and demonstration, handling objectives, closing, and follow-up. Although training criteria for personal sales forces may vary from one organization to another, most will include some version of these steps.

Prospecting and qualifying involve finding potential customers and determining whether they are in a buying position. Prospecting, or lead generation, can be as simple as asking current customers for names of acquaintances, or as sophisticated as using a database or mailing list. Often the salesperson's company provides leads, but a truly successful salesperson will also be able to generate his or her own leads. Generally, prospecting involves an element of cold-calling—calling an unknown potential customer and introducing yourself and your product. Often this is the least favorite part of a salesperson's job but ultimately one of the most important. In addition to prospecting for clients, a salesperson needs to qualify the customer. Is the potential customer financially in a decision-making position? Does this customer need the product or service? It is not atypical that a salesperson may need to contact many, many prospects before making a sale.

The preapproach is the step salespeople take when they are researching their prospective customer—often another company. They may read up on the company, talk to other vendors, or find out more about the industry. The salesperson will also take time to set sales-call objectives and try to determine the best time to call.

The next step is the approach, which is crucial for a salesperson to start out on the right foot. The salesperson should introduce himself or herself, the company represented, and the product or service being offered. It is also important that he or she listen carefully to the prospect and respond appropriately.

Once the approach has been made the salesperson should be ready to launch into the demonstration or presentation. Depending on the company and the product or service, there are generally three types of presentations. The canned approach is a tightly scripted talk that is either memorized or read. The formula approach is less rigid and, depending on the buyer's response to some carefully asked questions, will be tailored to meet the customer's needs. The third presentation style is the need-satisfaction approach, in which the seller tries to find out the customer's needs mostly by listening.

Presentations and demonstrations may involve any number of visual aids, such as flip-charts or demonstrations of the products themselves. One of the keys to a successful presentation is product knowledge. The more the salesperson knows about the product or service, the more relaxed he or she will be, and the more able to answer questions, fill the customer's need, and handle objections.

Handling objections is the next phase of selling. Almost every customer will present objections to making a purchase, whether real or not. A good salesperson is not flustered by these objections and handles them in a positive, confident manner. One approach to objections, used frequently with canned presentations, is to simply acknowledge the objection and continue with the presentation. In the more tailored presentations the salesperson can handle the objection by turning them into reasons to buy.

The next step of a sale is often identified by novice salespeople as the toughest step: closing, or asking the buyer to purchase. Some new salespeople are so reluctant to appear aggressive that they never try to close, and the customer may become annoyed and decide not to purchase for just that reason. Customers must be given the chance to purchase. Salespeople need to learn to look for signals that a closing is appropriate. Common signals that customers give include asking questions, making comments, leaning forward or nodding, and asking about price or terms.

The last step of a sale, the follow-up, is often neglected but is important for many reasons. The follow-up can be done in person or by telephone. This gives the customer the chance to ask questions and reinforce his or her buying decision. The salesperson can review how to use the product, go over instructions and payment arrangements, and make sure the product has arrived in proper working order. This step encourages repeat business, is a good opportunity to get referrals, and increases the chances that subsequent payments will be made.

The increasing trend toward long-term buyer-seller relationships entails a shift in the concerns of the personal salesperson from influencing buyer opinion and behavior to managing the dynamics of the buyer-seller relationship itself. This process is sometimes called ''relationship marketing,'' and refers to a variety of activities, including building and mediating relationships between businesses. In this ''partnering role,'' the salesperson attempts to keep in check the inevitable conflict of interest that will arise in a long-term relationship in which, for one party to do comparatively better, the other must do comparatively worse. In other words, he or she must use all the personal seller's available resources and tactics to turn this conflict of interest in to a mutual advantage.

Unfortunately, however, personal selling is often perceived as being a less-than-reputable field of work. Unethical salespersons, aggressive or hard-sell tactics, and misleading sales pitches have made many buyers wary of personal sellers. Fortunately, much has been done to address this issue. Selling associations such as the Direct Selling Association have adopted codes of ethics that dictate standards of behavior that all members are to follow. Most organizations with large personal sales forces have also adopted their own codes of ethics that provide guidelines regarding the type of sales pitch that can be made, the hours a sales call may be made, and the prohibition of incorporating misleading information or pressure tactics to make a sale. Much progress has been made in making personal selling a more reputable field, and efforts toward that goal will continue.

[Judith A. Zimmerman]

FURTHER READING:

Marks, Ronald B. *Personal Selling: A Relationship Approach.* Englewood Cliffs, NJ: Prentice Hall, 1996.

Sellars, David. *Role Playing: The Principles of Personal Selling.* Orlando, FL: Dryden Press, 1997.

Weitz, Barton A. and Kevin D. Bradford. ''Personal Selling and Sales Management: A Relationship Marketing Perspective.'' *Academy of Marketing Science,* Spring 1999, 241-254.

PERT

SEE: Performance Evaluation and Review Technique

PETER PRINCIPLE

Co-written in 1969 by Dr. Laurence J. Peter and Raymond Hull, *The Peter Principle: Why Things Always Go Wrong* was a slim, 167-page management self-help book that became a best seller. It also added a catch phrase to business management that has been regularly quoted over the three decades since it was first published. Some aspects of the theory were revived in the 1990s by the cynical business cartoon *Dilbert* by Scott Adams.

The anecdotal book, co-written by a Canadian writer and a British-born education professor, stated and restated in a number of ways the observation that Peter, who died in 1988, had made in his contact with store clerks, actors, business managers and other people he met outside the academic world he occupied. The Peter Principle: ''In a hierarchy every employee tends to rise to his own level of incompetence.''

THE THEORY AND ITS APPLICATIONS

The Peter Principle states that a good employee who is fulfilled doing a particular job may become a poor employee if promoted to a new position without evidence that he or she has the desire, ability and training to handle the job. Peter's observations and theories apply equally to the lowest level of undertalented employees and to top corporate officers who may spend their time on trivial matters because their well-promoted underlings are doing all the interesting work.

Peter's book was hailed as an explanation of why top producing salesmen sometimes make mediocre sales managers. It also explains today why founders of hot entrepreneurial companies frequently sell out to larger corporations because their skills at managing growing concerns have been overmatched by the task's requirements. The frustrated entrepreneurs sell out, then happily start building new companies, which was the strength they exhibited in the first place.

Peter and Hull filled the book with 19 other theories, including ''Peter's Corollary,'' which says ''In time, every post in a hierarchy tends to be occupied by an employee who is incompetent to carry out its duties.'' So, if that is true, how do corporations or any organizations accomplish anything? Peter's explanation is that all of the work is completed by people who have not yet reached their level of incompetence.

Peter also handles exceptions to his principle, such as the person who is ''kicked upstairs,'' promoted from a job where he is incompetent to a job where he will be even more incompetent. In Peter's view this promotion was made so to keep other employees thinking that the person really does know what he is doing and that if he can be promoted, they can too. Such promotions are supposedly given to keep incompetents who know how the business operates from joining the competition.

One of the unexpected theories in the book is that people in charge of hierarchies dislike super-competents as much as they dislike incompetents. According to Peter, simple incompetence is not always a reason for dismissal from a company because the employee can probably find a job he can do. However, super-competents, the men and women who seem to know everything and do everything well at all levels in anticipation of always moving up, are more likely to be fired because they disrupt the hierarchy. In Peter's view, these people attract too much attention to themselves, worrying others in the organization so much that they derail the super-competent's climb to the top.

Peter's book unabashedly champions finding a patron within the organization who will provide the ''pull'' necessary to create job opportunities for the competent person wishing to advance. On the other hand, he thinks ''push'' strategies—that is, self-initiative and self-promotion—have been given too much emphasis. He claims that no amount of push can overcome an employee who is on the rung of the ladder above, and push might be interpreted by superiors as not having focus in the current job.

In another attack on the inertia of hierarchies, Peter asserts that higher ranks frequently dislike leaders coming from the lower ranks because they are usually disruptive to the hierarchy. Disruption translates to insubordination, which translates to incompetence. He says those whom most take as leaders are really followers moving to the head of the following crowd. They are obeying precedents set before them by still higher leaders, who do not want or need anyone changing the rules of how to run the organization.

What happens when a person rises to the top of an organization without reaching a level of incompetence Peter says is inevitable? He sometimes changes jobs to find other ''challenges.'' Peter sites as examples military men who join industry or retired politicians who go into higher education. Peter's explanation is that these successful people did not spend enough time in their previous careers to find their own level of incompetence.

The other possibility for the top-level person is that they reach the top and then become almost instantly incompetent. Peter cites corporate board members who tell jokes rather than deal with company problems, or who spend their time rearranging reporting responsibilities instead of planning future successes.

CRITIQUES OF THE PETER PRINCIPLE

The book has been criticized because it is not based on case studies of real companies. Many examples in the book are of teachers and principals, reflecting Peter's background as a former teacher and a college professor. Also betraying its academic origins is the book's frequent use of obscure and elevated jargon. Examples include ''hierarchal exfoliation'' (the firing of both super-competent and super-incompetent employees) and ''Peter's Circumbendibus'' (a ''veiled'' detour up the corporate ladder around a ''super incumbent'' who is entrenched in a comfortable staff position and who has no intention of moving up the ladder by promotion so an eager underling can fill his slot in the hierarchy).

However, the most powerful critique of the Peter Principle is that in many instances it's simply inaccurate. Critics charge that it completely ignores employees' potential to learn on the job and develop new competencies—ironic given that Peter was an education professor rather than a management scholar—even if they weren't well equipped for it when they assumed the position.

FURTHER READING:

Blotnick, Srully. ''The Peter Principle Revisited.'' *Forbes,* 9 September 1985.

Crainer, Stuart. ''The Peter Principle.'' *Management Today,* October 1998.

Peter, Dr. Laurence J., and Raymond Hull. *The Peter Principle.* William Morrow & Company, 1969.

Schafer, Susan. ''Plugged into the Peter Principle.'' *Inc.,* 18 March 1997.

PHYSICAL DISTRIBUTION MANAGEMENT (TRANSPORTATION)

Part of logistics management, physical distribution is concerned with the transporting of merchandise, raw materials, or by-products, such as hazardous waste, from the source to the customer. A manager of physical distribution must also assess and control the cost of transporting these goods and materials, as well as to determine the most efficient way to store them, which usually involves some form of warehousing. Hence, physical distribution (PD) is concerned with **inventory control**, as well as with **packaging** and handling. **Customer relations**, order processing, and **marketing** are also related activities of PD.

In essence, physical distribution management (PDM) involves controlling the movement of materials and goods from their source to their destination. It is a highly complex process, and one of the most important aspects of any business. PDM is the ''other'' side of marketing. While marketing creates demand, PDM's goal is to satisfy demand as quickly, capably, and cheaply as possible.

One could maintain that PD is as old as civilization. Even merchants in ancient times had to move goods and raw materials to their destination, and to engage in storage and inventory control. Until the Industrial Revolution, however, these activities were carried out inefficiently: goods usually were replenished slowly, and there were far fewer goods than in the era of mass production. If marketing was conducted at all, it was usually done at the point of purchase.

The Industrial Revolution ushered in mass production and, by the late 19th century, the beginnings of mass marketing. Goods and raw materials also were conveyed over greater distances. Nonetheless, until World War II, PD was far less important than production and marketing. Physical distribution of goods and materials also remained basically unchanged, carried out as separate, unrelated activities—transportation and handling, storage, and inventory control.

The postwar years witnessed an unprecedented explosion of consumer goods and brands, thanks to modern mass marketing, the population explosion, and the increasing sophistication of the average consumer. The sheer volume and variety of goods enormously complicated their distribution and storage. A wholesaler of breakfast cereals, for instance, no longer handled a few cereal brands, but dozens of them, and with the proliferation of supermarkets, was confronted with the problem of greater demand and continuous product turnover. The cost of distribution escalated as well, further adding to the complexity of distribution. A seminal article on physical distribution (''New Strategies to Move Goods''), appearing in a September 1966 issue of *Business Week,* for the first time fostered an awareness of PD as a separate category of business. This eventually generated textbooks on physical distribution management, as well as courses in business schools. For the first time, PD, as well as **cost control**, became central concerns of upper management.

By this time, computers had slowly entered the realm of PD, at least in the United States. It was not until the 1970s, however, that computers were fully utilized. Their effect over time was to integrate the hitherto disparate categories of PD—transportation, storage, inventory, and distribution—into closely related activities.

Currently, computerization is performing the major functions of physical distribution management, from long-range strategic planning to day-to-day logistics, inventory, and market forecasting. The best of these systems are tightly integrated with inventory and other logistics systems, and may even be linked to customers' systems, as is the case with efficient consumer response (ECR) systems. ECR systems, which some have criticized as being to narrowly focused, attempt to maximize distribution efficiency by delivering inventory on a just-in-time basis. Advanced distribution systems may employ satellite tracking and routing of trucks, electronically tagged pallets or cargo containers, and elaborate data monitoring and storage capabilities. Data collected from these activities are used to identify weak spots in the chain and benchmark improvements.

Often upstart companies, and even some large ones as well, rely on third-party distributors for at least some of their physical distribution, and hence there is an entire industry of third-party logistics services. These and other outsourcing services received a great deal of attention during the 1990s, as manufacturing companies sought to eliminate peripheral activities when they could do so at cost savings. Smaller companies, on the other hand, frequently lack the expertise or resources to perform their own distribution. Nonetheless, some distribution analysts criticize the outsourcing movement because the net cost savings may be less than anticipated and the quality of the logistics service may be hard for the manufacturer to control.

Up to now, PDM has been concerned with the movement of physical objects. In the future, however, it will have to accommodate itself to the increasing shift of the economy away from manufacturing and toward service industries. In this new realm, environmental cleanup and the disposal of waste undoubtedly will be increasingly important to PDM. The expansion of global markets is also affecting PDM, requiring enormous technical and operational refinement.

SEE ALSO: Business Logistics; Channels of Distribution; Supply Chain Management

FURTHER READING:

Bachelor, Charles. "Buzzword or the Way of the Future?" *Financial Times,* 1 December 1998.

Cooke, James Aaron. "To Outsource or Not to Outsource?" *Logistics Management Distribution Report,* October 1998.

Distribution, monthly.

Logistics Management and Distribution Report, monthly.

Tompkins, James A., and Dale A. Harmelink, eds. *The Distribution Management Handbook.* New York: McGraw-Hill, 1993.

Wood, Donald F., et al. *Contemporary Logistics.* Upper Saddle River, NJ: Prentice Hall, 1998.

PLANNING

SEE: Business Planning; Financial Planning

POISON PILLS

A poison pill is a type of financial or structural maneuver that a company may make to frustrate an attempted takeover by a hostile bidder. The poison pill affords directors of a company sufficient latitude to restructure or acquire **debt** or sometimes sell assets, specifically to make the company a much less attractive takeover target. If the poison pill is effective, the acquiring company will abandon its takeover and allow the target company to remain independent.

For all the criticism directed at **takeovers**, it has been suggested that they perform a highly useful task: they motivate the directors of potential target companies to consistently maximize shareholder value and to restructure underperforming companies into profitable, competitive, and usually smaller enterprises.

HISTORY AND BACKGROUND

Poison pills have existed in various forms for many decades, but they were viewed merely as anomalies in **corporate finance**. Over an approximately ten-year period beginning in the late 1950s, several large conglomerates were formed out of the philosophy that any company involved in one industry would be ravaged by periodic downturns in that industry. Diversification would enable companies to maintain consistent profitability by offsetting losses in struggling operations with profits from other unrelated and more successful operations.

Conglomerates such as LTV, Textron, General Dynamics, TRW, General Electric, Teledyne, and Tenneco built enormous corporate empires that had interests in several major industries, specifically to achieve diversification. In the process, many companies lost their independence to these conglomerates, because few among them were able to mount successful defenses against unwelcome bids.

The rash of conglomerate activity and the pace of **mergers and acquisitions** caused concern that takeovers were causing excessive concentration in certain industries and were being allowed to proceed without sufficient notification or care. This led to congressional lobbying by business federations, **labor unions**, and **institutional investors** that culminated in passage of the Williams Act in 1968.

The Williams Act obliged parties to a takeover to fully disclose the terms of an impending acquisition and to allow a period in which competing offers for a target company could be made. The act became the basis for other federal laws regarding corporate mergers and acquisitions and established a basis for legal challenges using arguments such as bad faith, misrepresentation, and antitrust concerns.

During the period that followed, many state legislatures passed more specific and restrictive legislation on takeovers, based on the Williams Act. This, for the first time, involved legislators in corporate mergers and acquisitions and required companies to maintain strong government relations.

The Williams Act and the various state laws that were modeled after it caused many companies to alter their articles of incorporation by changing their legal domiciles to states with more favorable environments. By far, the most attractive was Delaware (and this explains why most companies today are incorporated in that state). State laws—particularly those in Delaware—provided grounds for statutory and legal defenses that could frustrate all but the least unwelcome takeovers. By the late 1970s, the pace of acquisitions nearly ground to a halt.

But in 1982 the U.S. Supreme Court passed a landmark ruling in the case of *Edgar v. MITE Corp.,* which invalidated the basis for antitakeover laws in 37 states. Helped to some degree by a noninterventionist U.S. Department of Justice under the Reagan administration, restrictive takeover laws were severely weakened. No longer able to take shelter in statutory and legal defenses, many firms were once again vulnerable to takeover offers; hence, the need for companies to develop their own antitakeover measures in the form of poison pills.

TYPES OF POISON PILLS

Poison pills typically discourage hostile takeovers by letting companies sell large amounts of **stock** to existing shareholders at cheap prices. The hostile bidder is not allowed to purchase any of the new stock, and his or her total holdings are capped at an arbitrary amount, often 15 percent of the company's total shares. As a result, the hostile bidder's holdings in the takeover target become diluted and are worth less.

The most common type of poison pill—used by more than nine out of ten companies—is the shareholder **rights**, or "flip-over," plan. Such a plan commonly allows a company facing an unwelcome bid to declare a special stock **dividend** consisting of rights to purchase additional, newly created shares. The exercise price to these rights is purposely set far above market value, so that a suitor company would have to spend substantially more to acquire control. The company may redeem the rights after the bid has been abandoned, but usually at only five cents per share.

If the takeover bid is successful, the shareholder rights may be transferred, or "flipped over," to the successor firm. The rights would entitle shareholders to purchase shares in the surviving firm at a discount of as much as 50 percent, causing tremendous dilution of the surviving firm, and possibly even placing control of that firm in jeopardy.

A variation of the flip-over is the "flip-in" plan. This plan is designed to hasten the exit of a suitor with a substantial minority of shares who cannot, or will not, affect a merger—and who may be playing the shareholders for a gain through **greenmail**. The flip-in offers shareholders in the target company—but not the suitor—rights to buy additional discounted shares.

As these rights are exercised, the suitor's position is diluted and share value drops. The suitor is faced with mounting losses the longer he or she hesitates, and is motivated to liquidate his or her holdings as quickly as possible.

Both poison pill plans enable a company to thwart all but the most determined and deep-pocketed suitors, while allowing shareholders to benefit greatly if the suitor succeeds. Nevertheless, no poison pill or any other type of defense is ever meant to be used. Their greatest utility is in their deterrent influence; a company is unlikely to launch a takeover of a firm whose defenses are sufficiently formidable.

THE EFFECTS OF POISON PILLS ON COMPANIES

Few companies have been able to maintain their independence indefinitely after employing a poison pill. While effective at fending off unwelcome bids, poison pills have tended to indicate to the financial community that the companies using them suffer from some financial or structural weakness and are ripe for some form of merger.

Many shareholder activists, concerned with the potential abuses that might result, have sponsored proposals that would require shareholder approval prior to including a poison pill in the corporate charter or activating an existing poison pill. Their argument is that by preserving the independence of firms, poison pills have the effect of perpetuating inefficiencies and poor **management** that result in declining productivity and competitiveness that is reflected in lower share value.

Another type of poison pill that has particularly angered shareholder activists is the so-called "dead-hand" poison pill. Dead-hand poison pills can be redeemed only by the incumbent **board of directors**. Such a plan is designed to keep the existing board and current management in place, sometimes at the expense of existing shareholders or in opposition to a majority of shareholders. It eliminates shareholders' ability to act by written consent. A variation on the dead-hand poison pill is the no-hand poison pill, which cannot be altered by anyone for at least one year or some specified time.

Chief executive officers (CEOs) and boards of directors frequently argue that poison pills have exactly the opposite effect on share value. They maintain that poison pills are brutally effective bargaining tools that may be used to extract only the most favorable terms from potential suitors. Negotiating positions can only be strengthened by poison pills, they say, and this will lead to more favorable bids. CEOs also see them as a way to have some control over their companies' future, especially if the **stock market** were to fall sharply and opportunistic buyers began hostile takeovers of undervalued companies.

While there is merit to both arguments, it is most often the case that these effects cancel each other out and have little or no effect on share value. Shareholder activists, however, remain increasingly vigilant about possible abuses that may arise from poison pill plans, and takeover defenses in general. Meanwhile, state legislatures have spent the years since the Supreme Court ruling on *Edgar v. MITE Corp.* gradually reconstructing restrictive antitakeover laws.

Despite opposition from shareholder activists, poison pills appeared to be growing in popularity in the 1990s. In 1998 some 530 companies extended or adopted new shareholder rights plans. In 1999 as many as 20 percent of all poison pill plans were expected to come up for renewal. At least 40 major corporations would be affected, and shareholder activists were calling for more public debate on and repeal of poison pill plans. In many cases boards of directors were not required to consult with shareholders regarding the renewal or lapsing of existing poison pill plans.

Leading the shareholder activists was the Teachers Insurance and Annuity Association-College Retirement Equities Fund (TIAA-CREF), the world's largest **pension fund** with an equity portfolio of about

2,600 companies. TIAA-CREF was in the process of going through its entire portfolio looking for companies with poison pill provisions. In addition to attacking dead-hand poison pills, TIAA-CREF called for letting shareholders vote on whether or not their company's poison pill plan should be renewed. Another leading shareholder activist, Guy Wyser-Pratte of New York City, proposed a ''chewable'' pill that would entitle shareholders to vote on any takeover proposal before the poison pill went into effect. If shareholders approved the takeover, the board would be required to stop using the pill.

[John Simley, updated by David P. Bianco]

FURTHER READING:

Crangle, Rick. ''Replacing Poison Pills with Vitamins.'' *Global Finance,* July 1998, 15.

Elofson, John. ''Should Dead Hand Poison Pills Be Sent to an Early Grave?'' *Securities Regulation Law Journal,* fall 1997, 303-43.

Feinberg, Phyllis. '''Deadhand' Pills a Major Proxy Issue.'' *Pensions and Investments,* 19 October 1998, 3.

Griffin, Ricky W., and Ronald J. Ebert. *Business.* 2nd ed. Englewood Cliffs, NJ: Prentice-Hall, 1991.

''Hundreds of Companies Targeted by Activists: Shareholder Group Threatens Binding Proposals on Poison Pills.'' *Investor Relations Business,* 7 December 1998, 1.

Norris, Floyd. ''Poison Pills Are Still Popular, but Their Purpose Has Changed.'' *New York Times,* 19 December 1996, C8/D10.

Norton, Leslie P. ''If This Stock Market Falters, Poison Pills Could Become a Hot Topic Again.'' *Barron's,* 6 July 1998, 17-18.

''Poison Pills Gain in Popularity.'' *Directorship,* March 1999, 12.

''Poison Pills: Let Shareholders Decide.'' *Business Week,* 17 May 1999, 104.

POLICIES AND POLICY MAKING

Policy at one time was the term used to describe top-level **decision making** in organizations. In recent years, however, this managerial function has been extended and refined in both the academic and practitioner literature and taken on more elegant designations, such as **strategy** formulation and implementation or strategic management. Policy making now, more aptly, simply describes the development of organizational policies. Some policies appertain at the highest levels and are essential elements of the organization's strategy. But, the vast majority of policies apply at lower levels and are operational in nature.

THE NATURE OF POLICIES

Very simply, policies are standing plans that provide guidelines for decision making. They are guides to thinking that establish the boundaries or limits within which decisions are to be made. Within these boundaries, judgment must be exercised. The degree of discretion permitted will vary from policy to policy. Some policies are quite broad and allow much latitude, whereas others are narrowly constructed and leave little room for judgment. To illustrate, a policy of selecting the best qualified candidate for a managerial position permits more discretion than a policy of promoting the best qualified candidate from within the organization. The latter is a narrower policy because it limits the choices to current employees. A policy of promoting from within the organization based on standardized test scores and seniority would, of course, be an even more restrictive policy.

To better comprehend the nature of policies, it is useful to differentiate them from other standing plans—i.e., plans designed to deal with recurring issues—such as rules, standard operating procedures, and standard methods. Rules are specific statements of what must or must not be done in a given situation. Unlike policies, they provide no room for managerial discretion. ''No smoking in the work area'' and ''Wash your hands before leaving the restroom'' are examples of company rules. Rules by their very nature are designed to suppress thinking whereas policies require varying degrees of judgment.

Standard operating procedures (SOPs) are detailed instructions for the execution of a particular operation. They specify an exact chronological sequence of steps to be followed and permit little room for discretion. Most procedures cut across departmental lines and involve several employees. SOPs are frequently used to support the implementation of major policies. For example, a policy of purchasing from the qualified bidder with lowest price might be routinely implemented through a prescribed SOP.

Standard work methods are established ways of performing specific tasks. Like SOPs, they designate an exact sequence of actions but, unlike SOPs, they are concerned only with the task of a single worker. The prescribed set of steps in ironing and folding shirts at a commercial laundry is an example of a standard work method.

FUNCTIONS OF POLICIES

Policies perform several important functions in organizations. First and foremost, they simplify decision making. They delimit the area of search for possible alternatives and preclude the need for repeated, in-depth analysis of recurring, similar problems. Consequently, they promote efficiency in the utilization of managerial time.

Policies also permit managers to delegate to subordinates more decisions and more important decisions than they would otherwise. Thus, if a manager establishes a policy governing a specific class of decisions, he or she will feel more comfortable delegating these decisions to subordinates because they will have set guidelines within which to make choices. The delegation of decision-making authority is important because it frees up managerial time for activities such as opportunity finding and planning that typically are put off.

Finally, policies help secure consistency and equity in organizational decisions. Thus, if several managers make decisions in a particular policy area, their decisions will be consistent within the limits established by the governing policy. Equity is also promoted through the policy mechanism, especially with regard to personnel and vendors. For example, an announced policy of permitting the company employees with the greatest seniority to have first choice of vacation times would tend to be viewed as more equitable than allowing managers to make these decisions without guidelines. By the same token, a policy stating that supply **contracts** will be awarded to the lowest qualified bidder would normally be viewed as fair by vendors.

FORMULATION OF POLICIES

Policies can emerge in four very different ways. First, and most commonly, they may be originated by **management**. Managers originate policies to ensure that decisions within the organization will be in line with its objectives. Generally, they are written and embodied in the company's policy manual, if it has one.

The second way policies come about is through appeal. The appeal process typically works something like this. A situation develops where an executive is uncertain whether he or she has the authority to make a decision. Consequently, he or she appeals to higher-level management for the decision. Once the decision is made, it becomes precedent for similar decisions in the future. The process is analogous to the way common law develops in the Anglo-American judicial system. There is a danger, however, of allowing too many policies to be made through appeal. A set of unwritten, incomplete, and uncoordinated policies may emerge because the various appealed decisions will, in all likelihood, be made on the basis of the individual merits of the particular situations without regard for their broader implications.

Third, policies may be implied from the decisions and actions of the company's executives. In fact, it is not uncommon to find that some of the ''real'' policies of a company differ from its stated policies. For example, a company may have a stated policy of promoting strictly on the basis of merit whereas in reality, relatives and personal friends of top management are given priority.

Finally, policies can be externally imposed. Not infrequently, outside institutions, such as various departments of government, trade unions, and trade associations, impose requirements on organizations. Labor contracts and federal regulations are familiar examples. Consider how the equal opportunity employment laws have led to major modifications in the personnel policies of many firms.

HIERARCHAL STRUCTURE OF POLICIES

Policies are found at all levels of organizations. At the very top, key policies may be important elements of the company's overall strategy and help define how it differentiates itself from its rivals and competes in the marketplace. Such policies are commonly called functional strategies because they guide strategic decision making at the functional level. Consider Polaroid's principal functional strategies under its founder, Edwin Land. In the financial area, there were two atypical policies: no long-term **debt** and growth strictly through internal development (i.e., no acquisitions). The company's product policy was to bring only unique, high-tech products to the market. A key marketing policy called for very heavy initial **advertising** of new products. Other strategic marketing policies emphasized the introduction of successively less expensive camera models and the pricing of instant film as a high margin **cash cow**. Production policy dictated subcontracting of high-volume, repetitive manufacturing work and keeping technically critical, high value-added work in-house. Taken together, these policies defined, to a large extent, Polaroid's competitive posture during its ''glory years.''

High-level policies typically must be interpreted and narrowed at lower organizational levels. This reality results in a hierarchical structure of policies within organizations. To explicate, a company might have a functional strategy of aggressive price **competition**. At the sales manager level, this policy might be refined to state that the company will meet competitors' prices on all of the firm's nonproprietary products. And, at the district level, the policy might be narrowed again to read that district sales managers can make price concessions up to 10 percent on their own authority but, beyond that, they must get approval from above. As the example illustrates, policies tend to be broad at higher organizational levels and become successively more restrictive as they move down the hierarchy.

POLICY AUDITS

Organizational policies have a tendency to become obsolete. Stated policies commonly change much more slowly than do the conditions that led to them. One approach to dealing with this problem is to conduct periodic reviews or audits of the organization's policies. These audits can help identify and eliminate outmoded policies. This regimen, however, tends to result in a time lag between the actual need for policy changes and the recognition of that need. It is therefore prudent for managers also to review policies on a more or less ongoing basis by asking questions such as, "What is the purpose of this policy?" and "Does it still make sense?" If the answers are negative or ambiguous, the policy may be a candidate for modification or elimination before the next scheduled audit. The astute manager will particularly be on the lookout for appealed and implied policies that may not be contributing to the achievement of the firm's goals.

POLICIES AND EMPOWERMENT

Thus far, the discussion has assumed a traditional hierarchical organization. But one might ask about the role of policies in the increasingly prevalent "empowered" organization where employees are encouraged to take ownership of their jobs and be entrepreneurial and innovative. In such organizations, there are typically fewer policies but those that are in place play an important role in establishing boundaries that place broad limits on employee behavior. Many of these policies will focus on legal and ethical behavior. For instance, a consulting firm might have a strict policy forbidding the disclosure of information about clients to outsiders. Establishing strategic boundaries represents a second crucial area of policy development in empowered organizations. To illustrate, a high-tech company might limit its product development opportunities to a defined set of technologies as a mean of reducing its risk and focusing its **research and development** initiatives.

SUMMARY

Policy making is concerned with the formulation of general statements or understandings that guide or channel managerial decisions. Policies, whether written or implied, are essential components of a company's planning framework because they simplify the making of recurring decisions and facilitate the delegation of these decisions. Successive delegations tend to result in a hierarchy of policies within traditional organizations. In organizations where **empowerment** is practiced, the principal function of policies is to provide essential limits to otherwise broad employee discretion.

It is not overly far-fetched to suggest that without policies, because of excessive analysis and the concentration of decisions at the top, corporate decision making in the hierarchical firm could be slowed to the point of bringing operations to a virtual standstill. Conversely, in the empowered organization, there would be the potential for complete lack of control and chaos. Yet, in today's fast-moving business world there is also the great danger of policies becoming rapidly outmoded. For this reason, audits and ongoing reviews are a must if a company's policies are to remain effective decision guides.

[Edmund R. Gray]

FURTHER READING:

Gray, Edmund R., and Larry R. Smeltzer. *Management: The Competitive Edge.* 2nd ed. Kendall/Hunt, 1993.

Koontz, Harold, and Heintz Weihrich. *Management.* 9th ed. New York: McGraw-Hill, 1988.

Newman. William H. *Administrative Action: The Technique of Organization and Management.* 2nd ed. Prentice-Hall, 1963.

Simons, Robert. "Control in an Age of Empowerment." *Harvard Business Review* 73, no. 2 (March/April 1995): 81-88.

POLLUTION

SEE: Business and Society; Clean Air Act; Clean Water Act; Comprehensive Environmental Response, Compensation and Liability Act (CERCLA) of 1980 (Superfund); Corporate Identity; Environmental Law and Business; Environmental Protection Agency; Global Warming; Recycling

PONZI SCHEMES

A Ponzi scheme is an investment swindle whereby some early investors are paid returns from the money acquired from new investors; eventually the scheme collapses when there is not enough new investment to continue the payouts. Each year in the United States several such fraudulent schemes are uncovered and prosecuted by the Securities Exchange Commission (SEC).

The original Ponzi scheme began in Boston in 1919. Charles Ponzi, a dapper 37-year-old Italian immigrant, conceived a unique arbitrage system. Member nations of the Universal Postal Union had agreed to a permanent exchange rate not affected by currency fluctuations. Ponzi saw he could buy depressed liras and francs, turn them into International Reply coupons, and then convert the coupons into U.S. dollars for a profit of up to 250 percent. He began paying investors 50 percent interest in 45 days.

This bonanza started a frenzy that went beyond the Italian North End and spread throughout New England. When Ponzi was exposed by the Boston *Post,* he had taken in $10,000,000 and purchased less than $30 worth of International Reply coupons. He had been redeeming his promissory notes with new funds from would-be greedy investors standing in block-long lines to reach his 16 clerks.

In 1920 Ponzi went to federal prison for using the mails to defraud and later to Massachusetts state prison for grand larceny. Receivers for his bankrupt Securities Exchange Company paid back about 35 cents on the dollar after puzzling over his bookkeeping for years. Ponzi died a pauper in Brazil in 1949.

Modern Ponzi scheme victims are less likely to be ignorant immigrants but are still vulnerable because they are preoccupied with other concerns. Doctors, entertainers, and retirees, for example, are frequent targets of Ponzi-scheme promoters.

Use of the term ''Ponzi scheme'' has broadened considerably since the 1920s. For example, the Drexel/Milken junk-bond craze of the 1980s, which fueled an unprecedented wave of corporate **takeovers** and contributed to the collapse of the savings and loan industry, has been described, with some justification, as a Ponzi scheme.

The term is often applied to the practices of certain third world governments—and more recently Russia—that borrow billions from the **International Monetary Fund** and then more billions to pay back the billions previously borrowed. The word ''Ponzi'' implies that these governments have no intention of repaying in full.

Social Security has frequently been called a Ponzi scheme by conservatives who claim that young workers will be cheated because the fund must inevitably go bankrupt. The word ''Ponzi'' in this context suggests that irresponsible politicians are looting the fund to disguise budget deficits and pyramiding benefits in the form of COLA entitlements to win votes from elderly recipients at the expense of future generations.

But perhaps the biggest true Ponzi scheme was that of Bennett Funding Group Inc., a billion-dollar operation involving some 12,000 investors. The company, which collapsed in 1996, sold unregistered securities on office equipment leases, an otherwise legal practice, but falsified and double-counted the underlying leases to make it appear it was properly investing all of the money it took in. Meanwhile, officers at the private family-owned business, based in Syracuse, New York, were squandering hundreds of millions on ill-fated real estate ventures and other unreported speculative pursuits. The company promised high returns on investments, some of which it actually delivered, and misled investors about how their money was being used and about the company's finances in general. The company ultimately failed under the heat of an SEC investigation, by which time it had taken in $1 billion and only had $300 million in assets to cover it. Among the victims were retirees, doctors, lawyers, and hundreds of banks.

What distinguishes a true Ponzi scheme is motive. If the promoters intend to milk investors by paying for borrowed money with more borrowed money, fully realizing that the pyramid must collapse, then it can correctly be characterized as a Ponzi scheme.

SEE ALSO: White Collar Crime

FURTHER READING:

Dunn, Donald H. *Ponzi! The Boston Swindler.* New York: McGraw-Hill, 1975.

Rapoport, Michael. ''On Cross-Exam, Govt Hammers Away at Bennett Funding Ex-CFO.'' *Dow Jones Newswires,* 9 February 1999.

Schonfeld, Erick. ''Caution: They're Out to Steal Your Money.'' *Fortune,* 18 August 1997.

PORTFOLIO MANAGEMENT THEORY

The theory of portfolio management describes the resulting **risk and return** of a combination of individual assets. A primary objective of the theory is to identify asset combinations that are efficient. Here, efficiency means the highest expected rate of return on an investment for a specific level of risk. The primary starting point for portfolio theory requires an assumption that investors are risk averse. This simply means that they will not consider a portfolio with more risk unless it is accompanied by a higher expected rate of return.

Modern portfolio theory was largely defined by the work of Harry Markowitz (1927-) in a series of articles published in the late 1950s. This theory was extended and refined by William Sharpe (1934-), John Lintner (1916 1983), James Tobin (1918-), and others in the subsequent decades. Portfolio theory integrates the process of efficient portfolio formation to the pricing of individual assets. It explains that some sources of risk associated with individual assets can be eliminated, or diversified away, by holding a proper combination of assets.

To begin the development of a theory of effective portfolio management, consider the following set of four individual **securities** as shown in Figure 1.

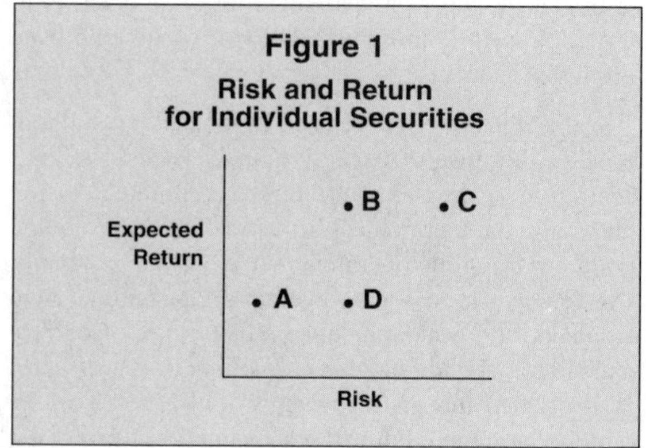

Figure 1
Risk and Return for Individual Securities

If investors are restricted to holding a single security, and since they prefer higher returns to lower returns, they will prefer B to C. Likewise, investors prefer less risk to more risk, so they will prefer B to D and A to C. Thus no rational, risk-averse investor will hold C or D. But what about the remaining portfolios A and B? The decision here is less clear. Neither portfolio is dominated by any of the others. Thus, investors must decide whether the additional expected return of B is adequate compensation for the additional risk it also exhibits. If these are the only four alternatives, then A and B are efficient portfolios since they exhibit the highest return for a given risk level. Rational investors, however, may now disagree on which of the two portfolios to select.

Now, suppose that investors can apportion their investment into A, B, or some of each. The expected return of this new set of two security portfolios will be a simple weighted average of the expected returns of the individual elements. For example, if the expected return on A were 12 percent and the expected return on B were 20 percent, then a portfolio with an equal proportion of each would be expected to return 16 percent. If the proportion of B was increased, the expected return would rise. Conversely, it would decline if the proportion of A was enhanced. Determining the risk inherent in these two security portfolios is somewhat more complex. There is a risk component contributed from A, another from B, and a third that results form the comovement of A and B. Statistically, this third component is referred to as covariance, or correlation. This comovement term can be strong or weak. It can also positive, indicating that the returns from A and B tend to move in the same direction, or negative, indicating that A and B tend to move in opposite directions.

Although the comovement component makes risk analysis of portfolios more complicated, it also represents the source of risk **diversification** and provides superior investment alternatives for many investors than can be attained by holding A or B in isolation. This is the insight that Markowitz was able to formalize. For example, if the returns generated by A and B exhibit moderate and positive comovement (or correlation), then portfolios of A and B would have expected return and risk characteristics as illustrated in Figure 2.

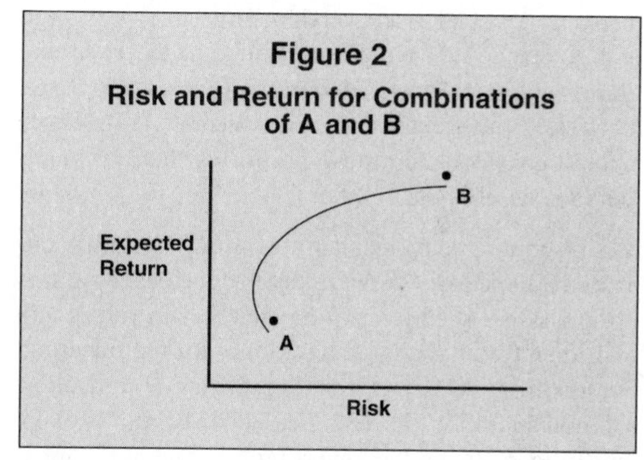

The set of combinations of A and B illustrated in Figure 2 are referred to as the opportunity set. Note that some portfolios that are attainable would not be desirable to a savvy risk-averse investor. For example, no investor will hold a 100 percent A portfolio since there is a combination containing some B that has the same level of risk and greater expected return. In fact, this is true for all portfolios represented on the lower half of the curve. The efficient frontier is the name given to the subset of the opportunity set containing the highest expected return portfolio for every possible level of risk. The shape of the graph and the resulting efficient frontier are both a function of the strength and direction of the correlation between the two securities. If the correlation were stronger and more positive, the curve would flatten and eventually become a straight line connecting the two points if the correlation became perfect. On the other hand, the curve would become more pronounced and approach the vertical axis of the graph if the correlation became weaker and possibly negative.

Next, consider this same problem with more than two securities to consider. The expected return of any combination of any number of securities remains a weighted average of the expected returns of the individual components, but the risk calculation must now contain a comovement, or correlation term for each unique pair of securities under consideration. Even though this requires a large amount of calculation, it can be accomplished. The resulting opportunity set is now represented by the area behind the curve in Figure 3. The efficient frontier of combinations of these risky individual securities, however, are the portfolios represented along the upper edge of the curve itself.

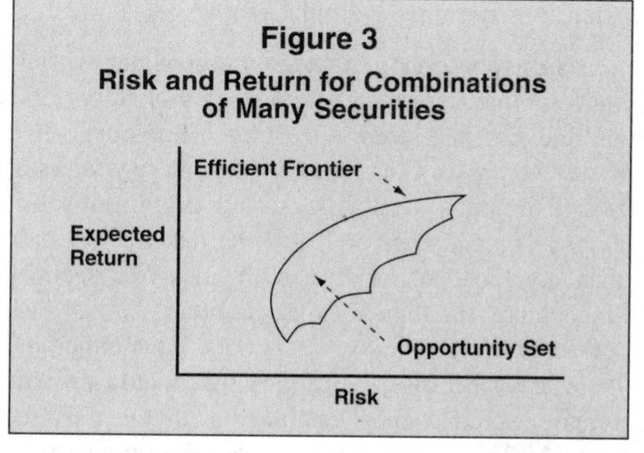

Which of these efficient portfolios is best for an individual investor? It depends upon that investor's personal level of risk aversion. Investors with high risk tolerance will choose portfolios to the right and those with low levels of risk tolerance will choose portfolios toward the left. Regardless, all investors should consider only those portfolios that are members of the efficient frontier.

A further refinement in this analysis can be obtained if there is a risk-free asset to consider as well. A truly riskless security will have a certain return and will therefore have no correlation with the uncertain returns from other individual securities or portfolios. Combinations of the risk-free security and a risky portfolio, Y, lie on the lowest broken line in Figure 4.

Figure 4
Risk and Return for Combinations of Risky Portfolios and a Risk Free Security

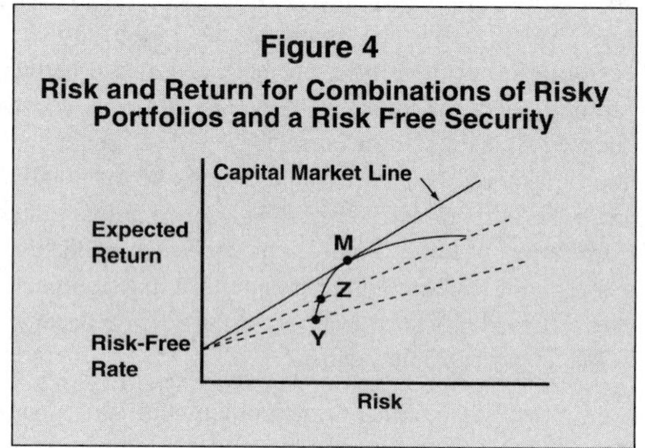

Note that investors can now achieve lower risk positions than are possible by holding only combinations of risky securities. Investors choosing to place a portion of their **wealth** in Y and the rest in the risk-free security will attain a portfolio that appears on the straight-line segment connecting those two components. If it were possible to borrow at the risk-free rate, investors could actually attain higher returns (for higher risk). These portfolios are represented by points on the broken line to the right of Y. These combinations, however, would not be efficient since there are pure combinations of risky securities that offer higher returns at similar risk levels.

Since portfolio Y is not unique, consider a different combination of risky assets, Z. Combinations of Z and the risk-free security lie upon a line connecting these two points. Clearly, any investors, regardless of their attitude toward risk, would prefer to select among combinations of Z and the risk-free security than combinations of Y and the risk-free security since there are higher expected returns at all risk levels. Portfolio Z, however, is not unique either and there are other risky portfolios that would provide superior returns when combined with the risk-free security. This process can be repeated until a particular portfolio M is identified. The line defining the expected returns and risk of combinations of M and the risk-free security is tangent to the former efficient frontier. Risky portfolios with higher expected return than M would not offer superior alternatives in conjunction with the risk-free security. Therefore, M is a unique combination. Investors who prefer a level of risk below that of M will hold a combination of M and the risk-free security. Their portfolios would plot between these two points on the graph. Investors who desire a risk level in excess of M can borrow at the risk-free rate and invest more than 100 percent of their original wealth in M. This will allow them to position themselves at points on the line above and to the right of M. In this scenario, the new efficient frontier is the solid line in Figure 4.

While M is unique in geometric terms, it is also unique in economic terms. Once this portfolio is identified, every investor, regardless of risk preferences, should choose combinations of M and the risk-free security. All investors should be allocating their wealth between M and the risk-free security. This has several important implications. First, all risky assets must be included in M. If not, then the price of excluded assets will quickly fall to a point where its rate of return will suggest membership in M. Since all assets are included in M, it is commonly referred to as the market portfolio.

The line passing through M is called the capital market line (CML). The slope of this line represents the price of additional units of expected return per unit of additional risk. Once the CML is defined, the next step is to determine the implications of portfolio M in deriving proper required returns for the individual securities it contains. One model that does this is the **capital asset pricing model** (CAPM). The CAPM indicates that the proper expected return for an individual security is related to its risk relative to the overall risk level of M. This relationship can be defined in the following equation.

$$\text{Expected Return for an Individual Security} = \text{Risk-free rate} + \beta\,(\text{Expected Return on M} - \text{Risk-free rate})$$

The return a security (or portfolio) is expected to generate in excess of the risk-free rate is called a risk premium. The expected return for a security must include a risk premium that is some multiple of the risk premium for the entire market. In this equation, β (or beta) is the risk of the individual security relative to the overall risk level of the market. A security with above-average risk would have a β in excess of 1 and a below-average risk security would have a β below 1. Since the aggregate of individual securities is the market itself, β for portfolio M is exactly 1.

Recall that the main benefit of forming portfolios is the potential to create combinations with lower risk and possibly higher expected returns than can be obtained from individual securities. Now consider the risk associated with an individual security as the sum of two parts. One part is represented by risk factors that are truly unique to the specific security. The other part is represented by risk factors that are essentially common with all other securities. For example, the potential for a key employee to leave the firm unexpectedly or the possibility of discovering gold under corporate headquarters are unique risk factors that are not shared with other firms. On the other hand, risk factors concerning the potential for unexpected and rapid growth in the national (or international) economy or the enactment of new legislation that affects the operating costs for all firms represent examples of common risk factors. While portfolio formation reduces the influence of unique risks associated with individual securities, it cannot eliminate exposure to common risk factors. Stated differently, properly constructed portfolios allow for diversification of unsystematic (unique) risk, but not for systematic (market) risk.

Using this latest interpretation, β represents the level of systematic risk of an individual security. Since investors have the potential to eliminate unsystematic risk from their portfolios, the return they expect should only include compensation for the systematic risk component. This is the underlying message of the CAPM.

There are other theories that attempt to explain how individual securities are priced. One prominent one is **arbitrage** pricing theory (APT). While CAPM essentially uses the market's risk premium as the sole determinant of a security's return, APT allows for multiple systematic risk factors. A simple representation of the APT model is provided below.

$$\begin{aligned}\text{Expected Return on an Individual Security} = {} & \text{Risk-free rate} \\ & + \beta 1 \text{ (Risk premium on M)} \\ & + \beta 2 \text{ (Change in inflation rate)} \\ & + \beta 3 \text{ (Change in GNP growth)}\end{aligned}$$

Systematic risk is now measured with respect to a variety of factors, not just market returns. While three factors are listed here, there may be more or fewer. Furthermore, the factors themselves are not specified by the theory. This means that any application of the theory requires the user to commit to a specific set of factors that can be justified both economically and statistically.

This is a good place to review the implications of portfolio theory. First, investors are risk averse and will accept more risk only if there is the expectation of higher return as well. This suggests that they will seek and hold only efficient combinations of securities. These efficient combinations have exploited the role of comovement among the individual securities to eliminate all diversifiable, or unsystematic risk. The returns expected from individual securities will therefore include no premium for diversifiable risk since it can be eliminated. The only source of risk requiring compensation is systematic, or market, risk.

It is also worth noting that if a risk-free asset is also available, there is a single risky portfolio (referred to as M, or the market portfolio) that is optimal for all investors. Investors will seek their desired level of risk exposure by selecting the proper proportions of the risky portfolio, M, and the risk-free asset.

As a practical matter, it is difficult to identify the true market portfolio since it, by definition, must contain proportions of all assets that have value. This means that investors and portfolio managers must create proxies for the market portfolio from some subset of all possible investments. Even if this proxy can be identified and created, the efficient frontier moves around as expected return and risk of the individual securities, and correlation among these elements, change over time. Moreover, it is impossible to estimate future risk and return without error. This leads some practitioners to view the efficient frontier as "fuzzy."

Three alternative approaches to portfolio management arise from these considerations. Many investors default to a passive portfolio strategy. A passive strategy requires the investor to buy and hold some replica of the market portfolio and accept an expected return equal to the market. For example, an investor may choose to hold a portfolio of stocks that is identical to the Standard & Poor's 500 or some other broad market index. This becomes the risky component of the portfolio and is combined with a proportion of a risk-free security (e.g., **U.S. Treasury bills**) to achieve the desired risk level. Underlying this strategy is the assumption that markets are reasonably efficient and that any attempt to improve the rate of return from risky securities is not likely to succeed. The broad market index is likely to reside within the "fuzzy" domain of the efficient frontier.

Active portfolio management strategies attempt to "beat the market" by identifying "mispriced" securities and forming efficient portfolios from those securities. This strategy clearly requires more effort from the investor. If such securities can be identified and the market eventually prices them properly, the active portfolio will generate returns in excess of those provided by the market on a risk adjusted basis.

A third approach relies on intensive quantitative analysis of securities specified by an investor. An optimization algorithm can provide an efficient allocation of funds among a given set of alternatives. This approach can be applied to an existing passive or active strategy.

In summary, portfolio management theory assesses risk and return relationships for combinations of securities. While the expected return of a portfolio is the simple weighted average of the expected returns of its component securities, portfolio risk must also consider the correlation among the returns of individual securities. Since part of the price fluctuation of a security is unique, it does not relate to price fluctuations of other securities held. This allows the investor to diversify, or eliminate, a portion of each security's risk. With additional analysis, the subset of portfolios with the highest expected return for a given risk level can be identified. If a risk-free asset can also be purchased or sold, then there is a unique combination of risky securities that will allow all investors to achieve superior returns for a given risk level. The capital asset pricing model and other models use this result to infer the risk-return relationship for individual securities. Although there is imprecision when attempting to implement these theories, they provide a useful way to evaluate and improve a variety of investment strategies.

[Paul Bolster]

FURTHER READING:

Bodie, Zvi, Alex Kane, and Alan J. Marcus. *Investments.* 4th ed. Boston: Irwin/McGraw-Hill, 1999.

Grinold, Richard C., and Ronald N. Kahn. *Active Portfolio Management.* 2nd ed. New York: McGraw-Hill, 1999.

Markowitz, Harry. *Portfolio Selection: Efficient Diversification of Investments.* 2nd ed. Cambridge, MA: Basil Blackwell, 1991.

Michaud, Richard O. *Efficient Asset Management.* Boston: Harvard Business School Press, 1998.

PREFERRED STOCK

Preferred stock is a form of corporate hybrid financing having characteristics of both **debt** and **common stock**. The financial markets view it as a form of debt, but accountants typically place it on the **balance sheet** as an equity account. Preferred stock units are called shares, with a par value per share and usually no maturity. When preferred stock has a maturity, usually 20 years, it also has a **call** feature. The shares may have a **dividend** (fixed) rate or dividend per share specified on a per annum basis but paid prorated quarterly. As preferred stock with a constant dividend per share with no maturity is a perpetuity, the valuation of it is based on the following formula:

$$P = \frac{D}{i}$$

where P = the price per share,
D = the annual dividend,
i = the interest rate in decimal form.

When the dividend rate is different from current market rates, the preferred stock price per share deviates from its par value. The dividend can change relative to current market **interest rates**. If so, the preferred stock is called adjustable rate (or variable rate) preferred stock. The mechanism detailing the calculation and frequency of adjustment of the dividend rate would be stated in the indenture (**contract**). As adjustable rate preferred stock continuously provides a return comparable to prevailing market conditions, the valuation of it is approximately par value. An advantage to the corporation issuing preferred stock is that the dividend is not an obligation as are debt interest payments. If preferred stock dividends are not paid, the consequence to the firm is not insolvency and bankruptcy. When the firm's preferred stock dividend is not paid, it accumulates (cumulative clause) as dividends in arrears. No common stock dividend can be paid until the arrearage has been made up. Most preferred stocks issues provide for voting rights enabling the preferred stockholders as a class to elect at least one director on the board if the preferred stock dividend has been foregone for six consecutive quarters or more. Otherwise, preferred stock has no voting rights. Approximately one-half of the preferred stock in the United States has a convertible put option. This gives convertible preferred stockholders the right to exchange their preferred stock to the company in return for its common stock within a conversion period of several years. When the preferred stock is convertible, a call feature is usually included giving the firm the right to buy back the convertible preferred stock for cash.

The tax implications of owning and selling preferred stock have largely determined the lack of interest in preferred stock in the United States. For the issuing corporation the preferred stock dividend payments are not **tax** deductible. Thus, the after-tax cost is the same as the before-tax cost. This tax-code ruling makes preferred stock an expensive form of financing, especially when it is viewed as a form of debt that allows interest expense to be used as a tax deduction.

In the United States, the negative tax ruling on preferred stock dividends is mitigated by a 70 percent dividend income exclusion on the tax returns of corporations. That is, if a corporation owns preferred stock, it can exclude 70 percent of dividend income and pay income taxes on only 30 percent of dividend income, both preferred and common stock. This feature of the tax code has caused a clientele effect whereby the vast majority of preferred stock is owned by corporations as opposed to individuals. On average, preferred stock is only about 4 percent of the total source of funds for U.S. firms and is concentrated in the **banking** and public utility industries. Nevertheless, the popularity of any instrument can fluctuate with changing market conditions, tax code, and specific features included in the preferred stock indenture.

[Raymond A. K. Cox]

FURTHER READING:

Chandy, P. R., L. Paul Hsueh, and Y. Angela Liu. "Effects of Preferred Stock Re-rating on Common Stock Prices: Further Evidence." *Financial Review* 28, no. 4 (November 1993): 449-67.

Houston, Arthur L., Jr., and Carol Olson Houston. "Financing with Preferred Stock." *Financial Management* 19, no. 3 (autumn 1990): 42-54.

Wansley, James W., Fayez A. Elayan, and Brian A. Maris. "Preferred Stock Returns, CreditWatch, and Preferred Stock Rating Changes." *Financial Review* 25, no. 2 (May 1990): 265-85.

PRESENT VALUE

The present value (PV) of an amount to be received in the future is the discounted face value considering the length of time the receipt is deferred and the required rate of return (or appropriate **discount rate** under the circumstances). The notion of present value presumes that money has a time value—today's dollar is worth more than the same dollar received at a future point in time—deriving from inflation, interest, and other considerations. This idea is used commonly when planning a **capital budget**.

This notion can be demonstrated by examining three common financial transactions:

- Money invested in bank certificates of deposit may earn interest at 5 percent. At that rate, $1,000 deposited on January 1 will accumulate $50 of interest by December 31, making the total available to the investor $1,050. Since this investor is willing to lend his money to the bank for 5 percent annual interest, that rate may be viewed as the required rate of return, or the discount rate. The $1,050 to be received on December 31 had a PV to that investor at January 1 of exactly $1,000 ($1{,}050/(1+.05)^1$).
- Annuity contracts can be bought from insurance companies whereby a single payment is made to the insurance company in exchange for a defined series of annual (or monthly) payments made back to the buyer. In these cases the simple sum of the periodic repayments from the insurance company to the buyer exceed the original annuity purchase price, in absolute terms. However, when considering the deferred repayment and the implied rate of return on the money loaned, the amounts exactly equate, on a present value basis.
- Mortgage loans are basically the reverse of the above described annuity contract. Here, the individual borrows the money, promising to make scheduled repayments to the lender. Again, due to the differential timing of cash flows, and the fact that the bank requires interest to be paid on the borrowed funds, the PVs equate. That is, the PV of the sum of the future mortgage payments is exactly equal to the amount borrowed (which by definition is at the PV on the date of the loan).

CALCULATING PRESENT VALUE

The formula for calculating the present value of a series of future receipts is:

$$PV = CF_1/(1+i)^1 + CF_2/(1+i)^2 + \ldots + CF_n/(1+i)^n$$

where CF_1 to CF_n = future receipts
i = the interest or discount rate appropriate for the stated period
n = the number of periods over which future receipts occur

RATE OF RETURN. The interest or discount rate used in PV calculations is a key element in determining the PV. This importance is emphasized when the future amounts occur over an extended period of time, due to the power of compounding. For example, the final payment on a 30-year loan at 7 percent interest would be worth approximately 13.1 percent of its face amount on a present value basis at the date of loan origin [$1/(1 + .07)^{30}$]. By contrast, the 30th payment on a loan with a 9 percent interest rate would be worth only 7.5 percent [$1/(1 + .09)^{30}$] of its face amount in present value terms at the origin. This simple example shows the power of compounding when time periods are long.

The discount rate used in a given circumstance must provide for compensation to the lender of funds for three elements of return:

1. Inflation: just to keep even in terms of buying power, the return of money at a future date must be appended by the rate of general price inflation as measured by the Consumer Price Index (CPI). In other words, if a person lends an amount of money adequate to buy a loaf of bread at time $t=0$, he will require repayment at $t=1$ of the original amount plus the fraction of that amount representing the CPI increase over the period. That way he will be able to buy the same loaf of bread at $t=1$.
2. Time value of money (TVM): beyond simply keeping even with inflation, the investor

or lender has a basic preference for consumption sooner rather than later. The cost of compensating for this aspect of human nature has been found to be about 1 to 2 percent per year. That is, the real rate of return on risk-free assets has averaged about 1.5 percent.

3. Risk: in addition to postponing the preferred immediate consumption and having to reimburse for inflation's erosion of buying power, many types of investment involve a risk of default. That is, the investor may never again see his funds, for example if the company goes bankrupt. Compensating for this element of required return can be considerably more expensive than the first two combined. For example, junk bonds may be paying interest at 12 percent, while anticipated inflation is only 4 percent and TVM is about 1.5 percent. This would mean that the risk premium component of the overall interest rate is 6.5 percent (12 percent − 4 percent − 1.5 percent).

NET PRESENT VALUE

An important extension of present value is net present value (NPV), which is simply the sum of present values for an investment's anticipated returns over time offset by its up-front costs. This is an important decision-making tool because an investment may appear lucrative in today's money, but once its returns are discounted it may reveal the investment would yield a net loss for the company compared to other options.

Imagine a company that has an opportunity to invest in a five-year joint venture with another firm beginning in 2002. The company would have to put up $100,000 at the start to fund its share, but the annual returns to the company are expected be $30,000 a year for five years. On the surface, it appears that the company would reap a 50 percent return on its investment, since $30,000 × 5 = $150,000.

Net present value paints a different scenario, however. Recall from the time value of money theory that $50,000 in five years is worth less than the same nominal figure today. There are also opportunity costs and capital acquisition costs to consider. What is the company losing by not using the $100,000 elsewhere? and how much does it cost the company to obtain new capital?

The latter question forms the basis for determining a minimum required rate of return on such an investment; if the returns on capital don't at least match the costs of obtaining it, the investment is losing money.

Table 1

Using Present Value to Evaluate Investment Returns

The expected returns on the hypothetical investment below indicate a poor investment because the net present value at the end of the period is negative.

Year	Nominal Return	Present Value at Year End
2002	30,000	25,863
2003	30,000	22,296
2004	30,000	19,221
2005	30,000	16,569
2006	30,000	14,283
Gross return	150,000	98,232
Minus cost		(100,000)
Net present value		(1,768)

With that in mind, suppose the company determines that its minimum rate of return is 16 percent given current interest rates, inflation, the risks associated with the investment, and so forth. Table 1 shows how the net present value of the venture would be computed. As the figures indicate, once the annual returns are discounted based on the company's capital costs and other factors, their present values as of 2002 would yield a negative NPV, a signal to management that the venture is probably not worthwhile. Not only would management expect a positive NPV, but if it has several options it would likely choose the one with the highest positive NPV.

SEE ALSO: Discounted Cash Flow

FURTHER READING:

Birrer, G. Eddy, and Jean L. Carrica. *Present Value Applications for Accountants and Financial Planners.* Westport, CT: Quorum Books, 1990.

Robison, Lindon J., and Pete J. Barry. *Present Value Models and Investment Analysis.* East Lansing, MI: Michigan State University Press, 1998.

PRICE/EARNINGS (P/E) RATIO

The price/earnings ratio (P/E ratio) provides a comparison of the current market price of a share of **stock** and that stock's earnings per share, or EPS (which is figured by dividing a company's net **income** by its number of shares of **common stock** outstanding). For example, if a company's stock sold for $30 per share and it posted earnings per share of $1.50, that company would have a P/E ratio of 15. A company's P/E ratio typically rises as a result of increases in its stock price, an indicator of the stock's popularity.

"The price-earnings ratio is part of the everyday vocabulary of investors in the stock market," noted

Richard A. Brealey and Stewart C. Myers in *Principles of Corporate Finance,* because a company's P/E ratio is often viewed as an indicator of future stock performance. "The high P/E shows that investors think that the firm has good growth opportunities, that its earnings are relatively safe and deserve a low **capitalization rate**, or both."

John B. Thomas observed in the *Indianapolis Business Journal,* however, that "while accepting that a high P/E ratio is usually a sign of high expectations, analysts and brokers nonetheless are quick to caution that the ratios are only part of the puzzle." A company may post an artificially high P/E ratio as a result of factors that can either boost stock prices or diminish earnings per share. Restructuring charges, **merger and acquisition** rumors (whether true or false), and high **dividend** yields all have the capacity to push a company's P/E ratio upward. In other instances, legitimately high P/E ratios can be adversely impacted down the road by such factors as market conditions, technology, and increased **competition** from new rivals (who may, in fact, be drawn to the industry by the company's previously posted P/E ratios).

Conversely, while a low P/E ratio is often a good indication that a company is struggling, appearances can again be deceiving. In addition, different industry sectors often have diverse P/E ratio averages. A company may have a fairly low P/E ratio when compared with all other corporations; when compared with the other companies within its industry, however, it may be a leader.

Finally, a company that posts a loss has no earnings to compare with its stock price. As a result, no P/E ratio can be determined for the company. Still, these companies may remain viable choices for investment if an investor decides that the company under examination is headed toward future profitability.

Since so many factors can influence a company's P/E ratio, industry analysts caution against relying on it too heavily in making investment decisions. As one analyst remarked to the *Indianapolis Business Journal,* while a company's P/E ratio is a valuable and often accurate investment tool, "if you're going to buy and sell stocks based on a P/E ratio, you're not going to make money. You'd better look at why it is high or low."

The P/E ratio became even trickier for investors to interpret in the late 1990s, as the **stock market** continually reached all time highs and numerous large-company stocks were traded at valuations more than two times their five-year expected growth rates. A general rule of thumb for investing states that a stock should sell at about its expected growth rate. For example, if a company's earnings were expected to grow at 12 percent per year, its stock should carry a P/E ratio of 12. "In normal times, investors preferred to buy shares in companies whose fortunes were expected to improve in coming years. They'd shop for companies whose future earnings-growth rates were expected to exceed current price/earnings multiples," Gretchen Morgenson wrote in *Forbes.* "But these are not normal times. The folks who are buying these shares are closing their eyes to ordinary standards of value. Call them see-no-evil stocks."

As an example, Morgenson noted that Procter & Gamble shares were trading at 28 times the company's latest 12-month earnings as of late 1997, and this high figure was hardly exceptional. While some analysts argued that the high P/E ratios were justified due to falling long-term **interest rates** and low **inflation**, others warned that they left no room for a downturn in earnings at the companies boasting high stock prices. "Buying overpriced stocks because you think they'll become even more expensive—the Greater Fool theory—has worked out pretty well in recent markets," Morgenson admitted. "But don't bet on it continuing to work forever. As the P/Es mount higher, the game gets riskier."

EARNINGS PER SHARE (EPS)

Earnings per share is one of the two factors that determine a company's P/E ratio; the other is the price of the company's stock. EPS is derived by dividing a corporation's net income by the number of shares of common stock that are outstanding. A company with 30,000 outstanding shares of common stock and a net income of $270,000 would thus have an earnings per share of $9.

An essential part of determining the P/E ratio, earnings per share has also come to be regarded as an important piece of information for the investment community in and of itself. "A primary concern of investors is how profitable a company is relative to their investment in the company," wrote Jay M. Smith Jr. and K. Fred Skousen in *Intermediate Accounting.* "The investor is concerned with how net income relates to shares held and to the market price of the stock. . . . Only by converting the total amounts to per share data can a meaningful evaluation be made," because EPS figures can illustrate the degree to which a company's net income is keeping pace with its **capital structure**. In recognition of the importance of this information, corporations are required to report EPS amounts on their **income statement** (the requirement was suspended for nonpublic entities in 1978).

[Laurie Collier Hillstrom]

FURTHER READING:

Bierman, Harold, Jr., and Seymour Smidt. *Financial Management for Decision Making.* New York: Macmillan, 1986.

Brealey, Richard A., and Stewart C. Myers. *Principles of Corporate Finance.* 5th ed. New York: McGraw-Hill, 1996.

''Don't Get Burned by Hot Stocks.'' *Money,* October 1994, 72.

Ip, Greg. ''The New Math: Are Some High P/E Stocks 'Bargains'?'' *Wall Street Journal,* 1 December 1997, C1.

Laderman, Jeffrey M. ''They're Not as Loony as They Look: P/E Ratios Are Loftier than Ever, but Don't Bail Out Just Yet.'' *Business Week,* 18 May 1998, 148.

Morgenson, Gretchen. ''See-No-Evil Stocks.'' *Forbes,* 22 September 1997, 252.

Smith, Jay M., Jr., and K. Fred Skousen. *Intermediate Accounting.* 9th ed. Cincinnati: South-Western Publishing, 1987.

Thomas, John B. ''P/E Ratios Driven by Variety of Factors, Carry Variety of Meanings.'' *Indianapolis Business Journal,* 23 May 1994, 10B.

PRICE INDEXES

Price indexes are used to measure the rate of inflation in the economy. There are three key price indexes that are routinely calculated and reported to the public by government agencies in the United States. These three measures differ with respect to the number of items they take into account. Before discussing these measures, it is worthwhile to explain why an index is needed to calculate the rate of inflation.

THE NEED FOR AN INDEX

Most economic variables are measured in absolute terms. For example, it was reported that 12 million cars were produced in 1994 in the United States and that the gross output of goods and services in the United States was estimated at $8.7 trillion during 1998. It is not possible, however, to measure the price associated with a group of **commodities** in absolute terms; only the price for one commodity can be measured in absolute terms. For example, we can thus say that the average price of a loaf of bread in the United States, was $1.75 in 1998. The difficulty arises when we have to deal with a number of commodities together. So, once we start asking what happened to Joe Smith's cost of living in 1998 compared to 1997, it is no longer logical to compute the average price of all the goods and services bought by him in 1997 and compare it with the average price of all the goods and services bought by him in 1998. After all, what meaning can we attach to the average of prices paid for, for instance, a fancy stereo system and a pound of hamburger? An index helps us out of this quandary. In the most basic terms, an index attaches weights to the prices of items whose collective price movement we are interested in. Below is a detailed discussion of the three main price indexes used widely in the United States and how they are constructed.

THREE MAIN PRICE INDEXES AND THE INFLATION RATE

The inflation rate is derived by calculating the rate of change in a price index. A price index, in turn, measures the level of prices of goods and services at a particular time. The number of items included in a price index varies depending on the objective of the index. Government agencies periodically report three types of price indexes, each having particular advantages and uses. The first, the **consumer price index (CPI)**, measures the average retail prices paid by consumers for goods and services. A couple thousand products, grouped into 207 sets of items, are included in this index. These items are selected on the basis of their inclusion in the household budget of a consumer. Each of the product prices is assigned a weight based on the importance of the item in the household budget. As a result, the CPI reflects changes in the cost of living of a typical urban household. The CPI is considered the most relevant **inflation** measure from the point of view of consumers, as it measures the prices of goods and services that are part of their budgets. Nevertheless, the CPI will not precisely measure changes in the cost of living of every consumer due to differences in consumption patterns.

A second price index used to measure the inflation rate is called the producer price index (PPI). It is a much broader measure than the consumer price index. The PPI measures the wholesale prices of approximately 3,000 items. The items included in this index are those that are typically used by producers (manufacturers and businesses) and thus include many raw materials and semi-finished goods. A change in the PPI reflects a change in the cost of production, as encountered by producers. Since producers may pass a part or all of the increase in the cost of production to consumers, movements in the PPI indicate future movements in the CPI. The producer price index can thus forewarn consumers of coming increases in the cost of living.

The **implicit price deflator** is the third measure of inflation. This index measures the prices of all goods and services included in the calculation of the current output of goods and services in the economy, known as **gross domestic product** (GDP). It is the broadest measure of price level. This index includes prices of fighter planes purchased by the Defense Department as well as paper clips used in any office. Thus, the implicit price deflator is a measure of the overall or aggregate price level for the economy. Movements in the implicit GDP price deflator capture the inflationary tendency of the overall economy.

The three measures of the inflation rate are most likely to move in the same direction, even though not to the same extent. Differences can arise due to the differing number of goods and services included in compiling the three indexes. The preceding three price indexes are discussed in further detail below.

CALCULATIONS OF THE CONSUMER PRICE INDEX AND THE INFLATION RATE

The construction of the consumer price index employs an index number technique in which a fixed basket of commodities (a collection of goods and services considered relevant to the index) is valued using prices at different points of time. This type of index is technically known as a Laspeyres index, named after the statistician who invented the method.

First, a point of reference is selected, commonly known as the base year. Normally, a particular year is selected as the base year—prices prevailing in the selected base year are used in comparing changes in the price level. Currently, however, the 1982-84 period (rather than a single year) is used as the base in the construction of the consumer price index in the United States. In this case, the average price of a commodity over the three-year period is used as the base price for the commodity. This implies that the average of 1982, 1983, and 1984 prices for any given item included in the CPI is used in comparing the prices of that commodity in successive months and years. The price of each item in the basket of commodities selected is attached a weight in accordance with its importance in the budget of a typical urban family. In other words, the government first identifies the goods and services that are used by a typical urban consumer. Then, it assigns a weight to each of the items in the fixed basket—the basket thus contains a collection of goods and services in quantities that, presumably, a representative consumer consumes. Next, the government evaluates the fixed basket of commodities using prices at successive points and compares its costs (or values) with the cost to buy the same basket in the base period. This results in a series of price ratios that are usually multiplied by 100 for convenience. Thus, the price index is 100 in the base period and its value at other points reflect movements in the price level, which can be used to calculate the inflation rate between any two points of time.

For example, the CPI in the United States for 1982 was 96.5, for 1983 it was 99.6, and for 1984 it was 103.9. The average of the CPI numbers for these three years is equal to 100, since the 1982-84 period is used as the base period or point of reference. The consumer price index stood at 141.9 at the end of 1992, and at 145.8 at the end of 1993. The latter two values of the CPI imply that the cost of the fixed basket of commodities, compared to the 1982-84 period, had gone up by 41.9 percent by the end of 1992, and by 45.8 percent by the end of 1993. They also imply that the inflation rate during 1993 was roughly 2.7 percent on an annual basis (inflation rate = {(145.8 - 141.9)/141.9}*100).

ITEMS INCLUDED IN THE CONSUMER PRICE INDEX. The consumer price index is calculated by the U.S. Bureau of Labor Statistics (BLS) and is published on a monthly basis. The broad categories of items that are included in construction of the CPI, in a highly simplified form, are: food and beverages, housing, apparel and upkeep, transportation, medical care, entertainment, and other goods and services. In reality, however, the CPI is based on a couple thousand products that are grouped into 207 sets of items. BLS employees visit thousands of stores in 85 geographical areas every month and collect more than 100,000 prices. Then the average prices of related items, such as poultry and honey are combined to yield group indexes—in this particular case, food and beverages. Next, the group indexes are combined to yield the overall price index called the ''all-items CPI.''

THE MEASUREMENT ERROR IN THE CONSUMER PRICE INDEX. Until 1983, the consumer price index data inflated the extent of true inflation, due to a measurement error. This error arose from the treatment of mortgage interest rates. The BLS attached excessive weights to this item, which rose quite rapidly during the 1970s. The government agency, in calculating price statistics, assumed that increased mortgage rates led to higher housing costs for homeowners—this is incorrect, since homeowners do not take out new **mortgages** every month. The mention of this measurement error is important, since the CPI series, unlike many other economic statistics, is not revised to correct for errors. Thus, the measurement error is still present in the CPI series and it can lead to misleading impressions. For example, consumer price index data suggest that real earnings (earnings adjusted for inflation) fell between 1972 and 1982, but according to another price index—also published by the federal government—real earnings grew slightly from 1972 to 1982.

THE USEFULNESS OF THE CONSUMER PRICE INDEX. The consumer price index is widely used, both in the private and public sectors. The CPI is most commonly used in calculating the inflation rate for general purposes. The movement in the CPI reflects changes in the cost of living for urban consumers. **Labor unions** often use the CPI in bargaining for wage increases. Also, most government pensions, including the level of Social Security benefits, are indexed to the consumer price index.

CALCULATIONS OF THE PRODUCER PRICE INDEX AND THE INFLATION RATE

The producer price index (PPI) is also published by the U.S. Bureau of Labor Statistics (BLS) on a monthly basis. For the PPI, the BLS collects prices on more than 3,000 commodities that are not bought by consumers directly but instead are purchased by businesses. In a simplified form, the producer price index can be thought of as having the following broad categories: finished goods; intermediate materials, supplies, and components; and crude materials for further processing. Each of these broad categories is further subdivided in smaller groups. For example, the finished goods category consists of foods, energy, and finished goods excluding food and energy (the last subcategory includes capital equipment).

The PPI uses an index number construction methodology similar to at used for the CPI. While price data are directly collected by the BLS workers, the actual prices for the PPI index are obtained from questionnaires that are mailed to thousands of firms that sell products included in the PPI.

Currently, 1982 is used as the base year for the producer price index series. The interpretation of the PPI series is similar to the CPI series—the PPI can also be used to calculate the inflation rate.

USEFULNESS OF THE PRODUCER PRICE INDEX. One should recognize that the producer price index serves as an index relevant to the producers' cost. In other words, the PPI tells what is happening to the cost of production. If the cost of production is rising, however, producers may also increase the prices at which they sell. This, in turn, is likely to increase the retail prices that consumers pay in stores across the nation. The importance of the producer price index, then, is that it forewarns of changes in the consumer price index and, therefore, the cost of living of ordinary households.

CALCULATIONS OF THE IMPLICIT PRICE DEFLATOR AND THE INFLATION RATE

The implicit price deflator is arrived at in an indirect manner, thus the adjective ''implicit.'' Calculation of the consumer price index (CPI) and the producer price index (PPI) are explicit—or direct—indexes calculated from price data on the items included. The implicit price deflator, on the other hand, is inferred indirectly from the estimates of gross domestic product (GDP) in nominal terms (in current dollars) and in real terms (the nominal value of GDP adjusted for inflation by reevaluating the GDP in prices that prevailed during a chosen base year).

Currently, 1992 is used as the base year for calculating the real value of GDP in the United States. For example, the 1998 U.S. output of goods and services is first evaluated at prices prevailing in 1998. Then, the 1998 output of goods and services is also evaluated at prices that prevailed in 1992 (thus the term ''GDP in 1992 dollars'' or ''GDP in constant dollars.'' One can easily see how the ratio of GDP in 1998 prices and GDP in 1992 prices would yield a measure of the extent of the rise in price level between 1992 and 1998. According to federal government statistics, this ratio is estimated at 1.1307 or 113.07 when multiplied by 100 (as is customarily done to be able to see the extent of price increase more conveniently). The value of the implicit price deflator of 113.07 in 1998 implies that the price level increased by 13.07 percent from 1992 to 1998 (note that the value of the implicit price deflator in the 1992 base year, is equal to 100).

The above method of expressing nominal or current gross domestic product into its value in 1992 prices is routinely done every year (of course, sometimes the base year itself, may be changed to a later year to keep the data series closer to the current period). Thus, we have 1997, 1996, 1995 (and so on) gross domestic products expressed in 1992 prices. This helps to calculate the inflation rate between subsequent years. For example, the implicit price deflator stood at 112.08 at the end of 1997. Given that the deflator was at 113.07 at the end of 1998, we arrive at the annual inflation rate of roughly 0.88 percent during 1998 (1998 inflation rate = [(113.07 - 112.08) / 112.08] * 100).

One should also notice that the term ''deflator'' is not used in the CPI or PPI. This is because, if you know the implicit price deflator, say, for 1998 and the 1998 GDP in current prices, you can arrive at the GDP in 1992 prices by deflating the 1998 GDP in current prices by the deflator for 1998 (expressed in plain ratio form, rather than the one multiplied by 100). Despite the use of term ''deflator,'' one should not lose sight of the fact the implicit price deflator is essentially a price index.

USEFULNESS OF THE IMPLICIT PRICE DEFLATOR. As was pointed out earlier, the implicit price index is the broadest measure of price level. Although this index is all-inclusive and changes in it reflect inflation pressure underlying the whole economy, it may not be directly useful to ordinary households and even businesses—the CPI and PPI are more relevant to these units.

USEFULNESS OF THE THREE PRICE INDEXES

As mentioned earlier, all three price indexes can be used to calculate the inflation rate. There are, however, two important differences among these indexes. First, the consumer and producer price indexes are published every month, whereas the implicit price deflator figures are reported on a quarterly basis. Thus, more frequent users of inflation data would be inclined to use the CPI or the PPI. Second, the coverage of the three indexes differs dramatically. Thus, one of these price index series can be more suitable than another in a particular case. To measure the cost of living for an urban consumer, for example, the CPI will be overwhelmingly preferred to the PPI and the implicit price deflator. Nevertheless, one must be aware that even the

CPI is an average price measure that is based on certain weights. While the CPI may reflect the cost of living changes for the average consumers, it cannot precisely reflect changes in the actual cost of living for a particular consumer—his or her consumption pattern may be quite different from that assumed in assigning weights to the fixed basket of commodities. One thus needs to interpret the price index numbers carefully.

Despite the slight caution one must exercise in interpreting the price indexes, a good understanding of the inflation rate is important for every individual and household. Most economies face positive rates of inflation year after year. If the inflation rate is positive and an individual's income remains constant, his or her real standard of living will fall since the individual's income will be worth less and less in successive periods. For example, a household earns $50,000 per year and its income remains fixed at this level in the future. If the inflation rate persists at 10 percent per year, the purchasing power of the household income will also keep declining at the rate of 10 percent per year. At the end of a five-year period, prices will be one and a half times greater. This will lead to the household being able to buy only two-thirds of the goods and services it was able to buy at the beginning of the period.

An understanding of inflation is also crucial in making plans to save for retirement, college education, or a boat. One must use an appropriate price index in calculating the funds required for a given purpose. The CPI is a good guide for retirement purposes. But if one is saving to buy a boat, even the CPI may not produce a good result—the individual may want to specifically know the way boat prices are increasing. Nevertheless, an understanding of price indexes prepares an individual adequately to explore such questions further.

SEE ALSO: Consumer Price Index; Implicit Price Deflator

[Anandi P. Sahu, Ph.D.]

FURTHER READING:

Froyen, Richard T. *Macroeconomics: Theories and Policies.* 6th ed. Upper Saddle River, NJ: Prentice Hall, 1998.

Gordon, Robert J. *Macroeconomics.* 7th ed. Reading, PA: Addison-Wesley, 1998.

Sommers, Albert T. *The U.S. Economy Demystified.* Lexington, MA: Lexington Books, 1985.

PRIME RATE

The prime rate has different meanings in different contexts. It most commonly refers to a commercial bank's prime lending rate, or the interest rate charged by **banks** for short-term **commercial loans** to their most creditworthy customers. Different banks may have different prime rates, and specific **loans** may vary from the prime rate due to a number of factors. Banks use the prime rate as a benchmark in setting the rates for a wide range of loans, including small business loans, home equity loans, and credit card balances. Banks also refer to their prime rate as their base lending rate.

In the context of **interest rates** in general, the prime rate refers to the rate of interest that would be charged on a riskless loan. In a sense it represents the "pure" cost of money in the absence of financial risk. Comparing yields on a riskless investment, such as U.S. government **securities**, with those of other investments, such as corporate **bonds**, provides a measure of the interest rate premium that must be paid for assuming some financial risk.

In the case of **Federal Reserve** banks, their prime rate is the **discount rate** they charge to member banks for advances that are secured by U.S. government securities. The Federal Reserve Board, through its Federal Open Market Committee, may raise or lower its discount rate as a matter of monetary policy. The prime lending rate of commercial banks is sensitive to the Fed's monetary policies; increases in the discount rate are usually followed by major banks raising their prime rates. It should be noted, however, that when the Federal Reserve Board raises its discount rate, it is not actually raising what is commonly called the prime rate. Rather, it is individual banks that raise or lower their prime rates in response to changes in the Federal Reserve's discount rate.

Changes in the prime rate are usually made first by the nation's largest banks, after which other banks follow suit. In some cases a few smaller banks may raise or lower their prime rates on their own, but normally other banks do not follow along. Most of the large banks tend to have the same prime rate, and changes in the prime rate affect the interest rates charged by banks on other types of loans and **credit** as well as the interest paid on investments such as certificates of deposit. While rates on loans tend to rise quickly in response to increases in the prime rate, they are generally much slower to respond to decreases in the prime rate.

The Federal Reserve Board can influence the prime rate through its monetary policy. In general the Fed increases its discount rate in times of economic growth in order to slow the economy's growth and reduce inflationary pressures. In slow economic times, the discount rate is likely to go down. As was noted, banks tend to raise or lower their prime rates in response to the announced monetary policies of the Federal Reserve Board.

Since 1965 the prime rate has reached a low of approximately 5 percent in 1965 and a high of more than 22 percent in 1980. Depending on economic conditions the prime rate may be relatively stable, or it may change frequently. In 1965, for example, the prime rate changed once, while in 1980 it changed 37 times as it fluctuated from just under 12 percent to just over 22 percent. Between March 1989 and March 1994, the prime rate charged by banks declined steadily to a low of 6 percent before it began to rise again. It reached 8.5 percent in March 1997 and stayed there until October 1998, when it was lowered to 8.25 percent in response to the Federal Reserve Board lowering its discount rate to 5.25 percent.

[David P. Bianco]

FURTHER READING:

Doherty, Jacqueline. "Ready for Prime Time?" *Barron's,* 28 September 1998, 19.

Dugas, Christine. "Rate Flux Has Far-Reaching Potential." *USA Today,* 26 March 1997, B10.

Murray, Matt. "Prime Rate Cut by 0.25 Percentage Point." *Wall Street Journal,* 1 October 1998, A3.

Selz, Michael. "Financing Small Business: Gap with Prime Rate Grows on Smallest Business Loans." *Wall Street Journal,* 11 February 1997, B2.

PRISONER'S DILEMMA

The prisoner's dilemma is only one of many illustrative examples of the logical reasoning and complex decisions involved in **game theory**. The prisoner's dilemma takes the form of a situation or game where two people must separately make decisions that will have consequences not only for their own self, but also for each other. When stuck in the situation or when playing the game, people confront a dilemma concerning their decisions, because when motivated solely by self-interest, they face more severe consequences than when motivated by group interests, as illustrated below. In order to make the best choice, each player would have to know what the other will do, but the structure of prisoner's dilemma prohibits players from having such knowledge, unless the situation or game is repeated. The prisoner's dilemma also is generally characterized by its lack of a single optimal strategy and the reliance of both parties on each other to achieve more favorable results.

When understood properly, this dilemma can multiply into hundreds of other more complex dilemmas. The mechanisms that drive the prisoner's dilemma are the same as those that are faced by marketers, military strategists, poker players, and many other types of competitors. The simple models used in the prisoner's dilemma afford insights on how competitors will react to different styles of play, and these will reveal suggestions on how those competitors can be expected to act in the future. A plethora of disciplines have studied the game, including **artificial intelligence**, biology, business, mathematics, philosophy, sociology, and political science.

Based on the game-theory research of Merrill Flood and Melvin Dresher for the Rand Corporation in 1950, Albert Tucker presented their findings in the form of the prisoner's dilemma scenario or game, using it to illustrate the failure of lowest-risk strategies and the potential for conflict between individual and collective rationality. Tucker suggested a model in which two players must choose an individually rational strategy, given that each player's strategy may affect the other player.

In the example, two suspects are apprehended by police for robbing a store. Prosecutors cannot prove either actually committed the robbery, but have enough evidence to convict both on a lesser charge of possession of stolen property.

Both suspects are isolated with no means of communication and offered an opportunity to plea bargain. Each is asked to confess and testify against the other. If both prisoners refuse to confess, they will be convicted of the lesser charge based on circumstantial evidence and will serve one year in jail. If both confess and implicate each other, they will be convicted of robbery and sentenced to two years in jail.

If, however, prisoner A refuses to confess while prisoner B confesses and agrees to testify against A, prisoner B will be set free. Meanwhile, prisoner A may be convicted on the basis of prisoner B's testimony and be sentenced to six years in jail. The reverse applies if prisoner A confesses and prisoner B remains silent.

The choices available to the prisoners, and the consequences for those choices, may be represented in the matrix shown in Figure 1 (numbers are years sentenced to jail).

Figure 1

	Prisoner A	
	Confess	Stay Silent
Prisoner B		
Confess	A: 2 B: 2	A: 6 B: 0
Stay Silent	A: 0 B: 6	A: 1 B: 1

If the prisoners hope to avoid spending six years in jail, and are willing to risk serving two years to guarantee this, they will be motivated to confess. A confession for either will ensure serving no more than two years, regardless of what the other does.

This strategy of confession is called a dominating strategy because it yields a better outcome for the prisoner—in this case, avoiding a six-year jail term—regardless of what the other prisoner does. It is also known as the ''sure-thing'' principle, because the prisoners who confess know for certain that they will not serve more than two years.

But where the dominating strategy of confession is individually rational, an even more optimal outcome may be gained from a strategy that is collectively rational. For example, if prisoners A and B can be assured that neither will confess, and both are willing to serve a year in prison as a result of this decision, they will be motivated not to confess.

This strategy, which yields the prisoners the lowest total number of years in jail, two, is called a cooperative strategy. The matrix in Figure 2 illustrates collectively optimal choices. It repeats the choices presented earlier, but shows the total number of years that will be served by both in each instance.

Figure 2

	Prisoner A: Confess	Prisoner A: Stay Silent
Prisoner B		
Confess	4	6
Stay Silent	6	2

Obviously, if the two prisoners are very loyal and refuse to implicate the other, they will both opt to remain silent and minimize the number of years they both must serve. In order to achieve this outcome, the two prisoners must have an agreement that is reasonably enforceable and effective or sufficient confidence in each other.

If the agreement is not effective, the prisoners may be motivated to adopt the dominating strategy because they can improve their situation by relying on it. One prisoner may be allowed to go free, while the other partner spends the next six years behind bars, or they both may spend one year in prison.

Indeed, one of the prisoners may be motivated to construct an agreement not to confess, specifically to cheat his or her partner and ensure his or her own freedom. This scenario demonstrates how uncooperative play can subvert cooperative strategies, and why knowledge is absolutely essential to making an individually optimal decision.

The prisoner's dilemma provides even more insights when examined in a series of cases where the dynamics change. For example, assume that prisoners A and B are arrested and A stays silent while prisoner B confesses, after both had agreed not to confess if caught. Prisoner B goes free while prisoner A marks the next six years in jail. Clearly, prisoner A has misjudged prisoner B.

Meanwhile, prisoner B returns to a life of crime and is picked up under identical circumstances with another partner, prisoner C. Prisoner C is aware of what B did to A last time, and has no intention of remaining silent, because C knows B cannot be trusted and C does not want to join prisoner A for six years.

Prisoner C possesses something A did not: superior knowledge about how prisoner B might act. Prisoner B knows prisoner C has this information, and like C will be motivated to confess. Hence, both are sentenced to two years in this scenario.

The fact that the game is repeated, or iterated, affords the players indications of each other's style of play based on past performance. By allowing opportunities for retribution, iterated play provides indications of how players will interact and how they will react to the consequences of uncooperative strategies.

For example, prisoner B would be well advised to retire from crime or to take considerable pains not to get caught, because B's past actions are likely to doom the chances that another partner who knows prisoner B's history will ever cooperate with prisoner B.

Iterated play against a programmed player—one whose decisions are predictable—will indicate how a player will react to opportunities to exploit the other. Assume that a player named Bob merely repeats the moves of another named Ray. Ray knows that whatever he does, Bob will do on the next move. Therefore, if Ray takes advantage of Bob on one move, Bob will reciprocate on the next move. This destructive cycle will continue until both can be convinced that they would benefit more from a cooperative style of play.

For example, if Bob and Ray are prisoners A and B, they might realize that repeatedly confessing against each other in a series of crimes is causing more damage than if they were to cooperate. This is illustrated in the tables, where both get two years if they confess, but only one if they cooperate and stay silent.

Examples of iterated play show that, as long as the benefits of cooperation outweigh the benefits of antagonism, players will eventually adopt a cooperative style of play. Both players will decide to cooperate because, over a series of repeated games, collective rationality becomes analogous to individual rationality.

Computer simulations of the prisoner's dilemma game have resulted in the discovery of what could be the optimal strategy for the game: the "tit for tat" approach. This strategy calls for playing cooperatively at first. But when the other player plays selfishly, it recommends reciprocating the opponent's moves. This research demonstrated that the tit for tat approach produces better results than the competing "golden rule" strategy, which stipulates that players make their decisions based on what they would like other players to choose.

APPLICATIONS OF THE PRISONER'S DILEMMA

The prisoner's dilemma may be extended to competitive market situations. Assume for instance that there are only two grocers in a given market, grocer Bill and grocer Mary. Bill decides to attack Mary by undercutting her prices. Mary reciprocates by matching the price cuts. Both forsake profits, and even incur losses, hoping to force the other into submission.

Finally, Bill gives up and raises his prices. Mary who can no longer afford underpricing Bill, raises her prices as well. Now neither is at a disadvantage. They have reached a cooperative agreement after learning that the consequences of antagonism are mutually deleterious.

As this example shows, business **competition** often involves the tit for tat strategy. Businesses begin by "playing" cooperatively and setting their prices with reasonable **profit margins**. After that, they match their competitors' last move. Hence, they offer discounts if their competitors offer discounts and added value if their competitors offer added value. Unlike the example, however, businesses hope that their competitors will realize they cannot "win" unless they cooperate before they begin to suffer losses. Consequently, the prisoner's dilemma suggests that business may profit more from being less competitive (in terms of price at least) and less from being more competitive.

A real-world example of the extended prisoner's dilemma exists in the fishing industry, where the rate of catches by fishers has increased faster than the ability of the fish to reproduce. The result is a depleted supply that has caused every fisher greater hardship.

The individually optimal strategy for fishers is to cooperate with each other by restraining the volume of their catches. Fishers forgo higher profits in the near term, but are assured of protecting their livelihood in the long term.

These examples directly contradict the accepted principle in economics that the individual pursuit of self-interest in a freely competitive market yields an optimal aggregated equilibrium. They demonstrate the application of diminishing returns to a finite resource.

The claim that cooperative strategies will prevail over uncooperative ones in iterated games gained support from a most unusual source: theoretical biology. Scientists concerned with evolutionary dynamics postulated that species that fight to the death work their way toward extinction.

It seems elementary that an animal determined to kill others of its kind would eventually cease to exist. Although contests within species are common, particularly in the selection of a mate, they often do not result in the death of one of the opponents. These contests reward the winner with a mate and reward the loser with survival for accepting defeat and walking away.

Assuming that the male and female of a species are produced randomly in equal numbers, repeated situations in which two males fight to the death for a single mate will yield a population in which females will outnumber males. If these deaths limit the reproduction of the species because of a lack of males, the population growth of this species will be retarded.

If two males under the same conditions fight only for supremacy, rather than to the death, the loser may prevail in another contest with another yet weaker opponent, and still be allowed to reproduce. Thus, nonlethal combat may be viewed as cooperative in the collective sense.

The prisoner's dilemma becomes relevant in evolutionary biology when one constructs a matrix to analyze the outcomes of contests between animals that are killers and those that are nonkillers (see Figure 3).

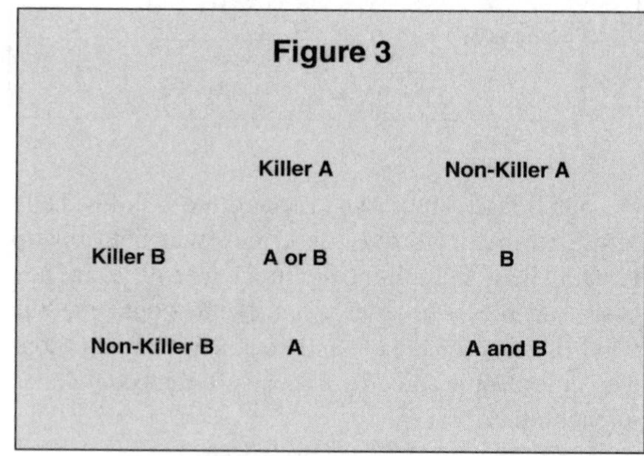
Figure 3

	Killer A	Non-Killer A
Killer B	A or B	B
Non-Killer B	A	A and B

A single killer will prevail in three of the four contests, while two nonkillers will survive in one of the four. In iterated play, the killers will eventually destroy all the nonkillers. In a population left only with killers, successive contests between killers will yield fewer and fewer killers until the species cannot sustain itself.

Meanwhile, populations in which there are no killers will suffer no decrease in the male population due to lethal contests. A roughly equal distribution of males and females will remain, and the animals will pair off and reproduce the species. This example once again proves that cooperative strategies are dominant in iterated play.

One instance where uncooperative play may benefit a player is in the case where the highest penalty is removal from the game. For example, if the two prisoners are implicated in a murder, but prosecutors can't determine who was the hit man, they may offer a plea bargain (see Figure 4).

Figure 4

	Prisoner A: Confess	Prisoner A: Stay Silent
Prisoner B		
Confess	A: 25 B: 25	A: Executed B: 12
Stay Silent	A: 12 B: Executed	A: 8 B: 8

If both confess, each gets 25 years. If they refuse to cooperate, they each get eight years. But, if prisoner A testifies that B actually did the murder, and B remains silent, prisoner B will be executed. While extreme, such a model by its nature precludes iteration because prisoner B will be dead.

Another case where uncooperative strategies may prove dominant is where the penalties to each player are insufficient to provide cooperative motivations. Consider the following example in Figure 5.

Figure 5

	Prisoner A: Confess	Prisoner A: Stay Silent
Prisoner B		
Confess	A: 2 B: 2	A: 3 B: 2
Stay Silent	A: 2 B: 3	A: 2 B: 2

Here, prisoners A and B are indifferent about confessing or staying silent because in either case they would get two years. But each is aware that if he remains silent while the other agrees to implicate him, he might face a third year in jail. Thus, in order to avoid the heavier penalty, both will adopt an uncooperative defensive strategy and confess.

The prisoner's dilemma may be extended to contests between more than two players. Assume for example that three prisoners, rather than two, are apprehended for robbery. Each prisoner must now weigh the possible outcomes of cooperation and antagonism with two counterparts. This scenario may be represented in a three-dimensional matrix with eight, rather than four possible outcomes.

If there was a fourth partner, the matrix would require a fourth dimension, or array, with 16 possible outcomes. The number of outcomes in a multiple-player dilemma may be expressed as a formula: $(C)^n$, where C is the number of choices available to each player and n represents the number of players.

Tests with multiple-prisoner dilemmas support the position that cooperative strategies remain individually optimal, particularly in iterated play.

[John Simley, updated by Karl Heil]

FURTHER READING:

Felkins, Leon. "The Prisoner's Dilemma." 5 September 1995. Available from www.magnolia.net/~leonf/sd/pd-brf.html.

Johnson, Robert R., and Bernard Siskin. *Elementary Statistics for Business.* PWS Pub. Co., 1985.

Maynard Smith, John. *Evolution and the Theory of Games.* Cambridge: Cambridge University Press, 1982.

Poundstone, William. *Prisoner's Dilemma: John Von Neumann, Game Theory, and the Puzzle of the Bomb.* New York: Anchor, 1993.

Rapoport, Anatol, and Albert M. Chammah. *Prisoner's Dilemma: A Study in Conflict and Cooperation.* Ann Arbor, MI: University of Michigan Press, 1965.

Spector, Jerry. "Strategic Marketing and the Prisoner's Dilemma." *Direct Marketing,* February 1997, 44.

PRIVATELY HELD COMPANY

A company may be publicly owned or privately owned. In the case of a privately owned, or closely held, company, all of the **stock** is concentrated in the hands of a few individuals. When the privately held company first issues its stock, it is not offered for sale to the general public. On the other hand, the stock of a **publicly held company** is offered to the general public for sale. A privately held company may decide to "go public." That is, it may make a stock offering to the general public in order to raise capital. The first public stock offering of a company is known as its initial **public offering** (IPO).

In order for a company to be privately held, it must be organized as a corporation. A corporation is a legal form of business that is established by a corporate charter granted by a particular state. The corporate charter establishes the corporation as a separate legal entity from its owners. The corporation is said to be a ''legal person'' and may enter into agreements, make **contracts**, and sue or be sued.

The owners of a corporation, whether public or private, are its common stockholders. There are two types of stock, common and preferred. Preferred stockholders generally receive a stated **dividend** of a specific amount. Common stockholders receive a dividend based on **corporate profits**, although in some cases **common stock** pays no dividend. The corporation's charter specifies how many shares and what types of stock it is allowed to issue. While both preferred stockholders and common stockholders are investors in the corporation and provide it with capital, it is the common stockholders who actually own the firm.

In a privately held corporation, the owners and managers may be the same individuals. In the case of a small grocery store organized as a corporation, for example, it would not be uncommon for the owners of the store to also run it. The president of a small manufacturing firm that is privately held may be the sole stockholder or hold a majority of the stock.

The corporate form of business organization allows a distinction to be made between a corporation's owners and its managers. In a large, privately held corporation, the shareholders who own the firm are likely to be different from the managers, executives, and directors who run the firm. In that case, the company's **board of directors** would be responsible for running the corporation to maximize profits for the shareholders. The directors may themselves be the sole shareholders. In practice the corporate directors establish corporate policy, make major decisions, and hire managers and others to oversee the daily operations of the corporation. Shareholders can express their satisfaction or displeasure with the board of directors of a corporation by voting them in or out of office.

Whether publicly held or privately held, corporations provide their owners with a degree of limited liability. The shareholders of a publicly held corporation may lose their investment in a company, but they have no personal liability beyond that. The same is also true for privately held corporations. If an owner of a privately held corporation, however, is also actively engaged in managing and directing the operations of the company, then he or she may be held personally liable in a lawsuit against the firm. The concept of limited liability still applies to some extent in that situation, so that in the case of multiple owners or shareholders, one shareholder is not personally liable for the wrongdoings of another shareholder. A parallel situation exists for publicly held companies, where a company's directors may be held personally liable for specific cases of wrongdoing.

Unlike publicly held companies, privately held companies are not required to make public their profits and other financial results. Of course, they are also not able to raise capital by selling shares of stock to the general public. Successful and relatively young privately held companies often attempt to facilitate their growth by becoming publicly held companies and making an IPO. It must be remembered, however, that not all privately held corporations are small; there are some very large corporations that remain privately held, such as Levi Strauss & Co. and Hallmark Cards, Inc.

SEE ALSO: Closely Held Corporations; Going Public; Preferred Stock

[David P. Bianco]

FURTHER READING:

Anderson, Hershal, et al. *Financial Accounting and Reporting.* 4th ed. Medford, NJ: Malibu Publishing, 1995.

Mann, Richard A. *Business Law and the Regulation of Business.* 6th ed. Cincinnati: SouthWestern Publishing, 1998.

Spiro, Herbert T. *Finance for the Nonfinancial Manager.* 4th ed. New York: John Wiley & Sons, Inc., 1996.

PRIVATELY PLACED SECURITIES

Privately placed securities are those that are sold directly to **institutional investors** instead of being offered for sale to the general public. Privately placed securities are usually bond issues, including corporate **bonds**; they also include other **debt** instruments as well as equity **securities**. Privately placed securities are issued primarily by smaller companies, although even Fortune 500 companies occasionally make use of the private placement market. The major purchasers of privately placed securities are life insurance companies, with other institutional investors such as **mutual funds**, **pension funds**, **banks**, **savings and loan associations**, and limited **partnerships** also participating in buying private placements.

Certain securities offerings, including privately placed securities, are exempt from the registration requirements of the **Securities and Exchange Commission** (SEC). These include securities that are purchased for investment rather than for distribution. Exempt securities must be offered through direct communication with the purchaser without general **advertising**. Such investors are assumed to have access to significant financial information concerning the issuer and the issue and thus do not require the guarantee of full disclosure afforded by SEC registration. Accordingly, exemption from SEC registration applies to the sale of securities involving a limited number of financially sophisticated purchasers.

While companies may not need to register their private placements with the SEC, they must comply with the SEC's Regulation D, which governs the private placement of securities. Instead of registering a prospectus with the SEC, companies prepare a private placement memorandum (PPM) for prospective investors. The PPM typically includes a description of the business, with a scenario covering anticipated **business conditions** and financial projections.

Privately placed securities are generally considered less liquid than comparable public issues. That is, it is easier for a purchaser to resell publicly issued securities than privately placed securities. This is due to the conditions under which private placements are issued as well as the restrictions that exist on resales. As a result of this liquidity risk, privately placed securities generally pay higher rates of interest than comparable public issues.

In 1990 bonds represented 87 percent of all privately placed securities, with equity securities accounting for the remaining 13 percent. Approximately $87 billion of privately placed bonds were issued in 1990, representing 29 percent of the $299 billion of new bonds issued in the United States that year. The $87 billion in privately placed bonds represented a decline from the high of $128 billion issued in 1988. One factor accounting for the decline was the desire of life insurance companies, the primary purchaser of private placements, to find more liquid investments to better cope with changing financial conditions.

Private placements proved to be very popular in the 1990s, as low yields in the public market sent investors to private placements. According to Securities Data Co., the market volume of private placements rose to $201 billion in 1996, a 50 percent increase over 1995. During 1995 44 percent of all private placements were led by **investment banks**, with commercial banks leading in 33 percent of the transactions.

Private placement offers several advantages to both borrowers (issuers) and lenders (purchasers). Since private placement is based on direct negotiations, it is possible to tailor the **loan** terms to fit the needs of both parties. Direct negotiation also makes it easier to structure complex offerings that would not be easily understood by the public. For lesser-known firms and smaller companies, private placements may represent their only source of long-term capital. For larger firms, private placements offer less expensive borrowing than with registered **public offerings**. Private placement also provides the issuer with some confidentiality regarding its financial records. In the case of public offerings and SEC registration, sensitive financial data must be disclosed.

Restrictive covenants are commonly used in private placements to protect the lender and ensure that the borrower conducts its business in a manner that will protect the value of the privately placed securities. While covenants are also written into loan agreements affecting public issues, they are generally more detailed in private placements. Among the areas covered by covenants are provisions for collateral to the security, delivery of financial data to the lender, and restrictions regarding the amount of additional long-term debt the borrower may take on. In addition the loan agreement may contain provisions limiting the issuer's ability to call in the security during times of falling **interest rates** and other restrictions designed to protect the purchaser's investment.

[David P. Bianco]

FURTHER READING:

Ben-Amos, Omri. "Clamor for Private Placements Limits Some Investors." *American Banker,* 2 December 1996, 28.

Evanson, David R. "Balancing Act." *Entrepreneur,* February 1996, 52-54.

"Finding the Best Advisers: Private Placements." *Inc.,* November 1994, 136.

Hirt, Geoffrey A. and Stanley B. Block. *Fundamentals of Investment Management.* 6th ed. Homewood, IL: Richard D. Irwin, 1998.

Keller, Stanley. "Current Issues in Private Placements." *Annual Institute on Securities Regulation,* spring 1995, 151-86.

Perlmuth, Lyn. "Scavenger Hunt." *Institutional Investor,* May 1997, 33.

Picker, Ida. "Private Placements' Growing Global Public." *Institutional Investor,* October 1992, 147-50.

Toal, Brian A. "The Bridges to Private Capital." *Oil and Gas Investor,* April 1998, 34-45.

PRIVATIZATION

The term "privatization" describes a shift in the ownership of assets or the provision of services from the government or public sector to the private sector. The scope of privatization, however, varies greatly in different parts of the world. In the former Soviet bloc countries of Eastern Europe, privatization means changing the ownership and control of all major industries and utilities from the national government to the private sector. These industries can range from telephone companies to automobile manufacturers. In western Europe—and especially in the United Kingdom—industries deemed vital to the welfare of the citizenry, such as coal, are returning to private sector ownership. In the United States, where there has been comparatively little government control or ownership of the means of production, privatization has had its greatest impact on traditional local or state services, such as trash collection and prisoner incarceration. As the privatization trend gains momentum in the United States, however, many services traditionally provided by the federal government, such as Social Security, are increasingly being considered for privatization.

On a scale grander than, for instance, municipal trash collection, privatization is viewed by its proponents as a rediscovery of the free enterprise philosophies of Scottish economist Adam Smith (1723-1790), and a repudiation of German political philosopher Karl Marx (1818-1883) and English economist John Maynard Keynes (1883-1946). Under Marxism the state dominated all areas of economic activity; Keynesian economics called for state intervention in market economies so as to manipulate **business cycles**, especially **recessions**. Smith, on the other hand, is identified with what came to be known as **laissez-faire** economics—''laissez-faire'' being a French phrase meaning ''allow to do.'' Tibor Machan (1939-), a philosophy professor at Auburn University, viewed the privatization movement as springing from a long held vision of Western liberalism. ''This vision conceived individuals and their voluntary institutions—churches, corporations, professional associations, labor unions, and the like—as the source of the values of civilization,'' he wrote. ''The State is a supporting mechanism, as referees are to sporting events. The work of living and developing life's values are tasks for free human beings. The State serves them when conflicts arise.'' Privatization detractors, however, claim there are downsides to privatization such as accountability, employee dislocation, and a compromised response to the needs of the citizenry. Privatization, especially in the United States, has come to encompass a variety of economic and political changes including the transfer of assets, services, and responsibilities from the state to the private sector; a lessening in the regulatory powers of government; and an increase in the individual's responsibility in meeting his or her own needs. Regardless of definition, privatization is driven by both specific public policy decisions and general socioeconomic trends.

FORMS OF PRIVATIZATION

CONTRACTING OUT. Privatization, especially as implemented in the United States by local governing bodies, generally takes one of four forms. The first and probably the most prevalent is ''contracting out,'' which can be described as public sector choice and public sector financing, with private sector production of the selected service. Under contracting out, the citizenry makes elected officials aware of a collective need such as trash pickup. The government then generally chooses via competitive bidding a private contractor to provide the service. The government is also responsible for financing these respective services—generally through its taxing powers. Hence, the government finances the service while the private sector provides it. The government determines the service level and pays the amount specified in the **contract**, but leaves production decisions to the private contractor. Although the service is ultimately paid for by the taxpayer, the government makes the actual payment to the provider. This scenario usually happens when a municipal or state government for various reasons seeks to contract out, to the private sector, a service it has traditionally provided. The government workers who had previously performed the job often undergo ''employee dislocation''—a polite term for **layoffs**, transfers to less desirable positions, etc.

Foremost amongst critics of contracting out are the state and city employee unions, which must contend with shrinking membership rolls, a lessening of dues, and angry, dislocated members. For instance, one of the traditional government services being increasingly contracted out is the incarceration of criminals in prisons owned and operated by private corporations such as Corrections Corporation of America (CCA). So prevalent has this practice become that in 1998 CCA began building a 2,304-bed prison in California without a firm commitment from the state to use the facility. The prison was built in anticipation of a future California need for more correctional facilities. CCA staffs its prisons not with state correctional employees but with CCA employees. As to be expected the California Correctional Peace Officers Association, the **labor union** representing California prison guards, is fighting any attempt by CCA to house state prisoners. According to an article in the *Wall Street Journal,* ''The powerful and politically savvy California prison-guards union is dead set against expanding the use of private-sector prisons much beyond the state's current contracts for about 5,000 beds.'' Union president Don Novey vowed to ''fight like hell'' any CCA attempt to house state prisoners. ''They can do anything they want with the feds,'' he added. The unions may be bucking a trend difficult to reverse. CCA, which was founded in 1983 and went public in 1986, was operating 77 prison facilities nationwide by 1998. The federal government also makes use of private for-profit prisons, housing 1 of every 20 federal prisoners in such facilities.

Surprisingly, services may be contracted out to other government agencies if the price is right. According to the *Wall Street Journal,* in 1998 the Federal Aviation Administration sought bids for contracting out the operation of its payroll **computers**. The lowest bidder, beating out IBM and two other private companies, was the U.S. Department of Agriculture.

Contracting out for services is the most popular form of privatization for state and local governments. The number of state and local governments contracting out with private firms to provide final services to consumers and intermediate services to the government has increased substantially in the past decade. The *Wall Street Journal* reported on a 1998 survey that found 73 percent of local governments using private janitorial services and 54 percent using private trash collectors, up from 52 and 30 percent, respectively, a decade earlier. In most cases contracting out has resulted in the same level of service but at a substantially lower cost—generally in the range of 10 to 30 percent lower.

FRANCHISING. Franchising is another form of privatization according to E. C. Pasour Jr., a professor at North Carolina State University. Franchising is a monopoly privilege awarded to a private firm that provides the service but with the price of the service being regulated and determined by the state. Most utilities, such as gas, electricity, and telephone service, are provided under the franchise form of privatization. A relatively recent service, cable TV, is also generally awarded as a monopoly privilege. Another important distinction of monopoly franchising is that the consumer makes direct payments to the provider for the service.

USER FEES. A variation on franchising and contracting out is user fees. Under this system of privatization, the consumer pays a set fee to cover all or part of the service **costs**. A municipality may, for instance, charge a set fee per household for trash collection rather than pay for that service out of a general **tax** pool.

LOAD-SHEDDING. The last form of privatization is ''load-shedding,'' whereby the government steps aside entirely. The consumer is responsible for deciding whether or not to make use of the service, the selection of the provider, and all payments for the service. Load-shedding is most often associated with trash collection. An extreme example of load-shedding, however, is the privately owned section of Route 91 in California. Tolls for traveling this stretch of road range from 60 cents at night to $3.20 during peak rush hours. There are of course alternate routes maintained by state and local road commissions for drivers wishing to avoid the toll.

ARGUMENTS FOR PRIVATIZATION

Proponents of privatization argue that government providers have no real incentive to hold down costs or to provide quality service. Private firms, on the other hand, are motivated by a profit motive that depends on holding costs down. The lower the cost incurred by the firm in satisfying the contract, the greater the realized profit. Private providers are also motivated by **competition** from other potential service providers. Competition between potential private suppliers to win a contract generally results in the lowest cost to the government and the taxpayer for the specified level of service. ''Competitive markets are rooted in private property, and there is no way to stimulate competitive conditions under conditions of government financing or government production,'' Pasour wrote.

Political ideology aside, traditional government services are generally privatized in hopes of saving money. While there is no large body of empirical evidence supporting or refuting the idea that privatization saves money, the literature is replete with anecdotal evidence that it does in fact save tax dollars. Some of this savings is due to the generally lower wages and fringe benefits paid by private firms but much of it comes from increased productivity. Lower labor costs resulting from privatization can arise from either lower wages or less labor input. The first reason would indicate that the government, prior to privatization, was paying wages higher than necessary for a given skill, while the second reason would indicate that the government was hiring more workers then necessary to complete the given tasks. Government agencies are normally less productive per paid labor hour than private firms. Private firms also generally have more flexibility than governmental agencies to use part-timers to meet peak loads, to fire unsatisfactory workers, and to allocate workers across a variety of tasks. Moreover, in contrast to its private sector counterparts, governments tend not to reward individual initiative or punish aberrant behavior, contributing to lower productivity. In other words, government is not motivated by profit and loss. According to Pasour, ''Government agencies are generally not profit-seeking enterprises, and profit and loss considerations have relatively little effect on (their) production and marketing decisions. That is, bureaucrats and politicians do not face incentives that foster good performance.''

Private firms may also be more innovative, using different approaches to providing a service. Government, by contrast, tends to stick with known approaches since changes often create problems, especially with an entrenched bureaucracy or a strident municipal union. Private firms may also use earnings to finance research or to purchase capital equipment relating directly to the service, while governments may not be able or willing to allocate revenue in the same manner given the many competing demands for tax dollars.

Another contributing factor to this cost disparity is the general overall efficiency of the private sector. The private sector has a strong incentive to operate efficiently. Private firms spending more money and employing more people to do the same amount of work will have lower **profit margins** and decreased profits. In the long run they will no longer be able to compete in a market economy. The disciplining effect of competition, however, does not affect the public sector. Government agencies generally operate in a noncompetitive environment and therefore can charge more for their services and be less concerned with consumer satisfaction. Government services that are provided in a noncompetitive market also deny the consumer comparability. The consumer or taxpayer has no real way of evaluating the price of a government service. This tends to make government less responsive to consumer needs. The private sector generally offers the consumer a higher quality of service while keeping costs under control.

OPPOSITION TO PRIVATIZATION

Ultimately privatization is a political process. As such any move toward privatization, no matter the economic benefits, will have political repercussions especially if privatization causes worker displacement. The burden of privatization falls most heavily on the public **workforce**. Because their jobs and **income** are at risk, public employees and their unions strongly oppose privatization. A 1992 survey of the 24 largest American cities showed that the greatest political opposition to privatization came from public employees and the unions representing them. Although it is not unusual for privatization to result in layoffs of public sector employees, seldom do the layoffs reach the level that workers and their unions predict. When layoffs are inevitable governments can often employ a number of strategies to lessen the burden on public employees while making the privatization process more palatable. Governments may assign displaced workers to other government jobs and positions or they may encourage or require contractors to hire laid-off workers or offer them first consideration when jobs open up. Governments may also offer early retirement incentives to workers facing a layoff.

Another tactic is to allow the affected employee union to bid on jobs—that is, compete head-to-head with the private sector. A similar tactic is employee ownership whereby the displaced workers are offered an ownership interest in a private company or offered financial assistance in forming their own company. The latter strategy proved to be popular in the United Kingdom but less so in the United States.

In spite of privatization's accelerated growth at the local level in the United States, there have been many backlashes and not just from employee unions. Consumer and institutional dissatisfaction with privatization most often occurs when the service directly affects people's welfare as opposed to such services as trash pickup. Charges of brutality and mistreatment of prisoners in for-profit prisons are not uncommon. Likewise, consumers complain about the higher and higher prices associated with various managed health care plans and for-profit hospitals. Also under attack is the privatization of a wide variety of government services designed to help the country's poorer citizens. In 1997 the administration of President Bill Clinton stopped Texas from turning over to Lockheed-Martin the procedure for deciding which applicants are eligible for Medicaid, food stamps, and welfare. In 1998 Florida sought, amid much controversy, federal approval to privatize, on an experimental basis, the management of welfare and Medicaid in five counties. Social worker and child-welfare advocate Sky Westerflund, head of the Kansas chapter of the National Association of Social Workers, worried that private companies overseeing welfare would be more concerned with the well-being of their bottom line than the well-being of children. ''Every single decision is based on that capitated rate,'' Westerflund told the *Wall Street Journal.* ''Their question is: Can we afford this.''

A 1998 *Wall Street Journal* article posed the question, ''Is making a profit by serving the poor a terrible notion that smacks of a Dickens novel, or is it a welcome move towards efficiency?'' Representative Barney Frank of Massachusetts answered in part. ''Private citizens should not have life-or-death power over other private citizens when you're talking about basic necessities. The financial motive should not be at work when we're talking about benefits.'' Joseph Stiglitz, a former economic adviser to President Clinton, disagreed. ''Wal-Mart makes profits off poor people, but it makes them better off. It's providing high quality and low price,'' he countered. Stiglitz went on to argue that it makes little difference if social services are provided by for-profit companies or non-profit government agencies. ''Rather, the key is whether the ultimate consumers can choose between competing providers. It is competition, not private ownership, that makes the market work well.''

U.S. GOVERNMENT PRIVATIZATION

While much privatization in the United States has taken place at the state and local level, the federal government is also turning over some of its operations to the private sector. In mid-summer 1998 the U.S. government finalized the $2.4 billion privatization of the U.S. Enrichment Corporation (USEC). USEC was a government-run corporation responsible for U.S. uranium enrichment operations. The U.S. Department of the Treasury received $1.9 billion from the public sale of 100 million USEC shares and $500 million in cash, which was borrowed by USEC from various **banks**. USEC controls 75 percent of the North American uranium enrichment market and 40 percent of the world market. USEC will also broker the purchase of Russian uranium for the federal government. The move to privatize the government's uranium enrichment operations was started by President Richard M. Nixon in 1969. In 1993 Congress passed legislation creating USEC as an independent government-owned corporation. President Clinton approved plans for privatization in 1997.

The federal government has also privatized the 750 former employees of its Office of Personnel Management (OPM) responsible for doing background checks on potential government employees. The former federal workers are now shareholders in and employees of US Investigation Services Inc. (USIS). USIS now does background checks for the federal government but is free to contract for the same type of work on the open market. USIS now counts as its customers state and local governments, casinos, and airlines. When James King took over OPM in 1993 he found the investigation unit overstaffed and underworked. OPM was required to charge other federal agencies for investigative work done on their behalf on a break-even basis. But because of federal downsizing, the number of new federal employees was declining and OPM's investigation unit was losing about $1.5 million a month. In 1994 King laid off 400 workers and began turning the unit into a private employee-owned company. In 1996 the new company took over with an exclusive contract protecting itself from competition for three years. Employees now own 90 of USIS while **management**, which was recruited from the outside, owns the rest. OPM estimates that in the first 15 months of operation USIS has saved taxpayers nearly $20 million.

One of the most hotly debated privatization issues in the United States in the 1990s revolved around Social Security. Begun in 1935 with passage of the Social Security Act, coverage of U.S. citizens had become nearly universal by 1956. In 1983 legislation was passed assuring the financial health of the Social Security system well into the 21st century. But because a large number of baby boomers will be retiring in the first decade of the new century, some analysts predicted a severe depletion of social security funds by 2030. Emboldened by spectacular gains in equity markets in the 1980s and 1990s, proponents of privatization argued that everyone would be better served if workers had more freedom in determining where their payroll taxes go. The *Wall Street Journal* divided Social Security privatizers into two groups: part-way privatizers and hard-core privatizers. The former would prefer payroll taxes going into **individual retirement accounts** and Social Security accounts. The latter would opt for workers being allowed to put most if not all of their Social Security contributions into individually chosen accounts similar to **mutual funds**. As of 1999, all Social Security taxes were invested in U.S. Treasury **bonds**. President Clinton was in favor of investing 15 percent of the Social Security trust fund in **stocks**, but **Federal Reserve** Chairman Alan Greenspan opposed any such move. Greenspan worried about Social Security taxes being allocated for political rather than economic considerations, as well as wondering what would happen if the bull market of the 1980s and 1990s turned into a bear market in the 21st century. As pointed out in a *Fortune* article, all mutual fund advertisements contain the disclaimer, ''Past performance cannot guarantee future results.''

PRIVATIZATION OUTSIDE THE UNITED STATES

The privatization movement began not in the United States but in the United Kingdom—and it began with a vengeance. During her administration, Margaret Thatcher, prime minister from 1979 to 1990, privatized gas, electricity, telephones, trains, and most other state-owned companies in an effort to overhaul Great Britain's socialized and centralized economy, reversing a trend started by the post-World War II defeat of Winston Churchill by Clement Attlee. Attlee and his Labour Party took over the leadership of Britain's government and ''sought to scale and control the commanding heights of their national economies,'' according to Daniel Yergin and Joseph Stanislaw, authors of *The Commanding Heights: The Battle between Government and the Marketplace that Is Remaking the World.* Attlee's Labourites favored a **mixed economy** marked by strong and direct government involvement in the nation's economy via fiscal management, state-owned and state-run companies, and an expanded welfare state. But by the 1980s the British economy and British productivity had become moribund. The *Guardian,* although an British left-of-center newspaper, nevertheless praised Thatcher's revitalization of her country's economy. ''With her privatizations, she slimmed down a state that had become flabby and overstretched, reconciling Britain forever to the market,'' it said. ''She effected the change brutally, and with great pain, but it was a change we had to make.''

In the former Marxist economies of Eastern Europe, major privatization efforts have taken place following the fall of the Berlin Wall in 1989. Privatization in the West has been gradual and it has left the basic structure of the Western countries intact. In Eastern Europe, however, the social, political, and economic **infrastructure** has been overturned; privatization has been both a part and a cause of this dramatic change. Prior to the fall of the Berlin Wall the socialist state totally dominated each country's economy. The government dictated production, cost, and the distribution of resources, goods, capital, and labor. ''We pretend to work while they pretend to pay us,'' was a common saying. Privatization in Eastern Europe has changed all this while ushering in free enterprise and market determination of economic factors.

SEE ALSO: International Privatization

[Michael Knes]

FURTHER READING:

Eggers, William D., and John O'Leary. ''Overcoming Public Employee Opposition to Privatization.'' In *Private Cures for Public Ills: The Promise of Privatization,* edited by Lawrence W. Reed. Irvington-on-Hudson, NY: Foundation for Economic Education, 1996.

Feigenbaum, Harvey, Jeffrey Henig, and Chris Hamnett. *Shrinking the State: The Political Underpinnings of Privatization.* Cambridge: Cambridge University Press, 1998.

Georges, Christopher. ''Social-Security 'Privatization' Effort Makes Headway.'' *Wall Street Journal,* 22 June 1998.

''Government Finishes Privatization Sale of U.S. Enrichment.'' *Wall Street Journal,* 29 July 1998.

Lipsher, Marc. ''Busting into the Prison Business.'' *Wall Street Journal,* 27 May 1998.

Manikaw, N. Gregory. ''How to Screw up Social Security.'' *Fortune,* 15 March 1999.

Miller, Marjorie. ''Thatcher's Influence Still Felt in Britain.'' *Detroit News,* 14 May 1999.

Pasour, E. C., Jr. ''Privatization: Is It the Answer?'' In *Private Cures for Public Ills: The Promise of Privatization,* edited by Lawrence W. Reed. Irvington-on-Hudson, NY: Foundation for Economic Education, 1996.

Reed, Lawrence W., ed. *Private Cures for Public Ills: The Promise of Privatization.* Irvington-on-Hudson, NY: Foundation for Economic Education, 1996.

Sharpe, Anita. ''Psyched Up: More States Turn Over Mental-Health Care to the Private Sector.'' *Wall Street Journal,* 24 January 1997.

Wessel, David, and John Harwood. ''Selling Entire Stock!: Capitalism Is Giddy with Triumph; Is It Possible to Overdo It?'' *Wall Street Journal,* 14 May 1998.

Yergin, Daniel, and Joseph Stanislaw. *The Commanding Heights: The Battle between Government and the Marketplace that Is Remaking the World.* New York: Simon & Schuster, 1998.

PRO FORMA STATEMENT

Pro forma, a Latin term meaning ''as a matter of form,'' is applied to the process of presenting financial projections for a specific period in a standardized format. Businesses use pro forma statements for **decision making** in planning and control, and for external reporting to owners, investors, and creditors. Pro forma statements can be used as the basis of comparison and analysis to provide **management**, investment analysts, and **credit** officers with a feel for the particular nature of a business's financial structure under various conditions. Both the American Institute of Certified Public Accountants (AICPA) and the **Securities and Exchange Commission** (SEC) require standard formats for businesses in constructing and presenting pro forma statements.

Pro forma statements are an important tool for new business ventures, as well. ''Anyone thinking of going into business should prepare pro forma statements, both income and cash flow, before investing time, money, and energy,'' James O. Gill wrote in his book *Financial Basics of Small Business Success.* As a vital part of the planning process, pro forma statements can help minimize the risks associated with starting and running a new business. They can also help persuade lenders and investors to provide financing for a start-up firm. But Gill emphasized that pro forma statements must be based upon objective and reliable information in order to create an accurate projection of a small business's profits and financial needs for its first year and beyond. To ensure the credibility of underlying information, the entrepreneur must conduct careful research. Gill suggested speaking with owners of similar businesses, lawyers, accountants, customers, suppliers, and federal agencies during the information-gathering stage. After preparing initial pro forma statements and getting the business off the ground, a small business owner should update the projections monthly and annually.

USES OF PRO FORMA STATEMENTS

BUSINESS PLANNING. A company uses pro forma statements in the process of **business planning** and control. Because pro forma statements are presented in a standardized, columnar format, management employs them to compare and contrast alternative business plans. By arranging the data for the operating and **financial statements** side-by-side, management analyzes the projected results of competing plans in order to decide which best serves the interests of the business.

In constructing pro forma statements, a company recognizes the uniqueness and distinct financial characteristics of each proposed plan or project. Pro forma statements allow management to:

1. Identify the assumptions about the financial and operating characteristics that generate the scenarios.
2. Develop the various sales and **budget** (revenue and expense) projections.
3. Assemble the results in profit and loss projections.
4. Translate this data into cash-flow projections.
5. Compare the resulting **balance sheets**.
6. Perform ratio analysis to compare projections against each other and against those of similar companies.
7. Review proposed decisions in **marketing**, production, **research and development**, etc., and assess their impact on profitability and liquidity.

Simulating competing plans can be quite useful in evaluating the financial effects of the different alternatives under consideration. Based on different sets of assumptions, these plans propose various scenarios of sales, production **costs**, profitability, and viability. Pro forma statements for each plan provide important information about future expectations, such as sales and **earnings forecasts**, cash flows; balance sheets, proposed capitalization, and **income statements**.

Management also uses this procedure in choosing among budget alternatives. Planners present sales revenues, production expenses, balance sheet and **cash flow statements** for competing plans with the underlying assumptions explained. Based on an analysis of these figures, management selects an annual budget. After choosing a course of action, it is common for management to examine variations within the plan.

If management considers a flexible budget most appropriate for its company, it would establish a range of possible outcomes generally categorized as normal (expected results), above normal (best case), and below normal (worst case). Management examines contingency plans for the possible outcomes at input/output levels specified within the operating range. Since these three budgets are projections appearing in a standardized, columnar format and for a specified period, they are pro forma.

During the course of the fiscal period, management evaluates its performance by comparing actual results to the expectations of the accepted plan using a similar pro forma format. Management's appraisal tests and retests the assumptions upon which it based its plans. In this way pro forma statements are indispensable to the control process.

FINANCIAL MODELING. Pro forma statements provide data for calculating financial ratios and for performing other mathematical calculations. Financial models built on pro form projections contribute to the achievement of corporate goals if they (1) test the goals of the plans, (2) furnish findings that are readily understandable, and (3) provide time, quality, and cost advantages over other methods.

Financial modeling tests the assumptions and relationships of proposed plans by asking ''What If'' questions regarding the effect on company performance of: changes in the prices of labor, materials, and overhead; an increase or decrease in the cost of goods sold; a change in the cost of borrowing money; an increase or decrease in sales volume; or a change in inventory **valuation**. Computer-assisted modeling has made assumption testing more efficient. The use of powerful processors permits online, real-time decision making through immediate calculations of alternative cash flow statements, balance sheets, and income statements.

ASSESSING THE IMPACT OF CHANGES. A company prepares pro forma financial statements when it expects to experience or has just experienced significant financial changes. The pro forma financial statements present the impact of these changes on the company's financial position as depicted in the income statement, balance sheet, and cash-flow statement. For example, management might prepare pro forma statements to gauge the effects of a potential **merger** or **joint venture**. It also might prepare pro forma statements to evaluate the consequences of **refinancing** debt through issuance of **preferred stock**, **common stock**, or other **debt**.

EXTERNAL REPORTING. Businesses also use pro forma statements in external reports prepared for owners (stockholders), creditors, and potential investors. For companies listed on the stock exchanges, the SEC requires pro forma statements with any filing, registration statements, or proxy statements. The SEC and organizations governing **accounting** practices require companies to prepare pro forma statements when essential changes in the character of a business's financial statements have occurred or will occur. Financial statements may change because of:

1. Changes in accounting principles due to adoption of a generally accepted accounting principle different from one used previously for financial accounting.
2. A change in accounting estimates dealing with the estimated economic life and net residual value of assets.
3. A change in the business entity resulting from the acquisition or disposition of an asset or investment, and/or the pooling of interests of two or more existing businesses.
4. A correction of an error made in a report or filing of a previous period.

Management's decision to change accounting principles may be based on (1) the issuance of a new accounting principle by the **Financial Accounting Standards Board** (FASB), (2) internal considerations taking advantage of revised valuations or tax codes, or (3) the accounting needs of a new business combination. By changing its accounting practices, a business might significantly affect the presentation of its financial position and the results of its operations. The change also might distort the earnings trend reported in the income statements for earlier years. Some examples of changes in accounting principles might include valuation of inventory via a first-in, first-out (FIFO) method or a last-in, first-out method (LIFO), or recording of **depreciation** via a straight-line method or an accelerated method.

When a company changes an accounting method, it uses pro forma financial statements to report the cumulative effect of the change for the period during which the change occurred. To enable comparison of the pro forma financial statements with previous financial statements, the company would present the financial statements for prior periods as originally reported, show the cumulative effect of the change on net **income** and retained earnings, and show net income on a pro forma basis as if the newly adopted accounting principle had been used in prior periods.

A change in accounting estimate may be required as new events occur and as better information becomes available about the probable outcome of future events. For example, an increase in the percentage used to estimate doubtful accounts, a major write-down of inventories, a change in the economic lives of plant assets, and a revision in the estimated liability for outstanding product **warranties** would require pro forma statements.

THE SEC FORMAT

The SEC prescribes the form and content of pro forma statements for companies subject to its jurisdiction in circumstances such as the above. Some of the form and content requirements are:

1. An introductory paragraph describing the proposed transaction, the entities involved, the periods covered by the pro forma information, and what the pro forma information shows.
2. A pro forma condensed balance sheet and a pro forma condensed income statement, in columnar form, showing the condensed historical amounts, the pro forma adjustments, and the pro forma amounts. Footnotes provide justification for the pro forma adjustments and explain other details pertinent to the changes.
3. The pro forma adjustments, directly attributable to the proposed change or transaction, which are expected to have a continuing impact on the financial statements. Explanatory notes provide the factual basis for adjustments.

PRO FORMA STATEMENTS FOR CHANGES IN ENTITY AND FOR BUSINESS COMBINATIONS

The FASB, the AICPA, and the SEC have provided significant directives to the form, content, and necessity of pro forma financial statements in situations where there has been a change in the form of a business entity. Such a change in form may occur due to changes in financial structure resulting from the disposition of a long-term liability or asset, or due to a combination of two or more businesses.

The purpose of pro forma financial statements is to facilitate comparisons of historic data and projections of future performance. In these circumstances users of financial statements need to evaluate a new or proposed business entity on a basis comparable to the predecessor business in order to understand the impact of the change on cash flow, income, and financial position. *Pro forma adjustments* to accounting principles and accounting estimates reformat the statements of the new entity and the acquired business to conform with those of the predecessor.

Occasionally, a **partnership** or sole proprietorship will sell all or part of the business interest. Sometimes it is necessary, especially if the business is ''**going public**,'' to reorganize into a corporation. The financial statements on a corporation with a very short history are not helpful in a thoughtful analysis of future potential. Similarly, because of the differences in federal income tax **liabilities**, a restatement of the predecessor business in historical terms only confuses the picture. Since the financial statements of the predecessor business do not contain some of the expense items applicable to a corporation, the pro forma financial statements make adjustments to restate certain expenses on a corporate basis. In particular these would include:

1. Stating the owners' salaries in terms of officers' salaries.
2. Calculating the applicable federal **taxes** on the predecessor business as though it were a corporation.
3. Including corporate state franchise taxes.
4. For partnerships acquired through the pooling of interests, adding the balance of the partners' capital to contributed capital in the combined company rather than to retained earnings.

S corporations exercise the tax-option of the shareholders to individually assume the tax liability rather than have it assumed by the corporation as a whole. If the shareholders choose to go public or change their qualifications, the corporation loses the tax-option. Therefore, in addition to the pro forma statement showing historical earnings, the new company will make pro forma provision for the taxes that it would have paid had it been a regular corporation in the past. When acquisition of an S corporation is accomplished through the pooling of interests, the pro forma financial statement may not include any of the retained earnings of the S corporation in the pooled retained earnings.

When presenting the historical operations of a business previously operated as a partnership, the accountant would make adjustments to bring the statement in line with the acquiring corporation. Historical data listed would include net sales; cost of sales; gross profit on sales; selling, general, and administrative expenses; other income; other deductions; and income before taxes on income. Pro forma adjustments would restate partnership operations on a corporate basis, including estimated partnership salaries as officers and estimated federal and state taxes on income, as well as pro forma net income and pro forma net income per share. Accountants make similar adjustments to pro forma statements for businesses previously operated as sole proprietorships and S corporations.

ACQUISITION OR DISPOSAL OF PART OF A BUSINESS

For a company that decided to acquire part of a new business or dispose of part of its existing business, a meaningful pro forma statement would adjust the historical figures to demonstrate how the acquired part would have fared had it been a corporation. Pro forma statements would also set forth conventional financial statements of the acquiring company, and pro forma financial statements of the business to be acquired. Notes to the pro forma statements explain the adjustments reflected in the statements.

A pro forma income statement would combine the historical income statement of the acquiring company and a pro forma income statement of the business to be acquired for the previous five years, if possible. Pro forma adjustments would exclude **overhead expenses** not applicable in the new business entity, such as division and head office expenses.

The purchase of a sole proprietorship, partnership, S corporation, or business segment requires pro forma statements for a series of years in order to reflect adjustments for such items as owners' or partners' salaries and income taxes. In this way, each year reflects the results of operations of a business organization comparable with that of the acquiring corporation. The pro forma statements giving effect to the business combination should be limited, however, to the current and immediately preceding periods.

SUMMARY

Pro forma statements are an integral part of business planning and control. Managers use them in the decision-making process when constructing an annual budget, developing long-range plans, and choosing among capital expenditures. Pro forma statements are also valuable in external reporting. Public accounting firms find pro forma statements indispensable in assisting users of financial statements in understanding the impact on the financial structure of a business due to changes in the business entity, or in accounting principles or accounting estimates.

Although pro forma statements have a wide variety of applications for ongoing, mature businesses, they are also important for **small businesses** and start-up firms, which often lack the track record required for preparing conventional financial statements. As a planning tool, pro forma statements help small business owners minimize the risks associated with starting and running a new business. The data contained in pro forma statements can also help persuade lenders and investors to provide financing for a start-up firm.

[Roger J. AbiNader, updated by Laurie Collier Hillstrom]

FURTHER READING:

Gill, James O. *Financial Basics of Small Business Success.* Menlo Park, CA: Crisp Publications, 1994.

Livingstone, John Leslie, ed. *The Portable MBA in Finance and Accounting.* 2nd ed. New York: Wiley, 1997.

Merrill, Ronald E., and Henry D. Sedgwick. *The New Venture Handbook.* Updated ed. New York: AMACOM, 1993.

Mosich, A. N. *Intermediate Accounting.* 6th ed. New York: McGraw-Hill, 1989.

Rappaport, Louis H. *SEC Accounting Practice and Procedure.* 3rd ed. New York: Ronald Press, 1972.

PROBLEM-SOLVING STYLES

Problem-solving styles are the different ways companies and individuals attempt to solve problems. The various problem-solving styles can help alleviate deviations from what is expected or planned, including anything from technical problems to employee-relations problems. Despite the various approaches, these styles address some or all of the stages of the problem-solving process. These stages can be divided into:

1. Problem identification
2. Identification of potential solutions
3. Evaluation of potential solutions
4. Anticipation of negative consequences
5. Overcoming obstacles to carrying out a solution
6. Detailed plan for carrying out a solution

PROBLEM IDENTIFICATION

Problem identification includes two different kinds: before the fact and after the fact. Before-the-fact problem identification entails discovering deficiencies before they have an impact on performance, before they result in deviations. This kind of problem finding requires a forward-looking problem-solving style and generally includes a change audit, a decision audit, an implementation audit, a resource audit, and an activity audit, according to Alfred W. W. Schoennauer in *Problem Finding and Problem Solving.* The change audit examines changes in a company's environment, decisions, resources, and tasks to uncover any aspects that might lead to future problems. For example, the entry of a competitor in the business environment could lead to reduced sales and hence reduced profits.

The decision audit reviews company decisions for their consistency with the environment, resources, and activities as well as with each other. Using the implementation audit, a company can determine if it thoroughly implements its ideas and policies and if it effectively communicates information about its implementations. The resource audit can identify potential problems by detecting any inadequate resource allocations that may impede company goals and expectations. Finally, the activity audit seeks to determine if company activities are conducted in conformance with plans and goals.

Because of the difficulty associated with identifying problems before they occur, most companies do not attempt to identify problems until after they experience their effects. Companies attempt to discover the problems at this point to avoid recurrence. After-the-fact problem identification usually focuses on company operations: production, sales, **training**, research, and so on. This kind of problem identification typically involves five steps:

1. Results analysis: determining the deviations from the goals and expectations.
2. Activity-interaction analysis: discovering inadequate activities and conduct that could cause the deviations.
3. Resource analysis: uncovering resource deficiencies.
4. Environmental analysis: discovering environmental constraints and threats.
5. Decision analysis: determining if decisions fail to account for various environmental, resource, and activity factors.

The Ishikawa fishbone or cause and effect diagram can be used to represent the problems and to help identify their causes. All of the possible major and minor causes of the end effect are enumerated along the "bones" of the diagram. Major causes might be environment, equipment, funds, methods, personnel, or training. Then all of the possible causes are evaluated to see if they might cause the problem under consideration. A potential difficulty is that it may be difficult to identify the actual cause of a specific problem with this diagram. Figure 1 shows an example of a fishbone diagram.

Whatever method a company uses to identify problems, it must make sure that it discovers actual causes and not "red herrings" or things that superficially resemble causes at first glance. Hence, the first step of problem solving involves ruling out possible causes to arrive at actual causes, which may entail sorting through a quagmire of possible causes and effects.

Figure 1
Fishbone Diagram

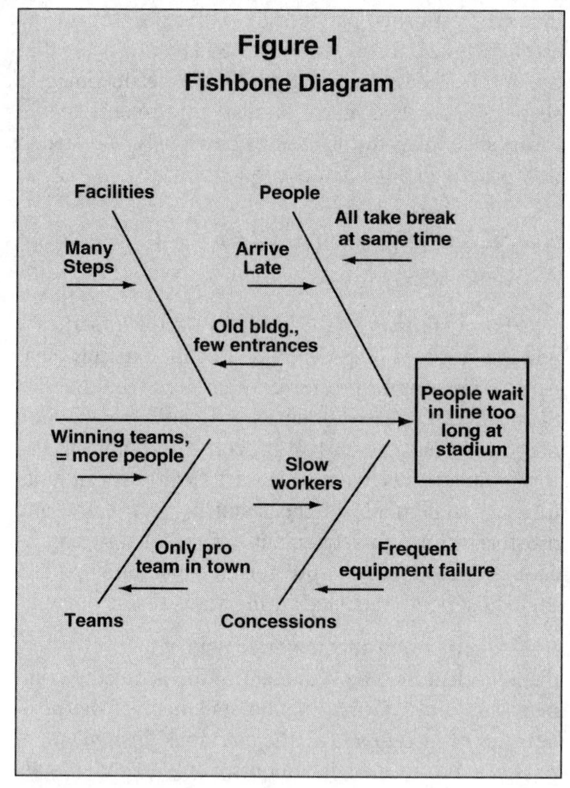

DEVELOPING AND CHOOSING POTENTIAL SOLUTIONS

At the heart of finding the best solution is weighing the pros and cons of possible solutions, by finding potential solutions to a problem, identifying the positive and negative aspects of each solution, and choosing the best solution based on these considerations. This method assumes that both the problem and the potential solutions are already well identified. While using a list of pros and cons is simple and requires little expertise, more complex problems require more sophisticated approaches.

A more intricate method of identifying potential solutions is Fritz Zwicky's morphological approach, in which a two- or three-dimensional matrix is used to force the consideration of possible solutions that might otherwise be overlooked. Also employed to identify solutions is Edward de Bono's use of "lateral thinking" to generate unconventional new ideas. This has some similarity to Roger Von Oech's "whack on the side of the head" approach to thinking of problems and their effects in unconventional terms.

De Bono summarizes traditional approaches to problem solving as digging a hole deeper, and lateral thinking and related approaches as digging a hole elsewhere. In *The Act of Creation,* Arthur C. Koestler explained these approaches using the concept of "bisociation," which refers to the intersection of two incompatible but internally consistent frames of reference that can lead to a solution that would otherwise not be discovered. He showed how all of humor, most of literature and art, and nearly all breakthrough scientific discoveries can be traced to the occurrence of bisociation on the part of the creator. Hence, lateral thinking and related approaches to problem solving develop alternative problem-solving strategies, whereas vertical approaches simply follow a single strategy.

Synectics, developed by William J. J. Gordon and George M. Prince, is an approach that deals with the stages of identifying solutions and overcoming obstacles to carrying out a solution. In the synectics approach, a **team** working on possible solutions to a problem takes an ''excursion'' into a fantasy environment somehow related to the problem. The ideas developed in the fantasy environment, using an open form of team participation, are then translated back into the real-world environment of the problem to become potential solutions. This consideration of the problem in a fantasy context allows the team to develop solutions that would otherwise not be discovered. Synectics also involves using analogies and metaphors to develop creative ways of developing solutions.

The use of **decision trees** can help problem solvers determine the merits of competing solutions. Decision trees show, in detail, the sequence of actions and events that will follow from an initial decision point, where one of a number of alternative actions can be taken (see Figure 2). They present different solutions and their implications in a manner that allows problem solvers to compare easily the costs and benefits of each decision. Decision trees include two elements: squares, which represent decision nodes, and circles, which represent chance nodes. The chance nodes refer to the points where decision makers do not have control over the outcome. Hence, the squares represent points where decision makers have choices and the circles represent points where they have no choices. The decisions and chance outcomes are arranged so that they represent the order they could occur in. The sequences of decisions and chance events can then be evaluated using expected monetary values based on the probability of the various outcomes.

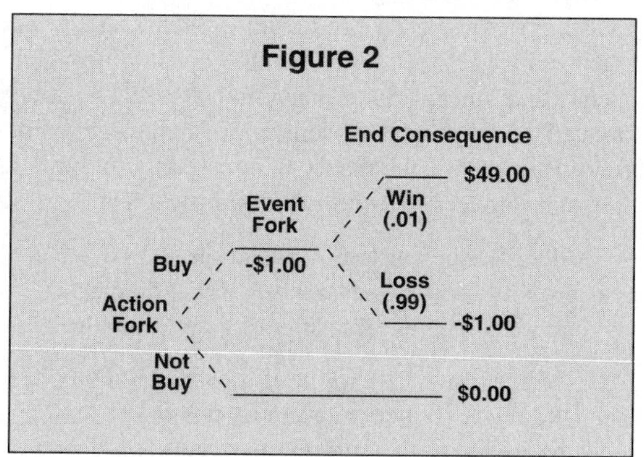

KEY APPROACHES TO PROBLEM SOLVING

While there are numerous formal and informal, theoretical and anecdotal, approaches to problem solving, the Kepner-Tregoe method, the theory of inventive problem solving (Triz), and the **theory of constraints** ''thinking process'' approaches stand out as either widely accepted (Kepner-Tregoe method) or growing in popularity (Triz and the theory of constraints).

THE KEPNER-TREGOE APPROACH TO PROBLEM SOLVING. In 1965 Charles H. Kepner and Benjamin B. Tregoe wrote a book, *The Rational Manager: A Systematic Approach to Problem-Solving and Decision Making,* that documented the problem-solving approach they had developed. They updated this work in 1981 with the publication of *The New Rational Manager,* to reflect the latest developments in their approach. The Kepner-Tregoe approach was in use at more than 3,000 corporations worldwide as of 1981, and had been accepted as a proven approach to problem solving in industry, government, and other applications. In fact, the authors detailed the use of their problem-solving approach by the National Aeronautics and Space Administration (NASA) to successfully diagnose the problems encountered by the *Apollo 13* astronauts and bring about their return. NASA personnel credited the Kepner-Tregoe approach with enabling them to discover the cause of the problem and find a solution under extraordinary time pressure with no tolerance for mistakes and no second chances available.

The Kepner-Tregoe approach covers stages one through five of the problem-solving process. The components of the Kepner-Tregoe approach are: situation appraisal, problem analysis, decision analysis, and potential problem analysis/potential opportunity analysis.

Situation appraisal entails organizing and clarifying complex situations as well as identifying problems or concerns, establishing priorities, and devising measures to solve problems or address concerns. In addition, situation appraisal also requires determining the key personnel to be involved in implementing the solution. The primary task of this step is examining the business environment in order to locate potential threats (problems or concerns) and opportunities, which means determining if company standards and goals are not being met, if areas need improvement, if company changes will create problems or opportunities, and so forth. After the problems have been identified, companies must figure out which ones are to be solved first, determine possible solutions, and set up teams to implement the solutions.

Problem analysis is used to ''identify, describe, analyze, and resolve a situation in which something has gone wrong without explanation,'' according to

Charles Kepner. The process uses cause-and-effect thinking to isolate the problem from the confusing mass of detail that usually surrounds problem situations. The concepts of identity, location, timing, and magnitude are used to home in on the cause of the problem's effects. Ultimately, problem analysis involves describing the problem, finding potential causes, evaluating potential causes, and determining the actual cause.

Decision analysis is used to examine the purpose behind making a decision, the possible options to achieve that purpose, and the risks for each of those alternatives. Once these factors are outlined, the alternative with the best balance between positive and negative factors can be chosen.

Potential problem analysis/potential opportunity analysis is used to analyze the consequences of a decision. If a decision might result in problems or might lead to trouble, this analysis can be used to foresee what could possibly go wrong and to develop measures that could either head off the problems altogether, or could deal with the problems once they actually arise. On the other hand, decisions also might have unforeseen consequences that are beneficial and this analysis helps identify these implications and maximize their effect. This process involves four steps: identifying potential problems or opportunities, determining probable causes, taking action to prevent or promote the causes, and planning action to minimize or maximize the effects.

THEORY OF INVENTIVE PROBLEM SOLVING. The theory of inventive problem solving, or Triz, is a small but growing approach to problem solving; it was developed in the 1940s by a patent investigator of the Soviet navy, Genrich Altshuller. This technique largely helps solve problems related to product design, although the principles have been transferred to other areas as well. At the foundation of the theory is the idea that the solution to 90 percent of all engineering problems can be found in other disciplines where the problems have already arisen. While researching **patents**, Altshuller discovered a pattern of **innovation**, which he believed could be applied to any problem. The Triz problem-solving technique requires engineers to have knowledge of 39 engineering parameters and 40 principles of invention, according to Rochelle Garner in *Electronic Business Today*. These parameters and principles derive from Altshuller's study of 1.5 million patents worldwide and are used repeatedly in the problem-solving process, according to Altshuller.

Triz also rests on the principle that inventions require overcoming contradictions. For example, if an auto manufacturer decides to increase the thickness of a car's body in order to enhance its durability, the car will become less efficient as a result of the added weight.

When using Triz, problem solvers identify the parameters they want to use and enhance and the parameters they want to bypass, and arrange them along the X and Y axes to create a contradiction table. The intersecting parameters will provide problem solvers with new ideas for overcoming their obstacles. In addition, Triz involves seeking solutions in outside disciplines. For example, removing shells from sunflower seeds, cleaning filters, and splitting diamonds along natural fractures can all be done using the same technique: placing these items in sealed chambers, increasing the pressure, and then suddenly decreasing the pressure.

Like other problem-solving methods, Triz begins by identifying the root of the cause and eliminating apparent causes. Then using the engineering parameters and inventive principles as well as contradiction tables, problem solvers review how other disciplines have confronted similar problems and develop potential solutions. Finally, the most effective solution given company needs, goals, and resources is selected, evaluated, and implemented.

THE THEORY OF CONSTRAINTS THINKING PROCESS APPROACH. The most complete and most advanced problem-solving style yet developed to solve complex problems is the logic-based theory of constraints thinking process. It encompasses all six of the stages of the problem-solving process. Although most of it is based on commonly known methods from the field of informal logic that began in the 1970s, this approach has much to offer as an integrated set of techniques that can be used to solve the most complex and difficult-to-grasp problems. It offers a means of creatively breaking through a seemingly unsolvable problem and then evaluating the solution to make sure that positive results occur and any negative results are avoided.

The thinking process was developed by Eliyahu M. Goldratt (1948-) as an outgrowth of the theory of constraints that he previously developed. The theory of constraints originally was intended to alleviate problems encountered in manufacturing. This approach concentrates on the constraint that limits the ability of a system to get things done. The main idea is that a system (e.g., a production system) should be managed to get the most from the constraint, which means that other parts of the system should be subordinated to the way the constraint is managed. For physical systems, the theory of constraints suggests a five-step process of continuous improvement:

1. Identify the system's constraint(s). (Constraints could be machines, market demand, policies, procedures, or corporate thinking.)
2. Decide how to exploit the system's constraint(s). (Squeeze the most possible from the limits of the current constraint.)

3. Subordinate everything else to the decisions made in step 2. (Avoid keeping nonconstraint resources busy doing unneeded work.)
4. Elevate the system's constraint(s). (If possible, reduce the effects of the constraint. Offload some of its demand, or expand its capability. Make sure everyone in the firm knows what the constraint is and what its effects are. **Marketing**, engineering, sales, and other functions should know about it and make decisions based on its effects.)
5. If the constraint is overcome in step 4, go back to step 1 and determine the next thing constraining the system. (This process is a continuum: over time solutions become constraints and need new solutions.)

For any system, the constraint is defined as anything that limits the system from achieving a higher level of performance relative to its goal. Obviously, this means that the system's goal must be defined before the constraint can be identified. Constraints can be either physical or nonphysical. A physical constraint could be the speed of a machine or the capacity of a vehicle, while a nonphysical constraint could be a policy or procedure based on someone's way of thinking.

The five-step improvement process described above is oriented toward solving problems in a system with physical constraints. If the constraint in a system is nonphysical, however, such as a policy that has outlived its usefulness, the five-step process above should be replaced by the five-component thinking process. The five components are: the current reality tree, evaporating cloud, future reality tree, prerequisite tree, and transition tree. The current reality tree is used to diagnose the core problem from its symptoms by using a form of cause-effect logic flowcharting. The evaporating cloud approach is used to creatively develop potential solutions to problems that seem intractable. The future reality tree is used to identify the results of the potential solution, both the positive results hoped for and the negative consequences that otherwise would not be anticipated and headed off. The prerequisite tree is used to overcome obstacles that stand in the way of accomplishing the solution. The transition tree is a logical form of implementation plan for carrying out the solution.

In developing a current reality tree, a list of symptoms that apply to a specific problem situation is developed. From this list of symptoms, called undesirable effects, one of the symptoms is chosen as a starting point. For this effect, its immediate cause is hypothesized, and the relationship is shown with an arrow connecting the statement of the cause to the statement of the effect. It is read in the following fashion: "If the cause, then the effect." This cause-effect relationship can be confirmed, if need be, by looking for another effect from the same cause. If this effect is observed, this tends to confirm that the cause-effect analysis is aimed in the right direction. If the effect does not occur, this is sufficient to disconfirm the original cause-effect hypothesis, and indicate that the analysis should aim in a different direction.

Once the original cause-and-effect relationship is deemed satisfactory, the cause can be considered as an effect, and its immediate cause can be hypothesized in turn. This process is repeated until the core problem is identified. The core problem is considered to be the cause that results in a sufficient number of the original symptoms of the problem. The current reality tree in Figure 3 shows an example of the use of this approach. An ellipse joining arrows from cause to effect is an indicator that all of the causes joined are required to produce the effect. Otherwise, a cause is considered

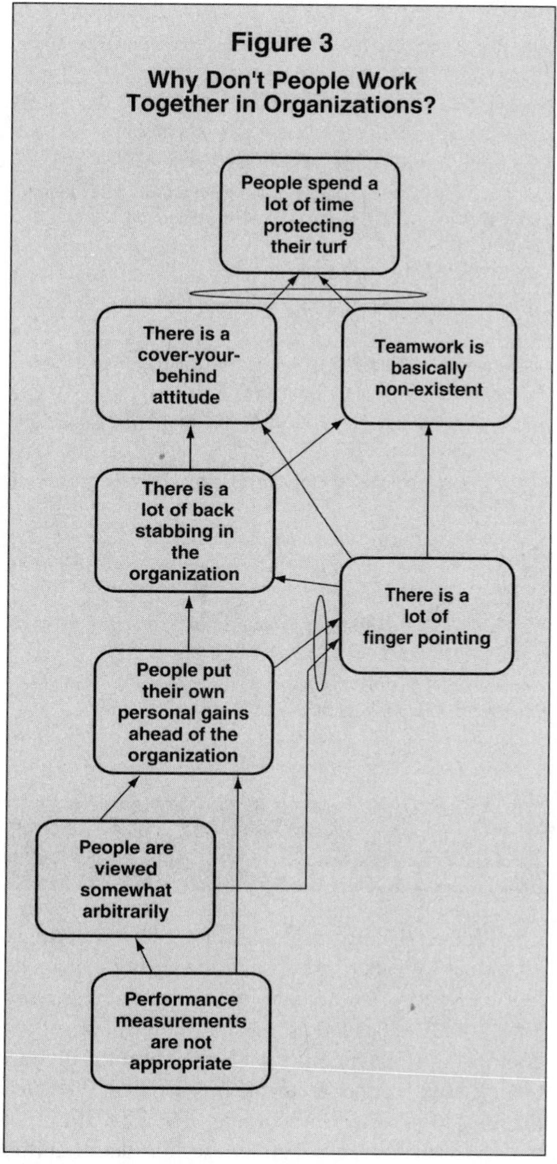

sufficient to result in the effect by itself. In Figure 3, note the effect of inappropriate performance measurements on the behavior of people in organizations.

SEE ALSO: Decision Making

[James T. Low, updated by Karl Heil]

FURTHER READING:

de Bono, Edward. *New Think: The Use of Lateral Thinking in the Generation of New Ideas.* New York: Avon Books, 1971.

Dettmer, William H. *The Theory of Constraints: A Systems Approach to Continuous Improvement.* Los Angeles: University of Southern California, 1995.

Garner, Rochelle. ''Triz of the Trade.'' *Electronic Business Today,* September 1997, 72.

Goldratt, Eliyahu M. *It's Not Luck.* Great Barrington, MA: North River Press, 1994.

Gordon, William J. J. *Synectics: The Development of Creative Capacity.* New York: Harper, 1961.

Kepner, Charles Higgins, and Benjamin B. Tregoe. *The New Rational Manager.* Princeton, NJ: Princeton Research Press, 1981.

Koestler, Arthur C. *The Act of Creation.* London: Hutchinson, 1964.

Noreen, Eric, Debra Smith, and James T. Mackey. *The Theory of Constraints and Its Implications for Management Accounting.* Great Barrington, MA: North River Press, 1995.

Osborn, Alexander Faickney. *Applied Imagination: Principles and Procedures of Creative Thinking.* Rev. ed. New York: Scribner, 1957.

Prince, George M. *The Practice of Creativity: A Manual for Dynamic Group Problem-Solving.* New York: Collier Books, 1972.

Schoennauer, Alfred W. W. *Problem Finding and Problem Solving.* Chicago: Nelson-Hall, 1981.

Spitzer, Quinn, and Ron Evans. *Heads, You Win!* New York: Simon & Schuster, 1997.

——. ''New Problems in Problem-Solving.'' *Across the Board,* April 1997, 36.

Von Oech, Roger. *A Whack on the Side of the Head: How to Unlock Your Mind for Innovation.* Menlo Park, CA: Creative Think, 1983.

Watzlawick, Paul. *Change: Principles of Problem Formation and Problem Resolution.* New York: Norton, 1974.

Zwicky, Fritz. *Discovery, Invention, Research through the Morphological Approach.* New York: Macmillan, 1969.

PRODUCT LIABILITY

Product liability issues have become increasingly important to manufacturers and marketing managers. In the last 20 years the liability of a manufacturer has been greatly expanded as a result of the spread of the doctrine of strict liability and the adoption of new theories that permit recovery in so-called ''delayed manifestation'' cases. According to Section 102(2) of the Uniform Product Liability Act, product liability includes ''all claims or action brought for personal inquiry, death, or property damage caused by the manufacture, design, formula, preparation, assembly, installation, testing, warnings, instructions, marketing, packaging, or labeling of any product.''

In the early history of law affecting issues of product liability, responsibility was based in the law of contract, as shown in the British case *Winterbottom v. Wright.* In 1840, a coachman for the royal mail was injured when the coach overturned due to insecurely bolted axles. The coachman sued the man who had contracted with the postmaster general to keep the coaches in good working condition. The court found that the coachman was not a party to the contract and, therefore, ruled against him.

In time, social policy changed with respect to this strict interpretation of contract law. The courts began to argue that there was a ''duty'' owed to users by sellers to provide reasonable care in the manufacture of goods. After the mid-1800s, sellers were held liable to third parties for manufacturing or sales negligence of goods inherently dangerous to human safety. Product examples included food, beverages, drugs, firearms, and explosives.

By 1962, the changes in social policy resulted in the application of tort principles to product liability. The landmark case of *MacPherson v. Buick Motor Co.* (1961) concerned liability of the auto manufacturer to the buyer of a car sold through a dealer. Although the concept of ''inherently dangerous'' goods was still held to be significant, there was a shift from the analysis to negligence (tort) principles in this case—that is, the producer was required to apply ''due care'' in the marketing of goods to users. *MacPherson v. Buick Motor Co.* first applied the theory of negligence to product liability. The opinion, written by Judge Cardozo of the New York Court of Appeals, had an immediate and widespread effect on the state of law. The principles laid down in *MacPherson* are now accepted throughout the country, followed by all American courts and adopted by the Restatement (Second) of Torts. Eventually, the concept of ''inherently dangerous'' products fell into disuse and the concept of negligence expanded beyond production to include labeling, installation, inspection, and design.

The *MacPherson* decision took legal thinking a step beyond previous rulings on inherently dangerous goods. It established that, because manufacturers knowingly market products that affect the interests of consumers, they owe a legal duty of caution and prudence to consumers. Because manufacturers may foresee potentially harmful product effects, they are responsible for attempting to minimize harm. Establishing this legal duty between the manufacturer and the consumer made it possible for plaintiffs to argue the negligent breach of that duty.

A weakness in the negligence approach to product liability results in burdening the plaintiff with having to prove the defendant's negligence. The concept of warranty was developed in an effort to limit this problem. A warranty is an assurance made by the producer to the user regarding safety and soundness of the product. In this case, only the original purchaser of an item could bring an action, and it could be against only the person who sold the product to him. This provided more limitations because most merchandise passes through many hands en route to the consumer.

Again the courts began to find exceptions to the rule. For example, during the early 20th century, the discovery of substandard sanitary conditions resulted in a public hysteria about adulteration and mislabeling of foods. Food marketers had long been held to special responsibilities, but in order to protect the public welfare, food businesses were held to an absolute responsibility to provide unadulterated food products. Soon after, the position was expanded to include drugs, beverages, and cosmetics.

The four elements of a negligent tort as applied to product liability cases are as follows:

1. A duty owed by the particular defendant to the particular plaintiff to act as a reasonably prudent person under the same or similar circumstance.
2. A breach of such a duty (by the defendant) that constitutes a failure to act reasonably.
3. Injury, including personal injury or property damage.
4. A causal link between the defendant's breach of duty and injuries sustained by the plaintiff.

The concept of negligence is applicable to every activity preceding a product's availability in the market. So everything from product design, the inspection and testing of materials, the manufacture and assembly of the product, the packaging, the accompanying instructions and warnings, through the inspection and testing of the final product are all susceptible to negligence. Negligence can result from omission as well as commission—failure to discover a flaw is as negligent as creating one. Similarly, failure to provide adequate warnings about potential dangers in the use of a product is a violation of duty.

Still it may be difficult to prove negligence in product liability cases. Defendants only must meet the general standards of reasonable behavior as judged against the behavior of a reasonably careful competitor who demonstrates the standard skills and expertise of the industry. In reality, a manufacturer must only show that ''ordinary care under the circumstances'' was applied to avoid liability for negligence. This is easy compared to the task of consumers showing evidence to the contrary.

Insurance companies are increasing their demand for scientific standards in product liability litigation. They argue that, without a rigorous, scientific analysis, using preordained standards and procedures, litigation would be unfairly biased against defendants, because unreliable information could be introduced, leaving the scientific merit to be judged by the jury. In the case of *Kumho v. Carmichael,* the 11th Circuit Court of Appeals distinguished between ''scientific'' evidence, which must meet standards set by the Supreme Court in *Daubert v. Merrell Dow,* and ''engineering'' evidence, which need not. ''Engineering'' refers to technical evaluations offered by expert witnesses, without a systematic examination of the specific materials involved in the case. In the oral argument at the Supreme Court for *Kumho,* this distinction was rigorously questioned. Though the Supreme Court upheld the Circuit Court's verdict in the case, the arguments furthered the debate over scientific standards and seemed to provide insurers with some ammunition.

Many products, even the most ordinary, pose some level of risk, and the law recognizes that it is often not possible to design a totally safe product. However, manufacturers are legally obligated to warn consumers about known dangers. Manufacturers may be found negligent if:

(1) they fail to warn users about recognized risk,

(2) the warning is too vague to be adequate, or

(3) the warning is not brought to the user's attention.

There is no duty to warn against misuse that is so rare or unusual that it cannot be foreseen. This poses a unique difficulty for manufacturers who must not only provide warnings, but must communicate them such that a reasonable person will find and understand them. In some cases a warning buried in an instruction ID may be judged inadequate; in other situations, a warning sticker on the product may be considered sufficient.

STRICT PRODUCT LIABILITY

The most recent evolution in tort law, strict liability, has transformed the very nature of inquiry because it eliminates the entire question of negligence, i.e., fault. Strict liability requires only demonstrating that a product caused an injury because it was defective; the reason for the defect is irrelevant. The product itself, not the defendant's use, is under investigation.

Under strict liability, the manufacturer is held liable for allowing a defective product to enter the marketplace. The issue is a matter of public policy, not the manufacturer's unreasonable or negligent conduct. The introduction of a defective product into the marketplace brings each member of the product's distribution channel into liability for negligence. The theory of strict liability holds that manufacturers

1. have the greatest control over the quality of their products;
2. can distribute their costs by raising prices; and
3. have special responsibilities in their role as sellers.

The tort of negligence at least provided the responsible person a standard by which to measure negligence, although it imposed the added burden of proving that the defendant was negligent. (According to Section 282 of the *Restatement (Second) of Torts,* negligence includes any ''conduct which falls below the standard established by law for the protection of others against unreasonable risk of harm.'') Although strict liability eases those burdens for the plaintiff and improves chances of recovery, it does not provide a universally accepted standard for measuring failure.

Section 402A of the *Restatement (Second) of Torts* relies on what has become known as the ''consumer-expectation'' test:

1. One who sells any product in a defective condition unreasonably dangerous to the user or consumer or to his property is subject to liability for physical harm thereby caused to the ultimate user or to consumer, or to his property if

(a) the seller is engaged in the business of selling such a product, and

(b) the product is expected to and does reach the user or consumer without substantial change in the condition in which it is used.

Though the definition is a source of some controversy, some analysts define ''unreasonably dangerous'' as dangerous beyond the reasonable expectation of the consumer with ordinary knowledge as to the product's characteristics. Despite its great influence, this definition has not been universally accepted. In California, for example, the court has rejected the necessity to prove unreasonable danger, arguing that such an expectation defeats the purpose of strict liability by imposing a negligence-like burden of proof on the plaintiff.

The *Restatement (Second) of Torts* recognizes that some products beneficial to society cannot be made entirely safe. Prescription drugs and vaccines are notorious examples. Such a product is not held defective simply because of its inevitable hazards; something else must be wrong with it also. Therefore, the *Restatement* does not hold drug companies strictly liable for a properly manufactured product accompanied by appropriate directions and warnings. In sum, design defects are not the same as manufacturing defects.

One defense manufacturers have employed with controversy is called ''state of the art.'' This means that manufacturers should be held accountable only for information available to them at the time of manufacture. Flaws or defects which arose due to unavailable knowledge are not considered in questions of liability. The problem of interpreting this defense concerns the variation of knowledge and its applications across the country.

The **Uniform Commercial Code** has provided alternatives for persons injured by products. This code contains warranty provisions. Recall that a warranty is an assurance made to the buyer of a product. Three types are most common: express warranties, implied warranties of merchantability, and implied warranties of fitness for a particular purpose.

Express warranties affirm facts about a product and become part of the sales bargain. They may be written with or without the words ''guarantee'' or ''warranty'' or may be implied by samples that demonstrate certain characteristics, such as a genuine leather binding. The implication is that all pieces in the lot purchased will have the same type of leather binding. Express warranties are defined and governed by Section 2-313 of the UCC.

Implied warranties pertain to the applicability of the goods purchased. The implied warranty of merchantability suggests that professional sellers have special skill or knowledge of their goods and sell goods which are ''fit for the ordinary purpose for which such goods are used.'' When the buyer is dependent on the seller's expertise (having indicated specific needs and the need to rely on the seller's advice), the seller is then liable to provide the right product. These warranties were created to serve public policy and did not result from agreement between parties to a sale. The courts construe implied warranties to protect buyers. The warranty of merchantability is governed by Section 2-314 of the UCC and is only applicable to merchants. The warranty of fitness for a particular purpose is governed by Section 2-315.

PRIVITY

Historically, a plaintiff had to have a relationship or connection, called privity, with a defendant in order to legally challenge that defendant. This factor became a defense used by manufacturers to avoid product liability cases of all kinds. The erosion of this defense has been important to the development of product liability, especially implied warranties.

Three types of privity exist. Horizontal privity refers to all persons making use of a product. Vertical privity concerns a product's channel of distribution. Market share privity stems from the notion of collective liability whereby an entire industry is liable for product injury. In this case, the specific manufacturer causing the product defect leading to injury cannot be determined.

[John Burnett]

FURTHER READING:

Jasper, Margaret. *The Law of Product Liability.* Dobbs Ferry, NY: Oceana Publications, 1996.

Owen, David G. *Product Liability and Safety: Cases and Materials.* Westbury, NY: The Foundation Press, 1996.

PRODUCT SAFETY

Product safety is part of a broad consumer movement commonly referred to as **consumerism**. Consumerism refers to a number of activities designed to protect consumers from a wide range of practices that can infringe on their rights and in some cases their safety in the marketplace. The consumer movement is generally supported by consumers, many business organizations, and various levels and branches of government—most especially the judicial branch, but also in the executive and legislative branches to varying degrees.

Product safety refers to the production, distribution, and sale of products that from various perspectives are either potentially unsafe or inherently unsafe to consumer use. Reasons for a product being unsafe include design defects, misrepresentation as to use, or the absence of adequate warnings as to potential dangers and hazards of the product even when it is used as intended. Product safety and product liability are inseparable. Product liability is concerned with the legal responsibility for injuries caused by one or more of the above factors. If an injury occurs through the use of a product the producer is offered, as prescribed by law and judicial precedent, various defenses. Generally speaking sellers and manufacturers are expected, as also prescribed by law and judicial precedent, to provide adequate instructions and warnings regarding a products use.

Consumer protection per se is not a current phenomena. There are references in the Bible to merchants maintaining fair standards and there are similar references in Hammurabi's code of ancient Babylonia. The ancient Romans had laws to protect consumers and they have come to be known in consumer and business circles for the Latin phrase *caveat emptor*—''let the buyer beware.'' Consumers have always, to one degree or another, been concerned about the products they buy in the marketplace. In terms of the development of consumer protection in the United States there are three distinct periods that ultimately led to the current status of product safety.

The first period, between 1879 and 1905, is often referred to as the Muckraking Era. The name is taken from the term *muckrakers,* which was coined to describe newspaper reporters who exposed various business abuses and violations. As a result of these exposés a number of bills were introduced in Congress to regulate the sale of food and drugs. These bills, however, resulted from the work of small groups of consumer advocates and were met with apathy by the general public and Congress. This apathy, coupled with the political and judicial clout enjoyed by business, meant that no significant legislative action was taken on the consumer front during these years. Much of this apathy dissipated in 1905, however, with publication of *The Jungle* by Upton Sinclair. Sinclair's book, although fiction, was a sordid exposé of the Chicago meat packing industry. The book provided gruesome details of the way meat was processed under dangerous and unsanitary conditions. This book, more than any other single event, jolted the public out of its apathy and made the need for consumer protection apparent to many people. Congress responded by passing the following public policy measures: Pure Food and Drug Act (1905); Federal Meat Inspection Act (1907); Federal Trade Commission Act (1914); and the Water Power Act (1920).

The next era, known as the Information Era, began in the 1930s, and was sparked by a book called *Your Money's Worth* written by Stuart Chase and F.J. Schlink. This book pictured the consumer as sort of an ''Alice'' in a ''Wonderland'' of conflicting product claims and bright promises. It focused on the advertising and packaging that inundated the consumer with information designed to sell a product rather than help the consumer make an intelligent decision. (In 1957 and 1960 Vance Packard would write *The Hidden Persuaders* and *The Wastemakers,* both best selling exposés of the advertising industry.) *Your Money's Worth* made a plea for impartial product testing agencies that had no vested interest in the product and thus could supply the consumer with objective and trustworthy information about the performance of the product. The 1930s, then, saw the development of independent product testing agencies, such as Consumers Union, that would test products and publish the results. In addition, the following important public policy measures were also passed in the 1930s: Food, Drug, and Cosmetic Act (1938); and the Wool Products Labeling Act of 1939.

The modern consumer movement began in 1965 with the publication of another book, Ralph Nader's *Unsafe at Any Speed.* Nader's book severely criticized the Chevrolet Corvair and accused its maker, General Motors, of a lack of concern for automobile safety and the safety of its automobile's occupants. The issue received national attention when it became public knowledge that General Motors had hired private investigators to follow Nader and investigate him while he was a witness before a Senate subcommittee. The time was ripe for a new consumer movement concerned with a range of issues that affected an increasingly affluent and educated populace, a technologically sophisticated marketplace, and a society that had high expectations and aspirations for the fulfillment of its needs. The increasing complexity of many modern products made it difficult for the average consumer to make rational choices, and many products were virtually impossible for the average consumer to repair should they break. During the latter half of the 1960s and early 1970s, Congress passed dozens of pro-consumer laws. The most significant piece of consumer legislation was the Consumer Product Safety Act, which was signed into law on October 27, 1972 by President Richard Nixon. This act created the **Consumer Product Safety Commission**, an independent federal agency intended to protect the public against unreasonable risk of injury associated with a wide range of consumer products.

Consumer rights and product safety as a legal concept pre-dates by centuries the creation of the Consumer Product Safety Commission. The theologian Aquinas (1225-1274 A.D.) asks, ''Is a sale rendered unlawful by a defect in the thing sold?'' He answers that a defect in kind, quantity, or quality if known by the seller and not revealed to the buyer voids the sale and is fraud and sin. The seller is thus bound to recompense the buyer. If the defect was unknown to the seller then it is not fraud but the seller must still make good to the buyer. The seller is also obliged to reveal secret flaws in the good ''. . . that may occasion loss through a decrease in value of the article or danger through the ware becoming harmful in use.'' If the flaw, however, is ''manifest'' the seller is not bound to reveal it as according to the ancient adage ''a buyer's eye is his merchant where the defect is obvious.''

In the United States a significant body of law has come into being that is concerned with product safety and product liability and the legal rights of both the consumer and the producer or seller of the product. Product safety law is regulatory law and consists of a system of rules and regulations promulgated by legislation and administrative agencies. All levels of government—local, state, and federal—contribute to the body of product liability and product safety law. Municipal authority, for instance, may require a minimum gauge of electrical wire to be used in new building construction, while states often regulate usage of such things as life preservers on its waters. Numerous federal agencies regulate standards for everything from automobiles to meat, poultry, and eggs. Product safety law operates *ex ante* by seeking to prevent accidents, injuries, or disease before they occur. Product liability law, however, regulates the private litigation of accidents and injury due to product defects, et al. and thus functions *ex post,* or after an accident or injury has occurred, according to David Owen, Professor of Law at the University of South Carolina.

Generally speaking, a product is considered to be tangible personal property often referred to as a ''good'' or ''chattel.'' Product liability, however, also includes such intangible goods as electricity coursing through the wires in a home, natural products such as a pet skunk, and ''writings'' such as aircraft navigational charts. Liability is generally imposed against a product's supplier when injuries are caused by a defective product. Product liability also applies to products that are not defective but are involved in ''negligent entrustment.'' Selling a knife or slingshot to a small child could, for instance, make a merchant liable for negligent entrustment. Product liability also applies to situations in which a product's capabilities are misstated or when a supplied product constitutes an abnormally dangerous activity. A shattered windshield that was said to be shatterproof is an example of the former and delivering gasoline in a leaky container could constitute an abnormally dangerous activity. ''A product that is harmful—because of defendant's negligence, misrepresentation, or abnormally dangerous conduct—is a defective product in the context of its use,'' according to Jerry Phillips, Professor of Law, University of Tennessee.

There are generally three types of defective products: those with manufacturing or production flaws, those with design defects, and those accompanied by defective or insufficient warnings or instructions. Manufacturing or production flaws may be attributed to physical flaws in the raw materials or components used to make the product or mistakes made in assembling the product. When product failure results in an injury and a product liability case results the crucial issue is: ''Whether the product's defective condition is attributable to mismanufacture or to some other cause—such as normal wear and tear, abuse by the user, or perhaps even to the accident itself,'' according to Owen.

Defective design is a troubling aspect of product liability law and the question: ''How safe is safe enough?'' goes to the heart of the matter. It is troubling for the consumer side because it raises social issues such as personal responsibility and it is troubling to manufacturers because there is a potential to condemn an entire production line unlike manufacturing or production flaws which can be more easily corrected. Most design defect cases are brought over the absence of or deficiency in safety devices such as guards on power tools or lawn mowers. Design defect cases may, however, be concerned with other things such as the absence of flame retardant chemicals on clothing, unnecessarily caustic chemicals in products such as drain cleaners, or metals that are lacking temper and thus prone to failure due to softness.

A lack of adequate warnings and instructions accompanying a product also falls under the purview of product liability. A manufacturer is obligated to provide such material with products being sold. Ironically, it is often less expensive for manufacturers to provide warnings than it is to redesign a product with safety problems, and conversely it is often easier for a plaintiff to successfully attack a manufacturer's warnings and instructions as being deficient than it is to prove a product has an inherently defective design. Another aspect, however, is the growing concept in product liability law of the right of the consumer to ''determine his own fate'' vis-a-vis product warnings. The rationale for this reasoning was given in a 1974 court decision: ''The user or consumer is entitled to make his own choice as to whether the product's utility or benefits justify exposing himself to the risks of harm. Thus, a true choice situation arises, and a duty to warn attaches, whenever a reasonable man would want to be informed of the risk in order to decide whether to expose himself to it.'' (see Owen: *Borel v. Fibreboard Paper Products Corp.*) Thus a consumer who is fully informed as to the risks of using a product may choose to modify or limit usage, use the product with full knowledge of the risks involved, or not use the product at all.

''Every transaction,'' according to Owen, ''implies a decision about safety costs and benefits.'' Consumers are generally more concerned with cost, performance, ease of use, and appearance then they are with safety—at least until an injury occurs. Manufacturers are of course concerned with the production and marketing cost of a product and subsequent salability. Both the consumer and the producer thus trade off certain costs and benefits. ''Because absolute safety is unattainable and because every product presents some risks, the seller and buyer are compelled to decide what level of hazard is acceptable,'' Owen writes. Product safety and product liability laws and regulations seek to ameliorate this hazard.

SEE ALSO: Consumer Product Safety Commission

[Michael Knes]

FURTHER READING:

Fischoff, Baruch, Riley, Donna, and Daniel Kovacs. ''What Information Belongs in a Warning?'' *Psychology & Marketing,* October 1998.

Owen, David G., Montgomery, John E., and W. Page Keeton. *Products Liability and Safety: Cases and Materials.* Westbury, NY: The Foundation Press, 1996.

Phillips, Jerry J. *Products Liability: In a Nutshell.[/I] 5th ed. St. Paul, MN: West/Wadsworth, 1998.*

PROFESSIONAL AND TRADE ORGANIZATIONS

Professional and trade associations are membership organizations, usually nonprofit, which serve the interests of members who share a common field of activity. Professional organizations—also called professional societies—consist of individuals of a common profession, whereas trade associations consist of companies in a particular industry. However, the distinction is not uniform; some professional associations also accept certain corporate members, and conversely, trade associations may allow individual members. The activities of both trade and professional associations are similar and the ultimate goal is to promote, through cooperation, the economic activities of the members while maintaining ethical practices. Trade and professional associations do not include **labor unions**.

Professional associations have the additional objectives of expanding the knowledge or skills of its members and providing professional standards. The definition of a profession is an occupation that requires considerable education and specialized training, such as medicine, law, **accounting**, and engineering. However, many use the term more loosely to encompass any coherent occupation class. There is a fine line between professional associations and scientific or academic societies, especially in certain fields, such as the applied sciences or education. Academic societies aim exclusively at advancement of the discipline, rather than being concerned with the methods of practice and economic well-being of the members. At the other end of the spectrum, the differentiation between professional associations and trade unions can be blurred, as some unions claim the added distinction of being professional associations.

The definition of an industry, as far as trade associations are concerned, is very flexible. Some associations deal with a specific activity, such as paper manufacturing, whereas others consist of company members involved in all aspects of a given product, such as the publishers, printers and marketers of calendars. Associations exist for both specialized sectors of an industry, e.g., independently owned drug stores, as well as very broad industry categories, e.g., manufacturing.

The membership figures for trade associations, unlike professional associations, are not a good indicator of size, for the companies belonging to a trade association may be very large and the associations may have multimillion-dollar budgets. A good example was the former American Automobile Manufacturers Association, the powerful lobbying voice of the U.S. auto industry, which consisted of General Motors Corporation, Ford Motor Company, and Chrysler

Table 1

Largest U.S. Professional Associations

Association	Members
National Association of Realtors	720,000
American Bar Association	380,000
American Institute of Certified Public Accountants	330,000
American Medical Association	300,000
Institute of Electrical and Electronics Engineers	274,000
American Registry of Radiologic Technologists	221,000
National Council of Teachers of Mathematics	215,000
American Nurses Association	210,000
National Association of Female Executives	200,000
Association for Supervision and Curriculum Development	198,000
National Association of Professional Insurance Agents	180,000
American Chemical Society	155,000
National Association of Social Workers	155,000
American Psychological Association	151,000
National Notary Association	150,000
American Dental Association	142,000

Largest U.S. Trade Associations

Trade Associations	Members
U.S. Chamber of Commerce	200,000
National Association of Home Builders	190,000
American Management Association	85,000
U.S. Hispanic Chamber of Commerce	70,000
American Library Association	57,000
American Hospital Association	55,000
American Advertising Federation	50,000
American Small Business Association	50,000
National Apartment Association	40,000
National Association of Wholesaler Distributors	40,000

Based on data from *Association Management,* May 1998; the *Encyclopedia of Associations,* 1998 ed.; and self-reporting by individual associations.

Corporation and operated on a $30 million budget. (The AAMA was disbanded in 1998 in the wake of Chrysler's merger with Germany's Daimler Benz AG.) Other influential trade associations include the AAMA's successor, the Alliance of Automobile Manufacturers; the National Association of Manufacturers; the Consumer Electronics Manufacturers Association; the American Bankers Association; and the Pharmaceutical Research and Manufacturers of America.

The activities of professional and trade associations often include some or all of the following:

- providing public relations for the field
- collecting and publishing statistics on the industry or profession
- advising members on technological or management issues
- promoting research
- sponsoring conferences
- monitoring regulations in the field
- lobbying government

Associations typically publish a newsletter or magazine distributed to members and many produce additional publications for the public. Some compile proprietary market data and analysis that is available only to members. Members may also receive special discounts on publications or other association materials.

Activities particular to trade associations include sponsoring trade shows and awards, providing market statistics for their members, promoting research on new products or manufacturing methods, offering scholarships or fellowships, and encouraging ethical business practices. Professional associations are uniquely involved in sponsoring or certifying training programs or examinations for individuals in the field. Almost all professional associations hold conferences or seminars to discuss techniques of practice. Professional associations also provide opportunities for personal networking and job information for members. Many associations can also supply experts to the media for discussion of industry or profession news and trends.

Both professional and trade associations set their own membership requirements and charge membership dues. Full members may vote in association affairs and run for office. Professional associations usually require specialized training or certification as a requirement for membership. National organizations with large memberships—which is typically the case for professional associations—often have local chapters to which their members also belong. The proliferation of organizations in both narrow and broad fields makes it common for a company or an individual to belong to more than one association.

[Heather Behn Hedden]

FURTHER READING:

American Society of Association Executives. *Gateway to Associations.* Chicago, 1999. Available from www.asaenet.org.

Association Management, monthly. Available from www.asaenet.org.

Encyclopedia of Associations, annual.

PROFIT MARGIN

The profit margin is an **accounting** measure designed to gauge the financial health of a business, firm, or industry. In general, it is defined as the proportion of profit, or revenue leftover after the firm's expenses are deducted, to total sales receipts over some defined period. Profit margins may be calculated at the enterprise level—how profitable is the business overall?—or on an individual product or service basis—how profitable is a particular line of business? The margin indicates how much profit a firm accrues from each dollar of sales and can be a measure of a company's cost efficiency, since a lower cost per unit of sales will yield a greater profit. Because both revenues and costs can be categorized in different ways, several forms of profit margin figures are used in business, the most common of which is the net profit margin, or net margin.

As a measure of the competitive success of a business, the profit margin is very important because it captures the firm's unit costs. A low-cost producer in an industry would generally have a higher profit margin. This is because firms tend to sell the same product at roughly the same price (adjusted for quality differences); therefore, lower costs would be reflected in a higher profit margin. Lower-cost firms also have a potentially deadly strategic advantage in a competitive price war because they have the leverage to undercut their competitors by cutting prices in order to gain market share and potentially drive higher-cost (and hence lower margin) firms out of business.

If costs rise and prices do not rise to keep up, then the profit margin will fall. In times of business cycle upturns, prices tend to rise; in business cycle downturns, prices tend to fall. Of course, many factors, and not only costs, will affect the profit margin, namely, industry-specific factors that relate to investment requirements, pricing, type of market, and conditions of production (including production turnover time).

As these dynamics suggest, however, comparing profit margins of different companies is most meaningful when the companies are in the same line of business or when there is reason to believe one's cost structure is analogous to another's. For instance, as Table 1 illustrates, companies in the pharmaceutical industry bring in, on average, a profit margin four times that of paper manufacturers. Thus, to expect a paper company to perform in the range of a pharmaceutical company would in most cases be unrealistic.

Corporations continually seek to expand their profit and, while a growing absolute dollar amount of profit is desirable, by itself it has limited significance unless it is placed in the context of the revenue from which it was derived. To a small entrepreneur, for example, a $2 million profit might be perceived as an enormous return and might represent a substantial proportion of sales. To General Motors, on the other hand, a net profit of $2 million would equal one-thousandth of one percent (.001 percent) of sales—it would be barely breaking even. This is why firms use measures such as the profit margin and the profit rate to show proportionality.

TYPES OF PROFIT MARGINS. Profit is a flow concept and the profit margin measures the flow of profits over some period compared with the costs, or sales incurred over the same period. Thus, one could compute the profit margin on costs (profits divided by costs), or the profit margin on sales (profit margin divided by sales). Other specific profit margin measures often calculated by businesses are

gross profit margin—(gross profit divided by net sales), the broadest measure of corporate profitability, where gross profit is the amount of revenue in excess of basic costs but before subtracting nonproduction expenses, such as the costs of sales and administration, taxes, and **depreciation**;

operating profit margin—(operating profit divided by net sales), where operating profit includes all revenue from ongoing operations (but excludes interest earned on assets, one-time sales of assets, and other peripheral sources of income) minus production, sales, and administrative costs;

net profit margin—(net profit divided by net sales), where net profit (also known as net income or net earnings) is operating profit minus interest, taxes, and depreciation.

PROFIT RATE. The profit margin is related to other measures, such as the rate of profit (sometimes called the rate of return), which comprise various measures of the amount of profit earned relative to the total amount of capital invested (or the stock of capital) required to generate that profit. Thus, while the profit margin measures the amount of profit per unit of sales, the rate of profit on total assets indicates the efficiency of the total investment. Or, put another way, while the profit margin measures the amount of profit per unit of capital (labor, **working capital**, and depreciation of plant and equipment) consumed over a particular period, the profit rate measures the amount of profit per unit of capital advanced (the entire stock of capital required for the production of the good). As an example, if a $1,000 investment in plant and equipment were required to produce a $100 television set, then a profit margin of 10 percent would translate into a profit rate on total investment of only 1 percent. Thus, in this scenario, the unit costs are low enough to generate 10 percent profit (profit margin) on the capital consumed (assuming some market price) to produce the TV, set but in order to achieve that margin, a total capital expenditure of $1,000 must be made.

The difference between the profit margin measure and the profit rate concept then lies in the rate at which the capital stock depreciates; and the rate at which the production process repeats itself, or turnover time. In the first case, if, say, the entire capital stock for a particular firm or industry is completely used up during one production cycle, then the profit margin would be exactly the same as the profit rate. In the case of turnover, if a firm succeeds in, for example, doubling the amount of times the production process repeats itself in the same period, then twice as much profit would be made on the same capital invested even though the profit margin might not change. More formally, the rate of return may be expressed as

$$\frac{\text{rate of}}{\text{return}} = \frac{\text{profit}}{\text{margin}} \times \text{sales} \div \frac{\text{average}}{\text{assets}}$$

where average assets is the total capital stock divided by the number of times the production process turns over. Thus, the rate of return can be increased by increasing the profit margin or shortening the production cycle. Of course, this will largely depend on the conditions of production in particular industries or firms.

PROFITS BY SECTOR. To give a broad view of the spectrum of profit margins for U.S. manufacturing sectors, shown in Table 1 are after-tax profit margins (net margins) on sales as reported to the U.S. Bureau of the Census for the third quarter of 1998.

Table 1

Net Margins by Manufacturing Sector

Sector	Net margin
Aircraft and aerospace equipment	5.6%
Apparel	5.4%
Chemicals	9.6%
Drugs	15.5%
Electrical machinery	7.0%
Fabricated metals	5.7%
Food and tobacco	7.7%
Furniture and fixtures	4.9%
Industrial chemicals and synthetics	3.8%
Instruments	4.9%
Iron and steel	4.8%
Lumber and wood products	3.3%
Machinery	5.3%
Motor vehicles and equipment	2.1%
Nonferrous metals	5.2%
Paper	3.4%
Petroleum	7.4%
Primary metals	5.0%
Printing	8.5%
Rubber	3.6%
Stone, clay, and glass	9.7%
Textiles	4.2%
Transportation equipment	3.4%
Manufacturing average	**6.2%**

Source: *Quarterly Financial Report,* U.S. Census Bureau, December 1998

For U.S. manufacturing firms as a whole, although absolute levels of profits are continually reaching new peaks (firms would hardly be induced to invest if their investment gained them the same profit—or less profit—each year), the profit margin can be cyclical, particularly over the short term. In general, after-tax margins at U.S. manufacturing companies in recent decades have averaged 4-6 percent annually. Profit margins in the retail sector tend to be much narrower, typically closer to 2 percent on an annual basis.

SEE ALSO: Income and Revenue; Income Statement

FURTHER READING:

Mueller, Dennis C., ed. *The Dynamics of Company Profits: An International Comparison.* New York: Cambridge University Press, 1990.

U.S. Census Bureau. *Quarterly Financial Report for Manufacturing, Mining, and Trade Corporations.* Series QFR-98-3. Washington: GPO, 1998. Available from www.census.gov.

PROFIT SHARING

Profit sharing refers to the process whereby companies distribute a portion of their profits to their employees. Profit-sharing plans are well established in American business. The annual U.S. Chamber of Commerce Employee Benefits Survey indicates that somewhere between 19 and 23 percent of U.S. companies have offered some form of profit sharing since 1963. Other estimates place the number of companies offering profit-sharing plans in the 1990s somewhere between one-fourth and one-third of all U.S. firms. Some companies combine profit sharing with their **401(k) plans**.

Historically, profit-sharing plans have their roots in the 19th century, when companies such as General Foods and Pillsbury distributed a percentage of their profits to their employees as a bonus. The first deferred profit-sharing plan was developed in 1916 by Harris Trust and Savings Bank of Chicago. There was a sharp increase in profit-sharing plans during World War II, when wages were frozen. Deferred profit-sharing plans enabled wartime employers to provide additional compensation to their employees without actually raising their wages.

The Employee Retirement Income Security Act of 1974 (ERISA) provided a further boost in the use of profit-sharing plans. ERISA regulates and sets the standards for pension plans and other employee benefit plans. Many employers found that a simple profit-sharing plan avoided many of ERISA's rules and regulations that affected **pension** plans.

Many companies have turned to profit-sharing plans during hard economic times, when they are unable to provide guaranteed wage increases. Chrysler Corporation, for example, introduced profit sharing for its union and nonunion employees in 1988 during an economic recession. Its profit-sharing plan was offered as part of its union contract in exchange for wage concessions made by its **workforce**. Corporate earnings at the time were weak, so profit-sharing payouts were small. By 1994, however, Chrysler had recovered and was paying an average profit-sharing bonus of $4,300 per person, to 81,000 workers, a total outlay of approximately $348 million.

TYPES OF PROFIT-SHARING PLANS

Companies may use any number of different formulas to calculate the distribution of profits to their employees and establish a variety of rules and regulations regarding eligibility, but there are essentially two basic types of profit-sharing plans. One type is a cash or bonus plan, under which employees receive their profit-sharing distribution in cash at the end of the year. The main drawback to cash distribution plans is that employee profit-sharing bonuses are then taxed as ordinary income. Even if distributions are made in the form of company **stock** or some other type of payment, they become taxable as soon as employees receive them.

To avoid immediate taxation, companies are allowed by the **Internal Revenue Service** (IRS) to set up qualified deferred profit-sharing plans. Under a deferred plan, profit-sharing distributions are held in individual accounts for each employee. Employees are not allowed to withdraw from their profit-sharing accounts except under certain, well-defined conditions. As long as employees do not have easy access to the funds, money in the accounts is not taxed and may earn tax-deferred interest.

Under qualified deferred profit-sharing plans, employees may be given a range of investment choices for their accounts. Such choices are common when the accounts are managed by outside investment firms. It is becoming less common for companies to manage their own profit-sharing plans due to the **fiduciary duties** and **liabilities** associated with them.

A 1998 survey conducted by Coopers & Lybrand found that 20 percent of all respondents provided a qualified deferred profit-sharing plan. Such plans were more prevalent among larger companies, with 30 percent of the respondents with 10,000 or more employees offering a qualified deferred profit-sharing plan.

OTHER ISSUES CONCERNING PROFIT-SHARING PLANS

Deferred profit-sharing plans are a type of defined contribution plan. Such employee benefit plans provide for an individual account for each employee. Individual accounts grow as contributions are made to them. Funds in the accounts are invested and may earn interest or show capital appreciation. Depending on employees' investment choices, their account balances may be subject to increases or decreases reflecting the current value of their investments.

The amount of future benefits that employees will receive from their profit-sharing accounts depends entirely on their account balance. The amount of their account balance will include the employer's contributions from profits, any interest earned, any **capital gains** or losses, and possibly forfeitures from other plan participants. Forfeitures result when employees leave the company before they are vested, and the funds in their accounts are distributed to the remaining plan participants.

Employees are said to be vested when they become eligible to receive the funds in their accounts. Immediate vesting means that they have the right to funds in their account as soon as their employer makes a profit sharing distribution. Companies may establish different time requirements before employees become fully vested. Under some deferred profit-sharing plans, employees may start out partially vested, perhaps being entitled to only 25 percent of their account, then gradually become fully vested over a period of years. A company's vesting policy is written into the plan document and is designed to motivate employees and reduce employee turnover.

In order for a deferred profit-sharing plan to gain qualified status from the IRS, it is important that funds in employee accounts not be readily accessible to employees. Establishing a vesting period is one way to limit access; employees have rights to the funds in their accounts only when they become partially or fully vested. Another way is to establish strict rules for making payments from employees accounts, such as at retirement, death, permanent disability, or termination of **employment**. Less strict rules may allow for withdrawals under certain conditions, such as financial hardship or medical emergencies. Nevertheless, whatever rules a company may adopt for its profit-sharing plan, such rules are subject to IRS approval and must meet IRS guidelines.

The IRS also limits the amount that employers may contribute to their profit-sharing plans. The precise amount is subject to change by the IRS, but recent **tax** rules allowed companies to contribute a maximum of 15 percent of an employee's salary to his or her profit sharing accounts. If a company contributed less than 15 percent in one year, it may exceed 15 percent by the difference in a subsequent year to a maximum of 25 percent of an employee's salary. According to a 1998 survey by *Employee Benefits Journal,* companies with profit sharing plans contributed an average of 8.6 percent of their employees' earnings to their plans.

Companies may determine the amount of their profit-sharing contributions in one of two ways. One is by a set formula that is written into the plan document. Such formulas are typically based on the company's pretax net profits, earnings growth, or some other measure of profitability. Companies then plug the appropriate numbers into the formula and arrive at the amount of their contribution to the profit-sharing pool.

Rather than using a set formula, companies may decide to contribute a discretionary amount each year. That is, the company's **board of directors**—at its discretion—decides what an appropriate amount would be.

Once the amount of the company's contribution has been determined, different plans provide for different ways of allocating it among the company's employees. The employer's contribution may be translated into a percentage of the company's total payroll, with each employee receiving the same percentage of his or her annual pay. Other companies may use a sliding scale based on length of service or other factors. Profit-sharing plans also spell out precisely which employees are eligible to receive profit-sharing distributions. Some plans may require a certain length of employment, for example.

[David P. Bianco]

FURTHER READING:

''Annual Survey of Profit Sharing and 401(k) Plans.'' *Employee Benefits Journal.* June 1998, 41.

Hansen, Fay. ''Profit Sharing and ESOPs Are Down, but ESPPs Are on the Rise.'' *Compensation and Benefits Review.* March/April 1998, 11.

''The Network Discusses: Global Recruiting, Profit Sharing, and Succession.'' *Compensation and Benefits Review.* March/April 1998, 38-40.

''The Network Discusses: Improving Visibility of Profit Sharing Plans.'' *Compensation and Benefits Review.* November/December 1997, 30-31.

PROGRAM EVALUATION AND REVIEW TECHNIQUE (PERT)

Program Evaluation and Review Technique (PERT) is a scheduling method originally designed to plan a manufacturing project by employing a network of interrelated activities, coordinating optimum cost and time criteria. PERT emphasizes the relationship between the time each activity takes, the **costs** associated with each phase, and the resulting time and cost for the anticipated completion of the entire project.

PERT is an integrated **project management** system. These systems were designed to manage the complexities of major manufacturing projects, the extensive data necessary for such industrial efforts, and the time deadlines created by defense industry projects. Most of these management systems developed following World War II, and each has its advantages.

PERT was first developed in 1958 by the U.S. Navy Special Projects Office on the Polaris missile system. Existing integrated planning on such a large scale was deemed inadequate, so the Navy pulled in the Lockheed Aircraft Corporation and the management consulting firm of Booz, Allen, and Hamilton. Traditional techniques such as line of balance, Gantt charts, and other systems were eliminated, and PERT evolved as a means to deal with the varied time periods it takes to finish the critical activities of an overall project.

The line of balance (LOB) management control technique collected, measured, and analyzed data to show the progress, status, and timing of production projects. It was introduced at Goodyear Tire and Rubber Company in 1941 and fully utilized during World War II in the defense industry. Even older is the Gantt chart, developed during World War I by Harvey Gantt, a pioneer in the field of scientific management. It is a visual management system, on which future time is plotted horizontally and work to be completed is indicated in a vertical line. The **critical path method** (CPM) evolved parallel to PERT. CPM is a mathematically ordered network of planning and scheduling project management; it was first used in 1957 by E.I. du Pont de Nemours & Co. PERT borrows some CPM applications. PERT proved to be an ideal technique for one-of-a-kind projects, using a time network analysis to manage personnel, material resources, and financial requirements. The growth of PERT paralleled the rapid expansion in the defense industry and meteoric developments in the space race. After 1960, all defense contractors adopted PERT to manage the massive one-time projects associated with the industry. Smaller businesses, awarded defense related government contracts, found it necessary to use PERT. At the same time, du Pont developed CPM, which was particularly applied in the construction industry. In the last 30 years, PERT has spread, as has CPM, as a major technique of integrated project management.

PERT centers on the concept of time and allows flexible scheduling due to variations in the amount of time it takes to complete one specific part of the project. A typical PERT network consists of activities and events. An event is the completion of one program component at a particular time. An activity is defined as the time and resources required to move from one event to another. Therefore, when events and activities are clearly defined, progress of a program is easily monitored, and the path of the project proceeds toward termination. PERT mandates that each preceding event be completed before succeeding events, and thus the final project, can be considered complete.

One key element to PERT's application is that three estimates are required because of the element of uncertainty and to provide time frames for the PERT network. These three estimates are classed as optimistic, most likely, and pessimistic, and are made for each activity of the overall project. Generally, the optimistic time estimate is the minimum time the activity will take—considering that all goes right the first time and luck holds for the project. The reverse is the pessimistic estimate, or maximum time estimate for completing the activity. This estimate takes into account Murphy's law—whatever can go wrong will—and all possible negative factors are considered when computing the estimate. The third is the most likely estimate, or the normal or realistic time an activity requires. Two other elements comprise the PERT network: the path, or critical path, and slack time. The critical path is a combination of events and activities that will necessitate the greatest expected completion time. Slack time is defined as the difference between the total expected activity time for the project and the actual time for the entire project. Slack time is the spare time experienced in the PERT network.

A vital aspect of PERT is the formula used for the calculation of expected project time. The project reads:

$$T = \frac{A + 4M + B}{6}$$

where T = expected completion time,
A = optimistic estimate,
M = most likely estimate,
B = pessimistic estimate.

Applying real numbers to the PERT formula, the result is as follows, where A (optimistic time) = 7 weeks; M (most likely time) = 11 weeks; B (pessimistic time) = 15 weeks:

$$\frac{7 + (4 \times 11) + 15}{6} = 11 \text{ weeks}$$

(or T, expected completion time)

Once the expected time is computed, the critical path is established. The PERT network considers all potential variables, thus quantifying the scheduling and planning of the project. In a comprehensive view of PERT, it becomes clear that despite the fact that some steps of the process are independent, the next step will depend on the successful completion of prior steps.

Another key to PERT is to analyze and revise the data owing to a constant state of flux. Factors influencing project management take many forms, including personnel, materials, equipment and facilities, utilities, and environmental conditions. For example, **absenteeism**, sickness, vacations, and even strikes can affect personnel supply, or sudden changes in climatic conditions (snow, flooding from rains, etc.) may have an environmental impact. Various methods have been established to adjust the PERT network in order to allow for unpredictable situations. In recent years, **computers** have provided one major means of network analysis and revision, especially on larger projects. Computers are significantly useful for computations of the critical path and slack time. Smaller networks can generally be managed with manual computations and are usually developed, evaluated, and revised without great difficulty.

The basic difference in PERT and CPM is in how the diagrams are drawn. In PERT, events are placed in circles (or rectangles) to emphasize a point in time. Tasks are indicated by the lines connecting the network of events. In CPM the emphasis is on the tasks, which are placed in circles. The circles are then connected with lines to indicate the relationship between the tasks. CPM use has become more widespread than the use of PERT applications.

PERT has advantages as well as disadvantages, but time has seemingly not diminished its applicability. Planning a major network reveals potential problem areas and interdependent events that are not so obvious in conventional project development methods. One advantage is the three time estimate process, again useful in identifying difficulties as well as more effective interrelated processes. When utilizing the latest computer applications to PERT networks, managers have additional benefits with which to plan. A final advantage is the use of what is termed the management-by-exception principle, whereby data accumulated and analyzed by various means can be applied to the planning and execution of a major project. When managers have used PERT in integrated project management, experience gained is reapplied to future projects, especially in developing bids for project estimates. When appropriate costing techniques are implemented with PERT networking, the project sponsors realize significant financial benefits.

The PERT/cost system was developed to gain tighter control over actual costs of any project. PERT/cost relates actual costs to project costs. Job cost estimates are established from an activity or a group of activities on the basis of a time network. Labor and nonlabor estimates are developed for the network targeting the control of time and costs and identifying potential areas where time and cost can be traded off—all aimed at more effective, efficient project management.

As with all aspects of business, the **Internet** has become a powerful tool with respect to PERT. Managers can now locate PERT applications on the World Wide Web and apply them directly to the appropriate manufacturing project. In most instances, PERT diagrams are available that eliminate the estimating process and make PERT a more useful and convenient tool.

Clearly PERT is a manufacturing-based project planning and scheduling network. In many instances, managers have attempted to apply PERT principles to other types of projects, including hospital planning for such issues as costs and social security, educational planning and development, various **accounting** functions, and even **real estate** development.

[Boyd Childress]

FURTHER READING:

Evarts, Harry F. *Introduction to PERT.* Allyn and Bacon, 1964.

Fair, Martin L. "A Comparative Study of Critical Path Method (CPM), Program Evaluation and Review Technique (PERT), and Graphic Evaluation and Review Technique (GERT)." Master's thesis, Indiana University of Pennsylvania, 1994.

Horsley, F. William. *Means Scheduling Manual: On-Time, On Budget Construction, Up-to-Date Computerized Scheduling.* 3rd ed. Kingston, MA: R.S. Means Co., 1991.

Moder, Joseph J. *Project Management with CPM, PERT, and Precedence Diagramming.* 3rd ed. New York: Van Nostrand Reinhold, 1983.

PERT, CPM, and Gantt. San Ramon, CA: Center for Project Management, 1990.

Soroush, H. M. "The Most Critical Path in a PERT Network." *Journal of the Operational Research Society,* May 1994, 89-99.

Spinner, M. Pete. *Elements of Project Management.* 2nd ed. Englewood Cliffs, NJ: Prentice-Hall, 1992.

Wiest, Jerome D., and Ferdinand K. Levy. *A Management Guide to PERT/CPM.* 2nd ed. Englewood Cliffs, NJ: Prentice-Hall, 1977.

PROJECT MANAGEMENT

Many times a business must implement a systematic change, such as constructing a building, installing a new computer system, merging with another company, developing a new product, entering a new market, etc. These changes are the results of projects.

A project is an organized undertaking intended to produce a specific outcome subject to limitations of people, time, and money. Projects usually require coordinated work from multiple groups of people, exist for only a limited time, and have goals that become more detailed over time.

Project management consists of processes to initiate, plan, execute, control, and close work on the project. During these processes, tradeoffs must be made between the amount of work (scope), acceptability of the work (quality), cost, and schedule so the project results are useful, timely, and affordable.

HISTORY OF PROJECT MANAGEMENT

Projects, sometimes of massive size, have occurred through human history. Early construction projects included the building of pyramids, cities, and medieval cathedrals. Other early projects included waging wars and building empires. While the results of these projects were often impressive, the human cost and time to complete them were sometimes staggering. Many thousands of workers and decades of time were often required.

In the 20th century, project managers have had to learn to manage **costs** and schedules much more closely, yet still achieve desired results. In the 1950s and 1960s techniques for planning and controlling schedules and costs were developed, primarily on huge aerospace and constructions projects. Much of this development was based on the concept of determining precedence relationships (that is, identifying which work activities must be completed before other work activities). Modern project management builds upon this. In the 1980s and 1990s many **software** companies offered ever more powerful and easy ways to plan and control project costs and schedules. The **information technology** and **telecommunications** industries especially have fueled massive growth in the use of project management in the 1990s. Now project management is commonly used in a wide variety of industries.

The trend in increasing use of project management is likely to continue. Business is faced with the challenges of more complex products and services, demands for higher quality outputs, more cost-conscious customers, faster development cycles, stiffer international **competition**, and increased use of **joint ventures** to share **risk** and leverage expertise. These challenges force business to quickly and inexpensively develop complex solutions. Project management is designed to help business leaders do just that.

RELATED CONCEPTS AND TERMS

There are many terms that can be confused with project management. The differences are usually one of size or organization. For example, enormous projects are often called programs. A program can usually be divided into multiple projects. For example, the multibillion-dollar development of a new aircraft can be described as a program composed of many projects that involve systems such as avionics of engines. Alternatively, the new aircraft program could have separate projects for various stages such as design or testing.

Projects, in turn, can be broken down into smaller sets of activities. These smaller sets of work are sometimes called subprojects, hammock activities, or work breakdown structure summary activities. These can, in turn, be broken down into still smaller sets of work called activities, tasks, or work packages. Responsibility for smaller sets of work is often assigned to one person or department while the project itself often requires multiple people, departments, or even companies to complete. Project management techniques can be applied to planning and managing both these larger and smaller undertakings.

As stated previously, project management is the set of processes used to accomplish a goal. The term ''task force'' is sometimes used interchangeably with project management. Functional, matrix, and project forms of organization refer to how a business is structured. While companies that have many projects are sometimes structured as matrix or project organizations, projects can be managed in any form of organizational structure.

A DETAILED LOOK AT PROJECT MANAGEMENT

All projects are performed to achieve a specific desired output. This output can be described both by its amount, size, or performance characteristics (scope) and by how well it serves its intended purpose and pleases its customers (quality). Scope and quality collectively are the project goals.

All projects have finite amounts of time, money, people, and other resources. They are also limited by technology and legal requirements. All of these limitations must be taken into account when managing project activities. There are many tools for planning, scheduling, monitoring, and reporting project activities. Business managers accomplish project goals—subject to the limitations faced—by using these tools, collectively referred to as project management tools.

Projects face different challenges than ongoing operations because of their defined start and stop points, unique output, and unique mix of workers. All nine of the following areas need to be planned and managed differently on projects: scope, time, cost, quality, risk, procurement, human resources, communications, and integration.

All project activities occur in a predictable pattern called the project life cycle. There are several distinct stages in the project life cycle. By understanding and planning for the events at each of these stages, a project manager has more chance for project success since important work will not be neglected and progress can be checked while there is still an opportunity to replan if necessary. Different industries and professional groups have defined project life cycles with four or more stages and with some variation in specific activities that reflect the unique demands of their industry. A simplified generic description of the project life cycle with typical names for the various stages and key activities associated with each stage follows.

The first project life cycle stage is often titled definition, initiate, or conceive. This stage starts with establishing the need for the project output. Then a project manager and possibly other core team members are assigned. The scope (desired output) is defined and approximate time and resource estimates are made to determine if it is feasible to achieve the desired output. Different strategies or alternative approaches are explored and one is selected. Finally, approval to proceed to the next phase is obtained. This often is in the form of a project charter that summarizes the results of the work in the definition stage; it is agreed to by both the project team and the organization's management.

The second stage is called planning, design, or development. Sometimes this stage is broken into two or more stages such as preliminary planning and detailed planning. Additional project team members may be assigned. Scope, quality standards, risks, interim deliverables, work activities, a schedule, resource needs, and responsibilities are defined or further refined. Once this planning is complete, approval to proceed to the next stage is obtained.

The next stage—often called execution, implementation, or construction—is when most of the actual project work is completed. Goods and services needed to complete the project are procured. (This procurement is sometimes defined as a separate stage.) The project organization, procedures, and reporting mechanisms are established. Project work activities are directed, monitored, and redirected, always keeping the project goals and limitations in mind. The output of the project frequently needs to be accepted in order to proceed to the last stage.

The final stage is phase-out, turnover, or start-up. Activities include transferring responsibility for the project outcome to the user, reassigning workers and other resources, and evaluating the project with an eye toward improving future projects.

Project management is a process that includes initiating, planning, executing, controlling, and closing work activities so that the project goals can met while taking into consideration limitations such as time, money, people, and other resources. Many work endeavors are already managed as projects. Increasing competitive pressures, improving software, and improving knowledge of project management concepts and techniques are likely to mean more work will be managed as projects in the future.

SEE ALSO: Matrix Management and Structure

[Timothy J. Kloppenborg, Ph.D.]

FURTHER READING:

Cleland, David I., ed. *Field Guide to Project Management.* New York: Van Nostrand Reinhold, 1998.

Duncan, William R. *A Guide to the Project Management Body of Knowledge.* Upper Darby, PA: Project Management Institute, 1996.

Kloppenborg, Timothy J., and Samuel J. Mantel Jr. ''Tradeoffs on Projects: They May Not Be What You Think.'' *Project Management Journal,* March 1990.

Martin, Paula, and Karen Tate. *Project Management Memory Jogger.* Methuen, MA: GOAL/QPC, 1997.

Meredith, Jack R., and Samuel J. Mantel Jr. *Project Management: A Managerial Approach.* 3rd ed. New York: Wiley, 1995.

Shtub, Avraham, Jonathon F. Bard, and Shlomo Globerson. *Project Management: Engineering, Technology, and Implementation.* Englewood Cliffs, NJ: Prentice Hall, 1994.

PROMISSORY NOTE

A promissory note is a written agreement from one party to another that promises the payment of a specific amount of money on a specified date. A promissory note is an alternative means of obtaining **credit** that is not widely used; it is more common to obtain business credit through an open account with a line of credit. A promissory note may be negotiable, so that the holder can sell or transfer the note to another party by endorsing it. In such cases the transferred note would usually be discounted somewhat from its face value.

Promissory notes of large corporations are also known as commercial paper. Commercial paper offers large corporations an alternative means of obtaining short-term financing. Most commercial paper is due in two to six months. It is usually sold to other business firms, insurance companies, **pension funds**, and **banks**. There is also an open market of commercial paper dealers. These kinds of promissory notes are usually issued in denominations of at least $1 million. The **interest** paid on prime commercial paper is usually slightly lower than that charged for prime business **loans**, so large firms with good credit ratings often choose to issue commercial paper rather than obtain a bank loan or use their line of credit.

The use of commercial paper on the open market is generally limited to large firms that are good credit risks. Purchasers often require that the issuer have enough open credit to back the note. Otherwise, payment of the promissory note may be dependent on the issuer having excess funds on hand. It is possible for a company's promissory notes to go into **default** if the company declares bankruptcy.

SEE ALSO: Credit; Debt

[David P. Bianco]

PROPERTY MANAGEMENT

Property management, also called real estate management, is the business of overseeing income-producing properties for third parties in exchange for a fee. A property manager typically has responsibility either directly or indirectly for the following aspects of a building's operations: **marketing**; financial administration and **budgeting**; **leasing**; tenant or resident relations; maintenance; property analysis; and **risk management**. The buildings property managers oversee are commonly categorized as residential, office, shopping center, or industrial.

Property management became a recognized profession after 1890 when the construction of urban **real estate** shifted from single family homes and two- or three-unit dwellings to larger, multi-family buildings. Construction of early urban multi-family residences was at its height in the mid-1920s. Another trend that gave rise to the need for third-party fee managers of real estate was the advent of the skyscraper in cities such as Chicago, Illinois, where soon after the Great Fire of 1871, the cityscape transformed itself—from horizontal to vertical. High-rise, multi-tenant office space required specialized skills, particularly in the area of leasing.

From 1920 to 1922, investors in real estate found themselves awash in profits. Faced with the quandary of how to spend so much extra income and at the same time manage their assets, many investors turned to real estate agents, asking them to collect rents, pay for building maintenance and utilities, maintain heating systems, and send in net profits at the end of the month. Building managers did not usually make extraordinary expenses without express instructions to do so, and owners were usually present during the leasing season. Real estate agencies often provided management services in order to obtain sales clients. Management business volume, however, started to become important in areas with high rents and large numbers of multi-family properties.

During the 1920s, split **mortgages** became popular. These finance instruments broke large **loans** into smaller **bonds** available to the investing public. Overlending on real estate, about which investors were quite often ignorant, was an ominous prelude to the decade that followed. With the Great Depression of the 1930s came mass foreclosures and, for all intents and purposes, the liquidation of individual ownership of investment properties.

What most in the industry today describe as the field of property management ironically has its roots in this disastrous failure of real estate as an investment vehicle for the common citizen in the years preceding the depression. With defaults on the mortgages of the vast majority of the income-producing properties in the nation, banks, insurance companies, **savings and loan associations**, trust companies, and investment protective committees were suddenly saddled with large numbers of multi family and commercial properties. They in turn formed management departments to oversee the operations of their real estate assets.

By the time the United States entered World War II in 1941, demand for urban property was high enough to diminish the need for specialists who could rent buildings under difficult conditions and create profit scenarios. During the war, moreover, federal rent controls applied to residential properties, so there was no longer a need for someone who could apply successful rental increases. With what was basically a captive market, building owners often neglected building upkeep. These market conditions generally lasted until the end of 1957.

The scenario changed after a construction boom from 1946 to 1956 created a housing surplus. Suburbs sprang up where there was once farmland or woods, and by the end of 1963 rental space was more readily available, rental rates were more stable, and occupancy rates were falling. Property managers experienced greater demand for their services.

A voracious demand for office space also colored the post-war period. Greater employment levels in the areas of government, retailing, and services were partly responsible. Another contributing factor was increased prosperity, which led many businesses to seek more space. Specialized space needs, e.g., for computing functions, also opened a market for office space with plus value.

During the 1960s and 70s, the onslaught of condominiums created another source of demand for property management services. Many condominiums were second homes in buildings under multiple ownership in resort areas, and their owners needed full-time managers. Also, an increase in the mortgage money supply allowed for the development of large income-producing properties. The popularization of **Real Estate Investment Trusts (REITs)**, which offered investments in real estate in the form of securities, and the subsequent collapse of many of these trusts from 1974 to 1975, created another period of high demand for property management services.

Since the real estate development boom years of the 1980s, the office market has been glutted with space in most regions. During the late 1980s and early 1990s, an important market for many property managers consisted of banks with real-estate-owned properties (REOs) on their books. As in the early years of the depression, financial institutions in the early 1990s needed outside specialists to manage real estate assets while they sought to sell them. By the late 1990s, property managers were enjoying the lowest vacancy rates for all types of properties in over 20 years alongside rising property rates and a healthy economy.

More promising prospects were on the horizon, as well. The increasing trend toward the privatization of public housing marked a tremendous opportunity for property management firms. In 1999, more than 3,400 public housing authorities in the U.S. administered 1.3 million units. Centralized regulation made penetration into these markets difficult, but for those firms who could develop a relationship with the Housing and Urban Development Department and negotiate the complex bureaucracy, an emerging market awaited. Requirements for a private company to take over a public housing project include a proven ability to effectively manage property; effective maintenance and security policies and capabilities; and healthy records in dealing with residents and dispute management.

During the early 1990s, some property management firms targeted their services at large corporations that had downsized their organizations and were outsourcing services, such as facilities management, previously provided in-house. Facilities managers offer property management services for a corporation's headquarters or other owner-occupied space. Other property management firms have branched into asset management services, through which they manage and maximize the value of the real property held by a client.

Another topic that is increasingly important in property management for all building types is risk management, through which managers analyze the real or potential risks at a piece of property and control them by reducing or transferring them to third parties through insurance or indemnification clauses in legal contracts. Risks property managers often assess and manage relate to emergencies, negligence, security, general liability, negligent hiring or other employment issues, and environmental liability.

RESIDENTIAL MANAGEMENT

Property managers of residential buildings often administer the financial, budgeting, and reporting functions for a portfolio of properties, and oversee site managers at individual buildings who perform other tasks. A site manager frequently lives in an apartment on the premises of the property managed and usually supervises leasing, maintenance, and employees who work on the grounds of the building. A property manager usually reports directly to the owner or owners of properties in the portfolio; a site manager usually reports directly to a property manager. The 1995 Property Owners and Managers Survey conducted by the U.S. Census Bureau found that 58 percent of multifamily properties either registered a profit or broke even, with greater success found in smaller properties.

A typical job description for a site manager includes responsibilities for the following: budget preparation assistance; purchase order and **inventory control**; oversight of building maintenance and physical operations; supervision of on-site employees; management of resident relations and retention; assistance in the design and implementation of marketing programs; administration of resident selection and application processes; rental payment collection; and record keeping.

OFFICE BUILDING MANAGEMENT

Office building managers frequently have the following responsibilities for the buildings they manage: budgeting and financial administration; reporting and owner relations; publicity and tenant relations; leasing and lease administration; emergency-procedures planning; supervision of contractors or in-house employees for maintenance, security, cleaning, elevators, landscaping; and other services. For leasing functions, property managers use either in-house leasing staffs or outside brokers.

SHOPPING CENTER MANAGEMENT

Shopping centers fall into the following categories: community, regional, specialty, mall, and convenience. Managers of shopping centers generally have the same responsibilities as managers of office buildings: budgeting, reporting, and financial administration; publicity and tenant relations; leasing and lease administration; emergency-procedures planning; supervision of contractors for maintenance, security, and other services.

Leasing of shopping centers differs from that of office buildings in that leases are often at least partially percentage-based. This usually means that after a tenant begins to generate a certain amount of money per square foot, a percentage of this income is paid as rent. In part because of percentage-based leases, shopping center managers must pay close attention to the profitability of tenants. Managers usually seek to provide tenant synergies by bringing tenants to the center who draw business for each other rather than compete with each other. Tenants are sometimes concerned with obtaining lease clauses that give them the exclusive right to provide a particular service or product at the center. The stable presence of an anchor tenant such as a large department store or supermarket is usually crucial to the profitability of a shopping center.

Finally, a trend in real estate development of the 1980s and early 1990s was to construct mixed-use developments, referring to properties that may have office, shopping, residential or other space all under the same roof. An important role of a property manager of a mixed-use development is to capitalize on marketing and functional synergies among the building uses present in the complex.

[Dorothy Walton]

FURTHER READING:

Decardo, Joseph W. *Property Management.* Englewood Cliffs, NJ: Prentice Hall, 1996.

Evans, Mariwyn. "Privatization of Public Housing." *Journal of Property Management,* March/April 1998. Available from www.irem.org/jpm.htm.

Fennel, Lawrence and John H. Lombardi. *Spotlight on Security for Real Estate Managers.* Institute of Real Estate Management, 1997.

Kyle, Robert C., Floyd M. Baird, and Marie S. Spodek. *Property Management.* 6th ed. Chicago: Dearborn Publishing, 1999.

PROPRIETARY INFORMATION

Proprietary information, also known as a trade secret, is information that a company wishes to keep confidential or secret from those outside the company. Proprietary information may include secret formulas, processes, and methods used in production. It may also include a company's **business plans**, **marketing** strategies, salary structure, customer lists, **contracts**, and computer system. In some cases the special knowledge and skills that an employee has learned on the job are considered to be a company's proprietary information.

There is no single standard by which to determine if information is proprietary or not. Some 39 U.S. states have laws that define a trade secret and the conditions under which it is considered to have been stolen. In general, for information to be considered proprietary, companies must treat it as such. Information that is readily available in public sources will not be treated by the courts as proprietary. The body of case law covering proprietary information and trade secrets recognizes a company's right to have proprietary information and provides it with remedies when its trade secrets have been misused or appropriated illegally.

There are several ways for a company to protect its proprietary information. Key employees with access to proprietary information may be required to sign restrictive covenants, also called noncompete agreements, that prohibit them from competing with their employer for a certain period after leaving the company. These restrictive covenants are usually enforced by the courts if they are reasonable with respect to time and place and do not unreasonably restrict the former employee's right to employment. In some cases the covenants are enforced only if the employee has gained proprietary information during the course of his or her employment.

Companies may also develop security systems to protect their proprietary information from being stolen by foreign or domestic competitors. Business and industrial espionage is an ongoing activity that clandestinely seeks to obtain trade secrets by illegal methods. A corporate system for protecting proprietary information would include a comprehensive plan ranging from employee education to data protection to securing phone lines and meeting rooms. In some cases a **chief information officer** would be responsible for implementing such a plan.

An employee who divulges a trade secret is committing a tort by violating a duty of loyalty that includes nondisclosure of proprietary information. Once the employee leaves the company, however, that duty no longer exists. For this reason companies often require employees to sign a restrictive covenant, or noncompete agreement.

In addition, the courts generally consider it unfair competition for one company to induce employees of another company who have acquired unique technical skills and secret knowledge during their employment, to terminate their employment and use their skills and knowledge for the benefit of the competing firm. In such a case the plaintiff company could seek an **injunction** to prevent its former employees and the competing company from using the proprietary information.

Case law has given rise to the doctrine of "inevitable disclosure," which recognizes that certain key employees have learned proprietary information and will carry it with them when they leave their employer. In cases where a key employee has left one company to work for a competitor, the courts have attempted to balance the original employer's right to protect its proprietary information against the former employee's fundamental freedom to change employers.

After a high-profile case involving the vice president and group executive in charge of purchasing for General Motors, who left GM to work for Volkswagen in Germany, the U.S. Congress passed the Economic Espionage Act of 1996. This act made it a federal criminal offense to steal trade secrets. According to the American Society for Industrial Security, theft of proprietary information and trade secrets costs U.S. companies approximately $300 billion a year.

[David P. Bianco]

FURTHER READING:

Mathiason, Garry. "What's in Your Head Can Hurt You." *Fortune,* 20 July 1998, 153.

Seglin, Jeffrey L. "Boundaries to Stealing All Those Bright Ideas." *New York Times,* 17 January 1999, 6.

Shook, Carrie. "Information Is Property." *Forbes,* 23 February 1998, 104.

Silverman, Rachel Emma. "The Millennium—Trade and Commerce: Stop, Thief!—Business Espionage Has Been Common for as Long as There Have Been Secrets Worth Stealing." *Wall Street Journal,* 11 January 1999, R50.

PUBLIC DEBT

Public debt, sometimes called national debt, is the cumulative amount a national government has borrowed to finance its outlays. Usually a result of deficit spending, public debt is distinct from a budget deficit in that it is cumulative, whereas deficit refers to a particular budget year's shortfall. Large public debts are common to many governments throughout the world, but none is larger than that of the United States.

The U.S. government finances its debts by borrowing in international credit markets and floating **bonds** through the U.S. Department of the Treasury and the **Federal Reserve System**. Federal borrowing is administered by the Treasury Department.

HISTORY AND BACKGROUND

The politics of public debt in the United States date back to the birth of the nation. In 1790, Alexander Hamilton (1755-1804) called the repayment of the **national debt** (then at $75 million) stemming from the Revolutionary War a "sacred obligation." War, in fact, traditionally has been the cause of surges in public debt. The public debt jumped from $65 million in 1860 to $3 billion in 1865 because of the Civil War, and to $24 billion after World War I. During the World War II years of 1940-45, the public debt increased sixfold from $43 billion to $259 billion.

The debt remained in the upper $200 billion range through the early 1960s, when it broke $300 billion, but it then accelerated briskly under the Johnson administration, in part due to the Vietnam War. By the first year of the Nixon administration it had reached $365 billion, and by the time President Nixon resigned the debt had risen to $484 billion. That figure doubled during the next six years, so that by President Reagan's first year in office the public debt hovered just below $1 trillion. Under the Reagan presidency, deficit spending rocketed to unprecedented peacetime levels, amassing a 188 percent increase in the national debt for the years in which the Reagan administration participated in the budget process. During the first Bush administration budget year (1990), the debt figure surpassed the $3 trillion mark for the first time. And by the end of fiscal 1994, the first Clinton budget year, the tally had surged to $4.6 trillion.

THE POLITICS OF PUBLIC DEBT

The public debt is one component of a far larger political question: the role, scope, and prerogatives of the federal government. The problem of the public debt becomes intertwined with questions about global and domestic priorities, the administration of the income tax system, and the function of the Federal Reserve. Federal spending can promote global prosperity, stimulate the domestic economy, develop the national **infrastructure**, provide access to education, and protect disadvantaged populations, among other things. Escalating interest payments on debt, however, ultimately crowd out vital expenditure and investment, sap energy from the business sector, and stifle economic productivity and growth. In addition, as Alexander Hamilton recognized, there are moral objections to passing on debt to future generations.

THE CONTEMPORARY PUBLIC DEBT

The U.S. government's fiscal 1998 was the first deficit-free year in nearly three decades, meaning that all government expenses for the budget year were funded through taxes and other receipts rather than debt. (The last balanced budget was in 1969.) This historic achievement was the product of a series of legislation and policy initiatives that reduced federal expenditures to a number of programs and trimmed the government's operating costs.

While great strides were made to erase the annual deficit, the public debt continued to swell entering the late 1990s, albeit at a slower pace. At the end of fiscal 1998, for example, the debt stood at approximately $5.54 trillion, representing a 3.2 percent increase from year-earlier levels. Significantly, interest payments on this debt totaled $364 billion that year alone. Annual interest payments from 1990 to 1998 grew by an average of $12 billion per year, although year-to-year amounts fluctuated widely.

Not only has the U.S. public debt risen in absolute terms, it has also grown disproportionately in relation to the broader economy. To illustrate, in 1980 the debt measured at just under one-third of the gross domestic product (GDP); in 1990 it weighed in at nearly 56 percent; and by 1997 it represented two-thirds. This was not the highest proportion on record, as the national debt actually exceeded GDP in the years immediately following World War II, but it represented a level last tested during the 1950s.

FURTHER READING:

Stabile, R. Donald, and Jeffrey A. Cantor. *The Public Debt of the United States: An Historical Perspective, 1775-1990.* Westport, CT: Praeger, 1991.

Thompson, Kenneth W., ed. *The Budget Deficit and the National Debt.* Lanham, MD: University Press of America, 1997.

U.S. Department of the Treasury. Bureau of Public Debt. *Monthly Statement of the Public Debt of the United States.* Washington, monthly. Available from www.publicdebt.ustreas.gov.

PUBLIC OFFERING

In order to raise capital, corporations offer their securities for sale to the general public. An initial public offering (IPO) is the first instance in which a corporation offers a specific, registered security for sale. A corporation whose securities are already trading publicly may also offer a new block of stock from its treasury stock or from a large investor in a secondary, or follow-up, offering. Another alternative is a direct public offering (DPO), a relatively uncommon practice in which a small company sells a limited number of its shares (less than $5 million) directly to investors rather than listing them on an exchange. Public offerings are in contrast to private offerings, in which a handful of individuals, many times with personal ties to the business owners or management, is approached directly with an offer to sell shares.

An IPO of **common stock** converts a business owned by one person or several persons into a business owned by many. Taking a company public serves two main purposes:

1. It provides an immediate injection of cash that can be used to enhance the possibilities of successful growth, to buy out and/or to retire the owners, and to establish a base value for estate purposes.
2. It expands the equity base and thereby increases the possibility of stock value appreciation.

There are disadvantages, however. The registration process is expensive and cumbersome, and requires not only the extensive disclosure of the inner workings of the business but also intense scrutiny of the owners and executive officers. Sharing ownership also means dilution of earnings and loss of control.

Secondary public offerings and IPOs involve the transfer of wealth from suppliers of capital to demanders of capital in exchange for (1) direct ownership of the business through stock ownership, and/or (2) a claim on future earnings through debt securities.

THE CAPITAL MARKETS

Public offerings are thus a means for businesses to participate in the **capital markets**, which consist of a diverse set of firms that perform the function of bringing together the suppliers and demanders of capital. The primary U.S. marketplaces are the New York Stock Exchange, the Nasdaq Stock Market, and various smaller exchanges and other over the-counter securities markets.

Securities issuing and trading is highly regulated in the United States. The **Securities Act of 1933** prohibited market players from unscrupulous dealings by requiring disclosure statements, and imposing criminal and civil penalties for inadequate and inaccurate disclosure of ''material fact,'' i.e., information that would likely cause potential investors to reconsider the feasibility of the investment. In 1934 the **Securities and Exchange Commission** was granted the authority to implement and enforce the 1933 act.

The SEC is a quasi-judicial administrative agency authorized to regulate securities industry personnel and the trading of public companies. The SEC is responsible for a formal system of underwriting securities, offering them to the public, raising funds in the public markets, and supervising the continuing trading of securities. For very small securities offerings, often within one state, the issuing firm may not be required to register with the SEC; however, unregistered securities offered to general investors are regarded with great suspicion.

The SEC requires the education, testing, and licensing of individuals engaged in the sale of securities. To keep the investing public properly informed, the SEC has established a series of periodic reports to be filed by publicly listed companies. To oversee public offerings, the SEC has a long and involved registration, disclosure, and review process.

BLUE-SKY LAWS. In order to prevent securities fraud, each state has legislation to prevent the sale of dubious investments, the proverbial one being an offer to sell the blue sky. The term ''blue sky laws'' generally refers to all state securities laws, and when a company has duly registered and complied with state laws, in addition to federal, it is said to comply with the blue sky laws. These laws are more or less similar to SEC rules and regulations, but there are some differences. Issuers of securities must comply with the blue-sky laws in each state in which they expect to offer the securities; if they are planning to be traded on a national market such as the Nasdaq, they effectively must comply with the laws of all 50 states.

THE SECURITIES PLACEMENT PROCESS

INITIAL PUBLIC OFFERING. The process of going public, i.e., making an initial public offering, is complex and costly. It begins with the process of incorporation, if necessary, for only corporations are publicly listed.

The corporation secures a financial adviser to consult on the feasibility of going public and in what manner to do so. After the decision has been made to go forward, the corporation seeks the services of a person who has access to funds. An investment banker serves as the liaison between investors and the company.

The company assembles an experienced team of accountants, auditors, and attorneys along with the investment banker. Together they complete and submit the registration forms and the initial offering prospectus required by the SEC. The prospectus provides a detailed discussion of the company, its performance and profitability, the **management**, and the intended uses for the funds raised.

Meanwhile, the company works with the underwriters to determine the appropriate offering price for the new securities, the underwriter's compensation, the size and timing of the offering, and the method of distributing the securities to the public.

The company and all of its team members are to honor a ''quiet period'' of 90 days from the date of commencing the work on the financial planning to the effective date of the registration statement. The SEC prohibits any publicity during the registration period other than the distribution of the preliminary prospectus. In practice, this means the company is not permitted to release publicity statements (e.g., drumming up interest in its shares) or other commentary about its impending offering up through the time it begins trading.

The SEC review determines the consistency and completeness of the statements to insure full disclosure of material facts. If incomplete, the company performs a ''cleanup'' to resolve SEC concerns.

In order to determine the public's interest in the IPO, the underwriter circulates an attention getter called a ''red herring,'' whose cover page is printed in red as a warning that it is merely a preliminary prospectus. The red herring usually does not give an offering date, price, or number of shares but inside the red herring is a wealth of company information, **financial statements**, and notes.

Upon approval of the registration statements and the prospectus, the SEC notifies the company, and the security may then be listed on an exchange and sold to the public. SEC approval does not constitute a statement of investment merit or fairness of the offering price, but only that full disclosure of relevant facts has been made.

If there are changes to the initial prospectus, the company will revise, reprint, and redistribute it. Sales are permitted only after the potential investor has had a prospectus in hand long enough for adequate review. In the instance where only the price and share information is needed, the company merely sticks a completed label on the cover sheet.

The lead investment banker supervises the public sale of the security. For a larger offering, the lead investment banker will form a syndicate of other investment bankers to underwrite the issue as well as a selling group to assist with the distribution. During the offering period, investment bankers are permitted to ''stabilize'' the price of the security in the secondary market by purchasing shares in the secondary market. This process is called pegging, and it is permitted to continue for up to ten days after the official offering date.

After a successful offering, the underwriter meets with all parties to distribute the funds and settle all expenses. At that time the transfer agent is given authorization to forward the securities to the new owners.

An IPO closes with the transfer of the stock, but the terms of the offering are not completed. The SEC requires the filing of a number of reports (Form SR) that document the appropriate use of the funds as described in the prospectus. If the offering is terminated for any reason, the underwriter returns the funds to the investors.

INVESTOR ISSUES

Public offerings, especially those by innovative new companies, are extremely popular with many investors. In the 1990s this interest was fueled by a regular supply of Internet start-up companies whose unlikely shares enjoyed meteoric run-ups in the stock markets. While some IPOs earn their investors handsome returns, investing in new public offerings, particularly with new companies, is highly speculative and therefore entails a great deal of risk for investors.

Despite the risks, many investors clamor to get in on conventional IPOs and other kinds of public offerings. In the late 1990s, one area under exploration both by investment banks and government regulators was the use of the Internet for various nontraditional securities transactions, including direct public offerings and direct trading without use of an exchange. According to investor advocates, such immediate and relatively informal trading venues underscore the need for investor education to minimize the risk of falling for fraudulent deals.

IMPORTANT SEC FORMS

- S-K: Standard Instructions for Filing Forms under the Securities Act of 1933, the **Securities Exchange Act of 1934**, and the Energy Policy and Conservation Act of 1975, which specifies the requirements for the nonfinancial portion of the registration.
- S-X: Form and Content of and Requirements for Financial Statements, the Securities Exchange Act of 1933, the Securities Act of 1934, the Public Utility Holding Company Act of 1935, and the Energy Policy and Conservation Act of 1975, which specifies the financial statements required and denotes the form, content, and time periods for submission of the information.
- Reg C: Describes the proper procedure for filing a registration statement, the mechanics and paper size, the number of copies, the size of the type, and the definition of terms.

SEE ALSO: Corporate Finance; Privately Placed Securities; Underwriting (Securities); Venture Capital

[Roger J. AbiNader]

FURTHER READING:

Arkebauer, James B., and Ron Schultz. *Going Public.* 3rd ed. Chicago: Dearborn Financial Publishing, 1998.

Halloran, Michael J. *Venture Capital and Public Offering Negotiation.* 3rd ed. New York: Aspen Law & Business, 1997.

Taulli, Tom. *Investing in IPOs.* New York: Bloomberg Press, 1999.

PUBLIC RELATIONS

The term ''public relations'' is practically self-explanatory, yet over the years it has meant different things to different people. To some the term conjures up negative images of publicity ''hacks,'' press agents, and propagandists. To others public relations means making corporations and other types of organizations more responsive to the demands of public opinion. In its simplest form, public relations means relating to the public. As practiced in the first years of the 20th century before the term ''public relations'' was coined, it meant one-way communications from an organization to its audience, or simple publicity. As public relations evolved during the 20th century, it recognized the importance of public opinion and its impact on the organization, and thus the necessity for two-way communication between an organization and its publics.

Edward L. Bernays (1891-1995), an important founding father of modern public relations, began practicing public relations in 1920. He coined the term ''public relations counsel'' and taught the first university course on public relations in 1923 at New York University. That same year his book, *Crystallizing Public Opinion,* was published and became the first book on public relations. In an interview that was published in the winter 1956 issue of *Public Relations Quarterly,* Bernays described public relations as ''a field of activity which has to do with the interaction between an individual, a group, an idea, or other unit with the public on which it depends. A counsel on public relations is an expert who advises on relations with these publics. He attempts to define the socially sound objectives of his client or project. He attempts to find out by research what the adjustments or maladjustments are between his client and the publics on which he depends.''

Philip Lesly (1918-), a leading authority on public relations and editor of *Lesly's Handbook of Public Relations and Communications,* succinctly defined public relations as ''helping an organization and its public adapt mutually to each other.'' Other definitions of public relations point to its role in protecting and developing goodwill or characterize it as how one organization or group tells other organizations or groups about itself. Yet public relations involves more than words; it also requires an organization to act. The effect of good public relations is to lessen the gap between how an organization sees itself and how others outside the organization perceive it.

Bernays, Lesly, and other experts agree that public relations involves two-way communication between an organization and its public. It requires listening to the publics on which an organization is dependent as well as analyzing and understanding the attitudes and behaviors of those audiences. Only then can an organization undertake an effective public relations campaign consisting of actions as well as words.

Public relations involves many different types of audiences and organizations. Public relations is practiced not only by companies and business firms, but also by trade associations on behalf of specific industries, professional associations on behalf of their members, and other nonprofit organizations as well as cities, states, countries, and a variety of government agencies.

The publics with which these organizations are concerned are also quite varied. Depending on the type of organization, they include its stockholders and investors, employees or members, customers and consumers, government regulators, the media, and the community in which it is located.

PUBLIC RELATIONS: A MULTIFACETED ACTIVITY

If we examine some of the goals and objectives of public relations, it becomes clear that it is a multifaceted activity involving many different functions. Topping the list of objectives, public relations seeks to create, maintain, and protect the organization's reputation, enhance its prestige, and present a favorable image. Studies have shown that consumers often base their purchase decision on a company's reputation, so public relations can have a definite impact on a company's sales and revenue. Public relations can be an effective part of a company's overall **marketing** strategy. In the case of a for-profit company, public relations and marketing may be coordinated to be sure they are working to achieve the same objectives.

Another major public relations goal is to create goodwill for the organization. This involves such functions as employee relations, stockholder and investor relations, media relations, community relations, and relations with the many other publics with whom the organization interacts, affects, or is affected by.

Public relations also has an educational component that can help it achieve such goals as outlined above. Public relations may function to educate certain publics about many things relevant to the organization, including educating them about business in general, new legislation, and how to use a particular product as well as to overcome misconceptions and prejudices. A nonprofit organization may attempt to educate the public regarding a certain point of view. Trade associations may undertake educational programs regarding particular industries and their products and practices.

PUBLIC RELATIONS AND TWO-WAY COMMUNICATION

Effective public relations requires a knowledge, based on analysis and understanding, of all the factors that influence perception of and attitudes toward the organization. The development of a specific public relations campaign follows these basic steps, which can be visualized as a loop that begins within the organization, extends to the target audience(s), and returns back to the organization.

While a specific public relations project or campaign may be undertaken proactively or reactively, the first basic step in either case involves analysis and research to identify all the relevant factors of the situation. In this first step the organization gains an understanding of the key factors that are influencing the perceptions of the organization and the nature of the publics involved.

The second step, policy formation, builds on the first. Here the organization establishes an overall policy with respect to the campaign, including defining goals and the desired outcome as well as the constraints under which the campaign will operate. It is necessary to establish such policy guidelines in order to evaluate proposed strategies and tactics as well as the overall success of the campaign.

In step three strategies and tactics are outlined. Here the organization brings into play its knowledge of its target audiences and develops specific programs consistent with established policies to achieve the desired objectives. Then the organization is ready for step four, actual communication with the targeted publics. Specific public relations techniques, such as press conferences or special events, are employed to reach the intended audience.

Up to this point the public relations loop has gone in one direction from the organization to its target audiences. In step five the loop turns back toward the organization as it receives feedback from its publics. How have they reacted to the public relations campaign? Are there some unexpected developments? Here the organization listens to its publics and, in the final step, assesses the program and makes any necessary adjustments.

PUBLIC RELATIONS PRACTICES AND TECHNIQUES

Public relations is a multifaceted activity involving different publics and audiences as well as different types of organizations, all with different goals and objectives. Specific areas of public relations will be reviewed next, with examples of practices and techniques and their use in effective campaigns covering a variety of situations. Many of the examples cited first appeared as case studies in the weekly *PR News* and were later collected in the *PR News Casebook.*

PRODUCT PUBLIC RELATIONS. Public relations and marketing work together closely when it comes to promoting a new or existing product or service. Public relations plays an important role in new product introductions by creating awareness, differentiating the product from other similar products, and even changing consumer behavior. For example, when the Prince Matchabelli division of Chesebrough-Pond's USA introduced a new men's cologne, there were 21 other men's fragrances being introduced that year. To differentiate its new offering, called Hero, Prince Matchabelli created a National Hero Awards Program honoring authentic male heroes and enlisted the participation of Big Brothers/Big Sisters of America to lend credibility to the program. When Coleco introduced its Cabbage Patch Kids, public relations helped increase awareness through licensed tie-in products, trade show exhibits, press parties, and even window displays in Cartier jewelry stores. When one bank began using **automated teller machines** (ATMs), it created a friendly new image of the new customer-operated machines by introducing them first to children. Public relations can also help introduce new products through staging a variety of special events and in the handling of sensitive situations.

Public relations is often called on to give existing products and services a boost by creating and renewing visibility. The California Raisins Advisory Board organized a national tour featuring live performances by the California Dancing Raisins to maintain interest in raisins during a summer-long advertising hiatus. The tour generated national and local publicity through media events, advance publicity, trade promotions, and media interviews with performer Ray Charles. Before denim became fashionable, the Denim Council helped gain public acceptance of the fabric with a multifaceted campaign that included a range of special events, book tie-ins, promotional giveaways, and specially designated "Denim Weeks," resulting in high-profile magazine and newspaper feature stories.

Other public relations programs for existing products involve stimulating secondary demand, as when Campbell Soup Co. increased overall demand for soup by publishing a recipe booklet. Identifying new uses for the product, as when Rit Household Dyes took advantage of the tie-dyeing craze of the 1960s and 1970s to increase demand for its products, is another way to stimulate interest in an existing product. Public relations can interest the media in familiar products and services in a number of ways, including holding seminars for journalists, staging a special media day, and supplying the media with printed materials ranging from "backgrounders" (in-depth news releases) to booklets and brochures. Changes in existing products offer additional public relations opportunities to focus consumers' attention. An effective public relations campaign can help to properly position a product and overcome negative perceptions on the part of the general public.

EMPLOYEE RELATIONS. Employees are one of the most important publics a company has, and an ongoing public relations program is necessary to maintain employee goodwill as well as to uphold the company's image and reputation among its employees. The essence of a good employee relations program is keeping employees informed and providing them with channels of communication to upper levels of **management**. Bechtel Group, a privately held complex of operating companies, published an **annual report** for its employees to keep them informed about the company's operations. The company used employee surveys to determine what information employees considered useful. A range of other communication devices were used, including a monthly tabloid and magazine, a quarterly video magazine, local newsletters, bulletin boards, a call-in telephone service, and "brown bag" lunches where live presentations were made about the company. **Suggestion systems**, which originated in World War II, are another effective way to improve employee-management communications.

Other public relations programs for employees include **training** them as company public relations representatives; explaining benefits programs to them; offering them educational, volunteer, and citizenship opportunities; and staging special events such as picnics or open houses for them. Other programs can improve performance and increase **employee motivation** and pride. Public relations also plays a role in recruiting new employees; handling reorganizations, relocations, and **mergers**; and resolving labor disputes.

FINANCIAL RELATIONS. Financial relations involves communicating not only with a company's stockholders, but also with the wider community of financial analysts and potential investors. An effective investor relations plan can increase the value of a company's **stock** and make it easier for it to raise additional capital. One successful plan involved financial presentations in ten major cities, mailings to the financial community, and financially oriented advertisements, resulting in the stock price increasing 50 percent and the **price-earnings ratio** doubling. In some cases special meetings with financial analysts are necessary to overcome adverse publicity, negative perceptions about a company, or investor indifference. Such meetings may take the form of full-day briefings, formal presentations, or luncheon meetings. A tour of a company's facilities may help generate interest among the financial community. Mailings and ongoing communications can help a company achieve visibility among potential investors and financial analysts.

Annual reports and stockholder meetings are the two most important public relations tools for maintaining good stockholder relations. Some companies hold regional or quarterly meetings in addition to the usual annual meeting. Other companies reach more stockholders by moving the location of their annual meeting from city to city. Annual reports can be complemented by quarterly reports and dividend check inserts. Companies that wish to provide additional communications with stockholders may send them a newsletter or company magazine. Personal letters to new stockholders and a quick response to inquiries ensure an additional measure of goodwill.

COMMUNITY RELATIONS. Comprehensive, ongoing community relations programs can help virtually any organization achieve visibility as a good community citizen and put the organization on the receiving end of the goodwill of the community in which it is located. **Banks**, utilities, radio and television stations, and major retailers and corporations are some of the types of organizations most likely to have ongoing programs that might include supporting urban renewal, performing arts programs, social and educational programs, children's programs, community organizations, and construction projects. Support may be financial or take the form of employee participation.

Organizations have the opportunity to improve goodwill and demonstrate a commitment to their communities when they open new offices, expand facilities, and open new factories. One company increased community awareness of its presence by converting a vacant building into a permanent meeting place. Another company built its new headquarters in an abandoned high school that it renovated. Mutual of Omaha scheduled an anniversary celebration and awards dinner to coincide with the dedication of its new underground office building to generate additional media coverage.

One of the more sensitive areas of community relations involves plant closings. A well-planned public relations campaign, combined with appropriate actions, can alleviate the tensions that such closings cause. Some elements of such a campaign might include offering special programs to laid-off workers, informing employees directly about proposed closings, and controlling rumors through candid and direct communications to the community and employees.

Organizations conduct a variety of special programs to improve community relations, including providing employee volunteers to work on community projects, sponsoring educational and literacy programs, staging open houses and conducting plant tours, celebrating anniversaries, and mounting special exhibits. Organizations are recognized as good community citizens when they support programs that improve the quality of life in their community, including crime prevention, **employment**, environmental programs, clean-up and beautification, **recycling**, and restoration.

Sometimes it is necessary for an organization to gain community support for a particular action, such as a new development or factory. One **real estate** developer elicited favorable media coverage and brought praise from local government by preserving a historic estate that was on a site that had been proposed for development. A utility company mobilized its employees to win community support for a proposed nuclear power plant. They participated in a telephone campaign, attended council meetings in area communities, and volunteered as guides for plant open houses.

CRISIS COMMUNICATIONS. Public relations practitioners become heavily involved in crisis communications whenever there is a major accident or natural disaster affecting an organization and its community. Other types of crises involve bankruptcy, product failures, and management wrongdoing. After the San Francisco earthquake of 1989, the Bank of America utilized its public relations department to quickly establish communications with customers, the financial community, the media, and offices in 45 countries to assure them the bank was still operating. When faced with bankruptcy, Chrysler Corp. embarked on an extensive public relations campaign under the direction of its public affairs department to persuade Congress to approve a $1.2 billion government loan guarantee. In some cases, crises call for an organization to become involved in helping potential victims; in other cases, the crisis may require rebuilding an organization's image.

GOVERNMENT AND POLITICAL PUBLIC RELATIONS. Public relations in the political arena covers a wide range, including staging presidential debates, as the League of Women Voters has done, holding seminars for government leaders, influencing proposed legislation, and testifying before a congressional committee. Political candidates engage in public relations, as do government agencies at the federal, state, and local levels.

Trade associations and other types of organizations attempt to block unfavorable legislation and support favorable legislation in a number of ways. The liquor industry in California helped defeat a proposed **tax** increase by taking charge of the debate early, winning endorsements, recruiting spokespersons, and cultivating grassroots support. A speakers bureau trained some 240 industry volunteers, and key messages were communicated to the public through printed materials and radio and television commercials.

In another example, many cities considered adopting legislation that banned the sale of spray paint to retail customers because of a rash of graffiti. The National Paint and Coatings Association launched a campaign that focused on the crime of vandalism. The collective research that went into the campaign resulted in an ongoing legislative monitoring operation through which the industry is alerted to new developments.

PUBLIC RELATIONS IN THE PUBLIC INTEREST. Organizations attempt to generate goodwill and position themselves as responsible citizens through a variety of programs conducted in the public interest. Some examples are environmental programs that include water and energy conservation, antipollution programs, and generally publicizing an organization's environmental efforts. Health and medical programs are sponsored by a wide range of nonprofit organizations, health care providers, and other businesses and industries. These range from encouraging other companies to develop **AIDS in the workplace** policies to the American Cancer Society's Great American Smokeout.

A variety of programs for young people may be conducted in the public interest. These range from providing educational materials to schools to sponsoring a radio program for students and teachers. International Paper developed a program to help older students and recent graduates improve their reading and writing skills by having celebrities write ''how-to'' articles that were printed as advertisements in popular magazines and major newspapers. Other programs offer political education, leadership and self-improvement, recreational activities, contests, and safety instruction.

CONSUMER EDUCATION. Organizations have undertaken a variety of programs to educate consumers, building goodwill and helping avoid misunderstandings in the process. Some examples of trade association activity in this area include the Soap and Detergent Association preparing a guide on housecleaning to be used in educational programs for new public housing residents. The National Association of Manufacturers held local open houses to educate the public about local businesses. The general public was allowed to make **toll-free telephone calls** to a pesticide symposium conducted by two agricultural associations. The automotive industry established the Automobile Information Council as a source of industry news and information. An association of accountants undertook to educate the public concerning new tax laws.

Other opportunities for educating consumers include sponsoring television and radio programs, producing manuals and other printed materials, producing materials for classroom use, and releasing the results of surveys. In addition to focusing on specific issues or industries, educational programs may seek to inform consumers about economic matters and business in general.

OTHER PUBLIC RELATIONS PROGRAMS. Other types of programs that fall under the umbrella of public relations include **corporate identity** programs ranging from name changes and new trademarks to changing a company's image and identity. Milestones and anniversaries are observed in a variety of ways to improve an organization's public relations.

Special events may be held to call attention to an organization and focus the public's goodwill. These include anniversary celebrations, events related to trade shows, special exhibits, fairs and festivals, and other types of events.

Speakers bureaus and celebrity spokespersons are effective public relations tools for communicating an organization's point of view. Speakers bureaus may be organized by a trade association or an individual company as well as by virtually any other type of organization. The face to-face communication that speakers can deliver is often more effective than messages carried by printed materials, especially when the target audience is small and clearly defined.

The examples of public relations practices given here indicate the range of activities and functions that fall within public relations. It is clear that while communication is the essence of public relations, an effective public relations campaign is based on action as well as words. Whether it is practiced formally or informally, public relations is an essential function for the survival of any organization.

PUBLIC RELATIONS AND THE INTERNET

The **Internet** and the World Wide Web and the use of **electronic mail** has given public relations practitioners a new tool for communicating with journalists and editors in the media. According to Paul Krupin, compiler of *The U.S. All Media E-Mail Directory,* "Media executives are increasingly adapting to the use of e-mail as a preferred method for receiving news releases." Electronic public relations is most effective for those companies whose products and services are web- or computer-oriented, and even though media contacts may prefer to receive news releases via e-mail, they still evaluate each release on the basis of its content. Krupin also noted in a 1998 article for *Directory World,* "The lion's share of media still rely on faxes, telephones, and street mail, pretty much in that order."

Also affected by the World Wide Web are press kits, which used to consist of a large folder filled with glossy photos, corporate bios, and narrative press releases. More effective for the World Wide Web are online press kits, which consist of video news releases, still images, and a wealth of background information—all available online at a company's Web site or e-mailed to media contacts. Benefits to using an online press kit include lower costs and making more information available to journalists. Photographs and news releases can be easily downloaded, saving valuable time for the user.

In addition to including current information, corporate Web sites often contain an archive of news releases going back in time. They may also contain other public relations items, such as a corporate history or timeline, annual reports, and profiles of corporate officers. Companies with an interest in public relations will be using the World Wide Web to find new opportunities to communicate their messages to their publics.

[David P. Bianco]

FURTHER READING:

Bernays, Edward L. *The Later Years: Public Relations Insights, 1956-1986.* Rhinebeck, NY: H&M Publishers, 1986.

Bianco, David, ed. *PR News Casebook: 1,000 Public Relations Case Studies.* Detroit: Gale Research, 1993.

Krupin, Paul. "Fine-Tune Your New Media Publicity Tools." *Directory World,* March/April 1998, 5-6.

Lesly, Philip, ed. *Lesly's Handbook of Public Relations and Communications.* New York: AMACOM, 1991.

Sutlip, Scott M. *Effective Public Relations.* 7th ed. Paramus, NJ: Prentice Hall, 1994.

Tye, Larry. *The Father of Spin: Edward L. Bernays and the Birth of Public Relations.* New York: Crown, 1998.

Wilcox, Dennis L., and others. *Public Relations: Strategies and Tactics.* 4th ed. Reading, MA: Addison-Wesley, 1995.

PUBLICLY HELD COMPANY

A publicly held company exists when that company's **stock** is owned by members of the general public. The stock of a publicly held company is openly traded. In order for a company to be publicly held, it must be organized as a corporation. A corporation is a legal form of business that is established by a corporate charter granted by a particular state. The corporate charter establishes the corporation as a separate legal entity from its owners. The corporation is said to be a "legal person" and may enter into agreements, make **contracts**, and sue or be sued.

A corporation may be publicly or privately owned. In the case of a privately owned, or closely held, corporation, all of the stock is concentrated in the hands of a few individuals. When the privately held corporation first issues its stock, it is not offered for sale to the general public. On the other hand, the stock of a publicly held corporation is offered to the general public for sale. A **privately held company** may decide to "go public." That is, it makes a stock offering to the general public in order to raise capital. The first public stock offering of a company is known as its initial **public offering** (IPO).

The owners of a corporation, whether public or private, are its common stockholders. There are two types of stock, common and preferred. Preferred stockholders generally receive a stated **dividend** of a specific amount. Common stockholders receive a dividend based on **corporate profits**, although in some cases **common stock** pays no dividend. The corporation's charter specifies how many shares and what types of stock it is allowed to issue. While both preferred stockholders and common stockholders are investors in the corporation and provide it with capital, it is the common stockholders who actually own the firm.

In a privately held corporation, the owners and managers may be the same individuals. That is not the case with a publicly held company. A distinction is made between a publicly held corporation's owners and its managers. While the shareholders own the firm, the company's managers, executives, and directors run the firm. The **board of directors** is responsible for running the corporation to maximize profits for the shareholders. In practice the corporate directors establish corporate policy, make major decisions, and hire managers and others to oversee the daily operations of the corporation. Shareholders can express their satisfaction or displeasure with the board of directors of a publicly owned firm by voting them in or out of office.

While the shareholders of a publicly owned company are its owners, they are not liable for the actions of the company. Through the concept of limited liability, the shareholders may lose their investments in a company, but they have no personal liability beyond that. For example, they are not personally responsible for the **debts** of the corporation. Although they are owners of the corporation, the shareholders have in effect agreed to give up immediate control of the corporation. As a result, they are not held personally liable for the actions of the corporation.

Publicly held companies must follow the financial reporting and disclosure requirements of the **Securities and Exchange Commission** (SEC). The SEC regulations are designed to keep stockholders informed of the financial condition of the corporation. In addition, the SEC regulates all stock offerings and requires that new stock offerings be registered and fully described in a document called a prospectus. Privately held corporations, on the other hand, are not required to make public their profits and other financial results.

Publicly held companies are responsible for much of the business activity of the United States. Corporations that have the ability to raise capital by selling shares of stock to the general public can accumulate large amounts of capital for use in their business. Successful and relatively young privately held companies often attempt to become publicly held companies when their **management** believes there is enough public confidence in their ability to turn a profit. It must be remembered, however, that not all corporations are publicly held, and there are some very large corporations that remain privately held.

SEE ALSO: Going Public; Preferred Stock

[David P. Bianco]

FURTHER READING:

Arkebauer, James. *Going Public: Everything You Needed to Know to Take Your Company Public or Invest in an IPO or DPO.* Chicago: Dearborn Trade, 1998.

Field, Drew. *Direct Public Offerings: The New Method for Taking Your Company Public.* Naperville, IL: Sourcebooks, 1997.

Lipman, Frederick D. *Going Public: Everything You Need to Know to Successfully Turn a Private Enterprise into a Publicly Traded Company.* Upland: DIANE Publishing, 1998.

PURCHASING POWER

Purchasing power refers to the amount of goods and services a fixed amount of money can purchase. The purchasing power of the dollar is related to changes in prices for different goods and services. Published price indices periodically measure the prices of commodities, retail prices, and prices for the economy as a whole. When prices for commodities increase, the purchasing power of the commodity dollar decreases. When retail prices increase, the purchasing power of the retail dollar decreases. And when prices for the economy as a whole, as reported in the **consumer price index (CPI)**, increase, then the purchasing power of the consumer dollar decreases.

Individuals living on fixed incomes are those who are most affected by price increases and corresponding decreases in purchasing power. Payments to such individuals, including government Social Security payments and a variety of **pension** payments from private industry, are often tied to changes in the consumer price index. When the consumer price index rises and the purchasing power of the dollar decreases, pension and Social Security payments typically add what is known as a *cost of living* factor. These additional payments are made to individuals living on fixed incomes in an attempt to maintain the level of purchasing power when prices go up.

In order to more accurately reflect the purchasing power of the dollar, economic statistics are usually reported in current dollars and in constant dollars. Constant dollars are measured against a base year in which a current dollar equals a constant dollar. Then for years before and after the base year, a current dollar is multiplied by a figure known as an implicit deflator to obtain the equivalent value in constant dollars. The deflator takes into account price increases and, depending on the behavior of prices, may change from year to year.

Reporting economic statistics in terms of constant dollars enables economists to compare economic performance from one year to another. Increases of such economic measures as the **gross national product (GNP)** or disposable personal income that are reported in current dollars would not accurately measure increases in productivity or in real income. Rather, much of the increase in GNP and disposable personal income would simply be due to inflationary factors, such as price increases. However, when such statistics are reported in constant dollars, then the effect of price increases is eliminated and a truer picture of actual production or purchasing power is given.

Economists refer to income reported in current dollars as money income, and income reported in constant dollars as real income. Real income provides a measure of purchasing power, since it takes into account the effect of price changes. When people speak of a dollar not being what it used to be, they mean that it no longer has the purchasing power it once had.

SEE ALSO: Consumer Price Index (CPI)

[David P. Bianco]

FURTHER READING:

Derks, Scott, ed. *The Value of a Dollar: Prices and Incomes in the United States, 1860-1989.* Detroit: Gale Research, 1994.

May, Robert G., et al. *Accounting.* Cincinnati, OH: South-Western Publishing Co., 1994.

Munn, Glenn G., et al. *Encyclopedia of Banking and Finance.* 9th edition. Rolling Meadows, IL: Bankers Publishing Co., 1991.

PUT-CALL PARITY

Put-call parity helps to define the relative values of an option to buy a **security** and the option to sell the same security. For example, suppose Microsoft **stock** is selling for $93 per share. Investors will pay something for the right, or option, to buy a share of Microsoft stock for $95 during the next 90 days. Suppose this amount is $8. Hence, purchasers of this "call" option expect the price to rise significantly above $95 by the end of this period. Likewise, other investors may pay $5 for the option to sell a share of Microsoft for $95 during the next 90 days. Purchasers of this "put" option expect the price to fall below $95.

Now consider two portfolios. Portfolio 1 consists of one put option and one share of Microsoft stock. This portfolio would cost $98 to create ($5 + $93). Portfolio 2 consists of one call option and one bank deposit that will grow to $95 in 90 days. If **interest rates** on such bank deposits are 6 percent per year, then an investor would earn about 1.5 percent in 90 days and must deposit $93.60 today. The total cost of Portfolio 2 is $101.60 ($8 + $93.60).

Since an option will be exercised only if it is beneficial to the holder, there are only two possible outcomes. Either Microsoft sells for $95 or more at the end of 90 days or it doesn't. Let's examine the payoffs for each portfolio at the end of 90 days. If Microsoft stock is selling for more than $95, say $110, then the put is worthless and the call is worth $15. Portfolio 1 will pay $110 ($0 + $110) and Portfolio 2 will pay $110 ($15 + $95). The payoffs for the two portfolios will be equal for any given price of Microsoft in excess of $95. If Microsoft is selling for less than $95, say $88, then the put is worth $7 and the call is worthless. Portfolio 1 will pay $95 ($7 + $88) and Portfolio 2 will pay $95 ($0 + $95) as well. Again, the payoffs for the two portfolios will be equal for any given price of Microsoft below $95.

What does this mean? Since the two portfolios always produce the same cash flows at the end of 90 days, they should have the same value today. In this example, however, Portfolio 1 is less expensive than Portfolio 2. This suggests an **arbitrage** opportunity. If an investor can buy Portfolio 1 and sell Portfolio 2, then an immediate profit of $3.60 can be achieved. An investor could sell Portfolio 2 by selling a call option and borrowing $93.60. Since each portfolio produces the same cash flow in 90 days, buying one and selling the other will result in a net cash flow of zero. But all of this pricing information is known today! Hence, many investors will be buying puts and selling calls to capture the arbitrage profit. This will eventually increase the price of the put and decrease the price of the call to a point where the arbitrage profit will vanish and the two portfolios will be priced identically.

The put-call parity relationship is a powerful economic result. It holds true in any reasonably efficient market and keeps investor optimism or pessimism from spiraling out of control.

SEE ALSO: Call and Put Options

[Paul Bolster]

FURTHER READING:

Brigham, Eugene F., Louis C. Gapenski, and Michael C. Ehrhardt. *Financial Management: Theory and Practice.* 9th ed. Fort Worth, TX: Dryden Press, 1999.

Hull, John C. *Options, Futures, and Other Derivatives.* 3rd ed. Upper Saddle River, NJ: Prentice Hall, 1997.

Kolb, Robert W. *Understanding Options.* New York: John Wiley & Sons, Inc., 1995.

QUALITY CIRCLES

The interest of U.S. manufacturers in quality circles (or quality control circles) was sparked by the dramatic improvements in the quality and economic competitiveness of Japanese goods in the post-World War II years. In their volume *Japanese Quality Circles and Productivity,* Ross and Ross defined a quality circle as follows: "A quality circle is a small group of employees doing similar or related work who meet regularly to identify, analyze, and solve product-quality and production problems and to improve general operations. The circle is a relatively autonomous unit (ideally about ten workers), usually led by a supervisor or a senior worker and organized as a work unit."

Under ideal circumstances these voluntary groups of problem solvers focus on measurable indicators of quality that impact the company's costs, productivity, or other business interests. Such indicators are usually industry- or process-specific. So, for example, quality circles at a manufacturing company might focus on finding ways to minimize product defects, as measured in the amount of product with a particular defect per thousand or million; meanwhile, those at an insurance company might seek methods to reduce the frequency of billing errors.

BACKGROUND

Quality circles are generally associated with Japanese management and manufacturing techniques. The introduction of quality circles in Japan in the postwar years was inspired by the lectures of W. Edwards Deming (1900-1993), a statistician for the U.S. government. The newly formed Union of Japanese Scientists and Engineers was familiar with Deming's work and heard that he would be coming to Japan in 1950 to advise the Allied occupation government. Accepting JUSE's invitation, Deming addressed Japanese industry's top 50 executives.

Deming based his proposals on the experience of U.S. firms operating under wartime industrial standards during World War II. Noting that American management had typically given line managers and engineers about 85 percent of responsibility for quality control and only about 15 percent to production workers, Deming argued that these shares should be reversed. Production processes should be redesigned to more fully account for quality control, and all employees in a firm from top down should understand statistical control technologies and undergo continuous education on quality control. Quality circles were the means by which this continuous education was to take place for production workers.

Were Japanese firms to adopt the system of quality controls he advocated, Deming predicted that nations around the world would be imposing import quotas on Japanese products within five years. His prediction was vindicated. Deming's ideas became very influential in Japan, and in 1951, JUSE established the annual corporate and individual Deming awards for achievements in quality improvement. Deming was also awarded the Second Order Medal of the Sacred Treasure from Emperor Hirohito for his contributions to the Japanese economy. A 1954 lecture series in Japan by American quality control expert Dr. J.M. Juran gave further impetus to the development of quality control circles.

The principles of quality circles emphasized the importance of preventing defects from occurring rather than relying on product inspection following a production process. Quality circles also attempted to minimize the scrap and downtime that resulted from part and product defects. Deming's idea that improving quality could increase productivity led to the development in Japan of the Total Quality Control (TQC) concept, in which quality and productivity are viewed as two sides of a coin. TQC also required that a manufacturer's suppliers make use of quality circles.

Quality circles often rely on visual representations such as scatter diagrams, flow charts, and cause-and-effect diagrams. In one common format, various aspects of the production process were categorized by materials, manpower, methods, and machines. The reliance on statistical representations of the production process and statistical production controls was another of Deming's legacies in Japan.

Quality circles in Japan were part of a system of relatively cooperative **labor-management relations**, involving company unions and lifetime employment guarantees for many full-time permanent employees. Consistent with this decentralized, enterprise-oriented system, quality circles provided a means by which production workers were encouraged to participate in company matters and by which management could benefit from production workers' intimate knowledge of the production process.

Recommendations from employees played an important role in Japan, and two associations, the Japanese Association of Suggestion Systems and the Japan Human Relations Association, were developed to improve the process. These associations reported that in 1980 alone changes resulting from employee suggestions resulted in savings of $10 billion for Japanese firms and bonuses of $4 billion for Japanese employees.

Active U.S. interest in Japanese quality control began in the early 1970s, when U.S. aerospace manufacturer Lockheed organized a tour of Japanese industrial plants. This trip marked a turning point in the previously established pattern, in which Japanese managers had made educational tours of industrial plants in the United States. Lockheed's visit resulted in the gradual establishment of quality circles in its factories beginning in 1974. Within two years, Lockheed estimated that its 15 quality circles had saved nearly $3 million, with a ratio of savings to cost of six to one.

As Lockheed's successes became known, other firms in the aerospace industry began adopting quality circles, including Hughes Aircraft, Northrop, Sperry Vickers, Martin Marietta, and Westinghouse. Thereafter quality circles spread rapidly throughout the U.S. economy; by 1980, over one-half of firms in the *Fortune* 500 had implemented or were planning on implementing quality circles. By the early 1980s, General Motors Corp. had established about 100 quality circles among its Buick, Oldsmobile, Cadillac, Chevrolet, and Fisher Body divisions.

A TARNISHED IMAGE

In the early 1990s, however, the U.S. **National Labor Relations Board (NLRB)** made important rulings regarding the legality of certain forms of quality circles. These rulings were based on the 1935 Wagner Act's prohibition of company unions and management-dominated labor organizations.

In December of 1992, the NLRB ruled that Electromation Inc. of Elkhart, Indiana, was operating unlawful quality circles and employee-involvement programs, referred to as "action committees" by the firm. These programs were found unlawful in that they were established by the firm, that their agendas were dominated by the firm, and that they addressed the conditions of employment within the firm. The NLRB stated that its ruling was not a general indictment against quality circles and labor-management cooperation programs, but was aimed specifically at the practices of Electromation. Electromation had been a nonunion firm, but was unionized by the Teamsters shortly after the "action committees" were eliminated.

The NLRB made a similar ruling against E.I. Du Pont de Nemours & Co., a unionized firm, in June of 1993. The NLRB ruled that Du Pont's seven labor-management committees in its Deepwater, New Jersey, plant were in effect labor organizations that were used to bypass negotiations with the plant's union, the Chemical Workers Association. The NLRB stated once again that its ruling was limited to the facts in the case at hand. Nonetheless, a number of employer representatives expressed their concern that the ruling would hinder the development of labor-management cooperation programs of all kinds.

The chilling effect from the NLRB rulings made many human resources departments wary of initiating new quality circle programs for fear of legal repercussions. This climate coincided what appeared to be a general waning of interest in quality circles among U.S. companies since the 1980s. By the mid-1990s the topic all but disappeared from discussions in the mainstream business press, and even academic journals gradually lost interest in quality circles.

Indeed, two Columbia Business School researchers, Eric Abrahamson and Gregory Fairchild, published a study characterizing quality circles in the United States as little more than a management fad. Abrahamson and Fairchild's work, based in large part on an analysis of periodical articles on the subject published over a 19-year span, suggested that the short-lived popularity of quality circles was a product of U.S. corporations' knee-jerk decisions in reaction to a perceived competitive disadvantage versus Japanese firms. The U.S. companies grasped, the professors argued, for easy ways to emulate the successful practices of their Japanese competitors, and the notion of quality circles appeared to many at the time to be one such way.

Despite quality circles' decline in popularity in the United States, the practice continues to enjoy support in Japanese firms.

SEE ALSO: Japanese Management Techniques; Quality Control; Total Quality Management (TQM)

[David Kucera]

FURTHER READING:

Griffith, Victoria. ''Ammunition for Fighting the Fad.'' *Financial Times,* 15 August 1997.

Journal for Quality and Participation, bimonthly.

Noble, Barbara Presley. ''Worker-Participation Programs are Found Illegal.'' *New York Times,* 8 June 1993.

Ross, Joel E., and William C. Ross. *Japanese Quality Circles and Productivity.* Reston Publishing Company, 1982.

Sasaki, Naoto and David Hutchins. *The Japanese Approach to Product Quality.* Pergamon Press, 1984.

QUALITY CONTROL

The American Society for Quality Control (ASQC), in its *Glossary and Tables for Statistical Quality Control,* defines quality control as:

> the operational techniques and the activities which sustain a quality of product or service that will satisfy given needs; also the use of such techniques and activities . . . the aim of quality is to provide quality that is satisfactory, e.g., safe, adequate, dependable, and economical. . . . [This requires] integrating several related steps including proper specification . . . design of the product . . . to meet the requirements; production [processes that] . . . meet the specification; inspection to determine [the degree of conformance] . . . to specification; and review of usage to provide for revision of specification [if necessary].

These steps are required for a firm to design, produce, market, and profit from a quality product. Control charts are one technique used in implementing, sustaining, and improving quality control. Statistical process studies are also an important tool in improving quality by reducing process variation. Other important techniques are experimental design and **Taguchi methods**. Total quality control (TQC) or **total quality management** (TQM) refers to quality control beyond the ''sustaining'' of quality. These last two concepts may lead to continual increases in quality.

Dr. Kaoru Ishikawa (1915-), recipient of many awards, including the Deming Prize, defined total quality control as a system of introducing and implementing quality technologies into various departments of a company, such as engineering, production, sales, and service, for the purpose of satisfying customers. He stated that viewed chronologically, TQC is only the first stage of company-wide quality control (CWQC). CWQC incorporates quality function deployment (QFD), whereas TQC does not. QFD is a design procedure that introduces quality control in product development. It is a formal mechanism that guarantees that ''the voice of the customer'' is heard throughout all the phases of manufacturing a product or providing a service.

As Dale Besterfield stated in his book *Quality Control,* the deliverance of a quality product or service requires the responsible integration of all the firm's departments—**marketing**, product engineering, purchasing, manufacturing engineering, manufacturing, inspection and testing, packaging and shipping, and product service. TQC or TQM is far more than sustaining quality, as it may include control systems, employee relations and **organizational behavior**, **statistical process control**, and Japanese management techniques.

Quality control techniques and standards, affecting almost all aspects of a business, have now been adopted at both national and international levels. The Malcolm Baldrige National Quality Award exemplifies the former. President Ronald Reagan signed the Malcolm Baldrige National Quality Improvement Act on August 20, 1987. The act was the culmination of a national campaign to improve the quality of goods and services in the United States. The award represents the highest level of recognition that an American company can receive.

On an international level, the **ISO 9000** series of quality standards was first published in 1987. These standards reflect the importance of quality and reliability as critical factors for achieving and maintaining worldwide competitive advantage. Another example is the international environment management standard, ISO 14001. Companies worldwide use this standard as a blueprint to develop and refine internal environmental management systems.

HISTORICAL BACKGROUND

Beginning in the Middle Ages, the maintenance of quality was generally guaranteed by the guilds. They required long periods of training, which instilled in craftsmen a strong pride in the quality of their work.

The Industrial Revolution initiated the specialization of labor. Consequently, workers no longer produced the whole product, only a part. This transformation led to a decline in workmanship. At first, quality was not greatly diminished since manufacturing processes were simple in the early days of the Industrial Revolution. As manufacturing processes became more complicated and work more specialized, however, the trend toward post-manufactured product inspection began.

During the 19th century, modern industrial systems arose. At this time in the United States, Frederick W. Taylor's (1856-1915) "scientific management" dominated. His philosophy placed work and production planning exclusively in the hands of **management** and industrial engineers. (The ultimate expression of Taylorism was Henry Ford's (1863-1947) moving assembly line.) Before scientific management, quality was manufacturing's responsibility. Since meeting production deadlines became the production manager's main priority, the responsibility for quality was placed increasingly in the hands of the "chief inspector" and the quality control department.

In 1924, at Bell Telephone Laboratories, Walter A. Shewhart (1891 1967) developed statistical control charts. These charts pinpointed the sources of variation within processes and were used to control the quality of, and to improve the processes that delivered, the output. It is a total quality management principle that, generally, quality is maintained and improved through the detection and reduction of process variation. Of course, it is assumed that the target value of the process has been obtained and maintained.

The introduction and implementation of Shewhart's control charts inaugurated statistical quality control. The value of statistical quality control became obvious during World War II. Unfortunately, American management failed to understand this value, and its brief and limited application was abandoned after the war as many companies viewed quality control as a wartime effort only. It seemed unnecessary in the booming postwar years when quantity was deemed to be all that mattered.

In 1946 the ASQC was founded. Under its auspices, quality professionals developed failure analysis methods to problem-solve, quality engineers became engaged in early product design, and a number of companies began to test the environmental performance of products.

In 1950 W. Edwards Deming (1900-1993), a statistician who had worked with Shewhart at Bell Labs, was invited by the Union of Japanese Scientists and Engineers (JUSE) to speak to Japan's leading industrialists. Deming presented a series of lectures on statistical quality techniques and on the responsibilities of top management for delivering quality products and services. The Japanese industrialists and engineers embraced Deming's teaching, and Japanese quality, productivity, and competitive position significantly increased. Under Deming, Joseph M. Juran (1904), and Armand V. Feigenbaum (1920-), the concept of quality control, no longer viewed as principally a corrective activity, was extended to all areas, from design to sales.

During the last four decades Japanese management and engineering professionals such as Ishikawa, Masaaki Imai, and Genichi Taguchi—the latter having formulated new statistical designs of experiment for quality—have expanded the theories of Deming, Juran, and R. A. Fisher. And in turn, American managers and statisticians have advanced the contributions of their Japanese counterparts.

SUSTAINING QUALITY: KAIZEN TECHNOLOGY

A crucial aspect of CWQC is maintaining the quality of existing processes, of processes pertaining to new products or services, and of processes resulting from innovative technologies (discoveries based on new scientific principles). Of course, design of experiments can assure that the new product has quality built into it. Then the problem becomes one of maintaining and improving the quality. An example of an innovative technology is **computer-aided design and computer-aided manufacturing** (CAD CAM). These projects have revolutionized production systems.

A Japanese approach of improving and sustaining the quality of processes is known as *kaizen* (continuous improvement) technology. The activity of improving is included because kaizen technology assumes that any process based on innovative technology or other technology, is subject to steady deterioration (entropy) unless constant efforts are made to maintain and improve the process's standards. Kaizen technology is the accumulation of small technological improvements continually made upon the production or service process.

Dr. Donald J. Wheeler, coauthor of *Understanding Statistical Process Control,* further describes entropy: "Entropy is relentless. Every process will naturally and inevitably migrate toward the state of chaos. The only way this migration can be overcome is by continually repairing the effects of entropy." Having the ability to repair a process assumes that its effects are known. This knowledge can be achieved through control charts and process capability studies. Unlike today's common U.S. management practices, which are based on the Taylor model, kaizen technology requires virtually every employee's personal contribution and effort to quality. This requires a substantial management commitment of time and effort; infusions of capital are no substitute for this investment in time, effort, and people. Unlike the Taylor model, kaizen technology assumes that all employees can contribute to the improvement of the production processes both in terms of quality and productivity.

Taylor argued that all-important knowledge and information was known by management, and it was the exclusive responsibility of management to use "science" to establish an optimal production system. This optimal system was to be based on the close supervision of all work procedures. Workers were to follow, without deviation, the procedures proscribed by management. Their performances were to be judged on the basis of the standards of these procedures.

Cooperation within such a system meant that the workers would adhere to the directives of management. Taylor argued that if any deviations occurred, they were caused by the worker's failure to adhere to his job specifications. Many in management believe this is not "science" because there are sources of variation outside of the worker's control.

It is the opinion of a number of managers and scientists that management based on the Taylor model is incompatible with achieving, as kaizen technology does, long-run and long-lasting (but undramatic) quality improvements because such improvements come about only when workers are actively involved in the production processes. The kaizen approach asserts that those closest to the work have a great deal of skill, energy, and knowledge that must be tapped. Many believe the Taylor model ignores this **workforce** potential; it does not support the **empowerment** of employees. The kaizen approach stresses gradual and consistent changes and improvements as a result of both labor and management slowly learning more and more about the processes and systems in which they are involved. Kaizen technology has affected many other areas of business practices. In the field of **accounting**, Y. Kato has developed three cost categories to analyze and measure kaizen improvements. Such interactions among a company's departments are an essential element of CWQC.

Consequently, Japanese firms are committed to the notion that the customer comes first. For most U.S. firms, however, there is considerable doubt that this is so. Authors Kenneth Delavigne and J. Daniel Robertson state that, "despite lip service to the importance of the customer, observations still show that most companies concentrate on what they can get from customers (money, profits) than on what they are going to provide to the customer (the quality of the product, and extensions to the product such as spare parts, courteous support, a product line that grows with the customer's needs, and so on)."

Delavigne and Robertson use the term "neo-Taylorism" in describing current U.S. management practices, and conclude that "the state of management was even worse at the end of the 1980s than when the decade began." During the 1990s there was some improvement overall in U.S. management practices. At this time, however, all the evidence is not in to adequately evaluate U.S. management practices in the 1990s.

SUSTAINING AND IMPROVING QUALITY: TWO ILLUSTRATIVE CASES OF KAIZEN TECHNOLOGY

CALSONIC CORPORATION. The first case is the Calsonic Corporation. Calsonic manufactures a "uniquely-designed flat motor" for automobiles. Instead of wire-wound magnetic cores, Calsonic uses laminated copper sheets that are perforated by high-speed stamping machines to form the electromagnetic circuitry. A French engineer conceived this technology used by Calsonic more than 25 years ago. He sold the rights to an American firm that was not able to commercialize it. Calsonic then purchased the rights and through a **joint venture** with the Yaskawa Electric Company found a way to manufacture the motor.

Calsonic feels that this manufacturing success was possible only due to kaizen technology. Many Calsonic employees made technological improvements on the original idea, especially in the areas of production engineering, precision stamping technology, product quality, assembly design, and machine maintenance.

The Calsonic Corporation's application of kaizen technology underlines Imai's observation that kaizen technology "includes those actions which make the best use of the resources at hand (such as people, machines, facilities, technology and so forth) . . . to improve little by little—the point is not to use money (unnecessarily)." Sustaining and improving the quality of output means quality control. For a firm to have the ability to do so requires TQM, and the application of such techniques as control charts and process capability studies. This is different from the common American managerial approach of attempting to find a quick fix, e.g., the attempt to find a new optimal situation by some new capital expenditure.

In the Calsonic example, employee involvement was critical. Kaizen technology, however, does not assume that workers and management have identical roles. Certainly, both labor and management spend time on quality improvement activities, with first-line supervisors and middle management spending the most time. But the kaizen approach asserts that workers spend the most time on maintenance activities that sustain quality. As one moves up the management ladder, that time decreases. Middle and top management spend far more time on innovative technology and new product development.

This is in contrast to the Taylor model, which asserts that workers must spend their time exclusively on maintenance and none on improvement. Therefore, management based on the Taylor model, according to many administrators, fails to tap the tremendous pool of information, knowledge, skill, and energy of workers.

DRAMS. The second example of sustaining and improving quality is dynamic random-access memory chips (DRAMs). Most of the technology for this high tech product was developed in the West, but today Japanese companies hold 75 percent of the world market.

The most important break-even factor for the manufacture of this product is the defective percentage. To control this factor, kaizen technology is necessary since any minor change in the manufacturing environment must be checked with great care to guarantee uniform production. At one Japanese plant, a small increase in the defective rate was noticed for a few hours one day. But, at first, no abnormal manufacturing conditions were discovered. Further investigation revealed the problem. A truck had parked by a ventilation tunnel for the DRAM plant's air conditioning system. The defective chips were caused by particles from the truck's exhaust. A new standard was introduced at the plant that prevented the problem from recurring. This new standard, obviously, resulted in sustaining and improving the quality of the output.

SUMMARY

For quality control to occur, the top management of any company must have totally committed itself to TQC, and then CWQC. Sustaining and improving the quality of manufacturing or service processes require such tools as control charts, process capability studies, experimental designs, **business ethics**, organizational change and development, and excellent employee relations. Finally, to compete internationally a company has to adopt international quality standards.

[Peter B. Webb, Ph.D.]

FURTHER READING:

Aeppel, Timothy. ''More, More, More: Rust-Belt Factory Lifts Productivity, and Staff Finds It's No Picnic.'' *Wall Street Journal,* 18 May 1999, A1.

American Society for Quality Control. Statistics Division. *Glossary and Tables for Statistical Quality Control.* Milwaukee, WI: American Society for Quality Control, 1983.

Besterfield, Dale H. *Quality Control.* New York: Prentice Hall, 1990.

Bossert, James L. *Quality Function Deployment: A Practitioner's Approach.* Madison, WI: ASQC Quality Press, 1991.

Box, G. E. P., William G. Hunter, and J. Stuart Hunter. *Statistics for Experimenters: An Introduction to Design, Data Analysis, and Model Building.* New York: John Wiley & Sons, 1978.

DeCarlo, Neil J., and W. Kent Sterett. ''History of the Malcolm Baldrige National Quality Award.'' *Quality Progress,* March 1990, 21-27.

Delavigne, Kenneth T., and J. Daniel Robertson. *Deming's Profound Changes: When Will the Sleeping Giant Awaken?* Englewood Cliffs, NJ: PTR Prentice Hall, 1994.

Deming, W. Edwards. *Out of the Crisis.* Cambridge, MA: MIT Center for Advanced Engineering Studies, 1986.

DeVor, Richard E., and others. *Statistical Quality Design and Control.* New York: Macmillan, 1992.

Feigenbaum, Armand V. *Total Quality Control.* Madison, WI: American Society for Quality Control, 1991.

Gitlow, Howard, and others. *Tools and Methods for the Improvement of Quality.* New York: Irwin, 1989.

Hemenway, Caroline G., and Gregory J. Hale. ''The TQEM-ISO Connection.'' *Quality Progress,* June 1996, 29-32.

Imai, Masaaki. *GEMBA Kaizen: A Common Sense, Low-Cost Approach to Management.* New York: McGraw-Hill, 1997.

——. *Kaizen: The Key to Japan's Economic Success.* New York: Random House Business Division, 1986.

Ishikawa, Kaoru. *Guide to Quality Control.* Boston: Asian Productivity Organization, 1987.

——. ''Quality and Standardization Programs for Economic Success.'' *Quality Progress,* January 1984, 16-20.

Kato, Y. ''Target Costing Support Systems: Lessons from Leading Japanese Companies.'' *Management Accounting Research,* April 1993, 43-44.

Lochner, Robert H., and Joseph E. Matar. *Designing for Quality: An Introduction to the Best of Taguchi and Western Methods of Statistical Experimental Design.* Madison, WI: ASQC Quality Press, 1990.

O'Neil, James P. ''Using ISO 9000 to Go beyond Industrial Norms.'' *Quality Progress,* December 1998, 43-44.

Taylor, Frederick W. *The Principles of Scientific Management.* New York: Harper & Row, 1911.

Thurow, Lester C. ''A Weakness in Process Technology.'' *Science,* 18 December 1987, 1659-63.

Wheeler, Donald J., and David S. Chambers. *Understanding Statistical Process Control.* Knoxville, TN: Statistical Process Controls, 1986.

Wilson, Lawrence A. ''Eight-Step Process to Successful ISO 9000 Implementation: A Management System Approach.'' *Quality Progress,* January 1996, 37-40.

Yoshida, Shuichi. ''Two Technological Developments.'' *Kaizen Communique,* January 1990, 3.

QUEUING THEORY

In its broadest sense, queuing theory is the study of contention for the use of a shared, but limited, resource. It is comprised of models and formulas that describe the relationships between service requests, congestion, and delay.

Queuing theory may be extended to cover a wide variety of contention situations, such as how customer check-out lines form (and how they can be minimized), how many calls a telephone switch can handle, how many computer users can share a mainframe, and how many doors an office building should have. More generally, queuing theory is used in business settings primarily in **operations management** and research problems such as production scheduling, logistics/distribution, and computer network management. These are diverse applications, but their solutions all involve the same dynamics.

The nature of the queue is one of cost shifting and burden averaging. A provider of some service whose resources are limited may serve only a small number of people at a time. Any number of people beyond that are obliged to wait their turn.

Assuming everyone's time is worth something, those who must wait for service are expending a valuable possession—their time. By waiting in line, the service provider is ensured that none of his resources will stand idle. In effect, the waiting customer is forced to pay in time for the privilege of being served, shifting costs from the service provider to the customer.

In a post office, where there is usually one line but several clerks, the next person to be served is the one who has stood longest in line. The burden of the wait is shared by all those in line—the larger the line, the longer the average wait.

The burden is less equally shared in a grocery store, where each clerk has a line. If one line happens to have five simple orders, and another has five patrons with large orders, coupons, and fruit to weigh, the simple line will probably move much faster. Those lucky enough to be in that line will be served before those in the complex line. Thus, grocery shoppers will not share the burden of the wait as equally as in the post office.

The question for the service provider is simple: how to provide good service. Indeed, the highest level of service would be achieved by providing resources equal to the number of patrons; a cashier for every shopper. However, this would be extremely costly and logistically impractical; dozens of cashiers would stand idle between orders.

To minimize costs, the manager may provide only one cashier, forcing everyone into a long, slow-moving line. Customers tiring of the wait would be likely to abandon their groceries and begin shopping at a new store. The question arises: what is an acceptable level of service at an acceptable cost to the provider.

These examples seem simple, but the questions they raise extend far beyond the average grocery store. Queuing theory is the basis for traffic management—the maintenance of smooth traffic flow, keeping congestion and bottlenecks to a minimum. Once the nature of the traffic flow is understood, solutions may be offered to ease the demands on a system, thereby increasing its efficiency and lowering the costs of operating it.

HISTORICAL DEVELOPMENT OF QUEUING THEORY

The first to develop a viable queuing theory was the French mathematician S.D. Poisson (1781-1840). Poisson created a distribution function to describe the probability of a prescribed outcome after repeated iterations of independent trials. Because Poisson used a statistical approach, the distributions he used could be applied to any situation where excessive demands are made on a limited resource.

The most important application of queuing theory occurred during the late 1800s, when telephone companies were faced with the problem of how many operators to place on duty at a given time. At the time, all calls were switched manually by an operator who physically connected a wire to a switchboard. Each customer required the operator only for the few seconds it took to relay directions and have the plug inserted and the time recorded. After the call was set up, the operator was free to accept another call. The problem for an early telephone traffic engineer was how many switchboards should be set up in an area.

Beyond that, supervisors were faced with the problem of how many operators to keep on the boards. Too many, and most operators would remain idle for minutes at a time. Too few, and operators would be overwhelmed by service requests, perhaps never catching up until additional help was added.

Often, callers who were unable to gain an operator's attention simply hung up in frustration and, suspecting it was a busy time for the operators, would wait several minutes before trying again. Others stayed on the line, waiting their turn to talk to the operator. Yet others would call repeatedly, hoping the operator would be sufficiently annoyed by repeated calls to serve them next.

These behavioral discrepancies caused problems for traffic engineers because they affected the level of demand for service from an operator. A call turned away was lost, not to come back until much later, and was effectively out of the system. Callers who held were more predictable, while repeat callers only increased demands on the system by appearing as several requests. Poisson's formula was meant only for the latter situation.

Because few callers acted as aggressively as the Poisson formula assumed, systems were often overengineered, resulting in a substantial waste of resources. Operator offices were equipped with 24 switchboards when they never used more than 20.

A Danish mathematician named A.K. Erlang developed a different approach to traffic engineering based on Poisson's work. He established formulas for calls that are abandoned (called Erlang-B) and for those that are held until service is granted (Erlang-C).

The Poisson and two Erlang formulas made some basic assumptions about the system. Because user behavior is unpredictable, the types of calls that are received are assumed to be randomly distributed. That is, unusual calling characteristics in one period are likely to be normalized over time yielding a more normal distribution.

QUEUING MODELS

The most basic model of a queue is known as the M/M/1 system. This notation means that items (persons, data packets, product units) arrive in the queue following a random Poisson distribution (also called Markovian, yielding the first ''M''), that the distribution of service intervals is first-in/first-out and exponential (second ''M''), and that the queue processes or services only one item at a time (numeral ''1''). This model corresponds to an ordinary queue, such as a grocery store line, where customers arrive at random times, are served one at a time in the order they come (no one receives priority), and one server is handling everyone. Without further information, this model also implicitly assumes there is no upper limit on the system capacity (at least none that can be specified) or on the population of items that may enter the queue, two assumptions that are of course erroneous in many real-life applications. An M/M/1 queue with capacity constraint *c* and population constraint *p* would be represented by the notation M/M/1/c/p.

Based on average arrival rates and average service rates, formulas describing the M/M/1 model, or any other queuing model, can be used to calculate important system measurements such as capacity utilization, average waiting times for servicing, or the average number of items in the queue at a given time. Using the M/M/1 model, for example, we can determine the average customer-processing speed necessary for a grocery store to maintain its promise that no more than three persons will wait in a given grocery line at any time (assuming that each line is an independent M/M/1 queue). To maintain an average of approximately three customers in the system at any given time, the store would need to check out 1.33 customers for every one who arrived per unit of time. If, for the sake of simplicity, we assume one customer arrives per minute, this would mean an average wait of just over three minutes per customer. At this level, the store is using approximately 75 percent of its server (cashier) time, or capacity.

If the store wanted to save on staffing dollars by increasing its capacity usage to 90 percent, its effective rate of service would have to slow to an effective rate of 1.1 customers a minute. Of course, this doesn't mean that employees would work more slowly, but that the system as a whole (which would require a more elaborate model to fully articulate) is processing the same number of customers at lower staffing levels. At the 90 percent utilization level, there would be an average of nine customers in the queue at any time, and the average wait would be about 9 minutes. In effect, a 20 percent gain in the store's utilization rate would cost the average customer a threefold increase in waiting time.

A different—and more accurate—model of the store's queuing system would yield different values, but this example illustrates how models may be applied to real-life problems. Other queuing models vary in the arrival patterns, servicing patterns, number of servers, and other constraints. Examples of other arrival and servicing patterns include deterministic patterns (e.g., D/D/1), where events occur at known rather than random intervals, and general patterns (e.g., G/G/1), where events may be random or deterministic. These patterns may be used in different combinations in the same model, as in M/D/1 or D/G/1. The order of processing/servicing can also vary. In the M/M/1 it is assumed that the order is first-in, first-out (FIFO), but any model may specify alternatives such as last-in, first-out (LIFO), serve in random order (SIRO), and various kinds of priority orders where certain items in the queue are processed sooner than others based on some criteria.

EXAMPLES OF QUEUING THEORY APPLICATIONS

The most unusual recurring period is the ''busy hour,'' that provides a pattern upon which the system should be engineered. For example, if a system receives its highest number of calls between 9 and 10 a.m., the office should be equipped with enough switchboards to handle that level of requests. The issue of how many operators to assign depends on calling patterns from one hour to the next.

What is interesting about the Poisson and Erlang formulas is that the relationship between operators and congestion is not parallel. For example, assume that 10 operators are inundated by 30 percent more calls than they usually handle. A supervisor calls in an eleventh operator and, even though the rate of incoming service requests remains constant, the backlog will gradually fall. After the backlog is eliminated, the eleventh operator may actually force others to go idle for extended periods.

We might assume that 10 operators handling 130 percent of their normal volume would require 13 operators. In fact, the addition of only one is more than enough to resolve the problem. This is because repeated calls are disposed of, and the aggregate wait of everyone holding (which grows geometrically) is reduced one factor at a time. The backlog simply cannot regenerate itself fast enough.

Put differently, 11 operators may be able to dispose of service requests at a faster rate than they are coming in. It may take a few minutes to eliminate the backlog, but the backlog will decline eventually.

Consider the situation in a grocery store where there are five lines open and 12 people in each line. The addition of only one extra cashier will quickly reduce the lines to one or two people, even though the same number of people are entering checkout lines. When the backlog is eliminated, the sixth cashier may be taken off and put on some other job.

As well as a system may be engineered, unusual nonrandom disturbances can cause the system to collapse in spectacular fashion. This was demonstrated by a problem with the New York water system during the 1950s. Engineers discovered that water pressure dropped significantly—and for firemen, perilously—during a period of hours every Sunday evening. A study revealed an unusual culprit: Milton Berle.

The comedian hosted an immensely popular weekly television show every Sunday that was watched by nearly everyone with a set. When the show went to a commercial break, tens of thousands of people, having finished dinner, retreated to their bathrooms at the same time.

With thousands of toilets being flushed within minutes of each other, sewers were inundated. More importantly, toilet tanks were refilling, each consuming two or three gallons of fresh water. The coordinated demand for water in a brief period of time virtually eliminated water pressure. In fact, some toilets took a half hour to refill, and water pressure took hours to recover.

Serious consideration was given to canceling the show. The solution, however, was relatively simple. The addition of only a few more water towers was sufficient to maintain adequate water pressure. In essence, the system was reengineered to handle more demanding peaks.

This situation may be repeated in a telephone system when everyone is motivated to place a call at the same time. During the 1989 San Francisco earthquake, vast numbers of people in the metropolitan area attempted to make a call at the same time—immediately after the quake subsided—hoping to learn whether friends and relatives were safe. Although the switching systems were automated, they were completely unable to handle the volume of requests for dial tone.

Only a small percentage of calls (enough to meet the capacity of the system) were allowed to go through. Indeed, radio and television reporters urged people to stay off the lines so that emergency calls could be handled.

There was no need to reengineer the system because the occurrence of earthquakes, while random, are not consistently repeated. It would be uneconomic to engineer the telephone network for peak usages that occur only once every decade or so. As a result, every earthquake yields a temporary breakdown in the telephone network.

Other slightly less offensive instances occur every time a radio host offers a prize to "caller number x." Telephone companies and public officials have convinced many radio stations to discontinue the practice.

FUTURE APPLICATIONS OF QUEUING THEORY

The most relevant and promising future applications of queuing theory are likely to occur in the areas of computer science and manufacturing systems. In computer science, queuing is a necessary consideration in contention for processing resources. Given that the highest-cost component in advanced computation is processing power, systems are moving increasingly toward network solutions in which processing power is distributed. The result of this trend toward greater distribution is that systems will contend for access to a network and to diverse processors and files.

In manufacturing, queuing is a necessary element of flexible systems in which factors of production may be continually adjusted to handle periodic increases in demand for manufacturing capacity. Excess capacity in periods of low demand may be converted into other forms of working capital, rather than be forced to spent those periods as idle, nonproductive assets.

The concept of **flexible manufacturing systems** is very interesting. Consider that today a company such as Boeing endures long periods of low demand for its commercial aircraft (a result of cycles in the air transportation industry), but must quickly tool up for expanded production when demand rises. The company must alternately open and mothball millions of dollars worth of manufacturing capacity (and hire and lay off thousands of workers) through every demand cycle.

During periods of low demand, floor space, machinery and inventories remain tied up. If, on the other hand, demand flows could be better managed, Boeing could convert these assets to more productive applications. The primary focus of queuing theory on flexible manufacturing remains centered on machine reliability and depreciation and processing and cycle times.

[John Simley]

FURTHER READING:

Gross, Donald, and Carl M. Harris. *Fundamentals of Queuing Theory.* New York: John Wiley & Sons, 1998.

Hall, Randolph W. *Queueing Methods: For Services and Manufacturing.* Englewood Cliffs, NJ: Prentice Hall, 1991.

R

R & D

SEE: Research and Development

RANDOM WALK THEORY

The random walk theory, in its simplest form, states that stock prices follow no predictable pattern. A controversial proposition, the theory, when taken to its extreme, counters the many forms of security analysis—including fundamental and **technical analysis**—that purport to positively identify price and risk trends.

The notion of a ''random walk'' is a mathematical concept for a variable, in this case share price, whose future values are unrelated to those past. The idea has been applied to many financial and nonfinancial phenomena, but in the business world it is most associated with scholarship on stock prices that began in the 1950s and climaxed in the 1970s.

During that period, a number of academic studies were advanced to describe an observed randomness in stock prices. Important contributions included Maurice Kendall's 1953 article ''The Analysis of Economic Time Series,'' published in the *Journal of the Royal Statistical Society,* and the 1964 book *The Random Character of Stock Market Prices* by Paul H. Cootner. But the theory's application to stock market pricing is perhaps best associated with Princeton economist Burton G. Malkiel's 1973 classic *A Random Walk Down Wall Street.*

The theory is seemingly borne out by a casual comparison of how highly managed **mutual funds** or other professionally selected stock portfolios regularly underperform the market as a whole. Consequently, random walk proponents recommended wide diversification to mirror the entire market's breadth, such as by choosing stocks based on indexes like the Standard & Poor's 500 or, more recently, the Wilshire 5000.

The theory is deeply intertwined with the efficient market theory, which holds that markets are constantly and immediately correcting prices based on new information. When markets are efficient, the theory posits, no stock is undervalued or overvalued at a particular moment, and once information becomes available that a stock may not be priced accurately in relation to the company's performance or growth prospects, the markets quickly correct that condition. Both theories were greeted with skepticism early on, but quickly grew to exert influence on both academics and professionals.

However, even as Malkiel and like-minded analysts continued to carry the random walk banner in the 1990s, since the 1970s there has been mounting evidence that stock prices aren't entirely random and markets aren't perfectly efficient. Large studies on U.S. and international stock data have suggested that technical price indicators such as moving averages are indeed positively correlated with accurate predictions of future price movements. Thus, critics of the random walk theory conclude that studies showing random walk tendencies were unsophisticated or failed to ask the right questions about price patterns.

Opponents to random walk point out the inefficiencies of the market that make it possible, as they see it, to anticipate with better than random accuracy what a stock might do under certain circumstances. These inefficiencies include incomplete or even conflicting information about companies as well as the market's propensity to under- and overreact to different types of new information.

Nonetheless, because many aspects of price movements remain ambiguous, the general tenets of the random walk theory continue to hold sway with many stock analysts and economists, and will continue to fuel new research and debate for the foreseeable future.

FURTHER READING:

Brock, William, Josef Lakonishok, and Blake LeBaron. ''Simple Technical Trading Rules and the Stochastic Properties of Stock Returns.'' *Journal of Finance,* December 1992.

Hulbert, Mark. ''A Random Walk Down Wall Street.'' *Forbes,* 21 October 1996.

Koretz, Gene. ''A Less-Than-Random Walk.'' *Business Week,* 21 December 1998.

Lo, Andrew W., and Archie Craig MacKinlay. *A Non-Random Walk Down Wall Street.* Princeton, NJ: Princeton University Press, 1999.

Musgrave, Gerald L. ''A Random Walk Down Wall Street.'' *Business Economics,* April 1997.

RANKING

A business ranking is one in which different companies or products are listed, or ranked, in order based on specific criteria. Within a particular industry, companies are typically ranked by criteria appropriate to that industry. **Banks** would be ranked in terms of their dollar volume. **Advertising** agencies are ranked according to their annual billings. Insurance companies may be ranked according to premiums earned. General businesses could be ranked by sales volume, profits, number of employees, and other criteria.

A ranking tells at a glance who the top performers are in a given category. *Business Rankings Annual* contains approximately 10,000 different rankings that have been published during the year. Examples include the top ten advertisers, the top ten retailers, and the top ten **mutual funds**. Firms may be ranked according to one or more criteria. In the case of retailers, they may be ranked according to profits per employee, sales, return on equity, or some other measure. Each criterion is used to compile a separate ranking. In some cases, multiple criteria may be combined to create a single ranking. The ranking of mutual funds tends to be based on several criteria, resulting in a more complex indexing procedure to determine each fund's performance.

Dun & Bradstreet Business Rankings, published annually, ranks U.S. companies by size. Two separate national rankings are compiled, one on the basis of sales volume, the other on the number of employees. In addition to the national rankings, the book ranks firms within each state and within industry category.

Perhaps the most well-known business ranking is the *Fortune* 500. Published annually in an April issue of *Fortune* magazine, the *Fortune* 500 ranks the top 500 U.S. companies by sales for the previous year. Through 1994, the *Fortune* 500 included only industrial companies. Starting in 1995, the list included service and retail firms. *Fortune* editors said the change was made to reflect the growing importance of those sectors of the economy. *Fortune* also publishes the Service 500 (May), the Global Industries 500 (July), and the Global Services 500 (August).

While such rankings are based on objective criteria, such as sales figures or number of employees, other types of rankings are based on a wide range of information collected from surveys and other types of research. These types of rankings include ''best places to work'' and ''best cities to raise a family.'' *Fortune* publishes its ''100 Best Companies to Work for in America'' every January. *Computerworld* surveys the 1,000 largest public companies and the 40 largest consultants for its annual ranking of the ''Best Places to Work in Information Systems.'' *Working Mother* magazine's annual survey of the ''100 Best Companies for Working Mothers'' is another well-known ranking of employers.

Product rankings are also more complex, being based on multiple measures of performance. A ranking of personal **computers**, for example, might be based on such performance measures as the speed of its central processing unit, the speed at which it writes to and reads a file from a disk, and the time required to copy a file from one disk to another. Then, using a mathematical process called multidimensional scaling, it would be possible to obtain a single ranking of different computer models on the basis of all the relevant performance criteria.

Rankings are also used in the physical and social sciences. Rankings help interpret the results of survey research and are used in manufacturing quality control, for example. In whatever field they are used, rankings allow for the comparison of similar entities on the basis of fair and consistent criteria.

[David P. Bianco]

FURTHER READING:

Business Rankings Annual. Farmington Hills, MI: Gale Group, (annual).

Dun & Bradstreet Business Rankings. Bethlehem, PA: Dun & Bradstreet, (annual).

''Ranking the Health Plans.'' *Newsweek,* 28 September 1998, 67-69.

Shellenbarger, Sue. ''Those Lists Ranking Best Places to Work Are Rising in Influence.'' *Wall Street Journal,* 26 August 1998, B1.

World Business Rankings Annual. 2nd ed. Farmington Hills, MI: Gale Group, 1998.

RATIOS

SEE: Financial Ratios; Information Ratio; Price/Earnings Ratio

REAL ESTATE

Real estate is land and all that is either on or under it, including water, trees, buildings, minerals, and oil. ''Real estate,'' also called ''real property,'' is a term that developed in medieval times. When contests were held over the title of a piece of land, the person judged as rightful owner received the real (actual) property as the settlement of the dispute.

The term ''real estate'' is used today to refer to land and the property on it, and to the real estate industry—including the sale and leasing of both domestic and commercial land, appurtenant property, and the financing of and investment in real properties.

In the selling and renting of both domestic and commercial real estate, brokers buy and sell and appraisers fix value. Property managers and a host of others arrange rentals. Another set of persons is involved with the financing of real estate purchases or rentals and **mortgage** issues for purchase.

Because of the many facets of the industry, determining which are the largest firms requires asking further questions. What part of the industry? By what measure? Volume of sales? Number of brokers? Number of offices? The industry itself is at odds on ranking issues. Regardless of the ranking system used, Century 21 and ReMax are indisputably the two largest players in the domestic residential real estate market.

Residential real estate sales were strong throughout the mid-to-late 1990s, but profits for real estate brokers fell during the same period. In response to market and business pressures, real estate companies adopted measures to increase agent productivity and streamline operations through reducing listings. Smaller firms also tended to consolidate during the period, and firms of all sizes became more willing to share information to boost overall sales in the residential real estate market.

Century 21 is one of the largest franchise real estate brokers in the United States, with Weichart Realtors operating nationally as one of the largest independent realtors. Although its parent company, Cendant Corp., was found guilty in 1998 of fraudulent **accounting** that falsely inflated corporate revenues to raise **stock** prices, Century 21 retained its standing in the market, in part by focusing its efforts on the growing Spanish-speaking market in the United States. Trends in 20th-century realty brokerage include the development of mortgage financing companies that handle financing and refinancing for domestic real estate sales, the increased training and professionalism of real estate broker, and the use of the term ''realtor,'' developed by the National Association of Realtors.

Real estate sales grew consistently and **capital markets** became increasingly lucrative during the mid-to-late 1990s, producing a boom in the real estate debt financing industry. Real estate debt financing also became increasingly competitive during the period, and insurance companies, long the main providers of mortgages, began to withdraw from the market. A variety of firms, including community banks and independent credit companies, emerged to replace insurance companies as providers of real estate debt financing. This proliferation of credit providers resulted in increased reliance on title insurance by mortgage finance **underwriters**, leading to creation of a national rating of title insurance firms by **Fannie Mae** in spring 1998. Not all insurance companies abandoned the real estate debt financing industry, however, as Prudential Insurance Co. created the Prudential Mortgage Capital Co. in August 1997 to serve as a conduit for the provision of commercial real estate loans.

As a force in the economy, the real estate industry holds power in its own right. Real estate brokers and managers form the seventh-largest industry by receipts (nearly $75 billion in 1992) in the nation among nonmanufacturing and **service industries**. Investment in real estate development by individuals and businesses, for their own use or as a speculative venture, grew to be a significant force in the 1990s. **Real estate investment trusts** (REITs) are, according to the Standard & Poor's *Industry Survey* of November 3, 1994, a ''formidable economic force.'' After a short downturn during the second half of 1995, REITs rebounded and by spring 1998 total market capitalization of REITs reached $1.3 trillion, and the number of REITs in the United States grew to 216. Some of the major players in the REIT market are Starwood Lodging Trust, Equity Office Properties Trust, Crescent Real Estate Equities Inc., Rouse Company, and the Simon DeBartolo Group.

The two largest foreign investors in U.S. real estate are Canada and Japan, although the Japanese recession of the late 1990s drastically reduced participation by Japanese investors. The outlook for the future of real estate—both commercial and domestic—is tied to the fate of **interest rates**, to changes in **tax** laws that make investment trusts easier to set up, and to the activities of REITs both in the stability of their investments and their activity in the stock market. **Capital gains** rates, which applied to real estate, were reduced from 28 to 20 percent in 1997; this, along with the increased use of REITs to facilitate **mergers and acquisitions**, seems likely to spur real estate sales and keep prices high for some time.

[Joan Leotta, updated by Grant Eldridge]

FURTHER READING:

"Banking." *Industry Surveys.* 3 December 1994, B59-60.

Bergsman, Steve. "Choosing the REIT Stuff." *Black Enterprise,* February 1995, 57-58.

Eckman, Katy. "Century 21 Eyes No. 1 Realtor Role in Spanish Language Marketing." *Adweek* 19, no. 41 (13 October 1997): 5.

Frantz, James B. "Borrowers Win Big in Today's Lending Frenzy." *National Real Estate Investor* 39, no. 10 (October 1997): 52.

Hylton, Richard D. "Why Real Estate Stays Grounded." *Fortune,* 13 December 1993, 141-43.

Jacobs, Barry G. "Balanced-Budget Package Provides Some Real Estate Relief." *National Real Estate Investor* 39, no. 10 (October 1997): 40.

Kimelman, John. "What Recovery?" *Financial Planner,* 21 February 1995, 68-69.

Levin, Gary. "Realty Firms Wage War over Ads." *Advertising Age,* 22 March 1993, 8.

Marshall, William T. "Breaking with Tradition." *America' s Community Banker* 7, no. 1 (January 1998): 16.

Nelson, Emily, and Mark Maremont. "Cendant Cites Wider Accounting Fraud: Bogus Revenue Over 3 Years Neared $300 Million." *Wall Street Journal,* 15 July 1998, A3.

Richards, Geoffrey. "Rating Title Firms: A Trend that Keeps Growing." *National Real Estate Investor* 40, no. 5 (May 1998): 102.

Schneider, Howard. "Ripple Effects Real Estate." *Mortgage Banking* 57, no. 1 (October 1996): 42.

Shaughnessy, Andy. "REIT Pulse." *National Real Estate Investor* 40, no. 8 (August 1998): 24.

Silver, Michael. "Corporate America Uses REIT Growth to Leverage Real Estate." *National Real Estate Investor* 40, no. 5 (May 1998): 120.

Slatin, Peter. "The Ground Floor: Opportunity Funds Vie with REITs in Hot Market." *Barron's,* 2 March 1998, 28.

Taub, Stephen. "REITs that Have the Wrong Stuff." *Financial World,* 2 January 1996, 18.

Tessler, Joelle. "REITs Use Offerings for Buying Spree." *Wall Street Journal,* 29 November 1996, A3C.

"Two Real Estate Investment Trusts Agree to Merge." *New York Times,* 28 February 1995, D4.

REAL ESTATE INVESTMENT TRUSTS (REIT)

A real estate investment trust (REIT), is a corporation or trust that combines the capital of many investors to acquire or provide financing for forms of **real estate**. A corporation or trust that qualifies as a REIT generally does not pay corporate income tax to the **Internal Revenue Service**; most states, in turn, honor this federal treatment and do not require REITs to pay state income tax either. This means that nearly all of a REIT's income is distributed to shareholders, without double taxation on the income. Unlike a partnership, a REIT cannot pass its tax losses onto its investors.

President Dwight D. Eisenhower signed the Real Estate Investment Trust Act of 1960, creating an industry that grew over the next 40 years to more than 215 REITs with a combined $160 billion market capitalization. The basic provisions of the law have changed little since it was enacted, although several modifications have been made. REITs were created to provide investors with the opportunity to participate in the benefits of ownership of larger-scale commercial real estate or mortgage lending and receive an enhanced return, since the income is not taxed at the REIT level.

In order for a corporation or trust to qualify as a REIT, it must comply with certain provisions within the Internal Revenue Code. As required by the tax code, a REIT must: be a corporation, business trust, or similar association; be managed by a **board of directors** or board of trustees; have shares that are fully transferable; have a minimum of 100 shareholders; have no more than 50 percent of the shares held by five or fewer individuals during the last half of each taxable year; invest at least 75 percent of the total assets in real estate; derive at least 75 percent of gross income from rents generated from either real property or interest on mortgages on real property; derive no more than 30 percent of gross income from the sale of real property held for less than four years, securities held for less than one year, or certain prohibited transactions; and pay dividends of at least 95 percent of REIT taxable income.

This last criteria has drawn criticism from industry players, who state that such a high rate of payment makes it difficult to retain the earnings necessary to pay for capital improvements. Legislation to mitigate this predicament was introduced in the House of Representatives in 1997, but stalled in committee.

The REIT industry started off slowly, following its 1960 inception. By 1968, industry assets totaled only $1 billion. By 1974, however, total assets exceeded $20 billion. But rising **interest rates**, a national **recession**, and an overbuilt real estate market affected the performance of the early REITs, and the industry experienced its first general shakeout. Exacerbating the problem, REITs were prohibited from operating or managing real estate; they could only own it. This forced REITs to work through third-party managers who were likely to have independent and, sometimes, conflicting interests, an arrangement investors were reluctant to buy into.

A restructuring and stabilization period followed. The Tax Reform Act of 1986 reduced tax-shelter opportunities in the real estate market, making competitive, tax-motivated real estate syndications less attractive and ensuring that real estate investment would become more income oriented. The reforms resulted in renewed growth in REITs. In addition, the law permitted the management of properties directly by the REIT.

In the late 1980s, however, competitors to REITs, such as banks and insurance companies, maintained a high level of real estate financing. The recession of the early 1990s, both in the broader economy and in the real estate market in particular (largely a result of excess construction in the 1980s) increased the appeal of the more conservative REITs to investors. As a result, REITs boomed through the mid-1990s.

Mergers, historically unattractive to REITs due to family-oriented ownership structures and asset-holdings restrictions, became popular as a part of this expansion. REIT managers in search of critical mass, geographical diversification, and long-term shareholder value have focused increasingly on consolidation. In turn, many mid-size and small REITs are being swallowed up by larger competitors or forced out of the market. Those larger firms with diversified, stable assets are more capable of drawing investors and commanding market share.

Industry analysts classify REITs by three investment categories: equity REITs, mortgage REITs, and hybrid REITs. Equity REITs own real estate, and their revenue principally derives from rent. Mortgage REITs lend money to real estate owners, and their revenue primarily springs from interest earned on mortgage loans. Some mortgage REITs also invest in residuals of mortgage-backed securities. Hybrid REITs combine the investment strategies of both equity REITs and mortgage REITs. The overwhelming majority of REITs (191) currently in operation are equity REITs.

Pension funds, endowment funds, insurance companies, bank trust departments, **mutual funds**, and investors—both U.S.-based as well as non-U.S.-based—own shares of REITs. An individual who chooses to invest in a REIT seeks to achieve current income distributions and long-term stock appreciation potential. REIT shares typically are purchased for $2 to $40 each, with no minimum purchase required.

Over 80 percent of the REITs operating in the United States in 1999 were traded on the national stock exchanges, including the New York Stock Exchange, the American Stock Exchange, and the NASDAQ National Market System. Dozens of REITs, however, are not traded on a stock exchange.

Analyzing the performance and current value of a REIT is not an easy task. Asset values may be derived using different rent multipliers and capitalization rates; but these values are derived from appraisal reports, which do not always reflect the same standards.

Rather than using asset values to analyze performance, the following elements are recommended for scrutiny: (1) **management** (prospective investors in a particular REIT should carefully examine the experience level of the management team); and (2) future growth (which is contingent on the future income from the REIT's holdings). **Income**, in turn, depends on rent, which is influenced by vacancy levels, regional economic growth, and units available in an area; and to some degree on the sales level of the REIT's properties.

SEE ALSO: Banks and Banking; Dividends; Mortgages/Mortgage-Backed Securities; Stocks; Taxes and Taxation; Trusts and Trustees

[Susan Bard Hall]

FURTHER READING:

Mount, Steven F. *Real Estate Investment Trusts.* Washington: Tax Management, Inc., 1996.

Mullaney, John A. *REITs: Building Profits with Real Estate Investment Trusts.* New York: John Wiley, 1998.

Practicing Law Institute. *REITs: Using Financing and Legal Techniques to Capitalize on the Expanding Market.* New York: Practicing Law Institute, 1999.

REBATES

Rebates, widely known as refunds, are a popular tool used by businesses to promote their products and services. The term "rebate" derives from the Middle English *rebaten,* meaning "to deduct." Rebates are distinct from **coupons** and other forms of discounting in that they reimburse a customer for part of the purchase price after rather than at the time of sale. Rebating evolved in the latter half of the 20th century from the marketing technique of offering coupons, which had proved broadly successful. Rebates were initially offered by producers of grocery-store goods and subsequently by manufacturers of nonfood items. Currently, businesses making use of rebates are diverse and include the manufacturers of health and beauty aids, household supplies, small and large appliances, automobiles, wine and liquor, and computers. The cash amounts these companies offer their customers is similarly wide ranging and can be less than a dollar or as much as $50 or more, depending on the retail price and nature of the product being promoted.

The first step in rebating, as outlined by Susan J. Samtur in *Cashing In at the Checkout,* is for the manufacturer to issue an offer of a rebate to all who purchase its product; typically the offer expires after six to eight months. The purchaser then completes a form provided by the manufacturer and mails it—along with any other items the manufacturer may require, such as a cash-register receipt or the Universal Product Code (UPC) snipped from the packaging—to the address specified on the form.

Most commonly, the purchaser sends the rebate form and related (''proof of purchase'') items not to the manufacturer but to one of several large clearinghouses hired by the manufacturer to handle these transactions—for instance, the Young America Corporation in Minnesota or the Nielson Clearing House in Texas. The clearinghouse then processes the form and sends the purchaser a check in the manufacturer's name, usually within four to eight weeks from the time the purchaser mails in the required information.

Companies use a number of means to get their rebate forms into the hands of customers. Many companies supply a pad of tear-off rebate forms to the stores selling their products; others print the form directly on the packaging or on a tag hanging from the merchandise; a few instruct the purchaser to write in for the form. To announce the rebate offer and distribute the forms, companies may also place advertisements in newspapers and magazines, utilize home mailers, and/or place ads in the myriad refunders' newsletters developed by consumers to avail themselves of these offers. In addition, companies frequently use television and radio advertisements to publicize their rebate promotions.

Rebating is highly attractive to consumers, offering a partial cash reimbursement for their purchases that is tax-free, since the **Internal Revenue Service** views rebates as a reduction in the price paid for a product, rather than as income. For manufacturers, rebating provides numerous advantages: it induces prospective customers to try their products; it boosts company sales and visibility; and it attracts interest from retailers, who often help promote the offer and expand the shelf space allotted to the manufacturer's goods accordingly. Rebate promotions can thus help a company increase its leverage with retailers and develop brand loyalty and repeat business among consumers over the long run—not just a one-time incentive to buy. This is most readily seen in seasonal industries such as that for small batteries. Battery industry sources estimate that 39 percent of their sales occur during the holiday season, so major battery manufacturers, including Rayovac, Duracell, and Panasonic, all announced ongoing rebate programs to extend from the holiday season into the spring and summer of 1997.

Indeed, a study conducted by United Marketing Services (UMS) found that participating in a rebate promotion makes customers better able to remember a product than is the case with other promotional methods. UMS also found the rate of consumer participation in rebate promotions to be on the rise. Despite this fact, consumer participation in rebating ranges from just 25 to 40 percent, and most participants request only two or three refunds per year. Hence, because the number of purchasers who actually request the refunds is relatively small, the dollar outlay in cash refunds for the manufacturer may be minimal in comparison with the sales and other benefits generated by the promotion.

Given the low rate of customer participation in rebate programs, some companies have neglected rebate requests, or even offered fraudulent rebate schemes. Many consumer complaints arose in 1997 when several computer companies, including CompUSA and Iomega, dedicated too few resources to rebate reimbursals, causing delays in rebate payments.

In the mid-1990s, industries that had traditionally made use of rebates to promote their products began to make use of new techniques. General Motors Corp., for instance, shifted $30 million in resources from its rebate programs to **advertising** and marketing initiatives in 1996. Even as traditional rebating seemed to lose some of its appeal, however, several innovative offshoots of rebating began to emerge. Among these were the linking of customer purchases to rebates in the form of contributions to retirement plans, tuition costs, and air-mileage credits. Other variations on rebate promotions include offering to refund a fixed percentage of the purchase price, rather than a set dollar amount; providing a ''bounceback coupon'' that can be redeemed on a later purchase; and making contributions to charitable causes based on customer participation in the promotion. Perhaps the most popular recent variation on rebating is the cobranded credit card, issued by a manufacturer and allowing its users to dedicate a percentage of their credit card purchases toward the purchase of the issuing companies products. Many large companies, including General Motors, Ford, Mobil, Texaco, and General Electric, adopted cobranded credit cards by the end of 1996.

The resiliency of traditional rebating and its future as a marketing and promotion tool remains undoubted, as even companies such as General Motors, which had appeared ready to abandon its old-line rebate programs in 1996, reinitiated them in the fall of 1998.

[Roberta H. Winston, updated by Grant Eldridge]

FURTHER READING:

Cruz, Humberto. "Mature Money: Limit Use of Co-Branded Credit Cards." *Detroit News,* 18 November 1996, F8.

Foster, Ed. "Customers Whose Rebate Checks Aren't in the Mail Are Beginning to Fight Back." *InfoWorld,* 9 February 1998, 62.

——. "Very Few Rebates Actually End Up Cutting the Real Cost of Computer Products." *InfoWorld,* 5 January 1998, 58.

"How Rebates Affect Purchases Behavior." *Adweek's Marketing Week,* 16 January 1989, SP11.

Joyce, Marion. *The Frugal Shopper.* New York: Perigree Books/Berkeley Publishing Group, 1986.

Samtur, Susan J., with Tad Tuleja. *Cashing In at the Checkout.* New York: Stonesong Press, 1979.

Smith, Anne Kates. "Buying Shopper Loyalty." *U.S. News and World Report,* 27 April 1992, 77.

"Tricks of the Trade." *Discount Merchandiser* 37, no. 2 (February 1997): 42.

Warner, Fara. "GM Launches Blitz to Boost Market Share." *Wall Street Journal,* 16 September 1998, A3.

RECESSION

A recession is a downturn in the **business cycle** that occurs when the real **gross national product** (GNP)—the total output of goods and services produced by the U.S. population—declines for two consecutive quarters, or six months. Recessions are usually characterized by a general decrease in output, **income**, **employment**, and trade lasting from six months to a year. A more severe and long-lasting economic crisis is known as a depression.

Virtually all advanced world economies that are not controlled centrally have experienced recurring cycles of slump and recovery in business activity since the Industrial Revolution. The United States suffered through four severe depressions in the 1800s, as well as the Great Depression in the 1930s. These crises cost a great deal in terms of national **wealth** and personal hardship. Since then, however, sophisticated analysis of economic trends has combined with increased government intervention to prevent such extreme fluctuations in economic activity. In fact, no depressions have occurred in industrialized nations since World War II, although many recessions have occurred. Governments monitor the business cycle closely and take various steps to stabilize the economy before it reaches extreme peaks and troughs. Formerly, the typical stages in the business cycle were depression, recovery, prosperity, and recession. Today, the phases are usually defined using the more moderate terms upswing, peak, recession, and trough.

THE BUSINESS CYCLE

Prior to entering the recession phase of the business cycle, the economy reaches the peak of its expansion. When it nears the full-employment level of output, its rate of growth begins to slow. Prices are generally rising, so consumers demand fewer products and services. As a result, companies begin to hire fewer new workers, and demand falls even further with the reduction in incomes. Productivity and output begin to decline as **costs** increase, and companies respond by decreasing investment. Gradually, the overall economy contracts, as the decrease in investment reduces production and employment. Eventually, government intervention and the natural progression of the business cycle cause the recession to end, or reach a trough or turning point, and the upswing stage begins.

Though the general pattern of the business cycle is understood, in reality the situation is not usually so clearly defined. The economy progresses through the stages very gradually, and not all regions, sectors, or businesses are affected in the same way at the same time. In addition, there are many other patterns of economic activity that interact with and complicate the business cycle. For example, economists often observe seasonal variations in output and sales in some sectors of the economy. Retail sales tend to pick up around Christmas, while construction tends to increase during the summer months. Economists also describe independent cycles of investment in certain industries, such as shipbuilding or agriculture. Finally, the overall level of economic activity tends to expand every year. These factors combine to make recessions difficult to predict or define.

Over the years, a number of changes have taken place or been instituted by the government to stabilize fluctuations in economic activity, and thus reduce the incidence and severity of recessions. For example, the growth of the service sector, with its relatively stable demand and its tendency to employ salaried personnel, has been a stabilizing influence. The corporate trend toward stable **dividend** policies has also helped, as has increased federal regulation of the **stock market** and the banking industry. Some experts claim that instituting a progressive income tax and an unemployment insurance program have also worked to moderate fluctuations in the business cycle. Finally, the government often intervenes directly with monetary or fiscal controls to prevent **inflation**, and with job **training** programs and public welfare to reduce the negative effects of unemployment.

THE U.S. RECESSION OF 1990-91

Despite such measures, however, recessions still occur in the United States and worldwide. During the U.S. recession that lasted from July 1990 through

March 1991, the economy showed the lowest growth rate since the Great Depression. *U.S. News and World Report* called the recession "unlike any the country has experienced in the post-World War II era, the result of years of profligacy and irresponsible government policies," and claimed it was responsible for the loss of 1.9 million jobs through early 1992. In fact, some analysts stated that this recession could have been as bad as the Great Depression if not for increased government spending—which represented 25 percent of GNP in 1991 as opposed to 3 percent in 1930—and federal deposit insurance for **banks**.

Still, economists disagreed on what caused the recession and the slow recovery, how long the recession officially lasted, and how a similar situation could best be prevented in the future. Some experts attributed the prolonged recession to industrial overcapacity, which led to falling asset values for many businesses. Others claimed that an overall decrease in consumption was responsible, whether in response to an increase in oil prices following the Persian Gulf War or because of a slowdown in the rate of population growth. Some analysts blamed technology, stating that the proliferation of electronically controlled credit cards led consumers to build up personal **debt**. Whatever the reasons for the recession, however, it seemed that businesses needed to be prepared for more downturns in the future.

A GLOBAL RECESSION IN OUR FUTURE?

The American economy showed remarkable growth during the mid-to-late 1990s, aided by low unemployment, low inflation, high business investment spending, and a government budget surplus. In addition, spending by American consumers grew at a healthy rate of 6 percent for first six months of 1998. Still, the economic crisis that began in Asia soon spread to Russia and Latin America, causing turmoil in the U.S. stock market during the second half of the year. Analysts began to debate whether this situation would lead to reductions in consumer spending and result in another recession.

Thanks to the strong probability that the U.S. government would cut **interest rates** and **taxes**, or increase public spending, in order to boost the economy, the *Economist* predicted a slowdown rather than a recession for 1999. "For the U.S. economy to go into a significant recession, never mind a depression," former Federal Reserve vice-chairman Alan Blinder stated, "important decision-makers would have to take leave of their senses." But other experts—pointing to the crash in stock and **bond** markets outside the United States and western Europe, shockingly low prices on **commodities** such as oil, an overvalued U.S. stock market, and high levels of individual and corporate debt—placed the likelihood that the American economy would enter a recession in 1999 at 50 to 80 percent.

[Laurie Collier Hillstrom]

FURTHER READING:

"America's Sluggish Recovery." *Economist,* 5 June 1993, 18.

Blanchard, Olivier. "Consumption and the Recession of 1990 1991." *American Economic Review* 83, no. 2 (May 1993): 27.

"Brightening Up: The Economy." *Economist,* 11 December 1993.

Caballero, Ricardo J., and Mohamad L. Hammour. "The Cleansing Effect of Recessions." *American Economic Review* 84, no. 5 (December 1994): 135.

Geroski, P. A., and P. Gregg. "What Makes Firms Vulnerable to Recessionary Pressures?" *European Economic Review* 40, no. 3-5 (April 1996): 551.

Hall, Robert E. "Macro Theory and the Recession of 1990-1991." *American Economic Review* 83, no. 2 (May 1993): 275.

Hansen, Gary D., and Edward C. Prescott. "Did Technology Shocks Cause the 1990-1991 Recession?" *American Economic Review* 83, no. 2 (May 1993): 280.

Littmann, David L. "Worry about Slow Growth, Not Recession." *Wall Street Journal,* 4 August 1998, A18.

"No Longer Boom, but Not Yet Doom." *Economist,* 17 October 1998, 25.

"On Understanding the History of Capitalism." *Monthly Review* 44, no. 5 (October 1992): 1.

Phillips, Michael M. "Risk of Global Recession Is 'Substantial,' World Bank Says in an Annual Report." *Wall Street Journal,* 3 December 1998, A4.

Rohwer, Jim. "Why the Global Storm Will Zap the U.S. Economy." *Fortune,* 28 September 1998, 34.

Ulan, Michael. "Is the Current Business Cycle Different? Does How We Measure Matter?" *Business Economics* 29, no. 2 (April 1994): 41.

Weinstein, Michael M. "Relax. Stocks Rarely Steer the Economy." *New York Times,* 3 September 1998, C1.

RECIPROCITY (COMMERCIAL POLICY)

In the area of international trade, reciprocity refers to an agreement between two or more countries to mutually reduce tariffs and **duties** on goods traded between them. Reciprocity has played an important role in the trade policy of the United States since 1934, when the Reciprocal Trade Agreements Program was initiated to lower tariffs and other **trade barriers**. Under that program the United States negotiated bilateral trade agreements with other countries. In the years following World War II, the **General Agreement on Tariffs and Trade** (GATT) took effect. It provided for multilateral trade agreements to be negotiated in a series of "rounds," the most recent of which was the Uruguay Round that concluded in 1993. GATT represents overall reciprocity, where the consenting nations agree to mutual and equivalent reductions of trade barriers.

In the United States, tariffs had reached a peak in the early 1930s as a result of the country's protectionist policy. In 1934 the Reciprocal Trade Agreements Program went into effect. Under that program the United States sought to increase its **exports** and pull the country out of the Great Depression. The president was empowered to negotiate bilateral treaties with other nations to reduce tariffs by as much as 50 percent of their 1934 levels. For such a treaty to be concluded with another country, it was necessary for the other country to reciprocate, or agree to an equivalent tariff concession.

Countries with which the United States had negotiated reciprocal tariff reductions were given **most-favored nation** (MFN) status. All countries with MFN status were then eligible to receive the same tariff reductions that were negotiated in the bilateral agreements. In the case of **commodities**, the United States often granted the MFN tariff reduction only to the chief supplier of the commodity to the United States.

Two amendments introduced in the late 1940s modified the original Reciprocal Trade Agreements Program and gave the United States more flexibility in granting and withdrawing tariff reductions. An escape clause introduced in 1947 allowed the United States to reimpose tariffs on any **imports** that caused unforeseen damage to domestic producers. In 1948 the peril-point clause was added; it gave the **U.S. International Trade Commission** the power to recommend maximum permissible tariff reductions that would not damage domestic producers.

Reciprocal trade agreements may encompass more than the lowering of tariffs. Equivalent market access is a type of reciprocity in which trading partners agree to allow each other's firms to operate in each other's countries. Reciprocity may involve the extension of restricted nationalistic treatment by one nation to another country's firms operating in its country, but only to the extent that its firms are allowed to operate in the other country. National treatment, another type of reciprocity also known as equivalent treatment, is the treatment of goods produced in another country as if they were domestic goods.

Reciprocity is generally considered a politically safe policy as well as an economically safe one. Economically, reciprocity eliminates the risks associated with unilaterally reducing tariffs, such as a balance of-payments deficit. Politically, reciprocity makes all tariff reductions appear as exchanges rather than concessions.

In the United States multilateral trade agreements involving reciprocity are negotiated by the president and the executive branch of government, but they must be approved by Congress. Since 1974, under procedures developed by the administration of President Richard Nixon, U.S. presidents have had "fast-track authority" to negotiate new trade agreements to open foreign markets. Such authority prevented the U.S. Congress from adding amendments and otherwise changing such agreements after they had been negotiated by the president. But when President Bill Clinton attempted to renew this traditional authority by introducing fast-track trade legislation in 1997, it was defeated by Congress. As a result, new reciprocal trade agreements may be more difficult for the United States to negotiate in the future.

[David P. Bianco]

FURTHER READING:

Davis, Bob, and others. "Costly Reversal: Defeat on Trade Bill May Weaken Clinton in Last Three Years; without Fast Track, U.S. Faces Obstacles in Talks on Tariffs, Other Barriers." *Wall Street Journal,* 11 November 1997, A1.

Weisberger, Bernard A. "When Tariffs Were in Flower." *American Heritage,* July/August 1998, 14-16.

RECRUITING

SEE: Employment Services

RECYCLING PROGRAMS

Recycling programs comprise three elements in a continuum represented by the "chasing arrows" symbol: collection of recyclable materials from the waste stream, processing the **commodities** into new products, and purchasing products containing recycled materials. It has been estimated that each office worker in America produces from one-half to one and one-half pounds of solid waste each day, of which 70 to 90 percent is paper. Whereas paper comprises at least 40 percent of the American waste stream and businesses contribute one-third of the nation's solid waste, recycling programs in the business world commonly address waste paper. Corporate recycling programs, however, have come to include other types of waste, including glass, chemicals, oils, plastics, and metals.

HISTORICAL PERSPECTIVE

Although the word "recycle" was not coined until the late 1960s, recycling has been a trash disposal option for centuries. Native Americans and early settlers routinely reused resources and avoided waste. Materials recovery was also a significant contributor to the U.S. effort during World War II, when businesses and citizens alike salvaged metal, paper, rubber, and other scarce commodities for military use. But the emergence of the ''throwaway society'' of the 1950s helped extinguish any residual recycling impetus. With seemingly unlimited landfill space, disposable and single-use products and packaging became the norm in the ensuing decades. Recycling did not regain popularity until the late 1960s and early 1970s, when environmental concerns rose to the fore in a ''green revolution.'' The first national Earth Day celebration in 1970 heralded antilitter campaigns, the creation of the federal **Environmental Protection Agency** (EPA), and some municipal and corporate recycling programs.

Legislation during that period provided an additional impetus for recycling programs, especially at the federal level. The Solid Waste Disposal Act established resource recovery goals as a priority for U.S. environmental and energy conservation programs. The Resource Recovery Act of 1970 amended the previous legislation by mandating paper recycling and procurement of recycled products in federal agencies wherever economically feasible. The well-known **Resource Conservation and Recovery Act** of 1976 completely revised both acts, imposing requirements regarding hazardous waste disposal and mandating the recycling of nonhazardous waste in federal facilities. The legislation included the requirement that federal agencies ''purchase items that contain the highest percentage of recovered materials practicable given their availability, price and quality.'' Deposit laws enacted around the country encouraged recycling of glass beverage bottles and aluminum cans; recycling of aluminum cans reached an all-time high of 66.5 percent in 1997.

The EPA and the **General Services Administration**, which were jointly charged with administration of federal government recycling programs, launched ''Use It Again, Sam,'' an earnest and widespread federal office paper recycling initiative, in 1976. Within two years, 90 federal agencies and their 115,000 employees were recycling, enjoying the support of President Jimmy Carter and guided by a comprehensive, EPA-issued manual. The recycling program declined in the 1980s, however, due to a lack of enforcement and oversight, budget cuts, apathy, and the EPA's concentration on administration of the **Comprehensive Environmental Response, Compensation & Liability Act of 1980** (Superfund) hazardous waste cleanup program. Many state and local governments around the country stepped in to fill this void in the ensuing decade. Overall, however, low disposal costs relegated recycling to little more than an afterthought of solid-waste management in the 1970s and early 1980s.

In the late 1980s, however, several factors converged to revive interest in recycling as an attractive alternative to traditional disposal. Evidence of toxic leaks from, and dangerous buildups of methane gas in, landfills around the country brought closures, increased regulation, and public opposition to location and expansion of landfills. Incineration was briefly tested as an expedient solution to the mounting solid-waste crisis, but problems with stack emissions and the disposal of toxic ash undermined that option. Public recognition of the crisis crested in 1987, when a garbage barge originating from New York City traveled to six states and three countries before dumping its load back in its home state. The number of operating landfills in the United States decreased from 18,500 in 1979 to 6,500 in 1988, and it was projected that by the year 2000 only 3,250 landfills would be open for business. The dearth of disposal options in the latter years of the 1980s caused disposal expenses to rise dramatically: landfill costs in some regions (especially the Northeast and Northwest) doubled and tripled within a few years. At the same time, some states (e.g., Rhode Island, New Jersey, Connecticut) adopted mandatory recycling legislation. These factors combined with increasing consumer demand for environmental responsibility to prompt a second green revolution that swept the country—including the business world—in the 1990s.

In the late 1980s and early 1990s, all but five states implemented recycling and waste reduction programs in response to the landfill crisis. Although the majority of states with recycling programs failed to meet their goals, solid-waste disposal was reduced to the point that, by 1997, most regions of the United States reported adequate landfill availability, and landfill tipping fees were on the decrease nationwide.

Increased globalization of business in the 1990s, along with the ever increasing strength of the environmental movement worldwide, also stimulated the development of recycling programs outside the United States. The adoption of the **North American Free Trade Agreement**, for instance, spurred the Mexican government to announce plans to develop a formal recycling industry by 1997. Other national economies, including those of France, Germany, Japan, Korea, the People's Republic of China, and Taiwan, either renewed or expanded their commitments to the recycling of paper, steel, plastics, and other solid-waste materials, in response to both international pressures and internal political developments.

BUSINESSES GET INVOLVED

Recycling programs emerged as ''good business for business'' in the last decade of the 20th century for a variety of reasons. Perhaps most importantly, recycling holds out the ''bottom line'' benefit of reducing waste disposal expenses. It also offered substantial, positive benefits for the local and global environment:

recycling one ton of office paper saves 17 trees, conserves enough energy to meet the requirements of at least 4,000 people, and saves three cubic yards of landfill space. Futhermore, the use of recycled materials can reduce the production costs of glass, aluminum, and paper products. Also, businesses that market materials salvaged from discarded equipment and materials have emerged. Recyclers have discovered, for example, that metals including gold, silver, and platinum can be extracted from discarded telecommunications and electronic equipment.

Fort Howard Corporation (which is now known as Fort James Corporation following a merger), is a sterling example of the practicability of recycling programs. Established in 1919, the company made its first official commitment to the environment in 1930. Recycling became an economic imperative during the 1940s, when a shortage of pulp pushed Fort Howard to reprocess waste paper. By the late 1970s the paper manufacturer had reduced its use of virgin pulp to "an almost negligible percentage," according to a 1993 article in *Managing Office Technology.* Fort Howard worked with municipal governments near plants to collect household and office waste paper, winning the EPA's first Administrator's Award for Recycling Leadership in 1990 and keeping more than one million tons of waste paper out of landfills each year in the 1990s.

Although the paper industry greatly increased its recycling capacity, the proliferation of **direct mail** promotional pieces ("junk mail") led to a perceived increase in the amount of waste paper being generated in the late 1990s. According to industry statistics, however, direct mail **advertising** accounts for only 2.1 percent of municipal solid waste, and 13.9 percent of direct-mail pieces are recycled.

Adopting a recycling program can enhance a company's reputation with its customers, employees, and surrounding community. As environmentalism gained ascendancy in the 1990s, a corporate recycling program also offered a substantial basis for **green marketing**. IBM Corporation focuses its recycling programs on environmental and public relations benefits. Like so many other American concerns, IBM got its first shot at recycling by salvaging metals during World War II. The oil crisis of the 1970s provided the impetus for the corporation's energy conservation programs. The company undertook its office paper recycling program around that time, but still found room for improvement in the early 1990s. By that time, almost two-thirds of IBM's more than 9,000 employees worked in an office environment. Internal investigations estimated that high quality white bond and computer paper constituted 70 percent (or 512 tons annually) of its office waste. With participation rates of about 80 percent, IBM expected to recover 480 tons of wastepaper annually, and set a goal of 50 percent waste reduction. In the 1990s the corporation expanded its program to include wooden pallets, lawn clippings, and corrugated cardboard.

If for no other reason, many firms were compelled to reduce their solid waste to comply with legislation. AT&T undertook paper recycling in New Jersey in 1984, three years before mandatory recycling legislation took effect in that state. The model program's waste-paper sales earned $372,000 in 1987 alone, in addition to saving disposal costs. The program was expanded nationwide in the 1990s, and set a 60 percent recycling goal. In 1992 the company recycled 12,565 tons of waste.

Some firms report the best success rates with a comprehensive recycling program encompassing their entire waste stream. Veryfine Products, Inc. of Littleton, Massachusetts, started its recycling program in 1982 with copy and computer paper. In 1989, with the enforcement of EPA waste-water treatment and source reduction standards imminent, the company designed a "state-of-the-art," $8.5 million water purification plant, as well as water-conserving cooling towers. By the early 1990s Veryfine was recycling 90 to 95 percent of all solid waste generated in the juice making process, including glass, aluminum, paper, plastic, pulp, cardboard, wood, and steel. The program included an environmental newsletter, recycling committee, and suggestion system. Veryfine's president, Samuel Rowse, played a vital leadership role in these programs. In 1993 he noted that the corporation's programs had not only avoided nearly $400,000 in landfill costs in recent years, but also gained $158,000 through the recovery and sale of aluminum and glass. Rowse asserted that "Fragmented attempts at recycling, source reduction and environmentally friendly packaging are not enough to make a significant difference in the years ahead. Rather, comprehensive environmental efforts should be integrated into every facet of the business—from the front office to the shipping and-receiving dock."

Other food industries also saw the economic and social benefits of recycling. By 1998 two secondary markets for recycled cooking oil had emerged in the United States. The first, serving restaurants, merely reprocessed the oil for further use in cooking. The second, serving operators of diesel engines and equipment, modified the used cooking oil to create "biodiesel" fuel, which burns more efficiently and with less emission of pollutants than traditional diesel fuel.

FIVE BASIC RECYCLING PROGRAM COMPONENTS

The federal government's 1993 *Office Recycling Program Guide* notes five basic, interconnected components of a comprehensive recycling program: education, collection, **marketing**, procurement, and monitoring and evaluation.

Education encompasses training of both leaders and participants in a recycling program. Studies have shown that the most successful recycling programs involve top-level **management** and require employee participation. Experts advise the appointment of a recycling coordinator or committee responsible for setting up, implementing, and monitoring the program. Some organizations employ environmental consultants to perform this function. Any recycling coordinator's first order of business is self-education. There are a wide variety of resources available to personnel charged with organizing recycling programs. Regional EPA offices and state-affiliated natural resource departments throughout the country offer information packets and recycling kits.

While recycling technically encompasses collecting, processing, and marketing, experts urge source reduction as an integral aspect of successful corporate recycling programs. Source reduction precludes waste management and its costs. Experts suggest several simple ways to reduce waste and reuse resources. Copy and write on both sides of a sheet of paper. Use coffee mugs instead of disposable cups. Reuse packing material and/or make it from shredded waste paper. Ensure that office equipment has a long life by negotiating strong service contracts. Route documents, or use **electronic mail**, instead of disseminating multiple copies. Have laser printer and copier toner cartridges refilled. Sears, Roebuck and Company's packaging reduction program, implemented in the early 1995, saved the retailer an estimated $5 million annually. McDonald's well-publicized partnership with the Environmental Defense Fund greatly reduced its packaging. ''Pollution Prevention Pays,'' a source reduction program started in 1975 by 3M Company, generated enough employee suggestions to save more than $500 million in operational costs by 1989.

After learning about recycling in general, recycling coordinators should acclimate themselves to the particulars of their company's waste-management program through a waste audit. A waste audit should note the sources, amounts and types of trash generated; the current methods and cost of disposal; and the volume of potentially recyclable trash. Based on these findings, leaders of recycling programs can determine which materials to target. Some experts advise beginning recyclers to limit their programs to one type of waste, usually high-quality bond and computer paper. Once participants have grown accustomed to recycling, the program can be expanded to include aluminum, newspaper, plastics, glass, and cardboard, for example. Some companies eventually recycle virtually all their waste. The types and volumes of materials to be recycled will govern the methods of collection employed.

Collection comprises the nuts-and-bolts logistics of separating, gathering, and storing recyclables from trash at their source. The most common methods are the desktop container, a series of designated containers, or a central collection area, but some businesses employ vendor sorting, where mixed recyclables are stored together and sorted off-site by the waste hauler. These containers are usually brought by janitorial or mailroom staff to a storage area, where the containers are kept until pickup by the waste-paper dealer. Some companies dealing with sensitive, proprietary, or confidential information may also need to consider destruction (by shredding, for example) as part of this step. Maintenance of quality standards is paramount in this aspect of a successful recycling program. Similar materials, such as white and colored paper, may have a market separately, but are nearly worthless when mixed. Processors of most types of paper discourage commingling of ''stickies'' (labels, stickers, and tape), food, and other contaminants. Although source separation has proven to be the best collection method, a new technology from Fort James Corporation marketed under the trade name Office Pack will allow businesses to collect virtually all grades of paper in one container. Such technological advances characterize the field of recycling, and are sure to continue as recycling enters the mainstream.

Marketing the recyclable materials to a processor involves research and contracting. Waste-paper dealers can be found in local phone directories or through contact with the Paper Stock Institute of America. *The EI Environmental Services Directory,* ''the nation's largest, most in-depth directory of environmental service providers,'' lists and describes more than 2,000 vendors. This component of the program obviously incorporates outside forces, including the solvency of the contractor and vagaries of the waste-paper market. It holds out the prospect, however, of converting disposal expenses into profits from scrap marketing.

Procurement helps ''close the recycling loop'' by arranging for the purchase and use of supplies made from recycled materials. These can include newsprint, tissue products, paperboard, and printing and writing papers. Some recycling experts suggest that companies purchase only materials that they can recycle, for example, only white paper or envelopes without plastic windows. *The Environmental Products Guide,* published by the federal government's General Services Administration, lists nearly 3,000 products that meet or exceed the EPA's guidelines for recycled content products. First published in 1989, *The Official Recycled Products Guide* includes nearly 4,000 entries on recycled products, with indexes, classifications, and cross-references. Although sometimes overlooked, procurement is a vital component of recycling programs. Some purchasing officers, in fact, report returns of 10 to 25 percent of materials' original purchase price. More importantly, however, without sufficient demand for recycled products, there will be no incentive for recyclers to reprocess waste. This aspect of office recycling in America appears to be lacking. A 1991 *Purchasing World* survey noted that while 87 percent of respondents collected used or excess materials for recycling, only half of the respondents' companies purchased products made from recycled materials for use in their own operations. This shortfall has been called ''recycling's greatest problem'' in the 1990s. In fact, the market for recycled paper products has been characterized by meteoric rises and falls. Between January and June 1994, for instance, the cost of recyclable paper rose from $18 to $110 per ton before falling to $80 per ton in November of the same year. The price rose once again to a peak of $200 per ton in June 1995, and then plummeted to $25 per ton by the following December. In the face of such shifts, manufacturers of recycled paper products often have difficulty competing with those using virgin materials.

Each aspect of the recycling program must be monitored and evaluated for efficiency and progress. A **cost benefit analysis** of the program can strengthen management support and encourage expansion to other areas of the company and/or other products in the waste stream. Periodic bulletins noting the number of trees, kilowatts of energy, and gallons of water saved by the program can keep enthusiasm high.

ENVIRONMENTAL ISSUES

Another issue facing recyclers today is the liability assumed by manufacturers of environmentally hazardous products, such as oils, chemicals, and batteries. The Institute of Scrap and Recycling Industries (ISRI) provides a variety of services for manufacturers of environmentally hazardous recycled products in an effort to ensure that recyclers stay abreast of manufacturing and environmental regulations affecting their present and future operations.

Recycling industries have increasingly been subject to public scrutiny as awareness of environmental issues increases. Manufacturers and recyclers of plastics have, in particular, come in for criticism, as many forms of plastics that bear the chasing arrow symbol are very difficult to recycle, and usually are used only once. Increased scrutiny has led to industrial response, however, and the rate of recycling of plastics polymers in the United States has risen from just 1 percent in the early 1990s to an estimated 50 percent by the year 2000.

In light of the economic, political and social influences that came to bear on the solid waste issue in the late 20th century, hundreds of major American businesses have launched recycling and waste reduction programs. Although the concept has received widespread media attention, the EPA reported in 1993 that less than 5 percent of offices in the United States participated in office paper recycling programs.

SEE ALSO: Environmental Law and Business

[April Dougal Gasbarre, updated by Grant Eldridge]

FURTHER READING:

''Aluminum Can Recycling Hits a Record.'' *Metal/Center News* 38, no. 5 (April 1998): 99.

Beverly, Dawn. *Business Recycling Manual.* New York: INFORM, Inc. and Recourse Systems, Inc., 1991.

Brown, Robert. ''Cooking Oil Recycling Projects Are Moving into the Mainstream.'' *Chemical Market Reporter* 253, no. 12 (23 March 1998): 8.

Curry, Gloria. ''Increasingly Cost-Effective, Recycling Programs Continue to Grow.'' *Office* 118 (August 1993): 30-31, 51, 55.

Erdmann, Bobbi. ''Old Electronic Equipment Worth Its Weight in Gold.'' *World Wastes* 41, no. 8 (August 1998): 6.

Fernberg, Patricia M. ''No More Wasting Away: The New Face of Environmental Stewardship.'' *Managing Office Technology* 38, no. 8 (August 1993): 12-19.

Goldstein, Nora, and Jim Glenn. ''The State of Garbage in America.'' *Biocycle* 38, no. 5 (May 1997): 71.

Grogan, Peter L. ''China Syndrome.'' *BioCycle* 37, no. 5 (May 1996): 86.

——. ''European Influence.'' *BioCycle* 38, no. 9 (September 1997): 86.

Hoeffer, El. ''ISRI Priorities: Superfund, Quality, Safety.'' *Iron Age New Steel* 12, no. 7 (July 1996): 39.

Hoke, Henry R. ''Junk Mail: Waste Not, Want Not.'' *Direct Marketing* 59, no. 4 (August 1996): 80.

Kornegay, Jennifer. ''Security Goes Green.'' *Security Management* 35 (August 1991): 95-96.

Larane, Andre. ''Recycling Is Standard in French Auto Industry.'' *World Wastes* 41, no. 1 (January 1998): 8.

MacEachern, Diane. *Save Our Planet.* New York: Dell Publishing, 1990.

''More Mixing, Better Paper Diversion.'' *BioCycle* (August 1993): 60-61.

Office Paper Recycling Guide. St. Louis: Federal Executive Board, 1992.

Ortbal, John. ''How to Cultivate an Office Recycling Program.'' *Modern Office Technology* (April 1991): 32-36.

Rowse, Samuel. ''A Veryfine Approach to Environmental Awareness.'' *Beverage World* 112 (October 1993): 76-78.

''The Seven Myths of 'Recycled' Plastic.'' *Earth Island Journal* 11, no. 4 (fall 1996): 26.

Steuteville, Robert. ''Corporate Recycling Reaps Savings.'' *BioCycle* 34 (August 1993): 34-36.

Strong, Debra L. *Recycling in America: A Reference Handbook.* 2nd ed. Santa Barbara, CA: ABC-CLIO, 1997.

Stundza, Tom. ''Treat Scrap as Trash and You Throw Money Away.'' *Purchasing* 11 (18 July 1991): 66-69.

U.S. Federal Supply Service. *The Environmental Products Guide.* Washington: U.S. General Services Administration, 1994.

U.S. General Accounting Office. *Wastepaper Recycling: Programs of Civil Agencies Waned During the 1980s.* Washington: U.S. General Accounting Office, [1989].

U.S. Office of Administrative and Management Services. *Office Recycling Program Guide.* Washington: U.S. Office of Administrative and Management Services, [1993].

Webb, Nan. ''Recycling Tasks Are Part of the Job.'' *Purchasing World* 35 (March 1991): 42-43.

REENGINEERING

SEE: Corporate Restructuring

REFINANCING

Refinancing is the refunding or restructuring of **debt** with new debt, equity, or a combination of both. The refinancing of debt is most often undertaken during a period of declining **interest rates** in order to lower the average cost of a firm's debt. Sometimes refinancing involves the issuance of equity in order to decrease the proportion of debt in the borrower's **capital structure**. As a result of refinancing, the maturity of the debt may be extended or reduced, or the new debt may carry a lower interest rate, or a combination of both.

Refinancing may be done by any issuer of debt, such as corporations, governmental bodies, or holders of **real estate**, including home owners. When a borrower retires a debt issue, the payment is in cash and no new security takes the place of the one being paid-off. The term ''refunding'' is used when a borrower issues new debt to refinance an existing one.

CORPORATE OR GOVERNMENT DEBT REFINANCING

The most common incentive for corporations or governmental bodies to refinance their outstanding debt is to take advantage of a decline in interest rates since the time the original debt was issued. Another trigger for corporate debt refinancing is when the price of their **common stock** reaches a level that makes it attractive for a firm to replace its outstanding debt with equity. Aside from reducing interest costs, this latter move gives a firm additional flexibility for future financing because by retiring debt they will have some unused debt capacity. Regardless of the reason for the refinancing, the issuer has to deal with two decisions: (1) is the time right to refinance, and (2) what type of security should be issued to replace the one being refinanced?

If a corporation or governmental body wishes to refinance before the maturity date of the outstanding issue, they will need to exercise the call provision of the debt. The call provision gives the borrower the right to retire outstanding **bonds** at a stipulated price, usually at a premium over face amount, but never less than face. The specific price that an issuer will need to pay for a call appears in the bond's indenture. The existence of a call premium is designed to compensate the bondholder for the firm's right to pay off the debt earlier than the holder expected. Many bond issues have a deferred call, which means the firm cannot call in the bond until the expiration of the deferment period, usually five to ten years.

The cash outlay required by exercising the call provision includes payment to the holder of the bond for any interest that has accrued to the date of the call and the call price, including premium, if any. In addition, the firm will need to pay a variety of administrative costs, including a fee to the bond's **trustee**. Of course, there will be flotation costs for any new debt or equity that is issued as part of the refinancing.

Sometimes an issuer may be prohibited from calling in the bonds (e.g., during the deferred call period). In these instances, the issuer always has the opportunity to purchase its bonds in the open market. This strategy may also be advantageous if the outstanding bond is selling in the market at a price lower than the call price. Open market purchases involve few administrative costs and the corporation will recognize a gain (loss) on the repurchase if the **market value** is below (above) the amount at which the corporation is carrying the bonds on its books (face value plus or minus unamortized premium or discount).

The major difficulty with open market purchases to effect a refinancing is that typically the market for bonds, especially municipals, is ''thin.'' This means that a relatively small percentage of an entire issue may be available on the market over any period. As a result, if a firm is intent on refinancing a bond issue, it almost always needs to resort to a call. This is why virtually every new bond that is issued contains a call provision.

If an outstanding issue does not permit a call or has a deferred call, the issuer can seek tenders (offers to sell) from current bondholders. This is an offer to have the bondholders sell their bonds back to the issuing corporation either at a predetermined price or one set through an auction. To be sure the **tender offer** is financially feasible to the issuer, boundaries will be set on the repurchase price.

Yet another tactic is available to ''retire'' a bond issue. This process is called defeasance and is popularly used in the not-for profit sector. It involves placing into trust, generally with a **bank,** a portfolio of **securities**, usually U.S. Treasuries with maturities at least as long as the time to the first call or maturity, whichever is earlier. If the transaction is structured properly, the interest and principal from the portfolio deposited in trust will equal or exceed the amount needed to service the bonds (interest, principal, and call premium, if any). Since for all practical purposes the bond issue has been retired, if the deal meets the necessary **accounting** requirements, the bond issue can be removed from the issuer's **balance sheet**.

The new debt instrument issued in refinancing can be simple or complex. A corporation could replace an existing bond with traditional bonds, serial bonds (which have various maturity dates), zero coupon bonds (which have no periodic interest payments), or corporate shares (which have no maturity date, but which may have associated **dividend** payments). One factor that a firm needs to consider is that the administrative and flotation costs of issuing either common or preferred shares are higher than for new debt. Furthermore, dividend payments, if any, are not **tax** deductible, while interest payments are.

The decision to refinance is a very practical matter involving time and money. Over time the opportunity to refinance varies with changing interest rates and **economic conditions**. When a corporation anticipates an advantageous interest rate climate, it then analyzes the cash flows associated with the refinancing. Calculating the **present value** of all the cash outflows and the interest savings assists in comparing refinancing alternatives that have different maturity dates and capitalization schemes.

Exhibit 1 demonstrates the type of computation that needs to be made to determine the financial feasibility of refinancing alternatives. We are assuming a call premium (tax deductible) of 5 percent and a tax rate of 40 percent. The **discount rate** used in the present value computations is the after-tax interest/dividend cost of the respective alternative. For simplicity, we are assuming annual interest payments.

As can be seen, the most favorable alternative is to refinance with the 30-year debt. This results in a net present value savings of $26,288. The other alternatives each have a net present value cost.

MORTGAGE REFINANCING

The above method of analyzing the refinancing decision is also applicable to **mortgage** refinancing for residential or commercial real estate. To decide which refinancing alternative is the best, the analysis would be similar to the corporate decision illustrated above. For a mortgage one would:

1. Calculate the present value of the after-tax cash flows of the existing mortgage.
2. Calculate the present value of the after-tax cash flows of the proposed mortgage.
3. Compare the outcomes and select the alternative with the lower present value. The

Exhibit 1
Example of Analysis Required for Refinancing

Original Issue:			
Outstanding principal	$300,000		
Call premium (5%)	15,000		
Annual interest	30,000		
Years remaining to maturity	30		
Refinancing Alternatives:	Cash	New 8% Debt 30 Year	Preferred Stock-9%
New amount	$ 0	$300,000	$300,000
Flotation costs	0	27,000	45,000
Annual interest		24,000	
Annual dividend			27,000
Initial cost of refinancing:			
Face amount of old issue	300,000	300,000	300,000
Call premium, net of taxes	9,000	9,000	9,000
New issue proceeds, net of costs		275,000	255,000
Initial cost	$309,000	$34,000	$54,000
Annual savings, net of taxes (@ 40%)	18,000	3,960	-9,000
Net present cost (savings) of refinancing	$106,356	$-26,288	$146,466

interest rate to be used in steps one and two is the after-tax interest cost of the proposed mortgage.

All of this needs to be tempered by how long the home owners believe they will be staying in their current home.

Whether it pays to refinance involves a different approach. Previously, in residential real estate the conventional wisdom applied the ''2 2-2 rule'': if interest rates have fallen two points below the existing mortgage rate, if the owner has already paid two years of the mortgage, and if the owner plans to live in the house another two years, then refinancing is feasible. Because of the tremendous varieties of mortgage options available today, however, this approach is no longer used. In fact, many home owners find it prudent to refinance if interest rates have fallen just 0.25 percent, especially if the refinancing can be done without the payment of points or closing costs.

A much easier approach involves three steps by determining: (1) the reduction in your monthly payment from refinancing, (2) the after-tax cash outflows required to refinance (usually points plus closing costs), and (3) how much longer you anticipate living in your current house. You then do a simple payback computation by dividing the costs from step two by the monthly savings in step one and comparing the result to the time in step three.

[Ronald M. Horwitz]

FURTHER READING:

Arsan, Noyan, and Eugene Poindexter. ''Revisiting the Economics of Mortgage Refinance.'' *Journal of Retail Banking* 15, no. 4 (winter 1993-1994); 45-48.

Bierman, Harold, Jr., and Seymour Smidt. *Financial Management for Decision Making.* New York: Macmillan, 1986.

Haugen, Robert A. *Introductory Investment Theory.* Englewood Cliffs, NJ: Prentice Hall, 1987.

Sharpe, William F., Gordon J. Alexander, and Jeffery V. Bailey. *Investments.* 6th ed. Upper Saddler River, NJ: Prentice Hall, 1998.

Short, Daniel G. *Fundamentals of Financial Accounting.* 7th ed. Homewood, IL: Irwin, 1993.

REGRESSION ANALYSIS

Regression analysis employs algebraic formulas to estimate the value of a continuous random variable, called a dependent variable, using the value of another, independent, variable. Statistical methods are used to determine the most correct estimate of that dependent variable, and whether the estimate is valid at all.

Regressions may be used for a wide variety of purposes where estimation is important. For example, a marketer may employ a regression to determine how sales of products might be affected by investments in **advertising**. An employer may perform a similar analysis to estimate an employee's job evaluation scores based on the employee's performance on an aptitude test. A biologist can even use a regression to see how temperature changes might affect the rate of reproduction in frogs.

While closely related, regression differs from correlation analysis in an important way. Where regression is used to estimate the value of a dependent variable, correlation measures the degree of relationship between two variables. In other words, correlation analysis can indicate the strength of a linear relationship between variables, but it is left to regression analysis to provide predictions of the dependent variable based on values of an independent variable.

A simple regression analysis is one in which a single independent variable is used to determine a dependent variable. The relationship between the variables is assumed to be consistent, or linear. Figure 1 shows examples of linear, nonlinear, and curvilinear scatter diagrams, as well as one where there is no consistent relationship between *X* and *Y* variables.

The equation that represents the simple linear regression is

$$Y_i = \alpha + \beta X_i + e_i$$

where Y_i = the value of the dependent variable in a certain observation, *i*;
X_i = the value of the independent variable in the observation *i*;
α = the value of *Y* when *X* is equal to zero, and may be thought of as the intercept (sometimes denoted β_0);
β = the slope of the regression line;
e_i is the random error in the observation *i*.

The values of both the independent variable *X* and the dependent variable *Y* are provided by a survey, or set of observed numerical samples. These sets of numbers are maintained as ordered pairs—a range of values of *Y* is indicated for each value of *X*. The value e_i represents the sampling error associated with the dependent random variable *Y*.

Some assumptions must be satisfied to perform the regression analysis. First, if we plot the values of *X* on a scatter diagram, the sampling error e_i, or variance from a mean, must be reasonably consistent for all values of *X*. In other words, for each value of *X*, the variation in values of *Y* must be reasonably consistent. This quality is called homoscedasticity.

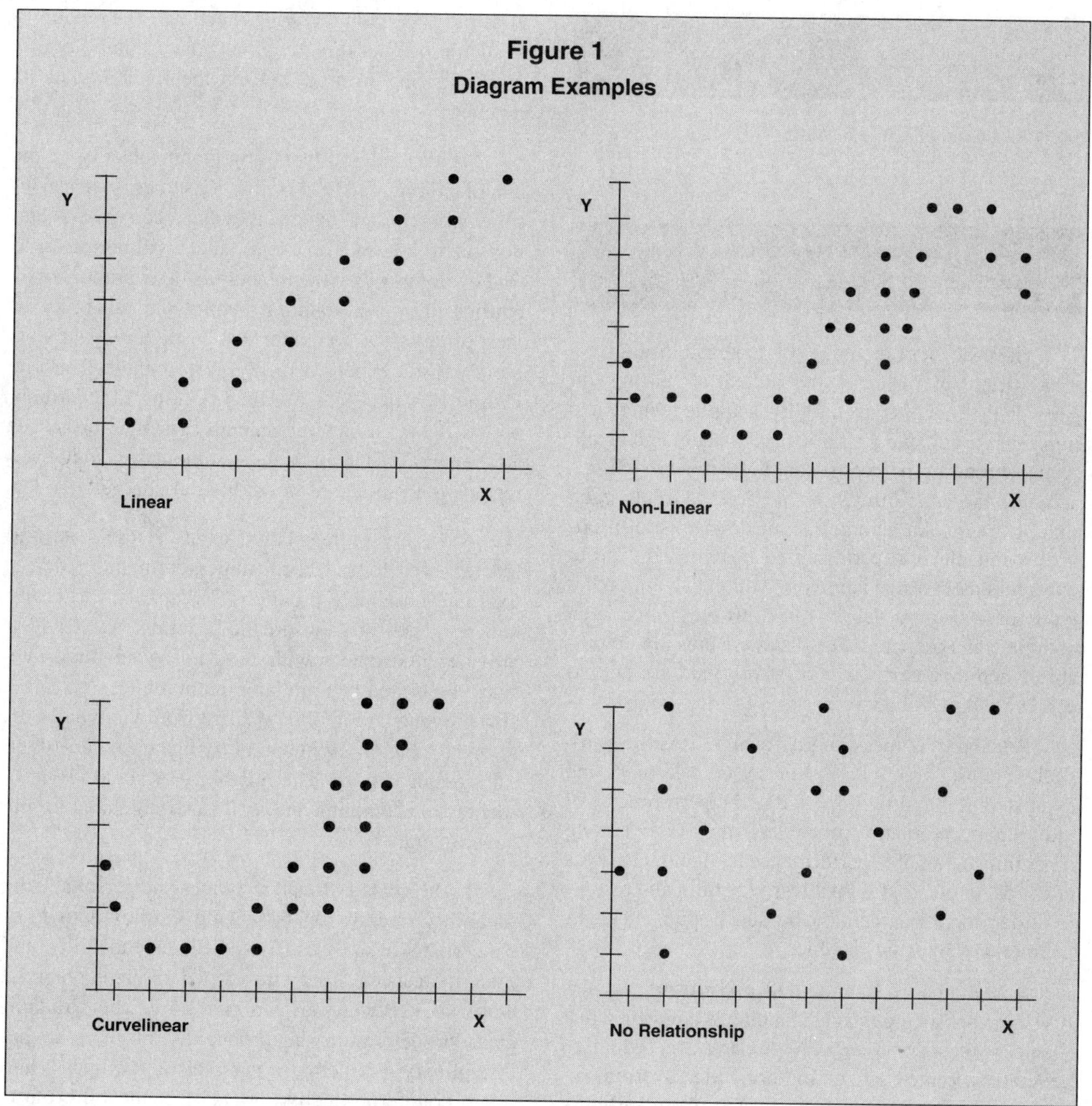

Second, observed values of the random variable and amounts of random error must be uncorrelated, a condition usually satisfied by random sampling of the dependent value.

A simple regression analysis uses only one independent variable. There are many situations, however, where a dependent variable is determined by 2, 3, 5, or even 100 independent variables. As a result, it becomes difficult to represent the relationships between the variables in a visual model.

For example, a simple regression with two variables can be represented on a graph, with one variable measured on the X axis and the other on the Y axis. But add a third variable, and the graph requires a third dimension, X_2. As a result, the regression line becomes a regression plane.

Add a fourth variable, and the regression can no longer be represented visually. Conceptually, it has four dimensions, also called hyperplanes or arrays. The same applies for regressions with even more variables; eight variables require eight dimensions.

These relationships can be expressed in complex mathematical formulas. They are no longer simple regressions, but multiple regressions.

[John Simley, updated by Kevin J. Murphy]

FURTHER READING:

Foster, D. P., R. A. Stine, and R. P. Waterman. *Business Analysis Using Regression.* New York: Springer-Verlag, 1998.

Golberg, M. *Introduction to Regression Analysis.* Computational Mechanics Inc./WIT Press, 2000.

Rawlings, John O., G. Sastry, and David A. Dickey. *Applied Regression Analysis.* New York: Springer-Verlag, 1998.

REIT

SEE: Real Estate Investment Trust

RELIABILITY

The concept of reliability or dependability is used in a variety of business and industrial settings. In general, the concept of reliability is applied where it is important to achieve the same results again and again. A manufacturing process is said to be reliable when it achieves the same results, within defined limits, each time it occurs. An automobile, or other type of product, is reliable if it performs consistently and up to expectations. The reliability of financial and other types of data may depend on how they have been compiled and prepared. Personnel are considered reliable when they perform consistently and are able to achieve defined objectives.

Reliability is measured by results. It is the yardstick against which performance is measured and evaluated. Reliability is applied to the performance of individuals, products, processes, and data, among other things. Reliable performance in all of these areas is critical to successful **business planning** and results. In order for a business to be successful, all of its components must be reliable.

In the area of **finance** and **accounting**, data is reliable when an independent audit has confirmed that financial records have been prepared according to generally accepted accounting principles. **Annual reports** and other financial disclosures from **publicly held companies** generally contain a statement from the **auditing** firm as to the reliability of the data contained therein. The statement of reliability affirms that the information contained in the financial report is free from error and bias and reasonably reflects the facts of the business operation.

Accounting data can be reliable without necessarily being verifiable. In order for such data to be verifiable, it must be possible to reconstruct the financial data and achieve the same results. In addition, two or more accountants working independently must be able to achieve the same results for financial data to be verifiable.

Reliability is also an important concept in manufacturing and engineering. Plants, processes, materials, and a host of other aspects of the manufacturing process are continually tested for reliability. Since reliability does not necessarily mean perfection, constant attention is paid to improving the reliability of a wide range of manufacturing functions. The reliability of such processes directly affects the profitability of a manufacturing firm as well as the reliability of its products.

Product reliability is important not only to the manufacturer, but also to the consumer. When consumers purchase products, they have certain expectations as to how well those products will perform and for how long. When manufacturers offer product **warranties**, they are standing behind the reliability of their products. A computer that has a three-year warranty can be expected to be more reliable than one with only a two-year warranty. During the warranty period, the manufacturer generally assumes the cost of any repairs or defects and, in some cases, may even replace the product at no additional charge.

A variety of legislation exists at the state and federal levels to protect consumers from faulty, defective, and unreliable products. Perhaps the most well known is California's so-called "lemon law," which provides consumers with remedies when they purchase consistently unreliable automobiles. That law also prevents automobile dealers from knowingly reselling a "lemon" without notifying consumers of the car's repair history. The reliability of some services, such as telecommunications, is also regulated by the government.

In the area of human resources and personnel, the reliability of individuals seeking **employment** is of concern to businesses. So-called dependability and integrity tests have been developed to screen potential employees. Businesses can give these tests to applicants to determine the probability of their having disciplinary problems, **absenteeism**, tardiness, and other counterproductive traits. Dependability tests complement mental and physical ability tests to provide employers with a better evaluation of potential new hires.

SEE ALSO: Product Liability

[David P. Bianco]

FURTHER READING:

Ellis, Ed. "Trains Must Achieve Reliability, but Can They?" *Trains Magazine,* August 1996, 14-15.

Hashim, Mohammad. "Measuring Reliability in Service Industries." *Management Decision,* July 1987, 46-51.

Ippolito, Richard A. "A Study of Wages and Reliability." *Journal of Law and Economics,* April 1996, 149-89.

Radford, Bruce W. "Electric Reliability: Sanctions or Commerce?" *Public Utilities Fortnightly,* 1 May 1998, 52-57.

Radosevich, Lynda. "ISP Performance Remains Steady." *InfoWorld,* 27 October 1997, 79-80.

REORGANIZATION

SEE: Corporate Restructuring

REPLACEMENT COST

Under generally accepted **accounting** principles, the value of a company's assets is based on its historical costs. The present book value of an asset is determined by its acquisition, or historical, cost, less any **depreciation**. A company's **financial statements** will reflect this, usually valuing its assets at their present book value.

Replacement costs provide an alternative way of valuing a company's assets. The replacement, or current, cost of an asset is the amount of money required to replace the asset by purchasing a similar asset with identical future service capabilities. In replacement cost accounting, assets and **liabilities** are valued at their cost to replace.

If replacement costs are used to establish the value of assets, then the replacement method of depreciation is also used to adjust the value of an asset as it is used over time. Under the replacement method of depreciation, an anticipated replacement cost for the asset is estimated. The depreciation expense is then calculated as the sum of the depreciation based on the historical cost, plus a percentage of the difference between the historical cost and the replacement cost. Using the replacement method, the depreciation expense associated with an asset is based on a combination of its historical cost and its replacement cost.

When an acquiring company seeks to obtain an estimate of a target company's value before making a purchase offer, the replacement costs of the company's assets often provide a more accurate value than does the present book value of the assets. The value of an asset is intended to reflect its earnings potential. Present book value, calculated on the basis of historical costs and depreciation, does not take into account such factors as **inflation**, for example. Replacement costs, on the other hand, are more likely to accurately reflect **economic conditions** that can affect the value of a company's assets.

SEE ALSO: Cost Accounting

[David P. Bianco]

REPURCHASE AGREEMENTS

Repurchase agreements are considered to be money market financial instruments. Money market financial instruments, in turn, consist of short-maturity or short-term financial instruments. A financial instrument is considered ''short-term'' if it matures within one year. This definition of ''short-term'' as used for money market purposes is different from that used by the **Internal Revenue Service**, which uses six months as the cut-off between short and long terms. Among the many **money market instruments**, repurchase agreements are among those that have the shortest maturity periods. Based on maturity period, repurchase agreements are usually classified under two sub-groups—overnight repurchase agreements and long-term repurchase agreements.

OVERNIGHT REPURCHASE AGREEMENTS

Repurchase agreements, or RPs, are essentially short-term loans backed by Treasury bills as collateral. Usually, the maturity period of a repurchase agreement is less than two weeks, overnight RPs being the shortest maturity repurchase agreement instrument. A repurchase agreement transaction can be illustrated as follows: corporation *A* has some idle cash and corporation *B* wants to borrow funds overnight to make up for the shortfall in the amount of required reserves that it must have at the Federal Reserve. Assume that corporation A uses $10 million to buy Treasury bills from corporation B, which agrees to buy back (repurchase) Treasury bills the next morning at a price slightly higher than corporation A's purchase price. The higher price that corporation B pays is a form of interest on the overnight use of corporation A's $10 million. Thus, in effect, corporation B borrows $10 million from corporation B for overnight use at a specified interest (implied in the purchase and repurchase prices of Treasury bills). Should corporation B not buy back the Treasury bills that corporation A is holding, the latter can sell those bills to its loan. Transferred Treasury bills thus serve as collateral, which the lender receives if the borrower does not pay back the loan.

Repurchase agreements are a relatively new financial instrument. They have been in existence only since 1969. However, they constitute an important source of funds for banks, where large corporations are considered the most important lenders.

Because of extremely short maturity, overnight repurchase agreements are considered very liquid—the instrument turns back into cash the very next day. Since RPs are liquid, but less liquid than currency or checkable deposits, they are included, by the **Federal Reserve**, in broader definitions of money supply.

LONGER-TERM REPURCHASE AGREEMENTS

Repurchase agreements that have maturity periods of more than one night are called long-term repurchase agreements, or term RPs. Thus, long term repurchase agreements also facilitate borrowing and lending in which Treasury bills are essentially used as collateral. By nature, long-term repurchase agreements are less liquid than overnight repurchase agreements.

[Anandi P. Sahu, Ph.D.]

FURTHER READING:

Mishkin, Frederic S. *The Economics of Money, Banking, and Financial Markets.* 5th ed. Reading, PA: Addison-Wesley, 1998.

Ritter, Lawrence S., William L. Silber, and Gregory F. Udell. *Principles of Money, Banking, and Financial Markets.* 9th edition. Reading, PA: Addison-Wesley, 1997.

REQUEST FOR PROPOSAL

Request for proposal (RFP) is the process by which a corporate department or government agency prepares bid documents to acquire equipment or services. The RFP is frequently published in the legal documents section of pertinent newspapers or in trade journals covering the industry in which the department operates. The RFP can also be distributed to a list of qualified potential bidders who have already been contacted and prequalified as eligible by the agency or department.

Qualification, a key concept in the RFP procedure, frequently depends on follow-up investigation on the part of the hopeful bidder, and careful wording of the original RFP. A company that deals only in Macintosh **computers** and **software** written for Apple Computer, Inc., for instance, could not hope to win the RFP bid and fulfill the needs of a government agency that is equipped with IBM personal computers. On the other hand Dell Computer, which sells IBM clones, may indeed fill the needs of the same department if it can prove that its computers can mesh with the existing IBM machines and MS-DOS software.

Private corporations sometimes employ the practice of issuing RFPs, usually when purchasing **commodities** or services that do not bear directly on the company's own products or services. Government agencies are closely associated with preparing and evaluating RFPs since their responsibility to get equipment and consulting talent at the lowest possible price is closely monitored by the press and **tax** watchdogs. This attention to low cost as monitored by the RFP process is exemplified by an old joke in which astronauts are asked how they feel about sitting on top of a rocket designed and built by a long string of low bidders.

Developments in public and private sector businesses and organizations have led some to doubt the continuing efficacy of RFPs. Many contractors are less than totally truthful in their responses to RFPs, a practice that can lead to nasty surprises for the contracting business or agency. Furthermore, the accelerated pace of business today makes the traditional RFP process too slow to allow agencies and businesses to respond to changes in technology and the marketplace. In light of these obstacles, many businesses and agencies are turning to the use of a streamlined RFP, known as a request for information (RFI), to identify qualified contractors. Many businesses are also eliminating the RFP process entirely by developing their own prototypical products and services in-house, where they are better able to maintain quality and scheduling control.

Even among corporations and agencies that continue to make use of RFPs, problems can arise. Under the Freedom of Information Act, all RFPs presented to government agencies are part of the public record, and can yield information useful to competitors. Finally, agencies and businesses issuing RFPs frequently know more about the products and services they require than do any potential contractors, and are therefore obliged to educate all parties responding to RFPs, a time-consuming process.

In response to these and other criticisms of the RFP process, the Society of Professional Administrators and Recordkeepers (SPARK) began development of national standards for RFPs in 1996. Through the creation of a model RFP, SPARK hopes to streamline the process while retaining the main strength of the RFP, namely, the in-depth information it can provide. Further efforts to modernize the RFP process are driven by computer software companies, including Microsoft, which launched its Exchange software to compete with Lotus Development Corporation's venerable Notes package in 1996.

PREPARING GOOD RFPs

There are some elements that an issuing agency should make sure to include in a good RFP:

- Be specific when describing what is needed to fulfill the agency needs. A request for ''five Pentium II computers'' is not specific. ''Five Pentium II computers, each powered by 350 megahertz microprocessors with 32

MB of RAM and expandable to 128 MB of RAM with 4 gigabyte hard drives with 3.5 inch (1.44 MB) floppy disk drives,'' on the other hand, is much more specific and useful to potential contractors. Such intricate description is needed to make sure that every potential vendor is bidding on the same equipment. Some companies may even want to specify the manufacturers of components that will be inside the computers. This would eliminate the potential problem of a vendor substituting a poor quality component that meets the specifications on paper, but is known for problems. In any case, managers issuing RFPs should have a good working knowledge of the technologies, products, and techniques to be used in their project as a further defense against misunderstanding and misinformation.

- Make sure the potential vendors understand the nature of the RFP agency—what it does, how the equipment will be used, the problem that is being addressed by the RFP, and any future goals that the agency plans that might relate to the equipment. Potential contractors should be asked for examples of similar projects they have undertaken, whether or not their existing infrastructure will support the proposed project, and for precise and complete billing information and cost overflow policies and procedures.
- Look as far into the future as possible. A successful RFP will inform contractors of a company or agency's long-term plans. Providing such speculative information may make a difference sometime in the future, and it does not hurt to see how the bidders respond to the possibility.
- Alert bidders regarding any environmental situations that the equipment might face. If the equipment is being purchased to go to Europe or South America, for example, tell them. Foreign standards might be entirely different from what is acceptable in the United States. If the equipment is intended to go into an old building on the second floor, check with the bidders to ensure that the equipment is not too heavy. Bidders might assume that the RFP agency knows that the item weighs a ton, while the RFP agency might not even have thought about where it will be used.
- Give vendors plenty of time to study the RFP before the deadline. Some companies give vendors as much as one month from the time the RFP is published before the bids are due. This allows bidders time to tinker with their bids, possibly allowing them to seek out new vendors of their own to help meet the needs of the RFP.
- Enforce standards on replying bidders. For instance, if a company returns a bid for ''five Pentium II computers with 200 megahertz microprocessors,'' return it to the company, or throw it out without comment, since the vendor did not follow the RFP's specifications for Pentium II computers running at 350 megahertz.
- Enforce deadlines on vendors. When buying off-the-shelf equipment, an agency should be suspicious of any vendor claiming to need more time than the contract requires in order to meet the needs of the agency. Why does the vendor need more time to deliver Pentium II computers when that type of computer is a commodity? If the RFP is for equipment that is ''cutting edge,'' the RFP agency should require the winning vendor to sign a performance bond that guarantees it will deliver by a certain date. Such bonds carry a monetary penalty that the vendor agrees to pay if it misses the delivery date.
- Try to limit the number of vendors since every bid requires staff scrutiny. Who makes the list? Who doesn't? That is up to the agency staff to determine. Many government agencies and some corporate departments are reluctant to cut vendors off bid lists out of fear of favoritism charges. One way to keep the list manageable is to require potential vendors to refile every few years and to meet certain criteria, such as listing past sales and experience or number of employees available to service the account. Shaky companies that would not be good vendors are unlikely to keep up with such refiling requirements.
- Make sure replying companies specifically address the problem that was the original purpose of issuing the RFP. Bids that address both the company's current problems and future needs carry more weight than those that just cover the minimum the company asked. As such, bids that emphasize **quality control** and assurance while taking account of workflow, electronic capacities (where applicable), production capabilities, shipping options, and cost, and supply ample references, should be given the most serious consideration.

A lawyer may be needed to make sure the RFP and the equipment or services it seeks are legal under local, state, and federal laws. For example, a company advertising for bids for fuel-oil storage tanks should make absolutely sure that the tanks offered by companies responding to the RFP fit all federal environmental standards as set down by the **Environmental Protection Agency**.

ANSWERING RFPs

Companies wishing to bid on RFPs should monitor the legal notices in local newspapers and trade magazines, and contact the purchasing departments of corporations and government agencies likely to request services and equipment. Investigate the requirements to be added to the "bid list."

There may be more to answering the RFP than just providing the lowest cost or the highest level of customer service. Some corporations and government agencies give special consideration on their bid lists to minority- and women-owned companies with "set-asides," a certain percentage of a job predetermined to go to companies that are usually smaller and newer to business.

Read the RFP carefully, paying particular attention to deadlines and performance clauses. Some RFPs may require that the winning bidder provide the service by a certain date. If that date is missed, the bidder might be forced to return cash to the organization that issued the RFP.

Determine if the RFP is for both equipment and service. Companies that sell equipment might not be able to adequately service it, yet that service performance may be written into the RFP in a separate section from the equipment specifications. Responders must know they can fulfill the entire contract before answering it.

[Clint Johnson, updated by Grant Eldridge]

FURTHER READING:

Bergsman, Steve. "Setting an Industry Standard for RFPs." *Pension Management* 32, no. 2 (February 1996): 29.

Cohen, Jason. "The ABCs of RFPs: Developing a Request for Proposal for Your Data Conversion Projects." *Inform* 12, no. 2 (February 1998): 34.

Greenbaum, Joshua M. "Truth, Lies, and RFPs." *Software Magazine,* May 1997, 12.

Lewis, Bob. "Are RFPs Only Requests for Punishment, or Can They Actually Help You?" *InfoWorld,* 22 January 1996, 62.

O'Connell, Sandra E. "An Alternative to the RFP." *HRMagazine* 41, no. 9 (September 1996): 36.

Schrage, Michael. "RFPs: May They Rest in Peace." *Computerworld,* 1 April 1996, 37.

Shah, Nirav. "Four Steps to Writing a Successful RFP." *American City and County* 113, no. 8 (July 1998): 24.

Shanoff, Barry. "How to Prevent Your Government Bids from Becoming Public Record." *World Wastes* 41, no. 10 (October 1998): 15.

Snyder, Joel. "Put More 'Ability' into Your E-mail RFP." *Network World* 13, no. 23 (3 June 1996): 53.

Stein, Murry. "Don't Bomb Out When Preparing RFPs." *Computerworld,* 15 February 1993, 102.

RESEARCH AND DEVELOPMENT

Research and development (R&D) represents a large and rapidly growing effort in both industrialized and semi-industrialized nations. In 1997 the United States spent $151 billion on industrial R&D and $32 billion on military R&D, for a total of $183 billion, equal to 2.5 percent of the **gross national product** (GNP). Similar ratios exist for economically advanced countries, such as Germany, France, the United Kingdom, and Japan. In order to compete in the international marketplace, rapidly industrializing countries such as South Korea, Indonesia, and Brazil have national policies in place for developing indigenous R&D. The goal is substitution of strategic **imports** and development of **exports**. Major countries not politically aligned with the Western powers—notably Russia, China, and India, and to a certain extent, France and Israel—perform significant levels of R&D for defense purposes, in order (1) to be technologically and logistically independent from Western sources, and (2) to export arms to third world countries. South Africa, Iraq, and North Korea spent inordinate amounts of their limited GNPs for military purposes in the 1990s.

The reason for this increased emphasis on R&D is that it creates new or improved technology that in turn can be converted through **technology management** into a competitive advantage at the business, corporate, and national level. While the process of technological **innovation** (of which R&D is the first phase) is complex and risky, the rewards can be very high, as witnessed, for example, by GE Engineering Plastics. Started in 1957 and based on R&D, the business grew to $7 billion in sales by 1997.

The relationship between R&D and economic growth is complex, but several economic studies have come to the conclusion that it is very significant. The "social" rate of return of industrial and agricultural R&D is on the order of 50 to 70 percent, while the "private" rate of return is on the order of 25 to 50 percent. The reason that the private rate is approximately half the social rate is that the originator of R&D cannot appropriate all the benefits of innovations and must share them with customers, the public, and even competitors. The Strategic Management Institute determined that, at the business level, the return of R&D for 42 major U.S. corporations was 33 percent in 1978. Therefore, R&D is a good investment for business, but a risky one—the majority of R&D projects fail to provide the expected financial results, and the successful projects (25 to 50 percent) must also pay for the projects that are unsuccessful or terminated early by **management**.

OBJECTIVES AND TYPES OF R&D

The objective of academic and institutional R&D is to obtain new knowledge, which may or may not be applied to practical uses. In contrast, the objective of industrial R&D is to obtain new knowledge *applicable to the company's business needs,* that eventually will result in new or improved products, processes, systems, or services that can increase the company's sales and profits.

The National Science Foundation defines three types of R&D: basic research, applied research, and development. Basic research has as its objective a fuller knowledge or understanding of the subject under study, rather than a practical application thereof. As applied to the industrial sector, basic research is defined as research that advances scientific knowledge but does not have specific commercial objectives, although such investigation may be in the fields of present or potential interest to the company.

Applied research is directed towards gaining knowledge or understanding necessary for determining the means by which a recognized and specific need may be met. In industry, applied research includes investigations directed to the discovery of new specific knowledge having specific commercial objectives with respect to products, processes, or services.

Development is the systematic utilization of the knowledge or understanding gained from research toward the production of useful materials, devices, systems, or methods, including design and development of prototypes and processes.

At this point, it is important to differentiate development from engineering, which can be defined as utilization of state-of-the-art knowledge for the design and production of marketable goods and services. In other words, research creates knowledge, and development develops and builds prototypes and proves their feasibility. Engineering then converts these prototypes into products or services that can be offered to the marketplace or into processes that can be used to produce commercial products and services.

In modern industrial practice, the distinction between R (research) and D (development) is not always clear. At General Electric's (GE) R&D Center, a relatively small percentage (5 to 10 percent) of the total effort is devoted to ''exploratory research,'' with results expected within a span of 10 to 15 years and no specific commercial applications. All the remaining efforts are lumped together and accounted for as R&D. Also, the relative importance of R&D varies according to a company's **strategy** and culture. Some companies, such as E.I. du Pont de Nemours & Co. and Sony, still rely heavily on research to eventually develop new products such as Kevlar or the VCR. Other companies prefer to conduct little or no research and instead develop new products from the results of research generated by others that may be generally available in the public domain or acquired legally. In the United States, Apple Computer Inc. and Microsoft Corp. conduct relatively little research but are exceptionally creative at development. The Japanese consumer electronics industry initially utilized the results of American and European research creatively and effectively to enter the international marketplace through new low-cost, high-quality products, which were developed, designed, and manufactured in a relatively short time. As technology became harder to acquire, many Japanese companies switched from development to research. For instance, in the 1950s, Toshiba was heavily dependent on GE's technology, but it now has a major independent R&D laboratory. Thanks to this change in R&D strategy, several Japanese firms have become world leaders in specific technological areas, for instance Canon in ink-jet printers, Toray in carbon fibers, Honda in small internal combustion engines, Fanuc in factory **automation**, and Toshiba in portable **computers**.

R&D AND TECHNOLOGY ACQUISITION

In many cases, technology required for industrial purposes is available in the marketplace, usually for a price. Before embarking on the lengthy and risky process of performing its own R&D, a company should perform a ''make or buy'' analysis and decide whether or not the new R&D project is strategically and economically justified.

The following influencing factors should be considered: proprietariness, timing, **risk**, and cost.

PROPRIETARINESS. If a technology can be safeguarded as proprietary, and protected by **patents**, trade secrets, nondisclosure agreements, etc., the technology becomes the exclusive property of the company and the value is much higher. In fact, a valid patent grants a company a temporary monopoly for 20 years to use the technology as it sees fit, usually to maximize sales and profits. In this case, a high level of R&D effort is justified for a relatively long period (up to ten years) with an acceptable risk of failure. Typical examples are the pharmaceutical companies and some high-tech materials producers. For instance, more than ten years and expenditures in excess of $1 billion dollars were required by Pfizer to develop Viagra, a treatment for male impotence, but the potential market is very large and will continue for a long time. Similarly, GE developed man-made industrial diamonds in its research laboratory in the early 1950s. Although the original patents have expired, GE is still the world's leading supplier. Its major competitor, De Beers, acquired a GE license in the late 1950s and still produces diamonds with the GE process.

On the contrary, if the technology cannot be protected, as is the case with certain **software** programs, expensive in-house R&D is not justified since the software may be copied by a competitor or "stolen" by a disloyal employee. In this case, the secret of commercial success is staying ahead of the **competition** by developing continuously improved software packages, supported by a strong **marketing** effort. MapInfo, a new venture founded in 1986, developed the first software program for displaying maps and related databases on a personal computer. They are still the world leader, thanks to the improved and expanded versions of the original mapping system and to a broad spectrum of application packages issued regularly since first commercialization.

TIMING. If the market growth rate is slow or moderate, in-house or contracted R&D may be the best means to obtain the technology. On the other hand, if the market is growing very fast and competitors are rushing in, the "window of opportunity" may close before the technology has been developed by the new entrant. In this case, it is better to acquire the technology and related know-how, in order to enter the market before it is too late. For instance, in December 1998 America Online acquired Netscape, the company with the most expertise in **Internet** browser software, in order to be able to compete effectively with Microsoft, Yahoo!, and many other Internet providers. Because of the Internet explosion, America Online had neither the people nor the time to develop its own proprietary software, and was consequently willing to pay $4.21 billion for Netscape.

RISK. Inherently, technology development is always riskier than technology acquisition because the technical success of R&D cannot be guaranteed. There is always the risk that the planned performance specifications will not be met, that the time to project completion will be stretched out, and that the R&D and manufacturing **costs** will be higher than forecasted. On the other hand, acquiring technology entails a much lower risk, since the product, process, or service, can be seen and tested before the **contract** is signed. This is the reason why rapidly industrializing countries represent a major fast-growing market for technology available from the more advanced nations. In the past such countries acquired older, obsolescent versions of technology, but now they demand the latest, in order to be competitive in the global marketplace.

Regardless of whether the technology is acquired or developed, there is always the risk that it will soon become obsolete and be displaced by a superior technology. This risk cannot be entirely removed, but it can be considerably reduced by careful technology **forecasting** and planning. If market growth is slow, and no winner has emerged among the various competing technologies, it may be wiser to monitor these technologies through "technology gatekeepers" and be ready to jump in as the winner emerges. For instance, in the development of nonimpact magnetic printers, several technologies were researched and developed: lasers, laser xerography, electrostatic, magnetic, and ink jet. In the 1970s, GE jumped on the magnetic technology bandwagon without considering alternative technologies; after spending nearly $10 million and ten years to develop its product, the company found no takers for its poor performing printer. In the meantime IBM, Xerox, Honeywell, and several Japanese companies had developed successful printers using the other technologies listed above. In retrospect, GE could have reduced its risk by monitoring the various competing technologies through gatekeepers in its R&D center and by starting a crash program (as it did with computerized axial tomography, a medical diagnostic imaging system) as soon as the market was ready and the winning technology had emerged.

COST. For a successful product line with a relatively long life, acquisition of technology is more costly, but less risky, than technology development. Normally, royalties are paid in the form of a relatively low initial payment as "earnest money," and as periodic payments tied to sales. These payments continue throughout the period of validity of the **licensing agreement**. Since these royalties may amount to 2 to 5 percent of sales, this creates an undue burden of continuing higher cost to the licensee, everything else being equal. On the other hand, R&D requires a high front-end investment and therefore a longer period of negative cash flow. There are also intangible costs involved in acquiring technology: the licensing agreements may have restrictive geographic or application clauses, other businesses may have access to the same technology and compete with lower prices or stronger marketing. Finally, the licensee is dependent upon the licensor for technological advances, or even for keeping up to date, and this may be dangerous. As a typical example, GE gave a general design and manufacturing license for heavy electrical equipment (hydraulic turbines, transformers, circuit breakers) to its **subsidiaries** in Italy, CGE (Compagnia Generale di Elettricità), and in Spain, GEE (General Eléctrica Española), for only 1.5 percent of sales. The problem arose when GE Power Systems decided to abandon the three businesses and drastically cut back R&D on steam turbines. The GE subsidiaries were stuck with obsolescent technologies and had to scramble to find other sources, since they lacked the resources and the time to perform in-house R&D.

MOVING AHEAD WITH R&D

Once the decision has been made to perform R&D, the company should decide where and how such R&D should be carried out. There are various possibilities: in-house R&D in the company laboratories, externally contracted R&D, and joint R&D. In-house R&D commands a strategic advantage, since the company is the sole owner of the technology and can protect it from unauthorized uses. In addition, since R&D is basically a learning process, the company can develop a group of experienced scientists and engineers that can be employed in developing more advanced products and processes and in transferring the results of their R&D to operations and to customers. Since R&D personnel do not like to work alone and are stimulated by peers, however, the laboratory should have a critical mass in the core technologies and support services. In some cases, critical mass may exceed the company resources, and external R&D will have to be contracted.

External R&D is usually contracted out to specialized nonprofit research institutions, such as Battelle Memorial Institute or SRI International in the United States, or to universities. The advantages are that these institutions may already have experienced personnel in the disciplines to be researched, as well as the necessary laboratory and test equipment. This will save money and especially time in comparison with in-house R&D. The disadvantages are that the company will not benefit from the learning experience, and may become overly dependent on the contractor. Also, the **technology transfer** may be difficult and there is always the possibility of leaks to competitors. In the case of universities, costs are usually lower and there is the additional benefit of identifying graduate students who may be hired later and researchers who may be employed as consultants when needed.

Joint R&D has been carried out systematically in Europe and Japan and has now become popular in the United States after **antitrust laws** were relaxed and tax incentives offered to **research and development consortia**. In a consortium, several companies with congruent interests join together to perform R&D, either in a separate organization (such as SEMATECH, the Semiconductor Manufacturing Technology Consortium), or in a university. The advantages are lower costs, since each company does not have to invest in similar equipment; a critical mass of researchers; and the interchange of information among the sponsors. The disadvantages are that all the sponsors have access to the same R&D results. Because of antitrust considerations, however, the R&D performed must be precompetitive, and each participant in the joint R&D must separately apply to its products, processes, and services the information obtained. In some countries (for example, Japan), this joint research is sponsored, if not imposed, by the government and the companies have no choice but to comply with the ''directives'' of MITI, the Ministry of Technology and Industry.

R&D LABORATORY ORGANIZATION AND FUNDING

For reasons of efficiency and control and to facilitate communications and synergy among researchers, R&D is usually performed within R&D laboratories, also called R&D centers. The organizational positioning and the funding of these laboratories is often a controversial matter and is still evolving. There have been three phases in the evolution of R&D in large and medium companies since the 1950s.

PHASE I. After World War II, it was believed that R&D was the key to the success of a technology-based company. All that was needed was to have the ''best'' (in terms of creativity and **training**) scientists available, give them well-equipped research laboratories, plenty of money, maximum freedom to do their own research, and wait for the inevitable scientific discoveries. According to the director of research of Eastman Kodak Co. ''the best person to decide what research shall be done is the man who is doing the research.'' The laboratory, in order to ensure full independence, was part of the corporate staff and was entirely funded by the corporation, which ''assessed'' its cost to operations. Little attention was given to how to transfer the research results to operations, or how to couple R&D activities with the company business strategies. In effect, technology management was not practiced.

Unfortunately, this **laissez-faire** management approach produced few useful results. In some cases, the scientists met insurmountable technical barriers (for instance, high-efficiency low-cost solar cells) or made important discoveries unrelated to the firm's strategic and business thrust (for instance, Nobel prizes in astrophysics and cosmology awarded to a telephone company). Some laboratories were unable to transfer their new technologies to the company operations and, in frustration, turned to more receptive audiences, including competitors. A well-publicized example is the development of the STAR PC by the Xerox Palo Alto Research Center (PARC). The computer business unit of Xerox was interested only in mainframe computers and disdained the STAR as a toy. Steve Jobs, the founder of Apple Computer, visited PARC, realized the potential of the new technology, hired the PARC researchers, developed the Lisa and Macintosh personal computers, and made a fortune.

PHASE II. As a reaction to these problems, operations were encouraged to set up their own laboratories, mostly to do development for a specific business. GE, for instance, had two central laboratories: the Research Laboratory and the General Engineering and Consulting Laboratory (later renamed the Advanced Technology Laboratory), both located in Schenectady, New York. These were later joined to form the present GE R&D Center. In addition, GE set up an Electronics Lab in Syracuse, New York, a Space Sciences Lab in Valley Forge, Pennsylvania, an Appliance Lab in Louisville, Kentucky, and a Plastics Application Lab in Pittsfield, Massachusetts. The R&D Center's mission was to perform research and longer term development of benefit to several operating units. The mission of the other laboratories was to perform shorter term research and mostly development for the businesses to which they were organizationally responsible and from which they received funding. To ensure closer coupling between the R&D Center and operations, only about two-thirds of the required funds came from the corporation through assessments. The remaining one-third was obtained through contracts that had to be negotiated with the interested operations. Naturally, operations would fund contracts only for short- or medium-term results, usually less than three years, and would not renew the contract annually unless they were satisfied. A separate ''liaison office'' was set up in the R&D Center to ensure close coupling with operations, to listen to their requirements (market pull) and to persuade them to adopt the new technologies (technology push), and to help sell the R&D contracts.

PHASE III. This system worked relatively well until the economic crises of the 1980s and the intensification of **international competition**. Many large and medium-sized corporations, faced with staggering losses and major reductions in **employment**, questioned the need for, and the role of, the corporate laboratory, especially its funding. Some central labs were simply eliminated, or drastically reduced in size, with their mission restricted to R&D for developing new businesses at the corporate level. Most researchers were transferred to operations, where the climate was less benign, others resigned, moving to universities or starting their own businesses. In the case of GE, there was a major cutback in the support functions of the R&D Center, and the liaison function was eliminated. The laboratory and section managers are now responsible for coupling with operations. At the same time, the funding sources of the laboratory were reversed. Before 1982, the corporation was contributing 67 percent of the **budget** in assessed funds, and contracts with operations amounted to the remaining 33 percent. Under the new president, Jack Welch, contract funds now amount to 75 percent and assessed funds to 25 percent. In theory, assessed funds are for exploratory research and for new business development. In practice, some may be shared with operations, for projects of longer range impact or higher risk, which operations are unwilling to fund alone. This new funding approach does ensure close coupling with operations, but targets the R&D Center activities towards the larger, and richer, GE businesses, such as plastics, medical systems and aircraft engines, while neglecting the poorer, less glamorous core businesses, such as power systems.

An R&D laboratory can be organized internally according to three patterns: by functions, by projects, and matrix. In the functional organization, all researchers working in a specific discipline, for instance laser optics or polymers, are grouped in a unit and report to a manager, who is a recognized expert in the field. This organization is similar to the various academic departments of a university. The advantages are close interaction with peers and competent evaluations of the scientific value of the researchers' work. The main disadvantage is that most industrial R&D projects require the contributions of different disciplines, and there is often nobody responsible for managing the project and integrating the work of the researchers.

In the project organization, all researchers working on a given project report to a project manager, who is usually not an expert in the researchers' specific disciplines. The project manager evaluates the researchers on the basis of practical results, time, and money, rather than on the value of their scientific and technical contributions. The advantages are that the project can be professionally managed and corrective actions taken if the results expected are not forthcoming or budgets are not met. The main disadvantage is that projects have, by definition, a limited life. A project **team**, as an organization, is disbanded as soon as the work has been completed. The researchers now have no ''home'' and must look for work on new projects, which may or may not be forthcoming.

The matrix organization attempts to combine the best features of the functional and project organizations, by assigning every researcher to two supervisors: a functional manager and a project manager. The functional manager is responsible for evaluating the scientific value of the researcher's work, planning his or her **career development**, and providing a ''home'' between projects. The project manager is responsible for evaluating the researcher's contributions to the project and giving him or her the resources needed to get the job done. Obviously, the two managers must work closely together in assigning the duties of the researchers, integrating their evaluations, and reporting them to higher management.

In practice, small and shorter term projects are run according to a functional organization, with one researcher taking on the project administration (*not* management) duties. Larger, longer range projects, such as the GE CAT (computerized axial tomography) and MRI (magnetic resonance imaging) medical diagnostic imaging systems projects, are organized as independent projects with strong professional **project management**. When project responsibility is transferred to operations, some of the researchers move too, thereby ensuring an effective transfer of technology. In other cases, engineers from operations are invited to join the R&D team, and they transfer back home with the project.

R&D PROJECT SELECTION, MANAGEMENT, AND TERMINATION

Industrial R&D is generally performed according to projects (i.e., separate work activities) with specific technical and business goals, assigned personnel, and time and money budgets. These projects can either originate ''top down''—for instance, from a management decision to develop a new product, such as the first IBM PC—or ''bottom up'' from an idea originated by an individual researcher, such as the Toshiba Japanese language word processor. The size of a project may vary from a part-time effort of one researcher for a few months with a budget of tens of thousands of dollars, to major five- or ten-year projects with large multidisciplinary teams of tens of researchers and budgets exceeding millions of dollars. Therefore, project selection and evaluation is one of the more critical and difficult subjects of R&D management. Of equal importance, although less emphasized in practice, is the subject of project termination, particularly in the case of unsuccessful or marginal projects.

Normally, a company or a laboratory will have requests for a greater number of projects than can be effectively implemented. Therefore, R&D managers are faced with the problem of allocating scarce resources of personnel, equipment, laboratory space, and funds to a broad spectrum of competing projects. Since the decision to start on an R&D project is both a technical and a business decision, R&D managers should select projects on the basis of the following objectives, in order of importance:

- maximizing the long-term return on investment
- making optimum use of the available human and physical resources
- maintaining a balanced R&D portfolio and controlling risk
- fostering a favorable climate for creativity and innovation

Project selection is usually done once a year, by listing all ongoing projects and the proposals for new projects, evaluating and comparing all these projects according to quantitative and qualitative criteria, and prioritizing the projects in ''totem pole'' order. The funds requested by all the projects are compared with the laboratory budget for the following year and the project list is cut off at the budgeted amount. Projects above the line are funded, those below the line delayed to the following year or tabled indefinitely. Some experienced R&D managers do not allocate all the budgeted funds, but keep a small percentage on reserve to take care of new projects that may be proposed during the year, after the laboratory's official budget has been approved. These unallocated amounts are often purposely disguised as ''proposal'' or ''exploratory'' funds, or made available by overbudgeting some ''safe'' projects, or even hidden by working on ''underground projects'' without the knowledge of headquarters. For instance, the highly successful Toshiba laptop computer was vetoed twice by Tokyo headquarters, and was developed in the Ome factory by ten engineers who, protected by the general manager, pretended to be working on budgeted military computer projects.

Since R&D projects are subject to the risk of failure, the **expected value** (EV) of a project can be evaluated *ex ante* according to the following statistical formula:

$$EV = P \times p_t \times p_c \times p_f$$

where P is the payoff if the project is successful, that is, the stream of net income accruing to the company over the life of the new product (or process or service) resulting from the project. The payoff P is then multiplied by the probability of success, which is the product of three separate probabilities:

1. p_t is the probability of technical success, i.e., that the new product or process will meet the technical and functional specifications
2. p_c is the probability of commercial success, i.e., that the new product will be accepted by the marketplace and will achieve the forecasted market share
3. p_f is the probability of financial success, i.e., that the new product will achieve the forecasted financial goals, in terms of profits, return on investment, and cash flow.

Consequently, project evaluation must be performed along two separate orthogonal real dimensions: technical evaluation, to establish the probability of technical success, and business evaluation, to establish the payoff and the probabilities of commercial and financial success. Once the expected value (EV) of a project has been determined, it should be divided by the forecasted cost C of the project, in order to obtain a benefit/cost ratio R of the form $R = EV/C$. Obviously the higher this ratio, the more desirable the project.

For more advanced and longer term projects, leading to major (rather than incremental) innovation, it may be difficult to establish reliable values of P, C, p_t, p_c, and p_f. In this case, a ''relative'' comparison of projects is made based on their respective ''technical quality'' and ''potential business value.''

Technical quality is evaluated by analyzing and rating the clarity of the project goals; the extent of the technical, institutional, and market penetration obstacles that must be overcome; the adequacy of the skills and facilities available in the laboratory for carrying out the work; and, finally, how easily the project results can be transferred to an interested business unit.

The potential business value of a project is defined in terms of the market share of an existing market that can be captured by the new product, or by the size of a new market that can be developed by the new product, or by the value of new technology that can be sold by the company or transferred to its customers.

After the first tentative list of projects has been established in order of priority, it is ''matched'' with the existing laboratory human and physical resources to make sure that these resources are well utilized. In fact, creative human resources are the laboratory's most valuable asset, and these should not be wasted by asking researchers to do work outside their disciplines and interests. Also, it is difficult, in a short time, to change the ''mix'' of available disciplines and equipment, and to hire and fire researchers as is done for labor. Thus, a shift towards new disciplines should be done gradually, avoiding the underutilization or overloading of the existing resources.

Once the tentative list of prospects has been modified according to the above, the entire ''project portfolio'' of the R&D laboratory should be balanced, in order to control risk, according to the three types of probabilities listed above.

Technical risk is controlled in two ways: (1) by having a spectrum of projects ranging from low to medium to high technical risk; and (2) by avoiding ''bunching'' too many projects in the same technology, particularly if the technology could be replaced by a superior technology during the expected lifetime of the new product.

Commercial risk can be controlled by not having ''too many eggs in one basket''—that is, by targeting different market segments (e.g., government, capital equipment, consumer, industrial, international) and attacking different competitors, since directly targeting a major competitor may trigger a dangerous counteroffensive and a price war.

Financial risk is controlled by having a majority of small and medium-size projects (in terms of R&D expense), a few large projects, and no projects that, in case of failure, could bankrupt the company. Financial risk, in terms of cash flow, is also controlled by having a spectrum (in time to payoff) of more short and medium-term projects than long-term projects. This type of spectrum is also psychologically important to maintain the credibility of the R&D laboratory in the face of upper-level executives who keep asking ''What have you done for me lately?''

By definition, R&D is a risky activity, and there are no ''zero-risk'' R&D projects, since these would then be engineering projects. While the majority of the projects in an R&D portfolio should be categorized as low-risk, some medium-risk projects are justified, and even a few high-risk projects, provided their expected value is high. In other words, the higher the risk, the higher the expected payoff if the project succeeds.

Finally, project evaluation and selection should be made objectively, in order to develop and maintain a favorable climate for creativity and innovation. Researchers will be naturally disappointed when their projects are not approved. Some may even suspect that other projects were preferred for subjective reasons, such as the ''halo'' effect (the past track record and prestige of other, more senior, researchers), the reluctance of management to terminate less-deserving projects, and especially political influences to select ''pet'' projects of executives. If there is a feeling that project selection is not done objectively, many researchers, particularly the junior ones, will lose their enthusiasm and renounce proposing new projects of a high potential value for the company. Eventually, if this situation persists, the laboratory will lose its creativity and concentrate on routine low-risk (but also low-payoff!) or ''political'' projects, and it will have difficulty in keeping and attracting the best researchers. Therefore, it is desirable that the project evaluation and selection criteria be properly explained and that all researchers be asked to participate in the evaluation process. Also, the final project portfolio should be presented to, and discussed with, all the researchers.

The management of R&D projects basically follows the principles and methods of project management. There is, however, one significant caveat in relation to normal engineering projects: R&D projects are risky, and it is difficult to develop an accurate budget, in terms of technical milestones, costs, and time to completion of the various tasks. Therefore, R&D budgets should be considered initially as tentative, and should be gradually refined as more information becomes available as a result of preliminary work and the learning process. Historically, many R&D projects have exceeded, sometimes with disastrous consequences, the forecasted and budgeted times to completion and funds to be expended. A typical example is the Concorde supersonic aircraft, a high-visibility ''national prestige'' project of the French and British governments. The original budget was

£150 million and 5 years to completion, while the actual expenditures were £1.1 billion and 12 years. As a consequence, the Concorde was a great technical success and a financial disaster! Although the Concorde was still flying in 1999, only the operating expenses were covered, and there was no prospect of recovering the initial investment. Therefore, in R&D, measuring technical progress and completion of milestones is generally more important than measuring expenditures over time.

Finally, termination of projects is a difficult subject because of the political repercussions on the laboratory. Theoretically, a project should be discontinued for one of the following three reasons:

1. There is a change in the environment—for instance, new government regulations, new competitive offerings, or price declines—that make the new product less attractive to the company.
2. Unforeseen technical obstacles are encountered and the laboratory does not have the resources to overcome them.
3. The project falls hopelessly behind schedule and corrective actions are not forthcoming.

Due to organizational inertia, and the fear of antagonizing senior ''prima donna'' researchers or executives with pet projects, there is often the tendency to let a project continue, hoping for a miraculous breakthrough that seldom happens.

In theory, an optimal number of projects should be initiated and this number should be gradually reduced over time to make room for more deserving projects. Also, the monthly cost of a project is much lower in the early stages than in the later stages, when more personnel and equipment have been committed. Thus, from a financial risk management viewpoint, it is better to waste money on several promising young projects than on a few maturing ''dogs'' with low payoff and high expense. In practice, in many laboratories it is difficult to start a new project because all the resources have already been committed, and just as difficult to terminate a project, for the reasons given above. Thus, an able and astute R&D manager should continuously evaluate his or her project portfolio in relation to changes in company strategy, should continuously and objectively monitor the progress of each R&D project, and should not hesitate to terminate projects that have lost their value to the company in terms of payoff and probability of success.

In conclusion, by assuring a close coupling with the company's strategic goals and by maintaining close contacts with operations, the laboratory and the R&D function will maintain credibility and strengthen their strategic value for the corporation.

[Pier A. Abetti]

FURTHER READING:

Hampton, John J., ed. *AMA Management Handbook.* AMACOM, 1994.

Levy, N. S. *Managing High Technology and Innovation.* Upper Saddle River, NJ: Prentice Hall, 1998.

Martin, Michael J. C. *Managing Technological Innovation and Entrepreneurship in Technology-Based Firms.* Reston, 1994.

Roussel, Philip. A., Kamal N. Saad, and Tamara J. Erikson. *Third Generation R&D.* Cambridge, MA: Harvard Business School Press, 1991.

Twiss, Brian. *Managing Technological Innovation.* 3rd ed. Pitman, 1985.

RESEARCH AND DEVELOPMENT CONSORTIA

Research and development (R&D) consortia are formed by manufacturing companies, often with the support of government, for the purpose of conducting shared research on new technologies for the benefit of the consortium's member companies. Government-supported R&D consortia (*kumaia*) have been common in Japan since the 1960s, and now number more than 200. In the United States, however, the formation of industry specific R&D consortia was hindered by **antitrust laws** that penalized cooperation among competitors until Congress passed the National Cooperative Research Act of 1984 (NCRA). In 1993 the NCRA was amended to include cooperative production and redesignated the National Cooperative Research and Production Act of 1993 (NCRPA). These legislative acts reflected a new technology policy aimed at reducing governmental obstacles to the commercialization of new technology.

Under the NCRPA, firms within an industry may form consortia to conduct ''precompetitive'' research. Precompetitive research is research that is considered generic to the development of multiple products of basic value to all participants. By forming R&D consortia, manufacturing firms can avoid duplicating basic research tasks and share the results more cost effectively. As a result they are able to compete more effectively in the global marketplace.

Research and development consortia are required by the NCRPA to register with the U.S. Department of Justice, which recorded more than 600 new consortia from 1985 to 1996. While the NCRPA does not provide exemption from antitrust laws, it limits the damages that may be assessed if an antitrust violation occurs. Where antitrust laws provide for triple damages to be assessed, the NCRPA limits liability to single damages. In addition, any alleged antitrust violations would be judged under a rule of reason standard, rather than assuming they were illegal per se. In the years since NCRPA was passed, however, no antitrust proceedings have been brought against registered consortia.

Research and development consortia can provide member companies with many benefits. They are formed to share expenses and resources and to pool talent and expertise. Consortia that are formed in the United States to compete globally are eligible for government funding. The most common type of consortia are horizontal, consisting of competing firms within an industry. Vertical consortia include firms ranging from materials suppliers to finished product manufacturers.

Companies form research and development consortia for different reasons. Among the reasons cited are market pressures, **international competition**, the increased pace of new product development, cutbacks in corporate research and development budgets, and shared concerns about meeting new regulatory or safety requirements. According to a survey conducted in 1993 by the *Economist* magazine, the three reasons most commonly cited were to gain access to a market, to exploit complimentary technologies, and to reduce the time taken for innovation.

Following the passage of the NCRA, research and development consortia were most frequently formed in the electronics, semiconductor, and pharmaceutical industries. In the chemical industry, companies more frequently entered into dual-company alliances rather than multicompany consortia.

Research and development consortia have been successful in spurring innovation. SEMATECH, a Texas-based consortia of major semiconductor manufacturers founded in 1987, has had dramatic success in helping its member companies regain dominant market shares in the international semiconductor equipment and silicon-chip markets. Another consortia, the U.S. Council for Automotive Research (USCAR), was formed to accelerate technological innovation among the major automobile manufacturers.

After manufacturing companies have agreed to form a consortium and have registered with the U.S. Department of Justice, they then assign personnel and budget funds to it. Joint research is usually conducted at a single specified site. Under the NCRPA, the research must be precompetitive, concerning areas generic to the products of each member company. As the consortium develops new technologies and improves on existing ones, individual companies may begin to apply those technologies to their own products. At a certain point, the companies may agree to dissolve the consortium to focus on their own applications.

Research and development consortia may consist exclusively of companies from a single nation, or they may be international in scope. Japan's Ministry of International Trade and Industry (MITI), which supports and directs R&D consortia in Japan, began opening some of its R&D consortia to foreign companies in 1990. In the **European Union**, U.S. companies are allowed to participate in publicly supported R&D consortia. In the United States, consortia that receive government funds are limited to domestic companies.

In the United States, **joint ventures** between private industry and federal laboratories offer similar research sharing and development opportunities as R&D consortia. Called Cooperative Research and Development Agreements (CRADAs), they are becoming more commonplace as federal laboratories refocus their efforts away from Cold War defense projects to help domestic industries develop new technologies.

[David P. Bianco]

FURTHER READING:

Corey, E. Raymond. *Technology Fountainheads: The Management Challenge of R&D Consortia.* Boston: Harvard Business School Press, 1997.

Hemphill, Thomas A. ''U.S. Technology Policy, Intraindustry Joint Ventures, and the National Cooperative Research and Production Act of 1993.'' *Business Economics,* October 1997, 48-54.

''Holding Hands.'' *Economist,* 27 March 1993, 14 16.

Jorde, Thomas M., and David J. Teece, eds. *Antitrust, Innovation, and Competitiveness.* New York: Oxford University Press, 1992.

Vandendorpe, Laura. ''Capitalizing on Consortia: Cooperation Bolsters Research.'' *Research and Development,* October 1997.

RESOLUTION TRUST CORPORATION (RTC)

The Resolution Trust Corporation (RTC) was a temporary federal agency established in 1989 to oversee the disposal of assets from failed savings and loan (S&L) institutions. It was created by Congress in the wake of the 1980s S&L crisis, in which hundreds of depository institutions slipped into insolvency due to unsound banking practices. By the time the RTC closed in December 1995, it had managed some 747 S&L closures and sell-offs valued at $460 billion in assets and $225 billion in deposit liabilities. The RTC's work affected no less than 25 million U.S. bank accounts, and while it was in operation, it operated the federal government's fourth-largest off-site records system.

FUNCTIONS

The RTC functioned by becoming either a conservator or a receiver for an insolvent S&L when the Office of Thrift Supervision (OTS) determined the S&L was being operated unsoundly. If the RTC became conservator, the S&L's financial condition was further evaluated and was prepared for sale with designated assets. The S&L's deposits and franchises were marketed to prequalified bidders. Once the question of the failed S&L's ownership was resolved, any remaining assets were held in receivership for disposition and were sold according to RTC guidelines.

The RTC was established on 9 August 1989, when the Financial Institutions Reform, Recovery and Enforcement Act (FIRREA) was signed into law. The law provided for a major restructuring of the nation's thrift industry and a reorganization of the federal agencies that oversaw the industry. These reforms were necessary not only because of widespread insolvency in the private sector, but also because the federal safety net, the Federal Savings and Loan Insurance Corporation (FSLIC), had been bankrupted by the crisis. The RTC's mission was threefold:

- to sell defunct S&L assets to recoup as much money as possible
- to minimize the impact of such transactions on local real estate and financial markets
- to maximize the availability and affordability of residential real estate for low- and moderate-income individuals.

The RTC created the Small Investor Program (SIP) in June 1993 to meet the needs of investors with moderate levels of investment capital. Under the SIP, the RTC offered real estate assets on an individual basis for at least 120 days, either through a broker, auction, or sealed bid sale. Assets marketed under SIP were offered with an emphasis on geographic focus to attract small investors who wanted to invest in their local market.

The RTC sold its real estate owned properties (REOs), loans, and other assets (including subsidiaries, mortgage servicing rights, and furniture, fixtures and equipment) depending upon product type, geographic location, complexity, market demand and marketing, and holding costs. Individual sale, sealed bid sale, open outcry auctions, and securitization were among the strategies the RTC used.

Some select assets, including short-term loans, were held to maturity. Loans were packaged and sold primarily through open outcry auctions, sealed bid sales, or securitization. Individual sale was the strategy the RTC uses to make real estate assets that were immediately deliverable upon closing available to the public. The sealed bid sale method was often selected when two or more parties were interested in the same asset or when a sealed bid sale could effectively establish a high level of competition that could command a higher sale price.

Open outcry auctions were used to sell REOs, loans, and furniture, fixtures, and equipment (FF&E). Auctions provided the opportunity to expose a large volume of assets to the marketplace and dispose of them quickly. Minimum bids or reserve prices were usually established, although the RTC also conducted absolute auctions or auctions with no minimum reserve on some of its smaller assets and FF&E. Securitization is the process of restructuring cash flows from pools of whole loans into securities that are liquid assets.

Among the assets in the RTC's inventory were:

- Commercial: Office complexes; retail shopping centers; bank branches; mobile home parks; storage facilities/mini-warehouses; industrial park/warehouses; restaurants; parking garages/lots; medical facilities/private hospitals; nursing/retirement homes; hotels/motels; resorts/golf courses; apartments; office condominiums; and mixed-use zoned land.
- Residential: Single-family detached (1 to 4); townhouse; condominium; co-op; and timeshare.
- Land: Unimproved, commercial and residential; developed, commercial and residential; agricultural; and ranch/pastures.
- Financial instruments: Residential/commercial mortgages; consumer loans (secured and unsecured); judgments/deficiencies; business loans; leasing portfolios; and securities.
- Subsidiaries: Mortgage banking/servicing; title; insurance; and real estate development.
- Furniture, fixtures & equipment (FF&E): Art; banking equipment; computers; gallery/restaurant equipment; office equipment; heavy equipment; and vehicles.

CLOSURE

Overall, the RTC was considered a successful mechanism for disposing of assets and recovering funds for depositors, although critics claimed that it didn't obtain particularly high returns on the assets it sold. It also completed its work faster than anticipated. As the RTC's work was drawing to a close, Congress passed the RTC Completion Act of 1993 to structure its dismantling. The act called for a transition of records and responsibilities from the RTC to the **Federal Deposit Insurance Corporation** (FDIC), which assumed all of the RTC's assets and liabilities.

SEE ALSO: Banks and Banking; Savings and Loan Associations

FURTHER READING:

Barrese, Edward F. "The Resolution Trust Corporation at Sunset: Transferring a Records Management Function." *Records Management Quarterly,* October 1996.

Gupta, Atul, Richard L.B. LeCompte, and Lalatendu Misra. "Taxpayer Subsidies in Failed Thrift Resolution: The Impact of FIRREA." *Journal of Monetary Economics,* July 1997.

"Treasury Secretary Says RTC Will Close Early." *Journal of Accountancy,* September 1995.

RESOURCE CONSERVATION AND RECOVERY ACT

In 1976 the Resource Conservation and Recovery Act (RCRA) was enacted as an amendment to the Solid Waste Disposal Act. RCRA regulates both household and hazardous solid wastes, with regulations covering hazardous wastes that are particularly detailed and are described as being "cradle to grave." ("Cradle to grave" refers to regulation from the point of generation of the waste through and including its ultimate point of "disposal" or storage.) The act was amended by Congress in 1978, 1980, 1984, 1986, 1988, and 1996, with the 1984 amendments making the most substantial additions to the program. The 1984 amendments, called the Hazardous and Solid Waste Amendments, expanded RCRA's coverage and requirements significantly to deal with hazardous industrial wastes.

Most of RCRA's programs are designed to be proactive; that is, they are designed to provide for safe handling and containment of both hazardous and nonhazardous wastes as they are generated. RCRA does not address the problems associated with inactive or abandoned dump sites or those associated with chemical spills or releases requiring immediate, emergency response. Those problems are dealt with under the **Comprehensive Environmental Response, Compensation, and Liability Act** (CERCLA), commonly known as Superfund. Both RCRA and CERCLA are administered by the federal **Environmental Protection Agency** (EPA). RCRA's programs regulating businesses are administered by regional offices of the EPA except in states that have been authorized to administer their own RCRA programs. In such states, businesses deal directly with a state counterpart to the EPA.

HISTORY—THE NEED FOR RCRA

Prior to 1965, regulation of solid wastes was considered to be the responsibility of state and local governments. When the Solid Waste Disposal Act was enacted in 1965, a great deal of our waste (garbage) disposal was through open dumping or in local "landfills." The Solid Waste Disposal Act was the first federal statute dealing with the effects of such dumping on our environment. The act's goal was to promote better solid waste disposal methods. It did so primarily by providing grants to states and local governments for research on waste disposal.

The Solid Waste Disposal Act was amended in 1970 by the Resource Recovery Act and in 1976 by RCRA. RCRA was designed to eliminate "the last remaining loophole in environmental law, that of unregulated land disposal of discarded materials and hazardous wastes," according to a report issued by the U.S. House of Representatives. In its enactment of RCRA in 1976 and in the 1984 and 1986 amendments to RCRA, Congress addressed three sets of needs and concerns. First, it focused on the need for a *system* for management of solid wastes. Second, it recognized the need for special provisions for dealing with hazardous wastes. Third, it included provisions to encourage resource conservation and recovery (recycling and reuse of resources).

Prior to enactment of RCRA, a great deal of the hazardous waste in the United States was "disposed of" or dumped at or near the site at which it was generated. In other cases, generators of hazardous waste hired transporters to take the wastes to off-site disposal areas. A lack of record-keeping and lack of efforts to contain wastes at disposal sites created serious problems for today and for future generations. When on-site disposal was used, records were not kept and property was often sold to parties who had no information about the presence of hazardous materials on the premises or buried on the property. When off-site disposal was used, generators often knew nothing about the location of or operations of the site to which transporters took hazardous wastes. Typically, a disposal site went through several changes of ownership during its period of operation, which averaged about 20 years. A site usually received hazardous wastes from numerous transporters and generators, and site operators had few or no records documenting the kinds of wastes located there. Further, after a site was closed, it was often sold (or occasionally donated) to purchasers who had no idea of its prior use. An example of this is the Love Canal site near Niagara Falls, New York, where in the late 1970s about 200 families experiencing unusually high rates of cancer, birth defects, and other health-related problems discovered that their homes and their children's elementary school had been built on top of a former waste dump for hazardous chemicals. Land for the school had been donated to the local school district.

RCRA'S PROVISIONS AND PROGRAMS

RCRA includes four distinct programs designed to implement its goals. First, it encourages states to develop plans to manage nonhazardous (household) waste. Second, it establishes a "cradle to grave" system for monitoring and controlling the disposal of hazardous waste. The system of paperwork for monitoring such disposal is called a manifest system. Third, it regulates underground storage tanks through a program called the Underground Storage Tank (UST) program. Fourth, the EPA has conducted a new demonstration program to track medical wastes from generation through disposal.

In Subtitle D of RCRA, states are encouraged to implement their own solid waste management plans. This has become increasingly difficult for states due to at least two factors. First, with population growth and the increased use of ''disposable'' products, the amount of waste being generated each year is increasing dramatically. Second, there is a phenomenon that has been labeled the ''NIMBY Syndrome.'' (''NIMBY'' stands for ''Not In My Back Yard.'') Our present solid waste disposal sites are being filled quickly; most are filled to capacity within 20 (or fewer) years after their opening. Yet, because of opposition of local residents, it has become extremely difficult for private waste disposal companies or local municipalities to find locations for and open new facilities for disposal of such wastes. No one wants to live next to or near such a site. As a result, in the 1984 Hazardous and Solid Waste Amendments, Congress authorized the EPA to take a more active role in assisting the states in handling nonhazardous waste landfills. The EPA has been working on strategies to deal with disposal of household wastes.

In Subtitle C of RCRA, Congress established a cradle to grave system for management of hazardous wastes. Pursuant to Subtitle C, the EPA has issued criteria for identifying hazardous wastes, and, in turn, it has used those criteria to issue a list of those wastes that are considered to be ''hazardous'' for purposes of administration of RCRA. That list is published in the Federal Register and is updated periodically. As a part of this cradle to grave system, the EPA was directed to issue three sets of standards regulating three sets of parties: (1) generators who produce hazardous waste, (2) transporters of the waste, and (3) those who own or operate disposal sites. The EPA has issued standards regulating how generators handle, label, and store hazardous wastes. Similar standards cover transporters of hazardous wastes. A transporter must obtain a license (permit) for hauling of wastes and that license will cover only specified types of waste, depending on whether the transporter has met the EPA's requirements for each type. Similarly, any facility accepting hazardous wastes for disposal must obtain a license (permit) from the EPA in which the EPA specifies which kinds of hazardous waste can be accepted by the facility. Such facilities are subject to extensive regulation by the EPA covering location and construction of the site as well as its ongoing operation. As a precondition to issuance of licenses (permits) to transporters or owners or operators of sites, the EPA applies extensive standards (regulations) to those parties.

Tying together the EPA's regulation of generators, transporters, and owners or operators of sites is the ''manifest system.'' A manifest is a set of paperwork that accompanies each ''batch'' of hazardous waste from the generator, through any and all transporters, and to the site of ultimate disposal. The disposal site might be better conceptualized as the site of ''permanent storage,'' because such wastes never ''go away.'' (In some cases, however, wastes may be treated to reduce hazards or to recover materials for reuse.) The RCRA and the EPA refer to disposal sites as ''treatment, storage and disposal facilities.''

The manifest is a form that is obtained from the EPA or its state counterpart in states that have been authorized to administer RCRA. The manifest form includes five or six copies of a form with copying materials in-between. The generator fills out his or her portion of the form, identifying the wastes to be hauled; keeps a copy; and conveys the remaining copies to the transporter. It should be noted that this manifest system affects most businesses in this country. Any company generating one-half of a 50-gallon barrel of hazardous wastes or more per month must comply with the manifest system.

Next, the transporter completes the remaining forms, giving the transporter's EPA-assigned identification number. The transporter keeps one copy. If there is a second transporter, he or she does the same. Finally, the disposal site owner or operator completes the remaining forms with his or her EPA-assigned identification number. The owner or operator keeps one copy, sends one to the EPA or its state counterpart, and sends one to the generator. The result is a complete paper record of a batch of hazardous wastes from the point of generation to its ultimate ''disposal'' site. Generators of waste can be held liable for civil or criminal penalties for failure to complete a manifest, for failure to hire an EPA-licensed transporter, or if the wastes are not placed in an EPA-licensed facility. There are also civil or criminal penalties for transporters or facilities that are either unlicensed or that handle or accept wastes not allowed under their licenses.

Subtitle I of RCRA, regulating underground storage tanks, was added to RCRA through 1984 amendments. Pursuant to the program, states are required to inventory all underground storage tanks containing hazardous substances or petroleum products. Testing of all such tanks is required and use of tanks that are subject to leaking should have been discontinued by 1997. If an owner or operator of the tank can be identified, he or she is required to undertake and pay for cleanup of the tank and contamination caused by the tank. When an owner or operator cannot be identified or is insolvent, funding may be available from a $500 million Leaking Underground Storage Tank Trust Fund that was established through the 1986 amendments to RCRA. The program is funded by federal **taxes** on motor fuels. The program has become controversial, however, because various states have run out of funds without having finished testing and cleanup of the numerous leaking tanks within their borders.

Subtitle J was added to RCRA in 1988 when U.S. citizens became alarmed in response to reports about medical wastes being washed up on beaches in the United States and in other parts of the world. Pursuant to Subtitle J, the EPA conducted a two-year demonstration project designed to track medical waste from generation to disposal, following the model of Subtitle C, which regulates disposal of hazardous wastes. To this date, Congress has not enacted a nationwide program for medical waste regulation. Some states, however, are regulating such wastes.

The most recent amendments to RCRA are in the Land Disposal Program Flexibility Act of 1996. The law allows decharacterized wastes from centralized wastewater management systems to be disposed of on land so long as they are not hazardous wastes at the point of disposal. The law also allows more flexibility for the states as they regulate small landfills (defined as those receiving less than 20 tons of waste per day), allowing them to exempt those small landfills from groundwater monitoring requirements under certain conditions.

Sanctions for violations of the various requirements of RCRA include civil and criminal penalties. Civil penalties range up to $25,000 per day per violation. Criminal penalties can include up to one year in prison, fines of up to $25,000 per day per violation, or both.

CRITICISMS OF RCRA AND ITS FUTURE

Corporate managers have been frustrated by the amount of paperwork required under RCRA, the minute details of operation covered by RCRA regulations, and by the EPA's slow action in reviewing applications for permits. RCRA limits the duration of permits to ten years, yet it may take up to four years to obtain a permit from the EPA. Thus, operators of a facility may feel as though they are continuously involved in the process of applying for permits. Some critics allege that as a consequence of this process the most reputable companies that make good-faith efforts and devote substantial resources to waste minimization and waste handling are unduly burdened by the EPA's regulation of their activities pursuant to RCRA. Those critics allege that at the same time RCRA's burdensome requirements encourage other less reputable companies to avoid the regulatory process altogether. Such companies dispose of their wastes in illegal ways creating hazards to which the public will be exposed.

Further, as the United States is becoming more involved in a global economy, its handling of hazardous waste has taken on global consequences. As a result of a scarcity of sites for disposal of both nonhazardous and hazardous wastes, new companies have been established in the United States that make a business of shipping our wastes abroad. Such waste is reportedly being hauled to sites in the Caribbean, the South American country of Guyana, various countries in Africa, and to other sites throughout the world. The attention of the world was captivated when from 1988 to 1990 a shipment of ash from Philadelphia spent two years traveling from country to country—including the Bahamas, Bermuda, Honduras, the Dominican Republic, Guinea-Bissau, and Haiti—trying to find a place to dump its cargo of waste. Environmentalists fear that impoverished Third World countries are becoming dumping grounds for the hazardous wastes of more prosperous, industrialized countries. As a consequence, traffic in international wastes has become the subject of international agreements, including, for example, the 1989 Basel Convention.

A sound environmental policy for the United States must include provisions for management of hazardous wastes. Environmentalists agree that businesses must be encouraged to develop innovative programs for management of hazardous waste. The current RCRA program may be discouraging such innovation by placing substantial costs and inconvenience on responsible businesses. Yet, our businesses must behave in a responsible manner in the international area and avoid taking advantage of citizens of Third World countries that may be coerced to accept hazardous wastes due to financial need. Thus, it is likely that Congress will give serious consideration to proposals for amendments to RCRA as it considers its reauthorization in the near future. In addition, issues related to management of wastes will extend beyond RCRA into negotiation of international agreements and treaties as our interconnections with other countries expand.

[Paulette L. Stenzel]

FURTHER READING:

Dufour, Jean-Paul, and Corinne Denis. "The North's Garbage Goes South." *World Press Review,* November 1988, 30-31.

Feder, Miriam. "Failures of the Current Waste Management Policy." *Environmental Law* 18 (1988): 671-81.

Findley, Roger W., and Daniel A. Farber. *Environmental Law in a Nutshell.* 4th ed. St. Paul, MN: West Publishing, 1996.

Kummer, Katharina. "The International Regulation of Transboundary Traffic in Hazardous Wastes: The 1989 Basel Convention." *International and Comparative Law Quarterly* 41 (1992): 530-62.

Sheppard, Nathaniel, Jr. ''West Shipping Waste Woes to Third World.'' *Chicago Tribune,* 11 July 1988.

U.S. Department of Energy. Office of Environmental Policy and Assistance. ''OEPA Environmental Law Summary: Land Disposal Program Flexibility Act of 1996 (P.L. 104-119).'' Washington: U.S. Department of Energy, 1997. Available from tis-nt.eh.doe.gov/oepa/law_sum/ldpfa.htm.

RESTRAINT OF TRADE

''Restraint of trade'' is a phrase from the Sherman Antitrust Act of 1890, a historic piece of legislation designed to halt the excessive monopolistic and anticompetitive activities of the then burgeoning industrial combinations and **trusts**. Specifically it was meant to curtail two types of anticompetitive behavior: the growth of giant monopolies through **mergers** and various price-fixing schemes and agreements. The act's key phrase, which appears in the first section is: ''Every contract, combination in the form of trust or otherwise, or conspiracy, in restraint of trade or commerce among the several states, or with foreign nations, is hereby declared to be illegal.'' Although the act was named after Senator John Sherman of Ohio, it was written primarily by Senators George Edmunds of Vermont and George Hoar of Massachusetts.

The years between the Panic of 1873 and the passage of the Sherman Antitrust Act witnessed a steady growth of monopolistic combinations and trusts. This monopolistic trend was particularly evident in heavy industry and railroads. There was a worrisome feeling in many circles that trusts were harming the economy by reducing or eliminating **competition**, which would subsequently lead to a slowdown in economic output. A strident antimonopolistic fervor soon developed that demanded the curtailment of trust activity through legal reform. There is contradictory evidence, however, as to the economic harm of trusts and monopolistic behavior in 19th-century America. Many economists felt that although a lack of competition tended to drive prices up, the inherent efficiency and cost effectiveness of trusts tended to drive prices down. Much of the antitrust fervor came from the so-called ''muckrakers'' and ''yellow journalists'' and was often based on emotion rather than empirical evidence. By the late 1880s the outcry for reform was growing unabated and by 1890 15 states had enacted antimonopolistic legislation. Pressure continued to mount for more effective and comprehensive federal legislation. The Sherman Antitrust Act was subsequently enacted by a large bipartisan congressional majority on July 2, 1890.

Prior to the Sherman Antitrust Act there was no legislation dealing specifically with anticompetitive business behavior. While contracts that allegedly restrained trade were unenforceable under certain circumstances, there were no laws allowing for punitive action or sanctions against the offending parties. Until this legislation, monopolies and trusts were also quite legal. The act's authors, however, purposefully declined to define ''trust'' and ''combination'' (the act likewise does not include intrastate commerce or restraint of production in its prohibitions).

A ''combination,'' however, is generally regarded as an association made up of individuals or corporations for the furtherance of a project. This association may include such formal or informal gatherings and methods as: **cartels**, ''gentlemen's agreements,'' and interlocking directorates. Devices such as purchase and sale contracts, leases, trusts, and **holding companies** can also fall under the definition of a ''combination.'' A ''trust'' is likewise regarded as a business combination created for the purpose of eliminating competition usually by controlling a significant number of manufacturing facilities, stores, etc. It is believed that the act was purposefully vague in these regards so as to curb monopolistic power without thwarting economic growth.

Likewise the authors of the act were believed to be purposefully vague so as to have the courts decide what constitutes restraint of trade. Over the decades the courts have come up with three different legal standards to be used in determining restraint of trade: the rule of reason, the per se test, and the truncated rule of reason.

''Rule of reason'' is the traditional test and the one most often applied in antitrust cases. It emanates from a number of cases including: *Standard Oil Company of New Jersey v. United States* (1911), *American Tobacco Company v. United States* (1911), and *Board of Trade of City of Chicago v. United States* (1918). In the first two cases, the U.S. Supreme Court found that not all but only unreasonable restraints of trade were illegal. In reaching a decision in the 1918 case the Court stated: ''Every agreement concerning trade, every regulation of trade, restrains. To bind, to restrain, is of their very essence. The true test of legality is whether the restraint imposed is such as merely regulates and perhaps thereby promotes competition or whether it is such as may suppress or even destroy competition.'' The Court went on to say that the condition of the particular business, both before and after the imposition of restraints, must be examined and a determination of the actual and probable effect of the restraint realized. Inherent in rule of reason cases is the ability of the violator to manipulate output or prices beyond the threshold that would be imposed naturally by the marketplace.

In *Northern Pacific Railroad Co. v. United States* (1958), the U.S. Supreme Court found that illegal restraints can sometimes fall outside a rule of reason analysis. In such cases carefully defined categories of restraint are illegal per se because "their pernicious effect on competition and lack of any redeeming virtue are conclusively presumed to be unreasonable and therefore illegal without elaborate inquiry as to the precise harm they have caused." Related is the *Socony Vacuum Oil Company* case (1940) in which the Court found that even though there were previous specific exceptions, tampering with price structure is nonetheless illegal, and stated "raising, depressing, fixing, pegging, or stabilizing the price of a commodity in interstate and foreign commerce is illegal per se."

The truncated rule of reason test is used in cases where the per se test is not applicable but where nonetheless "no elaborate industry analysis is required to demonstrate the anticompetitive character" of the restraint (*NCAA v. Board of Regents of the University of Oklahoma*).

There are two general categories of restraint of trade practices: vertical restraints and horizontal restraints. Vertical restraints occur when a company purchases or otherwise acquires control over another company that is either its supplier or customer. The controlling company is then in a position to impose various anticompetitive restraints on its former supplier or customer. Horizontal restraints deal with price-fixing agreements and are highly illegal. Similar to price-fixing agreements and likewise illegal are other practices such as "bid rigging," **boycotts**, territorial impositions, and imposed minimum fee schedules. In a 1997 case, a **Federal Trade Commission** judge ruled that Toys 'R' Us, a toy-products retailer, entered into illegal vertical agreements with toy manufacturers that resulted in restricted sales to competing wholesale clubs. Toys 'R' Us was also found by the judge to be guilty of forming horizontal agreements with other toy manufacturers in an effort to thwart the same wholesale clubs from obtaining popular toys.

SEE ALSO: Antitrust Acts and Laws

[Michael Knes]

FURTHER READING:

Bork, Robert. *The Antitrust Paradox.* Boston: Little, Brown, 1988.

Sfikas, Peter M. "What Is a Conspiracy? A Review of the Nation's Antitrust Laws." *Journal of the American Dental Association* 126 (October 1995): 1438-39.

——. "What Is Restraint of Trade? A Review of the Nation's Antitrust Laws." *Journal of the American Dental Association* 126 (November 1995): 1547-49.

Shaffer, Butler D. *In Restraint of Trade: The Business Campaign against Competition, 1918-1938.* Lewisburg, PA: Bucknell University Press, 1997.

Shenefield, John H. *The Antitrust Laws: A Primer.* Washington: AEI Press, 1998.

"TRU Restraint Case: More to Come. FTC's Ruling against Toys 'R' Us May Significantly Impact the Entire Retail Industry." *Discount Store News,* 20 October 1997, 8+.

RESTRICTIVE COVENANTS

Creditors use protective covenants in bond indentures to protect their interests by restricting certain activities of the issuer that could endanger the creditor's position. Similarly, **banks** employ loan covenants to ensure that the borrower uses the funds for the stated purpose. Auditors (or trustees, in the case of bond issues) must certify that the borrowing firm has not violated the covenants. If a covenant is violated, then the debtor is in technical default, and the creditor can require immediate repayment of the bond issue or the loan.

COVENANTS IN BOND AGREEMENTS

The American Bar Association's *Commentaries on Debentures* provides a summary of the typical covenants found in bond agreements. These covenants can be divided into four basic categories: (1) those restricting the issuance of new **debt**; (2) those restricting dividend payments; (3) those restricting **merger** activities; and (4) those restricting the disposition of the firm's assets. Bond covenants that restrict subsequent debt financing are by far the most common type. The provisions are typically stated in terms of **accounting** measures in order to make them easier to monitor. The issuance of debt may require any new bond issue to be subordinate to existing debt. This restriction is designed to prevent the firm from increasing the riskiness of existing debt by issuing new bonds with a superior, or equal, claim on the firm's assets. Other covenants may prohibit outright the issuance of additional debt unless the firm maintains certain prescribed financial ratios between tangible net worth and long-term debt, tangible assets and long-term debt, and income and interest charges.

Creditors also attempt to limit stockholders' ability to transfer assets to themselves through dividend restrictions. Bond covenants that restrict **dividends** are necessary to protect bondholders against the payout of assets that serve as collateral. In the extreme case, shareholders could vote to pay themselves a liquidating dividend leaving only an empty corporate shell. Most dividend restrictions refer not only to cash dividends, but also to share repurchases. Payout restrictions generally require that dividends can be paid only from earnings generated subsequent to the borrowing or earnings above a given amount. There are also frequently restrictions on a borrower's ability to increase dividends from existing levels.

Bond covenants allow merger activity only if certain conditions are met. Mergers can have a negative effect on existing bondholders if the acquiring firm has more debt in its **capital structure** than the target firm, or if the debt of the acquiring firm matures sooner than the debt of the target firm. Thus, bond covenants allow mergers only if the net tangible assets of the combined firms meet a certain minimum dollar amount or are greater than a certain fraction of long-term debt. The merger-related covenants could also make the merger contingent on the absence of **default** after the transaction is completed.

Debt covenants that restrict asset disposition decisions take the following forms: (1) restrictions on **common stock** investments, **loans**, and extensions of **credit**; (2) restrictions on the disposition of assets; and (3) covenants requiring the maintenance of minimum levels of assets. Assets that provide collateral cannot be disposed of under the provisions of the indenture agreement.

In addition to restrictions on the activities of the firm, covenants may also be expressed in the maintenance of certain levels of accounting-based measures, such as retained earnings, **working capital**, net assets, and debt-to-equity ratios. These affirmative covenants are generally related to the restrictions above by limiting a certain activity if the accounting variable drops below a certain level.

LOAN COVENANTS

To protect the surety of their **loans**, banks also require covenants in loan agreements. Loan covenants are similar to those found in bond issues, and are of two primary types. Affirmative covenants describe actions that a firm agrees to take during the term of the loan. These include such activities as providing **financial statements** and cash budgets, carrying insurance on assets and against insurable business risks, and maintaining minimum levels of net working capital. Negative covenants describe actions that a firm agrees not to take during the term of the loan. These may include agreements not to merge with other firms, not to pledge assets as security to other lenders, or not to make or guarantee loans to other firms. Another common restriction, especially with closely held companies, is a limit on officers' compensation. The covenants in private lending agreements often modify generally accepted accounting principles. For example, off-the-balance-sheet debt may be included in calculating the debt-to-equity ratio.

[Robert T. Kleiman, updated by Ronald M. Horwitz]

FURTHER READING:

Copeland, Thomas E., and J. Fred Weston. *Financial Theory and Corporate Policy.* 3rd ed. Reading, MA: Addison-Wesley, 1988.

Helfert, Erich A. *Techniques of Financial Analysis: A Modern Approach.* 9th ed. Irwin Professional Publishing, 1996.

Kester, W. Carl, William F. Fruhan, and Thomas Piper. *Case Problems in Finance.* 11th ed. Richard D. Irwin Publishing, 1997.

RESTRUCTURING

SEE: Corporate Restructuring

RESUMES

A resume is a document submitted to a potential employer by a job applicant outlining and summarizing that person's qualifications for **employment**. Generally speaking, resumes are written with a particular job objective in mind and include data on the applicant's education, previous work experience, and, to a lesser extent, personal information. The resume is formatted so as to make the applicant appealing as a potential employee. A resume should be accompanied by a cover letter that briefly introduces the applicant and the resume to the potential employer. The purpose of a resume is to be called for a job interview—not to land a job. This is an important distinction. Whether or not a person is hired for a particular position is largely determined by what transpires during the interview, not by the resume. A cover letter and resume are nonetheless extremely important as they are responsible for the employer's first impression of the job seeker. From this first impression a decision is made as to whether or not to proceed with the interview.

Resumes are looked at, read, and interpreted from two perspectives: the physical document itself and the content of the resume as it relates to the applicant. In the former, the potential employer at first reading will quickly notice any typographical errors, smudges, poor grammar, and the like. Many resumes also use a number of gimmicks to attract attention and set them apart from the competition. Such gimmicks can include odd sized or garishly colored sheets of paper, parchment paper, or unconventional type. One resume book, however, advises against thick or heavily textured paper—it might just jam an interviewer's copying machine! Many prospective employers feel that such tactics are an attempt to draw attention away from weaknesses in the applicant's background. Employers prefer resumes printed on white paper or another conservative color, such as ivory, light tan, or light gray. The color of the ink should also be conservative—black or navy. The paper should be at least 20 weight and have a slight texture. If, however, the job applicant is seeking a creative position in fields such as commercial art, graphic design, or advertising, some creativity might be in order. Regardless of the design of the resume it needs to be accompanied by a cover letter.

The content of the resume falls into three broad categories: education, previous work experience, and personal and social data. Personal and social data include such things as address and telephone number and, if relevant, club memberships, military status, and references. Educational information and previous work experience are arranged chronologically with the most contemporary information appearing first. Some professional resume writers believe the educational information should be foremost on the resume while others prefer work experience appearing first. There are those, however, who believe that a resume's format should be flexible enough so as to be tailored to fit one's own personal job hunt.

Job seekers may opt to use a professional resume service rather than prepare their own resumes. There is some disagreement among employers concerning professionally prepared resumes. Many such resumes are so standardized as to make their source apparent. Prospective employers often prefer resumes in the applicants' own words and style so as to better judge their communication skills.

For those who choose to prepare their own, there is a bewildering number of handbooks currently on the market dealing with resumes, cover letters, job interviews, and the like. Some are rather straightforward, such as *The Resume Makeover* (''50 Before and After Resumes Teach You How to Create the Most Effective Resume'') and *High Impact Resumes and Letters: How to Communicate Your Qualifications to Employers.* Others, although loaded with good information, are somewhat whimsical, such as *Sweaty Palms: The Neglected Art of Being Interviewed* and *The Complete Idiot's Guide to the Perfect Resume.* Others, such as *Best Resumes for Scientists and Engineers* and *Best Resumes for Attorneys,* are tailored to specific careers. Most of these and other titles provide a multitude of resume examples and helpful advice in a straightforward manner. The *Idiot's Guide,* for example, offers its readers the ''five commandments'' of resume writing: ''Thou Shalt Not Write about Your Past—Thou Shalt Write about Your Future''; ''Thou Shalt Not Confess''; ''Thou Shalt Not Write about Job Descriptions—Thou Shalt Write about Achievements''; ''Thou Shalt Not Write about Stuff You Don't Want to Do Again''; and finally, ''Thou Shalt Not Lie.''

Resume and job-hunting advice is also available on numerous **Internet** sites. Like resume handbooks, there are a large number of handbooks that serve as a guide to the ''information highway.'' *Career-X-Roads,* for example, is a directory to ''500 best job, resume, and career management sites on the World Wide Web.'' Another source is *The On-Line Job Search Companion,* which is a ''guide to hundreds of career planning and job hunting resources available via your computer.''

All of these and other titles offer practical and anecdotal information but offer little empirical evidence as to what makes a good resume. A 1984 survey, although somewhat dated, offers just such hard data. Personnel administrators of 500 large corporations and organizations in the United States were surveyed as to preferred resume content. A summary of the survey shows that the administrators wanted information on educational qualifications and previous work experience (92 percent), professional job objectives (90 percent), special aptitudes such as foreign-language skills (78 percent), special interests related to one's vocational field (75 percent), personal information (72 percent), and finally, social data (57 percent). The survey also demonstrated that content was more important than format and showed no support for the need to mention personality traits, little support for the inclusion of information on hobbies and outside activities, and a strong feeling that specific references to race, religion, and gender should not appear. There was mixed and sometimes contradictory support for information relating to age, marital status, and dependents.

It is generally agreed that potential employers are looking for hard data and information on resumes. Resumes without dates are often seen as indicators of excessive job changes or attempts to hide large gaps in one's employment history. Nebulous phrases such as ''exposed to'' or ''assisted in'' indicate a lack of depth in one's work experience as does excess space devoted to education, personal, and social information. Employers are also on the lookout for deliberately falsified information and often hire outside firms to verify information appearing on resumes.

[Michael Knes]

FURTHER READING:

Allen, Jeffrey G. *The Resume Makeover.* New York: Wiley, 1995.

Crispin, Gerry, and Mark Mehler. *Career-X-Roads.* Kendall Park, NJ: MMC Group, 1998.

Fondell, Joan, and Mary Jo Russo. *Best Resumes for Attorneys.* New York: Wiley, 1994.

Gonyea, James C. *The On-Line Job Search Companion.* New York: McGraw-Hill, 1995.

Hutchinson, Kevin L. ''Personnel Administrators' Preferences for Resume Content.'' *Journal of Business Communications,* fall 1984, 5-13.

Ireland, Susan. *The Complete Idiot's Guide to the Perfect Resume.* New York: Alpha Books, 1996.

Krannich, Ronald L., and William J. Banis. *High Impact Resumes and Letters.* Manassas Park, VA: Impact Publications, 1998.

Lewis, Adelle, and David J. Moore. *Best Resumes for Scientists and Engineers.* New York: Wiley, 1993.

Medley, H. Anthony. *Sweaty Palms: The Neglected Art of Being Interviewed.* Berkeley, CA: Ten Speed Press, 1995.

RETAIL TRADE

Retailing is the sector of the economy that offers goods and services for sale directly to the ultimate consumers, usually private individuals. It is related to wholesale trade, which is the purchase of goods or services in bulk by businesses or persons who may add something to those goods or services, or use them in production. Wholesalers usually do not deal directly with the end user.

By definition, retailers are primarily marketing and distribution organizations. In conventional merchandise retailing, they typically provide a conduit between a host of companies that specialize in producing goods and consumers who require those goods all at one site, the store. For more service-oriented retail operations, e.g., restaurants, the supplier relationship is somewhat different, but many of the same market dynamics still hold. As such, retailers are only effective to the degree they create convenience and value—broadly defined—for both customers and suppliers. In an era when some manufacturers would just as soon use the Internet to reach their markets directly—and do—retailers must redouble their efforts to create compelling value propositions and other enticements for customers. These may take the form of low prices, innovative product/service mixes, rewarding shopping experiences, customer perks, or any number of other marketing strategies.

ORGANIZATIONAL AND STATISTICAL PORTRAIT

The retail industry represents a major component of industrial, market based economies. In the United States, retailing consistently employed around one-fifth of the labor force, or well over 22 million workers, as of 1999. In 1998, U.S. retail trade was worth nearly $2.7 trillion in annual sales. However, sales growth at the aggregate level has been fairly slow in this mostly mature sector, and profit margins in many retail categories tend to be very thin. Adjusting for inflation, the entire retail sector's sales grew by less than 14 percent for the nine year period of 1990-98. Indeed, a boom year for retailers is 5 or 6 percent growth—a rate that in the high-tech sectors would cause investors to frantically liquidate their shares.

Retail trade has always been an important factor in the nation's economy and **credit** outlook. Retailers purchase items for sale with no guarantee of selling them, often borrowing large sums to make the goods available to customers. Customers, in turn, often purchase items on credit, using store or national credit cards.

RETAIL CATEGORIES

There are more than one million retail companies in the United States. For statistical and market analysis purposes, these retailers are usually categorized by what they sell. Using classification systems such as the **Standard Industrial Classification** (SIC) or the newer **North American Industry Classification System** (NAICS), the Census Bureau groups these establishments according to their principal merchandise line—the line that accounts for the largest share of store sales. Thus in general studies, a store such as Kmart which carries furniture, but sells far more clothing, might have its furniture sales reported under the principal line, clothing. This is, of course, a distortion, and professional analysts often seek to separate sales by each product line in order to create a more accurate profile.

The most general statistical categories for retailing are durable and nondurable goods. The conventional distinction between them is that durable goods are expected to have a life span of one year or more, whereas nondurables last less than a year (though this is not literally true in all cases). Durable goods include items like home appliances, electronics, furniture, motor vehicles, and so forth. Examples of nondurables include food, pharmaceuticals, toiletries, and paper products. Nondurable goods as a whole tend to be the larger sales category; as of 1998 nondurables represented 58 percent of retail sales compared to 42 percent for durables.

NONSTORE RETAILING. Retailers are also classified by whether or not they sell their wares in physical stores. While the vast majority do sell at physical outlets, nonstore retailing in the United States is a robust $80 billion industry—and one that has been growing more than twice as fast as conventional retailing. Net nonstore sales growth from 1990 to 1998 was in excess of 35 percent after inflation. Mail order services make up 70 percent of nonstore retailing by sales volume, although the category also includes vending machine operators and direct selling businesses (e.g., **telemarketing**, door-to-door).

E-COMMERCE. The latest form of nonstore retailing is over the **Internet and World Wide Web**. In **electronic commerce**, or e-commerce, the distinction between retailers and manufacturers (or even wholesalers) can be minimal to the end user. Behind the interface the differences remain, for electronic retailers still aggregate merchandise that others produce and market it to end users. But here, in theory at least, the added costs of having a middleman can be more apparent to consumers and, with consumers having equally convenient access to both retailer and manufacturer, place retailers at a competitive disadvantage. In practice, thus far at least, manufacturers have tended not to compete with retailers on price. In fact, many retailers on the Internet offer better prices than the producer does, for example, in packaged software sales, because software vendors tend to sell their products only at list price, whereas e-commerce retailers may offer discounts.

The importance of the electronic marketplace over the long run cannot be understated. A major study released in 1999 by two University of Texas economists indicated that the economic value of Internet-related activity was worth some $302 billion in 1998. Of this amount, $102 billion came from e-commerce, a level consistent with other analysts' estimates. While much of this was business-to-business trade, and technically outside the scope of retailing by conventional definition, consumer online purchases were reckoned at more than $10 billion by other researchers. In another gauge of consumer Internet commerce, some analysts estimated that during the 1998 holiday shopping season 8.5 million households bought gift items over the Internet, a more than fourfold increase from a year earlier.

HISTORY AND TRENDS

In the late 18th century in Europe, and slightly later in the United States, the mix of ample goods and enough people with disposable income to purchase those goods reached the critical mass needed to fuel the rise of a merchant class and a multitude of shops. Colonial American towns were lined with shops where the purchase of goods and the exchange of social niceties was a way of life. Frontier settlers were treated to ''portable'' stores in the form of peddler wagons until enough people lived in one area to support a store. This pattern continued well into the 20th century with a cluster of stores downtown that sold many goods, and a few food and general merchandise stores in the neighborhoods.

In the 1960s, retailing began to take on a new face. Retailers followed their customers to the suburbs with an array of strip malls; then in the 1970s and 1980s giant indoor shopping malls; and in the 1990s, the return of the strip mall and the emergence of the electronic shopping place.

One of the most pervasive U.S. retail trends over the second half of the 20th century was consolidation and the rise of large chain stores to replace smaller, local ones. This occurred perhaps earliest in the grocery store arena with the so-called supermarket revolution, extending roughly from the 1950s to the 1970s, which drove many smaller, independent grocery sellers out of business. A parallel movement that originated in the same period was the rise of the so-called category killer, epitomized by stores such as Toys 'R' Us, Inc. First appearing in the 1950s, Toys 'R' Us offered a very wide selection of items in its market category and sometimes at lower prices than smaller retailers. In theory, the category killer exhausted consumers' need to shop around for a particular item of interest because one store carried nearly everything.

Both consolidation and the growth of large-format chain stores continued and in many retail segments accelerated in the 1980s and 1990s. The category killer or ''superstore'' format was adopted in such diverse areas as hardware and home repair, office supplies, consumer electronics, and books. At the same time, **mergers and acquisitions** were a regular feature on the retail landscape, with a handful of stores in each category competing for market share as the top-tier national and superregional chains. Table 1 compares the size and geographic scope of some of the leading chains in several retail categories.

Retailing is highly competitive and large discount chains and specialty retailers alike compete aggressively for consumer dollars. As an example, food retailing has witnessed the discount/warehouse wars, enticing customers to buy in bulk at a discount. Retailers have sought to tailor their methods to reach consumers who are increasingly short of time, looking to get the best buy for their dollar, and demanding superior customer service.

At the same time, the very act of shopping has undergone change in a number of ways. Shopping is increasingly viewed as a utilitarian task, and the once-vaunted suburban shopping malls have actually experienced declining sales net of inflation. In women's retailing, where the traditional store concept is most alive, inroads have been made by electronic shopping, shopping in catalogs, and shopping by television and phone—all time-saving efforts.

Part of the reason for these changes in retailing is that the demographics of the U.S. market changed significantly in the last quarter of the 20th century. Single-parent families, dual-income families, and smaller families are just a few of the socioeconomic trends influencing retail markets. Cultural diversity and tolerance have also greatly affected the sector. Recognizing a diversified market, many retailers now target their ad campaigns to segments of the market once ignored. There have been, for example, campaigns for larger-sized women's clothing, ads targeted specifically toward Hispanics or African Americans, and the plethora of media efforts to gain the dollars of the fickle but lucrative teen market.

Table 1
Size and Scope of Selected Major Retailers by Market

Company	Sales	No. of Outlets	Geographic Scope
		Supermarkets	
Kroger Co.	$28.2 billion	1,400	Midwestern and southern states
Safeway Inc.	$24.5 billion	1,497	Western, midwestern, and mid-Atlantic states with some Canadian and Mexican holdings
Albertson's	$16 billion	983	In 25 western, midwestern, and southern states
		General Merchandise	
Wal-Mart Stores, Inc.	$137.6 billion	3,600	World's largest retailer with stores in all 50 states and heavy presence in many foreign countries
Kmart Corporation	$33.6 billion	2,150	National with stores in all 50 states and some international
		Consumer Electronics	
Circuit City Stores, Inc.	$10.8 billion	590	National with stores in 44 states
Best Buy Co., Inc.	$10.1 billion	311	In 36 states, mostly midwestern, southern, and western
		Books and Music	
Barnes & Noble, Inc.	$3 billion	1,009	National in 49 states
Borders Group, Inc.	$2.6 billion	1,176	National spread throughout the U.S. and a moderate presence in the U.K.

Notes: Sales and store count figures are based on company reporting as of 1998 or early 1999. Albertson's figures are from before its merger with American Stores Company.

On the management side of retailing, three important themes have been: (1) **inventory control** and other forms of **cost control** to improve profitability and cash flow; (2) related efficiencies gained from electronic ordering and management, such as reducing paperwork and inaccuracies; and (3) strategic relationships with vendors to control source costs and implement high-tech **supply chain management**.

RETAIL THEORY AND PUBLICATIONS

As in most major economic sectors, there is a strong body of literature and theories covering the methods and processes used in corporate retailing. Several academic and trade journals exist for retailing in general, as well as for specific segments, such as supermarkets, drug stores, or apparel stores. Topics addressed include pricing theory, business philosophy and strategy, consumer behavior, innovative practices, and current trends and issues facing the industry.

EMPLOYMENT PROFILE

Employment prospects in the retail store sector have always been most abundant in sales, and the majority of that workforce has been, traditionally, female. Sales persons, one of the industry's largest occupational groups, represent approximately 20 percent of the retail workforce, and cashiers make up an additional 15 percent. Each of these categories was expected to add several hundred thousand new positions in the United States over the period 1996-2006, according to Bureau of Labor Statistics projections. In fact, cashier positions were expected to be the single largest occupational growth category in terms of the number of new jobs added.

Despite the copious job openings in these areas of retailing, they are mostly unskilled and relatively low-paying positions, at least until workers reach management level. Approximately two of every five retail sales employees were part-time workers. This is significant because many part-time workers do not earn pension or health benefits. In addition, the use of many part-time workers means that merchants do not have to pay overtime to stay open seven days a week.

The retail corporate staff also includes buyers (usually college educated), financial managers, human resource specialists, finance and accounting staff, advertising and marketing personnel, and display specialists.

To prepare for careers in retail management, many colleges and universities offer associate and bachelor degrees in retail-related studies. A few offer advanced degrees, most notably the University of Arizona, which has a doctoral program. Common academic specializations include retail marketing, merchandising, and retail management.

FURTHER READING:

Berman, Barry, and Joel R. Evans. *Retail Management: A Strategic Approach.* Upper Saddle River, NJ: Prentice Hall, 1998.

''Key Success Factors from Leading Retailers.'' *International Journal of Retail & Distribution Management,* June-July 1997.

Levy, Michael, and Barton A Weitz. *Retail Management.* Chicago: Richard Irwin, 1998.

National Retail Federation. *National Retail Federation: The World's Largest Retail Trade Association.* Washington, 1999. Available from www.nrf.com.

"Report Quantifies Economic Impact of U.S. Internet-Related Companies." *Wall Street Journal,* 10 June 1999.

Reynolds, Jonathan. "Retailing on the Net." *International Journal of Retail & Distribution Management,* February-March 1999.

U.S. Bureau of Labor Statistics. *Occupational Outlook.* Washington: GPO, biannual. Available from www.bls.gov.

Wakefield, Kirk L., and Julie Baker. "Excitement at the Mall: Determinants and Effects on Shopping Response." *Journal of Retailing,* winter 1998.

RETIREMENT PLANNING

Retirement planning has become among the most important of a person's financial considerations, for several reasons. First, life expectancy has drastically increased. Where workers once had to survive for 5 to 10 years on retirement **income**, today's citizens can reasonably expect to live for 15 to 19 years after retirement. And because of lengthened life expectancy for men and women, the age at which Social Security can be collected has gradually been raised, meaning Americans will need to work longer before any benefits can be collected.

Inflation is another important factor in planning for retirement. At 6 percent inflation per year, what cost $1,000 in 1999 would cost $4,292 in 2024; or in 2024, $1,000 would have the purchasing power of $233 today. Money must be invested in places it can achieve the growth necessary to support the increased expenses that will be encountered at retirement age. And **taxes** make it difficult to keep returns on investment from diminishing. An investment that earns 5 percent actually loses money once taxes have been paid on the interest and inflation has been accounted for. At 6 percent inflation, taxpayers in the 28 percent tax bracket need to earn 11.1 percent on investments to realize a 2 percent gain. Because of statistics such as these, tax-deferred investments and retirement plans have become increasingly important to retirement planing.

In the late 20th century Americans were also accused of having a faulty view of how their retirement is likely to be funded. Most Americans between 45 and 64 expected their **pensions** to cover the majority of expenses after retirement, followed by Social Security and personal savings. For most retirees over the age of 65, however, personal savings is the primary source of income, followed by any money earned post-retirement, and then pension plans. The Social Security Administration estimated that personal savings, including **individual retirement accounts** (IRAs) and **401(k) plans**, would account for 44 percent of retirement income for those retiring between 1994 and 2004. Social Security ranked fourth in total annual income for retired persons, according to the U.S. Department of Health and Human Services. And debate continues over whether Social Security will even be available as retirement income for the youngest members of the current **workforce**.

GROWTH OF RETIREMENT PLANNING

Retirement is defined by *Barron's* as "leaving active employment permanently, for the remaining years of life, with income being provided through Social Security, pensions, and savings." Retirement age is the earliest age at which an employee can retire and receive full benefits, and is usually determined by age and length of service at a company. Some individuals choose early retirement, leaving active **employment** sooner than would normally be the case. This can be done as long as minimum age and service requirements are met, but often results in a proportionate reduction in benefits. Some might choose to defer retirement for some time (without a corresponding increase in benefits, usually), and some companies actually enforce automatic retirement when certain milestones have been reached.

Retirement benefits have been available to employees in the United States for a number of years. Private pension plans in the United States are a result of the Industrial Revolution in the late 1800s, as the industrial base shifted from agriculture to manufacturing. The Social Security Administration was created in the 1930s as a part of Franklin D. Roosevelt's New Deal. Shortly after the creation of Social Security, private pension plans grew, offering tax-deferred retirement income to millions of employees. Additional, subsequently introduced options for tax-deferred savings include the 401(k) plan, introduced in 1981, and IRAs, created in 1974. The insurance industry also began billing certain types of life insurance policies as retirement planning options, selling "whole life" and "variable universal life" policies which offered tax-deferred growth that would also be nontaxable upon withdrawal.

To provide a similar tax-deferred option for the self-employed, the Self-Employed Individuals Retirement Act was enacted in 1962 through the efforts of New York Congressman Eugene J. Keogh. This act established tax-deferred retirement plans—known as Keogh plans—with withdrawals starting between ages 59.5 and 70.5 years. The plan is for the self-employed and those who have income from **self-employment** on the side (freelancers, moonlighters, etc.).

RETIREMENT PLANNING VEHICLES

SOCIAL SECURITY. Social Security was conceived as a government-sponsored means of ensuring older U.S. citizens would be able to meet minimum retirement and medical insurance expenses. Employers and employees both contribute equally to the Social Security system throughout an employee's work life. Once the minimum age is reached, most U.S. citizens can begin withdrawing from the Social Security system. In 1998 reduced benefits were available at age 62, and full benefits could begin as early as age 65. The amount paid to each person depended on the amount contributed (earning levels) and whether the recipient was married or single. The amount paid is also adjusted for inflation when payment occurs. The age at which full benefits would be available was increased by a couple of months for each year after 1938 that a person was born. Those born in 1960 or later would not be eligible for full Social Security benefits until they reach 67. (Eligibility for Medicare, however, remained at age 65.)

PENSION PLANS. Defined-benefit and defined-contribution plans are both common examples of ''retirement plans,'' all of which are considered ''pension plans.'' These can be set up by corporations, **labor unions**, governments, or other organizations to provide retirement benefits. In defined-benefit plans, employees are entitled to specified payments at retirement, the amount having been determined by the employee's pay level and length of service. Money for these funds is set aside in a group fund, with no separate accounts for individual employees. Defined-benefit plans must conform to minimum funding and insurance requirements as set through the Pension Benefit Guaranty Corporation (established by the Employee Retirement Income Security Act of 1974), which can administer plans and place liens on corporate assets for non-funded pension **liabilities**. Generally, employees must become ''vested'' over a period of five years to be eligible for these benefits.

Defined-contribution plans are those in which an employee has his or her own account and both employer and employee contribute to the plan, usually an amount calculated as a percentage of the employee's pay. Contributions and interest earned accumulate in this account either until retirement or until an employee rolls the balance over into a different account with a new employer. Before being paid out, pension funds are usually invested in stock and bond markets. For both plans, maximum contribution rates are set for pretax dollars to avoid retirement plans becoming tax shelters for the most highly paid contributors. In the 1980s and 1990s, defined-benefit plans lost popularity in favor of defined-contribution plans, most commonly 401(k)s and 403(b)s. This is probably due in large part to similar changes in the U.S. corporate climate; more options were made available to employees, along with more control and additional responsibility for making decisions.

Perhaps the most significant difference between defined-benefit and defined-contribution plans is the voluntary nature of the latter. Defined-benefit plans are generally automatic, reserved for union and salaried employees. Defined-contribution plans are fully voluntary plans in which an hourly or salaried employee elects to have a certain percentage of money deducted—before taxes—from the paycheck. Adding to the financial pressure on employers resulting from defined-benefit plans, nondiscrimination rules were enacted in 1996. These rules state that public sponsors must offer the same benefits to all employees regardless of compensation. Many state and local municipalities moved to defined-contribution plans to avoid this new mandate. Also, the voluntary nature of defined-contribution plans makes detractors wonder if ill-informed employees will have less money at retirement than if the defined-benefit plans had been available.

THE 401(K). The 401(k) is a defined-contribution plan introduced in 1981; more than $1 trillion rests in 401(k) plans. The popularity of 401(k) and 403(b) plans is partially attributed to the ease with which such plans can be set up in comparison with defined-benefit plans; employees decide how to invest funds within a given set of options defined by the employer. Employees are allowed to contribute up to $10,000 each year to 401(k) plans, all of which is tax deductible, as are earnings accumulated in the plan. Most plans allow contributors to select which of several offered investment vehicles they would like to place their money in, such as **mutual funds**, company stock, and government **bonds**. An additional benefit of these plans is that companies often match voluntary employee contributions, meaning that by participating in company-sponsored 401(k) plans employees already realize significant financial growth.

Contributions to 401(k) plans are subject to penalty if withdrawn before age 59.5, unless the withdrawal is due to death or disability. **Loans** can be made against these plans, but employees must generally pay themselves back, with interest, and stand to lose—temporarily, until the loan is paid back in full—whatever earnings that money would have made had they left it in the 401(k). If an employee leaves the company, 401(k) balances (once vested) can be rolled over into IRAs or other 401(k) accounts. 403(b) plans work very similarly to 401(k) plans, but are available to educational institutions and other non-profit organization.

KEOGH (HR-10) AND SEP PLANS. Keogh plans were designed for self-employed people to save for retirement with the same tax savings as employed workers. Keogh plans offer benefits such as tax-deferred contributions and earnings and income-based contributions, just as standard pension plans do. In order to contribute, the contributing ''business'' must show a profit and demonstrate that it does not discriminate against other employees. The Keogh plan allows contributors to invest in **stocks**, bonds, precious coins, annuities, and cash value life insurance, and is available to all full-time employees of that person's business. Contributors are generally subject to vesting, which occurs after five years of full-time service (partial vesting can occur earlier). Withdrawals are subject to a 10 percent penalty plus income tax if taken before the age of 59.5.

An alternative option to the Keogh plan is the simplified employee pension (SEP) plan, which is easier for **small businesses** or self-employed individuals to administer. Up to 15 percent of pay can be contributed for each employee, and contributions are tax deductible from pretax profits. Income earned by SEP plans is tax deferred, but the maximum contribution is $22,500 per year, compared to $30,000 for Keogh plans. Any kind of business can open an SEP, and contributors do not have to wait to be vested. SEP plans are subject to the same early withdrawal penalties as Keogh plans, however.

INDIVIDUAL RETIREMENT ACCOUNTS. Individual retirement accounts (IRAs) were created in 1974 by Congress to encourage retirement savings on the part of individuals. Any person who makes below a certain income level can contribute up to $2,000 tax-free each year to IRAs, with a 6 percent penalty on additional money that is contributed. All earnings, however, are tax deferred. Since IRA contributions are made by the individual, and are not part of a company-sponsored plan, no vesting in required. Also, IRAs can be opened by anyone, even if self-employed. IRA investment options are selected by the person opening the account, and money may be placed in stocks, bonds, or mutual funds.

Except for allowable exemptions (such as death or disability), money invested in IRAs cannot be withdrawn until the contributor reaches the age of 59.5; early withdrawals result in a 10 percent penalty (as well as income tax) on the withdrawal amount. Once withdrawals begin, they are treated as ordinary income and taxed as any other income received. After a person reaches the age of 70.5, contributors must take minimum withdrawals or pay a 50 percent penalty (plus income tax) on the IRA.

In 1998 Congress authorized the Roth IRA, which differs substantially from the traditional IRA. While single people must make less than $40,000 to utilize the advantages of a traditional IRA, the Roth IRA allows contributions by single people making up to $110,000. In addition, money placed in a Roth IRA can be withdrawn anytime after the account has been opened for at least five years or the person is 59.5 years old, and allows for contributions to continue after the age of 70.5. Roth IRA contributions, however, are not tax deductible. Also, if money from a Roth IRA is rolled over into a traditional IRA, the proceeds are taxable.

LIFE INSURANCE. Many life insurance companies are now billing their policies as retirement planning vehicles as well. While standard term life insurance policies are by far the cheapest option, they offer no financial reward for paying into the policy. But other policies—such as whole life, universal life, and variable universal life—offer options for cash growth, customized investment, and the ability to make cash withdrawals after the policy had been in effect for a specified period. These also pay the face value of the policy in full in case of death. While life insurance premiums are paid with after-tax dollars, investment earnings are not taxed, nor were withdrawals taken upon retirement as of 1999. While not as beneficial to retirement planning as pension plans, to which contributions can be made before taxes (and to which the employer *and* employees contribute), these policies are another potential tax shelter for people who have already maximized 401(k) and pension contributions.

INVESTMENT VEHICLES

Once a person selects an IRA, 401(k), pension plan, or an investment-oriented life insurance policy, he or she often faces multiple investment options within the given plan. Most plans categorize the various options as growth funds, growth and income funds, income funds, balanced funds, and capital preservation funds. These categorizes indicate the purpose of that fund and how money within the fund will be invested. For example, growth funds focus completely on capital appreciation and invest in corporate stocks that are expected to realize substantial growth rates. These stocks probably fluctuate more than most, but offer the highest potential to increase investment value and outpace inflation. Because these funds stand to ''grow'' the most in value, they are termed ''growth'' funds. Growth and income funds also focus on capital appreciation, but also on generating income. They invest primarily in the **stock market**, but focus on those stocks that will also pay high **dividends**. These funds also generate high long-term returns.

Balanced funds try to ''balance'' the goals of income and capital appreciation by investing in both stocks and bonds. The income portion of the fund is derived from the interest paid on bonds, while appreciation is realized when stock prices rise, further increasing the investment's value. Balanced funds have higher returns than income and capital appreciation funds, but do not generally fluctuate as much as growth funds. Income funds focus more on income than appreciation, investing primarily in **debt** securities that pay interest, such as government or corporate bonds. While values do fluctuate, income funds often produce decent returns, in part by reinvesting dividends. Finally, capital preservation funds seek to stabilize investments, minimizing the risk of losing money on the principal invested. Capital preservation funds invest in **securities** that consistently earn returns at current **interest rates**; investment income is automatically reinvested, compounding the investment's value. These funds usually provide comparatively low returns, but the principal witnesses little or no fluctuation.

How much a person should contribute to different types of funds and investment vehicles varies depending on the individual's age and investment style. In general, younger investors can afford to take more risks (potentially realizing more growth) with their money, since it is not an active source of income. People in their 20s through mid-30s should be seeking maximum growth through investment, and can accept short-term volatility in exchange for long-term growth. More simply put, investors in this age group can afford short-term losses in the stock market in order to realize long-term gains. Most retirement plans advise that people between the ages of 20 and 35 place around 70 percent of their investments in growth funds, maximizing long-term growth. The remaining money can be distributed in growth and income or balanced funds and in income or capital preservation funds.

Once people attain the age of 35 and through their late 40s, investments should become slightly more stabilized and less prone to fluctuation. People in this age group, however, still usually have an increasing income, so the amount invested in growth funds need only be reduced by about 10 percent. That money can then be placed in a capital preservation fund to stabilize some of the principal invested. People in their early 50s through early 60s again need to reduce investment fluctuation, but still want to realize growth in their investments. More emphasis is placed on income and capital preservation as retirement grows nearer. Leaving about 40 percent of invested funds in growth funds should maintain fund growth goals, while investing the other 20 percent in growth and income or balanced funds should help reduce volatility.

Finally, for retired persons, investments need to maximize current income and grow only enough to outpace inflation. Little volatility in investment performance is desired, and income is more important as people are likely not actively earning any income on their own. Only a third of the investment amount needs to be placed in growth funds, while more can be invested in growth and income or balanced funds, income funds, and capital preservation funds.

CALCULATING RETIREMENT NEEDS

Determining how much income will be required at retirement is at best an educated guess. There are, however, several ''rules of thumb'' and many retirement ''calculators'' available for planning. *Kiplinger's Personal Finance Magazine* offers a retirement planning calculator on its **Internet** web site, as does *Money* magazine. Many advisors recommend having between 70 and 100 percent of pre-retirement income to live on, while others say a minimum of 80 percent will be necessary to maintain a pre-retirement lifestyle. This depends in part on how each person wants to spend his or her retirement years—homebodies will need less to live on than people who plan to spend the bulk of their time traveling. Other considerations include whether the retiree will remain in his or her own home or move to a new domicile. Most expect that expenses such as **mortgages**, car payments, and college tuition will be behind them at this point, but it may be necessary to plan for such things as well.

In order to complete most retirement planning calculators, a person needs to know how much income they would like each year after retirement; this number will be adjusted to account for inflation. Additional information required to get a good ballpark estimate includes how many more years of work remain until retirement, how much Social Security benefits are expected annually, marital status, value of current savings and assets, annual pension benefits, and life expectancy. This information is used to calculate the dollar value of assets needed at retirement. All of these together, in combination with information about each person's individual investment style, help illustrate how much that person needs to save by the time they retire, how much they need to save each month to attain that goal, and the best way for them to go about doing so.

Every person in the United States is entitled to Social Security and Medicare benefits. The Social Security Administration provides information on personal earnings and benefit estimates to anyone requesting the information. This can be done by contacting the agency directly via phone, mail, or through its web site. Obtaining accurate figures greatly aids in effectively calculating retirement resources and needs. Another benefit people will need to quantify is their pension. Many companies distribute annual benefits statements describing how much each employee has earned toward their pension at a given point and how much they can expect to receive as income at retirement based on their time invested in the company up to that date.

When planning and investing for retirement, it is important to assess current and future financial goals, i.e., how much money needs to be liquid or available at present, and how much can be invested for future use. This is important because many retirement plans assess penalties for funds withdrawn before the age of 59.5 years. If funds will be needed to purchase a home or meet educational expenses, an appropriate amount of money should remain where it can be readily accessed.

[Valerie E. Wilson, updated by Wendy H. Mason]

FURTHER READING:

Adams, David P., and David J. Glencer. "Investment Fundamentals: Retirement Plans." 1998.

Baldwin, Ben G. *The New Life Insurance Investment Advisor.* Chicago: Irwin, 1994.

Connor, John B., Jr. "Pay Me Later." *Small Business Reports,* July 1994, 44.

Elgin, Peggie R. "Uncle Sam Prepares to Block Fat Cats' Age-Weighted Plans." *Corporate Cashflow Magazine,* January 1994, 5.

Ippolito, Richard. "Toward Explaining the Growth of Defined Contribution Plans." *Industrial Relations,* January 1995, 1-20.

Malaspina, Margaret A. *Don't Die Broke.* Bloomberg Press, 1999.

Philip, Christine. "Value of Defined Contribution Plans Debated." *Pensions and Investments,* 20 February 1995, 39.

Putnam Investments. "Build Your Future Financial Security with Your Tax-Deferred Savings Plan." Putnam Mutual Funds Corp., 1993.

Reilly, Meegan M. "Metzenbaum Pension Bill Would Expand Coverage Requirements." *Tax Notes,* 31 October 1994, 589-90.

Siegel, Alan M., Morris, Virginia B., et al. *The Wall Street Journal Guide to Planning Your Financial Future.* Revised ed. Fireside, 1998.

Silverstein, Ken. "DC Plans." *Pension Management,* November 1994, 9.

Sloane, Leonard. *The New York Times Book of Personal Finance.* New York: Times Books, 1992.

Sollinger, Andrew. "Defined-Contribution Plans: In the Public Interest?" *Institutional Investor,* June 1993, 159.

"Work Force Mobility Lends Itself to Defined Contribution Approach." *Employee Benefit Plan Review,* June 1994, 55.

RETRAINING

SEE: Occupational Mobility and Retraining; Vocational Rehabilitation

REVENUE

SEE: Income and Revenue

RIGHT OF PRIVACY

At no time in American history has the "right of privacy" generated such heated controversy and been the focus of so much attention as at present. The Watergate scandal in the 1970s focused public attention for the first time on the damaging effects of sophisticated electronic technology on privacy. Watergate provided the impetus for the landmark Privacy Act of 1974, which limits the federal government's ability to disclose information about a citizen. This law was itself based on the Fair Information Standards (FIS) adopted by the U.S. Department of Health, Education, and Welfare in 1973, which stipulated that "there shall be no personal record system whose existence is secret; individuals have rights of access, inspection, review, and amendment to systems containing information about them." In 1978 Congress strengthened the law on illegal government wiretapping. States have followed the federal government's lead in passing laws protecting the privacy of their residents. Nevertheless, the computerization of business and government since the 1970s has made relentless onslaughts on the individual's privacy, most often without his or her knowledge or consent.

In American history, "privacy" traditionally has meant the right to be left alone. The Bill of Rights guarantees freedom of speech, press, and religion; prohibits the government from conducting "unreasonable searches and seizures"; and protects the individual from self-incrimination and "cruel and unusual punishment." These constitutional guarantees, while not defining privacy outright, implicitly uphold the sanctity and autonomy of the individual.

For the first hundred years of this country's history, constitutional guarantees respecting privacy adequately protected it. Information files were few, and the proximity of the frontier made surveillance virtually impossible. Late 19th-century technology, in the form of telegraphs and telephones, however, began to make inroads into privacy, and drew the attention of future Supreme Court Justice Louis D. Brandeis (1856 1941) and his law-firm colleague Samuel D. Warren (1852-1910). In 1890 their article, "The Right to Privacy," appeared in the *Harvard Law Review,* focusing primarily on the invasion of the individual's "right to be left alone" by the popular press. The ensuing legal debate over privacy contributed to the evolution of the concept of privacy in American law. In 1923 the Supreme Court struck down a Nebraska law that prohibited the teaching of any language other than English on the grounds that it violated personal autonomy, which was recognized for the first time as a legal principle. In 1965 the Supreme Court, in the case of *Griswold v. Connecticut,* held that the Constitution implicitly guaranteed the right of sexual privacy. The Griswold case as well as the 1973 *Roe v. Wade* decision, recognizing a woman's right to an abortion, personified for many the individual's right to personal privacy. Although individual privacy has generally received increased protection under the law, in all such cases there exists a tension between the right of society to intervene to stop or prevent illegal activity and the right of individuals to personal autonomy.

The clash between society—usually government and business interests—and the individual's right to personal autonomy has heightened since *Roe v. Wade,* thanks in large part to the "information revolution." The sophistication of surveillance technology and the invasion of **computers** into all realms of life, including churches and schools, have heightened the assault on individual autonomy to a degree undreamed of when the Constitution was written. The government's abuse of electronic surveillance to spy on its citizens during the Nixon administration drew national attention to the misuse of technology and the need for legal curbs. The result was the Privacy Act of 1974. This law was meant to empower the individual by giving him or her access on demand to any personal records held by a federal agency; the law also limited the power of any federal agency to "swap" records with another agency, as well as to disclose information on an individual.

Critics of the law since its passage cite its lax enforcement, loopholes, and exceptions, as well as the near absence of committed oversight and enforcement. Following on the heels of this law was the 1976 Supreme Court case, *United States v. Miller,* in which the court ruled that an individual's bank records belong to the bank, and not to the individual, who "surrenders" his or her right to privacy upon becoming a bank customer. This ruling also meant that individuals "surrendered" their right of privacy to insurance and credit card companies, and many other businesses and government agencies that provide services. Computerization of business and government has also invaded the workplace, in which millions of Americans may be monitored by computers, telephone tapping, and closed-circuit cameras.

Advancements in surveillance technology and the proliferation of computerization has undermined the authority of the Privacy Act of 1974. The FIS standards from which the law was derived were drafted in response to the technological reality of the late 1960s, and are proving inadequate to prevent misuse of surveillance techniques available today. Furthermore, recent rulings by the Supreme Court have undermined privacy protection, stating in one case that "You have little privacy from government snooping in an open field, in a telephone booth, or from technologically remote electronic eavesdropping; if you are homeless, your effects may be searched without a warrant." Such rulings have implied that an individual is safe from public scrutiny only in the privacy of his or her own home. Lower courts seem to be taking a more mixed view, with a 1997 ruling finding federal protection of state driver's license information unconstitutional, but a 1998 ruling finding that employers cannot maintain a list of employees with AIDS and HIV. Despite such advancements, further erosion of the individual's right to privacy seems inevitable. Beginning in October 1997, for instance, employers were required to report the name, address, and social security number of all new hires to facilitate the establishment of a National Directory of New Hires as a support to welfare reform and an aid to law enforcement agencies pursuing parents failing to meet their child support obligations.

Developments in medical science have also raised privacy issues. Computerization of health records enable physicians to track an individual's health in minute detail throughout his or her life. This information could easily be misused by insurance and health-care providers to exclude otherwise eligible individuals from coverage or treatment. The ability of physicians to identify potential health risks by examining an individual's genetic makeup could also enable insurance and health care providers to exclude individuals based on the probability of future ailments, something that has heretofore been impossible. In response to these new threats to privacy, Congress passed the Health Insurance Portability and Accountability Act (HIPAA) in 1996, although this measure was viewed as temporary in nature. Since the passage of HIPAA, however, Congress has been unable to agree on permanent guidelines for the protection of an individual's health records but has blocked, at least for the near future, a plan to issue every American a medical identification number and establish a national medical database. If Congress proves unable to act before August 1999, the U.S. Department of Health and Human Services is authorized to issue health-privacy regulations no later than February 2000.

New aspects of the right to privacy continue to capture public attention. In the late 1990s the legality of assisted suicide was widely debated in the political arena and tried in the courts. Although this legal and political dispute is far from concluded, initial federal court rulings imply that the 14th Amendment as currently worded does not allow assisted suicide, and that each state must decide its own law on the subject through passage of referenda.

The "right to privacy," guaranteed by the Constitution and buttressed by state and federal law, has required constant vigilance as it is increasingly being identified with the essence of democracy itself. Hence the issue of privacy will not diminish, but will loom larger in the future.

[Sina Dubovoy, updated by Grant Eldridge]

FURTHER READING:

American Civil Liberties Union. *Your Right to Privacy: A Basic Guide to Legal Rights in an Information Society.* Carbondale, IL: Southern Illinois University Press, 1990.

Ceniceros, Roberto. "Lawsuit over Employer's AIDS, HIV List Upheld." *Business Insurance,* 17 August 1998, 240.

Childs, Kelvin. "License Secrecy Law Struck Down." *Editor and Publisher,* 20 September 1997, 18.

Conlan, Michael F. "Privacy Concerns Delay Patient ID Number Proposal." *Drug Topics,* 17 August 1998, 87.

Dowd, Ann Reilly. "Alert: New Threats to Your Privacy—And Some Help." *Money,* 11 November 1997, 30.

Hershey, Robert D., Jr. "I.R.S. Staff Is Cited in Snoopings." *New York Times,* 19 July 1994, D1.

"I Spy (Congress Is Considering Bill to Limit Electronic Workplace Surveillance)." *Inc.,* April 1994, 110.

Katz, David M. "Health Risks Outweigh Privacy Worries." *National Underwriter,* 3 August 1998, 17.

Laundon, Kenneth C. "Markets and Privacy." *Association for Computing Machinery* 39, no. 9 (September 1996): 92.

Linowes, David F. *Privacy in America: Is Your Private Life in the Public Eye?* Champaign-Urbana, IL: University of Illinois Press, 1989.

Nelson, Corey L. "Is E-mail Private or Public? Employers Have No Right to Snoop through Mail." *Computerworld,* 27 June 1994, 135.

Troy, Edwin S. Flores. "The Genetic Privacy Act: An Analysis of Policy and Research Concerns." *Journal of Law, Medicine, and Ethics* 25, no. 4 (winter 1997): 256.

RIGHT-SIZING

SEE: Corporate Restructuring

RIGHTS (SECURITIES)

In order to raise money, **publicly held companies** sometimes offer additional **securities** (shares traded in the **stock market**) to their common stockholders, which allows shareholders to preserve their interest in a company. Companies seeking to raise money this way will issue the new securities at a rate lower than the **market value** and will enable stockholders to purchase them in proportion to the amount they own, i.e., to purchase a "pro rata" share. By issuing the securities at a low price, companies ensure they will sell a sufficient amount to raise the needed funds and they will offer stockholders the privilege of acquiring additional **stock** at a low price, which functions like a special **dividend**. This privilege is called a "preemptive right" and the document a company issues offering this privilege is known as a "right" or a "stock right." Since these stocks are offered below their market value, rights are imbued with a value of their own and are often actively traded. Stockholders must exercise their rights, however, within a specific period stipulated by the issuer, which is usually two to ten weeks. After the deadlines passes, rights expire and become worthless.

The rights offering allows current shareholders to maintain their relative control and to prevent the dilution of the value of their shares. The number of new shares that needs to be issued is calculated as the total amount of new funds to be raised divided by the subscription price per new share. The subscription price is the amount that current shareholders must pay to purchase one new share. The number of rights needed to purchase one new share is equal to the ratio of the number of old shares outstanding divided by the number of new shares to be issued, which is called the "rights exchange ratio."

For example, if a firm currently has 1,000 shares outstanding at a market price of $10 per share, the market value of the firm is $10,000. If the firm decides to sell $4,000 of new stock with a rights offering and if the subscription price is set at $8, the firm needs to issue 500 new shares. One new share may be purchased for each two old shares. Two rights are needed to buy one new share. The value of each share after the rights issue is equal to the new total market value, 10,000 plus 4,000 divided by the new number of shares outstanding, 1,000 plus 500. The new price per share, ex rights, is $9.33 = (10,000 + 4,000)/(1,000 + 500).

Prior to the rights issue, the rights and the share sell as one unit. The share is said to be selling rights on. After the holder of record date, the rights and the shares sell separately. The share is said to be selling ex rights.

The value of each right is equal to the difference between the current market price of the stock, rights on, and the subscription price of the rights issue divided by the number of rights needed to purchase one new share plus one. In this example, that is equal to $0.67 = (10 - 8)/(2 + 1). The value of the rights can be determined from the ex rights price. The value is equal to the ex rights market price minus the subscription price divided by the number of rights required to buy one new share, $0.67 = (9.33 - 8.00)/2. The value of the right is equal to the difference between the rights on share price and the ex rights price per share, $0.67 = ($10.00 - 9.33).

Prior to the rights offering ten shares represented a market value of $100 = ($10 × 10 shares). Assuming that a shareholder exercises all rights, this shareholder will have ten old shares and five new shares worth $140 = ($9.33 × 15 shares). The shareholder will have purchased the five new shares for $40. The value of the shareholder's 10 shares holding from prior to the rights issue is $100.

If a shareholder chose not to exercise the 10 rights but sold them, the shareholder would still have $100. Ten shares would be worth $93.33 = ($9.33 × 10 shares). Ten rights would be worth $6.67 = ($0.67 × 10 shares). The total is $100.

The ten shares prior to the rights offering represented 1 percent of the old total outstanding shares. The 15 shares after the rights offering represents 1 percent of the new total outstanding shares. Thus, both relative control and value are maintained.

Although issuing rights requires investors to buy new stocks in a short period, this technique for raising funds remains common and popular with many investors. Investors benefit from rights offerings because they can purchase additional shares at a low price and without broker fees, because they can retain their control in a company, because they stand to profit greatly if the relevant stock price increases during the rights period, and because they can sell the rights if they are unable to use them. Nevertheless, small investors may not receive enough rights to allow them to purchase whole shares or sell the rights economically. In addition, large investors may find this technique disadvantageous because the additional investment would be too substantial. Frequently, shareholders who receive rights are unable to use them and hence many rights are sold. Moreover, some stockholders, especially small ones, ignore their rights, let them expire, and take losses on them. Companies try to avoid these problems by having securities underwriters to buy rights and sell them to investors.

Because rights are short-term privileges to purchase securities at a price below market value, they often trade on a when-issued basis before companies issue the rights. That is, the trade of rights involves when-issued **contracts** that promise the future delivery of the rights at a specified price after the sellers receive them. Some brokers require sellers to make a deposit to ensure that they will in fact deliver the rights. Investors trade rights on both **over-the-counter securities markets** (e.g., **Nasdaq**) and stock exchanges.

[Carl B. McGowan, Jr., updated by Karl Heil]

FURTHER READING:

Christy, George A., and John C. Clendenin. *Introduction to Investments.* New York: McGraw-Hill, 1982.

Hagin, Robert. *The Dow Jones-Irwin Guide to Modern Portfolio Theory.* Homewood, IL: Dow Jones-Irwin, 1979.

Mittra, Sid, and Chris Gassen. *Investment Analysis and Portfolio Management.* New York: Harcourt Brace Jovanovich, 1981.

Reilly, Frank K. *Investment Analysis and Portfolio Management.* 3rd ed. Chicago: Dryden Press, 1989.

Springsteel, Ian. ''Right-of-Way.'' *CFO,* January 1998, 24.

RISK AND RETURN

The term ''risk and return'' refers to the potential financial loss or gain experienced through investments in **securities**. An investor who has registered a profit is said to have seen a ''return'' on his or her investment. The ''risk'' of the investment, meanwhile, denotes the possibility or likelihood that the investor could lose money. If an investor decides to invest in a security that has a relatively low risk, the potential return on that investment is typically fairly small. Conversely, an investment in a security that has a high risk factor also has the potential to garner higher returns. Return on investment can be measured by nominal rate or real rate (money earned after the impact of **inflation** has been figured into the value of the investment).

Different securities—including common **stocks**, corporate **bonds**, government bonds, and Treasury bills—offer varying rates of risk and return. As Richard A. Brealey and Stewart C. Myers noted in their book *Principles of Corporate Finance,* ''Treasury bills are about as safe an investment as you can get. There is no risk of default and their short maturity means that the prices of Treasury bills are relatively stable.'' Long-term government bonds, on the other hand, experience price fluctuations in accordance with changes in the nation's **interest rates**. Bond prices fall when interest rates rise, but they rise when interest rates drop. Government bonds typically offer a slightly higher rate of return than Treasury bills.

Another type of security is corporate bonds. Those who invest in corporate bonds have the potential to enjoy a higher return on their investment than those who stay with government bonds. The greater potential benefits, however, are available because the risk is greater. ''Investors know that there is a risk of default when they buy a corporate bond,'' commented Brealey and Myers. Those corporations that have this **default** option, though, ''sell at lower prices and therefore higher yields than government bonds.'' In the meantime, investors ''still want to make sure that the company plays fair. They don't want it to gamble with their money or to take any other unreasonable risks. Therefore, the bond agreement includes a number of **restrictive covenants** to prevent the company from purposely increasing the value of its default option.''

Investors can also put their money into **common stock**. Common stockholders are the owners of a corporation in a sense, for they have ultimate control of the company. Their votes—either in person or by proxy—on appointments to the corporation's **board of directors** and other business matters often determine the company's direction. Common stock carries greater risks than other types of securities, but can also prove extremely profitable. Earnings or loss of money from common stock is determined by the rise or fall in the stock price of the company.

There are other types of company stock offerings as well. Companies sometimes issue **preferred stock** to investors. While owners of preferred stock do not typically have full voting rights in the company, no **dividends** can be paid on the common stock until after the preferred dividends are paid.

RISK AND RISK AVERSION

Many types of risk loom for investors hoping to see a return on their money, noted Jae K. Shim and Joel G. Siegel in their *Handbook of Financial Analysis, Forecasting, and Modeling.* Business risk refers to the financial impact of basic operations of the company. Earnings variables in this area include product demand, selling price, and cost. Liquidity risk is the possibility that an asset may not be sold for its **market value** on short notice, while default risk is the risk that a borrower company will be unable to pay all obligations associated with a **debt**. Market risk alludes to the impact that marketwide trends can have on individual stock prices, while interest rate risk concerns the fluctuation in the value of the asset as a result of changes in interest rate, **capital market**, and money market conditions.

Individual risk aversion is thus a significant factor in the dynamics of risk and return. Cautious investors naturally turn to low-risk options such as Treasury bills or government bonds, while bolder investors often investigate securities that have the potential to generate significant returns on their investment. Certain types of common stock that fit this description include speculative stocks and penny stocks.

Many factors can determine the degree to which an investor is risk averse. William B. Riley Jr. and K. Victor Chow contended in *Financial Analysts Journal* that ''relative risk aversion decreases as one rises above the poverty level and decreases significantly for the very wealthy. It also decreases with age—but only up to a point. After age 65 (retirement), risk aversion increases with age.'' Riley and Chow note that decreases in risk aversion often parallel higher degrees of education as well, but speculate that ''education, income and wealth are all highly correlated, so the relationship may be a function of wealth rather than education.''

Economically disadvantaged families are, on the surface, often seen as risk-averse; in actuality, however, decisions by these households to avoid investment risk can be traced to a lack of discretionary **income** or **wealth**, rather than any true aversion. As Riley and Chow noted, ''risk aversion can . . . be expected to decrease as an individual's wealth increases, independent of income. Someone whose stock of wealth is growing can be expected to become less risk averse, as her tolerance of downside risk increases.''

[Laurie Collier Hillstrom]

FURTHER READING:

Becker, Gary S. ''You Want High Returns? Brace Yourself for High Risk.'' *Business Week,* 19 October 1998, 15.

Brealey, Richard A., and Stewart C. Myers. *Principles of Corporate Finance.* 5th ed. New York: McGraw-Hill, 1996.

Riley, William B., Jr., and K. Victor Chow. ''Asset Allocation and Individual Risk Aversion.'' *Financial Analysts Journal* 48, no. 6 (November/December 1992): 32.

''Risk and Return: Keeping a Level Head.'' *Financial Times,* 10 October 1998, WFT7.

Shim, Jae K., and Joel G. Siegel. *Handbook of Financial Analysis, Forecasting, and Modeling.* Englewood Cliffs, NJ: Prentice-Hall, 1988.

Simon, Ruth. ''Bonds Let You Sleep at Night, but at a Price.'' *Wall Street Journal,* 8 September 1998, C1.

RISK MANAGEMENT

Risk management is the identification, appraisal, and prevention or minimization of exposures to accidental loss for an organization or individual. Since **risk** offers not only the opportunity for growth but also for harm, risk managers must predict and prevent or control any potential harm. Risk management is essential for companies to avoid costly mistakes and business losses. The practice of risk management utilizes many tools and techniques, including insurance, to manage a wide variety of risks facing any entity, from the largest corporation to the individual. The term ''risk management'' has usually referred to property and casualty exposures to loss but recently has come to include financial risk management, e.g., **interest rates**, **foreign exchange** rates, **derivatives**, etc.

The term ''risk management'' is a relatively recent evolution of the term ''insurance management,'' and originated in the mid-1970s. The reason for this evolution is that the concept of risk management encompasses a much broader scope of activities and responsibilities than does insurance management. Risk management is now a widely accepted description of a discipline within most large companies as well as a growing number of smaller ones. The myriad risks faced by most businesses today necessitate a department solely devoted to managing these risks. Basic risks such as fire, windstorm, flood, employee injuries, and automobile accidents, as well as more complex exposures such as **product liability**, environmental impairment, and **employment** practices, are the province of the risk management department in a typical corporation.

These risks stem from various aspects of doing business and they generally fit into the following categories, according to Kevin Dowd in *Beyond Value at Risk:*

1. Business risks: risks associated with a company's particular market or industry.
2. Market risks: risks stemming from changes in market conditions, such as changes in prices, interest rates, and exchange rates.
3. Credit risks: risks arising from the possibility of not receiving payments promised by debtors.
4. Operational risks: risks resulting from internal system failures because of mechanical problems (e.g., machines breaking down) or human errors (e.g., poor management of funds).
5. Legal risks: risks stemming from the potential for other parties not to fulfill their contractual obligations.

Generally, risk managers are insurance brokers who advise clients on insurance and risk, independent **consultants** on risk who work for a fee, or salaried employees—frequently **treasurers** and **chief financial officers** (CFOs)—who manage risk for their companies. Because risk management has become an increasing part of insurance brokers' responsibilities, many work for fees instead of for commissions.

According to C. Arthur Williams Jr. and Richard M. Heins, authors of *Risk Management and Insurance,* the risk management process includes six steps. These steps are: (1) determining the objective of the organization, (2) identifying exposures to loss, (3) measuring those same exposures, (4) selecting from alternative methods of risk management, (5) implementing a method or set of methods as a solution, and (6) monitoring the results. The objective of an organization—growth, for example—will determine the **strategy** for managing various risks. Identification and measurement are relatively straightforward. The possibility of an earthquake, for instance, may be identified as a potential exposure to loss, but if the exposed facility is in New York the probability of an earthquake is very low and will have a low priority as a risk to be managed.

There are many alternative methods available for the management of risk, including loss prevention, loss reduction, risk avoidance, and risk financing. Loss prevention involves preventing a loss from occurring, via such methods as employee safety training. Loss reduction is concerned with reducing the severity of a loss, through, for example, the installation of fire sprinklers. While sprinklers will not prevent fire from occurring, they will reduce the damage it may cause. Risk avoidance is another available tool for managing risk. An example of this method is a drug company deciding not to market a drug because of potential liability claims.

Risk managers also may opt to use risk financing, which refers to paying for losses by retention or transfer. Retention of risk—sometimes referred to as self-insurance—is the last resort for managing risk. If there is no other way to manage a particular risk, a company bears the losses resulting from its risks, or retains its losses. For example, the deductible of an insurance policy is a retained loss. In addition, companies may establish special funds to cover any losses.

Transferring risk is when the risk is shared by a party other than the company ultimately responsible for the risk, such as a contractor or a consultant who may contribute to a company's risk, or by an insurance provider. Companies can transfer their losses through insurance by obtaining insurance policies that cover various kinds of risk that are insurable; insurance constitutes the leading method of risk management. Insurance typically covers property risks such as fire, natural disasters, and vandalism, liability risks such as employer's liability and **workers' compensation**, and transportation risks covering air, land, and sea travel as well as transported property and transportation liability.

Some companies choose to finance their risk by acquiring insurance companies to cover all or part of their risks. Such insurance companies are known as "captive insurers." Awareness of, and familiarity with, various types of insurance policies is necessary for the risk management process.

Furthermore, risk financing is commonly classified as preloss or postloss financing. Preloss financing refers to financing secured in anticipation of loss, such as an insurance policy. Here, companies pay insurance premiums prior to suffering losses. In contrast, postloss financing is securing funds after losses when companies obtain financing in response to losses. For example, taking out a **loan** and issuing **stocks** are forms of postloss financing.

In the implementation step, combinations of the above tools may be used. Indeed, the basic risk management techniques—retention, reduction or avoidance, and transfer—are complementary and risk managers often must use a variety of methods to adequately manage a company's risks. The final step, called monitoring, is necessary to determine if the solution employed actually obtained the desired result or if that solution requires modification.

KEY TRENDS IN RISK MANAGEMENT

The Risk and Insurance Management Society (RIMS), the primary trade group for risk managers, predicts that the key areas for risk management in the 21st century will be **operations management**, environmental risks, and ethics. RIMS also believes more small- and medium-size companies will focus on risk management and will hire risk managers or assign risk management tasks to treasurers or CFOs.

As RIMS predicted, corporate risk managers began concentrating more on ensuring their companies' compliance with federal environmental regulations during the 1990s. According to *Risk Management,* risk managers started to assess environmental risks such as those associated with pollution, waste management, and environmental liability in order to help companies bolster profitability and competitiveness. In addition, stricter environmental regulations also prompted companies to have risk managers review their compliance with environmental policies to avoid any penalties for failing to comply.

Furthermore, *Risk Management* indicated that there were five times as many natural disasters in the 1990s as the 1960s and that insurers paid 15 times what they paid in the 1960s. For instance, there were a record 600 catastrophes worldwide in 1996, which caused 12,000 deaths and $9 billion in losses from insurance. Some experts attribute the increase in natural disasters to **global warming**, which they believe will lead to more and fiercer crop damage, droughts, floods, and windstorms in the future.

The trend towards mergers in the 1990s also affected risk management. More and more companies called on risk managers to assess the risks involved in these mergers and to join their **merger and acquisition** teams. Buyers and sellers both use risk managers to identify and control risks. Risk managers on the buying side, for instance, review a selling company's expenditures, insurance policies, loss experience, and other aspects that could result in losses. After that, they develop a plan for preventing or controlling the risks they identify.

A final trend in risk management has been the advent of nontraditional insurance policies, providing risk managers with a new tool for preventing and controlling risks. These insurance policies cover financial risks such as corporate profits and currency fluctuation. Consequently, such policies ensure a level of profit even if a company experiences unexpected losses from circumstances beyond its control, such as natural disasters or economic problems in other parts of the world. In addition, they guarantee profits for companies operating in international markets, preventing losses if a currency appreciates or depreciates.

[Louis J. Drapeau, updated by Karl Heil]

FURTHER READING:

Dowd, Kevin. *Beyond Value at Risk: The New Science of Risk Management.* New York: John Wiley & Sons, Inc., 1998.

Feldman, Paul. ''Risk Managers' 'Global' Concerns.'' *Risk Management,* June 1998, 64.

Head, George L., and Stephen Horn II. *Essentials of Risk Management.* Vols. I-II. Insurance Institute of America, 1991.

Katz, David M. ''Cost Managers About to Become Asset Managers.'' *National Underwriter Property and Casualty—Risk and Benefits Management,* 2 December 1996.

——. ''New RIMS President Delillo Sees RM Future in Operations, Not Finance.'' *National Underwriter Property and Casualty—Risk and Benefits Management,* 27 April 1998, 3.

Kroll, Karen M. ''Covering Non-traditional Risks.'' *Industry Week,* 1 February 1999, 63.

Mills, Evan. ''The Coming Storm: Global Warming and Risk Management.'' *Risk Management,* May 1998, 20.

Risk and Insurance Management Society, Inc. ''Risk and Insurance Management Society, Inc. (RIMS) Website.'' Risk and Insurance Management Society, Inc., 1999. Available from www.rims.org.

Williams, C. Arthur, Jr., and Richard M. Heins. *Risk Management and Insurance.* New York: McGraw-Hill, 1989.

Wojcik, Joanne. ''Gaining a Higher Profile.'' *Business Insurance,* 5 October 1998, 2.

ROBOTICS

The Robotic Industries Association, the leading trade group for the robotics industry, defines a robot as follows: it is a ''reprogrammable, multifunctional manipulator designed to move material, parts, tools or specialized devices through variable programmed motions for the performance of a variety of tasks.'' This definition has become generally accepted in the United States and other Western countries. The most common form of industrial robot is made up of a single automated arm that resembles a construction crane.

ORIGINS OF THE NAME

The word ''robot'' was coined by Czech playwright Karel Capek (1890-1938) in his 1921 play *R.U.R.* (Rossum's Universal Robots). Robot is spelled *robota* in Czech and means forced labor. The word found its way into English-language dictionaries by the mid-1920s. The word ''robotics'' was first used by science fiction writer Isaac Asimov (1920-92) in his 1942 story ''Runaround,'' in which he wrote what became known as Asimov's Three Laws of Robotics: ''1. A robot may not injure a human being, or, through inaction, allow a human being to come to harm. 2. A robot must obey the orders given it by human beings except where such orders would conflict with the First Law. 3. A robot must protect its own existence as long as such protection does not conflict with the First or Second Law.'' Though fictional, these laws and Asimov's robot stories were influential to Joseph Engelberger, who is arguably the most important figure in the development of industrial robots. Though the word ''robot'' is relatively new, the concept is centuries old, and prior to the 1920s robot-like mechanisms were called automatons. In one of Noah Webster's earliest dictionaries, an automaton is defined as ''A self-moving machine or one which moves by invisible springs.''

DISTINGUISHING CHARACTERISTICS

In a number of respects, robots are like numerically controlled automated machine tools, such as an automated lathe, since they are both reprogrammable to produce a number of different objects. What distinguishes robots is their flexibility regarding both range of tasks and motion. In one typical manufacturing application, robots move parts in their various stages of completion from one automated machine tool to the next, the system of robots and machine tools making up a flexible manufacturing workcell. Robots are classified as soft automata, whereas automated machine tools are classified as hard automata. The Japanese Industrial Robot Association also classifies manually operated manipulators and nonreprogrammable, single-function manipulators as robots, and one must bear this in mind when comparing data on robot use between Japan and the United States.

Since robots are defined by their capacity to move objects or tools through space, key issues in robotic control are location and movement, referred to in the industry as kinematics and dynamics. The position of an object in a three-dimensional space can be defined relative to a fixed point with three parameters via the Cartesian coordinate system, indicating placement along x, y, and z axes. The orientation of an object requires three additional parameters, indicating rotation on these axes. These parameters are referred to as degrees of freedom. Together these six parameters and the movement among them make up the data of kinematic control equations. Robots carrying out simpler tasks may operate with fewer than six degrees of freedom, but robots may also operate with more than six, which is referred to as redundancy. Redundancy gives a robot greater mobility, enabling it to more readily work around obstructions and to choose among a set of joint positions to reach a given target in less time.

Two types of joints are commonly used in robots, the prismatic or sliding joint, resembling a slide rule, and the revolute joint, a hinge. The simplest type of robot to control is one made up of three sliding joints, each determining placement along a Cartesian axis. Robots made solely of revolute joints are more complex to control, in that the relation of joint position to control parameters is less direct. Other robots use both types of joints. Among these, a common type uses a large sliding joint for vertical placement of an arm made of revolute joints. The vertical rigidity and horizontal flexibility of such robots make them ideal for heavy assembly work (this configuration is referred to as SCARA for Selectively Compliant Arm for Robot Assembly). Robots may also be made of a system of arms each with restricted movement (i.e., with relatively few degrees of freedom) but which together can perform complex tasks. These are referred to as distributed robots. Such robots have the advantage of high speed and precision, but the disadvantage of restricted range of movement.

Robots are activated by hydraulic, pneumatic, and electrical power. Electric motors have become increasingly small with high power-to-weight ratios, enabling them to become the dominant means by which robots are powered. The hand of a robot is referred to in the industry as an end effector. End effectors may be specialized tools, such as spot welders or spray guns, or more general-purpose grippers. Common grippers include fingered and vacuum types.

One of the central elements of robotics control technology involves sensors. It is through sensors that a robotic system receives knowledge of its environment, to which subsequent actions of the robot can be adjusted. Sensors are used to enable a robot to adjust to variations in the position of objects to be picked up, to inspect objects, and to monitor proper operation. Among the most important types are visual, force and torque, speed and acceleration, tactile, and distance sensors. The majority of industrial robots use simple binary sensing, analogous to an on/off switch. This does not permit sophisticated feedback to the robot about how successfully an operation was performed. Lack of adequate feedback also often requires the use of guides and fixtures to constrain the motions of a robot through an operation, which implies substantial inflexibility in changing operations.

Robots may also be able to adjust to variations in object placement without the use of sensors. This is enabled by arm or end effector flexibility and is referred to as compliance. Robots with sensors may also make use of compliance.

Robots are programmed either by guiding or by off-line programming. Most industrial robots are programmed by the former method. This involves manually guiding a robot from point to point through the phases of an operation, with each point stored in the robotic control system. With off-line programming, the points of an operation are defined through computer commands. This is referred to as manipulator level off-line programming. An important area of research is the development of off-line programming that makes use of higher-level languages, in which robotic actions are defined by tasks or objectives.

Robots may be programmed to move through a specified continuous path instead of from point to point. Continuous path control is necessary for operations such as spray painting or arc welding a curved joint. Programming also requires that a robot be synchronized with the automated machine tools or other robots with which it is working. Thus robot control systems are generally interfaced with a more centralized control system.

MAJOR USES

Industrial robots perform both spot and electric arc welding. Welding guns are heavy and the speed of assembly lines requires precise movement, thus creating an ideal niche for robotics. Parts can be welded either through the movement of the robot or by keeping the robot relatively stationary and moving the part. The latter method has come into widespread use as it requires less expensive conveyors. The control system of the robot must synchronize the robot with the speed of the assembly line and with other robots working on the line. Control systems may also count the number of welds completed and derive productivity data.

Industrial robots also perform what are referred to as pick and place operations. Among the most common of these operations is loading and unloading pallets, used across a broad range of industries. This requires relatively complex programming, as the robot must sense how full a pallet is and adjust its placements or removals accordingly. Robots have been vital in pick and place operations in the casting of metals and plastics. In the die casting of metals, for instance, productivity using the same die-casting machinery has increased up to three times, the result of robots' greater speed, strength, and ability to withstand heat in parts removal operations. In 1992, CBW Automation Inc. of Colorado announced the development of the world's fastest parts-removal robot for plastics molding. Their robot moves through a four-foot stroke in under one-fifth of a second.

Assembly is one of the most demanding operations for industrial robots. A number of conditions must be met for robotic assembly to be viable, among them that the overall production system be highly coordinated and that the product be designed with robotic assembly in mind. The sophistication of the control system required implies a large initial capital outlay, which generally requires production of 100,000 to 1,000,000 units per year in order to be profitable. Robotic assembly has come to be used for production of printed circuit boards, electronic components and equipment, household appliances, and automotive subassemblies. As of 1985, assembly made up just over ten percent of all robotic applications.

Industrial robots are widely used in spray finishing operations, particularly in the automobile industry. One of the reasons these operations are cost-effective is that they minimize the need for environmental control to protect workers from fumes. Most robots are not precise enough to supplant machine tools in operations such as cutting and grinding. Robots are used, however, in machining operations such as the removal of metal burrs or template-guided drilling. Robots are also used for quality control inspection, to determine tightness of fit between two parts, for example. The use of robots in nonindustrial applications such as the cleaning of contaminated sites and the handling and analysis of hazardous materials represent important growth markets for robotics producers.

THE ROBOTICS INDUSTRY

EARLY DEVELOPMENT. The first industrial robot was developed in the mid-1950s by Joseph Engelberger (1925-), who has been referred to as the father of industrial robots. Engelberger also founded Unimation, Inc., which became the largest producer of industrial robots in the United States.

His early research involved touring Ford, Chrysler Corp., General Motors, and 20 other production plants. Engelberger observed that men performed the higher-paying jobs in which they lifted heavy objects with two hands simultaneously, while women performed tasks in which they used their hands asynchronously. Economic and technical considerations thus led Engelberger to focus on the development of a one-armed robot. Engelberger developed his first prototype in 1956, the design of which is very similar to Unimation robots produced decades later.

General Motors purchased a test model in 1959, though by 1964, Unimation had sold only 30 robots. It was not until the late 1960s that sales increased strongly and not until 1975 that the firm turned a profit. Together with number-two producer Cincinnati Milacron, Unimation accounted for 75 percent of the U.S. robotics market in 1980. Unimation Inc. became a wholly owned subsidiary of Westinghouse in 1982. By 1983, the firm had sales of $43 million.

TEPID DEMAND AND CYCLICAL SALES. Generally, there was much greater reluctance to adopt the use of robots in the United States than in places like Japan, which led the world in robot production and use. Among other apprehensions, U.S. companies balked at the heavy investments required and were sensitive to opposition from organized labor. Other times, when robots were ordered, they failed to deliver what manufacturers anticipated, due to unrealistic expectations of flawless operations and dramatic labor savings—ignoring the heavy maintenance robots required—and to the limitations of the machines themselves.

While the early 1980s saw promising growth, yielding some predictions that robotics would be a multibillion-dollar business by 1990, the U.S. robotics industry suffered a severe setback in the mid-1980s, largely the result of declining orders from the automobile industry. At the time, the auto industry still supplied over 70 percent of all U.S. robot orders. This resulted in a number of firms leaving the industry, including deep pocketed players such as General

Electric and Westinghouse, and left many of the remaining firms to merge or be acquired. The value of new orders fell from their 1984 high of $480 million for 5,800 units to a 1987 low of just 3,800 units worth $300 million.

RESURGENCE IN THE 1990s. After staging a strong recovery in the late 1980s, the industry faced another setback during the recession of the early 1990s. Orders stagnated in 1990 at $510 million based on 5,000 units industry-wide, and slumped to 4,000 units at $410 million the following year. However, following the general economic recovery, business picked back up in 1992, and by 1993 the industry received record orders for some 6,800 robots valued at $630 million. Solid orders and shipments continued throughout the remainder of the 1990s, often at double-digit growth rates, and surpassed in 1997 the billion-dollar mark for the first time. That year, companies ordered 12,149 robots worth $1.1 billion. Though orders slowed slightly in 1998, they remained strong into 1999. As of 1999, more than 92,000 robots were in operation in U.S. industrial settings.

A corollary to the industry's robust economic performance in the 1990s was that the industry was now building and marketing its products differently. Whereas earlier robots were ambitiously designed to take on giant tasks, but couldn't necessarily do so with great precision and reliability, designers increasingly focused their robots on performing more manageable tasks with greater consistency. They also made robots easier to operate and maintain. As reliability and ease of use were—and are—some of the biggest concerns companies have about robots, this helped fuel demand and improved the robotics industry's image. Robot manufacturers were also more careful not to promise more than their devices could deliver, a common complaint lodged against them during the 1980s.

Lower prices also contributed to the sales surge. Whereas in 1984 the average robot cost an estimated $82,758 (net value of orders divided by the number of units), by early 1999 the average had fallen to $76,669, not accounting for inflation. After inflation is factored in, the real reduction in prices was more than 40 percent over the 15-year period.

The robotics industry has also diversified its customer base. While automotive-related manufacturing still accounted for about half of the U.S. market in 1999, inroads were being made in non-automotive materials handling, **flexible manufacturing systems**, and service-oriented uses. Some of the other major industry sectors purchasing robots include electronics manufacturing, food and beverage production, pharmaceutical manufacturing, and the aerospace industry.

Some of the largest robotics companies operating in the United States include ABB Flexible Automation, Adept Technology, Inc., and Fanuc Robotics. As of the late 1990s, Adept Technology was the only major U.S.-based manufacturer, while ABB was part of a Swiss-based conglomerate and Fanuc, the world's largest robotics company, was based in Japan. Fanuc also had a U.S. joint venture with General Electric called GE Fanuc Automation North America.

JAPANESE TRENDS. Meanwhile, Japan has continued to dominate the world robotics arena. Prior to 1978, the largest user of industrial robots in Japan was the automobile industry, after which the electric and electronics industries became most important. Its production of industrial robots quadrupled from the mid-1980s to 1990, when it possessed over 40 percent of all industrial robots in use worldwide. By the late 1990s, annual Japanese orders for new robots still outpaced U.S. orders by a nearly four to one ratio. Unlike the United States, Japan makes extensive use of SCARA configuration robots, which offer substantial advantages in assembly work.

RECENT INNOVATIONS

Recent research and development has addressed a number of aspects of robotics. Robotic hands have been developed which offer greater dexterity and flexibility. Most visual sensors in use were designed for television and home video, and do not process information quickly for optimal performance in many robotics applications. Consequently, solid-state vision sensors came into increased use, and developments were also made with fiber optics. The use of superconducting materials offered the possibility of substantial improvements in the electric motors that drive robotic arms. Attempts were made to develop lighter robotic arms and also to increase their rigidity. Standardization of software and hardware to facilitate the centralization of control systems was also an important area of development, as was miniaturization of parts to create smaller devices.

One example of a relatively successful service robot is a series called HelpMate by Helpmate Robotics Inc., headed by industry patriarch Joseph Engelberger. The HelpMate serves as an in-house courier in hospitals, delivering reports and lab samples to various destinations throughout the building. Each unit has the building's floor plan stored in memory, and includes sensors so it doesn't run into people or other objects. In 1999 HelpMate units had been installed in approximately 70 U.S. hospitals. Other service-related areas of robotics under development include surgical devices and in-home personal-care assistants for elderly and disabled persons.

[David Kucera]

FURTHER READING:

Asimov, Isaac, and Karen Frenkel. *Robots: Machines in Man's Image.* New York: Harmony Books, 1985.

Loizos, Constance. ''Domo Arigato, Mr. Roboto.'' *Red Herring,* May 1998. Available from www.herring.com.

''Robot Orders Rocket to New Record in First Quarter.'' *Robot Times,* summer 1999.

Roush, Matt. ''Robot Industry Expands from Manufacturing.'' *Crain's Detroit Business,* 19 April 1999.

Vincent, Donald. ''The Robotics Industry: Leading the Charge to a Productive 21st Century.'' Ann Arbor, MI: Robotic Industries Association, 1999. Available from www.robotics.org.

Winter, Drew. ''The Droid Void Is Ending.'' *Ward's Auto World,* January 1994, 56.

RTC

SEE: Resolution Trust Corporation

S

S CORPORATIONS

Known formally as subchapter S corporations, a name derived from the section of the U.S. tax code dealing with them, S corporations are small business corporations specially designated by the **Internal Revenue Service** (IRS). They must meet several criteria in order to qualify.

Like all corporations, S corporations are distinct legal entities from their owners, and thus provide limited liability protection to the owners and officers during bankruptcies, lawsuits, and other claims against the company's revenue or assets. The primary advantage that an S corporation has over an ordinary C corporation is that its profits are not taxed separately, at least under federal law, from its owners' personal incomes (some states do not recognize S corporations for purposes of state corporate taxes). By contrast, net profits at C corporations are liable for the federal corporate income tax, which in 1999 ranged from 15 to 35 percent, depending on the amount of net income. Shareholder **dividends** from C corporations are also taxed as income, leading to double taxation. In exchange for the benefit of escaping the corporate income tax, S corporations are subject to relatively stringent ownership and organization standards set forth by the IRS.

QUALIFYING FOR "S" STATUS

All S corporations start as conventional C corporations, at least for a brief moment in their existence. All corporations are registered in a particular state, usually for a fee, and are governed by the laws of that state; in each additional state where they need to conduct substantive business (e.g., hold bank accounts, hire employees, execute contracts) corporations must also register, or qualify, to do business.

Once a corporation is formed under state law, it may petition the IRS for S status by filing a Form 2553: Election by a Small Business Corporation. The company must show that it meets IRS guidelines. The basic rules to qualify as an S corporation are as follows:

- It can't have more than 75 shareholders (married couples are treated as one).
- Its shareholders must all be individuals or certain kinds of trusts or nonprofit entities (other for-profit corporations generally can't be shareholders).
- It must not be a foreign (non-U.S.) company.
- It can only have one class of stock.
- Its tax year must be on a calendar-year basis unless it can show a business need to do otherwise.
- It can't be involved in certain restricted activities, including some forms of banking, insurance, and international sales.
- It must obtain at least 75 percent of its income from operations or ''active'' sources rather than passive investments, interest, and so forth, otherwise the excess income from passive sources can be taxed.

There are also restrictions on when a corporation must file in order to gain S status in an intended tax year. Generally, corporations must abide by all of these rules during the entire tenure of their S status, and if they break the rules the IRS may revoke the S privilege. Companies whose S status has terminated may requalify for it if they meet certain criteria. However, the IRS has proven rather equivocal about how strictly some of these must be observed; examples abound of cases in which the IRS ignored the breach of some S corporation rules, particularly when the breach was short-lived.

S CORPORATIONS VS. OTHER STRUCTURES

Although they are intended for small businesses, S corporations may not be the ideal choice of organization for several reasons. Most importantly, they can be substantially more complex (and in most places more expensive) to operate than partnerships or sole proprietorships. For example, accounting in corporations is usually expected to be much more rigorous than in other business structures. In addition, corporations must pay state registration and renewal fees, and in some states they are not exempt from a state corporate tax. Fulfilling such obligations adds to the cost of doing business and may require the assistance of an accountant or an attorney. As a result, small business owners may find that the protections and tax savings an S corporation provides in theory are not compelling or even practical reasons to justify their legal complexity.

The popularity of S corporations has ebbed and flowed to some degree with the vagaries of tax legislation. For example, after the sweeping 1986 tax code revisions, which established the S corporation in its present form, S status was popular because the highest tax bracket for individuals was lower than that for corporations. Thus, by passing their profits through the S corporation as personal income, high-income business owners could shave a few percentage points off their effective tax burdens. In 1993, however, another tweaking of the federal tax laws tipped the scale in the other direction: the maximum personal income tax became nearly five points higher than the maximum corporate tax. Subsequent reforms in the mid-1990s made S corporations more versatile for other purposes, such as allowing retirement plans and charitable organizations to be shareholders.

The utility of S corporations has also been affected by the rising popularity of some non-corporate, or perhaps semi-corporate, business structure alternatives, especially limited liability partnerships (LLPs) and limited liability companies (LLCs). The latter, in particular, can serve a similar tax-sheltering function to an S corporation, but LLCs aren't subject to as many restrictions. Under some circumstances both LLPs and LLCs can also be taxed as corporations. Both forms first gained widespread acceptance in the 1990s.

SEE ALSO: Corporate Ownership; Partnerships; Taxes and Taxation

FURTHER READING:

Cooke, Robert A. *How to Start Your Own (Subchapter) S Corporation.* New York: John Wiley & Sons, 1995.

Fay, Jack R. "What Form of Ownership Is Best?" *CPA Journal,* August 1998.

Jamison, Robert W. *1999 S Corporation Taxation Guide.* New York: Harcourt Brace Professional Publishing, 1998.

SAFETY

SEE: Industrial Safety

SALES CONTRACTS

A sales contract is an agreement between a buyer and seller covering the sale and delivery of goods, **securities**, and personal property other than goods or securities. In the United States domestic sales contracts are governed by the **Uniform Commercial Code** (UCC). International sales contracts fall under the **United Nations** Convention on Contracts for the International Sale of Goods (CISG), also known as the Vienna Sales Convention.

Under Article 2 of the UCC, which has been adopted by every state (except Louisiana), the District of Columbia, and the U.S. Virgin Islands, a contract for the sale of goods for more than $500 must be in writing in order to be enforceable (UCC 2-201). The sale of securities is a special case covered in Article 8 (UCC 8-319); to be enforceable a contract for the sale of securities must be in writing regardless of the amount involved. For the sale of other kinds of personal property, a minimum of $5,000 must be involved before an enforceable contract must be in writing. Otherwise, an oral agreement is enforceable as a binding contract.

Contracts that must be in writing to be enforceable are said to be within the Statute of Frauds. The Statute of Frauds dates back to 1677, when the English Parliament decreed that certain types of contracts must be in writing. The applicable parts of the UCC effectively define the types of sales contracts that must be in writing. In addition, every state has its own version of the Statute of Frauds.

Under the UCC a written sales contract should specify the parties involved, the subject matter to be sold, and any material or special terms or conditions. Some states also require that the consideration—the amount and type of payment for what is purchased—be specified. The UCC does not require a formal sales contract, though. In many cases a memorandum or collection of papers is sufficient compliance. The courts have held that a written check can be considered a written memorandum of a sales agreement. The UCC allows a written sales contract to be enforced even if it leaves out material terms and is not signed by both parties. One party, however, may not create a sales contract on its own that is binding against another party, and an enforceable contract must be signed by the defendant, or the one against whom the contract is sought to be enforced.

Although Article 2 of the UCC has not been revised since the 1950s, it was reviewed during the 1990s for possible changes to reflect changing ways of doing business. Five specific issues were addressed in the review of Article 2:

- repeal of the Statute of Frauds, which requires contracts to be in writing; over the years numerous exceptions to this rule have been adopted
- **electronic data interchange** (EDI) and the enforceability of standard form terms; where the standard forms of buyers and sellers differ, a proposed revision would default to the UCC's standard provisions, especially regarding implied **warranties** and consequential damages
- general provisions concerning the formation and modification of sales contracts were proposed
- express warranties made by advertising were addressed
- it was proposed that the ability of remote commercial buyers to recover on warranties be limited

In many cases a purchase order, pro forma invoice, or order acknowledgment may serve in place of a formal sales contract. A purchase order is issued by the buyer and sent to the seller, stating the type and amount of goods to be purchased, the price, and any other material terms such as a time limit on filling the order. A pro forma invoice is issued by the seller and sent to the buyer, often in response to a purchase order or oral agreement. In international transactions, the pro forma invoice may enable the buyer to open a line of **credit** with which to pay for the goods ordered. The pro forma invoice typically includes relevant terms and conditions that apply to the sale.

A formal order acknowledgment is useful for establishing the seller's position in case a dispute should arise. The order acknowledgment is drawn up by the seller in response to a received purchase order. It does not necessarily repeat the details of the purchase order, but it may clarify details such as delivery schedules. When a formal order acknowledgment is countersigned by the buyer, it becomes a type of sales contract.

For international transactions, the Vienna Sale Convention is binding on signatory countries, of which the United States is one. Each of the nations that has signed the convention may state up to five reservations. For example, the United States has stipulated that it shall apply to U.S. companies only when the transaction involves another signatory country. Much of the convention parallels the UCC, with these notable exceptions: (1) acceptance of an offer that includes a request for additions or modifications constitutes a counteroffer; (2) there is no provision requiring a contract be written in order to be enforceable; and (3) the period for discovering defective merchandise may be as long as two years.

Sales contracts are useful in providing for a common understanding between buyer and seller, minimizing disputes. When a dispute does occur, the sales contract can help provide for a fair settlement.

[David P. Bianco]

FURTHER READING:

Brinkman, Daren R. ''Unsecured Creditors' Rights in Sales and Secured Transactions: Is the Revised UCC 'New and Improved' or Just 'New'?'' *Business Credit,* September 1998, 34-37.

Fraser, Jill Andresky. ''Around the World in 180 Days (Collecting International Receivables).'' *Inc.,* April 1997, 107-8.

SALES FORCE

A company's sales force consists of its staff of salespeople. The role of the sales force depends to a large extent on whether a company is selling directly to consumers or to other businesses. In consumer sales, the sales force is typically concerned simply with taking and closing orders. Salespeople don't call on customers; the days of the door-to-door salesperson are long past. Salespeople don't create demand for the product, since demand for the product has already been created by **advertising** and promotion. They may provide the consumer with some product information, but individuals involved in consumer sales are often not concerned with maintaining long-term customer relationships. Examples of consumer sales forces include automobile salespersons and the sales staffs found in a variety of retail stores.

The sales force takes on a completely different role in business-to business sales. Industrial sales forces, for example, may be required to perform a variety of functions. These may include prospecting for new customers and qualifying leads, explaining who the company is and what its products can do, closing orders, negotiating prices, servicing accounts, gathering competitive and market information, and allocating products during times of shortages.

Within the business-to-business market, a distinction can be made between selling to retailers, industrial sales, and other types of business to-business sales and **marketing**. The concerns and activities of the sales force tend to vary in each type of business market. What they have in common, however, is the desire of the sales force to establish a long-term relationship with each of its customers and to provide service in a variety of ways.

In selling to retailers, for example, the sales force is not concerned with creating demand. Since consumer demand is more a function of advertising and promotion, the sales force is more concerned with obtaining shelf space in the retailer's store. The sales force may also attempt to obtain more promotion support from the retailer. The sales force relies on sophisticated marketing data to make a convincing presentation to the retailer in order to achieve its sales and marketing objectives.

The sales force may be organized around traditional geographic territories or around specific customers, markets, and products. An effective sales force consists of individuals who can relate well to decision makers and help them solve their problems. A sales manager or supervisor typically provides the sales force with guidance and discipline. Within the company the sales force may receive support in the form of specialized training, technical backup, inside sales staff, and product literature. **Direct mail** and other types of marketing efforts can be employed to provide the sales force with qualified leads.

The largest sales forces are involved in industrial selling. According to a survey published in the December 1998 issue of *Sales and Marketing Management,* however, the average company's sales force decreased by 26 percent from 166 people in 1996 to 123 in 1998. Reasons offered for the decline included an increase in **mergers** resulting in cutbacks in sales forces, more sales through technological advances such as **Internet** Web sites, and fewer customers accounting for a larger percentage of sales.

SALES FORCE AUTOMATION

Since the mid-1990s many companies have introduced sales force automation (SFA) programs. These programs provide mobile sales personnel with state of-the-art technologies, including laptop **computers** with CD-ROMs capable of making onsite product demonstrations. Some sales forces are able to use their laptop or palmtop computers for remote access to sales and other company data, **electronic mail**, and other functions. Sales forces that have adopted these technological advances are able to check order status, product information, and marketing plans quickly and efficiently from the field. Companies with successful SFA programs consider them an important factor in their sales growth.

SALES FORCE EFFICIENCY

Since the early 1970s, the cost of a single business-to-business industrial sales call has risen from less than $60 in 1971 to more than $250 at the end of the 1980s. Consequently, companies are very concerned about the efficiency of their sales force. Sales managers and supervisors can measure the efficiency of their sales force using several criteria. These include the average number of sales calls per salesperson per day, the average sales-call time per contact, the average revenue and cost per sales call, and the percentage of orders per 100 sales calls. The sales force can also be evaluated in terms of how many new customers were acquired and how many customers were lost during a specific period. The expense of a sales force can be measured by monitoring the sales-force-to-sales ratio, or sales-force cost as a percentage of total sales.

Using such criteria to evaluate the effectiveness of the sales force allows companies to make adjustments to improve its efficiency. If the sales force is calling on customers too often, for example, it may be possible to reduce the size of the sales force. If the sales force is servicing customers as well as selling to them, it may be possible to shift the service function to lower-paid personnel.

In industrial and other business-to-business sales, the sales force represents a key link between the manufacturer and the buyer. The sales force is often involved in selling technical applications and must work with several different contacts within a customer's organization. Industrial salespeople tend, on average, to be better educated than their consumer counterparts, and to be better paid. Their cost as a percentage of sales, however, is lower than in consumer sales, because industrial and business-to-business sales generally involve higher-ticket items or a larger volume of goods and services.

SALES FORCE COMPENSATION

The sales force may be compensated in one of three ways: straight salary, straight commission, or a combination of salary plus commission. From 1950 through 1990 more companies began using a combination of salary plus commission to compensate their sales forces, and fewer companies based their sales force compensation on straight commission. It appears that, as a percentage of all sales forces, the use of straight salaries remained constant. Whatever type of compensation system is used for the sales force, the important consideration is that the compensation adequately motivates the sales force to perform its best.

SEE ALSO: Sales Letter

[David P. Bianco]

FURTHER READING:

Campbell, Tricia. ''Beating Sales Force Technophobia.'' *Sales and Marketing Management,* December 1998, 68-72.

Colt, Stocktoh B., ed. *The Sales Compensation Handbook.* 2nd ed. New York: AMACOM, 1998.

Donnolo, Mark A. ''Expand Your Sales Force without Adding Headcount.'' *Marketing News,* 18 August 1997, 15-17.

Galea, Christine. ''What Makes a Sales Force Great?'' *Sales and Marketing Management,* October 1997, 70-71.

Garofalo, Gene. *Fundamentals of Sales and Marketing Management.* Paramus, NJ: Prentice Hall, 1998.

Ligos, Melinda. ''The Incredible Shrinking Sales Force.'' *Sales and Marketing Management,* December 1998, 15.

SALES FORECASTING

Sales forecasts are common and essential tools used for business planning, marketing, and general management decision making. A sales forecast is a projection of the expected customer demand for products or services at a specific company, for a specific time horizon, and with certain underlying assumptions.

A separate but related projection is the market forecast, which is an attempt to gauge the size of the entire market for a certain class of goods or services from all companies serving that market. Sales and market forecasts are often prepared using different methods and for different purposes, but sales forecasts in particular are often dependent at least somewhat on market forecasts. Although the focus of this discussion will be on sales forecasting, a brief summary of market forecasting will help provide context.

A special term in studying sales and market forecasts is the word ''potential.'' This refers to the highest possible level of purchasing, whether at the company level or at the industry or market level. In practice, full potential is almost never reached, so actual sales are typically somewhat less than potential. Hence, forecasts of potential must be distinguished from forecasts that attempt to predict sales realized.

MARKET FORECASTING

Assessing market potential involves observing and quantifying relationships among different social and economic factors that affect purchasing behaviors. Analysts at the industry level look for causal factors that, when linked together, explain changes (upward or downward) in demand for a given set of products or services. This may be done on the local level, the national level, or even the international level. The economic and social variables that are deemed most important—those that historically have shown the most influence on demand—are then incorporated into some type of formula or mathematical model that attempts to predict future purchasing activity based on expected changes in the causal factors.

The simplest example would be to consider the influence of widely observed macroeconomic indicators such as gross domestic product (GDP) and employment rates. A simplistic model of market growth might indicate that based on time-series data from the past decade the restaurant market tends to grow at one and one-tenth times the rate of GDP when the national unemployment rate is less than 7 percent, and at four-fifths of the GDP growth rate when unemployment is greater than 7 percent.

Suppose an analyst wishes to create a two-year forecast for the national restaurant business. Using published estimates from government or private sector economists, the analyst might learn that next year's GDP is expected to grow at 2.9 percent and unemployment is expected to register at 6.7 percent. The following year, however, GDP growth is expected to slow to 1.9 percent and unemployment is expected to rise to 7.6 percent. Using the simple model outlined, the forecast for next year's restaurant sales growth would be based on the first condition observed, namely that market growth is somewhat (10 percent) higher than GDP growth when unemployment is relatively low. In other words, the first year's forecast would be 1.1 × 2.9, or 3.19 percent restaurant market growth. In the second year, the second condition would come into play—market growth is slower than GDP growth—since unemployment is expected to surpass 7 percent. Thus the forecast would be 0.8 × 1.9 percent, or 1.52 percent growth in demand for restaurant services.

While this example illustrates the basic process of forecasting, serious market forecasts would of course consider many more factors than GDP and unemployment. For instance, more sophisticated models might look at the changing demographics of the customer base (size, average income, and other attributes), the rate of inflation, changes in interest rates, and changes in related markets that could affect the market under consideration. Consequently, the formulas for obtaining market forecasts are considerably more complex. But, as in this example, many market forecasts do rely on economic or demographic data from government or other sources; the forecaster often doesn't need to come up with from scratch his or her own projections for, say, GDP and population growth. Many market forecasts also rely on published indexes, ratios, and averages for various economic and social factors that have been compiled in databases or in reference books.

SALES POTENTIAL AND FORECASTING

Sales forecasting is an attempt to predict what share of the market potential identified in a market forecast a particular company expects to have. For very small companies that serve only a fraction of the total market, the company forecast may not even explicitly consider the market forecast or share, although implicitly, of course, the company's sales are subsumed under the total market size. In the other extreme, a monopoly's sales forecast is essentially the same as the market forecast.

Forecasts of different kinds are often prepared at different levels of a corporate enterprise. Managers of different stripes use forecasts for a variety of purposes, including marketing planning, resource/investment allocation, production scheduling, and labor recruitment. In some cases the uses are simply informational, but in many cases forecasts are the basis for major decisions like:

- what product lines to pursue
- how much to spend on production and in what ways
- how aggressively to advertise or promote the products
- how best to get the products to market in order to fulfill the projected demand

Yet sales forecasts are conditional in that they are only estimations and are highly interdependent with corporate strategy and actions. Some forecasts are developed before strategies and action plans are formulated; others are created to gauge the anticipated effects of an existing strategy.

A sales forecast may cause management to adjust some of its assumptions or decisions about production and marketing if the forecast indicates that (1) the current production capacity is grossly inadequate or excessive and (2) sales and marketing efforts are inconsistent with the expected outcomes. Management therefore has the opportunity to examine a series of alternate plans for changes in resource commitments (such as plant capacity, promotional programs, and market activities), changes in prices, or changes in production scheduling. Indeed, when a company is evaluating different courses of action it may develop separate forecasts for each option in order to assess the implications of each.

THE HISTORICAL PERSPECTIVE. As a starting point, management analyzes previous sales experience by product lines, territories, classes of customers, or other relevant categories. This analysis is often on a detailed level, such as on a month-by-month, quarterly, or seasonal basis, in addition to looking at overall annual trends. Such detailed views will allow management to look for seasonality in new forecasts or even to devise strategies to improve sales during slow seasons.

Management needs to consider a time line long enough to detect significant patterns in its sales history. This period is typically five to ten years. If the company's experience with a particular product class is shorter, management might also examine discernible experiences of similar companies. The longer the view, the better management is able to detect patterns that follow cycles. Patterns that repeat themselves, no matter how erratically, are considered "normal," while variations from these patterns are "deviant." Some of these deviations may have resulted from temporary or fluke conditions, such as bad weather or uncommon events. Depending on the circumstances, figures may need to be normalized to remove the influence of such factors.

MARKET POSITION. Forecasting may also consider how the company rates against its competitors in terms of market share, research and development, quality, pricing and sales financing policies, and overall public image. In addition, forecasters may evaluate the quality and size of the customer base to determine brand loyalty, response to promotions, economic viability, and credit worthiness.

PRICE INDEX. If prices for products have changed significantly over the years, changes in dollar volume of sales may not correlate well with unit sales. To adjust for such discrepancies, a price index may be developed showing the relative prices of goods for a given year versus some reference year. Perhaps the simplest case would be if the company's prices moved exactly at the rate of inflation, in which case it could use the historical tables from the Consumer Price Index or Producer Price Index, depending on what market it serves, to adjust its figures. Using this information, the company can establish more stable projections that are not unduly skewed by price fluctuations or inflation trends.

GENERAL ECONOMIC CONDITIONS AND SECULAR TRENDS. The condition of the overall economy often influences the rate of growth (or decline) for particular markets and firms. Sales forecasters may consider any number of macroeconomic trends that have been shown to correlate with company sales, including GDP and inflation. General indicators like these can be essential in interpreting a sales forecast or recent sales history, as they will show, for example, whether the company's dollar sales are rising faster than the rate of inflation or whether the company is growing more rapidly than the economy on average.

Similarly, the company may consider its performance relative to its industry, the secular trend.

While the secular trend represents the average for the industry, it may not be "normal" for a particular company. A comparison of the company's trends to the industry pattern may highlight that the company is serving a specialized market within the broader industry or that the company isn't keeping up well with its competitors. The forecast of such patterns may lead management to alter its strategies if such trends are unfavorable, or to concentrate more on a strategy that appears to be working well.

PRODUCT TRENDS. Forecasters may also analyze sales trends of individual products. This may include the use of price indexes. Such trends are important for understanding product life cycles and separating the performance of similar products (e.g., two different lines of shampoo from the same company) to evaluate strengths and weaknesses.

DEVELOPING A SALES FORECAST

Forecasting involves more uncertainties than most other management activities. For instance, while management exerts a good deal of control over expenditures, it has little ability to direct the buying habits of its customers. Thus, even while sales trends depend on the vagaries of the marketplace, management must make a reasonable estimate of what the future holds in order to plan corporate affairs effectively.

The process managers or analysts go through to create a sales forecast is similar to this:

1. Determine the purposes of the forecast (e.g., for purchasing, strategic planning, etc.).
2. Divide the company's products into homogeneous (or at least relevant) categories.
3. Determine the major factors affecting the sales of each product group and their relative importance.
4. Choose one or more forecasting methods based on the kind of data available and the sophistication needed in the forecast.
5. Gather all necessary data.
6. Analyze the data.
7. Check and cross-check any adjustments to the data (e.g., price indexing or seasonal adjustments).
8. Make assumptions regarding any effects of the various factors that can't be measured or forecast.
9. Convert deductions and assumptions into specific product and territorial forecasts and quotas.
10. Apply forecasts to company operations.
11. Periodically review performance and revise forecasts.

While forecasting is still neither effortless nor flawless, the gap between forecasts and reality has steadily narrowed over time. There are several ways that a company can improve the likelihood of creating an accurate sales forecast and using it effectively:

- using more than one forecasting technique
- abandoning or modifying a specific technique when it has proven unreliable for the company's needs
- remembering that forecasts are highly conditional
- carefully monitoring market developments for changes that contradict the underlying assumptions of the forecast
- conducting periodic reviews and making changes when necessary

OVERVIEW OF FORECASTING APPROACHES

A variety of approaches can be used to surmise the future growth of sales. Some are highly dependent on statistics and mathematical relationships, while others are more inferential or speculative. The choice of approach depends on how accurate or precise the forecast needs to be, how long of a period it's for, the availability of past or supporting data, the funding available for forecasting activities, and other considerations.

CAUSAL APPROACH. In the causal approach, forecasters identify the underlying variables that have a causal influence on future sales. For instance, new computer sales generally have a direct influence on software application sales. In the consumer software market, other causal factors might be population growth, the expansion of computer-based activities such as electronic commerce, and trends in work and school practices like working at home and computer-based education initiatives. Still other more general factors might be the growth of personal income, employment levels, patterns in international trade (new market opportunities or new competitive threats), and so forth.

To first assess the market trends, the task of the forecaster is to establish (if it has not already been reliably by others) how these factors relate to one another and to sales of software. Some will have a direct (positive) relationship with sales, while others will have an inverse or negative relationship. In statistical parlance, the forecaster is identifying a set of correlations. Upon further examination, some of these correlations will appear causal (population growth causes higher sales), while others will be indirect or coincidental (inflation growth may cause both rising interest rates and rising sales, but rising interest rates may have nothing to do with rising sales). The sum of all this information is a formula or model that, given a certain set of conditions characterizing the underlying factors, will indicate the future behavior of sales.

On the next level the forecaster must assess the company's position in the industry and how that is likely to change over the forecast period. If no change at all were expected (i.e., it retains the exact same share of the market over the period) the company's sales would grow at the exact same rate as the broader market. Since this is uncommon, however, the forecaster must surmise whether the firm's recent or intended actions—as well as those of its competitors—will result in rising or falling market share. Again, there are a variety of causal variables to be considered, such as advertising expenditures, promotional efforts, new product introductions, and technological changes, to name a few.

Eventually, through data analysis, model construction, and statistical methods, the forecaster will arrive at a causal model of company sales based on external factors and internal actions. When changes in those factors occur (or are expected to), the implications for the company's sales can be determined by recalculating the forecast using the same model but different inputs. As this description suggests, causal approaches to forecasting tend to be complex analyses of a wide array of potential influences on sales.

A **regression analysis** is a specific forecasting tool that identifies a statistical relationship between sales, the dependent variable in the analysis, and one or more influencing factors, which are termed the independent variables. When just one independent variable is considered (say, population growth), it is called a linear regression, and the results can be shown as a line graph predicting future values of sales based on changes in the independent variable. When more than one independent variable is considered, it is called a multiple regression and can't be represented with a simple line graph. Regression analysis is related to correlation analysis, where the latter is concerned with the strength of relationships between the independent and dependent variables.

Another causal model is life-cycle analysis. Here product sales growth rates are forecast based on analysts' projections of the phases of product acceptance by various segments of the market—innovators, early adapters, early majority, late majority, and laggards. Typically, this method is used to forecast new product sales. Analysts' minimum data requirements are the annual sales of the product being considered or of a similar product. It is often necessary to do market surveys to establish the cause-and-effect relationships that signal the different phases of the product life cycle.

NONCAUSAL APPROACHES. The most common noncausal approaches are time-series models, in which patterns are extrapolated from standardized historical data in order to reach a future projection. (Elaborate time series may also be used in causal models as well.) Analysts plot these patterns in order to project future sales. Because no attempt is made to identify and evaluate the underlying causes of sales patterns, the analyst implicitly assumes that the underlying causes will continue to influence future sales in roughly the same manner as in the past. Consequently, while it is easier to use and understand, this approach tends to be relatively simple and may not produce as reliable results as other methods.

One common method of forecasting based on time series is the use of moving averages. There are a number of specific methods that incorporate moving averages. All of these assume in some way that future sales will reflect an average of past performances rather than, for example, following a linear percentage increase trend. Moving average methods minimize the impact of random outcomes that could skew a forecast.

Exponential smoothing is a similar time-series technique. Rather than relying on equally weighed historical averages, however, exponential smoothing adds weight exponentially to the most recent values in the series. This assumes that the most recent figures are the best indicators of current trends and market forces, whereas older figures may represent an inaccurate or out-of-date picture of the sales trend.

Any sophisticated time-series technique also includes some provision for filtering out random noise or chance occurrences in the data that aren't part of the underlying sales trend. In a mathematical formula this takes the form of an error or noise term that is calculated into the forecast.

QUALITATIVE AND JUDGMENTAL APPROACHES. A number of approaches rely on the informed opinions of various individuals, who may consider past trends, causal factors, their personal observations, or any number of other factors to arrive at a forecast. Usually this involves asking a number of knowledgeable people from inside or outside the company what they expect will happen during the forecast period. The forecasters may be customers (intention-to-buy survey), sales staff, or outside industry experts who are familiar with the company and its competitors.

Aside from relatively informal internal surveys, perhaps the most widely known judgmental approach is the **Delphi technique**, which convenes a panel of (usually) outside experts who each come up with independent forecasts and then revise their projections until they reach a consensus position. Another important judgmental method is the **program evaluation and review technique** (PERT), in which optimistic, pessimistic, and most likely scenarios are developed (usually by one or more experts) and then weighed to produce an average expected scenario. A third general qualitative technique is called the probability assessment method (PAM), in which relevant internal staff members are asked to rate the probability of achieving a certain range or ranges of sales volume. The probabilities (given in percentages) are then translated into a cumulative probability curve that can be further analyzed to arrive at a forecast.

An intention-to-buy survey measures a target market's plans to buy a product within a given time period. Market analysts frequently conduct such surveys before introducing a new product or service. If it isn't a product they already purchase, respondents are given a neutral and reasonably detailed description of the product with the hope they will provide honest answers. When surveying the general public, care must be taken to ensure respondents don't provide unrealistically positive feedback on new product ideas, otherwise the results will be meaningless.

Such qualitative or judgmental methods are often preferred when (1) the variables influencing buying habits are changing or hard to determine, (2) enough data isn't available to support a statistical approach, (3) quantitative methods have given poor results in this forecasting situation, (4) the planning horizon is too far into the future for normal statistical methods to be useful, or (5) there is a need to consider technological breakthroughs which may only be in the early stages of development but will have impact during the forecasting period.

DIRECT VERSUS INDIRECT. When forecasters first consider the broader market and then winnow it down to the company level, it is known as the indirect approach. When they only work with company data, it is called the direct approach. While indirect obviously lends itself more to causal analysis and direct more to noncausal, in theory direct and indirect approaches can be used in both causal and noncausal models. While for many sales forecasters the direct approach is most practical, it can be a revealing exercise to go through the indirect approach, since it requires that the forecaster consider the entire market potential for a product. Through this process the forecaster—or a recipient of the forecast—may discover unmet needs or other indications that the product's sales are performing well below potential.

SEE ALSO: Business Conditions; Business Planning; Statistical Analysis for Management; Time Series Analysis

FURTHER READING:

Kress, George, and John Snyder. *Forecasting and Market Analysis Techniques: A Practical Approach.* Westport, CT: Quorum Books, 1994.

Mentzer, John T., and Carol C. Bienstock. *Sales Forecasting Management.* Thousand Oaks, CA: Sage Publications, 1997.

SALES LETTERS

The sales letter is the most important element of the standard direct mail package. It takes the place of a salesperson and provides sellers with the opportunity for personal, one-on-one communication with their prospects. In addition to their use in **direct mail**, sales letters are also used by salespeople in a variety of situations—from customer communications to internal letters written for others on the **sales force**.

A standard direct-mail package usually includes an outer envelope, a reply envelope, a brochure, and a response device in addition to the sales letter. The direct-mail letter is a sales letter and provides the opportunity to directly address the interests and concerns of the recipient. In a sense the letter replaces the salesperson in face-to-face selling. The letter typically spells out the benefits of the offer in detail. The more personal the sales letter, the more effective it generally is. To be successful the letter writer must be intimately familiar with not only the product or service and its benefits, he or she must know and understand the person to whom the letter is addressed.

A sales letter can be analyzed and discussed in terms of its components, including the letterhead and size of the letter, the salutation, the lead or opening, the body of the letter and its close, the signing of the letter, and the postscript. The look of a direct-mail sales letter is also important. Typeface selection, use of a second color, frequent indents and bullets, and other ways to highlight or emphasize certain parts of the letter play an important role in a sales letter's success.

Successful sales letters usually begin by spelling out some of the benefits of the product or service being sold. This is done in a way that captures the reader's attention. It may involve placing a lead sentence over the salutation or inside what is known as a Johnson Box, so named after 20th-century copywriter Frank Johnson who effectively used boxed messages to sell magazine subscriptions. Once the letter's lead has grabbed the reader's attention, the body of the letter follows to generate interest and motivate the reader to action. This is often accomplished by addressing the reader in a direct, personal manner and spelling out additional benefits that match the reader's known interests and needs. A successful sales letter may be as long as four pages or as short as one. There is no rule covering the length of a sales letter, only that it be long enough to tell an effective sales story.

The postscript, or P.S., is one of the most effective parts of a sales letter. Studies have shown that people who don't spend time reading the entire letter usually glance at the end of the letter and read the postscript—if there is one. Good letter writers know that the postscript is likely to be read, so they manage to include an especially attractive restatement of the offer, a key benefit, or other inducements to action in the postscript.

A ''lift letter'' is a variant of the direct-mail sales letter that is often added to a direct-mail package to ''lift'' the response rate. The lift letter often carries the message, ''Read this only if you've decided not to accept our offer,'' or something similar to grab the recipient's attention one more time.

Another variant of the direct-mail sales letter is the testimonial, or endorsement, letter. While some sales letters may incorporate testimonials into the body of the letter, in other cases it becomes desirable to include an entire letter that serves as a testimonial for the product or service being sold. Product endorsements from real people are used to provide credibility and overcome the reader's reluctance to accept **advertising** or sales copy at face value.

Outside the realm of direct mail, sales letters are used by salespeople to deal with a variety of situations. They may send sales letters to customers and prospects as a lead-in or follow-up to a telephone call or appointment, to confirm an appointment, as a letter of introduction, as a ''reminder'' to buy, and to cover a variety of other selling situations. Sales letters help salespeople build relationships with their customers. The letters are used to sell and service accounts. Customers often perceive letters as being more thoughtful than telephone calls.

Sales letters can also be used effectively to build a marketing team or sales force. Letters from the sales manager can be used to provide encouragement and inform the sales staff in a variety of ways. Sales letters are used to announce changes in territories or commissions, incentive award offers, recognition of achievement, and other business matters affecting the sales force.

[David P. Bianco]

FURTHER READING:

Lewis, Herschell Gordon. *World's Greatest Direct Mail Sales Letters.* Lincolnwood, IL: NTC/Contemporary Publishing, 1995.

SALES MANAGEMENT

Sales **management** refers to the administration of the personal selling component of an organization's **marketing** program. It includes the planning, implementation, and control of sales programs, as well as recruiting, training, motivating, and evaluating members of the sales force. The fundamental role of the sales manager is to develop and administer a selling program that effectively contributes to the achievement of the goals of the overall organization. The term ''sales manager'' may be properly applied to several members of an organization, including: marketing executives, managers of field sales forces, district and division managers, and product line sales administrators. This text emphasizes the role of managers that oversee a field sales force.

BACKGROUND

The discipline of marketing management emerged during the Industrial Revolution, when mass production resulted in the creation of large organizations, and technological advances related to transportation and communication enhanced access to geographic markets. The two developments contributed to a growing need for the management of groups of sales people in large companies.

During the 20th century, some observers have described four evolutionary stages of sales and marketing management. The first stage, which lasted until the beginning of the Great Depression, was characterized by an emphasis on engineering and production. Managers in those functional areas generally determined the company's goals and plans. They developed products and set prices with the assumption that the customers would naturally buy whatever they could get to the market. The job of the sales departments, then, was simply to facilitate the smooth flow of goods from the company to the consumer.

The maxim ''build a better mousetrap and the people will come,'' was effectively dashed by the Depression, when producers found that selling products could be much more difficult than churning them out. Sales people and managers were elevated to a new status, and their input into product planning and organizational goal setting increased. It was also during this period that ''hard sell'' tactics, which still embody the stereotype often ascribed to automobile and aluminum siding salesmen, were developed. The hard sell philosophy reflected the propensity of most organizations to focus on getting the customer to want the product that was being offered rather than delivering what the customer desired. This second evolutionary stage extended from the 1930s into the 1950s.

During the 1960s and 1970s, companies in the United States began to embrace the concept of marketing, which initiated a shift of the organizational focus from selling to customer satisfaction and more efficient advertising and promotional practices. The adoption of marketing techniques essentially involved the integration of the selling side of business into related functions, such as budgeting, inventory control, warehousing, and product development. Despite the emergence of the marketing philosophy, however, most manufacturing companies continued to emphasize the production side of their business.

Sales management at U.S. companies entered a fourth evolutionary stage during the 1980s, characterized by a marked shift from a supply-side marketing orientation to customer orientation. Several factors prompted this change. Increased foreign competition, particularly from Japan, posed a serious threat to American companies, which were comparatively inefficient and unaware of customer wants. In addition, a slowdown in U.S. market growth resulted in greater competition between domestic rivals. Finally, a change in social orientation demanded that companies focus on creating and selling products that would provide a better quality of life, rather than a higher material standard of living. This change was evidenced by the proliferation of laws protecting the environment and mandating product safety.

The result of changes during the 1980s and early 1990s was that sales and marketing specialists were forced to concentrate their efforts on determining precisely what customers wanted, and efficiently providing it. This change necessitated greater involvement by sales managers in the goal-setting and planning activities of the overall organization. This broadened scope meant that sales managers were expected to develop a more rounded body of knowledge that encompassed finance, operations, and purchasing.

At the same time, sales managers were forced to deal with other pivotal economic and social changes. Chief among socioeconomic trends of the 1980s and early 1990s was the evolution of marketing media. As the cost of the average industrial sales call rocketed from less than $100 in 1977 to more than $250 by the late 1980s, marketing and sales managers began to stress other sales tools. **Direct mail** and telephone sales became efficient **direct marketing** alternatives to face-to-face selling. They also surfaced as important media that sales managers could use to augment the efforts of their sales people in the field.

Costs have been contained somewhat in the intervening years. As of 1997, according to a survey by the trade journal *Sales & Marketing Management,* the average sales call across all industry segments and for sales agents of all levels of experience cost $113.25. Manufacturing continued to be the industry sector with the most expensive sales structure, with costs averaging $159 per call. Wholesaling was at the other end of the spectrum, averaging just $80 per call. As a percentage of total revenues, sales calls in the service industries tend to be highest, representing 13 percent on average. Sales call expenses in manufacturing, retailing, and wholesaling all averaged between 6 percent and 7 percent, according to the study.

Nonetheless, in the late 1990s sales cost cutting continued to be a priority at many companies. Among the methods increasingly used to trim selling overhead were having sales reps work out of their own homes, at least until they built up a certain amount of sales volume, and eliminating (more accurately, distributing) some of the functions of the traditional sales manager. Indeed, some companies boasted that they could operate without sales managers, as sales forces were becoming increasingly mobile and decentralized and as information technology provided the essential linkages between management and the sales force. Automation of sales-related activities was a major—and often frustrating—drive during the second half of the 1990s. This so-called sales force automation (SFA) was intended to maximize the efficiency of sales agents' work and to better coordinate sales activities with other functions in the business. However, as many as half of these software systems installed did not live up to the companies' expectations. Despite this, most in the field now see automation as a baseline requirement for nearly any sales force.

THE ROLE OF SALES MANAGEMENT

Although the role of sales management professionals is multidisciplinary, their primary responsibilities are: (1) setting goals for a sales-force; (2) planning, **budgeting**, and organizing a program to achieve those goals; (3) implementing the program; and (4) controlling and evaluating the results. Even when a sales force is already in place, the sales manager will likely view these responsibilities as an ongoing process necessary to adapt to both internal and external changes.

GOAL SETTING

To understand the role of sales managers in formulating goals, one must first comprehend their position within the organization. In fact, sales management is just one facet of a company's overall marketing strategy. A company's marketing program is represented by its marketing mix, which encompasses strategies related to products, prices, promotion, and distribution. Objectives related to promotion are achieved through three supporting functions: (1) **advertising**, which includes direct mail, radio, television, and print advertisements, among other media; (2) **sales promotion**, such as contests and coupons; and (3) personal selling, which encompasses the **sales force** manager.

The overall goals of the sales force manager are essentially mandated by the marketing mix. The mix coordinates objectives between the major components of the mix within the context of internal constraints, such as available capital and production capacity. For example, the overall corporate marketing strategy may dictate that the sales force needs to increase its share of the market by five percent over two years. It is the job of the sales force manager, then, to figure out how to achieve that directive. The sales force manager, however, may also play an important role in developing the overall marketing mix strategies that determine his objectives. For example, he may be in the best position to determine the specific needs of customers and to discern the potential of new and existing markets.

One of the most critical duties of the sales manager is to accurately estimate the potential of the company's offerings. An important distinction exists between market potential and sales potential. The former is the total expected sales of a given product or service for the entire industry in a specific market over a stated period of time. Sales potential refers to the share of a market potential that an individual company can reasonably expect to achieve. According to Irwin, a sales forecast is an estimate of sales (in dollars or product units) that an individual firm expects to make during a specified time period, in a stated market, and under a proposed marketing plan.

Estimations of sales and market potential are often used to set major organizational objectives related to production, marketing, distribution, and other corporate functions, as well as to assist the sales manager in planning and implementing his overall sales strategy. Numerous **sales forecasting** tools and techniques, many of which are quite advanced, are available to help the sales manager determine potential and make forecasts. Major external factors influencing sales and market potential include: industry conditions, such as stage of maturity; market conditions and expectations; general business and economic conditions; and the regulatory environment.

PLANNING, BUDGETING, AND ORGANIZING

After determining goals, the sales manager must develop a strategy to attain them. A very basic decision is whether to hire a sales force or to simply contract with representatives outside of the organization. The latter strategy eliminates costs associated with hiring, training, and supervising workers, and it takes advantage of sales channels that have already been established by the independent representatives. On the other hand, maintaining an internal sales force allows the manager to exert more control over the salespeople and to ensure that they are trained properly. Furthermore, establishing an internal sale force provides the opportunity to hire inexperienced representatives at a very low cost.

The type of sales force developed depends on the financial priorities and constraints of the organization. If a manager decides to hire salespeople, he needs to determine the size of the force. This determination typically entails a compromise between the number of people needed to adequately service all potential customers and the resources made available by the company. One technique sometimes used to determine size is the ''work load'' strategy, whereby the sum of existing and potential customers is multiplied by the ideal number of calls per customer. That sum is then multiplied by the preferred length of a sales call (in hours). Next, that figure is divided by the selling time available from one sales person. The final sum is theoretically the ideal sales force size. A second technique is the ''incremental'' strategy, which recognizes that the incremental increase in sales that results from each additional hire continually decreases. In other words sales people are gradually added until the cost of a new hire exceeds the benefit.

Other decisions facing a sales manager about hiring an internal sales force are what degree of experience to seek and how to balance quality and quantity. Basically, the manager can either ''make'' or ''buy'' his force. Young hires, or those whom the company ''makes,'' cost less over a long term and do not bring any bad sales habits with them that were learned in other companies. On the other hand, the initial cost associated with experienced sales people is usually lower, and experienced employees can start producing results much more quickly. Furthermore, if the manager elects to hire only the most qualified people, budgetary constraints may force him to leave some territories only partially covered, resulting in customer dissatisfaction and lost sales.

After determining the composition of the sales force, the sales manager creates a budget, or a record of planned expenses that is (usually) prepared annually. The budget helps the manager decide how much money will be spent on personal selling and how that money will be allocated within the sales force. Major budgetary items include: sales force salaries, commissions, and bonuses; travel expenses; sales materials; training; clerical services; and office rent and utilities. Many budgets are prepared by simply reviewing the previous year's budget and then making adjustments. A more advanced technique, however, is the percentage of sales method, which allocates funds based on a percentage of expected revenues. Typical percentages range from about two percent for heavy industries to as much as eight percent or more for consumer goods and computers.

After a sales force strategy has been devised and a budget has been adopted, the sales manager should ideally have the opportunity to organize, or structure, the sales force. In general, the hierarchy at larger organizations includes a national or international sales manager, regional managers, district managers, and finally the sales force. Smaller companies may omit the regional, and even the district, management levels. Still, a number of organizational considerations must be addressed. For example:

- Should the force emphasize product, geographic, or customer specialization?
- How centralized will the management be?
- How many layers of management are necessary?

The trend during the 1980s and early 1990s was toward flatter organizations, which possess fewer levels of management, and decentralized decision-making, which empowers workers to make decisions within their area of expertise.

IMPLEMENTING

After goal setting, planning, budgeting, and organizing, the sales force plan, budget, and structure must be implemented. Implementation entails activities related to staffing, designing territories, and allocating sales efforts. Staffing, the most significant of those three responsibilities, includes recruiting, training, compensating, and motivating sales people.

Before sales managers can recruit workers to fill the jobs, they must analyze each of the positions to be filled. This is often accomplished by sending an observer into the field. The observer records time spent talking to customers, traveling, attending meetings, and doing paperwork. The observer then reports the findings to the sales manager, who uses the information to draft a detailed job description. Also influencing the job description will be several factors, chiefly the characteristics of the people on which the person will be calling. It is usually important that salespeople possess characteristics similar to those of the buyer, such as age and education.

The manager may seek candidates through advertising, college recruiting, company sources, and employment agencies. Candidates are typically evaluated through personality tests, interviews, written applications, and background checks. Research has shown that the two most important personality traits that sales people can possess are empathy, which helps them relate to customers, and drive, which motivates them to satisfy personal needs for accomplishment. Other factors of import include maturity, appearance, communication skills, and technical knowledge related to the product or industry. Negative traits include fear of rejection, distaste for travel, self-consciousness, and interest in artistic or creative originality.

After recruiting a suitable sales force, the manager must determine how much and what type of training to provide. Most sales training emphasizes product, company, and industry knowledge. Only about 25 percent of the average company training program, in fact, addresses personal selling techniques. Because of the high cost, many firms try to reduce the amount of training. The average cost of training a person to sell industrial products, for example, commonly exceeds $30,000. Sales managers can achieve many benefits with competent training programs, however. For instance, research indicates that training reduces employee turnover, thereby lowering the effective cost of hiring new workers. Good training can also improve customer relations, increase employee morale, and boost sales. Common training methods include lectures, cases studies, role playing, demonstrations, on-the-job training, and self-study courses.

After the sales force is in place, the manager must devise a means of compensating individuals. The main conflict that must be addressed is that between personal and company goals. The manager wants to provide sufficient incentives for salespeople but also must meet the division's or department's goals, such as controlling costs, boosting market share, or increasing cash flow. The ideal system motivates sales people to achieve both personal and company goals. Good salespeople want to make money for themselves, however, a trait which often detracts from the firm's objectives. Most approaches to compensation utilize a combination of salary and commission or salary and bonus.

Although financial rewards are the primary means of motivating workers, most sales organizations employ other motivational techniques. Good sales managers recognize that sales people, by nature, have needs other than the basic physiological needs filled by money: they want to feel like they are part of winning team, that their jobs are secure, and that their efforts and contributions to the organization are recognized. Methods of meeting those needs include contests, vacations, and other performance based prizes in addition to self-improvement benefits such as tuition for graduate school. Another tool managers commonly use to stimulate their workers is quotas. Quotas, which can be set for factors such as the number of calls made per day, expenses consumed per month, or the number of new customers added annually, give salespeople a standard against which they can measure success.

In addition to recruiting, training, and motivating a sales force to achieve the sales manager's goals, managers at most organizations must decide how to designate sales territories and allocate the efforts of the sales team. Many organizations, such as real estate and insurance companies, do not use territories, however. Territories are geographic areas such as cities, counties, or countries assigned to individual salespeople. The advantage of establishing territories is that it improves coverage of the market, reduces wasteful overlap of sales efforts, and allows each salesperson to define personal responsibility and judge individual success.

Allocating people to different territories is an important sales management task. Typically, the top few territories produce a disproportionately high sales volume. This occurs because managers usually create smaller areas for trainees, medium-sized territories for more experienced team members, and larger areas for senior sellers. A drawback of that strategy, however, is that it becomes difficult to compare performance across territories. An alternate approach is to divide regions by existing and potential base. A number of computer programs exist to help sales managers effectively create territories according to their goals.

CONTROLLING AND EVALUATING

After setting goals, creating a plan, and setting the program into motion, the sales manager's responsibility becomes controlling and evaluating the program. During this stage, the sales manager compares the original goals and objectives with the actual accomplishments of the sales force. The performance of each individual is compared with goals or quotas, looking at elements such as expenses, sales volume, customer satisfaction, and cash flow. A common model used to evaluate individual sales people considers four key measures: the number of sales calls, the number of days worked, total sales in dollars, and the number of orders collected. The equation below can help to identify a deficiency in any of these areas:

$$\text{Sales} = \text{Days Worked} \times \frac{\text{Calls}}{\text{Days Worked}} \times \frac{\text{Orders}}{\text{Calls}} \times \frac{\text{Sales (\$)}}{\text{Orders}}$$

An important consideration for the sales manager is profitability. Indeed, simple sales figures may not reflect an accurate image of the performance of the overall sales force. The manager must dig deeper by analyzing expenses, price-cutting initiatives, and long-term contracts with customers that will impact future income. An in-depth analysis of these and related influences will help the manager to determine true performance based on profits. For use in future goal-setting and planning efforts, the manager may also evaluate sales trends by different factors, such as product line, volume, territory, and market.

After the manager analyzes and evaluates the achievements of the sales force, that information is used to make corrections to the current strategy and sales program. In other words, the sales manager returns to the initial goal-setting stage.

ENVIRONMENTS AND STRATEGIES

The goals and plans adopted by the sales manager will be greatly influenced by the industry orientation, competitive position, and market strategy of the overall organization. It is the job of sales managers, or people employed in sales-management-related jobs, to ensure that their efforts coincide with those of upper-level management.

The basic industry orientations are industrial goods, consumer durables, consumer nondurables, and services. Companies or divisions that manufacture industrial goods or sell highly technical services tend to be heavily dependent on personal selling as a marketing tool. Sales managers in those organizations characteristically focus on customer service and education, and employ and train a relatively high-level sales force. Sales managers that sell consumer durables will likely integrate the efforts of their sales force into related advertising and promotional initiatives. Sales management efforts related to consumer nondurables and consumer services will generally emphasize volume sales, a comparatively low-caliber sales force, and an emphasis on high-volume customers.

Michael Porter's well-received book *Competitive Strategy* lists three common market approaches that determine sales management strategies: low-cost supplier; differentiation; and niche. Companies that adopt a low-cost supplier strategy are usually characterized by a vigorous pursuit of efficiency and cost controls. A company that manufactures nails and screws would likely take this approach. They profit by offering a better value than their competitors, accumulating market share, and focusing on high-volume and fast inventory turn-over. Sales management efforts in this type of organization should generally stress the minimizing of expenses—by having sales people stay at budget hotels, for example—and appealing to customers on the basis of price. Sales people should be given an incentive to chase large, high-volume customers, and the sales force infrastructure should be designed to efficiently accommodate large order-taking activities.

Companies that adhere to a differentiation strategy achieve market success by offering a unique product or service. They often rely on brand loyalty or a patent protection to insulate them from competitors and, thus, are able to achieve higher-than-average profit margins. A firm that sells proprietary pharmaceuticals would likely use this method. Management initiatives in this type of environment would necessitate selling techniques that stressed benefits, rather than price. They might also entail a focus on high customer service, extensive prospecting for new buyers, and chasing customers that were minimally sensitive to price. In addition, sales managers would be more apt to seek high-caliber sellers and to spend more money on training.

Firms that pursue a niche market strategy succeed by targeting a very narrow segment of a market and then dominating that segment. The company is able to overcome competitors by aggressively protecting its niche and orienting every action and decision toward the service of its select group. A company that produced floor coverings only for extremely upscale commercial applications might select this approach.

Sales managers in this type of organization would tend to emphasize extensive employee training or the hiring of industry experts. The overall sales program would be centered around customer service and benefits other than price.

In addition to the three primary market strategies, Raymond Miles and Charles Snow claim that most companies can be grouped into one of three classifications based on their product strategy: prospector, defender, and analyzer. Each of these product strategies influences the sales management role. For example, prospector companies seek to bring new products to the market. Sales management techniques, therefore, tend to emphasize sales volume growth and market penetration through aggressive prospecting. In addition, sales people may have to devote more time to educating their customers about new products.

Defender companies usually compete in more mature industries and offer established products. This type of firm is likely to practice a low-cost producer market strategy. The sales manager's primary objective is to maintain the existing customer base, primarily through customer service and by aggressively responding to efforts by competitors to steal market share.

Finally, analyzer companies represent a mix of prospector and defender strategies. They strive to enter high-growth markets while still retaining their position in mature segments. Thus, sales management strategies must encompass elements used by both prospector and defender firms.

REGULATION

Besides markets and industries, another chief environmental influence on the sales management process is government regulation. Indeed, selling activities at companies are regulated by a multitude of state and federal laws designed to protect consumers, foster competitive markets, and discourage unfair business practices.

Chief among anti-trust provisions affecting sales managers is the Robinson-Patman Act, which prohibits companies from engaging in price or service discrimination. In other words, a firm cannot offer special incentives to large customers based solely on volume, because such practices tend to hurt smaller suppliers. Companies can give discounts to buyers, but only if those incentives are based on savings gleaned from manufacturing and distribution processes.

Similarly, the Sherman Act makes it illegal for a seller to force a buyer to purchase one product (or service) in order to get the opportunity to purchase another product, a practice referred to as a ''tying agreement.'' A long-distance telephone company, for instance, cannot necessarily require its customers to purchase its telephone equipment as a prerequisite to buying its long-distance service. The Sherman Act also regulates reciprocal dealing arrangements, whereby companies agree to buy products from each other. Reciprocal dealing is considered anticompetitive because large buyers and sellers tend to have an unfair advantage over their smaller competitors.

Also, several consumer protection regulations impact sales managers. The Fair Packaging and Labeling Act of 1966, for example, restricts deceptive labeling, and the Truth in Lending Act requires sellers to fully disclose all finance charges incorporated into consumer credit agreements. Cooling-off laws, which commonly exist at the state level, allow buyers to cancel contracts made with door-to-door sellers within a certain time frame. Additionally, the Federal Trade Commission (FTC) requires door-to-door sellers who work for companies engaged in interstate trade to clearly announce their purpose when calling on prospects.

SALES MANAGEMENT CAREERS

In many ways, sales managers are similar to other marketing managers in the organization in that they are assigned a profit center for which they are ultimately responsible and for which they are expected to oversee all activities. Naturally sales manager's jobs also differ from other marketing-related management positions. Foremost among the differences is the geographical positioning of subordinates. In order to cut sales costs, companies attempt to disperse their sales forces evenly throughout the entire selling zone. This division reduces the sales manager's ability to directly oversee their work. As a result, sales managers must spend much more of their time traveling than other managers.

Another distinguishing characteristic of sales management positions is their high exposure. Sales managers are usually on the ''front lines'' of their company's war in the competitive market. And, because of detailed weekly, or even daily, reports showing sales and profit data, their performance can be easily judged by superiors and coworkers. A corollary of the ease in measuring their performance is that their compensation plans typically differ from managers in areas such as finance or operations. Often, much of their compensation comes in the form of bonuses linked to statistics indicative of the success of the overall sales force. Based on published estimates, the typical senior sales representative in 1998 earned $68,000 a year, excluding bonuses and incentive pay, which were likely to put the figure at closer to $90,000. A typical salary for a district sales manager was $75,000, and for a regional sales manager, $80,000. Sales executives earned on average of $110,000. Importantly, online sales managers such as individuals who manage Internet sales activities for a company took in an impressive $117,000 in the middle category of earners, with top online sales managers averaging $150,000.

Despite their administrative orientation, many sales managers continue to spend much of their time selling. In fact, at least one study made during the 1970s indicated that sales managers spend about 35 percent of their time engaged in sales activities, including making important sales calls with their sales people and dealing with problem accounts. The study also revealed that about 20 percent of the managers' time, on average, was used to train people, establish performance standards, and handle other personnel matters. The remainder of the time was dedicated mostly to marketing, administrative, and financial tasks. How sales managers spend their time continues to be a subject of controversy at cost-conscious companies as they seek to maximize the value generated by all employees and managers.

POSITIONS

Sales managers commonly begin their careers as salespeople. In some instances, particularly in companies that sell products and services directly to customers, sales people may assume a management role in as little as six months. Typically, however, at least a few years of field sales experience is required to become eligible for a management position. In the case of firms that market highly technical industrial products, a competent sales person may have to work in the field for five or ten years before being promoted.

A common progression for a manager of a field sales force is district, regional, and then national sales manager. Some companies also have unit managers, who are typically placed in charge of four or five sales people. All of these territorial management positions are usually in direct authority over the sales force and generally entail the responsibilities outlined in this text. Most companies have a chief sales executive, or the equivalent thereof. Regardless of his or her title, that person is ultimately in charge of overseeing the successful operation of the entire field sales force program.

Some companies organize their sales forces by markets, products, or customer types, rather then territories. In those instances, sales force managers are commonly referred to as market sales managers or product sales managers. Furthermore, high-level field sales force managers, particularly in large organizations, may employ one or several assistant sales managers to handle budgeting, forecasting, research, and other duties. Finally, in addition to field sales force management positions, there are a number of sales management professionals who do not oversee sales people in the field. Such jobs include managers of sales training, customer service, and research departments.

SEE ALSO: Marketing; Training and Development

[Dave Mote]

FURTHER READING:

Dalrymple, Douglas J., and William L. Cron. *Sales Management: Concepts and Cases.* 6th ed. New York: John Wiley & Sons, 1997.

Keenan, William, Jr. ''Death of the Sales Manager.'' *Sales & Marketing Management,* April 1998.

Lee, Dick. ''Why Sales Automation Software Systems Fail.'' *Business Marketing,* June 1998.

Marchetti, Michele. ''Hey Buddy, Can You Spare $113.25?'' *Sales & Marketing Management,* August 1997.

Miles, Raymond and Charles C. Snow. *Organizational Strategy, Structure, and Process.* New York: McGraw-Hill, 1978.

Porter, Michael E. *Competitive Strategy.* New York: The Free Press, 1980.

Robertson, Dan H. *Sales Management: Decision Making for Improved Profitability.* 2nd ed. Upper Saddle River, NJ: Prentice Hall, 1999.

SALES PROMOTION

Sales promotion is an important component of a company's **marketing** communication strategy along with **advertising**, **public relations**, and **personal selling**. At its core, sales promotion is a marketing activity that adds to the basic value proposition behind a product (i.e., getting more for less) for a limited time in order to stimulate consumer purchasing, selling effectiveness, or the effort of the sales force. As this definition indicates, sales promotion may be directed either at end consumers or at selling intermediaries such as retailers or sales crews.

Sales promotion stems from the premise that any brand or service has an established perceived price or value, the ''regular'' price or some other reference value. Sales promotion is believed to change this accepted price-value relationship by increasing the value and/or lowering the price. Familiar examples of consumer sales promotion tools include contests and sweepstakes, branded give-away merchandise, bonus-size packaging, limited-time discounts, rebates, coupons, free trials, demonstrations, and point-accumulation systems.

Three issues clarify sales promotion. First, sales promotion ranks in importance with advertising and requires similar care in planning and strategy development. Second, three audiences can be targeted by sales promotion: consumers, resellers, and the sales force. And third, sales promotion as a competitive weapon provides an extra incentive for the target audience to purchase or support one brand over another. This last factor distinguishes sales promotion from other promotional mix tactics. For example, unplanned purchases may be directly related to one or more sales promotion offers.

In order to understand the basic role and function of sales promotion, one must differentiate between sales promotion and other components of the marketing mix. Sales promotion usually operates on a short timeline, uses a more rational appeal, returns a tangible or real value, fosters an immediate sale, and contributes highly to profitability. The idea of contribution to profitability may be confusing. It is simply the ratio between what is spent on a promotional mix compared to the direct profitability generated by that expenditure. A few exceptions to the above characteristics do exist. For example, a sweepstakes might use a very emotional appeal, while a business-to-business ad may be very rational.

THE STATE OF SALES PROMOTION

Various estimates from the mid-1990s placed annual spending on sales promotion in the United States at $30 billion a year to well over $100 billion, depending on how it is defined. In any case, there is wide consensus that sales promotion enjoyed fairly rapid growth from the 1980s through at least the mid-1990s, rising by more than 10 percent a year for much of the period. There is some evidence that growth slowed after the mid 1990s; promotional spending in the business-to-business arena was being outstripped by advertising spending as of 1997, a reversal from the trend just two years earlier. Still, the steep growth of media costs for traditional advertising has offered an ongoing incentive for marketers to use sales promotions.

Several factors contribute to the strength of sales promotion in the United States. First, consumers have accepted sales promotion as part of buying- decision criteria. Primarily, sales promotion offers consumers the opportunity to get more than they thought possible. Product sampling, for example, allows consumers to try the product without buying it. Furthermore, many people are reluctant decision makers who need some incentive to make choices. Sales promotion gives them the extra nudge they need in order to become active customers. Finally, sales promotion offers have become an integral part of the buying process, and consumers have learned to expect them.

The progression of sales promotion has been spurred by business, especially big business. Top managers and product managers have played direct roles in encouraging the recent growth of sales promotion. The product manager's goals and desires have provided the initial impetus. Product managers are challenged to differentiate their product in a meaningful way from competitors' products because buyers have many choices among brands and products offering similar satisfactions. Sales promotion techniques provide solutions to this dilemma. Heads of companies today focus increasingly on short-term results. They want sales tomorrow, not next quarter or next year. Sales promotions can provide immediate hikes in sales.

New technology, especially the computer, has also created greater acceptance of sales promotion by managers wanting to measure results. For example, scanning equipment in retail stores enables manufacturers to get rapid feedback on the results of promotions. Redemption rates for coupons or figures on sales volume can be obtained within days.

The growth in power of retailers has also boosted the use of sales promotion. Historically, the manufacturer had the power in the channel of distribution. Mass marketers utilized national advertising to get directly to consumers, creating a demand for the heavily advertised brands which stores couldn't ignore. With consolidation, retailers have gained access to sophisticated information. For example, use of computers and bar codes on packages is shifting the balance of power in their favor. Custom designed programs will help retailers to complete and increase sales in their market area. Sales promotion is an effective and satisfying response to the demand for account-specific marketing programs. Increased sales volume provided through sales promotion enhances small profit margins. Retailers also benefit from the immediate feedback of sales promotion that readily reveals unsuccessful programs.

LIMITATIONS

Although sales promotion is a competent strategy for producing quick, short-term, positive results, it is not a cure for a bad product, poor advertising, or an inferior sales team. After a consumer uses a coupon for the initial purchase of a product, the product must then take over.

Sales promotion activities may bring several negative consequences, primarily clutter from increased competitive promotions. New approaches are promptly cloned by competitors, with efforts to be more creative, more attention grabbing, or more effective in attracting the attention of consumers and the trade.

Another increasingly perceived drawback occurs with distributed manufacturers' coupons, such as those inserted in Sunday newspapers. While ideally these are offered as an incentive for new or occasional customers to try the product in hopes of making them regular buyers, research has suggested that most coupons are redeemed by individuals who would normally buy the products anyway. In effect, the manufacturers are subsidizing their existing sales, as only a relatively narrow segment of the consumer market actively uses clipped coupons from the newspapers.

To address this problem, manufacturers have found that in-store coupon devices or displays reach a wider cross-section of buyers and are more likely to entice targeted customers (in addition to the regular customers who will likely also use the coupons).

Also, consumers and resellers have learned how to milk the sales promotion game. Notably, consumers may wait to buy certain items knowing that eventually prices will be reduced. Resellers, having learned this strategy long ago, are experts at negotiating deals and manipulating competitors against one another, so that, for example, one company's product may be on sale one week and its competitor's the following week. Value-minded consumers then can regularly find an equivalent product on sale, which may increase their loyalty to the store at the cost of the manufacturers.

TECHNIQUES OF CONSUMER PROMOTIONS

Consumer sales promotions are steered toward the ultimate product users—typically individuals—especially shoppers in the local supermarket. Some of the same general techniques may be used to promote business-to business sales, although they tend to be implemented in different ways given the contrasts between the consumer and the corporate markets. In addition, trade sales promotions target resellers—wholesalers and retailers—who carry the marketer's product. Following are some of the key techniques in the storehouse of varied consumer-oriented sales promotions.

PRICE DEALS

A consumer price deal saves the buyer money when a product is purchased. The price deal hopes to encourage trial use of a new product or line extension, to recruit new buyers for a mature product, or to reinforce existing customers' continuing their purchasing, increasing their purchases, accelerating their use, or purchasing of multiple units of an existing brand. Price deals work most effectively when price is the consumer's foremost criterion or when brand loyalty is low. Four main types of consumer price deals are used: price discounts, price pack deals, refunds or **rebates**, and **coupons**.

PRICE DISCOUNTS. Buyers learn about price discounts and cents-off deals either at the point of sale or through advertising. At the point of sale, price reductions may be posted on the package or signs near the product or in storefront windows. Ads that notify consumers of upcoming discounts includes fliers, newspaper and television ads, and other media. Price discounts are especially common in the food industry, where local supermarkets run weekly specials.

Price discounts may be initiated by the manufacturer, the retailer, or the distributor. For instance, a manufacturer may ''pre-price'' a product and then convince the retailer to participate in this short term discount through extra incentives. Effectiveness of national price reduction strategies requires the support of all distributors. When such support is lacking, consumers may find that the manufacturer's price is covered by the retailer's price, bearing witness to the power of retailers.

Existing customers perceive discounts as rewards and often then buy in larger quantities. Price discounts alone, however, usually don't induce first time buyers. Other appeals must be available, such as mass media ad exposure or product sampling.

PRICE PACK DEALS. A price pack deal may be either a bonus pack or a banded pack. When a bonus pack is offered, an extra amount of the product is free when the product is bought at the regular price. This technique is routinely used for cleaning products, food, and health and beauty aids to introduce a new or larger size. A bonus pack rewards present users but may have little appeal to users of competitive brands. It is also a way to ''load'' customers up with the product.

When two or more units of a product are sold at a reduction of the regular single-unit price, a banded pack offer is being made. Sometimes the products are physically banded together, such as in toothbrush and toothpaste offers. More often, the products are simply offered in a two-for, three for, or ten-for format. In other cases, a smaller unit of the product may be attached to one of the regular size.

REFUNDS AND REBATES. A refund or rebate promotion is an offer by a marketer to return a certain amount of money when the product is purchased alone or in combination with other products. Refunds aim to increase the quantity or frequency of purchase, to encourage customers to load up. This dampens competition by temporarily taking consumers out of the market, stimulates purchase of postponable goods such as major appliances, and creates on-shelf excitement or encourages special displays. Consumers seem to view refunds and rebates as a reward for purchase. They appear to build brand loyalty rather than diminish it.

COUPONS. Coupons are legal certificates offered by manufacturers and retailers. They grant specified savings on selected products when presented for redemption at the point of purchase. Manufacturers sustain the cost of advertising and distributing their coupons, redeeming their face values, and paying retailers a handling fee. Retailers who offer double or triple the amount of the coupon shoulder the extra cost. Retailers who offer their own coupons incur the total cost, including paying the face value. Retail coupons are equivalent to a cents-off deal. In 1859, Grape-Nuts cereal created this promotional technique by offering a $.01 coupon.

Manufacturers disseminate coupons in many ways. They may direct deliver by mailing, dropping door to door, or delivering to a central location such as a shopping mall. They may distribute them through the media—magazines, newspapers, Sunday supplements, or freestanding inserts (FSI) in newspapers. They may insert a coupon into a package, attach it to, or print it on a package. Coupons may also be distributed by a retailer who uses them to generate store traffic or to tie in with a manufacturer's promotional tactic. Retailer-sponsored coupons are typically distributed through print advertising or at the point of sale. Sometimes, specialty retailers such as ice cream or electronics stores or newly opened retailers will distribute coupons door to door or through **direct mail**.

CONTESTS AND SWEEPSTAKES

Historically, a great deal of confusion about the terms contests and sweepstakes has existed. Simply, a contest requires the entrant, in order to be deemed a winner, to perform a task (for example, draw a picture, write a poem) that is then judged. This is termed a contest of skill. On the other hand, a sweepstakes is a random drawing or chance contest which may or may not have a requirement such as buying a ticket or purchasing a product. A contest requires a judging process; a sweepstakes does not.

The use of sweepstakes has grown dramatically in recent decades, thanks largely to changes in the legal distinctions that determine what is and is not a lottery. A lottery is a promotion that involves the awarding of a prize on the basis of chance with a consideration required for entry. Before these changes, being associated with a lottery carried negative stereotypes of gamblers or organized crime. In a sales promotion, the consideration is the box top or other token asked for by the advertiser. For many years, advertisers employed contests, thus eliminating the element of chance and removing the lottery stigma. The familiar "25 words or less" contest and many other similar devices were common. The liberalization of legal interpretations, including the ability to ask for a sales receipt as proof of purchase, made sweepstakes feasible.

Besides legal changes, concern for costs favored a switch to sweepstakes; in some cases sweepstakes can be cheaper to run than contests. In addition, participation in contests is very low compared to that of sweepstakes. Contests require participants to compete for a prize or prizes based on some sort of skill or ability. Sweepstakes, on the other hand, require only that participants submit their names for a drawing or another type of chance selection. Although the figures are rough, an estimated $87 million was spent on contests and sweepstakes in 1977, and $175 million in 1989.

Nonetheless, according to one estimate fewer than 20 percent of all households have ever entered a contest or sweepstakes. Even worse, some consumers feel conned when sweepstakes make aggressive or overly ambitious claims, such as that a particular individual is very close to winning. In the late 1990s some of the best-known U.S. sweepstakes such as American Family and Publishers Clearinghouse, firms that market magazine subscriptions alongside their much-touted sweepstakes, were under scrutiny by a number of state attorneys general and federal legislators, raising the possibility that new federal legislation would place limits on what sweepstakes could claim and in what manner.

SPECIAL EVENTS

By some estimates companies around the world spent over $15 billion a year as of 1997 to link their products and corporate identities with everything from jazz festivals to golf tournaments to stock car races. In fact, a number of large corporations have special divisions or departments that handle nothing but special events sponsorships. One of the world's largest agencies, Saatchi & Saatchi DFS Compton, has a group called HMG Sports that manages sports events, including the Olympics, a ski tour for Sanka and Post Cereals, bass-fishing contest for Hardee's, and a worldwide yacht-racing event for Beefeater's Gin.

Several good reasons explain why so many marketers have jumped on the special events bandwagon. First, events tend to attract a homogeneous audience very appreciative of the sponsors. Therefore, if a product fits with the event in terms of the expected stereotypical homogeneity of the audience, the impact of the sales promotion dollars will be quite high. To illustrate, Lalique Crystal should not sponsor a tractor pull, but Marlboro should. Second, events sponsorship may build support from trade and from employees. Those employees who manage the event may receive acknowledgment and even awards. Little is more appealing to the president of Kemper Insurance than presenting a $300,000 check to the winner of the Kemper Open on national television. Finally, compared to producing a series of ads, event management is simple. Many elements of events are prepackaged. For example, a firm can use the same group of people to manage many events. It can use booths, displays, premiums, and ads repeatedly by simply changing names, places, and dates.

PREMIUMS

A premium is tangible compensation, an incentive, given for rendering a particular deed, usually buying a product. The premium may be free, or, if not, the cost is well below the usual price. Getting a bonus amount of the product is a premium, as is receiving the prize in a cereal box, a free glass with a purchase of detergent, or a free atlas with a purchase of insurance.

Incentives given free at the time of a purchase are called direct premiums. With such bonuses there is no confusion about costs, returning coupons or box tops, clipping weight circles or bar codes, or saving proofs. Plus there is instant gratification.

Four variants of direct premium programs may be identified. First, the simple direct premium provides an incentive given separately as a product is purchased. For instance, when a shopper pays for a new coat, she learns it has a direct premium—a hanging travel bag. Second, in-packs may be enclosed with a package at the factory. A snack food company, for example, may include a serving tin inside its holiday package. On-packs are another type of factory-added packaging that lies outside the package, well attached by a plastic strip, wrapper, or other apparatus. Free dental floss attached to toothpaste is an example. Fourth, container premiums reverse the presentation of the in-pack by placing the product inside the premium such as fancy liquor decanters which often hold the goods at Christmas.

Other types of direct premium are traffic builders, door-openers, and referral premiums. The traffic-builder premium is an incentive—such as a gift of a small garden tool—to lure a prospective buyer to a store. A door-opener premium is directed to customers at home or business people in their offices. Door-opening favors are a staple device in the direct-sales field. The use of this premium type may create a subtle entry during house-to-house canvassing or a clincher when telephoning for an appointment. Door-openers serve similar functions in many other industries. For example, an electronics manufacturer offers free software to an office manager who agrees to an on-site demonstration. The final category of premiums is the referral provided by the purchaser. Sales leads from satisfied customers are awarded to sellers along with rewards for their assistance.

Mail premiums, unlike direct premiums, require the customer to perform some act in order to obtain a premium through return mail. The self-liquidator is the basic type of mail premium. It was created during the Great Depression of the 1930s, a time of enforced economy. Savings counted to the penny were vital to the ordinary consumer. Since promotion budgets were usually tight, the premium which cost the advertiser nothing was most appealing. The self-liquidator fit the bill. Self-liquidating meant the price the customer paid for the premium was the same as the cost paid by the advertiser. That is, the costs canceled themselves. A self-liquidating premium may be available in exchange for one or more proofs-of-purchase and a payment or charge covering the cost of the item plus handling, mailing, packaging, and taxes, if any. The premium represents a bargain because the customer cannot readily buy the item for the same amount.

CONTINUITY PROGRAMS

Continuity programs retain brand users over a long period by offering ongoing motivations; in this sense, long-term continuity programs differ somewhat from most other forms of sales promotions since they are relatively permanent. Self-liquidating premiums are one-time opportunities, whereas continuity programs demand that consumers keep saving something in order to get the premium in the future. Trading stamps, popularized in the 1950s and 1960s, such as S&H and Gold Bond, are prime examples. The bonus was usually one stamp for every dime spent at a participating store. The stamp company provided redemption centers where the stamps were traded for merchandise. A catalog listing the quantity of stamps required for each item was available at the participating store.

Today, airlines' frequent-flyer clubs, hotels' frequent-traveler plans, as well as bonus-paying credit card programs have replaced trading stamps continuity programs. Looking back, it seems that when competing brands have reached parity, continuity programs have provided the discrimination factor among those competitors. Continuity programs have also opposed a new threatening competitor by rewarding long-standing customers for their continuing loyalty. A continuity program is all about sustaining brand loyalty through continuous reward. Retail-driven frequent-shopper plans focus on core customers to solidify store loyalty; manufacturer sponsored programs usually encourage product loading and repeat purchase from stores.

SAMPLING

A sign of a successful marketer is getting the product into the hands of the consumer. Sometimes, particularly when a product is new or is not a market leader, an effective strategy involves giving a sample product to the consumer either free or for a small fee. The first rule is to use sampling only when a product can virtually sell itself. Thus, the product must have benefits or features obvious to the consumer. Also, the consumer must be given enough of the product to enable an accurate judging of its value. Trial sizes of a product dictate how much will be received.

There are several means of disseminating samples to consumers. The most popular has been through the mail. Increases in postage costs and packaging and bundling requirements, however, have made this method less attractive. An alternative is door-to-door distribution, particularly when the items are bulky and/or when reputable distribution organizations exist. The product may simply be hung on the doorknob or delivered face to face. This method permits selective sampling of neighborhoods, dwellings, or even people.

Another method is distributing samples in conjunction with advertising. An ad may include a coupon that the consumer can mail in for the product, or an address or phone number for ordering may be mentioned in the body of an ad. Direct sampling is achieved through prime media using scratch 'n'-sniff cards and slim foil pouches.

Products can also be sampled directly through the retailer who sets up a display unit near the product or hires a person to give the product to consumers as they pass by. This technique may build goodwill for the retailer and be effective in reaching the right consumers. Some retailers resent the inconvenience and require high payments for their cooperation.

The last form of distribution deals with specialty types of sampling. For instance, some companies specialize in packing samples together for delivery to a homogeneous consumer group such as newlyweds, new parents, students, or tourists. Such packages may be delivered at hospitals, hotels, or dormitories.

TRADE PROMOTIONS

A trade sales promotion is pointed toward resellers who distribute products to ultimate consumers. The term "trade" traditionally refers to wholesalers and retailers who handle or distribute marketers' products. Other terms for wholesalers and retailers include "resellers" and "dealers."

Commonly, a senior marketing officer or product manager is responsible for planning a trade promotion. Decisions about the nature of the deal and its timing are made jointly by the marketing officer, sales manager, and campaign manager. Because such deals have direct bearing on the pricing strategy and resulting profitability, they may require clearance by top management as well.

The objectives of sales promotions aimed at the trade are different from those directed to consumers. Trade sales promotions hope to accomplish four overall goals:

1. Develop in-store merchandising support or other trade support. Strong retail support at the store level is the key to closing the loop between the customer and the sale.
2. Control inventory. Sales promotions are used to increase or deplete inventory levels and to eliminate seasonal peaks and valleys.
3. Expand or improve distribution. Sales promotions can open up new areas or classes.
4. Motivate channel members. Sales promotions can generate excitement about the product among those responsible for selling it.

TYPES OF TRADE SALES PROMOTIONS

POP DISPLAYS. Manufacturers provide point-of-purchase (POP) display units free to retailers in order to promote a particular brand or group of products. The forms of POP displays include special racks, display cartons, banners, signs, price cards, and mechanical product dispensers. Probably the most effective way to ensure that a reseller will use a POP display is to design it to generate sales for the retailer.

High product visibility is the basic goal of POP displays. In industries such as the grocery field where a shopper spends about three-tenths of a second viewing a product, anything increasing product visibility is valuable. Beyond getting attention for a product, POP displays also provide or remind about important information such as the product name, appearance of the product, and sizes. Consumers may have seen or heard some of the information in ads before entering the store. The theme of the POP should be coordinated with the theme used in ads and by salespeople.

SALES CONTESTS. For salespeople, sales contests can be an effective motivation. Typically, a prize is awarded to the organization or person who exceeds a quota by the largest percentage. For example, Cepacol Mouthwash offered supermarket managers cash prizes matched to the percentages by which they exceeded the sales quota, plus a vacation to Bermuda for the manager who achieved the highest percentage. Often such programs must be customized for particular reseller groups.

TRADE SHOWS. Thousands of manufacturers display their wares and take orders at trade shows. In the United States companies were spending some $13 billion each year on trade shows as of the late 1990s. For many companies, maximum planning effort and much of the marketing budget are directed at the trade show. Success for an entire year may hinge on how well a company performs there.

Trade shows provide unique opportunities. First, trade shows provide a major opportunity to write orders for products. Second, they are a chance to demonstrate products, provide information, answer questions, and be compared directly with competitors. Since typically at least several direct competitors will be pitching their products to potential customers under the same roof, buyers have the opportunity to quickly judge quality, features, prices, and technology at these events. Similarly, such events also provide sellers with a chance to size up the competition and fortify their **competitive intelligence**.

SALES MEETINGS. Related to trade shows but less elaborate are sales meetings sponsored by manufacturers or wholesalers. Whereas trade shows are open to potential customers, sales meetings are targeted to the company sales force and/or independent sales agents. These meetings are usually conducted regionally and directed by sales managers and their field force. Sometimes a major marketing officer from corporate headquarters directs the proceedings. The purposes of sales meetings vary. The meetings may occur just prior to the buying season and are used to motivate sales agents, to explain the product or the promotional campaign, or simply to answer questions.

PUSH MONEY. An extra payment given to salespeople for meeting a specified sales goal is called push money; it is also known as spiffs or PM. For example, a manufacturer of refrigerators might pay a $30 bonus for sales of model A, a $25 bonus for model B, and a $20 bonus for model C between March 1 and September 1. At the end of that period, the salesperson would send evidence of these sales to the manufacturer and receive a check in return. Although push money has a negative image since it hints of bribery, many manufacturers offer it.

DEAL LOADERS. A deal loader is a premium given by a manufacturer to a retailer for ordering a certain quantity of product. Two types of deal loaders are most typical. The first is a buying loader which typically is a gift given for making a specified order size. The second is a display loader which means the display is given to the retailer after the campaign. For instance, General Electric may have a display containing appliances as part of a special program. When the program is over, the retailer receives all the appliances on the display if a specified order size was achieved. Trade deals are often special price concessions superseding, for a limited time, the normal purchasing discounts given to the trade. Trade deals include a group of tactics having a common theme—to encourage sellers to specially promote a product. The attention may be generated by special displays, purchase of larger-than-usual amounts, superior in-store locations, or greater advertising effort. In exchange, retailers may receive special allowances, discounts, goods, or money.

TRADE DEALS. Money spent on trade deals is considerable. In many industries, trade deals are the primary expectation for retail support. There are two main types of trade deals: buying allowances and advertising/display allowances.

A buying allowance is a bonus paid by a manufacturer to a reseller when a certain amount of product is purchased during a specific time. All the reseller has to do is meet the criteria of the deal. The payment may be a check or a reduction on the face value of an invoice. For example, a reseller who purchases ten to 15 cases receives a buying allowance of $6.00 off per case; a purchase of 16 to 20 cases would result in $6.75 off per case, and so forth.

In order to enjoy a buying allowance, some retailers engage in forward buying, a practice very common in grocery retailing. In essence, more merchandise than needed during the deal period is ordered. The extra merchandise is stored to be sold later at regular prices. The savings gained through the buying allowance must be greater than the cost of warehousing and transporting the extra merchandise.

The count and recount technique is an approach used in the buying allowance strategy. It involves a certain amount of money for each unit moved out of the wholesaler's or retailer's warehouse during a specified period.

A buy-back allowance is another type of buying allowance. It immediately follows a previous trade deal and offers a specified bonus for new purchases of the product related to the quantity of purchases from the first deal. The purpose is to motivate repurchase immediately after the first trade deal once the product has depleted warehouse stock.

The slotting allowance is the most controversial form of buying allowance. Slotting allowances are fees retailers charge manufacturers for each space or slot on the shelf or warehouse that new products will occupy. The controversy stems from the fact that in many instances this allowance amounts to little more than paying a bribe to the retailer.

The final type of buying allowance is a free goods allowance. The manufacturer offers a certain amount of product to wholesalers or retailers at no cost if they purchase a stated amount of the same or a different product. The bonus is in the form of free merchandise instead of money. For example, a manufacturer might offer a retailer one free case of merchandise for every 20 purchased.

An advertising allowance is a common method exercised primarily for consumer products. The manufacturer pays the wholesaler or retailer a dividend for advertising the manufacturer's product. The money can only be used to purchase advertising. Controlling this scheme may be difficult. Some resellers may view the advertising allowance as a type of personal bonus and engage in devious behavior such as billing the manufacturer at the much higher national rate rather than at a lower local rate. Therefore, many manufacturers require some verification.

A display allowance is the final form of promotional allowance. Some manufacturers pay retailers to select their display from the many available every week. The payment can be in the form of cash or goods. Retailers must furnish written certification of compliance with the terms of the contract before they are paid. Retailers tend to select displays that are easy to assemble and yield high volume and profits.

SUMMARY

Sales promotion techniques are distinct from most other forms of marketing in that they directly link the strategy and execution of a marketing campaign. They are geared toward creating an immediate boost in sales volume in response to a substantive offer in the promotion (discount, premium, etc.). As opposed to advertising to build brand image or name recognition, sales promotion is nearly always tied directly to the act of buying the product or service in question. As such, sales promotion is considered an efficient and effective vehicle for marketing communications. For consumers, sales promotion provides a direct and often rational motivation to purchase the product or service being promoted.

Given the many forms sales promotions may take, marketers must plan carefully which approach is best for their intended audience and the intended result of the campaign. In some cases this will be guided by precedence in particular industries; for example, soft-drink makers tend to rely on sweepstakes and continuity programs (often fostering accumulation in order to obtain merchandise) rather than bonus sizing or free samples. In this case, odd-sized beverage containers may present logistical troubles, and for established soft drinks, presumably most potential customers already know how they taste. As with any marketing communication, in sales promotions companies must be careful not to violate their brand image with the promotion. A classic example is with luxury or status products. In these categories discounting and even sweepstakes may send mixed messages to customers, as the assumption is usually that being able and willing to pay the full price is an intrinsic component of buying a status product. If the company violates its luxury brand by "cheapening" it (symbolically or economically), the promotion may alienate the established client base. Instead, the luxury marketer may wish to offer as a premium another luxury item or establish a continuity program.

SEE ALSO: Brands and Brand Names; Marketing; Merchandising

[John Burnett]

FURTHER READING:

Blattberg, Robert C., and Scott Neslin. *Sales Promotion: Concepts, Methods, Strategies.* New York: Simon & Schuster, 1995.

Bunish, Christine. "Sales: Expanded Use of Collateral Material, Catalogs Boosts Sales Promotion." *Business Marketing,* 1 May 1999.

LaRonca, Frank. "Dismantling the Wall Between Strategy, Execution." *Brandweek,* 16 December 1996.

Schultx, Don E., William A. Robinson, and Lisa A. Petrison. *Sales Promotion Essentials.* 3rd ed. Lincolnwood, IL: NTC Business Books, 1998.

Trivedi, Elizabeth, and Gardener Minakshi. "A Communications Framework to Evaluate Sales Promotion Strategies." *Journal of Advertising Research,* May-June 1998.

SALES REPRESENTATIVES

SEE: Manufacturers' Representatives; Sales Force

SALES TAX

A sales tax is a tax that is levied on the sales of goods and, in some cases, services. Sales taxes apply to transactions and are based on expenditures. Depending on what types of exemptions are allowed, businesses as well as individuals pay sales taxes. The retail sales tax and the **value-added tax** are the two most common types of sales tax that are applied to a broad range of goods. The **excise tax** is a type of sales tax that is applied to a specific commodity or type of goods, such as cigarettes, gasoline, and alcoholic beverages.

Since World War II sales and excise taxes have become a major source of revenue for state and local governments. In the United States 45 states and the District of Columbia have a general sales tax. Mississippi became the first state to apply a general sales tax in 1930. During the 1930s 24 states adopted a sales tax, followed by 6 states in the 1940s, 5 states in the 1950s, and 11 states in the 1960s. Currently Alaska, Delaware, Montana, New Hampshire, and Oregon do not have a state sales tax. In addition, 31 states permit local governments to levy their own sales tax.

In the United States the general sales tax is strictly the function of state and local governments. The United States is the only developed nation that does not levy some type of federal general sales tax. A national sales tax usually takes the form of a value-added tax (VAT). VATs are common in Western Europe, Canada, and other developed countries. A VAT is assessed on the value added at every stage of production and distribution. At each stage the seller pays a tax on the value added, or the difference between the seller's cost and the selling price. Then, the purchaser applies for a credit on that portion of the VAT that has already been paid by the seller. At the retail level, the different VATs that have been paid along the way are incorporated into the selling price to the consumer. The net result is that all of the businesses involved in production and distribution receive credits for the VAT they have paid, and the cost of the VAT is passed along to the consumer.

While the VAT is a multistage tax, the general sales tax that is collected at the retail level is a single-stage tax. The sales tax is usually an ad valorem, or flat-rate, tax that is based on the price of the goods or services being taxed. A VAT is also usually an ad valorem tax. On the other hand, excise taxes are usually assessed on a per unit basis (e.g., per gallon of gasoline or per package of cigarettes).

The tax base for sales tax was originally confined to merchandise or tangible goods. More recently, sales tax has been applied to services as well. One reason for adding services to the sales tax base is that services are accounting for a greater portion of the U.S. economy each year. The size of a state's sales tax base is further affected by any exemptions that have been granted. Sales of goods that will be resold are usually exempt from sales tax. States that have adopted a component part rule exempt ingredients and component parts of products that are manufactured for sale. A direct-use rule extends the sales tax exemption to the sales of machinery, equipment, fuels, lubricants, and similar items used directly in industrial or agricultural production.

Another area that may be exempt from sales tax in some jurisdictions is that of necessities. More than half of all states with a sales tax exempt prescription drugs, for example. Many states do not charge sales tax on food unless it is purchased in a restaurant or has already been prepared as a meal for carry-out. For every exemption granted, a state or local government loses a certain amount of revenue. In addition, a long list of exemptions may make it difficult for the state to administer the tax and for retailers to properly collect it.

Exemptions of specific categories of goods and services from the sales tax are often made in an attempt to make the sales tax more equitable. It is generally recognized that a sales tax is regressive. That is, individuals and families with lower incomes pay a greater proportion of their income for sales taxes than people with higher incomes. By exempting food and other necessities from the sales tax, it is argued, lower-income families are relieved from part of their tax burden.

Businesses as well as individuals pay sales taxes. To date there has been no attempt to exclude interbusiness transactions from sales taxes. To attempt to do so would greatly complicate the administration of the tax. While businesses in states that have adopted a component-part rule or direct-use rule may enjoy exemptions, and goods purchased for resale are also usually exempt, nevertheless businesses and individuals alike must pay the same sales tax on the goods and services they purchase.

SALES TAX AND THE INTERNET

Under the Internet Tax Freedom Act (ITFA) passed in 1998, Internet transactions are free from any new federal, state, and local taxes for a period of three years. With the rise of **electronic commerce**, state governments had been looking at sales taxes on **Internet** transactions as a possible new source of revenue. When Congress passed the ITFA, which was opposed by the National Conference of State Legislatures, it prevented states from collecting sales tax on Internet transactions for three years. In addition, under the U.S. Supreme Court's 1992 decision in *Quill Corp. v. North Dakota,* states are not allowed to collect sales tax on electronic purchases from companies that do not reside in the state.

[David P. Bianco]

FURTHER READING:

Fox, William F., and Matthew N. Murray. ''The Sales Tax and Electronic Commerce: So What's New?'' *National Tax Journal,* September 1997, 573-92.

Hamilton, Amy. ''Nation's State Lawmakers Delve into Internet Taxation Issues.'' *Tax Notes,* 18 August 1997, 888-90.

Houghton, Kendall L., and Jeffrey A. Friedman. ''Lost in (Cyber)space?'' *Tax Notes,* 15 September 1997, 1483-85.

Lukas, Aaron. ''Don't Bash Internet Tax Freedom.'' *Nation's Cities Weekly,* 15 February 1999, 4.

''Sales Tax Revenue.'' *Governing,* January 1999, S14.

Sheppard, Doug. ''Quill Nexus Protection May Not Last Forever.'' *Tax Notes,* 26 October 1998, 422-23.

SALVAGE VALUE

All assets have a salvage value, which is the estimated value each asset will have after it is no longer going to be used in the operation of a business. Also known as the residual value or scrap value, the salvage value may be zero or a positive amount. An asset's salvage value is arrived at based on estimates of what it could be sold for or, more likely, a standard figure.

The salvage value of an asset is used in **accounting** to determine its net cost, which is its acquisition, or historical, cost minus its salvage value, if any. An asset's net cost is used as the basis for most **depreciation** methods, except the double-declining balance method. For each accounting period, a percentage of the net cost of the company's assets is used to calculate depreciation expense. For example, if an asset has a useful life of five years, the annual depreciation expense using the straight-line method would be 20 percent of its net cost. Some accelerated methods of calculating depreciation are also based on the net cost of assets.

On the other hand, the double-declining balance method is based on the historical cost of an asset. For each accounting period, a rate double that of the straight-line method is applied to the historical cost of the asset minus any accumulated depreciation. Thus, the salvage value of the asset has no effect on depreciation when the double-declining balance method is used.

The salvage value is necessarily an estimate of an asset's value after it has been used over a period of time. A common method of estimating an asset's salvage value is to estimate how much the asset could be sold for. Its salvage value in this case would be based on its estimated market value after it had been in use for a certain length of time. Since different owners might estimate different market values for an asset, standard values that have achieved industry acceptance are often used for salvage values. The use of standard values in certain situations eliminates discrepancies that may arise from individual estimates.

It is clear that the amount of wear and tear on an asset can significantly affect its salvage value. In other words, it is not simply the length of time an asset is in use that affects its potential resale value. The way an asset has been operated, used, and otherwise maintained during its useful life can have a real effect on its future market value. Such considerations may affect a company or individual's decision whether to lease or buy an asset. In the case of a decision whether to lease or purchase a new car, for example, the dealer's estimate of the market value of the car at the end of the lease period affects the amount of the monthly lease payments. An individual may decide it is better financially to purchase a car than lease it if he or she believes it will have a higher resale value than is assigned by the dealer. The individual may calculate that at the end of the lease period, the car would be worth more than the resale value assigned by the car dealer, especially if he or she plans to take good care of it and generally does not drive a lot of miles. In that case a higher resale value should result in lower lease payments, and if the dealer will not lower the lease payments the individual would be better off financially to purchase the car and then resell it in the future for more than the dealer's resale value.

[David P. Bianco]

FURTHER READING:

Anderson, Hershal, et al. *Financial Accounting and Reporting.* 4th ed. Medford, NJ: Malibu Publishing, 1995.

Anthony, Robert N., et al. *A Review of Essentials of Accounting.* 7th ed. Upper Saddle River, NJ: Prentice-Hall, 1999.

Diamond, Michael A. *Financial Accounting.* 4th ed. Cincinnati: South-Western Publishing, 1995.

Eskew, Robert K., and Daniel L. Jensen. *Financial Accounting.* 5th ed. New York: McGraw-Hill, 1995.

Solomon, Lanny M., Larry M. Walther, and Richard J. Vargo. *Accounting: The Foundation for Business Success.* 5th ed. South-Western, 1996.

SANCTIONS

Sanctions involve the deliberate withdrawal, or threat of withdrawal, of customary trade or financial assistance by one or more countries against another country. Also known as embargoes, economic sanctions refer to measures taken by one or more nations against another country to halt trade with the target country. Sanctions may be imposed on **exports** or **imports** of specific products, financial assistance, and specific methods of transportation. When a government imposes a sanction, businesses that violate the sanction are subject to legal penalties.

There are a variety of political and economic reasons for imposing sanctions, or embargoes, against other countries. Under international law, the **United Nations** may impose economic sanctions on a nation that is deemed to be a threat to international peace and security. When the United Nations imposes an embargo or sanction, as it has done against such countries as Southern Rhodesia, South Africa, and the former Yugoslavia, member nations are requested to stop trading with the specified country. The embargo or sanction may cover all trade, or it may be limited to specific goods, such as the arms embargo that was in effect against South Africa.

Under the **General Agreement on Tariffs and Trade** (GATT), economic sanctions can be imposed by the **World Trade Organization** (WTO). GATT members could request that sanctions be imposed on countries they felt were obstructing trade. It remained to be determined how such powers would be used to affect a country's nontariff barriers. For example, the United States was concerned that such powers to impose sanctions could affect its food labeling and pollution standards laws, for example, if they were regarded by other nations as obstructing international trade.

Outside of the United Nations and the WTO, sanctions may be imposed unilaterally by a single country, as the United States did against Nicaragua in the 1980s, or multilaterally by a group of countries, as the Arab States have done against Israel. Imposing economic sanctions puts economic pressure on a country to change its political or economic policies. Unilateral and multilateral sanctions, however, may be broken by rival countries that do not agree with them. The United States has had an embargo on trade with Cuba since the early 1960s, but its effect was diminished by the massive aid Cuba received from the Soviet Union during the Cold War.

Unilateral sanctions are typically imposed by one country on another for the purpose of applying pressure or in retaliation for certain economic or political policies. The United States first imposed sanctions for the purpose of opening another country's market to American products in 1988. In an effort to open the Japanese market for cellular telephones, the United States resorted to trade sanctions against selected Japanese products in 1994. In 1994 the United States also imposed economic sanctions on Taiwan to protest that nation's illegal trade in tigers and rhinoceroses. Thus, the objective of a particular sanction may be very limited, or it may be very ambitious, as in the case of sanctions imposed during wartime between hostile nations.

More than 100 sanctions were applied between the end of World War II and the United Nations embargo against Iraq during the Gulf War. The United States took a leading role in approximately two-thirds of them. For the United States, economic sanctions were a major foreign policy tool during that period. They continued to be used during the Clinton administration, when the United States imposed more than 60 sanctions, more than half of all U.S. sanctions in the 20th century. Examples include those mentioned as well as sanctions against Russia and India for selling missile technology, expanded sanctions against Cuba, and sanctions against Myanmar (Burma) for human rights abuses. As of mid 1998 the United States had sanctions in effect against more than 70 countries, and the U.S. Congress was considering 30 additional sanctions.

While the United States has imposed sanctions more often than any other nation, sanctions can sometimes have a negative effect on domestic businesses. While tariffs are designed to protect domestic industries, sanctions prohibit domestic companies from doing business in the targeted countries. When other countries fail to support U.S. sanctions, then it is foreign competitors doing business in the targeted countries who benefit. Other negative effects of trade sanctions include making it difficult for domestic businesses to forecast where the next sanctions will be imposed and making it seem as if U.S. suppliers are unreliable when they can no longer do business in a targeted country.

Sanctions, like tariffs, are a barrier to **free trade**. Although some sanctions have resulted in the desired political or economic objectives, their effectiveness as a foreign policy tool can also be called into question. Sanctions can be imposed to express disfavor with a country's political or economic policies, allowing one country to take action against another short of going to war. Yet, in the case of sanctions imposed against Cuba and Iraq, studies have shown that is it not the political leaders of the country who suffer, it is the general population.

[David P. Bianco]

FURTHER READING:

Omestad, Thomas. ''Addicted to Sanctions.'' *U.S. News and World Report,* 15 June 1998, 30-31.

Peterson, Scott. ''The Crisis over Iraq: Iraqis Already Pay the Price of One 'Weapon.' '' *Christian Science Monitor,* February 1998, 6-7.

Roberts, Paul Craig. ''A Growing Menace to Free Trade: U.S. Sanctions.'' *Business Week,* 24 November 1997, 28.

Zunes, Stephen. ''Confrontation with Iraq: A Bankrupt U.S. Policy.'' *Middle East Policy,* June 1998, 87-108.

SAVINGS AND LOAN ASSOCIATIONS

The nature of savings and loan associations (S&Ls) has changed over time. S&Ls, along with savings **banks** and **credit unions**, are known as thrift institutions. Thrifts and commercial banks are also known as depository institutions and are distinguished from nondepository institutions such as **investment banks**, insurance companies, and **pension funds**. S&Ls traditionally have taken savings, time, and demand deposits as their primary liability, and made most of their income from lending deposits out as **mortgages**.

The first savings and loan association was organized in 1831 as the Oxford Provident Building Association of Philadelphia. Like the building societies of England and the credit cooperatives of Europe, it was a membership organization that took savings deposits from its members and in turn made home **loans** to them. S&Ls soon accepted deposits from the general public and became public depository institutions. They also became the primary source of credit for working individuals to purchase their own homes at a time when commercial banks did not offer mortgages. By the end of the 19th century there were nearly 6,000 S&Ls in existence.

S&Ls may be member owned, or they may be owned by stockholders. Member owned S&Ls are known as mutual associations. Individual states may allow S&Ls to incorporate under general corporation laws and issue **stock**. An S&L may have a federal charter or a state charter. Federal charters became available to S&Ls in 1933 with the passage of the Home Owners' Loan Act. Federal charters are issued by the Home Loan Bank Board (HLBB) and may be obtained by new institutions or by converting from a state charter. Since the start of 1934, savings deposits at S&Ls have been insured by the Federal Savings and Loan Insurance Corporation (FSLIC). The establishment of both the HLBB and the FSLIC came in the aftermath of the Great Depression.

The S&L industry thrived in the postwar era of the 1950s and 1960s until the interest rate volatility of the 1970s and early 1980s exposed it to losses on its holdings of long-term, low-interest-rate mortgages. As **interest rates** rose, investors were able to obtain a better return on their investments by purchasing money market certificates that were tied to the higher rates. The assets of money market funds increased from $12 billion in 1979 to $230 billion by the end of 1982. A lot of that money came from deposit accounts at S&Ls as well as from low-paying accounts at commercial banks.

It wasn't only rising interest rates, however, that brought on the S&L crises of the 1980s. By their very nature, S&Ls were always in a position of borrowing short and lending long. That is, the deposits they took in could be withdrawn on short notice, but their assets were tied up in long-term mortgages for the most part. In an era of stable interest rates, that formula worked fine, allowing S&Ls to increase their assets from just $17 billion in 1950 to $614 billion in 1980. During that period S&Ls were not allowed by law to pay an interest rate higher than 5.5 percent on demand deposits.

With 85 percent of all S&Ls losing money in 1981, the S&L industry was entering its first crisis of the decade. The federal government responded by lowering the capital standards for S&Ls while at the same time increasing the deposit insurance ceiling per account from $40,000 to $100,000. It was an era of federal deregulation in many industries, and in effect many S&Ls were not subject to rigorous examinations for years at a time.

In an attempt to keep S&Ls competitive with other financial institutions, many of the regulations were changed during the 1980s. S&Ls were allowed to engage in a variety of banking activities that had previously been prohibited. They could offer a wider range of financial services and were given new operating powers. Two key pieces of legislation were the Garn-St. Germain Depository Institutions Act of 1982 and the Depository Institutions Deregulation and Monetary Control Act of 1980.

While the government's policies were intended to encourage growth in the S&L industry, the effect was entirely different. The increase in deposit insurance meant that it was the FSLIC and not the S&L managers who were at risk when bad loans were made. As a result of the lowering of capital standards, many insolvent and weakly capitalized S&Ls made risky loans that eventually led to the second S&L crisis in the late 1980s.

In 1988 more than 200 S&L failures were resolved by the HLBB selling the S&Ls to individuals and firms. In 1989 Congress passed the Financial Institutions Reform, Recovery and Enforcement Act (FIRREA), which among other things established the **Resolution Trust Corporation** (RTC) to seize control of an estimated 500 insolvent S&Ls. In addition to selling insolvent S&Ls and otherwise trying to resolve them, the RTC also had the power to prosecute S&L officials for criminal wrongdoing. The RTC was supervised by the newly created Thrift Depositor Protection Oversight Board, part of the U.S. Department of the Treasury.

The RTC was abolished December 31, 1995, after completing its cleanup of the savings and loan industry. Between 1989 and 1991 the RTC floated $50 billion worth of **bonds** to fund the S&L bailout. During its tenure from 1989 to 1995 the RTC closed or merged 747 savings and loan institutions and sold nearly $450 billion in assets, including 120,000 pieces of **real estate**. According to *Business Week,* the agency recouped 86 percent of the assets of failed S&Ls, or $395 billion of a total of $456 billion in assets. Incidentally, under federal guidelines any RTC contract for $500,000 or more required a minority or female subcontractor, resulting in $1.6 billion worth of service and legal **contracts** for women- and **minority-owned businesses**. As a cost-saving measure, the Thrift Depositor Protection Oversight Board was abolished in October 1998. Its only remaining task, the retirement of the RTC bonds, was taken over by the U.S. Department of the Treasury.

Before Congress enacted FIRREA, the FSLIC and HLBB encouraged healthy S&Ls to take over failing institutions rather than have them declared insolvent and have to pay off their depositors. Under a system known as "supervisory goodwill," healthy S&Ls that acquired failing S&Ls were able to carry the difference between the failing S&Ls' assets and liabilities as capital on their books. That helped healthy S&Ls meet their minimum capital requirements. When Congress enacted FIRREA in 1989, it reduced the allowable period for carrying that "goodwill" from 40 years to five years. The S&L industry considered that a breach of contract on the government's part, and there resulted a series of lawsuits and appeals throughout the 1990s. By 1998 it appeared that the healthy S&Ls that incurred financial damages as a result of acquiring failing S&Ls would finally win their cases after the government had exhausted the appeals process.

In 1996 the S&L industry recapitalized its deposit insurance fund, making it safer to own an S&L. By 1998 the S&L industry was healthy, and there was an increase in the number of applications for S&L charters. Large insurance companies and brokerage firms that wanted to build an integrated financial services company were interested in owning an S&L, because that was the only way they could get into full-service banking. S&Ls could do virtually everything a bank could do except service large corporate customers and actively trade bonds. Thrifts could be owned by any type of company, and they faced less regulation from the Office of Thrift Supervision than banks did from their regulatory agencies.

[David P. Bianco]

FURTHER READING:

Anason, Dean. "U.S. Closes Office that Oversaw S&L Bailout." *American Banker,* 28 October 1998.

Domi, Olaf De Senerpont. "Court Says 24 Goodwill Suits Really Weren't Filed Too Late." *American Banker,* 16 January 1997, 2.

"Four . . . Three . . . Two . . . One (Resolution Trust Corp. Ends)." *Building Design and Construction,* February 1996, 9.

Fox, Justin. "Thrifts Readying Goodwill Claims: U.S. Seen Unlikely to Settle Up Fast." *American Banker,* 6 September 1995, 4.

Glancz, Ronald R., and others. "Why Insurers Are Buying Thrifts Now." *National Underwriter—Life and Health/Financial Services Edition,* 2 March 1998, 31-32.

LaFemina, Lorraine. "The Thrifts Strike Back and Banks Remain Strong." *LI Business News,* 5 August 1996, 21.

McNamee, Mike. "Hear the Banks Howling?: The S&Ls Are Back." *Business Week,* 7 December 1998, 54.

"RTC Shuts Its Doors: Lucrative Program Helped Many Black Owned Firms." *Black Enterprise,* March 1996, 22.

"The RTC's Epitaph: It Worked." *Business Week,* 15 January 1996, 29.

SBA

SEE: Small Business Administration

SCANNING SYSTEMS

Digital scanning refers to optical and electronic processes that capture and convert printed materials to digital format. Scanning is one component of a larger document imaging system that includes image-capture, storage, display, and retrieval capabilities. Document imaging systems typically differentiate between page imaging and text imaging, the most common types. Increasingly, however, the scanning industry has been leaning toward enhanced functionality, whereby single scanning systems are capable of scanning images, text documents, and even positive and negative film. Page scanners rely on bitmap images while text images rely on **optical character recognition** (OCR).

Bitmap images are arrays of horizontal and vertical dots or pixels that carry information about light and dark components of the image. A pixel in a simple black and white scanner carries one bit of information—whether the pixel is black-or-white. The number of available pixels or dots per inch determines the resolution of the image. The more dots per inch, the greater the resolution or level of visual sharpness of the image. These two critical concepts in digital scanning are called gray scale and resolution. Gray scale refers to the differentiated intensity of light and dark, while resolution refers to the level of detail available for display.

Scanning technology relies on photoelectric measures of light and dark to create bitmapped displays. The number of total photoelectric sensors and the amount of information contained about each pixel combine to create gray scale and resolution. The conversion of sensor data to digital format is obtained through the use of an analog-to-digital converter. The resulting digital information may be manipulated, stored, retrieved, or displayed on request as a digital mirror image of the original.

Scanner components typically include document input or reading devices, scan engines, and scanning software. Desktop digital scanners rely on either flatbed or sheet-fed operations to input hard-copy printed materials into digital form. Scanning engines incorporate cylinders and drums to record digital information, and frequently use charge-coupled devices (CCDs). Scanning software enables manipulation of both text and images. Using special scanning software, text recognition or optical character recognition (OCR) translates printed alphabetical symbols to digital words. These digital words may be edited or manipulated with a word processing software package.

Among the most significant, and long-awaited, developments in scanning technology is the ability to read handwritten data and transform it into digital format. Early uses of such technology included the scanning of addressed envelopes by postal departments for tracking mail, but the potential impact of this new technology is enormous. The latest versions improve on prototypes' poor resolution output by utilizing dual resonant lasers, which pivot along oscillating mirrors to capture optimal positioning and character recognition, producing superior digitization rates. Furthermore, the newest versions of these electro-optical systems use simple algebraic math for calculating the scan position and the angle of the laser beam's contact, rather than using the highly technical and specialized calculation functions employed by many other scanning systems, thereby resulting in relatively quick scan times.

Increasingly in the late 1990s, new developments in the scanning system market have focused less on breakthrough technology than on physical design, the aesthetics and utility of the user interface, and the integration of popular features and multi-imaging capabilities. At times, such developments range into the area of novelty, such as tiny scanning systems that can be worn on the hand or even fingers, or scanners the size of pens that can scan and store up to 3,000 pages of text. The latter, developed by the Swedish firm C Technologies AB, operates without a wire, and thus is highly portable, and can upload data to a standard personal computer. In the late 1990s, however, this technology was still in the experimental stages. In addition, many of the newer scanners come equipped with a wide range of software designed for sophisticated, often professional, editing, and with extensive archiving or storage capabilities, such as internal Zip drives.

Several considerations affect business use of scanners, including evaluation of needs, potential hazards, and maintenance activities. Advantages of scanning include reductions in both direct costs, such as materials required for manual reproduction of images and text, and indirect costs, such as the time an individual may spend, for example, retyping text rather than scanning it. Disadvantages include hardware investment and lack of industry standards. Purchasing a scanner involves assessing speed, resolution, gray scale, color, type, and special-features requirements.

HISTORY OF DIGITAL SCANNING

In 1925, AT&T produced the wirephoto scanning service, and with it the first commercial image scanning system. Used by the news media, this service allowed photos taken around the world to be transmitted and printed in other newspapers. Additional experimentation and development resulted in the first color scanner patented by Alexander Murray and Richard Morse in 1937. Lacking digital processing and storage capabilities, however, scanning remained unchanged within the news media and undeveloped commercially. In the late 1960s, the National Aeronautics and Space Administration (NASA) spurred the use of image scanning in lunar explorations. Original lunar images were created and transmitted to Earth in analog (continuous) signals for later digitization. The Jet Propulsion Laboratory, under contract with NASA, developed a system to convert these images to digital form for computer processing. During the same period, analog facsimile scanners were developed for use in the business sector and, within ten years, were converted to digital facsimile scanners (fax). Medical uses of scanning increased and heralded the development of computerized tomography (CT scan) and magnetic resonance imaging (MRI) during the late 1960s. With the advent of personal computers in the early 1980s, scanning devices dropped in price and were actively marketed for use with home and business applications. A number of companies have incorporated scanning to improve insurance records and customer service, while others, such as Northwest Airlines, effectively use scanners in accounting and auditing. In 1993 almost 876,000 scanners were installed in the United States.

DOCUMENT IMAGING SYSTEMS

Document imaging systems facilitate the initial input, storage, retrieval, and display of digital images. Specialized image processing systems additionally provide for image enhancement, image restoration, image analysis, image compression, and image synthesis. Image enhancement activities include, for example, sharpening edges and adjusting contrast. Restoration activities, like photometric correction, adjust images to compensate for conversion errors. Image analysis may extract features or classify objects within an image, while image compression concerns itself with decreasing the overall size of a digital image file. Finally, image synthesis may incorporate activities like visualization and image mergers. Scanning software may incorporate features of an image processing system for user convenience and effectiveness.

Document imaging systems capture information based on full or partial pages of data or based on text or optical character recognition. Full or partial pages of information are converted to bitmap images using a digital process that creates software addresses for each small component of the image. OCR scanners map bitmaps to character symbols to convert text to digital format. In both cases, the beginning point of all document imaging systems is typically the initial input using a scanner.

GRAY SCALE AND RESOLUTION

Two of the most important concepts in digital scanning are resolution and gray scale. Resolution refers to the level of detail available in a printed image or the relative degree of visual sharpness. The number of pixels per inch or dots per inch (dpi) determines the quality of the image resolution. A common resolution for high-quality images is 300 dpi, though scanners have incorporated optical resolution as high as 5,600 dpi. Gray scale information for any pixel is a relative value of light intensity and is determined by the number of bits allowed for each pixel (a bit is a binary digit or the smallest element of the binary language). Frequent configurations include 4 bits per pixel (16 levels of gray scale) and 8 bits per pixel (256 levels of gray scale). Although gray scale creates better resolution, however, trade-offs to resolution include increased scan time and increased storage requirements. Many companies were competing for the greatest bit-depth technology in the late 1990s, though that trend is likely to slow for a very practical reason: the human eye is incapable of distinguishing any difference in the color palate beyond about 30 or 36 bits.

Gray scale is necessary to provide automatic scaling without loss or distortion. Scaling is the process of adding or removing pixels from an image. Because image resolution and image size are reciprocal functions, they are related by a scaling factor—scanner resolution multiplied by scanned size. Imaging continuous tone art and photographs requires gray scaling to accommodate shades. While print media represent shades with different sizes of dots, pixels are all the same size and must be manipulated by controlling the size or configuration of groups of pixels. Two methods (dithering and true gray-scaling) simulate shades. Black and white images may be converted to gray scale using a process called dithering. Dithering creates a simulated number of gray tones using geometric groupings of pixels that form patterns. These patterns represent shades of gray. Dithered images are often grainy and poor. True gray scaling, on the other hand, uses pixels that contain gray scale information. These pixels are grouped into symmetric patterns.

SCANNING TECHNOLOGY

Scanners reflect light onto a printed page to illuminate light and dark areas of the page. These light and dark areas are recorded to a logical grid within the computer. Using a charge-coupled device (CCD), scanners record information by accumulating a charge proportional to the light intensity in a solid-state array of wells. Scanning and recording cylinders preserve photoelectric charges. The resolution at which an image can be scanned depends on the number of light sensors or CCDs in the scanner. Functionally, a CCD breaks up the scanned image into thousands of pixels. Each CCD photoreceptor cell converts light or dark into electrical voltage proportional to the light intensity. Exporting these voltages creates a bitmapped image. Raster scanning, line by line from top to bottom and left to right, yields a bitmap image.

A bitmap treats an image or document as a rectangular array of pixels by using a binary digital technique to represent the black-and-white pixels. Black pixels, represented by 1s, and white pixels, represented by 0s, are mapped to a grid to represent the light and dark areas of an image or document. When pixels hold information about a scale of light or dark (as opposed to simply black or white), they are consider to have gray scale definitions.

Digital scanners capture images (pictures and text) and convert them to computer files. These computer files represent the 0s and 1s of the binary language that the computer understands. Image scanners identify a picture as thousands and thousands of individual elements. These individual elements are known as pixels or pels and vary in density and pattern to accurately reproduce a graphic image. A picture element, or pel, is used when each element contains only black or white elements, while a pixel is used when the element contains intermediate shades of gray. Pixels are the smallest element of a display surface that hold information about color or light intensity. Bitmaps are the mapped pixel location and intensity necessary to recreate the original document or image.

SCANNER COMPONENTS

There are three main subsystems to a digital scanner: the document feed, the scan engine, and the scanning software. First, the document feed system provides a means by which the printed material is entered into the computer. The scan engine consists of a light source, such as mirrors and lenses, a light intensity sensor, and recording medium. Finally, the scan control system is typically a software program that manages and directs the scanning process including resolution and gray scale detection.

DOCUMENT FEED. Document feed systems ensure that paper documents or images enter the scanning device for digitization. Four scanner designs are available with different document feed formats. The flatbed scanner (or full-page scanner) resembles a photocopier with a flat glass area on which to lay documents. Almost any document type including books, heavy card stock, paste-ups, or other materials may be scanned on a flatbed scanner. By comparison, the document feed scanner can only handle single sheets and operates like a fax machine. While document feed scanners cannot scan a book, they can handle multiple sheets of paper automatically. Contemporary scanners frequently offer both flatbed and document feed in the same design. A third type of document feed system, the overhead scanner, is more specialized and used for three-dimensional objects. The scanning cylinder is usually encased above the scan bed and the light source points downward and is reflected upwards. The fourth, and increasingly popular, document feed system is the handheld scanner. Handheld scanners provide inexpensive scanning capabilities for small digitization activities. Most cover a four-inch swath of the document.

SCAN ENGINE. Scanning engines are the nuts and bolts of the digital scanner. Consisting of a light source (a moveable or fixed path of mirrors and lenses) and a light intensity sensor (a charge-coupled device), a document is scanned line by line. The light source, often fluorescent lamps, illuminates the document, and the reflected light is focused on a CCD by a mirror or prism. The resolution at which an image can be scanned depends on the number of CCDs in the scanner. For example, a 300-sensor-per-inch scanner can provide an image at 300 dots per inch. When the scan is in progress, either the sensors themselves or the document move at a fixed rate. As these sensors or CCDs are exposed to light, they generate a charge related to each pixel's level of light intensity or gray scale. One line at time, an image is produced that consists of an array of horizontal and vertical dots with varying intensity of light. An analog-to-digital converter generates digital information from the CCD's continuous analog signal. This information contains data about individual pixel elements and gray scale. The scan engine relays this information to the scanning software for processing, displaying, filing, or printing.

SCANNING SOFTWARE. Scanning software frequently incorporates interactivity with the user. In addition to determining how the image is scanned, scanning software manipulates files, scales images, edits, rotates, and performs a wide variety of other functions including image enhancement and alteration. Scanning parameters such as page contrast, gray scale, thresholds, area dimensions, scaling, and resolution are all set up using scanning software, and are normally set according to the preferences of the user. In addition to the scanning set-up parameters, scanning software may also include programs to manipulate, edit, and save images. Specialized software is available to convert file formats for import or export. One special type of scanning software, optical character recognition (OCR), is specifically designed for use with textual materials.

OPTICAL CHARACTER RECOGNITION (OCR). OCR breaks down a bitmapped image into smaller bitmaps of individual character cells. Assuming that each character is unbroken and surrounded by space, OCR scanning software identifies text characters using pattern and feature recognition, and saves them as individual letters and words. In pattern recognition, a preexisting library of symbols is compared to the bitmapped character. The closest match determines the character code. In feature recognition, curves and lines and their relationships are derived from a sample character. Again, the closest match determines the character code. Errors occur when incomplete or unknown matches are encountered. Error rates in OCR range from 1 to 5 percent.

The simplest and most popular application of OCR is as a replacement for keyboard entry. In high-volume fields, such as law and business, OCR scanners speed document entry appreciably. Forms may also be used with OCR to capture questions and responses more accurately. OCR is a processor-intensive function best suited to high-end work stations. With the advent of inexpensive, powerful microcomputers, OCR applications are increasingly effective and available. Particularly as more paper texts are transferred into World-Wide-Web-readable HTML format, OCR applications play a vital role in the dissemination of information.

COLOR SCANNERS

Color scanners require detecting, processing, and storing three pixels to accommodate red, blue, and, green colors within each range of gray scale. A four-bit color scanner provides only 16 colors. Typical color scan engines use an illumination system of fluorescent red, blue, and green lamps and filters. Balance and adjustment tables are provided by the computer and may be updated and altered using scanning software. Color scanners are processor-intensive and, while decreasing in price, remain somewhat specialized and expensive. For that reason, companies need to seriously consider their functional needs when investing in a color printer; a 24-bit scanner, for example, can reproduce 16.7 million colors, which can be quite useful for printers who produce glossy magazines, but would most likely be a waste in a firm that merely needs to reproduce simple bar graphs and pie charts.

MANAGERIAL CONSIDERATIONS

Evaluating the potential and practical use of a scanner includes evaluation of needs, consideration of environmental hazards, and discussion of maintenance activities. Needs evaluation includes performance goals, user access, and identification of materials to be scanned. Environmental hazards such as temperature, humidity, dust, static electricity, and power supply present critical issues in the location and use of digital scanners. Even ensuring that the scanner rests on a level surface can be crucial, as the system can fall out of calibration. Cleaning and maintaining the scanning and recording cylinders, lenses, and mechanical components are additional factors in evaluating the potential use of scanners in the workplace.

Considerations in the purchase of a scanner include speed, resolution, gray scale, color, type, and special features. Speed refers to the scan speed of both black-and-white and gray scale images. Resolution refers to the optical resolution range given in dots per inch (dpi). The number of detectable gray levels and color capabilities impact both cost and capability. Many scanners now incorporate both flatbed and sheet feed types. Special features include paper size, supported printers, documentation and support, and image-editing options. The two initial steps in selecting a scanner are: (1) determining the type of scanning to be done (OCR versus image) and (2) determining the best scanner system. Price range and compatibility with current computer resources are additional factors to consider when selecting a scanner.

Image processing offers many advantages, although not all business will benefit all the time. Direct cost savings are available when scanning systems free storage space and permit reductions in workforce. These savings may be offset, however, by higher skill levels required for existing personnel. Fast retrieval, concurrent access, processing and distribution control, and reductions in lost documents can all contribute to improved productivity and competitive advantage. Nevertheless, initial costs for large-scale scanning operations can be expensive. Additionally, because image processing and scanning applications are relatively new applications, few experts or reputable vendors may exist. Incompatibility with current computerized resources and a lack of industry-wide standards may also create problems in installation, exchange, and use of digitized images. Companies in the credit industry such as American Express have capitalized on the advantages of scanning and minimized the disadvantages. By effectively using scanning technology, American Express Co. improved the aesthetic quality of the billing statement, reduced mailing time, reduced funding costs, and reduced document entry errors. Likewise, British Airways has improved cabin crew services by using scanning to facilitate the creation and entry of the voyage report. For these and other companies, image scanning and processing is a powerful tool in the management of critical information.

STATE OF THE INDUSTRY

The 1990s were a good time for product sales and shipments, though not necessarily for firms. As prices have continually been forced downward, increased sales have often failed to keep pace with production and shipment costs, forcing many companies into bankruptcy or the sale of their product lines. Some major players in the late 1990s included Hewlett Packard, Microtek, Epson, and Umax Technologies. Industry analysts predict sustained growth in shipments well into the next decade, reaching about 38.9 million scanners, mostly flatbed, by 2003, according to International Data Corp.; this figure would be roughly three times the total shipments in 1998. However, by that time, vendors will scarcely be able to rely on large volume sales, as the market will be flooded with inexpensive flatbed scanners. As more consumers become familiar with scanning technology, firms will find their greatest hopes for achieving economies of scale in product innovation and upgrades.

[Tona Henderson]

FURTHER READING:

Baxes, Gregory A. *Digital Image Processing: Principles and Applications.* New York: John Wiley & Sons, 1994.

Gann, Robert G. *Desktop Scanning: Image Quality Evaluation.* Englewood Cliffs, NJ: Prentice Hall, 1998.

Green, William B. *Digital Image Processing: A Systems Approach.* New York: Van Nostrand Reinhold, 1989.

Pepper, Jon. ''Scanners Reborn.'' *Informationweek,* 26 October 1998, 97-100.

Richter, Uwe. ''Scanning the Chaos.'' *Novum,* December, 1998, 23-7.

Szabados, David. ''The Next Step in the Scanner Industry? It's Not More Bit Depth and Resolution. . . . '' *Computer Technology Review,* April 1998, 24-26.

Toth, Debora. ''Desktop Scanners Gain Wide Acceptance'' *Graphic Arts Monthly,* January 1999, 66-70.

Wetzler, Fred U. *Desktop Image Scanners and Scanning.* Silver Spring, MD: Association for Information and Image Management, 1989.

SEC

SEE: Securities and Exchange Commission, U.S.

SECURITIES ACT OF 1933

The Securities Act of 1933, sometimes referred to as the truth-in securities act, is primarily concerned with the initial issuance of **securities** from enterprises to the investing public in the United States. The intention of the 1933 act is to ensure that all relevant information about the security be disclosed to potential investors. This information must be registered with the **Securities and Exchange Commission** (SEC) prior to issuance of the securities. In fact, it is unlawful to offer securities unless a registration statement is filed and in effect with the SEC. Some securities are exempt from this registration, such as government securities, nonpublic offerings, intrastate offerings, and certain **public offerings** not exceeding $1.5 million. In the event that a securities registration statement contains erroneous information, the statement's effectiveness may be refused or suspended, based on a public hearing.

The key to the registration statement is that it provides the investor with information necessary to make an ''informed and realistic evaluation of the worth of the securities.'' Registration of the securities, however, does not imply approval of the issue by the SEC, or that the SEC has found the registration disclosures to be accurate. Those individuals found guilty of intentionally filing false securities with the SEC are at risk for fines, prison terms, or both. Additionally, those who are found to be connected with the securities, such as directors, accountants, and any other experts, may also be held liable and subject to discipline as well. Secondary parties involved in the issuance of fraudulent securities, such as brokerage firms and other financial institutions, cannot be sued for conspiracy or aiding and abetting under a Supreme Court ruling issued in the case of *Central Bank of Denver v. First Interstate Bank of Denver* in 1994.

SEC regulations also limit the amount of publicity issuers of new securities are able to provide. This provision was adopted to curb speculation such as that seen prior to the **stock market** crash of 1929, and to prevent use of securities issues to influence future market conditions. While succeeding in its initial goals, changes in the marketplace have rendered the act's publicity regulations difficult to enforce. For instance, companies fulfilling the disclosure portions of the act may at the same time be violating its publicity regulations. Furthermore, the increased globalization of securities markets makes the publicity regulations of the act unenforceable, as legal publicity overseas is rapidly communicated to the U.S. market, where it may be in violation of SEC regulations. In response to this and other problems, the SEC established a team of experts in the summer of 1998 to revamp the act and make it more responsive to modern business practices and technological advancement.

PURPOSE OF SECURITIES REGISTRATION

Securities registration requires, but does not guarantee, accuracy in the registration statement and prospectus. Investors who ultimately suffer economic losses after the purchase of securities do have important recovery rights under the law, if they can prove either incomplete or inaccurate disclosure of material facts in the registration statement or prospectus. In the event that investors wish to exercise these rights, they must be handled through the appropriate federal or state court, as the SEC has no power to award damages.

The only standard that must be met when registering securities is adequate and accurate disclosure of required material facts concerning the company and the securities it is proposing to offer. The issue of fairness of terms, the issuing company's potential success, and other factors that affect the merits of investing in the securities (regardless of price, potential profits, or other factors) has no bearing on the question of whether or not securities may be registered.

JUSTIFICATION PROCESS

Registration forms to be filed with the SEC must contain specific information such as: description of the registrant's properties and business; description of the significant provisions of the security to be offered for sale and its relationship to the registrant's other capital securities; information about the management of the registration; and **financial statements** certified by independent public accountants.

Registration statements and prospectuses on securities become public immediately upon filing with the SEC. Following the filing of the registration statement, securities may be offered orally or by certain summaries of the information in the registration statements as permitted by SEC rules. It is unlawful, however, to sell the securities until the effective date.

Most registration statements become effective on the 20th day after the filing. The SEC, however, may move ahead a security's effective date if it is deemed appropriate given the ''interests of investors and the public, the adequacy of publicly available information, and the ease with which the facts about the new offering can be disseminated and understood.''

EXEMPTIONS FROM REGISTRATION

As a general rule, registration requirements apply to securities of both foreign and domestic issuers, and to securities of foreign governments sold in domestic securities markets. Exemptions include private offerings to a limited number of persons or institutions who have access to the kind of information that registrations would disclose and who do not propose to redistribute the securities; offerings restricted to residents of the state in which the issuing company is organized and doing business; securities of municipal, state, federal, and other governmental instrumentalities as well as charitable institutions, **banks**, and carriers subject to the Interstate Commerce Act; and offerings of small business investment companies made in accordance with rules and regulations of the commission.

Exemptions are available when certain specified conditions are met. These conditions include the prior filing of a notification with the appropriate SEC regional office and the use of an offering circular containing certain basic information in the sale of the securities. Supplementary reporting rules adopted by the SEC in November 1998 require even exempt equities offerings to file reports with the SEC within the quarter following their issuance.

SEC standards developed in 1997 and put in force in 1998 also relieve certain responsibilities formerly faced by large securities issuers under the original provisions of the act. These new regulations require large securities issuers to register with the SEC as always, but no longer require the mailing of a prospectus to potential investors. Instead, securities issuers may mail a greatly abbreviated prospectus to potential investors, while merely exhibiting the more exhaustive information online at the website of the SEC.

Regardless of whether the securities are exempt from registration, antifraud provisions apply to all sales of securities involving interstate commerce or the U.S. postal system.

SEE ALSO: Securities Exchange Act of 1934

[Arthur DuRivage, updated by Grant Eldridge]

FURTHER READING:

Illiano, Gary. ''SEC Announces New Reporting Rules for Unregistered Equity Sales.'' *CPA Journal* 67, no. 2 (February 1997): 71.

Lee, Peter. ''SEC Rules Not OK.'' *Euromoney,* July 1997, 64.

McTague, Jim. ''D.C. Current: A Stealth Bill for Freddie.'' *Barron's,* 19 October 1998, 36.

Picker, Ida. ''Mending the Rules.'' *Institutional Investor* 32, no. 9 (September 1998): 41.

SECURITIES AND INVESTMENTS

''Investments'' refers to the process of applying resources so as to increase **wealth**. Direct investment is the actual acquisition and management of assets by the individual. For many assets such **direct investment** is cumbersome and unavailable to smaller investors. Direct investments are often difficult to manage, are of limited liquidity, and require expertise on the part of the investor. For larger direct investments, the required concentration of investor wealth in a few ventures increases risk. Consequently, investors using this direct form of investment demand higher return and are hesitant to undertake new ventures without substantial safeguards. If this were the only form of investment, formation of new ventures would be difficult and economic growth would be slow.

Many of these problems can be reduced or avoided by indirect investment through securities. Securities are instruments that represent an interest in, or claim on, other assets. Use of securities separates ownership from possession and management of assets. This separation allows widespread ownership and easy transfer, dispersion of wealth over investments, use of professional **management**, and access to broader sources of capital. This in turn helps create **capital markets** with more efficient allocation of resources, encouraging economic growth. The advantages of the security form of investment are not limited to physical assets. The appeal of securities over direct acquisition is evidenced by the recent ''securitization'' of financial assets. In this process normally illiquid assets are pooled, and shares in this diversified pool are then issued.

Securities simplify the investment process, but do not remove all problems. Analysis of securities, and their combination into portfolios, is a complicated problem requiring a high level of expertise. The investor must be concerned with both the level of and uncertainty about the anticipated returns. Investment theory is not so much directed toward the actual physical assets, or even to the predicted cash flows from the investments. Instead it is concerned with investment return, which is increasingly treated as a random variable described by a probability distribution. Securities exhibit a ''risk return tradeoff''—i.e., assets with greater uncertainty about the actual outcome (higher risk) must on average provide a higher anticipated return to induce investors to accept the risk. Over the period 1926 to 1995, a study by Ibbotson Associates indicated that **U.S. Treasury bills** (T-bills), the asset class with the most uncertain returns, had an average annual return of 3.7 percent, while small capitalization **stocks** had the highest uncertainty and an average annual return of 17.7 percent. As uncertainty of returns increased over asset classes, returns also increased. It is commonly accepted that greater risk accompanies greater anticipated return. Finally, the investor must consider the interactions between securities, combining them into portfolios that reduce risk through **diversification**.

SECURITIES

An amazing diversity of securities has developed over time, and there are variations on the general types of securities described here. The pace of **innovation** has increased in recent years with the development of quantitative analysis and investment models. New types of securities are being created, and old types modified, at an unprecedented pace. **Financial engineering**, which is the design of new and often very complex instruments and strategies, has emerged as a separate new discipline. Some standard forms of securities are apparent, however, and are typically classified according to various common characteristics into equity, fixed income, and **derivatives**. It should be noted that there are exceptions to every common characteristic—investors must carefully consider each individual security.

FIXED-INCOME SECURITIES—BONDS

Despite the greater publicity given to stock, firms in the United States obtain much more of their financing through issuing **bonds**. The cash flows to fixed income securities are fixed or specified in advance. In the case of bonds, these cash flows are a contractual obligation. The cash flows are the interest payments, generally paid semiannually, and the repayment of principal at maturity. Thus, a bond with a principal amount of $1,000, a 20-year life, and a 12 percent coupon rate will make 40 semiannual payments of $60, plus one payment of $1,000 at the end of 20 years. The principal amount and the coupon rate are not the price of and rate of return on the bond. The bond must provide the market return available from other, similar bonds. Since the cash flow is fixed, the only way that the rate of return on the bond can adjust to new conditions is through price change. The bond price will increase if **interest rates** decrease, but will decrease if interest rates increase. The effect of interest rates on prices is greater for longer bonds or for lower coupon bonds. Bondholders thus face ''interest rate risk'' or ''price risk.'' Since bonds vary as to coupon rate, principal amount, and other features, the bond price is often described in terms of the rate of return or yield of the bond rather than a dollar amount. Zero coupon bonds or ''zeroes'' are a variant from the usual coupon bonds in that there is no interest payment. Zeroes provide a return by being sold at a discount to the principal amount, and are particularly sensitive to changes in the required rate of return.

Callable bonds can be called in, or repurchased, by the issuing firm. The price at which the forced repurchase is carried out is the principal plus a call premium. The call premium may vary over the life of the bond, typically becoming smaller as maturity nears. This feature is to the benefit of the firm, primarily if the firm desires to refund the issue by replacing it with an issue with lower interest cost. Refunding will occur when recall is to the firm's advantage—i.e., when yields are low. Despite the attraction of receiving the call premium, a call is not welcomed by investors, who face the prospect of being forced to replace the investment with a security of lower yield. Further, the call price becomes in effect an upper limit to the price of the bond. This call risk is disagreeable to investors, so that callable bonds typically have a higher yield than similar noncallable bonds. Bonds are often "call protected" for a certain period to make the feature more acceptable to investors and allow issue at a higher price (lower yield). At the other extreme is the putable bond, which may be sold back to the issuer at the option of the investor. This feature is attractive to investors, and putable bonds will have a lower yield than similar nonputable bonds.

The maturity of a bond issue is a time of some concern. While the firm may be able to make the periodic interest payment, the repayment of principal at principal may be beyond the ability of the firm. Normally, an issue will simply be replaced by a new issue, but this may prove difficult or impossible under some conditions. A **sinking fund** is a way of avoiding this end of life crisis. Originally, a sinking fund requirement actually created a fund to which the firm made payments, so that all or at least a portion of the maturity payments were provided by the fund. More recent sinking fund provisions usually require that a certain amount of bonds be retired each year. If the bonds are selling below the call price, the requirement will be met through purchase on the open market. If the bonds are above the call price, they will be called. Often the call premium for purchases to meet sinking fund requirements is less than the call premium for refunding. This feature is thus a mixed blessing for investors. On the one hand the possibility of end of life crisis is lessened, the effective life of the issue is shortened, and it is also thought that sinking fund repurchases will support the value of the bonds. On the other hand, the investor faces the possibility of call at a reduced premium.

Because the cash flows are specified and contractual, bonds are considered to be among the safest investments. In addition to interest rate risk and call risk, however, bondholders face **default** risk and **inflation** risk. Because the cash flows are fixed in advance and will not change if costs rise, bondholders are exposed to the risk of loss of purchasing power resulting from inflation. Default may be total or may be a partial interruption in the specified cash flows, and even in bankruptcy bondholders typically recover at least a portion of principal. Risk of default is called "credit risk" or "quality risk," and is reflected in bond quality ratings, which are provided for a fee by independent external rating agencies. Bonds are classified by the rating agencies into broad classes depending on the probability of default at the time of the rating. A particular bond issue may be rated by several agencies, and ratings are normally consistent. Bond ratings may be reevaluated and changed if conditions change. The bond rating is an important determinant of the required yield, and a rating change can significantly affect the bond price.

The legal document under which the bond is issued is called the indenture, and this document spells out the characteristics and arrangements that affect the value and risk of the bond. There are a large variety of characteristics that have been written into the bond indenture, so that individual bond issues within a given type can vary widely. In some cases the bond indenture will contain various restrictions intended to reduce the risk of default (increase the bond quality). These restrictions often take the form of minimum required **accounting** ratios, although other restrictions on management occur.

CORPORATE BONDS. Corporates are simply bonds issued by corporations, and are typically callable. The credit risk of a corporate bond is a reflection of the viability of the issuer and the arrangements contained in the indenture, and variations are wide. One important characteristic of a bond is the collateral. Mortgage bonds are secured by a claim on a specific asset, usually real property. Mortgage bonds may be described as "open end," "limited open end," or "closed end," depending on the extent to which the collateral can be used as security for other issues. Equipment trust certificates are a variation of mortgage bond using equipment as security, while collateral trust certificates use securities of other entities as collateral. In bankruptcy, the asset would be sold and the proceeds used to pay the claims of the mortgage bondholders. Any excess proceeds would go the claimants of the next highest priority. If the proceeds were insufficient, the mortgage bondholders' claims for the balance would simply be joined to the next highest priority claimants, typically holders of debenture bonds. Debenture bonds are secured by a general, nonspecific claim on the firm's assets. In some cases the security of mortgage bonds or debentures may be augmented by the existence of subordinated debentures. In case of bankruptcy the holders of subordinated debentures must subordinate their claims to another specific class of bonds, and will receive payments only after the claims of the other class have been met in full.

Convertible corporate bonds are bonds that can be converted into the **common stock** of the issuing firm. They are considered attractive because the fixed cash flows set a minimum return, but the conversion allows the bondholder to participate in increases in stock price. Because of the attraction of this feature, convertible bonds sell at a higher price and so have a lower yield.

GOVERNMENT BONDS. Government bonds are securities issued by the U.S. Treasury and by U.S. government agencies. Treasury securities are obligations of the U.S. government, and are considered to have no credit risk. Treasury securities with original maturities ranging up to 10 years are called **U.S. Treasury notes**, while Treasury securities with original maturities from 10 to 30 years are called U.S. Treasury bonds. Treasury bonds are sometimes callable in the last 5 years before maturity. Treasury securities enjoy one of the most active markets, and are highly liquid. The market is an over-the-counter market where government securities dealers stand ready to buy or sell, providing continuous quotes.

Notes and bonds are issued on regular cycles for various maturities. Competitive bids specify the yield and the amount of securities desired. Noncompetitive bids specify only the amount of securities desired. The total amount of noncompetitive bids is first subtracted from the size of the offering, and the remaining amount is then allocated among the competitive bids by ascending yield. All noncompetitive bids are then accepted at the average price paid by the competitive bidders. Competitive bidders run the risk of winner's curse (overpaying) or of not having the bid accepted if the price is too low. Noncompetitive bidders avoid the winner's curse of overbidding and know that the order will be filled, but do not know the price and may miss the chance of buying at a low price.

Agencies are bonds issued by government agencies, with fixed interest payments and maturity value. These securities are not technically direct obligations of the U.S. government. Nonetheless, it is widely assumed that the U.S. government would support the obligation, and agency bonds are considered to have very low credit risk.

MUNICIPAL BONDS. Municipal bonds are issued by state and local governments. Interest payments on municipal bonds are generally exempt from federal **taxes**, and from state and local taxes for bondholders residing within the state of issue (but not for bondholders residing in other states). Because of this tax-exempt feature, these bonds tend to have a lower pretax yield than taxable bonds. The desirability of these bonds to an investor depends on the tax rate of the investor, with the tax exemption of greater value to investors in higher tax brackets. **Capital gains** on municipal bonds are fully taxable. It is important to recognize, however, that not all bonds issued by state and local governments qualify for this tax treatment, and the investor is advised to use caution.

General obligation municipal bonds are supported by the full faith and **credit** of the issuer. In reality, this means that the bonds ultimately rely on the taxing power of the municipality. The credit risk of a given issue is thus a function of the prosperity and existing tax load of the municipality. Revenue municipal bonds, on the other hand, are bonds issued to finance a particular project, such as a bridge or sewer line. Revenue bonds are meant to be paid by the proceeds from the project, such as bridge tolls or fees, and are not backed by the municipality itself. The credit risk of a particular issue depends on the viability of the project being financed. Various maturities are available, usually up to 30 years. Municipals are sometimes issued as serial bonds. A serial bond issue has staggered maturities, so that a certain number of the bonds will mature in any given year. The effect is the same as a sinking fund, except that the maturity of an individual bond is exactly known, and the investor can choose from a variety of maturities.

ASSET-BACKED SECURITIES

Asset-backed securities are backed by a pool of financial assets that, by themselves, are relatively illiquid. The assets are "securitized" by combining them into a portfolio and issuing securities that use the portfolio as collateral. **Mortgage-backed securities**, or pass-throughs, are securities that represent a claim to proceeds from a pool of mortgages. Ownership of an individual mortgage would be quite risky and would have high default risk, but ownership of a pool spreads default risk over all investors holding securities based on the pool. The cash flows from the instrument are the principal and interest payments of the mortgages, which are passed through to the bondholders. Although the default risk is reduced by the pooling, the cash flows to mortgage-backed securities are uncertain. Mortgagees have the right to repay the mortgages before maturity. Prepayment may result from relocation or similar individual circumstances, or from refinancing of mortgages at lower interest. The effect of the prepayment option is similar to the call feature of corporate bonds, except that it occurs continually in small amounts. The cash flows from mortgage-backed securities have also been repackaged in various ways to appeal to different investors. Other forms of asset-backed securities are backed by automobile **loans** or credit card receivables.

FIXED-INCOME SECURITIES—PREFERRED STOCK

Cash flows to **preferred stock** are also specified in advance. These cash flows take the form of a fixed dividend to be paid at set intervals. While some preferred stock has a maturity with a final payout, often there is no fixed maturity. The stock is said to be preferred for two reasons. The first is that no **dividends** may be paid on common stock unless the dividend on preferred stock has been paid. Second, in bankruptcy the preferred stockholders have a higher priority for payment than the common stockholders. Balancing these preferences is the characteristic that preferred stock usually has no voting power.

Although the cash flow to preferred stock is very similar to the cash flow to bonds, there is a major difference in the nature of the cash flows to preferred. The dividends are a promise, rather than a contractual obligation. Dividends are declared at the discretion of the directors. The directors have no legal obligation to declare scheduled dividends, and preferred stockholders cannot legally force payment. There are several reasons, however, why it is unlikely that the directors will fail to declare the dividend. First, the dividend is usually cumulative. This means that any undeclared scheduled dividend is not forgotten but is due and payable. Second, no dividends may be paid to common stockholders while preferred dividends are in arrears. Finally, the preferred stockholders are often granted voting power if preferred dividends are in arrears. Thus, theoretically, the directors will declare the dividends, if possible, to avoid the wrath of the now-voting and annoyed stockholders. In reality, given the difficulties of mounting a challenge to an entrenched management, this may not be all that powerful a motivation. It may be that investor antipathy to a firm in arrears on preferred dividends, and the resulting isolation from capital markets, is more important.

It has been suggested that preferred stock may not be a desirable investment for individual investors. This suggestion arises because 70 percent of intra-corporate dividends are excluded from taxable income. This rule arises because, unlike interest on bonds, dividends on preferred stock are not tax deductible to the firm. The earnings behind the preferred dividend face double taxation—once when earned by the firm, and once again when paid to the investor. If the dividend is passed through another firm that then pays the dividend earnings as a dividend, the earnings would have been subject to triple taxation. The tax treatment is intended to reduce this multiple taxation effect. As a result of this tax treatment, the after-tax return on preferred is greater for firms than for individuals. Demand from firms thus results in overpricing from the individual, fully taxable, viewpoint.

EQUITY SECURITIES

Equity securities, or stocks, are simply evidence of a partial share in the ownership of an enterprise. Thus, individual common stocks are referred to as ''shares.'' Sale of shares is more attractive to the firm than seeking direct investment. Since many shares can be issued for the same enterprise, the firm has access to a much wider pool of capital. This enables the firm to raise larger amounts and so consider larger projects.

Sale of shares is also attractive to management, at least in part, because it has more control over the firm due to the diffusion of ownership. The holder of a share does not have a direct voice in the management of the enterprise, but has an indirect control through the election of the directors, who in turn choose the management of the firm. Voting for directors may be through simple majority voting or through cumulative voting. In the majority system, each investor may cast one vote per position for each share held, and the director receiving more than 50 percent of the votes wins. Under majority voting, a group holding more than 50 percent of the voting stock could lock out minority groups. In the cumulative system, each investor receives one vote per position for each share held, but may cumulate the votes received by casting them all for one candidate. Under cumulative voting, fewer shares are required to guarantee election of a director, so that excluding minority stockholder groups is more difficult. Managements of firms that are **takeover** targets or are facing challenges from stockholders prefer to be under majority voting. Even under cumulative voting mounting a successful dissident drive faces formidable hurdles, however, since management may dominate the **board of directors** and controls the assets of the firm. If there is a disagreement with management, the conventional wisdom of Wall Street has been to sell the stock rather than mount a challenge. This conventional wisdom has changed somewhat in recent times because of a willingness of stockholders to take on the role of activists. Also, large positions held by institutions such as **mutual funds** or **pension funds** make challenges to management easier to pursue.

The cash flows to an equity investor are not specified in advance. They depend on the success of the enterprise, are uncertain or risky, and are properly described in terms of probability distributions. As part owner of the firm, the owner shares in the success or failure of the firm in two ways. The first way is through returns from capital gains and capital losses arising from increases or decreases in the value of the stock. The second way is through cash flows arising from the distribution of earnings in the form of dividends. The distribution of earnings through dividends is not automatic. Dividends are not an obligation, but instead are declared at the discretion of the board of directors. In practice, dividends are usually not just a function of earnings. Dividends are thought to be a signal to investors as to firm performance. Management prefers to present positive signals, smoothing dividends by avoiding decreases and increasing dividends only if it is likely that the higher level can be maintained. In some cases, firms have raised funds in the capital markets so as to maintain the dividend. An exception is the ''extraordinary'' dividend, so labeled by management as a sign that the increase is not permanent.

Despite the fact that shares are evidence of part ownership of a firm, common stock has limited liability in bankruptcy. Legally, the firm is considered to be an individual, able to assume its own **liabilities** separately from the shareholders. As a result, liability is separated from ownership. Limited liability means that the investor is not liable for the **debts** of the firm, and should the firm fail the investor's loss will be limited to no more than the amount invested. The development of this limited liability form of investment was a major factor in the rise of the corporate form of business, and greatly encourages investment in productive undertakings by individuals because of the risk limitation. In bankruptcy the various claims on the firm follow a well-defined priority, with common stockholders assigned the lowest priority. It is for this reason that the common stockholders are sometimes called the ''residual owners'' of the firm.

There are other characteristics of equity that are less universal, and there are other exceptions to these general properties of equity securities. Some firms have multiple classes of stock with different voting power and/or share of dividends. Other stock may be restricted as to trading. Common stocks are traded in both organized securities exchanges and over the counter. The size of the underlying firm, and the trading volume of the stock, vary widely. Consequently, the liquidity and the amount of information available on a stock also vary widely.

MONEY MARKET SECURITIES

Money market securities are instruments that are highly marketable, have low credit risk, and are of short maturity, usually one year or less. These securities generally trade on a discount basis, much like a zero coupon bond where the only cash flow is the final repayment of principal. The instruments provide a return by selling at a discount from maturity value. They are usually used by large institutions and mutual funds, and are seldom held by individual investors. Negotiable CDs are large certificates of deposit that can be traded among investors. Banker's acceptances are simply drafts on a bank, to be paid at some future date, which the bank has promised to honor or ''accept.'' These banker's acceptances are traded on a discount basis. Commercial paper is simply an unsecured loan to the issuing firm—they are sometimes called corporate IOUs. Only a small number of firms are able to use this instrument. T-bills, short-term govern securities having original maturities of 91 days or 182 days, are issued weekly, while 52-week maturities are issued monthly. Eurodollars are dollar-denominated deposits at foreign **banks** or at the foreign branches of American banks. The ''Euro'' prefix is historic in origin, and the deposits may be in banks worldwide. Both these and the similar eurodollar CDs escape regulation by the U.S. Federal Reserve Board. Repos are the purchase of government securities, with an agreement by the seller to repurchase the securities back at a set higher price—in effect, a very short-term collateralized loan.

DERIVATIVE SECURITIES

Derivatives are securities that provide payoffs according to the values of other assets such as **commodities**, stock prices, or values of a market **index**. They are often called ''contingent claims'' because their value is contingent on or derived from the value of other assets.

OPTIONS. **Options** grant the holder the right to decide whether or not a particular action will be taken. A call option grants the right to buy a fixed amount of assets, at a fixed price, for a fixed period, a put option grants the right to sell a fixed amount of an asset, at a fixed price, for a fixed period. The buyer of the option literally buys the right to decide whether or not the trade will be executed (the option exercised): the seller or writer of the option must comply with the decision of the buyer. Most trading is in standardized options traded on an exchange, although individualized contracts are available. Options contracts are available on common stock, commodities, foreign currency, and bonds. Some options are actually written on futures rather than directly on the asset in question, although there is no practical difference. Since delivery of a market index is infeasible, the delivery on index options is made in cash rather than the underlying asset. Options provide tremendous flexibility in creating financial strategies, and are often used to create synthetic securities. Options permit high **leverage** and may be very speculative, but can also be used to reduce exposure to some types of risk.

FUTURES AND FORWARD CONTRACTS. A forward contract is simply a commitment to trade a fixed amount at a fixed price at some future date. A **futures contract** is simply a standardized form of forward contract that is traded on an exchange. The futures contract has the added feature of a clearinghouse that guarantees performance, and the daily marking to market, or payment of gains or losses. Futures may be used by both producers and users of an asset to hedge against price changes, or they can be used as speculative investments.

SWAPS. A swap is simply an agreement to exchange cash flows. In an interest rate swap, one cash flow is typically at a fixed rate, while the other is at a floating rate. The rates are referenced to a nominal principal in the same currency, but the principal is not exchanged. In a currency swap the cash flows swapped are in different currencies and the rates may be fixed or floating. The principal amount in a currency swap is exchanged at the start and end of the swap. Swaps are relatively new, but have become widely used in corporate risk management to match the characteristics of assets and liabilities.

MUTUAL FUNDS

Mutual funds have become increasingly important as investment vehicles. Mutual funds pool the funds of many investors to invest in stocks, bonds, or other assets. This provides the benefits of professional management and allows wider diversification than can usually be achieved by the individual investor. The fund will often restrict its investment to specified types of securities, such as government bonds, corporate bonds, or large company stocks. Most mutual funds follow a specified investment style or strategy, and a wide spectrum of styles and strategies is available. Styles include growth (attempting to find stocks that will exhibit high future growth), value (attempting to purchase stocks that are undervalued), and index funds that attempt to simply replicate the returns to an index. So-called load funds require a commission at purchase, while no-load funds invest the entire amount. Open-end funds increase or decrease in size as investors buy or redeem shares in the fund, while closed-end funds have a limited number of shares and are publicly traded.

OTHER INSTRUMENTS

There are other instruments that separate ownership from possession and use, and provide limited liability. For various reasons, however, these instruments lack liquidity or other characteristics of securities. An example is the limited **partnership**, in which only the managing partner exercises management control and assumes full risk. The rest of the partners are called limited partners. The limited partners have no say in the management of the partnership, but in exchange have limited liability. This arrangement has been widely used in **real estate** investing. The major drawbacks to limited partnerships are the almost total reliance on the ability of the managing partner and the lack of liquidity. Another alternative is the **real estate investment trust** (REIT). REITs issue publicly traded shares against a portfolio of real estate that is managed by the REIT. This brings the benefits of greater liquidity than limited partnerships.

INVESTMENTS

The process of investing in securities can be visualized in terms of three problems. The first problem is choice—which of the individual assets will be acquired. The second problem is allocation—how the assets will be combined into a portfolio. The final problem is one of timing—how to respond to changing market conditions. This description is helpful in understanding the process, but in practice all three problems are interrelated and must be solved together.

CHOICE. The problem of choosing among the many securities is called security analysis. The traditional advice of "buy low, sell high" does not answer the question of what is high and what is low—security analysis attempts to answer this question. While three general philosophies can be identified—fundamental analysis, indexing, and **technical analysis**. Few investors, however, adhere solely to one philosophy. All three are relevant in some way, and there are in reality as many approaches to security analysis as there are security analysts.

FUNDAMENTAL ANALYSIS. The origin of fundamental analysis is often identified with J. B. Williams's suggestion that securities could be valued as the **present value** of the anticipated cash flows. This suggestion prompted the application of quantitative economic analysis to securities. Fundamental analysis is based on the belief that it is possible to identify mispriced securities using information about the underlying conditions in the economy, industry, and company—the fundamentals. Analysts using this approach gather and evaluate information about all facets of a firm and its industry. This includes sources such as accounting data, items published in the financial press, information from trade publications, and almost any other source that can be accessed. Professional security analysts usually specialize in one industry or sector of the economy, often maintaining a relationship with the management of the firms under analysis. Using this information and forecasts of **economic conditions**, fundamental analysts attempt to evaluate the intrinsic value, or the economically rational, correct value for the firm. Similar to bond price quotes in terms of yield, this intrinsic value is often indirectly expressed on the basis of expected return, rather than on dollar price. The return approach is optimal as a technique for comparison across similar firms, where the intent is to identify mispriced assets. Statistical concepts can be applied to provide probabilistic estimates of value or return.

Outside this common philosophy, there is often little in common among the techniques or strategies applied. One common approach is to analyze **price/earnings ratios** (or P/E ratios). The difficulty of this approach is that it requires specification of the suitable P/E ratio, which is in turn a function of the fundamentals. Somewhat more specific are the **discounted cash flow** techniques. Essentially, these techniques estimate the future cash flows from the asset, and take the intrinsic value of the asset as the present value of the cash flows. The present value is the amount that, if invested today at the required rate of return on the investment, would just re-create the estimated cash flows. This in turn raises the question of the required rate of return, which is defined as the rate of return on other, similar securities. There are numerous variations of these approaches. Another classification of fundamental analysis is based on management style, the strategy followed in choosing assets. Value managers, for instance, attempt to identify undervalued firms, while growth managers attempt to identify firms that will grow more rapidly than average.

INDEXING. This approach is identified with the efficient markets hypothesis arising from modern portfolio theory. Indexing is based on the belief that not only can analysts correctly identify mispriced assets, but also they are so efficient at this endeavor that very few stocks will be mispriced, and then only fleetingly. This implies that at any given time the best estimate of the value of an asset is the market price, and the expensive search for mispriced stocks will be unlikely to produce unusually high returns. Under this belief, the optimal course is to purchase a well-diversified portfolio of assets. The approach is called indexing because the portfolio is usually created in such a way as to mimic some market index, such as the Standard & Poor's 500. This approach is most often used for those common stocks that are widely traded.

TECHNICAL ANALYSIS. Technical analysis has its origins in the Dow theory. It agrees with the belief that stock values depend on the fundamentals. Due to the complexity of the relationships, the constantly changing conditions, and uncertain investor psychology, however, technicians believe that fundamental analysis is futile. Instead, this approach assumes that prices and investor sentiment adjust slowly, producing trends in security prices over time. The emphasis of technical analysis is thus on the detection of trends based on observance of price and trading data. The original theory has over time come to encompass a wide array of possible detection devices.

ALLOCATION

This is the problem of **portfolio management**. The idea of diversification—holding multiple assets—has always been stressed as correct investment procedure. Historically, however, this was based on an intuitive reasoning such as ''Don't put all of your eggs into one basket,'' and diversification was primarily a matter of the number of different assets to be held. A more exact, quantitative analysis of the nature of diversification was first provided by Harry M. Markowitz in the early 1950s. Markowitz noted that a combination of assets that are not perfectly correlated produce **risk and return** combinations that are superior to those available from the individual assets. The lower the correlation between the assets, the larger the effect. For example, all other things being equal, the owner of a ski resort would be better off investing in a beach resort than in another ski resort. The reason is the relationship of the pattern of earnings of the investment as compared to the earnings of the ski resort. If the owner acquires another ski resort, in cold years with good snow both would do well; in warm years with poor snow both would do poorly. The result would be a highly variable, risky total earnings stream. If the beach resort is purchased, however, it will do well in warm years and poorly in cold years. This pattern of earnings would balance out the fluctuations of the ski resort earnings, and produce a predictable, less risky total earnings flow.

This analysis led to the development of what is called modern portfolio management, and the understanding that asset correlations strongly affect the diversification process. The implication is that the decision to include an asset in a portfolio depends not only on the asset, but also on its relationship with the other assets in the proposed portfolio. Finally, for a given set of assets there are many combinations, and the risk and return of the combinations can vary greatly. The task of the portfolio manager is thus to choose both assets and proportions that will result in a portfolio with a suitable risk and return profile. The task can be visualized in the risk return space of Figure 1. The portfolio manager will avoid a portfolio such as F because portfolio F is dominated by portfolios B, C, and D. Portfolio F is said to be dominated because there are alternatives that are unarguably better. In this case, portfolio B has less risk but provides the same return, portfolio C provides more return for less risk, and portfolio D has more return for the same risk. An economically rational investor would always prefer B, C, or D to F. None of the other portfolios can be said to dominate one another. Portfolio E has higher return than portfolio A, but it also has higher risk. While a young doctor might prefer portfolio E because of its high return, and a widow with several children might prefer portfolio A because of its low risk—this is a

Figure 1

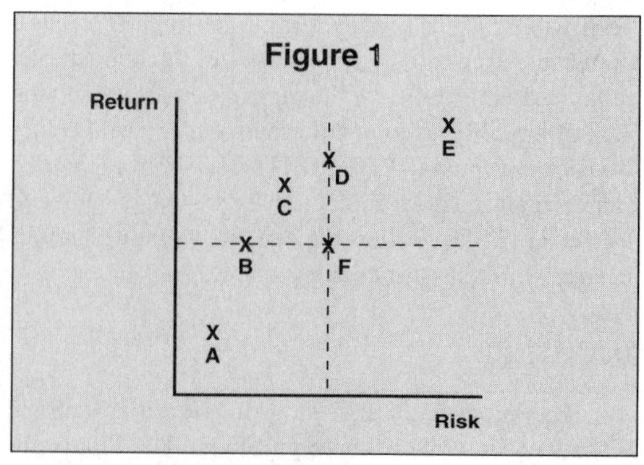

matter of personal choice, not of dominance. Portfolios A, B, C, D, and E are said to be efficient, where an efficient portfolio is simply a portfolio that is not dominated. The role of the portfolio manager, then, is to choose asset proportions that produce an efficient portfolio with appropriate risk and return.

Study of the effect of diversification led to a new way of thinking about risk itself. It became apparent that the risk of an asset had two components. Part of the risk, called diversifiable risk, could be reduced or eliminated through diversification. The reduction of risk through diversification has a natural limit. Although risks that affect individual assets or limited groups of assets can be reduced or eliminated by diversification, risks that affect all assets cannot be diversified. These nondiversifiable risks are those that cause entire capital markets to go through bull and bear phases—i.e., they affect the entire economic system. Another name for the nondiversifiable risk is thus systematic risk, while another name for diversifiable risk is nonsystematic risk. If an investor holds a well-diversified portfolio, it is only the nondiversifiable, systematic risk that is of concern. This systematic risk is measured by the beta of the asset. Modern portfolio theory suggests that the beta of a security is the determinant of the required return on an asset. This analysis, and the use of beta as a risk measure, is most often applied to common stock analysis. The underlying analysis of the nature of diversification, however, is applicable to all investment problems. Finally, this analysis points out a major reason for the growth of international investing. Foreign economies do not move directly with the domestic economy, and provide the opportunity to diversify beyond the domestic systematic risk.

The **capital asset pricing model** (CAPM) was developed based on the insights of modern portfolio theory, and, unfortunately, modern portfolio theory and the CAPM have become the same in the minds of many investors. This is incorrect—the insights of Markowitz and the resulting importance of diversification are not dependent on the CAPM, and are valid regardless of the validity of the model.

TIMING

Given that the market exhibits bull and bear stages, timers focus on buying and selling according to the market stages. Thus, a timer who anticipates a bull market would increase the proportion of stocks in the portfolio and decrease the amount of cash, and vice versa for a bear market. Cash in this usage is taken to mean money market securities rather than cash itself, since these securities provide return with nearly the liquidity and safety of cash itself. The timer might use either fundamental analysis of economic variables or technical analysis to form expectations. A pure timer would buy or sell an index portfolio, but the strategy is more often combined with fundamental or technical analysis. Timing may also take other forms. A bond portfolio manager might lengthen the maturity of the portfolio if interest rates are expected to decrease, or shorten the maturity if interest rates are expected to increase. Another version of timing is to attempt to buy stocks ahead of the **business cycle**, or sector rotation.

PROFESSIONAL DESIGNATIONS

There are a number of professional designations in the field of securities analysis. These include:

1. Registered representative stockbroker. Brokers are essentially the salespeople of the securities industry. Brokers must successfully complete the Series Seven examination given by the National Association of Security Dealers. The examination covers the basics of securities and markets, and is roughly equivalent in content to a college-level investments course.
2. Certified financial planner. This designation is relevant to professionals who provide financial guidance to individuals. This includes brokers, insurance representatives, and others dealing in investment products. The designation is granted by the College of Financial Planners, and requires successful completion of a ten-part examination covering an array of topics relevant to **financial planning** for individuals. The content would be equivalent to several college level courses.
3. Chartered financial analyst. This designation has become widely accepted as a requirement in the **investment management** industry. The designation is granted by the Institute of Chartered Financial Analysts after successful completion of three six-hour examinations covering various aspects of securities analysis and portfolio management, plus three years of experience in investment **decision making**. The content is equivalent to a master's degree.

SEE ALSO: Call and Put Options; Money Market Instruments

[David E. Upton]

FURTHER READING:

Bodie, Zvi, Alex Kane, and Alan J. Marcus. *Investments.* 4th ed. Boston: Irwin/McGraw-Hill, 1999.

Ellis, Charles D. *Winning the Loser's Game: Timeless Strategies for Successful Investing.* 3rd ed. New York: McGraw-Hill, 1998.

Fischer, Donald E., and Ronald J. Jordan. *Security Analysis and Portfolio Management.* Englewood Cliffs, NJ: Prentice Hall, 1995.

Malkiel, Burton G. *A Random Walk down Wall Street.* New York: Norton, 1996.

Reilly, Frank K., and Keith C. Brown. *Investment Analysis and Portfolio Management.* 5th ed. Fort Worth, TX: Dryden Press, 1997.

Stocks, Bonds, Bills, and Inflation: 1996 Yearbook. Chicago: Ibbotson Associates.

SECURITIES EXCHANGE ACT OF 1934

The Securities Exchange Act (SEA) of 1934 was enacted on June 6, 1934, and was meant to oversee and regulate trading on the various U.S. securities markets. Coming on the heels of the stock market crash of 1929, the act was meant to restore investor confidence in securities trading. It was widely believed that the market crash, which heralded the Great Depression, was due in part to deceit, duplicity, and ineptitude on the part of many bankers and stock brokers; structural weaknesses of the institutions they represented; and a lack of government oversight and regulation. Regarded by some economists as one of the best pieces of legislation to come out of President Franklin D. Roosevelt's New Deal, the SEA sought to end securities misrepresentation and manipulation. To this end the act authorized the creation of the **Securities and Exchange Commission** (SEC). Organized on July 2, 1934, the SEC was meant to promote "just and equitable principles of trade which would be conducive to open, fair, and orderly markets." Prior to the creation of the SEC, the **Federal Trade Commission** had some regulatory authority over securities trading.

The SEA was preceded by the **Securities Act of 1933**, which is often referred to as the "truth in securities act." This act required that significant financial information concerning securities being offered in interstate commerce be made available to potential investors, while outlawing fraud, deceit, and misrepresentation in securities offerings. Other similar legislation includes the Public Utility Holding Company Act of 1935, the Trust Indenture Act of 1939, the **Investment Advisers Act of 1940**, and the Investment Company Act of 1940.

The SEA assigns the SEC broad regulatory and oversight powers. The SEC's responsibilities include: securities markets, self-regulatory organizations, and the conduct of personnel—such as brokers, dealers, and investment advisers—involved in security trading. The SEC has the authority to investigate cases of suspected fraudulent behavior and oversees **takeovers** and proxy fights for violations. Regulation of **mutual funds** falls under the purview of the SEC per the Investment Company Act of 1940. The SEC is a quasi-judicial agency and its decisions may be appealed in federal court.

The SEA also provides for the regulation of various trading practices including short sales, wash sales, matched orders, and insider trading. Short sales involve the "borrowing" of a security lot from a broker. Anticipating a drop in the price of the security, the borrower covers the sale by agreeing to buy a future lot of the same security at a hoped-for lower price. The anticipated drop in price represents a profit for the borrower. An increase in the price of the stock, however, represents a loss for the borrower. Selling short is legal but closely regulated by the SEC. By contrast, matched orders, wash sales, and insider trading are all illegal. Matched orders involve a person buying a security lot from one broker while simultaneously selling an identical security lot through another broker. When done on a large-enough scale, matched orders give the appearance of the stock being active and such orders are executed with the intention of driving up the value of the stock. Wash sales are similar to matched orders except the collusion in the buying and selling of the security is between two or more brokers. Inherent in a wash sale is the agreement that neither party will be responsible for actually paying for or delivering the security being manipulated.

Insider trading involves a person profiting from the buying or selling of securities as the result of being privy to nonpublic information. Insiders are allowed to trade in securities issued by the institution in which they are involved, but must register their stock portfolios with the SEC and report all purchases and sales on a monthly basis. Rules governing insider trading are meant to minimize the unfair advantage that insiders have because of their privileged access to strategic nonpublic information.

An insider had always been generally regarded as an officer, director, a 10-percent-plus owner, or anyone having a **fiduciary duty** to the particular issuer of the securities. In 1997, however, the U.S. Supreme Court endorsed a broadly expanded definition of "insider" to include virtually anyone who trades on the basis of sensitive nonpublic information. As of the decision, the insider need not have a fiduciary duty to the issuer of the security. The six-to-three ruling involved a lawyer who worked for a firm advising a client attempting a planned takeover of the Pillsbury Co. Although the lawyer in question was not involved with the client, he learned through duplicity of the proposed takeover and began trading in Pillsbury stock, making $4.3 million. The Court found that even though the lawyer had no fiduciary duty to the company issuing the stock (Pillsbury), he still violated the "insider" prohibitions of the Securities Exchange Act of 1934. The SEC has also prosecuted a psychiatrist who profited from knowledge of a takeover bid gleaned from a patient and a printer whose security trading was based on a job involving a **tender-offer** document that had been printed but not yet released to the public. The SEC began prosecuting such cases in 1988 with mixed success until the 1997 ruling.

In 1996 Congress passed, and President Bill Clinton subsequently signed, legislation (PL104-290) that made a multitude of changes to the Securities Act of 1933, the Securities Exchange Act of 1934, the Investment Advisers Act of 1940, and the Investment Company Act of 1940. The new legislation was meant to rectify overlapping state/SEC rules regulating mutual funds, **capital markets**, investment advisers, and SEC registration fees and budget. The bill had widespread support throughout the security industry.

SEE ALSO: Securities and Investments; Stocks

[Michael Knes]

FURTHER READING:

Benston, George J. ''Required Disclosure and the Stock Market: An Evaluation of the Securities Exchange Act of 1934.'' *American Economic Review* 63, no. 1 (March 1973): 132-54.

''Bill Streamlines Securities Law.'' *Congressional Quarterly* 54, no. 49 (14 December 1996): 3406-8.

Ellenberger, Jack S. *Legislative History of the Securities Act of 1933 and Securities Exchange Act of 1934.* South Hackensack, NJ: F. B. Rothman, 1973.

Felsenthal, Edward. ''Big Weapon against Insider Trading Is Upheld.'' *Wall Street Journal,* 26 June 1997, C1.

Kose, John, and Ranga Narayanan. ''Market Manipulation and the Role of Insider Trading Regulations.'' *Journal of Business* 70, no. 2 (April 1997): 217-47.

Skousen, K. Fred. *An Introduction to the SEC.* Cincinnati: South-Western Publishing, 1991.

U.S. Securities and Exchange Commission. ''U.S. Securities and Exchange Commission.'' Washington: U.S. Securities and Exchange Commission, 1998. Available from www.sec.gov.

SECURITIES AND EXCHANGE COMMISSION, U.S.

The U.S. Securities and Exchange Commission (SEC) is responsible for administering federal securities laws written to provide protection for investors. The SEC also ensures that securities markets are fair and honest, and if necessary, the SEC may provide for the means to enforce securities laws through the appropriate sanctions. The SEC may further serve as adviser to the federal courts in Chapter 11 cases (corporate reorganization proceedings under Chapter 11 of the Bankruptcy Reform Act of 1978).

The SEC was created by Congress in 1934, under the **Securities Exchange Act**, as an independent, nonpartisan, quasi-judicial regulatory agency. At first, its main function was to revive public confidence in the securities markets, which had been destroyed by the 1929 stock market crash that triggered the Great Depression. The commission is made up of five members: one chairman and four commissioners. Each member is appointed to by the president to a five-year term. These terms are staggered such that each June 5th an appointed member's term expires. It is a policy that no more than three of the commissioners may be of the same political party.

The chairman and commissioners are responsible for ensuring that publicly held entities, broker-dealers in securities, investment companies and advisers, and other participants in the securities markets comply with federal securities law. These securities laws were designed to provide for informed investment analysis and decision making by the public investors—principally by ensuring adequate disclosure of material information (as directed in the **Securities Act of 1933**).

The commission's staff is made up of lawyers, accountants, financial analysts, engineers, investigators, economists, and other professionals. The SEC staff is divided into divisions and offices, which includes 12 regional and branch offices, each directed by officials appointed by the SEC chairman.

LAWS ADMINISTERED BY THE SEC

There are six major laws that the SEC is responsible for administering:

- Securities Act of 1933
- Securities Exchange Act of 1934
- Public Utility Holding Company Act of 1935
- Trust Indenture Act of 1939
- Investment Company Act of 1940
- Investment Advisers Act of 1940

The Securities Act of 1933, also known as the ''truth in securities'' law, has two primary objectives, both of which the SEC must ensure occurs: (1) to require that investors be provided with material information concerning securities offered for public sale; and (2) To prevent misrepresentation, deceit, and other fraud in the sale of securities.

In 1934 the U.S. Congress enacted the Securities Exchange Act in which the ''disclosure'' doctrine (from the Securities Act of 1933) was extended to securities listed and registered for public trading on the U.S. securities exchanges. In 1964, the Securities Act Amendments extended disclosure and reporting provisions to equity securities in the over the-counter market. The act seeks to ensure (through the SEC) fair and orderly securities markets by prohibiting certain types of activities and by setting forth rules regarding the operation of the markets and participants.

The SEC also administers the Public Utility Holding Company Act of 1935. Subject to regulation under this act are interstate holding companies engaged in the electric utility business or in the retail distribution of natural or manufactured gas. Reports to be filed with the SEC by these **holding companies** include detailed information concerning the organization, financial structure, and operations of the holding company and its subsidiaries. Holding companies are subject to SEC regulation in areas such as structure of the system, acquisitions, combinations, and issue and sale of securities.

The Trust Indenture Act of 1939, under the watchful eye of the SEC, applies to bonds, debentures, notes, and similar debt securities offered for public sale and issued under trust indentures with more than $7.5 million of securities outstanding at any one time. Other provisions of the act include prohibiting the indenture trustee from conflicting interest; requiring the trustee to be a corporation with minimal combined capital and surplus; and imposing high standards of conduct and responsibility on the trustee.

The SEC must ensure that the intentions of the Investment Company Act of 1940 are followed. The Investment Company Act seeks to regulate the activities of companies engaged primarily in investing, reinvesting, and trading in securities, and whose own securities are publicly offered. It is important for potential investors to understand that although the SEC serves as a regulatory agency in these cases, the SEC does not supervise the company's investment activities, and the mere presence of the SEC as a regulatory agency does not guarantee a safe investment.

The Investment Advisers Act of 1940 establishes a style, or a system, of regulating investment advisers (for the SEC). The main thrust of this act is simply its requirement that all persons, or firms, that are compensated for advising anyone about securities investment opportunities be registered with the SEC and conform to the established standards of investor protection. The SEC has the power and ability to strip an investment adviser of his or her registration if a statutory violation has occurred.

Finally, the SEC is given some responsibility connected with corporate reorganizations, commonly referred to as Chapter 11 proceedings. Chapter 11 of the Bankruptcy Code in the U.S. grants the SEC permission to become involved in any proceedings, but the SEC is primarily concerned with proceedings directly involving a large portion of public investor interest.

The main thrust of the SEC's activities is its disclosure-enforcement duties. This framework developed over the course of many years since, at its inception, the Commission simply lacked the muscle and resources to directly oversee industry activities. The disclosure of financial records thus became the bedrock of the SEC's attempt to secure investments and maintain investor confidence and economic stability.

The prominence of the SEC on the national economic scene has also grown over time. In particular, the merger- and takeover-intensive 1980s brought the SEC into the limelight at an unprecedented level. Long admired as one of the most efficient and respectable of government agencies, the SEC stepped up its enforcement priorities by waging a crusade against insider trading. Moreover, the Reagan administration recommended that the commission's role be expanded to include the direct encouragement of capital investment and accumulation. Amidst all this, and while facing down such sensational cases as the Ivan Boesky scandal, in which investors were taken for millions of dollars as a result of unsavory trading on non-disclosed information, the commission's primary duties centered on disclosure enforcement, a pattern that continued into the 1990s.

At the end of the 1990s, these duties underwent a severe escalation in order to safeguard investor knowledge regarding the infamous Y2K problem. In 1998, President Clinton signed the Year 2000 Information and Readiness disclosure Act. At issue is the protection of investors' capital and whether it could be materially affected by a lack of companies' preparedness for the Year 2000 computer crisis.

Years of labor by various business interests finally paid off in 1995 when the Private Securities Litigation Reform Act was passed over President Clinton's veto. This legislation severely limited private litigation brought under the Securities Exchange Act. The business community had lobbied for such reforms since the early 1990s, in large part to curtail what they saw as "frivolous" private securities lawsuits. The reforms grant large shareholders greater leverage in class action lawsuits and requires more detailed information about settlements to be disclosed to them. The provisions do not, however, apply to actions brought *by* the SEC. The law expands the commission's authority to provide exemptions from provisions of the Securities Exchange Act, and to modify accepted auditing standards.

[Art DuRivage]

FURTHER READING:

Hall, Billy Ray. *A Legal Solution to Government Gridlock: The Enforcement Strategy of the Securities and Exchange Commission.* New York: Garland Publishing, 1998.

Hamilton, James. *Year 2000: SEC Disclosure.* Chicago: CCH, Inc., 1998.

Practicing Law Institute. *Sweeping Reform: Litigating and Bespeaking Caution Under the New Securities Law.* New York: Practicing Law Institute, 1996.

SELF-EMPLOYMENT

Classification of someone as employed or self-employed depends on several factors, including degree of independence, the freedom to hire others to do the work taken on, the freedom to work for others, and the assumption of risks. Courts have held that the individual does not necessarily have to provide the equipment to do the job, as in the case of independent television and film mixers working on equipment owned by client production companies.

A worker's status as a self-employed worker can be reinforced by having multiple clients, being paid based on work done instead of on hours worked, or obtaining an employer identification number from the Internal Revenue Service (IRS) by filing form SS-4. Working under a business name also helps reinforce this status. For some self-employed workers, their business name is simply their own name. Stipulating in written contracts that either party can be dismissed on 30 days' notice helps differentiate self-employed workers from employees, who often cannot be fired at will. Printing invoices, business cards, and stationery also help identify a worker as being self-employed. In addition, employees have more statutory rights, benefits, and protections than self-employed workers, who must generally negotiate protections and obtain their own insurance, retirement plans, etc. In other words, self-employed workers typically do not receive fringe benefits or pay Social Security, Medicare, and income tax installments directly.

Variations of the term include ''independent contractors,'' ''free agents,'' ''freelancers,'' ''consultants,'' ''sole proprietors,'' and, creatively, ''soloists,'' ''virtual employees,'' ''corporate refugees,'' ''corporate mutineers,'' ''lone wolves,'' ''lone rangers,'' and ''lone eagles.''

While agencies and organizations did not collect accurate and consistent statistics of employed versus self-employed workers until the Decennial Census in 1940, the data available from the late 19th century and the early 20th century suggest that a significant portion of the work force was self-employed. Furthermore, the systematic survey and classification of the self-employed in 1940 indicated that 10 million people were self-employed as unincorporated businesses largely performing agricultural, fishing, and forestry tasks. These 10 million self-employed workers accounted for about 20 percent of the work force in 1940. In contrast, there were still around 10 million self-employed workers in mid-1999 (10.1 million as of May 1999), but they accounted for only about 9 percent of the total work force. Moreover, the percentage of self-employed agricultural workers has plummeted: whereas self-employed agricultural workers represented 90 percent of the self-employed in 1940, they represented about 8 percent in 1999. Instead, service and executive/administrative occupations supplanted farming-related ones as the primary occupations of the self-employed, together accounting for almost 30 percent of all self-employed workers in the mid- to late 1990s, according to the U.S. Bureau of Labor Statistics (BLS).

Self-employment declined after World War II, dropping to under 7 percent of the labor pool by 1969, but it began to increase slowly by the mid-1970s. Self-employment received increased attention in the 1980s and 1990s as many large firms responded to the growth of competition and a lingering recession by ''downsizing,'' or reducing the size of their ''permanent'' staffs and hiring temporary employees and contracting with self-employed workers to reduce overhead. Some such groups of businesses have been called ''virtual corporations,'' as they perform functions formerly grouped under a single corporation, but legally do not exist under one ownership. While in the past a large company using freelancers seemed to imply a crisis, it became a commonplace way to control costs and try out new talent in the 1990s.

The increase in self-employment, moreover, can be attributed partially to **workers' compensation**, social security, and job protection laws, which have made employers cautious about hiring full-time employees. In addition, sometimes smaller companies only can afford to temporarily hire professionals who have had experience at larger, more sophisticated companies.

While self-employment has a number of benefits such as independence and job flexibility, it also has some drawbacks. Intermittent income is one of the most important difficulties the newly independent businessperson must face. Downtime can be avoided by overscheduling or moonlighting, working a salaried job, also. New business owners are advised not to rely on their enterprises for income for at least the first six months; comfortable returns may not follow for months afterward.

SELF-EMPLOYMENT DATA

One of the primary sources for statistics on self-employment in the United States is the monthly Current Population Survey (CPS). The CPS was launched in 1940 as part of an effort to determine monthly unemployment levels, because the Great Depression still affected the country at the time. This survey includes data on different classes of workers—as well as on other aspects of employment such as industry and occupation—which refers to the distinction between agricultural and nonagricultural workers and between wage and self-employed workers, in addition to other classes of workers not relevant here.

The CPS tracks whether people over the age of 16 are employed, unemployed (seeking employment), or not in the work force at all. Those who have jobs are then classified as employed by government, private companies, or nonprofit organizations, or as self-employed. Workers indicating they are employed by government, private companies, or non-profit organizations are classified as wage and salary workers, whereas workers indicating they are self-employed are classified as self-employed, if their business is not incorporated. If self-employed workers have incorporated businesses, they are classified as wage and salary workers, because they are technically employees of their own businesses according to the law. (Incorporation establishes a company as a legal entity—the corporation—which is permitted to enter into contracts and open bank accounts. A corporation also has tax advantages.) This method of questioning has largely been consistent since 1948, with the exception of the distinction between being self-employed and owning an incorporated business, which was adopted in 1967.

The BLS also has another relevant survey: the Contingent and Alternative Work Arrangements Supplement to the Current Population Survey. This survey is conducted every two years and it tracks self-employed workers classified as independent contractors. Respondents who indicated they were self-employed but not incorporated in CPS survey are asked if they are self-employed as independent contractors, independent consultants, or freelance workers.

TYPES OF SELF-EMPLOYMENT

The Bureau of Labor Statistics distinguishes between two types of self-employed workers: independent contractors and business owners who have not incorporated their businesses (as mentioned above, owners of incorporated businesses are not classified as self-employed according to BLS criteria). Independent contractors include workers who are self-employed on a contract basis. The contracts they receive contracts specify the type and amount of work they are to perform as well as work-related arrangements and legal issues. There are many different types of independent contractors: professionals leaving corporate life, youngsters delivering papers, single parents stuffing envelopes at home, and construction-related workers. Professional and white collar self-employment services include editing, developing and running training programs, writing, graphic design, consulting, and financial services.

On the other hand, self-employed business owners (e.g. family and home business owners) refer to operations that have not been incorporated, which generally have few employees. Self-employed business owners take the form of anything from restaurant owners to store owners. The overall number of self-employed workers in the United States in the late 1990s stood at about 10 million.

In general, male independent contractors tended to work as managers, construction workers, writers and artists, and real estate and insurance agents in the late 1990s, whereas female independent contractors tended to work as managers, writers and artists, real estate and insurance agents, salespeople, and child-care providers, according to the BLS. Overall, about 17 percent of self-employed workers performed executive, administrative, and managerial tasks during this period. These workers either ran their own businesses or were self-employed as accountants and other professionals. By 2006, the BLS expects the percentage of self-employed professionals to reach 18.7. Self-employed workers performing service-related tasks such as providing child care or home health care services accounted for 11.5 percent of all self-employed workers during this period and the percentage of self-employed service workers is forecast to reach 12.6 percent by 2006.

CHARACTERISTICS OF THE SELF-EMPLOYED

Various personal characteristics seem to steer people into self-employment, such as being the oldest child or having parents who were self-employed. In addition, individuals are more likely to become self-employed if they have been fired from more than one job, have been previously employed in small businesses, are college graduates, are realistic risk takers, and are well-organized and good at organizing others. Furthermore, many are immigrants or children of immigrants. Some personality requirements for success as a self-employed worker are confidence, a positive outlook, friendliness, and the determination to succeed.

Self-employed individuals as a whole tend to work longer hours (an additional 4 hours per week, according to the Bureau of Labor Statistics) and work harder than their wage and salary counterparts—and they do it for irregular pay and, frequently, fewer benefits. About 26 percent of all independent contractors worked less than 35 hours a week, while 30 percent worked 49 hours a week in the late 1990s. The average work for all independent contracts was 46.3 hours. In addition, the income and assets of self-employed workers are dependent on their work contributions in a more intimate way than are those of their wage and salary counterparts. Not surprisingly, a study of certified public accountants in 1986 found the self-employed ones to have higher levels of organizational commitment.

In addition, self-employed workers who were independent contractors earned more on average than their wage and salary counterparts. For example, the BLS reported that independent contractors earned an average of $587 per week in 1997, whereas wage and salary workers averaged $510 per week. Studies concerning the amount of education of self-employed individuals point out that higher education generally may lead to higher pay. The BLS indicated that college graduate independent contractors averaged $752 per week, while high school graduate independent contractors averaged $512 per week. Independent contractors who did not graduate from high school averaged even less: $398 per week.

Furthermore, education also can play a key role in whether or not a worker is self-employed, although it depends to some extent on how being self-employed is defined. A common assumption has been that those with a higher level of education are more apt to be self-employed. Studies based on unincorporated self-employed workers have confirmed this belief to some extent by showing a moderate correlation between education level and self-employment. For example, a higher proportion of independent contractors have four years of college or more than wage and salary workers do, according to the Bureau of Labor Statistics. Approximately 34 percent of independent contractors between the age of 25 and 64—who make up about 50 percent all self-employed workers—had college degrees in the late 1990s, while 29 percent of their wage and salary counterparts had college degrees.

The self-employed have been found to report lower absences, which has been attributed not to superior health but the feeling of being indispensable. In fact, their jobs tend to be more physically and psychologically stressful due to the investments in energy the jobs demand. Yet certain stress factors are generally absent from self-employment—such as corporate meetings and employee discipline problems, although dealing with clients presents its own stress, such as rush orders and negotiations.

Age is a significant characteristic when examining self-employment trends. As workers get older, their chances of being self-employed increases. For example, 2.5 percent of workers 20-24 years old are self-employed, whereas 10.5 percent of workers 45-54 years old and 26 percent of workers 65 and over are self-employed, according to BLS statistics from the mid-1990s. The BLS attributes this trend to the greater prevalence of self-employment when older workers first entered the work force and to the inclination of older workers to launch post-retirement careers or second careers. Moreover, younger workers often lack the necessary skills and funds to become self-employed. Based on numbers, the largest group of self-employed workers is the group of workers 35-44 year old, which totals about 1.9 million. In addition, about 7 percent of working women are self-employed, whereas 10 percent of working men are self-employed.

SMALL BUSINESSES AND HOME BUSINESSES

Small business ownership is a significant part self-employment, which accounts for about 50 percent of self-employed workers. As previously mentioned, the BLS does not classify such business owners who have incorporated their businesses as self-employed. A study of small businesses by Robert L. Aronson indicated that 31 percent of the small businesses in the retail industry employed no workers and 67 percent in the construction industry employed no workers, indicating a significant amount of self-employment among small businesses. The self-employed small business owner must make many management decisions, such as keeping precise accounting and tax records, projecting cash flow, and making purchasing decisions. More successful individuals can—and frequently must—hire another professional to take on some of these tasks, particularly accounting, but also sometimes filing, manufacturing, billing, maintaining databases, mailing brochures, or selling.

Self-employment is often associated with working at home. However, wage and salary workers also work at home under various arrangements with their employers, so this characteristic is not exclusive to self-employed workers. In 1997, managers and professionals accounted for the largest share of home-based self-employed workers—1.7 million workers—according to the BLS. Other leading fields of home-based self-employment that year included sales, service, and precision production. The service industry accounted for 2.1 million home-based workers, followed by construction workers with 726,000 and retail workers with 532,000.

The personal computer and communications technology have made working at home more feasible throughout the 1980s and 1990s. Mastering these technologies has become essential for those without staffs. Through cellular telephones and pagers, the self-employed professional can stay in touch with clients throughout the day. Fax machines and modems make business over a large geographic area feasible and help the one-person office get work out quickly. Computerized spreadsheet and database programs are necessary to deal with administrative tasks quickly and efficiently. In addition, on-line services and electronic bulletin boards made instantaneous local, cross-country, and international networking and research feasible. Consultants can also use their **computers** to ''manufacture'' or ''distribute'' their work product. In most cases, they make their work process more efficient, as well. About 55 percent of all home-based self-employed workers used a computer for their work in 1997.

BECOMING SELF-EMPLOYED

Many articles and books on self-employment urge people to systematically plan their foray into self-employment, whether they intend to be independent contractors or business owners. The first step is developing a business plan, which includes determining individual interests, skills, strengths, weaknesses, and so on. This step also involves figuring out who the potential customs and competitors will be as well as researching the market for the intended line of business. In addition, part of planning for self-employment should include establishing contacts—potential clients—in the intended market.

Next, those preparing for self-employment must begin marketing themselves. One technique, while time-consuming and expensive, is making cold calls and using mailing lists to introduce services and skills. In addition, self-employed workers should emphasize their individual expertise, which marketers refer to as "unique selling propositions." Speaking at conventions and writing for trade journals on topics of professional competence are effective ways of going about emphasizing individual expertise. However, marketing is not only essential in the beginning but also throughout a career as a self-employed worker.

Self-employed workers also must set competitive fees. However, they often make the mistake of undercharging for their services or products at the beginning of their enterprises, at times even doing work for free with the hope of impressing new clients. This is partly due to a lack of confidence and partly because of their justified concerns about competing in the marketplace. This can pose a serious dilemma, as underpricing may not necessarily lead to more contracts; in fact, it can suggest a lack of quality. The best way of setting prices is finding out how much other self-employed workers in the same field are charging and basing fees on this information.

As they begin their enterprises, self-employed individuals feel compelled to accept a variety of assignments due to sheer scarcity of work. However, specialization can help ensure their long-term survival. For one thing, corporate clients can often find a generalist's abilities in-house. Also, specialization may allow professionals to broaden their client base geographically—freeing their fortunes from fluctuations in the local economy. These factors can enable the specialist to earn higher fees and work more consistently. Paradoxically, one's work as a specialist can garner referrals outside one's specialty, so specialization might not be as limiting as a strict definition would imply. The self-employed should be cautioned against changing their specialties too often, as this can confuse clients and make their own operations inefficient.

Depending on the line of business, self-employed workers may also have to obtain financing for supplies and equipment. Hence, research of various methods of financing may be necessary. Finally, being self-employed requires attention to administrative matters such as record keeping, accounting, insurance, and maintaining equipment.

TAX AND BENEFIT ISSUES IN SELF-EMPLOYMENT

Self-employment has long been a focus of the **Internal Revenue Service** (IRS). The IRS estimated that the self-employed underpay about $20 billion a year in taxes. Independent contractors and sole proprietors generally must pay taxes on all business profits—sales over business expenses. These self-employed workers usually may deduct expenditures for work-related equipment such as computers, telephones, trucks, tools, and other such expenses. To reduce taxes owed, forming a subchapter **S corporation** is an option, particularly when income before expenses and taxes exceeds $150,000. In an S corporation, income is not subject to self-employment taxes.

Nevertheless, self-employment provides some tax advantages, such as retirement plans and home-office and transportation deductions. In the simplified employee pension plan (SEP-IRA), a maximum of 13.1435 percent of net income can be contributed to these accounts annually, up to $30,000. A portion of the home dedicated exclusively to business use may be depreciated over 31 1/2 years. A standard deduction, 30 cents per mile, may be used for business-related transportation costs, or actual fuel and maintenance costs. Also, up to 25 percent of medical insurance premiums may be deducted for sole proprietors, partners, and more-than-2 percent S corporation shareholders; also, the self-employed pay Federal Insurance Contributions Act (FICA) tax on net, not gross, earnings. For these reasons, it is essential to keep an accurate record of expenses.

However, there are other tax disadvantages for unincorporated businesses besides the ones mentioned above. For example, owners of such businesses are not able to fully deduct employee contributions to health insurance. Not surprisingly, this discourages the self-employed from getting health insurance for themselves and their employees. Health insurance may be available through one's prior employer. The Consolidated Omnibus Budget Reconciliation Act(COBRA) requires companies with more than 50 employees to offer health care coverage up to 18 months after an employee leaves; this may be the only option for people with preexisting conditions that preclude new insurance coverage. Under this plan, however, employees must pay 102 percent of their insurance premiums (including a two percent administrative fee). Under COBRA, the departing employee is also credited with deductibles already paid, while temporary plans reset deductibles. Other options include a spouse's company plan, a trade organization plan, or individual coverage.

Independent life insurance plans tend to give better coverage than company plans that are converted within 30 days of leaving a job. Disability coverage typically can't be converted, but it can be necessary to cover business overhead during an out-of-work period. A single-premium insurance policy, where only one premium payment is required, is one solution to the problem of pensions that irregular earnings creates.

SELF-EMPLOYMENT AND JOB GROWTH

While self-employment contributed the country's job growth in the 1980s, it appeared to have no appreciable effect in the 1990s, according to the BLS. Between 1989 and 1997, self-employment accounted for only 0.7 percent of employment growth in the United States. In contrast, it led to 79 percent of job growth in Canada, whose economy is linked to the United States', during this period. This contribution to overall job growth marks a substantial drop in influence of self-employment on U.S. job growth, because between 1979 and 1989 self-employment was responsible for over 13 percent of the country's job growth. During the same period, self-employment accounted for about 17 percent job growth in Canada.

SEE ALSO: Small Businesses

[Frederick C. Ingram]

FURTHER READING:

Bregger, John E. "Measuring Self-Employment in the United States." *Monthly Labor Review,* January-February 1996.

Cohany, Sharon R. "Workers in Alternative Employment Arrangements: A Second Look." *Monthly Labor Review,* November 1998.

Manser, Marilyn E., and Garnett Picot. "The Role of Self-Employment in U.S. and Canadian Job Growth." *Monthly Labor Review,* April 1999.

Smith, Brian R. *How to Become Successfully Self-Employed.* Holbrook: MA, 1997.

SEP

SEE: Simplified Employee Pension

SERVICE INDUSTRIES

Definitions of which activities constitute the service sector vary somewhat, but by all definitions services are a massive and growing segment of the U.S. economy. One of the broadest definitions of service industries includes all areas of the economy except goods-producing industries (manufacturing, construction, agriculture, and mining) and government. By this definition, services in 1997 made up nearly two-thirds of total U.S. gross domestic product (GDP). When defined more narrowly to exclude areas such as retail and wholesale trade, communications and transportation, finance and real estate, and utilities, the "pure" services sector still accounted for approximately 22 percent of private-sector GDP and, at more than 34 million workers, employed twice as many people as all of U.S. manufacturing. Similar patterns have been observed in other leading industrial economies.

All of these figures are testimony to the rising importance of service industries in an era of so-called post-industrial economies. The trend is not particularly new. Indeed, it has characterized the U.S. economy since at least the post-World War II period. Shortly after the war, services broadly defined represented slightly less than 50 percent of U.S. GDP. By the 1980s, the proportion was in the 60 percent range.

The employment transition has been more dramatic. The narrowly defined service sector (**Standard Industrial Classification** codes 7011-8999) provided only 5.4 million U.S. jobs in 1950, compared to 15.2 million in manufacturing. By 1970, service employment had more than doubled to 11.5 million, while manufacturing had edged up only to 19.3 million. Services nearly doubled again by 1985, reaching 22 million workers, whereas manufacturing had stalled at 19.2 million, after having peaked briefly in the late 1970s at 21 million. Since the mid-1980s the manufacturing workforce has hovered around 17-19 million, while services continued to climb toward the 40 million mark, crossing 35 million by the late 1990s.

CONCERNS OVER EMPLOYMENT QUALITY

A perennial concern about the growth of service industries is that they tend to create lower-paying, lower-skilled jobs than those in manufacturing. There is some evidence to support this, particularly when the largest growth occupations in the service sector are considered. According to U.S. Bureau of Labor Statistics projections, some of the service occupations expected to offer the most new jobs in the late 1990s and early 2000s were retail clerks and cashiers, home health care workers, teachers' aides, and truck drivers. All of these positions require minimal training, experience high turnover, and generally don't pay very well. However, on the same list of high-growth occupations are registered nurses, systems analysts, teachers, database administrators, and sales supervisors, all of which are considered good jobs requiring moderate skill.

The forecasts envision that the most jobs will be created in relatively low paying jobs, yet some of the fastest growth (and not an insignificant number of jobs) will be in high-skilled, high-paying jobs. An early 1990s study concluded that the median service wage was only slightly less than the median goods producing wage, a difference of between 3 percent and 4 percent. Hence, while there is some substance to the claim that the so-called service economy produces less desirable jobs, the claim may be overstated in some cases.

LARGEST SERVICE SEGMENTS

The service sector comprises a very diverse set of activities. Under the **North American Industry Classification System** (NAICS), a relatively new and service-oriented nomenclature for describing economic activities, 14 of the 20 broad sectors can be considered services:

1. Utilities
2. Wholesale Trade
3. Retail Trade
4. Transportation and Warehousing
5. Information
6. Finance and Insurance
7. Real Estate and Rental and Leasing
8. Professional, Scientific, and Technical Services
9. Administrative and Support and Waste Management and Remediation
10. Educational Services
11. Health Care and Social Assistance
12. Arts, Entertainment, and Recreation
13. Accommodation and Foodservices
14. Other Services

The last seven categories on this list, sometimes along with information, are typically defined as the narrower service industry sector. Among these eight, health services are by far the largest category in terms of annual receipts, which in 1997 totaled an estimated $890 billion, based on advance figures from the Census Bureau's 1997 Economic Census. Information was second largest that year, with $642 in revenues, followed by professional and technical services ($609 billion), administrative and waste management services ($303 billion), and general private-sector "other" services ($270 billion). Food and accommodation services (primarily restaurants and hotels) also had sales in the upper range—probably falling in between professional/technical and administrative services—but the 1997 census data were not yet available at the time of publication.

TRADE IN SERVICES

Services have not only been a significant portion of the domestic economy, but they are also a major area of U.S. foreign trade. As of 1998, services accounted for approximately 28 percent all U.S. exports by value and 16 percent of imports by value. In total, service exports were worth $264 billion in 1998, while imports registered at $181 billion. Thus, unlike in merchandise trade, the United States has maintained a healthy trade surplus in services, worth nearly $83 billion in 1998. Some of the largest service export areas are travel and tourism (when foreign visitors spend money in the United States their travel is considered an export, and when U.S. residents spend money abroad it is recorded as an import), professional and technical services, and royalties from **intellectual property** rights licensed abroad (e.g., software, musical recordings, films).

ECONOMIC THEORIES ON THE RISE OF SERVICES

A variety of theories exist to explain service industry dominance. Michael V. Maciosek provided a helpful overview of the competing ideas in his 1995 paper "Behind the Growth of Service Industries," published in the *Illinois Business Review.* The conventional explanation centers around three notions. First, the rising efficiency of manufacturing means that it takes fewer workers and less capital to produce the equivalent amount of goods as before. Second, countries with lower labor costs can produce manufactured goods more cheaply than the United States, so U.S. imports rise and domestic production doesn't rise as quickly or may even decline. And third, some believe that as a society becomes more affluent and urban, an increasing share of income is spent on services rather than on goods. In the case of affluence this increase is fueled by convenience or indulgence, and in the case of urbanization it is brought about by specialization of labor, working outside the home, and related lifestyle changes. On the surface, there is some statistical evidence to support each of these claims.

However, an alternative perspective is that the service industry growth has been in large part a statistical construct that belies underlying trends. One argument for this viewpoint is that the appearance of service industry growth was caused by the separation and specialization of tasks previously performed all within one company, such as accounting or maintenance. In this sense, at least part of the service growth has merely been a reclassification of activities that once fell under manufacturing.

Another alleged distortion of service industry growth can be traced to productivity and pricing. Services, the theory goes, have not witnessed the high rate of productivity growth over the last several decades that manufacturing has. As a result, Maciosek reported, price inflation for services has been much greater than that for goods, and when industry specific inflation is factored in, the growth of services in relation to manufacturing all but vanishes.

Clearly, no single theory explains the service phenomenon entirely, and the various proposals are not mutually exclusive.

FURTHER READING:

Chmura, Christine. ''Are Service Jobs Creating a Second-Rate Economy?'' *ABA Banking Journal,* November 1996.

Daniels, P.W. *Service Industries in the World Economy.* Cambridge, MA: Blackwell, 1993.

Herzenberg, Stephen, John A. Alic, and Howard Wial. *New Rules for a New Economy: Employment and Opportunity in Postindustrial America.* Ithaca, NY: Cornell University Press, 1998.

Illeris, Sven. *The Service Economy: A Geographical Approach.* New York: John Wiley & Sons, 1996.

Maciosek, Michael V. ''Behind the Growth of Services.'' *Illinois Business Review,* fall 1995.

U.S. Bureau of Labor Statistics. ''Occupations with the Largest Job Growth, 1996-2006.'' *Employment Projections.* Washington, 1997. Available from www.bls.gov.

U.S. Census Bureau. ''Advance Summary Statistics for the United States.'' *1997 Economic Census.* Washington, March 1999. Available from www.census.gov.

SERVICE MARKS

Service marks are a special type of trademark designating a service instead of a product. In practice, the terms ''service mark'' and ''trademark'' are often used interchangeably; the terms ''trademark'' and simply ''mark'' may also be used to indicate both product and service marks. Examples of well-known service marks include American Express, Hilton Hotels, and American Airlines.

As with all other trademarks, service marks exist to differentiate a unique class of services offered by one organization from similar services offered by others. They provide all the same protections as conventional trademarks, but since services can be harder to define than physical products, registering a service mark can require slightly more rigorous evidence that the underlying activity is indeed a valid business operation. Service marks need not be registered, though, to carry legal force, in which case they are called common law service marks.

Service marks offer several advantages to their users. By providing a name or symbol that consumers can readily identify, they aid in word of-mouth **advertising** and help build customer loyalty. By constituting a distinctive mark customers associate with a company's services, service marks foster goodwill—the tendency for customers to repurchase services from that company. Service marks attract attention from consumers and help them distinguish among competitors and find the services sold under a particular mark.

THE NAME

The essential components of a typical service mark are a name, a visual representation of the name (logo) and, possibly, the look of the environment in which the service is performed. The name is simply whatever a company calls its service. It may be a common word or phrase, or it may be a unique or original name created by the company. Generally, the more unique a name, the stronger the protection it will enjoy. (Choosing a unique name can also be a wise decision from a marketing standpoint; see **brands and brand names**.) Companies should also avoid marks bearing similarity to others' marks; McDonald's restaurants, for instance, won an infringement suit against a chain of motels using the name McSleep.

THE VISUAL PRESENTATION

The design or logo concerns how the name appears in advertising or other company materials, and includes the color, type style, and any graphical representation of the name or graphic accompanying the name. The concept of unique design in service marks also extends to a broader class of visual elements known as *trade dress,* or the overall visual presentation of a product or service. For example, a restaurant's distinctive decor, in addition to its other unique traits, was upheld by the U.S. Supreme Court as protected trade dress for a service in the 1992 case *Two Pesos Inc. v. Taco Cabana Inc.* Though each may be protected separately from infringement by others, the name and design/presentation are often considered jointly when allegations of infringement arise.

REGISTRATION

Under the federal Trademark Act of 1946, service marks are afforded protection from illegal use by others—a form of unfair competition known as trademark infringement. While any company can gain some protection by merely using a mark in the course of selling or advertising its services, most authorities advise registering the mark at the federal level, preferably with the Patent and Trademark Office (PTO) of the U.S. Department of Commerce, to gain the fullest possible protection against piracy. Among the many benefits to the owners of federally registered service marks are the right to exclusive, nationwide use of their marks (within a limited scope of activities); the right to sue in federal court for trademark infringement; and a basis for applying to use the mark in foreign countries, as well as to prevent foreign competitors from using the mark in the United States. Moreover, federal registration can last indefinitely, so long as the registrant—the owner of the mark—meets certain requirements, such as continuing to use the mark and periodically renewing registration with the PTO.

States too offer trademark protection, generally simpler, quicker, and cheaper to obtain than federal registration. Not all states offer registration for service marks, however, and legal protection is limited to the particular state, rather than to the entire United States and its territories and possessions. Furthermore, federal registration usually takes precedence over state registration when legal disputes arise. On the other hand, state registration can be useful for businesses that don't meet the requirements for federal registration.

Obtaining federal registration for a service mark is a lengthy—often lasting a year or more—and complex process that begins with filing a written application with the PTO. To be eligible for filing such an application, a company must either have established prior use of the service mark (including foreign use for non-U.S. companies) or have a bona fide intention of using it on services rendered in federally regulated commerce, defined by the PTO as "all commerce that may lawfully be regulated by the U.S. Congress, for example, interstate commerce or commerce between the U.S. and another country." This stipulation is important and has resulted in numerous legal claims and lawsuits, such as a case in which Bookbinder's Restaurant in Philadelphia was found ineligible to register its name as a service mark because it was only a local business operating within state lines, whereas a pit-barbecue restaurant located on an interstate highway was found eligible.

Companies meeting these criteria submit a written application form (obtainable from the PTO in print or online), along with a filing fee and a drawing of the service mark; those businesses basing their application on prior use must also submit samples—brochures, advertisements, business cards—of the mark's use in commerce. The PTO then reviews the application, gives it a serial number, and assigns an examining attorney to determine whether the mark can be registered; if it can, the PTO publishes a notice of the mark in the weekly *Official Gazette,* giving other parties a chance to oppose the registration. Barring any opposition, successful applicants are issued a certificate of registration.

The PTO maintains two registers, principal and supplemental, the former conferring more rights than the latter. The PTO also specifies eight categories of services for which applicants can apply for registration of a service mark.

The PTO's examining attorneys can refuse registration for various reasons—among them that a mark is merely ornamental or descriptive, that it's disparaging or deceptive, or that it too closely resembles a mark already registered. Thus, a key part of the examining attorney's job is to search the PTO's library of existing and pending service marks to ascertain whether an applicant's mark conflicts with marks already in use.

Companies in the process of choosing a service mark are advised to conduct a preliminary search to verify that the mark hasn't already obtained national, state, or other rights. To aid in such efforts, the PTO maintains a trademark search library in Arlington, Virginia. Alternatively, companies can conduct a search through a patent and trademark depository library, available in most states, or hire an attorney or search firm to conduct the search.

Once registration is granted, a firm is entitled to use the registered trademark symbol (®) or, as alternatives, the phrases "Registered in U.S. Patent and Trademark Office" or "Reg. U.S. Pat. & Tm. Off."

DEFENDING A SERVICE MARK

Even once they're registered, service marks and other trademarks are in large measure only protected to the extent that they are used continuously and that the owner defends them against encroachment. The first step to defending a service mark occurs before registration through use of the (℠) symbol on company marketing. This act, which may done regardless of whether the service mark proprietor ever intends to register the mark, alerts other businesses and individuals that a claim is being made to the name, logo, and so forth. Aside from obvious cases of infringement, when a competitor uses a deceptively similar name or logo to tap into another company's business, service mark holders must also police against "genericization" or dilution of their name. This occurs when people routinely use the name to refer to an entire class of products or services, and not necessarily the particular ones being offered by the owner of the name. Well-known historical examples of trademarked products that became generic labels include fiberglass and styrofoam. While to some extent this is eventually out of the company's control, it can potentially be reduced by careful marketing that emphasizes the proprietary nature of the service and by sending warnings to media outlets if the name is being used generically in the mass media.

INTERNET SERVICE MARKS

One of the more important recent developments concerning service marks is the handling of Internet domain names. Domain name registration for technical purposes (i.e., creating a site name that can be looked up online) has nothing to do with trademark registration in itself, but the choice of names and who chooses them does matter. While no hard rules are yet in place, in general it is possible for companies to register Internet addresses as trademarks with the PTO, in addition to their regular business marks. Nonetheless, a number of trademark conflicts can arise with these names because of the separate registration systems.

First, a company that otherwise has no legitimate claim on a well known name may purchase that name through the technical domain registration process, which occurs solely on a first-come, first-serve basis. Usually the company only wants to resell the name to the company that holds the trademark, e.g., if a person bought the rights to the domain ''mcdonalds.com'' before the fast-food restaurant chain did, they might try selling it to the company for a profit. This would not necessarily be illegal, although McDonald's Corp. might well be able to prove it had an active trademark and force the upstart owner to give up the name without even going through a full federal court proceeding. While there was a rash of these sorts of conflicts as commercial use of the Internet exploded in the mid-1990s, more recently such abuses have been effectively reduced, in part because of the Trademark Dilution Act of 1996, which strengthened trademark holders' rights in such cases.

Still, trademark protection in that case might be ambiguous if the domain registrant had some coincidental relation to a more famous name, e.g., a nonfood business called McDonald's Plumbing, regardless of their intentions for it. Also, if it were a subtle but obvious variation on a name, it might not be so easily protected from the upstart company without going to court. However, if the upstart decided to start selling hamburgers, it would be a clear-cut example of infringement, as would be names that closely imitate the Internet-based businesses whose domain name is nearly identical to their company name, such as Amazon.com, Inc.

Because of such considerations, trademark attorneys have recommended that businesses register a trademark on a name before obtaining a matching Internet domain name to minimize the risk of claims against the name.

SEE ALSO: Intellectual Property; Trademark

FURTHER READING:

Borchard, William. *Trademark Basics.* New York: International Trademark Association, 1995.

Maguire, William E. ''Understanding the Fundamentals of Culinary Trademark Law.'' *Nation's Restaurant News,* 30 September 1996.

Posch, Robert J., Jr. ''Trademark Protection for Internet Domain Names.'' *Direct Marketing,* July 1998.

U.S. Department of Commerce. Patent and Trademark Office. *Basic Facts about Registering a Trademark.* Washington, 1995. Available from www.uspto.gov.

SEX DISCRIMINATION

SEE: Gender Discrimination

SEXUAL HARASSMENT

Sexual harassment is a term used to describe a variety of illegal, discriminatory actions—from unwelcome sexual advances to verbal conduct of a sexual nature—that create a hostile or abusive work environment. The **Equal Employment Opportunity Commission** (EEOC) defines sexual harassment as follows: ''Unwelcome sexual advances, requests for sexual favors, and other verbal or physical contact of a sexual nature constitute sexual harassment when: (1) Submission to such conduct is made either explicitly or implicitly a term or condition of an individual's employment. (2) Submission to or rejection of such conduct by an individual is used as the basis for employment decisions affecting such individuals. (3) Such conduct has the purpose or effect of unreasonably interfering with an individual's work performance or creating an intimidating, hostile, or offensive working environment.'' But legal experts warn managers and business owners that definitions of sexual harassment extend beyond the above borders. ''Most people think that sexual harassment necessarily involves conduct of a sexual nature,'' wrote Theresa Donahue Egler in *HRMagazine.* ''But, sexual harassment includes conduct that is not overtly sexual but is directed at an individual based on his or her gender. Thus, conduct such as profanity and other rude behavior . . . may give rise to liability so long as it is based on gender.''

Savvy business owners and managers will adopt a proactive stance to make certain that employees know that inappropriate behavior—whether taking the form of displaying sexually explicit photographs, using offensive language, making suggestive or otherwise inappropriate comments, badgering an employee for dates or other interactions outside the workplace, or suggesting that one gender is inferior to another—will not be tolerated in their company. Indeed, firms that do not do so leave themselves open to financial loss via lawsuits as well as other problems (low morale, **employee turnover**, **absenteeism**, etc.) that can ultimately affect financial performance. As EEOC guidelines state, "with respect to conduct between fellow employees, an employer is responsible for acts of sexual harassment in the workplace where the employer (or its agents or supervisory employees) knows or should have known of the conduct, unless it can show that it took immediate and appropriate corrective action."

A 1998 U.S. Supreme Court ruling pushed the envelope even further. The Court ruled—under Title VII of the Civil Rights Act of 1964—that an employer can be held liable for sexual harassment even if the employer is unaware of the incident. "The stakes are high and getting higher," concluded Ellen J. Wagner in *Sexual Harassment in the Workplace.* "In an increasingly litigious society and in an era of ever-increasing employee rights and employer responsibilities, sexual harassment allegations are particularly hazardous." *Nation's Business* contributors Robert T. Gray and Donald H. Weiss agreed. "All the signs point to sexual harassment becoming a more complex issue in the courts as well as in the workplace, and employers must be ready to respond accordingly," they wrote. "While that response can be prolonged and even difficult, the experts say that the depth of a company's commitment to preventing such conduct can be determined by one step at the moment of the filing of a complaint. That step: Take it seriously."

HARASSMENT AND EMPLOYEE RIGHTS

Sexual harassment has become a subject of considerable discussion during the 1990s. Previous generations of business owners and managers rarely had to address the issue. Business historians and social observers point to several possible factors for this. Some note that women used to comprise a much smaller component of the **workforce**, and that various societal pressures may have made them less likely to come forward with complaints. Others point out that many of the legal protections that are now in place against harassment have only developed over the last 30 years. Still other observers contend that the rise in sexual harassment claims simply reflects a general decline in civility in American society. Whatever the reasons, sexual harassment complaints have risen steadily in recent years. In fact, the number of sexual harassment claims that were filed with the EEOC increased from 6,883 in 1991 to 15,889 in 1997. "Because an agency complaint is a prerequisite to suit under federal and many state laws, these numbers forecast a corresponding increase in sexual harassment lawsuits in the coming years," wrote Egler. "When it is considered that many more potentially explosive situations are quietly resolved (some at substantial cost) before reaching the complaint stage, it is readily apparent that sexual harassment is a risk that requires proactive management."

But business owners and managers need to make sure that in their zeal to protect the legitimate rights of employees not to be harassed in the workplace, they do not trample on the rights of those accused of misbehavior. "While sexual harassment is clearly a pervasive reality, every case needs to be reviewed on its own merit," said Wagner. "Just because harassment is a significant social and corporate problem does not mean it has in fact occurred in a particular instance." Indeed, an employee who is punished or dismissed on the basis of a frivolous sexual harassment claim has the same recourse to the law as the victim of sexual harassment who is left unprotected by indifferent managers/owners. Business owners and managers thus need to consider the rights of all parties involved when investigating sexual harassment complaints.

CHANGING DEMOGRAPHICS OF SEXUAL HARASSMENT VICTIMS

Over the past several years, human resource professionals and business consultants alike have pointed to some fundamental changes in sexual harassment demographics. The overwhelming number of employees who are victims of sexual harassment continue to be women, but increasing numbers of men have found themselves targeted as well. From 1990 to 1994, for instance, the number of men who filed sexual harassment complaints with the EEOC tripled. Same-sex harassment charges have been on the rise as well. Observers note that some companies have been slow to treat such complaints as seriously as the more prevalent woman-as-victim, man-as-harasser complaints, with sometimes disastrous financial consequences for the businesses.

Some analysts expect women-as-harasser complaints to continue to rise, as the number of women business owners and executives grows. "Many would say that sexual harassment is nothing but an issue of power—that is, one person exercising power over another and using sex as the tool of power," attorney Gary Oberstein told *Industry Week*'s Michael Verespej. "[Women are now] in a position to see this as a tool, just as men have seen it as a tool for years." Verespej points out, however, that the nature of sexual harassment does seem to vary with the gender of the harasser. "When a male is the victim of harassment by a female, more than 50% of the cases allege a demand for sex—quid pro quo—in order to retain a job or receive a promotion," he reported. "By contrast, less than 15% of the cases in which a female is the victim of harassment by a male is there a demand for sex; the majority allege a hostile work environment."

The attention given to high-profile sexual harassment cases in the late 1990s has created an increase in other types of harassment cases. For example, employees have brought successful lawsuits against employers charging harassment based on age, AIDS, ethnic group, and activity by a union official. ''The prevalence of harassment suits in a variety of contexts indicates an enormous area of potential liability for companies and individuals in supervisory positions,'' Mary-Kathryn Zachary wrote in an article for *Supervision.*

DEVELOPING AND MAINTAINING SEXUAL HARASSMENT POLICIES

Ellen Wagner points out in *Sexual Harassment in the Workplace* that ''a well-drafted, carefully thought-out policy statement on sexual harassment can be valuable to an organization in at least three major ways: (1) as an employee relations tool, (2) as basic education for both managers and employees on the subject of sexual harassment, and (3) as a way of minimizing legal liability to the organization in hostile-environment sexual harassment cases . . . Not only is such a policy statement evidence of an organization's good-faith effort to provide a work environment free of harassment but, coupled with a proper investigation that successfully ends illegal or inappropriate conduct, it provides a major offensive weapon in employer efforts to demonstrate that all reasonable steps were taken and that they were effective.''

Indeed, business consultants universally counsel both small businesses and multinational corporations to establish formal written policies that make it explicitly clear that no forms of sexual harassment will be tolerated. Some companies prefer to disseminate this information as part of their larger general policy statements because of their sensitivity to giving extra attention to a sometimes awkward subject. But others reason that doing so can effectively bury the company's sexual harassment policies under the weight of all its other statements; these latter business owners and managers claim that dissemination of a separate policy statement not only better informs employees of the policy itself, but also underlines the company's serious approach to the subject.

Whether a business chooses to distribute its policies on sexual harassment via general information sources (such as an employee handbook) or separate statements, its policies should list all the various forms that sexual harassment can take (sexually loaded ''compliments,'' sexual advances, denigration of a person's gender, etc.) and explain how the company proceeds when confronted with a sexual harassment complaint. The policy statement should also discuss possible disciplinary consequences for workers who are found guilty of engaging in harassment. Finally, lawyers and consultants counsel their business clients to make sure that their policy statement is distributed to all employees. As Wagner noted, ''the most carefully drafted, best-written policy on sexual harassment is useless if it is not communicated throughout the organization.''

Other steps that businesses can take to establish a harassment-free workplace include: establishing internal procedures that address complaints promptly and thoroughly; establishing **training** programs that educate workers—especially managers, supervisors, and other people wielding power—about components of sexual harassment and their responsibilities when exposed to such behavior; and establishing alternative routes for workers to lodge complaints (in instances where their supervisor is the alleged harasser, for instance).

BUILDING A COMPREHENSIVE POLICY

Legal experts warn businesses that they need to make certain that their policies reflect a true understanding of the legal responsibilities of the employer, and a full recognition of the multitude of forms that sexual harassment can take. They point out that some companies have put together policies that, while sensible and effective in some or even most areas, are flawed in other areas, either because their policies did not adequately cover all the ways in which sexual harassment can occur, or because their understanding of sexual harassment was incomplete from the outset. For example, many people have long operated under the misconception that for sexual harassment to occur, the harasser must have a bad intent. The reality, however, is that ''what may be viewed as perfectly harmless by most men, may be viewed as offensive by most women,'' wrote Egler. ''In recognition of gender differences in perception, the courts have developed a new standard for analyzing claims of sexual harassment. In lieu of the traditional gender-neutral reasonable person standard, which is thought to be biased toward the male viewpoint, sexual harassment claims are analyzed in many jurisdictions from the perspective of a reasonable person of the same sex.''

Another important factor that is not always sufficiently appreciated by employers is that they can be held liable for harassing conduct by a third party such as a customer or vendor. Egler explained that ''even though these people are not employed by, and thus, not under the direction and control of the employer, the employer can be held responsible for harassment of its employees by such third parties.'' This mostly occurs in instances where the employer does not respond to such situations. Finally, Egler pointed out that some companies have been slow to recognize that ''what appears to be a consensual relationship by both parties may be regarded by the subordinate as an unwelcome obligation necessary for the protection of his or her job, whether or not this is actually the case.''

INVESTIGATING SEXUAL HARASSMENT COMPLAINTS

As one business attorney told *Industry Week,* companies "must take every complaint seriously, treat every complaint confidentially, investigate every complaint thoroughly, and take appropriate and immediate disciplinary action." Indeed, employers have a legal duty to investigate such complaints. "The objective of that review is simple," wrote Wagner. "To determine to the extent possible what happened, resolve the situation appropriately, and bring any illegal conduct to an end so that the workplace is once again free of any form of harassment."

Businesses need to make certain that the person who will investigate the complaint has credibility with the workforce. Ideally, the individual will be knowledgeable about the legal dimensions of sexual harassment, experienced in handling employee issues, familiar with the organization's policies, and socially and organizationally distant from both the alleged victim and the alleged harasser (the investigator should not be friends with the alleged victim, nor directly report to the alleged harasser, or vice versa). With smaller companies, however, it can be more difficult to adhere to such guidelines. If a small business owner has only four employees, and two of them become embroiled in a harassment case, finding an investigator with the above qualities is next to impossible. The owner may be tempted to look into the complaint him or herself in such instances, but business advisers often counsel against this. Instead, they recommend that the owner turn to an outside counsel or external consultant to pursue the complaint.

Whether the person doing the investigating is a third party, an employee, or the owner of the business, he or she should have a focused, carefully thought-out investigation plan designed to settle the issue in as timely a fashion as possible. This typically includes a review of relevant organizational records, including the complainant's personnel file, the alleged harasser's personnel file, performance reviews, and promotional and salary records. Such reviews can turn up everything from prior disciplinary warnings aimed at the accused to possibly relevant indications that the involved parties had previously competed against one another for promotions or other job opportunities. Such data may well be completely irrelevant to the legitimacy of the complaint, but it is the investigator's duty to check into all possible aspects of the complaint.

Every claim should be treated seriously, no matter how unusual or seemingly frivolous it might first appear, until an informed decision can be made. Conversely, an investigator should also suspend judgment on complaints that seem obviously legitimate until a thorough investigation has been completed. As Wagner remarked, "when sexual harassment is alleged, defamation is never very far away. . . . Since sexual harassment investigations almost always involve matters that might go to the heart of a person's reputation and good name, attention must be paid to minimizing the risks of defamation throughout the investigation and once it is concluded."

The first step in an investigation usually involves an in-depth interview of the complainant. Areas that should be pursued during this interview include the cultural background of the complainant (if dramatically different from that of the accused), a detailed reconstruction of the incident(s) that prompted the complaint, the context and circumstances in which it occurred, the involved parties' prior relationship (if any), the nature of the allegations against each individual in instances where incidents involved the participation of more than one person (common in hostile workplace complaints), and the complainant's expectations regarding how the alleged offender should be disciplined.

The investigation then turns to getting the accused's account of events. This step has different nuances, depending on whether the alleged harasser is a supervisor, a coworker, or a third party such as a customer, but basically this part of the investigation aims to secure the accused's perspective. In some instances, the accused may appear angry or shocked when confronted with a sexual harassment charge, so the investigator needs to allow time for the return of some measure of emotional equilibrium. When the initial reaction has subsided, wrote Wagner, the investigator should ask the worker to relate "what he believed happened during the incidents the complainant has cited. Allow him to relate his understanding of the situation through once, then return to it for specific, step-by-step review. As with the complainant, make sure the discussion is specific and detailed enough to provide the information you need to make an informed judgment later on. Note dates, times, places, circumstances, dress, words exchanged, as well as the specifics of the alleged acts." Again, issues such as prevailing work environment, prior relationships, etc., should be discussed.

Once the investigator has finished gathering information from the principal parties, he or she should then turn to possible witnesses. These could range from coworkers who were present when the alleged incident took place to those who have relevant information about either or both of the parties involved. The investigator should not be concerned with unsubstantiated rumors at this juncture; rather, he or she should concentrate on gathering factual data. This can be a very important part of the investigation, for accusations that turn into basic "he said, she said" disputes can be profoundly difficult for employers to resolve. "Immediate action may be difficult when an employer is faced with unsubstantiated accusation on one side and a categorical denial on the other,'' wrote Gray and Weiss. ''In such cases, [attorney Stephen] Bokat says, it is important to realize that 'these things tend not to occur in isolation. If there has been harassment, often someone else has seen or heard the conduct or speech involved or there will be repetitions that will indicate a pattern.' ''

Employers need to interview these witnesses carefully, however. ''You must assess the credibility and believability of all persons corroborating some aspect of the complainant's or accused's contention,'' confirmed Wagner. ''Consider the issue of witness motivation and the relationship between each witness and the individual whose word is being corroborated. Make sure you understand what each witness might stand to gain from the situation, as well as what genuine feelings are at work here.'' Witnesses also need to understand that the subject should not be discussed with coworkers or other individuals; sexual harassment charges are both serious and sensitive, and they should be regarded as such.

Human resources experts also recommend that investigators not rely wholly on interviews. Ideally, the investigator should secure written statements from all parties—complainant, accused, and witnesses—as part of this information-gathering process.

Once the investigation into the sexual harassment complaint has been completed, corrective action (if any) needs to be implemented. When corrective action is warranted, it can range from counseling to transfer to dismissal. The key factors that usually determine the severity of the corrective action are: (1) the nature of the offense, (2) the desires of the complainant, and (3) the impact that the incident had on the workplace as a whole.

HARASSMENT OF THE SELF-EMPLOYED

Self-employed individuals who work as **independent contractors** enjoy fewer legal protections from sexual harassment at the hands of clients. Experts recommend that self-employed people confronted with such unpleasantness react strongly and decisively. They should make it immediately clear that the harassment (which in these situations typically takes the form of unwanted sexual advances) is unwelcome, and that they would prefer to keep their association with their client a professional one. If this line of defense does not work, self-employed workers may wish to consult an attorney about their state's tort law, which regulates conduct between people and provides monetary damages. In addition, national women's organizations can often provide guidance and legal assistance in these matters. Finally, some observers believe that additional legal protections in this area may be on the way. They point out, for instance, that a bill has been introduced in California that would expressly prohibit sexual harassment against self-employed individuals providing contracted-for services. Violators of this proposed bill would be subject to considerable damages.

TAKING SEXUAL HARASSMENT POLICIES TOO FAR

The confusing array of rules about sexual harassment—as well as the threat of expensive litigation—was having a negative effect on the culture of some companies by the late 1990s. Some employers created repressive working environments in which employees were reluctant to tell jokes or pat each other on the back, let alone enter into romantic relationships, for fear of violating company policies about sexual harassment.

Many companies willingly spend thousands of dollars each year to train employees about sexual harassment in order to avoid the potential for million-dollar lawsuits later. In fact, an entire industry has grown up to assist companies in training workers to avoid inappropriate behavior and compromising situations. The lawyers, consultants, and therapists working in this field help companies to interpret ever-changing legal pronouncements on the issue and adapt their policies accordingly. ''In fearful executive suites around the nation, this vast new antiharassment industrial complex has found a ready market for a host of products and services that promise not simply to resolve but to prevent harassment, and, indeed, the conditions that give rise to it,'' according to an article in *U.S. News and World Report.*

Some experts have claimed that it is possible to take company policies about sexual harassment too far. After all, only 4 percent of companies have experienced sexual harassment lawsuits over the past five years, according to a 1998 survey conducted by the Society for Human Resource Management. It is important to weigh the risk of lawsuits against the negative effect of excessively strict or invasive policies that may make it difficult to attract and retain qualified employees. ''Corporate America is advancing into the treacherous territory of establishing rules, procedures, and guidelines that, in the name of preventing harassment, also establish a framework for romance,'' according to *U.S. News and World Report.*

It can be extremely difficult for employers to discourage or control romantic relationships between employees. After all, from six to eight million Americans enter into workplace romances each year. Some companies try to ban such behavior, particularly between supervisors and subordinates. But this approach can backfire. If a company terminates one employee for a romantic involvement with a coworker, and then that employee discovers that another employee had engaged in similar behavior and had not been fired, then the company may be subject to a lawsuit for wrongful termination rather than sexual harassment.

In recent years, some companies have developed innovative new ways to allow workplace romance while also protecting themselves against sexual harassment litigation. One example is a date-and-tell policy, which generally applies to supervisor-subordinate relationships. Upon entering into a romantic relationship with a subordinate, the supervisor is required to tell a designated person. This person then advises the subordinate of his or her rights under sexual harassment laws. In this way, the employer gains some protection from knowing that the relationship is consensual. Another example is a love contract, which often applies to a top executive or someone who has a sexual harassment complaint pending already. The contract documents the relationship and gives the company some measure of protection from litigation.

SEE ALSO: Gender Discrimination

[Kevin Hillstrom, updated by Laurie Collier Hillstrom]

FURTHER READING:

Bahls, Steven C., and Jane Easter Bahls. ''Hands-Off Policy.'' *Entrepreneur,* July 1997, 74+.

Barrier, Michael. ''Sexual Harassment.'' *Nation's Business,* December 1998, 14.

''Cupid's Cubicles.'' *U.S. News and World Report,* 14 December 1998, 44.

Egler, Theresa Donahue. ''Five Myths about Sexual Harassment.'' *HRMagazine* 40, no. 1 (January 1995): 27+.

''Facts about Sexual Harassment.'' Washington: U.S. Equal Employment Opportunity Commission, 1997.

Gray, Robert T., and Donald H. Weiss. ''How to Deal with Sexual Harassment.'' *Nation's Business,* December 1991, 28+.

Kimble-Ellis, Sonya, and Gerda D. Gallop. ''Safeguard against Sexual Harassment.'' *Black Enterprise,* December 1998, 36.

Lawlor, Julia. ''Stepping Over the Line.'' *Sales and Marketing Management* 147, no. 10 (October 1995): 90+.

Petrocelli, William, and Barbara Kate Repa. *Sexual Harassment on the Job: What It Is and How to Stop It.* 4th ed. Berkeley, CA: Nolo Press, 1998.

Verespej, Michael J. ''New Age Sexual Harassment: An Increasing Number of Victims Are Men or Same-Gender Workers.'' *Industry Week,* 15 May 1995, 64+.

Wagner, Ellen J. *Sexual Harassment in the Workplace: How to Prevent, Investigate, and Resolve Problems in Your Organization.* New York: AMACOM, 1992.

Zachary, Mary-Kathryn. ''Harassment: The Other Varieties Are on the Upswing.'' *Supervision,* January 1999, 21+.

SIC

SEE: Standard Industrial Classification System

SIMPLE INTEREST

Interest can be an expense or a revenue. Interest expense is the cost of borrowed money. Interest income is the earnings on money that has been lent or invested. The sum against which interest is calculated is known as the principal. Interest on the principal may be calculated as simple interest or compound interest.

The primary difference between simple interest and compound interest is the treatment of the length of time for which interest is paid or earned. In simple interest calculations, the number of time periods is disregarded. For example, $100 earning 10 percent simple interest results in interest income of $10 per year regardless of how many years are involved. That is, the amount of interest equals the **interest rate** times the principal. The accumulated interest and the number of time periods do not enter into the calculation.

On the other hand, in compound interest calculations, each time period affects the amount of interest earned or paid. That is because the accumulated interest itself earns interest, or is said to be compounded. For example, $100 earning 10 percent compound interest results in interest income of $10 in the first year. In the second year, interest income increases to 10 percent of $110, or $11, because the first year's interest is added to the principal. In the third year the interest payment increases to $12.10, or 10 percent of $121.

Thus, it can be seen that using simple interest, a $100 investment would earn $30 over three years at 10 percent. Using compound interest, the same investment would result in interest income of $33.10. Compound interest is widely used in **financial planning**, because it is assumed that interest on the principal would earn the same interest rate as the principal does. Simple interest is useful in situations where the interest payments are not being reinvested.

SEE ALSO: Interest Rates

[David P. Bianco]

SIMPLIFIED EMPLOYEE PENSION (SEP)

A simplified employee pension (SEP), also known as an SEP-IRA (**individual retirement account**), can be defined as a **pension plan** for **small business** owners and their employees and the self-employed. Created by Congress and monitored carefully by the **Internal Revenue Service** (IRS), SEPs are designed to give small business owners and employees the same ability to set aside money for retirement as traditional large corporate pension funds.

The Small Business Job Protection Act of 1996 also established the Savings Incentive Match Plan for Employees (SIMPLE), a streamlined SEP that is exempt from certain government reports and tests, provided that employers contribute 2 percent of each eligible employee's salary or match employee contributions up to 3 percent of wages. Employee contributions into a SIMPLE plan cannot exceed $6,000 per year, and employer contributions or matching funds cannot exceed $2,000 per year.

SEPs can also be much more flexible and attractive than corporate pensions. They can even be used to supplement such pensions and corporate **401(k) plans**. Many full-time employees use SEPs as a way to save and invest more money for retirement than they might normally be expected to put away under IRS rules. *Forbes* magazine described SEPs as a "moonlighter's delight" in a 1993 article. The reason for the magazine's enthusiasm is that SEPs, while created for the self-employed and small business people, also allow full-time employees to contribute a portion of **self-employment** income from consulting or freelancing.

The rules governing SEPs are fairly simple, but are subject to change with any Congressional action, so yearly checks of IRS publications 560 (retirement plans for the self-employed) and 590 (IRAs) are necessary. Through 1994, SEPs could be set up with a simple form and did not require any separate trustee, which is required of larger, more complicated pension plans. The maximum allowable tax-deductible SEP contribution per employee is 15 percent of salary or income (up to a maximum income of $150,000) or $22,500, whichever is less. The maximum amount an employer can contribute to his or her own plan is 13.0435 percent of income. Still, compared to the $2,000 allowable standard IRA contribution, which has not been fully tax deductible for all contributors since 1986, the advantages of SEPs are obvious. SEPs can also be combined with **variable annuities** as a strategy to avoid outliving retirement savings. Variable annuities are established when investors entrust their money to an insurance company for investment, with the insurance company agreeing to repay the investors at a set rate and time according to contractual terms. Furthermore, people can contribute to their existing IRAs and 401(k)s and still hold an SEP. SEPs were made still more attractive in January 1996 by amendments to the IRS code that prohibited states from imposing "source taxes" on the pensions and other retirement funds of their former residents now residing elsewhere.

One word of caution for small business owners: SEP plans must be set up for everyone in the company, including part-time employees. This does not mean that the SEP must be funded each year. If the company is experiencing a lean year, funding of the SEP may be skipped. All of the SEP's funding is deductible as a business expense in the year it is made.

A similar program is the salary reduction simplified employee pension (SARSEP). SARSEPs are similar to 401(k) plans, in which employees defer part of their annual compensation into an IRA. Any employer contributions to the program are deductible as business expenses. The employer can still establish a separate SEP to handle employer contributions. SARSEPs are available to businesses with 25 or fewer employees, but at least 50 percent of a company's employees must elect to participate in the program to launch it.

[Clint Johnson, updated by Grant Eldridge]

FURTHER READING:

Blakely, Stephen. "Are Variable Annuities for You?" *Nation's Business,* December 1997, 20.

Janicki, Michael. "New Federal Law Restricts State Taxation of Nonresidents' Pensions." *Tax Adviser* 27, no. 5 (May 1996): 279.

"Pensions Made Simple." *HR Focus* 74, no. 4 (April 1997): 9.

Rowland, Mary. "Pension Options for Small Firms." *Nation's Business,* March 1994, 25-27.

Silverstein, Kenneth. "Simple Pensions: Pension Simplification Efforts Continue to Be an Issue." *Pension Management* 32, no. 6 (June 1996): 9.

Turville, Mary A. "Pension Provisions in the 1996 Tax Acts." *National Public Accountant* 41, no. 12 (December 1996): 21.

SINKING FUND

To raise funds for expansion, product development, research, and other purposes, companies sometimes borrow money by issuing **bonds**, which are long-term **promissory notes** issued by companies to investors. Bond agreements or indentures generally require corporations to make regular interest payments—often semiannually—during the term of the bond. Corporations then must pay the maturity value or face value—the amount an investor initially paid—on the date of maturity. In addition, a bond agreement may contain a sinking fund provision that requires a corporation to repay a certain number of bonds in certain years, or for a corporation to retire part of a bond issue annually until fully repaid.

Traditionally under a sinking fund provision companies retired bonds by creating a special fund. Funds were transferred to a trustee who set up the fund and retired the bonds. Such arrangements, however, are not as common nowadays. Instead, the sinking fund provision simply refers to a company's obligation to buy back a certain number of bonds each year. The retirement of bond **debt** under the sinking fund provision may take the form of either paying a price at or above the face value of the bonds—which is referred to as calling the bonds—or buying them in the open market. Once in a while, a company will create a fund by transferring money to a trustee who invests it and initially uses money plus interest to retire the bonds once they mature.

A sinking fund provision may require either uniform annual payments, uniform increments over time, or contributions determined by the level of earnings. Since a bond issue with a sinking fund provision is generally considered to be safer than a similar bond issue without one, a sinking fund provision has the effect of lowering the **interest rate** on a bond issue. Consequently, a sinking fund provision is a trade off between safety and profitability from the investor's perspective.

A sinking fund may be illustrated as follows: if a company issued $10 million of ten-year bonds on June 1, 1990, with a sinking fund provision, it might have to retire 10 percent or ($1 million) of the bonds each year beginning in 1991 through June 1, 2000, when the bonds mature. Alternatively, since sinking fund provisions vary greatly, the company might have to retire 5 percent annually beginning in 1995.

BENEFITS OF A SINKING FUND

Sinking funds carry some risk, because failure to fulfill sinking fund requirements puts the bond issue into **default**, which might lead to bankruptcy. Hence, sinking funds might cause cash shortages. Nevertheless, an issuer may accept sinking fund provisions for the following reasons:

1. If the creditworthiness of the issuer is in question, lenders may not grant **credit** without a sinking fund since it provides a measure of protection for the creditor. The **opportunity costs** of the sinking fund requirement may be the inability to secure long-term debt needed to purchase highly profitable equipment.
2. The accumulation of funds in a special account also provides the issuer with security against future business conditions that may be detrimental to its ability to retire the debt.
3. The insurance provided by a sinking fund decreases the interest rates, therefore, the interest expenses. This results in increased cash flow.
4. When the purchase of productive assets requires a sinking fund, the sinking fund mirrors the **depreciation** schedule of those assets. The issuer benefits in two ways. Depreciation allows the issuer to recover the costs while simultaneously retiring the debt of equipment going out of service.
5. The issuer can book **capital gains** on debt retirement if it purchases bonds in the open market below book value.
6. A sinking fund enhances the **tax** benefits of financial **leverage**. First, interest expense and depreciation are tax deductible. The issuer can use the tax savings to fund part of the annual sinking fund payment. Second, the sinking fund could earn compounded interest, helping to reduce the cost of borrowing. Finally, the interest expense decreases proportionately to the amount of bonds outstanding. If the sinking fund accumulates and compounds, the earnings grow geometrically. At some point the issuer will benefit from a positive after-tax cash flow.

[Roger J. AbiNader, updated by Karl Heil]

FURTHER READING:

Brigham, Eugene F. *Fundamentals of Financial Management.* 7th ed. Fort Worth, TX: Dryden Press, 1995.

Fabozzi, Frank J. *Bond Markets, Analysis and Strategies.* 3rd ed. Upper Saddle River, NJ: Prentice Hall, 1995.

Schall, Lawrence D., and Charles W. Haley. *Introduction to Financial Management.* 6th ed. New York: McGraw-Hill, 1991.

SMALL BUSINESS ADMINISTRATION (SBA)

The Small Business Administration (SBA) was established with the passage of the Small Business Act of 1953. The SBA succeeded the small business loan program of the Reconstruction Finance Corporation. The purpose of the SBA is to help Americans start, run, and expand **small businesses**, as well as aiding, counseling, assisting, and protecting the interests of small business concerns.

Intrinsic to the SBA is the question: What is a small business? This question does not have a specific answer but Sec. 3(a) of the Small Business Act gives the following guidelines. A small business includes but is not limited to the production of food and fiber, ranching and the raising of livestock, aquaculture and all other farming and agriculture related industries. A small business is likewise independently owned and operated and not dominant in its field of operation. Agricultural enterprises are deemed to be small business concerns if they, and their affiliates, do not have annual receipts exceeding $500,000. The number of employees, the volume of business, net worth, net income, or any combinations of these factors may be utilized to determine if an enterprise is a ''small business.'' There are also restrictions on using a size standard for categorizing a business concern as a small business by a federal department or agency.

Based on its own information as well as data from the U.S. Department of Labor and the **U.S. Department of Commerce**, the SBA easily documents the enormous contribution small businesses make to the U.S. economy. The SBA estimates that in 1996 there were approximately 23 million small businesses in the United States, including the 842,357 new employer firms created that year alone. This represented a 2.8 percent increase over the figure for new firms in 1995. Also in 1996, industries dominated by small business concerns were responsible for 64 percent of the 2.5 million new jobs created that year. Small businesses also generally hire approximately 67 percent of first-time workers and provide them with initial job **training** in basic skills. Small businesses employ 53 percent of the private **workforce**; provide 47 percent of all sales in the United States; receive 35 percent of federal contract dollars; support 28 percent of high technology jobs; and are responsible for 51 percent of private sector output.

With small business concerns playing such a vital role in the U.S. economy, the SBA offers many services and programs designed to encourage small business start-ups, promote growth, and provide protection within this economic sector. The SBA provides disaster assistance for nonfarm, private sector losses that result from natural catastrophes such as floods, as well as damage from riots and civil unrest. The SBA also has a comprehensive array of financial programs for start-up as well as established small business concerns. Most of these programs offer loan guarantees to private lending institutions. Surety bond guarantees and **export** financing can also be provided to small business concerns. The SBA also ensures that small business concerns receive an equitable portion of government purchases, **contracts**, subcontracts, and sales of government property. Loan guarantees can be made by the SBA to state and local development authorities. In addition, the SBA is authorized to license, regulate, and make loan guarantees to investment companies falling within the SBA's definition of a small business.

The SBA also provides guidance in preparing a **business plan**, widely considered the most important step in starting a new business. A business plan is a blueprint that focuses the goals and helps gauge the progress of the new endeavor. It details the planned business and its major products or services, outlines the **management** team, and defines targets for sales, growth, new product development, etc.

Additionally, the SBA promotes business initiatives through its counseling, education, and training programs. One such program is SCORE (Service Corps of Retired Executives). SCORE is a free service consisting of thousands of retired volunteers who span the full range of business management—office managers, accountants, **advertising** and **public relations** experts, and sales managers. Many district offices also hold pre-business workshops for aspiring entrepreneurs. These sessions offer advice to those who want to start small retail and service businesses.

The SBA assures women, veterans, and minority groups full access to programs and services through its Office of Women's Business Ownership, Office of Veteran's Affairs, and Minority Enterprise Development Program. Another innovative SBA program is the bringing together of small business concerns and former welfare recipients turned job seekers. This program is in relation to the ''President's Welfare to Work Initiative'' and the Personal Responsibility and Work Opportunity Reconciliation Act of 1996.

Aida Alvarez was appointed to head the SBA by President Bill Clinton in early 1997. Under her administration the SBA arranged for 6,360 lenders to make 45,288 start-up and expansion **loans** worth $9.46 billion 1997. There were also 4,131 long-term fixed asset financing loans valued at $1.44 billion for a record $10.9 billion in loan guarantees.

SEE ALSO: Minority-Owned Businesses; Small Businesses; Women Entrepreneurs

[Michael Knes]

FURTHER READING:

Alvarez, Aida. ''A Record Year for SBA.'' *Credit World,* January/February 1998, 31-33.

Godfrey, Nicola. ''Aida Alvarez.'' *Working Woman,* July/August 1998, 26+.

Small Business Administration. *Borrower's Guide.* Washington: Small Business Administration, 1996.

——. ''U.S. Small Business Administration: Learn about the SBA.'' Washington: Small Business Administration, 1998. Available from www.sba.gov.

SMALL BUSINESSES

Small businesses and entrepreneurs form the backbone of the American economy. Without one, there would not be the other. Certainly, not all small businesses are owned by entrepreneurs, but it is entrepreneurs who generate the ideas that lead to opportunities for people to begin their own companies. That has been the case since the early days of American history, and will no doubt continue to be for the foreseeable future.

SMALL BUSINESSES IN THE U.S. ECONOMY

By various definitions, anywhere from 70 to 99 percent of American businesses fall into the ''small'' category. This range places the actual count of small businesses somewhere between 15 and 20 million firms, the vast majority of which are sole proprietorships. The exact percentage is difficult to estimate, since there is no clear-cut definition of what constitutes a small business. For example, the U.S. Chamber of Commerce defines a small business as a company that employs fewer than 500 people. Another definition suggests that a small business is one that employs fewer than 100 people. Yet a third definition eschews numbers and states simply that a small business is one that is independently owned, i.e., not a subsidiary of a large company. Whatever definition applies, one thing is certain: small businesses account for the bulk of businesses in the United States. That has been the case since the first settlers set foot on American soil in the early 1600s.

THE HISTORY OF SMALL BUSINESS

Small businesses were the lifeblood of the American economy between the time the first settlers arrived in the early 1600s and the Industrial Revolution. In almost every early American community, small business owners abounded. For example, a profile of Northampton, Massachusetts, in 1773 shows that workers other than farmers were not day laborers who toiled for wages. Rather, they were skilled artisans who worked for themselves. They comprised blacksmiths, goldsmiths, tanners, weavers, tailors, traders, barbers, or any other specialist whose services were needed by others. This situation continued until the Industrial Revolution.

The proliferation of machines and assembly line processing altered the way Americans did business, but, contrary to what many people predicted at the time, it did not eliminate the need for small business owners. That has never changed. Even today, when corporations are undergoing massive changes in their work structures, the need for small business owners has remained steady or even increased.

In the late 1980s, corporations began divesting themselves of large numbers of employees, particularly those in middle management. Many of these displaced workers opted to start their own businesses rather than take a chance on working for corporations and being downsized again. So, in the early 1990s, there began a trend toward more small business ownership. Many of the people who started these new businesses were merely exercising entrepreneurial skills that had either been dormant or simply never used. These were the new breed of entrepreneurs, whose presence is necessary if any economy is to flourish.

ENTREPRENEURS

Entrepreneurs are generally innovative people who turn new ideas into thriving businesses. Often, the businesses they start based on a simple idea turn into major corporations. Their endeavors pave the way for less innovative people with shrewd business minds to run small businesses of their own. Thus, entrepreneurs and business operators feed off one another—and feed the American economy.

As is the case with the term ''small business,'' entrepreneur is hard to define. To some people, an entrepreneur is simply an individual who starts a new enterprise. To others, the word connotes an individual who organizes and manages natural resources, labor, and capital in order to produce goods and services with the intention of making a profit—but who also runs the risk of failure. However the word is defined, entrepreneurs are the linchpin of the American economy. They make it possible for small business owners to survive, in whatever form of operation they choose.

SMALL BUSINESS RISKS

Running a successful small business requires a tremendous amount of dedication and a variety of skills. A successful small business owner must have a wide range of entrepreneurial skills, e.g., a knowledge of financing, selling, accounting, bookkeeping, regulatory procedures—in short, just about every facet of business. But, knowledge of the various business activities alone does not guarantee an owner success. There are other factors involved, such as location and luck. The bottom line is that small business operators must be dedicated to succeed—and not all of them do. Many small business owners fall victim to the pitfalls of the economy and fail due to no fault of their own. At other times, they end up in bankruptcy because they do not adhere to the basic rules of business.

TYPES OF SMALL BUSINESS

There exist several forms of small business—**S corporations**, sole proprietorships, general partnerships, **franchises**, and others. Regardless of what type of business owners choose, their goals are the same: to make provide returns on the owner's investment.

SOLE PROPRIETORSHIPS. The most common form of small business is the sole proprietorship, a business owned and usually operated by one person who is personally responsible for the firm's debts. According to Census Bureau figures, approximately three-quarters of all businesses are sole proprietorships. Nonetheless, because the tend to be so small, they account for less than six percent of total business revenues in the country. Individual sole proprietorships may be small, but from them grow some major corporations. Many of today's large companies (for example, Sears,

Roebuck & Co. and Ford Motor Co.), began as sole proprietorships.

One of the reasons sole proprietorships are so popular is because they offers many advantages to small business owners. The biggest advantages are they are simple to establish and offer many freedoms for the owner. Sole proprietors answer only to themselves. They alone enjoy the profits. On the other hand, they are solely responsible for debts. Another advantage is the privacy involved in running a sole proprietorship. The owner does not have to reveal information regarding the business to anyone, aside from tax reporting to the government.

Sole proprietorships are relatively simple to start up. While certain professions or trades require certification or licensure, there is otherwise no formal requirement for creating a sole proprietorship: it exists at the will of its owner. People interested in starting their own businesses often need do no more than hang out a sign. The lack of complex regulations governing the opening of a small business is extremely appealing to entrepreneurs, many of whom thrive on starting businesses and then divesting them. Perhaps the biggest advantage, though, is that owners of sole proprietorships can dissolve them as easily as they start them. That is why many sole proprietorships are designed to be short-lived.

There are people who form sole proprietorships to run a single athletic event or rock concert. As soon as the event is over, the business is terminated. Because of the ease of starting such a business, promoters can—and often do—''open'' and ''close'' such businesses frequently. This is possible for several reasons, not the least of which is the low cost of starting such a business.

Low start-up costs encourage many people to open their own businesses. In many cases, there are no legal fees involved. Often, a person starting a sole proprietorship need only register it with a state agency as protection against another person using the business' name. There are some sole proprietorships that require the owners to have licenses, for example, hair salons or bars. Depending on the business activity, the owner may have to comply also with local zoning and business permit requirements.

Consider a writer who wishes to start a business. There are no licenses involved, thus no fees to pay. The need for legal assistance is rare—possibly only for cases where copyright infringement is involved. Generally, writers can work out of office space in their homes without worrying about zoning regulations. And, comparatively speaking, there is very little equipment for a writer to purchase—writers need little more than a computer, a fax machine, a printer, a telephone, and a modem. They also need sundry items like paper and reference books. Thus, to start a writing business, all that is needed is a pronouncement that ''I am a small business owner'' and a desire to succeed. Most importantly, writers enjoy the ultimate benefits of a sole proprietorship: they keep the profits and get tax breaks.

There are, of course, cases when sole proprietors (and other business owners) suffer losses in the early stages of their operations. Tax laws allow sole proprietors to treat the sales revenues and operating expenses of the business as part of their personal finances. As a result, sole proprietors can reduce their taxes by deducting allowable operating losses from income earned from sources other than the business. This can be an important means of reducing tax liabilities that an individual would otherwise incur.

The possibility of losing money is but one of the disadvantages of a sole proprietorship. One major disadvantage is the fact that sole proprietors are responsible for all debts incurred by their businesses. This unlimited liability is a deterrent to some people seeking to start their own businesses. If a business doesn't generate the projected income in its existence, owners must pay any debts incurred out of their own pockets. If they do not—or cannot—creditors can claim the owners' personal property such as cars and houses. (Laws vary from state to state. Some states do allow business owners to protect some of their personal property.)

Another disadvantage associated with sole proprietorships is the lack of continuity. If an owner dies, the business is not passed down automatically to heirs or family members. A sole proprietorship is dissolved legally when the owner dies. Of course, there is nothing to stop other people from reorganizing the business if there is a successor available who is trained and willing to take over the business. If there is not, the deceased owner's executors or heirs must liquidate the assets of the business. The effects of an owner's death indicate another major disadvantage to a sole proprietorship: it is frequently dependent on the resources of one person.

Often, sole proprietors are responsible for all of the operations involved in running a business. They alone are responsible for the firm's cash flow and finances. Often, they find it difficult to borrow money through formal channels such as banks when they need it. This applies to money for starting and expanding businesses. Banks, for example, are sometimes reluctant to lend money to sole proprietors for fear they will not recover it if the owners die or become disabled. Therefore, proprietors usually must rely on the cash generated by the business, personal savings, or family loans to finance their operations, although the **Small Business Administration** does help small businesses secure outside loans by guaranteeing loans and providing other support programs.

GENERAL PARTNERSHIPS. General partnerships are fairly common in the world of small business even though they are legally one of the least popular form of business organization. There are over a million U.S. partnerships in existence, which generate less than 5 percent of total U.S. sales revenues. A general partnership is a business with two or more owners who share in the operation of a firm and in financial responsibility for its debts. There is no legal limit to the number of partners allowed. The number can run from two to hundreds. Partners do not have to invest equal amounts of money. They may earn profits that bear no relationship to the amount they have invested in the business. It is up to the partners to arrange the financial dealings and other management aspects of the organization.

Sometimes partnerships are created when sole proprietors can no longer run their businesses as one-person operations. Or, sole proprietors may simply want to expand, and taking on a partner or partners is the best way to accomplish it. A general partnership can be a start-up operation, too.

Like any other type of business, general partnerships have their advantages and disadvantages. One of the advantages is that partnerships can add talent and money as they go along. They also have an easier time borrowing money. Normally, banks and other lending institutions prefer to loan money to businesses that do not depend on one person. Another advantage is that partners in a business have access to one another's funds. This is especially important in a business that has a large number of partners.

Another advantage is that partnerships are easy to organize. There are few legal requirements involved in forming a general partnerships. Wise partners, however, will draft some type of agreement among themselves. The agreement may be written, oral, or unspoken. The important thing is that one must exist. Some of the questions that might be asked include general ones such as who invests what sums of money in the partnership, who receives what share of the partnership's profits, who does what and who reports to whom, and how the partnership may be dissolved if the need arises. What is included in the agreement is up to the individuals involved. The document is not a legal requirement; it is strictly a private document that no government agency needs to see.

A partnership is not a legal entity in the eyes of the law. It is simply an agreement between two or more people working together. From an Internal Revenue Service standpoint, partners are taxed as individuals. That, too, is an advantage for partnerships. But, there are the inevitable disadvantages, too.

Unlimited liability is a major drawback for partnerships, just as it is for sole proprietors. By law, each partner may be held personally liable for all debts occurred in the partnership's name. If any partner incurs a debt, even if the other partners do not know about it, they are all liable for it if the responsible partner cannot pay it. This legal stipulation remains even if the partnership agreement states that all notes and bills are to endorsed by the other partners.

Again, as is the case with the sole proprietorships, lack of continuity can be a disadvantage in partnerships. If one partner dies or withdraws from the business, the partnership may dissolve legally. This can happen even if the other partners agree to stay. They can, however, form a new partnership immediately if they wish, and retain the old firm's business. This arrangement prevents the loss of revenues that might otherwise affect the partners. The lack of continuity problem is closely associated with the difficulty of transferring ownership.

In a general partnership, no individual may sell out without the permission of the other partners. In addition, partners who want to retire or transfer their interests in the firm to family members cannot do so without the express permission of all the remaining partners. As a result, the continuation of a partnership may depend on the ability of retiring partners to find someone acceptable to the other partners to buy their shares. If retiring partners cannot find such a person, the partnership may have to be liquidated. As an alternative, the remaining partners may buy out a retiring partner.

Another major problem involved frequently with partnerships is the lack of conflict resolution. When sole proprietors have problems with the way their businesses are being run, they resolve the problems themselves. That is not the case with partners. If one partner or group of partners wants to expand a business, and another partner or group does not, there is a conflict. That conflict may be difficult to resolve, especially if the partners are evenly divided. Conflicts may involve virtually anything, ranging from partners' personal habits to personnel matters. The lack of resolution can lead to dissolution.

CORPORATIONS. Another type of small business is the corporation, which is normally associated with large businesses. Indeed, even though only 20 percent of the nation's businesses (about 3.6 million firms) are corporations, they generate 90 percent of the revenues. Nevertheless, a corporation does not have to be a large business.

Any business owner can incorporate. In legal terms, a corporation is a legal entity separate from its owners with many of the legal rights and privileges a person has. It is a form of business organization in which the liability of the owners is limited to their investment in the firm. Corporations may sue and be sued; buy, hold, and sell property; make and sell products to consumers; and commit crimes and be punished for them. As far as small businesses go, many of the attributes associated with corporations may be inappropriate. For example, a writer or a newsstand owner may not want to sell stock in their businesses, form boards of directors, or deal in proxy votes. Nevertheless, small business owners can incorporate to take advantage of benefits endemic to corporations.

The biggest advantages corporations experience include limited liability, continuity, greater likelihood of professional management, and easier access to money. On the other hand, there are disadvantages. For example, corporations may undergo stockholder revolts, experience high start-up costs, be subjected to excessive regulation, and pay high taxes.

S CORPORATIONS. A special form of corporation is the S corporation, so named because it is part of the Subchapter S of the U.S. Internal Revenue Code. Congress created the S corporation in 1958 to help small businesses compete better and to provide them with some relief from excessive taxation and regulation, both of which have increased since World War II.

The S corporation allows businesses to avoid double taxation. It is based on the premise that owners enjoy the limited liability benefits of corporate ownership but the taxation advantages of a partnership. Stockholders of an S corporation are taxed simply as if they were partners. As with other forms of small business, the corporations do not pay income taxes on earnings and the stockholders do not pay income taxes or tax on their dividends. Of course, there are limitations on the S corporation.

First, in order to qualify as an S corporation, a business must meet some stiff legal requirements. For example, it must be a domestic corporation that is independently owned and managed and not part of any other corporation. It cannot have any more than 35 stockholders. The stockholders that do exist may only be estates or individuals. They cannot be nonresident aliens. Lastly, no more than 25 percent of the firm's sales revenues may come from dividends, rent, interest, royalties, annuities, or stock sales, and no more than 80 percent of sales revenues may come from foreign markets. Despite these restrictions, S corporations do offer small business owners significant advantages.

LIMITED PARTNERSHIPS. Limited partnerships are businesses that have both active and inactive partners. They exist mainly so owners can avoid the problem of unlimited liability. The active partners run the company. The limited partners have no active role in the company's operations. (For this reason, they are sometimes called silent partners.) Should the business fail, they are liable only to the extent of their investment. They can invest their money without being held liable for the active partners' debts. There are legal stipulations that affect how a limited partnership is run. For example, each limited partnership must have at least one active partner designated as the general partner. This is primarily for liability purposes. In most cases, the general partner oversees the day-to-day operations of the company and holds the responsibility for its survival and growth.

In a master limited partnership, the business is organized much like a corporation. However, all the profits are paid out to investors. The company is run by a single "master" partner, who holds a majority of the stock. The major advantage to a master limited partnership is that it helps owners avoid double taxation. In this arrangement, the company sells shares to investors, just as a corporation does.

Corporations retain some portion of any profits for growth and expansion. They pay income taxes on these profits, and the stockholders must pay income taxes on the dividends they receive from the company. Under the master limited partnership arrangement, this double taxation is avoided. There are disadvantages, though. For instance, since more of the earnings are paid to investors than is normally the case in a corporation structure, per-share prices for **stocks** are higher. This dissuades potential investors from buying into the company. Nevertheless, the master limited partnership form of ownership is growing in popularity.

FRANCHISES

Generally, small business owners are on the lookout for any advantages that will help them survive in the increasingly competitive business environment. One of the most sought after advantages is security. That is why many business owners invest in franchises, which offer a reasonable amount of security. However, franchisees (the individuals who purchase franchises) give up a lot for that security. In fact, many experts do not consider franchise owners to be small business operators at all.

A franchised business may be any of the legal forms listed above; they are unique in that the basis for the business is a contract between the franchisee and the corporate franchisor. The franchising agreement is a continuing arrangement between a franchisor, the manufacturer or sole distributor of a trademarked product or service who typically has considerable experience in the line of business being franchised, and a franchisee, the local business operator. The franchisee purchases a license to operate an outlet bearing the franchisor's name and following its standard practices. In the process, the franchisee receives the opportunity to enter a new business, hopefully with an enhanced chance of success. That is not always the case, although failure rates among franchises run at less than 5 percent. By contrast, the Small Business Administration has reported that 65 percent of business start-ups fail within five years.

People who operate franchises forego independence in running their business. They cannot make major modifications to their facilities without corporate approval and they are subject to monitoring from the franchisor's office. Another disadvantage is that they may be locked into long-term contracts with suppliers that are dictated by the corporation. Whether or not franchisors can live with such restrictions is for them to decide. Restrictions, aside, however, purchasing a franchise is a good way for people to start their own businesses.

STARTING A SMALL BUSINESS

Franchising is one of the three basic ways people can start their own businesses. The other two are starting a new firm from the ground floor and buying an existing business.

A start-up firm is one that a business owner builds from scratch. The process usually takes a lot of work. Owners have to obtain financing, choose an appropriate location, hire trustworthy personnel, plan for continuity, etc. They must make major decisions regarding all aspects of the operation. For example, should they finance continuing operations through debt capital (financing that involves a loan to be repaid, usually with interest) or equity capital (financing which usually requires that the investor be given some form of ownership in the venture)? Who will manage the company if the owner dies or is disabled? These are critical questions for small business operators.

The loss of key employees hurts small business owners much more than it does large corporations. It is problems like these that differentiate between small business owners and their large corporation counterparts. That is why these problems must be addressed in the early stages of a business' existence. The solutions can mean the difference in whether a small business survives or fails. It is problems like these that often prompt small business owners to buy existing businesses, rather than starting their own.

Some people buy existing businesses with an eye toward keeping them in basically the same form and avoiding growing pains. Other owners, basically those who fall into the entrepreneurial category, may buy an existing business with the intention of changing it dramatically so they can take it in new directions. Some entrepreneurs will purchase existing businesses they know are in financial trouble just for the challenge of reviving them. This is another approach that differentiates entrepreneurs from small business owners. For whatever reason a person buys an existing business, there are several key questions that must be considered before the purchase is made.

One of the key issues is whether the product or service the business provides falls into the prospective owner's areas of expertise and interests. Another is whether the purchase price is reasonable. A third addresses the business' turnaround prospects. Then there is the question of the target firm's financial condition: is it favorable or poor? Naturally, the most salient question deals with how to finance the purchase and continuing operations.

FUNDING SMALL BUSINESSES

There exist several sources through which small business owners can finance their operations. These include, but are not limited to, Small Business Administration (SBA) loan programs, commercial banks, venture capitalists, business development corporations, and stock shares.

The SBA offers a variety of loan programs for small businesses that cannot borrow from other sources on reasonable terms. The SBA normally places limits on the amount of money that can be borrowed, but interest rates are usually slightly lower than those on commercial loans. Usually SBA loans take the form of loans by participating banks that are backed by the SBA in the event of default.

Commercial banks are good sources of loans for existing small businesses, but they are often reluctant to fund start-up firms that have no track record or cannot demonstrate adequate assets. Banks generally require security and guarantees before they will make start-up loans. They sometimes impose other stringent restrictions on borrowers. Hence, commercial banks are not a major source of loans for start-up businesses.

Venture capitalists are institutional risk takers who tend to specialize in certain types of businesses. They usually have formulas for evaluating a business and prefer strong minority ownership positions, as opposed to lending money in the form of a loan or some other debt instrument. Still, venture capitalists may structure deals with both equity and debt financing. They can be lucrative sources of funds, but competition for venture capital is fierce and thus very few who seek it actually receive any.

Business development corporations are privately owned companies chartered by states to make small business loans. They can develop creative financing packages. The most attractive facet of these corporations is that their loans are generally guaranteed by the SBA.

Another way of funding a small business is by issuing shares. In order to bring in capital from outside investors, business owners sell shares in the business through private or public offerings. Usually for very small businesses selling shares is not an option, as few independent investors will be interested unless there's potential for significant growth. In addition, such offerings are highly technical and usually require expert legal help to conform to state and federal securities laws. The share process also removes a large part of business owner's independence, however, since stockholders are given a say in how the business is run and receive a portion of the profits. Thus, selling equity in a company is mostly done by aggressive businesses that are committed to growing into larger organizations, and not by the typical home-based or one-person business.

PRACTICAL DETAILS

Small business owners often must also concern themselves with advertising, public relations, the legal aspects of operating a business, and other operational and management details. There are expenditures like insurance and personnel costs to be considered. There are business policies and procedures to establish. Inattention to these details can lead a small business to failure and possible bankruptcy.

It is an unfortunate fact of small business that many companies don't survive. There are several reasons. The most prominent are economic recessions, ineffective management, insufficient capital, bad-debt losses, competition, decline in the value of assets, and poor business location. Some of these are not within a small business owner's control. Most, however, are. It is essential, then, that small business owners pay strict attention to every aspect of their operations. Attention to details is the key to success in any type of business—small businesses in particular.

SEE ALSO: Entrepreneurship

[Arthur G. Sharp]

FURTHER READING:

Hatten, Timothy S., and Mary Coulter. *Small Business: Entrepreneurship and Beyond.* New York: Simon & Schuster, 1996.

Longenecker, Justin G., Carlos W. Moore, and Bill Petty. *Small Business Management.* 10th ed. Cincinnati: South-Western, 1996.

Ray, Robert J., Gail P. Hiduke, and J.D. Ryan. *Small Business: An Entrepreneur's Guide.* 4th ed. Fort Worth, TX: Dryden Press, 1996.

SOCIALISM AND COMMUNISM

While once used interchangeably, socialism and communism now have discrete meanings and each term is open to various interpretations. Nevertheless, communism generally refers to the theories and ideas stemming from Karl Marx and Friedrich Engels and their successors. At the crux of communism is a call for the abolition of capitalism—i.e., private ownership of the means of production and private profit—by force if necessary. After the communist revolution in Russia, Russian leaders such as Vladimir Lenin and Leon Trotsky further developed the tenets of communism as did Mao Tse-tung in China.

Socialism, on the other hand, is a political and economic approach that calls for state-owned businesses and state-controlled distribution of wealth brought about by democratic means. The doctrines of socialism also include demands for major industries, banking, utilities, and natural resources to be nationalized as well as for nationalized social services such as health care.

BACKGROUND

The word ''socialism'' was coined in 1832 by Pierre Leroux, editor of the Parisian journal, *Le Globe.* From then on, ''socialism'' took on many different meanings as the varieties of socialism grew and expanded, from western Europe to Russia, America, Asia, and Australia. It is mistakenly believed that Russians invented both socialism and communism and exported them, when in fact they borrowed these theories of political economy from western Europe and eventually developed their own versions of them.

Socialism, as distinct from ''socialistic'' ideas and practices that are evident as far back as biblical times, is a set of ideas, or theories, at the heart of which is a strong belief in social justice. All socialist theories are critical of wealth and the concentration of wealth in private hands; all of them advocate the elimination of poverty by equalizing the distribution of wealth, most often by some degree of collective (i.e., public) ownership. Only the most extreme socialist creeds have advocated the total elimination of private property. Because socialism also advocates some form of collective action, it can be defined not only as a theory but also as a movement.

The many varieties of socialism evolved in part from the disagreement on the means by which a more equitable distribution of wealth in society is to be achieved, a point on which no two socialist philosophies seemed to agree. Marxist socialism proposed the forceful establishment of a workers' dictatorship; conservative social democrats advocated parliamentary reform and trade unions; syndicalists favored a general strike of the workers; Christian socialists advocated a stringent application of the principles of the Bible (and also trade unions, or ''associations,'' as they called them). Furthermore, no two socialist creeds could agree on why poverty existed or how it had come about in the first place.

In short, the goal of a more just society based on an elimination of poverty is shared by virtually all socialist theories, including communism; how to achieve that goal led to the evolution of many different varieties of socialism. Finally, to make matters more difficult, socialism in theory often differed significantly from socialism in practice. Marxist socialism (that is, communism) in theory espoused workers' control of the means of production; Marxism in practice, however, be it in Russia, Cuba, or Cambodia, involved a communist-led government taking control of the means of production. Ironically, this produced permanent poverty for the mass of working people.

While socialistic ideas and practices have existed for thousands of years (the biblical Jesus was highly critical of wealth, defended the poor, and practiced a communal lifestyle), modern socialism was not born until the Industrial Revolution arrived in western Europe in the late 18th and early 19th centuries. The degrading poverty of the factory workers was nothing new—poverty has always been around—but their crowding into cities and their wretched living conditions made their particular kind of poverty so much more glaring and difficult to avoid. In addition to this new kind of poverty were two other important elements that would give rise to modern socialism: widespread literacy and the critical spirit that was the legacy of the Enlightenment. The difference therefore between a modern socialist and pre-modern socialist thinking was in the attitude towards poverty: Jesus, for example, took for granted that there always would be poverty; a modern socialist questioned the necessity of poverty, was convinced it could be abolished, and had a program to achieve this goal.

HISTORICAL ORIGINS OF SOCIALISM AND COMMUNISM

Socialist and communist theories grew out of the events and social conditions of the late eighteen century and early 19th century. This was the period when the Industrial Revolution swept across Western Europe. The Industrial Revolution brought about the rapid expansion of industries through mass production. The industrialization of Western Europe, however, led to deleterious consequences as companies competed ferociously without regulation and exploited the growing class of industrial workers. As a result, the living conditions of industrial workers deteriorated substantially by the middle of the 19th century as poverty, squalor, and degradation grew.

Consequently, bitter critiques of private wealth and intellectual theories about poverty became especially frequent preceding and during the French Revolution of 1789-99. Jean Jacques Rousseau (1712-78) was one of the earliest-known proponents of the state's responsibility for the equal distribution of wealth, but did not go so far as to advocate the dispossession of the rich. During the French Revolution, the supporters of the radical Jacobins in power demanded greater social justice and the equalization of wealth, but were not opposed to private property.

One of these French agitators, Gracchus Babeuf (1760-97), has frequently been cited as the "father" of modern communism for evolving a socialist creed (embodied in the *Manifesto of the Equals* written by a follower of Babeuf's) based on the belief that poverty was caused by class differences. The solution to poverty, according to Babeuf, was for the lower classes to overthrow the propertied class by force, establish themselves in power (i.e. create a "commonwealth" of equals), and proceed to distribute all property equally and hold it collectively. When Babeuf's secret organization, "The Conspiracy of the Equals," staged an abortive uprising in Paris in 1796, it was mercilessly crushed, his movement was outlawed, and Babeuf himself was guillotined.

Babeuf had been a poor, but highly literate, rural laborer, whose legacy was carried on by a number of disciples who were forced to live in permanent exile throughout western Europe. His followers came to be known as anarchists. The most famous names associated with anarchist socialism were August Blanqui (1805-81), who coined the term "dictatorship of the proletariat," and Pierre-Joseph Proudhon (1809-65), whose famous dictum, "property is theft," identified what many anarchist socialists by then believed was the primary cause of poverty.

Anarchism was the most extreme socialism before Karl Marx's *Capital,* the bible of Marxist socialism, was first published in London in 1867. Long before then, anarchism would move away from its roots in rural poverty to embrace the cause of the exploited factory worker during the Industrial Revolution. Blanqui believed in a violent insurrection of the proletariat (factory workers), who afterwards would establish a dictatorship during which time the workers would dispossess the rich and distribute their wealth equally among all. Blanqui referred to socialism as "communism," and his anarchist followers were popularly referred to as "communists," although this communism had nothing to do with Marxism, which was a later development. Because anarchists rejected centralized government and some advocated violence, they were considered by the public to be dangerous radicals. They were in fact among a small minority of socialists.

There were at the same time, in the first half of the 19th century, far "milder" versions of socialism. These creeds had their roots in the Enlightenment as well, but were spawned largely by the misery and poverty engendered by the early stages of the Industrial Revolution. They disdained violence and did not believe in dispossessing the propertied.

A milder variant of socialism was embodied in the almost quaint ideas of Charles Fourier (1772-

1837). This dreamy French intellectual disdained crowded cities and technology, advocating instead rural, self-sufficient agricultural communes, or phalansteries, where all property would be held in common, all inhabitants would do useful work but according to their own capacity and enjoyment (children, he reasoned, who loved playing in dirt, should be assigned garbage collecting), and adult love would be ''free'' and not chained by marriage. Women were to be absolutely equal and free (and could seek their own partners). Too poor to establish such a commune himself, many of his devoted followers brought his ideas to the United States, where they set up utopian communities in the Midwest. Similar ideas were espoused by the Welsh owner of Scottish factories, Robert Owen (1771-1858), whose followers also set up a utopian community in New Harmony, Indiana.

Christian socialism, most often associated with Anglican author and activist Charles Kingsley (1819-75), developed in the 1850s and advocated a practical Christianity with the church involved in the improvement of workers lives. This version of socialism had the greatest impact in England, but also had a significant influence in Germany by the late 19th century.

The German Karl Marx (1818-83) would scoff at all of these socialisms as ''utopian,'' although he would not admit how heavily they influenced him, especially anarchism. Marx's own variant of socialism was known as dialectical materialism, based on a dialectical model borrowed from the German historian Georg Hegel (1770-1831), who had taught at the University of Berlin shortly before Marx became a student there. The dialectic, acted out in a pattern of thesis, antithesis, and synthesis, gave form and logic to history, and explained how history evolved from one stage to the next.

KARL MARX AND MARXISM. Unlike Hegel, who believed ideas were as the primary in the historical process and that economic conditions stemmed from them, Marx held that economic processes—the production and distribution of goods and services—were the primary forces behind the historical process and economic conditions. However, like Hegel, Marx believed that history was evolving to a superior state, although Marx believed the superior state was greater balance between economic forces. Hence, Marx's theory is know as Materialism or Dialectical Materialism. The two central concepts of Marx's theory were the means of production (technology and know-how) and the relations of production (social institutions). Marx argued that the dialect works in such a way that a balance is temporarily struck between means of production and the relations of production. However, technology evolves more quickly than social institutions, according to Marx. The lag between the means and relations of production inevitably cause social revolution. Under the relations of production of the feudal system, social revolution sprang up of necessity because feudalism's market controls, property distribution, taxes, tariffs, and so on impeded the use of the productive forces associated with capitalism.

Marx's materialism owed much to the writing of the German intellectual, Ludwig Feuerbach (1804-72). In fact, Marx's dialectical materialism, fully expressed in his popular 1848 treatise, *The Communist Manifesto,* was thoroughly German. By borrowing the dialectical model (and logic) of Hegel, Marx set out to prove that the driving force throughout history has been the class struggle between the owners of the means of production (the thesis), and those who labored for them (the antithesis). In ancient times, the laborers were slaves; in Marx's own time, they were the proletariat. The tension, the class struggle, between laborers and private property owners, would be resolved only in the final stage of the dialectic. This would occur when the class-conscious proletariat united to overthrow the ''bourgeois'' or capitalist state by means of revolution. The workers would then proceed to establish a temporary dictatorship in order to forcibly dispossess the capitalist bourgeoisie of its property, and hence, of the means of production. With the means of production in the hands of the actual producers for the first time in history, a classless society would result. Consequently, the class struggle would end, and the final stage of the dialectic (and of history) would be achieved.

With occasional financial support from his friend and mentor Friedrich Engels (1820-95), Karl Marx was able to spend years doing research in the British Museum (he was forced into exile in 1848, spending the next 35 years in London, where he died). He buttressed his dialectical theory with statistics of industrial growth in Great Britain, the most advanced capitalist country, and with current British economic theories. One of these was promulgated by David Ricardo (1772-1823), who argued that labor was the source of all value. Marx interpreted this to mean that capitalist profits were really wages stolen from the workers. Marx predicted that capitalism in Great Britain would lead to greater impoverishment of the workers, with wages continuously falling; in time, capitalism would collapse. The result of his intensive study was his two volume work in German, *Das Kapital,* which was quickly translated into English (*Capital*) and eventually into Russian (it escaped Russian censorship because of its highly theoretical content).

Marxism (that is, dialectical materialism) is only an economic theory. Instead of being regarded in this light, it became in a few years a secular religion. A generation of educated Europeans were won over by the ''scientific'' logic of dialectical materialism, next to which all other existing socialist creeds seemed infantile and utopian. Until well into the 20th century, true believers of Marxism referred to it as ''scientific socialism.''

Since dialectical materialism is not a political theory, there is nothing about it that suggests the kind of totalitarianism with which the world has come to be associated with communism (a word Marx and Engels used loosely). Moreover, dialectical materialism or Marxism was put into practice for the first time in the least likely country, Russia. Marx and Engels would not have dreamed that a communist state would arise in an agrarian country.

Nonetheless, this economic theory of Karl Marx, together with other writings of Marx and Engels besides *Capital,* eventually led to totalitarian interpretations of Marxism: the proletariat and it alone would own all property (which is to say, the state); peasants, businessmen, professional people, would be dispossessed forcibly, since they were considered bourgeois, or petty bourgeois (as the peasants). Moreover, Marx and Engels had contempt for civil and political rights, which they also considered ''bourgeois'' and a means by which the bourgeoisie asserted its control. Finally, Marx adopted Blanqui's idea of the ''dictatorship of the proletariat'' as a necessary final (but temporary) stage of the dialectic, when the bourgeoisie would be compelled to give up their property, and capitalism would come to an end. Hence the necessity of compulsion and of a dictatorship, however temporary, are ominous indications that dialectical materialism, even in theory, was antidemocratic. Marx would have scoffed at this, insisting that a worker's state, where all were equal, could only be democratic. Of the rights of minorities he had not a clue, while due process of law was ''bourgeois.''

THE INFLUENCE OF MARXISM. Even before Marx's *Capital* was published and disseminated, factory workers in many countries in Europe were being organized into unions and demanding better working conditions and wages. Many labor leaders had been influenced by the socialist creeds popular before Marx, and had even organized a ''Worker's International'' (the First International) in which Marx himself had become briefly involved. It is not surprising that Marxism, wholly concerned with the factory worker and predicting the ultimate triumph of labor, would make a deep impact on labor leaders as well as dissatisfied intellectuals.

It was in Marx's native Germany that Marxist socialism made its greatest impact before World War I; German Marxism in turn would have enormous impact on the socialist movements in Scandinavia and Russia, as well as on the Polish, Bulgarian, and Serbian labor movements. The first Marxist party in the world was the German Social Democratic Workers' Party, founded by August Bebel (1840-1913) in 1868, at a time when Germany was politically divided and still largely agrarian (that would change after 1871). ''Social Democratic'' and ''Socialist'' meant the same thing to most Germans, and the name stuck. In the 1870s and 1880s, Marxist labor parties, or ''social democratic labor parties,'' sprang up throughout Europe. Unlike the American trade unions which arose independently of political parties, European trade unions were established by labor parties; hence, **labor unions** as a rule were closely tied to a political party. More often than not, the party was Social Democratic (meaning Marxist).

By 1889, Marxism as a movement had made such headway that Social Democratic party leaders throughout western Europe gathered in Paris and established the Second Socialist International (the First International had expired in London in the 1860s). The Second International had a permanent headquarters in Brussels called the ISB (International Socialist Bureau), and held periodic congresses every two years. During its brief history, from 1889 to 1914, the Second International was extremely successful in its role as promoter of Social Democracy throughout the world. Its leaders, such as Karl Kautsky (1854-1938) of the German Social Democratic Labor Party, Rosa Luxembourg (1870-1919; who was Polish, but most active in the German labor movement), Jean Jaures (1859-1914) in France, and Belgian Camille Huysmans (1871-1968; head of the ISB), gave the world the impression that the ''socialist'' (that is, Marxist) movement was invincible.

In fact, it was far from that. With the spread of universal male suffrage throughout western Europe, heretical voices within the Social Democratic parties and trade unions were questioning whether the lot of the worker was really getting worse, as Karl Marx had predicted, and whether the ballot box would not be a better means of serving the worker than the violent overthrow of the bourgeois state. Furthermore, most workers in the Social Democratic trade unions were not very interested in class struggle or the theoretical issues of dialectical materialism. Finally, by 1901, a respected leader of the German Social Democratic Labor Party, Eduard Bernstein (1850-1932), had broken with Marxism altogether. Having lived for years in England, he was impressed by what parliamentary democracy could do for workers who had the vote, and he observed that the quality of their lives and their wages had improved steadily over the years. Nevertheless, his break with Marxism was not a break with socialism. Rather, he was siding with a less dogmatic, more liberal socialism of the kind that had taken root in England, and that was best represented by the Fabian socialists (not a political party, but an eclectic group of men and women—George Bernard Shaw was one of their most famous members).

While Bernstein was condemned within the International and by his own party, his dramatic break with Marxism heralded a schism in Social Democracy between the right wing (or ''revisionists''), increasingly drawn to parliamentary democracy and to working within the system, and the left wing. Leftists were the hard-core Marxists, usually from eastern Europe and the Russian Empire, where democracy was weakest. This split between the left and right wings of the Social Democratic movement affected all the members of the International, including the American Social Democrats (led by Eugene Debs and Daniel De Leon). With the outbreak of World War I in 1914, it became permanent.

COMMUNISM IN RUSSIA. The self-appointed leader of the left-wing Social Democrats was Vladimir Lenin (1870-1924). He headed the Russian Social Democratic Labor Party's bolshevik wing (which had split off from the majority party in 1903), which he already was calling the ''Bolshevik'' party. In 1920, Lenin demanded that any Marxist party which joined the Third Communist International (or Comintern, headquartered in Moscow) shed the name ''social democratic'' and adopt the name ''communist'' to distinguish it from those parties that retained the name ''social democratic'' after World War I, but had shed Marxism.

It is ironic that the first communist government to be established in the world was in Russia, at the its height World War I. In the Russian Empire more so than in the other belligerent states, the unbearable strain of total war had undermined the shaky political regime. When popular pressure forced the tsar to abdicate in March 1917, the provisional government which replaced him doomed the country to chaos because of its efforts to promote democracy and civil liberties in the midst of total war. The newly amnestied Bolshevik leaders took advantage of the liberal atmosphere to undermine the democratic regime. With the help of the paramilitary Red Guards, they succeeded in toppling the new liberal government by force on November 7, 1917.

Even before he became head of state, Lenin had shifted the Marxist position on the peasantry (which Marx and Engels had lumped with the property-owning bourgeoisie) in order to win the support of Russia's vast mass of peasants. He declared that the peasantry were future proletariat; backed by plentiful statistics, Lenin proved in his writings that urbanization and industrialization in Russia were inevitable, and that the peasants were proletariat in the making. Nevertheless, only the Communist Party, and not the peasantry-turned-factory workers, could lead Russia along the path to a workers' state.

This emphasis on the primary and exclusive role of the party distinguishes ''Leninism'' from traditional Marxism. Traditional Social Democratic parties before World War I had not considered the party to be the ''vanguard'' of the revolution, nor did this concept of the party's leadership role fit into the scheme of the dialectic. Lenin's variant of Marxism, however, caught on especially in economically backward areas, where there were few factories and, hence, almost no proletariat.

Under Lenin, all enterprises, large and small, including the banking system, were nationalized. While small farmers could keep their land, this exception was meant to be only temporary. The Communist Party under Lenin felt too weak to directly challenge the majority of Russia's population.

Lenin also believed in rule by terror, which meant the secret police. This, too, would have horrified Social Democratic parties before World War I. To Lenin (who was a lawyer by profession), terror was justified since Russia was the only ''worker's state'' in the world, surrounded by capitalist enemies.

The Soviet Union (Russia and its satellite republics in the Caucasus and Central Asia) officially came into being in the 1920s. Lenin's successor, Joseph Stalin (1879-1953), became General Secretary of the Communist Party of the Soviet Union in 1928, and assumed complete control in 1929, turning the Soviet Union into one of the world's most totalitarian countries. Democracy had no tradition or roots in Russia, and Soviet-style (Marxist-Leninist) communism took root subsequently in areas of the world where democratic traditions were weak or nonexistent. Communism held sway until its collapse with the breakup of the U.S.S.R. in 1991.

COMMUNISM AND SOCIALISM IN THE 1990s

Communism has virtually disappeared 120 years after Karl Marx declared the imminent collapse of capitalism and is only loosely practiced in a few countries such as China, Cuba, and North Korea. However, China has been slowly moving away from communism and Marxism-Leninism since the 1980s, when the Communist Party declared these doctrines did not contain all the answers to political, economic, and social problems. Furthermore, North Korea has suffered from extreme poverty and has relied on aid from non-communist countries. Hence, its days as a communist nation may be numbered. Even Cuba considered economic reforms in the 1990s to stave off its economic problems stemming from the demise of the Soviet-bloc that provided aid and was a major trading partner.

Various forms of socialism or social democracy were adopted by Western European countries such as France, Germany, and Italy, which provided citizens with an array of social services. Advocates of socialism have striven to separate themselves as far as possible from communism and the communist regimes that established themselves under the name of socialism. Some have even parted ways with the principles of Marx and Engels, considering them idealistic and untenable. Instead, they focus more on practical and realizable ways of improving social and economic conditions and bringing about equality through democratic processes.

[Sina Dubovoy]

FURTHER READING:

Barber, Benjamin R. ''An Epitaph for Marxism.'' *Society,* November-December 1995, 22.

Carver, Terrell. ed. The Cambridge Campanion to Marx. New York: Cambridge University Press, 1991.

Lichtheim, George. *Marxism, An Historical and Critical Study.* New York: Columbia University Press, 1982.

Meyerson, Adam. ''The Ash Heap of History. Why Communism Failed.'' *Policy Review.* Fall, 1991, 4.

SOFTWARE

Software is the collective term for computer programs, which are instructions in code telling a computer what to do in response to specific user inputs. Software is part of a functioning computer system, which also consists of hardware, the actual computer machinery and equipment.

Although computers were commercially introduced in the early 1950s, the term software did not appear until the early 1960s. Originally, commercial software was either developed and sold exclusively by computer hardware manufacturers and their value-added resellers as part of a computer system, or it was custom-written by computer programmers for individual clients. It was only in the 1970s, once the mainframe and minicomputer market had sufficiently grown and microcomputers had appeared, that independent software companies emerged.

Two types of software—systems software and applications software—are needed to perform most common functions on a computer.

SYSTEMS SOFTWARE

OPERATING SYSTEMS. Operating systems software is the basic set of instructions for how a computer operates; most types perform similar functions. Operating systems may be either proprietary—that is designed and sold only with a specific computer hardware brand—or they may be sold independently of a computer brand, as long as the operating systems and the computers meet certain industry standards. During the course of the 1980s operating systems became increasingly independent of hardware.

Widely used proprietary system software include MVS and OS/390 for IBM mainframe computers, Unix for Sun Microsystems Inc.'s workstations, and VMS for Digital Equipment Corp.'s VAX minicomputers. MacOS is the proprietary operating system of Apple Macintosh computers, although for a brief stint in the mid-1990s it was licensed to outside developers who made Mac clones. In the 1990s Microsoft Corp.'s Windows became the dominant operating system for microcomputers, specifically IBM-compatible PCs, covering as much as 90 percent of the market. Other common nonproprietary operating systems for desktop computers include MS-DOS, OS/2, and the various versions—sometimes termed ''flavors''—of Unix, including the increasingly popular Linux open standard. Generally, applications software must be designed to run on a given operating system, although some operating systems, such as OS/2, can execute software designed for other operating systems.

Figure 1
Major Classes of Computer Software

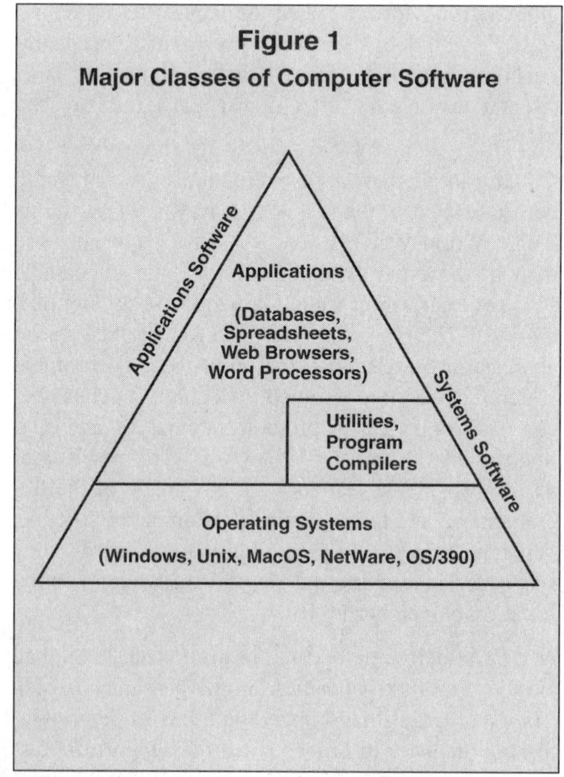

The operating system is often closely associated with the user interface; however, the two are technically separate. In many cases, particularly with PCs, the operating system includes an interface that serves as a template for application interfaces running on that system, but individual applications each have their own interfaces and may diverge substantially from the standard look and feel, often to the chagrin of users. Windows in its early versions was essentially an elaborate **graphical user interface** (GUI) running on top of MS-

DOS, the core operating system at that time, yet DOS's own interface was decidedly ungraphical. Similarly, interface and operating system are divorced from one another on many systems. Windows NT and the Windows 9x versions, on the other hand, were operating systems in their own right which also had GUIs.

NETWORK OPERATING SYSTEMS. A special category of systems software is network operating systems. This software, in conjunction with network adapter hardware, allows multiple computers to be connected together and share data and the use of peripheral equipment. These software systems are designed to cope with the special problems involved in linking multiple users, including file sharing, device sharing, traffic management, and security. The most common network operating systems for **local area networks (LANs)** are Novell, Inc.'s NetWare and Microsoft Windows NT. The rise of corporate Web sites and e-commerce activities has spawned a special breed of network operating systems, known as server operating systems or sometimes simply servers, for hosting and managing Web site activities.

UTILITIES AND OTHER SYSTEMS SOFTWARE. Systems software also includes a large class of often narrowly focused programs that are used to help manage computer resources. Many of these fall under the collective heading of utilities, which include such programs as virus checkers, system backup programs, and disk management and error recovery tools. These are particularly prevalent on desktop computers, but they exist for nearly all kinds of systems. Most utilities serve as a means to make the computer run smoothly for other applications, rather than as an end in themselves. A related class of software is file management tools, often considered a special set of utilities, which are specialized programs to facilitate more powerful file manipulations than the operating system's generic interface provides. Such file management activities might include browsing and modifying the computer's file and directory structure, renaming large groups of files in batches, or performing advanced searches for files that meet certain criteria.

The other major branch of systems software includes various programming tools that are used mainly by specialists on midrange or mainframe computers. While some of the newer software development suites for PC users like Microsoft's Visual C++ may be closer to applications software than systems software, other programming tools serve a more basic purpose for the system and may be considered systems software. On higher-end systems, on which programmers may write or customize any number of small programs or routines, the system is typically equipped with a compiler and possibly a debugger or an assembler. A compiler transforms source code written in a human-readable language, such as C or Ada or FORTRAN, into a machine readable language that can be executed as a program. Thus, after the programmer writes or modifies a program to be run on the system, it must be compiled in order to work. Debuggers are tools to help programmers identify and fix logical or syntax errors in their source code. In some cases an assembler may be used to create machine language from an intermediate form of a program known as assembly language. Assembly language, which is specific to a computer's type of processor, allows for a more nuanced handling of the program code than conventional programming languages provide.

APPLICATIONS SOFTWARE

Whereas systems software provides behind-the-scenes coordination and support, applications are front-end resources people use to get things done. Applications software may be custom-designed by or for an individual corporate user, developed and sold as part of a computer hardware system with its own proprietary operating system, or developed and marketed independently for use on one or more of the standard operating systems, also referred to as off-the-shelf software. The trend has been toward off-the-shelf software packages.

GENERAL USE APPLICATIONS. Software applications used in business may be of a generic type, sometimes called horizontal software, or be tailored to the very specific needs of an industry segment, which is referred to as vertical software. Common horizontal software categories include:

- **word processing** (Microsoft Word, WordPerfect, Word Pro)
- **spreadsheets** (Lotus 1-2-3, Microsoft Excel)
- **database management systems** (Oracle, Sybase)
- **electronic mail** (Lotus Notes, Microsoft Outlook)
- Web browsers (Netscape, Internet Explorer)

One of the biggest trends in general application software has been the integration of common task-oriented programs such as the above into so-called productivity suites. Widely held brands include Microsoft Office, Lotus SmartSuite, and Corel WordPerfect Office. While early iterations of these suites were little more than a set of discrete programs marketed as a bundle, refinements and innovations have begun to prove the power of integration. Some of the more useful innovations include multiple item clipboards for copying and pasting within suite programs (e.g., a user could copy a paragraph from a word processor and a table from a spreadsheet and paste them both into an e-mail message in one step), central configuration consoles for customizing all the programs in a suite from one menu, and integrating small Web browser windows into the desktop alongside non-Web resource windows.

HIGH-END SOFTWARE. Certain software applications, while not industry-specific, are designed mostly for business applications because of their capabilities to handle large volumes of data. One example is database management software, especially transaction processing software. This includes payroll and billing processing software and software used in retail and wholesale trade. Such software is typically developed for larger, more powerful computers, such as mainframes and minicomputers. Other examples of high-end software products include **management information systems**, human resource management systems (HRMSs), enterprise resource planning (ERP) systems, and executive information systems.

SPECIALIZED SOFTWARE. Software for a specific industry, or vertical software, is at its core a combination of generic software types, such as database management plus communications software, often with the addition of certain data and features. Examples of vertical software include transaction processing software used by banks, computer reservations software used by travel agents to book airline flights and hotel rooms, appointment scheduling software used in medical offices, software that monitors customer orders in mail-order houses, and software that keeps track of parts and labor for appliance repair contractors. Vertical software is more often proprietary than horizontal software, but it, too, is becoming increasingly available in off-the-shelf packages as its respective markets expand.

Other kinds of industry-specific software are those that facilitate engineering, manufacturing, and other production needs. **Computer-aided design** (CAD) software, for instance, is widely used in engineering and industrial design fields. Automated industrial machinery, such as in manufacturing or materials handling, uses software to control the machinery and processes. **Desktop publishing** software, used for publications design and typesetting, is regularly used not only by publishing and printing companies but also by many organizations and individuals wishing to create attractive documents.

The ability to integrate different software applications is a growing trend in business software. Different activities of a company have historically used independent software programs, such as one for accounts receivable, another for inventory management, another for manufacturing process control, and yet another for product design. Newer software tends to offer expanded features or the ability to ''interface'' with, or be connected to, other software programs. Similarly, various ''add-in'' software has been developed to add features to specific existing software packages. For example, in the retail/wholesale industries, the same software is now being used to record retail sales, keep track of inventories, and place orders with suppliers. In engineering, a CAD program can be linked to a database of information on component prices and labor costs to provide instant cost estimates for a specific design, which aids in budget planning. In some kinds of manufacturing, process control software not only automatically adjusts the flow of additives into product for desired quality, but also keeps track of the amount and rate of additive use; this data can be analyzed on a connected spreadsheet program to keep track of costs.

SEE ALSO: Database Management Systems; Graphical User Interface (GUI); Spreadsheets; Word Processing

[Heather Behn Hedden]

FURTHER READING:

Slater, Derek. ''Software Essentials.'' *CIO,* 15 February 1999. Available from www.cio.com.

Tanenbaum, Andrew S., and Albert S. Woodhull. *Operating Systems: Design and Implementation.* 2nd ed. Upper Saddle River, NJ: Prentice Hall, 1997.

Wailgum, Tom. ''Your OS at Work.'' *CIO,* 15 August 1998.

''Work Smart.'' (Buyer's Guide.) *Fortune,* summer 1998.

SOGO SHOSHA

A sogo shosha is a form of industrial organization and a kind of vertically integrated trading company that originated in Japan and for the most part has remained unique to Japan. At the center of these organizations is a trading company that arranges financing, coordinates activities, and handles **marketing** functions for the companies in its group of companies. These subordinate companies may be considered operating companies, because they specialize in certain types of business. Since World War II, Japan has emerged as one of the dominant world traders in part because of the sogo shosha.

While the term *sogo shosha* is Japanese for ''general trading company,'' the term generally refers to the entire group of operating companies that comprise the conglomerate or sogo shosha. Unlike typical Western trading companies and Japan's some 9,000 other trading companies, the sogo shosha are distinguished by their international networks, their trade of numerous **commodities**, and their large market shares. For example, a sogo shosha may control about 10 percent of Japan's trade, handle a range of 10,000 to 20,000 products including food, clothing, automobiles, and appliances, and have a network of over 200 offices throughout the world. Although developing and industrial countries have experimented with the sogo shosha system, few, if any, have succeeded in completely replicating the Japanese organization. The major sogo shosha include Mitsubishi, Mitsui, C. Itoh, Sumitomo, Marubeni, Nichimen, Kanematsu-Gosho, and Nissho Iwai Corp. In the late 1990s the sogo shosha controlled about 10 percent of the world's exports and over 50 percent of Japan's overall trade, according to *Marketing Intelligence and Planning*.

The sogo shosha are also characterized by their ability to issue large volumes of credit and to help small manufacturers buy and sell goods in the global market. These trading companies serve as intermediaries for distribution at home and abroad for Japanese companies. Nevertheless, the sogo shosha's responsibilities extend beyond trading because they take active measures to ensure stable levels of supply and demand over long periods. In addition to their ability to make the greatest use of the marketing intelligence network, the sogo shosha work on extremely thin margins, commonly little more than 1.5 percent. It is therefore necessary for these companies to maintain very high sales volumes and remain focused on long-term business development.

STRUCTURE OF THE SOGO SHOSHA

Typically, as the head of the several companies that comprise a group, the trading company is the primary shareholder of operating companies in its group. The trading company commonly places several of its own officials on the boards of these companies, while senior officials of the largest companies in the group maintain seats on the trading company's **board of directors**. This arrangement includes a loose system of interlocking directorships.

The sogo shosha differs from classical conglomerates, such as those in the United States and Europe, in that no single entity in the group owns more than a small percentage of any other company in the group. But taken together, the trading company and several of the other companies in its group may own a majority of shares in one of these companies, in effect, comprising a controlling interest.

All the companies in a typical sogo shosha own aggregate majority shares in each other, forming a complex system of cross-ownership. As a result, companies in a sogo shosha cannot technically be considered **subsidiaries** in the classic sense. Subordinate companies are merely "associated" with the sogo shosha because they are independently listed and substantial minority interests are held by investors outside the sogo shosha. Some sogo shosha include as few as a half dozen companies, while other larger organizations might contain as many as 150 or more subordinate companies.

This form of cross-ownership and board representation is not permitted in the United States, where strict **antitrust laws** preclude this type of control. For example, General Motors Corp. may hold shares in its EDS subsidiary, but EDS may not simultaneously hold shares in General Motors. Similarly, neither company's board may include more than one or two directors from the other company. In Japan, however, these are common features of a sogo shosha. This form of organization is allowed for several reasons.

First, the sogo shosha system has been in existence for more than a hundred years and has become a traditional, if not essential, feature of industrial organization in Japan. Second, the Japanese government recognizes that sogo shosha are highly efficient and synergistic: each company has a stake in the financial success of every other company and concentrates its resources to realize that success.

Third, sogo shosha generally are not anticompetitive. There are about a dozen such conglomerates in Japan, each of which is highly diversified and competes in specific industrial sectors against other sogo shosha and independent companies. For the most part, no sogo shosha dominates any of the industries in which it is involved—and it is likely that none would even if it could.

If, through expansion and acquisition, a sogo shosha built a large market share in a certain industry, the resulting concentration would enable that company to frustrate **competition** within that industry. Government regulators would require the company to reduce its presence in that market, specifically to preserve competition and protect the investments of other companies in that industry.

Such brash moves to dominate certain industries could seriously disrupt the business of competitors. While concern for the welfare of competitors is not particularly important in the United States, it would be treated gravely in Japan, where social mores demand a high level of respect for competitors, because many are capable of retribution that might prove destructive to the business of other enterprises in the group.

The government maintains a powerful agency—the Japanese Ministry of International Trade and Industry—to regulate and coordinate the actions of the conglomerates. In addition, the conglomerates have established an executive council called the Keidanren specifically to prevent such actions and maintain industrial harmony. This "coordination" among major producers would clearly constitute collusion in the United States.

The sogo shosha are populated with largely homogeneous personalities. They are male-dominated organizations whose staff are culled from the finest universities and placed on extensive socialization programs that include years of cultural preparation. By this process, a profound **team** mentality is established among the **workforce**. Employees of one company may deal with counterparts elsewhere in the organization free from cultural barriers and acclimated to a common code of conduct.

DEVELOPMENT OF THE SOGO SHOSHA

Before World War II, the term *sogo shosha* was not used; instead companies such as Mitsubishi Shoji and Mitsui Bussan were referred to as *boeki shosha,* or foreign trading companies. Nevertheless, the sogo shosha system has its origin with the political rebellion in 1868, in which the Tokugawa government was replaced by a restoration of the Meiji emperor. The new government initiated an ambitious industrial modernization program in which large state enterprises were established, using the British East India Company, Jardine Matheson, and other firms as models.

But because government officials lacked the managerial expertise to run these companies, the government was forced to turn the enterprises over to existing companies that, while small, had nonetheless demonstrated strong **management** skills.

These family-run businesses—which included Sumitomo, Mitsui, Mitsubishi, Ono, and Shimada—were primarily involved in **import** and **export** trading. Most were not manufacturers; their primary function was marketing products made by other companies and international trade, bearing characteristics of sogo shosha from the very beginning.

During the 1870s, many of these companies grew tremendously. Mitsui became Japan's leading trading firm, while Mitsubishi grew to dominate the shipping industry, and Sumitomo the mining industry. Ono and Shimada eventually dissolved, but were replaced by Yasuda, which became Japan's largest **bank**. Mitsui in particular quickly established itself as a major trading institution, because the Mitsui merchant family had sponsored the Meiji leadership. Consequently, Mitsui was given the privilege of entering into banking, mining, and trading and attained a semiofficial status. The government granted these favors not just to repay supporters but more importantly to advance Japan's industrialization.

These trade enterprises continued to grow in scope and scale, helped by strong relationships with local and national political figures and their involvement in Japan's military conquests of Korea, Manchuria, Taiwan, and China. So dominant were these companies in Japanese trade and industry, that they became known as *zaibatsu,* or money cliques.

The zaibatsu commonly consisted of a primary enterprise—usually a sogo shosha—surrounded by subsidiaries engaged in banking, insurance, shipping, mining, **real estate**, food processing, and manufacturing. By virtue of their assets in human and fixed capital, as well as their considerable political power and technological expertise, the zaibatsu became essential components of Japan's economic modernization, and remained so through the 1920s, when they reached the peak of their power.

Japanese colonial interests in Korea, Manchuria, and China were developed mainly by zaibatsu companies. They provided their homeland with a wealth of natural resources from these areas, including lumber, coal, and agricultural and animal products. Several of these areas became highly developed industrial centers.

During this period, the majority of Japan's import and export trade was conducted through the zaibatsu companies. This placed them in positions to identify promising new industries and either capitalize them for an equity interest or purchase them outright. In either case, growth companies were quickly made captive to a zaibatsu very early in their development stages.

The zaibatsu gradually lost their independence from political forces during the 1930s, after a nationalist military faction gained power over government and political organs. The zaibatsu were made targets of this faction, which denounced the companies as monopolist (in fact, Mitsui's chairman was assassinated by military fanatics).

For the most part, this was a valid criticism. The zaibatsu benefited greatly from **recessions** and other public crises, and exercised extensive control over government and public resources.

In 1937 the militarists launched a war of conquest against China. Despite their disdain for the zaibatsu, the military leaders recognized that these enterprises were essential to a successful prosecution of the war. By 1941 the zaibatsu had become synonymous with the Japanese military-industrial complex.

That year, the war expanded to include Britain, the United States, and the Netherlands. Far from reducing the companies' influence, the military leaders placed the zaibatsu in charge of large areas of the economy, resulting in tremendous concentration of the industrial sector. During this period, major trading companies largely acquired and distributed products according to government directives.

When the war ended in 1945, government authority was assumed by the American-led military occupation authority, known by its acronym SCAP. The first priority of SCAP was to prosecute war criminals, including senior officials of the zaibatsu who had been sympathetic to military and then to implement economic, political, and social reforms.

SCAP saw the zaibatsu companies not only as the core of Japan's ability to wage war, but also as an impediment to democratization. Furthermore, the high concentration of manufacturing capacity in the zaibatsu was incompatible with the American tradition of antitrust law.

As a result, SCAP decreed the establishment of antimonopoly laws that necessitated the dissolution of the zaibatsu into thousands of independent companies, none of which was allowed to retain its association through the old zaibatsu or even use the zaibatsu name. Consequently, Mitsui Bussan was divided into over 200 separate companies and Mitsubishi into 139, and so sogo shosha activities all but ceased during the period of occupation.

Despite the mandate, the captains of the defunct zaibatsu established in 1946 a loose federation called the Keidanren to coordinate reconstruction projects with the government. After the occupation ended in 1950, the Keidanren lobbied for the relaxation of antimonopoly laws that limited contact between former zaibatsu affiliates. This was largely achieved by 1952, and over the ensuing years, Mitsui, Mitsubishi, Sumitomo, and others gradually reestablished their groups around the banks that had been members of their groups.

At this stage, the relationships were merely commercial. As the former zaibatsu companies expanded the scope and volume of their business, they became known as *keiretsu,* banking conglomerates, and *zaikai,* financial circles.

The banks provided a legitimate medium for association between former affiliates, but the cross-ownership and interlocking directorships that had been features of the prewar zaibatsu were still prohibited. Several of the old groups reconstituted themselves through acquisitions, but also used the opportunity to expand into completely new lines of business.

The government recognized that the old zaibatsu groups could be very effective at rebuilding the shattered Japanese economy. They were best positioned to provide capital to small start-up enterprises and, given Japan's lack of natural resources, to develop a neomercantilist economy that would generate growth through exports.

They established foreign offices to sell goods in new markets, generating capital to develop primary industries, such as steel making, ship building, oil refining, automobile manufacturing, power generation, and road building.

The new sogo shosha conglomerates—again led by Mitsui, Mitsubishi, Sumitomo, and others—participated in the construction of a modern industrial **infrastructure** that facilitated the growth of thousands of smaller enterprises, fueling economic expansion through exports as they had 60 years earlier.

Through the Keidanren, the new sogo shosha worked closely with the government's Ministry of International Trade and Industry (MITI) to develop industries in which Japan had a distinct international competitive advantage. They brought products such as textiles, handicrafts, and simple electronics to markets in the United States, Europe, and Asia.

The cycle of investment enabled many of the sogo shosha to capitalize new ventures in heavy industry. By the 1960s Japan was positioned to enter international markets for automobiles, electronics, steel, and maritime products.

The sheer size of the sogo shosha made them essential partners in carrying through government policies. They employed most of the available managerial talent, and their banks had more capital than any other source.

The sogo shosha helped to create an environment in which independent companies were able to grow. Companies such as Honda, Hitachi, Kubota, Toyota, Sony, Ricoh, Canon Inc., Matsushita, Minebea, and Hino—none of which were officially associated with sogo shosha—built their own marketing networks independent of the sogo shosha. This forced many of the sogo shosha into increasingly risky ventures.

Despite their size, the sogo shosha operated on such narrow margins that the failure of even a small venture was catastrophic. Indeed, a medium-size sogo shosha called Ataki was forced into insolvency when its Canadian oil venture failed.

By 1978 Japan had nine major sogo shosha, led by Mitsubishi and Mitsui, and followed by C. Itoh, Marubeni, Sumitomo, Nissho-Iwai, Kanematsu-Gosho, Tomen, and Nichimen. Smaller groups included Chori, Itoman, Okura, and Toshoki.

THE CONTEMPORARY SOGO SHOSHA

Modern sogo shosha remain loosely organized. There is no powerful central parent company as there was before World War II. Contact between the principals of operating companies usually takes place in informal weekly or monthly gatherings, called clubs. The sogo shosha still concentrate on three core activities: (1) acting as an intermediary for marketing, import, and export transactions; (2) providing financial intermediary services; and (3) collecting economic, legal, political, and social information from their networks.

Despite the reemergence of limited cross-ownership and interlocking directorships and the collusory nature of the Keidanren and the club system, the concentration of industrial capacity in Japan is little different from that in the United States. In fact, in many cases there are fewer competitors in certain American markets than in Japanese ones.

The sogo shosha form of organization is by no means monolithic; groups vary in scale, scope and degrees of cross-ownership. While some sogo shosha are very tightly knit (to the extent of sharing strategies, names, and even chairmen), others are little more than associations of convenience whose companies may not even hold shares in each other.

The government maintains a strong degree of control over the sogo shosha through MITI, although its relationship with the companies is almost exclusively cooperative. MITI and the Keidanren frequently hold panels to study the companies' investment plans as part of an effort to coordinate production.

There are, however, patterns of price leadership in certain markets. This feature of **cartel** organization is allowed, and sometimes even condoned, by the government as a measure of demand control. While the sogo shosha frequently cooperate in certain areas, they avoid oligopolistic patterns by mounting rivalries that produce high rates of investment in new industries, often yielding low-cost products in brief cycles.

As more independent Japanese companies have grown in sales and volume, they have outgrown the need for representation and capitalization by the sogo shosha and established their own international marketing networks. To some extent, this has forced the sogo shosha "down market" into lower-technology goods in declining industries. This stems from the fact that most of the sogo shosha are historically concentrated in basic industries, handling low-margin primary—rather than higher-margin finished—products.

In addition, the sogo shosha tend to lack experience in marketing products—automobiles, electronics, and cosmetics—that require extensive consumer research and sales support. Firms in these industries are less likely to do business through a sogo shosha because the trading companies lack the necessary expertise—a deficit in experience that is self-perpetuating.

Despite the difficulties encountered by many sogo shosha during the late 1980s and 1990s, it is unlikely that any will meet their demise. The sogo shosha remain the largest companies in Japan and are sufficiently diversified to withstand periodic downturns in certain sectors of the economy. Even still, the market share of the sogo shosha has declined because numerous manufacturers in a variety of industries have opened up plants in countries with weaker currencies and because Japanese companies have started to manage their own international trade.

In the 1980s and 1990s the sogo shosha found themselves at a crossroads again, needing to adapt to new market conditions and opportunities. These opportunities include biotechnology, **computer** technology, information technology, and telecommunications. Furthermore, the sogo shosha have had to prepare themselves for the increasing **globalization** of the world market. The sogo shosha have responded to the new opportunities and the globalization by diversifying and investing. The sogo shosha have turned to stable albeit expanding regions such as South America and invested in new and growing areas of businesses such as telecommunications, according to the Japanese Chamber of Commerce and Industry.

SOGO SHOSHA EFFORTS IN COUNTRIES OTHER THAN JAPAN

One of the closest modern equivalents to the sogo shosha in other countries occurs in South Korea, where conglomerates such as the LG Group, Samsung, Hyundai, Ssangyong, and others—called *chaebol*—have been encouraged to follow the example of Japanese companies. While there are obvious differences between sogo shosha and *chaebol,* they have produced strikingly similar forms of industrial organization and economic growth. South Korea is today approximately where Japan was 20 years ago.

In addition, China, with the assistance of Japanese companies, began to establish sogo-shosha-style trading companies in the mid-to-late 1990s. These efforts gave rise to the **joint venture** Lansheng Daewoo Co., between Lansheng Corp. and Daewoo Corp. The sogo shosha also have helped a variety of companies set up general operations in China.

The United States tried to replicate the sogo shosha in the early 1980s with the signing of the Export Trading Company Act of 1982. This legislation was designed to facilitate the establishment of trade intermediaries and to encourage U.S. exports. The act's architects envisioned small and medium-sized companies joining export trading companies backed by banks offering financing. Such export companies, however, never developed for the most part. Suspicion of government-sponsored programs and the lack of publicity are often cited as reasons for the act's failure to produce the intended results, according to Paul Herbig and Alan T. Shao in *Marketing Intelligence and Planning.* Moreover, some of the trading companies that formed because of the act, such as Sears World Trade Organization and General Electric Trading Company, wound up defunct by the mid-1980s.

SEE ALSO: China, Doing Business in; Japan, Doing Business in; Korea, Doing Business in the Republic of

[John Simley, updated by Karl Heil]

FURTHER READING:

Allen, George Cyril. *A Short Economic History of Modern Japan.* New York: St. Martin's Press, 1981.

Herbig, Paul, and Alan T. Shao. "American Sogo Shosha: American Trading Companies in the Twenty-First Century." *Marketing Intelligence and Planning,* June/July 1997, 28.

Iwao, Ichiishi. "Sogo Shosha: Meeting New Challenges." *Journal of Japanese Trade and Industry,* January/February 1995, 16-18.

Oppenheim, Phillip. *Japan without Blinders.* Tokyo: Kodansha International, 1992.

Richardson, Bradley, and Taizo Ueda. *Business and Society in Japan.* New York: Praeger Publishers, 1981.

Tsurumi, Yoshi. *Sogoshosha: Engines of Export-Based Growth.* Montreal: Institute for Research on Public Policy, 1980.

Yamazaki, Taketoshi. "Sogo Sosha Hoping to Take Lead in Multimedia." *Tokyo Business Today,* January 1996, 20.

Yonekawa, Shin'ichi, ed. *General Trading Companies: A Comparative and Historical Study.* Tokyo: United Nations University Press, 1990.

Yoshihara, Kunio. *Sogo Sosha: The Vanguard of the Japanese Economy.* Tokyo: Oxford University Press, 1983.

Young, Alexander. *The Sogo Shosha: Japan's Multinational Trading Companies.* Boulder, CO: Westview Press, 1979.

SOUTH AMERICA, DOING BUSINESS IN

SEE: Andean Pact Nations, Doing Business in; Argentina, Doing Business in; Brazil, Doing Business in

SPECTRAL ANALYSIS

Spectral analysis is an advanced mathematical technique for studying phenomena that occur in cycles. As used in business and economics, it is concerned with forecasting outcomes based on time-series data, such as quarterly sales, exchange rates, stock prices, or growth in the gross domestic product. Spectral analysis is also widely used in engineering and sciences in fields like signal processing. Understanding the underlying mathematics requires intermediate-level undergraduate course work in statistics and calculus. Spectral methods are related to a broader class of time-series models known as autoregressive integrated moving average (ARIMA) models.

Although it has wide-reaching applications in the sciences, the beginnings of spectral analysis lie in the observance of nature. Ancient humans became aware of cycles with the changing of the seasons, the rising of tides, and the movement of the stars. Early astronomers and people living in agriculture-based civilizations first learned the values of recognizing patterns and of being able to make predictions and forecasts based on empirical observations of cyclic trends.

The foundations of spectral analysis lie in the broader area of times series analysis. The Fourier theorem, named for Baron J.B.J. Fourier (1768-1830), a French geometrician and physicist, states that periodic functions can be defined by the mathematical components of cyclical series decomposed, or broken down, into multiples of the functions sine and cosine. These are the components which create the spectrum which is analyzed. Astronomers, physicists, mathematicians, and other scientists grasped this concept and have used it extensively ever since, but it did not readily lend itself to economic studies.

Another major step in the development of time series analysis came with the work of Sir Arthur Shuster from 1898 to 1906. Shuster popularized the use of the periodogram method. In the 1920s, further advances were made by grappling mathematically with the ideas of the ebbs and flows of business economics. E. Slutsky and G.U. Yule made advances on previous methods with the idea of an auto regressive moving average.

FUNDAMENTALS OF SPECTRAL ANALYSIS

Waves on a pond have the physical shape characteristic of cycle, or wave, phenomena. By using this pond wave model, one can observe that while the waves are constant, they vary in their pitch, or distances apart, and their heights. These variations are termed wave frequency and amplitude, respectively. Frequency is measured in cycles per time unit, also referred to as the time period of a cycle. Amplitude is measured in the indexes relative to the variable of interest, such as unemployment expressed as a percentage, interest rates also expressed as a percentage, capital expenditures expressed in currency, and so on. By plotting historical data, it can be seen that variables change relative to the constant measure of time. A point can be found on the wave by a given value of one variable when the equation is used that describes the function of the sine wave. This equation expresses the effect of change on one variable relative to the other, or codependency with, the functions of sine and cosine. Nevertheless, business or economic conditions do not behave in a smooth, regular, cyclic pattern. They are irregular and, like the pond wave model, are stochastic, or random.

Economic statisticians plot variables of business interest against time and through the use of mathematical refinement techniques—such as smoothing and filtering—that produce the sine wave cycles. Some of the items or occurrences the statistician would be likely to filter out are cycles with wildly exaggerated amplitude, or noise, such as the price of steel during World War II. Noise can be compared to someone throwing a stone into the pond wave model. It cannot be predicted or taken into account in plotting general trends.

Analysis can be undertaken considering the entire time plot limits or at specific times or time intervals. These are termed the continuous spectrum and

Figure 1

Spectral Analysis in a Hypothetical Cyclical Market Prediction

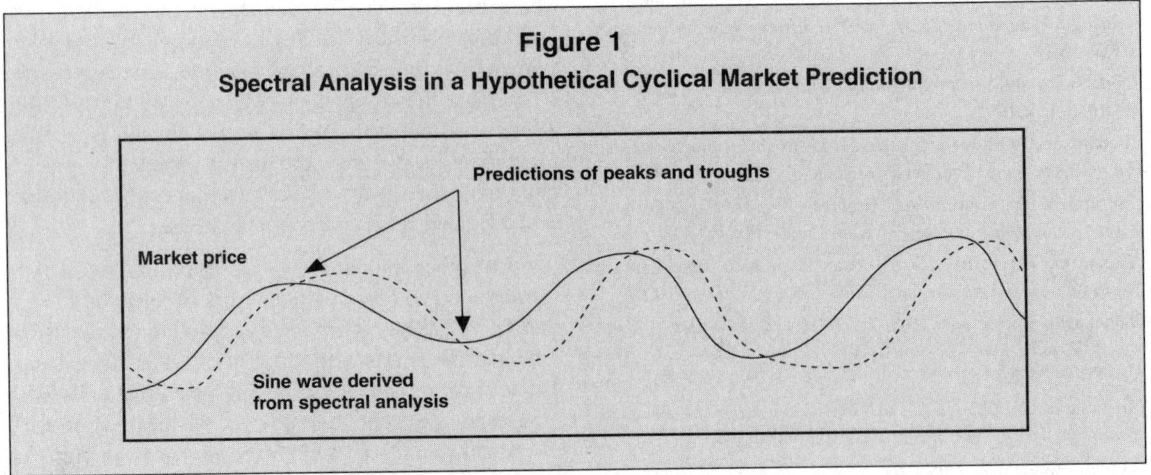

the discrete spectrum, respectively. Once a clarified sine wave cyclic pattern emerges from the plot of all the data, the statistician performs a regression analysis of the plot to determine the pattern of a trend. A projection can then be made by extending the variable of interest out along the trend line to a given time in the future.

SAMPLE APPLICATION

As with all forecasting models, spectral analysis does not always yield accurate predictions, but it has been used in a wide number of business and economic applications that involve time-series data. One of the simplest, and perhaps least scientific, uses is in software designed to signal optimal trading times in financial markets, i.e. buying near the lowest price and selling near the high point in a cycle. Experts debate the validity of such methods, which have no consistent track record of success, but proponents claim that under the right conditions spectral based systems can be useful trading aids. Figure 1 shows in simplified terms how such software might approach a cyclical pricing problem. In this example, mathematical properties of the real price cycle are assumed to be useful in determining its future path, and in particular, its peaks and troughs. Theoretically, a real up-down cycle can be identified by ignoring white noise or random movements. This method is of course far from foolproof, as the forecast peaks or troughs may never pan out. Indeed, some have argued that stock price movements are nearly all random and that no such cycles can be accurately calculated or predicted.

SEE ALSO: Forecasting; Stochastic Processes

[Karen L. Boyd]

FURTHER READING:

Horn, Robert V. *Statistical Indicators for the Economic and Social Sciences.* New York: Cambridge University Press, 1993.

Kennedy, Peter. *A Guide to Econometrics.* 4th ed. Cambridge, MA: MIT Press, 1998.

Ruggiero, Murray A. ''Forget the Dream: Now You Can Predict Tops and Bottoms.'' *Futures,* April 1997.

Stoica, Peter, and Randolph J. Moses. *Introduction to Spectral Analysis.* Upper Saddle River, NJ: Prentice Hall, 1997.

SPECULATION

Speculation is when a person or firm takes a long (ownership) or short (sell something without previous ownership) position in an investment. The person or firm is then called a speculator. The long speculator benefits when the price of the investment increases, whereas the short speculator gains when the price of the investment decreases. Both long and short positions are following the buy-low sell-high strategy except that the short speculator is reversing the time sequence of trades selling high (that which he or she does not own) and buying low (covering his or her short position) if all goes well. Either speculating strategy is based on a price forecast that can come from various sources or analytical methods. Some people distinguish the speculator from the true investor. It is thought investors have a more substantive fundamental rationale to base their investment decisions on, contrasted to the (naive) speculator who makes a trade more or less as a gambler would place a bet on the outcome of a roulette wheel.

Speculation may also be differentiated to that of a hedged (risk reducing) position. For example, corn farmers' **wealth** depends heavily on the price of corn. At the time of planting corn seed, the farmers do not know what the corn price will be when they sell it at harvest time. The farmers as producers are essentially speculating on a high corn price favorable to them compared to their production costs. Likewise the supermarket may be the buyer of the corn and desires low corn prices for its planned purchases so as to be able to offer low prices to its customers. The supermarket could speculate on corn by acquiring inventory now for sale later. In contrast to speculation, the farmers selling corn and supermarket buying corn could enter into transactions that reduce or eliminate their price risk in corn. An example of such a transaction would be for the farmers to sell corn **futures contracts** and the supermarket to buy corn futures contracts for a later date in the growing season.

Speculators may be classified as to type with respect to the time of their holding period. Speculators who invest in a position, long or short, for only a few minutes are called scalpers, for a day at a time are day traders, and for beyond a day are named position traders. These terms are more commonly used in the futures markets whereas the **stock market** would distinguish between short-term versus long-term speculators. Regardless of the category that speculators are placed in, their capital is placed at risk in an investment with the belief (or hope) that the price will subsequently go up (if long) or down (if short) in order to make a profit.

Speculation has been attributed as the cause of some spectacular crashes in the markets over the years. Some of these speculative markets are referred to bubbles. The tulip bulb market in the Netherlands in the early 1600s represents a speculative market. Tulip bulbs, of all colors, were sold in the Netherlands as part of the agricultural market beginning at an approximate equivalent of $5. As individuals saw the price of tulip bulbs climb, the market attracted an increasing number of investors who speculated on the future price of bulbs. The value of tulip bulbs is purely based on the forecast of its price determined by supply and demand. There is no use for the bulbs except for flower gardens. That is, the intrinsic fundamental value of future cash-flow-generation ability does not exist with tulip bulbs.

Nevertheless, people witnessed a forever rising tulip bulb price market and speculated that if they were to buy now, even though the bulb had no value but for resale, a greater fool would come by later to purchase it for an even higher price. This speculative bubble finally burst, around a $5,000 price per bulb, and tulip prices came tumbling down. Those speculators who bought a bulb at a high price were stuck with it. Of course, they could plant the bulbs and have a pretty garden. Similarly, speculators have been blamed, at least in part, for the downfall of other bull markets, where prices increase without apparent financial reason. The famous stock market crash of 1929 and the Japanese **real estate** and stock market crash of the early 1990s have been attributed to the frenzy caused by speculators speculating on the investments.

[Raymond A. K. Cox]

FURTHER READING:

Kolb, Robert B. *Futures, Options, and Swaps.* 2nd ed. Malden, MA: Blackwell Publishers, 1997.

SPILLOVER EFFECTS

SEE: Externalities

SPIN-OFFS

Spin-offs occur when a parent corporation distributes all or most of its holdings of stock in a subsidiary to the parent's shareholders based on the proportion to their holdings in the parent company, i.e. on a *pro rata* basis. As a result, the subsidiary company is no longer owned or controlled by the parent company and there are two separate publicly traded companies. Prior to the spin-off, shareholders only own the parent company's stock, whereas after the spin-off they own shares in both the parent and the subsidiary. In these transactions, no funds change hands, and the assets of the subsidiary are not revalued. The transaction is considered to be a stock dividend and a tax-free exchange under Internal Revenue Code Section 355.

It is important to distinguish corporate spin-offs from three types of related transactions—equity carve-outs, split-offs, and split-ups. Under an equity carve-out, a portion of the subsidiary's shares are offered for sale to the general public. This has the effect of injecting cash into the parent firm without the loss of control. Under a split-off, shareholders exchange their parent stock for the shares of the subsidiary. These transactions provide the company an opportunity to dispose of a subsidiary in a tax-free manner, and even to relieve itself of an unwanted shareholder. A split-up occurs when the parent distributes shares in each of its subsidiaries, and the parent firm liquidates and ceases to exist.

Spin-offs come in two forms: voluntary and involuntary. Voluntary spin-offs typically yield benefits to the stockholders of the parent company, because companies tend to spin off successful subsidiaries that are not core companies and thus not essential to the parent companies. Corporation may have a number of reasons for spinning off subsidiaries such as to improve the value of a subsidiary or to take advantage of tax benefits as discussed below. On the other hand, involuntary spin-offs generally result from complaints by federal and state regulatory agencies. For example, the Federal Trade Commission or the U.S. Department of Justice might file complaints against a parent company for antitrust violation if it acquired a competitor and thereby eliminated a substantial amount of competition. AT&T's divestiture of Lucent Technology (formerly Bell Laboratories) in 1996 is an example of a voluntary spin-off, whereas CBS Inc.'s divestiture of Viacom International, Inc. to comply with the Federal Communications Commission's rules is an example of an involuntary spin-off.

Although tax rules have permitted spin-offs since the mid-1950s, spin-offs did not occur with as much frequency and within major corporations until the 1980s, when a trend was ushered in by the spin-off of seven regional Bell companies by AT&T between 1982 and 1983. Since the 1980s, the number and value of corporate spin-offs has escalated. By 1996, the value of all U.S. spin-offs totaled $85.3 billion, according to David Sadtler et al. in *Breakup!*. In contrast, the value of U.S. spin-offs was only $16.6 billion in 1992 and under $5 billion in the 1980s. Furthermore, whereas spin-offs accounted for under 10 percent of U.S. divestitures in the 1980s, they accounted for almost 50 percent by the late 1990s.

KEY MOTIVATIONS FOR SPIN-OFFS

According to Ronald J. Kudla and Thomas H. McInish in *Corporate Spin-offs,* corporations have a variety of motivations for spin-offs, including management reasons, capital market factors, risks, tax benefits, marketing factors, and regulatory/legal reasons. Spin-offs can alleviate management problems of both parent companies and spun-off companies, because both kinds of companies often have different lines of business and different business environments. Since the parent companies generally are large diverse operations, they cannot provide the kind of management, financial, and resource support that the subsidiary needs for continuous growth. Moreover, parent companies usually focus their attention and resources on their core operations. Consequently, the spin-off allows the spun-off company to negotiate management, finance, and resource issues with its own board of directors and to make decisions for itself. The parent company benefits from the transaction because it can concentrate on its most important operations unencumbered by the spun-off company.

Furthermore, spin-offs may result after major shifts in the economic environment affecting corporations and their subsidiaries. While a combined organizational structure may have been optimal in the past, the separation of operations may now be appropriate. In particular, management synergy may be nonexistent for firms in unrelated businesses. Spin-offs enable managers to focus on the specific operating and financial characteristics of the subsidiary rather than being overly concerned with the impact of subsidiary decisions on the performance of the parent company.

Incentive contracts tied to the performance of the **common stock** of the parent company may not be meaningful for managers in the subsidiary. On the other hand, a spun-off subsidiary has the advantage of an independent stock price which should reflect the capital market's assessment of management's performance. Thus, compensation can be more directly related to performance with the existence of the spun-off unit.

Some parent companies decide to spin-off subsidiaries because they believe that all their lines of business are not accurately valued in the capital market. Spin-offs enable each company to obtain capital consistently based on its own operations and each company can raise capital according to the way capital markets affect each company's business. In essence, the motivation here for spinning-off a company is to give investors a clearer view of each company's business operations. The spin-off might attract new investors to the spun-off company and it might improve the parent company's value because the undervalued subsidiary is no longer associated with it.

In addition, many portfolio managers prefer ''pure play'' companies. Investment professionals may be interested in one or the other of a company's basic businesses, but not both. To the extent that financial markets are incomplete, spin-offs provide investors with a wider range of investment opportunities appealing to different investor clienteles. In addition, the issuance of separate financial reports on the operations of the subsidiary facilitate the evaluation of the firm's performance. Thus, this technique enables managers to uncover the hidden value of the subsidiary.

Since parent companies and some subsidiaries often unrelated business lines, they also have different business risks, which affect operating earnings. Parent companies sometimes spin-off subsidiaries to protect both companies from each other's risks, which generally stabilizes the earnings of the parent company. The spin-off of a riskier subsidiary allows each company to finance its expansion based on its own growth rates and projections.

Marketing concerns also prompt parent companies to spin off subsidiaries. The first concern is that consumers and suppliers will think parent company is not committed to its core line of business if it has an unrelated subsidiary. The second concern is the association of lines of business that are perceived as being incompatible. Hence, having diverse business lines may cause confusion among customers, investors, and suppliers who perceive a company as offering inconsistent products or services.

Another important motive for corporate spin-offs is to take advantage of tax benefits. Tax advantages can be achieved by the creation and spin-off into natural resource royalty trusts or real estate investment trusts. As long as these entities pay out 90 percent of their earnings to shareholders, they are tax exempt, permitting the parent company to shield income from taxes.

Finally, laws and regulations may cause companies to spin-off subsidiaries voluntarily or involuntarily. As previously mentioned, laws and regulations sometimes lead to involuntary spin-offs when complaints are filed to federal and state agencies. Nevertheless, parent companies sometimes spin off their subsidiaries to split up regulated and unregulated companies or to avoid legal hurdles associated with ownership of certain kinds of companies. A spin-off in such scenarios allows the unregulated companies to operate and expand unfettered by regulation.

However, David Sadtler et al. argue in *Breakup!* that the release of latent value is the ultimate motivation for spin-offs and that spin-offs generally result in increased value because they remove factors that impede the growth of value, according to Sadtler et al. These authors contend that simply being split up often enables subsidiaries to increase their value, because the spin-off frees them from the constraints of belonging to another company. Despite the possible advantages of being a subsidiary such as lower costs for borrowing, savings on administrative costs, expert management, and reduced costs through centralized purchasing, the subsidiary status also has possible disadvantages such as lack of knowledge of subsidiary needs, loss of freedom to operate as the subsidiary sees fit, and unnecessary and inhibiting policies. When the value of these disadvantages exceeds the value of the advantages, a subsidiary is better off operating as a separate company. Hence, both parent and subsidiary companies are free to realize their full potential value after a spin-off.

Sadtler et al. estimate that on average corporations inhibit about 10 percent their subsidiaries' potential value and that in the case of most spin-offs the amount of value inhibited is much greater. This loss of value stems from the costs associated with corporate centers, bureaucracy, ineffectual guidance, and investor preference for less diversified companies.

SPIN-OFF PROCEDURES

After a company decides to spin-off a subsidiary, it generally begins to prepare a work plan, which provides detailed information on the steps leading up to the completion of the spin-off, the projected dates for each step, and the parties responsible for the timely completion of each step.

A spin-off also involves the preparation of a plan of reorganization, which serves as the agreement between the parent and subsidiary for the specifics of the spin-off. Consequently, both boards of directors must approve of the plan of reorganization. This plan also includes information on the relationship between the parent and subsidiary companies during and after the spin-off process and it indicates any transfers of assets or liabilities from one company to another. If the company being spun off is going to be greatly restructured, the plan of reorganization will go into considerable detail describing the intended changes. The plan also provides information on the number of shares to be distributed and the key dates for distribution and payment.

Shareholders of the parent company generally receive an outline of the plan and a copy of the agreement in the proxy statement, which informs shareholders of the meeting where they will vote on the plan. The proxy statement and the prospectus for the plan of reorganization provide balance sheets and income statements of both the parent and subsidiary companies. These financial statements show how assets and liabilities will be divvied between the companies.

The parent company also must prepare a registration statement, which indicates the shares to be distributed in the spin-off. These shares generally are registered with the Securities and Exchange Commission and all shareholders who will receive shares of the spin-off company are sent a copy of the registration statement. Much of the information in this statement is the same as that in the proxy statement.

IMPACT OF CORPORATE SPIN-OFFS.

As indicated above, parent companies sometimes spin-off subsidiaries to increase the value of both parent and subsidiary companies. Nevertheless, different studies report different results from companies involved in spin-offs. Studies by the investment firm Oppenheimer and Co. indicate that companies increase their value at the time of the spin-off announcement, but also show that value may stagnate or decrease over a longer period. According to one such study of 19 spin-offs, 16 companies experienced increased value at the time of the announcement, 1 company's value decreased, and 2 companies' value did not change. However, only 11 companies and the companies they spun off had increased in value six months after the spin-off, whereas eight declined—although the combined value each company and the company it spun off still was greater than it was at the time of the spin-off announcement.

Other studies produced similar findings. Constantinos Markides found in his 1995 study *Diversification, Refocusing and Economic Performance* that spin-off announcements are accompanied by increases in share prices and that share prices of highly diversified or unprofitable companies showed the most dramatic increases. Over a longer period of time, Markides reported that spin-offs led to greater profitability for highly diversified companies. Moreover, in another 1995 study, Robert Comment and Gregg Jarrell examined companies involved in spin-offs over a three-year period and discovered that companies that spun-off subsidiaries performed about 7 percent better than companies that diversified.

However, other studies present a different view of spin-off effects. A Clarus Research Performance Database study of spin-offs by the world's 500 largest companies between 1996 and 1998 indicated that companies involved in spin-offs tended to underperform the market by 17 percent two after the spin-off announcement. This study suggests that spinning a subsidiary off will not lead to an increase in value in and of itself. Instead, the Clarus Research Performance Database study revealed that the companies whose value increased implemented restructuring and refocusing initiatives in addition to the spin-offs. Spin-offs fail to increase share prices alone because they are usually dependent on factors other than the spin-off.

SEE ALSO: Corporate Restructuring

[Robert T. Kleiman]

FURTHER READING:

Pearson, Michael. ''Spin-offs: Breaking up Is Hard to Do.'' *Journal of Business Strategy,* July-August 1998, 31.

Sadtler, David, et al. *Breakup!* New York: The Free Press, 1997.

SPREADSHEETS

A spreadsheet, at its most basic level, is essentially a matrix of rows and columns, used to record amounts and perform calculations. Spreadsheet rows and columns are composed of individual cells where users enter data. In most electronic spreadsheets, letters (A, B, C, etc.) identify columns, while numbers identify rows (1, 2, 3, etc.). Therefore, combinations of letters and numbers such as A1 or B2 identify individual cells. Usually the entries across a given row will have something in common (e.g., sales dollars), while the entries filling a given column will have another dimension of common element (e.g., the year 1999). Electronic spreadsheets—such as Excel, Quattro Pro, and Lotus 1-2-3—combine the capabilities of a calculator with a word processor, enabling users to perform various analyses and calculations and represent numeric information.

The manual form of the spreadsheet has been used in **accounting** for many years, and involved pencils, erasers, adding machines, tedium, and mistakes. Making a change used to be particularly painful when the item rippled through other sections or other spreadsheets. These factors motivated Dan Bricklin, a Massachusetts Institute of Technology graduate and a student at Harvard Business School at the time, to create the first spreadsheet program in 1978. Although not user friendly, the program facilitated calculations with its matrix of five columns and 20 rows. To improve the program, Bricklin enlisted the help of Bob Frankston and together they developed VisiCalc, short for ''visible calculator,'' which they released in 1979. Because of its success, other companies such as Lotus and Microsoft began producing their own spreadsheet applications.

Contemporary electronic spreadsheets are created by popular, user friendly **software** that runs on personal **computers**. Interrelated spreadsheet calculations can be ''linked'' so that making a change will automatically update other derivative or related calculations. Making editorial changes with electronic spreadsheets is quick and painless in that they allow users to cut, copy, and paste information with simple keystrokes or mouse gestures. In addition, every cell in an electronic spreadsheet can communicate with every other cell through rules defined by the users.

Users can perform basic functions by entering a formula for addition, subtraction, multiplication, division, or exponentiation and then selecting the rows and columns the formula will apply to. For example, a user can enter a formula for adding the contents of the cells A1 through F1. Furthermore, multiyear calculations can quickly be programmed, and recalculated under a variety of different assumptions. Sensitivity or ''what-if'' analyses have become enormously easier and more ubiquitous due to the advent of the electronic spreadsheet. Such analyses are facilitated by having the spreadsheet be ''driven'' by a number of input variables located in one section of the matrix. Spreadsheet ''what if'' analysis, for example, allows a user looking for a new house to plug in the prices of different houses and immediately view the effect on other variables, such as **tax** and **mortgage** payments.

Business estimates or projections using discounted **cash flow** analysis is another example of a task facilitated by the electronic spreadsheet. The basic cash flow model can be set up with variables established for revenue growth rate, market share, cost of goods sold, operating expenses, **discount rate**, the length of time to which to discount, etc. Any of the variables can then be modified, serially or concurrently, to quantify the effect on calculated value.

Electronic spreadsheets are especially useful, as compared to their manual predecessors, when doing complex calculations, such as certain statistical measures variances, regression coefficients of determination, and confidence intervals for sample results. They are also most useful when dealing with large volumes of data. Most electronic spreadsheets provide three main types of functionality:

1. Mathematical calculations, in column and row format.
2. Database features, including filling a row or column with sequential numbers, sorting a table of data in a defined alpha or numeric order, and selecting items meeting certain criteria.
3. Graphic presentation of the data, in a variety of formats, including line, bar, and pie charts.

More recent versions of the electronic spreadsheets have incorporated a print-enhancing capability whereby the user can set different font sizes and styles, boldface or underline selected items, create shaded areas for emphasis, and make other stylistic improvements to the hard copy output. It is now possible to compress large spreadsheets to fit on regular size paper, number sequential pages, add header or footer comments, and generally make the output look neat and professional. Spreadsheet programs are the second-best-selling application behind word-processing programs. Microsoft's Excel is the leading spreadsheet application followed by Corel's Quattro Pro and Lotus 1-2-3. These spreadsheet programs largely have the same features and capabilities, but they differ in style and commands.

SEE ALSO: Software

[Christopher C. Barry, updated by Karl Heil]

STAKEHOLDER THEORY

Stakeholder theory has been articulated in a number of ways, but in each of these ways stakeholders represent a broader constituency for corporate responsibility than stockholders. Discussions of stakeholder theory invariably present contrasting views of whether a corporation's responsibility is primarily (or only) to deliver profits to the stockholders/owners. Milton Friedman's (1912-) now-famous pronouncement that the only social responsibility of corporations is to provide a profit for its owners stands in direct contrast to those who claim that a corporation's responsibilities extend to non-stockholder interests as well.

One very broad definition of a stakeholder is "any group or individual which can affect or is affected by an organization." Such a broad conception would include suppliers, customers, stockholders, employees, the media, political action groups, communities, and governments. A more narrow view of stakeholder would include employees, suppliers, customers, financial institutions, and local communities where the corporation does its business. But in either case, the claims on corporate conscience are considerably greater than the imperatives of maximizing financial return to stockholders.

Stakeholder theories have grown in number and type since the term stakeholder was first coined in 1963. According to R. Edward Freeman, whose work in stakeholder theory is well known, the stakeholder concept was originally defined as including "those groups without whose support the organization would cease to exist." As a part of management theory and practice, stakeholder theory takes a number of forms. Descriptively, some research on stakeholder theory assumes that managers who wish to maximize their firm's potential will take broader stakeholder interests into account. This gives rise to a number of studies on how managers, firms, and stakeholders do in fact interact. Normatively, other management studies and theories will discuss how corporations ought to interact with various stakeholders.

From an analytical perspective, a stakeholder approach can assist managers by promoting analysis of how the company fits into its larger environment, how its standard operating procedures affect stakeholders within the company (employees, managers, stockholders) and immediately beyond the company (customers, suppliers, financiers). Freeman suggests, for example, that each firm should fill in a "generic stakeholder map" with specific stakeholders. General categories such as owners, financial community, activist groups, suppliers, government, political groups, customers, unions, employees, trade associations, and competitors would be filled in with more specific stakeholders. In turn, the rational manager would not make major decisions for the organization without considering the impact on each of these specific stakeholders. As the organization changes over time, and as the issues for decision change, the specific stakeholder map will vary.

Again, the contrast with Friedman's view should be evident: if the corporate manager looks only to maximize stockholder **wealth**, other corporate constituencies (stakeholders) can easily be overlooked. In a normative sense, stakeholder theory strongly suggests that overlooking these other stakeholders is (a) unwise or imprudent and/or (b) ethically unjustified. To this extent, stakeholder theory participates in a broader debate about business and ethics: will an ethical company be more profitable in the long run than a company that looks only to the "bottom line" in any given quarter or year? Those who claim that corporate managers are imprudent or unwise in ignoring various non-stockholder constituencies would answer "yes." Others would claim that overlooking these other constituencies is not ethically justified, regardless of either the short-term or long-term results for the corporation.

Inevitably, fundamental questions are raised, such as "What is a corporation, and what is the purpose of a corporation?" Many stakeholder theorists visualize the corporation not as a truly separate entity, but as part of a much larger social enterprise. The corporation is not so much a "natural" individual, in this view, but is rather constructed legally and politically as an entity that creates social goods. Robert Reich has noted that for many years, the tacit assumption of both corporate chiefs and U.S. political leaders was that "the corporation existed for its shareholders, and as they prospered, so would the nation." Yet that "root principle" may no longer be valid, according to many critics of corporate aims and activities in a global economy.

Moreover, the assumption that the corporate pursuit of profit would inevitably lead to social gain is a fairly recent one. In the first century of the United States, it was widely assumed that the corporate form could only be used for public purposes. Charters were not given out by legislatures as a matter of right, but only for public convenience or necessity. Sometime in the 1880s, states (such as New Jersey and Delaware) began to grant charters for nonpublic purposes, enhancing state revenues in the process. For most of the 20th century, the assumption has been that what is good for corporate America is also good for America. But, as Reich has noted, that assumption is being reconsidered.

Half the states in the United States have put into law "corporate constituency statutes" that make it permissible (but not mandatory) for corporate managers to take non-stockholder constituencies (stakeholders) into account. The legal effect of such laws may be to insulate officers and directors from liability for failing to maximize profits to shareholders, though it may be too early to predict the impact of such statutes. Moreover, such statutes are fairly open-ended, as they do not specify the weights that managers ought to assign to various corporate stakeholders. In this respect, the statutes are much like stakeholder theory itself: beyond the basic insight that corporations ought (as a matter of profitable prudence or morality) to consider non-shareholder interests, the competing claims and priorities of various constituencies are seldom defined or prioritized.

On an even more general level, there are various proposals and studies on reinventing the corporation, requiring federal charters for corporations, or adding a social responsibility amendment to the U.S. Constitution to require corporations to prove that their activities serve the common good. Legally, such proposals will have little momentum as long as corporate activities are perceived to provide social goods (jobs, new and useful products) without excessive social harms (pollution, socially suspect messages, harmful products). The public perceptions of the ethics or business in general and corporations in particular have gone through several cycles in U.S. history, and further restrictions on U.S. corporations are unlikely as long as most Americans participate in economic gains.

In the meantime, business managers may beneficially consider non-shareholder constituencies. The motivation for doing so may be pragmatic (for the long-term well-being of the company) or normative (for moral reasons), but the law does not currently require corporations or their managers to implement stakeholder theory.

SEE ALSO: Business Ethics

[Donald O. Mayer]

FURTHER READING:

Barnet, Richard J., and John Cavanagh. *Global Dreams: Imperial Corporations and the New World Order.* New York: Simon & Schuster, 1995.

Donaldson, T. J., and L. E. Preston. "The Stakeholder Theory and the Corporation: Concepts, Evidence, and Implications." *Academy of Management Review* 20 (1995).

Fort, Timothy L. "The Corporation as Mediating Institution: An Efficacious Synthesis of Stakeholder Theory and Corporate Constituency Statutes." *Notre Dame Law Review,* November 1997.

Friedman, Milton. "The Social Responsibility of Business Is to Increase Its Profits." *New York Times Magazine,* 13 September 1970.

Greider, William. *One World, Ready or Not: The Manic Logic of Global Capitalism.* New York: Simon and Schuster, 1997.

Lerner, Michael. "Social Responsibility Amendment to the U.S. Constitution." *Tikkun,* 17 July 1997.

Longstreth, Bevis. "Corporate Governance: Warren E. Buffet on Corporate Constituency Laws and Other Newfangled Ideas: An Imaginary Conversation." *Cardozo Law Review,* September/November 1997.

Reich, Robert B. "Corporation and Nation." *Atlantic Monthly,* May 1988.

Rowe, Jonathan. "Reinventing the Corporation." *Washington Monthly,* April 1996.

Steiner, George A., and John F. Steiner. *Business, Government, and Society: A Managerial Perspective.* 8th ed. McGraw-Hill Companies, 1997.

STANDARD INDUSTRIAL CLASSIFICATION SYSTEM (SIC)

The Standard Industrial Classification (SIC) system is a hierarchical coding structure developed by the U.S. government and used widely in government and private-sector data. It attempts to classify all forms of economic activity—including government and nonprofit entities—in order to provide a common statistical and conceptual framework for data collection and analysis. Most commonly this involves associating a particular company with one or more SIC codes based on the activities it performs; company data aggregated under SIC categories is said to describe an industry. Although it is gradually being replaced by a new classification tool called the **North American Industry Classification System (NAICS)**, the SIC system is still widely used in both current and historical contexts.

BACKGROUND

The SIC system traces its roots to the New Deal era, when the Interdepartmental Committee on Industrial Classification was established in 1937 to develop a classification system. It released its first classification of manufacturing industries in 1941, followed by a non-manufacturing classification in 1942. Revisions were made to the system in 1958, 1963, 1967, 1972, 1977, and 1987, the last version. These periodic changes were intended to keep pace with changes in the economy so that the system would recognize significant new categories and eliminate ones for trades that were nearly extinct. With inputs from such data-gathering agencies as the U.S. Census Bureau and the Bureau of Labor Statistics, the Office of Management and Budget oversaw the latter revisions of the system.

THE STRUCTURE

The SIC system uses letters and digits to represent the hierarchy and relation among categories of economic activity. Although they are often omitted from data using SICs, the letters A through K define the broadest categories in the system, called divisions:

A. Agriculture, forestry, and fishing

B. Mining

C. Construction

D. Manufacturing

E. Transportation, communications, and utilities

F. Wholesale trade

G. Retail trade

H. Finance, insurance, and real estate

I. Services

J. Public administration (government)

K. Nonclassifiable establishments

Within these divisions, in descending hierarchical order, are two-digit (known as the major group), three-digit (known as the industry group), and four-digit (known as the industry) classifications that progressively narrow the scope of the category. For example:

48 Communications

481 Telephone communications

4812 Radiotelephone communications

The four-digit level is considered the most specific; although some government agencies and private database services have created more elaborate systems detailed to six or eight digits, these aren't considered part of the official classification. Sometimes trailing zeros are used at the two- and three-digit levels to round the codes out to four digits, as in ''4800,'' another unofficial adaptation. No official four-digit SIC code ends with zero. There are approximately 1,000 official four-digit categories.

USAGE

Four-digit SICs are officially assigned on what the system terms an ''establishment'' basis, that is, at each physical location of a company. Thus, if a company has a headquarters, a manufacturing plant, and a distribution center, each might be assigned a different SIC code based on their activities. For locations involved in more than one line of business, and for corporate headquarters in general, one four-digit primary SIC is assigned based on the activity from which the company derives the greatest revenue. In SIC language, this company is said to be ''principally engaged'' in that activity, even if it represents a minority of sales. Secondary SICs may also be recorded. The U.S. government attempts to classify every establishment in the country using these principles, but the official classification of any particular firm is considered confidential and not disclosed to the public.

While government disclosure of a company's SIC is normally forbidden, there are no restrictions on dissemination by the private sector. Indeed, there are company databases sold to the public containing literally millions of company SICs and other information. Popular usage again deviates somewhat from government specifications. Database publishers and information services routinely compile and sell company data that include one or more SICs based on all of a company's activities or those it is best known for.

Frequently, a company's appropriate SIC can be readily learned from a simple description of what it does and a glance through a table of SIC codes. Thus, if one knows that General Motors Corporation is primarily an automobile manufacturer, one may be assured that SIC 3711: Motor Vehicles and Passenger Car Bodies is GM's primary SIC code.

Company information, particularly financial statistics, is also often combined within SIC categories to produce industry-level data. One of the most important publications to offer such data—and arguably one of the most important publications using SICs—had been the economic census taken every five years by the Census Bureau. Within the census, which occurs in years ending in two and seven, separate and voluminous documents, such as the Census of Manufactures, were produced for all of the major divisions of the SIC.

However, as of the 1997 census, the SIC organization was beginning to be phased out in favor of NAICS. All previous data from the census were presented in SICs.

THE FUTURE OF THE SIC

Most observers concede that the SIC system is slowly growing obsolete because of the introduction of NAICS. Still, a large body of historical and time-series data exists in SIC categories, and the transition to NAICS codes from SIC codes in new publications, from both the public and the private sector. Some government agencies and commercial publishers have developed so-called bridge tools that cross-reference data in NAICS categories with equivalent SICs. Others simply use both systems side by side, and a few commercial organizations made no immediate plans to convert to NAICS. Thus, the transition was expected to continue into the early 2000s, and even then SICs were unlikely to be eliminated altogether because there was little chance of all historical data using SICs being republished in NAICS versions.

While NAICS is the primary heir to the legacy of the U.S. SIC system, several similar classification schemes are used to organize economic and trade data. Among these are the Standard International Trade Classification (SITC), a United Nations-sanctioned system used to classify merchandise; the Harmonized System (HS), a highly detailed product classification also used by the United Nations and national governments to categorize merchandise trade; and the International Standard Industrial Classification (ISIC), is another industry-based system developed under the aegis of the United Nations.

SEE ALSO: North American Industry Classificaiton System

FURTHER READING:

North American Industry Classification System - United States, 1997. Washington: GPO, 1998. Available from www.ntis.gov.

Standard Industrial Classification Manual 1997. Washington: GPO, 1987. Available from www.ntis.gov.

STANDARDIZATION

Standardization refers to the creation and use of guidelines for the production of uniform, interchangeable components, especially for use in mass production. It also refers to the establishment and adoption of guidelines for conduct. In global **marketing**, the term is used to describe the simplification of procurement and production to achieve economy.

The concept of standardization originated near the turn of the 19th century. Before that time, products were made individually, with unique, hand-fitted parts. Eli Whitney (1765-1825), inventor of the cotton gin, has been credited with developing the concept of standardization, which he first applied to rifle manufacture in 1797. Instead of handcrafting each weapon, he produced components of uniform size in quantity, then assembled the parts into finished products. The concept saved time and money in production, and allowed for easy repair.

By the mid-1800s standardization joined the division of labor and machine-assisted manufacturing as well-established principles of mass production, but they were not widely applied for decades to come. Twentieth century industrialist Henry Ford (1863-1947) was a great proponent and beneficiary of mass production. He organized the Ford Motor Co. around its principles, taking standardization to a high level. His plants manufactured only one type of car at a time. Each auto that came off the production lines was identical, even down to the color—black. Standardization not only saved on production costs, but also benefited consumers, who no longer had to have replacement parts machined by hand.

Ford's success contributed to the proliferation of mass-production principles, including standardization, throughout the developed world. The concept has promoted a dramatic increase in manufacturing productivity, which in turn improved living standards. The concept of standardization has been applied in many ways since.

In general, standardization determines and promulgates criteria to which objects or actions are expected to conform. Standardization for manufacturing may entail the creation of production standards, tolerances, and/or specifications. These can be expressed as formulas, drawings, measurements, or definitions. Standards delineate the limits within which products or components must fall in order to be useful and interchangeable. Components that do not adhere to such limits are "nonstandard" or, more commonly, "rejects." Virtually any aspect of a product or component can be standardized. Quality control and testing are used to measure achievement of standards. The use of such standards promotes clear communication within and among organizations. It can also lower the costs of labor, production, and repair. In the current business climate, businesses have demanded ever-increasing standardization from their suppliers as well as from their own production.

Individual industries may have distinct sets of standards that promote communication among participants and discourage duplication of effort. George Westinghouse (1846-1914), inventor of the air brake and founder of Westinghouse, was an early advocate of the standardization of railway equipment. In the world of scientific inquiry, for example, the metric system is the standard of measurement. In the American construction industry, architects, suppliers, and builders have established standards for prefabricated buildings and construction components.

Organizations and professions may also be held up to standards of practice or conduct, such as safety and ethical standards. For example, government agencies such as the U.S. Food and Drug Administration and the U.S. **Consumer Product Safety Commission** set and enforce safety standards in their respective fields. The Hippocratic oath is a well-known ethical standard that physicians follow.

National and international organizations have also evolved to synthesize the diverse standardization efforts of the individual groups and promote acceptance of and adherence to basic standards. In the United States, the American National Standards Institute (ANSI) has taken up this cause. Although this organization does not normally compose standards, it does compile national engineering, safety, and industrial standards. ANSI diverged from its traditional role in 1998 by collaborating with the Human Factors and Ergonomics Society to establish national ergonomic standards for video display terminal workstations. In September 1998 ANSI also established an interactive website containing national and international standards and related information, and outlining U.S. participation in the International Organization of Standardization (ISO). Since its 1946 establishment in Geneva, Switzerland, the ISO has emerged as a powerful advocate of global standards for specifications, testing, approval, and certification. More than 80 nations are counted among its membership. Companies large and small strive for certification by the ISO, which has helped provide a basis of comparison and cooperation among companies around the world, especially as global trade has become increasingly vital to success. The standards set by such organizations often evolve with technological innovation.

The ISO issued its **ISO 9000** series of standards and guidelines governing quality management and assurance in 1987, and issued its **ISO 14000** series of standards for environmental management, policies, tools, and systems in 1998. Sets of voluntary standards such as these are known as metastandards, and provide universal guidelines and models for entire industries, groups of industries, and other areas of activity. Metastandards are also often used by public agencies forming industrial, professional, environmental, and technical regulations. Many industrial organizations, particularly those representing manufacturers of high technology products, feel that metastandards are irrelevant to their field, given the rapid pace of technical innovation. In 1998, as a response to this sentiment, the Council for Economic Priorities Accreditation Agency (CEPAA) formulated its own set of standards and registrations for use by high-technology industries.

Globalization of business has brought about new definitions and uses of standardization. As companies have begun to compete on a global scale, they have sought out "standardized" suppliers—those that offer the most economical, convenient, and dependable service. Thus, adherence to the standards promulgated by ANSI, ISO, and other national and international standards organizations can assist corporations wishing to do business globally. Ford Motor Co., an early proponent of standardization for mass production, has been praised for its successful use of standardization as it applies to global manufacturing and marketing.

Although standardization tends to lead to inflexibility, it can also allow for customization. When basic elements of a product are standardized, other aspects can be more flexible. For example, autos on an **assembly line** may use the same standard of wheel attachment, but different size wheels. Micromanagement takes this theory to its ultimate end. This theory attempts to apply standardization to all aspects of an operation, be it manufacturing or service. It seeks to identify the smallest aspects of a function, make them as efficient as possible, and then apply them throughout the operation. Clearly, standardization in all its forms will continue to be applied in new ways in the future.

[April Dougal Gasbarre, updated by Grant Eldridge]

FURTHER READING:

"ANSI On-Line Service Speeds Up Search for Standards." *Purchasing,* 17 April 1997, 23.

"ANSI's Office Ergonomics Standard Is Here: Now What?" *Safety and Health* 157, no. 1 (January 1998): 56.

Caldeira, Edward. "How ISO 9000 Helps Build Quality." *Professional Builder* 63, no. 9 (June 1998): 40.

International Organization for Standardization. *Access to Standards Information: How to Enquire or Be Informed about Standards and Technical Regulations Worldwide.* Geneva: International Organization for Standardization, 1986.

Jackson, Suzan L. "ISO 14000: What You Need to Know." *Occupational Hazards* 59, no. 10 (October 1997): 127.

Mazza, Sergio. "The Significance of Standards." *Plant Engineering* 51, no. 1 (January 1997): 92.

Reichard, Robert S. "One-Stop Shopping for Global Standards." *Purchasing,* 1 September 1998, 67.

Ricci, Patricia. *Standards: A Resource and Guide for Identification, Selection, and Acquisition.* Pat Ricci Enterprises, 1992.

Struebing, Laura. "The Standards at a Glance." *Quality Progress* 29, no. 1 (January 1996): 24.

U.S. Congress. Office of Technological Assessment. *Global Standards: Building Blocks for the Future.* Washington: Office of Technological Assessment, 1992.

Uzumeri, Mustafa V. "ISO 9000 and Other Metastandards: Principles for Management Practice?" *Academy of Management Executive* 11, no. 1 (February 1997): 21.

Wingo, Walter. "EU Members Endorse ISO 14001 as Prime Environmental Standard." *Design News* 51, no. 23 (18 November 1996): 16.

Zuckerman, Amy. "Challenges Make 1998 a Very Tumultuous Year for International Standards." *Quality Progress* 31, no. 7 (July 1998): 17.

STATISTICAL ANALYSIS FOR MANAGEMENT

Statistical analysis provides a framework for organizing data, analyzing data, and examining business problems in a logical and systematic way. With the tremendous strides in **computer** technology that have taken place, businesses have greater access to and more data than ever before. Statistical analysis provides managers with the tools necessary to make sense of large quantities of data and to make ever more effective business decisions based on inferences drawn from data.

Statistical methods may be broken into two broad categories—methods of description and methods of inference. Descriptive statistics methods consist of a variety of techniques—both mathematical and graphical—by which to organize and describe data. Two characteristics of great interest in data description are the central tendency and degree of variation in a given variable. For example, a manager might be interested in what the average earnings of a group of workers is or might be interested in knowing whether there is much variation in the diameter of items produced in a production run.

In order to determine central tendency and variation graphically, the manager could chart data for a given variable using a frequency **histogram**. A histogram is a bar chart that breaks a variable into sub-ranges from lowest to highest values of the data and plots the frequency of occurrence in each sub-range (or class). Often it is the case that the most frequently occurring values of the variable will appear near the middle of the histogram, thus this sub-range will have the bar with the greatest height. Variation will be shown by how spread out the bars are. If categories at the lower and upper ends of the data have bars without much height, then the data are not very spread out or variable.

Though the frequency histogram is the most popular means by which to display data graphically, a variety of other techniques exist. These include stem and leaf plots, box plots, and pie charts. In addition to determining central tendency and variation of a given variable, the manager may in other instances be interested in determining movement in data over time or may be interested in ascertaining whether two variables bear any relationship with respect to each other. In each of these instances, a scatterplot would be used to represent the data graphically. In the former instance, the variable in question would be charted against time itself, while in the latter case one variable would be plotted against the other.

Mathematical techniques also exist by which to describe data. These methods are usually used in conjunction with rather than as an alternative to the graphical techniques noted above. The chief measures of central tendency are the mean, median, and mode of a variable. The mean is obtained by taking the sum of the observations on the variable and dividing by the number of observations. The mean is overly influenced by particularly large or particularly small values of the variable and for this reason the median is sometimes a better measure of central tendency than is the mean. The median is found by sorting values of the variable from lowest to highest and identifying the middle value in this ranking. The mode is the most easily obtained measure of central tendency and is simply the most frequently occurring value in the data.

Measures of variation are the variance, standard deviation, and range of the data. The variance is the sum of the squared deviations from the mean of the variable divided by the number of observations minus one (or, in other words, it is approximately the average squared deviation from the mean). The standard deviation is the square root of the variance. If the data are highly variable, then many observations will fall a considerable distance from the mean of the data and for this reason both the variance and the standard deviation will take on relatively large values. The range of the data is simply the largest value minus the smallest value. Though much easier to compute than the variance and standard deviation, the range can be misleading, particularly if the variable has a small number of large or small values that are unrepresentative of the general tendency of the data.

In many cases, a manager may wish to go beyond mere description of a variable and instead draw some larger inference regarding the variable based on the available data. This issue becomes relevant when the data at hand is a sample of data drawn from some larger population. For example, one might have hourly earnings for a random sample of 100 high school graduates in a metropolitan area. The mean hourly earnings of this group could be calculated. The question is, does the average for this sample help you infer the average for the population of high school graduates in the metropolitan area? It turns out that methods of statistical inference do indeed allow one to make inferences concerning the population (which is really the group of interest) on the basis of the information contained in the sample.

Statistical inference techniques may be broken into two broad categories—estimation and **hypothesis testing**. Underpinning both estimation and hypothesis testing are the concepts of the random variable and the probability distribution drawn from probability theory. With estimation, one is interested in estimating some population parameter (say, the mean of the population) on the basis of information in the sample of data. One could estimate the population parameter of interest using the analog of the corresponding concept for the sample (known as a statistic), but usually this is of only passing interest. This is because a sample may accidentally over represent the higher end (or the lower end) of the population due to the random nature of the sampling. In turn, the sample statistic usually either over- or underestimates the population parameter. Using results from probability theory, however, one can establish a range (known as a **confidence interval**) within which it is highly likely (usually 90 percent, 95 percent, or 99 percent, depending on the degree of confidence desired) that the population parameter of interest lies. As long as this range is reasonably narrow, then the inference will be highly informative. So, returning to the hourly earnings example from above, suppose average earnings in the sample is $9.25 per hour. One could not be very confident that this is average earnings for all high school graduates in the metropolitan area. But the methods of statistical inference allow one to take this measure (known as a point estimate) and use additional information concerning variation of data within the sample to make the inference that it is 95 percent likely that mean average earnings of high school graduates in the metropolitan area is, say, between $9.10 and $9.40 per hour.

In conducting a hypothesis test, one poses a null hypothesis that the population parameter in question equals some specific value against an open-ended alternative hypothesis that the parameter does not equal the value specified under the null (known as a two-tailed test), is greater than the value specified in the null (a one-tail test), or is less than the value specified in the null (also a one-tail test). Using information from the sample of data, one then determines whether or not enough evidence exists to conclusively reject the null hypothesis.

Confidence intervals and hypothesis tests are powerful tools and can be applied to a variety of questions. The example above showed how these tools may be used to make an inference about a population mean. One may also use these tools to make inferences about population proportions, about standard deviations of populations, and so forth.

Additional useful tools in the manager's statistical analysis tool kit include analysis of variance and **regression analysis**. Analysis of variance allows one to determine whether or not means of a number of populations (three or more) differ. Regression analysis allows one to determine the impact of any number of variables (called independent variables) on some variable of interest (called the dependent variable). Concepts of confidence interval and hypothesis testing are also used in the context of these techniques.

[Kevin J. Murphy]

FURTHER READING:

Albright, S. C., W. Winston, and C. J. Zappe. *Data Analysis and Decision Making with Microsoft Excel.* Pacific Grove, CA: Duxbury Press, 1999.

Freund, J. E., F. J. Williams, and B. M. Perles. *Elementary Business Statistics: The Modern Approach.* 6th ed. Englewood Cliffs, NJ: Prentice Hall, 1993.

Neter, J., W. Wasserman, and G. A. Whitmore. *Applied Statistics.* 4th ed. Boston: Allyn & Bacon, 1993.

STATISTICAL OFFICE OF THE EUROPEAN COMMUNITY

The Statistical Office of the European Community, also known as Eurostat, is a Directorate-General of the Commission of the European Communities, which in turn is an institution of the **European Union**. The European Union is an economic, political, social, and monetary union of 15 western European nations. The European Union can trace its history through the Treaty of Paris (1951), which created the European Coal and Steel Community; the Treaty of Rome (1957), which created the European Atomic Energy Community and the European Economic Community; the 1967 coming together of these three organizations to form the European Community; and the 1992 **Maastricht Treaty**, which, among many other things, changed the name of the European Community to the European Union (EU). The mission of Eurostat is to provide the EU with harmonized statistical information of the highest quality. Eurostat collects this data from the National Statistical Units of each EU member country. This data is then standardized and ''harmonized'' and then disseminated to the EU at large as well as members of the European Economic Area, and in some cases the United States and Japan.

Eurostat was founded in 1953 as the Statistics Division of the High Authority of the Coal and Steel Community. In 1958, following the Treaty of Rome, it became known as the Statistics Division of the European Communities, and in 1959 it adopted its present formal title.

Eurostat is guided by the belief that productive negotiations between member countries of the EU is dependent upon current and reliable statistical information. This information must be in a format that can be justified between the various countries using it. Of the EU members from which information is gathered, there is a wide variance in terms of data quality and uniformity. This is due to gathering techniques, budgetary restraints, concerns of confidentiality, and differences in the way the various countries view the utility of this information. Eurostat harmonizes this data to make it uniformly meaningful and to create a ''common statistical language within the EU.'' Besides being available to member nations and the above institutions, Eurostat data is also available to trade and industry groups, political offices, educational institutions, the media, and private individuals.

Eurostat data is divided into nine major statistical themes: general statistics; economy and finance; population and social conditions; energy and industry; agriculture, forestry and fisheries; external trade; distributive trade, services, and transportation; environment; and research and development. This information is then disseminated as databases, printed publications, and electronic products. The databases include New Cronos, which holds more than 70 million statistical items on the EU nations and their major non-European trading partners; Comext, which is a trade database detailing EU imports and exports; REGIO, which contains EU socioeconomic data; Eurofarm, which deals with agriculture; and GISCO, which combines statistical information with geo-referenced data. The large number of printed publications include statistical documents related to Eurostat's mission. Eurostat's electronic products in CD-ROM format include: Comext, which contains 10,000 product headings, geonomenclature of 200 countries worldwide, each previous year's data formatted by month, quarter, and year, and statistics on major trade partners; Eurostat Yearbook, which provides socioeconomic statistics on EU members; Panorama of European Industry, which profiles Europe's 500 largest companies in the private sector as well as major trends in 25 European industrial sectors; and Eurofarm, which is a specialist database of information dealing with European agriculture, including wine production.

This information is distributed through private hosts, a network of Eurostat Data shops, the national Statistical Institutes of EU member countries, various sales offices, European Documentation Centres, and Euro-info-centres.

A major goal of the Maastricht Treaty was to move the members of the European Community towards the Economic and Monetary Union, which among other things would integrate the monetary policies of member countries and establish a common currency (the **euro**). Eurostat is playing a major role in this undertaking by being responsible for providing a harmonized index of consumer prices; providing standards for calculating **debt** and **deficits**; harmonizing the calculation of member countries' **gross domestic product** (GDP) and **gross national product** (GNP); and harmonizing the calculation of economic indicators. Eurostat will also gather data related to the measurement of **inflation**, public finances, and indicators of prices, wages, labor costs, external trade, industrial output, balance of payments, and the like. Eurostat is charged with gathering this relevant data in a timely manner and making it comparable.

[Michael Knes]

FURTHER READING:

De Michelis, Alberto. "The Statistics Corner" (EMU and Statistics). *Business Economics* 33, no. 3 (July 1998): 57-60.

"One-off Measures: Lessons in Massaging the Figures." *Banker,* May 1998, 29.

Statistical Office of the European Communities. "Eurostat: Statistical Office of the European Communities." Luxembourg: Statistical Office of the European Communities, 1998. Available from europa.eu.int/en/comm/eurostat/serven/home.htm.

STATISTICAL PROCESS CONTROL

Traditional **quality control** is designed to prevent the production of products that do not meet certain acceptance criteria. This could be accomplished by performing inspection on products that, in many cases, have already been produced. Action could then be taken by rejecting those products. Some products would go on to be reworked, a process that is costly and time consuming. In many cases, rework is more expensive than producing the product in the first place. This situation often results in decreased productivity, customer dissatisfaction, loss of competitive position, and higher cost.

To avoid such results, quality must be built into the product and the processes. Statistical process control (SPC), a term often used interchangeably with statistical quality control (SQC), involves the integration of quality control into each stage of producing the product. In fact, SPC is a powerful collection of tools that implement the concept of prevention as a shift from the traditional quality by inspection/correction.

SPC is a technique that employs statistical tools for controlling and improving processes. SPC is an important ingredient in continuous process improvement strategies. It uses simple statistical means to control, monitor, and improve processes. All SPC tools are graphical and simple to use and understand, as shown in Figure 1.

UNDERSTANDING VARIATION

The main objective of any SPC study is to reduce variation. Any process can be considered a transformation mechanism of different input factors into a product or service. Since inputs exhibit variation, the result is a combined effect of all variations. This, in turn, is translated into the product. The purpose of SPC is to isolate the natural variation in the process from other sources of variation that can be traced or whose causes may be identified. As follows, there are two different kinds of variation that affect the quality characteristics of products.

COMMON CAUSES OF VARIATION. Variation due to common causes are inherent in the process; they are inevitable and can be represented by a normal distribution. Common causes are also called chance causes

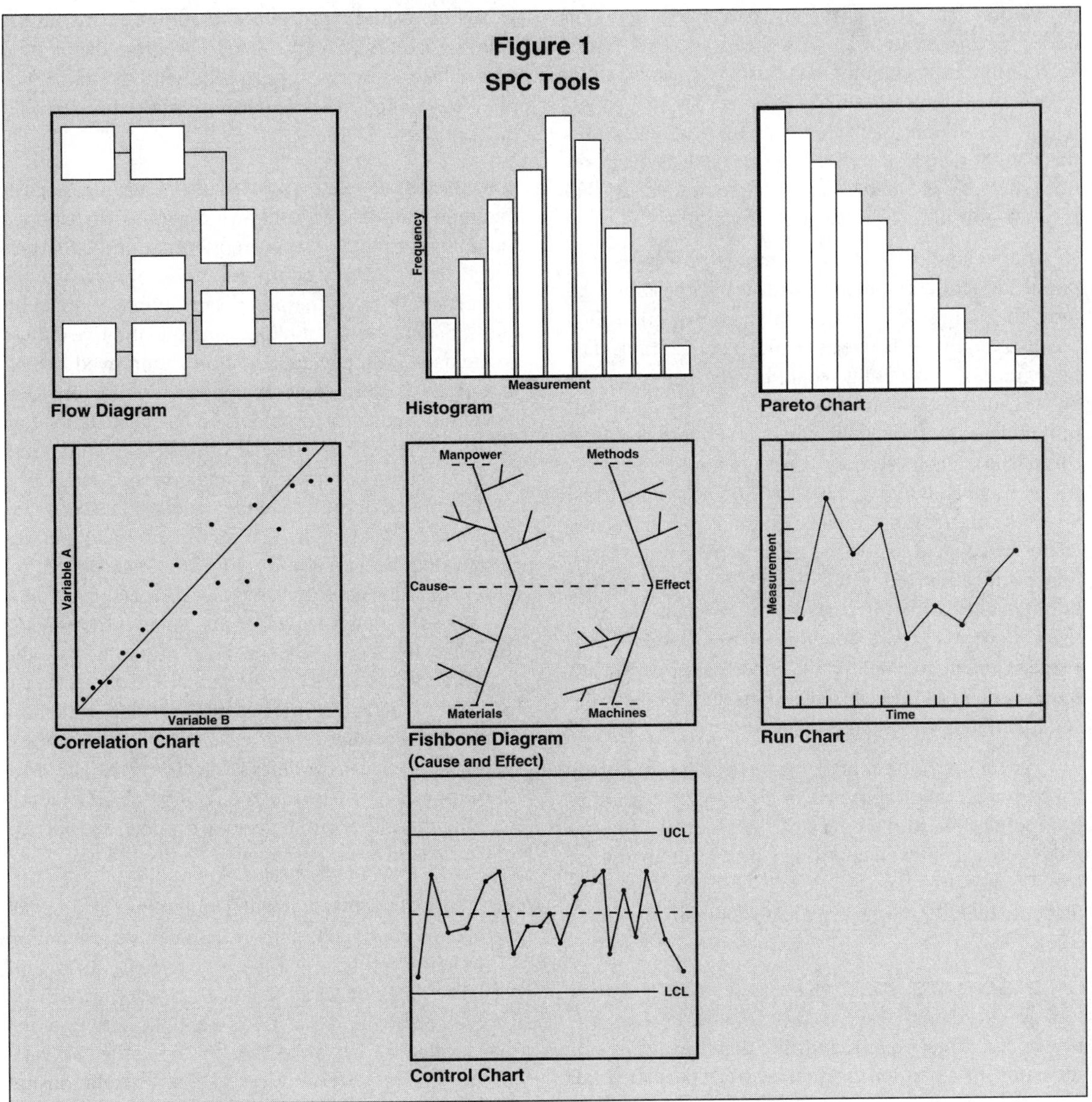

Flow Diagram

Histogram

Pareto Chart

Correlation Chart

Fishbone Diagram (Cause and Effect)

Run Chart

Control Chart

of variation. A stable process exhibits only common causes of variation. The behavior of a stable process is predictable or consistent, and the process is said to be in statistical control.

SPECIAL CAUSES OF VARIATION. Special causes, also called assignable causes of variation, are not part of the process. They can be traced, identified, and eliminated. Control charts are designed to hunt for those causes as part of SPC efforts to improve the process. A process with the presence of special or assignable cause of variation is unpredictable or inconsistent, and the process is said to be out of statistical control.

STATISTICAL PROCESS CONTROL (SPC) TOOLS

Among the many tools for quality improvement, the following are the most commonly used tools of SPC:

- histograms
- cause-and-effect diagrams
- Pareto diagrams
- control charts
- scatter or correlation diagrams
- run charts
- process flow diagrams

Figure 1 shows the seven basic tools of statistical process control, sometimes known as the "magnificent 7."

HISTOGRAMS. Histograms are visual charts that depict how often each kind of variation occurs in a process. As with all SPC tools, histograms are generally used on a representative sample of output to make judgments about the process as a whole. The height of the vertical bars on a histogram shows how common each type of variation is, with the tallest bars representing the most common outcomes. Typically a histogram documents variations at between 6 and 20 regular intervals along some continuum (i.e., categories made up of ranges of process values, such as measurement ranges) and shows the relative frequency that products fall into each category of variation.

For example, if a metal-stamping process is supposed to yield a component with a thickness of 10.5 mm, the range of variation in a poorly controlled process might be between 9 mm and 12 mm. The histogram of this output would divide it into several equal categories within the range (say, by each half millimeter) and show how many parts out of a sample run fall into each category. Under a normal distribution (i.e., a bell curve) the chart would be symmetrical on both sides of the mean, which is normally the center category. Ideally, the mean is also well within the specification limits for the output. If the chart is not symmetrical or the mean is skewed, it suggests that the process is particularly weak on one end. Thus, in the stamping example, if the chart is skewed toward the lower end of the size scale, it might mean that the stamping equipment tends to use too much force.

Still, even if the chart is symmetrical, if the vertical bars are all similar in size, or if there are larger bars protruding toward the edges of the chart, it suggests the process is not well controlled. The ideal histogram for SPC purposes has very steep bars in the center that drop off quickly to very small bars toward the outer edges.

PARETO CHARTS. Pareto charts are another powerful tool for statistical process control and quality improvement. They go a step further than histograms by focusing the attention on the factors that cause the most trouble in a process. With Pareto charts, facts about the greatest improvement potential can be easily identified.

A Pareto chart is also made up of a series of vertical bars. However, in this case the bars move from left to right in order of descending importance, as measured by the percentage of errors caused by each factor. The sum of all the factors generally accounts for 100 percent of all errors or problems; this is often indicated with a line graph superimposed over the bars showing a cumulative percentage as of each successive factor.

A hypothetical Pareto chart might consist of these four explanatory factors, along with their associated percentages, for factory paint defects on a product: extraneous dust on the surface (75 percent), temperature variations (15 percent), sprayer head clogs (6 percent), and paint formulation variations (4 percent). Clearly, these figures suggest that, all things being equal, the most effective step to reduce paint defects would be to find a procedure to eliminate dust in the painting facility or on the materials before the process takes place. Conversely, haggling with the paint supplier for more consistent paint formulations would have the least impact.

CAUSE-AND-EFFECT DIAGRAMS. Cause-and-effect diagrams, also called Ishikawa diagrams or fishbone diagrams, provide a visual representation of the factors that most likely contribute to an observed problem or an effect on the process. They are technically not statistical tools—it requires no quantitative data to create one—but they are commonly employed in SPC to help develop hypotheses about which factors contribute to a quality problem. In a cause-and-effect diagram, the main horizontal line leads toward some effect or outcome, usually a negative one such as a product defect or returned merchandise. The branches or ''bones'' leading to the central problem are the main categories of contributing factors, and within these there are often a variety of subcategories. For example, the main causes of customer turnover at a consumer Internet service provider might fall into the categories of service problems, price, and service limitations. Subcategories under service problems might include busy signals for dial up customers, server outages, e-mail delays, and so forth. The relationships between such factors can be clearly identified, and therefore, problems may be identified and the root causes may be corrected.

SCATTER DIAGRAMS. Scatter diagrams, also called correlation charts, show the graphical representation of a relationship between two variables as a series of dots. The range of possible values for each variable is represented by the X and Y axes, and the pattern of the dots, plotted from sample data involving the two variables, suggests whether or not a statistical relationship exists. The relationship may be that of cause and effect or of some other origin; the scatter diagram merely shows whether the relationship exists and how strong it is. The variables in scatter diagrams generally must be measurable on a numerical scale (e.g., price, distance, speed, size, age, frequency), and therefore categories like ''present'' and ''not present'' are not well suited for this analysis.

An example would be to study the relationship between product defects and worker experience. The researcher would construct a chart based on the number of defects associated with workers of different levels of experience. If there is a statistical relationship, the plotted data will tend to cluster in certain ways. For instance, if the dots cluster around an upward-sloping line or band, it suggests there is a positive correlation between the two variables. If it is a downward-sloping line, there may be a negative relationship. And if the data points are spread evenly on the chart with no particular shape or clustering, it suggests no relationship at all. In statistical process control, scatter diagrams are normally used to explore the relationships between process variables and may lead to identifying possible ways to increased process performance.

CONTROL CHARTS. Considered by some the most important SPC tool, control charts are graphical representations of process performance over time. They are concerned with how (or whether) processes vary at different intervals and, specifically, with identifying nonrandom or assignable causes of variation. Control charts provide a powerful analytical tool for monitoring process variability and other changes in process mean or variability deterioration.

Several kinds of control charts exist, each with its own strengths. One of the most common is the $\overline{X}$ chart, also known as the Shewhart $\overline{X}$ chart after its inventor, Walter Shewhart. The $\overline{X}$ symbol is used in statistics to indicate the arithmetic mean (average) of a set of sample values (for instance, product measurements taken in a quality control sample). For control charts the sample size is often quite small, such as just four or five units chosen randomly, but the sampling is repeated periodically. In an $\overline{X}$ chart the average value of each sample is plotted and compared to averages of previous samples, as well as to expected levels of variation under a normal distribution.

Four values must be calculated before the $\overline{X}$ chart can be created:

1. The average of the sample means (designated as $\overline{Xd}$ since it is an average of averages)
2. The upper control limit (UCL), which suggests the highest level of variation one would expect in a stable process
3. The lower control limit (LCL), which is the lowest expected value in a stable process
4. The average of range R (labeled $\overline{R}$), which represents the mean difference between the highest and lowest values in each sample (e.g., if sample measurements were 3.1, 3.3, 3.2, and 3.0, the range would be 3.3 − 3.0 = 0.3)

While the values of $\overline{Xd}$ and $\overline{R}$ can be determined directly from the sample data, calculating the UCL and LCL requires a special probability multiplier (often given in tables in statistics texts) A_2. The UCL and LCL approximate the distance of three standard deviations above and below the mean, respectively. The simplified formulas are as follows:

$$UCL_{\overline{X}} = \overline{Xd} + (A_2 \times \overline{R})$$

$$LCL_{\overline{X}} = \overline{Xd} - (A_2 \times \overline{R})$$

where $\overline{Xd}$ is the mean of the sample means
A_2 is a constant multiplier based on the sample size
$\overline{R}$ is the mean of the sample ranges

Graphically, the control limits and the overall mean $\overline{Xd}$ are drawn as a continuum made up of three parallel horizontal lines, with UCL on top, $\overline{Xd}$ in the middle, and LCL on the bottom. The individual sample means ($\overline{X}$) are then plotted along the continuum in the order they were taken (for example, at weekly intervals). Ideally, the $\overline{X}$ values will stay within the confines of the control limits and tend toward the middle along the $\overline{Xd}$ line. If, however, individual sample values exceed the upper or lower limits repeatedly, it signals that the process is not in statistical control and that exploration is needed to find the cause. More advanced analyses using $\overline{X}$ charts also consider warning limits within the control limits and various trends or patterns in the $\overline{X}$ line.

Other widely used control charts include *R* charts, which observe variations in the expected range of values and cumulative sum (CUSUM) charts, which are useful for detecting smaller yet revealing changes in a set of data.

RUN CHARTS. Run charts depict process behavior against time. They are important in investigating changes in the process over time, such as predictable cycles. Any changes in process stability or instability can be judged from a run chart. They may also be used to compare two separate variables over time to identify correlations and other relationships.

FLOW DIAGRAMS. Process flow diagrams or **flow charts** are graphical representations of a process. They show the sequence of different operations that make up a process. Flow diagrams are important tools for documenting processes and communicating information about processes. They can also be used to identify bottlenecks in a process sequence, to identify points of rework or other phenomena in a process, or to define points where data or information about process performance need to be collected.

PROCESS CAPABILITY ANALYSIS

Process capability is determined from the total variations that are caused only by common causes of variation after all assignable causes have been removed. It represents the performance of a process that is in statistical control. When a process is in statistical control, its performance is predictable and can be represented by a probability distribution.

The proportion of production that is out of specification is a measure of the capability of the process. Such proportion may be determined using the process distribution. If the process maintains its status of being in statistical control, the proportion of defective or nonconforming production remains the same.

Before assessing the capability of the process, it must be brought first to a state of statistical control. There are several ways to measure the capability of the process:

USING CONTROL CHARTS. When the control chart indicates that the process is in a state of statistical control, and when the control limits are stable and periodically reviewed, it can be used to assess the capability of the process and provide information to infer such capability.

NATURAL TOLERANCE VERSUS SPECIFICATION LIMITS. The natural tolerance limits of a process are normally these limits between which the process is capable of producing parts. Natural tolerance limits are expressed as the process mean plus or minus z process standard deviation units. Unless otherwise stated, z is considered to be three standard deviations.

There are three situations to be considered that describe the relationship between process natural tolerance limits and specification limits. In case one, specification limits are wider than the process natural tolerance limits. This situation represents a process that is capable of meeting specifications. Although not desirable, this situation accommodates, to a certain degree, some shift in the process mean or a change in process variability.

In case two, specification limits are equal to the process natural tolerance limits. This situation represents a critical process that is capable of meeting specifications only if no shift in the process mean or a change in process variability takes place. A shift in the process mean or a change in its variability will result in the production of nonconforming products. When dealing with a situation like this, care must be taken to avoid producing products that are not conforming to specifications.

In case three, specification limits are narrower than the process natural tolerance limits. This situation guarantees the production of products that do not meet the desired specifications. When dealing with this situation, action should be taken to widen the specification limits, to change the design of the product, and to control the process such that its variability is reduced. Another solution is to look for a different process altogether.

SEE ALSO: Total Quality Management (TQM)

FURTHER READING:

Fine, Edmund S. "Use Histograms to Help Data Communicate." *Quality,* May 1997.

Juran, Joseph M., and A. Blanton Godfrey, eds. *Juran's Quality Handbook.* 5th ed. New York: McGraw-Hill, 1998.

Maleyeff, John. "The Fundamental Concepts of Statistical Quality Control." *Industrial Engineering,* December 1994.

Schuetz, George. "Bedrock SQC." *Modern Machine Shop,* February 1996.

STATISTICS

SEE: Financial Statistics; Nonparametric Statistics; Statistical Analysis for Management; Statistical Office of the European Community; Statistical Process Control

STOCHASTIC PROCESSES

In probability theory, random phenomena that result from processes governed by probabilistic laws (such as the growth of a bacterial colony or the fluctuation of electric current in a circuit) are stochastic processes, according to Emanuel Parzen in *Stochastic Processes.* From a mathematical perspective, stochastic processes are collections of random variables and they involve events or phenomena with random outcomes. Random variables refer to variables whose values (e.g., true or false, yes or no) are determined by probabilistic laws. Stochastic processes include one or more random variables observed in multiple steps, or iterations, whose outcomes are not independent. In other words, the outcomes, while random, are related and can indicate a pattern of behavior. Consequently, stochastic processes can help eliminate some of the uncertainty associated with achieving various goals, because they take randomness into consideration.

Stochastic processes are commonly used in **game theory** examples, polling, tracking, probability calculations, and **statistical analysis**. In each case and at every step, an outcome may depend on any one of several random factors. Stochastic processes most often come into play for analyzing random yet predictable phenomena such as those of meteorology, business **management**, engineering, biology, and medicine.

Because of the existence of at least one random variable in stochastic processes, outcomes can never be predicted for certain according to deterministic laws. But because outcomes tend to indicate patterns of behavior, stochastic processes can yield knowledge in the form of predictions and they can indicate parameters of likely outcomes.

Stochastic processes may involve studying and measuring outcomes and patterns over a period of time for continuous phenomena. In a study involving the value of a **stock**, for example, a given variable A (which could represent a factor such as low **unemployment**) may be observed to increase value in 75 percent of past iterations. The variable B (which could represent a factor such as high unemployment) may be observed to decrease value in 75 percent of the cases. As a result, when A occurs, the observer may assume a 75 percent likelihood that value will increase.

The solution is not certain, because there is still a 25 percent chance that value will decrease. But past occurrences indicate a pattern of behavior suggesting that value is likely to increase when A is present and decrease when B is present. Repeated occurrences of variables and results may provide additional precision to the prediction, or identify the effects of other variables.

For single shot events, stochastic processes involve the measurement of a host of factors that can affect the outcome before and after each occurrence. Consider, for example, shooting a projectile toward a target 800 yards away. Measurement must be taken for and assumptions must be made about the weight of the projectile, amount of launch explosive, trajectory and direction of launch, wind direction and speeds, and even humidity.

If a single shot overshoots its target by 100 yards, adjustments must be made to gain accuracy. If additional shots are possible, variables such as trajectory, direction, and launch explosive may be adjusted to gain accuracy. The cycle is repeated on a third shot, then the fourth, until the target is hit.

Independent variables, such as atmospheric conditions, may change during the course of firings. They remain independent because changing wind speeds cannot be predicted with total accuracy. As a result, the projectile may be brought to land closer to the target, but unless conditions remain static, complete accuracy cannot be attained.

BUSINESS APPLICATIONS

Stochastic processes can play an important role in managing a business and they have been applied to a few aspects of managing business operations, including sales strategies and inventory control. Stochastic processes in business work in a similar fashion to other fields. First, if a sales strategy for a product fails to produce an intended outcome, dependent variables may be adjusted. But independent variables, governed by the actions of competitors, remain unpredictable. This is especially relevant because competitors may alter their own actions based on the results of the first strategy.

Second, retailers, wholesalers, and manufacturers face two major inventory control problems: determining when to order additional stock items and determining how many to order. To operate one of these businesses efficiently, managers must consider the uncertain amount of items that will be needed in a given period as well as the uncertain amount of time it will take to have the items delivered after they are ordered. Because of these two uncertainties, companies must maintain an inventory of items so that they have them when they need them. Since having an inventory requires significant investment, companies strive to keep their inventories to a minimum to reduce overhead. Stochastic process would involve identifying the current policies on when to order and how much to order. If these policies are not successful—if a company frequently has too much or not enough inventory—then the company would have to alter them and reevaluate them until they yielded a more favorable outcome. This reevaluation might include consideration of seasonal fluctuations, changes in product movement because of **economic conditions**, demand levels for the different days of the week, and so on until a more precise picture of these factors had been obtained.

[John Simley, updated by Karl Heil]

FURTHER READING:

Biswas, Suddhendu. *Applied Stochastic Processes.* New York: John Wiley & Sons, Inc. 1995.

Chou, Ya-lun. *Statistical Analysis for Business and Economics.* Amsterdam: Elsevier Science Publishing, 1989.

Johnson, Robert R. *Elementary Statistics.* 3rd ed. North Scituate, MA: Duxbury Press, 1980.

Parzen, Emanuel. *Stochastic Processes.* San Francisco: Holden-Day, 1962.

Wang, Yunzeng, and Yigal Gerchak. "Periodic Review Production Models with Variable Capacity, Random Yield, and Uncertain Demand." *Management Science,* January 1996, 130.

STOCK EXCHANGE

SEE: Stock Market

STOCK INDEX FUTURES

A contract for stock index futures is based on the level of a particular stock **index** such as the S&P 500 or the Dow Jones Industrial Average. The agreement calls for the contract to be bought or sold at a designated time in the future. Just as hedgers and speculators buy and sell **futures contracts** and options based on a future price of corn, foreign currency, or lumber, they may—for mostly the same reasons—buy and sell **contracts** based on the level of a number of stock indexes.

Stock index futures may be used to either speculate on the equity market's general performance or to hedge a stock portfolio against a decline in value. It is not unheard of for the expiration dates of these contracts to be as much as two or more years in the future, but like commodity futures contracts most expire within one year. Unlike **commodity futures**, however, stock index futures are not based on tangible goods, thus all settlements are in cash. Because settlements are in cash, investors usually have to meet liquidity or income requirements to show that they have money to cover their potential losses.

VALUING STOCK INDEX FUTURES

All stock index futures contracts have a value equal to their price multiplied by a specified dollar amount. To illustrate, the price of a stock index futures contract based on the New York Stock Exchange (NYSE) Composite Index is derived by multiplying the index level value by $500. This value results because each futures contract is equal to $500 times the quoted futures price. So, if the index level is determined to be 200, the corresponding stock index future would cost $100,000. The index level is marked-to-market, meaning that at the end of each day its value is adjusted to reflect changes in the day's share prices.

In stock index futures contracts, there are two parties directly involved. One party (the short position) must deliver to a second party (the long position) an amount of cash equaling the contract's dollar multiplier multiplied by the difference between the spot price of a **stock market** index underlying the contract on the day of settlement (IP_{spot}) and the contract price on the date that the contract was entered (CP_0).

$$\text{Cash} = \text{Contract Dollar Multiplier} \times (IP_{spot} - CP_0)$$

If an investor sells a six-month NYSE Composite futures contract (with a multiplier of $500 per index point) at 444 and, six months later, the NYSE Composite Index closes at 445, the short party will receive $500 in cash from the long party.

$$\text{Cash} = \$500\ (445 - 444) = \$500$$

Similarly, if an investor shorts a one-year futures contract at 442 and the index is 447 on the settlement day one year later (assuming that the multiplier is at $500), the short seller has to pay the long holder $2,500.

$$\text{Cash} = \$500\ (447 - 442) = \$2{,}500$$

Thus, positive differences are paid by the seller and received by the buyer. Negative differences are paid by the buyer and received by the seller.

BUYING AND SELLING STOCK INDEX FUTURES

When an investor opens a futures position, he or she does not pay the entire amount of the equity underlying the futures contract. The investor is required to put up only a small percentage of the value of the contract as a margin. A margin is the amount of money required for investors to give to their brokers to maintain their futures contracts. Unlike margins paid for stock purchases, margins paid for stock index futures are not purchases or sales of actual **securities**. Instead, they represent agreements to pay or receive the difference in price between the index underlying the contract on the day of settlement (IP_{spot}) and the contract price on the date that the contract was entered (CP_0). The exact amount of money needed to cover the margin is determined by two formulas. Both formulas are a function of the market price, the price of the index, and the strike price. The amount of money required for the margin is the greater result of the two formulas.

If the index moves against the sellers, they will be required to add to the margin amount. Known as a maintenance or variation margin, it is the minimum level to which investors' account equity can fall before they receive a margin call. When investors' equity in a stock index futures account falls below the maintenance level, they receive a margin call for enough money to bring the account up to the initial margin level. This margin requirement mandates that holders of futures positions settle their realized and unrealized profits and losses in cash on a daily basis. These profits and losses are derived by comparing the trade price against the daily settlement price of the futures contract. The settlement price is broadcast by the exchanges soon after the markets close; it represents the pricing of the last 30 seconds of the day's trading.

USES OF STOCK INDEX FUTURES

Investors can use stock index futures to perform myriad tasks. Some common uses are: to speculate on changes in specific markets (see above examples); to change the weightings of portfolios; to separate market timing from market selection decisions; and to take part in index **arbitrage**, whereby the investors seek to gain profits whenever a futures contract is trading out of line with the fair price of the securities underlying it.

Investors commonly use stock index futures to change the weightings or risk exposures of their investment portfolios. A good example of this are investors who hold equities from two or more countries. Suppose these investors have portfolios invested in 60 percent U.S. equities and 40 percent Japanese equities and want to increase their systematic risk to the U.S. market and reduce these risks to the Japanese market. They can do this by buying U.S. stock index futures contracts in the indexes underlying their holdings and selling Japanese contracts (in the Nikkei Index).

Stock index futures also allow investors to separate market timing from market selection decisions. For instance, investors may want to take advantage of perceived immediate increases in an equity market but are not certain which securities to buy; they can do this by purchasing stock index futures. If the futures contracts are bought and the **present value** of the money used to buy them is invested in risk-free securities, investors will have a risk exposure equal to that of the market. Similarly, investors can adjust their portfolio holdings at a more leisurely pace. For example, assume the investors see that they have several undesirable **stocks** but do not know what holdings to buy to replace them. They can sell the unwanted stocks and, at the same time, buy stock index futures to keep their exposure to the market. They can later sell the futures contracts when they have decided which specific stocks they want to purchase.

Investors can also make money from stock index futures through index arbitrage, also referred to as program trading. Basically, arbitrage is the purchase of a security or commodity in one market and the simultaneous sale of an equal product in another market to profit from pricing differences. Investors taking part in stock index arbitrage seek to gain profits whenever a futures contract is trading out of line with the fair price of the securities underlying it. Thus, if a stock index futures contract is trading above its fair value, investors could buy a basket of about 100 stocks composing the index in the correct proportion—such as a **mutual fund** comprised of stocks represented in the index—and then sell the expensively priced futures contract. Once the contract expires, the equities could then be sold and a net profit would result. While the investors can keep their arbitrage position until the futures contract expires, they are not required to. If the futures contract seems to be returning to fair market value before the expiration date, it may be prudent for the investors to sell early.

USING INDEXES TO HEDGE PORTFOLIO RISK

Aside from the above uses of indexes, investors often use stock index futures to hedge the value of their portfolios. To implement a hedge, the instruments in the cash and futures markets should have similar price movements. Also, the amount of money invested in the cash and futures markets should be the same. To illustrate, while investors owning well-diversified investment portfolios are generally shielded from unsystematic risk (risk specific to particular firms), they are fully exposed to systematic risk (risk relating to overall market fluctuations). A cost-effective way for investors to reduce the exposure to systematic risk is to hedge with stock index futures, similar to the way that people hedge commodity holdings using **commodity futures**. Investors often use short hedges when they are in a long position in a stock portfolio and believe that there will be a temporary downturn in the overall stock market. **Hedging** transfers the price risk of owning the stock from a person unwilling to accept systematic risks to someone willing to take the risk.

To carry out a short hedge, the hedger sells a futures contract; thus, the short hedge is also called a ''sell-hedge.'' For example, consider investors who own portfolios of securities valued at $1.2 million with a dividend of 4 percent. The investors have been very successful with their stock picks. Therefore, while their portfolios' returns move up and down with the market, they consistently outperform the market by 6 percent. Thus, the portfolio would have a beta of 1.00 and an alpha of 6 percent. Say that the investors believe that the market is going to have a 15 percent decline, which would be offset by the 1 percent received from dividends. The net broad market return would be -14 percent but, since they consistently outperform the market by 6 percent, their estimated return would be -8 percent. In this instance, the investors would like to cut their beta in half without necessarily cutting their alpha in half. They can achieve this by selling stock index futures. In this scenario, the S&P 500 index is at 240. The contract multiplier is $500, and therefore each contract represents a value of $120,000. Since the investors want to simulate the sale of half of their $1.2 million portfolios, they must sell five contracts (5 × $120,000 = $600,000). Thus, their portfolios would be affected by only half of the market fluctuation. While the investors could protect their portfolios equally well by selling half of their shares of stock and buying them again a short time later, using a short hedge on stock index futures is much cheaper than paying the **capital gains** tax plus the broker commissions associated with buying and selling huge blocks of stock.

At the extreme, stock index futures can theoretically eliminate the effects of the broad market on a portfolio. Perfect hedges are very unusual because of the existence of basis risk. The basis is the difference between the existing price in the futures market and the cash price of the underlying securities. Basis risk occurs when changes in the economy and the financial situation have different impacts on the cash and futures markets.

TRANSACTION COSTS

Whenever investors trade securities, they must pay transaction costs. Clearly, there is an explicit commission that investors must give their brokers for executing and clearing their trades. While investors can negotiate the commissions paid for stock index futures transactions with their broker, generally, they will pay their brokers around $25 per contract. (This commission varies somewhat with the investors' trading volume and the type of support they receive.) The commission usually covers the opening and the liquidation of the contracts and is paid at the time of their liquidation.

One of the largest attractions that trading stock index futures has is the relatively small transaction costs associated with them, especially when compared with other ways of attaining the same investment goals. For instance, the commissions paid to brokers for stock index futures transactions are much cheaper than the commissions paid for trading an equally large dollar amount of stocks underlying the index. Often, each futures contracts often represents more than $100,000 in stocks, and the associated commission would amount to about $25. For stocks, the commission paid on each share of stock would be about five cents. This could amount to hundreds of dollars commission depending on price per share.

LIMITS ON PRICE MOVEMENTS

For every contract, the exchange on which it is based establishes a limit on the amount the price can change. For each stock index futures contract the minimum price fluctuation, also called the "tick," is .05. So, a one point move in a futures contract means a gain or loss of one dollar times the dollar multiple of the specific contract, say $500. Therefore, the minimum amount that a price can change is .05 multiplied by the contract's dollar multiple, or .05 times $500, which is $25.

POPULAR STOCK INDEXES

Three of the most popular stock index for futures contracts are: The New York Stock Exchange Composite Index (traded on the New York Futures Exchange), the Value Line Composite Index (traded on the Kansas City Board of Trade), and the Standard & Poor's 500 Index (traded on the Chicago Mercantile Exchange). Furthermore, investors can also purchase options on stock index futures; for instance, the Standard & Poor's 500 Stock Index futures options are traded on the Chicago Mercantile Exchange.

SEE ALSO: Derivative Securities; Futures/Futures Contracts

[Kathryn Snavely, updated by Michael Knes]

FURTHER READING:

Barron's Finance and Investment Handbook. 2nd ed. New York: Barron's, 1987.

"Beating the S&P, Using Bonds." *Kiplinger's Personal Finance Magazine,* July 1997.

Bodie, Zvi, Alex Kane, and Alan J. Marcus. *Investments.* 4th ed. Boston: Irwin/McGraw-Hill, 1999.

Chicago Mercantile Exchange. "Chicago Mercantile Exchange: Getting Started." Chicago: Chicago Mercantile Exchange, 1998. Available from www.cme.com/market/mercwork.html.

Derack, Arthur. *Trade the OEX.* 3rd ed. Chicago: Bonus Books, 1996.

Fabozzi, Frank J., and Gregory M. Kipnis. *Stock Index Futures.* Homewood, IL: Dow Jones-Irwin, 1984.

Luskin, Donald L. *Index Options and Futures: A Complete Guide.* New York: Wiley, 1987.

Millers, John. *Stock Index Options and Futures.* London: McGraw-Hill, 1992.

Reilly, Frank K., and Keith C. Brown. *Investment Analysis and Portfolio Management.* 5th ed. Fort Worth, TX: Dryden Press, 1997.

——. *Investments.* 2nd ed. New York: Dresden Press, 1986.

Ritter, Jay R. "How I Helped Make Fischer Black Wealthier." *Financial Management* 25, no. 4 (winter 1996).

Weiner, Neil S. *Stock Index Futures: A Guide for Traders, Investors, and Analysts.* New York: Wiley, 1984.

Wilmott, Paul. *Derivatives: The Theory and Practice of Financial Engineering.* New York: John Wiley & Sons, Inc., 1998.

STOCK MARKET

In financial terms the word "market" has a meaning that is conceptual: a market is the interaction of offers to buy ("bids") and offers to sell ("asks"). Physical location is a detail, and the market may not have a single location—buyers and sellers may never meet face to face. The critical component is the existence of the offers. A market maker is said to make a market in an item by simply standing ready to buy or sell the item. In the extreme there are as many markets as market makers, but markets can be grouped in various ways. One common grouping is by the item traded. We will focus on the stock markets, as a part of the broader **securities** markets, using the plural to indicate that there are many trading mechanisms.

Philadelphia was originally the leading financial center of the United States, with New York and Boston as less important locations. In New York, trading was conducted in an area near the site of the wall erected to separate the original Dutch colony from the indigenous inhabitants. Trading in financial instruments was sparse and haphazard, often occurring through personal contact in the area coffee houses. In the late 1700s, however, there was increased trading in the Continental and Colonial war bonds that had been issued to finance the American Revolution. Brokerage services were offered by some merchants as a secondary activity. On May 17, 1792, 24 New York brokers signed an agreement to trade a restricted list of securities among themselves, and to charge a fixed commission of 0.25 percent. This was referred to as the buttonwood agreement because the designated meeting place was in the open near a buttonwood tree. The arrangement worked, and in the next year the association built the Tontine Coffee House and moved trading to one of the rooms inside the building. Trading was conducted as a ''call'' market. Several times each day the brokers would gather, each in an assigned seat, and the names of the traded securities would be called out one at a time. As the name of a security was read, the brokers would orally exchange offers to buy and sell in an ''auction'' process, until a price was agreed on.

The buttonwood brokers faced considerable **competition** from other similar groups and was at times overshadowed. By the 1860s, 11 exchanges had evolved in New York from outdoor trading in the ''curb markets''—outdoor markets where trading literally took place at the curbstones, with different **stocks** being traded at particular lampposts or other similar, agreed upon locations. In 1869 the original buttonwood association merged with the larger Open Board and adopted continuous auction trading, rather than the periodic call system originally used. The much-changed buttonwood association has endured, and still meets near the location of the wall and the buttonwood tree—the location is now on Wall Street. It uses the name adopted in 1863: New York Stock Exchange (NYSE). The NYSE is now the dominant, but not the only, U.S. stock exchange. The remaining New York curb markets went through various associations and combinations, eventually moving trading inside and merging into what is today the American Stock Exchange (AMEX). The exchanges in Philadelphia and Boston continue, and a number of other regional exchanges have come into existence.

Internationally, many exchanges were in existence before the beginning of U.S. markets. Some of the foreign exchanges are large, and compete with U.S. exchanges for international investments. The creation of new exchanges continues, particularly in emerging countries.

In addition to the formal, organized exchanges, stocks also trade in an extensive informal **over-the-counter (OTC) securities market**. This market does not have a physical location: buyers and sellers interact electronically. In fact, the number of stock issues traded is larger than the number of issues traded on the organized exchanges, although both the volume of trades and the size of the firms traded is generally smaller. For some securities, such as **bonds** or stock of small firms, these informal markets are the principal trading mechanism.

THE ROLE OF THE STOCK MARKETS

Securities markets may be classified by role into primary and secondary markets. The primary market is the process by which new securities are issued and marketed. After the distribution period, trading of the issue among investors is referred to as the secondary market.

THE PRIMARY MARKET. Capital for growth and new investments is the lifeblood of the firm. Large investors with the means to invest directly are scarce and difficult to attract. By issuing securities, a firm has access to a larger number of investors of varying means. This allows the firm to raise larger amounts of capital at less cost than through seeking **direct investment** by individuals or from bank **loans**. Without a primary securities market, new projects are difficult to finance, **innovation** slows, and **economic development** stagnates.

The process of selling stock to the general public for the first time is called an initial public offering (IPO). If the firm has previously issued stock to the general public, a new issue is called a seasoned new issue. Given the infrequency of a stock issue for a firm, and the unfamiliarity of the corporate financial officers with the complex process, it is logical for the firm to turn to an **investment banker**. The investment banker is an expert in **public offerings** who provides three services to the issuing firm. The first service is advice. The investment banker knows the extensive legal requirements and other arrangements surrounding registration and sale of securities, and guides the firm through the process. The investment banker is familiar with the securities markets, and can help the firm choose the optimal form of security and design its terms. The second service is **marketing** and distribution. The originating banker also provides price support or stabilization for the issue during the distribution phase, standing ready to buy the security to prevent or reduce price drops due to temporary imbalances. Notice of a public offering in the financial press is in the form of tombstones, so named because of the similarity of appearance. The tombstone describes the security and lists the originating banker and the members of the syndicate.

The third service provided by the investment banker is reduction of **risk** through the process of **underwriting**. This is perhaps the most important service provided. A public offering is an important event for a firm, and failure of an offering would be disastrous. In underwriting, the investment banker guarantees the success of the issue by simply buying the entire issue from the firm, accepting the risk that the security will not sell at the expected price. There are two reasons the investment banker can accept the risk of underwriting. First, a syndicate, or temporary association of investment bankers, is formed to underwrite, market, and distribute the issue. The originating banker retains a larger portion of the issue and the accompanying risk than other syndicate members, but this is often a small fraction of the total. Second, although the firm has only one issue underway, the investment banker is able to diversify, spreading the risk by participating in many issues. In some cases the investment banker will not accept the risk of the offering by underwriting. Although underwriting appears to be part of the marketing and distribution service, it is separable. In some cases the investment banker will decide that the risk is unacceptable and refuse to underwrite the issue, providing instead a best efforts offering.

In a secondary distribution the stock being sold is not issued by the firm, but is a large amount of previously issued stock held by an investor. The public offering may be accomplished more rapidly and perhaps at better prices than piecemeal selling. There are some variations on the issue process. Since 1982 firms have been permitted to register securities and then sell them gradually over a two-year period. This shelf registration, so called because the securities are ''on the shelf'' awaiting sale, is attractive because it is a ready source of capital. Shelf registration is also thought to have lower flotation costs, because the sale can be timed to take advantage of attractive market conditions, and small sales avoid the possible depression of prices associated with large offers. An alternative to a public offering is private placement. In private placement, the issue is placed with a limited number of investors, usually institutions, instead of being offered to the general public. This alternative is sometimes attractive to the issuing firm because the security and its conditions can be negotiated, the issue can be accomplished in less time, and there are fewer disclosure requirements. Notices of private placements are published in the financial press.

THE SECONDARY MARKET. The firm is not directly affected by trading in securities after issue, and only receives proceeds from the original issue of the security. As a result, it is sometimes thought that the secondary markets are somewhat irrelevant, a place where investors gamble without any real economic impact. This view is absolutely wrong. The secondary markets provide the liquidity and price discovery that are necessary for the existence of an effective primary market.

Liquidity refers to the ability to convert an asset to cash quickly at a price reflecting the fair (economically rational) value. Both conditions must be fulfilled, since any asset could be converted to cash quickly if offered at a low enough price. Liquidity in turn depends on three qualities. Depth is the presence of orders to trade at prices closely surrounding the market price. Breadth requires that the size of these orders be sufficient to prevent wide price swings, given trading volume. Resiliency refers to the speed with which mispricing due to temporary supply and demand imbalances call forth new orders. If these qualities are lacking, the resulting poor liquidity increases the risk of the buyer, since asset prices will fluctuate around fair value and the asset may have to be sold at a price below fair value. Under such conditions, investors are hesitant to invest, will demand a higher rate of return, and often require extensive safeguards. These conditions are often apparent in the **venture capital** market, in which firms that do not have access to the primary securities markets seek funding. In short, without secondary market liquidity a primary market for securities would not function well. Even the venture capital market is aided by the secondary market, since one factor in investing is the likelihood that the firm will grow enough to accomplish a public offering, so that the stock will become liquid. The possibility of a secondary offering also encourages participation in public offerings by large investors. The liquidity provided by an effective secondary market not only supports, but indeed enables, an effective primary market. It is not surprising that developing countries establish securities markets, since this mobilizes capital and facilitates economic growth.

Price discovery is the **valuation** of assets. Through trading, an equilibrium price that represents the consensus of the markets is established. This price is the result of information entering the market, and it is also information in itself. It is a signal both to investors and to the firm's **management** as to the expected future of the firm. The secondary market affects access to the primary through the signals from price discovery. If a firm's securities are given a low value, signaling low expectations, issue of new securities is difficult if not impossible. Even if a primary issue is possible, the cost of capital for the firm will be high, and the **capital budget** of the firm will be small, slowing growth. In essence, by deciding which firms will receive capital for new projects, the price discovery function of the secondary markets serves as the capital budgeting process of the economy, setting its goals, priorities, and future. Rather than being irrelevant gambling, secondary markets are a vital mechanism in the economy.

MARKET STRUCTURE

Another way of classifying securities markets is by the trading arrangements and rules. An organized exchange is characterized by a definite physical location and a restricted list of securities and traders. The OTC market, on the other hand, is simply a net of brokers and dealers who maintain contact and trade through various means of communication. A broker trades for the client as an agent without entering the trade as a principal, and is compensated by a commission. A dealer trades with the client as a principal. The dealer trades from inventory and receives no commission, compensation comes from trading gains and losses and the spread between the bid and ask prices. The distinction is by form of participation only. A given individual may function as both a dealer and a broker, but is not allowed perform both functions in the same transaction.

ORGANIZED EXCHANGES. The NYSE and the AMEX are examples of an organized exchange. In terms of numbers of companies, the NYSE is small, listing (in 1995) just over 3,000 stock issues of about 2,600 companies. These are large firms that meet the listing requirements, however, and in terms of value traded the NYSE is huge, accounting for about 85 percent of the value traded on U.S. exchanges. The AMEX is national in scope but has less stringent listing requirements, and the firms tend to be smaller than on the NYSE. Within the United States there are also regional stock exchanges that list firms that do not meet the listing requirements of the national exchanges.

Both the NYSE and the AMEX provide continuous trading in an auction process. Each stock trades at a designated trading post on the trading floor. Only members, who are said to hold a seat on the exchange (the term arises from the original buttonwood association practice of call trading from assigned seats) are allowed to trade. The public has access to trading through commission brokers who represent brokerage houses, executing trades for the firm's clients. The commission brokers may be assisted by independent two-dollar brokers, the name arising from the amount once charged for this assistance. Two-dollar brokers may also be floor traders, trading for their own account, but they may not fill both roles in the same stock in the same day, to avoid **conflict of interest**. An exchange member called a specialist will be present at the designated trading spot. The specialist makes a market in the stock by providing firm bid and ask offers. Normally, there is only one specialist for a given issue, although there have been exceptions. The specialist also handles the several types of away-from-the-market or limit orders left by brokers, which specify trading at a price other than the immediate market price. To fill this role, the specialist maintains the order book. The order book, now a computer, is simply a listing of clients' away-from-the-market orders left with the specialist by floor brokers. The specialist will execute these orders if and when the order flow permits. The execution of the orders preserves price priority, i.e., execution of highest bid or lowest offer to sell. The system does not necessarily preserve time priority, or execution in the order received, since order size is taken into account.

The specialist has the responsibility to maintain an orderly market, i.e., to avoid wide fluctuations in trading price. In order to do this, the specialist must stand ready to buy and sell on the firm's own account, and is subject to various trading rules to avoid conflict of interest. The possibility of large market movements makes market maintenance very risky, and the sharp market decline of 1987 caused large losses to specialists. Specialists must meet requirements to assure that they will have sufficient capital to maintain an orderly market. Despite the risks and limitations, being a specialist is rewarding. One source of specialist income is the commission on handling away-from-the-market orders. Prices were historically quoted in "eighths," or $0.125 increments (the increment is sometimes called the "tick"). In 1997, trading in 16ths was permitted, and it is likely that decimalization (penny tick) will follow.

It must be noted that the specialist does not control or set the price. The trading edge comes only from superior information of probable price movements. Indeed, many trades do not involve the specialist but are instead the product of the simultaneous crowd trading. The crowd is the group of traders and brokers present at the trading post. New offers are announced publicly, and may be accepted or responded to by a member of the crowd independently of the specialist and the book. This may occur at a price inside the specialist's bid ask spread, although price priority must be maintained.

Block trades are transactions of more than 10,000 shares, and account for about half of all transactions on the NYSE. Specialists are prohibited from soliciting orders in the stock in which they make a market. In order to maintain an orderly market in the face of such an order, the specialist would be forced to absorb much of the order into inventory. Understandably, specialists are reluctant to assume the risk of so large an inventory. As a result, block trades are not sent directly to the trading floor. Instead, a brokerage firm called a block house will undertake to find matching orders in what is sometimes called the upstairs market. The block and matched orders are then taken to the specialist and crossed, or executed, on the floor of the exchange.

Organized exchanges exist throughout the world, and compete with each other and with U.S. exchanges for international capital flows. Trading arrangements on these exchanges may differ from those used on domestic exchanges. The Tokyo Stock Exchange, for instance, is a pure agency market, in which the price is set by orders without exchange influence. Rather than using specialists, the order book is maintained by officials who may not trade in the stocks assigned to them. Trading on the Paris Bourse and the German and Austrian exchanges are call markets. In call markets orders are accumulated over time and crossed or executed at intervals, as in the original NYSE buttonwood trading. Investors considering international investment on foreign exchanges must be careful to understand the differing exchange arrangements. Another difference is that U.S. stock exchanges are private, while other exchanges such as the Paris Bourse are public exchanges under the authority of the government. Another arrangement is the bankers bourse used in Germany, where banks are the major securities traders. These arrangements will undergo rapid change with the introduction of the **euro**.

OVER-THE-COUNTER MARKETS. The OTC markets are sometimes defined as any securities trade that does not take place on an organized exchange. The name originates from the time when stock trading was a sideline for merchants and bankers, and securities were literally sold over a counter. Stocks trading OTC tend to be smaller and younger firms, although there are exceptions. The quality of the securities varies widely. As indicated by the plural, the OTC is properly viewed as a group of submarkets sharing certain characteristics. One characteristic is that this market has no central meeting place. It is instead an informal network of brokers trading for clients and dealers who make a market in the securities. There may multiple market makers for a given security, typically between 2 and 20. Brokers and dealers communicate and trade with each other by various means. The price of a trade is set by negotiation, rather than by the auction process of the NYSE. A broker receiving an order will contact the market makers and receive bid and ask quotations, and may choose the best offer or attempt to negotiate a better offer. There is no specialist or specific mechanism to maintain an orderly market, and price fluctuations depend on the breadth, depth, and resiliency of the market for the particular security. Trades executed OTC for stocks not listed on an exchange are referred to as the second market. Stocks listed on an exchange may also be traded OTC, and such trades are sometimes referred to as the third market.

One OTC subgroup consists of stocks listed on the **Nasdaq** exchange. This system provides electronic display of dealer bids and asks, allowing the broker to obtain the best price. Listing on Nasdaq is restricted to about 3,500 of the more widely traded stocks that also meet other listing requirements. As with NYSE listings on the exchanges, Nasdaq stocks are a minority in numbers but a majority in value and trading among OTC stocks. A step down from Nasdaq stocks are the pink-sheet stocks. The pink sheets were printed bid and ask quotations that were distributed daily; the name derives from the color of the paper used. This system has been supplanted by computerized quotation systems. Unlike Nasdaq quotes, these quotes are more in the nature of workout quotes or estimates, rather than firm quotes at which a trade can be executed. Although some large firms are included in this group, most are smaller firms. Trading in pink-sheet stocks tends to be relatively thin, or lacking in order depth and breadth, so that it is often difficult to move more than small amounts of stock without price concessions. Recently the fourth market has seen increased volume. This market consists of trading directly between institutions, without involving brokers.

MARKET EFFICIENCY

Among the first applications of **computers** was a search for the trends in stock prices postulated by the Dow theory. Various tests detected only very weak trends that were incapable of supporting investment strategies. Although the tests do not definitively disprove the existence of trends, the empirical observations led to the conclusion that stock prices are best described as a **random walk**, i.e., that changes in stock prices are random variables. The efficient markets hypothesis (EMH) arose as an explanation of this empirical observation. The EMH suggests that information is fully reflected in stock prices. If information is fully reflected, price changes will be the result of the arrival of new information. The arrival of new information will be random, since anything known would already be reflected in the price. This random arrival of information will result in random price fluctuations: informationally efficient markets will result in a random walk in stock prices. Two important possible misconceptions must be mentioned. The first misconception is that the random walk and the efficient markets hypotheses suggest that stock prices are random. Quite the opposite, the EMH suggests that information is fully and accurately reflected in prices, so that prices will be close estimates of true intrinsic value. The random walk refers to price changes, not to the prices themselves. The second misconception is that the hypotheses imply that nothing can be known about the price changes. This is wrong. Although a random walk implies that price changes cannot be exactly predicted, it is still possible to describe the probability distribution of price changes.

Market efficiency is closely related to both liquidity and price discovery. An efficient market is one in which price discovery is rapid and accurate, and the requirements for efficiency include the breadth, depth, and resiliency required for support of liquidity. Aside from the importance of efficiency for the capital budgeting role of the secondary markets, the question of market efficiency is important to investor strategy. If information is fully reflected in stock prices, that information cannot be used to generate excess returns, i.e., returns greater than could be expected without using the information. Definition of excess returns requires a definition of normal profits as a standard for comparison. A large number of tests of market efficiency have used the **capital asset pricing model** (CAPM) to establish a level of expected return on a risk adjusted basis. In this approach, risk is defined as the beta or systematic, nondiversifiable variation. More recently, the CAPM has been found to be inadequate in several ways. Some researchers have instead used a multifactor approach based on the **arbitrage** pricing theory. Unfortunately, the factors are not defined by the theory, and there is no theoretically supported and generally accepted set of factors. While there is no entirely satisfactory theory to specify expected returns, this does not make testing impossible, merely less precise. The effect of information can be detected by testing not for ''excess'' but for ''unusual'' returns, where unusual returns are returns that differ from observed historical returns relative to market returns.

The question of which information is reflected is treated by defining three levels of market efficiency based on the information set reflected. The lowest level of efficiency is called the weak form. This form of the EMH holds that investors cannot use historical market trading data (such as prices and volume) to increase returns over what would otherwise be expected. The next level of efficiency is the semi-strong form. This form applies to all publicly available data, such as **annual reports**, published brokerage reports, or newspaper articles, and all weak-form information. The highest level of efficiency is the strong form, which holds that all information, both public and private, is fully reflected in stock prices.

Studies of the weak form of the EMH include the original trend studies and numerous tests of trading rules. The majority of evidence to date supports weak-form efficiency. This would seem to rule out **technical analysis** as an investment approach. Proponents of the technical approach argue, however, that the tests are inadequate and that application of mechanical rules without human judgment would, of course, be useless. Tests of the strong form have indicated that this extreme form is violated by exclusive information such as the specialist's knowledge of the order book. Finally, tests of the semi-strong form have provided mixed results, revealing the presence of anomalies that indicate that at least some forms of public information are not fully reflected. The tests have several shortcomings. One problem is that they tend to use computer-accessible data that deal with the markets we would expect to be efficient. Another shortcoming is the time frame, with the majority of studies using daily or longer data.

The question of efficiency is best thought of as one of degree, rather than kind. Efficiency is not so much a matter of all stocks being correctly priced at all times, but of most stocks being close to intrinsic value most of the time. Markets are relatively efficient if mispricing is small, infrequent, and short-lived. Further, the question of efficiency depends on the market, the investor, and the time frame. The NYSE is relatively efficient, as is the AMEX. When we move to the OTC, we must consider the subgroup. For widely traded Nasdaq stocks, the markets are likely quite efficient. But the bond market is often described as less efficient, and market efficiency for low-volume pink-sheet stocks can be expected to be below Nasdaq efficiency. This would indicate an indexing (i.e., purchase of a portfolio of stocks mirroring a market **index**) approach on the NYSE, but fundamental analysis might be more appropriate for pink-sheet investors. Investor expertise and position in the information chain must also be considered. The market seems much more efficient for part-time amateur investors in the countryside than for full-time investment professionals on Wall Street. Finally, investors who are slow to act on information, or face trading delays, will find that information has already caused price adjustment. For these investors, the market is relatively efficient. Rather than present market efficiency as an absolute quality, the idea of ''grossly efficient'' or ''approximately efficient'' markets seems to predominate.

MARKET REGULATION

Given the importance of securities markets to the economy, and the spectacular profits that can be gained from abuse, regulation of securities markets is surprisingly recent and somewhat informal. There was little market regulation until 1911, when individual states began to enact blue sky laws regulating securities. The name comes from a court ruling that noted that some investment schemes promised little more than a patch of blue sky. These state laws were insufficient, inadequately enforced, and easily circumvented. Pools, or small groups of investors, cooperating in manipulation of stock prices and other unethical practices were not unusual. Financial information was difficult to obtain. Although organized exchanges required the disclosure of some financial information for traded stocks, this information was not always reliable. Federal regulation did not appear until after the market fluctuations of 1929. The major regulatory framework was constructed by the **Securities Act of 1933** and the **Securities Exchange Act of 1934**. The 1933 act required that firms issuing new stock register and disclosure financial information about the issue, and included antifraud provisions. The 1934 act extended the disclosure requirements to publicly traded securities, and established the **Securities and Exchange Commission** (SEC) to administer and revise the securities regulations. The OTC market was not brought into the regulatory structure until the Maloney Act of 1938. The Securities Investor Protection Act of 1970 established the Securities Investor Protection Corporation (SIPC) to protect against failure of brokerage firms, similar to protections against bank failure. It is important to note that the SIPC does not protect against investment losses, only against losses due to failure of brokerage firms.

It is interesting to note that the disclosure requirements of the organized exchanges had an important impact on the field of public **accounting**, and that the 1933 and 1934 acts added the requirement that **financial statements** be audited by an independent accountant. The auditor's opinion and the acceptance of registration of a securities issue by the SEC are similar in that neither is an endorsement of investment value. Instead, both simply indicate that all required information is included and presented according to accepted standards. Judgment of investment value is left to the informed investor. Registration of a new issue is automatic unless the SEC specifically rejects the statement within 20 days. The 1934 act granted the SEC approval of commission rate changes and power to change and formulate trading rules. It left the SEC out of some areas, granting control over minimum margin to the Federal Reserve Board and discipline of exchange members to the exchanges. The resulting structure is one that relies heavily on self-regulation by the exchanges, and by the National Association of Securities Dealers for the OTC market. Several professional organizations, such as the Institute of Chartered Financial Analysts, also set forth ethical codes governing those holding the designation.

Insider trading is an important issue that has not been satisfactorily resolved. Insider trading is trading on private information about a firm that has not been released to the general public. As a form of control, the SEC requires that insiders such as corporate officers and directors of publicly held firms report all transactions in the firm's stock. While some cases of insider trading are clear, such as buying by a corporate officer based on knowledge of unannounced increased earnings, there is no exact definition of insider trading. Present interpretations involve not only the nature of the information, but how and by whom it was obtained. Accidental acquisition of confidential information does not confer a fiduciary obligation, and the information can be used. Simply holding inside information does not preclude trading if the information is part of an overall mosaic of reasoning behind the trade, but was not by itself the primary reason for the trade.

THE FUTURE OF THE MARKETS

Since the days of buttonwood trading, the securities markets have been constantly changing. The introduction of the telegraph in the 1840s and the 1850s opened up trading on exchanges countrywide, and local newspapers began to list Wall Street price quotations. The 1870s saw the introduction of stock tickers and the telephone. In 1883 a two-page leaflet called the *Customer's Afternoon Letter* started publication; in July 1889 the leaflet was expanded and the name changed to the *Wall Street Journal.* The assets traded also changed, from mining and railroad stocks to industrial issues. After the market crash of 1929, trading practices changed remarkably, although trading did not recover to its previous level until the 1960s.

Recent changes have been perhaps even more rapid. As trading volume expanded during the 1960s Wall Street experienced a back office crisis. A number of firms failed because they were unable to keep up with the paperwork. Trading by institutions began to increase, and these institutions began to work outside the usual market procedures to avoid fixed commissions. In 1975, Congress passed the Securities Act Amendments. The amendments obligated the SEC to block anticompetitive exchange rules, precluded fixed commissions, and mandated the development of a National Market System (NMS). Although various steps have been taken that have resulted in closer integration of the markets, the controversy over how to achieve the NMS continues. The role of the specialist has been challenged by those who point to the OTC and to foreign markets such as the Tokyo exchange as proof that the specialist is an anachronism.

Regulation is only one source of pressure for change, however, and competition and technological innovation may be a bigger factor. Quotes from, and rapid execution on, all of the U.S. exchanges are available online. This has led to the phenomenon of "day traders," individuals who trade online on a very short-term basis, often changing position in a stock within minutes. While for various reasons these arrangements are still of relatively low trading volume, that volume is increasing rapidly. The presence of the alternatives itself is a powerful force. Although computer trading moves through the existing market system, it is likely that trading will become more direct, and the impact on the market structure is uncertain. Computerization and electronic communication makes trading on foreign exchanges not only feasible but easy, and, for some purposes, preferable. While on a year-to-year basis change may seem slow, it is likely that the next decade will see major changes in trading mechanisms and practices.

SEE ALSO: Disclosure Laws and Regulations; Nasdaq Stock Market; Over-the-Counter Securities Markets; Stocks

[David E. Upton]

FURTHER READING:

Bodie, Zvi, Alex Kane, and Alan J. Marcus. *Investments.* 4th ed. Boston: Irwin/McGraw-Hill, 1999.

Ellis, Charles D. *Winning the Loser's Game: Timeless Strategies for Successful Investing.* 3rd ed. New York: McGraw-Hill, 1998.

Malkiel, Burton G. *A Random Walk down Wall Street.* New York: W.W. Norton & Co., 1996.

Reilly, Frank K., and Keith C. Brown. *Investment Analysis and Portfolio Management.* 5th ed. Fort Worth, TX: Dryden Press, 1997.

Schwartz, Robert A. *Equity Markets: Structure, Trading, and Performance.* New York: Harper & Row, 1988.

Teweles, Richard J., and Edward S. Bradley. *The Stock Market.* 7th ed. New York: John Wiley & Sons, Inc., 1998.

STOCKS

An **entrepreneur** with a good idea can do nothing without capital to act on that idea. As a start, the entrepreneur can use personal resources to form a sole proprietorship. In this form the entrepreneur and the business are indistinguishable, and the amount of capital is limited to the personal **wealth** and borrowing power of the entrepreneur. The entrepreneur is personally liable for all obligations. If the business grows and prospers even more capital will be required, often rapidly outrunning the resources of the entrepreneur. Forming a **partnership** with other parties solves some of the problems, adding the personal resources of one or more partners. This form of organization dilutes the claim and authority of the entrepreneur. Partnerships do not work well if large amounts of capital are required since potential investors with large amounts of capital are hard to find. Once found, they are reluctant to enter partnerships for three reasons. The first reason is that all partners are equally and totally responsible for the obligations of the partnership. This **risk** exposure may easily exceed the original investment. The second reason is that the partnership is a temporary alliance. Partners may withdraw at any time. Finally, partnership interests are not liquid. Liquidity is the ability to convert an asset to cash quickly and at a fair price. Potential investors are reluctant to enter partnerships because of the difficulties of disposing of the investment and realizing a return. Many of these problems are avoided by the corporate form of ownership.

THE CORPORATE FORM

In the corporate form, a business is set up as legal entity that has the power to act as an individual, and for legal purposes is considered to be a real person. This entity by itself has no net legal value, as recognized in the basic **accounting** equation: ''Assets equals liabilities plus owners equity.'' What the firm owns as assets is owed to creditors and others as **liabilities**, and to the owners as equity. This creation of a legal person, however, separates the liabilities of the corporation from the liabilities of the owners. This results in ''limited liability'': should the firm fail, the obligations of the firm are not the obligations of the owners. The value of owning the firm may go to zero, but the investors' loss is limited to their original investment. Limited liability greatly reduces investor risk, so that investors are willing to consider more and riskier investments and will not require as great an anticipated return. This increased willingness to undertake new projects encourages **innovation**. Limited liability of investors has been an important factor encouraging economic growth. Another attraction of the corporate form is that ownership is subdivided into shares of stock. Shares may be sold to many investors, in varying amounts. The ease with which shares are transferred results in higher liquidity, and this higher liquidity reduces investor risk. The stockholder can exit the investment for another investment, or realize a return, more easily than is possible with a partnership interest. Finally, the investor can take a much smaller position through stock, which allows **diversification** over many ventures. The pool of potential investors becomes much larger, and raising capital becomes easier. Given these advantages, it is not surprising that many business ventures choose the corporate form, either at first or after growth makes the other forms overly cumbersome.

The corporate form does have some disadvantages. One disadvantage is double taxation of earnings. The earnings of sole proprietorships and partnerships are taxed once, as the earnings of the proprietor. The firm is a legal entity, however, and its earnings are taxed. Any distribution of the already once-taxed earnings is considered **income** of the investor, and the earnings are taxed a second time. Another disadvantage is that as ownership becomes wider, it becomes more diverse. Entrepreneurs remaining as managers may be distracted more often by fellow owners and more formal requirements. A different style of **management** may be required. On the positive side, the corporate form facilitates separation of ownership and management. This separation is a mixed blessing—it allows professional management and the application of expertise not yet developed by the entrepreneur, but raises the agency, or control, problem. The professional manager is now an agent of the stockholders, not necessarily part of the ownership, and may have different goals and agenda. Finally, ownership may be diluted, and control limited to less direct, impersonal procedures.

Securities issued by a corporation are classified as **debt** or as equity, equity being an ownership claim. Under the corporate form, ownership may be complicated. The main types of equity claims are common and **preferred stock**. These equity claims may take many forms. There are related claims, such as **rights**, **warrants**, and convertible securities. The securities also may be divided into those that are publicly traded, and those that are not. Although the underlying securities are in the same class, public trading implies a much wider ownership and liquidity, and often a much different set of problems and considerations. Securities of firms that are closely held, or have few shareholders, look quite different from an investment viewpoint.

COMMON STOCK

A share of **common stock** is quite literally a share in the business, a partial claim to ownership of the firm. Owning a share of common stock provides a number of rights and privileges. These include sharing in the income of the firm, exercising a voice in the management of the firm, and holding a claim on the assets of the firm.

DIVIDENDS. Stockholders share directly in the income of the firm in the form of cash **dividends**. The firm is not obligated to pay dividends, which will be paid only if declared by the **board of directors**. As a result, the size and timing of the dividends is uncertain. Although higher earnings are desired, the dividend policy of the firm—which is the long-run or average fraction of earnings that will be paid as dividends—is sometimes argued to be irrelevant. One argument is that in a perfect economic environment, dividends would be considered as a ''residual.'' This is because the stockholders may share indirectly in the income of the firm through **capital gains**—an increase in the stock price. In this view, management must choose between paying dividends now, or investing in projects that will increase stock price. Dividends would be paid only if the firm had no better use for the funds. Note that in this case, it could be argued that declaring or increasing dividend payout would be a negative signal, since the firm would be admitting that it lacked attractive investments and indicating lessened possibilities for growth. Another argument is that investors can change the dividend policy to suit themselves, selling stock to create dividends if higher payout is desired, or reinvesting dividends in the firm if lower payout is desired. It is also argued that investors form clienteles, investing in firms with the dividend policy they prefer. Tax considerations, on the other hand, suggest that stockholders are better off with low dividend policy. This is because capital gains are taxed at a lower rate than dividends, and capital gains are not taxed until realized, so that it is better to retain and reinvest earnings to produce capital gains.

For widely held, publicly traded firms there are a number of indications that stockholders and investors have a positive view of dividends and dividend increases. The explanation is that dividends are taken as a signal that the firm is healthy, and can afford to pay dividends. An increase would signal an improvement and the ability to pay higher dividends. A decrease in dividends would indicate inability to maintain the level of dividends, signaling a decline in prospects. The signal from a dividend increase is strong because management would be hesitant to increase dividends unless they could be maintained. The signal from a dividend decrease is strong because management would wish to give only positive signals by at least maintaining the dividend, and would cut the dividend only when absolutely necessary. The signaling nature of dividends is supported by cases in which the dividend is maintained in the face of declining earnings, sometimes even using borrowed funds. It is also supported by the occurrence of ''extraordinary'' or one-time-only dividends arising from a temporary excess of cash. This label is applied by management in an attempt to avoid signaling a higher earnings level. Note, however, that this argument does not deal with dividend policy, but instead with increasing or decreasing the size of the dividend under a constant dividend policy or payout ratio.

The signaling approach is not applicable to **closely held corporations**, which have few stockholders. In this situation, communication between management and shareholders is more direct and signals are not required. When owners are also the managers, sharing in earnings may take the indirect form of perks. In fact, shareholders in closely held firms may prefer that dividends be reinvested, even in relatively low return projects as a form of tax protection. The investment is on a pretax (before personal tax) basis for the investor, avoiding immediate double taxation and converting the income to capital gains that will be paid at a later date.

Dividends are declared for stockholders at a particular date, called the date of record. Since stock transactions ordinarily take several business days for completion, the stock goes ''ex-dividend'' before the date of record, unless special arrangement is made for immediate delivery. Since the dividend removes funds from the firm, it can be expected that the per share price will decrease by the amount of the dividend on the ex-dividend date.

Stock dividends are quite different in form and nature from cash dividends. In a stock dividend, the investor is given more shares in proportion to the number held. A stock split is similar, with a difference in accounting treatment and a greater increase in the number of shares. The use of the word ''dividends'' in stock dividends is actually a misuse of the word, since there is no flow of cash, and the proportional and absolute ownership of the investor is unchanged. The stockholder receives nothing more than a repackaging of ownership: the number of shares increases, but ceteris paribus share price will drop. There are, however, some arguments in favor of stock dividends. One of these is the argument that investors will avoid stocks of unusually high price, possibly due to required size of investment and round lot (100 share) trading. Decreasing price through stock dividends attracts more investors and results in wider ownership. Wider ownership is sometimes issued to thwart **takeovers**. On the other hand, stocks with unusually low price are also avoided, perhaps perceived as ''cheap.'' The price drop accompanying stock dividends can be used to adjust price. Stock dividends have also been suggested as a way to make cash dividends elective while also providing tax-advantaged reinvestment. With a cash dividend, an investor who wishes to reinvest must pay **taxes** and then reinvest the reduced amount. With a stock dividend, the entire amount is reinvested. Although taxes will ultimately be paid, in the interim a return is earned on the entire pretax amount. This is the same argument as that for low dividends in a closely held firm. Investors who wish cash dividends can simply sell the stock. Using stock dividends in this way faces restriction from the **Internal Revenue Service**.

CONTROL. The corporate form allows the separation of management and ownership, with the manager serving as the agent of the owner. Separation raises the problem of control, or what is termed the "agency" problem. Stockholders have only indirect control by voting for the directors. The directors in turn choose management and are responsible for monitoring and controlling management's conduct. In fact, the stockholder's ability to influence the conduct of the firm may be quite small, and management may have virtually total control within very broad limits.

Voting for the directors takes either of two forms. The first form is majority voting. In this form, each stockholder receives votes for each open position according the number of shares held, and may cast those votes for candidates for that position only. The winning candidate is the candidate winning a majority of the votes cast. The second form is called cumulative voting. In this form, stockholders again receive votes for each open position according to the number of shares held, but may apportion the votes among the positions and candidates as desired. The candidates receiving the most votes are elected. Excluding minority stockholders from representation on the board is more difficult under cumulative voting. If there are four directors to be elected and 1 million shares eligible to vote at one vote per share, a stockholder with 500,001 shares would control the election. Under majority voting a dissident stockholder with 200,001 shares could cast only 200,001 votes apiece for candidates for each of the four positions, which would not be sufficient to ensure representation on the board. Under cumulative voting, a dissident stockholder with a minimum of 200,001 shares could be sure of representation by electing one candidate of choice, casting a cumulative 800,004 votes for that candidate. The remaining 799,999 shares could be sure of electing three chosen candidates, but could not command sufficient votes to exceed the cumulative dissident vote four times.

Although the board of directors is supposedly independent of management, the degree of independence is sometimes small. Typically, some members of the board are "insiders" drawn from management, while others are "outside" directors. Even the outside directors may not be completely independent of management for several reasons. One reason is that few shareholders can afford the time and expense to attend the annual meetings, so that voting is done through the mail. This usually takes the form of a "proxy" giving management the power to vote for the shareholder, as instructed. While the shareholder may instruct management on how to vote, the choices may be few and are controlled by management. Management will tend to nominate safe candidates for directorship, who will not be likely to challenge the status quo. As a result, directorship is at times an honor or sinecure, treated as having few real obligations. Dissidents may mount opposition and seek the proxy votes, but such opposition is liable to face legal challenges and must overcome both psychological barriers and shareholder apathy. Many shareholders do not vote or routinely vote for management. Further, dissidents must spend their own money, while management has the resources of the firm at its disposal. Another reason for a lack of independence on the part of directors is the practice of interlocking boards of directors, who are likely to reach a tacit agreement. Conventional wisdom on Wall Street has long been to sell the stock rather than oppose an entrenched management.

In addition to controlling the proxy system, managements have instituted a number of other defensive mechanisms in the face of takeover threats. It is not unusual to find several "classes" of stock with different voting power, some classes having no voting power at all. A number of firms have changed from cumulative to majority voting. Staggered boards, with only a portion of the board terms expiring in a given year, and supermajority voting for some questions have also been used. Takeover defenses include the **golden parachute**, or extremely generous severance compensation in the face of a takeover, and the **poison pill**, an action that is triggered by a takeover and has the effect of reducing the value of the firm. While Sidney Cottle, Roger F. Murray, and Frank E. Block may have gone too far in saying that "The shareholder has become an ineffectual nuisance to be pacified by self-congratulatory reports and increasing dividends," it would appear that stockholder power has become more tenuous.

There has been some recent movement toward greater stockholder power. One factor in this movement is the increasing size of **institutional investors** such as **pensions** and **mutual funds**. This has led to a more activist stance, and a willingness to use the power of large stock positions to influence management. Another factor is a renewed emphasis on the duties of the directors, who may be personally liable for management's misconduct. At least part of this movement may be the result of takeover activities. The takeover and breakup or consolidation of firms, with accompanying job loss, has been much criticized. This activity showed that challenging management was possible, however, and encouraged dissident groups. It also sent a message to management that mediocre performance might not be tolerated. It has been suggested that the threat of takeover may have done much to reinforce the rights of stockholders. The use of defense mechanisms detrimental to the stockholder has called attention to managerial abuses. The appropriate level of salary and of management perks, such as use of the corporate jet and limousines, has come under scrutiny in the financial and popular press.

RESIDUAL OWNERSHIP. The common stockholder has a claim on the assets of the firm. This is an undifferentiated or general claim that does not apply to any specific asset. The claim cannot be exercised except at the breakup of the firm. The firm may be dissolved by a vote of the stockholders, or by bankruptcy. In either case, there is a well-defined priority in which the liabilities of the firm will be met. The common stockholders have the lowest priority, and receive a distribution only if prior claims are paid in full. For this reason the common stockholder is referred to as the residual owner of the firm.

PREEMPTIVE RIGHT. The corporate charter will often provide common stockholders with the right to maintain their proportional ownership in the firm, called the preemptive right. For example, if a stockholder owns 10 percent of the stock outstanding and 100,000 new shares are to be issued, the stockholder has the right to purchase 10,000 shares (10 percent) of the new issue. This preemptive right can be honored in a rights offering. In a rights offering, each stockholder receives one right for each share held. Buying shares or subscribing to the issue then requires the surrender of a set number of rights, as well as payment of the offering price. The offering is often underpriced in order to assure the success of the offering. The rights are then valuable because possession of the rights allows subscription to the underpriced issue. The rights can be transferred, and are traded. Rights will be given to the owner of the stock on the date of record. During the time that a purchase will be completed before the date of record, the stock is said to be trading with rights or rights on. During this period the price of the stock reflects both the value of the stock and the value of the (to-be-issued) right. When purchase of the stock will not be completed until after the date of record, but before the offering, the stock is said to be trading ex-rights or rights off. Similar to the ex-dividend date, the ex-rights date will be four days before the date of record. At the ex-rights day the price of the stock will drop by the value of the right, since the stock purchase will not include the right.

A rights offering may be attractive to management because the stockholders, who thought enough of the firm to buy its stock, are a presold group. The value of the preemptive right to the common stockholders, however, is questionable. The preemptive right of proportional ownership is important only if proportional control is important to the stockholder. The stockholder may be quite willing to waive the preemptive right. If the funds are used properly, the price of the stock will increase, and all stockholders will benefit. Without buying part of the new issue, the stockholder may have a smaller proportional share, but the share will be worth more. While rights are usually valuable, this value arises from underpricing of the issue rather than from an inherent value of rights. The real question is whether the issue should be undertaken at all—i.e., what is to be done with the funds from the offering? If the funds are to be used in a way that the market perceives as having little value, the price of the stock will decline. If the funds are to be used in a way that the market perceives as having great value, the price of the stock will increase. The value of the rights ultimately depends on the use of the funds.

VALUATION. In investment practice, decisions are more often expressed and made in terms of the comparative expected rates of return, rather than on price. A number of models and techniques are used for **valuation**. A common approach to valuation of common stock is **present value**. This approach is based on an estimate of the future cash dividends. The present value is then the amount that, if invested at the required rate of return on the stock, could exactly re-create the estimated dividends. This required rate of return can be estimated from models such as the **capital asset pricing model** (CAPM), using the systematic risk of the stock, or from the estimated rate of return on stocks of similar risk. Another common approach is based on the **price/earnings ratio**, or P/E. In this approach, the estimated earnings of the firm are multiplied by the appropriate P/E to obtain the estimated price. This approach can be shown to be a special case of present value analysis, with restrictive assumptions. Since various models and minor differences in assumptions can produce widely different results, valuation is best applied as a comparative analysis.

In some cases, such as estate valuation, the dollar value of the stock must be estimated for legal purposes. For assets that are widely publicly traded, the market price is generally taken as an objective estimate of asset value for legal purposes, since this is sale value of the stock. For stock that is not widely traded, valuation is based on models such as present value, combined with a comparison with similar publicly traded stock. Often, however, a number of discounts are applied for various reasons. It is widely accepted that, compared to publicly traded stock, stock that is not publicly traded should be valued at a discount because of a lack of liquidity. This discount may be 60 percent or more. Another discount is applied for a minority position in a closely held stock or a family firm, since the minority position would have no control This discount does not apply if the value is estimated from the value of publicly traded stock, because the market price of a traded stock is already the price of a minority position. There is an inverse effect for publicly traded stock in the form of a control premium. A large block of stock that would give control of the firm might be priced above market.

Finally, it should be noted that the accounting book value is only rarely more than tangentially relevant to market value. This is due to the use of accounting assumptions such as historic cost. While accounting information may be useful in a careful valuation study, accounting definitions of value differ sharply from economic value.

PREFERRED STOCK

Preferred stock is sometimes called a hybrid, since it has some of the properties of equity and some of the properties of debt. Like debt, the cash flows to be received are specified in advance. Unlike debt, these specified flows are in the form of promises rather than of legal obligations. It is not unusual for firms to have several issues of preferred stock outstanding, with differing characteristics. Other differences arise in the areas of control and claims on assets.

DIVIDENDS. Because the specified payments on preferred stock are not obligations, they are referred to as dividends. Preferred dividends are not tax-deductible expenses for the firm, and consequently the **cost** to the firm of raising capital from this source is higher than for debt. The firm is unlikely to skip, or fail to declare the dividend, however, for several reasons. One of the reasons is the dividends are typically (but not always) cumulative. Any skipped dividend remains due and payable by the firm, although no interest is due. One source of the preferred designation is that all preferred dividends in arrears must be paid before any dividend can be paid to common stockholders (although bond payments have priority over all dividends). Failure to declare preferred dividends may also trigger restrictive conditions of the issue. A very important consideration is that, just as for common dividends, preferred dividends are a signal to stockholders, both actual and potential. A skipped preferred dividend would indicate that common dividends will also be skipped, and would be a very negative signal that the firm was encountering problems. This would also close off access to the **capital markets**, and lenders would be wary.

There is also a form of preferred stock, called participating preferred, in which there may be a share in earnings above the specified dividends. Such participation would typically occur only if earnings or common dividends rose over some threshold, and might limited in other ways. A more recent innovation is adjustable-rate preferred stock, with a variable dividend based on prevailing **interest rates**.

CONTROL. Under normal circumstances preferred stockholders do not have any voting power, resulting in little control over or direct influence on the conduct of the firm. Some minimal control would be provided by the indenture under which the stock was issued, and would be exercised passively, i.e., the trustees for the issue would be responsible for assuring that all conditions were observed. In some circumstances, the conditions of the issue could result in increased control on the part of the preferred stockholders. For instance, it is not unusual for the preferred stockholders to be given voting rights if more than a specified number of preferred dividends are skipped. Other provisions may restrict the payment of common dividends if conditions such as required liquidity ratios are not met. Preferred stockholders also may have a preemptive right.

CLAIM ON ASSETS AND OTHER FEATURES. Another source of the preferred designation is that preferred stock has a prior claim on assets over that of common stock. The claim of **bonds** is prior to that of the preferred stockholders. Although preferred stock typically has no maturity date, there is often some provision for retirement. One such provision is the call provision, under which the firm may buy back or recall the stock at a stated price. This price may vary over time, normally dropping as time passes. Another provision is the **sinking fund**, under which the firm will recall and retire a set number of shares each year. Alternately, the firm may repurchase the shares for retirement on the open market, and would prefer to do so if the market price of the preferred is below the call price. Preferred stock is sometimes convertible, i.e., it can be exchanged for common stock at the discretion of the holder. The conversion takes place at a set rate, but this rate may vary over time.

VALUATION. The par value of a preferred stock is not related to market value, except that it is often used to define the dividend. Since the cash flow of dividends to preferred stockholders is specified, valuation of preferred is much simpler than for common stock. The valuation techniques are actually more similar to those used for bonds, drawing heavily on the present value concept. The required rate of return on preferred stock is closely correlated with interest rates, but is above that of bonds because the bond payments are contractual obligations. As a result, preferred stock prices fluctuate with interest rates. The introduction of adjustable-rate preferred stock is an attempt to reduce this price sensitivity to interest rates.

FOREIGN STOCK

Purchases of foreign stock have greatly increased in recent years. One motivation behind this increase is that national economies are not perfectly correlated, so that greater diversification is possible than with a purely domestic portfolio. Another reason is that a number of foreign economies are growing, or are expected to grow, rapidly. Additionally, a number of developing countries have consciously promoted the development of secondary markets as an aid to economic development. Finally, developments in communications and an increasing familiarity with international affairs and opportunities has reduced the hesitance of investors to venture into what once was unfamiliar territory.

Foreign investment is not without problems. International communication is still more expensive and sometimes slower than domestic communication. Social and business customs often vary greatly between countries. Trading practices on some foreign exchanges are different than in the United States. Accounting differs not only in procedures, but often in degree of information disclosed. Although double taxation is generally avoided by international treaties, procedures are cumbersome. Political instability can be a consideration, particularly in developing countries. Finally, the investor faces exchange rate risk. A handsome gain in a foreign currency can be diminished, or even turned into a loss, by shifting exchange rates. These difficulties are felt less by professional managers of large institutions, and much of the foreign investment is through this channel.

An alternative vehicle for foreign investing is the American Depositary Receipt (ADR). This is simply a certificate of ownership of foreign stock that is deposited with a U.S. trustee. The depository institution also exchanges and distributes any dividends, and provides other administrative chores. ADR's are appealing to individual investors. It has also been suggested that the benefits of international investing can be obtained by investing in international firms.

INVESTMENT CHARACTERISTICS

As a class, common stock has provided the highest rate of return to investors. A study by R. G. Ibbotson & Associates found that, over the period 1926-96, large company common stock provided an arithmetic average annual return of 12.7 percent. This compares with an average annual return of 6 percent for long-term corporate bonds, and 3.8 percent for **U.S. Treasury bills** (T-bills). Annual **inflation** over the period averaged 3.2 percent. Common stock also provided the highest risk, with returns having a standard deviation of 20.3 percent, as compared to 8.7 percent for long-term corporate bonds and 3.3 percent for T-bills. Although the data point out the desirability of common stock investment, these long-run averages must be interpreted carefully. Hidden within these averages were some extended loss periods, and some short periods of sharp losses. Also, the returns reflect the effects of diversification. The historical returns of individual stocks or small portfolios could have quite different average returns, and would almost certainly exhibit greater risk. Finally, the disclaimer so frequently found in investment advertisements that future performance may differ from past performance is applicable.

While the above observations give a general idea of the comparative returns to stocks overall, stocks are diverse in nature and can be classified many ways for investment purposes. One such classification has been the discussion of small cap stocks. These are stocks of smaller firms. Ibbotson & Associates found that, over the 1926-96 period, small cap stocks had an average annual return of 17.7 percent, but with a standard deviation of 34.1 percent. It must be noted that the sample used was the stocks in the lowest quintile of the New York Stock Exchange, when ranked on capitalization (shares outstanding times price per share). While small by comparison to the other quintiles, these firms are still sizable. Findings such as these have led to an investment strategy of purchasing such stocks to earn the historical higher return. Indicative of the problems of long-run averages, many such investors have been disappointed.

Stocks are also classified according to the level of risk. Thus risky stocks are sometimes referred to as aggressive or speculative. If risk is measured by the beta (systematic or nondiversifiable risk), then the term applies to a stock with a beta greater than one. These stocks are quite sensitive to the economic cycle, and are also called cyclical. Contrasted are the blue chip stocks, high-quality stocks of major firms that have long and stable records of earnings and dividends. Stocks with low risk, or a beta of less than one, are referred to as defensive. One form of investment strategy, called timing, is to switch among cyclical and defensive stocks according to expected evolution of the economic cycle. This **strategy** is sometimes refined to movement among various types of stock or sectors of the economy. Another stock category is income stocks, stocks that have a long and stable record of comparatively high dividends.

Common stock has been suggested as a hedge against inflation. This suggestion arises from two lines of thought. The first is that stocks ultimately are claims to real assets and productivity, and the prices of such claims should rise with inflation. As pointed out by Lawrence J. Gitman and Michael D. Joehnk, however, in real terms the Dow Jones Industrial Average (DJIA) fell almost without interruption from 1965 to 1982. The second line of thought is that the total returns to common stock are high enough to overcome inflation (the DJIA measures only the capital gains or price change component of returns). While this is apparently true over longer periods, as shown in the Ibbotson & Associates study, it has not held true over shorter periods.

Preferred stock is generally not considered a desirable investment for individuals. While as noted the junior position of preferred stockholders as compared to bonds indicates that the required rate of return on preferred will be above that of bonds, observation indicates that the yield on bonds has generally been above that of preferred of similar quality. The reason for this is a provision of the tax codes that 70 percent of the preferred dividends received by a corporation are tax exempt. This provision is intended to avoid double taxation. Because of the tax exemption, the effective after-tax yield on preferreds is higher for corporations, and buying of preferreds by corporations drives the yields down. The resulting realized return for individuals, who cannot take advantage of this tax treatment, would generally be below acceptable levels.

[David E. Upton]

FURTHER READING:

Bodie, Zvi, Alex Kane, and Alan J. Marcus. *Investments.* 4th ed. Boston: Irwin/McGraw-Hill, 1999.

Cottle, Sidney, Roger F. Murray, and Frank E. Block. *Graham and Dodd's Security Analysis.* 5th ed. New York: McGraw-Hill, 1988.

Gitman, Lawrence J., and Michael D. Joehnk. *Fundamentals of Investing.* 5th ed. New York: HarperCollins, 1993.

Hirt, Geoffrey A., and Stanley B. Block. *Fundamentals of Investment Management.* 6th ed. Boston: Irwin/McGraw-Hill, 1999.

R. G. Ibbotson & Associates. *Stocks, Bonds, Bills, and Inflation 1997 Yearbook.* Chicago.

STRATEGIC ALLIANCES

A strategic alliance is a business arrangement in which two or more firms cooperate for their mutual benefit. Firms may combine their efforts for a variety of purposes including, but not limited to, sharing knowledge, expertise, and expenses as well as to gain entry to new markets or to gain a competitive advantage in one. Further, creation of a strategic alliance may turn actual or potential competitors into partners working toward a common goal. Use of strategic alliances has become a major tool for businesses that are internationalizing their operations. Therefore, use of strategic alliances has expanded dramatically over the past decade, and their use will continue to increase as we enter the 21st century.

This article provides an introduction to strategic alliances. First, characteristics of a strategic alliance are examined and examples are given. Second, the benefits of strategic alliances are discussed, and, third, choices involved in formation of a strategic alliance are explored. Finally, the special considerations for international strategic alliances are discussed.

CHARACTERISTICS

JOINT VENTURE-BASED STRATEGIC ALLIANCES. A strategic alliance is often, but not always, in the form of a **joint venture**. A joint venture is created when two or more firms work together to form a new business entity that is separate from its "parents." (Not all joint ventures fit this definition, joint ventures by acquisitions are exceptions. See below.) Ownership may be in equal or unequal shares, and may provide for changes in ownership of shares.

The most common kind is the joint venture through a **subsidiary**. In such an instance, two entities create a third separate entity with its own legal existence. For example, American Motors Corp. has formed a joint venture with government-owned Beijing Automotive Works, creating a third entity called Beijing Jeep.

Another is the joint venture by acquisition. It is created when one business purchases all or part of the shares of another. For example, in the 1990s, the Lear Corp. acquired interior components producer Masland Corp.

A third is the joint venture by **merger**. This is created when two or more companies are dissolved and incorporated into one surviving entity. For example, corporations A and B merge and their assets are conveyed to a newly created corporation C. After the merger, corporation C continues but corporations A and B are dissolved. It should be noted, however, that this legal mechanism is seldom used for international joint ventures.

STRATEGIC ALLIANCES NOT BASED ON JOINT VENTURES. In general, a strategic alliance that is not in the form of a joint venture is formed for a limited purpose and is more narrow in its operations than the joint venture. Non-joint venture strategic alliances tend to be less stable and last for shorter terms than joint ventures. For example, United Airlines and British Airlines formed a strategic alliance for the purpose of **marketing** their North American and European routes in 1988. They did so because they were losing part of their market share to Delta and American Airlines. Within a year, however, the market shifted and they terminated the agreement.

LINKAGES THAT ARE NOT STRATEGIC ALLIANCES. It is important to note that not all linkages between national or international businesses are strategic alliances. Examples of arrangements that do not create strategic alliances include **licensing**, **exporting**, **franchising**, and foreign **direct investment** agreements.

BENEFITS

The **Internet**, advances in telecommunications, and improved transportation systems have helped firms enter foreign markets and have contributed to the **globalization** of business. Simultaneously, they have facilitated the creation of strategic alliances.

The decision to form a strategic alliance depends on the needs and goals of the companies involved and on the laws of the countries in which the companies are doing business. (It should be noted, however, that discussion of the specific laws of various countries is beyond the scope of this article.) The auto industry is an example of an industry that relies heavily on strategic alliances. In the 1990s the auto industry began to rely heavily on joint venture strategic alliances as it expanded its operations in Mexico and Latin America. Auto makers began to demand more complete systems from their suppliers in Mexico, and engineering responsibility was transferred from the auto makers to their suppliers. In conjunction with this trend, auto makers are identifying Tier II and Tier III "partners" for the Tier I supplier. They are encouraging Tier I suppliers to enter joint ventures with other companies. And, in general, the Tier I suppliers have the authority to select their own suppliers and joint ventures partners except in areas such as safety and regulatory matters where control is crucial.

MARKET ENTRY. A strategic alliance can ease entry into a foreign market. First, the local firm can provide knowledge of markets, customer preferences, distribution networks, and suppliers. This is especially true in Eastern Europe. Bestfoods is a food-processing firm that sells products such as Mazola corn oil. Bestfoods has formed strategic alliances with firms in several Eastern European countries that, in turn, market its products. A strategic alliance between British Airways and American Airlines was created in 1993 and designed to give the two airlines increased access to North American and European markets, respectively.

Sometimes, foreign countries require that a certain percentage of ownership remain in the hands of its citizens. For example, in Mexico, **foreign investment** is limited by law to 49 percent in specified areas, including bonding companies, firms that print and publish periodicals for national distribution, engine and car repairs, and operation of railway terminals. Thus, foreign firms cannot enter such markets alone; a joint venture is required.

SHARING RISKS AND EXPENSES. Another major benefit of a strategic alliance is that the firms involved can share risks. For example, in the early 1990s, film manufacturers Kodak and Fuji joined with camera manufacturers Nikon, Canon, and Minolta to create cameras and film for an "Advanced Photo System." The strategic alliance (which was not based on a strategic alliance) was terminated in 1996 after the film and camera were developed. But it benefited the parties, because, by developing a common product for the market, they shared expenses and they minimized the risks that would have been involved if two or more of them had developed new, but noncompatible, formats. They avoided the potential for the kinds of losses suffered by the Sony Corp. when its Betamax format for videocassette recorders was rejected by the public in favor of the VHS format.

SYNERGISTIC EFFECTS OF SHARED KNOWLEDGE AND EXPERTISE. A strategic alliance can help a firm gain knowledge and expertise. Further, when partners contribute skills, brands, market knowledge, and assets, there is a synergistic effect. The result is a set of resources that is more valuable than if the firms had kept them separate. For example, in the early 1990s, Motorola initiated an alliance among various partners, including Raytheon, Lockheed Martin, China Great Wall, and Nippon Iridium, to develop and build a global satellite-based communications network. This new network, called Iridium, allowed the partners to develop and implement a worldwide, space-based communications network.

GAINING COMPETITIVE ADVANTAGE. Similarly, a strategic alliance can help a firm gain a competitive advantage. For example, a strategic alliance can be used to take advantage of a favorable **brand** image that has been established by one of the partners. (Establishing a brand image is a lengthy, expensive process.) It can also be used to gain shelf space for products. For example, PepsiCo formed a joint venture with the Thomas J. Lipton Co. to market ready-to-drink teas throughout the United States. Lipton contributed brand recognition in teas and manufacturing expertise. PepsiCo, as the world's second-largest soft-drink manufacturer, shared its extensive distribution network.

FORMING A STRATEGIC ALLIANCE

After the decision is made to enter a strategic alliance, a firm faces many choices. Some of them relate to **management** and others relate to the law.

SELECTING A PARTNER. A firm must consider many factors as it selects a partner. First, it must select a firm with a compatible management style. For example, it is said that an alliance between the United Kingdom-based General Electric Corp. and a German firm called Siemens failed because their management styles were incompatible. On the other hand, a strategic alliance between General Mills and Nestlé, through a firm called Cereal Partners Worldwide (CPW), is viewed as a success because of the compatible styles of their managers.

Second, it is important to consider the partner's products and services. A strategic alliance will probably work best if the firms involved complement but do not compete directly with each other. This is true in the case of General Mills and Nestlé. Both produce foods, but the CPW joint venture is for the marketing of cereal in Europe. Nestlé has marketing expertise and distribution networks in Europe, but it does not make breakfast cereals.

Third, the potential risks of the alliance should be considered. To do so, the two potential parties must gather as much information about each other as possible before entering an agreement. For example, has the potential partner entered other strategic alliances? Did they succeed or fail? Why? Is the potential partner financially stable? Do the potential partners share common strategic goals (a common vision) for the alliance?

Finally, it should be noted that there are situations in which a privately owned firm may form a joint venture with a government as its partner. This has occurred in Latin America in lumbering and in the discovery, exploration, and development of oil fields. The government controls the resource, but it wants the expertise of a firm that has experience in developing that resource. Similarly, with the collapse of communism in Central and Eastern Europe, in 1989 and the early 1990s, privately owned firms from Europe and the Western Hemisphere formed joint ventures with state-owned firms in the formerly communist countries.

MANAGEMENT DECISIONS. In strategic alliances based on joint ventures, division of management must be carefully planned. There are various mechanisms through which management of such a strategic alliance can be shared. One involves shared management in which each party participates fully in management. This requires a high degree of cooperation.

A second mechanism is through assignment of management to one party. In such arrangements, the responsibility is usually assigned to the partner that owns the majority of the **stock** in the joint venture.

A third mechanism is through delegation to executive managers of the joint venture. In such an arrangement, executives are hired to run the joint venture. They may be hired from the outside or transferred from the firms that own the joint venture. The executive managers are responsible for day-to-day operations and decisions. The firms that own the joint venture do not get involved in day-to-day operations.

FORM OF OWNERSHIP. In the case of a strategic alliance based on a joint venture, a form for doing business must be chosen. Usually the joint venture is created as a corporation, but the laws of each country vary as to types of corporations that are available and the legal requirements imposed on each. Usually, a joint venture is created under the corporate laws of the country in which it will be doing business. But this is not always true. For example, sometimes, a different country may be selected because it offers tax or other legal advantages. Countries that are sometimes selected for tax reasons include, for example, the Bahamas, Lichtenstein, and Monaco. It should also be noted that not all joint ventures involve a corporation. Occasionally, there may be legal reasons to create a joint venture under a form such as the limited **partnership**.

A lawyer or lawyers must be consulted with regard to the choice of business organization and its formation. And, in the case of an international strategic alliance, lawyers licensed to practice in each of the nations involved should be involved. For example, there is no reciprocity with regard to legal practice under the **North American Free Trade Agreement**. The laws and legal systems of the United States and Mexico differ significantly. Therefore, an agreement between a Mexican and a U.S. firm should be reviewed by Mexican as well as U.S. lawyers. Within the **European Union** (EU), in contrast, there is reciprocity with respect to legal licensing and it is possible, legally, for a lawyer licensed in one EU country to handle an agreement in another EU country. Even in the EU, however, the need for expertise with respect to applicable laws may compel a party to hire a team that includes lawyers trained in the legal jurisdictions of each country whose laws may affect the agreement.

In addition to specifying a form for the business organization, the agreement on which the strategic alliance is based covers topics such as management responsibilities, financial matters, and **decision making**. Other clauses depend on the needs of the individual parties.

SPECIAL CONSIDERATIONS IN DESIGNING AN INTERNATIONAL STRATEGIC ALLIANCE

There are some special concerns that must be faced by firms entering international strategic alliances, especially if a joint venture is involved. One area relates to **intellectual property** rights (IPR). IPR includes **technology transfer** as well as **patent**, trademark, and **copyright** protection. IPR rights are often transferred or shared in the context of an international joint venture. Yet, this can be a particularly risky area for a U.S. partner, because U.S. IPR laws are far more protective than is the case with respect to IPR laws in other countries. Host-country laws may allow IPR rights to lapse more quickly than is true under U.S. law. Also, lax enforcement of IPR laws in host countries may lead to problems. This is an area in which the advice of legal counsel and careful drafting of documents are crucial.

A second area of concern relates to finance. At least three sets of concerns should be addressed with respect to currency and exchange rates. First, exchange rates may fluctuate dramatically. For example, when Mexico faced a financial crisis in 1995-96, it caused major concerns for U.S. companies involved in joint ventures with Mexican firms, because exchange rates between the United States and Mexico changed dramatically. In November 1994, the Mexican peso was trading for slightly over three pesos per U.S. dollar. The exchange rate had dropped to a low of 7.7 pesos per U.S. dollar as of March 1995. As of June 1999, the Mexican peso is trading for just over ten pesos per U.S. dollars. Therefore, the form of currency to be used in payments between companies from two countries must be addressed. Second, the potential for **inflation** must be considered. For example, inflation in Mexico reached an annualized rate of 64 percent as of February 1995. Although economic reforms have reduced Mexico's inflation to an annualized rate of 22 percent (comparing January 1999 to January 1998), inflation in Mexico continues to be much higher than in the United States. Third, **interest rates** can be affected by financial instability. For example, as of 1999 Mexico was still dealing with the aftermath of its **debt** crisis. Interest rates were relatively high as compared to those in the United States, and **loans** were difficult to obtain through Mexican banks. Such problems are not unique to dealing with Mexico. Exchange rates, payment (in whose currency?), the potential for varying rates of inflation in the two (or more) countries involved, and sources of loans are important considerations when an international strategic alliance is created.

A third area of concern relates to the potential for political instability. Instability in Yugoslavia in 1999 means that the companies of that country are not likely to be selected as potential partners for strategic alliances. Similarly, concerns about the need for democratic reform causes businesses to proceed carefully when investing in the People's Republic of China. That is one of the reasons why U.S. businesses are encouraging the Clinton administration to support the admission of China to the **World Trade Organization**.

LOOKING AHEAD

Strategic alliances have become increasingly popular in international business. They provide businesses with various benefits including access to markets, sharing of risks and expenses, synergistic effects of shared knowledge and expertise, and competitive advantages in the marketplace. There are risks to be considered and cautions to be exercised as a firm enters a strategic alliance. But, as businesses continue to globalize, strategic alliances will continue to be a major tool for the firms involved.

[Paulette L. Stenzel]

FURTHER READING:

Doz, Yves L., and Gary Hamel. *Alliance Advantage: The Art of Creating Value through Partnering.* Cambridge, MA: Harvard Business School Press, 1998.

Griffin, Ricky W., and Michael W. Pustay. Chapter 12 of *International Business: A Managerial Perspective.* 2nd ed. Reading, PA: Addison-Wesley, 1999, 448-71.

Lorange, Peter, and Johan Roos. *Strategic Alliances: Formation, Implementation, and Evolution.* Cambridge, MA: Blackwell Business, 1993.

STRATEGIC PAY/NEW PAY

The terms ''strategic pay'' and ''new pay'' became established through book titles—Edward Lawler's *Strategic Pay* in 1990, and J. R. Schuster and Patricia Zingheim's *The New Pay* in 1992. The concept of strategic pay looks at wages and benefits as one instrument through which an organization can meet its current business goals. Schuster and Zingheim provide the following definition of new pay: ''Under new pay, . . . pay programs respond to specific business and human resource challenges. . . . New Pay requires the use of all the possible 'communication' to hit the proper performance targets. . . . base pay, variable pay, indirect pay. . . . The centerpiece of new pay is variable pay (which) facilitates the employee-organization partnership by linking the fortunes of both parties in a positive manner.'' New pay programs specifically place portions of all employee pay ''at risk.'' If specified goals are met, all share in the gains; if not, all lose. This simple concept represents a paradigm shift in thinking about pay—from a cost to employers, to an investment by employers.

THE OLD PAY SYSTEM

For many years pay has been handled mechanically. Jobs were evaluated, and points were assigned for ''compensable factors'' in the job (such as responsibility, skill, mental effort, and working conditions). This approach is called the ''point-factor'' system. Pay was then related to the points in the job. Bands of jobs were developed in similar point ranges. Naturally, this system resulted in long lists of jobs at many companies (and in the federal government). Apart from the annual raise, one could get more money only by moving up in the point system. This ''pay the job'' approach had the obvious strengths of objectivity and impersonality. It did not really ask, however, whether anyone actually produced anything, and did not distinguish well between high- and low-performing persons. The concept of ''broad banding''—collapsing the long lists of jobs into broader ''bands''—was an attempt to address some of the difficulties of extensive job categories and provide a way around the potential lockstep of the point-factor system.

''Pay the person'' was an attempt to bring the person more directly into the pay equation. It did so by providing additional money for additional competencies learned on or through the job. ''Pay for knowledge'' and ''pay for skills'' systems allowed employees to earn more money if they acquired and demonstrated competence in additional skills. Employers liked this because employees became more broadly capable. Difficulties arose, however, because employees sometimes never got to use their new skills. These approaches lacked a focus on the results as well.

There were some other problems with the old pay system, aside from bureaucratization (pay the job) and disconnection between what people learned and what they could do (pay the person)—misalignment and annuitization. Existing pay practices tend to be unaligned with results. The rhetoric of linkage is used—as in the concept of the ''merit raise''—but in many actual cases, there is no merit involved. Somehow, in some way, a raise is determined. Of course alignment with firm goals assumes—wrongly in too many cases—that the firm *has* goals. Many compensation consultants find that their first job is to help an organization develop the things they wish to pay for. Reward systems were often best described through the title of the classic piece by Steve Kerr, ''On the Folly of Rewarding A while Hoping for B.'' The new pay emphasis requires that organizations define goals and review performance in a competent manner. Accomplishing these objectives is essential for organizational high performance today, regardless of the pay system. Companies could improve at objective setting and **performance appraisal**. Thus, initiating a new pay system is one way to usher in needed change. Nevertheless, achieving both of these objectives is difficult, particularly the development of staff skills in the area of performance appraisal. Tales abound of appraisal avoidance, cursory reviews, and unhelpful comments aimed at the person of the employee rather than at the employee's behavior. Without objectives and review, the total compensation idea will not work well.

Annuitization is another problem. Conventional ''raises'' go into the base. Hence, employers are paying for past performance year after year.

In spite of the fact that compensation **costs** are a large portion of most business operations, neither employees or employers thought of compensation as a total package. While the businessperson may have had a sense of total compensation costs, the employees lacked the idea of total compensation as something for which they worked. And both the business and the employees lacked the *idea* of total compensation (benefits especially were not seen as ''pay'' by employees). Rather, it was broken up into components. There was base pay and indirect pay (fringe benefits), as well as a range of bonuses, overtime, perks, and allowances. Yet it was difficult to get all the numbers in one place.

These components were often administered by different parts of the organization. Frequently, base salary was determined under one unit of the organization, using one theory, or a combination of theories. Benefits were often developed and administered under another department with different rationales and philosophies. Bonuses and special pay were often in yet another place. Something new was needed.

THE TOTAL COMPENSATION PACKAGE

New pay begins with a view that one should think about compensation as a complete, ''total'' package. Total compensation includes the nine elements outlined in Table 1.

BASE PAY. Base pay is what many think of as ''pay.'' It can be paid ''at market,'' below, or above market. In the future, base pay will likely become a smaller fraction of total compensation than it is now, and may be targeted at ''below market.'' Individuals and **teams** can add to their pay through increments in the variable pay area.

VARIABLE PAY. Variable pay is the portion of pay linked to results. A variety of types of performance goals—individual, team, unit, and total company—can become components of the variable pay amount. While such elements have been present—**profit sharing**, gain sharing, etc.—they have not usually been linked into a total compensation framework. Employees will be able to add a considerable amount to their ''pay,'' depending upon how they and the firm performs. The structuring of variable pay in this way means that ''the paycheck'' may vary a good bit more in the future than in the past. Also, variable pay does not go into the base; it is a year-by-year phenomenon.

INDIRECT PAY. Indirect pay—fringe benefits—has traditionally been viewed as an entitlement program within the company. In *New Pay,* Schuester and Zingheim stated that the ''view of indirect pay is to contain indirect pay costs to free dollars to spend on direct pay, particularly variable pay.'' Defined-contribution plans are becoming more popular than defined-benefit plans in retirement programs; health care costs are being closely examined. Rather than simply being willing to pick up additional costs, companies are defining the amount of money they wish to convey through indirect pay. This approach frees up dollars which, in previous years, might have gone to benefits automatically. It can now go into variable pay. If they wish, employees can purchase augmented benefits with variable pay dollars, but they can also do other things with the money. Cafeteria benefits is a name for this approach.

PERKS-PAY. Perks, as a component of pay, are declining. They tend to emphasize status distinctions in

Table 1

COMPENSATION DIMENSION	THUMBNAIL
Base Pay	Guaranteed Salary
Variable Pay	Overtime, Bonus, Stock Option, Variable Pay, any "one-time" payment
Indirect Pay	Benefits
Perks-pay	$ Values of prestige cars, accessories
Works-pay	Uniform allowance, cell phone
Opportunity for Growth	Can I learn on this job?
Opportunity for Advancement	Can I advance on this job?
Psychic Income	The emotional quality of the workplace (this can be negative)
Quality of Life	Can I balance my life on this job?

an era of more flattened, team-oriented firms. There has also been increased **tax** interest in perks.

WORKS-PAY. Works-pay is perhaps the most difficult area, as companies try to define what costs of business to employees, such as a uniform or car allowance, should be considered for employee reimbursement. Assembling these components creates learning for employer and employee alike, as each sees the amount of money involved.

OPPORTUNITY FOR GROWTH. Opportunity for growth addresses the direct and indirect ways employers support personal learning. One way is if the organization itself is a learning organization, and the employee feels that he or she can benefit from mentorship and instruction on the job. More directly, organizations pay for education, sometimes even advanced degrees, such as an MBA or Ph.D.

OPPORTUNITY FOR ADVANCEMENT. Opportunity for advancement reflects the extent to which the organization has ''room at the top.'' Employees may ''sacrifice'' higher salary (or ''invest'' the difference between their highest possible salary and the salary they can get at ''opportunimax'') in the hope of achieving a high position sooner rather than later.

PSYCHICINCOME. Psychic income involves the emotional rewards of the job/career. Priests and nuns, for example, emphasize psychic income, as do Peace Corps volunteers and many in the nonprofit sector. Psychic income can be negative, however, as in the case of a ''toxic workplace'' that pays well but pays no attention to any other aspects of the employees' lives.

QUALITY OF LIFE. Some employees seek quality of life, involving a workplace that integrates life in the organization with life outside of the organization. For example, jobs with firms in Los Angeles are likely to require a commute. For some this is fine; for others not. If one wants to ski to work in the winter, only a few firms will be suitable.

One interesting feature about the total compensation package just discussed is that individuals weigh the kind of compensation they prefer differently. Table 2 allows readers to explore this possibility.

In column 1 is the compensation dimensions. In column 2 individuals can record the importance of each of the dimensions in their ideal job. These weights, of course, may vary over time as individuals are at different points in their career path.

Column 3 asks for the same kind of rating for the individual's current job. Comparisons are achieved by taking the sum of the absolute differences between columns 2 and 3 for each row, and dividing by 2. The result—the index of difference—shows how much space there is between what one would ideally like and what one has at the moment. These numbers can become quite large.

The point of this exercise is not only to create information, but to suggest to employers that the

Table 2

Compensation Dimension 1	Ideal Job [IJ] Weight,in %, of total comp 2	My Job [MJ] Weight, in %, of total comp 3	Absolute Difference IJ-MJ % 4
Base Pay			
Augmented Pay			
Indirect Pay			
Works-pay			
Perks-pay			
Opportunity for Growth			
Opportunity for Advancement			
Psychic Income			
Quality of Life			
TOTAL	100%	100%	Sum
Index of Difference Sum of Column 4/2			

compensation plans of the future will be more cafeteria-like in nature. That is, individuals will, to a degree anyway, configure their compensation the way many of us now configure our benefits.

IMPLEMENTING A NEW PAY SYSTEM

If an employer or business is considering implementing a new pay system, there are several helpful tips. First, one should get information about the current system and the way it actually works. One needs to look carefully at the current practice; securing information from the full range of employees is likely to be more accepted if it is done by an outside consultant. A company-wide committee of employees might also be helpful.

It is clear that communication with employees is a key element. Overcommunication is usually needed in an organizational effort, and especially when issues of compensation are involved. Communication in a variety of media are helpful (video, print, oral, etc.). Candor in communication, as well as level and mode, is vital. Employees will think that employers are reducing their pay, rather than realigning it. Clarity about the total compensation package, and the ability of employees to affect some of their own compensation through variable pay is essential.

Step-by-step movement is important. Shifting from so-called merit raises to a variable pay raise system is a difficult change. One method is to develop a strategy by which all increments to base and indirect pay are ''market related'' and anything else is variable, driven by year-to-year performance.

Employers might want to move step by step, however, by allowing some of the variable pay increment to go into base, especially as a transition to a more fully operating variable pay system. The approach below suggests an arrangement of the relation of base increments to variable pay to the employees' percentile position in the range (1/100 indicates the first percentile; 50/100 the 50th, 100/100 the top of the range). For employees at the bottom of the range (1/100), 99 percent of the raise goes in base, and 1 percent to bonus; for employees in the middle of the range, it is half and half; for employees at the top of the range (100/100), all is variable pay. Assume that a particular employee's raise is $2,000. For the person in the tenth percentile, 90 percent of the money, or $1,800, would be an addition to base, while 10 percent, or $200, would be bonus. For the person at the top of the range, it would all be bonus. Over time, the decision points could be adjusted to move more toward a completely variable pay system.

Finally, it is helpful to emphasize the flexibility of the new pay system. The company needs to be as efficient and effective with total compensation as with other expenditures.

Employees need to be motivated through pay. In theory, one does not worry how much staff are paid—what they produce is what counts. In speaking about the new mind-set of organizations, Charles Handy refers to the 1/2 × 2 × 3 formula. It is "shorthand for one executive's goal that in five years there will be half as many people in the core of the company, paid twice as well, and producing three times as much value." As Hal Lancaster wrote, new pay is part of a new social contract between employers and employees that includes "meaningful work, learning opportunities, career management skills, honest communications and no-fault exits."

SEE ALSO: Compensation Administration

[John E. Tropman]

FURTHER READING:

Abernathy, William B. *The Sin of Wages: Where the Conventional Pay System has Led Us and How to Find a Way Out.* Abernathy & Assoc., 1996.

Handy, Charles. "The New Mind-Sets of Organizations." *Insights Quarterly,* winter 1992, 69-70.

Henderson, Richard L. *Compensation Management: Rewarding Performance.* 6th ed. Englewood Cliffs, NJ: Prentice Hall, 1994.

Kerr, Steve. "On the Folly of Hoping for A while Rewarding B." *Academy of Management Executive* 9, no. 1 (1995): 7-14.

Lancaster, Hal. "A New Social Contract to Benefit Employer and Employee." *Wall Street Journal,* 24 November 1994, B1.

Lawler, Edward E., III. *Strategic Pay.* San Francisco: Jossey Bass, 1990.

Lowman, Don. "'New Pay': Compensation for People, Not Jobs." *Employment Relations Today* 20, no. 1 (spring 1993): 37-445.

Schuster, J. R., and Patricia Zingheim. *The New Pay: Linking Employee and Organizational Performance.* New York: Lexington, 1992.

STRATEGY

Strategy—the firm's choice concerning how to deploy its resources—has content and timing. The strategy of each business unit defines which are its preferred customers to serve and which product/technological parameters are most appropriate for satisfying this demand (content). Judgments about its competitive environment suggest whether a business unit's early implementation of actions will be more advantageous than letting competitors take pioneering risks—whether a first-mover advantage exists for the firm that preempts another's product introductions, for example (timing).

Formulation of the multibusiness firm's corporate strategy assigns a mission to each of its business units that is consistent with the organization's goals; each business unit's mission defines the timing of cash flows to be generated (or a responsibility to support other business units that, in turn, generate cash). Because corporate-level strategy integrates the activities of its mix of businesses, its totality defines the firm's "personality" and risk-taking attitudes in its quest to create value for its stakeholders. Although corporate strategy has previously been focused on the timing of cash flows generated by astute investment in short-term projects, concerns about competitiveness and the challenges of managing people-based sources of competitive advantage have forced managers to participate in longer-term projects, as well. Where business units once developed individual distinctive competences appropriate to the unique opportunities and threats they faced, corporate managers now nurture the development and sharing of core competencies across organizational boundaries to cope with converging industry boundaries and to leverage the benefits of resource expenditures across several marketplaces.

Strategy (from *strategos,* the art of the general) has its roots in traditional military tactics and logistics such as those described in Sun Tzu's *Art of War.* Modern business practices have appropriated some of the tenents of the ancient military codes and applied them to business transactions in order to acquire a great market share, to improve efficiency, and to increase profit margins. Access to the vast computational power of mainframe **computers** in the late 1960s linked corporate strategy formulation issues inextricably with those of financial analyses, especially in matters of diversification where covariance terms were calculated to assess **risk** preferences. Promulgation of the 1970s strategic planning practices of General Electric Company popularized the use of strategic business units (SBUs), which assign "bottom line responsibility" to the use of resources within organizational units smaller than divisions (or with customer/technological responsibilities that transcend divisional boundaries). General Electric was also an early user of objective criteria, such as the growth/share matrix, to direct strategic investments. (Demand growth rates and relative market shares were typical criteria in such frameworks; low market-share businesses facing slow demand growth—dogs—were candidates for divestiture.) Troubled lines of business are candidates for turnarounds to improve liquidity; firms in turnarounds cut back in markets where they are overextended (retrenchment) and reduce noncontributing activities to improve their cash flows.

Strategy implementation issues have become inextricably linked with the design of effective **management information systems** and empowerment of organizational resources, particularly where corporate level managers seek to manage relationships among their firm's ongoing mix of business units effectively (operating synergies) as well as pick the best businesses to invest in (financial synergies). As strategic planning processes have sought to elicit support from personnel who must implement the firm's strategy, the power of strategic planners who once generated armchair analyses—complete with alternative scenarios that anticipated every contingency—has migrated to the "troops in the trenches" who must make the plan succeed. Line personnel in all aspects of operations have initiated suggestions for reengineering the process by which firms create value for their customers. Ongoing managers have voluntarily downsized their organizations to create value for shareholders, lest the managers be replaced by outsiders with the same mandate of value creation (the "market for **corporate control**").

Each business-level strategy matches firm's discretionary investments to existing (and future) market conditions in light of competitors' strategies for serving chosen customers in anticipation of creating value for investors (competitive strategy). Some industries have greater profitability potential than others at a particular time in a particular country. The five-forces model—which considers whether an industry's structural traits support high profitability margins—suggests which lines of business to enter (or exit). Using the tools of **microeconomic** analysis, the model indicates that the most profitable industries will sustain high entry barriers, low supplier and customer bargaining power, no perfect substitute products, and little price **competition**. Forecasts of future industry conditions are critical to justify new (or continued) funding of business units when using the five-forces model because competition is dynamic. Business unit managers must devise entry strategies appropriate to overcome the entry barriers in operation when their firm's products are introduced, and must remain ever-vigilant to overcome the response of competitors' **innovations**.

While corporate-level managers are charged with finding the best uses for resources, managers responsible for each business unit are charged with sustaining a basis for competitive advantage in serving the most attractive customers as their markets evolve. Although cost-based strengths are fundamental to becoming a preferred vendor, the evolving requirements of sophisticated customers mean that competitive advantage is a constantly moving target and effective managers must anticipate how industry success requirements will change and make expenditures to preempt competitors from improving their relative positions vis-à-vis key customers. When industries seem attractive, cash is often reinvested to maximize market share (**economies of scale**). Implicit in such reinvestment policies is the expectation that postponed profits can be harvested later by surrendering market share. Because the "first to exit" liquidates more of its investment than firms that procrastinate, however, business unit managers must also assess the changing costs of overcoming exit barriers when competitive conditions sour and declining demand no longer justifies continuing investment. In volatile markets, dominant market share is no longer a virtue. Strategic flexibility is more-highly valued as environments devolve to hypercompetition.

Because corporate-level (headquarters or corporate staff) managerial activities are justified by making particular combinations of business units more valuable than if each line of business were a separate company held in a financial portfolio, corporate strategy is centrally concerned with the nature of relationships between business units. Resource allocation among a multitude of business units is also a central concern of corporate level strategy; corporate managers often proactively intervene in business level decisions by deciding in which lines of business the firm should (1) enter; (2) exit; (3) expand (or shrink) by funding the capacity of a business unit's geographic plants; (4) encourage coordination among a business unit's geographic plants (or encourage autonomy among them instead); and/or (5) encourage coordination among the resources and facilities of related (but separate) business units more overtly than if decisions to share expenses, transfer knowledge, participate in each other's value-creation chains, or other relationships were left to chance. (In a "bottom-up" strategic planning process, these same decisions might surface when corporate-level managers arbitrate between competing uses of resources when resources are rationed.) Corporate strategy accounts for the differences between the two types of strategic planning processes (top-down versus bottom-up) with regard to which business unit initiates the need for headquarters to make trade-offs among competing uses of capital. Although business-unit managers typically compete across the firm for capital allocations, processes for enhancing the firm's core competencies increasingly make human resource allocations across business units a strategic concern that is coordinated by headquarters, as well.

Core competencies arising from an organization's accumulated technical knowledge and management systems can be shared more easily when its corporate strategy encourages intrafirm interactions (**economies of scope**) than when each business unit throughout a firm's international system of operations goes its own way (**laissez-faire**). While business unit managers often champion shorter-term interests that favor the market segments they have chosen to serve, product attributes they believe will best serve their customers, and technological postures that will develop competencies that best suit their respective lines of business, corporate level managers champion ''big-picture,'' corporate-wide interests and legitimize internal schemes of cross-subsidization by providing budgetary relief for activities that could enhance the longer-term priorities of the firm through the funding of (1) ''corporate development'' divisions, (2) strategic alliances that expose the firm to desired competencies without requiring equity ownership (virtual firm arrangements), or (3) other forms of corporate venturing, including internal alliances.

Although business-unit managers are concerned with optimizing their internal value-creating chains of relationships (by forging effective competitive strategies), corporate-level managers are responsible for arranging (and monitoring) the best system of value-creating relationships among sister business units, as well as with outsiders—which may include international suppliers (and distributors), locally competent suppliers (and distributors) within each site of international operations, competitors, local governments that build and support local infrastructures, and customers, among others. Doing so requires firms to maintain strategic flexibility since strategy implementation may involve cross-licensing (or other forms of information exchange), **joint ventures** (or other forms of equity participation), or **direct investments** through acquisition.

Within flexible organizations, corporate-level strategy initiates and audits competitive advantages based on organizational attributes. In particular, effective vertical strategies require a continuous process of redesigning task responsibilities (in collaboration with suppliers and customers) to create more value-added opportunities internally while continually weeding-out activities (and customers) that do not fit the firm's choice regarding what businesses it wants to be in (vertical integration), hence what competencies it wants to develop to sustain its competitive advantage. Vertical relationships can be secured through contractual ties, strategic alliances, or equity ownership, depending upon the competitive environments where transactions must occur. Disinvestment (or the severing of vendor-customer relationships) must occur when necessary, even where both business units are owned by the same corporate parents. Thus corporate-level oversight is mandatory—especially where sister business units are linked in such buyer-supplier relationships—to avoid perverting the firm's strategic vision.

Strategic flexibility requires organizations to gain new capabilities—through acquisition or internal development, depending upon the timing requirements of effective implementation—before competitors reach similar conclusions. Strategic flexibility may require firms to relocate stages of their value chain where national cost advantages in factors of production are short-lived. Where easy international flows of information make competitive imitation inevitable and timing advantages based on proprietary information are increasingly short-lived, flexible organizations need a corporate strategy that moves them from less-competitive businesses to those where opportunities to prosper are greater and success requirements are more compatible with the strengths they have developed internally.

[Kathryn Rudie Harrigan]

FURTHER READING:

Porter, Michael E. *Competitive Strategy: Techniques for Analyzing Industries and Competitors.* New York: Free Press, 1980.

STRATEGY FORMULATION

Strategy formulation is vital to the well-being of a company or organization. There are two major types of strategy: (1) corporate strategy, in which companies decide which line or lines of business to engage in; and (2) business or competitive strategy, which sets the framework for achieving success in a particular business. While business strategy often receives more attention than corporate strategy, both forms of strategy involve planning, industry/market analysis, goal setting, commitment of resources, and monitoring.

IMPORTANCE OF STRATEGY

The formulation of a sound strategy facilitates a number of actions and desired results that would be difficult otherwise. A strategic plan, when communicated to all members of an organization, provides employees with a clear vision of what the purposes and objectives of the firm are. The formulation of strategy forces organizations to examine the prospect of change in the foreseeable future and to prepare for change rather than to wait passively until market forces compel it. Strategic formulation allows the firm to plan its capital **budgeting**. Companies have limited funds to invest and must allocate capital funds where they will be most effective and derive the highest returns on their investments.

On the other hand, a firm without a clear strategic plan gives its decision makers no direction other than the maintenance of the status quo. The firm becomes purely reactive to external pressures and less effective at dealing with change. In highly competitive markets, a firm without a coherent strategy is likely to be outmaneuvered by its rivals and face declining market share or even declining sales.

The formulation of sound strategy may be seen as having six important steps:

1. The company or organization must first choose the business or businesses in which it wishes to engage—in other words, the corporate strategy.
2. The company should then articulate a ''mission statement'' consistent with its business definition.
3. The company must develop strategic objectives or goals and set performance objectives (e.g., at least 15 percent sales growth each year).
4. Based on its overall objectives and an analysis of both internal and external factors, the company must create a specific business or competitive strategy that will fulfill its corporate goals (e.g., pursuing a market niche strategy, being a low-cost, high-volume producer).
5. The company then implements the business strategy by taking specific steps (e.g., lowering prices, forging partnerships, entering new distribution channels).
6. Finally, the company needs to review its strategy's effectiveness, measure its own performance, and possibly change its strategy by repeating some or all of the above steps.

DEFINING THE BUSINESS

While this would appear to be the easiest of the six steps listed above, the simplicity of this first step is deceptive. Businesses must be defined in terms of their customers. Without customers, there is no business. They are a firm's only real source of revenue and, hence, of power. Successful businesses are those that create profitable customers. With this in mind, it makes sense to define any business in terms of its customers. Some companies achieve success by concentrating on product development, product quality, efficient production, and other product related functions. However, it is important to remember that the success of these companies is entirely dependent upon customers valuing a firm's products above others, or appreciating the lower prices provided through the firm's abilities to produce at lower costs. One cannot assume that customers always want to pay less for their goods and services. In the markets for luxury goods like perfumes, for example, few companies have been successful in pursuing the strategy of being the low-cost supplier, whereas in other markets this is a highly coveted industry status.

INDUSTRY DEFINITION BY END BENEFIT. Business scholars have long urged corporate leaders to define their businesses broadly and in terms of the end benefits their customers receive. Hence, oil companies should not view themselves as being in the ''oil business,'' but in terms of the broader category of ''energy,'' when attempting to market oil as a fuel. Automobile drivers don't necessarily have a strong preference for exactly what fuels their vehicle. If ethanol could power their vehicle as conveniently as gasoline, the consumer would have little preference between the two systems. If ethanol were more convenient and less expensive than gasoline, consumers would buy ethanol and not gasoline. Drivers aren't buying gasoline for its own sake when they visit a service station; rather, what they are buying is energy to facilitate transportation.

An example of an effectively broad industry definition comes from Charles Revson (1906-1975), founder of Revlon cosmetics, who often said he was in the business of selling ''the promise of hope.'' This insightful business definition led Revson to concentrate his efforts on meticulously creating advertising depicting feminine images that were unrealistic to the vast majority of his customers, yet were perfectly consistent with their deepest hopes for themselves. Lotteries operate on the same principles. Few people expect to win, so the benefit is the hope of winning. Hope can be a very profitable business to be in even if it is difficult to imagine as an industry.

DEFINITION BY CUSTOMERS SERVED. Many successful companies have defined themselves in terms of their customers. A general store in a remote area would do well to define its business as serving the customers in its trading area. While such a business definition might lead the firm in directions that would be at the whim of the local clientele, that business should remain profitable as long as customers are happy. An example of such a business is L.L. Bean, which was started when Leon L. Bean developed a superior hunting boot well suited for his native Maine and sold it through the mail to a mailing list of Maine residents who had purchased hunting licenses. The mail order company grew by first serving the needs of hunters and later by expanding the concept to all wilderness activities. While this might seem to be a definition based upon an activity, careful examination of L.L. Bean shows that the firm has identified a psychographic market segment to which it continually caters. Many of its buyers really don't care for wilderness sports as much as they simply identify with the targeted market segment and wish to buy products that conform to the segment's norms.

DEFINITION BY TECHNOLOGY. Genentech Inc. is a firm engaged in the development of genetic research and biotechnology for pharmaceuticals: it has defined itself as being in the biotech business. Business definition by technology leads to a very tumultuous corporate existence, as the business enterprise turns direction every time there's a new invention.

STRATEGIC MISSION

The strategic mission of an organization embodies a long-term view of what sort of organization it wishes to become. The value to management of having a lucid mission statement—the second step in strategy formulation—can be in rendering tangible the firm's long-term course and in guiding decisions toward a rational design. Among the elements that are key to a good mission statement are a statement of corporate values and philosophy, a statement of the scope and purpose of the business, an acknowledgement of special competencies, and an articulation of the corporate vision for its future.

STRATEGIC OBJECTIVES

Clearly stated strategic objectives, the third step of strategy formulation, outline the position in the marketplace that the firm seeks. Performance targets state the measurable milestones that the firm needs to reach or obtain to achieve its strategic objectives.

Some strategic objectives relate to the positioning of goods and services in the competitive marketplace while others concern the structure of the company itself and how it plans to produce goods or manage its operations. Typical strategic objectives involve profitability, market share, return on investment, technological achievement, customer service level, revenue size, and diversification.

In order to make strategic planning work, the goals, missions, objectives, performance targets, or other hopes of top management must somehow be made real by others in more distant locations down the organizational chart. Merely communicating to each member of the business the vision that top management has for the firm is not sufficient. Strategic objectives and performance targets should penetrate every corner of the organizational chart. There should be a hierarchy of strategic formulation starting with the highest levels of the firm, from which it is consistently translated from level to level so that each department knows what its contribution to the overall mission of the firm is to be. This process should end with each individual in the firm having strategic objectives and performance targets tailored to their specific role in the firm.

ORGANIZATION-WIDE STRATEGY LEVEL. This is top management's plan for achieving its aims. These strategies are for the entire organization and should not concern the specific affairs of individual business units.

Organization-wide strategy requires schemes for overseeing the extent and combinations of companies' assorted actions in order to achieve a superior corporate performance. When numerous activities are being managed simultaneously, there are interactive effects in managing the group of activities as a whole. Such a group of activities is often referred to as the "business portfolio." Proper management of the business portfolio demands actions and decisions about how and when the firm should enter new ventures and what areas the firm needs to exit. Further, in all management, timing is crucial. Top management needs to set the timetable for business entry, exit, growth, and downsizing. Often a sound strategy goes awry when management attempts to move too quickly, too slowly, or just fails to set any timetable for action allowing for little temporal coordination of the firm's efforts. Further, organization-wide strategy should address the balance of resources across the firm's various activities. These resources need to be allocated to direct the company's activities toward the strategic objectives of the organization. Through these activities at the corporate-wide level, decisions about balancing business risks can maximize security for the firm.

BUSINESS STRATEGY

The fourth step in strategy formulation requires developing the business or competitive strategy. Business strategy refers to the strategy used in directing one coherent business unit or product line. The most crucial question business strategy should address is how the unit plans to be competitive within its specific business market. Important logistical issues to consider include (1) what role each of the functional areas within the business unit will play in creating this competitive advantage in the marketplace; (2) what the potential responses are to prospective changes in marketplace; and (3) how to allocate the business unit's resources between its various divisions.

The overall competitive strategy should take into account three main factors: (1) the status, make-up, and prognosis of the industry as a whole and its market(s); (2) the firm's position relative to its competitors; and (3) internal factors at the firm, such as particular strengths and weaknesses.

INDUSTRY ANALYSIS. An industry or market analysis should consider the structure of the industry, the forces compelling change within the industry, the cost and price economics of the industry, elements critical to success in the industry, and imminent problems and issues in the industry.

A review of the industry's structure should evaluate factors such as these:

- the size of the total market
- the growth rate of the market
- profitability of the firms in the industry
- whether the industry is producing at capacity or there is excess capacity already in place
- the entry barriers to the industry
- whether the industry's products are commodity goods or highly unique

Change in an industry may occur along several lines, and the direction of change often has major implications for the competitive strategy. In an obvious example, if a manufacturing industry is facing in the medium term a massive technological overhaul due to phase-in of environmental regulations, it would probably make little sense to bring a major new factory on line using the older technology, even if for the moment it is still more widely used. Other noteworthy industry changes to consider include what stage of development the industry and its market are at (developing, mature, declining), what technological advances could impact the industry, what regulatory changes are new or on the horizon, and whether there are major patents about to expire that will allow cheaper entry into the market.

It is also important to examine in detail the economics of doing business in a particular industry. One area of particular concern is the cost structure. For instance, industries characterized by a high percentage of fixed costs are subject to extreme price wars during competitive times in the market. Airlines are an example of a high-fixed-cost industry. Industries with high variable costs tend to have smaller swings in their pricing structure. Cost structure also has implications for capital and cash flow requirements, as well as for the overall entry barriers to participating in the industry.

Production costs tend to decline over time in proportion to the total quantity of goods produced. This is mainly due to two factors: learning and experience. Each has its own curve, the ''learning curve'' and the ''experience curve.'' While each of these effects might be diagnosed separately, the end effect of both may be the same: the firm that produces the most goods in the industry tends to have the lowest cost of production in the long term. All things being equal, this will give that firm the long term cost advantage in the industry for the life of the product.

In a typical scenario, being the low-cost producer allows the firm to receive not only the greatest margin on its products when all firms in the market participate in an established price structure, but when price competition arises the low-cost producer can make a profit or break even on its goods, while its competitors lose money. This is a key strategic advantage. This is why many firms during the development of a new and potentially large long-term market will forgo a profitable, small, prestige niche strategy for a less profitable market penetration strategy that demands heavy investment and expansion of production. This second strategy can yield a long-term advantage in the industry by allowing the firm to gain from the learning and experience effects. Competitors later may not be able to catch up since they lack the cumulative production experience and assets of the pioneer in the industry.

One alternative to the low-cost strategy is a high-value strategy, in which customers pay more but also expect to receive a product or service somehow better than that offered by the low-cost supplier. The improvement may be tangible in durability and features, or it may be an appeal to status, image, or lifestyle that makes the product or service more compelling to some consumers.

However, even industry leaders must guard against complacency; they might be on top in the traditional market paradigm, but there may be a new paradigm emerging that will make them obsolete if they fail to change. The accumulation of learning and experience does little good if these assets are directed at the wrong vision of the market. This has strategic implications not only for the market leader, but also its competitors, who may be able to benefit from the leader's slow rate of change. A real-life example was the rise of Wal-Mart Stores, Inc. from a regional discount chain to the world's largest retailer. Arguably its older competitors like Kmart had more experience, but they failed to adapt to the market changes, technologies, and aggressive management practices that helped propel Wal-Mart to market dominance. Wal-Mart embodied a new paradigm in general consumer merchandise retailing, a model that the former market leaders have since tried to emulate.

COMPETITORS. A fundamental part of developing a business strategy is to understand in detail who the main competitors are and where their strengths and weaknesses lie. Competitors can be analyzed by the type of goods they produce, their price, markets served, or channels of distribution used. Many industries have clear niching, with each firm or group of firms avoiding direct competition through some combination of product differentiation or **market segmentation**. Other industries are characterized by large-scale head-on competition. Coca-Cola and Pepsi, in the soft drink industry, are a highly visible example.

Not all future competition originates from present competitors, however. New market entrants are most often found lurking on the sidelines of the firm. For example, suppliers are often looking to forward integrate into an industry. Suppliers of the raw materials that go into a product may have a competitive cost advantage through such vertical integration. Suppliers are often motivated in such moves by the assurance of having a guaranteed market for their output.

On the flip side, customers may decide to backward integrate into business. Customers considering backward integration usually first attempt to establish their own ''private labeled'' product prior to integration. When customers put considerable time and effort into their private label version of a product, it may well be a sign of a growing intent to backward integrate. The notion of private label is most associated with retailing, where, for example, grocery stores have house labels, but may or may not actually manufacture the products bearing their labels. However, similar practices exist in many other lines of business.

Firms that produce either substitutes for a product or complementary goods to a product may also be a competitor. These firms have experience in the market, and a competitor's product niche in the market represents a simple product line extension for their firm. Often the threat of competitive retaliation into these firms' product areas is useful in deterring such moves.

Barriers to market entry are often responsible for setting the level of competition in an industry. Historically, retail has tended to be a competitive industry due to the relatively low costs of entry into the market (although this has changed somewhat as large chains consolidate and have significant price and marketing advantages over smaller competitors). But compared to manufacturing heavy industrial goods, retail still has relatively few barriers. American auto manufacturers probably worry very little about other American firms entering the market of passenger automobiles, because both the financial and regulatory barriers to entry are far too high. Not all barriers are financial. Drug firms enjoy oligopoly status due to their abilities to interface with the U.S. Food and Drug Administration in getting new drugs approved. New firms would have great difficulty in developing the same working relationships. Military suppliers also enjoy an oligopoly status due to political barriers to entering the market. Each firm must analyze what factors keep its competitors at bay when assessing the potential for others to want to share in their profits.

IMPLEMENTING STRATEGIES

A strategy is of course only as good as its implementation. A company may have an impressive strategy for conquering the market, but if it fails to take the right steps the strategy is meaningless. The means of implementing strategies are called tactics. The tactical execution, while crucial to the success of any strategy, is not a traditional part of the formulation of that strategy. However, many firms have been successful in discovering successful tactics and building their strategies about ''what works.'' The implementation experience, whether favorable or unfavorable, also directly informs the strategy revision process or any new strategies, as the company will take into account its successes and failures when choosing future paths.

MONITORING AND ASSESSMENT

Strategy formulation should be done on a regular basis, as often as required by changes in the industry. Firms need to track the company's progress, or lack thereof, on the key goals and objectives outlined in the strategic plan. The company must be objective and flexible enough to realize whether the strategy is no longer appropriate as it was first conceived, and whether it needs revision or replacement. In other cases, the strategy itself may be fine, but the communication of the strategy to employees has been inadequate or the specific steps to implementation haven't worked out as planned. This evaluation and feedback of the strategy formulation, the final step, provides the foundation for successful future strategy formulation.

FURTHER READING:

Aspesi, Claudio, and Dev Vardhan. ''Brilliant Strategy, But Can You Execute?'' *McKinsey Quarterly,* winter 1999.

Bache, Alan, and Mike Freeman. ''Is Our Vision Any Good?'' *Journal of Business Strategy,* March-April 1999.

Bart, Christopher. ''Mission Matters.'' *CPA Journal,* August 1998.

Faulkner, David, and Cliff Bowman. *The Essence of Competitive Strategy.* Hertfordshire, UK: Prentice Hall International, 1995.

Ghemawat, Pankaj. ''Building Strategy on the Experience Curve.'' *Harvard Business Review,* March-April 1985, 143-49.

Peters, Thomas J., and Robert H. Waterman. *In Search of Excellence: Lessons from America's Best-Run Companies.* New York: Harper & Row, 1982.

Porter, Michael E. *Competitive Strategy: Techniques for Analyzing Industries and Competitors.* New York: Free Press, 1980.

———. ''How Competitive Forces Shape Strategy.'' *Harvard Business Review,* March-April 1979, 137-45.

Ulwick, Anthony W. *Business Strategy Formulation: Theory, Process, and the Intellectual Revolution.* Westport, CT: Quorum Books, 1999.

STRESS IN THE WORKPLACE

Generally defined as a negative physical or emotional reaction to a demanding environment, stress in workplaces is considered a significant and costly problem for the business world. Its impact extends from the immediate human toll on those who experience it to many costs and inefficiencies that can diminish business effectiveness. Estimates place the annual price tag of workplace stress in the United States at somewhere between $200 and $300 billion, owing to health care claims, **workers' compensation** claims, absenteeism, **employee turnover**, productivity losses, and other direct and indirect costs. Some research suggests, for instance, that health benefits for highly stressed employees cost some 40 percent more than average. One study has even suggested that stress greatly contributes to unethical employee behavior such as lying to customers and cutting corners on work tasks.

Specialists actually define two forms of stress, which may be loosely termed positive stress and negative stress. The difference is based largely on individuals' perceptions of the stressor, the situation causing stress. Some workers find certain kinds of stress exhilarating, such as working toward a goal or performing tasks that have some intrinsic reward to them. In other cases, stress looms over workers as a burden of demands, pressures, unreasonable expectations, conflict, and ill-treatment.

The simplistic judgment that workers who experience high levels of negative stress merely have bad attitudes or poor coping skills has been rejected by many businesses, and moreover, the courts. This is not to suggest that employees never contribute to their own misery, but there are a number of factors and situations that seem to universally produce negative responses. Five commonly cited factors include (1) poor working conditions, (2) workplace discrimination, (3) how much control or autonomy the worker has over the situation, (4) what kinds of demands are placed on him or her, and (5) whether the worker receives support from coworkers and supervisors. When workers suffer bad conditions or discrimination, or experience little control, heavy demands, and minimal support, conditions are ripe for stress.

EMPLOYER STRATEGIES

Employers have developed a number of tactics to help alleviate stress. There are two main categories of stress-reduction policies:

- programs to treat and reduce the effects of stress once it has already occurred
- programs to prevent stress from happening in the first place

Stress treatment initiatives were the earliest response to stress complaints when the issue began to gain momentum in the 1980s. These programs range from providing more generous health and wellness benefits—including access to fitness centers—to offering specific assistance to employees who experience stress, such as through counselors and employee assistance programs. Other programs have offered yoga sessions, massage therapy, and meditation classes. By one estimate, in 1985 27 percent of U.S. workplaces had some form of stress-reduction program. This figure was expected to be closer to 40 percent as of 2000.

More recently, reformers have placed growing emphasis on job design, so that preventing stress is built into the way a company structures its work activities. Suggestions for preventative stress techniques include formally breaking up the workday into several smaller segments punctuated by breaks for relaxation, more realistic and humane scheduling of tasks to be completed, and giving workers more voice in their arrangements.

LITIGATION

There has not always been a clear direction in the court cases, laws, and regulations addressing employee stress. Certainly litigants have been able to win large sums in court or wage costly legal battles, but there have been dual trends of lowering the burden of proof in some areas and raising the burden elsewhere. The latter approach has been more common.

Mental/emotional stress damages can be sought in one of four ways. First, if the claimant believes he or she has been specifically targeted with unreasonable job pressures because of his or her race, sex, or other protected status, an equal employment opportunity (EEO) lawsuit may be brought. As with any EEO suit, the claimant must demonstrate that the employer's actions (or inactions) had differential impact based on workers' membership in a protected class.

Second, in a special application of discrimination laws, employees may file suit under the Americans with Disabilities Act (ADA) that the employer has failed to make a reasonable accommodation for some disability and the result has been undue stress. In a variation on the theme, some have claimed an inability to handle stress as a disability in itself, but the courts have generally not supported such claims. One worker sued, for instance, on grounds that he was entitled to a stress-free work environment because he couldn't handle any amount of stress; he lost in court, as have litigants with similar claims.

Third, a worker can bring a general civil lawsuit alleging that the employer either (1) was negligent and allowed known stress-causing conditions to persist without taking reasonable measures to prevent them, or (2) intentionally inflicted mental or emotional suffering on the employee. In both cases there is typically a heavy burden for showing that the employer acted unreasonably, or even ''outrageously,'' in the language of some court decisions.

Fourth, and by far most common, employees may make claims through the state workers' compensation system. In some states, including California and Massachusetts, this is virtually the only legal avenue, outside of federal discrimination lawsuits, because emotional stress cases are not heard in the tort system.

In the mid-1980s, stress claims accounted for as much as 14 percent of workers' compensation cases, but legal reforms from the early 1990s in a number of states retooled how stress-based workers' compensation claims are handled. In most cases, the laws got tougher, requiring greater specificity and evidence for various aspects of the claim. For example, in California claimants formerly could bring cases when as little as 10 percent of their stress-related condition was attributed to their work. The new law required that the majority (more than 50 percent) of their condition must be caused by work in order to qualify. Not surprisingly, stress-based claims dropped by 40 percent in two years. Other states made similar revisions. Another example of tightening the requirements has been to uphold the legitimacy of normal business practices that may simply have unpleasant consequences for individuals, such as **employee dismissals**, **performance appraisals**, and disciplinary actions, so long as these are not unusually harsh or unfounded and are not discriminatory.

However, a number of states still have vague or broad standards in these areas, so employers must stay abreast of local trends. One area of broadening has been in what stress effects are considered sufficient evidence of damages incurred. Previously, many state courts held that mental or emotional effects from stress were insufficient because the laws made no mention of them. Instead, they required that a physical illness be shown in order to qualify under the law. In some cases the laws were revised to cover mental or emotional workplace stress, but in many places the standards remain ambiguous.

FURTHER READING:

Caudron, Shari. ''On the Contrary, Job Stress is in Job Design.'' *Workforce*, September 1998.

DeFrank, Richard S., and John M. Ivancevich. ''Stress on the Job: An Executive Update.'' *Academy of Management Executive*, August 1998.

''Depression, High Stress Most Costly Health Risk Factors: Study.'' *Employee Benefit Plan Review*, December 1998.

Dutton, Gail. ''Cutting-Edge Stressbusters.'' *HR Focus*, September 1998.

Krohe, James, Jr. ''Workplace Stress.'' *Across the Board*, February 1999.

Mann, Sally E. ''Employee Stress an Important Cost in Mergers.'' *Business Insurance*, 25 November 1996.

McShulskis, Elaine. ''Job Stress Can Prompt Unethical Behavior.'' *HRMagazine*, July 1997.

SUBSIDIARY

When one company acquires more than 50 percent of the voting stock of another company, thereby obtaining control of its operations, the acquired company becomes a subsidiary of the acquiring company. The acquiring company becomes the subsidiary's parent company. Together, the parent and the subsidiary form a corporate affiliation. Sometimes the parent company is organized expressly for the purpose of holding stock in other corporations; such parents are called **holding companies**. If the parent owns all of the voting stock of another company, that company is a wholly owned subsidiary of the parent company. A company may become a subsidiary through acquisition, or it may be established as a subsidiary to begin with. Controlling interest in a company's stock may be obtained through purchasing the **stock** or exchanging it for shares of the parent company's stock. A company may establish a subsidiary by forming a new corporation and retaining all or part of its stock.

Companies choose to acquire or establish subsidiaries for a variety of financial and managerial reasons. From a management point of view, subsidiaries allow for the advantages of decentralized **management**, where each subsidiary has its own management team. Each subsidiary is responsible to the parent company on a profit and loss basis. Unprofitable subsidiaries can more easily be sold off than can divisions of a consolidated business. Subsidiaries retain their corporate identities, and the holding company benefits from any goodwill and recognition attached to the subsidiary's name.

Subsidiaries can be acquired or established with less investment than would be required in a merger or consolidation. Where a **merger** would require obtaining complete interest in another company, a subsidiary can be acquired with the purchase of only a controlling interest in the company. In deciding whether to establish a subsidiary or a separate operating division, the parent company often takes into account the funds that could be raised by selling some of the new subsidiary's stock. There are also tax and other financial advantages to establishing or acquiring a subsidiary. Parent companies and their subsidiaries are considered separate legal entities, so that the assets of the parent company and the individual subsidiaries are protected against catastrophic and creditors' claims against one of the subsidiaries. Another advantage is that the stock in the subsidiary company is held as an asset on the books of the parent company and can be used as collateral for additional **debt** financing. In addition, one company can acquire stock in another company without approval of its stockholders; mergers and consolidations typically require stockholder approval.

Subsidiaries typically file financial reports on their operations with their parent companies. While subsidiaries and their parents are considered separate legal entities for the purpose of determining liability, they may be considered as a single economic entity for the purpose of filing financial statements. For tax purposes, the parent company must own at least 80 percent of the voting stock in another company in order to be able to file a consolidated tax return. In that case, the parent company and its subsidiaries are considered a single economic entity. The tax advantage here is that losses from one subsidiary can be used to offset profits from another subsidiary and reduce the overall taxable corporate income on the consolidated tax return. A significant disadvantage occurs when a company holds less than 80 percent of the subsidiary's voting stock; in that case separate tax returns must be filed for the parent and the subsidiary, and intercorporate dividends become subject to an additional tax.

SEE ALSO: Holding Companies; Mergers and Acquisitions

[David P. Bianco]

FURTHER READING:

Woelfel, Charles, ed. *Fitzroy Dearborn Encyclopedia of Banking and Finance.* 10th ed. Fitzroy Dearborn Publishers, 1998.

SUBSIDIES

A subsidy is a government payment to individuals, businesses, other governments, and other domestic institutions and organizations. Unlike government purchases, for which the government receives goods or services, subsidies do not provide the government with any goods or services in return. The purpose of government subsidies is to ensure the availability of necessary goods and services.

A wide range of domestic businesses, individuals, and other organizations in the United States are eligible for government subsidies. A complete listing of all federal subsidies can be found in the government publication, *Catalog of Federal Domestic Assistance.* Among the areas receiving government subsidies are agriculture, maritime industries, and mass transportation.

A subsidy may take the form of direct payments from the government, as is the case in a variety of agricultural crop and livestock production programs. The purpose of direct payments to wheat, cotton, wool, and other agricultural producers is to ensure adequate production to meet domestic and foreign demand and to protect or supplement the **income** of farmers.

A subsidy may also be in the form of a project grant. While direct payments may be used by the recipient for virtually any purpose, project grants usually carry stipulations regarding how the subsidy may be applied. The federal government provides project grants for a wide range of projects ranging from rural housing to urban mass transportation. Project grants and other federal subsidies that are given directly to state or local governments are also called grants-in-aid.

The federal government also subsidizes a range of services that its own agencies provide below cost to the public. When a government agency provides services to the public at a loss, the agency's income does not correspond to the value of the agency's output. Consequently, when calculating national income and **gross national product**, subsidies less surpluses of government enterprises are added to the value of output to arrive at national income.

In the area of international trade, export subsidies are government subsidies that are given to domestic producers of goods that will be exported. Export subsidies may take the form of a variety of government benefits, including direct payments, support prices, tax incentives, and funds for training. Export subsidies are given on the condition that the goods being produced will be exported. In the **European Union** (EU), export subsidies are called variable subsidies. Rules affecting variable subsidies of EU countries are found in the Common Agricultural Policy of the EU.

The **General Agreement on Tariffs and Trade** (GATT) contains restrictions on the use of export subsidies. Developed countries are forbidden to use subsidies to support the **export** of most manufactured goods, for example. Under GATT, less-developed nations are permitted to subsidize manufactured goods that will be exported, provided the subsidies do not significantly damage the economies of developed countries. GATT also provides for remedies, such as countervailing **duties**, when it has been determined that one trading partner is unfairly using export subsidies.

[David P. Bianco]

FURTHER READING:

Collins-Williams, Terry, and Gerry Salembier. "International Discipline on Subsidies: The GATT, the WTO, and the Future Agenda." *Journal of World Trade,* February 1996, 5-17.

SUCCESSION PLANNING

SEE: Management Succession Planning

SUGGESTION SYSTEMS

Suggestion systems are a form of employee-to-management communication that benefit employees as well as employers. They provide a two-way channel of communication between employees and **management**, with management accepting or rejecting employee suggestions and in some cases commenting on them. Suggestion systems give employees a voice and a role in determining company policies and operating procedures.

Employee suggestions can help increase efficiency, eliminate waste, improve safety, and improve the quality of a company's products and services. The company benefits not only in terms of cost savings realized as a result of employee suggestions, but also in terms of better employee morale. In many cases suggestion systems can help develop teamwork among employees. While the goal of a suggestion system is for cost savings to exceed expenses associated with the program, there are also intangible benefits to be realized from suggestion systems.

One of the first suggestion systems was started at General Electric in 1906. It consisted of a suggestion box in each department with a pad of blank paper on which employees were instructed to write practical suggestions for improving the company's manufacturing and other operations. The system was put into place only after an employee was fired for developing and proposing an idea for improving a manufacturing operation. Today, suggestion systems are common not only in manufacturing companies, but in businesses of all sizes and types.

A successful suggestion system must be promoted to the company's employees. Employees are typically given a handbook that explains the company's suggestion system. Such handbooks usually contain a statement of management support that encourages workers to ''speak up'' and make practical suggestions for improving operations. The handbook also spells out who is eligible for awards and what awards are given. In some companies certain levels of management are not eligible to receive awards for their suggestions. The handbook also defines what constitutes a suggestion, since some ''suggestions'' are simply considered part of doing one's job or routine maintenance and repair. Finally the handbook will usually contain one or more standardized forms on which suggestions can be submitted. Additional forms are usually made available in various ways to employees.

The administration of a suggestion system requires one or more plan administrators. A separate handbook may be prepared for company executives and supervisors, instructing them on their role in encouraging employees to participate in the suggestion system. In addition, each suggestion system requires certain individuals to be designated as suggestion evaluators. Usually the evaluator of a particular suggestion is someone with expertise in an area related to the suggestion. The evaluator's comments are then usually passed on to a committee that determines which suggestions will receive awards.

Suggestion systems typically provide some kind of reward to employees who have made suggestions that are adopted by the company. The rewards may be based on a percentage of cost savings realized as a result of the suggestion, or they may be a fixed amount with no relation to the savings involved. The awards may be given in cash or merchandise. The awards are usually heavily publicized within the company, and major awards are often publicized within the community. Such publicity serves as an incentive to other employees to come up with cost saving ideas and win awards on their own.

Suggestion systems may be continuous or conducted for a limited period. Some companies conduct annual suggestion contests that may last for a month. During that time, employees are encouraged to come up with as many suggestions as possible. In some cases employees may be divided into **teams** representing individual departments. Such teams compete against each other and try to produce the most suggestions. Prizes are then awarded to the teams making the most suggestions that can be used by the company. In the case of continuous suggestion systems, periodic contests can be used to stimulate employee interest in the existing program.

Businesses recognize that their employees' knowledge and ideas represent a valuable resource. Suggestion systems are one way to tap this resource. They are most effective as part of a broader work environment that encourages systematic participation by employees in problem solving and **decision making**.

SEE ALSO: Employee Motivation

[David P. Bianco]

FURTHER READING:

Allnoch, Allen. ''Closing the Participation Gap.'' *IIE Solutions,* November 1997, 6.

Bell, Robert F. ''Constructing an Effective Suggestion System.'' *IIE Solutions,* February 1997, 22.

Darragh-Jeromos, Peggy. ''A Suggestion System that Works for You.'' *Supervision,* November 1996, 6.

Teitelbaum, Richard. ''How to Harness Gray Matter.'' *Fortune,* 9 June 1997, 168.

Waxler, Caroline. ''The Million-Dollar Suggestion Box.'' *Forbes,* 7 September 1998, 171.

SUMMIT OF THE AMERICAS

A Summit of the Americas was held in Miami, Florida, on December 9-11, 1994, and was attended by U.S. President Bill Clinton and the heads of 34 other participating governments. The primary purpose of the summit was to plan for a Free Trade Area of the Americas (FTAA) to be established by the year 2005. The meeting addressed a set of 23 initiatives and resulted in a plan of action designed to ensure the implementation of the initiatives. The goal was to establish a new set of relationships among the nations and the people of the Americas.

The Miami summit made progress toward an FTAA, but it left a great deal of work to be done. The work is to be accomplished through an inter-American system supported by three ''pillars'' or sets of actors. The first pillar is international organizations. The three named in the plan of action are the Inter-American Development Bank (IADB), the **Organization of American States** (OAS), and the **United Nations** Economic Commission on Latin America and the Caribbean (ECLAC). A Tripartite Cooperation Committee established in the plan of action coordinates their activities. The second pillar includes government ministries and various working groups established through ministerial meetings. The third pillar is made up of non-state actors. (Some commentators refer to them as the nongovernmental organizations, or NGOs.) They include nonprofit groups and private businesses. The plan of action provides for participation by the non-state actors with respect to 14 of the 23 initiatives. The various actors have been working to implement the plan of action through meetings held since 1994.

Four years after the Miami summit, another Summit of the Americas was held in Santiago, Chile, on April 18-19, 1998. At that meeting, various actors met, measured their progress, and made further plans to achieve their goal of an FTAA by the year 2005. This article provides an overview of the two summits.

BACKGROUND

SUMMITS IN 1956 AND 1967. The Miami and Chile summits were not the first ever held in the Western Hemisphere. Summits were held in 1956 and 1967, but they produced few results. In contrast, the 1994 and 1998 summits are producing visible changes, due to the fact that the governments of the Western Hemisphere and their policies changed substantially during recent decades.

CHANGES IN LATIN AMERICA. In the 1950s and 1960s, at least half of the leaders of countries of the Western Hemisphere were backed by military organizations; democracy was not the ''norm'' in countries of Central and South America. In contrast, by 1993, most countries of the Western Hemisphere were democratic, albeit to varying degrees. Cuba is the only stronghold of communism and dictatorship today, and it was the only country of this hemisphere that was not included in the Miami and Chile summits.

CHANGES IN U.S. POLICY. As governments in Latin America have changed, U.S. policy toward Latin American countries has shifted. In the 1950s and 1960s, U.S. relations with Latin America focused on U.S. aid programs and concerns about U.S. national security. There was a sharp division between the industrial Northern Hemisphere, including the United States and Canada, and the Southern Hemisphere. With the end of the Cold War, the United States began to shift its efforts to policies designed to support democracy and human rights in Central and South America. The United States also began to shift its economic policies and became receptive to bilateral and regional trade agreements. Thus, by 1994, the **North American Free Trade Agreement** (NAFTA) was adopted by the United States, Canada, and Mexico. The United States had come to view Mexico as an important political ally, and trade partner.

OTHER TRADE PACTS. By the 1994, the Western Hemisphere was covered by a variety of bilateral and multilateral **free trade** areas and trading blocs, each of which continues to operate as we enter the 21st century. They include at least five major groups: (1) the Southern Cone Common Market, more commonly known as **Mercosur** (the *Mercado Común del Sur*), (2) NAFTA, (3) the **Caribbean Community and Common Market** (CARICOM), (4) the System of Central American Integration (SICA), and (5) the Association of Caribbean States (ACS).

MIAMI SUMMIT, DECEMBER 1994

GOALS. The Miami summit had various goals, only one of which was to establish the FTAA. The FTAA is designed to unite the Western Hemisphere and its various regional trade areas into one hemispheric-wide free trade area by the year 2005. The area has tremendous potential for expanded trade. For example, the region is the fastest-growing market for U.S. exports, and U.S. exports to Latin America are expected to exceed its exports to Europe by the year 2000. An FTAA will include more than 800 million people and have a **gross domestic product** (GDP) of over

US$7 trillion, an amount that is almost one-third of the world's GDP. Other topics and goals of the summit relate to supporting democracy, dealing with poverty and discrimination, the need for education, and the need for **sustainable development**.

DECLARATION OF PRINCIPLES AND PLAN OF ACTION. The Miami summit produced a declaration of principles and a plan of action. The plan of action included 23 initiatives and more than 150 action items. The initiatives and the action items provide an implementation strategy for the new inter-American system. The initiatives and the action items, in turn, were divided into four sets.

The first is ''Preserving and Strengthening the Community of Democracies of the Americas.'' Brazil and Canada are coordinating a working group that covers matters including reforming electoral laws, supervision of elections, local conflict resolution, and peace-building in Haiti and Central America.

The second is the goal of creating the FTAA by the year 2005. To achieve that goal, the trade ministers of the Western Hemisphere have met on a continuing basis. For example, they met in Denver, Colorado, in June 1996; Cartagena, Colombia, in March 1996; Belo Horizonte, Brazil, in May 1997; and San José, Costa Rica, in March 1998. Negotiations for the FTAA were officially launched at the Santiago, Chile, summit in 1998.

The third set of initiatives is designed to eradicate poverty and discrimination in the Western Hemisphere. Much of the work being done in this area is being done by international, nongovernmental organizations. Universal access to health services is one initiative, and is being coordinated by the Pan-American Health Organization. The OAS, ECLAC, and the IADB have worked together on issues related to the status of women. They are working to identify needs and develop strategies to meet those needs. Educational needs were included within this group of initiatives at the Miami summit, but they were been identified as a separate set for the Santiago summit.

A fourth set of initiatives related to the need for sustainable development, with emphasis on energy, pollution prevention, and biodiversity. Two energy initiatives were jointly led by Venezuela (through its Ministry of Energy and Pétroleos de Venezuela) and the U.S. government (through its Department of Energy).

AFTERMATH, 1994-98. During the four years following the Miami summit, results were mixed according to Richard Feinberg, a former Clinton adviser on Latin America and the person who is viewed as the ''architect'' of the Miami summit. He asserted that progress was made on the war on drugs and money laundering in Latin America, but the needs to strengthen democracy, protect human rights, improve education, and protect biodiversity need greater efforts.

Further, in the aftermath of the Miami summit, many countries of Latin America believe that their commitment and work toward establishing the FTAA have been greater than those of the United States. For example, at the close of the Miami summit, the United States, Canada, and Mexico announced their goal that Chile was to become the next member of (an expanded) NAFTA by the year 1996. That goal, however, has not been met. Chile stipulated that ''fast track'' legislation in the United States was a prerequisite to its negotiations with the United States. (Fast track legislation allows the U.S. president to negotiate a trade agreement and present it to the U.S. Congress for a ''yes or no'' vote, without amendment. It was in effect in the United States from 1974 to 1994.) Since fast track legislation expired in 1994, the U.S. Congress has refused to reauthorize it, and negotiations with Chile have stalled. Thus, the United States is viewed as ''dragging its feet'' with respect to Chile.

SANTIAGO SUMMIT, APRIL 1998

The Santiago, Chile, summit was held April 18-19, 1998. At that summit, three of the original four sets of initiatives were addressed, with the addition of consideration of education as a separate, fourth set of initiatives. First, progress in the area of democracy was documented and commitment to the various initiatives was reaffirmed. The IADB, the **World Bank**, and the **Agency for International Development** (AID) promised a total of $5.9 billion over a period of three years to support reform of justice systems, improve working conditions (including elimination of **child labor**), strengthen local governments, and other initiatives.

Second, in the area of economic integration, negotiations for the FTAA were launched. The IADB, the World Bank, and AID pledged a total of $18.8 billion over a three-year period. Those funds will be used to promote stable financial markets, protect the environment, develop clean energy sources, promote integrated transportation and telecommunication systems, as well as other projects.

Third, poverty-related initiatives were addressed. Discussion focused on assistance to micro enterprises, the need for poverty registration for the poor, the needs of women and other vulnerable groups, health care including immunization projects and the need for clean drinking water, and programs to fight hunger and malnutrition. The IADB, the World Bank, and AID pledged a total of US$12.5 billion for three years to work to meet these needs.

Fourth, education issues were addressed in a fourth set of initiatives, separate from poverty and discrimination issues. The need to strengthen primary and secondary education through teacher **training**, provide more text books, increase international exchange, and other programs was emphasized. To help fund projects, the IADB and the World Bank agreed to supply US$8.3 billion in **loans** over a three-year period.

Sustainable development, which was one of the four main initiatives at the Miami summit, was not a major area of discussion at the Santiago summit. It was dealt with separately, however, at the Santa Cruz Summit of the Americas on Sustainable Development held in December 1996, in Santa Cruz, Bolivia. Representatives of all 34 countries involved in the Miami and Santiago summits participated. They produced a plan of action that included 65 action items to be implemented in the hemisphere and to be funded, at least in part, by the Work Bank, OAS, and IADB.

LOOKING AHEAD

The Summit of the Americas in Miami in 1994 and the summit in Santiago in 1998 produced an ambitious plan of action covering democracy, education, economic integration, poverty and discrimination, and sustainable development. Economic integration, with the goal of an FTAA by the year 2005, was the centerpiece of the two summits and the goal that received the most media attention. And, as we move into the 21st century, trade integration is likely to continue to be the yardstick most frequently used to measure the results of the two summits. Yet, the challenge that lies ahead is for the 34 nations to move forward to meet the multiple important goals of the two summits.

[Paulette L. Stenzel]

FURTHER READING:

Carter, Tom. ''Miami Summit 'Architect' Sees Gains: Feinberg Urges 'Fast Track' for Clinton.'' *Washington Times,* 6 May 1997, A15.

Feinberg, Richard E. *Summitry in the Americas: A Progress Report.* Institute for International Economics, 1997.

''The Road to the Summit: From Miami to Santiago.'' Available from www.americasnet.net/eng/index.html.

Robins, Linda, and others. ''Reaching for New Heights.'' *U.S. News and World Report,* 12 December 1994, 68.

Rosenberg, Robin, and Steve Stein, eds. *Advancing the Miami Process: Civil Society and the Summit of the Americas.* North-South Center Press, University of Miami, 1995.

SUPERFUND

SEE: Comprehensive Environmental Response, Compensation and Liability Act (CERCLA) of 1980

SUPERVISION

Supervision is a somewhat misunderstood term in its business context. Generally, supervision applies to **management** of first-level, or production, employees. Many people use it interchangeably with management. The terms are not always synonymous.

Supervision is managing others through **leadership** and personal influence. Management means simply getting things done, not necessarily through coordination of the efforts of other people. Thus, an individual can be a good manager without ever dealing with people. A supervisor, however, exercises hands-on influence and leadership skills to guide others. Effective supervisors share many qualities, including the ability to maintain distance from their employees without losing awareness of their activities, yet still caring about their productiveness and well-being. Similarly, effective supervisors are direct and fair in their dealings with employees under their direction. When supervisors discharge their duties effectively, productivity rises and employees enjoy greater job satisfaction.

HISTORICAL OVERVIEW

Historically, supervisors were not trained to deal with subordinates. Rather, they managed by force and intimidation. It was not until the early part of the 20th century that supervision became a subject of study among management theorists.

In the early 1900s, researchers such as Frederick W. Taylor (1856-1915), Frank Gilbreth (1868-1925) and Lillian Gilbreth (1878-1972), and Chester Barnard (1886-1961) began analyzing what motivated workers. Taylor, who is often called the ''Father of Scientific Management,'' published two books, *Shop Management* (1903) and *Principles of Scientific Management* (1911), in which he said it was management's job to set up methods and standards of work and to provide incentives to workers to increase production. A few years later, the Gilbreths began to concentrate on time and motion studies and the improvement of methods of work. The Gilbreths' approach was to seek the best way to produce a certain product and then have managers teach all workers that best way. Barnard developed what is known as the acceptance theory, which suggested that if managers were to be effective, workers had to accept their authority. Conversely, management must also take steps to ensure effective supervision of employees. Supervisors require **training**, should be provided with personal and professional development goals, need the full backing of the corporate hierarchy, and are well served by the maintenance of a corporate supervisory resource center.

THE THREE LEVELS OF MANAGEMENT

There are three levels of management: executive, middle, and supervisory. Technically speaking, management is the process by which an individual or group directs the use of resources—for example, money, people, and things—toward common goals. Generally, the executive managers are responsible for overall planning, **strategy**, structure, etc. It is their role to oversee total operations, and usually they do not have much to do with the actual production process. They establish the company's mission and goals and leave the management of production to the next two levels.

Managers at the middle level manage other managers, i.e., the supervisors. They generally have less technical training than first-level supervisors. They are evaluated more on their managerial skills than their technical skills. Since they spend more of their time managing, production supervision is left to the first-level managers, the supervisors.

THE SUPERVISOR'S ROLE AND FUNCTIONS

Supervisors play an important role in the business environment. Their primary job is to see that the work performed by employees is completed on time and at the highest level of quality. In order to complete this task, they must know the production process and have an understanding of human behavior. Theirs is a pressure-filled job.

Supervisors perform a wide range of functions, all of which are closely intertwined. For example, they must be excellent communicators. It is their job to write reports, letters, memos, performance appraisals, and the gamut of documents that businesses need to operate. They must be equally comfortable in communicating with **chief executive officers** and assembly-line production workers. They must be able to run effective meetings. They must carefully monitor the organization's goals, strategies, tactics, and production schedules. They must be cognizant of union rules where applicable. They must be trainers, confidants, computer experts, goal setters—in short, supervisors must be well-rounded employees who are willing to accept the responsibilities required to keep a company running.

SUPERVISOR AS COMMUNICATOR. Supervisors are required to communicate with a variety of personnel in the course of their jobs. Approaches that might improve the productivity of people in their 20s, for example, are not generally applicable to people in their 50s. Similarly, supervisors must deal with people with a wide range of personal styles, regardless of their ages and backgrounds. Supervisors must be able to write and speak concisely, clearly, consistently, and courteously with senior managers, production workers, customers, suppliers, and other people who have an interest in the organization's activities. It is the supervisor's responsibility to start the upward communication process to inform middle and senior managers about production problems, adherence to production schedules, budget variances, and other matters. Furthermore, supervisors must be able to react to downward communications from senior managers in order to address problems as quickly and efficiently as possible.

Supervisory reporting mechanisms most commonly involve oral and written reports needed to protect their workers, the organization, and themselves from legal actions. For instance, supervisors must know when and in what form to document problems with personnel, which regulatory forms must be completed, to whom they must be submitted, and how frequently they should be done. Supervisors must also understand laws and ethical guidelines governing employee surveillance as they endeavor to monitor employee performance. Privacy issues play an increasingly large role in the workplace, as practices including drug testing, videotaping of employees, reviewing the computer files of employees, and monitoring the phone conversations of employees become commonplace in the business world. A large part of a supervisor's time is spent communicating. In fact, some estimates suggest that supervisors spend as much as 70 percent of their time communicating in one form or another.

SUPERVISOR AS TRAINER. An effective supervisor must be a polished trainer. It is part of the supervisor's responsibility to demonstrate to workers exactly how certain procedures are performed. Supervisors must also be excellent learners. Workers expect their supervisors to be doers as well as teachers. Therefore, supervisors must be able to master the tasks that workers are assigned to perform. This ability is much more critical for first line supervisors than those in middle and senior management, especially in industries using production processes. A thorough understanding of all jobs involved in a given production process is essential to effective supervision, as supervisors are ultimately responsible for deploying their **workforce** in the most productive and efficient manner possible.

SUPERVISOR AS STUDENT. For supervisors, life is a learning process. Not only must they learn the rudiments of their subordinates' jobs, but they must also learn basic supervisory skills. They must take courses in management, **computers**, communications, and other skills that will help them in their supervisory roles. If they do not continually update their skills, they will fail as supervisors, which is something neither they nor their organizations can afford.

SUPERVISOR AS GOAL SETTER. Supervisors are responsible for setting goals for themselves and their subordinates. In addition, they are charged with ensuring that unit and individual goals set by senior management are met. They must sit down with their subordinates and work together to set goals and monitor progress. This function requires full employment of the supervisor's communications skills.

Supervisors cannot simply set goals and then ignore them. First, they must set realistic goals for themselves and their staff members. Then, they must establish communications channels through which they and their subordinates monitor progress. This involves constant feedback between supervisors and subordinates, without which supervisors cannot be effective.

SUPERVISOR AS EVALUATOR. It is the supervisor's job to evaluate workers on a regular basis. Workers appreciate feedback on their progress. Generally, they want honest and frequent appraisals of their work and suggestions from their supervisors on how to improve their performance.

SUPERVISOR AS HUMAN RESOURCES SPECIALIST. Supervisors need to be aware of the needs of their subordinates. For example, they must know how to motivate people, how to reward them, how and when to discipline them, and when and how to refer them to **employee assistance programs**. They may have the assistance of human resources specialists in some of these areas, but the basic responsibility is the supervisor's. Given their daily presence among their employees, supervisors play a critical role in maintaining good moral among the workforce. Employees who are happy and take pride in their work are more productive, loyal, and responsive to overall corporate goals and projects.

SUPERVISOR AS COMPUTER EXPERT. In today's business environment, supervisors must be computer proficient. Many of today's management functions are tied closely to computers. For example, computers are used extensively in **decision making**, production scheduling, and product design. Supervisors are not responsible for many of the functions facilitated by computers, but they must have a working knowledge of how computers operate and their role in the production process.

In the production end of business, organizations are relying more and more on computer-integrated manufacturing (CIM). CIM comprises several types of systems, such as **computer-aided design** (CAD), **computer-aided manufacturing** (CAM), and **flexible manufacturing systems** (FMS) to aid in the manufacturing process. CAD uses computers to geometrically prepare, review, and evaluate product designs. CAM uses computers to design and control production processes. Finally, FMS is a manufacturing system that uses computers to control machines and the production process automatically so that different types of parts or product configurations can be handled on the same production line. It is essential that supervisors understand how these computerized systems work if they are to remain technologically current. First-level supervisors in particular must stay abreast of developments in computerized production systems. They must also be in positions to advise senior management as to what computerized systems are applicable in particular environments and what are not.

SUPERVISOR AS PRODUCER. The supervisor is inextricably linked to the production of goods and services. First, supervisors must be knowledgeable about the production process they control. They are responsible for a large variety of simultaneous activities in the ongoing production process. For example, to a large extent they control the production schedule. Supervisors are invariably involved in product planning design, project staffing, employee training, simplification of work methods, maintenance of equipment, and organization of tasks and activities while striving to keep relations with workers as amicable as possible. While performing these tasks, supervisors must keep the object of meeting organizational or corporate goals in the forefront.

The supervisor's tasks in the production process also include equipment and materials management, such as establishing guidelines for layout of the work being performed and selecting the right equipment for each job. Supervisors must schedule carefully to ensure that time is not wasted. It is a fact of business that idle time and workers are unproductive, costly, and a waste of capital investment. Thus, supervisors must be effective time managers and employee motivators. They must also keep an eye on technological developments, since innovative advancements in machinery and work performance techniques are constantly being made.

Supervisors must keep one eye on the future when performing their tasks. For example, a punch machine in a factory may become outdated and need to be replaced. It is an axiom in the manufacturing world that what is right for a particular job today may be outdated tomorrow. Therefore, supervisors may not only need to recommend new equipment, but might also be required to do economic analyses to justify the purchase of new machinery. In some cases, they might also be asked to maintain machinery or upgrade computer **software** systems. At the least, they must be effective communicators who can convince senior management of the need for upgraded machinery and the justification for capital expenditure outlays.

SUPERVISOR AS ADVISER. Supervisors must be particularly effective in an advisory role. Supervisors who can advise senior managers, middle managers, and subordinates on topics that affect their work activities are valuable. The problem is to restrict advice only to those areas directly related to individuals' needs at a particular time. More often than not, the supervisor does not provide detailed advice on particular issues. Generally, the supervisor's role is to point employees toward qualified professionals who can be of assistance. That in itself requires that supervisors be aware of where the proper professionals can be found.

There is seemingly no end to the areas in which supervisors become advisers. In whatever area the advice is provided, it must be aimed at improving individuals' performance and meeting organizational goals. As such, supervisors are called on to advise staff members' regarding their job performance and their personal lives as they relate to the organization's goals.

Many organizations today sponsor employee assistance programs (EAPs). These programs provide constructive responses to employees' substance abuse, psychological, family, and other personal problems. Through such programs, employers help employees overcome personal problems that adversely affect their performance and interfere with the achievement of organizational goals. Supervisors play an important role in EAP programs.

It is often the supervisor's responsibility to recognize problems that interfere with employees' work. Once such a problem is identified, the supervisor must refer the affected employees to EAP counselors or outside counselors who can assist in finding or providing treatment for the individuals' problems.

Skill development is yet another area in which the supervisor becomes an adviser. Supervisors who do not encourage their subordinates to develop their personal and work-related skills are defeating their own purposes and depriving employees of valuable training and advancement opportunities. Supervisors must have a grasp of what training is available, how it relates specifically to individual employees' needs, and where such training can be completed.

It is imperative that supervisors work with their employees to set up individual continuing development and training programs. To be able to do so, supervisors must know each employee's strengths and weaknesses and structure individual development programs accordingly. It is of no benefit to supervisor or employee to randomly select training courses that may be of no value to the individual or the organization. For example, sending a computer-illiterate machine operator whose communications skills are weak to a spreadsheet training session is of no value. Supervisors must be able to assess which continuing training programs will benefit which individuals. This can only be done by supervisors who are themselves well-trained and active participants in continuing development programs. Again, supervisors are merely advisers in the continuing education process, but their advice can make or break individuals and the organization.

SUPERVISOR AS IDEA CHAMPION. An idea champion is an individual who generates a new idea or believes in the value of a new idea and supports it in the face of potential obstacles. Generally, idea champions are members of the lower supervisory levels. They typically are creative people who are willing to take risks. Consequently, they frequently have trouble convincing senior managers that a particular idea or system will be beneficial to the organization. Thus, idea champions must often coordinate their activities with sponsors, who are more often than not middle-level managers.

SUPERVISOR AS ENVIRONMENTAL WATCHDOG. Contemporary supervisors exemplify the prototypical knowledge workers that the business world is beginning to demand. They must be knowledgeable about a wide range of environmental issues and workplace safety programs. Today's supervisors must be aware of public policy issues that were of no concern to their predecessors, but which are taking on added importance today.

Businesses today are corporate citizens. As such, their leaders must be aware of statutes and administrative laws affecting business. Additionally, ethical standards, changes in ideologies and values, and the involvement of the media in corporate affairs must be considered. Finally, society's attitudes toward business have changed dramatically over the past few years. These changes have had a profound effect on supervisors at all levels and have made their jobs more complex. For example, supervisors today must have a broader knowledge of legislation affecting production than did their predecessors. They must be careful to regulate the amount of air, water, and ground pollution released by the machinery and processes they oversee. In particular, they must have some knowledge of the reporting mechanisms that provide governmental regulatory agencies with the information they need to ensure statutory compliance. It is the first-level supervisors who are closest to the production process. Therefore, it is primarily their responsibility to make sure the production process is safe for their workers and the public.

Supervisors must also have a working knowledge of federal regulations administered by the Food and Drug Administration, the **Environmental Protection Agency**, the **National Labor Relations Board**, **Equal Employment Opportunity Commission**, the **Consumer Product Safety Commission**—the list is a long one. It is virtually impossible for individual supervisors to familiarize themselves with all the governmental regulations affecting their jobs today. To compound matters, many supervisors are working in the international arena as global **competition** expands. This requires them to widen their knowledge and experience even more.

SUPERVISOR AS INTERNATIONAL MANAGER. The emergence of large international businesses is creating a new demand for supervisors who can manage effectively in difficult circumstances. Contemporary supervisors are well-advised to learn new languages and become aware of cultural differences among workers. They must learn international trade laws and regulations and the differences in reward and punishment systems. They have to learn how to motivate workers in different countries and differentiate between what is ethical and legal in one country but not in another. There is no doubt that acquiring the knowledge and experience to supervise an international business is placing even more pressure on managers, but it is also opening new opportunities for supervisors.

THE NEW CHALLENGE FOR SUPERVISORS

The future holds much potential for supervisors. They have long been an important part of the business world. It would be impossible to conduct business on any scale were it not for the presence of qualified supervisors who can lead production workers. Supervisors function as leaders, trainers, goal setters, environmental watchdogs, facilitators, communicators, and more. Simply put, they are the backbone of the business world, and will continue to be as long as there is business to conduct.

SEE ALSO: Goal Setting; Human Resource Management; Leadership; Management

[Arthur G. Sharp, updated by Grant Eldridge]

FURTHER READING:

Chapman, Elwood N. *Supervisor's Survival Kit.* New York: Macmillan, 1990.

Daresh, John C. *Supervision as a Proactive Process.* Prospect Heights, IL: Waveland Press, 1991.

Eigen, Barry. *How to Think Like a Boss and Get Ahead at Work.* New York: Carol Publishing Group, 1990.

Fulmer, Robert M., and Stephen G. Franklin. *Supervision: Principles of Professional Management.* New York: Macmillan, 1982.

Giesecke, Joan, ed. *Practical Help for New Supervisors.* Chicago: American Library Association, 1992.

Hartman, Laura Pincus. ''The Rights and Wrongs of Workplace Snooping.'' *Journal of Business Strategy* 19, no. 3 (May/June 1998): 16.

Hubbard, Andrew S. ''Supervisory Development.'' *Mortgage Banking* 57, no. 1 (October 1996): 166.

Lambert, Clark. *The Complete Book of Supervisory Training.* New York: John Wiley & Sons, Inc., 1984.

Lowery, Robert C. *Supervisory Management: Guides for Application.* Englewood Cliffs, NJ: Prentice Hall, 1985.

Oradat, Greg D. ''A Supervisor's Responsibility in a Gainsharing and Continuous Improvement Environment.'' *Supervision* 59, no. 5 (May 1998): 3.

Radde, Paul O. *Supervising: A Guide for All Levels.* Austin, TX: Learning Concepts. 1981.

Satava, David, and Jim Weber. ''The ABCs of Supervision.'' *Journal of Accountancy* 185, no. 2 (February 1998): 72.

Seidenfeld, Martin. ''The Art of Supervision.'' *Supervision* 59, no. 4 (April 1998): 14.

Shulman, Lawrence. *Skills of Supervision and Staff Management.* Itasca, IL: F. E. Peacock Publishers, 1981.

Steinmetz, Lawrence L. *Supervision: First Line Management.* Homewood, IL: Irwin, 1992.

Weiss, W. H. ''Employee Involvement, Commitment, and Cooperation: Keys to Successful Supervision.'' *Supervision* 59O, no. 11 (November 1998): 12.

SUPPLY CHAIN MANAGEMENT

Supply chain management—a term that first appeared in the late 1980s—refers to the management of a distribution channel across organizations. All the members of the channel, from suppliers to end users, coordinate their business activities and processes to minimize their total costs and maximize their effectiveness in the market. The goal is to achieve the coordination and continuity of a vertically integrated channel without centralized ownership of the entities comprising the channel. The firms in the channel form a long-term partnership or strategic alliance in order to improve service to the end consumer, reduce channel costs, and create a competitive advantage.

Supply chain management can be contrasted with a traditional distribution channel in which firms deal with one another on a short-term, arm's-length basis, with each one trying to maximize their own gain from each transaction. Without supply chain management, the relationship between firms in the channel lasts only from transaction to transaction. Most organizations in the traditional channel do not really see themselves as part of a vertically integrated channel. They only see themselves as independent businesses that buy from suppliers at the lowest possible price and sell to customers at the highest possible price. Diseconomies caused by redundancies, particularly of inventory, are common in such a channel. By looking across the entire channel, supply chain management tries to eliminate these redundancies.

There are a number of key characteristics of supply chain management. One of the most important is that the firms involved see themselves as part of the channel and understand that their future depends to a large extent on the success of the whole channel. The relationships are viewed as long term, and the **corporate cultures**, philosophies, and missions are similar. There is joint planning of products, locations, and quantities of inventory to be kept in the system. There is also a great deal of information sharing between firms in order to coordinate the efficient flow of goods through the channel. Modern computing and communication technology, such as **electronic data interchange**, is used to rapidly provide information within the channel as needed. Cost advantages are exploited wherever possible. For example, the production of a product requiring a great deal of human labor would be produced by the member with the lowest labor costs.

Performance of a company's supply chain management can be analyzed in terms of cost control, customer service, and asset productivity. A study of leading supply chain management companies, conducted by William C. Copacino in association with the Massachusetts Institute of Technology, suggests there are several areas in which the leaders excel. These include functional excellence in such areas as procurement, manufacturing, transportation and distribution, and customer service, with a highly developed level of skills and integrated management. Leaders are also skilled at managing complexity, especially the management of surge and uncertainty in such areas as new product introductions, product-line complexity, and seasonal variations. Leading supply chain managers also employ the best information technology for applications, **data management**, decision-support tools, and communications. They are able to leverage the distinctive capabilities of supply chain providers as well as to create an extended supply chain with visibility and collaboration across the channel.

The rapid growth of **electronic commerce** is expected to have an effect on supply chain management. Benefits include process efficiency, with greatly reduced costs made possible by utilizing the power of the **Internet** to enhance efficiency and effectiveness of various supply chain processes from order entry to supplier management. Electronic commerce will also result in channel restructuring, the elimination of some intermediaries, and a drastic reduction of channel inventories, handling costs, and transition costs. Companies will be able to better integrate electronically with their suppliers and customers to lower transaction costs, manufacturing costs, and supply costs, among other benefits.

SEE ALSO: Business Logistics; Channels of Distribution; Physical Distribution Management

[George C. Jackson, updated by David P. Bianco]

FURTHER READING:

Copacino, William C. "A Cost-to-Serve Analysis Can Be an Eye-Opener." *Logistics Management Distribution Report,* 30 April 1999, 33.

——. "Electronic Commerce: How It Will Affect Logistics." *Logistics Management,* March 1997, 39.

——. "eSupplyChain.com." *Logistics Management Distribution Report,* 28 February 1999, 30.

——. "A Growing Tidal Wave of Supply-Chain Outsourcing." *Logistics Management Distribution Report,* September 1998, 38.

——. "The IT-Enabled Supply Chain: Key to Future Success." *Logistics Management Distribution Report,* April 1998, 36.

——. "Masters of the Supply Chain." *Logistics Management Distribution Report,* 31 December 1998, 23.

——. "Sell What You Make, Stupid!" *Logistics Management Distribution Report,* 31 January 1999, 34.

——. *Supply Chain Management.* Boca Raton, FL: Saint Lucie Press, 1997.

——. "Surge and Uncertainty: The Real Supply-Chain Test." *Logistics Management Distribution Report,* June 1998, 32.

Robeson, James F., and William C. Copacino, eds. *The Logistics Handbook.* New York: Free Press, 1994.

SUSTAINABLE DEVELOPMENT

The term "sustainable development" is used widely throughout the world today, and it is used in many contexts. Yet, it has become almost a buzz word, used by many people without a clear articulation of its meaning. Therefore, it is important to begin with a definition. The **United Nations (UN)** is credited with developing the term, which was defined by a UN body called the World Commission on the Environment and Development in a 1987 report titled *Our Common Future.* The World Commission defined sustainable development as development which, "meets the needs of the present without compromising the ability of future generations to meet their own needs." Since *Our Common Future* was released, the goal of sustainable development has been embraced by environmentalists, governments, and businesses throughout the world.

Sustainable development needs to be viewed in the context of a global economy in which goods, people, information, and ideas are moving across borders at an unprecedented pace. It is a far-reaching overall concept that encompasses multiple social, economic, and environmental goals.

The world's population doubled between 1950 and 1990, and it is expected to have doubled again early in the 21st century, demonstrating the social needs of sustainable development. Yet, much of the world lives in poverty. Hundreds of millions lack access to clean drinking water and suffer from malnutrition. Sustainable development can help up the basic needs of the world's population.

Economic growth can help reduce poverty. In Latin America, Asia, and elsewhere, economic growth has created new industrial centers. But, increased industrialization leads to environmental problems including air, water, and ground pollution.

Further, increased population and economic development have led to destruction of habitats and species. It is said that 80 percent of the world's forests have been destroyed, and deforestation continues in India, China, Latin America, and elsewhere. The amounts of ocean species such as whales, salmon, and cod have been seriously depleted by fishing. Irreplaceable coral reefs are being destroyed through human use as well as pollution. Further, by burning fossil fuels, we are depleting limited natural resources at the same time that we are causing imbalances in the atmosphere that lead to global warming and climate changes.

Overall, sustainable development requires a shift in thinking around the world. It is an underlying goal that can only be met through attention to social needs, **economic development**, and environmental protection. Sustainable development is often articulated as policy, but it must also be translated into action in our daily lives.

The various aspects of sustainable development can fill volumes, and therefore this article will provide only an introduction to some of the topic's many facets. First, it summarizes the history of the concept. Next, it discusses the pursuit of sustainable development in the United States. And finally, it examines three differing, yet interrelated, avenues through which the goal of sustainable development is being pursued: trade agreements, programs established by non-governmental organizations, and environmental law.

ARTICULATION OF THE CONCEPT AND GOALS

The United Nations (UN) has become increasingly involved in environmental issues since the late 1960s. In 1968, the UN passed a resolution in which it pledged to work to find solutions to environmental problems. In 1972, it held a Conference on the Human Environment in Stockholm, Sweden, and, as a result of that conference, the UN General Assembly established the United Nations Environmental Programme. In 1983, the General Assembly took another major step by establishing the World Commission on the Environment and Development (World Commission).

THE WORLD COMMISSION—OUR COMMON FUTURE. The World Commission conducted an in-depth, four-year study addressing interlocking ecological and economic threats and resulting concerns for the earth. As a result of its study, the Commission released a 1987 report titled *Our Common Future,* which is sometimes referred to as the Brundtland Report. In that report, the Commission defined sustainable development and its pursuit as important goals for the nations of the world. The Commission discussed the interrelationships among various crises facing citizens throughout the world. ''[A]n environmental crisis, a development crisis, an energy crisis. They are all one. . . . Ecology and economy are becoming ever more interwoven—locally, regionally, nationally, and globally—into a seamless net of causes and effects.''

RIO DE JANEIRO SUMMIT. The United Nations Conference on the Environment and Development (UNCED), was held in Rio de Janeiro (the Rio Conference) in 1992 and attended by representatives of over one hundred nations. As a result of the Rio Conference, UNCED issued ''Agenda 21,'' which is a statement of principles for implementing sustainable development in industrialized and developing countries around the world. Agenda 21 recommends that each country create a national council for sustainable development. As of late 1997, nearly 100 such councils had been created around the world including the President's Council on Sustainable Development (PCSD), created by President Bill Clinton in the United States.

THE PRESIDENT'S COUNCIL ON SUSTAINABLE DEVELOPMENT

President Clinton appointed leaders of major corporations, environmental groups, labor organizations, civil rights groups, and others to serve on the PCSD. Also serving were the Secretaries of Agriculture, Energy, and Commerce, as well as the Administrator of the Environmental Protection Agency.

After meetings held around the United States, the PCSD delivered a report to President Clinton in which it adopted the World Commission's definition of sustainable development and set out principles, 10 national goals, and 59 policy recommendations designed to promote sustainable development in the United States. The policy recommendations cover topics including population, agriculture, natural resource management, environmental regulation, strengthening communities, and public education. In its report, the PCSD emphasized the need for an integrated approach at the community level. Each person must be provided with opportunities to participate in decisions that will affect his or her future. The report emphasizes that knowledge is a key component in economic development, solving environmental problems, and working toward sustainable development.

SUSTAINABLE DEVELOPMENT AND TRADE NEGOTIATIONS

NAFTA. The North American Free Trade Agreement (NAFTA) took effect on January 1, 1994. It includes more provisions related to the environment than any international agreement or treaty entered into by the United States prior to that date. Environmentalists and labor leaders had a major influence on NAFTA. They worked together during debate on NAFTA, and their actions led to the negotiation of an Environmental Side Agreement and a Labor Side Agreement that were appended to NAFTA before it was considered by the U.S. Congress. NAFTA has been hailed as taking a major step forward for the environment, even though its provisions are limited. The Environmental Side Agreement mentions the pursuit of sustainable development three times, however, it is named only as a goal. NAFTA does not require pursuit or attainment of sustainable development. The body of NAFTA does, however, include numerous provisions related to environmental protection. For example, it covers phytosanitary measures (related to protection of human, animal, or plant life) and standards-related measures. The Side Agreement does not create new environmental laws, but the United States, Canada, and Mexico each promise to enforce their own environmental laws.

SUMMIT(S) OF THE AMERICAS. In December of 1994, President Clinton and leaders of 33 other Western Hemisphere countries met in Miami, Florida for the first **Summit of the Americas** since 1967. The purpose of the Summit was to plan for a Free Trade Area of the Americas (FTAA) to be established by the year 2005. The Miami Summit produced a Declaration of Principles and a Plan of Action. The Plan of Action included 23 initiatives, divided among four sets. The first set concerns strengthening democracy in the Americas. The second set outlines steps toward creating the FTAA, and the third set includes measures designed to eliminate discrimination and poverty in the Western Hemisphere. The fourth set is titled, ''Guaranteeing Sustainable Development and Conserving Our Natural Environment for Future Generations'' and includes three initiatives covering sustainable energy use, biodiversity, and pollution prevention.

Efforts have continued since the 1994 Summit. Sustainable development was addressed in a separate summit: the Santa Cruz Summit of the Americas on Sustainable Development held in December 1996 in Santa Cruz, Bolivia. Representatives of all of the 34 Miami Summit countries participated and produced a Plan of Action that includes 65 action items. In addition, funding was promised by the **World Bank**, the Organization of American States (OAS), and Inter-American Development Bank (IADB).

SUSTAINABLE DEVELOPMENT AND NON-GOVERNMENTAL ORGANIZATIONS (NGOs)

Business leaders are involved in the pursuit of sustainable development through various avenues. In some cases, they work with coalitions of environmentalists and other citizens. Other cases, they have incorporated discussion of sustainable development in the programs of privately-run organizations.

COALITIONS. Coalitions of environmental groups such as the Sierra Club, Greenpeace, and the Natural Resources Defense Council (NRDC) are credited with encouraging professional business organizations to develop guidelines on environmental management practices. One example is the Responsible Care(r) (CARE(r)) Program, adopted by the Chemical Manufacturers' Association (CMA). The program is designed to improve handling and disposal of chemicals. All members of the CMA are required to participate in the CARE(r) program. Another example is found in the activities of the Coalition for Environmentally Responsible Economies (CERES), a coalition of environmental groups, government agencies, investors, and economists that convened in the aftermath of a March 1989 accident in which the Exxon Valdez oil tanker spilled 11 million gallons of crude oil into Alaska's Prince William Sound. The CERES group a set of ten principles for environmental management that were first named the *Valdez Principles* and later renamed the *CERES Principles.* The group's initiatives have encouraged businesses to disclose environmental performance records to the public.

ISO 14000. The efforts of the CMA, CERES, environmental groups, and others set the stage for action by the **International Organization for Standardization (ISO)**. The ISO is a private standards organization that has been in operation since 1947. In 1996, the ISO issued its new **ISO 14000** Series International Environmental Management Standards. Those standards name attainment of sustainable development as a major goal, and they include standards for environmental management systems (EMSs) that can be adopted by companies around the world. Provisions within the ISO 14000 Series allow companies to obtain certification for environmental management standards, thus providing a way for companies to demonstrate environmental efforts to governments, environmentalists, consumers, and other companies. The standards and their widespread implementation are viewed evidence of a major shift in corporate attitudes and practices with respect to environmental protection.

SUSTAINABLE DEVELOPMENT THROUGH ENVIRONMENTAL LAW

Finally, individual countries continue to pursue sustainable development through national environmental law. In the United States such laws include, but are not limited to, the Clean Air Act, the Clean Water Act, the Toxic Substance Control Act, the Comprehensive Environmental Response, Clean-up and Liability Act (CERCLA, also known as Superfund), and the regulations implementing those statutes. The U.S. Endangered Species Act, passed in 1973, predates worldwide discussion of sustainable development, but its importance is underscored as we work toward sustainable development. In addition, new laws are needed to deal with concerns about biotechnology and biodiversity. For example, while some scientists promote biotechnology as a tool for developing a sustainable global environment, others fear that genetically modified organisms pose a threat to the environment.

A few U.S. laws are mentioned here by way of example, but discussion of the environmental laws of individual countries is beyond the scope of this article. Nevertheless, it is important to acknowledge that such laws are part of the overall set of tools that will continue to be used by citizens and governments around the world in the pursuit of sustainable development.

CONCLUSION

Sustainable development involves the pursuit of myriad social, economic, and environmental goals. Thus, it must be pursued through many avenues, by millions of people, and through thousands of organizations.

Since the UN's World Commission defined sustainable development in *Our Common Future* in 1987, progress has been made. For example, coalitions of business people and citizens worked to develop the *CERES Principles* in 1989. Those principles, and the efforts of those who developed them, have prompted businesses to work to voluntarily develop environmental management systems (EMSs). In connection with that impetus, the ISO 14000 Series Environmental Management Standards have been developed. As a result, over 200,000 companies around the world have developed EMS systems that have been certified pursuant to the ISO 14000 Series standards.

Simultaneously, governments have agreed to name sustainable development as a goal in trade agreements, in international agreements, and in national-level statutes. Thus, sustainable development is named as a goal in NAFTA, and it is a primary topic of discussion among the nations of the Western Hemisphere as they work toward a Free Trade Area of the Americans. And, it is considered, and often incorporated, as new environmental laws are drafted and existing laws are revised.

Sustainable development requires the efforts of all of us working as individuals and as groups. As coalitions of various interest groups work on various levels within the community, nationally, and globally, a synergy is created. That synergy is essential if we are to create a world economy based on sustainable development.

In closing, it is important to acknowledge that sustainable development is not a target that can be set, pursued, and reached. Instead it represents a goal that is still being defined, and it will continue to be redefined during the decades to come. We cannot foresee the state of our world decades from now, but we can work toward a point at which the essential needs of the world's citizens are being met without compromising the ability of future generations to meet their own needs.

SEE ALSO: Economic Development; Global Warming; International Organization for Standardization (ISO); ISO 14000; Summit of the Americas

[Paulette L. Stenzel]

FURTHER READING:

Dernbach, John C. ''Pollution Control and Sustainable Industry.'' *Natural Resources And Environment,* Fall 1997.

Feinberg, Richard E. *Summitry In The Americas: A Progress Report.* Institute for International Economics, 1997.

Lash, Jonathon. ''Toward a Sustainable Future,'' *Natural Resources And Environment,* Fall 1997.

Redick, Thomas P. ''Biotechnology, Biosafety, and Sustainable Development.'' *Natural Resources And Environment,* Fall 1997.

Robinson, Nicholas A. ''Attaining Systems for Sustainability through Environmental Law,'' *Natural Resources And Environment,* Fall 1997.

Stenzel, Paulette, L. ''Can NAFTA's Environmental Provisions Promote Sustainable Development?'' *Albany Law Review,* 1995.

World Commission On Environment And Development, Our Common Future. Oxford, England: Oxford University Press, 1987.

SUSTAINABLE GROWTH

The concept of sustainable growth was originally developed by Robert C. Higgins. The sustainable growth rate (SGR) of a firm is the maximum rate of growth in sales that can be achieved, given the firm's profitability, asset utilization, and desired dividend payout and **debt** (financial **leverage**) ratios. The variables in the model include: (1) the net profit margin on new and existing revenues (P); (2) the asset turnover ratio, which is the ratio of sales revenues to total assets (A); (3) the assets to beginning of period equity ratio (T); and (4) the retention rate, which is defined as the fraction of earnings retained in the business (R).

To compute a firm's SGR, multiply the four variables together, or, in other words, the SGR = PRAT. Alternatively, the SGR equals the retention ratio times the return on beginning of period equity. An examination of the SGR equation indicates that the SGR increases when the **profit margin** increases, the assets to beginning of period equity increases, asset turnover increases, or the retention rate increases.

The sustainable growth model assumes that the firm wants to: (1) maintain a target capital structure without issuing new equity; (2) maintain a target dividend payment ratio; and (3) increase sales as rapidly as market conditions allow. Since the asset to beginning of period equity ratio is constant and the firm's only source of new equity is retained earnings, sales and assets cannot grow any faster than the retained earnings plus the additional debt that the retained earnings can support. The SGR is consistent with the observed evidence that most corporations are reluctant to issue new equity and instead rely on the reinvestment of earnings to finance growth. Over the last decade, the **market value** of shares extinguished through repurchase or acquisition for cash by American corporations far exceeded the value of shares issued. If, however, the firm is willing to issue additional equity, there is in principle, no financial constraint on its growth rate.

USING THE SUSTAINABLE GROWTH RATE

The concept of sustainable growth can be helpful for planning healthy **corporate growth**. This concept forces managers to consider the financial consequences of sales increases and to set sales growth goals that are consistent with the operating and financial policies of the firm. Often, a conflict can arise if growth objectives are not consistent with the value of the organization's sustainable growth.

If a company's sales expand at any rate other than the sustainable rate, one or some combination of the four ratios must change. If a company's actual growth rate temporarily exceeds its sustainable rate, the required cash can likely be borrowed. When actual growth exceeds sustainable growth for longer periods, **management** must formulate a financial **strategy** from among the following options: (1) sell new equity; (2) permanently increase financial leverage (i.e., the use of debt); (3) reduce **dividends**; (4) increase the profit margin; or (5) decrease the percentage of total assets to sales.

In practice, firms may be reluctant to undertake these measures. Firms are reluctant to issue equity because of high issue costs, possible dilution of earnings per share, and the unreliable nature of equity funding on terms favorable to the issuer. A firm can increase financial leverage only if it has unused debt capacity with assets that can be pledged and its debt/equity ratio is reasonable in relation to its industry. The reduction of dividends typically has a negative impact on the company's stock price. Companies can attempt to liquidate marginal operations, increase prices, or enhance manufacturing and distribution efficiencies to improve the profit margin. In addition, firms can outsource more activities from outside vendors or lease production facilities and equipment, which has the effect of improving the asset turnover ratio. Increasing the profit margin is difficult, however, and large sustainable increases may not be possible. Therefore, it is possible for a firm to grow too rapidly, resulting in reduced liquidity and the need to deplete financial resources.

The sustainable growth model is particularly helpful in the situation in which a borrower requests additional financing. The need for additional **loans** creates a potentially risky situation of too much debt and too little equity. Either additional equity must be raised or the borrower will have to reduce the rate of expansion to a level that can be sustained without an increase in financial leverage.

Mature firms often have actual growth rates that are less than the sustainable growth rate. In these cases, management's principal objective is finding productive uses for the cash flows in excess of their needs. Options are to return the money to shareholders through increased dividends or **common stock** repurchases, reduce debt, or increase lower-earning liquid assets. Note that these actions serve to decrease the sustainable growth rate. Alternatively, these firms can attempt to enhance their actual growth rates through the acquisition of rapidly growing companies.

Growth can come from two sources: increased volume and **inflation**. The inflationary increase in assets must be financed as though it were real growth. Inflation increases the amount of external financing required and increases the debt/equity ratio when this ratio is measured on a historical cost basis. Thus, if creditors require that a firm's historical cost debt/equity ratio stay constant, inflation lowers the firm's sustainable growth rate.

SEE ALSO: Financial Ratios

[Robert T. Kleiman,
updated by Ronald M. Horwitz]

FURTHER READING:

Charan, Ram, and Noel M. Tichy. *Every Business Is a Growth Business.* Times Books, 1998.

Galpin, Timothy J. *Making Strategy Work: Building Sustainable Growth Capability.* San Francisco: Jossey-Bass, 1997.

Higgins, Robert C. "How Much Growth Can the Firm Afford?" *Financial Management,* fall 1977, 7-16.

Jones, Charles I. *Introduction to Economic Growth.* New York: W.W. Norton & Co., 1997.

T

T-BILLS

SEE: U.S. Treasury Bills

T-NOTES

SEE: U.S. Treasury Notes

TACTICAL ASSET ALLOCATION

Tactical asset allocation is an investment strategy that centers on altering investment proportions to take advantage of differences in expected performance of various asset classes. As an asset allocation strategy, the technique attempts to evaluate the expected performance of broad asset classes (such as **stocks**, **bonds**, and cash), rather than predicting which individual **securities** are likely to outperform in the upcoming period. Money managers evaluate the relative performance of each asset class, then adjust the exposure of their investment portfolios to each of the classes. In making investment decisions, proponents of tactical asset allocation often buy securities in out-of-favor asset classes.

INVESTMENT STRATEGIES

Most investment strategies divide decisions into two categories: asset allocation and security selection. Numerous studies have shown that the vast majority of a portfolio's performance is explained by the asset allocation decision. Thus, most individuals and institutions making investment decisions begin by setting a policy asset allocation that determines the long-term proportions to be invested in each class. This policy asset allocation must be suitable for the investor in terms of risk exposure and expected return. Asset classes can be defined simply (stocks, bonds, and cash) or more precisely by subdividing stocks, for example, into categories for large and small, growth and value, foreign and domestic companies. Additional asset classes such as **real estate**, **commodities**, and **derivatives** can be included as well.

In deciding the specific policy asset allocation, investors must assess their own aversion to risk and their required rate of return. Risk is the possibility of an investment losing or not gaining value. Expected return is the percentage gain that an investment must produce for an investment to be made. Normally, an investment with low risk is an investment with a low return. People who are risk averse require higher expected returns from securities that have higher risk. Additionally, most investors have an overall tolerance for risk that they prefer not to exceed. The proportion of the portfolio in each asset class should reflect these **risk and return** issues.

Once a portfolio with the proper asset allocation has been established, the investor must still monitor its overall risk. Even a passive buy and-hold strategy will eventually deviate from the desired policy asset allocation. Asset classes that perform well during a particular period will increase their proportion in the portfolio at the expense of other asset classes. This may result in a change in risk exposure that differs markedly from that desired. Also, changes in investor age, **wealth**, income, or lifestyle may require reevaluation of the policy asset allocation.

TACTICAL ASSET ALLOCATION TECHNIQUES

Like other asset allocation strategies, tactical asset allocation seeks to determine the best asset allocation using the standard approach of getting the best rate of return given an investor's risk tolerance. Adherents of tactical asset allocation forecast behavior of broad asset classes and alter these allocations based upon their expectations for performance. Since it is tactical in nature, it requires short-term deviations from the policy asset allocation and focuses on improving return at some expense to risk management. It assumes that an investor's risk tolerance is relatively stable over the long run and is flexible in the short run. A typical tactical asset allocation strategy will carefully delineate the extent to which asset class proportions may differ from the long-term policy asset allocation.

As a short-term investment strategy, tactical asset allocation is often considered a market timing strategy. This implicitly assumes that markets are inefficient (at least in the short term) and that over- and undervalued asset classes can be identified and exploited. Decisions made under this strategy are therefore driven by changes in predictions for the returns of the various asset classes.

Tactical asset allocation can also be described as a contrarian strategy. This approach assumes that out-of-favor asset classes, such as those that have performed poorly in a recent period, are likely to revert to their long-term average performance. Obviously, this strategy can make some investors very uncomfortable. While most investors tend to move away from out-of-favor asset classes, investors using tactical asset allocation tend to favor the unpopular markets. If the contrarian logic is correct, such a strategy should provide superior performance relative to a more passive investment approach.

While there are many adherents to tactical asset allocation, there is no strong consensus concerning its effectiveness to improve portfolio performance. Empirical studies suggest that it is possible to forecast asset class returns over long time periods, but that it becomes more difficult as the time period shortens. Tactical asset allocation can add value only if it is driven by effective forecasting of the relative performance of asset classes over a fairly short time horizon.

[Paul Bolster]

FURTHER READING:

Ehrhardt, Michael C., and John M. Wachowicz Jr. ''Tactical Asset Allocation.'' *Review of Business* 12, no. 3 (winter 1990): 9+.

Elgin, Peggy R. ''Tactical Asset Allocation Isn't for the Weak-Hearted.'' *Pension Management* 31, no. 3 (March 1995): 26.

Fabozzi, Frank J. *Investment Management.* 2nd ed. Upper Saddle River, NJ: Prentice Hall, 1999.

Jacques, William E. ''Con: Tactical Asset Allocation: A Sure Fire Investment Technique or Just a Fad?'' *Financial Executive* 5, no. 2 (March/April 1989): 43+.

Kinsley, Ralph L., Jr. ''Pro: Tactical Asset Allocation: A Sure-Fire Investment Technique or Just a Fad?'' *Financial Executive* 5, no. 2 (March/April 1989): 42+.

Lincoln, Sandy. ''Asset Allocation and the Time Horizon Complete the Picture.'' *Pension Management* 31, no. 3 (March 1995): 22+.

TAFT-HARTLEY ACT

Passed in 1947, the Taft-Hartley Act remains the cornerstone of United States labor law today. This act amended the Wagner Act of 1935. Commonly called the Labor Management Relations Act of 1947, this legislation reflects the attitudes of post-World War II America towards labor. Due to ''national emergency'' strikes during the war, postwar strikes, and the advantages given to unions by the Wagner Act, a Republican-controlled Congress passed the Act in an attempt to restore the balance of power between labor and management. The Act restricts the activities of unions in four ways by:

1. prohibiting unfair labor practices by unions,
2. listing the rights of employees who are union members,
3. listing the rights of employers, and
4. empowering the president of the United States to suspend labor strikes that may constitute a national emergency.

UNFAIR LABOR UNION PRACTICES

The Taft-Hartley Act prohibited several labor practices judged to be ''unfair.'' First, the Taft-Hartley Act made it illegal for unions to restrain employees from exercising their guaranteed bargaining rights. Therefore, a union cannot threaten the jobs of employees who vote against the union, once the union is recognized. Employees who criticize the union or testify against it in hearings or court cases cannot be punished.

Second, the act named as unfair any action by the union that would result in employers' discrimination against employees in order to encourage or discourage membership in a union. Exceptions to this include ''closed'' or ''union'' shop situations in which union membership is a prerequisite for employment. A closed shop is one in which the employer can hire only union members. Closed shops were outlawed in 1947, but still exist in some industries, largely left to the discretion of state governments. A union shop is one in which the employer can hire non-union employees, but employees must join the union within a certain period of time. If an employee does not join the union and pay dues, he or she can be terminated. In either situation, the union cannot force the employer to dismiss an employee for any other cause.

Third, the Taft-Hartley Act required unions to bargain ''in good faith'' with employers, and outlawed ''wildcat'' strikes (refusing to work while a valid contract exists). Bargaining in good faith requires both the union and management to communicate and initiate counter proposals, and make every reasonable effort to reach an agreement. The parties are not required to make concessions, only to meet and to discuss proposals.

Finally, the Act made ''featherbedding'' illegal. Featherbedding is the practice of making employers pay salaries to individuals who perform no work.

RIGHTS OF EMPLOYEES

The Taft-Hartley Act also protected employees' rights against their unions. Closed shops that forced employees to join unions were considered to violate an individual's right to freedom of association. Without the Taft-Hartley Act, states could not have enacted ''right-to-work'' legislation, which guarantees employees will not have to join a union as a condition of employment.

Right-to-work laws prohibit closed shops. Many states in the southern United States have enacted such laws. In the North, however, where unions have traditionally been strong, most states have not enacted right-to work legislation.

Critics of right-to-work laws point out that, since unions in a bargaining situation with a company are compelled to represent all employees in that company (as opposed to just those that belong to the union), non-unionized employees are in fact receiving the benefits of union representation for free. Such employees, these critics argue, benefit at the expense of the union. For this and other reasons, organized labor opposes right-to-work laws.

RIGHTS OF EMPLOYERS

Under the Taft-Hartley Act, employers have the right to express their views and opinions concerning unions and the results of unionization. Employers may say anything they wish about unions as long as they avoid threats, promises, coercion, and direct interference. For example, employers can claim that unionization might result in a plant closing; but cannot say that a particular plant will be closed if the union is voted in.

NATIONAL EMERGENCY STRIKES

The Taft-Hartley Act gives the president of the United States the power to intervene when a strike becomes a ''national emergency strike.'' National emergency strikes are those that can endanger national health or safety. The president may appoint a board of inquiry charged with making a report of the situation. Based upon this report, the president could apply for an injunction restraining the strike for 60 days. If there has been no resolution at the end of 60 days, the injunction can be extended for another 20 days. During this period, employees are polled in a secret ballot to determine their willingness to comply with the terms of their employer's last offer.

NATIONAL LABOR RELATIONS BOARD (NLRB)

The Taft-Hartley Act amended the Wagner Act of 1935. The Wagner Act was commonly referred to as the National Labor Relations Act (NLRA), created the National Labor Relations Board (NLRB), whose function was to monitor the collective bargaining process.

The NLRB is composed of five members, all of whom are appointed to five-year terms by the president of the United States, with the consent of the U.S. Senate. The general counsel of the NLRB is also appointed by the president, to a four year term. The board is charged with running over fifty different offices throughout the United States.

The responsibilities of the NLRB include:

1. Preventing unfair labor practices, whether they involve employers, labor unions, or representatives.
2. Determining appropriate grouping for collective bargaining. (That is, whether all company employees should be represented by a single union, or should unionization be further divided by craft area or plant location).
3. Conducting secret ballot elections to determine a bargaining representative; also determining if employees want an agreement that requires union membership as a condition of employment.

The NLRB can issue cease-and-desist orders for unfair labor practices. These orders are then enforced, upon appeal, by the U.S. Court System.

Any person or organization may file a charge of unfair labor practice with the NLRB. In addition, the NLRB accepts petitions to either certify or decertify an employee representative, with respect to collective bargaining issues. The NLRB will then conduct secret ballots of employees to determine the certification or decertification of a union.

LANDRUM-GRIFFIN ACT (1959)

Officially listed as the Labor Management Reporting and Disclosure Act of 1959, the Landrum-Griffin Act amended the Wagner Act (1935), and further enumerated unfair labor practices not named in the Taft-Hartley Act. The clear purpose of this Act was to further protect union members from possible wrongful acts on the part of their union leaders and officers. This legislation affords union employees with a number of rights within the framework of their union. The election processes were made more open through requirements that eliminated closed nomination systems. Union employees were assured of their right to sue their union for just damages without fear of retaliation. Union employees cannot be fined or suspended by the union without due process. Such due process includes a list of specific charges, a fair hearing, and time in which to prepare a defense. This Act also required unions to provide copies of the applicable collective bargaining agreement to all members working under that contract.

In addition, unions were banned from engaging in secondary boycotts, and from making agreements that forced employers to deal exclusively with other union shops or buy only union-made goods. Picketing an employer who had a valid collective bargaining contract with another union was also forbidden.

UNIONS AND THE LAW

The greatest period of growth for unions occurred between the Wagner Act of 1935 and the Taft-Hartley Act of 1947. During these years, union membership increased from approximately 3.5 million to 15 million. It is clear that the Taft-Hartley Act slowed the growth of union membership in the years following its passage. The issue of the proper balance of power between employers and employees continues, for which the Taft-Hartley Act functions as a historical backdrop.

SEE ALSO: Labor Law and Legislation; Labor Unions

[Bruce D. Buskirk and John E. Oliver]

FURTHER READING:

Jacoby, Daniel. *Laboring for Freedom: A New Look at the History of Labor in America.* Armonk, NY: M.E. Sharpe, 1998.

Kovach, Kenneth A. *Strategic Labor Relations.* Boston: University Press of America, 1997.

Nelson, Daniel *Shifting Fortunes: The Rise and Decline of American Labor, from the 1820s to the Present.* Chicago: Ivan R. Dee, 1997.

TAGUCHI METHODS

There has been a great deal of controversy about Genichi Taguchi's methodology since it was first introduced in the United States. This controversy has lessened considerably in recent years due to modifications and extensions of his methodology. The main controversy, however, is still about Taguchi's statistical methods, not about his philosophical concepts concerning quality or robust design. Furthermore, it is generally accepted that Taguchi's philosophy has promoted, on a worldwide scale, the design of experiments for quality improvement upstream, or at the product and process design stage.

Taguchi's philosophy and methods support, and are consistent with, the Japanese **quality control** approach that asserts that higher quality generally results in lower cost. This is in contrast to the widely prevailing view in the United States that asserts that quality improvement is associated with higher cost. Furthermore, Taguchi's philosophy and methods support the Japanese approach to move quality improvement upstream. Taguchi's methods help design engineers build quality into products and processes. As George Box, Soren Bisgaard, and Conrad Fung observed: "Today the ultimate goal of quality improvement is to design quality into every product and process and to follow up at every stage from design to final manufacture and sale. An important element is the extensive and innovative use of statistically designed experiments."

TAGUCHI'S DEFINITION OF QUALITY

The old traditional definition of quality states quality is conformance to specifications. This definition was expanded by Joseph M. Juran (1904-) in 1974 and then by the American Society for Quality Control (ASQC) in 1983. Juran observed that "quality is fitness for use." The ASQC defined quality as "the totality of features and characteristics of a product or service that bear on its ability to satisfy given needs."

Taguchi presented another definition of quality. His definition stressed the losses associated with a product. Taguchi stated that "quality is the loss a product causes to society after being shipped, other than losses caused by its intrinsic functions." Taguchi asserted that losses in his definition "should be restricted to two categories: (1) loss caused by variability of function, and (2) loss caused by harmful side effects." Taguchi is saying that a product or service has good quality if it "performs its intended functions without variability, and causes little loss through harmful side effects, including the cost of using it."

It must be kept in mind here that "society" includes both the manufacturer and the customer. Loss associated with function variability includes, for example, energy and time (problem fixing), and money (replacement cost of parts). Losses associated with harmful side effects could be market shares for the manufacturer and/or the physical effects, such as of the drug thalidomide, for the consumer.

Consequently, a company should provide products and services such that possible losses to society are minimized, or, "the purpose of quality improvement . . . is to discover innovative ways of designing products and processes that will save society more than they cost in the long run." The concept of reliability is appropriate here. The next section will clearly show that Taguchi's loss function yields an operational definition of the term "loss to society" in his definition of quality.

TAGUCHI'S LOSS FUNCTION

We have seen that Taguchi's quality philosophy strongly emphasizes losses or costs. W. H. Moore asserted that this is an "enlightened approach" that embodies "three important premises: for every product quality characteristic there is a target value which results in the smallest loss; deviations from target value always results in increased loss to society; [and] loss should be measured in monetary units (dollars, pesos, francs, etc.)."

Figure 1 depicts Taguchi's typically loss function. The figure also contrasts Taguchi's function with the traditional view that states there are no losses if specifications are met.

Figure 1
Taguchi's Loss Function

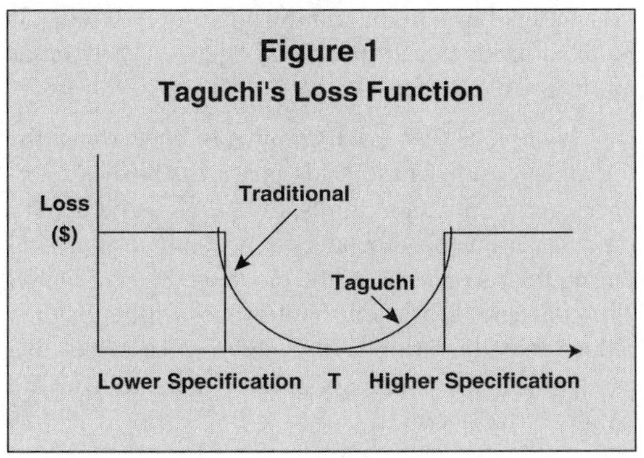

It can be seen that small deviations from the target value result in small losses. These losses, however, increase in a nonlinear fashion as deviations from the target value increase. The function shown above is a simple quadratic equation that compares the measured value of a unit of output Y to the target T:

$$L(Y) = k(Y - T)^2$$

where $L(Y)$ is the expected loss associated with the specific value of Y.

Essentially, this equation states that the loss is proportional to the square of the deviation of the measured value, Y, from the target value, T. This implies that any deviation from the target (based on customers' desires and needs) will diminish customer satisfaction. This is in contrast to the traditional definition of quality that states that quality is conformance to specifications. It should be recognized that the constant k can be determined if the value of $L(Y)$ associated with some Y value are both known. Of course, under many circumstances a quadratic function is only an approximation.

Since Taguchi's loss function is presented in monetary terms, it provides a common language for all the departments or components within a company. Finally, the loss function can be used to define performance measures of a quality characteristic of a product or service. This property of Taguchi's loss function will be taken up in the next section. But to anticipate the discussion of this property, Taguchi's quadratic function can be converted to:

$$L(Y) = k[\sigma^2 + (\mu - T)^2]$$

This can be accomplished by assuming Y has some probability distribution with mean μ and variance σ^2. This second mathematical expression states that average or expected loss is due either to process variation or to being off target (called "bias"), or both.

TAGUCHI, ROBUST DESIGN, AND THE DESIGN OF EXPERIMENTS

Taguchi asserted that the development of his methods of experimental design started in Japan about 1948. These methods were then refined over the next several decades. They were introduced in the United States around 1980. Although, Taguchi's approach was built on traditional concepts of design of experiments (DOE), such as factorial and fractional factorial designs and orthogonal arrays, he created and promoted some new DOE techniques such as signal-to-noise ratios, robust designs, and parameter and tolerance designs. Some experts in the field have shown that some of these techniques, especially signal-to-noise ratios, are not optimal under certain conditions. Nonetheless, Taguchi's ideas concerning robust design and the design of experiments will now be discussed.

DOE is a body of statistical techniques for the effective and efficient collection of data for a number of purposes. Two significant ones are the investigation of research hypotheses and the accurate determination of the relative effects of the many different factors that influence the quality of a product or process. DOE can be employed in both the product design phase and production phase.

A crucial component of quality is a product's ability to perform its tasks under a variety of conditions. Furthermore, the operating environmental conditions are usually beyond the control of the product designers, and, therefore robust designs are essential. Robust designs are based on the use of DOE techniques for finding product parameter settings (e.g., temperature settings or drill speeds), which enable products to be resilient to changes and variations in working environments.

It is generally recognized that Taguchi deserves much of the credit for introducing the statistical study of robust design. We have seen how Taguchi's loss function sets variation reduction as a primary goal for quality improvement. Taguchi's DOE techniques employ the loss function concept to investigate both product parameters and key environmental factors. His DOE techniques are part of his philosophy of achieving economical quality design.

To achieve economical product quality design, Taguchi proposed three phases: system design, parameter design, and tolerance design. In the first phase, system design, design engineers use their practical experience, along with scientific and engineering principles, to create a viably functional design. To elaborate, system design uses current technology, processes, materials, and engineering methods to define and construct a new ''system.'' The system can be a new product or process, or an improved modification of an existing product or process.

The parameter design phase determines the optimal settings for the product or process parameters. These parameters have been identified during the system design phase. DOE methods are applied here to determine the optimal parameter settings. Taguchi constructed a limited number of experimental designs, from which U.S. engineers have found it easy to select and apply in their manufacturing environments.

The goal of the parameter design is to design a robust product or process, which, as a result of minimizing performance variation, minimizes manufacturing and product lifetime costs. Robust design means that the performance of the product or process is insensitive to noise factors such as variation in environmental conditions, machine wear, or product to-product variation due to raw material differences. Taguchi's DOE parameter design techniques are used to determine which controllable factors and which noise factors are the significant variables. The aim is to set the controllable factors at those levels that will result in a product or process being robust with respect to the noise factors.

In our previous discussion of Taguchi's loss function, two equations were discussed. It was observed that the second equation could be used to establish quality performance measures that permit the optimization of a given product's quality characteristic. In improving quality, both the average response of a quality and its variation are important. The second equation suggests that it may be advantageous to combine both the average response and variation into a single measure. And Taguchi did this with his signal-to-noise ratios (S/N). Consequently, Taguchi's approach is to select design parameter levels that will maximize the appropriate S/N ratio.

These S/N ratios can be used to get closer to a given target value (such as tensile strength or baked tile dimensions), or to reduce variation in the product's quality characteristic(s). For example, one S/N ratio corresponds to what Taguchi called ''nominal is best.'' Such a ratio is selected when a specific target value, such as tensile strength, is the design goal.

For the ''nominal is best'' case, Taguchi recommended finding an adjustment factor (some parameter setting) that will eliminate the bias discussed in the second equation. Sometimes a factor can be found that will control the average response without affecting the variance. If this is the case, our second equation tells us that the expected loss becomes:

$$(k \times \sigma^2)$$

Consequently, the aim now is to reduce the variation. Therefore, Taguchi's S/N ratio is:

$$\text{S/N} = -10 \log_{10} S^2$$

where S^2 is the sample's standard deviation.

In this formula, by minimizing S^2, $-10 \log_{10} S^2$ is maximized. Recall that all of Taguchi's S/N ratios are to be maximized.

Finally, a few brief comments concerning the tolerance design phase. This phase establishes tolerances, or specification limits, for either the product or process parameters that have been identified as critical during the second phase, the parameter design phase. The goal here is to establish tolerances wide enough to reduce manufacturing costs, while at the same time assuring that the product or process characteristics are within certain bounds.

EXAMPLES AND CONCLUSIONS

As Thomas P. Ryan has stated, Taguchi at the very least, has focused ''our attention on new objectives in achieving quality improvement. The statistical tools for accomplishing these objectives will likely continue to be developed.'' Quality management ''gurus,'' such as W. Edwards Deming (1900-1993) and Kaoru Ishikawa (1915-), have stressed the importance of continuous quality improvement by concentrating on processes upstream. This is a fundamental break with the traditional practice of relying on inspection downstream. Taguchi emphasized the importance of DOE in improving the quality of the engineering design of products and processes. As previously mentioned, however, "his methods are frequently statistically inefficient and cumbersome." Nonetheless, Taguchi's design of experiments have been widely applied and theoretically refined and extended. Two application cases and one refinement example will now be discussed.

K. N. Anand, in an article in *Quality Engineering,* discussed a welding problem. Welding was performed to repair cracks and blown holes on the cast-iron housing of an assembled electrical machine. Customers wanted a defect-free quality weld, however the welding process had resulted in a fairly high percentage of welding defects. Management and welders identified five variables and two interactions that were considered the key factors in improving quality. A Taguchi orthogonal design was performed resulting in the identification of two highly significant interactions and a defect-free welding process.

The second application, presented by M. W. Sonius and B. W. Tew in a *Quality Engineering* article, involved reducing stress components in the connection between a composite component and a metallic end fitting for a composite structure. Bonding, pinning, or riveting the fitting in place traditionally made the connections. Nine significant variables that could affect the performance of the entrapped fiber connections were identified and a Taguchi experimental design was performed. The experiment identified two of the nine factors and their respective optimal settings. Therefore, stress levels were significantly reduced.

The theoretical refinement example involves Taguchi robust designs. We have seen where such a design can result in products and processes that are insensitive to noise factors. Using Taguchi's quadratic loss function, however, may provide a poor approximation of true loss and suboptimal product or process quality. John F. Kros and Christina M. Mastrangelo established relationships between nonquadratic loss functions and Taguchi's signal-to-noise ratios. Applying these relationships in an experimental design can change the recommended selection of the respective settings of the key parameters and result in smaller losses.

[Peter B. Webb, Ph.D.]

FURTHER READING:

American Society for Quality Control. Statistics Division. *Glossary and Tables for Statistical Quality Control.* Milwaukee, WI: American Society for Quality Control, 1983.

Anand, K. N. "Development of Process Specification for Radiographic Quality Welding." *Quality Engineering,* June 1997, 597-601.

Barker, T. B. "Quality Engineering by Design: Taguchi's Philosophy." *Quality Progress* 19, no. 12 (1986), 32-42.

Box, G. E. P., and others. "Quality Practices in Japan." *Quality Progress,* March 1988, 37-41.

Byrne, Diane M., and Shin Taguchi. "The Taguchi Approach to Parameter Design." *ASQC Quality Congress Transaction,* 1986, 168-77.

Daniel, Cuthburt. *Applications of Statistics to Industrial Experimentation.* New York: Wiley, 1976.

Farnum, Nicholas R. *Modern Statistical Quality Control and Improvement.* New York: Duxbury Press, 1994.

Kackar, R. N. "Off-Line Quality Control, Parameter Design, and the Taguchi Method." *Journal of Quality Technology* 17, no. 4 (1985): 176-88.

Kros, John F., and Christina M. Mastrangelo. "Impact of Nonquadratic Loss in the Taguchi Design Methodology." *Quality Engineering* 10, no. 3 (1998): 509-19.

Lochner, Robert H., and Joseph E. Matar. *Designing for Quality: An Introduction to the Best of Taguchi and Western Methods of Statistical Experimental Design.* Milwaukee, WI: ASQC Quality Press, 1990.

Phadke, M. S. *Quality Engineering Using Robust Design.* New York: Prentice Hall, 1989.

Quinlan, J. "Product Improvement by Application of Taguchi Method." In *Third Supplier Symposium on Taguchi Methods.* Dearborn, MI: American Supplier Institute, 1985.

Ross, P. J. *Taguchi Techniques for Quality Engineering.* New York: McGraw-Hill, 1988.

Ryan, T. P. "Taguchi's Approach to Experimental Design: Some Concerns." *Quality Progress,* May 1988, 34-36.

Sonius, M. W., and B. W. Tew. "Design Optimization of Metal to Composite Connections Using Orthogonal Arrays." *Quality Engineering* 9, no. 3 (1997): 479-87.

Taguchi, Genichi. *Introduction to Quality Engineering.* White Plains, NY: Asian Productivity Organization, UNIPUB, 1986.

——. "The Development of Quality Engineering." *ASI Journal* 1, no. 1 (1988): 1-4.

TAKEOVERS

In the market for **corporate control**, management teams vie for the right to acquire and manage corporate assets and strategies. If an outside group acquires control of a target corporation, the transaction is termed a takeover. There are two basic methods of effecting a corporate acquisition: a friendly takeover and a hostile takeover. In a friendly takeover, the **board of directors** of the target firm is willing to agree to the acquisition. By contrast, a hostile takeover occurs when the board of directors is opposed to the acquisition. Friendly takeovers often involve firms with complementary skills and resources in growing industries. Hostile offers generally involve poorly performing firms in mature industries. In these cases, the suitor desires to replace the existing **management** team and sell off underperforming business units.

FRIENDLY TAKEOVERS

Friendly takeovers can involve either the acquisition of the assets of the company or the purchase of the **stock** of the target. There are several advantages associated with the purchase of assets. First, the acquiring firm can purchase only those assets that it desires. Second, the buyer avoids the assumption of any contingent **liabilities** of the target. Third, the purchase of assets is easier to negotiate since only the board of directors, and not the shareholders, need approve the acquisition.

The second type of friendly takeover involves the purchase of the stock of the target. In this instance, the acquiring firm does assume the liabilities of the target firm. The target firm continues to operate as an autonomous **subsidiary** or it may be merged into the operations of the acquiring firm. The approval of the target's shareholders is necessary for this type of acquisition.

HOSTILE TAKEOVERS

Hostile takeovers occur when the board of directors of the target is opposed to the sale of the company. In this instance, the acquiring firm has two options if it chooses to proceed with the acquisition: a **tender offer** or a proxy fight. A tender offer represents an offer to buy the stock of the target firm either directly from the firm's shareholders or through the secondary market. This method tends to be an expensive way of acquiring the stock since the share price is bid up in anticipation of a takeover. Often, acquiring firms will first propose an offer to buy the company's stock to the target company's board of directors, with an indication that if the offer is turned down, it will then attempt a tender offer.

Federal securities regulations require the disclosure of the acquiring firm's intent with respect to the acquisition. Under the Williams Act, the acquiring firm must give 30 days notice to both the management of the target firm and the **Securities and Exchange Commission**. This enables the target firm to formulate a defensive strategy to maintain its independence.

In a proxy fight, the acquirer solicits the shareholders of the target firm in an attempt to obtain the right to vote their shares. The acquiring firm hopes to secure enough proxies to gain control of the board of directors and, in turn, replace the incumbent management. Proxy fights are expensive and difficult to win, since the incumbent management team can use the target firm's funds to pay all the costs of presenting their case and obtaining votes.

FORM OF THE TAKEOVER

The form of the takeover is often heavily influenced by income tax laws. A simple exchange of shares of **common stock**, while rarely used in takeovers, is considered a nontaxable exchange. The tax basis of the new shares is simply that of the old. Should the takeover use cash and/or debt to pay for the target's common shares, however, this generates a taxable transaction and the target's shareholders will be subject to **capital gains** taxes.

DEFENSIVE TACTICS

There are a number of maneuvers that can be used to ward off an unwanted suitor. These can be divided into two basic categories: preoffer tactics and postoffer tactics. Preoffer tactics are those that may be employed prior to the receipt of a hostile bid. For example, private companies are almost invulnerable to takeovers since blocking stakes of more than 50 percent of the outstanding shares are usually held by an individual or an affiliated group.

Hostile takeovers are often generated by investors who believe the shares of the target firm are undervalued. Therefore, a high stock price will also fend off many potential acquirers since it will be difficult for the acquirer to earn a sufficiently high return on its investment in the target. In other cases, size alone may pose a valid defense. Also, high-tech firms in the defense industry may be immune to takeovers because of the political ramifications.

Target companies can also decrease the likelihood of a takeover though charter amendments. With staggered terms for the board of directors, the board is divided into three groups, with only one group elected each year. Thus, a suitor cannot obtain control of the board immediately even though it may have acquired a majority ownership of the target via a tender offer. Under a supermajority amendment, a higher percentage than 50 percent, generally two-thirds or 80 percent is required to approve a merger. A fair price amendment prohibits two-tier bids, where the first 80 percent of the shares tendered receive one price, whereas the last 20 percent receive a lower price for their stock.

Other preoffer tactics include **poison pills** and dual class recapitalizations. With poison pills, existing shareholders are issued **rights** that, if a bidder acquires a certain percentage of the outstanding shares, can be used to purchase additional shares at a bargain price, usually half the market price. Dual class recapitalizations distribute a new class of equity with superior voting rights. This enables the target firm's managers to obtain majority control even though they do not own a majority of the shares.

Postoffer tactics occur after an unsolicited offer is made to the target firm. The target may file suit against the bidder alleging violations of **antitrust** or securities laws. Alternatively, the target may engage in asset and liability restructuring to make it an unattractive target. With asset restructuring, the target purchases assets that the bidder does not want or that will create antitrust problems or sells off the ''crown jewels,'' the assets that the suitor desires to obtain. Liability restructuring maneuvers include issuing shares to a friendly third party to dilute the bidder's ownership position or leveraging up the firm through a **leveraged recapitalization** making it difficult for the suitor to finance the transaction. Other postoffer tactics involve targeted share repurchases (often termed ''**greenmail**'' in which the target repurchases the shares of an unfriendly suitor at a premium over the current market price) and **golden parachutes**, which are lucrative supplemental compensation packages for the target firm's management. These packages are activated in the case of a takeover and the subsequent resignations of the senior executives.

SEE ALSO: Mergers and Acquisitions

[Robert T. Kleiman, updated by Ronald M. Horwitz]

FURTHER READING:

Auerbach, Alan J. *Corporate Takeovers: Causes and Consequences.* Chicago: University of Chicago Press, 1991.

Coffee, John C., Jr., Louis Lowenstein, and Susan Rose-Ackerman, eds. *Knights, Raiders, and Targets: The Impact of the Hostile Takeover.* New York: Oxford University Press, 1988.

Weston, J. Fred, Kwang S. Chung, and Juan A. Sui. *Takeovers, Restructuring, and Corporate Governance.* 2nd ed. New York: Prentice Hall, 1998.

TARIFF

SEE: Duty

TAXES AND TAXATION

To claim that taxes and taxation always have been unpopular is to state the obvious. Every American schoolchild learns about the Stamp Act of 1765 and how widespread resentment against ''taxation without representation'' precipitated the American Revolution. Few are aware of the fact that taxation with representation was just as unpopular: the Articles of Confederation of 1781 deprived the central government of the power of taxation. When a new constitution empowered Congress in 1791 to tax whiskey and other products, the Whiskey Rebellion ensued, nearly toppling the new government.

TAX HISTORY

Taxation—the raising of revenue—is about power, a subject that has excited much controversy throughout history. The Magna Carta of 1215, considered a watershed in the evolution of representative government, came about because of an English king's arbitrary imposition of taxes, without the consent of those being taxed. The issue was not about taxes themselves, but how they were being imposed. From then on, English rulers were deprived of the ''power of the purse,'' which, for the most part, shifted to the taxpayers as represented by Parliament.

The concept of consent endured, elevated by English philosopher John Locke (1632-1704) into a constitutional principle. Locke maintained that government existed in order to protect liberty and the right of property; even so, it had no inherent right to tax without consent. Hence, since the Magna Carta the matter of taxation—the power to raise revenue—continued to buttress representative government. In 1689 the English ''Bill of Rights'' explicitly guaranteed the right of taxation only to parliament. This was a dramatic departure in the 5,000-year history of taxation.

Another significant change has been the shared responsibility of all segments of society in the payment of taxes. In the United States, everybody from George Washington to the humble distiller of whiskey paid taxes. In medieval Europe and Russia, those least able to pay—the oppressed peasantry—carried most or all of the tax burden. Taxes were a social stigma. This changed with the evolution of the concept of taxation with representation, and its corollary: the responsibility of all to pay. In the early years of the American republic, so firmly entrenched was the idea that those who paid were those who ruled that the payment of property taxes (the only form of personal, individual tax in those days) became a more important voting criterion than mere citizenship.

Finally, the concept that those who are most able to afford to pay tax should pay the most—the ''progressive'' concept of taxation—is perhaps the most recent evolution in the history of taxation. It is nevertheless limited to the income tax, which in itself is the embodiment of the concept of everyone's responsibility to shoulder the tax burden.

Despite these changes over time, taxation is as old as recorded history. Today as in ancient times, all taxes fall into broad categories: direct and indirect, internal and external. A direct tax is one that a person pays directly, as with income tax. An indirect tax is one that is usually figured into the price of a product, with the purchaser often unaware of its existence. External taxes usually refer to tariffs, or taxes on **imports**, including food products. Internal taxes are those, such as **excise taxes** or **sales taxes**, added on to the price of a product produced or grown in this country (many foods are exempt from sales taxes).

Once the principle of taxation with representation was firmly established in the Constitution—which granted both the federal and state governments the right to tax—federal, state, and local taxes proliferated steadily in the United States. This was not only in the number and types of taxes, but also in the numbers of those who paid them. Moreover, taxes that were meant to be temporary—such as income tax and sales taxes—ended up becoming permanent.

That taxes are as unpopular as ever, despite their proliferation in the 20th century, is beyond dispute. Beginning in the late 1970s, promises to lessen individual and corporate tax burdens provided the political fuel for conservative candidates, who met with unprecedented success throughout the 1980s. By the mid-1990s candidates representing all points of the political spectrum found that opposition to taxation had become a prerequisite to election. Opposition to federal taxation aroused particular fervor, bringing the continued existence of the **Internal Revenue Service** into question within the federal legislature. While proposals to abolish the IRS were never seriously debated, the House of Representatives did hold public hearings on the IRS and its practices in the spring of 1998, and promised to reform the service in due time. In any event, Americans today sacrifice as much as, and sometimes more than, one-third of their income to taxes. How this came to be is the story of taxation in America.

There are roughly two periods of taxation in the United States: post 1913, which saw the adoption of the income tax (first by the federal government, then by the states) and the birth of Social Security, Medicare, and the state sales tax; and the pre-1913 years, which is largely the story of the poll, property, tariff, and other nonincome taxes.

POLL AND PROPERTY TAXES

In the pre-1913 period, while there were attempts to impose a personal income tax, taxes were non-income taxes. The oldest tax revenue sources, and the traditional fiscal bedrock of local and state government, were poll and property taxes. These concepts were brought over from England, and were direct taxes. The poll tax was a fixed, regressive tax (one in which everyone paid the same amount) that all adult males paid. It was this tax that writer Henry David Thoreau (1817-1862) refused to pay, and for which he was jailed. Because the poll tax had so many limitations and fell hardest on the poor, state after state discontinued it by the Civil War. Southern states revived it after 1870 in order to deprive newly enfranchised African Americans of the right to vote (with the payment of poll taxes becoming a voting requirement). In 1964 the 24th amendment made this practice illegal, but did not outlaw the poll tax itself.

The largest share of revenue for state and local governments prior to 1913 derived from property taxes, which, before the Civil War, included not only land and buildings but also slaves and cattle. In those days of limited government expenditures, revenue from property went to the federal government as well. By the time of the panic of 1893, property revenues became inadequate for most states, and other sources of income had to be devised (the first business tax, followed in 1911 by the first mandatory income tax, inaugurated in Wisconsin). Nevertheless, property taxes continued to be a major source of revenue.

The wave of political conservatism that swept the United States from the late 1970s to the early 1990s was triggered, in part, by opposition to property taxes. In 1978 California voters adopted Proposition 13, which restricted increases in property taxes and marked the first tangible manifestation of what was to become known as the taxpayer revolt. By 1996, 37 states had followed California's suit and placed restrictions on increases in property taxes. Although such measures were politically popular, the traditional tying of public school funding to property tax assessments ensured that any loss in property tax revenue would be most directly felt by school systems.

In order to maintain adequate school funding in the face of decreased property tax revenues, states turned to a variety of alternative means of funding public education. Michigan, for example, initiated a state lottery whose profits were in large measure channeled into public education; Michigan also raised sales taxes to recover lost property tax revenues. In fact, the great irony of the taxpayer rebellion of the late 20th century was that although certain taxes that were troublesome to the well-to-do were eliminated or reduced, taxation overall remained relatively unchanged. The main effect of the rebellion was, in the end, to shift the tax burden from the wealthy to the poor by reducing property and income taxes and raising sales and excise taxes.

EXCISE TAXES

The most important sources of income for the federal government prior to 1913, with one or two exceptions, were excise taxes and above all, tariffs. Alexander Hamilton (1755-1804), the treasury secretary under George Washington, favored a rational system of taxation and effective collection of taxes. The result was the Revenue Act of 1791, which imposed a variety of excise taxes (i.e., sales taxes) on ''luxury'' products, such as distilled liquor, refined sugar, snuff (including tobacco), horse drawn carriages, and more. The very significant sum of $210,000 was collected by the 400 revenue collectors a year later, though these taxes were extremely unpopular. They were discontinued and the revenue officials dismissed from their jobs when Hamilton's nemesis, Thomas Jefferson, took the oath of office in 1801. Jefferson was a staunch proponent of little government and maximum freedom of the individual. Thereafter, excise taxes were most often used by the states to raise revenue and by the federal government before the Civil War only as an expedient. After 1865 the only excise taxes that continued in force were on alcohol and tobacco.

Today, excise taxes exist on a variety of ''luxury'' goods produced in this country; they are indirect taxes, that is, usually the consumer is unaware that he or she is paying them (unlike sales taxes). The producer or manufacturer adds the tax to the price of the product. Other excise taxes are levied against tax-deferred retirement funds such as **401(k) plans** and **individual retirement accounts** (IRAs). Finally, excise taxes are applied to special products such as hunting and fishing equipment and airline tickets.

Excise taxes have generally been raised in recent years as a means of replacing revenues lost by politically motivated cuts in other forms of taxation. The growing popularity of salary-reduction retirement savings plans, such as 401(k) plans and IRAs, led the IRS to waive a 15 percent excise tax on retirement savings account withdrawals in 1997.

Excise taxes can, and often have been, used by governments to encourage or discourage certain public behaviors. Recent examples of this use of excise taxes include: the 1995 reduction of excise taxes on fuels using ethanol in their composition; increased excise taxes levied, beginning in 1995, against chemical manufacturers to offset future environmental cleanup costs; and the 1998 campaign to raise excise taxes on tobacco products to discourage smoking.

TARIFFS

In the early year of the Republic, excise taxes were not nearly as lucrative a source of federal revenue as tariffs. Particularly after 1816 the federal government raised much revenue on the taxes Congress imposed on imports, in opposition to **free trade**. Tariffs prevailed as the biggest source of federal revenue until the income tax appeared in 1913. After 1913 tariffs declined in importance, but never entirely disappeared.

Tariffs have had a long and stormy history down to the present day. As part of the federal government's revenue package in 1791, Congress added tariffs on a few imports. Alexander Hamilton wanted more, for he was strongly ''protectionist,'' that is, favoring taxes on imports in order to protect fledgling American industries from foreign **competition**. Yet even then there was controversy over this view, with ''free traders'' opposed to any restraints on trade with foreign nations, in the belief that they would retaliate against American goods. Hamilton was aware of the downside of his arguments, and therefore advocated temporary tariffs, only until American industry was on more solid competitive ground.

Because tariffs were so controversial, the initial ones were selective and limited. When the destructive Napoleonic Wars came to an end in 1815 and European industry threatened to recover rapidly, however, Congress gave in to pressure from northern business interests to pass a specific tariff act the following year.

The Tariff Act of 1816 called for moderate tariffs, but these were too few and too low to satisfy northern industrialists. But southern cotton planters opposed any tariffs, which would raise prices on goods that they imported for their own use. When the Civil War resulted in a northern-controlled Congress, raising tariffs was a foregone conclusion. The Morrill Act of 1861 raised tariffs to the highest level in American history, followed by even higher rates during each successive year of the Civil War.

Even with the restoration of the southern states to the Union, northerners continued to control Congress. By the 1870s the federal budget was bloated with a huge surplus, far exceeding expenditures. Instead of lowering the high tariffs, Congressmen siphoned off the surplus to their own particular ''pork barrels,'' with costly Civil War veterans' pensions on top of the list of every Congressman. Manufacturers as well as veterans were pleased. In the short run, the economy seemed to grow from high tariffs, and wealth appeared to be ''trickling down'' to the ordinary citizen.

At the same time, the downside of excessive protectionism was more and more in evidence. Prices rose precipitously on woolens and cottons, sugar, and sugar products, affecting mostly the poor. Monopolies gobbled up their competitors, and were themselves inefficient monoliths because of the absence of competition at home or abroad. By the time Democrat Grover Cleveland was reelected president in 1892, free trade was becoming an important issue. He persuaded Congress to slash tariffs by 40 percent. Before the benefits of a much lower tariff could be felt, a severe depression, the panic of 1893, struck, and four years later, the Republican Congress under William McKinley once again raised tariffs to an all-time high. Not until Woodrow Wilson was elected president in 1912 were tariffs once again lowered significantly. Nonetheless, they continued to zigzag from all-time lows, as during Wilson's two terms, to all-time highs, as during Calvin Coolidge's administrations in the 1920s. By then, international trade had all but shriveled up, as European countries enacted their own high tariffs in a belated revival of modern **mercantilism**. This only paved the way for the Great Depression to come.

What was becoming apparent in the first third of the 20th century was the declining importance of tariffs as revenue, compared with personal and corporate incomes taxes. By 1920 income tax revenues totaled over $5 billion—ten times more than tariffs. Nonetheless, despite the warnings of over 1,000 economists, President Herbert Hoover satisfied powerful business interests by signing the Smoot-Hawley Tariff Act of 1930, considered to be the highest tariff in American history. Even when the Great Depression accelerated during Hoover's administration, Congress stubbornly refused to lower tariff rates. Economists and historians alike have cited the Smoot-Hawley Tariff Act as a major contributing factor to the country's swift economic decline in the 1930s.

The undeclared war between protectionists and free trade advocates eventually was won by the free traders with consequences that have reverberated to the present time, with the passage of the **North American Free Trade Agreement** (NAFTA). Franklin D. Roosevelt, the first Democratic president in 12 years, took advantage of his enormous clout to get Congress to pass the Reciprocal Trade Agreements Act of 1934. **Reciprocity** was at the heart of this act: that is, if foreign governments would agree to lower their high tariffs, the United States would lower its tariffs accordingly. By the end of World War II, 29 countries had signed reciprocal trade agreements with the United States. This was enough to encourage the formation of a loose, free trade alliance in 1947 centered around the **General Agreement on Tariffs and Trade** (GATT). Thereafter, more and more countries joined GATT, and by 1990, 90 countries, accounting for 75 percent of the world's trade, had agreed to eliminate barriers to international trade. The adoption of the Uruguay Round of the GATT in 1994 pledged 100 signatory countries to reductions in overall tariffs to 6.3 percent by 1998, down from 40 percent in 1947. Most notably, overall global tariffs on pharmaceuticals, farm machinery, home and office furniture, medical equipment, paper products, and steel were to be reduced by one-third.

GATT may be a final nail in the coffin of protectionism, but opponents of total free trade are still heard from. Farmers the world over resent **international competition**, as do automakers and computer chip producers. International competition, aided by the artificially high dollar maintained by the administration of President Ronald Reagan, opened the door to the virtual takeover of whole industries by the Japanese in the 1970s and 1980s. Under pressure from U.S. automakers, GATT negotiations resulted in a trade pact in the early 1990s between the United States and Japan to limit the number of Japanese cars sold in the United States, and to enable more American cars to be sold in Japan. Vestiges of protective tariffs still exist, but these are disappearing in favor of regional free trade blocks, such as the **European Union** and NAFTA.

The history of tariffs as a tax on imported, foreign-made goods reveals how a tax, once considered indispensable, can decline in importance over time, and nearly disappear. In fact, the reduction of tariffs can sometimes be essential to a nation's participation in the global economy. This was seen in the case of the People's Republic of China, whose reentry into the **World Trade Organization** (WTO) in 1996 was made contingent upon its lowering its overall tariff rate from 35 percent to 23 percent. As tariffs have lessened in importance during the 20th century, income taxes have grown increasingly important and replaced revenue no longer generated from other sources.

Although tariffs have lost much of their revenue-raising importance, they are still widely used by governments wishing to influence the economic or political behavior of other nations. Threats of greatly increased tariffs were used by the United States in 1995 to force Japan to increase its importation of U.S.-made automotive parts and to pressure the People's Republic of China to crack down on the theft and unauthorized production of **intellectual properties**, including musical recordings and computer software. The unwillingness of governments and industries to abandon tariffs altogether was seen again in 1998, when the WTO nations were unable to agree on tariff reductions on paper and forest products.

INCOME TAXES

Income tax is unique in that it is one of the few major types of taxes that has philosophical underpinnings. Adam Smith (1723-1790), an 18th century Scottish economist whose 1776 treatise, *The Wealth of Nations,* has gone down in history as a work of genius, proposed the radical idea that income should be taxed regularly and permanently. Smith was of the same opinion as John Locke when it came to government: that it defended liberty and property rights; to Smith, government should be limited to those functions. Moreover, in order for the "wealth of a nation" to increase, government must spend only what it needed to run itself and nothing more. The revenue to run itself should be derived from a tax on income that must be fair and made clear to all well in advance of being levied.

Even before Smith's treatise was written, the colony of Massachusetts had been the first in the New World to impose an income tax in 1634, even though the property tax still remained the most important source of revenue. Nevertheless, the idea had evolved (and been taken for granted by Smith's day) that wealth was more than just property consisting of land and buildings. That is, a person had certain skills and knowledge that could produce income, even if he had no concrete property. Hence in addition to the property tax, the colony imposed a tax on the income of artisans, doctors, and other professionals. The difficulty that the colony faced with income tax is an old one: taxpayers concealed their taxable income and paid as little as possible. How to collect income taxes efficiently became the chief problem, one that was not resolved until mandatory payroll deductions were introduced in the 19th century.

The concept of an income tax and its philosophical justification were thus in place by the time the United States came into being. In addition, income tax is considered by tax historians and economists alike as the most advanced form in the long history of taxation. In the Articles of Confederation, however, the concept of taxation was surprisingly absent, and apparently had not caught on with the general public. The central government was all but deprived of any power to tax, while state governments taxed as little as possible. Property and poll taxes continued to hold sway, as did excise taxes on various goods.

Under the Constitution's explicit guarantee of the central government's power to tax in Article I, Section 8, a tax on income was not mandated but was not rejected altogether, either. In fact, the first U.S. treasury secretary, Alexander Hamilton, highly favored the idea. But in matters of taxation, Hamilton is considered by 20th-century historians as ahead of his time. The Revenue Act of 1791, Hamilton's brainchild, did not go down well with the public. What is most noteworthy about this act was its creation of the office of Commissioner of Revenue, forerunner of today's Internal Revenue Service. This, too, was Hamilton's idea. The revenue commissioner and his agents would administer the tax law, which mostly stipulated excise taxes and selected tariffs.

After Thomas Jefferson, who had led the opposition to the Revenue Act, became president in 1801, the act was repealed and the office of the Commissioner of Revenue was disbanded. Far from collapsing, the federal government grew wealthy on the lucrative revenues derived from tariffs, and the treasury recorded surpluses annually until the eve of the Civil War.

In July 1862 President Abraham Lincoln signed into law the largest revenue bill in U.S. history up to that point. With $2 million a day going to fund the public debt incurred by war, the need for more revenue was desperate. The bill restored the office of Commissioner of Internal Revenue. The commissioner was empowered to establish a system to collect a progressive income tax based on mandatory income withholding (with a tax return form duly created), as well as to collect numerous other internal taxes. For the first time, failure to comply with the tax laws could result in punishment—prosecution and confiscation of assets in the most extreme cases. Tax returns had to be signed under oath.

By the end of fiscal year 1863, the new revenue bureau took in, through its assessors and collectors, nearly $40 million. By war's end, the Bureau of Internal Revenue had grown from one employee to more than 4,000. Despite the huge sums garnered, the public deficit stood at an unprecedented $3 billion in 1865.

The income tax was discontinued after the Civil War, despite the large sums it had taken in. Wartime patriotism had ensured compliance with the income tax law, but public perception of the law was that it was a wartime exigency. Nevertheless, the Bureau of Internal Revenue was not dismantled after the war, but was put in charge of collecting other taxes, notably the excise taxes on distilled liquor and tobacco.

The post-Civil War period, until 1913, witnessed the growth of huge corporate monopolies and the stifling of competition. Populists and Progressives criticized the lack of social responsibility on the part of the extremely wealthy, and lobbied on behalf of a graduated income tax which would ensure that the wealthy paid their dues. In 1894 Congress revived the income tax, only to see it struck down by the Supreme Court a year later. The problem lay in the vagueness of Article I, Section 8, of the Constitution which gave the federal government the right to tax; according to the Supreme Court decision in *Pollock v. Farmers Loan and Trust Co.,* such a tax would have to be apportioned among the states according to population—and not just targeted to those with the most income. Since the intent of income tax proponents was to pressure those with the most income to pay the most, this decision was a resounding setback for their cause. Only an amendment to the Constitution could make income tax legal.

The Court's ruling precipitated a concerted movement toward adoption of an income tax amendment. Congress took the initiative in 1909, mainly in order to ensure the legality of its recently mandated 1 percent tax on corporate incomes over $5,000, which it disguised as an excise tax rather than as a tax on income. The amendment took nearly four years to be approved by three-quarters of the states, but finally, in February 1913, the 16th amendment was added to the Constitution. It invested Congress with authority to "lay and collect taxes on incomes, from whatever source derived, without apportionment among the several States, and without regard to any census or enumeration." The Bureau of Internal Revenue, a division of the U.S. Department of the Treasury, would administer and collect the new income tax, as it had during the Civil War. Nine years later, the bureau established an Intelligence Division for the surveillance of possible income tax evaders.

The graduated income tax was hailed by the reform-minded everywhere as a sound blow to "special interests." On October 13, 1913, an income tax bill was passed, the first since the abortive 1894 bill. It stipulated that all incomes above $3,000 would be taxed. An annual salary of over $3,000 in those days was a generous middle-class income; below that, no one paid income tax. Hence, less than 1 percent of working people would file tax returns. The new income tax bill repealed the 1909 excise tax on corporate incomes and levied a new corporate income tax on businesses. Mandatory withholding of income was reintroduced for the first time since the Civil War, but Congress repealed this measure in 1916 in favor of voluntary compliance.

The Revenue Act of 1916 raised income tax rates to new highs, and made more people eligible to file. A year later, incomes taxes were raised still more by the War Revenue Act of 1917. Nevertheless, as late as 1940 only 11 percent of working people were required to file, despite the huge cost of the preceding New Deal social legislation and the imposition of the Social Security Act of 1935.

The New Deal, however, had made deficit spending a respectable fiscal practice for the first time in American history. From then on, federal government spending would outstrip income, despite the increasing amounts of revenue derived from the income tax. In fact, mandatory payroll deductions, permanently enacted in 1943, increased revenue income tremendously—to $45 billion in 1945, from a mere $7.4 billion in 1941. Nevertheless, unlike the Civil War period when payroll deductions were introduced for the first time, mandatory payroll deductions remained in force after the end of World War II in 1945. The additional categories of new taxpayers also were not discontinued after World War II, when virtually all working people filed income tax returns. Forty years later, revenue rose to almost $1 trillion, still too inadequate to reduce the deficit, fund the government overall, and pay for the costly Cold War.

The story of internal revenue since World War II is one of increasingly higher taxes (despite tax cuts under President Dwight D. Eisenhower), the expanding size and power of the Internal Revenue Service (the name the Bureau of Internal Revenue adopted in 1953), and the growing deficit burden, in large part because of the need to finance the Cold War. By the end of the Cold War, the "peace dividend" had all but been swallowed up by the federal deficit, which amounted to hundreds of billions of dollars.

In 1952 Congress passed what it regarded as the most sweeping tax law since the 16th amendment inaugurated the income tax. In retrospect, this new tax code reform did more to streamline and make the Internal Revenue Service (IRS) more efficient than to alter personal income tax. Henceforth, all politically appointed posts within the bureau, except for commissioner and deputy commissioner, were replaced by civil service positions; the agency was also significantly decentralized, with headquarters in Washington determining policy, and field offices given wide latitude in decision making. In addition, electronic machines were introduced—predecessors of computers—to speed up processing of forms, which in turn were further simplified.

The consequence of decentralizing the IRS and giving decision-making power to field offices has been a lack of uniformity in interpreting and enforcing tax laws: no two field offices are required to interpret the same tax law similarly, and there are often wide variations from field office to field office, for which the IRS is often criticized. The power of the IRS to enforce the tax laws has been increased. While in 1954 the IRS could impose only 13 penalties on an errant taxpayer, by 1990, the number of penalties had escalated to 150, including seizure of a taxpayer's assets. The IRS made nearly 3 million such seizures in 1990 alone. Moreover, the IRS has the legal authority to request information from any **bank**, and to inquire into any type of vehicle registration or business activity. This uncovers a huge range of information on a business, individual, or married couple. The size of the IRS has grown to more than 100,000 employees, making it the largest government agency in the world.

Ninety-five percent of Americans file tax returns. The federal government derives approximately 55 percent of its revenue from income tax, individual as well as corporate. In 1990 this revenue amounted to nearly $1 trillion. Excise taxes, or "consumption" taxes, on fuel, cigarettes, alcohol, and selected luxury items account for another 4.4 percent. Despite these and other sources of income, the deficit in the national treasury rose continuously; in 1994 it stood at over $250 billion. To service this debt, the government borrowed money and was forced to pay interest on the loans, adding billions to the deficit. The rising deficit more than offset the tax cuts of the Eisenhower and Reagan administrations.

Under President Reagan, tax reform became a high priority. The deficit was too big, taxes were too high, tax forms too complicated, and tax evasion too simple, Reagan concluded. In 1986 his tax reform package inaugurated the most sweeping changes in American income tax since 1913.

In essence, Reagan's tax measure slashed individual income taxes and drastically cut government spending on social programs, in the hope of putting more money into the consumer's pocket. Individual tax brackets were reduced to two: all incomes up to

$17,600 were taxed 15 percent; over that amount, 27 percent. Six million low-income working people were exempt from paying any federal income taxes. Dozens of deductions were eliminated. The reform package also ended ''revenue sharing,'' a program introduced in President Richard Nixon's administration that involved the federal treasury ''refunding'' some federal tax monies to the states. While the bill slashed individual taxes and doubled the personal exemption, corporate taxes were raised, business exemptions were reduced, and loopholes were plugged. The business and corporate world would carry the tax burden, according to the 1986 tax reform bill, and not the individual.

Reagan's tax reforms created reductions in government spending, but were more than offset by the highest military expenditures in U.S. history. Furthermore, the significant increases in corporate income taxes were passed on to the consumer in the form of higher prices; and the elimination of revenue sharing forced states to significantly raise their income taxes for individuals as well as for businesses. In the end, the federal deficit rose to unprecedented levels under the Reagan administration, and his successor, George Bush, was forced to raise income taxes in 1991.

Tax reform continues to bedevil presidents. Following his move to increase income taxes, Bush instituted a deficit reduction plan that placed a ceiling on the deficit—automatic spending cuts would go into effect if this ceiling were exceeded. President Bill Clinton's deficit reduction plan, passed by Congress in August 1993, sought to reduce the federal deficit by $500 billion over a period of five years through a special 4.4 percent fuel tax and reduced government spending. In addition, his tax reform measure hiked taxes for the wealthy (individuals with annual income exceeding $115,000) and corporations. Critics believed that the consequences of the Clinton tax bill would be higher consumer prices, a reduction in capital spending, and a reduction in the already low level of private savings. Despite these trepidations, a booming economy enabled Clinton to reduce the deficit well ahead of schedule and hold inflation in check through the late 1990s.

During the economic boom of the mid-to-late 1990s, individual income tax reform efforts centered on **estate taxes**, **capital gains** taxes, and retirement savings. The Taxpayer Relief Act of 1997 (TRA) included provisions that reduced capital gains taxes (taxes on gains in value of equities, properties, or other holdings) on equities held for more than 18 months; created the Roth IRA, which allowed investors to withdraw their original investment from an IRA without taxation or penalty (although the original investment was not tax deductible, unlike a ''regular'' IRA); and altered the rules governing estate taxes to reduce the taxation of small inheritances (those under $1 million). Income taxes on businesses were also altered by the TRA. Operators of **home offices** and other **small businesses** were allowed to claim federal income tax deductions for office expenses under the new tax law. This measure essentially reestablished a principle that had existed until 1993: that home office expenses were deductible (that year, the Supreme Court had greatly narrowed the definition of what constituted a home office, and the ability of small businesses to deduct office expenses had been eroded). Further tax relief for businesses was also contemplated by Congress in 1998, which debated exempting Internet and information technology industries from income taxation, but the growing revenue potential of this sector of the economy rendered its complete exemption from income taxation a remote possibility.

SOCIAL SECURITY TAXES

Social Security taxes were the next major new tax after 1913 to follow income tax, and were deducted from payrolls simultaneously with income taxes. Meanwhile, like income tax, social security taxes have been steadily on the rise since they were first introduced in 1935.

Although income tax and social security taxes (which include Medicare) are both collected by the Internal Revenue Service, income tax monies make up general federal revenues, while social security taxes go straight into the Social Security trust fund. Social security taxes are the next biggest tax that individuals must pay annually, and for some of the 39 million self-employed, they may be higher than income tax.

The most enduring social legislation to emanate from the New Deal was social security. In 1935 the Social Security Act instituted federally administered old age **pensions**, **unemployment** insurance, and aid to the handicapped as well as to dependent children. These benefits would be paid equally by the employer and the employee, making Social Security theoretically immune to the vicissitudes of the economy or to the size of budget deficits.

In 1950 Social Security benefits were extended to the self-employed, who, however, were compelled to pay not only their own share of the Social Security taxes but the employer's as well, all lumped into one tax called **self-employment** tax. In that same year, Congress raised the Social Security tax by an additional 2 percent (split between employer and employee) in order to fund disability medical insurance, which was added to Social Security benefits. Currently, Social Security taxes are 7.15 percent of gross annual income; the self-employment tax is 15.3 percent. Many economists believe, in fact, that most workers pay the full 15.3 percent of their wages to maintain social security, since their employers make up their portion of the payments by offering reduced wages and benefits.

Whatever is not paid out in the form of pensions from the Social Security fund is invested in government notes. This ''surplus'' has been growing steadily to the point where in 1994 alone, $56 billion was added to it.

In 1965 Medicare was inaugurated, providing government medical insurance mostly for the elderly; it does not, however, cover all medical costs, such as prescription medicine and doctor's fees. The government does cover these costs for the indigent elderly, although these costs are paid out of general federal revenue, rather than from the Social Security trust fund.

STATE TAXES

While federal taxes, including Social Security and Medicare, ate up an average 28 percent of individual incomes in 1993, this did not include state income tax, local taxes, or property taxes. Forty-three states require everyone to file income tax returns. Reliance on state income tax for state treasuries increased dramatically after revenue sharing was discontinued under President Reagan. The rising cost of education and the expanding role of the state in funding primary and secondary education was the original impetus for state income tax. By the time most states required income tax returns, payroll deductions already were used by the federal government, a practice adopted by the states.

Most states also rely heavily on the sales tax, which Mississippi was the first to adopt in 1932. The Great Depression magnified the need for social services, and to finance these, state after state began to inaugurate sales taxes. Between 1933 and 1938, a total of 27 states had instituted a sales tax, that is, a tax on goods and services. Today, 45 states have sales taxes, the highest sales tax being in the state of Connecticut. Half of a state's revenue derives from the sales tax in the states that have this tax. In the aftermath of the taxpayer revolt, many states have raised their sales tax rates further to make up for revenues lost to property and income tax reductions.

Sales taxes vary: in some states, only luxuries are taxed, similar to an excise or consumption tax. Food items, except for food prepared for immediate consumption, rarely are taxed; some states exempt from sales taxes not only food but also clothing. The reasons for this lack of uniformity in applying the sales tax is that it is a regressive tax, and hence falls hardest on those with the least income. So popular and necessary have sales taxes become that many cities have enacted sales taxes as well.

TAX EVASION AND AVOIDANCE

The willingness to risk not paying or underpaying taxes is prevalent today, despite vastly superior techniques of ferreting out the miscreant taxpayer. Of the two types of tax evasion, noncompliance (failure to submit a return or misrepresenting one's taxable income), is illegal, while ''tax avoidance'' is legal. Since the IRS audits only 10 percent of the 200 million tax returns it receives annually, many people are willing to risk noncompliance. Tax avoidance, on the other hand, is mainly the resort of middle- and upper-income Americans; a few of the many ways that individuals and businesses avoid taxes include establishing tax shelters, such as foreign bank deposits, which are not taxed and have strict privacy laws; deferring income into the following year; setting up business on an island that is a tax haven; and investing in a bankrupt business in order to claim the investment on one's tax return.

Corporations and small businesses take yet another route in avoiding huge and burdensome taxes, especially employment taxes: hiring part-time rather than full-time employees, or resorting to temporary workers. To many observers, this has become a worrisome trend, since part-time and temporary workers usually receive no benefits or health insurance and are among the most insecure and vulnerable members of the American **workforce**.

Income tax, federal as well as state, Social Security taxes, and sales taxes have been the primary new taxes of the 20th century in the United States, while taxes enforced in the 19th century have not disappeared (with the exception of the poll tax). The 20th century, unlike the 19th, also has witnessed an unprecedented rise in taxes in many other countries.

[Sina Dubovoy, updated by Grant Eldridge]

FURTHER READING:

Bartlett, Donald L., and James B. Steele. *America: Who Really Pays the Taxes?* New York: Simon & Schuster, 1994.

Brennan, William G. ''Choosing the Right IRA.'' *Financial World,* September/October 1997, 115.

Burnham, David. *A Law unto Itself: The IRS and the Abuse of Power.* New York: Vintage Books, 1989.

Church, George J. ''Launch of an Economic Cold War.'' *Time,* 3 July 1995, 30.

Curatola, Anthony P. ''Be Specific: Calculate Your Gains Carefully.'' *Management Accounting* (U.S.) 79, no. 9 (March 1998): 16.

Daly, Michael, and Hiroaki Kuwahara. ''The Impact of the Uruguay Round on Tariff and Non-Tariff Benefits to Trade in the 'Quad.''' *World Economy* 21, no. 2 (March 1998): 207.

Doris, Lillian, ed. *The American Way in Taxation: Internal Revenue, 1862-1963.* Englewood Cliffs, NJ: Prentice Hall, 1963.

Downing, Neil. ''New Tax Laws Restore Deduction for Home-Based Businesses.'' *Knight-Ridder/Tribune Business News,* 7 August 1997.

Emert, Carol. ''U.S. Tariff Targets Listed for China Policy Sanctions.'' *WWD,* 6 February 1995, 2.

''Ethanol Gets a Tax Break in IRS Ruling.'' *Platt's Oilgram News,* 7 August 1995, 1.

Godfrey, John. ''House, Senate Approve Airline Ticket Tax Measure.'' *Tax Notes* 74, no. 9 (3 March 1997): 1098.

Halstead, Ted. ''Why Tax Work?'' *Nation,* 20 April 1998, 19.

Keiser, Laurence. ''Estate and Gift Tax Provisions of TRA '97.'' *CPA Journal* 67, no. 12 (December 1997): 30.

Kuhn, Susan E. ''Footloose and Tax-Free.'' *Fortune,* 3 February 1997, 147.

McKinnon, John D. ''Faulty Appraisal.'' *Florida Trend* 38, no. 8 (December 1995): 22.

Moore, W. Henson. ''Singapore Round Leaves Tariffs in Place.'' *Pulp and Paper* 71, no. 3 (March 1997): 158.

Morton, Roger. ''Michigan's Taxing Solution.'' *School and College* 33, no. 4 (April 1994): 50.

Mosk, Milton S., and Jeffrey W. Rankin. ''Environmental Excise Taxes Imposed on Chemicals and Substances.'' *Tax Adviser* 26, no. 5 (May 1995): 276.

Plotkin, Hal. ''Prop 13 Time Bomb Explodes: Start-Ups Hit.'' *Inc.,* October 1996, 19.

Rockland, David B. ''A Taxing Development.'' *Field and Stream,* March 1998, 8.

Shafroth, Frank. ''Hi-Tech Commerce Surges: Still Tax Protection Issue Won't Go Away.'' *Nation's Cities Weekly,* 20 April 1998, 1.

''Sunsetting the Internal Revenue Code.'' *Tax Executive* 50, no. 2 (March/April 1998): 141.

''Uruguay Round Will Fuel More U.S. Export Success Stories.'' *Business America* 115, no. 5 (June 1994): 4.

Webber, Carolyn, and Aaron Wildavsky. *A History of Taxation and Expenditure in the Western World.* New York: Simon & Schuster, 1986.

Young, Douglas J. ''Montana Property Taxes Since I-105.'' *Montana Business Quarterly* 32, no. 4 (winter 1994): 22.

Zarocostas, John. ''Chinese Expected to Expand Tariff Cuts in WTO Entry Talks.'' *Journal of Commerce and Commercial,* 21 March 1996, 5A.

TEAMS

The concepts of teamwork, team building, and self-directed work teams have penetrated nearly every segment of the business world in recent decades. More and more businesses are introducing or expanding teamwork as part of their production processes, with varying results. Registering a dramatic change from the more overtly authoritarian structure of traditional firms, companies have focused on more effectively utilizing their human resources by reorganizing them into more autonomous, creative units and harnessing the most productive aspects of their competitive *and* cooperative instincts.

A team is a temporary or ongoing task group whose members work together to identify problems, form consensuses about actions to be taken, and implement the most viable ones. Their purposes and goals often differ. For example, they may be formed to develop new products, act as liaisons between and among different departments within a corporation, or resolve problems. Teams are not, however, intended to be a panacea to all business problems, nor do they always work smoothly.

Teams are not appropriate for all organizations or in all types of businesses. Behavioral scientists are still working to determine exactly when teams will be most effective, what motivates team members, what types of business can best benefit from the implementation of teams, etc. The study of the philosophy and psychology of teamwork is still in its infancy. While effective teams can produce extraordinary results, studies have found that an estimated 50 percent of self-directed work teams result in failure. But as more and more businesses introduce the team concept, the wrinkles in the process are being ironed out and team popularity is growing. Teamwork seems to be the wave of the future in the business world.

THE TEAM PHILOSOPHY

The philosophy behind teamwork is simple: to mesh workers into cohesive groups in order to attain a common goal. The key word is ''cohesive.'' If group members are not properly matched, they will be neither cohesive nor productive. A nonproductive team does not benefit the organization or the individuals. It becomes management's responsibility, then, to assure that teams are well managed and composed of individuals who manifest the necessary characteristics for group work.

Theoretically, if properly managed, people who work in groups will be more productive. In reality, the teamwork approach does not always work well. For example, the right type of team may not be created. One of the keys to success in the team approach is to select the precise type of team best suited to accomplish the intended task. There is a wide variety of teams available from which to choose.

TYPES OF TEAMS

Many different types of teams exist in the business world. There are, for example, functional, task, project, ad hoc, and standing committees; interest and friendship groups; autonomous, integrated, and entrepreneurial work teams; quality circles; and others. Often, people lose sight of the fact that some of these entities are actually teams. But that is just what a committee is: a team put together for a specific purpose. Placed in that context, virtually every business uses one form of team or another.

Groups fall into two categories, formal and informal. Formal groups are those given legitimacy by the organization. Informal groups tend to be more social in nature. Nevertheless, they are sometimes sanctioned by the organization in order to stimulate innovation or increase employee morale. The type of group utilized by individual companies depends to a large extent on the business, the problems to be solved, and the level of participation (e.g., executive, managerial, supervisory, etc.). That is why it is so important that management choose the right team format.

FORMAL GROUPS

A *functional group,* also called a command group, is a formal group consisting of a manager and his or her subordinates, all of whom share a common specialty. For example, all the members of a functional group may be in the marketing department of an organization or the science department of a university. Functional groups tend to stay in existence for long periods of time. The type of organization the functional group serves generally determines the group's objectives, interactions, interdependencies, and performance levels.

A *task group,* or project group, is a formal group created for a specific purpose, usually to identify and resolve problems. Task groups generally work toward a definite project completion date in accordance with well defined parameters and within set budgets. Usually a prepared master plan governs their tasks and schedules.

Task groups supplement or replace work normally done by functional groups. They are frequently utilized in industries such as construction, petroleum, chemical, and aerospace, where workers tend to labor in teams assigned to complete specific projects. The teams might consist of a project manager, who oversees the team's activities, and specialists like engineers, research and development scientists, quality control technicians, etc., all of whom report to the project manager.

Closely related to the task group is the *task force,* also known as an ad hoc committee, which is a temporary team formed to address a specific issue. The task group does not actually perform the work required to resolve a problem, but is an advisory group. The group makes recommendations on an issue, then disbands. It is a distant cousin of the *standing committee,* which is a permanent group responsible for handling recurring matters in a narrowly defined subject area over an indefinite, generally long, timeframe.

INFORMAL GROUPS

There are two categories of informal groups, both of which play an important role in business: *interest* and *friendship* groups. An interest group facilitates employee pursuits of common concerns. A friendship group evolves mostly to meet employees' social needs. The leaders in both groups may differ from those appointed by the organization. However, the characteristics of both formal and informal types of groups are basically the same.

The relationships among the members are based on some common characteristics, e.g., personal interests or political beliefs. Often, but not always, the group's goals may be the same as the organization's. There are times when either or both types of groups can be formal, i.e., legitimized by the organization. The legitimacy is bestowed by astute executives because they realize that informal groups play a vital role in employees' work lives by boosting morale and facilitating communication. These are also keys to the success of more legitimate groups such as autonomous and integrated teams.

THE GROWTH OF TEAMS

Generally, when the term ''teams'' is used in the business context, people think of formal groups such as work teams, integrated work teams, and autonomous work teams. That is because such formal work units are becoming more popular in the workplace today and receive more attention from researchers than do the more traditional teams.

A *work team* is simply a group of individuals who cooperate in completing a set of tasks. Work teams fall into one of two categories: integrated and autonomous.

An *integrated work team* is a group that accomplishes many tasks by making specific assignments to members and rotating jobs among them as the tasks require. The team decides the members' specific assignments and how and when to rotate jobs among them as the tasks require. An integrated team has an assigned supervisor who oversees its activities. Such teams are used frequently in business areas such as building maintenance and construction.

An *autonomous* (or *self-managing*) *work team* is given almost complete autonomy in determining how a task will be done. Autonomous work teams have a wider range of discretion than integrated teams. The organization provides the autonomous team with a goal. From that point on, the team members determine work assignments, rest periods, schedules, quality control procedures, and other matters associated with the job. Fully autonomous teams may decide who is hired, who is fired, and perform one another's evaluations. Often, there are no supervisors in autonomous teams. All members of the group share equal responsibility for the leadership.

Autonomous work teams have proven especially effective in auto manufacturing and associated industries. For example, Goodyear Tire and Rubber experienced success with them in its Lawton, Oklahoma radial-tire plant. The work force included 164 teams made up of 5 to 27 members. Each team set its own production schedule and goals and screened applicants to decide on new members. Goodyear's management discovered that by using the team concept, the plant doubled its daily volume of comparable-sized, traditionally designed plants. More importantly, it beat the cost of comparable tires made by its foreign competitors.

The idea of matching or exceeding foreign competition's prices is essential to the success of American businesses. In adopting the team concept, American businesses are simply borrowing from foreign companies, like Volvo, which apply the team approach with a great deal of success.

A. B. Volvo is perhaps the best known model when the team approach is discussed. Its plants in Sweden are designed to produce cars without using assembly lines. Volvo's new plant in Kamar, Sweden, uses autonomous work teams consisting of about 20 workers each. The members are responsible for constructing entire units of cars, e.g., the engine or the electric system. Each member performs a series of tasks in a few minutes, which differs a bit from the procedures American assembly line workers in auto plants carry out. American workers will more likely perform a single task in a few seconds.

In the Volvo team environment, members learn several jobs to enable them to cover for sick or vacationing individuals. As efficient as the system became, it did not work well at first. There were problems in coordinating the team's multiple tasks, but constant refinements made the system work more effectively. Within a few years, it enabled Volvo to reduce the labor hours involved in producing one car by 40 percent, and increased the inventory turnover from nine times per year to 22. Most importantly, it sliced the number of defects by 40 percent, which is a tremendous cost saver for the company. Just how successful the autonomous team approach has been at Volvo is indicated by the fact that the company soon after opened a new plant at Uddevalla, where work teams will perform an even larger variety of tasks.

Yet another type of team is the *entrepreneurial team,* which comprises a group of individuals with diverse expertise and backgrounds. The members are assembled to develop and implement innovative ideas aimed at creating new products or services or improving existing ones. One of the best examples of an entrepreneurial team's worth is the development of the Ford Taurus automobile.

During the 1980s, the Ford Motor Company was suffering from lagging auto sales and severe competition from foreign manufacturers. Company executives decided to capitalize on their foreign competitors' strengths. They formed an entrepreneurial group as one step in their new approach.

First, they sidestepped the normal five-year process involved in designing, building, and producing a new automobile. Ordinarily, product planners would start the process with a basic concept. Then, designers would develop the look. Their ideas would be translated by engineers into specifications. Next, suppliers and manufacturers would process the design. Each group worked in a vacuum. There was little, if any, contact among the various groups.

Ford's executives decided on a radical new approach to producing the Taurus. The company allocated $3 billion to fund a new group, called Team Taurus. The project involved a team approach in which representatives from all the participating functional departments, e.g., planning, designing, engineering, and manufacturing, cooperated. The team had the ultimate responsibility for developing the new auto. The advantages of the team approach became apparent immediately.

For one thing, any problems with the design could be resolved quickly, since each department involved in the process had representation on the team. And, the team could—and did—create sub-teams to perform investigative work. For example, one sub-team was responsible for designing comfortable, easy-to-use seats. Another studied how to effectively reduce the number of parts used in the production process. The biggest contribution of the team, however, was in its approach to the workers who would actually build the cars.

Team members asked the assembly workers and suppliers for advice early in the design process. The workers were happy to participate. They suggested, for example, that the number of parts in a door panel be reduced from eight to two for easier handling and to ensure that all the bolts contained therein had the same size head. The idea was to eliminate the need for different-sized wrenches. Suppliers also presented some valuable ideas.

Quality circles are closely associated with the total quality management (TQM) process. TQM is a systematic approach to emphasizing organization-wide commitment, integration of quality improvement efforts with organizational goals, and inclusion of quality as a factor in performance appraisals. Quality circles represent one method toward achieving the goal of TQM.

Quality circles, also called quality improvement teams, comprise small groups of employees who work on solving specific problems related to quality and productivity, often with stated targets for improvement. Monsanto formed such a team several years ago in response to a problem reported to it by the Ford Motor Company.

Ford told Monsanto that a Monsanto product, Saflex, which was used to make laminated windshields, was experiencing problems. The dimensions of the materials changed between the time the products left Monsanto's plants and arrived at Ford's facilities. Monsanto immediately assembled a quality control group. Within two months, the team traced the problem to packaging, designed a new prototype, tested it, and implemented a new packaging process. Monsanto's response satisfied Ford. The quick problem resolution was made possible in part because Monsanto's management adhered to one of the cardinal rules of team building: select the right people to perform the work. Achieving positive results is the ultimate goal for any team. It is paramount, then, if business executives hope to reach that goal, and any others for which they strive, that they exercise great care in forming their teams.

For those firms with substantially team-oriented structures, increasingly a company will eliminate its product-based teams in favor of groups with a customer-oriented focus. The philosophy behind this move is that a team can develop a long-term relationship with a certain customer or group of customers. Procter & Gamble and IBM are examples of firms who have eschewed industry based sales forces in favor of teams that specialize on this customer oriented approach.

PUTTING THE TEAM TOGETHER

Forming a team involves a great deal more than just throwing several people together and assigning them a goal. Consideration must be given to motivation, conformity, rewards, intragroup relationships, and norms. Most importantly, a clear and meaningful mission statement must clearly state the team's shared vision at the outset.

Extensive research has demonstrated that the effectiveness of a team begins to diminish over 12 members. The ideal size is typically centered around 6 and can drift as high as 9. Some groups encompass as many as 25 members. With more members, of course, the possibility of fracturing and redundancy escalates. Usually, when formal groups are established with large numbers, they inevitably partition into subgroups. While the specific size determination is obviously best tailored to the specific needs of the company and project, most analysts agree that a tight, cohesive group will generally outperform a large, less associative team.

However, when considering the size of a team, a firm must also be conscious of the necessity of assembling a diversity of skills and functional expertise, which can help foster creative solutions and techniques and avoid stagnation. Conversely, however, it can lead just as easily to animosity and division. Therefore, the authority structure of the team must be carefully designed, implemented, and mediated.

One element that can make or break a team's effectiveness is the degree of mutual accountability. Teams must be fostered to ensure that their loyalty and accountability are directed toward the team and its overall performance, rather than toward the boss. The equal sharing of and dependence on the entire team's outcome is a crucial factor if a team is going to prove worth the trouble of its assembly.

There are two basic types of groups: homogeneous and heterogeneous. Homogeneous groups comprise people who have similar needs, motives, and personalities. They are generally effective at handling simple, routine tasks. Their members' compatibility usually leads to high levels of cooperation and effective communications. The hallmark of the homogeneous group is the fact that the members have few interpersonal problems. Their group harmony is conducive to high group effectiveness—although that is not always the case. At times, the members of homogeneous groups tend to overconformity, which makes it difficult for them to deal effectively with non-routine matters.

Heterogeneous groups, on the other hand, are most often effective at handling complex tasks, especially those requiring innovative approaches to problem solving. For the most part, the members possess different backgrounds and areas of specialization. What one member may lack in training and background, another has. And because they tend to have different types of personalities, they are not afraid to ask questions of one another or to differ on issues. They will challenge one another's conclusions, hypotheses, ideas, etc. Their willingness to confront other group members leads to a valuable exchange of ideas, which in turn leads to innovative solutions to problems. Of course, that is not always a positive thing. It can also lead to intra-group conflict, which is a barrier to productivity.

NORMS IN THE TEAM CONCEPT

Teams cannot work effectively to accomplish their goals if they do not establish norms by which they will operate, i.e., behavioral rules of conduct. Norms provide each individual in a group with guidelines on how to predict the behavior of the other members of the group.

Group norms are not designed to cover every conceivable situation in which a team might become involved. Rather, they address only those situations which are significant to the team. Similarly, not all norms apply to every team member. For example, all team members may have to adhere to norms regarding how much work they should do individually to help the group attain its goals. Perhaps only one member would be responsible for alerting the others to starting and ending times for a group session. There are times, however, when team members may deviate from norms, which can create dissension among them.

Once teams set norms, it is expected that each member will adhere to them. However, not all team members are willing at all times to contribute 100 percent to the group's efforts. Some are free riders, who exert less effort in groups than they do when working alone because they realize that when the team reaches its goal they will share in the glory and the rewards without regard to who actually completed the work.

Teams that include free riders must develop procedures to discipline individuals who do not perform their share of the work. Discipline can range from verbal warnings to firing or transferring the free rider. (Some teams, especially autonomous teams, have the power to hire and fire as they see fit without consulting management. Thus, it is within their province to handle free riders without overwhelming bureaucratic intervention.) The key to success for a team, then, is to get individual members to conform to the norms as closely as possible.

CONFORMITY TO NORMS

Individuals conform to team norms for a variety of reasons. Among them are personal factors, ambiguity, situational factors, and intragroup relationships.

People generally feel more comfortable in groups whose members share some common personal factors, e.g., age and intelligence. However, most people in the American workplace tend to be nonconformists. It is important, then, that groups be assembled with conformity in mind if they are to accomplish their tasks.

Intelligence is also an important factor in group conformity, too. Researchers have determined that the more intelligent people are, the more inclined they will be to go their own way. This is closely tied to ambiguity in the team setting. If the more intelligent members of a team clearly understand the instructions, alternatives, etc., involved in a group project, while other members see only ambiguity, then the latter faction will conform to the lead of those who seem to know what is going on. This can sway the power of balance among team members and lead to groupthink, i.e., social conformity to group ideas by members of the team. Groupthink can be hazardous for a team seeking diverse and innovative ideas to resolve a problem, create new products, etc.

Situational factors are also integral in the team concept. Such factors include the size of the group, unanimity of the majority, and structure. The people who form a group must consider carefully its optimum size in order to reduce friction as much as possible. They must also take into account the group's structure. Normally, the more decentralized a group is, the better it will perform. That is because contact and communications are limited to some extent, which lessens the possibility of groupthink. It is also essential that each member of a team knows his or her role within the group.

Everyone on a team is expected to act in a certain way. Those expectations constitute roles. Often, there is a direct connection between individual team members' functions and their roles. For instance, a marketing representative on a design team is expected to offer advice on how best to sell a new product. The quality control specialist is expected to oversee techniques designed to assure that the product is durable and performs as intended. That does not mean, though, that individuals' roles are limited to their particular areas of expertise. They are also expected to contribute in other ways, as devils' advocates, for example.

TEAM DEVELOPMENT

There are five widely recognized steps involved in the team-development process. They are forming, storming, norming, performing, and adjourning. Not all teams will go through all five stages. Some may pass through several and then regress. All teams go through some of the stages, though.

Forming is the stage in which team members attempt to assess the ground rules that will apply to a task and to group interaction. Team members seek basic information about the group's goals and their roles in the project. They begin to test the extent to which their individual input will be assessed. Individuals may also try to analyze interpersonal behaviors within the group. Basically, forming is a feeling-out process, in which the members test the waters through extensive dialogue and try to make sense of the ground rules, assessing one another's characteristics before carrying out the team's primary mission.

Once the forming stage is completed, the members go on to *storming*. This is the stage in which individuals initiate conflict with one another as they identify possible areas of disagreement. They also attempt to resolve differences of opinion regarding key issues. Areas of disagreement might include task requirements, possible resistance to them, and interpersonal relationships. The larger the team, the more likely are the chances of interpersonal conflicts. The storming stage is also the time in which leadership struggles begin, and thus listening to one another and trying to find mutually acceptable resolutions to disagreements is vital. If issues cannot be resolved, the team's chances of achieving its goals diminish greatly. Once the sorting out process is completed, the third stage, norming, begins.

In *norming*, the team members begin to build cohesion and develop a consensus about norms for performing tasks and relating to one another. By this time, the team members are aware of individuals' idiosyncrasies and are better able to cope with them. They are also clear as to what individual members' roles are and exhibit a greater appreciation for problem-solving techniques. Harmony is the watchword in the norming stage, which is the final step toward performing. Not all groups reach the performing stage, though.

During the *performing* stage team members actually channel their energy toward the completion of the group's task. If team members have not achieved harmony through the first three steps, they may either disband or regress until they do. Those that do reach the performing stage, however, apply the problem-solving solutions or innovative product ideas generated in the previous stages. By this time, the individual team members' roles have been clarified and the group exhibits positive synergy, i.e., the force that results when the combined gains from group interaction are greater than group process losses. Weaknesses have been identified, and efforts are channeled toward their strengths. Teams that reach this stage will most likely remain effective—as long as they continue to devote their energies toward completing the task and maintain harmonious interpersonal relationships. They may continue to do both until the inevitable fifth stage, adjournment, arrives.

Adjournment should be a happy stage, but it is not for some teams. It is the stage in which team members prepare for disengagement as the group nears successful completion of its goals. Members may be pleased with their efforts. However, they may feel some regrets at the team's imminent break-up. This, of course, depends on how long the team has been in operation. Adjournment is more often experienced by teams put together for short-term projects, e.g., ad hoc committees and temporary task groups. Nevertheless, adjournment is a part of the group development process—and often the most traumatic.

THE FUTURE OF TEAMS

Individual teams may adjourn, but teams in general will not. The Center for the Study of Work Teams (CSWT) reported in a recent study that, by the year 2000, roughly 80 percent of Fortune 500 firms will have half their employees working in teams. Proven to be capable of extraordinary success in the workplace, teams will no doubt remain vital in the future. More and more companies are resorting to teams as a way of resolving problems, designing innovative new products, or enhancing old ones. In many cases, teams lower companies' costs in accomplishing these goals. As long as teams have a positive impact on the bottom line, they will continue to be a part of the business environment.

[Arthur G. Sharp]

FURTHER READING:

Aranda, Eileen K., Luis Aranda, and Kristi Conlon. *Teams: Structure, Process, Culture, and Politics.* Englewood Cliffs, NJ: Prentice Hall, 1998.

Katzenbach, Jon R., ed. *The Work of Teams.* Cambridge, MA: Harvard Business School Press, 1998.

McDermott, Lynda, Nolan Brawley, and William Waite. *World Class Teams.* New York: John Wiley & Sons, 1998.

Stewart, Greg L., Charles C. Manz, and Henry P. Sims. *Team Work and Group Dynamics.* New York: John Wiley & Sons, 1998.

TECHNICAL ANALYSIS

Technical analysis is research into the supply and demand of investments based on historic trade information, in terms of both price and volume. Technical analysts, often called chartists, believe that it is possible to detect the onset of a movement in stock or market value from one equilibrium condition to another. To do this, they use charts and computer programs of past stock, commodity, and market movements to identify trends that they believe will predict pricing movements. Chartists are not concerned about why conditions are changing, they only want to identify the beginning of the change to take advantage of short- and intermediate-term gains. While most of these analysts predict short and intermediate pricing trends, some also forecast long-term market cycles based on their data.

Like many professionals in the security industry, chartists believe that the value of the market is determined by supply and demand for **stocks**. Furthermore, like others, chartists think that the supply and demand is influenced by many factors, not always rational, which are weighed continuously and subjectively by the market. Technical analysis differs from other schools of security **forecasting**, however, in the timing of stock price changes. Chartists believe that stocks move in trends lasting over long periods and that astute investors can profit from these trends if they act when the trends first begin. This supposition is based on two beliefs. First, chartists contend that information about stocks leaks into the market over extended periods. Stock prices change gradually as information moves from industry insiders to analysts and finally to investors. Second, chartists believe that a further time lag occurs because investors do not unanimously agree about the validity of the information or its impact upon the **security** in question. The gradual nature of price changes gives investors time to act to take advantage of a trend.

Thus, it is the job of the technical analyst to develop a system that can detect the beginning of a movement from one equilibrium price to a new higher or lower price. It must be underscored that chartists are overwhelmingly concerned with detecting the onset of a change in the supply and demand of a stock (or other investment) so that they can benefit from the price changes associated with finding a new equilibrium.

HISTORY AND BACKGROUND

Technical analysis is, perhaps, the oldest form of security analysis. It is believed that the first technical analysis occurred in 17th century Japan, where analysts used charts to plot price changes in rice. Indeed, many present-day Japanese analysts still rely on technical analysis to forecast prices in their stock exchange, which is the second largest in the world. In the United States, technical analysis has been used for more than 100 years. This form of analysis was especially helpful at the turn of the century when **financial statements** were not commonly available to investors.

In recent years, the ever-increasing use of personal **computers** has led to substantial growth in technical analysis, and numerous **software** packages have been developed to meet these increased needs. Thus, technical analysis can be applied not only to stocks and their markets but also to **bonds, commodities**, fixed-income markets, industries within markets, and currencies. Moreover, one of the most popular current applications of technical analysis is for **futures** derivatives.

TRADING RULES

Technical analysts rely on many rules, often using several at once when deciding whether to buy, sell, or do nothing with an investment. Some of the best-known rules are contrary opinion rules, rules that follow sophisticated investors, and rules that follow the market prices and volume. As with other types of forecasting, however, these rules can be interpreted in a variety of ways, leading to a variety of forecasts using the same information.

The first type, contrary opinion rules, maintains that the majority of investors are incorrect about stock decisions most of the time, but especially at market highs and lows. Thus, when the majority of investors are very bearish, a chartist using this rule would say that it is a good time to buy; conversely, when the majority of investors are bullish, the contrary opinion rule would dictate that selling is the best course of action. A specific example of a contrary rule is the odd-lot theory. In this theory, analysts watch transactions involving amounts less than a round lot (usually 100 shares) called an odd lot. Because this theory contends that small investors are usually wrong in forecasting pricing peaks and troughs, analysts recommend doing the opposite of those actions taken by people purchasing odd lots.

In addition to contrary rules, some chartists follow the activities of investors that they consider smart and savvy. An indicator of such activities is Barron's confidence index, which is a bond index comparing Barron's average yield on ten high-grade corporate bonds to the average yield of 40 average bonds on the Dow Jones. This comparison results in a ratio that should never exceed 100 because the 10 high-grade bonds on the numerator should always a have lower average yield than the average bonds on the denominator. In bullish markets, investors tend to take increased risks and buy lower-quality bonds to reap the higher yields; doing this eventually decreases the low-quality yields and, thus, the ratio increases. Conversely, when investors are bearish, they buy safer, high-quality bonds forcing their yield still lower, and the ratio decreases. While this indicator has merit, it can give analysts false information because it is solely based on the demand for bonds and in no way accounts for fluctuations in their supply. If the bond supply suddenly changes, their subsequent yields will also change with little regard to investor preference.

In addition to using some of the above rules, chartists often take into account stock prices and trading volume when making their purchasing decisions. The Dow theory asserts that stock prices move in three different fashions: (1) major, longer-term trends; (2) intermediate trends; and (3) short-run movements. When analyzing stock prices, chartists try to discern which way the long-term pricing trends are heading, realizing that there will be short-lived trends in the opposite direction. In addition to having an interest in stock price changes, chartists are also interested in stocks' trading volumes relative to their normal trading volumes. While a change in stock price indicates the net effect of trading activity, it gives no information on how widespread the public interest is about the stock. Thus, if a stock price increases in an environment of heavy trading and then has a setback in lighter trading, chartists would probably still view it as a bullish stock, thinking that only a few investors were selling to make a profit.

Technical analysts also use the breadth of market measure to influence their decisions. This is a measure that compares the number of stocks that have increased in price, the number that have decreased, and the number that have remained stable. Similarly, the advance-decline series is an aggregated examination of the net stocks gaining and declining each day.

ADVANTAGES AND DISADVANTAGES

As stated earlier, technical analysts make decisions by examining market and security trends with little regard to the cause of those trends. Conversely, fundamental analysts make their decisions by relying on accurate information about companies and markets before it becomes available to the general public. Because technical analysts do not believe that it is possible to receive and process this information quickly enough, many of the advantages relating to technical analysis correspond directly with the disadvantages of fundamental analysis.

For example, to project risks and future returns, fundamental analysts depend heavily on financial statements for information on a company's or industry's past performance. Technical analysts believe that there are inherent shortcomings in relying on these statements. First, the incredible variety of **accounting** methods makes it difficult to compare firms within the same industry and almost impossible to compare those in different industries. Second, financial statements do not contain all of the information that investors need to make sound decisions, such as information on sales of specific products or on the firm's customers. Finally, financial statements do not include any psychological aspects, such as goodwill, that influence stock prices. By observing patterns and information derived by the **stock market** itself, technical analysts avoid the trappings that often snare fundamental analysts.

In an efficient market, prices quickly and fully reflect all available information. Therefore, technical analysis can work only if security markets are in some way inefficient. Numerous studies testing the efficacy of simple technical trading rules have failed to provide compelling evidence of superiority over a simple buy-and-hold strategy. More recent studies suggest, however, that small benefits can be gleaned from more complex technical trading rules. Yet, past pricing patterns are not always repeated in the future. A forecasting technique can work for a time but later miss a major market turn. Another disadvantage of technical analysis is that pricing forecasts can be self-fulfilling prophesies. Thus, if a stock price is predicted to increase when it passes a given price, it sometimes will do so purely because people will buy the stock at the threshold price, expecting it to continue to increase. In this situation, the stock price typically returns to its real equilibrium value at a later time. A final problem is that there is a great deal of subjective judgment involved in making predictions. Two analysts can look at the same pricing history and arrive at very different pricing projections.

Technical analysis is a method of forecasting security prices by examining past price movements and other observable indicators of market activity. This technique rejects the more conventional mode of fundamental valuation based on financial statements. Technical analysis also requires a lack of efficiency in the pricing process although many studies indicate that major security markets are highly, if not perfectly, efficient.

[Kathryn Snavely, updated by Paul Bolster]

FURTHER READING:

Argenti, Paul A. *The Portable MBA Desk Reference.* New York: Wiley, 1994.

DeMark, Thomas R. *The New Science of Technical Analysis.* New York: Wiley, 1994.

Downes, John, and Jordan Elliot Goodman. *Barron's Finance and Investment Handbook.* 2nd ed. New York: Barron's, 1987.

Fabozzi, Frank J. *Investment Management.* 2nd ed. Upper Saddle River, NJ: Prentice-Hall, 1999.

Levine, Sumner N., ed. *Financial Analyst's Handbook.* 2nd ed. Homewood, IL: Dow Jones-Irwin, 1988.

Reilly, Frank K., and Keith Brown. *Investment Analysis and Portfolio Management.* 5th ed. Fort Worth, TX: Dryden Press, 1997.

TECHNOLOGY MANAGEMENT

Technology has become the key strategic resource needed for the success, indeed the survival, of a business, corporation, or nation. The Persian Gulf War was won by **United Nations** forces in a short time (a ground attack lasting 100 hours in February 1991), due to the technological sophistication of U.S. weapons and logistic support systems. By contrast, the U.S. consumer electronics industry, with $8 billion in sales and 80,000 employees in the 1960s, has been practically destroyed by Japanese **competition**, because of the latter's continuous **innovation** in products and manufacturing processes, lower **costs**, and higher quality.

DISEMBODIED AND EMBODIED TECHNOLOGY

Technology is the body of knowledge, tools, and techniques derived from science and practical experience used in the development, design, production, and application of products, processes, systems, and services. Technology is generally available in two forms: disembodied and embodied. Disembodied technology is knowledge and practical expertise recorded in written and electronic form, such as technical papers, drawings, databases, **patents**, and trade secrets. The value of disembodied technology depends upon its transferability from donor to recipient, and its protection from unauthorized uses. An example of income from disembodied technology is royalties generated from patents.

Embodied technology is incorporated in new or improved products, processes, systems, and services, that are offered to the marketplace. The value of embodied technology depends upon the ability of its producer and marketer to obtain a sustainable advantage over competitors, thereby achieving higher share, sales, and profits.

The following five examples illustrate businesses that profited from embodied technology:

1. Incorporating advanced technology in new products. Texas Instruments developed the Speak and Spell toy to teach the intricacies of English grammar to children and adults for whom English is a second language. A simple product that sells in toy and retail stores for a few dollars, it has a sophisticated microchip and voice synthesizer that "spells" and "speaks" words from its very large dictionary. This proprietary technology was the unique advantage that made Speak and Spell user friendly, inexpensive, and very popular.
2. Incorporating new or improved technology into a manufacturing process. Italian sweaters, designed and knitted by hand, were very popular in the post-World War II era. At that time, the wages and benefits of Italian garment workers increased rapidly, becoming ten times higher than those of workers in Taiwan, the Philippines, and other Asian countries, where the Italian designs were quickly copied. Recently, Italian engineers mastered the techniques of designing new patterns on personal **computers** using **computer-aided design** (CAD) programs, speeding up the design process. They then directly coupled the output of the CAD program to the input of the knitting machines using computer-aided manufacturing (CAM) programs. In the past, setting up the sweater-knitting robots to produce a new pattern was a lengthy and complicated process, requiring long runs of the same pattern to keep production costs down. Now the set up is done very rapidly by computer, producing one-of-a-kind patterns. Because many fashion-conscious customers are willing to pay premium prices for these exclusive patterns, the profitability of the producer is assured. In this case, proprietary process technology was applied to a **commodity** in order to raise its value and gain a competitive advantage over lower-cost competitors.
3. Having new information immediately available wherever needed. Andorra is a small principality of 54,000 inhabitants located in a remote section of the Pyrenees Mountains between France and Spain. Except for a small statistical tax on imported goods, it is virtually a tax-free market. In addition, its bank-secrecy laws make it a haven for money deposits. Andorra's principal **bank** offers competitive **interest rates** and a sophisticated computer system with up-to-the-minute information on interest and exchange rates worldwide. Taking advantage of such factors and the time zone differences between major exchanges such as New York, London, and Tokyo, short-term investment officers electronically move billions of dollars continuously, resulting in profits for investors and banks.
4. Using new technologies to provide rapid, accurate, and secure advanced services, from legal expert systems to credit card accounting. General Electric (GE) tried in vain to enter the mainframe computer business in competition with IBM, and probably lost $1 billion in the process from 1960 to 1970. GE, however, was able to utilize its hardware and **software** to develop the worldwide GE Information System Business for international customers. The system consists of three large computer centers in the United States and Europe, connected by cable and satellite communications and accessible by local direct-dialing from 90 percent of the world's phones. Multinational corporations can use this system for online information retrieval, accounting, inventory control, and **management information systems**. This case illustrates GE's use of proprietary hardware and software to provide a high-value-added service worldwide.
5. Serving new expanding markets created by technology. The **Internet** has opened the market for online information retrieval and electronic commerce. Netscape was founded in 1994 and achieved a market value of $7 billion after two years, thanks to the Navigator browser software developed by Marc Andreessen. Other successful Internet new ventures are Yahoo! and America Online; the latter acquired Netscape in December 1998 for $4.2 billion. Nevertheless, nimble established companies may benefit equally from these market explosions, as witnessed by Microsoft, which developed its Explorer browser software in six months to compete successfully with Netscape.

TECHNOLOGY MANAGEMENT CATEGORIES

Technology is a highly sophisticated and rapidly changing resource. The average life of a new PC product line is less than three years. As with any business resource, technology must be managed effectively and closely linked to corporate or national strategies and policies. This enables it to create **wealth** for a corporation or a nation; to improve the quality of life; to minimize physical, economic, and ecological ill effects; and to prevent disasters.

Technology management can be divided into the following categories:

1. Technology assessment, planning, and **forecasting**.
2. Technology development (research and development and engineering, R&D&E), acquisition, and integration.
3. **Technology transfer**, application, and sales.
4. Selection of the most appropriate technological strategies in relation to the specific environment, capabilities, and competitive position of the organization.

TECHNOLOGY ASSESSMENT AND PLANNING

For meaningful and effective technology planning, a business or a corporation needs to evaluate the following:

1. its technological position in relation to its competition (technology assessment)
2. the technologies required, in order of priority, to achieve its business objectives (technology planning)
3. the most appropriate technological strategies for achieving its business objectives in relation to trends in the environment, market, competition, government regulation, and the evolution of technology.

Technology assessment should address two questions: (1) Are we working on the ''right'' technologies for our business? (2) What is our competitive position?

Technology assessment should be a continuous effort by R&D&E personnel acting as ''technology gatekeepers,'' that is, following the evolution of technologies of interest to the business, as inferred from technical meetings and journals, new patents, new product announcements, and similar sources. Formal technology assessment should be conducted annually, during the preparation of the business's strategic plan, and should include 5- to 15-year projections, depending on the industry (for example, 5 years or less for computer games and 10 years or more for aircraft engines and pharmaceuticals).

Technology assessment should not be performed exclusively by R&D&E personnel, because of possible ''not invented here'' (NIH) biases, and the need to relate to other business functions. **Chief executive officers** (CEOs) have the option of appointing a corporate multifunctional **team**. Team members would report directly to the CEO and be augmented by independent **consultants** who have no NIH bias and have access to information that may not be readily available to the corporation.

Technology assessment can be accomplished in three steps:

1. identification of core technologies,
2. construction of a product/technology matrix,
3. construction of a technology importance/competitiveness matrix.

STEP ONE: CORE TECHNOLOGIES. The core technologies of a business are those critical technologies necessary for advancing the key performance parameters of a company's products, processes, and services. Performance parameters establish a product's value to the customer, and, therefore, influence a company's position in the marketplace. For example, the key performance parameters of a commercial aircraft jet engine are: thrust, weight, fuel consumption, noise, and pollution. Aircraft engine R&D&E has established the following technologies as keys to producing jet engines with high thrust, low weight, and acceptable fuel consumption: high-temperature high-strength alloys, ceramic coatings to reduce corrosion, powder metallurgy, fluid flow, heat transfer, and noise abatement.

STEP TWO: PRODUCT/TECHNOLOGY MATRIX. Once the core technologies have been identified, the importance of each technology for each product line is established. In the case of aircraft engines, product lines might include military jet engines, commercial jet engines, helicopter engines, and stationary gas turbines that produce electric power from oil or natural gas. For example, noise abatement is not important for military aircraft engines, quite important for commercial aircraft engines, and less important for stationary gas turbines, which can be provided with baffles, surrounded by isolating walls, and located in power generating stations, away from residential areas.

Once the ratings for the importance of each core technology for each product line have been determined, they are then ranked according to the relative weight of each product line for the company (as measured by sales, for example), to determine the rating of the technology for the company. Normally, four levels of importance are adequate: high, medium, low, or none.

STEP THREE: THE TECHNOLOGY IMPORTANCE/ COMPETITIVENESS MATRIX. Next, an assessment is made of the relative competitive position of the company in each core technology. This is done by comparing key product-performance parameters of the company and of the principal competitors. The business collects such data by talking to customers, manufacturers, representatives, dealers, and consultants, and by relying on its "technology gatekeepers." Three rating levels are sufficient: the company leads, is equal to, or follows the competition in the specific technology.

We now have two ratings for each core technology: importance to the company and relative competitive position. These ratings are plotted in Table 1, where the diameter of each circle is proportional to the amount of money budgeted for that specific technology. The aggregate position of the core technologies in the matrix of Table 1 shows the overall competitive standing of the company. A company with more circles in the upper left-hand corner (high-lead) is in a more competitive position than a company with circles scattered all over the matrix or bunched in the lower right-hand corner (low-follow).

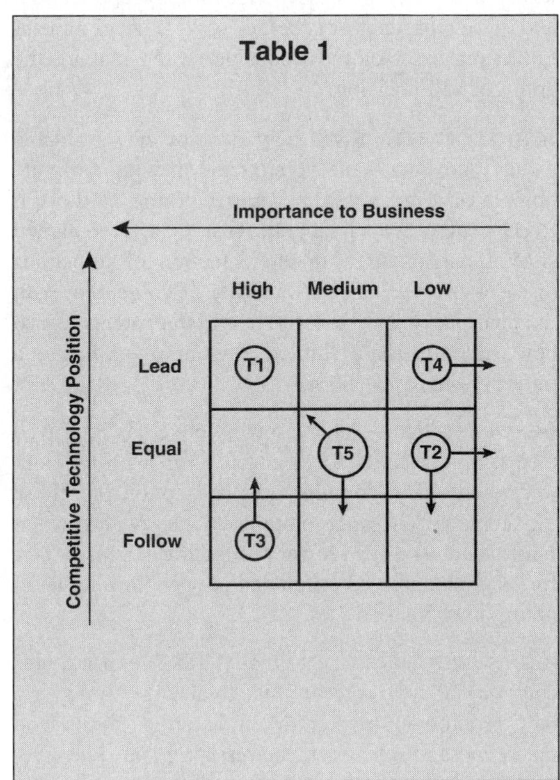

The purpose of technology planning is to achieve company objectives through the proper allocation of limited technological, human, physical, and financial resources. In Table 1, the goal is to shift the circles towards the upper left-hand corner (high-lead) of the matrix, and to drop or starve technologies of lesser importance to the company. Following are some examples, taken from the core technologies of GE Medical Systems.

In the case of T1, the company leads in this technology, which has high importance for the business. The company's business plan should allocate sufficient effort to maintain this lead and strengthen the company's competitive position in the marketplace. An example of a high-lead technology is GE's magnetic resonance imaging (MRI) product line where GE has been the world leader since 1984.

T2 represents a technology of low importance for the company, although its competitive position is equal to competition. In this case, the company should sell the technology to a business where it is of high or medium importance; otherwise, it will die of starvation and drift out of the matrix. Except for this **marketing** effort, no further resources should be allocated to this technology. Such was the case of with GE's ultrasound product line, which was transferred to a **joint venture** with the Japanese company Yokogawa Electric. GE now sells the systems developed by this joint venture worldwide.

T3 represents a technology of high importance but in a noncompetitive market position. To meet this challenge, the company must focus its efforts in **research and development** (R&D), or acquire the means needed to make the technology competitive. This was the case at GE Medical Systems in 1974. At that time GE was the market leader in conventional X-ray equipment, which was being replaced by a new advanced technology, computerized axial tomography (CAT), developed by the British firm Electrical and Musical Industries (EMI). Stung by a staggering loss of market share and the prospect of falling behind the competition, GE started a crash program in the corporate R&D center in order to overtake EMI's lead. Utilizing assets lacking at EMI—manufacturing, marketing, sales, and service—GE Medical Systems met its goal in three years, making it a worldwide leader in CAT. EMI eventually sold what was left of its medical business to GE.

T4 depicts a company leading in a technology that is of low importance to the company. This company has two options: sell the technology or develop a new product line, which could generate substantial sales and profits. Technological superiority does not guarantee new product success (as happened in the case of EMI). The company must establish the manufacturing, marketing, and financial resources required for successfully launching a new product line. This was the situation at GE when its R&D center developed MRI technology without the concurrence of GE Medical Systems **management**; eventually they adopted the technology.

Finally, T5 represents a technology whose value to the company is unclear. Both technical and strategic planning should be continued, in order to determine whether it warrants additional technical effort.

Up to now, the discussion of technology assessment and planning has been based on current core technologies. Each technology, however, has a limited life cycle, which could last only 2 or 3 years (for certain types of semiconductors) or as long as 40 years (for steam turbines). It is necessary, therefore, to include future core technologies in the technology assessment and planning processes. These are the technologies that have a strong potential of displacing and replacing current core technologies. Computers, for example, initially used electromechanical relays, and later, vacuum tubes. These were replaced first by transistors, then by integrated circuits, currently by microchips, and, in the future, possibly by superconducting Josephson junctions or laser optics. In practice, the three-step assessment and planning exercise described above would be done twice every year: once for today's markets, products, and technologies; and once for the markets and technologies projected for a certain number of years in the future (with the number varying, depending on the nature of the business).

The following process is recommended for this long-range technology plan. The strategic plan of the company or business unit includes a descriptive scenario of the markets targeted, for example, five years into the future, and the products and services to be developed to serve these markets. R&D&E personnel then develop a ''technology road map'' specifying the new or improved technologies that will be required in five years and the R&D competencies required to develop these technologies. Then, the company's current R&D competencies are compared to the competencies of its competitors, and specific plans are made for enhancing current competencies, developing new competencies in-house, or sourcing them through **licensing**, recruiting of specialists, or even acquiring other companies.

TECHNOLOGY APPLICATION AND SALES

As an asset, technology may be acquired or sold, stolen, wasted, made obsolete, or applied for company growth and profitability. Once technology has been developed or procured, it is part of a company's assets, and, as such, has value. Technology can be an **intangible asset**, hard to define, evaluate, or safeguard; therefore, it is difficult and risky to manage. **Intellectual property**, for example, can be lost if the holder leaves a company without transferring the technology to others or worse, is employed by a competitor. Thus, technology has no value for the company unless it is applied through embodiment in new or improved products, processes, systems, and services, or sold or transferred to other parties. In established companies, the originator of the technology, usually the R&D division, is separate from the user of the technology, usually the manufacturing and marketing departments. Therefore, the technology must be transferred across human, geographical, and organizational barriers, not a simple or smooth process.

Technology application is the practical utilization of technological assets to achieve customer satisfaction, to gain a competitive advantage in the market, and/or to improve the quality of life. In the past, the time span from technology development to application was lengthy. For example, it took 12 years for scientists to develop the first commercial application of the laser after its discovery in 1960. There is evidence that the time span between technology development and application is shortening, as evidenced by the Japanese electronic and electro-optical consumer industry and by the U.S. biotechnology industry.

Just as any company faces a make-or-buy alternative for obtaining technology, it also faces an apply-or-sell alternative for converting its technological assets into profits. Selling technology may be an attractive alternative for a company to cash in on its technological assets, rather than going through the costly and risky process of technology application, and of new product, process, or service development. Following are factors to consider when making the apply-or-sell decision.

STRATEGIC FIT. R&D may develop new valuable technologies that have no strategic fit with corporate objectives. For example, while working at the GE R&D center, Nobel laureate Ivar Giaever obtained several patents used in the detection of infectious diseases. As GE had no intention of competing with the pharmaceutical industry, it sold the patents to two new ventures for a limited amount of cash and a minority equity position.

OBSOLESCENCE. As a company develops improved technology, it must decide what to do with its older technology. The company has the option of selling the technology to a developing country with less sophisticated needs and lower production expenses. GE, for example, sold its outmoded copper forming technology to Poland.

HIGH INVESTMENTS. Normally, R&D expenditures comprise 10 to 30 percent of the total cost of bringing a new product to market. Manufacturing investment, marketing and sales costs, **advertising** and **sales promotion**, and customer education usually constitute higher costs than R&D. If a company has difficulty raising additional financing, it may sell the technology to, or enter into a joint venture with, a large, well-established company with plenty of liquid assets. Many emerging biotechnology companies contribute only the technology to a joint venture, with the established company providing cash and marketing expertise.

CLOSED MARKETS. For various reasons (**trade barriers**, for example), some markets may be closed to the company that developed the technology. For example,

GE Power Systems developed heavy-duty gas turbines as an alternative technology for electric power generation, and had the leading market share in the United States. GE wanted to expand its market to Europe, where the demand for electricity was growing rapidly. In most European countries, however, power utilities are government-owned and, for political reasons, buy only from local suppliers. GE, therefore, had no choice but to enter into cooperative agreements with leading French, Italian, German, and Spanish electrical-equipment manufacturers. The high-technology rotor was built in the United States and shipped to the customer site; the lower technology stator and housing were manufactured by local partners, who were also responsible for sales, installation, and maintenance. GE did not license its rotor technology and thus avoided possible leaks to European competitors. GE guaranteed the performance of the entire system, however.

PREEMPTING COMPETITORS. Once a proprietary technology has been developed, there is always the risk of a competitor developing an equal or better technology. To preempt the competitor, a company may sell the technology to the competitor at a reasonable price. The seller is at an advantage since the competitor will have increased production costs; may have to pay royalties, which can amount to a significant percentage of sales; and will abandon the idea of developing a superior technology. In such agreements, there is often a cross-licensing clause, giving the licensor company direct access to any improvements made by the licensee, and the right to visit the buyer's plants and **audit** their books. For instance, GE developed and held a manufacturing-technology patent for the first man-made industrial diamonds, which could be produced at much lower costs than mined diamonds. Nonetheless, GE decided to license its main competitor, South African diamond-mining company De Beers, to preempt them, increase their costs, and, of course, make a profit.

STANDARDS. As a product and an industry matures, rigid standards are established to facilitate interconnection of equipment and parts replacement, and to reduce operating costs. Various companies aggressively seek to have their specific technologies adopted as industry standards, at times giving away technology free to competitors in order to speed up the adoption process. Sun Microsystems, the leading producer of workstations, once sent engraved invitations to competitors to visit their display booths at trade fairs and obtain a free copy of the proposed standards. Sun wanted to convince competitors to adopt its standards, thereby expanding the market for compatible workstations and related software applications.

MULTIPLE SOURCING. No company or organization is comfortable when dependent on a single supplier for vital components or products. Therefore, large buyers, such as the U.S. military or IBM, insist that their preferred supplier license other potential suppliers to ensure a steady flow of goods in cases of strikes, calamities, shortages of materials, and so forth. Having multiple sources also can prevent arbitrary price escalations by the initial supplier.

CROSS-LICENSING. New technologies being developed by businesses may violate existing patents held by competitors. To avoid costly litigation and royalty payments, several large corporations may enter into cross-licensing agreements that exempt their core technologies. For many years GE, AT&T, and IBM had royalty-free cross-licensing agreements for patents not pertaining to core technologies. GE excluded new alloys for jet engines, and steam and gas turbines; AT&T, switching systems; and IBM, computer architecture.

ANTITRUST. While a patent is a legal monopoly for 20 years, the U.S. government contends that a patent cannot be used to violate **antitrust acts and laws**. Therefore, if a company achieves a dominant market position because of its unique technology, it may be subject to antitrust investigations and litigation. For example, the U.S. Antitrust Division forced the Xerox Corp. to license its copier patents to its weaker U.S. competitors (this occurred long before the Japanese moved in the U.S. copier market). As a result, many companies today prefer to license to their competitors, to avoid such a problem.

JOINT VENTURES. In some cases, a company does not have the expertise needed to market a new technology. As a result, one company may contribute the technology; and a second, the marketing know-how, **channels of distribution**, local sales and service, and so forth, creating a joint venture. GE Medical Systems entered into such an agreement with a Japanese company, Yokogawa Electric, to develop the Japanese and Far Eastern markets.

In conclusion, the main reasons for selling technology rather than incorporating it into new products are the desires to reduce exposure and **risk**, and to make a quick profit, even if the gain is less than one realized over a technology life cycle or patent validity.

TECHNOLOGICAL STRATEGIES

Technology is a valuable asset that a corporation can and should employ to gain a competitive advantage in the market. This can be achieved by utilizing business strategies in which technology is a major component. The choice of the most appropriate technological **strategy** for a business depends upon the environment, its strengths and weaknesses in relation to the competition, and the resources available—not only technological but also manufacturing, marketing, sales, distribution, and financial. Mixed strategies are utilized, but may cause organizational problems when implemented. Four basic technological strategies are: (1) first to market; (2) fast follower and . . . overtaker; (3) cost minimization; and (4) market niche or specialist.

FIRST TO MARKET. The first to market strategy is offensive, with a high-risk and high-reward potential. This strategy is implemented after a radically innovative technology is discovered by chance or by design, and then is embodied in a product of high functional utility for the customer. It is often used by high-tech new ventures, such as the MapInfo company, for PC map displays; and by progressive, established firms with plenty of resources, such as GE, for man-made diamonds and engineering plastics. If the company's competitive advantage can be maintained, the company enjoys a temporary monopoly or quasi-monopoly that can be exploited to optimize sales and profits. This was the case for GE's man-made diamonds and its first engineering plastic, Lexan. Scientists discovered these products in GE's R&D center while researching the behavior of simple elements, such as carbon, under high pressure and temperature; and a hard enamel for insulating copper wires. GE recognized the potential value of these inventions, devoted plenty of resources to their development and application, and waited patiently (ten years, in the case of Lexan) for the cash flow to become positive. Due to this strategy, GE Plastics, launched in 1957, had grown into a $7 billion business by 1998.

Long-term first-to-market strategy success requires more than a technology breakthrough. It is also necessary either to continue producing new products based on technological and market innovation, or to maintain market leadership through continuous price reduction, which in turn, depends upon cost reductions. This is not always easy, as shown by VisiCalc, a pioneering company that developed the first **spreadsheet** software program for personal computers. After the initial success, VisiCalc was not willing or able to develop an improved version or a second product; it was overtaken by Lotus Development Corporation, and is now bankrupt.

MapInfo is a case in contrast. It was founded by four Rensselaer Polytechnic Institute students who had developed, as part of their computer science project, the first program for displaying maps on a PC. While other programs used on mainframes cost $5,000 to $20,000, MapInfo offered their first software package in 1987 for only $750, making it affordable to the 30 million IBM-compatible PC owners worldwide. To stay ahead of the competition, every few months MapInfo introduces advanced versions of the first program, and new packages with additional functions. It has grown rapidly from $60,000 sales in 1987 to $60 million in 1998.

FAST FOLLOWER . . . AND OVERTAKER. After a pioneer has demonstrated that a technology actually works, and that the market is receptive to the innovation, a fast follower can move in rapidly, capture a large market share, and even overtake the first entrant. To succeed with this strategy, the fast follower should not duplicate the product of the pioneer and rely on lower production costs, as is practiced by some companies in the Pacific Rim. Rather, the fast follower should practice innovative imitation by offering a similar product that can be differentiated from the first entrant's offering. Fast followers capitalize on their existing complementary assets, such as production facilities, marketing channels, customer contacts, company image, and so forth, in order to achieve a substantial market share and even surpass the leader.

This was the case with the first IBM personal computer. Stung by the unexpected success of the Apple II, IBM started a crash program to develop its personal computer. Director Don Estridge was given a blank check to secure all the needed resources, make or buy the technology, and organize his project team. In less than one year, his team developed the IBM PC, more or less equivalent in performance and price to Apple II. IBM's PC, however, was painted ''bright blue''; that is, IBM relied on its strong image in the marketplace, and a large base of loyal customers, thereby commanding a market share equal to Apple's.

GE presents another example of a fast follower. In the field of computerized axial tomography, GE differentiated its offerings from developer EMI's not only through improved performance but also through its well-respected trademark, extended **warranties**, application engineering, customer training, and endorsements by leading doctors and clinics.

COST MINIMIZATION. The cost minimization strategy is effective for mass-produced goods, where significant **economies of scale** can be realized through process innovation. This strategy has been successfully used by the Japanese and other Pacific Rim countries to gain dominant market share in consumer electronics, IBM-compatible PC clones, and even the fashion industry.

As a technology matures, products become standardized, functional differences between various brands decline in importance, **personal selling** is replaced by mass marketing, and price becomes the dominant factor in the customer's decision to buy. To minimize production costs, product innovation is gradually replaced by process innovation, utilizing the learning curve, which projects declining unit costs as volume increases. Similarly, marketing and distribution costs are reduced—for instance, by **telemarketing**, **direct mail** sales, and discount stores. Utilizing the cost minimization strategy, the company strives to become the lowest cost producer and, therefore, the price leader. By reducing selling price and production costs according to the learning curve, the company forces less efficient competitors to withdraw, the market stabilizes, and the company increases its market share and profits.

In some cases, the company can practice ''forward pricing'' below actual costs, in anticipation of the learning curve; this will ''shake out'' competition, but also, more importantly, will discourage more powerful potential competitors from entering the market. Because of possible antitrust litigation, this practice is more common in Japan—particularly among computer and consumer electronics manufacturers—than in the United States.

To succeed with cost minimization, a business needs superior process-engineering and value analysis skills. In addition, a company must strive to reduce its total costs, not just manufacturing costs, while maintaining a high level of quality. Most customers will not, however, trade lower costs for lower quality. Detroit discovered this when it produced compact cars after the first oil crisis, to compete with the Europeans and Japanese. While Detroit's prices were 15 to 20 percent lower than their foreign competitors, the quality of its cars—measured by the number of defects in a new car—was one-third to one-half of foreign competitors. As a result, American consumers were willing to pay premiums of $1,000 to $1,500 per car and wait several months for the Japanese models, while the American versions sat unsold in dealers' lots.

MARKET NICHE OR SPECIALIST. The market niche or specialist strategy is generally adopted by new high-tech ventures that are searching for ''a place in the sun'' in competition with established dominant suppliers. In the early days of the computer industry, Digital Equipment Corp., Wang, and Control Data Corp. all adopted this strategy to compete with IBM. Normally the selected market niche is initially of little or no interest to the dominant supplier, who is willing to let competitors develop it. For instance, IBM avoided serving the R&D laboratories, and university scientific computing and data acquisition markets, because of their limited size. In addition, laboratory researchers and university professors demanded special features, nonstandard components, and complex application engineering that IBM was unable or unwilling to provide. Digital Equipment and Control Data were willing and able to provide specialist services for this small but rapidly growing market. Similarly, Wang developed the word processor market niche, a hybrid of electronic typewriters and small computers, and for a while, competed successfully with IBM and Olivetti.

To succeed, a market niche must be carefully selected and followed. If the market niche is too small, it will be saturated within a relatively short time, since the opportunity for growth is limited. For example, Control Data, to increase sales, was forced to abandon its original profitable but limited niche of data acquisition and control systems and compete directly with IBM in data processing, an area with low profits and fluctuations in market share.

Conversely, if the niche becomes too large, it becomes an attractive target for competitors. Cray Research illustrates this point. Cray was the original leader in the then-limited, but highly profitable market niche for supercomputers. Seymour Cray founded the company in 1972 with a mission ''to design and build a larger more powerful computer than anyone now has.'' Initially the market niche was quite small, estimated at 80 users worldwide in 1976. The niche grew to a $1 billion market by 1990, with large companies, such as Control Data, IBM, Fujitsu, and Hitachi entering the market. Cray Research lost market share, encountered serious cash flow problems, had to cut back on its advanced R&D efforts, and was swallowed up in an acquisition by Silicon Graphics in 1997.

Another danger of the market niche strategy is that the niche may be destroyed by new technology. For instance, Wang's word processor market was eliminated by the rapid progress in **microcomputer** technology. While word processors are limited in their functions, the PC's features include computations, spreadsheet calculations, graphics, and **word processing**, making them the preferred office tool.

To succeed with the market niche or specialist strategy, a company should be very selective in accepting orders that entail too much specialization. Such orders require excessive and expensive efforts in development and design engineering to meet the customer's unique specifications. Thus a company eventually becomes a ''job shop,'' adapting its designs to serve various customers, but unable to reduce costs according to the learning curve. The secret is to have one or two basic designs that can be easily and rapidly adapted to meet customer requirements, while utilizing standardized factory and software processes.

CONVERGENT AND DIVERGENT TECHNOLOGICAL AND APPLICATION STRATEGIES

A company or strategic business unit may gain a sustainable competitive advantage in a targeted market by utilizing convergent or divergent technological strategies for the design and application of its products and services:

1. A convergent technological strategy is defined as the development and synergistic integration of all technologies necessary to achieve worldwide leadership for a new product, process, or service. A typical example is the first laptop computer by Toshiba, in which the goal of hardware and software de-

velopment was to produce a small, lightweight laptop computer fully compatible with the IBM personal computer and its clones.

2. A divergent technological strategy is defined as the development of alternative technologies, related or unrelated, that will assure leadership in a given market. A typical example is GE Medical Systems which has achieved leadership in the medical imaging diagnostic market through a variety of product lines based on different technologies: conventional X rays, CAT scanners, MRI, and ultrasound.
3. A divergent application strategy is defined as targeting a broad spectrum of customers across many industries, with a great variety of diverse applications. A typical example is the Toray Company of Japan which has achieved worldwide leadership in the application of carbon fibers for aerospace to automobile brake linings and consumer products such as fishing rods.

Following are three examples of such technological strategies, which illustrate different ways of managing technology to achieve global leadership.

TOSHIBA LAPTOP COMPUTER: CONVERGENT TECHNOLOGIES. The first truly portable, IBM-compatible personal computer was the Toshiba laptop, an ''under-the-table'' project of a small team of passionate Japanese engineers led by Tetsuya Mizoguchi. The process of conceiving, designing, developing and building prototypes of this radical innovative product was driven by the ''back to the future'' approach, which can be summarized as follows.

The product concept is first developed based on an intensive market study in the field and on the factors that will ensure product leadership five years later. Considering the fast progress of the core technologies of personal computers, this is a difficult forecast that must be based, in part, on an intuitive feel for the marketplace. Then the engineering design process begins, based on stringent specifications. These are given to the engineers as design constraints that cannot be changed. The design is improved through subsequent iterations and optimized to satisfy the dominant constraint. (This constraint was size and weight for the laptop computer.) After market launch, improved or new models are developed to remain at least two years ahead of the competition.

In this case, all technologies to be embodied into the final product must *converge* to meet the design specifications. All components must work together as a system, and trade-offs must be made continuously in order to optimize the performance, and meet the dominant constraints, such as price, size, and weight of the final product. The engineers and scientists of the design team may be specialists in different disciplines—computer architecture, circuit design, design and manufacture of integrated circuits, heat transfer, mechanical design, liquid crystal and plasma displays, semiconductor and optical memories, ergonomics, etc.—but they are all working toward the common goal of optimizing the product. Future enhancements and new models, such as Toshiba's notebook, build on the established core competencies as the learning process continues and the market evolves towards miniaturization and ease of use.

GE MEDICAL SYSTEMS: DIVERGENT TECHNOLOGIES. The customers and users of GE Medical Diagnostic Systems products are medical doctors, radiologists, and hospital or clinic administrators. The required functional specifications are: a diagnostic imaging system that will yield high-quality images, in a very short time, with minimum hazard and discomfort to the patient, at a reasonable cost. The equipment should be reliable, rugged, and easy to operate. The value of meeting these specifications is very high: accurate and fast imaging can save human lives, help select the most appropriate diagnosis, and avoid unnecessary surgery and treatments.

The customers do not care, and often do not even understand, the technologies by which images are produced. In fact, there are many competing technologies to produce medical images of the human body: X rays, CAT, MRI, ultrasound, nuclear medicine (where the patient drinks a radioactive liquid), single photon emission computer tomography, etc. These technologies are both competitive and complementary, that is, they partially overlap (X rays, CAT, and MRI) and partially have their own preferred applications (ultrasound for pregnant women). In addition, the boundaries between application areas are constantly shifting and new models are under development. Consequently, a manufacturer cannot arbitrarily select one technology and hope that it will prevail in the marketplace. To achieve and maintain global leadership it is necessary to offer a broad spectrum of technical solutions, and constantly monitor the emergence of new competing technologies, in conjunction with the evolving functional requirements of the marketplace.

GE Medical, a leader in conventional X-ray radiography, found this out the hard way when EMI emerged as an unexpected competitor with the first CAT scanner. GE reacted with a crash program in the R&D center to follow and overtake EMI in technology and market leadership. Having learned the lesson well, GE was then a pioneer in developing MRI. In ultrasound, however, GE lagged behind in technology and especially cost. Yet a survey in 1994 showed that one out of three hospitals was in the market for additional ultrasound equipment. Consequently, GE could not afford not to be in this market segment. GE first had the product redesigned by another company, and then decided to produce a lower-cost version in a joint venture with a Japanese partner, Yokogawa Electric. We conclude that, in the case of medical diagnostics, we are faced with *divergent* technologies, with few common core competencies. The management challenge is to select and orchestrate these technologies for optimum customer benefits and company profitability.

TORAY CARBON FIBERS: DIVERGENT APPLICATIONS. The origin of Toray's carbon fiber business goes back to a ''happy accident'' that was exploited by company management's long-range vision and determination to achieve global leadership. In 1966, when Toray was producing rayon and nylon, one researcher had discovered a new monomer. His manager suggested carbonizing it to develop an acrylic textile fiber. Instead, the monomer turned into a strong and stiff carbon fiber, in one-tenth of the normal processing time. Fifteen years later, about 45 percent of all carbon fibers produced in the world were produced or licensed by Toray. In 1993 Toray had more than 50 percent of the market and built a new pre-preg plant near Seattle, Washington, to supply at least 20 percent of the structural components for the Boeing 777 aircraft. At the same time, its major competitors—Courtaulds, BASF, Amoco, Hercules, and Hitco—were downsizing their plants or offering them for sale.

How did Toray achieve this global market leadership? First, the product was positioned correctly on the price-performance scale, 20 to 30 times more expensive than commodities such as glass fibers, which are sold on price, but 3 to 8 times cheaper than specialized super-strength materials such as boron fibers, which are sold in very limited quantities.

Second, the applicability of carbon fibers was greatly expanded by:

1. offering the fibers not as basic material but as fabrics that are easier to incorporate into the final product, such as noncrimp woven, welded, triaxial, mesh, and stitching threads.
2. finding other materials that can be significantly strengthened with carbon fibers, such as organic resins, aluminum, steel, copper, magnesium, and high-strength engineering plastics. For example, lightweight, high-strength bicycle frames are made of plastic tubes reinforced by carbon fibers, as are nose cones of spaceships.

Third, all possible markets for fibers and composites were explored by finding market niches where carbon fibers could contribute a high added-value in terms of strength, stiffness, reduced weight, and resistance to shocks, abrasion, heat, and contamination. Table 1 presents a list of applications of Toray's advanced composite materials.

Table 1

Applications of Toray's Composites

Sports	**Tennis rackets, golf clubs, fishing rods, recreational boats, bicycles**
Energy	**Solar cells and mirrors, windmills, fuel cells, flywheels, centrifuges for uranium enrichment**
Aerospace	**Structural components for aircraft and spacecraft, rockets, ballistic linear motors, satellites, nose cones**
Automotive	**Structural parts (bumpers, doors, dashboards), spring leaves, shock absorbers, cardanic shafts, brake discs**
Marine and mechanical equipment	**High-performance cables, anticorrosion equipment, high-speed moving parts, wear-resistant parts, gears, medical equipment components**

As can be seen from this list, the targeted markets are extremely different in terms of customers and distribution channels. We can therefore define Toray's applications and markets as *highly divergent.* The management challenge is to develop sufficient engineering competencies to explain to the varied potential users the advantages of Toray's products for their specific applications.

In conclusion, the most important factor for effective technology management is the close coupling of technology and business strategies, the cooperation of the R&D&E functions with the manufacturing, marketing, and financial functions, and close contact with internal and external users.

[Pier A. Abetti]

FURTHER READING:

Abetti, Pier A. *Linking Technology and Business Strategy.* New York: American Management Association, 1989.

Betz, Frederick. *Strategic Technology Management.* New York: McGraw Hill, 1993.

Burgelman, Robert A., Modesto A. Maidique, and Steven C. Wheelwright. *Strategic Management of Technology and Innovation.* 2nd ed. Homewood, IL: Irwin, 1996.

Levy, Nino S. *Managing High Technology and Innovation.* Upper Saddle River, NJ: Prentice Hall, 1998.

Martin, Michael J. C. *Managing Technological Innovation and Entrepreneurship in Technology-Based Firms.* Reston, VA: Reston, 1994.

Tushman, Michael L., and Philip Anderson. *Managing Strategic Innovation and Change.* New York: Oxford University Press, 1997.

TECHNOLOGY TRANSFER

Technology transfer is the dissemination of technical knowledge, skills, and products from a point of origin into a broader sphere of use. The term can describe any number of such actions, but the main two stages of technology transfer are as follows:

1. *Noncommercial to commercial*—the transfer of knowledge from research settings such as universities, institutes, and government laboratories to the commercial sector.
2. *Industrial economy to developing economy*—the spread of knowledge from wealthier, developed economies to less developed economies.

In general, these stages occur in this sequence, although they can also happen in reverse order or simultaneously.

As the definitions above highlight, the most important aspect of technology transfer is the underlying knowledge of how technology works and how it can be applied to real-life problems. The skills needed to implement this knowledge in a practical form are also crucial, and it may be beneficial to physically transfer technology as well, but the physical transfer is usually least important from a technology-transfer perspective.

MECHANISMS FOR TECHNOLOGY TRANSFER

Technology transfer takes place through a number of different channels. Key among these are foreign **direct investment**, **licensing agreements**, **joint ventures**, and research collaboration between private companies and universities or government agencies. The choice of mechanism for individual companies depends largely on business strategy, risk tolerance, and available resources. A combination strategy may also be used. For instance, when technology has implications for more than one industry, the originating company or research center may choose to license its innovation for certain uses outside its expertise while directly developing the technology for those areas it is most competent in. In addition, multinational corporations, particularly those based in the United States, Western Europe, and Japan, act as major transferrers of technology to LDCs.

NONCOMMERCIAL TO COMMERCIAL TRANSFER

Universities, research institutes, and government-sponsored agencies are a major source of new technology that is ultimately exploited in the commercial realm. By one late 1990s estimate, university technology transfer alone is worth more than $21 billion a year in the United States.

ENCOURAGED BY LEGAL REFORMS. Since the late 1970s, American universities have played an increasingly important role in the development and transfer of new technologies. This shift was strongly encouraged by the 1980 passage of the Bayh-Dole Technology Transfer Act, which allowed nongovernmental organizations (universities, companies, nonprofits) to use federal dollars for research and still retain the patents to their innovations. Before then, government agencies commonly claimed at least some of the rights to such inventions and proved lethargic and inefficient managers of the **intellectual property**, impeding technology transfer.

A series of additional laws throughout the 1980s helped to further stimulate research for technology transfer to the commercial sector. Noteworthy acts included the National Cooperative Research Act of 1984, which loosened restrictions governing research collaboration between for-profit competitors, and the Technology Transfer Act of 1988, which enabled government research laboratories to form cooperation agreements with private-sector organizations to facilitate technology transfer.

UNIVERSITIES CENTRAL TO THE PROCESS. The emphasis of the top U.S. research universities on the commercial applications of research also resulted in part from a widespread perception that the United State was losing out to its international competitors in both basic and applied research. This led government, industry, and university representatives to undertake initiatives to develop new linkages between companies and top research universities. Among these linkages were university ownership of equity in firms established on the basis of university research, liaison or technical assistance programs, research partnerships, and the establishment by universities of patent and technology licensing offices. Many top research universities in the United States took the route of equity ownership in start-up companies. It was argued that this method facilitated technology transfer, created the possibility of large financial gain for universities, and helped to attract and retain faculty who might otherwise be tempted to join the commercial venture themselves.

Federal funding to universities continues to play a paramount role. Of the 1,500 or more patents in all fields issued to universities each year, some 80 percent come from projects that receive federal funds. The federal government has provided two-thirds of total university research funds, with private industry providing a relatively small though rapidly growing share. To a lesser extent, federal funds also target small businesses through such initiatives as the Small Business Administration's Small Business Technology Transfer (STTR) program.

DEVELOPED ECONOMY TO DEVELOPING ECONOMY

While technology is transferred internally in developed countries and LDCs alike, studies of technology transfer are often concerned specifically with transfers *from* the more advanced economies *to* LDCs. In this sense, technology transfer is central to the study of newly developing economies.

In his essay ''International Business and the Transborder Movement of Technology,'' Denis Simon defined three classes of technology transfer: material transfer, design transfer, and capacity transfer. Material transfer refers to physical goods ranging from product parts to fully operational plants. Design transfer refers to blueprints or other types of information used to build products or production facilities. Capacity transfer refers to education and training not only to operate existing plants but also to develop innovations in products and processes.

Japan is often referred to as a case of an advanced country that developed in large part through technology transfer. Previously developed capitalist countries such as Britain, the United States, and Germany relied to a larger extent on domestically produced technologies.

Japan's developmental success in the postwar years provides a contrast with the patterns observed in many LDCs. In particular, many LDCs have depended heavily on exports of raw materials, which often suffer from unstable prices in world markets, and have consequently run up large trade deficits and suffered from crushing debt burdens. Part of the appeal of technology transfer is that it creates the possibility for development that is less reliant on native sources of raw materials and is more self-sustaining. The newly industrialized countries of the Pacific Rim—including Taiwan, Hong Kong, South Korea, and Singapore—along with Brazil and India have recently emerged as significant beneficiaries of transferred technologies.

APPROPRIATENESS OF TECHNOLOGY TRANSFER. One of the central problems regarding technology transfer is whether the technology is ''appropriate'' for the recipient country. For example, technologies that are highly capital intensive may be transferred to a country in which there is substantial underemployment of labor. Transferred technologies may also require technically sophisticated workers and managers or natural resources that are in short supply in the recipient country. The problem of appropriate technologies suggests that substantial planning is generally required for technology transfer to be beneficial. At the same time, the problem highlights the potential conflicts between the interests of multinationals and the long-term development of recipient countries.

Thus, the viability of technology transfer is determined by the general level of industrial development in LDCs. New technologies are more readily able to be implemented if similar or complementary technologies have been previously established. Key among these considerations is the capacity of producers within an LDC to serve as suppliers of parts or services. Whether a transferred technology can be supported by suppliers within the country has a potentially large impact on the competitiveness of production, given the potentially higher costs of relying on parts from abroad as well as the greater lead times involved. In addition, toxin-producing industrial processes are potentially much more problematic in LDCs. In order to control environmental damage, these processes require pollution-abatement technologies, which are generally less developed in LDCs.

IMPORTANCE OF EDUCATION. Education is a vital part of the technology-transfer process and of the development process more generally. A gap often exists between the technical education levels in source and recipient countries. Employees must have sufficient training to efficiently operate and maintain machinery. More than that, **innovation** and **research and development** typically require highly educated technicians. LDCs often attempt to minimize their technical dependence on outside sources such that they are able to generate innovation from within, creating the possibility of a more self-sustaining development process.

The role of education becomes increasingly critical with the expansion of electronics-based and other medium- to high-tech goods. Accordingly, new product and process development generally requires a higher level of technical knowledge. At the same time, a larger share of all manufacturing production is beginning to be controlled by computers in highly integrated processes.

ROLE OF MULTINATIONAL CORPORATIONS. Multinational firms engage in technology transfer through licensing arrangements with non-affiliated firms or through foreign direct investment with affiliated firms. These are sometimes referred to as external and internal technology transfer, respectively. Multinationals generally prefer internal technology transfer. In his essay ''Contractual Agreements and International Technology Transfer,'' Bernard Bonin described this preference as follows: ''Foreign direct investment is normally preferred since the owner of the technology is thus in a position to capture all the rents attached to his technological advantage, while licensing is more risky in this regard. Contractual agreements will be entered into only when the potential benefit from intangible assets cannot be otherwise exploited.''

There are a number of factors that impede technology transfer within a firm, making external transfer more viable. Smaller firms may lack the resources to engage in direct investment. Firms may have inadequate managerial experience in overseas production and marketing. In other cases, the host country may restrict foreign direct investment, leaving licensing as the only option. More generally, firms are more inclined to license older products and processes, for which the relative technological advantage and profitability are generally less.

EVALUATING TECHNOLOGY TRANSFER'S SUCCESS. One of the contentious issues surrounding technology transfer is the means by which the success of such transfers should be evaluated. Traditionally the success of development has been measured in terms of the growth rate of **gross national product** (GNP) or per capita gross national product. This measure has been criticized on several grounds. For one, it does not take into account income distribution. In his *Strategic Planning in Technology Transfer to Less Developed Countries,* Christian Madu summarized other limitations of national income measures as follows: "Understanding the LDC's socio-economic structure and how it differs from that of the developed countries will help in the development of appropriate standards for measuring growth. For example, a major flaw of GNP is that it fails to take into account social costs due to industrial waste, crime, congestion, and different perceptions of the inhabitants about their changing environment in evaluating the nation's performance." New "quality of life" measures have been developed in recent years to complement GNP-based measures in evaluating technology transfer and other economic development policies.

The pace of technology transfer increased rapidly after the 1970s. This resulted from the growth of foreign direct investment by multinational corporations as well as from the increased outsourcing of product components in the international market. More generally, the growth of technology transfer reflects the increasingly international perspective of corporations. The growth in recent years was also an outcome of earlier technology transfers, in that those transfers enabled a greater number of countries to act as important sources of technology. Technology transfer has been greatly facilitated by improvements in international transport and communications, enabling firms to more readily control operations across the globe. Finally, the establishment of free trade agreements within North America, Europe, and Southeast Asia created more favorable financial environments for technology transfer.

RESTRICTED TECHNOLOGIES. Government policy plays a large role in technology transfer. The advanced capitalist countries typically have policies that restrict the outflow of certain technologies. Among these are military equipment or technologies with potential military applications. **Exporting** technologies may also be restricted in an effort to protect competitive advantages in certain high-tech goods. Among these goods are supercomputers and superconductors. The government policies of LDCs vary widely in the extent to which they regulate technology transfers. While many LDCs compete with each other to accommodate multinational corporations, others restrict foreign ownership, **foreign investment**, and joint ventures.

U.S. government regulation of technology transfer in the postwar years was shaped in large part by the Cold War. The Export Control Act of 1949 authorized the president to regulate exports on the grounds of short supply and national security, as well as to achieve foreign policy objectives. In that same year, the United States and six European countries formed the **Coordinating Committee for Multilateral Export Controls** (COCOM) in an effort to carry out strategic embargoes, particularly against China and the Soviet Union. COCOM was not strongly effective in Cold War years since some of these European countries sought to increase trade with the Communist powers. Consequently the United States relied on the Export Controls Act to attach restrictions to technologies licensed to allied and neutral countries in an effort to control the re-export of these technologies. Congress extended the act in 1953.

Exports to the Warsaw Pact countries increased during the Nixon administration with the Export Administration Act of 1969 and with détente. With the Soviet invasion of Afghanistan in 1979 and the election of Ronald Reagan in 1980 came the move toward greater restriction of technology transfers. The U.S. Department of Commerce came to play a leading role in the regulation of nonmilitary exports, and the staff of the Export Administration unit of the department increased by fourfold through the 1980s. Similar expansions occurred in the export-control divisions of U.S. Customs and the departments of Defense and State. Many U.S. businesses complained that these regulations substantially hurt their sales and their capacity to develop new technologies. Restrictions on technology transfer were progressively loosened in trade legislation enacted after the mid-1980s. New laws and regulations sought to situate the issue of export controls in light of general trade considerations as well as national security interests. Entering the 1990s, the collapse of the Eastern Bloc and the expansion of U.S. trade with China created possibilities for substantial increases of technology transfer from the United States and other advanced capitalist countries. However, particularly in the case of China, which in the late 1990s was embroiled in a scandal involving spying on U.S. defense laboratories and contractors for military technology secrets, the dichotomy between permissible and impermissible technology transfer remained a cornerstone of the U.S. foreign relations regime.

SEE ALSO: Intellectual Capital; Intellectual Property

[David Kucera]

FURTHER READING:

Bonin, Bernard. ''Contractual Agreements and International Technology Transfers: the Empirical Studies.'' In *Multinationals, Governments, and International Technology Transfer*, edited by A. E. Safarian, and Gilles Bertin. New York: St. Martin's Press, 1987.

Bremer, Howard. ''University Technology Transfer: Evolution and Revolution.'' Washington: Council on Governmental Relations, 1998. Available from www.cogr.edu.

Buckley, Peter J., et al, eds. *International Technology Transfer by Small and Medium-Sized Enterprises: Country Studies.* New York: St. Martin's Press, 1997.

Cooke, Ian, and Paul Mayes. *Introduction to Innovation and Technology Transfer.* New York: Artech House, 1996.

''Defining Technology Transfer.'' *Texas Business Review*, June 1998.

Keithly, Joseph P. ''Tapping Technology Transfer.'' *Electronic Business*, November 1997.

Madu, Christian N. *Strategic Planning in Technology Transfer to Less Developed Countries.* Westport, CT: Quorum Books, 1992.

Rein, Barry. ''Legal Basics of Tech Transfer Licensing.'' *R&D*, February 1996.

Simon, Denis. ''International Business and the Transborder Movement of Technology: A Dialectic Perspective.'' In *Technology Transfer in International Business*, edited by Tamir Agmon and Mary Ann von Glinow. New York: Oxford University Press, 1991.

TELECOMMUNICATIONS

SEE: Telephony (Voice Telecommunications)

TELECOMMUTING

Telecommuting is generally defined as using technology to travel to one's job, rather than physically commuting to it. For instance, telecommuters might log onto home **computers** and dial in to their company's computer system to perform the normal tasks of their jobs. But it is important to note that telecommuters are still employees of a company. Those who work from home running their own businesses are not telecommuters; they are more appropriately referred to as home-based business owners. Telecommuters and home-based business owners share many of the same needs, however, such as ready access to customers and reliable connectivity to the outside world.

Telecommuting is a rapidly growing trend in American business. The number of companies offering telecommuting as an option to employees increased from 6 percent in 1993 to 33 percent in 1998, according to a survey in *Business Week.* Telecommuting is expected to continue to grow as new occupations that are shaped by modern communications come into existence. ''Workers in newly emerging jobs won't have to fight past patterns or expectations,'' Peter Coffee wrote in *PC Week.* '' 'Telepresence' via fax, e-mail and (increasingly) video will be their norm and not an awkward innovation.'' In fact, some experts believe that telecommuting may be only the first step in the creation of increasingly sophisticated working environments, as **information technologies** continue to change the way people work.

A number of factors have contributed to the trend toward telecommuting. Lisa Shaw, author of *Telecommute! Go to Work without Leaving Home,* wrote that ''the labor pool of employees with specific talents will shrink, making employers more willing to make concessions to keep valued employees happy. A smaller labor pool combined with an increasing demand for highly skilled laborers has fueled employee-driven change in working environments. Scarce, highly skilled workers have begun to demand more flexible work arrangements, especially as they choose to live farther and farther from their employers.''

Shaw and other observers also note that demographic changes within the American **workforce** are a factor in the growth of telecommuting. These experts contend that new generations of workers are less willing to sacrifice time with family than their counterparts of previous eras. This desire to spend more time at home and avoid long commutes has made telecommuting an increasingly attractive option.

Perhaps the most important factor in the growth of telecommuting is that improved technology has made working from home viable. With the advent of high-speed modems, fax machines, voice mail, powerful personal computers, **electronic mail**, and the like, workers can now perform their jobs virtually anywhere without losing touch with employers and customers. Indeed, *PC Week* reported that ''virtual office'' technology allowed more than 11 million workers to telecommute at least one day per month in 1998.

ADVANTAGES OF TELECOMMUTING

Both employers and employees have found telecommuting beneficial, often mutually so. Among the advantages cited by workers is the ability to avoid long, stressful commutes. The sheer convenience of commuting across the hall rather than across town is compelling reason enough for some. In addition, staying at home to work means the telecommuter's workday is shorter, leaving more time for pleasurable activities and more flexibility for changeable tasks such as **child and elder care**. A study conducted by AT&T

showed that 75 percent of telecommuters felt increased satisfaction with their personal and family lives. Employers find these advantages work for them, too, by making it easier to retain valuable employees.

According to *Nation's Business,* another advantage of telecommuting is increased employee effectiveness. Initially, employers feared productivity downturns with home-based workers, but actually the opposite has been true (although there are exceptions, of course). Telecommuters face fewer distractions from hectic office environments and spend less time in meetings. They also tend to have increased morale, which translates to fewer sick days and lower turnover rates for employers.

Another quantifiable benefit for employers is the reduced need for space. Office space and parking space requirements can be curtailed if a portion of one's staff telecommutes. Jack Nilles, president of JALA International, a Los Angeles-based management consulting firm, estimates that companies can save $11,000 per year for each employee who telecommutes two days a week. Of course, companies may incur some costs upon implementing a telecommuting program. For example, they may need to supply workers with computers, modems, remote access **software**, fax machines, and additional phone lines for their home offices. But these one-time costs are likely to be much smaller than the potential annual savings.

OVERCOMING POTENTIAL TELECOMMUTING PITFALLS

Although telecommuting offers numerous potential advantages to both employers and employees, it is not appropriate for everyone. For example, some people lack the self-discipline that is needed for working at home. They may be distracted by children and spouses who find it difficult to understand that telecommuters are still working even though they are at home. Other people may go to the opposite extreme and find that nonwork activities are crowded out of their lives. In effect, their home becomes their office so they work all the time. This problem is most likely to occur when telecommuting is considered an experiment. In that case, Coffee explained, home workers may feel ''constant pressure to make up for perceived lack of commitment to the job by outproducing coworkers.'' Finally, some telecommuters find that they miss the social interaction that takes place in an office environment.

It is important to realize that telecommuting affects the entire office, not just the employees who spend some or all of their time working from home. It transforms the social interactions between coworkers and requires adjustments from people still in the office. Telecommuting also presents challenges for supervisors. Some managers tend to feel suspicious toward telecommuters. If they cannot physically observe an employee at work, they are concerned that that employee is not really working. In addition, some managers worry that by allowing their staffs to telecommute, they will eliminate the need for their own jobs. After all, when top executives visit an office and see mostly empty cubicles, they might wonder why they are paying someone to supervise a nonexistent staff.

As Lin Grenshing-Pophal explained in an article for *HRMagazine,* **training** can help companies overcome the potential pitfalls involved in telecommuting. She recommends training the telecommuters, training their supervisors, and then training both groups together. Ideally, telecommuters and managers should discuss their expectations for their new working relationship and figure out exactly how the arrangement will work before a telecommuting program is implemented. The main challenge for supervisors involves learning to manage for results rather than for time spent on the job. ''In a telecommuting relationship, time is not important, and this is one of the harder lessons for supervisors to learn,'' Grenshing-Pophal wrote. ''In training managers to supervise telecommuters, experts say that learning to make the transition from managing time to managing projects is critical and will determine the success of an organization's telecommuting program.'' It may also be helpful to train employees who will remain in the office in order to prevent them from feeling jealous and help them be supportive of telecommuters.

In an article for *Entrepreneur,* Heather Page noted that companies should create a written policy to cover telecommuting. This document should detail who is eligible for the program, outline what is expected of telecommuters, and provide a list of the equipment and services that the company will supply. It may also be helpful to include a checklist to help employees determine whether their job—and personality—is well suited to telecommuting. Finally, Page recommends that companies create systems for measuring the effectiveness of their telecommuting programs and making changes as needed.

SUMMARY

Telecommuting will have far-reaching implications for all business owners in the future. As the labor pool shrinks, businesses large and small will compete for workers, many of whom will ask for the telecommuting option. Fortunately, telecommuting has advantages for everyone involved. It saves businesses money by reducing space needs, turnover, and sick time, and improves employee morale by increasing personal time and flexibility. Of course, telecommuting also involves some potential pitfalls. For example, supervisors may find it difficult to deal with employees who rarely come to the office. But training sessions and written policies can help companies overcome the problems and reap the benefits associated with telecommuting.

SEE ALSO: Supervision

[Kristin Kahrs, updated by Laurie Collier Hillstrom]

FURTHER READING:

Baig, Edward C. "Saying Adios to the Office." *Business Week,* 12 October 1998, 152+.

Coffee, Peter. "More Time at Home or Less Time at Work?" *PC Week,* 18 January 1999, 47.

Ditlea, Steve. "Home Is Where the Office Is: Technology Improvements Have Made the Home Office an Effective Workplace Alternative." *Nation's Business,* November 1995, 41+.

Grensing-Pophal, Lin. "Training Supervisors to Manage Teleworkers." *HRMagazine* 44, no. 1 (January 1999): 67+.

Kugelmass, John. *Telecommuting: A Manager's Guide to Flexible Work Arrangements.* New York: Lexington Books, 1995.

Page, Heather. "Home Work: Telecommuting Can Improve Employee Morale and Increase Productivity." *Entrepreneur,* December 1998, 50+.

"Remote Possibilities." *Fortune,* summer 1998, 192+.

Shaw, Lisa. *Telecommute! Go to Work without Leaving Home!* New York: Wiley, 1996.

Tergesen, Anne. "Making Stay-at-Homes Feel Welcome." *Business Week,* 12 October 1998, 155+.

TELEMARKETING

Telemarketing is a direct market technique for selling goods and services, making appointments, and generating sales leads over the telephone. Although the telephone has been used as a sales tool for nearly a century, the term *telemarketing* was first used by AT&T in the early 1980s in conjunction with a long-distance phone service sales campaign. Telemarketing may be *in-bound* or *out-bound.* With in-bound telemarketing the consumer responds to advertisements, usually featuring toll-free 800-numbers, and calls a company or a company's telephone service and orders products directly. Out-bound telemarketing involves a company's sales force calling consumers, usually at their residence, and soliciting orders or making appointments. Out-bound telemarketing as such is proactive, with the telemarketing company taking the initiative. Out-bound telemarketing has as of late become controversial because of privacy issues and questionable if not outright fraudulent telemarketing schemes. In spite of this controversy, in 1996 approximately 304,000 Americans were employed in telemarketing or telemarketing related jobs as reported by the *Occupational Outlook Quarterly. Management Review* estimates that telemarketing generates about $424.5 billion in annual revenue.

The telemarketing industry dates back to the early part of the 20th century, when the financial services industry used the telephone as a marketing technique. Stock brokers have traditionally made extensive use of the phone, a practice that continues today. In the 1930s and 1940s, telemarketing units—commonly known as inside sales operations, because the sales reps remained "inside" the office—began to emerge in wholesale distribution organizations. This trend accelerated during World War II as much of the nation's sales force was drafted into service and travel was restricted due to rationing of gasoline and tires.

Magazine publishers began to use telemarketing extensively in the 1940s and 1950s, trying to sign up new subscribers as well as re-sign former subscribers. In 1955 Reuben H. Donnelley began a major telemarketing success story when he started a telephone sales program to sell advertising in the Yellow Pages to small businesses. In 1985, the most profitable publishing entity in the state of California was the Pacific Telephone's Yellow Pages—and approximately 60 percent of the adds and one-third of the revenue were generated by phone.

The introduction in 1960 of the Wide Area Telephone Services (WATS) lines helped increase business use over the telephone. This opened the way for high volume outbound calling at low cost, so it became cost-effective to have large regional or national call centers. Similarly, with the 1967 unveiling of 800 numbers, inbound WATS lines paved the way for direct response capability, where consumers could respond to national advertising toll free.

The telemarketing industry is rapidly growing in the United States, tripling between 1988 and 1998 to about 2,500 companies. In 1995 about 81 million Americans bought goods and services from telemarketers. Consumer sales totaled about $186 billion with business-to-business sales reaching over $238 billion. Telemarketing has grown because it is so cost-effective. One telemarketer, sitting at a phone with a telephone list of sales leads, can reach many more potential customers in eight hours than can a salesperson on the road. It is estimated that face-to-face field calls to potential customers cost about $250 each with outside sales people making four to six contacts a day. An outbound telemarketer, however, can make 90-100 calls a day with 35-50 of these calls ending up as full presentations. Wages in the telemarketing industry are also relatively low. Again citing the *Occupational Outlook Quarterly,* in 1996 the median wage for workers in the telemarketing category was $7.77. Training for telemarketers takes only a day or two before the trainee makes his or her first sales call. Even faster and cheaper but probably less effective are automatic dialing machines with a pre-recorded sales message.

The telephone, as an ''intimate'' means of communication, also contributes to the success of telemarketing. ''The telephone is one of the few mediums that allow you to have a dialogue with prospective or existing customers. You have the ability to deliver or fine-tune the message and respond based on what you're hearing over the phone,'' Jon Kaplan, past president of the American Telemarketing Association told *Management Review* during an interview. People are also more and more comfortable doing business over the phone, especially those with hectic schedules. Andrew Wetzler, president of Wetzler & Associates, a consulting company specializing in telemarketing sales, also has great belief in the telephone as an effective tool for sales. ''Everyone thought you had to have face-to-face contact for selling. In reality, there aren't a lot of things that can't be sold over the phone. Some big-ticket items are the exception, but in most cases, product upgrades and smaller items are perfect for phone sales,'' said Wetzler when interviewed for the same article.

Telemarketing programs can either be handled in-house by a company or farmed out to service bureaus. Operations can range from extremely small to major corporations or service centers that have more than 1,000 telephone stations. Although telemarketing can be used as a stand-alone operation, it often works best when part of an overall marketing effort. Companies considering the use of telemarketing have to look at such factors as which products and services are good candidates for telephone sales; whether telemarketing can be used to increase volume through upgrading the sale; how the process can help qualify prospects, define the market, and help service existing accounts; and whether telemarketing can help generate new business. Some of the roles telemarketing can be used to fulfill include: selling, the generation of sales leads, information gathering on such things as advertising effectiveness, and finally telemarketing can be used to improve customer service.

Telemarketing, like any other business or industry also has a downside. The success of any telemarketing operation is dependent on a list of customers in potential need of the good or service being sold. It is, for instance, a waste of time and money for a home improvement company to telephone people living in apartment buildings. Throughout the 1990s many laws and regulations went into effect curtailing telemarketing operations, especially the Telemarketing and Consumer Fraud and Abuse Prevention Act of 1994.

Technology works both for and against telemarketers. The growing popularity of telephone answering machines, for instance, allows consumers to screen calls often denying the telemarketer a ''foot in the door.'' Making use of expanding technology, however, telemarketers have started using predictive dialers which dial a high volume of numbers in such a way as to avoid dead time which can be caused by busy signals and answering machines. Predictive dialers allow operators to dial 80 calls an hour instead of the usual 45. Predictive dialers often go awry, however, and can ''hang up'' as soon as a telephone receiver is picked up leaving the consumer waiting for a person to answer or in some cases leaving the consumer with the feeling that they are being harassed or stalked by telephone. Juanita Abbott, who is a manager for the regional annoyance-call bureau for Bell Atlantic told *Fortune* magazine that much of their time is spent explaining predictive dialers to worried or frightened telephone customers. ''The calls run the gamut. People say, 'I know it's my neighbor because I parked my car to close.' They think the worst.'' *Fortune* magazine estimates that 40 percent of telemarketers use predictive dialers, which means that 141 million calls can be dialed each day or about 5.5 percent of the total daily volume of calls in the United States. Telemarketers claim that abandoned calls remain low at between 1 and 2 percent (even so this is over 768,000 abandoned calls a day) but consumer advocacy groups claim the number can be as high as 10 percent.

Telemarketing also has a bad reputation because of fraudulent schemes that plague the industry. According to *Black Enterprise* American consumers lose $40 billion annually to fraudulent telemarketing scams. It is estimated by Cleo Manuel of the National Consumers League in Washington D.C. that 14,000 or 10 percent of the 140,000 telemarketing firms in the U.S. may be fraudulent. ''Boiler-Room'' scam operations are run out of motel rooms and low rent buildings that can be vacated quickly and just as quickly set up somewhere else. These fraudulent operators, however, never abandon their ''mooch'' list which is sort of an underground directory of consumers who have already fallen victim to fraudulent schemes making them likely to be targeted again. ''They hit you up for $100 and then three months later, hit you up for a couple thousand,'' according to Tim Healey, an FBI supervisory special agent for economic crime and telemarketing fraud. Healey advises consumers to be wary of offers for free vacations, business opportunities, credit cards, magazine sales, and solicitations for charitable donations.

To discourage and prevent telemarketing fraud the Telemarketing and Consumer Fraud and Abuse Prevention Act became law in 1994. The act gave law enforcement agencies powerful tools with which to combat telemarketing fraud while giving consumers protection and guidance in separating fraudulent telemarketing schemes from legitimate offers. Under authority of the act the **Federal Trade Commission (FTC)** adopted the Telemarketing Sales Rule (which quickly became known as the ''Rule'') in 1995. The Rule contains a number of key provisions aimed directly at achieving the hoped for goals of the 1994 legislation. The Rule has language covering: specific disclosures; the prohibition of misrepresentations; times when telemarketers can and cannot call consumers; the prohibition of calls after a consumer asks not to be called; the setting of payment restrictions for the sale of certain goods and services; and the requirement that specific business records be kept for two years. It is important to note that the Rule does not supersede more stringent state and local telemarketing laws. Another telemarketing law in place is the Telephone Consumer Protection Act, which is enforced by the Federal Communications Commission (FCC).

Under its authority the Rule defines telemarketing as any plan, program, or campaign to sell goods or services through interstate telephone calls. With a few technical exceptions, all telemarketers must comply with the Rule whether or not the telemarketer initiates or receives the call and whether or not the telemarketer is actually the party supplying the goods or services. Not covered under the rules are: banks, federal credit unions, and federal savings and loans; common carriers; non-profit organizations; and companies engaged in the business of insurance, to the extent that the business is regulated by state law. Telephone calls not covered by the Rule generally include: calls placed by consumers in response to a catalog; 900-number calls; calls relating to franchising; unsolicited consumer calls; calls made in relation to a face-to-face sales transaction; business-to-business calls not involving the retail sale of nondurable office or cleaning supplies; calls made in response to general media advertising; and calls made in response to direct mail advertising (for important exceptions to the above see *Complying with the Telemarketing Sales Rule.*) The Rule also prohibits credit card laundering. This occurs when a telemarketer who is unable to establish a legitimate *merchant account* with a financial institution that issues credit cards employs the unlawful services of a launderer or factor who provides access to a merchant account and thus the whole credit card collection and payment system.

In addition to federal legislation there is a growing body of state law regulating telemarketing. Georgia, for instance, passed a ''do-not-call-list'' law in 1999 which provides for the implementation of a list that consumers can add their names to. Telemarketers are forbidden from calling names on this list. Georgia became the fourth state to pass such a law that is stricter than present federal regulations. Similar pending legislation is on the calendar for 21 other states. In Georgia and Kentucky consumers can register their names on these lists for a $5 fee and the list is available to telemarketers for $10. Telemarketing data files must then be reconciled with updated lists. Other states such as Florida and Oregon require phone directory publishers to print a black dot next to the names of people wishing not to be called by telemarketers. Telemarketers again buy the list from the publisher and reconcile their files. In Georgia violating the list can result in a fine up to $2000. Growing ''do-not-call-list'' legislation means rising costs for telemarketing industry. ''I estimate that telemarketing companies will need to hire one person for each two states to administer the do-not-call-rules,'' Tyler Prochnow, a legislative consultant for the American Teleservices Association, told *Marketing News.* ''These new employees would be needed to get the updated lists from the states on time, format them properly and push them through the computer.''

Expanding technology is also causing problems for telemarketers. Ameritech, for instance, introduced in 1998 a telephone screener called *Privacy Manager.* Costing under $4 per month, Privacy manager requires a caller ID display box that allows ''normal'' calls to pass through it. Calls originating from numbers classified as ''private,'' ''blocked,'' ''out of area,'' ''unavailable,'' or ''unknown'' are stopped and without the phone ringing a recorded message asks the caller to reveal their name. If a name is forthcoming the phone rings and upon picking up the phone the resident hears the message: ''This is Privacy Manager, you have a call from . . . '' The customer then can either accept the call, hang up, or choose to play a message saying: ''We don't accept telemarketing calls. Please add me to your do-not-call list.''

Ameritech's Richard Notebart is enthusiastic about Privacy Manager. ''We have never had a product test this good, including voice mail and caller ID. It satisfied a need that consumers have just been pleading to have resolved,'' Notebart told the *Wall Street Journal.* Telemarketing consultant Rudy Oetting thinks that devices like Privacy Manager will only make telemarketers work harder. ''It will cause marketers who use the telephone channel to become more selective and creative in their approach so that people who do receive calls will be interested in what they are being call about.'' Oetting did admit, however, that telemarketing calls reaching into homes is rapidly approaching the saturation level.

Telemarketers, however, are also making use of evolving technology to reach consumers, especially with the growth of the Internet and e-mail. Ron Weber, of Ron Weber and Associates expects e-mail business to grow by half in 1999 and Gene Gray of APAC Teleservices told *Marketing News* that telemarketers should be less concerned with the means of communication and more concerned with communicating. ''It's not important that it come from an e-mail or a fax or an inbound call. The task is to be prepared to do all that.'' Telemarketing and direct marketing insiders also predict that the Internet will play a major role in that industry's future.

"Traditional phone and mail distribution of literature can be supplemented or augmented by the Web site," according to Warren Hunter, president of the Philadelphia office of DMW Worldwide. Michael Osborn of Catalyst Direct also views technology as the future of the industry. "Companies are also feeling the pressure, because of declining response rates, to target better and get down to one-to-one communications. As we start to market more one-to-one, a lot of technology and computer power is required," Osborn told *Marketing News.* Those companies that aren't equipped with the proper technology will not only find it more difficult to compete in the coming year but, over the long haul, "it will become virtually impossible," Osborn went on to say.

Working to promote telemarketing as an industry that will benefit the consumer and be good for the economy is the American Telemarketing Association (ATA). The ATA lobbies on behalf of the telemarketing industry, publishes a code of ethics for its members, and works with such groups as the FBI, the Federal trade Commission, and the National Consumers League to combat telemarketing fraud.

[Michael Knes]

FURTHER READING:

"ATA: American Telemarketing Association." North Hollywood, CA: American Telemarketing Association, 1997. Available from: www.atancal.com.

Barragan, Napoleon. *How To Get Rich With A 1-800 Number.* New York: HarperCollins, 1997.

Beatty, Sally. "Ameritech's New Phone Service Aims to Keep Telemarketers At Bay." *Wall Street Journal,* 23 September 1998.

Briones, Maricris. "IT, Privacy Issues Will Challenge Direct Marketers." *Marketing News,* 7 December 1998.

——. "Technology—The Key In Teleservices." *Marketing News,* 7 December 1998.

Geller, Lois K. *The Complete Guide to Profitable Direct Marketing.* New York: The Free Press, 1996.

Harlan, Ray, and Walter M. Woolfson, Jr. *Interactive Telemarketing.* Bradenton, FL: McGuinn & McGuire, 1996.

Heckman, James. "How Telemarketers are Coping with Rising Tide of State Regs." *Marketing News,* 12 April 1999.

Jones, Joyce. "The Telemarketing Hoax: How To Protect Yourself From Fraudulent Phone Sales." *Black Enterprise,/* September 1998.

Mariani, Matthew. "You're A What? Telemarketer." *Occupational Outlook Quarterly,* Spring 1999.

Romano, Catherine. "Telemarketing Grows Up." *Management Review,* June 1998.

Shaw, Karen L. "States Hang Up On Telemarketers." *Marketing News,* 1 March 1999.

U.S. Federal Trade Commission. *Complying With The Telemarketing Sales Rule.* Washington DC: Federal Trade Commission, 1996.

Vinzant, Carol. "Telemarketers Find a Whole New Way to Be Annoying." *Fortune.*

TELEPHONY (VOICE TELECOMMUNICATIONS)

Telephony or voice telecommunications refers to the communication of sound over a distance using wire or wireless telephones and related technology. Telephony is one domain of telecommunications, which includes:

1. Data communications, which involves the transfer of numbers and text through **computer** networks.
2. Video communications, which refers to the transfer of images through broadcast, cable, and satellite television.
3. Voice communications, which involves the transfer of sounds—especially the human voice—through telephone systems.

These domains are not mutually exclusive, however, because the differences between various kinds of telecommunications are beginning to disappear. For example, telephone lines are used for telephones, fax machines, and modems. Despite the overlap, the distinction between these kinds of telecommunication remains useful, since each may employ separate technology and serve different purposes.

Telephony has played and is expected to continue to play a significant and increasing role in business and has become just as essential to companies as personnel, capital, and **marketing**. Not surprisingly, voice communications is the most important form of telecommunications for businesses, because of its use for communication among employees and between employees and customers and for the dissemination of information. Consequently, voice communications is a business resource that can improve internal and external communication, maintain good internal and external relationships, save time and money, and even help earn money. Key business applications of telephony include **telemarketing**, teleconferencing, and **telecommuting**.

HISTORICAL DEVELOPMENT OF TELEPHONY

Telephony has its origin with telegraphy in 1844, when Samuel Morse (1791-1872) developed the capability to send pulses of electric current over wires that spanned distances farther than one could shout, walk, or ride. The mechanics involved a battery power source, a key switch to pass or interrupt the flow of current, wires to carry the signal to another location, and a receiving device that used current to operate a magnet that pulled on a metal armature to produce an audible click.

Morse developed the first application of discrete signals for telegraphy, using a lexicon of multiple long and short closures of the circuit to represent letters and numbers—known as Morse code. Telegraph operators used Morse code to send messages between stations located in different cities.

Due to the costs involved in setting up this network of operators linked by wires, the commercialization of telegraphy required that the service be offered at a price that only businesses could afford. Thus the first telecommunications network, using telegraphy, was largely a business-to-business enterprise whose dominant provider was the Western Union company.

Even with extremely fast key operators and massive networks consisting of hundreds of wires between locations, telegraph companies were unable to meet the rising demand for their services. This is because each wire could carry only one message at a time. In order to maximize the capacity of the wires already in place, several entrepreneurs tried to develop a system in which several messages could be sent over the same circuit using several harmonically discrete signals.

One of these experimenters was Alexander Graham Bell (1847-1922) who, in developing such a system, stumbled on the principle of telephony—transmission of a voice signal. When Bell's assistant Thomas Watson (1854-1934) flicked a telegraph armature to release it from its magnet, Bell heard the ring of the armature. This convinced him that sounds could be made to influence a magnetic field, and that these fluctuations in the magnetic force could be translated into an electrical signal that could operate a speaker.

In the celebrated event of his discovery, Bell set up his device, but spilled battery acid on his lap. He called for Watson, who was in a laboratory down the hallway. When Watson arrived, he reported that he had heard Bell's cry over the wires.

The two worked diligently to prepare a patent application, but in the oddest coincidence, filed their **patent** the very same day as Elisha Gray (1835-1901), another inventor who had developed a similar but slightly superior device. After an acrimonious 17-year legal battle, Bell was awarded the patent in 1876.

But Bell had tremendous difficulty selling his invention. He failed to interest Western Union, which maintained that there was no use for such a toy when key operators could communicate faster than people could talk. To raise money, Bell demonstrated his invention in sideshows, and eventually raised enough to set up the Bell Telephone Company with networks in Boston and New York, and even acquired Gray's rival Western Electric Company.

As the telephone grew in popularity, it became obvious that Western Union had failed to appreciate the greatest asset of the telephone: *anyone,* not just skilled key operators, could use it. With the prospect of serving a thousand times as many accounts, Western Union scrambled to get in on the business and hired Thomas Edison (1847-1931) to develop a superior telephone unrelated to Bell's patent. Bell sued and won, winning the right to acquire Western Union's telephone network and the patent rights on Edison's vastly improved telephone.

Bell's American Telephone & Telegraph Company (AT&T) unfairly muscled hundreds of other independent telephone companies into lopsided **mergers**. This invited U.S. Department Justice intervention in 1914, whereby AT&T was enjoined from further acquisitions and was declared a regulated monopoly.

During this time, a Kansas City undertaker named Almon Strowger noted a steady decline in his business. He suspected the culprit was the local operator, who was married to a competing mortician. Telephony was impractical as a strictly point-to-point system; it required operators to switch calls from one person to any number of others on the network. Strowger set out to develop an automatic switching system that used a dial on the telephone to mechanically switch calls without intervention from an operator. Thus, the automatic switch was born.

The telephony network remained basically unchanged for half a century. Due to its pre-1914 acquisitions, AT&T had monopolized the nation's largest markets and ran the only long distance network. During the 1960s, AT&T developed a touch-tone dialing system, using audible signaling tones, to replace the dial and its electromechanical switches.

More importantly, in 1968 the Carterfone company won the right to connect its own brand of equipment to the AT&T-dominated network. This cleared the way for other competing manufacturers to enter the market.

But also that year, an upstart company called MCI Communications Corp. established a long distance network separate from AT&T's, using microwave communications. Others followed, including GTE, which built another long distance network out of the Southern Pacific Railroad's sprawling private telephone system—an enterprise called Sprint.

In 1982 several decades of **antitrust** action against AT&T by the U.S. Department of Justice culminated in a consent decree in which AT&T agreed to divest its 22 local service Bell companies. The divestiture, which took place in 1984, created seven independent "Baby Bells" and left AT&T with only its long distance operations, its Bell Labs research group, and the Western Electric manufacturing division. It also cleared the way for **competition** in the long distance market.

RECENT TELECOMMUNICATIONS REFORM

The initial reform of the telecommunications industry had the immediate effect of splitting up AT&T, but it also paved the way for additional telecommunications reform. The most significant kind of reform since the breakup of AT&T was the passage of the Telecommunications Act of 1996. The primary purpose of the act was to promote competition within the telecommunications industry by eliminating obstacles and offering incentives for companies to enter the market. The act also was designed to bring about the integration of various telecommunications services: telephone, cable, wireless, and **Internet** access services.

In the telephony sector, the act opened up local and long distance phone markets to competition and replaced any state laws prohibiting competition in these markets. Under the act, local telephone companies can enter long distance markets and long distance companies can enter local markets. In addition, local exchange carriers are still able to operate their long distance networks, but they must allow competitors to connect to these networks.

The act also allows cable companies to offer telephony and related services even if they do not own local franchises and replaced rules prohibiting cross-ownership, permitting telephone companies to own cable companies and vice versa.

Nevertheless, little progress had been made in realizing this more competitive telecommunications market by the end of the decade. Although many telephone companies announced their plans to enter new markets before the Telecommunications Act was signed into law, they were unable to execute their plans because they became embroiled in lawsuits and disputes over opening up their own markets and entering new ones. Consequently, the Bell spin-offs still dominated the local market and the big-three long distance phone companies (AT&T, MCI, and Sprint) still controlled the long distance market. Nevertheless, there was at least one new competitor in the top 100 phone markets and 165 new telephone companies by 1999, according to the *National Journal.* Moreover, Supreme Court rulings have upheld the **Federal Communications Commission**'s authority to establish national telecommunications rules and prices that will encourage competition—powers that had been blocked since 1996.

TELEPHONE SYSTEMS AND COMPONENTS

A telephone system is a system that allows private, two-way voice and data communication. Phones are interconnected at local central offices, which use solid-state switches controlled by digital logic circuitry or by computers. The switches are integrated systems that direct calls to other locations and prepare the signals for transmission. Local central offices are connected with ''trunks,'' which consist of wires, fiber-optic cables, and radio links and are also largely controlled by computers. The different components of the telephone system are connected to each other by countless miles of wire—including copper wire, coaxial cable, and fiber-optic cable—as well as radio waves. This network of wires, phones, and switches enables any telephone subscriber to call any other telephone subscriber.

Each piece of voice communications equipment is connected to the network with inside wire or building cable. This wire is connected to the public network at a terminal box, or ''point of presence,'' where it meets telephone company wires that lead it to a central office.

Each of these connections is called a local loop, because it consists of a single pair of wires from a subscriber's phone to a local central office. One wire sends current from the central office to the terminal equipment, and the other carries it back to the central office. One central office serves each ''exchange.'' An exchange is the group of all phones with the same first three digits as part of the phone number. The circuit is broken until a telephone is lifted off its switch hook. This allows current to flow through the circuit, signaling the central office switch that a request for service has been made.

The switch then provides dial tone, indicating that it is ready to receive instructions from the caller. These instructions are an address, or telephone number, which tell the switch where to send the call. If the call is to another number served by the same central office, the switch simply sets up a connection between the caller and the person being called.

If the call is to a number served by another central office, the switch sends the call over an interoffice trunk to the central office serving that number, and the switch at that location makes the final connection.

If the call is going a great distance, such as to another state, it will direct the call over another type of trunk to a tandem toll office, which will send the call over long distance lines to a counterpart, and direct the call to another local office serving the party being called. This hierarchy of switching systems is necessary to support the immense number of telephone numbers that have been assigned.

Calls fall into roughly four billing categories, based on the mileage involved. Local calls generally run up to 8 miles, while zone calls cover distances up to 15 miles. Local long distance runs up to 40 miles or so, and distances beyond that are long distance calls. All but local calls are billed according to the duration of the call.

With the divestiture of the Bell System, the Federal Communications Commission established local access transport areas, or LATAs. These LATAs comprise the areas in which the Bell companies or local exchange carriers may complete calls alone. A call to someone in another LATA must be carried by a long distance company, or interexchange carrier (sometimes called an IXC).

LATAs were created to ensure that local Bell companies do not compete in the long distance market. But in addition to the Bell companies, several hundred independent telephone companies exist that are not bound by LATA restrictions because their presence is not nearly as ubiquitous. In most cases, they have no choice but to hand the call off to an IXC or another local telephone company.

The basic telephone circuit is engineered to carry a voice grade level of bandwidth, which ranges from 300 to 3300 Hertz. Several conversations may be carried over the same pair of wires through various forms of multiplexing.

Frequency division multiplexing literally stacks different conversations by changing their frequency, much like an FM radio signal. Filtering equipment can "tune in" to whichever conversation it is supposed to hear. Time division multiplexing gives each conversation one twenty-fourth of a given transmission period to pass over the wires. Sampling equipment can reconstruct all 24 conversations with completely adequate quality.

The wires used to transmit the calls are called facilities. An ordinary twisted wire pair can support several dozen voice grade conversations. Coaxial cable has greater bandwidth capacity, and can carry up to 10,800 different conversations. Fiber-optic cable, which operates on the concept of digital light pulses, rather than analog waveforms, has an even greater capacity, handling millions of signals simultaneously.

By and large, digital systems are more accurate than analog because they allow error correction. Over great distances, analog signals must be amplified. But in amplifying the conversation, intermediate transmission equipment also amplifies electrical "noise" that enters the circuit.

By contrast, digital signals are regenerated, meaning that transmission equipment hears the message being sent, but rather than amplifying it, it repeats what it has heard. Included in the stream of information are signals that ensure the transmission equipment has heard correctly. If it has not, the system will ask to hear it again and make adjustments, such as changing its timing, to correct the error. The result is a transmission of nearly perfect quality. This is why a long distance call from Hong Kong to Chicago can sound as clear as a call from next door.

In handling a call, telephone switching equipment determines billing information by reading the identity of the line in use. As it switches the call to interoffice trunks, it provides that identity along with the number being dialed. This information is called automatic number identification, or ANI.

ANI allows every carrier associated in completing the call to properly assign charges. Recently, telephone companies have allowed consumers to use ANI by providing a service called Caller ID, that reveals the billing number on a small display device. Caller ID enables the called party to see the number, and in some cases the billing name, of the person calling even before answering the phone.

A more invasive use of ANI is made by inbound telemarketing organizations. By calling the telemarketer's **toll-free telephone** number, customers can reveal their ANI code. The company's computer can be instructed to match a customer record with the incoming call so that when an attendant answers, he or she already has the customer's purchasing and **credit** history on a computer screen.

These types of business systems are highly complex and always involve the use of private branch exchanges (PBXs). The PBX is a miniature telephone switch owned and operated by a company for its own use. It allows calls to be completed between offices without using telephone company facilities. PBXs can span several buildings and, with connections provided by telephone companies, can even link sites in different states or countries.

In some instances, a PBX will connect two different sites with a point-to-point connection that is not switched, called a dedicated circuit. These lines are constantly connected between the two points to ensure that access between the sites is always available. Dedicated circuits use telephone company facilities and are billed at a special rate.

For all practical purposes, PBXs, like telephone switches, are computers. Their job is to administer and complete requests for connections and monitor the system for trouble. They can assign billing to specific users—ending unauthorized use of the telephone for personal calls—and can be made to restrict certain types of calls, such as long distance or 900 numbers. PBXs can also be programmed to know which long distance company offers the lowest rate for a given destination and time, and automatically switch outgoing calls to that carrier.

But despite its cost-containment features, the PBX is primarily a tool for maximizing efficiency. A typical office of 100 people does not need 100 telephone lines, but perhaps the 24 offered by T-1 cables. This is because, depending on the employees' calling characteristics, no more than 15 or 20 people will be using a phone at any one time. The PBX can be used to match requests for service with available resources, with a minimum of waste. In addition, most PBXs are endowed with diagnostic features that allow the system operator to locate wiring faults and determine the nature of terminal equipment failures.

PBXs with an automated attendant feature can handle call-answering tasks, greeting the caller and requesting an extension number to complete the call. If the called party does not answer, the PBX will switch the caller to a voice mail system to leave a message for that party. Automated attendant systems also handle routine menial tasks, such as providing hours of operation, a mailing address, fax number, or other frequently requested information.

For offices with a high amount of inbound calling, such as an order-processing center, the PBX may be matched with an automatic call distributor (ACD). These devices distribute incoming sales calls among a pool of operators, and may even direct calls to those who it knows are least busy. This ensures that operators share the workload evenly. PBXs range in size from as few as 5 lines to as many as 10,000. Usually, the larger the system, the more sophisticated its capabilities.

Other types of voice communications equipment, specifically designed for the mobile market, are pagers and cellular phones. While not voice communications devices themselves, pagers are radio receivers that are programmed to display simple messages, such as a caller's telephone number, thereby facilitating voice communication. In contrast, cellular phones are actual telephones, connected to the network not by wires, but by a radio signal. Each cellular phone operates off a host antenna located nearest to it. As the caller moves from one area, or ''cell,'' to another, the system hands the call over to another antenna in an adjacent cell. This allows a caller to roam anywhere within a service area without losing the connection.

TRENDS IN TELEPHONY

Traditionally, businesses have been served by a single local telephone company authorized to provide service in a given area. In addition, all calls between the business and other parties on the network have been switched through this local exchange carrier, or LEC.

But competition will soon be extended to the local market, because of the Telecommunications Act of 1996. Local telephone companies face the loss of significant portions of market share to competing cellular telephone companies, digital wireless radio, bypass operators, and even cable television companies.

Bypass operators are among the most important new competitors in the business market. They establish alternate connections between a company's PBX and its long distance carrier, completely bypassing the local telephone company. In practice, companies do not transfer all their communications traffic to a bypass operator, but choose to split it between them and the local telephone company to leverage each on price and service reliability.

With the new telecommunications legislation, cable companies are poised to provide significant competition to local telephone companies. For example, Time Warner's cable operations compete with Nynex in parts of New York. Cable companies are well positioned because they have hundreds of miles of cable running through neighborhoods, are connected to millions of households, and have armies of repair and installation workers. Perhaps most importantly, their wiring consists of coaxial cable, which can provide high-speed data and computer networking as well as television programs and telephone calls.

Because of the deregulation of the local telephone market and the competition forecasted to ensue, analysts expect lower-cost and higher-quality telecommunications services, which should benefit businesses, according to *Telephony.* The expanding competition in the telephony market also is predicted to lead to new methods for data, video, and voice services.

Furthermore, some analysts expect satellite-based wireless telephony to become a major component of wireless telephony, because of the plans for several telecommunications satellite systems, such as Iridium and Globalstar in the late 1990s. These systems are linked through ground stations to wireless **infrastructure** already in place and are designed to allow users to place and receive calls and paging from anywhere in the world. Iridium became the first worldwide mobile telecommunications service in 1998.

BUSINESS APPLICATIONS OF VOICE COMMUNICATIONS

While the number of business telephone connections is substantially smaller than the number of residential connections, business traffic volume is far greater than residential traffic. While telecommunications services and technology have been viewed, like office equipment, as playing a supporting role, contemporary businesses have begun to place greater emphasis on telecommunications, including voice communications, and have recognized that telecommunications contributes to a company's competitive advantage by increasing productivity and facilitating marketing.

Telephone use and service constitutes the largest business application of telecommunications and most likely will continue to. Because basic telephone use has matured, telephone companies have introduced a host of features to benefit telephone users, such as call waiting, caller ID, and voice- or text-guided phones.

The importance of the telephone for business also helped bring about voice mail, which allows callers to leave messages in voice mailboxes if someone is away from the phone or on another line. This service not only strengthens a company's internal communication but also its external communication with suppliers and customers. In addition, telephone companies provide businesses with direct inward dial and direct outward dial. Direct inward dial enables an outside caller to dial a called party's extension and reach him or her directly, whereas direct outward dial allows a user with an extension to dial directly outside the system.

The growth of business use of telephony also led to the rise of telemarketing and call centers. Telemarketing is an offshoot of **direct marketing** and the practice of making cold calls to consumers in an effort to introduce them to and sell them products or services. Telemarketers often obtain lists of phone numbers of consumers who meet a number of criteria that indicate their potential in having an interest in a company's offerings. For many companies, the telephone has become an indispensable marketing tool and telemarketing has become a significant component of their overall marketing mix. In 1998, for example, companies spent $62 billion on telemarketing and garnered revenues of $482 billion from telemarketing efforts, according to the Direct Marketing Association.

Call centers are professional operations or company divisions that handle large numbers of incoming and outgoing calls for companies and thereby help businesses provide efficient and more affordable telephone service to their customers. Call centers allow companies to offer telephone services 24 hours a day, seven days a week. Furthermore, they can help companies build solid relationships with customers by providing them with both specialized and personalized service. In addition, some call centers also perform telemarketing. Telephone equipment makers have developed technology especially for call centers, creating phones that automatically route callers to the next available representative, match callers with subject experts, and match callers' phones numbers to their accounts.

Furthermore, telephone technology makes possible one-to-one and group audio-conferencing, enabling managers, executives, and other workers to ''meet'' via the telephone. Teleconferencing saves companies time and effort, especially when conference participants would have to travel great distances to participate in person. According to a survey by Advanstar Communications, more than 30 million office workers in the United States have access to audio, video, and data conferencing technology or services and 88 percent of these workers say that these forms of teleconferencing enhance productivity and efficiency.

Telecommuting is another business application of telecommunications technology, although it involves data communications technology to a greater extent than voice communications technology. Telecommuting refers to working from home and ''commuting'' to the office through telecommunications equipment such as computers, fax machines, and telephones. Despite the importance of computers to telecommuting, telephones are still effective ways of contacting a working site from home. Home telephones and cellular phones allow workers to teleconference, check voice mail, schedule meetings, make sales calls, and so forth from home.

[John Simley, updated by Karl Heil]

FURTHER READING:

Bates, Regis J., and Donald W. Gregory. *Voice and Data Communications Handbook.* New York: McGraw-Hill, 1998.

Brooks, John. *Telephone: The First Hundred Years.* New York: Harper & Row, 1976.

Green, Harry James. *The Business One Irwin Handbook of Telecommunications.* 2nd ed. Homewood, IL: Business One Irwin, 1991.

''Key Telecom Act Provisions.'' *Television Digest,* 12 February 1996, 7.

Misra, Jay, and Byron Belitsos. *Business Telecommunications: Concepts, Technologies, and Cases in Telematics.* Homewood, IL: Irwin, 1998.

Mullins, Brody. ''Critics, Backers of '96 Act Joust on Phone Markets.'' *National Journal,* 13 March 1999, S3.

Porter, Tom. ''Call Centers—The New World of Business.'' *Los Angeles Business Journal,* 14 July 1997, 27.

Yokell, Larry J. ''Building the Business Case for Cable Telephony.'' *Business Communications Review,* March 1996, 39.

TEMPORARY EMPLOYMENT

Temporary employees typically work for firms for brief and often fixed periods, in contrast with permanent full- and part-time workers. Temporary employees are part of the category contingent workers, which also includes part-time employees and contract workers, and temporary employees are either hired directly or are provided to client firms by temporary employment agencies, as is most often the case. In the 1990s, roughly 90 percent of U.S. businesses and 95 percent of Fortune 500 firms used some form of temporary employment, according to temporary employment agencies. Among the areas of most rapid growth are the use of temporaries in professional, technological, and service occupations. Companies typically use temporary help for employee absences, special assignments, seasonal work increases, and temporary worker shortages.

Temporary employment firms typically undertake hiring and firing decisions, issue paychecks, and also withhold payroll taxes and make contributions for unemployment insurance, workers' compensation, and Social Security. In the late 1990s, there were approximately, 15,000 temporary employment agencies in the United States. The industry is served by the National Association of Temporary Services (NATSS), which has 1,500 members. According to NATSS, 72 percent of assigned workers eventually move to permanent positions. Furthermore, a study by the Upjohn Institute for Employment Research indicated that over 50 percent of the companies that expanded their use of temporary workers in the 1990s did so in an effort to find permanent workers.

Temporary workers generally receive hourly wages that range from $5.50 an hour for unskilled jobs to $15 an hour for skilled jobs. Moreover, some highly skilled workers receive over $75 an hour for technology- and knowledge-based. The mean hourly rate was $10.11 in the late 1990s, according to NATSS. Temporary job assignments generally last anywhere from 1 day to several months. However, some managerial and executive assignments may last as long as a few years.

The first temporary employment firms began operations in the 1940s. It was not until the 1980s and 1990s, however, that temporary employment grew rapidly. Annual average temporary employment grew from 340,000 in 1978 to 695,000 by 1985, increasing three times faster than total service sector employment and eight times faster than total nonagricultural employment. The temporary employment industry experienced its most explosive growth in the early 1990s, expanding by an average of 17 percent a year. Annual average temporary employment rose to 2.2 million workers by 1996 and to nearly 2.8 million by 1998 with an annual growth rate of about 9 percent. Between 1992 and 1998, 18.4 million non-agricultural jobs were added to the U.S. economy. Temporary employment accounted for 1.4 million of these jobs, according to the U.S. Bureau of Labor Statistics (BLS). The BLS predicts that the temporary employment will increase by 53 percent by 2006, making it one of the most rapidly expanding industries. Overall, temporary employment accounts for about 2 percent of the country's employment.

In the late 1990s, temporary employment agencies began investing greater more in training employees for their assignments. A NATSS survey from 1998 reported that temporary employment agencies spent $720 million on training 1997, in contrast to only $260 million in 1995. The survey also indicated that 4.8 million workers participated in the training programs and that about 90 percent of all temporary employment agencies provide training for free.

Temporary workers exhibit a variety of demographic characteristics. About 40 percent have completed at least a two-year college program and roughly 20 percent attend school while working. In addition, 21 percent use temporary employment as a path to permanent employment, going directly from being a student to being a temporary employee. Furthermore, the segment of temporary workers between 18 and 24 years old has continued to grow.

The administrative and clerical category has been the leading temporary employment category for decades. However, the BLS predicts that this category will decline through 2006, while skilled and professional occupations increase. The professional occupations—including accountants, managers, engineers, and computer programmers and technicians, lawyers, and marketing professionals—already constitute a significant and growing sector of the industry. These temporary positions accounted for about 11 percent of the industry's total placements in the late 1990s, according to the BLS.

The manufacturing sector also made up a growing proportion of the demand for temporary workers in recent years. A large number of manufacturers made increasing use of the just-in-time system, which minimized inventories. Temporary employment provided flexibility, which suited it to the conditions of the just-in-time production. The U.S. Department of Labor estimated that about 33 percent of all temporary employees worked for manufacturers and temporary agencies provided about 400,000 temporary workers per day to the manufacturing sector in mid-1990s. An example was Nike's repackaging facility in Memphis. Nike employed 120 permanent employees, who received at least $13 per hour plus benefits. This core labor force worked alongside 60 to 225 temporaries provided by Norrell Services. Norrell received $8.50 per hour for each temporary, who in turn received $6.50 per hour. These temporaries did not receive health insurance, though Norrell did cover workers' compensation and Social Security.

REASONS FOR THE GROWTH OF TEMPORARY EMPLOYMENT

A confluence of factors fueled the growth of temporary employment including corporate downsizing or restructuring, low unemployment rates, outsourcing, and increased employment regulation. Downsizing refers to the corporation practice of reducing the size of their core workforce. In the 1980s, for example, Fortune 500 firms cut three million jobs. What's more, companies averaged about 600,000 layoffs annually in the mid- to late 1990s. Companies substitute temporary for permanent employees because temporaries receive hourly wages that average 75 percent of the wages of permanent employees, and generally receive fewer benefits. Temporary workers contracting directly with firms are generally not eligible for unemployment insurance or workers' compensation. In addition, temporary employees provided firms with a great deal of flexibility in the face of changing business conditions. The trend of substitution of temporary for permanent workers is reflected in the fact that the decline in temporary employment was substantially less in the recession of the early 1980s than in the recessions of the 1970s.

Unemployment rates in the mid- to late 1990s remained some of the lowest in three decades. For example, the unemployment rate staid below five percent in 1998—a 28-year low. Since some economists generally argue that a natural unemployment rate for the United States is about 5 or 6 percent, they suggest that companies face greater difficulty finding and retaining employees when the unemployment rate drops below the natural rate. Consequently, temporary employment agencies were poised to help companies overcome their staffing shortages. Simultaneously, temporary employment agencies assist unemployed workers providing them with temporary positions until they locate permanent ones and thereby helping reduce the unemployment rate.

Related trend to corporate downsizing has been outsourcing where companies contract with outside workers or agencies to perform non-core tasks. As a result, temporary employment agencies received some of the outsourcing business from these companies. Finally, increased regulation requiring employers to pay taxes on and provide various benefits to permanent employees also contributed to the demand for temporary employment so that companies could bypass the additional measures or effort needed to comply with these regulations.

In his 1988 volume, *Alternative Staffing Strategies,* David Nye argued that the expanded use of temporary employment was likely to persist. He wrote that factors that caused the growth of temporary employment are expected to continue exerting an influence on the labor market. According to Nye, these factors include the decline of manufacturing jobs and the growth information, technology, and service jobs, employer reliance on temporary employment to help cope with possible business slowdowns, the growth of technology that requires specialization, and the presence workers with adequate skills who by choice or of necessity seek temporary employment.

LEGAL ISSUES

One area of concern for temporary workers is the extent to which they are protected by labor legislation. Temporary employment firms are required to abide by the **Fair Labor Standards Act of 1938**, the Equal Employment Opportunity Act of 1972, and the Occupational Safety and Health Act of 1970. Temporary workers are often ineligible for unemployment insurance. This results in part from their inability to meet the minimum earnings requirements specified in state laws. In addition, temporary employment firms may offer unemployed temporaries a one-day assignment just prior to their eligibility for unemployment benefits, thus minimizing firms' contribution to unemployment insurance.

The Employee Retirement Income Security Act of 1974 (ERISA) requires firms with pension plans to offer them to all employees working 1,000 or more hours per year. Firms can consequently minimize these costs by working temporaries a lesser number of hours. Labor legislation makes it difficult for short-term workers to engage in collective bargaining, and the **National Labor Relations Board (NLRB)** determines on a case-by-case basis whether temporaries can be included in bargaining units.

KEY TEMPORARY EMPLOYMENT AGENCIES

The largest temporary employment firm in the United States in 1998 was Manpower Inc., with $8.8 billion in revenues—a $6 billion increase over 1992. Manpower employed over 2 million workers worldwide in 1998. Manpower was founded in Milwaukee in 1948 and originally provided unskilled temporary workers for industrial employment. Soon the company diversified into providing temporary office workers. Because of the volume of temporary workers it places, Manpower is considered the largest employer in the United States—with more employees than IBM and AT&T combined. About one-third of Manpower's workers receive permanent positions each year as a result of their temporary employment. The firm not only provides secretarial and factory workers, but also accountants and doctors. This is part of an overall trend in temporary employment in which professional occupations, including executives, lawyers, engineers and scientists, are among the fastest growing. Furthermore, with demand for technical workers, Manpower established Manpower Technical, which specializes in helping high-tech companies solve their staffing problem for everything from computer programming to engineering to biotechnology. Manpower Technical reports providing temporary help to about 94 percent of the 500 companies.

In terms of revenue, Manpower Inc. was followed by the Olsten Corporation, with $4.6 billion and 701,000. Olsten provides a wide array of temporary staffing services, including office, professional, and health care help. Olsten has separate subsidiaries that handle some its specialty fields such as Co-Counsel and Olsten Health Care Services. Kelly Services Inc. was the third leading company with $4 billion in revenues and 750,000 workers, out of an industry total of about $58.6 billion in 1998. In contrast, total industry revenues were $20 billion in 1990.

SEE ALSO: Outsourcing

[David Kucera]

FURTHER READING:

Brogan, Timothy W. "Staffing Services Annual Update." May 1999. Available from www.natss.org/staffingservicesupdate.html.

Melchiomo, Rich. "The Changing Temporary Work Force: Managerial, Professional, and Technical Workers in the Personnel Supply Services Industry." *Occupational Outlook Quarterly,* spring 1999, 24.

Stone, Martha L. "Companies Turn to Marketing Temps." *Business Marketing,* October 1998, 10.

TENDER OFFERS

A tender offer asks the stockholders of a firm to submit, or tender, their shares for an established price. While tender offers may be made for any type of **securities**, they are usually made for **common stock**. A tender offer may be made by the firm that originally issued the stock, or by another company or group of investors. Tender offers are commonly used by issuing firms to repurchase a quantity of their stock. They are also used to acquire a controlling interest in a firm.

A tender offer must specify an offer price, the maximum number of shares that will be purchased, the beginning and expiration dates of the offer, and the last day when tendered stock can be withdrawn by shareholders. When a tender offer is made, it must remain open for a specified time period. During this time, shareholders have the right to withdraw shares they have already tendered. If the tender offer is oversubscribed—that is, more shares are tendered than are going to be purchased—then purchases must be made on a prorated basis. If the offer terms are amended to provide for a higher price, then shares already tendered automatically receive the higher price.

A tender offer that is made by the firm that originally issued the stock is known as a stock repurchase, or self-tender offer. This often occurs when **management** believes the company's **stock** is undervalued on the market. While a self-tender offer reduces the firm's liquidity—as it uses up some of its cash reserves—it also sends the message that management is confident of strong cash flows in the future. Consequently, a self-tender offer often has the effect of increasing the value of the company's stock.

A tender offer may be used to acquire controlling interest in a company. When one company seeks to gain control over another, it will usually approach the target company's management with a **merger** proposal. If an agreement cannot be reached with management, then a **takeover** bid can be initiated by making a tender offer to the company's stockholders.

In a two-tier tender offer, the acquiring company will make a tender offer to obtain voting control of the target company. In a second stage or tier, the acquiring company votes its controlling interest to obtain merger approval at a shareholders' meeting. Typically, the target company's shareholders would receive higher compensation for their shares in the first tier (tender offer), than in the second tier (merger).

High stock prices and increased competition to acquire desirable companies resulted in a surge in the number and value of tender offers transacted during 1997, the last year for which statistics were available. In 1997 there were 208 transactions involving tender offers worth a total of $111.4 billion, compared to 154 successful tender offers worth $75.2 billion in 1996 and 161 tenders worth $76.1 billion in 1995. The 1997 figure was the highest since 1989, when there were 208 tender offers worth $156.1

There are antitakeover measures a company may use to counter the threat of a two-tier tender offer. For example, a company may add fair price and super majority amendments to its corporate charter. A fair price amendment stipulates that an acquiring company must pay a fair price for all of the target company's shares that it purchases, which is usually the highest price the acquiring company has paid. A super majority amendment increases the necessary majority to approve an acquisition or merger from one-half to two-thirds. Companies may also attempt to thwart hostile takeovers by obtaining "marriage proposals," or more favorable tender offers, from other firms.

As a result of Congressional investigations, tender offers were placed under the jurisdiction of the **Securities and Exchange Commission** (SEC) by the Williams Act of 1968, which also established disclosure rules and other requirements for tender offers. The acquiring firm must provide 30 days' notice of its intention to make an acquisition to the management of the target firm and to the SEC. Another requirement is that the beneficial owner of the stock, as well as the party financing the acquisition, must be disclosed when substantial amounts of stock are being acquired with the intent to gain control of a firm. In addition, anyone making a tender offer that would result in ownership of more than 5 percent of a class of securities is required to file a report with the SEC.

[David P. Bianco]

FURTHER READING:

"A Good Way to Win a Prize Target." *Mergers and Acquisitions,* March/April 1997, 20-21.

"Viable Deal Format in a Hot Market: Intensifying Competition and Pricey Deals Boost the Use of Tender Offers." *Mergers and Acquisitions,* March/April 1998, 22-23.

TERM STRUCTURE OF INTEREST RATES

The term structure of **interest rates** describes the differing yields to maturity (YTM) on similar debt securities, with yields typically being higher the longer the period until maturity. For instance, a **U.S. Treasury bill** with a 6-month maturity might carry a 4.5 percent yield, while a 30-year Treasury bond bought at the same time may yield a 5.5 percent return. When such a difference exists, it is known as a term premium. In the United States, Treasury securities are generally used to map the term structure of interest rates (i.e., the **yield curve**) because they are virtually free of **default** risk. However, term structures may be computed and analyzed for any number of interest bearing instruments.

Economists and financial analysts employ term structure analysis, which frequently involves creating or using mathematical models, for a variety of applications. Some of the most common include

- forecasting future interest rates
- estimating the cost of capital for discounting future cash flows
- building predictive models of general economic growth (e.g., to project gross domestic product)
- formulating monetary policy
- estimating future inflation
- understanding dynamics in financial markets
- constructing a portfolio or **hedging** strategy

The shape of the term structure may change from period to period, being either upward sloping (i.e., long-term rates higher than short-term rates), downward sloping (i.e., long-term rates lower than short-term rates), or flat (long-term rates equal to short-term rates). Most frequently, however, the term structure is upward sloping. In addition to the direction of the slope, term structure analysis is concerned with the steepness of the slope at any particular time, where a greater slope signifies a larger disparity between interest rates over some period of time. The yield curve in Figure 1 illustrates the nominal term structure (that is, using the current face value and not adjusting for future inflation) for U.S. Treasury securities based on current rates as of mid-1999.

NOMINAL VERSUS REAL RATES

For many detailed analyses of term structure, the nominal or observed interest rates (e.g., those shown in the figure) are only a starting point, and may not be very meaningful if they cannot be adjusted for infla-

Figure 1
Nominal Term Structure of U.S. Treasury Interest Rates

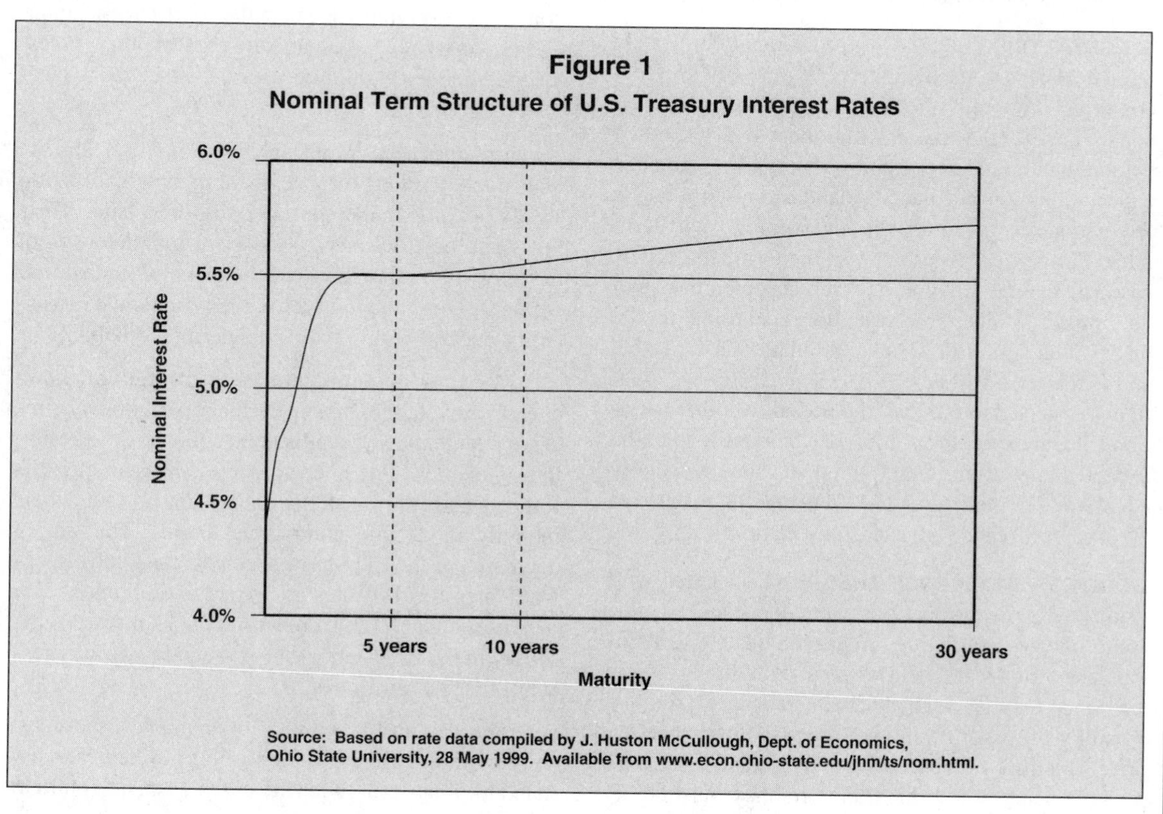

Source: Based on rate data compiled by J. Huston McCullough, Dept. of Economics, Ohio State University, 28 May 1999. Available from www.econ.ohio-state.edu/jhm/ts/nom.html.

tion somehow. A simple model of the relationship between nominal rates, real rates, and inflation is given by the formula

$$1 + R = (1 + r) \times (1 + h)$$

where R = the nominal interest rate,
r = the real interest rate net of inflation, and
h = the inflation rate

For example, if the nominal rate on a bond is 4.5 percent, and a reliable estimate suggests that inflation over the term will average 2.7 percent, the real rate could be estimated as follows:

$$\begin{aligned} 1 + 0.045 &= (1 + r) \times (1 + 0.027) \\ 1.045 &= 1.027 + 1.027r \\ 0.0175 &= r \end{aligned}$$

Thus, the real rate of return in this case is just 1.75 percent.

TERM STRUCTURE THEORIES

Several theories have been developed to explain the shape and behavior of term structures. While there is no general consensus on these theories among economists, the general trend has been toward more complex theories that address issues like volatility in bond prices. Three main perspectives on term structure are the expectations theory, the liquidity preference theory, and the market segmentation theory.

EXPECTATIONS THEORY. Expectations theory, also termed expectations hypothesis, is one of the most common economic theories of term structure. It comes in several variations, the most widely known being the unbiased expectations theory. The unbiased expectations theory contends that the long-term rate is the geometric mean of the intervening short-term rates. Further, it suggests that if the term structure is upward sloping, inflation rates are expected to rise in the future. A flat term structure, according to the theory, indicates little change in inflation is expected, and if the term structure is downward sloping, inflation is expected to fall over the period. Another variation is local expectations theory, which posits that the expected rate of return on future maturities is actually equal to the short-term risk-free rate (e.g., current Treasury bill yield) adjusted for inflation.

LIQUIDITY PREFERENCE THEORY. Concerned with risk-aversion investment behaviors, the liquidity preference theory asserts that lenders anticipate the potential need to liquidate an investment earlier than expected. Since for a given change in interest rates, the price volatility of a short-term investment is lower than the price volatility of a long-term investment, investors prefer to lend short term. Therefore, they must be offered a risk premium to induce them to lend long-term. Borrowers, on the other hand, often prefer long-term bonds because they eliminate the risk of having to refinance at higher interest rates in future periods. Furthermore, the fixed costs of frequent refinancing can be quite high. Therefore, borrowers are willing to pay the premium necessary to attract long-term financing.

The liquidity preference theory, in conjunction with the unbiased expectations theory, suggests that an upward sloping term structure would be expected to occur more often than a downward sloping term structure. In fact, as stated earlier, this is the most common situation.

MARKET SEGMENTATION THEORY. Market segmentation theory (MST) is also known as institutional hedging or habitat theory. This theory sees two separate maturity habitats or segments—one long and the other short. Each segment has a schedule of supply (lenders) and demand (borrowers) for loanable funds. The point at which the demand and supply intersect determines the prevailing rate for that sector.

MST recognizes that there are institutional restrictions on the asset side and hedging pressures on the liability side which allow for very little substitutability between **bonds** of different maturities. Some of these restrictions result from government regulation, company policy, **Securities and Exchange Commission** regulations, goals and objectives, and fiscal and operational considerations.

Commercial **banks** and nonfinancial corporations generally supply loans in the short-term segment of the market. Nonfinancial corporations invest (hedge) their excess liquidity until it is needed to meet cash distributions.

Life insurance companies, pension funds, and the like supply the long term segment in anticipation of a steady stream of income over the long haul. Their goals and objectives seem to differ completely from the short-term suppliers except that, for each to be successful over the long-term, they each must consistently operate within their predetermined habitat.

The flow of funds into these institutions, however, is not static. Customers make withdrawals, receive payments, and reallocate resources. As a result, the supply schedule in each market shifts among different institutions. Pensioners may place their monthly funds into commercial banks. The supply decreases in the long-term segment, thus putting upward pressure on rates to attract more funds. The increase of capital in commercial banks increases the supply in the short-term, thus putting downward pressure on short-term rates.

The demand schedules for loanable funds also shifts with changes in the economic cycles. The demand for long-term funds increases when an upturn in the economy is perceived, putting upward pressure on rates. As a business cycle matures, the need to expand inventories creates upward pressures on short-term rates, thus attracting additional supply to the short segment.

The market segmentation model proposes that the spread between long and short-term rates depends largely on the relative supply and demand for these instruments by transactors in their preferred habitats.

SEE ALSO: Bonds; Valuation

[Roger J. AbiNader]

FURTHER READING:

Brown, Roger. ''Mastering Management: Term Structure of Interest Rates.'' *Financial Times,* 3 May 1996.

Dodds, J.C., and J.L. Ford. *Expectations, Uncertainty, and the Term Structure of Interest Rates.* Reprint ed. New York: Gregg International Publishers, 1993.

Russell, Steven. ''Understanding the Term Structure of Interest Rates.'' *Federal Reserve Bank of St. Louis Review,* July-August 1992.

Van Deventer, Donald R., and Kenji Imai. *Financial Risk Analytics: A Term Structure Model Approach for Banking, Insurance, and Investment Management.* Chicago: Irwin Professional Publishing, 1996.

THAILAND, DOING BUSINESS IN

Thailand, formerly known as Siam, is one of the most important trading nations in Southeast Asia. At just under 200,000 square miles, Thailand is approximately three-fourths the size of Texas. Thailand has a population of approximately 57 million (or 3.3 times Texas's population). This makes Thailand among the world's most densely populated nations.

THE THAI ECONOMIC CRISIS

Thailand, until 1997, was one of the most rapidly developing nations in the world. In July 1997, however, the Thai economy was shaken to its foundations. The July 1997 collapse of the baht (Thailand's currency) soon spread beyond Thailand, where it became known as the East Asian economic crisis.

Thailand's economic collapse resulted from several factors, not the least of which was that virtually no one had thought a collapse was possible. Because of Thailand's historic stability, the 1997 economic collapse caught most observers by surprise. Thailand had for decades shown remarkable growth. Thus, while in the 1980s Thailand emerged as one of the strongest developing economies in world trade, its growth was not unprecedented.

Beginning in the 1960s and throughout the 1970s Thailand sustained an annual economic growth rate exceeding 7 percent. Following the double-digit growth of the 1980s, Thailand had seemingly stabilized at the still quite respectable annual **gross domestic product** (GDP) of 8 percent. Moreover, even during the political instability in the nation in 1991 and 1992, the Thai economy remained healthy.

During the last decade before the crash, Thailand's exports more than doubled, making major inroads in the global marketplace in manufactured goods ranging from textiles to integrated circuitry. Even in agriculture, the nation had shown a shift from rice to processed food exports such as canned fruit and fish.

It was, however, during the last four years of the 1980s that Thailand took its role as one of Asia's economic tigers. During those four years, Thailand's averaged annual economic growth rate had reached 10 percent, with a growth in GDP of 18.2 percent. While political difficulties had reduced that GDP by the 1990s, Thailand still averaged over 8 percent for most of the decade. By the end of 1997 that figure had fallen to -0.4 percent.

The signs of trouble were difficult to see before 1997. At the beginning of the 1990s, Thailand's **banks** and larger companies began to borrow in dollars and did not maintain fallback positions. They adopted this position precisely because the nation was economically so robust that few people recognized the possibility of any exchange rate risk. The resultant investment capital was, in turn, used to fuel a **real estate** boom. Within a few years, the property speculation leveled out.

The slowing of the overheated real estate market, however, was not in itself a bad sign, and had in fact been anticipated to some extent. The timing of the downturn, however, was significant. By the mid-1990s many foreign investors began to grow cautious of investment throughout Southeast Asia as they waited to see the results of Hong Kong's repatriation with China in 1997. This caution, in turn, began to slow Thailand's export growth, the engine that drove the Thai economic miracle.

By 1996 many financial analysts began to question whether the Bank of Thailand could continue to tie the baht to the U.S. dollar. In response, the Bank of Thailand attempted to shore up the exchange rate, seriously compromising its foreign exchange reserves. Finding this course of action untenable, the Bank of Thailand in 1997 floated the exchange rate. What followed was one of the most dramatic currency readjustments in history, with the baht falling by 27 percent against the dollar in a single day.

The result was a dramatic leap in foreign **liabilities** that Thai firms could not repay. The result in July 1997 was the Thai economic collapse.

Thailand's prime minister at the time, Chavalit Yongchaiyudh entered into a $14 billion agreement with the **International Monetary Fund** (IMF) to rebuild economic stability and to augment foreign exchange reserves. The economy, however, continued to weaken, and Chawalit Yongchaiyudh resigned. His successor as prime minister, Chuan Likphai, strictly followed the IMF program. By February 1998 the Thai economy seemed to have stabilized.

THE CURRENT THAI ECONOMY

While the East Asian economic crisis began in Thailand, it is notable that Thailand was among the first nations to have at least moderately begun to recover. This can be attributed to a number of factors too, ranging from strictly adhering to the IMF program to confidence in the king. Most significantly, though, is that, despite the collapse of its currency, Thailand's economy remained basically sound.

Thailand has long held a reputation as the world's leading rice exporter, and it still controls more than a third of all rice exports. Additionally, Thailand remains a major producer of tapioca (second in the world), as well as sugar, coconuts, and cotton. As a result, two-thirds of the nation's labor force still remains tied to agriculture. Also, Thailand is a leading producer of gemstones, notably sapphires. All of these areas have remained stable.

The economic crisis affected primarily the manufacturing and service sectors that had fueled Thailand's spectacular growth. By 1998 Thailand's economy had once again stabilized but the nation remains in deep **recession**.

ETHNICITY

Thailand is not a homogeneous nation. Approximately 75 percent of Thailand's population are ethnic Thais. This group itself is not homogeneous—dividing into the dominant central Thais (or Siamese) of the Chao Phraya Delta and the nearly equally populous Thai-Lao of the northeastern part of the country near the border with Laos. The ethnic Thais also include the less numerous Northern Thais as well as several ethnically distinct Thai-speaking groups, such as the Shan, the Phuan, and the Yaw peoples. Each of these groups has its own dialect and, to some extent, its own business behavior and cultural variations. Still the vast majority of interaction that the *farang*—foreigner—will have in business will be among the culturally and economically dominant central Thais.

THE ETHNIC CHINESE. Much more important for the *farang*—at least in terms of business—than the distinctions among Thai-speaking groups is Thailand's important Chinese minority. Between 12 and 14 percent of Thailand's population is comprised of ethnic Chinese. As with Thailand's neighbors in Southeast Asia, the ethnic-Chinese presence and influence in business far exceeds their numbers in the population. In distinct contrast to the Philippines, Malaysia, Indonesia, and other Asian nations where the Chinese play a significant economic role, however, Thailand has experienced very little ethnic tensions between the two groups, and ethnic-Chinese groups have been harmoniously integrated into day-to-day life in Thailand. This is particularly significant when compared to neighboring Indonesia where anti-Chinese riots and persecutions took place in 1997 and 1998, when the Thai economic crisis spread there.

Both of Thailand's two major business cultures, the Thais and the ethnic Chinese, have their own customs, traditional dress, and usually distinctive names. It is, however, important to note that the ethnic Chinese in Thailand have assimilated into Thai culture at a level unequaled in anywhere else in Southeast Asia. In part this assimilation may be explained on the Thai side by the cultural value Thais place on tolerance of any *farangs,* not just the Chinese. Equally important are the two cultures' common ties to Buddhism. In part, assimilation may be explained on the Chinese side by the fact that the Chinese in Thailand never experienced prolonged persecution. Moreover, while the Chinese were traditionally prohibited from owning land or participating in government in Thailand, such bans are no longer practiced. In short, the Chinese may have assimilated more readily in Thailand than elsewhere in Southeast Asia simply because the ability to do so was open to them.

Indeed, intermarriage between Thais and ethnic Chinese is not uncommon and many leading Thai families have at least some Chinese ancestry. Even King Taksin, the 18th-century Thai military leader (and later monarch), who was the avenger of the sack of Ayutthaya, had a Chinese mother. Such Chinese-Thai unions have made it more difficult (and arguably less important) to define clearly who is ethnically pure Thai or pure Chinese. Today, the two cultures live together harmoniously in Bangkok and other cities with large Chinese communities.

Despite harmonious ties and religious similarities with the ethnic-Thai majority, Thailand's ethnic Chinese remain a distinctive group. Because of laws that were in force well into the 20th century prohibiting ethnic-Chinese land ownership and participation in government service, Thailand's Chinese gravitated toward trade and **service industries**, where they still play a force far disproportionate to their numbers.

Regardless of their position in society, the Chinese are not newcomers to Thailand. The Thais themselves came to Thailand in the tenth century A.D. from southwest China. Throughout the thirteenth through 19th centuries, Chinese had been present in small numbers in Thailand for trade purposes and as a counterbalance first to Burmese then later Portuguese threats.

It was not until 1824, however, that Chinese immigrants came in large numbers to Thailand. It was in that year that Rama III granted the Chinese tin-mining and sugar plantation rights to counterbalance British and U.S. colonial schemes in the region. While this laid the foundation for the Chinese presence in Thailand, the Chinese still entered Thailand from a position of a strong home nation. By contrast, most Chinese emigration to Thailand came only after China's social and economic collapse that followed the European, Japanese, and U.S. colonial incursions there in the second half of the 19th century. This massive Chinese immigration to Thailand continued unabated throughout the 19th and early 20th centuries and did not end until World War II and the closing of postrevolutionary China's borders.

The Chinese themselves are not a single ethnic group. Five major Chinese subcommunities exist in Thailand, each speaking mutually unintelligible dialects. These, in turn, form their own subcommunity ties and loyalties. The five major groups are Hokkien, Yueh or Cantonese, Hakka, Wu or Shanghaiese, and Hainanese. Additionally, many members of the other Chinese dialect groups are present in smaller numbers as well.

OTHER GROUPS IN THAILAND. An additional 3.5 percent of the population consists of ethnic Malays, most of whom are Moslems and most of whom live near Thailand's border with Malaysia. While numerous, Thailand's ethnic Malays have not played a major role in business and are regionally isolated, and so will not be addressed in this article. Their behavior follows that of ethnic Malays.

Another 5 percent of the population consists of small non-Thai-speaking communities. These consist of non-Thai regional groups such as the Semang, the Htin, the Khamu, and the Moken (or "sea gypsies"—*chao leh*). This figure would also include the hundreds of thousands of refugees from Vietnam, Kampuchea (Cambodia), and Burma (Myanmar) to whom since 1975 Thailand has maintained an open-door policy of political asylum. For its provision of such asylum, Thailand has received widespread praise from numerous international humanitarian organizations. Moreover, these groups are of some marginal importance in regional trade, and may prove more so as the communist nations such as Vietnam enter more into the global trade arena.

Finally, just over 3 percent of the people consist of the members of the 20 or so hill tribes of the north, such as the Hmong, the Akha, the Karen, the Lisu, the Lahu, and the Yao peoples. These groups are important in Thailand's growing tourism industry and in the manufacture of handcrafted items, but aside from these two areas play little part in the business world. While each of these groups represent unique and important cultures, with different customs, languages, and religions, they remain relatively unimportant in international trade and so are not addressed further in this article.

NAMES AND TITLES

THAI NAMES AND TITLES. As with English names, Thai names have a first name that is the individual's personal name and a second surname that is the family name. Unlike English names, however, Thai names attach the title to the first or personal name, not to the surname.

The standard Thai title is *Khun.* Unlike English titles, *Khun* applies equally to men or women. Moreover, while Thai women do take on their husband's surnames, they will continue to be addressed by their first names. Thus, a woman named Rungludi Kasetsiri would be addressed as *Khun* Rungludi. Her husband Anand Kasetsiri would be addressed as *Khun* Anand.

Unlike the English titles of Mr. or Ms., however, *Khun* is not clearly an indicator of formality. One uses *Khun* when speaking of someone in the third person as a sign of respect and one uses *Khun* directly in conversation with another person when that person is a relative stranger. Thais quickly move to drop *Khun* when speaking with those they know well. In such cases, they use only the person's first or personal name. This use of the first name, however, does not have the same level of informality of first-name use in English because *Khun* itself is always attached to the person's first name.

Additionally, *Khun* is not used when the individual addressed has a professional or academic title. Thus if a man named Prasert Pibulsonggram were a Ph.D. or M.D., he would be addressed as *Dokter* Prasert. If he were a military officer he would be *Muad'* Prasert, and so on. These titles, unlike *Khun,* do carry additional formality and respect and would be less likely to be dropped as quickly as *Khun* among those of lower status.

Many Thais, particularly in government, have royal titles. Preceding Thai royal names are (listed here in descending rank) the abbreviations M.C. (*Mom Chao*), M.R. (*Mom Rachawong*) and M.L. (*Mom Luang*). All of these royal titles are nonhereditary so that the child of one rank is born at the next lowest rank. Thus the child of someone with the title *Mom Rachawong* will have the next lowest title *Mom Luang*. The child of someone with the lowest title, in turn, will be born with no royal title at all.

Additionally, all Thais have nicknames. Unlike English, in which some people have nicknames and others do not, Thais without exception have a nickname. Also, unlike English, Thai nicknames are much less a sign of informality than English nicknames. English nicknames are used only among close friends and in relatively informal situations. Thai nicknames are used by even casual acquaintances and are used in all but the most formal settings. Thai nicknames mean something in Thai and some Thais will translate their names for use in English. This can be disquieting since the meanings often seem insulting in English, ranging as they do from animals (such as Pig or Cow) to physical features (such as Fat One or Shorty). Thai nicknames are, in general, shorter than Thai first names and so actually make names a bit simpler for *farangs.*

When addressing *farangs,* Thais will usually use the foreigner's first name or *Khun* with the foreigner's first name. Thais well acquainted with English-speakers, however, may attempt to use English naming practice. This is particularly the case with Thais acquainted with *farangs* who do not come from the United States or Australia, where first name use is as common as in Thailand. Thus, a person named Ralph Griffiths would customarily be addressed as *Khun* Ralph or simply Ralph. As a sign of cross-cultural sensitivity, however, a Thai might address him as Mr. Griffiths. The Thai, would, in either case, still expect to be addressed in the Thai manner back, using his or her personal name. The *farang,* even if addressed by Mr. or Ms. and a last name, should address the Thai by his or her first (personal) name, probably preceded by *Khun.*

CHINESE NAMES AND TITLES. The large ethnic-Chinese community of Thailand poses an additional naming problem for the foreigner. This is particularly so in the case of those in Thailand for business, in which the Chinese community plays so dominant a position.

Due to government pressure to make the ethnic Chinese adopt Thai names (by making a Thai name a prerequisite to obtaining government documents, scholarships, and so forth), many ethnic Chinese have done so. Indeed, a number of Chinese and those of Chinese-Thai mixed ancestry may have only Thai names. As a result, unlike other ethnic-Chinese communities in the rest of Southeast Asia, many Chinese in Thailand use the same address system as the rest of the country. Thus most ethnic Chinese use the Thai title *Khun* or professional titles in the same manner as the ethnic Thais.

Nevertheless, one title, *Aa-sia',* is used in the Thai naming system specifically to show respect for important or powerful Chinese merchants. Thus an ethnic-Thai merchant named Prasert Tantiyanon, even if important or powerful, would still be addressed as *Khun* Prasert while his or her Chinese counterpart even with the identical Thai name might likely be addressed as *Aa-sia'* Prasert.

It should not be assumed, however, that all ethnic Chinese have or even prefer Thai names. Many ethnic Chinese have two names. They are likely to have Thai names with which they conduct business with ethnic Thais and with foreigners and a second Chinese name that they use in the Chinese community. *Farang* businesspeople may in fact achieve an advantage not readily open to ethnic Thais in using the Chinese name of such person. The Thai would be expected to use the Thai addressing system. *Farangs,* by contrast, can show respect for their ethnic-Chinese counterpart's traditions and community because they have chosen to use the Chinese address system. Finally, as with the rest of Southeast Asia, many ethnic Chinese do not follow the local naming system, and have only a Chinese name. In the Chinese naming system, the person using a Chinese name should be aware that the individual's family name comes first. After this comes the generation name and the personal name, usually hyphenated when written in English. Thus, Wu Kwok-wen is Mr. Wu. Calling him Mr. Kwok-wen would be very insulting. Because Chinese traditionally are extremely reluctant to use personal names in any but the most intimate relationships, many ethnic Chinese have adopted additional Thai nicknames or—for foreigners—English names so that their ethnic Thai or U.S. counterparts can have the illusion of being on a first name basis without insulting anyone. Thus, Wu Kwok-wen may select the English name Ralph. His English-language card might even show the name as ''Ralph'' Wu Kwok-Wen. His U.S. business counterparts would then know to call him Ralph, *Khun* Ralph, or Mr. Wu, as they felt appropriate.

Most Chinese women do not adopt the names of their husbands after marriage. Thus, Lee Mei-Ling could easily be the wife of Wu Kwok-Wen. For business purposes, with English-speakers, she may allow herself to be called Mrs. Wu, but most people will know her as Ms. Lee or by her Thai name.

THE ENVIRONMENT

ATTITUDES TOWARD TECHNOLOGY. The attitudes of both of Thailand's major ethnic groups regarding technology significantly differs from that of the United States. The United States is a control culture, meaning that U.S. culture views technology as consistently positive and reinforces a belief that people can control their environment to conform to their needs. By contrast, both ethnic-Thai and ethnic-Chinese culture in Thailand are more accurately described as a harmonization culture. Here the emphasis is on one's integration into a natural order rather than one's control of that order. This is most evident in the Thai concept of spirit forces, ghosts, and the charms and rites used to placate or direct these forces. The Thai Buddhist concept of karma pervades Thai life as well and has within it the notion of a harmony between good and evil. This notion is summarized in the commonly used Thai proverb: ''Do good, get good; do evil, get evil.'' As a result, in Thai culture, the environment is not (as it is in U.S. culture) something to be conquered, but something to be kept in balance.

This harmonization orientation toward technology and the environment is even more clearly expressed by the ethnic Chinese following of *feng shui* (ancient geomancy dealing with the balance of spiritual forces). The importance of location, lucky or unlucky dates, and numerous other factors determined by *feng shui* experts guide most of Thailand's traditional Chinese community. For example, many Chinese would confer with a *feng shui* expert before deciding on an office location or signing an important agreement.

Considerations for maintaining good relations with spirits, balancing karma, and following *feng shui* are often looked down on by ethnocentric or religiously bigoted foreigners unfamiliar with them. Regardless of the foreigner's own beliefs, however, he or she should be aware that such practices are important to those who adhere to them. These practices should be accorded the same respect one would give to any Western religious practice, rather than be misinterpreted as the equivalent of minor superstition.

ENVIRONMENTAL ISSUES. Following World War II, approximately 70 percent of Thailand was still covered in forest and woodlands. By the late 1980s, only 20 to no more than 30 percent could be considered forested. Deforestation had been conducted so haphazardly that in 1988 a major disaster occurred when hundreds of tons of cut lumber slid down hillsides cleared of their trees and buried several villages. Hundreds were killed and more were left homeless. In 1989, responding to the disaster, Thailand outlawed all logging and related industries. Timber imports are strictly monitored and the construction industry must even request government approval to use timber salvaged from existing structures.

SOCIAL ORGANIZATION

Social organizational factors in Thailand affecting business include the political structure and climate of the nation, the importance of the king, the role of Buddhism in all aspects of life, and the concept of the work ethic.

THE POLITICAL STRUCTURE AND CLIMATE. Thailand's political system has never been particularly stable since the 1932 coup d'état that overthrew King Pokklao (Rama VII), Thailand's last absolute monarch. Since the advent of constitutional monarchy, Thailand has undergone ten successful coups, nine unsuccessful coup attempts, and a partial occupation by the Japanese (during World War II). Yet the stability of the Thai legal courts and the unifying respect for the monarchy—constitutionally limited or otherwise—have customarily sustained Thai economic stability and political consistency on the day-to-day level until fairly recent times.

On February 23, 1991, Thailand's longest modern period of stability was shaken when the government was overthrown by a bloodless military coup. In May 1992 antigovernment demonstrators demanded the military leader's resignation. The military killed dozens of the protesters and hundreds more were injured in the incident. These incidents have raised concerns among foreign investors and manufacturers regarding Thailand's political stability.

THE IMPORTANCE OF THE KING. The power of the absolute monarchy of the Thai king was ended with the forced abdication of King Pokklao in the 1932 pro-democracy coup. While theoretically the king holds little direct power (he appoints the members of the Supreme Court and advises in a ceremonial capacity), in reality the monarchy is far stronger than any other constitutional monarchy in the world.

The king and the royal family are revered by the vast majority of Thailand's people, who view the monarch as a sort of demigod. Even the Thai constitution expressly indicates that the monarch be ''enthroned in a position of revered worship.'' Not only is open criticism of the monarch and royal family illegal, but the vast majority of the Thai people will not tolerate even mildly negative comments regarding them. As a result, the foreigner conducting business in Thailand should avoid all negative comments regarding Thai royalty.

One side point to this is the unintentional insult many U.S. movie fans often make in referencing the unfortunate U.S. motion picture *The King and I.* This classic Hollywood musical was newly released in a cartoon version in 1999. Both versions of the film depict the Thai monarch Rama IV (King Mongkut the Great) as backward and naive, and needing to be educated to behave in a civilized manner by his Western tutor. Thais universally consider the film or reference to it to be an insult to the monarchy and Thailand.

The current king, Bhumibol Adulyadej (Rama IX) celebrated his 73rd birthday in December 1998. While the king is nearly universally revered, the issue of his age has increasingly become an issue since his son, the Crown Prince Maha Vajiralongkorn, may not share the same popularity. As a result, the king agreed to modify the royal succession law to enable his highly popular second daughter, Princess Chakri Sirindhorn, to succeed him if the court of regents so chooses at the time of the king's death. Consequently, the princess has been given the same status as the crown prince.

The decision is not a light one, since the king personally restored the respect and strength of the monarchy. Moreover, while the king constitutionally has little direct power, in reality his influence is difficult to overestimate. Many attribute his intervention for calm as having helped avert an even worse disaster during the 1997 economic crisis.

Relatedly, Thais are highly patriotic. It is a serious offense to belittle the nation or insult shows of nationalism. For instance, the Thai national anthem is played each morning and each early evening through loudspeakers set up for the purpose in most Thai villages. Thais stop their activities and stand to show respect. For the foreigner, failure to stand may show lack of respect. While this widespread practice is not carried on in much of Bangkok, its counterpart exists when the anthem is played in movie theaters and other public gatherings.

THE ROLE OF BUDDHISM

Approximately 95 percent of Thailand's population—ethnic Thai, ethnic Chinese, and others—practice Buddhism. As Buddhism is a lifestyle as much as a religion, its near universal practice in Thailand has an effect on business as it does on all aspects of life. While Buddhism cannot adequately be summarized in a few paragraphs here, it is possible at least to point to areas where Buddhism will have an influence on business that would contrast with standard U.S. business practice.

First, the United States emphasizes to a large degree the importance of individual achievement. The average U.S. businessperson is motivated by a desire to succeed and a craving to get ahead. This a very foreign notion to Buddhism, which teaches that all desires result only in suffering. What one achieves is the sum total of one's meritorious and evil behavior in both this life and stored up from past life—this state of what happens to one is called karma. A Thai's success (or failure), therefore, is usually viewed as entirely apart from what one actually does—it is a function of good or bad karma. Thus, the U.S. notion of making one's own opportunities contrasts with the Thai notion of making the most of situations as (or if) they present themselves.

The Buddhist concept of the process of change also contrasts markedly with how change is viewed in the United States. Both Thai and U.S. cultures embrace change—but for entirely different reasons. The United States is a culture primarily of immigrants who believed in the positive nature of change. In the United States, however, change must be created; the average U.S. businessperson is—by Thai standards—almost obsessed with trying to change things as they are by force of will. For Thais, by contrast, change is inevitable. In Buddhism, change is the most fundamental principle—all things must change. As a result, Thais feel much less concerned than their U.S. counterparts precisely because change will occur regardless of one's efforts. To attempt to direct the change would be futile—whether that change is trying to stop the change of state from death to life or in any other event, including business.

Thailand and the United States are both nations with a strong emphasis on tolerance. This too, however, differs fundamentally between the two cultures. Those from the United States emphasize tolerance on the belief that all people are of equal importance. Thais do not share in the U.S. belief in equality. Instead, Thais emphasize tolerance based on the opposite rationale—the Buddhist precept that all things, including people, are essentially unimportant.

Finally, most Thai men, even fairly Westernized or relatively secularized Thais, will have spent a period as a monk. This explains the throngs of orange-robed monks one sees throughout the country from the most urban parts of Bangkok to the most rural northern villages. Again, while many monks *buat phra* (enter the monkhood—*sangha*) for a lifetime, it is the average people—not the exceptionally religious individuals—who make up the majority of the monks in the nation. Many Thais *buat phra* for only a few days, but the majority *buat phra* for at least three months, and many for considerably longer. One usually enters the monkhood just before marriage or before taking on a first major job. Monkhood is often seen as a sort of way to enter into the more responsible positions of work and family life. Nevertheless, Thais may enter the monkhood several times in their lives and for any number of reasons. The practice is so common that banks and government jobs are required to give leave for employees to make merit as monks, a practice followed by many Thai companies as well. Leaves are taken for men to undergo the Buddhist monkhood to fulfill parental obligations, for *dukkha* (or mourning), and to give recognition for *kae bon* (to achieve goals in the Thai sense of the phrase).

THE WORK ETHIC IN THAILAND

The nature of the work ethic among ethnic Thais and ethnic Chinese differ from one another and both differ from that practiced generally in the United States.

ETHNIC-THAI WORK ETHIC. Most ethnic Thais are good and loyal workers. They are not, however, motivated, as are most people from the United States, by work itself as a prime object. For most North Americans, work in and of itself is considered to be a good thing. Most Americans identify themselves by their jobs and a common introductory question in North America is "What do you do?"—a rather un-Thai question.

Ethnic Thais see work as a part of life, but not an end in itself. Work per se is not good of its own accord. Work—as all things—must have an element of enjoyment in it. This need to have a good time—called *sanu'ke*—has almost the same attribute of being considered good in itself as North Americans tend to give the notion of work. In short, work without *sanu'ke* is unacceptable, while *sanu'ke* without work is acceptable. For Americans, work without fun is not only acceptable but arguably the norm and possibly even culturally preferable. A Thai, in short, must enjoy his or her job. The foreign manager must take this into account to manage a Thai **workforce** well.

ETHNIC-CHINESE WORK ETHIC. The ethnic Chinese do not share the ethnic-Thai drive for *sanu'ke*. Assuredly, the average Chinese will not eschew enjoyment in the workplace, but it is not a prerequisite there or in any other arena of life.

The ethnic Chinese, though Buddhist, are markedly influenced by the ethical principles of Confucianism. The Confucianist obligations to family and clan are strong in the workplace. These obligations tie family member to family member and clan member to clan member in a web of obligations known in Chinese as *guanxi*. This web of relationships motivates the ethnic Chinese to fulfill the needs of those to whom he or she is tied. *Guanxi*, also leads to a greater group identification than is practiced among ethnic Thais and (even more so) than U.S. businesspeople. The Confucianist influence on Chinese life tends to lead the individual Chinese to see himself or herself first as a member of a larger kinship structure and only secondly as an individual. This is exactly the opposite notion of U.S. individualism, where the individual is always seen as primary and motivation is at its highest form in reaching self-actualization of one's individual goals. Such U.S.-style individualism is very foreign to most of Thailand's ethnic Chinese.

A second Confucianist notion differentiates ethnic-Chinese behavior from ethnic-Thai or U.S. behavior. This is the notion that one lives on in the memory of others after death, and that attachment to the memory of one's ancestors is good. In traditional Buddhism as practiced by ethnic Thais, any attachment is bad—including attachment to the memory of one's ancestors. In customary U.S. Judeo-Christian notions, one goes to heaven after one dies. One lives on in heaven, not in the memory of one's descendants. Being remembered after death is generally perceived as good in the United States, but it is not a religious precept. For the Confucianist-influenced Chinese, however, being remembered is one's afterlife. As a result, the traditional Chinese practice is to do as much as possible while alive so that one will be more likely to be remembered. The notion of overwork does not, per se, exist in the Chinese conception. One can work too much so that, by exhaustion, one becomes ill or one overlooks important obligations—but overwork as a state is not an understandable concept. By contrast, the U.S. notion of work rests on the Judeo-Christian notion of work as a punishment for sin in the Garden of Eden. Adam's punishment upon his banishment from Eden was work. When one works too much, in the United States, one is said to be a "glutton for punishment." Such notions traditionally have no counterpart in the ethnic-Chinese community.

CONTEXTING

Thailand is a high context society and the United States is a low context culture. This means that Thais are more likely to rely on implicit communication rather than on explicit messages. Thais as a result read more into what is said than the words themselves may actually mean. For most Thais, what is meant matters more than what is actually said.

In Thailand, meaning is usually communicated indirectly, especially in the delivery of bad news. As a result, Thais are likely to agree to things with which they disagree, allowing the context of the discussion or past relationship to convey their disagreement. This is clear to Thais but to those from low context cultures such as the United States, such indirect communication is often misread as dishonesty. Conversely, the direct style of communication practiced by most U.S. businesspeople in Thailand is perceived as rude and often causes others to lose face.

Thais, as a high context culture, place a strong value on value on face-saving, while most Americans place little emphasis on face-saving. Most Thais are motivated by a desire to maintain surface harmony, even if disagreement brews beneath the surface. By contrast, low context U.S. business practice encourages individuals to say exactly what they think.

This also affects the U.S. and Thai approach to the law. U.S. business behavior is controlled by following the law and adherence to written agreements. In Thailand, one commonly holds to a **contract** to maintain harmony in the workplace rather than from fear of a lawsuit. The American businessperson in Thailand is thus viewed as threatening to this carefully balanced harmony. Additionally, U.S. low context businesspeople are viewed as lacking tact (and are therefore unpleasant to deal with), having no sense of face, and being needlessly litigious. The Thais in turn are viewed by their American counterparts as dishonoring their promises and ignoring their own laws. In reality both perceptions are accurate when viewed through the contexting values of the other's culture.

Still, to succeed in business in Thailand, the foreigner will need to view contracts and other legally binding arrangements as ongoing rather than definitive. Moreover, the foreigner will have to be willing to allow some inconsistencies to stand at times to maintain appearance and avoid shaming the Thais who would otherwise terminate the business relationship.

TEMPORAL CONCEPTION

Thailand is a polychronic culture. Time is more fluid than in monochronic societies such as the United States. The Thais value friendship, personal commitments, and the completion of tasks at hand at the expense of preset schedules.

Time is seen as malleable. Appointment times are approximate. Work hours are variable. Consequently, the monochronic foreigner needs to adjust his or her concepts of scheduling, deadlines, and other time-linked activities in Thailand.

Additionally, many North Americans hold a short-term view of time. U.S. and Canadian business practice is driven by a sense of urgency. In part, this is motivated by the needs for quarterly progress built into the system of stockholdership in the United States and Canada. In part, however, quarterly reports have little to do with this urgency—it is a cultural impatience for immediate gratification and the individual drive to bring about visible change.

By contrast, both of Thailand's major business ethnic groups hold a long-term view of time, although for different reasons. The ethnic-Chinese view of time is essentially Confucianist. Time is viewed in generational—not quarterly—terms. The ethnic Chinese view commitments and needs over a long-term view of actions spanning a lifetime as remembered by one's descendants. The ethnic-Thai view of time is equally long-term, but more Buddhist in motivation. Everything is in constant change as part of the endless life cycle that has always gone on before one was born and will continue to go on after one dies. Change is inevitable so one feels no need to force the change ahead of time. Generally Thais believe that things have a way of working out, so there is no need to pressure the end result. To do so would be presumptuous and probably disruptive.

SEE ALSO: China, Doing Business in; Cross-Cultural/International Communication

[David A. Victor]

FURTHER READING:

Cooper, Robert, and Nanthapa Cooper. *Culture Shock! Thailand.* Singapore: Times Books International, 1982.

Fieg, John Paul. *Thais and North Americans.* 2nd ed. Yarmouth, ME: Intercultural Press, 1989.

Henderson, Callum. *Asia Falling: Making Sense of the Asian Currency Crisis and Its Aftermath.* New York: McGraw-Hill, 1998.

Holmes, Henry, and Suchada Tangtongtavy. *Working with the Thais: A Guide to Managing in Thailand.* Bangkok: White Lotus, 1996.

Leppert, Paul. *Doing Business with the Thais.* Chula Vista, CA: Patton Pacific Press, 1992.

O'Reilly, James, and Larry Habegger, eds. *Travelers' Tales: Thailand.* San Francisco: Travelers' Tales, 1993.

Schlossstein, Steve. *Asia's New Little Dragons: The Dynamic Emergence of Indonesia, Thailand, and Malaysia.* Chicago: Contemporary Books, 1991.

Sharples, Jennifer, and William Timmons. *The Bangkok Expats Handbook.* Bangkok: Success Media, 1996.

Victor, David A. *International Business Communication.* New York: HarperCollins, 1992.

Welty, Roger. *Thai and I: Successful Living in Thailand.* Bangkok: Community Services Association of Thailand, 1996.

Wyatt, David K. *Thailand: A Short History.* New Haven, CT: Yale University Press, 1984.

Yee, Kenny, and Catherine Gordan. *Do's and Don'ts in Thailand.* 2nd ed. Bangkok: BPS Publications, 1995.

THEORY OF CONSTRAINTS

Sometimes known as constraint analysis, the theory of constraints (TOC) is a systematic and iterative approach to management that emphasizes adapting business practices in order to best cope with limitations, or constraints, that stand in the way of key objectives. The goal of TOC is to maximize the efficiency of a process selectively at the most critical points and thereby maximize profitability, quality, or other corporate objectives. TOC is often contrasted with traditional **cost accounting** or margin contribution approaches to problem solving, which, according to TOC proponents, may not truly optimize profits and the use of resources because they tend to have a unit focus rather than a system/process focus like TOC.

TOC is related to a wider set of management philosophies that center around continuous improvement. W. Edwards Deming (1900-93) was credited with revolutionizing business in Japan by effectively introducing concepts of continuous improvement. Out of Deming's teachings, management practices such as just-in-time (JIT) manufacturing, **total quality management** (TQM), **statistical process control** (SPC), and employee involvement (EI) were created. While each of these philosophies has merit, their actual benefits, as measured over time, have generally been less than what was originally assumed. This is because very few organizations that attempt to implement these various "improvement opportunities" have done so in an organized fashion that targets the operating factors with the greatest impact.

Companies should ask the following critical questions of themselves before pursuing an improvement strategy:

- What are the key areas within the organization for competitive improvement?
- What are the key technologies and techniques that will improve these key competitive areas at the least cost?
- How do these improvement and investment opportunities relate (i.e., how can they be applied in an integrated, supportive, and logical manner)?
- In what sequence should these opportunities be addressed?

Although Deming has passed on, the spirit of his work remains alive and well. TQM, JIT, EI, and the like influence more recent theories such as the theory of constraints.

TOC: A MANAGEMENT PHILOSOPHY

As a management philosophy, TOC focuses on a company's most critical issues (obstacles or constraints) and the effects of those constraints on the rest of the system (company). TOC allows a company to use its constraints as leverage by which it can improve its subject system. A constraint is anything that limits a company's ability to achieve a higher level of performance; usually this translates ultimately into impediments to profits.

TOC was developed by Israeli physicist Eliyahu M. Goldratt, of the Goldratt Institute in New Haven, Connecticut. After marketing a proprietary scheduling software package that scheduled tasks based on his constraint principles, Goldratt turned to educating people on those principles—TOC—so they could apply the concepts to any number of business problems. Goldratt introduced TOC in his 1984 novel *The Goal,* which was followed by a number of other books and articles on the subject.

At its core, TOC assumes that any company is composed of a number of subsystems. If each of these subsystems is optimized individually, overall company performance may actually be considered disappointing because such an approach doesn't take into account how the subsystems interact and what their collective limitations are in the production process. Instead, the idea is to optimize the system as a whole, even if it means certain nonessential components aren't optimally efficient. The company must identify its core problems (or constraints) first. These constraints can involve

- product quality
- product cost
- product engineering effectiveness
- materials procurement
- production planning and control
- marketing

These constraints are most likely to directly affect the company's profitability and cash flow. Such a constraint on profitability and cash flow serves as the platform for the TOC management philosophy.

TOC views an organization as a chain composed of many links (resources). The contribution of a link in the chain is heavily dependent upon the performance of its other links. The organization must be successful in its effort to synchronize the various chain links it requires to satisfy the organization's predetermined purpose, whatever that purpose may be. In order for a company to improve its performance, it must learn to identify and manage its weakest link. By doing this, the company answers a critical question tied to performance improvement: What to change? Logically, the organization must then answer, "to what should they change the constraint," and finally, "how to cause this change." This is accomplished by applying a five-step TOC process:

1. Identify the system's constraints
2. Decide how to exploit the constraints
3. Subordinate everything else to the constraints
4. Elevate the system's constraints
5. After breaking the constraint, repeat the five-step process

OVERLAP OF TOC PHILOSOPHY. TOC does in fact borrow from many of Deming's progressive management philosophies. TOC, however, goes well beyond Deming's approaches, and differs from them in many ways. This is what is making TOC a leading "contender" for the next generation of management theory for U.S. business, and indeed the business world abroad. Areas of TOC that overlap with other management approaches include the following:

- It stresses ongoing continuous improvement.
- It seeks employee involvement and empowerment.
- It stresses company-wide education and cultural transformation.
- It establishes clearly defined quality measurements.
- It breaks down departmental barriers, stressing global rather than local goals.
- It calls for shrinking the supplier base and reducing inventories.

Differences with TOC versus other management approaches include: (1) TOC focuses on identifying and exploiting constraints as the way to achieve ongoing improvement and increased profitability; and (2) it replaces cost accounting (which according to Goldratt, is ''the number one enemy of productivity'') with a new measurement system.

TOC maintains that cost-based management mentality invariably leads to flawed decisions, focusing on artificial targets, and masking root causes of problems.

According to chief operating officer Larry Webb of Stanley Furniture, for a company dedicated to the implementation of TOC, the biggest difference between TOC and other philosophies is that ''the others basically try to fix the whole company at once, which is a physical impossibility. By focusing on the constraint, everyone in the company is allocating resources in the right place. What TOC does in a succinct way is make sure you work on the right things rather than just doing things right.''

MEASUREMENTS OF TOC

To understand TOC and to apply it effectively to an organization, one must completely understand the goal of the organization (for this essay, it is assumed that organization refers to a profit-seeking entity, as opposed to a nonprofit one). Goldratt, in *The Goal,* emphasized that the goal of any organization is to make money. It is important therefore to create a set of measurements that honestly and accurately allow an organization to monitor its performance as it relates to its goal. Professor James Cox of Georgia University contended that the traditional cost accounting system used by businesses for nearly 70 years ''doesn't lend itself to tracking the impact of decisions on revenues and profits.''

With TOC, the ''cost world'' is replaced by the ''throughput world,'' which is driven by these three key components:

1. Throughput: The rate at which the system generates new money through sales.
2. Inventory: Money the system has invested in things it intends to sell, which would include plant, property, and equipment.
3. Operating expense: The money spent to convert inventory into throughout.

Using these measurements in combination with TOC ''scientific'' problem-solving methods allows management to focus on critical issues and root causes rather than symptoms of problems.

A major difference in the cost world and the TOC throughput world is that the cost world focuses on reducing operating expenses as the primary means to improvement, whereas the throughput world views cutting operating expenses as the least important of the three key improvement measurements. The throughput world emphasizes increasing throughput, reducing inventory, and reducing operating expenses.

Tradition in the cost world indicates that, to save money or reduce costs, a company must explore laying people off as downturns occur. A TOC-driven company, however, will not view layoffs as an option, as they would rather seek alternatives than to disrupt employee morale and loyalty.

TOC emphasizes reducing inventory as a way to expedite response time. In the throughput world, inventory is seen as a liability, not as an asset (as it is viewed in the cost world). Common-sense reasoning suggests that if a company reduces its inventories, the following occurs:

- Increased responsiveness to the market
- Improved ''promise-date'' performance
- Decreased obsolescence cost
- Increased quality

TYPES OF CONSTRAINTS

Constraints limit the ability to improve throughput. In TOC, a constraint can take various forms. These include capacity constraint (bottleneck or physical), market constraint, policy constraint, logistical constraint, and behavioral constraint.

A capacity constraint is simply a situation where market demand for a product exceeds the amount of the product that the system is able to supply. Some general examples of capacity constraints include skewed investment policies toward a specific type of unit production process, ''cost world'' focus, traditional manning practices, and personnel hiring guidelines. The reverse of capacity constraint is considered a market constraint whereby an organization is capable and willing to sell more products than the market is willing to buy. Market constraints include pricing based upon product standard costs, sales commission policies, product technology development guidelines, and market segmentation practices. When a company issues a ''no-overtime'' policy, it is placing a policy constraint upon the system.

Perhaps the easiest constraint to illustrate is a physical constraint (bottleneck). Physical constraints are resources, either human or mechanical, whose capacity is less than or equal to the demand placed on them. The challenge therefore becomes to identify and utilize physical constraints to control the flow of product through the plant or store into the hands of the consumer. TOC proves that physical constraints control the pace of any system, so therefore an hour gained at the physical constraint is an hour gained for the entire system. An hour gained elsewhere, at a nonconstraint, is therefore meaningless.

TOC holds that investments made to support a nonconstraint are unwise. The TOC manager must ask herself if an investment made will (1) be directed at a constraint; (2) increase throughout; (3) reduce inventory expense; and (4) reduce operating expense.

EXAMPLES OF TOC IN PRACTICE

TOC is practiced in many different industries, including automotive, computers, telecommunications, furniture, retail food, consumer goods, and apparel. Practitioners have ranged from *Fortune* 500 companies like Procter & Gamble Co. and General Electric Co. to small local businesses.

In a widely cited small business example, Kent Moore Cabinets of Bryan, Texas, used TOC in the late 1980s to address employee turnover caused by the seasonal nature of its business. The company's main production and selling season was spring through fall, when the construction industry is most active, and thus winter was its slow season. Previously the company laid off some of its employees during the winter, but found it was hard to attract the better workers year after year when lay-offs were always imminent. Using TOC, the company identified seasonality as its biggest constraint. Throughput analysis suggested that the company could maximize profits and fight worker turnover by keeping a full staff year round and offering builders an incentive (a 20 percent discount) to buy cabinets during the winter. The strategy succeeded and the new orders generated more than enough revenue to cover the additional labor during the winter. The company credited TOC with helping boost revenues by two-thirds in just two years.

More recently, many larger companies have sought to unite TOC concepts with the newer cost accounting methods known as activity-based costing (ABC) or activity based management (ABM). Similar to TOC, these accounting techniques examine production costs from a process standpoint, e.g., marking which steps of a production process (activities) require the largest investments and which contribute the most profit.

Many other companies continue to see the benefits that the TOC management approach can provide. It is not considered an overnight process, although in certain manufacturing environments, companies may enjoy quick, short-term results. TOC is rather a long-term approach to how an organization, or a system, operates. As Deming's work revolutionized management practices, so too does the theory of constraints continue the transition.

SEE ALSO: Critical Path Method

[Art DuRivage]

FURTHER READING:

Bushong, J. Gregory, and John C. Talbott. ''An Application of the Theory of Constraints.'' *CPA Journal,* April 1999.

Cooper, Robin, and Regine Slagmulder. ''Integrating Activity-Based Costing and the Theory of Constraints.'' *Management Accounting,* February 1999.

Gardiner, Stanley C., John H. Blackstone Jr., and Lorraine R. Gardiner. ''The Evolution of the Theory of Constraints.'' *Industrial Management,* May/June 1994.

Osten, Sam, and Mike C. Peterson. ''A Theory of Constraints Fable,'' parts 1 and 2. *Industrial Management,* March/April 1996; May/June 1996.

THIRD WORLD, DOING BUSINESS IN THE

The term ''third world'' came into use in grouping countries by their economic status. The industrialized countries located mainly in the West were categorized as the ''first world,'' the once-communist countries of the East as ''second world,'' and the rest of the developing countries as the ''third world.'' With the dismantling of the Soviet Union and the discarding of communism by the Eastern European countries, the ''second world'' has lost its meaning and the term ''third world'' has become a misnomer. The term is still being used as a synonym to describe the developing countries, but according to the **International Monetary Fund** (IMF) there are only two groupings of countries by their economic status—the 23 industrialized countries and the 138 developing countries. For the purposes of this article, third world countries are taken to be the same as the developing countries as loosely grouped by the IMF.

HISTORICAL PERSPECTIVE

Most of the third world countries are former colonies of European powers and gained their independence after the World War II. Colonialism was as much an economic domination as it was political. The main features of a colonial economy were twofold. First, the natural resources of the colonies were exploited and depleted by the colonial powers. Secondly, the colonies were used as the market for the manufactured goods. In both ways the economic interests of the colonial countries prevailed.

When the colonies gained their independence, most of them had to overcome this adverse economic situation created by colonialism. Economic discipline, good **management**, strategic planning, and above all, competent political leadership are some of the attributes required to reverse such a condition. Unfortunately, most newly independent countries lack these necessary characteristics.

A legacy of colonialism is mistrust of the colonial powers. The emphasis on economic self-reliance by many former colonies can be traced to this mistrust. Protectionism is a by-product of this policy of self-reliance. **Foreign investment** is suspect. Fear of foreign profits draining the economy is prevalent. The post-independent economic growth, or lack of it, in many countries is conditioned by this colonial past.

POLITICAL BACKGROUND

Most third world countries do not enjoy a democratic political system. Dictatorships, of one kind or other, are a common feature of most countries. There are a few notable exceptions, such as India, that have managed to maintain an unbroken record of democratic governments. In an undemocratic system there are no checks on corruption or unilateral **decision making**. Dictatorships often distort the economic system. Efficiency and the need for quick decision making are reasons given by dictators for seizing power. Dictatorships rarely live up to their promise. Political stability and consistent government policies are preconditions for businesses to operate successfully. In the absence of these conditions in many third world countries, doing business involves added risk.

ECONOMIC CONDITIONS

National **debt** is a common characteristic among third world countries. Often the economy of a country is based on a few **commodities**, making it vulnerable to price fluctuations. Even when the commodity is oil, countries are unable to make use of the profits to overcome economic backwardness because of poor economic management. The economies of many countries revolve in a vicious circle. To develop the economy these countries need to borrow capital, thereby increasing their debt. It becomes difficult to service the debt unless there is sustained export surplus and it is seldom possible to achieve this surplus in a fluctuating world commodity market. When commodity prices are low, exports do not generate enough trade surplus to service the debt.

The developing countries require capital and skilled human resources to transform a colonial economy into a modern industrial economy. Most countries do not possess either, again with some exceptions. The internal savings are inadequate to mount an ambitious development program. Technical and managerial skills are in short supply due to the slow growth in higher education. In the absence of political will and direction, economic management becomes even more difficult. Poverty and economic drift are generally the consequence. Even when foreign investment is welcome, the economic uncertainties stand in the way of attracting capital.

In recent years, increased **globalization**, a breakdown of protectionism, expanded **free trade**, collapse of the Soviet system and the popularity of the free market economy have allowed a group of third world countries to emerge as newly industrialized states. These countries, in spite of their political systems, have embraced the capitalist path of development. They have trained enough skilled people to utilize the capital generated by domestic savings and foreign investment. These countries are the most entrepreneurial among the developing countries. South Korea, Taiwan, Hong Kong, Singapore, Thailand, Brazil, Chile, and Mexico are, in varying degrees, examples of newly industrialized countries. Unfortunately the discrediting of socialism led to unrestrained acceptance of free market and free flow of capital. Bad investment decisions and a decrease in the demand for goods in Western countries for the products of the newly industrialized countries, especially electronic goods, caused an economic downfall. The financial sector in the East Asian countries—including in Japan, one of the economic giants in the world—nearly collapsed. Beginning with Thailand in 1997, the financial crisis spread quickly to other East Asian countries. Measures are under way through the efforts of the IMF and Western **banking** institutions to stabilize the situation. In early 1999 Brazil became the latest country to be hit by a financial crisis. These events point out the need for keeping a sensible balance between a regulated economy and an unrestrained free market economy.

Commensurate with the high risks involved are the prospects of higher returns in doing business in these developing countries and especially so in the newly industrialized countries. The countries provide cheap labor that is skilled enough to perform many operations. As these countries become more prosperous, they also provide a growing market for goods and services. Their large population base is a potential market as their purchasing power increases. Many of the developing countries offer attractive incentives for establishing businesses and for investing. It is in the interest of the industrialized countries to take advantage of this situation. In a highly competitive global economy, many industries can diversify manufacturing and keep costs to the minimum by moving operations to developing countries. In many of the third world countries, the policy of nationalistic self-reliance is being replaced by a policy of pragmatic economic interests. Generating **employment** and prosperity even at the cost of some of the profits being repatriated is gaining support. The need of the industrialized countries to expand economically is consistent with the need of developing countries to industrialize and improve the standard of living of their people. In this context, the economic interests of both groups of countries are fulfilled.

BUSINESS ENVIRONMENT

It is inaccurate to generalize the **business conditions** prevailing in the third world countries. Conditions vary greatly especially between the newly industrialized countries and the rest of the developing countries. Some common features, however, can be noted. Political stability is wanting, especially in those countries where democratic roots are not strong. Investment capital is scarce. Wages and benefits tend to be low. Availability of skilled workers is limited. Educational levels are low, especially if high technology is involved in the business. Environmental regulations are few and not seriously enforced. The judicial system is often unpredictable and severe. Bureaucratic hurdles, such as obtaining licenses and permits, have to be overcome. Communication is difficult in an unfamiliar linguistic and cultural environment. Value systems tend to be different, which might cause misunderstandings. Instruction in the language and culture of the country is a prerequisite to doing business. **Infrastructure** necessary to operate a business—such as communication facilities, transportation, and energy supply—may not be adequate. These factors have to be borne in mind before embarking on any business venture in the third world.

INFORMATION SOURCES

The **United Nations** Industrial Development Organization located in Vienna, Austria, is a major source of additional information on developing countries. It publishes the periodical *Industrial Development Abstracts.* The **World Bank** in Washington, D.C., is another source of information. One of its publications, *World Development Indicators,* incorporates two of its earlier publications, *Social Indicators of Development* and *World Tables.* The World Bank web site is an excellent source for concise and up-to-date country statistics. The UN Economic Commissions for Latin America and for Asia and the Pacific publish the *Economic Survey of Latin America and the Caribbean* and the *Economic Bulletin for Asia and the Pacific,* respectively. The **Association of South East Asian Nations** publishes annual surveys and statistical data on member countries. The *Asia Yearbook,* published by the *Far Eastern Economic Review,* and *Latin America,* an annual published by Stryker-Post publications in Washington, D.C., are examples of private publications providing country-based information in their respective regions.

[Divakara K. (Dik) Varma]

TIME MANAGEMENT

''Time management'' refers to making the most productive use of a set period of time—be it days, hours, weeks, or months. In business the principle of time management is to use the time available to complete a project wisely and to work ''smarter, not harder'' in order to get more accomplished within that fixed period.

For centuries people used the general measurement of sunrise to sunset to gauge time, but with the development of the clock attention began to focus on the hours within a day as well. By the 17th century the clock had been perfected and become so well-established in society that the French mathematician and philosopher René Descartes (1596 1650) used the clock as a model for humanity in his writings.

But it was during the Industrial Revolution that the clock really came of age. Frederick W. Taylor (1856-1915), an American engineer, undertook the first time and motion studies. Taylor subjected each aspect of the work process to a stopwatch measurement, then studied the results to look for ways to reduce the number of steps needed to accomplish a particular task or job. This concept of time management as something that managers did for line workers held sway until the 1930s, when managers began to find their own tasks so overwhelming that they too sought ways to manage time more efficiently.

In the 1930s Ivy Lee, a **management** consultant, initiated a simple ''6-Step'' process that became the standard for measuring the productivity of managers. The Ivy Lee plan was simple. Managers needed only to list the six most important things to be done that day, in order of importance, the most important being first. Then, the manager was to work on those tasks in order, not proceeding from one task to the next until the preceding task had been accomplished.

In the last half of the 20th century time came to be described as a ''commodity, a resource to be used, hoarded, traded, and exploited.'' Despite changes in the way that businesses view time, time management for managers remains, in large measure, a matter of simplifying and compartmentalizing tasks to avoid diffuseness of effort. Making schedules and lists of the type recommended by Lee is still the most common method employed by managers wishing to improve their time management. Other simple and commonsense techniques, such as keeping meetings to a minimum and keeping them as short as possible, are all that is required in many cases to free a manager's time for more productive activities.

After World War II, studies of management began to broaden to look at time management in all aspects of business and life. Use of time became a focal area of management seminars in the 1960s and 1970s. In 1967 Peter Drucker proposed a chronological record-keeping method for managers, which was refined by Alec Mackenzie into an executive time directory in 1972. The following year saw the release of Alan Lakein's book, *How to Get Control of Your Time and Your Life,* which reflected recognition by business educators of public concern with time management. Some of the best-known resources on time management include *The One Minute Manager* by Dr. Kenneth H. Blanchard and Spencer Johnson, and its sequel by Blanchard and Robert Lorber, *Putting the One Minute Manager to Work.* In the late 1990s, businesses began looking at the development of new partnerships and alliances, streamlining of corporate procedures and processes, and increased use of consultants, as means to more effective time management.

Critical path accountability, a new time management technique for managers, emerged in the mid-to-late 1990s. Managers making use of critical path accountability involve all members of a business transaction, including manufacturers, distributors, customers, and their employees in the production and delivery process. Keeping all parties to a transaction informed as to its progress leads to mutual accountability and the establishment of a system of checks and balances within the production process.

The essentials of time management involve recognition of goals and organization of one's efforts so that all steps taken follow a path toward achieving that goal and are not wasted or diverted from that purpose. Many of the barriers to efficient time management are flaws of human nature—the desire to procrastinate, to pursue pleasure rather than purpose, perfectionism that will not accept a job as complete, and insecurity that does not allow a person to delegate tasks to others. As such, a time management strategy often begins with an assessment of one's personal habits, including the ability to "just say no" to certain requests for demands upon your time that will not contribute to achievement of your basic goals. Mackenzie, in *The Time Trap,* said that time management is not just about the use of an abstract commodity—time. Mackenzie posited that time management is about what we can accomplish with time.

Good time management also reaches into other areas of management, including planning and **goal setting**, communication with others in order to effectively delegate, and assessment skills to determine if the goals were reached and how work can be done better in the future.

Many experts feel that current attitudes toward time management will evolve significantly in the near future. According to Diana Scharf-Hunt and Pam Hart, just as the clock—a mechanical tool in a mechanical age—led industry to respond to needs for time management in a mechanistic way with time and motion and lists and plans for steps to reach goals, the computer information age has broadened our understanding of time and created different needs to which management must respond.

Scharf-Hunt, a respected management consultant and specialist in time management, put forth the idea that as the 20th century draws to a close, the seconds and minutes of a clock are no longer the final arbiters of time. The computer calculates in nanoseconds—the blink of an eye. Scharf-Hunt and Hart found "Just as the clock tolled hours, minutes and seconds for the Industrial age, now the computer measures intervals in fleeting blips of time so infinitesimal that we cannot experience, let alone absorb them. As the clock once revolutionized work and society, the computer is revolutionizing how we work and live with time."

Scharf-Hunt and Hart formulated a time management style for the 21st century that involves a more thorough understanding of who we are, a more holistic approach to time that blends an outlook on work and life and the need to balance personal choices of all types—not just career choices—and philosophy with work. While appointments and meetings need to be viewed as relevant to the work goal, one needs also to consider their relevancy to total purpose. The broader basis for control is the belief that the mind is the ultimate control or site of management activity and the whole mind must be considered. On the other hand Charles Fine, in his 1997 book, *The Quick and the Dead,* makes the more traditional point that industries (in this case, the U.S. automobile industry) must respond to the faster pace of business in the computer age by increasing their flexibility and ability to respond to new markets, industrial procedures, and products.

Modern electronics are also revolutionizing personal time management. Many companies have begun allowing employees to make use of "just in-time" electronic communications to discharge their personal duties while on the job, a move that in the long run allows employees to spend more time at work and less time attending to personal matters. Other organizations have turned to their employees' internal state-of-mind as a time management device, setting up meditation and other consciousness raising programs to help employees deal with the limitations of time. Despite such novel methods, common sense prevails in employee as well as managerial time management. Designing offices to minimize lines of sight to personal workspaces, for instance, can reduce talking among employees and increase productivity.

But while the foundation of time management may shift and go beyond the business setting to life as a whole, the premise remains that time management in business seeks to use time and structure it to enable managers to reach the goals of efficiency and effectiveness.

SEE ALSO: Critical Path Method

[Joan Leotta, updated by Grant Eldridge]

FURTHER READING:

Blanchard, Kenneth H., and Spencer Johnson. *The One Minute Manager.* New York: Berkley Books, 1982.

Blanchard, Kenneth H., and Robert Lorber. *Putting the One Minute Manager to Work.* New York: William Morrow, 1984.

Drucker, Peter. *The Effective Executive.* New York: Harper, 1967.

Farrant, Don. "A New Look at Time Leaks." *Supervision* 58, no. 5 (May 1997): 3.

Federico, Richard F. "A Blur of Work Bites and Life Bites: A New Corporate Strategy?" *Communication World* 14, no. 3 (February 1997): 42.

Harung, Harald S. "Reflections: Improved Time Management through Human Development." *Journal of Managerial Psychology* 13, no. 5-6 (May/June 1998): 406.

Lakein, Alan. *How to Get Control of Your Time and Your Life.* New York: New American Library, 1973.

Lorge, Sarah. "Improving Time Management." *Sales and Marketing Management* 150, no. 2 (February 1998): 112.

Mackenzie, Alec. *The Time Trap.* 3rd ed. New York: AMACOM, 1997.

Main, Bill. "Managing Critical Path Accountability." *ID: The Voice of Foodservice Distribution* 32, no. 12 (1 November 1996): 31.

Mancini, Marc. *Time Management.* New York: Business One Irwin/Mirror Press, 1994.

Ridlehuber, Ted R. *The 30-Day Plan: A Performance-Enhancing Time Management Tool.* Intertech Publishing Company, 1997.

Scharf-Hunt, Diana, and Pam Hart. *The Tao of Time.* New York: Simon & Schuster, 1990.

Sneed, Paula A. "Carpe Diem: Take Advantage of Time." *Journal of Advertising Research* 37, no. 1 (January/February 1997): RC2.

Straub, Joseph T. "Your Time: Manage It to the Max." *Getting Results* 41, no. 7 (July 1996): 62.

Vasilash, Gary S. "The Quick and the Dead." *Automotive Manufacturing and Production* 110, no. 10 (October 1998): 8.

Weber, Rose A. *Time Is Money.* New York: Free Press, 1980.

TIME SERIES ANALYSIS

Time series analysis is a branch of the field of **econometrics**. Time series analysis proceeds from the premise that much can be deduced about a particular variable on the basis of the past behavior of that variable. As is generally true in econometrics, a key objective of time series analysis is prediction of future values of the variable of interest. In the case of time series analysis, however, such prediction often is based on some form of extrapolation of the past behavior of the variable.

The distinguishing characteristic of a time series of a variable is that observations are ordered along the dimension of time. Thus one might have monthly sales data for a business from January 1991 to May 1999. In this case, the analyst has 101 observations ([8 × 12] + 5) on the firm's sales ordered from the beginning to the end of the observation period. A graph of this data might reveal that the firm's sales have trended upward over time. Other characteristics of the series might reflect periodic bursts and lulls in sales, as might be the case if the firm's sales picked up particularly in holiday seasons or, say, over the summer months. In addition, the firm's sales might be related to general business conditions (i.e., the **business cycle**). Finally, some part of movement in the series will simply appear to be random, as the firm's sales are influenced by a variety of external factors that cannot easily be accounted for. The important point to note in this discussion is that some movement in a time series is systematic and some movement is random. The systematic factors in our hypothetical firm's sales are the upward trend, the dependency on **business conditions**, and the seasonal behavior of sales. More formally, a time series can be thought of as having a trend component, a cyclic component, a seasonal component, and a random component.

A variety of techniques of varying levels of sophistication have developed over the years by which to conduct time series analysis. The simplest and least costly to apply techniques are deterministic. That is, these techniques do not attempt to account for the random (or stochastic) nature of a time series at all. Such models fall under the heading of extrapolation models. Two of the most commonly used extrapolation models are the linear trend model and the moving average model.

A linear trend model might be used when a time series exhibits steady increase over time. Such a model is typically fit by regressing the variable of interest against a trend variable (which begins with a value of 1 and increases by 1 unit for each time period). The resulting regression coefficient found for the trend variable gives the change in the dependent variable per time period. Such models are easy to create, but the danger inherent in their use is that while many economic series do trend up over time, they do not trend up at a steady rate. As a result, the linear trend model may account well for movement in the variable of interest in the middle of the sample period, but may significantly under- or overstate the variable at the end of the sample period. Consequently, the model will not do an adequate job of predicting the future position of the variable (i.e., outside of the sample period). In some instances, this nonlinearity in the movement of the dependent variable can be adequately dealt with by use of a more sophisticated trend variable. This can be accomplished by using a polynomial rather than a linear trend and can also be accomplished by a suitable transformation (e.g., logarithmic) of the dependent variable. Nevertheless, these extensions do force a high degree of determinism on the future path of the dependent variable and for this reason may lead to inadequate forecasts.

A second class of deterministic time series model is the moving average model. The simplest type of moving average model states the dependent variable as an average of past values of itself. So, for example, we might expect sales at a business to equal average sales at the business over the last four quarters or over the last 12 months. A more sophisticated approach would give heavier weight in the averaging of past values of the dependent variable to more recent occurrences. A model that accomplishes this task is the exponentially weighted moving average model. The reader should note that moving average models are mechanical and nonstatistical. As a result, it is not possible to determine the degree of confidence one could have in the **forecasting** ability of the model as would be the case with a statistical model (even one as simple as the linear trend model). The benefit of using a moving average model, however, is the ease with which it may be applied.

More sophisticated, statistical models of time series can be attributed to the seminal work of G. E. P. Box and G. M. Jenkins, who developed the autoregressive integrated moving-average (ARIMA) technique. This technique incorporates the random element of time series in the estimation process. Box-Jenkins methodology relies on four distinct steps—identification of a suitable model for the series at hand, estimation of the model, diagnostic checking and re-estimation of the model if necessary, and forecasting future values of the series. Though ARIMA modeling constitutes an important step forward in time series analysis, it is worth noting that such models are limited in the sense that forecasts are obtained only on the basis of past behavior of the series in question and lagged random disturbances in that series.

Work in time series analysis in the 1980s and 1990s concentrated on development of time series models that merge the causal framework of econometrics with the univariate approach of ARIMA modeling. This work led to a variety of important developments such as transfer function modeling, vector autoregression models, unit root tests, error correction models, and structural time series models. Though application of these techniques can be rather complicated, their adoption has led to significant improvements in understanding of time series processes and in forecasting ability. It is fair to say that the biggest advancements in the field of econometrics in recent years have occurred in the area of time series analysis.

[Kevin J. Murphy]

FURTHER READING:

Box, George E. P., G. M. Jenkins, et al. *Time Series Analysis: Forecasting and Control.* 3rd ed. Upper Saddle River, NJ: Prentice Hall, 1994.

Granger, C. W. J. *Forecasting in Business and Economics.* 2nd ed. Boston: Academic Press, 1989.

Hamilton, James D. *Time Series Analysis.* Princeton, NJ: Princeton University Press, 1994.

Harvey, Andrew. C. *Time Series Models.* 2nd ed. Cambridge, MA: MIT Press, 1993.

Pindyck, R. S., and D. L. Rubinfield. *Econometric Models and Economic Forecasts.* 3rd ed. New York: McGraw-Hill College Div., 1997.

TOLL-FREE TELEPHONE CALLS (800 NUMBERS)

Toll-free numbers allow their users to call long-distance free of charge, and instead the receiving party pays. They are considered an important tool for maintaining contact with customers and gaining information about them; by nature toll-free numbers reveal the number of the person placing the call, and unlike Caller ID systems, this cannot be blocked on a toll-free line. In the United States toll-free numbers begin with the prefixes 800, 888, and 877 (with additional expansion prefixes likely to appear in the early 2000s). Typically, a monthly fee and a per-minute fee are charged to the holder of the number.

BACKGROUND AND TECHNICAL STRUCTURE

Then-monopoly AT&T Corp. introduced the first toll-free service in 1967, although it was not quick to catch on. This was due to both technical limitations and market apprehension toward subsidizing incoming calls, a practice some viewed as laughable at the time.

Until 1980, toll-free calls were routed through an arcane and inflexible system that didn't enable nationwide dialing to the same number. Companies that needed toll-free numbers thus had to maintain multiple numbers for different regions. A major breakthrough came in 1980 when AT&T brought the 800-number system into a digital switching environment designed by AT&T computer scientist Roy Weber. His innovation, still employed today, used the seven digits after 800 as a unique computer file name that instructed the telephone network how to route the call. In other words, modern toll-free numbers are simply aliases used in the telephone switching network to direct a call to a local line somewhere.

As a result, switching instructions for toll-free numbers can be customized for time of day, calling volume, geographic origin of caller, and other variables. In the simplest case, the computer file tells the network to dial one number, for example, the company's main local line, all the time. More complicated schemes could direct the computer to dial the company's main line during its normal business hours, to a support center during off hours, and to a different support center if calling volume ever exceeds a specified level.

AT&T maintained its monopoly on toll-free service even after it was forced in 1984 to spin off local phone service, the move that created the regional Bell operating companies. In 1985 the **Federal Communications Commission** (FCC) ordered local phone companies to provide equal access for other carriers of toll-free service. Other major long-distance and regional carriers, such as MCI Communications Corp. and Sprint Corp., then began to offer toll-free service, but AT&T retained the leading market share. In fact, vestiges of AT&T's toll-free monopoly continued into the late 1990s in the form of its lock-hold on toll-free directory assistance. Because the FCC has affirmed AT&T's ownership of the well-known information number 1-800-555-1212—even though FCC regulators have expressed the wish to open the service to competition—it receives virtually all such calls. Challengers began to emerge in the mid-1990s, however, notably Universal Directory Services, Inc. of Hurst, Texas.

RAMPANT GROWTH

After the limitations of the early system were overcome, businesses warmed to the public relations potential of offering free calls to their customers. This was coupled with a broader explosion in demand for telecommunications devices such as fax machines, pagers, and dial-up computer networking. A climate was set for tremendous growth in the use of toll-free numbers.

By 1990, toll-free service had also become affordable to consumers, who saw it as a alternative to expensive calling cards and collect calls. Small businesses sought the same cost savings for sales representatives and other personnel in the field. The numbers also made it relatively inexpensive for small businesses to implement national marketing efforts.

All of these factors converged to create a run on toll-free numbers in the 1990s. The 800 prefix could support 8 million numbers, and as of 1993 only 3 million were in use. By mid-1995, though, more than 90 percent of the numbers were taken and new requests were set to overtake the available numbers well before the planned expansion to 888 was in place. The FCC was forced to step in and mandate the rationing of numbers until 1996, when 888 was unveiled. In 1997 it was estimated that 11 million U.S. toll-free numbers were in use to support some 34 billion calls, two-thirds of which were handled by AT&T.

Such volume promised to rapidly consume all 888 numbers as well, particularly because companies that used their 800 numbers as trademarks—indeed, even their names in cases like 1-800 CONTACTS, Inc.—many sought to obtain the 888 version of their number as well. This hastened the introduction of the prefix 877 in 1998, while further expansions were planned for the following years.

GLOBAL DIALING

Just as 800 numbers were drying up in the United States, the United Nations-affiliated International Telecommunication Union (ITU) launched in 1997 the first-ever ''global 800'' numbers. Looking identical to conventional toll-free numbers, these special numbers enabled callers in one participating country to dial an 11-digit number to reach a company in another country—eliminating the need for country codes and other hassles of international calling.

FURTHER READING:

Engebretson, Joan. ''What's That Number Again?'' *Telephony,* 13 October 1997.

Fishman, Charles. ''Inside the 1-800 Factory.'' *Los Angeles Times,* 3 August 1997, 14.

TOTAL QUALITY MANAGEMENT (TQM)

Total quality management (TQM) refers to **management** methods used to enhance quality and productivity in organizations, particularly businesses. TQM is a comprehensive system approach that works horizontally across an organization, involving all departments and employees and extending backward and forward to include both suppliers and clients/customers.

TQM is only one of many acronyms used to label management systems that focus on quality. Other acronyms that have been used to describe similar quality management philosophies and programs include CQI (continuous quality improvement), SQC (statistical **quality control**), QFD (quality function deployment), QIDW (quality in daily work), and TQC (total quality control). Despite the ambiguity of the popularized term ''TQM,'' that acronym is less important than the substance of the management ideology that underlies it. TQM provides a framework for implementing effective quality and productivity initiatives that can increase the profitability and competitiveness of organizations.

ORIGINS OF TQM

Although TQM techniques were adopted prior to World War II by a number of organizations, the creation of the total quality management philosophy is generally attributed to Dr. W. Edwards Deming (1900-1993). In the late 1920s, while working as a summer employee at Western Electric Company in Chicago, he found worker motivation systems to be degrading and economically unproductive; incentives were tied directly to quantity of output, and inefficient postproduction inspection systems were used to find flawed goods.

Deming teamed up in the 1930s with Walter A. Shewhart (1891-1967), a Bell Telephone Company statistician whose work convinced Deming that statistical control techniques could be used to supplant traditional management methods. Using Shewhart's theories, Deming devised a statistically controlled management process that provided managers with a means of determining when to intervene in an industrial process and when to leave it alone. Deming got a chance to put Shewhart's statistical quality-control techniques, as well as his own management philosophies, to the test during World War II. Government managers found that his techniques could easily be taught to engineers and workers, and then quickly implemented in overburdened war production plants.

One of Deming's clients, the U.S. State Department, sent him to Japan in 1947 as part of a national effort to revitalize the war-devastated Japanese economy. It was in Japan that Deming found an enthusiastic reception for his management ideas. Deming introduced his **statistical process control**, or statistical quality control, programs into Japan's ailing manufacturing sector. Those techniques are credited with instilling a dedication to quality and productivity in the Japanese industrial and service sectors that allowed the country to become a dominant force in the global economy by the 1980s.

While Japan's industrial sector embarked on a quality initiative during the middle 1900s, most American companies continued to produce mass quantities of goods using traditional management techniques. America prospered as war-ravaged European countries looked to the United States for manufactured goods. In addition, a domestic population boom resulted in surging U.S. markets. But by the 1970s some American industries had come to be regarded as inferior to their Asian and European competitors. As a result of increasing economic **globalization** during the 1980s, made possible in part by advanced **information technologies**, the U.S. manufacturing sector fell prey to more competitive producers, particularly in Japan.

In response to massive market share gains achieved by Japanese companies during the late 1970s and 1980s, U.S. producers scrambled to adopt quality and productivity techniques that might restore their competitiveness. Indeed, Deming's philosophies and systems were finally recognized in the United States, and Deming himself became a highly sought-after lecturer and author. The "Deming Management Method" became the model for many American corporations eager to improve. And total quality management, the phrase applied to quality initiatives proffered by Deming and other management gurus, became a staple of American enterprise by the late 1980s. By the early 1990s, the U.S. manufacturing sector had achieved marked gains in quality and productivity. By the late 1990s several American industries had surpassed their Japanese rivals in these areas.

TQM PRINCIPLES

Specifics related to the framework and implementation of TQM vary between different management professionals and TQM program facilitators, and the passage of time has inevitably brought changes in TQM emphases and language. But all TQM philosophies share common threads that emphasize quality, teamwork, and proactive philosophies of management and process improvement. As Howard Weiss and Mark Gershon observed in *Production and Operations Management,* "the terms quality management, quality control, and quality assurance often are used interchangeably. Regardless of the term used within any business, this function is directly responsible for the continual evaluation of the effectiveness of the total quality system." The authors went on to delineate the basic elements of total quality management as expounded by the American Society for Quality Control: (1) policy, planning, and administration; (2) product design and design change control; (3) control of purchased material; (4) production quality control; (5) user contact and field performance; (6) corrective action; and (7) employee selection, **training**, and motivation.

For his part, Deming pointed to all of these factors as cornerstones of his total quality philosophies in his book *Out of the Crisis.* He contended that companies needed to create an overarching business environment that emphasized improvement of products and services over short-term financial goals. He argued that if such a philosophy was adhered to, various aspects of business—ranging from training to system improvement to manager-worker relationships—would become far more healthy and, ultimately, profitable. But while Deming was contemptuous of companies that based their business decisions on statistics that emphasized quantity over quality, he firmly believed that a well-conceived system of statistical process control could be an invaluable TQM tool. Only through the use of statistics, Deming argued, can managers know exactly what their problems are, learn how to fix them, and gauge the company's progress in achieving quality and organizational objectives.

MAKING TQM WORK

Joseph Jablonski, author of *Implementing TQM,* identified three characteristics necessary for TQM to succeed within an organization: participative management; continuous process improvement; and the utilization of **teams**. Participative management refers to the intimate involvement of all members of a company in the management process, thus deemphasizing traditional top-down management methods. In other words, managers set policies and make key decisions only with the input and guidance of the subordinates who will have to implement and adhere to the directives. This technique improves upper management's grasp of operations and, more importantly, is an important motivator for workers who begin to feel as if they have control and ownership of the process in which they participate.

Continuous process improvement, the second characteristic, entails the recognition of small, incremental gains toward the goal of total quality. Large gains are accomplished by small, sustainable improvements over a long term. This concept necessitates a long-term approach by managers and the willingness to invest in the present for benefits that manifest themselves in the future. A corollary of continuous improvement is that workers and management develop an appreciation for, and confidence in, TQM over time.

Teamwork, the third necessary ingredient for the success of TQM, involves the organization of cross-functional teams within the company. This multidisciplinary team approach helps workers to share knowledge, identify problems and opportunities, derive a comprehensive understanding of their role in the overall process, and align their work goals with those of the organization.

Jablonski also identified six attributes of successful TQM programs:

- Customer focus (includes internal customers such as other departments and coworkers, as well as external customers)
- Process focus
- Prevention versus inspection (development of a process that incorporates quality during production, rather than a process that attempts to achieve quality through inspection after resources have already been consumed to produce the good or service)
- Employee **empowerment** and compensation
- Fact-based **decision making**
- Receptiveness to feedback

In addition to identifying three characteristics that need to be present in an organization and six attributes of successful TQM programs, Jablonski offers a five-phase guideline for implementing total quality management: preparation, planning, assessment, implementation, and diversification. Each phase is designed to be executed as part of a long-term goal of continually increasing quality and productivity. Jablonski's approach is one of many that has been applied to achieve TQM, but contains the key elements commonly associated with other popular total quality systems.

PREPARATION. During preparation, management decides whether or not to pursue a TQM program. They undergo initial training, identify needs for outside **consultants**, develop a specific vision and goals, draft a corporate policy, commit the necessary resources, and communicate the goals throughout the organization.

PLANNING. In the planning stage, a detailed plan of implementation is drafted (including budget and schedule), the **infrastructure** that will support the program is established, and the resources necessary to begin the plan are earmarked and secured.

ASSESSMENT. This stage emphasizes a thorough self-assessment—with input from customers/clients—of the qualities and characteristics of individuals in the company, as well as the company as a whole.

IMPLEMENTATION. At this point, the organization can already begin to determine its return on its investment in TQM. It is during this phase that support personnel are chosen and trained, and managers and the **workforce** are trained. Training entails raising workers' awareness of exactly what TQM involves and how it can help them and the company. It also explains each worker's role in the program and explains what is expected of all the workers.

DIVERSIFICATION. In this stage, managers utilize their TQM experiences and successes to bring groups outside the organization (suppliers, distributors, and other companies that have an impact on the business's overall health) into the quality process. Diversification activities include training, rewarding, supporting, and partnering with groups that are embraced by the organization's TQM initiatives.

TQM INTO THE FUTURE

Total quality management—first popularized in the 1950s in Japan—swept through American businesses in the 1980s and resulted in significant improvements in quality, productivity, customer satisfaction, and competitiveness in many companies by the 1990s. The basic principles of TQM are intended to achieve continuous organizational improvement through the participation and commitment of workers throughout a company. TQM focuses all the resources of an organization upon meeting the needs of customers (both internal and external), using statistical tools and techniques to measure results and aid decision making.

Despite the impressive results many companies have achieved through TQM, its future popularity is still in doubt. By the late 1990s some experts began to question whether TQM was a fad that would soon be superseded by yet another management technique. At the same time, however, other experts sought to apply TQM to emerging business problems, such as making **computer** systems compliant in the year 2000. It appears as if the underlying principles of TQM may find continued applications in business, even if they are eventually incorporated into a new movement for management innovation and organizational change.

[Dave Mote, updated by Laurie Collier Hillstrom]

FURTHER READING:

De Cock, Christian, and Ian Hipkin. "TQM and BPR: Beyond the 'Beyond' Myth." *Journal of Management Studies* 34, no. 5 (September 1997): 659+.

Deming, W. Edwards. *Out of the Crisis.* Cambridge, MA: MIT Center for Advanced Engineering Study, 1982.

Hiam, Alexander. *Closing the Quality Gap: Lessons from America's Leading Companies.* Englewood Cliffs, NJ: Prentice Hall, 1992.

Hunt, V. Daniel. *Quality in America: How to Implement a Competitive Quality Program.* Homewood, IL: Business One Irwin, 1992.

Jablonski, Joseph R. *Implementing TQM.* 2nd ed. Albuquerque: Technical Management Consortium, 1992.

Roberts, Harry V., and Bernard F. Sergesketter. *Quality Is Personal: A Foundation for Total Quality Management.* New York: Free Press, 1993.

Scheuermann, Larry, Zhiwei Zhu, and Sandra B. Scheuermann. "TQM Success Efforts: Use More Quantitative or Qualitative Tools?" *Industrial Management and Data Systems* 97, no. 7-8 (July/August 1997): 264+.

Spencer, Michael S., and Leslie K. Duclos. "TQM Stresses MIS: The Ache of Continuous Change." *Mid-American Journal of Business* 13, no. 1 (spring 1998): 59+.

Ward, James A. "TQM and the Year 2000 Crisis." *Information Systems Management* 15, no. 2 (spring 1998): 60+.

Weiss, Howard J., and Mark E. Gershon. *Production and Operations Management.* Boston: Allyn and Bacon, 1989.

TQM

SEE: Total Quality Management

TRADE BARRIERS

Trade barriers may occur in international trade when goods have to cross political boundaries. A trade barrier is a restriction on what would otherwise be **free trade**. The most common form of trade barriers are tariffs, or duties (the two words are often used interchangeably in the context of international trade), which are usually imposed on imports. There is also a category of nontariff barriers, also known as nontariff measures, which also serve to restrict global trade.

There are several different types of duties or tariffs. An export **duty** is a **tax** levied on goods leaving a country, while an import duty is charged on goods entering a country. A duty or tariff may be categorized according to how it is calculated. An ad valorem tariff is one that is calculated as a percentage of the value of the goods being imported or exported. For example, a 20 percent ad valorem duty means that a duty equal to 20 percent of the value of the goods in question must be paid. Duties that are calculated in other ways include a specific duty, which is based on the quantity, weight, or volume of goods, and a compound duty (also known as a mixed tariff), which is calculated as a combination of an ad valorem duty and a specific duty.

Duties and tariffs are also categorized according to their function or purpose. An antidumping duty is imposed on imports that are priced below fair market value and that would damage domestic producers. Antidumping duties are also called punitive tariffs. A countervailing duty, another type of punitive tariff, is levied after there has been substantial or material damage done to domestic producers. A countervailing duty is specifically charged on imports that have been subsidized by the exporting country's government. The purpose of a countervailing duty is to offset the **subsidy** and increase the domestic price of the imported product.

A prohibitive tariff, also known as an exclusionary tariff, is designed to substantially reduce or stop altogether the importation of a particular product or commodity. It is typically used when the amount of an imported good exceeds a certain permitted level. It may be used to protect domestic producers. Another type of tariff is the end-use tariff, which is based on the use of an imported product. For example, the same product may be charged a different duty if it is intended for educational use as opposed to commercial use.

In addition to duties and tariffs, there are also nontariff barriers (NTBs) to international trade. These include quantitative restrictions, or quotas, that may be imposed by one country or as the result of agreements between two or more countries. Examples of quantitative restrictions include international commodity agreements, voluntary export restraints, and orderly marketing arrangements.

Administrative regulations constitute a second category of NTBs. These include a variety of requirements that must be met in order for trade to occur, including fees, licenses, permits, domestic content requirements, financial bonds and deposits, and government procurement practices. The third type of NTB covers technical regulations that apply to such areas as packaging, labeling, safety standards, and multilingual requirements.

In 1980 the Agreement on Technical Barriers to Trade, also known as the Standards Code, came into effect for the purpose of ensuring that administrative and technical practices do not act as trade barriers. By the end of 1988 the agreement had been signed by 39 countries. Additional work on promoting unified standards to eliminate these NTBs was conducted by the **General Agreement on Tariffs and Trade** (GATT) Standards Committee, which in 1994 was succeeded by the newly created **World Trade Organization** (WTO). As a result more than 131 governments accepted the provisions of the Technical Barriers to Trade (TBT) Agreement enforced by the WTO.

Standards and testing practices can become technical barriers to trade when they are developed by national or regional interests and then imposed on the international trading. The **U.S. Department of Commerce**'s 1998 report, "National Export Strategy," identified "the global manipulation of international standards and testing practices by governments and regional economic blocs" as a major threat to U.S. competitiveness abroad. Under the TBT Agreement the WTO is supposed to guarantee due process and transparency in the establishment of international standards. The Department of Commerce, however, has presented examples where narrow regional or market interests have resulted in standards forced on international trade, and governments and regional economic blocs such as the **European Union** (EU) have openly used standards and related practices to achieve market domination. The United States was among those countries calling for technology- and trade neutral standards, especially for markets in Latin America and Asia.

Other types of existing technical trade barriers include environmental, health, and safety certification requirements. In Europe such requirements range from banning imported beef from cattle raised with hormones to not allowing older airplanes to land because of noise pollution concerns.

Since the passage of the Omnibus Trade and Competitiveness Act of 1988, the U.S. State Department periodically submits reports to Congress called "Country Reports on Economic Policy and Trade." These reports detail significant barriers to U.S. exports. Such barriers include not only tariffs, sanctions, embargoes, and technical regulations, they can also cover local conditions such as fuel shortages, lack of a modern telecommunications system, backward **banking** systems, and low purchasing power.

Tariffs and other trade barriers have a definite effect on consumption and production. They serve to reduce consumption of the imported product, because the tariff raises the domestic price of the import. They also serve to stimulate domestic production of the product when that is possible, also because of the higher domestic price. Proponents of tariffs argue that such an increase in domestic production is desirable, while opponents argue that it is inefficient from an economic standpoint. The overall effect of tariffs and trade barriers on international trade is to reduce the volume of trade and to increase the prices of imports. Proponents of free trade argue that both of those results are undesirable, while proponents of protectionism argue that tariffs may be necessary for a variety of reasons.

There are several reasons advanced for imposing trade barriers. These include protecting domestic producers against foreign competitors (especially infant industries), improving a nation's terms of trade, reducing domestic **unemployment**, and improving a nation's balance of-payments position. Those who would argue against imposing trade barriers point to the possibility of retaliation by other nations, leading to a trade war. The more trade barriers there are, the lower the volume of international trade and the higher the domestic prices of imported goods. As a result, global resources are less efficiently allocated and the level of world **income** and production is reduced. It has been the recognition of the negative effects of trade barriers on international trade that has led to international agreements, such as GATT, designed to reduce or eliminate them.

SEE ALSO: Dumping

[David P. Bianco]

FURTHER READING:

Biederman, David. "Trade Barriers: Everywhere." *Traffic World,* 7 September 1998, 33.

Sanger, David E. "Miffed at Europe, U.S. Raises Tariffs for Luxury Goods." *New York Times,* 4 March 1999, C1+.

"World Trade Survey." *Economist,* 3 October 1998.

Zuckerman, Amy. "Experts See Standards as Threat to U.S. Competitiveness in World Marketplace." *Quality Progress,* May 1998, 16.

——. "Using Standards as Barriers to Trade." *New Steel,* May 1997, 90.

TRADE CREDIT

Trade credit refers to the **credit** that one business extends to another in the course of doing business with each other. Trade credit may be extended by a purchasing firm to its supplier, or vice versa. If prepayment is made, then the purchaser is extending trade credit to the seller. Where the seller allows a certain time period for payment to be made, then the seller is extending trade credit to the buyer.

Trade credit may either be long term or short term. Examples of long term trade credit may be found in the automotive and petroleum industries, where it is common practice for manufacturers to extend long-term, low interest **loans** to their dealers. Trade credit, however, is most commonly short term, anywhere from 30 to 120 days, and is typically extended by a seller to a buyer.

A seller typically extends trade credit to a buyer by offering the buyer a specified time to pay for the goods that were purchased. The trade credit may be offered on net terms, which means that no interest will be charged if payment is made within the specified period, usually 30, 60, 90, or 120 days. A two-part offer of trade credit adds a discount period during which the purchaser may take a discount if payment is made within an even shorter period. For example, a ''2/10 Net 30'' offer means that the buyer has the option of taking a 2 percent discount if payment is made within ten days. Otherwise, full payment is expected within 30 days.

Two-part trade credit offers have an implicit interest charge built in. That is, if the purchaser chooses the ''Net 30'' option over the ''2/10'' option and fails to take the trade discount offered, then the purchaser is in effect paying an interest charge on the 30 days of credit that has been extended. When annualized, the **interest rate** on most trade credit far exceeds that offered by **banks** and other financial institutions. Consequently, some theorists hold that two-part trade credit offers provide sellers with information about the creditworthiness of their customers. It is argued that creditworthy customers would always take the trade discount, because they could find third-party financing at better rates than are offered by the two-part trade credit offer.

The actual credit terms of trade credit offers appear to be standardized within industries, although they may vary from industry to industry. They tend to remain constant and not be affected by supply and demand. The extending of trade credit can serve a business firm's informational and financial needs. In addition to providing sellers with information on the creditworthiness of their customers, trade credit offers can serve to bond relationships between buyers and sellers. Sellers who offer trade credit generally have a financial interest in maintaining a continuing relationship with their buyers. The extending of trade credit also gives the purchaser time to verify the quality of the goods purchased and evaluate the seller's performance.

Financially, the handling of trade credit offers and payments are part of a business firm's accounts receivable and accounts payable decisions. Financial decisions about extending two-part trade credit offers take into account the trade-off between offering a discount and receiving less money on the one hand, and receiving payment sooner and improving cash flow on the other. In terms of accounts payable, it is expected that all creditworthy firms would take advantage of trade discounts whenever possible. If no trade discount is offered, then simply being able to withhold payment for 30 to 120 days without paying interest improves the purchaser's cost of funds and provides greater control over cash flow.

SEE ALSO: International Finance

[David P. Bianco]

TRADE DEFICIT

A trade deficit is a condition in the **balance of trade** between a country's exports and imports. If the value of a country's **imports** exceeds the value of its **exports**, then that country is said to have a trade deficit. When the value of a country's exports exceeds the value of its exports, then it has a trade surplus. Trade deficits and surpluses may be measured in terms of the international trade between two nations, or between one nation and the rest of the world.

For the United States, the balance of international transactions is reported on a regular basis in the monthly *Survey of Current Business* by the U.S. Bureau of Economic Analysis in the Economics and Statistics Administration of the **U.S. Department of Commerce**. The current account balance of U.S. international transactions consists of four types of transactions: merchandise, services, investment income, and unilateral transfers. When the current account balance is positive, the United States has a trade surplus. When it is negative, there is a trade deficit.

While the Bureau of Economic Analysis reports on the four major categories of international transactions to determine the current account balance for the United States, oftentimes discussions of the current U.S. trade deficit do not take all four categories of transactions into account. In some discussions, the trade deficit is cited only as the balance of trade in merchandise, or goods. In other cases, the trade deficit refers to the balance of international trade in goods and services. Adding to the confusion is the fact that the Department of Commerce reports several versions of the trade deficit, including several revisions, before the most definitive number is released.

Nevertheless, the current account balance as reported by the Bureau of Economic Analysis also includes international transactions in investment income and unilateral transfers. In this context investment income includes interest paid abroad to foreign investors and interest received by public and private sectors in the United States from foreign sources. Unilateral transfers include outflows for net U.S. purchases of foreign **securities** and inflows for net foreign purchases of U.S. securities, U.S. **banks**' claims against foreigners and **liabilities** to foreign sources, and net outflows for U.S. **direct investment** abroad and net inflows for foreign direct investment in the United States. All of these transactions affect the current account balance.

Looking at the recent history of the U.S. trade deficit in terms of all four categories of international transactions, the U.S. trade deficit peaked at $168 billion in 1987, when the dollar was seriously overvalued. An economic **recession** followed, and by 1991 the current account balance showed a deficit of $4.4 billion. From 1992 to the end of the decade the trade deficit swelled from $56 billion to a projected $236 billion for 1998 and $300 billion for 1999. For 1997 the trade deficit was reported to be $155 billion, consisting of a $198 billion trade deficit in goods, a $88 billion trade surplus in services, a $5 billion deficit in investment income, and a $40 billion deficit in unilateral transfers.

The $5 billion deficit in investment income for 1997 was the first deficit in that category in decades. It meant that for the first time in decades foreign investors received more payments on their investments in the United States than U.S. investors received on their investments abroad.

In terms of international trade in goods and services only, the United States enjoyed a rising trade surplus in services and experienced a rising trade deficit in merchandise during the 1990s. The surplus in services increased from $27 billion in 1990 to $88 billion in 1997. Trade in services is reported in seven categories, including travel, royalties and license fees, education, financial services, professional services, military sales, and telecommunications trade.

In terms of international merchandise trade with specific countries, the United States has a trade surplus with some countries and a trade deficit with others. From 1991 to 1993, the United States had an increasing trade deficit in goods with Canada, Germany, Japan, Asia (excluding Japan), and China. For the same period, the United States had a merchandise trade surplus with England, Latin America, and Mexico. Merchandise trade with Western Europe went from a surplus in 1991 and 1992 to a deficit in 1993.

A variety of factors determine the size of a country's trade deficit or surplus. Since the balance of trade is measured by the value of imports and exports, the quantity of trade as well as its price affects the size of a particular trade deficit or surplus. When a country's currency is weak, for example, exports are valued lower and imports cost more, thus tending to increase the size of a trade deficit and reduce the size of a trade surplus.

The strength of a country's economy as well as the condition of the international economy also affect trade deficits and surpluses. When there is a worldwide recession, with a weakening of many countries' economies, there is a reduced demand for a given country's exports. A lower international demand for exports tends to increase a country's trade deficit. When a country's domestic economy is expanding, then that economy's demand for exports tends to increase, also tending to increase a country's trade deficit. Thus, an increasing trade deficit could be the result of a growing domestic economy, a worldwide recession, or a weak currency.

[David P. Bianco]

FURTHER READING:

Biederman, David. "U.S. Exports: Doom, Meet Gloom." *Traffic World,* 12 October 1998, 56.

Cohen, Warren. "Up, Up, and Away: The U.S. Trade Deficit Is Poised to Hit an All-Time High. But There's a Silver Lining." *U.S. News and World Report,* 2 November 1998, 50.

Goldman, David P. "Buy Dollars." *Forbes,* 8 February 1999, 161.

Hanke, Steve H. "Good-Bye Goldilocks." *Forbes,* 14 December 1998, 102.

Koretz, Gene. "Exchange Rate Flu: How Bad?" *Business Week,* 23 November 1998, 27.

Taylor, Timothy. "Untangling the Trade Deficit." *Public Interest,* winter 1999, 82-83.

TRADEMARK

SEE: Brands and Brand Names; Copyright; Patents/Patent Law

TRAINING AND DEVELOPMENT

Training and development refer to programs designed to help new employees adjust to the workplace successfully. In addition, they include the formal ongoing efforts of corporations and other organizations to improve the performance and self-fulfillment of their employees through a variety of methods and programs. In the modern workplace, these efforts have taken on a broad range of applications, from training in highly specific job skills to long-term professional development, and are applicable to all sorts of employees ranging from line workers to the **chief executive officer**. Training and development have emerged as formal corporate functions, integral elements of corporate **strategy**, and are recognized as professions with distinct theories and methodologies as companies increasingly acknowledge the fundamental importance of employee growth and development, as well as the necessity of a highly skilled **workforce**, in order to improve the success and efficiency of their organizations.

For the most part, training and development are used together to bring about the overall acclimation, improvement, and education of an organization's employees. While closely related, there are important differences between the terms and the scope of each. In general, training programs have very specific and quantifiable goals, such as operating a particular piece of machinery, understanding a specific process, or performing certain procedures with great precision. On the other hand, developmental programs concentrate on broader skills that are applicable to a wider variety of situations, such as **decision making**, **leadership** skills, and **goal setting**. In short, training programs are typically tied to a particular subject matter and are applicable to that subject only, while developmental programs center on cultivating and enriching broader skills useful in numerous contexts.

HISTORY OF TRAINING PROGRAMS

The apprenticeship system emerged in ancient cultures to provide a structured approach to the training of unskilled workers by master craftsmen. This system was marked by three distinct stages: the unskilled novice, the journeyman or yeoman, and finally, the master craftsman. Together, they formed an ''organic'' process whereby the novice ''grew'' into a master craftsman over a period of years.

With the onset of the Industrial Age, the training of the unskilled underwent a dramatic transformation in which **vocational education** and training emerged to replace the traditional apprentice system. The division of labor in an industrial factory resulted in specific job tasks that required equally specific training in a much shorter time span. As training activities grew more methodical and focused, the first recognizable modern training methods began to develop during the 19th and early 20th centuries: gaming simulations became an important tool in the Prussian military during the early 1800s and pyschodrama and role playing were developed by Dr. J. L. Moreno of Vienna, Austria, in 1910.

The early 20th century witnessed the emergence of training and development as a profession, resulting in the creation of training associations and societies, the advent of the **assembly line** requiring greater specificity in training, and the dramatic training requirements of the world wars. Important groups forming during this period include the American Management Association in 1923 (which began as the National Association of Corporation Schools in 1913), and the National Management Association in 1956 (which began as the National Association of Foremen in 1925). At the same time, Henry Ford (1863-1947) introduced the assembly line at his Highland Park, Michigan, plant. Because the assembly line created an even greater division of labor, along with an unprecedented need for precision and teamwork, job tasks and assignments required more highly specific and focused training than ever before.

The enormous production needs of the World War I and II created a heavy influx of new workers with little or no industrial education or skills to the workplace, thereby necessitating massive training efforts that were at once fast and effective. In particular, the heavy demand for shipping construction during World War I resulted in a tenfold increase in workers trained on-site by instructors who were supervisors using a simple four-step method: show, tell, do, check. During World War II, large numbers of trained industrial workers left their jobs to enter the armed forces, severely limiting the organizational support normally provided by coworkers in training their replacements. Heavy demands were placed on foremen and supervisors, and the training within industry (TWI) service was formed to train supervisors as instructors. Job instruction training (JIT) was employed to train defense-plant supervisors in instructing new employees in necessary job skills as quickly as possible. Other programs included job relations training (JRT), job methods training (JMT), and job safety training (JST). During this time, the American Society for Training and Development (ASTD) was formed.

By the end of World War II most companies and organizations realized the importance of training and development as a fundamental organizational tool. Training programs that originally were developed in response to national crises had become established corporate activities with long-term strategies working toward improving employee performance. In the mid-1950s gaming simulations gained popularity. Trainers began giving serious consideration to the efficacy of their training programs, and interest in the evaluation of training programs grew. The 1960s witnessed an explosion of training methods as the number of corporations using **assessment centers** increased from one to 100 by the end of the decade. Government programs to train young men for industrial jobs, such as the Job Development Program 1965 and the Job Corps, were initiated to improve the conditions of the economically disadvantaged. New methods included training laboratories, sensitivity training, programmed instruction, **performance appraisal** and evaluation, needs assessments, **management** training, and **organizational development**.

By the 1970s a new sense of professionalism emerged in the training community. Training programs grew dramatically, and the ASTD produced the *Professional Development Manual for Trainers*. Government programs were aimed increasingly at minorities as a group and required corporations to increase their efforts to recruit minorities. With the rise of organizational development, the focus of training shifted away from the individual and toward the organization as a whole. Technological advances in training programs included the use of videotapes, satellites, and **computers**.

The 1980s and early 1990s saw important social, economic, and political changes that have had a profound effect on the way corporations do business, resulting in an ever increasing need for effective training. In a time of economic constraints coupled with increasing **international competition**, training and development programs needed to respond more quickly and effectively to technological change. Increasing governmental regulations also require a greater breadth of training programs to reflect the greater diversity of employees.

Furthermore, computers became an integral part of business and industry in the 1980s and 1990s, making knowledge of computer use essential for many workers. As a consequence, companies launched computer training and development programs to ensure that their employees possessed the needed computer skills. In addition, companies used computers as a training method known as computer-based training, relying on specially designed computer programs to impart knowledge and skills needed for a host of tasks.

CONTEMPORARY TRAINING AND DEVELOPMENT TECHNIQUES

While new instructional methods are under continuous development, several training methods have proven highly effective and are widely used to acclimate new employee, impart new skills, and improve existing skills. They include structured **on-the-job training**, role playing, self-instruction, team building games and simulations, computer-based training, mentoring, and job rotation.

ON-THE-JOB TRAINING. One of the most common and least expensive methods of training and development is on-the-job training (OJT). OJT refers to the process of learning skills while working where workers—especially new workers—obtain the knowledge and skills they need to complete their tasks through a systematic training program. Research indicates that employees acquire approximately 80 percent of their work-related knowledge and skills on the job, making consideration and implementation of successful OJT programs indispensable for employers. While OJT dates back to ancient **apprenticeship programs**, much 20th-century OJT remained uncodified and unstructured until the 1980s and 1990s.

The structured forms of OJT that emerged promised to remedy problems associated with unstructured OJT by relying on a planned process designed and proven to impart the necessary skills by the end of the OJT period. Nevertheless, like unstructured OJT, structured OJT involves having an experienced employee train a new employee at the work site and having the new employee receive feedback, advice, and suggestions from coworkers and trainers. Structured OJT generally assumes that new employees lack certain skills and the goal of the OJT program is to instill these skills. Therefore, employers design the training programs so that new employees do not initially perform these new tasks in order to learn. Instead, they gain knowledge and experience that will facilitate the performance of these tasks at the appropriate time and gradually work toward performing these tasks. Moreover, trainers assist and intervene at structured intervals, rather than intervening at random points in the training program as can occur with unstructured OJT.

Implementing a structured OJT program involves five basic steps: (1) analyzing the tasks and skills to be learned; (2) selecting, training, and supervising trainers; (3) preparing training materials; (4) conducting an OJT program; and (5) evaluating the program and making any necessary improvements or modifications.

ROLE PLAYING. In role playing, trainees assume various roles and play out that role within a group to learn and practice ways of handling different situations. A facilitator creates a scenario that is to be acted out by the participants and guided by the facilitator. While the situation might be contrived, the interpersonal relations are genuine. Furthermore, participants receive immediate feedback from the facilitator and the scenario itself allowing better understanding of their own behavior.

SELF-INSTRUCTION. Self-instruction refers an instructional method that emphasizes individual learning. In self-instruction programs, the employees take primary responsibility for their own learning. Unlike instructor- or facilitator-led instruction, trainees have a greater degree of control over topics, the sequence of learning, and the pace of learning. Depending on the structure of the instructional materials, trainees can achieve a higher degree of customized learning. Forms of self-instruction include programmed learning, individualized instruction, personalized systems of instruction, learner-controlled instruction, and correspondence study. For self-instruction programs to be successful, employers must not only make learning opportunities available, but also must promote interest in these learning opportunities. Self-instruction allows trainees to learn at their own pace and receive immediate feedback. This method also benefits companies that have to train only a few people at a time.

TEAM BUILDING. Team building is the active creation and maintenance of effective work groups with similar goals and objectives. Not to be confused with the informal, ad-hoc formation and use of **teams** in the workplace, team building is a formal and methodological process of building work teams with objectives and goals, facilitated by a third-party consultant. Team building is commonly initiated to combat ineffectual group functioning that negatively affects group dynamics, **labor-management relations**, quality, or productivity. By recognizing the problems and difficulties associated with the creation and development of work teams, team building provides a structured, guided process whose benefits include a greater ability to manage complex projects and processes, flexibility to respond to changing situations, and greater motivation among team members.

GAMES AND SIMULATIONS. Games and simulations are structured competitions and operational models used as training situations to emulate real-life scenarios. The benefits of games and simulations include the improvement of **problem-solving** and decision-making skills, a greater understanding of the organizational whole, the ability to study actual problems, and the power to capture the student's interest.

COMPUTER-BASED TRAINING. In computer-based training (CBT), computers and computer-based instructional materials are the primary medium of instruction. Computer-based training programs are designed to structure and present instructional materials and to facilitate the learning process for the student. Primary uses of CBT include instruction in computer hardware, **software**, and operational equipment. The last is of particular importance because CBT can provide the student with a simulated experience of operating a particular piece of equipment or machinery while eliminating the risk of damage to costly equipment by a trainee or even a novice user. At the same time, the actual equipment's operational use is maximized because it need not be utilized as a training tool. The use of computer-based training enables a training organization to reduce training **costs**, while improving the effectiveness of the training. Costs are reduced through a reduction in travel, training time, amount of operational hardware, equipment damage, and instructors. Effectiveness is improved through standardization and individualization. In recent years, videodisc and CD-ROM have been successfully integrated into PC platforms allowing low-cost personal computers to serve as multimedia machines, increasing the flexibility and possibilities of CBT.

MENTORING. Mentoring refers to programs in which companies select mentors—also called advisers, counselors, and role models—for trainees or let trainees choose their own. When trainees have questions or need help, they turn to their mentors, who are experienced workers or managers with strong communication skills. Mentors offer advice not only on how to perform specific tasks, but also on how to succeed in the company, how the company's **corporate culture** and politics work, and how to handle to delicate or sensitive situations. Furthermore, mentors provide feedback and suggestions to assist trainees in improving inadequate work.

JOB ROTATION. Through job rotation, companies can create a flexible workforce capable of performing a variety of tasks and working for multiple departments or teams if needed. Furthermore, employees can cultivate a holistic understanding of a company through job rotation and can learn and appreciate how each department operates. Effective job rotation programs entail more than a couple of visits to different departments to observe them. Rather, they involve actual participation and completion of actual duties performed by these departments. In addition, job rotation duties encompass typical work performed under the same conditions as the employees of the departments experience. Because of the value some companies place on job rotation, they establish permanent training slots in major departments, ensuring ongoing exposure of employees to new tasks and responsibilities.

TYPES OF TRAINING AND DEVELOPMENT PROGRAMS

Companies can apply these different methods of training and development to any number of subjects to ensure the skills needed for various positions are instilled. Companies gear training and development programs towards both specific and general skills, including technical training, sales training, clerical training, computer training, communications training, organizational development, **career development**, supervisory development, and management development. The goal of these programs is for trainees to acquire new knowledge or skills in fields such as sales or computers or to enhance their knowledge and skills in these areas.

TECHNICAL TRAINING. Technical training seeks to impart technical knowledge and skills using common training methods for instruction of technical concepts, factual information, and procedures, as well as technical processes and principles. Likewise, sales training concentrates on the education and training of individuals to communicate with customers in a persuasive manner and inculcate other skills useful for sales positions.

COMMUNICATIONS TRAINING. Communications training concentrates on the improvement of interpersonal communication skills, including writing, oral presentation, listening, and reading. In order to be successful, any form of communications training should be focused on the basic improvement of skills and not just on stylistic considerations. Furthermore, the training should serve to build on present skills rather than rebuilding from the ground up. Communications training can be taught separately or can be effectively integrated into other types of training, since it is fundamentally related to others disciplines.

ORGANIZATIONAL DEVELOPMENT. Organizational development (OD) refers to the use of knowledge and techniques from the behavioral sciences to analyze existing organizational structure and implement changes in order to improve organizational effectiveness. OD is useful in such varied areas as the alignment of employee goals with those of the organization, communications, team functioning, and decision making. In short, it is a development process with an organizational focus to achieve the same goals as other training and development activities aimed at individuals. OD practitioners commonly practice what has been termed ''action research'' to effect an orderly change that has been carefully planned to minimize the occurrence of unpredicted or unforeseen events. Action research refers to a systematic analysis of an organization to acquire a better understanding of the nature of problems and forces within an organization.

CAREER DEVELOPMENT. Career development of employees covers the formal development of an employee's position within an organization by providing a long-term development strategy and training programs to implement this strategy and achieve individual goals. Career development represents a growing concern for employee welfare and the long-term needs of employees. For the individual, it involves stating and describing career goals, the assessment of necessary action, and the choice and implementation of necessary actions. For the organization, career development represents the systematic development and improvement of employees. To remain effective, career development programs must allow individuals to articulate their desires. At the same time, the organization strives to meet those stated needs as much as possible by consistently following through on commitments and meeting the expectations of the employees raised by the program.

MANAGEMENT AND SUPERVISORY DEVELOPMENT. Management and supervisory development involves the training of managers and supervisors in basic leadership skills enabling them to function effectively in their positions. For managers this typically involves the development of the ability to focus on the effective management of their employee resources, while striving to understand and achieve the strategies and goals of the organization. Management training typically involves individuals above the first two levels of **supervision** and below senior executive management. Managers learn to effectively develop their employees by helping employees learn and change, as well as by identifying and preparing them for future responsibilities. Management development may also include programs that teach decision-making skills, creating and managing successful work teams, allocating resources effectively, **budgeting**, communication skills, **business planning**, and goal setting.

Supervisory development addresses the unique situation of the supervisor as a link between the organization's management and workforce. It must focus on enabling supervisors to deal with their responsibilities to both labor and management, as well as coworkers, and staff departments. Important considerations include the development of personal and interpersonal skills, understanding the management process, and productivity and quality improvement.

DESIGNING TRAINING PROGRAMS

The design of training programs covers the planning and creation of training and development programs. Like the training programs themselves, the development of training programs has evolved into a profession that utilizes systematic models, methods, and processes of instructional systems design (ISD). Instructional systems design includes the systematic design and development of instructional methods and materials to facilitate the process of training and development and ensure that training programs are necessary, valid, and effective. Although the instructional design process can take on variety of sequences, the process must include the collection of data on the tasks or skills to be learned or improved, the analysis of these skills and tasks, the development of methods and materials, delivery of the program, and finally the evaluation of the training's effectiveness. Table 1 describes the process in greater detail.

Training and development programs often rely on the principles and theories of various behavioral sciences such as psychology and sociology. The behavioral sciences provide useful theories on individual behavior, motivations, organizational dynamics, and interpersonal relationships, which the developers of training programs can draw on when creating their programs. Similarly, the development of a distinctive

Table 1
A Typical Instructional Systems Design Model

STEP	DESCRIPTION
Needs analysis	Measuring the disparity between current and desired skill levels
Task assessment	Collection of data on job tasks and the subsequent identification of learning requirements and possible difficulties
Stating objectives	Creation of concise statement of objectives and purpose as a benchmark
Assessment/testing	Development of testing materials designed to measure the performance of the objectives
Development of materials	Selection of effective instructional strategies followed by the development of materials based on the chosen strategies
Pilot programs	Piloting the program to gauge the effectiveness of the materials as well as identify potential weaknesses through subsequent evaluation
Evaluation	Evaluation of the efficacy of the methods and materials

adult educational model has influenced the development of training programs, giving them an exclusive focus on adults. According to this model, adults learn best through goal-oriented instruction, unlike children, who learn best through instruction based on the subject matter itself. Hence, given the goal-oriented needs of adult education, the design and development of training materials have taken on a much higher level of structure and methodology than traditional methods for instructional development.

EVALUATING TRAINING PROGRAMS

Once a company implements a training program, it must evaluate the program's success, even if it has produced desired results for other companies and even if similar programs have produced desires for it. Companies first must determine if trainees are acquiring the desired skills and knowledge. If not, then they must ascertain why not and they must figure out if the trainees are failing to acquire these skills because of their own inability or because of ineffective training programs.

In order to evaluate training programs, companies must collect relevant data. The data should include easily measurable and quantifiable information such as costs, output, quality, and time, according to Jack J. Phillips in *Recruiting, Training, and Retraining New Employees.*

1. Costs: budget changes, unit costs, project cost variations, and sales expenses.
2. Output: Units produced, units assembled, productivity per hour, and applications reviewed.
3. Quality: Error rates, waste, defective products, customer complaints, and shortages.
4. Time: On-time shipments, production or processing time, overtime, training time, efficiency, and meeting deadlines.

Companies also can use qualitative data such as work habits, attitudes, development, adaptability, and initiative to evaluate training programs. Most companies, however, prefer to place more weight on the quantitative data previously outlined.

Furthermore, according to Phillips, companies tend to evaluate training and development programs on four levels: behavior, learning, reaction, and results. Businesses examine employee behavior after training programs in order to determine if the programs helped employees adjust to their environment; also, companies can obtain evidence on employee behavior via observation and interviews. Throughout the training process, employers monitor how well trainees are learning about the company, the atmosphere, and their jobs.

To evaluate training and development programs effectively, employers also gauge employee reactions to the programs. This feedback from trainees provides companies with crucial information on how employees perceive their programs. Using questionnaires and interviews, companies can identify employee attitudes toward various aspects of the training programs. Finally, employers attempt to determine the results of their training programs by studying the quantifiable data addressed earlier as well as by considering the **employee turnover** rate and job performance of workers who recently completed a training and development program.

[Bradley T. Bernatek, updated by Karl Heil]

FURTHER READING:

Craig, Robert L., ed. *Training and Development Handbook: A Guide to Human Resource Development.* 3rd ed. New York: McGraw-Hill, 1987.

Fallon, William K., ed. *AMA Management Handbook.* 2nd ed. New York: AMACOM, 1983.

Goldstein, Irwin L., ed. *Training and Development in Organizations.* 2nd ed. San Francisco: Jossey-Bass, 1989.

Jacobs, Ronald L., and Michael J. Jones. *Structured On-the-Job Training.* San Francisco: Berret-Koehler Publishers, 1995.

McCarthy, Elizabeth. ''Firms Realize Training Is the Only Way to Keep Up.'' *Sacramento Business Journal,* 29 May 1998, E6.

Phillips, Jack J. *Recruiting, Training, and Retraining New Employees.* San Francisco: Jossey-Bass, 1987.

''Stop Us if You've Heard This Before . . . : A Surgical Counterstrike against Myths and Cliches in the Training World.'' *Training,* September 1997, 24.

Tobin, Daniel R. *The Knowledge-Enabled Organization.* New York: AMACOM, 1998.

TRANSACTION COSTS

In a widely used but limited sense, transaction costs refer to the cost of transferring ownership or property rights. Transaction costs are associated with buying and selling different kinds of property, including **real estate**, **stocks** and **bonds**, and currencies. Examples of such transaction costs include brokers' fees and salespeople's commissions, among others. In calculating the transaction costs of buying and selling any kind of property, both the costs to the seller and those of the buyer are considered.

In another sense, transaction costs as discussed in **economic theory** refer to the cost of anything that might be defined as a transaction. Whenever goods exchange hands, there are transaction costs. Broadly defined, transaction costs include that which would have been saved had the goods not exchanged hands. Many transaction cost studies have been conducted to determine their effect on different aspects of economic behavior and performance.

In a simple bilateral exchange, it is generally easy to quantify transaction costs. When there are complex contracts calling for exchanges among many different parties, however, transaction costs become so complex that it may be impossible to quantify them. Studies of such complex transactions often rely on a qualitative discussion of transaction costs.

Depending on the situation, transaction costs may be independent of the quantity or value of goods transferred. In other cases there may be pronounced **economies of scale**, where larger transactions incur relatively smaller transaction costs on a cost per unit basis. It is clear, however, that the existence of transaction costs serves to reduce the overall volume of transactions in an economy. As the cost of transferring of goods increases, traders have a stronger incentive to minimize the number of their transactions.

Transaction costs have an interesting effect on currency trading. If there were no transaction costs in the foreign currency market, then each currency could be traded against any other currency using consistent rates. That is, the value of the dollar against the yen would equal the value of the yen against the British pound multiplied by the value of the British pound against the dollar. Since there are transaction costs involved, however, it is not possible to calculate consistent rates among the many different currencies. That is, one cannot in practice calculate the value of the dollar against the yen by measuring the values of the dollar and the yen against a third currency.

Transaction costs also influence the structure of markets and the nature of intermediary networks. When transaction costs are low, a more complex intermediary network tends to arise. This is the case for financial assets such as **securities**, **foreign exchange**, commodity contracts, and gold, among others. The markets for these assets tend to move to where the transaction costs are lowest. As technological advances affect financial transactions and lower the transaction costs involved, it is anticipated that the financial system will become more elaborate, with greater specialization or division of labor and an increase in the number of transactions relative to the volume of traded assets.

It is also theorized that transaction costs determine what will be used as money, or a medium of exchange, in a particular economy. If one imagines that there are several **commodities** that could serve as a medium of exchange, the ones that will be chosen are those that involve the lowest transaction costs. The one that is selected as money, then, is the one with the lowest transaction cost (and holding cost). Thus, it can be seen that money serves to conserve resources that would otherwise disappear as transaction costs.

SEE ALSO: Stock Index Futures

[David P. Bianco]

TRANSFER AGENT

The function of a transfer agent is to maintain up-to-date records of the ownership of a corporation's **securities** and to execute transfers of the corporation's **stock** and other securities. A transfer agent may be an officer or clerk of the corporation, or an outside individual, **bank**, or trust company. Larger corporations may have their own transfer departments. It is common practice for corporations to utilize the services of a bank's transfer department to fulfill the duties of a transfer agent.

A transfer agent is responsible for seeing that stock and other securities transfers are properly executed. When a corporation's stock is sold, the transfer agent reregisters the securities that are to be transferred. The securities that have been sold must be canceled, and the transfer agent must establish the validity of the securities to be canceled. The transfer agent then cancels the old certificates and issues new certificates following transfer instructions. The transfer agent records the certificate numbers of the new stock, the new registration information, and the old certificate numbers and date of cancellation. At the end of each business day the transfer agent verifies all transactions by matching the number of shares canceled with the number of shares issued.

In the final step of a securities transfer, the transfer agent delivers the new securities according to instructions. The securities may be delivered to an individual, a brokerage firm, a bank, or a depository institution. It normally takes four working days for a stock transfer to be completed following the transaction date.

State laws governing the activities of a transfer agent are based on the **Uniform Commercial Code** (UCC), Article 8, which covers investment securities. The UCC spells out the rights and **liabilities** of the buyer, seller, and transfer agent in transactions involving securities. In addition, transfer agents are regulated by the **Securities and Exchange Commission** (SEC). SEC regulations are designed to ensure that transfer agents act promptly and accurately. Transfer agents for corporations listed on the New York Stock Exchange (NYSE) must meet additional requirements of the NYSE, among which is the requirement to maintain an office on Manhattan in New York City.

SEE ALSO: Banks and Banking

[David P. Bianco]

TRANSFER PRICING

Transfer pricing is the value placed on goods and services exchanged between affiliates or divisions within a company. The transactions are not truly at arm's length, and therefore do not represent a market price for the goods or services provided. Because the organization may want to properly measure efficiency, productivity, or profitability at the division level, transfer prices must be established when one part of a company does business with another.

The need to track exchanges can occur for a variety of reasons. For example, a company might want to keep track of how its legal department's resources are consumed by various user groups. By charging other departments for use of legal department services, the company can rationally allocate the cost to the area utilizing those services (and responsible for the expense). An obvious side effect of such a policy is that users may think twice about using the legal department, thereby limiting unnecessary demands. On the other hand, management may want to be sure that various decisions—hiring, firing, ad copy, contract terms, etc.—are approved by the legal staff before being completed, which may not happen if user groups restrict use because of the charges incurred.

Beyond the question of staff department chargebacks are the issues of: interdepartment or intercompany transfers of product or services that ultimately will be sold to third parties, and the allocation of costs between subsidiaries. A common example is where one division manufactures a product and another sells it. Although the parent company's goal may be to report true profitability at each level, the management teams responsible at the plant and at the sales office will have opposing agendas, with the former arguing for relatively high transfer prices and the latter lobbying for lower transfer prices.

The best rule to follow is to let market prices be the guide; the factory would ''sell'' to the sales division at a price they could receive if selling to a third-party distributor. That way the manufacturing results are judged based on profits from market price transactions combined with manufacturing efficiency and know-how, while the sales division is tracked on how well they are able to manage the interplay of market forces on demand and pricing. This criterion is known as the ''Basic Arm's Length Standard (BALS)'' and is the preferred standard by which transfer prices are set.

Another important issue concerning transfer pricing arises with respect to income tax jurisdiction. Companies with international or interstate operations will often have separate subsidiaries in each jurisdiction, sometimes for legal and/or political reasons. The affiliates will likely be subject to differential tax rates in the various jurisdictions in which they do business. In these cases, the transfer price issue becomes the concern of an interested third party—the tax authorities. Here the motivation would be to shift profits from a high tax-rate location to a lower one; this can be easily accomplished by manipulating the transfer prices. Obviously the **Internal Revenue Service** is aware of this practice, and will challenge inappropriate transfer prices in the course of audits. Section 482 of the Internal Revenue Code was written to set tax rules and guidelines for acceptable transfer pricing and cost allocations between affiliates.

Transfer pricing within multinational corporations (MNCs) can be fairly complex, requiring different strategies for different transactions and markets. Foreign tax systems, exchange controls, and competition all need to be taken into account. Where two countries, such as the United States and Canada, might have similar substantive laws but differing compliance and reporting rules, companies might use advance pricing agreements (APAs) to ensure compliance. An APA defines an acceptable transfer price calculation method before being implemented, thus avoiding problems with a transfer price audit.

SEE ALSO: Cost Accounting

[Christopher C. Barry, updated by David P. Bianco]

FURTHER READING:

Alles, Michael, and Srikant Dakar. ''Strategic Transfer Pricing,'' *Management Science,* April 1998.

Atrill, Peter, and E.J. McLaney. *Management Accounting for Non-Specialists.* Paramus, NJ: Prentice Hall, 1999.

Baldo, Anthony. ''Avoiding the Transfer Pricing Bite,'' *Treasury and Risk Management,* January-February 1999.

Brealey, Richard A., and Stewart C. Myers. *Principles of Corporate Finance.* Fifth edition. New York: McGraw-Hill Cos., 1996.

De Breyne, Stephanie. ''Transfer Pricing: Get it in Writing!'' *CMA: The Management Accounting Magazine,* February 1998.

Downes, John, and Jordan Elliot Goodman. *Dictionary of Finance and Investment Terms.* 4th ed. Hauppauge, NY: Barron's Educational Series, 1995.

Fraedrich, John P., and Connie Rae Bateman. ''Transfer Pricing by Multinational Marketers: Risky Business,'' *Business Horizons,* January-February 1996.

Horngren, Charles T. *Management and Cost Accounting.* Paramus, NJ: Prentice Hall, 1999.

Moles, Peter, and Nicholas Terry. *The Handbook of International Financial Terms.* New York: Oxford University Press, 1997.

''The Real World of Transfer Pricing,'' *Taxes: The Tax Magazine,* March 1999.

Shapland, Rick, and Bill Major. ''40 Percent of Transfer Pricing Penalty Upheld,'' *The Tax Adviser,* April 1999.

TRANSPORTATION OF GOODS

SEE: Physical Distribution Management

TRAVEL

SEE: Business Travel

TREASURER

The treasurer is the person responsible for the custody and supervision of a business's funds. The office of the treasurer had its antecedent in English government which codified the organization, purposes, and general responsibilities of the business corporation during the 17th century when activities in worldwide colonization and trade exploded.

Corporate law, among other things, provided for a tripartite executive branch of president, secretary, and treasurer. States of the United States adopted this model, modifying it as necessary. All 50 states require the inclusion of these three officers. The corporate bylaws more specifically define their powers and responsibilities.

Ordinarily, the treasurer provides for the custody and supervision of all funds. Through a system of **accounting** controls and procedures, the treasurer tracks, in detail, the origin and utilization of funds. The treasurer employs, at a minimum, a series of standardized reports and analyses, integrating the dollars, volume of sales or production, number of employees, and financial costs into a series of ratios and percentages that assist **management** in evaluating progress and profitability.

Many businesses separate the reporting from the funds management functions. The resulting specialization has the **controller** performing tasks for the treasurer. The controller oversees the reporting and analysis of the sources and utilization of funds. Reporting directly to the treasurer, the controller is responsible for the accounting function. In this situation the treasurer manages the actual funds.

As an officer of the corporation, the treasurer has various corporate and accounting responsibilities. On the corporate level, the treasurer may transfer capital stock. The treasurer also maintains unissued (treasury) capital stock, performs **due diligence** (an evaluation) on financial and **debt** instruments, and records and transfers **bonds** on the company's books.

Accountable to the stockholders, the treasurer maintains capital stock records, signs checks for deposit, makes deposits, develops and maintains relations with financial and **banking** institutions, serves on the **board of directors**, and performs other duties that promote the profitability and objectives of the business. In conjunction with the other officers, the treasurer may transfer **stock**, sign checks for payment, borrow money, make long-term investments, sign **contracts**, repay debt, and distribute **dividends**. The treasurer may also be responsible for the administration of **employee benefits** plans, such as **pension funds**, **401(k) plans**, employee stock purchase plans, and **employee stock options**.

In the capacity of chief accountant, the treasurer protects, from a ''book'' standpoint, the business assets by keeping track of their use and disposition. To prevent fraud and to ensure profit, the treasurer exercises a plethora of controls. These include the detailed recording (accounting) of all financial activities, the discharging of all **liabilities** arising from debt, **credit**, and **taxation**, and the overseeing of a management risk policy including **interest rate** risk, foreign currency risk, and insurance coverage. The treasurer also directs the tax accounting and the **auditing** functions. For **budget** and **business planning** purposes the treasurer disseminates accounting and financial reports as appropriate.

As custodian, the treasurer supervises the collection and recording of cash receipts, manages the securing of credit, arranges debt financing and repayment, and invests excess funds. Through various planning and analytical tools, the treasurer ascertains cash balances, forecasts future needs, arranges for debt financing, invests excess funds, establishes the sales credit policy, and ensures the collection of receivables. In addition the treasurer signs and distributes the payroll.

An unincorporated business assigns concomitant duties to its treasurer where applicable. In either situation, the treasurer's office is the central processing area of the financial and personnel data required to construct intelligent budgets, to efficiently manage credit and excess funds, to establish long-term financial plans and strategies, and to identity the degree of operational productivity.

Because of the complexities of business and financial markets, businesses seeking a treasurer look for a qualified employee with substantial experience as an accountant, preferably as a **certified public accountant** (CPA). In addition, even the smallest business needs a computer literate employee able to maintain computer accounting systems, perform **spreadsheet** analyses, create analytical models, and dabble in **desktop publishing**.

[Roger J. AbiNader, updated by David E. Salamie]

FURTHER READING:

Gotthilf, Daniel L. *Treasurer's and Controller's Desk Book.* 2nd ed. New York: AMACOM, 1997.

Malburg, Christopher R. *Controller's and Treasurer's Desk Reference.* New York: McGraw-Hill, 1994.

TRUSTS AND TRUSTEES

A trust is a tool that an individual or institution uses to transfer property to a beneficiary. The party that grants the property is called the trustor. The trustor gives the property to the trustee, who, in turn, is charged with the task of disbursing the property to the beneficiary according to the instructions of the trustor. As of 1997 U.S. banks managed an estimated $3.3 trillion in discretionary trust assets, or assets banks control as trustees, according to reporting by federal oversight agencies.

One important advantage that a trust has over a simple gift is that the trustor can exercise control over the disbursement of funds or property over time, even after his or her death (or dissolution, in the case of an institutional trustor). For example, a trustor may stipulate that funds periodically transferred to an all-female academy must be terminated if the school begins enrolling males. A second, and perhaps more important, advantage is that trusts can be used to minimize tax burdens incurred when transferring wealth.

The two main categories of trusts are non-charitable and charitable, they are differentiated from one another primarily by tax status. Charitable trusts are organized for nonprofit beneficiaries, such as educational, religious, and charitable organizations. Examples of major charitable trusts include the Ford Foundation and the Pew Charitable Trusts. Beneficiaries of noncharitable trusts typically include individuals or groups—particularly relatives or employees of the trustor—or profit-seeking organizations. Examples include pension and investment funds and personal estates.

Most trustees in the United States are banks' trust departments. However, other types of financial institutions act as trustees, and some companies specialize in trust management. Firms in the latter category are sometimes known as independent trust companies. Furthermore, for very large trusts, such as those created through **corporate philanthropy**, the trustees are separate entities that have been set up as foundations (e.g. Ford Foundation, Lilly Foundation, Wal-Mart Foundation) to manage the trust funds.

HISTORY OF TRUSTS

Trusts date back to about ancient Egypt, circa 4000 B.C., when the equivalent of today's trust officers were charged with holding, managing, and caring for other people's property. Various prototypes of trust institutions were later developed in second-century Rome, some of which involved the use of property for charitable purposes. Trusts began to evolve into their present form during the eighth century, when English clergymen acted as executors of wills and trusts. Throughout the Middle Ages and into the 17th century, trusts developed under English common law to resemble their current legal structure in the United States.

Legalized trusts began in the United States in 1822, when Farmer's Fire Insurance and Loan Company of New York became the first institution chartered in the trust business. Corporate trusts developed in 1830 to help raise money for new business ventures. During the next half century, the number and types of institutions engaged in the trust business rose rapidly. Most of these entities maintained a separate department devoted exclusively to trust services.

In 1906, Congress enacted laws that allowed banks to act as trustees, resulting in approximately 1,300 such institutions offering trust services by 1920. After the Great Depression, many trustees were prevented from conducting business by legislation that essentially restricted institutions other than banks and trust companies from serving as trustees. Legislation also established what became known as the "Chinese Wall," which refers to measures that forbade bank trust departments from sharing customer credit or investment information.

The Depression also helped change American attitudes about saving and investing, and consequently, trusts. Employee benefit trusts, for example, became popular in the 1940s and proliferated so rapidly, that Congress enacted the Employee Retirement Income Security Act of 1974 (ERISA), to define the responsibilities of trustees managing such funds. By 1980, more than 4,000 banks, along with hundreds of trust companies, were managing $229 billion in employee benefit trusts. In 1986, employee benefit trusts represented over 40 percent of all U.S. trust assets.

Investments in individual and charitable trusts also escalated after the Depression. Wealthy individuals, in particular, increasingly used trusts as a way to invest their savings and to transfer wealth. Increases in tax benefits that allowed trustors to avoid estate and gift taxes boosted the utilization of trusts.

In the late 1970s and early 1980s, due to a number of economic and regulatory influences, trusts began to change. High interest rates and the deregulation of certain sectors of financial markets, for instance, prompted trust departments to invest their assets in a multitude of new instruments. Instead of traditional T-bills and commercial paper, trustees began investing money in certificates of deposit, money market funds, variable-rate notes, and other options many analysts deemed risky. (Ironically, these investment vehicles are quite conservative by today's standards, to the extent that many bank trust departments seek to shed their conservative image.) In addition, a strong economy in the mid-1980s generated an influx of investment in trusts, much of which went into charitable trust funds. Between 1980 and 1986, the total amount of money invested in trusts jumped from $571 billion to $1.07 trillion.

Although assets under trustee management continued to climb through the mid-1980s, trustees faced a variety of setbacks in the late 1980s. The Tax Reform Act of 1986, for instance, increased costs and paperwork, and created some confusion for trustees, the end result of which was to discourage the use of trusts and estates as devices to accumulate and transfer wealth. Investment in trusts slowed in the late 1980s and early 1990s. Between 1987 and 1989, the number of trustees in the U.S. decreased from 6,285 to 4,283, and total employment by those trustees fell from 32,491 to 25,853.

TYPES OF TRUSTS

Several different kinds of charitable and noncharitable trusts are legally recognized. Generally, they all serve the same basic function, which is to transfer wealth from the trustor to the beneficiary(s) by means of a trustee. In addition to transferring wealth in the form of dollars, trusts may also include the following gifts: income-producing property, business inventory or equipment, securities, life insurance, works of art, real estate, or jewelry.

NONCHARITABLE TRUSTS

INDIVIDUAL TRUSTS. Noncharitable trust accounts that banks and trust companies manage are categorized as either individual or institutional (corporate). Individual accounts can be further classified into personal agencies or trusts. Personal agency accounts are different from ordinary trust accounts in that property does not actually change hands. Instead, the trust company simply manages assets under the direction of its client, often acting as a safekeeping agent, custodian, manager, or escrow agent. The company may provide complete investment management and reporting services as well.

In contrast to personal agencies, individual trust accounts involve a beneficiary. The trustor establishes an account with a trustee that manages, invests, and distributes the property. Income from the assets is then used to benefit dependents, organizations, or other parties. The trust may also be used to indirectly benefit the trustor. Many trust structures allow trustors various tax benefits and varying degrees of control over account assets.

Two types of individual trusts are guardianships and estate settlement accounts. In the first category, the trustee acts as a guardian to a minor or mentally incompetent individual, caring for the property that benefits that person. Estate settlements, on the other hand, involve securing and valuing a client's assets, distributing assets in accordance with a will, and representing the client's wishes at death.

Individual trusts are also classified as either revocable or irrevocable. Revocable trusts are used to distribute wealth while the grantor is alive, and can be amended at any time. In an irrevocable trust, the trustor relinquishes all control over account assets.

INSTITUTIONAL TRUSTS. Like individual trusts, institutional (or corporate) trusts can be divided into agency and trust accounts. Institutional trusts, though, exist to raise capital for businesses, to reward employees, or to provide income for retired employees. The two most common types of corporate agencies are transfer agencies and registrarships. Trustees in agency relationships simply serve to transfer and register stocks and bonds.

In a corporate trust, the trust company acts as a trustee for a group of people who have lent money to a corporation through bonds or other obligatory instruments. Employee benefit accounts are another form of corporate trust. These trusts provide full custody services, compliance reporting, investment management, and special record keeping for each participating employee's interest in pension, profit-sharing, and other benefit accounts.

CHARITABLE TRUSTS

Donors may use a variety of trusts to transfer wealth to nonprofit causes. Each type of trust offers different advantages regarding the amount of control the trustor may exercise over the gift, various tax benefits that accrue to the trustor, and the method of compensation bestowed upon the beneficiary.

Charitable trusts, as opposed to all other forms of trusts, are usually enforced by the U.S. government. Furthermore, the entire trust industry is closely regulated by the U.S. government. For example, beneficiaries may reclaim property if trustees violate their fiduciary duty (or trust) by making unlawful or reckless investments.

The charitable remainder annuity trust (CRAT) periodically distributes a fixed amount of property to noncharitable parties—often the trust's grantor. After the recipient(s) die, the remainder of the CRAT passes to a charitable organization. Among other advantages, the CRAT allows the grantor charitable income tax deductions equal to the present value of the remaining interest that will ultimately be received by the charity. These deductions are used to offset income from the trust during the grantor's life.

The wealth replacement trust is used in conjunction with a charitable gift. This technically complex type of trust is used to replace assets given to a charity, while benefiting specific noncharitable parties—often the grantor's family members. The grantor may receive valuable tax benefits related to capital gains, gift, and estate taxes. Survivors of the grantor's estate typically benefit from reduced inheritance taxes.

Charitable lead trusts distribute income to philanthropic entities for a fixed term. At the end of the term, the remaining trust is transferred to a noncharitable beneficiary, such as a spouse or child. A benefit of a charitable lead trust is that the grantor avoids estate taxes on the value of assets that defaults to the beneficiaries.

A pooled income fund is a trust maintained by a charitable organization. Each donor who transfers income to the pool may be eligible to receive significant income tax and gift-tax deductions, as well as estate tax benefits. Charitable gift annuities, which became popular in the 1980s, have similar donor benefits. This type of trust, however, is arranged so that grantors receive specified sum of money each year for the remainder of the donor's life.

Other charitable trusts include ''bargain sales,'' in which donors sell property to charities for below-market prices, and ''charitable stock bailouts,'' in which a donor contributes closely held stock to a charity, thereby deriving various tax and/or business benefits.

TRUSTEES

Although trust companies and banks expect to profit in their role as trustee, they have a legal responsibility to act in the best interests of both the beneficiary and the trustor, and to conduct their activities with skill and care. Responsibilities include:

- protecting trust assets from attack by outside parties
- dispensing property to beneficiaries
- investing trust assets in a prudent manner
- keeping accurate records
- being accountable to the beneficiary as specified by the trustor.

Most importantly, the trustee is obliged to faithfully execute the wishes of the trustor. In return for their services, trustees are compensated by one of several methods. A common pricing schedule is a percentage of the market value of assets under management in a trust account. Under this arrangement, trustees typically charge from 0.1 to 0.5 percent, and in some cases as much as 1 percent per year of the total value of assets in the trust. For example, a $2 million trust fund might yield $5,000, or 0.25 percent, in annual fees.

Similarly, some trustees charge a ''gross income receipts fee,'' which is a percentage of income collected from interest and dividends on the account. For instance, if the trustee earned interest and dividends of $50,000 by investing account assets for a period of one year, the trustee might receive 5 percent of those proceeds, or $2,500 dollars. In addition to these charges, some trustees also charge minimum annual management fees or activity fees for special services.

For many financial institutions, fees from trust services are a major revenue center. Government data indicate that in 1997 U.S. banks took in approximately $23.8 billion in fiduciary income derived from commissions and other fees for managing trust account assets. When banks' $19.7 billion in management expenses that year were deducted, they were left with $3.9 billion in operating income, or a comfortable 16 percent net operating margin. The two largest fee categories by account type are personal/estate trusts and general agency accounts. These two groups were responsible for more than half of all bank fiduciary income in 1997. The largest expenses involved in operating a bank trust department are typically staffing costs, including salaries and benefits, which may account for anywhere from a third to more than half of all trust management expenses.

BUSINESS STRATEGIES. In order to maintain profitability in trust operations, many banks impose minimum account sizes. Formerly only the largest regional and national banks had such policies. Emphasis on the bottom line, however, has impelled smaller banks to do likewise. Large banks, for example, might require that trust accounts be worth at least $1 million. As an alternative, some smaller banks have instituted steep minimum annual fees rather than specifying a minimum account size. Smaller banks may also stratify their service offering by account size, offering only minimal services for the smallest accounts (say, those under $100,000), and additional services for each successive asset bracket.

Conventional wisdom holds that small trusts demand an inordinate amount of resources for very minimal returns to the bank. By extension, for smaller banks it is generally not profitable to maintain a trust department if the total discretionary assets aren't of a certain magnitude; some industry veterans believe the minimum assets size should be in the $70 million to $100 million range.

Another strategy for bank trust departments has been to outsource various parts of the trust management process. The level of outsourcing can range from sending out routine and technical activities like transaction processing or accounting to bringing on board an outside firm to run the trust business entirely. Bank executives believe such approaches help control costs and allow the executives to focus on sales and customer service. Some of the largest outside services firms for trust-department outsourcing include SEI Investments Company, DST Systems, Inc., and UAM Trust.

LARGEST TRUST BANKS. For personal trust accounts, the largest U.S. banks as of year-end 1997, as reported by *American Banker,* were NationsBank Corp., with 65,392 trust accounts and $126 billion in assets; Wells Fargo & Co., with 65,271 accounts and $62 billion in assets; and PNC Bank Corp, with 37,132 accounts and $38 billion in assets.

In the general institutional trust category, State Street Corp. was the largest bank based on 1997 figures, with over 40,000 accounts and $423 billion in assets. Some trust industry analysts rank State Street as the largest trust bank overall because of its asset size, but technically a few large commercial banks that administer corporate trusts have more in trust assets. Other general institutional trustee banks include Bank of New York, with 39,074 accounts; and Bankers Trust of New York, with 21,444 accounts.

[Dave Mote]

FURTHER READING:

Clarke, John M., Jack W. Zalaha, and August Zinsser III. *The Trust Business.* Washington: American Bankers Association, 1988.

Federal Financial Institutions Examination Council. *Trust Assets of Financial Institutions - 1997.* Washington, 1998. Available from www2.fdic.gov/structur/trust/.

Fraser, Katharine. ''Profit-Conscious Trust Departments Raising Account Minimums.'' *American Banker,* 6 October 1997.

Luhby, Tami. ''More Banks Outsourcing Their Trust Processing.'' *American Banker,* 6 October 1998.

Namjestnik, Kenneth J. *The Trust Risk Management Manual.* Chicago: Probus Professional Publishing, 1995.

Nemer-Wilfong, Tara. ''Bank Trust Departments Increasing Outsourcing.'' *Trusts & Estates,* October 1998.

Phillips, James A. ''Think about Not Calling It a Trust Department.'' *American Banker,* 18 October 1996.

Shenkman, Martin M. *The Complete Book of Trusts.* 2nd ed. New York: John Wiley & Sons, 1997.

''Top Fiduciary Trust Accounts.'' *American Banker,* 21 July 1998.

TRW REPORTS

SEE: Commercial Credit Reporting; Consumer Credit Reporting

TURNOVER

SEE: Employee Turnover

U

U.S. DEPT. OF COMMERCE

The ideological underpinnings of the U.S. Department of Commerce lay in the preamble to the U.S. Constitution, which says that the purpose of the Constitution is in part to "promote the general welfare" of this "more Perfect Union." The Department of Commerce (DoC) has thus viewed as its mission the promotion of the general welfare of the United States and its citizens. Since its founding in 1913 the DoC has sought to achieve this goal through a plethora of seemingly disparate activities—though all ultimately aimed at supporting commerce and thus the general welfare of America. No more succinct description of these multitudinous activities exists than the one found in the *U.S. Government Manual:* "The Department of Commerce encourages, serves, and promotes the Nation's international trade, economic growth, and technological advancement. The Department provides a wide variety of programs through the competitive free enterprise system. It offers assistance and information to increase America's competitiveness in the world economy; administers programs to prevent unfair foreign trade competition; provides social and economic statistics and analyses for business and government planners; provides research and support for increased use of scientific, engineering, and technological development; works to improve our understanding and benefits of the Earth's physical environment and oceanic resources; grants patents and registers trademarks; develops policies and conducts research on telecommunications; provides assistance to promote domestic economic development; and assists in the growth of minority businesses."

Even before the Constitution was adopted in 1787 there had been various efforts to bring together government and commercial interests for their mutual benefit. One such attempt was the Mount Vernon conference of 1785, which was a 13-point agreement between Virginia and Maryland that dealt with commerce on the shared waterways of the Potomac River. As the United States grew and prospered, both politically and commercially, so did the role of government expand. In 1798 the Navy Department was created; in 1829 the postmaster general joined the cabinet under President Andrew Jackson; in 1849 the Department of the Interior was established, as was the Department of Justice in 1870. In 1888 the Bureau of Labor became a separate department and the Department of Agriculture came into being in 1889. As the government continued to expand, so did pressure for it to establish some sort of "Department of Commerce and Industry." This pressure gained new impetus in the aftermath of the economic Panic of 1893 and the then newly formed National Association of Manufacturers.

Finally in 1903 Congress passed legislation creating the Department of Commerce and Labor and the bill was signed into law by President Theodore Roosevelt. In the process it downgraded the previously formed Department of Labor to the Bureau of Labor. The new department was initially responsible for ten areas of activity ranging from the Bureau of Census and Coast and Geodetic Survey to the Steamboat Inspection Service and Bureau of Standards. As the U.S. economy continued to expand, labor began pressuring the government for a return of its own department, but this time with cabinet status. On William Taft's last day as president, March 4, 1913, he signed legislation giving labor cabinet status and changing the Department of Labor and Commerce to the Department of Commerce. The following day, March 5, newly elected President Woodrow Wilson appointed William C. Redfield (1858-1932) as the first secretary of commerce. The new secretary oversaw the Coast and Geodetic Survey, the Steamboat Inspection Service, and the Bureaus of Corporations, Census, Lighthouses, Standards, Navigation, Fisheries, and Foreign and Domestic Commerce. By 1998 the DoC had grown to be one of the government's largest and most diverse cabinet departments, with 33,000 employees and a $4.9 billion budget.

The secretary of commerce is a cabinet position and oversees all the functions and authorities assigned to the DoC. Offices under the secretary include the Business Liaison Office, the Consumer Affairs Office, and the Office of Small and Disadvantaged Business Utilization. The latter functions as an advocate for guaranteeing that **small businesses** and businesses owned by women and minorities receive their maximum fair share of DoC **contracts** and subcontracts. The undersecretary for economic affairs advises the secretary and other government agencies and officials on microeconomic and macroeconomic trends. The undersecretary is also the administrator of the Economics and Statistics Administration and in that role supervises the Bureau of the Census and the Bureau of Economic Analysis.

The Bureau of the Census was established as a permanent office in 1902 to conduct a population census every ten years, a census of state and local governments and various commercial activities every five years, as well as monthly, quarterly, and annual surveys on a wide variety of subjects and activities. The Bureau of Economic Analysis is known as the ''nation's economic accountant.'' The bureau attempts, through the integration and interpretation of economic data, to compile a comprehensive picture of the U.S. economy. The Bureau of Export Administration promotes and controls the export of U.S. goods and the Economic Development Administration targets federal resources to economically distressed areas and local areas in need of economic development.

The largest bureau within the DoC is the National Oceanic and Atmospheric Administration (NOAA). The mission of NOAA is to provide the DoC with an overall assessment of those environmental issues and environmental phenomena that affect the country and its economy. This is accomplished through the National Weather Service; the National Environmental Satellite, Data, and Information Service; the National Marine Fisheries Service; the National Ocean Service; the Office of Oceanic and Atmospheric Research; and the Office of NOAA Corps Operations. The latter is responsible for maintaining NOAA's fleet of ships and planes used in fulfillment of its mission.

Other DoC agencies having self-describing titles include the International Trade Administration, the Minority Business Development Agency, the National Telecommunications and Information Administration, and the Patent and Trademark Office.

The Office of Technology Policy, the National Institute of Standards and Technology, and the National Technical Information Service fall under the purview of the DoC's Technology Administration.

[Michael Knes]

FURTHER READING:

Greenberger, Robert S. ''Commerce Department Admits It Erred in Matter of Hughes Report to China.'' *Wall Street Journal,* 9 July 1998, B7.

——. ''U.S. Faces Probe of Role in Aiding China in Analyzing 1995 Rocket-Launch Crash.'' *Wall Street Journal,* 24 June 1998, A8.

Magnusson, Paul. ''Commerce: Keep the Business, Lose the Sleaze.'' *Business Week,* 10 February 1997, 38.

Miller, William H. ''Commerce Back on Track.'' *Industry Week,* 20 July 1998, 46+.

''The New Daley Machine.'' *Economist,* 1 February 1997, 34.

U.S. Department of Commerce. *From Lighthouse to Laserbeams: A History of the U.S. Department of Commerce.* Washington: U.S. Department of Commerce, Office of the Secretary, 1995.

——. ''U.S. Department of Commerce.'' Washington: U.S. Department of Commerce, 1998. Available from www.doc.gov.

U.S. Government Manual. Washington: GPO, 1998.

U.S. INFLATION-ADJUSTED SECURITIES

INFLATION-PROTECTED U.S. TREASURY NOTES

Beginning in 1997, the U.S. Treasury began issuing a new series of savings **securities** that have their returns linked to the rate of **inflation**. For many years, **risk**-averse investors have been purchasing U.S. savings bonds as a safe-haven from credit risks and the risks of the **stock market**. These new securities, called ''inflation-protected securities'' or TIPS, provide investors protection against not only both of these risks, but inflation as well. Like other Treasury instruments, TIPS are guaranteed by the U.S. government so they are free from **default** risk.

The new securities, which were promoted by Treasury Secretary Robert Rubin, carry a fixed rate of interest, which is set when the securities are originally sold and is paid semiannually. The security's principal is adjusted semiannually by the change in the nonseasonally adjusted U.S. City Average All Items Consumer Price Index for All Urban Consumers (CPI-U) causing the semiannual interest payment to be a function of the fixed rate multiplied by the adjusted face amount of the security. It is this adjustment in the principal that affords investors the inflation protection.

A major component in the determination of any **interest rate** is the premium for inflation. At the time of issuance, the coupon rates on traditional Treasury instruments, so-called ''risk-free'' rates, reflect this premium. Because of their inflation adjustment, however, the coupon rate offered on TIPS is lower than other Treasury securities with comparable maturities. If the coupon rate reflected the inflation premium, there would be, in essence, double payment for the inflation premium.

To illustrate how this works, assume a $1,000 face inflation-indexed note was sold with a 3.5 percent yield. If there were no change in the CPI-U from the time the security was issued, the investor would receive a semiannual interest payment of $17.50 ($1,000 × .035 ÷ 2). If the CPI-U were to increase by 2 percent, the principal of the note would increase to $1,020 ($1,000 × 1.02) and the semiannual interest payments would rise to $17.85 ($1,020 × .035 ÷ 2). The interest payment is based on the immediately adjusted principal. So, using our example, if inflation rose 2 percent during the first six months of a TIPS existence, the first interest payment the investor would receive would be $17.85. Further, at maturity the investor would receive the final inflation-adjusted principal amount or the par amount at original issue, whichever was greater. Recently, due to the low rate of inflation, concern has arisen that we may enter a period of deflation. Should the CPI-U decrease, the principal amount of TIPS will also decrease, but not below the original principal.

This does not come without a **tax** cost, however. The interest payments are subject to federal income taxes in the year received, plus, the amount of the periodic principal inflation adjustment is treated as ordinary income and is taxable in the year of adjustment, even though the principal will not be paid until maturity. Like all U.S. Treasury securities, the interest on inflation-adjusted securities is exempt from state and local taxes. Because of the tax treatment of the principal adjustment, many financial planners recommend using TIPS only in tax deferred retirement accounts such as **individual retirement accounts** (IRAs). The wisdom of this can be appreciated if inflation should return to the higher rates of the 1980s. It would then be mathematically possible for the tax bill on a TIPS to be greater than the annual cash interest payments received!

TIPS are sold at quarterly auctions held the first month of each calendar quarter. As is true with all Treasury security auctions, winning competitive bids are awarded at a single price. Noncompetitive tenders are accepted in the range of $1,000 to $5,000,000 and are also issued at the single price. Because of the inflation adjustment to a TIPS' principal, their coupon interest rate tends to be lower than regular Treasury securities. For example, the TIPS maturing in July 2002 have a coupon rate of 3.625 percent; the Treasury note maturing the same month has a coupon rate of 6 percent. Thus, the coupon rate on these securities comes very close to being an estimate of the so-called ''real'' interest rate. Because of the recent budget surplus, the Treasury has announced plans to cut the amount of inflation-indexed securities sold at periodic auctions. In addition, the Treasury is considering the frequency of some new issues.

All sales are in book-entry form—no actual securities are issued. All TIPS are eligible for stripping into their principal and interest components. To date, TIPS have been sold as notes with maturities of five and ten years and as bonds with a 30-year maturity. TIPS can be purchased through a broker for a fee or directly from the Treasury Department, similar to other Treasury notes and bonds.

There is a very active secondary market for TIPS. As a result, they can be resold before maturity through a broker or the Treasury's Sell Direct program. Like other debt instruments, TIPS are subject to interest rate risk. Therefore, as market interest rates change, the market value of TIPS will fluctuate. TIPS are included in the daily government securities quotation in the leading financial press. They are typically reported in a separate section entitled inflation-indexed treasury securities. Like other Treasury instruments, they trade in 32nds of a dollar. The quotations include the coupon rate and the inflation-adjusted (accrued) principal. The reported yield to maturity is based on the adjusted principal (see Table 1).

These securities are an ideal way for investors to avoid inflation risk and therefore protect purchasing power. With traditional **bonds**, both corporate and governmental, real returns to investors decrease as inflation increases. With TIPS, however, because the principal is adjusted by the CPI-U, inflation risk disappears. The relative attractiveness of TIPS depends on the general level of interest rates vis-à-vis the rate of inflation and the shape of the **yield curve**. On the negative side, the yield of TIPS will likely remain below the long-term average for equity investments. As a result, investors should seek vehicles other than TIPS if they are concerned about the impact of inflation on items whose rate of increase in cost has typically been greater than the CPI-U.

INFLATION-INDEXED SAVINGS BONDS

Because of the booming stock market in the late 1990s, sales of traditional U.S. savings bonds have fallen from their peak of $17.5 billion annually to slightly over $5 billion. In an attempt to attract small investors back to savings bonds, the U.S. Treasury in

Table 1
Quotations of Inflation-Indexed Treasury Securities As of January 29,1999

Rate	Maturity	Bid/Asked	Change	Yield*	Accrued Principal
3.625	07/02	99-28/29	+0.01	3.634	1024
3.375	01/07	97-07/08	-0.02	3.773	1035
3.625	01/08	98-27/28	. . .	3.766	1015
3.875	01/09	100-28/29	-0.02	3.757	1000
3.625	04/28	98-25/26	-0.05	3.690	1014

*Yield to maturity on accrued principal.

September 1998 began offering U.S. savings bonds that have their returns tied to the rate of inflation (I-bonds). These bonds are sold at their principal amounts, unlike Series EE bonds, which are sold at discounts. The face amounts of I-bonds range from $50 to $10,000. Fixed interest rates for new purchases are set twice a year, in May and November, and prevail for all purchases during the six-month period and remain for the life of the bond. In addition to the fixed rate, there is an inflation component derived from the CPI U (see above). This component is adjusted twice a year, also in May and November. The total yield on the bond is the sum of the fixed rate and the inflation component. The bonds can be purchased at **banks**, **savings and loan associations**, and other authorized **financial institutions**. Purchases are also available through some payroll savings plans. These bonds are seen as attractive alternatives to those investors still keeping savings in low-yielding bank accounts.

I-bonds do not pay periodic cash interest payments. Instead, the interest is compounded semiannually and paid when the bond is redeemed. I-bonds can earn interest for up to 30 years. Unlike other savings bonds, they cannot be exchanged for other series of savings bonds. Like Series EEs, the bonds must be held at least six months before redemption and if they are redeemed less than five years after purchase, investors must forfeit one quarter's interest. In the event of a negative CPI-U (i.e., deflation) the inflation adjustment is reduced and if deflation is severe, the adjustment can cause a negative inflation component, driving the total return below the fixed return. The Treasury has announced, however, that the combined interest rate will not be allowed to go below zero. So, to that extent, investors in I-bonds are not only protected against inflation, but deflation, as well.

Unlike TIPS, but similar to Series EE bonds, investors may elect to have the income from I-bonds taxed on either the cash or accrual basis. If the cash basis is elected, any increase in principal value will not be taxed until the bonds are redeemed. Should an investor elect the cash basis, the cash basis must be used for all I-bonds and any other savings bonds purchased on a discount basis (e.g., Series EE). I-bonds are eligible for tax benefits upon their redemption when the proceeds are used for qualifying education expenses.

SEE ALSO: U.S. Treasury Notes

[Ronald M. Horwitz]

FURTHER READING:

Lexington Software Corporation. ''United States Savings Bond Public Information Pages.'' Milwaukee: Lexington Software Corporation, 1999. Available from www.savingsbond.com.

U.S. Department of the Treasury. ''Welcome to the U.S. Department of Treasury.'' Washington: U.S. Department of the Treasury, 1999. Available from www.ustreas.gov.

U.S. INTERNATIONAL TRADE COMMISSION

The International Trade Commission (ITC) of the United States is an independent federal agency charged with providing foreign trade analysis and recommendations concerning foreign trade to the legislative and federal branches of the U.S. government. The ITC is bipartisan and objective in its operations.

The ITC was established in 1916 as the U.S. Tariff Commission. The agency took its present name in 1974. The ITC's goal is to determine the effect of imports on American industry. ITC economists also gather data on international trade and disseminate this information to various government branches and agencies, as well as the public. The ITC serves only in an advisory capacity. It cannot negotiate with foreign governments nor does it set policy. The ITC can, however, direct action against unfair trade practices relating to **copyright**, **patent**, and trademark infringement, and the ITC also revises and publishes the Harmonized Tariff Schedule of the United States. The responsibilities and duties of the ITC are defined in numerous legislative acts including the Tariff Act of 1930, the Trade Expansion Act of 1962, the Trade Act of 1974, the Trade Agreements Act of 1979, and the Omnibus Trade and Competitiveness Act of 1988.

A tariff is a **duty** or **tax** imposed by a government on imports and occasionally exports. The purpose of a tariff is to protect home markets. In the United States, Congress is the sole authority for regulating commerce with foreign countries. Since its inception, the U.S. government had been under pressure to create some sort of a tariff commission. As the economy grew and trade expanded so did the pressure for such a commission. It was felt by many that a nonpolitical independent agency could best provide the unbiased technical information required by the government to make sound trade and tariff decisions. In 1882 Congress created a temporary trade commission and in 1888 legislation was introduced to make the commission permanent. The bill passed the Senate but failed in the House in 1889. During President William Howard Taft's term in office (1909-13) he created a Tariff Board, but like its predecessor, it proved to be temporary. President Woodrow Wilson, under pressure from the U.S. Chamber of Commerce, the American Federation of Labor, and the Tariff Commission League, asked Congress to pass legislation creating a permanent tariff agency. The Tariff Commission was subsequently created in 1916. Under the Trade Act of 1974 it became the U.S. International Trade Commission with expanded powers and greater independence. The 1974 act removed the ITC's budget from the purview of the executive branch and gave the commission the power to review and issue remedies to trade infractions, subject to court review.

The ITC has many responsibilities and activities including: determining whether U.S. industries are being damaged by imports subsidized by a foreign government or imports priced less than their fair value; taking action against various unfair trade practices such as patent, trademark, or copyright infringement—subject to presidential approval; determining whether agricultural imports interfere with U.S. Department of Agriculture price-support programs; conducting surveys and gathering information on trade and tariff levels; monitoring import levels; developing uniform statistical data on imports, exports, and domestic production; and being involved in the establishment of an international harmonized commodity code. It is important to remember that the ITC does not make policy, negotiate trade agreements, or serve as a judicial body.

Two of the most important responsibilities of the ITC are determinating whether or not the fair importation of foreign goods is hurting a domestic industry and whether or not **dumping** is taking place. A domestic industry faces injury if competing foreign goods were to be brought into the country in overwhelming quantities. In such a scenario the ITC has the responsibility to recommend to the executive branch a rise in the tariff or an adjustment in the import quota of the good in question so as to protect the home industry. Dumping involves the importation and selling of foreign goods at less than the fair market price or the unfair subsidization of that imported good by a foreign government. Both actions could ultimately result in the home industry being forced out of business. In such a case increased duties equal to the dumping margin could be imposed. In matters of dumping allegations the ITC works closely with the **U.S. Department of Commerce**. The Commerce Department generally investigates whether or not dumping takes place while the ITC investigates as to whether or not a U.S. industry has been injured by the dumping practice.

Complaints of such unfair trade practices can be lodged with the ITC by representatives of an American industry. The commission has 30 days to decide whether or not to pursue the investigation. If the ITC chooses to investigate, it has one year to reach a decision. Complainants must show a relationship between the import and the injury and the relationship must be clearly documented. Such a complaint would be investigated by the commission's Unfair Import Investigation Division. The case could be tried before an administrative law judge and eventually appealed to a federal court. In such trials safeguards are often instituted so as to protect confidential technical information and marketing strategies.

The ITC is headed by six commissioners who are nominated by the president and confirmed by the U.S. Senate. From these six commissioners, no more than three of whom can be from any one political party, the president designates a chairman and vice-chairman. These two officers must be from different political parties and the chairman must be of a different political party than the preceding chairman. Both officers serve terms of two years while commissioners serve overlapping terms of nine years.

The ITC also has a Trade Remedy Assistance Office that aids small businesses and the public with relief from or benefits of U.S. trade laws. This office offers general information on the above as well as technical advice and legal assistance. The ITC also maintains its National Library of International Trade and the ITC Law Library.

[Michael Knes]

FURTHER READING:

Dobson, John M. *Two Centuries of Tariffs: The Background and Emergence of the U.S. International Trade Commission.* Washington: International Trade Commission, 1976.

Hansen, Wendy L., and Thomas J. Prusa. "The Economics and Politics of Trade Policy: An Empirical Analysis of ITC Decision Making." *Review of International Economics* 5, no. 2 (May 1997): 230-45.

United States International Trade Commission. "U.S. International Trade Commission." Washington: United States International Trade Commission, 1998. Available from www.usitc.gov.

U.S. SECURITIES AND EXCHANGE COMMISSION

SEE: Securities and Exchange Commission, U.S.

U.S. TREASURY BILLS

Popularly known as T-bills, U.S. Treasury bills are short-term debt securities issued by the U.S. Department of the Treasury. They generally come in three maturities: 13 weeks (also cited as three months or 91 days), 26 weeks (six months or 182 days), and 52 weeks (one year or 364 days). Along with other longer-term Treasury instruments such as **U.S. Treasury notes** (1- to 10-year maturities) and bonds (30-year maturities), T-bills are widely held, highly liquid, and low-risk investments. Most trading in T-bills, however, is done by institutional investors such as **banks**, brokerages, investment funds, and other types of firms.

Two markets exist for T-bills and other Treasury securities: the primary market and the secondary market. The primary market is through periodic auctions by the U.S. Treasury. They may then be resold any number of times on the secondary market, where they often serve as **money market instruments**, or short-term, low-risk, low-yield repositories for large sums of money. Interest earned on T-bills is tax-exempt at the state and local levels. Another attractive feature of T-bills is that they may be purchased in denominations as low as $10,000, which is considerably smaller than the minimum denominations of many other money market instruments, which may be $1 million or more apiece. This active secondary market ensures that Treasuries are highly liquid and flexible investments.

PRIMARY MARKET

The Treasury holds auctions for the 13-week and 26-week T-bills every Monday (or the next business day when the financial markets are closed on Monday). Auctions for the 52-week bill occur on Tuesdays every fourth week. Details on all upcoming auctions, including the total face value to be issued of each maturity, are announced weekly on Thursdays. New T-bills are actually issued a few days after the auction, typically on Thursdays.

Investors submit bids on either a competitive or noncompetitive basis. Competitive bidders state the price they are willing to pay, and noncompetitive bidders agree to accept the average price of all accepted bids. At the auction, the Treasury first accepts all noncompetitive bids, and then accepts competitive bids in descending order of price until the total face value of that maturity is sold. For example, if the Treasury wishes to issue $10 billion in 13-week bills and $6 billion in noncompetitive bids has been received, only the first $4 billion in competitive bids, beginning with the highest, will be accepted.

The price paid by the noncompetitive bidders is equal to the weighted average of the competitive bids; in the example, the weighted average bid for the $4 billion worth of bills. The results of each auction are summarized in the *Wall Street Journal* and on numerous Internet sites, including the Treasury's Web site.

T-bills are sold at a discount, and prices are quoted as a percentage of the maturity value. The discount is the difference between the face value and the purchase price, and represents the interest earned on the investment. Unlike Treasuries with longer maturities, T-bills don't pay periodic interest payments; the full value of the interest is factored into the discount and earned if the bill is held to maturity.

The *discount rate,* also called the discount yield, on T-bills is determined by the competitively determined purchase price and may be calculated using the bank-discount method as follows:

$$r = \left(\frac{M - P}{M}\right) \times \left(\frac{360}{D}\right)$$

where r = discount rate
M = maturity (face) value
P = purchase (discount) value
D = days to maturity

For example, if the average purchase price at auction for a 13-week bill is $98.835 per $100 of par value, the discount yield would be found as follows:

$$r = \left(\frac{\$100 - \$98.835}{\$100}\right) \times \left(\frac{360}{91}\right) = 4.608\%$$

However, for some purposes the discount rate is believed to underestimate the real return on investment because it is the rate of return on the face value of the bill, rather than the return on the amount actually invested (i.e., the purchase price). As an alternative, some prefer to calculate the *investment rate* as follows:

$$r = \left(\frac{M - P}{P}\right) \times \left(\frac{365}{D}\right)$$

where r = investment rate
M = maturity (face) value
P = purchase (discount) value
D = days to maturity

Note that the investment rate formula uses 365 days (or 366 in a leap year) instead of 360 (which is based on 12 30-day months) as the numerator over time to maturity. In the example above, the investment rate would be determined as follows:

$$r = \left(\frac{\$100 - \$98.835}{\$98.835}\right) \times \left(\frac{365}{91}\right) = 4.728\%$$

Thus, the investment rate, also known as the equivalent coupon yield or the effective yield, tends to show a return that is 10 to 20 basis points higher than the discount yield indicates. Summary reports of Treasury auctions often show both the discount yield and the investment yield.

A quick estimation of a T-bill yield may be done by taking the discount value per $100 (so if the purchase price is $98.835, the discount is $1.165), and multiplying it by the number of maturities that make up a year for that kind of bill (e.g., there are four 13-week and two 26-week maturities in a year). Hence, a rough estimate of the yield on the 13 week T-bill bought at $98.835 would be $1.165 × 4, or 4.66 percent. In this case, the estimate falls in between the calculated discount rate and the investment rate.

Money center banks, securities dealers, and other institutional investors submit the majority of competitive bids in T-bill auctions. Individuals may purchase new issues of T-bills in several ways: (1) from the Treasury's Bureau of Public Debt or one of the Federal Reserve Banks (a paper bid can be mailed); (2) over the phone or the Internet through the TreasuryDirect system; or (3) through a broker or bank.

SECONDARY MARKET

Government securities dealers are responsible for providing an active secondary market in all U.S. government securities, and especially in Treasury securities. The price at which dealers are willing to buy is called the bid price and the price at which they are willing to sell is called the asked price. The difference between these prices is called the spread, which is the dealer's compensation for brokering the transaction.

Secondary market trading of T-bills is typically reported in the financial news in terms of the discount rate bid and asked, instead of the purchase and selling prices per unit of face value, as is done in the primary market. For example, a secondary market listing may show that a T-bill with 30 days left to maturity was bid at 3.87 percent and asked at 3.83 percent. Both the bid and asked price are calculated using the bank-discount method given by

$$P = M - \left(M \times r \times \frac{D}{360}\right)$$

where P = purchase (discount) value
M = maturity (face) value
r = discount rate
D = days to maturity

In the example above, the bid price on a $10,000 T-bill with 30 days left to maturity would be

$$P = \$10{,}000 - \left(\$10{,}000 \times 0.0387 \times \frac{30}{360}\right) = \$9{,}967.75$$

and the asked price would be

$$P = \$10{,}000 - \left(\$10{,}000 \times 0.0383 \times \frac{30}{360}\right) = \$9{,}968.08$$

Since the spread is the asked price less the bid price, in this example the dealer's spread is $9,968.08 − $9,967.75, or a modest $0.33 per $10,000. Since the dealer is likely handling millions of dollars worth of T-bills, this would amount to a more substantial profit when the total value of the bills is considered. For the buyer who pays the asked price, the yield if held to maturity would be calculated by the investment return rate formula above, which would equal 3.896 percent. Financial papers typically publish this amount under the heading ''ask yield'' or something on that order.

In order for the dealer to have a positive spread, i.e., to make a profit, the asked price is always higher than the bid price. Because price and discount rate have an inverse relationship, this means the asked discount rate is always slightly lower than the bid rate, typically by just a few basis points. Spreads tend to be more narrow the longer the time left to maturity.

SEE ALSO: Bonds; U.S. Treasury Notes

FURTHER READING:

Federal Reserve Bank of New York. ''Fedpoint 28: Estimating Yields on Treasury Securities.'' *Fedpoints.* New York, 1998. Available from www.ny.frb.org/pihome/fedpoint.

U.S. Department of Treasury. Bureau of Public Debt. *T-Bills, Notes, and Bonds.* Washington, 1999. Available from www.publicdebt.treas.gov/sec/sec.htm.

U.S. TREASURY NOTES

U.S. Treasury notes (T-notes) are **debts** with intermediate maturities of one to ten years issued by the U.S. Department of the Treasury. The Treasury issues T-notes in minimum denominations of $1,000. T-notes (and **bonds**) are issued in book entry form, which requires the Treasury to establish an account for the owner.

Treasury notes are sold at auction with both competitive and noncompetitive bids accepted. Noncompetitive bids are handled identically to Treasury bills auctions and are limited to a maximum of $5 million from a single bidder. Noncompetitive bids can now be made over the **Internet**, by phone, or by paper forms.

Unlike bill auctions where a rate of discount is indicated, bidders in T-note auctions indicate a yield to maturity. Now, T-notes, like all Treasury **securities**, are sold at a single price auction. The practice of awarding winning bids at multiple prices has been discontinued. Each successful competitive and noncompetitive bidder is now awarded securities at the price equivalent to the highest accepted rate or yield (i.e., lowest price) of accepted competitive tenders. Given the yield from an auction, accepted at auction, the Treasury sets the stated **interest rate** on new notes at the nearest 1/8 percentage point that produces an average auction price slightly below par.

T-notes are issued on a rotational basis throughout the year as follows: two-year maturities are issued monthly; five- and ten-year notes are issued quarterly during the second month of the calendar quarter. Because of the recent large budget surplus, the Treasury has announced it will be reducing the size of five- and ten-year Treasury note auctions and possibly reducing the frequency of the two-year note auctions.

Unlike **U.S. Treasury bills** (T-bills) which have no coupon or stated rate of interest, Treasury notes (and bonds) do carry stated rates as determined at the time of sale; they also pay interest semiannually. While T-bills will always sell at a discount, the market prices of T-notes will change in the same way as corporate **bonds**. Therefore, T-notes will sell at a discount or premium depending upon whether market interest rates move above, or below, the note's stated rate. Currently, all outstanding Treasury notes are noncallable.

There is also an extremely active market in T-note **futures contracts**. The Chicago Board of Trade began trading in Treasury note futures in June 1979. The basic trading unit is $100,000 of face value. T-note futures have become one of the most popular forms of interest rate futures. They are widely used to hedge against adverse interest rate movements.

PROS AND CONS OF T-NOTE INVESTING

Treasury notes, like other U.S. Treasury debt, have several advantages. The interest received is subject to federal income **taxes**, but exempt from state and local income taxes. Like other debt securities, the longer the maturity of a T-note, the greater its interest rate risk. T-notes also enjoy an extremely active secondary market, similar to other Treasury issues. Security firms and commercial depositories offer a wide variety of notes in amounts and maturities to accommodate a broad range of investors. Government securities dealers are charged with maintaining the liquidity of this market.

Since T-notes are available in the secondary market in a wide variety of maturities, an investor can select a maturity (and yield) corresponding to the investor's requirements. Given the shape of the **yield curve**, the existence of T-notes frequently offers investors the opportunity to take advantage of intermediate term yields, which are just a few basis points lower than long-term rates. In the fall of 1998, however, intermediate term T-notes were actually yielding less than shorter term T-bills. Thus, the investor cannot, in today's volatile money markets, make any assumption regarding the yields of T-notes relative to shorter or longer maturities.

T-note rates are often used as bellwether indicators for rates on home **mortgages**. Traditionally, changes in the ten-year maturity T-note rates were the best indicators of changes in mortgage rates. Recently, however, with the dramatic increase in the pace of mortgage **refinancing**, yields on shorter-term T-notes, usually with around three- to five-year maturities, are thought to be better indicators.

TREASURY NOTE QUOTATIONS

T-note prices are reported daily in the *Wall Street Journal,* together with their yields to maturity. Since they are listed with Treasury bonds, most quotation sources use the letter *n* after the instrument's year of maturity to designate a note. T-notes trade in 32nds of a dollar. Hence, a price quotation of 98:16 (note the use of the colon to designate 32nds) equals $985.00. Table 1 presents the prices and yields of selected T-notes based on January 29, 1999 trades. Quotations used by traders often include a "+" which raises the price to the next 64th (e.g., 98:12+ = 98 25/64).

The yields to maturity are computed like any other debt instrument, being equal to that interest rate, which compares the **present value** of the remaining interest payments and the face amount of the note to the current price of the T-note.

STRIPS

To accommodate a huge market demand for risk-free zero coupon bonds, the Treasury initiated Separate Trading of Registered Interest and Principal of Securities Notes (STRIPS). Financial institutions and

Table 1
U.S. Treasury Note Quotations
As for January 29,1999

Stated Interest Rate	Maturity Mo/Yr	Asked Price	Yield Based on Asked Price
4 1/2%	Jan 01n	99:27	4.58%
4 1/4%	Jan 03n	98:24	4.54%
5 7/8%	Nov 05n	106:24	4.70%
4 3/4%	Nov 08n	100:25	4.65%

government securities brokers and dealers may request that the Treasury book the interest and principal separately to facilitate the timely payment of a wide variety of zero bond rates and maturities. Quotations for STRIPS appear with those for other Treasury instruments in the *Wall Street Journal.* Instruments that are stripped principal of T-notes are indicated by ''np''; stripped interest is indicated by ''ci.'' Strips are subject to the taxation features of **original issue discount** instruments.

FOREIGN-TARGETED NOTES

In October 1984 the Treasury instituted securities designed especially for foreign institutions and foreign branches of U.S. banks who certify that, on the day of issuance, they will place these notes only with non-U.S. citizens. After a 45-day period, foreign investors may exchange these notes for comparable domestic issues, or sell them to U.S. citizens. The Treasury sets the interest rate according to the results of the auction of the companion domestic issue and provides book-entry form during the 45-day waiting period. Afterwards, the Treasury makes registered notes available.

SEE ALSO: U.S. Treasury Bills

[Ronald M. Horwitz]

FURTHER READING:

Board of Governors of the Federal Reserve. *The Federal Reserve System: Purposes and Functions.* 7th ed. Washington DC: Board of Governors of the Federal Reserve, 1984.

——. *1989 Historical Chart Book.* Washington DC: Board of Governors of the Federal Reserve, 1990.

Kahn, Milton. *The Complete Guide to Buying U.S. Treasury Bills, Notes, and Bonds from the Federal Government.* Denver: Klondike Publishing, 1995.

Kleege, Steven. ''Does Treasury Know How to Make a Buck.'' *Business Week,* 17 October 1994.

Ricchiuto, Steve R. *The Rate Reference Guide to the U.S. Treasury Market.* Probus Publishing, 1990.

Ricchiuto, Steve R., and Barclays de Zoete Wedd. *The Rate Reference Guide to the U.S. Treasury Market.* 2nd ed. Chicago: Irwin Professional Publishing, 1996.

Rosen, Jan M. ''U.S. Easing the Route to Buying Treasuries.'' *New York Times,* 9 August 1998.

U.S. Department of the Treasury. Bureau of Public Debt. ''T-Bills, Notes, and Bonds.'' Washington: Bureau of Public Debt, U.S. Department of the Treasury, 12 August 1998. Available from www.treasurydirect.gov.

U.S.-CANADA FREE TRADE AGREEMENT OF 1989

The U.S.-Canada Free Trade Agreement of 1989 (FTA) represented a bilateral agreement between the world's largest trading partners. The United States and Canada have more trade between them than any other two countries on earth. At the time of the agreement, the United States and Canada traded roughly $150 billion worth of goods a year.

Negotiations on the FTA began in 1985, and the pact actually was agreed to on 4 October 1987. Following approval by the legislative bodies of both nations in 1988, the agreement officially took effect on 1 January 1989. The historic pact was the culmination of more than 100 years of on-again, off-again talk of **free trade** between the United States and its northern North American neighbor.

The issue actually caused much more of a stir in Canada than in the United States. Polls taken at the time of the debate indicated that more than 40 percent of Americans were not even aware that the two nations had signed such an agreement, compared with just 3 percent of Canadians. In the United States, the FTA did not garner nearly as much press as did the **North American Free Trade Agreement** (NAFTA), the pact between the United States, Canada, and Mexico that came about five years later, and which incorporated most FTA provisions into its framework.

In Canada, however, the FTA was the subject of long and heated debate. The Liberal party in Canada even used the FTA to force an election—with free trade virtually the only subject of the campaign. The reason for the disparity in emotion on the issue becomes readily apparent upon examination of the comparative economic situations. For the United States, while trade with Canada is significant, it is not all that large when taken as a portion of the whole economy. From the Canadian standpoint, though, United States investment and trade is a fairly hefty percentage of the economy.

After all the talk and debate, the FTA was adopted and took effect on time—with the understanding that the agreement was an evolving document with mechanisms for changing and problem solving. What the FTA tried to do is put simply in the objectives agreed to by the two nations:

- eliminate barriers to trade in goods and services between the two countries;
- facilitate conditions of fair competition within the free trade area;
- significantly expand liberalization of conditions for cross-border investment;
- establish effective procedures for the joint administration of the agreement and the resolution of disputes; and
- lay the foundation for further bilateral and multilateral cooperation to expand and enhance the benefits of the agreement.

On the last point, the FTA apparently has been successful, as it helped lay the foundation for NAFTA, although certain differences do exist between the two agreements.

HISTORY AND BACKGROUND

When the FTA finally took effect in 1989, the issue of free trade talk between the two nations had a history that went back into the 1850s. In 1854, there actually was a reciprocal free trade agreement signed that lasted until 1866, when the United States terminated the pact.

That agreement actually was negotiated between the United States and Great Britain, because the five British colonial provinces that existed back then had not yet become nations. The agreement basically covered commodities such as natural resources and agricultural products. Although manufactured products were not part of the pact, about two-thirds of trade between the then-30 United States and the Canadian provinces were covered.

There were attempts to make this agreement into a common market—where both areas would set unified tariffs for all third parties—but those efforts came to an end when the United States terminated the agreement in 1866. The United States appeared to take this action as protectionism began to develop in the United States during and after the Civil War.

During the next 45 years, first Canada and then the United States tried to bring back the free trade agreement, but protectionism on one or the other's part stalled progress each time. An informal agreement that was never ratified came about in 1911 after a tariff war that took place in 1907. Canada started by adopting a three-tiered tariff system that greatly affected the United States, which retaliated in 1909. An oral agreement on a free trade pact was reached in January 1911, put into a formal letter by the Canadian delegates, and then replied to formally by the United States Secretary of State, Philander Knox. But the Liberal party in Canada that negotiated the agreement was defeated in an election held because of the proposed free trade agreement, and the pact was never implemented.

The two nations held no further bilateral talks until 1935, when they agreed to what was termed a modest most-favored nation agreement. The two sides held negotiations again in 1948 but the Canadian government broke off the discussions.

Why the 1988 agreement succeeded where some of these earlier attempts did not is unclear, although a number of issues—including the **globalization** of the business world—no doubt had some impact. Some Canadians also wanted their nation protected from possible protectionist legislation they feared the United States might implement. Although most of the protectionist actions in the United States were aimed at Japan and the Far East, Canada thought it could be affected if the United States implemented emergency action under rules of the **General Agreement on Tariffs and Trade (GATT)**. Under GATT, all nations must be treated alike, and Canadians were afraid of the possibility of such measures from its largest trading partner.

DIFFERING OBJECTIVES

Leading up to the signing of the agreement, both the Canadian and American sides had objectives they wished to achieve. On one side, Canada had its high tariffs that encouraged foreign manufacturers to build plants in Canada for the Canadian market, as it would be more cost efficient than to service the market with exports. During the 1950s and 1960s the Canadian economy grew extensively and the nation had few programs that influenced market conditions. But in the 1970s and 1980s, Canadians became more concerned about the extensive control and possible influence of the United States multinationals that had operations in Canada. The Canadian government began screening foreign direct investment and adopted policies aimed at making Canada less dependent on the United States and more competitive on its own. Although the ownership and control of the United States in Canada's industry did lessen, the United States share of Canada's trade remained high and Canadian competitiveness did not improve.

Canadians who favored free trade began to believe that Canada's resource products would no longer sustain the nation, so the country should focus on its competitiveness in the manufacturing arena. Canada's tariffs, following seven rounds of GATT talks, were no longer high enough to shield it from foreign competition. What was keeping Canada from being competitive were nontariff barriers in foreign nations, and the threat of further such barriers, particularly in the United States

The Canadian government articulated four main objectives heading into discussions on the FTA: access to the United States market by limiting the effects of United States trade laws; enhance access to the United States market by eliminating tariffs and achieving more liberal nontariff barriers; ensure any gains through a strong agreement with an effective dispute settlement mechanism; and maintain policy discretion in cultural industries and foreign investment in some sensitive sectors.

From the United States side, officials saw the FTA as beneficial in several ways. Limitations of the GATT agreement had affected United States access to foreign markets for United States high-technology products. Various things such as trade-related investment policies, subsidies, treatment of intellectual property rights, government procurement practices, and product standards had limited the United States in trade.

In addition, the United States, by reaching this agreement with Canada, would be showing the **European Union**, Japan, and other nations that it was open to other trade possibilities if the ongoing Uruguay Round of the GATT talks did not bring substantial results.

The FTA also brought the United States a chance to eliminate the higher Canadian tariffs and to secure improvements made in the trade and investment climate. In nontariff barriers, the United States could get rid of or at least lessen discrimination of federal and provincial procurement practices along with barriers caused by technical standards and testing requirements.

BASIC TERMS

Over a ten-year period, the FTA was to eliminate tariffs, duty drawbacks, and most import restrictions. The phase-in was aimed at allowing certain industries to get used to the realization of competition in a free market environment.

There were three options for tariff removal. As of 1 January 1989, duties were eliminated in full on about 15 percent of all dutiable goods traded between the two nations. Some of the industries and products included skis, whiskey, vending machines, needles, fur, and computers.

Products that covered another 35 percent of dutiable goods were placed on a five-year elimination program, with the tariffs reduced by 20 percent each year beginning 1 January 1989. Aftermarket auto parts, chemicals, furniture, explosives, paints, some meats, paper, subway cars, and telecommunication equipment were some of the covered products.

The final 50 percent of dutiable products were put on a ten-year tariff reduction path, with 10 percent of the duty taken off each year, with the process ending 1 January 1998. Those products included: most agricultural products, appliances, beef, pleasure craft, railcars, softwood plywood, steel, textiles and apparel, and tires. With regard to automotive products, tariffs were phased out on vehicles that meet a 50-percent content rule, where half the content must come from the two nations.

The FTA also prohibits restrictions on exports, export taxes and subsidies, and the dual pricing of exports. There were, however, a few safeguards. During the ten-year phase-in period, duties could be restored for up to three years if domestic producers prove suffering because of the reductions.

Also included were measures to standardize environmental provisions, such as pesticide and emissions regulations, usually by lowering Canadian protection standards to more lenient U.S. levels.

Both nations also will give each other's subsidiaries what is known as ''foreign treatment'' with regard to foreign investment. Canada did reserve the right to screen direct purchases of its largest nonfinancial corporations and financial institutions. That nation's cultural industries were exempted from most provisions of the agreement.

For settling disputes, the FTA set up a five-person panel with two members from the United States, two from Canada, and one decided by the other four members or chosen at random from an approved list. Issues will be referred when either side feels the other has made an unfair judgment under trade laws. The dispute-settlement process was expected to develop a set of mutually agreed rules about what constitutes dumping and subsidies, among other things.

GETTING IT APPROVED

In the United States the process was relatively quiet. President Reagan put the FTA on the fast-track process for congressional approval. That meant the Congress had only so many days to debate it and then had to either accept it or reject it in its entirety. They could not amend the agreement in any way. The United States House of Representatives approved it 9 July 1988, while the Senate followed suit on 9 September. Neither vote was close.

In Canada, however, there was no equivalent to the fast-track process. Under its parliamentary form of government, the House of Commons passed the matter easily because the majority of seats were held by the Progressive Conservative party, was led by Prime Minister Brian Mulroney.

But the Canadian Senate is not an elected body. Senators are appointed for life by the prime minister. Because the Liberal party had been in power for most of the 15 years prior to the FTA, that party had a majority of Senate seats and blocked passage. The Liberals used the debate to force a general election to break the impasse, and the election became an emotional debate on free trade and its impact on Canada. When the votes were counted, the conservatives still had a majority, although reduced, and the Liberal party did not oppose the voice of the people and allowed the FTA to go through.

Canadians were so aware of the debate because the impact on them was far greater than on United States citizens. Exports accounted for 28 percent of the Canadians' **gross national product**, compared with just 7 percent in the United States. And 80 percent of Canada's exports were destined to go to the United States.

Many Canadian critics felt vindicated in the years following the passage of the FTA, eyeing the contraction of employment across all industries between 1989 and 1993. The Canadian Labour Congress reported the loss of over 250, 000 jobs in the first two years of the Agreement, along with a wave of takeovers of Canadian-based countries. Some commentators, however suggest that the FTA was hardly a crucial factor in these numbers, and attribute them instead to other domestic economic policies like the fight against inflation.

DIFFERENCES WITH NAFTA

Besides bringing Mexico into the arena for free trade, the North American Free Trade Agreement (NAFTA) also broadened the parameters of the FTA between United States and Canada in many respects. Areas where NAFTA expounds upon FTA include **intellectual property** rights, land transportation, the environment, and several others. Below is a summary of some of the differences:

MARKET ACCESS. NAFTA makes no changes in the three-stage phase-out of tariffs for items traded between the United States and Canada.

RULES OF ORIGIN. NAFTA clears up many of the questions regarding rules of origin in the FTA and also integrates the administration of the rules. It includes a provision that allows up to 7 percent of the value of North American products to originate outside the continent. It also mandates that cars and light trucks have 62.5 percent of costs derive from North America to qualify for preferential treatment. For other vehicles, NAFTA specifies 60 percent North American content after a phase-in period.

NAFTA also makes the rules of origin simpler for certain electronics products and strengthens it for textiles. Fabric and yarn for garments must now come from North America, although there is a quota that allows a certain number of garments to qualify as North American in origin although they do not meet the rule.

CUSTOMS ISSUE. NAFTA extended by two years the deadline for elimination of duty drawback to 1 January 1996. Duty drawback is the refund of duties on imported inputs incorporated into products for export. NAFTA also allows trade and professional equipment duty-free treatment when brought in on a temporary basis by professionals covered by the provisions.

GOVERNMENT PROCUREMENT. NAFTA raises the guidelines on federal procurement of goods and services valued at over $50,000 ($25,000 on goods alone) and construction contracts that are valued at over $6.5 million. The provisions also cover certain government-owned corporations for contracts over $250,000 on goods and services and $10 million on construction contracts. These items are intended to allow firms from all three countries to compete on equal footing for government contracts over the threshold. For example, under the FTA, firms from the United States won 535 Canadian contracts worth in excess of $20 million between 1 January 1989 and 30 June 1992.

SERVICES. Under NAFTA, the provisions covering services are expanded to most every service sector. The agreement also eliminates federal and local restrictions on partner country access to services markets except in some instances, as well as citizenship or permanent-residency requirements on the licensing of professional service providers.

FINANCIAL SERVICES. NAFTA sets up a series of rules on trade and investment in financial services. It also ensures that United States firms in Canada can process financial data in the United States and gives access to NAFTA dispute settlement mechanisms for financial services firms.

INVESTMENT. NAFTA broadens guidelines regarding investors so that the definition includes non-NAFTA individuals who operate in a NAFTA country. NAFTA also covers real estate, stocks, bonds, and certain contracts and technologies, and provides binding arbitration in disputes between investors and any of the three governments involved in NAFTA.

INTELLECTUAL PROPERTY RIGHTS. Addressing a topic not detailed by the FTA, NAFTA extends patent protection to a minimum of 20 years; provides **copyright** protection for products such as computer programs, sound recordings, motion pictures, and satellite signals; and bolsters trademark protection, service markets, trade secrets, and other intellectual property rights.

LAND TRANSPORTATION. Another area not covered by FTA, NAFTA makes certain that future Canadian laws and policies will not discriminate unfairly against land transportation service providers in the United States.

ENVIRONMENT. In another new provision, NAFTA allows the three nations to keep their existing health, safety, and environmental standards and to impose new standards that can be scientifically justified and are not discriminatory.

[Bruce Meyer]

FURTHER READING:

Feinberg, Susan E., Michael P. Keane, and Mario Frank Bognanno. ''Trade Liberalization and 'Delocalization': New Evidence from Firm-Level Panel Data.'' *Canadian Journal of Economics,* October 1998, 749-777.

Gaston, Noel, and Daniel Trefler. ''The Labour Market Consequences of the Canada-U.S. Free Trade Agreement.'' *Canadian Journal of Economics,* February 1997, 18-41.

Siddiqui, Fakhari, ed. *The Economic Impact and Implications of the Canada-U.S. Free Trade Agreement.* Lewiston, NY: Edwin Mellen Press, 1991.

UN

SEE: United Nations

UNDERGROUND ECONOMY

The term ''underground economy'' refers to the part of the economy that generates income, but goes untaxed. According to Tibbett Speer in *American Demographics,* each year as much as $1 trillion of income goes unreported to the **Internal Revenue Service**. Moreover, the unreported amount appears to be growing, due partly to a rapid increase in small service companies and a large influx of illegal immigrants, according to Speer. Roughly 83 percent of the **taxes** Americans owe the government are paid voluntarily. Audits and other enforcement methods generate an additional 4 percent. However, the remaining 13 percent of potential tax revenue slips through the cracks.

A number of hypotheses have been advanced to explain the increasing practice of tax evasion. Some academic economists have studied the relationship between the tax rate and tax revenue collected. Young H. Jung, et al Arthur Snow, and Gregory Trandel suggest in the *Journal of Public Economics* that under certain assumptions regarding the risk-taking behavior of individuals, a rise in the tax rate increases the number of individuals who avoid paying taxes in that sector of the economy in which tax evasion is possible. The tax rate level, consequently, also affects the total amount of tax revenue evaded. Thus, Jung et al suggest that the design of tax policy itself sows seeds of the inevitability of tax evasion. Therefore, tax policy makers have to take care to craft a tax system that provides incentives to pay taxes and severely discourages the avoidance of tax payments.

One cannot put all the blame of underground economy on illegal immigrants or the design of the tax structure, however. The structure of the economy is itself to blame to a great extent. As mentioned earlier, the rapid growth of small service companies has contributed to the growing size of the underground economy. Some sections of the underground economy are truly ''underground,'' i.e., their activities are considered illegal. Thus, one does not pay taxes on what one cannot admit to doing. David Fettig points out in *Fedgazette* that illegal income is part of the underground economy in the United States. This hidden sector includes illegal drug dealing, illegal prostitution, unlawful gambling, and other criminal activity. Fettig argues that while the amount of money involved in criminal activity, and the subsequent tax revenue lost, is of interest to economists and policymakers, it is largely considered unrecoverable. Thus, if one considers the underground economy to be comprised of legal and illegal segments, policymakers realize that they can recover taxes only from the legal segment of the underground economy. Therefore, policymakers' attention is focused more towards the size of the underground economy as it relates to otherwise legal enterprises, like ''off-the-books'' hiring or unrecorded retail sales. These are activities that normally appear above ground and part of normal business activities, but sometimes go unreported or unrecorded—most often to avoid tax payments or the costs of meeting regulatory requirements. Fettig emphasizes that the underground economy's impact on economic statistics and on government programs are foremost in policymakers' minds when they think about this, because the goals of new policies may be thwarted in some way if they fail to consider the underground section of the economy.

[Anandi P. Sahu, Ph.D.]

FURTHER READING:

Benson, Ragnar. *Ragnar's Guide to the Underground Economy.* Paladin Press, 1999.

Fettig, David. "You Can't Tax What You Can't See." *Fedgazette,* April 1994.

Jung, Young H, Arthur Snow, and Gregory A. Trandel. "Tax Evasion and the Size of the Underground Economy." *Journal of Public Economics,* July 1994.

Lippert, Owen, and Michael Walker, eds. *The Underground Economy: Global Evidence of Its Size and Impact.* Fraser, 1997.

Pozo, Susan. *Exploring the Underground Economy: Studies of Illegal and Unreported Activity.* W.E. Upjohn, 1996.

Speer, Tibbett L. "Digging Into the Underground Economy." *American Demographics,* February 1995.

UNDERWRITING (INSURANCE)

In the insurance industry, the practice of underwriting refers to the process of accepting or rejecting risks. It is the very heart of insurance and is the first step taken by an insurance company to generate premiums. Originally, insurance and underwriting were synonymous. That is, underwriting referred to the operation of the insurance business. As the insurance industry developed, underwriting took on a more specialized meaning.

In the early days insurance was more personal than it is today. A contract was drawn up between a property owner and a second party, who was willing to insure the specified property, or between the insured and the insurer. The contract specified the terms under which the property would be insured. The property owner placed his name at the top of the contract, stating that he was the owner of the property and beneficiary of the contract if the property was subsequently damaged. The other party, who guaranteed the contract and was the insurer, signed his name below, at the bottom of the contract. Literally, he "underwrote" the contract.

An underwriter is the person who decides whether or not to insure **risks** for which applications have been submitted. The underwriter's task is to evaluate a risk, estimate the potential exposure, determine the likelihood of loss, then make a decision whether or not to accept the application for insurance.

The term "underwriter" developed in the early days of marine insurance. It was common practice for individuals seeking insurance for a ship and its cargo to meet with those desiring to write such insurance in coffeehouses. A person seeking insurance for his ship and its cargo would bring a paper describing the ship, its contents, crew, and destination to the coffeehouse. The paper would circulate, with each individual who wished to assume some of the obligation signing his name at the bottom and indicating how much exposure he was willing to assume. An agreed-upon rate and terms were also included in the paper. Since these people signed their named under the description of the risk, they became known as underwriters.

As insurers changed from individual to companies, signatures on insurance contracts became those of company officers. The term underwriter continued to be used in a more restrictive sense; it applied only to the person who performed the process of selecting risks and determining the terms of insurance. Risk selection and determination of policy terms continue to be the basic duties of underwriters today.

Underwriters work for insurance companies. In addition to on-the-job training, they may earn an Associate in Underwriting designation from the Insurance Institute of America. In the life insurance segment, underwriters may enter a program of study that leads to the designation of Chartered Life Underwriter (CLU). Most CLU's are engaged in some aspect of insurance sales as well. In the property and casualty insurance segment, underwriters may work toward the designation of Chartered Property Casualty Underwriter (CPCU).

UNDERWRITING'S FOUR BASIC FUNCTIONS

The process of underwriting involves four basic functions: 1) selection of risks, 2) classification and rating, 3) policy forms, and 4) retention and reinsurance. By performing these four functions the underwriter increases the possibility of securing a safe and profitable distribution of risks.

RISK SELECTION. In this step the underwriter decides whether or not to accept a particular risk. It involves securing factual information from the applicant, evaluating that information, and deciding on a course of action. The underwriter is typically aided by a list of acceptable and prohibited risks.

CLASSIFICATION AND RATING. Once the risk has been accepted, the underwriter then classifies and rates the policy. Several tentative classifications are usually assigned before a final decision on classifying the risk is reached. The purpose of using classifications is to separate risks into homogeneous groups to which rates can be assigned. Insurers may have their own classification and rating system, or they may obtain a system from a rating bureau.

POLICY FORMS. After determining the acceptability of an applicant and assigning the proper classification and rating, the underwriter is ready to issue an insurance policy. The underwriter must be familiar with the different types of policies available as well as be able to modify the form to fit the needs of the applicant.

The first three underwriting functions—risk selection, classification and rating, and policy selection—are interdependent. That is, the underwriter determines that a certain risk is acceptable when specified rates and forms are used. The underwriter also performs a fourth separate function on every risk before the underwriting is complete: reinsurance.

RETENTION AND REINSURANCE. Reinsurance involves protecting the insurance company against a certain portion of potential losses. Every risk presents the possibility of loss that will equal or exceed the policy limits. It is up to the underwriter to protect his or her company from undue financial strain. The underwriter does this by retaining only a certain portion of the risk and securing reinsurance for the remainder of the risk.

[David P. Bianco]

FURTHER READING:

Dearborn Financial Institute Staff. *Introduction to Life Underwriting*. 11th edition. Chicago: Dearborn Financial Publishing, 1998.

Morgan, Joseph F. *Underwriting Commercial Property*. 2nd ed. Malvern, PA: Insurance Institute of America, 1997.

Randall, Everett. *Introduction to Underwriting*. 2nd ed. Malvern, PA: Insurance Institute of America, 1994.

UNDERWRITING (SECURITIES)

Underwriting involves the orderly process of security registration for the financial sourcing of a **public offering** through the purchase of securities for resale to the public. The underwriting may be a firm commitment to purchase the entire amount of the company's **securities** regardless of the ability to resell them. The underwriting of such a low-priced initial public offering (IPO) and other less-well-known stock (e.g., over-the-counter stock) may be done on a best-efforts basis where the underwriter acts only as an agent and accepts no financial **liabilities**.

A successful underwriting not only sells the securities, but does so at a fair price. In addition, underwriters maintain a stable, liquid aftermarket for the trading of securities.

Until the 1950s, underwriting was the only function performed by a number of specialty houses. Thereafter, underwriters merged their talents with retail and institutional sales in order to bolster their sagging bottom lines. Today there is little distinction between wholesale underwriting, which serves institutional clients including broker-dealers, and retail underwriting, which sells directly to individual investors.

Most underwriting in the 1990s was handled by investment banks and brokerage firms. In 1996 the Federal Reserve Board lifted the revenue limit on securities underwriting by commercial **banks** and their **subsidiaries** from 10 to 25 percent. Although the ruling represented another falling barrier between **investment banking** and commercial banking, it was expected to have little effect on the underwriting industry.

Large underwriting firms assist the largest corporations with secondary offerings and maintain a financial advisory role for the long term. As full-service houses, large firms need to handle IPOs in excess of $15 million for the fees to be profitable.

Medium-size underwriting firms generally serve regional interests and handle offerings within the $5 to $15 million range. Although established companies, they lack the full range of services and number of personnel dedicated to underwriting and distribution. These firms are not likely to maintain a financial advisory capacity to their clients.

There are few remaining small underwriting firms. Some handle only small offerings called ''penny stocks.'' Others specialize in a particular segment of the market. Offerings are usually under $7 million.

LETTER OF INTENT

A letter of intent (LOI) is an agreement to proceed with the registration of securities with the **Securities and Exchange Commission** (SEC). The contents of the LOI state, as clearly as possible, the duties and obligations of the parties.

A nonbinding letter of intent requires a good-faith deposit from the company to demonstrate its financial capacity to complete the costly and cumbersome process of **going public**. In a binding LOI the entrepreneur is responsible for payment of certain **costs** whether or not the securities are actually issued.

LOIs contain an adverse-change clause, allowing the underwriter to pull out if there are material adverse changes in the financial position of the company or in **business conditions**.

UNDERWRITING AGREEMENT

The underwriting agreement finalizes the terms of the underwriting **contract**, except for the final price of the security to be offered and the amount of the security to be offered. The parties usually sign this agreement a day or two before the actual public offering.

For a firm commitment, the underwriting may include a ''green shoe'' provision, which is an allotment option of up to 15 percent of additional stock for the account of the underwriter. When a public offering goes particularly well, the underwriter executes the green shoe to increase the amount of securities for sale.

Underwriting on a best-efforts basis uses a number of variable options to conclude the offering. An all-or-none offering will be canceled if all the securities are not sold. A mini-max offering establishes acceptable upper and lower ranges.

UNDERWRITING COSTS

Underwriters are paid commissions, securities, or through a combination of fees and securities. In a firm commitment the price underwriters pay the company for the securities is expected to be less than the price offered to the public. This ''underwriter's spread'' compensates the underwriter for conducting the offering. The spread averages 10 percent or less and is dependent on the anticipated complexity and size of the offering. The maximum spread allowed by the National Association of Securities Dealers (NASD) is 10 percent.

There are certain ''nonaccountable expenses'' that cannot be construed as an integral part of the offering, but which were necessitated by the preliminary steps to bring the company to the registration process. The NASD is the only exchange that requires an accounting of these expenses.

UNDERWRITING SYNDICATES

When offerings are too large for one firm to digest, the lead underwriter forms a temporary syndicate of other underwriters and broker-dealers to assist with the initial fund raising and the distribution of the securities. The participation of other firms in the underwriting minimizes the risks for all participants.

The originator of the offering is the managing underwriter and acts as the financial adviser to the syndicate. The managing underwriter keeps 30 percent of the underwriting spread, allowing 70 percent for the other participants.

At the time of the offering, a rectangular advertisement with a bold outline, called a ''tombstone ad,'' appears in the business pages announcing the offering. It names the issues, describes the security offered, and lists all the participating firms.

SEE ALSO: Underwriting (Insurance)

[Roger J. AbiNader, updated by David P. Bianco]

FURTHER READING:

Arkebauer, James. *Going Public: Everything You Need to Know to Take Your Company Public or Invest in an IPO or DPO.* Chicago: Dearborn Trade, 1998.

Barker, William W. *SEC Registration of Public Offerings under the Securities Act of 1933.* Chicago: American Bar Association, 1997.

Brown, Meredith, ed. *Mechanics of Global Equity Offerings: Structuring the Offering and Negotiating the Underwriting Agreement.* Cambridge, MA: Kluwer Law and Taxation Publishers, 1995.

Goldblatt, Jennifer. ''Market Ho-Hum about New Revenue Limit on Securities Underwriting.'' *American Banker,* 26 December 1996, 20.

Johnson, Hazel J. *The Banker's Guide to Investment Banking: Securities and Underwriting Activities in Commercial Banking.* New York: McGraw-Hill Professional Book Group, 1996.

Lipman, Frederick D. *Going Public: Everything You Need to Know to Successfully Turn a Private Enterprise into a Publicly Traded Company.* Upland, PA: DIANE Publishing, 1998.

Shillinglaw, Gordon. *Accounting: A Management Approach.* 9th ed. New York: McGraw-Hill Higher Education, 1992.

UNEMPLOYMENT

SEE: Employment

UNIFORM COMMERCIAL CODE

The Uniform Commercial Code (UCC) is a collection of modernized, codified, and standardized laws that apply to all commercial transactions with the exception of real property. The UCC was developed under the direction of the National Conference of Commissioners on Uniform State Laws (NCCUSL), the American Law Institute (ALI), and the American Bar Association (ABA). The purpose of the UCC was to introduce uniformity into state laws affecting business and commerce. To date, all 50 states (Louisiana has adopted articles 1, 3, 4, and 5), the District of Columbia, and the U.S. Virgin Islands have adopted the UCC as state law.

The UCC has a permanent editorial board, and members of the ALI and NCCUSL meet to consider changes to the UCC. Amendments and revisions to the UCC are made to cover new developments in commerce, ranging from electronic funds transfers and the leasing of personal property to electronic filing systems and **information technology**. Once a revision has been approved by the NCCUSL and the ALI, it is submitted in a form suitable for adoption by individual state legislatures. Each state then has the option of adopting the amendments and revisions to the UCC as state law.

The need for a UCC was recognized as early as 1940, and work on the UCC began in 1945. In 1952 a draft was approved by the NCCUSL, the ALI, and the ABA. Pennsylvania became the first state to enact the UCC, on April 6, 1953, effective July 1, 1954. The UCC editorial board issued a new code in 1957 in response to comments from various states and a special report by the Law Revision Commission of New York State. By 1966 48 states had enacted the code.

The UCC consists of ten articles. Article 10 provides for states to set the effective date of enactment and lists specific acts that should be repealed once the UCC has been enacted. Individual states may also add to the list of repealed acts. When enacted, the UCC replaced the following acts, which are listed in Article 10: Uniform Negotiable Instruments Act, Uniform Warehouse Receipts Act, Uniform Sales Act, Uniform Bills of Lading Act, Uniform Stock Transfer Act, Uniform Conditional Sales Act, and Uniform Trust Receipts Act. In addition, Article 10 recommends repealing any acts regulating **bank** collections, bulk sales, chattel **mortgages**, conditional sales, factor's lien acts, farm storage of grain and similar acts, and assignment of accounts receivable. These are all areas covered in the UCC.

Article 1, General Provisions, gives principles of interpretation and general definitions that apply throughout the UCC. Article 2, Sales, superseded the Uniform Sales Act and covers areas such as **sales contracts**, performance, creditors, good faith purchasers, and remedies. Article 3, Commercial Paper, replaced the Uniform Negotiable Instruments Act and covers transfer and negotiation, rights of a holder, and liability of parties, among other areas. Article 4, Bank Deposits and Collections, incorporated much of the Bank Collection Code developed by the American Bankers Association and covers such areas as collections and deposits and **customer relations**.

Article 5 is devoted to **letters of credit**. Article 6 covers bulk transfers. Article 7 covers warehouse receipts, bills of lading, and other documents of title. Article 8, Investment Securities, replaced the Uniform Stock Transfer Act and covers the issuance, purchase, and registration of **securities**. Article 9 is devoted to secured transactions, sales of accounts, and chattel paper. It replaced the Uniform Trust Receipts Act, the Uniform Conditional Sales Act, the Uniform Chattel Mortgage Act, and a variety of other acts.

REVISIONS TO THE UCC

During the 1990s several revisions made by the ALI and the NCCUSL were accepted by many state legislatures. These included a 1990 revision of Article 2A, a revised Article 3, and 1995 revisions to Article 5. In addition, the ALI and the NCCUSL recommended that Article 6 be repealed; 37 jurisdictions had done so by mid-1998. Alternative recommended revisions to Article 6 were adopted by five jurisdictions. A 1994 revision of Article 8 was adopted by 50 jurisdictions.

Perhaps the most controversial proposed amendment was the writing of Article 2B, which attempted to establish the legal groundwork for transactions involving information and intangible goods such as **software**. Some analysts felt that the proposed Article 2B unfairly favored the software industry, protecting it from a wide range of **product liability** issues. In 1997 a coalition of 18 industry associations voiced its opposition to Article 2B, and a vote on final approval by the NCCUSL and the ALI was postponed until 1999. Article 2B, which dealt specifically with the licensing of information and software **contracts**, would have far-reaching consequences for the way information is accessed, used, and exchanged.

Changes and interpretations of the Uniform Commercial Code appear in *Business Lawyer*'s "Uniform Commercial Code Annual Survey."

[David P. Bianco]

FURTHER READING:

Brinkman, Daren R. "Unsecured Creditors' Rights in Sales and Secured Transactions: Is the Revised UCC 'New and Improved' or Just 'New'?" *Business Credit,* September 1998, 34 37.

Jamtgaard, Laurel. "Licenses and Information Wares: An Update on UCC Article 2B." *Information Outlook,* November 1998, 31.

"More Suits?" *Industry Week,* 23 June 1997, 68.

Patchel, Kathleen. "The Uniform Commercial Code Survey: Introduction." *Business Lawyer,* August 1998, 1457-59.

Williamson, Miryam. "Eye on the Government: IT and the Feds." *Computerworld,* 29 June 1998, 76-78.

UNIONS

SEE: Labor Unions

UNIT INVESTMENT TRUST

A unit investment trust (UIT) is a type of investment fund. A UIT consists of a fixed portfolio of securities—usually **bonds**—in which the selection of stocks or bonds remains constant during the life of the trust and new securities are not added to the portfolio. UITs may sell nonperforming investments, but the money from the sale is distributed to unit holders rather than being reinvested. Unlike other types of investment funds, such as open-end and closed-end **mutual funds**, the portfolio is not managed. Instead, it is established for a specified period—typically 20 to 30 years—and is placed under the management of a trustee. After the trust is created, ownership shares, or units, that reflect the value of the underlying assets are sold to investors. The assets cannot be redeemed until maturity. Throughout the holding period, however, unit owners can sell their shares for whatever the market will bear.

As with other investment funds, UITs come with a variety of investment objectives and portfolio options. Some of the major categories include:

- tax-exempt municipal bonds
- corporate bonds
- stocks
- mortgage-backed securities
- U.S. Treasury securities

Although the vast majority of domestic UITs—over 90 percent—concentrate on tax-exempt bonds, that category only represents around 43 percent of total UIT market value. The bull market of the 1990s created strong interest in stock UITs, which has been the fastest-growing category, increasing tenfold for the period 1990-97. In fact, by 1997 stock UITs overtook tax-free bonds in terms of invested market value, amassing close to 49 percent of all UIT dollars. Based on figures from the Investment Company Institute, a trade association for investment firms, as of 1997 there were 11,595 UITs in the United States representing $86 billion in market value.

While equity UITs have flourished, investment in UITs in general has been soft compared to their heyday in the 1980s. The market value of UITs peaked in 1989 at $131 billion, but fell into a protracted decline through the mid-1990s, bottoming out at $73 billion in 1995. At their peak, the value of bond UITs alone topped $100 billion. Since 1995, they have begun to grow once again, and all of that growth can be attributed to stocks. Investment rates in UITs continue to be dwarfed by interest in mutual funds, which boast a collective market value in excess of $3 trillion.

Unlike managed funds, UITs do not have a **board of directors** or investment managers. The trustee simply collects the interest income and cash flow from the repayment of the bonds, and distributes the funds to the unit holders until all bonds mature or are called. Because the investments are not directed, annual fees charged to maintain the trust are sometimes lower than fees charged for managed funds. In addition to lower management fees, UITs may provide investors with a diversified portfolio of bonds that offer different maturity dates and an average holding period that complements their financial needs. Indeed, because most UIT assets are invested in bonds, UIT participants purchase shares with the expectation of earning a steady, monthly income and then receiving most of their principal back at expiration. Investors theoretically get the benefit of holding bonds until maturation without the volatility and risks inherent in short-term trading. Thus, unlike in managed funds, UIT shareholders know exactly what they are buying.

Among the drawbacks of UITs are that their investment portfolios are unresponsive to changing market conditions. An individual investment that looks good when the trust is formed, for example, may sour soon afterward. Nevertheless, it cannot be removed from the trust. In addition to that handicap, many UIT holders find that their shares are difficult to liquidate in the open market. Because no one tracks and compares the performance of all UITs on the market, moreover, investors may also have a difficult time comparing UIT alternatives. Finally, the UIT industry is characterized by a lack of standards for advertising and marketing, which dilutes the efficiency of UIT investing for many fund investors.

UITs usually charge a sales fee of 3 percent to 4 percent, although it can range from 1 percent to 5 percent. Shareholders may also pay a supervisory fee of $1.50 to $1.75 per $1,000 per month. These fees, which are high in comparison to competing no-load funds, have caused some analysts to consider UITs an unwise investment. UIT fees are low to moderate compared to mutual funds with front or back loads. Despite those detractions, UITs, as rejuvenated by stocks, continue to be popular investment vehicles in the United States.

FURTHER READING:

Investment Company Institute. *A Guide to Unit Investment Trusts.* Washington, 1997. Available from www.ici.org.

Renberg, Werner. "Bye, Bye Bonds: Sales of Unit Investment Trusts Are Up, and So Is Their Focus on Equities." *Barron's,* 3 August 1998.

UNITED NATIONS (UN)

The United Nations (UN) is the world's preeminent organization working toward global peace, harmony among nations, and the betterment of all the peoples of the world. The only sovereign nations of the world not counted among the UN's 187 member nations are Kiribati, Nauru, Switzerland, Taiwan, Tonga, Tuvalu, and Vatican City. Since its founding in 1945 the United Nations, which is headquartered in New York City, has had many successes and failures in striving to achieve its four purposes as set forth in the UN Charter. The four purposes are to: "save succeeding generations from the scourge of war"; "reaffirm faith in fundamental human rights"; "establish conditions under which justice and respect for the obligations arising from treaties and other sources of international law can be maintained"; and "promote social progress and better standards of life in larger freedom.''

The charter of the United Nations was signed June 26, 1945, in San Francisco, California. The charter was derived in part from deliberations held between the United States, the Soviet Union, China, and Great Britain at the Dumbarton Oaks estate in Washington, D.C., in 1944. These deliberations led to the United Nations Conference on International Organization which was held in San Francisco between April 25 and June 25, 1945. The 50 nations attending the conference became founding members of the UN. Poland did not send a delegation but shortly thereafter signed the charter and is generally regarded as a founding member. On October 24, 1945, following the devastation of World War II, the UN became a viable entity with the charter being ratified by the governments of the United States, China, France, the Soviet Union, Great Britain, and other signatories. October 24 has since been declared United Nations Day. China was until 1971 represented by the Nationalist government in Taiwan. The delegation from the People's Republic of China was, however, seated in its stead in October of that year. The name ''United Nations'' originated with President Franklin Roosevelt and was first used in the ''Declaration by United Nations'' issued during a 1942 meeting between the 26 nations fighting Germany and the Axis powers during World War II. The United Nations succeeded the ill-fated League of Nations that was established following World War I.

While pursuing international peace, harmony, and cooperation between the nations of the world, the UN is concurrently involved in human-rights concerns as well as economic, cultural, health, and social issues. The UN Charter serves as the UN's constitution and besides enumerating that body's four purposes, also lists seven principles: equality of membership, member responsibilities, peaceful settlement of disputes, when force or various sanctions may or may not be used, responsibilities related to attaining the goals enumerated in the charter, noninterference in the internal affairs of member countries, and relations with and expectations concerning nonmember countries.

The UN is divided into six principal organs: the General Assembly, the Security Council, the International Court of Justice, the Economic and Social Council, the Trusteeship Council, and the Secretariat. All members belong to the General Assembly which is the UN's deliberative body. The assembly makes recommendations but has no power of enforcement. The Security Council is responsible for the maintenance of peace through military intervention, economic sanctions, and various peacekeeping activities. It has five permanent and six nonpermanent members. The countries comprising the ''Big Five'' are: the United States, France, Great Britain, the People's Republic of China, and Russia. Prior to 1971 and 1991 respectively, the last two seats were held by Taiwan and the Soviet Union. The six nonpermanent seats are held for two years by nations chosen by the General Assembly on the basis of geographical distribution, contributions to world peace, and attainment of general UN goals. The International Court of Justice is the only principal UN body not headquartered in New York City. Residing at the Hague, the Netherlands, the court seats 15 judges appointed to nine-year terms by the General Assembly and the Security Council. The court issues advisory opinions and settles member disputes that fall within the court's limited jurisdiction. The Economic and Social Council has 54 members elected by the General Assembly to three year terms and issues advice and opinions related to social and economic issues. The Trusteeship Council administers non-self-governing territories dating back to the League of Nations.

The United Nations Secretariat is headed by a secretary-general and is the UN's chief administrative body. The Secretariat is responsible for settling international disputes, carrying out peacekeeping activities, gathering information related to political and economic trends, and in general overseeing activities relating to the goals of the UN while directing the activities of the various UN special agencies.

UN specialized agencies and agencies related to the UN are many and varied. Some of the more notable agencies are:

- The **International Monetary Fund**, which stabilizes currency exchange rates between countries thus making trade easier while minimizing balance of payment problems.
- The United Nations Educational, Scientific, and Cultural Organization (UNESCO), which encourages various projects in these areas so as to increase international cooperation and understanding.
- The **World Bank** (more formally known as the International Bank for Reconstruction and Development) which lends funds for infrastructure projects.
- The World Health Organization, which deals with health and related problems on both a local and global level.
- The Food and Agricultural Organization, which combats world hunger by working to improve agriculture and fisheries.

There are also special bodies associated with the General Assembly including the United Nations Conference on Trade and Development, the United Nations Development Programme, and the United Nations Environment Program. The best-known special body is the United Nations Children's Fund (UNICEF) which funds and administers child health and welfare programs in many areas of the world, but especially the developing countries of the **Third World**.

One of the most controversial and often divisive roles of the UN has been its peacekeeping efforts through cease-fire negotiations, the deployment of peacekeeping forces, or UN-sanctioned military intervention. Some of the UN's major efforts in these regards have been: the 1949 cease fire interventions in unrelated disputes between the Netherlands and Indonesia, and between Pakistan and India; military intervention in Korea in 1950; a 1964 peacekeeping force that intervened in a conflict between Greek and Turkish forces over ethnic tensions on Cyprus; a UN peacekeeping force sent to Lebanon in 1978 to stop fighting between Israel and the Palestine Liberation Organization; a 1991 military coalition spearheaded by the United States that ousted Iraqi forces from Kuwait in what became known as the Persian Gulf War; and various interventions, starting in 1992, in Central Europe to help resolve ethnic-driven conflict in the former Yugoslavia.

In its ongoing effort to promote world peace the UN and its organizations have been the recipients of five Nobel Peace Prizes: the Office of the United Nations High Commissioner for Refugees—awarded in 1954 and 1981; UNICEF—1965; the **International Labor Organization**—1969; and the United Nations Peace-Keeping Forces, for various peacekeeping operations—1988.

The Nobel Peace Prize has also been awarded to various individuals associated with the UN: U.S. ex-Secretary of State Cordell Hull (1871-1955), for his efforts to establish the UN—awarded in 1945; Lord John Boyd Orr (1880-1971) of the United Kingdom, the first director-general of the Food and Agriculture Organization—1949; Ralph Bunche (1904-1971) of the United States, for mediating a 1948 armistice agreement between Israel, Jordan, Lebanon, Syria, and Egypt—1950; Lester Pearson (1897-1972) of Canada, president of the seventh session of the UN General Assembly, for his work in resolving the 1956 Suez Crisis—1957; Dag Hammarskjöld (1905-1961) of Sweden, UN secretary-general, for his intervention in the Congo crisis—1961; and Ireland's Seán MacBride (1904-1988), for his role as the United Nations High Commissioner for Refugees—1974.

Despite these many successes the UN is a troubled and often ineffectual organization. Since the Persian Gulf War, for instance, the UN has been unable to stop Iraq's continual and seemingly endless cat-and-mouse game with UN weapons inspectors. Over the decades an ideological rift has developed between the UN's Third World members (known as the ''South'') and the industrialized and developed nations (known as the ''North'') and shows no signs of healing. Currently the United States owes the UN almost $1.5 billion in back dues (total arrears among all members is approaching $2.5 billion) and Congress refuses to release these funds until the UN institutes major reforms (i.e., downsizing.) The current annual assessment for U.S. dues ($298 million) represents 25 percent of the UN's regular budget while 10 of the 185 members nations are responsible for 75 percent of the UN's $1.3 billion annual budget. The UN is also a bloated bureaucracy even after a 14 percent reduction (to 8,800 employees) in the central bureaucracy since 1994. There is, however, unrealized momentum within the organization to reduce the administrative portion of the central budget from 38 percent to 25 percent. Finally, regional bickering is hampering a needed move toward increasing the permanent membership of the Security Council (Pakistan versus India, Italy versus Germany, Argentina versus Brazil, etc.).

In an effort to reform the UN, Secretary-General Kofi Annan (1938) has instituted a ''quiet revolution'' which in part is attempting to establish greater rapport with the world's business community. The UN feels that with its expertise in **cross-cultural communication** and cooperation it is uniquely able to help business meet the challenges of **globalization** and global interdependence. The UN also strongly believes that business can greatly profit from expanded markets that will grow concurrently with a world free from strife, chaos, and war.

[Michael Knes]

FURTHER READING:

Alger, Chadwick F., ed. *The Future of the United Nations System: Potential for the Twenty-First Century.* Tokyo: United Nations University Press, 1998.

Europa World Year Book 1998. London: Europa Publications, 1998.

Hillen, John. *Blue Helmets: The Strategy of UN Military Operations.* Washington: Brassey's, 1998.

Hoopes, Townsend. *FDR and the Creation of the UN* New Haven: Yale University Press, 1997.

Meisler, Stanley. *United Nations: The First Fifty Years.* New York: Atlantic Monthly Press, 1995.

''Reforming the United Nations.'' *Economist,* 8 August 1998, 19-22.

Robbins, Carla Anne. ''UN Council Denounces Iraq but Looks Too Divided to Act.'' *Wall Street Journal,* 7 August 1998, A9.

United Nations. ''United Nations.'' New York: United Nations, 1998. Available from www.un.org.

UPC (UNIVERSAL PRODUCT CODE)

SEE: Bar Coding

UTILITARIANISM

Utilitarianism is a highly secular philosophy that originated in Great Britain in the late 18th century, but whose influence continues down to the present day. It is one of several common philosophies used to evaluate **business ethics**.

HISTORICAL DEVELOPMENT

Utilitarianism is most often associated with Jeremy Bentham (1748-1832), James Mill (1773-1836), and his son, John Stuart Mill (1806-1873). Of the three, John Stuart Mill is considered the most brilliant exponent of utilitarianism, although he also is known for other significant contributions to 19th century intellectual thought.

Jeremy Bentham finished his law studies at Oxford University in 1763 but never practiced law. His intellect was probing and highly analytical and concerned more with reforming injustices (such as the penal system and penal law) than with conforming to the status quo. In this respect he was typical of philosophers of the Enlightenment, which was at its zenith when Bentham began his singular career. Bentham's disciple, James Mill, did much to publicize his radical ideas in England.

Bentham was much influenced by the secularism of the age. Rejecting Christianity as too intuitive and untenable, he sought a material explanation for right and wrong, good and evil. He found his answers in the writings of such theorists as Scottish philosopher David Hume (1711-76) and French *philosophe* Claude-Adrien Helvétius (1715-71), who posited that true justice was synonymous with the good of the whole. Bentham made this principle, dubbed the ''greatest happiness'' principle, a moral criterion and the basis for his philosophy of reform.

In *An Introduction to the Principles of Morals and Legislation* (1789), Bentham introduced his ''utilitarian'' doctrine: mankind has two masters, pleasure and pain; nothing is good except pleasure, or bad except pain. To advance pleasure is the aim of human nature, and therefore the goal of every person; by extension, it should be the goal of society as well. But since individual interests clash within every society, the aim of legislation and government should be to harmonize these clashing interests for the good of the whole.

In time Bentham's philosophy would be criticized (by none other than John Stuart Mill) for being excessively narrow, reducing human nature to almost instinctual pain and pleasure, and making no allowance for an individual's spiritual strivings or emotions. Therefore, although Bentham intended utilitarianism (a word he used only once) to be applicable to both the individual and to society, it seemed most persuasive as a social philosophy. In this respect, utilitarianism has had the most profound impact in the development of legal thought.

Bentham became convinced that the British government, controlled by a handful of leading families, was influenced solely by narrow self-interest. In time he came to advocate the abolition of the monarchy, universal male suffrage, and rule by parliament. In so doing he was not a promoter of democracy; rather, he viewed these changes (radical for his day and age) strictly from the perspective of utility, or what was best for the whole.

Bentham became the leader in England of a group of reform-minded radicals, including James Mill. A dissatisfied clergyman who came to abandon his religion, Mill became Bentham's ardent disciple and a rigid interpreter of ''Benthamism.'' His unique contribution was *Analysis of the Phenomena of the Human Mind* (1829), in which Mill attempted to analyze the ''pleasure principle,'' which many non-utilitarians rejected as hedonistic and selfish, a position he attempted to disprove. This unusual psychological study was saturated with ''Benthamite'' ideology—it was not original—but did much to disseminate Bentham's ideas.

James Mill's greatest contribution to the development of utilitarianism appears to have been his son, John Stuart Mill. The younger Mill became a rigid utilitarian in his teen years, but after suffering a nervous breakdown at age 20, he came to the conclusion that utilitarianism was a sterile, over-intellectualized moral theory that left no room for intuition or feelings.

John Stuart Mill never rejected the philosophy of his boyhood, but in his seminal work, *Utilitarianism* (1863), written in his middle years, he so revised the basic doctrine of Bentham that his book appeared to almost reject it. He proposed that goodness was not necessarily pleasurable; that quality of pleasure was more important than quantity; and that there were ''lower'' and ''higher'' pleasures, such as intellectual, spiritual, and emotional ones.

The most striking departure from traditional or classical utilitarianism was in John Stuart Mill's rejection of **laissez-faire** economics. While Jeremy Bentham advocated political and social reform rather than economic reform, a disciple of his, David Ricardo (1772-1823), expressed in 1817 the utilitarian view of economics in his *Principles of Political Economy.* Ricardo advocated free economic competition, without any legislative constraints, as leading to the greatest good for the greatest number. John Stuart Mill rejected this classic statement of laissez-faire economics. His readings of French socialist thinkers led him to question the sanctity of private property and to advocate a more equitable distribution of wealth and equal opportunity for all. Despite his considerable revision of classical utilitarianism, John Stuart Mill never abandoned this doctrine, which as a social and legal philosophy has remained influential to this day.

BUSINESS APPLICATIONS

Utilitarianism may be employed in any business decision-making process that seeks to maximize positive effects (especially morally, but perhaps also financially and so forth) and minimize negative outcomes. As with Bentham's formulation, utilitarianism in business ethics is primarily concerned with outcomes rather than processes. If the outcome leads to the greatest good (or the least harm) for the greatest number of people, then it is assumed the end justifies the means.

Just as John Stuart Mill objected to the coldest, most basic version of the theory, modern business ethicists decry utilitarianism's limits as an instructive ethical analysis. For example, Reitz, Wall, and Love argued that utilitarianism isn't an appropriate tool when outcomes affect a large number of separate parties with different needs or in complex processes whose outcomes and side effects can't be readily foreseen, e.g., implementing new technology.

There are a number of alternative ethical philosophies to utilitarianism also used in business. Formalism, associated with the philosopher Immanuel Kant (1724-1804), is a rule-based system of ethical principles that are applied to each step of the process leading up to—and including—the outcome. In other words, the end is only just if the means are as well. This is sometimes also termed universalism, since the method attempts to apply universal ethical standards consistently across business practices, as contrasted with the relativism of utilitarian ethics. Although scholars disagree about its exact relation to utilitarianism (some argue they may coexist), formalism is frequently cited as the opposite of utilitarianism. Under formalism, a business action that passes the ethical tests at every stage is considered ethical; if the rules or principles are violated along the way, the action is unethical regardless of the outcome.

SEE ALSO: Business Ethics

[Sina Dubovoy]

FURTHER READING:

Brady, F.N. *Ethical Managing: Rules and Results.* New York: Macmillan, 1990.

Ebenstein, Alan O. *The Greatest Happiness Principle: An Examination of Utilitarianism.* New York: Garland, 1991.

Jackson, Julius. *A Guided Tour of John Stuart Mill's Utilitarianism.* Mountain View, CA: Mayfield Publishing Co., 1993.

Reitz, H Joseph, James A. Wall Jr., and Mary Sue Love. ''Ethics in Negotiation: Oil and Water or Good Lubrication?'' *Business Horizons,* May-June 1998.

Schminke, Marshall, Maureen L. Ambrose, and Terry W. Noel. ''The Effect of Ethical Frameworks on Perceptions of Organizational Justice.'' *Academy of Management Journal,* October 1997.

V

VALUATION

Valuation involves putting a price on a piece of property, whether it be **real estate**, **intellectual property** (**patents**, **copyrights**, trademarks, and other intangibles), personal property, or a business. In the context of a business valuation the appraiser considers many factors, including financial attributes (such as sales and profitability trends, noncash expenses, capital expenditures, tangible and intangible assets, the implications of long-term **contracts**, nonrecurring profit and loss statement items, related party transactions, and contingent **liabilities**), **marketing** attributes (including location, **competition**, barriers to entry, distributor relationships) and macroeconomic attributes (regulatory constraints, labor relations, **interest rates**, general **economic conditions**, the state of the art for the company's products, and others). A thorough understanding of the subject company's background and circumstances is critical to the appraiser's ability to assess the reasonableness of various assumptions that will underlie the valuation.

VALUATION APPROACHES

There are many different valuation methodologies, some more suited to certain types of property than others. The main approaches include liquidation, asset value, market comparable, and discounted cash flow.

LIQUIDATION APPROACH. This method assumes a company will cease operations and that the value will simply be the sum of the individual assets that can be sold; no goodwill for the company's name, location, customer base, or other accumulated experience is captured. This level is further divided into forced liquidations (as in a bankruptcy) and orderly liquidations, with values generally placed higher in the latter.

ASSET VALUE APPROACH. This approach starts with the company's book values per its **balance sheet** (at historical cost), and makes adjustments thereto to bring them in line with market values. For example, real estate acquired long ago is frequently worth more than its historical cost. Alternatively, some intangible assets may have no continuing value in certain situations, or may be worth much more than book value in others. This method is most often used in companies where much of the assets are **commodity** like.

MARKET COMPARABLE APPROACH. This approach looks to comparable companies—in terms of industry, size, growth rates, capitalization, and other factors—for which a **market value** is known or observable (e.g., **publicly held companies**) to establish a gauge. Then, a ratio of value is calculated for the comparable(s)—such as market to book, market to earnings, and market to **cash flow**—which is applied to the target company's parameters. In some cases a comparable private company may have recently changed hands under similar terms and circumstances. Here, the particular transaction may be useful as an indicator of value.

DISCOUNTED CASH FLOW (DCF) APPROACH. This method uses projections of future cash flows from operating the business or using the asset, and requires detailed assumptions about future operations, including volumes, pricing, costs, and other factors. DCF usually starts with forecast income, adding back noncash expenses, deducting capital expenditures, and adjusting for **working capital** changes to arrive at expected cash flows. The appropriate **discount rate**

must be determined and used to bring the future cash flows back to their present value at the as-of date of the valuation. DCF in its single-period form is known as capitalization of earnings, which usually involves normalizing a recent measure of income or cash flow to reflect a steady-state or going forward amount that can be capitalized at the appropriate multiple.

VALUATION ISSUES AND STANDARDS

It is important to recognize and deal properly with certain subtleties and standards in the field of valuation. Issues and standards to be aware of include:

- Treatment of **debt**: if the methodology applied uses a pre-debt-service income measure, then debt must usually be subtracted from the resulting figure.
- Control premiums: if the methodology is based on **price/earnings ratios** of comparable public companies and the interest being valued is the entirety of a company, a control premium may be applicable. Conversely, if the starting point is from a controlling perspective and the interest being valued is ''minority,'' then a discount for lack of control may be indicated.
- Discount for lack of marketability: also known as the liquidity discount, this involves whether or not the property can be readily sold. For example, publicly traded companies are highly marketable, and their shares can be quickly turned into cash. **Closely held corporations**, on the other hand, are more difficult (and in some cases by agreement, impossible) to sell. Depending on the reference point of the valuation, it may be necessary to subtract a discount for lack of marketability, or add a premium for the presence of marketability.
- The standard of value must be clearly defined. That is, whether the valuation is based on book value, fair market value, fair value, liquidating versus **going concern** value, investment value, or some other defined perspective of value. The distinction is important because of adjustments that are necessary under some, but not all, of these standards (e.g., control premiums, discounts for illiquidity).
- The as-of date must be specified and maintained. Values of property vary over time, and it is critical to state the date reference for any valuation. Further, the information used by the appraiser should be limited to that which would have been available at the as-of date; that is, subsequent information is generally excluded from the equation when doing valuations.
- The form of organization is important. Different legal forms of entity—corporations, **S corporations**, and **partnerships**—are subject to different **tax** rules, which affect the value of the enterprise.
- The focus of the valuation must be clearly identified. The portion of the enterprise being acquired, the type(s) of **securities** involved, whether the transaction is a **stock** purchase or an asset purchase deal, and how the transaction may affect existing relationships, such as related party transfers, can all affect the value.

[Christopher C. Barry, updated by Wendy H. Mason]

FURTHER READING:

Copeland, Tom, Tim Koller, and Jack Murrin. *Valuation: Measuring and Managing the Value of Companies.* New York: Wiley, 1995.

Damodaran, Aswath. *Investment Valuation: Tools and Techniques for Determining the Value of Any Asset.* New York: Wiley, 1996.

Pratt, Shannon P. *Valuing a Business.* Homewood, IL: Dow Jones-Irwin, 1989.

West, Tom, and Jeffrey D. Jones, eds. *Handbook of Business Valuation.* New York: Wiley, 1992.

VALUE-ADDED TAX (VAT)

A value-added tax (VAT) is a **tax** levied on the value added to goods or services produced by businesses. Such a tax is collected in stages from each business that contributes to the final market value of goods and services. While VAT is paid by businesses, the actual tax burden is typically passed along to consumers. While **sales tax** is easily perceived by consumers, VAT is generally considered invisible to consumers because retailers add little value to the goods they sell, so there is little or no VAT charged to retailers. By the time goods reach the retail level, the VAT that has been charged along the way to companies in the manufacturing and distribution sectors has been incorporated into the selling price.

The concept of ''value added'' in manufacturing is used to measure the productive activity of a business. The tax base on which VAT is calculated is the difference between the selling price of a firm's output and the purchase price for intermediate products. That difference is known as the value added by the firm. Value added consists of productive activity, such as labor done by workers and manufacturing operations performed by machines.

In countries that have a VAT, such as Canada and member states of the **European Union**, the tax generally affects goods bought and sold within the country as well as imports into the country, while exports from the country receive a credit on the VATs that have been paid or assessed. Goods that are exempt from the VAT are said to be zero-rated. In addition to exports, goods that may be zero-rated typically include food and other necessities. Countries may also charge a "luxury" rate on certain goods that is higher than their standard VAT.

In the EU, each country has a different VAT rate. Thus far, there has been little or no progress made on standardizing the different rates among the member countries, especially in terms of trade between member countries. As of 1992-93, the standard VAT rates varied from a low of 15 percent charged in Germany, Luxembourg, and Spain, to high rates of 21 percent in Ireland and 25 percent in Denmark. The United Kingdom was charging businesses a 17.5 percent VAT. In 1997-98 the European Commission took the lead in proposing a common system of VAT within the EU.

Canada adopted a national VAT in 1991, called the federal goods and services tax (GST). It replaced the federal manufacturers' sales tax, which was based on the total resale value of a manufacturer's goods, not just the value added. The Canadian GST is imposed on every recipient of a taxable good or service made in Canada, with the vendor being responsible for collecting the tax and paying the government. A GST taxable good or service is considered made in Canada only if it is delivered or made available to the recipient in Canada; if delivered outside of Canada, then no GST is applied. In at least one Canadian court case, mail-order goods shipped from New York into Canada were ruled subject to the GST.

The United States considered adding a VAT in the early 1980s as part of a general tax reform, and proposals to introduce a VAT resurfaced in the late 1990s. It was argued that a VAT would result in balance-of-payments stability in international trade and that it would provide the government with enough revenue to reduce **income taxes**. The United States did not adopt a VAT, however, in part because it is considered a regressive tax that places a proportionally larger tax burden on lower-income consumers.

[David P. Bianco]

FURTHER READING:

David, Irene, and Alison Pavlin. "Professional Taxing." *CA Magazine,* June/July 1998, 34-35.

Gale, William G. "What Can America Learn from the British Tax System?" *National Tax Journal,* December 1997, 753-77.

Seaton, Peter. "Westminster, VAT Are You Playing At?" *Accountancy,* March 1998, 65.

Zink, Bill. "The Long Arm of the Canadian Goods and Services Tax." *Tax Adviser,* February 1998, 82.

VARIABLE ANNUITY

Annuities are typically **contracts** sold by companies whereby the buyer agrees to make payments over a specified period. For example, $100 paid each year for three years is a three-year annuity. In a fixed annuity payments are for a fixed, predetermined amount, in a variable annuity the amount of money paid out each period varies. Normally, the amount fluctuates according to some outside influence, such as the return on an investment. For example, a three-year variable annuity may pay $70, $128, and $97 in years one, two, and three, respectively.

The term "annuity" is most commonly used to describe a contract between an insurance company and an individual or entity. Various annuity products proliferated in the insurance industry during the 1980s following increased competition for traditional life insurance dollars from investment vehicles such as **mutual funds** and **individual retirement accounts** (IRAs). Typically, an investor in an annuity gives a sum of money to an insurance company in return for that insurer's promise to supply a series of payments for a fixed number of years during his or her lifetime. The person can elect to have the payments begin immediately after the initial payment of the premium (immediate annuity) or at some future date (deferred annuity). Disbursements for deferred annuity contracts start at least one year after the premium payment.

The most common type of annuities are deferred, because interest that accrues on the investment is not taxed until the money is disbursed. The advantage of such an arrangement is that the investor can time the payouts to reduce total **tax** liabilities. For example, a young investor in a high-income tax bracket could invest money in a deferred annuity with plans to withdraw the investment in the form of annual payments after retirement, when he or she would be in a lower-income tax bracket. Deferred annuities can be fixed or variable.

Investors in variable annuities can usually move their money around into different mutual funds offered by the insurance company—usually five to ten different funds, including bond, stock, and money-market funds. A younger investor, for example, has the option of gradually adopting a more conservative underlying investment portfolio as time passes. The arrangement is similar to investing in an IRA. The key difference is that the maximum amount of money one can invest in an IRA is limited by federal law, and the initial IRA investment is tax-deductible. The amount that one can contribute to a deferred annuity, in contrast, is unlimited but not tax-deductible. Potential drawbacks of variable annuities include annual management fees, early-withdrawal penalties, and the risk of a negative return in a given year, unlike the minimum rate of return determined by fixed annuities.

Variable annuities are often combined with life insurance products to form variable life insurance. Variable life insurance offers the advantages provided by variable annuities that are described above as well as the benefits of life insurance. Typically, an individual (the insured) pays a single premium or a series of premiums. The insured can then select from a number of options to convert the policy into an income stream, which entails a stated death benefit. The basic options include: (1) taking the market value of the investment as a lump-sum payment; (2) receiving a variable periodic payment; and (3) receiving a fixed annuity. Variable life insurance gives the insured more control over his or her investment than do other types of life insurance, and the surviving beneficiary is not subject to income tax on the death benefit.

Actuaries at insurance companies determine benefits and payments related to life annuities by consulting mortality tables. These tables of historical data show the probability for life expectancy for specific individuals based on demographic and behavioral attributes. Using that information, the insurer effectively structures the variable annuity so that the insured bears the investment risk of the underlying investment portfolio. For example, assume that Jim retires at age 60 with $100,000 in his variable annuity contract. Mortality tables suggest that Jim, a motorcycle rider and heavy smoker, will likely die within five years. Assuming that the insurance company can expect to get an average investment return of 5 percent annually (the assumed investment return, or AIR), the insurer can calculate Jim's annual benefit payment with the following formula:

$$B_t = B_{t-1}\left(\frac{1 + R_t}{1 + .04}\right)$$

where B equals the benefit payment in each year t, and R_t is the actual return on Jim's portfolio in year t. The first payment is determined by simply calculating a constant payment that, over five years, would equal $100,000 given a discount rate equal to the AIR. In this case, the formula yields a first payment of $23,097 assuming a discount rate equal to the AIR of 5 percent. Thus, if Jim's portfolio returned 6 percent in the second year after his retirement, his annual payment would be $23,317, or $23,317 = $23,097[1.06/1.05].

Thus, each year's benefit is calculated by multiplying the previous year's benefit by a factor that reflects the actual investment performance of the portfolio. The formula guarantees that Jim will continue to receive a relatively substantial annual benefit throughout his life, regardless of how long he actually lives. If Jim lives 15 years the insurance company will obviously lose money on his annuity contract. Theoretically, however, the mortality tables will ensure that the company profits from the average performance of its large pool of annuity contracts—some of those insured will die earlier than expected, and some will die later.

In the 1990s, variable annuities were continually threatened by efforts of Congressional Republicans to lower the capital gains tax. The Budget Reconciliation Act of 1997 finally succeeded, reducing the capital gains tax rate from 28 to 20 percent. As a result, tax-deferred variable annuities carry a relatively greater tax burden than previously, limiting their appeal to investors.

[Dave Mote]

FURTHER READING:

Holmes, Phil. *Investment Appraisal.* Boston, MA: International Thomson Business Press, 1998.

Kosnett, Jeffrey R. ''Tracking Variable Life.'' *Life Association News,* May 1999, 69-79.

VAT

SEE: Value-Added Tax

VENTURE CAPITAL

The term ''venture capital'' (VC) usually refers to third-party private equity capital for new and emerging enterprises. Companies that specialize in providing this funding are known as venture capital firms or simply venture capitalists. In practice, venture capital firms often provide the entrepreneur with more than just money; since they usually become part owners in the firm, they frequently take an active role in shaping the company's business strategy and its **management**—including possibly installing one or more experienced executives from the outside.

While the venture capital firm may be affiliated with **banks** or other lending institutions, most are independent and privately managed. Their efforts are focused; business activity is limited to working with start-ups or young organizations. Venture capital organizations provide their clients with capital through direct equity investments, **loans**, or other financial arrangements. Due to the highly speculative nature of their investments, venture capitalists take big risks by working with new ventures. Indeed, the majority of companies they finance don't pan out. In exchange for the high level of risk, venture capitalists expect a high return on their investments from the few that do turn into successful enterprises.

FORMATION OF VENTURE CAPITAL FIRMS

All businesses need some financial resources to begin activity. The exchange between someone with a good idea (an entrepreneur) and someone with the resources to help make a business out of the idea (a banker, a rich uncle, or a venture capitalist) is as old as business itself. However, venture capital as a distinct form of business financing arose only recently. John Wilson, in his book *The New Ventures, Inside the High Stakes World of Venture Capital,* marks 1946 as the year the venture capital industry originated in the United States. J.H. Whitney brought together partners from the East Coast for the first venture capital fund, working with an initial capitalization of approximately $10 million. The structure of the first fund—a partnership between those contributing to the initial capitalization—was the model for a majority of venture capital organizations that followed as the industry grew.

One of the first venture capital funds was created by city leaders in Boston. The American Research and Development Corporation was headed by General George Doriot, one of the early leaders in the industry. The successful investments made by this group helped to legitimize the new form of financing. Burill and Norback, in their book *The Arthur Young Guide to Raising Venture Capital* argue that Doriot's leadership set the course for future venture capital organizations. ''Doriot . . . is famous for instituting the ethos of the venture capital industry—the venture capitalist as one who guides and manages a growing company through times thick and thin.'' ADR, and Doriot, gained attention because of the success of one of their first clients, Digital Equipment Corp. (DEC). The American Research and Development Corporation's initial investment of $67,000 grew into more than $600 million.

The passage of the Small Business Investment Act of 1958 by the federal government was an important incentive for would-be venture capital organizations. The act provided venture capital firms organized as Small Business Investment Companies (SBICs) and Minority Enterprise Small Business Investment Companies (MESBICs) with an opportunity to increase the amount of funds available to entrepreneurs. The privately managed SBICs and MESBICs had access to federal money through the Small Business Administration which could then be leveraged four dollars to one against privately raised funds. The SBICs and MESBICs, in turn, made the financial resources available to new ventures and entrepreneurs in their communities.

In recent decades, the venture capital industry has become big business. According to a widely cited annual estimate published by VentureOne Corporation, venture capital firms in 1998 disbursed approximately $12.5 billion in funds to approximately 1,800 new or continuing ventures. This level of funding was nearly double that just three years earlier. Part of the trend has been to invest more money in the typical new venture: the average size of investment in 1998 was approximately $6.8 million, compared with $5.4 million per deal as of 1995. These figures don't include so-called angel investors and venture capital provided by sources outside the mainstream venture capital industry, such as when large corporations provide equity funding to small strategic business partners.

As more capital has entered the VC arena, the focus of venture capital firms has also gradually shifted. Whereas the first venture capitalists provided money to organizations for very basic initial start-up activities, the industry increasingly looks for firms that are somewhat further along in their development. As a result, there is a tendency for venture capital organizations to shy away from early stage and start-up financing. Rather than provide the entrepreneur or new venture with money early on in the growth of the business (in the first year of business, for instance), venture capital firms increasingly provide funds for products and services with proven markets and a higher chance of success in the marketplace.

INSTITUTIONALIZATION

What may have started out as a relatively loose partnership of individuals with money to invest has become a set of organizations with formalized structures and business activities. Venture capital firms, or financial firms that offer venture funds along with other financing options, have become accepted parts of the business world, finding their own niche as providers of capital for higher risk situations.

As the industry matures, two types of organizations predominate those disbursing venture capital. The structure of the venture organization usually dictates the means through which the organization makes a profit. Leveraged firms borrow money from other financial institutions, the government or private sources and, in turn, lend the funds to entrepreneurs and new ventures at a higher rate of interest. Leveraged firms make money by charging their clients a higher interest rate than they pay for the use of the funds. Because leveraged firms rely on interest income, they make most of the disbursements in the form of loans to new ventures. This practice is less common among firms that are dedicated to providing venture capital.

Equity firms sell stock in the venture capital organization to individual or institutional investors, in effect pooling investors' money, and then use the proceeds to purchase equity in new ventures. Equity venture capital firms build portfolios of investments in companies. This kind of venture capital company tries to resell the stock of its portfolio businesses at a later date for a profit. Whereas a leveraged firm can expect a relatively steady stream of interest income, an equity firm may not experience a return on their investment for years. The return usually comes as a result of the sale of their equity in the new venture. Venture capital organizations can either sell their equity back to the company itself or on the public stock exchanges (like the New York Stock Exchange) in an initial public offering (IPO).

There are a variety of ownership structures for venture capital firms. A few firms are publicly traded on the stock exchanges. Because of the nature of the ownership, these firms tend to be larger than most venture capital organizations. However, the overwhelming majority of firms are private companies. The firms may have been formed by individuals, families, or small groups of investors. Some are also limited partnerships formed by insurance companies or pension funds. These organizations generally form the venture capital organizations to achieve a greater rate of return than most of their other investments. Other firms are organized as bank subsidiaries as a way for the banks to own equity in small businesses. These organizations are independent of other bank activities. Some firms have been set up by corporations, although these are relatively rare. In other cases, corporations looking to gain high returns on their funds invest in existing venture capital limited partnerships where risk can be shared and **liabilities** are limited.

FORMS OF VENTURE CAPITAL FINANCING

Venture capital firms invest at different stages in the development of the enterprise, often according to their own particular investment strategy. The managers of a venture capital firm may prefer to invest in brand new companies or their strategy may dictate investment in businesses that are much more developed. Because the business is unproven, early investments are inherently more risky and the firm can demand a higher return. Later investments are more stable and bring a more modest return. Most venture capital firms try to diversify their holdings by investing in a variety of enterprises at various stages of development.

''Seed capital'' is given to individuals or groups in the idea stage, the point at which there is a good idea for a business but no formal organization. At this stage, the entrepreneur is likely to use the money provided by a venture capital organization to conduct further **market research**, assemble a management team, or develop a prototype.

More often than not, those who look for seed capital are turned down by venture firms and must rely on their own resources to find the needed capital. However, after they have developed a prototype and proved their idea will be viable, new enterprises may approach a venture capital in order to gather funds needed to begin operations. In such cases, venture capital organizations provide ''start-up'' or ''first-round'' financing to give the growing business sufficient capital to meet the demands of defining and developing customer base and creating solid relationships with suppliers. First-round financing usually comes in the form of an equity investment. Venture firms will expect a higher rate of return for first-round investments.

As a new venture prospers, it may require additional financing to meet the capital needs inherent in expansion. Venture firms can provide second-round or ''expansion-round'' financing to their clients whose markets or sales are growing at such a rate that potential for profit looks good. At this point, the venture is usually heading towards success. Assuming the venture's early sales or sales commitments and general market prospects still appear strong, those seeking expansion financing are in a better bargaining position than those seeking first-round or seed money.

If the expansion stage is successful, the new venture may begin a period of fast growth. At this point, the company may be making money, but not enough to finance the rapid expansion. Additional ''growth stage'' or third-round capital may be solicited from venture capital firms. In other cases, the new venture may consider ''going public,'' or offering equity on the public markets as a means of gaining a cash infusion.

In addition to financing different stages of growth, venture capital firms can be of service to entrepreneurs in other, related situations. Some venture firms will assist management in a merger, acquisition, or other form of buyout, where the stock of a company is purchased by a management team or a group of other entrepreneurs with the help and financial support of the venture capital firm's managers. In such a case, the money used to purchase the business is loaned to the buyout team by the venture capital firm. Another area of activity for some venture capital firms is ''turnaround financing'' for businesses that have suffered serious setbacks or are nearing bankruptcy. Funds provided by a venture capital firm are used to finance recovery efforts or launch new programs aimed at turning the business around. Although few firms undertake the risk inherent in financing a turnaround situation, most are willing to consider them as part of their business strategy.

THE SCREENING PROCESS

Competition for venture capitalists' limited funds is extremely intense, and often less than 1 percent of companies that solicit funds actually receive any. Generally only firms with significant growth potential are considered, and thus venture capital is not an option for small, individual-based businesses with less ambitious plans. A typical recipient of venture capital will expect sales in the tens of millions of dollars within the first couple years of their product or service reaching the market, and much larger long-term potential.

Other factors that influence the investment decision include:

- the venture capital firm's confidence in the business management
- how clearly and concisely the business proposition is presented
- the nature of the business and its intended market
- how quickly the company is likely to begin making sales, and especially, profits
- what other individuals or companies are backing the new venture
- personal referrals on the management or business in general

The screening process usually begins formally when the business seeking capital submits a business plan to the venture capital firm, although in practice often there is some form of interpersonal networking leading up to the submission, such as by word of mouth among mutual friends or business associates. Often, start-up firms enlist the support of experienced and well-placed attorneys or accountants who have worked with venture capitalists in the past. Indeed, there are law firms that specialize in this sort of practice. At the very least, usually the head of the start-up firm makes personal contact with a decision maker at the venture capital company via a phone call around the time the plan is submitted.

Venture capitalists scrutinize the business plan and the company submitting it thoroughly before proceeding any further. The venture capital firm must be confident that the claims made by the entrepreneur are realistic and attainable in general, and that the particular company and management team at hand is capable of pulling it off. In both the plan and any subsequent meetings, the venture capitalist attempts to size up the management's clarity of purpose, ability to cope with adversity, and market focus, among other things.

The venture capital firm must also have confidence the investment will pay out according to the plans offered by the entrepreneur. Before a venture capital firm makes an investment, it thoroughly investigates the client and the client's business in a process called **due diligence**. Due diligence simply means extensive research into the industry, the entrepreneur's background and experience, and the reliability of the financial projections supplied by the client. In addition, the due diligence process may include a visit to the client's place of business or questions about the client's personal and professional history. By conducting research into the client, the venture capital firm tries to maximize its understanding of the opportunity and its potential risks and rewards. By accumulating information, the venture capital firm better prepares itself to make the best possible decision about the investment.

After the venture capital firm is confident in the abilities and claims of the entrepreneur, it must be certain that it understands the market in which the new venture will operate. The experience and specialties of the firm's management will dictate whether or not the firm will narrow the focus of their business. Some venture capital firms specialize in certain industries or specific technologies. There are firms that only invest in, for instance, computer network technology businesses. Other firms only work with businesses in the biotechnology field. Consequently, VC firms that have such specialties turn away those businesses that don't fit into their area of expertise.

In recent years in there has been a pronounced emphasis on emerging technology—especially computer-related—by venture capitalists. In 1998, for example, almost two-thirds of all venture capital, or $7.8 billion, was devoted to **information technology** (IT) ventures, according to a VentureOne report. In particular, much of this money was funneled into IT communications applications, including Internet-based technologies. Health-related ventures (often also technological in nature) were a distant second, at $2.7 billion, or 21 percent of all venture capital.

FURTHER READING:

Burrill, G. Steven, and Craig T. Norback. *The Arthur Young Guide to Raising Venture Capital.* Billings, MT: Liberty House, 1988.

Gibson, Paul. ''The Art of Getting Funded.'' *Electronic Business,* March 1999.

Gladstone, David J. *Venture Capital Handbook.* Rev. ed. Englewood Cliffs, NJ: Prentice Hall, 1988.

Littman, Jonathan. ''The New Face of Venture Capital.'' *Electronic Business,* March 1998.

VentureOne Corporation. ''1998 Investment Highlights.'' *Industry Data.* San Francisco, 1999. Available from www.ventureone.com.

VIOLENCE IN THE WORKPLACE

SEE: Workplace Violence Program

VIRTUAL REALITY COMPUTER SIMULATION

Virtual reality (VR) is a computer-generated three-dimensional environment that generally provides real-time interactivity for the user. Within this broad construct are many different forms of VR simulations, some quite simple and others extremely sophisticated. The technology is still quite new—in many cases practical implementations have only been in place since the early and mid-1990s—and relatively underdeveloped. For business uses, some successful applications of VR have been in such areas as product design and modeling, employee training, data visualization, and management decision-making aids. Consumer-oriented applications of VR include games and VR-enabled interactive Internet sites. Overall, in the first years of the 21st century design and education/training applications are seen as the most important for VR technology.

These and other uses are still mostly under development, but already some companies, notably in transportation equipment design, have reported significant cost and planning advantages to using VR versus conventional design methods. For example, automotive designers can use a simulation of proposed car design to pretest usability concerns like the driver's range of view through the windshield, the impact of glare on the windshield, how well the headlight design functions in different driving conditions, and a host of other design factors. If the simulation shows unfavorable results, the design can be changed at a relatively low cost compared to finding these problems only after a physical prototype is made. Thus, the VR design process can not only create a more ergonomic or user-friendly product, but also improve the technical design to reduce the cost of manufacturing, speed up the design phase, increase quality, and so forth.

Just as the uses of VR vary widely, so too do the software programs and hardware that run VR simulations. Most software applications must be at least partially customized by a developer, but increasingly there are off-the-shelf programs that facilitate building and navigating virtual environments. Hardware may range from a relatively recent desktop computer (older PCs would struggle with the graphics and processing demands of VR software) to a headset or even a room that creates a full 3-D sensory experience for the user.

EARLY HISTORY

Although the technology for computer simulation was not actually implemented until the early 1980s by Jaron Lanier in Foster City, California, the concept first received wide publicity in the novel *Brave New World* (1932) by Aldous Huxley. In this novel, set some 600 years in the future, mankind has built the perfect Utopia—complete with ''Feelies,'' movies which give the viewer the ultimate sensation of interacting with the characters and events on the screen. This concept, however, remained just that until the 1960s, when Ivan Sutherland of Stanford University experimented with computer graphics and wrote a software program called SketchPad while working toward his doctoral degree. In an era when most people thought that **computers** were only for crunching numbers, Sutherland used clever software to make the computer manipulate engineering drawings. With SketchPad in the 1960s, Sutherland created the field of computer graphics and demonstrated an entirely new way of talking to the computer—interactive computing. In 1965, Sutherland realized that computers could conjure up powerful visual illusions, illusions that did not have to be confined to a flat, two-dimensional screen. He realized that computers held the key to a much richer kind of visualization and wondered what would happen if he could reach through the screen itself and surround himself in a simulated world. He then built an experimental helmet that gave the user the illusion of being inside a three-dimensional world. As the user moved his or her head, the pictures changed accordingly. But the technology was barely able to handle a simple geometrical world in those days.

More than two decades later, a group of scientists at the University of North Carolina, following Sutherland's academic theories, brought the art of simulation to a level where it could be demonstrated. A head-mounted display (HMD), consisting of a pair of small TV displays, was connected to a helmet and a small tracking system that allowed the computer to determine where the helmet was in position and orientation at every instant. Using these two technologies, scientists were able to program computers to impart to the individual wearing the helmet the feeling of being immersed in a computer-simulated environment. So, instead of looking at a computer-generated image on a standard television set on a table top, the user seemed to be inside that world. And, instead of walking through the world by knobs, buttons, and rotators, the user was able to walk through that world just by looking around. The effect was made all the more vivid because the user was performing those actions he was performing in everyday life.

Jaron Lanier first brought the commercial applications of virtual reality to the public's attention. He almost certainly was influenced by the work of the United States government in flight simulation for the training of astronauts in its aerospace program. Believing that people should be able to create their own media products through interactive computer networks, Lanier founded VPL Research, Inc., as a vehicle for his research into ''virtual reality,'' a term he invented. Virtual reality used the appeal of the simulated experiences of computer games to ''sell'' its multi-sensory data that combined sight, sound, and touch and its interactive capabilities which gave the user greater control. Over the ensuing years, the company introduced many virtual-space hardware products, such as the Datasuit and the Dataglove.

TYPES OF VR ENVIRONMENTS

VR environments can be divided into four categories: (1) total immersion, (2) partial immersion, (3) augmented reality, and (4) desktop. Total immersion, the most elaborate and expensive form, attempts to put the user completely into a computer-generated world. Many total immersion systems are installed in their own rooms or in special modules so that the user may be surrounded by visual, audio, and any other sensory experiences being simulated. Partial immersion includes some special sensory devices, such as goggles or gloves, but is not as extensive as full immersion. Next, augmented reality creates images and sounds that are merged with real-life images or sounds. Augmented reality is sometimes seen as a hybrid or bridge environment between VR and the physical world. Finally, desktop VR is the most basic form, typically a 3-D interactive application on a desktop computer; in most cases this involves only standard computer equipment and no special viewing or other sensory devices. Desktop VR is generally the least costly VR environment.

Telepresence, a form of augmented reality, allows users to create or recreate distant events by being part of the action. Through the user of virtual reality, telepresence can simulate objects, sounds, worlds, and people. The essence of the distant event is conveyed to the user via network links. Real objects and sound are output to a head-mounted display (HMD) from digital data bases, which minimize the amount of information that has to be sent to the user via the communications pipeline. Indeed, telepresence, via microscopic television cameras and fiber optics, is already being used to show doctors how to use virtual reality to perform microscopic surgery.

APPLICATIONS OF VIRTUAL REALITY

Some of the key business and commercial fields that have deployed VR technology include aviation, engineering, medicine, law, and general management functions.

AVIATION APPLICATIONS. As early as 1988, the Simmod (Simulation Module) Air Traffic Control System was helping American Airlines to rank at or near the top as far as on-time performance. Simmod was a microcomputer-based air traffic model that simulated landings, ground movements, and take-offs at any airport in the world. American Airlines was the first to test the Federal Aviation Administration's (FAA) project. At that time, the FAA planned to make the Simmod module available as public-domain software. American Airlines found that senior management believed that Simmod was a crucial planning tool to identify bottlenecks and to predict how factors affected flight schedules.

A related area of aviation in which VR simulation has proven particularly significant is flight training, since it requires many hours of practice and to use real planes for all training is both expensive and more dangerous. Flight simulators are widely used in private industry as well as in military settings.

ENGINEERING APPLICATIONS. Virtual reality has proven a particularly useful tool in engineering and design. Major automotive, aerospace, and other machinery companies, for examples, have eagerly added VR capabilities to their product development processes. Although some see VR as a replacement for **computer-aided design** (CAD), in practice it is used to supplement CAD. Some companies have found it not only useful for the designers to use for themselves, but also for designers to communicate with non-engineers and non-technical decision makers who otherwise would learn very little from looking at a CAD representation of a product.

MEDICAL APPLICATIONS. Although VR technology was deficient in tactile control—haptics—until the early 1990s, great strides were made in the technology that year as it related to medicine. For instance, one basic virtual reality system manipulates abstract objects via a disembodied hand that floats in space. The hand's movements are then translated into commands that can control the visual display. For more complex applications, such as surgery, however, information obtained from tactile manipulation is essential for precise maneuvers. Virtual reality researchers are experimenting with various approaches to solve such tactile deficiencies. One approach utilizes tactors, or tiny switches (created from a ''shape memory'' nickel-titanium alloy) that are sensitive to touch.

Other medical innovations also occurred in the early 1990s. In 1992, computer science professor Henry Fuchs and two graduate students superimposed ultrasonic images of a fetus onto a video image of a pregnant woman's abdomen to provide an accurate and unique perspective for guiding physicians as they inserted and manipulated probes in the body. In 1993, gastroenterologist Duncan Bell and his team of surgeons developed an imaging technique that allowed a physician to use computer-generated images of the patient's tissue to guide the performance of a colonoscopy.

This technology, some doctors believe, might one day permit surgeons to perform procedures from remote sites, bringing specialized care to small communities and rural hospitals. In addition, virtual reality enables superior medical visualization, based on data from CAT imaging systems, and better visualization of diagnostic scans. More immediately, however, a key use of VR simulations is in surgical training, enabling surgeons to hone their skills in an interactive environment without the risk of compromising a patient's health.

LEGAL APPLICATIONS. The legal profession has benefited from the technology's versatility, too. Law students investigating courtroom procedures and argumentation can vicariously interact with "individuals" in a fabricated courtroom. By testing several avenues of debate on the same case, prospective attorneys can see beforehand the results of various approaches to a case. Separately, virtual reality enables accident scenes and other critical events to be reconstructed in the courtroom.

MANAGEMENT APPLICATIONS. Some interesting applications of VR since the mid-1990s have been directed at testing management decisions and strategies. For example, in 1998 *Business Week* reported that the retailer Macy's was having a store simulation model that would allow it to test layout and **merchandising** alternatives before physically implementing them. In this case, the VR system employs a series of so-called adaptive agents, which are computer simulations of individuals given general traits believed to exist in a certain population. These on-screen agents are programmed to make decisions on their own using logic supplied by the programmer.

The whole model depends heavily on the accuracy and comprehensiveness of the logic sets included in the program. Ideally the agents' collective "thoughts" and "actions" would be analogous to those of a representative sample of the real population. Thus, in the store setting, the agents move around the store, respond to different stimuli, and ultimately make purchases or fail to make purchases. The management can then make changes to the virtual store environment and see how the agents' behavior changes over some period, say, a week or a month (which is accelerated on the computer). Once the model is shown to have external validity, i.e., it accurately predicts real human behavior, the company can then use it as a tool for testing policies before they are put into action. Similar customer-response models have been developed in a variety of industries.

General training is another area VR systems are increasingly devoted to. While in activities such as flight simulation the training exercise is directed at hard skills, some of the more recent VR training simulations have focused on soft skills like interpersonal relations. One application, for example, takes participants through a difficult project in which they must secure cooperation from virtual agents, or avatars, who respond in different ways depending on their programmed personalities and on the trainee's behavior toward them.

FURTHER READING:

Byrne, John A. "Virtual Management." *Business Week,* 21 September 1998.

Stamps, David. "One the Road to Virtual Reality." *Training,* September 1998.

Theirauf, Robert J. *Virtual Reality Systems for Business.* Westport, CT: Quorum Books, 1995.

Vince, John. *Essential Virtual Reality Fast.* Berlin: Springer Verlag, 1998.

Watts, Tim, G.M. Peter Swann, and Naresh R. Pandit. "Virtual Reality and Innovation Potential." *Business Strategy Review,* autumn 1998.

Wimsatt, Alison. "Virtual Reality Software Really Flies." *IIE Solutions,* November 1998.

VOCATIONAL EDUCATION

Vocational education is the **training** and retraining of individuals for particular crafts or trades, including training for mechanical and technical careers. This instruction can take place at the secondary or postsecondary level, or as part of **on-the-job training** and retraining programs. Vocational educators seeks to train workers for jobs that do not require degrees from four-year colleges—which account for 65 to 70 percent of all the jobs in the United States.

Vocational education—sometimes referred to as alternative education—is practical education geared towards developing the skills needed for any number of trades and careers. The length of vocational training varies depending on the skills required to perform a particular job.

HISTORY AND BACKGROUND

Vocational education in America can be traced back to the colonial era, when youngsters learned skilled trades through **apprenticeship programs**. Congressional support of vocational education as part of the public school system emerged in 1862, with the passage of the Morrill Tariff Act, which encouraged the establishment of land grant colleges to teach agricultural and mechanical skills. Vocational education began to filter down to the secondary level shortly thereafter, led by Professor Calvin Woodward (1837-1914) of St. Louis's Washington University. Woodward discovered that his engineering students were "woefully inept at the use of simple tools," and therefore urged secondary schools to add training in carpentry, printing, drafting, bricklaying, machine work, and home economics. Woodward hoped to arrive at a curriculum that balanced theoretical and practical knowledge, but the system actually evolved separately from academic schools in the form of manual training and trade schools.

In 1895 the National Association of Manufacturers was founded. This group promoted vocational education as a technique for making the United States globally competitive. The association's leaders based their logic on the performance of the global economic leader of the time, Germany, which supported trade schools and apprenticeship programs. Labor leaders hoped that vocational education would keep children in school longer, thereby protecting them from harsh work environments and simultaneously shrinking the labor force, leading to wage increases. Agriculturists continued to encourage a curriculum that included scientific and technological courses that would help students advance in their field. Social reformers, largely proponents of the Progressive movement, hoped that vocational education would imbue destitute people with the Protestant work ethic and help lift them from poverty. Educational leaders were often trapped in the midst of these diverse interests: many worried that vocational education would interfere with the public school goal of "providing a common education for all students."

In the first decade of the 20th century, forces in these diverse groups formed the National Society for the Promotion of Industrial Education. They lobbied for, and were successful in having Congress pass, legislation launching a public vocational education system in America. The Smith-Hughes Act of 1917 appropriated $1.7 million for secondary-level programs and established a Federal Board of Education. States that chose to participate in the federal vocational plan had to match federal contributions, appoint state directors and boards of vocational education, and formulate local guidelines for use of the funds.

Charles A. Prosser (1871-1952), the first federal administrator of vocational education, had a lasting influence on the program. Prosser maintained that courses at vocational high schools should be job specific, and that the enabling legislation limited training to the fields of agriculture, trade and industry, and home economics. Prosser also encouraged the division of vocational training programs from mainstream public education, thereby creating a system that vocational educator and author Charles Law later characterized as separate and unequal, in part because vocational and academic teachers even had separate certification programs. Over the ensuing six decades, secondary vocational programs grew separately and focused on specific skill training, taking priority over academics. By the late 1970s, combined federal, state, and local expenditures on such programs totaled over $6.6 billion, and enrollment topped 19.5 million.

At this point, serious questions about the rationale behind, and the effectiveness of, vocational education emerged. The U.S. Department of Health, Education, and Welfare had released its critical *Work in America* report in 1972. The study charged that more than 50 percent of the graduates of secondary vocational education programs did not find **employment** related to their specialization, that unemployment statistics for program graduates were not significantly lower than those of traditional grads, that the programs cost from 50 to 75 percent more than traditional curricula, and that the skills taught in such programs were generally obsolete. After an initially defensive reaction, professionals in the field began to question their own practices and objectives.

The issue was thrust upon the general public when the National Commission on Excellence in Education published *A Nation at Risk* in 1983. The report criticized America's public education system (including vocational education) for "offering little or no direction or assistance" to the 50 percent of high school graduates who either did not go on to college or dropped out. Dubbed "forgotten youths," these students were characterized by: having poor basic skills (including communication, math, problem-solving, and teamwork skills), the incapability to link theory and practice, the lack of participation and interest in school activities, and lack of movement from high school to college or the workplace.

Other factors—including military and corporate downsizing, a shrinking labor pool, intensifying **international competition**, and rising college tuition costs—have combined with public calls for change, to prompt reform efforts at all levels of education. In order to revitalize vocational education, schools and industries launched new programs or revamped traditional approaches.

VOCATIONAL EDUCATION IN THE 1990S

Generally, there have been three methods of improving vocational education: integration of academic and vocational high schools, renewed interest in apprenticeship programs and community and technical colleges, and a plethora of private initiatives across the country.

INTEGRATION OF ACADEMIC AND VOCATIONAL PROGRAMS. Integration of academic and vocational high schools was promoted by the Carl D. Perkins Vocational Education and Applied Technology Act of 1990. This legislation encouraged the combination of academic and vocational curricula so that students could obtain both academic and occupational knowledge and abilities. The objective of such programs reflect the goal established by Calvin Woodward for his 19th-century manual-training schools: the union of the finest curricular and instructional practices of academic and vocational education into a single learning experience. Pilot integration programs funded by the Perkins Act generally have four themes in common: promotion of academic and generic skills through an engaging curricula, activity-based motivational and practical teaching methods, interdisciplinary cooperation, and a focus on skills and knowledge needed by students to make the transition to employment or college. Such programs have been undertaken in Ohio, Kentucky, California, Oregon, and Virginia.

APPRENTICESHIPS. Apprenticeships, which have existed in the United States since the colonial era, have also received increased attention among today's vocational educators. Due to shortages of skilled workers in many fields, apprenticeships became a method for industries to help ensure they had a sufficient supply of skilled workers. Apprenticeship is a contractual relationship between an employer and an employee that lasts a specific length of time during which the apprentice worker learns all aspects (including techniques and theory) of a trade. Apprenticeships range in length from one to six years, averaging four years, and may be cosponsored by trade unions. An apprentice's pay usually amounts to half that of an experienced skilled worker, and increases over the course of the program. Individuals who successfully complete one of over 830 federally registered apprenticeships receive certification. According to the *Occupational Outlook Quarterly,* ''About 100,000 new apprentices are registered each year,'' mostly in construction.

Although a high school diploma or its equivalent is usually a prerequisite to entry into an apprentice program, complaints from industries that high school students lacked sufficient skills for certain jobs prompted the growth of school-to-apprenticeship programs in which high school students split their days between academics and part-time apprenticeships. They are graduated to full-time apprenticeships and eventually reach the skilled tradesperson status. In 1990 the U.S. Department of Labor (USDL) inaugurated Apprenticeship 2000, a series of pilot school-to-work programs based on Germany's dual-educational system. The USDL also set up state and regional bureaus of apprenticeship and training around the country. These have expanded the application of the apprenticeship concept from traditional blue-collar fields such as plumbing and bricklaying, to areas including food services, health care, and the hospitality industry.

SCHOOL-TO-WORK PROGRAMS. The School-to-Work Opportunity Act of 1994 officially ushered in the federal government's promotion of school and industry partnerships through five-year grants. Since the enactment of this legislation, 37 states, about 2,000 schools, 135,000 employers, and 500,000 students have participated in school-to-work programs sponsored by the act. Nevertheless, numerous school-to-work programs predated the act. For example, the Boston Private Industry Council's ''Project Protech'' began matching four urban high schools with some of the city's most renowned teaching hospitals in 1991. With funding from the U.S. Department of Labor's Office of Work-Based Learning, the four-year program begins in a student's junior year in high school, gradually phases in on the-job training, and then segues into community college coursework after high school graduation. In addition, many other employers participate in school-to-work programs, including high-tech companies in the **computer** and communications industries.

Other aspects of school-to-work programs entail having students visit work sites, attend career seminars and workshops, take inventory of their skills and interests, and shadow workers. Through these programs, participating employers provide information sessions at schools and schools conduct various career workshops and seminars and offer courses on cultivating different work skills. Schools and participating employers also arrange student visits to work sites and allow students to shadow workers—or observe and follow workers as they perform their tasks.

COMMUNITY COLLEGES AND TECHNICAL COLLEGES. Community and technical colleges have also become important centers of preparatory and remedial vocational education. The first community colleges opened around the turn of the century and by 1990s there were roughly 900 public two-year colleges with over 4 million students enrolled. Community colleges, especially in the second half of the century, have played an instrumental role in training students for a host of vocations. Technical colleges such as DeVry, Inc. developed later in the 20th century. DeVry, for instance, was established in 1931 as an electronics trade school with two campuses, in Chicago and Toronto. It began a period of rapid expansion in the late 1960s, and by the early 1980s the DeVry chain of schools boasted 30,000 students. Displacement of workers from the military and the defense industry, combined with rising tuition costs at liberal arts colleges have benefited community colleges such as DeVry. In the 1990s, the chain responded to industries needs for remedial worker education with on-site training programs.

Some businesses have taken vocational education upon themselves to survive. For example, the Will-Burt Co., a steel manufacturing and assembly concern in Orrville, Ohio, was faced with a myriad of problems. Declining profits and sales, employee turnover of more than 30 percent, and a product reject rate of 35 percent threatened the company's future. Remediating faulty work, in fact, consumed about 25,000 hours annually at the plant. In cooperation with

Wayne College, a branch campus of the University of Akron, CEO Harry Featherstone (1929-) developed a mandatory educational course that included practical applications of math, blueprint reading, geometry, and statistics. The program was undertaken on company time at full pay. Featherstone reflected on the project's success, noting that within a few years, employee turnover was reduced to 2.5 percent, product rejects plummeted to 7 percent, and manufacturing efficiency increased over 95 percent. He estimated that the program cost $200,000.

SKILLED WORKER SHORTAGES. Because of many factors, including a low national unemployment rate and public perception of skilled trade jobs, there was shortage of skilled trade workers in the 1990s. Consequently, companies, **labor unions**, and schools considered ways of making the skilled trades more appealing and attracting more people to them, as well as ways of training workers to perform tasks in high-tech environments. For example, the National Tooling and Machining Association reported that related job vacancies totaled about 20,000 in 1998, and the National Institute of Metalworking Skills predicted that this number would reach 40,000 by 2003.

Some solutions to the shortage include: (1) joint apprenticeship and training programs where students work as apprentices for companies while completing courses at community colleges, (2) skilled trade certification programs through community colleges, and (3) augmented high school metalworking and machine shop courses. Like other apprenticeship programs, this one allows students to hold a job in fields they are learning and gain hands on experience. In addition, it provides students with necessary classroom training in math, science, and shop skills.

Proposals for certification in the skilled trades recommend four-year cooperative programs modeled after the joint apprenticeship programs that provide students with academic preparation as well as hands-on experience. This program, however, would confer an associate's degree on students after completion of the program. Advocates of this program suggest that companies and unions should determine how many students participate in it based on present and projected market demand for skilled tradespersons, which would ensure graduates employment after completing the program.

Finally, high schools will have to improve their metalworking and shop classes in order train enough skilled trade workers to fill all the empty positions. High schools in California, however, tended to reduce and terminate their skilled trade programs instead of strengthening and modernizing them in the 1990s due to limited and shrinking school budgets.

SEE ALSO: Apprenticeship Programs

[April Dougal Gasbarre, updated by Karl Heil]

FURTHER READING:

''Apprenticeship.'' *Occupational Outlook Quarterly* 35 (winter 1991/1992): 26-40.

Byrne, Harlan S. ''DeVry Inc.'' *Barron's,* 8 February 1993, 36-38.

Gardner, Greg. ''Crunch Time for Skilled Trades.'' *Ward's Auto World,* August 1998.

Law, Charles J., Jr. *Tech Prep Education: A Total Quality Approach.* Lancaster, PA: Technomic Publishing, 1994.

Matthes, Karen. ''Apprenticeships Can Support the Forgotten Youth.'' *HR Focus* 68 (December 1991): 19.

McClure, Arthur F., James Riley Chrisman, and Perry Mock. *Education for Work: The Historical Evolution of Vocational and Distributive Education in America.* Cranbury, NJ: Associated University Presses, 1985.

''Partners in Progress: Early Steps in Creating School-to Work Systems.'' *Spectrum: The Journal of State Government* 70, no. 4 (fall 1997): 15+.

Sharf, Stephen. ''Wake-Up Call: A Solution to Skilled-Trades Shortage.'' *Ward's Auto World,* August 1998.

VOCATIONAL REHABILITATION

Vocational rehabilitation refers to any programs that seek to restore disabled individuals to their optimal physical, mental, social, vocational, and economic ability. In a legal sense, vocational rehabilitation is a **workers' compensation** benefit in some states, which involves programs designed to help workers who have become physically or mentally disabled and who can no longer hold the same jobs they had prior to their disabilities. Most vocational rehabilitation programs—whether part of workers' compensation or not—aid the disabled in receiving training for new occupations, locating jobs, retaining jobs, and building permanent careers.

The Social Security Administration defines a disability generally as a limitation in the type or quantity of work someone can perform, stemming from a chronic condition with a duration of six months or more. Hence, this definition includes those who cannot work regularly or at all and are considered ''severely disabled'' as well as those who must seek new occupations because of their limitations and those who can continue to perform the same job but not the same amount of work.

Both public and private vocational rehabilitation programs exist. Each state has its own joint federally and state-funded vocational rehabilitation program with similar eligibility requirements, policies, and offerings. Eligibility requirements tend to be general and allow anyone with a disability who needs job assistance to take advantage of these programs. In addition, state veterans departments offer analogous services to veterans who became disabled as a result of their military duties. Furthermore, a host of private companies and organizations offer vocational rehabilitation services. These private providers include everything from charitable organizations to insurance companies.

HISTORY OF VOCATIONAL REHABILITATION

The roots of vocational rehabilitation in America can be traced to the diffuse development of disability-specific workshops in the early 19th century. The first of these was the Perkins Institute, incorporated in Boston in 1829 to train blind individuals for manufacturing jobs. Efforts such as this were few and far between, however, until turn-of-the-century Progressivism strengthened the impetus. Social justice was a key concern of the Progressive political movement, and many forward-looking vocational rehabilitation organizations were established during the era. Some programs, such as Goodwill Industries, the Salvation Army, the Society of St. Vincent de Paul, and the Jewish Vocational Service Agencies, evolved under the sponsorship of religious organizations. Others—such as the groundbreaking Sunbeam Circle (now known as Vocational Guidance and Rehabilitation Services) in Cleveland, Ohio; the National Society for Crippled Children and Adults (also known as the Easter Seals Society) in Elyria, Ohio; and the Red Cross Institution for Crippled and Disabled Men (ICD Rehabilitation and Research Center) in New York City—were the result of private altruism. All these programs have since expanded nationwide.

By far the greatest stimulus to vocational rehabilitation arose after World War I, when the influx of disabled veterans from overseas battlefields proved too much for private institutions to bear. There were philosophical and practical motives for inauguration of the public program of vocational rehabilitation. Soldiers had fulfilled their obligation to the country; the nation owed its disabled veterans the opportunity to return to work and productivity. In this pre-welfare era, private social support was simply not sufficient to support the millions of potential dependents. These factors compelled the passage of the Smith-Hughes Act of 1917, which created the Federal Board for Vocational Education of Veterans. The Soldier Rehabilitation Act of 1918 expanded Smith-Hughes to provide vocational training to disabled veterans. Ratification of the Vocational Rehabilitation (Smith-Fess) Act two years later extended services to disabled civilians. Vocational rehabilitation marked a significant landmark in the thirties, when the passage of the Social Security Act of 1935 established the first permanent base for the federal program.

These various pieces of legislation set up a federal/state cooperative whose budget was evenly shared. States that wanted to participate submitted a plan of action for federal approval and reported annually to the Federal Board for Vocational Education. The state agencies were prohibited from using funds for buildings, equipment, or physical restoration. A network of federal, state, and private agencies evolved through the passage of over a dozen pieces of legislation throughout the ensuing decades. These laws expanded the definition of eligibility and increased the amount of expenditures toward the program. By 1923, 36 states participated in the $1.3 million program. The federal government's role was to set administrative procedures and techniques, provide funding, and promote the program. Responsibility for actual programming fell to the states. In practice, state agencies usually evaluated client eligibility and potential for rehabilitation, provided counseling, and managed job placement. State agencies often contracted with private organizations for medical treatment, physical rehabilitation, and occupational training. In his text *Introduction to Rehabilitation,* James A. Bitter characterized the public-private vocational rehabilitation partnership as "perhaps the most successful human service program in the United States."

The public vocational rehabilitation program grew dramatically during the late 1950s and throughout the 1960s. Federal expenditures increased from $23 million in 1954 to $600 million by 1970. Funding for buildings, maintenance, and research was permitted, and definitions of eligibility were expanded during the period to include those developmentally disabled by epilepsy, cerebral palsy, and other neurological impairments.

Vocational rehabilitation came to the attention of the business community during the 1970s, when state governments, led by California, began to make it a mandatory part of the resolution of workers' compensation cases. A concurrent nationwide study of on-the-job injuries emphasized the failures of workers' compensation programs and spurred public and union pressure to make vocational rehabilitation part of disability management programs across America. Predictably, many employers resented and resisted vocational rehabilitation as yet another expensive bureaucracy. By the late 1980s, some states, including Georgia, Minnesota, and New Mexico, repealed the requirement. But two circumstances soon converged to make vocational rehabilitation more viable in the eyes of business leaders. By the early 1990s, abuse of the workers' compensation system had pushed annual national costs over $60 billion. Once again, California led the way: stress claims alone increased 700 percent from 1982 to 1992.

Perhaps the most important legislation affecting vocational rehabilitation since 1935 was the 1990 **Americans with Disabilities Act** (ADA). This mandate built upon the foundation laid by the Rehabilitation Act of 1973, which prohibited federal agencies, programs, and contractors from discriminating against people with disabilities. The ADA also incorporated the nondiscriminatory ideals of the Civil Rights Act of 1964, ruling that ''no employer shall discriminate against a qualified individual with a disability because of the disability of such individual in regard to job application procedures, the hiring or discharge of employees, employee compensation, advancement, job training, and other term and conditions of employment.'' The law requires that all employers, public and private, of more than 25 people make ''reasonable accommodations'' (in terms of expense and degree of change) for disabled employees. The ADA also dramatically broadened the definition of disability to include any ''physical or mental impairment that substantially limits one or more of the major life activities,'' (including work) a history of having such an impairment, or even the perception of having an impairment.

The combined impact of skyrocketing workers' compensation costs and the legal requirements of the ADA compelled employers and insurers to turn to vocational rehabilitation as a cost containment technique. The alternative was the courtroom, for example: from October 1992 to October 1993, approximately 3,300 cases filed with the **Equal Employment Opportunity Commission** were concerned with employers' failure to provide reasonable accommodation to disabled workers.

Congress strengthened the right of the disabled to work when it passed the Rehabilitation Act Amendments of 1992. These amendments included the requirements that even the severely disabled receive vocational rehabilitation and that people with disabilities must be given the opportunity to seek gainful **employment**. Six years later the Rehabilitation Act was reauthorized with the Rehabilitation Act Amendments of 1998. These amendments called for the establishment of the Interagency Committee on Disability Research to encourage and coordinate research projects related to vocational rehabilitation among government agencies and departments. The amendments of 1998 also created the National Institute on Disability and Rehabilitation Research to carry out vocational rehabilitation research within the U.S. Department of Education.

PRACTICAL APPLICATIONS OF VOCATIONAL REHABILITATION

Aside from the legal requirements of the ADA, there are many practical justifications for the application of vocational rehabilitation. Moreover, there is an ample supply of working-age people with disabilities. The President's Committee on Employment of People with Disabilities reported that there were about 30 million working-age people with disabilities in the United States in 1994. Of these disabled people, about 52 percent or 15.39 million were employed. In contrast, 82 percent of the general working-age population is employed, indicating the additional progress vocational rehabilitation efforts must make to reach a comparable level of employment for the disabled. What's more, a study released by Northwestern National Life in 1994 estimated that more than 25 percent of 25-year-old workers would be disabled for one year before they reached retirement age. In purely economic terms, these individuals represent hundreds of billions of dollars in welfare expenditures and lost productivity every year. In purely human terms, citizens of a democracy such as ours can claim ''an inherent right to earn a living,'' as asserted by Bitter in *Introduction to Rehabilitation.* Since 1918, vocational rehabilitation has existed as a tool for both cost containment and **empowerment**.

Vocational rehabilitation can help solve other workplace dilemmas as well. Marriott Corporation, a food service company, turned to vocational rehabilitation as a solution to its problems of high **employee turnover** and a dwindling labor pool. The company tapped into the largely neglected supply of workers with disabilities through an in-house program called Pathways to Independence. Pathways incorporated job matching, social and occupational training, and ongoing support. The leading fast food chain, McDonald's, initiated its McJobs program in 1981 for similar reasons. The six- to eight-week program recruits, trains, and employs an average of 900 mildly to severely disabled people annually.

Technological **innovations** have further promoted placement of rehabilitated employees. IBM Corp.'s National Support Center for Persons with Disabilities, for example, opened in 1985. It features more than 800 devices and tools that can ease the transition to work, including voice synthesizers, adapters for people with impaired mobility, and voice-activated **computers**. Contrary to popular belief, disabled workers are not typically expensive or difficult to accommodate. The President's Committee on Employment of People with Disabilities released a survey in 1996 that indicated 20 percent of workplace modifications cost nothing, and 51 percent cost between $500 and $1, and only 4 percent cost over $5,000. Furthermore, Sears, Roebuck and Co. has noted that 90 percent of its accommodations have cost nothing. The survey by the President's Committee on Employment of People with Disabilities also reported that the average accommodation expenditure was $200 and that for every dollar spent on accommodation of the disabled, companies saved $34 in costs stemming from workers' compensation, insurance, and **training**.

In addition to the potential bottom-line benefits of vocational rehabilitation, such programs can promote positive employee relations. Communicating the benefits of the program, keeping in contact with workers on disability leave, and establishing light- and alternate-duty occupations can help show all employees that they are valued contributors to a business.

HOW VOCATIONAL REHABILITATION WORKS

Vocational rehabilitation is a very individualized, goal-oriented process with the ultimate objective of employing its clientele. The delivery of this service is comprised of several steps, including diagnosis, compilation of an individualized written rehabilitation program, counseling and guidance, physical and mental restoration, training, job placement, and post-employment services. Vocational rehabilitation clients are often referred to rehabilitation agencies by schools, hospitals, welfare agencies, and other agencies or organizations, yet many are self-referred or referred by a physician.

Usually at the outset the disabled are assigned a counselor who conducts the diagnosis by gathering various kinds of information to determine eligibility. Diagnosis occurs at several levels. A preliminary diagnostic study determines a prospective client's eligibility for rehabilitation services in the public program. A medical evaluation identifies a client's disabilities and functional limitations. This very vital assessment may incorporate a physical examination as well as investigation of the client's medical and vocational history. A psychological evaluation of mental and emotional abilities and limitations, both historical and current, can also be included. A sociocultural evaluation includes compilation of identifying information; personal, family, and home life histories; educational and work histories; and assessment of personality, habits, and economic situation. The vocational evaluation is an assessment of the client's occupational aptitudes and potential; work history, habits, interests, attitudes, and responsibilities; as well as the tenor of previous work relationships. Finally, the educational evaluation relates the client's skills to his or her vocational potential. It includes information on the level of education (including special areas of interest and achievement), as well as learning capacity and study habits. Clearly, many aspects of the diagnostic study overlap, just as the individual aspects of people's lives converge. The findings of these diagnoses are utilized in the next step, compilation of the individualized written rehabilitation program with the client.

The individualized written rehabilitation program is jointly developed by the rehabilitation counselor and the client (or the client's representative, in the case that the client is unable to contribute to the discussion). At this point, the client and the counselor plan a program of services based on the client's needs and objectives. This ''plan of attack'' includes:

1. a justification of the client's eligibility for treatment,
2. a long-range employment goal,
3. intermediate goals,
4. identification of the services necessary to reach those goals,
5. projected beginning dates for each service and the duration of each,
6. a procedure and schedule for the evaluation of the individual program.

After the both parties agree to a program of services, the counselor makes arrangements for providing the client with the services needed. The services a client receives may include counseling, education, job placement, physical or mental restoration, career training, and work modification or accommodation.

Counseling and guidance are ongoing aspects of vocational rehabilitation. Called ''the synthesizing function of the rehabilitation process,'' counseling promotes the entire program. Physical and mental restoration works to alleviate the physical or mental conditions that impede a client's fullest potential functioning. This step may include medical, physical, and therapeutic treatment; prosthetics and/or orthotics; occupational or communication therapy; and psychiatry.

There are four types of training that a client of vocational rehabilitation may undergo: personal adjustment training, prevocational training, compensatory skill training, and vocational training. Personal adjustment training refers to the development of pro-work attitudes and habits such as dependability, responsibility, and consistency. Prevocational training endows the background knowledge necessary to choose and prepare for occupational skill development. This may include tours of job sites, study of industries, and learning to fill out job applications and use public transportation. Compensatory skill training refers to the development of skills that make up for a disability, i.e., speech or lip reading for the hearing impaired and mobility training for the visually impaired. Vocational training alludes to the development of specific job skills, usually at trade and vocational schools, colleges and universities, rehabilitation facilities, sheltered workshops, and **apprenticeship programs**, or on the job.

Before entering the job market or receiving job placement services, clients, especially those with severe physical or mental disabilities, may participate in sheltered workshops designed to prepare clients for the competitive labor market. The sheltered workshop is a not-for-profit enterprise that can use the services of workers with restricted abilities and limited skills. Workshops tend to employ the disabled to perform assembly, collating, custodial, mailing, packaging, and **telemarketing** tasks. These workshops include Goodwill Industries, Citizens Development Center, and Ennis Association for Retarded Citizens, among others.

Job placement is the climax of the entire rehabilitation process. This complicated and underrated step matches client and job. Just as no two work environments are exactly alike, no two vocational rehabilitation clients are exactly alike. Job placement often entails cooperation between the vocational rehabilitation agency and the potential employer, including modification of a job and/or the work environment. Computerization has helped facilitate the placement process. The Occupational Access System is an example of ''transferable skills analysis'' **software**. This job-matching software package based on the U.S. Department of Labor's *Dictionary of Occupational Titles* can help mate a client's skills, work history, and interests with occupations. Databases of adaptive equipment can also facilitate a return to work.

Placement is not the end of the vocational rehabilitation story. Some clients require postemployment services such as continued counseling, supplementary training, health services, assistance with transportation, or other rehabilitation services.

[April Dougal Gasbarre, updated by Karl Heil]

FURTHER READING:

Bitter, James A. *Introduction to Rehabilitation.* C.V. Mosby, 1979.

Callahan, Michael J., et al. *Keys to the Workplace.* Baltimore: Paul H. Brookes Publishing, 1997.

Gice, Jon. ''The Relevance of the Americans with Disabilities Act to Workers Compensation.'' *CPCU Journal,* June 1992, 79-83.

Heine, Alicia. ''Killing Two Birds with One Stone.'' *Business Insurance.* 16 May 1994, 33-34.

Jones, David C. ''Co. Using Technology in Vocational Rehabilitation.'' *National Underwriter,* 8 November 1993, 2, 13.

Levitan, Sar A., and Robert Taggert. *Jobs for the Disabled.* Baltimore: Johns Hopkins University Press, 1977.

Madeja, Peter C. ''Return-to-Work Programs: Employers Should Re-examine Vocational Rehabilitation.'' *Business Insurance,* 28 September 1992, 47-48.

Mulcahy, Colleen. ''Rehab Saves $35 for Every $1 Spent, Study Finds.'' *National Underwriter,* 9 May 1994, 17.

Obermann, C. Esco. *A History of Vocational Rehabilitation in America.* Arno Press, 1980.

Weiss, Joseph W. *The Management of Change: Administrative Logics and Actions.* Praeger Publishers, 1986.

Wiley, Carolyn. ''Programs that Lead the Way in Enabling People with Disabilities to Work.'' *Employment Relations Today,* spring 1992, 31-38.

W

WAN

SEE: Wide Area Networks

WARRANTIES AND GUARANTEES

A warranty or guarantee is given to the purchaser by a product manufacturer or provider of a service with the understanding that the manufacturer or provider will replace or repair a defective product or make good an ineffective service within a predetermined span of time. Popularized by national retailers and automobile manufacturers over the last few decades, written or implied warranties have become virtually standard and necessary to secure the trust of consumers. Few things are sold these days without some form of warranty—with the stereotypical exception of used cars where the original manufacturer's warranty has lapsed and dealers often choose not to offer one of their own.

New cars are a different story, however, and provide the most visible use of warranties by manufacturers. Every television commercial for automobiles today touts the length of the warranty. In the 1960s Chrysler Corp. emphasized its generous warranty over the features of its cars, when it created an advertising jingle proclaiming that its cars were covered for ''five long years or 50,000 miles—whichever comes first.'' Korean automobile manufacturer Hyundai also offered generous warranties on its 1998 models in an effort to counteract a reputation for mechanical unreliability. Used car purchasers are sometimes able to enjoy warranty protection, as a secondary industry arose in the late 1990s to sell extended service contracts covering certain repairs on used and leased cars.

In the 1980s and 1990s, consumer activists greatly expanded car warranty coverage with the passage of ''lemon laws'' in many state legislatures. These laws hold that automobiles should at least work reliably beyond the manufacturers' written warranties. If a consumer buys an automobile that undergoes continuous and unreasonable mechanical problems, lemon laws give the consumer the leverage to force the dealer to remedy the problems. Sometimes the simplest remedy for the dealer is to buy the vehicle back or offer the consumer a reduced price on a new car. This imposes a serious financial burden on dealers, and a dealership of the Ford Motor Company in New Jersey successfully sued the parent company in 1996, claiming that Ford inflated the price of its cars to cover warranty repair costs, to the detriment of the dealers' business. Controversy has also arisen within the automobile industry regarding the responsibility of off-site suppliers of parts for warranty-related customer claims, although many small suppliers claim that they could not survive if made to pay for a portion of automotive warranty claims.

The manufacturers of high-cost electronic products such as computers have incorporated longer warranties as selling points against their competition, implying that any equipment sold with a shorter warranty must be of lesser quality. Often warranties can be extended for a full year for as little as $100, giving peace of mind to computer users while bringing in millions of dollars to computer manufacturers confident that their equipment will function well past the extended warranty date. One study estimated that nearly 40 percent of buyers of electronic products purchase extended warranties as do more than half of car buyers.

New types of warranties were developed in the late 1990s in response to changes in the marketplace and new environmental regulations. The use of home warranties by builders and developers to boost housing sales also became commonplace, and in 1998 the State of California considered extending warranty coverage to automotive emissions inspections and services.

While manufacturers would like consumers to think of warranties as something they provide as evidence of their faith in their products, the truth is that most warranties are covered by local, state, and federal laws. The final judge in this country is the **Federal Trade Commission**, which uses the Magnuson-Moss Warranty-Federal Trade Commission Improvement Act of 1975 as its guideline. This law requires stores to provide consumers with copies of written warranties for products costing more than $15 if the customer requests them before making a purchase. The retailer should keep a binder or folder of warranties for all the products it carries.

States require that the manufacturer or seller of a product offer an implied warranty—some sort of guarantee that the product will work once it is out of the box and that it will work in the way that its manufacturer says it will. A wet vacuum that is supposed to suck up water from the garage floor has to perform that job, or the consumer has a legal right to return it for one that does. The length of time that these implied warranties are in effect varies from state to state.

There are two types of written warranties: full and limited. A manufacturer offering a full warranty must grant it for a specific length of time, must make repairs at no charge in a reasonable length of time, and cannot require the customer to jump through any hoops in order to invoke the warranty. Limited warranties, which must be labeled so in writing, limit the liability of the manufacturer. A limited warranty may offer to replace defective parts free while still levying high labor charges or require that the consumer ship the product to a manufacturer-approved service center. The distinctions between full and limited warranties and the obligations of manufacturers to honor them vary from state to state so it is up to the consumer to carefully read the literature and understand what is covered before the purchase. Fortunately for consumers, manufacturers are required to follow any implied warranties created by local laws.

What some consumers wish would be part of a warranty might not be. The warranty might cover direct damages such as fixing a broken refrigerator but exclude indirect damages such as the cost of replacing ruined food that was in the refrigerator when it broke down. Some implied warranties exist that manufacturers leave consumers to discover on their own. One example is fixing paint on cars. Automobile manufacturers do not advertise that they can sometimes be persuaded that paint should not flake off a car after the warranty has expired. It may take persistence to get past the local dealer, but every year hundreds of dissatisfied car owners receive new paint jobs, sometimes after negotiations have failed and the car owners have threatened to publicize their cases or purchase competing models.

Extended warranties remain controversial. Manufacturers sell them betting that the extended warranty will not be needed or used, thereby resulting in profits. Consumers buy them for peace of mind, under the assumption that they are protecting their initial outlay of money. The controversy revolves around what the warranties cover. Some extended warranties are actually service agreements, resulting in higher charges than might be expected under a warranty. In other cases the fine print in the warranties exclude the very things that the consumer assumes would be covered. Automobile extended warranties usually require that consumers keep meticulous service records. For example, car owners who do not keep their receipts for oil and transmission fluid changes could find that they have invalidated the extended warranty purchased when the car was new.

Do consumers need extended warranties? One survey found only 38 percent of consumers who had bought extended warranties had ever had anything repaired under them. Of the manufacturers responding to the same survey, 62 percent reported offering extended warranties, but only 13 percent of the warranty work they performed was for a customer holding an extended warranty. By 1996, misuse of extended warranties led more than 30 states to consider or enact regulation of extended service businesses. Manufacturers and contractors in certain industries also began to question the efficacy of extended warranties, with 76 percent of heating and cooling contractors reporting in 1996 that their extended service contract programs were losing money. In fact, difficulties encountered by manufacturers and contractors offering extended warranties and service contracts have given rise to a new industry, in which insurance companies offer companies protection against unexpected levels of extended warranty and service contract claims.

Small, local manufacturers and service providers who believe that adding warranties will make their sales pitches more attractive should carefully review local, state, and federal laws such as the Magnuson Moss Act. Governments take the issuing of warranties very seriously as should any company that issues them.

[Clint Johnson, updated by Grant Eldridge]

FURTHER READING:

Caplin, Joan. "Home Buying: How Valuable Is a Warranty?" *Money,* October 1998, 210.

Clay, Jordan E. "Home Warranties Require Close Buyer, Seller Scrutiny." *Dallas Business Journal* 20, no. 46 (18 July 1997): C16.

Conley, Keri. "Home Warranties Are More Popular as Home Buyers Become Cost Wary." *Pittsburgh Business Times* 14, no. 30 (27 February 1995): 12.

"Contractors Can Offer Extended Warranties." *Contractor* 44, no. 3 (March 1997): 5.

Drury, Tracey. "Used Cars Treated Like New Under Terms of Warranty." *Business First of Buffalo* 13, no. 50 (22 September 1997): 32.

"Great Warranty Debate." *Ward's Auto World* 34, no. 7 (July 1998).

Heyler, Jack. "Emission Warranties Expanding." *Motor Age* 117, no. 10 (October 1998): 76.

Mahoney, Thomas A. "Long-Term Warranties Don't Work, Industry Tells the News in Survey." *Air Conditioning, Heating and Refrigeration News* 197, no. 14 (1 April 1996): 1.

Sawyers, Arlena. "Ford to Appeal Ruling that Holds Makers Responsible for Warranties." *Automotive News,* 25 March 1996, 3.

"Service Contract Bills in 30 States." *HFN: The Weekly Newspaper for the Home Furnishing Network,* 12 June 1995, 58.

Simison, Robert L. "Hyundai Plans Turbo-Charged Warranty to Beat the Rap of Problems with Quality." *Wall Street Journal,* 23 September 1998, A4.

Turpin, Joanna R. "Many HVACR Contractors Use Home Warranties to Help Boost Business." *Air Conditioning, Heating and Refrigeration News* 197, no. 10 (4 March 1996): 22.

WARRANTS (SECURITIES)

Warrants are options to purchase a fixed number of shares for a fixed price, known as the warrant-conversion price. Warrants typically have an expiration date, although some are issued in perpetuity. Warrants may be sold either with a bond or **stock** issue. If the underlying stock price rises substantially, the warrant holder can exercise the warrants at the fixed price and participate in the stock's growth. When issued with **bonds**, warrants reduce the bonds' coupon rate. Warrants are typically issued to entice investors with a no-risk opportunity to participate in future growth.

The intrinsic value of a warrant is equal to the market price of one share of common stock, minus the exercise price of the warrant, times the number of shares that can be purchased with each warrant. If the current market price per share of common stock is $10 and the warrant exercise price is $2, and if each warrant allows the investor to purchase two shares, the warrant has an intrinsic value of $16.

The actual market value of a warrant may be higher than the intrinsic value. The difference between the market value and the intrinsic value is the premium. The market value of the warrant can never be less than zero. The premium depends on the warrant's leverage effect, the time to maturity, and the volatility of the price of the underlying stock. The warrant's leverage depends on the difference between the market price of the underlying stock and the warrant exercise price; the greater the difference in price, the higher the leverage and the greater the potential for gain or loss. The longer the time to maturity, the higher the premium, because the probability that the underlying stock will increase in price is greater. The greater the volatility of the underlying stock, the higher the premium, again because the probability that the underlying stock will increase in price is greater.

The warrant premium is a negative function of the cash dividend paid on the underlying stock. Since the owner of the warrant does not own the underlying stock, he/she is not entitled to the cash dividend paid. The larger the dividend that is paid on the underlying stock, the lower the premium on the warrant.

Some restrictions may apply to stock acquired through warrants. In the case of ordinary warrants, the **Securities and Exchange Commission (SEC)** requires investors who have exercised warrants to delay selling their stock until the expiration of a holding period-usually two years. To bypass this restriction companies began issuing net-issuance warrants, in which no cash is exchanged when the warrants are exercised. If the net-issuance warrant entitled an investor to purchase $5,000 worth of stock at a $2,000 warrant-conversion price, the company would subtract the cost of the conversion and issue $3,000 worth of stock to the investor.

[Carl B. McGowan, Jr., updated by David P. Bianco]

FURTHER READING:

Carlsen, Clifford. "Document Uses Warrants as Lure in Stock Offering," *San Francisco Business Times,* 1 November 1991.

Ehrhardt, Michael C., and Ronald E. Shrieves. "The Impact of Warrants and Convertible Securities on the Systematic Risk of Common Equity," *The Financial Review,* November 1995.

McHattie, Andrew. *The Investor's Guide to Warrants: Capitalize on the Fastest Growing Sector of the Markets.* Financial Times Management, 1996.

Reilly, Frank K., and Keith C. Brown. *Investment Analysis and Portfolio Management.* 5th ed. Fort Worth, TX: Dryden Press, 1996.

Spiro, Herbert T. *Finance for the Nonfinancial Manager.* 4th ed. New York: John Wiley & Sons, 1996.

WEALTH

The concept of wealth refers to the value of the total quantity of goods or assets in existence at a particular time. Private wealth, or the wealth of an individual, consists of the value of things owned, including money and other claims against goods and services such as **stocks** and **bonds**. In the case of national wealth, however, money and other claims against goods and services are not included as part of a country's wealth. Rather, national wealth consists of the goods in existence that are available for use. Thus, a distinction is made between private wealth and national wealth. If an individual destroys a $100 bill, that person loses wealth, but the national wealth remains unaffected.

Wealth is a measurement of a stock of goods at a particular time. Wealth is said to be a stock concept. In contrast, **income** and **gross national product** are flow concepts. That is, production and income measure the rate at which goods and services are produced over a period of time. While national wealth may be measured in terms of dollars, it is important to realize that national wealth consists of a supply of goods, not money or claims against goods.

Real or national wealth consists of two types of goods, natural wealth and produced wealth. Natural wealth includes the value of a country's natural resources, such as minerals, farm land, and construction sites. Produced wealth, or capital goods, consists of machinery, buildings, equipment, and inventories of raw materials and finished products. Capital goods, in turn, include both consumer capital, producer capital, and government capital. Consumer capital includes such items as automobiles, appliances, and furniture. Producer capital consists of buildings, productive equipment, inventory, and other goods that are owned by business firms. Government capital includes those goods owned by various governments, such as police and fire vehicles, highways, sewers, schools, and jails.

The capital stock portion of national wealth may be increased through investment. Gross private domestic investment is that part of the gross national product that is spent on nonresidential structures, producer durable equipment, residential structures, and increases in business inventories. Gross investment includes the replacement of older equipment as well as additions to the total amount of capital goods. Net investment, or the net addition to the stock of capital goods, is calculated by subtracting capital consumption allowances from gross investment.

[David P. Bianco]

FURTHER READING:

Blanchard, Olivier. *Macroeconomics.* Upper Saddle River, NJ: Prentice Hall, 1997.

Froyen, Richard T. *Macroeconomics: Theories and Policies.* 6th ed. Upper Saddle River, NJ: Prentice Hall, 1998.

Hess, Peter, and Clark G. Ross. *Economic Development, Theories, Evidence, and Policies: Theories, Evidence, and Policies.* HBJ College and School Div., 1997.

Mansfield, Edwin. *Principles of Microeconomics.* 7th ed. New York: W. W. Norton & Company, 1992.

WHITE COLLAR CRIME

The term *white collar crime* was first used in 1939 during an address delivered by Professor Edwin Sutherland of Indiana University to the American Sociological Society. Sutherland sought to expand the definition of crime beyond the generally held belief that crime was an activity, often violent, perpetrated by members of the socio-economic under class. Sutherland felt that viewing crime from this old perspective ignored the fact that ''persons of the upper socio-economic class engage in much criminal behavior; that this behavior differs from the criminal behavior of the lower socio-economic classes principally in the administrative procedures used in dealing with the offenders,'' (see Rosoff). American business history is, of course, replete with violations of law by the so called ''robber barons'' and ''captains of industry.'' White collar crime was used metaphorically by Sutherland to differentiate between crimes committed by people working in office buildings and crimes committed by those who were either unemployed or occupied in the ''blue collar'' trades. To Sutherland, a white collar crime was a crime ''committed by a person of respectability and high social status in the course of his occupation.'' Sutherland thus sought to connect the social status of the white collar criminal with the ''occupational mechanism'' by which his or her crime is committed.

White collar crime has come to be a generic term for a broad and ever expanding range of non-violent criminal activity including but not limited to: embezzlement, bribery, money laundering, illegal lobbying activities, consumer fraud, price fixing, income tax fraud, and computer ''hacking'' or computer break-ins. Because white collar crimes are so varied, it is difficult to come up with hard data on both the number of white collar crimes committed in the United States each year and the dollar amount involved. Governmental agencies such as the U.S. Justice Department, for instance, do not have a data category that collectively encompasses all offenses generally considered to constitute white collar crime.

Nevertheless various organizations often attempt to arrive at monetary estimates of the problem. The **U.S. Department of Commerce**, for instance, estimated in 1974 that white collar crime was a $40 billion ''industry.'' By 1996, however, the Association of Certified Fraud Examiners felt that the figure for occupational fraud and abuse—internal fraud—topped $400 billion. That organization's 1996 *Report to the Nation on Occupational Fraud and Abuse* also estimated that organizations generally lose about six percent of revenue to white collar crime.

White collar crime, although not identified as such until the mid-20th century, is not a recent phenomena. White collar crime has existed in business since the first entrepreneurs opened shop. Cases of fraud date back as far as 360 B.C., when Xenothemis and Hegestratos, two residents of Syracuse, then a Greek colony, conspired to bilk a commodity broker through a deceitful scheme. They asked the unsuspecting broker for an advance on a shipment of corn they claimed was loaded on a vessel owned by Hegestratos. Their intention was to sink the vessel at sea and keep the money for the non-existent corn. Hegestratos, however, when caught by passengers in the act of scuttling the ship, panicked and drowned when he jumped overboard.

In U.S. business history much of what is now considered white collar crime was then considered a normal, if somewhat underhanded, part of doing business. For example, some of the best known ''captains of industry'' in the late 19th century were known to stretch their business ethics. Among some of the more notorious were Jay Gould, Jim Fiske, Schuyler Colfax (who was Ulysses S. Grant's vice-president), and James Garfield, the 20th president of the United States.

Colfax and Garfield were involved in the infamous Credit Mobilier scandal of the mid-1800s. Credit Mobilier was the construction company for the Union Pacific Railroad. The U.S. government lent the company $16,000 per mile for that part of the railroad built on level ground, $32,000 per mile for track laid on difficult terrain, and $48,000 per mile for rail laid in the mountains. Credit Mobilier charged the Union Pacific huge sums for its services, much of it for work never completed. The major stockholders owned stock in both companies and earned $23,000,000 in profits—much of it government money.

The *New York Sun* suspected financial corruption in the building of the railroad and revealed such in 1872. The paper discovered that Oak Ames, a member of the Pacific Railroad Committee in the House of Representatives, had ''sold'' stock in Credit Mobilier to several Congressman, including the future President Garfield and Vice-President Colfax, in an effort to stave off a corruption investigation. Ultimately, however, a senate investigating committee absolved the politicians of any wrongdoing.

Neither were Jay Gould and Jim Fiske saints. In the 1870s they watered stock in the Erie Railroad by printing phony stock certificates, which they then sold to Cornelius Vanderbilt, a railroad magnate who operated the New York Central Railroad—and a man who was no stranger to shady financial dealings. Their manipulation cost Vanderbilt millions of dollars and threw the Erie railroad into bankruptcy in 1875. That was not the first time Fiske and Gould had created havoc in the United States through their financial wheeling and dealing.

In 1869, the pair tried to corner the nation's available gold supply. President Grant had told them the government was not planning to sell gold on the open market. With that ''insider information'' in hand Fiske and Gould then set out to purchase large amounts of gold, thus driving up the price. Their actions forced business owners who required gold to settle international transactions to sell stocks and bonds and call in debts to gather enough money to purchase gold. Grant reacted quickly and authorized the sale of $4 million of the Treasury's gold supply. Somehow, Fiske and Gould learned of the sale before it occurred. They were amongst the first to sell their gold—and at a tremendous profit. These scandals, however, had no adverse affect on Fiske and Gould, who brought 19th century white collar crime to new heights.

Nearly every decade of the 20th century produced a white collar criminal who made newspaper headlines. The 1920s saw the rise of Charles Ponzi whose name lives on in the term ''Ponzi Scheme.'' Ponzi's firm, the Financial Exchange Company, took pyramid investing to new heights by promising, and delivering to the first few investors, an astounding 50 percent return on their investment in 45 days. Although bilking later investors for over $10 million, Ponzi died a pauper in Brazil, where he ran a hot dog stand, in 1949.

In the 1950s the politically connected Billy Sol Estes parlayed empty and non-existent storage tanks into $175 million by claiming they were full of liquid fertilizer and salad oil. In 1963 he was sentenced to 15 years in a federal prison. Estes is remembered for his quote: ''You borrow enough from a banker and you no longer have a creditor. . . . You get into somebody deep enough, and you've got a partner.'' The go-go years of the 1980s also saw a number of white collar criminals who made the headlines and became media sensations. In 1981 Barry Minkow, a 16-year-old Los Angeles high school student, borrowed $1,500 to start ZZZZBest, a carpet cleaning company. By 1987 the company's paper value, all based on fraudulent or non-existing assets, was nearly $200 million. Later that year Minkow's mythical holdings collapsed and what was worth $200 million on paper was auctioned off for $62,000. Minkow was convicted on 57 counts of bank, stock, and mail fraud, money laundering, racketeering, conspiracy, and tax evasion, all at 22 years of age. Minkow received a 25-year jail sentence.

The best known white collar criminal of the 1980s is undoubtedly Michael Milken, the ''junk bond king'' and the ultimate inside trader who, with his cohort in crime Dennis Levine, made $500 million in one year. Milken made Ivan Boesky, another trader whose stock speculations were based on inside information, look like a piker as Boesky only managed to make $50 million in one year from his nefarious deals. All three spent time in federal prison. People like Milken and Boesky often become folk heroes of a sort because their offenses are non-violent and their ''victims'' are often institutions or ethereal concepts.

White collar crimes are committed by individuals ranging from company clerks to CEOs of multinational corporations as well as people working on their own to rob private citizens. White collar crimes can also be perpetrated by corporations, through the actions of individuals or groups of employees. More often than not, however, corporations are the targets of white collar criminals, rather than the perpetrators of crimes. These crimes can result in monetary losses of a few cents to tens of millions of dollars, depending on their complexity and the expertise and intentions of the perpetrators. They can be committed by employees seeking only to embezzle a ''few dollars'' to executives siphoning off corporate funds under the guise of outlandish salaries.

According to Michael Gips, senior editor of *Security Management,* occupational fraud is the most common and rapidly growing type of white collar crime. Occupational fraud refers to an employee using his or her occupation for self-benefit at the expense of the employer. In essence the employer is the victim of the crime as opposed to fraud perpetrated against private citizens by such schemes as credit card fraud, ''identity takeover,'' etc. Included under the heading occupational fraud are such activities as bribery, conflict of interest scenarios, and kickbacks. Owners and equity executives account for only about 12 percent of occupational fraud. More and more occupational fraud, however, is being committed by high-level executives, and although their numbers are small the monetary impact of their crimes is staggering. The Association of Certified Fraud Examiners reported that the median loss due to white collar crimes inflicted on companies by their owners and high level executives is 16 times greater than crimes perpetrated by lower level employees. These high level executives are able to keep fraudulent transactions well hidden because of access to companies' money and books.

Occupational fraud is also growing in the nonprofit sector amongst educational and tax-exempt institutions such as foundations, universities, and also not-for-profit hospitals. Such institutions and organizations are often lax in checking the backgrounds of potential employees and are reluctant to report white collar crime for fear of estranging donors, benefactors, and their reputation in the community.

The rapid growth of computerization has added to the problem of occupational fraud, according to Gips. ''Many of the schemes are now conducted with the aid of a computer, where information can more easily be hidden, altered, or deleted.'' Employee downsizing is also a contributing factor as terminated employees, who easily rationalize their actions, seek revenge on employers. Another result of downsizing is the reduction in security and auditing employees.

Fraud is especially prevalent in financial institutions and takes up about 40 percent of the time and resources of the FBI's financial crime section according to FBI section chief Charles Owen. Owen reports that in 1991 the FBI pursued 7,163 fraud cases in financial institutions but by late 1997 that figure had jumped to 8,300 cases. Much of this rise is due to check and mortgage loan fraud.

The electronic age has also issued in unique opportunities for white collar criminals especially as our society moves more and more towards a cashless society. Electronic transfer fraud is a growing problem as more and more consumers and companies are charging goods and services over the Internet on their credit cards. ''Most companies are struggling to develop secure payment methods, such as the Secure Electronic Transaction (SET) system, designed to prevent theft of credit card numbers on the Internet,'' Gips writes. Other areas of concern are health care fraud, telemarketing fraud, and investment fraud.

It is estimated by the U.S. General Accounting Office that healthcare fraud in 1995 alone tallied up to somewhere between $30 and $100 billion, much of this in the government Medicare program. To combat Medicare fraud the GAO has set up an Internet site entitled FraudNET through which people can report fraud, mismanagement, or other abuses perpetrated by the public and government employees. Telemarketing fraud targets businesses and private citizens, especially the elderly, through a wide variety of fraudulent schemes. A favorite business scam is to bill companies for low priced items that were never ordered in the hopes that a busy accounts payable clerk will issue a check without questioning the invoice.

Security regulators in New York estimate that investment fraud that gets reported cost the American public approximately $6 billion in 1996. By mid-1997, however, there was a 25 percent increase in stock market fraud complaints. Much fraudulent activity in the stock market is due to the extraordinary bull market of the 1990s. Surprisingly, **stock market** fraud is most likely under reported as good economic times generates fewer complaints and fewer investigations. ''Usually those frauds are not uncovered until bad economic times, like the S&L crisis in the late eighties,'' according to Joseph Wells of the Association of Certified Fraud Examiners.

There is a growing effort to combat increasing white-collar crime. Law enforcement agencies are becoming more sophisticated in their approach to the problem as is the FBI. Both are hiring personnel trained in areas such as embezzlement, fraud against the elderly, cellular phone theft, computer crime, and the list of crime specialties continues to grow. The FBI for instance was instrumental in the creation of a subgroup of the Interagency Bank Fraud Working Group, which looks into computer related fraud in financial institutions. Under the Health Insurance Portability and Accountability Act, the FBI received $47 million in 1997 to investigate healthcare fraud. By 2003 funding is expected to reach $114 million to combat the growth of fraud in the healthcare industry. Private agencies such as the already mentioned Association of Certified Fraud Examiners and the National White Collar Crime Center also contribute to fighting white collar crime.

The National White Collar Crime Center, which is part of the Institute for Intergovernmental Research, operated from 1978 to 1992 as part of the Leviticus Project. This undertaking was a multi-state association of law enforcement, prosecution, and regulatory agencies which joined together to fight crime and corruption in the coal and eventually in the oil, natural gas, and precious metals industries. In 1992 the goal was expanded to fight all economic crimes. The Center's mission includes, ''providing investigative support services to assist in the fight against economic crime, operating a national training and research institute focusing on economic crime, developing partnerships with public and private agencies to address economic crime issues, and developing the Center as a national resource in combating economic crime.'' The Center provides services to local and state law enforcement, prosecution, and regulatory agency members in the U.S.

Companies can also develop and enforce measures to combat white collar crime. In writing for *Managing Office Technology* Donald Bucklin offers the following steps that companies should take to head off white collar crime problems: establish compliance standards and procedures for employees and company representatives; assign specific high-level employees to monitor implementation and compliance of these standards and procedures; communicate these standards and procedures to all employees through training programs, seminars, and the like; do not delegate discretionary authority to crime-prone employees; make use of monitoring and auditing systems and procedures; establish disciplinary mechanisms for standards enforcement; and respond appropriately to detected offenses. Bucklin feels that the above steps, if instituted and enforced, will be a major step in preventing white collar crime—before such a crime is uncovered by an outside organization such as a government regulatory agency. ''An effective program can help you conduct internal compliance audits of target activities from the point of view of a prosecutor, and insure that adequate controls exist to prevent white collar criminal activities,'' Bucklin concludes.

White collar crime will not disappear any time soon. Criminals will continue to devise new and more elaborate schemes to take advantage of ever changing technology in order to bilk their victims. Corporations, law enforcement officials, and others will continue to develop sophisticated measures to detect fraud and apprehend criminals. White collar crime did not begin with Xenothemis and Hegestratos, nor did it end with Michael Milken and Dennis Levine. It has been part of society since the dawn of business and will remain so. However, as more and more people become aware of its detrimental effects on individuals and society as a whole, the efforts to combat it will increase.

[Arthur G. Sharp, updated by Michael Knes]

FURTHER READING:

Bologna, Jack and Paul Shaw. *Corporate Crime Investigation.* Boston: Butterworth-Heinemann, 1997.

Bucklin, Donald. ''Worried That White Collar Crime is Afoot?'' *Managing Office Technology,* June 1997.

Cole, Richard B. *Management of Internal Business Investigations: A Survival Guide.* Springfield, IL: Charles C. Thomas, Publisher Ltd., 1996.

Gips, Michael A. ''Where Has All The Money Gone?'' *Security Management,* February 1998.

National White Collar Crime Center. ''National White Collar Crime Center.'' Tallahassee, FL: Institute For Intergovernmental Research, 1999. Available from: www.iir.com/nwccc/nwccc.htm.

Riddle, Kelly E. ''Unbuttoning White Collar Crime.'' *Security Management,* January 1999.

Rosoff, Stephen M., Pontell, Henry N., and Robert Tillman. *Profit Without Honor: White Collar Crime and the Looting of America.* Upper Saddle River, NJ: Prentice Hall, 1998.

Sutherland, Edwin H. *White Collar Crime.* New York: Holt, Rinehart and Winston, 1961.

WHOLESALING

Wholesaling, also known as distributing, is an intermediate stage between the origin of a good or service and its ultimate distribution to an end user through **retail trade** channels. Despite the emergence of so-called wholesale clubs aimed at the consumer market, wholesale trade typically involves business-to-business transactions. Traditionally, wholesaling is associated with physical product distribution, but wholesale markets also exist for other economic sectors such as energy and telecommunications services.

According to the U.S. Census Bureau under the **North American Industry Classification System** (NAICS), wholesale trade as of 1997 was carried out by more than 450,000 U.S. business establishments employing 5.8 million workers. More dramatic evidence of wholesaling's impact on the economy is that in 1997 these activities generated more than $4 trillion in sales, an amount equal to one-half of U.S. gross domestic product.

In terms of value, merchandise wholesaling is split almost evenly between trade in durable goods and trade in nondurables. However, durable goods involve more businesses, more workers, and higher payrolls.

TYPES OF WHOLESALERS

Strictly speaking, although a wholesaler may own or control retail operations, wholesalers do not sell to end customers. Indeed, many wholesale operations are themselves owned by retailers or manufacturers. Wholesalers are extremely important in a variety of industries, including automobiles, grocery products, plumbing supplies, electrical supplies, and raw farm produce.

Wholesaling involves that part of the **marketing** process in which intermediaries, i.e., those between the producer and end consumer, buy and resell goods, making them available to an expanded buyer's market over an expanded geographical market area. As middle agents, wholesalers are only effective when the price they charge for goods and services is less than the value placed by customers. By facilitating the transfer of title of goods, they are involved in the bulking and distributing of goods.

Although there are a number of ways to classify wholesalers, the categories used by the Census of Wholesale Trade are employed most often. The three types of wholesalers are:

- merchant wholesalers;
- agents, brokers, and commission merchants; and
- manufacturers' sales branches and offices.

MERCHANT WHOLESALERS. Merchant wholesalers are firms engaged primarily in buying, taking title to, storing (usually), and physically handling products in relatively large quantities and reselling the products in smaller quantities to retailers, industrial, commercial, or institutional concerns, and to other wholesalers. They go under many different names, such as wholesaler, jobber, distributor, industrial distributor, supply house, assembler, importer, exporter, and many others.

BROKERS. Agents, brokers, and commission merchants are also independent middlemen who do not (for the most part) take title to the goods in which they deal, but instead are actively involved in negotiatory functions of buying and selling while acting on behalf of their clients. They are usually compensated in the form of commissions on sales or purchases. Some of the more common types go under the names of manufacturers' agents, commission merchants, brokers, selling agents, and import and export agents.

MANUFACTURERS' AGENTS. Manufacturers' sales branches and offices are owned and operated by manufacturers but are physically separated from manufacturing plants. They are used primarily for the purpose of distributing the manufacturers' own products at wholesale. Some have warehousing facilities where inventories are maintained, while others are merely sales offices. Some of them also wholesale allied and supplementary products purchased from other manufacturers.

BENEFITS OF WHOLESALING

Wholesaling provides an expanded consumer market potential in terms of geographical locations and consumer purchasing power while at the same time providing a cash flow for the manufacturer. There are several major reasons for the importance of wholesaling. First, all goods and necessary supplies for their production pass through some form of middle agent and wholesaling system. For this reason, the effective functioning of wholesale linkages contributes directly to the economic well-being of a society.

Secondly, for most small producers, an immediate geographic location is typically insufficient to provide and maintain an on-going customer base for their operations. As a means to sell their goods, smaller producers must have avenues to develop market segments of potential customers and must make sure their goods are of the quality customers want at prices they are willing to pay. The role of wholesalers is to provide links to an expanded market base, i.e., to discover where customers are located and how best to reach them. In this sense, wholesaling uses time and place as it relates to information and availability. Wholesalers create utility through holding goods that can be drawn upon by buyers at a cost lower than direct exchange.

Finally, wholesalers act as distribution channels and interface with markets and producers within markets. Whereas wholesaling and retailing provide similar functions in that they receive, store, and distribute goods, the importance of wholesaling is in its ability to moderate supply and demand fluctuations and cope with larger transactions with less emphasis on selling techniques and services and product promotion. Wholesaling has the capability to adjust the distribution of goods from surplus to deficit areas.

Wholesalers are successful only if they are able to serve the needs of their customers, who may be retailers or other wholesalers. Some of the marketing functions provided by wholesalers to their buyers are:

- providing producer's goods in an appropriate quantity for resale by buyers
- providing wider geographical access and diversity in obtaining goods
- ensuring and maintaining a quality dimension with the goods that are being obtained and resold
- providing cost-effectiveness by reducing the number of producer contacts needed
- providing ready access to a supply of goods
- assembling and arranging goods of a compatible nature from a number of producers for resale
- minimizing buyer transportation costs by buying goods in larger quantities and distributing them in smaller amounts for resale
- working with producers to understand and appreciate **consumerism** in their production process.

OUTLOOK

New technology, global competition, and retail consolidation have been forcing many wholesalers to modify their business practices in order to remain competitive. While some experts have gone so far to say that these factors will eliminate certain kinds of wholesaling altogether, even a cautious prognosis would anticipate that the number of wholesalers will continue to fall as the largest and most efficient—which are not necessarily the same—are best able to cope with market changes.

TECHNOLOGICAL CHANGE. Two general classes of technology have had a major impact on wholesaling: logistics management technologies and the **Internet**. Logistics technology is a broad category of devices and **software** used to make distribution more efficient and reliable. These include implementation of sophisticated **automatic identification systems** for tracking stock, personnel, and equipment; satellite tracking systems for wholesalers who must manage a fleet of delivery trucks; and integrated computer systems to manage inventory, distribution, and customer services. The best of these technologies, although they require substantial investments, help keep costs down while improving the quality of service. Meanwhile, the Internet is having a profound effect of giving wholesalers' customers more opportunities to compare prices and obtain goods from alternative sources, making wholesaling more price competitive and signaling danger for inefficient wholesalers who may have enjoyed a near monopoly in local markets. The Internet also feeds on a general wish by both manufacturers and retailers to cut out the middlemen in the distribution process. If wholesalers fail to use **electronic commerce** to their advantage, they risk granting that wish.

GLOBAL COMPETITION. Related to the Internet's leveling power are the benefits and drawbacks of heightened **international competition**, which is likely to be aided by the Internet. Again, competition from abroad will tend to add downward pressure on prices and hurt inefficient and low-margin wholesalers the most. Conversely, however, when wholesalers are able to expand into new markets while keeping costs under control, they may be able to at least recoup any loss of sales domestically and possibly improve sales and profits overall.

RETAIL CONSOLIDATION. A significant threat to wholesalers has been the rise of large and lean national retailers in sectors such as supermarkets, home electronics, office supplies, and do-it-yourself supplies. These large chain stores tend to rely less on wholesalers for their own inventories, and at any rate are gradually snuffing out the independent retailers who are more likely to need wholesalers. Wholesalers have little hope of gaining the big chains as customers because often the chains have cost advantages of both scale and scope over wholesalers. As retail consolidation is expected to continue, a concomitant drop in the number of wholesalers serving those markets can be expected. As some analysts see it, two kinds of wholesalers are likely to weather the changes best: those that will continue growing larger and serving a diverse client base, and those that will focus on specialty markets and excel in those niches.

SEE ALSO: Retail Trade

FURTHER READING:

Keough, Jack. ''E-Commerce: A Strategic Weapon.'' *Industrial Distribution,* December 1998.

Merrefield, David. ''Wholesale Changes.'' *Supermarket News,* 21 September 1998.

Olorunniwo, Festus, and Donna Wood. ''Reengineering in the Wholesale and Retail Industries.'' *Industrial Management,* May-June 1998.

Rosenbloom, Bert, ed. *Wholesale Distribution Channels: New Insights and Perspectives.* Binghamton, NY: Haworth Press, 1994.

U.S. Census Bureau. *1997 Economic Census.* Washington, 1999. Available from www.census.gov.

WIDE AREA NETWORKS (WANS)

A wide area network (WAN) is a telecommunications network, usually used for connecting **computers**, which spans a wide geographical area, such as between different cities, states, or even countries. WANs typically are used by corporations or organizations to facilitate the exchange of data between their computers in dispersed offices. Across all industries, most large corporations with facilities at multiple locations use WANs, and even small businesses with just two remote sites increasingly use WANs. Most WANs link two or more **local area networks** (LANs), and the **Internet** is in essence a very large WAN.

WANS VERSUS OTHER NETWORKS

Although WANs serve a purpose similar to that of LANs, WANs are structured and operated quite differently. The user of a WAN usually does not own the communication lines that connect the remote computer systems but instead subscribes to a service through a telecommunications provider. Unlike LANs, WANs typically do not link individual computers, but rather are used to link LANs in what are known as internetworks, using devices called routers and remote bridges. WANs also transmit data at much slower speeds than LANs, most commonly at about 1.5 megabits per second (Mbps) or less, instead of the tens, hundreds, or even thousands of Mbps achieved by LANs. WANs are structurally similar to metropolitan area networks (MANs), but are typically slower and provide communications links for distances greater than 50 kilometers.

WANs have existed for decades, but new technologies, services, and applications have developed over the years. WANs were originally developed for digital leased-line services carrying only voice, rather than data. As such, they connected the private branch exchanges (PBXs) of remote offices of the same company. WANs are still used for voice services, but are used most heavily for data and, recently, also for images, such as video conferencing. WAN usage is growing, as more companies have installed LANs and as more affordable internetworking equipment has become available.

TECHNOLOGICAL PROFILE

WAN technology is diverse and complex. There are any number of ways to establish a network connection between two points, ranging from systems based on traditional metal wires or cables to fiber-optic or radio-frequency communications. In addition to the connection medium, there are a variety of networking protocols to choose from based on the kinds of networks being connected and the capacity and reliability requirements for the data.

WANs are either point-to-point, involving a direct connection between two sites, or operate across packet-switched networks, in which data is transmitted in packets over shared circuits. Point-to-point WAN service may involve either analog dial-up lines, using a modem to connect the computer to the telephone line, or dedicated leased digital telephone lines, also known as ''private lines.'' Analog lines, which may be either part of a public-switched network or leased lines, are suitable for batch data transmissions, such as nonurgent order entry and point of-sale transactions. Dedicated digital phone lines permit uninterrupted, secure data transmission at fixed costs. Point-to-point WAN service providers include both local telephone companies and long distance carriers, such as AT&T and MCI WorldCom.

POINT-TO-POINT SERVICES. A leading type of point-to-point WAN technology in North America is T1, which is based on a method of dividing a digital line service with a rate of 1.544 Mbps into 24 channels of 64 Kbps each. By modern standards this rate is relatively slow compared to LAN technology and compared to the increasing corporate demands placed on LANs. The cost of setting up and leasing a T1 (or the faster T3) represents a sizable outlay for companies. In the early 1990s nearly all WANs used T1 or other leased lines, which are leased from a telecommunications carrier, but this changed rapidly as cheaper and faster alternatives emerged. Many observers have forecast the sharp decline of leased-line services once infrastructure is in place to better support the newer, less expensive alternatives. Other point-to-point services available include fractional T1, T3, dataphone digital services, switched 56 Kbps, integrated services digital network (ISDN), and asymmetric digital subscriber line (ADSL). ADSL and similar DSL technologies drew a great deal of attention from corporate network managers in the late 1990s because they were considerably less expensive than leased lines—as much as 60 percent less—and delivered similar or better performance.

In addition to their typical high costs, another drawback to point to-point configurations is that they aren't well suited to accommodate mobile users, e.g., business travelers. Since the services are linked only to specific locations, companies must find alternative modes of network access for mobile users. Packet-switched networking provides this ability, among other benefits.

PACKET-SWITCHED SERVICES. WAN technologies that rely on public networks via packet-switching, a method of encoding data into small, uniquely identified chunks known as packets, have been increasingly popular over the past decade. Two of the most important packet-based technologies are frame relay and asynchronous transfer mode (ATM).

Frame relay is the older of the two, coming into general use in the early 1990s. It was in large part a replacement to the slower X.25 standard that had been around since the mid-1970s. Most frame relay WANs are hosted by commercial network operators that charge flat rates based on the speed of service or volume of data required. Supported by relatively inexpensive networking hardware, frame relay is based on establishing a logical or virtual circuit across a network with another computer. In frame relay, the packets, or frames, of data may vary in size, and no attempt is made to correct errors. This latter feature is based on the assumption that frame relay is run over relatively high quality, digital networks and the data is less susceptible to errors. This also improves speed since the network protocol isn't trying to correct the data. The stability of this connection allows frame relay service providers to guarantee a certain minimum level of service. The comparative low cost and high quality of service made frame relay one of the most popular WAN technologies in the 1990s.

ATM services, which were introduced commercially in the mid-1990s, are based on similar principles. Many have touted ATM as a break-through technology, but as of the late 1990s it had only a modest impact on the WAN market. ATM employs a concept called cell relay to transmit data. Cells are uniformly sized, small packets of data; in the case of ATM, just 53 bytes each, including a 5-byte header. By contrast, a frame relay packet may range up to several thousand bytes. As with frame relay, ATM transfers data over a defined virtual path rather than allowing packets to follow any number of paths to their destinations, as occurs in TCP/IP protocols used in Internet applications. This highly stable connection lends itself to video and other applications that require a steady, predictable flow of data. The drawbacks to this certainty are that the constant level of service may be low compared to other options, and ATM may not be well equipped to manage short-term spikes in demand for network resources.

FIBER-OPTIC CONNECTIVITY. Fiber-optic connectivity for WANs is another major research and growth area. Fiber optics, which involves sending light signals through glass or plastic fibers, can support very fast and extremely high quality data transfer. Most fiber-optic networks use one form or another of packet switching technology, such as ATM.

One emerging standard in this arena is synchronous optical network (SONET), a set of protocols adopted by the American National Standards Institute (ANSI) for high-bandwidth fiber-optic networking. The international analog to SONET is known as the synchronous digital hierarchy (SDH). While its technical merits have been lauded by some, others note that the economics of SONET are less appealing. It has proven expensive to implement, and some critics claim it wasn't designed properly to handle heavy data traffic that businesses want such services for. Nonetheless, large corporations with heavy throughput requirements have begun to hook up to SONET-based services.

A competing, and more economically compelling, standard is dense wavelength division multiplexing (DWDM). DWDM is a method for efficiently sharing signals over a fiber by altering the portion of the light spectrum for each different stream of data. By using each fiber more efficiently, DWDM allows significantly higher bandwidths for data than SONET, which is based on time division multiplexing (TDM), or allotting time to each separate stream of data on a fixed rotation. This translates into substantial cost savings on hardware as well. DWDM technology was being rapidly deployed by a number of network operators because of such advantages.

THE FUTURE

While the Internet and other networking developments have changed the face of WANs and have threatened some older forms of WAN technology, a number of experts believe they will become more important rather than less, as trends like globalization and telecommuting create new demand for high-power long-distance networking. Demand for network bandwidth will continue to swell. One technology forecast saw corporate WAN traffic rising by as much as 30 percent a year through 2002, and much of this traffic will increasingly be routed through public networks using virtual private network technology rather than the closed private networks of the past.

[Heather Behn Hedden]

FURTHER READING:

Held, Gilbert. *Internetworking LANs and WANs: Concepts, Techniques, Methods.* 2nd ed. New York: John Wiley & Sons, 1998.

Machlin, Robert. "The Internet: Redefining the WAN." *Telecommunications,* January 1998.

Sullivan, Kristina B. "Companies Reach for High-Speed Alternative to Leased Lines for Access to the LAN." *PC Week,* 16 November 1998.

WOMEN ENTREPRENEURS

According to the National Foundation for Women Business Owners, the number of businesses owned by women jumped 78 percent from 1988 to 1998. By the year 2000, reports estimate over one-half of all **small businesses** will be owned by women. The increasing role women are playing as business owners is part of the overall impact women are having on society today. Women in the media are bringing new insights in reporting; women in the movies are featured in expanded roles beyond those of wife, girlfriend, or mother; women in medicine are offering new dimensions to caring for patients and more research on women's health issues; women in law are seeking justice for crimes committed against women; and women in politics today represent the largest constituency in history.

While the trend of women owning businesses is growing, it is certainly not new. Women have owned and operated businesses since the beginnings of American history and much earlier in other parts of the world. They rarely were recognized, however, or given credit for their efforts. Often women were invisible as they worked side by side with their husband in business and may have only stepped into the leadership position when their husband died. Many recognizable businesses today are owned and operated by the wife or daughter of the founder. Two well-known examples are Tootsie Roll, which is controlled by a woman and her four daughters, and the Playboy empire, taken over by Hugh Hefner's daughter, Christie Hefner.

In other cases, women began a business on their own or they were given the impetus to begin one. Lila Bell Acheson Wallace helped to start *Reader's Digest.* Knox Gelatin was started by Mrs. Knox. Pepperidge Farms was started by a mother to create food products to help her asthmatic son. Josephine Dickson and her husband created Band-Aids. Susan Hoover gave the name to Hoover Vacuum Sweepers. Elizabeth and Olivia Norris brought William Procter and James Gamble together, and Alice Marriott ran a root beer stand with her husband Bill, which was the beginning of the Marriott hotel and food business. Eleanor Roosevelt operated her own school.

TRENDS IN INDUSTRIES

Most operated businesses are in the service sector, which coincides with most new women-owned businesses being started today. Women tend to launch businesses in the industry where they have had direct experience, mostly in traditional fields. This explains the lack of women business owners in nontraditional fields such as manufacturing. This is slowly changing, however. From 1980 to 1989, women-owned sole proprietorships increased over 175 percent in mining, construction, manufacturing, and transportation.

In the late 1990s, 60 percent of women-owned businesses were concentrated in retail and service sectors and in traditional industries such as cosmetics, food, fashion, and personal care. Famous women business owners in these industries include: Mary Kay Ash, Mrs. Fields, Estée Lauder, and Donna Karan.

Unfortunately, U.S. Census Bureau statistics lag by several years and many questions about women entrepreneurs are still unanswered due to the lack of available data. Today, women-owned businesses are a vital economic force which, according to the National Association of Women Business Owners, employ more people than the Fortune 500 firms. Also, most women conduct business as sole proprietors. According to Sarah Gracie in *Management Today,* women founded almost one-third of all new businesses in 1997 in the small and medium-sized business sector.

More and more women are becoming role models each year. Today, numerous women own and manage billion-dollar businesses in a variety of industries with several thousand employees.

REASONS TO START

Women start businesses for different reasons than their male counterparts, most citing independence as their key motivator (men most commonly cite money as their primary goal). Women start businesses about ten years later then men. Motherhood, lack of **management** experience, and traditional socialization can all be reasons for delayed entry into a career as a business owner. Most women never plan to own a business or even consider business ownership as a career option. In fact, over 30 percent started a business due to some traumatic event such as divorce, discrimination due to pregnancy or the corporate **glass ceiling**, the health of a family member, or economic reasons such as a **layoff**.

A new talent pool of women entrepreneurs today is coming from those leaving corporate America to chart their own destiny. Many of these women have developed financial expertise and bring experience in manufacturing or nontraditional fields. Armed with more management experience and business savvy, these women will be the trendsetters of tomorrow.

Family businesses may indeed be the best training ground for women entrepreneurs as 78 percent of women business owners polled in the mid-1990s mentioned some type of family business connection. While men start businesses for growth opportunities and profit potential, women most often found businesses for personal goals such as achievement, accomplishment, or stepping in to ''help'' their family. Women consider financial success as an external confirmation of their ability rather than a primary goal or motivation to start a business. According to Joline Godfrey, author of *Our Wildest Dreams,* women gave the following reasons for starting businesses:

- Happiness/Self Fulfillment: 38%
- Achievement/Challenge: 30%

- Helping Others: 20%
- Sales Growth/Profit: 12%

THE DEVELOPMENT OF A MANAGEMENT STYLE

Despite gains, women business owners still have many barriers to overcome before obtaining truly equal opportunity in the marketplace. Many of these challenges are rooted in childhood socialization, which plays a critical role in the choices adults make throughout their lifetime. These early experiences are the beginnings of a management style developed by both males and females.

The realms of family and business have been separated since the Industrial Revolution. This has resulted in different gender roles and expectations based on different socialization experiences. Men and women in families and in business are still struggling with the results of these forces today because these roles carry deep-rooted emotions that are slow to change. Gender socialization has been described as the lifelong process of developing attitudes, skills, expectations, behaviors, and values. The study of gender focuses on people's perceptions and how males and females differ socially rather than biologically.

This process begins at birth when little girls are dressed in pink and boys in blue. Girls are described as cute and boys as strong. Girls are given baby dolls and household items and boys receive combat and sports items. Parents then begin to reward the "right" behavior and punish "unacceptable" behavior according to their preconceived ideas developed from society.

The management style people use as adults is developed at this early time in their lives. Girls begin to learn skills that are not conducive to today's business world. Females are taught to be sensitive and tactful; they learn to be "helpless" and to be dependent on their fathers, rather than to be self-assertive and self-reliant. They are taught to be economically dependent. Parents also protect their daughters rather than prepare them and are reluctant to give females much freedom to take risks.

During this early period, females learn to collaborate and work toward the good of the group, and they nurture and serve as peacemakers. They do not learn about winners and losers but rather they learn to feel responsible for the welfare of the group. Girls also attribute their own success to luck, effort, and ease of the task; whereas they attribute failure personally, ascribing it to their lack of ability. In March 1992, the American Association of University Women released a study titled "How Schools Shortchange Girls," documenting how girls are called on less, encouraged less, and overall get unequal treatment in the classroom setting.

Research during the 1990s revealed that many fathers aim to protect their daughters rather than prepare them for the realities of today's world. Women business owners are succeeding despite the negative comments from their fathers such as: "Don't worry your pretty little head about business," "Business is not for women, marry a good businessman," "Women should not be too smart or compete too much."

In contrast, boys learn traits such as aggressiveness, competitiveness, and dominance—particularly when playing with war toys and sporting games. They learn strategy and tactics needed to win. And they learn that if they lose, there is always another opportunity. They are called on more in the classroom and guess more often.

Family, siblings, and peer groups have been identified as additional settings in which unequal socialization takes place. Stereotypes are reinforced daily through television, magazines, and radio song lyrics. Families also set rules that are gender based. Female roles are inside the house with cooking, cleaning, and laundry. Male roles are outside with grass cutting and taking out the trash.

Women organize their lives around the needs of the family, whereas men organize their lives around the demands of their work. Women's work roles have been second to executing the material, emotional, and social life of the family. It is not surprising then that women consider business ownership as a way to have more flexible time with their family.

CHALLENGES FACED BY WOMEN BUSINESS OWNERS

This lifelong socialization process provides a basis for most of the challenges women business owners face in the marketplace. The process does not provide most women with the skills and traits needed to compete as men do in today's business world, nor does it educate most men about how the natural talents of women can be used to advantage in business. Until now, women have been led to believe that they are the ones who need to cope and adjust. Since women business owners have gained an economic clout over the past 20 years, however, now firms that have traditionally done business with males are beginning to recognize they should also make adjustments toward the needs of women.

Since this socialization process has taught women not to think big, to be risk averse, and to fear financial issues, most are undercapitalized in their businesses and have limited access to resources such as financing know-how and the male network. It is not surprising then to learn that three out of four women-owned businesses started out with their own financing of less than $5,000. Today 38 percent still have no bank financing; 52 percent have used credit cards in their business as compared to 18 percent of all business owners.

Study after study confirms women business owners are not getting equal treatment at financial institutions. Sixty-seven percent of women business owners report difficulty in working with financial institutions as compared to 55 percent of all firms. Over one-half of women business owners believed they faced **gender discrimination** when dealing with a **loan** officer; therefore, most women business owners actually grow their businesses by reinvesting profits.

Women often believed their professional advisers did not expect them to know a lot and spoke down to them, particularly when they were starting in business. The women felt an unjustified request was made of them when they were required to obtain their husband's guarantee in order to procure a **bank** loan. Women felt bankers were patronizing and this interfered with building relationships with their bankers. Many women said their personal ability to manage the venture was continually being questioned by male bankers. Women declared they wanted more details from their advisers, they wanted options and alternatives—not prescriptive advice, and not lectures.

Most women business owners do not have business degrees and most were never exposed in college to business ownership as a career option. Even today students have access to relatively few resources such as books, lectures, or role models of women business owners.

Furthermore, in business schools where most of the professional advisers today were trained, the male model of business is still being taught by an overwhelming majority of male professors. Examples of women entrepreneurs have been left out of textbooks, and rarely is a female business owner used as the example or case study. Neither the women nor the men students are learning about the natural abilities and talents women are using to succeed as business owners today. Unfortunately, without some very strong initiatives on the part of educators, the process will be slow to change.

Another area where women business owners are getting shortchanged is in the area of procurement, or the selling of their goods and services to city, state, and federal governments. Fewer than five percent of the women-owned firms in the United States are certified to do business with their state government and only 1.5 percent of the billions of dollars in federal contracts go to women-owned firms.

If a company is 51 percent woman-owned and controlled by a woman, it can obtain certification and bid on government contracts. Many women, however, may have heard it is difficult to do business with the government or believe the government will not be interested in what they are selling. Another myth is that government contracts are too large for small businesses (especially women-owned businesses) and one needs to be a legal and contract expert to bid on government contracts. In actuality, many governments have created set-aside programs that specifically help women-owned businesses in the process.

STRENGTHS OF WOMEN BUSINESS OWNERS

Despite the many challenges women face, this early socialization has given women specific traits and abilities that define the female model of business ownership. This different management style can be an asset and one from which men can learn. The style can be described as more cooperative than the competitive male model now taught in business schools. This style is often further developed through volunteer activities in early adulthood.

The cooperative style naturally used by most women comes from their early experiences and focuses on the welfare of the group. Participation is shared among the employees with attention paid to their ideas and needs. The style often extends to social issues that are frequently driving forces within the company. The business strategy is formed through active listening and educational experiences and focuses on issues—not just the bottom line. The ability to build relationships is an asset with customers and suppliers, and in the international marketplace. In order to overcome the obstacles they face, women often come up with creative, out-of-the-ordinary methods to help further their goal.

These variables help define the cooperative style that has developed from early socialization of females. Once aware of these traits they become more apparent to observation. This cooperative style is easier to recognize in women business owners where the women are not conforming to a culture set by males in a large corporation. This new, distinctive business is one from which we all can learn. The new model of business for the next century will combine the talents of this cooperative style used by women with the more traditional business approach.

THE FUTURE

With more and more women opening businesses every day, the future for the next generation of business owners is bright. While the business world is normally slow to change, economic advantages of women-owned firms will help speed the process. As more young women see a wider range of women business owner role models, they will be more encouraged. As mothers socialize their daughters to the business world during their preadolescent years, more are likely to choose business ownership as a career option.

RESOURCES

A number of resources now exist to support women entrepreneurs. In 1988 Congress authorized the **Small Business Administration** (SBA) Office of Women's Business Ownership. They recently created a "Low-Doc" loan program that makes it easier for women entrepreneurs to obtain SBA financing. The SBA also has established a Women's Network for Entrepreneurial Training that links women mentors with protégées. Small Business Development Centers (SBDC) are also cosponsored by the SBA and operate in every state. They offer free and confidential counseling to anyone interested in small business. The SBA also posts resources for women business owners on the **Internet**. The site has corporate sponsors and provides information on financing, **marketing**, and management techniques.

Many states now have a Women's Business Advocate to promote women entrepreneurs within the state. These advocates are represented by an organization called the National Association of Women Business Advocates.

A number of trade associations now represent women entrepreneurs. The National Association of Women Business Owners is the largest group throughout the country. There are also some smaller regional groups that can be located through the Yellow Pages or local **chambers of commerce**. The American Business Women's Association provides leadership, networking, and educational support. The National Association of Female Executives makes women aware of the need to plan for career and financial success. In addition, a growing number of Yellow Page directories throughout the country list women-owned businesses as a special classification.

SEE ALSO: Entrepreneurship; Family-Owned Businesses; Women in Business

[Cynthia Iannarelli, updated by Wendy H. Mason]

FURTHER READING:

Dogar, Rana. "The Top 500 Women-Owned Businesses." *Working Woman,* May 1998.

Duff, Carolyn S. *When Women Work Together: Using Our Strengths to Overcome Our Challenges.* Berkeley, CA: Conari Press, 1993.

Godfrey, Joline. *Our Wildest Dreams: Women Entrepreneurs Making Money, Having Fun, Doing Good.* New York: Harper-Business, 1992.

Gracie, Sarah. "In the Company of Women." *Management Today,* June 1998.

Heim, Pat, and Susan Golant. *Hardball for Women: Winning at the Game of Business.* Los Angeles: Lowell House, 1992.

Landrum, Gene N. *Profiles of Female Genius: Thirteen Creative Women Who Changed the World.* Amherst, NY: Prometheus Books, 1994.

Larkin, Geraldine A. *Woman to Woman: Street Smarts for Women Entrepreneurs.* Englewood Cliffs, NJ: Prentice Hall, 1993.

Moore, Dorothy P., and E. Holly Buttner. *Women Entrepreneurs: Moving beyond the Glass Ceiling.* Thousand Oaks, CA: Sage Publications, 1997.

Silver, A. David. *Enterprising Women: Lessons from 100 of the Greatest Entrepreneurs of Our Day.* New York: American Management Association, 1994.

Steel, Dawn. *They Can Kill You, but They Can't Eat You: Lessons from the Front.* New York: Pocket Books, 1993.

Zuckerman, Laurie. *On Your Own: A Women's Guide to Building a Business.* 2nd ed. Dover, NH: Upstart Publishing, 1993.

WOMEN IN BUSINESS

From the beginning of time, women have worked at home, as well as outside of the home, to contribute to the greater economic well-being of family. Even in colonial America, characterized by rural and self sufficient communities, women assumed roles in the manufacture and sale of goods. Beginning with the textile mills and the shoemaking industry of postrevolutionary America, the first real explosion of women into business appeared at the turn of the century in secretarial and take-home work situations. By World War I, women were poised to enter the **workforce** in great numbers and spurred into the workplace by the absence of men on the homefront. As men returned from the war and the economy gradually worsened into the Great Depression, women suffered displacement from the business world. World War II created a similar growth of women in business. Without a serious economic depression and as a result of changing societal norms, women's roles and functions in business have steadily increased in the years since World War II. In 1991 women represented 45 percent of the U.S. workforce.

Blue-collar workers traditionally evoke images of trades and manufacturing employees. White-collar employees hold positions of professional and managerial importance. Women in business, while represented in both, create a third category called pink-collar workers. Pink-collar workers are commonly associated with clerical, sales, and service positions. In each of these roles, women participate and create a presence. In trade and manufacturing jobs particularly, the relationship between women and **labor unions** has been noteworthy. In professional and managerial jobs, women are directly exposed to ideas and conceptions of power and control. And, in service jobs, women, as the dominant labor force, deal with effects of technology daily in a compelling way.

The sum total of this historical record and increasing participation in the workforce brings to light the controversial matter of a woman's work and worth. In particular, **gender discrimination** and pay inequity demonstrate the difficult transition of women into the business world. Protective legislation is one demonstration of governmental attempts to prevent and discourage sex discrimination on the job. Legal redress for salary inequities is another method of controlling pay discrimination. Other contributing concerns that women bring to business include issues about benefits. **Child care/elder care** needs accompany women into the business world as do preferences for flexible scheduling and **family leave**. These issues reflect the dual role that women hold in both the business world and the family/personal world. Married women, mothers, and older women benefit from workplace accommodations to individual needs and conflicting priorities when benefits are tailored accordingly.

HISTORY

In 17th- and 18th-century America, women worked at home with their husbands to contribute to the family's economic support. Employment opportunities for women were scarce. In this essentially self supporting rural lifestyle, centers of commerce emerged as small towns and cities. Working out of necessity, women became shopkeepers, artisans, and merchants. The most frequent reason for working was widowhood. Examples of working women in colonial America are often associated with the clothing trade. Women printers, however, illustrate a particularly significant departure from textile-based employment. **Women entrepreneurs** such as Elizabeth Timothy (c. 1700-1757) and Cornelia Smith Bradford (d. 1755) operated as independent printers and bookbinders in South Carolina and Boston, respectively, in 18th-century America. The employment of women in the printing trades was well-regarded and common at the time. Frequently, a woman would inherit her husband's printing business at the time of his death. As proprietors and purveyors of the printed word, women printers enjoyed a small but significant minority role in colonial America. The impending war with England created a demand for goods made in America, thus opening business opportunities to women engaged in the production of cloth and food. Even as women worked, however, they still worked out of necessity. The prevailing societal attitude projected the ideal woman as family oriented, not business oriented.

As a logical conclusion, postrevolutionary America found women engaged in the business of working at home. Piecework or take-home work formed roots during this time that continue to modern day. In conjunction with increased industrialization, textile mills in the northeastern states sought women out as a source of cheap labor and the organized movement of women into the workforce first appeared. Combined with the endeavors of early women's rights activists such as Elizabeth Cady Stanton (1815-1902), the idea of women in the workplace began to gain approval. Yet, the outspoken cultural preference was still towards the ideal woman and ''spheres of influence.'' Spheres of influence refers to a prevailing theory that women belonged in the private sphere of family while men belonged in the public sphere of business. As cities grew and transportation improved, work and business were increasingly conducted from a centralized location. As a result, homework or piecework decreased. The influx of immigration from 1840 on increased the labor force. Society began to embrace the idea of the ideal woman and diminished the expectation for a woman's contribution to family financial health. Instead, men assumed the burden of sole provider while women stayed at home more and more frequently. With the advent of the Civil War, this model changed.

Clerical and teaching opportunities opened to women during the Civil War. Nursing began to assume a professional component due to the casualties of the war. As a result of the great many deaths in the Civil War, thousands of women were left to fend for themselves financially and economically. A conflict arose between the economic need for survival and the cultural expectations of family responsibility. Even among wealthy women, the move from private to public sphere accelerated in voluntary and charitable outlets.

By the turn of the 19th century, women altered the cultural landscape by creating the idea of a new woman to replace the ideal women. Changing ideas of women included the central role of woman as partner to the economic well-being of the family and society as a whole. By 1900, more than 20 percent of women worked for a wage. The range and variety of employment in the 1900 census indicates that women held jobs in law, journalism, dentistry, medicine, engineering, mining, and other typical occupations. Women were counted in 295 of the 305 occupations listed on the census. The increasing industrialization of the United States resulted in a surge in factory work. More than one million women worked in factories in 1900. Most of these women were young, single, and foreign-born. They worked for low wages and knew no job security. Factories were unsafe and dirty. As a result, the businesswoman's first association with labor unionism appeared. In the Uprising of the 20,000 in 1909, women banded together and struck to protest working conditions and wages in the clothing industry. Many other labor unions appeared that either solely represented or incorporated the female employee during the early 1900s.

Even as women worked in industry to fuel its growth, the outcome created new business opportunities for women in clerical jobs. Between 1900 and 1920, the number of women clerical workers grew from 187,000 to 1,421,000. Women entered professional and managerial jobs during this time as well. Health, education, and caring professions emerged to alleviate suffering caused by industrialization while simultaneously expanding professional opportunities for women. During World War I, women assumed many of the roles and jobs of men during their absence. After the war, however, women were expected to return to familial pursuits. Still considered a secondary labor force, women were encouraged to engage in volunteer and charity work. Many who chose to remain in the workforce took lower-paying jobs as men returned from military service.

During World War II, women again entered the workforce in great numbers. In response to a need for new workers and new production, six million women went to work during the war. Society's approval of this phenomena was reflected in posters of Rosie the Riveter and other cultural signals. Magazines and movies and other media all reinforced a woman's patriotic duty to work. Again, however, at the end of the war, women were encouraged to leave the workplace and return to the family environment. While half the women in the workplace left between 1945 and 1946, by 1947 the employment rate of women had regained its wartime levels. And, by 1950, almost one third of all women worked outside the home.

From the end of World War II to present, women continued to gain a significant presence in the work world. In the 1960s, the women's movement articulated a number of issues that concerned women employees, including low pay, low status, and sexual discrimination. Gaining steam, women networked and organized and successfully lobbied for governmental protections such as the Equal Pay Act of 1963 and the Pregnancy Discrimination Act of 1978. Through a series of redress such as court decisions, laws, and **affirmative action**, women found new rights and opportunities in the workplace. During this time, married women and mothers continued to participate in employment outside the home in increasing numbers. Spurred by consumerism and the need to make more money to buy more things, married women composed almost two-thirds of the female labor force in the mid-1970s. And, as more women emerged as single parents, mothers also entered the workforce in increasing numbers as a matter of economic survival.

WORKING WOMEN

Women work in the trades and labor jobs, in professional and managerial jobs, and in the **service industry**. Although women's work is as varied as the women themselves, these traditional categories of workplace employment serve as a useful framework to evaluate women in business. In trade and labor employment, women find themselves at particular odds with male-dominated occupational patterns. For example, blue-collar jobs are often associated with male-dominated unions. In professional and managerial jobs, women continue to enter business only to encounter a phenomena called the **glass ceiling**. The glass ceiling documents the rise of women only to a certain point within a business (i.e., middle **management**) and points to sex discrimination as the cause of this limited advancement. As a result of more equal access to higher education and professional programs, women continue to advance themselves within the professional and managerial fields. In the service sector, women dominate business at the lowest levels. Almost 45 percent of all working women are employed within the low-paying and low-status jobs of the service sector.

TRADES AND UNIONS. Although women have been members of labor unions since the early 1800s, their significant participation has been hampered by economic, cultural, and social reasons. Until wartime, women and their employers typically viewed the female workforce as temporary employees. These perceptions made women appear to be easily replaced, and diluted the effectiveness of any combined or unionized activities. Additionally, many of the unions' strongest tactics, including the strike, were perceived by society and women workers as unfeminine and undesirable. In 1900 only about 2 percent of the female workforce were unionized. Nevertheless, the harsh conditions of early industrial America prevailed upon women to organize and unionize for better working conditions. One of the earliest, the International Ladies Garment Workers Union (ILGWU) represented women in the textile and garment industries. The 1909 Uprising of the 20,000 saw women flexing their union muscles and striking. Throughout the next several decades, women participated more frequently in unions, including the American Federation of Labor (AFL) and Congress of Industrial Organizations (CIO). Of the two, the CIO is historically seen as more sympathetic to women. Fearful that low wages for women would decrease wages for men as well, both the AFL and CIO invited women to join and advocated equal pay. Mary Kenney was the first AFL woman organizer in 1891. The major unions, however, often exhibited ambivalent attitudes and actions toward women, including refusal to take actions against affiliates that excluded women from membership.

PROFESSIONS AND MANAGEMENT. As women gained more access to education and professional programs, their presence began to be felt in professional and managerial fields. Historically, graduate programs in business denied entry to women. In 1963,

Harvard began to admit women into the Graduate School of Business Administration. By 1989, women received almost half the undergraduate degrees awarded in business nationally and almost a third of all MBAs. Historically, women gained admittance to managerial and professional positions in traditionally female fields such as librarianship and **human resource management**. Other more male-dominated professions, however, such as law and medicine, more frequently reflect women's entrance and success. As early as 1869, Arabella Mansfield (1846-1911) took and passed the Iowa bar exam. In 1981, Sandra Day O'Connor (1930-) became the first female Supreme Court judge. In the interim century, women advanced in law and by 1996, women accounted for roughly half of all law students and almost one-third of practicing lawyers. Similarly, in medicine, women such as Elizabeth Blackwell (1821-1910; M.D., 1849) proved that women were competent and capable of performing within the professional fields. The American Medical Association began accepting women as members as early as 1876. Yet, until the 1970s, women were poorly represented in all medical fields except nursing. In 1996 women comprised 20 percent of all physicians and more than 40 percent of medical students. Within 15 years, women were expected to account for one-third of practicing physicians in the United States. Today, women are present in accounting, architecture, engineering, medicine, journalism, psychology, and other professional endeavors. Yet, they remain stymied by the glass ceiling.

The glass ceiling is a theory that attempts to explain why women do not advance into the uppermost professional and managerial jobs in business. For example, in medicine, only about 10 percent of women faculty members are full professors while almost a third of their male colleagues are full professors. Similar statistics in nearly every managerial or professional category point to the same inequity. In an apparent self-fulfilling pattern, productivity seems connected to the number of senior female positions within the company. Companies such as Motorola, Inc. programatically approach this problem by setting goals and structuring promotion and advancement opportunities that meet their goals. Like Deloitte and Touche, these and other companies recognize women's worth to the profession and competitive advance therein.

One result of the glass ceiling has been the rise of women entrepreneurs. By establishing their own businesses, women entrepreneurs hope to avoid discriminatory factors and measures that impair their success in the traditionally male business world. Women form businesses at nearly twice the rate of men. And, in the United States, about 6.5 million businesses are owned or controlled by a woman. Some, such as Elizabeth Arden (1878-1966), Helena Rubinstein (1870-1965), and Estée Lauder, made their fortunes in cosmetics while others, such as Olive Ann Mellor-Beech (1903-1993), inherited their businesses when their husbands died. By 1996, 3.5 million home-based businesses were owned by women, and those businesses provided work for approximately 14 million people. Discrimination is not absent, however, in the entrepreneurial world. In April 1994 Congress set a goal for the U.S. government to put 5 percent of its procurement dollars into women-owned businesses. Still, during the late 1990s, less than 2 percent of government procurement spending went to women's firms.

SERVICE INDUSTRY. The service industry, so thoroughly dominated by the female labor force, represents another category of employment frequently called the pink-collar jobs. These pink-collar jobs are characterized by low pay and low status. Clerical positions are perhaps the most widely recognized of these positions in the business world. With the advent of the typewriter in the late 1800s, women came forward to apply for and receive employment as typists. While previous male clerical workers had seen these entry level jobs as an effective means to move up within the organization, female workers soon discovered that management relied on breaking down clerical tasks so that workers would be interchangeable. In 1990, 80 percent of all clerical workers were women and more than 25 percent of all working women found themselves in clerical jobs. Retail sales workers account for another large segment of the service sector employment. Since the early 1900s, retail sales clerks have been transformed to cashiers with the restructuring of retail from full-service to self-service format.

WOMEN'S WORTH AND WORK

Early cultural consensus held that women and men enjoyed two different spheres of influence. Men moved within the public sphere of influence, including business and commerce, while women were confined to the private or family sphere of influence. More than any other factor, the issue of sex discrimination influences current promotion and pay practices within the workplace. Sex discrimination emerges from a strong past belief that women belonged in the home environment and not in the business environment. Two central tenants of sex discrimination hold that women do not need the money of employment since they will be supported by a man and that women are not as qualified as men. The Equal Pay Act of 1963 and the Civil Rights Act of 1964 provided protective legislation for women and enabled them to legally contest discriminatory practices in pay and promotion. As a result of these and other laws, bona fide occupational qualifications exist to define and determine the extent to which sex relates to ability to successfully complete a job. The **Equal Employment Opportunity Commission** is the watchdog governmental agency set up to deter sex discrimination in the workplace. Nevertheless, both historically and in modern settings, women earn less than men for the same work. **Comparable worth**, or the principle that equal work deserves equal pay, continues to evoke considerable controversy since many fear that male wages will decline rather than women's wages increase.

Three factors account for the origins of the low pay of women. First, women workers were always seen as merely supplementing their husband's pay. Even unmarried women were perceived to be transitional and on their way to domestic life. Under these assumptions, women did not warrant the **training** or education to move to higher-paying jobs even if they had been available. Second, early professional positions in nursing, education, and librarianship were outgrowths of charitable and philanthropic work. Done for charity and ''good works,'' the pay for these jobs reflected remuneration as an irrelevant part of employment. Finally, the historical involvement of women in domestic or housework type employment (e.g., sewing, cleaning) tied women's employment to traditional household duties. These household duties, since they were unpaid in a familial situation, received low pay in a commercial situation.

WOMEN'S ISSUES IN BUSINESS

Married women, mothers, older women, and women of color are all present in the business world along with their single, white counterparts. In 1998 more than 30 million married women worked outside the home and women represented 49 percent of the professional, managerial, and administrative workforce. In the coming years, women of color will compose the fastest growing segment of the labor force. Because of their dual role in the home and at work, women bring to the job new and previously unconsidered issues in **employment**. Some of these issues include child care, elder care, scheduling, and financial considerations.

As more and more single female parents enter the business world, the need for child care increases. From a business perspective, this is imperative to ensure the continued supply of female workers. In the early 19th century, women were normally left to their own devices to arrange for child care. Neighbors and relatives filled this need and, when unavailable, children were simply left home alone. At the turn of the century, women such as Josephine Dodge spearheaded philanthropic efforts to establish child care centers for working mothers. Dormant until the 1970s, the lack of available child care reflected society's preference for women to stay at home rather than work. Only during wartime did the government intervene with subsidized child-care arrangements to further the employment of women. With the advent of the 1960s, societal attention turned seriously to child-care efforts. And, in the 1970s, the White House Conference on Children addressed child-care issues by recommending federal funding. Rather than directly subsidizing child-care needs, federal tax reform in 1976 and 1978 offered tax relief for funds spent on child care. A relatively small number of businesses provide child-care arrangements as part of an employment package. Companies such as Boeing Corporation offer 24-hour hotline services, and others such as Apple Computer, Inc. offer on-site facilities. For small businesses, subsidization of child care can be prohibitively expensive. In 1990 child care accounted for the fourth-largest expense in most working families.

As life expectancy increases, working women are often faced with a situation called ''the sandwich generation.'' Caring for children and aging parents, female workers also bring to the workplace the issue of elder care. Similar in many ways—economically and socially—to child care, elder care is expensive and often requires specialized medical attendants. Almost three-quarters of all caregivers of aging relatives are women. The Family and Medical Leave Act of 1993 addresses both child and family needs by allowing up to 12 weeks of unpaid leave annually for the birth or adoption of a child or the serious illness of a family member.

As a result of conflicting family roles and responsibilities, women embrace the idea of flexible scheduling. Flexible scheduling allows women to set their own hours within limits set by corporate policy or practice. While companies must bear the costs of complicated schedules, they reap the benefits of increased productivity as women arrange schedules to meet their familial responsibilities. Almost 60 percent of all women would prefer a job with flexible hours. Other arrangements, such as job sharing, allow women to share jobs with other women in order to accommodate home demands.

Pension plans that incorporate early vesting and portability accommodate women's more frequent entries and exits from the business world. Since women have not, however, typically received the same benefits, at retirement many women find themselves with considerably less financial security than their male counterparts. Pension plans that require women to pay more to participate than men are illegal since the 1978 Supreme Court ruling on *Los Angeles v. Manhart.*

SEE ALSO: Gender Discrimination; Glass Ceiling; Women Entrepreneurs

[Tona Henderson, updated by Wendy H. Mason]

FURTHER READING:

Amott, Teresa. *Caught in the Crisis: Women and the U.S. Economy Today.* New York: Monthly Review Press, 1993.

——, and Julie A. Matthaei. *Race, Gender, and Work.* Boston: South End Press, 1991.

Baron, Ava, ed. *Work Engendered: Toward a New History of American Labor.* Ithaca, NY: Cornell University Press, 1991.

Boris, Eileen. *Home to Work: Motherhood and the Politics of Industrial Homework in the United States.* Cambridge: Cambridge University Press, 1994.

Bullock, Susan. *Women and Work.* London: Zed Books, 1994.

Chauvin, Keith W., and Ronald A. Ash. "Gender Earnings Differentials in Total Pay, Base Pay, and Contingent Pay." *Industrial Labor Relations and Review* 47, no. 4 (July 1994): 634-39.

Cook, Alice H., Val R. Lorwin, and Arlene Kaplan Daniels. *The Most Difficult Revolution: Women and Trade Unions.* Ithaca, NY: Cornell University Press, 1992.

Coolidge, Leslie, and Danielle D'Angelo. "Family Issues to Shape the Profession's Future." *CPA Journal* 64, no. 5 (May 1994): 16-21.

"Dependent Care Is Valuable Support Tool for Employers, Employees." *Employee Benefit Plan Review,* August 1993, 54-55.

Dogar, Rana. "The Top 500 Women-Owned Businesses." *Working Woman,* May 1998, 35+.

"Equal Partners: September Is Women in Medicine Month." *American Medical News,* 2 September 1996, 39.

Glazer, Nona Y. *Women's Paid and Unpaid Labor: The Work Transfer in Health Care and Retailing.* Philadelphia: Temple University Press, 1993.

Guteman, Roberta. "Changing the Face of Management." *Working Woman,* November 1994, 21-23.

Hand, Shirley, and Robert A. Zawacki. "Family-Friendly Benefits: More Than a Frill." *HR Magazine,* October 1994, 79-84.

Karsten, Margaret Foegen. *Management and Gender: Issues and Attitude.* Westport, CT: Quorum Books, 1994.

Kassam, Shayde. "The Changing Face of the Workforce." *Plant Engineering and Maintenance,* winter/spring 1994, 12.

Koziara, Karen Shallcross, Michael H. Mosckow, and Lucretia Tanner. *Working Women: Past, Present, and Future.* Washington: Bureau of National Affairs, 1987.

Kwolek-Folland, Angel. *Engendering Business: Men and Women in the Corporate Office, 1870-1930.* Baltimore: Johns Hopkins University Press, 1994.

"Law and Order: Women Sit on the High Court, but on the Beat, It's a Man's World." *Working Woman,* November/December 1996, 53.

Nelton, Sharon. "Women Owners and Uncle Sam." *Nation's Business,* April 1998, 53+.

Nichols, Nancy A. "Whatever Happened to Rosie the Riveter?" *Harvard Business Review* 71, no. 4 (July/August 1993): 54-62.

Perkins, Anne G. "Women in the Workplace: The Ripple Effect." *Harvard Business Review* 72, no. 6 (November/December 1994): 15.

Schneider, Dorothy, and Carl J. Schneider. *Women in the Workplace.* Santa Barbara, CA: ABC-CLIO, 1993.

Wellington, Sheila. "Cracking the Ceiling: Barriers Frustrated Women This Century." *Time,* 7 December 1998, 187.

Zellner, Wendy. "Women Entrepreneurs." *Business Week,* 18 April 1994, 104-10.

WORD PROCESSING

Word processing technology refers to various kinds of electronic text storage and manipulation devices, primarily through use of a computer **software** application. Although there are many specific computer programs and other devices available for word processing functions, as a class these have become one of the most basic and ubiquitous tools in the contemporary business world.

HISTORY OF WORD PROCESSING

The first machines able to record typed information for reuse were the automatic typewriters of the 1930s, which used rolls of paper tape to record keystrokes. The next major advance came in the 1960s when IBM introduced a typewriter capable of storing information that could later be revised. Released in 1964, the MT/ST (Magnetic Tape/Selectric Typewriter) used magnetic tape rather than paper to store data. However, this typewriter only allowed minimal editing in the middle of a document, as anything changed had to occupy the same number of characters as the original text. This limitation was surmounted shortly afterward with the development of IBM's MC/ST (Mag Card Selectric Typewriter), which allowed full document editing and soon became the industry standard for word processing devices.

Word processing technology evolved swiftly during the 1970s as such companies as Wang Laboratories, Olivetti, and Digital Equipment Corporation (DEC) entered the field. Notably, virtually all of the major developers also had ties to the nascent computer industry, and the creation of dedicated word processing machines often followed a parallel course to that of microcomputers.

Technical developments such as cathode-ray-tube (CRT) monitors and microchips—also used in computers—advanced the capabilities of word processors far beyond any typewriter. A noteworthy innovation was Xerox's Bravo model of the mid-1970s. It allowed users to make font face, formatting, and graphical changes easily using a mouse-like pointer.

Large metropolitan newspapers were among the first to embrace word processors. Law and real estate offices were also prime customers because they generated lengthy, largely standard documents such as contracts that lent themselves to storage and manipulation in order to save labor.

By the 1980s dedicated word processing devices and personal computers began to diverge, and computers running word processing software began to take a growing share of the market. While top-of-the-line word processing machines were sometimes better equipped to deliver highly formatted and easily manipulated text, computers offered businesses the ability to run a much wider range of applications, including spreadsheets and databases, in addition to document management.

Some stand-alone word processors also mimicked simple spreadsheet and related functions, but by the early 1990s personal computers were increasingly sought instead of such devices. By this time, some estimates suggest that as much as 95 percent of all secretaries were using some form of word processing software. As PC use continued to soar, stand-alone word processing units were relegated to mostly niche markets; and for business purposes word processing became synonymous with a category of computer software and the associated functions.

APPLICATIONS OF WORD PROCESSING

The production of printed documents before word processing was a comparatively arduous task. Standard contracts had to be typed individually, or preprinted forms had to be carefully fed through a typewriter in order to align the typewriter text with the appropriate blanks on the form. Minor corrections could require whole pages to be retyped. Word processing software on computers all but eliminated much of this tedium, and it has been estimated that a secretary using a word processor may be three times more efficient than one using a typewriter.

In addition to merely storing documents for later manipulation and retrieval, modern word processing software applications offer general features such as:

- spelling and grammar checks
- thesauri
- word counts
- search-and-replace functions.

As word processors have grown more sophisticated, they have advanced from the arena of creating simple documents to the realms of **desktop publishing** and integrated office information processing. All modern word processors contain extensive options for formatting text—be it choosing a font face, a point size, or a justification style. Off-the-shelf word processing packages by leading software publishers also routinely include the following capabilities:

- the ability to create spreadsheet tables with embedded formulas for automated calculations
- the ability to create a form letter and merge it with a list of recipient names and addresses for producing a mass mailing
- tools for placing custom shapes, colors, and graphics to produce highly formatted documents
- integration with certain spreadsheet and database programs to enable cross-use of structured data
- a facility for storing regularly used text formats as user-specified ''styles''
- the ability to automatically generate indexes and table of contents
- the ability to store user-defined sets of keystrokes and procedures, often called macros, to automate repetitive tasks.

Since the mid-1990s most word processing software has also included modest provisions for e-mail and **Internet** use. For instance, Internet addresses might be specially encoded in documents so that when a user selects the address it launches a web browser. Some programs have even added utilities for creating simple web pages.

PLANNED OBSOLESCENCE?

A corollary to the development of complex word processing software has been the rate at which programs on the market have been rendered obsolete by newer versions. Cynics describe this phenomenon as planned obsolescence or as a money-making scheme by software publishers. Whether or not either of these charges is valid, among the major word processing packages, such as Microsoft Word, WordPerfect (Corel Corporation), and Word Pro (Lotus Development Corporation), new releases have been issued at approximately two-year intervals. Owners of previous versions are usually offered a discount for upgrading. While these upgrades typically are compatible with the next most recent version, backwards compatibility erodes quickly with each new version. This is not to suggest that the new versions have not had their merits. On the contrary, a single upgrade can streamline an awkward program into an intuitive and efficient application, although such a radical improvement tends to be the exception. In addition to making existing functionalities more accessible and efficient, most word processor upgrades boast some kind of new functions. As an example, in the late 1990s a couple of the leading publishers were touting voice recognition features in their programs as a substitute for typing.

FURTHER READING:

Miller, Susan, and Kyle Knowles. ''New Ways of Writing: A Handbook for Writing with Computers.'' New York: Prentice Hall, 1996.

Picarille, Lisa. ''More Roads Lead to the 'Net.'' *Computerworld,* 19 February 1996, 59.

''Work Smart.'' *Fortune,* summer 1998, 168.

WORK SCHEDULES

SEE: Family Leave; Hours of Labor

WORKERS' COMPENSATION

Approximately every 19 seconds someone is injured in an on-the-job accident. But whether or not the injured individual has health insurance, if the injury occurred on the job it is very likely that the injury will be cared for and the worker's lost income replaced under the workers' compensation insurance system.

The workers' compensation system developed to provide medical coverage and/or income replacement for workers (or the families of workers) who were injured or became ill or died as a result of workplace conditions or accidents. These laws, which require an employer to purchase insurance that provides care and income replacement, were developed in the early industrial age. During that period machine industry workers were being injured at a high rate. Their only remedy for medical care and to replace income lost due to days off of work was to sue the employer in court for negligence. For many this was financially impossible and when it could happen, the cost to employers was very high. Both employers and employees found that a legal system of compensation whereby the employee gave up the right to sue, but was guaranteed legal protection and coverage for the injuries, was preferable.

The first workers' compensation law was passed in Germany in 1883. The rest of industrialized Europe quickly followed suit. The first U.S. state law that passed and remained in force was in Wisconsin in 1911. By 1949 every state had a workers' compensation law on the books.

In 1916, the U.S. Congress passed the Federal Employees Compensation Act providing protection to federal workers. The passage of this law, while it had no legal impact on any private, state, or local workers, aided the cause of state workers' compensation laws by providing a national example of caring for employees. Today the federal government also administers the provisions of the Longshoremen's and Harbor Workers' Compensation Act, which provides benefits for longshoremen, and the Black Lung Act, which provides benefits for coal mine workers who suffer from Black Lung disease. Aside from these three exceptions, the rest of the more than 93.7 million wage and salary workers (as of 1989) are covered under the varying provisions of the 50 state laws and those of the District of Columbia.

Each State has its own workers' compensation law and administration. Although the provisions of each State law differ greatly, the underlying principle is the same—that employers should assume the costs of injuries, illnesses, and deaths that occur on the job, without regard to fault, and partially replace wage income lost. While income replacement under workers' compensation is usually a percentage of the actual wage, is it counted as a transfer payment and, as such, is not subject to federal income tax.

Except for a few states, coverage is compulsory for all private employers. Employers who reject coverage also lose the common law defense for suits filed by employees for negligence. Some state laws exempt certain categories of employees from coverage. Those most likely to be excluded from coverage are domestics, agricultural workers, and manual laborers.

In 1995 employers paid $26.1 billion in premiums, 9.4 percent less than was paid in 1994. The general downward trend (the figure in 1990 was $30.9 billion) is further registered in the primary measure of compensation costs: the cost as a percentage of business payrolls. The Bureau of Labor Statistics estimated that in 1998 this figure measured 36 cents per hour worked, down from 38 cents in 1997. In manufacturing industries, the Bureau found that compensation insurance costs decreased an average of nine percent per year between 1994 and 1998. While workers' compensation represents the only aspect of employee compensation and benefit costs that has continually decreased through the 1990s as states have slashed benefits, many analysts expect the typically cyclical pricing for workers' compensation to be on the verge of another increase.

Increasing costs have led employers to a deeper interest in on-the job safety since insurance premiums for workers' compensation are often based on loss ratio. A loss ratio is defined by the Social Security Administration as the proportion of the premium dollar that is returned to the worker as cash or medical benefits.

Generally, there are three different methods available for employers to insure workers for the required workers' compensation protection. These are state insurance funds, private insurance, and self-insurance. The latter is seen as a cost-saving method for many safety-oriented firms. Where states permit it, many large employers now self-insure and many small employers form groups to insure themselves and decrease the risks. Premiums paid out reflect the payment of benefits and the cost of administering the program, policy writing, claims investigations and adjustments, allocation of reserves for long-term accrued disabilities, and other administrative costs.

Managed care, in which health maintenance organizations or other licensed entities pre-pay for health services and administer the financial and medical details for a defined insured population, is the most common avenue by which workers' compensation-related medical insurance is provided. There exists a good deal of controversy relating to these organizations, however; these administrations, often with enormous bureaucracies, generate disfavor among much of the public (and many doctors) because, in order to safeguard their financial bottom line, HMOs often discourage and deny extensive or aggressive treatments that doctors and patients often feel is necessary, but that is considered inconsistent with the HMO's financial concerns.

First popular in the 1980s, ''employee leasing'' represents an alternative to managed care. It refers to an arrangement in which employees of a business known as a leasing firm are sent to a client firm for a fee, usually based on the workers' wages. This arrangement eliminates a degree of the client firm's payroll, thereby mitigating insurance premiums.

Another emerging issue is how workers' compensation regulations will meet the increasing trend toward telecommuting, whereby many workers are choosing to take advantage of improved office and telecommunications technology by working at home. Just how hours spent working at home will be determined in terms of employer liability for workers' safety and compensation is yet to be settled.

Changes to state workers' compensation laws are made by state legislatures. In 1993, changes mandated by states included measures to implement managed health care as a way to save money for employers, reduce fraud, and improve safety in the workplace.

Fraud is always a concern. But under the workers' compensation program there is also the question not only of legitimacy of the injury but of legitimacy of the place of injury. The system only covers injuries at the workplace or injuries related to workplace activity. If a worker injures his or her back over the weekend while doing yard work he or she is not covered, even though the injury may cost time from the job. The extension of workers' compensation into the full life of the worker and into caring for the family as a whole has been under study by many. In 1992 four states—Alabama, Georgia, California, and Maine—began to examine ways in which workers' compensation might be added to a health insurance plan for the general population.

In 1999 insurance companies lauded the U.S. Supreme Court's decision in the case of *American Manufacturers Mutual v. Sullivan.* The 3rd Circuit Court of Appeals in Pennsylvania had determined an aspect of that state's workers' compensation reform legislation, which stated that insurers could suspend payments to medical providers pending review, illegitimate on the grounds that, as ''state actors,'' insurers were bound to afford beneficiaries full constitutional protections, including a notice and a hearing before the suspension of payments. The Supreme Court, however, overturned that ruling, upholding the provisions of Pennsylvania's reforms. Similar laws around the country, both current and prospective, now seem more secure, much to the delight of insurers, who will be afforded greater leverage in assessing the appropriateness of beneficiaries' medical treatments.

[Joan Leotta]

FURTHER READING:

Hansen, Fay. ''Workers' Compensation: Hard Times Ahead.'' *Compensation and Benefits Review.* May/June 1999, 15-20.

Hood, Jack B. *Workers' Compensation and Employee Protection Laws.* St. Paul, MN: West Group, 1999.

Jasper, Margaret. *Workers' Compensation Law.* Dobbs Ferry, NY: Oceana Publications, 1997.

Lenscis, Peter M. *Workers' Compensation: A Reference and Guide.* London: Quorum Books, 1998.

WORKFORCE

Workforce refers to both the total number of all workers and of workers available to a nation, project, or industry. The U.S. Department of Labor (DOL) and U.S. industry also use this definition.

The U.S. Bureau of Labor Statistics (BLS) conceptualizes the workforce, also known as the ''labor force,'' as ''all employed and unemployed civilians.'' Children below the age of 16 are not included in the count. Other groups that are not included in the calculation of the workforce are students; homemakers; those unable to work due to illness, disability, or other cause; retirees; and individuals who have left the workforce voluntarily, including discouraged workers.

The U.S. Bureau of the Census collects data that is analyzed and tabulated by the BLS, which publishes them in a monthly periodical entitled *Employment and Earnings.* In addition, the June edition of the publication provides data on nearly 600 industries for which monthly data is unavailable. Many times, articles or even entire issues of *Monthly Labor Review,* published by the DOL, are devoted to workforce data. This publication compares the U.S. workforce to that of other countries, analyzes the workforce in particular industries, and looks at the workforce by subcategories including education, race, age, and ethnic group.

Workforce data is also reported by occupation. The Occupational Employment Statistics (OES) is a periodic survey mailed to a number of nonfarm commercial establishments. In the survey, actual employee hours worked are reported by occupation. The occupations are categorized according to the **Standard Industrial Classification** (SIC) code for each industry and workplace surveyed. The BLS *SIC Manual* is available at most public libraries.

Studies of the composition of the workforce benefit both industries and individuals. The current method of defining the workforce was introduced in the 1930s. Prior to that time there was no measurement of workforce available, although a count of the number of workers on particular jobs was tabulated. Modern measurements of the workforce provide industries with insight into the location, skills, and availability of various types of workers, and provide a crucial aid in **employee recruitment**.

The National Association of Manufacturers (NAM) joined with the DOL in November 1991 in a project known as ''A Partnership in Work Force Readiness.'' The project's goal was to shape policies that help **management** and workers deal with predicted industrial and demographic changes and make the U.S. manufacturing sector more competitive globally. Jerry Jasinowski, then president of NAM, stated that reports submitted by the project in 1992 discussed ''the results of our current efforts to assist companies in meeting specific challenges to achieving high performance workplaces in America's manufacturing sector.'' The key elements noted in these reports were the need for industry to keep pace with technological changes; to achieve higher productivity by showing readiness to reorganize work, training patterns, and education; and for overall flexibility in the workplace. The report also acknowledged the need of workers, line managers, and upper management to understand, monitor, and enhance the skills of a culturally diverse workforce to improve the global competitiveness of U.S. industries.

Workforce 2000, a DOL study undertaken to predict workforce needs in the next century, showed that the greatest future demand will be for workers with technical skills. BLS statistics released in 1996 show that the highest number of new jobs were created by the health-care and computer industries, and project that this trend will continue through 2005. Further BLS studies in 1997 revealed that administrative, professional, and service occupations will account for the majority of new employment opportunities created in the United States through 2006. Other projections show that Hispanic males will comprise the fastest-growing segment of the national workforce, although the mixture of ethnic and racial groups present in the workforce will remain virtually unchanged through 2006. These findings point to a need to ensure that Hispanic males receive the technical training required to prepare them for the jobs of the future, and show the policy value of workforce statistics and related projections.

Data revealing that more mothers with young children were remaining in the workforce, with projections of further increases in this segment of the population, underscore the need for expanded public and private sector child-care facilities and helped substantiate arguments used to pass the Family and Medical Leave Act of 1993.

Recent BLS surveys and projections indicate that the workforce will undergo fundamental changes in the early 21st century as the so-called baby boomers reach retirement age. The large number of baby boomers currently of working age enabled the participation rate, that is the percentage of the nation's total population currently employed, to reach a record 67 percent in 1996. The changing demographics of the workforce were also revealed by the fact that the participation rate for males declined by nearly 1 percent between 1982 and 1993, and was projected to drop a further 2.2 percent by the year 2005. This loss of male workers was more than compensated for by an increase in the participation rate of women during the same period. Longer-term forecasts for the workforce include a gradual aging of the working population as the baby boomers approach retirement, followed by a sharp reduction in the participation rate as the ''boomers'' actually retire. The gradual but accelerating aging of the workforce has given rise to increased emphasis on protecting the availability of Social Security benefits, provision of elder care, and related public policies.

SEE ALSO: Child Care/Elder Care; Family Leave

[Joan Leotta, updated by Grant Eldridge]

FURTHER READING:

Bowman, Charles. ''BLS Projections to 2006: A Summary.'' *Monthly Labor Review* 120, no. 11 (November 1997): 3.

Edmondson, Brad. ''Work Slowdown.'' *American Demographics,* March 1996, 4.

Kolberg, William, and F. Smith. *Rebuilding America's Workforce.* Homewood, IL: Business One Irwin, 1992.

''Labor Force.'' *Occupational Outlook Quarterly* 41, no. 4 (winter 1997): 25.

National Association of Manufacturers. *Workforce Readiness: How to Meet Our Greatest Competitive Challenges.*

National Association of Manufacturers. U.S. Department of Labor. *Workforce Readiness: A Manufacturing Perspective.*

Schiff, Lenore. ''The Growing Labor Force.'' *Time,* 3 March 1997, 34.

WORKING CAPITAL

Working capital is the difference between current assets and current **liabilities** on a company's **balance**

sheet. Current assets include such things as cash, accounts receivable, marketable **securities**, inventory, and prepaid expenses. Examples of current liabilities are accounts payable, accrued expenses, and the near-term portion of **loan** or lease payments due. ''Current'' is generally defined as those assets or liabilities that will be liquidated within the course of one business cycle, typically a year.

Working capital is one measure of liquidity; creditors will often be interested in a company's working capital as one indicator of the debtor's ability to make payments on a timely basis. The components of working capital are used to calculate several **financial ratios**, including the current ratio, which is current assets divided by current liabilities. **Banks** will often write into their loan **contracts** covenants requiring the maintenance of prescribed levels of working capital or current ratio. The importance of these measures to **credit** analysts is what makes the determination of current versus noncurrent status so important on a company's balance sheet. Because of this, much thought goes into the classification of assets and liabilities.

Working capital is also of interest in the context of a business **valuation**, for at least two reasons. First, when using a **discounted cash flow** approach, the appraiser will often consider changes expected in working capital over the projected periods to convert income figures into cash flows. Second, an excess amount of working capital, particularly cash, is sometimes grounds for additional value being quantified, above and beyond that which would result from the income capitalization component of the valuation. This is because companies of a given standard industrial classification code, or industry type, are commonly thought of as requiring a certain level of working capital to operate under normal circumstances. Companies that vary significantly from the norm may be considered to have excess or inadequate working capital, and therefore warrant an adjustment.

Working capital can be provided by several sources:

1. Net income, plus noncash expenses;
2. Financing activities, including loans and equity infusions;
3. Decrease in noncurrent assets, e.g., the sale of fixed assets.

Most business activities affect working capital, either consuming or generating it. Sales made at a positive margin increase working capital, as they increase one current asset (accounts receivable or cash) more than they decrease another current asset (inventory). Starting up a new product line may require higher levels of working capital, as inventory and receivables must be built up to some steady-state level. Changes in credit terms, either that the company gives on its receivables, or that it gets on its payables, will affect working capital. For example, extending more favorable credit terms to one's customers will require higher amounts of working capital, as accounts receivable will build without any compensating changes to make up the difference. The repayment of a long-term **debt** (**bonds**, capital leases, etc.) will result in a reduction, or use of working capital. This occurs as a current asset (cash) is used to reduce a noncurrent liability.

[Christopher C. Barry, updated by David P. Bianco]

FURTHER READING:

Anderson, Hershal, and others. *Financial Accounting and Reporting*. 4th ed. Medford, NJ: Malibu Publishing, 1995.

Anthony, Robert N., and others. *Accounting: Text and Cases*. 9th ed. NP: McGraw-Hill Higher Education, 1994.

Diamond, Michael A. *Financial Accounting*. 4th ed. Cincinnati: South-Western Publishing, 1995.

Eskew, Robert K., and Daniel L. Jensen. *Financial Accounting*. 5th ed. New York: McGraw-Hill, 1995.

Solomon, Lanny M., Larry M. Walther, and Richard J. Vargo. *Financial Accounting*. 3rd ed. New York: West Publishing, 1992.

WORKPLACE VIOLENCE PROGRAM

The 1990s have seen workplace violence (WPV) receive unparalleled attention in the popular press and among safety and health professionals. Much of the reason for this publicity has been the reporting of data by nationally recognized agencies regarding the magnitude of this problem. In 1994 the U.S. Department of Justice warned that the workplace is the ''most dangerous place to be in America''; and in 1996 the National Institute for Occupational Safety and Health (NIOSH) proclaimed homicide the leading cause of occupational injury or death for women, and the second-leading cause (behind motor-vehicle accidents) for men. As a result, companies are now confronting their ethical and legal responsibilities to respond to these increased risk factors with *increased awareness* of the issue of workplace violence, and *decreased tolerance* for behaviors that, even as little as a decade ago, may have been considered acceptable. And regardless of the statistical analyses performed on this issue, or the causes assigned to its trends, violence in the workplace is a universal problem, and one that must be addressed proactively by every business, regardless of its commodity, geographical setting, or history of violence. What follows is designed to present a ''practical'' guide to meeting these demands by generating an effective workplace violence program that documents WPV risk factors, prevention strategies, and response protocols.

KEY STATISTICS

In NIOSH's 1996 *Current Intelligence Bulletin* (*CIB*) on violence in the workplace, the institute first pointed out that ''sensational'' acts of coworker violence (which constituted a relatively small subset of the total picture) were often emphasized by the media to the exclusion of the daily murders and assaults committed by strangers during crimes against particular industries, and that 17 percent of the occupational assaults against women were perpetrated by former husbands or boyfriends.

The *CIB* then went on to chart the ''occupational clustering'' associated with workplace violence statistics. According to the report, 56 percent of the fatal assaults, more than 1,000 annually, occurred in the following retail and public order industries (in order of decreasing frequency): taxicabs, liquor stores, gas service stations, security, law enforcement, grocery stores, jewelry stores, hotels/motels, barber shops, and eating establishments. Conversely, accounting for 85 percent of nonfatal workplace assaults were primarily **service industries**, namely nursing homes, social service organizations, and hospitals, followed (at a distance) by two retail industries, grocery stores and eating establishments.

Additionally, the *CIB* stated that between 1992 and 1994, between 73 and 82 percent of the circumstances that surrounded workplace homicides were related to robbery or other crimes, followed by business disputes with work associates (9.5 percent), fellow/former employee disputes (5 percent), customer disputes (4.5 percent), police in the line of duty (6.5 percent), security guards in the line of duty (6 percent), and personal disputes with acquaintances (4 percent).

Finally, aside from the unquestionable pain and suffering endured by victims and witnesses of workplace violence, the following figures (provided in 1999 by the National Safe Workplace Institute) tabulate the monetary losses associated with it: A single episode of workplace violence averages $250,000 in lost work time and legal expenses. Productivity decreases as much as 80 percent for up to two weeks after an incident, due to a range of factors including the absence of impacted workers and interruptions due to police investigations, facility damage, the effects of posttraumatic stress syndrome, and time spent debriefing or counseling employees.

CAUSES AND ASSOCIATED PREVENTION

Statistics plainly indicate that the greatest risk of workplace violence is associated with robbery or other crimes. Clearly then, as the general crime rate increases, so too shall crimes perpetrated in the workplace. Consequently, great potential exists for workplace-specific assessment and prevention efforts related to workplace violence from outside perpetrators (e.g., cash-handling policies, physical separation of workers from customers, lighting, security devices, escort services, employee **training**, and so forth).

Conversely, NIOSH also revealed that over 100 supervisors and coworkers were murdered by fellow employees in 1997, and, according to a Northeastern Facility criminologist who tracks workplace violence nationwide, the number of workers who killed their bosses doubled from 1982 to 1992. Concurrently, shop ''culture'' has begun to reflect this overall trend. Key departures are: (1) Fighting incidents are more intense than they were in the past, wherein there seems to be an increased willingness to use greater levels of force; (2) the level of discourse is increasingly coarse—harsh words and gross profanity are commonplace; and (3) as a corollary, in order to get attention, vocalized threats have become more specific and more threatening. And while no single cause appears to be forthcoming from experts regarding this trend, several plausible possibilities exist.

One theory suggests that, whereas the workplace was once a source of security, comfort, or even ''extended family,'' many have now have become breeding grounds for anxiety and contentiousness, where **layoffs** and downsizing are matched in frequency only by hostile **takeovers**, buyouts, and **mergers**. Herein, personal integrity, dignity, and humanity have been lost; and with this undercurrent of ''impersonalization'' may come a growing propensity for acts of violence against the administrative ''machine,'' or against coworkers who have become little more than ''inanimate'' sources of competition, suspicion, and resentment.

Another theory is that as violence increases, so does the ''theatrical'' coverage thereof (via the media, television, movies, etc.), thereby desensitizing all of us to its horrors and making it a more conceivable option to those who are already upset or angry at work. And while acts of violence perpetrated by fellow or former employees comprise only 5 percent of total workplace violence incidents, the resulting paranoia, anger, and depression that results from observing peers harming peers is considered to be far more severe in witnesses and survivors than that which results from observing violence perpetrated by strangers. Accordingly, examining possible precursors to this type of violence in the workplace, regardless of how abstract or dynamic the postulates may appear, and using this information as part of a comprehensive workplace violence prevention program, is critical to minimizing these types of incidents.

Every employer's workplace violence program will be distinctly different. This author, however, suggests that each program contain the following four parts and corresponding sections.

PART I—EMPLOYEE PERPETRATORS

Part I of the WPV program should address those components that are dedicated to preventing and responding to violence in the workplace perpetrated by existing or former employees.

BEHAVIORS PROHIBITED IN THE WORKPLACE. This section of the WPV program should list the company's prohibited behaviors that constitute workplace violence; key examples are below. Note that since regulating language can be a slippery slope, the italicized phrases in the first three prohibitions below may be useful as clarifiers to assist with differentiating between improper, or even offensive, versus truly threatening communications.

1. Threats (whether veiled or unveiled, specific or general, serious or facetious) of significant harm to company persons or property, *which evoke fear or concern in witnesses or victims*
2. Communication, verbal or otherwise, *intended to raise fear for personal safety*
3. Obscene communication or racial epithets *used as mechanisms of verbal insult or abuse*
4. Physical assault
5. Stalking
6. Unauthorized penetration or sabotage of electrical, mechanical, or computer systems, or deliberate damage to facility property
7. Unauthorized transporting of weapons onto the premises

Please note that of those prohibitions, all but the first two are already covered by existing policies in nearly every company. Nevertheless, the remaining behaviors are commonly included as ''WPV Prohibited Behaviors'' in order to illustrate the various types of workplace violence, and thereby integrate the concept of workplace violence, and all that it implies, into the company culture.

Also note that the first two prohibitions will undoubtedly provoke anger, fear, and resentment among employees who will voice grave concerns regarding potential McCarthyism, witch-hunts, First Amendment violations, reckless or malicious reporting, and so forth. A legitimate response to these types of apprehensions is threefold:

1. The punitive measures associated with these prohibited behaviors are: (a) decided on a case-by-case basis, (b) follow a multidisciplinary investigation (described in the WPV program), and (c) range from negligible to severe, thereby allowing for a fair and measured response to each prohibited behavior.
2. Sexual harassment policies were met with virtually identical concerns, and have been successfully upheld since their inception.
3. Statistics bear out the fact that past perpetrators of workplace violence have notoriously threatened to commit their violent crimes (often in startling detail) prior to carrying them out. Thus, until a zero tolerance against threats is invoked, employers are unable to employ an objective and uniform response to what may have otherwise been valid predictors of violence, and employees have no means to report threatening behavior without the risk of appearing paranoid or oversensitive. Moreover, the repercussions of ignoring this type of historical evidence, and thereby risking serious injury or death to employees, must necessarily outweigh the (as-yet-unsubstantiated) concerns voiced by objectors to the policies.

WPV OBLIGATIONS—EMPLOYER AND EMPLOYEE. This section of the WPV program should identify what the company considers to be the employer's and the employees' obligations related to preventing and responding to WPV.

It is advisable for employers to have in place the following:

1. Preventive prehire and layoff practices
2. A statement of zero tolerance against violent threats and behaviors in the workplace
3. Policies and procedures presenting consequences that can result when WPV occurs
4. A policy regarding employee responsibility to report violent threats or behaviors and procedures for how to do so
5. A TMT that will investigate all reports of violent threats or behavior
6. A description of possible intervention strategies and who will perform follow-up
7. Training programs for employees and their supervisors that include warning signs of potential violence and guidelines for de-escalating potentially violent behavior
8. A trauma plan that addresses emergency measures to be taken during a WPV incident, including an emergency signal or code to be used.

On the other hand, key employee obligations are to:

1. Understand and agree to the terms and conditions of this policy/program
2. Familiarize themselves with this WPV program and/or attend WPV awareness training
3. Understand and accept that a consequence of the facility's duty to provide a safer working environment is that actions of individuals are regulated in a more conservative manner
4. Refrain from participating in any of the prohibited behaviors described in this program
5. Report persons engaging in any of the prohibited behaviors identified in this program, or report any behavior that constitutes threats or potential/actual acts of violence that they have witnessed, received, or discovered through a third party.

GENERAL RISK ASSESSMENT AND ASSOCIATED PREVENTION STRATEGIES. This section of the WPV program should document the company's area(s) of greatest risk for employee violence (without regard to particular incidents or individuals), and briefly describe general mechanisms in place for lowering these risks.

General areas of high risk often include: (1) poorly executed **hiring practices**; (2) poorly conceived firing practices; and (3) discrete areas (e.g., offices, departments, divisions) that employ especially disgruntled employees and/or present a history of workplace violence. Accordingly, this section may identify prehire practices for supervisors that include explicit screening for prior violent acts/crimes or dis-

Table 1a

Model for Reporting, Investigating, Accessing, & Responding to WPV Incidents at XYZ Company

I. REPORTING WPV (OR POTENTIAL WPV) INCIDENTS AT XYZ
   A. XYZ employees have a "duty to warn" XYZ administrators that they have been victim to, witnessed, or otherwise discovered persons engaging in any of the WPV behaviors prohibited by the company.
   B. XYZ employees have four options available for reporting actual or potential WPV:
      1. Inform their supervisors, or
      2. inform a higher level administrator, or
      3. inform a member of XYZ's Threat Management Team (TMT) directly, or
      4. leave a message on the "WAVE" (Workplace Act of Violence Expected) Hotline, ext. 1234 or (999) 555-1234.
   C. The "Workplace Violence Threat/Incident Report". Anyone who takes a formal "Workplace Violence Threat/Incident Report" shall ask two sets of questions found on the Workplace Violence Report Form (seeTable II):
      1. The first set of questions will specifically address the threatening incident or behavior of concern
      2. The second set of questions are based on a group of "warning signs", identified in Table III, that has been described for individuals who have historically become violent in the workplace.

II. THREAT/INCIDENT MANAGEMENT - Upon receipt of a formal Threat/Incident Report, the TMT member must convene the "core" TMT, plus ad-hoc members as necessary, to perform any/all of the following 3 steps (each as deemed appropriate by the TMT):
   A. Threat/Incident Investigation (in recommended order):
      1. Review the WPV log and files to determine if other Threat/Incident Reports have been filed against this individual;
      2. Review personnel records to determine if any disciplinary notices, etc. have been logged in this individual's personnel file;
      3. XYZ Police inspects personal belongings on XYZ property if weapons or other instruments of violence are suspected;

(cont. Table 1b)

Table 1b

Model for Reporting, Investigating, Accessing, & Responding to WPV Incidents at XYZ Company

(cont. from Table 1a)

4. Using the "warning signs of potential violence" (Table III), the TMT member interviews witnesses identified on the Report, and/or the individual's past or present supervisor(s), for their impressions or any information that may be helpful;
5. Using the "warning signs of potential violence" (Table III), the TMT member interviews co-workers, and any additional individuals who may have insight into, or relevant experience with, the alleged perpetrator's behaviors.
6. TMT psychologist, or a member who has consulted with the TMT psychologist, interviews the subject of allegation(s);
7. Subject of the allegation(s) may be placed on administrative leave with pay pending further review and notification to return.

B. Threat/Incident Assessment:

1. TMT then reviews the information obtained to determine whether a "substantial risk of harm to persons or property" exists.
2. Assessing Threats. The following criteria can be used in combination to determine whether a threat, including abusive or obscene communication, presents a substantial risk of harm to persons or property:
   a. Presence of "warning signs";
   b. Context in which threats were made (e.g., was alleged perpetrator victim of long-term bullying or discrimination?);
   c. Tone with which threatening language or behavior was presented;
   d. Apprehension or fear created in the person being threatened;
   e. Whether the threat was "conditional" or "unconditional", the latter being more serious;
   f. How specific the threat was (the more specific the threat, the more it is considered a risk);
   g. Known history of violent or threatening behavior at work or home.

(cont. Table 1c)

proportionate workplace anger. Likewise, this section could provide various mechanisms for notifying subordinates of layoffs that are less likely to result in violence. Finally, some companies conduct cultural assessments to measure their employees' attitudes and beliefs in order to isolate (and address) those locales of higher risk; a description of the nature and frequency of these assessments can be described in this section.

PROCEDURES FOR REPORTING, INVESTIGATING, ASSESSING, AND RESPONDING TO INCIDENTS. This section of the WPV program should provide the explicit procedures for reporting, investigating, assessing, and responding to WPV incidents. Obviously, this section will vary the most significantly from facility to facility. Nevertheless, Table 1 (and associated Tables 2-4) constitute a detailed example of this section in order to accomplish two goals: (1) streamline the various guidelines and recommendations of a broad assortment of WPV research/literature into a practical process; and (2) provide a working model of how an actual WPV investigation might be approached.

For purposes of drafting this section of the WPV program, it may serve the company to include a great deal of step-by-step detail, much like writing an ''administrative recipe'' (see Table 1). And, while this approach may superficially appear to offer inadequate levels of administrative flexibility, it actually offers each of the TMT members more protection by limiting independent judgments and decisions (based on a personal history with the employee, a Polyanna nature, and so forth), which may later prove disastrously erroneous. And, as the model in Table 1 shows, any and all steps of the threat/incident management process *may* be eliminated by consensus (and documenta-

Table 1c

Model for Reporting, Investigating, Accessing, & Responding to WPV Incidents at XYZ Company

(cont. from Table 1b)

3. Assessing Physical Fighting. The criteria in Table IV can be used to determine whether those engaged in physical fighting present a substantial risk of harm to persons or property.
4. Four classifications commonly used, alone or in combination, to describe offenses and their perpetrators are:
   a. "Non-Dangerous" Act or - falls into one of the following 3 categories but evidence does not support a "substantial risk of harm to persons or property":
      1) "False alarm:" a misunderstanding or misinterpretation has occurred;
      2) "Bully:" alleged perpetrator attempted to browbeat individuals to get his/her own way;
      3) "Ventilator:" alleged perpetrator used inappropriate verbal or body language to "blow off steam."
   b. "Dangerous Act or Actor:" Evidence supports a "substantial risk of harm to persons or property."

C. Threat/Incident Response

1. Based on the conclusions drawn in the Threat Assessment phase, the core TMT shall proceed in one of two directions:
   a. Enter Report in the TMT log as "non-actionable" (with brief explanation and/or "non-dangerous" classification)
   b. Deem that Report is "actionable." This consensus often requires the assistance of "ad hoc" team members, e.g., attorneys, psychologists, etc., in order to establish solid information regarding, e.g., the institution's legal rights and responsibilities, police and security issues and options, and psychological perspective and potential ramifications
2. Consequences to employees who commit an "actionable" WPV offense can include, but are not limited to:
   a. Referral to appropriate health care professionals for indefinite care and follow-up;
   b. written reprimand;
   c. short-term removal from the workplace; and/or
   d. long-term separation from the workplace, up to and including suspension, dismissal and arrest.

tion) of the core TMT. Overall then, this approach inherently affords the company better and more uniform risk management.

The company may also want to include in this section frequently asked questions regarding the WPV reporting process. The following are two of the most common questions posed by individuals who are considering filing WPV threat/incident reports. Legitimate responses follow.

Q. If I file a report, will I be notified of the precise outcome of the TMT's investigation?

A. The TMT shall *not* generally divulge to any reporting employees the explicit course of action taken in response to a threat/incident report; as a result, reporting employees are strongly encouraged to contact the TMT immediately if threatening or violent behavior is repeated at any time following the initial report.

Q. If I file a report, will I be guaranteed absolute anonymity?

A. The TMT will handle all matters brought to its attention with due regard for your confidentiality, privacy rights, and concerns for safety, but if you disclose your identify to a TMT member, that member cannot guarantee absolute or permanent anonymity. An anonymous WPV reporting hotline, however, *has* been set up for individuals who desire anonymity.

TRAINING. In this section, the WPV program should list, at a minimum, the following:

1. The primary topics that will be covered in this training. Key topics are as follows:
   a. How to recognize the danger signs of potential workplace violence

Table 2a
Model of a WPV Threat/Incidence Report

1. Check any/all of the following that describe what is being reported, (referred to hereafter in this report as "incident"): threat of harm to persons/property___ verbal/non-verbal intimidation ___ physical assault ___ obscene communication____ stalking ___ penetration/sabotage of proprietary systems and/or deliberate damage to university property. ____ transporting of weapons onto premises ____ other (describe briefly):
2. Individual making report (check one): was a recipient/victim of the incident _____ was a witness to incident ______ heard about incident from recipient/victim or witness ______
3. Name of individual perpetrating the incident:
4. Department of individual perpetrating the incident:
5. Job classification of individual perpetrating the incident:
6. Name of recipient, victim or potential victim of incident:
7. Date/time of the incident:
8. Describe what happened, and/or any triggering events, just prior to the incident:
9. Describe any history leading to the incident:
10. If incident involved verbal or written discourse, describe specific language used:
11. If incident involved any physical conduct, describe specific behavior:
12. If incident involved any non-verbal communication, describe specific behavior:
13. Describe the physical and emotional appearance of the alleged perpetrator:
14. Names of others who were directly involved with or witnessed the incident:
15. Describe how the incident ended:
16. Describe the victim's response(s) following the incident: (a) physical response(s) (e.g., went back to work, exited area, sat down, kicked or pounded inanimate objects, etc.); (b) emotional response(s) (e.g., angry, crying, laughing, afraid, etc.) and/or (c) verbal response(s) (including whether they were spoken or shouted) of the victim following the incident:
17. Describe what happened to the alleged perpetrator after the incident ended:
18. Names of any supervisory staff involved in the incident (during or afterwards):
19. To the best of your knowledge, were any employees (including the alleged perpetrator) reprimanded or disciplined as a result of the incident? ______ (Y/N) Describe:
20. Steps which have already been taken to ensure incident does not escalate or repeat itself:

(cont. Table 2b)

   b. How to file a workplace violence report
   c. How to diffuse a potentially violent individual
2. How often the training is held
3. Who will present the training
4. Who is required to attend
5. Who is encouraged to attend
6. How to obtain additional copies of the written WPV program.

COMPOSITION OF THE FACILITY'S THREAT MANAGEMENT TEAM. In this section, the WPV program should briefly reiterate the function and purpose of the TMT, and then list the names, positions, and complete contact information for every individual on the team.

Generally, a TMT will be comprised of a core team, supplemented by ad hoc team members, who are brought in on an as-needed basis. The core team would include a representative from the risk management department, a representative from the occupational safety department, a representative from the police department, and representative(s) from the human relations department (including a representative from bargaining, as well as the **employee assistance program**, whenever possible). Ad hoc team members include a representative from the general counsel's office, psychologist(s) and/or psychiatrist(s), a representative from media/**public relations**, and outside (the company) experts as necessary.

PART II—NONEMPLOYEE PERPETRATORS

Part II of the WPV program should address those components that are dedicated to preventing and re-

Table 2b

Model of a WPV Threat/Incidence Report, cont.

(cont. from Table 2a)

Did/Does alleged perpetrator demonstrate any of the following warning signs of potential violence: (check √ all that apply)

1. Instills fear in co-workers/supervisors _____
2. Irrational beliefs, ideas or obsessions (Place 2 √s if of a romantic nature) _____
3. Expressions of a desire to hurt oneself, or other signs of impending suicide (e.g., giving personal items to others, hinting ominously of an unspecified departure) _____
4. Expressions of desire to hurt others _____
5. Expressions of hopelessness or futility _____
6. Litigious behavior, i.e. filing numerous grievances or lawsuits _____
7. Feelings of being victimized, picked on or persecuted _____
8. Violence toward inanimate objects and/or animals _____
9. Uncharacteristic stealing or sabotaging of projects, supplies or equipment _____
10. History of violence _____
11. History of inappropriate or disproportionate anger _____
12. Attendance problems _____
13. Inordinate impact on supervisor's time (coaching/counseling etc.) _____
14. Markedly decreased or widely fluctuating productivity or performance _____
15. Concentration problems (poor memory, etc.) _____
16. Behavioral signs of stress (e.g. heightened anxiety, sudden inexplicable and unpredictable mood swings, depression) _____
17. Persistent blaming of others and inability to accept constructive criticism _____
18. "Surveillance" of co-workers/supervisors (e.g. notes, lists, private investigator activity) _____
19. Obsession with: guns/weapons; police, fascist, military or survivalist strategies/causes; or known violent perpetrators _____
20. Poor or slipping hygiene and/or health _____
21. Reckless or uncharacteristic disregard for safety precautions _____

sponding to violence in the workplace perpetrated by individuals never employed by the company.

GENERAL RISK ASSESSMENT AND ASSOCIATED PREVENTION STRATEGIES. This section of the WPV program should document the company's area(s) of greatest risk for nonemployee workplace violence, and briefly describe the general mechanisms in place for lowering these risks.

General areas of high risk include work sites that: (1) are primarily staffed by women, which introduces a higher risk of domestic violence; (2) are located in areas where one or more crimes are particularly common (e.g., robbery, gang-related crimes, rape, arson); (3) have a history of workplace violence; (4) handle cash or other valuable **commodities**; (5) have individuals who work alone; and (6) are removed (indefinitely or intermittently) from the general population. Accordingly, this section may identify any number of general preventive strategies, such as badge-only entry, security cameras, enhanced night lighting, domestic violence education and counseling, cash-handling policies, physical separation of workers from customers, escort services, and so forth.

TRAINING. This section of the WPV program should list, at a minimum, the following:

1. The primary topics that will be covered in this training. Key topics are as follows:
   a. How to recognize the danger signs of potential workplace violence
   b. How to diffuse a potentially violent individual
   c. The facility's emergency signal or code word

Table 3
Warning Signs of Potential Violence

The following behaviors (presented in no particular order) can be used as potential indicators of impending workplace violence:

[NOTE: By their very nature, these predictive profiles can be under- or over-inclusive of people likely to commit violent acts. Determining whether any/all of these behaviors serve as valid indicators of potential violence is a case-by-case judgement call, based upon the knowledge and experience of the appraiser(s) combined with all other factors revealed during the corresponding WPV investigation phase]

1. Instills fear in co-workers and/or supervisors
2. Irrational beliefs, ideas or obsessions
3. Expressions of a desire to hurt oneself, or other signs of impending suicide (e.g., giving personal items to others, hinting ominously of an unspecified departure)
4. Expressions of desire to hurt others
5. Expressions of hopelessness or futility
6. Litigious behavior, i.e. filing numerous grievances or lawsuits
7. Feelings of being victimized, picked on or persecuted
8. Violence toward inanimate objects or animals
9. Uncharacteristic stealing or sabotaging of projects, supplies or equipment
10. History of violence (witnessed directly, or described by alleged perpetrator or others)
11. History of inappropriate or disproportionate anger
12. Attendance problems
13. Inordinate impact on supervisor's time (coaching, counseling, etc.)
14. Markedly decreased or widely fluctuating productivity or performance
15. Concentration problems (poor memory, etc.)
16. Behavioral signs of stress (e.g., heightened anxiety, sudden inexplicable and unpredictable mood swings, depression)
17. Persistent blaming of others and inability to accept constructive criticism
18. "Surveillance" of co-workers/supervisors (e.g., notes, lists, private investigators)
19. Fascination or obsession with: weapons; police, fascist, military or survivalist strategies or causes; or known violent perpetrators
20. Poor or slipping hygiene or health
21. Reckless or uncharacteristic disregard for safety precautions

d. How and why to best utilize the general WPV prevention strategies and equipment provided by the company

2. How often the training is held
3. Who will present the training
4. Who is required to attend
5. Who is encouraged to attend
6. How to obtain additional copies of the written WPV program

RESPONSE TO POTENTIAL OR ACTUAL INCIDENTS. This section of the WPV program should present mechanisms for summoning emergency assistance in the wake of a potential or actual WPV incident. It would include information about any emergency signals or code words that are to be used under these circumstances. It would further differentiate, if necessary, the discrete response measures for each type of perpetrator (e.g., an enrolled student versus a ''trespasser'' on a college campus, a patient versus a visitor in a hospital).

OBTAINING PERSONAL PROTECTION ORDERS. This section of the WPV program should describe in detail the following:

1. Purpose and function of a personal protection order (PPO)
2. How to obtain a PPO (and what part the employer can play in this process)
3. The legal criteria considered when issuing a PPO
4. Who at the facility can assist with questions regarding PPOs

Table 4

Criteria Used to Consider "Risk" of Those Engaged in Physical Fighting

The following criteria can be used to consider whether those engaged in a physical fight present a "substantial risk of harm to persons or property":

1. Length of employment of alleged perpetrator(s) and overall work record(s), including history of prior violence
2. Whether conduct consisted of single unpremeditated blow, or series of deliberate acts
3. Whether blow(s) were struck with clenched fists or open hands
4. Whether fight was unusual "spur-of-the-moment" affair, or result of continuing bad blood between participants;
5. Severity and duration of fight
6. Location of fight
7. Effect of altercation on morale, safety and work habits of others
8. Whether fight was between two employees, or between an employee and his/her supervisor
9. Whether a reasonable or prudent employee would have been inclined to react in a similar manner
10. Whether the event is closed or likely to be repeated
11. The presence of other mitigating circumstances not listed here, such as provocation or discrimination
12. Whether the misconduct evinces a dangerous propensity, a vicious tendency, or a serious emotional instability
13. Whether the misconduct will lead to refusal, reluctance or inability of other employees to work with the alleged perpetrators

TRAUMA PLAN. This section of the WPV program should either present all information pertaining to critical incident response, or should refer readers to an existing company document that provides said information (e.g., the company's ''emergency response plan'' or ''**crisis management** plan''). Key examples of topics to include are:

1. Coordination of personnel from police, emergency response, medical, security, evacuation, and buildings and grounds
2. Management of key communications with employees, media, customers, victims' families, counselors, etc.

POSTTRAUMA RESPONSE. This section of the WPV program should present the company's policy and procedures following a violent incident (including resources and funding). Key examples of topics to include are:

1. Crisis intervention and debriefing of victims and witnesses within 24 hours of the incident
2. Treatment of posttraumatic stress syndrome
3. Grief management services

WPV PROGRAM APPENDICES

FORMAL POLICY REGARDING WPV. Given the controversial nature of any WPV policy, it must first be reviewed by the facility's general counsel, and subsequently approved, endorsed, and delivered from the top down, i.e., by the company's president, cabinet, and/or **board of directors**; otherwise effective implementation is unrealistic. This policy should include at least the following elements:

1. Prohibited behaviors that constitute violence in the workplace.
2. The steps that will be followed to address employees who allegedly engage in one or more prohibited behaviors (e.g., incident investigation, risk assessment, and response).
3. The range of punitive responses that may be employed in response to acts of workplace violence (e.g., referral to appropriate health care, written reprimand, short-term removal from the workplace, long-term separation from the workplace, dismissal).
4. The penalty for making false or misleading WPV reports.
5. The penalty for retaliating against those who have made good-faith WPV reports.

COPY OF WORKPLACE VIOLENCE THREAT/INCIDENT REPORT. Employees should be able to examine a WPV threat/incident report prior to making the decision to file a report. A model of a WPV threat/incident report is provided in Table 2.

INSTRUCTIONS FOR ACCESSING/USING THE WPV ''HOT LINE'' Assuming that the facility has set up a ''hot line'' for reporting potential or actual WPV incidents, the following information should be provided regarding its access and use:

1. The telephone number to dial from inside or outside the facility
2. What the caller can expect to hear on the recorded message, and what information he/she is expected to provide at the tone
3. A statement about caller anonymity

CONCLUSION

The days of operating without a workplace violence program are over. Every company's program and associated policies and procedures will undoubtedly be carefully scrutinized by myriad governing agencies, not to mention hungry attorneys, after a violent incident. Furthermore, employers are obligated under the Occupational Safety and Health Act's "General Duty Clause" to furnish a workplace "free from recognized physical harm." According to the **Occupational Safety and Health Administration** (OSHA), this section of the act may be invoked where the employer fails to keep the workplace free from a hazard to which its employees were exposed, the hazard was recognized, the hazard caused or was likely to cause death or serious physical harm to workers, and a feasible or useful method for correcting the hazard existed. More specifically, on January 13, 1994, the head of OSHA announced a goal to address workplace violence via this section of the act by citing employers who do not adequately protect their employees from workplace violence. Consequently, OSHA has begun citing workplaces where one or more of the following is not present (regardless of whether histories of violence exist at those workplaces): (1) a workplace violence policy/program, (2) mandatory training to staff in the key components of that program, and (3) documented enforcement of the WPV policies therein.

Admittedly, the process of drafting a practical and useful WPV program is arduous and controversial. The risks associated with *not* doing so, however, clearly imply a social, moral, legal, and economic irresponsibility that cannot be overlooked.

[Rikki B. Schwartz]

FURTHER READING:

Baron, S. Anthony. *Violence in the Workplace: A Prevention and Management Guide for Businesses.* Ventura, CA: Pathfinder Publishing of California, 1993.

——, and Eugene D. Wheeler. *Violence in Our Schools, Hospitals, and Public Places.* Ventura, CA: Pathfinder Publishing of California, 1994.

Blythe, Bruce, and Rick Gardner. "Eye on Workplace Violence." *Risk Management,* April 1999, 43.

Dobry, Stanley T. "Legal Aspects of Workplace Violence." 21st Annual Labor and Employment Law Seminar, sponsored by the Institute of Continuing Legal Education. 26 December 1996. 13: 21-77.

Doering, Barbara W. "Violence and Fear of Violence in the Workplace." *Labor Arbitration Institute,* 1996, 103.

Nuyen, Donna R. "Resolving Violence in the Workplace: A Management Perspective." Fundamentals of Michigan Employment Law Workshop, sponsored by the Institute of Continuing Legal Education. 21 July 1995. 3: 3-24.

U.S. Department of Justice. Office of Justice Programs. "Workplace Violence, 1992-1996." *National Crime Victimization Survey.* Washington: GPO, 1998. Available from www.ojp.usdoj.gov/bjs.

U.S. National Institute for Occupational Safety and Health. Division of Safety Research. *Current Intelligence Bulletin 57: Violence in the Workplace/Risk Factors and Prevention Strategies.* DHHS (NIOSH) Publication No. 96-100. Cincinnati: National Institute for Occupational Safety and Health, 1996. Available from www.cdc.gov/niosh/violcont.html.

WORKS COUNCIL

An important feature of European **labor-management relations**, works councils are committees of labor representatives within companies which consult with management and may even have certain decision-making powers. They take on a number of forms, but in general they are seen as democratic bodies that give voice to worker concerns and interests. In their strongest form, works councils are said to have co-determination rights with management in some areas of corporate policy. In the broader context, works councils are conventionally credited with reducing labor conflicts and promoting harmonious labor practices, particularly concerning changes in the workplace.

Under **European Union** law since the mid-1990s, large multinational companies operating in EU countries generally must sponsor transnational councils or so-called European Works Councils (EWCs), which bring together members of an enterprise's **workforce** from each country it has operations in. These relatively recent creations have historical roots in national and regional works councils, which have been prevalent in parts of Europe, notably Germany, for decades. Similar entities exist outside Europe, but the concept is mostly closely associated with European practices. Within the United States there has been periodic interest in instituting such a practice.

Works councils in Europe are generally separate from collective bargaining activities and don't involve wage negotiations, although actions taken in works councils may be complementary to collective bargaining efforts. Legally, works councils are required to be formally independent of industrial **labor unions**, creating, symbolically at least, a dual system of labor representation. In theory, unions are supposed to deal with issues such as wages and working hours, while works councils take up issues such as working conditions, safety and health, and general policy communications. In practice, however, a high percentage (approaching three-quarters according to one study) of workers who are representatives in works councils are also active in trade unions, and the interests of the two labor organizations are closely aligned.

DEVELOPMENT OF WORKS COUNCILS

THE GERMAN SYSTEM. Works councils flourished in various countries of western Europe in the immediate post-World War II period (later losing momentum in many places), but they have always been strongest in Germany. German industrial unions were first legally recognized in 1918 and works councils in 1920 under the Works Councils Act. After World War II, the legal foundation for works councils was reestablished by the Works Constitution Acts of 1952 and 1972.

The 1972 act called for all German businesses with five or more permanent employees to establish a works council, although in practice not all companies did. Councils were normally organized at the plant or establishment level. The number of employees on the council and its exact powers were dictated by the company's size. For instance, a firm with 5 to 20 employees would have a one-person council, while a workforce of 9,000 would have 31 representatives. Representatives on the councils served four-year terms, and all elections within companies were held at the same time throughout the country. Further, works council activities were financed by the company and conducted on company time.

The law also specified employment policy domains in which the councils were to have codetermination rights—the right to veto proposed corporate policies. If the council didn't approve a management proposal, the issue was to be settled by a special committee consisting of an equal number of workers and managers. Ultimately, if the dispute couldn't be resolved internally, it might be taken to a special labor court. Areas where works councils enjoyed codetermination rights included working hours (e.g., **hours of labor**, overtime, employee leave), health and safety, and performance monitoring and appraisal. Councils also had lesser rights (right of consent, right of consultation) in other policy domains.

At the same time, works councils were given incentives to help them cooperate with management to reach mutually beneficial solutions to disagreements. For example, larger works councils formed economic committees that received regular briefings and data from management concerning the company's sales, investment plans, marketing, and other strategic concerns. The councils were required to keep this information confidential, but they used it to help inform their positions on corporate policies. Theoretically, if the data showed that the company risked losing money, the council members would be more sympathetic to management's reforms or other changes. In this role, works councils have sometimes been seen as a moderating influence on labor unions.

EUROPEAN COUNCILS. While most of that system still remains intact in Germany, the modern resurgence of works councils elsewhere in Europe began in the 1970s under the auspices of the European Community (EC), forerunner to the European Union. An early proposal for a worker consultation system in large companies was circulated starting in the mid-1970s, but the idea was quite unpopular and the measure was rejected by the EC member governments. In the mid-1980s a new thrust for worker representation came about as EC was beginning assert its influence more strongly on social affairs in member states. The EC began to facilitate dialogs between labor and corporate partisans, even funding these initiatives. Ultimately, the effort succeeded in the wake of the Maastricht Treaty of 1993, which created the European Union and thereby enhanced the powers of the European Commission, the EC agency that had been pressing for works councils.

In 1994 the commission's proposal was adopted by the Council of the European Union as the Directive on European Works Councils (EWCs). Applying to multinational firms with at least 1,000 employees in EU countries generally and having at least 150 employees in two EU countries, the rules for EWCs were much looser than those in the German system. Altogether, this requirement affected some 15 million workers at about 1,500 companies, including a number of U.S. firms with large European operations.

The directive called for these transnational firms to create EWCs or ''a procedure for informing and consulting employees'' that would transcend national boundaries. The latter alternative left open the possibility for a collaborative body that didn't fit the conventional mold of a works council. As in the German model, management was responsible for funding an EWC or similar body, and both sides were bound to hold sensitive information that arose during the process in confidence. The exact rules governing each company's works council were to be negotiated by the management and a special workers' negotiating committee. As a result, the directive did not ascribe any particular rights or functions to the works councils beyond information and consultation. Rollout of the EWC rule was gradual, with the first deadline in 1996 and full implementation not required across the board until 1999.

EVALUATING WORKS COUNCILS

Supporters of works councils commonly cite a number of benefits they bring. Among these are:

- better flow of information between management and labor
- more say for workers in corporate decisions
- decreased labor-management conflict
- potentially higher productivity and profitability when labor's interests are aligned with management's

Scholarly research provides some support for the claim that works councils improve labor-management relations, at least as measured by how each side perceives the other. For example, a few attitudinal studies, particularly of managers, found that European managers were much more receptive to works councils in the 1990s than they were in the 1970s, and executives were more likely to see them as positive influences.

However, the claim that works councils confer economic advantages to companies is not well supported by academic research. Indeed, a number of researchers during the early to mid-1990s found, if anything, the opposite. By measures such as total factor productivity and profitability, several studies have suggested that works councils have at best no significant effect on corporate economic performance. Moreover, a couple studies indicated that works councils might even have negative implications for corporate profitability.

Data and research on works councils were still fairly limited as of the late 1990s, though, especially concerning EWCs since they're so new. In 1999 the European Commission, as provided under the directive, began conducting a comprehensive assessment of the EWC rule and its effects thus far. Depending on the outcome of that assessment, the commission was considering proposing modifications to the rule. Separately, the commission was already circulating a proposal that would create a more uniform framework—in other words, tighter restrictions—for how EWCs would operate in different companies and countries.

While Europe has continued to experiment with works councils, the United States largely has watched from the sidelines. Most notably, the Commission on the Future of Worker-Management Relations (better known as the Dunlop Commission) released in the mid-1990s a report that was generally favorable toward works councils as a means to improve worker participation. However, the commission, apparently divided over the issue, did not come out strongly in favor of works councils and the issue remains controversial on both pragmatic grounds—some critics maintain they're ineffective—and ideological grounds.

FURTHER READING:

Addison, John, Claus Schabel, and Joachim Wagner. ''On the Determinants of Mandatory Works Councils in Germany.'' *Industrial Relations,* October 1997.

Ramsay, Harvie. ''Fool's Gold? European Works Councils and Workplace Democracy.'' *Industrial Relations Journal,* December 1997.

Rogers, Joel, and Wolfgang Streeck. *Works Councils: Consultation, Representation, and Cooperation in Industrial Relations.* Chicago: University of Chicago Press, 1995.

Walsh, Janet. Review of *Innovation and Employee Participation Through Works Councils: International Case Studies,* edited by Raymond Markey and Jacques Monat. *Industrial Relations,* June 1998.

WORLD BANK

The World Bank was created along with its sister institution, the **International Monetary Fund** (IMF), at Bretton Woods, New Hampshire, in 1944. World leaders gathered at the Bretton Woods conference to ensure the economic recovery and economic stabilization of a world economy ravaged by World War II. They created the World Bank, which over the decades has evolved into a lending institution working to foster the long-term growth of less-developed countries while integrating their economies into the global economy. The IMF, on the other hand, works to stabilize currency exchange rates and provides aid for countries with balance of payment problems.

The World Bank is more formally known as the International Bank for Reconstruction and Development (IBRD). It is affiliated with four other organizations: the International Development Association, the International Finance Corporation, the International Centre for the Settlement of Investment Dispute, and the Multi-Lateral Investment Guarantee Agency. The World Bank Group is an umbrella organization comprised of these four institutions and the IBRD. Although ''World Bank'' and ''International Bank for Reconstruction and Development'' are often used interchangeably, the term ''World Bank'' more properly describes an organization jointly comprising the IBRD and the International Development Association. The IBRD is also a designated ''special agency'' of the **United Nations**.

The immediate purpose of the Bretton Woods conference was to formulate a plan for post-World War II international economic cooperation. President Franklin Roosevelt and U.S. Treasury Secretary Henry Morgenthau Jr. both believed that a stabilized world economy would be invaluable in preventing a reoccurrence of the Great Depression of the 1930s and perhaps an ensuing global war. Establishment of the IBRD was an integral part of their plan.

Over the decades, the emphasis of the IBRD has shifted from its immediate and short-term purpose of rebuilding war-ravaged economies to the promotion of economic growth in developing countries. In fact the IBRD makes **loans** only to developing or transitional countries, unlike the IMF which makes no such distinction amongst its client nations. The IBRD makes loans directly to governments of member nations and to large private development projects that are backed by guarantees of member nation governments. Loans made directly to governments are generally to ease balance of payment problems, promote trade, and solve social sector problems related to such things as primary education, nutrition, and programs targeting the rural poor. The IBRD also helps governments in the promotion of "social safety nets" such as social security and **pension** systems. Private loans have traditionally been made for large building projects of high productivity and employment that will benefit the citizens of the host country. Environmental quality also figures in the IBRD's scheme of things; in 1998 it had a portfolio of 166 environmental projects totaling approximately $11 billion. To all of these ends the IBRD commits about $20 billion in new loans to approximately 100 developing countries annually. Although these loans are made at low **interest rates**, the IBRD is often criticized by the borrowing countries for imposing severe austerity measures as a condition of the loan.

The IBRD raises capital by borrowing from world capital markets and from members' subscriptions to capital shares. The IBRD, which regards itself as a fiscally conservative and prudent institution, accounts for nearly three-fourths of monies lent by the World Bank. Most of this money is raised by selling AAA-rated **bonds** and other debt **securities** to individuals and institutional investors such as corporations, insurance companies, and pension funds. The IBRD lends money at three-quarters of a percent above what its own borrowing rate is. Loans are financed for 15 to 20 years with a three-to-five-year grace period before repayment of principal must begin. A borrowing country has never defaulted on a loan, because of the IBRD's rule requiring that outstanding loans and disbursements not exceed the combined capital and reserves of the borrowing country.

In order to better align itself with the economic needs of a changing world, the IBRD has instituted a Strategic Compact designed to carry the institution well into the 21st century. The Strategic Compact will, it is hoped, make the IBRD more efficient by lowering costs, improving products and processes, and impacting more on its customer countries.

The 1997 Asian monetary crisis, which began with currency turmoil in Thailand and quickly grew to global proportions, has been the World Bank's greatest challenge. Between January and March 1997, however, the IBRD was able to quickly and with much efficiency raise $14.9 billion through 69 bond offerings in 17 different currencies. This speaks to the sophistication and ease with which the IBRD is able to move through world financial markets. Some of this is due to World Bank President James Wolfensohn who has held that position since 1995. Wolfensohn, in an effort to make the governments of developing countries politically as well as economically responsible, is changing the emphasis of the World Bank's lending priorities. Wolfensohn is shifting the exclusivity of lending policies away from such civil engineering projects as big dams and superhighways and more towards projects that will implement educational institutions, political reform, effective tax collection systems, and environmental regulation. Wolfensohn feels that such programs, if implemented, will encourage private-sector investment.

The chief governing authority of the IBRD is the Board of Governors, with one governor being appointed by each member country. The appointed governor is usually a finance minister or a person holding a comparable office in the represented country. Daily operations of the IBRD are administered by 24 executive directors who represent the interests of their respective countries while overseeing the implementation of IBRD policy and project management.

SEE ALSO: Development Banks

[Michael Knes]

FURTHER READING:

Doherty, Jacqueline. "World Bank's Treasury: A Force in the Market." *Barron's,* 25 May 1998, 30.

Dudley, Nigel. "Most Professional Borrower: World Bank." *Euromoney,* June 1998, 104+.

Kapur, Devesh. *The World Bank: Its First Half Century.* Washington: Brookings Institution, 1997.

McTague, Jim. "It's a New World: An Aussie-Born Wall Street Veteran Shakes Up a Big Multinational Lender." *Barron's,* 25 May 1998: 27-30.

Sender, Henny. "The Storm Intensifies: Asia's Still-Growing Problems May Drag down the Rest of the World." *Far Eastern Economic Review,* 1 October 1998, 44-50.

World Bank. "World Bank." Washington: International Bank for Reconstruction and Development, 1998. Available from www.worldbank.org.

WORLD TRADE ORGANIZATION (WTO)

The World Trade Organization (WTO) is an international organization founded in 1995 to promote global trade in goods, services, and **intellectual prop-**

erty. It is the successor to the **General Agreement on Tariffs and Trade** (GATT), which since 1947 sought to promote international economic growth through the establishment of legally binding rules governing trade between countries. In 1993 GATT held its Uruguay Round negotiations at which it was decided that its final act would further liberalize trade measures and establish a permanent structure, the WTO, to manage international trading procedures and protocols. Ministers meeting in Marrakesh, Morocco, in 1994 agreed to the final act. Concurrently in Marrakesh, a majority of GATT countries approved the establishment of the WTO. In 1998, 132 countries, including the United States, belonged to the WTO.

The WTO provides a framework used by national governments to implement trade legislation and regulations and the WTO provides a forum for collective debate, negotiation, and adjudication of trade disputes. In this regard the WTO has five essential functions: to administer and implement the multilateral and plurilateral trade agreements that make up the WTO; to provide a forum for trade negotiations; to provide a forum for the resolution of trade disputes; to monitor trade policies of member countries; and to cooperate with other international organizations involved in global trade, commerce, and economic policy making.

Although the WTO shares many of the same goals as GATT, it is much more than just an extension of GATT—its scope is much broader and the nature of the new organization is much different. GATT was a collection of trade rules bound together by multilateral agreements but lacking a real institutional foundation. The WTO, on the other hand, is a permanent institution with a large staff and secretariat. Although GATT had been in existence for a number of decades, its application was on a "provisional basis," while the WTO was created as a permanent institution. GATT rules applied only to "merchandise goods" or tangible products. WTO agreements apply to merchandise goods but also cover intellectual property and trade in services. Many of the GATT arrangements were plurilateral and therefore selective in nature. Most of the WTO arrangements are multilateral and involve the entire WTO membership. The WTO has also instituted a more efficient system for settling disputes that is much less susceptible to blockage as was the GATT system.

The highest authority of the WTO is the Ministerial Conference, which is made up of ministerial representatives from member countries. The conference meets at least once every two years and has the authority to make decisions on all matters of the multilateral trade agreements. The WTO General Council is composed of representatives from member countries and is responsible for day-to-day WTO activities and operations. The General Council reports to the Ministerial Conference. The General Council convenes as the Dispute Settlement Body, which oversees the settlement of trade disputes between members, and as the Trade Policy Review Body, which reviews the trade policies of member countries. The WTO's Council for Trade in Goods, Council for Trade in Services, and the Council for Trade-Related Aspects of Intellectual Property are subsidiary bodies of the council.

The WTO decision-making process utilizes consensus, at least initially, rather than voting. This continues the GATT decision-making process and seeks to ensure that all members' needs and interests receive attention and consideration. When agreement cannot be reached via consensus, however, there is a voting procedure. In the voting procedure decisions are based on a simple majority with every member country having one vote. The WTO agreement anticipates four specific voting situations. An interpretation of any WTO multilateral trade agreement can be adopted by a majority vote of at least three-quarters of WTO members. WTO's Ministerial Conference can, by a majority vote of three-quarters of its members, waive a member country's obligation under a multilateral trade agreement. Multilateral trade agreement provisions can be amended by an approval vote of all members, or under certain circumstances, a two-thirds majority vote of the members. Finally, a two-thirds majority vote of the Ministerial Conference is necessary for the admission of new members.

A central feature of the WTO is its dispute settlement process. This process is especially important because it adds security and predictability to the world trading system and prevents member countries from taking unilateral preemptive action. The first stage of the process requires bilateral discussions between members on each side of the dispute. If after 60 days a settlement has not been reached, the complainant may ask the General Council, convening as the Dispute Settlement Body (DSB), to set up an independent panel to review the case. Both parties submit arguments to the panel followed by a presentation of their respective cases. If scientific or technical expertise is required, then an expert review group can be appointed. The panel submits an interim report to both parties and within three to six months, depending on the circumstances of the case, a final report is submitted. The DSB usually adopts the report in 60 days. Appeals to the final report are allowed on matters of law and legal interpretation only and can be presented to three members of the Appellate Body but only within 90 days of the report's submission. The Appellate Body has the final authority on the case and its decision must be accepted by both parties unless there is a DSB consensus against it. If the decision of the Appellate Body is not instituted within a reasonable period, then the conflicting members are required to negotiate mutually acceptable compensation. The DSB is also responsible for overseeing the implementation of the final decision.

Since the WTO's founding in 1995, it has adjudicated approximately 150 trade dispute cases, as opposed to GATT's 300 cases in 47 years.

Despite this elaborate system for settling disputes, the WTO has come under severe criticism from various U.S. organizations and businesses that feel that the WTO is perpetuating rather than eliminating **trade barriers**—at the expense of U.S. companies. Most of the criticism centers on three very large U.S. defeats in the late 1990s. On appeal the WTO has allowed Britain, Ireland, and the **European Union** to reclassify U.S. **local area network** computer equipment as **telecommunication** hardware. This decision nearly doubles the duty on this equipment from 3.9 percent to 7.5 percent, making it less competitive in European markets. The WTO also ruled that U.S. attempts to protect endangered sea turtles from shrimp nets violated world trading rules. The largest loss, in terms of U.S. dollars, was the much publicized U.S. case brought on behalf of Eastman Kodak against Japan. The United States and Kodak charged that Japan violated WTO agreements by protecting its home film market in favor of the Fuji Photo Film Co. Some analysts feel that the United States presented a weak case based on dated information. Nevertheless, these same analysts faulted the WTO for giving implicit support to Japan's protective home distribution system by claiming it fell outside the purview of WTO trade agreements. In bringing trade complaints before the WTO the United States seems to win the small cases but lose the major ones.

The WTO is also under attack by environmentalists who claim that the WTO's dispute resolution panels favor international trade at the expense of environmental protection. Cases cited by WTO critics include the aforementioned U.S./sea turtle dispute and a WTO ruling that the European Union could not ban hormone-treated beef from its markets. The WTO has also ruled that the state of Massachusetts cannot put a pricing penalty on state procurement bids from companies doing business with Myanmar (formerly Burma) because of that nation's human rights violations. Although not an environmental decision, activists fear that the WTO may use this case as a precedent to invalidate multilateral environmental agreements. Particularly worrisome would be an invalidation of the so called Basel ban. The Basel ban, which is an amendment to the Basel convention, deals with international shipments of hazardous wastes and prohibits the shipping of hazardous waste from **Organisation for Economic Co-operation and Development** countries to developing countries. The WTO is also criticized for attacking the use of "eco-labels." These labels, which are required by some governments, provide environmental claims and environmental information on product labels.

[Michael Knes]

FURTHER READING:

Blackhurst, Richard. "The WTO and Global Economy." *World Economy* 20 (August 1997): 527-44.

Das, Bhagirath Lal. *Trade and Development Issues and the World Trade Organisation.* London: Zed Books, 1997.

Hileman, Bette. "WTO and the Environment." *Chemical and Engineering News* 76, no. 4 (2 November 1998): 17-18.

Hoekman, Bernard M. *The Political Economy of the World Trading System: From GATT to WTO.* New York: Oxford University Press, 1995.

International Monetary Fund. "World Trade Organization." Washington: International Monetary Fund, 1998. Available from www.imf.org/external/np/sec/decdo/wto.htm.

Jackson, John H. *The World Trade Organization: Constitution and Jurisprudence.* London: Royal Institute for International Affairs, 1998.

Magnussoon, Paul. "Why the WTO Needs an Overhaul." *Business Week,* 29 June 1998, 35.

Siegmund, John E. "Services in the WTO: Recent Developments and Overview." *Business America* 119, no. 4 (April 1998): 12 14.

WORLD WIDE WEB (WWW)

SEE: Internet and World Wide Web

WORLD WIDE WEB CONSORTIUM (W3C)

The World Wide Web Consortium (W3C) is an international group of **Internet** researchers, **software** developers, **computer** manufacturers, and universities founded by the pioneer of the Internet's World Wide Web, Tim Berners-Lee, in 1994. Berners-Lee established the W3C in collaboration with the European Laboratory for Particle Physics (CERN) and initially received support from the U.S. Defense Advanced Research Project Agency (DARPA) and the European Commission.

The goal of the W3C is to help the World Wide Web (also known as the Web) evolve by developing common languages and formats that will allow users with different hardware and software to enjoy similar features of the Web. In essence, its objective is to make the Web accessible to all and not dependent on the technology of any single company. Consequently, the consortium serves as one the Web's governing bodies. The consortium is backed by a variety of companies including rivals such as Microsoft and Netscape, but it remains vendor neutral in keeping with the philosophy of the World Wide Web.

Three universities—Massachusetts Institute of Technology Laboratory for Computer Science (MIT/LCS), the Institut National de Recherche en Informatique et en Automatique (INRIA), and the Keio University Shonan Fujisawa Campus (KEIO)—host the consortium, representing the United States, Europe, and Japan, respectively.

The consortium's basic organization—called a team—includes a director, a chairman, an advisory committee, and staff. Berners-Lee still heads the W3C as the director and Jean-François Abramatic serves as the W3C's chairman. The team works out of the three host universities. The consortium's some 300 members—including America Online, Apple Computer, AT&T, IBM, Intel, and Microsoft—fund its operations. Although the W3C includes members from many different industries as well as for-profit and nonprofit companies and organizations from around the world, it is not an open group. Instead, members must pay fees to join and membership is not available to individuals. Because of its closed-door policies and its power to determine the fate of the Web, critics have argued that the W3C should become an open group and adopt more democratic policies, according to the *Technology Review.* Nevertheless, the W3C's members are generally satisfied with consortium's ability to help members reach agreements and implement standards. Moreover, the W3C has attempted to work more with outside companies, organizations, and experts.

THE WORLD WIDE WEB

The World Wide Web is the information distribution ''service'' of the Internet where information is stored, linked together, presented, and retrieved. The Web also supports multimedia: graphics, music, and video. The Internet is the network of computer networks through which users can access the Web. Prior to the development of the Web, the Internet was largely used by academia and the military in part because it was difficult to navigate, forced users to download all information they wanted read, and lacked links to related items. But Berners-Lee conceived of software and protocols (commands and sequences used by computers to communicate in networks) in the late 1980s and early 1990s, which became known as the World Wide Web when implemented.

This combination of software and protocols can support multimedia as well as hypertext, text that is connected in a nonlinear order, allowing users to browse through a group of related topics in whatever order they choose. In addition, the Web also uses uniform resource locators (URLs), which are unique addresses of the sites or documents on the Web and the Web enables users to peruse information online. Perhaps the most dramatic piece of software that helped skyrocket the popularity of the World Wide Web is the Web browser, which was developed in 1993. With the advent of the Web and the Web browser, business use of the network increased exponentially as businesses hurried to set up company Web sites. In 1993 there were only two business Web sites, but by May 1999 more than 4,600,000 company domains were registered, according to the organization Domainstats.

THE W3C'S FOCUS AND SERVICES

Because other standards bodies exist for the Internet such as the Internet Engineering Task Force, the W3C concentrates mostly on the user interface of the Web and the architecture of the Web, which refers to the Web's **infrastructure**. This area encompasses defining the Web, Web documents, and the protocols for accessing and disseminating Web documents. Furthermore, the consortium also addresses issues of intellectual ownership of Web documents, rating systems for Web documents, and Internet privacy.

The W3C provides a venue for members to discuss and negotiate issues related to the Web and the consortium assists members by hosting discussions and helping members reach agreements, plan meetings, and develop consistent and timely approaches to improving and advancing the World Wide Web. The W3C strives to help bring about consensus among its members and its negotiation process requires participants to address other participants' perspectives and objections in an effort to resolve disputes and help members reach agreements.

To promote a standardized Web, the consortium tries to develop common specifications for the World Wide Web to enable companies and organizations to develop Web technology in their own fields. Because Web technologies change quickly, the W3C maintains a flexible process of adopting new features for the World Wide Web or new policies for the consortium itself.

The consortium's efforts to standardize the Web usually involve encouraging members to compromise and reach agreements about patenting and licensing their products. Members often license their Web technologies to each other at no cost in exchange for free licensing rights to the technology of other members.

When the consortium involves itself in an aspect of Web technology or policy, it launches an ''activity'' in that area, which means it allocates resources and staff to that area. The director proposes activities and the W3C's advisory committee reviews the proposal. Based on the recommendations of the committee, the consortium makes a decision as to whether it should initiate the activity. If the W3C decides to launch an activity, it will form groups to carry it out.

In addition, the W3C is charged with approving new Web authoring languages and developing Web standards. Furthermore, it offers the public a library of information and Web specifications helpful for developers and users, sample codes, and demonstration software to showcase new technology.

RECENT W3C RATIFICATIONS

In the late 1990s the W3C approved two new Web protocols: extensible markup language (XML) and document object model level one (DOM). Based on hypertext markup language (HTML)—the original language for Web development—as well as HTML's predecessor, standard generalized markup language (SGML), XML promises to be the next-generation Web authoring language. XML allows users to create Web sites with different segments that are structured in different ways, which is difficult to do using HTML. DOM is a Web interface that is not dependent on a specific Web authoring language or computer platform and is designed for revising the content and layout of Web sites. DOM enables developers to create language-independent software, too. Both Microsoft and Netscape plan for their 5.0 Web browsers to support DOM.

[Karl Heil]

FURTHER READING:

''About the World Wide Web Consortium.'' 14 April 1999. Available from www.w3.org/Consortium/Overview.html#Membership.

''Domainstats.'' May 1999. Available from www.domainstats.com.

Garfinkel, Simson L. ''The Web's Unelected Government.'' *Technology Review,* November/December 1998, 38.

Hannon, Brian. ''W3C Eyes DOM, XSL.'' *PC Week,* 24 August 1998, 10.

——. ''XML Gets Nod from the W3C.'' *PC Week,* 16 February 1998, 24.

Reid, Robert H. *Architects of the Web.* New York: JohnWiley & Sons, Inc., 1997.

''World Wide Web Consortium Process Document.'' Available from www.w3.org/Consortium/Process/#GAProcess.

WTO

SEE: World Trade Organization

WWW

SEE: Internet and World Wide Web

Y

Y2K

SEE: Year 2000 Compliance

YEAR 2000 COMPLIANCE

Year 2000 (Y2K) compliance refers to the complex process whereby governments, businesses, and individuals upgrade computer systems so that 2000 is recognized by those systems as a valid date. The Y2K problem was developed beginning in the late 1960s when the modern computer industry began, i.e., when computers began to be able to store data in addition to processing it. The problem will occur because many computer programs and applications were written to store data in only two digits, so that 1999 would be stored as ''99'' and 2000 as ''00.'' Computers programmed to understand years using only two digits were expected to misread 2000 as 1900 (or some other date), causing many computers to crash or malfunction.

The Y2K problem affects not only computer programs and applications, but also operating systems, computer hardware, and other products and systems that rely on embedded chips and/or utilize computerized technology.

Why were dates written with two instead of four digits? When many programs were written and stored on mainframe computers in the 1960s, the cost of computer resources and storage space were at a premium. Memory was expensive, hard drive space was expensive, and computer time was expensive. In order to conserve costly storage space, the date field was truncated from four digits to two digits as a standard for most applications and operating systems. As a result, millions of programs, millions of computers, and millions of embedded systems that utilize computer technology are expected to malfunction when they are required to accept date information beginning with January 1, 2000.

WHAT WILL BE AFFECTED?

The Y2K problem is expected to affect virtually every computer program and application written since the 1960s and not updated to correct the problem. To correct the problem, billions of lines of computer code need to be examined. As one Y2K expert put it, ''The code has been broken.'' Fixing this aspect of the problem requires massive amounts of manpower and the time to do it. General Motors projected it would spend between $710 million and $780 million to prepare its computer systems for the year 2000.

As difficult as code auditing is, embedded system remediation may pose an even greater problem. Remediation is the process by which applications or embedded systems are inventoried, assessed, reprogrammed, tested, and re-implemented. When one takes into account the scope and complexities of embedded systems throughout the world, the magnitude of the Y2K problem becomes more apparent. The prevalence of embedded computer systems reflects just how deeply computers have become integrated into everyday life. For example, computer systems are imbedded in the following everyday processes:

- Electricity and billing

- Radio and television communications
- Telephone call routing and billing
- Shipping and distribution of important commodities, including imports and exports
- Checking and savings accounts, money transfers, and ATM transactions
- Processing, ordering, and shipping of packaged goods and food
- Admission of patients to hospitals, billing, dispensing prescription medicines, and diagnostic machinery
- Airlines reservations systems, air traffic control systems, and airplane maintenance systems
- Benefit payments
- Defense systems

Embedded systems are those devices that perform an automated function or process using a built-in microprocessor, program, and computerized clock (also known as a RTC or real time clock). These devices are sometimes called PLCs, or process logic controllers. Embedded systems are found in devices ranging from VCRs to satellite control systems. There are an estimated 25 billion embedded systems worldwide. Of those, it is not known how many are date sensitive and prone to Y2K failure, although estimates range from .25 percent to 10 percent.

Many of the embedded systems that are date sensitive may or may not be mission critical, depending on the industry and the application. In one case involving Kraft Foods, the company tested 832 PLCs and found 10 percent of them to be date sensitive. PLCs at Kraft control safety and food production and so were mission critical. In what was possibly a related incident, Kraft had to destroy several million dollars worth of food, because its expiration date was after January 1, 2000.

CAN THE Y2K PROBLEM BE FIXED?

Several factors have made it difficult to examine and remediate embedded systems. Since many of the embedded systems are continuously ''live,'' testing can only take place in a simulated environment, without integration with other systems. In addition, it would be impossible to test embedded systems that have been upgraded until all such systems were in place, and the upgraded systems would not be ready to test at the same time. In other cases remediation cannot be accomplished, because the microprocessors themselves can no longer be manufactured.

In theory the Y2K problem can be fixed, and Y2K compliance can be achieved. In practical terms, though, several factors prevent full compliance. These boiled down to two key factors: manpower and time. On a worldwide basis there are not enough people to examine and rewrite programs. An estimated 400 computer languages have been used, with COBOL accounting for about 30 percent of non-compliant languages. In addition, many businesses and government agencies were running out of time. Large organizations needed to begin addressing the problem well before 1999. Small to medium-sized companies are even further behind in remediation and replacement of non-compliant systems. As of March 1999, an estimated 22 million small businesses, or approximately 50 percent, had done nothing to prepare for Y2K, according to one survey.

Another factor to be considered as January 1, 2000, approached was the fact that it was an absolute deadline. Historically, complex information technology (IT) projects have not been completed on time. There was no reason to expect that a project as complex as Y2K compliance would be completed on time either.

WHAT BUSINESSES ARE EXPECTED TO DO

Since businesses might not have the resources to make sure every piece of equipment is Y2K compliant, they are urged to prioritize all processes and deal with those that are the most critical. One method called ''triage'' was adopted from emergency medical procedures, whereby soldiers with critical injuries were categorized into three classes based on whether or not they would survive with or without medical treatment. The term has been applied to Y2K systems to determine whether or not they are ''mission critical.'' Using this method, businesses can allocate limited resources to saving the most critical systems first.

In order to determine which systems are mission critical, an organization must first complete an asset inventory of all computers, software, and other equipment with embedded chips. These include personal computers, software, fax machines, heating and ventilation equipment, communications equipment, modems, security systems, and safes. This process can be aided by forming search committees to take an asset inventory and assess what areas are mission-critical to the operation of the business.

The asset inventory then prepares an organization for a Y2K audit, a several-step process to identify potential Y2K problems and takes steps to fix them. Potential problems could occur in the following areas:

1. Hardware, including imbedded chips and processors in fax machines and other office equipment.
2. Standard software applications, including spreadsheets, databases, and word processors
3. Operating systems

4. Custom-written software
5. Outside vendors and other third parties
6. Sources of power and other basic resources

Customers, suppliers, and vendors also need to be contacted. Any with non-compliant systems can potentially contaminate a business's systems and become open to Y2K litigation. Businesses are urged to contact suppliers or equipment manufacturers in order to assess the possibility that inventoried items will not function properly. Businesses also needed to consider the impact of critical outside service providers, including telephone, electricity, water, gas, and possible raw material suppliers. Such suppliers should be contacted to confirm Y2K readiness in writing.

In some cases businesses need to develop contingency plans for critical services and products, in case there is a Y2K malfunction, especially for service providers who appeared to be lagging in Y2K compliance efforts. Businesses are also urged to review all legal contracts and insurance policies to determine coverage for Y2K-related problems. Finally, a disaster plan should be developed to cover scenarios involving utilities or a lack of supplies.

To get the ball rolling, organizations need to make high-level management decisions regarding what to fix and what to risk not fixing. Management also needs to make business decisions regarding time and resource allocation to address the problem. Small business owners can seek assistance on the Web, where there are sites tailored to the small business owner that provided self-assessment checklists and programs.

1999 PROVIDES A PREVIEW

Several key 1999 dates represented potential failure points for embedded systems. Some analysts predicted that one-fourth of all Y2K-related problems would occur in 1999. The Gartner Group predicted that only 8 percent of all Y2K problems would happen on January 1, 2000. Taskforce 2000, a privately funded organization, predicted in April 1999 that 60 percent of computer errors and data disruption would occur during 1999, and 30 percent would occur after January 1, 2000. The group estimated only 5-10 percent of the problem would occur on January 1 because of the rollover from 1999 to 2000.

Two key dates in 1998 passed without noticeable effects. These were July 1, 1998, which was the start of fiscal 1999 for 46 states, and October 1, 1998, the beginning of fiscal 1999 for the federal government. These were dates when computers began to look forward into fiscal 2000 to calculate benefits. While errors were expected, no significant interruption of government service occurred.

January 1, 1999, was the date that many computer applications, such as inventory, benefits, and banking and credit systems, began looking ahead to 2000. On this date the chances were high that an undetected Y2K problem could trigger a variety of results: miscalculation of expiration dates on time-sensitive inventories; errors in check payments to employees, beneficiaries, or suppliers; under- or over-estimation of interest on credit accounts; and others. Some 13 states and the District of Columbia applied short-term patches to computer systems to ensure they would be able to issue benefit checks on or after January 1, 1999.

January 4, 1999, was the first working day of the year. On this day new data was entered into systems looking ahead to 2000. While older files may have been isolated from database calculations, new data was subject to risks associated with potential Y2K problems. Other 1999 dates related to Y2K included those dates on which fiscal 2000 began for various governments, including April 1 (Canada, Japan, and New York), July 1 (46 states), and October 1 (U.S. government). Y2K problems on these dates could affect the earnings reports of companies that are highly dependent on government for revenues as well as the credit and bond ratings for those governments.

August 22, 1999, was the date that the Global Positioning System reached the end of its built-in calendar and rolled over to start a new calendar for 20 years. If a company was using an older CPS receiver, it was possible that the rollover would affect traffic management. However, most commercial users of GPS had already upgraded their systems, including the Federal Aviation Administration (FAA) and the airlines.

GOVERNMENT EFFORTS TO SOLVE THE Y2K PROBLEM

The "Year 2000 Information and Readiness Disclosure Act" was signed into law on October 19, 1998. The purpose of the law was to encourage business-to-business communication on readiness, strategies, tools, and any other information related to Y2K compliance. However, businesses were reluctant to discuss Y2K compliance actions, even after the bill was passed. A 1999 survey by the California Public Employees' Retirement System, which had more than $35 billion invested in 2,469 companies, garnered a response from only 600 of those firms. A mere 13.5 percent provided meaningful information. One reason for such reluctance might have been the fact that there were several class action lawsuits filed in 1997 and 1998 against information technology vendors based in part on Y2K statements made to customers and to the public.

The federal law contained provisions and guidelines regarding "Year 2000 Readiness Disclosures." It also provided a limited temporary exemption from federal and state antitrust laws to permit businesses to exchange Y2K data between and among traditional competitors, for the purpose of correcting or avoiding Y2K processing problems. While the law did not lessen the liability of companies if there were to be a Y2K product or service failure or defect, it did establish a high but fair and consistent standard of proof for a claimant to use an entity's "Year 2000 Statement" as the basis for legal action. The overall purpose of the law was to establish uniform legal standards in the disclosure of Y2K information; it did not in any way lessen the ability of wronged parties to take legal action against entities with whom they had a contractual relationship, for failures, fraud, or breaches of contract.

A subsequent piece of legislation, known as The Y2K Act or The McCain-Dodd Y2K Act, passed the House and Senate of the U.S. Congress by mid-1999, and was headed for conference. The bill was supported by a wide range of businesses, industry associations, and the high-tech community, while being opposed by attorney groups such as the Trial Bar. The Y2K Act sought to discourage Y2K litigation and encourage remediation. Its provisions were aimed at discouraging frivolous lawsuits related to Y2K by preserving existing contracts, establishing a cure period for Y2K disputes, and allowing a reasonable efforts claim into evidence in contractual disputes.

Many small businesses simply did not have the resources to address the Y2K problem in a timely manner. To assist small businesses in becoming Y2K compliant, the U.S. Congress passed the Small Business Year 2000 Readiness Act, which set up a $500 million guaranteed loan program in 1999 for small businesses trying to fix the Y2K problem. The program was to be administered by the U.S. Small Business Administration.

Other federal resources included the Presidential Council on Year 2000 Conversion headed by John Koskinen, which devoted most of its efforts to providing information to the public about Y2K compliance. It said that national systems such as power grids, telecommunication networks, and air traffic were Y2K compliant, but it warned of localized, temporary disruptions. It created 25 working groups to facilitate communication between industries and developed a Y2K toolkit to promote community involvement. It also helped to develop a "Year 2000 Investor Kit" to help investment firms, markets, regulators, and the media provide information to the public about the Y2K readiness of the financial services industry. It also set up a toll-free information line for consumers.

The Federal Emergency Management Agency (FEMA) conducted a series of ten regional workshops in February and March 1999 for emergency management and fire services officials. The workshops covered initial Y2K compliance assessments, potential consequences of Y2K disruptions, and the coordination of responses among local, state, and federal agencies.

Also addressing the Y2K problem was a Senate special committee, headed by Sen. Robert Bennett and Sen. Christopher Dodd. Various reports were issued by the U.S. Office of Management and Budget (OMB) and the Government Accounting Office (GAO).

Y2K compliance of federal government agencies was under constant scrutiny. An Office of Management and Budget report listed 43 high impact government systems, of which only two were Y2K compliant in early 1999. The Federal Aviation Administration (FAA) said it was 99 percent Y2K compliant in September 1998. However, by June 1999 it was reportedly only 92 percent compliant and was faced with a string of control system failures at major airports, including La Guardia (New York), O'Hare (Chicago), Dallas/Forth Worth, and San Diego, among others. FAA expected to achieve Y2K compliance by July 1999. The agency said its air traffic control computers passed a major test in April 1999. Compounding the problem for the FAA was the fact that most of the nation's 670 domestic airports began their Y2K compliance efforts too late.

U.S. Representative Christopher Horn (R-CA) issued a quarterly report card on Y2K compliance by federal agencies. His June 1999 report card found that the federal government's mission-critical systems were 94 percent compliant. However, the report noted that two critical systems—the FAA's air traffic control system and the payment management system of the Department of Health and Human Services—were not yet Y2K compliant. Also of concern were systems with December 1999 completion dates, which covered areas such as child nutrition, food stamps, child care, child support enforcement, child welfare, and more.

Individual states set up Y2K project offices to provide support and information. City governments were expected to do their own auditing and compliance checking. Key areas of concern were being able to provide basic services such as water and electricity as well as 911 and other emergency services.

BUSINESS EFFORTS TO SOLVE THE Y2K PROBLEM

While many major corporations began Y2K compliance programs before 1999, not all industries appeared able to achieve Y2K compliance before the year 2000. Heavily regulated fields, such as banking, insurance, and finance, were the furthest ahead. Among the industries lagging behind were health care, where some two-thirds of all hospitals had no plans to test their systems for Y2K compliance, and oil, where computer links to foreign suppliers were a concern. Food processing, farming, agriculture, construction, and education were other areas that had fallen behind schedule in their Y2K compliance efforts. Following are a few example of how different industries were dealing with the Y2K problem.

SOFTWARE. In early 1999 Microsoft was saying that it had tested 2000 of its software applications and found 93 percent of them "Y2K ready." However, "ready" did not mean "compliant." In some cases, a patch upgrade was needed for the software to be Y2K compliant. In addition, Microsoft made PC Analyzer available as a free software tool to determine Y2K compliance. While the company faced some litigation with regard to Y2K-related problems, one such suit concerning its FoxPro database software was dismissed "with prejudice," meaning that it could not be appealed.

Microsoft also had to provide patch upgrades for its Windows NT Terminal Server Edition (TSE), which it first released in mid-1998 in a non-compliant version. Patches promised for September and December 1998 were not delivered. Patches posted in January 1999 were later admitted to be inadequate, with the result that some companies mistakenly believed that TSE deployments were Y2K compliant. Customers were left wondering if an NT Service Pack scheduled for March 1999 delivery would provide adequate Y2K compliance.

SECURITIES INDUSTRY. The Securities Industry Association (SIA) ran a series six weekend tests during March and April 1999. More than 400 U.S. securities firms, stock exchanges, and asset managers tested how well computers would handle stock, bond, and mutual fund trades at the end of the year. The tests simulated conditions on December 29, 1999, the last trading day of the year.

THE OPTIONS CLEARING CORPORATION (OCC). The Options Clearing Corporation began its computer conversion process in 1985 and became Y2K compliant in 1996. The OCC expected its Y2K team to continue to be active well into the year 2000. As the clearinghouse for the American Stock Exchange, the Chicago Board Option Exchange, the Pacific Stock Exchange, and the Philadelphia Stock Exchange, the OCC typically had a daily liability of $30 billion. It could not afford to have any downtime at all, so not surprisingly it invested heavily in Y2K compliance. After achieving software compliance, it focused on the embedded chips residing in its servers and mainframe computers. Other efforts included contacting its power company, telephone company, and building management to ensure that communications and electricity would not be cut off and that the elevators in its building would continue to operate.

AIRLINES. Northwest Airlines has been addressing the Y2K problem since 1991. The company's efforts involved examining more than 34 million lines of computer code and testing 14,000 pieces of equipment at 130 sites in the United States. The airline spent some $45 million to become Y2K compliant and assigned about 200 employees to the task.

RETAIL INDUSTRY. Efforts at Y2K compliance among the nation's retailers has been coordinated by the National Retail Federation since February 1997. Its efforts included risk assessment, the development of best practices guidelines, and contingency planning.

Y2K EFFECT ON BANKING AND CREDIT

In early 1999 *USA Today* reported that banks were beginning to tighten credit standards for companies that seemed to be lagging in their Y2K compliance efforts. Banks were starting to ask companies to show that computers were Y2K compliant, or that they would be compliant in time. For companies that were not Y2K compliant, some banks were requiring more collateral to back loans or would not add to existing credit lines. Regulators were encouraging banks to tighten credit on business loans to companies who were not Y2K compliant to minimize losses in case the Y2K bug disrupted the companies' business and made it more difficult for them to repay loans.

The Federal Deposit Insurance Corporation (FDIC) planned to tour several cities to talk to newspapers and other media in an effort to calm people's fears about the effect of Y2K on banking operations. A March 1999 Gallup poll revealed that more than half of all Americans believed that banking systems would fail on January 1, 2000. The FDIC reported that 97 percent of banks had done a satisfactory job of dealing with the Y2K problem, with the remaining 3 percent (about 320 banks) being mostly small banks. Industry analysts and banking experts tended to agree with the FDIC's assessment, saying that banks seemed to be on top of the problem.

Federal banking regulators, operating under very stringent guidelines from the federal government and FDIC, conducted numerous bank examinations to make sure the banking industry would be Y2K compliant. As a result, federal officials were not especially concerned about the banking industry's Y2K preparedness as of late March 1999. The regulators had made sure that banks had Y2K compliance plans as well as teams and resources in place. A second phase of examination involved determining whether individual banks had been successful in correcting their systems. Banks were required not only to test their own systems, but also their interfaces with important third parties. The final phase of federal oversight involved reviewing contingency plans.

Also of concern was the public's confidence in the banking system. People who did not have a lot of confidence in technology in the first place were likely to run to the bank and take their money out. Several programs were being conducted to educate the public and boost its confidence in the banking system. In addition, the Federal Reserve significantly increased its currency order to ensure that an adequate supply of cash would be available in case of a run on banks.

The President's Council on Year 2000 Conversion developed a "Year 2000 Investor Kit" to help investment firms, markets, regulators, and the media provide information to the public about the Y2K readiness of the financial services industry. The Kit was developed jointly with the **Securities and Exchange Commission (SEC)**, National Association of Securities Dealers (NASD), and Securities Industry Association (SIA). It contained a review of the financial services industry's efforts to prevent Y2K computer problems, a list of frequently asked questions (FAQs), a Y2K checklist, and information about checking personal computers and other equipment for potential Y2K problems.

Investors could also check on the Y2K readiness of registered broker-dealers, mutual funds, and investment advisors at the SEC Web site.

CONCLUSION

Preparing computer systems for Y2K has been a costly exercise requiring billions of dollars worldwide. While no accurate estimate of the total cost is available, some companies have reported how much they expected to spend. General Motors announced it would spend between $710 million and $780 million to prepare its computer systems for the year 2000. Boston's State Street Bank and Trust spent an estimated $200 million preparing for Y2K. Just to be on the safe side, State Street told its employees not to plan on taking a vacation over the New Year's weekend. Like the employees of many other companies, some 1,500-2,000 employees at State Street will be at their desks watching the clock tick past midnight to ensure that the bank's computers don't crash.

[David P. Bianco]

FURTHER READING:

Abrams, Jim. "Y2K Alerts a Test for Government." *Detroit Free Press,* 9 June 1999.

Balas, Janet L. "Preparing the Library for the Year 2000." *Computers in Libraries,* March 1999.

Boyko, Allan. "A Y2K Checklist." *Edmonton Sun,* 29 March 1999.

Center for Strategic and International Studies. "Y2K: A Global Ticking Time Bomb?" Conference Proceedings, 2 June 1998.

"FDIC Plans Campaign to Calm Y2K Fears." *Knight Ridder Newspapers,* 29 March 1999.

"Federal Y2K GPA up Slightly." *ITAA Year 2000 Outlook,* 18 June 1999.

"FEMA Regional Y2K Workshops Begin." FEMA Press Release, 26 January 1999.

Gallagher, John. "Northwest Spends Millions to Make Sure that the Dreaded Y2K Bug is Just a Blip." *Detroit Free Press,* 27 April 1999.

"GM Forecasts Year 2000 Costs at $710-780 Million." Reuters, 12 March 1999.

Healy, Beth. "Party? Hardly. Financial Staffers on Full Y2K Alert." *BusinessToday.com,* 12 March 1999.

Information Technology Association of America. "ITAA Guide to the 'Year 2000 Information and Readiness Disclosure Act.'" 28 June 1999.

——. "ITAA Summary of Key Provisions of Interest to the IT Industry: The Year 2000 Information and Readiness Disclosure Act - S.2392." 28 June 1999.

MacDonald, Michael. "Y2K Grief Hits Early for Some." *The London Free Press,* 29 March 1999.

Mcdonald, Susan. "Federal Regulators Ensure Banks' Readiness for Y2K." *Business First,* 29 March 1999.

Miller, Rich. "Y2K Fears Tighten Credit." *USA Today,* 19 April 1999.

Mukherjee, Sougata. "Y2K Loans May Spell Trouble." *The Denver Business Journal,* 29 March 1999.

"National Retail Federation Supports the Y2K Act." *PR Newswire,* 8 June 1999.

Pettitt, Jo. "Microsoft in Trouble over Year 2000 Again." VNU Business Publications, 12 March 1999.

Rankin, Robert A. "Y2K Problems Inevitable, Senate Panel Says." *Detroit Free Press,* 24 February 1999.

Ratcliffe, Mitch. "Y2K in 1999: Plumbing the Reality of the Problem." 29 December 1998. Available from www.zdnet.com..

"Report: Y2K Bug Will Hit Early, Reverberate." *Yahoo! News,* 21 April 1999.

"Securities Industry Y2K Test Surpasses Expectations." *BusinessToday,* 8 March 1999.

Sowinski, Jay. "Do You Want to Risk Chaos for Your Firm? Ignore Y2K." *Kansas City Business Journal,* 29 March 1999.

Stewart, Julie. "As Calendar Winds Down, Cities Zero in on 2000 Woes." *Arkansas Democrat-Gazette,* 29 March 1999.

"U.S. Warns Airlines Insurance Must Cover 2000 Bug." *Yahoo! News,* 20 April 1999.

"Y2K Legislation." *Information Week,* 8 March 1999.

"Y2K Litigation Bill Passes Senate; Conference Could be Sticky." *ITAA Year 2000 Outlook,* 18 June 1999.

"Y2K News Site Issues Air Travel Public Safety Notice; Documents Timeline of FAA Failures." *PR Newswire,* 9 June 1999.

"Y2K Stats: The Options Clearing Corporation." *PC Week,* 6 July 1998.

YIELD CURVE ANALYSIS

Yield curve analysis involves the measurement of differences in **interest rates** between notes that have a different term to maturity. To evaluate the term to maturity effect, one examines the same issuer (for example, **U.S. Treasury bills**) with various **debt** notes and maturity. The typical yield curve is upward sloping, meaning short term to maturity notes have low interest rates and longer term to maturity notes have higher interest rates. Of course, one strategy to maximize investment return would be to invest in the longer term, higher yielding notes. This strategy presumes there are no immediate liquidity needs and that the shape and level of the yield curve will not change. In fact, the shape and level of the yield curve itself can be used to develop an interest rate forecast using an expectations theory model. This theory as it applies to yield curve analysis states that the interest rate for a longer time period is a product of the interest rates for the total of the shorter time intervals that comprise the longer time period. The increase in investment yield with the longer term notes is not present if the yield curve shape is flat (same rate for all maturities), downward sloping (short-term notes have high interest rates whereas long term notes have low rates) and humped (a combination upward sloping and flat) yield curve.

Another aspect of yield curve analysis is the comparison of yields between issuers of a different quality (determined by **bond** ratings) or sector (for example, corporates versus federal government). The spread (difference) between the two issuers may vary by term to maturity. Opportunities to earn higher returns may occur when the spread between the notes is not the normal amount. For example, the spread between the 91-day U.S. Treasury bill and 3-month bank certificates of deposit (CD) usually is about 40 basis points (0.40 percent). If the present spread is 70 basis points that would favor investment in CDs, whereas a spread of 15 basis points would tilt the advantage towards U.S. Treasury bills. The spread between the two issuers will vary with other term to maturity comparisons causing a more complicated investment strategy to be employed.

Another yield curve strategy is ''riding the yield curve.'' This technique is the most profitable with upward sloping yield curves. The investors acquire a longer term to maturity debt note than their planned holding period, and sell the debt note at the date when they had initially desired to cash out. The reason for doing so is to earn a higher interest rate on the longer term note at purchase plus a **capital gain** on the sale of the higher return note. The end result is a higher total investment return.

[Raymond A. K. Cox]

FURTHER READING:

Cox, Raymond A. K., and Daniel E. Vetter. ''Money Market Returns and Risk, 1938-1989.'' *Journal of Midwest Finance* 22 (1993): 50-54.

——, and James M. Felton. ''Performance from Riding the Yield Curve, 1980-1992.'' *Journal of Business and Economic Perspectives* 20 (1994): 128-32.

Z

Z SCORE

The Z Score is a statistical measure used by financial traders to determine whether there is a dependency, or correlation, among their trades. A trader might suspect a dependency if he or she experiences a run of several consecutive profitable trades, or a run of several consecutive unprofitable trades. "Obviously, there was some kind of dependency or serial correlation among your trades [in this case], where winners were followed by winners and losers were followed by more losers," Thomas Stridsman wrote in the April 1998 issue of *Futures*. "If this happens again, you'll want to exploit the good times and perhaps avoid trading altogether in bad times."

Traders can verify the existence of a dependency among their trades by calculating the Z Score of their trading system or strategy. The Z Score indicates whether the trading system results in more or fewer streaks of consecutive wins or losses than would occur randomly. Ideally, traders can apply this information to future trades in order to increase profits and decrease losses by adjusting the amount of money invested in each trade, depending on the results of the previous trade. It is important to note, however, that the Z Score is useful only to traders who use a trading system, and only when that system is working on a particular market.

The formula for calculating the Z Score of a trading system is:

$$Z = \left(\frac{N(R - .5) - X}{\frac{X(X - N)}{N - 1}} \right)^{1/2}$$

where N = the total number of trades (for the formula to work effectively, the Z Score must be calculated for a minimum of 30 trades),

R = the total number of runs (a new run begins each time a profitable trade is followed by an unprofitable one, or vice versa),

$X = 2 \times W \times L$,

W = the total number of winning trades,

L = the total number of losing trades.

If this calculation results in a negative Z Score, it means that the trading strategy has fewer streaks or runs than would occur randomly. In other words, there is some dependency or correlation among trades because winners tend to follow winners and losers tend to follow losers. If the calculation results in a positive Z Score, it indicates that the trading strategy has more streaks than would occur randomly. There is a reverse correlation among trades because winners tend to follow losers and losers tend to follow winners.

The closer the Z Score to zero, the lower the likelihood that the trader will be able to rely on a dependency among trades to increase profits or decrease losses. On the other hand, traders are likely to be able to take advantage of a high or low Z Score (above $+2$ or below -2) to improve their results. For example, a trader with a Z Score of -2 should increase the size of his or her next trade after a winner, because the correlation between trades indicates that the next trade should also be a winner. Similarly, a trader with a Z Score of $+2$ should increase the size of his or her next trade following a loser, because the correlation indicates that the next trade should be a winner.

The majority of trading systems yield a Z Score between 1 and −1, showing a limited dependency between trades. But this is not necessarily a bad thing. "What do you do if you don't know your system's Z Score or serial correlation, or if you find out they aren't high enough to be exploited profitably?" Stridsman noted. "Investigate whether you can further improve your system because—and it may sound strange—the truth is that a system or a trading strategy that shows signs of any kind of dependency or correlation among its trades is not optimized to its maximum potential."

A DIFFERENT Z SCORE PREDICTS BANKRUPTCY

The most current definition of Z Score is the one used by financial traders to determine whether there is a dependency among their trades. It is worth noting, however, that another definition exists. Financial economist Edward I. Altman developed a Z Score for predicting commercial bankruptcy in 1968. Altman's model determines the probability that a company will enter bankruptcy within any 12-month period, using five **financial ratios** that can be calculated from basic financial reports.

The formula for manufacturing companies is:

$$Z = 1.2A + 1.4B + 3.3C + 0.6D + E$$

where A = working capital divided by total assets,
B = retained earnings divided by total assets,
C = earnings before interest and taxes (EBIT) divided by total assets,
D = market value of preferred stock and common stock divided by total **liabilities**,
E = sales divided by total assets (for nonmanufacturing companies, element E is omitted from the formula).

This Z Score provides an objective measure of a firm's financial health that can be used for **credit** evaluation, **investment analysis**, insurance **underwriting**, legal analysis, and turnaround management. It was 95 percent accurate in predicting bankruptcy in Altman's initial study, and between 82 and 85 percent accurate in independent follow-up studies.

[Laurie Collier Hillstrom]

FURTHER READING:

Auchterlonie, David L. "A Paean to the Z Score and Its Commercial Bankruptcy Prediction." *Journal of Lending and Credit Risk Management,* September 1997, 50.

Stridsman, Thomas. "If It's Broke, Don't Fix It." *Futures,* May 1998, 44.

——. "Scoring High and Low." *Futures,* April 1998, 46.

ZERO ECONOMIC GROWTH

Zero economic growth is an **economic condition** that may be the result of a nation's public policy, or it may be caused by a **recession**. When several Asian economies experienced economic and financial crises in 1998, some countries, including Japan, were expected to experience zero economic growth during the following year. A number of factors may be used to measure a nation's economic growth. The largest overall measure of economic output is a country's **gross national product** (GNP), which is an annual measure of the goods and services produced in the country. When the GNP increases from year to year, economic growth is occurring. Should the GNP decrease, then there is said to be negative growth. Under zero economic growth, the GNP would remain constant over time. For most countries zero economic growth is perceived as a worst-case scenario.

As a matter of public policy, most nations strive for moderate economic growth from year to year. Two types of policies, monetary and fiscal, can be implemented to affect a country's economic performance. Fiscal policy refers to the use of government spending and taxation to affect the overall demand for goods and services. Increased government spending increases the size of the GNP. Higher **tax** rates reduce the amount of disposable personal income, with a corresponding reduction in demand. Using these two fiscal tools, a government can raise or lower the demand in the economy, with corresponding effects on the GNP and economic growth.

Monetary policy refers to the use of controls over **interest rates**, the **money supply**, and the ability of **banks** to make **loans**. In the United States monetary policy is established by the Federal Reserve Board. Monetary policies can help reduce **unemployment** and slow **inflation**. For example, when the Federal Reserve Board makes it easier for banks to make loans, thus increasing the money supply, businesses are thereby encouraged to make more investments and hire more workers. By increasing the **discount rate**, on the other hand, the Federal Reserve Board can restrict the money supply and help reduce inflation. Restricting the money supply tends to reduce the size of the GNP, while measures to expand the money supply tend to increase the size of the GNP.

Zero economic growth may be an unwanted condition that a country experiences as the result of a recession or another set of economic circumstances. While fiscal and monetary policies can have some effect on economic performance, it is quite possible to experience unintended zero economic growth. Factors that could contribute to a flat or declining GNP might include high unemployment, inflation and higher prices, high interest rates and little business expansion, a general recession, and anything else that would lessen demand and business production.

Zero economic growth has been discussed in academic circles as a desirable goal of public policy. It is argued that an ever-expanding economy will sooner or later become too large for the finite world we live in. If the world's economies become too large, they will make too great a demand on our planet's finite resources. The ultimate effect of economic growth would thus be the collapse of the ecological, social, political, and economic systems as we know them.

The no-growth argument may be countered by pointing to the adaptability of existing social, economic, and political systems. As economic growth continues, new alternatives are likely to become available. Technological innovations may provide new solutions to the problems caused by economic growth. While economic growth has its costs and benefits, public policy will likely continue to attempt to minimize the costs and maximize the benefits without abandoning the concept of stable economic growth as a policy objective.

[David P. Bianco]

FURTHER READING:

Davis, Bob. ''IMF Expects 'Moderate Rebound' in Asia in '99.'' *Wall Street Journal,* 14 April 1998, A2.

Melzer, Thomas C. ''To Conclude: Keep Inflation Low and, in Principle, Eliminate It.'' *Federal Reserve Bank of St. Louis Review,* November/December 1997, 3-7.

Stephen, Andrew. ''Party Goes on While Clouds Loom.'' *New Statesman,* 24 July 1998, 24.

Tiglao, Rigoberto. ''Mixed Prognosis: The Islands Show Some Resilience to Asia's Malaise.'' *Far Eastern Economic Review,* 19 February 1998, 58.

INDEX